THE EUROPEAN FOOTBALL YEARBOOK

2000 2001

General Editor **MIKE HAMMOND**   Published by **SPORTS PROJECTS LTD**

www.sportsprojects.com

ICELAND

Arctic Circle

FAROE
ISLANDS

N
O
R
W
A
Y

S
W
E
D
E
N

F
I
N
L
A
N
D

NORTHERN
IRELAND

SCOTLAND

North
Sea

DENMARK

Baltic
Sea

ESTONIA

LATVIA

LITHUANIA

RUSSIA

BELARUS

REPUBLIC
OF
IRELAND

WALES

ENGLAND

HOLLAND

BELGIUM

LUXEMBOURG

G
E
R
M
A
N
Y

POLAND

CZECH
REPUBLIC

SLOVAKIA

Bay of
Biscay

F
R
A
N
C
E

LIECHTENSTEIN

SWITZERLAND

AUSTRIA

HUNGARY

ROMANIA

SLOVENIA

CROATIA

YUGOSLAVIA

BULGARIA

PORTUGAL

S P A I N

MONACO

ANDORRA

I
T
A
L
Y

SARDINIA (It)

CORSICA (Fr)

VATICAN
CITY

SAN MARINO

BOSNIA-
HERZEGOVINA

ALBANIA

MACE-
DONIA

GREECE

M e d i t e

SICILY

MALTA

r r a n e a n   S e a

THE EUROPEAN FOOTBALL YEARBOOK 2000/2001

ACKNOWLEDGEMENTS

The European Football Yearbook 2000/2001
First Published in Great Britain by Sports Projects Ltd
November 2000

Copyright Sports Projects Ltd
188 Lightwoods Hill, Smethwick, Warley, West Midlands,
B67 5EH, England
website: www.sportsprojects.com
email: info@sportproject.u-net.com

ISBN 0 946866 55 4 (paperback)
ISBN 0 946866 56 2 (hardback)

Printed in Great Britain

General Editor
Mike Hammond

Editorial and Research Co-ordinators
Lakis Avraamides, Mert Aydin, Nikolai Belov, José Del Olmo,
Tamás Dénes, Gerry Desmond, Dimcho Dimitrov Ivanov,
Marshall Gillespie, Miron Goihman, Michael Hansen,
Peter Hekkema, Romeo Ionescu, Valery Karpoushkin,
Daniel Kolbusch, Jean-Paul Kolbusch, Igor Kramarsich,
Zdenek Kucera, George Kusunelos, Esko S. Lahtinen, Tarmo Lehiste,
Dag Lindholm, Robert McElroy, Goran Mancevski, Fatmir Meneri,
Kazimierz Oleszek, Olexandr Pauk, Humberto M. Pereira Silva,
Zdravko Reic, Mike Ritter, Revaz Shengelia, Vidir Sigurdsson,
Jesper Krogshede Sørensen, Andrej Stare, Algis Staskevicius,
Edouard Stutz, Matej Széher, Mel ap ior Thomas, Razvan Toma,
Serge Van Hoof, Victor Vassallo, Stefan Welte, Jacob Zelazo,
Luciano Zinelli.

Special thanks to
Susan Hammond

Photographs:
Empics Ltd and courtesy of featured clubs

Design, layout and graphics:
Nadine Goldingay, Phil Lees and Vic Millward, Mikhail Sipovich

Cover design:
Bernard Gallagher

INTRODUCTION

As the *European Football Yearbook* completes its first decade, it is interesting to look back at our very first edition.

The burning topic of debate in 1991? Nothing more contentious than the use of the penalty shoot-out to settle important matches.

"It is high time," stormed the *Yearbook's* editorial, "that FIFA and UEFA... think again about the damaging effect it is having on the game."

Ten years on, however, the shoot-out is still with us, and if truth be told, we would all be delighted if it still represented the extent of European football's controversies.

Sadly, the continental game now has bigger fish to fry. Concern grows in some quarters at the level to which the Champions' League overshadows domestic and even international competition, and as we go to press, there is a threat of chaos within the game should the transfer system be ruled illegal by the European Union.

A vibrant Euro 2000 showed what football can still be capable of, however, and while the game as we know it prevails, the *European Football Yearbook* remains constant as your definitive guide to football around the continent, placing at your fingertips the facts and figures on last season for European teams, club and national strips and emblems and a comprehensive account of the season for each nation.

BERNARD GALLAGHER

Publisher

COMMENT

A bright beginning to the new century

The stature of Euro 2000 rose with every passing day. It was a tournament that began well, got better and reached a crescendo with a dramatic final. David Trezeguet's glorious golden goal was the perfect climax to a competition that will live long in the memory.

Some observers were so taken with events in the Low Countries that they even drew comparisons with the great World Cup of 1970, long considered to be the Utopian prototype of all major international football tournaments.

The common denominator of Mexico '70 and Euro 2000 is that they both ran to the same, classic format - 16 teams at the start, an opening group phase, eight quali-

fiers, then straight knockout through to the final. It is the perfect system. The process is simple and straightforward, with no complicated mathematics and no overcrowded fixture schedule.

The European Championship will never attain the glamour and appeal of the World Cup, but it is likely to produce a superior standard of football quite simply because there are so few makeweights in its field. World Cups, on the other hand, tend to include half a dozen or so qualifiers whose presence is justified by not much more than geographical expedience and whose realistic ambition stretches no further than making up the numbers and adding colour to the party.

The structure of Euro 2000 was no different from Euro '96 but it was a more enjoyable tournament, and the main reason for that was the superior quality of the leading participants. France, Italy, Holland and Portugal were all top-class international teams. Each would have been worthy winners, and it was wholly appropriate that all four should reach the semi-finals - though a disappointment, perhaps, that the Italians should eliminate the Dutch in such a negative fashion in the semi-final.

Mercifully, that game in Amsterdam was the only one of the seven knockout ties which ran its maximum two-hour

Celebration time for the French, newly crowned European Champions.

COMMENT

course and resulted in trial by penalty shoot-out. The other semi-final and - for the second European Championship running - the final were both resolved by the golden goal. It remains a contentious rule. The 'sudden death' principle certainly makes for great tension and drama, but when the decisive goal is a controversial one - as in the France v Portugal semi-final - it is just as cruel and unforgiving as a missed spot-kick in a shoot-out and has the same devaluing effect on the overall spectacle.

Nevertheless, it has to be said that the officials got that particular decision exactly right, and it was especially pleasing to see the referee, Günter Benkö, actually taking the advice of his assistant before he signalled for the all-important penalty.

Some years ago FIFA's rulemakers deemed it mandatory for the benefit of the doubt to be given to the attacking team in tight offside decisions. But it seldom happens. On several occasions at Euro 2000 the man on the line not only failed to favour the attacker when he was level with the defender but, worse still, penalised him when he was clearly in an onside position. As many as five or six goals were prevented at Euro 2000 by hastily raised flags. In fact, one of the tournament's most treasured goals - Patrick Kluivert's equaliser against France - came about only because one linesman bucked the trend and allowed play to continue after a close call. Video replays proved - as they almost always do - that his decision not to intervene was correct.

Overall, the standard of refereeing at Euro 2000 was not too bad. There were some rash penalty decisions at the start, which, alas, encouraged players to take a dive in subsequent matches, but in general the referees used their authority sensibly and, more importantly, most of them operated on the same wavelength, which brought a greater level of consistency than had been witnessed at previous tournaments. For this UEFA deserve a pat on the back. Their decision to limit the number of referees to an elite group and house them together for the duration of the tournament paid off.

One ugly scar that worked its way onto the otherwise smiling face of Euro 2000 was the fighting and property-wrecking that went on in the streets of Brussels and Charleroi.

While the English domestic game has largely rid itself of football-related violence - incidents nowadays are on a fraction of the scale that was once the norm - for some reason the England team continues to be accompanied abroad by some fans who are unable to make the distinction between national pride and rampant xenophobia. Many of those who misbehaved in Belgium were known

Belgian fans pose in front of the Atomium before the start of the first game of the Championship.

troublemakers whose names were on the files of the National Criminal Intelligence Service but who, through lack of adequate legislation, were allowed to make the short trip across the North Sea free and unhindered.

The British Government clearly failed in their duty to prevent these hooligans from travelling to the Low Countries and deserved the castigation which came their way, but, even so, there was genuine astonishment when UEFA, responding to a televised, stage-managed, seat-throwing scene of mayhem in Charleroi's main square, issued a threat to expel England from the competition if there were any further scenes of violence.

In the event, there was no need for them to transfer those words into deeds. England were beaten a couple of days later by Romania and went home early anyway.

Still, at least football made an encouraging start to the new century on the pitch. Euro 2000 was a delight. Let there be more of its kind in the future.

MIKE HAMMOND

EURO 2000 FINALS   Group A

Reputations ruined by perfect Portugal

Group A was difficult to call. Germany, the defending champions, and England had the history and the reputation, while Portugal and Romania, who had both come through the same qualifying group, appeared to have the better teams. Nobody gave the Germans much chance of defending the trophy they had won four years earlier. They were clearly a fading force, and with criticism weighing heavily on coach Erich Ribbeck and the players, the team's usual confidence appeared to have drained away. England, too, had their problems - an insipid qualifying

campaign and a manager, Kevin Keegan, who seemed ill-equipped tactically to cope at the highest level. Romania were an unknown quantity, with many of their veteran stars coming to the end of their days, while the ongoing concern for Portugal was whether their multi-talented team could be effective as well as exciting to watch.

Group A's opening matches took place on the third day of competition. First into action were Germany and Romania in Liège. It was not a great game. Strewn with unforced errors and untidy play, it ended in a 1-1 draw, which was just about the right result. It could have been much worse for the Germans. For the first 20 minutes they looked hopelessly disorganised in defence. The game was only five minutes old when Romania took the lead, Viorel Moldovan rifling the ball into the roof of the net from close range after Adrian Ilie had robbed Thomas Linke and rolled the ball invitingly across the box into his path. The German defence was there for the taking. The odd system they played, with veteran Lothar Matthäus operating in no man's land in front of two markers, bordered on the suicidal, allowing the Romanians to create one-on-one situations simply by hoisting balls over the midfield.

GROUP A MATCH DETAILS

12/06/2000, Liège
GERMANY 1 Scholl (20)
ROMANIA 1 Moldovan (5)
referee - Nielsen (DEN)
GERMANY - Kahn; Linke (Rehmer 46), Nowotny, Matthäus (Deisler 77); Babbel, Hässler (Hamann 73), Jeremies, Scholl, Ziege; Bierhoff, Rink.
ROMANIA - Stelea; Ciobotariu, Popescu, Filipescu, Chivu; Petrescu (Contra 69), Galca, Munteanu; Hagi (Mutu 75); Ilie, Moldovan (Lupescu 84).

12/06/2000, Eindhoven
PORTUGAL 3 Figo (22), João Pinto (38), Nuno Gomes (60)
ENGLAND 2 Scholes (3), McManaman (18)
referee - Frisk (SWE)
PORTUGAL - Vítor Baía; Abel Xavier, Jorge Costa, Fernando Couto, Dimas; Paulo Bento, Vidigal; Figo, Rui Costa (Beto 84), João Pinto (Sérgio Conceição 75); Nuno Gomes (Capucho 90).
ENGLAND - Seaman; Neville G., Adams (Keown 81), Campbell, Neville P.; Beckham, Ince, Scholes, McManaman (Wise 57); Shearer, Owen (Heskey 46).

17/06/2000, Arnhem
ROMANIA 0
PORTUGAL 1 Costinha (90)
referee - Veissière (FRA)
ROMANIA - Stelea; Contra, Popescu, Filipescu, Chivu; Petrescu (Petre 64), Galca, Munteanu; Hagi; Moldovan (Ganea 69), Ilie (Rosu 78).
PORTUGAL - Vítor Baía; Secretário, Fernando Couto, Jorge Costa, Dimas; Paulo Bento, Vidigal; Figo, Rui Costa (Costinha 87), João Pinto (Sérgio Conceição 56); Nuno Gomes (Sá Pinto 56).

17/06/2000, Charleroi
ENGLAND 1 Shearer (53)
GERMANY 0
referee - Collina (ITA)
ENGLAND - Seaman; Neville G., Keown, Campbell, Neville P.; Beckham, Ince, Scholes (Barmby 72), Wise; Shearer, Owen (Gerrard 61).
GERMANY - Kahn; Babbel, Matthäus, Nowotny; Deisler (Ballack 72), Hamann, Scholl, Jeremies (Bode 78); Ziege; Jancker, Kirsten (Rink 70).

20/06/2000, Charleroi
ENGLAND 2 Shearer (40p), Owen (45)
ROMANIA 3 Chivu (22), Munteanu (48), Ganea (88p)
referee - Meier (SUI)
ENGLAND - Martyn; Neville G., Keown, Campbell, Neville P.; Beckham, Ince, Scholes (Southgate 81), Wise (Barmby 75); Shearer, Owen (Heskey 67).
ROMANIA - Stelea; Contra, Popescu (Belodedici 32), Filipescu, Chivu; Petrescu, Galca (Rosu 68), Munteanu; Mutu; Moldovan, Ilie (Ganea 74).

20/06/2000, Rotterdam
PORTUGAL 3 Sérgio Conceição (35, 54, 71)
GERMANY 0
referee - Jol (HOL)
PORTUGAL - Pedro Espinha (Quim 89); Beto, Jorge Costa, Fernando Couto, Rui Jorge; Sérgio Conceção, Costinha, Paulo Sousa (Vidigal 71), Capucho; Pauleta (Nuno Gomes 66), Sá Pinto.
GERMANY - Kahn; Rehmer, Nowotny, Linke; Matthäus; Deisler, Ballack (Rink 46), Scholl (Hässler 59), Hamann; Bode, Jancker (Kirsten 69).

EURO 2000 FINALS   Group A

However, just when it seemed that the Germans might be turned over, they suddenly came back into the game. A patient build-up resulted in Mehmet Scholl gaining possession on the edge of the penalty area. His left-foot shot was true and precise, leaving Romanian goalkeeper Bogdan Stelea rooted to the spot.

Moldovan's early goal - which, in truth, he almost missed - did not fill him with confidence, and he somehow manufactured a glaring double miss midway through the second half. After that let-off the suspicion rose that the Germans might return to type by grabbing a late winner. Oliver Bierhoff was unfortunate to have a goal disallowed for offside, but that marginal decision counterbalanced Romania's earlier rejected penalty claim, when Ilie was clearly clipped in the area by Jens Nowotny.

The second match of the group, between Portugal and England in Eindhoven, proved to be far more spectator-friendly. Dramatic and unpredictable from first moment to last, it was won in thrilling fashion by the Portuguese, who, inspired by their two brilliant playmakers, Luís Figo and Rui Costa, recovered from an early two-goal deficit to take the game 3-2. England made a sensational start. Twice in the opening 18 minutes David Beckham was allowed space on the right flank to swing in his trademark crosses, and on each occasion the accuracy of his delivery was matched by that of the finish. Paul Scholes, England's hero in qualifying, headed in the first goal, and Steve McManaman, recent star of the Champions' League final, netted the second with an immaculately struck half-volley.

Despite England's lead, it was Portugal who had begun the game with the more impressive style and rhythm, and, sure enough, the deficit was rapidly halved when Figo was allowed to run at a retreating England defence and wallopped in an unstoppable, slightly deflected 25-yard shot into the top corner of England's net. Before an exhilarating first half was over, Portuguese managed to draw level. It was a goal of millimetric precision, a superb glancing header from João Pinto preceded by a perfectly delivered cross from Rui Costa,

The force was now with the Portuguese, whose gifted midfield technicians were causing the England defence untold problems, forcing them onto the back foot with their clever movement and one-touch passing. The third Portuguese goal was another example of craft and ingenuity getting the better of an overworked defence. Rui Costa, in sublime form, threaded a magnificent diagonal pass into the England penalty area and Nuno Gomes, reacting with more haste and urgency than Adams and David Seaman, nipped in first to clip the ball home for his first international goal.

England's Paul Ince is tackled by Germany's Ulf Kirsten.

England did not give up. Scholes continued to pose a threat up front, and one of his efforts would probably have entered the net had it not struck Alan Shearer on the way. But Portugal were not to be denied and they successfully held on for a magnificent victory.

More of the same was expected from Humberto Coelho's thrill-seekers when they faced Romania in Arnhem five days later. But it proved to be a featureless match which Portugal were lucky to win thanks to a goal in the fourth minute of stoppage-time when substitute midfielder Costinha rose in a crowded area to head home a Figo free-kick.

Portugal might have opened the scoring much earlier but for two awful offside decisions which deprived Nuno Gomes and João Pinto after they had been put clean through by Rui Costa. The closest Romania came to scoring was with a late thunderbolt from Gheorghe Hagi. The Romanian skipper had earlier picked up his second yellow card of the tournament and thus had to sit out the final group game against England.

The England v Germany match in Charleroi had been preceded by endless hype and also, unfortunately, the predicted violence between rival fans, both in Charleroi and in Brussels. England were seeking revenge for their heartbreaking semi-final penalty shoot-out defeat at Euro '96, but for the first half-hour it was Germany who ran the game, with England looking all at sea. It was only the lack of forward thrust - with skipper Bierhoff missing after injuring a calf in training - that prevented the Germans from going ahead, but after 35 minutes, with their first chance of the game, England almost drew first blood when a Michael Owen header was turned onto the post by Oliver Kahn.

Early in the second half England did go ahead. Once again the provider was Beckham. His clever outswinging

EURO 2000 FINALS   Group A

Portugal's Paulo Bento gets the ball away from Romania's Gheorghe Hagi.

free-kick found its way through a host of bodies to Alan Shearer, who, left in space, showed admirable technique to meet the bouncing ball with a stooping header which flew past Kahn into the net. That was to be the end of England as an attacking force. For the rest of the game, whether by accident or design, they were camped in retreat in their own half. Germany wasted three clear chances, the worst of them when Carsten Jancker snatched at his shot from eight yards out and screwed it wide. England defended with more conviction after that, but it was real backs-to-the-wall stuff, the pressure on the defence intensifying because of the team's inability to hold onto the ball for any meaningful length of time.

The tension was unrelenting, but when the final whistle came, it brought massive relief and much celebration for the England players and their fans. It had been 34 years since the last competitive victory over Germany. But the truth was that England had won playing poorly - and against a team that, while unfortunate to lose, were a pale shadow of the illustrious German sides of the past.

Germany's decline was confirmed in their final match when a second-string Portuguese XI destroyed them 3-0 in Rotterdam. With Portugal already confirmed as group winners and Germany still in with a chance - albeit a slim one - of reaching the quarter-finals, there was every incentive for Erich Ribbeck's team to go for broke. Instead they capitulated. Portugal, having rested Figo, Rui Costa and several others, found a new midfield star in Sérgio Conceição, who helped himself to a hat-trick as Germany slithered towards a catastrophic 3-0 defeat.

The battle for the runners-up spot was therefore decided by the England v Romania game in Charleroi. The odds seemed to be stacked in England's favour. They needed only a draw to go through. They had already played in Charleroi. They had beaten Germany at last. And Romania were without their suspended skipper Hagi. But, as against the Germans, Keegan's team began dreadfully. Romania were completely on top as England once more found themselves incapable of retaining possession under pressure. Romania deserved to go ahead, but it was a fluke goal which allowed them to do so, full-back Christian Chivu's intended cross to the back post spinning into the net beyond England 'keeper Nigel Martyn.

Romania created further chances but just before half-time England scored not one but two goals to take a thoroughly ill-deserved half-time lead. Shearer scored the first of them from the penalty spot, after Paul Ince had been fouled, and Michael Owen beat the offside trap and the advancing 'keeper to slot home the second.

England had 15 minutes to digest their good fortune and make plans for an improved performance in the second half. But the cardinal sins continued, the first enabling Romania to grab a quick equaliser when a catalogue of defensive errors presented Dorinel Munteanu with the chance to score from the edge of the area. After that England resorted to the modus operandi that had carried them through the game against Germany. It was ghastly to watch but it nearly worked. Keegan's men were just two minutes away from getting the draw they needed when full-back Phil Neville attempted a foolish tackle in the area on Moldovan and got it horribly wrong, taking both of the Romania striker's legs instead of the ball.

It was the break Romania deserved, and Ioan Viorel Ganea showed nerves of steel to step up and slot the ball into the corner of the net. It gave Romania their first-ever European Championship victory and put them into the quarter-finals. For England, it spelt utter humiliation. Like the Germans, they were going home early, with only rage and vilification to greet them on their return.

		Pd	W	D	L	F	A	Pt	GD
GROUP A FINAL TABLE									
1	Portugal	3	3	0	0	7	2	9	5
2	Romania	3	1	1	1	4	4	4	0
3	England	3	1	0	2	5	6	3	-1
4	Germany	3	0	1	2	1	5	1	-4

TOP SCORERS
3   SÉRGIO CONCEIÇÃO (Portugal)
2   Alan SHEARER (England)

EURO 2000 FINALS

Group B

Co-hosts Belgium bite the dust

Group B was headed by joint-hosts Belgium, but the strongest team in the section was undoubtedly Italy. Despite a troubled build-up, during which they had actually lost at home to the Belgians, the 'Azzurri' were fortunate to find themselves in a relatively hazard-free first-round group.

None of Belgium, Sweden or Turkey had pretensions beyond reaching the quarter-finals. While the Belgians had made considerable improvements during the ten-month reign of new coach Robert Waseige, they still lacked genuine star quality. The Swedes, despite a near-flawless

qualifying campaign, were missing several key players through injury. And the Turks, though buoyed by Galatasaray's unexpected UEFA Cup victory, were still relative novices in major tournament football.

Initially it looked as if the outcome of the opening match, between Belgium and Sweden in Brussels, might well determine which of those two countries would go through to the next round with Italy. As tournament openers go, Euro 2000's was certainly up there among the best. Preceded by a pleasantly brief, no-nonsense Opening Ceremony, Belgium v Sweden turned out to be a game rich in entertainment and packed with incident - if not exactly overflowing with exceptional quality.

The Swedes manufactured a shot on target after barely 13 seconds, and the man who struck it, Kennet Andersson, came even closer to scoring a few minutes later when he headed just wide from a corner. The match began with a bright tempo and that was maintained throughout the first half, during which the Belgians gradually came into the picture, with right-winger Gert Verheyen invariably at

GROUP B MATCH DETAILS

10/06/2000, Brussels
BELGIUM 2 Goor (42), Mpenza E. (46)
SWEDEN 1 Mjällby (53)
referee - Merk (GER)
BELGIUM - De Wilde; Deflandre, Valgaeren, Staelens, Léonard (Van Kerckhoven 73); Verheyen (Peeters 88), Vanderhaeghe, Wilmots, Goor; Strupar (Nilis 69), Mpenza E..
SWEDEN - Hedman; Nilsson (Lucic 46), Björklund, Andersson P., Mellberg; Alexandersson, Mjällby, Andersson D. (Osmanovski 70), Ljungberg; Andersson K., Pettersson (Larsson 50).

11/06/2000, Arnhem
TURKEY 1 Okan (61)
ITALY 2 Conte (52), Inzaghi (70p)
referee - Dallas (SCO)
TURKEY - Rüstü; Alpay, Ogün, Fatih; Ümit (Tugay 76), Sergen (Arif 81), Tayfun, Tayfur, Okan (Ergün 66), Abdullah; Hakan Sükür.
ITALY - Toldo; Nesta, Cannavaro, Maldini; Zambrotta, Albertini, Conte, Pessotto (Iuliano 61); Fiore (Del Piero 74); Totti (Di Livio 82), Inzaghi.

14/06/2000, Brussels
ITALY 2 Totti (6), Fiore (66)
BELGIUM 0
referee - García Aranda (ESP)
ITALY - Toldo; Cannavaro, Nesta, Iuliano; Zambrotta, Conte, Albertini, Fiore (Ambrosini 83), Maldini; Inzaghi (Delvecchio 77), Totti (Del Piero 64).
BELGIUM - De Wilde; Deflandre, Valgaeren, Staelens, Van Kerckhoven (Hendrikx 44); Verheyen (Mpenza M. 67), Wilmots, Vanderhaeghe, Goor; Strupar (Nilis 57), Mpenza E..

15/06/2000, Eindhoven
SWEDEN 0
TURKEY 0
referee - Jol (HOL)
SWEDEN - Hedman; Lucic, Mellberg, Björklund, Sundgren; Mild, Mjällby, Ljungberg, Alexandersson (Andersson A. 62); Andersson K. (Pettersson 46), Larsson (Svensson 78).
TURKEY - Rüstü; Fatih, Ogün (Tugay 59), Alpay; Ümit (Tayfun 44), Izzet (Sergen 57), Suat, Okan, Hakan Ünsal; Arif, Hakan Sükür.

19/06/2000, Brussels
TURKEY 2 Hakan Sükür (45, 70)
BELGIUM 0
referee - Nielsen (DEN)
TURKEY - Rüstü; Fatih, Ogün, Alpay; Tayfun, Okan (Ergün 77), Tugay (Tayfur 37), Suat, Abdullah; Hakan Sükür, Arif (Osman 87).
BELGIUM - De Wilde; Deflandre, Staelens, Valgaeren, Van Kerckhoven; Verheyen (Strupar 63), Vanderhaeghe, Wilmots, Goor (Hendrikx 58); Nilis (De Bilde 76), Mpenza E..

19/06/2000, Eindhoven
ITALY 2 Di Biagio (39), Del Piero (88)
SWEDEN 1 Larsson (77)
referee - Melo Perreira (POR)
ITALY - Toldo; Ferrara, Iuliano (Cannavaro 50), Maldini (Nesta 42); Negro, Di Livio (Fiore 64), Di Biagio, Ambrosini, Pessotto; Montella, Del Piero.
SWEDEN - Hedman; Mellberg, Andersson P., Björklund, Gustafsson (Andersson K. 75); Mild, Mjällby (Andersson D. 56), Ljungberg, Svensson (Alexandersson 52); Larsson, Osmanovski.

EURO 2000 FINALS   Group B

Belgium's Lorenzo Staelens (left) goes in high on Sweden's Kennet Andersson.

the source of their most threatening moves. The Swedish defence, so assured during the qualifying competition, seemed slow and ponderous, and two minutes before half-time a glaring error by veteran right-back Roland Nilsson allowed Belgium's left-wing raider Bart Goor to race goalwards and beat Magnus Hedman with a precise left-foot finish.

1-0 became 2-0 in the first minute after the interval. It was a contentious goal. Although there was nothing wrong with Emile Mpenza's explosive finish - a rising right-foot drive that zoomed past the helpless Hedman - it did appear that he controlled the ball with his left arm before letting fly. If there was any sense of injustice, however, that was cancelled out later in the half when Belgian skipper Lorenzo Staelens had a perfectly good goal ruled out for a non-existent foul on the 'keeper.

By that stage Sweden were back in the game. In a match of many defensive deficiencies, the biggest error of all belonged to Belgian 'keeper Filip De Wilde, who clumsily stood on the ball while attempting to field a back-pass and presented Johan Mjällby with a gift of a goal that allowed the Swedes an unexpected escape route back into the contest. To De Wilde's credit, he did redeem himself soon afterwards with a fine save from Fredrik Ljungberg and then again in the closing minutes when he tipped over a Mjällby header. On the balance of play, though, it was Belgium who should have added to their total. Following Patrik Andersson's 81st-minute red card - his punishment for two over-the-top sliding tackles - the home side created a plethora of chances, but they failed to convert one of them. That led to a tense climax in what had generally been a fine game, sensibly refereed, for the most part, by German Markus Merk.

A poor refereeing decision, however, was to determine the outcome of Group B's second encounter, between Turkey and Italy in Arnhem. The two teams were level at 1-1 when, with 20 minutes to go, Scottish official Hugh Dallas gifted the Italians a penalty. Ogün's gentle shoulder-brush with Filippo Inzaghi was sufficient to send the Italian striker sprawling to the turf. It was an exaggerated fall but the referee was taken in by it, and, to heighten the injustice, Inzaghi himself stepped up to convert the spot-kick.

Although the manner of their defeat was difficult to take, Turkey did not really deserve anything from the game. They defended well, with centre-back Alpay a prominent figure, but were negligible as an attacking force. They fought their way back into the match bravely following Antonio Conte's spectacular overhead kick, but Okan's headed equaliser came from a rare foray forward, and for almost the whole of the second half the 'Azzurri' laid siege to their goal. After the penalty the Italians had ample opportunity to kill the Turks off and would have done so but for the frame of the goal and Inzaghi's wasteful finishing.

Still, a win was a win, and in Italy's second game, against Belgium in Brussels, it took them only six minutes to get off the mark. Francesco Totti, still preferred to Alessandro Del Piero despite the latter's excellent cameo performance against Turkey, headed the Italians in front from Demetrio Albertini's free-kick, and the pattern for the match was set. It might have been different had Goor's superb left-foot drive moments later not been tipped onto the bar by Francesco Toldo. But, once ahead, the Italians were free to indulge in their favourite brand of absorb-and-counter football, with their defence and midfield ranged barrier-like across the pitch and their attack only coming into life on the break.

Belgium enjoyed the lion's share of possession and they also created openings, but Toldo was superb in the Italian goal, making two excellent saves at full stretch to deny Staelens and Luc Nilis before Italy extended their advantage with a sumptuous second goal, scored by midfielder Stefano Fiore with a curling right-foot shot after a neat one-two with Inzaghi. The Italians should have had a third goal after a mix-up in the Belgian defence resulted in Joos Valgaeren heading the ball into his own net, but the Spanish referee showed pity by cancelling it out for a barely noticeable shove by substitute Marco Delvecchio.

Although their team were defeated, the Belgian fans showed very little sign of discontent at the final whistle. In the image of their best player, Marc Wilmots, Belgium worked hard enough but just didn't possess the skill or the cunning to find a way through the well-staffed and well marshalled Italian defence.

The co-hosts' chances of reaching the quarter-finals

EURO 2000 FINALS

Group B

Italy's Stefano Fiore (left) tries to flick the ball over Turkey's Alpay Özalan.

were boosted 24 hours later when Sweden and Turkey played out a stultifying goalless draw in Eindhoven. It was a thoroughly depressing match, devoid of any structure, substance or style. Neither team deserved to win, and the only positive thing about the game was the result, which increased the probability of both teams departing early. Apart from Kennet Andersson's powerful third-minute free-kick, brilliantly saved by Turkish 'keeper Rüstü, the entertainment value was virtually nil. It was a brutal game, too, with Dutch referee Dick Jol showing far too much lenience. Turkey's Suat - a persistent fowler - and Sweden's Mjällby - who nearly broke Turkish débutant Muzzy Izzet's ankle with one horrific challenge - should both have been red-carded.

The draw meant not only that Italy were through to the last eight but that Sweden and Turkey both still had a chance of joining them. The ball, however, was very much in Belgium's court. If they drew at home to Turkey in their final game, then, irrespective of the Italy v Sweden result, they would be through to the quarter-finals.

It did not seem like a difficult task. Judged on the first two matches, Belgium were a far better side than Turkey. But on the night when they had to prove as much, Robert Waseige's team were found wanting. Above all, it was another case of missed chances. As with their previous two performances, the Belgians were determined to make the running, and did so in some style. But when it came to delivering the final blow, they lacked the necessary coolness and concentration.

Worse still, Turkey made them pay. Not once, but twice. With the first half in stoppage time, a high ball was hoisted into the Belgian penalty area. There seemed to be no apparent danger, but as goalkeeper De Wilde rose to collect it, his hands were beaten to the ball by Hakan

Sükür's head, which directed it into the empty net. With the initiative lost, Belgium threw everything at the Turks in the second half. Initially they created some decent chances, the best of them when Mpenza, set up by Nilis's perfect cross, sent a bullet header straight at the impressive Rüstü. But as the half went on, the Belgians became all too desperate. They left holes at the back and on 70 minutes Turkey broke clear into their half, Suat squaring the ball for Hakan to blast the ball home with his left foot and give his team a seemingly unassailable lead.

Belgium came again but the Turkish rearguard stood solid and firm, getting in vital blocks, tackles and headers to intensify the frustration of their increasingly desperate opponents. Gradually Belgium's efforts dwindled to nothing, and when De Wilde was sent off after a dreadful challenge on Arif, forcing defender Eric Deflandre to take over in goal, the Belgians had nothing left to offer except fading hope. Their fate was sealed, and they had become the first European Championship hosts ever to be eliminated in the first round.

As for Turkey, their delight at winning a match for the first time in a major tournament was significantly enhanced by the news that Sweden had simultaneously lost 2-1 to Italy in the other game.

While Turkey, against all odds, had reached the last eight, the Swedes were left to reflect on a tournament of woeful underachievement. Even a deliberately under-strength Italy were too good for them, although they had chances aplenty to reverse the scoreline, notably when Fredrik Ljungberg missed a sitter in the first half and Patrik Andersson was denied at close range by Toldo's brilliant save. The best moment of the match was Italy's winning goal from Alessandro Del Piero - a wonderful solo effort from the Juventus striker that not only maintained his team's's 100 per cent record but also provided Italy coach Dino Zoff with a major selection dilemma for the quarter-final to come...

		Pd	W	D	L	F	A	Pt	GD
1	Italy	3	3	0	0	6	2	9	4
2	Turkey	3	1	1	1	3	2	4	1
3	Belgium	3	1	0	2	2	5	3	-3
4	Sweden	3	0	1	2	2	4	1	-2

GROUP B FINAL TABLE

TOP SCORER
2   HAKAN Sükür (Turkey)

EURO 2000 FINALS   Group C

Positions undecided until final kick

Spain, so strong and convincing in the qualifying competition, had good reason to feel happy with their first-round draw. The only team actually seeded on merit (Germany were the defending champions, Holland and Belgium the co-hosts), Spain found themselves grouped with two European Championship débutants - Norway and Slovenia - and another team - Yugoslavia - which had not participated in the finals since 1984.

Nevertheless, all three opponents had proved their worth during the qualifying competition. Norway, like Spain, had run away with their group, winning every one of their away fixtures; Yugoslavia had finished on top of a section including Croatia and the Republic of Ireland; and Slovenia had caused a major sensation in defeating Ukraine over two legs in the play-offs.

Spain's first assignment was against Norway in Rotterdam. José Camacho's team were expected to make their superior talent count, but against a strong and committed Norwegian defence they encountered major problems. Right from the opening minutes it was obvious that the Norwegians' priority was to sit back and soak up the pressure. But Spain's response was so limp and uninspired that the first clear chance actually belonged to Norway, with Ole Gunnar Solskjaer being foiled only by the crossbar as he glanced on full-back André Bergdølmo's cross. Urzaiz and Raúl had chances at the other end but by half-time the game was still goalless and in need of a lift.

GROUP C MATCH DETAILS

13/06/2000, Rotterdam
SPAIN 0
NORWAY 1 Iversen (66)
referee - El Ghandour (EGY)
SPAIN - Molina; Míchel Salgado, Hierro, Paco, Aranzábal; Etxeberria (Alfonso 71), Guardiola, Valerón (Helguera 79), Fran (Mendieta 71); Urzaiz, Raúl.
NORWAY - Myhre; Heggem, Berg (Eggen 59), Bragstad, Bergdølmo; Iversen (Riseth 90), Bakke, Skammelsrud, Mykland, Solskjaer; Flo (Carew 70).

13/06/2000, Charleroi
YUGOSLAVIA 3 Milosevic (67, 73), Drulovic (70)
SLOVENIA 3 Zahovic (23, 57), Pavlin (52)
referee - Melo Perreira (POR)
YUGOSLAVIA - Kralj; Dudic, Djukic, Mihajlovic, Nadj; Stankovic D. (Stojkovic 36), Jokanovic, Jugovic, Drulovic; Kovacevic (Milosevic 52), Mijatovic (Kezman 83).
SLOVENIA - Dabanovic; Milanic, Galic, Milinovic; Novak, Ceh, Pavlin (Pavlovic 74), Karic (Osterc 78); Zahovic, Rudonja; Udovic (Acimovic 64).

18/06/2000, Amsterdam
SLOVENIA 1 Zahovic (59)
SPAIN 2 Raúl (4), Etxeberria (60)
referee - Merk (GER)
SLOVENIA - Dabanovic; Milanic (Knavs 68), Galic, Milinovic; Novak, Ceh, Pavlin (Acimovic 82), Karic; Zahovic, Rudonja; Udovic (Osterc 46).
SPAIN - Cañizares; Míchel Salgado, Hierro, Abelardo, Aranzábal; Etxeberria, Valerón (Engonga 88), Guardiola (Helguera 80), Mendieta; Raúl, Alfonso (Urzaiz 70).

18/06/2000, Liège
NORWAY 0
YUGOSLAVIA 1 Milosevic (7)
referee - Dallas (SCO)
NORWAY - Myhre; Heggem (Bjørnebye 35), Eggen, Bragstad, Bergdølmo; Iversen (Carew 71), Bakke (Strand 76), Skammelsrud, Mykland, Solskjaer; Flo.
YUGOSLAVIA - Kralj; Komljenovic, Saveljic, Djukic, Djorovic; Stojkovic (Nadj 83), Jokanovic (Govedarica 86), Jugovic, Drulovic; Mijatovic (Kezman 85), Milosevic.

21/06/2000, Bruges
YUGOSLAVIA 3 Milosevic (32), Govedarica (51), Komljenovic (76)
SPAIN 4 Alfonso (38, 90), Munitis (51), Mendieta (90p)
referee - Veissière (FRA)
YUGOSLAVIA - Kralj; Komljenovic, Djukic, Mihajlovic, Djorovic (Stankovic J. 15); Stojkovic (Saveljic 68), Jokanovic, Jugovic (Govedarica 46), Drulovic; Milosevic, Mijatovic.
SPAIN - Cañizares; Míchel Salgado (Munitis 46), Abelardo, Paco (Urzaiz 64), Sergi; Mendieta, Guardiola, Helguera, Fran (Etxeberria 22); Raúl, Alfonso.

21/06/2000, Arnhem
SLOVENIA 0
NORWAY 0
referee - Poll (ENG)
SLOVENIA - Dabanovic; Milinovic, Galic (Acimovic 83), Knavs; Novak, Ceh, Pavlin, Karic; Zahovic, Rudonja; Siljak (Osterc 86).
NORWAY - Myhre; Bergdølmo, Eggen, Bragstad, Bjørnebye; Carew (Bakke 61); Strand 82), Iversen, Solbakken, Mykland, Solskjaer; Flo.

EURO 2000 FINALS   Group C

When the tedium was finally broken by a goal, midway through the second half, surprisingly it was Norway who scored it. Unsurprisingly, however, it came about as a result of route-one football, with goalkeeper Thomas Myhre's long punt being met in the opposing penalty area by the head of Steffen Iversen, who redirected the ball into the empty net after Spain's goalkeeper Molina had senselessly come out to intercept. Having gone in front, Norway worked even more tirelessly to cling onto their advantage. Again, Spain offered little in reply, although their cause was belatedly assisted by Alfonso and Mendieta, who at last brought a touch of subtlety to the attack after their introduction as substitutes. The Norwegian defence came under severe pressure in the last ten minutes, but, led by goalkeeper Myhre, centre-back Bjørn Otto Bragstad and midfielder Erik Mykland, the underdogs held on for a famous win.

If the fare in Rotterdam was generally unappetising, the lingering disappointment was swiftly erased a few hours later by a quite remarkable match in Charleroi between Yugoslavia and Slovenia. With an hour gone, the unheralded Slovenians, amazingly, were 3-0 up and about to register one of the greatest upsets in European Championship history. But then the Yugoslavs went down to ten men and, equally amazingly, came back to score three goals in six minutes to complete one of the competition's greatest-ever comebacks. By the end Slovenia were clinging on by their fingernails to the draw but still came close to staging a dramatic finale when an effort from defender Zeljko Milinovic was cleared off the line in the final minute.

Slovenia's collapse was totally unexpected because until their opponents were reduced to ten men following Sinisa Mihajlovic's idiotic dismissal, Srecko Katanec's team played quite wonderfully. Zlatko Zahovic carried on where he had left off in the qualifying tournament, scoring two goals and providing the assist for another. His opening header was exquisitely placed, and he showed admirable composure in converting his second goal after intercepting Mihajlovic's suicidal crossfield pass. It was his well flighted free-kick that led to Slovenia's other goal, expertly headed in by the team's other skilful left-footed midfielder, Miran Pavlin.

For two thirds of the match the Slovenians worked tremendously hard and passed the ball beautifully, but it only took a few minutes for their world to fall apart. Yugoslavia's first shot in anger, from left-winger Ljubinko Drulovic after 66 minutes, suddenly stunned them back into life, and incredibly their next three attacks all produced goals – two tap-ins from substitute Savo Milosevic sandwiching a firmly-struck left-footer from Drulovic.

Going into their second match, against Slovenia in Amsterdam, seeds Spain were stuck at the bottom of the group. Prior to the tournament this looked to be the most one-sided encounter of the first round, but Slovenia's 'finest hour' against Yugoslavia and Spain's woeful efforts against Norway had led to a significant re-evaluation of the pre-match odds.

Spain were given the perfect start when their first attack brought a goal, Raúl lifting a beautiful left-foot shot into the top corner after full-back Míchel Salgado's run had been blocked. Liberated by this early breakthrough, Spain were able to control the match, and although the style of their play was less than captivating, they appeared to have the measure of the Slovenians throughout. Even when Slovenia, on a rare counter-attack, scored an equaliser, bundled home by Zahovic from Mladen Rudonja's cross, the Spaniards drove immediately downfield and retook the lead. The architect of the goal was Gaizka Mendieta, whose magnificent run and pass took out as many as five Slovenian defenders, enabling Joseba Etxeberria to rifle the ball past Mladen Dabanovic at the near post and restore an advantage that Spain held - albeit with the odd scare - through to the final whistle.

Yugoslavia's match with Norway in Liège was decided by a freak early goal from Savo Milosevic, now on at the start after his match-saving performance against Slovenia. The big striker managed to get a slight deflection onto Drulovic's inswinging free-kick and give his team an early advantage that they never surrendered.

That quickfire goal should have enticed the Norwegians out of their customary shell, but they never looked comfortable chasing the game. In truth, it would not have flattered the Yugoslavs had they added to their margin of victory. Inspired by their veteran skipper Dragan Stojkovic, Yugoslavia pieced together some tantalising moves, but there was also a hard and unappealing edge to their play. There seemed to be ill feeling between the two sets of players from the start, and referee Hugh Dallas had his patience tested on a number of occasions before he finally produced the red card, the unfortunate victim being substitute Mateja Kezman, who had barely been on the pitch for a minute before he received his marching orders after a reckless lunge on Norway's best player, Erik Mykland. Yugoslavia almost paid for the reduction in their number when in the final minute John Carew was sent clean through by Solskjaer, but the young striker put Norway's best chance of the game wide of the goal.

With a draw and a victory, Yugoslavia were on top of the group and requiring just a draw against Spain in their final game to accede to the quarter-finals. All four teams

EURO 2000 FINALS   Group C

Yugoslavia's Sinisa Mihajlovic (right) and Spain's Alfonso battle for the ball.

still had a chance of progress, with Norway and Spain also having their fate in their own hands. A victory for each of them would ensure further progress. Slovenia, on the other hand, could only make it through if they and Spain both won.

The stage was set. The permutations and possibilities were endless, but generally each of the four teams knew what they had to do. It was a case of who dares, wins, but against Slovenia the Norwegians refused to alter their habits and press for the victory that would have guaranteed their safe passage, and that, ultimately, was to end their interest in the competition - even though, 99 times out of 100, their calculated gamble of going for a draw would have paid off.

The Norwegians were undone by a quite sensational climax to the match in Bruges between Yugoslavia and Spain. 2-3 down and seemingly dead and buried as the game entered its third minute of injury time, Spain incredibly came back to win 4-3 and steal a place in the quarter-finals as group winners.

There could be no denying that the group favourites never gave up in their quest to reach the next round - they had, after all, twice come from behind earlier in the match - but it was certainly a stroke of luck that enabled them to get their third equaliser, in the 93rd minute. Defender Abelardo fell to the deck virtually unchallenged as he tried to meet Raúl's chip, but French referee Gilles Veissière ruled that he had been fouled and pointed to the penalty spot. Mendieta rolled the spot-kick home, and suddenly everything was up for grabs again.

With 95 minutes on the clock Spain flung the ball into the area one last time. Amidst a crowd of bodies the ball

fortuitously dropped to a player in space, and Alfonso, with one swing of his white boot, drilled the ball low into the corner of the Yugoslav net. It was a brilliant strike, a goal worthy of winning such an epic match, but while it was received with joyous pandemonium among the Spanish players and fans, the Yugoslav supporters, who had seen their team play splendidly for most of the game, scoring three fine goals through Milosevic (again), Dejan Govedarica and Slobodan Komljenovic, were seething with anger.

The target of their wrath was the referee, who, aside from awarding Spain their controversial penalty and adding on those crucial minutes of stoppage time, had also earlier sent off Slavisa Jokanovic - Yugoslavia's third red-card victim in as many games. One particularly enraged Yugoslav follower ran onto the pitch with the obvious intention of assaulting the French official before being restrained by matchwinner Alfonso, and another hurled a coin which hit M. Veissière just above the eye.

These scenes, though despicable, did prove one thing: that Yugoslavia and Spain had not been guilty of collusion at Norway's expense. For the fact was that both Spain and Yugoslavia were still in the competition, whereas Norway were on their way home.

The Norwegians' game with Slovenia had already finished, at 0-0, when the humdinger in Bruges entered its 91st minute. Norway felt comfortable in the knowledge that anything other than a Spanish win would see them through...but then came the dramatic dénouement that ultimately left them distraught.

The universal feeling among neutrals, however, was that the two best teams had gone through. Spain and Yugoslavia had between them produced the game of the tournament - a seven-goal thriller that would go down in European Championship legend.

		Pd	W	D	L	F	A	Pt	GD
GROUP C FINAL TABLE									
1	Spain	3	2	0	1	6	5	6	1
2	Yugoslavia	3	1	1	1	7	7	4	0
3	Norway	3	1	1	1	1	1	4	0
4	Slovenia	3	0	2	1	4	5	2	-1

TOP SCORERS
4   Savo MILOSEVIC (Yugoslavia)
3   Zlatko ZAHOVIC (Slovenia)
2   ALFONSO Pérez (Spain)

EURO 2000 FINALS

Group D

No problems for Holland and France

No major tournament would be complete without its Group of Death, and Group D, containing four previous winners, was chosen to bear the title. Whether it merited the billing was debatable, given that France, the world champions, and Holland, the co-hosts, were the clear favourites to qualify at the expense of Denmark and the Czechs.

The Czechs were highly rated because of their perfect record during the qualifying competition, whereas Denmark had ensured their place at the finals with victories in each of their last six qualifying matches. But as France and Holland were generally fancied not only to qualify for the quarter-finals but also to contest the final, there seemed little hope at the outset for the two outsiders.

France hit the ground running with an impressive opening win against Denmark. Although the World Cup winners began edgily, with goalkeeper Fabien Barthez being forced into emergency action twice in the first 12 minutes, they soon settled down and went on to play with supreme confidence, demolishing their opponents with slick interplay in midfield and exceptional speed and movement up front.

At the heart of France's performance was the masterful Zinedine Zidane. Always inventive, always unpredictable, always involved, he bestrode the match with his unique talent, protecting and passing the ball like no other and effectively carrying on where he had left off in his last big match for France - the 1998 World Cup final.

It was France's major absentee from that final, Laurent Blanc, who got his team's Euro 2000 campaign up and running when he scored after 16 minutes, sidefooting the ball into an empty net after Nicolas Anelka had used his pace to cause problems for Peter Schmeichel. The French did not create many more clear chances in the first half but after the break they broke loose and gave the Danish defence persistent problems. Thierry Henry missed one straightforward chance but made up for it soon after when,

GROUP D MATCH DETAILS

11/06/2000, Bruges
FRANCE 3 Blanc (16), Henry (65), Wiltord (90)
DENMARK 0
referee - Benkö (AUT)
FRANCE - Barthez; Thuram, Blanc, Desailly, Lizarazu; Djorkaeff (Vieira 58), Deschamps, Petit; Zidane; Anelka (Wiltord 82), Henry.
DENMARK - Schmeichel; Colding, Henriksen, Schjønberg, Heintze; Bisgaard (Jørgensen 72), Nielsen A., Tøfting (Gravesen 72), Grønkjaer; Sand, Tomasson (Beck 79).

11/06/2000, Amsterdam
HOLLAND 1 De Boer F. (89p)
CZECH REPUBLIC 0
referee - Collina (ITA)
HOLLAND - Van der Sar; Reiziger, Stam (Konterman 74), De Boer F., Van Bronckhorst; Seedorf (De Boer R. 57), Cocu, Davids, Zenden (Overmars 78); Bergkamp, Kluivert.
CZECH REPUBLIC - Srnicek; Latal (Bejbl 69), Repka, Rada, Gabriel; Poborsky, Nedved (Lokvenc 90), Nemec, Rosicky, Smicer (Kuka 83); Koller.

16/06/2000, Bruges
CZECH REPUBLIC 1 Poborsky (35p)
FRANCE 2 Henry (7), Djorkaeff (60)
referee - Poll (ENG)
CZECH REPUBLIC - Srnicek; Repka, Rada, Gabriel (Fukal 46); Nedved, Bejbl (Lokvenc 50), Rosicky (Jankulovski 62), Nemec; Smicer, Koller.
FRANCE - Barthez; Thuram, Blanc, Desailly, Candela; Vieira, Deschamps, Petit (Djorkaeff 46); Zidane; Henry (Wiltord 90), Anelka (Dugarry 54).

16/06/2000, Rotterdam
DENMARK 0
HOLLAND 3 Kluivert (57), De Boer R. (66), Zenden (77)
referee - Meier (SUI)
DENMARK - Schmeichel; Colding, Henriksen, Schjønberg (Helveg 82), Heintze; Bisgaard, Nielsen A. (Tøfting 61), Gravesen (Nielsen B.S. 67), Grønkjaer; Sand, Tomasson.
HOLLAND - Van der Sar (Westerveld 89); Reiziger, Konterman, De Boer F., Van Bronckhorst; Zenden, Cocu, Davids, Overmars (De Boer R. 61); Bergkamp (Winter 76), Kluivert.

21/06/2000, Amsterdam
FRANCE 2 Dugarry (8), Trezeguet (30)
HOLLAND 3 Kluivert (14), De Boer F. (51), Zenden (59)
referee - Frisk (SWE)
FRANCE - Lama; Karembeu, Leboeuf, Desailly, Candela; Dugarry (Djorkaeff 68), Vieira (Deschamps 90), Micoud, Pires; Trezeguet, Wiltord (Anelka 80).
HOLLAND - Westerveld; Bosvelt, Stam, De Boer F., Numan; Overmars (Van Vossen 89), Cocu, Davids, Zenden; Bergkamp (Winter 78), Kluivert (Makaay 60).

21/06/2000, Liège
DENMARK 0
CZECH REPUBLIC 2 Smicer (64, 67)
referee - El Ghandour (EGY)
DENMARK - Schmeichel; Helveg, Henriksen, Schjønberg, Heintze (Colding 68); Goldbaek, Tøfting, Nielsen B.S., Grønkjaer; Tomasson, Beck (Molnar 74).
CZECH REPUBLIC - Srnicek; Fukal, Rada, Repka; Poborsky, Nedved, Bejbl (Jankulovski 61), Berger, Nemec; Koller (Kuka 73), Smicer (Lokvenc 78).

EURO 2000 FINALS   Group D

Holland's Edgar Davids (right) is challenged by the Czech Republic's Radoslav Latal.

set free by Zidane, he sprinted half the length of the field before tucking the ball past Schmeichel with a precise finish. That was the end of the contest but not the end of France's commitment to attack, and in the second minute of stoppage time they grabbed a deserved third goal, one that should probably have been disallowed as goalscorer Sylvain Wiltord had been offside in the build-up

The French had been a joy to watch and their opening display certainly threw down the.gauntlet to the Dutch, who went into battle later that evening against the Czech Republic in Amsterdam.

But while the French were formidable, the Dutch were to play disastrously, the only sweetener being the fact that they actually won the game. How they did so will forever remain a mystery, because they were a clear second best to a Czech Republic side which produced a team performance superior to anything they had managed in becoming Europe's vice-champions four years earlier.

Winning football matches, however, can often dependent more on luck than judgment, and this was very much a case in point. Holland, who created barely a notable goalscoring chance all evening, were handed victory one minute from time when Italian referee Pierluigi Collina, supposedly one of the world's best officials, fell for the oldest trick in the book and gifted them a penalty. Technically, perhaps, Collina felt justified in pointing to the spot after Czech skipper Jiri Nemec gave a slight tug to Ronald de Boer's shirt. But the Dutchman's theatrical leap into the air was a deliberate attempt to dupe the official. He knew he couldn't reach Marc Overmars' cross so threw himself to the ground instead. Collina took the bait and Ronald's brother Frank whacked in the penalty. 1-0 to Holland.

Sympathy for the Czechs was overwhelming but they

also deserved huge applause. Coach Jozef Chovanec's game plan was so nearly perfect. In the first half his ploy was to squeeze the confidence out of the Dutch by pulling everybody back and cutting off their supply lines. It worked a treat, because as soon as the second half started the Czechs, having lulled their opponents into a false sense of security, went in for the kill. Holland did not know what had hit them but they somehow survived four clear goal attempts in 15 minutes. Pavel Nedved, playing the game of his life, came closest to scoring, heading against the inside of the post and across the goal-line, while Jan Koller, only marginally less impressive, also hit the frame of the goal with another fine header.

A goal then and the Dutch would have struggled to get back into the game. But even without the deserved break-through, it was the Czechs who continued to play the classier, more refined football. Then came the decisive penalty, but even after that the Czechs were not finished, creating another golden chance which substitute Radek Bejbl somehow put wide with the goal at his mercy.

For the poor Czechs there was no respite. Their next fixture was against France, and their task was made even more onerous when a stray backpass from defender Petr Gabriel allowed Thierry Henry to nip in and score after just seven minutes. The pacy frontman should have made it 2-0 when a majestic Zidane pass put him through but he slid his shot just wide. The Czechs, knowing that another defeat would be fatal, pressed hard for an equaliser and were driven forward by Euro '96 hero Karel Poborsky, who had a marvellous first half.

Fittingly it was the Benfica midfielder who brought the Czechs level, albeit from a penalty that should not have been awarded. The luck that had deserted the Czechs in Amsterdam returned when Didier Deschamps's shove from behind on a goalbound Nedved was deemed to have taken place in the penalty area when, in fact, the initial point of impact was well outside. Morally, perhaps, it was worthy of the ultimate sanction, but, leaving the debate for others, Poborsky blasted the spot-kick past Barthez to put the Czechs level.

1-1 was a just half-time scoreline. Both teams were playing well, and the skill levels were high. It was anyone's game, but two incidents early in the second half were to decide the outcome. Firstly, Nedved was sent clean through on goal but his shot was well saved by Barthez. Then, with their first chance of the half, France scored, Youri Djorkaeff despatching Henry's pass with a crisp, decisive finish.

Once behind, the Czechs lost their shape and their heart. For the second match running Koller was unlucky

EURO 2000 FINALS

Group D

to see a header come back off the crossbar, but otherwise the Eastern Europeans created very little, Despite the presence of two giant strikers in Koller and Vratislav Lokvenc, the Czechs could not make effective use of their height, and as the match wore on, it became all too easy for the French to protect their lead.

France's qualification and the Czech Republic's elimination were confirmed a few hours later as Holland finally got their act together with a 3-0 victory over Denmark in Rotterdam - a result which also put the co-hosts through and the Danes out. For 45 minutes, however, Frank Rijkaard's team were no better than they had been for the full 90 against the Czechs. Despite the mass of orange-bedecked fans in the stands, the Dutch could find no inspiration. Although the bulk of the possession was theirs, they were too predictable going forward, and at half-time the jeers and whistles of the fans were wholly appropriate. In fact, a minute earlier Holland were lucky to avoid going behind when Danish midfielder Thomas Gravesen, fed by the excellent Jesper Grønkjaer, curled a measured shot against the Dutch crossbar.

Everything changed on 57 minutes, though, when a move initiated in his own half by Edgar Davids resulted in Patrick Kluivert sidefooting a loose ball into the corner of the hitherto defiant Peter Schmeichel's net. Once in front, Holland found another couple of gears, going from static to vibrant at a stroke. A brilliant cross from Boudewijn Zenden created a second goal for Ronald de Boer and then it was Zenden himself who clipped in goal number three after a dynamic forward surge from Michael Reiziger.

Denmark had the chance of a late consolation when Edwin van der Sar brought down Ebbe Sand for the first clear-cut penalty of the tournament, but Michael Schjønberg put his spot-kick wide. It was irrelevant within the context of the match and the tournament, but it served to heighten the Danes' depression as they exited the competition with a second 3-0 defeat. They would subsequently go on to lose again, 2-0 to the Czech Republic, in their meaningless final fixture.

With the main issue of qualification resolved, the final matches held little real interest. However, Holland were eager to beat France in Amsterdam because that was the only result which would keep them on Dutch soil.

Many believed that Holland v France would be a dress rehearsal for the final, but with the French withholding most of their key players and the Dutch considering it prudent to rest some of theirs, the fixture lost some of its appeal. That was the theory. In practice, though, it was a wonderful game, a true spectacle, with both teams playing delightful, high-grade football. For the first time, pre-tournament

France's Christian Karembeu tackles Holland's Arthur Numan.

favourites Holland looked like the genuine article, and although they twice fell behind, they had the courage to fight back and claim the victory they desired and deserved.

France were not too disheartened that they lost but they didn't stand aside and let the Dutch through. Although in arrears for the final half-hour, the world champions kept plugging away and even in stoppage time they were still throwing men forward in an attempt to salvage a point. Holland, though, were tremendous. Kluivert, Ronald de Boer and Zenden each scored their second goals of the tournament, all of them spectacularly executed, and Edgar Davids was back to his brilliant 1998 World Cup form. All of a sudden Holland seemed transformed, oozing class and confidence with every touch and pass. For the co-hosts, the tournament was beginning to hot up. They had taken a while to get going, but now it looked as if they would take some stopping...

GROUP D FINAL TABLE

		Pd	W	D	L	F	A	Pt	GD
1	Holland	3	3	0	0	7	2	9	5
2	France	3	2	0	1	7	4	6	3
3	Czech Republic	3	1	0	2	3	3	3	0
4	Denmark	3	0	0	3	0	8	0	-8

TOP SCORERS
2   Frank DE BOER (Holland)
    Patrick KLUIVERT (Holland)
    Boudewijn ZENDEN (Holland)
    Thierry HENRY (France)
    Vladimir SMICER (Czech Republic)

EURO 2000 FINALS   Quarter-finals

QUARTER-FINALS

With the possible exception of Turkey, Euro 2000 had its ideal quarter-final line-up, with the eight strongest and most spectator-friendly teams still involved. Three of the ties clearly favoured the group winners, with Portugal, Italy and Holland, all protecting 100 per cent records, expected to progress at the expense of Turkey, Romania and Yugoslavia, respectively, while Spain's reward for claiming top spot in Group C was a tough assignment against world champions France

Portugal and Turkey began the knockout phase of the competition when they met in Amsterdam. The roof of the ArenA was closed for the occasion, and for the first 15 minutes or so the strange atmosphere seemed to stifle the ambition of both teams. Slowly but surely, though, Portugal began to seize the initiative, and their first potent attack forced Turkish goalkeeper Rüstü into making a brave and spectacular save to deny Costinha.

The first action of note at the other end led to the game's major flashpoint - the sending-off of Turkey's best defender, Alpay Özalan. It was a controversial decision. Although Alpay had a swing at Fernando Couto while both were grounded after an awkward aerial challenge, the reason the Portuguese centre-back lay writhing with his hands to his face was because his defensive colleague Jorge Costa had caught him in the face accidentally with his knee. Unfortunately, Dutch referee Martin Jol added two and two and got five. Had he consulted his assistant, he might

Portugal's Sérgio Conceição (left) and Arif Erdem of Turkey wrestle for possession.

have been less hasty to jump to the wrong conclusion.

There was a degree of poetic justice for the Turks when Jol later awarded them a penalty after Fernando Couto had slid in rashly on Arif, but the Turkish striker fired his spot-kick straight at Vítor Baía and Fernando Couto cleared the danger on the follow-up. That was the last action of the half and came shortly after Portugal had taken a deserved lead, with Nuno Gomes heading in sublimely from Figo's deflected cross.

The Portuguese striker tapped in a second goal 11 minutes into the second half, after more brilliant approach

QUARTER-FINALS MATCH DETAILS

24/06/2000, Amsterdam
TURKEY 0
PORTUGAL 2 Nuno Gomes (44, 56)
referee - Jol (HOL)
TURKEY - Rüstü; Fatih, Ogün (Sergen 84); Alpay; Tayfun, Tayfur, Ergün, Okan (Oktay 62), Hakan Ünsal; Arif (Suat 62), Hakan Sükür.
PORTUGAL - Vítor Baía; Sérgio Conceição, Fernando Couto, Jorge Costa, Dimas; Costinha (Paulo Sousa 46); Paulo Bento; João Pinto, Rui Costa (Capucho 87), Figo; Nuno Gomes (Sá Pinto 74).

24/06/2000, Brussels
ITALY 2 Totti (34), Inzaghi (43)
ROMANIA 0
referee - Melo Perreira (POR)
ITALY - Toldo; Cannavaro, Nesta, Iuliano; Zambrotta, Conte (Di Biagio 55), Albertini, Maldini (Pessotto 46); Fiore; Totti (Del Piero 75), Inzaghi.
ROMANIA - Stelea; Filipescu, Belodedici, Ciobotariu, Chivu; Petre, Hagi, Galca (Lupescu 68), Munteanu; Moldovan (Ganea 54), Mutu.

25/06/2000, Rotterdam
HOLLAND 6 Kluivert (24, 38, 54), Govedarica (51og), Overmars (78, 90)
YUGOSLAVIA 1 Milosevic (90)
referee - García Aranda (ESP)
HOLLAND - Van der Sar (Westerveld 65); Bosvelt, Stam, De Boer F., Numan; Overmars, Cocu, Davids, Zenden (De Boer R. 80); Bergkamp, Kluivert (Makaay 60).
YUGOSLAVIA - Kralj; Saveljic (Stankovic J. 61), Mihajlovic, Djukic; Komljenovic, Stojkovic (Stankovic D. 51), Govedarica, Jugovic, Drulovic (Kovacevic 69); Milosevic, Mijatovic.

25/06/2000, Bruges
SPAIN 1 Mendieta (38p)
FRANCE 2 Zidane (32), Djorkaeff (44)
referee - Collina (ITA)
SPAIN - Cañizares; Míchel Salgado, Abelardo, Paco, Aranzábal; Mendieta (Urzaiz 56), Guardiola, Helguera (Gerard 77), Munitis (Etxeberria 72); Alfonso, Raúl.
FRANCE - Barthez; Thuram, Blanc, Desailly, Lizarazu; Djorkaeff, Deschamps, Vieira; Dugarry, Zidane (Henry 81); Anelka.

EURO 2000 FINALS

Quarter-finals

play by Figo, and from that moment onwards the pre-match favourites freewheeled to victory, toying with the Turks and creating a myriad of gilt-edged chances but somehow failing to add to their total. Rüstü was defiant to the last, making telling saves from Nuno Gomes, Rui Costa and Paulo Bento, but there were bad misses too, especially from Jorge Costa, who failed to convert a simple chance from almost on the goal-line.

But while Portugal's old finishing woes came back to haunt them, their passing and movement in midfield continued to be of the highest quality. Figo, in addition to creating both goals, showed some memorable flashes of skill, while Rui Costa impressed once more with his ability to tame the ball in an instant, carry it towards defenders and then pick out colleagues with measured through-balls.

In the end it was all too easy for Portugal, and the 2-0 final scoreline did them scant justice. Turkey, having done what they set out to do by reaching the quarter-finals, looked a bedraggled and jaded bunch in the closing stages and the final whistle probably came to them as a pleasant relief.

Italy joined Portugal in the last four with a comfortable victory of their own. The 'Azzurri' were fortunate to be facing a Romanian side that had lost three key players through suspension - Dan Petrescu, Cosmin Contra and Adrian Ilie - as well as veteran sweeper Gica Popescu through injury. The Romanians did, however, welcome back their skipper Gheorghe Hagi, and he was to have a profound impact on proceedings in the King Baudouin Stadium.

It was Hagi's 125th international, but he failed to last the distance. He was sent off after 57 minutes for taking a dive in the area and trying to win a penalty. That was his second yellow-card offence in just three minutes and he had to go. Indeed he ought to have seen red for his first misdemeanour - a vicious stamp on Antonio Conte's ankle that forced the Italian midfielder out of both the game and the tournament. Hagi had shown the other side of his character in the first half when his sweet lob from Adrian Mutu's magnificent long diagonal pass agonisingly came back off the post.

Had that effort gone in, the pattern of the game might have been totally different, but it didn't and that allowed Italy to take complete command. Only two minutes earlier the Italians had taken the lead when, having drawn the Romanian defence out of position at a free-kick, they worked the ball back into the area, where Francesco Totti beat Bogdan Stelea with a neat volley. Two minutes before half-time their advantage was doubled when Filippo

Inzaghi, for once avoiding the offside trap that had ensnared him on countless occaions before, latched onto Demetrio Albertini's pass and slid the ball low past Stelea.

2-0 up at half-time, Italy appeared to be in the clear, and when Hagi received his marching orders 12 minutes into the second period, the contest was effectively over. Stung by the loss of their captain, Romania provided a courageous initial response, with midfielder Dorinel Munteanu and defender Liviu Ciobotariu both coming close to scoring, but the threat was only brief, and with the Italian rearguard standing predictably firm and resilient, the final quarter of the match proved to be nothing more than a slow, uneventful countdown to the final whistle.

Italy, like Portugal, had made it four wins out of four and demonstrated once again that they were the masters at defending a lead. With Toldo, Nesta and Cannavaro showing unbreachable form at the back and their forwards beginning to offer a greater menace in front of goal, the 'Azzurri' suddenly had the look of potential champions.

So, too, did Holland. The following day Frank Rijkaard's team were to maintain their game-by-game improvement with a truly breathtaking exhibition of attacking skills against Yugoslavia. Their semi-final place was never in danger as they ripped their opponents to pieces. 6-1 was the final score as the Dutch ran riot, producing by far the best team performance of the entire competition.

Holland came very close to establishing two new tournament records - the highest winning margin and the record individual goalscoring haul in one game - but ultimately failed in both. 6-0 became 6-1 in stoppage-time when Savo Milosevic netted Yugoslavia's consolation, and the four goals which the dynamic Patrick Kluivert appeared to have scored became a mere three when the Dutch striker

Yugoslavia's Predrag Mijatovic is sandwiched by Arthur Numan and Edgar Davids.

EURO 2000 FINALS   Quarter-finals

later confessed what his body language had indicated at the time - thet the third of his four goals had in fact gone in off a Yugoslav defender.

Kluivert was in awesome form. He provided two wonderful finishes to convert Dennis Bergkamp and Edgar Davids passes in the first half, and the goal which completed his hat-trick showed marvellous technique as well as tremendous positional awareness as he skilfully angled his first-time shot into the corner. Kluivert was withdrawn from the action soon afterwards and deserved his standing ovation, but the goals did not stop there. Marc Overmars added two more late in the game as the Dutch continued to make mincemeat of the beleaguered Yugoslav defence.

It was a mesmering performance. Yugoslavia simply had no answer to the Dutch as they passed and moved the ball with a mixture of rhythmic efficiency and balletic beauty. Everybody in an orange shirt appeared to be on the same wavelength, and the big Dutch crowd lapped up every minute of a captivating display.

The great entertainment of Rotterdam was matched later the same evening in Bruges, where Spain and France, as expected, engaged in the most closely-contested of the four quarter-finals.

Both teams began brightly, with Zinedine Zidane making an early impression with a wonderful run down the left. France's genial number ten showed that he was human midway through the half when he swung and missed at an excellent cross from the recalled Christophe Dugarry, but within a few minutes he redeemed himself by putting France into the lead with a majestic free-kick.

But while Zidane was continuing to rival Portugal's Figo for the Player of the Tournament tag, another illustrious Frenchman, defender Lilian Thuram, was having a torrid time trying to cope with Spain's lively left-winger Pedro Munitis, and eight minutes after France had gone in front, Thuram conceded a penalty, taking Munitis's legs from under him as he checked back skilfully in the area. Gaizka Mendieta did the rest, slotting the ball home with the same dead-eye precision he had shown a few days earlier against Yugoslavia.

A thrilling first half was concluded in France's favour when Youri Djorkaeff, unmarked on the right, latched onto Patrick Vieira's neat lay-off and fired a ferocious shot past Cañizares at the near post.

Spain almost equalised for the second time immediately after the interval when Fabien Barthez saved at Alfonso's feet following more excellent work from Munitis, and as the second half progressed they looked more likely to score the next goal than France. The French worked diligently

France's Thierry Henry (right) battles with Spain's Iván Helguera.

to retain their advantage and should have been assisted in their efforts when Paco deliberately and maliciously brought down a goalbound Thierry Henry with 20 minutes to go. However, referee Pierluigi Collina showed the Spanish defender yellow instead of the red he deserved.

Collina appeared to side with Spain a second time when, in the very last minute, following an extended spell of pressure on the French goal, Abelardo fell to the ground on the dead-ball line after Barthez had allowed the ball to spill from his hands. It was clear that the French 'keeper made a foolish attempt to grab the ball at the defender's feet but whether there was any contact was questionable.

No matter. The penalty was given and Raúl stepped up to take it. Normally it would have been Mendieta's duty, but the Valencia man had been substituted. It was a death-or-glory moment for Spain's superstar striker. Elimination or extra-time beckoned. He took careful aim but blazed his left-foot shot horribly over the bar. Even then Spain were not finished for just seconds later they created another golden opportunity, when Urzaiz leapt to meet Alfonso's cross, but his header sailed over the bar.

France, who had been pegged back for virtually the whole of the last 15 minutes, were relieved more than elated at the final whistle. They had played some fine football and had every reason to feel satisfied with their performance, but they had also needed some luck to survive. Spain, on the other hand, had failed once again to deliver at a major tournament, and poor Raúl, his head clasped mournfully in his hands, summed up the feeling of a team that, having experienced the ecstasy of the dramatic victory over Yugoslavia, now knew what it felt like to be on the receiving end of last-minute agony.

EURO 2000 FINALS

Semi-finals

SEMI-FINALS

There could be no argument that the four most deserving teams had reached the semi-finals. Portugal, Italy, Holland and France had all stamped their class on a high-quality, entertaining tournament. But now it was time to get serious. Each of the quartet believed that they could win the Henri Delaunay trophy. They were all in form and all just one step away from the final. But only two of them could make it through. Something had to give.

The first semi-final, between France and Portugal in Brussels, was billed as Zidane v Figo. Memories were also dredged up of the epic semi-final between the two countries in Marseilles 16 year earlier. On paper it was a hugely attractive tie, with both sides known to favour an open, positive, attack-minded approach.

Yet for the first 15 minutes the two teams virtually cancelled each other out. The beginning was extremely cagey, with neither side willing to show their hand. What the game needed was a goal and suddenly, out of the blue, it got one. Portugal's Nuno Gomes was the scorer, latching onto a loose ball on the edge of the area and beating Fabien Barthez with a fierce left-foot snapshot.

Still the match struggled to come alive. The midfield was densely packed, with Sérgio Conceição, Costinha and Vidigal all working feverishly hard to deny Zidane room for manoeuvre and Didier Deschamps, Patrick Vieira and Emmanuel Petit doing likewise to reduce the effectiveness of Figo and Rui Costa. The flair players, for once, were being crowded out.

Shortly after the interval, with almost their first proper chance, France equalised. Like Nuno Gomes's earlier effort, it came almost without warning. Nicolas Anelka was put through by Lilian Thuram and his pull-back was turned in by Thierry Henry for his third goal of the competition.

Goalscoring chances continued to be few and far between. Only in the final few minutes did the action hot up, with the French getting behind the Portuguese defence

twice and Portugal going extremely close to grabbing a last-minute winner when Abel Xavier's goalbound header from Figo's free-kick was acrobatically tipped over by Barthez.

For the first time in the tournament extra-time was required, bringing the 'golden goal' rule into force. The impasse continued, but with five minutes remaining, an incident of huge controversy was to decide the outcome in France's favour.

French substitute David Trezeguet raced into the area. He was foiled by Vítor Baía and the ball ran loose to Sylvain Wiltord who fired in a shot from almost on the byline, which Abel Xavier blocked at the near post. France were preparing to take the corner when referee Günter Benkö ran across to see why his Slovakian assistant, Igor Srumka, was furiously waving his flag. At once the truth was revealed as Benkö, amidst chaotic scenes, pointed to the penalty spot. The linesman had ruled that Abel Xavier used his hand to deflect the ball wide - and television images showed that he was indeed correct. The Portuguese players did not, of course, have access to those images and many of them went berserk, pushing and shoving the officials as they pleaded for the decision to be reversed.

For two long minutes utter pandemonium reigned, but there was still the small matter of France actually taking the penalty. There was only one man for the task. Zinedine Zidane, who had never been on the losing side for France in a competitive match, stepped forward amidst intense pressure and with one glorious swing of his right leg drove the ball hard and firm into the top corner to win the match and put his country into the final.

It was a dramatic conclusion to a generally uninspiring match. Although Portugal continued to protest in undignified fashion long after their fate had been sealed, they had no right to declare themselves moral victors.

The manner of their exit was cruel, and in some respects their overheated reaction was understandable, but on

---

SEMI-FINALS MATCH DETAILS

28/06/2000, Brussels
FRANCE 2 Henry (51), Zidane (117p)
PORTUGAL 1 Nuno Gomes (19)
(golden goal)
referee - Benkö (AUT)
FRANCE - Barthez; Thuram, Blanc, Desailly, Lizarazu; Vieira, Deschamps, Petit (Pires 87); Zidane; Anelka (Wiltord 71), Henry (Trezeguet 105).
PORTUGAL - Vítor Baía; Abel Xavier, Fernando Couto, Jorge Costa, Dimas (Rui Jorge 91); Costinha, Vidigal (Paulo Bento 60); Sérgio Conceição, Rui Costa (João Pinto 76), Figo; Nuno Gomes.

29/06/2000, Amsterdam
ITALY 0
HOLLAND 0
(aet; 3-1 on pens.)
referee - Merk (GER)
ITALY - Toldo; Cannavaro, Nesta, Iuliano; Zambrotta, Albertini (Pessotto 77), Di Biagio, Maldini; Fiore (Totti 82); Inzaghi (Delvecchio 66), Del Piero.
HOLLAND - Van der Sar; Bosvelt, Stam, De Boer F., Van Bronckhorst; Overmars, Cocu (Winter 95), Davids, Zenden (Van Vossen 77); Bergkamp (Seedorf 86), Kluivert.

EURO 2000 FINALS   Semi-finals

Francesco Toldo saves Frank de Boer's penalty.

balance France deserved their place in the final.

The second semi-final, between Holland and Italy in Amsterdam, was also to be settled from the penalty spot but in different circumstances altogether.

Almost from the outset Italy's intention appeared to be to drain the game of spectacle and drag it through two hours of tedium into a penalty shoot-out. While Italy's great strengths clearly lay in their defensive organisation and resilience, their earlier performances had also shown that they were excellent going forward. Yet against Holland, whom they clearly feared after their six-goal drubbing of Yugoslavia, Italy chose only to defend.

The onus was on the Dutch to break them down. It was the first true test for Frank Rijkaard and his players. But despite being given every opportunity available to take their place in the final, Holland could not seize the moment.

It turned out to be a night of utter torment for the rows and rows of orange-clad fans in the Amsterdam ArenA. Holland did their level best to break down the blue barrier ranged in front of them, but the writing was on the wall from the moment that Francesco Toldo saved Frank de Boer's penalty after 39 minutes. Even though Italy had already been reduced to ten men by this stage, with Gianluca Zambrotta seeing red after two scandalous lunges on Boudewijn Zenden, the Italian players could sense that their strategy of caution and attrition was going to pay dividends.

The second half was all one-way traffic, with Italy utterly disinterested in entering Holland's half. On 62 minutes the Dutch won another penalty when Edgar Davids was tripped by Mark Iuliano. Had referee Markus Merk adhered strictly to the rules he would have sent the Italian defender off as well as awarding the penalty, but the Italians' luck held on both counts. Iuliano stayed on and Patrick Kluivert rolled his penalty against the foot of the post.

After that, Holland barely created another meaningful

opening. For all their smart, patient, technically adroit build-up play, most of it engineered by the persistent Davids, their attack was blunt and impotent. What Holland needed was some variation but they refused even to try speculative crosses or shots from distance, which was surprising as Italy seemed quite content to hand possession straight back to them.

The nightmare conclusion which all Dutch fans feared almost came to fruition in stoppage-time when substitute Marco Delvecchio scampered free and forced Edwin van der Sar into his first meaningful intervention of the evening. Then, ten minutes into extra-time Delvecchio was through again, forcing Van der Sar into a brilliant save with his left foot. Meanwhile the Dutch plodded on, getting nowhere. The three substitutes introduced by Rijkaard were all totally ineffective, and with no further chances created at either end, the game stumbled towards the conclusion that had seemed inevitable all along.

Once it went to penalties, there was only going to be one winner. Holland had already shown their fallibility from the spot and, sure enough, their nerve failed them again in the shoot-out. Luigi Di Biagio, Gianluca Pessotto and Francesco Totti all scored for Italy while Frank de Boer and Japp Stam missed Holland's first two kicks. Kluivert kept Dutch hopes alive by converting penalty number three and so did Paolo Maldini when he missed for Italy. But then Toldo saved his third spot-kick of the game, from Paul Bosvelt, and Holland's dream was over.

The Dutch could have no complaints. The match had been theirs for the taking but they had been unable to handle the pressure. As for Italy, they had defended magnificently, with Toldo, Alessandro Nesta and Fabio Cannavaro playing out of their skins to keep the Dutch at bay, but the hope was that this was just a one-off and that they would not adopt the same exclusively negative approach in the final.

FINAL

And so to Rotterdam. History beckoned the French, who were aiming to become the first team to follow up a World Cup win with victory in the European Championship. Italy were appearing in their first major final since the 1994 World Cup and, now as then, were widely perceived as the unattractive underdogs.

The pre-match fear was that the game would run along similar lines to the turgid World Cup quarter-final of two years earlier. The manner of Italy's semi-final victory over Holland exaggerated the concerns, as did the fact that they had not beaten France for 22 years.

There were no real surprises in the French line-up, with Roger Lemerre reverting to the starting XI that had beaten

EURO 2000 FINALS

Final

FINAL MATCH DETAILS

02/07/2000, Rotterdam
FRANCE 2 Wiltord (90), Trezeguet (103)
ITALY 1 Delvecchio (56)
(golden goal)
referee - Frisk (SWE)
FRANCE - Barthez; Thuram, Blanc, Desailly, Lizarazu (Pires 85); Vieira,
Deschamps; Djorkaeff (Trezeguet 75), Zidane, Dugarry (Wiltord 57); Henry.
ITALY - Toldo; Cannavaro, Nesta, Iuliano; Pessotto, Albertini, Fiore (Del Piero
52), Di Biagio (Ambrosini 65), Maldini; Totti, Delvecchio (Montella 85).

France celebrate Euro 2000 victory.

Spain in the quarter-final. Nine of Lemerre's chosen team had appeared in the World Cup final two years earlier, the exceptions being Laurent Blanc (suspended for that match) and Thierry Henry.

Italy made three changes. One of them was enforced, with Gianluca Pessotto replacing the suspended Gianluca Zambrotta, but the other two appeared to be an attempt by Dino Zoff to revitalise his attack, with Roma pair Francesco Totti and Marco Delvecchio coming in for Juventus duo Inzaghi and Del Piero.

It was a positive sign of intent, and, sure enough, Totti and Delvecchio were both prominent in an enterprising opening ten minutes from the 'Azzurri'. France, too, began boldly, with Thierry Henry looking very sharp, clipping in one early shot that hit the foot of the post. After those opening exchanges the match gradually settled into the predicted pattern, with the Italians hanging back and muscling the French out of their usual rhythm. Zidane could barely get into the game, and by half-time the world champions had fashioned only one further chance.

Italy brought Del Piero on for Fiore early in the second half, and shortly afterwards they broke the deadlock. Totti skilfully fed Pessotto on the right and his measured cross found Delvecchio, who blasted home on the volley from close range. Italy now had the bit between their teeth, and another chance was created when Totti put Del Piero through in the inside-left channel. The substitute had a clear sight of goal but his left-foot shot was woefully inaccurate, scuttling harmlessly wide of the goal.

That should have been game over, but France came back and Toldo was forced to make two good saves, from substitute Sylvain Wiltord and the ever-dangerous Henry. As the game headed towards its conclusion Zidane at last emerged from his shell and began to

drive his team forward. The danger, however, was that Italy would hit them on the break, and on 84 minutes Del Piero was sent through again, only to hit a tame shot which Barthez comfortably saved.

The minutes ticked away. Stoppage-time arrived, but France kept applying the pressure. The Italian fans pleaded with referee Anders Frisk to blow for full-time, but the action continued...and then came the extraordinary climax.

The game was into its fourth additional minute when Barthez launched a long kick upfield. David Trezeguet, another substitute, headed it on into the area, where Wiltord was waiting. The Bordeaux striker shaped to hit it first time but he concentrated, waited and then struck the ball low and hard past Toldo into the far corner. Amazingly, with virtually the last kick of the game, France were level.

Their resistance finally broken, Italy's confidence seemed shot to pieces as extra-time began. It was all France, and it took just 13 minutes for them to finish the Italians off. A rare error by Fabio Cannavaro allowed Robert Pires, France's third substitute, to scamper skilfully to the byline, and his cut-back was met with a left-footed volley of stunning force and accuracy from Trezeguet. Toldo stood no chance whatsoever as the ball thundered into the netting behind him.

It was all over. For the second European Championship in a row, a 'golden goal' had decided the final. But, unlike in 1996, this one was a gem - arguably the best goal of the entire tournament and the perfect way for such an enjoyable, exciting competition to end.

France were the new European champions. Although blessed by good fortune at key moments, they were nevertheless the most complete and consistent team in the tournament and thoroughly deserved to take their proud and unique place in history.

TOP SCORERS

5	Patrick KLUIVERT (Holland)
	Savo MILOSEVIC (Yugoslavia)
4	NUNO GOMES (Portugal)
3	SÉRGIO CONCEIÇÃO (Portugal)
	Zlatko ZAHOVIC (Slovenia)
	Thierry HENRY (France)

APPEARANCES - Group by Group

GROUP A - GERMANY

No.	Player	P	Ap	(s)	Gls
1	Oliver KAHN	G	3		
2	Markus BABBEL	D	2		
3	Marko REHMER	D	1	(1)	
4	Thomas LINKE	D	2		
5	Marco BODE	A	1	(1)	
6	Jens NOWOTNY	D	3		
7	Mehmet SCHOLL	M	3		1
8	Thomas HÄSSLER	M	1	(1)	
9	Ulf KIRSTEN	A	1		
10	Lothar MATTHÄUS	D	3		
11	Paulo Roberto RINK	A	1	(2)	
12	Jens LEHMANN	G			
13	Michael BALLACK	M	1	(1)	
14	Dietmar HAMANN	M	2	(1)	
15	Dariusz WOSZ	M			
16	Jens JEREMIES	M	2		
17	Christian ZIEGE	M	2		
18	Sebastian DEISLER	M	1	(1)	
19	Carsten JANCKER	A	2		
20	Oliver BIERHOFF	A	1		
21	Carsten RAMELOW	M			
22	Hans-Jörg BUTT	G			
● Coach - Erich RIBBECK					

GROUP A - ROMANIA

No.	Player	P	Ap	(s)	Gls
1	Bogdan LOBONT	G			
2	Dan PETRESCU	D	3		
3	Liviu CIOBOTARIU	D	2		
4	Iulian FILIPESCU	D	4		
5	Constantin GALCA	M	4		
6	Gheorghe POPESCU	D	3		
7	Adrian MUTU	A	2	(1)	
8	Dorinel MUNTEANU	M	4		1
9	Viorel MOLDOVAN	A	4		1
10	Gheorghe HAGI	M	3		
11	Adrian ILIE	A	3		
12	Bogdan STELEA	G	4		
13	Cristian CHIVU	D	4		1
14	Florentin PETRE	M	1	(1)	
15	Ionut LUPESCU	M		(2)	
16	Laurentiu ROSU	M		(2)	
17	Miodrag BELODEDICI	D	1	(1)	
18	Ioan Viorel GANEA	A		(3)	1
19	Erik LINCAR	M			
20	Catalain HALDAN	M			
21	Florian PRUNEA	G			
22	Cosmin CONTRA	D	2	(1)	
● Coach - Emeric IENEI					

GROUP A - PORTUGAL

No.	Player	P	Ap	(s)	Gls
1	VÍTOR BAÍA	G	4		
2	JORGE COSTA	D	5		
3	RUI JORGE	D	1	(1)	
4	VIDIGAL	M	3	(1)	
5	FERNANDO COUTO	D	5		
6	PAULO SOUSA	M	1	(1)	
7	FIGO	M	4		1
8	JOÃO PINTO	M	3	(1)	1
9	SÁ PINTO	A	1	(2)	
10	RUI COSTA	M	4		
11	SÉRGIO CONCEIÇÃO	M	3	(2)	3
12	PEDRO ESPINHA	G	1		
13	DIMAS	D	4		
14	ABEL XAVIER	D	2		
15	COSTINHA	M	3	(1)	1
16	BETO	D	1	(1)	
17	PAULO BENTO	M	3	(1)	
18	PAULETA	A	1		
19	CAPUCHO	M	1	(2)	
20	SECRETÁRIO	D	1		
21	NUNO GOMES	A	4	(1)	4
22	QUIM	G		(1)	
● Coach - HUMBERTO COELHO					

GROUP A - ENGLAND

No.	Player	P	Ap	(s)	Gls
1	David SEAMAN	G	2		
2	Gary NEVILLE	D	3		
3	Philip NEVILLE	D	3		
4	Sol CAMPBELL	D	3		
5	Tony ADAMS	D	1		
6	Martin KEOWN	D	2	(1)	
7	David BECKHAM	M	3		
8	Paul SCHOLES	M	3		1
9	Alan SHEARER	A	3		2
10	Michael OWEN	A	3		1
11	Steve McMANAMAN	M	1		1
12	Gareth SOUTHGATE	D		(1)	
13	Nigel MARTYN	G	1		
14	Paul INCE	M	3		
15	Gareth BARRY	D			
16	Steven GERRARD	M		(1)	
17	Dennis WISE	M	2	(1)	
18	Nick BARMBY	M		(2)	
19	Emile HESKEY	A		(2)	
20	Kevin PHILLIPS	A			
21	Robbie FOWLER	A			
22	Richard WRIGHT	G			
● Coach - Kevin KEEGAN					

APPEARANCES - Group by Group

GROUP B - BELGIUM

No.	Player	P	Ap	(s)	Gls
1	Filip DE WILDE	G	3		
2	Eric DEFLANDRE	D	3		
3	Joos VALGAEREN	D	3		
4	Lorenzo STAELENS	D	3		
5	Philippe CLEMENT	M			
6	Yves VANDERHAEGHE	M	3		
7	Marc WILMOTS	M	3		
8	Bart GOOR	M	3		1
9	Emile MPENZA	A	3		1
10	Branko STRUPAR	A	2	(1)	
11	Gert VERHEYEN	M	3		
12	Geert DE VLIEGER	G			
13	Frédéric HERPOEL	G			
14	Johan WALEM	M			
15	Jacky PEETERS	D		(1)	
16	Luc NILIS	A	1	(2)	
17	Philippe LEONARD	D	1		
18	Nico VAN KERCKHOVEN	D	2	(1)	
19	Eric VAN MEIR	D			
20	Gilles DE BILDE	A		(1)	
21	Mbo MPENZA	A		(1)	
22	Marc HENDRIKX	D		(2)	
● Coach - Robert WASEIGE					

GROUP B - SWEDEN

No.	Player	P	Ap	(s)	Gls
1	Magnus HEDMAN	G	3		
2	Roland NILSSON	D	1		
3	Patrik ANDERSSON	D	2		
4	Joachim BJÖRKLUND	D	3		
5	Teddy LUCIC	D	1	(1)	
6	Gary SUNDGREN	D	1		
7	Håkan MILD	M	2		
8	Tomas GUSTAFSSON	D	1		
9	Fredrik LJUNGBERG	M	3		
10	Jörgen PETTERSSON	A	1	(1)	
11	Niclas ALEXANDERSSON	M	2	(1)	
12	Magnus KIHLSTEDT	G			
13	Magnus SVENSSON	M	1	(1)	
14	Olof MELLBERG	D	3		
15	Daniel ANDERSSON	M	1	(1)	
16	Anders ANDERSSON	M		(1)	
17	Johan MJÄLLBY	M	3		1
18	Yksel OSMANOVSKI	A	1	(1)	
19	Kennet ANDERSSON	A	2	(1)	
20	Henrik LARSSON	A	2	(1)	1
21	Marcus ALLBÄCK	A			
22	Mattias ASPER	G			
● Coaches - Tommy SÖDERBERG & Lars LAGERBÄCK					

GROUP B - TURKEY

No.	Player	P	Ap	(s)	Gls
1	RÜSTÜ Reçber	G	4		
2	TAYFUR Havutçu	M	2	(1)	
3	OGÜN Temizkanoglu	D	4		
4	FATIH Akyel	D	4		
5	ALPAY Özalan	D	4		
6	ARIF Erdem	A	3	(1)	
7	OKAN Buruk	M	4		1
8	TUGAY Kerimoglu	M	1	(2)	
9	HAKAN Sükür	A	4		2
10	SERGEN Yalçin	M	1	(2)	
11	TAYFUN Korkut	M	3	(1)	
12	ÖMER Çatkiç	G			
13	OSMAN Özköylü	D		(1)	
14	SUAT Kaya	M	2	(1)	
15	Muzzy IZZET	M	1		
16	ERGÜN Penbe	M	1	(2)	
17	OKTAY Derelioglu	A		(1)	
18	AYHAN Akman	M			
19	ABDULLAH Ercan	M	2		
20	HAKAN Ünsal	D	2		
21	FEVZI Tuncay	G			
22	ÜMIT Davala	M	2		
● Coach - Mustafa DENIZLI					

GROUP B - ITALY

No.	Player	P	Ap	(s)	Gls
1	Christian ABBIATI	G			
2	Ciro FERRARA	D	1		
3	Paolo MALDINI	D	6		
4	Demetrio ALBERTINI	M	5		
5	Fabio CANNAVARO	D	5	(1)	
6	Paolo NEGRO	D	1		
7	Angelo DI LIVIO	M	1	(1)	
8	Antonio CONTE	M	3		1
9	Filippo INZAGHI	A	4		2
10	Alessandro DEL PIERO	A	2	(4)	1
11	Gianluca PESSOTTO	M	3	(2)	
12	Francesco TOLDO	G	6		
13	Alessandro NESTA	D	5	(1)	
14	Luigi DI BIAGIO	M	3	(1)	1
15	Mark IULIANO	D	5	(1)	
16	Massimo AMBROSINI	M	1	(2)	
17	Gianluca ZAMBROTTA	M	4		
18	Stefano FIORE	M	5	(1)	1
19	Vincenzo MONTELLA	A	1	(1)	
20	Francesco TOTTI	A	4	(1)	2
21	Marco DELVECCHIO	A	1	(2)	1
22	Francesco ANTONIOLI	G			
● Coach - Dino ZOFF					

APPEARANCES - Group by Group

GROUP C - SPAIN

No.	Player	P	Ap	(s)	Gls
1	Santiago CAÑIZARES	G	3		
2	MICHEL SALGADO	D	4		
3	Agustín ARANZABAL	D	3		
4	Josep GUARDIOLA	M	4		
5	ABELARDO Fernández	D	3		
6	Fernando HIERRO	D	2		
7	Iván HELGUERA	D	2	(2)	
8	FRAN González	M	2		
9	Pedro MUNITIS	A	1	(1)	1
10	RAUL González	A	4		1
11	ALFONSO Pérez	A	3	(1)	2
12	SERGI Barjuán	D	1		
13	Iker CASILLAS	G			
14	GERARD López	M		(1)	
15	Vicente ENGONGA	M		(1)	
16	Gaizka MENDIETA	M	3	(1)	2
17	Joseba ETXEBERRIA	M	2	(2)	1
18	Francisco Jémez PACO	D	3		
19	Juan VELASCO	D			
20	Ismael URZAIZ	A	1	(3)	
21	Juan Carlos VALERON	M	2		
22	José Francisco MOLINA	G	1		
● Coach - José Antonio CAMACHO					

GROUP C - NORWAY

No.	Player	P	Ap	(s)	Gls
1	Thomas MYHRE	G	3		
2	André BERGDØLMO	D	3		
3	Bjørn Otto BRAGSTAD	D	3		
4	Henning BERG	D	1		
5	Trond ANDERSEN	D			
6	Roar STRAND	M		(2)	
7	Erik MYKLAND	M	3		
8	Ståle SOLBAKKEN	M	1		
9	Tore André FLO	A	3		
10	Kjetil REKDAL	M			
11	Bent SKAMMELSRUD	M	2		
12	Frode OLSEN	G			
13	Morten BAKKE	G			
14	Vegard HEGGEM	D	2		
15	John Arne RIISE	M			
16	Dan EGGEN	D	2	(1)	
17	John CAREW	A	1	(2)	
18	Steffen IVERSEN	M	3		1
19	Eirik BAKKE	M	2	(1)	
20	Ole Gunnar SOLSKJAER	A	3		
21	Vidar RISETH	M		(1)	
22	Stig Inge BJØRNEBYE	D	1	(1)	
● Coach - Nils Johan SEMB					

GROUP C - YUGOSLAVIA

No.	Player	P	Ap	(s)	Gls
1	Milorad KORAC	G			
2	Ivan DUDIC	D	1		
3	Goran DJOROVIC	D	2		
4	Slavisa JOKANOVIC	M	3		
5	Miroslav DJUKIC	D	4		
6	Dejan STANKOVIC	M	1	(1)	
7	Vladimir JUGOVIC	M	4		
8	Predrag MIJATOVIC	A	4		
9	Savo MILOSEVIC	A	3	(1)	5
10	Dragan STOJKOVIC	M	3	(1)	
11	Sinisa MIHAJLOVIC	D	3		
12	Zeljko CICOVIC	G			
13	Slobodan KOMLJENOVIC	D	3		1
14	Nisa SAVELJIC	D	2	(1)	
15	Goran BUNJEVCEVIC	D			
16	Dejan GOVEDARICA	M	1	(2)	1
17	Ljubinko DRULOVIC	M	4		1
18	Darko KOVACEVIC	A	1	(1)	
19	Jovan STANKOVIC	M		(2)	
20	Mateja KEZMAN	A		(2)	
21	Albert NADJ	M	1	(1)	
22	Ivica KRALJ	G	4		
● Coach - Vujadin BOSKOV					

GROUP C - SLOVENIA

No.	Player	P	Ap	(s)	Gls
1	Marko SIMEUNOVIC	G			
2	Spasoje BULAJIC	D			
3	Zeljko MILINOVIC	D	3		
4	Darko MILANIC	D	2		
5	Marinko GALIC	D	3		
6	Aleksander KNAVS	D	1	(1)	
7	Dzoni NOVAK	M	3		
8	Ales CEH	M	3		
9	Saso UDOVIC	A	2		
10	Zlatko ZAHOVIC	M	3		3
11	Miran PAVLIN	M	3		1
12	Mladen DABANOVIC	G	3		
13	Mladen RUDONJA	M	3		
14	Sasa GAJSER	D			
15	Rudi ISTENIC	M			
16	Anton ZLOGAR	M			
17	Ermin SILJAK	A	1		
18	Milenko ACIMOVIC	M		(3)	
19	Amir KARIC	M	3		
20	Milan OSTERC	A		(3)	
21	Zoran PAVLOVIC	M		(1)	
22	Dejan NEMEC	G			
● Coach - Srecko KATANEC					

APPEARANCES - Group by Group

GROUP D - HOLLAND

No.	Player	P	Ap	(s)	Gls
1	Edwin VAN DER SAR	G	4		
2	Michael REIZIGER	D	2		
3	Jaap STAM	D	4		
4	Frank DE BOER	D	5		2
5	Boudewijn ZENDEN	M	5		2
6	Clarence SEEDORF	M	1	(1)	
7	Phillip COCU	M	5		
8	Edgar DAVIDS	M	5		
9	Patrick KLUIVERT	A	5		5
10	Dennis BERGKAMP	A	5		
11	Marc OVERMARS	M	4	(1)	2
12	Giovanni VAN BRONCKHORST	D	3		
13	Bert KONTERMAN	D	1	(1)	
14	Peter VAN VOSSEN	M		(2)	
15	Paul BOSVELT	D	3		
16	Ronald DE BOER	M		(3)	1
17	Pierre VAN HOOIJDONK	A			
18	Ed DE GOEY	G			
19	Arthur NUMAN	D	2		
20	Aron WINTER	M		(3)	
21	Roy MAKAAY	A		(2)	
22	Sander WESTERVELD	G	1	(2)	
● Coach - Frank RIJKAARD					

GROUP D - CZECH REPUBLIC

No.	Player	P	Ap	(s)	Gls
1	Pavel SRNICEK	G	3		
2	Tomas REPKA	D	3		
3	Radoslav LATAL	M	1		
4	Pavel NEDVED	M	3		
5	Milan FUKAL	D	1	(1)	
6	Petr VLCEK	D			
7	Jiri NEMEC	M	3		
8	Karel POBORSKY	M	3		1
9	Pavel KUKA	A		(2)	
10	Jan KOLLER	A	3		
11	Tomas ROSICKY	M	2		
12	Vratislav LOKVENC	A		(3)	
13	Radek BEJBL	M	2	(1)	
14	Pavel HORVATH	M			
15	Marek JANKULOVSKI	M		(2)	
16	Ladislav MAIER	G			
17	Vladimir SMICER	A	3		2
18	Jiri NOVOTNY	D			
19	Karel RADA	D	3		
20	Patrik BERGER	M	1		
21	Petr GABRIEL	D	2		
22	Jaromir BLAZEK	G			
● Coach - Jozef CHOVANEC					

GROUP D - FRANCE

No.	Player	P	Ap	(s)	Gls
1	Bernard LAMA	G	1		
2	Vincent CANDELA	D	2		
3	Bixente LIZARAZU	D	4		
4	Patrick VIEIRA	M	5	(1)	
5	Laurent BLANC	D	5		1
6	Youri DJORKAEFF	M	3	(2)	2
7	Didier DESCHAMPS	M	5	(1)	
8	Marcel DESAILLY	D	6		
9	Nicolas ANELKA	A	3	(2)	
10	Zinedine ZIDANE	M	5		2
11	Robert PIRES	M	1	(2)	
12	Thierry HENRY	A	5		3
13	Sylvain WILTORD	A	1	(4)	2
14	Johan MICOUD	M	1		
15	Lilian THURAM	D	5		
16	Fabien BARTHEZ	G	5		
17	Emmanuel PETIT	M	3		
18	Frank LEBOEUF	D	1		
19	Christian KAREMBEU	M	1		
20	David TREZEGUET	A	1	(2)	2
21	Christophe DUGARRY	A	3	(1)	1
22	Ulrich RAME	G			
● Coach - Roger LEMERRE					

GROUP D - DENMARK

No.	Player	P	Ap	(s)	Gls
1	Peter SCHMEICHEL	G	3		
2	Michael SCHJØNBERG	D	3		
3	René HENRIKSEN	D	3		
4	Jes HØGH	D			
5	Jan HEINTZE	D	3		
6	Thomas HELVEG	D	1	(1)	
7	Allan NIELSEN	M	2		
8	Jesper GRØNKJAER	M	3		
9	Jon Dahl TOMASSON	A	3		
10	Martin JØRGENSEN	M		(1)	
11	Ebbe SAND	A	2		
12	Søren COLDING	D	2	(1)	
13	Martin LAURSEN	D			
14	Brian Steen NIELSEN	M	1	(1)	
15	Stig TØFTING	M	2	(1)	
16	Thomas SØRENSEN	G			
17	Bjarne GOLDBAEK	M	1		
18	Miklos MOLNAR	A		(1)	
19	Morten BISGAARD	M	2		
20	Thomas GRAVESEN	M	1	(1)	
21	Mikkel BECK	A	1	(1)	
22	Peter KJAER	G			
● Coach - Bo JOHANSSON					

QUALIFYING GROUP 1

Italian celebrations delayed by Danes

Favourites Italy duly finished on top of Group One, but the 'Azzurri' were made to sweat before they sealed their automatic qualification for the finals.

With six of their eight matches played, the Italians appeared to have an impregnable lead, six points ahead of closest pursuers Denmark. Their position was so strong that they even had the luxury of going into their penultimate match, at home to the Danes, knowing that a 0-1 defeat would be enough for them to take the automatic qualifying berth.

Denmark arrived in Naples with confidence high after winning three qualifiers in a row, the last of them just four days earlier against Switzerland in Copenhagen, where a late winner from Jon Dahl Tomasson had given them a crucial lifeline.

On a night of incessant rain in the Stadio San Paolo, it looked as if Denmark's hopes had gone when Italy went in front through a spectacular Diego Fuser free-kick after ten minutes and doubled their lead through Christian Vieri (after a rare Peter Schmeichel error) later in the first half. But the match was com-

pletely turned on its head by a highly contentious penalty awarded to the Danes just before half-time. Fabio Cannavaro's innocuous clash with Tomasson was deemed worthy of a spot-kick, which Italian-based Martin Jørgensen converted to put his team back in the game.

After the interval it was all Denmark. The Italian defence appeared to switch off for the evening as time and again the visitors plotted their way through. Shortly before the hour the Danes were deservedly level as Morten Wieghorst volleyed home from close range following an excellent pull-back by Ebbe Sand. Seven minutes later the miraculous comeback was complete when Tomasson saw his mishit left-foot shot squirm into the net via a defender's foot. Even then the Danes continued to attack. No further goals ensued but there were two red cards as Wieghorst was booked twice in as many minutes late on and Italian substitute Giuliano Giannichedda quickly followed suit.

The 3-2 victory was crucial for the Danes as it guaranteed their place in the play-offs, but it was a sickener for Wales and Switzerland, who, having both

TOP SCORERS

3   Filippo INZAGHI (Italy)
    Christian VIERI (Italy)
    Jon Dahl TOMASSON
    (Denmark)
    Stéphane CHAPUISAT
    (Switzerland)
    Kubilay TÜRKYILMAZ
    (Switzerland)

GROUP 1 FINAL TABLE

			Home				Away				Total					
		Pd	W	D	L	F	A	W	D	L	F	A	W	D	L	F	A	Pt	GD
1	Italy	8	2	1	1	9	4	2	2	0	4	1	4	3	1	13	5	15	8
2	Denmark	8	2	0	2	5	5	2	2	0	6	3	4	2	2	11	8	14	3
3	Switzerland	8	2	2	0	5	1	2	0	2	4	4	4	2	2	9	5	14	4
4	Wales	8	1	0	3	3	8	2	0	2	4	8	3	0	5	7	16	9	-9
5	Belarus	8	0	2	2	1	3	0	1	3	3	7	0	3	5	4	10	3	-6

QUALIFYING GROUP 1

defeated Belarus, had been banking on an Italian win to keep their own chances alive. As for Italy, they now required at least a draw in their final qualifier, away to Belarus, to move back ahead of Denmark, whose programme was complete.

Belarus, though yet to record a win, had proved difficult opponents for the Italians earlier in the tournament, drawing 1-1 in Ancona, so the visit to Minsk was no formality. Given the state of play, a goalless draw was the most predictable outcome, and so it proved. Dino Zoff's team did not play well but they were marginally the better side and did what they had to.

Vieri came closest to bringing them victory when he struck a post with a powerful left-foot shot, but in the end it didn't matter. A draw was enough.

Switzerland beat Wales 2-0 in Wrexham on the final day to move level on points with the Danes, but it was

Italy's Christian Vieri (centre) plays the ball between Denmark's Jes Høgh (left) and Allan Nielsen (right).

Denmark's superior head-to-head record (1-1 in Zürich, 2-1 in Copenhagen) that had already ensured their place in the play-offs.

GROUP 1 MATCH DETAILS 1999/2000

04/09/99, Minsk
BELARUS 1 Baranov (30)
WALES 2 Saunders (42), Giggs (85)
referee - Øvrebø (NOR)
BELARUS - Tumilovich, Tarlovskiy, Lavrik, Lukhvich, Ostrovskiy, Gurenko, Baranov, Chaika, Kulchiy, Makovskiy, Orlovskiy (Romashchenko 60).
WALES - Jones P., Page, Barnard, Melville, Coleman, Pembridge (Robinson C. 80), Robinson J., Saunders, Blake, Speed, Giggs.

04/09/99, Copenhagen
DENMARK 2 Nielsen A. (54), Tomasson (81)
SWITZERLAND 1 Türkyilmaz (80)
referee - Wojcik (POL)
DENMARK - Schmeichel, Goldbaek (Colding 51), Henriksen, Høgh, Heintze, Helveg, Nielsen A. (Nielsen B.S. 80), Tøfting, Tomasson (Wieghorst 88), Jørgensen, Sand.
SWITZERLAND - Huber, Jeanneret, Di Jorio (Türkyilmaz 60), Müller P., Hodel, Vogel, Sesa (Müller S. 77), Wicky (Wyss 89), Chapuisat, Sforza, Bühlmann.

08/09/99, Lausanne
SWITZERLAND 2 Türkyilmaz (68, 87p)
BELARUS 0
referee - Irvine (NIR)
SWITZERLAND - Huber, Henchoz, Di Jorio, Müller P. (Wolf 78), Hodel, Vogel, Bühlmann (Sesa 71), Wicky, Chapuisat (Comisetti 63), Sforza, Türkyilmaz.
BELARUS - Afanasenko, Yakimovich, Lavrik, Lukhvich, Ostrovskiy, Gurenko, Baranov, Chaika, Kulchiy (Kachuro 55), Makovskiy (Romashchenko 69), Tarlovskiy.

08/09/99, Naples
ITALY 2 Fuser (10), Vieri (34)
DENMARK 3 Jørgensen (39p), Wieghorst (57), Tomasson (64)
referee - Jol (HOL)
ITALY - Buffon, Panucci, Cannavaro, Nesta, Pancaro, Fuser, Di Francesco (Conte 70), Albertini, Baggio D. (Giannichedda 46), Vieri (Totti 77), Inzaghi.
DENMARK - Schmeichel, Helveg (Goldbaek 52), Henriksen, Høgh, Heintze, Colding, Tøfting (Wieghorst 52), Nielsen A., Jørgensen, Tomasson (Schjønberg 86), Sand.

09/10/99, Minsk
BELARUS 0
ITALY 0
referee - Colombo (FRA)
BELARUS - Shantalosov, Yakhimovich, Tarlovskiy, Lukhvich, Ostrovskiy, Gurenko, Baranov, Orlovskiy, Chaika, Romashchenko (Makovskiy 46), Gerasimets (Kulchiy 79).
ITALY - Buffon, Panucci, Maldini, Di Biagio, Cannavaro, Nesta, Moriero, Conte, Inzaghi, Vieri (Del Piero 81), Zambrotta.

09/10/99, Wrexham
WALES 0
SWITZERLAND 2 Rey (16), Bühlmann (60)
referee - Papadakos (GRE)
WALES - Jones P., Delaney, Barnard, Page, Coleman, Savage, Robinson J., Saunders (Hartson 66), Blake (Roberts 77), Speed, Oster (Jones M. 67).
SWITZERLAND - Zuberbühler, Haas, Di Jorio, Henchoz, Hodel, Vogel, Sesa, Jaquet (Wyss 70), Rey (Comisetti 66), Jeanneret, Bühlmann.

QUALIFYING GROUP 2

Norway through with perfect away record

Norway made sure of their first ever European Championship qualification with a match to spare as they won back-to-back home games against Greece and Slovenia at the beginning of September.

The Norwegians had previously struggled in Oslo, but the 1-0 victory over the Greeks not only put them into a commanding position but also ensured the elimination of their vanquished opponents.

Slovenia strengthened their position with two successive home wins over Albania and Georgia thanks to winning goals from the ever-prolific Zlatko Zahovic - his seventh and eighth of the competition - but they travelled to Oslo still two points behind and knowing that they had to win the match in order to take control of the group and give themselves a realistic chance of finishing first. In the event, the Slovenians were swamped as Norway treated a packed house in the Ullevaal stadium to their most convincing performance of the competition. Two early goals set them on their way, and by the final whistle they and their fans were celebrating an historic qualification with a comprehensive 4-0 victory.

It was not all bad news for the Slovenians, however. Latvia's failure to win in Georgia meant that Srecko Katanec's side were certain of finishing second. For that reason they rested several key players (Zahovic among them) for the final encounter at home to Greece, which resulted in a 0-3 defeat.

There was no let-up from Norway, who managed to grab a late winner to beat Latvia 2-1 in Riga and maintain their remarkable 100 per cent record away from home. The game's goalscorers were all from the English Premiership, with Ole Gunnar Solskjaer and Tore André Flo netting for Norway and Marian Pahars finding the target for Latvia.

TOP SCORERS

8	Zlatko ZAHOVIC (Slovenia)	
5	Tore André FLO (Norway)	
	Ole Gunnar SOLSKJAER (Norway)	
4	Steffen IVERSEN (Norway)	
3	Nikos MAHLAS (Greece)	Marian PAHARS (Latvia)
	Andrey SHTOLCERS (Latvia)	Alban BUSHI (Albania)
	Shota ARVELADZE (Georgia)	

GROUP 2 FINAL TABLE

		Pd	Home W	D	L	F	A	Away W	D	L	F	A	Total W	D	L	F	A	Pt	GD
1	Norway	10	3	1	1	9	5	5	0	0	12	4	8	1	1	21	9	25	12
2	Slovenia	10	3	0	2	6	6	2	2	1	6	8	5	2	3	12	14	17	-2
3	Greece	10	2	1	2	8	6	2	2	1	5	2	4	3	3	13	8	15	5
4	Latvia	10	1	2	2	3	4	2	2	1	10	8	3	4	3	13	12	13	1
5	Albania	10	1	2	2	6	7	0	2	3	2	7	1	4	5	8	14	7	-6
6	Georgia	10	1	2	2	6	9	0	0	5	2	9	1	2	7	8	18	5	-10

QUALIFYING GROUP 2

GROUP 2 MATCH DETAILS 1999/2000

18/08/99, Ljubljana
SLOVENIA 2 Zahovic (49), Osterc (80)
ALBANIA 0
referee - Da Silva (POR)
SLOVENIA - Dabanovic, Osterc, Rudonja, Milanic (Milinovic 69), Galic, Knavs, Novak (Istenic 90), Ceh, Udovic (Acimovic 46), Zahovic, Pavlin.
ALBANIA - Strakosha, Pinari, Shulku, Xhumba, Vata, Bellai, Haxhi, Murati (Halili 58), Kola, Rraklli (Bogdani 60), Tare.

04/09/99, Oslo
NORWAY 1 Leonhardsen (35)
GREECE 0
referee - Merk (GER)
NORWAY - Olsen, Berg, Bergdølmo, Hoftun, Heggem, Leonhardsen (Riseth 74), Mykland, Skammelsrud, Solskjaer (Rudi 69), Flo T.A., Iversen.
GREECE - Atmatsidis, Mavrogenidis, Kasapis, Dabizas, Uzunidis, Pursanidis, Zagorakis (Mahlas 50), Niniadis (Yanakopoulos 46), Yeorgatos, Limberopoulos, Nikolaidis.

04/09/99, Tirana
ALBANIA 3 Bushi (29, 78), Muka (90)
LATVIA 3 Astafyev (21, 63), Shtolcers (70)
referee - Hamer (LUX)
ALBANIA - Strakosha, Lala, Shulku, Xhumba, Vata, Fakaj (Bogdani 67), Haxhi, Bushi, Bellai, Murati (Dalipi 46), Tare (Muka 78).
LATVIA - Kolinko, Stepanov, Astafyev (Babichev 82), Zemlinsky, Lobanyov, Lukashevich, Ivanov (Blagonadezhdin 60), Bleidelis, Rubins, Shtolcers (Boulders 85), Mikholap.

04/09/99, Ljubljana
SLOVENIA 2 Acimovic (48), Zahovic (80)
GEORGIA 1 Arveladze S. (56)
referee - Wegereef (HOL)
SLOVENIA - Simeunovic, Osterc (Acimovic 46), Rudonja, Milinovic, Galic, Knavs, Novak, Ceh, Udovic (Karic 75), Zahovic (Istenic 90), Pavlin.
GEORGIA - Gvaramadze, Kobiashvili, Tskitishvili, Didava, Sichinava, Akhvlediani (Shekiladze 46), Kaladze, Potskhveria, Kavelashvili, Arveladze A., Arveladze S.

08/09/99, Tbilisi
GEORGIA 2 Arveladze S. (30), Kavelashvili (52)
LATVIA 2 Bleidelis (62), Stepanov (90)
referee - Radoman (YUG)
GEORGIA - Gvaramadze, Didava, Kaladze, Tsereteli, Tskitishvili (Sichinava 70), Nemsadze, Jamarauli, Kobiashvili, Shekiladze, Kavelashvili (Arveladze A. 75), Arveladze S. (Demetradze 72).
LATVIA - Kolinko, Stepanov, Laizans (Boulders 83), Zemlinsky, Lobanyov, Rubins, Pahars, Isakov (Babichev 59), Bleidelis, Shtolcers (Sharando 74), Ivanov.

08/09/99, Oslo
NORWAY 4 Istenic (16og), Iversen (18), Solskjaer (30), Leonhardsen (68)
SLOVENIA 0
referee - Veissière (FRA)
NORWAY - Olsen, Berg, Bergdølmo, Hoftun, Heggem, Leonhardsen, Mykland, Skammelsrud (Sørensen 78), Solskjaer (Riseth 79), Flo T.A. (Lund 89), Iversen.
SLOVENIA - Simeunovic (Dabanovic 46), Knavs, Milinovic, Novak, Rudonja, Pavlin, Zahovic, Ceh, Osterc (Acimovic 81), Udovic (Karic 39), Istenic.

06/10/99, Athens
GREECE 2 Tsartas (1), Yeorgiadiss (88)
ALBANIA 0
referee - Ivanov (RUS)
GREECE - Atmatsidis, Amanatidis, Yeorgatos (Niniadis 68), Uzunidis, Katsiambis, Zagorakis (Yeorgiadis 46), Dabizas, Zikos, Mahlas, Tsartas, Nikolaidis.
ALBANIA - Strakosha, Murati (Duro 54), Haxhi, Lala, Xhumba, Vata, Bushi, Bellai (Bogdani 84), Rraklli, Kola, Tare (Muka 68).

09/10/99, Maribor
SLOVENIA 0
GREECE 3 Tsartas (36), Yeorgiadis (42), Nikolaidis (80)
referee - El Ghandour (EGY)
SLOVENIA - Simeunovic, Bajrektarevic, Rudonja, Vugdalic (Englaro 86) Galic, Seslar, Novak, Ceh, Udovic (Karic 46), Acimovic, Simundza (Osterc 60).
GREECE - Atmatsidis, Amanatidis, Zikos, Dabizas, Antzas (Zagorakis 71), Poursanidis, Yeorgiadis, Konstandinidis, Limberopoulos, Tsartas (Niniadis 68), Nikolaidis (Mahlas 81).

09/10/99, Riga
LATVIA 1 Pahars (53)
NORWAY 2 Solskjaer (52), Flo T.A. (86)
referee - Drabek (AUT)
LATVIA - Kolinko, Lukashevich (Laizans 82), Astafyev, Zemlinsky, Blagonadezhdin, Ivanov, Bleidelis, Pahars, Rubins, Shtolcers.
NORWAY - Olsen, Bergdølmo, Hoftun, Berg, Heggem, Iversen (Lund 46), Mykland (Solbakken 80), Leonhardsen, Flo T.A., Solskjaer (Riseth 89), Skammelsrud.

09/10/99, Tirana
ALBANIA 2 Rraklli (30), Kola (36)
GEORGIA 1 Arveladze S. (52)
referee - Micallef (MLT)
ALBANIA - Beqaj, Duro, Shulku, Xhumba, Vata, Fakaj, Lala, Bushi (Murati 54), Kola, Rraklli (Muka 73), Tare (Bogdani 90).
GEORGIA - Chanturia, Kobiashvili, Gokhokidze, Didava, Shekiladze, Chichveishvili, Nemsadze, Jamarauli, Kaladze, Arveladze A. (Janashia 83), Arveladze S.

QUALIFYING GROUP 3

Lucky Germans let off the hook

As expected, the private battle for first place between Germany and Turkey went down to the final head-to-head showdown in Munich.

For a long while it looked as if the Germans would have to win that match in order to claim top spot, but when Turkey dropped two points unexpectedly in a 1-1 draw away to Moldova, the picture altered. Now it was the Turks who had to win, with Germany, the defending European champions, needing only a draw to ensure their progress.

Erich Ribbeck's team went into the Munich decider fortified by successive victories away to Finland at home to Northern Ireland.

Captain Oliver Bierhoff was their matchwinner in Helsinki, scoring two early goals in the 2-1 win, while recalled wing-back Christian Ziege took centre stage in Dortmund against the Northern Irish, setting up another early Bierhoff strike and then scoring three excellent goals of his own to complete the first

TOP SCORERS

7	Oliver BIERHOFF (Germany)
4	HAKAN Sükür (Turkey)
	TAYFUR Havutçu (Turkey)
3	Marco BODE (Germany)
	Ulf KIRSTEN (Germany)
	Christian ZIEGE (Germany)
	ARIF Erdem (Turkey)
	Jonatan JOHANSSON (Finland)
	Joonas KOLKKA (Finland)
	Mika-Matti PAATELAINEN (Finland)
	Igor OPREA (Moldova)

hat-trick of his career and seal an easy 4-0 victory.

Turkey had a hat-trick hero of their own in their game against Northern Ireland, with front-runner Arif Erdem putting the ball in the net three times in five minutes to give his team a 3-0 win. It would have been better for the Turks had Arif saved one of those goals for the following match in Chisinau four days later. Trailing 0-1 for most of the game, Turkey finally drew level late in the game when midfielder Tayfur drove the ball powerfully home from the edge of the area. But when Hakan Sükür had a diving header spectacularly saved by the Moldovan 'keeper in the closing moments, the Turks were forced to settle for a draw.

It was a point that mattered little in the context of finishing first, but it meant that Turkey could still reach the finals as the best runners-up even if they drew against Germany - provided that in Group Seven Portugal did not defeat Hungary by three goals.

Victory, of course, was Turkey's first

GROUP 3 FINAL TABLE

		Pd	Home W	D	L	F	A	Away W	D	L	F	A	Total W	D	L	F	A	Pt	GD
1	Germany	8	3	1	0	12	1	3	0	1	8	3	6	1	1	20	4	19	16
2	Turkey	8	3	0	1	7	3	2	2	0	8	3	5	2	1	15	6	17	9
3	Finland	8	2	0	2	10	9	1	1	2	3	4	3	1	4	13	13	10	0
4	Northern Ireland	8	1	1	2	3	8	0	1	3	1	11	1	2	5	4	19	5	-15
5	Moldova	8	0	3	1	2	4	0	1	3	5	13	0	4	4	7	17	4	-10

QUALIFYING GROUP 3

priority and, backed by a huge following in the Olympiastadion, they went for the German jugular right from the start. Three times in the opening eight minutes the Turks created clear chances to score. Midfielder Sergen Yalçin wasted the first of them when he skied over with his weaker right foot, but he then turned creator with two sublime passes to set up Tayfur and Tayfun, each of whom could not convert the chance.

Throughout the first half Turkey were the superior team but they could not make the all-important breakthrough. A scandalous offside decision denied Hakan Sükür early in the second half as he raced clear onto another excellent Sergen through-ball, but in the last half-hour Turkey visibly tired and Germany - a very mediocre Germany - just held on for the point that saw them through to the finals.

As for Turkey, their valiant efforts proved to be in vain on two counts. With Portugal beating Hungary 3-0, the only reward for Mustafa Denizli's men was a second bite of the qualification cherry in the play-offs - a prize already promised to them after the victory in Belfast.

Turkey's Tugay Kerimoglu (right) dives in to tackle Northern Ireland's Jon McCarthy.

GROUP 3 MATCH DETAILS 1999/2000

04/09/99, Belfast
NORTHERN IRELAND 0
TURKEY 3 Arif (45, 46, 49)
referee - Sars (FRA)
NORTHERN IRELAND - Taylor, Hughes A., Horlock, Lomas, Williams, Hunter, McCarthy (Gillespie 63), Lennon, Dowie (Quinn 73), Hughes M., Kennedy.
TURKEY - Rüstü, Ali Eren, Ogün, Tayfur, Alpay, Arif (Okan 79), Abdullah (Hakan Ünsal 75), Tugay, Hakan Sükür, Sergen (Ümit 89), Tayfun.

04/09/99, Helsinki
FINLAND 1 Salli (63)
GERMANY 2 Bierhoff (2, 17)
referee - López Nieto (ESP)
FINLAND - Niemi (Laaksonen 46), Ylönen (Kuqi 46), Kuivasto, Hyypiä, Salli, Riihilahti, Wiss, Saastamoinen, Kottila, Tainio, Johansson.
GERMANY - Lehmann, Babbel, Ziege, Linke, Nowotny, Jeremies, Scholl (Nerlinger 79), Neuville (Strunz 85), Bierhoff, Matthäus, Kirsten (Schneider 32).

08/09/99, Dortmund
GERMANY 4 Bierhoff (2), Ziege (16, 33, 45)
NORTHERN IRELAND 0
referee - Bikas (GRE)
GERMANY - Lehmann, Nowotny (Wörns 46), Matthäus, Linke, Babbel (Strunz 30), Scholl, Jeremies, Ziege, Neuville (Schneider 66), Bierhoff, Bode.
NORTHERN IRELAND - Taylor, Nolan, Williams, Morrow, Horlock, McCarthy, Lomas, Lennon (Gillespie 46), Kennedy, Dowie (Quinn 46), Hughes M.

08/09/99, Chisinau
MOLDOVA 1 Epureanu (3)
TURKEY 1 Tayfur (76)
referee - Schluchter (SUI)
MOLDOVA - Dinov, Fistican, Stroenco, Guzun (Sischin 78), Oprea, Osipenco, Epureanu, Gaidamasciuc (Stratulat 46), Boret, Rebeja, Clescenco (Kirilov 82).
TURKEY - Rüstü, Ali Eren, Alpay, Fatih (Ayhan 46), Ogün, Tayfur, Hakan Ünsal, Sergen (Ümit 88), Hakan Sükür, Arif, Okan (Tugay 46).

09/10/99, Helsinki
FINLAND 4 Johansson (9), Hyypiä (63), Kolkka (72, 82)
NORTHERN IRELAND 1 Whitley Je. (59)
referee - Ancion (BEL)
FINLAND - Viander, Lehkosuo, Kuivasto, Hyypiä, Tihinen, Wiss (Ylä-Jussila 86), Kolkka, Riihilahti (Valakari 86), Litmanen, Paatelainen, Johansson.
NORTHERN IRELAND - Taylor, Jenkins (Whitley Ji. 79), Williams, Morrow, Nolan, McCarthy, Whitley Je., Lennon, Kennedy, Hughes M. (Johnson 74), Quinn (Coote 68).

09/10/99, Munich
GERMANY 0
TURKEY 0
referee - Collina (ITA)
GERMANY - Kahn, Babbel, Ziege (Bode 76), Linke, Schneider (Dogan 89), Jeremies, Scholl, Hamann (Nerlinger 46), Bierhoff, Matthäus, Neuville.
TURKEY - Rüstü, Ali Eren, Ogün, Fatih, Alpay, Abdullah (Ergün 69), Tayfur (Oktay 85), Hakan Sükür, Sergen, Okan (Arif 72).

QUALIFYING GROUP 4

Russian goalkeeper lets in France

This was the most closely-contested of all the qualifying groups and, fittingly, the outcome was not settled until the final whistle had sounded in each of the two decisive last-day encounters in Moscow and Paris.

France and Ukraine had seemed the likeliest qualifiers until Russia came storming back into contention with a burst of six consecutive victories. Iceland, too, were not out of it until they lost their penultimate match at home to Ukraine. With Russia and France also obtaining narrow away wins on the same day, it left the situation at the top of the group delicately poised with just one round of matches remaining.

Unbeaten Ukraine had one point more than both Russia and France but their final fixture was away to the in-form Russians. France, meanwhile, were at home to the tenacious Icelanders, who still had a theoretical chance of reaching the play-offs if they were to win in Paris. The French themselves needed a win to ensure that they remained in the competition, but only a draw in Moscow, allied to that result, would give them first place. A win

for either Russia or Ukraine would also be a guarantee of automatic qualification (unless, in Russia's case, France beat Iceland by six goals).

There were a whole host of permutations before kick-off, and it remained that way throughout the course of the 90 minutes. France went 2-0 up against Iceland, only to be sensationally pegged back by two strikes early in the second half. At that stage the match in Moscow was goalless and France were eliminated. But then came the twists. Firstly, substitute David Trezeguet pounced on a loose ball and put France 3-2 up. Secondly, Russian midfielder Valeriy Karpin rifled a free-kick through the Ukrainian wall and into the net.

That was still the state of play with three minutes remaining, and it meant that Russia were through to the finals, with France in the play-offs. But then came the final, fateful act of a dramatic evening. Ukraine, desperate for a goal, won a free-kick on the left touchline. Andriy Shevchenko swung it into the crowded area with his right foot. It was heading for the hands of Russian goal-

GROUP 4 FINAL TABLE

			Home					Away					Total					
		Pd	W	D	L	F	A	W	D	L	F	A	W	D	L	F	A	Pt	GD
1	France	10	3	1	1	9	5	3	2	0	8	5	6	3	1	17	10	21	7
2	Ukraine	10	3	2	0	10	3	2	3	0	4	1	5	5	0	14	4	20	10
3	Russia	10	3	1	1	12	5	3	0	2	10	7	6	1	3	22	12	19	10
4	Iceland	10	3	1	1	7	2	1	2	2	5	5	4	3	3	12	7	15	5
5	Armenia	10	1	2	2	5	7	1	0	4	3	8	2	2	6	8	15	8	-7
6	Andorra	10	0	0	5	1	10	0	0	5	2	18	0	0	10	3	28	0	-25

QUALIFYING GROUP 4

keeper Aleksandr Filimonov, but he completely misjudged the flight and ended up helping the ball on its way and dropping it over the goal-line. It was a bizarre goal but a hugely significant one. Now the picture had completely changed. Russia, instead of being poised for automatic qualification, were out. Ukraine were in the play-offs. And France, scarcely able to believe their luck, were through to the European Championship finals.

GROUP 4 MATCH DETAILS 1999/2000

04/09/99, Kiev
UKRAINE 0
FRANCE 0
referee - Dallas (SCO)
UKRAINE - Shovkovskyi, Luzhnyi, Popov, Holovko, Vashchuk, Dmitrulin (Mykytyn 46), Gusin (Tsykhmeistruk 79), Maximov (Konovalov 66), Kosovskyi, Shevchenko, Rebrov.
FRANCE - Barthez, Thuram, Lizarazu, Vieira, Blanc, Djorkaeff (Pires 69), Deschamps, Desailly, Anelka (Laslandes 52), Zidane, Karembeu.

04/09/99, Moscow
RUSSIA 2 Beschastnykh (8p), Karpin (70)
ARMENIA 0
referee - Agius (MLT)
RUSSIA - Filimonov, Khlestov, Khokhlov, Smertin, Alenichev, Beschastnykh, Onopko, Karpin, Titov (Semak 80), Panov (Shirko 78), Tikhonov (Yanovskiy 73).
ARMENIA - Berezovski, Mkrchyan, Khachatryan V., Hovsepyan, Hovhannisyan, Vardanyan, Khachatryan R. (Petrosyan T. 84), Harutyunyan (Kakosyan 54), Voskanyan, Shahgeldyan (Delani 77), Mikaelyan.

04/09/99, Reykjavík
ICELAND 3 Gudjónsson Th. (28), Hreidarsson (32), Gudjohnsen (90)
ANDORRA 0
referee - Liba (CZE)
ICELAND - Kristinsson B., Helgason, Hreidarsson, Jónsson, Sigurdsson L. (Vidarsson 29), Gudjónsson B., Gunnarsson, Gudmundsson, Sigurdsson H. (Helguson 57), Gudjónsson Th., Dadason (Gudjohnsen 75).
ANDORRA - Koldo, García A.M. (Godoy Ar. 59), Escura, Ramírez, Txema, Sonejee, Pol (Buxo 90), Emiliano, Jiménez, Sánchez, Godoy Al. (García G. 67).

08/09/99, Yerevan
ARMENIA 2 Mikaelyan (6), Shahgeldyan (90p)
FRANCE 3 Djorkaeff (45p), Zidane (67), Laslandes (74)
referee - Uzunov (BUL)
ARMENIA - Berezovski, Mkrchyan, Khachatryan V., Hovsepyan, Khachatryan R. (Kocharyan 74), Yesayan, Petrosyan T., Harutyunyan (Grigoryan 63), Sarkisyan, Shahgeldyan, Mikaelyan (Delani 67).
FRANCE - Barthez, Thuram, Lizarazu, Karembeu, Blanc, Djorkaeff, Deschamps, Desailly, Laslandes, Zidane (Déhu 72), Wiltord (Robert 66).

08/09/99, Reykjavík
ICELAND 0
UKRAINE 1 Rebrov (43p)
referee - Vítor Pereira (POR)
ICELAND - Kristinsson B., Helgason, Hreidarsson, Jónsson (Vidarsson 84), Sigurdsson L., Kristinsson R., Gunnarsson, Kolvidsson (Helguson 58), Marteinsson, Gudjónsson Th., Dadason (Gudjohnsen 72).

UKRAINE - Shovkovskyi, Luzhnyi (Mykytyn 79), Popov, Holovko, Vashchuk, Dmitrulin, Maximov, Konovalov (Tsykhmeistruk 66), Kosovskyi, Shevchenko, Rebrov.

08/09/99, Andorra La Vella
ANDORRA 1 Ruiz (39p)
RUSSIA 2 Onopko (23, 57)
referee - Larsen (DEN)
ANDORRA - Koldo, Ramírez, Escura, Txema, Sonejee, Lima I., Emiliano, Godoy Al. (Pol 59), Jiménez, Sánchez (Godoy Ar. 89), Ruiz.
RUSSIA - Filimonov, Khlestov, Onopko, Smertin, Khokhlov (Bezrodnyi 65), Karpin, Alenichev (Yanovskiy 61), Titov, Tikhonov, Beschastnykh (Panov 46), Shirko.

09/10/99, Saint-Denis
FRANCE 3 Dadason (17og), Djorkaeff (38), Trezeguet (71)
ICELAND 2 Sverrisson E. (47), Gunnarsson (56)
referee - Heynemann (GER)
FRANCE - Lama, Thuram, Blanc, Desailly, Lizarazu, Deschamps, Boghossian (Vieira 90), Zidane, Djorkaeff, Laslandes (Trezeguet 63), Wiltord (Vairelles 90).
ICELAND - Kristinsson B., Helgason, Sigurdsson L., Marteinsson (Kolvidsson 80), Hreidarsson, Sverrisson E., Kristinsson R., Gunnarsson, Gudjónsson Th., Sigurdsson H. (Helguson 65), Dadason (Gudjohnsen 54).

09/10/99, Moscow
RUSSIA 1 Karpin (75)
UKRAINE 1 Shevchenko (87)
referee - Elleray (ENG)
RUSSIA - Filimonov, Khlestov, Khokhlov, Smertin, Alenichev, Drozdov, Onopko, Karpin, Titov, Panov (Semak 76), Tikhonov (Beschastnykh 61).
UKRAINE - Shovkovskyi, Luzhnyi, Mizin, Holovko, Vashchuk, Dmitrulin (Kovalev 76), Maximov (Moroz 76), Gusin, Skachenko (Mykytyn 42), Shevchenko, Rebrov.

09/10/99, Andorra La Vella
ANDORRA 0
ARMENIA 3 Petrosyan A. (26), Yesayan (59), Shahgeldyan (63)
referee - Jones (ENG)
ANDORRA - Koldo, Ramírez, Escura, Sonejee, Txema (Jonas 58), Lima, Godoy Al. (Pol 56), Emiliano (Soria 62), Jiménez, Sánchez, Ruiz.
ARMENIA - Abrahamyan, Sukiasyan, Voskanyan, Mkrchyan, Khachatryan R., Vardanyan, Petrosyan A. (Hakopyan Ara 79), Petrosyan T. (Kocharyan 82), Sarkisyan, Shahgeldyan (Minasyan 78), Yesayan.

QUALIFYING GROUP 5

Sweden give England a helping hand

Sweden, unbeaten and unchallenged, made light work of their qualification. They clinched their place at the finals with back-to-back 1-0 wins against Bulgaria and Luxembourg...and then found themselves in the position of independent arbiter as England and Poland, their distant pursuers, sought salvation with a place in the play-offs.

Both teams had the chance to settle their own fate when they came face to face in Warsaw in September. A win for either would ensure a play-off spot whereas a draw would resolve nothing. England travelled to the Polish capital fuelled with confidence after slaughtering Luxembourg 6-0 at Wembley, with captain Alan Shearer scoring a hat-trick. But Poland were a considerably tougher test, and they genuinely fancied their chances of gaining the victory that would send their old adversaries spinning out of the competition.

It was a fairly even match, but not one of any great aesthetic value. Its appeal was its tension and the knowledge of what was at stake. England created the clearer openings but Robbie Fowler spurned two good chances in the first

half. England were denied a blatant penalty after 57 minutes when Paul Scholes was brought down in the area, but they could have no complaints with the referee's decision when he sent off midfielder David Batty for a crude challenge six minutes from time. Shortly afterwards Andrzej Juskowiak was persented with a glorious chance to win the match but his header was directed straight at England goalkeeper Nigel Martyn, who saved.

It was a stalemate, but the reactions at the final whistle indicated that the Poles were the happier with the result. They still had one game left to play - away to already qualified Sweden - whereas England, their progamme completed, had left themselves completely at the mercy of the group winners. Only a Swedish victory would save them.

And so to the Råsunda stadium. For 45 minutes almost nothing happened, and the suspicion was raised - certainly from an English standpoint - that the two teams had made prior arrangement for a mutual stand-off. This was England's great fear. But midway through the second half the match came alive when Kennet Andersson latched on to a superb pass from Fredrik Ljungberg

TOP SCORERS

6	Alan SHEARER (England)
3	Henrik LARSSON (Sweden)
	Paul SCHOLES (England)
	Tomasz IWAN (Poland)

GROUP 5 FINAL TABLE

			Home				Away					Total						
		Pd	W	D	L	F	A	W	D	L	F	A	W	D	L	F	A	Pt	GD
1	Sweden	8	4	0	0	7	1	3	1	0	3	0	7	1	0	10	1	22	9
2	England	8	2	2	0	9	1	1	2	1	5	3	3	4	1	14	4	13	10
3	Poland	8	2	1	1	5	1	2	0	2	7	7	4	1	3	12	8	13	4
4	Bulgaria	8	1	1	2	4	5	1	1	2	2	3	2	2	4	6	8	8	-2
5	Luxembourg	8	0	0	4	2	9	0	0	4	0	14	0	0	8	2	23	0	-21

QUALIFYING GROUP 5

and slid a shot under the Polish goalkeeper to put Sweden in front.

Poland almost came back and equalised straight away but a couple of half-chances went begging. English frustration mounted soon afterwards after a terrible close-range miss from Andersson, who tried to chest Henrik Larsson's cross into the net when a simple header would have done the trick. Finally, though, the Poles petered out, and a stoppage-time goal from Larsson completed yet another Swedish victory - their seventh of the campaign.

With just one goal conceded and two points dropped, Sweden were comprehensive victors. England - a desperately grateful and relieved England - were now faced with the chance to redeem themselves in the play-offs. Theirs had been a woeful campaign, but their one satisfactory performance - the 3-1 victory at home to Poland - ultimately saved their bacon. Poland had the same number of points, but England's superioriority in head-to-head combat tipped the balance in their favour.

England's Martin Keown is blocked by a wall of Luxembourg players.

GROUP 5 MATCH DETAILS 1999/2000

04/09/99, Solna
SWEDEN 1 Alexandersson (65)
BULGARIA 0
referee - Koren (ISR)
SWEDEN - Hedman, Nilsson, Andersson P., Björklund, Kåmark, Andersson D., Mild (Svensson Ma. 83), Mjällby, Ljungberg (Alexandersson 63), Larsson, Andersson K.
BULGARIA - Ivankov, Stoilov (Gruev 88), Zagorcic (Yankov 25), Petkov I., Markov, Kirilov, Borimirov, Petrov S., Hristov M., Petkov M., Todorov (Yovov 46).

04/09/99, Wembley
ENGLAND 6 Shearer (12p, 27, 33), McManaman (29, 43), Owen (89)
LUXEMBOURG 0
referee - Shmolik (BLS)
ENGLAND - Martyn, Dyer (Neville G. 46), Keown, Adams (Neville P. 65), Pearce, McManaman, Beckham (Owen 65), Batty, Parlour, Shearer, Fowler.
LUXEMBOURG - Felgen, Ferron, Schauls, Birsens, Funck, Saibene, Theis, Vanek, Schneider (Alverdi 46), Posing (Deville F. 82), Christophe (Zaritski 62).

08/09/99, Warsaw
POLAND 0
ENGLAND 0
referee - Benkö (AUT)
POLAND - Matysek, Klos (Bak 89), Zielinski, Waldoch, Siadaczka, Iwan, Nowak, Hajto, Michalski, Gilewicz (Juskowiak 64), Trzeciak (Swierczewski 60).
ENGLAND - Martyn, Neville G. (Neville P. 13), Keown, Adams, Pearce, Scholes, Beckham, Batty, McManaman (Dyer 79), Fowler (Owen 65), Shearer.

08/09/99, Luxembourg
LUXEMBOURG 0
SWEDEN 1 Alexandersson (39)
referee - Hanacsek (HUN)
LUXEMBOURG - Felgen, Strasser, Schauls, Birsens, Funck, Vanek, Posing, Saibene (Holtz 87), Schneider (Zaritski 46), Alverdi (Theis 72), Christophe.
SWEDEN - Hedman, Nilsson, Andersson P., Mjällby, Lucic, Schwarz (Sundgren 81), Mild, Alexandersson, Svensson Ma. (Zetterberg 46), Larsson, Andersson K.

09/10/99, Solna
SWEDEN 2 Andersson K. (64), Larsson (90)
POLAND 0
referee - Meier (SUI)
SWEDEN - Hedman, Nilsson (Sundgren 46), Andersson P., Björklund, Kåmark, Schwarz, Alexandersson, Mjällby, Ljungberg (Mild 83), Larsson, Andersson K.
POLAND - Matysek, Klos, Waldoch, Siadaczka, Zielinski, Hajto, Swierczewski (Wichniarek 89), Michalski, Juskowiak (Kryszalowicz 81), Czereszewski (Nowak 73), Trzeciak.

10/10/99, Sofia
BULGARIA 3 Borimirov (40), Petkov I. (68), Hristov (78)
LUXEMBOURG 0
referee - Gadoski (SVK)
BULGARIA - Zdravkov, Zagorcic (Ivanov 82), Stoilov, Petkov I., Yordanov, Markov, Borimirov, Petrov S., Hristov M. (Todorov 64), Aleksandrov, Bachev (Hristov R. 50).
LUXEMBOURG - Felgen, Vanek, Schauls, Birsens, Strasser, Saibene, Alverdi (Theis 70), Posing (Deville F. 58), Christophe, Cardoni (Holtz 86), Zaritski.

QUALIFYING GROUP 6

Goal-crazy Spain leave rivals standing

GROUP 6 RESULTS - 98/99

AUSTRIA 1, ISRAEL 1	CYPRUS 4, SAN MARINO 0
CYPRUS 3, SPAIN 2	SPAIN 9, AUSTRIA 0
CYPRUS 0, AUSTRIA 3	ISRAEL 3, CYPRUS 0
SAN MARINO 0, ISRAEL 5	SAN MARINO 0, SPAIN 6
ISRAEL 1, SPAIN 2	AUSTRIA 7, SAN MARINO 0
SAN MARINO 1, AUSTRIA 4	SPAIN 9, SAN MARINO 0
SAN MARINO 0, CYPRUS 1	ISRAEL 5, AUSTRIA 0

Spain, fully recovered from their shock opening defeat in Cyprus, completed their campaign with three comprehensive victories to run away with Group Six. Their home record was extraordinary. After the two 9-0 victories over Austria and San Marino the previous season, José Camacho's team also put Cyprus and Israel to the sword. The final goal-balance from their four home games was a staggering 29 for, none against.

It was the team's third successive away victory, however, which ensured that Spain would finish on top of the pile. Austria had every reason to fear the Spaniards after their earlier drubbing in Valencia, but for much of the re-match in Vienna the Austrians were actually on top. Unlucky not to take an early lead when Christian Mayrleb struck the inside of the post, they came back to level 1-1 early in the second half when Spain's captain, Fernando Hierro, volleyed into his own net from Ivica Vastic's free-kick. Not long afterwards, however, Hierro

TOP SCORERS

11	RAUL González (Spain)
6	Ismael URZAIZ (Spain)
5	Fernando HIERRO (Spain)
	Alon MIZRAHI (Israel)
	Ivica VASTIC (Austria)
4	Joseba ETXEBERRIA (Spain)
	LUIS ENRIQUE (Spain)
	Haim REVIVO (Israel)
	Yossi BENAYOUN (Israel)
	Milenko SPOLJARIC (Cyprus)
3	Julen GUERRERO (Spain)
	Avi NIMNI (Israel)
	Christian MAYRLEB (Austria)

made amends when he curled in a beautifully measured free-kick, and it was left to Luis Enrique to seal Spain's victory with a brilliant header two minutes from time.

Austria's elimination was confirmed a few days later when Israel, who had surprisingly gone down 2-3 in Cyprus, destroyed San Marino 8-0 in Tel-Aviv. Spain's victory over Cyprus by the same scoreline - featuring hat-tricks from the Athletic Bilbao pair Urzaiz and Guerrero - also ensured their qualification as group winners.

The only issue still to be settled by the final round of matches was the identity of the group runners-up. Israel had a one-point advantage over Cyprus, but they had to travel to Albacete to take on mighty Spain - a guaranteed home-banker given what had gone before - which left Cyprus needing to win their final fixture away to Austria in order to pip the Israelis for the play-off spot.

It was a tough enough propsition to start with, but when Cyprus conceded a

GROUP 6 FINAL TABLE

		Pd	Home					Away					Total					Pt	GD
			W	D	L	F	A	W	D	L	F	A	W	D	L	F	A		
1	Spain	8	4	0	0	29	0	3	0	1	13	5	7	0	1	42	5	21	37
2	Israel	8	3	0	1	17	2	1	1	2	8	7	4	1	3	25	9	13	16
3	Austria	8	2	1	1	12	5	2	0	2	7	15	4	1	3	19	20	13	-1
4	Cyprus	8	3	0	1	10	7	1	0	3	2	14	4	0	4	12	21	12	-9
5	San Marino	8	0	0	4	1	16	0	0	4	0	28	0	0	8	1	44	0	-43

QUALIFYING GROUP 6

soft goal after five minutes, then another midway through the first half, their hopes lay in tatters. Red cards for Costas Kaiafas and Milenko Spoljaric deepened the gloom, but there was an unexpected consolation for the visitors when defender Costas Costa broke free to score an exhiliarting solo goal - the perfect parting shot from a team that had greatly exceeded all expectations during the course of the competition.

Israel managed to restrict Spain to just three goals in their final match, but their defeat was academic thanks to Austria's win. The 42nd and last goal of Spain's prolific campaign was scored by Raúl, who, with a personal haul of 11, confirmed himself as the Euro 2000 qualifying competition's top scorer, three ahead of Slovenia's Zlatko Zahovic.

Gaizka Mendieta of Valencia came off the bench to star for Spain.

GROUP 6 MATCH DETAILS 1999/2000

04/09/99, Vienna
AUSTRIA 1 Hierro (54og)
SPAIN 3 Raúl (22), Hierro (55), Luis Enrique (87)
referee - Piraux (BEL)
AUSTRIA - Manninger, Hatz, Streiter, Winklhofer, Ibertsberger, Mählich (Schopp 60), Cerny, Kühbauer, Mayrleb, Vastic, Kirchler (Weissenberger 67).
SPAIN - Cañizares, Míchel Salgado, Sergi, Guardiola, Paco, Hierro, Etxeberria (Mendieta 80), Luis Enrique, Morientes (Guerrero 87), Raúl, Valerón (Engonga 72).

05/09/99, Limassol
CYPRUS 3 Engomitis(28), Spoljaric (53, 86p)
ISRAEL 2 Badir (33), Benayoun (82)
referee - Barber (ENG)
CYPRUS - Panayiotou, Costa, Pittas, Kaiafas (Aristocleous 80), Charalambous M., Melanarkitis, Engomitis, Spoljaric, Gogic (Constandinou 71), Papavassiliou (Christodoulou 65), Okkas.
ISRAEL - Davidovich, Harazi A., Ghrayeb, Shelach (Sivilia 64), Benado, Hazan, Banin, Revivo, Abuksis (Benayoun 55), Berkovic (Badir 16), Mizrahi.

08/09/99, Badajoz
SPAIN 8 Urzaiz (20, 25, 38), Guerrero (33, 42, 57), César (82), Hierro (89)
CYPRUS 0
referee - Trentalange (ITA)
SPAIN - Cañizares (Toni 78), Míchel Salgado, Hierro, César, Aranzábal, Etxeberria (Munitis 46), Guardiola, Guerrero, Luis Enrique (Mendieta 60), Raúl, Urzaiz.
CYPRUS - Panayiotou, Costa, Engomitis, Pittas (Theodotou 46), Luca, Melanarkitis, Christodoulou, Nicolaou (Aristocleous 46), Gogic (Yiasemakis 88), Papavassiliou, Okkas.

08/09/99, Tel-Aviv
ISRAEL 8 Benayoun (25, 46, 70), Mizrahi (38), Revivo (40, 69), Sivilia (83), Abuksis (89)
SAN MARINO 0
referee - Kaplan (TUR)
ISRAEL - Davidovich, Harazi A., Amsalem, Talker, Benado (Halfon 65), Hazan, Telesnikov, Revivo, Benayoun, Tikva (Abuksis 61), Mizrahi (Sivilia 46).
SAN MARINO - Gasperoni F., Tomassoni, Gennari, Bacciocchi S., Pelliccioni, Della Balda, Bacchiocchi N. (Selva R. 58), Gasperoni B., Montagna (De Luigi 80), Selva A., Zonzini (Della Valle 74).

10/10/99, Albacete
SPAIN 3 Morientes (30), César (37), Raúl (52)
ISRAEL 0
referee - Krug (GER)
SPAIN - Toni, Míchel Salgado, Hierro (César 24), Paco, Sergi, Etxeberria, Guardiola, Luis Enrique, Guerrero (Mendieta 69), Morientes (Urzaiz 77), Raúl.
ISRAEL - Auat, Gershon, Amsalem, Shelach, Benado (Halfon 50), Hazan (Telesnikov 81), Banin, Tal, Berkovic (Benayoun 67), Revivo, Turgeman.

10/10/99, Vienna
AUSTRIA 3 Glieder (5), Vastic (23), Herzog (81)
CYPRUS 1 Costa (63)
referee - Bazzoli (ITA)
AUSTRIA - Manninger, Vastic, Winklhofer, Neukirchner (Herzog 46), Cerny (Kauz 74), Kühbauer, Ibertsberger, Weissenberger (Wimmer 83), Kirchler, Glieder, Mayrleb.
CYPRUS - Panayiotou, Costa, Charalambous M., Alexandrou, Engomitis, Kaiafas, Melanarkitis (Dimitriou 82), Spoljaric, Christodoulou, Gogic (Agathocleous 25), Okkas (Theodotou 46).

QUALIFYING GROUP 7

Room for two as Romania and Portugal both qualify

Going into the final series of matches, Portugal held a one-point lead over Romania. But the positions were reversed on the first weekend of September when Romania crushed Slovakia 5-1 in Bratislava and Portugal, against all odds, were held 1-1 by Azerbaijan in Baku. In fact, Portugal were lucky to escape with a point, their equaliser, from Luís Figo, not arriving until the very last minute.

That altered the two teams' priorities for their direct confrontation a few days later in Bucharest. Now the onus was on Portugal, rather than Romania, to seek victory.

It was Romania who scored first with a goal that could only be described as a fluke. Adrian Ilie swung in a free-kick from the left touch-line, but nobody got a touch and the ball somehow found its way through the mass of bodies into the net. With the last kick of the first half Portugal equalised, courtesy of a rather more orthodox free-kick, brilliantly curled in by Figo. In the second half the Romanians elected to hold onto what they had, and as Portugal ran out of ideas, the game gradually petered out into the draw that the home side wanted.

TOP SCORERS

8	JOÃO PINTO (Portugal)
6	SÁ PINTO (Portugal)
	RUI COSTA (Portugal)
	Adrian ILIE (Romania)
4	Viorel MOLDOVAN (Romania)
	Vilmós SEBÖK (Hungary)
3	Ioan GANEA (Romania)
	Dorinel MUNTEANU (Romania)
	PAULO MADEIRA (Portugal)

The Romanian fans greeted the final result as if it was a victory, and for good reason. They had preserved their one-point lead and their last remaining fixture was away to lowly Liechtenstein.

All was not lost for Portugal, however. That one point gained in Bucharest put them into contention for the best runners-up spot. The Portuguese knew that if they won their final match, at home to Hungary, by four clear goals, they would be through to the finals.

In the end, with Italy avoiding defeat in Minsk against Belarus, they needed only three - and they got them. On a night of great passion and excitement in the Stadium of Light the Portuguese swarmed forward at every opportunity. A debatable penalty, converted by Rui Costa, sent them on their way, and within a couple of minutes that lead had been doubled by João Pinto's close-range header. The rest of the first half proved frustrating, with striker Pauleta adding to the increasing anxiety by getting himself bizarrely sent off. However, shortly before the hour substitute Abel Xavier scored the vital third goal, heading in Figo's perfect

GROUP 7 FINAL TABLE

		Pd	W	D	L	F	A	W	D	L	F	A	W	D	L	F	A	Pt	GD
1	Romania	10	3	2	0	14	1	4	1	0	11	2	7	3	0	25	3	24	22
2	Portugal	10	4	0	1	19	1	3	2	0	13	3	7	2	1	32	4	23	28
3	Slovakia	10	2	1	2	6	8	3	1	1	6	1	5	2	3	12	9	17	3
4	Hungary	10	2	1	2	10	5	1	2	2	4	5	3	3	4	14	10	12	4
5	Azerbaijan	10	1	1	3	5	7	0	0	5	1	19	1	1	8	6	26	4	-20
6	Liechtenstein	10	1	1	3	2	13	0	0	5	0	26	1	1	8	2	39	4	-37

QUALIFYING GROUP 7

cross. Despite their shortage in numbers Portugal continued to attack, believing that a fourth goal was necessary, but when the result from Minsk filtered through at the end of the game, the celebrations began.

Romania, meanwhile, also clinched their qualification with a 3-0 win, albeit in the decidedly less vibrant setting of Liechtenstein's Rheinpark stadium.

GROUP 7 MATCH DETAILS 1999/2000

04/09/99, Baku
AZERBAIJAN 1 Tagizade (51)
PORTUGAL 1 Figo (90)
referee - Gallagher (ENG)
AZERBAIJAN - Kramarenko, Agaev, Poshekhontsev, Akhmedov, Lychkin (Stukas 90), Getman, Kuliyev, Tagizade, Musayev (Kurbanov 58), Vasilyev (Kambarov 54), Niftaliyev.
PORTUGAL - Vítor Baía, Secretário, Dimas, Paulo Madeira, Fernando Couto, Paulo Sousa (Capucho 67), Figo, João Pinto, Sá Pinto (Sérgio Conceição 46), Rui Costa, Paulo Bento (Pauleta 30).

04/09/99, Vaduz
LIECHTENSTEIN 0
HUNGARY 0
referee - Kaldma (EST)
LIECHTENSTEIN - Jehle, Zech, Ospelt, Hasler, Hefti, Gigon, Stocklasa Ma., Telser (Ritter 60), Stocklasa Mi., Frick M. (Beck M. 90), Beck T. (Bicker 83).
HUNGARY - Király, Korsós G., Sebök V., Halmai, Mátyus, Fehér (Lendvai 46), Dárdai, Illés, Dombi (Sowunmi 60), Horváth (Herczeg 76), Egressy.

04/09/99, Bratislava
SLOVAKIA 1 Labant (22)
ROMANIA 5 Ilie (6), Hagi (30), Ciobotariu (66), Moldovan (88, 90)
referee - Cesari (ITA)
SLOVAKIA - König, Karhan, Nemeth P., Kratochvil (Hrabal 74), Varga, Labant, Valachovic, Balis (Jancula 68), Nemeth S., Janocko, Fabus (Ujlaky 81).
ROMANIA - Stelea, Petrescu, Ciobotariu, Filipescu, Galca, Popescu Gh., Sabau (Stinga 82), Munteanu D., Ganea (Moldovan 58), Hagi (Lupescu 76), Ilie.

08/09/99, Bratislava
SLOVAKIA 2 Nemeth S. (4), Karhan (56)
LIECHTENSTEIN 0
referee - Georgiou (CYP)
SLOVAKIA - Susko, Karhan, Janocko (Hrabal 42), Dzurik, Varga, Labant, Valachovic, Balis, Nemeth S. (Kozuch 76), Ujlaky, Fabus (Nemeth P. 61).
LIECHTENSTEIN - Jehle, Ospelt, Stocklasa Ma., Ritter, Zech, Stocklasa Mi., Beck T., Frick M. (Büchel 12; Beck M. 57), Hasler, Telser, Gigon (Wohlwend 57).

08/09/99, Bucharest
ROMANIA 1 Ilie (37)
PORTUGAL 1 Figo (45)
referee - Strampe (GER)
ROMANIA - Stelea, Petrescu (Nanu 46), Ciobotariu, Filipescu, Galca, Popescu Gh., Sabau, Munteanu D., Moldovan (Lupescu 67), Hagi, Ilie (Ganea 86).
PORTUGAL - Vítor Baía, Rui Bento, Dimas, Paulo Madeira, Fernando Couto, Paulo Sousa (Sérgio Conceição 69), Figo, João Pinto (Pauleta 80), Sá Pinto, Rui Costa, Paulo Bento.

08/09/99, Budapest
HUNGARY 3 Sebök V. (28), Egressy (51), Sowunmi (55)
AZERBAIJAN 0
referee - Lazarevski (MAC)
HUNGARY - Király, Hrutka, Korsós G., Mátyus, Sebök V., Halmai, Lendvai, Egressy, Sowunmi (Füzi 89), Illés, Herczeg (Horváth 74).
AZERBAIJAN - Gasanadze, Getman, Poshekhontsev, Asadov, Lychkin (Stukas 68), Kerimov (Kambarov 60), Kuliyev, Yadullayev, Musayev, Vasilyev (Ismailov 90), Niftaliyev.

09/10/99, Vaduz
LIECHTENSTEIN 0
ROMANIA 3 Rosu (25), Ganea (65, 74)
referee - Butenko (RUS)
LIECHTENSTEIN - Jehle, Ospelt, Stocklasa Ma., Hefti, Zech, Ritter, Frick C. (Wohlwend 89), Frick M., Beck T., Telser (Bicker 69), Beck M..
ROMANIA - Stelea, Petrescu, Nanu, Ciobotariu, Galca (Lupescu 75), Popescu Gh., Petre, Rosu, Moldovan (Ganea 61), Hagi (Stinga 77), Ilie.

09/10/99, Baku
AZERBAIJAN 0
SLOVAKIA 1 Labant (70)
referee - Vasaras (GRE)
AZERBAIJAN - Kramarenko, Agaev (Kerimov 80), Poshokhontsev, Akhmedov, Isaev (Ismailov 56), Getman, Yadullayev, Kambarov (Lychkin 46), Musayev, Vasilyev, Niftaliyev.
SLOVAKIA - Susko, Kozak, Suchancok, Kratochvil, Varga, Labant (Pinte 84), Timko, Karhan (Zeman 86), Nemeth P., Janocko (Kozuch 90), Fabus.

09/10/99, Lisbon
PORTUGAL 3 Rui Costa (14p), João Pinto (16), Abel Xavier (57)
HUNGARY 0
referee - Nielsen (DEN)
PORTUGAL - Vítor Baía, Secretário (Abel Xavier 46), Paulo Madeira, Jorge Costa, Dimas, Paulo Sousa, Rui Costa (Paulo Bento 84), Figo, Sérgio Conceição, João Pinto (Sá Pinto 89), Pauleta.
HUNGARY - Király, Korsós G., Dragóner, Lakos, Mátyus, Lendvai, Halmai, Pisont (Dárdai 25), Sowunmi (Kovács 82), Horváth (Herczeg 76), Egressy.

QUALIFYING GROUP 8

Yugoslavia profit from Ireland's late jitters

Because of the unsettled political situation in the Balkans almost half of the fixtures in Group Eight were crammed into the final two months, including the two long-awaited clashes between bitter rivals Yugoslavia and Croatia.

The first of them, in Belgrade, was a drab stalemate, interrupted for 45 minutes when the floodlights failed at the start of the second half. When Yugoslavia then went to Dublin for the second of their postponed fixtures and lost 2-1, the group became wide open.

Ireland's victory completed a perfect record at Lansdowne Road, but they were to suffer their second successive away defeat (albeit some ten months after the first one) when, four days later, they went down 1-0 in Zagreb to Croatia. It was a night of torment for Mick McCarthy's men, beaten by a Davor Suker strike - his 42nd goal in 52 internationals - four minutes into stoppage time.

Ireland's inability to hold out until the final whistle was to come back to haunt them in even more devastating circumstances on their return to the Balkans a month later.

Going into their final game, in Skopje, the Irish, having narrowly beaten Malta 3-2, trailed Yugoslavia, double winners over Macedonia, by a point, with Croatia a further point back. With the Croats and Yugoslavs meeting face to face in Zagreb, the Irish knew that unless Yugoslavia won that match, a victory for them over the Macedonians would be enough to win the group. Croatia were also still in the frame, knowing that victory would at the very least keep them in the competition.

It was an intriguing situation, and there was to be a dramatic twist right at the end when Ireland, leading 1-0 through an early Niall Quinn strike and on the brink of a place in the finals, allowed Macedonian defender Goran Stavrevski to steam unguarded into the Irish box and send an unstoppable header thudding into the net. The Irish were distraught, but if that was the bad news, the good news was soon to follow as they discovered that Croatia had been held to a 2-2 draw - despite playing the entire second half with a

TOP SCORERS

4   Savo MILOSEVIC (Yugoslavia)
    Robbie KEANE (Republic of Ireland)
    Davor SUKER (Croatia)
3   Predrag MIJATOVIC (Yugoslavia)
    Dejan STANKOVIC (Yugoslavia)
    Niall QUINN (Rep. Ireland)
    Artim SACIRI (Macedonia)
    Sasa CIRIC (Macedonia)

GROUP 8 FINAL TABLE

			Home					Away					Total					
		Pd	W	D	L	F	A	W	D	L	F	A	W	D	L	F	A	Pt	GD
1	Yugoslavia	8	3	1	0	8	2	2	1	1	10	6	5	2	1	18	8	17	10
2	Rep. Ireland	8	4	0	0	10	1	1	1	2	4	5	5	1	2	14	6	16	8
3	Croatia	8	3	1	0	8	5	1	2	1	5	4	4	3	1	13	9	15	4
4	Macedonia	8	1	2	1	8	6	1	0	3	5	8	2	2	4	13	14	8	-1
5	Malta	8	0	0	4	4	12	0	0	4	2	15	0	0	8	6	27	0	-21

QUALIFYING GROUP 8

one-man advantage following Yugoslav defender Zoran Markovic's sending-off.

Two almost identical Yugoslav goals, both sourced from Sinisa Mihajlovic free-kicks and both against the run of play, earned the vicitors the point that not only kept them ahead of their opponents but also, thanks to Stavrevski's late strike in Skopje, gave them automatic qualification as the group winners. Croatia, the bronze-medallists at France '98, were out, but the Irish at least had the chance to fight again in the play-offs.

GROUP 8 MATCH DETAILS 1999/2000

18/08/99, Belgrade
YUGOSLAVIA 0
CROATIA 0
referee - Nielsen (DEN)
YUGOSLAVIA - Kocic, Mirkovic, Mihajlovic, Djorovic (Drulovic 46), Jokanovic, Djukic, Stankovic J., Nadj, Mijatovic, Kovacevic (Milosevic 62), Stankovic D.
CROATIA - Ladic, Kovac R., Jarni, Soldo, Stimac, Simic D., Asanovic, Boban (Biscan 81), Stanic (Rapajc 46), Suker, Jurcic.

21/08/99, Zagreb
CROATIA 2 Stanic (34), Soldo (55)
MALTA 1 Carabott (61)
referee - Uzunov (BUL)
CROATIA - Mrmic, Biscan, Rapajc, Soldo, Stimac, Simic D., Asanovic, Stanic (Vlaovic 46), Suker, Boban (Saric 16), Simic J. (Boksic 46).
MALTA - Barry, Said, Carabott, Vella, Debono, Camilleri, Busuttil (Okonkwo 77), Saliba, Nwoko (Mifsud A. 90), Brincat, Agius (Sultana 83).

01/09/99, Dublin
REPUBLIC OF IRELAND 2 Keane Rob. (53), Kennedy (69)
YUGOSLAVIA 1 Stankovic D. (59)
referee - Collina (ITA)
REPUBLIC OF IRELAND - Kelly A., Irwin (Carr 66), Staunton, Breen, Cunningham, Keane Roy (Carsley 69), Kilbane, Kinsella, Quinn N. (Cascarino 78), Keane Rob., Kennedy.
YUGOSLAVIA - Kocic, Komljenovic, Mihajlovic (Saveljic 68), Bolic, Govedarica, Djukic, Stankovic D., Nadj (Kovacevic 76), Mijatovic, Milosevic, Savicevic (Drulovic 53).

04/09/99, Zagreb
CROATIA 1 Suker (90)
REPUBLIC OF IRELAND 0
referee - Díaz Vega (ESP)
CROATIA - Ladic, Simic D., Jarni, Soldo, Stimac, Bilic (Rukavina 46), Asanovic, Stanic (Simic J. 84), Suker, Rapajc, Kovac R..
REPUBLIC OF IRELAND - Kelly A., Carr, Staunton, Breen, Cunningham, Carsley, Kelly G. (Harte 73), Kinsella, Cascarino (Quinn N. 83), McLoughlin, Duff (Kilbane 57).

05/09/99, Belgrade
YUGOSLAVIA 3 Stojkovic (36, 54), Savicevic (77)
MACEDONIA 1 Ciric (65p)
referee - Frisk (SWE)
YUGOSLAVIA - Kralj, Mirkovic, Krstajic, Jokanovic, Djukic, Saveljic, Stankovic D. (Govedarica 74), Mijatovic, Milosevic (Kovacevic 83), Stojkovic (Savicevic 66), Drulovic.

MACEDONIA - Milosevski, Stavrevski, Jovanovski (Memedi 46), Lazarevski, Babunski, Savevski, Veselinovski, Micevski (Serafimovski 50), Hristov, Ciric (Gerasimovski 75), Saciri.

08/09/99, Ta' Qali
MALTA 2 Said (62), Carabott (68p)
REPUBLIC OF IRELAND 3 Keane Rob. (13), Breen (21), Staunton (73)
referee - Corpodean (ROM)
MALTA - Barry, Said, Chetcuti (Buhagiar 23), Carabott, Debono, Buttigieg (Vella 29), Busuttil, Saliba, Nwoko, Camilleri, Agius (Thewma 67).
REPUBLIC OF IRELAND - Kelly A., Carr, Staunton, Breen (Harte 75), Cunningham, Carsley, Kilbane (Duff 66), Kinsella, Quinn N., Keane Rob., Kennedy (McLoughlin 55).

08/09/99, Skopje
MACEDONIA 2 Saciri (59), Ciric (87)
YUGOSLAVIA 4 Milosevic (1), Babunski (4og), Stankovic D. (14), Drulovic (38)
referee - Lubos (SVK)
MACEDONIA - Milosevski, Stavrevski, Jovanovski, Lazarevski, Babunski, Savevski (Gerasimovski 46), Veselinovski (Serafimovski 40), Micevski (Sainovski 40), Hristov, Ciric, Saciri.
YUGOSLAVIA - Kralj, Mirkovic (Komljenovic 40), Krstajic, Mihajlovic, Djukic, Jokanovic, Drulovic, Stojkovic (Savicevic 46), Stankovic D., Mijatovic, Milosevic (Kovacevic 83).

10/10/99, Zagreb
CROATIA 2 Boksic (20), Stanic (47)
YUGOSLAVIA 2 Mijatovic (25), Stankovic D. (31)
referee - Garcia Aranda (ESP)
CROATIA - Ladic, Rukavina, Jarni, Soldo, Juric, Tudor (Rapajc 82), Asanovic, Stanic, Suker, Kovac R. (Biscan 62), Boksic (Simic J. 76).
YUGOSLAVIA - Kralj, Mirkovic, Djorovic, Mihajlovic, Jokanovic, Djukic, Stankovic D., Nadj (Drulovic 56), Mijatovic (Savicevic 74), Milosevic, Stojkovic (Bolic 53).

10/10/99, Skopje
MACEDONIA 1 Stavrevski (90)
REPUBLIC OF IRELAND 1 Quinn N. (18)
referee - Fernández Marín (ESP)
MACEDONIA - Filevski, Stavrevski, Jovanovski (Memedi 77), Sedloski, Babunski, Gerasimovski, Stojanoski (Beciri 56), Savevski, Hristov, Sainovski, Stanic (Zaharievski 70).
REPUBLIC OF IRELAND - Kelly A., Irwin, Staunton, Breen, Cunningham, McLoughlin, Kelly G., Kinsella, Quinn N. (Cascarino 78), Keane Rob. (O'Neill 66), Kennedy (Holland 85).

QUALIFYING GROUP 9

Ten out of ten for perfect Czechs

The Czech Republic, who had become the first team to qualify for the Euro 2000 finals when they beat Scotland in Prague at the end of the 1998/99 season, maintained their one hundred per cent record right through to the end. Three further victories, all achieved without conceding a goal, completed their perfect campaign.

The first of them, in Lithuania, was settled by a burst of three goals in eight second-half minutes, the first two from Pavel Nedved, the third from Jan Koller, who later completed a handsome 4-0 win with another goal in stoppage time. The big Anderlecht striker was on target again in the next two games as well - a 3-0 victory over Bosnia-Herzegovina in Teplice, followed by a 2-0 win against the Faroe Islands in Prague. Some of the gloss was taken off the Czechs' achievement in that final fixture when key midfielder Patrik Berger stupidly got sent off, thus picking up a two-match ban which he would have to carry into the finals the following summer.

While the Czechs disappeared into the distance at the top of the table, Scotland seized the runners-up spot. In the end they finished seven points clear of Bosnia-Herzegovina, Lithuania and Estonia, but it was not quite as easy as that for Craig Brown's team.

The key game took place in Sarajevo at the beginning of September. Scotland had not won a competitive match away from home for three years but they ended their barren run with a gutsy, patient 2-1 win against a skilful Bosnian side who badly missed injured Real Madrid striker Elvir Baljic. A goalless draw in Estonia four days later left Scotland requiring only two points from their last two qualifiers, both at home, to clinch second place.

A 1-0 victory in the first of them, against Bosnia-Herzegovina at Ibrox, allowed them to take it easy against Lithuania at Hampden, a game they also won, 3-0. Scotland were exceedingly fortunate to get the three points

TOP SCORERS

6	Jan KOLLER (Czech Republic)
	Elvir BALJIC (Bosnia-Herzegovina)
5	Patrik BERGER (Czech Republic)
4	Billy DODDS (Scotland)
	Elvir BOLIC (Bosnia-Herzegovina)
3	Vladimir SMICER (Czech Republic)
	Pavel NEDVED (Czech Republic)
	Valdas IVANAUSKAS (Lithuania)
	Sergei TEREHHOV (Estonia)
	Andres OPER (Estonia)

GROUP 9 FINAL TABLE

			Home				Away				Total						
		Pd	W	D	L	F	A	W	D	L	F	A	W	D	L	F	A	Pt	GD
1	Czech Republic	10	5	0	0	14	3	5	0	0	12	2	10	0	0	26	5	30	21
2	Scotland	10	4	0	1	10	5	1	3	1	5	5	5	3	2	15	10	18	5
3	Bosnia-Herzegovina	10	2	1	2	6	6	1	1	3	8	11	3	2	5	14	17	11	-3
4	Lithuania	10	1	2	2	5	8	2	0	3	3	8	3	2	5	8	16	11	-8
5	Estonia	10	1	1	3	7	8	2	1	2	8	9	3	2	5	15	17	11	-2
6	Faroe Islands	10	0	2	3	3	7	0	1	4	1	10	0	3	7	4	17	3	-13

QUALIFYING GROUP 9

against the Bosnians. They played poorly throughout but twice got lucky - firstly when John Collins converted a debatable penalty midway through the first half and secondly when fit-again Baljic drove a fantastic left-foot

shot against the crossbar five minutes from time. The same player was to be blessed with greater fortune a few days later when he scored all four goals in Bosnia's 4-1 victory away to Estonia.

GROUP 9 MATCH DETAILS 1999/2000

04/09/99, Sarajevo
BOSNIA-HERZEGOVINA 1 Bolic (23)
SCOTLAND 2 Hutchison (13), Dodds (45)
referee - Levnikov (ISR)
BOSNIA-HERZEGOVINA - Dedic, Joldic (Repuh 77), Mujdza (Demirovic 77), Konjic, Hibic, Besirevic, Bolic, Halilovic (Mujcin 62), Kodro, Barbarez, Topic.
SCOTLAND - Sullivan, Weir, Hopkin, Calderwood (Dailly 46), Hendry, Ferguson (Durrant 69), Dodds, Burley, McCann, Hutchison, Collins.

04/09/99, Toftir
FAROE ISLANDS 0
ESTONIA 2 Reim (88), Piiroja (90)
referee - Trivkovic (CRO)
FAROE ISLANDS - Mikkelsen, Johannesen, Hansen J.K., Thorsteinsson (Hansen Ø. 74), Hansen H.F., Joensen (a Borg 89), Arge (Jarnskor H. 89), Johnsson, Mørkøre A., Jonsson, Petersen.
ESTONIA - Poom, Piiroja, Kirs, Hohlov-Simson, Saviauk (Lemsalu 90), Alonen, Terehhov, Anniste (O'Konnel-Bronin 67), Kristal, Reim, Zelinski (Ustriski 75).

04/09/99, Vilnius
LITHUANIA 0
CZECH REPUBLIC 4 Nedved (60, 63), Koller (68, 90)
referee - Granat (POL)
LITHUANIA - Stauce, Semberas (Skerla 56), Zvirgzdauskas, Vencevicius, Zutautas D., Razanauskas, Preiksaitis (Danilevicius 80), Mikalajunas, Tereskinas, Ivanauskas (Ramelis 38), Jankauskas.
CZECH REPUBLIC - Srnicek, Repka, Rada, Nikl, Poborsky (Sloncik 79), Bejbl, Nedved (Baranek 78), Berger, Nemec (Horvath 71), Kuka, Koller.

08/09/99, Tallinn
ESTONIA 0
SCOTLAND 0
referee - Stuchlik (AUT)
ESTONIA - Poom, Kirs, Hohlov-Simson, Piiroja, Saviauk, Kristal, Anniste, Reim, Terehhov, O'Konnel-Bronin (Zelinski 46), Oper.
SCOTLAND - Sullivan, Weir, Hendry, Dailly, Johnston (McCann 54), Burley, Collins, Durrant (Ferguson 65), Davidson, Hutchison, Dodds.

08/09/99, Torshavn
FAROE ISLANDS 0
LITHUANIA 1 Ramelis (55)
referee - Romain (BEL)
FAROE ISLANDS - Mikkelsen, Johannesen, Hansen J.K., Thorsteinsson, Hansen H.F., Hansen Ø., Jarnskor H. (a Lakjuni 84), Johnsson (Benjaminsen 65), Mørkøre A., Jonsson, Arge (a Borg 46).
LITHUANIA - Stauce (Padimanskas 79), Zutautas D., Vencevicius, Tereskinas, Razanauskas (Skerla 77), Zvirgzdauskas, Semberas, Mikalajunas, Preiksaitis (Danilevicius 88), Skinderis, Ramelis.

08/09/99, Teplice
CZECH REPUBLIC 3 Koller (26), Berger (59p), Poborsky (67)
BOSNIA-HERZEGOVINA 0
referee - Nilsson (SWE)
CZECH REPUBLIC - Srnicek, Suchoparek, Nikl, Repka, Poborsky, Nedved (Hasek 83), Bejbl, Berger, Nemec, Kuka (Baranek 79), Koller (Lokvenc 59).
BOSNIA-HERZEGOVINA - Dedic, Joldic (Repuh 70), Besirevic, Konjic, Hibic, Ihtijarevic (Bolic 70), Varesanovic, Sabic, Barbarez, Kodro, Topic (Demirovic 70).

05/10/99, Glasgow
SCOTLAND 1 Collins (26p)
BOSNIA-HERZEGOVINA 0
referee - Sundell (SWE)
SCOTLAND - Sullivan, Weir, Davidson, Lambert, Hendry (Calderwood 37), Dailly, Dodds (McSwegan 90), Burley, Gallacher (Burchill 80), Hopkin, Collins.
BOSNIA-HERZEGOVINA - Guso, Kapetanovic, Besirevic, Hujdurovic, Varesanovic, Barbarez, Ihtijarevic (Topic 77), Sabic, Bolic, Mujcin (Avdic 84), Baljic.

09/10/99, Prague
CZECH REPUBLIC 2 Koller (11), Verbir (84)
FAROE ISLANDS 0
referee - Lica (ROM)
CZECH REPUBLIC - Srnicek, Repka, Suchoparek (Verbir 74), Baranek (Hornak 59), Rada, Bejbl (Horvath 66), Nemec, Poborsky, Koller, Smicer, Berger.
FAROE ISLANDS - Knudsen, Johannesen, Hansen J.K., Thorsteinsson, Hansen H.F., Joensen, Jarnskor H. (Hansen Ø. 89), Johnsson, Mørkøre A., Jonsson, Petersen (Jacobsen 71).

09/10/99, Glasgow
SCOTLAND 3 Hutchison (48), McSwegan (50), Cameron (88)
LITHUANIA 0
referee - Bré (FRA)
SCOTLAND - Gould, Weir, Davidson, Lambert, O'Neil, Ritchie, Dailly, Burley (Cameron 46), Burchill (Dodds 79), Hutchison, McSwegan (Gallacher 83).
LITHUANIA - Leusas, Zutautas D., Zvirgzdauskas, Skinderis, Skerla, Stumbrys (Vencevicius 54), Razanauskas, Mikalajunas, Tereskinas (Fomenko 64), Dancenka (Maciulevicius 54), Mikulenas.

09/10/99, Tallinn
ESTONIA 1 Oper (4)
BOSNIA-HERZEGOVINA 4 Baljic (42, 57, 67, 87)
referee - Luinge (HOL)
ESTONIA - Kaalma, Piiroja, Kirs, Hohlov-Simson, Anniste (Saviauk 61), Alonen, Terehhov (O'Konnel-Bronin 74), Oper, Kristal, Reim, Zelinski (Viikmäe 40).
BOSNIA-HERZEGOVINA - Guso, Joldic, Kapetanovic, Hujdorovic, Varesanovic, Besirevic, Ihtijarevic, Sabic (Duro 60), Bolic (Mujcin 80), Baljic (Avdic 89), Topic.

QUALIFYING PLAY-OFFS

Portugal took the solitary automatic qualifying berth available to the teams placed second in their group. The other eight runners-up were thrust into the do-or-die play-offs.

It was an open draw, and the pairing which inevitably stood out was Scotland v England. The two teams had not met since their first-round encounter at Euro '96, and inevitably the tie was billed locally as the 'Battle of Britain'.

The first leg, played before a capacity crowd of 52,000 at Hampden, belonged to England. Two first-half goals from Paul Scholes, both the product of untracked runs into the penalty area, gave Kevin Keegan's team what appeared to be an insurmountable advantage to take back to Wembley. England might have had a third goal at the start of the second half when Scholes was tripped in the area, but the Scots too had chances to score, notably when Billy Dodds hit the underside of the bar just seconds after England had gone 2-0 up.

England's performance in Glasgow did not justify total confidence for the return, but nobody could have predicted that they would play as shabbily as they did. The Scots, with nothing to lose, outplayed the Auld Enemy in every department, and it was no more than they deserved when Don Hutchison rose to meet a Neil McCann cross after 38 minutes and put his team 1-0 up on the night.

The Scots continued to dominate after the interval as an increasingly nervous England clung desperately to their first-leg lead. Late in the game Scotland thought they had scored the vital second goal when defender Christian Dailly sent a powerful header goalwards, but David Seaman, with one of the most important saves of his career, somehow kept it out. England had qualified, but embarrassingly so, and among the fans there was precious little celebration.

The Republic of Ireland, who so narrowly missed out on automatic qualification, were unable to make amends in the play-offs. They were evenly matched against Turkey, but the difference between the two sides proved to be the goal which the Irish sloppily conceded six minutes from time in the first leg at Lansdowne Road. Lee Carsley's needless handball gifted the Turks a penalty, which, with a crashing drive, Tayfur converted to cancel out Robbie Keane's splendid opener five minutes earlier. Keane was suspended for the second leg, in Bursa, and without him the Irish were unable to score the goal they needed to stay alive. In fact, Turkey

Dynamo Kiev's Serhiy Rebrov (now with Tottenham Hotspur) put Ukraine into the lead from the penalty spot in the play-off game at home to Slovenia.

were the better team on the night and deserved to go through, but the Irish were left to reflect on what might have been as they succumbed to their third qualifying play-off defeat in a row.

Israel never had any chance of reaching their first major tournament in 30 years. In-form Denmark annihilated them 5-0 in the first leg at Ramat-Gan, with Jon Dahl Tomasson scoring the first two goals to maintain his excellent scoring run in the competition. The second leg in Copenhagen was a formality, but the Danish players joined in the party mood and won again easily, scoring three further goals without reply.

The big shock was Slovenia's defeat of Ukraine. On paper this looked like a mismatch, but the Slovenians demonstrated in both games the giant strides they had made under coach Srecko Katanec and they thoroughly deserved their place at the finals following a 2-1 win in Ljubljana and a 1-1 draw in Kiev.

The home victory was achieved with possibly the best goal of the entire qualifying competition - an incredible 45-yard lob from substitute midfielder

TOP SCORERS	
11	RAUL González (Spain)
9	Zlatko ZAHOVIC (Slovenia)
8	JOÃO PINTO (Portugal)
7	Oliver BIERHOFF (Germany)
6	Jon Dahl TOMASSON (Denmark)
	Valeriy KARPIN (Russia)
	Alan SHEARER (England)
	Ismael URZAIZ (Spain)
	RUI COSTA (Portugal)
	SÁ PINTO (Portugal)
	Adrian ILIE (Romania)
	Jan KOLLER (Czech Republic)
	Elvir BALJIC (Bosnia-Herzegovina)

QUALIFYING PLAY-OFFS

Milenko Acimovic. The other two goals were also of a high quality, with Zlatko Zahovic's ninth goal of the tournament equalising a stupendous opener from Andriy Shevchenko.

The second leg, in Kiev, was played in farcical conditions, with the falling snow making decent football virtually impossible. However, Slovenia showed that they were a team armed with guts and determination as well as talent. Unlucky to go behind to a controversial Serhiy

Rebrov penalty, they came back strongly and silenced the huge crowd with a scrappy but hugely significant equaliser, scored by midfielder Miran Pavlin.

Slovenia, against all odds, had made it, whereas Ukraine joined Scotland, Ireland, Israel and the previously eliminated Croatia and Russia as the major absentees from the big summer extravaganza in Belgium and Holland.

PLAY-OFF MATCH DETAILS

13/11/99, Glasgow
SCOTLAND 0
ENGLAND 2 Scholes (21, 42)
referee - Díaz Vega (ESP)
SCOTLAND - Sullivan, Weir, Hendry, Ritchie, Dailly, Ferguson, Burley, Collins, Gallacher (Burchill 83), Hutchison, Dodds.
ENGLAND - Seaman, Campbell, Adams, Keown, Neville P., Beckham, Ince, Redknapp, Scholes, Shearer, Owen (Cole 67).

17/11/99, Wembley
ENGLAND 0
SCOTLAND 1 Hutchison (38)
referee - Collina (ITA)
ENGLAND - Seaman, Campbell, Adams, Southgate, Neville P., Beckham, Ince, Scholes (Parlour 90), Redknapp, Shearer, Owen (Heskey 63).
SCOTLAND - Sullivan, Weir, Hendry, Dailly, Davidson, Burley, Ferguson, Collins, Hutchison, McCann (Burchill 74), Dodds.

(ENGLAND 2-1)

13/11/99, Dublin
REPUBLIC OF IRELAND 1 Keane Rob. (79)
TURKEY 1 Tayfur (83p)
referee - Frisk (SWE)
REPUBLIC OF IRELAND - Kelly A. (Kiely 61), Carr, Irwin, Breen, Cunningham, Keane Roy, Delap (Duff 53), Carsley, Cascarino (Connolly 75), Keane Rob., Kilbane.
TURKEY - Rüstü, Ali Eren, Ogün, Tayfur, Alpay, Abdullah, Tayfun, Ümit (Arif 46), Hakan Sükür, Sergen (Mert 85), Hakan Ünsal (Tugay 67).

17/11/99, Bursa
TURKEY 0
REPUBLIC OF IRELAND 0
referee - Veissière (FRA)
TURKEY - Rüstü (Engin 38), Ali Eren, Ogün, Tayfur, Alpay, Arif (Ümit 84), Abdullah, Okan, Hakan Sükür, Sergen, Tayfun (Fatih 46).
REPUBLIC OF IRELAND - Kiely, Carr (Kenna 4), Cascarino 81), Irwin, Breen, Cunningham, Keane Roy, Delap, Kinsella, Quinn N., Connolly (Duff 78), Kilbane.

(1-1; TURKEY on away goal)

13/11/99, Tel-Aviv
ISRAEL 0
DENMARK 5 Tomasson (2, 34), Tøfting (67), Jørgensen (69), Nielsen B.S. (73)
referee - Elleray (ENG)
ISRAEL - Auat, Harazi A., Amsalem, Benado, Ben Shimon (Tal 37), Hazan, Banin (Telesnikov 76), Revivo, Turgeman, Berkovic, Abuksis (Benayoun 37).
DENMARK - Schmeichel, Tøfting (Goldboek 78), Henriksen, Høgh, Heintze, Helveg, Nielsen B.S., Grønkjær, Tomasson (Andersen 79), Jørgensen (Schjønberg 86), Sand.

17/11/99, Copenhagen
DENMARK 3 Sand (3), Nielsen B.S. (14), Tomasson (65)
ISRAEL 0
referee - Melo Pereira (POR)
DENMARK - Schmeichel (Sørensen 19), Tøfting, Henriksen, Høgh, Heintze, Helveg (Laursen J. 71), Nielsen B.S., Grønkjær (Schjønberg 83), Tomasson, Jørgensen, Sand.
ISRAEL - Elimelech, Harazi A., Amsalem (Badir 43), Shelach, Talker, Hazan, Banin, Tal (Telesnikov 28), Turgeman, Berkovic, Benayoun (Gershon 72).

(DENMARK 8-0)

13/11/99, Ljubljana
SLOVENIA 2 Zahovic (53), Acimovic (84)
UKRAINE 1 Shevchenko (33)
referee - Meier (SUI)
SLOVENIA - Dabanovic, Karic, Rudonja, Milanic (Osterc 75), Knavs, Novak, Ceh, Pavlin, Milinovic, Udovic (Acimovic 46), Zahovic.
UKRAINE - Shovkovskyi, Parfenov, Gusin, Holovko, Kandaurov (Kardash 57), Vashchuk, Dmitrulin, Popov, Kosovskyi, Shevchenko, Rebrov.

17/11/99, Kiev
UKRAINE 1 Rebrov (67p)
SLOVENIA 1 Pavlin (79)
referee - Heynemann (GER)
UKRAINE - Shovkovskyi, Luzhnyi, Fedorov, Holovko, Vashchuk, Dmitrulin, Kandaurov (Kovalev 46), Skachenko (Moroz 58), Kosovskyi (Popov 73), Shevchenko, Rebrov.
SLOVENIA - Dabanovic, Karic (Osterc 79), Rudonja, Milanic, Galic, Milinovic, Novak, Ceh, Udovic (Acimovic 56), Zahovic, Pavlin.

(SLOVENIA 3-2)

EUROPEAN QUALIFYING GROUPS

GROUP ONE

YUGOSLAVIA, RUSSIA, SWITZERLAND,
SLOVENIA, LUXEMBOURG, FAROE ISLANDS

2000/01 FIXTURES

02/09/00	Switzerland v Russia
03/09/00	Faroe Islands v Slovenia
	Luxembourg v Yugoslavia
07/10/00	Luxembourg v Slovenia
	Switzerland v Faroe Islands
	Yugoslavia v Russia
11/10/00	Russia v Luxembourg
	Slovenia v Switzerland
	Yugoslavia v Faroe Islands
24/03/01	Luxembourg v Faroe Islands
	Russia v Slovenia
	Yugoslavia v Switzerland
28/03/01	Russia v Faroe Islands
	Slovenia v Yugoslavia
	Switzerland v Luxembourg
02/06/01	Faroe Islands v Switzerland
	Russia v Yugoslavia
	Slovenia v Luxembourg
06/06/01	Faroe Islands v Yugoslavia
	Luxembourg v Russia
	Switzerland v Slovenia

2001/02 FIXTURES

01/09/01	Faroe Islands v Luxembourg
	Slovenia v Russia
	Switzerland v Yugoslavia
05/09/01	Faroe Islands v Russia
	Luxembourg v Switzerland
	Yugoslavia v Slovenia
06/10/01	Russia v Switzerland
	Slovenia v Faroe Islands
	Yugoslavia v Luxembourg

GROUP TWO

HOLLAND, PORTUGAL, REPUBLIC OF IRELAND,
CYPRUS, ANDORRA, ESTONIA

2000/01 FIXTURES

16/08/00	Estonia v Andorra
02/09/00	Andorra v Cyprus
	Holland v Republic of Ireland
03/09/00	Estonia v Portugal
07/10/00	Andorra v Estonia
	Cyprus v Holland
	Portugal v Republic of Ireland
11/10/00	Holland v Portugal
	Republic of Ireland v Estonia
15/11/00	Cyprus v Andorra
14/02/01	Portugal v Andorra
24/03/01	Andorra v Holland
	Cyprus v Republic of Ireland
28/03/01	Andorra v Republic of Ireland
	Cyprus v Estonia
	Portugal v Holland
25/04/01	Holland v Cyprus
	Republic of Ireland v Andorra
02/06/01	Estonia v Holland
	Republic of Ireland v Portugal
06/06/01	Estonia v Republic of Ireland
	Portugal v Cyprus

2001/02 FIXTURES

15/08/01	Estonia v Cyprus
01/09/01	Andorra v Portugal
	Republic of Ireland v Holland
05/09/01	Cyprus v Portugal
	Holland v Estonia
06/10/01	Holland v Andorra
	Portugal v Estonia
	Republic of Ireland v Cyprus

EUROPEAN QUALIFYING GROUPS

GROUP THREE	GROUP FOUR

CZECH REPUBLIC, DENMARK, BULGARIA, ICELAND, NORTHERN IRELAND, MALTA

SWEDEN, TURKEY, SLOVAKIA, MACEDONIA, AZERBAIJAN, MOLDOVA

2000/01 FIXTURES

02/09/00	Bulgaria v Czech Republic	
	Iceland v Denmark	
	Northern Ireland v Malta	
07/10/00	Bulgaria v Malta	
	Czech Republic v Iceland	
	Northern Ireland v Denmark	
11/10/00	Denmark v Bulgaria	
	Iceland v Northern Ireland	
	Malta v Czech Republic	
24/03/01	Bulgaria v Iceland	
	Malta v Denmark	
	Northern Ireland v Czech Republic	
28/03/01	Bulgaria v Northern Ireland	
	Czech Republic v Denmark	
25/04/01	Malta v Iceland	
02/06/01	Denmark v Czech Republic	
	Iceland v Malta	
	Northern Ireland v Bulgaria	
06/06/01	Czech Republic v Northern Ireland	
	Denmark v Malta	
	Iceland v Bulgaria	

2000/01 FIXTURES

02/09/00	Azerbaijan v Sweden
	Turkey v Moldova
03/09/00	Slovakia v Macedonia
07/10/00	Macedonia v Azerbaijan
	Moldova v Slovakia
	Sweden v Turkey
11/10/00	Azerbaijan v Turkey
	Moldova v Macedonia
	Slovakia v Sweden
24/03/01	Azerbaijan v Moldova
	Sweden v Macedonia
	Turkey v Slovakia
28/03/01	Macedonia v Turkey
	Moldova v Sweden
	Slovakia v Azerbaijan
02/06/01	Macedonia v Moldova
	Sweden v Slovakia
	Turkey v Azerbaijan
06/06/01	Azerbaijan v Slovakia
	Sweden v Moldova
	Turkey v Macedonia

2001/02 FIXTURES

01/09/01	Denmark v Northern Ireland
	Iceland v Czech Republic
	Malta v Bulgaria
05/09/01	Bulgaria v Denmark
	Czech Republic v Malta
	Northern Ireland v Iceland
06/10/01	Czech Republic v Bulgaria
	Denmark v Iceland
	Malta v Northern Ireland

2001/02 FIXTURES

01/09/01	Macedonia v Sweden
	Moldova v Azerbaijan
	Slovakia v Turkey
05/09/01	Azerbaijan v Macedonia
	Slovakia v Moldova
	Turkey v Sweden
06/10/01	Macedonia v Slovakia
	Moldova v Turkey
	Sweden v Azerbaijan

EUROPEAN QUALIFYING GROUPS

GROUP FIVE

NORWAY, UKRAINE, POLAND, WALES, ARMENIA, BELARUS

2000/01 FIXTURES

02/09/00	Belarus v Wales
	Norway v Armenia
	Ukraine v Poland
07/10/00	Armenia v Ukraine
	Poland v Belarus
	Wales v Norway
11/10/00	Belarus v Armenia
	Norway v Ukraine
	Poland v Wales
24/03/01	Armenia v Wales
	Norway v Poland
	Ukraine v Belarus
28/03/01	Belarus v Norway
	Poland v Armenia
	Wales v Ukraine
02/06/01	Armenia v Belarus
	Ukraine v Norway
	Wales v Poland
06/06/01	Armenia v Poland
	Norway v Belarus
	Ukraine v Wales

2001/02 FIXTURES

01/09/01	Belarus v Ukraine
	Poland v Norway
	Wales v Armenia
05/09/01	Belarus v Poland
	Norway v Wales
	Ukraine v Armenia
06/10/01	Armenia v Norway
	Poland v Ukraine
	Wales v Belarus

GROUP SIX

BELGIUM, SCOTLAND, CROATIA, LATVIA, SAN MARINO

2000/01 FIXTURES

02/09/00	Belgium v Croatia
	Latvia v Scotland
07/10/00	Latvia v Belgium
	San Marino v Scotland
11/10/00	Croatia v Scotland
15/11/00	San Marino v Latvia
14/02/01	Belgium v San Marino
24/03/01	Croatia v Latvia
	Scotland v Belgium
28/03/01	Scotland v San Marino
25/04/01	Latvia v San Marino
02/06/01	Belgium v Latvia
	Croatia v San Marino
06/06/01	Latvia v Croatia
	San Marino v Belgium

2001/02 FIXTURES

01/09/01	Scotland v Croatia
05/09/01	Belgium v Scotland
	San Marino v Croatia
06/10/01	Croatia v Belgium
	Scotland v Latvia

EUROPEAN QUALIFYING GROUPS

GROUP SEVEN

SPAIN, AUSTRIA, ISRAEL,
BOSNIA-HERZEGOVINA, LIECHTENSTEIN

2000/01 FIXTURES

02/09/00	Bosnia-Herzegovina v Spain
03/09/00	Israel v Liechtenstein
07/10/00	Liechtenstein v Austria
	Spain v Israel
11/10/00	Austria v Spain
	Israel v Bosnia-Herzegovina
24/03/01	Bosnia-Herzegovina v Austria
	Spain v Liechtenstein
28/03/01	Austria v Israel
	Liechtenstein v Bosnia-Herzegovina
02/06/01	Liechtenstein v Israel
	Spain v Bosnia-Herzegovina
06/06/01	Austria v Liechtenstein
	Israel v Spain

2001/02 FIXTURES

01/09/01	Bosnia-Herzegovina v Israel
	Spain v Austria
05/09/01	Austria v Bosnia-Herzegovina
	Liechtenstein v Spain
07/10/01	Bosnia-Herzegovina v Liechtenstein
	Israel v Austria

GROUP EIGHT

ROMANIA, ITALY, LITHUANIA, HUNGARY,
GEORGIA

2000/01 FIXTURES

03/09/00	Hungary v Italy
	Romania v Lithuania
07/10/00	Italy v Romania
	Lithuania v Georgia
11/10/00	Italy v Georgia
	Lithuania v Hungary
24/03/01	Hungary v Lithuania
	Romania v Italy
28/03/01	Georgia v Romania
	Italy v Lithuania
02/06/01	Georgia v Italy
	Romania v Hungary
06/06/01	Hungary v Georgia
	Lithuania v Romania

2001/02 FIXTURES

01/09/01	Georgia v Hungary
	Lithuania v Italy
05/09/01	Georgia v Lithuania
	Hungary v Romania
06/10/01	Italy v Hungary
	Romania v Georgia

GROUP NINE

GERMANY, ENGLAND, GREECE, FINLAND, ALBANIA

2000/01 FIXTURES

02/09/00	Finland v Albania
	Germany v Greece
07/10/00	England v Germany
	Greece v Finland
11/10/00	Albania v Greece
	Finland v England
24/03/01	England v Finland
	Germany v Albania
28/03/01	Albania v England
	Greece v Germany
02/06/01	Finland v Germany
	Greece v Albania
06/06/01	Albania v Germany
	Greece v England

2001/02 FIXTURES

01/09/01	Albania v Finland
	Germany v England
05/09/01	England v Albania
	Finland v Greece
06/10/01	England v Greece
	Germany v Finland

UEFA CHAMPIONS' LEAGUE

The ever-expanding UEFA Champions' League underwent its most dramatic transformation yet with the introduction of a secondary group phase and an increase in the number of first-round participants from 24 to 32, i.e. eight groups instead of six.

The winners and runners-up of those eight groups were to qualify for the second group phase, and there was even a get-out clause for the third-placed teams, who dropped 'down' into the UEFA Cup. Only eight teams were therefore eliminated from European competition altogether at the end of the first phase.

The expansion of the competition forced upon its participants a massive fixture overload which, while guaranteeing the increase in revenue and sponsorship benefits that the big clubs had requested, placed considerable demands on the players.

In 1998/99 the two finalists, Manchester United and Bayern Munich, were required to play a total of 13 Champions' League matches. In 1999/2000 that figure had increased to 19 (17 for clubs given exemption to the first phase) - the equivalent of half a season of domestic competition.

So, effectively, in warding off the threat of the rival European Super League, UEFA had created their own tournament in its image. Now, instead of games played exclusively on Wednesdays on alternate weeks, the Champions' League took place on Tuesdays and Wednesdays (with the UEFA Cup shunted into the Thursday slot) and, at some stages of the competition, on a weekly basis.

PRELIMINARY ROUNDS

Before the Champions' League proper could begin, the original entry of 71 clubs (which included all of Europe's domestic champions except those from Andorra and San Marino as well as up to four representatives from other nations) had to be pruned down to 32. As 16 teams were exempt anyway, that left 55 teams vying for the remaining 16 qualifying places. UEFA's chosen process of elimination was to stage three separate qualifying rounds, with the first of them taking place in mid-July.

The draws for the first two preliminary rounds were made at the same time, so the 37 teams involved knew what they had to do in advance to reach the promised land of the qualifying round, where, win or lose, their European participation would be guaranteed one way or another until the end of September.

Of the nine teams who made it through the first preliminary round, only three were to reach the qualifying round - Partizan Belgrade, Zimbru Chisinau

PRELIMINARY ROUND 1 RESULTS

(July 14/21, 1999)

ÍBV 1 (Johannesson S. 45), **SK Tirana 0**
SK Tirana 1 (Bulku S. 79), **ÍBV 2** (Johanesson S. 32, Sigurdsson 44)
(ÍBV 3-1)

Barry Town 0, Valletta 0
Valletta 3 (Agius G. 41, 45, Chetcuti 56), **Barry Town 2** (Sloan 44, 56)
(Valletta 3-2)

HB 1 (a Lakjuni 47), **FC Haka 1** (Popovich 64)
FC Haka 6 (Salli 26, Reynders 44, Nyyssönen 47, Wilson 62, Popovich 80, Torkkeli 90), **HB 0**
(FC Haka 7-1)

Jeunesse Esch 0, Skonto Riga 2 (Astafyev 67, Mikholap 73)
Skonto Riga 8 (Bleidelis 38, 50, Mikholap 40, 54, 61, 84p, 90p, Kolesnichenko 77), **Jeunesse Esch 0**
(Skonto Riga 10-0)

Liteks Lovech 3 (Hadji 12, Bushi 35p, Petrov 82), **Glentoran 0**
Glentoran 0, Liteks Lovech 2 (Haxhi 65, Bushi 90)
(Liteks Lovech 5-0)

Partizan Beograd 6 (Ilic S. 12, Pekovic 25, 71, Ivic 37, 75, Kezman 56),
FC Flora Tallinn 0
FC Flora Tallinn 1 (Viikmäe 52),
Partizan Beograd 4 (Kezman 10, 69, Ilic S. 20, Tomic 82)
(Partizan Beograd 10-1)

St. Patrick's Athletic 0,
Zimbru Chisinau 5 (Berco 30, 43, Epureanu 36, 84, Boret 71)
Zimbru Chisinau 5 (Tropanet 25, 40, Boret 31, 75, Oprea 83p),
St. Patrick's Athletic 0
(Zimbru Chisinau 10-0)

Sloga Jugomagnat Skopje 1 (Memedi 66),
Kapaz Ganja 0
Kapaz Ganja 2 (Mamedov 20, Rzaev 90p),
Sloga Jugomagnat Skopje 1 (Arif 34)
(2-2; Sloga Jugomagnat Skopje on away goal)

Zalgiris Vilnius 2 (Stesko I. 45, Stesko A. 87),
Tsement Ararat 0
Tsement Ararat 0,
Zalgiris Vilnius 3 (Novikovas 7, Joksas 31, Vasiliauskas 65)
(Zalgiris Vilnius 5-0)

UEFA CHAMPIONS' LEAGUE

and Skonto Riga, all of whom racked up ten goals in their opening ties, with Skonto striker Mikhail Mikholap scoring five goals at home to Jeunesse Esch.

The second preliminary round was chock-full of surprises, with exactly half of the 14 seeded teams failing to progress. The biggest surprise was Maribor's 5-1 victory at home to Genk. Although the Belgian champions came back to win the second leg, it was not enough to save them. Besiktas were also surprise fallers, going out on the away-goals rule to Hapoel Haifa, while Norwegian league runners-up Molde staged a brilliant second-leg comeback to dispose of their Russian equivalent, CSKA Moscow. The closest-fought tie saw Widzew Lodz, deputising for the suspended Polish champions Wisla Krakow, recover from a 4-1 first-leg defeat in Bulgaria to reverse the scoreline at home to Liteks Lovech and take the tie in a penalty shoot-out.

QUALIFYING ROUND

That Dynamo Kiev, the previous season's beaten semi-finalists, were forced to enter the competition in the second preliminary round showed that there was a loophole in UEFA's seeding system, but the perennial Ukrainian champions only just scraped into the Champions' League proper thanks to a last-minute goal from their new Uzbekistan international striker Maxim Shatskikh at home to Danish champions AaB.

But while Kiev went through to the lucrative group phase, many other fancied teams failed to make it. One was Parma, the UEFA Cup holders, who were forced to defend that trophy after losing 2-1 on aggregate to Scottish champions Rangers. Mallorca, the 1998/99 Cup-winners' Cup finalists, also missed out on the Champions' League challenge when they conceded a late penalty at home to Molde.

PRELIMINARY ROUND 2 RESULTS

(July 28, August 4, 1999)

Anorthosis Famagusta 2 (Obiku 26, 88p),
Slovan Bratislava 1 (Hrncar 51)
Slovan Bratislava 1 (Timko 60), **Anorthosis Famagusta 1** (Obiku 58)
(Anorthosis Famagusta 3-2)

Besiktas 1 (Ayhan 90), **Hapoel Haifa 1** (Rosso 76)
Hapoel Haifa 0, Besiktas 0
(1-1; Hapoel Haifa on away goal)

CSKA Moskva 2 (Sischin 7, Khomukha 85), **Molde FK 0**
Molde FK 4 (Tessem 47, Berg Hestad 65, Hoseth 67, 81), **CSKA Moskva 0**
(Molde FK 4-2)

Dinamo Tbilisi 2 (Tsitaishvili 81, Khomeriki 90),
Zimbru Chisinau 1 (Berco 68)
Zimbru Chisinau 2 (Dodul 24, Epureanu 90), **Dinamo Tbilisi 0**
(Zimbru Chisinau 3-2)

Dnepr-Transmash Mogilev 0, AIK 1 (Tjernström 89)
AIK 2 (Corneliusson 54, Gustafsson 77), **Dnepr-Transmash Mogilev 0**
(AIK 3-0)

Dynamo Kyiv 2 (Shatskikh 38, 78), **Zalgiris Vilnius 0**
Zalgiris Vilnius 0, Dynamo Kyiv 1 (Rebrov 35)
(Dynamo Kyiv 3-0)

FC Haka 1 (Niemi 51), **Rangers 4** (Amoruso 17, Mols 26, 41, Moore 86)
Rangers 3 (Wallace 15, Johansson 28, Amato 66), **FC Haka 0**
(Rangers 7-1)

ÍBV 0, MTK Hungária FC 2 (Halmai 18, Preisinger 73)
MTK Hungária FC 3 (Ilea 4, Kuttor 25, Illés 41), **ÍBV 1** (Bjarklind 89)
(MTK Hungária FC 5-1)

Liteks Lovech 4 (Todorov 40, 78, Zivkovic 82p, Kondev 90),
Widzew Lodz 1 (Wichniarek 89p)
Widzew Lodz 4 (Gesior 15, Wichniarek 52, 62, Michalski 74),
Liteks Lovech 1 (Todorov 30) (aet)
(5-5; Widzew Lodz 3-2 on pens.)

NK Maribor 5 (Balajic 24, Galic 62, Karic 69p, Simundza 76, Djuranovic 90),
KRC Genk 1 (Strupar 37)
KRC Genk 3 (Gudjónsson Th. 45, 61, Horváth 64), **NK Maribor 0**
(NK Maribor 5-4)

Partizan Beograd 3 (Ilic S. 10, Krstajic 22, 87), **Rijeka 1** (Sztipánovics 56)
Rijeka 0, Partizan Beograd 3 (Kezman 7, 82, Ivic 19)
(Partizan Beograd 6-1)

Rapid Bucuresti 3 (Barbu 15, Schumacher 53, Mutica 72),
Skonto Riga 3 (Chaladze 4, 33, Astafyev 60)
Skonto Riga 2 (Laizans 77, Rubins 87), **Rapid Bucuresti 1** (Raducan 33)
(Skonto Riga 5-4)

SK Rapid Wien 3 (Dowe 54, Savicevic 74, Penksa 86), **Valletta 0**
Valletta 0, SK Rapid Wien 2 (Dowe 70, Lagonikakis 88)
(SK Rapid Wien 5-0)

Sloga Jugomagnat Skopje 0, Brøndby IF 1 (Daugaard 15)
Brøndby IF 1 (Daugaard 4p), **Sloga Jugomagnat Skopje 0**
(Brøndby IF 2-0)

UEFA CHAMPIONS' LEAGUE

Fiorentina and Valencia both won through comfortably to ensure that there would be three Italian and three Spanish sides present in the first group phase, but the only country which succeeded in taking two teams through the qualifying round was Germany. Borussia Dortmund and Hertha Berlin joined Bayern Munich and Bayer Leverkusen in a four-pronged Champions' League assault after both claiming 2-0 aggregate victories.

For the second season running the biggest upset came at the expense of a team from France. A year earlier HJK Helsinki had put out Metz and now Lyon's Champions' League dreams died an equally painful death as they lost home and away to magnificent Maribor, who thus ensured a Slovenian presence in Europe's premier club competition for the very first time.

The qualifying round proved to be the end of the road for the three teams that had entered the competition at the start. Partizan Belgrade, Zimbru Chisinau and Skonto Riga fell, respectively, to Spartak Moscow, PSV and Chelsea, scoring just one goal between them.

Chelsea were among half of the 16 qualifiers who had never previously competed in the Champions' League. The other seven licking their lips in anticipation of the glamour and riches to come were Fiorentina, Valencia, Hertha Berlin, Maribor, Molde, AIK and Boavista.

QUALIFYING ROUND RESULTS

(August 11/25, 1999)

AaB 1 (Strandli 55), **Dynamo Kyiv 2** (Rebrov 13, Shatskikh 40)
Dynamo Kyiv 2 (Gusin 74, Shatskikh 90), **AaB 2** (Oper 9, Gaarde 47)
(Dynamo Kyiv 4-3)

AEK 0, AIK 0
AIK 1 (Novakovic 57), **AEK 0**
(AIK 1-0)

Brondby IF 1 (Smith 65), **Boavista FC 2** (Mário Silva 24, Moreira 73)
Boavista FC 4 (Litos 12, Ahinful 99, 109, Rui Bento 116),
Brondby IF 2 (Christensen 47, Bjur 90) (aet)
(Boavista FC 6-3)

Chelsea 3 (Babayaro 76, Poyet 77, Sutton 84), **Skonto Riga 0**
Skonto Riga 0, Chelsea 0
(Chelsea 3-0)

Croatia Zagreb 0, MTK Hungária FC 0
MTK Hungária FC 0, Croatia Zagreb 2 (Simic 59, 83)
(Croatia Zagreb 2-0)

Fiorentina 3 (Adani 17, Cois 57, Rui Costa 90),
Widzew Lodz 1 (Adani 74og)
Widzew Lodz 0, Fiorentina 2 (Chiesa 39, Cois 66)
(Fiorentina 5-1)

Hapoel Haifa 0, Valencia CF 2 (López 68, Farinós 75)
Valencia CF 2 (Sánchez 59, 65), **Hapoel Haifa 0**
(Valencia CF 4-0)

Hertha BSC Berlin 2 (Daei 2, Preetz 58), **Anorthosis Famagusta 0**
Anorthosis Famagusta 0, Hertha BSC Berlin 0
(Hertha BSC Berlin 2-0)

Olympique Lyonnais 0, NK Maribor 1 (Filipovic 88)
NK Maribor 2 (Simundza 24, Balajic 45), **Olympique Lyonnais 0**
(NK Maribor 3-0)

Molde FK 0, RCD Mallorca 0
RCD Mallorca 1 (Stankovic 22p), **Molde FK 1** (Lund 85p)
(1-1; Molde FK on away goal)

Rangers 2 (Vidmar 33, Reyna 76), **Parma 0**
Parma 1 (Walem 67), **Rangers 0**
(Rangers 2-1)

SK Rapid Wien 0, Galatasaray 3 (Hakan Ünsal 34, Fatih 38, Hagi 90)
Galatasaray 1 (Okan 53), **SK Rapid Wien 0**
(Galatasaray 4-0)

Spartak Moskva 2 (Shirko 37, Tikhonov 73), **Partizan Beograd 0**
Partizan Beograd 1 (Kezman 73),
Spartak Moskva 3 (Shirko 20, 46, Titov 85p)
(Spartak Moskva 5-1)

SK Sturm Graz 2 (Vastic 33, Martens 45),
Servette FC Genève 1 (Lonfat 45)
Servette FC Genève 2 (Juarez 50, Thurre 90),
SK Sturm Graz 2 (Kocijan 54, Vastic 78)
(SK Sturm Graz 4-3)

FK Teplice 0, Borussia Dortmund 1 (Nerlinger 66)
Borussia Dortmund 1 (Herrlich 90), **FK Teplice 0**
(Borussia Dortmund 2-0)

Zimbru Chisinau 0, PSV 0
PSV 2 (Nilis 79, Ooijer 88), **Zimbru Chisinau 0**
(PSV 2-0)

UEFA CHAMPIONS' LEAGUE

FIRST PHASE GROUP A

Maribor's reward for becoming the least expected of all the 32 Champions' League participants was a place in an imposing group alongside Lazio, Bayer Leverkusen and Dynamo Kiev.

After one match, however, the Slovenians were actually leading the group. Not content with seeing off Genk and Lyon in the preliminaries, Maribor marked their Champions' League début with a sensational 1-0 victory in Kiev, Ante Simundza scoring the late winner after a superb pass from Albanian Kliton Bozgo. With Leverkusen and Lazio drawing 1-1, Maribor found themselves out in front with a two-point lead.

It didn't last. Maribor were beaten at home a week later by Leverkusen and then went on to suffer two successive 4-0 beatings at the hands of Lazio. The Italians chalked up their first victory when they came from behind to defeat Kiev 2-1 in the Stadio Olimpico. Chilean hitman Marcelo Salas scored a superb winner in that game and he was twice on target the following week to complete another home win, against Maribor.

Lazio's repeat performance in Slovenia virtually ensured their qualification for the next round, but an interesting battle was developing for second place between Leverkusen and Kiev. The first meeting between the two teams ended in a 1-1 draw at the BayArena, with Kiev 'keeper Olexandr Shovkovskyi securing the Ukrainians' first point with a fantastic save from a Stefan Beinlich free-kick. The return fixture was equally tense but

Kiev eventually came through to collect their first victory, with defenders Holovko and Vashchuk scoring decisive second-half goals.

On matchday five Lazio duly secured first place in the group - and with it seeded status for the second phase draw - thanks to a 1-1 draw at home to Leverkusen which was never in danger after Pavel Nedved bundled the ball across the line in the first minute. Ulf Kirsten's headed equaliser was important for Leverkusen because with Kiev beating Maribor 2-1 in their penultimate game (two goals from Serhiy Rebrov did the trick), Leverkusen knew that if they could win their final match at home to Maribor, the Ukrainians would have to end Lazio's unbeaten record to deny the Germans qualification in second place.

There was an unexpected final twist to the plot. While Kiev went down 0-1 to Lazio, they still managed to hang onto second place because Leverkusen could only draw 0-0 against Maribor. It was the third successive home draw for Christoph Daum's side and it proved costly because although they had the same number of points as Kiev, it was the latter who joined Lazio in the next round because of their superior head-to-head record.

FIRST PHASE GROUP B

On paper Group B looked very tough, especially for Swedish outsiders AIK. They knew they had very little chance of survival in the company of Barcelona,

CHAMPIONS' LEAGUE FIRST PHASE GROUP A

(September 14/22/29, October 19/27, November 2, 1999)

RESULTS

Bayer 04 Leverkusen 1 (Neuville 14), **Lazio 1** (Mihajlovic 18)

Dynamo Kyiv 0, NK Maribor 1 (Simundza 73)

Lazio 2 (Negro 70, Salas 72), **Dynamo Kyiv 1** (Rebrov 67p)

NK Maribor 0, Bayer 04 Leverkusen 2 (Zivkovic 82, Kirsten 90)

Bayer 04 Leverkusen 1 (Kirsten 52), **Dynamo Kyiv 1** (Gusin 71)

Lazio 4 (Inzaghi 60, Sérgio Conceição 62, Salas 70, 77), **NK Maribor 0**

Dynamo Kyiv 4 (Kosovskyi 4, Shatskikh 36, Holovko 61, Vashchuk 89), **Bayer 04 Leverkusen 2** (Kirsten 12, Neuville 48)

NK Maribor 0, Lazio 4 (Mihajlovic 36, Inzaghi 50, 73, Stankovic 62)

Lazio 1 (Nedved 1), **Bayer 04 Leverkusen 1** (Kirsten 44)

NK Maribor 1 (Balajic 50), **Dynamo Kyiv 2** (Rebrov 37, 84p)

Dynamo Kyiv 0, Lazio 1 (Mamedov 17og)

Bayer 04 Leverkusen 0, NK Maribor 0

FINAL TABLE			Home				Away				Total					
		Pd	W	D	L	F	A	W	D	L	F	A	W	D	L	F	A	Pt	GD
1	Lazio	6	2	1	0	7	2	2	1	0	6	1	4	2	0	13	3	14	10
2	Dynamo Kyiv	6	1	0	2	4	4	1	1	1	4	4	2	1	3	8	8	7	0
3	Bayer 04 Leverkusen	6	0	3	0	2	2	1	1	1	5	5	1	4	1	7	7	7	0
4	NK Maribor	6	0	0	3	1	8	1	1	1	1	4	1	1	4	2	12	4	-10

UEFA CHAMPIONS' LEAGUE

Fiorentina and Arsenal, but the glamour of the opposition at least guaranteed three bumper pay-days at the Råsunda stadium.

But if all seemed lost at the outset for the Swedes, the pessimism seemed misplaced when they matched mighty Barcelona all the way in their opening fixture. A sensation was in the offing when Yugoslav striker Nebojsa Novakovic gave AIK the lead with just 18 minutes to go, but Barça bounced back to win with two set-piece goals late in the game. AIK coach Stuart Baxter was incensed by the performance of French referee Marc Batta, claiming that he had been attempting to substitute two players at the time of the corner which led to Barcelona's equaliser.

Fiorentina and Arsenal drew their opening fixture 0-0. The English team played well and deserved victory but, as in the previous season's Champions' League campaign, they let themselves down by missing chances, most significantly when Kanu's lazy penalty was saved by Francesco Toldo ten minutes from time. A week later Toldo was beaten four times as Fiorentina went down 4-2 to a Rivaldo-inspired Barcelona in the Nou Camp. In the other game Arsenal did what they had to by taking all three points at home to AIK, but once again the Swedes conceded two late goals to end up with nothing after deserving more.

Arsenal's next match was in Barcelona. They had never played a competitive match in Spain, but having gone a goal behind after an error from Patrick Vieira let

in Luis Enrique, the Gunners came back strongly after the interval and won themselves an unexpected point when Kanu's low shot found the bottom corner with nine minutes remaining. Barcelona got their revenge three weeks later when they returned to Wembley, the scene of their 1992 European Cup triumph, and trounced Arsenal 4-2. Barça were in coruscating form but were aided and abetted by some hapless defending from the Londoners, whose captain, Tony Adams, had an evening to forget.

With Fiorentina taking just four points off AIK, Barcelona's victory meant that they became the first team to make mathematically certain of their place in the second phase. A week later they secured first place with a 5-0 thrashing of AIK. But it was the other match, between Arsenal and Fiorentina at Wembley, which attracted most of the attention.

Both teams knew that a victory would seal their place in the last 16. Arsenal, who had only won three out of 12 European games under Arsène Wenger, were under pressure to exorcise the ghost of Wembley. They tried their best to break the Fiorentina defence down but clear-cut chances were few and far between as the Italians stood firm. Then, with 15 minutes remaining, Fiorentina made a rare sortie into the Arsenal half. Jörg Heinrich fed Gabriel Batistuta on the right-hand side of the penalty area and with a truly world-class finish that scorched into the roof of the net the Argentinian put his team in front. Arsenal responded with force but with three

CHAMPIONS' LEAGUE FIRST PHASE GROUP B

(September 14/22/29, October 19/27, November 2, 1999)

RESULTS

AIK 1 (Novakovic 72), **FC Barcelona 2** (Abelardo 85, Dani 90)

Fiorentina 0, Arsenal 0

Arsenal 3 (Ljungberg 27, Henry 89, Suker 90), **AIK 1** (Nordin 53)

FC Barcelona 4 (Figo 7, Luis Enrique 10, Rivaldo 67p, 69), **Fiorentina 2** (Batistuta 50, Chiesa 79)

FC Barcelona 1 (Luis Enrique 16), **Arsenal 1** (Kanu 81)

AIK 0, Fiorentina 0

Arsenal 2 (Bergkamp 44, Overmars 84),
FC Barcelona 4 (Rivaldo 13p, Luis Enrique 15, Figo 55, Cocu 69)

Fiorentina 3 (Batistuta 5, Chiesa 36, Balbo 86), **AIK 0**

Arsenal 0, Fiorentina 1 (Batistuta 75)

FC Barcelona 5 (Kluivert 14, 33, Zenden 42, Gabri 53, Déhu 56), **AIK 0**

Fiorentina 3 (Bressan 14, Balbo 56, 69),
FC Barcelona 3 (Figo 19, Rivaldo 43, 73)

AIK 2 (Andersson A. 41, 68), **Arsenal 3** (Overmars 17, 52, Suker 56)

FINAL TABLE

		Pd	Home W	D	L	F	A	Away W	D	L	F	A	Total W	D	L	F	A	Pt	GD
1	FC Barcelona	6	2	1	0	10	3	2	1	0	9	6	4	2	0	19	9	14	10
2	Fiorentina	6	1	2	0	6	3	1	1	1	3	4	2	3	1	9	7	9	2
3	Arsenal	6	1	0	2	5	6	1	2	0	4	3	2	2	2	9	9	8	0
4	AIK	6	0	1	2	3	5	0	0	3	1	11	0	1	5	4	16	1	-12

UEFA CHAMPIONS' LEAGUE

minutes remaining they were denied an equaliser in an amazing goalmouth scramble, with Toldo saving magnificently at point-blank range from Kanu after Davor Suker had struck a post.

That was that. With one game still to go, all the positions had been resolved. Barcelona were through as group winners, Fiorentina as runners-up, Arsenal were into the UEFA Cup while AIK were guaranteed to finish bottom. The final matches, though both entertaining and full of goals, had mere cosmetic value.

FIRST PHASE GROUP C

The peculiarities of the Champions' League draw meant that all four teams in Group C were actually 'placed' rather than drawn there. It was an evenly-balanced section, with Boavista, the surprise qualifiers from Portugal, marginally less favoured than the other three - 1997 champions Borussia Dortmund and the two seeded teams, Rosenborg and Feyenoord.

Rosenborg were the first to get into the groove, celebrating their fifth successive Champions' League participation with their first away win in three years. Boavista had no answer to the Norwegians as they struck three goals without reply to claim the best opening-night performance of any of the 32 teams.

In the other match Feyenoord were held 1-1 in Rotterdam by Borussia Dortmund. Drawing matches they might have won was to become a frustrating habit for the Dutch champions over the following weeks.

Fine goalkeeping by Francesco Toldo kept Fiorentina in the game against Arsenal.

CHAMPIONS' LEAGUE FIRST PHASE GROUP C

(September 14/22/29, October 19/27, November 2, 1999)

RESULTS

Boavista FC 0, Rosenborg BK 3 (Sørensen 9, Berg Ø. 44, Strand R. 73)

Feyenoord 1 (Van Wonderen 68), **Borussia Dortmund 1** (Bobic 71)

Borussia Dortmund 3 (Möller 40, Bobic 52, 65),
Boavista FC 1 (Rui Bento 45)

Rosenborg BK 2 (Carew 21, 24), **Feyenoord 2** (Tomasson 11, Kalou 22)

Boavista FC 1 (Mário Silva 85), **Feyenoord 1** (Bosvelt 62)

Rosenborg BK 2 (Sørensen 35, Carew 68),
Borussia Dortmund 2 (Barbarez 11, Kohler 22)

Feyenoord 1 (Tomasson 76), **Boavista FC 1** (Timofte 82p)

Borussia Dortmund 0, Rosenborg BK 3 (Sørensen 17, 58, Winsnes F. 70)

Rosenborg BK 2 (Berg Ø. 61, Dahlum 66), **Boavista FC 0**

Borussia Dortmund 1 (Addo 44), **Feyenoord 1** (Van Vossen 73)

Boavista FC 1 (Pedro Emanuel 16), **Borussia Dortmund 0**

Feyenoord 1 (Somalia 86), **Rosenborg BK 0**

FINAL TABLE			Home				Away				Total					
		Pd	W	D	L	F	A	W	D	L	F	A	W	D	L	F	A	Pt	GD
1	Rosenborg BK	6	1	2	0	6	4	2	0	1	6	1	3	2	1	12	5	11	7
2	Feyenoord	6	1	2	0	3	2	0	3	0	4	4	1	5	0	7	6	8	1
3	Borussia Dortmund	6	1	1	1	4	5	0	2	1	3	4	1	3	2	7	9	6	-2
4	Boavista FC	6	1	1	1	2	4	0	1	2	2	6	1	2	3	4	10	5	-6

UEFA CHAMPIONS' LEAGUE

While sharing the spoils in a 2-2 draw away to Rosenborg was no great hardship, they twice allowed Boavista to score late equalisers, conceding a goal from all of 35 yards in the away fixture. That put Leo Beenhakker's side in a delicate position with two rounds to play, and when they made it five one-pointers out of five thanks to a memorable solo strike from Dutch international Peter van Vossen in Dortmund, it was possible that they might exit the tournament despite being unbeaten.

Rosenborg and Dortmund made the early running, but after a 2-2 draw in Trondheim the Norwegians took command with their second 3-0 away win of the competition, hammering the Germans into a state of surrender with an awesome display in the Westfalenstadion which many classed as the finest performance ever from a Norwegian team in Europe. Two goals from Jan Derek Sørensen made him the star of a scintillating show.

Rosenborg's place as group winners was settled when they won at home for the first time a week later, beating Boavista 2-0. But the issue of second place remained unresolved. With one game remaining Dortmund headed Feyenoord by a point. If they won away to Boavista, they would be through, but if they lost, Feyenoord could afford to draw at home to already-qualified Rosenborg and still qualify. If Dortmund drew, Feyenoord had to win.

Both games finished 1-0. Dortmund went behind early and could not recover, while Feyenoord pinched a late winner, through Brazilian import Somalia, to grab their first victory and simultaneously bring about Rosenborg's first defeat.

FIRST PHASE GROUP D

Manchester United, the reigning European champions, could have no complaints about the draw. Although they had never previously faced any of Marseille, Croatia Zagreb and Sturm Graz in European combat, there seemed little for them to worry about.

However, England's finest made rather a mess of their opening fixture, at home to a Croatia Zagreb side now coached by Argentinian anglophile Ossie Ardiles. Lacking the bulk of their first-choice team, United put up a lethargic first-half display, and although they got their act together after the interval, they were denied victory by Zagreb's veteran international goalkeeper Drazen Ladic, who had a splendid match.

United were in much better form a week later as they trounced Sturm Graz 3-0 in Austria. Captain Roy Keane set them up for a comfortable victory with a crashing shot from 30 yards, and further goals from Dwight Yorke and Andy Cole made the three points a certainty, even if Sturm did make life easier for them when their star, Ivica Vastic, missed a penalty early in the second half.

CHAMPIONS' LEAGUE FIRST PHASE GROUP D

(September 14/22/29, October 19/27, November 2, 1999)

RESULTS

Manchester United 0, Croatia Zagreb 0

Olympique Marseille 2 (Pires 9, Ravanelli 33), **SK Sturm Graz 0**

Croatia Zagreb 1 (Sokota 64),
Olympique Marseille 2 (Bakayoko 5, Pérez 77)

SK Sturm Graz 0, Manchester United 3 (Keane 17, Yorke 31, Cole 33)

Croatia Zagreb 3 (Rukavina 28, Sokota 34, 57p), **SK Sturm Graz 0**

Manchester United 2 (Cole 79, Scholes 83),
Olympique Marseille 1 (Bakayoko 40)

Olympique Marseille 1 (Gallas 69), **Manchester United 0**

SK Sturm Graz 1 (Mujcin 40og), **Croatia Zagreb 0**

Croatia Zagreb 1 (Prosinecki 90),
Manchester United 2 (Beckham 32, Keane 49)

SK Sturm Graz 3 (Mählich 18, Kocijan 61, 84),
Olympique Marseille 2 (Dugarry 53, 78)

Manchester United 2 (Solskjaer 56, Keane 69),
SK Sturm Graz 1 (Vastic 88p)

Olympique Marseille 2 (Bakayoko 53, Diawara 89),
Croatia Zagreb 2 (Mujcin 42, Mikic 83)

			Home				Away				Total					
		Pd	W	D	L	F	A	W	D	L	F	A	W	D	L	F	A	Pt	GD
1	Manchester United	6	2	1	0	4	2	2	0	1	5	2	4	1	1	9	4	13	5
2	Olympique Marseille	6	2	1	0	5	2	1	0	2	5	6	3	1	2	10	8	10	2
3	SK Sturm Graz	6	2	0	1	4	5	0	0	3	1	7	2	0	4	5	12	6	-7
4	Croatia Zagreb	6	1	0	2	5	4	0	2	1	2	3	1	2	3	7	7	5	0

FINAL TABLE

UEFA CHAMPIONS' LEAGUE

After two games Marseille were the group leaders with maximum points, having beaten Sturm 2-0 at home and Croatia Zagreb 2-1 away. The French side came to Old Trafford intent on holding their position and for most of the game looked set to do so. While United spurned a succession of first-half chances Marseille took a shock lead, Ibrahima Bakayoko exploiting an error from Henning Berg before violently shooting his team ahead. United were up against it but they had shown many times before that they did not readily accept defeat and, sure enough, they came back not only to equalise but to win the game with two late goals from Andy Cole and Paul Scholes. Cole's effort, a superb overhead kick, was one of the goals of the round.

Three weeks later Marseille regained first place when they beat United 1-0 on a mudheap of a pitch in the Stade Vélodrome, with defender William Gallas scoring the winner. It was United's first Champions' League defeat in 19 matches but it had no lasting effect because a week later they went to Zagreb and won 2-1 to book their place in the second phase. Marseille also made it through with one game remaining, albeit not quite so impressively. Sturm Graz beat them 3-2 but the margin of the Austrians' victory was not sufficient to give them a chance of overtaking Marseille.

The three points did, however, greatly improve Sturm's chances of finishing third, and although they lost their final match, 2-1 to Manchester United, Sturm

eventually claimed third place when Croatia Zagreb, needing victory away to Marseille, had it snatched away from them in the 89th minute by a close-range header from Kaba Diawara.

FIRST PHASE GROUP E

Norwegian débutants Molde found themselves in the company of three experienced Champions' League campaigners in Real Madrid, FC Porto and Olympiakos and inevitably entered the competition with little expectation other than to make the most of their brief flirtation with European football's élite.

It was tough luck on Molde when they lost their opening game against Porto to an 88th-minute winner, but that encounter was overshadowed by a spectacularly exciting 3-3 draw in Athens between Olympiakos and Real Madrid. It was the Greek side's two expensive summer acquisitions, Brazilian Giovanni and Slovenian Zlatko Zahovic, who led the fight against the 1998 champions, but Real rescued a point when Raúl tapped in a Roberto Carlos cross ten minutes from time.

Olympiakos had always struggled away from home in previous competitions, and they conformed to type by losing their second match, 2-0 in Oporto, with Esquerdinha's brilliant early free-kick initiating their downfall.

With two wins out of two, FC Porto held pole position but lost it when Real Madrid, who had thrashed Molde

CHAMPIONS' LEAGUE FIRST PHASE GROUP E

(September 15/21/28, October 20/28, November 3, 1999)

RESULTS

Molde FK 0, FC Porto 1 (Deco 88)

Olympiakos 3 (Giovanni 10, 64, Zahovic 67),
Real Madrid 3 (Sávio 24, Roberto Carlos 32, Raúl 80)

FC Porto 2 (Esquerdinha 6, Jardel 46), **Olympiakos 0**

Real Madrid 4 (Morientes 27, Sávio 60, 69p, Guti 81),
Molde FK 1 (Schei Lindbaek 80)

Olympiakos 3 (Giovanni 16, 70, Luciano 77), **Molde FK 1** (Lund 58)

Real Madrid 3 (Morientes 23, Helguera 37, Hierro 68p),
FC Porto 1 (Jardel 28)

Molde FK 3 (Lund 54, 59, Berg Hestad 74),
Olympiakos 2 (Mavrogenidis 35, Zahovic 40)

FC Porto 2 (Jardel 12, 34), **Real Madrid 1** (Peixe 68og)

FC Porto 3 (Deco 1, 28, Jardel 58), **Molde FK 1** (Berg Hestad 82)

Real Madrid 3 (Raúl 21, Morientes 64, Roberto Carlos 83), **Olympiakos 0**

Molde FK 0, Real Madrid 1 (Karembeu 43)

Olympiakos 1 (Yanakopoulos 55), **FC Porto 0**

FINAL TABLE			Home				Away					Total					
		Pd	W	D	L	F	A	W	D	L	F	A	W	D	L	F	A	Pt	GD
1	Real Madrid	6	3	0	0	10	2	1	1	1	5	5	4	1	1	15	7	13	8
2	FC Porto	6	3	0	0	7	2	1	0	2	2	4	4	0	2	9	6	12	3
3	Olympiakos	6	2	1	0	7	4	0	0	3	2	8	2	1	3	9	12	7	-3
4	Molde FK	6	1	0	2	3	4	0	0	3	3	10	1	0	5	6	14	3	-8

UEFA CHAMPIONS' LEAGUE

4-1, overtook them with another impressive victory in the Bernabéu. Three weeks later, however, the Portuguese champions were back on top, with Mário Jardel scoring twice in a revenge victory at the Estádio das Antas.

By exchanging victories, Real Madrid and FC Porto were effectively in the clear. This was because Olympiakos were unable to hold onto a two-goal half-time lead away to Molde. The Norwegians struck back with three goals after the interval, the first two from their qualifying-round hero Andreas Lund, to claim their first Champions' League victory.

Matchday five confirmed the two front-runners' qualification for the next round as they each maintained their perfect home records with trouble-free three-goal victories against opponents who were unable to win a single point away from home. Matchday six was all about the fight between Real and Porto to finish first and the subsidiary battle between Olympiakos and Molde to take the UEFA Cup spot. Real and Olympiakos both got what they wanted by winning 1-0.

FIRST PHASE GROUP F

Other groups may have been populated by no-hopers, but Group F contained no makeweights whatsoever. All four contestants had at least one European trophy in their roll of honour, and it was difficult to forecast which of Bayern Munich, Valencia, PSV and Rangers would make it through to the next round.

Bayern, the frustrated runners-up of the previous season, were high on motivation as they began their third successive Champions' League challenge, but it was a newcomer, Brazilian winger Paulo Sérgio, who got their campaign off to a winning start with a brace of goals in a 2-1 victory at home to PSV. The other opening game also resulted in a home win, with Valencia making nonsense of their lowly position in the Spanish league (no points after three matches) by blitzing Scottish Premier League leaders Rangers to claim a surprisingly easy 2-0 win.

Bayern and Valencia both consolidated their positions by drawing away from home in their next encounters, but while the Spaniards were very hard done by in Eindhoven, where the home side were gifted a hugely controversial penalty, the Germans were very lucky to come away with a point from Glasgow, Michael Tarnat's deflected free-kick in the 90th minute breaking Scottish hearts after Jörg Albertz had put his fellow countrymen in arrears with a typical left-foot shot midway through the first half.

Bayern were lucky to get another point in their next game, at home to Valencia. With the scoreline at 1-1, Claudio López broke clear in the final minute and was about to score when, outrageously, the referee blew the final whistle, thus ruling out the goal. Valencia protested their case in no uncertain terms, but nothing came of it. Three weeks later the Spaniards had the chance to make their point on the field of play, but the match ended in another 1-1 draw.

With Valencia and Bayern cancelling each other out, Rangers moved to the top of the table after doing the

---

CHAMPIONS' LEAGUE FIRST PHASE GROUP F

(September 15/21/28, October 20/28, November 3, 1999)

RESULTS

FC Bayern München 2 (Paulo Sérgio 11, 69), **PSV 1** (Khokhlov 59)

Valencia CF 2 (Moore 56og, Kily González 73), **Rangers 0**

PSV 1 (Van Nistelrooy 72p), **Valencia CF 1** (López 4)

Rangers 1 (Albertz 22), **FC Bayern München 1** (Tarnat 90)

FC Bayern München 1 (Élber 6), **Valencia CF 1** (Gerard 79)

PSV 0, Rangers 1 (Albertz 84)

Rangers 4 (Amoruso 19, Mols 34, 80, McCann 56), **PSV 1** (Van Nistelrooy 45p)

Valencia CF 1 (Ilie 11), **FC Bayern München 1** (Effenberg 18p)

PSV 2 (Van Nistelrooy 39, Nilis 57), **FC Bayern München 1** (Santa Cruz 51)

Rangers 1 (Moore 60), **Valencia CF 2** (Mendieta 35, López 45)

Valencia CF 1 (López 70), **PSV 0**

FC Bayern München 1 (Strunz 33p), **Rangers 0**

FINAL TABLE

		Home						Away					Total						
		Pd	W	D	L	F	A	W	D	L	F	A	W	D	L	F	A	Pt	GD
1	Valencia CF	6	2	1	0	4	1	1	2	0	4	3	3	3	0	8	4	12	4
2	FC Bayern München	6	2	1	0	4	2	0	2	1	3	4	2	3	1	7	6	9	1
3	Rangers	6	1	1	1	6	4	1	0	2	1	3	2	1	3	7	7	7	0
4	PSV	6	1	1	1	3	3	0	0	3	2	7	1	1	4	5	10	4	-5

UEFA CHAMPIONS' LEAGUE

'double' over PSV. Rangers boss Dick Advocaat made a triumphant return to his former club as Albertz again found the target with a late strike to claim an excellent 1-0 win over a team that, like Rangers, had a 100 per cent record in their domestic league. The return match at Ibrox was a breeze for Rangers as two-goal Dutchman Michael Mols led them to a convincing 4-1 win.

Rangers went into their penultimate fixture, at home to Valencia, knowing that a third successive victory would take them into the next phase. But, once again, Valencia were the better team, and goals from Gaizka Mendieta and Claudio López put the visitors in the driving seat. Rangers clawed one goal back, from Australian defender Craig Moore, but could not save the game.

It was not all doom and gloom for the Scots, though, because while they were going down to Valencia, Bayern were surprisingly losing their unbeaten record in Eindhoven, where Luc Nilis struck a fabulous winner. It was the gifted Belgian striker's 37th goal in European competition, taking him past such famous names as Johan Cruijff and Ferenc Puskás in the all-time rankings. It was a goal of great significance for the scorer and also for the Dutch fans, who never tired of putting one over the Germans. However, it did little for PSV's hopes of remaining in Europe.

Bayern's defeat meant that Valencia had qualified for the next stage. The Spaniards needed just one more point to claim first place, and they did so by beating PSV in their final game. The more significant action took place in Munich where Bayern needed victory to take the runners-up spot while Rangers required a draw to proceed in their place.

For Rangers it was to be a night on which everything that could go wrong did go wrong. Three times they struck the frame of the Bayern goal, but the ball just would not cross the line, and, to add insult to injury, the Germans stole victory with a disputed penalty which Rangers goalkeeper Stefan Klos so very nearly saved. A bad injury to Michael Mols completed a night of misery for Dick Advocaat's side as Bayern sneaked through to the second phase. It was a lucky win for the German champions but also a timely one as both Borussia Dortmund and Bayer Leverkusen had dropped out of the competition 24 hours earlier.

FIRST PHASE GROUP G

UEFA are proud of their ranking system but it occasionally throws up glitches. Group G was a case in point. Not only were there no previous European trophy-winners among the quartet, the group seeds were Spartak Moscow, who, paradoxically, were the only one of the four teams obliged to pre-qualify. Furthermore, Bordeaux and Willem II were exempt despite never having played Champions' League football before.

CHAMPIONS' LEAGUE FIRST PHASE GROUP G

(September 15/21/28, October 20/28, November 3, 1999)

RESULTS

Sparta Praha 0, Girondins de Bordeaux 0

Willem II 1 (Arts 56), **Spartak Moskva 3** (Tikhonov 27p, 37, 53p)

Girondins de Bordeaux 3 (Victoria 16og, Laslandes 21, Feindouno 83), **Willem II 2** (Abdellaoui 40, Sanou 70)

Spartak Moskva 1 (Bezrodnyi 73), **Sparta Praha 1** (Lokvenc 17)

Girondins de Bordeaux 2 (Wiltord 9, Micoud 56), **Spartak Moskva 1** (Bezrodnyi 64)

Sparta Praha 4 (Novotny J. 26, Prohaszka 29p, Rosicky 40, Jarosik 58), **Willem II 0**

Spartak Moskva 1 (Tikhonov 55p), **Girondins de Bordeaux 2** (Micoud 21, Wiltord 76)

Willem II 3 (Bombarda 1, Shukov 6, Schenning 50), **Sparta Praha 4** (Novotny J. 17, Labant 54p, 90p, Baranek 62)

Girondins de Bordeaux 0, Sparta Praha 0

Spartak Moskva 1 (Bezrodnyi 25), **Willem II 1** (Sanou 63)

Willem II 0, Girondins de Bordeaux 0

Sparta Praha 5 (Lokvenc 1, 65, Rosicky 10, Fukal 49, Labant 63p), **Spartak Moskva 2** (Bulatov 34, Bezrodnyi 45)

FINAL TABLE		Pd			Home				Away					Total					
		Pd	W	D	L	F	A	W	D	L	F	A	W	D	L	F	A	Pt	GD
1	Sparta Praha	6	2	1	0	9	2	1	2	0	5	4	3	3	0	14	6	12	8
2	Girondins de Bordeaux	6	2	1	0	5	3	1	2	0	2	1	3	3	0	7	4	12	3
3	Spartak Moskva	6	0	2	1	3	4	1	0	2	6	8	1	2	3	9	12	5	-3
4	Willem II	6	0	1	2	4	7	0	1	2	3	8	0	2	4	7	15	2	-8

UEFA CHAMPIONS' LEAGUE

Spartak made a promising early move when they won their opening match 3-1 away to Willem II. It was a difficult début for the Dutch outsiders, who conceded two penalties and were undone by an Andrei Tikhonov hat-trick. Bordeaux also conceded a spot-kick in their opening match away to Sparta Prague but Ulrich Ramé saved from Horst Siegl to preserve a goalless draw.

As expected, Bordeaux claimed all three points in their next match, at home to Willem II, but it was a late goal from Pascal Feindouno, their last-day hero in the previous season's French championship success, that brought them a 3-2 victory. Spartak wasted an opportunity to take control of the group when they had two players sent off in a disappointing 1-1 draw at home to Sparta Prague.

The Czechs, in turn, gained their first win at Willem II's expense, thrashing them 4-0 in Prague and then completing the 'double' with a highly entertaining 4-3 victory in Tilburg, clinched by Slovakian midfielder Vladimir Labant's last-minute penalty.

While Sparta were taking six points from Willem II, Bordeaux were doing likewise at Spartak Moscow's expense, with French internationals Johan Micoud and Sylvain Wiltord finding the net in each 2-1 triumph. With ten points in the bag, the Girondins were home and dry, their place in the next round already guaranteed with two matches still to play.

Bordeaux managed to maintain their unbeaten record through their last two games, but two goalless draws, at home to Sparta and away to Willem II, proved costly to them in terms of their final position. The Czechs, who were confirmed as Bordeaux's fellow qualifiers after Spartak Moscow failed yet again to win at home, against Willem II, took first place on goal difference after pummelling the Russians 5-2 in their final game. It was a brilliant performance from Sparta and ensured their status as seeds for the second phase draw.

FIRST PHASE GROUP H

Group B, featuring Arsenal and Fiorentina, was not the only first-phase section with a strong Anglo-Italian flavour. Group G contained Chelsea and Milan, two teams rich in Continental talent who were both favoured to progress to the second round at the expense of Galatasaray and Hertha Berlin.

The two favourites met on the opening matchday at Stamford Bridge. With Graeme Le Saux and Chris Sutton left out, captain Dennis Wise was the only Englishman in Chelsea's starting XI. Milan, for their part, had five nationals on show, but the best Italian on the pitch was Chelsea's Gianfranco Zola, who, perhaps miffed by his continued exclusion from the Italian national team, gave the watching Italian press a performance to remember. Serie A exiles Didier Deschamps and Marcel Desailly also shone in an excellent Chelsea performance that saw them bank a point from a 0-0 draw - the third of the opening week for England's Champions' League participants.

CHAMPIONS' LEAGUE FIRST PHASE GROUP H

(September 15/21/28, October 20/28, November 3, 1999)

RESULTS

Chelsea 0, Milan 0

Galatasaray 2 (Hakan Sükür 23, Hagi 86p),
Hertha BSC Berlin 2 (Preetz 12, Wosz 13)

Hertha BSC Berlin 2 (Daei 2, 70), **Chelsea 1** (Leboeuf 86p)

Milan 2 (Leonardo 44, Shevchenko 45), **Galatasaray 1** (Ümit 50)

Chelsea 1 (Petrescu 55), **Galatasaray 0**

Milan 1 (Bierhoff 74), **Hertha BSC Berlin 1** (Daei 69)

Galatasaray 0, Chelsea 5 (Flo 32, 49, Zola 54, Wise 79, Ambrosetti 87)

Hertha BSC Berlin 1 (Wosz 41), **Milan 0**

Hertha BSC Berlin 1 (Rekdal 35p),
Galatasaray 4 (Hakan Sükür 48, 66, Tugay 81, Okan 90)

Milan 1 (Bierhoff 74), **Chelsea 1** (Wise 76)

Chelsea 2 (Deschamps 11, Ferrer 44), **Hertha BSC Berlin 0**

Galatasaray 3 (Capone 27, Hakan Sükür 86, Ümit 90p),
Milan 2 (Weah 20, Giunti 51)

FINAL TABLE		Pd	Home					Away					Total					Pt	GD
			W	D	L	F	A	W	D	L	F	A	W	D	L	F	A		
1	Chelsea	6	2	1	0	3	0	1	1	1	7	3	3	2	1	10	3	11	7
2	Hertha BSC Berlin	6	2	0	1	4	5	0	2	1	3	5	2	2	2	7	10	8	-3
3	Galatasaray	6	1	1	1	5	9	1	0	2	5	4	2	1	3	10	13	7	-3
4	Milan	6	1	2	0	4	3	0	1	2	2	4	1	3	2	6	7	6	-1

UEFA CHAMPIONS' LEAGUE

Galatasaray and Hertha also opened up with a draw - 2-2 in Istanbul - but a week later there were home wins for both Hertha and Milan, the Germans gaining a rather fortunate 2-1 victory over Chelsea thanks to two goals from Iranian striker Ali Daei while the Italian champions overcame Galatasaray by the same scoreline following a burst of two goals in two minutes just before half-time.

Daei was on the mark again a week later to halt Milan in their tracks in the San Siro and give Hertha a precious 1-1 draw, but the Serie A side were aghast at the refereeing of Frenchman Gilles Veissière, who booked five Milan players and disallowed an injury-time effort from Leonardo for a debatable offside. Milan's anger was such that they filed an official complaint to UEFA. There were no protests about the referee from Chelsea as they registered their first Champions' League win, 1-0 against Galatasaray, having seen opposition goalkeeper Cláudio Taffarel red-carded for handling outside the area in the first half and also survived a goal-claim from the Turks when the ball appeared to have just crossed the line before Ed de Goey pawed it clear. With the visitors down to ten men, Chelsea took advantage, going ahead through Dan Petrescu and then dominating without scoring in the final half-hour as Zola missed four reasonable chances to improve the margin of victory.

Zola did get on the scoresheet in the return fixture three weeks later as Chelsea ran riot, destroying a Taffarel-less Galatasaray 5-0 in Istanbul. With Milan simultaneously going down to a 1-0 defeat in Berlin, it left the Italians with much to do in their final two matches.

The penultimate encounter, at home to Chelsea, was a must-win game for Milan. They did not play well but appeared to have done the necessary when Oliver Bierhoff headed in a Serginho cross 16 minutes from time. But Chelsea, who had gone close to taking the lead through Gustavo Poyet just seconds before Bierhoff's goal, struck back straightaway. Wise was the scorer, collecting Roberto Di Matteo's long pass with an excellent first touch and tucking the ball into the corner with an accurate left-foot shot.

Milan's discomfort was exacerbated by the news that Galatasaray had won 4-1 in Berlin. It meant the Turks still had something to play for when they faced the Italians at home in the final match. It also meant that Chelsea and Hertha could both squeeze Milan out by agreeing to a mutually beneficial draw. Milan's only chance of Champions' League survival was to beat Galatasaray and hope that there were winners and losers at Stamford Bridge, but the Turks also knew that a home win would

put them in the UEFA Cup and eliminate Milan from Europe altogether.

Group H was the only group which entered its final matchday with all major issues unresolved. Chelsea knew that a draw was enough to take them through but it was in their interests to win as topping the group would help their seeding for the next round. A brilliant early strike fom Didier Deschamps - his first goal in 73 European matches - put Gianluca Vialli's team in the driving seat and there was another unexpected goalscorer later in the half as Albert Ferrer, like Deschamps, struck his first goal for Chelsea to make it 2-0.

While Chelsea celebrated victory, Hertha waited on news from Istanbul. It proved to be good for them but disastrous for Milan. Leading 2-1 with only a few minutes remaining, the Italians conceded an equaliser when Hakan Sükür scored with a superb diving header. Shortly afterwards Hakan was poised to strike again when Milan defender Bruno Ngotty shoved him in the back. Amidst incredible tension midfielder Ümit nervelessly converted the ensuing penalty to win the game 3-2. Hertha's Champions' League place was safe, Galatasaray were in the UEFA Cup, while Milan, the champions of Italy, had lost their hold on two European competitions within the space of a few minutes. The first phase of the Champions' League could hardly have concluded in more dramatic circumstances.

SECOND PHASE GROUP A

Barcelona were installed as the tournament favourites after finding themselves in a second phase group that looked, on paper, to be significantly less daunting than the one from which they had just qualified. Sparta Prague, FC Porto and Hertha Berlin had all come through the previous round on merit but Barça were clearly a class apart.

However, it was the Portuguese champions who made the brighter start, taking maximum points from their first two encounters and entering the winter break with a two-point lead. They won their opening game 2-0 in Prague, with Brazilian goal-machine Jardel netting his sixth goal of the competition to move to the top of the Champions' League top-scorer listings. There then followed a 1-0 victory at home to Hertha, settled by a magnificent solo goal from Yugoslav winger Ljubinko Drulovic, who raced from deep within his own half before slotting the ball home with a calm finish.

Barcelona, meanwhile, went into the winter shut-down with four points. Their opening match, in Berlin, should not have been played. A swirl of freezing fog hung over

UEFA CHAMPIONS' LEAGUE

the stadium for the entire 90 minutes and visibility was negligible. Still, both teams managed to find their way to goal, with Kai Michalke equalising Luis Enrique's headed opener in a 1-1 draw. Barça were clearly more at home in the Nou Camp, where two weeks later they demolished Sparta 5-0, making the most of the Czechs' one-man disadvantage following the dismissal of midfielder Martin Hasek.

When the competition resumed three months later, Barcelona's Rivaldo was the European and World Footballer of the Year and he demonstrated why with an awesome display as the Catalans beat Porto 4-2 in the Nou Camp to take over at the top. It was a night of Brazilian glamour all round because both of Porto's goals were scored by Jardel, who struck twice with trademark headers. Rivaldo equalised Jardel's early opener with a typically deceptive free-kick and rounded off the win with a neat individual strike late on.

Barcelona thus became the only unbeaten team left in the competition. A week later Louis van Gaal's side became the first side to book their place in the quarter-finals when they completed the 'double' over Porto. A goal in each half gave the Catalans a 2-0 win. Defender Abelardo volleyed in after 38 minutes and Rivaldo sealed the victory with a free-kick just before the hour.

With two successive defeats, Porto's bid to join Barça in the next round had come under threat, especially as Sparta Prague had beaten Hertha with a spectacular

last-minute strike from their defender Milan Fukal. Porto entertained Sparta on matchday five and needed victory to ensure their safe passage, but despite going 2-0 up they could not hold on, and it was Fukal again who struck in the last minute to keep the issue open.

Porto were still the favourites to qualify. They needed a point away to winless Hertha, and even a defeat would not be fatal if Sparta failed to win at home to confirmed group winners Barcelona. At half-time, with the Czechs leading and Porto being held, everything was in the melting pot, but Porto and Barcelona both went on to win in the second half. Clayton scored a magnificent goal for Porto and there was an equally unheralded match-winner for Barcelona as Gabri struck twice to give his team a total of 16 points from their six matches - the highest in any group - and raise their total goal-tally to 36 in 12 games. No wonder everybody wanted to avoid the Catalans in the quarter-final draw.

SECOND PHASE GROUP B

Fiorentina, the conquerors of Arsenal, were again drawn to face English opposition, and they caused great consternation for holders Manchester United when they beat them 2-0 at home in their opening fixture. The Italians fully exploited two errors of judgment in the United defence to score a goal in each half and bag three important points. Once again Fiorentina's matchwinner was Gabriel Batistuta. It was he who pounced on Roy

CHAMPIONS' LEAGUE SECOND PHASE GROUP A

(November 23, December 8, 1999, March 1/7/15/21, 2000)

RESULTS

Hertha BSC Berlin 1 (Michalke 33), **FC Barcelona 1** (Luis Enrique 13)

Sparta Praha 0, FC Porto 2 (Drulovic 76, Jardel 83)

FC Barcelona 5 (Kluivert 44, 70, Luis Enrique 45, 76, Guardiola 60),
Sparta Praha 0

FC Porto 1 (Drulovic 77), **Hertha BSC Berlin 0**

FC Barcelona 4 (Rivaldo 15, 87, De Boer F. 22, Kluivert 44),
FC Porto 2 (Jardel 4, 79)

Hertha BSC Berlin 1 (Veit 45), **Sparta Praha 1** (Siegl 84)

FC Porto 0, FC Barcelona 2 (Abelardo 38, Rivaldo 58)

Sparta Praha 1 (Fukal 90), **Hertha BSC Berlin 0**

FC Barcelona 3 (Xavi 10, Gabri 49, Kluivert 82),
Hertha BSC Berlin 1 (Alves 7)

FC Porto 2 (Jorge Costa 16, Capucho 64),
Sparta Praha 2 (Lokvenc 64, Fukal 90)

Hertha BSC Berlin 0, FC Porto 1 (Clayton 70)

Sparta Praha 1 (Svoboda Z. 18), **FC Barcelona 2** (Gabri 52, 88)

FINAL TABLE			Home				Away				Total					
	Pd	W	D	L	F	A	W	D	L	F	A	W	D	L	F	A	Pt	GD
1 FC Barcelona	6	3	0	0	12	3	2	1	0	5	2	5	1	0	17	5	16	12
2 FC Porto	6	1	1	1	3	4	2	0	1	5	4	3	1	2	8	8	10	0
3 Sparta Praha	6	1	0	2	2	4	0	2	1	3	8	1	2	3	5	12	5	-7
4 Hertha BSC Berlin	6	0	2	1	2	3	0	0	3	1	5	0	2	4	3	8	2	-5

UEFA CHAMPIONS' LEAGUE

Keane's stray backpass to open the scoring on 24 minutes with a masterful right-foot finish. Then, early in the second half, the Argentinian maestro robbed Henning Berg of possession before teeing-up his compatriot Abel Balbo for the decisive second goal.

The other opening Group B fixture brought an even more decisive home win as Valencia maintained their unbeaten record with a comprehensive 3-0 victory over another previously undefeated side, Bordeaux. The French champions kept their goal unbreached for an hour but a superb left-foot shot from Francisco Farinós opened the floodgates for the Spanish side, and two further goals followed from Adrian Ilie and Kily González.

Bordeaux went a fourth successive game without scoring when they were held 0-0 at home by a Francesco Toldo-inspired Fiorentina. Manchester United, however, got their act together in decisive fashion, destroying Valencia 3-0 at Old Trafford. The atmosphere was livened up before the game by the announcement that Roy Keane had a agreed a new four-year contract, and it was fitting that the Irishman should open the scoring when he buried a low drive into the bottom corner. If Keane was the hero of the hour, David Beckham was the man of the match, and it was from two of his pin-point crosses that United increased their lead, through Ole Gunnar Solskjaer and Paul Scholes. It ended 3-0,

giving United their 50th victory in the European Cup/Champions' League.

When the competition resumed in March, United were looking to redeem themselves after underperforming in the FIFA Club World Championship in Brazil. They did so by beating Bordeaux home and away. Ryan Giggs was the star of the show in the first meeting, at Old Trafford, scoring the first goal and laying on the second for Teddy Sheringham in a 2-0 win. In the return at the Parc Lescure, Bordeaux finally ended their five-match drought when an error from Raimond van der Gouw gifted skipper Michel Pavon an early goal, but a controversial red card for Lilian Laslandes allowed the defending champions to pick up the tempo and it was that man Keane again who netted their equaliser. In the second half the game ebbed and flowed, but it was United who grabbed the winner thanks to a terrific late goal from substitute Ole Gunnar Solskjaer.

United's two victories took them to the top of the table as Fiorentina and Valencia exchanged victories. Fiorentina won 1-0 at home with a dubious penalty from ex-Valencia man Predrag Mijatovic. In the Mestalla, however, Valencia were much the stronger side and won 2-0, even if their decisive second goal did not arrive until the 94th minute - moments after a Rui Costa free-kick had been disallowed for offside.

United's fifth match was at home to Fiorentina and they

CHAMPIONS' LEAGUE SECOND PHASE GROUP B

(November 23, December 8, 1999, March 1/7/15/21, 2000)

RESULTS

Fiorentina 2 (Batistuta 24, Balbo 51), **Manchester United 0**

Valencia CF 3 (Farinós 60, Ilie 69, Kily González 90),
Girondins de Bordeaux 0

Girondins de Bordeaux 0, Fiorentina 0

Manchester United 3 (Keane 38, Solskjaer 47, Scholes 69), **Valencia CF 0**

Fiorentina 1 (Mijatovic 20p), **Valencia CF 0**

Manchester United 2 (Giggs 42, Sheringham 84),
Girondins de Bordeaux 0

Girondins de Bordeaux 1 (Pavon 9),
Manchester United 2 (Keane 33, Solskjaer 84)

Valencia CF 2 (Ilie 35, Mendieta 90p), **Fiorentina 0**

Girondins de Bordeaux 1 (Wiltord 54),
Valencia CF 4 (Djukic 41, Mendieta 48p, Kily González 72, Sánchez 90)

Manchester United 3 (Cole 20, Keane 33, Yorke 70),
Fiorentina 1 (Batistuta 16)

Fiorentina 3 (Chiesa 47p, Batistuta 60, Rui Costa 64),
Girondins de Bordeaux 3 (Wiltord 5, Zanotti 87, Battles 90)

Valencia CF 0, Manchester United 0

FINAL TABLE			Home				Away					Total						
		Pd	W	D	L	F	A	W	D	L	F	A	W	D	L	F	A	Pt	GD
1	Manchester United	6	3	0	0	8	1	1	1	1	2	3	4	1	1	10	4	13	6
2	Valencia CF	6	2	1	0	5	0	1	0	2	4	5	3	1	2	9	5	10	4
3	Fiorentina	6	2	1	0	6	3	0	1	2	1	5	2	2	2	7	8	8	-1
4	Girondins de Bordeaux	6	0	1	2	2	6	0	1	2	3	8	0	2	4	5	14	2	-9

UEFA CHAMPIONS' LEAGUE

knew that a fourth straight victory would guarantee their qualification. The match was delayed for 15 minutes because of an electricity failure but there were plenty of sparks on the field in a scintillating first half. Batistuta put Fiorentina ahead with a ferocious swerving shot but United responded swiftly with a fine goal from Andy Cole. The home side then took command with captain Keane's sixth goal of the competition. There was no let-up after the interval, and once Fiorentina were reduced to ten men following Fabio Rossitto's sending-off, United were in complete control, netting a third goal through Dwight Yorke's perfect header and finishing the game to deafening applause from the stands. It was United's best performance of the season and ensured their presence in the Champions' League quarter-finals for the fourth year in succession.

Fiorentina's misery was compounded when they learned that Valencia had trounced Bordeaux 4-1 in the Parc Lescure. Even without the suspended Claudio López the Spaniards were far too good for their hosts. The victory hoisted them into second place and they knew that a draw at home to already-qualified United would guarantee their qualification for the last eight.

In fact, United were in the comfortable position of travelling to Valencia knowing that first place (and, therefore, a seeding slot for the quarter-finals) was secure

unless they lost by more than two goals. It was out of Fiorentina's hands, and although Valencia and United engaged in an entertaining first half, the second period was a complete stand-off, with both teams happy to settle for the goalless draw that suited each of their requirements.

SECOND PHASE GROUP C

There was a chilly start to Group C as Real Madrid travelled to face Dynamo Kiev while Bayern Munich headed to the competiton's most northerly outpost, Trondheim, to take on Rosenborg.

Snow had to be cleared from the pitch in the Ukrainian capital as Kiev took on Real for the third time in 1999, having eliminated them from the previous season's quarter-finals. On this occasion the tables were turned as the Spaniards, lacking a coach following the recent dismissal of John Toshack, won the game 2-1 thanks to a couple of fine goals from their all-Spanish strikeforce of Morientes and Raúl. In the other game Rosenborg and Bayern shared a 1-1 draw.

Matchday two brought predictable but uneasy home wins for both Real and Bayern. In the Bernabéu the Norwegians were looking good value for a precious point with five minutes remaining. Giant young striker John Carew had headed in an equaliser to cancel out

---

CHAMPIONS' LEAGUE SECOND PHASE GROUP C

(November 24, December 7, 1999, February 29, March 8/14/22, 2000)

RESULTS

Dynamo Kiev 1 (Rebrov 85p), **Real Madrid 2** (Morientes 17, Raúl 48)

Rosenborg BK 1 (Skammelsrud 47), **FC Bayern München 1** (Jancker 10)

FC Bayern München 2 (Jancker 6, Paulo Sérgio 80),
Dynamo Kyiv 1 (Rebrov 50)

Real Madrid 3 (Raúl 18, Sávio 84, Roberto Carlos 90),
Rosenborg BK 1 (Carew 47)

Dynamo Kyiv 2 (Khatskevich 10, Rebrov 29), **Rosenborg BK 1** (Jakobsen 48)

Real Madrid 2 (Morientes 26, Raúl 47),
FC Bayern München 4 (Scholl 21, Effenberg 24, Fink 39, Paulo Sérgio 66)

FC Bayern München 4 (Scholl 2, Élber 30, Zickler 79, 90),
Real Madrid 1 (Helguera 69)

Rosenborg BK 1 (Berg Ø. 38), **Dynamo Kyiv 2** (Rebrov 32, 67)

FC Bayern München 2 (Scholl 10, Paulo Sérgio 39p),
Rosenborg BK 1 (Carew 64)

Real Madrid 2 (Raúl 13p, Roberto Carlos 71),
Dynamo Kyiv 2 (Khatskevich 42, Hierro 56og)

Dynamo Kyiv 2 (Kaladze 34, Demetradze 71), **FC Bayern München 0**

Rosenborg BK 0, **Real Madrid 1** (Raúl 3)

FINAL TABLE		Home					Away					Total					
	Pd	W	D	L	F	A	W	D	L	F	A	W	D	L	F	A	Pt	GD
1 FC Bayern München	6	3	0	0	8	3	1	1	1	5	5	4	1	1	13	8	13	5
2 Real Madrid	6	1	1	1	7	7	2	0	1	4	5	3	1	2	11	12	10	-1
3 Dynamo Kyiv	6	2	0	1	5	3	1	1	1	5	5	3	1	2	10	8	10	2
4 Rosenborg BK	6	0	1	2	2	4	0	0	3	3	7	0	1	5	5	11	1	-6

UEFA CHAMPIONS' LEAGUE

John Carew scored twice for Rosenborg during their second phase games.

Raúl's early tap-in. But a late rally from the Spaniards produced two goals from Brazilian imports Sávio and Roberto Carlos. Bayern also left it late before they claimed a 2-1 victory over Dynamo Kiev, the winning goal coming ten minutes from time when another Brazilian, Paulo Sérgio, netted from close range after a throw-in had been flicked into his path.

As the competition went into a three-month hibernation, Real and Bayern seemed uncatchable at the top, but Dynamo Kiev had recovered from a poor start in the first phase and they were to do so again, collecting all six points from their two matches with Rosenborg. The previous season's semi-finalists won the home game 2-1 thanks to two spectacular long-range strikes, the second of them from Serhiy Rebrov, who was the hero again a week later when he struck twice more in another 2-1 win to join Jardel and Rivaldo as the competition's joint-top scorer on eight goals.

Kiev's 'double' over Rosenborg put them level on points

with Real Madrid, who, remarkably, were turned over twice in six days by a rampant Bayern. The Germans' first win, 4-2 in the Bernabéu, came in the week of the club's Centenary and was heralded as one of their finest ever away performances in Europe. Bayern took a two-goal lead through Mehmet Scholl and Stefan Effenberg and responded to Real's comeback attempts with further strikes from Thorsten Fink and Paulo Sérgio. The following week Bayern needed a bit of good fortune to get them going when Scholl opened the scoring from a suspiciously offside position. Brazilian Giovane Élber increased their advantage with an impressive second goal, and although Real were stirred back to life with a stunning long-range strike from Iván Helguera, Bayern killed them off late in the game with two breakaway goals from Alexander Zickler.

Despite the blow to their pride, Real knew that a return to winning ways at home to Kiev would enable them to join Bayern in the quarter-finals. But the Ukrainians came to the Bernabéu full of confidence and they were the better team in a 2-2 draw which Real salvaged only with a fortuitous free-kick from Roberto Carlos.

That left the two contenders level on points, but Real had the superior head-to-head record, and that eventually proved to be the decisive factor as both teams won their final games. Kiev were given a helping hand by group winners Bayern, who rested nine first-teamers for the trip to the Ukrainian capital and went down 2-0. Real's task was more difficult but an early Raúl goal proved sufficient for a 1-0 victory away to Rosenborg, who thus exited the competition with a fifth consecutive defeat.

SECOND PHASE GROUP D

First phase group winners Lazio and Chelsea were the clear favourites to progress in this section, and that was borne out in the opening encounters as Chelsea ripped Feyenoord apart at Stamford Bridge while Lazio cruised to an impressive 2-0 victory away to Marseille.

Chelsea completely overpowered a woeful Feyenoord to inflict on the Dutch champions their first defeat of the competition. 3-1 was the final score but the victory should have been by a significantly greater margin such was the English side's dominance. Missed chances meant that Chelsea had to wait until first-half stoppage-time to take the lead, but Celestine Babayaro's close-range header eased the tension and Tore André Flo scored two scrappy second-half goals to seal the win.

Lazio went to the south of France smarting from a disastrous 4-1 defeat in the Rome derby - the first time

UEFA CHAMPIONS' LEAGUE

they had been beaten in 23 competitive matches - but despite resting several leading players they were still too strong for Marseille. Second-half goals from midfielders Dejan Stankovic and Sérgio Conceição paved the way to an important victory, which goalkeeper Luca Marchegiani protected with a miraculous one-handed save late in the game. After the match Marseille coach Rolland Courbis resigned, to be replaced by Bernard Casoni.

Casoni's first Champions' League match, against Feyenoord in Rotterdam, was not a memorable one. Two Marseille defenders, Yannick Fischer and Sébastien Pérez, were both red carded and the home side took full advantage to score three late goals, two of them from Argentine striker Julio Cruz, who had also netted Feyenoord's late consolation against Chelsea.

In Rome, Lazio and Chelsea shared a goalless draw, which took both teams into the winter break with four points from two games. It was the second time that the Londoners had returned from Italy with a precious point, having drawn 1-1 with Milan in the first phase. But there was a price to pay in the Stadio Olimpico when manager Gianluca Vialli was dismissed to the stands after arguing with the fourth official. In a game of few chances, which Chelsea governed in impressive style, the best opportunity fell late on to the visitors when Gianfranco Zola's chip was somehow scrambled off the line.

There was a surprise in store for both group favourites in the first week back after the winter break. Lazio's

1-2 defeat at home to Feyenoord was arguably the shock of the entire competition. It was their first defeat in Europe for almost two years and came about as a result of two late strikes from Jon Dahl Tomasson. The Danish international twice exploited hesitancy in the Italian defence to turn the match on its head after Juan Sebastián Verón had opened the scoring with a brilliantly opportunistic volley. Feyenoord's win put them top as Chelsea succumbed to a 1-0 defeat in Marseilles, victims of Robert Pires's stunning winner, which he crashed into the net from a tight angle via both goalposts.

Chelsea reversed that scoreline a week later thanks to a first-half strike from Dennis Wise, but Lazio could not make good their home defeat by Feyenoord, drawing 0-0 in Rotterdam. The Italians were back in second place after matchday five, however, thanks to a blockbusting 5-1 victory at home to Marseille - a match in which Simone Inzaghi equalled Marco van Basten's Champions' League record by scoring four goals in one match. He should have broken it but missed a penalty.

Chelsea, meanwhile, confirmed their presence in the last eight with their second comprehensive 3-1 victory over Feyenoord. The English side were on top throughout and could even afford the luxury of a missed Frank Leboeuf penalty and a sloppily conceded equaliser before they ran out convincing winners.

There was plenty still for Chelsea to play for on the final matchday. They required a draw at home to Lazio to ensure first place in the group. The Italians' need was for

CHAMPIONS' LEAGUE SECOND PHASE GROUP D

(November 24, December 7, 1999, February 29, March 8/14/22, 2000)

RESULTS

Olympique Marseille 0, Lazio 2 (Stankovic 64, Sérgio Conceição 77)

Chelsea 3 (Babayaro 45, Flo 67, 85), **Feyenoord 1** (Cruz 90)

Feyenoord 3 (Cruz 72, 90, Bosvelt 83), **Olympique Marseille 0**

Lazio 0, Chelsea 0

Lazio 1 (Verón 37), **Feyenoord 2** (Tomasson 78, 85)

Olympique Marseille 1 (Pires 16), **Chelsea 0**

Chelsea 1 (Wise 27), **Olympique Marseille 0**

Feyenoord 0, Lazio 0

Feyenoord 1 (Kalou 58), **Chelsea 3** (Zola 39, Wise 64, Flo 69)

Lazio 5 (Inzaghi 17, 37, 38, 71, Boksic 82),
Olympique Marseille 1 (Leroy 50)

Chelsea 1 (Poyet 45), **Lazio 2** (Inzaghi 54, Mihajlovic 66)

Olympique Marseille 0, Feyenoord 0

FINAL TABLE		Home					Away					Total						
	Pd	W	D	L	F	A	W	D	L	F	A	W	D	L	F	A	Pt	GD
1 Lazio	6	1	1	1	6	3	2	1	0	4	1	3	2	1	10	4	11	6
2 Chelsea	6	2	0	1	5	3	1	1	1	3	2	3	1	2	8	5	10	3
3 Feyenoord	6	1	1	1	4	3	1	1	1	3	4	2	2	2	7	7	8	0
4 Olympique Marseille	6	1	1	1	1	2	0	0	3	1	9	1	1	4	2	11	4	-9

UEFA CHAMPIONS' LEAGUE

a victory, because anything less would give Feyenoord the chance to qualify as group runners-up.

There was not one Englishman in the Chelsea starting XI. Dennis Wise was rested, and with Alessandro Nesta ruled out through injury, it meant that both captains were missing. Lazio coped better without theirs. Although they dominated the midfield in the first half it was Chelsea who took the lead on the stroke of half-time with a violent shot from Gustavo Poyet. After the interval Lazio reinforced their attack and the move paid off. Inzaghi turned in an equaliser from close range and Sinisa Mihajlovic put Lazio deservedly ahead with a perfectly executed free-kick. From then on Lazio's superior class told, and although Fernando Couto was sent off seven minutes from time, Sven Göran Eriksson's side confidently protected their lead.

With Feyenoord held 0-0 in Marseilles, Lazio only needed a draw, but the win was significant for two reasons. It enabled them to win the group, and it also made them the first team ever to beat Chelsea at Stamford Bridge in European competition - a record that had remained intact for over 40 years.

QUARTER-FINALS

The structure of the quarter-final draw rewarded the group winners, who not only avoided each other but had the advantage of playing the second leg at home. The pairings for the semi-finals were also made at the same time, and while the outcome ensured that there could be no repeat of the 1999 final between Manchester United and Bayern Munich, the possibilities remained for either an all-English final or a showdown between Spanish giants Barcelona and Real Madrid.

First up, though, were the quarter-finals, and the choice tie was the one between the last two winners of the

Lazio's Sérgio Conceição gets in a cross ahead of Valencia's Joachim Björklund.

competition, Real Madrid and Manchester United.

The first leg, in Madrid, ended goalless but it was full of incident. Real were the better team and created a number of chances against a full-strength United but they were unable to find a way past Mark Bosnich, who produced a memorable display, capping his evening with an outstanding save late on to deny Englishman Steve McManaman. United themselves made only rare attacking forays but they did create the best chance of the evening when Andy Cole headed a Beckham corner tamely over the bar from close range. 0-0 away from home is not necessarily a positive result, and United

QUARTER-FINAL RESULTS

(April 4/5 & 18/19, 2000)

FC Porto 1 (Jardel 46), **FC Bayern München 1** (Paulo Sérgio 80)
FC Bayern München 2 (Paulo Sérgio 14, Linke 90),
FC Porto 1 (Jardel 89)
(FC Bayern München 3-2)

Real Madrid 0, Manchester United 0
Manchester United 2 (Beckham 64, Scholes 88p),
Real Madrid 3 (Keane 20og, Raúl 50, 52)
(Real Madrid 3-2)

Chelsea 3 (Zola 30, Flo 34, 38), **FC Barcelona 1** (Figo 62)
FC Barcelona 5 (Rivaldo 23, 97p, Figo 44, Dani 83, Kluivert 104),
Chelsea 1 (Flo 60) (aet)
(FC Barcelona 6-4)

Valencia CF 5 (Angulo 2, Gerard 4, 40, 79, López 90),
Lazio 2 (Inzaghi 28, Salas 87)
Lazio 1 (Verón 52), **Valencia CF 0**
(Valencia CF 5-3)

Rivaldo shoots for goal as Chelsea's Didier Deschamps slides in.

UEFA CHAMPIONS' LEAGUE

discovered why just 21 minutes into the return at Old Trafford when a disastrous own-goal from Roy Keane gifted Real a priceless away goal. United peppered their opponents' goal for the remainder of the half but Real's young goalkeeper Iker Casillas would not be beaten. The defending champions knew they had to score twice and continued to drive forward after the interval but Real ruthlessly exploited the spaces they left at the back, and two sublime counter-attacks, the first led by McManaman, the second by Fernando Redondo, both resulted in goals for Raúl. There was no way back for United after that. They tried their best, pulling one goal back with a brilliant Beckham strike and then another, from a Paul Scholes penalty. But the final whistle came soon afterwards and the holders were out.

Real's victory completed an amazing 'treble' for Spanish football, because the previous evening both Barcelona and Valencia had already clinched their place in the semi-finals.

Barcelona also defeated English opposition, but the tournament favourites were taken to the very brink by Chelsea, who gave as good as they got in an engrossing, exciting quarter-final. Chelsea were in dreamland at half-time in the first leg at Stamford Bridge. Three excellent goals within the space of eight minutes - one from a Zola free-kick, the other two from Flo - put the Londoners in the clear, but Figo gave Barcelona a crucial away goal, and that was to prove the turning point of the tie.

There was a remarkable atmosphere in a sold-out Nou Camp for the second leg. Despite having lost their unbeaten record, Barcelona still scented a place in the semi-finals. 2-0 was the scoreline they sought and by half-time they had achieved it, with superstars Rivaldo

Valencia's Miguel Angel Angulo gets to grips with Barça's Phillip Cocu.

and Figo scoring the goals. But Chelsea were not out of it and on the hour an horrendous error from Barça 'keeper Ruud Hesp enabled Flo to score his third goal of the tie and put Chelsea right back in business. With seven minutes left, however, Barça struck back, through substitute Dani, and in the last minute they seemed to have scored the winner when Patrick Kluivert put the ball into the net after a goalmouth scramble. The referee, however, had already blown for a penalty. Rivaldo had the chance to finish Chelsea off...but put his penalty wide. Into extra-time the two teams went, and it was all Barça. They won another penalty, and this time Rivaldo scored. A few minutes later Kluivert made it 5-1 with a close-range header and Chelsea were beaten.

The exhiliartion of that performance was matched a couple of weeks earlier by Valencia as they sensationally crushed Lazio 5-2. The Italian side went into the game without an away defeat in Europe for three and a half years but Valencia tore that proud record to shreds with a fantastic display. With the game just four minutes old the home side were already 2-0 up, through Spanish U-21 internationals Angulo and Gerard. The latter went on to score a hat-trick, but Lazio kept in touch with goals from Simone Inzaghi and substitute Marcelo Salas and seemed happy to settle for a 4-2 defeat...until Claudio Lopez, a player set to join Lazio, increased Valencia's

Jens Jeremies of Bayern Munich cuts inside Porto's Ljubinko Drulovic.

UEFA CHAMPIONS' LEAGUE

lead to 5-2 with a superb left-foot shot in the very last minute.

Lazio, the lone remaining Serie A side in Europe, had a mountain to climb. They dominated the second leg from start to finish, but with Spanish international 'keeper Santiago Cañizares having a night to remember, they managed just the one goal, a 30-yard screamer from Verón. The first-leg defeat had simply left them with too much ground to make up.

Joining the three Spanish sides in the semi-finals were Bayern Munich, who scraped past FC Porto thanks to late goals in each leg. The Portuguese champions dominated the first game, but a Mário Jardel header was cancelled out ten minutes from time when the Porto defence went to sleep and allowed Paulo Sérgio to race clear and score. The same player put his team ahead early on in the return leg, but the Germans must have felt it was the Nou Camp revisited when Jardel yet again stung them with a brilliant header in the 90th minute. However, just as the referee was about to blow for full-time, Bayern took a free-kick and Mehmet Scholl's cross was headed in by defender Thomas Linke to put his team into the last four.

SEMI-FINALS

The first of the two semi-finals brought favourites Barcelona down the Mediterranean coast to Valencia. The Catalans would probably have preferred to play anywhere else because Valencia had long held an Indian sign over them on the domestic front.

Once again the Mestalla was bursting at the seams in anticipation. Barcelona were missing the suspended Luís Figo but they still had Rivaldo, and the great Brazilian was in vibrant form during the first half as Barça sought to recover from the concession of an early goal, slammed home by Angulo. Barcelona were level when Maurico Pellegrino, one of their former players, put the ball into his own net in trying to intercept a Boudewijn Zenden cross. Back, though, came Valencia, and before half-time they had taken a 3-1 lead. Angulo was a major thorn in Barcelona's side. He converted a Kily González cross to make it 2-1 and then earned his team a penalty after being fouled by Carlos Puyol. Captain Gaizka Mendieta calmly slotted home the spot-kick, sending Hesp the wrong way.

The second half was less dramatic but Valencia continued to dominate. With full-time looming, Barcelona had clearly settled for a 3-1 defeat, but, as against Lazio, Valencia kept going right up until the final whistle and concluded a magnificent performance wth a stunning stoppage-time strike from Claudio López. 92 minutes were on the clock when the Argentine crowned some diligent work on the left from Amedeo Carboni with a magnificent first-time shot which entered the net via the inside of the far post.

"Remontada" (fightback) was the message from the Nou Camp crowd to their players at the start of the second leg, but it was to go unheeded. Valencia were made of sterner stuff than Chelsea and they went on to boss the game with extraordinary conviction, barely

Real's Raúl finds himself surrounded by the Bayern defence.

UEFA CHAMPIONS' LEAGUE

giving Louis van Gaal's star-studded team a sniff of a chance to reduce the deficit. The way in which Valencia played their way out of trouble at the back was particularly impressive, and in Mendieta, López and veteran French full-back Jocelyn Angloma they possessed the three best players on the pitch. The goals all came late. Mendieta struck first for Valencia to kill the tie, and although Barça came back to win the game on the night with goals from Dutchmen Frank de Boer and Phillip Cocu it was the hollowest of victories. The sporting Nou Camp crowd applauded Valencia off the field. They were through to the final, and deservedly so.

Real Madrid and Bayern Munich had already met twice during the second group phase, and the Germans had soundly won both matches. But the Spaniards showed that they bore no scars because after just four minutes of the first leg in the Bernabéu they went ahead. The goalscorer was none other than Nicolas Anelka, the 'enfant terrible' who had only just returned from a club suspension. A second Real goal, inadvertently put into

Valencia's Mendieta beats Roberto Carlos to the ball.

his own net by Jens Jeremies after a penetrating run from Míchel Salgado, sent the Bernabéu crowd into raptures, and there would have been further additions to the score but for the goalkeeping of Oliver Kahn, who denied Morientes, Sávio and Raúl. Bayern's only clear chance came late in the game when Thorsten Fink headed fractionally wide from a corner.

60,000 fans attended the second leg on a warm night in Munich. 12 minutes in they were up on their feet as Carsten Jancker volleyed spectacularly into the roof of the net following a well-worked free-kick. Élber thought he had made it 2-0 to Bayern but English referee Graham Poll controversially disallowed it. Bayern were still bemoaning their luck when, up at the other end, Real sprung a rare counter-attack and scored. Sávio's perfect left-wing cross was met by a superb header from Anelka which flew past Kahn into the top corner. It was later revealed that the Frenchman had never previously scored with his head during his professional career.

Armed with a precious away goal, Real could afford to relax. Bayern now needed three goals to win. They got one of them when Élber glanced in a Stefan Effenberg free-kick early in the second half, but despite an intense effort from the Germans, Real's defence never looked likely to be breached again. Bayern's bid to reach a second successive final was over. Real, the 1998 champions, were through to face Valencia in an all-Spanish showdown at the Stade de France.

FINAL

Never before in the 44-year history of the European Cup/Champions' League had two clubs from the same country contested the final. This, however, was Spain's

Steve McManaman bagged his only goal of the tournament in the final.

UEFA CHAMPIONS' LEAGUE

year, and Real Madrid and Valencia were both accompanied to Paris by an armada of enthusiastic fans.

Having won the trophy seven times previously, Real knew all about the occasion and were the favourites to win. However, Valencia had shown in beating both Lazio and Barcelona that on their day they were a match for anyone.

Valencia had the added comfort of knowing that they had already qualified for the following season's Champions' League whereas Real could only get back into the competition if they were triumphant in the final.

The game began encouragingly with a brisk early pace and plenty of action at both ends. It was Real, however, who gradually took a grip on midfield, and one of their most diligent performers, Steve McManaman, came very close to opening the scoring when his controlled volley through a crowded penalty area was kept out with an excellent save by Cañizares. On 39 minutes the deadlock was broken as Fernando Morientes headed Real into a deserved lead following good work from Anelka and Míchel Salgado.

Valencia, kitted out all in orange, made a fiery start to the second half but they lacked the stealth and penetration of Real. The men in black - they, too, had been obliged to switch colours for the occasion - absorbed everything that Valencia threw at them and then, on 67 minutes, doubled their lead when McManaman adjusted his feet superbly to volley in a spectacular shot from the edge of the area.

Five minutes later Valencia missed their best chance of the game when Claudio López just failed to make contact with Mendieta's chipped pass. It was a pivotal moment because soon afterwards the game was all over as Raúl sped clear from Sávio's long pass and, having rounded Cañizares, clipped a right-foot shot back across the 'keeper and into the far corner beyond the despairing efforts of a backtracking defender. That was Raúl's tenth goal of the tournament, placing him level with FC Porto's Jardel at the top of the goal charts.

The final whistle could not come soon enough for both teams. Valencia had given up. There would be no repetition of the previous year's amazing climax. Real were the champions of Europe for a

FINAL

24/05/2000, Paris Saint-Denis
REAL MADRID 3 Morientes (39), McManaman (67), Raúl (75)
VALENCIA CF 0
referee - Braschi (ITA)
REAL MADRID - Casillas; Míchel Salgado (Hierro 84), Iván Campo, Helguera, Karanka, Roberto Carlos; Redondo, McManaman; Raúl; Anelka (Sanchis 79), Morientes (Sávio 71).
VALENCIA CF - Cañizares; Angloma, Pellegrino, Djukic, Gerardo (Ilie 68); Mendieta, Farinós, Gerard, Kily González; Angulo, López.

The celebrations begin for Real Madrid.

record eighth time and the first team to win the Champions' League twice. The 3-0 scoreline brooked no argument. They thoroughly deserved their win. New coach Vicente del Bosque, who had been confirmed in the position on the eve of the match, had won the tactical battle with his counterpart Héctor Cúper, and the best players on the field were all from Real, with McManaman arguably the pick of a fine bunch in which Redondo, Raúl and Iván Helguera were all prominent.

Fittingly, Real donned their traditional white shirts to collect the trophy, and they also handed the honour of lifting the trophy to veteran club captain Manuel Sanchis. It had been the longest and most gruelling European Cup tournament of all, but Real, the very first winners back in 1956, were back on the podium once again after a worthy, well-earned victory.

TOP SCORERS

(excluding Preliminary/Qualifying rounds)
10 Mário JARDEL (FC Porto)
    RAUL (Real Madrid)
9   Simone INZAGHI (Lazio)
8   RIVALDO (FC Barcelona)
    Serhiy REBROV (Dynamo Kyiv)
7   Tore André FLO (Chelsea)
    PAULO SÉRGIO (FC Bayern München)
6   Patrick KLUIVERT (FC Barcelona)
    LUIS ENRIQUE (FC Barcelona)
    Roy KEANE (Manchester United)
    Fernando MORIENTES (Real Madrid)
5   Gabriel BATISTUTA (Fiorentina)
    John CAREW (Rosenborg BK)
    Claudio LOPEZ (Valencia CF)
    Gaizka MENDIETA (Valencia CF)

UEFA CUP

QUALIFYING ROUND RESULTS

(August 12/26, 1999)

RSC Anderlecht 6 (Goor 18, 41, Gunnarsson 40og, Zetterberg 53, Baseggio 56, Radzinski 65), **Leiftur 1** (De Boeck 25og)
Leiftur 0, RSC Anderlecht 3 (Van Diemen 2, Zetterberg 41p, 62p)
(RSC Anderlecht 9-1)

Ankaragücü 1 (Ünal 15), **B36 0**
B36 0, Ankaragücü 1 (Hakan Keles 81)
(Ankaragücü 2-0)

APOEL Nicosia 0, Levski Sofia 0
Levski Sofia 2 (Sirakov 67, Pazin 75), **APOEL Nicosia 0**
(Levski Sofia 2-0)

FC BATE Borisov 1 (Lisovskiy 72), **Lokomotiv Moskva 7**
(Janashia 6, 34, 60, Loskov 24, Sarkisyan 55, Bulykin 73, 86)
Lokomotiv Moskva 5 (Chugainov 17, Loskov 23, Smertin 36, Kharlachyov 66, 75), **FC BATE Borisov 0**
(Lokomotiv Moskva 12-1)

Belshina Bobruisk 1 (Khripach 21), **Omonia Nicosia 5**
(Kalotheou 9, Mihajlovic 26, Rauffmann 33, Kaiafas 54, Constandinides 90)
Omonia Nicosia 3 (Rauffmann 64, 68, 75), **Belshina Bobruisk 0**
(Omonia Nicosia 8-1)

FK Bodo/Glimt 1 (Staurvik 27), **FC Vaduz 0**
FC Vaduz 1 (Wegmann 38), **FK Bodo/Glimt 2** (Saeternes 29, 83)
(FK Bodø/Glimt 3-1)

Cwmbran Town 0,
Celtic 6 (Berkovic 2, Tébily 19, Larsson 32, 59, Viduka 49, Brattbakk 84)
Celtic 4 (Brattbakk 8, Smith 60, Mjällby 65, Johnson 88), **Cwmbran Town 0**
(Celtic 10-0)

Ferencváros 3 (Horváth 36, Füzi 42, Kovács 73),
Constructorul Chisinau 1 (Comlionoc 78)
Constructorul Chisinau 1 (Zabolotnii 40), **Ferencváros 1** (Horváth 38)
(Ferencváros 4-2)

IFK Göteborg 3 (Andersson P. 36, Karlsson P. 74, 87), **Cork City 0**
Cork City 1 (Morley 30), **IFK Göteborg 0**
(IFK Göteborg 3-1)

Grasshopper-Club Zürich 4 (Chapuisat 30, 63, Isabella 78, 85),
Bray Wanderers 0
Bray Wanderers 0,
Grasshopper-Club Zürich 4 (Tikva 6, 39, De Napoli 53, Muff 65)
(Grasshopper-Club Zürich 8-0)

Hajduk Split 5 (Bulat 4, Baturina 44, Grdic 57, Leko 68, Deranja 90),
F91 Dudelange 0
F91 Dudelange 1 (Kabongo 49), **Hajduk Split 1** (Jazic 52)
(Hajduk Split 6-1)

HIT Gorica 2 (Mitrakovic 74p, Zlogar 83), **Inter Cardiff 0**
Inter Cardiff 1 (Mainwaring 57), **HIT Gorica 0**
(HIT Gorica 2-1)

HJK 2 (Rafael 21, Ilola 70), **Shirak Gyumri 0**
Shirak Gyumri 1 (Bernetsyan 28), **HJK 0**
(HJK 2-1)

Inter Bratislava 3 (Gerich 16, Kratochvil 28, Pernis 75),
Bylis Ballsh 1 (Jakupi 62)
Bylis Ballsh 0, Inter Bratislava 2 (Nemeth S. 34, 64)
(Inter Bratislava 5-1)

KÍ 0, Grazer AK 5 (Radovic 7, 37, Standfest 9, 85, 89)
Grazer AK 4 (Ramusch 47, Akwuegbu 74, Dmitrovic 81, Tutu 88), **KÍ 0**
(Grazer AK 9-0)

KR 1 (Hinriksson 87), **Kilmarnock 0**
Kilmarnock 2 (Wright 90p, Bagan 92), **KR 0** (aet)
(Kilmarnock 2-1)

Kryvbas Kryvyi Rih 3 (Ponomarenko 8, Palyanytsya 66, Moroz 80),
Shamkir 0
Shamkir 0, Kryvbas Kryvyi Rih 2 (Simakov 24, 70)
(Kryvbas Kryvyi Rih 5-0)

FC Lantana Tallinn 0, Torpedo Kutaisi 5
(Khvadagiani 2, Janashia D. 32, Ionanidze 38, Chkhetiani 54, Megreladze 65)
Torpedo Kutaisi 4 (Ionanidze 11, Megreladze 26, 29, 71),
FC Lantana Tallinn 2 (Leitan 37, Dolinin 56)
(Torpedo Kutaisi 9-2)

Lokomotivi Tbilisi 1 (Kebadze 23), **Linfield 0**
Linfield 1 (Larmour 67), **Lokomotivi Tbilisi 1** (Kebadze 79)
(Lokomotivi Tbilisi 2-1)

Lyngby FC 7 (Hermansen 29, 90, Jensen 33, Larsen 47, Magleby 68, Lüthje 82, Havlykke 87), **Birkirkara 0**
Birkirkara 0, Lyngby FC 0
(Lyngby FC 7-0)

Maccabi Tel-Aviv 3 (Kubica 13, 33, Basis 69),
FBK Kaunas 1 (Papeckys 19)
FBK Kaunas 2 (Pacevicius 29, 48), **Maccabi Tel-Aviv 1** (Basis 86)
(Maccabi Tel-Aviv 4-3)

Metalurgs Liepaya 3 (Boulders 36, Verpakovsky 53, Dragun 62),
Lech Poznan 2 (Zurawski 23, Najewski 59)
Lech Poznan 3 (Golinski 55, Kubicki 72, Mackiewicz 79),
Metalurgs Liepaya 1 (Boulders 87)
(Lech Poznan 5-4)

UEFA CUP

The side-effects of UEFA's new masterplan for the Champions' League were felt in the UEFA Cup. With the Cup-winners' Cup a thing of the past, the UEFA Cup welcomed into its vastly expanded number all of Europe's domestic Cup holders (or, in some cases, runners-up) as well as the usual teams who had finished just off the pace in their national championships.

It was also decided, controversially, to place Champions' League 'losers' into the UEFA Cup at two separate stages. As before, the 16 defeated teams in the Champions' League qualifying round were allowed in at the first-round stage, but in addition, for the first time, the eight teams finishing third in each of the eight first-phase Champions' League groups were entitled to a place in the UEFA Cup third round.

With so many teams to juggle around, it was perhaps surprising that the tournament organisers decided to dispense with the two-tier filtering system that had been used before. Now there was just one qualifying round, and it took place in August rather than July. This was quite a boon to teams from the less successful countries. It meant that they went into European action several weeks later than their Champions' League representatives, which allowed them to adhere more or less to their regular pre-season routine.

QUALIFYING ROUND RESULTS (CONTINUED)

FC Mondercange 2 (Christophe 38, Neves 90), **Dinamo Bucuresti 6** (Lupescu 21p, Petre F. 28, Mihalcea 49, Mutu 51, 78, Niculae 80)
Dinamo Bucuresti 7 (Mutu 8p, 19, Niculae 23, 29, 74, Fogel 71og, Petre T. 89), **FC Mondercange 0**
(Dinamo Bucuresti 13-2)

Neftchi Baku 2 (Vasilyev 27, 65),
Crvena zvezda Beograd 3 (Boskovic 68, Pjanovic 69, Pantelic 70)
Crvena zvezda Beograd 1 (Pantelic 76), **Neftchi Baku 0**
(Crvena zvezda Beograd 4-2)

Portadown 0, CSKA Sofia 3 (Manchev 1, Kovacevic 77, Bukarev 85)
CSKA Sofia 5 (Petkov 15p, Litera 29, 51, Hristov 63p, Simeonov 81),
Portadown 0
(CSKA Sofia 8-0)

FK Riga 0, Helsingborgs IF 0
Helsingborgs IF 5 (Andersson C. 4, Jonsson 16, Powell 43, Prica 66, Bakkerud 84), **FK Riga 0**
(Helsingborgs IF 5-0)

SCT Olimpija Ljubljana 1 (Moro 27), **Kareda Siauliai 1** (Fomenka 68)
Kareda Siauliai 2 (Fomenka 67, 70),
SCT Olimpija Ljubljana 2 (Moro 21, Kmetec 87)
(3-3; SCT Olimpija Ljubljana on away goals)

Serif Tiraspol 1 (Mudjiri 10), **Sigma Olomouc 1** (Kovac 20)
Sigma Olomouc 0, Serif Tiraspol 0
(1-1; Sigma Olomouc on away goal)

Shakhtar Donetsk 3 (Seleznev 60, Shtolcers 80, 89),
Sileks Kratovo 1 (Gokic 90)
Sileks Kratovo 2 (Ignatov 19p, Simovski 74),
Shakhtar Donetsk 1 (Seleznev 22)
(Shakhtar Donetsk 4-3)

Sliema Wanderers 0, FC Zürich 3 (Kavelashvili 36, Bartlett 80, Kebe 90)
FC Zürich 1 (Kebe 70), **Sliema Wanderers 0**
(FC Zürich 4-0)

Steaua Bucuresti 3 (Ilie 40, 89, Ciocoiu 79), **FC Levadia Maardu 0**
FC Levadia Maardu 1 (Olumets 29),
Steaua Bucuresti 4 (Reghecampf 53, Rosu 69, 80, Ilie 84)
(Steaua Bucuresti 7-1)

Tulevik Viljandi 0, Club Brugge KV 3 (Deflandre 50p, Jankauskas 58, 69)
Club Brugge KV 2 (Jankauskas 48, De Brul 69), **Tulevik Viljandi 0**
(Club Brugge KV 5-0)

Vardar Skopje 0, Legia Warszawa 5 (Mieciel 8, Czereszewski 19, Srutwa 58, 74, Wroblenski 66)
Legia Warszawa 4 (Czereszewski 5, Karwan 16, Sokolowski 53, Mieciel 77),
Vardar Skopje 0
(Legia Warszawa 9-0)

Viking FK 7 (Lunde Aarsheim 5, Svensson 17, 48, Dadason 40, 72, 82, Nygaard 64), **CE Principat 0**
CE Principat 0, Viking FK 11 (Dadason 37, 42, Berre 43, 61, 75, Berland 44, 45, Sanne 64, 65, 67, Mathiassen 83)
(Viking FK 18-0)

Vllaznia Shkodër 1 (Sinani 44), **Spartak Trnava 1** (Leitner 29)
Spartak Trnava 2 (Ujlaky 58, 89), **Vllaznia Shkodër 0**
(Spartak Trnava 3-1)

Vojvodina Novi Sad 4 (Suskavcevic 5, Jankovic 18p, 47, Jovic 62),
Újpest FC 0
Újpest FC 1 (Kovács Z. 56), **Vojvodina Novi Sad 1** (Bratic 87)
(Vojvodina Novi Sad 5-1)

VPS 1 (Pohja 41), **St. Johnstone 1** (Lowndes 76)
St. Johnstone 2 (Simão 87, 90), **VPS 0**
(St. Johnstone 3-1)

FK Yerevan 0, Hapoel Tel-Aviv 2 (Harazi 55, 58)
Hapoel Tel-Aviv 2 (Pisont 82, Antebe 90), **FK Yerevan 1** (Gogoladze 50)
(Hapoel Tel-Aviv 4-1)

UEFA CUP

QUALIFYING ROUND

76 teams took part in the qualifying round. These included teams from all of the lesser-ranked nations plus the three clubs that had qualified as the wild-card entrants through UEFA's Fair Play lucky dip.

There was only one champion club entered at this stage. That was Andorran team CE Princiat, who, for reasons best known to the competition planners, did not warrant a starting berth in the Champions' League. Perhaps UEFA felt sorry for them. That certainly wasn't the case with Norwegian side Viking FK, who mercilessly annihilated the mountainside minnows 18-0 on aggregate.

Even in a round full of one-sided mismatches, no other team could quite match Viking's performance, although three other teams managed to take their goal haul into double figures. Dinamo Bucharest overcame Luxembourg's Mondercange 13-2, with highly-rated youngster Adrian Mutu scoring four of the goals, while Lokomotiv Moscow thrashed Belarus's BATE Borisov 12-1 and Celtic dismantled their fellow Brits Cwmbran Town 10-0.

Celtic were not the only former European trophy-winners involved at this stage. Red Star Belgrade, Steaua Bucharest, IFK Gothenburg, Ferencváros and Anderlecht were also in action, and they all came through in some comfort.

In fact, with the draw heavily seeded, there was little scope for lesser teams to make it into the first round. Icelandic league leders KÍ came the closest to causing an upset. They were just seconds away from knocking out Kilmarnock when a debatable penalty saved the Scottish Premier League side, who went on to win in extra-time. Lithuanian side Kareda Siauliai also made life extremely hazardous for Olimpija Ljubljana, who eventually scraped home on the away-goals rule after a late equaliser in the second leg.

FIRST ROUND

The first round of the UEFA Cup had never been so large. The 96 participants included the 38 preliminary-round qualifiers, 39 exempt teams, 16 'second-chancers' from the Champions' League and the three escapees from the summer's InterToto competition.

There were some distinguished new arrivals, including the mighty Juventus, who had qualified via the InterToto (along with Montpellier and West Ham), and the UEFA Cup holders themselves, Parma, who had been dumped out of the Champions' League by Rangers.

Juventus and Parma were rapidly installed as the favourites to win the competition, but it was the team from Turin which made the better first impression. While Parma were pressed hard by Ukrainian side Kryvbas Kryvyi Rih (at least in the first leg, in Italy), Juve cruised past Omonia Nicosia, winning 10-2 on aggregate with new Yugoslav signing Darko Kovacevic carrying on where he had left off for Real Sociedad in the previous season's UEFA Cup by scoring four of the goals, including a hat-trick in the Stadio delle Alpi.

Other big-hitters were Ajax and PAOK, who both scored nine goals over the two legs, and Roma, who demolished Vitória Guimarães 7-0 at the Stadio Olimpico. Guimarães won the return 1-0 to save a bit of face but it was to be a bad couple of weeks all round for the Portuguese representation.

The biggest shock was Sporting's elimination by Viking. Blitzed 3-0 in Stavanger, where new recruit Peter Schmeichel played his first European match since lifting the Champions' Cup with Manchester United a few months earlier, Sporting could manage only a 1-0 win back in Lisbon and thus joined Guimarães and Beira Mar on the first-round scrapheap. Benfica might have made it a full house but they recovered from a 0-1 home defeat against Dinamo Bucharest to take the tie 2-1 on aggregate thanks to a splendid second-leg performance in the Romanian capital.

Comebacks were also needed by the two Galician sides, Celta Vigo and Deportivo La Coruña. Celta were 0-3 down at one stage to Swiss Cup winners Lausanne before they readdressed the situation, with South African striker netting a hat-trick in an easy second-leg victory. Deportivo were beaten 1-0 in Norway by Stabaek but got the two goals they needed back home at the Riazor.

One team unable to reverse a shock first-leg defeat, however, were Club Bruges, who lost out on away goals to Israeli champions Hapoel Haifa. On the eve of the first game, in Israel, the four Russian officials who were due to take charge of the match were replaced by a delegation from Romania after they were found to be drunk and disorderly on their arrival in the country.

Rapid Vienna, who lost their local 'derby' with Inter Bratislava, joined Sporting and Bruges as the most surprising first-round fallers, but the big five countries of England, France, Germany, Italy and Spain all carried their full complement into the next round.

UEFA CUP

FIRST ROUND RESULTS

(September 16/30, 1999)

AB 0, Grasshopper-Club Zürich 2 (Bjur 50og, Ekoku 82)
Grasshopper-Club Zürich 1 (Magno 79), **AB 1** (Daugaard 31)
(Grasshopper-Club Zürich 3-1)

Ajax 6 (Verlaat 25p, Reuser 26, Knopper 48, Mahlas 50, 64, Wamberto 72),
Dukla Banska Bystrica 1 (Verlaat 14og)
Dukla Banska Bystrica 1 (Malatinsky 44),
Ajax 3 (Arveladze 47, Bobson 64, Laudrup 90)
(Ajax 9-2)

Amica Wronki 2 (Dawidowski 22, Bosacki 70), **Brøndby IF 0**
Brøndby IF 4 (Madsen 35, 76, Da Silva 54, Christensen 78),
Amica Wronki 3 (Kryszalowicz 53, 68, Kukiela 65p)
(Amica Wronki 5-4)

RSC Anderlecht 3 (Bajrektarevic 21og, Radzinski 36, 68),
SCT Olimpija Ljubljana 1 (Ekmecic 54)
SCT Olimpija Ljubljana 0, RSC Anderlecht 3 (Koller 64, Radzinski 70, 72)
(RSC Anderlecht 6-1)

Anorthosis Famagusta 1 (Engomitis 83), **Legia Warszawa 0**
Legia Warszawa 2 (Mieciel 48, Czereszewski 68),
Anorthosis Famagusta 0
(Legia Warszawa 2-1)

Aris 1 (Mantzios 12p), **Servette FC Genève 1** (Petrov 88)
Servette FC Genève 1 (Lonfat 35), **Aris 2** (Andrioli 37, Kizeridis 97) (aet)
(Aris 3-2)

Atlético Madrid 3 (Gamarra 41, Hasselbaink 46, Paunovic 59), **Ankaragücü 0**
Ankaragücü 1 (Birol 85), **Atlético Madrid 0**
(Atlético Madrid 3-1)

SC Beira Mar 1 (Fary 41), **Vitesse 2** (Van Hooijdonk 50, Grozdic 82)
Vitesse 0, SC Beira Mar 0
(Vitesse 2-1)

SL Benfica 0, Dinamo Bucuresti 1 (Nastase 34)
Dinamo Bucuresti 0, SL Benfica 2 (Maniche 24, Chano 71)
(SL Benfica 2-1)

FK Bodø/Glimt 0,
SV Werder Bremen 5 (Pizarro 11, 70, Bogdanovic 44, 55, Maximov 60)
SV Werder Bremen 1 (Ailton 76), **FK Bodø/Glimt 1** (Staurvik 76)
(SV Werder Bremen 6-1)

Celtic 2 (Larsson 24, 49p), **Hapoel Tel-Aviv 0**
Hapoel Tel-Aviv 0, Celtic 1 (Larsson 60)
(Celtic 3-0)

Crvena zvezda Beograd 0, Montpellier HSC 1 (Loko 3)
Montpellier HSC 2 (Ouédec 35, Loko 52),
Crvena zvezda Beograd 2 (Jelic 48, Boskovic 55p)
(Montpellier HSC 3-2)

CSKA Sofia 0, Newcastle United 2 (Solano 51, Ketsbaia 77)
Newcastle United 2 (Shearer 36, Robinson 88),
CSKA Sofia 2 (Litera 29, Simeonov 90)
(Newcastle United 4-2)

Grazer AK 3 (Akwuegbu 12, 56, Tutu 34), **Spartak Trnava 0**
Spartak Trnava 2 (Muzlay 45, 70), **Grazer AK 1** (Standfest 14)
(Grazer AK 4-2)

Hajduk Split 0, Levski Sofia 0
Levski Sofia 3 (Ivankov 16p, Bachev 33, Dimitrov 85), **Hajduk Split 0**
(Levski Sofia 3-0)

Hapoel Haifa 3 (Turgeman 18, 32, Sivilia 44),
Club Brugge KV 1 (Jankauskas 65)
Club Brugge KV 4 (Verheyen 19, Borkelmans 26, Janssen 52, 90),
Hapoel Haifa 2 (Rosso 18, Turgeman 78)
(5-5; Hapoel Haifa on away goals)

Helsingborgs IF 1 (Jonsson 85), **Karpaty Lviv 1** (Hetsko 17)
Karpaty Lviv 1 (Hetsko 90), **Helsingborgs IF 1** (Jonsson 90) (aet)
(2-2; Helsingborgs IF 4-2 on pens.)

HIT Gorica 0, Panathinaikos 1 (Limberopoulos 14)
Panathinaikos 2 (Sigurdsson 38, Nasiopoulos 70), **HIT Gorica 0**
(Panathinaikos 3-0)

HJK 0, Olympique Lyonnais 1 (Vairelles 16)
Olympique Lyonnais 5 (Ânderson 11, Blanc 15, Linarès 17, Vairelles 71, 86),
HJK 1 (Lehkosuo 40)
(Olympique Lyonnais 6-1)

Inter Bratislava 1 (Lalik 45), **SK Rapid Wien 0**
SK Rapid Wien 1 (Zingler 65), **Inter Bratislava 2** (Suchancok 45, Babnic 64)
(Inter Bratislava 3-1)

Ionikos 1 (Dimitriadis 90), **FC Nantes 3** (Lièvre 56, Monterrubio 67, 83)
FC Nantes 1 (Da Rocha 48), **Ionikos 0**
(FC Nantes 4-1)

1.FC Kaiserslautern 3 (Koch H. 29, Djorkaeff 37, Marschall 39),
Kilmarnock 0
Kilmarnock 0, 1.FC Kaiserslautern 2 (Djorkaeff 22, Ramzy 29)
(1.FC Kaiserslautern 5-0)

Lausanne-Sports 3 (Kuzba 20, Mazzoni 22, 58),
RC Celta 2 (Revivo 61, Karpin 67p)
RC Celta 4 (McCarthy 11, 85, 89, Mostovoi 76), **Lausanne-Sports 0**
(RC Celta 6-3)

Lech Poznan 1 (Zurawski 44p), **IFK Göteborg 2** (Andersson P. 27, Mild 83)
IFK Göteborg 0, Lech Poznan 0
(IFK Göteborg 2-1)

Lokomotivi Tblisi 0, PAOK 7
(Yeorgiadis 17, 25, Sabry 43, Frousos 56, 62, Marangos 67, Frantzeskos 69)
PAOK 2 (Valencia 50, Salpingidis 87), **Lokomotivi Tbilisi 0**
(PAOK 9-0)

UEFA CUP

FIRST ROUND RESULTS (CONTINUED)

Lyngby FC 1 (Arifulin 69og),
Lokomotiv Moskva 2 (Chugainov 13, Bulykin 37)
Lokomotiv Moskva 3 (Kharlachyov 20, Drozdov 43, Janashia 44),
Lyngby FC 0
(Lokomotiv Moskva 5-1)

Maccabi Tel-Aviv 2 (Kubica 44, Ben Dayan 85), **RC Lens 2** (Sakho 39, Job 54)
RC Lens 2 (Nouma 77, Delporte 80), **Maccabi Tel-Aviv 1** (Basis 24)
(RC Lens 4-3)

AS Monaco 3 (Simone 69, 90, Trezeguet 73), **St. Johnstone 0**
St. Johnstone 3 (Léonard 5og, Dasovic 35, O'Neil 76),
AS Monaco 3 (Prso 9, Riise 25, Legwinski 69)
(AS Monaco 6-3)

MTK Hungária FC 0, Fenerbahçe 0
Fenerbahçe 0, MTK Hungária FC 2 (Kenesei 55, 63)
(MTK Hungária FC 2-0)

Omonia Nicosia 2 (Kontolefteros 76, 85),
Juventus 5 (Inzaghi 3, 17, Kovacevic 22, Esnáider 25, Del Piero 83)
Juventus 5 (Kovacevic 21, 47, 87, Tacchinardi 55, Conte 90),
Omonia Nicosia 0
(Juventus 10-2)

Parma 3 (Di Vaio 13, 20, Baggio 67),
Kryvbas Kryvyi Rih 2 (Palyanytsya 5, Monarev 74)
Kryvbas Kryvyi Rih 0, Parma 3 (Boghossian 38, Crespo 40, Di Vaio 67)
(Parma 6-2)

Partizan Beograd 1 (Tomic 21),
Leeds United 3 (Bowyer 26, 82, Radebe 39)
Leeds United 1 (Huckerby 55), **Partizan Beograd 0**
(Leeds United 4-1)

Roda JC 2 (Doomernik 18, Zafarin 26), **Shakhtar Donetsk 0**
Shakhtar Donetsk 1 (Benio 32),
Roda JC 3 (Tchoutang 28, Van der Luer 81, Van Dessel 88)
(Roda JC 5-1)

Roma 7 (Aldair 12, Montella 14, 73, Alenichev 16, 54, 76, Marcos Assunção 40),
Vitória Setúbal 0
Vitória Setúbal 1 (Maki 77), **Roma 0**
(Roma 7-1)

Sigma Olomouc 1 (Kobylik 64),
RCD Mallorca 3 (Engonga 11, Diego Tristán 51, Stankovic 75)
RCD Mallorca 0, Sigma Olomouc 0
(RCD Mallorca 3-1)

Skonto Riga 1 (Astafyev 31), **Widzew Lodz 0**
Widzew Lodz 2 (Wichniarek 1, Gesior 43), **Skonto Riga 0**
(Widzew Lodz 2-1)

Stabaek IF 1 (Finstad 57), **RC Deportivo 0**
RC Deportivo 2 (Jokanovic 37, Flávio Conceição 62), **Stabaek IF 0**
(RC Deportivo 2-1)

Steaua Bucuresti 2 (Ciocoiu 63, Danciulescu 82), **LASK Linz 0**
LASK Linz 2 (Stumpf 5, Sane 90),
Steaua Bucuresti 3 (Bordeanu 7, Ilie 30, Duro 61)
(Steaua Bucuresti 5-2)

FK Teplice 3 (Frydek 33, Kolomaznik 53, Rizek 71),
Ferencváros 1 (Tóth 15)
Ferencváros 1 (Mátyus 57p), **FK Teplice 1** (Rada 53)
(FK Teplice 4-2)

Torpedo Kutaisi 0, AEK 1 (Zikos 90)
AEK 6 (Ciric 7p, Bjekovic 21, Maladenis 24, Kopitsis 44, 88, Nikolaidis 73),
Torpedo Kutaisi 1 (Megreladze 73)
(AEK 7-1)

Tottenham Hotspur 3 (Leonhardsen 3, Perry 32, Sherwood 56),
Zimbru Chisinau 0
Zimbru Chisinau 0, Tottenham Hotspur 0
(Tottenham Hotspur 3-0)

Udinese 1 (Sottil 9), **AaB 0**
AaB 1 (Matovac 71), **Udinese 2** (Muzzi 52, Locatelli 90)
(Udinese 3-1)

Viking FK 3 (Svensson 57, Berre 70, Espevoll 78p), **Sporting CP 0**
Sporting CP 1 (Ayew 75p), **Viking FK 0**
(Viking FK 3-1)

Vojvodina Novi Sad 0, Slavia Praha 0
Slavia Praha 3 (Petrous 39, Dosek T. 73, Zelenka 80),
Vojvodina Novi Sad 2 (Belic 18, Bogdanovic 47)
(Slavia Praha 3-2)

West Ham United 3 (Wanchope 39, Di Canio 48, Lampard 58), **Osijek 0**
Osijek 1 (Bubalo 70),
West Ham United 3 (Kitson 27, Ruddock 83, Foé 90)
(West Ham United 6-1)

VfL Wolfsburg 2 (Akonnor 61, Juskowiak 87), **Debreceni VSC 0**
Debreceni VSC 2 (Sabo 54, 90), **VfL Wolfsburg 1** (Akpoborie 25)
(VfL Wolfsburg 3-2)

Zenit Sankt-Peterburg 0, Bologna 3 (Ventola 38, Signori 69, 90p)
Bologna 2 (Fontolan 38, Cipriani 75),
Zenit Sankt-Peterburg 2 (Panov 35, Kondrashov 89)
(Bologna 5-2)

FC Zürich 1 (Jamarauli 29), **K Lierse SK 0**
K Lierse SK 3 (Van Meir 17, Huysegems 72, Zdebel 83),
FC Zürich 4 (Jamarauli 2, Frick 59, Eydelie 88, Daems 90og)
(FC Zürich 5-3)

UEFA CUP

SECOND ROUND

English hopes of making a long-awaited impression in the UEFA Cup suffered a double blow as the two London sides, Tottenham and West Ham United, were both eliminated.

While the Hammers could not recover at home after an entertaining, error-strewn 2-0 defeat away to Steaua Bucharest, Spurs went out in harrowing fashion to Kaiserslautern. It was a case of payback time for the Germans after the previous season's Manchester United v Bayern Munich Champions' League final, with Kaiserslautern, inspired by French international Youri Djorkaeff, netting two last-minute goals at home in the second leg to turn the tie around completely after Tottenham had led 1-0.

Northerners Newcastle and Leeds were able to keep the English flag flying. While Bobby Robson's side won home and away against FC Zürich, David O'Leary's young, in-form team set a new club record of ten successive wins in the first leg of their tie with Lokomotiv Moscow, which they won surprisingly easily, 7-1 over the two matches.

French First Division strugglers Nantes just beat Leeds to the biggest aggregate winning margin, hammering Inter Bratislava 7-0. Lyon also progressed without conceding a goal in their three hours of play. They beat Celtic 1-0 home and away but the tie was overshadowed by a terrible injury to Celtic's Swedish striker Henrik Larsson, who broke his leg in two places early on in the first leg at the Stade Gerland.

Larsson's former club, Helsingborg, who had just been crowned Swedish champions, were no match for Parma, who won 3-1 in Sweden thanks to a hat-trick from stand-in striker Marco Di Vaio. Darko Kovacevic remained at the head of the scorers' charts, taking his total to seven in four games with three goals for Juventus in a 4-2 aggregate triumph over Levski Sofia.

All of the Italian teams progressed, although Bologna were outplayed for long periods in their tie with Anderlecht, while Udinese needed a goal in each game from Argentinian striker Roberto Sosa to survive against Legia Warsaw. Roma, like Parma, were much too strong for Swedish opposition, beating IFK Gothenburg comfortably after two away goals in the first leg from new signing Vincenzo Montella.

For the second round running Benfica managed to survive despite losing in the Stadium of Light. A late goal from defender Ronaldo enabled Jupp Heynckes' side to win 2-1 away to PAOK in a thrilling game on a dusty pitch in Salonika, but the scoreline was reversed

in Lisbon and Benfica were forced by the Greeks into a penalty shoot-out before they ultimately prevailed. There was happier news on the penalties front for the two other Greek sides as Panathinaikos and AEK both squeezed through on away goals thanks only to late spot-kicks in Athens from imported midfielders. Dragan Ciric was AEK's saviour against Hungary's MTK while Karlheinz Pflipsen left it until the very last minute before he saved Panathinaikos from an ignominious exit at the hands of Grazer AK.

The away-goals rule also came to the assistance of German Cup holders Werder Bremen. They had been easy winners against Norwegian side Bodø/Glimt in the first round but Viking proved far more obdurate and it was only after surviving a late onslaught in Stavanger that the Bundesliga side maintained their foothold in the competition.

THIRD ROUND

The 24 survivors from the second round were joined by eight fresh outcasts from the Champions' League - Arsenal, Bayer Leverkusen, Borussia Dortmund, Galatasaray, Olympiakos, Rangers, Spartak Moscow abd Sturm Graz. Surprisingly, only three of them would live to fight another day.

One of them was always bound to fall after Rangers and Borussia Dortmund were drawn against one another. The Scottish champions appeared to take command of the tie when they won the first leg 2-0 at a blustery Ibrox, with an own-goal from veteran German international Jürgen Kohler preceding a wonderfully constructed second goal from Rod Wallace. But two weeks later Rangers threw away a glorious chance of extending their European involvement beyond Christmas when they failed to exploit a number of counter-attacking opportunities to score a priceless away goal and finally conceded an 'equaliser' in the second minute of stoppage-time after Dortmund's goalkeeper Jens Lehmann joined in a desperate late rally. Lehmann was to become the hero of the evening half an hour or so later as he saved three successive penalties to bring Dortmund victory in the shoot-out.

There was another astonishing German comeback the same night as Werder Bremen, seemingly out for the count after losing 3-0 away to Lyon, won 4-0 in an almost deserted Weserstadion. All the Germans' fine work nearly came undone however, when Lyon striker Sonny Ânderson, a two-goal hero in the first leg, missed an easy chance to give his team the tie on away goals with the last kick of the game.

UEFA CUP

SECOND ROUND RESULTS

(October 21, November 2, 1999)

RSC Anderlecht 2 (Koller 17, 35), **Bologna 1** (Signori 90)
Bologna 3 (Crasson 45og, De Boeck 51og, Nervo 90), **RSC Anderlecht 0**
(Bologna 4-2)

Aris 2 (Andrioli 44, Kizeridis 68), **RC Celta 2** (Karpin 41, 42)
RC Celta 2 (Djorovic 66, Turdó 90), **Aris 0**
(RC Celta 4-2)

Atlético Madrid 1 (Baraja 86), **Amica Wronki 0**
Amica Wronki 1 (Jackiewicz 34),
Atlético Madrid 4 (Hasselbaink 30, Capdevila 44, Baraja 51, Correa 84)
(Atlético Madrid 5-1)

RC Deportivo 3 (Pauleta 17, Djalminha 50p, Makaay 53),
Montpellier HSC 1 (Delaye 6)
Montpellier HSC 0, RC Deportivo 2 (Makaay 45, Pauleta 83)
(RC Deportivo 5-1)

IFK Göteborg 0, Roma 2 (Montella 37, 52)
Roma 1 (Fábio Júnior 88), **IFK Göteborg 0**
(Roma 3-0)

Grazer AK 2 (Lipa 57, Pamic 80), **Panathinaikos 1** (Sypniewski 65)
Panathinaikos 1 (Pflipsen 90p), **Grazer AK 0**
(2-2; Panathinaikos on away goal)

Hapoel Haifa 0, Ajax 3 (Mahlas 3, Knopper 12, Laudrup 56)
Ajax 0, Hapoel Haifa 1 (Rosso 58p)
(Ajax 3-1)

Inter Bratislava 0, FC Nantes 3 (Sibierski 26p, Da Rocha 35, Carrière 86)
FC Nantes 4 (Sibierski 49, Monterrubio 60, Devineau 74, Da Rocha 82),
Inter Bratislava 0
(FC Nantes 7-0)

Leeds United 4 (Bowyer 27, 45, Smith 56, Kewell 83),
Lokomotiv Moskva 1 (Loskov 80)
Lokomotiv Moskva 0, Leeds United 3 (Harte 16p, Bridges 28, 45)
(Leeds United 7-1)

RC Lens 4 (Brunel 3, Nouma 17, Nyarko 74, Blanchard 87),
Vitesse 1 (Van Hooijdonk 73p)
Vitesse 1 (Kreek 64), **RC Lens 1** (Blanchard 90)
(RC Lens 5-2)

Levski Sofia 1 (Yofu 54), **Juventus 3** (Oliseh 23, Kovacevic 52, 89)
Juventus 1 (Kovacevic 79), **Levski Sofia 1** (Atanasov 15)
(Juventus 4-2)

Olympique Lyonnais 1 (Blanc 64), **Celtic 0**
Celtic 0, Olympique Lyonnais 1 (Vairelles 17)
(Olympique Lyonnais 2-0)

MTK Hungária FC 2 (Egressy 20, Erös 34), **AEK 1** (Ciric 61)
AEK 1 (Ciric 75p), **MTK Hungária FC 0**
(2-2; AEK on away goal)

PAOK 1 (Frantzeskos 89), **SL Benfica 2** (Nuno Gomes 67, Ronaldo 89)
SL Benfica 1 (Kandaurov 25), **PAOK 2** (Marangos 28, Sabry 44) (aet)
(3-3; SL Benfica 4-1 on pens.)

Parma 1 (Cannavaro F. 44), **Helsingborgs IF 0**
Helsingborgs IF 1 (Stavrum 86), **Parma 3** (Di Vaio 11, 42, 43)
(Parma 4-1)

Roda JC 0, VfL Wolfsburg 0
VfL Wolfsburg 1 (Akonnor 87), **Roda JC 0**
(VfL Wolfsburg 1-0)

Slavia Praha 3 (Ulich 20, 50, Kuchar 39),
Grasshopper-Club Zürich 1 (Yakin 23)
Grasshopper-Club Zürich 1 (Yakin 76), **Slavia Praha 0**
(Slavia Praha 3-2)

Steaua Bucuresti 2 (Rosu 39, Ilie 57), **West Ham United 0**
West Ham United 0, Steaua Bucuresti 0
(Steaua Bucuresti 2-0)

FK Teplice 1 (Verbir 68), **RCD Mallorca 2** (Diego Tristán 26, 31)
RCD Mallorca 3 (Nadal 30, Stankovic 58, Niño 68), **FK Teplice 0**
(RCD Mallorca 5-1)

Tottenham Hotspur 1 (Iversen 34p), **1.FC Kaiserslautern 0**
1.FC Kaiserslautern 2 (Buck 89, Carr 90og), **Tottenham Hotspur 0**
(1.FC Kaiserslautern 2-1)

Udinese 1 (Sosa 29), **Legia Warszawa 0**
Legia Warszawa 1 (Czereszewski 11), **Udinese 1** (Sosa 41)
(Udinese 2-1)

SV Werder Bremen 0, Viking FK 0
Viking FK 2 (Berland 3, Dadason 84),
SV Werder Bremen 2 (Wiedener 43, Herzog 63)
(2-2; SV Werder Bremen on away goals)

Widzew Lodz 1 (Wichniarek 6p), **AS Monaco 1** (Giuly 40)
AS Monaco 2 (Lamouchi 50, Trezeguet 85), **Widzew Lodz 0**
(AS Monaco 3-1)

FC Zürich 1 (Castillo 68), **Newcastle United 2** (Maric 51, Shearer 60)
Newcastle United 3 (Maric 33, Ferguson 58, Speed 61),
FC Zürich 1 (Jamarauli 16)
(Newcastle United 5-2)

UEFA CUP

While Dortmund and Bremen soldiered on, Germany's other two teams, Kaiserslautern and Leverkusen, found themselves on the receiving end of equally impressive comebacks from Lens and Udinese, respectively. The French side blitzed Kaiserslautern 4-1 in the Fritz-Walter-Stadion while Udinese, who had been eliminated by Leverkusen in the first round the previous season, gained their revenge with a 2-1 victory in the BayArena courtesy of two fine goals from unsung striker Massimo Margiotta.

Olympiakos and Sturm Graz were also bounced out at the first time of asking by Italian opposition. The Greeks actually went ahead against Juventus before suffering a rare home defeat, while Sturm, fresh from an improved bout of form in the Champions' League, took UEFA Cup holders Parma to extra-time in a six-goal thriller at the Arnold-Schwarzenneger-Stadion before they made their second European exit within a matter of weeks.

Spartak Moscow also bit the dust. Their home tie with Leeds United could not be played due to icy weather.

THIRD ROUND RESULTS

(November 25, December 9, 1999)

AEK 2 (Nikolaidis 45, 90), **AS Monaco 2** (Giuly 26, Simone 78)
AS Monaco 1 (Simone 32), **AEK 0**
(AS Monaco 3-2)

Ajax 0, RCD Mallorca 1 (Diego Tristán 34)
RCD Mallorca 2 (Soler F. 3, Biagini 70), **Ajax 0**
(RCD Mallorca 3-0)

Arsenal 3 (Overmars 13p, Winterburn 81, Bergkamp 90), **FC Nantes 0**
FC Nantes 3 (Sibierski 13, 58, Vahirua 79),
Arsenal 3 (Grimandi 24, Henry 31, Overmars 42)
(Arsenal 6-3)

Bologna 1 (Signori 67), **Galatasaray 1** (Hakan Sükür 82)
Galatasaray 2 (Hasan 5, Ümit 29), **Bologna 1** (Ventola 8)
(Galatasaray 3-2)

RC Celta 7 (Karpin 19p, 53, Makelele 29, Turdó 39, 50, Juanfran 42, Mostovoi 60), **SL Benfica 0**
SL Benfica 1 (Cáceres 79og), **RC Celta 1** (McCarthy 19)
(RC Celta 8-1)

RC Deportivo 4 (Olivares 7og, Pauleta 12, Djalminha 14, Donato 30), **Panathinaikos 2** (Warzycha 31, Galetto 67)
Panathinaikos 1 (Asanovic 78p), **RC Deportivo 1** (Makaay 90)
(RC Deportivo 5-3)

RC Lens 1 (Schjønberg 84og),
1.FC Kaiserslautern 2 (Sikora 31og, Wagner 37)
1.FC Kaiserslautern 1 (Hristov 21),
RC Lens 4 (Job 20, 40, Strasser 56og, Nyarko 90)
(RC Lens 5-3)

Olympique Lyonnais 3 (Ânderson 13, 45, Vairelles 77),
SV Werder Bremen 0
SV Werder Bremen 4 (Bode 16, Herzog 39p, Baumann 54, Pizarro 77),
Olympique Lyonnais 0
(SV Werder Bremen 4-3)

Olympiakos 1 (Yanakopoulos 14),
Juventus 3 (Tudor 27, Kovacevic 67, Inzaghi 87)
Juventus 1 (Kovacevic 2), **Olympiakos 2** (Djordjevic 37, 80p)
(Juventus 4-3)

Parma 2 (Di Vaio 16, Stanic 62), **SK Sturm Graz 1** (Schopp 21)
SK Sturm Graz 3 (Reinmayr 67, 95, Vastic 87),
Parma 3 (Stanic 5, 110, Crespo 120) (aet)
(Parma 5-4)

Rangers 2 (Kohler 18og, Wallace 44), **Borussia Dortmund 0**
Borussia Dortmund 2 (Ikpeba 28, Bobic 90), **Rangers 0** (aet)
(2-2; Borussia Dortmund 3-1 on pens.)

Roma 1 (Totti 51p), **Newcastle United 0**
Newcastle United 0, Roma 0
(Roma 1-0)

Slavia Praha 4 (Dostalek 1, 47, Horvath 35, Dosek T. 55),
Steaua Bucuresti 1 (Lutu 82)
Steaua Bucuresti 1 (Ciocoiu 45), **Slavia Praha 1** (Dostalek 50)
(Slavia Praha 5-2)

Spartak Moskva 2 (Shirko 38, Robson 65), **Leeds United 1** (Kewell 14)
Leeds United 1 (Radebe 84), **Spartak Moskva 0**
(2-2; Leeds United on away goal)

Udinese 0, Bayer 04 Leverkusen 1 (Ballack 76)
Bayer 04 Leverkusen 1 (Ballack 21), **Udinese 2** (Margiotta 9, 18)
(2-2; Udinese on away goals)

VfL Wolfsburg 2 (Juskowiak 21, Akonnor 83p),
Atlético Madrid 3 (Aguilera 6, 58, Hasselbaink 37)
Atlético Madrid 2 (Hasselbaink 4, Correa 86), **VfL Wolfsburg 1** (Akonnor 56p)
(Atlético Madrid 5-3)

UEFA CUP

It was switched, against the Russians' will, to Sofia and staged a week later than scheduled, but although Spartak came back strongly to claim a deserved 2-1 win - ironically, their first 'home' victory of the season in Europe - they were eventually eliminated by a rare goal from Leeds skipper Lucas Radebe late in the return at Elland Road. It gave David O'Leary's team their second Russian scalp in successive rounds following their earlier triumph over Spartak's chief domestic rivals Lokomotiv.

Arsenal made it two out of two for the English teams, comfortably disposing of Nantes after a fine first-leg display at Highbury, where they were happy to return after their Champions' League misadventures at Wembley. Two spectacular late goals from Nigel Winterburn and Dennis Bergkamp turned the second leg into a formality.

Galatasaray joined Dortmund and Arsenal as the only survivors from the Champions' League intake with an impressive victory over Bologna, who thus became their second successive Serie A victims (after Milan in the Champions' League) and the first Italian fallers in the UEFA Cup. Ajax also dropped out, beaten decisively home and away by Mallorca, but the most shocking scoreline of all was Celta Vigo's 7-0 thrashing of Benfica - the heaviest defeat ever suffered in Europe by the famous Lisbon club and one which ensured that while all of Spain's four teams marched on into the last 16, Portugal, like Scotland, Greece, Austria, Holland, Romania and Russia, had no further interest in the competition.

FOURTH ROUND

In previous editions of the UEFA Cup the fourth round had only ever existed under the guise of the quarter-finals. But now, thanks to the enlargement and revamping of the competition, there were still 16 teams involved.

Four of those were from Italy but, incredibly, not one of them was to go any further. The UEFA Cup had long been a guarantee of success for Serie A sides, but as the competition entered the new millennium, suddenly, one by one, Italy's finest all fell by the wayside.

There were to be extraordinary results all round. In fact, there was a case for claiming that the underdogs won every single one of the eight ties. The pairings for the quarter-finals had been made at the same time as the fourth-round draw, so the victors knew what awaited them next, and it would have been no surprise had the last-eight line-up looked like this: Monaco v Dortmund, Deportivo v Parma, Juventus v Atlético Madrid and Roma

v Udinese. As it turned out, not one of these teams made it through.

The collective demise of the Italians was truly astonishing. Udinese were the first to fall when they lost on away goals to Slavia Prague after a nerve-racking second leg which had been brought forward to the Tuesday. Two laters later the mighty threesome of Juventus, Parma and Roma all joined them on the casualty list after falling unexpectedly to defeats on foreign soil.

The big story was Juventus's sensational 4-0 mauling by Celta Vigo. 1-0 up from the first leg in Turin, where the ever-prolific Kovacevic had headed in his tenth goal

FOURTH ROUND RESULTS

(March 2/9, 2000)

Arsenal 5 (Dixon 5, Henry 30, 67, Kanu 78, Bergkamp 83),
RC Deportivo 1 (Djalminha 54p)
RC Deportivo 2 (Victor 69, 90), **Arsenal 1** (Henry 63)
(Arsenal 6-3)

Atlético Madrid 2 (Hasselbaink 24, 79), **RC Lens 2** (Dacourt 16, 78)
RC Lens 4 (Nouma 29, 53, Sakho 37, Brunel 71),
Atlético Madrid 2 (Hasselbaink 45, Kiko 64)
(RC Lens 6-4)

Borussia Dortmund 0, Galatasaray 2 (Hakan Sükür 32, Hagi 45)
Galatasary 0, Borussia Dortmund 0
(Galatasaray 2-0)

Juventus 1 (Kovacevic 50), **RC Celta 0**
RC Celta 4 (Makelele 1, Birindelli 30og, McCarthy 46, 69), **Juventus 0**
(RC Celta 4-1)

RCD Mallorca 4 (Stankovic J. 42, 53p, 63p, Diego Tristán 90),
AS Monaco 1 (Simone 2)
AS Monaco 1 (Simone 33), **RCD Mallorca 0**
(RCD Mallorca 4-2)

Parma 1 (Crespo 5), **SV Werder Bremen 0**
SV Werder Bremen 3 (Dabrowski 29, Bode 44, Ailton 66),
Parma 1 (Stanic 32)
(SV Werder Bremen 3-2)

Roma 0, Leeds United 0
Leeds United 1 (Kewell 67), **Roma 0**
(Leeds United 1-0)

Slavia Praha 1 (Zanchi 76og), **Udinese 0**
Udinese 2 (Fiore 23, Sosa 51), **Slavia Praha 1** (Koller 42)
(2-2; Slavia Praha on away goal)

UEFA CUP

of the competition, Juve's advantage was erased after just 28 seconds in Spain when Frenchman Claude Makelele fired in a deflected shot from the edge of the area. Stunned by this early setback, Juve lost their discipline and ended the half in a complete mess, with Antonio Conte and Paolo Montero both red-carded and Alessandro Birindelli red-faced after putting through his own net after a farcical mix-up with goalkeeper Edwin van der Sar. The Dutchman was at fault twice more after the interval as his ex-Ajax team-mate, South African striker Benni McCarthy, sealed Juve's humiliating fate with two further goals.

Parma also went to their second leg, in Bremen, with a 1-0 first-leg lead, but Werder had played well in the first game and, inspired by Brazilian forward Aílton, they did even better in the second, coming back from the dead for the second round running to enthrall their fans with a memorable, if nerve-shredding victory.

Roma completed a black Thursday for Italian football when they went down to Leeds, a team they had knocked out of the competition a year earlier. A goalless draw in the first leg was predominantly down to the heroic goalkeeping of Nigel Martyn, who produced a string of dazzling saves, most of them at the expense of Italian international Francesco Totti. Martyn was less occupied in the return at Elland Road, and Leeds deservedly won through thanks to a wonderful long-distance strike from their young Australian Harry Kewell. Roma, like Juventus, took their defeat badly, ending up with just nine players on the field.

Arsenal were never in danger of eliminaton after a fabulous first-leg performance at home to Spanish league leaders Deportivo La Coruña. Arsène Wenger's team produced their best display of the season to hammer the Galicians 5-1. Their last three goals came after the controversial dismissal of Brazilian midfielder Djalminha, but even with a full complement Deportivo would have struggled to contain their in-form opponents. The best goal of the night was scored by Nigerian striker Kanu, who sold the goalkeeper a couple of exquisite dummies before nonchalantly slotting the ball into the net with his left foot.

Only one other Champions' League refugee could join Arsenal in the quarter-finals as Galatasaray and Borussia Dortmund had been drawn together. It was no contest. The Turks destroyed their struggling opponents in the first leg at the Westfalenstadion. On a night of driving wind and rain Galatasaray treated their massive support to a magnificent display, outclassing their hosts in every department and cementing their superiority with two

goals at the end of the first half from Hakan Sükür and Gheorghe Hagi. The goalless draw in Istanbul a fortnight later was something of an anti-climax, but a sell-out crowd in the Ali Sami Yen stadium were not disappointed in the slightest by the final result.

The two Franco-Spanish ties produced one victor for each country, although not the ones anticipated. Mallorca saw off French league leaders Monaco thanks to a hat-trick of dead-ball strikes (one free-kick, two penalties) from their Yugoslav midfielder Jovan Stankovic in a 4-1 first-leg win, while Lens got the better of Atlético Madrid, winning 6-4 on aggregate after two brilliant goals from man-of-the-match Olivier Dacourt had earned them a well-deserved 2-2 draw from the first leg in Madrid. Three equally fine goals in the two games from Atlético's Jimmy Floyd Hasselbaink were not enough to save the previous season's semi-finalists from joining the other seven illustrious fourth-round fallers.

QUARTER-FINALS

With the Italians out of the way, the English and the Spanish scented long-lost UEFA Cup glory. England had not had a single semi-finalist in the competition since 1984, whereas Spain had not had their hands on the trophy since 1986. With Arsenal, Leeds, Celta and Mallorca all having avoided each other in the draw, an Anglo-Spanish clean sweep looked on the cards.

All four teams began their ties at home, but while the two English teams both managed to build a healthy first-leg advantage, Spain's remaining twosome both struggled, with Mallorca effectively bidding farewell to the competition after a comprehensive defeat.

Arsenal had it all their own way at Highbury against a dull and unimpressive Werder Bremen, who failed to manufacture a single goalscoring chance all evening.

Arsenal's Tony Adams and Werder Bremen goalkeeper Frank Rost vie for a loose ball.

UEFA CUP

QUARTER-FINAL RESULTS

(March 16/23, 2000)

Arsenal 2 (Henry 21, Ljungberg 77), **SV Werder Bremen 0**
SV Werder Bremen 2 (Bode 41, Bogdanovic 60),
Arsenal 4 (Parlour 8, 25, 70, Henry 59)
(Arsenal 6-2)

RC Celta 0, RC Lens 0
RC Lens 2 (Ismaël 62p, Nouma 72), **RC Celta 1** (Revivo 55)
(RC Lens 2-1)

Leeds United 3 (Wilcox 39, Kewell 54, Bowyer 59), **Slavia Praha 0**
Slavia Praha 2 (Ulich 53, 79p), **Leeds United 1** (Kewell 47)
(Leeds United 4-2)

RCD Mallorca 1 (Lauren 78),
Galatasaray 4 (Arif 44, Emre 48, Hakan Sükür 59, Okan 65)
Galatasaray 2 (Capone 34, Hakan Sükür 46),
RCD Mallorca 1 (Carlos 62)
(Galatasaray 6-2)

Thierry Henry notched his fifth goal in as many UEFA Cup games to give the Gunners the lead after 21 minutes, and Fredrik Ljungberg ensured that the scoreline accurately reflected the balance of play when he made it 2-0 13 minutes from the end. Arsenal boss Arsène Wenger reckoned that the two-goal lead gave his team a mere 50-50 chance of progress, but this time the Germans could not pull off a comeback. An early away goal from Ray Parlour tightened Arsenal's grip and when the blond midfielder added another midway through the second half, it was game, set and match to the Gunners.

Parlour went on to complete his first-ever hat-trick in a comprehensive 4-2 win, and although Henry also

Leeds striker Michael Bridges takes on Slavia Prague goalkeeper Radek Cerny.

maintained his goal-a-game ratio, his evening was spoiled when he was controversially sent off.

Leeds joined Arsenal in becoming England's first semi-finalists for 16 years. They were thoroughly dominant in their first leg at home to Slavia Prague. Several chances went begging before Jason Wilcox, beautifully fed by Lee Bowyer, made it 1-0 just before half-time, but David O'Leary's side were more precise with their finishing after the interval, and further goals from Harry Kewell and Bowyer gave the Czechs a massive uphill task for the return in Prague a week later. Although Slavia went into the second leg with a four-point lead in the Czech championship, Leeds were clearly a class above their domestic oppposition. Bad misses from Kewell and Michael Bridges let Slavia off the hook in the first half but the Australian made no mistake with a superb first-time shot just after the interval. The Czechs were now a beaten side but they came back strongly. Inspired by midfielder Ivo Ulich, who scored two goals, hit the bar and had another effort cleared off the line, Slavia went on to win the game, which, despite their elimination, earned them a raucous send-off from their supporters.

Celta Vigo went into their first leg at home to Lens bursting with confidence after the slaying of Juventus on the same ground a week earlier. But despite battering the French side for almost the entire 90 minutes, they could not convert any of the many chances they created. They did, however, survive a major scare at the end when Pascal Nouma put the ball in the net for Lens only to be flagged down for a non-existent offside. The big striker was to get his revenge the following week when he scored the decisive goal of the tie to give the French side a 2-1 victory in the Stade Bollaert. Lens were in big trouble when Celta's Israeli forward Haim Revivo broke the deadlock with a delightful free-kick, but a clumsily conceded penalty soon got them back on track, and it was left to Nouma to clip in the winner 18 minutes from time and give his team their second Spanish scalp in a fortnight.

Mallorca, the previous season's Cup-winners' Cup runners-up, were forced to abandon hope of another final appearance early on in their tie with Galatasaray. The Turks were magnificent in the first leg, totally outplaying the Spaniards on their own pitch and ruthlessly exploiting their superiority with four exquisite goals from their Turkish international quartet of Arif, Emre, Hakan Sükür and Okan. The first three goals were all lobs over the goalkeeper, with Emre's wonderful left-footed chip off the underside of the bar the pick of the bunch. Mallorca scored a goal of their own, through

UEFA CUP

Fredrik Ljungberg of Arsenal battles with Olivier Dacourt of Lens.

winger Lauren, near the end but it was all academic. In fact, the Spaniards acknowledged that they had given up on the tie when they rested several players for the second leg in Istanbul. Once again Galatasaray dominated and should have won by a greater margin than the final scoreline of 2-1.

SEMI-FINALS

The prospect of a first all-English UEFA Cup final since 1972 was maintained as Arsenal and Leeds avoided each other in the draw. The Londoners were paired with Lens while Leeds faced yet another long-haul trip, to face Galatasaray in Istanbul.

Before the action could begin, tragedy struck. On the night before the Galatasaray-Leeds game two visiting English fans were stabbed to death in the centre of Istanbul by Turkish thugs. The murders shocked everybody connected with Leeds but there was a distinct lack of respect shown by Galatasaray. Initially there was some doubt as to whether the match would take place, but UEFA eventually sanctioned it to go ahead - against a backdrop of hundreds of armed police. Scandalously, there was no minute's silence; worse still, the Galatasaray players did not wear black arm bands.

The Leeds players and fans were naturally subdued, and it was no great surprise that Galatasaray established a 2-0 half-time lead, with Hakan Sükür and Capone twice exploiting huge gaps in the centre of the Leeds defence to score. After the change-around Leeds came back into the contest, and as Galatasaray's attacking threat waned, Leeds created a string of chances. Michael Bridges wasted the best of them, on the hour, when, clean

through on goal, he could only fire his first shot straight at goalkeeper Taffarel and send the rebound wide. Harry Kewell later missed another glorious opportunity to grab a potentially crucial away goal when he sent a free header wide.

The build-up to the second leg was dominated by discussions over security. While Leeds wished to mourn their two dead fans in private, Galatasaray, still showing alarming insensitivity, insisted on the right to take visiting fans to Elland Road. Eventually common sense prevailed and the Turkish club backed down.

Even so, the feeling of resentment remained, and the match was to be bitter and at times brutal. Leeds, going through a bad run of form, desperately wanted to win but their hopes were crushed early on when Jonathan Woodgate hacked down Hakan Sükür and Gheorghe Hagi sent the ensuing penalty past Nigel Martyn. Now Leeds had to score four times without further reply to reach the final. They got one goal back fairly swiftly, through the head of Norwegian Eirik Bakke, but

Leeds' Ian Harte jumps into the action with Galatasaray's Gheorghe Hagi.

SEMI-FINAL RESULTS

(April 6/20, 2000)

Arsenal 1 (Bergkamp 2), **RC Lens 0**
RC Lens 1 (Nouma 73), **Arsenal 2** (Henry 43, Kanu 86)
(Arsenal 3-1)

Galatasaray 2 (Hakan Sükür 12, Capone 44), **Leeds United 0**
Leeds United 2 (Bakke 16, 68),
Galatasaray 2 (Hagi 5p, Hakan Sükür 42)
(Galatasaray 4-2)

UEFA CUP

Galatasaray ended the half by re-establishing their advantage with a wonderful individual goal from Hakan Sükür, who collected a pass from Hagi and showed great composure and skill to score his tenth European goal of the season. Soon afterwards Leeds had Kewell sent off for a rash challenge on Hagi (although he didn't actually make contact) and Emre was also red-carded in a tit-for-tat decision a minute or two later after he flew in on Bowyer. The second half brought a second equalising header from Bakke but not much more. Leeds were dismayed, but Galatasaray quietly celebrated the historic achievement of becoming the first Turkish team to reach a European final.

There they would meet another English team. Arsenal, like Galatasaray, had entered the UEFA Cup as Champions' League cast-offs, but they made the most of their second chance, comfortably seeing off Lens with victories in both legs of their semi-final.

It was not all plain sailing for Arsenal in the first leg, at Highbury, where they scored very early on, through a fine strike by Dennis Bergkamp, but missed the pace and goalscoring instinct of the suspended Henry and could not add to their total. In fact, they were fortunate to keep their goal intact when Nouma rattled a simple chance against the crossbar from point-blank range in the second half.

The second leg, in Lens, saw Arsenal at their very best. A run of seven successive wins had filled Arsène Wenger's side with tremendous confidence and they made most of the running in the Stade Bollaert. Just before half-time they deservedly went in front when Henry, back from suspension, scored a brilliant goal, turning superbly in the area before smashing a glorious rising right-foot shot into the top corner. Arsenal should have wrapped up the game early in the second half when Emmanuel Petit and Henry both missed good chances, but a goal from Lens, totally against the run of play, ensured a lively closing 17 minutes. Nouma was the player who scored it but ten minutes later he fashioned his second terrible miss of the tie when he screwed a shot wide with the goal at his mercy. It would have been unjust had Lens gone ahead because Arsenal had controlled the game, so when Kanu drove in Overmars' square pass to make it 2-1 with four minutes remaining, a sense of order was restored to the scoreline.

Gheorghe Popescu fires home Galatasaray's winning penalty past David Seaman.

FINAL

To many, it seemed perverse that two teams who had begun the season competing in another competition should be contesting the final of the UEFA Cup. Arsenal and Galatasaray had both skipped the first two rounds of the competition but here they were in the final, staged at the Parken stadium in Copenhagen.

Unfortunately, the match was preceded by outbreaks of violence in the city centre between English and Turkish hooligans. After the tragic events of Galatasaray's semi-final with Leeds it was inevitable that the bad feeling between the two sets of fans would linger. However, the carnage in Copenhagen's main square was sickening, particularly to the Danish locals, who could barely believe what they were witnessing.

At the ground, however, there was thankfully no trouble. Alas, there wasn't too much football, either. The two teams served up very little quality in a dull, uneventful first half. Caution appeared to be the name of the game as both sides refused to commit players forward. On the odd occasions that they did there was no punch up front. The best chance of the half fell to Galatasaray striker Arif, who shot badly wide after being set up well by Ümit.

Hakan Sükür came close to opening the scoring early in the second half when he struck the foot of the post, but a few minutes later Arsenal spurned an even better chance when Kanu lifted his shot over the bar from close range after being perfectly set up by Henry. From then on it was nip and tuck, with a few half-chances being created at both ends. If anything, Galatasaray were the better, more

THE EUROPEAN FOOTBALL YEARBOOK 2000-2001

TOP SCORERS		
(excluding Qualifying rounds)		
10	Darko KOVACEVIC (Juventus)	
7	Thierry HENRY (Arsenal)	
	Jimmy Floyd HASSELBAINK (Atlético Madrid)	
	Marco DI VAIO (Parma)	
6	HAKAN Sükür (Galatasaray)	
	Pascal NOUMA (RC Lens)	
	Marco SIMONE (AS Monaco)	
	Benni McCARTHY (RC Celta)	

UEFA CUP

FINAL

17/05/2000, Copenhagen
GALATASARAY 0 ARSENAL 0
(aet; 4-1 on pens.)
referee - López Nieto (ESP)
GALATASARAY - Taffarel; Capone, Popescu, Bülent; Okan (Hakan Ünsal 83), Suat (Ahmet 94), Ergün, Ümit; Hagi; Hakan Sükür, Arif (Hasan 95).
ARSENAL - Seaman; Dixon, Keown, Adams, Silvinho; Parlour, Vieira, Petit, Overmars (Suker 114); Bergkamp (Kanu 74), Henry.

Bülent Korkmaz lifts the UEFA Cup with team mate Hakan Sükür.

productive team, with Ümit, Okan and Suat all working diligently and confidently in midfield.

Goalless after 90 minutes, the match thus entered golden-goal extra-time. Just three minutes in Galatasaray were reduced to ten men when Gheorghe Hagi, the veteran Romanian, foolishly swung an arm at Arsenal skipper Tony Adams. That made life difficult for the Turks and as Arsenal began to increase the number of their attacks, Galatasaray virtually decided to shut up shop and play for penalties. Henry looked certain to score after 108 minutes when he headed goalwards from a Ray Parlour cross but goalkeeper Cláudio Taffarel made a stunning save to keep the ball out, and the Brazilian 'keeper was at it again a few minutes later, denying Kanu with a terrific double save.

It was one-way traffic through to the end but Arsenal could not make the breakthrough, so after two hours of largely uninspiring goalless football, the first European final of the 21st century went down to a penalty shoot-out.

Galatasaray had the advantage of taking the penalties at the end where the bulk of their supporters were massed. Ergün got them off to a good start by

Arsenal's Thierry Henry stretches for the ball with Bülent Korkmaz.

planting his kick into the corner. Arsenal's Davor Suker was next up but he struck the post. Hakan Sükür made it 2-0 to the Turks, and that lead became 3-1 when Parlour and Ümit both found the target. Patrick Vieira was next in line for Arsenal but his shot rattled back off the underside of the bar. That left Gheorghe Popescu, formerly of Arsenal's arch-rivals Tottenham Hotspur, with the chance to seal a first ever European trophy success for Turkish football. He stepped up...and buried his right-foot shot low into the corner.

The Galatasaray players and fans went wild with delight. They just about deserved their victory, having been marginally the better side until Hagi's dismissal. While Arsenal had to come to terms with the fact that they had gone a second successive season without a trophy, Galatasaray revelled in the completion of a unique 'treble'. They had already won the Turkish league and Cup and had now become the 16th different club to win the UEFA Cup, with Turkey joining England, Holland, Germany, Italy, Sweden, Belgium and Spain as only the eighth country to collect the trophy in the 29-year history of the competition.

EUROPEAN CUP QUALIFIERS 2000/2001

COUNTRY	UEFA CHAMPIONS' LEAGUE	UEFA CUP
ALBANIA	SK Tirana	Teuta Durrës, Tomori Berat
ANDORRA		Constelació Esportiva
ARMENIA	Shirak Gyumri	Mika Ashtarak, Ararat Yerevan
AUSTRIA	FC Tirol Innsbruck, SK Sturm Graz	Grazer AK, SK Rapid Wien
AZERBAIJAN	Shamkir	Kapaz Ganja, Neftchi Baku
BELARUS	FC BATE Borisov	Slaviya Mozyr, FC Gomel
BELGIUM	RSC Anderlecht	KRC Genk, Club Brugge KV, KAA Gent, K Lierse SK+
BOSNIA-HERZEGOVINA	Brotnjo Citluk	Zeljeznicar Sarajevo, Buducnost Banovici
BULGARIA	Levski Sofia	Neftochimik Bourgas, CSKA Sofia
CROATIA	Dinamo Zagreb, Hajduk Split	Osijek, Rijeka
CYPRUS	Anorthosis Famagusta	Omonia Nicosia, APOEL Nicosia
CZECH REPUBLIC	Sparta Praha, Slavia Praha	Slovan Liberec, Petra Drnovice
DENMARK	Herfølge BK, Brøndby IF	Viborg FF, AB
ENGLAND	Manchester United, Arsenal, Leeds United	Chelsea, Leicester City, Liverpool
ESTONIA	FC Levadia Maardu	Tulevik Viljandi, FC Flora Tallinn
FAROE ISLANDS	KÍ	B36, GÍ
FINLAND	FC Haka	FC Jokerit, HJK
FRANCE	AS Monaco, Paris Saint-Germain, Olympique Lyonnais	FC Nantes, FC Gueugnon, Girondins de Bordeaux
GEORGIA	Torpedo Kutaisi	Lokomotivi Tbilisi, Vit Georgia Tbilisi
GERMANY	FC Bayern München, Bayer 04 Leverkusen, Hamburger SV, TSV 1860 München	SV Werder Bremen, 1.FC Kaiserslautern, Hertha BSC Berlin, VfB Stuttgart*
GREECE	Olympiakos, Panathinaikos	AEK, OFI, PAOK, Iraklis
HOLLAND	PSV, SC Heerenveen, Feyenoord	Roda JC, Vitesse, Ajax
HUNGARY	Dunaferr SE	MTK Hungária FC, Vasas DH
ICELAND	KR	ÍA, ÍBV
ISRAEL	Hapoel Tel-Aviv	Beitar Jerusalem, Maccabi Haifa

EUROPEAN CUP QUALIFIERS 2000/2001

COUNTRY	UEFA CHAMPIONS' LEAGUE	UEFA CUP
ITALY	Lazio, Juventus, Milan, Inter	Parma, Roma, Fiorentina, Udinese*
LATVIA	Skonto Riga	Metalurgs Liepaya, FK Ventspils
LIECHTENSTEIN		FC Vaduz
LITHUANIA	Zalgiris Kaunas	Ekranas Panevezys, Zalgiris Vilnius
LUXEMBOURG	F91 Dudelange	Jeunesse Esch, CS Grevenmacher
MACEDONIA	Sloga Jugomagnat Skopje	Pobeda Prilep, Rabotnicki Kometal Skopje
MALTA	Birkirkara	Sliema Wanderers, Valletta
MOLDOVA	Zimbru Chisinau	Constructorul Chisinau, Serif Tiraspol
N. IRELAND	Linfield	Glentoran, Coleraine
NORWAY	Rosenborg BK	SK Brann, Molde FK, Lillestrøm SK
POLAND	Polonia Warszawa	Amica Wronki, Wisla Krakow, Ruch Chorzow
PORTUGAL	Sporting CP, FC Porto	SL Benfica, Boavista FC
REP. IRELAND	Shelbourne	Bohemians, Cork City
ROMANIA	Dinamo Bucuresti	Universitatea Craiova, Rapid Bucuresti
RUSSIA	Spartak Moskva, Lokomotiv Moskva	CSKA Moskva, Torpedo Moskva, Dinamo Moskva, Alania Vladikavkaz
SAN MARINO		Folgore
SCOTLAND	Rangers	Aberdeen, Celtic, Heart of Midlothian
SLOVAKIA	Inter Bratislava	1.FC Kosice, Slovan Bratislava
SLOVENIA	NK Maribor	SCT Olimpija Ljubljana, HIT Gorica
SPAIN	Real Madrid, RC Deportivo FC Barcelona, Valencia CF	RCD Espanyol, Real Zaragoza, Deportivo Alavés, Rayo Vallecano+, RC Celta*
SWEDEN	Helsingborgs IF	Orgryte IS, AIK, Halmstads BK, IFK Norrköping+
SWITZERLAND	FC St. Gallen	FC Zürich, Lausanne-Sports, FC Basel
TURKEY	Galatasaray, Besiktas	Antalyaspor, Gaziantepspor
UKRAINE	Dynamo Kyiv, Shakhtar Donetsk	Kryvbas Kryvyi Rih, Vorskla Poltava
WALES	Total Network Solutions	Bangor City, Barry Town
YUGOSLAVIA	Crvena zvezda Beograd	Napredak Krusevac, Partizan Beograd

N.B. + = Fair Play qualifiers; * = InterToto qualifiers

MISCELLANEOUS

EUROPEAN FOOTBALLER OF THE YEAR 1999

Zinedine ZIDANE (Juventus/FRANCE)

3   Mario BASLER (FC Bayern München/1.FC Kaiserslautern/GERMANY)

Ryan GIGGS (Manchester United/WALES)

2   Hernán CRESPO (Parma/ARGENTINA)

KANU (Arsenal/NIGERIA)

RONALDO (Inter/BRAZIL)

1   Claudio LOPEZ (Valencia CF/ARGENTINA)

Andy COLE (Manchester United/ENGLAND)

Edgar DAVIDS (Juventus/HOLLAND)

David GINOLA (Tottenham Hotspur/FRANCE)

ROBERTO CARLOS (Real Madrid/BRAZIL)

Marcelo SALAS (Lazio/CHILE)

Pts	Player
219	RIVALDO (FC Barcelona/BRAZIL)
154	David BECKHAM (Manchester United/ENGLAND)
64	Andriy SHEVCHENKO (Dynamo Kyiv/Milan/UKRAINE)
48	Gabriel BATISTUTA (Fiorentina/ARGENTINA)
38	Luís FIGO (FC Barcelona/PORTUGAL)
36	Roy KEANE (Manchester United/REPUBLIC OF IRELAND)
33	Christian VIERI (Lazio/Inter/ITALY)
30	Juan Sebastián VERON (Parma/Lazio/ARGENTINA)
27	RAUL González (Real Madrid/SPAIN)
16	Lothar MATTHÄUS (FC Bayern München/GERMANY)
14	Dwight YORKE (Manchester United/TRINIDAD & TOBAGO)
13	Jaap STAM (Manchester United/HOLLAND)
12	Sinisa MIHAJLOVIC (Lazio/YUGOSLAVIA)
9	Zlatko ZAHOVIC (FC Porto/Olympiakos/SLOVENIA)
8	Pavel NEDVED (Lazio/CZECH REPUBLIC)
7	Mário JARDEL (FC Porto/BRAZIL)
6	Peter SCHMEICHEL (Manchester United/Sporting CP/DENMARK)
5	Stefan EFFENBERG (FC Bayern München/GERMANY)
4	Oliver BIERHOFF (Milan/GERMANY)

N.B. The following players were pre-selected for the poll but did not receive any votes:

Fabien BARTHEZ (AS Monaco/FRANCE)

Dennis BERGKAMP (Arsenal/HOLLAND)

Laurent BLANC (Olympique Marseille/Inter/FRANCE)

Gianluigi BUFFON (Parma/ITALY)

Frank DE BOER (FC Barcelona/HOLLAND)

Marcel DESAILLY (Chelsea/FRANCE)

Giovane ÉLBER (FC Bayern München/BRAZIL)

Josep GUARDIOLA (FC Barcelona/SPAIN)

Filippo INZAGHI (Juventus/ITALY)

Patrick KLUIVERT (FC Barcelona/HOLLAND)

Paolo MALDINI (Milan/ITALY)

Fernando MORIENTES (Real Madrid/SPAIN)

Hidetoshi NAKATA (Perugia/JAPAN)

Emmanuel PETIT (Arsenal/FRANCE)

Gustavo POYET (Chelsea/URUGUAY)

Olexandr SHOVKOVSKYI (Dynamo Kiev/UKRAINE)

Lilian THURAM (Parma/FRANCE)

Sylvain WILTORD (Girondins de Bordeaux/FRANCE)

Gianfranco ZOLA (Chelsea/ITALY)

MISCELLANEOUS

Lazio's Sinisa Mihajlovic fends off Andy Cole of Manchester United.

EUROPEAN SUPER CUP 1999

27/08/99, Monaco
LAZIO 1 Salas (35)
MANCHESTER UNITED 0
referee - Wojcik (POL)

LAZIO - Marchegiani; Negro, Nesta, Mihajlovic, Pancaro; Stankovic, Verón, Almeyda, Nedved (Simeone 66); Mancini (Lombardo 83), Inzaghi (Salas 23).

MANCHESTER UNITED - Van der Gouw; Neville G., Stam (Curtis 57), Berg, Neville P.; Beckham (Cruijff 58), Keane, Scholes, Sheringham; Cole (Greening 76), Solskjaer.

WORLD CLUB CUP 1999

30/11/99, Tokyo
MANCHESTER UNITED 1 Keane (35)
PALMEIRAS 0
referee - Krug (GER)

MANCHESTER UNITED - Bosnich; Neville G., Stam, Silvestre, Irwin; Beckham, Butt, Keane, Scholes (Sheringham 74), Giggs; Solskjaer (Yorke 46).

PALMEIRAS - Marcos; Júnior Baiano, Roque Júnior, Arce; César Sampaio, Galeano (Evair 53), Júnior, Alex, Zinho; Asprilla (Oseas 56), Paulo Nunes (Euller 76).

Manchester United's Dwight Yorke swoops in to challenge Palmeiras's Roque Júnior.

INTRODUCTION TO NATIONS/CLUBS

The following pages contain individual reviews of each of the UEFA nations, including Statistics, a General Review, Photographs, Players of the Season and, in a separate section, Colour Team Strips and Emblems.

As a general guide, all Clubs are referred to by the names of their original language in statistical tables and headings. In narrative text, however, some will be referred to by their English names (e.g. Crvena zvezda Beograd = Red Star Belgrade; 1.FC Köln = Cologne)

The abbreviations and explanations below should act as a guide to assist the reader in understanding and appreciating the various items of information.

NATIONAL SECTION
LEAGUE CHAMPIONSHIP RESULTS
Home teams are listed, together with numbers, in the left-hand column. Away teams are ranged horizontally across the top of the table, with the team's corresponding number as reference. Teams are listed alphabetically.

LEAGUE CHAMPIONSHIP FINAL TABLE
This is the final table of the country's First, or Premier, Division championship, with clubs listed in official classification order. Home, Away and Total performance records are shown in separate columns.

KEY:
Pd = Played
W = Won
D = Drawn
L = Lost
F = Goals for
A = Goals against
Pt = Points
GD = Goal Difference

An unbroken line (————) indicates the relegation zone.

A dotted line (················) indicates the play-off zone.

Any irregularities from the standard formula of 3 points for a win, 1 point for a draw and 0 points for a defeat are stipulated at the foot of the table.

TOP SCORERS
These refer to league goals only.

DOMESTIC CUP
The rounds included are those in which the First, or Premier, Division clubs are involved.
For two-legged ties, the aggregate scores and qualifiers are shown in brackets.
(aet) = after extra-time
(asd) = after sudden-death

NATIONAL TEAM RESULTS
This covers all the official full international matches played by the country's national team from July 24, 1999 to July 2, 2000.

KEY:
(ECQ) = European Championship Qualifier
(ECF) = European Championship Finals
(CC) = Confederations' Cup
H = Home
A = Away
N = Neutral
p = penalty
og = own-goal

NATIONAL TEAM APPEARANCES
This lists all the players who have appeared in their national team during the 1999/2000 season, together with date of birth, club(s), match-by-match appearances and all-time appearance and goal totals.

KEY:
G = Goalkeeper
D = Defender
M = Midfielder
A = Attacker
s = substitute

The number after the letter indicates the time of substitution.

Cps = Total full international caps gained at the end of the season.

Gls = Total full international goals scored at the end of the season.

Three-letter codes have been used as column headings to indicate opponents. These are as follows:

EUROPE
ALB = Albania
AND = Andorra
ARM = Armenia
AUT = Austria
AZB = Azerbaijan
BLS = Belarus
BEL = Belgium
BOS = Bosnia-Herzegovina
BUL = Bulgaria
CRO = Croatia
CYP = Cyprus
CZE = Czech Republic
DEN = Denmark
ENG = England
EST = Estonia
FAR = Faroe Islands
FIN = Finland
FRA = France
GEO = Georgia
GER = Germany
GRE = Greece
HOL = Holland
HUN = Hungary
ISL = Iceland
ISR = Israel
ITA = Italy
LAT = Latvia
LIE = Liechtenstein
LIT = Lithuania
LUX = Luxembourg
MAC = Macedonia
MLT = Malta
MOL = Moldova
NIR = Northern Ireland
NOR = Norway
POL = Poland
POR = Portugal
IRL = Republic of Ireland
ROM = Romania
RUS = Russia
SMR = San Marino
SCO = Scotland
SVK = Slovakia
SLO = Slovenia
ESP = Spain
SWE = Sweden
SUI = Switzerland

INTRODUCTION TO NATIONS/CLUBS

TUR = Turkey
UKR = Ukraine
WAL = Wales
YUG = Yugoslavia

NON-EUROPE
ALG = Algeria
ANG = Angola
ARG = Argentina
AUS = Australia
BER = Bermuda
BOL = Bolivia
BRA = Brazil
BFA = Burkina Faso
BUR = Burundi
CMR = Cameroon
CAN = Canada
CAF = Central African Republic
CHD = Chad
CHL = Chile
COL = Colombia
CON = Congo
CRC = Costa Rica
CVD = Cape Verde Islands
DRC = Democratic Republic of Congo
EGY = Egypt
GAB = Gabon
GAM = Gambia
GHA = Ghana
GUI = Guinea
IRN = Iran
IRQ = Iraq
CIV = Ivory Coast
JAM = Jamaica
JOR = Jordan
JPN = Japan
KAZ = Kazakhstan
KEN = Kenya
LIB = Liberia
MAD = Madagascar
MLI = Mali
MWI = Malawi
MEX = Mexico
MAR = Morocco
MOZ = Mozambique
NAM = Namibia
NZL = New Zealand
NIG = Nigeria

OMN = Oman
PAN = Panama
PAR = Paraguay
PER = Peru
PHI - Philippines
RWA = Rwanda
STK = St. Kitts
STV = St. Vincent
SAU = Saudi Arabia
SEN = Senegal
SRL = Sierra Leone
SAF = South Africa
KOR = South Korea
SYR = Syria
TAD = Tadjikistan
TOG = Togo
TRI = Trinidad & Tobago
TUN = Tunisia
UGA = Uganda
UAE = United Arab Emirates
USA = United States
URU = Uruguay
UZB = Uzbekistan
VEN = Venezuela
ZAM = Zambia
ZIM = Zimbabwe

EUROPEAN CUPS

Results, goalscorers, goal-times and full line-ups are included

KEY:
H = Home
A = Away

The three-letter country codes used are the same as those shown above.

CLUB SECTION
LEAGUE RESULTS

This lists each club's league matches in chronological order, giving Date, Opponent, Venue, Result and Goalscorer(s)

KEY:
H = Home
A = Away
p = penalty
og = own-goal

APPEARANCES

The figures refer to league games only.

KEY:
P = Position
Ap = Number of appearances in starting line-up
(s) = Number of appearances as a substitute
Gls = Number of goals scored
G = Goalkeeper
D = Defender
M = Midfielder
A = Attacker

Foreign players are indicated using the same three-letter codes as shown above.

DIRECTORIES

Where more than one Coach/Manager has been used during the course of the season, these are all indicated. New Coaches/Managers for the 2000/01 season have been added where known at the time of going to press.

PROMOTED CLUBS

The clubs promoted to the First, or Premier, Division at the end of the 1999/2000 season are presented at the back of each national section, together with Second, or First, Division tables and Promotion/Relegation Play-off details. These tables use the same abbreviations as the LEAGUE CHAMPIONSHIP FINAL TABLE (see above), except that no Home and Away performance records are shown.

An unbroken line (——————) at the top of the table indicates the promotion zone.

A dotted line (················) at the top of the table indicates the promotion play-off zone

An unbroken line (——————) at the bottom of the table indicates the relegation zone

A dotted line (················) at the bottom of the table indicates the relegation play-off zone.

N.B. Where reference is made to the 1999/2000 domestic season, this should be understood as the 1999 season for Armenia, Belarus, Estonia, the Faroe Islands, Finland, Iceland, Latvia, Lithuania, Norway, Russia and Sweden.

ALBANIA

TOP PRIZES DECIDED BY PENALTIES

Double murder overshadows title thriller

FEDERATION DIRECTORY

Federata Shqiptarë e Futbollit
Rruga Dervish Hima Nr. 31, Tiranë

tel - (42) 50275/6/7
fax - (42) 27877

Year of Formation - 1930
President - Miço Papadhopulli
Secretary - Sulejman Starova

Stadium - Qemal Stafa, Tirana (18,000)

The most exciting and unpredictable Albanian championship in years was concluded in grisly fashion when a gunman walked into a café-bar close to the national stadium in Tirana and shot dead Adrian Çobo, the club president of surprise title challengers Tomori Berat, and Luan Zylfo, the country's most prominent referee.

The murders took place after an important match in Tirana between relegation-threatened Partizani and Tomori, which the latter won 1-0 to maintain their hopes of a first-ever championship triumph with one match remaining.

Even in a country that has grown accustomed to urban terrorism in recent years, the killings caused widespread shock, and a temporary suspension of the championship was called as a mark of respect to the two victims.

It would have been a fitting memorial to president Çobo had his team gone on to take the title, but although the Tomori players succeeded in lifting themselves sufficiently to win their final game of the campaign, 3-1 at home to Shkumbini, the result was only good enough to earn them a play-off with defending champions SK Tirana, who also won at home, 4-0 against city rivals Dinamo. Teuta Durrës, the long-time leaders, would have made it a three-way tie on 52 points had they not lost 3-2 to Shkumbini in their penultimate match - the team's fifth successive away game without a win.

The rules of the competition - copied from Italy - were that teams finishing level on points had to play off at a neutral venue. This was probably the most fitting solution given that Tirana had the better goal-difference and Tomori the superior head-to-head record. The deciding game was staged in Elbasan, a town situated between Tirana and Berat (though hardly equidistant) and it proved to be just as tight as the season-long struggle for supremacy. 1-1 at 90 minutes, there was no change to the scoreline in extra-time, so for the first time the Albanian championship was settled by a penalty shoot-out.

To the consternation of most neutrals, it was Tirana who won through, netting all five of their spot-kicks while Tomori missed one of theirs. Thus, the blue-and-whites from the capital celebrated their fifth championship triumph in six years and a record 19th in all. New to the victory rostrum, however, was the club's Egyptian president, El Sayed Metwali, who had arrived at the start of the season promising great things.

One of his coups had been to bring in Hungarian midfielder

LEAGUE CHAMPIONSHIP RESULTS 99/00

		1	2	3	4	5	6	7	8	9	10	11	12	13	14
1	Apolonia Fier		1-1	0-2	0-1	2-0	2-0	2-0	1-1	2-1	3-1	0-1	2-1	0-0	2-0
2	Bylis Ballsh	1-0		2-1	2-0	6-3	1-0	1-0	1-0	1-1	2-1	0-2	0-0	1-0	2-1
3	Dinamo Tiranë	0-1	0-0		2-1	1-0	2-0	2-1	3-0	2-1	1-0	1-2	1-2	3-3	0-2
4	Elbasani	0-2	3-1	2-1		0-0	2-1	1-1	1-0	0-0	0-0	2-1	1-0	0-1	1-2
5	Flamurtari Vlorë	3-1	1-0	0-0	3-0		0-3	1-2	2-1	1-0	3-1	1-0	1-0	0-1	3-1
6	Lushnja	2-0	1-1	3-1	4-0	2-0		1-0	0-1	1-0	3-2	3-2	2-0	1-1	1-1
7	Partizani Tiranë	3-1	0-0	1-0	2-1	1-0	1-1		1-1	1-2	2-3	2-0	0-0	0-1	2-2
8	Shkumbini Peqin	2-0	1-1	1-1	1-0	1-0	1-1	3-0		2-0	2-0	3-2	0-1	3-0	2-1
9	Shqiponja Gjirokastër	0-0	2-0	1-0	0-0	0-0	1-0	3-0	2-1		2-0	0-0	1-1	0-0	3-2
10	Skënderbeu Korçë	7-0	2-1	1-1	2-0	2-1	2-1	1-0	3-1	1-0		0-0	0-1	2-2	1-0
11	Teuta Durrës	4-0	2-0	1-1	1-0	3-0	2-0	4-0	2-0	1-0	2-0		1-0	2-0	1-0
12	SK Tirana	7-0	2-0	4-0	2-1	2-0	2-1	3-0	3-1	4-1	1-0	1-0		0-0	1-0
13	Tomori Berat	2-0	4-3	2-1	2-0	2-1	3-2	2-1	3-1	1-0	2-0	0-0	1-0		2-0
14	Vllaznia Shkodër	1-0	1-0	0-0	1-2	3-1	3-0	1-0	2-1	0-0	2-1	2-0	0-2	1-0	

LEAGUE CHAMPIONSHIP FINAL TABLE 99/00

		Pd	W	D	L	F	A	W	D	L	F	A	W	D	L	F	A	PT	GD
			Home					Away					Total						
1	SK Tirana	26	12	1	0	32	4	4	3	6	8	10	16	4	6	40	14	52	26
2	Tomori Berat	26	12	1	0	26	9	3	6	4	9	13	15	7	4	35	22	52	13
3	Teuta Durrës	26	12	1	0	26	1	3	3	7	10	15	15	4	7	36	16	49	20
4	Vllaznia Shkodër	26	9	2	2	17	7	2	2	9	12	21	11	4	11	29	28	37	1
5	Bylis Ballsh	26	10	2	1	20	9	0	5	8	8	20	10	7	9	28	29	37	-1
6	Lushnja	26	9	3	1	24	9	1	2	10	10	22	10	5	11	34	31	35	3
7	Shkumbini Peqin	26	9	3	1	22	7	1	2	10	9	24	10	5	11	31	31	35	0
8	Skënderbeu Korçë	26	9	3	1	24	8	1	1	11	9	25	10	4	12	33	33	34	0
9	Shqiponja Gjirokastër	26	7	6	0	15	4	1	3	9	6	17	8	9	9	21	21	33	0
10	Dinamo Tiranë	26	7	2	4	18	13	1	5	7	9	18	8	7	11	27	31	31	-4
11	Apolonia Fier	26	7	3	3	17	9	2	1	10	5	32	9	4	13	22	41	31	-19
12	Flamurtari Vlorë	26	9	1	3	19	10	0	2	11	6	25	9	3	14	25	35	30	-10
13	Elbasani	26	6	4	3	13	10	2	1	10	6	22	8	5	13	19	32	29	-13
14	Partizani Tiranë	26	5	5	3	16	12	1	1	11	5	25	6	6	14	21	37	24	-16

N.B. Championship play-off: SK Tirana 1, Tomori Berat 1 (aet; 5-4 on penalties).

Zoltán Kenesei towards the end of the campaign. The 27-year-old import proved to be an instant hit and effectively masterminded the team's progress through the tense closing weeks of the campaign. Goalkeeper Blendi Nallbani also shone in a team that had needed to be reconstructed at the start of the season by incoming coach Shqëlqim Muça following the departure of free-scoring young strikers Merkoçi, Muka and Zeqo. The team's leading marksman, with just eight goals, turned out to be Anesti Vito, an early-season capture from Flamurtari.

Tomori's Klodian Arbri was the top scorer in the entire

PLAYER OF THE SEASON

ERION BOGDANI

Young striker Erion Bogdani made big news in his homeland when he left Croatian club Zagreb in mid-season to join Italian side Reggina, thus becoming the first Albanian in modern times to play in Serie A. Not only that but he went on to play a significant role in Reggina's successful bid to avoid relegation, scoring two goals, including a crucial winner against Venezia. The Italian media reacted favourably to his contributions, as did coach Franco Colomba and the Reggina fans. The ex-Partizani and Dinamo Tirana spearhead should feature strongly for his country during the 2002 World Cup qualifiers, but first he has to break up the established German-based partnership of Altin Rraklli and Igli Tare.

EUROPEAN CUPS 99/00

CHAMPIONS' CUP

● SK TIRANA
Preliminary round 1 ÍBV (ISL)
H 1-2   Bulku S. (79)
Nallbani, Sina, Alimehmeti, Dede, Gallo (Bulku S. 46), Tafaj, Malko (Ruhi 46), Mema, Çoclli (Demneri 72), Prenga, Ishka.
A 0-1
Nallbani, Sina, Malko, Alimehmeti, Dede, Mema, Tafaj, Bulku S., Prenga, Ishka (Bulku E. 75), Çoçlli (Ruhi 65).

UEFA CUP

● BYLIS BALLSH
Qualifying round INTER BRATISLAVA (SVK)
H 0-2
Shehi, Dume, Pinari, Ahmataj, Osmani, Xhafa (Asllani K. 46; Rexha 63), Jupi, Qorri, Çuko (Haxhiaj 80), Jakupi, Elezi.
A 1-3   Jakupi (62)
Shehi, Dume, Pinari, Haxhiaj, Ahmataj, Osmani (Elezi 46), Çuko, Jupi. Qorri, Xhafa (Ymeri 81), Jakupi.

● VLLAZNIA SHKODER
Qualifying round SPARTAK TRNAVA (SVK)
H 1-1   Sinani (44)
Mustafa, Osja (Plori 87), Dibra, Premçi, Kotrri, Lici, Cungu, Miloti, Osmani (Ymeri 78), Sinani, Bano (Pisha 52).
A 0-2
Mustafa, Osja, Lici, Pisha, Dibra (Volumi 87), Kotrri, Osmani, Cungu, Shllaku (Bano 30), Miloti, Sinani.

INTERNATIONAL HONOURS

None.

DOMESTIC CUP 99/00

1/8 FINALS
Skënderbeu Korçë v Bylis Ballsh 1-0; 0-3
(Bylis Ballsh 3-1)
Shqiponja Gjirokastër v Tomori Berat 1-0; 0-1
(1-1; Tomori Berat on pens.)
Flamurtari Vlorë v Teuta Durrës 1-1; 0-3
(Teuta Durrës 4-1)
Besa Kavajë v Lushnja 1-2; 1-1
(Lushnja 3-2)
Partizani Tiranë v Shkumbini Peqin 1-1; 1-2
(Shkumbini Peqin 3-2)
Apolonia Fier v Vllaznia Shkodër 1-0; 0-3
(Vllaznia Shkodër 3-1)
Elbasani v Dinamo Tiranë 1-2; 0-3
(Dinamo Tiranë 5-1)
Kukësi v SK Tirana 1-1; 1-7
(SK Tirana 8-2)

QUARTER-FINALS
Dinamo Tiranë 2 (Galanxhi, Qorri), Tomori Berat 0
Tomori Berat 1 (Aliaj), Dinamo Tiranë 0
(Dinamo Tiranë 2-1)
Lushnja 0, Bylis Ballsh 0
Bylis Ballsh 1 (Jakupi), Lushnja 1 (Malko)
(1-1; Lushnja on away goal)
Shkumbini Peqin 1 (Gjoni), Vllaznia Shkodër 1 (Bizi)
Vllaznia Shkodër 1 (Osja), Shkumbini Peqin 1 (Gjoni)
(2-2; Shkumbini 5-3 on pens.)
Teuta Durrës 0, SK Tirana 0
SK Tirana 0, Teuta Durrës 0
(0-0; Teuta Durrës 4-3 on pens.)

SEMI-FINALS
Teuta Durrës 0, Dinamo Tiranë 1 (Pisha)
Dinamo Tiranë 1 (Ahmataj),
Teuta Durrës 2 (Muça, Stojku)
(2-2; Teuta Durrës on away goals)

Shkumbini Peqin 3 (Tosku, Xhetani, Kola), Lushnja 0
Lushnja 3 (Elezi, Malko, Bano), Shkumbini 0
(3-3; Lushnja 3-1 on pens.)

FINAL
05/05/2000, Tirana
TEUTA DURRËS 0
LUSHNJA 0
(aet; 5-4 on pens.)
referee - Zylfo
TEUTA DURRËS - Shehi, Xhai, Zëre, Lici, Tole, Muça,
Rexhepi (Çanaku 79), Prenga, Da Silva (Ceno 68),
Stojku (Bespalla 46), Babamusta.
LUSHNJA - Prençe, Manko, Hysko Al., Malko, Hasalla,
Toshëllari (Gazheli 115), Çuko, Muka, Bano,
Hysko Ar., Elezi.

league with 18 goals (over half his team's total), but that individual prize was scant consolation for his team's narrow failure to win the league. Coached by Theodhori Arbri, Tomori earned universal adulation for their adventurous, attacking style, but the tragic death of their president and the penalty shoot-out defeat in the championship 'final' ensured the most depressing of ends to what had otherwise been a memorable season.

Penalties were also the deciding factor in the outcome of the Albanian Cup, with Teuta taking the trophy at the expense of Lushnja following two hours of goalless football in the final. Teuta had also progressed without scoring against Cup holders Tirana in the quarter-finals, and they needed the away-goals rule to get past Dinamo in the semis. It might not have been the most comprehensive of Cup triumphs, but it was just reward for the ambitious input of the club's charismatic president, 36-year-old Edmond

Hasanbelliu, who in two years had transformed the coastal club from relegation candidates to title challengers and Cup winners. Like Tirana, Teuta boasted an influential foreigner during the latter stages of the season, with Giovanni da Silva, a Brazilian, causing quite a stir following his arrival in the spring.

While Teuta go from strength to strength, quite the reverse is true for Partizani Tirana. Generally regarded as the most glamorous and prestigious Albanian club, sufficiently so to attract major Italian sponsorship during the 1990s, Partizani plummeted to uncharted depths when they began the new millennium by dropping into the Second Division. It was a season of woe all round for the debt-ridden club, whose relegation was unavoidable despite the best efforts of their courageous young president Albert Xhani to arrest the decline.

Elbasani joined Partizani in Division Two after losing

NATIONAL TEAM RESULTS 99/00

18/08/99	Slovenia (ECQ)	A	Ljubljana	0-2	
04/09/99	Latvia (ECQ)	H	Tirana	3-3	Bushi (29, 78), Muka (90)
06/10/99	Greece (ECQ)	A	Athens	0-2	
09/10/99	Georgia (ECQ)	H	Tirana	2-1	Rraklli (30), Kola (36)
06/02/00	Andorra	N	Ta' Qali	3-0	Dalipi (63p), Vata (86), Zajmi (90)
08/02/00	Azerbaijan	N	Ta' Qali	1-0	Murati (37)
10/02/00	Malta	A	Ta' Qali	1-0	Sinani (23)
26/04/00	Macedonia	A	Prilep	0-1	

TOP SCORERS

18 Klodian ARBRI (Tomori Berat)
14 Vladimir GJONI (Shkumbini Peqin)
12 Daniel XHAFA (Flamurtari Vlorë/Bylis Ballsh)
   Rigels QOSA (Skënderbeu Korçë)
11 Anesti VITO (Flamurtari Vlorë/SK Tirana)
8 Alban REXHA (Partizani Tiranë)
   Fjodor XHAFA (Dinamo Tiranë)
   Edi MARTINI (Vllaznia Shkodër)
   Artan BANO (Lushnja)
   Justin BESPALLA (Teuta Durrës)

their end-of-season play-off with Besa Kavajë, who, in turn, accompanied Beslidhja Lezhë into the top flight. Beslidhja required two play-off victories themselves to assure promotion, the second of them against Besa, which - as with every other major issue during the season - was settled by a penalty shoot-out.

With two teams relegated and two promoted, the top division maintained the 14-team structure that had been introduced at the start of the season. Even with fewer teams than before, the remarkable home-team bias remained, with every one of the 14 clubs winning more home games than they lost and, likewise, losing more away games than

NATIONAL TEAM APPEARANCES 99/00

Coach - Astrit HAFIZI; Medin ZHEGA	SLO	LAT	GRE	GEO	AND	AZB	MLT	MAC	Cps	Gls
Foto STRAKOSHA (29/03/65) - Ionikos (GRE)	G	G	G					G	41	-
Luan PINARI (27/10/77) - Dinamo Tiranë	D								4	-
Ilir SHULKU (02/01/69) - Eintracht Nordhorn (GER)	D	D		D					41	1
Arian XHUMBA (07/09/68) - Paralimni (CYP)	D	D	D	D				D46	30	-
Rudi VATA (13/02/69) - FC Energie Cottbus (GER)	D	D	D	D	D	D		D46	51	4
Arian BELLAI (11/03/70) - Yanina (GRE)	M	M	D84						15	1
Altin HAXHI (07/06/65) - Lovech (BUL)	M	M	M					M	21	2
Edvin MURATI (12/11/75) - Paris Saint-Germain (FRA)	M58	M46	M54	s54		M	M	s46	8	1
Bledar KOLA (01/08/72) - Panathinaikos (GRE)	M		M	M				M70	29	5
Altin RRAKLLI (17/07/70) - SpVgg Unterhaching (GER)	A60		A	A73				A46	41	8
Igli TARE (25/07/73) - 1.FC Kaiserslautern (GER)	A	A78	A68	A90				A83	23	3
Mahir HALILI (30/06/75) - HIT Gorica (SLO)	s58								13	1
Erion BOGDANI (14/04/75) - Zagreb (CRO)	s60	s67	s84	s90					9	1
Ervin FAKAJ (15/07/76) - Hannover 96 (GER)		D67		D				s46	15	-
Altin LALA (18/02/74) - Hannover 96 (GER)		M	M	M				M46	14	-
Alban BUSHI (24/08/73) - Adanaspor (TUR)		A	M	M54				s46	25	6
Edmond DALIPI (03/03/72) - Apollon (GRE)		s46			M	M	M55	s70	16	1
Devi MUKA (21/12/76) - Varteks Varazdin (CRO)		s78	s68	s73	A	A	M	s46	9	1
Albert DURO (12/06/78) - Steaua Bucuresti (ROM)			s54	D				D	5	-
Arian BEQAJ (20/08/75) - OFI (GRE)				G		G	G		6	-
Armir GRIMA (16/06/74) - Dinamo Tiranë					G				4	-
Rezart DABULLA (24/10/79) - SK Tirana					D				2	-
Geri ÇIPI (22/02/76) - NK Maribor (SLO)					D	D	D	D	5	-
Suad LICI (20/03/74) - Teuta Durrës					D	M	D		3	-
Bledar DEVOLLI (15/01/78) - Shqiponja Gjirokastër					M46	s87			2	-
Altin RRICA (13/12/73) - Partizani Tiranë					M		s55		2	-
Kliton BOZGO (05/12/70) - NK Maribor (SLO)					A	A90	A		12	-
Vioresin SINANI (04/11/77) - Varteks Varazdin (CRO)					A46		s46	s83	3	1
Johan DRIZA (20/09/76) - SK Tirana					s46	D87	D		4	-
Roland ZAJMI (06/11/73) - Proodeftiki (GRE)					s46	A	A46		4	1
Ilir DIBRA (16/08/77) - Vllaznia Shkodër						D	D		2	-
Enkelejd DOBI (23/05/75) - Varteks Varazdin (CRO)						s90			2	1
Redi JUPI (31/05/74) - Dinamo Tiranë							M		5	-
Çlirim BASHA (05/02/71) - Alemannia Aachen (GER)								D	1	-

they won. Of the 182 matches played, there were 123 home wins, 37 draws and just 22 away wins. Hats off to Lushnja, whose 3-0 victory at Flamurtari in November was the most emphatic away from home all season.

Not surprisingly, Albanian clubs also struggled on their travels in international competition. The three European representatives all lasted just one round, and the national team succumbed to predictable European Championship qualifying defeats in Slovenia and Greece.

There was, however, a happy ending to the Euro 2000 campaign when Albania beat Georgia 2-1 in Tirana - a result which enabled Astrit Hafizi's team to swap places with their vanquished opponents and avoid the wooden spoon. The victory was not enough to keep Hafizi in his job, however. The Albanian FA decided that the team would be better off without him and, rather harshly, gave him the sack.

Even more surprising was the choice of his successor. The post was handed to 52-year-old Medin Zhega. A fine player in his time with Vllaznia, Dinamo and Albania, he had a spell as coach to the national Under-21 side but had spent several years in the wilderness and had not coached in club football for almost a decade.

Yet Zhega's first three matches all brought victories. By overcoming Andorra, Azerbaijan and hosts Malta successively over four days in February, a second-string, largely home-based Albania brought home the Rothmans Cup - a minor trophy, perhaps, but something for the new coach and his players to cherish as they looked ahead to the far more gruelling prospect of World Cup qualification.

Grouped alongside Germany, England, Greece and Finland, the Albanians know that they are unlikely to finish anywhere other than bottom, but that will not prevent them from seeking a few prized scalps along the way. The games against Germany and Greece will be especially interesting given the growing number of Albanian players now earning their living in those two countries.

PROMOTED CLUBS 99/00

SECOND DIVISION FINAL TABLES

GROUP A	Pd	W	D	L	F	A	Pt	GD
1 **Beslidhja**	16	12	2	2	48	11	38	37
2 Burreli	16	12	1	3	37	22	37	15
3 Kastrioti	16	12	0	4	40	26	36	14
4 Ilir V.	16	10	1	5	25	15	31	10
5 Shkodra	16	6	2	8	28	33	20	-5
6 Kukësi	16	5	1	10	19	31	16	-12
7 Korabi	16	4	1	11	15	35	13	-20
8 Erzeni	16	3	1	12	13	31	10	-18
9 Laçi	16	2	3	11	12	33	9	-21

GROUP B	Pd	W	D	L	F	A	Pt	GD
1 **Besa**	18	12	3	3	29	16	39	13
2 Memaliaj	18	11	2	5	28	20	35	8
3 Naftëtari	18	8	3	7	26	20	27	6
4 Pogradeci	18	8	2	8	24	13	26	11
5 Gramozi	18	8	2	8	25	24	26	1
6 Albpetrol	18	8	2	8	29	29	26	0
7 Tepelena	18	8	1	9	27	25	25	2
8 Sopoti	18	7	2	9	23	27	23	-4
9 Butrinti	18	5	3	10	25	39	18	-14
10 Devolli	18	4	2	12	18	41	14	-23

PROMOTION PLAY-OFFS
Beslidhja 2, Memaliaj 1
Besa 2, Burreli 1

Beslidhja 1, Besa 1 (aet; 4-2 on pens.)
Besa 2, Elbasani 1

CLUB DIRECTORIES

Klubi Sportiv Beslidhja
Lezhë
tel - (262) 3307
Year of Formation - 1928
President - Nikoll Lesi
Secretary - Pjetër Lesi
Coach - Luan Vukatana
Stadium - Beslidhja (3,000)

Klubi Sportiv Besa
Rruga Vangjel Thanasi, nr.7
Kavajë
tel - (57) 42617
Year of Formation - 1925
President - Flamur Kollozi
Secretary - Artan Lilamani
Coach - Ilir Gjyla
Stadium - Besa (8,000)

APOLONIA FIER

CLUB DIRECTORY

Klubi Sportiv Apolonia
Rruga 1 Maji, nr.73
Fier
tel - (64) 2183
Year of Formation - 1925
President - Fatmir Kajolli
Secretary - Besnik Veliu
Coach - Vangjel Capo
Stadium - Loni Papuçiu (6,000)

MAJOR HONOURS
Domestic Cup - (1) 1998.

APPEARANCES 99/00

	P	Ap	(s)	Gls
Kujtim BALLA	M	12	(5)	1
Artan BARE	M	18	(1)	2
Dashnor BITA	D	24		4
Dorian BUBEQI	A	8	(1)	6
Ermal CAKRANI	M	12	(7)	
Ledio CAPO	G	25		
Elidon ÇOBANI	A	11	(6)	
Ervin ÇUNI	D	6	(5)	
Ajet GURGURI	M	16	(2)	3
Erion HAZIZI	G	1		
Edmond KAÇELI	M	21	(2)	
Altin KORE	G		(1)	
Jurgen MALI	A	15	(1)	
Elton MARINI	A	18	(5)	
Melsi MERTIRI	M	8		
Bledar MUÇA	M	8	(2)	1
Orest MUZHA	M	2	(2)	1
Bledar OLLDASHI	M	4	(4)	
Edvin PASHOLLARI	M	21	(2)	
Artan POÇI	D	8	(1)	1
Dashnor POÇI	M	9	(3)	1
Viktor QENDRO	A	10		1
Bledar RISTANI	D	11	(8)	
Vaskë RUKO	A	8	(1)	
Endri YZEIRI	A	10		1

LEAGUE RESULTS 1999/2000

18/09/99	Teuta Durrës	A	0-4	
25/09/99	Tomori Berat	H	0-0	
02/10/99	Partizani Tiranë	A	1-3	Bita (p)
16/10/99	Shkumbini Peqin	H	1-1	Qendro
23/10/99	Lushnja	A	0-2	
30/10/99	Bylis Ballsh	H	1-1	Poçi A.
06/11/99	Elbasani	H	0-1	
13/11/99	Shqiponja Gjirokastër	A	0-0	
20/11/99	Dinamo Tiranë	H	0-2	
24/11/99	SK Tirana	A	0-7	
04/12/99	Flamurtari Vlorë	H	2-0	Gurguri 2
11/12/99	Vllaznia Shkodër	A	0-1	
18/12/99	Skënderbeu Korçë	H	3-1	Yzeiri, Bita, Gurguri
19/02/00	Teuta Durrës	H	0-1	
26/02/00	Tomori Berat	A	0-2	
04/03/00	Partizani Tiranë	H	2-0	Poçi D., Bita
11/03/00	Shkumbini Peqin	A	0-2	
18/03/00	Lushnja	H	2-0	Bubeqi 2 (1p)
25/03/00	Bylis Ballsh	A	0-1	
01/04/00	Elbasani	A	2-0	Bita, Bubeqi
08/04/00	Shqiponja Gjirokastër	H	2-1	Bubeqi, Balla
15/04/00	Dinamo Tiranë	A	1-0	Bare
22/04/00	SK Tirana	H	2-1	Bare (p), Bubeqi (p)
29/04/00	Flamurtari Vlorë	A	1-3	Muça
13/05/00	Vllaznia Shkodër	H	2-0	Muzha, Bubeqi
24/05/00	Skënderbeu Korçë	A	0-7	

BYLIS BALLSH

CLUB DIRECTORY

Klubi Sportiv Bylis
Bashkia
Ballsh
Year of Formation - 1972
President - Ismet Beqiri
Secretary - Xhemil Hoxha
Coach - Shpëtim Duro
Stadium - Ballshi (6,500)

APPEARANCES 99/00

	P	Ap	(s)	Gls
Klodian ASLLANI	M	11		3
Luan ASLLANI	D	25		3
Egert BAKALLI	M	23	(1)	1
Ferdinand BILALI	M	13	(9)	2
Elidon DEMIRAJ	M	19	(2)	
Kujtim DIVIA	G	1		
Dashnor DUME	D	18	(1)	
Alpin GALLO	D	11		
Romeo HAXHIAJ	A	15		3
Saimir HAXHIU	A	14		
Hekuran JAKUPI	A	17	(4)	6
Ilir KALARI	D	1	(2)	
Adriatik KANANI	D	8	(4)	
Kreshnik LUTAJ	D	2	(11)	1
Ardian NINI	M	1	(2)	
Altin PELARI	D	11	(10)	
Artjan POÇI	D	5		
Erton RESULI	M	10		
Nuri REXHA	M	14	(2)	1
Besion SHEHU	M	4	(4)	
Arben SINA	G	24		
Fatos SULAJ	M	16	(4)	
Daniel XHAFA	A	12		8

LEAGUE RESULTS 1999/2000

18/09/99	SK Tirana	H	0-0	
25/09/99	Shkumbini Peqin	A	1-1	Jakupi
02/10/99	Flamurtari Vlorë	H	6-3	Haxhiaj, Rexha, Bakalli, Lutaj, Jakupi, Bilali
16/10/99	Lushnja	A	1-1	Asllani L. (p)
23/10/99	Vllaznia Shkodër	H	2-1	Haxhiaj, Asllani L.
30/10/99	Apolonia Fier	A	1-1	Haxhiaj
06/11/99	Skënderbeu Korçë	H	2-1	Jakupi 2
13/11/99	Elbasani	A	1-3	Jakupi (p)
20/11/99	Teuta Durrës	H	0-2	(w/o)
24/11/99	Shqiponja Gjirokastër	A	0-2	
04/12/99	Tomori Berat	H	1-0	Jakupi
11/12/99	Dinamo Tiranë	A	0-0	
18/12/99	Partizani Tiranë	A	0-0	
19/02/00	SK Tirana	A	0-2	
26/02/00	Shkumbini Peqin	H	1-0	Asllani L. (p)
04/03/00	Flamurtari Vlorë	A	0-1	
11/03/00	Lushnja	H	1-0	Asllani K.
18/03/00	Vllaznia Shkodër	A	0-1	
25/03/00	Apolonia Fier	H	1-0	Asllani K.
01/04/00	Skënderbeu Korçë	A	1-2	Bilali
08/04/00	Elbasani	H	2-0	Xhafa 2
15/04/00	Teuta Durrës	A	0-2	
22/04/00	Shqiponja Gjirokastër	H	1-1	Xhafa
29/04/00	Tomori Berat	A	3-4	Xhafa 3
13/05/00	Dinamo Tiranë	H	2-1	Xhafa, Asllani K.
24/05/00	Partizani Tiranë	H	1-0	Xhafa

DINAMO TIRANË

CLUB DIRECTORY

Klubi Sportiv Dinamo
Rruga Dervish Hima, nr. 30
Tiranë
tel - (42) 23662
Year of Formation - 1950
President - Besnik Sulo
Secretary - Sokol Morina
Coach - Faruk Sejdini; Bujar Kasmi; Shpëtim Duro
Stadium - Selman Stërmasi (12,000)

MAJOR HONOURS
League Championship - (15) 1950, 1951, 1952,
1953, 1955, 1956, 1960, 1967, 1973, 1975,
1976, 1977, 1980, 1986, 1990.
Domestic Cup - (12)
1950, 1951, 1952, 1953, 1954, 1960, 1971,
1974, 1978, 1982, 1989, 1990.

APPEARANCES 99/00

	P	Ap	(s)	Gls
Julian AHMATAJ	D	20		
Elton DALIPI	A	7	(9)	
Paulin DHEMBI	M	20		1
Julian GALANXHI	M	8	(8)	
Armir GRIMA	G	13		
Gentian HAJDARI	D	23		1
Elton HASANI	A	4	(9)	1
Blendi HAXHIAJ	D	10		
Redi HOXHA	M	3	(4)	
Shpëtim IMERAJ	M	23		3
Redi JUPI	M	21	(1)	1
Thoma KOKURI	G		(1)	
Iljon LIKA	G	5	(1)	
Marian LITI	A		(11)	1
Erjon MATRAKU	M	10	(1)	
Artan MERGJYSHI	D	8		
Erion MUÇOLLARI	D	1	(2)	
Arjon MUSTAFA	G	8		
Genc NASTASI	A		(2)	
Arjan PISHA	D	23	(1)	1
Ilir QORRI	M	18		2
Sergei ROMANISHIN (UKR)	M	11		
Andi SHTREPI	A		(1)	
Ligoraq TIKO	A	11		3
Ermal VARFI	M	1	(1)	
Erald XHAFA	M		(1)	
Erion XHAFA	M	1	(1)	
Fjodor XHAFA	A	24	(1)	8
Fatjon YMERI	A	13		5

LEAGUE RESULTS 1999/2000

18/09/99	Flamurtari Vlorë	A	0-0	
25/09/99	Vllaznia Shkodër	H	0-2	
02/10/99	Skënderbeu Korçë	A	1-1	Xhafa F.
16/10/99	Teuta Durrës	H	1-2	Ymeri
23/10/99	Tomori Berat	A	1-2	Xhafa F.
30/10/99	Partizani Tiranë	H	2-1	Xhafa F., Imeraj
06/11/99	Shkumbini Peqin	A	1-1	Hasani
13/11/99	Lushnja	H	2-0	Ymeri 2
20/11/99	Apolonia Fier	A	2-0	Ymeri 2
24/11/99	Elbasani	H	2-1	Imeraj, Dhembi
04/12/99	Shqiponja Gjirokastër	A	0-1	
11/12/99	Bylis Ballsh	H	0-0	
18/12/99	SK Tirana	H	1-2	Xhafa F.
19/02/00	Flamurtari Vlorë	H	1-0	Qorri
26/02/00	Vllaznia Shkodër	A	0-0	
04/03/00	Skënderbeu Korçë	H	1-0	Xhafa F.
11/03/00	Teuta Durrës	A	1-1	Pisha
18/03/00	Tomori Berat	H	3-3	Tiko, Xhafa F., Hajdari
25/03/00	Partizani Tiranë	A	0-1	
01/04/00	Shkumbini Peqin	H	3-0	Jupi, Imeraj, Xhafa F.
08/04/00	Lushnja	A	1-3	Qorri
15/04/00	Apolonia Fier	H	0-1	
22/04/00	Elbasani	A	1-2	Liti
29/04/00	Shqiponja Gjirokastër	H	2-1	Tiko, Xhafa F.
13/05/00	Bylis Ballsh	A	1-2	Tiko
24/05/00	SK Tirana	A	0-4	

ELBASANI

CLUB DIRECTORY

Klubi i Futballit Elbasani
Bulevardi Qemal Stafa
Stadiumi KF Elbasani
Elbasan
tel - (42) 53253
Year of Formation - 1923
Secretary - Zamir Arapi
Coach - Astrit Sejdini; Luan Deliu
Stadium - Elbasani (13,500)

MAJOR HONOURS
League Championship - (1) 1984.
Domestic Cup - (2) 1975, 1992.

APPEARANCES 99/00

	P	Ap	(s)	Gls
Taulant BAKIU	D	17		
Saimir BARDHI	M		(3)	
Dorian BYLYKBASHI	A	13		2
Gentian BYLYKBASHI	M	11	(1)	
Mikel CENKO	A	2	(4)	
Daniel DALIPI	M	3	(8)	
Ridvan DISHA	D	10	(5)	
Muharrem DOSTI	G	23		2
Klodian DURO	M	11		
Ilirian FILE	D	24		1
Gjergj GJIKA	M	16	(3)	
Gentian GRABOCKA	A	15		4
Olsi HIDA	D	8	(8)	1
Isuf IBERSHIMI	M	20		4
Klevis JANI	M		(2)	
Elvis KOTORRI	G	3	(4)	
Eriol MERXHA	M	24		2
Dashamir MUÇA	D	13	(3)	
Oltion OSMANI	M	12		3
Kastriot SHAHINI	M	7	(1)	
Saimir SHENGJERGJI	D	25		
Alket SHIMA	D	1	(4)	
Armand STAMBOLLHXIU	A	13	(4)	
Elton VERÇANI	D	15	(1)	

LEAGUE RESULTS 1999/2000

18/09/99	Skënderbeu Korçë	A	0-2	
25/09/99	Teuta Durrës	H	2-1	Bylykbashi D., File
02/10/99	Tomori Berat	A	0-2	
16/10/99	Partizani Tiranë	H	1-1	Bylykbashi D.
23/10/99	Shkumbini Peqin	A	0-1	
30/10/99	Lushnja	H	2-1	Grabocka, Osmani
06/11/99	Apolonia Fier	A	1-0	Hida
13/11/99	Bylis Ballsh	H	3-1	Grabocka 2, Osmani
20/11/99	Shqiponja Gjirokastër	H	0-0	
24/11/99	Dinamo Tiranë	A	1-2	Merxha
04/12/99	SK Tirana	H	1-0	Grabocka
11/12/99	Flamurtari Vlorë	A	0-3	
18/12/99	Vllaznia Shkodër	H	1-2	Osmani (p)
19/02/00	Skënderbeu Korçë	H	0-0	
26/02/00	Teuta Durrës	A	0-1	
04/03/00	Tomori Berat	H	0-1	
11/03/00	Partizani Tiranë	A	1-2	Dosti (p)
18/03/00	Shkumbini Peqin	H	1-0	Dosti (p)
25/03/00	Lushnja	A	0-4	
01/04/00	Apolonia Fier	H	0-2	
08/04/00	Bylis Ballsh	A	0-2	
15/04/00	Shqiponja Gjirokastër	A	0-0	
22/04/00	Dinamo Tiranë	H	2-1	Ibërshimi 2 (2p)
29/04/00	SK Tirana	A	1-2	Merxha
13/05/00	Flamurtari Vlorë	H	0-0	
24/05/00	Vllaznia Shkodër	A	2-1	Ibërshimi 2 (1p)

FLAMURTARI VLORË

CLUB DIRECTORY

Klubi Sportiv Flamurtari
Rruga Perlat Rexhepi, nr.41
Vlorë
tel - (63) 24563
Year of Formation - 1923
President - Shkëlqim Selami
Secretary - Hajri Hasanaj
Coach - Edmond Liçaj
Stadium - Flamurtari (8,200)

MAJOR HONOURS
League Championship - (1) 1991.
Domestic Cup - (2) 1985, 1988.

APPEARANCES 99/00

	P	Ap	(s)	Gls
Ilir ALLIU	D	13		
Artur AVDULLAI	M	16	(6)	
Neritan BAJAZITI	A	2	(7)	1
Roland BEJLERI	G	5		
Estref BILLA	G	9	(1)	
Taulant ÇERÇIZI	D	24	(1)	5
Arnold ÇIPI	A	21	(1)	
Jorgaq DIAMANTI	D	2		
Erjon DINE	G	3		
Bardhyl DOSKU	G	9		
Edmir GJONI	M	3	(7)	
Dritan HALIBI	M	2	(6)	
Gentian IBRAHIMI	M	18	(3)	2
Sherif IDRIZI	M	22		2
Bledar ISARAJ	D		(2)	
Bledar LALA	M	22	(2)	
Klodian LIÇAJ	M	20		3
Elton LILA	A	20	(1)	1
Klardi MAHIRAJ	D		(1)	
Fation MALAJ	M	26		
Ardian NINI	M	9	(4)	1
Dritan RESULI	M	11		1
Artur SAKAJ	M	3	(8)	
Admir SEJFULLAI	A	6	(7)	1
Gentian SELAMI	M	3	(3)	
Dritan SELIMI	M		(1)	1
Oltion SINANI	D		(3)	
Anesti VITO	A	4		3
Daniel XHAFA	A	13		4

LEAGUE RESULTS 1999/2000

18/09/99	Dinamo Tiranë	H	0-0	
25/09/99	SK Tirana	A	0-2	
02/10/99	Bylis Ballsh	A	3-6	Liçaj, Vito 2
16/10/99	Vllaznia Shkodër	H	3-1	Vito (p), Ibrahimi, Xhafa
23/10/99	Skënderbeu Korçë	A	1-2	Xhafa
30/10/99	Teuta Durrës	H	1-0	Xhafa
06/11/99	Tomori Berat	A	1-2	Çerçizi
13/11/99	Partizani Tiranë	H	1-2	Çerçizi
20/11/99	Shkumbini Peqin	A	0-1	
24/11/99	Lushnja	H	0-3	
04/12/99	Apolonia Fier	A	0-2	
11/12/99	Elbasani	H	3-0	Nini, Xhafa, Resuli (p)
18/12/99	Shqiponja Gjirokastër	A	0-0	
19/02/00	Dinamo Tiranë	A	0-1	
26/02/00	SK Tirana	H	1-0	Çerçizi
04/03/00	Bylis Ballsh	H	1-0	Idrizi
11/03/00	Vllaznia Shkodër	A	1-3	Liçaj
18/03/00	Skënderbeu Korçë	H	3-1	Liçaj, Sejfullai, Bajaziti
25/03/00	Teuta Durrës	A	0-3	
01/04/00	Tomori Berat	H	0-1	
08/04/00	Partizani Tiranë	A	0-1	
15/04/00	Shkumbini Peqin	H	2-1	Lila, Çerçizi
22/04/00	Lushnja	A	0-2	
29/04/00	Apolonia Fier	H	3-1	Ibrahimi, Çerçizi, Selimi
13/05/00	Elbasani	A	0-0	
24/05/00	Shqiponja Gjirokastër	H	1-0	Idrizi (p)

LUSHNJA

CLUB DIRECTORY

Klubi Sportiv Lushnja
Lagjja Xh. Nepravishta
Lushnjë
tel - (42) 300
Year of Formation - 1927
President - Artur Çobani
Secretary - Agim Mone
Coach - Hysen Dedja
Stadium - Roza Haxhiu (12,000)

APPEARANCES 99/00

	P	Ap	(s)	Gls
Artan BANO	A	22	(1)	8
Saimir BENDO	D	4	(3)	
Elton BORIÇI	M	2	(2)	2
Arben CELA	A	17	(1)	2
Dritan ÇUKO	M	19	(2)	2
Enik DHIMA	M	11	(2)	
Aurel DUSHI	A	1	(4)	
Bardhyl ELEZI	A	11	(3)	4
Judmir GAZHELI	D	21	(2)	
Argenc GJERGJOVA	A	3	(6)	
Blerim HASALLA	D	17	(7)	1
Altin HYSKO	M	22		1
Arben HYSKO	M	16	(3)	
Elton KORRESHI	M		(2)	
Saimir MALKO	D	21		7
Bledar MANKO	D	19		
Orgert MUKA	M	18	(5)	1
Saimir MUSAI	G		(1)	
Dritan OMERI	M	12	(8)	3
Hektor PREMÇE	G	26		
Sokol PRIFTI	M	4	(2)	
Saimir QEFA	D	3	(1)	
Admir TOSHKELLARI	M	17	(2)	3

LEAGUE RESULTS 1999/2000

18/09/99	Tomori Berat	A	2-3	Çuko, Toshkëllari
25/09/99	Partizani Tiranë	H	1-0	Cela
02/10/99	Shkumbini Peqin	A	1-1	Bano
16/10/99	Bylis Ballsh	H	1-1	Bano
23/10/99	Apolonia Fier	H	2-0	Toshkëllari, Malko
30/10/99	Elbasani	A	1-2	Omeri
06/11/99	Shqiponja Gjirokastër	H	1-0	Bano
13/11/99	Dinamo Tiranë	A	0-2	
20/11/99	SK Tirana	H	2-0	Çuko, Bano
24/11/99	Flamurtari Vlorë	A	3-0	Malko (p), Bano, Hasalla
04/12/99	Vllaznia Shkodër	H	1-1	Cela
11/12/99	Skënderbeu Korçë	A	1-2	Toshkëllari
18/12/99	Teuta Durrës	H	3-2	Malko (p), Hysko Al., Muka
19/02/00	Tomori Berat	H	1-1	Malko (p)
26/02/00	Partizani Tiranë	A	1-1	Malko (p)
04/03/00	Shkumbini Peqin	H	0-1	
11/03/00	Bylis Ballsh	A	0-1	
18/03/00	Apolonia Fier	A	0-2	
25/03/00	Elbasani	H	4-0	Omeri, Malko (p), Bano, Elezi
01/04/00	Shqiponja Gjirokastër	A	0-1	
08/04/00	Dinamo Tiranë	H	3-1	Elezi 2, Malko (p)
15/04/00	SK Tirana	A	1-2	Omeri
22/04/00	Flamurtari Vlorë	H	2-0	Bano, Boriçi
29/04/00	Vllaznia Shkodër	A	0-3	
13/05/00	Skënderbeu Korçë	H	3-2	Elezi, Bano, Boriçi
24/05/00	Teuta Durrës	A	0-2	

PARTIZANI TIRANË

CLUB DIRECTORY

Klubi Sportiv Partizani
Rruga Frosina Plaku, nr.31, Tiranë
tel - (42) 25138
Year of Formation - 1946
President - Albert Xhani
Secretary - Neptun Bajko
Coach - Edmond Gëzdari; Genc Tomori
Stadium - Selman Stërmasi (12,000)

MAJOR HONOURS
League Championship - (15) 1947, 1948, 1949,
1954, 1957, 1958, 1959, 1961, 1963, 1964,
1971, 1979, 1981, 1987, 1993.
Domestic Cup - (14)
1948, 1949, 1957, 1958, 1961, 1964, 1966,
1968, 1970, 1973, 1980, 1991, 1993, 1997.

APPEARANCES 99/00

	P	Ap	(s)	Gls
Igli ALLMUÇA	D		(1)	
Artur AVDULLAI	D		(1)	
Fatmir BEGA	M	17	(5)	1
Ardit BEQIRI	D	16	(5)	
Marin BRAHO	M		(2)	
Gentian BRATJA	D	8	(8)	
Artan ÇIÇIKU	A		(4)	
Nikolin ÇOÇLLI	M	15		1
Xhelal FARUKU	A	8		1
Genti GJONDEDA	M	18	(2)	
Sokol ISHKA	A	2	(8)	1
Ilir KALARI	D	12	(1)	1
Maringlen KAPAJ	D	14	(5)	1
Edmond KAPLLANI	A	5	(8)	2
Xhevahir KAPLLANI	G	11		
Eriton KASMI	G	1		
Thoma KOKURI	G	9		
Ramiz KOLLCAKU	D	1	(2)	
Ilir KURTI	D	22		
Artan MERGJYSHI	D	12		
Ermal MERGJYSHI	G	5		
Sokol META	M	22	(1)	
Sulior MULLETI	A	8	(7)	1
Elion NUSHI	D	11		
Alban REXHA	A	24		8
Florian RIZA	A	2		
Altin RRICA	M	13		1
Nordik RUHI	D	2		
Arian SHETA	D	3		
Andi SHTREPI	A		(4)	1
Fation TAFAJ	M	2		
Alban THACI	M	4	(6)	
Ligoraq TIKO	A	13		2
Rigels TURTULLI	M	6	(1)	

LEAGUE RESULTS 1999/2000

18/09/99	Shkumbini Peqin	H	1-1	Mulleti
25/09/99	Lushnja	A	0-1	
02/10/99	Apolonia Fier	H	3-1	Rexha 2, Shtrepi
16/10/99	Elbasani	A	1-1	Rexha
23/10/99	Shqiponja Gjirokastër	H	1-2	Rexha
30/10/99	Dinamo Tiranë	A	1-2	Tiko
06/11/99	SK Tirana	H	0-0	
13/11/99	Flamurtari Vlorë	A	2-1	Tiko, Rexha
20/11/99	Vllaznia Shkodër	H	2-2	Rexha 2
24/11/99	Skënderbeu Korçë	A	0-1	
04/12/99	Teuta Durrës	H	2-0	Rrica, Çoçlli
11/12/99	Tomori Berat	A	1-2	Rexha (p)
18/12/99	Bylis Ballsh	H	0-0	
19/02/00	Shkumbini Peqin	A	0-3	
26/02/00	Lushnja	H	1-1	Kalari
04/03/00	Apolonia Fier	A	0-2	
11/03/00	Elbasani	H	2-1	Kapllani 2
18/03/00	Shqiponja Gjirokastër	A	0-3	
25/03/00	Dinamo Tiranë	H	1-0	Faruku
01/04/00	SK Tirana	A	0-3	
08/04/00	Flamurtari Vlorë	H	1-0	Bega
15/04/00	Vllaznia Shkodër	A	0-1	
22/04/00	Skënderbeu Korçë	H	2-3	Kapaj, Ishka
29/04/00	Teuta Durrës	A	0-4	
13/05/00	Tomori Berat	H	0-1	
24/05/00	Bylis Ballsh	A	0-1	

SHKUMBINI PEQIN

CLUB DIRECTORY

Klubi Sportiv Shkumbini
Pranë Bashkisë
Peqin
tel - (73) 4234
Year of Formation - 1924
President - Ferdinand Ibrahimi
Secretary - Sokol Branica
Coach - Ramadan Shehu
Stadium - Peqin (5,000)

APPEARANCES 99/00

		P	Ap	(s)	Gls
Elson BAHITI	M	13	(2)	1	
Aranit BALLHYSA	G	1	(2)		
Ervin BARDHI	A	24		6	
Klodian DERVISHI	D	18		2	
Roland DERVISHI	A	10	(7)		
Gerti DOMI	D		(2)		
Drinush ELEZI	A	7	(5)		
Klodian ELEZI	G	25			
Vladimir GJONI	A	23		14	
Gentian KAJA	D	20	(1)		
Besnik KOLA	M	24		3	
Gugash MAGANI	D	22	(1)		
Gentian MARKU	M	1	(4)		
Dritan MEHMETI	M	22	(2)		
Lorenc PASHA	M	17		1	
Çlirim SAJA	D	1	(3)		
Alferd SALLIU	M	8	(9)		
Erion STAVRE	D	20	(1)	1	
Kastriot TOSKU	D	17	(2)		
Kujtim XHAHYSI	M	1			
Saimir XHETANI	A	12	(4)	2	

LEAGUE RESULTS 1999/2000

18/09/99	Partizani Tiranë	A	1-1	Gjoni
25/09/99	Bylis Ballsh	H	1-1	Gjoni (p)
02/10/99	Lushnja	H	1-1	Gjoni
16/10/99	Apolonia Fier	A	1-1	Gjoni
23/10/99	Elbasani	H	1-0	Kola
30/10/99	Shqiponja Gjirokastër	A	1-2	Bahiti
06/11/99	Dinamo Tiranë	H	1-1	Bardhi
13/11/99	SK Tirana	A	1-3	Pasha
20/11/99	Flamurtari Vlorë	H	1-0	Stavre
24/11/99	Vllaznia Shkodër	A	1-2	Gjoni (p)
04/12/99	Skënderbeu Korçë	H	2-0	Gjoni, Bardhi
11/12/99	Teuta Durrës	A	0-2	
18/12/99	Tomori Berat	H	3-0	Dervishi K., Bardhi, Kola
19/02/00	Partizani Tiranë	H	3-0	Bardhi, Gjoni 2
26/02/00	Bylis Ballsh	A	0-1	
04/03/00	Lushnja	A	1-0	Gjoni
11/03/00	Apolonia Fier	H	2-0	Dervishi K., Gjoni
18/03/00	Elbasani	A	0-1	
25/03/00	Shqiponja Gjirokastër	H	2-0	Bardhi, og (Miho)
01/04/00	Dinamo Tiranë	A	0-3	
08/04/00	SK Tirana	H	0-1	
15/04/00	Flamurtari Vlorë	A	1-2	Xhetani
22/04/00	Vllaznia Shkodër	H	2-1	Kola, Bardhi
29/04/00	Skënderbeu Korçë	A	1-3	Gjoni (p)
13/05/00	Teuta Durrës	H	3-2	Gjoni 2, Xhetani
24/05/00	Tomori Berat	A	1-3	Gjoni (p)

SHQIPONJA GJIROKASTËR

CLUB DIRECTORY

Klubi Sportiv Shqiponja
Bashkia e qytetit
Gjirokastër
tel - (726) 3647
Year of Formation - 1930
President - Grigor Tavo
Secretary - Çaush Begaj
Coach - Faruk Sejdini
Stadium - Gjirokastra (5,000)

APPEARANCES 99/00

	P	Ap	(s)	Gls
Gentian BEGEJA	A	10		3
Klodian BRAHIMI	M	2	(2)	
Dorian BUBEQI	A	12		3
Mikel CENKO	D	15	(4)	1
Arben ÇONI	D	16	(2)	
Perparim DAIU	D	19	(1)	
Bledar DEVOLLI	M	20		2
Gentian HITAJ	M	3	(3)	
Aldrion ISLAMI	D	1	(11)	
Xhevahir KAPLLANI	G	13		
Edmond KODRA	A	19	(1)	3
Altin KORE	M	12		
Dritan KRISTIDHI	G	13		
Roland MIHO	D	23		
Dhiogjen MUÇO	M		(1)	
Astrit NEXHA	M	25		2
Nevil NORA	M	6	(16)	2
Neritan NOVI	M	22		
Kreshnik OSMANI	M	9		
Altin RRICA	M	6	(1)	
Gentian SADIKAJ	A	1	(6)	
Admir SHEHAJ	A	24	(1)	3
Altin XHUMBA	D	15		1

LEAGUE RESULTS 1999/2000

18/09/99	Vllaznia Shkodër	A	0-0	
25/09/99	Skënderbeu Korçë	H	2-0	Kodra, Bubeqi
02/10/99	Teuta Durrës	A	0-1	
16/10/99	Tomori Berat	H	0-0	
23/10/99	Partizani Tiranë	A	2-1	Devolli, Nexha
30/10/99	Shkumbini Peqin	H	2-1	Nora, Nexha
06/11/99	Lushnja	A	0-1	
13/11/99	Apolonia Fier	H	0-0	
20/11/99	Elbasani	A	0-0	
24/11/99	Bylis Ballsh	H	2-0	Xhumba, Bubeqi
04/12/99	Dinamo Tiranë	H	1-0	Bubeqi
11/12/99	SK Tirana	A	1-4	Kodra
18/12/99	Flamurtari Vlorë	H	0-0	
19/02/00	Vllaznia Shkodër	H	3-2	Shehaj, Begeja, Nora
26/02/00	Skënderbeu Korçë	A	0-1	
04/03/00	Teuta Durrës	H	0-0	
11/03/00	Tomori Berat	A	0-1	
18/03/00	Partizani Tiranë	H	3-0	og (Nushi), Shehaj, Begeja
25/03/00	Shkumbini Peqin	A	0-2	
01/04/00	Lushnja	H	1-0	Begeja
08/04/00	Apolonia Fier	A	1-2	Kodra
15/04/00	Elbasani	H	0-0	
22/04/00	Bylis Ballsh	A	1-1	Cenko
29/04/00	Dinamo Tiranë	A	1-2	Devolli
13/05/00	SK Tirana	H	1-1	Shehaj
24/05/00	Flamurtari Vlorë	A	0-1	

SKËNDERBEU KORÇË

CLUB DIRECTORY

Klubi Sportiv Skënderbeu
Rruga Gjergj Kastrioti
Korçë
tel - (824) 2241
Year of Formation - 1909
President - Vasfi Haruni
Secretary - Gjergj Ballço
Coach - Luan Deliu
Stadium - Skënderbeu (8,000)

MAJOR HONOURS
League Championship - (1) 1933.

APPEARANCES 99/00

	P	Ap	(s)	Gls
Dritan AGOLLI	G	5	(2)	
Ilir ALLIU	D	7		
Gjergj BALLÇO	A		(1)	1
Roland DEMBO	D	1	(1)	
Bardhyl DOSKU	G	10		
Altin DRITA	D	26		1
Festim FETOLLARI	M	23		1
Olsi GJIKA	G	11		
Olsi GJOKA	A	4	(3)	
Bledi KADIU	M	20	(3)	3
Edi KOLECI	M	2	(1)	
Ervin KOTOMELO	M	17	(5)	
Stavrion LAKO	D	24		
Gentian LIÇI	M	8		2
Klevis LLUKA	M	3	(9)	
Elton MALIQI	M	4	(4)	
Gjergj MEMELI	A	9	(10)	2
Rigels QOSA	A	21		12
Kastriot RUSTEMI	M	22		2
Bledi SHKEMBI	M	25		1
Gentian SPAHIU	A		(1)	
Marko THOMA	M	7	(7)	
Bledar VILA	D	11	(10)	4
Roland XHEMA	D	4		
Enkelejd ZYLA	A	22	(1)	4

LEAGUE RESULTS 1999/2000

18/09/99	Elbasani	H	2-0	Vila, Qosa
25/09/99	Shqiponja Gjirokastër	A	0-2	
02/10/99	Dinamo Tiranë	H	1-1	Qosa
16/10/99	SK Tirana	A	0-1	
23/10/99	Flamurtari Vlorë	H	2-1	Qosa, Memeli
30/10/99	Vllaznia Shkodër	A	1-2	Qosa
06/11/99	Bylis Ballsh	A	1-2	Zyla
13/11/99	Teuta Durrës	H	0-0	
20/11/99	Tomori Berat	A	0-2	
24/11/99	Partizani Tiranë	H	1-0	Rustemi
04/12/99	Shkumbini Peqin	A	0-2	
11/12/99	Lushnja	H	2-1	Kadiu, Qosa
18/12/99	Apolonia Fier	A	1-3	Qosa
19/02/00	Elbasani	A	0-0	
26/02/00	Shqiponja Gjirokastër	H	1-0	Vila
04/03/00	Dinamo Tiranë	A	0-1	
11/03/00	SK Tirana	H	0-1	
18/03/00	Flamurtari Vlorë	A	1-3	Kadiu
25/03/00	Vllaznia Shkodër	H	1-0	Zyla
01/04/00	Bylis Ballsh	H	2-1	Qosa (p), Drita
08/04/00	Teuta Durrës	A	0-2	
15/04/00	Tomori Berat	H	2-2	Fetollari, Qosa
22/04/00	Partizani Tiranë	A	3-2	Qosa 3
29/04/00	Shkumbini Peqin	H	3-1	Zyla, Qosa, Kadiu
13/05/00	Lushnja	A	2-3	Rustemi, Vila
24/05/00	Apolonia Fier	H	7-0	Memeli, Zyla, Liçi 2, Ballço, Vila (p), Shkembi

TEUTA DURRËS

CLUB DIRECTORY

Klubi Sportiv Teuta
Rruga Mujo Ulqinaku, nr.19
Lagja 12
Durrës
tel - (52) 23631
Year of Formation - 1920
President - Edmond Hasanbelliu
Secretary - Maksut Leshteni
Coach - Hasan Lika
Stadium - Niko Dovana (12,000)

MAJOR HONOURS
League Championship - (1) 1994.
Domestic Cup - (2) 1995, 2000.

APPEARANCES 99/00

	P	Ap	(s)	Gls
Neritan BABAMUSTA	M	18	(2)	1
Gentian BEGEJA	A	10		2
Justin BESPALLA	A	12	(12)	8
Gazmend ÇANAKU	D	12	(4)	
Elton CENO	A	5	(1)	
Giovanni DA SILVA (BRA)	A	8	(4)	3
Oert KOTE	D	15	(6)	1
Fatos KUCI	D	13	(3)	
Suad LICI	M	21		4
Edi LILA	D	1	(4)	
Kreshnik MANÇE	A		(9)	
Bujar MUÇA	M	24		3
Sokol PRENGA	M	17		2
Habib REXHEPI	M	19	(3)	
Orges SHEHI	G	25		
Arian SHETA	D	4	(6)	1
Gentian STOJKU	D	15	(2)	5
Afrim TOLE	A	20		1
Marenglen XHAI	M	24		3
Arian ZERE	D	12		

LEAGUE RESULTS 1999/2000

18/09/99	Apolonia Fier	H	4-0	Xhai, Muça, Bespalla 2
25/09/99	Elbasani	A	1-2	Stojku
02/10/99	Shqiponja Gjirokastër	H	1-0	Tole
16/10/99	Dinamo Tiranë	A	2-1	Begeja (p), Lici
23/10/99	SK Tirana	H	1-0	Begeja (p)
30/10/99	Flamurtari Vlorë	A	0-1	
06/11/99	Vllaznia Shkodër	H	1-0	Lici
13/11/99	Skënderbeu Korçë	A	0-0	
20/11/99	Bylis Ballsh	A	2-0	(w/o)
24/11/99	Tomori Berat	H	2-0	Stojku, Bespalla
04/12/99	Partizani Tiranë	A	0-2	
11/12/99	Shkumbini Peqin	H	2-0	Xhai, Sheta
18/12/99	Lushnja	A	2-3	Bespalla, Muça
19/02/00	Apolonia Fier	A	1-0	Bespalla
26/02/00	Elbasani	H	1-0	Muça
04/03/00	Shqiponja Gjirokastër	A	0-0	
11/03/00	Dinamo Tiranë	H	1-1	Xhai
18/03/00	SK Tirana	A	0-1	
25/03/00	Flamurtari Vlorë	H	3-0	Prenga 2, Da Silva
01/04/00	Vllaznia Shkodër	A	0-2	
08/04/00	Skënderbeu Korçë	H	2-0	Stojku, Da Silva
15/04/00	Bylis Ballsh	H	2-0	Stojku, Bespalla
22/04/00	Tomori Berat	A	0-0	
29/04/00	Partizani Tiranë	H	4-0	Da Silva, Stojku, Bespalla 2
13/05/00	Shkumbini Peqin	A	2-3	Lici, Babamusta
24/05/00	Lushnja	H	2-0	Lici, Kote

SK TIRANA

CLUB DIRECTORY

Klubi Sportiv Tirana
Stadiumi Selman Stërmasi
Tiranë
tel - (42) 33299
Year of Formation - 1920
President - El Sayed Metwali Abdel Rahman
Secretary - Sulejman Mema
Coach - Shkëlqim Muça
Stadium - Selman Stërmasi (12,000)

MAJOR HONOURS
League Championship - (19)
1930, 1931, 1932, 1934, 1936, 1965, 1966,
1967, 1968, 1970, 1982, 1985, 1988, 1989,
1995, 1996, 1997, 1999, 2000.
Domestic Cup - (9) 1963, 1976, 1977, 1983,
1984, 1986, 1994, 1996, 1999.

APPEARANCES 99/00

	P	Ap	(s)	Gls
Krenar ALIMEHMETI	D	26		4
Ervin BULKU	D	10	(10)	
Sokol BULKU	M	11	(5)	
Rezart DABULLA	D	23		1
Nevil DEDE	D	23	(1)	5
Johan DRIZA	D	11		
Alpin GALLO	D	2	(1)	
Isli HIDI	G		(1)	
Sokol ISHKA	A		(4)	
Julian KAPAJ	M		(2)	
Zoltán KENESEI (HUN)	M	10		
Matyós LAZAR (HUN)	M		(2)	
Gentian LIÇI	M	5	(5)	
Ardian MEMA	M	24		6
Enkli MEMISHI	M	10	(14)	2
Blendi NALLBANI	G	26		
Sokol PRENGA	M	5		1
Florian RIZA	A	5	(9)	1
Erion RIZVANOLLI	A	21	(5)	7
Nordik RUHI	D	1	(2)	
Elvis SINA	D	25		1
Péter SUTORI (HUN)	M	3	(2)	
Alban TAFAJ	D	22		1
Anesti VITO	A	19	(1)	8
László VUKOVICS (HUN)	A		(2)	
Fation YMERI	A	4	(4)	2

LEAGUE RESULTS 1999/2000

18/09/99	Bylis Ballsh	A	0-0	
25/09/99	Flamurtari Vlorë	H	2-0	Rizvanolli, Mema
02/10/99	Vllaznia Shkodër	A	2-0	Rizvanolli, Prenga
16/10/99	Skënderbeu Korçë	H	1-0	Mema
23/10/99	Teuta Durrës	A	0-1	
30/10/99	Tomori Berat	H	0-0	
06/11/99	Partizani Tiranë	A	0-0	
13/11/99	Shkumbini Peqin	H	3-1	Memishi, Dede, Vito
20/11/99	Lushnja	A	0-2	
24/11/99	Apolonia Fier	H	7-0	Alimehmeti 2 (1p), Rizvanolli 2, Dede 2, Vito
04/12/99	Elbasani	A	0-1	
11/12/99	Shqiponja Gjirokastër	H	4-1	Mema, Tafaj, Sina, Riza
18/12/99	Dinamo Tiranë	A	2-1	Alimehmeti (p), Dabulla
19/02/00	Bylis Ballsh	H	2-0	Vito 2
26/02/00	Flamurtari Vlorë	A	0-1	
04/03/00	Vllaznia Shkodër	H	1-0	Dede
11/03/00	Skënderbeu Korçë	A	1-0	Rizvanolli
18/03/00	Teuta Durrës	H	1-0	Memishi
25/03/00	Tomori Berat	A	0-1	
01/04/00	Partizani Tiranë	H	3-0	Ymeri, Vito, Mema
08/04/00	Shkumbini Peqin	A	1-0	Ymeri
15/04/00	Lushnja	H	2-1	og (Dhima), Rizvanolli
22/04/00	Apolonia Fier	A	1-2	Dede
29/04/00	Elbasani	H	2-1	Mema 2
13/05/00	Shqiponja Gjirokastër	A	1-1	Alimehmeti (p)
24/05/00	Dinamo Tiranë	H	4-0	Rizvanolli, Vito 3

TOMORI BERAT

CLUB DIRECTORY

Klubi Sportiv Tomori
Lagjja 30 vjetori
Stadiumi Tomori
Berat
tel - (623) 2627
Year of Formation - 1923
President - vacant
Secretary - Ismet Ajazi
Coach - Theodhori Arbri
Stadium - Tomori (14,750)

APPEARANCES 99/00

	P	Ap	(s)	Gls
Eduard ALIAJ	D	8	(1)	
Klodian ARBRI	A	25		18
Klodian ASLLANI	A	10		
Afrim ÇALA	M	16	(3)	
Altin ÇUKO	A	1	(3)	
Afrim DELIU	D	21		
Klodian DINO	D	18	(3)	1
Arben DURO	G	1		
Elton FANI	D	16	(3)	
Gëzim GEGA	M	13	(5)	
Edmond GJATA	A	14	(6)	
Besnik HASA	M	21	(2)	
Luan JAHJA	M	10	(3)	
Nurian KANANI	D	1	(2)	
Gentian LAKO	D	19		3
Gentian MALASI	M		(2)	
Sajmir MALOKU	A	25		7
Madrit MUZHAJ	G	24		2
Eljon NUSHI	M	7	(4)	
Shkëlzen RUSTEMI	M	11	(1)	
Ronaldo TABAKU	M	7	(13)	1
Arjan ZERE	M	7		1

LEAGUE RESULTS 1999/2000

18/09/99	Lushnja	H	3-2	Maloku, Arbri 2
25/09/99	Apolonia Fier	A	0-0	
02/10/99	Elbasani	H	2-0	Lako, Arbri
16/10/99	Shqiponja Gjirokastër	A	0-0	
23/10/99	Dinamo Tiranë	H	2-1	Maloku, Tabaku
30/10/99	SK Tirana	A	0-0	
06/11/99	Flamurtari Vlorë	H	2-1	Maloku, Arbri
13/11/99	Vllaznia Shkodër	A	0-1	
20/11/99	Skënderbeu Korçë	H	2-0	Arbri, Lako
24/11/99	Teuta Durrës	A	0-2	
04/12/99	Bylis Ballsh	A	0-1	
11/12/99	Partizani Tiranë	H	2-1	Zëre, Arbri
18/12/99	Shkumbini Peqin	A	0-3	
19/02/00	Lushnja	A	1-1	Arbri
26/02/00	Apolonia Fier	H	2-0	Arbri 2
04/03/00	Elbasani	A	1-0	Arbri
11/03/00	Shqiponja Gjirokastër	H	1-0	Lako
18/03/00	Dinamo Tiranë	A	3-3	Maloku, Arbri, Muzhaj (p)
25/03/00	SK Tirana	H	1-0	Muzhaj (p)
01/04/00	Flamurtari Vlorë	A	1-0	Arbri
08/04/00	Vllaznia Shkodër	H	2-0	(w/o)
15/04/00	Skënderbeu Korçë	A	2-2	Arbri, Dino
22/04/00	Teuta Durrës	H	0-0	
29/04/00	Bylis Ballsh	H	4-3	Maloku, Arbri 3
13/05/00	Partizani Tiranë	A	1-0	Arbri
24/05/00	Shkumbini Peqin	H	3-1	Maloku 2, Arbri

VLLAZNIA SHKODËR

CLUB DIRECTORY

Klubi Sportiv Vllaznia
Lagja Kongresi i Përmetit
Shkodër
tel - (224) 2305
Year of Formation - 1919
President - Myftar Çela
Secretary - Ismet Hoxha
Coach - Ramazan Rragami
Stadium - Loro Boriçi (15,000)

MAJOR HONOURS
League Championship - (8) 1945, 1946, 1972,
1974, 1978, 1983, 1992, 1998.
Domestic Cup - (5)
1965, 1972, 1979, 1981, 1987.

APPEARANCES 99/00

	P	Ap	(s)	Gls
Amarildo BELISHA	M	2	(7)	
Brikeno BIZI	M	13	(1)	2
Dorian BYLYKBASHI	A	10		7
Armando CUNGU	M	22		1
Ilir DIBRA	A	22	(1)	
Edmond DOÇI	D	1	(4)	
Klodian DURO	M	9		1
Armir GRIMA	G	11		
Shpëtim GRUDA	M	6	(3)	
Salvador KAÇAJ	M		(8)	
Uliks KOTRRI	M	1		
Elvis KRUJA	A	14	(3)	5
Edi MARTINI	A	6	(2)	8
Gjovalin MUÇIÇI	M	5		
Arjan MUSTAFA	G	13		
Edmir NDOJA	G	1	(1)	
Alban NEZIRI	M	4	(1)	
Alban NOGA	D	18		
Safet OSJA	D	25		1
Kreshnik OSMANI	A	11	(1)	
Leonard PERLOSHI	D	10	(1)	1
Elvis PLORI	M	6	(9)	1
Astrit PREMÇI	D	22		
Armando SHLLAKU	A	6		1
Alban VOLUMI	A	1	(6)	
Altin XHAHYSA	M	12	(5)	1
Luan ZMIJANI	D	24		

LEAGUE RESULTS 1999/2000

18/09/99	Shqiponja Gjirokastër	H	0-0	
25/09/99	Dinamo Tiranë	A	2-0	Kruja 2
02/10/99	SK Tirana	H	0-2	
16/10/99	Flamurtari Vlorë	A	1-3	Kruja
23/10/99	Bylis Ballsh	A	1-2	Shllaku
30/10/99	Skënderbeu Korçë	H	2-1	Martini 2
06/11/99	Teuta Durrës	A	0-1	
13/11/99	Tomori Berat	H	1-0	Perloshi
20/11/99	Partizani Tiranë	A	2-2	Martini 2
24/11/99	Shkumbini Peqin	H	2-1	Martini 2
04/12/99	Lushnja	A	1-1	Cungu
11/12/99	Apolonia Fier	H	1-0	Martini
18/12/99	Elbasani	A	2-1	Kruja, Martini
19/02/00	Shqiponja Gjirokastër	A	2-3	Bylykbashi 2
26/02/00	Dinamo Tiranë	H	0-0	
04/03/00	SK Tirana	A	0-1	
11/03/00	Flamurtari Vlorë	H	3-1	Bylykbashi 2, Plori
18/03/00	Bylis Ballsh	H	1-0	Bizi
25/03/00	Skënderbeu Korçë	A	0-1	
01/04/00	Teuta Durrës	H	2-0	Osja, Duro
08/04/00	Tomori Berat	A	0-2	(w/o)
15/04/00	Partizani Tiranë	H	1-0	Bylykbashi
22/04/00	Shkumbini Peqin	A	1-2	Xhahysa
29/04/00	Lushnja	H	3-0	Bylykbashi 2, Bizi
13/05/00	Apolonia Fier	A	0-2	
24/05/00	Elbasani	H	1-2	Kruja

ANDORRA

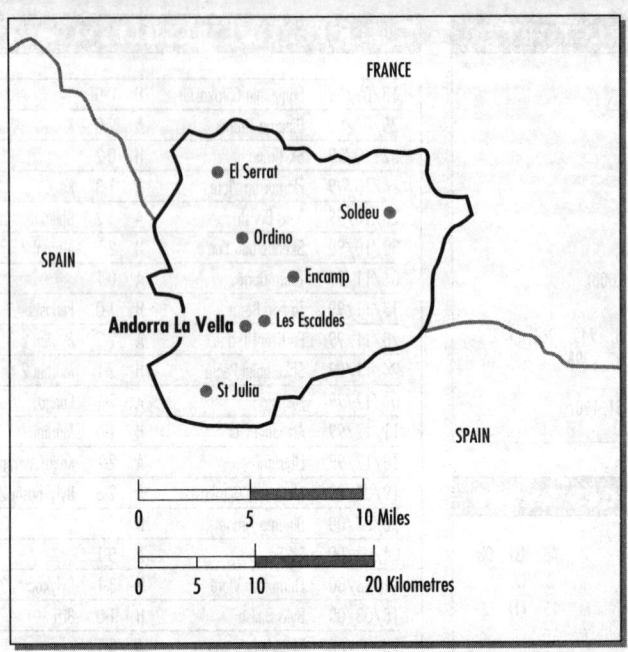

DIFFERENT CHAMPIONS, SAME TEAM

Andorra break duck with first win

FEDERATION DIRECTORY

Federació Andorrana de Futbol
C/ Sant Salvador 10 - 2 - 5, Edifici Galerias Plaza, Andorra la Vella

tel - (376) 862003
fax - (376) 862006

Year of Formation - 1994
President - Francesc Vila Circuns
Secretary - Tomás Gea

Stadium - Comunal (1,140)

It took them 25 matches to do it, but on April 26, 2000 the Andorran national team finally recorded their first victory. It came in a friendly at home to Belarus, with midfielder Jesús Lucendo and striker Juli Sánchez scoring twice within a five-minute purple patch around the hour mark to seal an historic 2-0 triumph.

Andorra were actually on something of a roll, having drawn each of their two previous internationals, against Malta (1-1) and Azerbaijan (0-0) at the Rothmans tournament. Prior to that three-match unbeaten run the team from the Principality had played 22 games and lost 20 of them.

Andorra duly completed their début European Championship campaign without a point, but they did give Russia quite a scare when they went down narrowly at home, 1-2, in their penultimate match. The late-season form intimated that Andorra's first World Cup qualifying campaign might not turn out to be another whitewash, especially with Lucenda, the country's only genuinely technically gifted player, having been successfully persuaded to return to the side by coach David Rodrigo.

The Andorran championship in 1999/2000 was a comical affair. The league authorities had reduced the top two divisions to eight teams each in a bid to make them more balanced and competitive. But, as far as the top flight was concerned, the change had the opposite effect. Constelació Esportiva won the title with a perfect record, playing 12 games and winning the lot. In reality, they actually won 13 out of 13, but a 7-0 victory over CE Benito was annulled when the latter withdrew during the winter break.

Constelació's success was not surprising because at the

LEAGUE CHAMPIONSHIP RESULTS 99/00

		1	2	3	4	5	6	7
1	Constelació Esportiva		10-0	2-0	6-2	5-0	2-1	11-0
2	FC Encamp	1-2		1-2	7-2	2-2	0-2	5-3
3	CM Inter d'Escaldes	1-8	1-1		3-1	2-1	0-6	5-1
4	CE Principat	0-5	1-4	0-5		2-3	0-3	1-0
5	UE Sant Julià	0-8	0-4	2-5	1-0		0-2	11-0
6	FC Santa Coloma	0-2	3-1	2-0	4-0	3-1		6-1
7	Sporting d'Escaldes	1-9	1-7	0-0	0-7	3-2	2-2	

LEAGUE CHAMPIONSHIP FINAL TABLE 99/00

		Pd	W	D	L	F	A	W	D	L	F	A	W	D	L	F	A	Pt	GD
1	Constelació Esportiva	12	6	0	0	36	3	6	0	0	34	3	12	0	0	70	6	36	64
2	FC Santa Coloma	12	5	0	1	18	5	4	1	1	16	4	9	1	2	34	9	28	25
3	CM Inter d'Escaldes	12	3	1	2	12	18	3	1	2	12	7	6	2	4	24	25	20	-1
4	FC Encamp	12	2	1	3	16	13	3	1	2	17	16	5	2	5	33	29	17	4
5	UE Sant Julià	12	2	0	4	14	19	1	1	4	9	17	3	1	8	23	36	10	-13
6	CE Principat	12	1	0	5	4	20	1	0	5	12	21	2	0	10	16	41	6	-25
7	Sporting d'Escaldes	12	1	2	3	7	27	0	0	6	5	39	1	2	9	12	66	5	-54

N.B. CE Benito withdrew during the winter break; all their matches were declared null and void.

NATIONAL TEAM APPEARANCES 99/00

Coach - David RODRIGO	POR	ISL	RUS	ARM	ALB	MLT	AZB	BLS	Cps	Gls
Alfonso SANCHEZ (27/09/74) - CF Tapia (ESP)	G								2	-
Agusti POL Pérez (13/01/77) - CF Santaboja (ESP)	D88	M90	s59	s56					18	1
Francisco Xavier RAMIREZ Palomo (07/09/76) - FC Andorra (ESP)	D	D	D	D	D	D	D	D	16	-
Antonio LIMA Sola (22/09/70) - CF Hospitalet (ESP)	D			D	D	D	D	D	18	1
José Manuel García Luena "TXEMA" (04/12/74) - FC Andorra (ESP)	D68	D	D	D58	D	D	D56	D	22	-
Ildefons LIMA Sola (10/12/79) - RCD Espanyol B (ESP)	M		M	M		M	M	M	19	-
EMILIANO González Arquez (20/09/69) - FC Andorra (ESP)	M73	M	M	M62	M71	M89	M64	M88	15	-
Oscar SONEJEE Masan (26/03/76) - FC Andorra (ESP)	M80	M	M	M	M	M	M	s85	21	1
Justo RUIZ González (31/08/69) - FC Andorra (ESP)	M		M	M	M	M	M	M	19	1
Manolo JIMENEZ (12/08/76) - FC Andorra (ESP)	A65	A	A	A	A77	A80	A	s75	17	-
Juli SANCHEZ Soto (20/06/78) - FC Andorra (ESP)	A	A	A89	A	A	A	A	A	21	2
Genis GARCIA Iscza (18/05/78) - FC Andorra (ESP)	s65	s67							9	-
Angel Martin GARCIA (25/11/78) - FC Andorra (ESP)	s68	D59							16	-
Alex GODOY - FC Andorra (ESP)	s73	M67	M59	M56					4	-
Jordi ESCURZA Aixas (19/04/80) - CF Europa Barcelona (ESP)	s80	D	D	D	D	D	D	D85	10	-
Jordi BENET - FC Andorra (ESP)	s88								1	-
Jesús Luis Alvarez de Fukate "KOLDO" (04/09/70) - FC Andorra (ESP)		G	G	G	G	G	G	G	20	-
Armand GODOY - FC Andorra (ESP)		s59	s89						2	-
David BUXO (1982) - FC Andorra (ESP)		s90		s71					2	-
Roberto JONAS Alonso (1977) - FC Andorra (ESP)					s58			D	3	-
Francisco Xavier SORIA - FC Andorra (ESP)					s62	s77	s56		3	-
Josep FELIX ALVAREZ Blazquez (10/07/66) - Constelació Esportiva					M85			s88	4	-
Marc PUJOL (1982)					s85	s89	s64		3	-
Gerard DIAZ Juanez (12/09/76)						s80			1	-
Jesús Julian LUCENDO Heredia (19/04/70) - FC Andorra (ESP)								A75	15	3

start of the season they looted previous champions CE Principat of just about all of their players. So, effectively, although Constelació became the new champions of Andorra, the players who took the title were largely the same ones who had triumphed 12 months earlier. Just to prove their massive supremacy over the rest, Constelació ended the season by thrashing FC Encamp 6-0 in the Cup final to complete the most comprehensive of 'doubles' - this despite playing most of the game with ten men and ending it, like their opponents, with nine.

NATIONAL TEAM RESULTS 99/00

18/08/99	Portugal	A	Lisbon	0-4	
04/09/99	Iceland (ECQ)	A	Reykjavík	0-3	
08/09/99	Russia (ECQ)	H	Andorra La Vella	1-2	Ruiz (39p)
09/10/99	Armenia (ECQ)	H	Andorra La Vella	0-3	
06/02/00	Albania	N	Ta' Qali	0-3	
08/02/00	Malta	A	Ta' Qali	1-1	Sonejee (2)
16/02/00	Azerbaijan	A	Ta' Qali	0-0	
26/04/00	Belarus	H	Andorra La Vella	2-0	Lucendo (57p), Sánchez (62)

DOMESTIC CUP 99/00

FINAL
04/06/2000, Andorra La Vella
CONSTELACIO ESPORTIVA 6 Barra (8), Bardina (13), Félix (45), Sivera (68), Aladino (87p), Sánchez (89), FC ENCAMP 0
referee - Mengual
CONSTELACIO ESPORTIVA - Iñaki, Pablo, Andrés, Coto, Sánchez, Félix, Richard (Sivera 46), Lorenzatti, Barra (Edu 69), Minguella, Bardina (Aladino 23).
FC ENCAMP - Paulo, Cristo (Rubén 45), Hugo, Juan, Jesús, Miguel (Zani 46), Santi, Osvaldo, Andrés (Felipe 46), Joao, Alex.

EUROPEAN CUPS 99/00

UEFA CUP
● CE PRINCIPAT
Qualifying round VIKING FK (NOR)
A 0-7
    Iñaki, Pablo (Guillamo 63), Andres, Coto, Luis, Patri, Richard (Guardiola 75), Felix, Paski (Villarubla 49), Minguella, Diego.

H 0-11
    Iñaki, Luis, Pablo, Coto (Roca 46), Canito, Richard, Lorenzati (Marin 73), Felix, Minguella, Patri, Paski (Titos 68).

ARMENIA

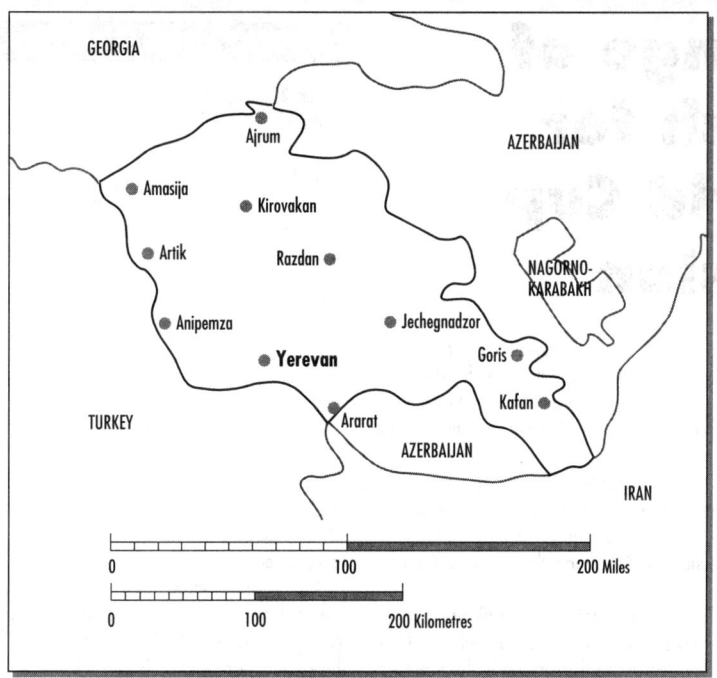

GEORGIA

Ajrum

AZERBAIJAN

Amasija

Kirovakan

Artik

Razdan

NAGORNO-
KARABAKH

Anipemza

Jechegnadzor

Yerevan

Goris

Kafan

TURKEY

Ararat

AZERBAIJAN

IRAN

| 0 | | 100 | | 200 Miles |

| 0 | 100 | 200 Kilometres |

SHIRAK TRIUMPH IN CHAOTIC FINALE

Change of coach for World Cup mission

FEDERATION DIRECTORY

Football Federation of Armenia
Saryun Street 38, 375010 Yerevan

tel - (3741) 535084
fax - (3741) 151573

Year of Formation - 1934
President - Suren Abrahamyan
Secretary - Armen Hovhannisyan

Stadium - Razdan, Yerevan (48,256)

Armenia ended the Euro 2000 qualifying campaign with a respectable total of eight points. They finished the ten-match series as they had begun it, with a three-goal victory over Andorra. In between, the only positive results had been two goalless draws at home to Iceland and Ukraine, but perhaps the greatest satisfaction was gained by the 2-3 defeat against eventual winners France - a match watched by 35,000 enthusiastic Armenians in which the home side led for almost the whole of the first half.

A new coach was appointed to the national side in December 1999 when Varuzhan Sukiasyan, who had led Tsement Ararat to three domestic trophies in the previous 18 months while also serving the Armenian FA as the national Under-21 coach, took over from Suren Barsegyan, whose contract was not renewed after the European Championship campaign. Sukiasyan's mission will be to collect as many points as possible from an evenly-balanced World Cup qualifying group that contains Norway, Ukraine, Poland, Wales and Belarus.

The crowds are sure to turn up in their continued thousands to watch the national team in the Razdan Stadium but there is very little interest in the domestic league, which is no wonder given the bizarre goings-on which discoloured the conclusion to the 1999 Premier League season.

An intriguing three-way contest between title-holders Tsement and the country's other two top clubs, Ararat Yerevan and Shirak Gyumri, ended in farce when in the penultimate round Tsement beat Shirak 1-0 with a penalty awarded ten minutes into stoppage-time. As it stood, the result effectively guaranteed Tsement the title (and a second successive calendar-year 'double'), but the league authorities decided that the referee had been

LEAGUE CHAMPIONSHIP RESULTS 1999

		1	2	3	4	5	6	7	8	9
1	Ararat Yerevan		3-0	1-0	3-0	2-1	0-4	1-0	1-0	3-0
			4-1	5-2	5-1	0-0	1-0	1-1	3-0	3-1
2	Dvin Artashat	0-2		1-3	2-1	1-1	1-3	0-3	0-5	0-3
		0-3		0-3	0-3	0-3	0-4	0-3	1-6	0-1
3	Erebuni Yerevan	0-2	2-0		3-0	5-0	0-3	0-3	0-0	0-0
		0-1	3-0		3-0	2-0	1-2	1-7	0-1	0-1
4	FK Gyumri	0-7	3-7	0-2		0-2	0-6	1-6	2-1	1-3
		1-2	1-1	0-6		0-2	3-4	0-3	2-2	1-2
5	Kilikia Yerevan	0-1	7-1	0-2	9-0		2-3	0-1	2-1	0-0
		1-4	5-0	2-0	5-0		0-3	1-0	2-4	1-2
6	Shirak Gyumri	1-2	4-1	1-0	5-0	3-1		0-1	1-0	2-1
		1-1	11-1	6-0	3-0	4-2		1-0	5-0	4-1
7	Tsement Ararat	2-0	5-1	1-2	3-1	3-1	2-0		1-1	1-0
		0-0	7-0	4-1	8-0	1-1	0-0		2-0	3-2
8	FK Yerevan	0-0	2-0	0-0	6-0	4-2	1-1	0-2		1-0
		1-0	3-0	3-0	6-2	5-3	2-1	1-2		2-3
9	Zvartnots Yerevan	1-1	6-1	0-0	1-0	1-0	4-6	1-0	1-2	
		2-1	3-0	0-0	2-0	2-1	1-1	1-3	4-0	

INTERNATIONAL HONOURS

None

DOMESTIC CUP 99/00

FINAL
27/05/2000, Abovyan
MIKA ASHTARAK 2 Mkrchyan (33), Nordikyan (75)
ZVARTNOTS YEREVAN 1 Avanesyan (44)
referee - Nalbandyan
MIKA ASHTARAK - Aslanyan, Petikyan, Dallakyan, Avanesyan, Babayan (Nordikyan 61), Hayrapetyan (Muradyan 54), Markosyan, Mkrchyan, Khashmanyan, Nikolyan (Hovhannisyan 84), Adjemyan.
ZVARTNOTS YEREVAN - Yeritsyan, Narimanyan, Mkrchyan, Mirijanyan, Adamyan (Nazaryan 25), Gevorgyan, Lobyan (Hovhannisyan 80), Asoyan, Arzumanyan, Khachmanyan, Avanesyan.

LEAGUE CHAMPIONSHIP FINAL TABLE 1999

		Pd	W	D	L	F	A	W	D	L	F	A	W	D	L	F	A	Pt	GD
1	Shirak Gyumri	32	13	1	2	52	11	10	3	3	41	18	23	4	5	93	29	73	64
2	Ararat Yerevan	32	13	2	1	36	11	9	4	3	27	10	22	6	4	63	21	72	42
3	Tsement Ararat	32	11	4	1	43	10	11	1	4	35	9	22	5	5	78	19	71	59
4	Zvartnots Yerevan	32	9	4	3	30	16	7	2	7	20	22	16	6	10	50	38	54	12
5	FK Yerevan	32	10	3	3	37	16	5	3	8	23	27	15	6	11	60	43	51	17
6	Erebuni Yerevan	32	6	2	8	20	20	6	3	7	21	24	12	5	15	41	44	41	-3
7	Kilikia Yerevan	32	7	1	8	37	22	3	3	10	20	33	10	4	18	57	55	34	2
8	Dvin Artashat	32	1	1	14	6	47	1	1	4	14	69	2	2	28	20	116	8	-96
9	FK Gyumri	32	1	2	13	15	56	1	0	15	8	64	2	2	28	23	120	8	-97

N.B. Karabakh Stepanakert expelled after 15 matches; all their results declared null and void.

Promotion/Relegation Play-off - Mika Ashtarak 1, Kilkia Yerevan 0

TOP SCORERS

21	Shirak SARIKYAN (Tsement Ararat)
20	Arman KARAMYAN (Kilikia Yerevan)
16	Ara ADAMYAN (Shirak Gyumri)
	Mher AVANESYAN (Zvartnots Yerevan)
	Kolia YEPRANOSYAN (Shirak Gyumri)
15	Artyom BERNETSYAN (Shirak Gyumri)
13	Artur PETROSYAN (Shirak Gyumri)
	Karen BARSEGYAN (Ararat Yerevan)
12	Varazdat AVETISYAN (FK Yerevan)
	Sergei ERZRUMYAN (Kilikia Yerevan)

NATIONAL TEAM RESULTS 99/00

18/08/99	Estonia	A	Pärnu	0-2	
04/09/99	Russia (ECQ)	A	Moscow	0-2	
08/09/99	France (ECQ)	H	Yerevan	2-3	Mikaelyan (6), Shahgeldyan (90p)
09/10/99	Andorra (ECQ)	A	Andorra La Vella	3-0	Petrosyan A. (26), Yesayan (59), Shahgeldyan (63)
09/01/00	Guatemala	N	Los Angeles	1-1	Manukyan (20)
02/02/00	Moldova	N	Larnaca	2-1	Nazaryan (45), Dokhoyan (95)
04/02/00	Cyprus	A	Nicosia	2-3	Petrosyan A. (50), Karamyan Arm. (74)
06/02/00	Georgia	N	Limassol	1-2	Khachatryan V. (44)
26/04/00	Georgia	H	Yerevan	0-0	
03/06/00	Lithuania	A	Kaunas	2-1	Movsesyan (5), Petrosyan A. (29)

EUROPEAN CUPS 99/00

CHAMPIONS' CUP
● **TSEMENT ARARAT**
Preliminary round 1 ZALGIRIS VILNIUS (LIT)
A 0-2
> Dadamyan, Hayrapetyan, Nazaryan, Simonyan, Hovhannisyan (Hokhoyan 46), Harutyunyan, Hakopyan Ara (Hakopyan H. 55), Khachatryan, Voskanyan, Minasyan (Melikyan 66), Asatryan.

H 0-3
> Avagyan, Hayrapetyan, Nazaryan, Simonyan, Grigoryan, Hakopyan Ara, Hakopyan H., Khachatryan (Asatryan 32), Voskanyan (Arzumanyan 36), Minasyan (Hokhoyan 56), Hakopyan Aram.

UEFA CUP
● **FK YEREVAN**
Qualifying round HAPOEL TEL-AVIV (ISR)
H 0-2
> Kuznetsov, Mkryan, Babayan, Yesayan (Gogoladze 85), Ladouce (Aptsiauri 46), Gvasalia, Avetisyan, Kocharyan, Dokhoyan K., Dokhoyan A. (Gamtsemliadze 78), Danielyan.

A 1-2 Gogoladze (50)
> Kuznetsov, Ayvazyan, Petikyan, Babayan, Yesayan (Dokhoyan A. 70), Ladouce, Gvasalia (Poghosyan 84), Dokhoyan K., Delani, Gamtsemliadze, Gogoladze.

● **SHIRAK GYUMRI**
Qualifying round HJK (FIN)
A 0-2
> Abrahamyan (Hovhannisyan 19), Margaryan, Demirtshyan, Artoyan, Aleksanyan, Tahmazyan, Yepranosyan (Tumasyan 90), Avanesyan, Bernetsyan, Khodgoyan, Harutyunyan (Badikyan 63).

H 1-0 Bernetsyan (28)
> Hovhannisyan, Margaryan, Demirtshyan, Nikolyan, Aleksanyan, Tahmazyan, Yepranosyan (Tumasyan 78), Avanesyan, Bernetsyan (Adamyan 67), Khodgoyan, Harutyunyan.

biased and ordered a re-match. Nine days later, with all the other matches completed, the two teams met again and drew 0-0. That was the result Shirak needed to take the title by one point from Ararat and two from Tsement.

None of the top three in the league made it into the final of the Cup five months later. Tsement (under their new name of Araks) and Ararat were both eliminated by newly-promoted Mika Ashtarak, who completed their unexpected triumph with a 2-1 victory over Zvartnots Yerevan in the final.

NATIONAL TEAM APPEARANCES 99/00

Coach - Suren BARSEGYAN; Varuzhan SUKIASYAN	EST	RUS	FRA	AND	GUA	MOL	CYP	GEO	GEO	LIT	Cps	Gls
Roman BEREZOVSKI (05/08/74) - Zenit Sankt-Peterburg (RUS)	G	G	G				G	G	s46		22	-
Karen BARSEGYAN (15/03/75) - Ararat Yerevan	D										2	1
Vardan KHACHATRYAN (29/10/68) - Rubin Kazan (RUS)	D	D	D			D	D	D			29	1
Artur MKRCHYAN (09/08/73) - Krylya Sovetov Samara (RUS)	D	D	D	D		D63	D			s67	15	-
Romik KHACHATRYAN (23/08/78) - Tsement Ararat	M	M84	M74	M	M	M	M	M	M	M	10	-
Artur PETROSYAN (17/12/71)												
- Lokomotiv Nizhniy Novgorod (RUS)/Shirak Gyumri	M83			M79	M	M	M89	M	M79	M	45	5
Tigran PETROSYAN (23/12/73) - Krylya Sovetov Samara (RUS)	M87	s84	M	M82	M				M56		8	-
Hovhannes TAHMAZYAN (11/01/70) - Shirak Gyumri	M										1	-
Karen ASATRYAN (21/12/74) - Tsement Ararat	M									s79	2	-
Tigran YESAYAN (02/06/72) - FK Yerevan	A77		A	A							20	4
Karapet MIKAELYAN (27/09/69) - Krylya Sovetov Samara (RUS)	A77	A	A67								20	2
Haik HAKOPYAN (26/12/80) - Tsement Ararat	s77										2	-
Artur KOCHARYAN (14/09/74) - Zvartnots Yerevan	s77		s74	s82							3	-
Karen DOKHOYAN (06/10/76) - FK Yerevan	s83					s57	M	M		M	5	1
Ara HAKOPYAN (04/11/80) - Tsement Ararat	s87		s79	A	s46		s78	A68			7	-
Sarkis HOVSEPYAN (02/11/72) - Zenit Sankt-Peterburg (RUS)		D	D			D	D	D	D		43	-
Sarkis HOVHANNISYAN (17/08/68) - Lokomotiv Moskva (RUS)		D									15	-
Harutyun VARDANYAN (05/12/70) - Fortuna Köln (GER)		D		D	D				D	D	37	1
Haik HARUTYUNYAN (10/12/74) - Tsement Ararat		M54	M63								6	-
Artur VOSKANYAN (13/08/76) - Uralan Elista (RUS)		M		M					M	M	8	-
Armen SHAHGELDYAN (28/08/73) - Lausanne-Sports (SUI)		A77	A	A78					A	A	27	4
Manuk KAKOSYAN (01/08/74) - Zhemchuzhina Sochi (RUS)		s54									3	-
Marcelo DELANI (22/06/76) - FK Yerevan		s77	s67								2	-
Albert SARKISYAN (15/05/75) - Lokomotiv Moskva (RUS)			M	M							14	-
Razmik GRIGORYAN (11/10/71) - Tsement Ararat			s63								14	2
Harutyun ABRAHAMYAN (28/08/71) - Ararat Yerevan				G	G			G46	G	G	20	-
Yervand SUKIASYAN (20/01/67) - BV Cloppenburg (GER)				D	D				D	D	27	-
Artur MINASYAN (04/06/77) - Ararat Yerevan				s78		M	M87				12	-
Armen PETIKYAN (19/02/72) - Mika Ashtarak					D					s78	2	-
Felik KHODGOYAN (22/12/75) - Shirak Gyumri					Mi				M	M	9	1
Gagik MANUKYAN (16/08/75) - Tsement Ararat					Mii		s102				4	1
Rafael NAZARYAN (26/03/75) - Tsement Ararat					M	M	s87	M			8	1
Artavazd KARAMYAN (17/11/79) - Kilikia Yerevan					si		M102	M	s56		4	-
Arman KARAMYAN (07/11/79) - Kilikia Yerevan					sii	s70	A96	s43	s68		5	1
Ararat HARUTYUNYAN (24/08/75) - Shirak Gyumri						M57	M44	s84			3	-
Armen SARGSYAN (03/10/75) - Tsement Ararat						A46	s96	A43			3	-
Aram HAKOPYAN (15/08/79) - Tsement Ararat						A70	s44	A84			3	-
Tigran KAZATZYAN (22/08/74) - Olympiakos Nicosia (CYP)						s63	s89	D78			3	-
Karen SIMONYAN (06/07/70) - Tsement Ararat										M67	2	1
Andrei MOVSESYAN (27/10/75)										A78	1	1

AUSTRIA

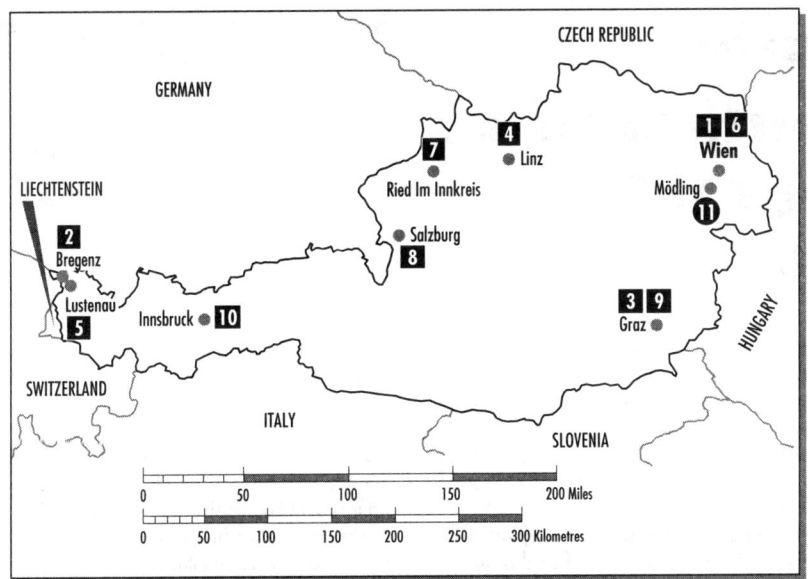

№		№	
1	**FK AUSTRIA WIEN**	130	
2	**SW BREGENZ**	131	
3	**GRAZER AK**	132	
4	**LASK LINZ**	133	
5	**SC AUSTRIA LUSTENAU**	134	
6	**SK RAPID WIEN**	135	

№		№
7	**SV RIED**	136
8	**SV SALZBURG**	137
9	**SK STURM GRAZ**	138
10	**FC TIROL INNSBRUCK**	139

Promoted club

11	**VFB ADMIRA MÖDLING**

WORLD CUP DRAW OFFERS DEJA VU

Sturm weathered as Tirol take title

FEDERATION DIRECTORY

Österreichischer Fussball-Bund
Ernst Happel Stadion, Meiereistrasse 7, 1020 Wien

tel - (01) 72718-0	Year of Formation - 1904
fax - (01) 72816-32	President - Beppo Mauhart
website - www.oefb.at	Secretary - Alfred Ludwig
email - oefb@asn.or.at	

Stadium - Ernst-Happel-Stadion, Wien (47,500)

Sturm Graz's dream of an Austrian championship hat-trick failed to come true. Although Ivica Osim and co. made a bold and determined bid during the spring to make up the ground they had lost during a fixture-overloaded autumn, they narrowly failed to bridge the gap on long-time frontrunners FC Tirol and ultimately had to settle for second place.

Tirol, who appeared to be galloping away with the title in the early weeks of the season, suffered a mid-term crisis, which left them just two points clear of Sturm at the winter break. But, refreshed by the lay-off, they came back with renewed vigour in the spring and, showing extraordinary persistence, maintained their challenge right through to the end. Nine wins in their last ten matches, including a sequence of five successive 1-0 victories, eventually carried the Tyroleans through to their first championship win in ten years. Final confirmation of their triumph was delayed until the final day of the season, when goals from local boys Roland Kirchler and Michael Baur brought a decisive 2-1 win over Austria Vienna.

The architect of Tirol's triumph was coach Kurt Jara, who in barely 18 months at the helm had completely transformed the club's fortunes. On taking control the former Austrian international had declared that he would return the title to Innsbruck within three years. He needed just half that time.

A man with very different ideas from those of his luckless predecessor, Frantisek Cipro, Jara rekindled the Tyrolean soul of the club by making local homegrown players (Kirchler, Baur, Robert Wazinger, Alfred Hörtnagl) the cornerstones of the team. He also brought the best out of the club's foreign contingent. 37-year-old Russian goalkeeper Stanislav Cherchesov was a picture of consistency and reliability, not to mention good health (he played in every game), while Polish striker Radoslaw Gilewicz simply carried on where he had left off the previous season, finishing up as the team's runaway top scorer with 18 goals. Austrian international defender Walter Kogler also performed with credit to earn himself a third championship-winner's medal with three different clubs, having previously reached the top podium with both Austria Vienna (1992/93) and Salzburg (1996/97).

Tirol's victory allowed them a first shot at the Champions' League, but it was Sturm's protracted involvement in Europe

LEAGUE CHAMPIONSHIP RESULTS 99/00

		1	2	3	4	5	6	7	8	9	10
1	FK Austria Wien		3-1	5-2	2-1	2-0	0-3	0-2	2-0	1-3	0-2
			2-5	2-0	3-1	1-0	3-0	1-0	2-2	0-1	2-0
2	SW Bregenz	1-1		0-1	2-1	2-0	1-1	1-2	0-0	1-4	0-3
		1-1		3-1	0-2	1-1	0-3	0-4	5-1	1-0	0-3
3	Grazer AK	0-2	3-0		0-1	2-3	3-1	0-0	0-0	1-0	1-1
		2-0	0-4		2-1	0-4	0-4	1-1	2-0	2-4	2-0
4	LASK Linz	1-1	3-0	1-3		3-0	0-1	1-0	2-4	0-2	3-0
		1-0	0-1	2-2		5-0	1-1	1-1	1-1	1-1	0-1
5	SC Austria Lustenau	1-0	3-0	1-4	1-1		0-1	0-1	1-0	1-2	1-3
		1-2	0-4	0-0	2-2		0-1	1-1	0-2	0-1	1-1
6	SK Rapid Wien	2-0	2-0	2-1	3-0	2-0		5-1	1-0	0-0	2-4
		1-0	4-1	2-0	0-1	4-0		1-0	5-0	2-3	0-0
7	SV Ried	0-0	5-1	0-1	2-1	1-1	1-2		3-0	2-0	5-0
		1-2	2-0	3-1	2-0	4-2	1-0		2-0	1-1	1-2
8	SV Salzburg	0-1	0-1	1-0	2-1	1-1	1-2	3-0		2-0	5-0
		2-1	4-1	5-1	1-2	2-0	0-0	2-1		0-0	0-1
9	SK Sturm Graz	2-2	4-0	5-0	0-0	5-1	1-0	2-1	0-2		0-1
		3-2	3-1	6-1	2-0	7-0	3-1	3-2	3-1		4-1
10	FC Tirol Innsbruck	0-2	4-0	1-0	5-0	3-0	2-1	1-0	0-0	1-0	
		2-1	2-0	1-0	1-0	1-0	1-0	3-1	2-1	1-1	

LEAGUE CHAMPIONSHIP FINAL TABLE 99/00

			Home					Away					Total						
		Pd	W	D	L	F	A	W	D	L	F	A	W	D	L	F	A	PT	GD
1	FC Tirol Innsbruck	36	15	2	1	31	7	9	3	6	23	23	24	5	7	54	30	77	24
2	SK Sturm Graz	36	14	2	2	53	16	8	6	4	24	16	22	8	6	77	32	74	45
3	SK Rapid Wien	36	13	2	3	38	11	7	4	7	21	18	20	6	10	59	29	66	30
4	FK Austria Wien	36	11	1	6	31	23	5	5	8	18	21	16	6	14	49	44	54	5
5	SV Ried	36	11	3	4	36	14	4	5	9	20	25	15	8	13	56	39	53	17
6	SV Salzburg	36	9	5	4	25	14	3	5	10	14	31	12	10	14	39	45	46	-6
7	Grazer AK	36	8	4	6	23	22	4	2	12	18	40	12	6	18	41	62	42	-21
8	LASK Linz	36	6	6	6	26	19	4	3	11	15	30	10	9	17	41	49	39	-8
9	SW Bregenz	36	5	5	8	19	29	5	0	13	20	44	10	5	21	39	73	35	-34
10	SC Austria Lustenau	36	3	5	10	14	26	1	2	15	8	48	4	7	25	22	74	19	-52

that arguably handed the Tyroleans the title. The previous season's 'double'-winners qualified for the first group phase of the Champions' League with a good win over Servette, and although they initially looked set to repeat their misadventure of a year earlier, they recovered from a poor start to register home wins against both Marseille and Croatia Zagreb. That was too little, too late to keep them in the Champions' League but good enough to maintain their European involvement in the UEFA Cup, where they were desperately unlucky to go down in extra-time to holders Parma.

The burden of competing intensely on two fronts during the autumn was too much for Osim and his players. Their league form went to pot, notably with three consecutive away defeats during the busy September/ October period.

Once the European interest ended, however, it was a different story. Sturm launched themselves furiously into their title defence, and before long they were nibbling at the heels of both Tirol and Rapid Vienna. They lost just one of their last 20 matches, but ultimately that unexpected 1-0 reverse at Bregenz seven rounds from the end was to seal their fate - even if, with one match remaining,

they still harboured hopes of entering hat-trick heaven.

Sturm did have the consolation, as runners-up, of joining Tirol in the 2000/01 Champions' League qualifying round. They also bettered their championship-winning points total of the previous season and scored five goals more. Ivica Vastic, the Croatian-born Austrian international, was, once again, the undisputed Bundesliga player of the season. He scored 32 goals, becoming the first player to pass the 30-goal mark in Austria's top division for a decade.

Rapid Vienna also possessed a brilliant Balkan in Dejan Savicevic. The veteran Yugoslav international, nicknamed "Il Genio" during his many years in Italy with Milan, arrived at Rapid amidst much debate, but he silenced the doubters with several exciting displays, notably against historical rivals FK Austria, when he scored twice in a 3-0 away win to give Rapid their 100th victory in the Vienna derby.

Sadly, Savicevic proved to be injury-prone, and without him Rapid lacked flair. A brilliant run of form at the start of the spring campaign powered the green-and-whites into title contention, but they were brusquely halted in their tracks by successive setbacks against title

TOP SCORERS

32	Ivica VASTIC (SK Sturm Graz)
21	Christian MAYRLEB (FK Austria Wien)
19	Ronald BRUNMAYR (SV Ried)
18	Radoslaw GILEWICZ (FC Tirol Innsbruck)
17	Rene WAGNER (SK Rapid Wien)
12	Benedict AKWUEGBU (Grazer AK)
11	Saso UDOVIC (LASK Linz)
	Dejan SAVICEVIC (SK Rapid Wien)

NATIONAL TEAM RESULTS 99/00

18/08/99	Sweden	A	Malmö	0-0	
04/09/99	Spain (ECQ)	H	Vienna	1-3	Hierro (54og)
10/10/99	Cyprus (ECQ)	H	Vienna	3-1	Glieder (5), Vastic (23), Herzog (81)
23/02/00	Greece	A	Kalamata	1-4	Vastic (44)
29/03/00	Sweden	H	Graz	1-1	Flögel (17)
26/04/00	Croatia	H	Vienna	1-2	Vastic (17)

rivals Tirol and Sturm, and when FK Austria made it three defeats in a row (with their first win over Rapid for five seasons), Heribert Weber's team knew that they would have to settle for third place.

Weber departed at the season's end, to be replaced by 'sports director' Ernst Dokupil, but he ought to have gone some eight months earlier. The Rapid directors' response to the club's UEFA Cup defeat by cross-border neighbours Inter Bratislava was to give Weber the sack, but he refused to go, and as the club could not afford a pay-off, he stayed put.

Although Rapid finished clear in third place to earn a return to the UEFA Cup, there was general dismay among the fans. Particularly aggravating was the team's inability to raise themselves for the big occasions. In addition to losing home and away to both Galatasaray and Inter Braztislava in Europe, Rapid took just one paltry point from four games against each of their championship rivals Tirol and Sturm.

Austria Vienna had another year in the doldrums. Not even the appointment of club icon Herbert Prohaska could revive them, and with nothing more than the perennial InterToto place to show for their efforts, the ex-national team boss was thrown out by rich new club president Frank Stronach, who decided to start afresh by appointing SV Ried's Heinz Hochhauser as a replacement and

NATIONAL TEAM APPEARANCES 99/00

Coach - Otto BARIC	SWE	ESP	CYP	GRE	SWE	CRO	Cps	Gls
Alex MANNINGER (04/06/77) - Arsenal (ENG)	G	G	G	s46			4	-
Michael STREITER (19/01/66) - FK Austria Wien	D	D					34	1
Thomas WINKLHOFER (30/12/70) - SV Salzburg	D	D	D	D	D	D	12	-
Michael HATZ (17/11/70) - SK Rapid Wien	D	D			D	D	6	-
Robert IBERTSBERGER (20/01/77) - SV Salzburg/Venezia (ITA)	M	M	M	D			4	-
Dietmar KÜHBAUER (04/04/71) - Real Sociedad (ESP)	M	M	M	M			38	4
Ivica VASTIC (29/09/69) - SK Sturm Graz	M	M	D	A46	A46	A	28	11
Alfred HÖRTNAGL (24/09/66) - FC Tirol Innsbruck	M68						20	1
Roland KIRCHLER (29/09/70) - FC Tirol Innsbruck	M89	M67	M	M46	s56	s46	8	-
Christian MAYRLEB (08/06/72) - FK Austria Wien	A	A	A	A64	s46	s67	14	3
Mario HAAS (16/09/74) - RC Strasbourg (FRA)	A46			s46			16	2
Markus WEISSENBERGER (08/03/75) - Arminia Bielefeld (GER)	s46	s67	M83	s64	A79	M67	6	-
Jürgen KAUZ (23/08/74) - LASK Linz	s68		s74				2	-
Gerd WIMMER (09/01/77) - SK Rapid Wien	s89		s83				2	-
Roman MÄHLICH (17/09/71) - SK Sturm Graz		M60					19	-
Harald CERNY (13/09/73) - TSV 1860 München (GER)		A	M74	M		s46	36	3
Markus SCHOPP (22/02/74) - SK Sturm Graz		s60			M	M46	24	1
Günther NEUKIRCHNER (02/12/71) - SK Sturm Graz			D46	D	D65	D67	9	1
Eduard GLIEDER (28/01/69) - SV Salzburg			A				5	2
Andreas HERZOG (10/09/68) - SV Werder Bremen (GER)			s46	M70	M56	M	79	18
Franz WOHLFAHRT (01/07/64) - VfB Stuttgart (GER)				G46	G	G	47	-
Gilbert PRILASNIG (01/04/73) - SK Sturm Graz				M	M	M46	8	-
Günter SCHIESSWALD (25/09/73) - SK Rapid Wien				s46			1	-
Martin AMERHAUSER (23/07/74) - Grazer AK				s70	s79		8	2
Martin STRANZL (16/06/80) - TSV 1860 München (GER)					M	M	2	-
Thomas FLÖGEL (09/06/71) - Heart of Midlothian (SCO)					M	M	11	1
Ernst DOSPEL (08/10/76) - FK Austria Wien					s65		1	-
Andreas LIPA (26/04/71) - Grazer AK						s67	1	-

EUROPEAN CUPS 99/00

CHAMPIONS' CUP
● SK RAPID WIEN
Preliminary round 2 VALLETTA (MLT)
H 3-0 Dowe (54), Savicevic (74), Penksa (86)
Maier; Wimmer, Schiesswald, Schöttel, Hatz (Szabo 46); Dowe, Lagonikakis (Penksa 68), Freund, Wetl; Savicevic, Wagner (Vier 81).
A 2-0 Dowe (70), Lagonikakis (88)
Maier; Wimmer, Schiesswald, Schöttel, Hatz; Dowe, Lagonikakis, Freund (Zingler 80), Heraf (Wetl 64); Penksa (Schwarz 71), Wagner.

Qualifying round GALATASARAY (TUR)
H 0-3
Maier; Wimmer, Schiesswald, Schöttel, Hatz (Wetl 75); Zingler (Szabo 46), Freund, Dowe, Lagonikakis; Penksa, Wagner.
A 0-1
Maier; Wimmer, Zingler, Schiesswald, Hatz; Penksa, Heraf (Savicevic 46), Dowe, Wetl (Freund 27); Schwarz, Lagonikakis.

● SK STURM GRAZ
Qualifying round SERVETTE FC GENEVE (SUI)
H 2-1 Vastic (33), Martens (45)
Schicklgruber; Foda; Milanic (Koutsoupias 80), Popovic, Korsós, Schupp, Reinmayr, Prilasnig (Minavand 90); Martens; Strafner (Kocijan 63), Vastic.
A 2-2 Kocijan (54), Vastic (78)
Schicklgruber; Foda; Milanic, Popovic (Mählich 46); Schopp (Korsós 66), Prilasnig (Reinmayr 85), Schupp, Martens, Neukirchner; Vastic, Kocijan.

Champions' League
1st match OLYMPIQUE MARSEILLE (FRA)
A 0-2
Schicklgruber; Feldhofer, Foda, Neukirchner (Koutsoupias 82); Prilasnig, Schupp, Mählich, Reinmayr (Korsós 46); Martens (Pantelic 46); Vastic, Kocijan.

2nd match MANCHESTER UNITED (ENG)
H 0-3
Sidorczuk; Foda; Prilasnig (Koutsoupias 72), Feldhofer (Korsós 72); Neukirchner, Mählich (Reinmayr 75), Vastic, Schupp, Martens; Strafner, Kocijan.

3rd match CROATIA ZAGREB (CRO)
A 0-3
Schicklgruber; Foda; Neukirchner, Milanic (Feldhofer 66); Schopp (Korsós 50), Martens, Mählich (Pantelic 73), Vastic, Prilasnig; Strafner, Kocijan.

4th match CROATIA ZAGREB (CRO)
H 1-0 Mujcin (40og)
Schicklgruber; Neukirchner; Prilasnig, Feldhofer; Schopp, Mählich, Schupp, Korsós, Martens (Strafner 90); Vastic, Kocijan (Reinmayr 81).

5th match OLYMPIQUE MARSEILLE (FRA)
H 3-2 Mählich (18), Kocijan (61, 84)
Schicklgruber; Neukirchner; Feldhofer (Strafner 39), Prilasnig; Schopp (Reinmayr 81), Mählich, Schupp, Martens, Minavand (Bardel 76); Vastic, Kocijan.

6th match MANCHESTER UNITED (ENG)
A 1-2 Vastic (88p)
Schicklgruber; Neukirchner; Strafner, Prilasnig; Schopp, Angibeaud (Bardel 71), Mählich, Martens (Reinmayr 71), Minavand; Vastic, Kocijan (Bochtler 73).

UEFA CUP
● GRAZER AK
Qualifying round KÍ (FAR)
A 5-0 Radovic (7, 37), Standfest (9, 85, 89)
Almer; Pötscher (Stückler 46), Lipa, Ehmann, Hartmann; Ramusch, Ceh, Kulovits (Aloisi 46), Standfest; Radovic (Tutu 72), Akwuegbu.
H 4-0 Ramusch (47), Akwuegbu (74), Dmitrovic (81), Tutu (88)
Schranz; Hübler, Stückler, Nilsen (Nørlund Andersen 74), Hartmann; Ramusch, Aloisi (Rader 64), Kulovits, Dmitrovic; Tutu, Pamic (Akwuegbu 59).

1st round SPARTAK TRNAVA (SVK)
H 3-0 Akwuegbu (12, 56), Tutu (34)
Almer; Hübler, Ehmann, Nilsen, Lipa; Ramusch (Kulovits 86), Ceh, Aloisi, Standfest (Dmitrovic 75); Akwuegbu, Tutu (Radovic 89).
A 1-2 Standfest (14)
Almer; Pötscher, Nilsen, Ehmann, Hartmann; Ramusch, Ceh, Aloisi, Standfest (Lipa 80); Akwuegbu (Tutu 64), Pamic (Sick 73).

2nd round PANATHINAIKOS (GRE)
H 2-1 Lipa (57), Pamic (80)
Almer; Lipa, Ehmann, Nilsen, Hartmann (Amerhauser 75); Ramusch, Ceh, Kulovits (Aloisi 90), Dmitrovic; Pamic, Akwuegbu (Tutu 81).
A 0-1
Almer; Lipa, Akoto, Nilsen, Hartmann; Ramusch, Ceh, Aloisi (Amerhauser 60), Kulovits, Dmitrovic (Pötscher 83); Akwuegbu (Pamic 76).

● LASK LINZ
1st round STEAUA BUCURESTI (ROM)
A 0-2
Pavlovic; Muhr; Ba, Milinovic; Brenner, Kauz, Pichorner, Bradaric (Mehlem 68), Panis; Stumpf (Jochum 59), Udovic (Kiesenebner 77).
H 2-3 Stumpf (5), Sane (90)
Wimleitner; Grassler, Milinovic, Jochum; Brenner, Kauz, Pichorner, Mehlem, Panis (Bradaric 14); Stumpf (Sane 61), Udovic (Lichtenwagner 63).

● SK RAPID WIEN
1st round INTER BRATISLAVA (SVK)
A 0-1
Maier; Schöttel; Schiesswald, Hatz; Wimmer, Heraf (Savicevic 46), Freund, Dowe, Wetl (Lagonikakis 61); Wagner, Penksa.
H 1-2 Zingler (65)
Maier; Hatz (Schwarz 75), Schiesswald, Schöttel, Lagonikakis; Wimmer, Wetl (Zingler 62), Freund, Dowe; Wagner, Penksa (Savicevic 46).

● SK STURM GRAZ
3rd round PARMA (ITA)
A 1-2 Schopp (21)
Schicklgruber; Foda; Milanic (Angibeaud 77), Neukirchner (Feldhofer 58); Schopp, Prilasnig, Mählich, Martens, Minavand; Kocijan (Reinmayr 84), Vastic.
H 3-3 (aet) Reinmayr (67, 95), Vastic (87)
Schicklgruber; Neukirchner (Angibeaud 64); Feldhofer (Reinmayr 57), Strafner (Foda 61); Schopp, Mählich, Korsós, Prilasnig, Minavand; Vastic, Kocijan.

drafting in almost a completely new playing squad.

Hochhauser arrived in the capital with a burgeoning reputation, having steered underdogs Ried into the top half of the table. His attractive team, led from the front by Ronald Brunmayr, scored more goals than Tirol and actually hammered the champions 5-0 in the early autumn, with Brunmayr claiming a hat-trick.

Salzburg and Grazer AK were both guilty of massively underperforming in the league, but they partially compensated for that by reaching the final of the Austrian Cup, with Graz emerging triumphant after a penalty shoot-out following an incident-packed 2-2 draw.

Salzburg, who had never won the Cup, were hoping to provide the perfect finale to the glorious career of veteran goalgetter Toni Polster, who, amidst considerable media interest, decided to return to his homeland (after a 13-year absence) for one final half-season hurrah. But Salzburg were unable to deliver, and the legendary Viennese hitman decided to call time on a remarkable career that had brought him an amazing total of 416 goals.

As Polster arrived in Salzburg from Germany, another Austrian legend, Hans Krankl, left in the opposite direction, to coach Fortuna Cologne. He was replaced at Salzburg by Miroslav Polak but with little success. Grazer AK, too, parted company with a much-heralded coach in mid-season when, just two days before the spring resumption, Klaus Augenthaler left for Nuremberg. His friend and replacement Rainer Hörgl did not last long, and it was Werner Gregoritsch, GAK's third coach of the campaign, who oversaw the Cup win.

INTERNATIONAL HONOURS

World Cup Finals appearances: 1934 (4th), 1954 (3rd), 1958, 1978 (2nd phase), 1982 (2nd phase),1990, 1998

European Championship appearances: 1960

DOMESTIC CUP 99/00

SECOND ROUND
ESK-GAK Amateure 0, SV Ried 2
SV Schwechat 0, FC Tirol Innsbruck 7
ASK Köflach 1, SK Vorwärts Steyr 1 (aet; 5-3 on pens.)
Union Vöcklamarkt 0, LASK Linz 2
ASKÖ Donau Linz 0, First Vienna 1
SV Würmla 0, FK Austria Wien 3
SV Gmunden 1, SV Wörgl 2
ASK Voitsberg 1, Grazer AK 3 (aet)
SV Rohrbach 0, FC Niederösterreich St. Pölten 3
SV Anger 0, DSV Leoben 4
ISS Landhaus 1, SW Bregenz 6
SC Krems 0, SC Untersiebenbrunn 3
Wolfsberger AC 1, SK Sturm Graz 4
SVG Reichenau 1, WSG Wattens 4
SV Ried Amateure 1, SV Austria Braunau 2
FC Waidhofen/Ybbs 0, SC Austria Lustenau 3
FC Wacker Innsbruck 1, FC Kärnten Austria VSV 2
SV Leibnitz 0, VfB Admira Wacker Mödling 2
WSV ATSV Ranshofen 1, SK Rapid Wien 1
(aet; 4-1 on pens.)
ASK Klingenbach 1, SV Salzburg 5
USV Hartberg Umgebung 0, ASKÖ Pasching 3
Polizei-Feuerwehr 2, Prater Austria Amateure 0
SEZ BSV Bad Bleiburg 3, SV Hundsheim 2
SK Eintracht Wels 2, SV Salzburg Amateure 5
FAC Avanti 2, Frastanzer FC Lustenau 1907 1
SAK 1914 3, TSV Hartberg 3 (aet; 4-5 on pens.)
SV Kukmirn 0, 1. Simmeringer Sportclub 0
(aet; 6-7 on pens.)
SC Rheindorf Altach 2, ASV Schrems 1
SV Stockerau 1, SV Seekirchen 2

ASK Kottingbrunn 4, FC St. Michael im Lavanttal 1
SV Spittal/Millstättersee 6, SV Mattersburg 2 (aet)
SV Oberwart 3, FC Hard 2

THIRD ROUND
SV Spittal/Drau 0, SV Salzburg 2
WSV ATSV Ranshofen 0, LASK Linz 3 (aet)
SEZ Bad Bleiburg 0, FC Kärnten Austria VSV 3
ASK Kottingbrunn 1, Grazer AK 5
ASKÖ Pasching 1, SK Sturm Graz 1 (aet; 5-4 on pens.)
SV Seekirchen 0, WSG Wattens 4
Polizei-Feuerwehr 0, DSV Leoben 5
SC Rheindorf Altach 0, VfB Admira Wacker Mödling 2
FAC Avanti 0, First Vienna 3
SV Oberwart 2, SV Wörgl 5
1. Simmeringer SC 2, SV Ried 1
SV Salzburg Amateure 3,
FC Niederösterreich St. Pölten 0 (w/o)
ASK Köflach 0, FC Untersiebenbrunn 3 (aet)
TSV Hartberg 0, FK Austria Wien 1
FC Tirol Innsbruck 2, SW Bregenz 0
SV Austria Braunau 4, SC Austria Lustenau 2

FOURTH ROUND
1. Simmeringer SC 0, SV Salzburg 1
First Vienna 0, FC Tirol Innsbruck 1
SV Salzburg Amateure 1,
VfB Admira Wacker Mödling 3
Grazer AK 3, SV Wörgl 1
SV Austria Braunau 1, SC Untersiebenbrunn 1
(aet; 4-3 on pens.)
ASKÖ Pasching 5, WSG Wattens 1

DSV Leoben 3, FC Kärnten Austria VSV 1
FK Austria Wien 1, LASK Linz 0

QUARTER-FINALS
SV Salzburg 5 (Szewczyk 26, Aufhauser 37,
Hütter 51, 78, Meyssen 67),
VfB Admira Wacker Mödling 0
ASKÖ Pasching 2 (Aslan 24, Zogovic 44),
FC Tirol Innsbruck 0
Grazer AK 2 (Kulovits 40, Aloisi 112),
SV Austria Braunau 1 (Schriebl 71) (aet)
FK Austria Wien 0, DSV Leoben 0 (aet; 5-3 on pens.)

SEMI-FINALS
SV Salzburg 3 (Polster 6, 75, Laessig 71),
FK Austria Wien 2 (Hopfer 17, Plassnegger 67)
ASKÖ Pasching 0, Grazer AK 1 (Akwuegbu 43)

FINAL
16/05/2000, Vienna
GRAZER AK 2 Pamic (3p, 34)
SV SALZBURG 2 Szewczyk (44), Aufhauser (90)
(aet; 4-3 on pens.)
referee - Schüttengruber
GRAZER AK - Almer; Lipa; Ehmann, Pötscher;
Ramusch, Kulovits, Ceh, Dmitrovic (Sick 79),
Standfest (Amerhauser 85); Pamic, Akwuegbu
(Tutu 66).
SV SALZBURG - Sáfár; Szewczyk (Lipcsei 97);
Winklhofer, Jank; Struber, Laessig, Hütter (Meyssen
71), Aufhauser, Nikolic, Kitzbichler; Polster
(Sabitzer 56).

PLAYER OF THE SEASON

MARTIN STRANZL

He has never played for an Austrian Bundesliga club, but 20-year-old Martin Stranzl is already being touted as one of the leaders of the next generation of Austrian internationals. The powerfully built youngster impressed on his national team début against Sweden in March 2000 with his nerveless application and robust, uncompromising defensive play. He also had a splendid season in Germany with 1860 Munich, helping the 'Lions' into a Champions' League qualifying berth and meriting high marks in the German press. He has made an excellent start but knows he still has a long way to go before he can even think of emulating the achievements of his idol, Paolo Maldini.

The battle for survival at the foot of the table proved shortlived, with Austria Lustenau suffering a nightmare run of 25 games without a win to drift out of touch with their regional rivals, newly-promoted SW Bregenz, and end their three-year stint in the top division. Their place was taken by merger club VfB Admira Mödling, clear winners of the Second Division, from which two former top-flight sides, St. Pölten and Vorwärts Steyr, were forced

to retire in mid-season due to financial disrepair.

Grey skies continue to circulate over the Austrian national team. A 1-3 home defeat by Spain quickly ended any hopes of qualifying for Euro 2000 via the play-offs, and there was precious little improvement thereafter. National coach Otto Baric maintains that he needs time to rebuild the team, but he may not survive if Austria fail in the World Cup qualifiers - which, given that they have to do battle once more with Spain and Israel, the teams which savaged them during the European Championship campaign, has to remain a distinct possibility.

Following a 4-1 defeat by Greece in February, Baric announced that he would no longer call on players who were not appearing regularly for their clubs. This initially ruled out foreign-based players Alex Manninger, Robert Ibertsberger, Didi Kühbauer and Mario Haas. Baric can hardly afford to be so selective given the modest resources at his disposal, but he has always been forthright and dogmatic and is quite prepared to stand or fall by his decisions.

These days Austria lack sufficient quality to outplay opponents so they have to rely on their fight and determination, but in Martin Stranzl, Markus Weissenberger and Thomas Flögel, Baric does at least have a few useful foundation stones with which to rebuild. Of the older, established names, Ivica Vastic remains a class act, and Andy Herzog is also still willing and able. But Austrian fans could be in for a long, long wait before another Toni Polster comes along...

PROMOTED CLUB 99/00

SECOND DIVISION FINAL TABLE

		Pd	W	D	L	F	A	Pt	GD
1	VfB Admira Mödling	36	23	8	5	70	29	77	41
2	DSV Leoben	36	19	9	8	50	32	66	18
3	SV Wörgl	36	17	11	8	58	41	62	17
4	Untersiebenbrunn	36	15	12	9	50	31	57	19
5	FC Kärnten	36	16	9	11	54	40	57	14
6	SV Braunau	36	14	9	13	42	37	51	5
7	First Vienna FC 1894	36	12	14	10	55	43	50	12
8	WSG Wattens	36	10	8	18	52	66	38	-14
9	FCN St. Pölten	36	9	5	22	25	58	30	-33
10	SK Vorwärts Steyr	36	1	3	32	13	92	4	-79

N.B. FCN St. Pölten and SK Vorwärts Steyr withdrew during season due to bankruptcy. All unfulfilled fixtures awarded 3-0 to opponents; direct matches awarded as 0-0 draws without points.

CLUB DIRECTORY

VfB Admira Mödling
Sportanlage Duursmagasse
2340 Mödling
tel - (02236) 48710
fax - (02236) 48710-35
website - www.admira-wacker-moedling.at
email - office@admira-wacker-moedling.at
Year of Formation - 1911
President - Hans Werner Weiss
Secretary - Norbert Plihal
Coach - Milan Miklavic
Stadium - Sportanlage Duursmagasse (6,000) or Bundesstadion Südstadt (12,000)

MAJOR HONOURS

League Championship - (9) 1927, 1928, 1932, 1934, 1936, 1937, 1939, 1947, 1966.
Domestic Cup - (6)
1928, 1932, 1934, 1947, 1964, 1966.

FK AUSTRIA WIEN

CLUB DIRECTORY

FK Austria-Memphis Wien
Franz Horr-Stadion, Matthias Sindelar-Tribüne
Fischhofgasse 12, 1100 Wien
tel - (01) 68801500 / fax - (01) 6880150380
website - www.fk-austria.at
email - fak@fk-austria.at
Year of Formation - 1911
President - Georg Sattler
Coach - Herbert Prohaska
(00/01 - Heinz Hochhauser)
Stadium - Franz Horr-Stadion (11,800)

MAJOR HONOURS
League Championship - (21) 1924, 1926, 1949,
1950, 1953, 1961, 1962, 1963, 1969, 1970,
1976, 1978, 1979, 1980, 1981, 1984, 1985,
1986, 1991, 1992, 1993.
Domestic Cup - (22) 1921, 1924, 1925, 1926,
1933, 1935, 1936, 1948, 1949, 1960, 1962,
1963, 1967, 1971, 1974, 1977, 1980, 1982,
1986, 1990, 1992, 1994.

APPEARANCES 99/00

	P	Ap	(s)	Gls
Thomas DARAZS	M	9	(16)	1
George DATORU (NIG)	A	28	(3)	5
Ernst DOSPEL	D	30	(2)	1
Ludwig ERNSTSSON (SWE)	A	1	(2)	
Wolfgang HOPFER	M	23	(4)	1
Mladen IVANCIC (CRO)	D	13	(3)	
Patrik JEZEK (CZE)	M	14	(1)	1
Patrick KASUBA	A		(1)	
Wolfgang KNALLER	G	33		
Bozo KOVACEVIC	M		(2)	
Gerald KRAJIC	A		(2)	1
Günther KREISSL	G	3		
Jürgen LEITNER	M	35		1
Christian MAYRLEB	A	33	(1)	21
Anton PFEFFER	D	25		
Gernot PLASSNEGGER	M	9	(10)	3
Rashid RAKHIMOV (RUS)	M	23	(2)	2
Manfred ROSENEGGER	A		(1)	
Paul SCHARNER	D	9	(3)	
Manfred SCHMID	M	19	(2)	1
Rafal SIADACZKA (POL)	M	11	(1)	
Pavel SOBCZAK (POL)	A	4	(14)	1
Roman STARY	A	3	(4)	
Peter STÖGER	M	23	(2)	4
Michael STREITER	D	16	(3)	
Christian TAMANDL	D	6	(1)	
Michael WAGNER	M	26	(3)	5

LEAGUE RESULTS 1999/2000

30/06/99	Grazer AK	A	2-0	Wagner, Mayrleb
06/07/99	SV Salzburg	H	2-0	Mayrleb 2 (1p)
14/07/99	LASK Linz	A	1-1	Datoru
21/07/99	FC Tirol Innsbruck	H	0-2	
31/07/99	SK Rapid Wien	H	0-3	
07/08/99	SK Sturm Graz	A	2-2	og (Milanic), Stöger
14/08/99	SV Ried	H	0-2	
21/08/99	SC Austria Lustenau	A	0-1	
24/08/99	SW Bregenz	A	1-1	Mayrleb
28/08/99	SC Austria Lustenau	H	2-0	Rakhimov, Mayrleb
11/09/99	Grazer AK	H	5-2	Dospel, Mayrleb 2, Datoru, Sobczak
17/09/99	SV Salzburg	A	1-0	Datoru
25/09/99	LASK Linz	H	2-1	Wagner, Stöger
01/10/99	FC Tirol Innsbruck	A	2-0	Rakhimov, Mayrleb
06/10/99	SW Bregenz	H	3-1	Mayrleb, Wagner, Darazs
16/10/99	SK Rapid Wien	A	0-2	
22/10/99	SK Sturm Graz	H	1-3	Mayrleb
30/10/99	SV Ried	A	0-0	
07/11/99	Grazer AK	A	0-2	
14/11/99	SV Salzburg	H	2-2	Hopfer, Stöger
27/11/99	LASK Linz	H	3-1	Mayrleb 2, Datoru
03/03/00	SK Rapid Wien	A	0-1	
07/03/00	SW Bregenz	A	1-1	Mayrleb
11/03/00	SC Austria Lustenau	H	1-0	Stöger
19/03/00	SV Ried	A	2-1	Leitner, Wagner
26/03/00	FC Tirol Innsbruck	H	2-0	Mayrleb 2 (1p)
01/04/00	SK Sturm Graz	A	2-3	Datoru, Mayrleb
08/04/00	SK Sturm Graz	H	0-1	
15/04/00	SW Bregenz	H	2-5	Mayrleb, Schmid
22/04/00	SV Salzburg	A	1-2	Mayrleb
29/04/00	Grazer AK	H	2-0	Plassnegger, Jezek
06/05/00	LASK Linz	A	0-1	
09/05/00	SK Rapid Wien	H	3-0	Mayrleb 2, Plassnegger
13/05/00	SC Austria Lustenau	A	2-1	Wagner, Krajic
20/05/00	SV Ried	H	1-0	Plassnegger
27/05/00	FC Tirol Innsbruck	A	1-2	Mayrleb (p)

SW BREGENZ

CLUB DIRECTORY

Casino SW Bregenz
Postfach 261, 6901 Bregenz
tel - (05574) 42795
fax - (05574) 53621
website - http://members.vol.at/swbregenz
email - sw.bregenz@vol.at
Year of Formation - 1920
President - Josef Fitz
Secretary - Markus Feldkircher
Coach - Srdjan Gemaljevic; Slavko Kovacic
(00/01 - Ove Flindt)
Stadium - Casino-Stadion (15,000)

APPEARANCES 99/00

	P	Ap	(s)	Gls
Emanuel AGBO (NIG)	A	4	(3)	
Emanuel AKWUEGBU (NIG)	A	10	(1)	1
Neno BAIANO (BRA)	M	6	(13)	
Thomas BERNTSEN (NOR)	D	2	(1)	
Matthias BLEYER	A	17	(3)	3
Manfred EISBACHER	M	6	(8)	
Bruno FRIESENBICHLER	A	6	(11)	5
Günter FRIESENBICHLER	A		(1)	
Holger GAISSMAYER (GER)	A	3	(4)	
Herbert GAGER	M	19		3
Ralph GEIGER	D	22	(5)	
Robert GOLEMAC (CRO)	D	25	(2)	
Slobodan GRUBOR	D	19	(3)	
Thomas HICKERSBERGER	D	16	(7)	1
Martin HILBERGER	M	1	(3)	
Sancho JANI	M	17	(5)	2
Johann KOGLER	M	10	(3)	1
Harald KORNEXL	M	17	(1)	
Roland KORNEXL	D	20	(1)	
Nedzad KURUSOVIC (CRO)	G	28		
Oliver MATTLE	A		(1)	
Marko MUTAPCIC (CRO)	M	28		1
Wolfgang OTT	G	8	(1)	
Jan Ove PEDERSEN (NOR)	M	16		4
David PRATS (ESP)	A	3	(6)	
Stefan RAPP	M	22	(7)	4
Hendrik Jan REGTOP (HOL)	A	15		7
Daniel SCHMID	D	1		
Tim SPERREVIK (NOR)	M		(1)	
Zoran TOMIC (YUG)	A	24	(10)	3
Lars UNGER (GER)	M	31	(3)	3

LEAGUE RESULTS 1999/2000

30/06/99	SV Ried	H	1-2	Tomic
07/07/99	SK Rapid Wien	A	0-2	
14/07/99	SK Sturm Graz	H	1-4	Friesenbichler B.
21/07/99	SC Austria Lustenau	A	0-3	
03/08/99	SV Salzburg	A	1-0	Akwuegbu
07/08/99	LASK Linz	H	2-1	Gager, Unger (p)
15/08/99	Grazer AK	A	0-3	
21/08/99	FC Tirol Innsbruck	A	0-4	
24/08/99	FK Austria Wien	H	1-1	Friesenbichler B.
28/08/99	FC Tirol Innsbruck	H	0-3	
11/09/99	SV Ried	A	1-5	Bleyer
19/09/99	SK Rapid Wien	H	1-1	Bleyer
25/09/99	SK Sturm Graz	A	0-4	
02/10/99	SC Austria Lustenau	H	2-0	Gager, Jani
06/10/99	FK Austria Wien	A	1-3	Bleyer
16/10/99	SV Salzburg	H	0-0	
23/10/99	LASK Linz	A	0-3	
30/10/99	Grazer AK	H	0-1	
13/11/99	SK Sturm Graz	A	1-3	Gager
16/11/99	SC Austria Lustenau	H	1-1	Rapp
27/11/99	SV Salzburg	A	1-4	Jani
04/03/00	LASK Linz	A	1-0	Regtop (p)
07/03/00	FK Austria Wien	H	1-1	Regtop (p)
12/03/00	SK Rapid Wien	H	0-3	
21/03/00	FC Tirol Innsbruck	A	0-2	
25/03/00	Grazer AK	H	3-1	Kogler, Rapp 2
01/04/00	SV Ried	A	0-2	
08/04/00	SV Ried	H	0-4	
15/04/00	FK Austria Wien	A	5-2	Pedersen, Regtop, Tomic (p), Mutapcic, Hickersberger
22/04/00	SK Sturm Graz	H	1-0	Pedersen
29/04/00	SC Austria Lustenau	A	4-0	Regtop 2, Friesenbichler B., Pedersen
06/05/00	SV Salzburg	H	5-1	Regtop (p), Friesenbichler B., Rapp, og (Laessig), Tomic
09/05/00	LASK Linz	H	0-2	
12/05/00	SK Rapid Wien	A	1-4	Friesenbichler B.
20/05/00	FC Tirol Innsbruck	H	0-3	
27/05/00	Grazer AK	A	4-0	Unger 2, Pedersen, Regtop

GRAZER AK

THE EUROPEAN FOOTBALL YEARBOOK 2000-2001

CLUB DIRECTORY

Liebherr Grazer Athletik-Klub
Stadionplatz 1, 8040 Graz
tel - (0316) 4830300
fax - (0316) 4830309
website - www.gak.at
email - office@gak.at
Year of Formation - 1902
President - Peter Svetits
Coach - Klaus Augenthaler; Rainer Hörgl;
Werner Gregoritsch
Stadium - Arnold Schwarzenegger-Stadion (15,428)

MAJOR HONOURS
Domestic Cup - (2) 1981, 2000.

APPEARANCES 99/00

	P	Ap	(s)	Gls
Eric AKOTO (GHA)	D	7	(1)	
Benedict AKWUEGBU (NIG)	A	21	(6)	12
Ross ALOISI (ITA)	M	12	(10)	
Martin AMERHAUSER	M	19	(5)	3
Franz ALMER	G	31		
Christian BINDER	A	1	(1)	
Ales CEH (SLO)	M	25	(1)	
Boban DMITROVIC (YUG)	M	11	(9)	2
Anton EHMANN	D	26	(3)	3
Jürgen HARTMANN	D	21	(4)	
Michael HÜBLER	M	7	(1)	
Bernd KAINTZ	M		(3)	
Enrico KULOVITS	M	29	(2)	1
Christian LEUCHTMANN	A		(1)	
Andreas LIPA	D	28	(1)	2
Roger NILSEN (NOR)	D	13		
Igor PAMIC (CRO)	A	19	(4)	9
Markus PFINGSTL	M	1	(1)	
Gregor PÖTSCHER	D	23	(1)	
David PREISS	M		(1)	
Wolfgang RADER	M		(1)	
Thomas RADLSPECK (GER)	M	6	(2)	
Zeljko RADOVIC	A	11	(1)	4
Doeter RAMUSCH	M	30		1
Andreas SCHRANZ	G	4	(1)	
Bernhard SCHUITEMAN (HOL)	D	6	(2)	
Gernot SICK	D	13	(6)	
Joachim STANDFEST	A	15	(12)	
Christoph STÜCKLER	D	3	(2)	
Tomas TOMIC (GER)	G	1		
Skelley Adu TUTU (GHA)	A	13	(14)	4

LEAGUE RESULTS 1999/2000

Date	Opponent	H/A	Score	Scorers
30/06/99	FK Austria Wien	H	0-2	
07/07/99	SV Ried	A	1-0	Radovic
14/07/99	SC Austria Lustenau	H	2-3	Pamic 2
21/07/99	SK Sturm Graz	A	0-5	
27/07/99	SV Salzburg	H	0-0	
03/08/99	LASK Linz	A	3-1	Radovic, Akwuegbu 2
06/08/99	FC Tirol Innsbruck	A	0-1	
15/08/99	SW Bregenz	H	3-0	Radovic 2, Ehmann
21/08/99	SK Rapid Wien	A	1-2	Ehmann
29/08/99	SK Rapid Wien	H	3-1	Dmitrovic, Akwuegbu 2
11/09/99	FK Austria Wien	A	2-5	Akwuegbu 2
19/09/99	SV Ried	H	0-0	
25/09/99	SC Austria Lustenau	A	4-1	Akwuegbu 2, Tutu, Dmitrovic
03/10/99	SK Sturm Graz	H	1-0	Pamic
06/10/99	SV Salzburg	A	0-1	
16/10/99	LASK Linz	H	0-1	
24/10/99	FC Tirol Innsbruck	H	1-1	Akwuegbu
30/10/99	SW Bregenz	A	1-0	Akwuegbu
07/11/99	FK Austria Wien	H	2-0	Pamic, Kulovits
13/11/99	SC Austria Lustenau	A	0-0	
23/11/99	FC Tirol Innsbruck	H	2-0	Ehmann, Tutu
27/11/99	SV Ried	A	1-3	Tutu
04/03/00	SV Salzburg	H	2-0	Amerhauser, Akwuegbu
10/03/00	SK Sturm Graz	A	1-6	Amerhauser
18/03/00	LASK Linz	H	2-1	Lipa, Pamic
25/03/00	SW Bregenz	A	1-3	Pamic
01/04/00	SK Rapid Wien	A	0-2	
07/04/00	SK Rapid Wien	H	0-4	
15/04/00	FC Tirol Innsbruck	A	0-1	
22/04/00	SC Austria Lustenau	H	2-0	Pamic, Ramusch
29/04/00	FK Austria Wien	A	0-2	
06/05/00	SV Ried	H	1-1	Tutu
09/05/00	SV Salzburg	A	1-5	Amerhauser
13/05/00	SK Sturm Graz	H	2-4	Pamic 2
20/05/00	LASK Linz	A	2-2	Akwuegbu, Lipa
27/05/00	SW Bregenz	H	0-4	

LASK LINZ

LASK Linz
Stadion der Stadt Linz, Ziegeleistrasse, 4020 Linz
tel - (0732) 603332 / fax - (0732) 6033329
website - http://www.lask.at
email - master@lask.at
Year of Formation - 1908
President - Peter-Michael Reichel
Secretary - Gottfried Leeb
Coach - Marinko Koljanin
Stadium - Linzer Stadion (25,138)

MAJOR HONOURS
League Championship - (1) 1965.
Domestic Cup - (1) 1965.

APPEARANCES 99/00

	P	Ap	(s)	Gls
Cheikh Sidy BA (SEN)	D	26	(2)	
Amir BRADARIC	M	14	(6)	2
Ewald BRENNER	A	28	(4)	6
Eugène DADI (FRA)	A	9	(4)	3
Herbert GRASSLER	D	28	(3)	1
Lukas HINTERSTEINER	M		(1)	
Karl IRNDORFER	M		(1)	
Hannes JOCHUM	D	24		
Jürgen KAUZ	M	27		2
Markus KIESENEBNER	M	3	(7)	
Armin LEITNER	D		(1)	
Christoph LICHTENWAGNER	M	8	(10)	5
Michael MEHLEM	D	22	(10)	
Almir MEMIC (BOS)	A	1	(4)	
Zeljko MILINOVIC (SLO)	D	31	(1)	2
Bernhard MUHR	D	23	(5)	
Pascal ORTNER	M	1	(8)	
Jürgen PANIS	M	32		3
Zeljko PAVLOVIC (CRO)	G	27		
Jürgen PICHORNER	M	26	(7)	2
Klaus ROHSEANO	M	18		
Souleymane SANE (SEN)	A		(10)	
Christian STUMPF	A	15	(7)	3
Saso UDOVIC (SLO)	A	20	(7)	11
Markus WEISSENBERGER	M	4		1
David WIMLEITNER	G	9	(2)	

LEAGUE RESULTS 1999/2000

30/06/99	SK Sturm Graz	H	0-2	
07/07/99	SC Austria Lustenau	A	1-1	Dadi
14/07/99	FK Austria Wien	H	1-1	Dadi
17/07/99	SV Salzburg	A	1-2	Weissenberger
27/07/99	FC Tirol Innsbruck	A	0-5	
03/08/99	Grazer AK	H	1-3	Udovic
07/08/99	SW Bregenz	A	1-2	Kauz
14/08/99	SK Rapid Wien	H	0-1	
21/08/99	SV Ried	A	1-2	Dadi
28/08/99	SV Ried	H	1-0	Udovic
10/09/99	SK Sturm Graz	A	0-0	
18/09/99	SC Austria Lustenau	H	3-0	Brenner, Udovic 2
25/09/99	FK Austria Wien	A	1-2	Stumpf
02/10/99	SV Salzburg	H	2-4	Stumpf, Kauz
06/10/99	FC Tirol Innsbruck	H	3-0	Bradaric 2, Stumpf
16/10/99	Grazer AK	A	1-0	Milinovic
23/10/99	SW Bregenz	H	3-0	Milinovic, Udovic 2
29/10/99	SK Rapid Wien	A	0-3	
05/11/99	SV Ried	H	1-1	Brenner
12/11/99	FC Tirol Innsbruck	A	0-1	
20/11/99	SK Sturm Graz	H	1-1	Brenner
27/11/99	FK Austria Wien	A	1-3	Grassler
04/03/00	SW Bregenz	H	0-1	
11/03/00	SV Salzburg	A	2-1	Panis, Udovic
18/03/00	Grazer AK	A	1-2	Lichtenwagner
25/03/00	SK Rapid Wien	H	1-1	Udovic
01/04/00	SC Austria Lustenau	A	2-2	Brenner, Lichtenwagner
08/04/00	SC Austria Lustenau	H	5-0	Udovic 2, Lichtenwagner 2, Pichorner
14/04/00	SK Sturm Graz	A	0-2	
22/04/00	FC Tirol Innsbruck	H	0-1	
29/04/00	SV Ried	A	0-2	
06/05/00	FK Austria Wien	H	1-0	Udovic
09/05/00	SW Bregenz	A	2-0	Panis, Lichtenwagner
13/05/00	SV Salzburg	H	1-1	Pichorner
20/05/00	Grazer AK	H	2-2	Brenner 2
27/05/00	SK Rapid Wien	A	1-0	Panis

SC AUSTRIA LUSTENAU

CLUB DIRECTORY

SC Austria Memphis Lustenau
Postfach 138, 6890 Lustenau
tel - (05577) 86250
fax - (05577) 85689
website - www.austria-lustenau.at
email - info@austria-lustenau.at
Year of Formation - 1914
President - Hubert Nagel
Secretary - Christian Ortner
Coach - Klaus Scheer; Goran Stanisavljevic
(00/01 - Wolffgang Schwarz)
Stadium - Reichshof-Stadion (11,750)

APPEARANCES 99/00

		P	Ap	(s)	Gls
Armand BENNEKER (HOL)	D	35			2
Danijel BREZIC (SLO)	M	25	(3)		1
Michael BUTREJ (GER)	M	29			2
Harald DÜRR	M		(3)		
Leeroy ECHTELD (HOL)	A	13	(7)		
Christian ENDER	A		(1)		
Marcus ENZENEBNER	D	1	(3)		
Samir GARCI (TUN)	A	2	(3)		
Theo GRÜNER	M	30	(2)		
Patrick JOVANOVIC	D	20	(8)		1
Harald KATEMANN (GER)	D	31	(2)		
Matthias KECK	M	3	(3)		
Mario KRASSNITZER	G	25			
Birkir KRISTINSSON (ISL)	G	7			
Ivan KRISTO	A	7	(11)		2
Martin LANG	M	4	(1)		
Jürgen MACCANI	M	5	(1)		
José Alex MARCELINO (BRA)	A	22	(11)		2
Michael Jide OLUGBODI (NIG)	M	16	(4)		
Richard PADMORE (GHA)	D	1	(1)		
Alexander PASTOOR (HOL)	D	32	(1)		
Marcelo PAVÃO Moreira (BRA)	M	5	(2)		
Roger PRINZEN (GER)	D	11	(1)		2
Hendrik Jan REGTOP (HOL)	A	18	(2)		3
Thomas RITTER (GER)	M	11			
Markus SCHNEIDHOFER	M	6	(21)		2
Goran STANISAVLJEVIC (YUG)	M	9	(3)		1
Tamás TIEFENBACH (HUN)	A	20	(1)		3
Martin UNGER	G	4			
Clemens ZWIJNENBERG (HOL)	D	4			

LEAGUE RESULTS 1999/2000

30/06/99	SV Salzburg	A	0-1	
07/07/99	LASK Linz	H	1-1	Stanisavljevic (p)
14/07/99	Grazer AK	A	3-2	Regtop, Brezic, Marcelino
21/07/99	SW Bregenz	H	3-0	Benneker, Tiefenbach, Schneidhofer
27/07/99	SV Ried	A	1-1	Butrej
03/08/99	FC Tirol Innsbruck	H	1-3	Tiefenbach
07/08/99	SK Rapid Wien	A	0-2	
14/08/99	SK Sturm Graz	H	1-2	Marcelino
21/08/99	FK Austria Wien	H	1-0	Jovanovic
28/08/99	FK Austria Wien	A	0-2	
11/09/99	SV Salzburg	H	1-0	Benneker
18/09/99	LASK Linz	A	0-3	
25/09/99	Grazer AK	H	1-4	Schneidhofer
02/10/99	SW Bregenz	A	0-2	
06/10/99	SV Ried	H	0-1	
15/10/99	FC Tirol Innsbruck	A	0-3	
23/10/99	SK Rapid Wien	H	0-1	
30/10/99	SK Sturm Graz	A	1-5	Regtop
13/11/99	Grazer AK	H	0-0	
16/11/99	SW Bregenz	A	1-1	Regtop
19/11/99	SK Rapid Wien	A	0-4	
04/03/00	SV Ried	H	1-1	Tiefenbach
11/03/00	FK Austria Wien	A	0-1	
14/03/00	FC Tirol Innsbruck	H	1-1	Prinzen
19/03/00	SK Sturm Graz	H	0-1	
25/03/00	SV Salzburg	A	0-2	
01/04/00	LASK Linz	H	2-2	Butrej, Prinzen
08/04/00	LASK Linz	A	0-5	
15/04/00	SK Rapid Wien	H	0-1	
22/04/00	Grazer AK	A	0-2	
29/04/00	SW Bregenz	H	0-4	
05/05/00	FC Tirol Innsbruck	A	0-1	
09/05/00	SV Ried	A	2-4	Kristo, og (Hujdurovic)
13/05/00	FK Austria Wien	H	1-2	Kristo
20/05/00	SK Sturm Graz	A	0-7	
27/05/00	SV Salzburg	H	0-2	

SK RAPID WIEN

CLUB DIRECTORY

Sportklub Rapid Wien
Keisslergasse 6, 1140 Wien
tel - (01) 91001 / fax - (01) 9111906
website - http://www.skrapid.at
email - skrapid pieber@master co.at
Year of Formation - 1899
Secretary - Werner Kuhn
Coach - Heribert Weber (00/01 - Ernst Dokupil)
Stadium - Gerhard-Hanappi (19,600)

MAJOR HONOURS
League Championship - (30) 1912, 1913, 1916,
1917, 1919, 1920, 1921, 1923, 1929, 1930,
1935, 1938, 1940, 1941, 1946, 1948, 1951,
1952, 1954, 1956, 1957, 1960, 1964, 1967,
1968, 1982, 1983, 1987, 1988, 1996.
Domestic Cup - (14) 1919, 1920, 1927, 1946,
1961, 1968, 1969, 1972, 1976, 1983, 1984,
1985, 1987, 1995.

APPEARANCES 99/00

	P	Ap	(s)	Gls
Martin BRAUN (GER)	M	1		
Jens DOWE (GER)	M	28	(4)	1
Stefan FEITSCH	M		(4)	
Oliver FREUND (GER)	M	31		3
Andreas IVANSCHITZ	M		(1)	
Michael HATZ	D	24	(1)	3
Raimund HEDL	G	1		
Andreas HERAF	M	8	(2)	
Thomas HIRSCH	D	1		
Andreas LAGONIKAKIS (GRE)	M	30	(1)	2
Oliver LEDERER	M	2	(5)	
Ladislav MAIER (CZE)	G	35		
Farhad MAJIDI (IRN)	A	8	(4)	2
Marek PENKSA (SVK)	A	14	(7)	3
Thomas PICHLMANN	A		(2)	
Zeljko RADOVIC	A	8	(4)	6
Krzysztof RATAJCZYK (POL)	D	10	(2)	1
Jürgen SALER	M	8	(10)	
Dejan SAVICEVIC (YUG)	M	19	(3)	11
Peter SCHÖTTEL	D	33		
Günter SCHIESSWALD	D	28	(2)	3
Florian SCHWARZ	A	3	(9)	
Otto SZABO (SLO)	M	5		
Angelo VIER (GER)	A	1	(2)	
René WAGNER (CZE)	A	34		17
Arnold WETL	M	23	(4)	
Roman WALLNER	A	1	(6)	1
Gerd WIMMER	M	29	(4)	3
Thomas ZINGLER	M	11	(7)	2

LEAGUE RESULTS 1999/2000

29/06/99	FC Tirol Innsbruck	A	1-2	og (Barisic)
07/07/99	SW Bregenz	H	2-0	Wagner, Savicevic (p)
13/07/99	SV Salzburg	H	1-0	Savicevic (p)
17/07/99	SK Sturm Graz	H	0-0	
21/07/99	SV Ried	A	2-1	Hatz, Penksa
31/07/99	FK Austria Wien	A	3-0	Savicevic 2, Wagner
07/08/99	SC Austria Lustenau	H	2-0	Freund, Wagner
14/08/99	LASK Linz	A	1-0	Schiesswald
21/08/99	Grazer AK	H	2-1	Wagner, Zingler
29/08/99	Grazer AK	A	1-3	Schiesswald
11/09/99	FC Tirol Innsbruck	H	2-4	Hatz, Wagner
19/09/99	SW Bregenz	A	1-1	Savicevic
25/09/99	SV Salzburg	A	1-1	Lagonikakis
03/10/99	SV Ried	H	5-1	Savicevic 2, Freund, Schiesswald, Wimmer
06/10/99	SK Sturm Graz	A	0-1	
16/10/99	FK Austria Wien	H	2-0	Zingler, Wagner
23/10/99	SC Austria Lustenau	A	1-0	Wagner
29/10/99	LASK Linz	H	3-0	Wagner 2 (1p), Penksa
07/11/99	FC Tirol Innsbruck	H	0-0	
13/11/99	SV Ried	A	0-1	
19/11/99	SC Austria Lustenau	H	4-0	Wagner, Savicevic (p), Dowe, Penksa
30/11/99	SK Sturm Graz	A	1-3	Wagner
03/03/00	FK Austria Wien	H	1-0	Freund
12/03/00	SW Bregenz	A	3-0	Majidi, Wagner, Radovic
17/03/00	SV Salzburg	H	5-0	Savicevic (p), Lagonikakis, Radovic 2, Hatz
25/03/00	LASK Linz	A	1-1	Wimmer
01/04/00	Grazer AK	H	2-0	Wagner, Radovic
07/04/00	Grazer AK	A	4-0	Wagner, Radovic 2, Ratajczyk
15/04/00	SC Austria Lustenau	A	1-0	Wagner
22/04/00	SV Ried	H	1-0	Wagner (p)
29/04/00	FC Tirol Innsbruck	A	0-1	
06/05/00	SK Sturm Graz	H	2-3	Savicevic 2
09/05/00	FK Austria Wien	A	0-3	
12/05/00	SW Bregenz	H	4-1	Majidi, Wallner, Wimmer, Wagner
20/05/00	SV Salzburg	A	0-0	
27/05/00	LASK Linz	H	0-1	

SV RIED

CLUB DIRECTORY

SV Josko Ried im Innkreis
Bahnhofstrasse 19, 4910 Ried/Innkreis
tel - (07752) 81100 / fax - (07752) 81102
website - www.svried.at
email - office@svried.at
Year of Formation - 1912
President - Wolfgang Deschberger
Secretary - Monique Schlegel
Coach - Heinz Hochhauser
(00/01 - Helmut Kronjäger)
Stadium - Stadion der Stadt Ried (9,500)

MAJOR HONOURS
Domestic Cup - (1) 1998.

APPEARANCES 99/00

	P	Ap	(s)	Gls
Michael ANGERSCHMID	M	26	(4)	2
Michael ANICIC (YUG)	M	22	(6)	5
Mario BROSER	M		(10)	
Ronald BRUNMAYR	A	30	(4)	19
Herwig DRECHSEL	M	19	(6)	3
Andreas FADING	A	5	(4)	3
Oliver GLASNER	D	32		4
Stefan HARTL	M		(3)	
Markus HIDEN	M	27	(8)	1
Faruk HUJDUROVIC (BOS)	D	29	(1)	
Alexander JANK	D	15	(10)	2
Boris KITKA (SVK)	D	14		
Christophe LAUWERS (BEL)	A	9	(12)	
Andrzej LESIAK (POL)	D	32		1
Thomas NENTWICH	D	4	(2)	
Mattias NYLUND (SWE)	M		(2)	
Milan ORAZE	G	35		
Manuel ORTLECHNER	M		(1)	
Elvis RAMAKIC	A	1	(6)	1
Manfred RAZENBÖCK	G	1		
Manfred ROTHBAUER	M	29	(6)	3
Günter STEININGER	D	33		2
Dominik STÖBICH	A		(1)	
Karoly SZANYO	M	4	(2)	
Marco VILLA (GER)	A	8	(14)	8
Helmut ZELLER	M	21	(4)	2

LEAGUE RESULTS 1999/2000

30/06/99	SW Bregenz	A	2-1	Rothbauer, Villa
07/07/99	Grazer AK	H	0-1	
14/07/99	FC Tirol Innsbruck	A	0-1	
21/07/99	SK Rapid Wien	H	1-2	Villa
27/07/99	SC Austria Lustenau	H	1-1	Steininger
03/08/99	SK Sturm Graz	A	1-2	Anicic
07/08/99	SV Salzburg	H	3-0	Anicic, Brunmayr, Drechsel (p)
14/08/99	FK Austria Wien	A	2-0	Rothbauer, Brunmayr
21/08/99	LASK Linz	H	2-1	Steininger, Villa
28/08/99	LASK Linz	A	0-1	
11/09/99	SW Bregenz	H	5-1	Drechsel, Rothbauer, Villa, Brunmayr 2
19/09/99	Grazer AK	A	0-0	
24/09/99	FC Tirol Innsbruck	H	5-0	Brunmayr 3, Villa, Zeller
03/10/99	SK Rapid Wien	A	1-5	Zeller
06/10/99	SC Austria Lustenau	A	1-0	Hiden
16/10/99	SK Sturm Graz	H	2-0	Glasner, Villa
23/10/99	SV Salzburg	A	2-2	Brunmayr 2 (1p)
30/10/99	FK Austria Wien	H	0-0	
05/11/99	LASK Linz	A	1-1	Glasner
13/11/99	SK Rapid Wien	H	1-0	Anicic
20/11/99	SV Salzburg	A	1-2	Villa
27/11/99	Grazer AK	H	3-1	Ramakic, Villa, Jank
04/03/00	SC Austria Lustenau	A	1-1	Glasner
11/03/00	FC Tirol Innsbruck	H	1-2	Anicic (p)
19/03/00	FK Austria Wien	H	1-2	Brunmayr
24/03/00	SK Sturm Graz	A	2-3	Glasner, Brunmayr
01/04/00	SW Bregenz	H	2-0	Fading, Jank
08/04/00	SW Bregenz	A	4-0	Angerschmid, Fading, Brunmayr 2
15/04/00	SV Salzburg	H	2-0	Brunmayr 2
22/04/00	SK Rapid Wien	A	0-1	
29/04/00	LASK Linz	H	2-0	Angerschmid, Drechsel
06/05/00	Grazer AK	A	1-1	Anicic
09/05/00	SC Austria Lustenau	H	4-2	Brunmayr 3, Lesiak
13/05/00	FC Tirol Innsbruck	A	1-3	Brunmayr
20/05/00	FK Austria Wien	A	0-1	
27/05/00	SK Sturm Graz	H	1-1	Fading

SV SALZBURG

CLUB DIRECTORY

SV Wüstenrot Salzburg
Alpenstrasse 61, 5033 Salzburg
tel - (0662) 433332 / fax - (0662) 430216
website - www.sv-wuestenrot-salzburg.co.at
email - office@sv-wuestenrot-salzburg.co.at
Year of Formation - 1933
President - Anton Pichler
Secretary - Rudi Mirtl
Coach - Johann Krankl; Miroslav Polak
(00/01 - Hans Backe)
Stadium - Casino Stadion Salzburg (14,457)

MAJOR HONOURS
League Championship - (3) 1994, 1995, 1997.

APPEARANCES 99/00

		P	Ap	(s)	Gls
Franz AIGNER	M		2	(1)	
Heinz ARZBERGER	G		2	(1)	
René AUFHAUSER	M		27	(6)	4
Amir BRADARIC	M		1	(4)	
Markus FÜRSTALLER	D			(1)	
Eduard GLIEDER	A		13	(3)	4
Mario HIEBLINGER	D		5	(2)	
Adolf HÜTTER	M		24	(4)	2
Robert IBERTSBERGER	D		20		1
Christoph JANK	D		25	(3)	
Florian KARASEK	D		3	(1)	
Newton Ben KATANHA (ZIM)	A			(1)	
Erwin KEIL	M			(1)	
Richard KITZBICHLER	M		22	(6)	3
Samuel KOEJOE (HOL)	A		11	(7)	2
Attila KORSÓS (HUN)	M		14	(3)	3
Heiko LAESSIG (GER)	M		28	(1)	2
Péter LIPCSEI (HUN)	M		17	(8)	
Harald MEYSSEN (BEL)	M		12	(1)	1
Sladjan NIKOLIC (YUG)	M		21	(6)	6
Manfred PAMMINGER	M		10	(10)	
Heimo PFEIFENBERGER	A		9	(2)	
Anton POLSTER	A		12		2
Werner PROMBERGER	A		2	(10)	3
Herfried SABITZER	A		13	(4)	1
Szabolcs SÁFÁR (HUN)	G		34		
Florian SCHWARZ	A		4	(5)	1
Gerhard STRUBER	A		7	(3)	2
Roman SZEWCZYK (POL)	D		27		
Bernd WINKLER	A			(1)	
Thomas WINKLHOFER	D		31		1

LEAGUE RESULTS 1999/2000

30/06/99	SC Austria Lustenau	H	1-0	Nikolic
06/07/99	FK Austria Wien	A	0-2	
13/07/99	SK Rapid Wien	A	0-1	
17/07/99	LASK Linz	H	2-1	Ibertsberger, Koejoe
27/07/99	Grazer AK	A	0-0	
03/08/99	SW Bregenz	H	0-1	
07/08/99	SV Ried	A	0-3	
14/08/99	FC Tirol Innsbruck	H	1-0	Aufhauser
21/08/99	SK Sturm Graz	A	2-0	Koejoe, Korsós
28/08/99	SK Sturm Graz	H	1-1	Korsós
11/09/99	SC Austria Lustenau	A	0-1	
17/09/99	FK Austria Wien	H	0-1	
25/09/99	SK Rapid Wien	H	1-1	Glieder
02/10/99	LASK Linz	A	4-2	Glieder 2, Korsós, Nikolic
06/10/99	Grazer AK	H	1-0	Glieder (p)
16/10/99	SW Bregenz	A	0-0	
23/10/99	SV Ried	H	2-2	Sabitzer, og (Lesiak)
31/10/99	FC Tirol Innsbruck	A	0-0	
06/11/99	SK Sturm Graz	H	0-0	
14/11/99	FK Austria Wien	A	2-2	Aufhauser, Promberger
20/11/99	SV Ried	H	2-1	Nikolic 2
27/11/99	SW Bregenz	H	4-1	Promberger 2, Kitzbichler, Winklhofer
04/03/00	Grazer AK	A	0-2	
11/03/00	LASK Linz	H	1-2	Laessig
17/03/00	SK Rapid Wien	A	0-5	
25/03/00	SC Austria Lustenau	H	2-0	Kitzbichler, Struber
01/04/00	FC Tirol Innsbruck	A	1-2	Nikolic
08/04/00	FC Tirol Innsbruck	H	0-1	
15/04/00	SV Ried	A	0-2	
22/04/00	FK Austria Wien	H	2-1	Laessig, Hütter
29/04/00	SK Sturm Graz	A	1-3	Hütter (p)
06/05/00	SW Bregenz	A	1-5	Polster
09/05/00	Grazer AK	H	5-1	Struber, Nikolic, Aufhauser 2, Meyssen
13/05/00	LASK Linz	A	1-1	Kitzbichler
20/05/00	SK Rapid Wien	H	0-0	
27/05/00	SC Austria Lustenau	A	2-0	Polster, Schwarz

SK STURM GRAZ

CLUB DIRECTORY

SK Puntigamer Sturm Graz
Eggenberger Gürtel 9/i, 8020 Graz
tel - (0316) 771771 / fax - (0316) 724811
website - www.sksturm.at
email - advisor@sksturm.at
Year of Formation - 1909
President - Gerhard Stroicz
Secretary - Heinz Schilcher
Coach - Ivica Osim
Stadium - Arnold Schwarzenegger-Stadion (15,428)

MAJOR HONOURS
League Championship - (2) 1998, 1999.
Domestic Cup - (3) 1996, 1997, 1999.

APPEARANCES 99/00

	P	Ap	(s)	Gls
Didier ANGIBEAUD (CMR)	M	1	(6)	
Georg BARDEL	M		(2)	
Michael BOCHTLER (GER)	D		(2)	
Ferdinand FELDHOFER	D	2	(6)	
Andrés FLEURQUIN (URU)	M	13		2
Franco FODA (GER)	D	33		
Thomas GRÖBL	M		(2)	
Tomislav KOCIJAN	M	23	(3)	9
György KORSÓS (HUN)	M	10	(10)	1
Georgios KOUTSOUPIAS (GRE)	D	1	(1)	
Roman MÄHLICH	M	19		
Jan-Pieter MARTENS (BEL)	M	18	(9)	4
Darko MILANIC (SLO)	D	18	(1)	
Mehrdad MINAVAND (IRN)	M	9	(14)	
Günther NEUKIRCHNER	D	32		3
Marko PANTELIC (YUG)	A	1	(2)	
Ranko POPOVIC (YUG)	D	6		2
Gilbert PRILASNIG	M	29	(5)	5
Hannes REINMAYR	M	22	(10)	6
Josef SCHICKLGRUBER	G	34		
Markus SCHOPP	M	27		6
Markus SCHUPP (GER)	M	33		2
Kazimierz SIDORCZUK (POL)	G	2		
Gerald STRAFNER	A	15	(12)	1
Imre SZABICS (HUN)	A	3	(11)	1
Ivica VASTIC	M	35		32
Sergei YURAN (RUS)	A	10	(1)	3

LEAGUE RESULTS 1999/2000

30/06/99	LASK Linz	A	2-0	Strafner, Martens
07/07/99	FC Tirol Innsbruck	H	0-1	
14/07/99	SW Bregenz	A	4-1	Vastic 3 (1p), Martens
17/07/99	SK Rapid Wien	A	0-0	
21/07/99	Grazer AK	H	5-0	Vastic 3 (1p), Reinmayr, Prilasnig
03/08/99	SV Ried	H	2-1	Popovic, Vastic (p)
07/08/99	FK Austria Wien	H	2-2	Neukirchner, Reinmayr
14/08/99	SC Austria Lustenau	A	2-1	Reinmayr, Vastic
21/08/99	SV Salzburg	H	0-2	
28/08/99	SV Salzburg	A	1-1	Kocijan
10/09/99	LASK Linz	H	0-0	
18/09/99	FC Tirol Innsbruck	A	0-1	
25/09/99	SW Bregenz	H	4-0	Kocijan, Korsós, Neukirchner, Vastic (p)
03/10/99	Grazer AK	A	0-1	
06/10/99	SK Rapid Wien	H	1-0	Prilasnig
16/10/99	SV Ried	A	0-2	
22/10/99	FK Austria Wien	A	3-1	Martens, Vastic, Schopp
30/10/99	SC Austria Lustenau	H	5-1	Vastic 4, Kocijan
06/11/99	SV Salzburg	A	0-0	
13/11/99	SW Bregenz	H	3-1	Kocijan 2 (1p), Szabics
20/11/99	LASK Linz	A	1-1	Schopp
30/11/99	SK Rapid Wien	H	3-1	Vastic 3
05/03/00	FC Tirol Innsbruck	A	1-1	Prilasnig
10/03/00	Grazer AK	H	6-1	Schopp, Neukirchner, Schupp, Vastic 2, Martens
19/03/00	SC Austria Lustenau	A	1-0	Fleurquin
24/03/00	SV Ried	H	3-2	Vastic 2 (1p), Reinmayr
01/04/00	FK Austria Wien	H	3-2	Vastic, Reinmayr, Kocijan
08/04/00	FK Austria Wien	A	1-0	Vastic
14/04/00	LASK Linz	H	2-0	Vastic 2
22/04/00	SW Bregenz	A	0-1	
29/04/00	SV Salzburg	H	3-1	Kocijan, Yuran, Fleurquin
06/05/00	SK Rapid Wien	A	3-2	Prilasnig, Reinmayr, Vastic
10/05/00	FC Tirol Innsbruck	H	4-1	Schopp, Vastic 2, Yuran
13/05/00	Grazer AK	A	4-2	Popovic, Yuran, Prilasnig, Schopp
20/05/00	SC Austria Lustenau	H	7-0	Kocijan, Schupp, Vastic 4, Schopp
27/05/00	SV Ried	A	1-1	Kocijan

FC TIROL INNSBRUCK

CLUB DIRECTORY

FC Tirol Milch Innsbruck
Resselstrasse 18/II, 6020 Innsbruck
tel - (0512) 33432   fax - (0512) 393288
website - www.fc-tirol.at
email - sekretariat@fc-tirol.at
Year of Formation - 1913
President - Martin Kerscher
Secretary - Siegmund Feistmantl
Coach - Kurt Jara
Stadium - Tivoli (18,100)

MAJOR HONOURS
League Championship - (8) 1971, 1972, 1973,
1975, 1977, 1989, 1990, 2000.
Domestic Cup - (7)
1970, 1973, 1975, 1978, 1979, 1989, 1993.

APPEARANCES 99/00

	P	Ap	(s)	Gls
Markus ANFANG (GER)	M	26	(1)	1
Zoran BARISIC	D	15	(2)	4
Michael BAUR	M	18	(1)	4
Bruno BERLOFFA	M		(1)	
Stanislav CHERCHESOV (RUS)	G	36		
Christoph DAMM	A		(1)	
Bernhard ERKINGER	M	2	(2)	
Radoslav GILEWICZ (POL)	A	30		18
Eduard GLIEDER	A	11	(1)	
Thomas GRUMSER	M	2	(5)	1
Paul HAFNER	D		(4)	
Alexander HÖRTNAGL	M	3	(9)	
Alfred HÖRTNAGL	M	28	(3)	1
Patrik JEZEK (CZE)	M	21		4
Roland KIRCHLER	M	34		8
Aleksander KNAVS (SLO)	D	28	(1)	1
Stefan KÖCK	D	2	(11)	
Walter KOGLER	D	34		
Wolfgang MAIR	A	9	(20)	3
Stefan MARASEK	M	21		2
Peter PAWLOWSKI	A	2	(9)	
Oliver PRUDLO	D	25	(6)	
Markus SCHARRER	M	23	(10)	6
Florian STURM	A	1	(1)	
Karel VACHA (CZE)	A		(5)	
Robert WAZINGER	M	25	(2)	1
Heinz WEBER	G		(1)	

LEAGUE RESULTS 1999/2000

29/06/99	SK Rapid Wien	H	2-1	Barisic, Gilewicz
07/07/99	SK Sturm Graz	A	1-0	Gilewicz
14/07/99	SV Ried	H	1-0	Gilewicz
21/07/99	FK Austria Wien	A	2-0	Kirchler, Knavs
27/07/99	LASK Linz	H	5-0	Gilewicz 3, Hörtnagl Alf., Scharrer
03/08/99	SC Austria Lustenau	A	3-1	Jezek, Gilewicz, Baur
06/08/99	Grazer AK	H	1-0	Gilewicz
14/08/99	SV Salzburg	A	0-1	
21/08/99	SW Bregenz	H	4-0	Baur, Gilewicz, Mair, Wazinger
28/08/99	SW Bregenz	A	3-0	Gilewicz, Kirchler, Mair
11/09/99	SK Rapid Wien	A	4-2	Gilewicz, Anfang, Barisic, Jezek
18/09/99	SK Sturm Graz	H	1-0	Barisic
24/09/99	SV Ried	A	0-5	
01/10/99	FK Austria Wien	H	0-2	
06/10/99	LASK Linz	A	0-3	
15/10/99	SC Austria Lustenau	H	3-0	Jezek, Barisic, Scharrer
24/10/99	Grazer AK	A	1-1	Scharrer (p)
31/10/99	SV Salzburg	H	0-0	
07/11/99	SK Rapid Wien	A	0-0	
12/11/99	LASK Linz	H	1-0	Jezek
23/11/99	Grazer AK	A	0-2	
05/03/00	SK Sturm Graz	H	1-1	Gilewicz
11/03/00	SV Ried	A	2-1	Marasek, Gilewicz
14/03/00	SC Austria Lustenau	A	1-1	Mair
21/03/00	SW Bregenz	H	2-0	Gilewicz, Scharrer
26/03/00	FK Austria Wien	A	0-2	
01/04/00	SV Salzburg	H	2-1	Marasek, Scharrer
08/04/00	SV Salzburg	A	1-0	Gilewicz
15/04/00	Grazer AK	H	1-0	Gilewicz
22/04/00	LASK Linz	A	1-0	Scharrer (p)
29/04/00	SK Rapid Wien	H	1-0	Kirchler
05/05/00	SC Austria Lustenau	H	1-0	Grumser
10/05/00	SK Sturm Graz	A	1-4	Gilewicz
13/05/00	SV Ried	H	3-1	Baur, Kirchler, Gilewicz
20/05/00	SW Bregenz	A	3-0	Kirchler 3
27/05/00	FK Austria Wien	H	2-1	Kirchler, Baur

AZERBAIJAN

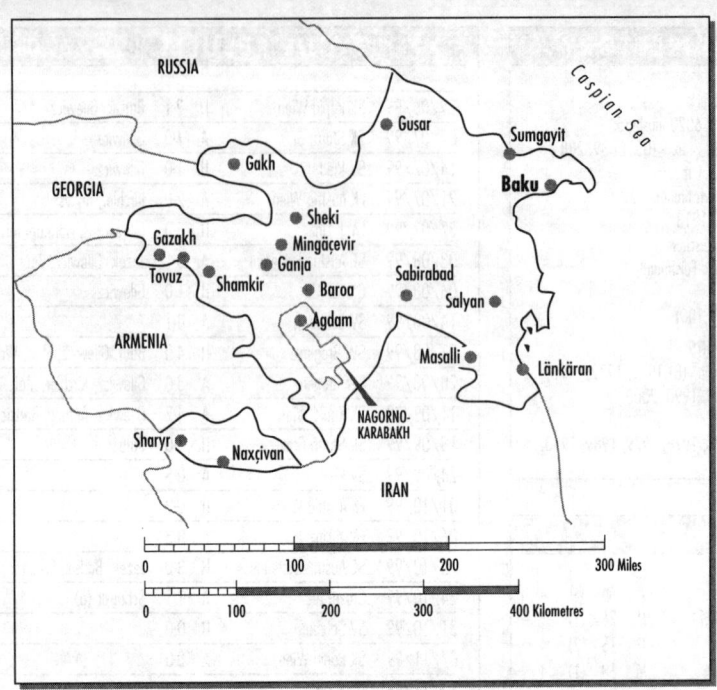

GEORGIAN FIRES SHAMKIR TO TITLE

Famous win snatched away by Figo

FEDERATION DIRECTORY

Azärbaycan Futbol Federasiyalari Assosiasiyasi
42 Hüsü Haciyev küç., 370009 Baku

tel - (12) 944916   Year of Formation - 1992
fax - (12) 989393   President - Fuad Musaev

Stadium - Tofik Bakhramov, Baku (36,080)

Azerbaijan's largely uneventful European Championship qualifying adventure nearly provided a highlight to treasure. The team's penultimate home fixture, against Portugal, was 90 minutes old when, with almost the last kick of the game, Azerbaijan were robbed of a famous victory by an equalising goal from superstar Luís Figo.

The Azerbaijanis had led since the 51st minute with a goal from young midfielder Zaur Tagizade but just couldn't quite resist the barrage of pressure that the Portuguese piled on their goal in the closing minutes. Nevertheless, a draw against such a strong and skilful team was regarded as an extremely positive result - especially as Portugal had blitzed them 7-0 in the reverse fixture.

Sadly, that game in Baku proved to be a flash in the pan because Azerbaijan were well beaten in their next two matches - 3-0 in Hungary and 1-0 at home to Slovakia. Those results led to the dismissal of Akhmed Aleskerov as national team coach.

LEAGUE CHAMPIONSHIP RESULTS 99/00

		1	2	3	4	5	6	7	8	9	10	11	12
1	ANS Pivani Baku		0-1	4-1	0-3	2-2	1-0	1-0	1-1	3-1	0-3	1-0	1-0
2	Dinamo Baku	1-0		3-1	0-2	1-0	0-1	0-2	4-0	0-0	0-2	2-0	2-1
3	Hazar Universiteti Baku	1-0	0-2		3-1	0-0	2-1	2-3	2-0	1-2	0-2	0-0	0-0
4	Kapaz Ganja	2-1	1-0	4-2		1-1	2-0	1-0	5-1	1-0	0-0	9-0	3-0
5	Karabakh Agdam	3-0	0-0	2-0	2-1		3-2	1-1	***	2-0	1-5	0-0	0-0
6	Kimyachi Sumgayit	0-1	1-0	1-0	2-3	1-0		1-2	2-0	4-2	***	4-1	1-3
7	Neftchi Baku	***	1-0	5-1	3-1	2-0	4-0		1-0	2-0	0-0	1-1	3-0
8	OIK Baku	2-1	0-0	0-2	1-2	1-1	2-1	1-2		0-1	0-3	1-0	0-2
9	Shafa Baku	0-2	0-3	1-0	3-2	2-2	2-0	0-0	3-0		0-2	1-0	3-1
10	Shamkir	1-0	2-0	6-0	2-1	1-0	0-0	2-0	3-1	2-0		2-1	2-0
11	Turan Tovuz	2-3	2-1	2-1	0-1	0-0	1-0	0-2	1-0	3-0	3-3		0-1
12	Vilash Masalli	1-2	1-1	2-0	3-0	2-1	2-1	2-1	1-0	2-1	1-3	3-0	

N.B. *** - match void; awarded as 0-3 defeat against both teams.

LEAGUE CHAMPIONSHIP FINAL TABLE 99/00

		Pd	W	D	L	F	A	W	D	L	F	A	W	D	L	F	A	Pt	GD
1	Shamkir	22	10	1	0	23	3	7	3	1	23	8	17	4	1	46	11	55	35
2	Kapaz Ganja	22	9	2	0	29	5	5	0	6	17	19	14	2	6	46	24	44	22
3	Neftchi Baku	22	8	2	1	22	6	5	2	4	13	11	13	4	5	35	17	43	18
4	Vilash Masalli	22	8	1	2	20	10	3	2	6	8	15	11	3	8	28	25	36	3
5	ANS Pivani Baku	22	6	2	3	14	12	4	0	7	10	16	10	2	10	24	28	32	-4
6	Dinamo Baku	22	6	1	4	13	9	3	3	5	8	8	9	4	9	21	17	31	4
7	Shafa Baku	22	6	2	3	15	12	2	1	8	7	20	8	3	11	22	32	27	-10
8	Karabakh Agdam	22	5	4	2	14	12	0	6	5	7	13	5	10	7	21	25	25	-4
9	Kimyachi Sumgayit	22	6	0	5	17	15	1	1	9	6	19	7	1	14	23	34	22	-11
10	Turan Tovuz	22	5	2	4	14	12	0	3	8	3	24	5	5	12	17	36	20	-19
11	Hazar Universiteti Baku	22	4	3	4	11	11	1	0	10	8	30	5	3	14	19	41	18	-22
12	OIK Baku	22	3	2	6	8	15	0	1	10	3	26	3	3	16	11	41	12	-30

NATIONAL TEAM APPEARANCES 99/00

Coach - Akhmed ALESKEROV; Asker ABDULLAYEV	POR	HUN	SVK	MLT	ALB	AND	GEO
Dmitriy KRAMARENKO (12/09/74) - Dinamo Moskva (RUS)	G		G				
Ermin AGAEV (16/07/73) - Torpedo-ZIL Moskva (RUS)	D		D80				D61
Tarlan AKHMEDOV (17/11/71) - Neftchi Baku	D		D	D	D	D	D
Igor GETMAN (06/07/71) - Neftchi Baku	D	D	D	D46			
Bakhtiyar MUSAYEV (04/08/73) - Neftchi Baku	D58	D	D	s46		D	s46
Vladimir POSHEKHONTSEV (23/05/67) - Neftchi Baku	M	M	M				
Vyacheslav LYCHKIN (30/09/73) - Torpedo-ZIL Moskva (RUS)	M90	M68	s46				M46
Kamal KULIYEV (14/11/76) - Neftchi Baku	M	M		M	M	M	M
Zaur TAGIZADE (21/02/69) - Neftchi Baku/Lelle SK (EST)	M			M	M	M46	
Vadim VASILYEV (17/05/72) - Neftchi Baku	A54	A90	A	A	A	A	A
Adagim NIFTALIYEV (07/09/76) - Neftchi Baku	A	A	A		A		
Elshan KAMBAROV (30/10/72) - Neftchi Baku	s54	s60	M46				s63
Makhmud KURBANOV (10/05/73) - Kapaz Ganka/Shamkir	s58			M46	D		
Alexei STUKAS (17/02/79) - Neftchi Baku	s90	s68					
Jangiv GASANZADE (04/08/79) - Neftchi Baku		G			G	G	
Aslan KERIMOV (01/01/73) - Baltika Kaliningrad (RUS)		D60	s80				s61
Arif ASADOV (18/08/70) - Karabakh Agdam		M		M	M	M	M
Ilgham YADULLAYEV (17/09/75) - Neftchi Baku		M	M	M	M	M	M
Farrukh ISMAILOV (30/08/78) - Neftchi Baku		s90	s56	s46		s46	
Mirbagir ISAEV (13/03/74) - Karabakh Agdam		M56					
Elkhan GASANOV (03/04/67) - KTP (FIN)		G					
Ruslan MUSAYEV (21/05/79) - Tulevik Viljandi (EST)			M	M	M	s85	
Elichin RAKHMANOV (18/01/79) - Neftchi Baku			M				
Abuzar IBRAGINOV (03/06/75) - Shafa Baku			D				
Kurban KURBANOV (13/04/72) - Baltika Kaliningrad (RUS)			M	M			
Gusein MAGOMEDOV (22/08/74) - Kapaz Ganja							G
Vidadi RZAEV (04/09/67) - Kapaz Ganja							M63
Elshat KULIYEV (04/11/76) - Kapaz Ganja							M85
Badri KVARATSHELIA (12/02/65) - Shamkir							A75
Ramiz MAMEDOV (15/08/68) - Kapaz Ganja							s75

His successor, Asker Abdullayev, made his bow at the Rothmans Cup in Malta but three disappointing, goalless performances there against fellow minnows Malta, Albania and Andorra did not bode well, and when another 0-0 draw followed in June at home to Georgia, Abdullayev went the same way as his predecessor, with former Soviet Union international Igor Ponomarev being appointed in his stead to oversee the 2002 World Cup qualifying campaign.

The match against Georgia was memorable chiefly for the international début of 35-year-old Badri Kvaratshelia. Although Georgian by birth, he was persuaded to take out Azeri citizenship and promptly made his first international appearance against his homeland.

Kvaratshelia was much in demand because of his outstanding season in the Azeri domestic championship, during which he not only claimed the top-scorer prize with 16 goals but also won a second successive championship winner's medal. Transferred from Kapaz Ganja to Shamkir at the start of the season, he formed a

TOP SCORERS

16	Badri KVARATSHELIA (Shamkir)	
12	Rovsan AKHMEDOV (Kapaz Ganja)	
	Viktor KULIKOV (Shamkir)	
10	Ramiz MAMEDOV (Kapaz Ganja)	

INTERNATIONAL HONOURS

None

NATIONAL TEAM RESULTS 99/00

04/09/99	Portugal (ECQ)	H	Baku	1-1	Tagizade (51)
08/09/99	Hungary (ECQ)	A	Budapest	0-3	
09/10/99	Slovakia (ECQ)	H	Baku	0-1	
06/02/00	Malta	A	Ta' Qali	0-3	
08/02/00	Albania	N	Ta' Qali	0-1	
10/02/00	Andorra	N	Ta' Qali	0-0	
04/06/00	Georgia	H	Baku	0-0	

DOMESTIC CUP 99/00

1/8 FINALS
Shafa-2 Baku v Neftchi Baku 0-3; 1-3
(Neftchi Baku 6-1)
Shamkir v Vilash Masalli 1-1; 0-0
(1-1; Vilash Masalli on away goal)
Kapaz Ganja v Kimyachi Sumgayit 5-0; 0-1
(Kapaz Ganja 5-1)
Turan Tovuz v Karabakh Agdam 0-1; 1-0
(1-1; Karabakh Agdam 5-4 on pens.)
Hazar Universitet Baku v Shafa Baku 2-2; 1-4
(Shafa Baku 6-3)
OIK Baku v ANS Pivani Baku 0-2; 0-1
(ANS Pivani Baku 3-0)
Deniz Neftchilari v Dinamo Baku 1-4; 1-10
(Dinamo Baku 14-2)
Azersun v Shahdag Guba 2-0; 3-0
(Azersun 5-0)

QUARTER-FINALS
ANS Pivani Baku v Neftchi Baku 0-1; 0-1
(Neftchi Baku 2-0)
Vilash Masalli v Azersun 2-0; 0-0
(Vilash Masalli 2-0)
Dinamo Baku v Kapaz Ganja 1-1; 0-0
(1-1; Kapaz Ganja on away goal)
Karabakh Agdam v Shafa Baku 0-0; 2-1
(Karabakh Agdam 2-1)

SEMI-FINALS
Kapaz Ganja v Neftchi Baku 1-0; 0-0
(Kapaz Ganja 1-0)
Karabakh Agdam v Vilash Masalli 1-0; 1-1
(Karabakh Agdam 2-1)

FINAL
28/05/2000, Baku
KAPAZ GANJA 2 Mamedov (53), Akhmedov (69)
KARABAKH AGDAM 1 Shaguliyev (90)
referee - Mamedov
KAPAZ GANJA - Huseynov Ma., Rzaev, Sahniyarov,
Veliyev V., Kuliyev, Sukurov, Huseynov Mu.
(Suleymanov 79), Mamedov, Jabbarov (Veliyev R.
87), Hasanov (Allakhverdiyev 88), Akhmedov.
KARABAKH AGDAM - Kuliyev Vur., Aliyev, Akhmedov
(Mustafayev 88), Asadov, Muslimov, Kuliyev Vug.,
Hankisiyev, Ismailov, Kurbanov A. (Bagirov 57),
Huseynov V. (Huseynov Y. 77), Sahguliyev.

lethal striking partnership with Ukrainian Viktor Kulikov, and together these two fired the goals which sped Shamkir to the first championship title in their history.

It was a very convincing triumph. The figures in the final table showed one defeat, but no team had actually beaten Shamkir. That 'defeat' was in fact a punishment which Shamkir shared with six other clubs who had all staged a boycott in the eighth round of matches following a conflict between the clubs and two rival governing bodies. With order restored, Shamkir went about their business in irresistible fashion and clinched the title two rounds before the end.

There was no joy for the champions in the Cup competitions. Well beaten by Ukrainian side Kryvbas in the qualifying round of the UEFA Cup, Shamkir also fell at the first hurdle of the domestic Cup, against Vilash Masalli. The trophy was eventually won by Kapaz Ganja, who overcame Karabakh Agdam 2-1 in a final watched by around 6,000 spectators in Baku's Tofik Bakhramov Stadium.

The country's best-known club, Neftchi Baku, were pleased to see Kapaz win because it meant that they joined them in qualifying for the UEFA Cup. Neftchi, who supplied several players to the national team during the season, could finish only third in the league. It was of minimal comfort to them that they were the best-placed of the six clubs from the capital, two of whom, student club Hazar Universiteti and army club OIK, were relegated.

EUROPEAN CUPS 99/00

CHAMPIONS' CUP
● **KAPAZ GANJA**
Preliminary round 1 SLOGA JUGOMAGNAT SKOPJE (MAC)
A 0-1
Magomedov, Sahniyarov, Veliyev, Kuliyev, Kurbanov, Mamedov,
Jabbarov, Akhmedov, Rzaev, Kerdzevadze (Sukurov 71), Huseynov
(Suleymanov 76).
H 2-1 Mamedov (20), Rzaev (90p)
Magomedov, Sahniyarov, Veliyev (Suleymanov 46), Kuliyev, Kurbanov,
Mamedov, Jabbarov (Parvarov 72), Akhmedov, Rzaev, Kerdzevadze
(Allakhverdiyev 68), Huseynov.

UEFA CUP
● **NEFTCHI BAKU**
Qualifying round CRVENA ZVEZDA BEOGRAD (YUG)
H 2-3 Vasilyev (27, 65)
Gasanzade, Getman, Akhmedov, Poshekhontsev (Yadullayev 74), Kuliyev,
Kambarov, Vasilyev, Musayev (Ismailov 77), Tagizade, Stukas
(Rakhmanov 41), Niftaliyev.

A 0-1
Gasanzade, Getman, Akhmedov, Kuliyev, Vasilyev, Musayev
(Ismailov 86), Yadullayev, Tagizade, Ismailov (Kambarov 46), Stukas,
Niftaliyev (Aliyev 90).

● **SHAMKIR**
Qualifying round KRYVBAS KRYVYI RIH (UKR)
A 0-3
Mekhdiev, Yunusov, Mamedov Az., Jabbarov, Abushev (Kulikov 58), Aliev
(Ibragimov 77), Mardanov, Mamedov I. (Orujuv 35), Kvaratshelia,
Mamedov Ar., Kurbanov.
H 0-2
Mekhdiev, Mamedov Ar. (Abushev 26), Yunusov, Mamedov Az., Jabbarov
(Odjaguevdiev 72), Kulikov, Aliev, Mardanov, Orujov, Mamedov I.
(Kurbanov 46), Kvaratshelia.

BELARUS

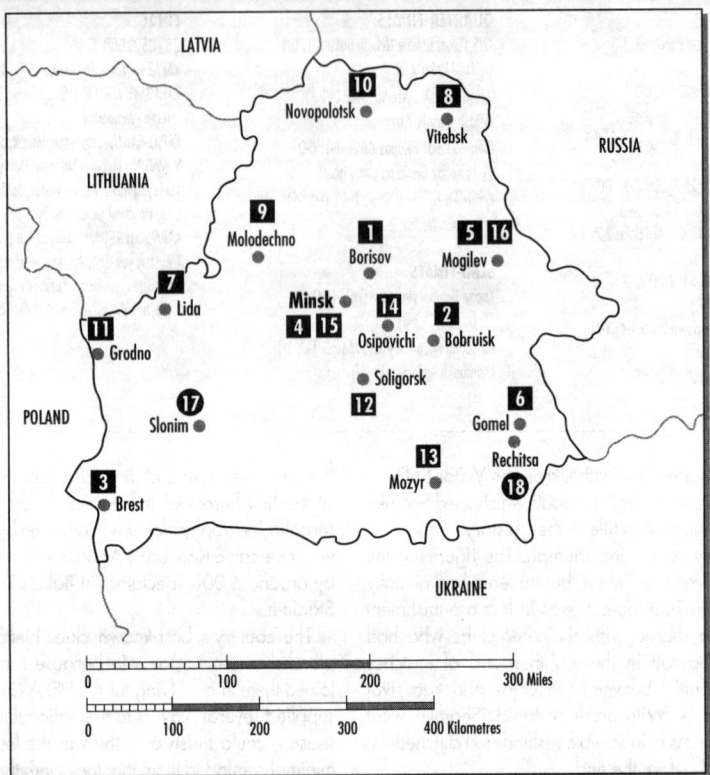

FIRST TITLE FOR BATE BORISOV

Depression right across the board

FEDERATION DIRECTORY

The Belarussian Football Federation
ul. S. Kirov 8/2, 220060 Minsk

tel - (017) 2272920/2272325/
2204540
fax - (017) 2272920/2273429
email - gambler@belpak.minsk.by

Year of Formation - 1992
President - Grigoriy Fedorov
Secretary - Viktor Ivanovskiy

Stadium - Dinamo, Minsk (42,375)

1999 was a year to forget for Belarussian football. The lingering worry, however, is that it wasn't just a one-off. The state of the game in this former Soviet republic is close to total disarray, with standards on the decline and very little interest being generated by supporters or sponsors.

Most footballers who take part in the Belarussian league survive on nothing much more than a hand-to-mouth existence, and it is the fervent ambition of every single one of them to earn a move abroad to neighbouring Russia or Ukraine where the standard of living and the level of pay are so much better.

The depth to which local football has sunk was demonstrated all too starkly by the collective capitulation of Belarus's three participants in the European club competitions. Dnepr-Transmash Mogilev, Belshina Bobruisk and FC BATE Borisov, all going reasonably well at home,

were destroyed by their foreign opponents, losing every game, scoring just two goals between them and conceding 23. Belshina's 8-1 aggregate loss to Omonia Nicosia of Cyprus said it all. Belarus had descended to the bottom of the European barrel.

It was a similar tale of woe for the national team. Though never disgraced in any of their European Championship qualifying matches, they were unable to claim a single victory and took just three points from a possible 24. The irony was that two of those points came at the expense of Italy, the group winners and, ultimately, runners-up at the Euro 2000 finals. The 0-0 draw with the 'Azzurri' in Minsk which concluded Belarus's campaign marked the return to the national team hot seat of Sergei Borovskiy, who, for the second time, replaced his former Dinamo Minsk team-mate Mikhail Vergeyenko as coach.

LEAGUE CHAMPIONSHIP RESULTS 1999

		1	2	3	4	5	6	7	8	9	10	11	12	13	14	15	16
1	FC BATE Borisov		3-1	3-1	2-0	1-1	3-1	1-1	3-2	2-1	7-1	4-1	2-1	1-1	2-0	2-1	4-0
2	Belshina Bobruisk	0-3		4-1	1-1	0-1	0-0	4-1	4-0	3-0	2-2	5-1	3-3	0-0	1-1	2-1	5-1
3	Dinamo Brest	2-4	2-0		2-1	1-1	1-2	1-0	3-0	7-0	3-2	1-1	1-1	2-7	2-0	2-1	4-0
4	Dinamo Minsk	1-0	2-1	3-2		2-1	3-4	5-0	4-0	2-0	2-1	1-1	0-0	0-0	7-0	5-0	1-1
5	Dnepr-Transmash Mogilev	0-0	3-0	4-1	2-1		2-1	3-1	1-0	1-1	0-2	1-1	3-1	3-0	3-1	1-0	5-2
6	FC Gomel	2-2	2-3	3-1	0-1	1-1		3-0	2-0	3-1	2-0	2-0	1-0	1-0	4-1	1-0	5-0
7	FC Lida	0-4	5-1	0-3	2-1	0-0	1-4		0-0	1-0	1-0	0-3	1-2	0-7	0-2	0-1	3-1
8	Lokomotiv-96 Vitebsk	0-1	1-2	0-1	1-0	1-1	2-0	1-1		1-2	2-0	1-1	1-1	0-4	6-1	2-0	4-1
9	FC Molodechno	0-3	1-2	0-3	1-2	1-1	0-1	0-2	1-4		1-3	1-1	0-1	2-5	1-2	2-2	0-5
10	Naftan-Devon Novopolotsk	0-4	1-2	0-5	1-1	1-2	1-2	4-1	3-1	1-2		3-1	0-2	0-3	2-1	4-0	2-0
11	Neman-Belkard Grodno	1-2	1-0	2-1	0-0	0-2	0-2	4-2	2-1	0-0	4-0		0-2	2-3	2-0	1-0	3-0
12	Shakhter Soligorsk	0-1	2-1	7-1	0-1	1-0	2-2	4-1	0-2	3-1	5-2	3-0		2-1	8-1	1-0	1-0
13	Slaviya Mozyr	1-3	1-0	2-1	4-0	4-0	1-1	3-0	3-0	1-0	2-0	3-1	0-2		2-1	2-0	5-0
14	Svisloch-Krovlya Osipovichi	0-5	0-1	1-3	0-0	0-2	1-3	0-3	2-2	3-0	1-1	0-1	0-1	2-3		0-2	3-2
15	Torpedo-MAZ Minsk	1-3	2-1	2-0	1-2	0-3	1-1	1-0	1-1	2-1	2-2	2-1	4-1	1-6	2-0		0-0
16	Torpedo-Kadino Mogilev	1-5	0-3	1-1	2-2	2-5	0-1	1-0	0-4	4-1	2-0	1-0	0-1	0-0	3-0	0-1	

LEAGUE CHAMPIONSHIP FINAL TABLE 1999

		Pd	Home W	D	L	F	A	Away W	D	L	F	A	Total W	D	L	F	A	PT	GD
1	FC BATE Borisov	30	12	3	0	40	13	12	2	1	40	9	24	5	1	80	22	77	58
2	Slaviya Mozyr	30	12	1	2	34	9	8	4	3	40	16	20	5	5	74	25	65	49
3	FC Gomel	30	11	2	2	32	10	8	4	3	25	18	19	6	5	57	28	63	29
4	Dnepr-Transmash Mogilev	30	11	3	1	32	12	6	6	3	21	15	17	9	4	53	27	60	26
5	Shakhter Soligorsk	30	11	1	3	39	14	7	4	4	19	16	18	5	7	58	30	59	28
6	Dinamo Minsk	30	10	4	1	38	11	4	5	6	13	19	14	9	7	51	30	51	21
7	Dinamo Brest	30	9	3	3	34	20	5	1	9	25	32	14	4	12	59	52	46	7
8	Belshina Bobruisk	30	7	6	2	34	16	6	0	9	18	26	13	6	11	52	42	45	10
9	Neman-Belkard Grodno	30	8	2	5	22	15	2	5	8	14	28	10	7	13	36	43	37	-7
10	Torpedo-MAZ Minsk	30	7	4	4	22	22	3	1	11	9	25	10	5	15	31	47	35	-16
11	Lokomotiv-96 Vitebsk	30	6	4	5	23	16	3	3	9	17	29	9	7	14	40	45	34	-5
12	Naftan-Devon Novopolotsk	30	6	1	8	23	27	2	3	10	16	36	8	4	18	39	63	28	-24
13	FC Lida	30	5	2	8	14	29	2	2	11	13	35	7	4	19	27	64	25	-37
14	Torpedo-Kadino Mogilev	30	5	3	7	17	24	1	2	12	13	45	6	5	19	30	69	23	-39
15	Svisloch-Krovlya Osipovichi	30	2	3	10	13	29	2	1	12	11	45	4	4	22	24	74	16	-50
16	FC Molodechno	30	0	3	12	11	37	2	2	11	10	34	2	5	23	21	71	11	-50

After that relatively positive start, hope reigned that Borovskiy might be able to lead the team to better results in the new millennium. But the worst was yet to come. Three spring friendlies away to Bulgaria, Andorra and Estonia all ended in comprehensive defeats.

How a team that could hold Italy to two draws could lose so limply to Andorra was difficult to understand, but the reason put forward by most was that the players simply didn't care about performing for the national team unless they could exploit the situation by showing themselves off to prospective foreign scouts. Money, rather than national pride, was apparently their chief, if not only, source of inspiration.

Of the players selected by Vergeyenko and Borovskiy in 1999/2000, a significant majority were Russian-based, with only a couple - Sergei Gurenko and Petr Kachuro -

EUROPEAN CUPS 99/00

CHAMPIONS' CUP
● **DNEPR-TRANSMASH MOGILEV**
Preliminary round 2 AIK (SWE)
H 0-1
　　Astapchik, Klimovich, Shuneiko, Sverdlov, Baranov, Likhtarovich, Lukashov, Kalachev (Bykov 90), Lanko, Ogorodnik (Kozlov 73), Solodukhin (Kapov 73),
A 0-2
　　Astapchik, Klimovich, Shuneiko, Sverdlov, Baranov, Likhtarovich, Lukashov, Kalachev, Lanko (Kozlov 75), Chumachenko, Solodukhin (Ogorodnik 65).

UEFA CUP
● **FC BATE BORISOV**
Qualifying round LOKOMOTIV MOSKVA (RUS)
H 1-7　Lisovskiy (72)
　　Fedorovich, Goncharenko, Skripchenko, Tikhomirov, Loshankov, Yermakovich (Lisovskiy 37), Arzamastsev (Baranov 21), Nevinskiy, Kutuzov, Kuznetsov (Miroshkin 63), Pjatrauskas.

A 0-5
　　Khomutovskiy, Rogozhkin (Kuznetsov 46), Skripchenko, Tikhomirov, Loshankov (Akulich 58), Divakov, Arzamastsev, Nevinskiy, Miroshkin, Baranov, Goncharik (Doroshkevich 46).

● **BELSHINA BOBRUISK**
Qualifying round OMONIA NICOSIA (CYP)
H 1-5　Khripach (21)
　　Zhemchugov, Razumovich, Shustikov (Kovalevich 58), Khripach, Shagoiko, Banul, Gradoboyev I., Gradoboyev E. (Smirnykh 56), Borisik (Mikhalev 35), Khlebosolov, Ulezlo.

A 0-3
　　Zhemchugov, Kovalevich, Kashkar, Khripach, Shagoiko, Banul, Gradoboyev I. (Migas 77), Gradoboyev E., Smirnykh (Mikhalev 50), Khlebosolov (Turchinovich 67), Ulezlo.

TOP SCORERS

22	Valeriy STRIPEIKIS (Slaviya Mozyr)
19	Vitaliy KUTUZOV (FC BATE Borisov)
17	Vitaliy ALESHCHENKO (Lokomotiv-96 Vitebsk)
	Roman VASILYUK (Dinamo Brest)
15	Alexandr VYAZHEVICH (Dinamo Minsk)
13	Dmitriy PODREZ (Shakhter Soligorsk)
12	Viktor BOREL (FC Gomel)
11	Dmitriy BESPANSKIY (Shakhter Soligorsk)
	Dmitriy CHALEI (Slaviya Mozyr)
	Dmitriy DENISYUK (Slaviya Mozyr)
	Dmitriy OGORODNIK (Dnepr-Transmash Mogilev)
	Vladimir SHUPILOV (Naftan-Devon Novopolotsk)

NATIONAL TEAM RESULTS 99/00

Date	Opponent		Venue	Score	
18/08/99	Russia	H	Minsk	0-2	
04/09/99	Wales (ECQ)	H	Minsk	1-2	Baranov (30)
08/09/99	Switzerland (ECQ)	A	Lausanne	0-2	
09/10/99	Italy (ECQ)	H	Minsk	0-0	
29/03/00	Bulgaria	A	Sofia	1-4	Skripchenko (57)
26/04/00	Andorra	A	Andorra La Vella	0-2	
04/06/00	Estonia	A	Tallinn	0-2	

belonging to Western clubs. Gurenko's transfer to Roma was viewed as a major step forward for Belarussian football, but the talented wing-back had a miserable time in the Eternal City, starting just one Serie A game. Still, at least he had the honour of becoming the first Belarussian to appear in Italy's top league since Sergei Aleinikov, the ex-USSR international who spent three years there with Juventus and Lecce.

DOMESTIC CUP 99/00

1/16 FINALS
Torpedo Zhodino 0, Neman-Belkard Grodno 3
Kommunalnik Slonim 0, FC Gomel 7
Zlin Gomel 2, Torpedo-Kadino Mogilev 0
FC Pinsk-900 0, Dinamo Brest 2
Ozertsy Glubokoye 1, Dinamo Minsk 4
Zabudova Chist 2, Lokomotiv-96 Vitebsk 4
FC Rogachev 1, Naftan-Devon Novopolotsk 3
Keramik-Bereza 1, Dnepr-Transmash Mogilev 2
Neman Mosty 0, Slaviya Mozyr 2
Vedrich-97 Rechitsa 1, Svisloch-Krovlya Osipovichi 1
(aet; 3-4 on pens.)
Granit Mikhashevichi 2, Shakhter Soligorsk 0
Polesiye Mozyrskiy r-n 0, Belshina Bobruisk 6
FC Luninets 3, FC BATE Borisov 4

1/8 FINALS
Dinamo Brest 1, Dnepr-Transmash Mogilev 0

Belshina Bobruisk 3, Zlin Gomel 1
Neman-Belkard Grodno 4, FC Molodechno 1
Svisloch-Krovlya Osipovichi 1, Torpedo-MAZ Minsk 3
FC Lida 2, Granit Mikhashevichi 0
Lokomotiv-96 Vitebsk 0, Dinamo Minsk 0
(aet; 4-3 on pens.)
FC BATE Borisov 0, FC Gomel 2
Slaviya Mozyr 3, Naftan-Devon Novopolotsk 2

QUARTER-FINALS
Belshina Bobruisk 2 (Balashov 59, Korolik 69),
Lokomotiv-96 Vitebsk 1 (Vekhtev 45)
Dinamo Brest 0, Slaviya Mozyr 6 (Stripeikis 20, 33, Vasilyuk 23, 43, Matveichik 68, Slesarchuk 90)
FC Gomel 3 (Kovalevich 93p, Afonasenko 102, Bliznyuk 109), FC Lida 0 (aet)
Torpedo-MAZ Minsk 0, Neman-Belkard Grodno 0
(aet; 4-2 on pens.)

SEMI-FINALS
Torpedo-MAZ Minsk 1 (Levitskiy 86),
Belshina Bobruisk 0
Slaviya Mozyr 3 (Denisyuk 13, 21, 54), FC Gomel 0

FINAL
28/05/2000, Minsk
SLAVIYA MOZYR 2 Stripeikis (77), Vasilyuk (90)
TORPEDO-MAZ MINSK 0
referee - Chikun
SLAVIYA MOZYR - Gayev, Balin, Lukashenko, Shutov, Pervushin (Apanas 24), Samatov, Matveichik, Karsakov (Lukashevich 57), Denisyuk (Chalei 12), Vasilyuk, Stripeikis.
TORPEDO-MAZ MINSK - Khomutovskiy, Sednev, Omelyanchuk, Kabelskiy, Smirnykh, Maleyev (Linev 76), Korytko, Kukar, Zenin (Levitskiy 46), Novitskiy, Yaromko (Lica 65).

PLAYER OF THE SEASON

VASILIY BARANOV
Of all the Belarus internationals exiled across the border in Russia, Vasiliy Baranov has probably done most to promote his nation's cause. The powerful 28-year-old midfielder began his career with FC Gomel and Vedrich Rechitsa before making his debut in the Russian league in 1996 with Baltika Kaliningrad. He joined Spartak Moscow halfway through the 1998 season and was there for the duration in 1999 to claim his second successive Russian national title. He has also gained considerable Champions' League experience, having appeared in all of Spartak's group games both in 1998 and 1999. A major asset to the Belarus national team, his industrious and skilful midfield play is supplemented by a formidable long-range shot. He scored his country's only home goal in the Euro 2000 qualifying campaign with just such a strike in the 1-2 defeat against Wales - a match in which he also twice struck the crossbar.

Only two home-based players were selected more than once for the national team during the season, and they were the 1999 championship's top scorer - Slaviya Mozyr striker Valeriy Stripeikis - and the champion club's outstanding individual - FC BATE Borisov defender Valeriy Skripchenko.

BATE won their first national title with room to spare. 12 points was their final margin of victory and nobody could argue that they were anything other than just and proper champions. They were beaten just once - 0-1 at fallen giants Dinamo Minsk - and scored more goals and conceded fewer than any other team. In many respects BATE were a shining example to the competition. Unlike others, they played with effort and determination in every match. They were also coached sensibly and shrewdly by Yuriy Puntus and led intelligently from the top by ambitious young president Anatoliy Kapskiy. Even when

INTERNATIONAL HONOURS

None.

NATIONAL TEAM APPEARANCES 99/00

Coach - Mikhail VERGEYENKO; Sergei BOROVSKIY	RUS	WAL	SUI	ITA	BUL	AND	EST	Cps	Gls
Gennadiy TUMILOVICH (03/09/71)									
- Zhemchuzhina Sochi (RUS)/Hapoel Irony Rishon Lezion (ISR)	G	G		s46		G	G	10	-
Sergei GURENKO (30/09/72) - Roma (ITA)	D	M	M	M	M	M70		40	2
Andrei OSTROVSKIY (13/09/73) - Dinamo Moskva (RUS)	D	D	D	D	s46	D	D	26	1
Alexandr LUKHVICH (21/02/70) - Torpedo Moskva (RUS)	D	D	D	D	D77	s46	D	11	-
Vyacheslav GERASHCHENKO (25/07/72) - Chernomorets Novorossiisk (RUS)	D				D46			15	-
Alexandr CHAIKA (27/01/76) - Alania Vladikavkaz (RUS)	M68	M	M	M		M		16	-
Vasiliy BARANOV (05/10/72) - Spartak Moskva (RUS)	M	M	M	M	M63		M46	23	3
Alexandr KULCHIY (01/11/73) - Dinamo Moskva (RUS)	M	M	M55	s79				22	2
Radislav ORLOVSKIY (09/03/70) - Torpedo Moskva (RUS)	M46	M60		M		s46	M	23	2
Maxym ROMASHCHENKO (31/07/76) - Dinamo Moskva (RUS)	A79	s60	s69	A46		A46	A	15	2
Petr KACHURO (02/08/72) - Sheffield United (ENG)	A54		s55					25	4
Boris GOROVOI (08/04/74) - Zenit Sankt-Peterburg (RUS)	s46					s70		3	-
Igor TARLOVSKIY (21/09/74) - Alania Vladikavkaz (RUS)	s54	M	M	M	M46	M		8	1
Konstantin KOVALENKO (02/05/75) - Zhemchuzhina Sochi (RUS)	s68							2	-
Vitaliy STRIPEIKIS (15/10/74) - Slaviya Mozyr	s79				A	A56		3	-
Andrei LAVRIK (07/12/74) - Lokomotiv Moskva (RUS)		D	D		s63			14	-
Vladimir MAKOVSKIY (23/04/77) - Baltika Kaliningrad (RUS)/Vorskla Poltava (UKR)		A	A69	s46		A		25	4
Yuriy AFANASENKO (19/08/73) - Dinamo Minsk			G					3	-
Erik YAKHIMOVICH (06/09/68) - Dinamo Moskva (RUS)			D	D		D	D	24	-
Valeriy SHANTALOSOV (15/03/66) - Lokomotiv Nizhniy Novgorod (RUS)					G	G46		23	-
Sergei GERASIMETS (13/10/65) - Zenit Sankt-Peterburg (RUS)				A79				25	7
Sergei YASKOVICH (11/01/72) - Anzhi Makhachkala (RUS)					D	D		8	-
Sergei SHTANYUK (13/08/73) - Dinamo Moskva (RUS)					D	D46	D	21	1
Valentin BELKEVICH (27/01/73) - Dynamo Kyiv (UKR)					M		M	30	5
Alexandr KHATSKEVICH (19/10/73) - Dynamo Kyiv (UKR)					M70		M	17	-
Vadim SKRIPCHENKO (26/11/75) - FC BATE Borisov					s46		s46	6	2
Nikolai RYNDYUK (02/02/78) - Lokomotiv Nizhniy Novgorod (RUS)					s70	s56	A46	6	1
Vladimir SHUNEIKO (22/04/74) - Dnepr-Transmash Mogilev					s77			1	-
Alexandr VYAZHEVICH (07/06/70) - Dinamo Minsk							s46	2	-

Lokomotiv Moscow humiliated them in the UEFA Cup qualifying round, BATE refused to buckle. Driven on by the goals of their young forward duo Vitaliy Kutusov (19 goals at 19 years of age) and Nikolai Ryndyuk (back from a spell with... Lokomotiv Moscow), BATE ensured an early conclusion to the title race and brought the club their first title just two years after promotion.

BATE were eliminated from the domestic Cup by FC Gomel, who, assisted by the mass recruitment of players from Lokomotiv 96 Vitebsk, succeeded in finishing third. Second place went to Slaviya Mozyr, who also went on to win the Cup, thus making up for their heartbreaking penalty shoot-out defeat by Belshina Bobruisk a year earlier. This time they came back from a goal behind in the final against Torpedo-MAZ Minsk to snatch victory with a last-minute goal from new signing Roman Vasilyuk. The same player had struck twice on his return visit to former club Dinamo Brest in the quarter-final, which Slaviya won 6-0.

Slaviya's runners-up spot in the league was achieved thanks to a sensational burst of form during the middle of the season when they won 11 matches on the trot, scoring 47 goals in the process, 13 of them to top scorer Stripeikis, a new arrival from Naftan-Devon Novopolotsk. A poor start, however, had left Slaviya with far too much ground to make up on BATE Borisov, and their faint hopes were completely extinguished when BATE ended their winning run with a 1-1 draw in Borisov.

Every club in Belarus had financial problems, but the plight of defending champions Dnepr-Transmash was harsher than most. They started the season like a train, going unbeaten for 17 games, but slowed almost to a standstill after that, with the obligatory sale of some of their better players eventually taking its toll. It was as much as coach Valeriy Streltsov and his remaining players could do to hold onto fourth place - a valiant effort in the circumstances.

The haemmorhage of Belarus's best footballers to Russia and Ukraine is unlikely to abate, but although the 'money rules' attitude is unquestionably a handicap to development, some young players with genuine talent are still emerging. The shafts of light which shone through the gloom during the 1999 campaign came from Kutuzov (BATE), Dmitriy Chalei (Slaviya), Alexandr Afonasenko (Gomel), Dmitriy Boriseiko (Neman), Vasilyuk and Andrei Razin (Dinamo Brest), Dmitriy Likhtarovich and Dmitriy Kolachev (Dnepr-Transmash).

If a bleak future is to be avoided, players such as these must learn to become more professional in their outlook and more deicated to their chosen trade. Only then can Belarus work its way back to a position of respectability in European football.

PROMOTED CLUBS 1999

SECOND DIVISION FINAL TABLE

		Pd	W	D	L	F	A	Pt	GD
1	**Kommunalnik Slonim**	**30**	**18**	**5**	**7**	**57**	**29**	**59**	**28**
2	**Vedrich-97 Rechitsa**	**30**	**16**	**10**	**4**	**56**	**30**	**58**	**26**
3	Dinamo-Yuni Minsk	30	16	8	6	50	36	56	14
4	Kommunalnik Svetlogorsk	30	16	8	6	45	31	56	14
5	Granit Mikashevichi	30	15	9	6	47	25	54	22
6	Neman Mosty	30	14	10	6	49	30	52	19
7	Torpedo Zhodino	30	11	11	8	55	43	44	12
8	Keramik-Bereza	30	11	10	9	37	38	43	-1
9	FC Orsha	30	10	9	11	46	37	39	9
10	FC Rogachev	30	9	11	10	49	44	38	5
11	Zlin Gomel	30	9	9	12	37	30	36	7
12	Zvezda-VA-BGU Minsk	30	8	9	13	38	57	33	-19
13	Polesiye Mozyrskiy r-n	30	7	6	17	32	61	27	-29
14	Veino-Dnepr Mogilevskiy r-n	30	6	8	16	31	57	26	-26
15	FC Pinsk-900	30	6	8	16	33	50	26	-17
16	Vitbich-Dinamo-Energo Vitebsk	30	0	5	25	26	90	5	-64

CLUB DIRECTORIES

Kommunalnik Slonim
ul. A. Pushkina 57 A
231800 Slonim
tel - (01562) 25776/26773
fax - (01562) 27402/42730
Year of Formation - 1996
President - Oleg Laktyushin
Coach - Alexei Shubenok
Stadium - Yunost (5,000)

Vedrich-97 Rechitsa
ul. 10 let Octyabrya 17
247500 Rechitsa
tel - (02340) 32230
fax - (02340) 41833
Year of Formation - 1997
President - Nikolai Zarezako
Secretary - Sergei Stashuk
Coach - Nikolai Goryunov; Sergei Gomonov
Stadium - Rachitsadrev (5,500)

FC BATE BORISOV

CLUB DIRECTORY

FC BATE Borisov
boulevard Komarov 28
222120 Borisov
tel - (277) 40510/45050
fax - (277) 62622/62621
email - fcbate@st.belpak.minsk.by
Year of Formation - 1996
President - Anatoliy Kapskiy
Coach - Yuriy Puntus
Stadium - City (6,000)

MAJOR HONOURS
League Championship - (1) 1999.

APPEARANCES 1999

	P	Ap	(s)	Gls
Dmitriy AKULICH	M		(17)	2
Alexandr ARZAMASTSEV	D	25	(1)	4
Alexandr Vasiliyevich BARANOV	M	16	(5)	6
Alexei BODE	M	1		
Andrei DIVAKOV	M	6	(5)	1
Yuriy DOROSHKEVICH	A	10	(6)	3
Alexandr FEDOROVICH	G	19		
Alexandr GLEB	M	1	(12)	1
Viktor GONCHARENKO	D	22	(2)	
Artem GONCHARIK	A	5	(11)	8
Vasiliy KHOMUTOVSKIY	G	11		
Vitaliy KUTUZOV	A	28		19
Sergei KUZNETSOV	D	6	(5)	
Leonid LAGUN	M		(1)	
Alexandr LISOVSKIY	M	23	(1)	6
Yevgeniy LOSHANKOV	M	22	(5)	3
Sergei MIROSHKIN	D	14	(3)	
Vladimir NEVINSKIY	M	25	(3)	4
Ionas PJATRAUSKAS (LIT)	D	4		
Vitaliy ROGOZHKIN	M	19	(5)	
Nikolai RYNDYUK	A	10	(1)	9
Kirill SAVOSTIKOV	D	1		
Dmitriy SILANTIYEV	A	1	(2)	1
Vadim SKRIPCHENKO	D	27		3
Yuriy TIKHOMIROV	D	10	(1)	2
Alexandr YERMAKOVICH	M	24	(3)	8

LEAGUE RESULTS 1999

Date	Opponent	H/A	Score	Scorers
11/04/99	Torpedo-MAZ Minsk	H	2-1	Kutuzov, Lisovskiy
17/04/99	FC Molodechno	A	3-0	Baranov, Akulich, Goncharik
24/04/99	Naftan-Devon Novopolotsk	H	7-1	Kutuzov 3, Arzamastsev, Doroshkevich, Baranov, Divakov
03/05/99	Svisloch-Krovlya Osipovichi	A	5-0	Gleb, Goncharik 2, Loshankov, Nevinskiy (p)
07/05/99	FC Gomel	A	2-2	Kutuzov, Nevinskiy
15/05/99	FC Lida	A	4-0	Kutuzov, Nevinskiy, Goncharik 2
21/05/99	Torpedo-Kadino Mogilev	A	5-1	Lisovskiy 2, Arzamastsev, Baranov, Akulich
25/05/99	Dinamo Brest	A	4-2	Lisovskiy, Tikhomirov (p), Arzamastsev, Goncharik
09/06/99	Slaviya Mozyr	A	3-1	Skripchenko, Tikhomirov (p), Doroshkevich
13/06/99	Lokomotiv-96 Vitebsk	H	3-2	Kutuzov, Yermakovich, Loshankov
17/06/99	Shakhter Soligorsk	H	2-1	Lisovskiy, Loshankov
23/06/99	Neman-Belkard Grodno	A	2-1	Kutuzov, Baranov
30/06/99	Dnepr-Transmash Mogilev	H	1-1	Kutuzov
06/07/99	Dinamo Minsk	A	0-1	
11/07/99	Belshina Bobruisk	H	3-1	Kutuzov, Lisovskiy, Yermakovich
23/07/99	Torpedo-MAZ Minsk	A	3-1	Ryndyuk, Kutuzov, Yermakovich
31/07/99	FC Molodechno	H	2-1	Ryndyuk, Arzamastsev
06/08/99	Naftan-Devon Novopolotsk	A	4-0	Ryndyuk, Yermakovich, Silantiyev, Baranov
16/08/99	Svisloch-Krovlya Osipovichi	H	2-0	Ryndyuk 2
21/08/99	FC Gomel	H	3-1	Kutuzov, Ryndyuk, Doroshkevich
31/08/99	Torpedo-Kadino Mogilev	H	4-0	Goncharik, Skripchenko, Nevinskiy, Yermakovich
06/09/99	FC Lida	H	1-1	Goncharik
11/09/99	Dinamo Brest	H	3-1	Ryndyuk, Kutuzov, Skripchenko
18/09/99	Belshina Bobruisk	A	3-0	Kutuzov 2 (1p), Yermakovich
22/09/99	Slaviya Mozyr	H	1-1	Kutuzov (p)
25/09/99	Lokomotiv-96 Vitebsk	A	1-0	Ryndyuk
04/10/99	Shakhter Soligorsk	A	1-0	Kutuzov
13/10/99	Neman-Belkard Grodno	H	4-1	Kutuzov (p), Ryndyuk, Yermakovich 2
23/10/99	Dnepr-Transmash Mogilev	A	0-0	
30/10/99	Dinamo Minsk	H	2-0	Baranov, Kutuzov (p)

BELSHINA BOBRUISK

CLUB DIRECTORY

FC Belshina Bobruisk
ul. Uyanovskaya 94A
213800 Bobruisk
tel - (02251) 40056/26705
fax - (02251) 40056
Year of Formation - 1996
President - Arkadiy Polyakov
Coach - Ivan Savostikov; Liudas Rumbutus;
Oleg Volokh
Stadium - Spartak (4,800)

MAJOR HONOURS
Domestic Cup - (2) 1997, 1999.

APPEARANCES 1999

		P	Ap	(s)	Gls
Ashot BAGIRYAN	A		6	(4)	1
Vyacheslav BANUL	M		21	(4)	2
Alexandr BORISIK	M		11	(5)	5
Vitaliy GAMANOVICH	M		11	(7)	1
Eduard GRADOBOYEV	M		26		3
Igor GRADOBOYEV	M		29		1
Gennadiy KASHKAR	D		11		
Andrei KHLEBOSOLOV	A		18	(1)	8
Andrei KHRIPACH	D		24		2
Igor KOVALEVICH	D		21	(2)	2
Alexandr LIS	M			(6)	
Dmitriy MIGAS	M		7	(11)	1
Vitaliy MIKHALEV	M		21	(4)	3
Vladimir PUTRASH	A		10		8
Sergei RAZUMOVICH	D		16	(1)	1
Vitaliy SEMERIKOV	M		1	(2)	
Alexandr SHAGOIKO	M		15	(3)	1
Sergei SHALAI	G		11	(2)	
Taras SHAMSHORIK	M		3	(8)	1
Igor SHUSTIKOV	D		12	(2)	1
Vasiliy SMIRNYKH	M		2	(5)	
Alexandr SYSOI	D			(1)	
Yevgeniy TIMOFEYEV	D		9	(2)	1
Andrei TURCHINOVICH	A		9	(10)	2
Sergei ULEZLO	A		17	(8)	7
Sergei ZHEMCHUGOV	G		19		

LEAGUE RESULTS 1999

11/04/99	Naftan-Devon Novopolotsk	H	2-2	Timofeyev, Gradoboyev E.
17/04/99	Svisloch-Krovlya Osipovichi	A	1-0	Borisik
24/04/99	FC Gomel	H	0-0	
03/05/99	FC Lida	A	1-5	Ulezlo
07/05/99	Torpedo-Kadino Mogilev	H	5-1	Khlebosolov (p), Mikhalev, Ulezlo 2, Borisik
15/05/99	Dinamo Brest	A	0-2	
21/05/99	Lokomotiv-96 Vitebsk	H	4-0	Khlebosolov 2, Shustikov, Borisik
25/05/99	Slaviya Mozyr	H	0-0	
09/06/99	Shakhter Soligorsk	H	3-3	Khlebosolov, Banul, Borisik
13/06/99	Neman-Belkard Grodno	A	0-1	
17/06/99	Dnepr-Transmash Mogilev	H	0-1	
24/06/99	Dinamo Minsk	A	1-2	Razumovich
30/06/99	Torpedo-MAZ Minsk	H	2-1	Khlebosolov, Turchinovich
07/07/99	FC Molodechno	A	2-1	Migas, Borisik
11/07/99	FC BATE Borisov	A	1-3	Shagoiko
24/07/99	Naftan-Devon Novopolotsk	A	2-1	Khlebosolov, Mikhalev
31/07/99	Svisloch-Krovlya Osipovichi	H	1-1	Khlebosolov (p)
06/08/99	FC Gomel	A	3-2	Gradoboyev I., Khlebosolov, Khripach
16/08/99	FC Lida	H	4-1	Gradoboyev E., Khripach, Bagiryan, Ulezlo
20/08/99	Torpedo-Kadino Mogilev	A	3-0	Gradoboyev E., Putrash, Shamshorik
31/08/99	Lokomotiv-96 Vitebsk	A	2-1	Putrash 2
06/09/99	Dinamo Brest	H	4-1	Mikhalev, Kovalevich (p), og (Khomko), Putrash
11/09/99	Slaviya Mozyr	A	0-1	
18/09/99	FC BATE Borisov	H	0-3	
22/09/99	Shakhter Soligorsk	A	1-2	Putrash
26/09/99	Neman-Belkard Grodno	H	5-1	Ulezlo, Gamanovich, Turchinovich, Banul, Kovalevich (p)
04/10/99	Dnepr-Transmash Mogilev	A	0-3	
13/10/99	Dinamo Minsk	H	1-1	Ulezlo
23/10/99	Torpedo-MAZ Minsk	A	1-2	Putrash
30/10/99	FC Molodechno	H	3-0	Putrash 2, Ulezlo

DINAMO BREST

CLUB DIRECTORY

Dinamo Brest
ul. N. Gogol 9
224075 Brest
tel - (0162) 263329/265221
fax - (0162) 264283
Year of Formation - 1976
President - Nikolai Shirinskiy
Coach - Alexandr Razin
Stadium - Dinamo (15,000)

APPEARANCES 1999

	P	Ap	(s)	Gls
Andrei ASHIKHMIN	G	5		
Alexandr GERASIMUK	D	11	(4)	2
Alexandr GOLOVCHIK	A	3	(4)	
Sergei GRIB	D	25		4
Yuriy KHOMKO	D	21	(6)	2
Sergei P. KOVALCHUK	M	20	(1)	1
Sergei KOVALYUK	M	3	(8)	
Mikhail LITVINCHUK	A	9	(8)	3
Sergei MALAKHOV	D	25		2
Vyacheslav MIKHALCHENKO	M	13	(1)	7
Vladimir MISHCHERUK	A	1	(2)	
Andrei PROKOPYUK	M	28		2
Andrei RAZIN	M	15	(10)	9
Vadim SAVCHUK	M	18	(6)	5
Andrei SLADINSKIY	D	19	(6)	
Vladimir SOROCHINSKIY (KAZ)	D	26		
Dmitriy STRACHKO	D	11	(1)	
Oleg STRAKHANOVICH	M	22	(4)	4
Roman VASILYUK	A	25	(2)	17
Dmitriy VIRKO	G	20		
Vitaliy YAKUSHIK	A	5	(3)	1
Andrei ZAROVSKIY	G	5		

LEAGUE RESULTS 1999

11/04/99	Svisloch-Krovlya Osipovichi	H	2-0	Yakushik, Vasilyuk
17/04/99	FC Gomel	A	1-3	Gerasimuk
24/04/99	FC Lida	H	1-0	Vasilyuk
03/05/99	Torpedo-Kadino Mogilev	A	1-1	Malakhov
07/05/99	Lokomotiv-96 Vitebsk	H	3-0	Malakhov (p), Grib, Savchuk
15/05/99	Belshina Bobruisk	H	2-0	Grib, Vasilyuk
21/05/99	Slaviya Mozyr	A	1-2	Khomko
25/05/99	FC BATE Borisov	H	2-4	Grib, Vasilyuk
09/06/99	Neman-Belkard Grodno	H	1-1	Grib
13/06/99	Dnepr-Transmash Mogilev	A	1-4	Litvinchuk
18/06/99	Dinamo Minsk	H	2-1	Strakhanovich, Vasilyuk
22/06/99	Torpedo-MAZ Minsk	A	0-2	
30/06/99	FC Molodechno	H	7-0	Strakhanovich 2, Vasilyuk, Savchuk, Razin 2, Kovalchuk
07/07/99	Naftan-Devon Novopolotsk	A	5-0	Khomko, Vasilyuk 2, Razin 2
11/07/99	Shakhter Soligorsk	A	1-7	Vasilyuk
24/07/99	Svisloch-Krovlya Osipovichi	A	3-1	Mikhalchenko 2, Prokopyuk
31/07/99	FC Gomel	H	1-2	Litvinchuk
07/08/99	FC Lida	A	3-0	Razin (p), Strakhanovich, Vasilyuk
14/08/99	Torpedo-MAZ Minsk	H	4-0	Vasilyuk 3 (1p), Razin
21/08/99	Lokomotiv-96 Vitebsk	A	1-0	Mikhalchenko
31/08/99	Slaviya Mozyr	H	2-7	Mikhalchenko, Razin
06/09/99	Belshina Bobruisk	A	1-4	Litvinchuk
11/09/99	FC BATE Borisov	A	1-3	Razin
18/09/99	Shakhter Soligorsk	H	1-1	Vasilyuk
22/09/99	Neman-Belkard Grodno	A	1-2	Razin
26/09/99	Dnepr-Transmash Mogilev	H	1-1	Vasilyuk
04/10/99	Dinamo Minsk	A	2-3	Savchuk 2
13/10/99	Torpedo-MAZ Minsk	H	2-1	Mikhalchenko 2
23/10/99	FC Molodechno	A	3-0	Savchuk, Mikhalchenko, Prokopyuk
30/10/99	Naftan-Devon Novopolotsk	H	3-2	Vasilyuk 2, Gerasimuk

DINAMO MINSK

CLUB DIRECTORY

Dinamo Minsk
ul. Vitebska 11, 220050 Minsk
tel - (017) 2064821/2064820/2064822/
2064823
fax - (017) 2064824
email - dinamo-minsk@mail.ru
Year of Formation - 1927
President - Yuriy Chizh
Secretary - Leonid Vasilevskiy
Coach - Veniamin Arzamastsev; Yuriy Kurnenin
Stadium - Dinamo (42,375)

MAJOR HONOURS
League Championship (USSR) - (1) 1982.
League Championship - (6) 1992, 1993, 1994,
1995 (spring), 1995 (autumn), 1997.
Domestic Cup - (1) 1992, 1994.

APPEARANCES 1999

		P	Ap	(s)	Gls
Yuriy AFANASENKO	G	12			
Anatoliy BAIDACHNYI	M	6	(7)	1	
Andrey BELOUSOV	D	22	(1)		
Artem CHELYADINSKIY	D	27			
Alexei DENISENYA	A	4	(6)		
Pavel DOVGULEVETS	D	13	(2)		
Alexandr KHRAPKOVSKIY	D	29		7	
Alexandr KHURSEVICH	M		(1)		
Sergei V. KOVALCHUK	M	28		7	
Vitaliy LEDENEV	A	4	(14)	6	
Andrei LEONCHIK	M	20	(3)	7	
Vyacheslav MARCHENKO	M	4			
Alexandr OSIPOVICH	M	15	(3)	1	
Alexandr OSTRIKOV	M		(7)		
Vladimir OSTRIKOV	M	18	(5)	4	
Pavel RODNENOK	D	19	(5)		
Andrei SATSUNKEVICH	G	18			
Andrei SHILO	D	13		1	
Sergei TARTOVSKIY	M	3	(3)		
Roman TREPACHKIN	M	25	(2)	1	
Andrei VETELKIN	A	5	(11)	1	
Alexei VERGEYENKO	M	4	(4)		
Vitaliy VOLODENKOV	M	16			
Viktor VRUBLEVSKIY	M	1	(1)		
Alexandr VYAZHEVICH	A	24	(2)	15	

LEAGUE RESULTS 1999

11/04/99	Shakhter Soligorsk	A	1-0	Khrapkovskiy
18/04/99	Neman-Belkard Grodno	H	1-1	Vetelin
24/04/99	Dnepr-Transmash Mogilev	A	1-2	Kovalchuk
03/05/99	Lokomotiv-96 Vitebsk	A	0-1	
07/05/99	Torpedo-MAZ Minsk	A	2-1	Ostrikov V., Vyazhevich
15/05/99	FC Molodechno	A	2-1	Trepachkin, Khrapkovskiy
21/05/99	Naftan-Devon Novopolotsk	H	2-1	Shilo, Kovalchuk
25/05/99	Svisloch-Krovlya Osipovichi	A	0-0	
09/06/99	FC Lida	A	1-2	Khrapkovskiy
14/06/99	Torpedo-Kadino Mogilev	H	1-1	Vyazhevich
18/06/99	Dinamo Brest	A	1-2	Vyazhevich
24/06/99	Belshina Bobruisk	H	2-1	Khrapkovskiy, Kovalchuk (p)
30/06/99	Slaviya Mozyr	A	0-4	
06/07/99	FC BATE Borisov	H	1-0	Vyazhevich
14/07/99	FC Gomel	H	3-4	Kovalchuk (p), Vyazhevich, Ledenev
24/07/99	Shakhter Soligorsk	H	0-0	
31/07/99	Neman-Belkard Grodno	A	0-0	
08/08/99	Dnepr-Transmash Mogilev	H	2-1	Ledenev, Leonchik
14/08/99	Lokomotiv-96 Vitebsk	H	4-0	Osipovich, Leonchik, Vyazhevich, Ledenev
22/08/99	Torpedo-MAZ Minsk	H	5-0	Leonchik, Kovalchuk, Ostrikov V., Khrapkovskiy, Ledenev
27/08/99	FC Molodechno	H	2-0	Ledenev, Leonchik
31/08/99	Naftan-Devon Novopolotsk	A	1-1	Leonchik
11/09/99	Svisloch-Krovlya Osipovichi	H	7-0	Kovalchuk, Khrapkovskiy, Vyazhevich 5
16/09/99	FC Gomel	A	1-0	Kovalchuk
24/09/99	FC Lida	H	5-0	Leonchik 2, Vyazhevich 2, Ostrikov V.
26/09/99	Torpedo-Kadino Mogilev	A	2-2	Vyazhevich, Ostrikov V.
04/10/99	Dinamo Brest	H	3-2	Vyazhevich, Khrapkovskiy, Ledenev
13/10/99	Belshina Bobruisk	A	1-1	Baidachnyi
23/10/99	Slaviya Mozyr	H	0-0	
30/10/99	FC BATE Borisov	A	0-2	

DNEPR-TRANSMASH MOGILEV

CLUB DIRECTORY

Dnepr-Transmash Mogilev
Zadorozhnoye shosse 21
212026 Mogilev
tel - (0222) 263485
fax - (0222) 263009
Year of Formation - 1998
President - Vladimir Brezhezinskiy
Secretary - Yuriy Kolochinskiy
Coach - Valeriy Streltsov
Stadium - Spartak (11,200)

MAJOR HONOURS
League Championship - (1) 1998.

APPEARANCES 1999

	P	Ap	(s)	Gls
Sergei ASTAPCHIK	G	30		
Olexandr BAHNYUK (UKR)	D	6	(3)	
Alexandr Vladimirovich BARANOV	D	15	(7)	
Mykola BENEVELSKYI (UKR)	D		(1)	
Eduard BOLTRUSHEVICH	D	17	(1)	2
Vitaliy BULYGA	M	5	(12)	1
Kirill BYKOV	D	3	(3)	
Ihor CHUMACHENKO (UKR)	M	27	(1)	9
Dmitriy KALACHEV	M	27	(1)	5
Ruslan KAPANTSOV	G		(1)	
Yevgeniy KAPOV	D	15	(8)	
Vladimir KLIMOVICH	D	16	(2)	3
Yevgeniy KOZLOV	A	2	(7)	
Vitaliy LANKO	A	20	(8)	7
Dmitriy LIKHTAROVICH	D	29	(1)	2
Yuriy LUKASHOV	M	24	(5)	1
Oleh MAVRENKOV (UKR)	M		(3)	
Dmitriy OGORODNIK	A	21	(7)	11
Dmitriy RADKOV	D		(1)	
Vladimir SHUNEIKO	D	27	(1)	1
Vladimir SOLODUKHIN	A	19	(10)	10
Yaroslav SVERDLOV	D	27		1

LEAGUE RESULTS 1999

11/04/99	Neman-Belcard Grodno	A	2-0	Ogorodnik, Kalachev
17/04/99	Lokomotiv-96 Vitebsk	A	1-1	Bulyga
24/04/99	Dinamo Minsk	H	2-1	Ogorodnik, Solodukhin
03/05/99	Torpedo-MAZ Minsk	A	3-0	Chumachenko 2, Kalachev
07/05/99	FC Molodechno	H	1-1	Solodukhin
15/05/99	Naftan-Devon Novopolotsk	A	2-1	Kalachev, Klimovich
21/05/99	Svisloch-Krovlya Osipovichi	H	3-1	Solodukhin, Ogorodnik, Lanko
25/05/99	FC Gomel	A	1-1	Ogorodnik
09/06/99	Torpedo-Kadino Mogilev	A	5-2	Solodukhin 2, Lanko 2, Ogorodnik
13/06/99	Dinamo Brest	H	4-1	Chumachenko, Klimovich, Ogorodnik 2
17/06/99	Belshina Bobruisk	A	1-0	Chumachenko
23/06/99	Slaviya Mozyr	H	3-0	Lanko, Solodukhin, Kalachev
30/06/99	FC BATE Borisov	A	1-1	Boltrushevich
07/07/99	Shakhter Soligorsk	H	3-1	Likhtarovich, Lukashov, Lanko
11/07/99	FC Lida	H	3-1	Shuneiko, Solodukhin, Boltrushevich (p)
23/07/99	Neman-Belkard Grodno	H	1-1	Ogorodnik
31/07/99	Lokomotiv-96 Vitebsk	H	1-0	Likhtarovich
08/08/99	Dinamo Minsk	A	1-2	Kalachev
14/08/99	Torpedo-MAZ Minsk	H	1-0	Ogorodnik
21/08/99	FC Molodechno	A	1-1	Solodukhin
27/08/99	Naftan-Devon Novopolotsk	H	0-2	
31/08/99	Svisloch-Krovlya Osipovichi	A	2-0	Chumachenko, Sverdlov
11/09/99	FC Gomel	H	2-1	Solodukhin, Lanko
17/09/99	FC Lida	A	0-0	
22/09/99	Torpedo-Kadino Mogilev	H	5-2	Ogorodnik, Lanko, Chumachenko 2, Solodukhin
26/09/99	Dinamo Brest	A	1-1	Klimovich
04/10/99	Belshina Bobruisk	H	3-0	Chumachenko 2, Ogorodnik
13/10/99	Slaviya Mozyr	A	0-4	
23/10/99	FC BATE Borisov	H	0-0	
30/10/99	Shakhter Soligorsk	A	0-1	

FC GOMEL

CLUB DIRECTORY

FC Gomel
ul. Bogdanova 7
246031 Gomel
tel - (0232) 524023/507773/555489
fax - (0232) 524019
email - green-white@newmail.ru
Year of Formation - 1995
President - Semen Voronchuk
Secretary - Sergei Boiko
Coach - Valeriy Yanochkin; Vyacheslav Akshayev
Stadium - Centralnyi (10,000)

APPEARANCES 1999

		P	Ap	(s)	Gls
Alexandr AFONASENKO	M	15	(6)	3
Gennadiy BLIZNYUK	A	3	(16)	5
Viktor BOREL	A	10	(13)	12
Oleg CHEREPNEV	D	21		
Alexandr DANILENKO	M	1		
Eduard DEMENKOVETS	M	29	(1)	9
Vasiliy DROZDOV	D	17	(2)	
Roman DZHAFAROV	D	1	(2)	
Sergei FEDOROVICH	D	1	(2)	
Vyacheslav LEVCHUK	D	24	(1)	1
Viktor MALYAVKO	D	4		
Vasiliy MAZUR	A	18	(8)	7
Sergei NIKITENKO	M	17	(2)	2
Serhiy NYKONCHUK (UKR)	M	4	(14)	2
Mikhail PATSKO	M	17	(5)	4
Maxim RAZUMOV	A	24	(4)	1
Vladimir RYZHCHENKO	G	2		
Vladimir SELKIN	G	28		
Andrei SIVKOV	M	17	(5)	
Andrei SKOROBOGATKO	M	2	(4)	
Oleg SYSOYEV	D	25		3
Dmitriy TROSKO	M	27		
Andrei YUSIPETS	M	23	(4)	8

LEAGUE RESULTS 1999

11/04/99	Torpedo-Kadino Mogilev	A	1-0	Yusipets (p)
17/04/99	Dinamo Brest	H	3-1	Yusipets 2 (1p), Borel
24/04/99	Belshina Bobruisk	A	0-0	
03/05/99	Slaviya Mozyr	H	1-0	Bliznyuk
07/05/99	FC BATE Borisov	H	2-2	Demenkovets, Bliznyuk
15/05/99	Shakhter Soligorsk	H	1-0	Borel
21/05/99	Neman-Belkard Grodno	A	2-0	Mazur, Borel
25/05/99	Dnepr-Transmash Mogilev	H	1-1	Nykonchuk
09/06/99	Torpedo-MAZ Minsk	H	1-0	Nykonchuk
13/06/99	FC Molodechno	A	1-0	Nikitenko
17/06/99	Naftan-Devon Novopolotsk	H	2-0	Sysoyev, Borel (p)
23/06/99	Svisloch-Krovlya Osipovichi	A	3-1	Borel, Bliznyuk 2
01/07/99	Lokomotiv-96 Vitebsk	A	0-2	
07/07/99	FC Lida	H	3-0	Mazur 2, Demenkovets
14/07/99	Dinamo Minsk	A	4-3	Borel, Afonasenko, Mazur 2
24/07/99	Torpedo-Kadino Mogilev	H	5-0	Yusipets 2, Demenkovets, Patsko 2
31/07/99	Dinamo Brest	A	2-1	Yusipets, Afonasenko
06/08/99	Belshina Bobruisk	H	2-3	Yusipets, Mazur
21/08/99	FC BATE Borisov	A	1-3	Sysoyev
27/08/99	Shakhter Soligorsk	A	2-2	Nikitenko (p), Levchuk
31/08/99	Neman-Belkard Grodno	H	2-0	Sysoyev, Mazur
11/09/99	Dnepr-Transmash Mogilev	A	1-2	Yusipets
16/09/99	Dinamo Minsk	H	0-1	
22/09/99	Torpedo-MAZ Minsk	A	1-1	Demenkovets
26/09/99	FC Molodechno	H	3-1	Razumov, Afonasenko, Demenkovets
01/10/99	Slaviya Mozyr	A	1-1	Demenkovets
04/10/99	Naftan-Devon Novopolotsk	A	2-1	Borel 2 (1p)
13/10/99	Svisloch-Krovlya Osipovichi	H	4-1	Borel (p), Patsko, Bliznyuk, Demenkovets (p)
23/10/99	Lokomotiv-96 Vitebsk	H	2-0	Patsko, Borel
30/10/99	FC Lida	A	4-1	Demenkovets 2, Borel 2

FC LIDA

CLUB DIRECTORY

FC Lida
ul. Kirov 32 A
231300 Lida
tel - (01561) 29761
fax - (01561) 21661
Year of Formation - 1997
President - Ivan Prokhorov
Coach - Ivan Prokhorov
Stadium - City (3,500)

APPEARANCES 1999

	P	Ap	(s)	Gls
Pavel BATYUTO	M	12		
Marat BELEZYAKO	M	1		
Alexandr BULOICHIK	M	30		
Zviad BURDZENIDZE (GEO)	A	13		5
Valentin BURNOS	G	25		
Alexei DEMIN	A	10	(1)	2
Dmitriy GRIGORUK	D	1	(3)	
Vitold KHOKHLACH	D	29		3
Oleg KOTIN	M	12		
Dmitriy KOZICH	D	1	(6)	
Valeriy LYANTSEVICH	M	13	(11)	
Maxim LYCHEV	G	5		
Valentin MIKHEYEV	A	13	(12)	3
Viktor MISKO	D	4		
Nikolai MOZHEIKO	A		(3)	
Sergei PETRUSHEVSKIY	M	25		1
Alexandr POZNYAK	M	29	(1)	4
Andrei PRIKHODKO	D	4	(2)	1
Vitaliy RASHKEVICH	D	6		
Dmitriy SAFRONOV	A	7		
Boris SAKUTA	D	22	(4)	
Pavel SHMIGERO	M	11	(3)	
Alexandr SKOPETS	D	11	(8)	
Olexandr YUREVYCH (UKR)	M	30		
Yuriy ZHIRUN	A	16	(10)	8

LEAGUE RESULTS 1999

11/04/99	Lokomotiv-96 Vitebsk	H	0-0	
17/04/99	Torpedo-Kadino Mogilev	H	3-1	Khokhlach, Zhirun 2
24/04/99	Dinamo Brest	A	0-1	
03/05/99	Belshina Bobruisk	H	5-1	Poznyak, Burdzenidze 3, Zhirun
07/05/99	Slaviya Mozyr	A	0-3	
15/05/99	FC BATE Borisov	H	0-4	
21/05/99	Shakhter Soligorsk	A	1-4	Petrushevskiy (p)
25/05/99	Neman-Belkard Grodno	H	0-3	
09/06/99	Dinamo Minsk	H	2-1	Burdzenidze, Poznyak
13/06/99	Torpedo-MAZ Minsk	A	0-1	
17/06/99	FC Molodechno	H	1-0	Mikheyev
23/06/99	Naftan-Devon Novopolotsk	A	1-4	Mikheyev
30/06/99	Svisloch-Krovlya Osipovichi	H	0-2	
07/07/99	FC Gomel	A	0-3	
11/07/99	Dnepr-Transmash Mogilev	A	1-3	Burdzenidze
24/07/99	Lokomotiv-96 Vitebsk	A	1-1	Demin
01/08/99	Torpedo-Kadino Mogilev	A	0-1	
07/08/99	Dinamo Brest	H	0-3	
16/08/99	Belshina Bobruisk	A	1-4	Zhirun
22/08/99	Slaviya Mozyr	H	0-7	
31/08/99	Shakhter Soligorsk	H	1-2	Khokhlach
06/09/99	FC BATE Borisov	A	1-1	Zhirun
11/09/99	Neman-Belkard Grodno	A	2-4	Demin, Zhirun
17/09/99	Dnepr-Transmash Mogilev	H	0-0	
21/09/99	Dinamo Minsk	A	0-5	
26/09/99	Torpedo-MAZ Minsk	H	0-1	
04/10/99	FC Molodechno	A	2-0	Prikhodko, Khokhlach
13/10/99	Naftan-Devon Novopolotsk	H	1-0	Poznyak
23/10/99	Svisloch-Krovlya Osipovichi	A	3-0	Poznyak, Mikheyev, Zhirun
30/10/99	FC Gomel	H	1-4	Zhirun

LOKOMOTIV-96 VITEBSK

CLUB DIRECTORY

Lokomotiv-96 Vitebsk
ul. Karl Marx 2A
210001 Vitebsk
tel - (0212) 378574/379173
fax - (0212) 379341/379173
Year of Formation - 1996
President - Igor Lobanov
Secretary - Eduard Verkhovskiy
Coach - Viktor Trubitsyn
Stadium - Dinamo (5,500)

MAJOR HONOURS
Domestic Cup - (1) 1998.

APPEARANCES 1999

	P	Ap	(s)	Gls
Alexei ABRAMOV	M		(2)	
Vitaliy ALESHCHENKO	A	25	(1)	17
Vyacheslav BELEI	D	30		
Sergei CHERNYSHOV	M	21	(5)	3
Vasiliy DYATLOV	D	23		2
Vyacheslav GORMASH	M	17	(3)	5
Andrei KARPOV	A		(4)	
Ivan KHOBRIN	M		(1)	
Yuriy KONOPLEV	D	24	(1)	1
Artem KOSAK	D	2	(6)	
Vladislav KOVRYGA	A	6	(3)	
Sergei KULANIN	D	2	(3)	
Sergei KUZMINICH	A	7	(12)	1
Andrei LYUBCHENKO	G	17		
Alexei POGE	G	13		
Alexei POZNYAK	M	11	(9)	3
Dmitriy PUTKIN	A	1	(7)	
Filipp SHALAYEV	A		(2)	
Vitaliy SIGOV	D	17		1
Alexei SOLDATOV	M	5	(3)	
Sergei TERIKHOV	M	22	(3)	
Igor TRUKHOV	M	30		6
Oleg VOROPAYEV	D	28		
Sergei YEREMEYEV	M	29	(1)	1

LEAGUE RESULTS 1999

Date	Opponent	H/A	Score	Scorers
11/04/99	FC Lida	A	0-0	
17/04/99	Dnepr-Transmash Mogilev	H	1-1	Konoplev
23/04/99	Torpedo-Kadino Mogilev	A	4-0	Aleshchenko, Poznyak, Chernyshov, Trukhov
03/05/99	Dinamo Minsk	H	1-0	Aleshchenko
07/05/99	Dinamo Brest	A	0-3	
15/05/99	Torpedo-MAZ Minsk	H	2-0	Aleshchenko 2
21/05/99	Belshina Bobruisk	A	0-4	
25/05/99	FC Molodechno	H	1-2	Aleshchenko
09/06/99	Naftan-Devon Novopolotsk	H	2-0	Aleshchenko 2
13/06/99	FC BATE Borisov	A	2-3	Yeremeyev, Sigov
16/06/99	Svisloch-Krovlya Osipovichi	H	6-1	Aleshchenko 3, Gormash 2, Trukhov
22/06/99	Shakhter Soligorsk	A	2-0	Aleshchenko 2
01/07/99	FC Gomel	H	2-0	Dyatkov, Poznyak
07/07/99	Neman-Belkard Grodno	A	1-2	Trukhov
11/07/99	Slaviya Mozyr	A	0-3	
24/07/99	FC Lida	H	1-1	Kuzminich
31/07/99	Dnepr-Transmash Mogilev	A	0-1	
07/08/99	Torpedo-Kadino Mogilev	H	4-1	Aleshchenko 3 (1p), Gormash
14/08/99	Dinamo Minsk	A	0-4	
21/08/99	Dinamo Brest	H	0-1	
27/08/99	Torpedo-MAZ Minsk	A	1-1	Aleshchenko
31/08/99	Belshina Bobruisk	H	1-2	Dyatlov
11/09/99	FC Molodechno	A	4-1	Trukhov 2, Chernyshov, Gormash (p)
18/09/99	Slaviya Mozyr	H	0-4	
22/09/99	Naftan-Devon Novopolotsk	A	1-3	Aleshchenko
25/09/99	FC BATE Borisov	H	0-1	
04/10/99	Svisloch-Krovlya Osipovichi	A	2-2	Poznyak, Gormash
13/10/99	Shakhter Soligorsk	H	1-1	Chernyshov
23/10/99	FC Gomel	A	0-2	
30/10/99	Neman-Belkard Grodno	H	1-1	Trukhov

FC MOLODECHNO

CLUB DIRECTORY

FC Molodechno
ul. M. Masherov 6 A
223310 Molodechno
tel - (273) 52444/73164
fax - (273) 54582
Year of Formation - 1993
President - Liudas Rumbutis
Coach - Vladimir Golubko; Boris Lazarchik
Stadium - Metallurg (5,500)

APPEARANCES 1999

	P	Ap	(s)	Gls
Vitaliy BYCHKOVSKIY	D	5	(4)	
Alexandr DANILENKO	A	9	(1)	
Vyacehslav DERBAN	M	19	(2)	
Vitaliy DIKOVICH	M	9	(11)	2
Sergei DOROKHOVICH	M	14		
Sergei FEDOROVICH	D	11		
Dmitriy KABELSKIY	D	22		
Sergei KABELSKIY	D	27		3
Alexei KATORGIN	M		(2)	
Dmitriy LABETSKIY	D	8	(5)	
Alexandr LEBEDEV	D	2		
Vitaliy MAKRITSKIY	A	10	(1)	2
Mikhail MARKHEL	A	6	(3)	2
Dmitriy MOLOSH	D	7	(1)	
Vladimir MURASHKO	A	2	(7)	
Alexandr NOVASH	M	4	(3)	
Valeriy PAVLOVETS	D	14	(2)	1
Maxim PESETSKIY	G	5	(1)	
Sergei PILETSKIY	M	2	(3)	
Pavel PLYUT	D	3	(4)	1
Andrei PORYVAYEV	M	3	(5)	
Vitaliy RAGUNOVICH	D	27		
Pavel RYZHEVSKIY	A		(3)	
Pavel SEDUN	D	1		
Taras SHAMSHORIK	M	15		4
Ivan SRIBNENKO	M	6	(7)	
Andrei TSYBULKO	M	2		
Alexandr VASILEVSKIY	G	25		
Sergei VOITOVICH	D	21	(1)	1
Dmitriy VOLCHEK	M	11		
Alexandr VOLSKIY	D	12	(2)	1
Pavel YEVSEYENKO	A	15	(9)	3
Valeriy ZHUKOVSKIY	M	13	(1)	1

LEAGUE RESULTS 1999

04/04/99	Slaviya Mozyr	A	0-1	
17/04/99	FC BATE Borisov	H	0-3	
24/04/99	Shakhter Soligorsk	A	1-3	Shamshorik (p)
03/05/99	Neman-Belkard Grodno	H	1-1	Yevseyenko
07/05/99	Dnepr-Transmash Mogilev	A	1-1	Shamshorik (p)
15/05/99	Dinamo Minsk	H	1-2	Plyut
21/05/99	Torpedo-MAZ Minsk	A	1-2	Shamshorik (p)
25/05/99	Lokomotiv-96 Vitebsk	A	2-1	Zhukovskiy, Kabelskiy S.
09/06/99	Svisloch-Krovlya Osipovichi	A	0-3	
13/06/99	FC Gomel	H	0-1	
17/06/99	FC Lida	A	0-1	
23/06/99	Torpedo-Kadino Mogilev	H	0-5	
30/06/99	Dinamo Brest	A	0-7	
07/07/99	Belshina Bobruisk	H	1-2	Pavlovets
11/07/99	Naftan-Devon Novopolotsk	H	1-3	Shamshorik (p)
24/07/99	Slaviya Mozyr	H	2-5	Volskiy, Markhel
31/07/99	FC BATE Borisov	A	1-2	Yevseyenko
07/08/99	Shakhter Soligorsk	H	0-1	
14/08/99	Neman-Belkard Grodno	A	0-0	
21/08/99	Dnepr-Transmash Mogilev	H	1-1	Makritskiy
27/08/99	Dinamo Minsk	A	0-2	
31/08/99	Torpedo-MAZ Minsk	H	2-2	Voitovich, Makritskiy
11/09/99	Lokomotiv-96 Vitebsk	H	1-4	Kabelskiy S. (p)
18/09/99	Naftan-Devon Novopolotsk	A	2-1	Yevseyenko, Dikovich
22/09/99	Svisloch-Krovlya Osipovichi	H	1-2	Markhel
26/09/99	FC Gomel	A	1-3	Kabelskiy S.
04/10/99	FC Lida	H	0-2	
13/10/99	Torpedo-Kadino Mogilev	A	1-4	Dikovich
23/10/99	Dinamo Brest	H	0-3	
30/10/99	Belshina Bobruisk	A	0-3	

NAFTAN-DEVON NOVOPOLOTSK

CLUB DIRECTORY

Naftan-Devon Novopolotsk
ul. Molodezhnaya 49 A
211440 Novopolotsk
tel - (02144) 57740/50605
fax - (02144) 54377
Year of Formation - 1995
President - Anatoliy Artyukh
Coach - Alexandr Traiduk
Stadium - Atlant (6,500)

APPEARANCES 1999

	P	Ap	(s)	Gls
Alexandr CHAPKOVSKIY	D	17		
Sergei DEMIDCHIK	A	19	(7)	5
Alexei DUBINA	D	5	(1)	
Svyatoslav GAVRILIN	M	7	(11)	1
Andrei GORNOSTAYEV	M	15	(11)	2
Ruslan GNEDKOV	D	17		1
Viktor IGNATIYEV	G	14	(1)	
Andrei KOZLOVSKIY	M	2	(9)	
Vitaliy KOZYAK	M	25	(4)	3
Artem OVODOV	M	1	(2)	
Igor POTAPOV	G	16		
Yuriy ROMANOVSKIY	M	24		
Sergei SALYGO	D	28		
Igor SHALAMOVSKIY	M	6	(2)	
Vladimir SHUPILOV	M	30		11
Oleg SIDORENKOV	D	14	(5)	1
Vitaliy TARAKANOV	M	29	(1)	5
Alexei TARASEVICH	A	17	(7)	5
Vladimir TERESHCHENKO	A	15	(5)	3
Vitaliy TIKHOMIROV	M	21	(2)	
Dmitriy TIMOFEYEV	M		(1)	
Mikhail ZHOROV	A	8	(10)	2

LEAGUE RESULTS 1999

11/04/99	Belshina Bobruisk	A	2-2	Shupilov, Demidchik
17/04/99	Slaviya Mozyr	H	0-3	
24/04/99	FC BATE Borisov	A	1-7	Shupilov
03/05/99	Shakhter Soligorsk	H	0-2	
07/05/99	Neman-Belkard Grodno	A	0-4	
15/05/99	Dnepr-Transmash Mogilev	H	1-2	Tarasevich
21/05/99	Dinamo Minsk	A	1-2	Tereshchenko
25/05/99	Torpedo-MAZ Minsk	H	4-0	Tarasevich, Shupilov 2, Demidchik
09/06/99	Lokomotiv-96 Vitebsk	A	0-2	
13/06/99	Svisloch-Krovlya Osipovichi	H	2-1	Tarasevich, Shupilov
17/06/99	FC Gomel	A	0-2	
23/06/99	FC Lida	H	4-1	Tarakanov 2, Kozyak, Shupilov
30/06/99	Torpedo-Kadino Mogilev	A	0-2	
07/07/99	Dinamo Brest	H	0-5	
11/07/99	FC Molodechno	A	3-1	Demidchik, Tarasevich, Gornostayev
24/07/99	Belshina Bobruisk	H	1-2	Gnedkov
31/07/99	Slaviya Mozyr	A	0-2	
06/08/99	FC BATE Borisov	H	0-4	
14/08/99	Shakhter Soligorsk	A	2-5	Demidchik, Kozyak
20/08/99	Neman-Belkard Grodno	H	3-1	Zhorov, Shupilov (p), Gornostayev
27/08/99	Dnepr-Transmash Mogilev	A	2-0	Kozyak, Zhorov
31/08/99	Dinamo Minsk	H	1-1	Sidorenkov
11/09/99	Torpedo-MAZ Minsk	A	2-2	Tarakanov, Shupilov
18/09/99	FC Molodechno	H	1-2	Tarakanov
22/09/99	Lokomotiv-96 Vitebsk	H	3-1	Tereshchenko 2, Shupilov
26/09/99	Svisloch-Krovlya Osipovichi	A	1-1	Demidchik
04/10/99	FC Gomel	H	1-2	Shupilov
13/10/99	FC Lida	A	0-1	
23/10/99	Torpedo-Kadino Mogilev	H	2-0	Gavrilin, Tarasevich
30/10/99	Dinamo Brest	A	2-3	Tarakanov, Shupilov (p)

NEMAN-BELKARD GRODNO

CLUB DIRECTORY

Neman-Belkard Grodno
ul. Kommunalnaya 3
230023 Grodno
tel - (0152) 723799
fax - (0152) 723799
Year of Formation - 1999
President - Vasiliy Pirozhnik
Secretary - Stanislav Ulasevich
Coach - Sergei Solodovnikov
Stadium - Neman (14,000)

MAJOR HONOURS
Domestic Cup - (1) 1993

APPEARANCES 1999

		P	Ap	(s)	Gls
Dmitriy BORISEIKO	A	19	(2)	3
Dmitriy DOLYGA	M		(4)	1
Anatoliy DRACHILOVSKIY	D	20		
Oleg KIRENYA	M	10	(10)	
Oleg KOTIN	M	3	(3)	
Artur KRIVONOS	D	25		
Yuriy MAMIDO	M	20	(7)	
Yuriy MAZURCHIK	A	24	(4)	6
Vladimir MOZOLOVSKIY	M	3	(1)	
Vitaliy NADIYEVSKIY	D	3	(7)	
Sergei NIKULIN (RUS)	M	19	(4)	6
Igor PETRASHEVICH	M	9	(8)	
Vladimir PETROV	M	26	(1)	1
Sergei Vasiliyevich POLYAKOV	M	26	(2)	6
Oleg RADUSHKO	D	22	(2)	6
Dmitriy ROVNEIKO	D	24		
Dmitriy RUTKO	D		(4)	
Albert RYBAK	G	21		
Dmitriy SAFRONOV	A		(2)	
Alexei SUCHKOV	A		(2)	
Alexandr SULIMA	G	9		
Sergei TARASHCHIK	A	16	(11)	1
Sergei TRASKEVICH	M		(4)	
Sergei TSYBUL	A	4	(7)	2
Yuriy TUPITSKIY	M	26		3
Nikolai YANKOVSKIY	D	1		

LEAGUE RESULTS 1999

11/04/99	Dnepr-Transmash Mogilev	H	0-2	
18/04/99	Dinamo Minsk	A	1-1	og (Khrapkovskiy)
24/04/99	Torpedo-MAZ Minsk	H	1-0	Tsybul
03/05/99	FC Molodechno	A	1-1	Radushko
07/05/99	Naftan-Devon Novopolotsk	H	4-0	Polyakov, Radushko, Boriseiko, Tsybul
15/05/99	Svisloch-Krovlya Osipovichi	A	1-0	Nikulin
21/05/99	FC Gomel	H	0-2	
25/05/99	FC Lida	A	3-0	Mazurchik 3
09/06/99	Dinamo Brest	A	1-1	Polyakov
13/06/99	Belshina Bobruisk	H	1-0	Radushko
17/06/99	Slaviya Mozyr	A	1-3	Polyakov
23/06/99	FC BATE Borisov	H	1-2	Tarashchik
30/06/99	Shakhter Soligorsk	A	0-3	
07/07/99	Lokomotiv-96 Vitebsk	H	2-1	Radushko, Tupitskiy
11/07/99	Torpedo-Kadino Mogilev	H	3-0	Radushko 2, Mazurchik
23/07/99	Dnepr-Transmash Mogilev	A	1-1	Tupitskiy
31/07/99	Dinamo Minsk	H	0-0	
06/08/99	Torpedo-MAZ Minsk	A	1-2	Nikulin
14/08/99	FC Molodechno	H	0-0	
20/08/99	Naftan-Devon Novopolotsk	A	1-3	Mazurchik
27/08/99	Svisloch-Krovlya Osipovichi	H	2-0	Boriseiko, Mazurchik (p)
31/08/99	FC Gomel	A	0-2	
11/09/99	FC Lida	H	4-2	Nikulin 2 (2p), Polyakov, Tupitskiy
18/09/99	Torpedo-Kadino Mogilev	A	0-1	
22/09/99	Dinamo Brest	H	2-1	Nikulin (p), Boriseiko
26/09/99	Belshina Bobruisk	A	1-5	Nikulin
04/10/99	Slaviya Mozyr	H	2-3	Petrov, Polyakov
13/10/99	FC BATE Borisov	A	1-4	Dolya
23/10/99	Shakhter Soligorsk	H	0-2	
30/10/99	Lokomotiv-96 Vitebsk	A	1-1	Polyakov

SHAKHTER SOLIGORSK

CLUB DIRECTORY

Shakhter Soligorsk
ul. Maxim Gorkiy 5
223710 Soligorsk
tel - (210) 20621
fax - (210) 20123
Year of Formation - 1963
President - Ivan Tupolskiy
Secretary - Sergei Cherevako
Coach - Ivan Shchekin
Stadium - Shakhter (5,000)

APPEARANCES 1999

	P	Ap	(s)	Gls
Alexei ADAMITSKIY	D	7		
Vadim ARTAMONOV	M	14	(4)	
Oleg AVGUL	D	1		
Dmitriy BESPANSKIY	M	28		11
Anatoliy BUDAYEV	D	30		
Oleg CHERNYAVSKIY	M	22	(1)	4
Andrei DOVNAR	M	14		4
Andrei DROZD	G	1		
Yuriy LAGODICH	A		(2)	
Vadim LASOVSKIY	D	3	(5)	
Andrei LYUBCHUK	D	1	(2)	
Andrei MILEVSKIY	M	1	(4)	
Alexandr MISHCHISHIN	D	21	(1)	
Vadim NARUSHEVICH	D	1	(2)	
Sergei NIKIFORENKO	A	20	(4)	4
Alexandr NOVIK	A	8	(17)	4
Sergei PETRUKOVICH	A		(1)	
Dmitriy PODREZ	M	30		13
Sergei SERGEL	A	6	(8)	1
Pavel SHAVROV	A	7	(12)	6
Maxim SHCHERBIN	A	7	(4)	2
Fedor SIKORSKIY	M	27	(1)	
Anatoliy TIKHONCHIK	A	17	(3)	7
Alexandr TISHKOV	D	4	(3)	
Oleg VERAXA	M	2	(9)	
Yuriy VERGEICHIK	M	1	(1)	
Vladimir VORONOV	D	28		2
Alexandr YEVNEVICH	G	29		

LEAGUE RESULTS 1999

Date	Opponent	H/A	Score	Scorers
11/04/99	Dinamo Minsk	H	0-1	
17/04/99	Torpedo-MAZ Minsk	A	1-4	Shavrov
24/04/99	FC Molodechno	H	3-1	Podrez, Tikhonchik, Shavrov
03/05/99	Naftan-Devon Novopolotsk	A	2-0	Bespanskiy, Tikhonchik
07/05/99	Svisloch-Krovlya Osipovichi	H	8-1	Tikhonchik 3, Bespanskiy 2, Shavrov, Podrez, Novik
15/05/99	FC Gomel	A	0-1	
21/05/99	FC Lida	H	4-1	Tikhonchik, Shavrov 3
25/05/99	Torpedo-Kadino Mogilev	A	1-0	Tikhonchik
09/06/99	Belshina Bobruisk	A	3-3	Shcherbin, Chernyavskiy, Novik
13/06/99	Slaviya Mozyr	H	2-1	Podrez, Novik
17/06/99	FC BATE Borisov	A	1-2	Novik
22/06/99	Lokomotiv-96 Vitebsk	H	0-2	
30/06/99	Neman-Belkard Grodno	H	3-0	Nikiforenko, Podrez 2
07/07/99	Dnepr-Transmash Mogilev	A	1-3	Podrez
11/07/99	Dinamo Brest	H	7-1	Podrez 4 (1p), Sergel, Bespanskiy, Voronov
24/07/99	Dinamo Minsk	A	0-0	
31/07/99	Torpedo-MAZ Minsk	H	1-0	Nikiforenko
07/08/99	FC Molodechno	A	1-0	Chernyavskiy
14/08/99	Naftan-Devon Novopolotsk	H	5-2	Dovnar, Podrez, Bespanskiy 2, Chernyavskiy
21/08/99	Svisloch-Krovlya Osipovichi	A	1-0	Voronov
27/08/99	FC Gomel	H	2-2	Dovnar, Nikiforenko
31/08/99	FC Lida	A	2-1	Podrez 2 (1p)
11/09/99	Torpedo-Kadino Mogilev	H	1-0	Shcherbin
18/09/99	Dinamo Brest	A	1-1	Dovnar
22/09/99	Belshina Bobruisk	H	2-1	Bespanskiy 2
26/09/99	Slaviya Mozyr	A	2-0	Nikiforenko, Chernyavskiy
04/10/99	FC BATE Borisov	H	0-1	
13/10/99	Lokomotiv-96 Vitebsk	A	1-1	Bespanskiy
23/10/99	Neman-Belkard Grodno	A	2-0	Bespanskiy, Dovnar
30/10/99	Dnepr-Transmash Mogilev	H	1-0	Bespanskiy

SLAVIYA MOZYR

CLUB DIRECTORY

Slaviya Mozyr
ul. Ya. Kolasa 26
247760 Mozyr
tel - (02351) 20194/23065
fax - (02351) 23881
email - slaviya@mail.ru/
Year of Formation - 1995
President - Mikhail Yuferev
Secretary - Igor Bobr
Coach - Alexandr Kuznetsov
Stadium - Yunost (7,500)

MAJOR HONOURS
League Championship - (1) 1996.
Domestic Cup - (2) 1996, 2000.

APPEARANCES 1999

	P	Ap	(s)	Gls
Yuriy ANTONOVICH	M	17	(1)	3
Valeriy APANAS	D	29		
Igor BALIN	D	26		1
Dmitriy CHALEI	M	25	(3)	11
Ruslan DANILYUK	D	3	(13)	
Dmitriy DENISYUK	M	23	(6)	11
Vladimir GAYEV	G	19		
Vadim GOPTAREVSKIY	D		(1)	
Dmitriy KARSAKOV (RUS)	M	27	(1)	7
Igor KHARLAN	G	3		
Vasiliy KUZHNIR	A	2	(7)	1
Fedor LUKASHENKO	M	29	(1)	6
Andrei LUKASHEVICH	D	9	(3)	
Oleg MALYUKOV	D	9		
Mikhail MARTOVICH	M		(1)	1
Artur MATVEICHIK	M	27	(2)	2
Oleg SAMATOV (RUS)	M	26		3
Alexandr SEMYANOV (RUS)	M	1	(6)	
Sergei SINITSYN	G	8		
Igor SLESARCHUK	A	3	(19)	4
Valeriy STRIPEIKIS	A	29		22
Maxim SUKHOVEYEV	A	1	(7)	
Mikhail VAVILOV	D	9	(6)	
Valeriy VYSOKOS (UKR)	M	5	(9)	1

LEAGUE RESULTS 1999

11/04/99	FC Molodechno	H	1-0	Chalei
17/04/99	Naftan-Devon Novopolotsk	A	3-0	og (Gnedkov), Samatov, Stripeikis
24/04/99	Svisloch-Krovlya Osipovichi	H	2-1	Stripeikis (p), Antonovich
03/05/99	FC Gomel	A	0-1	
07/05/99	FC Lida	H	3-0	Denisyuk, Lukashenko, Antonovich
15/05/99	Torpedo-Kadino Mogilev	A	0-0	
21/05/99	Dinamo Brest	H	2-1	Chalei, Stripeikis
25/05/99	Belshina Bobruisk	A	0-0	
09/06/99	FC BATE Borisov	H	1-3	Stripeikis
13/06/99	Shakhter Soligorsk	A	1-2	Stripeikis
17/06/99	Neman-Belkard Grodno	H	3-1	Chalei, Stripeikis, Kushnir
23/06/99	Dnepr-Transmash Mogilev	A	0-3	
30/06/99	Dinamo Minsk	H	4-0	Antonovich, Chalei (p), Stripeikis 2
07/07/99	Torpedo-MAZ Minsk	A	6-1	Stripeikis 3, Denisyuk, Lukashenko, Slesarchuk
11/07/99	Lokomotiv-96 Vitebsk	H	3-0	Denisyuk 2, Lukashenko
24/07/99	FC Molodechno	A	5-2	Chalei 2 (1p), Karsakov, Balin, Samatov
31/07/99	Naftan-Devon Novopolotsk	H	2-0	Chalei, Denisyuk
06/08/99	Svisloch-Krovlya Osipovichi	A	3-2	Stripeikis, Denisyuk 2
22/08/99	FC Lida	A	7-0	Stripeikis 2, Chalei, Matveichik, Slesarchuk, Denisyuk, Lukashenko
27/08/99	Torpedo-Kadino Mogilev	H	5-0	Chalei, Stripeikis, Denisyuk, Samatov, Martinovich
31/08/99	Dinamo Brest	A	7-2	Stripeikis, Karsakov 3, Vysokos, Denisyuk, Lukashenko
11/09/99	Belshina Bobruisk	H	1-0	Stripeikis
18/09/99	Lokomotiv-96 Vitebsk	A	4-0	Stripeikis 2, Matveichik, Lukashenko
22/09/99	FC BATE Borisov	A	1-1	Stripeikis (p)
26/09/99	Shakhter Soligorsk	H	0-2	
01/10/99	FC Gomel	H	1-1	Karsakov
04/10/99	Neman-Belkard Grodno	A	3-2	Chalei 2 (1p), Stripeikis
13/10/99	Dnepr-Transmash Mogilev	H	4-0	Karsakov 2, Slesarchuk 2
23/10/99	Dinamo Minsk	A	0-0	
30/10/99	Torpedo-MAZ Minsk	H	2-0	Stripeikis, Denisyuk

SVISLOCH-KROVLYA OSIPOVICHI

CLUB DIRECTORY

Svisloch-Krovlya Osipovichi
ul. V. Chapayev 11
213760 Osipovichi
tel - (02235) 22190/24635
fax - (02235) 24002
Year of Formation - 1994
President - Alexandr Konchits
Secretary - Vladimir Zavadskiy
Coach - Alexandr Konchits
Stadium - Yunost (2,200)

APPEARANCES 1999

	P	Ap	(s)	Gls
Oleg ALESHKEVICH	M	26	(3)	3
Vitaliy AZAROV (UKR)	M	14	(1)	2
Oleg BULOICHIK	D	24		1
Dmitriy DEGILEVICH	M		(1)	
Igor KAPACHENYA	M	3	(10)	
Dmitriy KIRDUN	M	1	(22)	
Sergei KROT	A	20	(4)	4
Yuriy LAGODICH	A	8		1
Alexei LITVINKO	A	21	(2)	3
Vladimir LOMAKO	D	13		1
Sergei MIKHAILOV	G	2		
Vitaliy PAVLOV	M	19	(5)	
Igor PORKULEVICH	M	10	(3)	4
Maxim SAMUSHCHIK	A	19	(6)	4
Gennadiy SHELEST	G	14	(1)	
Alexandr SOKOLOVSKIY	M	29		1
Igor SOROKA	M	22	(3)	
Ruslan SVIRIDENKO	D	4	(2)	
Andrei SVIRKOV	G	14		
Sergei TSINKEVICH	D	27	(1)	
Sergei VEREMEIKO	D	11	(3)	
Andrei VIKHROV	D	29		

LEAGUE RESULTS 1999

11/04/99	Dinamo Brest	A	0-2	
17/04/99	Belshina Bobruisk	H	0-1	
24/04/99	Slaviya Mozyr	A	1-2	Litvinko
03/05/99	FC BATE Borisov	H	0-5	
07/05/99	Shakhter Soligorsk	A	1-8	Aleshkevich
15/05/99	Neman-Belkard Grodno	H	0-1	
21/05/99	Dnepr-Transmash Mogilev	A	1-3	Buloichik (p)
25/05/99	Dinamo Minsk	H	0-0	
09/06/99	FC Molodechno	H	3-0	Aleshkevich, Lagodich, Samushchik
13/06/99	Naftan-Devon Novopolotsk	A	1-2	Krot
16/06/99	Lokomotiv-96 Vitebsk	A	1-6	Krot
23/06/99	FC Gomel	H	1-3	Samushchik
30/06/99	FC Lida	A	2-0	Samushchik, Aleshkevich
07/07/99	Torpedo-Kadino Mogilev	H	3-2	Lomako, Porkulevich, Krot
11/07/99	Torpedo-MAZ Minsk	A	0-2	
24/07/99	Dinamo Brest	H	1-3	Porkulevich (p)
31/07/99	Belshina Bobruisk	A	1-1	Samushchik
06/08/99	Slaviya Mozyr	H	2-3	Krot, Sokolovskiy
16/08/99	FC BATE Borisov	A	0-2	
21/08/99	Shakhter Soligorsk	H	0-1	
27/08/99	Neman-Belkard Grodno	A	0-2	
31/08/99	Dnepr-Transmash Mogilev	H	0-2	
11/09/99	Dinamo Minsk	A	0-7	
18/09/99	Torpedo-MAZ Minsk	H	0-2	
22/09/99	FC Molodechno	A	2-1	Porkulevich, Azarov
26/09/99	Naftan-Devon Novopolotsk	H	1-1	Azarov
04/10/99	Lokomotiv-96 Vitebsk	H	2-2	Litvinko 2
13/10/99	FC Gomel	A	1-4	Porkulevich
23/10/99	FC Lida	H	0-3	
30/10/99	Torpedo-Kadino Mogilev	A	0-3	

TORPEDO-MAZ MINSK

CLUB DIRECTORY

Torpedo-MAZ Minsk
ul. S. Lazo 10
220021 Minsk
tel - (017) 2430811/2429949
fax - (017) 2430771
Year of Formation - 1947
President - Viktor Bogmolov
Secretary - Valentina Lazebnaya
Coach - Yevgeniy Shabunya; Leonid Kuchuk;
Anatoliy Yurevich
Stadium - Torpedo (7,000)

APPEARANCES 1999

	P	Ap	(s)	Gls
Nikolai ABRAMOVICH	G	9		
Igor DOLINOV	M	2	(3)	
Andrei DOVNAR	M	14		2
Ivan GALUKHIN (RUS)	A	1	(9)	1
Vladimir GOLMAK	D	28		3
Igor GRIGORIYEV	A	6	(14)	3
Pavel KIRILCHIK	D	1	(2)	
Ivan KIRSANOV	M	5	(8)	
Oleg KONONOV	D	3		
Vladimir KONOVALOV	A		(1)	
Vladimir KORYTKO	M	20	(2)	
Viktor KUKAR	M	28		
Roman LEVITSKIY	M	16	(2)	1
Yevgeniy LINEV	D	21	(2)	
Sergei LYCHKOVSKIY	G	1	(1)	
Yuriy MALEYEV	M	26		
Nikita MALYI	A	5	(5)	1
Mikhail MARKHEL	A	9	(5)	
Antuan MAYOROV	M	1	(2)	
Pavel MIRONCHIK	D	4	(6)	
Sergei OMELYANCHUK	D	10	(8)	1
Artur SAAKYAN	M	9	(2)	
Alexandr SEDNEV	D	15		1
Denis SEMENOV	D	9	(1)	
Nikolai SHVYDAKOV	A	19	(3)	4
Alexandr SNEGIREV	M	1	(2)	
Yuriy SVIRKOV	G	20	(2)	
Sergei YAROMKO	A	29		8
Sergei YEVDOKIMENKO	M	4	(3)	
Alexei ZAKHAROV	M	2	(2)	
Sergei ZHURAVSKIY	M	12	(2)	6

LEAGUE RESULTS 1999

11/04/99	FC BATE Borisov	A	1-2	Golmak
17/04/99	Shakhter Soligorsk	H	4-1	Golmak 2, Dovnar, Yaromko
24/04/99	Neman-Belkard Grodno	A	0-1	
03/05/99	Dnepr-Transmash Mogilev	H	0-3	
07/05/99	Dinamo Minsk	H	1-2	Shvydakov
15/05/99	Lokomotiv-96 Vitebsk	A	0-2	
21/05/99	FC Molodechno	H	2-1	Levitskiy, Yaromko (p)
25/05/99	Naftan-Devon Novopolotsk	A	0-4	
09/06/99	FC Gomel	A	0-1	
13/06/99	FC Lida	H	1-0	Dovnar
18/06/99	Torpedo-Kadino Mogilev	A	1-0	Yaromko
22/06/99	Dinamo Brest	H	2-0	Shvydakov 2
30/06/99	Belshina Bobruisk	A	1-2	Yaromko
07/07/99	Slaviya Mozyr	H	1-6	Grigoriyev
11/07/99	Svisloch-Krovlya Osipovichi	H	2-0	Yaromko (p), Grigoriyev
23/07/99	FC BATE Borisov	H	1-3	Zhuravskiy
31/07/99	Shakhter Soligorsk	A	0-1	
06/08/99	Neman-Belkard Grodno	H	2-1	Yaromko, Grigoriyev
14/08/99	Dnepr-Transmash Mogilev	A	0-1	
22/08/99	Dinamo Minsk	A	0-5	
27/08/99	Lokomotiv-96 Vitebsk	H	1-1	Zhuravskiy
31/08/99	FC Molodechno	A	2-2	Malyi, Zhuravskiy
11/09/99	Naftan-Devon Novopolotsk	H	2-2	Sednev, Yaromko
18/09/99	Svisloch-Krovlya Osipovichi	A	2-0	Zhuravskiy, Yaromko
22/09/99	FC Gomel	H	1-1	Omelyanchuk
26/09/99	FC Lida	A	1-0	Shvydakov
05/10/99	Torpedo-Kadino Mogilev	H	0-0	
13/10/99	Dinamo Brest	A	1-2	Zhuravskiy
23/10/99	Belshina Bobruisk	H	2-1	Galukhin, Zhuravskiy
30/10/99	Slaviya Mozyr	A	0-2	

TORPEDO-KADINO MOGILEV

CLUB DIRECTORY

Torpedo-Kadino Mogilev
Avenue Vitebsk 43
212004 Mogilev
tel - (0222) 422447
fax - (0222) 422894
Year of Formation - 1974
President - Mikhail Bass
Secretary - Vadim Krasnov
Coach - Mikhail Bass
Stadium - Torpedo (7,000)

APPEARANCES 1999

	P	Ap	(s)	Gls
Sergei ALANTSOV	D	6	(4)	
Fedir ARTYUKHOV (UKR)	A	9	(1)	
Ivan BENEVELSKYI (UKR)	A	18	(3)	2
Christopher CHE (CMR)	D	15		
Mykhailo DEMIN (UKR)	M	15		1
Dmitriy GITSELEV	D	9	(3)	
Andriy GOLYAS (UKR)	A		(7)	
Igor GORBACHEV	M	23	(5)	1
Anatoliy ILINICH	M	1		
Yuriy KALASHNIKOV	M	6	(6)	
Vyacheslav KANASHEVICH	G	20		
Vyacheslav KANASHEVICH	M		(2)	
Gennadiy KARASEV	M	5	(7)	2
Dmitriy KISELEV	D	27		1
Sergei KOVALEV	G	2	(1)	
Sergei KOVALEV	M		(2)	
Igor KUTSENKO	A		(1)	
Vladimir KUZHELEV	M	10	(1)	4
Oleg KUZMENOK	A	26	(3)	8
Viktor MASYUK	D	7		
Alexei MAXIMENKO	D	9	(5)	
Alexei MITIN	G	8	(1)	
Olexandr MUZYKA (UKR)	D	14		
Anton OGANESOV (UKR)	A	9	(10)	4
Ruslan POKAZATSKIY	M	10	(3)	1
Vladislav SAVCHUK	M	3		
Andrei SKOROBOGATKO	M	12		2
Sergei TEPLYAKOV	M	28	(1)	1
Pavlo TSISLEVSKYI (UKR)	M	3		
Andrei VASILIYEV	M	13		
Andrei YAKUBOVICH	D	1		
Olexandr ZABARA (UKR)	M	10	(9)	2
Serhiy ZAKHAROV (UKR)	D	11		1

LEAGUE RESULTS 1999

11/04/99	FC Gomel	H	0-1	
17/04/99	FC Lida	A	1-3	Kuzmenok
23/04/99	Lokomotiv-96 Vitebsk	H	0-4	
03/05/99	Dinamo Brest	H	1-1	Kuzhelev
07/05/99	Belshina Bobruisk	A	1-5	Kuzhelev
15/05/99	Slaviya Mozyr	H	0-0	
21/05/99	FC BATE Borisov	H	1-5	Kuzhelev
25/05/99	Shakhter Soligorsk	H	0-1	
09/06/99	Dnepr-Transmash Mogilev	H	2-5	Oganesov, Skorobogatko
14/06/99	Dinamo Minsk	A	1-1	Kuzhelev
18/06/99	Torpedo-MAZ Minsk	H	0-1	
23/06/99	FC Molodechno	A	5-0	Zakharov (p), Benevelskyi,
				Oganesov, Karasev 2
30/06/99	Naftan-Devon Novopolotsk	H	2-0	Teplyakov, Skorobogatko
07/07/99	Svisloch-Krovlya Osipovichi	A	2-3	Pokazatskiy, Zabara
11/07/99	Neman-Belkard Grodno	A	0-3	
24/07/99	FC Gomel	A	0-5	
01/08/99	FC Lida	H	1-0	Kuzmenok
07/08/99	Lokomotiv-96 Vitebsk	A	1-4	Kuzmenok
14/08/99	Dinamo Brest	A	0-4	
20/08/99	Belshina Bobruisk	H	0-3	
27/08/99	Slaviya Mozyr	A	0-5	
31/08/99	FC BATE Borisov	A	0-4	
11/09/99	Shakhter Soligorsk	A	0-1	
18/09/99	Neman-Belkard Grodno	H	1-0	Kuzmenok
22/09/99	Dnepr-Transmash Mogilev	A	2-5	Kuzmenok, Zabara (p)
26/09/99	Dinamo Minsk	H	2-2	Kuzmenok, Kiselev
05/10/99	Torpedo-MAZ Minsk	A	0-0	
13/10/99	FC Molodechno	H	4-1	Oganesov, Gorbachev (p),
				Kuzmenok 2
23/10/99	Naftan-Devon Novopolotsk	A	0-2	
30/10/99	Svisloch-Krovlya Osipovichi	H	3-0	Oganesov, Benevelskyi, Demin

BELGIUM

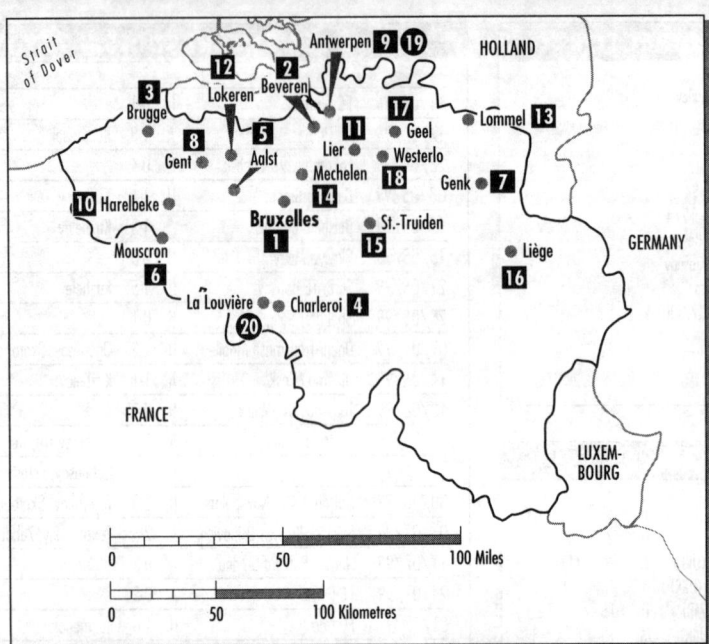

1	RSC ANDERLECHT	174	12	KSC LOKEREN	185
2	KSK BEVEREN	175	13	KFC LOMMELSE SK	186
3	CLUB BRUGGE KV	176	14	KV MECHELEN	187
4	RSC CHARLEROI	177	15	K ST.-TRUIDENSE VV	188
5	KSC EENDRACHT AALST	178	16	R STANDARD LIEGE	189
6	R EXCELSIOR MOUSCRON	179	17	KFC VERBROEDERING GEEL	190
7	KRC GENK	180	18	KVC WESTERLO	191
8	KAA GENT	181	**Promoted clubs**		
9	GERMINAL BEERSCHOT ANTWERPEN	182	19	ROYAL ANTWERP FC	
10	KRC HARELBEKE	183	20	RAA LA LOUVIERE	
11	K LIERSE SK	184			

ANDERLECHT BACK WHERE THEY BELONG

Hell on earth for the Red Devils

FEDERATION DIRECTORY

Union Royale des Sociétés de Football Association
Houba de Strooperlaan 145, 1020 Bruxelles

tel - (02) 4771211   Year of Formation - 1895
fax - (02) 4782391   President - Michel D'Hooghe
website - www.footbel.com   Secretary - Alain Courtois

Stadium - Roi Baudouin, Bruxelles (40,000)

Belgium were good enough to reach the quarter-finals of Euro 2000. They were entertaining co-hosts, a better team perhaps than many believed they might be. But a combination of missed chances, unforced errors and panic under pressure resulted in their elimination by Turkey in the third match of the group phase. In losing that match 2-0 in Brussels, Belgium earned themselves the unwanted record of becoming the first host nation of a European Championship or World Cup to fail to advance beyond the first round.

That statistic may well haunt Belgium for many years to come, but the truth of the matter is that Robert Waseige's team made a positive contribution to an excellent tournament. They played crowd-pleasing, attack-minded football in all three matches, and although the results - one

2-1 victory and two 0-2 defeats - do not look good on paper, especially for a team playing at home in front of capacity crowds, Belgium had no need to hang their heads in shame.

Even Filip De Wilde, the goalkeeper whose Euro 2000 included two terrible blunders which led to goals and an horrendous tackle which brought a red card, had his positive moments, notably the save of the tournament early on against Italy. Belgium's midfield was full of quality, with Gert Verheyen and Bart Goor showing commendable enterprise in their wide-midfield roles, and Marc Wilmots and Yves Vanderhaeghe dovetailing splendidly in the centre. Eric Deflandre was also one of the most consistently productive full-backs at the tournament and Emile Mpenza showed that he had the

LEAGUE CHAMPIONSHIP RESULTS 99/00

		1	2	3	4	5	6	7	8	9	10	11	12	13	14	15	16	17	18
1	RSC Anderlecht		5-2	1-1	3-0	4-1	3-2	1-3	1-2	2-2	2-0	2-0	5-0	3-3	5-0	2-1	2-0	4-0	3-0
2	KSK Beveren	0-0		2-3	1-1	0-2	1-1	1-4	0-1	1-4	2-2	1-1	2-1	1-0	2-1	3-4	0-2	1-1	4-0
3	Club Brugge KV	0-2	3-1		3-1	3-0	1-2	2-0	1-3	2-0	1-2	1-0	6-1	3-1	6-0	4-0	5-2	4-0	2-0
4	RSC Charleroi	1-1	2-3	0-2		0-1	2-1	2-1	1-2	3-0	2-1	1-1	2-4	1-1	1-4	1-1	1-4	1-3	1-2
5	KSC Eendracht Aalst	2-3	2-4	0-2	0-3		2-5	1-3	4-2	1-2	3-0	2-3	1-0	3-1	2-0	2-0	1-2	1-0	1-1
6	R Excelsior Mouscron	0-2	3-0	1-2	2-1	1-1		5-0	5-3	1-1	4-2	3-3	0-0	0-0	2-0	3-0	1-3	3-1	2-1
7	KRC Genk	1-4	4-1	1-0	1-2	2-1	2-2		0-1	4-0	4-3	2-2	1-1	1-2	3-1	0-2	4-0	1-0	1-1
8	KAA Gent	0-3	4-1	2-0	3-2	4-0	2-3	0-2		1-3	4-2	2-0	1-1	6-2	6-1	4-2	1-5	1-1	2-3
9	Germinal Beerschot Antwerpen	1-3	2-0	5-3	3-0	3-2	0-1	3-0	2-0		1-0	1-1	0-0	3-1	0-0	3-1	2-0	4-1	3-2
10	KRC Harelbeke	2-2	0-5	1-1	4-1	1-1	1-1	1-2	1-2	1-0		0-3	2-3	5-1	5-2	3-2	3-4	3-0	3-1
11	K Lierse SK	0-3	1-3	1-0	2-0	5-2	1-0	5-0	2-1	3-1	2-0		1-2	4-0	5-1	0-0	1-0	2-2	7-0
12	KSC Lokeren	2-3	5-2	2-5	1-1	5-1	3-2	1-2	0-4	1-1	2-0	5-1		2-1	0-2	3-0	5-3	0-0	0-0
13	KFC Lommelse SK	3-3	0-0	0-0	1-1	3-3	0-4	0-1	1-3	2-2	0-2	1-0	1-0		0-2	4-1	2-1	1-1	2-2
14	KV Mechelen	2-5	3-1	0-0	2-1	2-0	1-3	2-0	0-2	2-0	4-0	4-3	0-0	1-0		3-2	2-4	1-1	2-2
15	K St.-Truidense VV	0-4	0-2	0-1	2-2	1-5	0-0	0-5	0-0	2-0	2-0	2-1	1-1	2-0	3-1		2-0	1-1	2-1
16	R Standard Liège	0-0	3-1	0-1	1-3	3-1	2-0	5-1	0-2	1-0	1-3	3-1	1-2	4-1	2-1	2-1		3-0	4-0
17	KFC Verbroedering Geel	0-0	1-1	0-2	0-0	1-2	1-4	1-1	1-5	0-2	3-2	2-1	3-0	0-0	3-0	1-2	0-0		2-3
18	KVC Westerlo	5-0	3-2	1-0	1-1	3-2	3-0	6-6	4-2	3-2	4-1	0-2	3-3	1-0	8-0	3-2	2-1	4-1	

LEAGUE CHAMPIONSHIP FINAL TABLE 99/00

			Home				Away				Total						
		Pd	W	D	L	F	A	W	D	L	F	A	W	D	L	F	A	PT	GD
1	RSC Anderlecht	34	12	3	2	48	17	10	6	1	38	19	22	9	3	86	36	75	50
2	Club Brugge KV	34	13	0	4	47	15	8	4	5	23	17	21	4	9	70	32	67	38
3	KAA Gent	34	9	2	6	43	31	11	1	5	35	23	20	3	11	78	54	63	24
4	R Excelsior Mouscron	34	9	5	3	36	20	7	4	6	31	25	16	9	9	67	45	57	22
5	R Standard Liège	34	11	1	5	35	18	7	1	9	31	34	18	2	14	66	52	56	14
6	KVC Westerlo	34	13	3	1	54	25	3	5	9	19	41	16	8	10	73	66	56	7
7	Germinal Beerschot Antwerpen	34	12	3	2	36	15	4	4	9	20	30	16	7	11	56	45	55	11
8	KRC Genk	34	8	4	5	32	23	8	2	7	31	36	16	6	12	63	59	54	4
9	K Lierse SK	34	12	2	3	42	15	3	5	9	23	32	15	7	12	65	47	52	18
10	KSC Lokeren	34	8	4	5	37	28	4	7	6	19	30	12	11	11	56	58	47	-2
11	KV Mechelen	34	9	4	4	31	24	3	1	13	16	53	12	5	17	47	77	41	-30
12	KSC Eendracht Aalst	34	7	1	9	28	31	4	3	10	25	41	11	4	19	53	72	37	-19
13	K St.-Truidense VV	34	7	5	5	20	24	3	2	12	21	41	10	7	17	41	65	37	-24
14	KRC Harelbeke	34	7	4	6	36	31	3	1	13	20	41	10	5	19	56	72	35	-16
15	KSK Beveren	34	4	6	7	22	28	5	2	10	29	41	9	8	17	51	69	35	-18
16	RSC Charleroi	34	4	4	9	22	32	3	6	8	20	30	7	10	17	42	62	31	-20
17	KFC Verbroedering Geel	34	4	6	7	19	25	1	7	9	13	35	5	13	16	32	60	28	-28
18	KFC Lommelse SK	34	4	8	5	21	26	1	4	12	14	40	5	12	17	35	66	27	-31

N.B. Where teams are level on points, classification is determined by the number of victories.

pace and positional sense to worry top-class international defences, if not, alas, the finishing touch.

De Wilde, inevitably, headed the list of underperformers, although strikers Branko Strupar - the naturalised new boy - and Luc Nilis - the recalled veteran - were not far behind. Both players fell way short of their potential, and neither could score the goals which the team's overall play deserved.

Coach Waseige could not entirely escape criticism, either. He became too desperate too early in the crunch match against Turkey, piling players forward and launching speculative attacks when a more patient approach would probably have brought the draw Belgium needed to reach the quarter-finals. Nevertheless, Waseige deserved credit for the way in which he had revived the team during his year in charge. When he took over from Georges Leekens, in August 1999, Belgium were at rock bottom, devoid, it seemed, of any spirit or confidence. But Waseige, the wily francophone, soon arrested the slump.

A ridiculously entertaining 5-5 draw in Rotterdam got his reign off to a promising start, and when Morocco were routed 4-0 in Liège three days later, it meant that Belgium had scored more goals in two games under Waseige than they had managed in the previous 11 under Leekens. Throughout the build-up to Euro 2000 the Red Devils suffered just one defeat - against England in Sunderland.

They even made history by winning in Italy for the first time, beating the 'Azzurri' 3-1 in Lecce. Sadly, they were unable to repeat that scoreline against Dino Zoff's team on home soil at Euro 2000, and that opening-day victory over the Swedes ultimately counted for nothing.

Disenchantment with the national team was minimal, however, compared to that which followed another early mass exodus from Europe by Belgium's clubs. One after another they fell. Champions Genk set the pattern when they humiliatingly bowed out in the second qualifying round of the Champions' League to the Slovenians of Maribor. A few weeks later it was the turn of both Club

INTERNATIONAL HONOURS

World Cup Finals appearances: 1930, 1934, 1938, 1954, 1970, 1982 (2nd phase), 1986 (4th), 1990 (2nd round), 1994 (2nd round), 1998

European Championship appearances: 1972 (3rd), 1976, 1980 (runners-up), 1984, 2000

European Club Competitions
Cup-winners' Cup   RSC Anderlecht (1976, 1978)
                                 KV Mechelen (1988).

UEFA Cup   RSC Anderlecht (1983)

Super Cup   RSC Anderlecht (1976, 1978).

NATIONAL TEAM APPEARANCES 99/00

Coach - Georges LEEKENS; Robert WASEIGE	FIN	HOL	MAR	ENG	ITA	POR	HOL	NOR	DEN	SWE	ITA	TUR	Cps	Gls
Philippe VANDE WALLE (22/12/61) - Club Brugge KV	G	G40											8	-
Tjörven DE BRUL (22/06/73) - Club Brugge KV	D46												10	-
Carl HOEFKENS (06/10/78) - K Lierse SK	D	s78	s56										4	-
Lorenzo STAELENS (30/04/64) - RSC Anderlecht	D	D	D46		D	D	D	D	D	D	D	D	71	8
Marc HENDRIKX (02/07/74) - KRC Genk	D46	s72	s46				s46	s46		s44	s58		10	-
Yves VANDERHAEGHE (30/01/70) - R Excelsior Mouscron	M	M	M	M	M87	M	M	s46	M	M	M	M	15	-
Marc WILMOTS (22/02/69) - FC Schalke 04 (GER)	M81	M		M	M86	M	M83		M	M	M	M	49	17
Johan WALEM (01/02/72) - Parma (ITA)	M	s81	M	s46	s86		M						20	1
Bart GOOR (09/04/73) - RSC Anderlecht	M	M	M		M	M68	M	M	M	M	M	M58	19	3
Sandy MARTENS (23/12/72) - Club Brugge KV	A46												6	3
Jurgen CAVENS (19/08/78) - K Lierse SK	A46												4	-
Glen DE BOECK (22/08/71) - RSC Anderlecht	s46		s46										23	-
			/56											
Gert VERHEYEN (20/09/70) - Club Brugge KV	s46	M89	M73		s70	M77	M86	M	M86	M88	M67	M61	31	5
Branko STRUPAR (09/02/70) - KRC Genk/Derby County (ENG)	s46	A	A	A74	A80	A81	A62		A61	A69	A57	s61	11	5
Emile MPENZA (04/07/78) - R Standard Liège/FC Schalke 04 (GER)	s46	A81	A			A		A86	A	A	A		27	8
Walter BASEGGIO (19/08/78) - RSC Anderlecht	s81												3	-
Eric DEFLANDRE (02/08/73) - Club Brugge KV		D78	D46	D			D	s70	D46	D	D	D	24	-
Jacky PEETERS (13/12/69) - Arminia Bielefeld (GER)		D	D	D	D				s86	s88			6	-
Nico VAN KERCKHOVEN (14/12/70) - FC Schalke 04 (GER)		D72	D46	M	D				s46	s73	D44	D	26	2
Frédéric HERPOEL (16/08/74) - KAA Gent		s40											1	-
Toni BROGNO (19/07/73) - KVC Westerlo		s89		s74	s80	s81		A63					7	-
Geert DE VLIEGER (16/01/71) - RSC Anderlecht/Willem II (HOL)		G	G46					s32	s29				7	-
David BROCKEN (18/02/71) - RSC Anderlecht			s46										2	-
Mbo MPENZA (04/12/76) - R Standard Liège/Sporting CP (POR)			s73		M70	s77	s86				s67		19	-
Eric VAN MEIR (28/02/68) - K Lierse SK				D									17	1
Davy OYEN (17/07/75) - RSC Anderlecht				D									3	-
Stefaan TANGHE (15/01/72) - R Excelsior Mouscron				M46									7	1
Gilles DE BILDE (09/06/71) - Sheffield Wednesday (ENG)				A	A	A46	s62	s63	s86			s76	24	2
Ronny GASPERCIC (09/05/69) - CF Extremadura (ESP)				s46	G		G32						7	-
Régis GENAUX (30/08/73) - Udinese (ITA)					D	D	D70						22	-
Philippe CLEMENT (22/03/74) - Club Brugge KV					s87		M46						11	-
Filip DE WILDE (05/07/64) - RSC Anderlecht						G	G	G29	G	G	G	G	33	-
Joos VALGAEREN (03/03/76) - Roda JC (HOL)						D		D	D	D	D	D	6	-
Philippe LEONARD (14/02/74) - AS Monaco (FRA)						D	D	D46	D46	D73			18	-
Michael GOOSSENS (30/11/73) - R Standard Liège						s46	s83						13	1
Danny BOFFIN (10/07/65) - FC Metz (FRA)						s68							42	1
Bertrand CRASSON (05/10/71) - RSC Anderlecht							D						22	1
Luc NILIS (25/05/67) - PSV (HOL)							A	s61	s69	s57	A76		56	10

DOMESTIC CUP 99/00

1/16 FINALS
KSC Lokeren 1, Club Brugge KV 0
KVC Westerlo 3, KSK Beveren 1
RSC Charleroi 2, KSC Eendracht Aalst 6
KSV Waregem 1, KSV Cercle Brugge 0
KRC Genk 3, SK Tongeren 0
KV Mechelen 2, Hekelgem 1 (aet)
Royal Antwerp FC 4, Heusden-Zolder 0
KFC Lommelse SK 2, RWD Molenbeek 1
KFC Verbroedering Geel 1, AEC Mons 1
(aet; 3-4 on pens.)
K Lierse SK 6, Torhout 1
KAA Gent 3, Dessel Sport 1
K St.-Truidense VV 1, Francs Borains 0 (aet)
KV Oostende 0, Germinal Beerschot Antwerpen 1
RAA La Louvière 0, R Excelsior Mouscron 0
(2-3 on pens.)
R Standard Liège 3, KRC Harelbeke 2
RSC Anderlecht 1, SV Ingelmunster 4 (aet)

1/8 FINALS
R Standard Liège 2, KVC Westerlo 1
KSC Lokeren 4, KV Mechelen 0
R Excelsior Mouscron 0, K St.-Truidense VV 0
(aet; 1-4 on pens.)
KRC Genk 8, SV Ingelmunster 1
AEC Mons 2, KFC Lommelse SK 0
KSV Waregem 0, KAA Gent 2
KSC Eendracht Aalst 4, Germinal Beerschot Antwerpen 1
Royal Antwerp FC 1, K Lierse SK 2 (aet)

QUARTER-FINALS
R Standard Liège 1 (Mornar 16), AEC Mons 0
K Lierse SK 1 (Snoeckx 40), KSC Lokeren 0
K St.-Truidense VV 2 (Fiers 29, Teppers 82),
KSC Eendracht Aalst 1 (Claeys 47)
KRC Genk 3 (Gudjónsson Th. 30p, 65, Hendrikx 35),
KAA Gent 1 (Joly 58)

SEMI-FINALS
R Standard Liège 2 (Pierre 4, Goossens 20),
K Lierse SK 0
K Lierse SK 0, R Standard Liège 0
(R Standard Liège 2-0)
KRC Genk 0, K St.-Truidense VV 0
K St.-Truidense VV 0, KRC Genk 1 (Origi 2)
(KRC Genk 1-0)

FINAL
14/05/2000, Brussels
KRC GENK 4
Ban (19), Gudjónsson Th. (52, 75), Hasi (80)
R STANDARD LIEGE 1 Pierre (1)
referee - Piraux
KRC GENK - Brockhauser, Delbroek, Hendrikx, Kimoni,
Vangronsveld, Hasi (Olivieri 85), Skoko, Daerden,
Origi, Ban (Horváth 65), Gudjónsson Th..
R STANDARD LIEGE - Runje, Dimas, Wuillot, Van
Buyten, Brocken, Ciobotariu, Selymes (Lukunku 46;
Blay 60), Ernst, Pierre, Goossens (El Yamani 75),
Mornar.

Bruges and Lierse to depart in unflattering fashion from the UEFA Cup, the former going down on away goals (a common affliction) to Israeli champions Hapoel Haifa and the latter losing home and away to FC Zürich.

Only Anderlecht put up a half-decent fight. They were easy winners over Olimpija Ljubljana in round one and looked set to overcome Bologna as well when prolific new Czech striker Jan Koller put them 2-0 up at home to Bologna. But the concession of a last-minute goal provoked their downfall and the Italians came through to win, albeit with much less conviction than the 3-0 second-leg scoreline would suggest.

Unlucky in Europe, Anderlecht were unstoppable at home. Newly coached by Aimé Anthuenis, the man who brought the Belgian title to Genk the previous season, the 'Mauves' bestrode

NATIONAL TEAM RESULTS 99/00

18/08/99	Finland	H	Bruges	3-4	Martens (42), Wilmots (60), Mpenza E. (73)
04/09/99	Holland	A	Rotterdam	5-5	Strupar (8, 29), Goor (49), Wilmots (52),
					Mpenza E. (76)
07/09/99	Morocco	H	Liège	4-0	Staelens (7p), Walem (18), Mpenza E. (20),
					Strupar (88)
10/10/99	England	A	Sunderland	1-2	Strupar (14)
13/11/99	Italy	A	Lecce	3-1	De Bilde (6), Wilmots (69), Goor (85)
23/02/00	Portugal	H	Charleroi	1-1	Strupar (56)
29/03/00	Holland	H	Brussels	2-2	Verheyen (14), Mpenza E. (27)
26/04/00	Norway	A	Oslo	2-0	Verheyen (55, 90)
03/06/00	Denmark	A	Copenhagen	2-2	Staelens (51p), Wilmots (73)
10/06/00	Sweden (ECF)	H	Brussels	2-1	Goor (42), Mpenza E. (46)
14/06/00	Italy (ECF)	H	Brussels	0-2	
19/06/00	Turkey (ECF)	H	Brussels	0-2	

TOP SCORERS

30	Ole Martin ÅRST (KAA Gent)
	Toni BROGNO (KVC Westerlo)
20	Jan KOLLER (RSC Anderlecht)
19	David PAAS (KRC Harelbeke)
16	Eric VAN MEIR (K Lierse SK)
14	Tomasz RADZINSKI (RSC Anderlecht)
	Pär ZETTERBERG (RSC Anderlecht)
	Dante BROGNO (RSC Charleroi)
	Marcin ZEWLAKOW (R Excelsior Mouscron)
13	Remco TORKEN (KSK Beveren)
	Jochen JANSSEN (Club Brugge KV)
	Gert VERHEYEN (Club Brugge KV)
	Sven VERMANT (Club Brugge KV)
	Chris JANSSENS (KSC Lokeren)
	Vedran PELIC (KVC Westerlo)

EUROPEAN CUPS 99/00

CHAMPIONS' CUP
● KRC GENK
Preliminary round 2 NK MARIBOR (SLO)
A 1-5 Strupar (37)
Brockhauser, Kimoni, Olivieri, Van Geem (Gudjónsson B. 81), Delbroek, Jansson, Hasi, Gudjónsson Th. (Caushllari 66), Hendrikx, Strupar, Ban (Horváth 75).
H 3-0 Gudjónsson Th. (45, 61), Horváth (64)
Brockhauser, Van Geem (N'Sumbu 46), Olivieri, Kimoni, De Oliveira (Pereira 79), Delbroek, Gudjónsson Th., Hasi, Hendrikx, Oulare, Strupar.

UEFA CUP
● CLUB BRUGGE KV
Qualifying round TULEVIK VILJANDI (EST)
A 3-0 Deflandre (50p), Jankauskas (58, 69)
Vande Walle, Deflandre, Lesnjak, Lembi, Ilic, Borkelmans, Clement, Englebert, Martens (Janssen 74), Verheyen (Vermant 79), Jankauskas.
H 2-0 Jankauskas (48), De Brul (69)
Vande Walle, Deflandre, De Brul, Lesnjak, Borkelmans, Lembi, Englebert (Anic 70), Vermant, Martens (Janssen 46), Verheyen (Schockaert 82), Jankauskas.

1st round HAPOEL HAIFA (ISR)
A 1-3 Jankauskas (65)
Verlinden, Deflandre (Martens 46), Lesnjak, De Brul, Lembi, Borkelmans, Englebert, Clement, Vermant, Jankauskas (Schockaert 88), Verheyen.
H 4-2 Verheyen (19), Borkelmans (26), Janssen (52, 90)
Verlinden, De Brul, Lesnjak (Anic 83), Lembi, Borkelmans, Englebert (Fadiga 76), Clement, Vermant, Verheyen, Jankauskas (Martens 83), Janssen.

● K LIERSE SK
1st round FC ZÜRICH (SUI)
A 0-1
Deman, Shekiladze, Van Meir, Hofkens, Daems, Snoeckx, Leen, Zdebel, Somers, Cavens (Huysegems 70), Van de Weyer (Huysmans 80).

H 3-4 Van Meir (17), Huysegems (72), Zdebel (83)
Nys, Van Meir, Hoefkens, Daems, Leen (Shekiladze 46), Somers (Huysmans 64), Snoeckx, Zdebel, Huysegems, Van de Weyer, Cavens (Peelman 82).

● RSC ANDERLECHT
Qualifying round LEIFTUR (ISL)
H 6-1 Goor (18, 41), Gunnarsson (40og), Zetterberg (53), Baseggio (56), Radzinski (65)
De Vlieger, Brocken, Staelens (Crasson 85), De Boeck, Oyen, Van Diemen, Baseggio, Zetterberg (Stoica 73), Goor, Radzinski, Koller (Ekakia 78).
A 3-0 Van Diemen (2), Zetterberg (41p, 62p)
De Vlieger, Brocken, De Boeck, Staelens, Oyen, Goor, Van Diemen, Baseggio (Dheedene 66), Zetterberg (Stoica 72), Koller, Radzinski (Ekakia 46).

1st round SCT OLIMPIJA LJUBLJANA (SLO)
H 3-1 Bajrektarevic (21og), Radzinski (36, 68)
De Vlieger, Staelens, Verstraeten (Stoica 70), Oyen, Brocken, Van Diemen, Baseggio, Zetterberg, Goor, Koller, Radzinski (Ekakia 81).
A 3-0 Koller (64), Radzinski (70, 72)
De Vlieger, Brocken, De Boeck, Verstraeten, Oyen, Goor, Van Diemen, Baseggio, Zetterberg (Crasson 88), Koller (Ekakia 82), Radzinski (Soetaers 83).

2nd round BOLOGNA (ITA)
H 2-1 Koller (17, 35)
De Wilde, Brocken, Staelens, Crasson, De Boeck, Goor, Van Diemen, Zetterberg, Baseggio, Koller, Radzinski (Ekakia 78).
A 0-3
De Wilde, Brocken (Ekakia 50), De Boeck, Staelens, Crasson, Van Diemen (Scifo 75), Baseggio, Zetterberg, Goor, Koller, Radzinski.

the championship with a class and confidence that barely allowed the other teams a look-in.

For the first time in six seasons the Brussels club won their opening match - 3-2 against Mouscron - and they never looked back, racing clear with a 13-match unbeaten run that brought entertainment and goals galore. A 1-3 defeat by Anthuenis's old club Genk in their own backyard at the end of November halted the run, but a fortnight later, with the onset of the winter break, Anderlecht still had a lead of five points plus a game in hand, their match at Bruges having twice been postponed due to fears of hooliganism.

By the time that fixture did finally take place, at the end of February, Anderlecht had the title in their sights. By winning 2-0, with goals from Bart Goor and Alin Stoica, they not only registered their first win in Bruges for ten years but also extended their lead at the top to an

insurmountable ten points. In the end, the actual clinching of the championship turned out to be an anti-climax. Two weekends in succession Anderlecht had to put their victory celebrations on hold. The first occasion was when bogey side Westerlo slaughtered them 5-0 - a humiliation which proved too much for some Anderlecht fans, who invaded the pitch in protest. Seven days later Anderlecht had the chance to make amends and take the title in front of a full house in their home stadium. But once again they were found wanting, going down 2-1 to Gent despite having taken a half-time lead through veteran Enzo Scifo.

Anderlecht had to wait another five days before the championship was mathematically theirs, and they claimed it without kicking a ball thanks to Bruges's 0-1 defeat at Lierse. The following afternoon, with the tension removed, Anderlecht treated their travelling fans to a sumptuous

PLAYERS OF THE SEASON

YVES VANDERHAEGHE

The story of Yves Vanderhaeghe (pictured below) is both chilling and heartwarming. Ten years ago, at the age of 20, he was pronounced dead. During one of his club Roeselaere's fixtures the stadium speaker announced that he had died from a brain tumour. An obituary was also run in a local newspaper. But, in fact, Vanderhaeghe was to make a miraculous recovery from his critical illness. Four years later he made his top-flight début with Eendracht Aalst. Five years after that he became a Belgian international, and in 1999/2000 he was the best midfield anchorman in the country, his excellent season for Mouscron and Belgium culminating in three 90-minute appearances at Euro 2000 and a dream transfer to champions Anderlecht. The sheer will-power which saved Vanderhaeghe's life a decade ago is a quality which has remained with him and can be observed every time he ventures onto a football field.

TONI BROGNO

In scoring 30 goals for Westerlo, Toni Brogno became the first Belgian player to top the Eerste Klasse scoring charts since Edwin Vandenbergh in 1991. It wasn't good enough for the lively, diminutive striker to claim a place in Belgium's Euro 2000 squad - he was dropped from the preliminary pool on the eve of the tournament - but it certainly put the 27-year-old in the limelight for the first time in his career. The younger brother of Charleroi stalwart Dante Brogno, Toni also started out with his home-town club but it was the move to Westerlo that sent his career spinning into orbit. His 1999/2000 campaign began with four goals in a 6-6 thriller against champions Genk and he kept up a consistent strike-rate thereafter, peaking again with two goals in the stunning 5-0 victory over champions-elect Anderlecht. Westerlo were unable to retain his services, however, and in the summer he made the short move south to join French First Division club Sedan.

4-1 win at Genk. In some ways it was the perfect place for them to stage their victory party - on the ground of the defending champions and at the former home of their coach.

Anthuenis's second title in successive years confirmed him as the best coach in the country. Another equally influential new arrival in Brussels was Jan Koller, who maintained the prolific scoring form which had enabled him to take the league's top-scorer prize the previous season with Lokeren. He scored 20 goals and was well supported in that department by two other foreigners, Canadian forward Tomasz Radzinski and Swedish play-maker Pär Zetterberg. Veteran sweeper Lorenzo Staelens scored only one goal but he did earn himself the country's Player of the Year award, which many felt was long overdue.

Staelens' former club, Bruges, managed to take second place in the Eerste Klasse, eight points behind Anderlecht,

but it was not a memorable season for the Flemish club. Coach René Verheyen was sacked in mid-season only to be farcically reinstated a few days later when it transpired that his would-be successor, Gent's Trond Sollied, would not be available until the end of the season.

Gent joined Bruges in the UEFA Cup and were extremely satisfied with third place. Norwegian striker Ole Martin Årst evidently enjoyed working under his fellow countryman because he scored 30 goals to finish as the league's joint-top scorer alongside Westerlo's Toni Brogno. Årst was one of a vast array of foreigners at Gent, and in one match the club actually had no Belgian players at all on the teamsheet.

Standard Liège were the Jekyll and Hyde team of the season. In the early spring it looked inconceivable that the 'Rouches' would fail to land a European ticket. They were on an incredible roll, having put together ten straight wins during an extraordinary run which was accompanied by

36 goals - and all this in the wake of the sale abroad of the Mpenza brothers. The catalyst for their surge in form was the arrival of new coach Jean Thissen, who had substituted the veteran Tomislav Ivic. But by the end of the league campaign Thissen was no longer in charge and Ivic was back on the bench. Incomprehensibly, Standard's form had deserted them - they lost seven of their last eight games - and their only chance of a return to Europe was in the final of the Belgian Cup. But there, too, they were to suffer more embarrassment. A goal in the first minute proved useless as Genk came back to hammer them 4-1, thereby completing a remarkable hat-trick of trophy successes in consecutive years and making up for a miserable season in the league.

Mouscron, who lost the League Cup final on penalties to Anderlecht, were a joy to watch for much of the season but a poor closing run denied them a European place. Westerlo, too, gained the support of the neutrals for the gung-ho, attacking style adopted by their coach, the legendary Jan Ceulemans. They, like Mouscron, would have been worthy European participants, but the team which did make it into the UEFA Cup were Lierse. They had Belgium's Footballer of the Century, Paul Van Himst, to thank as he pulled their name out of the hat in the UEFA Fair Play lottery.

Royal Antwerp returned to Belgium's top flight by romping to victory in the Tweede Klasse. They finished 20 points ahead of the other promoted team, convincing play-off winners La Louvière, who thus ended a 21-year absence from the élite. Geel joined long-doomed Lommel in relegation, which was good news for Charleroi, who had already announced the arrival of local-boy-made-good Enzo Scifo as their new club president (as well as player) in 2000/01.

PROMOTED CLUBS 99/00

SECOND DIVISION FINAL TABLE

		Pd	W	D	L	F	A	Pt	GD
1	**Royal Antwerp FC**	34	24	8	2	84	29	80	55
2	KV Oostende	34	17	10	7	50	30	61	20
3	RAA La Louvière	34	18	6	10	58	29	60	29
4	FC Turnhout	34	17	5	12	64	46	56	18
5	RWD Molenbeek	34	15	10	9	50	38	55	12
6	KSV Cercle Brugge	34	14	12	8	54	36	54	18
7	SV Ingelmunster	34	16	6	12	64	47	54	17
8	Dessel Sport	34	16	6	12	43	48	54	-5
9	FC Denderleeuw	34	14	9	11	43	41	51	2
10	Maasland	34	13	11	10	53	54	50	-1
11	KSK Deinze	34	12	7	15	46	42	43	4
12	KV Tienen	34	11	7	16	35	52	40	-17
13	Hekelgem	34	12	4	18	36	60	40	-24
14	SV Roeselaere	34	11	6	17	50	58	39	-8
15	RTFC Liégeois	34	9	12	13	43	54	39	-11
16	KV Kortrijk	34	11	5	18	52	79	38	-27
17	Visé	34	5	7	22	46	73	22	-27
18	FC Kapellen	34	1	9	24	22	77	12	-55

PROMOTION PLAY-OFFS FINAL TABLE

		Pd	W	D	L	F	A	Pt	GD
1	**RAA La Louvière**	6	5	0	1	12	3	16	9
2	SV Ingelmunster	6	3	2	1	13	8	10	5
3	KV Oostende	6	1	2	3	7	12	6	-5
4	FC Turnhout	6	0	5	1	3	12	1	-9

CLUB DIRECTORIES

Royal Antwerp FC
Oude Bosuilbaan 54A
2100 Deurne
tel - (03) 3246406
fax - (03) 3260970
Year of Formation - 1880
President - Eddy Wauters
Coach - Regi Van Acker
Stadium - Bosuilstadion (13,649)

MAJOR HONOURS
League Championship - (4)
1929, 1931, 1944, 1957.
Domestic Cup - (2) 1955, 1992.

Royale AA La Louvière
Boulevard du Tivoli 80
7100 La Louvière
tel - (064) 211975/263713
fax - (064) 263525
Year of Formation - 1912
President - Filipo Gaone
Coach - Marc Grosjean
Stadium - Tivoli (13,072)

RSC ANDERLECHT

CLUB DIRECTORY

RSC Anderlecht
Avenue Théo Verbeeck 2
Anderlecht, 1070 Bruxelles
tel - (02) 5229400 / fax - (02) 5200740
website - www.rsca.be
Year of Formation - 1908
President - Roger Vanden Stock
Manager - Michel Verschueren
Secretary - Philippe Collin
Coach - Aimé Anthuenis
Stadium - Constant Vanden Stock (28,063)

MAJOR HONOURS
League Championship - (25)
1947, 1949, 1950, 1951, 1954, 1955, 1956,
1959, 1962, 1964, 1965, 1966, 1967, 1968,
1972, 1974, 1981, 1985, 1986, 1987, 1991,
1993, 1994, 1995, 2000.
Domestic Cup - (8) 1965, 1972, 1973, 1975,
1976, 1988, 1989, 1994.
European Cup-winners' Cup - (2) 1976, 1978.
UEFA Cup - (1) 1983.
European Super Cup - (2) 1976, 1978.

APPEARANCES 99/00

	P	Ap	(s)	Gls
Yanis ANASTASIOU (GRE)	A	4	(6)	4
Walter BASEGGIO	M	30	(1)	1
David BROCKEN	D	9	(1)	
Bertrand CRASSON	D	26	(2)	
Glen DE BOECK	D	26	(4)	1
Geert DE VLIEGER	G	8		
Filip DE WILDE	G	26	(1)	
Didier DHEEDENE	D	15	(10)	
Olivier DOLL	D	5	(8)	
Elonga EKAKIA (DRC)	A	14	(15)	11
Bart GOOR	M	31	(1)	7
Jan KOLLER (CZE)	A	33		20
Davy OYEN	D	7		
Tomasz RADZINSKI (CAN)	A	25		14
Enzo SCIFO	M	11	(9)	2
Tibor SELYMES (ROM)	D		(1)	
Tom SOETAERS	A		(3)	
Edrissa SONKO (GAM)	M		(6)	1
Lorenzo STAELENS	D	30		1
Stéphane STASSIN	D		(4)	
Alin STOICA (ROM)	A	4	(12)	6
Patrick VAN DIEMEN (HOL)	M	30	(2)	4
Mike VERSTRAETEN	D	5	(3)	
Oleh YASHCHUK (UKR)	A	1		
Pär ZETTERBERG (SWE)	M	34		14

LEAGUE RESULTS 1999/2000

08/08/99	R Excelsior Mouscron	H	3-2	Scifo, Zetterberg (p), Van Diemen
15/08/99	KSK Beveren	H	5-2	Koller 2, Radzinski 3
22/08/99	K Lierse SK	A	3-0	Radzinski, Zetterberg (p), Van Diemen
29/08/99	KFC Lommelse SK	H	3-3	Ekakia 2, Stoica
19/09/99	K St.-Truidense VV	H	2-1	Radzinski, Zetterberg
25/09/99	KSC Lokeren	A	3-2	Staelens, Radzinski, Ekakia
03/10/99	Germinal Beerschot Antwerpen	H	2-2	Koller, Radzinski
13/10/99	KSC Eendracht Aalst	A	3-2	Koller, Ekakia, Goor
24/10/99	KFC Verbroedering Geel	H	4-0	Zetterberg (p), Radzinski 2, Koller
28/10/99	KRC Harelbeke	H	2-0	Ekakia, De Boeck
06/11/99	KV Mechelen	A	5-2	Koller 3, Zetterberg 2
10/11/99	KVC Westerlo	H	3-0	Zetterberg 2, Ekakia
19/11/99	KAA Gent	A	3-0	Koller, Radzinski, Zetterberg
28/11/99	KRC Genk	H	1-3	Koller
05/12/99	R Standard Liège	A	0-0	
11/12/99	RSC Charleroi	H	3-0	Zetterberg (p), Koller 2
11/01/00	R Excelsior Mouscron	A	2-0	Goor, Van Diemen
15/01/00	KSK Beveren	A	0-0	
23/01/00	K Lierse SK	H	2-0	Koller, Ekakia
29/01/00	KFC Lommelse SK	A	3-3	Ekakia, Koller, Stoica
06/02/00	Club Brugge KV	H	1-1	Sonko
12/02/00	K St.-Truidense VV	A	4-0	Ekakia 2, Goor, Koller
19/02/00	KSC Lokeren	H	5-0	Anastasiou 2, Goor 2, Zetterberg (p)
27/02/00	Club Brugge KV	A	2-0	Goor, Stoica
05/03/00	Germinal Beerschot Antwerpen	A	3-1	Koller 2, Ekakia
11/03/00	KSC Eendracht Aalst	H	4-1	Zetterberg 2 (1p), Koller, Stoica
18/03/00	KFC Verbroedering Geel	A	0-0	
26/03/00	KRC Harelbeke	A	2-2	Van Diemen, Koller
01/04/00	KV Mechelen	H	5-0	Baseggio, Radzinski 2, Zetterberg, Anastasiou
09/04/00	KVC Westerlo	A	0-5	
16/04/00	KAA Gent	H	1-2	Scifo
22/04/00	KRC Genk	A	4-1	Goor, Radzinski 2, Koller
06/05/00	R Standard Liège	H	2-0	Stoica, Anastasiou
11/05/00	RSC Charleroi	A	1-1	Stoica

KSK BEVEREN

CLUB DIRECTORY

KSK Beveren
Klapperstraat 151 bis, 9120 Beveren
tel - (03) 7759000/7759697
fax - (03) 7550800
website - www.kskbeveren.be
President - Frans Van Hoof
Manager - Marc Pinson
Coach - Stani Gzil; Emilio Ferrera
Stadium - Freethiel (13,290)

MAJOR HONOURS
League Championship - (2) 1979, 1984.
Domestic Cup - (2) 1978, 1983.

APPEARANCES 99/00

	P	Ap	(s)	Gls
Christian ACEVEDO (ARG)	D	2	(1)	
Ricardo BONETTO (ITA)	A	10		1
Stéphane DEMETS	M	13	(4)	
Gunther DE MEYER	D	27	(1)	2
Kenny DE VUYST	D	21	(1)	1
Kris DE WREE	M	1		
Bert DHONT	M	24		
Gideon IMAGBUDU (NIG)	M	11	(2)	3
Kristof IMSCHOOT	D	3	(1)	
Arben NUHIJU (MAC)	A	21	(8)	11
Jószef NYIKOS (HUN)	M	3	(7)	1
Tristan PEERSMAN	G	14	(1)	
Gábor PUGLITS (HUN)	M	1	(1)	
Luigi RICCIO (ITA)	M		(1)	
Werry SELS	M	33	(1)	5
Jimmy SMET	D	27	(2)	
Lambert SMID (CZE)	M	26		1
Bartosz TARACHULSKI (POL)	A	17	(8)	3
Davy THEUNIS	M	17	(1)	
Paul TISDALE (ENG)	M		(1)	
Remco TORKEN (HOL)	A	19	(3)	13
Bart VAN DEN EEDE	A	10	(6)	2
Kris VAN DE PUTTE	G	20	(1)	
Martin VAN OPHUIZEN (HOL)	D	22		
Johan VAN RUMST	M	9	(9)	3
Stijn VLAMINCK	D	23	(4)	3

LEAGUE RESULTS 1999/2000

07/08/99	KSC Eendracht Aalst	H	0-2	
15/08/99	RSC Anderlecht	A	2-5	Van den Eede, Bonetto
21/08/99	KRC Harelbeke	H	2-2	Tarachulski, De Meyer
28/08/99	KV Mechelen	A	1-3	Imagbudu (p)
18/09/99	KAA Gent	A	1-4	Nuhiju
25/09/99	KRC Genk	H	1-4	Imagbudu
02/10/99	R Standard Liège	A	1-3	De Meyer
13/10/99	RSC Charleroi	H	1-1	Smid (p)
24/10/99	R Excelsior Mouscron	A	0-3	
30/10/99	KFC Verbroedering Geel	A	1-1	Nuhiju
06/11/99	K Lierse SK	H	1-1	Torken
10/11/99	KFC Lommelse SK	A	0-0	
20/11/99	Club Brugge KV	H	2-3	Nuhiju, Vlaminck
27/11/99	K St.-Truidense VV	A	2-0	Torken 2
04/12/99	KSC Lokeren	H	2-1	Vlaminck, Sels
08/12/99	KVC Westerlo	H	4-0	Nuhiju 4 (1p)
11/12/99	Germinal Beerschot Antwerpen	A	0-2	
12/01/00	KSC Eendracht Aalst	A	4-2	Sels 2, Torken 2
15/01/00	RSC Anderlecht	H	0-0	
23/01/00	KRC Harelbeke	A	5-0	(w/o; original result 3-6 Sels, Torken, Nuhiju)
29/01/00	KV Mechelen	H	2-1	Van Rumst, Tarachulski
05/02/00	KVC Westerlo	A	2-3	Imagbudu, Nuhiju
12/02/00	KAA Gent	H	0-1	
19/02/00	KRC Genk	A	1-4	Van den Eede
04/03/00	R Standard Liège	H	0-2	
11/03/00	RSC Charleroi	A	3-2	Nuhiju, De Vuyst, Tarachulski
19/03/00	R Excelsior Mouscron	H	1-1	Torken
25/03/00	KFC Verbroedering Geel	H	1-1	Nuhiju
01/04/00	K Lierse SK	A	3-1	Van Rumst, Torken, Nyikos
09/04/00	KFC Lommelse SK	H	1-0	Torken
16/04/00	Club Brugge KV	A	1-3	Sels
22/04/00	K St.-Truidense VV	H	3-4	Torken 2, Vlaminck
06/05/00	KSC Lokeren	A	2-5	Torken 2 (1p)
11/05/00	Germinal Beerschot Antwerpen	H	1-4	Van Rumst

CLUB BRUGGE KV

CLUB DIRECTORY

Club Brugge KV
Olympialaan 74, 8200 Brugge
tel - (050) 402121 / fax - (050) 381023
website - www.clubbrugge.com
Year of Formation - 1894
President - Michel Van Maele
Manager - Antoine Vanhove
Secretary - Jacques De Nolf
Coach - René Verheyen (00/01 - Trond Sollied)
Stadium - Jan Breydel (30,000)

MAJOR HONOURS

League Championship - (11)
1920, 1973, 1976, 1977, 1978, 1980, 1988,
1990, 1992, 1996, 1998.
Domestic Cup - (7)
1968, 1970, 1977, 1986, 1991, 1995, 1996.

APPEARANCES 99/00

	P	Ap	(s)	Gls
Darko ANIC (YUG)	M	3	(1)	1
Vital BORKELMANS	D	33		3
Philippe CLEMENT	M	31		4
Tjörven DE BRUL	D	25	(1)	1
Olivier DE COCK	D	17	(6)	3
Eric DEFLANDRE	D	28	(1)	
Jimmy DEWULF	D		(1)	
Nader Ibrahim EL SAYED (EGY)	G	2		
Gaëtan ENGLEBERT	M	25	(7)	3
Khalilou FADIGA (SEN)	A	15	(2)	2
Aleksandar ILIC (YUG)	D	4	(3)	
Edgaras JANKAUSKAS (LIT)	A	9	(6)	4
Jochen JANSSEN	A	28	(4)	13
Nzelo LEMBI (DRC)	D	32		2
Milan LESNJAK (YUG)	D	13	(5)	1
Sandy MARTENS	A	21	(8)	4
Andrés MENDOZA (PER)	A		(9)	1
Dalibor MITROVIC (YUG)	A		(1)	
Koen SCHOCKAERT	A		(2)	
Tim SMOLDERS	A		(5)	2
Philippe VANDE WALLE	G	4		
Gert VERHEYEN	M	28	(1)	13
Dany VERLINDEN	G	28		
Sven VERMANT	M	28	(4)	13
Dimitri WELLENS	M		(2)	

LEAGUE RESULTS 1999/2000

08/08/99	K St.-Truidense VV	H	4-0	Verheyen, Martens, Lesnjak, Vermant
15/08/99	KSC Lokeren	A	5-2	Englebert, Jankauskas 2, Clement, Verheyen
22/08/99	Germinal Beerschot Antwerpen	H	2-0	Verheyen 2
29/08/99	KSC Eendracht Aalst	A	2-0	Vermant (p), Janssen
19/09/99	KRC Harelbeke	A	1-1	Janssen
26/09/99	KV Mechelen	H	6-0	Janssen 3, Verheyen, Jankauskas, Vermant (p)
03/10/99	KVC Westerlo	A	0-1	
13/10/99	KAA Gent	H	1-3	Lembi
24/10/99	KRC Genk	A	0-1	
30/10/99	R Standard Liège	H	5-2	Martens, Anic, Fadiga, Vermant, Janssen
05/11/99	RSC Charleroi	A	2-0	Martens, Vermant (p)
10/11/99	R Excelsior Mouscron	H	1-2	Jankauskas
20/11/99	KSK Beveren	A	3-2	Borkelmans, Vermant 2
26/11/99	K Lierse SK	H	1-0	Janssen
04/12/99	KFC Lommelse SK	A	0-0	
11/12/99	KFC Verbroedering Geel	H	4-0	Verheyen, Borkelmans, Vermant, De Cock
12/01/00	K St.-Truidense VV	A	1-0	De Cock
16/01/00	KSC Lokeren	H	6-1	Vermant (p), Verheyen 2, Janssen 2, Smolders
21/01/00	Germinal Beerschot Antwerpen	A	3-5	Verheyen 2, Englebert
30/01/00	KSC Eendracht Aalst	H	3-0	Vermant (p), Mendoza, Smolders
06/02/00	RSC Anderlecht	A	1-1	Borkelmans
13/02/00	KRC Harelbeke	H	1-2	De Cock
19/02/00	KV Mechelen	A	0-0	
27/02/00	RSC Anderlecht	H	0-2	
05/03/00	KVC Westerlo	H	2-0	Janssen, Vermant
10/03/00	KAA Gent	A	0-2	
19/03/00	KRC Genk	H	2-0	De Brul, Verheyen
24/03/00	R Standard Liège	A	1-0	Verheyen
01/04/00	RSC Charleroi	H	3-1	Janssen, Vermant 2 (1p)
07/04/00	R Excelsior Mouscron	A	2-1	Clement, Janssen
16/04/00	KSK Beveren	H	3-1	Fadiga, Janssen, Clement
21/04/00	K Lierse SK	A	0-1	
06/05/00	KFC Lommelse SK	H	3-1	Lembi, Verheyen, Martens
11/05/00	KFC Verbroedering Geel	A	2-0	Clement, Engelbert

RSC CHARLEROI

CLUB DIRECTORY

Royal Charleroi Sporting Club
Boulevard Zoë Drion 19
6000 Charleroi
tel - (071) 328734/319126
fax - (071) 327514
website - www.sporting-charleroi.be
Year of Formation - 1904
President - Abbas Bayat
Secretary - Pierre-Yves Hendrickx
Coach - Luka Peruzovic; Raymond Mommens;
Manu Ferrera
Stadium - Pays de Charleroi (20,000)

APPEARANCES 99/00

	P	Ap	(s)	Gls
Philippe ALBERT	D	14		1
Enzo BIONDO	D	11	(2)	
Dante BROGNO	A	25	(2)	14
Zoran CILINSEK (YUG)	M	12	(8)	1
Fábio DA SILVA (BRA)	M	1	(2)	
Dimitri DE CONDE	M	32		3
Frank DEFAYS	D	31		
Luciano Ray DJIM (CAF)	M	1	(9)	
Istvan DUDAS (YUG)	G	10		
Grégory DUFER	M	15	(1)	1
Roch GERARD	D	13	(6)	1
Grégory GHISLAIN	D		(1)	
Nikola JERKAN (CRO)	D	25	(2)	
Alexandros KAKLAMANOS (GRE)	A	15	(5)	6
Mahamadou KERE (BFA)	M	19	(7)	
Slaven LALIC (CRO)	D	6	(1)	
Jean-François LECOMTE	G	16	(1)	
Marijan MRMIC (CRO)	G	8		
Christian NEGOUAI (FRA)	A	1	(8)	
Serhiy OMELIANOVICH (UKR)	M	17	(8)	
Alassane OUEDRAOGO (BFA)	A	5	(10)	2
Aziz RABBAH (MAR)	M	21	(2)	1
Sergio ROJAS (ARG)	A	21	(5)	9
Tomasz ROMANIUK (POL)	D	17	(3)	1
Sandro SOUZA (BRA)	M	15		2
Bertin TOKENE (CMR)	D	23		
Hari VUKAS (CRO)	A		(2)	

LEAGUE RESULTS 1999/2000

07/08/99	KRC Harelbeke	H	2-1	Brogno, Gérard
14/08/99	KV Mechelen	A	1-2	Rojas
21/08/99	KVC Westerlo	H	1-2	Brogno
28/08/99	KAA Gent	A	2-3	Rojas, Brogno
11/09/99	KRC Genk	H	2-1	De Condé, Brogno
17/09/99	R Standard Liège	A	3-1	Brogno, Albert, Souza
26/09/99	KFC Verbroedering Geel	A	0-0	
01/10/99	R Excelsior Mouscron	H	2-1	Brogno, Kaklamanos
13/10/99	KSK Beveren	A	1-1	Brogno (p)
23/10/99	K Lierse SK	H	1-1	Kaklamanos
30/10/99	KFC Lommelse SK	A	1-1	Ouédraogo
05/11/99	Club Brugge KV	H	0-2	
10/11/99	K St.-Truidense VV	A	2-2	Ouédraogo, Cilinsek
20/11/99	KSC Lokeren	H	2-4	Kaklamanos, Souza
27/11/99	Germinal Beerschot Antwerpen	A	0-3	
04/12/99	KSC Eendracht Aalst	H	0-1	
11/12/99	RSC Anderlecht	A	0-3	
12/01/00	KRC Harelbeke	A	1-4	Kaklamanos
15/01/00	KV Mechelen	H	1-4	Rojas
23/01/00	KVC Westerlo	A	1-1	Kaklamanos
29/01/00	KAA Gent	H	1-2	Kaklamanos
05/02/00	KRC Genk	A	2-1	Brogno, Dufer
13/02/00	R Standard Liège	H	1-4	Brogno (p)
19/02/00	KFC Verbroedering Geel	H	1-3	Rojas
04/03/00	R Excelsior Mouscron	A	1-2	Rabbah
11/03/00	KSK Beveren	H	2-3	Rojas, Brogno
18/03/00	K Lierse SK	A	0-2	
25/03/00	KFC Lommelse SK	H	1-1	Rojas
01/04/00	Club Brugge KV	A	1-3	Romaniuk
08/04/00	K St.-Truidense VV	H	1-1	Brogno
15/04/00	KSC Lokeren	A	1-1	Rojas
22/04/00	Germinal Beerschot Antwerpen	H	3-0	Rojas 2, De Condé
06/05/00	KSC Eendracht Aalst	A	3-0	Brogno 2, De Condé
11/05/00	RSC Anderlecht	H	1-1	Brogno

KSC EENDRACHT AALST

CLUB DIRECTORY

KSC Eendracht Aalst
Bredestraat 10
9300 Aalst
tel - (053) 769110
fax - (053) 779878
website - www.eendracht-aalst.be
Year of Formation - 1919
President - Luc Coppens
Manager - Jean-Paul Van Lieferinge
Secretary - Jean-Pierre Van Drogenbroeck
Coach - Barry Hulshoff (00/01 - Wim De Coninck)
Stadium - Pierre Cornelis (9,500)

APPEARANCES 99/00

	P	Ap	(s)	Gls
Georges ARTS	D	26		2
Geoffrey CLAEYS	M	28		1
Davy COOREMAN	M	27	(5)	4
Steve COOREMAN	A	19		7
Dirk DAELMANS	M	19	(3)	1
José DE OLIVEIRA Alexandre (BRA)	M	6	(6)	2
Patrick DIMBALA (DRC)	A	3	(11)	2
Predrag FILIPOVIC (YUG)	D	25	(6)	
Johan GROMMEN	A	14	(11)	6
Ringo JACOBS	D	4	(4)	
Kristof KESTENS	M		(7)	
Vladan KUJOVIC (YUG)	G	8		
Harald MEYSSEN	M	16	(1)	6
Ljubodrag MILOSEVIC (MAC)	D	7	(4)	
Jean-Claude MUKANYA (DRC)	D	4	(2)	
Christophe NEIRINCKX	D		(1)	
Cosimo SARLI (ITA)	A	10	(5)	5
Kris TEMMERMAN	M	32		
Gunter THIEBAUT	A	27	(5)	8
Sammy VAN DEN BOSSCHE	A	18	(2)	1
Peter VAN DER HEYDEN	M	26	(4)	4
David VAN HOYWEGHEN	D	24	(1)	2
Jan VAN STEENBERGHE	G	26		
Warry VAN WATTUM (HOL)	D		(3)	
Stijn VERGEYLEN	D	5	(9)	1

LEAGUE RESULTS 1999/2000

07/08/99	KSK Beveren	A	2-0	Cooreman D., Cooreman S.
15/08/99	K Lierse SK	H	2-3	Cooreman S. 2
22/08/99	KFC Lommelse SK	A	3-3	Cooreman S. 2, Thiebaut
29/08/99	Club Brugge KV	H	0-2	
11/09/99	K St.-Truidense VV	A	5-1	Grommen, Cooreman S., Thiebaut, Van den Bossche, Vergeylen
19/09/99	KSC Lokeren	H	1-0	Cooreman D.
25/09/99	Germinal Beerschot Antwerpen	A	2-3	Van der Heyden, Meyssen
03/10/99	KFC Verbroedering Geel	H	1-0	Daelmans
13/10/99	RSC Anderlecht	H	2-3	Grommen, Cooreman D.
24/10/99	KRC Harelbeke	A	1-1	Van Hoyweghen
31/10/99	KV Mechelen	H	2-0	Meyssen, Van der Heyden
06/11/99	KVC Westerlo	A	2-3	Van der Heyden, Meyssen
10/11/99	KAA Gent	H	4-2	Meyssen, Thiebaut, Van der Heyden, Grommen
20/11/99	KRC Genk	A	1-2	Grommen
28/11/99	R Standard Liège	H	1-2	Cooreman S.
04/12/99	RSC Charleroi	A	1-0	Meyssen
12/12/99	R Excelsior Mouscron	H	2-5	Thiebaut, De Oliveira
12/01/00	KSK Beveren	H	2-4	Meyssen, Grommen
15/01/00	K Lierse SK	A	2-5	Thiebaut, Cooreman D.
23/01/00	KFC Lommelse SK	H	3-1	Van Hoyweghen, Sarli 2
30/01/00	Club Brugge KV	A	0-3	
06/02/00	K St.-Truidense VV	H	2-0	Thiebaut, De Oliveira
12/02/00	KSC Lokeren	A	1-5	Sarli
20/02/00	Germinal Beerschot Antwerpen	H	1-2	Grommen
04/03/00	KFC Verbroedering Geel	A	2-1	Dimbala, Arts
11/03/00	RSC Anderlecht	A	1-4	Dimbala
19/03/00	KRC Harelbeke	H	3-0	Claeys, Thiebaut, Sarli
25/03/00	KV Mechelen	A	0-2	
01/04/00	KVC Westerlo	H	1-1	Sarli (p)
09/04/00	KAA Gent	A	0-4	
15/04/00	KRC Genk	H	1-3	Arts
22/04/00	R Standard Liège	A	1-3	og (Ciobotariu)
06/05/00	RSC Charleroi	H	0-3	
11/05/00	R Excelsior Mouscron	A	1-1	Thiebaut

R EXCELSIOR MOUSCRON

CLUB DIRECTORY

Royal Excelsior Mouscron
Rue du Stade 33
7700 Mouscron
tel - (056) 860600
fax - (056) 860570
website - www.excelsior.be
Year of Formation - 1964
President - Jean-Pierre Doutremmerie
Secretary - Jacques Vandewalle
Coach - Hugo Broos
Stadium - Le Canonnier (10,692)

APPEARANCES 99/00

	P	Ap	(s)	Gls
Mathieu ASSOU	A	1	(1)	
Olivier BESENGEZ	D	11		
Mohammed Farid BIHHI (MAR)	A	1	(5)	
BOTO-LOKI	A		(1)	
Marco CASTO	M	29	(2)	1
Adriano DA CRUZ (BRA)	D	1		
Thomas DEBENEST	G	7		
Koen DE VLEESCHAUWER	D	30	(1)	1
Steve DUGARDEIN	M	32		4
Mustapha EL IDRISSI (FRA)	A		(2)	
Botuly Trésor EMPOKE	A		(1)	
Axel LAWAREE	A	17	(5)	10
Tonci MARTIC (CRO)	M	23	(2)	4
Olivier Polo NZUZI (DRC)	A	4	(10)	
Kevin PECQUEUX	M	1	(1)	
Giovanni SEYNHAEVE	D	5	(7)	1
Stefaan TANGHE	M	31		11
Alexandre TEKLAK	D	27	(5)	1
Franck VANDENDRIESSCHE	G	27		
Yves VANDERHAEGHE	M	32		8
Gonzague VANDOOREN	A	18	(9)	4
Donald VAN DURME	D	2		
Gordan VIDOVIC	D	10		4
Marc WUYTS	A	4	(5)	1
Marcin ZEWLAKOW (POL)	A	29		14
Michal ZEWLAKOW (POL)	D	32		

LEAGUE RESULTS 1999/2000

08/08/99	RSC Anderlecht	A	2-3	Vandooren, Zewlakow Ma.
14/08/99	KRC Harelbeke	A	1-1	Vanderhaeghe (p)
21/08/99	KV Mechelen	H	2-0	Vanderhaeghe 2 (1p)
28/08/99	KVC Westerlo	A	0-3	
11/09/99	KAA Gent	H	5-3	Zewlakow Ma. 2, Tanghe 3
18/09/99	KRC Genk	A	2-2	Vidovic, Vanderhaeghe
24/09/99	R Standard Liège	H	1-3	Tanghe
01/10/99	RSC Charleroi	A	1-2	Dugardein
13/10/99	KFC Verbroedering Geel	A	4-1	Lawarée, Vandooren, Tanghe, Wuyts
24/10/99	KSK Beveren	H	3-0	Vandooren, Zewlakow Ma., Teklak
30/10/99	K Lierse SK	A	0-1	
06/11/99	KFC Lommelse SK	H	0-0	
10/11/99	Club Brugge KV	A	2-1	Zewlakow Ma., Vandooren
20/11/99	K St.-Truidense VV	H	3-0	Zewlakow Ma., Martic, Vanderhaeghe
27/11/99	KSC Lokeren	A	2-3	og (Vanhaezebrouck), Vanderhaeghe (p)
04/12/99	Germinal Beerschot Antwerpen	H	1-1	Zewlakow Ma.
12/12/99	KSC Eendracht Aalst	A	5-2	Vanderhaeghe, Lawarée 2, Zewlakow Ma. 2
11/01/00	RSC Anderlecht	H	0-2	
16/01/00	KRC Harelbeke	H	4-2	Dugardein, Vanderhaeghe (p), Zewlakow Ma. 2
22/01/00	KV Mechelen	A	3-1	Lawarée, Tanghe, Zewlakow Ma.
30/01/00	KVC Westerlo	H	2-1	Zewlakow Ma., Martic
05/02/00	KAA Gent	A	3-2	Martic 2, og (Ramcic)
11/02/00	KRC Genk	H	5-0	Tanghe, Lawarée 3, Zewlakow Ma.
18/02/00	R Standard Liège	A	0-2	
04/03/00	RSC Charleroi	H	2-1	Seynhaeve, Tanghe
11/03/00	KFC Verbroedering Geel	H	3-1	og (Daelemans), Lawarée, Tanghe
19/03/00	KSK Beveren	A	1-1	Vidovic
25/03/00	K Lierse SK	H	3-3	Lawarée, Vidovic, Tanghe
01/04/00	KFC Lommelse SK	A	4-0	Dugardein, De Vleeschauwer, Vidovic, Lawarée
07/04/00	Club Brugge KV	H	1-2	Tanghe
15/04/00	K St.-Truidense VV	A	0-0	
22/04/00	KSC Lokeren	H	0-0	
06/05/00	Germinal Beerschot Antwerpen	A	1-0	Castro (p)
11/05/00	KSC Eendracht Aalst	H	1-1	Dugardein

KRC GENK

CLUB DIRECTORY

KRC Genk
Stadionplein 4, 3600 Genk
tel - (089) 841608
fax - (089) 841708
website - www.krcgenk.be
Year of Formation - 1988
President - Edgard Troonbeeckx
Manager - Paul Heylen
Coach - Jos Heyligen; Johan Boskamp
Stadium - Feniksstadion (22,989)

MAJOR HONOURS
League Championship - (1) 1999.
Domestic Cup - (2) 1998, 2000.

APPEARANCES 99/00

	P	Ap	(s)	Gls
Zoran BAN (CRO)	A	13	(3)	7
István BROCKHAUSER (HUN)	G	31		
Ilir CAUSHLLARI (ALB)	M	2	(5)	
Koen DAERDEN	M	3	(2)	
Davide D'ANGELO	A		(1)	
Wilfried DELBROEK	D	8	(1)	1
Benjamin Rogério DE OLIVEIRA (BRA)	A	8	(5)	
Gert DOUMEN	G	3	(1)	
Bjarni GUDJÓNSSON (ISL)	M	13	(7)	
Thórdur GUDJÓNSSON (ISL)	M	30	(3)	10
Besnik HASI (CRO)	M	28	(2)	1
Marc HENDRIKX	M	27	(1)	5
Ferenc HORVÁTH (HUN)	A	14	(14)	8
Marco INGRAO	M	1		
Jesper JANSSON (SWE)	M	21	(3)	2
Daniel KIMONI	D	26	(3)	
Ngoy N'SUMBU (DRC)	A	3	(11)	4
Domenico OLIVIERI (ITA)	D	31		2
Mike Okoth ORIGI (KEN)	A	18	(6)	6
Souleymane OULARE (GUI)	A	2		2
Juha REINI (FIN)	D	14	(2)	1
Josip SKOKO (AUS)	M	8	(1)	1
Branko STRUPAR	A	15		9
Stefan TEELEN	D	10		
Rachid TIBARI	M	1		
Chris VAN GEEM	D	25	(1)	
Kevin VANBEUREN	D	1		
Cédric VAN DER ELST	M	1	(1)	
Marc VANGRONSVELD	D	16	(4)	1
Bart VANHEES	D	1		

LEAGUE RESULTS 1999/2000

07/08/99	KVC Westerlo	A	6-6	Strupar 3 (3p), Oulare, N'Sumbu, Gudjónsson Th.
14/08/99	KAA Gent	A	2-0	Oulare, Gudjónsson Th.
21/08/99	KFC Verbroedering Geel	A	1-1	og (Smits D.)
29/08/99	R Standard Liège	H	4-0	Hendrikx, Horváth 3
11/09/99	RSC Charleroi	A	1-2	Strupar (p)
18/09/99	R Excelsior Mouscron	H	2-2	Horváth, Strupar
25/09/99	KSK Beveren	A	4-1	Horváth, og (De Vuyst), Strupar, Gudjónsson Th.
03/10/99	K Lierse SK	H	2-2	N'Sumbu, Strupar
13/10/99	KFC Lommelse SK	A	1-0	og (Segers)
24/10/99	Club Brugge KV	H	1-0	N'Sumbu
30/10/99	K St.-Truidense VV	A	5-0	Vangronsveld, Janssen, Origi 2, Olivieri
06/11/99	KSC Lokeren	H	1-1	Olivieri
10/11/99	Germinal Beerschot Antwerpen	H	4-0	Strupar 2, Gudjónsson Th., Ban
20/11/99	KSC Eendracht Aalst	H	2-1	Ban, Hendrikx
28/11/99	RSC Anderlecht	A	3-1	Hendrikx, Gudjónsson Th., Origi
05/12/99	KRC Harelbeke	H	4-3	Gudjónsson Th., Hendrikx, Horváth, Jansson
11/12/99	KV Mechelen	A	0-2	
12/01/00	KVC Westerlo	H	1-1	Ban
15/01/00	KAA Gent	H	0-1	
22/01/00	KFC Verbroedering Geel	H	1-0	Reini
28/01/00	R Standard Liège	A	1-5	Origi
05/02/00	RSC Charleroi	H	1-2	Origi
11/02/00	R Excelsior Mouscron	A	0-5	
19/02/00	KSK Beveren	H	4-1	Hasi, Ban, Gudjónsson Th., Skoko
04/03/00	K Lierse SK	A	0-5	
11/03/00	KFC Lommelse SK	H	1-2	Hendrikx
19/03/00	Club Brugge KV	A	0-2	
25/03/00	K St.-Truidense VV	H	0-2	
01/04/00	KSC Lokeren	A	2-1	Ban, Gudjónsson Th.
08/04/00	Germinal Beerschot Antwerpen	A	0-3	
15/04/00	KSC Eendracht Aalst	A	3-1	Delbroek, Origi, Gudjónsson Th.
22/04/00	RSC Anderlecht	H	1-4	Ban
06/05/00	KRC Harelbeke	A	2-1	Ban, Gudjónsson Th.
11/05/00	KV Mechelen	H	3-1	N'Sumbu, Horváth 2

KAA GENT

THE EUROPEAN FOOTBALL YEARBOOK 2000-2001

CLUB DIRECTORY

KAA Gent
Bruiloftstraat 42, 9050 Gentbrugge-Gent
tel - (09) 2306610
fax - (09) 2302010
website - www.kaagent.be
Year of Formation - 1898
President - Ivan De Witte
Manager - Michel Louwagie
Coach - Trond Sollied (00/01 - Henk Houwaart)
Stadium - Jules Ottenstadion (18,215)

MAJOR HONOURS
Domestic Cup - (2) 1964, 1984.

APPEARANCES 99/00

	P	Ap	(s)	Gls
Ole Martin ÅRST (NOR)	A	32	(1)	30
Fabio BURGIO	M		(2)	
Cédric CARREZ (FRA)	D	21	(2)	1
Thomas CHATELLE	A		(12)	
Anders CHRISTENSEN (DEN)	D	31		
Tore André DAHLUM (NOR)	A	11	(1)	5
Frank DAUWEN	M	11	(1)	1
Ivica DRAGUTINOVIC (YUG)	M	11	(4)	4
Frédéric DUPRE	D		(7)	
Morten FALCH (DEN)	D		(1)	
Ronald FOGUENNE	M	9	(7)	
Saso GAJSER (SLO)	M	20	(7)	2
Frédéric HERPOEL	G	33		
Eric JOLY (FRA)	M	30	(3)	8
Tarik KHARIF (FRA)	A	25	(4)	6
Nasreddine KRAOUCHE (ALG)	M	2	(2)	1
Anders NIELSEN (DEN)	A	15	(6)	3
Morten PEDERSEN (NOR)	D	17		
Edin RAMCIC (BOS)	M	25	(2)	
Cédric ROUSSEL	A	1	(3)	3
Zoran SAVIC (YUG)	G	1		
Gunther SCHEPENS	M	18	(1)	7
Emil STERBAL (SLO)	D	13	(4)	
Tamás SZEKERES (HUN)	D	19	(2)	2
Ode THOMPSON (NIG)	A		(2)	
Tom VANDERVEE	D	3	(3)	
Tomas VASOV (YUG)	M	26		4

LEAGUE RESULTS 1999/2000

06/08/99	KFC Verbroedering Geel	A	5-1	Kharif, Vasov 2, Årst, Gajser
14/08/99	KRC Genk	H	0-2	
21/08/99	R Standard Liège	A	2-0	Schepens, Vasov
28/08/99	RSC Charleroi	H	3-2	Szekeres, Roussel 2 (1p)
11/09/99	R Excelsior Mouscron	A	3-5	Nielsen 2, Roussel (p)
18/09/99	KSK Beveren	H	4-1	Årst 3, Joly
25/09/99	K Lierse SK	A	1-2	Schepens
02/10/99	KFC Lommelse SK	H	6-2	Årst 2, Schepens 3, Joly
13/10/99	Club Brugge KV	A	3-1	Årst, Nielsen, Gajser
23/10/99	K St.-Truidense VV	H	4-2	Joly, Schepens, Årst 2
30/10/99	KSC Lokeren	A	4-0	Joly, Szekeres, Carrez, Årst
06/11/99	Germinal Beerschot Antwerpen	H	1-3	Schepens
10/11/99	KSC Eendracht Aalst	A	2-4	Årst 2
19/11/99	RSC Anderlecht	H	0-3	
28/11/99	KRC Harelbeke	A	2-1	Årst 2 (1p)
04/12/99	KV Mechelen	H	6-1	Kharif 2, Årst 3, Joly
11/12/99	KVC Westerlo	A	2-4	Årst, Joly
12/01/00	KFC Verbroedering Geel	H	1-1	Joly
15/01/00	KRC Genk	A	1-0	Dahlum
22/01/00	R Standard Liège	H	1-5	Årst
29/01/00	RSC Charleroi	A	2-1	Årst, Dahlum
05/02/00	R Excelsior Mouscron	H	2-3	Kharif, Joly
12/02/00	KSK Beveren	A	1-0	Dauwen
18/02/00	K Lierse SK	H	2-0	Vasov, Kharif
04/03/00	KFC Lommelse SK	A	3-1	Årst 3
10/03/00	Club Brugge KV	H	2-0	Dahlum, Årst (p)
18/03/00	K St.-Truidense VV	A	0-0	
26/03/00	KSC Lokeren	H	1-1	Dahlum
01/04/00	Germinal Beerschot Antwerpen	A	0-2	
09/04/00	KSC Eendracht Aalst	H	4-0	Årst 2, Dahlum, Dragutinovic
16/04/00	RSC Anderlecht	A	2-1	Årst, Dragutinovic
22/04/00	KRC Harelbeke	H	4-2	Årst 3, og (Verhoeven)
06/05/00	KV Mechelen	A	2-0	Dragutinovic 2
11/05/00	KVC Westerlo	H	2-3	Kraouche, Kharif

GERMINAL BEERSCHOT ANTWERPEN

CLUB DIRECTORY

Germinal Beerschot Antwerpen
Atletenstraat 80
2020 Antwerpen
tel - (03) 2484845
fax - (03) 2484846
website - www.germinal-beerschot.com
Year of Formation - 1999
President - Jos Verhaegen
Manager - Louis De Vries
Coach - Franky Van der Elst
Stadium - Olympic Stadion (12,500)

APPEARANCES 99/00

	P	Ap	(s)	Gls
Joël BARTHOLOMEEUSSEN	M		(4)	
Geert BRUSSELERS (HOL)	M	14	(15)	
Marc DEGRYSE	M	31		10
Andrei DEMKIN (RUS)	A	14	(16)	8
Philip HAAGDOREN	M	28	(3)	3
Tony HERREMAN	D	29	(1)	2
Gunther HOFMANS	A	31	(2)	10
Manu KARAGIANNIS	M	26		3
Ervin KOVÁCS (HUN)	D	10		
LEONARDO da Silva (BRA)	M	14	(10)	
Peter MAES	G	2	(1)	
Vinko MARINOVIC (YUG)	D	19	(1)	1
Jan MOONS	G	32		
Kurt MORHAYE	A		(2)	
Aleksandar MUTAVDZIC (YUG)	D	13	(2)	4
Justice SANDJON (CMR)	D	15	(5)	
Francis SEVEREYNS	A	6	(12)	2
Rudi SMIDTS	D	28	(2)	
Kristof SNELDERS	A		(1)	
Wesley SONCK	A	22	(7)	11
Djordje SVETLICIC (YUG)	D	16	(2)	
Stephan VAN DER HEYDEN	M	23		2
Bart VAN ZUNDERT	M	1	(2)	

LEAGUE RESULTS 1999/2000

07/08/99	K Lierse SK	A	1-3	Van der Heyden
14/08/99	KFC Lommelse SK	H	3-1	Demkin, Degryse, Severeyns
22/08/99	Club Brugge KV	A	0-2	
28/08/99	K St.-Truidense VV	H	3-1	Hofmans, Demkin, Haagdoren
11/09/99	KSC Lokeren	A	1-1	Degryse
18/09/99	KFC Verbroedering Geel	H	4-1	Hofmans, Degryse, Demkin, Marinovic
25/09/99	KSC Eendracht Aalst	H	3-2	Degryse 2, Hofmans
03/10/99	RSC Anderlecht	A	2-2	Hofmans, Degryse
13/10/99	KRC Harelbeke	H	1-0	Degryse (p)
23/10/99	KV Mechelen	A	0-2	
30/10/99	KVC Westerlo	H	3-2	Sonck, Demkin 2
06/11/99	KAA Gent	A	3-1	Herreman, Sonck, Mutavdzic
10/11/99	KRC Genk	A	0-4	
20/11/99	R Standard Liège	A	0-1	
27/11/99	RSC Charleroi	H	3-0	Demkin 3
04/12/99	R Excelsior Mouscron	A	1-1	Hofmans
11/12/99	KSK Beveren	H	2-0	Mutavdzic, Degryse
12/01/00	K Lierse SK	H	1-1	Karagiannis
15/01/00	KFC Lommelse SK	A	2-2	Sonck, Haagdoren
21/01/00	Club Brugge KV	H	5-3	Degryse, Karagiannis, Hofmans, Sonck 2
29/01/00	K St.-Truidense VV	A	0-2	
12/02/00	KFC Verbroedering Geel	A	2-0	Hofmans, Mutavdzic
20/02/00	KSC Eendracht Aalst	A	2-1	Sonck, Herreman (p)
01/03/00	KSC Lokeren	H	0-0	
05/03/00	RSC Anderlecht	H	1-3	Sonck
12/03/00	KRC Harelbeke	A	0-1	
18/03/00	KV Mechelen	H	0-0	
25/03/00	KVC Westerlo	A	2-3	Van der Heyden, Degryse
01/04/00	KAA Gent	H	2-0	Hofmans, Sonck
08/04/00	KRC Genk	H	3-0	Hofmans, Mutavdzic, Sonck
15/04/00	R Standard Liège	H	2-0	Sonck (p), Severeyns
22/04/00	RSC Charleroi	A	0-3	
06/05/00	R Excelsior Mouscron	H	0-1	
11/05/00	KSK Beveren	A	4-1	Haagdoren, Hofmans, Karagiannis, Sonck

KRC HARELBEKE

CLUB DIRECTORY

KRC Harelbeke
Stasegemsesteenweg 23
8530 Harelbeke
tel - (056) 739173
fax - (056) 718135
Year of Formation - 1930
President - Geert Sustronck
Manager - Marc De Smedt
Secretary - Jeroom Debrabandere
Coach - Henk Houwaart
(00/01 - Herman Helleputte)
Stadium - Forestiers (9,737)

APPEARANCES 99/00

	P	Ap	(s)	Gls
Kemokai CAMARA (GUI)	G	24	(1)	
Joris DE TOLLENAERE	A	8	(5)	
Maxime DHOORE	A	3	(5)	
Andrei DIATEL (RUS)	M	22	(1)	4
Nordine HAMEG (ALG)	D	10	(8)	1
Blessing KAKU (NIG)	M	25	(2)	5
Rene KLOMP (HOL)	M	24	(7)	6
Arkadiusz KUBIK (POL)	M	15	(3)	1
Lukasz KUBIK (POL)	D	33		1
Martinus LAAMERS (HOL)	M	30		1
Dmitri LUNIN (RUS)	M		(1)	
Daniel MAES	D	32		
Grégory MEILHAC (FRA)	A	3	(10)	
Dmitri MICHKOV (RUS)	M	13	(4)	2
David PAAS	A	31		19
Robbie PLETS	M		(4)	
Giovanni SANDRA	M		(3)	1
Ebou SILLAH (GAM)	A	27	(1)	4
Serge VANDEWALLE	D	9	(5)	2
Kurt VANDOORNE	G	10	(1)	
Kenny VERHOENE	D	24	(2)	5
Jeffrey VERHOEVEN	D	3	(10)	
Steven WOSTIJN	A	25	(7)	9
Rimantas ZVINGILAS (LIT)	A	3	(5)	1

LEAGUE RESULTS 1999/2000

07/08/99	RSC Charleroi	A	1-2	Diatel
14/08/99	R Excelsior Mouscron	H	1-1	Verhoene
21/08/99	KSK Beveren	A	2-2	Verhoene, Sandra
29/08/99	K Lierse SK	H	0-3	
11/09/99	KFC Lommelse SK	A	2-0	Paas, Michkov
19/09/99	Club Brugge KV	H	1-1	Paas (p)
25/09/99	K St.-Truidense VV	A	0-2	
03/10/99	KSC Lokeren	H	2-3	Paas, Verhoene
13/10/99	Germinal Beerschot Antwerpen	A	0-1	
24/10/99	KSC Eendracht Aalst	H	1-1	Wostijn
28/10/99	RSC Anderlecht	A	0-2	
07/11/99	KFC Verbroedering Geel	H	3-0	Verhoene, Paas, Kaku
10/11/99	KV Mechelen	H	5-2	Paas 2, Klomp, Hameg, Kaku
21/11/99	KVC Westerlo	A	1-4	Sillah
28/11/99	KAA Gent	H	1-2	Paas
05/12/99	KRC Genk	A	3-4	Paas 2, Sillah
12/12/99	R Standard Liège	H	3-4	Zvingilas, Kaku, Verhoene
12/01/00	RSC Charleroi	H	4-1	Paas, Kubik L., Kubik A., Klomp
16/01/00	R Excelsior Mouscron	A	2-4	Paas, Klomp
23/01/00	KSK Beveren	H	0-5	(w/o; original result 6-3
				Diatel 2, Wostijn 2, Paas, Sillah)
29/01/00	K Lierse SK	A	0-2	
06/02/00	KFC Lommelse SK	H	5-1	Paas 3 (1p), Wostijn, Kaku
13/02/00	Club Brugge KV	A	2-1	Klomp, Paas
20/02/00	K St.-Truidense VV	H	3-2	Klomp, Laamers, Paas
04/03/00	KSC Lokeren	A	0-2	
12/03/00	Germinal Beerschot Antwerpen	H	1-0	Vandewalle
19/03/00	KSC Eendracht Aalst	A	0-3	
26/03/00	RSC Anderlecht	H	2-2	Wostijn, Diatel
02/04/00	KFC Verbroedering Geel	A	2-3	Michkov, Sillah
09/04/00	KV Mechelen	A	0-4	
16/04/00	KVC Westerlo	H	3-1	Paas, Vandewalle, Wostijn
22/04/00	KAA Gent	A	2-4	Wostijn, Klomp
06/05/00	KRC Genk	H	1-2	Kaku
11/05/00	R Standard Liège	A	3-1	Wostijn 2, Paas (p)

K LIERSE SK

CLUB DIRECTORY

K Lierse SK
Voetbalstraat 4
2500 Lier
tel - (03) 4801370
fax - (03) 4880659
website - www.lierse/be
Year of Formation - 1906
President - Freddy Van Laer
Manager - Herman Van Holsbeeck
Secretary - Benny Van Dyck
Coach - Walter Meeuws
Stadium - Herman Vanderpoorten (14,538)

MAJOR HONOURS
League Championship - (4)
1932, 1942, 1960, 1997.
Domestic Cup - (2) 1969, 1999.

APPEARANCES 99/00

	P	Ap	(s)	Gls
Coen BURG (HOL)	M	2	(3)	
Jurgen CAVENS	A	26	(3)	11
Filip DAEMS	D	27		1
Tim DE KEYSER	D	9	(6)	1
Patrick DEMAN	G	7	(1)	
Carl HOEFKENS	D	31		
Stein HUYSEGEMS	A	9	(20)	5
Dirk HUYSMANS	A	4	(11)	2
Steve LAEREMANS	D	33		3
Frank LEEN	M	32		
Patrick NIJS	G	27		
Gert PEELMAN	A	3	(8)	
Jerry POORTERS	D	4	(1)	
Andrzej RUDY (POL)	M	12	(1)	1
Gela SHEKILADZE (GEO)	D	11	(9)	
Karel SNOECKX	M	30	(3)	4
Hans SOMERS	M	28		5
Joe SPITFRI (AUS)	A	7	(9)	3
Luc STRUYVEN	M	1	(1)	1
David VANDECAUTER	M		(1)	
Robby VAN DE WEYER	A	25	(8)	9
Eric VAN MEIR	D	27		16
Tomasz ZDEBEL (POL)	M	19	(1)	1

LEAGUE RESULTS 1999/2000

Date	Opponent	H/A	Score	Scorers
07/08/99	Germinal Beerschot Antwerpen	H	3-1	Cavens, Somers, Zdebel
15/08/99	KSC Eendracht Aalst	A	3-2	Van Meir 2, Cavens
22/08/99	RSC Anderlecht	H	0-3	
29/08/99	KRC Harelbeke	A	3-0	Cavens 2, Huysegems
11/09/99	KV Mechelen	H	5-1	Van Meir (p), og (Peytier), Van de Weyer 2, Huysegems
19/09/99	KVC Westerlo	A	2-0	Daems, Cavens
25/09/99	KAA Gent	H	2-1	Van Meir, Van de Weyer
03/10/99	KRC Genk	A	2-2	Van de Weyer, Huysmans
13/10/99	R Standard Liège	H	1-0	Snoeckx
23/10/99	RSC Charleroi	A	1-1	Snoeckx
30/10/99	R Excelsior Mouscron	H	1-0	Van Meir
06/11/99	KSK Beveren	A	1-1	og (Smet)
10/11/99	KFC Verbroedering Geel	A	1-2	Cavens
20/11/99	KFC Lommelse SK	H	4-0	Somers, Laeremans, Huysmans, Struyven
26/11/99	Club Brugge KV	A	0-1	
04/12/99	K St.-Truidense VV	H	0-0	
11/12/99	KSC Lokeren	A	1-5	Huysegems
12/01/00	Germinal Beerschot Antwerpen	A	1-1	Van Meir
15/01/00	KSC Eendracht Aalst	H	5-2	Van Meir 3 (1p), Van de Weyer 2
23/01/00	RSC Anderlecht	A	0-2	
29/01/00	KRC Harelbeke	H	2-0	Somers, Huysegems
05/02/00	KV Mechelen	A	3-4	Spiteri, Van Meir 2
12/02/00	KVC Westerlo	H	7-0	Cavens 2, Van de Weyer 2, Van Meir 2 (1p), Somers
18/02/00	KAA Gent	A	0-2	
04/03/00	KRC Genk	H	5-0	Cavens, Snoeckx, Van Meir, Somers, Spiteri
11/03/00	R Standard Liège	A	1-3	Cavens
18/03/00	RSC Charleroi	H	2-0	Van Meir, Van de Weyer
25/03/00	R Excelsior Mouscron	A	3-3	Laeremans, Rudy, Huysegems
01/04/00	KSK Beveren	H	1-3	Van Meir
07/04/00	KFC Verbroedering Geel	H	2-2	Laeremans, De Keyser
15/04/00	KFC Lommelse SK	A	0-1	
21/04/00	Club Brugge KV	H	1-0	Snoeckx
06/05/00	K St.-Truidense VV	A	1-2	Cavens
11/05/00	KSC Lokeren	H	1-2	Spiteri

KSC LOKEREN

CLUB DIRECTORY

KSC Lokeren
Daknamstraat 91
9160 Lokeren
tel - (09) 3483905
fax - (09) 3491243
website - www.kscl.be
Year of Formation - 1970
President - Roger Lambrecht
Secretary - Louis Horemans
Coach - Willy Reynders; Rudi Cossey;
Georges Leekens
Stadium - Daknam (12,000)

APPEARANCES 99/00

	P	Ap	(s)	Gls
Sam-Dominique ABOUO (CIV)	D	5	(3)	
Pola BAPO	A		(1)	
Jean-Paul BOEKA-LISASI (DRC)	A	16	(3)	2
Rigo BUYAI-KIDODA (DRC)	A	1		
Vaclav BUDKA (CZE)	M	7	(6)	2
Mladen DABANOVIC (SLO)	G	24		
Charles DAGO (CIV)	A	8	(3)	4
Davy DE BEULE	M		(1)	
Steven DE GEEST	D	16	(3)	
Karel DE SMET	D	12	(5)	
Sinisa DOBRASINOVIC (YUG)	M	2		
Chris JANSSENS	M	31		13
Suad KATANA (BOS)	D	16		
Papy KIMOTO (DRC)	M	7	(11)	4
Jan KOZAK (CZE)	A	1	(4)	
Ognjen MAJDOV (CRO)	D	3	(6)	
Marcel M'BAYO (DRC)	M	21	(2)	1
Zeljko MITRAKOVIC (SLO)	M	11	(3)	1
Camille MUZINGA (DRC)	D	5	(1)	
Novica NIKCEVIC (SLO)	A	2	(14)	4
Martin PENICKA (CZE)	M	13	(2)	2
Jurgen SIERENS	G	1		
Stefaan STAELENS	D	11	(3)	1
Stefan VAN DENDER	D	11	(8)	
Ronny VAN GENEUGDEN	M	29	(2)	6
Michael VAN HOEY	D	4	(4)	
Hein VANHAEZEBROUCK	D	16		
Arnar VIDARSSON (ISL)	M	28	(3)	1
Roman VONASEK (CZE)	M	27	(1)	5
Souleymane YOULA (GUI)	A	9	(5)	9
Patrice ZERE (CIV)	D	28		
Daniel ZYTKA (CZE)	G	9		

LEAGUE RESULTS 1999/2000

07/08/99	KFC Lommelse SK	A	0-1	
15/08/99	Club Brugge KV	H	2-5	Janssens 2
21/08/99	K St.-Truidense VV	A	1-1	Budka
28/08/99	KFC Verbroedering Geel	H	0-0	
11/09/99	Germinal Beerschot Antwerpen	H	1-1	Nikcevic
19/09/99	KSC Eendracht Aalst	A	0-1	
25/09/99	RSC Anderlecht	H	2-3	Van Geneugden (p), Penicka
03/10/99	KRC Harelbeke	A	3-2	Van Geneugden, Penicka, Janssens
13/10/99	KV Mechelen	H	0-2	
23/10/99	KVC Westerlo	A	3-3	Vonasek, Van Geneugden, Boeka-Lisasi
30/10/99	KAA Gent	H	0-4	
06/11/99	KRC Genk	A	1-1	Janssens
10/11/99	R Standard Liège	H	5-3	Janssens 2, Dago, Nikcevic 2
20/11/99	RSC Charleroi	A	4-2	Van Geneugden, Vidarsson, Boeka-Lisasi, Budka
27/11/99	R Excelsior Mouscron	H	3-2	Van Geneugden, Dago, og (De Vleeschauwer)
04/12/99	KSK Beveren	A	1-2	Vonasek
11/12/99	K Lierse SK	H	5-1	Vonasek, M'Bayo, Dago, Youla 2
12/01/00	KFC Lommelse SK	H	2-1	Nikcevic, Janssens
16/01/00	Club Brugge KV	A	1-6	Youla
22/01/00	K St.-Truidense VV	H	3-0	Youla 2, Staelens
29/01/00	KFC Verbroedering Geel	A	0-3	
12/02/00	KSC Eendracht Aalst	H	5-1	Dago, Janssens, Vonasek, Youla, Mitrakovic
19/02/00	RSC Anderlecht	A	0-5	
01/03/00	Germinal Beerschot Antwerpen	A	0-0	
04/03/00	KRC Harelbeke	H	2-0	Janssens, Youla
12/03/00	KV Mechelen	A	0-0	
18/03/00	KVC Westerlo	H	0-0	
26/03/00	KAA Gent	A	1-1	Youla
01/04/00	KRC Genk	H	1-2	Janssens
07/04/00	R Standard Liège	A	2-1	Janssens, Vonasek
15/04/00	RSC Charleroi	H	1-1	Youla
22/04/00	R Excelsior Mouscron	A	0-0	
06/05/00	KSK Beveren	H	5-2	Kimoto 2, Janssens 2, Van Geneugden
11/05/00	K Lierse SK	A	2-1	Kimoto 2

KFC LOMMELSE SK

CLUB DIRECTORY

KFC Lommelse SK
Gemeentelijk Sportcentrum
Speelpleinstraat 20
3920 Lommel
tel - (011) 559090
fax - (011) 559099
Year of Formation - 1932
President - Dirk Vanden Boer
Manager - Gaston Peeters
Coach - Jos Daerden; Harm Van Heldhoven
Stadium - Gemeentelijk Sportcentrum (12,500)

APPEARANCES 99/00

	P	Ap	(s)	Gls
Gert DAVIDTS	G	7	(1)	
Dieter DEKELVER	A	19	(7)	7
Kristján FINNBOGASON (ISL)	G	1		
Mark FORD (ENG)	M	15		
Sylvo GARCIA	A		(5)	
Louis GOMIS (SEN)	A	14	(6)	2
Kim GRANT (ENG)	A	17	(3)	3
Stijn HAELDERMANS	M	22		1
Kresimir MARUSIC (AUS)	M	13	(1)	
Jacky MATTHIJSSEN	G	26		
Wim MENNES	M	20	(1)	1
Daniël NASSEN	D	24	(1)	
Michel NOBEN	D	13	(2)	
Daniël SCAVONE	D	17	(1)	2
Twan SCHEEPERS (HOL)	A	7	(1)	2
Dirk SCHOOFS	M	19	(7)	1
Didier SEGERS	D	14	(2)	
Timmy SIMONS	D	32		4
Wim VAN DIEST	M	26	(5)	2
Eric VAN KESSEL (HOL)	D	6	(6)	
Tom VANRUYSSEVELDT	A		(4)	
Lima VIEIRA NIVALDO (BRA)	M	1	(6)	
Kris VINCKEN	M	24	(1)	
Miroslaw WALIGORA (POL)	A	20	(12)	9
Karim ZOUAOUI (FRA)	A	17	(10)	1

LEAGUE RESULTS 1999/2000

07/08/99	KSC Lokeren	H	1-0	Waligora
14/08/99	Germinal Beerschot Antwerpen	A	1-3	Van Diest
22/08/99	KSC Eendracht Aalst	H	3-3	Simons (p), Waligora, Dekelver
29/08/99	RSC Anderlecht	A	3-3	Grant, Dekelver 2
11/09/99	KRC Harelbeke	H	0-2	
18/09/99	KV Mechelen	A	0-1	
25/09/99	KVC Westerlo	H	2-2	Grant, Waligora
02/10/99	KAA Gent	A	2-6	Dekelver, Grant
13/10/99	KRC Genk	H	0-1	
23/10/99	R Standard Liège	A	1-4	Waligora
30/10/99	RSC Charleroi	H	1-1	Gomis
06/11/99	R Excelsior Mouscron	A	0-0	
10/11/99	KSK Beveren	H	0-0	
20/11/99	K Lierse SK	A	0-4	
27/11/99	KFC Verbroedering Geel	A	0-0	
04/12/99	Club Brugge KV	H	0-0	
11/12/99	K St.-Truidense VV	A	0-2	
12/01/00	KSC Lokeren	A	1-2	Van Diest
15/01/00	Germinal Beerschot Antwerpen	H	2-2	Dekelver, Simons
23/01/00	KSC Eendracht Aalst	A	1-3	Scavone
29/01/00	RSC Anderlecht	H	3-3	Dekelver 2, Simons (p)
06/02/00	KRC Harelbeke	A	1-5	Gomis
12/02/00	KV Mechelen	H	0-2	
19/02/00	KVC Westerlo	A	0-1	
04/03/00	KAA Gent	H	1-3	Simons (p)
11/03/00	KRC Genk	A	2-1	Mennes, Zouaoui
19/03/00	R Standard Liège	H	2-1	Scheepers, Schoofs
25/03/00	RSC Charleroi	A	1-1	Scheepers
01/04/00	R Excelsior Mouscron	H	0-4	
09/04/00	KSK Beveren	A	0-1	
15/04/00	K Lierse SK	H	1-0	Waligora
22/04/00	KFC Verbroedering Geel	H	1-1	Waligora
06/05/00	Club Brugge KV	A	1-3	Haeldermans
11/05/00	K St.-Truidense VV	H	4-1	Waligora 3, Scavone

KV MECHELEN

CLUB DIRECTORY

KV Mechelen
Kleine Nieuwedijkstraat 53, 2800 Mechelen
tel - (015) 218230 / fax - (015) 219033
website - www.kvmechelen.be
Year of Formation - 1904
President - Willy Van den Wijngaert
Manager - Ivan Buskens
Secretary - Jef Dinaer
Coach - Gunter Jacob (00/01 - Leo Clijsters)
Stadium - Achter de Kazerne (13,847)

MAJOR HONOURS
League Championship - (4)
1943, 1946, 1948, 1989.
Domestic Cup - (1) 1987.
European Cup-winners' Cup - (1) 1988.
European Super Cup - (1) 1989.

APPEARANCES 99/00

	P	Ap	(s)	Gls
Johan BAL	D	27		1
Chris BRUYNINCKX	A		(5)	1
Tom CALUWE	M	10	(4)	2
Ngom CAMARA (GUI)	M	12	(8)	
Daniël CAMUS	M	27	(2)	5
Thomas CHATELLE	A	4	(6)	2
Johan DARCON	D	1	(2)	
Benjamin DEBUSSCHERE	D	26		1
Drissa DIALLO (GUI)	D	17	(10)	1
João ELIAS (ANG)	A	28	(1)	10
Fritz EMERAN (FRA)	D	30		
Sammy GREVEN	D	21	(5)	2
Garret KUSCH (CAN)	A		(2)	
Johnny LEBEGGE	G		(1)	
Tom PEETERS	M	33		1
Geoffrey PEYTIER	D	8		
Steven RIBUS	A	21		7
Kevin STICKENS	M		(1)	
Birger VAN DE VEN	M		(3)	
Sven VANDENBROECK	M	29	(2)	1
Joris VAN HOUT	A	33	(1)	8
Matthias VAN STEENBERGHE	A	10	(10)	2
Kenny VERHOEVEN	D	2	(11)	1
Sam VERMEULEN	M	1		
Ivan WILLOCKX	G	34		

LEAGUE RESULTS 1999/2000

07/08/99	R Standard Liège	A	1-2	Van Hout
14/08/99	RSC Charleroi	H	2-1	Elias, Van Hout (p)
21/08/99	R Excelsior Mouscron	A	0-2	
28/08/99	KSK Beveren	H	3-1	Camus, Bal, Ribus
11/09/99	K Lierse SK	A	1-5	Ribus
18/09/99	KFC Lommelse SK	H	1-0	Van Hout
26/09/99	Club Brugge KV	A	0-6	
02/10/99	K St.-Truidense VV	H	3-2	Van Hout, Ribus, Elias
13/10/99	KSC Lokeren	A	2-0	Caluwé, Elias
23/10/99	Germinal Beerschot Antwerpen	H	2-0	Ribus 2
31/10/99	KSC Eendracht Aalst	A	0-2	
06/11/99	RSC Anderlecht	H	2-5	Greven, Verhoeven
10/11/99	KRC Harelbeke	A	2-5	Vandenbroeck, Van Steenberghe
20/11/99	KFC Verbroedering Geel	H	1-1	Van Steenberghe
27/11/99	KVC Westerlo	H	2-2	og (Michiels), Greven
04/12/99	KAA Gent	A	1-6	Caluwé
11/12/99	KRC Genk	H	2-0	og (Van Geem), Elias
12/01/00	R Standard Liège	H	2-4	Ribus, Camus (p)
15/01/00	RSC Charleroi	A	4-1	Elias, Chatelle, Diallo, Camus
22/01/00	R Excelsior Mouscron	H	1-3	Bruyninckx
29/01/00	KSK Beveren	A	1-2	Elias
05/02/00	K Lierse SK	H	4-3	Debusschere, Van Hout, Elias 2
12/02/00	KFC Lommelse SK	A	2-0	Camus, Chatelle
19/02/00	Club Brugge KV	H	0-0	
04/03/00	K St.-Truidense VV	A	1-3	Peeters
12/03/00	KSC Lokeren	H	0-0	
18/03/00	Germinal Beerschot Antwerpen	A	0-0	
25/03/00	KSC Eendracht Aalst	H	2-0	Van Hout, Elias
01/04/00	RSC Anderlecht	A	0-5	
09/04/00	KRC Harelbeke	H	4-0	Van Hout 2, Camus, Elias
16/04/00	KFC Verbroedering Geel	A	0-3	
22/04/00	KVC Westerlo	A	0-8	
06/05/00	KAA Gent	H	0-2	
11/05/00	KRC Genk	A	1-3	Ribus

K ST.-TRUIDENSE VV

CLUB DIRECTORY

K Sint-Truidense VV
Tiensesteenweg 170
3800 Sint-Truiden
tel - (011) 683829
fax - (011) 692380
website - www.stvv.com
Year of Formation - 1924
President - Leo Schepers
Secretary - Fernand Knaepen
Coach - Poll Peters; Willy Reynders
Stadium - Staaien (12,861)

APPEARANCES 99/00

	P	Ap	(s)	Gls
Samuel AERTS	D	2	(2)	
Dusan BELIC (YUG)	G	25		
Coen BURG (HOL)	M	10	(6)	3
Kris BUVENS	M	1		
Robrecht DECKERS	D	1		
Robbie DELLO	D	18	(4)	1
Peter DELORGE	M	24	(3)	
Eddy DIERICKX	M	30		1
Filip FIERS	A	30	(2)	10
Gunther GRAMMET	D	3	(1)	
Nicky HAYEN	D	23	(1)	1
Sascha HOLANS	M	2	(1)	
ISAÍAS Magalhães da Silva (BRA)	M	20	(10)	2
Philippe LENGLOIS	D	23	(4)	
Kurt MERTENS	A	13	(10)	3
Steven NIJS	D	7	(1)	
Mladen RUDONJA (SLO)	A	17	(5)	5
Davy SCHOLLEN	G	2	(1)	
Patrick TEPPERS	M	30	(2)	3
Genival de Oliveira VALDO (BRA)	A	5	(4)	3
Bram VANGEEL	A	5	(11)	2
Dirk VAN OEKELEN	D	19	(1)	2
Gunter VERJANS	M	4	(2)	
Peter VOETS	D	30	(1)	1
Robert VOLK (SLO)	G	7	(1)	
Wouter VRANCKEN	D	23	(6)	4

LEAGUE RESULTS 1999/2000

08/08/99	Club Brugge KV	A	0-4	
14/08/99	KFC Verbroedering Geel	H	1-1	Dello
21/08/99	KSC Lokeren	H	1-1	Voets
28/08/99	Germinal Beerschot Antwerpen	A	1-3	Vrancken
11/09/99	KSC Eendracht Aalst	H	1-5	Isaías
19/09/99	RSC Anderlecht	A	1-2	Mertens
25/09/99	KRC Harelbeke	H	2-0	Teppers, Fiers
02/10/99	KV Mechelen	A	2-3	Fiers, Mertens
13/10/99	KVC Westerlo	H	2-1	Fiers 2 (1p)
23/10/99	KAA Gent	A	2-4	Fiers, Teppers
30/10/99	KRC Genk	H	0-5	
06/11/99	R Standard Liège	A	1-2	Vrancken
10/11/99	RSC Charleroi	H	2-2	Vangeel 2
20/11/99	R Excelsior Mouscron	A	0-3	
27/11/99	KSK Beveren	H	0-2	
04/12/99	K Lierse SK	A	0-0	
11/12/99	KFC Lommelse SK	H	2-0	Mertens, Fiers
12/01/00	Club Brugge KV	H	0-1	
15/01/00	KFC Verbroedering Geel	A	2-1	Dierickx, Fiers
22/01/00	KSC Lokeren	A	0-3	
29/01/00	Germinal Beerschot Antwerpen	H	2-0	Vrancken, Isaías
06/02/00	KSC Eendracht Aalst	A	0-2	
12/02/00	RSC Anderlecht	H	0-4	
20/02/00	KRC Harelbeke	A	2-3	Burg, Hayen
04/03/00	KV Mechelen	H	3-1	Van Oekelen, Burg, Fiers
11/03/00	KVC Westerlo	A	2-3	Fiers 2 (1p)
18/03/00	KAA Gent	H	0-0	
25/03/00	KRC Genk	A	2-0	Van Oekelen, Rudonja
01/04/00	R Standard Liège	H	2-0	Teppers, Rudonja
08/04/00	RSC Charleroi	A	1-1	Rudonja
15/04/00	R Excelsior Mouscron	H	0-0	
22/04/00	KSK Beveren	A	4-3	Rudonja 2, Vrancken, Valdo
06/05/00	K Lierse SK	H	2-1	Valdo, Burg
11/05/00	KFC Lommelse SK	A	1-4	Valdo

R STANDARD LIEGE

Royal Standard de Liège
Rue de la Centrale 2, 4200 Liège
tel - (04) 2522122 / fax - (04) 2521469
website - www.standard.be
Year of Formation - 1900
President - André Duchêne
Coach - Tomislav Ivic; Zeljko Mijac; Jean Thissen;
Tomislav Ivic
Stadium - Sclessin (30,000)

MAJOR HONOURS
League Championship - (8) 1958, 1961, 1963,
1969, 1970, 1971, 1982, 1983.
Domestic Cup - (5)
1954, 1966, 1967, 1981, 1993.

APPEARANCES 99/00

	P	Ap	(s)	Gls
Rabiu AFOLABI (NIG)	D	20	(3)	1
Adrian ALIAJ (ALB)	M	2	(3)	
Theophilus AMUZU (GHA)	M		(1)	
Roberto BISCONTI	M	12	(1)	1
George BLAY (NIG)	D	12	(5)	1
David BROCKEN	D	16		
Liviu CIOBOTARIU (ROM)	D	23		
Pascal DIAS (FRA)	A	12	(14)	5
Manuel DIMAS (POR)	D	13		
Mohammed EL YAMANI (EGY)	A	1	(1)	1
Didier ERNST	D	31		2
FLORKIN	M		(1)	
Michael GOOSSENS	A	15		8
Ariel GRANA (ARG)	D	2		
Guy HELLERS (LUX)	M	4		
Ali LUKUNKU (FRA)	A	14	(10)	8
MAURY	D	1		
Ivica MORNAR (CRO)	A	21	(3)	8
Emile MPENZA	A	11		4
Mbo MPENZA	A	17		6
Moustapha OUSSALAH	M	1		
Frédéric PIERRE	M	26	(1)	5
Sébastien PIRON	M	1		
Gauthier REMACLE	D	5	(15)	1
Vedran RUNJE (CRO)	G	32		
SAGLAM	A		(1)	
Tibor SELYMES (ROM)	D	20		1
Filip SUSNJARA (CRO)	G	2	(1)	
Bernd THIJS	M	23	(6)	11
Onder TURACI	A	1		
Daniel VAN BUYTEN	D	22	(6)	3
Laurent WUILLOT	D	4	(3)	
Joseph YOBO (NIG)	M	10	(8)	

LEAGUE RESULTS 1999/2000

07/08/99	KV Mechelen	H	2-1	Mpenza M., Mpenza E.
14/08/99	KVC Westerlo	A	1-2	Mpenza M.
21/08/99	KAA Gent	H	0-2	
29/08/99	KRC Genk	A	0-4	
11/09/99	KFC Verbroedering Geel	A	0-0	
17/09/99	RSC Charleroi	H	1-3	Mpenza M.
24/09/99	R Excelsior Mouscron	A	3-1	Pierre, Mpenza E., Mpenza M.
02/10/99	KSK Beveren	H	3-1	Thijs 2, Mpenza M.
13/10/99	K Lierse SK	A	0-1	
23/10/99	KFC Lommelse SK	H	4-1	Mornar 2, Dias, Bisconti
30/10/99	Club Brugge KV	A	2-5	Pierre, Lukunku
06/11/99	K St.-Truidense VV	H	2-1	Thijs, Pierre
10/11/99	KSC Lokeren	A	3-5	Blay, Lukunku 2
20/11/99	Germinal Beerschot Antwerpen	H	1-0	Selymes
28/11/99	KSC Eendracht Aalst	A	2-1	Dias, Mpenza E.
05/12/99	RSC Anderlecht	H	0-0	
12/12/99	KRC Harelbeke	A	4-3	Thijs, Mpenza E., Afolabi, Mpenza M.
12/01/00	KV Mechelen	A	4-2	Goossens 2, Ernst, Mornar
15/01/00	KVC Westerlo	H	4-0	Lukunku 2, Goossens, Mornar
22/01/00	KAA Gent	A	5-1	Mornar 2, Goossens, Lukunku, Dias
28/01/00	KRC Genk	H	5-1	Van Buyten, Mornar, Lukunku, Thijs (p), Goossens
05/02/00	KFC Verbroedering Geel	H	3-0	Thijs 2 (1p), Goossens
13/02/00	RSC Charleroi	A	4-1	Pierre, Goossens, Ernst, Thijs (p)
18/02/00	R Excelsior Mouscron	H	2-0	Thijs, Mornar
04/03/00	KSK Beveren	A	2-0	Lukunku, Dias
11/03/00	K Lierse SK	H	3-1	Goossens, Van Buyten, Dias
19/03/00	KFC Lommelse SK	A	1-2	Van Buyten
24/03/00	Club Brugge KV	H	0-1	
01/04/00	K St.-Truidense VV	A	0-2	
07/04/00	KSC Lokeren	H	1-2	Pierre
15/04/00	Germinal Beerschot Antwerpen	A	0-2	
22/04/00	KSC Eendracht Aalst	H	3-1	Thijs 2 (1p), Remacle
06/05/00	RSC Anderlecht	A	0-2	
11/05/00	KRC Harelbeke	H	1-3	El Yamani

KFC VERBROEDERING GEEL

CLUB DIRECTORY

KFC Verbroedering Geel
Rauwelkoven 43
2440 Geel
tel - (014) 580126
fax - (014) 591097
Year of Formation - 1924
President - Vic Keersmakers
Manager - Dimitri M'Buyu
Coach - Paul Put; Dmitri M'Buyu; Sándor Popovics
(00/01 - Jos Heyligen)
Stadium - De Leunen (11,500)

APPEARANCES 99/00

	P	Ap	(s)	Gls
Davy ALENTIJNS	M	4	(5)	
Gudmundur BENEDIKTSSON (ISL)	A	8	(7)	4
Nico CURTO	A	6	(11)	2
Björn DAELEMANS	A	29	(3)	8
Jef DELEN	A	32	(2)	6
Csaba FEHÉR (HUN)	D	14		
Jo GEERINCKX	D	29		
Marc JANSSEN	D	13	(3)	
Miklós LENDVAI (HUN)	M	31		1
Peter MEEUSEN	A	21	(10)	
Tony MOLS	M	16		
Dalibor NOVCIC (YUG)	A	1	(5)	
Zoltán PETÖ (HUN)	D	13		
Sándor PREISINGER (HUN)	A	8	(6)	2
Ronny SCHUERMANS	G	34		
Björn SMITS	M	29		3
Dave SMITS	D	16	(4)	
Marc SYLVERMANS	D	11		
István SZEKÉR (HUN)	D	14		1
Georgica VAMESU (ROM)	D	10	(1)	
Bruno VERSAVEL	M	23		2
ZÉFILHO (BRA)	A	12	(8)	2

LEAGUE RESULTS 1999/2000

06/08/99	KAA Gent	H	1-5	Delen
14/08/99	K St.-Truidense VV	A	1-1	Lendvai
21/08/99	KRC Genk	H	1-1	Daelemans
28/08/99	KSC Lokeren	A	0-0	
11/09/99	R Standard Liège	H	0-0	
18/09/99	Germinal Beerschot Antwerpen	A	1-4	Curto
26/09/99	RSC Charleroi	H	0-0	
03/10/99	KSC Eendracht Aalst	A	0-1	
13/10/99	R Excelsior Mouscron	H	1-4	Curto
24/10/99	RSC Anderlecht	A	0-4	
30/10/99	KSK Beveren	H	1-1	Zéfilho
07/11/99	KRC Harelbeke	A	0-3	
10/11/99	K Lierse SK	H	2-1	Daelemans, Benediktsson
20/11/99	KV Mechelen	A	1-1	Benediktsson
27/11/99	KFC Lommelse SK	H	0-0	
04/12/99	KVC Westerlo	H	2-3	Smits B., Zéfilho
11/12/99	Club Brugge KV	A	0-4	
12/01/00	KAA Gent	A	1-1	Versavel
15/01/00	K St.-Truidense VV	H	1-2	Daelemans
22/01/00	KRC Genk	A	0-1	
29/01/00	KSC Lokeren	H	3-0	Versavel, Delen 2
05/02/00	R Standard Liège	A	0-3	
12/02/00	Germinal Beerschot Antwerpen	H	0-2	
19/02/00	RSC Charleroi	A	3-1	Preisinger, Delen, og (Keré)
04/03/00	KSC Eendracht Aalst	H	1-2	Daelemans
11/03/00	R Excelsior Mouscron	A	1-3	Delen
18/03/00	RSC Anderlecht	H	0-0	
25/03/00	KSK Beveren	A	1-1	Preisinger
02/04/00	KRC Harelbeke	H	3-2	Daelemans (p), Benediktsson, Delen
07/04/00	K Lierse SK	A	2-2	Szekér, Daelemans
16/04/00	KV Mechelen	H	3-0	Daelemans 2, Smits B.
22/04/00	KFC Lommelse SK	A	1-1	Benediktsson
06/05/00	KVC Westerlo	A	1-4	Smits B.
11/05/00	Club Brugge KV	H	0-2	

KVC WESTERLO

KVC Westerlo
De Merodedreef 189
2260 Westerlo
tel - (014) 545288
fax - (014) 542321
website - www.kvcwesterlo.be
Year of Formation - 1933
President - vacant
Manager - Herman Wijnants
Coach - Jan Ceulemans
Stadium - 't Kuipje (10,278)

APPEARANCES 99/00

	P	Ap	(s)	Gls
Sadio BA	D	17	(7)	
Toni BROGNO	A	32		30
Kristof DAEMS	M		(2)	
Björn DE CONINCK	D	13	(6)	3
Bart DEELKENS	G	3		
António DOS SANTOS (BRA)	D	6	(3)	
Franky FRANS	G	31		
Rudy JANSSENS	M	33		1
Sidney LAMMENS	D	15		2
Frank MACHIELS	D	30		3
Cvijan MILOSEVIC (BOS)	M	20	(7)	2
Dejan MITROVIC (YUG)	A	23	(6)	5
Tom MOONS	M		(5)	
Vedran PELIC (YUG)	A	17	(13)	13
Krist PORTE	M	3	(12)	2
Marc SCHAESSENS	D	29		2
Ives SERNEELS	M	31		3
Benoît THANS	M	27		
Dirk THOELEN	D	14	(15)	2
Kevin VANDENBERGH	A		(4)	
Mario VERHEYEN	D	13		1
Bart WILLEMSEN	D	8	(9)	
Lucas ZELENKA (CZE)	M	9	(8)	4

LEAGUE RESULTS 1999/2000

07/08/99	KRC Genk	h	6-6	Brogno 4 (2p), Pelic 2
14/08/99	R Standard Liège	H	2-1	Brogno 2 (1p)
21/08/99	RSC Charleroi	A	2-1	Mitrovic, Porte
28/08/99	R Excelsior Mouscron	H	3-0	Brogno 2 (1p), Mitrovic
19/09/99	K Lierse SK	H	0-2	
25/09/99	KFC Lommelse SK	A	2-2	Milosevic, Brogno
03/10/99	Club Brugge KV	H	1-0	Pelic
13/10/99	K St.-Truidense VV	A	1-2	Pelic
23/10/99	KSC Lokeren	H	3-3	Porte (p), Lammens, Thoelen
30/10/99	Germinal Beerschot Antwerpen	A	2-3	Schaessens, Brogno
06/11/99	KSC Eendracht Aalst	H	3-2	Brogno 3 (1p)
10/11/99	RSC Anderlecht	A	0-3	
21/11/99	KRC Harelbeke	H	4-1	Lammens, Brogno 2 (1p), Mitrovic
27/11/99	KV Mechelen	A	2-2	Mitrovic, Brogno
04/12/99	KFC Verbroedering Geel	A	3-2	Verheyen, Mitrovic, Brogno
08/12/99	KSK Beveren	A	0-4	
11/12/99	KAA Gent	H	4-2	Brogno, Janssens, Serneels, Milosevic
12/01/00	KRC Genk	A	1-1	Schaessens
15/01/00	R Standard Liège	A	0-4	
23/01/00	RSC Charleroi	H	1-1	Brogno (p)
30/01/00	R Excelsior Mouscron	A	1-2	Zelenka
05/02/00	KSK Beveren	H	3-2	Zelenka, Pelic, De Coninck
12/02/00	K Lierse SK	A	0-7	
19/02/00	KFC Lommelse SK	H	1-0	Machiels
05/03/00	Club Brugge KV	A	0-2	
11/03/00	K St.-Truidense VV	H	3-2	De Coninck 2, Brogno
18/03/00	KSC Lokeren	A	0-0	
25/03/00	Germinal Beerschot Antwerpen	H	3-2	Pelic, Zelenka, Brogno
01/04/00	KSC Eendracht Aalst	A	1-1	Pelic
08/04/00	RSC Anderlecht	H	5-0	Brogno 2, Zelenka, Machiels, Pelic
16/04/00	KRC Harelbeke	A	1-3	Brogno
22/04/00	KV Mechelen	H	8-0	Brogno 4 (1p), Pelic 2, Serneels, Thoelen
06/05/00	KFC Verbroedering Geel	H	4-1	Pelic 2, Serneels, Brogno
11/05/00	KAA Gent	A	3-2	Brogno, Pelic, Machiels

BOSNIA-HERZEGOVINA

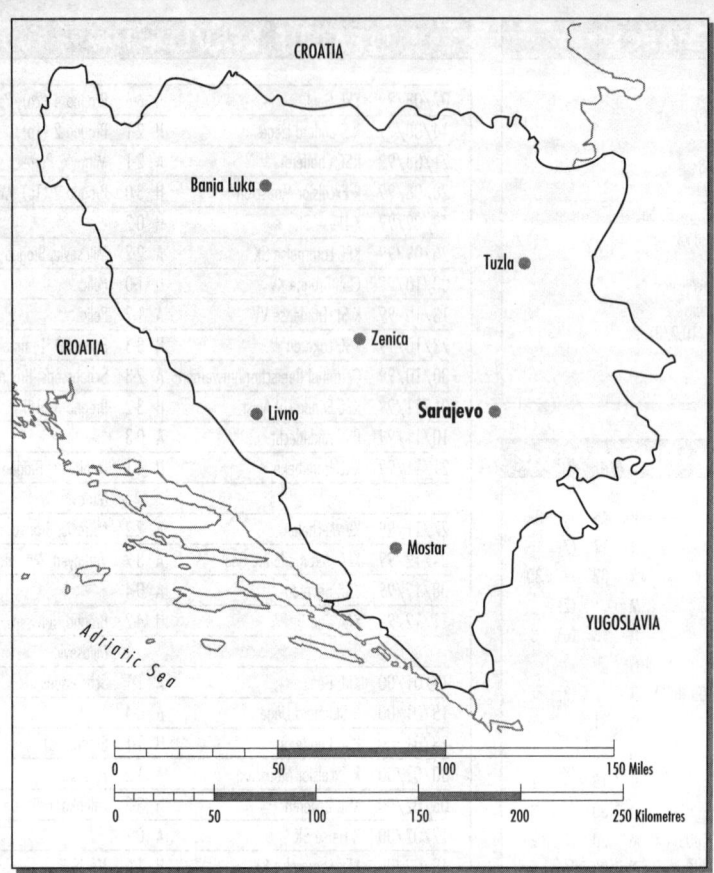

EUROPEAN FOOTBALL BACK ON THE AGENDA

Brotnjo Citluk take first unified title

FEDERATION DIRECTORY

Nogometni Savez Bosne i Hercegovine
Ulica Ferhadija 30, 71000 Sarajevo

tel - (033) 276676
fax - (033) 444332
website - www.crp.com.ba/nsbih

Year of Formation - 1992
President - Jusuf Pusina
Secretary - Munib Usanovic

Stadium - Kosevo, Sarajevo (20,000)

Following encouragement from UEFA, two of the three 'entities' which make up the footballing infrastructure of Bosnia and Herzegovina - those representing the Muslim and Croatian communities - agreed to join forces and stage a unified national championship, the first of its kind, in 1999/2000.

It was by no means the finished product. The Serbian authorities refused to join in and complete the unification. And the Muslims and Croatians only got together at the end of the season, in June, for a series of play-offs, having both staged their own private competitions from August through to May.

With the Serbs opting out, the agreed formula was for the top five teams from the Muslim league to be joined by the top three in the Croatian league. These eight teams were then split into two mini-league groups, the winners of which contested a two-legged championship final.

The play-offs produced some surprising results, with neither of the original league winners - Jedinstvo Bihac (Muslim) and Posusje (Croat) - going through. Group A was won by Buducnost Banovici, a mere fifth in the Muslim league, while Group B was topped by Croatian league runners-up Brotnjo Citluk. Both teams progressed by virtue of a superior head-to-head record. The final itself was equally tight, but it was Brotnjo who took the championship on the away-goals rule after drawing 1-1 away and 0-0 at home.

Brotnjo's victory earned them entry into the Champions' League, while Buducnost joined Cup winners Zeljeznicar Sarajevo in the UEFA Cup. There had been no Bosnian teams in the 1999/2000 competitions because of UEFA's

LEAGUE CHAMPIONSHIP RESULTS 99/00

MUSLIM LEAGUE	1	2	3	4	5	6	7	8	9	10	11	12	13	14	15	16
1 Bosna Visoko		2-0	4-1	4-0	1-1	0-0	0-0	1-0	1-2	2-0	1-1	4-0	2-3	1-0	1-1	1-3
2 Buducnost Banovici	4-0		0-0	3-0	1-0	2-0	2-1	1-0	2-1	2-1	1-0	0-0	1-0	3-1	0-0	1-0
3 Celik Zenica	3-0	1-1		2-0	3-1	5-0	2-1	3-3	1-0	1-0	4-1	1-0	0-0	1-1	2-0	1-1
4 Drina Zvornik	1-3	0-3	0-4		1-3	2-0	0-2	0-8	2-1	0-1	0-3	1-2	0-2	0-4	5-3	1-2
5 Dzerdelez Zenica	1-0	3-2	3-2	4-1		3-0	2-2	1-0	2-1	3-1	2-0	2-2	2-1	0-0	3-1	3-0
6 Gradina Srebrenica	3-1	0-4	0-0	2-1	1-3		1-0	0-1	1-0	0-0	0-1	1-5	2-1	1-0	0-3	2-6
7 Iskra Bugojno	1-0	0-0	3-0	4-0	2-0	2-0		0-1	2-1	1-1	3-1	0-0	2-3	2-1	1-2	1-0
8 Jedinstvo Bihac	1-0	2-1	2-0	4-1	1-1	4-0	2-0		1-0	4-1	2-0	0-2	2-1	2-0	2-1	1-0
9 Krajina Cazin	1-1	2-1	1-2	2-0	1-1	2-0	1-0	1-1		2-0	1-2	3-1	0-0	3-1	2-1	1-0
10 Lukavac	0-1	0-2	1-0	3-1	1-0	2-1	2-1	0-1	0-3		1-3	2-0	0-1	0-0	2-1	2-3
11 Rudar Kakanj	1-0	4-2	2-0	2-0	2-1	4-0	0-0	1-0	2-0	0-1		0-0	1-0	2-0	2-0	1-1
12 Sarajevo	1-0	2-0	3-1	5-0	1-1	4-0	0-0	1-0	3-0	3-0	1-1		4-0	3-0	5-1	4-1
13 Sloboda Tuzla	2-0	0-0	3-1	3-1	3-1	5-1	2-0	0-1	3-1	2-0	0-1	1-2		2-1	2-0	0-0
14 TOSK Tesanj	3-1	0-0	0-1	3-1	0-2	xxx	1-1	2-0	1-0	2-2	2-1	1-0	0-0		1-1	1-0
15 Velez Mostar	2-0	0-0	3-0	8-0	2-0	4-0	xxx	2-0	2-0	5-0	1-1	1-0	4-1	3-1		2-2
16 Zeljeznicar Sarajevo	1-3	1-0	2-2	5-0	4-1	3-0	3-1	2-0	2-0	2-1	4-1	2-0	2-0	2-0	4-1	

xxx - match void; awarded as home win.

CHAMPIONSHIP PLAY-OFFS

GROUP A	1	2	3	4		GROUP B	1	2	3	4
1 Buducnost Banovici		2-1	3-0	1-0		1 Brotnjo Citluk		3-0	4-0	2-1
2 Posusje	2-0		0-1	1-1		2 Jedinstvo Bihac	3-1		3-0	2-0
3 Siroki Brijeg	3-1	3-2		1-0		3 Rudar Kranj	1-2	0-1		1-7
4 Zeljeznicar Sarajevo	1-3	1-2	1-0			4 Sarajevo	2-0	2-1	2-0	

LEAGUE CHAMPIONSHIP FINAL TABLES 99/00

MUSLIM LEAGUE

		Pd	W	Home D	L	F	A	W	Away D	L	F	A	W	Total D	L	F	A	Pt	GD
1	Jedinstvo Bihac	30	13	1	1	30	8	5	2	8	16	15	18	3	9	46	23	57	23
2	Zeljeznicar Sarajevo	30	13	1	1	39	10	4	4	7	19	22	17	5	8	58	32	56	26
3	Sarajevo	30	12	3	0	40	5	4	4	7	14	19	16	7	7	54	24	55	30
4	Rudar Kakanj	30	11	3	1	24	5	5	3	7	17	23	16	6	8	41	28	54	13
5	Buducnost Banovici	30	12	3	0	23	4	3	5	7	16	17	15	8	7	39	21	53	18
6	Dzerdelez Zenica	30	12	3	0	34	13	3	4	8	16	24	15	7	8	50	37	52	13
7	Velez Mostar	30	12	3	0	39	5	2	3	10	16	32	14	6	10	55	37	48	18
8	Sloboda Tuzla	30	10	2	3	28	10	4	3	8	13	22	14	5	11	41	32	47	9
9	Celik Zenica	30	10	5	0	30	9	3	3	9	14	27	13	8	9	44	36	47	8
10	Iskra Bugojno	30	9	3	3	24	10	1	5	9	9	18	10	8	12	33	28	38	5
11	Krajina Cazin	30	9	4	2	23	11	2	0	13	10	25	11	4	15	33	36	37	-3
12	Bosna Visoko	30	7	5	3	25	12	3	1	11	10	25	10	6	14	35	37	36	-2
13	TOSK Tesanj	30	8	5	2	17	10	1	3	11	10	25	9	8	13	27	35	35	-8
14	Lukavac	30	7	1	7	16	18	2	3	10	9	29	9	4	17	25	47	31	-22
15	Gradina Srebrenica	30	6	2	7	14	26	0	1	14	2	42	6	3	21	16	68	21	-52
16	Drina Zvornik	30	3	0	12	13	41	0	0	15	6	54	3	0	27	19	95	9	-76

HERCEG-BOSNA LEAGUE

		P	W	D	L	F	A	Pt	GD
1	Posusje	26	19	4	3	54	14	61	40
2	Brotnjo Citluk	26	18	3	5	63	21	57	42
3	Siroki Brijeg	26	14	6	6	53	23	48	30
4	Capljina	26	13	5	8	42	34	44	8
5	Kiseljak	26	13	4	9	37	27	43	10
6	Zrinjski Mostar	26	12	7	7	45	30	43	15
7	Ljubuski	26	10	10	6	45	22	40	23
8	Orasje	26	11	2	13	39	32	35	7
9	Troglav Livno	26	10	1	5	27	40	31	-13
10	Vitez	26	6	7	13	17	42	25	-25
11	GOSK Gabela	26	7	4	15	25	62	25	-37
12	Zepce	26	7	2	17	24	52	23	-28
13	Redarstvenik Mostar	26	6	4	16	21	50	22	-29
14	Stolac	26	4	5	17	12	55	17	-43

SRPSKA LEAGUE

		Pd	W	D	L	F	A	Pt	GD
1	Boksit Milici	38	26	4	8	84	28	82	56
2	Rudar Ugljevik	38	23	9	6	91	24	78	67
3	Leotar Trebinje	38	22	9	7	80	33	75	47
4	Sloboda Novi Grad	38	21	8	9	71	32	71	39
5	Modrica	38	19	6	13	51	34	63	17
6	Radnik Bijeljina	38	16	11	11	67	35	59	32
7	Borac Banja Luka	38	16	11	11	70	40	59	30
8	BSK Banja Luka	38	18	5	15	59	42	59	17
9	Kozara Gradiska	38	17	6	15	51	40	57	11
10	Glasinac Sokolac	38	17	5	16	58	44	56	14
11	Ljubic Prnjavor	38	16	8	14	54	50	56	4
12	Mladost Gacko	38	16	7	15	52	50	55	2
13	Rudar Prijedor	38	17	4	17	47	45	55	2
14	Drina Zvornik	38	16	6	16	50	43	54	7
15	Borac Samac	38	15	5	18	47	55	50	-8
16	Sloga Doboj	38	15	1	22	46	65	46	-19
17	Jedinstvo Brcko	38	14	3	21	49	79	45	-30
18	Famos Srpsko Sarajevo	38	11	4	23	40	76	37	-36
19	Sloga Srbac	38	7	1	30	40	94	22	-54
20	Sloga Trn	38	1	1	36	15	211	4	-196

CHAMPIONSHIP PLAY-OFFS

GROUP A

		Pd	W	D	L	F	A	W	D	L	F	A	W	D	L	F	A	Pt	GD
1	Buducnost Banovici	6	3	0	0	6	1	1	0	2	4	6	4	0	2	10	7	12	3
2	Siroki Brijeg	6	3	0	0	7	3	1	0	2	1	4	2	1	3	8	8	7	0
3	Posusje	6	1	1	1	3	2	1	0	2	5	6	4	0	2	8	7	12	1
4	Zeljeznicar Sarajevo	6	1	0	2	3	5	0	1	2	1	3	1	1	4	4	8	4	-4

GROUP B

		Pd	W	D	L	F	A	W	D	L	F	A	W	D	L	F	A	Pt	GD
1	Brotnjo Citluk	6	3	0	0	9	1	1	0	2	3	6	4	0	2	12	7	12	5
2	Jedinstvo Bihac	6	3	0	0	8	1	1	0	2	2	5	4	0	2	10	6	12	4
3	Sarajevo	6	3	0	0	6	1	1	0	2	8	5	4	0	2	14	6	12	8
4	Rudar Kakanj	6	0	0	3	2	10	0	0	3	0	9	0	0	6	2	19	0	-17

FINAL
Buducnost Banovici 1, Brotnjo Citluk 1; Brotnjo Citluk 0, Buducnost Banovici 0 (1-1; Brotnjo Citluk champions on away goal)

refusal to accept clubs which were not representative of the whole country. However, even though the Serbs were not involved this time, European football's governing body appreciated the efforts that had been undertaken and made a concession. A full-scale joint Muslim-Croatian league in 2000/01 should ensure that there are no more blank seasons in the future.

Steps are also being taken to unify the Bosnia-Herzegovina national team. The all-Muslim side which competed in the Euro 2000 qualifiers was supplemented by a handful of 'Croatians' in a few low-key friendlies, most of them unofficial, that took place during the winter and early spring.

National team coach Faruk Hadzibegic quit the national team job at the end of the European Championship campaign after failing to agree on the terms of his contract renewal and was succeeded by ex-Zeljeznicar boss Drago Smajlovic. Despite the new intake, Bosnia-Herzegovina's bid to qualify for the 2002 World Cup will be shaped around the same players who faded badly at the end of the Euro 2000 campaign. The team did finish on a high when Real Madrid's expensive new acquisition, striker Elvir Baljic, scored all four goals in a 4-1 win over Estonia, but two earlier defeats by Scotland had already scuppered the team's chances of reaching the play-offs.

NATIONAL TEAM APPEARANCES 99/00

Coach - Faruk HADZIBEGIC; Drago SMAJLOVIC	SCO	CZE	SCO	EST	MAC	Cps	Gls
Mirsad DEDIC (04/02/68) - Sarajevo	G	G				26	-
Omer JOLDIC (01/01/77) - Sloboda Tuzla	D77	D70		D		10	-
Mirsad HIBIC (11/10/73) - Sevilla FC (ESP)	D	D			D	13	-
Muhamed KONJIC (04/05/70) - Coventry City (ENG)	D	D			D	19	2
Jasmin MUJDZA (02/03/74) - Hajduk Split (CRO)	M77					8	-
Marko TOPIC (10/01/76) - Monza (ITA)	M	M70	s77	M	M75	12	1
Sead HALILOVIC (16/03/69) - Altay (TUR)	M62					14	-
Bakir BESIREVIC (03/11/65) - Osijek (CRO)	M	M	D	M		18	-
Sergej BARBAREZ (17/09/71) - Borussia Dortmund (GER)	M	M	M		M	9	1
Elvir BOLIC (10/10/71) - Fenerbahçe (TUR)	A	s70	A	A80	A90	21	10
Meho KODRO (12/01/67) - Deportivo Alavés (ESP)	A	A			A46	13	3
Edin MUJCIN (14/01/70) - Croatia Zagreb (CRO)	s62		M84	s80		15	1
Senad REPUH (18/11/72) - Bursaspor (TUR)	s77	s70				14	1
Enes DEMIROVIC (13/06/72) - Istanbulspor (TUR)	s77	s70				10	-
Mirsad VARESANOVIC (31/05/72) - Bursaspor (TUR)	D	D	D	D		17	-
Nermin SABIC (21/12/73) - Croatia Zagreb (CRO)	M	M	M60	M55		20	-
Faruk IHTIJAREVIC (01/05/76) - Sarajevo	M70	M77	M	s55		6	-
Adnan GUSO (1975) - Erzurumspor (TUR)		G	G	G		3	-
Sead KAPETANOVIC (21/01/72) - Borussia Dortmund (GER)		D	D	D		14	-
Faruk HUJDUROVIC (14/05/70) - SV Ried (AUT)		D	D			2	-
Elvir BALJIC (08/07/74) - Real Madrid (ESP)		A	A89			15	6
Alen AVDIC (03/04/77) - FC Denderleeuw (BEL)		s84	s89			2	-
Samir DURO (18/10/77) - Sarajevo			s60	s75		2	-
Hasan SALIHAMIDZIC (01/01/77) - FC Bayern München (GER)					M46	16	4
Miro KLJAJIC (1978) - Brotnjo Citluk					s46	1	-
Bruno AKRAPOVIC (1976)					s46	1	-
Ivica HULJEV (1977) - Posusje					s90	1	-

DOMESTIC CUP 99/00

FINAL GROUP

Bosna Visoko 2, Zeljeznicar Sarajevo 2
Sloboda Tuzla 2, Bosna Visoko 1
Zeljeznicar Sarajevo 3, Sloboda Tuzla 1

(Zeljeznicar Sarajevo winners)

INTERNATIONAL HONOURS

None

TOP SCORERS

MUSLIM LEAGUE
25   Asmir DZAFIC (Velez Mostar)
     Dzemo SMJECANIN (Dzerdelez Zenica)

HERCEG-BOSNA LEAGUE
18   Robert RISTOVSKI (Kiseljak)
17   Nikola JURCIC (Brotnjo Citluk)

SRPSKA LEAGUE
29   ZDJELAR (Sloboda Novi Grad)
26   GAJIC (Drina Zvornik)

NATIONAL TEAM RESULTS 99/00

04/09/99	Scotland (ECQ)	H	Sarajevo	1-2	Bolic (23)
08/09/99	Czech Republic (ECQ)	A	Teplice	0-3	
05/10/99	Scotland (ECQ)	A	Glasgow	0-1	
09/10/99	Estonia (ECQ)	A	Tallinn	4-1	Baljic (42, 57, 67, 87)
29/03/00	Macedonia	H	Zenica	1-0	Konjic (88)

BULGARIA

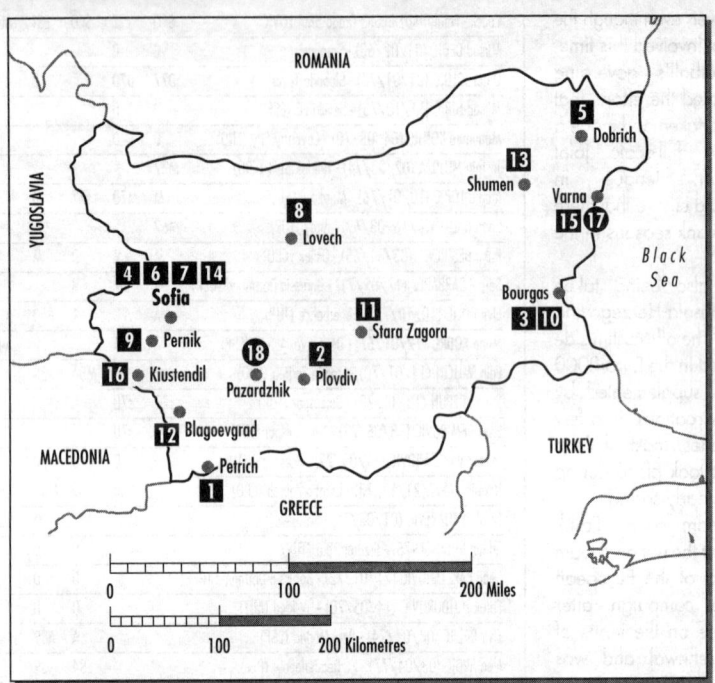

1	BELASITSA PETRICH	203
2	BOTEV PLOVDIV	204
3	CHERNOMORETS BOURGAS	205
4	CSKA SOFIA	206
5	DOBRUDZHA DOBRICH	207
6	LEVSKI SOFIA	208
7	LOKOMOTIV SOFIA	209
8	LOVECH	210
9	MINIOR PERNIK	211
10	NEFTOCHIMIK BOURGAS	212

11	OLYMPIC-BEROE STARA ZAGORA	213
12	PIRIN BLAGOEVGRAD	214
13	SHUMEN	215
14	SLAVIA SOFIA	216
15	SPARTAK VARNA	217
16	VELBAZHD KIUSTENDIL	218
Promoted clubs		
17	CHERNO MORE VARNA	
18	ISKAR-HEBAR PAZARDZHIK	

MLADENOV NAMED AS NATIONAL COACH

Levski stroll home to 21st title

FEDERATION DIRECTORY

Bulgarski Futbolen Soius
ul. Karnigradska 19, 1000 Sofia

tel - (02) 877490/874725
fax - (02) 9862538
website - www.bfu.online.bg

Year of Formation - 1924
Secretary - Ivan Vutsov
President - Ivan Slavkov

Stadium - Vasil Levski, Sofia (70,000)

After a five year gap the Bulgarian title returned to the blue half of the capital as Levski Sofia comfortably held off the challenge of rivals CSKA to register their 21st championship victory.

After two successive seasons in the runners-up spot, Levski made it third time lucky, and they did so without too much undue concern. Even a mid-season change of coach failed to deflect them from their course, and by the end of the campaign they were siting pretty with a ten-point lead, having won 23 of their 30 matches and lost just two.

Newly coached by Ljubomir Petrovic, the Serb who had taken Red Star Belgrade to European Cup glory in 1991, Levski carried on where they had left off the previous season, winning their opening six games and dropping just two points from the first 30 available. The first significant setback came at the end of October when they lost the derby match at CSKA, who thus leapfrogged them into top spot, but by the winter break they had regained the initiative with a three-point advantage.

That lead was trebled two matches into the spring campaign as CSKA stumbled to two heavy defeats, and from there on in Levski were effectively out on their own. They made things hard for themselves with three succesive draws and a shock defeat by lowly Minior Pernik, but a 1-0 'revenge' victory over CSKA in mid-May proved to be the decisive moment of the campaign.

The man in charge of Levski for the second half of the season was Dimitar Dimitrov, who had been tapped by club president Nasko Sirakov while he was still serving as the Bulgarian national coach and persuaded to sign an 18-month deal. A title-winner already with Liteks Lovech two years earlier, Dimitrov did not quite match the success rate of Petrovic in terms of points per matches, but in the closing weeks he brought his influence to bear as

LEAGUE CHAMPIONSHIP RESULTS 99/00

		1	2	3	4	5	6	7	8	9	10	11	12	13	14	15	16
1	Belasitsa Petrich		3-1	1-0	2-0	1-0	0-0	2-2	1-0	2-2	1-1	1-1	4-1	1-0	2-0	1-1	1-2
2	Botev Plovdiv	2-0		0-1	1-2	0-0	1-2	1-0	2-0	1-0	1-2	2-0	2-1	4-0	6-0	6-2	1-0
3	Chernomorets Bourgas	3-0	0-0		0-2	0-0	2-3	1-1	1-1	2-1	0-0	2-1	2-0	1-0	1-0	3-2	1-1
4	CSKA Sofia	3-0	4-0	3-0		4-1	1-0	3-2	2-0	6-1	1-4	3-0	1-1	4-0	3-1	1-0	3-1
5	Dobrudzha Dobrich	3-1	1-0	0-0	0-3		0-1	2-1	1-3	3-1	0-0	2-1	4-2	3-0	2-0	2-0	0-1
6	Levski Sofia	6-0	4-1	2-0	1-0	2-1		3-0	1-1	4-1	2-0	2-0	1-0	3-0	4-1	5-0	3-0
7	Lokomotiv Sofia	2-0	1-1	4-1	0-0	4-0	1-1		2-1	2-3	1-1	4-1	5-1	2-0	6-0	5-0	1-1
8	Lovech	8-0	2-0	2-0	3-2	4-1	1-1	3-2		6-3	0-1	2-0	1-1	6-0	0-1	4-1	3-1
9	Minior Pernik	4-0	1-1	2-1	1-2	4-0	3-2	0-1	4-3		1-0	2-0	2-0	2-0	0-3	1-1	0-2
10	Neftochimik Bourgas	3-0	0-1	2-0	2-1	3-1	1-1	3-2	2-1	4-1		3-0	1-1	1-0	0-0	4-0	1-0
11	Olympic-Beroe Stara Zagora	1-0	5-2	1-0	1-1	1-0	0-1	2-0	0-2	1-0	0-0		4-0	1-0	1-1	2-0	0-4
12	Pirin Blagoevgrad	1-0	3-1	2-3	0-1	2-1	0-1	1-0	0-1	2-0	1-0	2-1		3-1	1-4	2-0	1-0
13	Shumen	0-1	1-2	2-3	0-1	0-1	1-4	1-1	1-0	1-3	1-1	2-1	1-0		0-3	0-3	1-2
14	Slavia Sofia	5-1	3-2	1-0	0-0	2-1	0-2	1-0	1-0	4-1	1-1	1-2	3-1	1-0		0-0	1-2
15	Spartak Varna	3-1	2-1	4-2	1-2	2-0	0-1	2-1	1-0	1-0	1-1	4-0	2-1	4-0	0-0		5-3
16	Velbazhd Kiustendil	2-1	2-0	2-1	3-1	0-0	1-3	1-1	1-3	3-0	1-0	4-0	3-0	6-0	1-0	2-0	

LEAGUE CHAMPIONSHIP FINAL TABLE 99/00

			Home				Away				Total						
		Pd	W	D	L	F	A	W	D	L	F	A	W	D	L	F	A	PT	GD
1	Levski Sofia	30	14	1	0	43	5	9	4	2	23	12	23	5	2	66	17	74	49
2	CSKA Sofia	30	13	1	1	42	11	7	3	5	18	15	20	4	6	60	26	64	34
3	Velbazhd Kiustendil	30	11	2	2	32	10	6	2	7	20	22	17	4	9	52	32	55	20
4	Neftochimik Bourgas	30	11	3	1	30	9	3	8	4	12	12	14	11	5	42	21	53	21
5	Lovech	30	11	2	2	45	14	4	2	9	16	20	15	4	11	61	34	49	27
6	Slavia Sofia	30	9	3	3	24	13	4	3	8	14	27	13	6	11	38	40	45	-2
7	Spartak Varna	30	11	2	2	32	13	1	3	11	10	38	12	5	13	42	51	41	-9
8	Botev Plovdiv	30	10	1	4	30	10	2	3	10	13	32	12	4	14	43	42	40	1
9	Lokomotiv Sofia	30	9	5	1	40	11	1	4	10	14	26	10	9	11	54	37	39	17
10	Chernomorets Bourgas	30	7	6	2	19	12	3	1	11	12	28	10	7	13	31	40	37	-9
11	Minior Pernik	30	9	2	4	27	16	2	1	12	17	42	11	3	16	44	58	36	-14
12	Dobrudzha Dobrich	30	9	2	4	23	14	1	3	11	7	29	10	5	15	30	43	35	-13
13	Olympic-Beroe Stara Zagora	30	9	3	3	20	11	1	1	13	8	36	10	4	16	28	47	34	-19
14	Pirin Blagoevgrad	30	10	0	5	21	14	0	3	12	10	36	10	3	17	31	50	33	-19
15	Belasitsa Petrich	30	8	6	1	23	11	1	0	14	5	46	9	6	15	28	57	33	-29
16	Shumen	30	3	2	10	12	26	0	0	15	1	42	3	2	25	13	68	11	-55

Levski not only strode clear in the championship race but also came through to win the Bulgarian Cup, thereby completing the fourth 'double' in the club's history.

Two late goals in the final against Neftochimik Bourgas completed a nigh-on perfect season for Levski, who had also put up an impressive performance in the UEFA Cup, getting past both APOEL Nicosia and Hajduk Split with their goal unbreached before losing, predictably, to Juventus. Even then, they came within ten minutes of snatching an historic second-leg victory in Turin, albeit after they had already lost 3-1 in Sofia.

As with other recent Bulgarian champions, Levski were not wholly reliant on homegrown players. Their top goalscorer was an African, Ivory Coast striker Serge Yofu, who joined at the start of the season from Dobrudzha Dobrich. And two of the defensive mainstays were also foreigners - Scotsman John Inglis and Yugoslav Predrag Pazin. Of the Bulgarians, penalty-taking goalkeeper Dimitar Ivankov had an excellent season at both ends of the pitch, while Aleksandar Aleksandrov was the main man in midfield and the two Ivanovs, defender Biser and striker Georgi, also made outstanding contributions, not least with their goals in the Cup final.

CSKA, who were beaten home and away by Levski in the quarter-finals of the Cup, finished nine points clear of the third-placed team, Velbazhd Kiustendil, in the

NATIONAL TEAM RESULTS 99/00

18/08/99	Ukraine	A	Kiev	1-1	Petkov I. (90)
04/09/99	Sweden (ECQ)	A	Solna	0-1	
10/10/99	Luxembourg (ECQ)	H	Sofia	3-0	Borimirov (40), Petkov I. (68), Hristov R. (78)
17/11/99	Greece	A	Kozani	0-1	
09/02/00	Slovakia	N	Valparaíso	1-0	Chomakov (82)
12/02/00	Chile	A	Valparaíso	2-3	Berbatov (43), Stoilov (87)
15/02/00	Australia	N	Valparaíso	1-1	Ivanov G. (90)
29/03/00	Belarus	H	Sofia	4-1	Todorov (23), Donkov (42), Petkov I. (61), Petrov S. (80)
26/04/00	Ukraine	H	Sofia	0-1	

TOP SCORERS

20 Misho MIKHAILOV (Velbazhd Kiustendil)
19 Svetoslav TODOROV (Lovech)
16 Plamen TIMNEV (Spartak Varna)
14 Dimitar IVANOV (CSKA Sofia)
   Dimitar BERBATOV (CSKA Sofia)
   Anton EVTIMOV (Minior Pernik)
13 Serge YOFU (Levski Sofia)
12 Georgi IVANOV (Levski Sofia)
10 Anastas PETROV (Botev Plovdiv)

league, but it meant no more than a place in the UEFA Cup for the club which had drafted in ex-international striker Liuboslav Penev as club president the previous summer in a bid to recapture some of their former lustre. There was more than a touch of irony when Dimitar Penev, the CSKA coach and uncle to the president, was sacked after the team's wretched start to the spring campaign. By the end of the season Liuboslav Penev was declaring his readiness to return to the playing field, with former international strike-partner Emil Kostadinov proposing to rejoin him at the spearhead of the CSKA attack.

Defending champions Liteks Lovech had a poor season. They never truly recovered from their early European exit, when, after building a handsome 4-1 first-leg lead over Widzew Lodz in the second preliminary round of the Champions' League, they lost the return by the same score and ended up going out on penalties. Their elimination was doubly painful because it resulted in the loss of their sponsor. Hence the name change back to plain 'Lovech'.

The one consolation for Lovech might have been a Golden Boot crown for their Bulgarian international forward Svetoslav Todorov, but he was pipped at the post in highly dubious circumstances by Velbazhd Kiustendil's Misho Mikhailov, who lifted his total to 20 goals by scoring a hat-trick in his team's final fixture - a 5-3 defeat by Spartak Varna. Suspicions of a deliberate 'trade-off' were still lingering long after the season had ended.

Mikhailov's club, which had changed its name from Levski to Velbazhd in July 1999, did well to finish third and also reach the semi-finals of the Cup. Their reward was a place in the InterToto. The third bona fide European place went to Neftochimik, the unfortunate beaten Cup finalists, who might have finished higher than fourth in the

INTERNATIONAL HONOURS

World Cup Finals appearances: 1962, 1966, 1970, 1974, 1986 (2nd round), 1994 (4th), 1998

European Championship appearances: 1968, 1996

DOMESTIC CUP 99/00

1/16 FINALS
Golemi Vrakh Dolna Sekira 1, Spartak Varna 6
Cherno More Varna 2, Pirin Blagoevgrad 0
Yunak Shumen 1, Botev Plovdiv 4
Venets Oreshets 0, CSKA Sofia 4
Iskar Sofia 2, Levski Sofia 4
Vidima Rakovski Sevlievo 0, Lokomotiv Sofia 0
(aet; 3-4 on pens.)
Spartak Plovdiv 0, Neftochimik Bourgas 2
Velbazhd Kiustendil 1, Dunav Ruse 0
Iskar German 0, Shumen 0 (aet; 7-8 on pens.)
Slavia Sofia 3, Kremikovtsi 0
Maritsa Plovdiv 1, Chernomorets Bourgas 2
Belasitsa Petrich 1, Lokomotiv Plovdiv 0
Botev Vratsa 1, Minior Pernik 2
Spartak Pleven 0, Olympic-Beroe Stara Zagora 2
Dobrudzha Dobrich 10, Khaskovo 0
Lovech 3, Septemvri Sofia 1

1/8 FINALS
Cherno More Varna v Chernomorets Bourgas 0-2; 1-2
(Chernomortes Bourgas 4-1)
Velbazhd Kiustendil v Spartak Varna 3-0; 3-4
(Velbazhd Kiustendil 6-4)
Levski Sofia v Lovech 2-0; 1-3
(3-3; Levski Sofia on away goal)
Botev Plovdiv v Minior Pernik 2-0; 2-0
(Botev Plovdiv 4-0)
Neftochimik Bourgas v Olympic-Beroe Stara Zagora
3-0; 4-1
(Neftochimik Bourgas 7-1)

Slavia Sofia v CSKA Sofia 1-2; 1-1
(CSKA Sofia 3-2)
Dobrudzha Dobrich v Shumen 2-1; 0-4
(Shumen 5-2)
Lokomotiv Sofia v Belasitsa Petrich 4-1; 0-1
(Lokomotiv Sofia 4-2)

QUARTER-FINALS
CSKA Sofia 0, Levski Sofia 1 (Ivanov G. 78)
Levski Sofia 3 (Pavlov 17, Ivanov G. 35,
Ivankov 62p), CSKA Sofia 1 (Ivanov D. 86p)
(Levski Sofia 4-1)
Lokomotiv Sofia 3 (Mitov 38, 64, Peev 88p),
Velbazhd Kiustendil 1 (Stoichev 16)
Velbazhd Kiustendil 2 (Stoianov I. 4, Mikhailov 40),
Lokomotiv Sofia 0
(3-3; Velbazhd Kiustendil on away goal)
Shumen 5 (Hristianov 20, Paleikov 41, 55,
Miroslavov 52, 64),
Chernomorets Bourgas 1 (Georgiev 29)
Chernomorets Bourgas 6 (Banev 10, 77, 81,
Edinho 24, 45, Stoikov 76),
Shumen 0
(Chernomorets Bourgas 7-5)
Neftochimik Bourgas 3 (Yanchev 61, Branimirov 81,
Petkov 86),
Botev Plovdiv 0
Botev Plovdiv 1 (Georgiev G. 49),
Neftochimik Bourgas 1 (Kiselichkov 13)
(Neftochimik Bourgas 4-1)

SEMI-FINALS
Levski Sofia 6 (Ivanov G. 10, 90, Ivankov 26p,
Dimitrov 40, Aleksandrov 70, Milovanovic 72),
Velbazhd Kiustendil 1 (Hristev 74)
Velbazhd Kiustendil 1 (Yordanov 86), Levski Sofia 0
(Levski Sofia 6-2)

Chernomorets Bourgas 2 (Banev 4, 76),
Neftochimik Bourgas 2 (Dimitrov 28, Kiselichkov 90)
Neftochimik Bourgas 3 (Chilikov 31, 70,
Parushev 50p),
Chernomorets Bourgas 1 (Stoikov 22)
(Neftochimik Bourgas 5-3)

FINAL
31/05/2000, Plovdiv
LEVSKI SOFIA 2 Ivanov G. (85), Ivanov B. (89)
NEFTOCHIMIK BOURGAS 0
referee - Genov
LEVSKI SOFIA - Ivankov, Sirakov, Stoilov, Ivanov B.,
Pazin, Inglis, Aleksandrov (Vachev 90), Atanasov
(Milovanovic 62), Ivanov G., Telkiiski (Nikolov 46),
Topuzakov.
NEFTOCHIMIK BOURGAS - Gospodinov, Orachev
(Petrov 77), Branimirov, Ibraimov (Petkov 89),
Parushev, Hristov D., Yanchev, Dimitrov S., Chilikov,
Kiselichkov, Gruev.

league had they been able to transfer their form in the big matches ('doubles' over CSKA and Lovech, for example) to the lesser fixtures. They also struggled to score goals - a characteristic which would haunt them in the Cup final when a number of chances went begging, leaving coach Dimitar Stoichev and his players to rue the missed opportunity of a first significant trophy for the Black Sea club.

The fight to avoid relegation was more intense than usual, with as many as five clubs going down as a result

NATIONAL TEAM APPEARANCES 99/00

Coach - Dimitar DIMITROV; Stoicho MLADENOV	UKR	SWE	LUX	GRE	SVK	CHL	AUS	BLS	UKR	Cps	Gls
Yordan GOSPODINOV (15/06/78) - Neftochimik Bourgas	G					G37				2	-
Georgi PEEV (11/03/79) - Lokomotiv Sofia	D67				M68	s41	D46	s46	s10	6	-
Zlatomir ZAGORCIC (15/06/71) - Lovech	D46	D25	D82	D46						14	-
Ivailo YORDANOV (22/04/68) - Sporting CP (POR)	D		D	D						49	3
Ivailo PETKOV (07/12/75) - Istanbulspor (TUR)	D	D	D	D	D	D	D	D	D	27	3
Zlatko YANKOV (07/06/66) - Neftochimik Bourgas	M	s25								79	4
Daniel BORIMIROV (15/01/70) - TSV 1860 München (GER)	M	M	M	M	M77	M41	s46	D	M60	54	5
Stilian PETROV (05/07/79) - Celtic (SCO)	M67	M	M	M90	M	M	M75	M	M10	17	1
Milen PETKOV (12/01/74) - CSKA Sofia/AEK (GRE)	M	M		M				M60	M46	16	-
Marian HRISTOV (29/07/73) - 1.FC Kaiserslautern (GER)	A46	A	A64	A80						17	2
Hristo YOVOV (04/11/77) - 1.FC Köln (GER)	A60	s46								11	3
Rosen KIRILOV (04/01/73) - Adanaspor (TUR)	s46	D		s46						12	-
Svetoslav TODOROV (30/08/78) - Lovech	s46	A46	s64	s80	A	A	A89	A76	A55	15	1
Georgi BACHEV (18/04/77) - Levski Sofia	s60		A50							15	1
Georgi MARKOV (20/01/72) - Lokomotiv Sofia	s67	D	D	D			D	D	D	13	1
Ilia GRUEV (30/10/69) - Neftochimik Bourgas	s67	s88								13	1
Dimitar IVANKOV (30/10/75) - Levski Sofia		G								5	-
Stanimir STOILOV (13/02/67) - Levski Sofia		D88	D	D		D	D	s60		14	3
Zdravko ZDRAVKOV (04/10/70) - Adanaspor (TUR)			G	G	G	s37	G	G	G	33	-
Aleksandar ALEKSANDROV (19/01/75) - Levski Sofia			M	M65	s55	s70	M	s81	s60	8	-
Rumen HRISTOV (22/03/75) - CSKA Sofia			s50							1	1
Biser IVANOV (24/04/73) - Levski Sofia			s82		D	D	D		D	5	-
Dimitar BERBATOV (30/01/81) - CSKA Sofia				s65		A56	A46			3	1
Todor YANCHEV (19/05/76) - Neftochimik Bourgas				s90						1	-
Krasimir CHOMAKOV (08/06/77) - CSKA Sofia					D					3	1
Ilian ILIEV (02/07/68) - CS Marítimo (POR)					M55	M70		M46		31	2
Georgi IVANOV (02/07/76) - Levski Sofia					A56		s75	s46	s55	14	1
Martin PETROV (15/01/79) - Servette FC Genève (SUI)					s56	s56	s46	s76	s55	6	-
Veselin VELIKOV (19/03/77) - CSKA Sofia					s68	D	s89			3	-
Ilian STOIANOV (25/11/77) - Velbazhd Kiustendil					s77					8	-
Veselin BRANIMIROV (25/08/77) - Neftochimik Bourgas						D	D			2	-
Elin TOPUZAKOV (05/02/77) - Levski Sofia								D	s46	2	-
Krasimir BALAKOV (29/03/66) - VfB Stuttgart (GER)								M81	M	71	12
Georgi DONKOV (02/06/70) - 1.FC Köln (GER)								A46	A55	9	2
Deian DONCHEV (08/01/74) - Spartak Varna									D	1	-

EUROPEAN CUPS 99/00

CHAMPIONS' CUP
● **LITEKS LOVECH**
Preliminary round 1 GLENTORAN (NIR)
H 3-0 Haxhi (12), Bushi (35p), Petrov (82)
Vutov, Dimitrov N., Zagorcic, Kolev, Ibraimov, Johnston, Haxhi, Petrov,
Emilov (Rusev 46), Bushi (Motta 78), Todorov (Dimitrov V. 70).
A 2-0 Haxhi (65), Bushi (90)
Vutov, Ibraimov (Rusev 80), Zagorcic, Kolev, Zhelev, Dimitrov N., Haxhi,
Johnson, Petrov (Emilov 75), Bushi, Todorov (Dimitrov V. 71).

Preliminary round 2 WIDZEW LODZ (POL)
H 4-1 Todorov (40, 78), Zivkovic (82p), Kondev (90)
Vutov, Dimitrov N., Zagorcic, Kolev, Johnson, Ibraimov (Rusev 46), Bushi,
Petrov (Zivkovic 62), Todorov, Haxhi (Kondev 63), Jelenkovic.
A 1-4 (aet; 3-2 on pens.) Todorov (30)
Vutov, Dimitrov N. (Kishishev 66; Kondev 104), Zagorcic, Kolev, Zhelev,
Jelenkovic, Zivkovic, Johnson, Haxhi, Bushi, Todorov (Motta 66).

UEFA CUP
● **CSKA SOFIA**
Qualifying round PORTADOWN (NIR)
A 3-0 Manchev (1), Kovacevic (77), Bukarev (85)
Lukic, Kremenliev, Mrkic, Chomakov, Trenchev, Paskov (Deianov 64),
Hristov (Bukarev 81), Litera, Simeonov, Sarac, Manchev (Kovacevic 61).
H 5-0 Petkov (15p), Litera (29, 51), Hristov (63p), Simeonov (81)
Lukic, Kremenliev, Mrkic, Trenchev, Sarac, Litera (Paskov 82), Chomakov,
Petkov, Berbatov (Simeonov 65), Hristov, Kovacevic (Manchev 58).

1st round NEWCASTLE UNITED (ENG)
H 0-2
Lukic, Kremenliev (Ivanov G. 60), Mrkic, Sarac, Trenchev (Litera 55),
Velikov, Chomakov, Hristov (Ivanov D. 56), Berbatov, Petkov, Manchev.

A 2-2 Litera (29), Simeonov (90)
Lukic, Kremenliev, Mrkic, Tomash, Velikov, Antonov, Litera (Deianov 84),
Kiosev, Ivanov D. (Simeonov 55), Berbatov, Bukarev (Hristov 78).

● **LEVSKI SOFIA**
Qualifying round APOEL NICOSIA (CYP)
A 0-0
Ivankov, Topuzakov, Pazin, Dionisiev, Sirakov (Stankov 72), Inglis,
Stoilov, Ivanov B., Aleksandrov, Ivanov G., Lazarov (Atanasov 57).
H 2-0 Sirakov (67), Pazin (75)
Ivankov, Ivanov B., Stoilov (Genchev 90), Dimitrov, Pazin, Inglis,
Aleksandrov (Atanasov 79), Sirakov, Ivanov G., Topuzakov, Yofu
(Lazarov 69).

1st round HAJDUK SPLIT (CRO)
A 0-0
Ivankov, Stankov, Stoilov, Ivanov B., Pazin, Inglis, Aleksandrov
(Atanasov 90), Bachev (Yofu 80), Ivanov G., Sirakov, Topuzakov.
H 3-0 Ivankov (16p), Bachev (33), Dimitrov (85)
Ivankov, Stankov, Stoilov, Ivanov B. (Dimitrov 83), Pazin, Inglis
(Dionisiev 55), Aleksandrov, Bachev, Yofu (Georgiev 75), Sirakov,
Topuzakov.

2nd round JUVENTUS (ITA)
H 1-3 Yofu (54)
Ivankov, Stankov (Telkiiski 77), Pazin, Ivanov B., Dionisiev
(Dimitrov 71), Inglis, Aleksandrov (Atanasov 85), Yofu, Ivanov G.,
Sirakov, Topuzakov.
A 1-1 Atanasov (15)
Ivankov, Stoilov, Ivanov B., Dionisiev, Bachev, Dimitrov, Aleksandrov
(Telkiiski 90), Atanasov (Inglis 75), Ivanov G. (Yofu 55), Sirakov,
Topuzakov.

---

of the top division being reduced from 16 to 14 clubs. Shumen, who had been saved from relegation at the eleventh hour the previous summer due to Metalurg Pernik's enforced demotion for match-fixing, probably wished they had gone down anyway. They were cast adrift early on and finished up with a paltry eight points. For the other clubs in the basement, however, there was plenty of stress and tension. Ultimately, Belasistsa Petrich and Pirin Blagoevgrad both went down automatically and Dobrudzha followed them in the play-offs.

Dobrudzha looked a lost cause during the first half of the season after losing each of their opening eight matches, but a tremendous fightback in the spring almost earned them a miraculous escape from the drop. They made it as far as the play-offs, but unlike Olympic-Beroe Stara Zagora, who successfully came through their end-of-season death-or-glory encounter against Spartak Pleven, Dobrudzha ran out of steam and lost to newly merged Iskar-Hebar Pazardzhik, who thus joined Second Division champions Cherno More Varna in the new-look 14-team top flight. A further reduction will be carried out at the end

of the 2000/01 season in order to bring the First Division down to just 12 teams.

Like the domestic league, the Bulgarian national team is undergoing a period of transition. The abject failure of the Euro 2000 qualifying campaign, in which Bulgaria beat Luxembourg and nobody else, confirmed the end of a golden era for the team, which peaked of course at the 1994 World Cup in the United States when the so-called 'Stoichkov generation' finished in fourth place.

Dimitar Dimitrov's defection to Levski Sofia in December 1999 forced the Bulgarian FA to search anew for a coach capable of leading the team into the new millennium. Hristo Stoichkov himself seemed to be the obvious candidate. He had ended his playing career in Japan and had been appointed in a nebulous 'technical director' role only a few months earlier. However, it was felt that Stoichkov still had much to learn as a coach, and as the great man subsequently decided to relaunch his playing career in America with MLS side Chicago Fire, 43-year-old Stoicho Mladenov was promoted from the Under-21s to take charge of the national team.

Mladenov was one of Bulgaria's leading players during the 1980s. He appeared at the 1986 World Cup in Mexico and scored 15 goals in 59 international appearances. At club level he won three national titles with CSKA Sofia before ending his career in Portugal, which is where he first became a coach.

The new man's first test was a winter tour to Chile, which was followed up by an encouraging 4-1 victory at home to Belarus. The main feature of that game was the return from international exile of veteran playmaker Krasimir Balakov, and such was the Stuttgart schemer's impact that it seemed Mladenov would be relying heavily on him to lead an otherwise young and inexperienced team into the World Cup qualifiers.

With the Czech Republic, Denmark, Iceland, Northern Ireland and Malta to contend with, Bulgaria cannot be too pessimistic about their chances of reaching the World Cup finals for the third time in succession. With talented yougsters such as Stilian Petrov, Svetoslav Todorov, Martin Petrov and Dimitar Berbatov coming through, there is a possibility that the team could be regenerated in time for 2002. But Mladenov, more than anyone else, knows that the task will be anything but easy.

PLAYER OF THE SEASON

DIMITAR BERBATOV

It is inevitable that from now on every young Bulgarian forward with a touch of class will be compared to Hristo Stoichkov, but the view from Bulgaria during the 1999/2000 season was that one truly outstanding candidate to follow in the great man's footsteps has already emerged. Dimitar Berbatov was an 18-year-old fringe player at CSKA Sofia when the campaign began, but barely a few weeks into it the young striker was being afforded praise of the highest order. He scored seven goals in CSKA's first seven games and although he could only double that total by the season's end, he had done more than enough to merit inclusion in the Bulgarian national side. He celebrated his first international start with a goal against Chile in Valparaíso, and as news of his talent spread across Europe, it was Italian club Lecce who jumped to the front of the queue to secure his signature during the summer.

PROMOTED CLUBS 99/00

SECOND DIVISION FINAL TABLE

		Pd	W	D	L	F	A	Pt	GD
1	**Cherno More Varna**	**30**	**23**	**1**	**6**	**59**	**27**	**70**	**32**
2	Spartak Pleven	30	21	4	5	57	32	67	25
3	**Iskar-Hebar Pazardzhik**	**30**	**17**	**5**	**8**	**51**	**31**	**56**	**20**
4	Dunav Ruse	30	15	5	10	43	35	50	8
5	Botev Vratsa	30	14	3	13	48	48	45	0
6	Vidima Rakovski Sevlievo	30	12	5	13	40	40	41	0
7	Lokomotiv Plovdiv	30	12	3	15	28	38	39	-10
8	Metalurg Pernik	30	11	5	14	29	33	38	-4
9	Septemvri Sofia	30	10	8	12	44	49	38	-5
10	Svetkavitsa Targovishte	30	11	5	14	35	43	38	-8
11	Kremikovtsi Vidin	30	10	8	12	35	35	38	0
12	Haskovo	30	11	4	15	36	43	37	-7
13	Etar Veliko Tarnovo	30	10	7	13	32	38	37	-6
14	Antibiotik Ludogorets Razgrad	30	11	4	15	31	36	37	-5
15	Maritsa Plovdiv	30	9	6	15	29	39	33	-10
16	Beroe 2000 Stara Zagora	30	3	7	20	21	51	16	-30

PROMOTION/RELEGATION PLAY-OFFS
Iskar-Hebar Pazardzhik 1, Dobrudzha Dobrich 0
Olympic-Beroe Stara Zagora 2, Spartak Pleven 0

CLUB DIRECTORIES

FC Cherno More
Ticha stadion
Varna
tel - (052) 302243/303392/302777
Year of Formation - 1913
President - Krasen Kralev
Manager - Bozhil Kolev
Coach - Radi Zdravkov
Stadium - Ticha (4,000)

MAJOR HONOURS
League Championship - (4)
1925, 1926, 1934, 1938.

FK Iskar-Hebar
Pazardzhik
Year of Formation - 2000
President - Dimitar Dimitrov
Coach - Voin Voinov
Stadium - Georgi Benkovski (12,000)

BELASITSA PETRICH

CLUB DIRECTORY

FC Belasitsa
Ul. Stadionska 2, 2850 Petrich
tel - (0745) 23554
Year of Formation - 1923
President - Kostadin Hadzhiivanov
Director - Rumen Popov
Coach - Grigor Petkov; Dimitar Aleksiev; Petar Kurdov; Ilia Karadaliev
Stadium - Tsar Samuil (9,000)

APPEARANCES 99/00

		P	Ap	(s)	Gls
Georgi ALEKSANDROV	A	23	(1)		2
Dimitar ATANASOVSKI	G	1			
Mirko BABIC (YUG)	M	7			
Stoil BOIADZHIEV	D	17	(5)		
Nikolai BOICHEV	M	7			1
Hary BORISLAVOV	M	4	(4)		
Georgi CHAKAROV	D	3			
Andriy CHOPENKO (UKR)	A	10	(5)		1
Vevzi DAVLEDOV (UZB)	M	12			
Ivan DIMITROV	A	23	(1)		5
Shteriu DIMITROV	A	7	(7)		1
Engibar ENGIBAROV	D	21			6
Georgi GEORGIEV	A	3			
Ventsislav ILIEV	M	9			
Taso JOVANOVIC (YUG)	M	3	(3)		1
Vasil KAMBUROV	G	12	(1)		
Svetlan KONDEV	A	4			1
Ivan LIBOV	M	1			
Petar MALINOV	M	8	(15)		
Vladimir MANOLKOV	G	8			
Ivan MILANOV	A	17	(3)		2
Nesko MILOVANOVIC (YUG)	M	8	(2)		5
Yasin MISHAUI	A	14	(5)		2
Yulian NIKOLOV	D	7	(6)		
Koba NINOA	D	1			
Ilko OPRENOV	A		(4)		
Petko PETKOV	G	9			
Georgi PETROV	D	7	(3)		
Miodrag RADULOVIC (YUG)	M	2	(2)		
Emil SHALAMANOV	D	16	(1)		1
Valentin STANKOV	A		(2)		
Krasimir STOIANOV	M	16	(4)		
Rosen STOIANOV	D	10	(2)		
Tsanko STOICHKOV	A		(6)		
Liubomir UZUNOV	M	1	(2)		
Marko VASILIJEVIC (YUG)	M	10	(1)		
Anatoli VATEV	D	3	(1)		
Valentin YAKOV	D	26			

LEAGUE RESULTS 1999/2000

07/08/99	Dobrudzha Dobrich	H	1-0	Dimitrov I.
14/08/99	Botev Plovdiv	A	0-2	
20/08/99	Pirin Blagoevgrad	H	4-1	Dimitrov I., Milanov 2 (1p), Shalamanov (p)
28/08/99	Chernomorets Bourgas	A	0-3	
11/09/99	Shumen	H	1-0	Engibarov (p)
19/09/99	Levski Sofia	A	0-6	
25/09/99	Lokomotiv Sofia	H	2-2	Milovanovic, Dimitrov S.
02/10/99	Olympic-Beroe Stara Zagora	A	0-1	
17/10/99	Spartak Varna	H	1-1	Milovanovic
24/10/99	Lovech	H	1-0	Milovanovic
30/10/99	Neftochimik Bourgas	A	0-3	
06/11/99	Velbazhd Kiustendil	H	1-2	Dimitrov I.
20/11/99	Minior Pernik	A	0-4	
27/11/99	CSKA Sofia	H	2-0	Milovanovic 2
04/12/99	Slavia Sofia	A	1-5	Dimitrov I.
26/02/00	Dobrudzha Dobrich	A	1-3	Engibarov (p)
04/03/00	Botev Plovdiv	H	3-1	Mishaui, Aleksandrov, Dimitrov I.
11/03/00	Pirin Blagoevgrad	A	0-1	
18/03/00	Chernomorets Bourgas	H	1-0	Mishaui
25/03/00	Shumen	A	1-0	Jovanovic
31/03/00	Belasitsa Petrich	H	0-0	
08/04/00	Lokomotiv Sofia	A	0-2	
22/04/00	Olympic-Beroe Stara Zagora	H	1-1	Engibarov
29/04/00	Spartak Varna	A	1-3	Chopenko
06/05/00	Lovech	A	0-8	
13/05/00	Neftochimik Bourgas	H	1-1	Engibarov (p)
20/05/00	Velbazhd Kiustendil	A	1-2	Aleksandrov
27/05/00	Minior Pernik	H	2-2	Boichev, Engibarov
03/06/00	CSKA Sofia	A	0-3	
09/06/00	Slavia Sofia	H	2-0	Kondev, Engibarov

BOTEV PLOVDIV

CLUB DIRECTORY

FC Botev Plovdiv
Bul. Istochen 10, 4000 Plovdiv
tel - (032) 226375/225736
fax - (032) 226388
Year of Formation - 1912
President - Dimitar Hristolov
Director - Slavcho Horozov
Coach - Petar Zekhtinski; Marin Bakalov;
Dinko Dermendzhiev
Stadium - Hristo Botev (21,000)

MAJOR HONOURS
League Championship - (2) 1929, 1967.

APPEARANCES 99/00

	P	Ap	(s)	Gls
Armen AMBARZUMIAN	G	28		1
Kiril ANDONOV	D	27		1
Decho ARIZANOV	M		(1)	
Daniel ATANASOV	D	1		
Dian BOZHILOV	M	18	(7)	3
Aleksandar DIMITROV	A		(1)	
Geno DOBREVSKI	A	13	(7)	4
Georgi GEORGIEV	A	30		1
Manol GEORGIEV	M	11	(13)	3
Dimitar HADZHIEV	D	25	(4)	
Borislav IVANOV	M		(5)	
Krasimir KAMBUROV	A		(2)	
Asen KARASLAVOV	M	3	(2)	
Boris KHVOINEV	A	4		2
Nikolai KIROV	G	2		
Vasil KOLEV	D	13		
Plamen KRUMOV	A	11	(1)	
Evgeni KURDOV	A	1	(6)	1
Mario METUSHEV	M		(2)	
Nedko MILENOV	M		(2)	
Georgi MINKOV	D	1	(5)	
Benjamin NIETO (CMR)	M		(3)	
Petar PENCHEV	D	27	(1)	2
Anastas PETROV	A	23	(3)	10
Zaprian RAKOV	D	4	(1)	
Petar SHOPOV	D	11	(1)	
Todor SIMEONOV	D	17	(2)	1
Ivan TANCHOVSKI	M	11	(8)	
Vladimir TILEV	D	9	(1)	
Andrei TODOROV	D		(3)	
Kostadin VIDOLOV	M	22		8
Georgi VLADIMIROV	A	13	(1)	4
Ivan YOTOVSKI	M	5	(7)	1

LEAGUE RESULTS 1999/2000

07/08/99	Olympic-Beroe Stara Zagora	A	2-5	Dobrevski 2 (2p)
14/08/99	Belasitsa Petrich	H	2-0	Khvoinev, Dobrevski (p)
21/08/99	Lovech	A	0-2	
28/08/99	Neftochimik Bourgas	H	1-2	Khvoinev
11/09/99	Velbazhd Kiustendil	A	0-2	
18/09/99	Minior Pernik	H	1-0	Bozhilov
25/09/99	CSKA Sofia	A	0-4	
02/10/99	Slavia Sofia	H	6-0	Yotovski, Petrov 3, Vidolov, Bozhilov
17/10/99	Dobrudzha Dobrich	A	0-1	
23/10/99	Spartak Varna	A	1-2	Petrov
30/10/99	Pirin Blagoevgrad	H	2-1	Petrov (p), Georgiev M.
06/11/99	Chernomorets Bourgas	A	0-0	
20/11/99	Shumen	H	4-0	Georgiev M. 2, Petrov 2 (1p)
28/11/99	Levski Sofia	A	1-4	Penchev
04/12/99	Lokomotiv Sofia	H	1-0	Andonov
26/02/00	Olympic-Beroe Stara Zagora	H	2-0	Vidolov, og (Mirchev)
04/03/00	Belasitsa Petrich	A	1-3	Penchev
11/03/00	Lovech	H	2-0	Vladimirov, Petrov
19/03/00	Neftochimik Bourgas	A	1-0	Vladimirov
26/03/00	Velbazhd Kiustendil	H	1-0	Petrov
01/04/00	Minior Pernik	A	1-1	Dobrevski
09/04/00	CSKA Sofia	H	1-2	Vidolov
22/04/00	Slavia Sofia	A	2-3	Vidolov 2
29/04/00	Dobrudzha Dobrich	H	0-0	
06/05/00	Spartak Varna	H	6-2	Georgiev G. (p), Vidolov 3, Simeonov, Vladimirov
13/05/00	Pirin Blagoevgrad	A	1-3	Bozhilov
20/05/00	Chernomorets Bourgas	H	0-1	
27/05/00	Shumen	A	2-1	Vladimirov, Kurdov
03/06/00	Levski Sofia	H	1-2	Ambarzumian (p)
09/06/00	Lokomotiv Sofia	A	1-1	Petrov

CHERNOMORETS BOURGAS

CLUB DIRECTORY

FC Chernomorets
Ul. Industrialna 12
8000 Bourgas
tel - (056) 47787/47423
Year of Formation - 1919
President - Dimitar Terziev
Director - Rusi Gochev
Coach - Ivan Kiuchukov
Stadium - Chernomorets (22,000)

APPEARANCES 99/00

	P	Ap	(s)	Gls
ADRIANO Felício (BRA)	A	7	(4)	4
Marin BAICHEV	D	11	(2)	
Ilian BANEV	A	13	(8)	4
Ivan DONCHEV	D	8	(1)	
Kostadin DZHAMBAZOV	D	16	(6)	1
Carlos EDINHO (BRA)	D	15	(3)	3
Stanimir GEORGIEV	A	17	(7)	1
Yuri IVANIKOV	M	12	(10)	1
Petar KIUMIURDZHIEV	D	8	(1)	
Miroslav KOSEV	M	12	(9)	1
Petar KOSTADINOV	M	6	(12)	1
Ivan KURTEV	D	11		1
Milen PENCHEV	D	15	(1)	
Gergin PETROV	G	7	(1)	
Venko PETROV	D	11	(2)	
Todor POPOV	G	22		
Petar RAKHNEV	G	1		
Angel STOIKOV	A	28		5
Ivan TENEV	D	8		
Stefan TRAIKOV	D	13	(9)	
Atanas YANKOV	D	23		
Petar YANKOV	A	14	(8)	4
Slavi ZHEKOV	A	28	(1)	5
Stoian ZHELEV	M	21		
Ivo ZHELEZAROV	A	3	(3)	

LEAGUE RESULTS 1999/2000

06/08/99	Levski Sofia	A	0-2	
14/08/99	Lokomotiv Sofia	H	1-1	Zhekov
21/08/99	Olympic-Beroe Stara Zagora	A	0-1	
28/08/99	Belasitsa Petrich	H	3-0	Georgiev, Yankov, Dzhambazov
11/09/99	Lovech	A	0-2	
17/09/99	Neftochimik Bourgas	H	0-0	
25/09/99	Velbazhd Kiustendil	A	1-2	Banev
02/10/99	Minior Pernik	H	2-1	Yankov 2
17/10/99	CSKA Sofia	A	0-3	
23/10/99	Slavia Sofia	H	1-0	Kosev
30/10/99	Dobrudzha Dobrich	A	0-0	
06/11/99	Botev Plovdiv	H	0-0	
20/11/99	Pirin Blagoevgrad	A	3-2	Ivanikov, Yankov, Banev
27/11/99	Spartak Varna	A	2-4	Stoikov (p), Edinho
04/12/99	Shumen	H	1-0	Zhekov
26/02/00	Levski Sofia	H	2-3	Stoikov 2
04/03/00	Lokomotiv Sofia	A	1-4	Zhekov
11/03/00	Olympic-Beroe Stara Zagora	H	2-1	Zhekov, Stoikov (p)
18/03/00	Belasitsa Petrich	A	0-1	
25/03/00	Lovech	H	1-1	Kurtev
01/04/00	Neftochimik Bourgas	A	0-2	
08/04/00	Velbazhd Kiustendil	H	1-1	Zhekov
22/04/00	Minior Pernik	A	1-2	Adriano
28/04/00	CSKA Sofia	H	0-2	
06/05/00	Slavia Sofia	A	0-1	
13/05/00	Dobrudzha Dobrich	H	0-0	
20/05/00	Botev Plovdiv	A	1-0	Stoikov
27/05/00	Pirin Blagoevgrad	H	2-0	Kostadinov, Adriano
03/06/00	Spartak Varna	H	3-2	Adriano 2, Edinho
09/06/00	Shumen	A	3-2	Banev 2, Edinho

CSKA SOFIA

CLUB DIRECTORY

FC CSKA Sofia
Stadion Bulgarska Armia
Bul. Dragan Tsankov 3, 1504 Sofia
tel - (02) 9630998/9633965/9630632
Year of Formation - 1948
President - Liuboslav Penev
Directors - Rumen Yankov, Emil Kostadinov
Coach - Dimitar Penev; Spas Dzhevizov;
Aleksandar Stankov
Stadium - Bulgarska Armia (24,000)

MAJOR HONOURS
League Championship - (28) 1948, 1951, 1952,
1954, 1955, 1956, 1957, 1958, 1959, 1960,
1961, 1962, 1966, 1969, 1971, 1972, 1973,
1975, 1976, 1980, 1981, 1982, 1983, 1987,
1989, 1990, 1992, 1997.
Domestic Cup - (9) 1981, 1983, 1985, 1987,
1988, 1989, 1993, 1997, 1999.

APPEARANCES 99/00

	P	Ap	(s)	Gls
Stanislav ANGELOV	M	9	(1)	1
Georgi ANTONOV	D	8	(4)	1
Dimitar BERBATOV	A	26	(1)	14
Asen BUKAREV	A	10	(13)	5
Krasimir CHOMAKOV	D	22		6
Metodi DEIANOV	M	21	(6)	3
Rosen EMILOV	M	2	(6)	
Stefan GIGLIO (MLT)	A	4		3
Rumen HRISTOV	A	12	(5)	3
Dimitar IVANOV	A	19	(8)	14
Galin IVANOV	D	29		2
Ivailo IVANOV	G	8		
Rumen KALCHEV	A	2	(4)	1
Georgi KIOSEV	M	3	(6)	
Todor KIUCHUKOV	G	16	(1)	
Emil KREMENLIEV	D	26		
Ivan LITERA (YUG)	M		(1)	
Stefan LULCHEV	D	2	(2)	
Vladimir MANCHEV	A	12	(10)	3
Sasa MRKIC (YUG)	D	2	(2)	
Yevgeniy NEMODRUG (UKR)	G	6		
Ivan PASKOV	M	7	(3)	
Milen PEIKOV	M	13		1
Svetoslav PETROV	A	12	(1)	2
Stanislav RUMENOV	A		(3)	
Genadi SIMEONOV	A		(2)	
Aleksandar TOMASH	M	30		1
Ivo TRENCHEV	D	5	(2)	
Veselin VELIKOV	D	24		
Petar ZLATINSKI	M		(2)	

LEAGUE RESULTS 1999/2000

06/08/99	Neftochimik Bourgas	A	1-2	Chomakov (p)
15/08/99	Velbazhd Kiustendil	H	3-1	Ivanov D. 2, Berbatov
21/08/99	Minior Pernik	A	2-1	Hristov 2
29/08/99	Spartak Varna	A	2-1	Manchev, Berbatov
10/09/99	Slavia Sofia	H	3-1	Petkov (p), Berbatov, Ivanov D.
19/09/99	Dobrudzha Dobrich	A	3-0	Berbatov 2, Bukarev
25/09/99	Botev Plovdiv	H	4-0	Ivanov D., Bukarev, Berbatov 2
03/10/99	Pirin Blagoevgrad	A	1-0	Chomakov
17/10/99	Chernomorets Bourgas	H	3-0	Chomakov (p), Ivanov D., Bukarev
24/10/99	Shumen	A	1-0	Ivanov D.
30/10/99	Levski Sofia	H	1-0	Ivanov D.
07/11/99	Lokomotiv Sofia	A	0-0	
20/11/99	Olympic-Beroe Stara Zagora	H	3-0	Ivanov D. 2, Tomash
27/11/99	Belasitsa Petrich	A	0-2	
05/12/99	Lovech	H	2-0	Antonov, Hristov
27/02/00	Neftochimik Bourgas	H	1-4	Ivanov D.
04/03/00	Velbazhd Kiustendil	A	1-3	Deianov
12/03/00	Minior Pernik	H	6-1	Petrov, Ivanov D. 2, Chomakov 2, Berbatov
17/03/00	Spartak Varna	H	1-0	Ivanov D.
26/03/00	Slavia Sofia	A	0-0	
01/04/00	Dobrudzha Dobrich	H	4-1	Chomakov, Berbatov 2, Ivanov D.
09/04/00	Botev Plovdiv	A	2-1	Petrov, Ivanov G.
22/04/00	Pirin Blagoevgrad	H	1-1	Manchev
28/04/00	Chernomorets Bourgas	A	2-0	Berbatov, Kalchev
06/05/00	Shumen	H	4-0	Manchev, Berbatov 2 (2p), Angelov
13/05/00	Levski Sofia	A	0-1	
21/05/00	Lokomotiv Sofia	H	3-2	Deianov, Ivanov G., Berbatov
27/05/00	Olympic-Beroe Stara Zagora	A	1-1	Giglio
03/06/00	Belasitsa Petrich	H	3-0	Bukarev 2, Deianov
09/06/00	Lovech	A	2-3	Giglio 2

DOBRUDZHA DOBRICH

CLUB DIRECTORY

FC Dobrudzha
Bul 25 Septemvri 10
9300 Dobrich
tel - (058) 22591/28283
Year of Formation - 1919
President - Velichko Naidenov
Director - Dian Valchev
Coach - Ivan Manolov; Vasil Velikov;
Tzvetan Atanasov; Vasil Velikov
Stadium - Dobrudzha (20,000)

APPEARANCES 99/00

	P	Ap	(s)	Gls
Rumen BOEV	D	12		1
Anton DIMITROV	M	3		
Ivelin DIMITROV	D	1	(3)	
Sergei DIMITROV	D		(1)	
Kristian DOBREV	A	20	(3)	4
Ivo GESHEV	D	2		
Yulian IGNATOV	M		(2)	
Slavcho ILIEV	M	15		3
Iren KARAPETROV	A		(3)	
Vasil KOLEV	D	8		
Boris KONDEV	A		(5)	
Svetoslav KRASTEV	D	30		1
Svetoslav PETROV	M	14		
Desislav RUSEV	A	8	(1)	5
Svilen SIMEONOV	G	29		
Rumen SLAVOV	M	22		
Stefan SLAVOV	D	21	(1)	3
Nikolai SPASOV	D	14	(1)	
Stanislav STANKOV	A	6	(2)	
Stanimir STOIKOV	D		(1)	
Vasil USHEV	A	11	(12)	
Radoslav VARDAROV	A	26	(2)	7
Dimitar VASILEV	A	15		2
Stefan VASILEV	D	6	(16)	
Daniel VELICHKOV	D	14	(1)	
Velin VELIKOV	G	1	(2)	
Damian VELKOV	M	6	(14)	1
Ogust YOFU (CIV)	A	5	(2)	
Georgi ZDRAVKOV	A	25		2
Ventseslav ZHELEV	D	16	(7)	1
Veselin ZHIVKOV			(1)	

LEAGUE RESULTS 1999/2000

07/08/99	Belasitsa Petrich	A	0-1	
14/08/99	Lovech	H	1-3	Slavov S.
22/08/99	Neftochimik Bourgas	A	1-3	Dobrev
28/08/99	Velbazhd Kiustendil	H	0-1	
11/09/99	Minior Pernik	A	0-4	
19/09/99	CSKA Sofia	H	0-3	
25/09/99	Slavia Sofia	A	1-2	Vardarov
02/10/99	Spartak Varna	A	0-2	
17/10/99	Botev Plovdiv	H	1-0	Slavov S.
23/10/99	Pirin Blagoevgrad	A	1-2	Velkov
30/10/99	Chernomorets Bourgas	H	0-0	
06/11/99	Shumen	A	1-0	Boev
20/11/99	Levski Sofia	H	0-1	
27/11/99	Lokomotiv Sofia	A	0-4	
04/12/99	Olympic-Beroe Stara Zagora	H	2-1	Zdravkov 2
26/02/00	Belasitsa Petrich	H	3-1	Krastev, Iliev, Dobrev
04/03/00	Lovech	A	1-4	Dobrev
11/03/00	Neftochimik Bourgas	H	0-0	
18/03/00	Velbazhd Kiustendil	A	0-0	
25/03/00	Minior Pernik	H	3-1	Vasilev D., Iliev, Vardarov
01/04/00	CSKA Sofia	A	1-4	Vardarov
08/04/00	Slavia Sofia	H	2-0	Slavov, Rusev
22/04/00	Spartak Varna	H	2-0	Vardarov, Rusev
29/04/00	Botev Plovdiv	A	0-0	
06/05/00	Pirin Blagoevgrad	H	4-2	Dobrev (p), Rusev, Zhelev, Vardarov
13/05/00	Chernomorets Bourgas	A	0-0	
20/05/00	Shumen	H	3-0	Vardarov 2, Vasilev D.
27/05/00	Levski Sofia	A	1-2	Rusev
03/06/00	Lokomotiv Sofia	H	2-1	Rusev, Iliev
09/06/00	Olympic-Beroe Stara Zagora	A	0-1	

LEVSKI SOFIA

CLUB DIRECTORY

FC Levski Sofia
ulitsa Todorini Kukli 47
Kvartal Poduiene, 1517 Sofia
tel - (02) 459121/476064
fax - (02) 9454227
Year of Formation - 1914
President - Vladimir Grashnov
Director - Nasko Sirakov
Coach - Ljubomir Petrovic; Dimitar Dimitrov
Stadium - Georgi Asparuchov (45,000)

MAJOR HONOURS
League Championship - (21) 1933, 1937, 1942.
1946, 1947, 1949, 1950, 1953, 1965, 1968,
1970, 1974, 1977, 1979, 1984, 1985, 1988,
1993, 1994, 1995, 2000.
Domestic Cup - (9) 1942, 1982, 1984, 1986,
1991, 1992, 1994, 1998, 2000.

APPEARANCES 99/00

	P	Ap	(s)	Gls
Aleksandar ALEKSANDROV	M	26	(2)	6
Chavdar ATANASOV	M	13	(8)	4
Georgi BACHEV	A	5	(3)	3
Krasimir DIMITROV	D	12	(9)	
Aleksei DIONISIEV	D	8	(4)	2
Dalibor DRAGIC (YUG)	D	7	(2)	
Stanislav GENCHEV	M		(1)	
Georgi GEORGIEV	A	3	(11)	3
John INGLIS (SCO)	D	15	(2)	
Dimitar IVANKOV	G	27		5
Biser IVANOV	D	24	(2)	4
Georgi IVANOV	A	23		12
Todor KOLEV	A		(3)	
Hristo LAZAROV	A	1	(3)	
Nesko MILOVANOVIC (YUG)	M	3	(9)	1
Asen NIKOLOV	M	12		1
Victorio PAVLOV	M	5	(1)	
Predrag PAZIN (YUG)	D	23		1
Yuli PETKOV	D	2	(5)	
Georgi SHEITANOV	G	3		
Zakhari SIRAKOV	M	28	(1)	1
Martin STANKOV	D	13	(1)	
Stanimir STOILOV	D	24	(1)	3
Dimitar TELKIISKI	M	6	(10)	4
Elin TOPUZAKOV	D	22	(1)	3
Veselin VACHEV	D	4	(2)	
Serge YOFU (CIV)	A	21	(4)	13

LEAGUE RESULTS 1999/2000

06/08/99	Chernomorets Bourgas	H	2-0	Aleksandrov, Ivankov (p)
15/08/99	Shumen	A	4-1	Ivanov G. 2, Topuzakov, Aleksandrov
21/08/99	Spartak Varna	H	5-0	Ivanov B., Yofu 2, Ivanov G., Ivankov (p)
29/08/99	Lokomotiv Sofia	H	3-0	Yofu, Aleksandrov, Ivanov G.
11/09/99	Olympic-Beroe Stara Zagora	A	1-0	Ivanov B.
19/09/99	Belasitsa Petrich	H	6-0	Ivanov (p), Stoilov, Ivanov G., Bachev 2, Telkiiski
24/09/99	Lovech	A	1-1	Sirakov
03/10/99	Neftochimik Bourgas	H	2-0	Aleksandrov, Telkiiski
15/10/99	Velbazhd Kiustendil	A	3-1	Ivanov G., Yofu, Atanasov
23/10/99	Minior Pernik	H	4-1	Yofu 2, Ivankov (p), Dionisiev
30/10/99	CSKA Sofia	A	0-1	
07/11/99	Slavia Sofia	H	4-1	Yofu, Stoilov, Topuzakov, Telkiiski
20/11/99	Dobrudzha Dobrich	A	1-0	Yofu
28/11/99	Botev Plovdiv	H	4-1	Topuzakov, Aleksandrov, Georgiev, Telkiiski
04/12/99	Pirin Blagoevgrad	A	1-0	Bachev
26/02/00	Chernomorets Bourgas	A	3-2	Atanasov, Nikolov, Pazin
05/03/00	Shumen	H	3-0	Ivanov G. 2, Atanasov
12/03/00	Spartak Varna	A	1-0	Dionisiev
17/03/00	Lokomotiv Sofia	A	1-1	Ivankov (p)
25/03/00	Olympic-Beroe Stara Zagora	H	2-0	Yofu 2
31/03/00	Belasitsa Petrich	A	0-0	
08/04/00	Lovech	H	1-1	Ivanov B.
22/04/00	Neftochimik Bourgas	A	1-1	Ivanov G.
29/04/00	Velbazhd Kiustendil	H	3-0	Ivanov G., Atanasov, Milovanovic
06/05/00	Minior Pernik	A	2-3	Yofu, Stoilov
13/05/00	CSKA Sofia	H	1-0	Ivanov G.
21/05/00	Slavia Sofia	A	2-0	Aleksandrov, Ivanov G.
27/05/00	Dobrudzha Dobrich	H	2-1	Yofu 2
03/06/00	Botev Plovdiv	A	2-1	Georgiev, Ivanov B.
09/06/00	Pirin Blagoevgrad	H	1-0	Georgiev

LOKOMOTIV SOFIA

CLUB DIRECTORY

FC Lokomotiv
Bul. Rozhen 23, 1220 Sofia
tel - (02) 9360356 / fax - (02) 9360341
Year of Formation - 1929
President - Nikolai Gigov
Director - Boicho Velichkov
Coach - Gosho Petkov; Pavel Panov
Stadium - Lokomotiv (25,000)

MAJOR HONOURS
League Championship - (4)
1940, 1945, 1964, 1978.
Domestic Cup - (1) 1995.

APPEARANCES 99/00

	P	Ap	(s)	Gls
Ventsislav BONEV	D	1	(1)	
Georgi BORISOV	A	5	(7)	1
Simeon CHILIBONOV	M	4		1
Marcho DAVCHEV	M	17	(8)	3
Dejan DZURIC (YUG)	D	1		
Gancho EVTIMOV	D	25		5
Emil GARGAROV	M	9	(14)	7
Elton GASHI (ALB)	A	6	(1)	2
Deian GENCHEV	M	19	(5)	5
Hristo GEORGIEV	D	2	(1)	
Aleksandar GEROV	G	2	(1)	
Vladimir IVANOV	D	21		1
Rosen KAPTIEV	A	1	(9)	2
Georgi KARAKANOV	D	5	(5)	
Vladimir MANOLKOV	G	4		
Georgi MARKOV	D	22		
Dobri MITOV	D	12	(1)	2
MacDonald MUKASI (SAF)	A	17	(6)	7
Valentin NAIDENOV	D	4		
Anatoli NANKOV	M	12	(1)	1
Ivo PARGOV	A	7	(4)	3
Georgi PEEV	M	25		8
Yordan PETKOV	D	21		1
Milen RADUKANOV	D	7		
Ilian SIMEONOV	A	14	(9)	4
Petar STANEV	A	3	(3)	
Radostin STANEV	G	10		
Slavcho TOSHEV	G	5		
Stefan UCHIKOV	D	16	(1)	
Dimitar VASEV	D	6		1
Ilian VASILEV	G	9		
Bozhidar YANKOV	A	6		
Zlatko YANKOV	M	6	(1)	
Vladimir YONKOV	D	6	(2)	

LEAGUE RESULTS 1999/2000

08/08/99	Pirin Blagoevgrad	H	5-1	Mukasi 2, Genchev, Evtimov, Pargov
14/08/99	Chernomorets Bourgas	A	1-1	Peev
22/08/99	Shumen	H	2-0	Chilibonov (p), Peev
29/08/99	Levski Sofia	A	0-3	
11/09/99	Spartak Varna	H	5-0	Evtimov 2, Mukasi, Pargov (p), Genchev
18/09/99	Olympic-Beroe Stara Zagora	H	4-1	Genchev (p), Gargorov, Pargov, Borisov
25/09/99	Belasitsa Petrich	A	2-2	Genchev, Gargorov
03/10/99	Lovech	H	2-1	Genchev, Peev
17/10/99	Neftochimik Bourgas	A	2-3	Peev, Mukasi
23/10/99	Velbazhd Kiustendil	H	1-1	Vasev (p)
30/10/99	Minior Pernik	A	1-0	Mukasi
07/11/99	CSKA Sofia	H	0-0	
21/11/99	Slavia Sofia	A	0-1	
27/11/99	Dobrudzha Dobrich	H	4-0	Davchev, Simeonov (p), Gargorov, Mukasi
04/12/99	Botev Plovdiv	A	0-1	
26/02/00	Pirin Blagoevgrad	A	0-1	
04/03/00	Chernomorets Bourgas	H	4-1	Peev 2 (1p), Evtimov, Mitov
11/03/00	Shumen	A	1-1	Mitov
17/03/00	Levski Sofia	H	1-1	Gargorov
25/03/00	Spartak Varna	A	1-2	Nankov
01/04/00	Olympic-Beroe Stara Zagora	A	0-2	
08/04/00	Belasitsa Petrich	H	2-0	Davchev, Gargarov
22/04/00	Lovech	A	2-3	Peev, Davchev
29/04/00	Neftochimik Bourgas	H	1-1	Evtimov
06/05/00	Velbazhd Kiustendil	A	1-1	Petkov
13/05/00	Minior Pernik	H	2-3	Kaptiev 2
21/05/00	CSKA Sofia	A	2-3	Peev, Ivanov
27/05/00	Slavia Sofia	H	6-0	Simeonov 3, Gargolov 2, Gashi
03/06/00	Dobrudzha Dobrich	A	1-2	Mukasi
09/06/00	Botev Plovdiv	H	1-1	Gashi

LOVECH

CLUB DIRECTORY

FC Lovech
Stadion Lovech, 5500 Lovech
tel - (068) 29091/24420 / fax - (068) 20012
Year of Formation - 1921
President - Angel Bonchev
Coach - Aleksandar Zheliazkov; Ferario Spasov;
Cedomir Djurdjevic
Stadium - Lovech (7,000)

MAJOR HONOURS
League Championship - (2) 1998, 1999.

APPEARANCES 99/00

	P	Ap	(s)	Gls
Atanas BORNOSUZOV	M	2	(6)	
Kaloian CHENKOV	M	1		
Nikola DIMITROV	D	24	(4)	1
Georgi GEORGIEV	M	1		
GEORGIEV	D	1		
Stanimir GOSPODINOV	D	7		
Altin HAXHI (ALB)	M	23		3
Nebojsa JELENKOVIC (YUG)	M	17	(5)	3
Ibe JOHNSON (NIG)	D	6	(6)	
Dimitar KARADLIEV	D	10	(2)	
Radostin KISHISHEV	M	15		2
Yanek KIUCHUKOV	D	13		
Stefan KOLEV	D	6		
Svetlin KONDEV	A	6	(4)	1
Zvetan KRASTEV	D	3		
Luís Carlos MOTTA (BRA)	A	9	(12)	4
Valentin NAIDENOV	D	11		
NENKOV			(1)	
Kiril NIKOLOV	A	5	(7)	
Ivailo PETEV	M	8		4
Marin PETROV	A	20	(5)	5
Atanas POPOV	D	2	(1)	
Ivan RAICHEV	D	7	(5)	
Desislav RUSEV	A		(4)	1
Ivan RUSEV	M	5	(7)	1
Dragoljub SIMONOVIC (YUG)	A	7	(1)	1
Rumen STANKULOV	A		(2)	
Stoian STAVREV	G	14		
Svilen STOILOV	M	1	(1)	
Metodi STOINEV	A	10	(5)	2
Svetoslav TODOROV	A	26		19
Vitomir VUTOV	G	16		
Hristo YOVOV	A	11	(1)	9
Stefan YURUKOV	A	7		4
Zlatomir ZAGORCIC	D	8		
Zhivko ZHELEV	D	16	(2)	
Marian ZIVKOVIC (YUG)	M	12	(5)	

LEAGUE RESULTS 1999/2000

08/08/99	Slavia Sofia	H	0-1	
14/08/99	Dobrudzha Dobrich	A	3-1	Motta, Kondev, Petrov
21/08/99	Botev Plovdiv	H	2-0	Petrov 2
29/08/99	Pirin Blagoevgrad	A	1-0	Todorov
11/09/99	Chernomorets Bourgas	H	2-0	Dimitrov, Todorov (p)
19/09/99	Shumen	A	0-1	
24/09/99	Levski Sofia	H	1-1	Haxhi
03/10/99	Lokomotiv Sofia	A	1-2	Rusev D.
17/10/99	Olympic-Beroe Stara Zagora	H	2-0	Petrov, Rusev D.
24/10/99	Belasitsa Petrich	A	0-1	
30/10/99	Spartak Varna	H	4-1	Stoinev, Todorov 2, Simonovic
06/11/99	Neftochimik Bourgas	H	0-1	
20/11/99	Velbazhd Kiustendil	A	3-1	Jelenkovic 2, Todorov
27/11/99	Minior Pernik	H	6-3	Todorov 4, Motta, Stoinev
05/12/99	CSKA Sofia	A	0-2	
26/02/00	Slavia Sofia	A	0-1	
04/03/00	Dobrudzha Dobrich	H	4-1	Todorov 3 (1p), Kishishev
11/03/00	Botev Plovdiv	A	0-2	
18/03/00	Pirin Blagoevgrad	H	1-1	Yovov
25/03/00	Chernomorets Bourgas	A	1-1	Kishishev
01/04/00	Shumen	H	6-0	Jelenkovic, Yovov, Todorov 2, Motta, og (Vasilev Z.)
08/04/00	Levski Sofia	A	1-1	Yurukov
22/04/00	Lokomotiv Sofia	H	3-2	Petev 2, Todorov (p)
29/04/00	Olympic-Beroe Stara Zagora	A	2-0	Yovov 2
06/05/00	Belasitsa Petrich	H	8-0	Yurukov 2, Todorov 3, Haxhi 2, Motta
13/05/00	Spartak Varna	A	0-1	
20/05/00	Neftochimik Bourgas	A	1-2	Petrov
27/05/00	Velbazhd Kiustendil	H	3-1	Petev, Yovov 2
03/06/00	Minior Pernik	A	3-4	Petev, Yovov 2
09/06/00	CSKA Sofia	H	3-2	Todorov, Yurukov, Yovov

MINIOR PERNIK

CLUB DIRECTORY

FC Minior
ul. Fizkulturna 1
2300 Pernik
tel - (076) 24963
Year of Formation - 1919
President - Krasimir Mikhailov
Director - Kiril Nikolov
Coach - Yanko Dinkov; Yuri Vasev; Evlogi Banchev
Stadium - Minior (20,000)

APPEARANCES 99/00

	P	Ap	(s)	Gls
Nikolai ALEKSANDROV	A	18		
Vladimir ANDONOV	M		(1)	
Petar ANESTIEV	D	12	(2)	
Hristo ARANGELOV	M	5	(3)	
Vladimir ARNAUDOV	M	22	(1)	
Spas BOIANOV	M	7	(4)	2
Svetoslav BORISOV	D	2	(3)	
Velizar DIMITROV	A	3	(2)	2
Stoicho DRAGOV	G	6		
Kiril DZHOROV	D	8	(5)	2
Liudmil EVGENIEV	D	27	(1)	
Anton EVTIMOV	A	28		14
Dimitar GEORGIEV	A	30		7
Marian GEORGIEV	M	5	(10)	1
Svetoslav GEORGIEV	D		(1)	
Viktor GEORGIEV	G	15	(1)	
Georgi KARAKANOV	M	15		3
Angelo KIUCHUKOV	M	27		3
Metodi METODIEV	A		(3)	
Kiril NIKOLOV	M	9	(5)	1
Yakov PAPARKOV	D	24	(1)	2
Slavcho PAVLOV	M	10	(1)	2
Shaban SHEVKED	D	6		
Ivo SLAVCHEV	M	8		
Spas STOIMENOV	D	15	(1)	
Krasimir SVILENOV	A	8	(4)	3
TOSHEV	A		(3)	
Emil VARADINOV	G	9		
Vladislav VLADOV	D		(1)	
Yulian YANAKIEV	D	11	(7)	2
Ivailo YORDANOV	A		(2)	

LEAGUE RESULTS 1999/2000

Date	Opponent		Score	Scorers
07/08/99	Velbazhd Kiustendil	A	0-3	
15/08/99	Spartak Varna	A	0-1	
21/08/99	CSKA Sofia	H	1-2	Boianov
28/08/99	Slavia Sofia	A	1-4	Dzhorov
11/09/99	Dobrudzha Dobrich	H	4-0	Evtimov, Boianov, Dzhorov, Svilenov
18/09/99	Botev Plovdiv	A	0-1	
25/09/99	Pirin Blagoevgrad	H	2-0	Karakanov 2
02/10/99	Chernomorets Bourgas	A	1-2	Svilenov
17/10/99	Shumen	H	2-0	Nikolov, Georgiev D.
23/10/99	Levski Sofia	A	1-4	Evtimov
30/10/99	Lokomotiv Sofia	H	0-1	
06/11/99	Olympic-Beroe Stara Zagora	A	0-1	
20/11/99	Belasitsa Petrich	H	4-0	Svilenov, Evtimov (p), Kiuchukov, Karakanov
27/11/99	Lovech	A	3-6	Georgiev D. 2, Kiuchukov
04/12/99	Neftochimik Bourgas	H	1-0	Kiuchukov
26/02/00	Velbazhd Kiustendil	H	0-2	
03/03/00	Spartak Varna	H	1-1	Paparkov
12/03/00	CSKA Sofia	A	1-6	Evtimov
18/03/00	Slavia Sofia	H	0-3	
25/03/00	Dobrudzha Dobrich	A	1-3	Georgiev D.
01/04/00	Botev Plovdiv	H	1-1	Pavlov
08/04/00	Pirin Blagoevgrad	A	0-2	
22/04/00	Chernomorets Bourgas	H	2-1	Evtimov (p), Yanakiev
29/04/00	Shumen	A	3-1	Pavlov, Paparkov, Evtimov
06/05/00	Levski Sofia	H	3-2	Evtimov 3 (2p)
13/05/00	Lokomotiv Sofia	A	3-2	Dimitrov, Evtimov 2 (1p)
20/05/00	Olympic-Beroe Stara Zagora	H	2-0	Yanakiev, Evtimov
27/05/00	Belasitsa Petrich	A	2-2	Georgiev D., Georgiev M.
03/06/00	Lovech	H	4-3	Georgiev D. 2, Evtimov 2 (1p)
09/06/00	Neftochimik Bourgas	A	1-4	Dimitrov

NEFTOCHIMIK BOURGAS

CLUB DIRECTORY

FC Neftochimik
Stadium Neftochimik
zh.k. Lazur, 8000 Bourgas
tel - (056) 800320/800325
fax - (056) 24898
Year of Formation - 1932
President - Hristo Portochanov
Director - Erolin Kiuchukov
Coach - Dimitar Stoichev
Stadium - Neftochimik (22,000)

APPEARANCES 99/00

	P	Ap	(s)	Gls
Veselin BRANIMIROV	D	29		
Simeon CHILIBONOV	M	5	(1)	1
Georgi CHILIKOV	A	12	(9)	1
Krasimir DENEV	D	4	(3)	
Stanimir DIMITROV	A	22	(5)	4
Milen GEORGIEV	A	14	(1)	6
Yordan GOSPODINOV	G	28		
Ilia GRUEV	A	29		6
Daniel HRISTOV	D	10	(4)	
Milen HRISTOV	M	1	(4)	
Said IBRAIMOV	D	23	(1)	2
Todor KISELICHKOV	M	21	(4)	8
Nikolai KRASTEV	D	9	(3)	1
Marko MARKOV	D		(6)	
Blagomir MITREV	M	18	(3)	1
Malin ORACHEV	M	24	(1)	
Velian PARUSHEV	D	13	(1)	3
Dian PETKOV	M	5	(13)	1
Rasen PETROV	D	18	(2)	
Plamen RUSINOV	A	1	(5)	1
Stoiko SAKALIEV	A	4	(10)	1
Veselin SHULEV	G	2		
Plamen STOIANOV	M		(3)	
Mitko TRENDAFILOV	M	8	(5)	
Todor YANCHEV	A	30		3

LEAGUE RESULTS 1999/2000

06/08/99	CSKA Sofia	H	2-1	Gruev (p), og (Tomash)
13/08/99	Slavia Sofia	A	1-1	Georgiev
22/08/99	Dobrudzha Dobrich	H	3-1	Sakaliev, Georgiev 2
28/08/99	Botev Plovdiv	A	2-1	Kiselichkov, Yanchev
11/09/99	Pirin Blagoevgrad	H	1-1	Rusinov
17/09/99	Chernomorets Bourgas	A	0-0	
25/09/99	Shumen	H	1-0	Gruev (p)
03/10/99	Levski Sofia	A	0-2	
17/10/99	Lokomotiv Sofia	H	3-2	Dimitrov, og (Ivanov), Gruev (p)
24/10/99	Olympic-Beroe Stara Zagora	A	0-0	
30/10/99	Belasitsa Petrich	H	3-0	Gruev, Chilibonov, Yanchev
06/11/99	Lovech	A	1-0	Georgiev
20/11/99	Spartak Varna	H	4-0	Georgiev, Krastev, Yanchev, Dimitrov
27/11/99	Velbazhd Kiustendil	H	1-0	Mitrev
04/12/99	Minior Pernik	A	0-1	
27/02/00	CSKA Sofia	A	4-1	Parushev, Georgiev, Kiselichkov 2
04/03/00	Slavia Sofia	H	0-0	
11/03/00	Dobrudzha Dobrich	A	0-0	
19/03/00	Botev Plovdiv	H	0-1	
25/03/00	Pirin Blagoevgrad	A	0-1	
01/04/00	Chernomorets Bourgas	H	2-0	Ibraimov, Kiselichkov
08/04/00	Shumen	A	1-1	Chilikov
22/04/00	Levski Sofia	H	1-1	Parushev (p)
29/04/00	Lokomotiv Sofia	A	1-1	Kiselichkov
06/05/00	Olympic-Beroe Stara Zagora	H	3-0	Petkov, Dimitrov, Kiselichkov
13/05/00	Belasitsa Petrich	A	1-1	Gruev
20/05/00	Lovech	H	2-1	Dimitrov, Parushev
27/05/00	Spartak Varna	A	1-1	Gruev
03/06/00	Velbazhd Kiustendil	A	0-1	
09/06/00	Minior Pernik	H	4-1	Ibraimov, Kiselichkov 2, og (Evgeniev)

OLYMPIC-BEROE STARA ZAGORA

CLUB DIRECTORY

FC Olympic-Beroe
ul. Georgi Kiumurev 10
6000 Stara Zagora
tel - (042) 37277/20816
Year of Formation - 1999
President - Stanislav Tanev
Director - Stoiko Stoikov
Coach - Dragoslav Vekbalac; Ventsislav Kepov
Stadium - Beroe (22,000)

MAJOR HONOURS
League Championship - (1) 1986.

APPEARANCES 99/00

	P	Ap	(s)	Gls
Ivan BADALOV	M	3	(5)	
Dimitar BALABANOV	D	9	(2)	
Liubo BOZHINKOV	M	6	(2)	
Stoicho DRAGOV	G	12		
Rosen EMILOV	M	10		
Rumen GALABOV	A	20	(4)	3
Ekrem GENCH	A	4	(2)	1
Tencho GEORGIEV	M		(1)	
Marian GERASIMOV	A	20	(2)	
Georgi IVANOV	M		(1)	
Ivailo IVANOV	A		(5)	
Koicho IVANOV	D	8		
Zeljko KARANOVIC (YUG)	D	27		
Vasil KIROV	M	16	(7)	1
Vasil KUZMANOV	G	1		
Predrag MARKOVIC (YUG)	D	25	(1)	
Galin MINCHEV	A	4	(3)	
Gospodin MIRCHEV	M	18	(2)	2
NACHEV	A		(1)	
Ivailo PETROV	G	14		
Boris PETROVIC (YUG)	A	6	(2)	
Stilian POPCHEV	M	6	(4)	
Zoran RAJOVIC (YUG)	A	12	(8)	4
Dimitar RALCHEV	D	2	(3)	
Spas SPASOV	A		(2)	
Hristo TERZIEV	A	10	(10)	3
Ivan TODOROV	M		(1)	
Todor TODOROV	M	15	(5)	1
Ivan TONCHEV	A	9	(2)	4
Dimitar TOPALOV	G	2		
Petko VINKOV	D	27	(2)	1
Hristo YANEV	A	25	(1)	7
Velko YOTOV	A	4	(1)	
Boro ZAGORAC (YUG)	A	4	(2)	1

LEAGUE RESULTS 1999/2000

07/08/99	Botev Plovdiv	H	5-2	Rajovic 2, Yanev 2, Terziev
14/08/99	Pirin Blagoevgrad	A	1-2	Galabov
21/08/99	Chernomorets Bourgas	H	1-0	Mirchev
28/08/99	Shumen	A	1-2	Todorov T.
11/09/99	Levski Sofia	H	0-1	
19/09/99	Lokomotiv Sofia	A	1-4	Rajovic
25/09/99	Spartak Varna	H	2-0	Vinkov, Terziev
02/10/99	Belasitsa Petrich	H	1-0	Terziev
17/10/99	Lovech	A	0-2	
24/10/99	Neftochimik Bourgas	H	0-0	
30/10/99	Velbazhd Kiustendil	A	0-4	
06/11/99	Minior Pernik	H	1-0	Galabov
20/11/99	CSKA Sofia	A	0-3	
27/11/99	Slavia Sofia	H	1-1	Yanev
04/12/99	Dobrudzha Dobrich	A	1-2	Galabov
26/02/00	Botev Plovdiv	A	0-2	
04/03/00	Pirin Blagoevgrad	H	4-0	Tonchev 2, Zagorac, Yanev
11/03/00	Chernomorets Bourgas	A	1-2	Yanev
18/03/00	Shumen	H	1-0	Yanev
25/03/00	Levski Sofia	A	0-2	
01/04/00	Lokomotiv Sofia	H	2-0	Tonchev, Rajovic
08/04/00	Spartak Varna	A	0-4	
22/04/00	Belasitsa Petrich	A	1-1	Gench
29/04/00	Lovech	H	0-2	
06/05/00	Neftochimik Bourgas	A	0-3	
13/05/00	Velbazhd Kiustendil	H	0-4	(w/o)
20/05/00	Minior Pernik	A	0-2	
27/05/00	CSKA Sofia	H	1-1	Yanev (p)
03/06/00	Slavia Sofia	A	2-1	Kirov, Mirchev
09/06/00	Dobrudzha Dobrich	H	1-0	Tonchev

PIRIN BLAGOEVGRAD

CLUB DIRECTORY

FC Pirin
ul Dabravka 1
2700 Blagoevgrad
tel - (073) 27052/23090
Year of Formation - 1922
President - Ognean Krastev
Director - Valentin Chakarov
Coach - Boris Angelov; Petar Mikhtarski
Stadium - Hristo Botev (15,000)

APPEARANCES 99/00

	P	Ap	(s)	Gls
Blagoi ANDONOV	M	1		
Angel ANGELOV	D	2		
Petar ADZHOV	A	12	(5)	2
Anton BACHEV	M	6	(2)	1
Stanislav BACHEV	D	21		
Petar BANDEV	M		(3)	
Georgi BIZHEV	A	16	(7)	3
Vesko CHERGOV	A	5	(2)	2
Georgi DASKALOV	M	2	(6)	
Vlodko DAVIDKOV (MAC)	M	15	(10)	3
Stoimen DONCHEV	D	9	(7)	
Svetoslav GEORGIEV	D	9	(4)	
Kostadin GERGANCHEV	A	6	(3)	
Stoine ILIEV	D	21	(2)	
Ivo IVANIKOV	G	13		
Dimitar KOEMDZHIEV	D	12		
Atanas LIASKOV	A		(5)	
MARKOV	A		(1)	
Aleksandar METODIEV	A		(1)	
Petar MIKHTARSKI	A	15	(8)	5
Zvetan MILOTINOV	D	3	(1)	
Miroslav MITEV	G	9	(1)	
Ivailo PANCHEV	A	19	(2)	3
Venko POPOV	M	21		
Rumen RANGELOV	G	8		
Radostin RUSEV	D	23		
Veselin SARBAKOV	M	12	(2)	1
Petar SHOPOV	A	7	(3)	1
Lachezar SOTIROV	G		(1)	
Hristo VOINOV	D	23	(1)	7
Boris YANEV	A	3	(10)	1
Bozhidar YANKOV	A	14	(1)	1
Daniel ZHELIAZKOV	A	23		1

LEAGUE RESULTS 1999/2000

08/08/99	Lokomotiv Sofia	A	1-5	Mikhtarski
14/08/99	Olympic-Beroe Stara Zagora	H	2-1	Mikhtarski, Yankov
20/08/99	Belasitsa Petrich	A	1-4	Mikhtarski
29/08/99	Lovech	H	0-1	
11/09/99	Neftochimik Bourgas	A	1-1	Voinov
18/09/99	Velbazhd Kiustendil	H	1-0	Davidkov
25/09/99	Minior Pernik	A	0-2	
03/10/99	CSKA Sofia	H	0-1	
17/10/99	Slavia Sofia	A	1-3	Sarbakov
23/10/99	Dobrudzha Dobrich	H	2-1	Panchev, Mikhtarski
30/10/99	Botev Plovdiv	A	1-2	Shopov
06/11/99	Spartak Varna	A	1-2	Adzhov
20/11/99	Chernomorets Bourgas	H	2-3	Adzhov, Voinov
27/11/99	Shumen	A	0-1	
04/12/99	Levski Sofia	H	0-1	
26/02/00	Lokomotiv Sofia	H	1-0	Voinov
04/03/00	Olympic-Beroe Stara Zagora	A	0-4	
11/03/00	Belasitsa Petrich	H	1-0	Bizhev
18/03/00	Lovech	A	1-1	Bizhev
25/03/00	Neftochimik Bourgas	H	1-0	Bizhev
01/04/00	Velbazhd Kiustendil	A	0-3	
08/04/00	Minior Pernik	H	2-0	Voinov, Zheliazkov
22/04/00	CSKA Sofia	A	1-1	Davidkov
29/04/00	Slavia Sofia	H	1-4	Yanev
06/05/00	Dobrudzha Dobrich	A	2-4	Voinov 2
13/05/00	Botev Plovdiv	H	3-1	Chergov, Mikhtarski, Panchev (p)
20/05/00	Spartak Varna	H	2-0	Panchev, Chergov
27/05/00	Chernomorets Bourgas	A	0-2	
03/06/00	Shumen	H	3-1	Bachev A., Davidkov, Voinov
09/06/00	Levski Sofia	A	0-1	

SHUMEN

CLUB DIRECTORY

FC Shumen
ul. Preslav 6
9700 Shumen
tel - (054) 69894
Year of Formation - 1919
President - Kamen Kostadinov
Director - Emil Zankov
Coach - Georgi Tzvetkov; Todor Todorov;
Ivan Tankov; Rosen Mateev
Stadium - Panaiot Volov (20,000)

APPEARANCES 99/00

	P	Ap	(s)	Gls
Roman AHALKAZI	A		(4)	
Rumen ANGELOV	M	11	(9)	1
Boris BORISOV	D	16	(1)	
Ventsislav DIMITROV	A		(1)	
Asen GAIDARDZHIEV	M	10	(3)	1
Trifon GEORGIEV	D	1		
Kristian HRISTIANOV	M	14	(4)	
Stanislav ILIEV	M	14		
Ivan IVANOV	A	3		
Yordan KAMENOV	A		(5)	
Konstantin KOLEV	D	12	(13)	
Filip KRUMOV	D	10	(1)	
Angel MALINOV	D	2		
Samir MASTANOV	D	8		
Ivan MILCHEV	G	7	(1)	
Konstantin MIRCHEV	M	11		3
Miroslav MIROSLAVOV	A	17		2
Liubomir NIKOLOV	A	9	(4)	1
Liubomir PALEIKOV	A	8	(4)	1
Rumen RANGELOV	G	2	(1)	
Shener REMZI	A	17	(3)	
Mikhail SPASOV	A	9	(3)	
Stoiko STOIKOV	D	18	(1)	1
Vasil VASILEV	D	6	(2)	
Zahari VASILEV	M	14	(6)	
Rumen VENKOV	M	19	(4)	
Petar VOINOV	G	20	(1)	
Aleksandar YANAKIEV	D	1	(4)	
Milen YORDANOV	M	5	(2)	1
Yuksel YUMEROV	D	25	(1)	
Plamen ZENOV	D	5	(1)	
Nikolai ZHELIAZKOV	A	25		2

LEAGUE RESULTS 1999/2000

11/08/99	Spartak Varna	H	0-3	
15/08/99	Levski Sofia	H	1-4	Stoikov
22/08/99	Lokomotiv Sofia	A	0-2	
28/08/99	Olympic-Beroe Stara Zagora	H	2-1	Miroslavov (p), Yordanov
11/09/99	Belasitsa Petrich	A	0-1	
19/09/99	Lovech	H	1-0	Miroslavov (p)
25/09/99	Neftochimik Bourgas	A	0-1	
02/10/99	Velbazhd Kiustendil	H	1-2	Zheliazkov
17/10/99	Minior Pernik	A	0-2	
24/10/99	CSKA Sofia	H	0-1	
30/10/99	Slavia Sofia	A	0-1	
06/11/99	Dobrudzha Dobrich	H	0-1	
20/11/99	Botev Plovdiv	A	0-4	
27/11/99	Pirin Blagoevgrad	H	1-0	Angelov
04/12/99	Chernomorets Bourgas	A	0-1	
26/02/00	Spartak Varna	A	0-4	
05/03/00	Levski Sofia	A	0-3	
11/03/00	Lokomotiv Sofia	H	1-1	Zheliazkov
18/03/00	Olympic-Beroe Stara Zagora	A	0-1	
25/03/00	Belasitsa Petrich	H	0-1	
01/04/00	Lovech	A	0-6	
08/04/00	Neftochimik Bourgas	H	1-1	Mirchev
12/04/00	Velbazhd Kiustendil	A	0-6	
29/04/00	Minior Pernik	H	1-3	Gaidardzhiev
06/05/00	CSKA Sofia	A	0-4	
13/05/00	Slavia Sofia	H	0-3	(w/o)
20/05/00	Dobrudzha Dobrich	A	0-3	
27/05/00	Botev Plovdiv	H	1-2	Mirchev (p)
03/06/00	Pirin Blagoevgrad	A	1-3	Nikolov
09/06/00	Chernomorets Bourgas	H	2-3	Mirchev, Paleikov

SLAVIA SOFIA

CLUB DIRECTORY

FC Slavia
ul. Koloman 1, kvartal Ovcha Kupel, 1618 Sofia
tel - (02) 551137/550075
fax - (02) 555231/552137
Year of Formation - 1913
President - Ventseslav Stefanov
Director - Anton Grigorov
Coach - Stoian Kotzev; Miroslav Mironov
Stadium - Slavia (32,000)

MAJOR HONOURS
League Championship - (7)
1928, 1930, 1936, 1939, 1941, 1943, 1996.
Domestic Cup - (1) 1996.

APPEARANCES 99/00

	P	Ap	(s)	Gls
Vlado ANDONOV	M	2		
Stoian ATSAROV	D	21		
Georgi BACHEV	A	2		
Ivo BANKIN	A	2	(5)	
Kiril DZHOROV	D	11	(1)	1
Filip FILIPOV	D	6		
Blagoi GEORGIEV	M	18	(4)	3
Hristo GEORGIEV	D	11	(2)	
Marian GERMANOV	D	7		
Stanimir GOSPODINOV	D	11	(1)	1
Borislav ILIEV	M	6	(4)	1
Emil IVELINOV	A	2		
Atanas KIROV	A		(2)	
Stefan KOLEV	D	9		
Vlado KOLEV	A	2	(10)	1
Stefan KOSTADINOV	A	11	(11)	1
Martin KUSHEV	M	14		8
Hristo LAZAROV	A	20		6
Anton LICHKOV	D	4	(1)	
Dimitar NAKOV	M	11		
Neno NENOV	D	23		
Rumen NENOV	G	12		
Zvetan NIKOLOV	A	4	(8)	
Rumen PANAIOTOV	M	7		1
Ivelin PENEV	M		(1)	
Georgi PETKOV	G	11		
Rusi PETKOV	G	4		
Yasen PETROV	M	3	(8)	
Troian RADULOV	D	11	(2)	2
Dimitar RANGELOV	A		(1)	
Ivan REDOVSKI	A		(2)	1
Vlado SHALAMANOV	M	8		1
Petar SHOPOV	A	11	(2)	3
Robert SJOLIN (SWE)	D	1		
Ivo SLAVDHEV	M	5		
Stoian STOIANOV	G	2	(1)	
Vladimir STOIKOV	D	4	(1)	
Martin TOPUZOV	D	23	(1)	3
Spas URUMOV	A	1	(6)	1
Ljubomir VORKAPIC (YUG)	A	4	(2)	1
Mikhail ZAKHARIEV	D	15	(3)	

LEAGUE RESULTS 1999/2000

08/08/99	Lovech	A	1-0	Kolev V.
13/08/99	Neftochimik Bourgas	H	1-1	Kushev
21/08/99	Velbazhd Kiustendil	A	0-1	
28/08/99	Minior Pernik	H	4-1	Kostadinov, Panaiotov, Vorkapic, Kushev
10/09/99	CSKA Sofia	A	1-3	Shalamanov
18/09/99	Spartak Varna	A	0-0	
25/09/99	Dobrudzha Dobrich	H	2-1	Iliev, Kushev
02/10/99	Botev Plovdiv	A	0-6	
17/10/99	Pirin Blagoevgrad	H	3-1	Kushev 2, Lazarov
23/10/99	Chernomorets Bourgas	A	0-1	
30/10/99	Shumen	H	1-0	Radulov
07/11/99	Levski Sofia	A	1-4	Lazarov
21/11/99	Lokomotiv Sofia	H	1-0	Kushev
27/11/99	Olympic-Beroe Stara Zagora	A	1-1	Georgiev B.
04/12/99	Belasitsa Petrich	H	5-1	Topuzov, Kushev 2 (2p), Lazarov 2
26/02/00	Lovech	H	1-0	Lazarov
04/03/00	Neftochimik Bourgas	A	0-0	
11/03/00	Velbazhd Kiustendil	H	1-2	Georgiev B.
18/03/00	Minior Pernik	A	3-0	Radulov, Lazarov, Shopov
26/03/00	CSKA Sofia	H	0-0	
01/04/00	Spartak Varna	H	0-0	
08/04/00	Dobrudzha Dobrich	A	0-2	
22/04/00	Botev Plovdiv	H	3-2	Georgiev B., Dzhorov, Topuzov (p)
29/04/00	Pirin Blagoevgrad	A	4-1	Gospodinov, Shopov 2, Urumov
06/05/00	Chernomorets Bourgas	H	1-0	Topuzov
13/05/00	Shumen	A	3-0	(w/o)
21/05/00	Levski Sofia	H	0-2	
27/05/00	Lokomotiv Sofia	A	0-6	
03/06/00	Olympic-Beroe Stara Zagora	H	1-2	Redovski
09/06/00	Belasitsa Petrich	A	0-2	

SPARTAK VARNA

CLUB DIRECTORY

FC Spartak
ul. Seliolu 39
9002 Varna
tel - (052) 245020/225780/253090
fax - (052) 237541
Year of Formation - 1919
President - Nikolai Ishkov
Director - Ivan Slavov
Coach - Velislav Vutsov
Stadium - Spartak (15,000)

MAJOR HONOURS
League Championship - (1) 1932.

APPEARANCES 99/00

	P	Ap	(s)	Gls
Georgi ARNAUDOV	G	17	(1)	
Georgi BOGDANOV	A	20	(3)	
Dimitar DAMIANOV	A	1		
Traian DIANKOV	M	28		2
Slaveiko DIMITROV	D	7	(1)	
Slavoljub DJORDJEVIC (YUG)	D	9	(1)	
Deian DONCHEV	M	20	(2)	
Dejan DZURIC (YUG)	D	3	(3)	
Nikolai FILIPOV	A	16	(9)	3
Kaloian GENCHEV	M	1	(5)	1
Stanislav GENCHEV	M	7	(4)	1
Emil GEORGIEV	D	1	(5)	
Stefan GOSHEV	D	14		2
Borislav ILIEV	M		(2)	
Georgi IVANOV	M	25	(1)	1
Krasimir KOLEV	G	11	(1)	
Nasko KOSTADINOV	M	2	(11)	1
Georgi KOVACHEV	A	7	(1)	
Zlatin MIKHAILOV	D	14		
Dimitar MITOV	D		(3)	
Ivan PASKOV	M	11	(1)	3
Ivailo PETEV	M	17	(2)	2
Zdravko RADEV	D	1	(4)	
Raicho RAICHEV	G	2	(1)	
Ivan RUSEV	M	5		1
Nikolai STANCHEV	A	11	(1)	1
Metodi STOINEV	A	6	(2)	2
Yordan STOILOV	M	4	(2)	
Ilian TASHEV	D	3	(1)	
Plamen TIMNEV	A	27	(1)	16
Marian TODOROV	M	7	(4)	
Radomir TODOROV	M	4	(6)	
Anton VALCHANOV	D	18	(5)	
Stefan YURUKOV	A	11	(2)	6

LEAGUE RESULTS 1999/2000

11/08/99	Shumen	A	3-0	Timnev 2, Genchev K.
15/08/99	Minior Pernik	H	1-0	Stanchev (p)
21/08/99	Levski Sofia	A	0-5	
29/08/99	CSKA Sofia	H	1-2	Timnev
11/09/99	Lokomotiv Sofia	A	0-5	
18/09/99	Slavia Sofia	H	0-0	
25/09/99	Olympic-Beroe Stara Zagora	A	0-2	
02/10/99	Dobrudzha Dobrich	H	2-0	Timnev 2
17/10/99	Belasitsa Petrich	A	1-1	Filipov
23/10/99	Botev Plovdiv	H	2-1	Yurukov, Timnev
30/10/99	Lovech	A	1-4	Diankov
06/11/99	Pirin Blagoevgrad	H	2-1	Filipov, Yurukov
20/11/99	Neftochimik Bourgas	A	0-4	
27/11/99	Chernomorets Bourgas	H	4-2	Petev, Yurukov 2, Timnev (p)
04/12/99	Velbazhd Kiustendil	A	0-2	
26/02/00	Shumen	H	4-0	Timnev 3 (1p), Ivanov
04/03/00	Minior Pernik	A	1-1	Yurukov
12/03/00	Levski Sofia	H	0-1	
17/03/00	CSKA Sofia	A	0-1	
25/03/00	Lokomotiv Sofia	H	2-1	Yurukov, Petev
01/04/00	Slavia Sofia	A	0-0	
08/04/00	Olympic-Beroe Stara Zagora	H	4-0	Diankov, Timnev, Genchev S., Kostadinov
22/04/00	Dobrudzha Dobrich	A	0-2	
29/04/00	Belasitsa Petrich	H	3-1	Rusev, Timnev (p), Filipov
06/05/00	Botev Plovdiv	A	2-6	Timnev (p), Stoinev
13/05/00	Lovech	H	1-0	Timnev
20/05/00	Pirin Blagoevgrad	A	0-2	
27/05/00	Neftochimik Bourgas	H	1-1	Goshev
03/06/00	Chernomorets Bourgas	A	2-3	Stoinev, Timnev
09/06/00	Velbazhd Kiustendil	H	5-3	Paskov 3, Timnev, Goshev (p)

VELBAZHD KIUSTENDIL

CLUB DIRECTORY

FC Velbazhd
Stadium Osogovo
2500 Kiustendil
tel - (078) 248153
fax - (078) 48153
Year of Formation - 1920
President - Georgi Iliev
Director - Emil Nakov
Coach - Dimitar Sokolov
Stadium - Osogovo (11,000)

APPEARANCES 99/00

	P	Ap	(s)	Gls
Krasimir BISLIMOV	D	18	(2)	
Stefan GOSHEV	D	6	(5)	
Ivailo GRANCHARSKI	D		(1)	
Angel HARALAMPIEV	G		(1)	
Velko HRISTEV	D	24	(2)	2
Kiril KOLEV	A	1		
Petar KOLEV	D	12	(4)	1
Ivan LITERA (YUG)	M	10		5
Ivo MAKSIMOV	M	1	(1)	
Ilian MARKOVSKI	D	1		
Biser METODIEV	A	1		
Mario METUSHEV	M	3	(7)	2
Misho MIKHAILOV	A	23	(3)	20
Nedko MILENOV	M	5	(7)	
Daniel OSTROVSKI	A	17	(2)	2
Borislav PAVLOV	M	5	(3)	
Svetlin PENEV	A		(1)	
Krasimir PETKOV	G	18		
Georgi PETROV	D	19	(2)	
Rosen PETROV	D	6	(3)	
Plamen PETROV	A	9	(9)	1
Todor PRAMATAROV	A	13		3
Mikhail ROLEV	G	11		
Georgi SLAVCHEV	D	4	(1)	
Zdravko STANKOV	D	21	(3)	
Ivan STOICHEV	A	19		3
Asen STOIANOV	D	9	(5)	1
Ilia STOIANOV	M	19	(3)	1
Nikolai VAZELOV	M	9	(4)	
Boiko VELICHKOV	M	21	(4)	5
Daniel YORDANOV	D	12	(6)	1
Evgeni YORDANOV	A	2	(5)	1

LEAGUE RESULTS 1999/2000

07/08/99	Minior Pernik	H	3-0	Stoianov A., Metushev 2
15/08/99	CSKA Sofia	A	1-3	Hristev
21/08/99	Slavia Sofia	H	1-0	Velichkov
28/08/99	Dobrudzha Dobrich	A	1-0	Pramatarov
11/09/99	Botev Plovdiv	H	2-0	Mikhailov (p), Pramatarov
18/09/99	Pirin Blagoevgrad	A	0-1	
25/09/99	Chernomorets Bourgas	H	2-1	Mikhailov (p), Velichkov (p)
02/10/99	Shumen	A	2-1	Mikhailov, Hristev
15/10/99	Levski Sofia	H	1-3	Mikhailov
23/10/99	Lokomotiv Sofia	A	1-1	Ostrovski
30/10/99	Olympic-Beroe Stara Zagora	H	4-0	Mikhailov 3 (1p), Velichkov
06/11/99	Belasitsa Petrich	A	2-1	Velichkov, Mikhailov (p)
20/11/99	Lovech	H	1-3	Mikhailov
27/11/99	Neftochimik Bourgas	A	0-1	
04/12/99	Spartak Varna	H	2-0	Pramatarov, Mikhailov
26/02/00	Minior Pernik	A	2-0	Stoichev, Mikhailov
04/03/00	CSKA Sofia	H	3-1	Mikhailov, Ostrovski, Stoianov I.
11/03/00	Slavia Sofia	A	2-1	Litera, Mikhailov
18/03/00	Dobrudzha Dobrich	H	0-0	
26/03/00	Botev Plovdiv	A	0-1	
01/04/00	Pirin Blagoevgrad	H	3-0	Mikhailov, Stoichev, Yordanov E.
08/04/00	Chernomorets Bourgas	A	1-1	Mikhailov (p)
22/04/00	Shumen	H	6-0	Petrov P., Litera 3, Mikhailov, Kolev
29/04/00	Levski Sofia	A	0-3	
06/05/00	Lokomotiv Sofia	H	1-1	Velichkov
13/05/00	Olympic-Beroe Stara Zagora	A	4-0	(w/o)
20/05/00	Belasitsa Petrich	H	2-1	Stoichev, Yordanov D.
27/05/00	Lovech	A	1-3	Litera
03/06/00	Neftochimik Bourgas	H	1-0	Mikhailov
09/06/00	Spartak Varna	A	3-5	Mikhailov 3

CROATIA

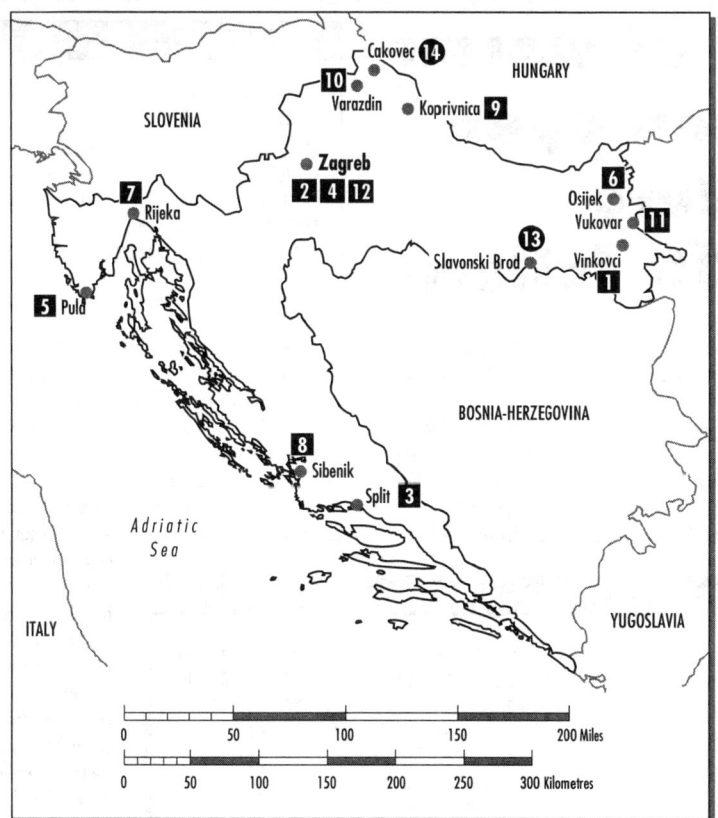

1	CIBALIA VINKOVCI	226
2	DINAMO ZAGREB	227
3	HAJDUK SPLIT	228
4	HRVATSKI DRAGOVOLJAC ZAGREB	229
5	ISTRA PULA	230
6	OSIJEK	231
7	RIJEKA	232
8	SIBENIK	233

9	SLAVEN BELUPO KOPRIVNICA	234
10	VARTEKS VARAZDIN	235
11	VUKOVAR '91	236
12	ZAGREB	237
Promoted clubs		
13	MARSONIA SLAVONSKI BROD	
14	CAKOVEC	

WHAT'S IN A NAME FOR PERENNIAL CHAMPIONS?

Can of worms prised open by Euro 2000 failure

FEDERATION DIRECTORY

Croatian Football Federation
Ilica 31, 10 000 Zagreb

tel - (01) 4831267
fax - (01) 4833346
website - www.hns-cff.hr
email - hns-ccf(monkey)zg.tel.hr

Stadium - Maksimir, Zagreb (45,000)

Year of Formation - 1991
President - Vlatko Markovic
Secretary - Zorislav Srebric

Bankruptcy, corruption and crowd disorder were the unpleasant watchwords of the 1999/2000 season in Croatia.

There were two pivotal moments which altered the face of Croatian football. The first was the national team's failure to qualify for the European Championship finals. The second was the death of state president - and unofficial national football supremo - Franjo Tudjman.

There is little doubt which event caused most grief to Croatia's football followers. It was the manner of the team's elimination which made it so painful. Needing victory at home to the 'evil enemy' from Yugoslavia in their final game, Croatia were held to a 2-2 draw - this despite having a one-man advantage for most of the game.

The misery of the capacity crowd in Zagreb was compounded by news that a late equaliser for Macedonia against Ireland in the other Group Eight match had handed Yugoslavia automatic qualification for the finals. Croatia had gone into the match buoyed by their previous three results and were fully expected (at least by their own fans) to win. But it wasn't to be, and the feeling of distress brought about by elimination resonated through the country. A mere 15 months earlier Croatia's footballers had been the pride of Eastern Europe, having finished third at the 1998 World Cup in France. Now they were destined to miss out on the Euro 2000 party, and it hurt.

There was to be no enforced departure, however, for the team's coach, Miroslav Blazevic. Early rumours of his resignation were quickly dispelled as he declared his firm intention to see out the remaining years of his contract through to the

LEAGUE CHAMPIONSHIP RESULTS 99/00

#	Team	1	2	3	4	5	6	7	8	9	10	11	12
1	Cibalia Vinkovci		1-4	2-2	2-0	3-1	2-3	0-0	3-0	0-0	3-1	0-1	0-0
				0-0				1-1	4-2	0-0	2-0	5-2	
2	Dinamo Zagreb	2-0		0-0	5-0	3-1	3-1	1-1	3-1	5-1	4-1	5-0	2-2
		3-0		3-1	3-0	2-0		2-0			0-1		
3	Hajduk Split	1-1	1-1		0-3	1-0	5-4	3-2	3-1	1-0	2-0	2-0	3-0
							1-0		0-3	0-0	0-0	4-0	5-0
4	Hrvatski dragovoljac Zagreb	2-0	2-4	0-5		1-0	3-0	0-4	1-1	2-2	0-1	1-1	1-2
		2-1		0-0		2-0		0-1		0-2			
5	Istra Pula	3-0	0-4	0-5	4-5		1-1	1-0	0-0	0-2	0-2	3-0	0-0
		0-1		1-1				2-1		0-1		4-3	
6	Osijek	1-1	1-3	2-0	2-1	1-0		3-2	3-0	2-1	1-1	2-1	0-0
		3-0	1-4		4-2	3-1		2-0			0-0		
7	Rijeka	1-3	3-1	1-2	4-2	4-1	0-1		3-1	1-1	2-0	2-0	2-0
				2-0					2-0	3-1	4-0	0-0	2-3
8	Sibenik	2-2	1-1	1-3	0-0	0-1	0-2	0-2		0-0	2-0	2-1	2-1
			2-1		2-0	3-0	1-1						2-1
9	Slaven Belupo Koprivnica	1-0	0-5	0-0	0-1	1-1	1-4	2-2	0-0		2-1	1-2	1-1
			2-0				5-2		2-1			1-0	2-0
10	Varteks Varazdin	0-3	0-3	3-2	0-0	4-1	2-0	2-1	0-0	0-1		2-0	1-1
					1-1	1-2			1-1	0-0		3-2	
11	Vukovar '91	0-0	0-0	0-2	1-0	1-3	3-1	0-0	3-0	0-0	2-2		3-4
			0-3			1-0		1-1		2-1			1-1
12	Zagreb	0-0	0-1	0-3	3-3	1-1	2-1	4-1	4-1	0-1	1-0	1-0	
		1-2	1-2		1-1	4-1	2-2					1-2	

LEAGUE CHAMPIONSHIP FINAL TABLE 99/00

			Home				Away				Total						
		Pd	W	D	L	F	A	W	D	L	F	A	W	D	L	F	A	PT	GD
1	Dinamo Zagreb	33	13	3	1	46	10	10	3	3	37	15	23	6	4	83	25	75	58
2	Hajduk Split	33	11	4	2	32	15	6	6	4	26	15	17	10	6	58	30	61	28
3	Osijek	33	11	4	2	31	17	4	4	8	24	32	15	8	10	55	49	53	6
4	Rijeka	33	11	2	4	36	16	3	5	8	18	23	14	7	12	54	39	49	15
5	Slaven Belupo Koprivnica	33	7	5	4	21	20	5	8	4	13	14	12	13	8	34	34	49	0
6	Cibalia Vinkovci	33	7	7	3	28	17	4	5	7	14	22	11	12	10	42	39	45	3
7	Varteks Varazdin	33	6	6	4	20	18	4	4	9	12	26	10	10	13	32	44	40	-12
8	Zagreb	33	6	5	6	26	22	3	7	6	16	27	9	12	12	42	49	39	-7
9	Sibenik	33	7	5	4	20	16	1	5	11	13	34	8	10	15	33	50	34	-17
10	Hrvatski dragovoljac Zagreb	33	5	4	7	17	24	3	5	9	19	34	8	9	16	36	58	33	-22
11	Istra Pula	33	5	4	7	19	26	3	2	12	14	35	8	6	19	33	61	30	-28
12	Vukovar '91	33	5	7	4	19	18	2	2	13	13	38	7	9	17	32	56	30	-24

N.B. Where two or more teams are level on points, classification is determined by the results of the matches between them.

summer of 2002. One man who did call it quits was team captain Zvonimir Boban. He had missed the big game in Zagreb through injury but he was back to bid farewell to the national team a month later when Croatia lost 3-0 to France in a friendly.

That fixture was the first of a delberately tough build-up campaign for the World Cup qualifiers, and it was perhaps unsurprising that Croatia should subsequently fail to win any of their three home fixtures in the spring against Spain (0-0), Germany (1-1) and France again (0-2). Their only positive result during that preparation period was a 2-1 victory in Austria.

Although Croatia should expect to finish in the top two of a World Cup qualifying group that includes Belgium, Scotland, Latvia and San Marino, they will need some of the mainstays of the team to make considerable improvements on their 1999/2000 form. Davor Suker, voted Croatia's 'Player of the Millennium', lasted just one season at Arsenal, where, as at Real Madrid the year before, he regularly kept the bench warm. Alen Boksic continued to struggle with injuries at Lazio before downgrading his status - if not his bank balance - with a transfer to Middlesbrough. Robert Jarni dropped into the Spanish Second Division after failing to impress at Real Madrid. And the likes of Zvonimir Soldo, Igor Stimac and Aljosa Asanovic all began to show their age. Of Croatia's many exiled stars, only the German-based Kovac brothers, Nico (Hamburg) and Robert (Leverkusen), could honestly claim to have enjoyed a genuinely rewarding season.

Slaven Bilic, another 'golden oldie', even took the retrograde step of returning home to Croatia, where, his

TOP SCORERS

21	Tomislav SOKOTA (Croatia/Dinamo Zagreb)
15	Bosko BALABAN (Rijeka)
14	Ivan BOSNJAK (Cibalia Vinkovci)
	Josip SIMIC (Croatia/Dinamo Zagreb)
13	Mate BATURINA (Hajduk Split)
	Stanko BUBALO (Osijek)
	Mario DODIK (Slaven Belupo Koprivnica)
10	Ivan LEKO (Hajduk Split)
	Vlatko DJOLONGA (Hrvatski dragovoljac Zagreb)
	Admir HASANCIC (Rijeka)
	Klaudio VUKOVIC (Sibenik)
	Amarildo ZELA (Vukovar '91)

NATIONAL TEAM RESULTS 99/00

18/08/99	Yugoslavia (ECQ)	A	Belgrade	0-0	
21/08/99	Malta (ECQ)	H	Zagreb	2-1	Stanic (34), Soldo (55)
04/09/99	Republic of Ireland (ECQ)	H	Zagreb	1-0	Suker (90)
09/10/99	Yugoslavia (ECQ)	H	Zagreb	2-2	Boksic (20), Stanic (47)
13/11/99	France	A	Saint-Denis	0-3	
23/02/00	Spain	H	Split	0-0	
29/03/00	Germany	H	Zagreb	1-1	Kovac N. (70)
26/04/00	Austria	A	Vienna	2-1	Boksic (28), Stanic (65)
28/05/00	France	H	Zagreb	0-2	

injury woes finally at an end, he rejoined his former club Hajduk Split and helped them to victory in the Croatian Cup.

Hajduk's first trophy in five years came about thanks to a two-legged 2-1 victory over arch-rivals Dinamo Zagreb in the final. It came at the cost of a three-match home-ground spectator ban, however, after major crowd disturbances forced the abandonment of the first leg in the Poljud stadium with four minutes still to play.

Hajduk were perhaps fortunate to have their 2-0 lead in that game confirmed as a final result, but they played supremely well in the second leg in Zagreb, particularly in defence (where Bilic and young goalkeeper Stipe Pletikosa were exceptional), to silence the home crowd and take the Cup.

Given the circumstances of Hajduk's victory, many in Croatia were entitled to wonder whether they would have won the Cup had Franjo Tudjman still been alive. For one

NATIONAL TEAM APPEARANCES 99/00

Coach - Miroslav BLAZEVIC	YUG	MLT	IRL	YUG	FRA	ESP	GER	AUT	FRA	Cps	Gls
Drazen LADIC (01/01/63) - Croatia/Dinamo Zagreb	G		G	G					G8	59	-
Zvonimir SOLDO (02/11/67) - VfB Stuttgart (GER)	D	D	M	M	D	D		M86	M	47	2
Igor STIMAC (06/09/67) - Derby County (ENG)/West Ham United (ENG)	D	D	D		D69	D	D	D	D	47	2
Dario SIMIC (12/11/75) - Inter (ITA)	D	D	D				D46		D	35	1
Robert KOVAC (06/04/74) - Bayer 04 Leverkusen (GER)	D		D	D62			D	D	D46	8	-
Mario STANIC (10/04/72) - Parma (ITA)	M46	M46	M84	M	M		M83	M86	M88	35	7
Zvonimir BOBAN (08/10/68) - Milan (ITA)	M81	M16			M85					51	12
Aljosa ASANOVIC (14/12/65) - Panathinaikos (GRE)	M	M	M	M	M	M84	M	M83	M58	62	3
Krunoslav JURCIC (26/11/69) - Croatia Zagreb (CRO)/Torino (ITA)	M					M			s58	19	-
Robert JARNI (26/10/68) - Real Madrid (ESP)/UD Las Palmas (ESP)	M		M	M	M	M			M	60	1
Davor SUKER (01/01/68) - Arsenal (ENG)	A	A	A	A	A	A	A		A	57	42
Milan RAPAJC (16/08/73) - Perugia (ITA)	s46	A	A	s82			s83	A75		13	-
Igor BISCAN (04/05/78) - Croatia/Dinamo Zagreb	s81	M		s62				s83		7	1
Marijan MRMIC (06/05/65) - RSC Charleroi (BEL)		G								14	-
Josip SIMIC (16/09/77) - Croatia/Dinamo Zagreb		A46	s84	s76				s86		7	1
Danijel SARIC (04/08/72) - Croatia/Dinamo Zagreb		s16			s84	M	s64	M	s46	17	-
Goran VLAOVIC (07/08/72) - Valencia CF (ESP)		s46								40	13
Alen BOKSIC (21/01/70) - Lazio (ITA)		s46	A76	A			A	A	A46	32	8
Slaven BILIC (11/09/68) - Everton (ENG)			D46							44	3
Tomislav RUKAVINA (14/10/74) - Croatia Zagreb			s46	M	M84					5	-
Goran JURIC (05/02/63) - Croatia Zagreb				D						16	-
Igor TUDOR (16/04/78) - Juventus (ITA)				D82				s86		15	-
Zeljko PAVLOVIC (02/03/71) - LASK Linz (AUT)					G			s46	s8	4	-
Stjepan TOMAS (06/03/75) - Croatia/Dinamo Zagreb					D	D	s46	D		8	1
Boris ZIVKOVIC (15/11/75) - Bayer 04 Leverkusen (GER)					s69		D64	s75		3	-
Nico KOVAC (15/10/71) - Hamburger SV (GER)					s85	M66	M	M	M	10	1
Stipe PLETIKOSA (08/01/79) - Hajduk Split						G	G	G46		6	-
Davor VUGRINEC (24/03/75) - Trabzonspor (TUR)					A					7	3
Jurica VUCKO (10/08/76) - Hajduk Split						s66			s46	3	-
Mario CVITANOVIC (06/05/75) - Dinamo Zagreb						s84				6	-
Stanko BUBALO (26/04/73) - Osijek									s88	2	-

thing, they would not have been playing 'Dinamo' Zagreb. It was after only after Tudjman's death, in December, that the club finally decided to shake off their unloved 'Croatia' prefix and return to their former name.

More significantly, Tudjman's death enabled proper investigations to be carried out into the allegations that he and his government had not only given special favours to his own club (Croatia/Dinamo) but had also 'protected' football clubs in general from having to meet their financial responsibilities.

Incidents of unpaid taxes were found to be widespread, with Dinamo Zagreb said to be around £50m in debt to the state, followed in the 'table of shame' by Hajduk (£20m) and Osijek and Rijeka (around £10m each).

Worse still, the findings of the investigators revealed that many functionaries had been placing club funds into personal bank accounts. The discovery of these slush-funds led to the imprisonment of a number of well-known names, among them Hajduk directors Vedran Rozic and Ivan Buljan.

An examination of the financial structure of Dinamo Zagreb showed that government handouts had inflated the wage bill to astronomical proportions, dwarfing the salaries on offer at other Croatian clubs.

But if the purpose of this state subsidisation was to turn Croatia/Dinamo Zagreb into a powerhouse of European football, then it proved to be an unsuccessful mission in 1999/2000. Although the club reached the Champions'

EUROPEAN CUPS 99/00

CHAMPIONS' CUP
● **CROATIA ZAGREB**
Qualifying round MTK HUNGÁRIA FC (HUN)
H 0-0
Ladic, Juric, Biscan, Tomas, Rukavina (Saric 69), Mujcin, Prosinecki, Jurcic, Cvitanovic M. (Kozniku 78), Simic, Mikic (Pavlovic 40).
A 2-0   Simic (59, 83)
Ladic, Juric, Tokic, Tomas, Rukavina, Biscan, Jurcic, Prosinecki (Jelicic 81), Cvitanovic M., Simic (Sokota 86), Kozniku (Mikic 46).

Champions' League
1st match MANCHESTER UNITED (ENG)
A 0-0
Ladic, Juric, Tokic, Tomas, Saric, Biscan, Jurcic, Rukavina (Sokota 89), Mujcin (Mumlek 69), Cvitanovic M., Simic (Mikic 68).

2nd match OLYMPIQUE MARSEILLE (FRA)
H 1-2   Sokota (64)
Ladic, Juric, Tokic (Sokota 46), Tomas, Saric, Biscan, Rukavina (Jelicic 76), Jurcic, Mujcin, Cvitanovic M. (Mumlek 46), Simic.

3rd match SK STURM GRAZ (AUT)
H 3-0   Rukavina (28), Sokota (34, 57p)
Ladic, Juric, Biscan, Tomas, Saric, Rukavina (Tokic 74), Jurcic, Mujcin (Prosinecki 67), Cvitanovic M., Sokota (Mikic 79), Simic.

4th match SK STURM GRAZ (AUT)
A 0-1
Ladic (Butina 13), Saric, Mujcin, Biscan, Juric, Tomas (Cvitanovic M. 46), Rukavina, Jurcic, Simic (Mikic 46), Prosinecki, Sokota.

5th match MANCHESTER UNITED (ENG)
H 1-2   Prosinecki (90)
Butina, Juric (Prosinecki 35), Sedloski, Tomas, Saric, Rukavina, Tokic, Mujcin, Cvitanovic M. (Mumlek 69), Sokota, Mikic (Simic 54).

6th match OLYMPIQUE MARSEILLE (FRA)
A 2-2   Mujcin (42), Mikic (83)
Butina, Rukavina, Tokic, Tomas, Saric, Prosinecki (Jelicic 70), Jurcic, Mujcin (Mumlek 67), Cvitanovic M., Sokota (Mikic 62), Simic.

● **RIJEKA**
Preliminary round 2 PARTIZAN BEOGRAD (YUG)
A 1-3   Sztipánovics (56)
Tafra, Tomisic, Matkovic, Milinovic, Cacic, Brajkovic, Hasancic, Agic, Viskovic (Pavic 46), Balaban (De Oliveira 70), Sztipánovics.
H 0-3
Tafra, Tomisic, Matkovic (Modric 46), Milinovic, Cacic, Brajkovic, Hasancic, Agic (Matulovic 69), Viskovic, Sztipánovics, Balaban (Peteh 80).

UEFA CUP
● **HAJDUK SPLIT**
Qualifying round F91 DUDELANGE (LUX)
H 5-0   Bulat (4), Baturina (44), Grdic (57), Leko (68), Deranja (90)
Pletikosa, Grdic, Djuzelov, Matic (Leko 46), Bulat, Pralija, Skoko, Musa (Miladin 73), Jazic, Baturina (Bilic M. 59), Deranja.
A 1-1   Jazic (52)
Sunara, Bulat, Jazic, Grdic, Mise, Matic (Miladin 62), Vucevic (Bilic M. 55), Skoko, Vucko, Leko (Lalic 58), Deranja.

1st round LEVSKI SOFIA (BUL)
H 0-0
Pletikosa, Lalic, Vukovic, Matic, Miladin (Bulat 54), Skoko, Leko (Vucevic 77), Jazic, Musa, Baturina (Deranja 67), Vucko.
A 0-3
Pletikosa, Lalic (Grdic 70), Matic (Mise 46), Vukovic, Bulat, Skoko, Leko, Jazic, Musa (Deranja 46), Baturina, Vucko.

● **OSIJEK**
1st round WEST HAM UNITED (ENG)
A 0-3
Galinovic, Beljan, Zebic, Vuica, Gaspar, Ergovic, Vranjes, Babic, Besirevic (Balatinac 79), Prisc (Mitu 62), Bubalo (Turkovic 82).
H 1-3   Bubalo (70)
Malovan, Beljan, Zebic, Vuica, Prisc (Jukic 63), Vranjes (Zrilic 79), Ergovic, Babic, Besirevic, Mitu, Bubalo (Turkovic 86).

PLAYERS OF THE SEASON

STIPE PLETIKOSA

21-year-old Stipe Pletikosa is considered to be the heir apparent to veteran Drazen Ladic as Croatia's national team goalkeeper. Those who have watched him develop his talent in Split have even spoken about him in the same breath as Hajduk and Yugoslavia legend Vladimir Beara. In 1999/2000 the youngster came on in leaps and bounds, both for club and country. He was Hajduk's star performer in the memorable Cup final victory over Dinamo Zagreb, and after playing a major part in qualifying the Croatian U-21 side for the European finals in Slovakia, he turned his hand successfully to the senior team, playing in three successive friendlies against Spain, Germany and Austria. His giant physical frame and armspan give him a commanding physical presence, but he also excels with his outstanding anticipation and reaction speed.

TOMISLAV SOKOTA

Without doubt the most impressive outfield player in Croatia's domestic league was 23-year-old Tomislav "Tomo" Sokota. His 21 goals for Dinamo Zagreb earned him the league's top-scorer prize and he also struck three times in the Champions' League. Not the quickest of forwards, he makes up for it with alertness in and around the box and a tremendously powerful shot. Naturally two-footed, he is confident enough to let fly with either foot and regularly finds the net from free-kicks or 'impossible' angles. A stalwart of the Croatian U-21 side, he is already being talked of as the natural successor to Davor Suker in the senior team. A big move abroad is his inevitable next step up the ladder.

DOMESTIC CUP 99/00

1/16 FINALS

Bjelovar 2, Dubrovnik 1
Neretva Metkovic 2, Inker Zapresic 1
Vukovar '91 0, Slaven Belupo Koprivnica 1
Moslavac Popovaca 0, Hajduk Split 8
Spansko Zagreb 1, Sibenik 2
Split 0, Marsonia Slavonski Brod 4
Uljanik Pula 0, Zagreb 2
Zagorec Krapina 3, Belisce 1
Sloboda Varazdin 1, Hrvatski dragovoljac Zagreb 2
Cazmatrans Cazma 1, Cibalia Vinkovci 2
Koprivnica 1, Varteks Varazdin 2
Radnik Velika Gorica 1, Rijeka 2
Mosor Zrnovnica 0, Segesta Sisak 0 (6-5 on pens.)
Nehaj Senj 2, Zadarkomerc Zadar 2 (3-2 on pens.)
BSK Bazinatours Pozega 0, Croatia Zagreb 10
Omladinac Novo Selo Rok 2, Osijek 3

1/8 FINALS

Cibalia Vinkovci 2, Hrvatski dragovoljac Zagreb 1
Nehaj Senj 0, Rijeka 1
Neretva Metkovic 0, Zagreb 6
Hajduk Split 3, Sibenik 1
Zagorec Krapina 0, Varteks Varazdin 1
Mosor Zrnovnica 0, Slaven Belupo Koprivnica 2
Bjelovar 1, Osijek 3
Croatia Zagreb 4, Marsonia Slavonski Brod 0

QUARTER-FINALS

Slaven Belupo Koprivnica 0, Hajduk Split 0
Hajduk Split 2 (Vucevic 6, Ribic 21),
Slaven Belupo Koprivnica 1 (Dodik 37)
(Hajduk Split 2-1)

Rijeka 1 (Balaban 21),
Dinamo Zagreb 2 (Pilipovic 2, Sokota 36)
Dinamo Zagreb 2 (Sokota 6, Bazina 86),
Rijeka 2 (Brajkovic 59, 90)
(Dinamo Zagreb 4-3)

Varteks Varazdin 2 (Sabolcki 49, Dobi 89),
Zagreb 1 (Peric 64)
Zagreb 2 (Bule 39, Popovic 54), Varteks Varazdin 0
(Zagreb 3-2)

Cibalia Vinkovci 2 (Bosnjak 46, Pernar 48),
Osijek 1 (Pernar 54og)
Osijek 0, Cibalia Vinkovci 0
(Cibalia Vinkovci 2-1)

SEMI-FINALS

Hajduk Split 2 (Musa 62, Bilic M. 87),
Zagreb 1 (Bule 40)
Zagreb 2 (Osibov 15, Kosic 34),
Hajduk Split 2 (Vucko 44, Mihacic 54og)
(Hajduk Split 4-3)

Cibalia Vinkovci 0,
Dinamo Zagreb 3 (Kozniku 25, Biscan 40, Mikic 80)

Dinamo Zagreb 3 (Cvitanovic I. 17, 45, Pilipovic 62),
Cibalia Vinkovci 1 (Mujcin 64og)
(Dinamo Zagreb 6-1)

FINAL

02/05/2000, Split
HAJDUK SPLIT 2 Vucko (38p, 53)
DINAMO ZAGREB 0
referee - Kovacic
HAJDUK SPLIT - Pletikosa, Djuzelov, Bilic S., Grdic,
Miladin, Musa, Mise (Andric 70), Leko, Jazic,
Baturina, Vucko (Bilic M. 75).
DINAMO ZAGREB - Ladic, Tokic, Juric, Tomas, Saric,
Mujcin, Biscan, Pavlovic (Sabic 65), Krznar, Simic
(Cvitanovic I. 54), Sokota (Mikic 78).

16/05/2000, Zagreb
DINAMO ZAGREB 1 Cvitanovic I. (90)
HAJDUK SPLIT 0
referee - Siric
DINAMO ZAGREB - Ladic, Saric (Bazina 74),
Cvitanovic M. (Krznar 66), Sedloski, Tokic, Tomas,
Biscan, Sabic, Sokota, Mujcin (Pavlovic 56),
Cvitanovic I..
HAJDUK SPLIT - Pletikosa, Miladin, Jazic, Djuzelov,
Bilic S., Grdic, Musa, Mise (Bulat 62), Vucko, Leko,
Baturina (Deranja 68; Bilic M. 71).

(HAJDUK SPLIT 2-1)

League, they were unable to build on the promise of an opening draw away to holders Manchester United and ended up bottom of the group, even below the modest Austrians of Sturm Graz.

The club had manifested their ambition at the start of the campaign by recruiting Osvaldo Ardiles, the ex-Argentinian World Cup winner, as coach, but after the Champions' League elimination he was swiftly ushered towards the exit door and replaced by his assistant (and previous incumbent) Marijan Vlak. Ardiles had been the first foreign coach employed by a Croatian club, but the experience was a negative one for all concerned.

With a former name and a former coach restored, Dinamo became a better team in the spring, and although the Croatian Cup was to elude them, they romped to victory in the league, winning the title for the fifth year in succession.

At the winter break Dinamo were neck-and-neck with Hajduk, and they even fell four points behind two games after the restart. But no sooner had they dropped back than they were out in front again, and a brilliant closing run of eight wins in nine games ensured that the title would be returning yet again to the capital - with or without assistance from men in high places.

14 points was Dinamo's ultimate margin of victory, and the players most responsible for establishing that level of

INTERNATIONAL HONOURS

World Cup Finals appearances: 1998 (3rd)

European Championship appearances: 1996

European Club Competitions
Fairs' Cup   Dinamo Zagreb (1967)

supremacy were striker Tomislav Sokota (with 21 goals, the league's top marksman), versatility man Igor Biscan and centre-backs Stjepan Tomas and Mario Tokic. The highly-paid Robert Prosinecki also had his moments, but his perpetual lack of fitness ensured that the Dinamo fans were treated only rarely to his vast potential, and at the end of the season the former world-class midfielder caused quite a stir when he announced that he was joining local side Hrvatski dragovoljac... before later revealing that this would only be a temporary stop before he journeyed on to Japan to join Gamba Osaka.

Like two other star names, Krunoslav Jurcic and Tomislav Rukavina, who had left Dinamo to join Italian Serie A clubs in mid-season, Prosinecki realised that, given the unsettled situation, it would be wise to get out while he could and pursue his career elsewhere.

PROMOTED CLUBS 99/00

SECOND DIVISION FINAL TABLE

		Pd	W	D	L	F	A	Pt	GD
1	**Marsonia Slavonski Brod**	32	19	7	6	52	18	64	34
2	**Cakovec**	32	18	9	5	62	38	63	24
3	Zadarkomerc Zadar	32	19	5	8	47	25	62	22
4	Pomorac Kostrena	32	17	9	6	49	26	60	23
5	Mosor Zrnovnica	32	17	8	7	55	26	59	29
6	Segesta Sisak	32	15	11	6	58	29	56	29
7	PIK Vrbovec	32	15	10	7	57	39	55	18
8	Solin Gradja	32	15	6	11	53	42	51	11
9	Orijent Rijeka	32	10	11	11	37	41	41	-4
10	Belisce	32	11	6	15	42	43	39	-1
11	Jadran Porec	32	11	5	16	37	53	38	-16
12	Croatia Sesvete	32	9	7	16	38	48	34	-10
13	Bjelovar	32	9	5	18	38	49	32	-11
14	Cazmatrans	32	7	8	17	33	50	29	-17
15	Split	32	6	8	18	29	68	26	-39
16	Zagorec Krapina	32	5	7	20	24	63	22	-39
17	Otok	32	6	4	22	28	81	22	-53

CLUB DIRECTORIES

NK Marsonia
Brace Radic 26
35000 Slavonski Brod
tel - (035) 231153
fax - (035) 231153
Year of Formation - 1909
President - Dragan Maric
Secretary - Simo Zirdum
Coach - Ilija Loncarevic
Stadium - Kraj Save (5,000)

NK Cakovec
Sportsko 2
40300 Cakovec
tel - (040) 315800
fax - (040) 315800
President - Stjepan Hamonajec
Secretary - Edo Pongrac
Coach - Drazen Besek
Stadium - Mladost (5,000)

CIBALIA VINKOVCI

CLUB DIRECTORY

HNK Cibalia
Ruzina 13
32100 Vinkovci
tel - (032) 332356
fax - (032) 332364
Year of Formation - 1947
President - Bozo Galic
Secretary - Ranko Zagorac
Coach - Srecko Lusic
Stadium - Mladost (15,000)

APPEARANCES 99/00

	P	Ap	(s)	Gls
Antun ANDRICEVIC	D	21		
Darko ANTIC	M		(1)	
Mladen BARTOLOVIC	A	29		9
Ivan BOSNJAK	A	31	(1)	14
Mario CUTURA	D	26		2
Tomislav DABRO	D	4	(7)	
Velimir GRGIC	A	3	(7)	
Oliver GUDELJ	D	2	(4)	
Ivica IVEZIC	M		(1)	
Admir JOLDIC (BOS)	M		(2)	
Jure JURIC	M	29	(1)	1
Mario JURIC	D	8	(3)	
Ante KELAVA	D		(3)	
Mario KRIZANOVIC	D	11	(10)	
Ivan LAJTMAN	M		(7)	
Boris LEUTAR	D	25		
Mario LUCIC	D		(1)	
Ivica MARIC	G	16		
Ivica MARINCIC	M	2	(10)	
Ivan MAROSLAVAC	M	28	(1)	2
Goran MESTROVIC	M	26		7
Mario MESTROVIC	M	18	(2)	2
Mario PAJIC	A		(1)	
Ilica PERIC	G	17		
Drazen PERNAR	D	30		1
Zlatko RAGUZ	D	8		
Ivan RAVLIC	D	6	(4)	
Igor TKALCEVIC	D	21	(4)	2
Hari VUKAS	A	2	(6)	

LEAGUE RESULTS 1999/2000

24/07/99	Croatia Zagreb	A	0-2	
31/07/99	Zagreb	H	0-0	
28/08/99	Varteks Varazdin	A	3-0	Maroslavac, Bartolovic, Mestrovic G.
07/09/99	Slaven Belupo Koprivnica	H	0-0	
11/09/99	Sibenik	A	2-2	Juric, Mestrovic G.
19/09/99	Osijek	H	2-3	Bosnjak 2 (1p)
26/09/99	Rijeka	A	3-1	Mestrovic G. 3 (3p)
02/10/99	Hrvatski dragovoljac Zagreb	H	2-0	Bosnjak, Bartolovic
12/10/99	Istra Pula	A	0-3	
16/10/99	Hajduk Split	H	2-2	Cutura, Tkalcevic
23/10/99	Vukovar '91	A	0-0	
06/11/99	Zagreb	A	0-0	
23/11/99	Varteks Varazdin	H	3-1	Bosnjak 2, Bartolovic
27/11/99	Slaven Belupo Koprivnica	A	0-1	
04/12/99	Sibenik	H	3-0	Bosnjak 2, Mestrovic G.
07/12/99	Croatia Zagreb	H	1-4	Bosnjak
19/02/00	Osijek	A	1-1	Bartolovic
26/02/00	Rijeka	H	0-0	
29/02/00	Hrvatski dragovoljac Zagreb	A	0-2	
04/03/00	Istra Pula	H	3-1	Cutura, og (Bozac), Bartolovic
07/03/00	Hajduk Split	A	1-1	Mestrovic M.
11/03/00	Vukovar '91	H	0-1	
18/03/00	Sibenik	H	4-2	Bosnjak 2, Pernar, Bartolovic
25/03/00	Varteks Varazdin	H	2-0	Mestrovic G. (p), Maroslavac
01/04/00	Zagreb	A	2-1	Bosnjak, Bartolovic
08/04/00	Rijeka	H	1-1	og (Tomisic)
11/04/00	Osijek	A	0-3	
15/04/00	Hajduk Split	H	0-0	
22/04/00	Dinamo Zagreb	A	0-3	
29/04/00	Slaven Belupo Koprivnica	H	0-0	
06/05/00	Hrvatski dragovoljac Zagreb	A	1-2	Tkalcevic
09/05/00	Vukovar '91	H	5-2	Bartolovic, Mestrovic M., Bosnjak 3
13/05/00	Istra Pula	A	1-0	Bartolovic

DINAMO ZAGREB

CLUB DIRECTORY

NK Dinamo
Maksimirska 128, 10 000 Zagreb
tel - (01) 2334111
fax - (01) 212316
Year of Formation - 1945
President - Mirko Barisic
Secretary - Ivan Bedi
Coach - Osvaldo Ardiles; Marijan Vlak
Stadium - Maksimir (45,000)

MAJOR HONOURS
League Championship - (6)
1993, 1996, 1997, 1998, 1999, 2000.
League Championship (Yugoslavia) - (4)
1948, 1954, 1958, 1982.
Domestic Cup - (4) 1994, 1996, 1997, 1998.
Domestic Cup (Yugoslavia) - (8) 1951, 1960,
1963, 1965, 1969, 1973, 1980, 1983.
Fairs' Cup - (1) 1967.

APPEARANCES 99/00

		P	Ap	(s)	Gls
Mario BAZINA	A	2	(7)	1
Igor BISCAN	M	28	(1)	6
Sasa BJELANOVIC	A		(1)	
Tomislav BUTINA	G	4	(2)	
Igor CVITANOVIC	A	10	(2)	6
Mario CVITANOVIC	D	19	(5)	1
Josko JELICIC	M	2	(2)	
Krunoslav JURCIC	M	13		4
Goran JURIC	D	20	(1)	
Ardian KOZNIKU	A	2	(6)	1
Damir KRZNAR	D	9	(3)	1
Drazen LADIC	G	28		
Mihael MIKIC	A	12	(14)	6
Grazvydas MIKULENAS (LIT)	A	1	(3)	1
Edin MUJCIN (BOS)	M	19	(6)	3
Miljenko MUMLEK	M	6	(3)	5
Zoran PAVLOVIC (SLO)	M	11	(4)	2
Renato PILIPOVIC	M	7	(12)	
Robert PROSINECKI	M	19		5
Tomislav RUKAVINA	M	8	(5)	1
Nermin SABIC (BOS)	M	7	(11)	1
Danijel SARIC	M	27	(1)	1
Goce SEDLOSKI (MAC)	D	10		1
Josip SIMIC	A	16	(4)	14
Tomislav SOKOTA	A	28	(2)	21
Mario TOKIC	D	24	(1)	1
Stjepan TOMAS	D	30		
Vladimir VASILJ	G	1		

LEAGUE RESULTS 1999/2000

24/07/99	Cibalia Vinkovci	H	2-0	Jurcic, Simic
31/07/99	Varteks Varazdin	H	4-1	Simic, Prosinecki (p), Mujcin, Jurcic
29/08/99	Sibenik	A	1-1	Prosinecki
07/09/99	Rijeka	H	1-1	Simic
10/09/99	Istra Pula	A	4-0	Simic 2, Mumlek, Mikulenas
17/09/99	Vukovar '91	H	5-0	Sokota, Mumlek 2, Simic 2 (1p)
25/09/99	Zagreb	A	1-0	Simic
02/10/99	Slaven Belupo Koprivnica	H	5-1	Sokota, Cvitanovic M., Biscan 2, Prosinecki
12/10/99	Osijek	A	3-1	Sokota 3
15/10/99	Hrvatski dragovoljac Zagreb	H	5-0	Sokota 2, Prosinecki, Simic, Rukavina
23/10/99	Hajduk Split	A	1-1	Sokota
06/11/99	Varteks Varazdin	A	3-0	Simic, Saric, Mikic
23/11/99	Sibenik	H	3-1	Simic, Jurcic, Mikic
27/11/99	Rijeka	A	1-3	Simic
04/12/99	Istra Pula	H	3-1	Simic, Sokota, Mumlek
07/12/99	Cibalia Vinkovci	A	4-1	Prosinecki, Sokota, Mujcin, Jurcic
19/02/00	Vukovar '91	A	0-0	
26/02/00	Zagreb	H	2-2	Sokota, Tokic
29/02/00	Slaven Belupo Koprivnica	A	5-0	Sokota 2, Cvitanovic I., Sabic, Mikic
04/03/00	Osijek	H	3-1	Pavlovic, Sokota, Cvitanovic I.
07/03/00	Hrvatski dragovoljac Zagreb	A	4-2	Cvitanovic I., Sokota, Mikic, Mumlek
11/03/00	Hajduk Split	H	0-0	
18/03/00	Varteks Varazdin	H	0-1	
25/03/00	Slaven Belupo Koprivnica	A	0-2	
01/04/00	Hrvatski dragovoljac Zagreb	H	3-0	Sokota (p), Mikic, Kozniku
08/04/00	Vukovar '91	A	3-0	Krznar, Bazina, Biscan
11/04/00	Istra Pula	H	2-0	Sokota, Simic
15/04/00	Sibenik	A	1-2	Sokota
22/04/00	Cibalia Vinkovci	H	3-0	Biscan 2 (1p), Mikic
29/04/00	Zagreb	A	2-1	Sokota, og (Biskup)
06/05/00	Rijeka	H	2-0	Cvitanovic I., Mujcin
09/05/00	Osijek	A	4-1	Cvitanovic I. 2, Pavlovic, Sokota (p)
13/05/00	Hajduk Split	H	3-1	Biscan, Sedloski, Sokota

HAJDUK SPLIT

CLUB DIRECTORY

HNK Hajduk
Poljudsko setaliste bb, 21 000 Split
tel - (021) 355444 / fax - (021) 585630
Year of Formation - 1911
President - Sime Luketin
Secretary - Fredi Fiorentini
Coach - Ivan Katalinic; Ivica Matkovic;
Petar Nadoveza
Stadium - Poljud (50,000)

MAJOR HONOURS
League Championship - (3) 1992, 1994, 1995.
League Championship (Yugoslavia) - (9)
1927, 1929, 1950, 1952, 1955, 1971, 1974,
1975, 1979.
Domestic Cup - (3) 1993, 1995, 2000.
Domestic Cup (Yugoslavia) - (9) 1967, 1972,
1973, 1974, 1976, 1977, 1984, 1987, 1991.

APPEARANCES 99/00

	P	Ap	(s)	Gls
Srdjan ANDRIC	M	8	(3)	
Mate BATURINA	A	29	(3)	13
Mate BILIC	A	12	(16)	6
Slaven BILIC	D	9		
Josip BULAT	D	17	(2)	1
Mario CAREVIC	A		(2)	
Zvonimir DERANJA	A	16	(3)	6
Igor DJUZELOV (MAC)	D	9	(3)	
Anthony GRDIC (AUS)	D	15	(3)	
Ante JAZIC (CAN)	D	20	(4)	1
Vik LALIC	D	18	(5)	2
Ivan LEKO	M	28		10
Stipe MATIC	D	17	(5)	
Darko MILADIN	D	21	(4)	
Ante MISE	M	5	(7)	
Jasmin MUJDZA (BOS)	D	8	(1)	1
Igor MUSA	M	28	(3)	6
Angelo PANOV (MAC)	D		(2)	
Tonci PIRIJA	D		(3)	
Stipe PLETIKOSA	G	32		
Nenad PRALIJA	M	1	(1)	1
Jurica PULJIZ	D	5	(3)	1
Mate RADELJIC	D	4	(4)	
Zoran RATKOVIC	A		(7)	
Josip RIBIC	A	1	(2)	
Goran SABLIC	D	5	(1)	1
Josip SKOKO (AUS)	M	15		
Dario SRNA	A		(2)	
Kresimir SUNARA	G	1		
Goran VUCEVIC	M	6	(3)	
Jurica VUCKO	A	20	(1)	6
Hrvoje VUKOVIC	D	13	(3)	

LEAGUE RESULTS 1999/2000

28/07/99	Varteks Varazdin	A	2-3	Sablic, Pralija
01/08/99	Sibenik	H	3-1	Baturina, Musa, Lalic
29/08/99	Rijeka	A	2-1	Musa, Bilic M.
07/09/99	Istra Pula	H	1-0	Jazic
11/09/99	Vukovar '91	A	2-0	Vucko (p), Bilic M.
19/09/99	Zagreb	H	3-0	Leko, Vucko 2 (1p)
25/09/99	Slaven Belupo Koprivnica	A	0-0	
03/10/99	Osijek	H	5-4	Mujdza, Leko, Vucko 2 (1p), Baturina
12/10/99	Hrvatski dragovoljac Zagreb	A	5-0	Baturina, Deranja 2, Vucko, Bulat
16/10/99	Cibalia Vinkovci	A	2-2	Musa, Bilic M.
23/10/99	Croatia Zagreb	H	1-1	Lalic
30/10/99	Varteks Varazdin	H	2-0	Deranja, Bilic M.
06/11/99	Sibenik	A	3-1	Deranja, Baturina, Leko
23/11/99	Rijeka	H	3-2	Baturina 2, Leko
27/11/99	Istra Pula	A	5-0	Baturina 2, og (Cernjul), Deranja, Puljiz
04/12/99	Vukovar '91	H	2-0	og (Sesar), Leko
19/02/00	Zagreb	A	3-0	Leko 2 (1p), Musa
26/02/00	Slaven Belupo Koprivnica	H	1-0	Musa
29/02/00	Osijek	A	0-2	
04/03/00	Hrvatski dragovoljac Zagreb	H	0-3	(w/o)
07/03/00	Cibalia Vinkovci	H	1-1	Baturina
11/03/00	Dinamo Zagreb	A	0-0	
18/03/00	Slaven Belupo Koprivnica	H	0-0	
25/03/00	Hrvatski dragovoljac Zagreb	A	0-0	
01/04/00	Vukovar '91	H	4-0	Musa, Leko, Baturina 2
08/04/00	Istra Pula	A	1-1	Leko
11/04/00	Sibenik	H	0-3	(w/o)
15/04/00	Cibalia Vinkovci	A	0-0	
22/04/00	Zagreb	H	5-0	Baturina 2, Bilic M. 2, Leko
29/04/00	Rijeka	A	0-2	
06/05/00	Osijek	H	1-0	og (Ergovic)
09/05/00	Varteks Varazdin	H	0-0	
13/05/00	Dinamo Zagreb	A	1-3	Deranja

HRVATSKI DRAGOVOLJAC ZAGREB

CLUB DIRECTORY

NK Hrvatski dragovoljac
Aleja pomoraca 25
10 000 Zagreb
tel - (01) 6555030
fax - (01) 6520341
Year of Formation - 1975
President - Stjepan Spajic
Secretary - Ivan Cvjetkovic
Coach - Branko Tucak; Milan Petkovic;
Milivoj Bracun
Stadium - Inker (15,000)

APPEARANCES 99/00

	P	Ap	(s)	Gls
Mario ANDRACIC	A	17	(3)	1
Mario BAZINA	A	5		1
Nevio BERDI	M	3	(6)	
Dragan BODUL	A	5	(8)	
Spomenko BOSNJAK	D	25		1
Igor CALO	A	23	(2)	9
Silvije CAVLINA	G	12		
Vlatko DJOLONGA	D	30		10
Antonio FRANJA	A	4	(16)	3
Andriy GRISCHENKO (UKR)	A	10	(4)	
Rajko GRLIC	D	4		
Oliver GUDELJ	D	2	(1)	
Bernard GULIC	M	10	(11)	
Branko JAGIC	M		(2)	
Predrag JURIC	M	19	(4)	
Davorin KABLAR	D	1		
Neno KATULIC	A	19	(8)	
Marin LALIC	M	12	(3)	1
Ivo MAGLICA	M	10	(2)	
Elvis MARGETA	D	17		1
Nikica MILETIC	M	28	(1)	
Frane PETRICEVIC	A	26	(4)	4
Anto PETROVIC	D	24		
Kresimir POLETI	D	12	(2)	
Branko PULJIC	M	9	(6)	
Zankarlo SIMUNIC	G	21	(1)	
Zeljko SKOPLJANAC	D	10	(1)	1
Robert SUSAC	D	5	(3)	

LEAGUE RESULTS 1999/2000

24/07/99	Sibenik	A	0-0	
24/08/99	Rijeka	H	0-4	
28/08/99	Istra Pula	A	5-4	Djolonga 3 (2p), Petricevic, Franja
07/09/99	Vukovar '91	H	1-1	Calo
11/09/99	Zagreb	A	3-3	Calo, Djolonga (p), Franja
18/09/99	Slaven Belupo Koprivnica	H	2-2	Djolonga 2 (1p)
25/09/99	Osijek	A	1-2	Petricevic
02/10/99	Cibalia Vinkovci	A	0-2	
12/10/99	Hajduk Split	H	0-5	
15/10/99	Croatia Zagreb	A	0-5	
23/10/99	Varteks Varazdin	H	0-1	
30/10/99	Sibenik	H	1-1	Djolonga
06/11/99	Rijeka	A	2-4	Bosnjak, Calo
23/11/99	Istra Pula	H	1-0	Bazina (p)
27/11/99	Vukovar '91	A	0-1	
04/12/99	Zagreb	H	1-2	Djolonga
19/02/00	Slaven Belupo Koprivnica	A	1-0	Djolonga
26/02/00	Osijek	H	3-0	Petricevic, Andracic, Calo
29/02/00	Cibalia Vinkovci	H	2-0	Calo, Franja (p)
04/03/00	Hajduk Split	A	3-0	(w/o)
07/03/00	Dinamo Zagreb	H	2-4	Calo, Djolonga
11/03/00	Varteks Varazdin	A	0-0	
18/03/00	Osijek	A	2-4	Calo, Margeta
25/03/00	Hajduk Split	H	0-0	
01/04/00	Dinamo Zagreb	A	0-3	
08/04/00	Slaven Belupo Koprivnica	H	0-2	
11/04/00	Varteks Varazdin	A	1-1	Skopljanac
15/04/00	Vukovar '91	A	0-2	
22/04/00	Istra Pula	H	2-0	Lalic, Petricevic
29/04/00	Sibenik	A	0-2	
06/05/00	Cibalia Vinkovci	H	2-1	Calo, og (Tkalcevic)
09/05/00	Zagreb	A	1-1	Calo
13/05/00	Rijeka	H	0-1	

ISTRA PULA

CLUB DIRECTORY

NK Istra
Marsovo polje 8
52100 Pula
tel - (052) 210870
fax - (052) 223856
Year of Formation - 1961
President - Mladen Ivancic
Secretary - Branko Bubic
Coach - Dragan Simeunovic; Rajko Magic
Stadium - Gradski (7,000)

APPEARANCES 99/00

	P	Ap	(s)	Gls
Zaim ALIBASIC	M	8	(3)	
Valter ANDROSIC	D	6	(2)	
Zelimir BAGAVAC	M	17	(7)	
Igor BERNOBIC	D	12	(1)	
Sasa BJELANOVIC	A	14		4
Dalibor BOZAC	D	30		2
Tomislav CERNJUL	D	13	(1)	
Miroslav DJOKIC (MAC)	A	6	(5)	1
Sandi DOBRIC	M	10	(3)	
Viktor DVIRNIK (UKR)	A	16	(1)	1
Nereo FATORIC	M	24	(5)	3
Mate GAZILJ	M		(1)	
Nedim HALILOVIC (BOS)	M		(1)	
Sergej JAKIREVIC	M	9	(1)	
Alen JURIC	A	1	(1)	
Ivica LANDEKA	D	4	(2)	
Ivica MILOS	M		(1)	
David MODRUSAN	G	5	(2)	
Antonio MOMCILOVSKI	A	13	(3)	
Tihomir NOSEK	A	12	(13)	9
Danijel OSTOVIC	M	5	(13)	1
Sasa PERSIC	D	9	(5)	
Ivan PETROVIC	G	26		
Kristijan POLOVANEC	M	13		2
Dragan RAKOVIC	D	25	(1)	5
Marko SAFRAN	D		(1)	
Elvis SCORIA	A	4	(3)	
Predrag SMOLCIC	D	3	(2)	
Kristijan STEKO	G	2		
Ognjen UGRCIC	D	29		
Igor ZIKOVIC	M	13	(8)	4
Andrej ZIVKOVIC	M	29		
Antonio ZUPAN	M	5	(5)	1

LEAGUE RESULTS 1999/2000

24/07/99	Slaven Belupo Koprivnica	H	0-2	
31/07/99	Osijek	A	0-1	
28/08/99	Hrvatski dragovoljac Zagreb	H	4-5	Rakovic (p), Zikovic, Bjelanovic 2
07/09/99	Hajduk Split	A	0-1	
10/09/99	Croatia Zagreb	H	0-4	
18/09/99	Varteks Varazdin	A	1-4	Fatoric
25/09/99	Sibenik	H	0-0	
02/10/99	Rijeka	A	1-4	Bjelanovic
12/10/99	Cibalia Vinkovci	H	3-0	Ostovic, Rakovic, Zikovic
16/10/99	Vukovar '91	H	3-0	Nosek 2, Rakovic
23/10/99	Zagreb	A	1-1	Zikovic
30/10/99	Slaven Belupo Koprivnica	A	1-1	Bozac
06/11/99	Osijek	H	1-1	Bjelanovic
23/11/99	Hrvatski dragovoljac Zagreb	A	0-1	
27/11/99	Hajduk Split	H	0-5	
04/12/99	Croatia Zagreb	A	1-3	Dvirnik
19/02/00	Varteks Varazdin	H	0-2	
26/02/00	Sibenik	A	1-0	Bozac
29/02/00	Rijeka	H	1-0	Nosek
04/03/00	Cibalia Vinkovci	A	1-3	Polovanec
07/03/00	Vukovar '91	A	3-1	Zikovic, Fatoric, Nosek
11/03/00	Zagreb	H	0-0	
18/03/00	Zagreb	A	1-4	Polovanec (p)
25/03/00	Rijeka	H	2-1	Nosek, Zupan
01/04/00	Osijek	A	1-3	Djokic
08/04/00	Hajduk Split	H	1-1	Nosek
11/04/00	Dinamo Zagreb	A	0-2	
15/04/00	Slaven Belupo Koprivnica	H	0-1	
22/04/00	Hrvatski dragovoljac Zagreb	A	0-2	
29/04/00	Vukovar '91	H	4-3	Rakovic, Nosek 3
06/05/00	Varteks Varazdin	A	2-1	Rakovic, Fatoric
09/05/00	Sibenik	A	0-3	
13/05/00	Cibalia Vinkovci	H	0-1	

OSIJEK

CLUB DIRECTORY

NK Osijek
Wilsonova bb
31 000 Osijek
tel - (031) 570300
fax - (031) 570500
Year of Formation - 1946
President - Antun Novalic
Secretary - Milan Spanjic
Coach - Stanko Poklepovic; Pavao Strugacevac;
Stanko Mrsic
Stadium - Gradski vrt (22,000)

MAJOR HONOURS
Domestic Cup - (1) 1999.

APPEARANCES 99/00

	P	Ap	(s)	Gls
Marko BABIC	M	13		
Josip BALATINAC	M	16	(14)	3
Mario BARISIC	M		(1)	
Ivica BELJAN	D	28		2
Bakir BESIREVIC (BOS)	M	23	(2)	1
Nenad BJELICA	M	16		7
Kresimir BRKIC	A		(1)	
Stanko BUBALO	A	31	(1)	13
Ivo ERGOVIC	D	32		3
Mario GALINOVIC	G	3		
Josip GASPAR	M	17	(5)	
Dejan GODAR	M	2	(1)	
Ronald GRNJA	M	14	(11)	2
Ivan JUKIC	M		(1)	
Stjepan JUKIC	M	9	(12)	
Jaksa KRSTULOVIC	M	4	(1)	1
Goran LJUBOJEVIC	A		(1)	
Domagoj MALOVAN	G	30		
Mario MIJATOVIC	A		(1)	
Dumitru MITU (ROM)	A	16	(13)	2
Igor OSTOPANJ	D	3	(4)	
Milan PAVLICIC	A	1	(7)	1
Mario PRISC	M	21	(5)	1
Almir TURKOVIC (BOS)	A	18	(1)	7
Jurica VRANJES	M	15		4
Damir VUICA	D	25		1
Dalibor ZEBIC	D	21	(2)	
Dubravko ZRILIC	A	5	(9)	5

LEAGUE RESULTS 1999/2000

24/07/99	Rijeka	A	1-0	Bubalo
31/07/99	Istra Pula	H	1-0	Zrilic
28/08/99	Vukovar '91	A	1-3	Zrilic
07/09/99	Zagreb	H	0-0	
11/09/99	Slaven Belupo Koprivnica	A	4-1	Vranjes, Ergovic, Mitu, Prisc
19/09/99	Cibalia Vinkovci	A	3-2	Balatinac, Vranjes, Grnja
25/09/99	Hrvatski dragovoljac Zagreb	H	2-1	Beljan, Balatinac
03/10/99	Hajduk Split	A	4-5	Vranjes 2, Bubalo, og (Vucko)
12/10/99	Croatia Zagreb	H	1-3	Bubalo
16/10/99	Varteks Varazdin	A	0-2	
23/10/99	Sibenik	H	3-0	Turkovic 2, Pavlicic
30/10/99	Rijeka	H	3-2	Turkovic, Ergovic, Bubalo
06/11/99	Istra Pula	A	1-1	Turkovic
23/11/99	Vukovar '91	H	2-1	Bubalo 2
27/11/99	Zagreb	A	1-2	Vuica
04/12/99	Slaven Belupo Koprivnica	H	2-1	Besirevic (p), Bubalo
19/02/00	Cibalia Vinkovci	H	1-1	Bjelica (p)
26/02/00	Hrvatski dragovoljac Zagreb	A	0-3	
29/02/00	Hajduk Split	H	2-0	Turkovic, Bubalo
04/03/00	Dinamo Zagreb	A	1-3	Bjelica
07/03/00	Varteks Varazdin	H	1-1	Turkovic
11/03/00	Sibenik	A	2-0	Bjelica, Zrilic
18/03/00	Hrvatski dragovoljac Zagreb	H	4-2	og (Skopljanac), Bubalo 2, Bjelica (p)
25/03/00	Vukovar '91	A	1-1	Beljan
01/04/00	Istra Pula	H	3-1	Bubalo 2, Turkovic
08/04/00	Sibenik	A	1-1	Ergovic
11/04/00	Cibalia Vinkovci	H	3-0	Balatinac, Zrilic 2
15/04/00	Zagreb	A	2-2	Mitu, Bjelica (p)
22/04/00	Rijeka	H	2-0	Krstulovic, Grnja
29/04/00	Varteks Varazdin	H	0-0	
06/05/00	Hajduk Split	A	0-1	
09/05/00	Dinamo Zagreb	H	1-4	Bjelica
13/05/00	Slaven Belupo Koprivnica	A	2-5	Bubalo, Bjelica (p)

RIJEKA

CLUB DIRECTORY

NK Rijeka
Portic 3
51 000 Rijeka
tel - (051) 261622
fax - (051) 261174
Year of Formation - 1946
President - Zarko Tomljanovic
Secretary - Nikola Tomac
Coach - Nenad Gracan
Stadium - Kantrida (21,000)

MAJOR HONOURS
Domestic Cup (Yugoslavia) - (2) 1978, 1979.

APPEARANCES 99/00

		P	Ap	(s)	Gls
Jasmin AGIC	M		28		3
Bosko BALABAN	A		29		15
Igor BERNOBIC	D			(1)	
Goran BRAJKOVIC	M		31		2
Bozidar CACIC	D		21		1
Kristijan CAVAL	D		6	(5)	2
Sérgio DE OLIVEIRA (BRA)	A			(1)	
Admir HASANCIC (BOS)	A		24	(1)	10
Darko HORVAT	G		3		
Sandro KLIC	M			(4)	
Slavko LINIC	M			(1)	
Damir MATULOVIC	M		28	(2)	
Andre MIJATOVIC	D		21		2
Ante MILICIC	A		8	(14)	5
Damir MILINOVIC	D		24		3
Josip MODRIC	D			(1)	
Dalibor PAULETIC	D		1	(1)	
Boris PAVIC	M		14	(5)	
Vedran PETEH	M		2	(1)	
Stipe REZIC	M		4	(3)	
Zdravko SIMIC	A			(1)	
Stjepan SKOCIBUSIC	D		13	(3)	1
Antonio STRILIC	M			(2)	
Barnabás SZTIPÁNOVICS (HUN)	A		28	(1)	5
Dzoni TAFRA	G		30		
Mauro TOMISIC	D		19	(2)	
Dalibor VISKOVIC	M		22	(2)	1
Kazimir VULIC	M		7	(4)	

LEAGUE RESULTS 1999/2000

24/07/99	Osijek	H	0-1	
24/08/99	Hrvatski dragovoljac Zagreb	A	4-0	Brajkovic, Milinovic, Balaban 2 (1p)
29/08/99	Hajduk Split	H	1-2	Agic
07/09/99	Croatia Zagreb	A	1-1	Milinovic
11/09/99	Varteks Varazdin	H	2-0	Viskovic, Balaban (p)
18/09/99	Sibenik	A	2-0	Skocibusic, Brajkovic
26/09/99	Cibalia Vinkovci	H	1-3	Balaban
02/10/99	Istra Pula	H	4-1	Hasancic, Milicic 2, Balaban (p)
12/10/99	Vukovar '91	A	0-0	
16/10/99	Zagreb	H	2-0	Balaban (p), Sztipánovics
23/10/99	Slaven Belupo Koprivnica	A	2-2	Balaban (p), Agic
30/10/99	Osijek	A	2-3	Agic, Hasancic
06/11/99	Hrvatski dragovoljac Zagreb	H	4-2	Balaban 3, Hasancic
23/11/99	Hajduk Split	A	2-3	Sztipánovics, Balaban
27/11/99	Croatia Zagreb	H	3-1	Balaban 2, Sztipánovics
04/12/99	Varteks Varazdin	A	1-2	Hasancic
19/02/00	Sibenik	H	3-1	Sztipánovics 2, Caval
26/02/00	Cibalia Vinkovci	A	0-0	
29/02/00	Istra Pula	A	0-1	
04/03/00	Vukovar '91	H	2-0	Balaban, Hasancic
07/03/00	Zagreb	A	1-4	Hasancic
11/03/00	Slaven Belupo Koprivnica	H	1-1	og (Kacic)
18/03/00	Vukovar '91	H	0-0	
25/03/00	Istra Pula	A	1-2	Cacic
01/04/00	Sibenik	H	2-0	og (Bakula), og (Budanovic)
08/04/00	Cibalia Vinkovci	A	1-1	Balaban
11/04/00	Zagreb	H	2-3	Milicic 2
15/04/00	Varteks Varazdin	H	4-0	Caval, Milicic, Milinovic, Mijatovic
22/04/00	Osijek	A	0-2	
29/04/00	Hajduk Split	H	2-0	og (Djuzelov), Hasancic
06/05/00	Dinamo Zagreb	A	0-2	
09/05/00	Slaven Belupo Koprivnica	H	3-1	Hasancic 3
13/05/00	Hrvatski dragovoljac Zagreb	A	1-0	Mijatovic

SIBENIK

CLUB DIRECTORY

HNK Sibenik
Bana Jelacica bb
22 000 Sibenik
tel - (022) 218163
fax - (022) 218406
Year of Formation - 1932
President - Miho Mioc
Secretary - Zvonko Vidacak
Coach - Stanko Mrsic; Andjelko Godinic;
Kresimir Goran Vidov; Zeljko Maretic;
Vjekoslav Lokica
Stadium - Subicevac (12,000)

APPEARANCES 99/00

	P	Ap	(s)	Gls
Ivica ANTOLIC	D	27	(1)	
Marijan BAKULA	M	28		1
Mladen BUDANOVIC	D	20	(2)	
Tonci BULAT	G	8	(3)	
Adis CVELJO	D		(1)	
Ivica DUSPARA	M	10	(2)	1
Ive GRANDO	M		(1)	
Mario HARMAT	A	10	(5)	2
Ante IVICA	D	16	(1)	
Danko JOVIC	A	3	(4)	
Nedo JOVIC	M	18	(3)	1
Sinisa JOZIC	D	2	(2)	
Anel KARABEG	M	23	(3)	1
Marko KARTELO	M	1	(9)	
Lucijan KLARIN	D	1	(3)	
Danijel KOVACEVIC	M	27	(2)	2
Mladen KOVACIC	M	25	(1)	2
Ognjen MAJDOV	D	7	(2)	
Ivo MARASOVIC	D	8	(6)	2
Armando MARENZI	M	3	(13)	
Paolo MATAS	A	3	(11)	2
Ivan MILAS	D	25	(3)	1
Ivica MILICEVIC	D	1	(1)	
Alen MRZLECKI	D	16		
Denis PUTNIK	D	13		2
Sinisa SEGOVIC	M	1		
Zoran SLAVICA	G	25		
Ivo SUPE	D	3		
Tomislav VINCELJ	A	12	(2)	3
Klaudio VUKOVIC	A	27	(3)	10

LEAGUE RESULTS 1999/2000

24/07/99	Hrvatski dragovoljac Zagreb	H	0-0	
01/08/99	Hajduk Split	A	1-3	Marasovic
29/08/99	Croatia Zagreb	H	1-1	Harmat
07/09/99	Varteks Varazdin	A	0-0	
11/09/99	Cibalia Vinkovci	H	2-2	Marasovic, Harmat
18/09/99	Rijeka	H	0-2	
25/09/99	Istra Pula	A	0-0	
02/10/99	Vukovar '91	H	2-1	Vukovic 2 (1p)
12/10/99	Zagreb	A	1-4	Karabeg
16/10/99	Slaven Belupo Koprivnica	H	0-0	
23/10/99	Osijek	A	0-3	
30/10/99	Hrvatski dragovoljac Zagreb	A	1-1	Kovacic
06/11/99	Hajduk Split	H	1-3	Putnik
23/11/99	Croatia Zagreb	A	1-3	Vukovic
27/11/99	Varteks Varazdin	H	2-0	Putnik, Duspara
04/12/99	Cibalia Vinkovci	A	0-3	
19/02/00	Rijeka	A	1-3	Vukovic
26/02/00	Istra Pula	H	0-1	
29/02/00	Vukovar '91	A	0-3	
04/03/00	Zagreb	H	2-1	Bakula, Jovic N.
07/03/00	Slaven Belupo Koprivnica	A	0-0	
11/03/00	Osijek	H	0-2	
18/03/00	Cibalia Vinkovci	A	2-4	Vukovic, Kovacic
25/03/00	Zagreb	H	2-1	Vukovic 2 (1p)
01/04/00	Rijeka	A	0-2	
08/04/00	Osijek	H	1-1	Vincelj
11/04/00	Hajduk Split	A	3-0	(w/o)
15/04/00	Dinamo Zagreb	H	2-1	Vukovic, Vincelj
22/04/00	Slaven Belupo Koprivnica	A	1-2	Matas
29/04/00	Hrvatski dragovoljac Zagreb	H	2-0	Vukovic, Vincelj
06/05/00	Vukovar '91	A	1-2	Vukovic
09/05/00	Istra Pula	H	3-0	Milas, Kovacevic, Matas
13/05/00	Varteks Varazdin	A	1-1	Kovacevic

SLAVEN BELUPO KOPRIVNICA

CLUB DIRECTORY

NK Slaven Belupo
Ante Starcevica 29
48 000 Koprivnica
tel - (048) 621203
fax - (048) 621203
Year of Formation - 1912
President - Damir Selak
Secretary - Robert Markulin
Coach - Luka Bonacic; Mladen Francic
Stadium - Gradski (6,000)

APPEARANCES 99/00

	P	Ap	(s)	Gls
Frano AMIZIC	D	21	(2)	
Leonard BISAKU	M	13	(8)	1
Petar BOSNJAK	D	22	(3)	
Stipe BOSNJAK	D	26		
Dario BRGLES	A	1	(9)	
Pavo CRNAC	D	18	(5)	4
Mario DODIK	A	31	(1)	13
Oliver DRVOSEK	A	1	(3)	
Roy FERENCINA	M	26	(1)	1
Marin GALIC	M	12	(2)	
Antun HAVAIC	M	19	(6)	2
Renato JURCEC	A	26	(2)	8
Hasan KACIC	D	29		1
Vladimir KOKOL (SLO)	D	2	(9)	
Grgica KOVAC	D	13		
Mario KOVACEVIC	M	28	(1)	
Ivica KRIZANAC	M	3	(5)	
Robert LISJAK	G	2	(1)	
Zdravko MEDJIMOREC	D	1	(3)	
Goran MIKOLAJ	M	1	(2)	
Zoran OGRIZOVIC	A	6	(3)	1
Alen PETROVIC	M	5	(7)	1
Danijel RADICEK	M	2	(3)	
Ivica RAGUZ	M	2	(7)	
Ivica SERTIC	M	10	(1)	1
Ivica SOLOMUN	G	15		
Dragan STOJKIC	G	16		
Slobodan SUDEC	D	5		
Josip TETEC	M	7	(8)	1

LEAGUE RESULTS 1999/2000

Date	Opponent		Score	Scorers
24/07/99	Istra Pula	A	2-0	Dodik, Tetec
31/07/99	Vukovar '91	H	1-2	Dodik
28/08/99	Zagreb	A	1-0	Jurcec
07/09/99	Cibalia Vinkovci	A	0-0	
11/09/99	Osijek	H	1-4	Ogrizovic
18/09/99	Hrvatski dragovoljac Zagreb	A	2-2	Jurcec, Havaic
25/09/99	Hajduk Split	H	0-0	
02/10/99	Croatia Zagreb	A	1-5	Bisaku
12/10/99	Varteks Varazdin	H	2-1	Kacic, Dodik (p)
16/10/99	Sibenik	A	0-0	
23/10/99	Rijeka	H	2-2	Dodik 2
30/10/99	Istra Pula	H	1-1	Jurcec
06/11/99	Vukovar '91	A	0-0	
23/11/99	Zagreb	H	1-1	Jurcec
27/11/99	Cibalia Vinkovci	H	1-0	Dodik (p)
04/12/99	Osijek	A	1-2	Jurcec
19/02/00	Hrvatski dragovoljac Zagreb	H	0-1	
26/02/00	Hajduk Split	A	0-1	
29/02/00	Dinamo Zagreb	H	0-5	
04/03/00	Varteks Varazdin	A	1-0	Havaic
07/03/00	Sibenik	H	0-0	
11/03/00	Rijeka	A	1-1	Dodik
18/03/00	Hajduk Split	A	0-0	
25/03/00	Dinamo Zagreb	H	2-0	Crnac, Dodik
01/04/00	Varteks Varazdin	A	0-0	
08/04/00	Hrvatski dragovoljac Zagreb	A	2-0	Dodik 2
11/04/00	Vukovar '91	H	1-0	Ferencina
15/04/00	Istra Pula	A	1-0	Jurcec
22/04/00	Sibenik	H	2-1	Crnac, Dodik
29/04/00	Cibalia Vinkovci	A	0-0	
06/05/00	Zagreb	H	2-0	Jurcec 2
09/05/00	Rijeka	A	1-3	Dodik
13/05/00	Osijek	H	5-2	Crnac 2, Petrovic, Dodik, Sertic

VARTEKS VARAZDIN

CLUB DIRECTORY

NK Varteks
Zagrebacka 96
42 000 Varazdin
tel - (042) 241332
fax - (042) 240250
Year of Formation - 1931
President - Andjelko Herjavec
Secretary - Nevenko Herjavec
Coach - Drazen Besek; Branko Janzek;
Luka Bonacic
Stadium - Gradski (12,000)

APPEARANCES 99/00

	P	Ap	(s)	Gls
Ivan ABAZA	M	1	(2)	
Andrija BALAJIC	M	19	(2)	1
Goran BOROVIC	D	9	(1)	
Tomo CIKOVIC	D		(2)	
Zlatko DALIC	M	10	(3)	1
Enkelejd DOBI (ALB)	A	2	(5)	1
Mirza GOLUBICA	A	8	(6)	1
Vjeran GRABANT	D		(4)	
Drazen HORVAT	A	3	(4)	1
Danijel HRMAN	M	17	(4)	
Faik KAMBEROVIC (BOS)	A	6	(3)	1
Veldin KARIC	A	9	(2)	4
Zoran KASTEL	D	23	(1)	
Grgica KOVAC	D	12		
Matija KRISTIC	D	16	(3)	
Ivica KRIZANAC	M	4	(1)	
Danijel MADJARIC	G	16		
Drazen MADUNOVIC	D	27		
Paolo MATAS	A	1	(4)	
Devi MUKA (ALB)	M	22	(1)	2
Miljenko MUMLEK	M	3		
Damir MUZEK	M	18	(4)	5
Mladen POSAVEC	M	29		3
Ivan REZIC	D	5	(3)	
Silvester SABOLCKI	D	28		3
Nikola SAFARIC	M	5	(11)	3
Vioresin SINANI (ALB)	A	17	(8)	5
Hrvoje SKLEPIC	D	8	(1)	
Ivica SOLOMUN	G	17		1
Nikola SRPAK	A	1	(3)	
Robert TEZACKI	M	16	(9)	
Josko TOPIC	A		(1)	
Dalibor TUKSER	D	11	(3)	

LEAGUE RESULTS 1999/2000

28/07/99	Hajduk Split	H	3-2	Golubica, Dalic, Safaric
31/07/99	Croatia Zagreb	A	1-4	Sabolcki
28/08/99	Cibalia Vinkovci	H	0-3	
07/09/99	Sibenik	H	0-0	
11/09/99	Rijeka	A	0-2	
18/09/99	Istra Pula	H	4-1	Muka, Kamberovic, Muzek 2 (1p)
25/09/99	Vukovar '91	A	2-2	Posavec 2
01/10/99	Zagreb	H	1-1	Sinani
12/10/99	Slaven Belupo Koprivnica	A	1-2	Sinani
16/10/99	Osijek	H	2-0	Muzek (p), Sabolcki
23/10/99	Hrvatski dragovoljac Zagreb	A	1-0	Muzek (p)
30/10/99	Hajduk Split	A	0-2	
06/11/99	Croatia Zagreb	H	0-3	
23/11/99	Cibalia Vinkovci	A	1-3	Sinani
27/11/99	Sibenik	A	0-2	
04/12/99	Rijeka	H	2-1	Sinani 2
19/02/00	Istra Pula	A	2-0	Muzek, Dobi
26/02/00	Vukovar '91	H	2-0	Solomun (p), Safaric
29/02/00	Zagreb	A	0-1	
04/03/00	Slaven Belupo Koprivnica	H	0-1	
07/03/00	Osijek	A	1-1	Karic
11/03/00	Hrvatski dragovoljac Zagreb	H	0-0	
18/03/00	Dinamo Zagreb	A	1-0	Muka
25/03/00	Cibalia Vinkovci	A	0-2	
01/04/00	Slaven Belupo Koprivnica	H	0-0	
08/04/00	Zagreb	A	2-1	Posavec, Safaric
11/04/00	Hrvatski dragovoljac Zagreb	H	1-1	Karic
15/04/00	Rijeka	A	0-4	
22/04/00	Vukovar '91	H	3-2	Balajic, Karic, Sabolcki
29/04/00	Osijek	A	0-0	
06/05/00	Istra Pula	H	1-2	Karic (p)
09/05/00	Hajduk Split	A	0-0	
13/05/00	Sibenik	H	1-1	Horvat

VUKOVAR '91

CLUB DIRECTORY

Vukovar '91
Borisa Kidrica bb
32000 Vukovar
tel - (032) 441284
fax - (032) 441283
President - Stipe Seremet
Secretary - Ivica Mise
Coach - Davor Mladina
Stadium - Gradski (6,000)

APPEARANCES 99/00

	P	Ap	(s)	Gls
Vladimir BALIC	G	32		
Zlatko BIJELIC	M	26		2
Miroslav BOJKO	A	16		3
Mato DADIC	D	19	(8)	3
Kresimir DRNASIN	M	21	(1)	
Ivan ILECIC	M	1	(6)	
Ivan JERKOVIC	M	12	(5)	1
Ivica JOZINOVIC	D	24	(2)	
Josip JURIC	A	7	(2)	
Matijas KNEZOVIC	M	29	(1)	2
Zeljko KOBAS	M	5	(4)	
Mladen MARJANOVIC	D	14	(5)	3
Igor MIKLOSEVIC	D	4	(2)	
Ivo MILIC	D	20	(1)	
Mario MLINARIC	D		(1)	
Ante PESIC	D	13		
Vladimir PRCE	D	1	(9)	
Zlatko RAGUZ	D	14		
Mario RIMAC	D	16	(3)	1
Sinisa SESAR	D	31		2
Stjepan SIMIC	G	1		
Slaven TOKIC	D	9	(6)	
Fatmir VATA (ALB)	A	13		2
Ivica VUKA	M	6	(11)	2
Marijan VUKA	A	7	(19)	1
Amarildo ZELA (ALB)	A	22	(6)	10
Mario ZIVKOVIC	A		(2)	

LEAGUE RESULTS 1999/2000

24/07/99	Zagreb	H	3-4	Marjanovic, Bijelic (p), Sesar
31/07/99	Slaven Belupo Koprivnica	A	2-1	Marjanovic, Dadic
28/08/99	Osijek	H	3-1	Vata 2, Dadic
07/09/99	Hrvatski dragovoljac Zagreb	A	1-1	Zela
11/09/99	Hajduk Split	H	0-2	
17/09/99	Croatia Zagreb	A	0-5	
25/09/99	Varteks Varazdin	H	2-2	Zela 2
02/10/99	Sibenik	A	1-2	Vuka I.
12/10/99	Rijeka	H	0-0	
16/10/99	Istra Pula	A	0-3	
23/10/99	Cibalia Vinkovci	H	0-0	
30/10/99	Zagreb	A	0-1	
06/11/99	Slaven Belupo Koprivnica	H	0-0	
23/11/99	Osijek	A	1-2	Zela (p)
27/11/99	Hrvatski dragovoljac Zagreb	H	1-0	Jerkovic
04/12/99	Hajduk Split	A	0-2	
19/02/00	Dinamo Zagreb	H	0-0	
26/02/00	Varteks Varazdin	A	0-2	
29/02/00	Sibenik	H	3-0	Bijelic (p), Zela 2
04/03/00	Rijeka	A	0-2	
07/03/00	Istra Pula	H	1-3	Dadic
11/03/00	Cibalia Vinkovci	A	1-0	Bojko
18/03/00	Rijeka	A	0-0	
25/03/00	Osijek	H	1-1	Zela
01/04/00	Hajduk Split	A	0-4	
08/04/00	Dinamo Zagreb	H	0-3	
11/04/00	Slaven Belupo Koprivnica	A	0-1	
15/04/00	Hrvatski dragovoljac Zagreb	H	2-0	Knezovic, Rimac
22/04/00	Varteks Varazdin	A	2-3	Zela (p), Vuka I.
29/04/00	Istra Pula	A	3-4	Zela, Sesar, Bojko
06/05/00	Sibenik	H	2-1	Bojko, Vuka M.
09/05/00	Cibalia Vinkovci	A	2-5	Knezovic, Marjanovic
13/05/00	Zagreb	H	1-1	Zela

ZAGREB

CLUB DIRECTORY

NK Zagreb
Kranjceviceva 4
10 000 Zagreb
tel - (01) 3668111
fax - (01) 338156
Year of Formation - 1949
President - Miroslav Marcinkovic
Secretary - Zlatko Dracic
Coach - Ivo Susak
Stadium - NK Zagreb (12,000)

APPEARANCES 99/00

	P	Ap	(s)	Gls
Ivica BANOVIC	M	24	(5)	8
Drazen BISKUP	D	28		
Erion BOGDANI (ALB)	A	10	(2)	2
Nino BULE	A	32	(1)	9
Jozo CACIC	M		(1)	1
Mario CIZMEK	M	5	(4)	1
Sorin COLCEAG (ROM)	G	9		
Goran DASOVIC	M	1		
Ivica FERENCEVIC	D	3	(1)	
Igor ILECIC	D	5	(4)	
Marko JURIC	M	4	(7)	
Domagoj KOSIC	M	31		6
Paul LAPIC (AUS)	G	1		
Kruno LOVREK	A	7	(15)	3
Vatroslav MIHACIC	G	19		
Mario OSIBOV	D	14		1
Benedikt PANIC	M		(1)	
Darko PERIC	M	18	(6)	1
Ivica PIRIC	D	6	(1)	
Josko POPOVIC	A	22	(2)	7
Krunoslav RENDULIC	M	31		
Predrag SIMIC	D	15	(4)	1
Goran STAVREVSKI (MAC)	D	27	(1)	
Jakov SURAC	M	15	(10)	
Sandro TOMIC	G	4		
Hrvoje VEJIC	D	17	(2)	2
Domagoj VERHAS	D	15	(11)	

LEAGUE RESULTS 1999/2000

24/07/99	Vukovar '91	A	4-3	Bule 2, Kosic, Vejic
31/07/99	Cibalia Vinkovci	A	0-0	
28/08/99	Slaven Belupo Koprivnica	H	0-1	
07/09/99	Osijek	A	0-0	
11/09/99	Hrvatski dragovoljac Zagreb	H	3-3	Vejic, Bule, Lovrek
19/09/99	Hajduk Split	A	0-3	
25/09/99	Croatia Zagreb	H	0-1	
01/10/99	Varteks Varazdin	A	1-1	Bogdani
12/10/99	Sibenik	H	4-1	Banovic, Bogdani, Kosic, Popovic
16/10/99	Rijeka	A	0-2	
23/10/99	Istra Pula	H	1-1	Kosic (p)
30/10/99	Vukovar '91	H	1-0	Bule
06/11/99	Cibalia Vinkovci	H	0-0	
23/11/99	Slaven Belupo Koprivnica	A	1-1	Banovic
27/11/99	Osijek	H	2-1	Popovic, Bule
04/12/99	Hrvatski dragovoljac Zagreb	A	2-1	Banovic, Kosic
19/02/00	Hajduk Split	H	0-3	
26/02/00	Dinamo Zagreb	A	2-2	Banovic, Lovrek
29/02/00	Varteks Varazdin	H	1-0	Banovic
04/03/00	Sibenik	A	1-2	Popovic
07/03/00	Rijeka	H	4-1	Popovic 3, Simic
11/03/00	Istra Pula	A	0-0	
18/03/00	Istra Pula	H	4-1	Bule 2, Popovic, Peric
25/03/00	Sibenik	A	1-2	Kosic
01/04/00	Cibalia Vinkovci	H	1-2	Osibov
08/04/00	Varteks Varazdin	H	1-2	Bule
11/04/00	Rijeka	A	3-2	Banovic 3
15/04/00	Osijek	H	2-2	Kosic (p), Cizmek
22/04/00	Hajduk Split	A	0-5	
29/04/00	Dinamo Zagreb	H	1-2	Lovrek
06/05/00	Slaven Belupo Koprivnica	A	0-2	
09/05/00	Hrvatski dragovoljac Zagreb	H	1-1	Cacic
13/05/00	Vukovar '91	A	1-1	Bule

CYPRUS

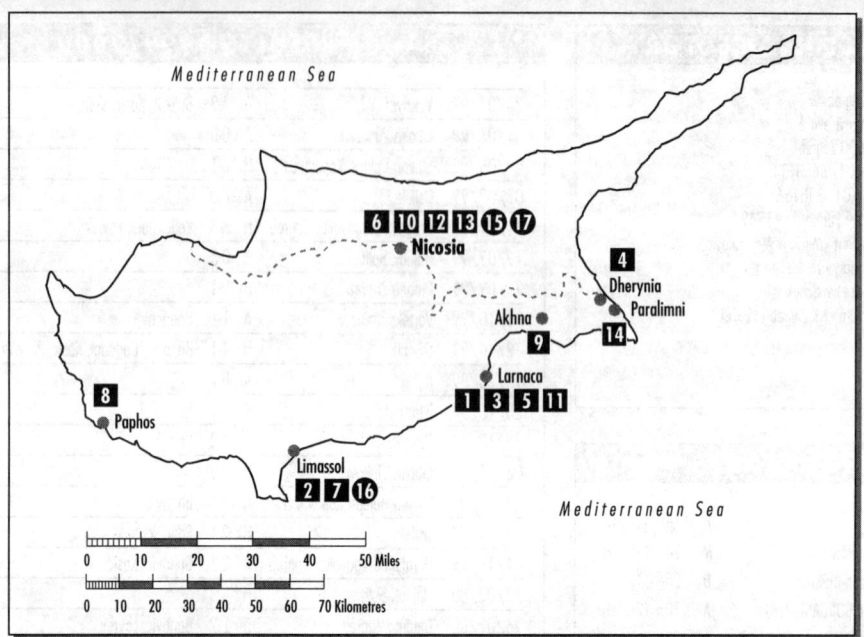

1	AEK LARNACA	244	10	ETHNIKOS ASHIA	253
2	AEL LIMASSOL	245	11	NEA SALAMINA FAMAGUSTA	254
3	ALKI LARNACA	246	12	OLYMPIAKOS NICOSIA	255
4	ANAGENNISIS DHERYNIA	247	13	OMONIA NICOSIA	256
5	ANORTHOSIS FAMAGUSTA	248	14	PARALIMNI	257
6	APOEL NICOSIA	249	**Promoted clubs**		
7	APOLLON LIMASSOL	250	15	DIGHENIS MORPHOU	
8	APOP PAPHOS	251	16	ARIS LIMASSOL	
9	ETHNIKOS AKHNA	252	17	DOXA KATOKOPIA	

TON UP FOR RAMPANT RAUFFMANN

Four in a row for Anorthosis

FEDERATION DIRECTORY

Cyprus Football Association
Stasinos Street 1, PO Box 5071, 2404 Nicosia

tel - (02) 352341   Year of Formation - 1934
fax - (02) 590544   President - Marios Lefkaritis
                                     Secretary - Lambros Adamou

The outcome was the same, but the storyline was very different. In each of the previous two seasons Anorthosis, the displaced club from Famagusta, had taken the Cypriot title on the final day of the season. In 1999/2000 they wrapped it up four weeks before the end.

It was only when the club's fourth successive championship triumph was all but secure that Anorthosis eased off. Their first 20 matches yielded an extraordinary tally of 19 wins and one draw. No other team could possibly live with that, not even Omonia Nicosia, who, for the third year running, had to settle for second place.

It is the custom in Cyprus for most clubs to change their coach at least once a year, but Anorthosis know a good man when they see one and have no inclination to part company with Dusan Mitosevic, whose four seasons at the club have all ended in championship wins.

The Yugoslav's magic touch was apparent right from the opening day of the season when Anorthosis, fuelled by some impressive showings in the Champions' League against Slovan Bratislava and Hertha Berlin, crushed Omonia 5-3. From then on the two title candidates traded victory for victory, but it was that early advantage which enabled Mitosevic's men to stay out in front for the duration of the season.

Anorthosis seemed poised to break the points record that they had set jointly with Omonia the season before, but a first defeat by Olympiakos (2-5) at the end of March suddenly brought their unbeaten run to an abrupt end, and after the title was made safe with a 5-0 home win against Ethnikos Ashia, Mitosevic decided to try out some of the younger players in the squad. The experimentation effectively cost Anorthosis the chance to break the 67-point record, notably when they lost their final home game 1-2 to AEK.

There was a further sting in the tail for the champions at the end of the season when it was announced that their two most important homegrown players, Cypriot internationals Yiotis Engomitis and Yiannakis Okkas, were being sold to top Greek side PAOK. Although this double deal brought a great deal of money to the club, it was not welcomed by the Anorthosis fans. Both players had been in excellent form all season, proving even more influential to the team than the three foreign imports, Vladan Tomic, Zoran Milinkovic and recalled Nigerian striker Mike Obiku, back at the club after a seven-year gap.

Omonia once again possessed the league's most impressive foreign player in the prolific German goal-poacher

LEAGUE CHAMPIONSHIP RESULTS 99/00

		1	2	3	4	5	6	7	8	9	10	11	12	13	14
1	AEK Larnaca		3-2	4-2	4-1	0-3	1-2	2-0	0-0	1-2	2-1	0-1	3-1	0-4	2-1
2	AEL Limassol	2-0		6-1	1-0	2-3	1-0	1-2	2-1	0-0	2-1	0-3	4-1	0-0	2-0
3	Alki Larnaca	2-7	1-3		1-3	1-5	1-4	0-6	2-3	0-4	0-2	0-9	1-2	0-3	2-1
4	Anagennisis Dherynia	0-1	1-3	3-1		0-4	0-5	0-1	3-1	1-3	1-5	0-4	1-2	0-7	0-3
5	Anorthosis Famagusta	1-2	6-1	4-0	4-1		1-1	3-1	4-0	3-1	5-0	1-0	3-0	5-3	4-1
6	APOEL Nicosia	1-0	2-0	6-0	5-0	0-2		2-1	2-2	2-1	3-2	1-2	8-2	3-3	3-2
7	Apollon Limassol	3-1	1-3	3-1	1-0	3-2	2-1		4-1	0-0	2-0	2-1	3-3	0-4	3-1
8	APOP Paphos	0-1	2-0	5-0	5-1	0-4	1-0	1-1		4-0	0-0	2-1	2-0	1-2	2-3
9	Ethnikos Akhna	0-2	1-2	5-1	5-0	2-3	1-0	1-3	3-1		1-1	2-0	3-3	0-1	3-1
10	Ethnikos Ashia	3-0	3-2	3-0	0-1	1-3	0-2	3-1	1-2	1-0		1-1	2-1	0-1	2-0
11	Nea Salamina Famagusta	2-1	0-2	6-0	7-3	1-4	3-1	3-2	1-1	0-1	2-1		2-2	0-1	2-1
12	Olympiakos Nicosia	2-2	3-3	5-0	2-1	5-2	0-2	5-3	5-0	1-0	2-2	3-1		1-3	3-5
13	Omonia Nicosia	0-3	1-0	4-1	8-1	2-2	3-2	3-0	5-0	2-0	2-0	1-1	0-3		6-2
14	Paralimni	3-0	6-1	3-2	4-0	0-1	0-0	2-1	2-1	3-3	2-0	1-5	2-0	2-2	

LEAGUE CHAMPIONSHIP FINAL TABLE 99/00

			Home					Away					Total						
		Pd	W	D	L	F	A	W	D	L	F	A	W	D	L	F	A	PT	GD
1	Anorthosis Famagusta	26	11	1	1	44	11	10	1	2	38	17	21	2	3	82	28	65	54
2	Omonia Nicosia	26	9	2	2	37	15	9	3	1	34	12	18	5	3	71	27	59	44
3	APOEL Nicosia	26	9	2	2	38	17	5	2	6	20	14	14	4	8	58	31	46	27
4	Nea Salamina Famagusta	26	7	2	4	29	20	6	2	5	29	14	13	4	9	58	34	43	24
5	Apollon Limassol	26	9	2	2	27	18	4	1	8	22	26	13	3	10	49	44	42	5
6	AEL Limassol	26	8	2	3	23	12	5	1	7	22	30	13	3	10	45	42	42	3
7	AEK Larnaca	26	7	1	5	22	20	6	1	6	20	19	13	2	11	42	39	41	3
8	Paralimni	26	8	3	2	30	16	3	0	10	21	34	11	3	12	51	50	36	1
9	Olympiakos Nicosia	26	7	3	3	37	24	3	3	7	20	34	10	6	10	57	58	36	-1
10	Ethnikos Akhna	26	6	2	5	27	18	4	3	6	15	18	10	5	11	42	36	35	6
11	APOP Paphos	26	7	2	4	25	13	2	3	8	13	34	9	5	12	38	47	32	-9
12	Ethnikos Ashia	26	7	1	5	20	14	2	3	8	15	24	9	4	13	35	38	31	-3
13	Anagennisis Dherynia	26	2	0	11	10	40	2	0	11	12	47	4	0	22	22	87	12	-65
14	Alki Larnaca	26	1	0	12	11	52	0	0	13	9	57	1	0	25	20	109	3	-89

Rainer Rauffmann. The former Cologne striker won the league's top-scorer title for the third year running, scoring a total of 34 goals, the same number as the rest of his team-mates put together.

Rauffmann reached his century of goals in record time, completing the ton in a 4-0 away win over Apollon Limassol in mid-January.

For the first time in his three-year sojourn on the island,

DOMESTIC CUP 99/00

FIRST ROUND
Nea Salamina Famagusta 3, Dighenis Akritas Morphou 1
Ethnikos Akhna 2, Doxa Katokopia 0
Paralimni 3, Ayia Napa 0
MEAP Pera Choriou 1, AEL Limassol 3
Iraklis Yerolakkos 1, Alki Larnaca 3
Kinyras Paphos 0, AEK Larnaca 3
Onisillos Sotira 2, AEK-Achilleas Ayiou Theraponta 1
Akritas Hloraka 0, Olympiakos Nicosia 4
PEFO Limassol 0, Apollon Limassol 8
Omonia Nicosia 6, AMEP 0
AEZ Zakaki 2, Anagennisis Dherynia 1
ASIL Lysi 0, APOEL Nicosia 3
APEP Kyperounta 2, Ethnikos Ashia 4
Ermis Aradippou 0, Anorthosis Famagusta 5
APOP Paphos 1, Achyronas Liopetri 0
Evaghoras Paphos 1, Aris Limassol 3

SECOND ROUND
AEK Larnaca v Nea Salamina Famagusta 2-0; 0-1
(AEK Larnaca 2-1)
Onisillos Sotira v APOP Paphos 1-1; 1-4
(APOP Paphos 5-2)
Anorthosis Famagusta v Paralimni 3-0; 5-1
(Anorthosis Famagusta 8-1)
Aris Limassol v Ethnikos Ashia 1-3; 1-2
(Ethnikos Ashia 5-2)
Olympiakos Nicosia v AEL Limassol 1-1; 0-0

(1-1; AEL Limassol on away goal)
Apollon Limassol v APOEL Nicosia 2-4; 3-2
(APOEL Nicosia 6-5)
Alki Larnaca v Ethnikos Akhna 1-1; 1-2
(Ethnikos Akhna 3-2)
Omonia Nicosia v AEZ Zakaki 3-0; 4-0
(Omonia Nicosia 7-0)

QUARTER-FINALS
AEK Larnaca 2 (Eleftheriou 14, 20), Ethnikos Ashia 0
Ethnikos Ashia 1 (Costaras 75),
AEK Larnaca 2 (Milenkovic 65, Kounnis 82)
(AEK Larnaca 4-1)
APOEL Nicosia 3 (Marcelo 27, Oreschuk 77, Yiasemakis 84), APOP Paphos 0
APOP Paphos 1 (Papadopoulos 21),
APOEL Nicosia 6 (Ioannou 7, 33, Yiasemakis 14, 23, Oreschuk 85, Charalambides 90)
(APOEL Nicosia 9-1)
Omonia Nicosia 2 (Panayiotou 11, Iosiphides 30og),
Anorthosis Famagusta 0
Anorthosis Famagusta 0, Omonia Nicosia 0
(Omonia Nicosia 2-0)
Ethnikos Akhna 1 (Adzic 36),
AEL Limassol 2 (Yarpozis 72, Chrysostomou 80)
AEL Limassol 3 (Christophi 65, Yarpozis 81, 87),
Ethnikos Akhna 0
(AEL Limassol 5-1)

SEMI-FINALS
Omonia Nicosia 3 (Kaiafas 66, Kontolefteros 85, Rauffmann 88), AEL Limassol 0
AEL Limassol 1 (Yarpozis 69),
Omonia Nicosia 4 (Konnafis 20, Malekkos 22, Kaiafas 37, Kontolefteros 58)
(Omonia Nicosia 7-1)

APOEL Nicosia 0, AEK Larnaca 0
AEK Larnaca 0,
APOEL Nicosia 2 (Charalambides 55, Yiasemakis 87)
(APOEL Nicosia 2-0)

FINAL
13/05/2000, Nicosia
OMONIA NICOSIA 4 Mihajlovic (36, 87p), Rauffmann (43, 62)
APOEL NICOSIA 2 Yiasemakis (64p), Oreschuk (85)
referee - Loizou
OMONIA NICOSIA - Yiallouris, Konnafis (Andreou S. 82), Georgiou, Ioakim, Panayiotou, Tittel, Nicolaou Ch. (Nicolaou N. 90), Kaiafas (Kalotheou C. 80), Rauffmann, Mihajlovic, Malekkos.
APOEL NICOSIA - Petrides, Petrou, Nicolaou (Charalambides 46), Misos, Christodoulou, Aristocleous, Satsias, Aloneftis, Ioannou, Yiasemakis (Hadjiloucas 46), Marcelo (Oreschuk 62).

the German also helped his club to win a trophy. The Cypriot Cup returned to Omonia after a six-year interval and was achieved with a sumptuous 4-2 win over local rivals APOEL in the final. Not unexpectedly, Rauffmann

got his name onto the scoresheet twice - as did his fellow import Vesko Mihajlovic, signed from Anorthosis the previous summer.

APOEL's defeat in the Cup final brought a sad end to

NATIONAL TEAM APPEARANCES 99/00

Coach - Stavros PAPADOPOULOS	ROM	ISR	ESP	AUT	LIT	ARM	ROM	IRN	ROM	Cps	Gls
Nicos PANAYIOTOU (06/12/70) - Anorthosis Famagusta	G	G	G	G	G46	G46	G		G	43	-
Costas KAIAFAS (22/09/74) - Omonia Nicosia	D	D80		M						6	1
Charis CHARALAMBOUS (25/03/71) - Anorthosis Famagusta	D				D	D		D	D	13	-
Ioakim IOAKIM (16/09/75) - Omonia Nicosia	D46				D	D	D	D71		10	1
Marios CHARALAMBOUS (18/06/69) - Apollon Limassol	D46	D	D					D	D73	48	2
Vassos MELANARKITIS (11/08/72) - Anorthosis Famagusta	M	M	M	M82	M	M	M46	M	M	24	2
Milenko SPOLJARIC (24/01/67) - Apollon Limassol	M	M		M		M	M	M46		17	7
Costas MALEKKOS (09/04/71) - Omonia Nicosia	M34				A46	s46	A74	A62		28	3
Yiotis ENGOMITIS (26/05/72) - Anorthosis Famagusta	A76	A	M	M		M		M	A63	31	6
Sinisa GOGIC (20/10/63) - Olympiakos (GRE)	A	A71	A88	A25						37	8
Yiannakis OKKAS (11/02/77) - Anorthosis Famagusta	A46	A	A	A46	A76	s46	A	A	A79	27	3
Nikodimos PAPAVASSILIOU (31/08/70) - Apollon Limassol	s34	M65	M							38	5
Pambos PITTAS (26/07/66) - Apollon Limassol	s46	D	D46							80	7
Philippos PHILIPPOU (24/06/75) - Apollon Limassol	s46									1	-
Michalis CONSTANDINOU (19/02/78) - Iraklis (GRE)	s46	s71			A	s46	A46	A57	A65	15	4
Aristos ARISTOCLEOUS (28/02/74) - APOEL Nicosia	s76	s80	s46					s46	M82	17	-
Costas COSTA (04/01/69) - Apollon Limassol		D	D	D						34	2
Marios CHRISTODOULOU (04/07/74) - Aris (GRE)		s65	M	M						21	2
Lucas LUCA (12/04/78) - Anorthosis Famagusta				D						1	-
Charis NICOLAOU (31/03/74) - Omonia Nicosia			M46							6	-
George THEODOTOU (01/01/74) - AEK Larnaca			s46	s46	D	s46	D46	s46	D	26	-
Yiasemis YIASEMAKIS (31/05/75) - APOEL Nicosia			s88			A46		s62	s65	4	-
Klimis ALEXANDROU (01/09/74) - AEK Larnaca				M						9	2
Marios AGATHOCLEOUS (08/09/74) - Aris (GRE)				s25		A46	s46	s57	s63	24	7
Marios DIMITRIOU (01/08/73) - AEL Limassol				s82			s74			4	-
Dimitris IOANNOU (12/08/68) - Anorthosis Famagusta					D				D	46	3
Petros KONNAFIS (28/08/79) - Omonia Nicosia					D46	D	s46		D	4	-
Andonis NICOLAOU (29/10/74) - Aris Limassol					M46					1	-
Marios KARAS (24/10/74) - Paralimni					s46		D	s71		3	-
Savvas CONSTANDINOU (28/08/71) - AEK Larnaca					s46		G			3	-
Dimitris ASHIOTIS (31/03/71) - Olympiakos Nicosia					s46					6	-
Dimitris LEONIS (13/11/77) - AEL Limassol					s46					1	-
Christos POYIATZIS (26/04/76) - Ethnikos Akhna					s76		M46		s73	3	1
Nicos K. NICOLAOU (05/08/73) - Nea Salamina Famagusta						M46	M	M46		4	-
Eleftherios ELEFTHERIOU (12/06/74) - AEK Larnaca						A46	s46		s79	3	-
Chrysis MICHAEL (26/05/77) - AEL Limassol						s46				1	-
Marios THEMISTOCLEOUS (01/04/75) - Olympiakos Nicosia							s46			1	-
Marinos SATSIAS (24/05/78) - APOEL Nicosia									s82	1	-

NATIONAL TEAM RESULTS 99/00

18/08/99	Romania	H	Limassol	2-2	Malekkos (14), Gogic (65)
05/09/99	Israel (ECQ)	H	Limassol	3-2	Engomitis (28), Spoljaric (53, 86p)
08/09/99	Spain (ECQ)	A	Badajoz	0-8	
10/10/99	Austria (ECQ)	A	Vienna	1-3	Costa (63)
02/02/00	Lithuania	H	Limassol	2-1	Constandinou M. (61, 88p)
04/02/00	Armenia	H	Nicosia	3-2	Melanarkitis (36), Spoljaric (42, 115p)
06/02/00	Romania	H	Nicosia	3-2	Okkas (4), Poyiatzis (69), Agathocleous (99)
23/03/00	Iran	H	Nicosia	0-0	
26/04/00	Romania	A	Constanta	0-2	

TOP SCORERS

34	Rainer RAUFFMANN (Omonia Nicosia)
21	Yiasemis YIASEMAKIS (APOEL Nicosia)
18	Serge HONI (Olympiakos Nicosia)
	Pambos CHARALAMBOUS (APOP Paphos)
16	Yiotis ENGOMITIS (Anorthosis Famagusta)
	Slavisa CULA (Paralimni)
14	Boban KITANOV (AEL Limassol)
	Sinisa JELIC (Nea Salamina Famagusta)
13	Zoran MASIC (Apollon Limassol)
12	Mike OBIKU (Anorthosis Famagusta)
	Yiannakis OKKAS (Anorthosis Famagusta)

a thoroughly dismal season. Although they were third in the league, they finished up a mammoth 19 points behind the champions, and even though that was sufficient to guarantee a place in Europe, it was no surprise that coach Andreas Michaelides, the former national team boss, was given the sack after the Cup defeat by Omonia.

With APOEL and Apollon both suffering unduly in the league and all but one of the three relegation places being booked early on - bottom club Alki set new negative records, losing 25 of their 26 matches and conceding 109 goals - the talk intensified about reducing the top division to 12 or ten clubs. However, a proposal to this end was turned down by the smaller clubs, who opted, rather masochistically, to retain the status quo.

EUROPEAN CUPS 99/00

CHAMPIONS' CUP
● ANORTHOSIS FAMAGUSTA
Preliminary round 2 SLOVAN BRATISLAVA (SVK)
H 2-1 Obiku (26, 88p)
Panayiotou, Engomitis, Charalambous (Ciric 84), Foukaris, Luca, Melanarkitis V., Neophytou (Iosiphides 61), Milinkovic, Okkas, Jovanovic (Kotsonis 68), Obiku.
A 1-1 Obiku (58)
Panayiotou, Engomitis, Charalambous (Kotsonis 48), Foukaris, Luca, Melanarkitis V., Pounas, Milinkovic, Okkas (Iosiphides 76), Jovanovic, Obiku (Melanarkitis A. 83).

Qualifying round HERTHA BSC BERLIN (GER)
A 0-2 Panayiotou, Charalambous, Foukaris (Iosiphides 67), Pounas, Okkas, Jovanovic (Neophytou 71), Luca, Engomitis, Melanarkitis A., Melanarkitis V., Obiku (Ciric 82).
H 0-0 Panayiotou, Engomitis (Iosiphides 88), Charalambous (Ciric 64), Luca, Foukaris, Melanarkitis A., Melanarkitis V., Milinkovic, Okkas, Neophytou (Jovanovic 71), Obiku.

UEFA CUP
● ANORTHOSIS FAMAGUSTA
1st round LEGIA WARSZAWA (POL)
H 1-0 Engomitis (83)
Panayiotou, Charalambous, Luca, Melanarkitis A., Kotsonis, Melanarkitis V., Okkas, Neophytou (Ciric 31), Milinkovic (Foukaris 46), Engomitis, Obiku (Sotiriou 58).
A 0-2 Panayiotou, Charalambous (Neophytou 71), Iosiphides (Ioannou 80), Foukaris, Melanarkitis V., Melanarkitis A., Ciric (Obiku 67), Kotsonis, Milinkovic, Engomitis, Okkas.

● APOEL NICOSIA
Qualifying round LEVSKI SOFIA (BUL)
H 0-0 Petrides, Satsias, Misos, Christodoulou, Stavrou, Timotheou, Aloneftis, Hadjiloucas (Aristocleous 56), Oreschuk, Ioannou (Yiasemakis 63), Marcelo (Phasouliotis C. 78).
A 0-2 Petrides, Satsias, Aloneftis, Christodoulou, Misos, Stavrou, Timotheou (Hadjiloucas 70), Aristocleous, Oreschuk, Ioannou 75), Yiasemakis, Marcelo (Pohouzouris 79).

● OMONIA NICOSIA
Qualifying round BELSHINA BOBRUISK (BLS)
A 5-1 Kalotheou (9), Mihajlovic (26), Rauffmann (33), Kaiafas (54), Constandinides (90)
Christophi, Nicolaou Ch. (Panayiotou G. 70), Nicolaou N., Ioakim, Tittel, Kalotheou C., Kaiafas (Constandinides 74), Rauffmann, Mihajlovic, Georgiou (Odysseos 36), Malekkos.
H 3-0 Rauffmann (64, 68, 75)
Yiallouris, Nicolaou N., Ioakim, Panayiotou G., Nicolaou Ch. (Andreou S. 69), Rauffmann, Tittel, Kalotheou C., Panayiotou Ch. (Constandinides 55), Kaiafas, Kontolefteros (Loizides 24).

1st round JUVENTUS (ITA)
H 2-5 Kontolefteros (76, 85)
Yiallouris, Nicolaou N., Ioakim, Tittel, Kalotheou C., Nicolaou Ch., Georgiou (Panayiotou G. 46), Constandinides (Malekkos 72), Kaiafas, Mihajlovic (Kontolefteros 75), Rauffmann.
A 0-5 Yiallouris, Constandinides, Ioakim, Tittel, Panayiotou, Odysseos (Kontolefteros 79), Kaiafas, Nicolaou Ch. (Andreou S. 46), Kalotheou, Mihajlovic (Georgiou 72), Rauffmann.

INTERNATIONAL HONOURS

None

Another blemish which refused to go away was the continued spectator violence, which forced several clubs into playing at neutral venues as the result of home-ground bans. The worst incident of all came after the Paralimni v Omonia match in November, when the visiting Omonia fans set fire to the stadium and then went on the rampage outside the ground, destroying dozens of cars in nearby showrooms.

There was a brief return to the bad old days for the Cypriot national team when they were hammered 8-0 by Spain in their penultimate Euro 2000 qualifier. Although Cyprus had expected to lose the match, the severity of the scoreline was difficult to stomach, especially after the team had put themselves back into play-off contention just three days earlier with a crucial 3-2 victory over Israel in Limassol.

Remarkably, despite the battering in Badajoz, Cyprus still had their fate in their own hands. A win in their final fixture, away to Austria, would have carried Stavros

PLAYER OF THE SEASON

YIOTIS ENGOMITIS
Together with Anorthosis team-mate Yiannakis Okkas, 28-year-old winger Yiotis Engomitis became the latest Cypriot international to head off to the Greek mainland when he joined PAOK of Salonika during the summer. Engomitis left after the best season of his career, during which he scooped the country's Footballer of the Year and Sportsman of the Year awards and netted a top-scoring 16 goals in Anorthosis's fourth successive title triumph. A very talented player who can operate in a variety of roles, his natural position is wide on the right but he has latterly been used further forward in attack. He is an established member of the Cypriot national team and scored in each of the famous 3-2 home wins over Spain and Israel during the Euro 2000 qualifying campaign.

Papadopoulos's side into the play-offs. But it was too much to ask and Austria, who were already eliminated, cruised to a straightforward 3-1 win.

PROMOTED CLUBS 99/00

SECOND DIVISION FINAL TABLE

		Pd	W	D	L	F	A	Pt	GD
1	**Dighenis Akritas Morphou**	26	20	2	4	77	20	62	57
2	**Aris Limassol**	26	19	3	4	71	31	60	40
3	**Doxa Katokopia**	26	17	6	3	62	25	57	37
4	APEP Pitsilia	26	14	4	8	51	36	46	15
5	Halkanoras Dhali	26	12	4	10	38	41	40	-3
6	Evaghoras Paphos	26	10	6	10	35	38	36	-3
7	Omonia Aradippou	26	9	6	11	42	43	33	-1
8	Ermis Aradippou	26	9	5	12	47	39	32	8
9	AEK-Achilleas Ayiou Theraponta	26	8	8	10	43	52	32	-9
10	Onisillos Sotira	26	8	7	11	39	45	31	-6
11	AEZ Zakakiou	26	7	6	13	36	46	27	-10
12	PAEEK Kerynia	26	6	4	16	23	60	22	-37
13	Anagennisis Germasoyia	26	5	5	16	23	64	20	-41
14	Iraklis Gerolakkos	26	3	4	19	27	74	13	-47

CLUB DIRECTORIES

Dighenis Akritas Morphou FC
PO Box 23548, 1684 Nicosia
tel - (02) 316800 / fax - (02) 316576
Year of Formation - 1931
President - Andreas Dionysiou
Secretary - Andreas Meraklis
Coach - George Savvides
Stadium - Makarion (20,000)

Aris FC
1 A. Sikelianou str., 3085 Limassol
tel - (05) 382075/381076
fax - (05) 379689
Year of Formation - 1930
President - Doros Ieropoulos
Secretary - Charalambos Illambas
Coach - Andreas Kissonergis
(00/01 - George Paraskeva)
Stadium - Tsirion (20,000)

Doxa Katokopia FC
PO Box 28293, 2092 Nicosia
tel - (02) 821929 / fax - (02) 368186
Year of Formation - 1954
President - Photis Yiannakas
Secretary - Stavros Loizou
Coach - Nicos Andronicou
Stadium - Kykkos (3,000)

AEK LARNACA

CLUB DIRECTORY

AEK FC
Kilkis str.
6015 Larnaca
tel - (04) 655999
fax - (04) 652464
Year of Formation - 1994
President - Dinos Lefkaritis
Secretary - Photis Photiou
Coach - Radmilo Ivanisevic; Marios Constandinou
(00/01 - Petros Ravousis)
Stadium - GS Zenon (16,000)

APPEARANCES 99/00

	P	Ap	(s)	Gls
Andreas ADAMOU	A	1	(12)	1
Alekos ALEKOU	M	2	(1)	
Klimis ALEXANDROU	A	8	(4)	2
Eleftherios ANDONIOU	M		(3)	
Christos BAKARIS	A	11	(4)	
Savvas CONSTANDINOU	G	20		
Goran DJORDJEVIC (YUG)	M	23	(2)	
Eleftherios ELEFTHERIOU	M	19	(2)	4
Christophoros FELLAS	D	2	(1)	
Aleksandar JANJIC (YUG)	A	15	(2)	7
Sergis KOUNNIS	A	7	(6)	5
George KOUNOUSHIS	D		(2)	
Pambos KOUTOURIS	M		(5)	
Neophytos LARKOU	D	21		2
Michalis MARKOU	M	23		
Andreas MAVRIS	G	6		
Bojan MILENKOVIC (YUG)	M	24		4
Costas MINA	M	1	(10)	
Dimitris PANAYIOTOU	D	22	(2)	3
Michalis PAPAIOANNOU	A	23	(2)	4
Stelios STYLIANIDES	D	17	(6)	3
George THEODOTOU	D	25		1
George VASSILIOU	D	2	(3)	
Panikos XIOUROUPPAS	A	14	(4)	4

LEAGUE RESULTS 1999/2000

18/09/99	Apollon Limassol	A	1-3	Papaioannou
25/09/99	Ethnikos Ashia	H	2-1	og (Andreou N.), Alexandrou
03/10/99	Anagennisis Dherynia	A	1-0	Xiourouppas
16/10/99	Olympiakos Nicosia	A	2-2	Adamou, Xiourouppas
24/10/99	Omonia Nicosia	H	0-4	
30/10/99	APOP Paphos	A	1-0	Panayiotou
06/11/99	Nea Salamina Famagusta	H	0-1	
13/11/99	AEL Limassol	A	0-2	
21/11/99	Paralimni	H	2-1	Panayiotou, Janjic
27/11/99	Alki Larnaca	A	7-2	Janjic 2, Xiourouppas, Larkou, Milenkovic, Eleftheriou, Papaioannou
04/12/99	APOEL Nicosia	H	1-2	Janjic
18/12/99	Ethnikos Akhna	A	2-0	Janjic, Milenkovic
09/01/00	Anorthosis Famagusta	H	0-3	
15/01/00	Ethnikos Ashia	A	0-3	
22/01/00	Anagennisis Dherynia	H	4-1	Eleftheriou, Panayiotou, Stylianides, Kounnis
30/01/00	Olympiakos Nicosia	H	3-1	Kounnis, Stylianides, Eleftheriou
12/02/00	Omonia Nicosia	A	3-0	Milenkovic, Kounnis, Papaioannou
26/02/00	APOP Paphos	H	0-0	
05/03/00	Nea Salamina Famagusta	A	1-2	og (Michael)
19/03/00	AEL Limassol	H	3-2	Kounnis 2, Eleftheriou
26/03/00	Paralimni	A	0-3	
01/04/00	Alki Larnaca	H	4-2	Stylianides, Milenkovic (p), Xiourouppas, Larkou
09/04/00	APOEL Nicosia	A	0-1	
16/04/00	Ethnikos Akhna	H	1-2	Papaioannou
22/04/00	Anorthosis Famagusta	A	2-1	Janjic, Alexandrou
06/05/00	Apollon Limassol	H	2-0	Janjic, Theodotou

AEL LIMASSOL

CLUB DIRECTORY

AEL FC
138 Glastonos str.
3032 Limassol
tel - (05) 362888
fax - (05) 373960
Year of Formation - 1930
President - Dimitris Solomonides
Secretary - Sakis Karapateas
Coach - Panikos Orphanides; Loizos Mavroudis
(00/01 - Andreas Michaelides)
Stadium - Tsirion (20,000)

MAJOR HONOURS
League Championship - (5)
1941, 1953, 1955, 1956, 1968.
Domestic Cup - (6)
1939, 1940, 1948, 1985, 1987, 1989.

APPEARANCES 99/00

		P	Ap	(s)	Gls
Andonis ANDONIOU	A	18	(6)	1	
Sozos ANDREOU	D	18			
Christos CHARALAMBOUS	M		(2)		
Christos CHRISTODOULOU	D	14	(4)	2	
Ermogenis CHRISTOPHI	D	21		2	
Chrysostomos CHRYSOSTOMOU	D	11	(9)		
George CONSTANDI	M	4	(12)		
Panayiotis CONSTANDINIDES (GRE)	D	13		1	
Marios DIMITRIOU	A	23		5	
George IOANNOU	D		(2)		
Boban KITANOV (YUG)	A	26		14	
Kyriakos KYRIAKOU	M	16	(1)		
Marios KYRIAKOU	D	21			
Dimitris LEONIS	G	23			
Chrisis MICHAEL	D	17	(4)	2	
Stelios NICOLAOU	A	4	(1)		
Christos PANAYIOTOU	G	3			
Milan PECELJ (YUG)	A	14	(5)	3	
Argiris PETROU	A	8	(6)	3	
Andreas SOPHOCLEOUS	M	22	(1)	1	
Panayiotis STAVRINOU	M	3	(11)		
Alexis YARPOZIS	A	7	(6)	10	

LEAGUE RESULTS 1999/2000

Date	Opponent	H/A	Score	Scorers
19/09/99	Alki Larnaca	A	3-1	Pecelj, Dimitriou 2
25/09/99	APOEL Nicosia	H	1-0	Michael
02/10/99	Ethnikos Akhna	A	2-1	Kitanov, Petrou
16/10/99	Anorthosis Famagusta	H	2-3	Kitanov, Christophi
23/10/99	Apollon Limassol	A	3-1	Kitanov (p), Christodoulou, Petrou
30/10/99	Ethnikos Ashia	H	2-1	Kitanov 2
07/11/99	Anagennisis Dherynia	A	3-1	Kitanov, Constandinides, og (Kosmas)
13/11/99	AEK Larnaca	H	2-0	Christophi, Dimitriou
20/11/99	Omonia Nicosia	A	0-1	
27/11/99	APOP Paphos	H	2-1	Sophocleous, Petrou
05/12/99	Nea Salamina Famagusta	A	2-0	Kitanov 2
19/12/99	Olympiakos Nicosia	A	3-3	Pecelj 2, Yarpozis
08/01/00	Paralimni	H	2-0	Dimitriou, Kitanov
16/01/00	APOEL Nicosia	A	0-2	
22/01/00	Ethnikos Akhna	H	0-0	
29/01/00	Anorthosis Famagusta	A	1-6	Dimitriou
12/02/00	Apollon Limassol	H	1-2	Michael
26/02/00	Ethnikos Ashia	A	2-3	Kitanov, Yarpozis
04/03/00	Anagennisis Dherynia	H	1-0	Yarpozis
19/03/00	AEK Larnaca	A	2-3	Yarpozis, Kitanov
25/03/00	Omonia Nicosia	H	0-0	
01/04/00	APOP Paphos	A	0-2	
08/04/00	Nea Salamina Famagusta	H	0-3	
15/04/00	Olympiakos Nicosia	H	4-1	Yarpozis 3 (1p), Andoniou
22/04/00	Paralimni	A	1-6	Kitanov
06/05/00	Alki Larnaca	H	6-1	Yarpozis 3, Kitanov 2, Christodoulou

ALKI LARNACA

CLUB DIRECTORY

Alki FC
23 Loukis Akritas str.
6015 Larnaca
tel - (04) 852955/654099
fax - (04) 628984
Year of Formation - 1948
President - Costas Nicolaides
Secretary - Christos Charalambous
Coach - Loizos Mavroudis (00/01 - Nedim Tutic)
Stadium - GS Zenon (16,000)

APPEARANCES 99/00

	P	Ap	(s)	Gls
Andonis ANDONIOU	M	6	(4)	
Andreas ANDREOU	G	1	(2)	
Justin BABKO (CMR)	M	23	(2)	1
Nicos CHARALAMBOUS	D	15	(4)	
Charis CHARI	G	2		
George CHIRAS	M	1	(5)	
Michalis CHRISTOU	A	12	(1)	
George CONSTANDINOU	M	9		
Dimitris COSTA	D	3	(2)	
Savvas DAMIANOU	M	10	(5)	3
Koulis EVANGELOU	D	5	(3)	
Christos GEORGIOU	D	20		
Marinos GEORGIOU	D	17	(1)	1
Kyriakos HAPERI	D	2	(2)	
Akis IOANNOU	A	14	(1)	3
Nicolas KARAYIORGIS	A	15	(4)	
Boris KHVOINEV (BUL)	A	24		4
Andonis KONNARIS	D	19		2
George KYRIAKOU	D	2	(7)	
Michalis MICHAEL	M	10	(4)	
Michalis MICHAELIDES	A	1	(5)	
Pambos MILTIADOUS	G	23		
Michalis NEROUPOS	D	5	(3)	
George PAKOULAS	D	6	(6)	
Andreas PARPAS	A	8		
Yasen PETROV (BUL)	A	12		3
Andreas YIATROU	M	21		3

LEAGUE RESULTS 1999/2000

19/09/99	AEL Limassol	H	1-3	Ioannou
25/09/99	Paralimni	A	2-3	Petrov (p), Khvoinev
02/10/99	Olympiakos Nicosia	H	1-2	Petrov (p)
17/10/99	APOEL Nicosia	H	1-4	Georgiou M.
24/10/99	Ethnikos Akhna	A	1-5	Konnaris
30/10/99	Anorthosis Famagusta	H	1-5	Yiatrou
06/11/99	Apollon Limassol	A	1-3	Ioannou
14/11/99	Ethnikos Ashia	H	0-2	
20/11/99	Anagennisis Dherynia	A	1-3	Khvoinev
27/11/99	AEK Larnaca	H	2-7	Petrov, Ioannou
05/12/99	Omonia Nicosia	A	1-4	Yiatrou
19/12/99	APOP Paphos	H	2-3	Khvoinev, Yiatrou
08/01/00	Nea Salamina Famagusta	A	0-6	
15/01/00	Paralimni	H	2-1	Khvoinev, Damianou
22/01/00	Olympiakos Nicosia	A	0-5	
29/01/00	APOEL Nicosia	A	0-6	
13/02/00	Ethnikos Akhna	H	0-4	
27/02/00	Anorthosis Famagusta	A	0-4	
04/03/00	Apollon Limassol	H	0-6	
19/03/00	Ethnikos Ashia	A	0-3	
26/03/00	Anagennisis Dherynia	H	1-3	Damianou
01/04/00	AEK Larnaca	A	2-4	Babko, Damianou
08/04/00	Omonia Nicosia	H	0-3	
15/04/00	APOP Paphos	A	0-5	
23/04/00	Nea Salamina Famagusta	H	0-9	
06/05/00	AEL Limassol	A	1-6	Konnaris

ANAGENNISIS DHERYNIA

CLUB DIRECTORY

Anagennisis FC
6 Ammohostou Street
PO Box 36081
5385 Dherynia
tel - (03) 821436
fax - (03) 730089
Year of Formation - 1920
President - Kyriakos Panayiotou
Secretary - Marios Pantelis
Coach - Adamos Adamou
(00/01 - Ayis Aiomamitis)
Stadium - Municipal (6,000)

APPEARANCES 99/00

	P	Ap	(s)	Gls
Andonis Ioannou AFXENTI	M	10		
Nicolas CHRISTOPHI	M	9	(2)	1
Panikos CONSTANDINOU	G	10		
Kyriakos DIMITRIOU	M	14	(8)	4
Demos DIMOSTHENOUS	M	9	(4)	
Yiannos KALOTHEOU	D	13		
Marios KARAYIANNIS	M	4	(2)	
Aristos KARAS	M	5		
Robert KOCIS (SVK)	A	14		4
George KOSMA	D	11	(4)	
Marios KYRIAKOU	G	4		
Lambros LAMBROU	D		(3)	
Costas LUCA	M	12	(10)	3
Nebojsa MLADENOVIC (YUG)	A	22		5
Nicos NICOLAOU	M	10	(6)	
George PAPASSAVAS	G	8	(1)	
Andreas PETROU	D	12	(4)	
Iacovos ROUSOS	D	22		2
Christos SHIAILIS	D	2	(2)	
Dimitris SHIAILIS	M	19	(3)	1
Jiovannis SHIEPIS	M	8	(2)	
Andreas STASIS	G	4	(1)	
Tasos STASIS	D	22	(1)	
Valentin STEFAN (ROM)	M	12	(1)	2
Christakis TRISOKKAS	M	16	(6)	
George TSOUKKAS	M	4	(7)	
George YIANNAKOU	D	10		

LEAGUE RESULTS 1999/2000

Date	Opponent	H/A	Score	Scorers
19/09/99	Ethnikos Ashia	A	1-0	Rousos
26/09/99	Olympiakos Nicosia	A	1-2	Kocis (p)
03/10/99	AEK Larnaca	H	0-1	
17/10/99	Omonia Nicosia	A	1-8	Mladenovic
23/10/99	APOP Paphos	H	3-1	Dimitriou 2, Kocis
31/10/99	Nea Salamina Famagusta	A	3-7	Mladenovic, Stefan 2
07/11/99	AEL Limassol	H	1-3	Mladenovic
14/11/99	Paralimni	A	0-4	
20/11/99	Alki Larnaca	H	3-1	Kocis 2, Luca
28/11/99	APOEL Nicosia	A	0-5	
04/12/99	Ethnikos Akhna	H	1-3	Dimitriou
18/12/99	Anorthosis Famagusta	A	1-4	Christophi
08/01/00	Apollon Limassol	H	0-1	
16/01/00	Olympiakos Nicosia	H	1-2	Mladenovic
22/01/00	AEK Larnaca	A	1-4	Luca
29/01/00	Omonia Nicosia	H	0-7	
12/02/00	APOP Paphos	A	1-5	Luca
27/02/00	Nea Salamina Famagusta	H	0-4	
04/03/00	AEL Limassol	A	0-1	
18/03/00	Paralimni	H	0-3	
26/03/00	Alki Larnaca	A	3-1	Mladenovic, Rousos, Shiailis D.
01/04/00	APOEL Nicosia	H	0-5	
08/04/00	Ethnikos Akhna	A	0-5	
15/04/00	Anorthosis Famagusta	H	0-4	
22/04/00	Apollon Limassol	A	0-1	
06/05/00	Ethnikos Ashia	H	1-5	Dimitriou

ANORTHOSIS FAMAGUSTA

CLUB DIRECTORY

Anorthosis FC of Famagusta
Andonis Papadopoulos Stadium
PO Box 40756
6307 Larnaca
tel - (04) 635834/639033
fax - (04) 635833
Year of Formation - 1911
President - Kikis Constandinou
Secretary - Christakis Pittas
Coach - Dusan Mitosevic
Stadium - Andonis Papadopoulos (9,500)

MAJOR HONOURS
League Championship - (11)
1950, 1957, 1958, 1960, 1962, 1963, 1995,
1997, 1998, 1999, 2000.
Domestic Cup - (6)
1949, 1962, 1963, 1971, 1975, 1998.

APPEARANCES 99/00

	P	Ap	(s)	Gls
Andonis ANDONIOU	M	1	(3)	
Kyriakos CHAILIS	M	4	(6)	3
Zacharias CHARALAMBOUS	D	23	(2)	2
Michalis CHRISTOPHI	D	1	(2)	
Yiotis ENGOMITIS	A	20		16
Stavros FOUKARIS	D	17	(6)	
Dimitris IOANNOU	D	17	(2)	3
George IOSIPHIDES	M	14	(4)	3
Anastasios KARSERAS	M	3	(3)	1
Christos KOTSONIS	M	26		5
Kyriakos KOURSAROS	M	1	(2)	
Lucas LUCA	D	7	(3)	1
Andreas MELANARKITIS	D	9	(2)	1
Vassos MELANARKITIS	M	24		3
Zoran MILINKOVIC (YUG)	M	19		2
Marios NEOPHYTOU	A	8	(5)	6
Mike OBIKU (NIG)	A	14	(2)	12
Yiannakis OKKAS	A	20	(2)	12
Nicos PANAYIOTOU	G	22		
Panikos POUNNAS	M	11	(11)	
Andros SOTIRIOU	A	2	(7)	3
Savvas THOUPOS	M		(7)	1
Vladan TOMIC (YUG)	M	19		6
Andonis YIORGALLIDES	G	4		

LEAGUE RESULTS 1999/2000

18/09/99	Omonia Nicosia	H	5-3	Okkas 3, Obiku, Milinkovic
25/09/99	APOP Paphos	A	4-0	Kotsonis, Engomitis, Ioannou, Melanarkitis A.
03/10/99	Nea Salamina Famagusta	H	1-0	Sotiriou
16/10/99	AEL Limassol	A	3-2	Engomitis, Melanarkitis V., Neophytou
23/10/99	Paralimni	H	4-1	Engomitis, Okkas, Iosiphides, Kotsonis
30/10/99	Alki Larnaca	A	5-1	Chailis 2, Tomic, Engomitis, Thoupos
07/11/99	APOEL Nicosia	H	1-1	Kotsonis
13/11/99	Ethnikos Akhna	A	3-2	Engomitis, Okkas, Tomic
20/11/99	Olympiakos Nicosia	H	3-0	Okkas, Engomitis, Sotiriou
28/11/99	Apollon Limassol	H	3-1	Obiku 2 (1p), Neophytou
04/12/99	Ethnikos Ashia	A	3-1	Iosiphides, Obiku, Okkas
18/12/99	Anagennisis Dherynia	H	4-1	Obiku, Kotsonis, Charalambous, Sotiriou
09/01/00	AEL Limassol	A	3-0	Ioannou, Okkas, Engomitis
16/01/00	APOP Paphos	H	4-0	Iosiphides, Tomic, Ioannou, Chailis
23/01/00	Nea Salamina Famagusta	A	4-1	Okkas 2, Obiku, Engomitis
29/01/00	AEL Limassol	H	6-1	Obiku 4, Kotsonis, Tomic
12/02/00	Paralimni	A	1-0	Engomitis
27/02/00	Alki Larnaca	H	4-0	Obiku 2, Charalambous, Okkas
05/03/00	APOEL Nicosia	A	2-0	(w/o; abandoned at 0-0)
18/03/00	Ethnikos Akhna	H	3-1	Engomitis 2, Milinkovic
26/03/00	Olympiakos Nicosia	A	2-5	Tomic, Karseras
01/04/00	Apollon Limassol	A	2-3	Melanarkitis V. 2 (1p)
09/04/00	Ethnikos Ashia	H	5-0	Engomitis 4, Neophytou
15/04/00	Anagennisis Dherynia	A	4-0	Engomitis, Tomic, Okkas, Neophytou
22/04/00	AEK Larnaca	H	1-2	Neophytou (p)
07/05/00	Omonia Nicosia	A	2-2	Neophytou, Luca

APOEL NICOSIA

CLUB DIRECTORY

APOEL Football Co.
PO Box 21133
1502 Nicosia
tel - (02) 394994
fax - (02) 379234
Year of Formation - 1926
President - Chris Triantaphillides
Secretary - Paris Spanos
Coach - Andreas Michaelides
(00/01 - Dusan Sapuric)
Stadium - GS Pancypria (23,000)

MAJOR HONOURS
League Championship - (16) 1936, 1937, 1938,
1939, 1940, 1947, 1948, 1949, 1952, 1965,
1973, 1980, 1986, 1990, 1992, 1996.
Domestic Cup - (17) 1937, 1941, 1947, 1951,
1963, 1968, 1969, 1973, 1976, 1978, 1979,
1984, 1993, 1995, 1996, 1997, 1999.

APPEARANCES 99/00

	P	Ap	(s)	Gls
Nectarios ALEXANDROU	A		(4)	
George ALONEFTIS	A	23	(1)	3
Aristos ARISTOCLEOUS	M	16	(1)	
Xenios ARISTOTELOUS	D	2		
Costas CHARALAMBIDES	A	7	(5)	1
Mohammed CHIAOUCH (MAR)	M		(4)	
George CHRISTODOULOU	D	24		2
Marios ELIA	D	5	(4)	2
Lucas HADJILUCAS	M	2	(9)	
Yiannos IOANNOU	A	12	(3)	9
MARCELO Veridiano (BRA)	A	19	(3)	6
Marios MARKOU	D	3	(5)	
Angelos MISOS	D	18		
Michalis MORPHIS	G	2		
Andonis NICOLAOU	M	20		2
Roman ORESCHUK (RUS)	A	16	(7)	5
Andros PETRIDES	G	24		
Petros PETROU	M	22	(1)	
Costas PHASOULIOTIS	M	3	(10)	1
Panayiotis PHASOULIOTIS	M	4	(7)	
Marios POUHOUZOURIS	M		(2)	
Marinos SATSIAS	D	25		3
Costas STAVROU	D	9	(2)	
Nicos TIMOTHEOU	D	6	(4)	1
Yiasemis YIASEMAKIS	A	24	(1)	21

LEAGUE RESULTS 1999/2000

18/09/99	Nea Salamina Famagusta	H	1-2	Yiasemakis
25/09/99	AEL Limassol	A	0-1	
03/10/99	Paralimni	H	3-2	Ioannou 2, Yiasemakis
17/10/99	Alki Larnaca	A	4-1	Oreschuk, Yiasemakis 2,
				Phasouliotis C.
23/10/99	Olympiakos Nicosia	H	8-2	Ioannou 4, Yiasemakis 3, Marcelo
31/10/99	Ethnikos Akhna	H	2-1	Yiasemakis, Aloneftis
07/11/99	Anorthosis Famagusta	A	1-1	Oreschuk
13/11/99	Apollon Limassol	H	2-1	Oreschuk, Yiasemakis
21/11/99	Ethnikos Ashia	A	2-0	Christodoulou, Nicolaou
28/11/99	Anagennisis Dherynia	H	5-0	Yiasemakis 3, Timotheou, Aloneftis
04/12/99	AEK Larnaca	A	2-1	Satsias, Yiasemakis
18/12/99	Omonia Nicosia	H	3-3	Aloneftis, Christodoulou, Ioannou
08/01/00	APOP Paphos	A	0-1	
16/01/00	AEL Limassol	H	2-0	Marcelo, Yiasemakis
22/01/00	Paralimni	A	0-0	
29/01/00	Alki Larnaca	H	6-0	Yiasemakis 3, Marcelo, Ioannou,
				Elia
13/02/00	Olympiakos Nicosia	A	2-0	Yiasemakis
26/02/00	Ethnikos Akhna	A	0-1	
05/03/00	Anorthosis Famagusta	H	0-2	
18/03/00	Apollon Limassol	A	1-2	Ioannou
25/03/00	Ethnikos Ashia	H	3-2	Nicolaou, Marcelo 2
01/04/00	Anagennisis Dherynia	A	5-0	Yiasemakis 2, Satsias, Elia,
				og (Stasis)
09/04/00	AEK Larnaca	H	1-0	Marcelo
15/04/00	Omonia Nicosia	A	2-3	Charalambides, Oreschuk
22/04/00	APOP Paphos	H	2-2	Satsias, Yiasemakis (p)
07/05/00	Nea Salamina Famagusta	A	1-3	Oreschuk

APOLLON LIMASSOL

CLUB DIRECTORY

Apollon Football Co.
1 Mesogion str.
PO Box 53206
3301 Limassol
tel - (05) 363702/379082
fax - (05) 359116
Year of Formation - 1954
President - George Papas
Secretary - Costas Solomou
Coach - Dieter Ferner (00/01 - Gunder Bengtsson)
Stadium - Tsirion (20,000)

MAJOR HONOURS
League Championship - (2) 1991, 1994.
Domestic Cup - (4) 1966, 1967, 1986, 1992.

APPEARANCES 99/00

	P	Ap	(s)	Gls
Stelios ANDONIOU	M	1		
Sofronis AVGOUSTI	G	21		
Marios CHARALAMBOUS	D	13		2
Chrisostomos Juras CHRISTOPHI	D	20	(2)	
Costas CONSTANDINOU	M	8	(8)	1
Costas COSTA	D	6		1
Paris EVRIPIDOU	A		(2)	
Christos GERMANOS	M	20		1
George KAIS	A	2	(10)	
Loizos KAKOYIANNIS	D	13		
Xenios KYRIAKOU	D	10	(2)	1
Zoran MASIC (YUG)	A	20	(2)	13
Alexandros MICHAEL	G	5		
Andreas PANAYIOTOU	M	8	(2)	
Marios PANAYIOTOU	D	14	(3)	2
Nikodimos PAPAVASSILIOU	M	12	(5)	9
Dejan PEKOVIC (YUG)	A	9	(10)	3
Philippos PHILIPPOU	D	7	(4)	1
Pambos PITTAS	D	23		1
Milenko SPOLJARIC	M	20	(1)	10
Amir TELJIGOVIC (YUG)	M	20	(2)	
Christos THEOPHILIOU	M	20	(2)	
Angelos TSOLAKIS	A	14	(3)	4

LEAGUE RESULTS 1999/2000

18/09/99	AEK Larnaca	H	3-1	Philippou, Spoljaric (p), Masic
25/09/99	Omonia Nicosia	A	0-3	
02/10/99	APOP Paphos	H	4-1	Spoljaric 2, Papavassiliou, Masic
16/10/99	Nea Salamina Famagusta	A	2-3	Charalambous, Papavassiliou
23/10/99	AEL Limassol	H	1-3	Pekovic
30/10/99	Paralimni	A	1-2	Tsolakis
06/11/99	Alki Larnaca	H	3-1	Tsolakis, Charalambous, Pekovic
13/11/99	APOEL Nicosia	A	1-2	Masic
20/11/99	Ethnikos Akhna	H	0-0	
28/11/99	Anorthosis Famagusta	A	1-3	Constandinou
04/12/99	Olympiakos Nicosia	H	3-3	Kyriakou, Spoljaric (p), Masic
18/12/99	Ethnikos Ashia	H	2-0	Spoljaric, Panayiotou M.
08/01/00	Anagennisis Dherynia	A	1-0	Pekovic
15/01/00	Omonia Nicosia	H	0-4	
22/01/00	APOP Paphos	A	1-1	Masic
29/01/00	Nea Salamina Famagusta	H	2-1	Masic, Tsolakis
12/02/00	AEL Limassol	A	2-1	Spoljaric, Costa
26/02/00	Paralimni	H	3-1	Papavassiliou, Germanos, Tsolakis
04/03/00	Alki Larnaca	A	6-0	Papavassiliou 4, Masic,
				Panayiotou M.
18/03/00	APOEL Nicosia	H	2-1	Masic 2
25/03/00	Ethnikos Akhna	A	3-1	Masic 2, Papavassiliou
01/04/00	Anorthosis Famagusta	H	3-2	Spoljaric 2 (1p), Pittas
08/04/00	Olympiakos Nicosia	A	3-5	Spoljaric 2 (2p), Masic
16/04/00	Ethnikos Ashia	A	1-3	Papavassiliou
22/04/00	Anagennisis Dherynia	H	1-0	Masic
07/05/00	AEK Larnaca	A	0-2	

APOP PAPHOS

CLUB DIRECTORY

APOP FC
PO Box 60080
8010 Paphos
tel - (06) 232004/235353
fax - (06) 237210
Year of Formation - 1953
President - Stathis Tourvas
Secretary - Panikos Phacontis
Coach - Milovan Ristivojevic; Andreas Kissonergis
Stadium - Paphiako (10,000)

APPEARANCES 99/00

	P	Ap	(s)	Gls
Ljubisa ALEKSIC (YUG)	D	21	(2)	
Ioannis Anthimou ANDREOU	D	4	(10)	
Polykarpos Andoniou ANIFTOS	M	12	(1)	2
Pambos CHARALAMBOUS	A	25		18
Costas CONSTANDINOU	G	8	(2)	
Costas CONSTANDINOU	A	1	(2)	
George GEORGIOU	M	13	(5)	
George Tsiartas GEORGIOU	D	5	(7)	3
Philippos GEORGIOU	M	16	(5)	
George IOANNOU	M	7		1
Nicolas KYRIAKOU	M	8		
Zoran MAJSTOROVIC (YUG)	A	23	(1)	2
Christos NIKITA	D	10	(3)	
Panikos PAPADOPOULOS	A	23		2
Andros PAPAIOANNOU	G	18		
Michalis PATOUNAS	M	21	(4)	1
Stelios SOPHOCLEOUS	M	24		4
Andreas STEPHANOU	M	14	(6)	3
Nicos TRYPHONOS	D		(7)	
Vrionis VRIONI	D	8	(11)	
Vladan VUKOVIC (YUG)	M	25		1

LEAGUE RESULTS 1999/2000

19/09/99	Ethnikos Akhna	A	1-3	Vukovic
25/09/99	Anorthosis Famagusta	H	0-4	
02/10/99	Apollon Limassol	A	1-4	Charalambous
16/10/99	Ethnikos Ashia	H	0-0	
23/10/99	Anagennisis Dherynia	A	1-3	Charalambous
30/10/99	AEK Larnaca	H	0-1	
07/11/99	Omonia Nicosia	A	0-5	
14/11/99	Olympiakos Nicosia	A	0-5	
20/11/99	Nea Salamina Famagusta	H	2-1	Sophocleous, Charalambous (p)
27/11/99	AEL Limassol	A	1-2	Charalambous
04/12/99	Paralimni	H	2-3	Sophocleous 2
19/12/99	Alki Larnaca	A	3-2	Aniftos, Stephanou, Charalambous
08/01/00	APOEL Nicosia	H	1-0	Charalambous
16/01/00	Anorthosis Famagusta	A	0-4	
22/01/00	Apollon Limassol	H	1-1	Papadopoulos
30/01/00	Ethnikos Ashia	A	2-1	Papadopoulos, Ioannou
12/02/00	Anagennisis Dherynia	H	5-1	Charalambous 3, Sophocleous, Patounas
26/02/00	AEK Larnaca	A	0-0	
04/03/00	Omonia Nicosia	H	1-2	Georgiou G.T. (p)
18/03/00	Olympiakos Nicosia	H	2-0	Stephanou 2
25/03/00	Nea Salamina Famagusta	A	1-1	Charalambous
01/04/00	AEL Limassol	H	2-0	Charalambous 2
09/04/00	Paralimni	A	1-2	Charalambous
15/04/00	Alki Larnaca	H	5-0	Charalambous 3 (1p), Aniftos, og (Haperis)
22/04/00	APOEL Nicosia	A	2-2	Charalambous 2
06/05/00	Ethnikos Akhna	H	4-0	Majstorovic 2, Georgiou G.T. 2

ETHNIKOS AKHNA

CLUB DIRECTORY

Ethnikos Akhna FC
Dasaki Akhna
tel - (04) 721320
fax - (04) 722060
Year of Formation - 1968
President - Kikis Philippou
Secretary - Costas Constantinides
Coach - Moca Vukotic
Stadium - Dasaki (8,000)

APPEARANCES 99/00

	P	Ap	(s)	Gls
Perica ADZIC (YUG)	D	16	(1)	2
Kyriakpos AGAPIOU	G	1	(2)	
Alexis ALEXANDROU	A	13	(5)	4
Stavros GEORGIOU	A	14	(7)	1
Borce GJUREV (MAC)	A	18	(6)	6
Petros HADJAROS	D		(2)	
Spyros KASTANAS	D	23	(2)	4
Andreas KATZIS	D	20		1
Lambros LAMBROU	M	22		4
Liasis LIASIS	M	10	(9)	2
Pavlos MARKOU	M	10	(4)	3
Dragan MUSIC (YUG)	A	20	(1)	10
Panikos NEOCLEOUS	A	10	(13)	2
Christos PASHIALIS	D	21	(5)	1
Marios PASHIALIS	D	24		
Christos PHOULIS	M	18	(2)	
Panayiotis PONTIKOS	M		(1)	
Christos POYIATZIS	M	20	(3)	2
Dimitris SERGIOU	M		(4)	
Michalis SHIMITRAS	G	25		
Nicos SOPHOCLEOUS	A	1	(8)	

LEAGUE RESULTS 1999/2000

19/09/99	APOP Paphos	H	3-1	Music 2, Gjurev
26/09/99	Nea Salamina Famagusta	A	1-0	Lambrou
02/10/99	AEL Limassol	H	1-2	Poyiatzis
16/10/99	Paralimni	A	3-3	Music 2, Adzic
24/10/99	Alki Larnaca	H	5-1	Lambrou 2, Georgiou, Alexandrou, Neocleous
31/10/99	APOEL Nicosia	A	1-2	Kastanas
06/11/99	Olympiakos Nicosia	H	3-3	Alexandrou 2, Pashialis Ch.
13/11/99	Anorthosis Famagusta	H	2-3	Poyiatzis, Music
20/11/99	Apollon Limassol	A	0-0	
27/11/99	Ethnikos Ashia	H	1-1	Music (p)
04/12/99	Anagennisis Dherynia	A	3-1	Music (p), Alexandrou, Kastanas
19/12/99	AEK Larnaca	H	0-2	
08/01/00	Omonia Nicosia	A	0-2	
15/01/00	Nea Salamina Famagusta	H	2-0	Adzic, Kastanas
22/01/00	AEL Limassol	A	0-0	
30/01/00	Paralimni	H	3-1	Music 2 (1p), Gjurev
13/02/00	Alki Larnaca	A	4-0	Gjurev 3 (1p), Lambrou
26/02/00	APOEL Nicosia	H	1-0	Liasis
04/03/00	Olympiakos Nicosia	A	0-1	
18/03/00	Anorthosis Famagusta	A	1-3	Music
25/03/00	Apollon Limassol	H	1-3	Liasis
01/04/00	Ethnikos Ashia	A	0-1	
08/04/00	Anagennisis Dherynia	H	5-0	Markou 2, Neocleous, Katzis, Kastanas
16/04/00	AEK Larnaca	A	2-1	Markou, Gjurev
23/04/00	Omonia Nicosia	H	0-1	
06/05/00	APOP Paphos	A	0-4	

ETHNIKOS ASHIA

CLUB DIRECTORY

Ethnikos Ashia FC
Kavaphi str.
2121 Aglatzia
PO Box 27735
2432 Nicosia
tel - (09) 621389/769292
fax - (02) 766559
President - Costas Leondiou
Secretary - Andonis Mavris
Coach - Nicos Andronicou
Stadium - Kykkos (3,000)

APPEARANCES 99/00

	P	Ap	(s)	Gls
Nicos ANDREOU	D	24		2
Dimitris COSTARAS	M	26		3
Dimos DASKALAKIS	M	25	(1)	1
George DIMITRIADES	A	1	(3)	
Pantelis DIMITRIOU	M	20	(3)	
Stevo DRAGISIC (YUG)	A	21	(5)	8
James ENAGWANA (NIG)	M	23		1
Stavros HADJIPSALTIS	M	1	(11)	
Kyriakos IOANNOU	G	6		
Elias KAPSALIS	M		(13)	
Stelios KITTOS	M	25		4
Yiannos LYMBOURIS	D		(1)	
Sotiris MAGAPHAS	M	6	(5)	
Nicos MAGNITIS	M	22		1
Socratis MARANGOS	G	20		
Arsen MIHAJLOVIC (YUG)	A	21	(1)	10
George PANTELAS	D	17	(4)	1
Ara PETROSYAN	A	10	(13)	1
George SAVVA	D	18	(3)	2
Lucas SOCRATOUS	A		(2)	
Evripides TSIAKLIS	A		(7)	1

LEAGUE RESULTS 1999/2000

18/09/99	Anagennisis Dherynia	H	0-1	
25/09/99	AEK Larnaca	A	1-2	Savva
02/10/99	Omonia Nicosia	H	0-1	
16/10/99	APOP Paphos	A	0-0	
24/10/99	Nea Salamina Famagusta	H	1-1	Dragisic
30/10/99	AEL Limassol	A	1-2	Andreou
06/11/99	Paralimni	H	2-0	Dragisic, Kittos
14/11/99	Alki Larnaca	A	2-0	Kittos, Costaras
21/11/99	APOEL Nicosia	H	0-2	
27/11/99	Ethnikos Akhna	A	1-1	Tsiaklis
04/12/99	Anorthosis Famagusta	H	1-3	Costaras
18/12/99	Apollon Limassol	A	0-2	
09/01/00	Olympiakos Nicosia	H	2-1	Dragisic, Mihajlovic
15/01/00	AEK Larnaca	H	3-0	Pantelas, Dragisic, Savva
23/01/00	Omonia Nicosia	A	0-2	
30/01/00	APOP Paphos	H	1-2	Costaras
12/02/00	Nea Salamina Famagusta	A	1-2	Mihajlovic
26/02/00	AEL Limassol	H	3-2	Kittos, Mihajlovic, Petrosyan
04/03/00	Paralimni	A	0-2	
19/03/00	Alki Larnaca	H	3-0	Daskalakis, Enagwana, Mihajlovic
25/03/00	APOEL Nicosia	A	2-3	Mihajlovic 2
01/04/00	Ethnikos Akhna	H	1-0	Dragisic
09/04/00	Anorthosis Famagusta	A	0-5	
16/04/00	Apollon Limassol	H	3-1	Andreou, Dragisic (p), Mihajlovic
23/04/00	Olympiakos Nicosia	A	2-2	Dragisic 2 (2p)
06/05/00	Anagennisis Dherynia	A	5-1	Mihajlovic 3, Kittos, Magnitis

NEA SALAMINA FAMAGUSTA

CLUB DIRECTORY

Nea Salamina FC
Stadio Ammohostos
4 Rangavi str.
6047 Larnaca
tel - (04) 652317/663090
fax - (04) 663228
Year of Formation - 1948
President - Demos Takis
Secretary - Pambos Stylianou
Coach - Slobodan Vucekovic
Stadium - Ammohostos (8,000)

APPEARANCES 99/00

	P	Ap	(s)	Gls
Adamos ADAMOU	D	9	(6)	
Michalis ANDREOU	G	7		
Pambos ANDREOU	A	24	(1)	11
Athos ANGELI	M	6	(11)	4
Dimitris Tofaris DIMITRIOU	D	10	(7)	
George ELIA	A	13	(7)	7
Paris ELIA	D	24	(1)	2
Stavros GEORGIOU	M		(2)	1
Andreas IOANNIDES	M	19	(3)	
Sinisa JELIC (YUG)	M	15	(7)	14
Sinisa JOVANOVIC (YUG)	D	21	(1)	1
Andreas LOUGRIDES	G	18	(1)	
Liasos LUCA	D	7	(5)	5
Marios LUCA	D	3	(8)	1
Michalis MICHAEL	D	14	(1)	
Mirko MIHIC (YUG)	A	17		6
Nicos A. NICOLAOU	D	23		
Nicos K. NICOLAOU	M	20		2
Andros PANAYIOTOU	D	11	(2)	
Panikos PHILIOTIS	M	19	(5)	3
Louis STEPHANI	M	5	(7)	
Velis SYGRASIDES	G	1	(1)	

LEAGUE RESULTS 1999/2000

18/09/99	APOEL Nicosia	A	2-1	Andreou P., Mihic
26/09/99	Ethnikos Akhna	H	0-1	
03/10/99	Anorthosis Famagusta	A	0-1	
16/10/99	Apollon Limassol	H	3-2	Elia P., Andreou P., Philiotis
23/10/99	Ethnikos Ashia	A	1-1	Elia P.
31/10/99	Anagennisis Dherynia	H	7-3	Jelic 4, Mihic 2, Andreou P.
06/11/99	AEK Larnaca	A	1-0	Mihic
13/11/99	Omonia Nicosia	H	0-1	
20/11/99	APOP Paphos	A	1-2	Angeli
27/11/99	Olympiakos Nicosia	A	1-3	Andreou P.
05/12/99	AEL Limassol	H	0-2	
18/12/99	Paralimni	A	5-1	Elia G. 2, Andreou P. 2 (1p), Philiotis
08/01/00	Alki Larnaca	H	6-0	Jelic 2, Nicolaou N.K., Andreou P., Mihic, Luca L.
15/01/00	Ethnikos Akhna	A	0-2	
23/01/00	Anorthosis Famagusta	H	1-4	Elia G.
29/01/00	Apollon Limassol	A	1-2	Elia G.
12/02/00	Ethnikos Ashia	H	2-1	Mihic, Andreou P.
27/02/00	Anagennisis Dherynia	A	4-0	Jelic, Andreou P. (p), Luca L., Elia G.
05/03/00	AEK Larnaca	H	2-1	Luca L. (p), Jelic
18/03/00	Omonia Nicosia	A	1-1	Jelic
25/03/00	APOP Paphos	H	1-1	Angeli
02/04/00	Olympiakos Nicosia	H	2-2	Jelic, Elia G.
08/04/00	AEL Limassol	A	3-0	Jelic 2, Nicolaou N.K.
15/04/00	Paralimni	H	2-1	Jelic, Elia G.
23/04/00	Alki Larnaca	A	9-0	Andreou P. 2 (2p), Luca L. 2, Angeli, Jelic, Luca M., Philiotis, og
07/05/00	APOEL Nicosia	H	3-1	Angeli, Jovanovic, Georgiou

OLYMPIAKOS NICOSIA

CLUB DIRECTORY

Olympiakos FC
6A Athinas str.
PO Box 22339
1021 Nicosia
tel - (02) 344080/348337
fax - (02) 344090
Year of Formation - 1931
President - Christos Hadjitophis
Secretary - George Hadjisavvas
Coach - Ronnie Whelan
Stadium - GS Pancypria (23,000)

MAJOR HONOURS
League Championship - (3) 1967, 1969, 1971.
Domestic Cup - (1) 1977.

APPEARANCES 99/00

	P	Ap	(s)	Gls
Alexandros ALEXANDROU	G	19		
Iacovos APOSTOLOU	D	18	(1)	
Dimitris ASHIOTIS	M	23		8
Andreas AVLONITIS	A	1	(6)	2
Elias CHRYSOSTOMOU	D	9	(1)	
Costas CONSTANDINOU	D	10	(10)	
George CONSTANDINOU	D	17	(2)	
Renos DIMITRIADES	D	7	(4)	1
Stephanos GEORGIOU	D	6	(4)	1
Serge HONI (CMR)	A	26		18
Michalis JAPOURAS	M	10	(2)	
Elias KAPSALIS	M	1	(5)	
Thomas KAPSALIS	A	3	(2)	
Digran KAZADJIAN	D	15	(3)	
Sladjan NIKOLIC (YUG)	D	24		2
Goran PETKOVSKI (MAC)	A	23		9
Philippos PHILIPPOU	M	7	(11)	
Andreas RIALAS	M	3	(12)	1
Petros SAVVA	G	7	(1)	
Nicos STAVROU	D	10		
Marios THEMISTOCLEOUS	M	24		5
Savvas TSIAKLIS	M	23		8

LEAGUE RESULTS 1999/2000

18/09/99	Paralimni	A	0-2	
26/09/99	Anagennisis Dherynia	H	2-1	Honi, Petkovski
02/10/99	Alki Larnaca	A	2-1	Ashiotis, Honi
16/10/99	AEK Larnaca	H	2-2	Honi, Ashiotis
23/10/99	APOEL Nicosia	A	2-8	Themistocleous, Ashiotis
30/10/99	Omonia Nicosia	H	1-3	Ashiotis
06/11/99	Ethnikos Akhna	A	3-3	Tsiaklis, Nikolic, Petkovski
14/11/99	APOP Paphos	H	5-0	Tsiaklis 3, Dimitriades, Petkovski (p)
20/11/99	Anorthosis Famagusta	A	0-3	
27/11/99	Nea Salamina Famagusta	H	3-1	Honi, Themistocleous, Ashiotis
04/12/99	Apollon Limassol	A	3-3	Honi 2, Tsiaklis
19/12/99	AEL Limassol	H	3-3	Petkovski, Honi, Tsiaklis
09/01/00	Ethnikos Ashia	A	1-2	Honi
16/01/00	Anagennisis Dherynia	A	2-1	Themistocleous
22/01/00	Alki Larnaca	H	5-0	Petkovski 2, Avlonitis 2, Nikolic
29/01/00	AEK Larnaca	A	1-3	Honi
13/02/00	APOEL Nicosia	H	0-2	
27/02/00	Omonia Nicosia	A	3-0	Honi (p), Tsiaklis, Themistocleous
04/03/00	Ethnikos Akhna	H	1-0	Petkovski
18/03/00	APOP Paphos	A	0-2	
26/03/00	Anorthosis Famagusta	H	5-2	Honi 3, Georgiou, Ashiotis
02/04/00	Nea Salamina Famagusta	A	2-2	Petkovski, Ashiotis
08/04/00	Apollon Limassol	H	5-3	Honi 2 (1p), Petkovski, og (Andoniou), Themistocleous
15/04/00	AEL Limassol	A	1-4	Honi (p)
23/04/00	Ethnikos Ashia	H	2-2	Tsiaklis, Honi
06/05/00	Paralimni	H	3-5	Rialas, Ashiotis, Honi

OMONIA NICOSIA

CLUB DIRECTORY

Omonia FC
5 Papanicoli str.
PO Box 20617
1077 Nicosia
tel - (02) 377377
fax - (02) 377496
Year of Formation - 1948
President - Doros Seraphim
Secretary - Savvas Nicolaou
Coach - Dusan Galis
(00/01 - Asparuch Nikodimov)
Stadium - GS Pancypria (23,000)

MAJOR HONOURS
League Championship - (17) 1961, 1966, 1972, 1974, 1975, 1976, 1977, 1978, 1979, 1981, 1982, 1983, 1984, 1985, 1987, 1989, 1993.
Domestic Cup - (11) 1965, 1972, 1974, 1980, 1981, 1982, 1983, 1988, 1991, 1994, 2000.

APPEARANCES 99/00

	P	Ap	(s)	Gls
Sakis ANDREOU	M	3	(10)	
George CONSTANDINIDES	D	1	(11)	
Nicolas GEORGIOU	A	20		
Ioakim IOAKIM	D	18		2
Costas KAIAFAS	M	17	(1)	1
Costas KALOTHEOU	D	13	(5)	
Petros KONNAFIS	D	17	(2)	1
Lefteris KONTOLEFTEROS	A	18	(8)	8
Nicos LOIZIDES	D	5	(5)	
Costas MALEKKOS	A	23		10
Vesko MIHAJLOVIC (YUG)	M	24		8
Charis NICOLAOU	M	12	(7)	
Nicos NICOLAOU	D	8	(10)	
Odysseas ODYSSEOS	M	2	(7)	
Christos PANAYIOTOU	M	2		
Yiotis PANAYIOTOU	D	26		3
Yiannakis PONTIKOS	A	2	(4)	
Rainer RAUFFMANN (GER)	A	26		34
Dusan TITTEL (SVK)	D	23		1
Tassos YIALLOURIS	G	26		

LEAGUE RESULTS 1999/2000

18/09/99	Anorthosis Famagusta	A	3-5	Ioakim, Rauffmann, Mihajlovic
25/09/99	Apollon Limassol	H	3-0	Rauffmann 3 (1p)
02/10/99	Ethnikos Ashia	A	1-0	Kontolefteros
17/10/99	Anagennisis Dherynia	H	8-1	Rauffmann 5, Malekkos 2, Kontolefteros
24/10/99	AEK Larnaca	A	4-0	Rauffmann 2, Kontolefteros, Malekkos
30/10/99	Olympiakos Nicosia	A	3-1	Rauffmann 2 (1p), Mihajlovic
07/11/99	APOP Paphos	H	5-0	Rauffmann 2 (1p), Konnafis, Malekkos, Mihajlovic
13/11/99	Nea Salamina Famagusta	A	1-0	Rauffmann
20/11/99	AEL Limassol	H	1-0	Rauffmann
28/11/99	Paralimni	A	2-2	Kontolefteros, Rauffmann
05/12/99	Alki Larnaca	H	4-1	Malekkos 2, Rauffmann, Mihajlovic
18/12/99	APOEL Nicosia	A	3-3	Rauffmann 2 (1p), Malekkos
08/01/00	Ethnikos Akhna	H	2-0	Tittel, Kontolefteros
15/01/00	Apollon Limassol	A	4-0	Rauffmann 2, Malekkos, Kaiafas
23/01/00	Ethnikos Ashia	H	2-0	Rauffmann (p), og (Daskalakis)
29/01/00	Anagennisis Dherynia	A	7-0	Panayiotou Y. 2, Malekkos 2, Mihajlovic 2, og (Stasi)
12/02/00	AEK Larnaca	H	0-3	
27/02/00	Olympiakos Nicosia	H	0-3	
04/03/00	APOP Paphos	A	2-1	Rauffmann 2
18/03/00	Nea Salamina Famagusta	H	1-1	Kontolefteros
25/03/00	AEL Limassol	A	0-0	
02/04/00	Paralimni	H	6-2	Rauffmann 4 (1p), og (Mastrou), Kontolefteros
08/04/00	Alki Larnaca	A	3-0	Rauffmann 2, Mihajlovic
15/04/00	APOEL Nicosia	H	3-2	Panayiotou Y., Mihajlovic, Kontolefteros
23/04/00	Ethnikos Akhna	A	1-0	Rauffmann
07/05/00	Anorthosis Famagusta	H	2-2	Rauffmann, Ioakim

PARALIMNI

CLUB DIRECTORY

Union of Paralimni FC
PO Box 30020
5310 Paralimni
tel - (03) 821352/827329
fax - (03) 826568
Year of Formation - 1936
President - George Koumas
Secretary - Andreas Papaefstathiou
Coach - Nenad Starovlach; Andonis Kleftis
(00/01 - Håkan Sandberg)
Stadium - Municipal (8,000)

APPEARANCES 99/00

	P	Ap	(s)	Gls
Nontas CHRISTINAKIS	G	18		
Slavisa CULA (YUG)	A	20		16
Michalis ECONOMOU	A	22		3
Costas ELIA	A	8	(8)	
George GAVRIEL	M	17		2
Dimos GOUMENOS	D	15	(3)	3
George KARAS	D	1	(1)	
Marios KARAS	D	19	(1)	2
Andonis KEZOS	M	10	(1)	
George KIZAS	M	14	(5)	1
George KOLANIS	M	1	(6)	
George LOIZOU	D	3	(3)	
Kyriakos MASTROU	D	17		
George MERTAKKAS	G	8	(1)	
Dusan MILUTINOVIC (YUG)	A	20	(4)	4
George NICOLAOU	M	1	(5)	
Andreas PITIRIS	D	4	(2)	
Martinos SOLOMOU	A	2	(5)	1
Panayiotis SPYROU	D	14	(4)	2
Andonis STYLIOTIS	D		(6)	
Marios THOMA	A	17	(2)	5
Pavlos TSIOLAKKIS	A	3	(10)	2
Costakis Loizou TSOUKKAS	M	13	(2)	
Arian XHUMBA (ALB)	M	14		4
Andonis ZEMBASHIS	M	25		6

LEAGUE RESULTS 1999/2000

18/09/99	Olympiakos Nicosia	H	2-0	Cula, Thoma
25/09/99	Alki Larnaca	H	3-2	Cula 2, Economou
03/10/99	APOEL Nicosia	A	2-3	Gavriel 2
16/10/99	Ethnikos Akhna	H	3-3	Thoma, Kizas, Xhumba
23/10/99	Anorthosis Famagusta	A	1-4	Karas M.
30/10/99	Apollon Limassol	H	2-1	Xhumba 2
06/11/99	Ethnikos Ashia	A	0-2	
14/11/99	Anagennisis Dherynia	H	4-0	Thoma, Cula, Goumenos, Tsiolakkis
21/11/99	AEK Larnaca	A	1-2	Economou
28/11/99	Omonia Nicosia	H	2-2	Cula 2 (1p)
04/12/99	APOP Paphos	A	3-2	Xhumba (p), Milutinovic, Zembashis
18/12/99	Nea Salamina Famagusta	H	1-5	Cula
08/01/00	AEL Limassol	A	0-2	
15/01/00	Alki Larnaca	A	1-2	Tsiolakkis
22/01/00	APOEL Nicosia	H	0-0	
30/01/00	Ethnikos Akhna	A	1-3	Cula
12/02/00	Anorthosis Famagusta	H	0-1	
26/02/00	Apollon Limassol	A	1-3	Cula
04/03/00	Ethnikos Ashia	H	2-0	Thoma, Milutinovic
18/03/00	Anagennisis Dherynia	A	3-0	Thoma, Karas M., Goumenos
26/03/00	AEK Larnaca	H	3-0	Goumenos, Milutinovic, Cula
02/04/00	Omonia Nicosia	A	2-6	Solomou, Milutinovic
09/04/00	APOP Paphos	H	2-1	Cula 2 (1p)
15/04/00	Nea Salamina Famagusta	A	1-2	Zembashis
22/04/00	AEL Limassol	H	6-1	Cula 3 (1p), Zembashis, Spyrou, Economou
06/05/00	Olympiakos Nicosia	A	5-3	Zembashis 3, Spyrou, Cula

CZECH REPUBLIC

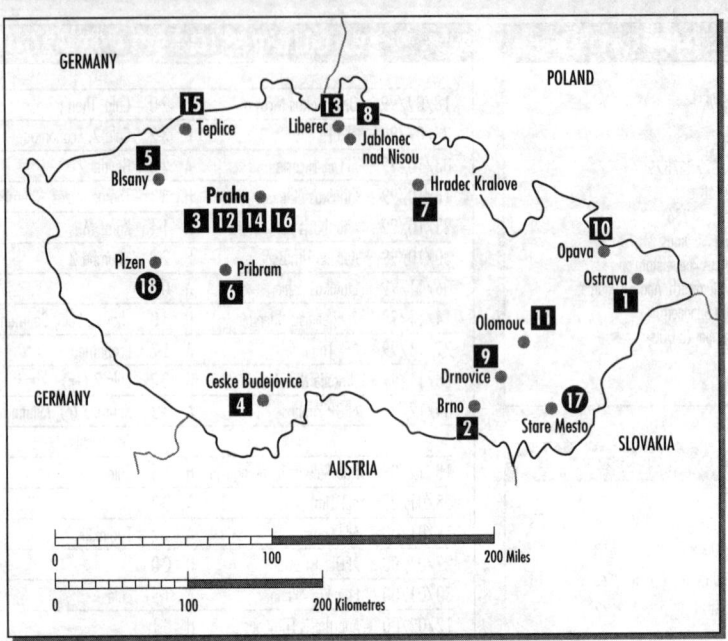

SPARTA AND SLAVIA A CLASS APART

Perfect qualifiers become luckless finalists

FEDERATION DIRECTORY

Ceskomoravsky Fotbalovy Svaz
Diskarska 100, 169 00 Praha 6 - Strahov

tel - (02) 20513575/   Year of Formation - 1990
20511194-96   President - Ing. Frantisek Chvalovsky
fax - (02) 33353107   Secretary - Ludek Macela
website - www.fotbal.cz
email - cmfs@fotbal.cz

Stadium - Strahov, Praha (20,000)

The Czech Republic's Euro 2000 challenge lasted just two matches, but it was widely acknowledged that they were the best and unluckiest of the eight teams which went home at the end of the first round.

Always up against it in a group that contained both the world champions and the pre-tournament favourites, the 1996 runners-up travelled to the Low Countries in good heart, having not only qualified with a flawless record of ten wins out of ten but also put together a string of fine performances in the build-up.

Their opening defeat to Holland in Amsterdam was a travesty of justice. Having kept the co-hosts at arm's length with all-out defence in the first half, coach Jozef Chovanec gave the order to attack after the interval and the result was a constructive 25-minute siege on the Dutch goal. The Czechs needed only a modicum of luck to take the lead

but they got none at all. There were bad misses, great saves by Dutch 'keeper Edwin van der Sar and two headers against the woodwork. But the ball just wouldn't go in. A point - the least the Czechs deserved - was then belatedly swiped away from them by a hugely controversial penalty decision, which enabled Holland to sneak probably the most ill-deserved victory in their footballing history.

Chovanec's men were in form again for the first 45 minutes against France in Bruges, but there too they lacked the killer punch and the only goal they scored came via a dubious penalty, coolly converted by man of the match Karel Poborsky. France, on the other hand, scored twice and the Czechs were unable to reassert themselves after the interval, their efforts being hindered by some rather desperate tactical changes introduced by the coach.

LEAGUE CHAMPIONSHIP RESULTS 99/00

		1	2	3	4	5	6	7	8	9	10	11	12	13	14	15	16
1	Banik Ostrava		1-0	1-1	1-1	6-1	2-0	2-2	1-1	3-1	2-2	2-2	1-3	3-0	0-3	2-2	1-1
2	Boby Brno	2-1		1-1	2-0	3-0	0-0	1-2	2-0	2-3	1-0	1-0	3-1	3-0	1-1	2-1	4-2
3	Bohemians Praha	0-0	0-0		0-1	1-1	2-0	1-0	2-0	3-1	1-0	1-3	0-1	2-0	0-1	0-0	1-0
4	SK Ceske Budejovice	2-2	1-0	1-2		2-2	5-0	2-1	2-0	2-0	1-0	1-2	0-1	0-1	1-4	3-1	1-0
5	Chmel Blsany	1-0	1-0	1-0	3-2		2-1	1-0	1-2	0-2	1-0	1-0	2-3	1-0	1-4	0-2	0-2
6	Dukla Pribram	2-0	1-2	3-0	1-0	1-0		1-0	2-1	1-1	1-0	0-2	1-1	1-1	1-3	3-0	5-2
7	SK Hradec Kralove	1-3	1-0	1-2	1-0	1-1	1-1		0-0	0-2	2-2	0-0	0-1	1-3	0-2	2-0	0-0
8	FK Jablonec 97	2-2	0-0	1-2	2-1	4-2	0-2	0-0		1-0	4-0	0-0	0-0	0-0	0-2	3-1	3-0
9	Petra Drnovice	1-0	2-0	3-0	2-0	2-0	2-1	1-0	3-0		1-1	1-0	0-1	1-1	0-1	1-1	1-0
10	SFC Opava	2-3	4-1	0-0	3-2	0-0	0-1	0-0	2-0	2-0		3-0	0-0	3-1	1-1	1-1	0-1
11	Sigma Olomouc	4-1	1-1	0-0	1-1	0-1	1-0	2-2	0-0	1-2	2-1		0-2	1-1	1-1	2-2	2-0
12	Slavia Praha	2-0	3-1	2-0	4-1	2-1	3-1	3-0	4-0	2-1	3-1	2-0		0-0	2-1	0-1	3-1
13	Slovan Liberec	1-0	0-1	2-0	2-0	1-1	0-0	1-0	0-0	0-0	1-0	0-0	0-1		1-2	2-0	1-0
14	Sparta Praha	2-0	3-0	0-0	7-0	3-1	2-1	3-1	3-0	5-0	4-0	6-0	5-1	2-1		3-2	2-1
15	FK Teplice	0-2	2-1	2-0	3-0	0-0	2-0	1-1	2-0	2-2	1-1	2-1	1-1	1-0	4-2		0-0
16	Viktoria Zizkov	3-1	1-0	2-2	1-1	1-1	1-1	2-1	0-0	2-0	3-2	3-3	3-1	0-0	2-3	3-1	

LEAGUE CHAMPIONSHIP FINAL TABLE 99/00

			Home				Away					Total					
		Pd	W	D	L	F	A	W	D	L	F	A	W	D	L	F	A	PT	GD
1	Sparta Praha	30	14	1	0	50	8	10	3	2	31	15	24	4	2	81	23	76	58
2	Slavia Praha	30	13	1	1	35	9	8	4	3	18	16	21	5	4	53	25	68	28
3	Petra Drnovice	30	10	3	2	21	6	4	3	8	15	26	14	6	10	36	32	48	4
4	Boby Brno	30	10	3	2	28	12	2	3	10	7	21	12	6	12	35	33	42	2
5	FK Teplice	30	8	6	1	23	11	2	5	8	15	27	10	11	9	38	38	41	0
6	Dukla Pribram	30	9	3	3	24	13	2	4	9	9	23	11	7	12	33	36	40	-3
7	Bohemians Praha	30	7	4	4	14	8	3	6	6	10	20	10	10	10	24	28	40	-4
8	Slovan Liberec	30	7	5	3	12	5	2	6	7	9	19	9	11	10	21	24	38	-3
9	Viktoria Zizkov	30	7	7	1	27	17	2	3	10	10	24	9	10	11	37	41	37	-4
10	Chmel Blsany	30	9	0	6	16	18	1	7	7	12	27	10	7	13	28	45	37	-17
11	Banik Ostrava	30	5	8	2	28	20	3	3	9	15	25	8	11	11	43	45	35	-2
12	Sigma Olomouc	30	4	8	3	18	15	3	5	7	13	23	7	13	10	31	38	34	-7
13	FK Jablonec 97	30	6	6	3	20	12	1	5	9	4	24	7	11	12	24	36	32	-12
14	SK Ceske Budejovice	30	8	2	5	24	16	1	3	11	10	33	9	5	16	34	49	32	-15
15	SFC Opava	30	6	6	3	21	11	0	4	11	10	28	6	10	14	31	39	28	-8
16	SK Hradec Kralove	30	3	6	6	11	17	1	5	9	10	21	4	11	15	21	38	23	-17

So, with two defeats in two games, the Czech Republic's European Championship was over. They still had the small matter of a third fixture, against Denmark, to fulfil, and although two Vladimir Smicer goals brought a welcome 2-0 victory, it was scant consolation for a side that knew they deserved better.

The Czechs encounter Denmark again on the road to the 2002 World Cup, and with Bulgaria, Iceland, Northern Ireland and Malta making up the group, there is a more than even chance that Chovanec and his players will qualify for the Far East without recourse to the play-offs. Not one of the present generation of Czech stars has played in a World Cup before, so they will not be short on incentive. The likes of Smicer, Poborsky, Pavel Nedved, Patrik Berger, Jan Koller and Tomas Repka would dearly love to crown their careers with an appearance at the game's showpiece tournament.

The European Championship finals apart, 1999/2000 proved to be an excellent season internationally for the Czech Republic. The U-21 side finished runners-up to Italy at the European finals in neighbouring Slovakia and thus

TOP SCORERS

22	Vratislav LOKVENC (Sparta Praha)
16	Marek KINCL (Slovan Liberec/ Viktoria Zizkov)
13	Stanislav VLCEK (Sigma Olomouc)
11	Vitezslav TUMA (Petra Drnovice)
	Tomas JANDA (SK Ceske Budejovice)
	Tomas DOSEK (Slavia Praha)
10	Radek ONDERKA (SFC Opava)
	Pavel VERBIR (FK Teplice)
	Miroslav BARANEK (Sparta Praha)
	Pavel HORVATH (Slavia Praha)
	Horst SIEGL (Sparta Praha)

NATIONAL TEAM RESULTS 99/00

18/08/99	Switzerland	H	Drnovice	3-0	Koller (48), Zwyssig (56og), Baranek (89)
04/09/99	Lithuania (ECQ)	A	Vilnius	4-0	Nedved (60, 63), Koller (68, 90)
08/09/99	Bosnia-Herzegovina (ECQ)	H	Teplice	3-0	Koller (26), Berger (59p), Poborsky (67)
09/10/99	Faroe Islands (ECQ)	H	Prague	2-0	Koller (11), Verbir (84)
13/11/99	Holland	A	Eindhoven	1-1	Koller (68)
08/02/00	Mexico	N	Hong Kong	2-1	Kolomaznik (50), Verbir (55)
23/02/00	Republic of Ireland	A	Dublin	2-3	Koller (3, 37)
29/03/00	Australia	H	Teplice	3-1	Fukal (9), Koller (53), Ulich (66)
26/04/00	Israel	H	Prague	4-1	Nedved (14, 57), Koller (37), Wagner (90)
03/06/00	Germany	A	Nuremberg	2-3	Kuka (54), Berger (80)
11/06/00	Holland (ECF)	A	Amsterdam	0-1	
16/06/00	France (ECF)	N	Bruges	1-2	Poborsky (35p)
21/06/00	Denmark (ECF)	N	Liège	2-0	Smicer (64, 67)

DOMESTIC CUP 99/00

SECOND ROUND
Roudnice nad Labem 0, Sparta Praha 8
Jiskra Trebon 3, SK Ceske Budejovice 1
VP Frydek-Mistek 0, SFC Opava 0 (1-4 on pens.)
Podjestedsky Cesky Dub 1, FK Jablonec 97 3
SK Hranice 3, FC Vitkovice 3 (2-4 on pens.)
Elserumo Brumov 0, Banik Ratiskovice 1
FC Chomutov 0, Slavia Praha 2
Dukla Sekopt Hranice 3, Banik Ostrava 3
(1-4 on pens.)
Slovan Breclav 1, Boby Brno 7
SK Smichov 1, Bohemians Praha 4
Slovan Pardubice 0, SK Hradec Kralove 6
Keramika Chlumcany 1, Chmel Blsany 2
Slovan Varnsdorf 0, Slovan Liberec 2
SK Strakonice 1908 1, Dukla Pribram 3
Unex Unicov 0, Sigma Olomouc 2
Technoplast Chropyne 0, Petra Drnovice 8
Spolana Neratovice 0, Viktoria Zizkov 2
Bela pod Bezdezem 1, MUS Most 1996 9
Aritma Praha 1, Xaverov Horni Pocernice 6
CZU Praha 0, Viktoria Plzen 3
Lokomotiva Petrovice 0, SK Detmarovice 2
Meteor Louny 1, Dropa CKD Kompresory Strizkov 4
MSA Dolni Benesov 2, Biocel Vratimov 1
Union Celakovice 0, Mlada Boleslav 0 (5-4 on pens.)
SK Semily 1, OEZ Letohrad 1 (5-4 on pens.)
Synot Stare Mesto 1, Svit Zlin 3
Roubina Dolni Kounice 2, VMG Kyjov 1
TJ Svitavy 1, FK Holice 1932 1 (1-3 on pens.)

Zeman Brno 1, PSJ Jihlava 1 (7-6 on pens.)
1.FC Polesovice 0, FK Kunovice 3
Zenit Caslav 1, Spartak Rychnov nad Kneznou 4
Tatran Kadan 1, FK Teplice 0

THIRD ROUND
Union Celakovice 1, Dukla Pribram 1 (6-5 on pens.)
Banik Ratiskovice 1, Petra Drnovice 0
Dropa CKD Kompresory Strizkov 1, Sparta Praha 2
Spartak Rychnov nad Kneznou 1, Viktoria Zizkov 2
Roubina Dolni Kounice 1, Slovan Liberec 3
FK Holice 1932 1, SFC Opava 3
SK Detmarovice 0, Sigma Olomouc 4
Svit Zlin 4, Banik Ostrava 2
FC Vitkovice 2, Bohemians Praha 2 (2-0 on pens.)
Zeman Brno 1, Slavia Praha 3
Xaverov Horni Pocernice 0, Chmel Blsany 1
MUS Most 1, FK Jablonec 97 1 (2-3 on pens.)
Tatran Kadan 0, MSA Dolni Benesov 3
FK Kunovice 1, Boby Brno 4
Jiskra Trebon 1, Viktoria Plzen 4
SK Semily 1, SK Hradec Kralove 3

FOURTH ROUND
Banik Ratiskovice 1, Chmel Blsany 0
SK Hradec Kralove 0, Viktoria Zizkov 0 (3-5 on pens.)
Sigma Olomouc 1, SFC Opava 0
Slovan Liberec 3, Boby Brno 1
Svit Zlin 0, FK Jablonec 97 2
MSA Dolni Benesov 1, FC Vitkovice 1 (1-3 on pens.)

Union Celakovice 0, Slavia Praha 4
Viktoria Plzen 1, Sparta Praha 0

QUARTER-FINALS
Viktoria Plzen 1 (Zapomnel 41),
Banik Ratiskovice 2 (Kulyk 16p, 37)
Sigma Olomouc 2 (Ujfalusi 60, Vlcek 98),
Viktoria Zizkov 1 (Kincl 63) (aet)
FC Vitkovice 0, FK Jablonec 97 0 (aet; 3-2 on pens.)
Slovan Liberec 2 (Lazzaro Liuni 63, Stajner 81),
Slavia Praha 0

SEMI-FINALS
Banik Ratiskovice 3 (Zemanek 39, 56, Orsula 73),
FC Vitkovice 0
Slovan Liberec 2 (Jiranek 50, Neumann 54),
Sigma Olomouc 0

FINAL
10/05/2000, Prague
SLOVAN LIBEREC 2 Lazzaro Liuni (24, 61)
BANIK RATISKOVICE 1 Hrotek (81)
referee - Liba
SLOVAN LIBEREC - Kinsky, Lexa, Johana, Jiranek,
Neumann, Capek (Pilny 90), Michalik (Kozuch 89),
Janu, Jun, Lazzaro Liuni, Stajner (Bakes 79).
BANIK RATISKOVICE - Barcuch, Urbanek, Svoboda,
Svestka, Babicek (Kosturik 83), Orsula (Toman 67),
Hrotek, Suran (Kordula 75), Kaloc, Kulyk, Zemanek.

---

qualified for the Sydney Olympics. On the club scene, too, there was plenty to celebrate as Prague duo Sparta and Slavia cobbled together lengthy runs in Europe, with the former reaching the second group phase of the Champions' League and the latter marching as far as the quarter-finals of the UEFA Cup.

Sparta, who benefitted from automatic Champions' League qualification, did tremendously well to win their first-round group ahead of Bordeaux, Spartak Moscow and Willem II. They were unbeaten in their six matches and really turned on the style at home to the Russian champions, producing a second-half display that will go down in Letna legend. A much tougher group awaited them in the second round but, remarkably, Sparta were still in contention for a quarter-final place by the final matchday thanks to two crucial last-minute goals in successive matches by defender Milan Fukal.

Slavia also fought to the bitter end in the UEFA Cup. It was only a late winner which carried them past Vojvodina Novi Sad in the first round and some very brave backs-to-the-wall defending which enabled them

to come out on top against Grasshopper and Udinese. Leeds United were too strong for them in the quarter-final, but even after going down 3-0 at Elland Road and falling further behind at home, Frantisek Cipro's team still had the guts to come back and win the return leg, with midfielder Ivo Ulich scoring twice to cap an excellent indivdual display.

The country's other two Euro combatants, Sigma Olomouc and Teplice, were unable to match the achivements of the big boys from the capital - they both fell to Spanish side Mallorca in successive rounds of the UEFA Cup - and that was pretty much the story of the domestic league as well, with Sparta and Slavia showing complete dominance to turn the fight for the championship into a private war.

The gulf in class between the top two and the rest was larger than ever. There were 16 teams in the league but they could be divided into three distinct brackets - title contenders (Sparta and Slavia), UEFA Cup chasers (Drnovice, Teplice and Brno) and the rest, all of whom at one stage or another were troubled by relegation fears.

NATIONAL TEAM APPEARANCES 99/00

Coach - Jozef CHOVANEC

Player	SUI	LIT	BOS	FAR	HOL	MEX	IRL	AUS	ISR	GER	HOL	FRA	DEN	Cps	Gls
Ladislav MAIER (04/01/66) - SK Rapid Wien (AUT)	G						G							6	-
Jan SUCHOPAREK (23/09/69) - Tennis Borussia Berlin (GER)	D		D	D74			s46							61	4
Marek NIKL (20/02/76) - 1.FC Nürnberg (GER)	D	D	D											4	-
Karel RADA (02/03/72) - Slavia Praha	D	D		D	D	D	D	D	D	D	D	D	D	37	4
Karel POBORSKY (30/03/72) - SL Benfica (POR)	M83	M79	M	M	M		M	M73	s63	M58	M	M	M	58	3
Radek BEJBL (29/08/72) - Atlético Madrid (ESP)	M	M	M	M66	M65		M	s73	M	M53	s69	M50	M61	50	3
Radek SLONCIK (29/05/73) - Banik Ostrava	M80	s79				M46								17	-
Pavel NEDVED (30/08/72) - Lazio (ITA)	M62	M78	M83		M		M82	M	M79	M66	M90	M	M	46	9
Jiri NEMEC (15/05/66) - FC Schalke 04 (GER)	M52	D71	M	M	M52		M62	M		M79	M	M	M	82	1
Pavel KUKA (19/07/68) - VfB Stuttgart (GER)	A66	A	A79	s76			s69	A70	s50	s83			s73	81	26
Jan KOLLER (30/03/73) - RSC Anderlecht (BEL)	A66	A	A59	A	A76		A69	A	A63	A73	A	A	A73	17	13
Roman TYCE (07/05/77) - TSV 1860 München (GER)	s52													1	-
Pavel HORVATH (22/04/75) - Slavia Praha	s62	s71		s66	M90	M70	s72		M72	s53				10	-
Vratislav LOKVENC (27/09/73) - Sparta Praha	s66		s59	s65	A70			s58	s70	s73	s90	s50	s78	31	3
Rene WAGNER (31/10/72) - SK Rapid Wien (AUT)	s66						s57	s76	s63					10	3
Tomas GALASEK (15/01/73) - Willem II (HOL)	s80													11	-
Miroslav BARANEK (01/11/73) - Sparta Praha	s83	s78	s79	M59					s79					12	2
Pavel SRNICEK (10/03/68) - Sheffield Wednesday (ENG)	G	G	G	G					G	G	G	G	G	34	-
Tomas REPKA (02/01/74) - Fiorentina (ITA)	D	D	D	D	D46				D	D	D	D	D	39	1
Patrik BERGER (10/11/71) - Liverpool (ENG)	M	M	M				M72			s79			M	40	18
Martin HASEK (11/10/69) - Sparta Praha			s83											11	-
Vladimir SMICER (24/05/73) - Liverpool (ENG)					A		A57			A50	M83	A	A78	44	18
Michal HORNAK (28/04/70) - Sparta Praha					s59									38	1
Pavel VERBIR (13/11/72) - FK Teplice					s74	A61	A58							9	2
Petr GABRIEL (17/05/73) - Sparta Praha					D	D	D	D38	D53	D	D	D46		10	1
Radoslav LATAL (06/01/70) - FC Schalke 04 (GER)					D58			s62	s53	s58	D69			55	3
Martin CIZEK (09/06/74) - TSV 1860 München (GER)						s52		M58						18	-
Ivo ULICH (05/09/74) - Slavia Praha						s58			s58	M63				8	1
Milan FUKAL (16/05/75) - Sparta Praha						s90			D	D	D	s46	D	8	1
Radek CERNY (18/02/74) - Slavia Praha						G								1	-
Petr VLCEK (18/10/73) - Slavia Praha						D		s38						14	-
Marek JANKULOVSKI (09/05/77) - Banik Ostrava						M						s62	s61	3	-
Jan POLAK (14/03/81) - Boby Brno						M85								2	-
Michal KOLOMAZNIK (20/07/76) - FK Teplice						M								1	1
Petr VESELY (07/06/71) - Banik Ostrava						s46								2	-
Marek KINCL (03/04/73) - Viktoria Zizkov						s61								1	-
Radim NECAS (26/08/69) - FK Jablonec 97						s70								4	-
Stanislav VLCEK (26/02/76) - Sigma Olomouc						s70								1	-
Erich BRABEC (24/02/77) - Petra Drnovice						s85								1	-
Tomas ROSICKY (04/10/80) - Sparta Praha								s82	M76	s72	s66	M	M62	6	-
Jaromir BLAZEK (29/12/72) - Sparta Praha						G								1	-
Jiri NOVOTNY (07/04/70) - Sparta Praha												D		24	2

PLAYERS OF THE SEASON

MILAN FUKAL

To English-speakers his surname may be the source of much juvenile merriment, but Milan Fukal (pictured right) was no laughing matter for his new club Sparta Prague in 1999/2000. Recruited shortly after the campaign had begun from his hometown club FK Jablonec - his parting gift was two goals in a 3-1 win against Teplice - the powerful centre-back proved to be the final piece in Ivan Hasek's jigsaw. He slotted in neatly alongside Jiri Novotny and Petr Gabriel in the Sparta back-three and offered a major attacking threat on his frequent forays upfield. In total, the 25-year-old scored seven goals in the league and three in the Champions' League, including two crucial last-minute efforts against Hertha Berlin and FC Porto. He also found the net nine minutes into his second international start and was included in Jozef Chovanec's Czech squad for Euro 2000. Much interest was shown in him by a cluster of foreign clubs and the departure to Germany of teammates Lokvenc, Gabriel and Baranek ultimately persuaded him to agree a

lucrative deal with Champions' League qualifiers Hamburg.

IVO ULICH

Along with Sparta Prague starlet Tomas Rosicky, Slavia's Ivo Ulich was the best midfielder on view in the Czech league during 1999/2000. He appeared in 28 of Slavia's league games, scoring six goals, and was also a regular in the club's European campaign, making his mark with a brace of goals against Grasshopper and then confirming his prowess with a virtuoso second-half display in the quarter-final second leg against Leeds, when, in addition to scoring two goals, he also hit the bar and had another shot kicked off the line. A pacy, artful schemer, he was set to leave Slavia for Teplice or Nuremberg in 1999 but remained in Prague and went on to reap the benefits. He was unlucky not to make the Czech Republic's Euro 2000 squad, but with in-form Serie A superstar Pavel Nedved earmarked for his favoured position, his chances of breaking into the team were always going to be severely restricted.

Sparta and Slavia both collected points with an ease that reflected badly on the opposition. Slavia went unbeaten for 23 games, while Sparta strung together 15 straight victories, a 'grand slam' which, completed by a glorious 5-1 thrashing of Slavia, secured Sparta's sixth Czech championship in seven years.

By the end of the season Sparta had chalked up 76 points - 16 more than the total which had won them the title a year earlier. Most of the club's fans were inclined to agree that Sparta had never been stronger. Ivan Hasek, who took over as coach at the start of the season after previously holding a position as assistant to Jozef Chovanec in the national side, won over an army of admirers with his style of play. He not only brought out the best of club stalwarts such as Vratislav Lokvenc (the league's top scorer, on 22 goals), Jiri Novotny and Miroslav Baranek, but also greatly assisted the development of the less experienced players, above all teenaged midfielder Tomas Rosicky, who performed with such flair and consistency

throughout the season that he earned a place in the Czech Republic's Euro 2000 squad alongside his teammates Fukal, Lokvenc, Novotny, Gabriel and goalkeeper Jaromir Blazek.

Slavia also had their fair share of national team members, with midfielder Pavel Horvath and defenders Karel Rada and Petr Vlcek making the trip to the Low Countries (and Ulich and 'keeper Radek Cerny narrowly missing out). Their 68-point total would probably have taken the title in any other season, but coach Frantisek Cipro and his charges were well aware that it should have been greater.

Four points ahead of Sparta at the winter break, Slavia were in command for three quarters of the season until they suffered their first defeat - 3-1 at Viktoria Zizkov. That appeared to knock the stuffing out of them, and the 5-1 hammering by Sparta three rounds from the end finished them off. Petra Drnovice, inspired by veteran libero Miroslav Kadlec, finished in third place - albeit 20 points

EUROPEAN CUPS 99/00

CHAMPIONS' CUP
● FK TEPLICE
Qualifying round BORUSSIA DORTMUND (GER)

H 0-1 Machacek, Rada, Rizek, Brabec, Fousek, Kolomaznik (Divecky 71), Frtala (Pikl 73), Bilek, Frydek (Jindracek 70), Tesarik, Verbir.

A 0-1 Machacek, Brabec, Rizek, Rada, Fousek, Frtala (Frydek 73), Bilek, Kolomaznik, Tesarik, Verbir (Vachousek 75), Divecky (Jindracek 82).

● SPARTA PRAHA
Champions' League
1st match GIRONDINS DE BORDEAUX (FRA)

H 0-0 Postulka, Fukal, Novotny J., Gabriel, Baranek, Svoboda Z. (Novotny P. 90), Hasek, Rosicky (Prohaszka 83), Labant, Siegl (Sionko 58), Lokvenc.

2nd match SPARTAK MOSKVA (RUS)

A 1-1 Lokvenc (17)
Postulka, Hornak, Novotny J., Fukal, Gabriel, Baranek (Prohaszka 85), Sionko, Hasek, Rosicky (Obajdin 75), Labant, Lokvenc.

3rd match WILLEM II (HOL)

H 4-0 Novotny J. (26), Prohaszka (29p), Rosicky (40), Jarosik (58)
Postulka, Fukal, Novotny J., Gabriel, Hornak, Sionko (Siegl 84), Hasek, Rosicky, Baranek (Obajdin 81), Labant, Prohaszka (Jarosik 36).

4th match WILLEM II (HOL)

A 4-3 Novotny J. (17), Labant (54p, 90p), Baranek (62)
Postulka, Fukal, Novotny J., Gabriel, Labant, Baranek (Obajdin 86), Svoboda Z., Hasek, Rosicky (Siegl 61), Sionko, Lokvenc (Jarosik 80).

5th match GIRONDINS DE BORDEAUX (FRA)

A 0-0 Postulka, Fukal, Novotny J., Gabriel, Hornak, Baranek (Svoboda Z. 89), Hasek, Rosicky (Jarosik 90), Labant, Sionko, Lokvenc (Siegl 81).

6th match SPARTAK MOSKVA (RUS)

H 5-2 Lokvenc (1, 65), Rosicky (10), Fukal (49), Labant (63p)
Postulka, Fukal, Novotny J., Gabriel, Hornak, Rosicky (Svoboda Z. 68), Hasek, Obajdin (Jarosik 75), Labant, Sionko (Siegl 85), Lokvenc.

7th match FC PORTO (POR)

H 0-2 Postulka, Fukal, Novotny J., Gabriel, Hornak, Obajdin (Jarosik 70), Hasek, Rosicky (Svoboda Z. 86), Baranek, Lokvenc, Sionko (Siegl 71).

8th match FC BARCELONA (ESP)

A 0-5 Postulka, Fukal, Novotny J., Gabriel, Svoboda V. (Bolf 17), Hornak, Hasek, Sionko (Jarosik 70), Baranek, Lokvenc.

9th match HERTHA BSC BERLIN (GER)

A 1-1 Siegl (84)
Blazek, Fukal, Novotny J., Bolf, Gabriel, Sionko, Rosicky, Jarosik, Baranek, Lokvenc (Siegl 68), Obajdin (Hapal 75).

10th match HERTHA BSC BERLIN (GER)

H 1-0 Fukal (90)
Blazek, Fukal, Novotny J., Bolf, Gabriel, Hapal (Siegl 65), Jarosik, Rosicky, Baranek, Lokvenc, Sionko (Svoboda Z. 74).

11th match FC PORTO (POR)

A 2-2 Lokvenc (64), Fukal (90)
Blazek, Fukal, Novotny J., Bolf (Hornak 81), Gabriel, Baranek, Svoboda Z. (Siegl 86), Jarosik, Rosicky, Sionko (Obajdin 56), Lokvenc.

12th match FC BARCELONA (ESP)

H 1-2 Svoboda Z. (18)
Blazek, Fukal, Novotny J., Bolf, Gabriel, Sionko, Svoboda Z. (Hapal 58), Jarosik, Rosicky, Lokvenc, Obajdin (Flachbart 71).

UEFA CUP
● FK TEPLICE
1st round FERENCVÁROS (HUN)

H 3-1 Frydek (33), Kolomaznik (53), Rizek (73)
Machacek, Rizek, Rada, Brabec, Fousek (Kukol 60), Frydek (Jindracek 65), Kolomaznik (Sourada 90), Frtala, Bilek, Tesarik, Verbir.

A 1-1 Rada (53)
Machacek, Rizek, Rada, Brabec, Kukol (Fousek 70), Kolomaznik, Frydek, Frtala, Tesarik, Verbir (Sourada 90), Divecky (Jindracek 82).

2nd round RCD MALLORCA (ESP)

H 1-2 Verbir (68)
Machacek, Rizek, Rada (Vachousek 79), Brabec, Kukol, Fousek (Sourada 39), Frtala, Frydek (Jindracek 57), Kolomaznik, Tesarik, Verbir.

A 0-3 Machacek, Bilek, Rada, Brabec, Fousek, Frtala, Jindracek, Frydek, Tesarik, Verbir (Kolomaznik 68), Divecky (Sourada 63).

● SIGMA OLOMOUC
Qualifying round SERIF TIRASPOL (MOL)

A 1-1 Kovac (20)
Skacel, Kovar, Machala, Kotulek, Kucera, Mucha, Ujfalusi, Kovac (Necas 90), Heinz (Kotrys 89), Fabus (Vlcek 56).

H 0-0 Bures, Kovar, Machala, Kotulek, Kucera, Mucha (Necas 80), Ujfalusi, Kovac, Urbanek, Heinz (Krohmer 89), Fabus (Vlcek 64).

1st round RCD MALLORCA (ESP)

H 1-3 Kobylik (64)
Havel, Kovar, Machala, Kotulek, Krohmer, Kovac, Necas, Urbanek (Rozehnal 13; Kobylik 21), Kucera, Vlcek, Fabus (Mucha 83).

A 0-0 Bures, Ujfalusi, Machala, Kotulek, Kucera, Krohmer, Mucha, Necas (Rozehnal 69), Kovac (Kobylik 64), Urbanek, Vlcek (Fabus 78).

● SLAVIA PRAHA
1st round VOJVODINA NOVI SAD (YUG)

A 0-0 Cerny, Vlcek, Rada, Koller, Dosek L., Ulich, Dostalek, Horvath (Dosek T. 71), Kuchar, Skala (Krejcik 55), Zelenka (Kucera 87).

H 3-2 Petrous (39), Dosek T. (73), Zelenka (80)
Cerny, Vlcek, Rada, Petrous, Dosek L. (Kucera 62), Ulich, Dostalek (Kuchar 50), Horvath, Krejcik (Vagner 48), Zelenka, Dosek T..

2nd round GRASSHOPPER-CLUB ZÜRICH (SUI)

H 3-1 Ulich (20, 50), Kuchar (39)
Cerny, Vlcek, Rada, Petrous, Dosek L., Ulich, Dostalek (Kucera 87), Horvath, Skala (Kuchar 29), Zelenka (Vagner 65), Dosek T..

A 0-1 Cerny, Petrous, Rada, Vlcek, Dosek L., Dostalek, Horvath, Kuchar (Lerch 90), Skala (Krejcik 67), Zelenka (Vagner 58), Dosek T..

3rd round STEAUA BUCURESTI (ROM)

H 4-1 Dostalek (1, 47), Horvath (35), Dosek T. (55)
Cerny, Vlcek (Krejcik 52), Rada, Petrous, Dosek L., Ulich, Dostalek, Horvath, Kuchar, Zelenka (Vagner 67), Dosek T. (Skala 86).

EUROPEAN CUPS 99/00 (CONT.)

A 1-1   Dostalek (50)
Cerny, Koller, Rada, Vlcek, Dosek L., Ulich, Dostalek, Horvath
(Lerch 90), Petrous, Dosek T. (Vagner 81), Zelenka (Krejcik 85).

4th round UDINESE (ITA)
H 1-0   Zanchi (76og)
Cerny, Rada, Petrous, Koller, Hysky, Lerch (Vagner 72), Ulich,
Dostalek, Horvath, Skala (Kuchar 51), Zelenka, Dosek T. (Kozel 90).
A 1-2   Koller (42)
Cerny, Rada, Vlcek (Hysky 34), Koller, Dosek L., Ulich, Dostalek,
Horvath, Petrous, Zelenka (Vagner 77), Dosek T. (Kuchar 90).

Quarter-final LEEDS UNITED (ENG)
A 0-3
Cerny, Rada, Vlcek (Vagner 57), Koller, Dosek L., Kuchar, Dostalek
(Hysky 65), Horvath, Ulich, Dosek T..
H 2-1   Ulich (53, 79p)
Cerny, Kozel, Koller, Hysky, Dosek L., Ulich, Kuchar (Vozabal 86),
Dostalek (Lerch 54), Skala, Zelenka, Dosek T. (Vagner 54).

INTERNATIONAL HONOURS

World Cup Finals appearances: 1934 (runners-up), 1938 (qtr-finals),
1954, 1958, 1962 (runners-up), 1970, 1982, 1990 (qtr-finals)
European Championship appearances: 1960 (3rd), 1976 (Winners),
1980 (3rd), 1996 (runners-up), 2000

import Leandro Lazzaro Liuni, gave Liberec a 2-1
victory in the final against Second Division side Banik
Ratiskovice - the first lower-division club to reach the final
since Dukla Prague in 1996/97. Liberec's victory earned
them a first major trophy and also made up for their extra-
time defeat by Slavia in the 1999 final.

At the bottom of the table SFC Opava and Hradek
Kralove were relegated and replaced by Synot Stare
Mesto and Viktoria Plzen. Stare Mesto matched Sparta
Prague's 76-point total in lifting the Second Division
championship while runners-up Plzen ensured the perfect
finale to an excellent season which had also featured a
1-0 victory over Sparta in the fourth round of the Cup -
a result which showed that even in a country where two
clubs have become so dominant, it is still possible, occasionally, for the underdogs to have their day.

behind Slavia - and thus qualified for Europe for the first
time. There was also a first visit to the UEFA Cup for
Slovan Liberec, who made up for a barren league campaign - just 21 goals in 30 games - by collecting the
Czech Cup. Two goals from their top scorer, Argentinian

PROMOTED CLUBS 99/00

SECOND DIVISION FINAL TABLE

		Pd	W	D	L	F	A	Pt	GD
1	**Synot Stare Mesto**	30	24	4	2	76	29	76	47
2	**Viktoria Plzen**	30	17	8	5	50	22	59	28
3	Banik Ratiskovice	30	14	9	7	48	33	51	15
4	MUS Most	30	10	15	5	43	32	45	11
5	NH Ostrava	30	11	10	9	46	39	43	7
6	AFK Atlantic Bohdanec	30	10	10	10	36	33	40	3
7	Spolana Neratovice	30	12	6	12	42	45	42	-3
8	FC Zlin	30	10	11	9	44	33	41	11
9	Xaverov Horni Pocernice	30	10	7	13	34	41	37	-7
10	Zelezarny Trinec	30	9	10	11	39	60	37	-21
11	FC Karvina	30	8	9	13	44	48	33	-4
12	LeRK Prostejov	30	8	9	13	39	47	33	-8
13	Mlada Boleslav	30	7	12	11	31	40	33	-9
14	FC Vitkovice	30	7	12	11	23	38	33	-15
15	Tatran Postorna	30	5	10	15	30	47	25	-17
16	VP Frydek-Mistek	30	4	4	22	26	64	16	-38

CLUB DIRECTORIES

1.FC Synot Stare Mesto
Velkomoravska 583, 686 03 Stare Mesto
tel - (0632) 551800
fax - (0632) 541202
website - www.fc.synot.cz
email - cadova@synot.cz
Year of Formation - 1927
President - Miroslav Valenta
Secretary - Milan Omelka
Coach - Frantisek Komnacky
Stadium - Siruch (4,300)

FC Viktoria Plzen
Struncovy sady 3, 301 12 Plzen
tel - (019) 7235180/7236038
fax - (019) 7236520
website - www.fcviktoriaplzen.cz
email - fcviktoria@titan.lapeco.cz
Year of Formation - 1911
President - Milan Masopust
Secretary - Vaclav Korinek
Coach - Lubos Urban
Stadium - Viktoria Plzen (28,218)

BANIK OSTRAVA

CLUB DIRECTORY

FC Banik Ostrava
Bukovanskeho 4/1028, 710 00 Ostrava
tel - (069) 6241687 / fax - (069) 6241827
website - www.fotbal.com/ostrava.htm
email - banik@idp.cz
Year of Formation - 1922
President - Erwin Gerö
Secretary - Libor Radimec
Coach - Werner Licka (00/01 - Milan Boksa)
Stadium - Bazaly (19,048)

MAJOR HONOURS
League Championship - (3) 1976, 1980, 1981.
Domestic Cup - (3) 1973, 1978, 1991.

APPEARANCES 99/00

		P	Ap	(s)	Gls
Jan BARANEK	M	22		(4)	1
Vit BARANEK	G	25			
Milan BAROS	A	23		(6)	6
Robert CAHA	M	17		(5)	
Vladimir CAP	D	19		(2)	3
Josef DVORNIK	M	15		(2)	
Josef HOFFMANN	D	1			1
Marek JANKULOVSKI	M	25		(2)	8
Rostislav KISA	D	8		(2)	1
Lubomir KUBICA	D	5		(2)	
Marcel LICKA	M	22		(5)	2
Martin LUKES	A	11		(8)	3
Milan PALENIK	M			(5)	
Marek POSTULKA	A	6		(13)	2
Milan POSTULKA	D	21			1
Martin RASKA	G	5			
Petr SAMEC	A	8		(12)	5
Michal SLACHTA	M	29			2
Radek SLONCIK	A	7		(4)	
Tomas STASTKA	D	20		(4)	
Petr VESELY	D	25			4
Radim WOZNIAK	D	11			
Libor ZUREK	A	5		(8)	3

LEAGUE RESULTS 1999/2000

01/08/99	Chmel Blsany	H	6-1	Baranek J., Vesely, Lukes, Jankulovski, Baros, Zurek
08/08/99	Slavia Praha	A	0-2	
15/08/99	Sigma Olomouc	H	2-2	Jankulovski, Samec
22/08/99	Petra Drnovice	A	0-1	
28/08/99	Viktoria Zizkov	H	1-1	Samec
12/09/99	SFC Opava	A	3-2	Licka (p), Zurek, Slachta
18/09/99	FK Jablonec 97	H	1-1	Samec
26/09/99	FK Teplice	A	2-0	Samec, Baros
02/10/99	Sparta Praha	H	0-3	
17/10/99	SK Ceske Budejovice	A	2-2	Baros, Zurek
22/11/99	Boby Brno	H	1-0	Licka
31/10/99	Bohemians Praha	A	0-0	
07/11/99	Dukla Pribram	H	2-0	Vesely, Slachta
20/11/99	SK Hradec Kralove	H	2-2	Lukes 2
28/11/99	Slovan Liberec	A	0-1	
05/12/99	Chmel Blsany	A	0-1	
19/02/00	Slavia Praha	H	1-3	Postulka Ma.
27/02/00	Sigma Olomouc	A	1-4	Jankulovski (p)
04/03/00	Petra Drnovice	H	3-1	Jankulovski 2, Cap
12/03/00	Viktoria Zizkov	A	1-3	Kisa
17/03/00	SFC Opava	H	2-2	Cap 2
25/03/00	FK Jablonec 97	A	2-2	Baros, Postulka Ma.
02/04/00	FK Teplice	H	2-2	Vesely, Baros
09/04/00	Sparta Praha	A	0-2	
16/04/00	SK Ceske Budejovice	H	1-1	Postulka Mi.
22/04/00	Boby Brno	A	1-2	Vesely
30/04/00	Bohemians Praha	H	1-1	Jankulovski (p)
07/05/00	Dukla Pribram	A	0-2	
13/05/00	SK Hradec Kralove	A	3-1	Jankulovski, Samec, Baros
17/05/00	Slovan Liberec	H	3-0	Hoffmann, Jankulovski, og (Jiranek)

BOBY BRNO

THE EUROPEAN FOOTBALL YEARBOOK 2000-2001

CLUB DIRECTORY

FC Boby Brno (now - FC Stavo Artikel Brno)
Drobneho 45, 602 00 Brno
tel - (05) 41233583/7272483
fax - (05) 41233581
website - www.fotbal.com/brno.htm
email - fc@boby.cz
Year of Formation - 1913
President - Ing. Jaroslav Bubla
Secretary - Radek Belak
Coach - Karel Jarusek
Stadium - Za Luzankami (50,000)

MAJOR HONOURS
League Championship - (1) 1978.

APPEARANCES 99/00

	P	Ap	(s)	Gls
Petr BASTAR	D	18	(4)	
Daniel BREZNY	D	3	(1)	
Zdenek CIHLAR	D	27		
Libor DOSEK	A	11		3
Patrik HOLOMEK	A	12	(4)	2
Pavel HOLOMEK	A	10		1
Petr KOCMAN	M	11	(11)	2
Jiri KOPUNEC	A		(5)	
Gökmen KORE (TUR)	M		(9)	
Martin KOTULEK	D	3		
Petr KRIVANEK	D	28		5
Jan MAROSI	M	21	(8)	4
Jan PALINEK	D	15	(3)	1
Jan POLAK	M	29		1
Lubos PRIBYL	G	30		
Patrik SIEGL	M	30		9
Pavel SUSTR	A	4	(19)	
Petr SVANCARA	A	29		4
Martin ZBONCAK	M	21	(4)	2
Marek ZUBEK	M	28		

LEAGUE RESULTS 1999/2000

30/07/99	Sigma Olomouc	H	1-0	Krivanek
09/08/99	Petra Drnovice	A	0-2	
14/08/99	Viktoria Zizkov	H	4-2	Holomek Pat., Palinek, Siegl (p), Holomek Pav.
20/08/99	SFC Opava	A	1-4	Marosi
28/08/99	FK Jablonec 97	H	2-0	Siegl (p), Marosi
12/09/99	FK Teplice	A	1-2	Siegl
18/09/99	Sparta Praha	H	1-1	Polak
26/09/99	SK Ceske Budejovice	A	0-1	
02/10/99	Dukla Pribram	H	0-0	
17/10/99	Bohemians Praha	H	1-1	Marosi (p)
22/10/99	Banik Ostrava	A	0-1	
29/10/99	SK Hradec Kralove	H	1-2	Kocman
07/11/99	Slovan Liberec	A	1-0	og (Marek)
21/11/99	Chmel Blsany	H	3-0	Siegl, Svancara, Holomek Pat.
29/11/99	Slavia Praha	A	1-3	Krivanek
05/12/99	Sigma Olomouc	A	1-1	Siegl (p)
19/02/00	Petra Drnovice	H	2-3	Krivanek, Zboncak
27/02/00	Viktoria Zizkov	A	0-1	
05/03/00	SFC Opava	H	1-0	Dosek
12/03/00	FK Jablonec 97	A	0-0	
19/03/00	FK Teplice	H	2-1	Kocman, Svancara
25/03/00	Sparta Praha	A	0-3	
31/03/00	SK Ceske Budejovice	H	2-0	Krivanek, Zboncak
09/04/00	Dukla Pribram	A	2-1	Marosi, Siegl
16/04/00	Bohemians Praha	A	0-0	
22/04/00	Banik Ostrava	H	2-1	Svancara, Dosek
30/04/00	SK Hradec Kralove	A	0-1	
07/05/00	Slovan Liberec	H	3-0	Dosek, Siegl 2 (2p)
13/05/00	Chmel Blsany	A	0-1	
17/05/00	Slavia Praha	H	3-1	Svancara, Krivanek, Siegl

BOHEMIANS PRAHA

CLUB DIRECTORY

CU Bohemians Praha
Vrsovicka 31, 101 00 Praha 10
tel - (02) 71721459   fax - (02) 71721459
website - www.fc-bohemians.cz/
email - bohemka@mbox.vol.cz
Year of Formation - 1905
President - Pavel Svarc
Secretary - Jiri Novak
Coach - Vlastimil Petrzela
Stadium - FC Bohemians (13,716)

MAJOR HONOURS
League Championship - (1) 1983.

APPEARANCES 99/00

	P	Ap	(s)	Gls
Jaromir BLAZEK	G	16		
Kamil CONTOFALSKY (SVK)	G	14		
Richard CULEK	M	23	(2)	1
Martin DANHEL	D		(1)	
Karel DOLEZAL	D	25	(1)	
Jan FLACHBART	A	5		1
Tomas FREISLER	D	11	(5)	
Petr GOTTWALD	A	1	(5)	
Michal HRBEK	D	12		
Libor JANACEK	M	14		1
Josef JINOCH	D	13	(2)	
Martin JIRANEK	D	16		
Roman JUN	M	11	(1)	4
Jaroslav KAMENICKY	D	6		
Karol KISEL (SVK)	M	7	(1)	
Marian KLAGO (SVK)	A	11	(3)	2
Ludek KLUSACEK	D	2		
Pavel KULIG	M	22	(7)	3
Tomas KULVAJT	A	4	(5)	
Pavel MARES	M	12	(1)	
Kamil MATUSZNY	M	5	(8)	1
Marcel MELECKY	M	12	(5)	
Tomas NAVRAT	M	12	(7)	
Jiri NOVAK	A	11	(1)	1
Miroslav OBERMAJER	D	5		
Michal PETROUS	D	23	(1)	1
Bohuslav SNAJDR	M	5	(16)	1
Pavel VASICEK	M	7	(3)	2
Pavel VELEBA	A		(2)	
Benjamin VOMACKA	M	11	(1)	1
Ludek ZDRAHAL	A	14	(2)	5

LEAGUE RESULTS 1999/2000

Date	Opponent	H/A	Score	Scorers
01/08/99	Slavia Praha	H	0-1	
08/08/99	Sigma Olomouc	A	0-0	
15/08/99	Petra Drnovice	H	3-1	Zdrahal, Matuszny, Kulig
22/08/99	Viktoria Zizkov	A	2-2	Culek, Flachbart (p)
29/08/99	SFC Opava	H	1-0	Vasicek
10/09/99	FK Jablonec 97	A	2-1	Jun 2
20/09/99	FK Teplice	H	0-0	
24/09/99	Sparta Praha	A	0-0	
01/10/99	SK Ceske Budejovice	H	0-1	
17/10/99	Boby Brno	A	1-1	Zdrahal
24/10/99	Dukla Pribram	H	2-0	Zdrahal, Novak
31/10/99	Banik Ostrava	H	0-0	
07/11/99	SK Hradec Kralove	A	2-1	Jun 2
19/11/99	Slovan Liberec	H	2-0	Zdrahal, Vasicek
28/11/99	Chmel Blsany	A	0-1	
03/12/99	Slavia Praha	A	0-2	
19/02/00	Sigma Olomouc	H	1-3	Janacek
25/02/00	Petra Drnovice	A	0-3	
03/03/00	Viktoria Zizkov	H	1-0	Snajdr
12/03/00	SFC Opava	A	0-0	
19/03/00	FK Jablonec 97	H	2-0	Zdrahal, Vomacka
24/03/00	FK Teplice	A	0-2	
02/04/00	Sparta Praha	H	0-1	
09/04/00	SK Ceske Budejovice	A	2-1	Klago 2
16/04/00	Boby Brno	H	0-0	
22/04/00	Dukla Pribram	A	0-3	
30/04/00	Banik Ostrava	A	1-1	Kulig (p)
07/05/00	SK Hradec Kralove	H	1-0	Petrous
13/05/00	Slovan Liberec	A	0-2	
17/05/00	Chmel Blsany	H	1-1	Kulig

SK CESKE BUDEJOVICE

CLUB DIRECTORY

SK Ceske Budejovice
Strelecky ostrov 3
370 21 Ceske Budejovice
tel - (038) 7312502-4
fax - (038) 7312503
website - www.skcb.cz/
email - budejovice@skcb.cz
Year of Formation - 1905
President - Ing. Lubomir Skala
Secretary - Milan Cadek
Coach - Pavel Tobias (00/01 - Jindrich Dejimal)
Stadium - Strelecky ostrov (12,000)

APPEARANCES 99/00

	P	Ap	(s)	Gls
Pavel BABKA	M		(1)	
Viktor DOLISTA	A		(1)	
Michal DRAHORAD	M	26	(1)	1
Jaroslav DROBNY	G	28		
Ladislav FUJDIAR	A	17	(9)	4
David HOREJS	D	5	(1)	
Tomas JANDA	A	25	(4)	11
Richard JUKL	M	19	(5)	4
Michal KANIK	M	23	(1)	
Marek KOPECKY	M	8	(15)	
Tomas KREJCA	M		(2)	
Karel KREJCI	M		(1)	
David LAFATA	A	3	(14)	
Roman LENGYEL	D	15		1
Martin LESTINA	D	1	(1)	
Ales MATOUSEK	A		(2)	
Michel NEHODA	A	4	(2)	1
Martin OBSITNIK (SVK)	M	24	(1)	4
Jan PEJSA	D	29		1
Pavel PENICKA	D	30		2
Miloslav PENNER	D	27		1
Libor POLOMSKY	M	6	(2)	1
Jiri POSPISIL	D	14		
Stanislav ROZBOUD	M	5	(12)	
Martin SILMBROD	D	2	(1)	
Pavol SVANTNER	G	2		
Karel VACHA	A	11	(2)	2
Martin VOZABAL	M	6	(8)	1

LEAGUE RESULTS 1999/2000

01/08/99	Petra Drnovice	H	2-0	Janda 2
08/08/99	Viktoria Zizkov	A	1-1	Jukl
14/08/99	SFC Opava	H	1-0	Obsitnik
22/08/99	FK Jablonec 97	A	1-2	Lengyel
29/08/99	FK Teplice	H	3-1	Janda 2, Jukl
12/09/99	Sparta Praha	A	0-7	
19/09/99	Dukla Pribram	H	5-0	Obsitnik 2, Fujdiar 2, Janda
26/09/99	Boby Brno	H	1-0	Janda
01/10/99	Bohemians Praha	A	1-0	Drahorad
17/10/99	Banik Ostrava	H	2-2	Janda, Fujdiar
24/10/99	SK Hradec Kralove	A	0-1	
31/10/99	Slovan Liberec	H	0-1	
07/11/99	Chmel Blsany	A	2-3	Vozabal, Penner
21/11/99	Slavia Praha	H	0-1	
26/11/99	Sigma Olomouc	A	1-1	Obsitnik
05/12/99	Petra Drnovice	A	0-2	
19/02/00	Viktoria Zizkov	H	1-0	Nehoda
27/02/00	SFC Opava	A	2-3	Polomsky, Penicka
05/03/00	FK Jablonec 97	H	2-0	Janda 2
10/03/00	FK Teplice	A	0-3	
18/03/00	Sparta Praha	H	1-4	Vacha
25/03/00	Dukla Pribram	A	0-1	
31/03/00	Boby Brno	A	0-2	
09/04/00	Bohemians Praha	H	1-2	Pejsa
16/04/00	Banik Ostrava	A	1-1	Vacha
22/04/00	SK Hradec Kralove	H	2-1	Janda, Penicka
30/04/00	Slovan Liberec	A	0-2	
05/05/00	Chmel Blsany	H	2-2	Janda, Jukl
13/05/00	Slavia Praha	A	1-4	Jukl
17/05/00	Sigma Olomouc	H	1-2	Fujdiar

CHMEL BLSANY

CLUB DIRECTORY

FK Chmel Blsany
U stadionu 14
439 88 Blsany
tel - (0399) 214523
fax - (0399) 214592
website - www.fotbal.com/blsany.htm
email - blsany@fkchmel.cz
Year of Formation - 1946
President - Ing. Jiri Hendrych
Secretary - Eva Sidova
Coach - Miroslav Beranek
Stadium - FK Chmel (4,600)

APPEARANCES 99/00

	P	Ap	(s)	Gls
Gunter BITTENGEL	A	12	(7)	
Jakub BURES	M	7	(4)	
Petr CECH	G	1		
Ales CHVALOVSKY	G	29		
Pavel DEVATY	M	3	(4)	
Libor DOSEK	A	11	(6)	3
Vaclav DROBNY	D	17	(3)	
Patrik GEDEON	M	27	(2)	3
Petr GRUND	D	4	(1)	
Michal HOFFMANN	A	1		
Roman HOGEN	A	15	(5)	3
Ondrej HOUDA	M		(3)	
Frantisek KOUBEK	A	18	(4)	3
Stanislav KREJCIK	M	8	(4)	
Jan KYKLHORN	A		(6)	
Martin PAZDERA	M	16	(3)	
Pavel PERGL	M	2	(4)	
Michal POSPISIL	A	22	(4)	3
Jan SIMAK	A	24	(4)	5
Michal SMARDA	M	17	(2)	2
Jiri SYKORA	M	20	(6)	2
Karel TICHOTA	D	27	(2)	2
Jan VELKOBORSKY	M	29		2
Jan VOREL	D	6	(5)	
Petr VRABEC	M	4	(5)	
Ivo ZBOZINEK	D	10	(1)	

LEAGUE RESULTS 1999/2000

01/08/99	Banik Ostrava	A	1-6	Tichota
08/08/99	SK Hradec Kralove	H	1-0	Sykora
14/08/99	Slovan Liberec	A	1-1	Dosek
22/08/99	Dukla Pribram	A	0-1	
27/08/99	Slavia Praha	H	2-3	Simak, Gedeon
12/09/99	Sigma Olomouc	A	1-0	Simak
19/09/99	Petra Drnovice	H	0-2	
26/09/99	Viktoria Zizkov	A	1-1	Sykora
02/10/99	SFC Opava	H	1-0	Simak
17/10/99	FK Jablonec 97	A	2-4	Simak, Smarda (p)
25/10/99	FK Teplice	H	0-2	
30/10/99	Sparta Praha	A	1-3	Dosek
07/11/99	SK Ceske Budejovice	H	3-2	Dosek, Smarda (p), Pospisil
21/11/99	Boby Brno	A	0-3	
28/11/99	Bohemians Praha	H	1-0	Gedeon
05/12/99	Banik Ostrava	H	1-0	Gedeon
19/02/00	SK Hradec Kralove	A	1-1	Hogen
27/02/00	Slovan Liberec	H	1-0	Hogen
05/03/00	Dukla Pribram	H	2-1	Tichota, Pospisil
12/03/00	Slavia Praha	A	1-2	Hogen
19/03/00	Sigma Olomouc	H	1-0	Velkoborsky
25/03/00	Petra Drnovice	A	0-2	
02/04/00	Viktoria Zizkov	H	0-2	
09/04/00	SFC Opava	A	0-0	
16/04/00	FK Jablonec 97	H	1-2	Koubek
22/04/00	FK Teplice	A	0-0	
30/04/00	Sparta Praha	H	1-4	Koubek
05/05/00	SK Ceske Budejovice	A	2-2	Velkoborsky, Simak (p)
13/05/00	Boby Brno	H	1-0	Pospisil
17/05/00	Bohemians Praha	A	1-1	Koubek

DUKLA PRIBRAM

CLUB DIRECTORY

FC Dukla Pribram (now - FC Marila Pribram)
Stadion Na Litavce
P.O. Box 65, 261 02 Pribram
tel - (0306) 26173   fax - (0306) 26173
website - www.fotbal.com/dukla.htm
email - DuklaPB@PBA.cz
Year of Formation - 1948
President - Jaroslav Starka
Secretary - Miloslav Jicha
Coach - Jiri Kotrba
Stadium - Na Litavce (7,000)

MAJOR HONOURS
League Championship - (11) 1953, 1956, 1958,
1961, 1962, 1963, 1964, 1966, 1977, 1979,
1982.
Domestic Cup - (8) 1961, 1965, 1966, 1969,
1981, 1983, 1985, 1990.

APPEARANCES 99/00

	P	Ap	(s)	Gls
Tonci BASIC (CRO)	M	3	(3)	
Jiri BIRHANZL	D	1	(2)	
Michal CALOUN	G	12		
Radek CIZEK	M	14	(12)	4
Ales HYNEK	D	10	(2)	
Peter JAKUBECH (SVK)	G	9		
Zdenek JANOS	G	6		
Lukas JAROLIM	M	27	(2)	2
Petr JENDRUSCAK	M		(1)	
Jan KLIMA	G	1		
Tomas KUCERA	A	6	(1)	
Marek KULIC	A	22	(3)	7
Marcel MACHA	D	27		
Jaroslav MASEK	M	12	(4)	2
Radek MYNAR	D	29		5
David NEHODA	D	4		
Robert NOVAK (SVK)	M	14		
Rudolf OTEPKA	M	10	(4)	3
Petr PODZEMSKY	D	28	(1)	1
Jiri RYCHLIK	M	10	(5)	1
Vlastimil RYSAVY	A	17	(6)	1
Jaroslav SCHINDLER	D	14		1
Michal SEMAN	A	25	(1)	5
Daniel SMEJKAL	M	4	(16)	
Martin SPINAR	D	15		
Michal SPIT	G	2		
Hynek TALPA	D	1	(1)	
Ivan VALACHOVIC (SVK)	M	2	(3)	
Ludek VYSKOCIL	A	5	(1)	
Jan ZUSTAK	A		(15)	1

LEAGUE RESULTS 1999/2000

31/07/99	FK Jablonec 97	A	2-0	Rysavy, Masek
08/08/99	Slovan Liberec	H	1-1	Seman
15/08/99	FK Teplice	A	0-2	
22/08/99	Chmel Blsany	H	1-0	Seman
28/08/99	Sparta Praha	A	1-2	Mynar
12/09/99	Slavia Praha	H	1-1	Kulic
19/09/99	SK Ceske Budejovice	A	0-5	
24/09/99	Sigma Olomouc	H	0-2	
02/10/99	Boby Brno	A	0-0	
17/10/99	Petra Drnovice	H	1-1	Seman
24/10/99	Bohemians Praha	A	0-2	
31/10/99	Viktoria Zizkov	H	5-2	Mynar 2, Jarolim, Kulic,
				Podzemsky (p)
07/11/99	Banik Ostrava	A	0-2	
21/11/99	SFC Opava	H	1-0	Cizek
28/11/99	SK Hradec Kralove	A	1-1	Mynar
05/12/99	FK Jablonec 97	H	2-1	Seman, Masek
19/02/00	Slovan Liberec	A	0-0	
27/02/00	FK Teplice	H	3-0	Jarolim, Mynar, Rychlik
05/03/00	Chmel Blsany	A	1-2	Cizek
11/03/00	Sparta Praha	H	1-3	Kulic
20/03/00	Slavia Praha	A	1-3	Cizek (p)
25/03/00	SK Ceske Budejovice	H	1-0	Cizek
02/04/00	Sigma Olomouc	A	0-1	
09/04/00	Boby Brno	H	1-2	Kulic
16/04/00	Petra Drnovice	A	1-2	Otepka
22/04/00	Bohemians Praha	H	3-0	Otepka, Zustak, Kulic
30/04/00	Viktoria Zizkov	A	1-1	Schindler
07/05/00	Banik Ostrava	H	2-0	Seman, Otepka
13/05/00	SFC Opava	A	1-0	Kulic
17/05/00	SK Hradec Kralove	H	1-0	Kulic

SK HRADEC KRALOVE

CLUB DIRECTORY

SK Hradec Kralove
Vsesportovni stadion, 500 09 Hradec Kralove 9
tel - (049) 551553 / fax - (049) 5511485
website - www.fotbal.com/hradec.htm
email - hkfotbal@hka.czn.cz
Year of Formation - 1905
President - Ing. Vladimir Voda
Secretary - Vaclav Kynos
Coach - Stanislav Kocourek
Stadium - Vsesportovni stadion (25,000)

MAJOR HONOURS
League Championship - (1) 1960.
Domestic Cup - (1) 1995.

APPEARANCES 99/00

	P	Ap	(s)	Gls
Ales BEDNAR	A		(8)	
Petr BILEK	A	3	(3)	
Vladimir BLÜMEL	D	13	(1)	
Tomas BOUSKA	A	8	(10)	2
Pavel CERNY	A	26	(3)	4
Josef CHALOUPKA	D		(1)	
Michal DOLEZAL	M	9	(7)	
Jaroslav DVORAK	M	12		
Patrik HOLOMEK	A	5	(1)	
David HOMOLAC	D	26		3
Roman JURACKA	D	15	(2)	
David KALOUSEK	D	18		1
Daniel KAPLAN	M	3	(4)	
Jan KRAUS	A	20	(7)	5
Pavel KUBES	M	3	(4)	
Michal LESAK	M	24		1
Karel NOVOTNY	G	14		
Radek OPRSAL	A	4	(4)	
Karel PITAK	M	18	(7)	3
Jaroslav PLASIL	M	3		
Karel PODHAJSKY	G	16		
Petr POKORNY	D	7		
Adrian ROLKO	D	11	(3)	
Petr SAMEK	M	1	(3)	
Zdenek SEVCIK	M	1		
Rudolf SKACEL	M		(3)	
Ondrej SZABO	M	22	(3)	1
Jiri WEISSER	A		(2)	
Miroslav ZEMANEK	M	25		
David ZOUBEK	M	23	(6)	

LEAGUE RESULTS 1999/2000

01/08/99	Slovan Liberec	H	1-3	Homolac (p)
08/08/99	Chmel Blsany	A	0-1	
13/08/99	Slavia Praha	H	0-1	
22/08/99	Sigma Olomouc	A	2-2	Kalousek, Szabo
28/08/99	Petra Drnovice	H	0-2	
12/09/99	Viktoria Zizkov	A	1-2	Kraus
19/09/99	SFC Opava	H	2-2	Kraus 2
26/09/99	FK Jablonec 97	A	0-0	
04/10/99	FK Teplice	H	2-0	Pitak, Homolac
15/10/99	Sparta Praha	A	1-3	Kraus
24/10/99	SK Ceske Budejovice	H	1-0	Bouska
29/10/99	Boby Brno	A	2-1	Cerny, Kraus
07/11/99	Bohemians Praha	H	1-2	Pitak
20/11/99	Banik Ostrava	A	2-2	Cerny, Bouska
28/11/99	Dukla Pribram	H	1-1	Cerny
05/12/99	Slovan Liberec	A	0-1	
19/02/00	Chmel Blsany	H	1-1	Homolac
26/02/00	Slavia Praha	A	0-3	
05/03/00	Sigma Olomouc	H	0-0	
12/03/00	Petra Drnovice	A	0-1	
19/03/00	Viktoria Zizkov	H	0-0	
25/03/00	SFC Opava	A	0-0	
02/04/00	FK Jablonec 97	H	0-0	
09/04/00	FK Teplice	A	1-1	og (Pokorny)
14/04/00	Sparta Praha	H	0-2	
22/04/00	SK Ceske Budejovice	A	1-2	Lesak
30/04/00	Boby Brno	H	1-0	Cerny
07/05/00	Bohemians Praha	A	0-1	
13/05/00	Banik Ostrava	H	1-3	Pitak
17/05/00	Dukla Pribram	A	0-1	

FK JABLONEC 97

FK Jablonec 97
U stadionu 5, 466 01 Jablonec nad Nisou
tel - (0428) 318943
fax - (0428) 319897
website - www.fotbal.com/jablonec.htm
email - fkjablonec@lbc.pvtnet.cz
Year of Formation - 1945
President - Pavel Marek
Secretary - Lubos Srejma
Coach - Juilius Bielik (00/01 - Jaroslav Hrebik)
Stadium - Strelnice (14,730)

MAJOR HONOURS
Domestic Cup - (1) 1998.

APPEARANCES 99/00

	P	Ap	(s)	Gls
Jozef ANTALOVIC (SVK)	D	5	(1)	
Milan BARTESKA	M	25	(4)	2
Vaclav BUDKA	M	3	(6)	
Vladimir CHALOUPKA	A	3	(8)	1
Tomas CIZEK	M	17	(7)	
Dejan DJURANOVIC (CRO)	M		(3)	
Milan FUKAL	D	1		2
Karel HAVLICEK	D	18		
Radim HOLUB	A	25	(3)	7
Jan HOMOLA	D	6	(1)	1
Petr HRUSKA	M	6		
Pavel JIROUSEK	M	21	(3)	1
Miloslav KORDULE	D	19	(5)	1
Josef LASTOVKA	A		(4)	
Jiri MASEK	M	4	(5)	
Lubomir MATI (SVK)	A	2	(4)	
Radim NECAS	M	27		2
Petr PAPOUSEK	M	18	(5)	2
Petr PIZANOWSKI	G	16		
Karel PODHAJSKY	G	14		
Tomas POZAR	D	4		
Martin PROCHAZKA	A		(5)	
Roman SKUHRAVY	D	29		3
Dalibor SLEZAK	A	12	(7)	1
Karel URBANEK	D	4		
Jiri VAVRA	A	15	(5)	
Martin VEJPRAVA	D	8	(3)	1
Josef WEBER	M	28		

LEAGUE RESULTS 1999/2000

Date	Opponent	H/A	Score	Scorers
31/07/99	Dukla Pribram	H	0-2	
06/08/99	FK Teplice	H	3-1	Fukal 2, Chaloupka
14/08/99	Sparta Praha	A	0-3	
22/08/99	SK Ceske Budejovice	H	2-1	Skuhravy, Barteska
28/08/99	Boby Brno	A	0-2	
10/09/99	Bohemians Praha	H	1-2	Necas (p)
18/09/99	Banik Ostrava	A	1-1	Skuhravy
28/09/99	SK Hradec Kralove	H	0-0	
02/10/99	Slovan Liberec	A	0-0	
17/10/99	Chmel Blsany	H	4-2	Slezak, Barteska, Vejprava (p), Holub
25/10/99	Slavia Praha	A	0-4	
31/10/99	Sigma Olomouc	H	0-0	
07/11/99	Petra Drnovice	A	0-3	
21/11/99	Viktoria Zizkov	H	3-0	Holub 2, Necas
28/11/99	SFC Opava	A	0-2	
05/12/99	Dukla Pribram	A	1-2	Holub
19/02/00	FK Teplice	A	0-2	
27/02/00	Sparta Praha	H	0-2	
05/03/00	SK Ceske Budejovice	A	0-2	
12/03/00	Boby Brno	H	0-0	
19/03/00	Bohemians Praha	A	0-2	
25/03/00	Banik Ostrava	H	2-2	Homola, Holub
02/04/00	SK Hradec Kralove	A	0-0	
09/04/00	Slovan Liberec	H	0-0	
16/04/00	Chmel Blsany	A	2-1	Papousek, Holub
21/04/00	Slavia Praha	H	0-0	
30/04/00	Sigma Olomouc	A	0-0	
07/05/00	Petra Drnovice	H	1-0	Jirousek
13/05/00	Viktoria Zizkov	A	0-0	
17/05/00	SFC Opava	H	4-0	Holub, Skuhravy (p), Kordule, Papousek

PETRA DRNOVICE

CLUB DIRECTORY

FC Petra Drnovice
Sportovni areal
683 04 Drnovice
tel - (0507) 353265/353547
fax - (0507) 353265
website - www.fotbal.com/drnovice.html
email - fc.petra@vy.gin.cz
Year of Formation - 1932
President - Jan Gottvald
Secretary - Pavel Holub
Coach - Karel Vecera
Stadium - Sportovni areal (9,500)

APPEARANCES 99/00

	P	Ap	(s)	Gls
Erich BRABEC	D	24		1
Bronislav CERVENKA	M	23	(2)	2
Vlastimil CHYTRY	A		(2)	
Marcel CUPAK	A	29	(1)	7
Rene FORMANEK	D	14	(8)	1
Zdenek GRYGERA	D	29		3
Miroslav HOLENAK	M	27	(2)	1
Miroslav KADLEC	D	28		
Vladimir KINDER (SVK)	M	9	(3)	
Jiri KAUFMAN	A	7	(19)	3
Ivan KOPECKY	M	3	(2)	1
Miloslav KUFA	M	26		1
Fotis MANIATIS	M	1	(10)	
Martin MÜLLER	D	18		1
Rudolf OTEPKA	M	5	(8)	
Martin PARIZEK	G	1		
Pavel PERGL	D	6	(3)	1
Jiri POSPISIL	D	11	(1)	1
Vitezslav TUMA	A	20	(2)	11
Zdenek VALNOHA	M	17	(9)	2
Martin VANIAK	G	29		
Pavel ZAVADIL	M	3	(6)	

LEAGUE RESULTS 1999/2000

01/08/99	SK Ceske Budejovice	A	0-2	
09/08/99	Boby Brno	H	2-0	Cupak, Valnoha
15/08/99	Bohemians Praha	A	1-3	Tuma
22/08/99	Banik Ostrava	H	1-0	Grygera
28/08/99	SK Hradec Kralove	A	2-0	Grygera, Tuma
12/09/99	Slovan Liberec	H	1-1	Grygera
19/09/99	Chmel Blsany	A	2-0	Pospisil, Kaufman
26/09/99	Slavia Praha	H	0-1	
04/10/99	Sigma Olomouc	A	2-1	Müller, Cupak
17/10/99	Dukla Pribram	A	1-1	Formanek
24/10/99	Viktoria Zizkov	H	1-0	Brabec
31/10/99	SFC Opava	A	0-2	
07/11/99	FK Jablonec 97	H	3-0	Tuma 2, Valnoha
21/11/99	FK Teplice	A	2-2	Tuma, Holenak
28/11/99	Sparta Praha	H	0-1	
05/12/99	SK Ceske Budejovice	H	2-0	Tuma (p), Cupak
19/02/00	Boby Brno	A	3-2	Cupak, Cervenka, Pergl
25/02/00	Bohemians Praha	H	3-0	Tuma, Cupak, Kufa
04/03/00	Banik Ostrava	A	1-3	Cervenka
12/03/00	SK Hradec Kralove	H	1-0	Tuma
19/03/00	Slovan Liberec	A	0-0	
25/03/00	Chmel Blsany	H	2-0	Cupak, Tuma
02/04/00	Slavia Praha	A	1-2	Cupak
09/04/00	Sigma Olomouc	H	1-0	Tuma
16/04/00	Dukla Pribram	H	2-1	Tuma, Kaufman
22/04/00	Viktoria Zizkov	A	0-2	
28/04/00	SFC Opava	H	1-1	Kopecky
07/05/00	FK Jablonec 97	A	0-1	
13/05/00	FK Teplice	H	1-1	Kaufman
17/05/00	Sparta Praha	A	0-5	

SFC OPAVA

CLUB DIRECTORY

Slezsky FC Opava
Lipova 2
746 01 Opava
tel - (0653) 211246
fax - (0653) 215125
website - www.fotbal.com/opava.htm
Year of Formation - 1907
President - Alois Sommer
Secretary - Jiri Berousek
Coach - Jiri Bartl
Stadium - Stadion v Mestskych sadech (15,000)

APPEARANCES 99/00

	P	Ap	(s)	Gls
Jiri FENCL	D	15	(1)	
Alois GRUSSMANN	M	10	(9)	1
Michal HAMPEL	A		(3)	
Pavel HARAZIM	D	8	(6)	
Roman HENDRYCH	A	6	(3)	1
Roman JANOUSEK	A	6	(13)	2
Miroslav KAMAS	D	27		
Jaroslav KOLINEK	M	26	(1)	1
Edvard LASOTA	M	13		1
Frantisek METELKA	M		(3)	
Radek MÜLLER	A		(1)	
Jan NEZMAR	A	18	(6)	8
Roman NOHAVICA	D	17	(4)	1
Radek ONDERKA	A	22	(2)	10
Zdenek POSPECH	M	6	(1)	
Radomir PRASEK	A	2	(4)	
Lubomir PUHAK (SVK)	A	6	(11)	1
Ivo SCHMUCKER	G	26		
Lumir SEDLACEK	M	18	(7)	2
Radek SPILACEK	M	24	(2)	1
Michal STEFKA	M	26	(2)	1
Ondrej SVEJDIK	M	1		
Igor SZKUKALEK (SVK)	M	28	(1)	
Michal VOREL	G	4		
Tomas VYCHODIL	D	21	(3)	

LEAGUE RESULTS 1999/2000

31/07/99	FK Teplice	A	1-1	Nezmar
07/08/99	Sparta Praha	H	1-1	Onderka
14/08/99	SK Ceske Budejovice	A	0-1	
20/08/99	Boby Brno	H	4-1	Nezmar 2, Hendrych, Sedlacek
29/08/99	Bohemians Praha	A	0-1	
12/09/99	Banik Ostrava	H	2-3	Onderka 2
19/09/99	SK Hradec Kralove	A	2-2	Nezmar, Onderka
26/09/99	Slovan Liberec	H	3-1	Nezmar 3
02/10/99	Chmel Blsany	A	0-1	
17/10/99	Slavia Praha	H	0-0	
24/10/99	Sigma Olomouc	A	1-2	Stefka
31/10/99	Petra Drnovice	H	2-0	Kolinek, Onderka
07/11/99	Viktoria Zizkov	A	2-3	Onderka, Nezmar
21/11/99	Dukla Pribram	A	0-1	
28/11/99	FK Jablonec 97	H	2-0	Onderka, Janousek
05/12/99	FK Teplice	H	1-1	Grussmann
19/02/00	Sparta Praha	A	0-4	
27/02/00	SK Ceske Budejovice	H	3-2	og (Karnik), Puhak, Onderka
05/03/00	Boby Brno	A	0-1	
12/03/00	Bohemians Praha	H	0-0	
17/03/00	Banik Ostrava	A	2-2	Onderka, Lasota
25/03/00	SK Hradec Kralove	H	0-0	
02/04/00	Slovan Liberec	A	0-1	
09/04/00	Chmel Blsany	H	0-0	
16/04/00	Slavia Praha	A	1-3	Nohavica
22/04/00	Sigma Olomouc	H	3-0	Sedlacek, Spilacek, Janousek
28/04/00	Petra Drnovice	A	1-1	Onderka
07/05/00	Viktoria Zizkov	H	0-1	
13/05/00	Dukla Pribram	H	0-1	
17/05/00	FK Jablonec 97	A	0-4	

SIGMA OLOMOUC

CLUB DIRECTORY

SK Sigma Olomouc
Legionarska 12
771 00 Olomouc
tel - (068) 5223380
fax - (068) 5220953
website - www.sajm.cz/sk sigma/
email - pois@telecom.cz
Year of Formation - 1919
President - Ing. Jaromir Gajda
Secretary - Dalibor Jarolim
Coach - Dan Matuska (00/01 - Leos Kalvoda)
Stadium - Andruv stadion (12,625)

APPEARANCES 99/00

	P	Ap	(s)	Gls
Jiri BARBORIK	M	11	(1)	1
Tomas BURES	G	21		
Martin FABUS (SVK)	A	13	(2)	1
Radomir HAVEL	G	5	(1)	
Roman HENDRYCH	A	6	(7)	
Marek HEINZ	A	14	(1)	4
David KOBYLIK	M	5	(11)	
Radim KÖNIG	M	8	(3)	1
David KOTRYS	M	1	(7)	
Martin KOTULEK	D	15		1
Radoslav KOVAC	D	27	(1)	
Michal KOVAR	D	16		3
Jiri KROHMER	M	3	(12)	
Radim KUCERA	M	24	(2)	2
Oldrich MACHALA	D	30		
Josef MUCHA	M	17	(7)	4
Emil NECAS	M	18	(8)	
Zdenek OPRAVIL	M		(2)	
David ROZEHNAL	D	1	(3)	
Jindrich SKACEL	G	4		
Martin SPACIL	A		(4)	
Tomas UJFALUSI	M	27	(2)	
Ales URBANEK	M	19	(8)	1
Stanislav VLCEK	M	29		13
Pavel ZBOZINEK	M	14		
Ludek ZDRAHAL	A	2	(2)	

LEAGUE RESULTS 1999/2000

01/08/99	Boby Brno	A	0-1	
08/08/99	Bohemians Praha	H	0-0	
15/08/99	Banik Ostrava	A	2-2	Vlcek 2
22/08/99	SK Hradec Kralove	H	2-2	Kovar (p), Kucera
29/08/99	Slovan Liberec	A	0-0	
12/09/99	Chmel Blsany	H	0-1	
20/09/99	Slavia Praha	A	0-2	
24/09/99	Dukla Pribram	A	2-0	Kotulek, Kucera
04/10/99	Petra Drnovice	H	1-2	Mucha
17/10/99	Viktoria Zizkov	A	3-3	Mucha, Fabus, Kovar (p)
24/10/99	SFC Opava	H	2-1	Mucha, Barborik
31/10/99	FK Jablonec 97	A	0-0	
08/11/99	FK Teplice	H	2-2	Vlcek 2
20/11/99	Sparta Praha	A	0-6	
26/11/99	SK Ceske Budejovice	H	1-1	Vlcek
05/12/99	Boby Brno	H	1-1	Vlcek
19/02/00	Bohemians Praha	A	3-1	Heinz 2 (1p), Vlcek
27/02/00	Banik Ostrava	H	4-1	Vlcek, König, Urbanek, Heinz
05/03/00	SK Hradec Kralove	A	0-0	
12/03/00	Slovan Liberec	H	1-1	Vlcek
19/03/00	Chmel Blsany	A	0-1	
26/03/00	Slavia Praha	H	0-2	
02/04/00	Dukla Pribram	H	1-0	Vlcek
09/04/00	Petra Drnovice	A	0-1	
16/04/00	Viktoria Zizkov	H	2-0	Mucha, Heinz
22/04/00	SFC Opava	A	0-3	
30/04/00	FK Jablonec 97	H	0-0	
07/05/00	FK Teplice	A	1-2	Vlcek
13/05/00	Sparta Praha	H	1-1	Kovar
17/05/00	SK Ceske Budejovice	A	2-1	Vlcek 2

SLAVIA PRAHA

CLUB DIRECTORY

SK Slavia Praha
Atleticka 2
169 00 Praha 6
tel - (02) 57213290
fax - (02) 57210868
website - www.slavia.cz/
email - martina.horakova@slavia.cz
Year of Formation - 1893
President - Ing. Vladimir Leska
Secretary - PaeDr. Zdenek Kudela
Coach - Frantisek Cipro
Stadium - Evzena Rosickeho (19,150)

MAJOR HONOURS
League Championship - (10) 1925, 1929, 1930,
1931, 1933, 1934, 1935, 1937, 1947, 1996.
Domestic Cup - (2) 1997, 1999.

APPEARANCES 99/00

	P	Ap	(s)	Gls
Radek CERNY	G	30		1
Lukas DOSEK	D	27	(2)	1
Tomas DOSEK	A	24	(4)	11
Richard DOSTALEK	M	25	(5)	4
Pavel HORVATH	M	25	(1)	10
Martin HYSKY	D	2	(3)	
Libor KOLLER	D	10	(4)	1
Lubos KOZEL	D	2	(2)	
Radek KREJCIK	M	2	(5)	
Tomas KUCERA	A		(7)	
Tomas KUCHAR	M	26	(3)	3
Jiri LERCH	D	4	(15)	
Adam PETROUS	D	25		
Karel RADA	D	28		
Jiri SKALA	M	13	(5)	2
Anton SOLTIS (SVK)	M		(4)	
Ivo SVOBODA	A		(1)	1
Ivo ULICH	M	28		6
Robert VAGNER	A	9	(18)	3
Petr VLCEK	D	24		1
Martin VOZABAL	M		(3)	
Ludek ZELENKA	A	26	(3)	9

LEAGUE RESULTS 1999/2000

01/08/99	Bohemians Praha	A	1-0	Horvath (p)
07/08/99	Banik Ostrava	H	2-0	Kuchar, Zelenka
13/08/99	SK Hradec Kralove	A	1-0	Vagner
22/08/99	Slovan Liberec	H	0-0	
27/08/99	Chmel Blsany	A	3-2	Dosek T. 2, Zelenka
12/09/99	Dukla Pribram	A	1-1	Zelenka
20/09/99	Sigma Olomouc	H	2-0	Dosek T., Zelenka
26/09/99	Petra Drnovice	A	1-0	Vlcek
04/10/99	Viktoria Zizkov	H	3-1	Horvath, Zelenka, Ulich
17/10/99	SFC Opava	A	0-0	
25/10/99	FK Jablonec 97	H	4-0	Dosek T., Skala, Dosek L., Cerny (p)
30/10/99	FK Teplice	A	1-1	Horvath (p)
08/11/99	Sparta Praha	H	2-1	Horvath, Vagner
21/11/99	SK Ceske Budejovice	A	1-0	Dosek T.
29/11/99	Boby Brno	H	3-1	Dosek T. 2, Dostalek
03/12/99	Bohemians Praha	H	2-0	Dosek T., Zelenka
19/02/00	Banik Ostrava	A	3-1	Dosek T., Ulich, Zelenka
26/02/00	SK Hradec Kralove	H	3-0	Kuchar, Svoboda, Horvath
03/03/00	Slovan Liberec	A	1-0	Horvath
12/03/00	Chmel Blsany	H	2-1	Zelenka, Dostalek
20/03/00	Dukla Pribram	H	3-1	Ulich, Kuchar, Horvath (p)
26/03/00	Sigma Olomouc	A	2-0	Dostalek, Skala
02/04/00	Petra Drnovice	H	2-1	Ulich, Zelenka
07/04/00	Viktoria Zizkov	A	1-3	Horvath
16/04/00	SFC Opava	H	3-1	Dosek T., Ulich, Horvath (p)
21/04/00	FK Jablonec 97	A	0-0	
30/04/00	FK Teplice	H	0-1	
06/05/00	Sparta Praha	A	1-5	Dostalek
13/05/00	SK Ceske Budejovice	H	4-1	Ulich, Vagner, Dosek T., Horvath
17/05/00	Boby Brno	A	1-3	Koller

SLOVAN LIBEREC

CLUB DIRECTORY

FC Slovan Liberec
Na Hradbach 1300, 460 01 Liberec
tel - (048) 5103714
fax - (048) 5103715
website - www.fotbal.com/liberec.htm
Year of Formation - 1958
President - Ing. Zbynek Stiller
Secretary - Pavel Jirous
Coach - Ladislav Skorpil
Stadium - Mestsky stadion (6,808)

MAJOR HONOURS
Domestic Cup - (1) 2000.

APPEARANCES 99/00

	P	Ap	(s)	Gls
Milan BAKES	D	2	(3)	
Martin BARBARIC	A	7	(6)	1
David BREDA	M	16	(8)	
Pavel CAPEK	M	20	(5)	
Martin CUPR	M	13	(1)	1
Petr DVORAK	A	1	(10)	
Zbynek HAUZR	G	25		
Michal HRBEK	D	10		1
Libor JANACEK	M	15	(1)	
Tomas JANU	M	14		
Martin JIRANEK	D	12	(1)	
Petr JOHANA	D	11		1
Roman JUN	M	10	(3)	
Marek KINCL	A	5	(1)	1
Antonin KINSKY	G	5		
Marian KLAGO (SVK)	A	8	(4)	1
Vladimir KOZUCH (SVK)	A	7	(6)	3
Leandro Hernán LAZZARO LIUNI (ARG)	A	26	(1)	8
Josef LEXA	D	21	(5)	1
Stanislav MAREK	D	19	(1)	
Kamil MATUSZNY	M	2	(5)	
Rastislav MICHALIK (SVK)	M	24		2
Jan NECAS	M	9	(9)	
Pavel NEGRU	A		(2)	
Robert NEUMANN	M	21	(7)	
Lukas NOVOTNY	D		(3)	
Bohuslav PILNY	D	17		
Petr SILNY	M	3		
Jiri STAJNER	A	7	(1)	1

LEAGUE RESULTS 1999/2000

01/08/99	SK Hradec Kralove	A	3-1	Cupr, Barbaric (p), Lexa
08/08/99	Dukla Pribram	A	1-1	Hrbek
14/08/99	Chmel Blsany	H	1-1	Kincl
22/08/99	Slavia Praha	A	0-0	
29/08/99	Sigma Olomouc	H	0-0	
12/09/99	Petra Drnovice	A	1-1	Lazzaro Liuni
17/09/99	Viktoria Zizkov	H	1-0	Lazzaro Liuni
26/09/99	SFC Opava	A	1-3	Klago
02/10/99	FK Jablonec 97	H	0-0	
17/10/99	FK Teplice	A	0-1	
23/10/99	Sparta Praha	H	1-2	Lazzaro Liuni
31/10/99	SK Ceske Budejovice	A	1-0	Michalik
07/11/99	Boby Brno	H	0-1	
19/11/99	Bohemians Praha	A	0-2	
28/11/99	Banik Ostrava	H	1-0	Lazzaro Liuni
05/12/99	SK Hradec Kralove	H	1-0	Lazzaro Liuni
19/02/00	Dukla Pribram	H	0-0	
27/02/00	Chmel Blsany	A	0-1	
03/03/00	Slavia Praha	H	0-1	
12/03/00	Sigma Olomouc	A	1-1	Lazzaro Liuni
19/03/00	Petra Drnovice	H	0-0	
25/03/00	Viktoria Zizkov	A	0-0	
02/04/00	SFC Opava	H	1-0	Stajner
09/04/00	FK Jablonec 97	A	0-0	
16/04/00	FK Teplice	H	2-0	Michalik, Lazzaro Liuni
22/04/00	Sparta Praha	A	1-2	Kozuch
30/04/00	SK Ceske Budejovice	H	2-0	Johana, Kozuch
07/05/00	Boby Brno	A	0-3	
13/05/00	Bohemians Praha	H	2-0	Lazzaro Liuni, Kozuch
17/05/00	Banik Ostrava	A	0-3	

SPARTA PRAHA

CLUB DIRECTORY

AC Sparta Praha
Milady Horakove 1066/68, 170 00 Praha 7
tel - (02) 20570323 / fax - (02) 20571665
website - www.sparta.cz/
email - Football@Sparta.cz
Year of Formation - 1893
President - Ing. Vlastimil Kostal
Secretary - David Simon
Coach - Ivan Hasek
Stadium - AC Sparta Praha (21,362)

MAJOR HONOURS

League Championship - (25) 1926, 1927, 1932, 1936, 1938, 1946, 1948, 1952, 1954, 1965, 1967, 1984, 1985, 1987, 1988, 1989, 1990, 1991, 1993, 1994, 1995, 1997, 1998, 1999, 2000.
Domestic Cup - (9) 1964, 1972, 1976, 1980, 1984, 1988, 1989, 1992, 1996.

APPEARANCES 99/00

	P	Ap	(s)	Gls
Miroslav BARANEK	A	25	(2)	10
Jaromir BLAZEK	G	13		
Rene BOLF	D	15	(1)	1
Jan FLACHBART	M	1	(10)	
Milan FUKAL	D	23	(3)	7
Petr GABRIEL	D	25		2
Pavel HAPAL	M	3	(3)	2
Martin HASEK	M	17	(1)	
Michal HORNAK	D	15	(5)	
Jiri JAROSIK	M	13	(8)	3
Tomas JUN	A		(1)	
Vladimir LABANT (SVK)	D	10	(2)	2
Roman LENGYEL	M	2	(3)	
Vratislav LOKVENC	A	25		22
Jiri NOVOTNY	D	26	(1)	1
Pavel NOVOTNY	M	7	(5)	1
Josef OBAJDIN	A	13	(9)	5
Tomas POSTULKA	G	17		
Martin PROHASZKA (SVK)	A	2	(5)	1
Tomas ROSICKY	M	20	(4)	5
Horst SIEGL	A	16	(9)	10
Libor SIONKO	M	19	(6)	5
Vlastimil SVOBODA	M	5	(1)	
Zdenek SVOBODA	M	18	(5)	3

LEAGUE RESULTS 1999/2000

30/07/99	Viktoria Zizkov	H	2-1	Sionko, Labant (p)
07/08/99	SFC Opava	A	1-1	Sionko
14/08/99	FK Jablonec 97	H	3-0	Lokvenc, Sionko, Prohaszka (p)
22/08/99	FK Teplice	A	2-4	Baranek, Fukal
28/08/99	Dukla Pribram	H	2-1	Gabriel, Fukal
12/09/99	SK Ceske Budejovice	H	7-0	Lokvenc 2, Rosicky 2, Svoboda Z., Sionko, og (Penner)
18/09/99	Boby Brno	A	1-1	Obajdin
24/09/99	Bohemians Praha	H	0-0	
02/10/99	Banik Ostrava	A	3-0	Baranek 2, Jarosik
15/10/99	SK Hradec Kralove	H	3-1	Obajdin, Baranek, Fukal
23/10/99	Slovan Liberec	A	2-1	Obajdin, Fukal
29/10/99	Chmel Blsany	H	3-1	Labant (p), Obajdin, Baranek
08/11/99	Slavia Praha	A	1-2	Novotny P.
20/11/99	Sigma Olomouc	H	6-0	Siegl 2, Baranek, Lokvenc, Bolf, Fukal
28/11/99	Petra Drnovice	A	1-0	Lokvenc
04/12/99	Viktoria Zizkov	A	3-2	Lokvenc 2, Svoboda Z. (p)
19/02/00	SFC Opava	H	4-0	Hapal, Obajdin, Sionko, Lokvenc
27/02/00	FK Jablonec 97	A	2-0	Hapal (p), Lokvenc
04/03/00	FK Teplice	H	3-2	Baranek 2, Fukal
11/03/00	Dukla Pribram	A	3-1	Lokvenc 2, Svoboda Z.
18/03/00	SK Ceske Budejovice	A	4-1	Lokvenc 4
25/03/00	Boby Brno	H	3-0	Fukal, Siegl, Lokvenc
02/04/00	Bohemians Praha	A	1-0	Siegl
09/04/00	Banik Ostrava	H	2-0	Siegl, Rosicky
14/04/00	SK Hradec Kralove	A	2-0	Jarosik, Siegl
22/04/00	Slovan Liberec	H	2-1	Siegl, Lokvenc
30/04/00	Chmel Blsany	A	4-1	Lokvenc 2, Jarosik, Siegl
06/05/00	Slavia Praha	H	5-1	Lokvenc 2, Gabriel, Baranek, Novotny J.
13/05/00	Sigma Olomouc	A	1-1	Baranek
17/05/00	Petra Drnovice	H	5-0	Siegl 2, Rosicky 2, Lokvenc

FK TEPLICE

CLUB DIRECTORY

FK Teplice
Na Stinadlech 2796
415 01 Teplice
tel - (0417) 43795/23224
fax - (0417) 29017
website - www.fkteplice.cz/
email - fkteplice@vol.cz
Year of Formation - 1945
President - Stepan Popovic
Secretary - Rudolf Repka
Coach - Josef Pesice (00/01 - Petr Rada
Stadium - Stadion Na Stinadlech (18,500)

APPEARANCES 99/00

		P	Ap	(s)	Gls
Michal BILEK	M	20	(4)	5
Petr BRABEC	D	28	(1)	1
Radek DIVECKY	A	18	(9)	7
Petr FOUSEK	M	20	(4)	1
Zdeno FRTALA (SVK)	M	24		
Martin FRYDEK	M	19	(6)	
Michal HAJEK	M		(1)	
Pavel HOLOMEK	A	12	(3)	4
Jaromir JINDRACEK	M	6	(20)	1
Michal KOLOMAZNIK	M	26	(3)	5
Pavel KUCERA	G		(1)	
Tomas KUKOL	M	12	(11)	
Libor MACHACEK	G	30		
Ales PIKL	D	2	(2)	
Petr POKORNY	D	16		
Miroslav RADA	D	14	(1)	
Zbynek RAMPACEK	D	14		
Marian RIZEK	D	13		1
David SOURADA	A	2	(8)	
Dusan TESARIK	M	25	(4)	3
Stepan VACHOUSEK	A		(5)	
Pavel VERBIR	A	29		10

LEAGUE RESULTS 1999/2000

31/07/99	SFC Opava	H	1-1	Tesarik
06/08/99	FK Jablonec 97	A	1-3	Kolomaznik
15/08/99	Dukla Pribram	H	2-0	Divecky, Kolomaznik
22/08/99	Sparta Praha	H	4-2	Bilek 3 (1p), Divecky
29/08/99	SK Ceske Budejovice	A	1-3	Rizek
12/09/99	Boby Brno	H	2-1	Tesarik, Kolomaznik
20/09/99	Bohemians Praha	A	0-0	
26/09/99	Banik Ostrava	H	0-2	
04/10/99	SK Hradec Kralove	A	0-2	
17/10/99	Slovan Liberec	H	1-0	Jindracek
25/10/99	Chmel Blsany	A	2-0	Verbir 2
30/10/99	Slavia Praha	H	1-1	Verbir (p)
08/11/99	Sigma Olomouc	A	2-2	Bilek, Divecky
21/11/99	Petra Drnovice	H	2-2	Holomek 2
28/11/99	Viktoria Zizkov	A	1-3	Verbir (p)
05/12/99	SFC Opava	A	1-1	Divecky
19/02/00	FK Jablonec 97	H	2-0	Bilek, Verbir (p)
27/02/00	Dukla Pribram	A	0-3	
04/03/00	Sparta Praha	A	2-3	Verbir, Holomek
10/03/00	SK Ceske Budejovice	H	3-0	Divecky, Brabec, Tesarik
19/03/00	Boby Brno	A	1-2	Divecky
24/03/00	Bohemians Praha	H	2-0	Divecky, Holomek
02/04/00	Banik Ostrava	A	2-2	Verbir 2 (1p)
09/04/00	SK Hradec Kralove	H	1-1	Fousek
16/04/00	Slovan Liberec	A	0-2	
22/04/00	Chmel Blsany	H	0-0	
30/04/00	Slavia Praha	A	1-0	Verbir (p)
07/05/00	Sigma Olomouc	H	2-1	Verbir (p), Kolomaznik
13/05/00	Petra Drnovice	A	1-1	Kolomaznik
17/05/00	Viktoria Zizkov	H	0-0	

VIKTORIA ZIZKOV

CLUB DIRECTORY

FK Viktoria Zizkov
Seifertova trida, 130 00 Praha 3
tel - (02) 22722045   fax - (02) 22716295
website - www.fotbal.com/zizkov.htm
Year of Formation - 1903
President - Jiri Steinbroch
Secretary - Jiri Jechoutek
Coach - Petr Ulicny
Stadium - FK Viktoria (8,000)

MAJOR HONOURS
League Championship - (1) 1928.
Domestic Cup - (1) 1994.

APPEARANCES 99/00

		P	Ap	(s)	Gls
Tomas BURGER	M	1			
Jan BURYAN	D	21	(3)	1	
Kennedy CHIHURI (ZIM)	M	23	(3)	2	
Martin CUPR	D	10	(3)		
Roman GIBALA	M	16	(6)	3	
Rostislav HERTL	M	9	(4)		
Petr HOLOTA	M	8	(8)		
Radovan HROMADKO	A	14	(5)	3	
Tomas HUNAL	D	21	(1)		
Marek KINCL	A	22		15	
Tomas KLINKA	A	2	(3)		
Jiri KOBR	G	16			
Miroslav MIKULIK	D	19	(2)		
Antonin MLEJNSKY	D	15			
Jaromir NAVRATIL	M	6	(3)	2	
Pavol PAVLUS (SVK)	D		(1)		
Ales PIKL	D	23		5	
Petr PIZANOWSKI	G	14			
Jaromir PLOCEK	M	16	(8)	2	
Jiri SABOU	M	9	(4)	1	
Miroslav SEBESTA	A	3	(10)		
Miroslav SOVIC (SVK)	M	5	(2)		
Michal STAREC	D	5	(2)		
Ludek STRACENY	A	21		3	
Karel VALKOUN	A	2	(6)		
Pavel VELEBA	A		(2)		
Jan ZAKOPAL	D	21	(2)		
Pavel ZBOZINEK	M	8	(3)		

LEAGUE RESULTS 1999/2000

30/07/99	Sparta Praha	A	1-2	Navratil
08/08/99	SK Ceske Budejovice	H	1-1	Hromadko
14/08/99	Boby Brno	A	2-4	Gibala (p), Plocek
22/08/99	Bohemians Praha	H	2-2	Chihuri, Plocek
28/08/99	Banik Ostrava	A	1-1	Gibala
12/09/99	SK Hradec Kralove	H	2-1	Gibala, Navratil
17/09/99	Slovan Liberec	A	0-1	
26/09/99	Chmel Blsany	H	1-1	Kincl
04/10/99	Slavia Praha	A	1-3	Hromadko
17/10/99	Sigma Olomouc	H	3-3	Kincl 3
24/10/99	Petra Drnovice	A	0-1	
31/10/99	Dukla Pribram	A	2-5	Kincl 2
07/11/99	SFC Opava	H	3-2	Kincl 2, Pikl
21/11/99	FK Jablonec 97	A	0-3	
28/11/99	FK Teplice	H	3-1	Hromadko, Pikl, Straceny (p)
04/12/99	Sparta Praha	H	2-3	Kincl 2
19/02/00	SK Ceske Budejovice	A	0-1	
27/02/00	Boby Brno	H	1-0	Buryan
03/03/00	Bohemians Praha	A	0-1	
12/03/00	Banik Ostrava	H	3-1	Straceny, Pikl, Kincl
19/03/00	SK Hradec Kralove	A	0-0	
25/03/00	Slovan Liberec	H	0-0	
02/04/00	Chmel Blsany	A	2-0	Chihuri, Kincl
07/04/00	Slavia Praha	H	3-1	Sabou, Straceny, Pikl
16/04/00	Sigma Olomouc	A	0-2	
22/04/00	Petra Drnovice	H	2-0	Pikl, Kincl
30/04/00	Dukla Pribram	H	1-1	Kincl
07/05/00	SFC Opava	A	1-0	Kincl
13/05/00	FK Jablonec 97	H	0-0	
17/05/00	FK Teplice	A	0-0	

DENMARK

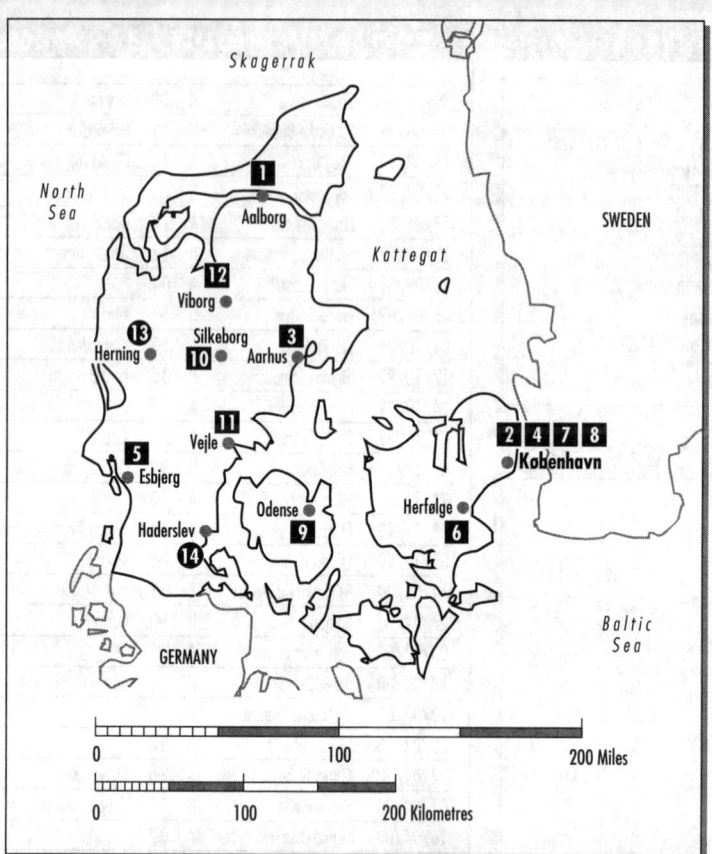

1	AAB	289
2	AB	290
3	AGF	291
4	BRØNDBY IF	292
5	ESBJERG FB	293
6	HERFØLGE BK	294
7	FC KØBENHAVN	295
8	LYNGBY FC	296

9	OB	297
10	SILKEBORG IF	298
11	VEJLE BK	299
12	VIBORG FF	300
Promoted clubs		
13	FC MIDTJYLLAND	
14	HADERSLEV FK	

POINTLESS AND GOALLESS AT EURO 2000

Miracle comes true for village 'nobodies'

FEDERATION DIRECTORY

Dansk Boldspil Union
Idraettens Hus, Brøndby stadion 20, 2605 Brøndby

tel - (43) 262222   Year of Formation - 1889
fax - (43) 262245   President - Poul Hyldgaard
website - www.dbu.dk   Secretary - Jim Stjerne Hansen

Stadium - Parken, København (41,641)

Herfølge BK's triumph in the first Danish championship of the 21st century was nothing short of miraculous. Even Hans Christian Andersen would have been hard pressed to put together a tale that contained so much fantasy and romance.

Not one of the 5,200 inhabitants of Herfølge, a small village near Copenhagen, could have imagined in their wildest dreams that their local club might one day become the national champions. Since the club's first promotion to the top division in 1981, Herfølge had never finished higher than fourth, never qualified for Europe, never won a thing.

Yet, in 1999/2000, against all conceivable odds, they landed the biggest prize of all. There can be no rational explanation for their success. The Superliga contained several clubs which dwarfed Herfølge in terms of professionalism, spending power and quality of personnel. But Brøndby, AaB and the rest were all powerless to prevent the minnows from carving their name in history.

The catalyst for Herfølge's rags-to-riches rise was unquestionably their coach, John "Faxe" Jensen, the only household name amidst a gathering of 'nobodies'. The former Danish international midfielder, goalscoring hero of the 1992 European Championship final, decided to leave Brøndby, where he had won eight Danish championships, and take up the position of Herfølge player/coach. His coaching experience was negligible, but straight away it was obvious that he possessed all the right characteristics for the job.

Herfølge first rose to the top of the table - as they had done, briefly, the previous season - after ten rounds, by which stage Jensen and co. had accumulated six wins, four draws and no defeats. It all looked very promising, but when the first defeat came - 0-4 away to defending champions AaB - two more soon followed, and that, so everybody thought, would be the end of Herfølge's challenge. But no sooner had they been written off than the minnows put together another

LEAGUE CHAMPIONSHIP RESULTS 99/00

		1	2	3	4	5	6	7	8	9	10	11	12
1	AaB		2-2	1-0	3-1	7-1	4-0	0-0	0-2	1-2	2-1	7-1	2-0
			0-2	1-1	3-1			1-1			1-0		1-2
2	AB	1-1		1-0	2-0	1-2	2-2	1-2	3-0	0-2	1-1	1-1	6-0
				2-3	2-0		3-0	0-2	2-2		2-0		
3	AGF	1-1	2-2		0-2	1-0	1-1	1-0	3-0	3-3	2-1	1-2	0-4
						4-3	2-3	1-0		0-1		2-0	
4	Brøndby IF	1-0	3-0	3-0		3-1	2-2	3-1	1-0	2-1	1-0	4-0	4-1
				2-0		2-3	5-0	1-1	2-2		0-0		
5	Esbjerg FB	0-0	0-1	0-1	2-0		1-2	2-0	2-3	2-0	0-3	1-1	1-2
		0-0	0-0							0-2		3-1	1-2
6	Herfølge BK	3-1	1-2	1-1	0-2	2-0		1-1	4-1	1-0	3-2	1-1	2-1
		0-2				3-2			3-3	4-1	3-1	3-2	
7	FC København	0-2	1-2	2-1	1-1	3-0	0-1		1-2	1-0	4-1	1-0	2-1
		0-0				3-1	2-0			1-1		1-4	
8	Lyngby FC	3-2	0-2	3-1	3-0	5-1	1-2	1-0		2-0	1-3	5-1	1-3
				3-0		4-6	1-0	0-4			0-0	0-1	
9	OB	2-2	0-3	4-0	2-1	4-1	0-1	2-0	0-0		0-4	1-1	1-1
		1-4	1-1		1-1				1-3				0-1
10	Silkeborg IF	1-1	1-0	2-0	1-1	4-0	1-1	0-0	3-0	0-1		2-2	1-1
				4-1		2-0		2-1	1-0				1-0
11	Vejle BK	2-2	0-0	1-1	0-4	2-1	0-2	2-7	4-0	1-1	0-4		2-3
		1-1	3-1	1-1						0-1	2-1		0-2
12	Viborg FF	7-2	1-3	1-1	2-0	2-3	1-0	2-1	2-0	2-4	1-1	3-0	
			2-1	1-1	2-2			1-1	0-2				

LEAGUE CHAMPIONSHIP FINAL TABLE 99/00

			Home				Away				Total					
		Pd	W	D	L	F	A	W	D	L	F	A	W	D	L	F	A	PT	GD
1	Herfølge BK	33	10	4	3	35	23	6	4	6	17	26	16	8	9	52	49	56	3
2	Brøndby IF	33	12	4	1	39	12	3	5	8	17	25	15	9	9	56	37	54	19
3	AB	33	7	5	5	30	18	7	5	4	22	17	14	10	9	52	35	52	17
4	Viborg FF	33	7	5	4	30	22	8	2	7	26	28	15	7	11	56	50	52	6
5	AaB	33	9	4	4	36	17	3	9	4	21	23	12	13	8	57	40	49	17
6	Silkeborg IF	33	9	6	1	26	9	4	4	9	23	24	13	10	10	49	33	49	16
7	Lyngby FC	33	9	1	7	33	26	5	4	7	18	29	14	5	14	51	55	47	-4
8	FC København	33	8	3	5	23	17	4	5	8	21	20	12	8	13	44	37	44	7
9	OB	33	4	6	6	20	24	7	4	6	22	20	11	10	12	42	44	43	-2
10	AGF	33	7	4	5	24	23	2	5	10	12	32	9	9	15	36	55	36	-19
11	Vejle BK	33	4	6	7	21	32	3	5	8	17	36	7	11	15	38	68	32	-30
12	Esbjerg FB	33	4	4	8	15	18	4	0	13	25	52	8	4	21	40	70	28	-30

sparkling run of victories - a run which lifted them a full six points clear of inconsistent pursuers Brøndby at the winter break.

It was only then that Herfølge began to be considered as serious championship contenders, but most pundits remained convinced that they would eventually crack. That prophecy seemed to come true when Jensen's men went through a torrid patch in March and April, losing six games out of nine, the last of them 5-0 away to Brøndby. Logically, that should have been the end of Herfølge's dream, but just as Brøndby had taken over pole position, they began to lose their form. The same applied to AaB, who had also slowly crept into contention.

And so it was that Herfølge came back to reclaim the lead and, ultimately, take the title. The championship was made mathematically safe in the penultimate round with a 1-1 draw away to Silkeborg thanks to Brøndby's simultaneous 0-2 defeat at AB. Brøndby would recover to beat AaB in their final fixture and take the cherished runners-up spot, but the big prize, and all the plaudits, went to the miracle men from Herfølge.

Jensen was showered with praise from all quarters as he celebrated yet another title. He had inspired his team to surpass themselves several times over, and players such as Jesper Falck, Kenneth Jensen, Jens Madsen and, especially, Steven Lüstü suddenly shed their 'journeyman' tags to become fêted throughout the land.

Commentators of a less romantic persuasion pointed out that Herfølge had won the title largely through the deficiencies of others. The figures backed them up. On an average of points won per games played, Brøndby had the worst record of any Danish champions. Their +3 goal

difference was smaller than that of any previous winner, and no team had ever scooped the title before with nine defeats.

There was another major shock as Viborg, who, like Herfølge, had never achieved anything of note, captured the Danish Cup. A single goal from their Swedish import Hans Eklund (runner-up to Silkeborg's Peter Lassen in the Superliga goal charts) was enough to take the spoils in the final against AaB, who thus ended the season empty-handed. The result of the final was not altogether surprising given that Viborg had thrashed AaB 7-2 in the league ten days earlier, but it was greeted with great dismay by the fans of the Aalborg club, beaten finalists also the previous year against AB.

AaB's best player in the closing weeks of the season was Danish international striker Mikkel Beck, who had arrived on loan from Derby County. Brøndby also borrowed a couple of foreign-based luminaries in Peter Møller (from Oviedo) and Stig Inge Bjørnebye (from Liverpool), while strugglers AGF reaped considerable dividends by temporarily recalling Stig Tøfting from MSV Duisburg. The beefy midfielder was a major factor in helping AGF to avoid the drop - something Vejle were unable to do despite the assistance of their foreign-based 'joker', Erik Bo Andersen, whose seven goals in 14 games

INTERNATIONAL HONOURS

World Cup Finals appearances: 1986 (2nd round), 1998 (qtr-finals)

European Championship appearances: 1964 (4th), 1984 (semi-finals), 1988, 1992 (Winners), 1996, 2000

TOP SCORERS

16	Peter LASSEN (Silkeborg IF)
15	Hans EKLUND (Viborg FF)
14	Søren ANDERSEN (OB)
	Søren FEDERIKSEN (AaB)
13	Bent CHRISTENSEN (Brøndby IF)
	Heine FERNANDEZ (Viborg FF)
	Henrik PEDERSEN (Silkeborg IF)
10	Jesper FALCK (Herfølge BK)
	Kenneth JENSEN (Herfølge BK)
	Ruben BAGGER (Brøndby IF)

NATIONAL TEAM RESULTS 99/00

18/08/99	Holland	H	Copenhagen	0-0	
04/09/99	Switzerland (ECQ)	H	Copenhagen	2-1	Nielsen A. (54), Tomasson (81)
08/09/99	Italy (ECQ)	A	Naples	3-2	Jørgensen (39p), Wieghorst (57), Tomasson (64)
10/10/99	Iran	H	Copenhagen	0-0	
13/11/99	Israel (ECQ)	A	Tel-Aviv	5-0	Tomasson (2, 34), Tøfting (67),
					Jørgensen (69), Nielsen B.S. (73)
17/11/99	Israel (ECQ)	H	Copenhagen	3-0	Sand (3), Nielsen B.S. (14), Tomasson (65)
29/03/00	Portugal	A	Leiria	1-2	Tomasson (4)
26/04/00	Sweden	H	Copenhagen	0-1	
03/06/00	Belgium	H	Copenhagen	2-2	Tomasson (37), Schmeichel (60p)
11/06/00	France (ECF)	N	Bruges	0-3	
16/06/00	Holland (ECF)	A	Rotterdam	0-3	
21/06/00	Czech Republic (ECF)	N	Liège	0-2	

proved to be in vain as his new team dropped out of the Superliga alongside Esbjerg.

It was AGF's ability to beat their fellow strugglers which kept them up. They were even obliged to replay a game in which they had controversially defeated Esbjerg 2-1 as a result of a bizarre refereeing decision. The re-staging of the match set a dangerous precedent but fortunately AGF won the second game too, 1-0, so the relegation issue was unaffected.

Returning to the fairytale theme, the Second Division produced another unlikely story with the promotion of Haderslev, a village club with a tiny stadium that possesses no floodlights and very few seats. The other newcomers to the Superliga were FC Midtjylland, the merger club formed from Ikast and Herning. They led the table from start to finish, winning 24 of their 30 matches.

There was a significant increase in Superliga attendances, with an average of 5,838 (compared to 4,975 the previous season) taking the aggregate to above one million for the first time. The main reason for this upturn was the large number of matches which had a significant bearing on the title race, European qualification or relegation. As ever, the biggest crowd attended the FC Copenhagen v Brøndby derby (28,818). The two reverse fixtures, at the Brøndby Stadion, attracted 16,163 and 19,283 (a stadium record).

DOMESTIC CUP 99/00

FOURTH ROUND
B1913 3, FC Midtjylland 6
BK Frem 1, Esbjerg FB 3
Haderslev FK 3, B93 4
AC Horsens 0, Aarhus Fremad 2
IF32 Glostrup 2, AGF 1
Kolding IF 0, FC København 5
Køge BK 2, Silkeborg IF 2 (aet; 2-4 on pens.)
Måløv BK 3, BK Fremad Amager 4
Svendborg FB 0, Viborg FF 2
Virum-Sorgenfri 0, OB 1
byes - AaB, AB, Brøndby IF, Herfølge BK, Lyngby FC, Vejle BK

FIFTH ROUND
FC Aarhus 3, Vejle BK 2 (aet)
AB 1, Herfølge BK 0
B93 0, Brøndby IF 4
Esbjerg FB 1, OB 0

BK Fremad Amager 3, Viborg FF 9
IF 32 Glostrup 2, Lyngby FC 4
FC København 2, Silkeborg IF 0
FC Midtjylland 0, AaB 0 (aet; 4-5 on pens.)

QUARTER-FINALS
FC Aarhus 0, Brøndby IF 1 (Christensen 85)
Esbjerg FB 1 (Alkhag 79),
AaB 2 (Gaarde 62, Frederiksen 68)
FC København 1 (Zuma 15),
AB 1 (Daugaard 70) (aet; 4-5 on pens.)
Lyngby FC 2 (August 63, Vinzents 93),
Viborg FF 3 (Conteh 87, 100, Fernandez 113) (aet)

SEMI-FINALS
AB 1 (Løvenkrands P. 49), AaB 1 (Andersson 80)
AaB 2 (Beck 8p, 76), AB 1 (Stokholm 28)
(AaB 3-2)

Viborg FF 1 (Fernandez 78p), Brøndby IF 0
Brøndby IF 1 (Frandsen 43og), Viborg FF 0 (aet)
(1-1; Viborg FF 5-4 on pens.)

FINAL
01/06/2000, Copenhagen
VIBORG FF 1 Eklund (9)
AAB 0
referee - Fisker
VIBORG FF - Onyszko, Hamm, Sørensen, Pedersen R.,
Larsen, Poulsen (Kaergaard 88), Frandsen, Nielsen
J.G., Winther (Kjaergaard 34), Eklund, Fernandez
(Nørlund 63).
AAB - Nielsen; Priske, Boye, Matovac, Jessen
(Boelum 87), Andersson (Frederiksen 61),
Solbakken, Rasmussen (Gaardsøe 46), Gaarde,
Oper, Beck.

NATIONAL TEAM APPEARANCES 99/00

Coach - Bo JOHANSSON	HOL	SUI	ITA	IRN	ISR	ISR	POR	SWE	BEL	FRA	HOL	CZE	Cps	Gls
Peter SCHMEICHEL (18/11/63) - Sporting CP (POR)	G	G	G	G	G	G19	G	G	G	G	G	G	124	1
Søren COLDING (02/09/72) - Brøndby IF	D	s51	D	D			s60	s81	D	D		s68	26	-
René HENRIKSEN (27/08/69) - AB/Panathinaikos (GRE)	D	D	D	D	D	D	D	D	D	D	D	D	20	-
Jes HØGH (07/05/66) - Chelsea (ENG)	D	D	D	D	D	D	D	D					57	1
Jan HEINTZE (17/08/63) - PSV (HOL)	D46	D	D	D46	D	D	D46	D	D	D	D	D68	65	2
Thomas HELVEG (24/06/71) - Milan (ITA)	M	D	M52	M	D	D71	D	D81			s82	D	52	2
Bjarne GOLDBAEK (06/10/68) - Chelsea (ENG)/Fulham (ENG)	M46	M51	s52	M85	s78		s46		s77			M	24	-
Stig TØFTING (14/08/69) - MSV Duisburg (GER)/AGF	M84	M	M52	M74	M78	M	M60	M56	s30	M72	s61	M	22	2
Martin JØRGENSEN (06/10/75) - Udinese (ITA)	M53	M	M		M86	M	M71			s72			24	3
Jon Dahl TOMASSON (29/08/76) - Feyenoord (HOL)	A58	A88	A86	A	A79	A	A46	A	A46	A79	A	A	21	8
Ebbe SAND (19/07/72) - FC Schalke 04 (GER)	A	A	A	A75	A	A	A	A46	A46	A	A		26	5
Michael SCHJØNBERG (19/01/67) - 1.FC Kaiserslautern (GER)	s46		s86	s46	s86	s83	s46	M81	s77	D	D82	D	44	3
Carsten FREDGAARD (20/05/76) - Sunderland (ENG)	s46												1	-
Morten WIEGHORST (25/02/71) - Celtic (SCO)	s53	s88	s52	s74									18	3
Peter MØLLER (23/03/72) - Real Oviedo (ESP)	s58												17	3
Jacob LAURSEN (06/10/71) - Derby County (ENG)	s84				s71								25	-
Allan NIELSEN (13/03/71) - Tottenham Hotspur (ENG)		M80	M	M					M	M	M61		35	7
Brian Steen NIELSEN (28/12/68) - AB		s80			M	M	M85	M	M30		s67	M	52	2
Søren ANDERSEN (31/01/70) - OB			s75	s79				s81					12	-
Per FRANDSEN (06/02/70) - Blackburn Rovers (ENG)			s85										19	-
Jesper GRØNKJAER (12/08/77) - Ajax (HOL)					M	M83	M46	M	M	M	M	M	12	-
Thomas SØRENSEN (12/06/76) - Sunderland (ENG)					s19								1	-
Miklos MOLNAR (10/04/70) - Kansas City Wizards (USA)								s46		s46		s74	18	2
Claus JENSEN (29/04/77) - Bolton Wanderers (ENG)							s71						1	-
Martin LAURSEN (26/07/77) - Verona (ITA)							s85	s56	D77				3	-
Mikkel BECK (12/05/73) - AaB								s46		s79		A74	19	3
Morten BISGAARD (25/06/74) - Udinese (ITA)									M77	M72	M		5	-
Thomas GRAVESEN (11/03/76) - Hamburger SV (GER)									s46	s72	M67		8	-

The domestic league might have pulled the crowds in but there was very little supplementary revenue generated by the European club competitions. It was a disastrous season all round for the Danish participants, with both AaB and Brøndby failing to reach the Champions' League and not one of the four teams managing to progress beyond the first round of the UEFA Cup.

The Danish national side managed to dispel some of the gloom by qualifying for their fifth successive European Championship finals. It looked a very tall order when they approached their final two fixtures needing victories against Switzerland at home and Italy away. But the signs of recovery which had emerged at the end of the previous

season were not misleading and after overcoming the Swiss 2-1 in Copenhagen, Denmark produced one of their greatest-ever performances by coming from two goals down in Naples to beat Italy 3-2.

Denmark's match-winner in both games was young Feyenoord striker Jon Dahl Tomasson, and he was on target twice more two months later to begin the rout of Israel which secured the Danes' passage to the Low Countries via the play-offs. Bo Johansson's team were on top of the world after adding a 3-0 home win to the spectacular 5-0 triumph in Tel-Aviv, and inevitably expectations grew that the team could go on to great things at the finals.

But then came the draw in Brussels and hopes quickly

faded. Denmark could not have been dealt a less appealing hand. Their task was to survive a first-round group that contained Holland, France and the Czech Republic. It was a mission improbable, if not impossible, and confidence was further drained by a poor run of results in the build-up, the only highlight of which was goalkeeper Peter Schmeichel earning a draw with Belgium by scoring his first international goal from the penalty spot.

Schmeichel, who had extended his massive personal haul of silverware by helping Sporting to their long-awaited Portuguese title, had a reasonable European Championship, but the only other Dane who looked up to the job was young Ajax winger Jesper Grønkjaer, who offered glimpses of the sort of individual talent once plentifully supplied by the Laudrup brothers.

Three defeats and a goal-balance of 0-8 told the full horror-story of Denmark's Euro 2000 campaign. They never stood a chance. Even if key men Martin Jørgensen, Jes Høgh and Thomas Helveg had been fully fit, the Danes would have had major difficulties against opponents of such quality. Nevertheless, it was a sad way for coach Johansson to end his time in office. He, after all, had been the architect of Denmark's best-ever World Cup performance two years earlier.

Now the baton has been passed on to the 'Dream Team' of Morten Olsen and his assistant Michael Laudrup. Qualification for the 2002 World Cup is their goal, but to achieve that the team will have to be strengthened in all areas, especially in attack where the hunt for that elusive "new Elkjaer" goes on and on and on...

EUROPEAN CUPS 99/00

CHAMPIONS' CUP
● AAB
Qualifying round DYNAMO KYIV (UKR)
H 1-2 Strandli (55)
Nielsen, Priske, Baelum, Matovac, Jessen, Gaarde, Thomsen (Frederiksen 78), Andersson, Gaardsøe (Rasmussen 66), Oper, Strandli.
A 2-2 Oper (9), Gaarde (47)
Nielsen. Priske, Baelum, Matovac, Jessen, Oper, Thomsen, Andersson, Gaarde, Gaardsøe, Strandli.

● BRØNDBY IF
Preliminary round 2 SLOGA JUGOMAGNAT SKOPJE (MAC)
A 1-0 Daugaard (15)
Krogh M., Colding, Da Silva, Nielsen, Smith, Bjur, Ravn (Olsen 77), Daugaard, Jensen M., Christensen (Madsen 62), Bagger (Krogh S. 81).
H 1-0 Daugaard (4p)
Krogh M., Colding, Da Silva, Nielsen, Smith, Ravn, Daugaard, Jensen M. (Olsen 86), Bjur, Madsen (Christensen 80), Bagger (Lindrup 75).

Qualifying round BOAVISTA FC (POR)
H 1-2 Smith (65)
Krogh M., Colding, Da Silva, Nielsen, Smith, Ravn (Olsen 79), Daugaard (Jensen M. 74), Madsen (Skarbalius 46), Bjur, Christensen, Bagger.
A 2-4 (aet) Christensen (47), Bjur (90)
Krogh M., Colding, Nielsen, Johansen, Smith, Bjur, Daugaard, Ravn, Bagger, Christensen (Krogh S. 84), Graulund (Madsen 71).

UEFA CUP
● AAB
1st round UDINESE (ITA)
A 0-1
Nielsen, Priske, Baelum, Matovac, Jessen, Thomsen, Solbakken, Andersson, Gaarde, Oper, Strandli.
H 1-2 Matovac (71)
Nielsen, Priske, Baelum, Matovac, Jessen, Thomsen, Solbakken, Andersson, Rasmussen (Gaarde 59), Frederiksen (Oper 59), Strandli.

● AB
1st round GRASSHOPPER-CLUB ZÜRICH (SUI)
H 0-2
Hoffmann, Olesen, Frank, Albrechtsen, Michaelsen, Bjur, Nielsen B.S., Stokholm, Sørensen, Daugaard, Sule.
A 1-1 Daugaard (31)
Hoffmann, Olesen, Frank, Albrechtsen (Metin 75), Daugaard, Rasmussen, Bjur, Nielsen B.S., Sørensen (Løvenkrands T. 46), Nielsen A. (Knudsen 64), Hermansen.

● BRØNDBY IF
1st round AMICA WRONKI (POL)
A 0-2
Krogh M., Colding, Johansen, Nielsen, Smith, Bjur, Lindrup (Olsen 60), Daugaard, Jensen, Bagger, Christensen (Graulund 69).
H 4-3 Madsen (35, 76), Da Silva (54), Christensen (78)
Krogh M., Colding, Da Silva, Nielsen, Smith, Bjur, Ravn (Jensen 71), Daugaard (Johansen 76), Lindrup (Bagger 69), Madsen, Christensen.

● LYNGBY FC
Qualifying round BIRKIRKARA (MLT)
H 7-0 Hermansen (29, 90), Jensen (33), Larsen (47), Magleby (68), Lüthje (82), Havlykke (87)
Fahlström, Vinzents, Birn, Petersen M. (Bidstrup 80), Larsen L.L., Hindsberg (Christensen 74), Jensen, Johansen (Lüthje 66), Magleby, Havlykke, Hermansen.
A 0-0
Fahlström, Vinzents, Andie, Marvits, Larsen L.L., Hindsberg, Lüthje (Christensen 23), Bidstrup, Magleby (Petersen R.B. 74), Tengstedt, Hermansen.

1st round LOKOMOTIV MOSKVA (RUS)
H 1-2 Arifulin (69og)
Fahlström, Vinzents, Birn, Petersen M., Larsen L.L., Hindsberg (Havlykke 45), Johansen, Bidstrup (Andie 78), Jensen, Hermansen.
A 0-3
Fahlström, Vinzents (Christensen 58), Birn, Petersen M., Larsen L.L., Hindsberg, Johansen, Bosun, Magleby, Tengstedt (Andie 58), Hermansen (Lüthje 76).

PLAYERS OF THE SEASON

STEVEN LÜSTÜ
Herfølge's championship victory was very much a team effort but if there was one prominent individual other than coach John Jensen who deserved a special mention, it was centre-back Steven Lüstü. An ever-present at the club since arriving from Naestved in 1993, he added the final happy ending to the fairytale of Herfølge's season by scoring his very first league goal for the club in the dying seconds of the last game of the season, against FC Copenhagen. It was a fitting finale, not just for the player but also for the team because it earned them a 1-1 draw and prevented their finest hour from being spoiled by a defeat. Lüstü was on the shortlist for Denmark's Euro 2000 squad but didn't quite make it. Some believed that his remarkable pace - he was Denmark's 100m champion in his youth - would have been an asset to the defence but it was not to be. Now he yearns for the chance to prove himself with a foreign club.

MARTIN LAURSEN
As one Laursen quit the Danish national team, another one arrived. No sooner had Derby defender Jacob Laursen voluntarily closed the chapter on his international career than Martin Laursen, of Italian club Verona, promptly announced himself as a prime candidate to replace him. Once he had settled in, the 23-year-old had a very impressive first season in Serie A, having joined Verona from Silkeborg, where, coincidentally, he learned his trade under coach Preben Elkjaer (an Italian championship-winner with Verona in 1985). He made his international début against Portugal in March and would have appeared at Euro 2000 but for an injury which prevented him from playing in any of Denmark's first-round games.

PROMOTED CLUBS 99/00

SECOND DIVISION FINAL TABLE

		Pd	W	D	L	F	A	Pt	GD
1	**FC Midtjylland**	30	24	4	2	78	17	76	61
2	**Haderslev FK**	30	19	5	6	67	42	62	25
3	B93	30	18	7	5	69	39	61	30
4	Køge BK	30	15	8	7	65	40	53	25
5	AC Horsens	30	14	8	8	57	31	50	26
6	Randers Freja FC	30	15	4	11	57	49	49	8
7	BK Frem	30	12	9	9	56	49	45	7
8	Farum BK	30	12	6	12	48	58	42	-10
9	Hvidovre IF	30	11	7	12	55	52	40	3
10	Ølstykke FC	30	9	9	12	42	60	36	-18
11	BK Fremad Amager	30	10	5	15	43	48	35	-5
12	FC Aarhus	30	8	11	11	38	43	35	-5
13	Dalum IF	30	8	8	14	35	57	32	-22
14	Svendborg FB	30	5	5	20	28	58	20	-30
15	FC Fredericia	30	4	5	21	24	61	17	-37
16	B1909	30	3	5	22	32	90	14	-58

CLUB DIRECTORIES

FC Midtjylland
Mercurvej 501, 7400 Herning
tel - (96) 271040
fax - (96) 271041
website - www.fc-mj.dk
Year of Formation - 1999
Chairman - Johnny Rune
Secretary - Jens Ørgaard
Coach - Ove Pedersen
Stadium - Ikast Stadion (15,000)

Haderslev Fodboldklub
Christiansfeldvej 37, 6100 Haderslev
tel - (74) 521499
fax - (74) 524699
website - www.hfk-haderslev.dk
email - post@hfk-haderslev.dk
Year of Formation - 1906
Chairman - Teddy Pedersen
Secretary - Poul Henriksen
Coach - Frank Andersen
Stadium - Haderslev Stadion (5,000)

AAB

CLUB DIRECTORY

Aalborg Boldspilklub A/S
Hornevej 2, 9220 Aalborg Øst
Year of Formation - 1885
tel - (98) 157222 / fax - (98) 153334
website - www.aalborg-bk.dk
email - aab@dbu.dk
Chairman - Ole Mølgaard
Secretary - Børge Bach
Coach - Hans Backe (00/01 - Peter Rudbaek)
Stadium - Aalborg Stadion (13,374)

MAJOR HONOURS
League Championship - (2) 1995, 1999.
Domestic Cup - (2) 1966, 1970.

APPEARANCES 99/00

	P	Ap	(s)	Gls
Anders ANDERSSON (SWE)	M	29		6
Thomas AUGUSTINUSSEN	A		(1)	
Thomas BAELUM	D	30		
Mikkel BECK	A	10		8
Torben BOYE	D	10	(6)	
Søren FREDERIKSEN	A	28	(5)	14
Allan GAARDE	M	26	(5)	3
Thomas GAARDSØE	M	3	(15)	2
Kent HANGAARD	A		(5)	
Jens JESSEN	D	30		4
Jacob KRÜGER	D	8	(1)	
Jacob LAURSEN	A		(1)	
Jozo MATOVAC (SWE)	D	29		2
Jimmy NIELSEN	G	33		
Andres OPER (EST)	A	18	(12)	7
Jari PEDERSEN	A	3	(4)	
Brian PRISKE	D	25	(2)	1
Henrik RASMUSSEN	M	24	(4)	2
Ståle SOLBAKKEN (NOR)	M	28		5
Frank STRANDLI (NOR)	A	12	(2)	
Lars THOMSEN	M	13	(3)	3
Peter TRANBERG	M	4	(10)	

LEAGUE RESULTS 1999/2000

25/07/99	Herfølge BK	A	1-3	Solbakken
02/08/99	Viborg FF	H	2-0	Matovac, Oper
06/08/99	FC København	A	2-0	Oper, Frederiksen
15/08/99	Silkeborg IF	H	2-1	Jessen 2
21/08/99	AGF	H	1-0	Gaarde
29/08/99	OB	A	2-2	Gaarde, Frederiksen
10/09/99	Lyngby FC	H	0-2	
19/09/99	Vejle BK	A	2-2	Andersson, Priske
26/09/99	Brøndby IF	H	3-1	Frederiksen 2, Matovac
06/10/99	AB	H	2-2	Thomsen, Frederiksen
13/10/99	Herfølge BK	H	4-0	Oper 2, Andersson, Solbakken
17/10/99	Lyngby FC	A	2-3	Thomsen, Frederiksen
20/10/99	Esbjerg FB	A	0-0	
24/10/99	Brøndby IF	H	3-1	Oper, Jessen, Thomsen
01/11/99	AGF	A	1-1	Jessen
08/11/99	Viborg FF	H	1-2	Frederiksen
21/11/99	Vejle BK	A	1-1	Solbakken
28/11/99	AB	A	1-1	Solbakken
12/03/00	FC København	H	0-0	
20/03/00	Silkeborg IF	A	1-1	Frederiksen
26/03/00	OB	H	1-2	Andersson
02/04/00	Esbjerg FB	A	0-0	
09/04/00	Lyngby FC	H	1-1	Gaardsøe
16/04/00	Herfølge BK	A	2-0	Beck, Gaarde
20/04/00	Esbjerg FB	H	7-1	Beck 3, Solbakken, Frederiksen, Andersson 2
23/04/00	OB	A	4-1	Frederiksen, Beck 2, Andersson
01/05/00	Silkeborg IF	H	1-0	Frederiksen
07/05/00	FC København	A	0-0	
10/05/00	AB	H	0-2	
14/05/00	Vejle BK	H	7-1	Rasmussen, Beck, Frederiksen 2, Oper 2, Gaardsøe
21/05/00	Viborg FF	A	2-7	Beck, Frederiksen
25/05/00	AGF	H	1-1	Rasmussen
28/05/00	Brøndby IF	A	0-1	

AB

CLUB DIRECTORY

Akademisk Boldklub
Skovdiget 1, 2880 Bagsvaerd
tel - (44) 989842 / fax - (44) 989733
website - www.ab.co.dk
Year of Formation - 1889
Chairman - Mogens Flagstad
Secretary - Per Frimann
Coach - Ole Mørch; Peter Frandsen
Stadium - Gladsaxe Idraetspark (13,800)

MAJOR HONOURS
League Championship - (9) 1919, 1921, 1937,
1943, 1945, 1947, 1951, 1952, 1967.
Domestic Cup - (1) 1999.

APPEARANCES 99/00

		P	Ap	(s)	Gls
Martin ALBRECHTSEN	D	30		(1)	1
Jan BJUR	D	29			3
Rasmus DAUGAARD	A	14		(12)	6
Peter FRANK	D	10		(1)	
René HENRIKSEN	D	5			
Chris HERMANSEN	A	16		(2)	5
Jan HOFFMANN	G	33			
Nikolaj HUST	D			(2)	
Michael JOHANSEN	D			(1)	
Rasmus JØRGENSEN	M			(1)	
Peter KNUDSEN	M	5		(11)	
Lars Bo LARSEN	D	17			
Peter LØVENKRANDS	A	8		(6)	5
Tommy LØVENKRANDS	A	13		(9)	3
Kaan METIN	A	3		(13)	3
Jan MICHAELSEN	M	25			6
Alex NIELSEN	A	5		(9)	1
Brian Steen NIELSEN	M	27			5
Allan OLESEN	D	32			
Peter RASMUSSEN	M	29			7
Nicolai STOKHOLM	M	19		(11)	
Abdul SULE (NIG)	A	25		(1)	6
Jesper SØRENSEN	M	18		(8)	1
Kristoffer AAGAARD	A			(1)	

LEAGUE RESULTS 1999/2000

25/07/99	AGF	H	1-0	Rasmussen
01/08/99	OB	A	3-0	Sule, Daugaard, Rasmussen
08/08/99	Lyngby FC	H	3-0	Rasmussen, Nielsen B.S., Hermansen
15/08/99	Vejle BK	A	0-0	
21/08/99	Brøndby IF	H	2-0	Bjur, Michaelsen
29/08/99	Esbjerg FB	A	1-0	Sørensen
12/09/99	Silkeborg IF	H	1-1	Daugaard
19/09/99	Herfølge BK	H	2-2	Hermansen, Rasmussen
26/09/99	Viborg FF	A	3-1	Rasmussen, Daugaard, Løvenkrands T.
03/10/99	FC København	H	1-2	Hermansen
06/10/99	AaB	A	2-2	Metin, Løvenkrands T.
13/10/99	Esbjerg FB	H	1-2	Rasmussen
18/10/99	Herfølge BK	A	2-1	Hermansen, Metin
24/10/99	Lyngby FC	H	2-2	Rasmussen, Sule
31/10/99	Brøndby IF	A	0-3	
07/11/99	AGF	H	2-3	Nielsen B.S. (p), Bjur
21/11/99	Viborg FF	A	1-2	Løvenkrands T.
28/11/99	AaB	H	1-1	Hermansen
12/03/00	Vejle BK	A	1-3	Bjur
19/03/00	FC København	A	2-1	Metin, Michaelsen
26/03/00	Silkeborg IF	H	2-0	Daugaard 2
02/04/00	OB	A	1-1	Michaelsen
09/04/00	Herfølge BK	H	3-0	Sule, Nielsen B.S. 2 (1p)
16/04/00	Esbjerg FB	A	0-0	
20/04/00	OB	H	0-2	
23/04/00	Silkeborg IF	A	0-1	
30/04/00	FC København	H	0-2	
07/05/00	Vejle BK	H	1-1	Albrechtsen
10/05/00	AaB	A	2-0	Sule, Michaelsen
14/05/00	Viborg FF	H	6-0	Løvenkrands P. 3, Michaelsen, Sule, Daugaard
21/05/00	AGF	A	2-2	Sule, Michaelsen
25/05/00	Brøndby IF	H	2-0	Løvenkrands P. 2
28/05/00	Lyngby FC	A	2-0	Nielsen B.S., Nielsen A.

AGF

CLUB DIRECTORY

Aarhus Gymnastik Forening af 1880
Fredensvang, Terp Skovvej 16-18, 8260 Viby J
tel - (86) 112733 / fax - (86) 145779
website - www.agf.co.dk
Year of Formation - 1880
Chairman - Preben Andersen
Secretary - Dan Iversen
Coach - Peter Rudbaek; Kent Nielsen &
Lars Lundkvist (00/01 - Ove Christensen)
Stadium - Aarhus Stadion (9,877)

MAJOR HONOURS
League Championship - (5)
1955, 1956, 1957, 1960, 1986.
Domestic Cup - (9) 1955, 1957, 1960, 1961,
1965, 1987, 1988, 1992, 1996.

APPEARANCES 99/00

	P	Ap	(s)	Gls
Kenneth AGGERHOLM	A		(2)	
Jesper ANDERSEN	D	10	(1)	
Lennart BAK	M	11	(2)	2
Filip BERGMAN (SWE)	D	4		
Anders BJERRE	D	17	(1)	2
Allan BORGVARDT	A		(3)	
Kenneth CHRISTIANSEN	M	14	(5)	1
Carsten HALLUM	A	7	(5)	2
Jes HØJEN	D	3		
Bjarne JENSEN	M		(7)	
John JENSEN	D	8	(7)	
Oli JOHANNESEN (FAR)	D	7	(2)	
Nocko JOKOVIC	A	11		7
Mads JØRGENSEN	M	28		2
Jacek KACPRZAK (POL)	M	4	(2)	1
Jakob KRAGH	G	15	(1)	
Ulrik KRISTENSEN	A		(2)	
Ólafur KRISTJÁNSSON (ISL)	D	14	(12)	1
Frank KROGSDAL	A	6	(6)	
Eric LIND	A	10	(6)	
Ken MARTIN	D	33		2
Johnny MØLBY	M	16	(1)	1
Bo NIELSEN	A	21	(7)	8
Tommy NIELSEN	D	10	(2)	
Michael NONBO	M	31		
Mads RIEPER	D	20	(1)	2
Dennis SIIM	D	15	(2)	
Kenny THORUP	A	3	(4)	
Tómas Ingi TÓMASSON (ISL)	A	12	(8)	2
Stig TØFTING	M	7		2
Gregers ULRICH	M	8	(1)	
Lars WINDFELD	G	18		

LEAGUE RESULTS 1999/2000

25/07/99	AB	A	0-1	
01/08/99	Herfølge BK	H	1-1	Bjerre
08/08/99	Viborg FF	A	1-1	Jørgensen
16/08/99	FC København	H	1-0	Nielsen
21/08/99	AaB	A	0-1	
29/08/99	Silkeborg IF	A	0-2	
12/09/99	OB	H	3-3	Christiansen, Bjerre, Tómasson
19/09/99	Lyngby FC	A	1-3	Kacprzak
26/09/99	Vejle BK	H	1-2	Kristjánsson
03/10/99	Brøndby IF	A	0-3	
13/10/99	Brøndby IF	H	0-2	
17/10/99	Vejle BK	A	1-1	Martin
24/10/99	Viborg FF	A	1-1	Rieper
01/11/99	AaB	H	1-1	og (Krüger)
07/11/99	AB	A	3-2	Nielsen 3
22/11/99	FC København	H	1-0	Rieper
28/11/99	Silkeborg IF	A	1-4	Nielsen
12/03/00	OB	H	0-1	
19/03/00	Esbjerg FB	A	1-0	Bak
26/03/00	Herfølge BK	H	2-3	Nielsen B., Mølby
30/03/00	Esbjerg FB	H	1-0	Tómasson
02/04/00	Lyngby FC	A	0-3	
10/04/00	Vejle BK	H	2-0	Jørgensen, Jokovic
16/04/00	Brøndby IF	A	0-2	
20/04/00	Lyngby FC	H	3-0	Jokovic 3
23/04/00	Herfølge BK	A	1-1	Jokovic
30/04/00	Esbjerg FB	H	4-3	Jokovic, Tøfting, Bak, Nielsen B.
03/05/00	FC København	A	1-2	Hallum
07/05/00	OB	A	0-4	
10/05/00	Silkeborg IF	H	2-1	Tøfting, Jokovic (p)
21/05/00	AB	H	2-2	Martin, Nielsen B.
25/05/00	AaB	A	1-1	Hallum
28/05/00	Viborg FF	H	0-4	

BRØNDBY IF

CLUB DIRECTORY

Brøndbyernes Idraets Forening
Gildhøjcentret
Brøndbyvester Boulevard 8, 2605 Brøndby
tel - (43) 630810 / fax - (43) 432627
website - www.brondby-if.dk
email - brondby@brondby-if.dk
Year of Formation - 1964
Chairman - Ole Borch
Secretary - Per Bjerregaard
Coach - Tom Køhlert; Åge Hareide
Stadium - Brøndby Stadion (18,500)

MAJOR HONOURS
League Championship - (8) 1985, 1987, 1988,
1990, 1991, 1996, 1997, 1998.
Domestic Cup - (3) 1989, 1994, 1998.

APPEARANCES 99/00

	P	Ap	(s)	Gls
Ruben BAGGER	A	29	(4)	10
Oumar BARRO (BFA)	A		(2)	
Ole BJUR	M	27	(2)	3
Stig Inge BJØRNEBYE (NOR)	D	13		2
Bent CHRISTENSEN	A	21	(9)	13
Søren COLDING	D	27		1
Morten CRAMER	G	1		
Vragel DA SILVA (BRA)	D	12	(3)	3
Kim DAUGAARD	M	24	(2)	4
Peter GRAULUND	A	2	(11)	4
Roger HELLAND (NOR)	D	12		
Mikkel JENSEN	M	16	(12)	1
Dan Anton JOHANSEN	D	15	(4)	
Mattias JONSSON (SWE)	A	12	(3)	2
Mogens KROGH	G	32		
Søren KROGH	M		(4)	
Thomas LINDRUP	M	12	(8)	1
Peter MADSEN	A	21	(7)	7
Peter MØLLER	A	2	(5)	3
Per NIELSEN	D	28		
Krister NORDIN (SWE)	M	9	(1)	1
Mads OLSEN	M		(1)	
Allan RAVN	M	9	(2)	1
Michael RIEBERS	D		(1)	
Aurelijus SKARBALIUS (LIT)	M	8	(3)	
Martin Ditlev SMITH	D	16	(1)	
Magnus SVENSSON (SWE)	M	15		

LEAGUE RESULTS 1999/2000

24/07/99	Lyngby FC	H	1-0	Bagger
01/08/99	Vejle BK	A	4-0	Da Silva, Daugaard, Bagger, Ravn
08/08/99	Silkeborg IF	H	1-0	Christensen
15/08/99	Esbjerg FB	H	3-1	Bagger, Bjur, Lindrup
21/08/99	AB	A	0-2	
29/08/99	Herfølge BK	H	2-2	Christensen, Graulund
12/09/99	Viborg FF	A	0-2	
20/09/99	FC København	H	3-1	Christensen 2, Madsen
26/09/99	AaB	A	1-3	Da Silva
03/10/99	AGF	H	3-0	Christensen 2, Bagger
06/10/99	OB	A	1-2	Madsen
13/10/99	AGF	A	2-0	Bjur, Madsen
17/10/99	Viborg FF	H	4-1	Da Silva, Madsen, Graulund, Daugaard (p)
24/10/99	AaB	A	1-3	Daugaard (p)
31/10/99	AB	H	3-0	Daugaard, Madsen, Christensen
07/11/99	FC København	A	1-1	Madsen
21/11/99	Silkeborg IF	H	0-0	
27/11/99	OB	A	1-1	Graulund
12/03/00	Esbjerg FB	H	2-3	Bagger, Colding (p)
19/03/00	Herfølge BK	A	2-0	Jonsson, Christensen
26/03/00	Lyngby FC	H	2-2	Bagger, Christensen
02/04/00	Vejle BK	A	1-1	Graulund
09/04/00	Viborg FF	A	2-2	Bjørnebye 2
16/04/00	AGF	H	2-0	Bjur, Christensen
20/04/00	Vejle BK	H	4-0	Bagger, Christensen, Madsen, Jensen
23/04/00	Lyngby FC	A	0-3	
30/04/00	Herfølge BK	H	5-0	Bagger 2, Christensen 2, Møller
07/05/00	Esbjerg FB	A	0-2	
10/05/00	OB	H	2-1	Møller, Nordin
15/05/00	Silkeborg IF	A	1-1	Møller
21/05/00	FC København	H	1-1	Jonsson
25/05/00	AB	A	0-2	
28/05/00	AaB	H	1-0	Bagger

ESBJERG FB

CLUB DIRECTORY

Esbjerg Forenede Boldklubber
Gl. Vardevej 88, 6700 Esbjerg
tel - (75) 453355 / fax - (75) 122833
website - www.efb.dk
email - esbjerg@dbu.dk
Year of Formation - 1924
Chairman - Jørgen L. Jensen
Secretary - Niels Erik Søndergaard
Coach - Viggo Jensen
Stadium - Esbjerg Idraetspark (16,630)

MAJOR HONOURS
League Championship - (5)
1961, 1962, 1963, 1965, 1979.
Domestic Cup - (2) 1964, 1976.

APPEARANCES 99/00

	P	Ap	(s)	Gls
Iddi ALKHAG	A	26		5
Hans Henrik ANDREASEN	M	24	(6)	2
Kenneth BJERRE	M		(1)	
Søren BORUP	A	2	(2)	
Marcelo de Souza BRAGA (BRA)	M	1	(6)	
Brian FAKKENOR	D	4	(8)	1
Benny GALL	G	31		
John HANSEN	A		(6)	
Johnny HANSEN	D	10		4
Thomas HANSEN	M	6	(14)	
Henrik IBSEN	D	33		
Lars JAKOBSEN	D	32		
Henrik JENSEN	D	24	(3)	1
Kim JENSEN	M	22	(8)	2
Martin JENSEN	D	30		
Carsten JØRGENSEN	M	1		
Simon KARKOV	M	25	(4)	6
Jan KRISTIANSEN	M		(1)	
Jan LADEFOGED	G	1		
Jerry LUCENA	M		(2)	
Henrik NIELSEN	A	5	(3)	3
Søren PALLESEN	M	22	(3)	1
Joakim PERSSON (SWE)	M	13		2
Morten SKYTTE	M	1	(2)	1
Kenni SOMMER	A	10	(9)	3
Ronnie SVENSSON	G	1	(1)	
Lars SØRENSEN	D	9	(3)	1
Jess THORUP	A	30	(1)	7

LEAGUE RESULTS 1999/2000

26/07/99	OB	H	2-0	Alkhag, Sørensen
01/08/99	Lyngby FC	A	1-5	Karkov
09/08/99	Vejle BK	H	1-1	Thorup
15/08/99	Brøndby IF	A	1-3	Alkhag
22/08/99	Silkeborg IF	A	0-4	
29/08/99	AB	H	0-1	
13/09/99	Herfølge BK	A	0-2	
19/09/99	Viborg FF	H	1-2	Skytte
26/09/99	FC København	A	0-3	
13/10/99	AB	A	2-1	Thorup 2
17/10/99	FC København	H	2-0	Alkhag, Karkov
20/10/99	AaB	H	0-0	
25/10/99	Silkeborg IF	A	0-2	
31/10/99	OB	H	0-2	
07/11/99	Vejle BK	H	3-1	Jensen K., Thorup, Andreasen
21/11/99	Herfølge BK	A	2-3	Pallesen (p), Jensen H.
28/11/99	Lyngby FC	H	2-3	Alkhag, Fakkenor
12/03/00	Brøndby IF	A	3-2	Hansen Johnny, Karkov, Persson
19/03/00	AGF	H	0-1	
26/03/00	Viborg FF	A	3-2	Sommer 3
30/03/00	AGF	A	0-1	
02/04/00	AaB	H	0-0	
09/04/00	FC København	A	1-3	Andreasen
16/04/00	AB	H	0-0	
20/04/00	AaB	A	1-7	Thorup
23/04/00	Viborg FF	H	1-2	Nielsen
30/04/00	AGF	A	3-4	Persson, Hansen Johnny (p), Alkhag
07/05/00	Brøndby IF	H	2-0	Hansen Johnny, Thorup
11/05/00	Lyngby FC	A	6-4	Hansen Johnny (p), Karkov 2, Thorup, Jensen K., Nielsen
14/05/00	Herfølge BK	H	1-2	og (Mikkelsen)
22/05/00	Vejle BK	A	1-2	Nielsen
25/05/00	OB	A	1-4	Karkov
28/05/00	Silkeborg IF	H	0-3	

HERFØLGE BK

CLUB DIRECTORY

Herfølge Boldklub
Vordingborgvej 124
Postbox 57, 4681 Herfølge
tel - (56) 276021 / fax - (56) 275575
website - www.hb.dk
email - hb@hb.dk
Year of Formation - 1921
Chairman - Martin Juul
Secretary - Flemming Brinkgaard
Coach - John Jensen
Stadium - Herfølge Stadion (8,500)

MAJOR HONOURS
League Championship - (1) 2000.

APPEARANCES 99/00

	P	Ap	(s)	Gls
Thomas ABEL	M		(2)	
Morten AVNSKJOLD	M		(1)	
Torben CHRISTIANSEN	D	6	(1)	
Jesper FALCK	A	33		10
Bo HENRIKSEN	A	7	(3)	1
Chris HERMANSEN	A	2	(4)	1
Jesper HEYDE	M	20	(5)	2
Thomas HØYER	M	21		2
Jesper JACOBSEN	A	11	(11)	6
Lars JAKOBSEN	M	16	(10)	1
John JENSEN	M	4	(12)	
Kenneth JENSEN	A	30	(2)	10
Kenneth KASTRUP	D	24	(3)	
Thomas KNUDSEN	A	6	(13)	5
Steven LUSTÜ	D	31		1
Dan LÜBBERS	D	18	(6)	
Henrik LYKKE	D	23		2
Jens MADSEN	M	26	(1)	3
Jakup MIKKELSEN (FAR)	G	31		
Gert NODIN	D	11		1
Henrik NØRREGAARD	M		(1)	
Tommy SCHRAM	M	20	(8)	5
Michael THOMSEN	D	15	(4)	
Claus UDENGAARD	G	2	(1)	
Iørn ULDBJERG	M	2	(3)	
Jeppe VESTERGAARD	D	4	(1)	

LEAGUE RESULTS 1999/2000

25/07/99	AaB	H	3-1	Schram 2, Falck
01/08/99	AGF	A	1-1	Schram
08/08/99	OB	H	1-0	Schram
15/08/99	Lyngby FC	A	2-1	Falck, Jensen K.
22/08/99	Vejle BK	H	1-1	Falck
29/08/99	Brøndby IF	A	2-2	Jensen K. 2
13/09/99	Esbjerg FB	H	2-0	Lykke, Jacobsen
19/09/99	AB	A	2-2	Knudsen, Jensen K.
27/09/99	Silkeborg IF	H	3-2	Jensen K., Nodin, Knudsen
03/10/99	Viborg FF	H	2-1	Henriksen, og (Hansen)
06/10/99	FC København	A	1-0	Madsen
13/10/99	AaB	A	0-4	
18/10/99	AB	H	1-2	Knudsen
24/10/99	FC København	A	0-2	
31/10/99	Silkeborg IF	H	4-1	Madsen, Jacobsen, Falck 2 (1p)
07/11/99	OB	A	1-0	Jensen K.
21/11/99	Esbjerg FB	H	3-2	Jensen K., Jacobsen 2
28/11/99	Vejle BK	H	3-1	Jacobsen, Lykke, Falck
13/03/00	Lyngby FC	A	0-1	
19/03/00	Brøndby IF	H	0-2	
26/03/00	AGF	A	3-2	Falck 2, Høyer
03/04/00	Viborg FF	H	3-2	og (Sørensen), Jacobsen, Falck
09/04/00	AB	A	0-3	
16/04/00	AaB	H	0-2	
20/04/00	Viborg FF	A	0-1	
23/04/00	AGF	H	1-1	Hermansen
30/04/00	Brøndby IF	A	0-5	
07/05/00	Lyngby FC	H	4-1	Heyde, Høyer, Knudsen, Jensen K.
10/05/00	Vejle BK	A	2-0	Schram, Knudsen
14/05/00	Esbjerg FB	A	2-1	Madsen, Falck
21/05/00	OB	H	3-3	Jensen K., Heyde, Jakobsen
25/05/00	Silkeborg IF	A	1-1	Jensen K.
28/05/00	FC København	H	1-1	Lustü

FC KØBENHAVN

CLUB DIRECTORY

FC København
Øster Allé 50, 2100 København Ø
tel - (35) 433131 / fax - (35) 433113
website - www.fck.dk
email - cm@fck.dk
Year of Formation - 1992
Chairman - Peter Norvig
Secretary - Charles Maskelyne
Coach - Kim Brink (00/01 - Roy Hodgson)
Stadium - Parken (41,641)

MAJOR HONOURS
League Championship - (1) 1993.
Domestic Cup - (2) 1995, 1997.

APPEARANCES 99/00

	P	Ap	(s)	Gls
Harald BRATTBAKK (NOR)	A	14		7
Peter CHRISTIANSEN	D	2	(2)	1
Clement CLIFORD	A	12	(2)	2
Kofi DAKINAH	M	5	(1)	1
Piotr HAREN	D	11	(6)	
Carsten HEMMINGSEN	M	19	(2)	2
Niclas JENSEN	M	29		1
Todi JONSSON (FAR)	A	24	(4)	3
Thomas KJAERBYE	M		(2)	
Martin Bill LARSEN	A	2	(12)	
Thomas LAURIDSEN	A	1	(5)	
Christian LØNSTRUP	D	14	(1)	1
Kim MADSEN	D	24	(2)	
Claus NIELSEN	M	8		
David NIELSEN	A	19	(7)	8
Lars Højer NIELSEN	M	1	(3)	
Michael "Mio" NIELSEN	D	30		1
Hjalte Bo NØRREGAARD	M	2	(5)	
Will ORBEN (USA)	A	2	(1)	
Yüsüf ÖZTÜRK	M	6	(11)	
Thomas RYTTER	D	20	(2)	
Michael STENSGAARD	G	16		
Bo SVENSSON	D	18	(2)	
Thomas THORNINGER	M	17	(8)	6
Diego TUR	D	18	(1)	1
Donatas VENCEVICIUS (LIT)	M	17	(2)	2
Mads Kjøller WESTH	A	2	(6)	2
Karim ZAZA	G	17	(1)	
Sibusisu ZUMA (SAF)	A	13	(2)	4

LEAGUE RESULTS 1999/2000

25/07/99	Viborg FF	A	1-2	Nielsen D.
01/08/99	Silkeborg IF	A	0-0	
06/08/99	AaB	H	0-2	
16/08/99	AGF	A	0-1	
23/08/99	OB	H	1-0	Nielsen D.
30/08/99	Lyngby FC	A	0-1	
12/09/99	Vejle BK	H	1-0	Jensen
20/09/99	Brøndby IF	A	1-3	Cliford
26/09/99	Esbjerg FB	H	3-0	og (Jakobsen), Nielsen D. 2
03/10/99	AB	A	2-1	Nielsen M., Thorninger
06/10/99	Herfølge BK	H	0-1	
13/10/99	OB	H	1-1	Thorninger
17/10/99	Esbjerg FB	A	0-2	
24/10/99	Herfølge BK	H	2-0	Thorninger, Cliford
31/10/99	Lyngby FC	A	4-0	Jonsson, Thorninger, Nielsen D., Vencevicius
07/11/99	Brøndby IF	H	1-1	Vencevicius
22/11/99	AGF	A	0-1	
28/11/99	Viborg FF	H	2-1	Westh, Jonsson
12/03/00	AaB	A	0-0	
19/03/00	AB	H	1-2	og (Albrechtsen)
26/03/00	Vejle BK	A	7-2	Brattbakk 3, Thorninger 2, Nielsen D. 2
02/04/00	Silkeborg IF	A	1-2	Dakinah
09/04/00	Esbjerg FB	H	3-1	Brattbakk, Hemmingsen (p), Christiansen
17/04/00	OB	A	0-2	
20/04/00	Silkeborg IF	H	4-1	Brattbakk 2, Zuma, Nielsen D.
23/04/00	Vejle BK	H	1-4	Zuma
30/04/00	AB	A	2-0	Hemmingsen (p), Zuma
03/05/00	AGF	H	2-1	Lønstrup, Tur
07/05/00	AaB	H	0-0	
10/05/00	Viborg FF	A	1-1	Jonsson
21/05/00	Brøndby IF	A	1-1	Brattbakk
25/05/00	Lyngby FC	H	1-2	Zuma
28/05/00	Herfølge BK	A	1-1	Westh

LYNGBY FC

CLUB DIRECTORY

Lyngby Fodbold Club
Lundtoftevej 61, 2800 Lyngby
tel - (45) 884060 / fax - (45) 874445
website - www.lyngby-fc.dk
email - lyngby-fc@lyngby-fc.dk
Year of Formation - 1921
Chairman - Poul Hedegaard
Secretary - Peter Packness & René Dupont
Coach - Poul Hansen
Stadium - Lyngby Stadion (12,000)

MAJOR HONOURS
League Championship - (2) 1983, 1992.
Domestic Cup - (3) 1984, 1985, 1990.

APPEARANCES 99/00

		P	Ap	(s)	Gls
Thomas ANDIE	M		8	(10)	
John Bradley AUGUST (SAF)	A		14	(1)	5
Stefan BIDSTRUP	M		23	(1)	7
Martin BIRN	D		31		
Ayeni BOSUN (NIG)	M		6	(3)	
Kim CHRISTENSEN	A		7	(11)	5
Per FAHLSTRÖM (SWE)	G		32		
Claus FALLENTIN	G		1		
Tobias GRAHN (SWE)	A			(3)	
Andreas HAVLYKKE	A		24		8
Søren HERMANSEN	A		24	(2)	9
Nichlas HINDSBERG	M		14	(2)	2
Carsten HOLBEK	G			(1)	
Mikkel Bo JENSEN	D		14	(1)	1
Martin JOHANSEN	M		27		1
Mads JUNKER	A		1	(6)	1
Lars LARSEN	M		7	(5)	
Lennart Lynge LARSEN	D		29	(1)	3
Jimmi LÜTHJE	M		11	(15)	2
Christian MAGLEBY	M		17	(2)	5
Rasmus MARVITS	M		1	(8)	1
Jari PEDERSEN	A		3	(6)	
Morten PETERSEN	D		32		
Ronny B. PETERSEN	A			(2)	
Frank SCHOEMAN (SAF)	D		3		
René TENGSTEDT	M		4	(11)	
Ulrich VINZENTS	D		30	(1)	1

LEAGUE RESULTS 1999/2000

24/07/99	Brøndby IF	A	0-1	
01/08/99	Esbjerg FB	H	5-1	Hermansen 2, Havlykke 2, Marvits
08/08/99	AB	A	0-3	
15/08/99	Herfølge BK	H	1-2	Jensen
22/08/99	Viborg FF	A	0-2	
30/08/99	FC København	H	1-0	Bidstrup
10/09/99	AaB	A	2-0	Hindsberg 2
19/09/99	AGF	H	3-1	Bidstrup, Magleby, Hermansen
26/09/99	OB	A	0-0	
03/10/99	Silkeborg IF	H	1-3	Hermansen
06/10/99	Vejle BK	H	5-1	Hermansen 2, Magleby 3
13/10/99	Viborg FF	A	2-0	Havlykke, Magleby
17/10/99	AaB	H	3-2	Havlykke, Hermansen, Bidstrup
24/10/99	AB	A	2-2	Havlykke, Bidstrup
31/10/99	FC København	H	0-4	
07/11/99	Silkeborg IF	A	0-3	
21/11/99	OB	H	2-0	Lüthje, Vinzents
28/11/99	Esbjerg FB	A	3-2	Johansen, Junker, Lüthje
13/03/00	Herfølge BK	H	1-0	Bidstrup
19/03/00	Vejle BK	H	0-1	
26/03/00	Brøndby IF	A	2-2	Hermansen, August
02/04/00	AGF	H	3-0	Hermansen, Bidstrup, August
09/04/00	AaB	A	1-1	Christensen
16/04/00	Viborg FF	H	1-3	Christensen
20/04/00	AGF	A	0-3	
23/04/00	Brøndby IF	H	3-0	Larsen L.L., Havlykke, Christensen
30/04/00	Vejle BK	A	0-4	
07/05/00	Herfølge BK	A	1-4	Havlykke
11/05/00	Esbjerg FB	H	4-6	Havlykke, Christensen 2, August
14/05/00	OB	A	3-1	Bidstrup, Larsen L.L. 2
21/05/00	Silkeborg IF	H	0-0	
25/05/00	FC København	A	2-1	August 2
28/05/00	AB	H	0-2	

OB

Odense Boldklub
Box 344, Sdr. Boulevard 172, 5100 Odense C
tel - (63) 119090 / fax - (63) 119080
website - www.ob.dk
email - ob@ob.dk
Year of Formation - 1887
Chairman - Fritz Bonde
Secretary - Kim Brink
Coach - Jens Plambech; Torben Storm
(00/01 - Troels Bech)
Stadium - Odense Stadion (15,633)

MAJOR HONOURS
League Championship - (3) 1977, 1982, 1989.
Domestic Cup - (3) 1983, 1991, 1993.

APPEARANCES 99/00

	P	Ap	(s)	Gls
Jesper ANDERSEN	D	2	(3)	
Søren ANDERSEN	A	27		14
Greger ANDRIJEVSKI (SWE)	A	6	(10)	1
Mads BARTRAM	D	1	(1)	
Jesper BENGTSSON	D		(1)	
Sune HEILBO	M	20	(8)	2
Michael HEMMINGSEN	D	28		3
Lars HØGH	G	33		
Lars JACOBSEN	D	26	(1)	1
Bjarne JENSEN	M	10	(9)	
Jann JENSEN	D	26		
Mads JENSEN	A	1	(3)	
Ulrik JOHANSEN	M	2	(1)	
Henrik JØRGENSEN	D	1		
Lars JØRGENSEN	M		(1)	
Ulrik Rosenløv LAURSEN	D	25		
Claus MADSEN	M	9	(6)	1
Mwape MITI (ZAM)	A	19	(2)	2
Steen NEDERGAARD	D	23	(3)	2
Morten PANDURO	A	5	(11)	2
Per PEDERSEN	A	1		
Ulrik Baerholm PEDERSEN	M	30	(1)	4
Morten RASMUSSEN	D	2	(4)	
Torben SABGILD	D	6	(14)	
Jonas D. SCHMIDT	A		(2)	
Andrew TEMPO (ZAM)	M	30		2
Nicolai WAEL	M	30		8

LEAGUE RESULTS 1999/2000

26/07/99	Esbjerg FB	A	0-2	
01/08/99	AB	H	0-3	
08/08/99	Herfølge BK	A	0-1	
15/08/99	Viborg FF	H	1-1	Andersen S.
23/08/99	FC København	A	0-1	
29/08/99	AaB	H	2-2	Andersen S., Nedergaard (p)
12/09/99	AGF	A	3-3	Pedersen U.B., Andrijevski,
				Andersen S.
19/09/99	Silkeborg IF	A	1-0	Andersen S.
26/09/99	Lyngby FC	H	0-0	
03/10/99	Vejle BK	A	1-1	Wael
06/10/99	Brøndby IF	H	2-1	Heilbo, Wael
13/10/99	FC København	A	1-1	Miti
17/10/99	Silkeborg IF	H	0-4	
24/10/99	Vejle BK	H	1-1	Wael
31/10/99	Esbjerg FB	A	2-0	Tempo, Madsen
07/11/99	Herfølge BK	H	0-1	
21/11/99	Lyngby FC	A	0-2	
27/11/99	Brøndby IF	H	1-1	Wael
12/03/00	AGF	A	1-0	Pedersen U.B.
19/03/00	Viborg FF	H	0-1	
26/03/00	AaB	A	2-1	Andersen S. 2
02/04/00	AB	H	1-1	Hemmingsen (p)
09/04/00	Silkeborg IF	A	0-1	
17/04/00	FC København	H	2-0	Hemmingsen, Andersen S.
20/04/00	AB	A	2-0	Heilbo, Miti
23/04/00	AaB	H	1-4	Andersen S.
30/04/00	Viborg FF	A	4-2	Andersen S.., Hemmingsen (p),
				Nedergaard, Pedersen U.B.
07/05/00	AGF	H	4-0	Andersen S. 3, Pedersen U.B.
10/05/00	Brøndby IF	A	1-2	Wael
14/05/00	Lyngby FC	H	1-3	Andersen S.
21/05/00	Herfølge BK	A	3-3	Wael 2, Panduro
25/05/00	Esbjerg FB	H	4-1	Panduro, Tempo, Wael, Jacobsen
28/05/00	Vejle BK	A	1-0	Andersen S.

SILKEBORG IF

CLUB DIRECTORY

Silkeborg Idraets Forening
Ansvej 110, 8600 Silkeborg
tel - (86) 804477 / fax - (86) 804647
website - www.sif-supoort.dk
email - sif@sif-support.dk
Year of Formation - 1917
Chairman - Ole Hansen
Secretary - Orla Madsen
Coach - Benny Johansen
Stadium - Silkeborg Stadion (11,000)

MAJOR HONOURS
League Championship - (1) 1994.

APPEARANCES 99/00

	P	Ap	(s)	Gls
Goodwin ATTRAM (GHA)	M	8	(5)	2
Morten BRUUN	D	15		
Lars BRØGGER	M	8	(9)	2
Johnny HANSEN	D		(2)	
Rasmus HANSEN	D	6	(6)	
Henrik IPSEN	G	2		
Nocko JOKOVIC	A	11	(7)	1
Jacob JUHL	D	19	(4)	2
Peter KJAER	G	31		
Peder KNUDSEN	M	14	(2)	2
Nicki KRISTENSEN	M	7	(4)	
Michael LARSEN	D	23		2
Thomas Røll LARSEN	M	26	(5)	2
Peter LASSEN	A	25		16
Kern LYHNE	M	12	(11)	
Kim NØRHOLT	A	2	(6)	
Jens OVERGAARD	D		(3)	
Brian PEDERSEN	M		(7)	
Henrik PEDERSEN	A	28		13
Christian Duus PETERSEN	D	26	(2)	
Thomas POULSEN	M	15	(1)	
Brian ROSENKVIST	A		(3)	
Rasmus SVENNINGSEN	M	6		
Peter SØRENSEN	M	25	(3)	
Jesper THYGESEN	M	22	(7)	5
Robert TOLLUND	G		(1)	
Bora ZIVKOVIC	D	32		1

LEAGUE RESULTS 1999/2000

25/07/99	Vejle BK	A	4-0	Pedersen 2, Lassen, Jokovic
01/08/99	FC København	H	0-0	
08/08/99	Brøndby IF	A	0-1	
15/08/99	AaB	A	1-2	Pedersen
22/08/99	Esbjerg FB	H	4-0	Thygesen, Pedersen 2, Lassen
29/08/99	AGF	H	2-0	Lassen, Pedersen
12/09/99	AB	A	1-1	Zivkovic
19/09/99	OB	H	0-1	
27/09/99	Herfølge BK	A	2-3	Lassen, Larsen M. (p)
03/10/99	Lyngby FC	A	3-1	Knudsen, Lassen, Thygesen
06/10/99	Viborg FF	H	1-1	Brøgger
13/10/99	Vejle BK	H	2-2	Lassen, Larsen M. (p)
17/10/99	OB	A	4-0	Pedersen 2, Lassen 2
25/10/99	Esbjerg FB	H	2-0	Lassen, Pedersen
31/10/99	Herfølge BK	A	1-4	Lassen
07/11/99	Lyngby FC	H	3-0	Knudsen, Lassen, Pedersen
21/11/99	Brøndby IF	A	0-0	
28/11/99	AGF	H	4-1	Brøgger, Lassen 3
12/03/00	Viborg FF	A	1-1	Lassen
20/03/00	AaB	H	1-1	Lassen
26/03/00	AB	A	0-2	
02/04/00	FC København	H	2-1	Juhl, Thygesen
09/04/00	OB	H	1-0	Juhl
16/04/00	Vejle BK	A	1-2	Pedersen
20/04/00	FC København	A	1-4	Larsen T.R.
23/04/00	AB	H	1-0	Attram
01/05/00	AaB	A	0-1	
07/05/00	Viborg FF	H	1-0	Pedersen
10/05/00	AGF	A	1-2	og (Nielsen B.)
15/05/00	Brøndby IF	H	1-1	Attram
21/05/00	Lyngby FC	A	0-0	
25/05/00	Herfølge BK	H	1-1	Thygesen
28/05/00	Esbjerg FB	A	3-0	Pedersen, Larsen T.R., Thygesen

VEJLE BK

CLUB DIRECTORY

Vejle Boldklub
Helligkildevej 2, 7100 Vejle
tel - (75) 727500 / fax - (75) 833033
website - www.vejle-boldklub.dk
email - vbe@vejle-boldklub.dk
Year of Formation - 1891
Chairman - Ole Vedel
Secretary - Henrik Lund
Coach - Ole Fritsen; Allan Michaelsen;
Poul Erik Andreasen (00/01 - Keld Bordinggaard)
Stadium - Vejle Stadion (15,332)

MAJOR HONOURS
League Championship - (5)
1958, 1971, 1972, 1978, 1984.
Domestic Cup - (6)
1958, 1959, 1972, 1975, 1977, 1981.

APPEARANCES 99/00

	P	Ap	(s)	Gls
Erik Bo ANDERSEN	A	14		7
René S. ANDERSEN	M	2	(4)	
Ulrik BALLING	A	25	(3)	2
Trond BJØRNDAL (NOR)	D		(8)	
Keld BORDINGGAARD	M	5	(9)	2
Erik BOYE	G	22		
Jerry BROWN	A	6	(10)	1
Peter CHRISTIANSEN	M	16		
Kaspar DALGAS	A	18	(11)	3
Allan DYRING	M	6	(3)	2
Klaus ESKILDSEN	D	14	(4)	
Calle FACIUS	M	26	(1)	1
Boye HABEKOST	G	5		
Henrik HOLM	M		(1)	
Danny JUNG	A	2	(1)	
Lars Lauth JØRGENSEN	M	2	(2)	
Nicolai JØRGENSEN	M	10	(4)	
Christian KELLER	A	11	(5)	1
Dick LAST (SWE)	G	6		
Jesper LJUNG (SWE)	M	23		2
Jens MADSEN	D	28	(2)	1
Michael MADSEN	D		(3)	
Jesper MIKKELSEN	M	17	(8)	5
Henrik RISOM	D	32		5
Kent SCHOLZ (GER)	D	30	(3)	
Jesper SØGAARD	M	7		1
Jan SØNKSEN	D	17	(1)	2
Dan SØRENSEN	D	19	(7)	2

LEAGUE RESULTS 1999/2000

25/07/99	Silkeborg IF	H	0-4	
01/08/99	Brøndby IF	H	0-4	
09/08/99	Esbjerg FB	A	1-1	Dalgas
15/08/99	AB	H	0-0	
22/08/99	Herfølge BK	A	1-1	Brown
29/08/99	Viborg FF	H	2-3	Dyring, Facius
12/09/99	FC København	A	0-1	
19/09/99	AaB	H	2-2	Sørensen, Mikkelsen
26/09/99	AGF	A	2-1	Sønksen, Dyring
03/10/99	OB	H	1-1	Madsen
06/10/99	Lyngby FC	A	1-5	Ljung
13/10/99	Silkeborg IF	A	2-2	Dalgas, Søgaard
17/10/99	AGF	H	1-1	Mikkelsen
24/10/99	OB	A	1-1	Sønksen
31/10/99	Viborg FF	H	0-2	
07/11/99	Esbjerg FB	A	1-3	Mikkelsen
21/11/99	AaB	H	1-1	Risom (p)
28/11/99	Herfølge BK	A	1-3	Ljung
12/03/00	AB	H	3-1	Balling, Andersen E.B., Bordinggaard
19/03/00	Lyngby FC	A	1-0	Dalgas
26/03/00	FC København	H	2-7	Risom (p), Sørensen
02/04/00	Brøndby IF	H	1-1	Keller
10/04/00	AGF	A	0-2	
16/04/00	Silkeborg IF	H	2-1	Risom (p), Andersen E.B.
20/04/00	Brøndby IF	A	0-4	
23/04/00	FC København	A	4-1	og (Svensson), Andersen E.B. 3
30/04/00	Lyngby FC	H	4-0	Risom, Andersen E.B. 2, Mikkelsen
07/05/00	AB	A	1-1	Risom
10/05/00	Herfølge BK	H	0-2	
14/05/00	AaB	A	1-7	Bordinggaard
22/05/00	Esbjerg FB	H	2-1	Mikkelsen, Balling
25/05/00	Viborg FF	A	0-3	
28/05/00	OB	H	0-1	

VIBORG FF

CLUB DIRECTORY

Viborg Fodsports Forening
Kirkebaekvej 94
Postbox 214, 8800 Viborg
tel - (86) 601066
fax - (86) 601046
website - www.viborgff.dk
email - ff-prof@post11.tele.dk
Year of Formation - 1896
Chairman - Bruno Jensen
Secretary - Morten Jensen
Coach - Kim Poulsen
Stadium - Viborg Stadion (15,000)

MAJOR HONOURS
Domestic Cup - (1) 2000.

APPEARANCES 99/00

	P	Ap	(s)	Gls
Denni CONTEH	A	5	(5)	2
Hans EKLUND (SWE)	A	32	(1)	15
Heine FERNANDEZ	A	26	(1)	13
Thomas FRANDSEN	M	27	(5)	4
Morten HAMM	D	25	(3)	
Dennis HANSEN	D	13	(1)	
Casper JACOBSEN	G		(1)	
Klaus KAERGAARD	M	1	(12)	1
Claus KJAERGAARD	M	6	(14)	
René KJAERSGAARD	D		(1)	
Jan LARSEN	D	7	(11)	
Jakob Glerup NIELSEN	M	30		
Martin NIELSEN	D	9	(2)	
Alex NØRLUND	M	14	(11)	4
Arkadiusz ONYSZKO (POL)	G	32		
Henrik PEDERSEN	M	2	(4)	
Ralf PEDERSEN	D	28		
Morten POULSEN	M	29	(2)	9
Asbjørn SENNELS	D	1		
Milan SIMPUNOVIC (YUG)	G	1		
Palle SØRENSEN	D	28	(1)	3
Thomas TENGSTEDT	D	21	(4)	1
Claus TROELSEN	A		(1)	
Andreas WINTHER	M	26	(3)	4

LEAGUE RESULTS 1999/2000

25/07/99	FC København	H	2-1	Fernandez, Poulsen
02/08/99	AaB	A	0-2	
08/08/99	AGF	H	1-1	Eklund
15/08/99	OB	A	1-1	Eklund
22/08/99	Lyngby FC	H	2-0	Fernandez (p), Winther
29/08/99	Vejle BK	A	3-2	Eklund 2, Frandsen
12/09/99	Brøndby IF	H	2-0	Fernandez (p), Eklund
19/09/99	Esbjerg FB	A	2-1	Fernandez 2
26/09/99	AB	H	1-3	Fernandez
03/10/99	Herfølge BK	A	1-2	Nørlund
06/10/99	Silkeborg IF	A	1-1	Winther
13/10/99	Lyngby FC	H	0-2	
17/10/99	Brøndby IF	A	1-4	Fernandez
24/10/99	AGF	H	1-1	Eklund
31/10/99	Vejle BK	A	2-0	Winther, Poulsen
08/11/99	AaB	A	2-1	Eklund, Fernandez
21/11/99	AB	H	2-1	Fernandez, Frandsen
28/11/99	FC København	A	1-2	Sørensen
12/03/00	Silkeborg IF	H	1-1	Nørlund
19/03/00	OB	A	1-0	Poulsen
26/03/00	Esbjerg FB	H	2-3	Tengstedt, Winther
03/04/00	Herfølge BK	A	2-3	Eklund, Fernandez
09/04/00	Brøndby IF	H	2-2	Eklund, Frandsen
16/04/00	Lyngby FC	A	3-1	Conteh, Nørlund, Poulsen
20/04/00	Herfølge BK	H	1-0	Poulsen
23/04/00	Esbjerg FB	A	2-1	Eklund, Fernandez
30/04/00	OB	H	2-4	Fernandez 2
07/05/00	Silkeborg IF	A	0-1	
10/05/00	FC København	H	1-1	Eklund (p)
14/05/00	AB	A	0-6	
21/05/00	AaB	H	7-2	Poulsen 2, Eklund 2, Nørlund, Kaergaard, Conteh
25/05/00	Vejle BK	H	3-0	Sørensen 2, Eklund
28/05/00	AGF	A	4-0	Frandsen, Poulsen 2, Eklund

ENGLAND

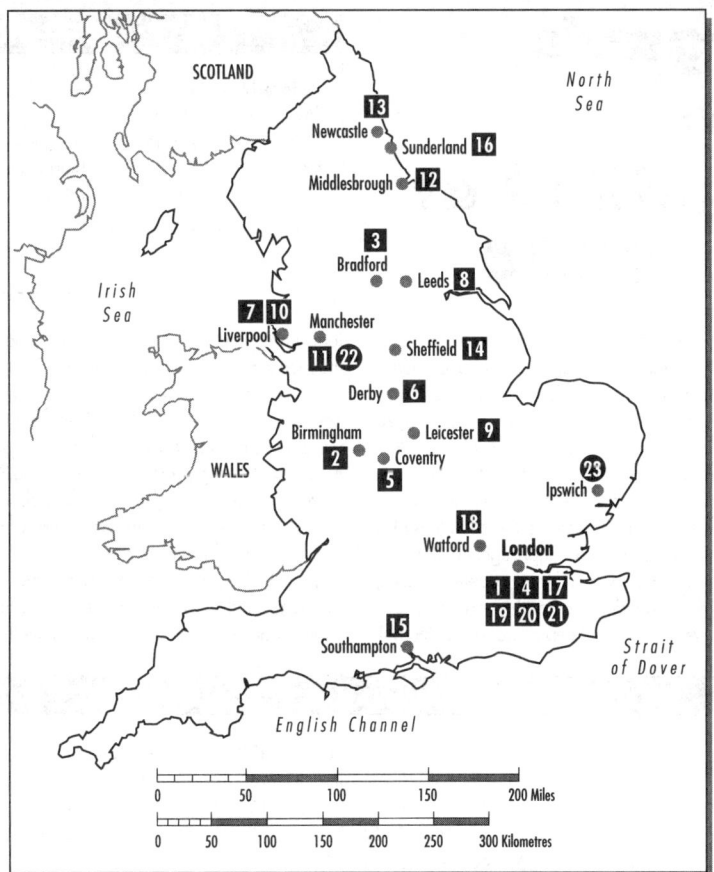

1	ARSENAL	313	13	NEWCASTLE UNITED	325
2	ASTON VILLA	314	14	SHEFFIELD WEDNESDAY	326
3	BRADFORD CITY	315	15	SOUTHAMPTON	327
4	CHELSEA	316	16	SUNDERLAND	328
5	COVENTRY CITY	317	17	TOTTENHAM HOTSPUR	329
6	DERBY COUNTY	318	18	WATFORD	330
7	EVERTON	319	19	WEST HAM UNITED	331
8	LEEDS UNITED	320	20	WIMBLEDON	332
9	LEICESTER CITY	321	**Promoted clubs**		
10	LIVERPOOL	322	21	CHARLTON ATHLETIC	
11	MANCHESTER UNITED	323	22	MANCHESTER CITY	
12	MIDDLESBROUGH	324	23	IPSWICH TOWN	

UNSTOPPABLE UNITED RETAIN PREMIERSHIP

Keegan's flaws magnified at Euro 2000

FEDERATION DIRECTORY

The Football Association
16 Lancaster Gate, London W2 3LW

tel - (020) 72624542/74027151
fax - (020) 74020486
website - www.the-fa.org

Stadium - Wembley, London (79,045)

Year of Formation - 1863
Chairman - Geoff Thompson
Chief Executive - Adam Crozier

England came within a couple of minutes of reaching the Euro 2000 quarter-finals, but it would have been a travesty of justice had they succeeded in qualifying for the knockout phase. They were a poor team, which played drab, unimaginative football, and when full-back Phil Neville committed the clumsy, unnecessary foul that enabled Romania to claim a 3-2 victory in the final group game, it restored a sense of order to the scoreline of a match in which England had been thoroughly outplayed.

It had been a similar story in England's opening match, against Portugal, when despite holding an early 2-0 advantage they were unable to keep possession of the ball

long enough to give themselves a chance of defending their lead. Even the historic, long-awaited 1-0 victory over Germany - England's first competitive triumph over the old enemy since the 1966 World Cup final - was achieved under considerable duress, with the Germans controlling the game for long periods but, unlike the Portuguese and Romanians, letting England off the hook with their lack of quality and precision in the final third of the pitch.

In short, England were a shambles. And the man most responsible for that was the team's head coach, Kevin Keegan. In the run-up to the tournament there was widespread concern about Keegan's ability to lead, guide

LEAGUE CHAMPIONSHIP RESULTS 99/00

		1	2	3	4	5	6	7	8	9	10	11	12	13	14	15	16	17	18	19	20
1	Arsenal		3-1	2-0	2-1	3-0	2-1	4-1	2-0	2-1	0-1	1-2	5-1	0-0	3-3	3-1	4-1	2-1	1-0	2-1	1-1
2	Aston Villa	1-1		1-0	0-0	1-0	2-0	3-0	1-0	2-2	0-0	0-1	1-0	0-1	2-1	0-1	1-1	1-1	4-0	2-2	1-1
3	Bradford City	2-1	1-1		1-1	1-1	4-4	0-0	1-2	3-1	1-0	0-4	1-1	2-0	1-1	1-2	0-4	1-1	3-2	0-3	3-0
4	Chelsea	2-3	1-0	1-0		2-1	4-0	1-1	0-2	1-1	2-0	5-0	1-1	1-0	3-0	1-1	4-0	1-0	2-1	0-0	3-1
5	Coventry City	3-2	2-1	4-0	2-2		2-0	1-0	3-4	0-1	0-3	1-2	2-1	4-1	4-1	0-1	3-2	0-1	4-0	1-0	2-0
6	Derby County	1-2	0-2	0-1	3-1	0-0		1-0	0-1	3-0	0-2	1-2	1-3	0-0	3-3	2-0	0-5	0-1	2-0	1-2	4-0
7	Everton	0-1	0-0	4-0	1-1	1-1	2-1		4-4	2-2	0-0	1-1	0-2	0-2	1-1	4-1	5-0	2-2	4-2	1-0	4-0
8	Leeds United	0-4	1-2	2-1	0-1	3-0	0-0	1-1		2-1	1-2	0-1	2-0	3-2	2-0	1-0	2-1	1-0	3-1	1-0	4-1
9	Leicester City	0-3	3-1	3-0	2-2	1-0	0-1	1-1	2-1		2-2	0-2	2-1	1-2	3-0	2-1	5-2	0-1	1-0	1-3	2-1
10	Liverpool	2-0	0-0	3-1	1-0	2-0	2-0	0-1	3-1	0-2		2-3	0-0	2-1	4-1	0-0	1-1	2-0	0-1	1-0	3-1
11	Manchester United	1-1	3-0	4-0	3-2	3-2	3-1	5-1	2-0	2-0	1-1		1-0	5-1	4-0	3-3	4-0	3-1	4-1	7-1	1-1
12	Middlesbrough	2-1	0-4	0-1	0-1	2-0	1-4	2-1	0-0	0-3	1-0	3-4		2-2	1-0	3-2	1-1	2-1	1-1	2-0	0-0
13	Newcastle United	4-2	0-1	2-0	0-1	2-0	2-0	1-1	2-2	0-2	2-2	3-0	2-1		8-0	5-0	1-2	2-1	1-0	2-2	3-3
14	Sheffield Wednesday	1-1	0-1	2-0	1-0	0-0	0-2	0-2	0-3	4-0	1-2	0-1	1-0	0-2		0-1	0-2	1-2	2-2	3-1	5-1
15	Southampton	0-1	2-0	1-0	1-2	0-0	3-3	2-0	0-3	1-2	1-1	1-3	1-1	4-2	2-0		1-2	0-1	2-0	2-1	2-0
16	Sunderland	0-0	2-1	0-1	4-1	1-1	1-1	2-1	1-2	2-0	0-2	2-2	1-1	2-2	1-0	2-0		2-1	2-0	1-0	2-1
17	Tottenham Hotspur	2-1	2-4	1-1	0-1	3-2	1-1	3-2	1-2	2-3	1-0	3-1	2-3	3-1	0-1	7-2	3-1		4-0	0-0	2-0
18	Watford	2-3	0-1	1-0	1-0	1-0	0-0	1-3	1-2	1-1	2-3	2-3	1-3	1-1	1-0	3-2	2-3	1-1		1-2	2-3
19	West Ham United	2-1	1-1	5-4	0-0	5-0	1-1	0-4	0-0	2-1	1-0	2-4	0-1	2-1	4-3	2-0	1-1	1-0	1-0		2-1
20	Wimbledon	1-3	2-2	3-2	0-1	1-1	2-2	0-3	2-0	2-1	1-2	2-2	2-3	2-0	0-2	1-1	1-0	1-1	5-0	2-2	

LEAGUE CHAMPIONSHIP FINAL TABLE 99/00

			Home				Away					Total						
		Pd	W	D	L	F	A	W	D	L	F	A	W	D	L	F	A	PT	GD
1	Manchester United	38	15	4	0	59	16	13	3	3	38	29	28	7	3	97	45	91	52
2	Arsenal	38	14	3	2	42	17	8	4	7	31	26	22	7	9	73	43	73	30
3	Leeds United	38	12	5	2	29	18	9	4	6	29	25	21	6	11	58	43	69	15
4	Liverpool	38	11	4	4	28	13	8	6	5	23	17	19	10	9	51	30	67	21
5	Chelsea	38	12	5	2	35	12	6	6	7	18	22	18	11	9	53	34	65	19
6	Aston Villa	38	8	8	3	23	12	7	5	7	23	23	15	13	10	46	35	58	11
7	Sunderland	38	10	6	3	28	17	6	4	9	29	39	16	10	12	57	56	58	1
8	Leicester City	38	10	3	6	31	24	6	4	9	24	31	16	7	15	55	55	55	0
9	West Ham United	38	11	5	3	32	23	4	5	10	20	30	15	10	13	52	53	55	-1
10	Tottenham Hotspur	38	10	3	6	40	26	5	5	9	17	23	15	8	15	57	49	53	8
11	Newcastle United	38	10	5	4	42	20	4	5	10	21	34	14	10	14	63	54	52	9
12	Middlesbrough	38	8	5	6	23	26	6	5	8	23	26	14	10	14	46	52	52	-6
13	Everton	38	7	9	3	36	21	5	5	9	23	28	12	14	12	59	49	50	10
14	Coventry City	38	12	1	6	38	22	0	7	12	9	32	12	8	18	47	54	44	-7
15	Southampton	38	8	4	7	26	22	4	4	11	19	40	12	8	18	45	62	44	-17
16	Derby County	38	6	3	10	22	25	3	8	8	22	32	9	11	18	44	57	38	-13
17	Bradford City	38	6	8	5	26	29	3	1	15	12	39	9	9	20	38	68	36	-30
18	Wimbledon	38	6	7	6	30	28	1	5	13	16	46	7	12	19	46	74	33	-28
19	Sheffield Wednesday	38	6	3	10	21	23	2	4	13	17	47	8	7	23	38	70	31	-32
20	Watford	38	5	4	10	24	31	1	2	16	11	46	6	6	26	35	77	24	-42

and organise a team at the highest level of international football. By his own admission he was no tactical genius. In fact, as Euro 2000 proved, he was much worse than that. England were found out tactically in all three games, submitting themselves on each occasion to the superior control and flexibility of the opposition. Keegan's predilection for a rigid 4-4-2 was exposed early on yet he stuck with it through to the bitter, tortuous end despite overwhelming evidence that it wasn't working.

Keegan asked to be judged at Euro 2000, and given that he had boldly claimed beforehand that England could actually win the tournament, his experience in Belgium and Holland could only be described as one of complete failure. Yet, in their wisdom, the FA backed him to the hilt, maintaining brashly that he was still "the right man for the job". Quite what grounds they had for making that statement was not immediately apparent.

Much was said and written after England's early exit about the team's lack of basic technique and flair, and clearly they were considerably less confident than other sides when it came to possessing, protecting and passing the ball under pressure - the three essential hallmarks of a successful international side. But the criticism strayed off beam when it tried to make out a case for branding all English players as deficient in this department. Players such

as David Beckham, Paul Scholes, Dennis Wise and Steve McManaman had all proved themselves up to the mark for their clubs in the Champions' League, so the fault was more collective than individual. England at Euro 2000 were badly prepared and badly organised. Good players underperformed primarily because the man who picked the team was unable to bring the best out of them.

England's failure should not, of course, have come as a surprise. After all, they had been exceedingly lucky to reach the finals in the first place. Sweden baled Keegan's men out when they beat Poland in the final qualifying tie, and then, in the play-offs against Scotland, England did their level best to squander a 2-0 first-leg lead with a performance at Wembley that was as abject as any ever witnessed from an England team in their traditional stronghold.

The 0-1 defeat should have been the wake-up call Keegan needed to get the team properly prepared for the following summer. But instead he agreed to just one warm-up fixture in the next six months - a 0-0 draw at home to Argentina - and then, when the matches did come thick and fast on the eve of the tournament, he chose to experiment with different selections and formations rather than fine-tune his chosen XI for the challenge ahead. In the end, Euro 2000 was a disaster waiting to happen. The victory over Germany in Charleroi? A source of great celebration for England fans at the time but rendered utterly meaningless by what followed on the same pitch against Romania three days later.

The more important games against Germany were to come in the qualifying campaign for the 2002 World Cup. With Greece, Finland and Albania also making up England's group, it will be no easy task for Keegan and his players to restore morale and confidence sufficiently to go on and qualify automatically for Japan and Korea. They must attempt to do so without their greatest goalscorer of recent years, Alan Shearer, now retired from international football with a proud record of 30 goals in 63 games. But with young players of genuine quality like Scholes, Beckham and Michael Owen to call on, the future for England should be a lot less bleak than it was portrayed during the dark days of Euro 2000.

English clubs gave the mother country of football plenty to cheer during the 1999/2000 season. While the only international trophy collected was the World Club Cup, won by Manchester United against South American champions Palmeiras in Tokyo, the overall performance in the European club competitions was better than for many years.

United were understandably disappointed to surrender their Champions' League crown, especially as they lost it at Old Trafford, where Real Madrid outplayed them to win 3-2 in the quarter-finals. However, United confirmed their new-found status among the giants of European football with some scintillating displays in the group games, notably those at home to Valencia and Fiorentina.

Chelsea also reached the last eight of the Champions' League and came close to eliminating favourites Barcelona. 3-0 up at half-time in the first leg at Stamford Bridge, they were still set to record the greatest result in the club's history with seven minutes to go in the Nou Camp,

but the Catalans finally pummelled them into submission in extra-time.

The UEFA Cup had long been a graveyard for English teams, but after a gap of 16 years England finally broke through the quarter-final barrier with not one but two clubs. Leeds got there the hard way, travelling from one unwelcome destination to another before they departed the competition under the most harrowing of circumstances, following the murder of two of their fans in Istanbul on the night before the first leg of the semi-final against Galatasaray. It was the Turkish side which also halted Arsenal in their tracks, although not until the conclusion of the penalty shoot-out in the final after two goalless hours in Copenhagen.

Arsenal, like their conquerors, had only qualified for the UEFA Cup after dropping out of the Champions' League at the end of the first group phase. For the second season running the Gunners fired blanks at their adopted home of Wembley in the Champions' League, but the return to Highbury in the UEFA Cup produced four successive first-leg wins, which paved the way for them to reach their fifth European final.

Arsenal, Leeds, Manchester United and Chelsea are all members of the newly-established 'big five' of English football, which also includes Liverpool (absent from European competition in 1999/2000). The term is used to associate the only teams with the financial muscle and pulling power capable of winning the Premiership. A more accurate and appropriate grading, however, would be to put four of the clubs in a subsidiary group behind Manchester United.

England's most prominent and successful club side of

TOP SCORERS

30 Kevin PHILLIPS (Sunderland)
23 Alan SHEARER (Newcastle United)
20 Dwight YORKE (Manchester United)
19 Michael BRIDGES (Leeds United)
    Andy COLE (Manchester United)
17 Thierry HENRY (Arsenal)
16 Paolo DI CANIO (West Ham United)
14 Niall QUINN (Sunderland)
    Steffen IVERSEN (Tottenham Hotspur)
    Chris ARMSTRONG (Tottenham Hotspur)

NATIONAL TEAM RESULTS 99/00

Date	Opponent		Venue	Score	Scorers
04/09/99	Luxembourg (ECQ)	H	Wembley	6-0	Shearer (12p, 27, 33), McManaman (29, 43), Owen (89)
08/09/99	Poland (ECQ)	A	Warsaw	0-0	
10/10/99	Belgium	H	Sunderland	2-1	Shearer (6), Redknapp (67)
13/11/99	Scotland (ECQ)	A	Glasgow	2-0	Scholes (21, 42)
17/11/99	Scotland (ECQ)	H	Wembley	0-1	
23/02/00	Argentina	H	Wembley	0-0	
27/05/00	Brazil	H	Wembley	1-1	Owen (38)
31/05/00	Ukraine	H	Wembley	2-0	Fowler (44), Adams (68)
03/06/00	Malta	A	Ta' Qali	2-1	Keown (23), Heskey (75)
12/06/00	Portugal (ECF)	N	Eindhoven	2-3	Scholes (3), McManaman (18)
17/06/00	Germany (ECF)	N	Charleroi	1-0	Shearer (53)
20/06/00	Romania (ECF)	N	Charleroi	2-3	Shearer (40p), Owen (45)

DOMESTIC CUP 99/00

THIRD ROUND

Cambridge United 2, Crystal Palace 0
Nottingham Forest 1, Oxford United 1
(replay) Oxford United 1, Nottingham Forest 3
Aston Villa 2, Darlington 1
Charlton Athletic 2, Swindon Town 1
Crewe Alexandra 1, Bradford City 2
Derby County 0, Burnley 1
Exeter City 0, Everton 0
(replay) Everton 1, Exeter City 0
Fulham 2, Luton Town 2
(replay) Luton Town 0, Fulham 3
Grimsby Town 3, Stockport County 2
Hereford United 0, Leicester City 0
(replay) Leicester City 2, Hereford United 1 (aet)
Hull City 1, Chelsea 6
Norwich City 1, Coventry City 3
Preston North End 2, Oldham Athletic 1
Queens Park Rangers 1, Torquay United 1
(replay) Torquay United 2, Queens Park Rangers 3
Reading 1, Plymouth Argyle 1
(replay) Plymouth Argyle 1, Reading 0
Sheffield Wednesday 1, Bristol City 0
Sunderland 1, Portsmouth 0
Tranmere Rovers 1, West Ham United 0
Walsall 1, Gillingham 1
(replay) Gillingham 2, Walsall 1
Watford 0, Birmingham City 1
West Bromwich Albion 2, Blackburn Rovers 2
(replay) Blackburn Rovers 2, West Bromwich Albion 0
Wigan Athletic 0, Wolverhampton Wanderers 1
Wimbledon 1, Barnsley 0
Wrexham 2, Middlesbrough 1
Chester 1, Manchester City 4

Huddersfield Town 0, Liverpool 2
Leeds United 2, Port Vale 0
Sheffield United 1, Rushden & Diamonds 1
(replay) Rushden & Diamonds 1, Sheffield United 1
(aet; 5-6 on pens.)
Tottenham Hotspur 1, Newcastle United 1
(replay) Newcastle United 6, Tottenham Hotspur 1
Arsenal 3, Blackpool 1
Ipswich Town 0, Southampton 1
Bolton Wanderers 1, Cardiff City 0

FOURTH ROUND

Aston Villa 1, Southampton 0
Charlton Athletic 1, Queens Park Rangers 0
Coventry City 3, Burnley 0
Everton 2, Birmingham City 0
Fulham 3, Wimbledon 0
Grimsby Town 0, Bolton Wanderers 2
Newcastle United 4, Sheffield United 1
Plymouth Argyle 0, Preston North End 3
Sheffield Wednesday 1, Wolverhampton Wanderers 1
(replay) Wolverhampton Wanderers 0,
Sheffield Wednesday 0 (aet; 3-4 on pens.)
Tranmere Rovers 1, Sunderland 0
Wrexham 1, Cambridge United 2
Arsenal 0, Leicester City 0
(replay) Leicester City 0, Arsenal 0 (aet; 6-5 on pens.)
Manchester City 2, Leeds United 5
Liverpool 0, Blackburn Rovers 1
Gillingham 3, Bradford City 1
Chelsea 2, Nottingham Forest 0

FIFTH ROUND

Cambridge United 1, Bolton Wanderers 3

Coventry City 2, Charlton Athletic 3
Everton 2, Preston North End 0
Fulham 1, Tranmere Rovers 2
Gillingham 3, Sheffield Wednesday 1
Aston Villa 3, Leeds United 2
Chelsea 2, Leicester City 1
Blackburn Rovers 1, Newcastle United 2

QUARTER-FINALS

Bolton Wanderers 1 (Gudjohnsen 47),
Charlton Athletic 0
Chelsea 5 (Flo 17, Terry 49, Weah 50, Zola 85p,
Morris 87), Gillingham 0
Everton 1 (Moore 20),
Aston Villa 2 (Stone 16, Carbone 45)
Tranmere Rovers 2 (Allison 45, Jones G. 78),
Newcastle United 3 (Speed 27, Domi 36, Ferguson 58)

SEMI-FINALS

Bolton Wanderers 0, Aston Villa 0 (aet; 1-4 on pens.)
Chelsea 2 (Poyet 16, 71), Newcastle United 1 (Lee 65)

FINAL

20/05/2000, Wembley
CHELSEA 1 Di Matteo (73)
ASTON VILLA 0
referee - Poll
CHELSEA - De Goey; Melchiot, Desailly, Leboeuf,
Babayaro; Di Matteo, Wise, Deschamps, Poyet; Zola
(Morris 89), Weah (Flo 87).
ASTON VILLA - James; Ehiogu, Southgate, Barry;
Delaney, Taylor (Stone 77), Boateng, Merson, Wright
(Hendrie 87); Dublin, Carbone (Joachim 77).

the 1990s began the new century just as they had ended the old one - as Premiership champions. The 1999/2000 season was no match, of course, for the historic 'treble'-winning campaign of a year earlier, but it did confirm United as being in a class of their own in the domestic arena. Their sixth league title in eight years was won with such ease that by the end of the season, following a closing sequence of 11 straight victories, Sir Alex Ferguson's team had established new Premiership records for points (91), goals (97), and the margin of victory (18 points).

Although United were accused of resting on their laurels at the start of the season when the only significant newcomers they brought in were replacement goalkeepers for the departed Peter Schmeichel, the squad they entered for Premiership combat proved to be vastly superior to anything else their rivals could come up with. Ferguson managed his resources extremely effectively, and although

the team had the odd pitfall - notably when Chelsea hammered them 5-0 to end a long unbeaten run in early October - they always looked capable, if pushed, of shifting up to a higher gear. Leeds stalked them bravely for two-thirds of the season, but when the defending champions won 1-0 at Elland Road in February, the last credible challenge to United's supremacy was extinguished. The title was duly secured five matches before the end with a 3-1 win at Southampton. It was the perfect pick-me-up for the United fans, coming as it did just a few days after the Champions' League defeat by Real Madrid.

There was no domestic 'double' for United. Indeed, it was never a possibility. Amidst huge controversy the club decided to withdraw from the FA Cup, the reason being that they could not jointly compete in that competition and the newly-formed FIFA Club World Championship, which took place in January and for which United had qualified

EUROPEAN CUPS 99/00

CHAMPIONS' CUP
● ARSENAL
Champions' League
1st match FIORENTINA (ITA)
A 0-0
Manninger; Luzhnyi, Keown, Adams, Winterburn, Ljungberg, Vieira, Grimandi, Overmars, Bergkamp (Henry 82), Suker (Kanu 61).

2nd match AIK (SWE)
H 3-1   Ljungberg (27), Henry (89), Suker (90)
Manninger, Dixon, Keown, Adams, Winterburn, Ljungberg (Henry 68), Vieira, Grimandi (Silvinho 55), Overmars (Kanu 68), Suker, Bergkamp.

3rd match FC BARCELONA (ESP)
A 1-1   Kanu (81)
Manninger, Dixon, Keown, Adams, Winterburn, Parlour (Henry 73), Vieira, Grimandi, Overmars (Ljungberg 79), Kanu, Bergkamp (Suker 73).

4th match FC BARCELONA (ESP)
H 2-4   Bergkamp (44), Overmars (84)
Seaman, Dixon, Keown (Upson 73), Adams, Winterburn, Parlour, Vieira, Ljungberg (Henry 76), Overmars, Kanu (Suker 76), Bergkamp.

5th match FIORENTINA (ITA)
H 0-1
Seaman, Dixon (Suker 74), Keown, Adams, Winterburn, Parlour (Ljungberg 58), Vieira, Petit (Vivas 60), Overmars, Bergkamp, Kanu.

6th match AIK (SWE)
A 3-2   Overmars (17, 52), Suker (56)
Manninger, Dixon, Luzhnyi (Vivas 77), Upson, Winterburn, Ljungberg, Vieira, Petit (Malz 77), Overmars, Suker (Hughes 77), Kanu.

● CHELSEA
Qualifying round SKONTO RIGA (LAT)
H 3-0   Babayaro (76), Poyet (77), Sutton (84)
De Goey, Ferrer, Leboeuf, Desailly, Le Saux, Petrescu (Goldbaek 79), Deschamps (Babayaro 65), Poyet, Wise, Sutton, Zola (Flo 65).

A 0-0
De Goey (Cudicini 78), Petrescu, Høgh, Desailly, Babayaro, Goldbaek (Harley 82), Morris, Poyet (Nicholls 64), Wise, Flo, Forssell.

Champions' League
1st match MILAN (ITA)
H 0-0
De Goey, Ferrer, Desailly, Leboeuf (Høgh 80), Babayaro, Petrescu, Wise, Deschamps, Poyet (Le Saux 79), Flo (Sutton 85), Zola.

2nd match HERTHA BSC BERLIN (GER)
A 1-2   Leboeuf (86p)
De Goey, Ferrer (Ambrosetti 64), Leboeuf, Desailly, Le Saux (Morris 73), Petrescu, Deschamps, Wise, Babayaro, Flo (Sutton 64), Zola.

3rd match GALATASARAY (TUR)
H 1-0   Petrescu (55)
De Goey, Ferrer, Leboeuf, Desailly (Høgh 62), Babayaro, Petrescu, Morris, Wise, Ambrosetti (Poyet 53), Sutton (Flo 85), Zola.

4th match GALATASARAY (TUR)
A 5-0   Flo (32, 49), Zola (54), Wise (79), Ambrosetti (87)
De Goey, Ferrer, Leboeuf, Desailly, Babayaro, Poyet (Wise 67), Morris, Deschamps (Petrescu 67), Le Saux, Flo, Zola (Ambrosetti 76).

5th match MILAN (ITA)
A 1-1   Wise (76)
De Goey; Ferrer, Desailly, Leboeuf, Babayaro, Petrescu (Morris 46), Deschamps, Wise, Poyet (Di Matteo 75), Zola (Ambrosetti 84), Flo.

6th match HERTHA BSC BERLIN (GER)
H 2-0   Deschamps (11), Ferrer (44)
De Goey, Ferrer, Høgh (Leboeuf 66), Desailly (Lambourde 85), Babayaro, Petrescu, Deschamps, Wise, Zola (Poyet 62), Flo, Sutton.

7th match FEYENOORD (HOL)
H 3-1   Babayaro (45), Flo (67, 85)
De Goey, Ferrer, Leboeuf, Desailly, Babayaro, Petrescu, Deschamps (Dalla Bona 86), Wise, Poyet (Di Matteo 86), Flo, Zola.

8th match LAZIO (ITA)
A 0-0
De Goey, Ferrer, Desailly, Leboeuf, Babayaro, Petrescu, Wise, Deschamps (Di Matteo 75), Poyet, Flo, Zola.

9th match OLYMPIQUE MARSEILLE (FRA)
A 0-1
De Goey, Ferrer (Morris 81), Leboeuf, Desailly, Harley, Petrescu, Deschamps (Di Matteo 61), Wise, Poyet, Flo (Sutton 81), Zola.

10th match OLYMPIQUE MARSEILLE (FRA)
H 1-0   Wise (27)
De Goey, Ferrer, Leboeuf, Desailly, Babayaro, Morris, Deschamps (Di Matteo 79), Wise, Poyet, Flo, Zola (Harley 79).

11th match FEYENOORD (HOL)
A 3-1   Zola (39), Wise (64), Flo (69)
De Goey, Petrescu, Leboeuf, Desailly, Babayaro, Di Matteo, Wise, Poyet (Morris 76), Flo, Zola (Ambrosetti 89).

12th match LAZIO (ITA)
H 1-2   Poyet (45)
De Goey, Ferrer, Desailly, Leboeuf (Høgh 62), Babayaro (Harley 74), Petrescu, Di Matteo (Morris 74), Deschamps, Poyet, Flo, Zola.

Quarter-final FC BARCELONA (ESP)
H 3-1   Zola (30), Flo (34, 38)
De Goey, Ferrer, Thome, Desailly, Babayaro, Petrescu (Di Matteo 71), Deschamps, Wise, Morris, Flo (Sutton 87), Zola.

A 1-5   (aet) Flo (60)
De Goey, Ferrer (Lambourde 46), Leboeuf, Desailly, Babayaro, Morris, Deschamps (Petrescu 101), Wise, Di Matteo, Flo, Zola (Poyet 105).

● MANCHESTER UNITED
Champions' League
1st match CROATIA ZAGREB (CRO)
H 0-0
Van der Gouw, Clegg (Fortune 75), Neville P., Berg, Wilson (Sheringham 60), Stam, Beckham, Scholes, Cole, Yorke, Giggs.

2nd match SK STURM GRAZ (AUT)
A 3-0   Keane (17), Yorke (31), Cole (33)
Van der Gouw, Neville P., Irwin, Berg, Keane (Wilson 62), Stam, Beckham, Scholes, Cole (Solskjaer 77), Yorke, Cruijff (Sheringham 67).

3rd match OLYMPIQUE MARSEILLE (FRA)
H 2-1   Cole (79), Scholes (83)
Van der Gouw, Irwin, Neville P., Berg (Sheringham 77), Scholes, Stam, Beckham, Butt, Cole (Clegg 86), Yorke, Solskjaer (Fortune 72).

EUROPEAN CUPS 99/00 (CONTINUED)

4th match OLYMPIQUE MARSEILLE (FRA)
A 0-1
Bosnich, Neville P., Irwin, Berg (Solskjaer 83), Keane, Stam, Beckham, Scholes, Cole, Yorke, Giggs.

5th match CROATIA ZAGREB (CRO)
A 2-1   Beckham (32), Keane (49)
Bosnich, Neville P., Irwin, Berg, Keane, Stam, Beckham, Scholes (Greening 67), Cole (Cruijff 78), Yorke (Solskjaer 59), Giggs.

6th match SK STURM GRAZ (AUT)
H 2-1   Solskjaer (56), Keane (69)
Bosnich, Neville G., Irwin (Higginbotham 76), Berg, Keane, May, Greening (Cruijff 65), Wilson (Neville P. 52), Cole, Solskjaer, Giggs.

7th match FIORENTINA (ITA)
A 0-2
Bosnich, Neville G., Stam, Berg (Neville P. 63), Irwin, Beckham, Keane, Scholes, Giggs, Cole (Sheringham 63), Yorke (Solskjaer 63).

8th match VALENCIA CF (ESP)
H 3-0   Keane (38), Solskjaer (47), Scholes (69)
Van der Gouw, Neville P., Irwin, Neville G., Keane, Stam, Beckham, Scholes (Butt 70), Cole (Yorke 70), Solskjaer, Giggs.

9th match GIRONDINS DE BORDEAUX (FRA)
H 2-0   Giggs (42), Sheringham (84)
Van der Gouw, Neville G., Irwin, Silvestre, Keane (Fortune 88), Stam, Beckham, Butt, Cole (Neville P. 81), Sheringham, Giggs (Solskjaer 88).

10th match GIRONDINS DE BORDEAUX (FRA)
A 2-1   Keane (33), Solskjaer (84)
Van der Gouw, Neville G., Irwin (Solskjaer 82), Silvestre, Keane, Stam, Beckham, Butt, Cole (Berg 85), Sheringham (Yorke 76), Giggs.

11th match FIORENTINA (ITA)
H 3-1   Cole (20), Keane (33), Yorke (70)
Bosnich, Neville G., Berg, Stam, Irwin, Beckham, Keane, Scholes, Giggs, Yorke, Cole.

12th match VALENCIA CF (ESP)
A 0-0
Bosnich, Neville G., Berg, Stam, Irwin, Beckham, Scholes, Keane, Fortune, Solskjaer (Cruijff 66), Sheringham.

Quarter-final REAL MADRID (ESP)
A 0-0
Bosnich, Neville G., Berg, Stam, Irwin (Silvestre 87), Beckham, Keane, Scholes (Butt 81), Giggs, Cole, Yorke (Sheringham 76).
H 2-3   Beckham (64), Scholes (88p)
Van der Gouw, Neville G., Berg (Sheringham 62), Stam, Irwin (Silvestre 46), Beckham, Keane, Scholes, Giggs, Cole (Solskjaer 62), Yorke.

UEFA CUP
● ARSENAL
3rd round FC NANTES (FRA)
H 3-0   Overmars (13p), Winterburn (81), Bergkamp (90)
Seaman, Vivas, Grimandi, Adams, Winterburn, Ljungberg (Henry 69), Vieira, Petit (Parlour 38), Overmars, Kanu (Suker 69), Bergkamp.
A 3-3   Grimandi (24), Henry (31), Overmars (42)
Manninger, Dixon, Grimandi, Adams, Winterburn, Ljungberg (Vivas 80), Vieira, Petit, Overmars (Silvinho 64), Kanu, Henry (Suker 71).

4th round RC DEPORTIVO (ESP)
H 5-1   Dixon (5), Henry (30, 67), Kanu (78), Bergkamp (83)
Seaman, Dixon, Luzhnyi, Keown, Silvinho, Ljungberg, Grimandi, Petit, Overmars (Kanu 65), Henry (Suker 76), Bergkamp (Parlour 82).
A 1-2   Henry (63)
Seaman, Dixon, Luzhnyi, Silvinho, Winterburn (Vernazza 83), Parlour, Vieira, Petit, Ljungberg, Kanu (Malz 82), Henry (Suker 78).

Quarter-final SV WERDER BREMEN (GER)
H 2-0   Henry (21), Ljungberg (77)
Seaman, Dixon, Luzhnyi, Adams, Silvinho, Parlour (Overmars 66), Grimandi, Vieira, Ljungberg, Henry (Suker 76), Bergkamp (Kanu 66).
A 4-2   Parlour (8, 25, 70), Henry (59)
Manninger, Dixon, Luzhnyi, Adams (Petit 61), Silvinho, Parlour, Vieira (Winterburn 76), Grimandi, Ljungberg, Kanu (Overmars 68), Henry.

Semi-final RC LENS (FRA)
H 1-0   Bergkamp (2)
Seaman, Dixon, Keown, Grimandi, Silvinho, Parlour, Vieira, Petit, Overmars (Ljungberg 74), Kanu, Bergkamp (Suker 82).
A 2-1   Henry (43), Kanu (86)
Seaman, Dixon, Keown, Adams, Silvinho, Parlour, Vieira, Petit, Ljungberg (Overmars 70), Henry (Grimandi 81), Bergkamp (Kanu 70).

Final GALATASARAY (TUR)
0-0   (aet; 4-1 on pens.)
Seaman, Dixon, Keown, Adams, Silvinho, Parlour, Vieira, Petit, Overmars (Suker 114), Henry, Bergkamp (Kanu 74).

● LEEDS UNITED
1st round PARTIZAN BEOGRAD (YUG)
A 3-1   Bowyer (26, 82), Radebe (39)
Martyn, Mills, Woodgate, Radebe, Harte, Kelly, Bowyer, Batty, Hopkin, Bridges (Smith 70), Kewell.
H 1-0   Huckerby (55)
Martyn, Kelly, Woodgate, Radebe, Harte, Hopkin (Bakke 80), Batty, Bowyer, Kewell (Jones 85), Huckerby, Bridges (Smith 67).

2nd round LOKOMOTIV MOSKVA (RUS)
H 4-1   Bowyer (27, 45), Smith (56), Kewell (83)
Martyn, Kelly, Woodgate, Radebe, Harte, McPhail, Batty, Bowyer, Kewell, Smith, Bridges (Huckerby 62).
A 3-0   Harte (16p), Bridges (28, 45)
Martyn, Kelly, Woodgate, Radebe, Harte, McPhail (Hopkin 80), Batty, Bowyer (Håland 46), Bakke, Bridges, Kewell (Huckerby 66).

3rd round SPARTAK MOSKVA (RUS)
A 1-2   Kewell (14)
Martyn, Kelly, Woodgate, Duberry, Harte, Håland, McPhail, Bowyer, Bakke, Bridges (Huckerby 55), Kewell.
H 1-0   Radebe (84)
Martyn, Kelly, Woodgate, Radebe, Harte, McPhail, Bowyer, Bakke, Kewell, Smith (Huckerby 72), Bridges.

4th round ROMA (ITA)
A 0-0
Martyn, Jones, Woodgate, Håland, Radebe, Kelly, Bowyer, Bakke, Harte, Bridges (Smith 70), Kewell.
H 1-0   Kewell (67)
Martyn, Kelly, Håland, Radebe, Harte, Bowyer, Bakke (Jones 84), McPhail (Huckerby 89), Wilcox, Kewell, Bridges (Smith 82).

EUROPEAN CUPS 99/00 (CONTINUED)

Quarter-final SLAVIA PRAHA (CZE)
H 3-0 Wilcox (39), Kewell (54), Bowyer (59)
Martyn, Kelly, Håland, Radebe, Harte, Bakke, Bowyer, McPhail (Huckerby 76), Wilcox, Bridges (Smith 86), Kewell.
A 1-2 Kewell (47)
Martyn, Kelly, Woodgate, Radebe, Harte, Håland, Bakke, McPhail, Jones, Bridges (Smith 48), Kewell.

Semi-final GALATASARAY (TUR)
A 0-2
Martyn, Kelly, Woodgate, Radebe, Harte, Bakke, McPhail, Jones (Wilcox 65), Bowyer, Kewell, Bridges (Huckerby 75).
H 2-2 Bakke (16, 68)
Martyn, Mills, Woodgate, Radebe, Harte (Huckerby 46), Bakke, Bowyer, McPhail, Wilcox, Bridges, Kewell.

● **NEWCASTLE UNITED**
1st round CSKA SOFIA (BUL)
A 2-0 Solano (51), Ketsbaia (77)
Harper, Barton, Dabizas, Goma, Domi, Solano (Hamilton 83), Dyer, Lee, Speed, Shearer, Ferguson (Ketsbaia 18).
H 2-2 Shearer (36), Robinson (88)
Harper, Barton, Dabizas, Goma, Marcelino, Domi, Lee (McClen 90), Solano, Maric (Robinson 72), Speed, Shearer.

2nd round FC ZÜRICH (SUI)
A 2-1 Maric (51), Shearer (60)
Harper, Barton, Dabizas, Hughes, Domi, Solano (McClen 88), Dyer (Serrant 64), Lee, Speed, Maric (Robinson 79), Shearer.
H 3-1 Maric (33), Ferguson (58), Speed (61)
Harper, Barton, Dabizas, Marcelino, Domi, Solano, Lee (McClen 82), Maric (Glass 86), Speed, Shearer, Ferguson (Robinson 82).

3rd round ROMA (ITA)
A 0-1
Harper, Charvet, Dabizas, Barton, Solano, Hughes, Lee, Speed, Pistone, Shearer, Ketsbaia (Robinson 81).

H 0-0
Harper, Dumas (Hughes 28), Charvet, Dabizas, Solano, Dyer (Ferguson 73), Lee, Speed, Pistone, Shearer, Ketsbaia (Glass 73).

● **TOTTENHAM HOTSPUR**
1st round ZIMBRU CHISINAU (MOL)
H 3-0 Leonhardsen (3), Perry (32), Sherwood (56)
Walker, Carr, Young, Perry, Taricco (Edinburgh 82), Leonhardsen, Freund, Sherwood, Ginola, Armstrong (Dominguez 76), Iversen.
A 0-0
Walker, Carr, Young, Perry, Taricco (Edinburgh 86), Leonhardsen, Freund, Nielsen, Clemence, Armstrong (Dominguez 76), Iversen.

2nd round 1.FC KAISERSLAUTERN (GER)
H 1-0 Iversen (34p)
Walker, Carr, Campbell, Perry, Taricco, Fox (Clemence 90), Freund, Sherwood, Leonhardsen, Ginola, Iversen.
A 0-2
Walker, Carr, Campbell, Perry, Edinburgh (Young 76), Leonhardsen, Freund, Sherwood, Clemence, Armstrong (Ginola 81), Iversen.

● **WEST HAM UNITED**
1st round OSIJEK (CRO)
H 3-0 Wanchope (39), Di Canio (48), Lampard (58)
Hislop, Sinclair, Potts, Stimac, Margas, Keller, Moncur (Foé 88), Lampard, Lomas, Wanchope, Di Canio (Kitson 85).
A 3-1 Kitson (27), Ruddock (83), Foé (90)
Hislop, Sinclair (Newton 46), Potts, Ferdinand (Ruddock 63), Stimac, Keller, Foé, Lampard, Lomas, Kitson, Di Canio (Wanchope 69).

2nd round STEAUA BUCURESTI (ROM)
A 0-2
Hislop, Sinclair, Potts (Margas 61), Ferdinand, Ruddock, Lomas, Moncur, Lampard, Foé, Wanchope, Di Canio (Cole 55).
H 0-0
Hislop, Sinclair, Margas, Ferdinand, Ruddock, Keller (Kitson 64), Lampard, Cole, Lomas, Wanchope, Di Canio.

as the reigning European champions. As it turned out, United played poorly in Brazil but the break certainly did them a power of good - as their results in the second half of the season demonstrated.

The usual suspects all played their part in United's Premiership triumph, with Beckham, Scholes, Ryan Giggs, Jaap Stam and Andy Cole battling it out for second place in the United hit-parade behind the team's indomitable captain Roy Keane, who was rewarded for his brilliant form in all competitions with both the Player of the Year and the Footballer of the Year prizes. Tha latter award, voted for by members of the press, was newly named in 2000 after the great Sir Stanley Matthews, who sadly passed away in February, aged 85.

Matthews owed much of his legend to the FA Cup - Blackpool's epic 4-3 victory over Bolton at Wembley in 1953 has always been referred to as the 'Matthews Final' - but the world's oldest knockout competition lost much of

its lustre in 1999/2000. Manchester United's decision not to defend the trophy was the major drawback, but the competition's organisers also played their part in devaluing it, firstly by bringing the third round forward from the traditional first weekend of January and then by staging the two semi-finals on alternate weekends at Wembley.

It was perhaps fitting, therefore, that the final, between Chelsea and Aston Villa, should be a dull, stagnant affair, livened up only by Roberto Di Matteo's winning goal (his second in this fixture) 17 minutes from time. Chelsea's victory brought their total number of trophies to five in three years, four of them won under the stewardship of manager Gianluca Vialli. However, the prize Chelsea wanted most - the Premiership - proved to be way beyond their reach. Vialli's team of big-name foreigners frequently excelled in the showpiece games, especially those in the Champions' League, but they were continually found wanting in the bread-and-butter league matches. Their failure to return to the Champions' League in 2000/01 was viewed as a major disappointment, but having finished 26 points behind the champions they could have no complaints. In fact, they needed that FA Cup final win to reach the UEFA Cup, otherwise they would have been serving mid-summer penance in the InterToto.

For the second year in a row the second automatic Champions' League place went to Arsenal. Arsène Wenger's team ensured a quick return to Europe's premier competition with a run of eight successive victories in the closing weeks of the campaign. Rather like Chelsea, they dropped far too many points in unexpected places, and they were always up against it after losing at home to Manchester United in August. The UEFA Cup run was

NATIONAL TEAM APPEARANCES 99/00

Coach - Kevin KEEGAN	LUX	POL	BEL	SCO	SCO	ARG	BRA	UKR	MLT	POR	GER	ROM	Cps	Gls
Nigel MARTYN (11/08/66) - Leeds United	G	G	s46					G				G	14	-
Kieron DYER (29/12/78) - Newcastle United	D46	s79	M58			M59		s81					5	-
Martin KEOWN (24/07/66) - Arsenal	D	D	D	D		D46	D		D59	s81	D	D	33	2
Tony ADAMS (10/10/66) - Arsenal	D65	D	D	D	D			D		D81			64	5
Stuart PEARCE (24/04/62) - West Ham United	D	D											78	4
Steve McMANAMAN (11/02/72) - Real Madrid (ESP)	M	M79						M	s69	M57			29	3
David BECKHAM (02/05/73) - Manchester United	M65	M		M	M	M73	M	M	M80	M	M	M	34	1
David BATTY (02/12/68) - Leeds United	M	M											42	-
Ray PARLOUR (07/03/73) - Arsenal	M				s90	s73	s59						7	-
							/90							
Alan SHEARER (13/08/70) - Newcastle United	A	A	A86	A	A	A78	A84	A	A51	A	A	A	63	30
Robbie FOWLER (09/04/75) - Liverpool	A	A65					s84	A46	s59				14	3
Gary NEVILLE (18/02/75) - Manchester United	s46	D13					D		D	D	D	D	39	-
Philip NEVILLE (21/01/77) - Manchester United	s65	s13	s58	D	D	s59	D	M73	D	D	D	D	29	-
Michael OWEN (14/12/79) - Liverpool	s65	s65	s58	A67	A63	A84			A46	A61	A67		22	7
Paul SCHOLES (16/11/74) - Manchester United		M		M	M90	M	M	M73	M69	M	M72	M81	27	10
David SEAMAN (19/09/63) - Arsenal			G46	G	G	G	G			G	G		59	-
Gareth SOUTHGATE (03/09/70) - Aston Villa		D		D	D		D	s59			s81		37	1
Paul INCE (21/10/67) - Middlesbrough			M	M	M	M59		s69	M	M	M		53	2
Jamie REDKNAPP (25/06/73) - Liverpool			M	M	M								16	1
Frank LAMPARD (20/06/78) - West Ham United			M76										1	-
Steve GUPPY (29/03/69) - Leicester City			M										1	-
Kevin PHILLIPS (25/07/73) - Sunderland			A58			s78	s84		A59				5	-
Dennis WISE (16/12/66) - Chelsea			s76			M	M		M69	s57	M	M75	19	1
Emile HESKEY (11/01/78) - Leicester City/Liverpool			s86		s63	A79		s46	s51	s46		s67	9	1
Sol CAMPBELL (18/09/74) - Tottenham Hotspur				D	D	D	D	D	D	D	D	D	36	-
Andy COLE (15/10/71) - Manchester United				s67		s79							7	-
Jason WILCOX (15/07/71) - Leeds United						M							3	-
Rio FERDINAND (07/11/78) - West Ham United						s46							9	-
Nick BARMBY (11/02/74) - Everton							s90	s73	M		s72	s75	15	3
Steven GERRARD (30/05/80) - Liverpool								M81			s61		2	-
Gareth BARRY (23/02/81) - Aston Villa								s73	s80				2	-
Richard WRIGHT (05/11/77) - Ipswich Town								G					1	-

PLAYERS OF THE SEASON

PAUL SCHOLES

England would not have qualified for Euro 2000 without Paul Scholes. It was his two smartly taken goals against Scotland at Hampden Park that gave England the first-leg cushion they needed to squeeze past the Auld Enemy in the play-offs. And, before that, it was his hat-trick at home to Poland which ultimately enabled Kevin Keegan's team to take second place in their qualifying group. The shy red-head has become a national treasure, a goalscoring midfielder to bear comparison with previous models of the genre Bryan Robson and David Platt. Like those two, he is excellent at arriving undetected into the penalty-box, but he is a superior passer of the ball and his link-up play, finely honed at Manchester United, is as good as anyone's. Scholes was one of United's top performers in 1999/2000, scoring nine goals in the Premiership, including two stunning long-range strikes against Bradford and Middlesbrough, and three in Europe.

KEVIN PHILLIPS

In the first four seasons of the 20-club Premiership, only one player, Alan Shearer, managed to hit the 30-goal barrier. Kevin Phillips joined him in 1999/2000, scoring precisely 30 goals to help newly-promoted Sunderland to a very satisfactory seventh place in the table. Although the lightweight striker had scored abundantly for the Wearsiders two years running in the First Division, very few people expected him to maintain a similar strike-rate in the Premiership. Yet he did just that, putting the ball in the net with such frequency and consistency that by the end of the season he had earned himself a place in England's party for the European Championship. In the two previous Premiership campaigns the top marksman had managed just 18 goals, but Phillips passed that milestone before Christmas. For a player who had never previously performed in the top division, it was a truly stunning achievement.

ANDY COLE

There was some debate about the real reason behind Andy Cole's exclusion from England's Euro 2000 squad. The official line was that he was injured, but it was common knowledge that Kevin Keegan didn't really rate him. Others, too, have shared the belief that the Manchester United striker misses too many chances at international level to merit the risk, but on the basis of his splendid club form it would seem only fair that he be given a decent chance to disprove the theory. Cole enjoyed probably the best of his six seasons at Old Trafford in 1999/2000. Although his friend and team-mate Dwight Yorke marginally outgunned him in the Premiership (20 goals to 19), Cole, unlike the previous season, was the more consistent partner. A four-goal salvo against his former club Newcastle set him off, and there were some equally classy performances to follow. He scored the crucial winner away to Leeds in the Premiership and delivered his most memorable performance yet for United in the brilliant 3-1 victory over Fiorentina in the Champions' League - a match in which he equalled Denis Law's club record of 14 European Cup goals.

DENNIS WISE

Dennis Wise looked all at sea for England at Euro 2000, but nobody could argue that he didn't deserve the international recognition after a season in which he performed heroically for his club. Surrounded by foreigners, the Chelsea captain was at times the only Englishman in the team, but he was their main pivot in midfield, frequently outclassing his more illustrious colleague, Frenchman Didier Deschamps, in that sector of the pitch. Small and fiery, Wise will never lose the natural aggression that is part of his game, but he tempered it well for Chelsea in the Champions' League, scoring four goals, including crucial strikes away to Milan and at home to Marseille. It was no coincidence that when the 33-

PLAYERS OF THE SEASON

year-old was controversially rested for the match against Lazio at Stamford Bridge, Chelsea went down 0-2, losing a European match at home for the first time in their history.

SAMI HYYPIÄ

It has been argued for many years that Finland will never qualify for a major international tournament until the majority of their players are engaged as professionals at major European clubs. Jari Litmanen was the standard-bearer, and now he has been joined by Sami Hyypiä, whose first season in the English Premiership, with Liverpool, could hardly have gone better. The giant centre-back was in majestic form almost from day one, his central defensive partnership with Swiss international Stéphane Henchoz solving the Merseysiders' well-documented defensive shortcomings almost at a stroke. Hyypiä's calmness, confidence and composure earned him the captain's armband, and none of the top-class strikers in the Premiership could honestly claim to have got the better of the big Finn, who deservedly won his country's Footballer of the Year award (thereby ending Litmanen's long hegemony) and was also shortlisted for the equivalent prize in England.

a very pleasant bonus and came at a time when new signing Thierry Henry was scoring goals at a phenomenal rate. Had the Frenchman found such form earlier, Arsenal's Premiership challenge would have been much stronger.

Thanks to a brief resurgence at the end of the season Leeds took the third Champions' League spot. David O'Leary's dashing young side had gone off the rails following the tragic events in Istanbul, but over the season they were good value for their third-place finish. They had been the only challengers to Manchester United, leading the table at halfway, and in dazzling young Australian Harry Kewell they possessed arguably the brightest and most spectacular talent in the Premiership.

Leeds were effectively gifted third place by Liverpool, who had an atrocious finish, taking just two points from their last 15 and failing to score a single goal in those last five fixtures, despite the presence in their ranks of three of the forwards set to represent England at Euro 2000 - Michael Owen, Robbie Fowler and new £12m signing Emile Heskey. The Merseysiders had made considerable

progress under Gérard Houllier, especially in defence, where newcomers Sami Hyypiä and Stéphane Henchoz formed a formidable central partnership, but the team's wretched finish ruined much of what had gone before.

Joining Liverpool and Chelsea in the UEFA Cup were Leicester City, who earned their European passport with a victory in the League Cup. Their third final appearance in four years brought a 2-1 victory over First Division Tranmere Rovers, with skipper Matt Elliott scoring the two headed goals which enabled Leicester to lift a major trophy at Wembley for the first time. With the final taking place in February, Leicester also became Europe's first trophy-winners of the new millennium. A superb season for Martin O'Neill's unfashionable, under-rated team was completed with an impressive eighth-place finish in the Premiership - the fourth year in a row that Leicester had finished in the top half of the table.

O'Neill, who left to join Celtic in the summer, was a strong candidate once again for the Manager of the Year award. Another was ex-national team boss Bobby Robson,

INTERNATIONAL HONOURS

World Cup Finals appearances: 1950, 1954 (qtr-finals), 1958, 1962 (qtr-finals), 1966 (Winners), 1970 (qtr-finals), 1982 (2nd phase), 1986 (qtr-finals), 1990 (4th), 1998 (2nd round)

European Championship appearances: 1968 (3rd), 1972, 1980, 1988, 1992, 1996 (semi-finals), 2000

European Club Competitions

Champions' Cup	Manchester United (1968, 1999)
	Liverpool (1977, 1978, 1981, 1984)
	Nottingham Forest (1979, 1980)
	Aston Villa (1982)
Cup-winners' Cup	Tottenham Hotspur (1963)
	West Ham United (1965)
	Manchester City (1970)
	Chelsea (1971, 1998)
	Everton (1985)
	Manchester United (1991)
	Arsenal (1994)
Fairs' Cup	Leeds United (1968, 1971)
	Newcastle United (1969)
	Arsenal (1970)
UEFA Cup	Tottenham Hotspur (1972, 1984)
	Liverpool (1973, 1976)
	Ipswich Town (1981)
Super Cup	Liverpool (1977)
	Nottingham Forest (1979)
	Aston Villa (1982)
	Manchester United (1991)
	Chelsea (1998)
World Club Cup	Manchester United (1999)

who successfully turned Newcastle United around after they had sunk to the depths of the table under previous manager Ruud Gullit. Newcastle's grim early-season fortunes were in direct contrast to those of north-east rivals Sunderland, who, freshly promoted from Division One, had a magnificent run in the autumn, even coming close at one stage to topping the table. Their great strength was the goalscoring of their deadly front pair, Kevin Phillips and Niall Quinn, with the former scoring 30 goals to win the Premiership's Golden Boot

The other two promoted sides, Bradford and Watford, both conformed to predictions by struggling against relegation. But while Watford, led by another former England manager, Graham Taylor, went down, Bradford survived. Their 1-0 victory at home to Liverpool on the final day condemned Wimbledon, after 14 years of gravity-defying resistance, to relegation, where they joined Sheffield Wednesday, condemned early on after a woeful start. The three vacant Premiership places were taken by First Division champions Charlton Athletic, runners-up Manchester City and - after finally breaking their play-off hoodoo - Ipswich Town.

PROMOTED CLUBS 99/00

FIRST DIVISION FINAL TABLE

		Pd	W	D	L	F	A	Pt	GD
1	**Charlton Athletic**	46	27	10	9	79	45	91	34
2	**Manchester City**	46	26	11	9	78	40	89	38
3	**Ipswich Town**	46	25	12	9	71	42	87	29
4	Barnsley	46	24	10	12	88	67	82	21
5	Birmingham City	46	22	11	13	65	44	77	21
6	Bolton Wanderers	46	21	13	12	69	50	76	19
7	Wolverhampton Wanderers	46	21	11	14	64	48	74	16
8	Huddersfield Town	46	21	11	14	62	49	74	13
9	Fulham	46	17	16	13	49	41	67	8
10	Queens Park Rangers	46	16	18	12	62	53	66	9
11	Blackburn Rovers	46	15	17	14	55	51	62	4
12	Norwich City	46	14	15	17	45	50	57	-5
13	Tranmere Rovers	46	15	12	19	57	68	57	-11
14	Nottingham Forest	46	14	14	18	53	55	56	-2
15	Crystal Palace	46	13	15	18	57	67	54	-10
16	Sheffield United	46	13	15	18	59	71	54	-12
17	Stockport County	46	13	15	18	55	67	54	-12
18	Portsmouth	46	13	12	21	55	66	51	-11
19	Crewe Alexandra	46	14	9	23	46	67	51	-21
20	Grimsby Town	46	13	12	21	41	67	51	-26
21	West Bromwich Albion	46	10	19	17	43	60	49	-17
22	Walsall	46	11	13	22	52	77	46	-25
23	Port Vale	46	7	15	24	48	69	36	-21
24	Swindon Town	46	8	12	26	38	77	36	-39

PROMOTION PLAY-OFFS

Bolton Wanderers 2, Ipswich Town 2
Ipswich Town 5, Bolton Wanderers 3 (aet)
(Ipswich Town 7-5)

Birmingham City 0, Barnsley 4
Barnsley 1, Birmingham City 2
(Barnsley 5-2)

Ipswich Town 4, Barnsley 2

CLUB DIRECTORIES

Charlton Athletic FC
The Valley, Floyd Road, Charlton, London SE7 8BL
tel - (020) 83334000 / fax - (020) 83334001
website - www.cafc.co.uk
Year of Formation - 1905
Chairman - M. A. Simons
Manager - Alan Curbishley
Stadium - The Valley (20,043)

MAJOR HONOURS
FA Cup - (1) 1947.

Manchester City FC
Maine Road, Moss Side, Manchester M14 7WN
tel - (0161) 2323000 / fax - (0161) 2328999
website - www.mcfc.co.uk
Year of Formation - 1887
Chairman - D. A. Bernstein
Secretary - J. B. Halford
Manager - Joe Royle
Stadium - Maine Road (34,026)

MAJOR HONOURS
League Championship - (2) 1937, 1968.
FA Cup - (4) 1904, 1934, 1956, 1969.
League Cup - (2) 1970, 1976.
European Cup-winners' Cup - (1) 1970.

Ipswich Town FC
Portman Road, Ipswich, Suffolk IP1 2DA
tel - (01473) 400500 / fax - (01473) 400040
website - www.itfc.co.uk
Year of Formation - 1878
Chairman - David Sheepshanks
Secretary - David Rose
Manager - George Burley
Stadium - Portman Road (22,700)

MAJOR HONOURS
League Championship - (1) 1962.
FA Cup - (1) 1978.
UEFA Cup - (1) 1981.

ARSENAL

CLUB DIRECTORY

Arsenal FC
Arsenal Stadium, Highbury, London N5 1BU
tel - (020) 77044000
fax - (020) 77044001
website - www.arsenal.co.uk
Year of Formation - 1886
Chairman - Peter Hill-Wood
Vice Chairman - David Dein
Manager - Arsène Wenger
Stadium - Highbury (38,500)

MAJOR HONOURS
League Championship - (11)
1931, 1933, 1934, 1935, 1938, 1948, 1953,
1971, 1989, 1991, 1998.
FA Cup - (7)
1930, 1936, 1950, 1971, 1979, 1993, 1998.
League Cup - (2) 1987, 1993.
European Cup-winners' Cup - (1) 1994.
Fairs' Cup - (1) 1970.

APPEARANCES 99/00

	P	Ap	(s)	Gls
Tony ADAMS	D	21		
Graham BARRETT	A		(2)	
Dennis BERGKAMP (HOL)	A	23	(5)	6
Tommy BLACK	M		(1)	
Luís BOA MORTE (POR)	A		(2)	
Ashley COLE	D	1		
Lee DIXON	D	28		4
Julian GRAY	M		(1)	
Gilles GRIMANDI (FRA)	D	27	(1)	2
Thierry HENRY (FRA)	A	26	(5)	17
Stephen HUGHES	M	1	(1)	
Martin KEOWN	D	27		1
Fredrik LJUNGBERG (SWE)	M	22	(4)	6
Oleh LUZHNYI (UKR)	D	16	(5)	
Brian McGOVERN (IRL)	D		(1)	
Stefan MALZ (GER)	M	2	(3)	1
Alex MANNINGER (AUT)	G	14	(1)	
Marc OVERMARS (HOL)	M	22	(9)	7
Ray PARLOUR	M	29	(1)	1
Emmanuel PETIT (FRA)	M	24	(2)	3
David SEAMAN	G	24		
Davor SUKER (CRO)	A	8	(14)	8
Matthew UPSON	D	5	(3)	
Paolo VERNAZZA	M	1	(1)	
Patrick VIEIRA (FRA)	M	29	(1)	2
Nélson VIVAS (ARG)	D	1	(4)	
Rhys WESTON (WAL)	D	1		
Nigel WINTERBURN	D	19	(9)	

LEAGUE RESULTS 1999/2000

07/08/99	Leicester City	H	2-1	Bergkamp, og (Sinclair)
10/08/99	Derby County	A	2-1	Petit, Bergkamp
14/08/99	Sunderland	A	0-0	
22/08/99	Manchester United	H	1-2	Ljungberg
25/08/99	Bradford City	H	2-0	Vieira, Kanu (p)
28/08/99	Liverpool	A	0-2	
11/09/99	Aston Villa	H	3-1	Suker 2, Kanu
18/09/99	Southampton	A	1-0	Henry
25/09/99	Watford	H	1-0	Kanu
03/10/99	West Ham United	A	1-2	Suker
16/10/99	Everton	H	4-1	Dixon, Suker 2, Kanu
23/10/99	Chelsea	A	3-2	Kanu 3
30/10/99	Newcastle United	H	0-0	
07/11/99	Tottenham Hotspur	A	1-2	Vieira
20/11/99	Middlesbrough	H	5-1	Overmars 3, Bergkamp 2
28/11/99	Derby County	H	2-1	Henry 2
04/12/99	Leicester City	A	3-0	Grimandi, Dixon, Overmars
18/12/99	Wimbledon	H	1-1	Henry
26/12/99	Coventry City	A	2-3	Ljungberg, Suker
28/12/99	Leeds United	H	2-0	Ljungberg, Henry
03/01/00	Sheffield Wednesday	A	1-1	Petit
15/01/00	Sunderland	H	4-1	Henry 2, Suker 2
24/01/00	Manchester United	A	1-1	Ljungberg
05/02/00	Bradford City	A	1-2	Henry
13/02/00	Liverpool	H	0-1	
26/02/00	Southampton	H	3-1	Ljungberg 2, Bergkamp
05/03/00	Aston Villa	A	1-1	Dixon
12/03/00	Middlesbrough	A	1-2	Bergkamp
19/03/00	Tottenham Hotspur	H	2-1	og (Armstrong), Henry (p)
26/03/00	Coventry City	H	3-0	Henry, Grimandi, Kanu
01/04/00	Wimbledon	A	3-1	Kanu 2, Henry (p)
16/04/00	Leeds United	A	4-0	Henry, Keown, Kanu, Overmars
23/04/00	Watford	A	3-2	Henry 2, Parlour
29/04/00	Everton	A	1-0	Overmars
02/05/00	West Ham United	H	2-1	Overmars, Petit
06/05/00	Chelsea	H	2-1	Henry 2
09/05/00	Sheffield Wednesday	H	3-3	Dixon, Silvinho, Henry
14/05/00	Newcastle United	A	2-4	Kanu, Malz

ASTON VILLA

CLUB DIRECTORY

Aston Villa FC
Villa Park, Trinity Road
Birmingham B6 6HE
tel - (0121) 3272299
fax - (0121) 3222107
website - www.avfc.co.uk
Year of Formation - 1874
Chairman - Doug Ellis
Secretary - Steven Stride
Manager - John Gregory
Stadium - Villa Park (39,217)

MAJOR HONOURS
League Championship - (7)
1894, 1896, 1897, 1899, 1900, 1910, 1981.
FA Cup - (7)
1887, 1895, 1897, 1905, 1913, 1920, 1957.
League Cup - (5)
1961, 1975, 1977, 1994, 1996.
European Champions' Cup - (1) 1982.
European Super Cup - (1) 1982.

APPEARANCES 99/00

	P	Ap	(s)	Gls
Gareth BARRY	D	30		1
Jonathan BEWERS	M		(1)	
George BOATENG (HOL)	M	30	(3)	2
Colin CALDERWOOD (SCO)	D	15	(3)	
Benito CARBONE (ITA)	A	22	(2)	3
Neil CUTLER	G		(1)	
Mark DELANEY (WAL)	M	25	(3)	1
Mark DRAPER	M		(1)	
Dion DUBLIN	A	23	(3)	12
Ugo EHIOGU	D	31		1
Peter ENCKELMAN (FIN)	G	9	(1)	
Najwan GHRAYEB (ISR)	D	1	(4)	
Lee HENDRIE	M	18	(11)	1
David JAMES	G	29		
Julian JOACHIM	A	27	(6)	6
Paul MERSON	M	24	(8)	5
Lloyd SAMUEL (TRI)	D	5	(4)	
Gareth SOUTHGATE	D	31		2
Steve STONE	M	10	(14)	1
Ian TAYLOR	M	25	(4)	5
Alan THOMPSON	M	16	(5)	2
Darius VASSELL	A	1	(10)	
Richard WALKER	A	2	(3)	2
Steve WATSON	D	13	(1)	
Alan WRIGHT	D	31	(1)	1

LEAGUE RESULTS 1999/2000

07/08/99	Newcastle United	A	1-0	Joachim
11/08/99	Everton	H	3-0	Joachim, Dublin, Taylor
16/08/99	West Ham United	H	2-2	Dublin 2
21/08/99	Chelsea	A	0-1	
24/08/99	Watford	A	1-0	Delaney
28/08/99	Middlesbrough	H	1-0	Dublin
11/09/99	Arsenal	A	1-3	Joachim
18/09/99	Bradford City	H	1-0	Dublin
25/09/99	Leicester City	A	1-3	Dublin
02/10/99	Liverpool	H	0-0	
18/10/99	Sunderland	A	1-2	Dublin
23/10/99	Wimbledon	H	1-1	Dublin
30/10/99	Manchester United	A	0-3	
06/11/99	Southampton	H	0-1	
22/11/99	Coventry City	A	1-2	Dublin
27/11/99	Everton	A	0-0	
04/12/99	Newcastle United	H	0-1	
18/12/99	Sheffield Wednesday	H	2-1	Merson, Taylor
26/12/99	Derby County	A	2-0	Boateng, Taylor
29/12/99	Tottenham Hotspur	H	1-1	Taylor
03/01/00	Leeds United	A	2-1	Southgate
15/01/00	West Ham United	A	1-1	Taylor
22/01/00	Chelsea	H	0-0	
05/02/00	Watford	H	4-0	Stone, Merson 2, Walker
14/02/00	Middlesbrough	A	4-0	Carbone, og (Summerbell), Joachim 2
26/02/00	Bradford City	A	1-1	Merson
05/03/00	Arsenal	H	1-1	Walker
11/03/00	Coventry City	H	1-0	Ehiogu
15/03/00	Liverpool	A	0-0	
18/03/00	Southampton	A	0-2	
25/03/00	Derby County	H	2-0	Carbone, Boateng
05/04/00	Sheffield Wednesday	A	1-0	Thompson
09/04/00	Leeds United	H	1-0	Joachim
15/04/00	Tottenham Hotspur	A	4-2	Dublin 2 (1p), Carbone, Wright
22/04/00	Leicester City	H	2-2	Thompson, Merson
29/04/00	Sunderland	H	1-1	Barry
06/05/00	Wimbledon	A	2-2	Hendrie, Dublin
14/05/00	Manchester United	H	0-1	

BRADFORD CITY

Bradford City FC
Bradford & Bingley Stadium
Valley Parade
Bradford
BD8 7DY
tel - (01274) 773355
fax - (01274) 773356
website - www.bradfordcity.co.uk
Year of Formation - 1903
Chairman - Geoffrey Richmond
Secretary - Jon Pollard
Manager - Paul Jewell (00/01 - Chris Hutchings)
Stadium - Bradford & Bingley (25,000)

MAJOR HONOURS
FA Cup - (1) 1911.

APPEARANCES 99/00

	P	Ap	(s)	Gls
Peter BEAGRIE	M	30	(5)	7
Robbie BLAKE	A	15	(13)	2
Jorge CADETE (POR)	A	2	(5)	
Matt CLARKE	G	21		
Aidan DAVISON (NIR)	G	5	(1)	
John DREYER	M	11	(3)	1
Gareth GRANT	A		(1)	
Gunnar HALLE (NOR)	D	37	(1)	
Wayne JACOBS	D	22	(2)	
Jamie LAWRENCE	M	19	(4)	3
Stuart McCALL (SCO)	M	33	(1)	1
Lee MILLS	A	19	(2)	5
Andy MYERS	D	10	(3)	
Andrew O'BRIEN	D	36		1
Isaiah RANKIN	A		(9)	
Neil REDFEARN	M	14	(3)	1
Bruno RODRIGUEZ (FRA)	A		(2)	
Dean SAUNDERS (WAL)	A	28	(6)	3
Lee SHARPE	M	13	(5)	
Neville SOUTHALL (WAL)	G	1		
Gary WALSH	G	11		
Ashley WESTWOOD	D	1	(4)	
David WETHERALL	D	38		2
Gareth WHALLEY	M	16		1
Dean WINDASS	A	36	(2)	10

LEAGUE RESULTS 1999/2000

07/08/99	Middlesbrough	A	1-0	Saunders
14/08/99	Sheffield Wednesday	H	1-1	Beagrie (p)
21/08/99	Watford	A	0-1	
25/08/99	Arsenal	A	0-2	
28/08/99	West Ham United	H	0-3	
12/09/99	Tottenham Hotspur	H	1-1	McCall
18/09/99	Aston Villa	A	0-1	
25/09/99	Derby County	A	1-0	og (Carbonari)
02/10/99	Sunderland	H	0-4	
16/10/99	Wimbledon	A	2-3	Mills, Windass
23/10/99	Leicester City	H	3-1	Blake, Mills, Redfearn
01/11/99	Liverpool	A	1-3	Windass
06/11/99	Coventry City	H	1-1	Mills
20/11/99	Leeds United	A	1-2	Windass
28/11/99	Chelsea	A	0-1	
04/12/99	Middlesbrough	H	1-1	Mills
18/12/99	Newcastle United	H	2-0	Saunders, Wetherall
26/12/99	Manchester United	A	0-4	
28/12/99	Everton	H	0-0	
03/01/00	Southampton	A	0-1	
08/01/00	Chelsea	H	1-1	Mills
15/01/00	Sheffield Wednesday	A	0-2	
22/01/00	Watford	H	3-2	Beagrie (p), Whalley, O'Brien
05/02/00	Arsenal	H	2-1	Windass, Saunders
12/02/00	West Ham United	A	4-5	Windass, Beagrie (p), Lawrence 2
26/02/00	Aston Villa	H	1-1	Windass
04/03/00	Tottenham Hotspur	A	1-1	Lawrence
12/03/00	Leeds United	H	1-2	Beagrie
18/03/00	Coventry City	A	0-4	
25/03/00	Manchester United	H	0-4	
01/04/00	Newcastle United	A	0-2	
08/04/00	Southampton	H	1-2	Blake
15/04/00	Everton	A	0-4	
21/04/00	Derby County	H	4-4	Windass 3, Beagrie (p)
24/04/00	Sunderland	A	1-0	Dreyer
30/04/00	Wimbledon	H	3-0	Beagrie 2 (1p), Windass
06/05/00	Leicester City	A	0-3	
14/05/00	Liverpool	H	1-0	Wetherall

CHELSEA

CLUB DIRECTORY

Chelsea FC
Stamford Bridge, London SW6 1HS
tel - (020) 73855545
fax - (020) 73814831
website - www.chelseafc.co.uk
Year of Formation - 1905
Chairman - Ken Bates
Managing Director - Colin Hutchinson
Manager - Gianluca Vialli
Stadium - Stamford Bridge (35,421)

MAJOR HONOURS
League Championship - (1) 1955.
FA Cup - (3) 1970, 1997, 2000.
League Cup - (2) 1965, 1998.
European Cup-winners' Cup - (2) 1971, 1998.
European Super Cup - (1) 1998.

APPEARANCES 99/00

	P	Ap	(s)	Gls
Gabriele AMBROSETTI (ITA)	M	9	(7)	
Celestine BABAYARO (NIG)	D	23	(2)	
Carlo CUDICINI (ITA)	G	1		
Samuele DALLA BONA (ITA)	D		(2)	
Ed DE GOEY (HOL)	G	37		
Marcel DESAILLY (FRA)	D	23		1
Didier DESCHAMPS (FRA)	M	24	(3)	
Roberto DI MATTEO (ITA)	M	14	(4)	2
Albert FERRER (ESP)	D	24	(1)	
Tore André FLO (NOR)	A	20	(14)	10
Bjarne GOLDBAEK (DEN)	M	2	(4)	
Jon HARLEY	D	13	(4)	2
Jes HØGH (DEN)	D	6	(3)	
Bernard LAMBOURDE (FRA)	M	12	(3)	2
Frank LEBOEUF (FRA)	D	28		2
Graeme LE SAUX	D	6	(2)	
Mario MELCHIOT (HOL)	D	4	(1)	
Jody MORRIS	M	19	(11)	3
Dan PETRESCU (ROM)	M	24	(5)	4
Gustavo POYET (URU)	M	25	(8)	10
Chris SUTTON	A	21	(7)	1
John TERRY	D	2	(2)	
Emerson THOME (BRA)	D	18	(2)	
George WEAH (LIB)	A	9	(2)	3
Dennis WISE	M	29	(1)	4
Robert WOLLEASTON	A		(1)	
Gianfranco ZOLA (ITA)	A	25	(8)	4

LEAGUE RESULTS 1999/2000

07/08/99	Sunderland	H	4-0	Poyet 2, Zola, Flo
14/08/99	Leicester City	A	2-2	Wise, og (Sinclair)
21/08/99	Aston Villa	H	1-0	og (Ehiogu)
28/08/99	Wimbledon	A	1-0	Petrescu
11/09/99	Newcastle United	H	1-0	Leboeuf (p)
18/09/99	Watford	A	0-1	
25/09/99	Middlesbrough	A	1-0	Lambourde
03/10/99	Manchester United	H	5-0	Poyet 2, Sutton, og (Berg), Morris
16/10/99	Liverpool	A	0-1	
23/10/99	Arsenal	H	2-3	Flo, Petrescu
30/10/99	Derby County	A	1-3	Leboeuf
07/11/99	West Ham United	H	0-0	
20/11/99	Everton	A	1-1	Flo
28/11/99	Bradford City	H	1-0	Flo
04/12/99	Sunderland	A	1-4	Poyet
19/12/99	Leeds United	H	0-2	
26/12/99	Southampton	A	2-1	Flo 2
29/12/99	Sheffield Wednesday	H	3-0	Wise, Flo, Morris
04/01/00	Coventry City	A	2-2	Flo 2
08/01/00	Bradford City	A	1-1	Petrescu
12/01/00	Tottenham Hotspur	H	1-0	Weah
15/01/00	Leicester City	H	1-1	Wise
22/01/00	Aston Villa	A	0-0	
05/02/00	Tottenham Hotspur	A	1-0	Lambourde
12/02/00	Wimbledon	H	3-1	Poyet, Weah, Morris
26/02/00	Watford	H	2-1	Desailly, Harley
04/03/00	Newcastle United	A	1-0	Poyet
11/03/00	Everton	H	1-1	Wise
18/03/00	West Ham United	A	0-0	
25/03/00	Southampton	H	1-1	og (Richards)
01/04/00	Leeds United	A	1-0	Harley
12/04/00	Coventry City	H	2-1	og (Hendry), Zola
15/04/00	Sheffield Wednesday	A	0-1	
22/04/00	Middlesbrough	H	1-1	Poyet
24/04/00	Manchester United	A	2-3	Petrescu, Zola
29/04/00	Liverpool	H	2-0	Weah, Di Matteo
06/05/00	Arsenal	A	1-2	Poyet
14/05/00	Derby County	H	4-0	Zola, Poyet, Di Matteo, Flo

COVENTRY CITY

THE EUROPEAN FOOTBALL YEARBOOK 2000-2001

CLUB DIRECTORY

Coventry City FC
Highfield Road Stadium
King Richard Street
Coventry CV2 4FW
tel - (024) 76234000
fax - (024) 76234099
website - www.ccfc.co.uk
Year of Formation - 1883
Chairman - Bryan Richardson
Secretary - Graham Hover
Manager - Gordon Strachan
Stadium - Highfield Road (23,611)

MAJOR HONOURS
FA Cup - (1) 1987.

APPEARANCES 99/00

	P	Ap	(s)	Gls
John ALOISI (AUS)	A	3	(4)	2
Robert BETTS	M		(2)	
Gary BREEN (IRL)	D	20	(1)	
David BURROWS	D	11	(4)	
Youssef CHIPPO (MAR)	M	33		2
Marc EDWORTHY	D	10		
John EUSTACE	M	12	(4)	1
Steve FROGGATT	M	21	(5)	1
Tomas GUSTAFSSON (SWE)	D	7	(3)	
Mustapha HADJI (MAR)	M	33		6
Marcus HALL	M	7	(2)	
Paul HALL (JAM)	A		(1)	
Magnus HEDMAN (SWE)	G	35		
Colin HENDRY (SCO)	D	9		
Darren HUCKERBY	A	1		
Robbie KEANE (IRL)	A	30	(1)	12
Muhamed KONJIC (BOS)	D	3	(1)	
Gary McALLISTER (SCO)	M	38		11
Gary McSHEFFREY	A		(3)	
Runar NORMANN (NOR)	M	1	(7)	
Steve OGRIZOVIC	G	3		
Carlton PALMER	M	15		1
Barry QUINN (IRL)	M	5	(6)	
Cédric ROUSSEL (BEL)	A	18	(4)	6
Richard SHAW	D	27	(2)	
Gavin STRACHAN (SCO)	M	1	(2)	
Paul TELFER (SCO)	M	26	(4)	
Noel WHELAN	M	20	(6)	1
Paul WILLIAMS	D	26	(2)	1
Ysrael ZUNIGA (PER)	A	3	(3)	2

LEAGUE RESULTS 1999/2000

07/08/99	Southampton	H	0-1	
11/08/99	Leicester City	A	0-1	
14/08/99	Wimbledon	A	1-1	McAllister (p)
21/08/99	Derby County	H	2-0	Keane 2
25/08/99	Manchester United	H	1-2	Aloisi
29/08/99	Sunderland	A	1-1	Keane
11/09/99	Leeds United	H	3-4	McAllister (p), Aloisi, Chippo
19/09/99	Tottenham Hotspur	A	2-3	Keane, Chippo
25/09/99	West Ham United	H	1-0	Hadji
02/10/99	Everton	A	1-1	McAllister
16/10/99	Newcastle United	H	4-1	Palmer, Williams, Keane, Hadji
23/10/99	Sheffield Wednesday	A	0-0	
31/10/99	Watford	H	4-0	Keane, Froggatt, Hadji, McAllister (p)
06/11/99	Bradford City	A	1-1	McAllister
22/11/99	Aston Villa	H	2-1	Roussel, Keane
27/11/99	Leicester City	H	0-1	
04/12/99	Southampton	A	0-0	
18/12/99	Liverpool	A	0-2	
26/12/99	Arsenal	H	3-2	McAllister, Hadji, Keane
04/01/00	Chelsea	H	2-2	Roussel, Keane
15/01/00	Wimbledon	H	2-0	McAllister (p), Keane
22/01/00	Derby County	A	0-0	
05/02/00	Manchester United	A	2-3	Roussel 2
12/02/00	Sunderland	H	3-2	Keane, Hadji, Roussel
19/02/00	Middlesbrough	A	0-2	
26/02/00	Tottenham Hotspur	H	0-1	
05/03/00	Leeds United	A	0-3	
11/03/00	Aston Villa	A	0-1	
15/03/00	Everton	H	1-0	McAllister
18/03/00	Bradford City	H	4-0	Roussel, Whelan, Eustace (p), Zuniga
26/03/00	Arsenal	A	0-3	
01/04/00	Liverpool	H	0-3	
12/04/00	Chelsea	A	1-2	McAllister
15/04/00	Middlesbrough	H	2-1	og (Ince), Keane
22/04/00	West Ham United	A	0-5	
29/04/00	Newcastle United	A	0-2	
06/05/00	Sheffield Wednesday	H	4-1	McAllister 2, Zuniga, Hadji
14/05/00	Watford	A	0-1	

DERBY COUNTY

CLUB DIRECTORY

Derby County FC
Pride Park Stadium
Derby DE24 8XL
tel - (01332) 202202
fax - (01332) 667519
website - www.dcfc.co.uk
Year of Formation - 1884
Chairman - Lionel Pickering
Secretary - Keith Pearson
Manager - Jim Smith
Stadium - Pride Park (33,597)

MAJOR HONOURS
League Championship - (2) 1972, 1975.
FA Cup - (1) 1946.

APPEARANCES 99/00

		P	Ap	(s)	Gls
Francesco BAIANO (ITA)	A	5	(4)	
Mikkel BECK (DEN)	A	5	(6)	1
Paul BOERTIEN	D		(2)	
Lars BOHINEN (NOR)	M	8	(5)	
Vasilios BORBOKIS (GRE)	D	6	(6)	
Craig BURLEY (SCO)	M	18		5
Deon BURTON (JAM)	A	15	(4)	4
Horacio CARBONARI (ARG)	D	29		2
Malcolm CHRISTIE	A	10	(11)	5
Rory DELAP (IRL)	M	34		8
Tony DORIGO	D	20	(3)	
Steve ELLIOTT	D	18	(2)	
Stefano ERANIO (ITA)	M	17	(2)	
Esteban FUERTES (ARG)	A	8		1
Kevin HARPER (SCO)	A		(5)	
Russell HOULT	G	10		
Richard JACKSON	D		(2)	
Seth JOHNSON	M	36		1
Giorgi KINKLADZE (GEO)	M	12	(5)	1
Jacob LAURSEN (DEN)	D	36		1
Lee MORRIS	A	2	(1)	
Adam MURRAY	M	1	(7)	
Avi NIMNI (ISR)	M	2	(2)	1
Mart POOM (EST)	G	28		
Darryl POWELL (JAM)	M	31		2
Spencer PRIOR	D	15	(5)	
Chris RIGGOTT	D		(1)	
Marvin ROBINSON	A	3	(5)	
Stefan SCHNOOR (GER)	D	22	(7)	
Branko STRUPAR (BEL)	A	13	(2)	5
Dean STURRIDGE	A	14	(11)	6

LEAGUE RESULTS 1999/2000

07/08/99	Leeds United	A	0-0	
10/08/99	Arsenal	H	1-2	Delap
14/08/99	Middlesbrough	H	1-3	Burton
21/08/99	Coventry City	A	0-2	
25/08/99	Sheffield Wednesday	A	2-0	Delap, Sturridge
28/08/99	Everton	H	1-0	Fuertes
11/09/99	Wimbledon	A	2-2	Carbonari, Johnson
18/09/99	Sunderland	H	0-5	
25/09/99	Bradford City	H	0-1	
04/10/99	Southampton	A	3-3	Delap, Laursen, Beck
16/10/99	Tottenham Hotspur	H	0-1	
25/10/99	Newcastle United	A	0-2	
30/10/99	Chelsea	H	3-1	Burton, Delap 2
06/11/99	Liverpool	A	0-2	
20/11/99	Manchester United	H	1-2	Delap
28/11/99	Arsenal	A	1-2	Sturridge
05/12/99	Leeds United	H	0-1	
18/12/99	Leicester City	A	1-0	Powell
26/12/99	Aston Villa	H	0-2	
28/12/99	West Ham United	A	1-1	Sturridge
03/01/00	Watford	H	2-0	Strupar 2
15/01/00	Middlesbrough	A	4-1	Christie 2, Burton, Burley
22/01/00	Coventry City	H	0-0	
05/02/00	Sheffield Wednesday	H	3-3	Strupar, Burley, Christie
12/02/00	Everton	A	1-2	Nimni
26/02/00	Sunderland	A	1-1	Christie
04/03/00	Wimbledon	H	4-0	Kinkladze, Christie, Sturridge, Burton
11/03/00	Manchester United	A	1-3	Strupar
18/03/00	Liverpool	H	0-2	
25/03/00	Aston Villa	A	0-2	
02/04/00	Leicester City	H	3-0	Burley, Delap, Sturridge
08/04/00	Watford	A	0-0	
15/04/00	West Ham United	H	1-2	Sturridge
21/04/00	Bradford City	A	4-4	Delap, Strupar, Burley 2 (2p)
24/04/00	Southampton	H	2-0	Powell, Christie
29/04/00	Tottenham Hotspur	A	1-1	Carbonari
06/05/00	Newcastle United	H	0-0	
14/05/00	Chelsea	A	0-4	

EVERTON

CLUB DIRECTORY

Everton FC
Goodison Park
Liverpool L4 4EL
tel - (0151) 3302200
fax - (0151) 2869112
website - www.evertonfc.co.uk
Year of Formation - 1878
Chairman - Sir Philip Carter
Vice Chairman - Bill Kenwright
Manager - Walter Smith
Stadium - Goodison Park (40,260)

MAJOR HONOURS
League Championship - (9) 1891, 1915, 1928, 1932, 1939, 1963, 1970, 1985, 1987.
FA Cup - (5) 1906, 1933, 1966, 1984, 1995.
European Cup-winners' Cup - (1) 1985.

APPEARANCES 99/00

		P	Ap	(s)	Gls
ABEL XAVIER (POR)	D		18	(2)	
Michael BALL	D		14	(11)	1
Nick BARMBY	M		37		9
Danny CADAMARTERI	A		3	(14)	1
Kevin CAMPBELL	A		26		12
Alex CLELAND (SCO)	D		3	(6)	
John COLLINS (SCO)	M		33	(2)	2
Richard DUNNE (IRL)	D		27	(4)	
Scot GEMMILL (SCO)	M		6	(8)	1
Paul GERRARD	G		34		
Richard GOUGH (SCO)	D		29		1
Tony GRANT	M			(2)	
Mark HUGHES (WAL)	A		9		1
Stephen HUGHES	M		11		1
Don HUTCHISON (SCO)	M		28	(3)	6
Francis JEFFERS	A		16	(5)	6
Phil JEVONS	M		2	(1)	
Tommy JOHNSON	A			(3)	
Jamie MILLIGAN	A			(1)	
Joe-Max MOORE (USA)	A		11	(4)	6
Thomas MYHRE (NOR)	G		4		
Mark PEMBRIDGE (WAL)	M		29	(2)	2
Terry PHELAN (IRL)	D			(1)	
Steve SIMONSEN	G			(1)	
David UNSWORTH	D		32	(1)	6
Mitch WARD	M		6	(4)	
Dave WATSON	D		5	(1)	
David WEIR (SCO)	D		35		2

LEAGUE RESULTS 1999/2000

08/08/99	Manchester United	H	1-1	og (Stam)
11/08/99	Aston Villa	A	0-3	
14/08/99	Tottenham Hotspur	A	2-3	Unsworth 2 (2p)
21/08/99	Southampton	H	4-1	Gough, og (Lundekvam), Jeffers, Campbell
25/08/99	Wimbledon	H	4-0	Unsworth, Barmby, Jeffers, Campbell
28/08/99	Derby County	A	0-1	
11/09/99	Sheffield Wednesday	A	2-0	Barmby, Gemmill
19/09/99	West Ham United	H	1-0	Jeffers
27/09/99	Liverpool	A	1-0	Campbell
02/10/99	Coventry City	H	1-1	Jeffers
16/10/99	Arsenal	A	1-4	Collins
24/10/99	Leeds United	H	4-4	Campbell 2, Hutchison, Weir
30/10/99	Middlesbrough	A	1-2	Campbell
07/11/99	Newcastle United	A	1-1	Campbell
20/11/99	Chelsea	H	1-1	Campbell
27/11/99	Aston Villa	H	0-0	
04/12/99	Manchester United	A	1-5	Jeffers
18/12/99	Watford	A	3-1	Barmby, Hutchison, Unsworth (p)
26/12/99	Sunderland	H	5-0	Hutchison 2, Jeffers, Pembridge, Campbell
28/12/99	Bradford City	A	0-0	
03/01/00	Leicester City	H	2-2	Hutchison, Unsworth (p)
15/01/00	Tottenham Hotspur	H	2-2	Campbell, Moore
22/01/00	Southampton	A	0-2	
06/02/00	Wimbledon	A	3-0	Campbell 2, Moore
12/02/00	Derby County	H	2-1	Moore, Ball (p)
26/02/00	West Ham United	A	4-0	Barmby 3, Moore
04/03/00	Sheffield Wednesday	H	1-1	Weir
11/03/00	Chelsea	A	1-1	Cadamarteri
15/03/00	Coventry City	A	0-1	
19/03/00	Newcastle United	H	0-2	
25/03/00	Sunderland	A	1-2	Barmby
01/04/00	Watford	H	4-2	Hughes M., Moore 2, Hughes S.
08/04/00	Leicester City	A	1-1	Hutchison
15/04/00	Bradford City	H	4-0	Pembridge, Unsworth (p), Barmby, Collins
21/04/00	Liverpool	H	0-0	
29/04/00	Arsenal	H	0-1	
08/05/00	Leeds United	A	1-1	Barmby
14/05/00	Middlesbrough	H	0-2	

LEEDS UNITED

CLUB DIRECTORY

Leeds United FC
Elland Road
Leeds LS11 OES
tel - (0113) 2266000
fax - (0113) 2266050
website - www.lufc.co.uk
Year of Formation - 1919
Chairman - Peter Ridsdale
Secretary - Ian Silvester
Manager - David O'Leary
Stadium - Elland Road (40,000)

MAJOR HONOURS
League Championship - (3) 1969, 1974, 1992.
FA Cup - (1) 1972.
League Cup - (1) 1968.
Fairs' Cup - (2) 1968, 1971.

APPEARANCES 99/00

	P	Ap	(s)	Gls
Eirik BAKKE (NOR)	M	24	(5)	2
David BATTY	M	16		
Lee BOWYER	M	31	(2)	5
Michael BRIDGES	A	32	(2)	19
Michael DUBERRY	D	12	(1)	1
Alf Inge HÅLAND (NOR)	M	7	(6)	
Ian HARTE (IRL)	D	33		6
Martin HIDEN (AUT)	D		(1)	
David HOPKIN (SCO)	M	10	(4)	1
Darren HUCKERBY	A	9	(24)	2
Matthew JONES (WAL)	M	5	(6)	
Gary KELLY (IRL)	D	28	(3)	
Harry KEWELL (AUS)	M	36		10
Stephen McPHAIL (IRL)	M	23	(1)	2
Nigel MARTYN	G	38		
Danny MILLS	D	16	(1)	1
Lucas RADEBE (SAF)	D	31		
Alan SMITH	A	20	(6)	4
Jason WILCOX	M	15	(5)	3
Jonathan WOODGATE	D	32	(2)	1

LEAGUE RESULTS 1999/2000

07/08/99	Derby County	H	0-0	
11/08/99	Southampton	A	3-0	Bridges 3
14/08/99	Manchester United	A	0-2	
21/08/99	Sunderland	H	2-1	Bowyer, Mills
23/08/99	Liverpool	H	1-2	og (Song)
28/08/99	Tottenham Hotspur	A	2-1	Smith, Harte
11/09/99	Coventry City	A	4-3	Bowyer, Huckerby, Harte (p), Bridges
19/09/99	Middlesbrough	H	2-0	Bridges, Kewell
25/09/99	Newcastle United	H	3-2	Bowyer, Kewell, Bridges
03/10/99	Watford	A	2-1	Bridges, Kewell
16/10/99	Sheffield Wednesday	H	2-0	Smith 2
24/10/99	Everton	A	4-4	Bridges 2, Kewell, Woodgate
30/10/99	West Ham United	H	1-0	Harte
07/11/99	Wimbledon	A	0-2	
20/11/99	Bradford City	H	2-1	Smith, Harte (p)
28/11/99	Southampton	H	1-0	Bridges
05/12/99	Derby County	A	1-0	Harte (p)
19/12/99	Chelsea	A	2-0	McPhail 2
26/12/99	Leicester City	H	2-1	Bridges, Bowyer
28/12/99	Arsenal	A	0-2	
03/01/00	Aston Villa	H	1-2	Kewell
23/01/00	Sunderland	A	2-1	Wilcox, Bridges
05/02/00	Liverpool	A	1-3	Bowyer
12/02/00	Tottenham Hotspur	H	1-0	Kewell
20/02/00	Manchester United	H	0-1	
26/02/00	Middlesbrough	A	0-0	
05/03/00	Coventry City	H	3-0	Kewell, Bridges, Wilcox
12/03/00	Bradford City	A	2-1	Bridges 2
19/03/00	Wimbledon	H	4-1	Bakke 2, Harte (p), Kewell
26/03/00	Leicester City	A	1-2	Kewell
01/04/00	Chelsea	H	0-1	
09/04/00	Aston Villa	A	0-1	
16/04/00	Arsenal	H	0-4	
23/04/00	Newcastle United	A	2-2	Bridges, Wilcox
30/04/00	Sheffield Wednesday	A	3-0	Hopkin, Bridges, Kewell
03/05/00	Watford	H	3-1	Bridges, Duberry, Huckerby
08/05/00	Everton	H	1-1	Bridges
14/05/00	West Ham United	A	0-0	

LEICESTER CITY

CLUB DIRECTORY

Leicester City FC
City Stadium
Filbert Street
Leicester LE2 7FL
tel - (0116) 2915000
fax - (0116) 2470585
website - www.lcfc.co.uk
Year of Formation - 1884
Chairman - John Elsom
Manager - Martin O'Neill (00/01 - Peter Taylor)
Stadium - Filbert Street (22,215)

MAJOR HONOURS
League Cup - (3) 1964, 1997, 2000.

APPEARANCES 99/00

		P	Ap	(s)	Gls
Pegguy ARPHEXAD (FRA)	G		9	(2)	
Stuart CAMPBELL (SCO)	M		1	(3)	
Stan COLLYMORE	A		6		4
Tony COTTEE	A		30	(3)	13
Lawrie DUDFIELD	A			(2)	
Darren EADIE	M		15	(1)	
Matt ELLIOTT (SCO)	D		37		6
Graham FENTON	A		1	(1)	
Tim FLOWERS	G		29		
Phil GILCHRIST	D		17	(10)	1
Tommy GOODWIN	D		1		
Arnar GUNNLAUGSSON (ISL)	M		2		
Steve GUPPY	M		29	(1)	2
Emile HESKEY	A		23		7
Andrew IMPEY	M		28	(1)	1
Muzzy IZZET (TUR)	M		32		8
Neil LENNON (NIR)	M		31		1
Ian MARSHALL	A		2	(19)	
Stefan OAKES	M		15	(7)	1
Robbie SAVAGE (WAL)	M		35		1
Frank SINCLAIR (JAM)	D		34		
Jordan STEWART	M			(1)	
Gerry TAGGART (NIR)	D		30	(1)	6
Danny THOMAS	D			(3)	
Steve WALSH	D		5	(6)	
Theo ZAGORAKIS (GRE)	M		6	(11)	1

LEAGUE RESULTS 1999/2000

07/08/99	Arsenal	A	1-2	Cottee
11/08/99	Coventry City	H	1-0	Izzet (p)
14/08/99	Chelsea	H	2-2	Heskey, Izzet (p)
21/08/99	West Ham United	A	1-2	Heskey
24/08/99	Middlesbrough	A	3-0	Heskey 2, Cottee
30/08/99	Watford	H	1-0	Izzet
11/09/99	Sunderland	A	0-2	
18/09/99	Liverpool	H	2-2	Cottee, Izzet
25/09/99	Aston Villa	H	3-1	Izzet, og (Southgate), Cottee
03/10/99	Tottenham Hotspur	A	3-2	Izzet 2 (1p), Taggart
16/10/99	Southampton	H	2-1	Guppy, Cottee
23/10/99	Bradford City	A	1-3	Impey
30/10/99	Sheffield Wednesday	H	3-0	Taggart 2, Cottee
06/11/99	Manchester United	A	0-2	
20/11/99	Wimbledon	H	2-1	Cottee 2
27/11/99	Coventry City	A	1-0	Heskey
04/12/99	Arsenal	H	0-3	
18/12/99	Derby County	H	0-1	
26/12/99	Leeds United	A	1-2	Cottee
28/12/99	Newcastle United	H	1-2	Zagorakis
03/01/00	Everton	A	2-2	Elliott 2
15/01/00	Chelsea	A	1-1	Taggart
22/01/00	West Ham United	H	1-3	Heskey
05/02/00	Middlesbrough	H	2-1	og (O'Neill), og (Schwarzer)
12/02/00	Watford	A	1-1	Elliott
05/03/00	Sunderland	H	5-2	Collymore 3, Heskey, Oakes
11/03/00	Wimbledon	A	1-2	Taggart
18/03/00	Manchester United	H	0-2	
26/03/00	Leeds United	H	2-1	Collymore, Guppy
02/04/00	Derby County	A	0-3	
08/04/00	Everton	H	1-1	Taggart
15/04/00	Newcastle United	A	2-0	Cottee, Savage
19/04/00	Tottenham Hotspur	H	0-1	
22/04/00	Aston Villa	A	2-2	Elliott, Lennon
29/04/00	Southampton	A	2-1	Cottee, Izzet
03/05/00	Liverpool	A	2-0	Cottee, Gilchrist
06/05/00	Bradford City	H	3-0	Elliott 2, Cottee
14/05/00	Sheffield Wednesday	A	0-4	

LIVERPOOL

CLUB DIRECTORY

Liverpool FC
Anfield Road, Liverpool L4 0TH
tel - (0151) 2632361 / fax - (0151) 2608813
website - www.liverpoolfc.net
Year of Formation - 1892
Chairman - David Moores
Chief Executive - Rick Parry
Manager - Gérard Houllier
Stadium - Anfield (45,362)

MAJOR HONOURS
League Championship - (18)
1901, 1906, 1922, 1923, 1947, 1964, 1966,
1973, 1976, 1977, 1979, 1980, 1982, 1983,
1984, 1986, 1988, 1990.
FA Cup - (5) 1965, 1974, 1986, 1989, 1992.
League Cup - (5)
1981, 1982, 1983, 1984, 1995.
European Champions' Cup - (4)
1977, 1978, 1981, 1984.
UEFA Cup - (2) 1973, 1976.
European Super Cup - (1) 1977.

APPEARANCES 99/00

	P	Ap	(s)	Gls
Patrik BERGER (CZE)	M	34		9
Titi CAMARA (GUI)	A	22	(11)	9
Jamie CARRAGHER	D	33	(3)	
Robbie FOWLER	A	8	(6)	3
Brad FRIEDEL (USA)	G	2		
Steven GERRARD	M	26	(3)	1
Dietmar HAMANN (GER)	M	27	(1)	1
Vegard HEGGEM (NOR)	D	10	(12)	1
Stéphane HENCHOZ (SUI)	D	29		
Emile HESKEY	A	12		3
Sami HYYPIÄ (FIN)	D	38		2
Dominic MATTEO	D	32		
Erik MEIJER (HOL)	A	7	(14)	
Danny MURPHY	M	9	(14)	3
John NEWBY	A		(1)	
Michael OWEN	A	22	(5)	11
Jamie REDKNAPP	M	18	(4)	3
Karlheinz RIEDLE (GER)	A		(1)	
Vladimir SMICER (CZE)	M	13	(8)	1
Rigobert SONG (CMR)	D	14	(4)	
Steve STAUNTON (IRL)	D	7	(5)	
David THOMPSON	M	19	(8)	3
Sander WESTERVELD (HOL)	G	36		

LEAGUE RESULTS 1999/2000

07/08/99	Sheffield Wednesday	A	2-1	Fowler, Camara
14/08/99	Watford	H	0-1	
21/08/99	Middlesbrough	A	0-1	
23/08/99	Leeds United	A	2-1	Camara, og (Radebe)
28/08/99	Arsenal	H	2-0	Fowler, Berger
11/09/99	Manchester United	H	2-3	Hyypiä, Berger
18/09/99	Leicester City	A	2-2	Owen 2 (1p)
27/09/99	Everton	H	0-1	
02/10/99	Aston Villa	A	0-0	
16/10/99	Chelsea	H	1-0	Thompson
23/10/99	Southampton	A	1-1	Camara
27/10/99	West Ham United	H	1-0	Camara
01/11/99	Bradford City	H	3-1	Camara, Redknapp (p), Heggem
06/11/99	Derby County	H	2-0	Murphy, Redknapp
20/11/99	Sunderland	A	2-0	Owen, Berger
27/11/99	West Ham United	A	0-1	
05/12/99	Sheffield Wednesday	H	4-1	Hyypiä, Murphy, Gerrard, Thompson
18/12/99	Coventry City	H	2-0	Owen, Camara
26/12/99	Newcastle United	A	2-2	Owen 2
28/12/99	Wimbledon	H	3-1	Owen, Berger, Fowler
03/01/00	Tottenham Hotspur	A	0-1	
15/01/00	Watford	A	3-2	Berger, Thompson, Smicer
22/01/00	Middlesbrough	H	0-0	
05/02/00	Leeds United	H	3-1	Hamann, Berger, Murphy
13/02/00	Arsenal	A	1-0	Camara
04/03/00	Manchester United	A	1-1	Berger
11/03/00	Sunderland	H	1-1	Berger (p)
15/03/00	Aston Villa	H	0-0	
18/03/00	Derby County	A	2-0	Owen, Camara
25/03/00	Newcastle United	H	2-1	Camara, Redknapp
01/04/00	Coventry City	A	3-0	Owen 2, Heskey
09/04/00	Tottenham Hotspur	H	2-0	Berger, Owen
16/04/00	Wimbledon	A	2-1	Heskey 2
21/04/00	Everton	A	0-0	
29/04/00	Chelsea	A	0-2	
03/05/00	Leicester City	H	0-2	
07/05/00	Southampton	H	0-0	
14/05/00	Bradford City	A	0-1	

MANCHESTER UNITED

CLUB DIRECTORY

Manchester United FC
Sir Matt Busby Way, Old Trafford
Manchester M16 ORA
tel - (0161) 8688000 / fax - (0161) 8688804
website - www.manutd.com
Year of Formation - 1878
Chairman - Peter Kenyon
Secretary - Ken Merrett
Manager - Sir Alex Ferguson
Stadium - Old Trafford (68,936)

MAJOR HONOURS
League Championship - (13) 1908, 1911, 1952,
1956, 1957, 1965, 1967, 1993, 1994, 1996,
1997, 1999, 2000.
FA Cup - (10) 1909, 1948, 1963, 1977, 1983,
1985, 1990, 1994, 1996, 1999.
League Cup - (1) 1992.
European Champions' Cup - (2) 1968, 1999.
European Cup-winners' Cup - (1) 1991.
European Super Cup - (1) 1991.
World Club Cup - (1) 1999.

APPEARANCES 99/00

	P	Ap	(s)	Gls
David BECKHAM	M	30	(1)	6
Henning BERG (NOR)	D	16	(6)	1
Mark BOSNICH (AUS)	G	23		
Nicky BUTT	M	21	(11)	3
Michael CLEGG	D		(2)	
Andy COLE	A	23	(5)	19
Jordi CRUIJFF (HOL)	A	1	(7)	3
Nick CULKIN	G		(1)	
John CURTIS	D		(1)	
Quinton FORTUNE (SAF)	M	4	(2)	2
Ryan GIGGS (WAL)	M	30		6
Jonathan GREENING	A	1	(3)	
Danny HIGGINBOTHAM	D	2	(1)	
Denis IRWIN (IRL)	D	25		3
Ronny JOHNSEN (NOR)	D	2	(1)	
Roy KEANE (IRL)	M	28	(1)	5
David MAY	D		(1)	
Gary NEVILLE	D	22		
Phil NEVILLE	D	25	(4)	
Paul SCHOLES	M	27	(4)	9
Teddy SHERINGHAM	A	15	(12)	5
Michaël SILVESTRE (FRA)	D	30	(1)	
Ole Gunnar SOLSKJAER (NOR)	A	15	(13)	12
Jaap STAM (HOL)	D	33		
Massimo TAIBI (ITA)	G	4		
Raimond VAN DER GOUW (HOL)	G	11	(3)	
Ronnie WALLWORK	D		(5)	
Mark WILSON	M	1	(2)	
Dwight YORKE (TRI)	A	29	(3)	20

LEAGUE RESULTS 1999/2000

08/08/99	Everton	A	1-1	Yorke
11/08/99	Sheffield Wednesday	H	4-0	Scholes, Yorke, Cole, Solskjaer
14/08/99	Leeds United	H	2-0	Yorke 2
22/08/99	Arsenal	A	2-1	Keane 2
25/08/99	Coventry City	A	2-1	Scholes, Yorke
30/08/99	Newcastle United	H	5-1	Cole 4, Giggs
11/09/99	Liverpool	A	3-2	og (Carragher) 2, Cole
18/09/99	Wimbledon	H	1-1	Cruijff
25/09/99	Southampton	H	3-3	Sheringham, Yorke 2
03/10/99	Chelsea	A	0-5	
16/10/99	Watford	H	4-1	Yorke, Cole 2, Irwin (p)
23/10/99	Tottenham Hotspur	A	1-3	Giggs
30/10/99	Aston Villa	H	3-0	Scholes, Cole, Keane
06/11/99	Leicester City	H	2-0	Cole 2
20/11/99	Derby County	A	2-1	Butt, Cole
04/12/99	Everton	H	5-1	Irwin (p), Solskjaer 4
18/12/99	West Ham United	A	4-2	Yorke 2, Giggs 2
26/12/99	Bradford City	H	4-0	Fortune, Yorke, Cole, Keane
28/12/99	Sunderland	A	2-2	Keane, Butt
24/01/00	Arsenal	H	1-1	Sheringham
29/01/00	Middlesbrough	H	1-0	Beckham
02/02/00	Sheffield Wednesday	A	1-0	Sheringham
05/02/00	Coventry City	H	3-2	Cole 2, Scholes
12/02/00	Newcastle United	A	0-3	
20/02/00	Leeds United	A	1-0	Cole
26/02/00	Wimbledon	A	2-2	Cruijff, Cole
04/03/00	Liverpool	H	1-1	Solskjaer
11/03/00	Derby County	H	3-1	Yorke 3
18/03/00	Leicester City	A	2-0	Beckham, Yorke
25/03/00	Bradford City	A	4-0	Yorke 2, Scholes, Beckham
01/04/00	West Ham United	H	7-1	Scholes 3 (1p), Irwin, Cole,
				Beckham, Solskjaer
10/04/00	Middlesbrough	A	4-3	Giggs, Cole, Scholes, Fortune
15/04/00	Sunderland	H	4-0	Solskjaer 2, Butt, Berg
22/04/00	Southampton	A	3-1	Beckham, og (Benali), Solskjaer
24/04/00	Chelsea	H	3-2	Yorke 2, Solskjaer
29/04/00	Watford	A	3-2	Yorke, Giggs, Cruijff
06/05/00	Tottenham Hotspur	H	3-1	Solskjaer, Beckham, Sheringham
14/05/00	Aston Villa	A	1-0	Sheringham

MIDDLESBROUGH

CLUB DIRECTORY

Middlesbrough FC
Cellnet Riverside Stadium
Middlesbrough
Cleveland
TS3 6RS
tel - (01642) 877700
fax - (01642) 877840
website - www.mfc.co.uk
Year of Formation - 1876
Chairman - Steve Gibson
Chief Executive - Keith Lamb
Manager - Bryan Robson
Stadium - Cellnet Riverside (35,049)

APPEARANCES 99/00

	P	Ap	(s)	Gls
Alan ARMSTRONG	A	3	(9)	1
Marlon BERESFORD	G	1		
Andy CAMPBELL	A	16	(9)	4
Colin COOPER	D	26		
Michael CUMMINS (IRL)	M		(1)	
Brian DEANE	A	29		9
Gianluca FESTA (ITA)	D	27	(2)	2
Curtis FLEMING (IRL)	D	27		
Paul GASCOIGNE	M	7	(1)	1
Jason GAVIN (IRL)	D	2	(4)	
Dean GORDON	D	3	(1)	
Paul INCE	M	32		3
Sean KILGANNON	M		(1)	
Neil MADDISON	M	6	(7)	
Carlos MARINELLI (ARG)	A		(2)	
Robbie MUSTOE	M	18	(10)	
Keith O'NEILL (IRL)	M	14	(2)	
Anthony ORMEROD	M		(1)	
Gary PALLISTER	D	21		1
Hamilton RICARD (COL)	A	28	(6)	12
Mark SCHWARZER (AUS)	G	37		
Phil STAMP	M	13	(3)	
Robbie STOCKDALE	D	6	(5)	1
Mark SUMMERBELL	M	16	(3)	
Andy TOWNSEND (IRL)	M	3	(2)	
Steve VICKERS	D	30	(2)	
Christian ZIEGE (GER)	M	29		6

LEAGUE RESULTS 1999/2000

07/08/99	Bradford City	H	0-1	
10/08/99	Wimbledon	A	3-2	Ziege, Ricard 2 (1p)
14/08/99	Derby County	A	3-1	Deane, Ziege, Ricard (p)
21/08/99	Liverpool	H	1-0	Deane
24/08/99	Leicester City	H	0-3	
28/08/99	Aston Villa	A	0-1	
11/09/99	Southampton	H	3-2	Pallister, Gascoigne (p), Deane
19/09/99	Leeds United	A	0-2	
25/09/99	Chelsea	H	0-1	
03/10/99	Newcastle United	A	1-2	Deane
17/10/99	West Ham United	H	2-0	Deane, Armstrong
24/10/99	Watford	A	3-1	og (Williams), Juninho, Ince
30/10/99	Everton	H	2-1	Ziege, Deane
06/11/99	Sunderland	H	1-1	Ricard
20/11/99	Arsenal	A	1-5	Ricard
27/11/99	Wimbledon	H	0-0	
04/12/99	Bradford City	A	1-1	Ricard
18/12/99	Tottenham Hotspur	H	2-1	Ziege, Deane
26/12/99	Sheffield Wednesday	A	0-1	
15/01/00	Derby County	H	1-4	Campbell
22/01/00	Liverpool	A	0-0	
29/01/00	Manchester United	A	0-1	
05/02/00	Leicester City	A	1-2	Campbell
14/02/00	Aston Villa	H	0-4	
19/02/00	Coventry City	H	2-0	Festa, Ricard
26/02/00	Leeds United	H	0-0	
04/03/00	Southampton	A	1-1	Ricard (p)
12/03/00	Arsenal	H	2-1	Ince, Ricard
18/03/00	Sunderland	A	1-1	Ziege
25/03/00	Sheffield Wednesday	H	1-0	Campbell
03/04/00	Tottenham Hotspur	A	3-2	og (Carr), Ricard 2
10/04/00	Manchester United	H	3-4	Campbell, Ince, Juninho
15/04/00	Coventry City	A	1-2	Ziege (p)
22/04/00	Chelsea	A	1-1	Ricard
29/04/00	West Ham United	A	1-0	Deane (p)
02/05/00	Newcastle United	H	2-2	Juninho, Festa
06/05/00	Watford	H	1-1	Stockdale
14/05/00	Everton	A	2-0	Deane, Juninho

NEWCASTLE UNITED

CLUB DIRECTORY

Newcastle United FC
St. James' Park, Newcastle-upon-Tyne, NE1 4ST
tel - (0191) 2018400 / fax - (0191) 2018600
website - www.nufc.co.uk
Year of Formation - 1881
Chairman - Freddy Shepherd
Manager - Ruud Gullit; Bobby Robson
Stadium - St. James' Park (52,167)

MAJOR HONOURS
League Championship - (4)
1905, 1907, 1909, 1927.
FA Cup - (6)
1910, 1924, 1932, 1951, 1952, 1955.
Fairs' Cup - (1) 1969.

APPEARANCES 99/00

	P	Ap	(s)	Gls
José ANTUNES (BRA)	A	1	(4)	
Warren BARTON	D	33	(1)	
David BEHARALL	D		(2)	
Laurent CHARVET (FRA)	D	1	(1)	
Nikos DABIZAS (GRE)	D	29		3
Didier DOMI (FRA)	D	19	(8)	3
Franck DUMAS (FRA)	D	6		
Kieron DYER	M	27	(3)	3
Duncan FERGUSON (SCO)	A	17	(6)	6
Kevin GALLACHER (SCO)	A	15	(5)	2
Diego GAVILAN (PAR)	M	2	(4)	1
Shay GIVEN (IRL)	G	14		
Stephen GLASS (SCO)	M	1	(6)	1
Alain GOMA (FRA)	D	14		
Andy GRIFFIN	D	1	(2)	1
Steve HARPER	G	18		
HÉLDER Cristovão (POR)	D	8		1
Steve HOWEY	D	7	(2)	
Aaron HUGHES (NIR)	D	22	(5)	2
John KARELSE (HOL)	G	3		
Temuri KETSBAIA (GEO)	M	11	(10)	
Robert LEE	M	30		
Jamie McCLEN	M	3	(6)	
MARCELINO Elena (ESP)	D	10	(1)	
Silvio MARIC (CRO)	M	3	(10)	
Alessandro PISTONE (ITA)	D	15		1
Paul ROBINSON	A	2	(9)	
Carl SERRANT	D	2		
Alan SHEARER	A	36	(1)	23
Nolberto SOLANO (PER)	M	29	(1)	3
Gary SPEED (WAL)	M	36		9
Tommy WRIGHT (NIR)	G	3		

LEAGUE RESULTS 1999/2000

07/08/99	Aston Villa	H	0-1	
09/08/99	Tottenham Hotspur	A	1-3	Solano
15/08/99	Southampton	A	2-4	Shearer (p), Speed
21/08/99	Wimbledon	H	3-3	Speed, Domi, Solano (p)
25/08/99	Sunderland	H	1-2	Dyer
30/08/99	Manchester United	A	1-5	og (Berg)
11/09/99	Chelsea	A	0-1	
19/09/99	Sheffield Wednesday	H	8-0	Hughes, Shearer 5 (2p), Dyer, Speed
25/09/99	Leeds United	A	2-3	Shearer 2
03/10/99	Middlesbrough	H	2-1	Shearer 2
16/10/99	Coventry City	A	1-4	Domi
25/10/99	Derby County	H	2-0	og (Eranio), Shearer
30/10/99	Arsenal	A	0-0	
07/11/99	Everton	H	1-1	Shearer (p)
20/11/99	Watford	A	1-1	Dabizas
28/11/99	Tottenham Hotspur	H	2-1	Glass, Dabizas
04/12/99	Aston Villa	A	1-0	Ferguson
18/12/99	Bradford City	A	0-2	
26/12/99	Liverpool	H	2-2	Shearer, Ferguson
28/12/99	Leicester City	A	2-1	Ferguson, Shearer
03/01/00	West Ham United	H	2-2	Dabizas, Speed
16/01/00	Southampton	H	5-0	Ferguson 2, Solano, og (Dryden), og (Monk)
22/01/00	Wimbledon	A	0-2	
05/02/00	Sunderland	A	2-2	Domi, Hélder
12/02/00	Manchester United	H	3-0	Ferguson, Shearer 2
26/02/00	Sheffield Wednesday	A	2-0	Gallacher, Shearer
04/03/00	Chelsea	H	0-1	
11/03/00	Watford	H	1-0	Gallacher
19/03/00	Everton	A	2-0	Hughes, Dyer
25/03/00	Liverpool	A	1-2	Shearer
01/04/00	Bradford City	H	2-0	Speed, Shearer
12/04/00	West Ham United	A	1-2	Speed
15/04/00	Leicester City	H	0-2	
23/04/00	Leeds United	H	2-2	Shearer 2
29/04/00	Coventry City	H	2-0	Shearer (p), Gavilan
02/05/00	Middlesbrough	A	2-2	Speed, Pistone
06/05/00	Derby County	A	0-0	
14/05/00	Arsenal	H	4-2	Speed 2, Shearer, Griffin

SHEFFIELD WEDNESDAY

CLUB DIRECTORY

Sheffield Wednesday FC
Hillsborough
Sheffield S6 1SW
tel - (0114) 2212121
fax - (0114) 2212122
website - www.swfc.co.uk
Year of Formation - 1867
Chairman - Howard Culley
Secretary - Alan Sykes
Manager - Danny Wilson; Peter Shreeves (00/01 - Paul Jewell)
Stadium - Hillsborough (39,859)

MAJOR HONOURS
League Championship - (4)
1903, 1904, 1929, 1930.
FA Cup - (3) 1896, 1907, 1935.
League Cup - (1) 1991.

APPEARANCES 99/00

	P	Ap	(s)	Gls
Niclas ALEXANDERSSON (SWE)	M	37		5
Peter ATHERTON	D	35		1
Andy BOOTH	A	20	(3)	2
Lee BRISCOE	M	7	(9)	
Benito CARBONE (ITA)	A	3	(4)	2
Steve CRESSWELL	A	2	(18)	1
Gilles DE BILDE (BEL)	A	37	(1)	10
Simon DONNELLY (SCO)	A	3	(9)	1
Steve HASLAM	M	16	(7)	
Andy HINCHCLIFFE	D	29		1
Barry HORNE (WAL)	M	7		
Wim JONK (HOL)	M	29	(1)	3
Mark McKEEVER (NIR)	A	1	(1)	
Jon NEWSOME	D	5	(1)	
Ian NOLAN (NIR)	D	28	(1)	
Phil O'DONNELL (SCO)	M		(1)	
Kevin PRESSMAN	G	18	(1)	
Alan QUINN (IRL)	M	18	(1)	3
Petter RUDI (NOR)	M	18	(2)	2
Philip SCOTT (SCO)	M	2	(3)	
Gerald SIBON (HOL)	A	12	(16)	5
Danny SONNER (NIR)	M	18	(9)	
Pavel SRNICEK (CZE)	G	20		
Emerson THOME (BRA)	D	16	(1)	
Des WALKER	D	37		

LEAGUE RESULTS 1999/2000

07/08/99	Liverpool	H	1-2	Carbone
11/08/99	Manchester United	A	0-4	
14/08/99	Bradford City	A	1-1	og (Dreyer)
21/08/99	Tottenham Hotspur	H	1-2	Carbone (p)
25/08/99	Derby County	H	0-2	
28/08/99	Southampton	A	0-2	
11/09/99	Everton	H	0-2	
19/09/99	Newcastle United	A	0-8	
25/09/99	Sunderland	A	0-1	
02/10/99	Wimbledon	H	5-1	Jonk, De Bilde 2, Rudi, Sibon
16/10/99	Leeds United	A	0-2	
23/10/99	Coventry City	H	0-0	
30/10/99	Leicester City	A	0-3	
06/11/99	Watford	H	2-2	De Bilde 2 (1p)
21/11/99	West Ham United	A	3-4	Rudi, Jonk, Booth
05/12/99	Liverpool	A	1-4	Alexandersson
18/12/99	Aston Villa	A	1-2	De Bilde (p)
26/12/99	Middlesbrough	H	1-0	Atherton
29/12/99	Chelsea	A	0-3	
03/01/00	Arsenal	H	1-1	Sibon
15/01/00	Bradford City	H	2-0	Alexandersson, og (O'Brien)
22/01/00	Tottenham Hotspur	A	1-0	Alexandersson
02/02/00	Manchester United	H	0-1	
05/02/00	Derby County	A	3-3	De Bilde, Sibon, Donnelly
12/02/00	Southampton	H	0-1	
26/02/00	Newcastle United	H	0-2	
04/03/00	Everton	A	1-1	Quinn
11/03/00	West Ham United	H	3-1	Cresswell, Hinchcliffe, Alexandersson
18/03/00	Watford	A	0-1	
25/03/00	Middlesbrough	A	0-1	
05/04/00	Aston Villa	H	0-1	
12/04/00	Wimbledon	A	2-0	De Bilde, Sibon
15/04/00	Chelsea	H	1-0	Jonk (p)
22/04/00	Sunderland	H	0-2	
30/04/00	Leeds United	A	0-3	
06/05/00	Coventry City	A	1-4	De Bilde
09/05/00	Arsenal	A	3-3	Sibon, De Bilde, Quinn
14/05/00	Leicester City	H	4-0	Quinn, Booth, Alexandersson, De Bilde

SOUTHAMPTON

CLUB DIRECTORY

Southampton FC
The Dell
Milton Road
Southampton SO15 2XH
tel - (023) 80220505
fax - (023) 80330360
website - www.soton.ac.uk/saints
Year of Formation - 1885
Chairman - Rupert Lowe
Secretary - Brian Truscott
Manager - Dave Jones; Glenn Hoddle
Stadium - The Dell (15,000)

MAJOR HONOURS
FA Cup - (1) 1976.

APPEARANCES 99/00

	P	Ap	(s)	Gls
Marco ALMEIDA (POR)	M		(1)	
James BEATTIE	A	8	(10)	
Francis BENALI	D	25	(1)	
John BERESFORD	D		(3)	
Luís BOA MORTE (POR)	A	6	(8)	1
Shayne BRADLEY	A		(1)	
Wayne BRIDGE	M	15	(4)	1
Patrick COLLETER (FRA)	D	8		
Kevin DAVIES	A	19	(4)	6
Jason DODD	D	30	(1)	
Richard DRYDEN	D	1		
Scott HILEY	D	3		
Mark HUGHES (WAL)	A	18	(2)	1
Paul JONES (WAL)	G	31		
Hassan KACHLOUL (MAR)	M	29	(3)	5
Matt LE TISSIER	M	9	(9)	3
Claus LUNDEKVAM (NOR)	D	25	(2)	
Chris MARSDEN	M	19	(2)	
Gary MONK	D	1	(1)	
Neil MOSS	G	7	(2)	
Matthew OAKLEY	M	26	(5)	3
Egil ØSTENSTAD (NOR)	A	3		1
Marian PAHARS (LAT)	A	31	(2)	13
Dean RICHARDS	D	35		2
Stuart RIPLEY	M	18	(5)	1
Danny RODRIGUES (POR)	A		(2)	
Trond Egil SOLTVEDT (NOR)	M	17	(7)	1
TAHAR El Khalej (MAR)	D	11		1
Jo TESSEM (NOR)	M	23	(2)	4

LEAGUE RESULTS 1999/2000

07/08/99	Coventry City	A	1-0	Østenstad
11/08/99	Leeds United	H	0-3	
15/08/99	Newcastle United	H	4-2	Kachloul 2, Pahars, Hughes
21/08/99	Everton	A	1-4	Pahars
28/08/99	Sheffield Wednesday	H	2-0	Kachloul, Oakley
11/09/99	Middlesbrough	A	2-3	Kachloul, Pahars
18/09/99	Arsenal	H	0-1	
25/09/99	Manchester United	A	3-3	Pahars, Le Tissier 2
04/10/99	Derby County	H	3-3	Pahars, Oakley, Ripley
16/10/99	Leicester City	A	1-2	Pahars
23/10/99	Liverpool	H	1-1	Soltvedt
30/10/99	Wimbledon	A	1-1	Pahars
06/11/99	Aston Villa	A	1-0	Richards
20/11/99	Tottenham Hotspur	H	0-1	
28/11/99	Leeds United	A	0-1	
04/12/99	Coventry City	H	0-0	
18/12/99	Sunderland	A	0-2	
26/12/99	Chelsea	H	1-2	Davies
28/12/99	Watford	A	2-3	Boa Morte, Davies
03/01/00	Bradford City	H	1-0	Davies
16/01/00	Newcastle United	A	0-5	
22/01/00	Everton	H	2-0	Tessem, Oakley
05/02/00	West Ham United	H	2-1	Pahars, og (Charles)
12/02/00	Sheffield Wednesday	A	1-0	Tessem
26/02/00	Arsenal	A	1-3	Richards
04/03/00	Middlesbrough	H	1-1	Pahars
08/03/00	West Ham United	A	0-2	
11/03/00	Tottenham Hotspur	A	2-7	Tessem, Tahar
18/03/00	Aston Villa	H	2-0	Davies 2
25/03/00	Chelsea	A	1-1	Tessem
01/04/00	Sunderland	H	1-2	Le Tissier (p)
08/04/00	Bradford City	A	2-1	og (Windass), Pahars
15/04/00	Watford	H	2-0	Davies, Pahars
22/04/00	Manchester United	H	1-3	Pahars
24/04/00	Derby County	A	0-2	
29/04/00	Leicester City	H	1-2	Kachloul
07/05/00	Liverpool	A	0-0	
14/05/00	Wimbledon	H	2-0	Bridge, Pahars

SUNDERLAND

CLUB DIRECTORY

Sunderland AFC
Stadium of Light
Sunderland
Tyne and Wear
SR5 1SU
tel - (0191) 5515000
fax - (0191) 5515123
website - www.sunderland-afc.com
Year of Formation - 1879
Chairman - Bob Murray
Chief Executive - John Fickling
Manager - Peter Reid
Stadium - Stadium of Light (48,300)

MAJOR HONOURS
League Championship - (6)
1892, 1893, 1895, 1902, 1913, 1936.
FA Cup - (2) 1937, 1973.

APPEARANCES 99/00

	P	Ap	(s)	Gls
Kevin BALL	M	6	(5)	
Steve BOULD	D	19	(1)	
Paul BUTLER (IRL)	D	31	(1)	1
Thomas BUTLER (IRL)	M		(1)	
Jody CRADDOCK	D	18	(1)	
Daniele DICHIO	A		(12)	
Carsten FREDGAARD (DEN)	A		(1)	
Michael GRAY	D	32	(1)	
Thomas HELMER (GER)	D	1	(1)	
Darren HOLLOWAY	D	8	(7)	
Kevin KILBANE (IRL)	M	17	(3)	1
Chris LUMSDON	M	1		
Gavin McCANN	M	21	(3)	4
Chris MAKIN	D	34		1
Andy MARRIOTT	G	1		
Milton NUÑEZ (HON)	A		(1)	
John OSTER (WAL)	M	4	(6)	
Kevin PHILLIPS	A	36		30
Niall QUINN (IRL)	A	35	(2)	14
Alex RAE (SCO)	M	22	(4)	3
Michael REDDY (IRL)	A		(8)	1
Eric ROY (FRA)	M	19	(5)	
Stefan SCHWARZ (SWE)	M	27		1
Thomas SØRENSEN (DEN)	G	37		
Nicky SUMMERBEE	M	29	(3)	1
Paul THIRLWELL	M	7	(1)	
Darren WILLIAMS	D	13	(12)	

LEAGUE RESULTS 1999/2000

07/08/99	Chelsea	A	0-4	
10/08/99	Watford	H	2-0	Phillips 2 (1p)
14/08/99	Arsenal	H	0-0	
21/08/99	Leeds United	A	1-2	Phillips
25/08/99	Newcastle United	A	2-1	Quinn, Phillips
29/08/99	Coventry City	H	1-1	Phillips
11/09/99	Leicester City	H	2-0	Butler P., McCann
18/09/99	Derby County	A	5-0	McCann, Phillips 3, Quinn
25/09/99	Sheffield Wednesday	H	1-0	Schwarz
02/10/99	Bradford City	A	4-0	Rae, Quinn, Phillips 2 (1p)
18/10/99	Aston Villa	H	2-1	Phillips 2 (1p)
24/10/99	West Ham United	A	1-1	Phillips
31/10/99	Tottenham Hotspur	H	2-1	Quinn 2
06/11/99	Middlesbrough	A	1-1	Reddy
20/11/99	Liverpool	H	0-2	
27/11/99	Watford	A	3-2	Phillips 2, McCann
04/12/99	Chelsea	H	4-1	Quinn 2, Phillips 2
18/12/99	Southampton	H	2-0	Phillips 2
26/12/99	Everton	A	0-5	
28/12/99	Manchester United	H	2-2	McCann, Quinn
03/01/00	Wimbledon	A	0-1	
15/01/00	Arsenal	A	1-4	Quinn
23/01/00	Leeds United	H	1-2	Phillips
05/02/00	Newcastle United	H	2-2	Phillips 2
12/02/00	Coventry City	A	2-3	Phillips, Rae
26/02/00	Derby County	H	1-1	Rae
05/03/00	Leicester City	A	2-5	Phillips, Quinn
11/03/00	Liverpool	A	1-1	Phillips (p)
18/03/00	Middlesbrough	H	1-1	Quinn
25/03/00	Everton	H	2-1	Summerbee, Phillips
01/04/00	Southampton	A	2-1	Quinn, Phillips (p)
08/04/00	Wimbledon	H	2-1	Quinn, Kilbane
15/04/00	Manchester United	A	0-4	
22/04/00	Sheffield Wednesday	A	2-0	Phillips 2
24/04/00	Bradford City	H	0-1	
29/04/00	Aston Villa	A	1-1	Quinn
06/05/00	West Ham United	H	1-0	Phillips
14/05/00	Tottenham Hotspur	A	1-3	Makin

TOTTENHAM HOTSPUR

CLUB DIRECTORY

Tottenham Hotspur FC
Bill Nicholson Way, 748 High Road
Tottenham, London N17 0AP
tel - (020) 83655000
fax - (020) 83655005
website - www.spurs.co.uk
Year of Formation - 1882
Chairman - Alan Sugar
Director of Football - David Pleat
Manager - George Graham
Stadium - White Hart Lane (36,236)

MAJOR HONOURS
League Championship - (2) 1951, 1961.
FA Cup - (8) 1901, 1921, 1961, 1962, 1967,
1981, 1982, 1991.
League Cup - (3) 1971, 1973, 1999.
European Cup-winners' Cup - (1) 1963.
UEFA Cup - (2) 1972, 1984.

APPEARANCES 99/00

		P	Ap	(s)	Gls
Darren ANDERTON	M	22			3
Chris ARMSTRONG	A	29	(2)	14
Sol CAMPBELL	D	29		
Stephen CARR (IRL)	D	34			3
Stephen CLEMENCE	M	16	(4)	1
Simon DAVIES	M	1	(2)	
Gary DOHERTY (IRL)	D		(2)	
José DOMINGUEZ (POR)	M	2	(10)	
Justin EDINBURGH	D	7	(1)	
Matthew ETHERINGTON	M	1	(4)	
Les FERDINAND	A	5	(4)	2
Ruel FOX	M	1	(2)	
Steffen FREUND (GER)	M	24	(3)	
David GINOLA (FRA)	M	36		3
Steffen IVERSEN (NOR)	A	36		14
Ledley KING	D	2	(1)	
Willem KORSTEN (HOL)	M	4	(5)	
Øyvind LEONHARDSEN (NOR)	M	21	(1)	4
Dave McEWEN	A		(1)	
Allan NIELSEN (DEN)	M	5	(9)	
Chris PERRY	D	36	(1)	1
John PIERCY	M	1	(2)	
John SCALES	D	3	(1)	
Tim SHERWOOD	M	23	(4)	8
Mauricio TARICCO (ARG)	D	29		
Ramon VEGA (SUI)	D	2	(3)	1
Ian WALKER	G	38		
Luke YOUNG	D	11	(9)	

LEAGUE RESULTS 1999/2000

07/08/99	West Ham United	A	0-1	
09/08/99	Newcastle United	H	3-1	Iversen, Ferdinand, Sherwood
14/08/99	Everton	H	3-2	Sherwood, Leonhardsen, Iversen
21/08/99	Sheffield Wednesday	A	2-1	Ferdinand, Leonhardsen
28/08/99	Leeds United	H	1-2	Sherwood
12/09/99	Bradford City	A	1-1	Perry
19/09/99	Coventry City	H	3-2	Iversen, Armstrong, Leonhardsen
26/09/99	Wimbledon	A	1-1	Carr
03/10/99	Leicester City	H	2-3	Iversen 2
16/10/99	Derby County	A	1-0	Armstrong
23/10/99	Manchester United	H	3-1	Iversen, og (Scholes), Carr
31/10/99	Sunderland	A	1-2	Iversen
07/11/99	Arsenal	H	2-1	Iversen, Sherwood
20/11/99	Southampton	A	1-0	Leonhardsen
28/11/99	Newcastle United	A	1-2	Armstrong
06/12/99	West Ham United	H	0-0	
18/12/99	Middlesbrough	A	1-2	Vega
26/12/99	Watford	H	4-0	Ginola, Iversen, Sherwood 2
29/12/99	Aston Villa	A	1-1	Sherwood
03/01/00	Liverpool	H	1-0	Armstrong
12/01/00	Chelsea	A	0-1	
15/01/00	Everton	A	2-2	Armstrong, og (Watson)
22/01/00	Sheffield Wednesday	H	0-1	
05/02/00	Chelsea	H	0-1	
12/02/00	Leeds United	A	0-1	
26/02/00	Coventry City	A	1-0	Armstrong
04/03/00	Bradford City	H	1-1	Iversen
11/03/00	Southampton	H	7-2	og (Richards), Anderton, Armstrong 2, Iversen 3
19/03/00	Arsenal	A	1-2	Armstrong
25/03/00	Watford	A	1-1	Armstrong
03/04/00	Middlesbrough	H	2-3	Armstrong, Ginola
09/04/00	Liverpool	A	0-2	
15/04/00	Aston Villa	H	2-4	Iversen, Armstrong
19/04/00	Leicester City	A	1-0	Ginola
22/04/00	Wimbledon	H	2-0	Armstrong, Anderton
29/04/00	Derby County	H	1-1	Clemence
06/05/00	Manchester United	A	1-3	Armstrong
14/05/00	Sunderland	H	3-1	Anderton (p), Sherwood, Carr

WATFORD

CLUB DIRECTORY

Watford FC
Vicarage Road Stadium
Watford
WD1 8ER
tel - (01923) 496000
fax - (01923) 496001
website - www.watfordfc.com
Year of Formation - 1881
Chairman - Sir Elton John
Secretary - Catherine Alexander
Manager - Graham Taylor
Stadium - Vicarage Road (20,800)

APPEARANCES 99/00

	P	Ap	(s)	Gls
Adrian BAKALLI (BEL)	M		(2)	
Alex BONNOT (FRA)	M	7	(5)	
Stephen BROOKER	M		(1)	
Alec CHAMBERLAIN	G	27		
Neil COX	D	20	(1)	
Chris DAY	G	11		
Clint EASTON	M	13	(4)	
Dominic FOLEY (IRL)	A	5	(7)	1
Nigel GIBBS	D	11	(6)	
Xavier GRAVELAINE (FRA)	A	7		2
Johann GUDMUNDSSON (ISL)	M	1	(8)	
Heidur HELGUSON (ISL)	A	14	(2)	6
Micah HYDE	M	33	(1)	3
Richard JOHNSON	M	20	(3)	3
Peter KENNEDY (NIR)	D	17	(1)	1
Des LYTTLE	D	11		
Charlie MILLER (SCO)	M	9	(5)	
Tommy MOONEY	A	8	(4)	2
Michel NGONGE (BEL)	A	16	(7)	5
Gifton NOEL-WILLIAMS	A	1	(2)	
Robert PAGE (WAL)	D	36		1
Steve PALMER	M	38		
James PANAYI	D	2		
David PERPETUINI	M	12	(1)	1
Paul ROBINSON	D	29	(3)	
Alan SMART (SCO)	A	13	(1)	5
Tommy SMITH	A	13	(9)	2
Darren WARD	D	7	(2)	1
Mark WILLIAMS (NIR)	D	20	(1)	1
Nordin WOOTER (HOL)	M	16	(4)	1
Nick WRIGHT	A	1	(3)	

LEAGUE RESULTS 1999/2000

07/08/99	Wimbledon	H	2-3	Kennedy (p), Ngonge
10/08/99	Sunderland	A	0-2	
14/08/99	Liverpool	A	1-0	Mooney
21/08/99	Bradford City	H	1-0	Mooney
24/08/99	Aston Villa	H	0-1	
30/08/99	Leicester City	A	0-1	
11/09/99	West Ham United	A	0-1	
18/09/99	Chelsea	H	1-0	Smart
25/09/99	Arsenal	A	0-1	
03/10/99	Leeds United	H	1-2	Williams
16/10/99	Manchester United	A	1-4	Johnson
24/10/99	Middlesbrough	H	1-3	Smith
31/10/99	Coventry City	A	0-4	
06/11/99	Sheffield Wednesday	A	2-2	Ngonge, Page
20/11/99	Newcastle United	H	1-1	Ngonge
27/11/99	Sunderland	H	2-3	Ngonge, Johnson (p)
04/12/99	Wimbledon	A	0-5	
18/12/99	Everton	H	1-3	Ngonge
26/12/99	Tottenham Hotspur	A	0-4	
28/12/99	Southampton	H	3-2	Perpetuini, Gravelaine 2
03/01/00	Derby County	A	0-2	
15/01/00	Liverpool	H	2-3	Johnson, Helguson
22/01/00	Bradford City	A	2-3	Hyde, Helguson
05/02/00	Aston Villa	A	0-4	
12/02/00	Leicester City	H	1-1	Wooter
26/02/00	Chelsea	A	1-2	Smart
04/03/00	West Ham United	H	1-2	Helguson
11/03/00	Newcastle United	A	0-1	
18/03/00	Sheffield Wednesday	H	1-0	Smart
25/03/00	Tottenham Hotspur	H	1-1	Smart
01/04/00	Everton	A	2-4	Smart, Hyde
08/04/00	Derby County	H	0-0	
15/04/00	Southampton	A	0-2	
23/04/00	Arsenal	H	2-3	Helguson, Hyde
29/04/00	Manchester United	H	2-3	Helguson, Smith
03/05/00	Leeds United	A	1-3	Foley
06/05/00	Middlesbrough	A	1-1	Ward
14/05/00	Coventry City	H	1-0	Helguson

WEST HAM UNITED

CLUB DIRECTORY

West Ham United FC
Boleyn Ground
Green Street
Upton Park
London E13 9AZ
tel - (020) 85482748
fax - (020) 85482758
website - www.westhamunited.co.uk
Year of Formation - 1895
Chairman - Terence Brown
Secretary - Peter Barnes
Manager - Harry Redknapp
Stadium - Upton Park (26,054)

MAJOR HONOURS
FA Cup - (3) 1964, 1975, 1980.
European Cup-winners' Cup - (1) 1965.

APPEARANCES 99/00

	P	Ap	(s)	Gls
Shaun BYRNE	D		(1)	
Stephen BYWATER	G	3	(1)	
Michael CARRICK	M	4	(4)	1
Gary CHARLES	D	2	(2)	
Joe COLE	M	17	(5)	1
Paolo DI CANIO (ITA)	M	29	(1)	16
Rio FERDINAND	D	33		
Ian FEUER (USA)	G	3		
Marc-Vivien FOE (CMR)	M	25		1
Craig FORREST (CAN)	G	9	(2)	
Shaka HISLOP	G	22		
Sasa ILIC (YUG)	G	1		
Frédéric KANOUTE (FRA)	A	8		2
Marc KELLER (FRA)	M	19	(4)	
Paul KITSON	A	4	(6)	
Frank LAMPARD	M	34		7
Steve LOMAS (NIR)	M	25		1
Javier MARGAS (CHL)	D	15	(3)	1
Scott MINTO	D	15	(3)	
John MONCUR	M	20	(2)	1
Adam NEWTON	D		(2)	
Ian PEARCE	D	1		
Stuart PEARCE	D	8		
Steve POTTS	D	16	(1)	
Neil RUDDOCK	D	12	(3)	
Trevor SINCLAIR	M	36		7
Igor STIMAC (CRO)	D	24		1
Paulo WANCHOPE (CRC)	A	33	(2)	12

LEAGUE RESULTS 1999/2000

07/08/99	Tottenham Hotspur	H	1-0	Lampard
16/08/99	Aston Villa	A	2-2	og (Southgate), Sinclair
21/08/99	Leicester City	H	2-1	Wanchope, Di Canio
28/08/99	Bradford City	A	3-0	Di Canio, Sinclair, Wanchope
11/09/99	Watford	H	1-0	Di Canio
19/09/99	Everton	A	0-1	
25/09/99	Coventry City	A	0-1	
03/10/99	Arsenal	H	2-1	Di Canio 2
17/10/99	Middlesbrough	A	0-2	
24/10/99	Sunderland	H	1-1	Sinclair
27/10/99	Liverpool	A	0-1	
30/10/99	Leeds United	A	0-1	
07/11/99	Chelsea	A	0-0	
21/11/99	Sheffield Wednesday	H	4-3	Wanchope, Di Canio (p), Foé, Lampard
27/11/99	Liverpool	H	1-0	Sinclair
06/12/99	Tottenham Hotspur	A	0-0	
18/12/99	Manchester United	H	2-4	Di Canio 2
26/12/99	Wimbledon	A	2-2	Sinclair, Lampard
28/12/99	Derby County	H	1-1	Di Canio
03/01/00	Newcastle United	A	2-2	Lampard, Stimac
15/01/00	Aston Villa	H	1-1	Di Canio
22/01/00	Leicester City	A	3-1	Wanchope 2, Di Canio
05/02/00	Southampton	A	1-2	Lampard
12/02/00	Bradford City	H	5-4	Sinclair, Moncur, Di Canio (p), Cole, Lampard
26/02/00	Everton	H	0-4	
04/03/00	Watford	A	2-1	Lomas, Wanchope
08/03/00	Southampton	H	2-0	Wanchope, Sinclair
11/03/00	Sheffield Wednesday	A	1-3	Lampard
18/03/00	Chelsea	H	0-0	
26/03/00	Wimbledon	H	2-1	Di Canio, Kanouté
01/04/00	Manchester United	A	1-7	Wanchope
12/04/00	Newcastle United	H	2-1	Wanchope 2
15/04/00	Derby County	A	2-1	Wanchope 2
22/04/00	Coventry City	H	5-0	Carrick, Margas, Di Canio 2, Kanouté
29/04/00	Middlesbrough	H	0-1	
02/05/00	Arsenal	A	1-2	Di Canio
06/05/00	Sunderland	A	0-1	
14/05/00	Leeds United	H	0-0	

WIMBLEDON

CLUB DIRECTORY

Wimbledon FC
Selhurst Park
South Norwood
London SE25 6PY
tel - (020) 87712233
fax - (020) 87680641
website - www.wimbledon-fc.co.uk
Year of Formation - 1889
Chairman - B.R. Gjelsten
Secretary - Steve Rooke
Manager - Egil Olsen; Terry Burton
Stadium - Selhurst Park (26,297)

MAJOR HONOURS
FA Cup - (1) 1988.

APPEARANCES 99/00

		P	Ap	(s)	Gls
Gareth AINSWORTH	M			(2)	2
Trond ANDERSEN (NOR)	D	35		(1)	
Martin ANDRESEN (NOR)	M	4		(10)	1
Neal ARDLEY	M	10		(7)	2
Walid BADIR (ISR)	M	12		(9)	1
Dean BLACKWELL	D	16		(1)	
Carl CORT	A	32		(2)	9
Kenny CUNNINGHAM (IRL)	D	37			
Robbie EARLE (JAM)	M	23		(2)	3
Jason EUELL	M	32		(5)	4
Damien FRANCIS	M	1		(8)	
Marcus GAYLE (JAM)	A	35		(1)	7
Wayne GRAY	A			(1)	
John HARTSON (WAL)	A	15		(1)	9
Paul HEALD	G	1			
Hermann HREIDARSSON (ISL)	D	24			1
Michael HUGHES (NIR)	M	13		(7)	2
Duncan JUPP (SCO)	M	6		(3)	
Alan KIMBLE	D	24		(4)	
Carl LEABURN	A	5		(13)	
Andreas LUND (NOR)	A	10		(2)	2
Tore PEDERSEN (NOR)	D	6			
Andy ROBERTS	M	14		(2)	
Neil SULLIVAN (SCO)	G	37			
Ben THATCHER	D	19		(1)	
Chris WILLMOTT	D	7			

LEAGUE RESULTS 1999/2000

07/08/99	Watford	A	3-2	Cort, Gayle, og (Johnson)
10/08/99	Middlesbrough	H	2-3	Cort, Hartson
14/08/99	Coventry City	H	1-1	Cort
21/08/99	Newcastle United	A	3-3	Hughes, Ainsworth 2
25/08/99	Everton	A	0-4	
28/08/99	Chelsea	H	0-1	
11/09/99	Derby County	H	2-2	Hartson, Euell
18/09/99	Manchester United	A	1-1	Badir
26/09/99	Tottenham Hotspur	H	1-1	Hartson
02/10/99	Sheffield Wednesday	A	1-5	Hartson
16/10/99	Bradford City	H	3-2	Hartson 2, Cort
23/10/99	Aston Villa	A	1-1	Earle
30/10/99	Southampton	H	1-1	Gayle
07/11/99	Leeds United	H	2-0	Hartson, Gayle
20/11/99	Leicester City	A	1-2	Gayle
27/11/99	Middlesbrough	A	0-0	
04/12/99	Watford	H	5-0	Cort, Eadie, Hartson, Euell, Gayle
18/12/99	Arsenal	A	1-1	Cort
26/12/99	West Ham United	H	2-2	Hreidarsson, Ardley
28/12/99	Liverpool	A	1-3	Gayle
03/01/00	Sunderland	H	1-0	Cort
15/01/00	Coventry City	A	0-2	
22/01/00	Newcastle United	H	2-0	Earle, Gayle
06/02/00	Everton	H	0-3	
12/02/00	Chelsea	A	1-3	Lund
26/02/00	Manchester United	H	2-2	Euell, Cort
04/03/00	Derby County	A	0-4	
11/03/00	Leicester City	H	2-1	Ardley (p), Cort
19/03/00	Leeds United	A	1-4	Euell
26/03/00	West Ham United	A	1-2	Hughes
01/04/00	Arsenal	H	1-3	Lund
08/04/00	Sunderland	A	1-2	og (Roy)
12/04/00	Sheffield Wednesday	H	0-2	
16/04/00	Liverpool	H	1-2	Andresen
22/04/00	Tottenham Hotspur	A	0-2	
30/04/00	Bradford City	A	0-3	
06/05/00	Aston Villa	H	2-2	og (Ehiogu), Hartson
14/05/00	Southampton	A	0-2	

ESTONIA

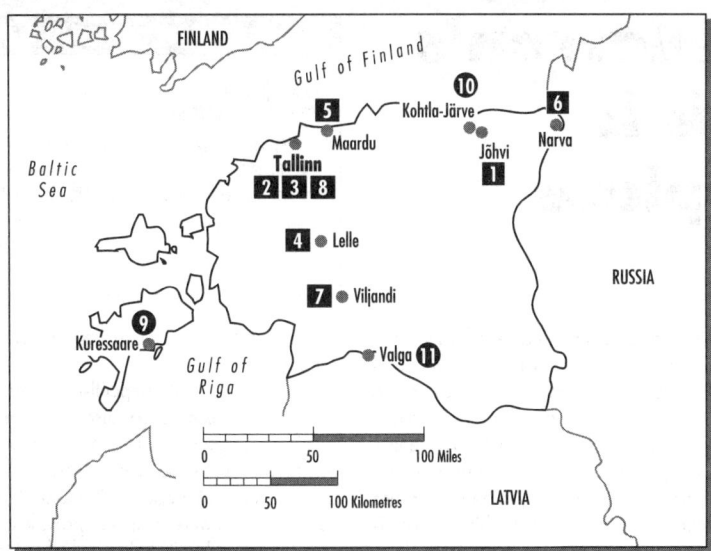

NEWCOMERS LEVADIA SCOOP TOP PRIZES

Thórdarson's work is complete

FEDERATION DIRECTORY

Eesti Jalgpalli Liit
Võidu 16, 11213 Tallinn

tel - (6) 542715/6/7
fax - (6) 542719
website - www.estfootball.ee

Stadium - Kadriorg (4,700)

Year of Formation - 1921
President - Peeter Küttis
Secretary - Tõnu Sirel

November 1999 marked the end of an era for Estonian football. It was the month in which the contract of Teitur Thórdarson - coach to the national team as well as 'feeder' club FC Flora Tallinn - ran its course. The Icelander had spent four years as the principal figure behind the development of professional football in his adopted country. He had done a magnificent job, but all parties came to the conclusion that it was time for him to take his leave.

During his time in office Thórdarson succeeded in winning the hearts of the Estonian fans. At his leaving ceremony he received a gift from the State, and when Estonia celebrated Independence Day three months later, on February 24, he was invited back from Norway, where he had found employment at SK Brann, to receive a commemorative medal from the president of the Estonian Republic.

Thórdarson's final competitive international in charge of the team was a hugely disappointing 1-4 defeat by Bosnia-Herzegovina in Tallinn. It was an inappropriate way to bow out for the man who had steered Estonia into contention for a European Championship play-off spot, but the players were unable to provide a fitting farewell performance - despite being in the lead for almost all of the first half.

That game had been rendered academic by previous results, but when Estonia took the field at home to Scotland a month earlier, there was still a genuine chance that they might reach the play-offs. September 8 1999 was viewed by most Estonians as the most important day in the country's footballing history. The Kadriorg Stadium was full and people were parked in front of television sets all over the country. In the event, Estonia gave as good as they got but could not quite grab the victory that would have meant so much. It finished goalless and Estonia's high hopes of European Championship qualification had all but evaporated.

Thórdarson's place as national team coach was taken by his assistant, Tarmo Rüütli, who also had a club job at Tulevik Viljandi. There was some irony, therefore, that Rüütli's Tulevik should finish the 1999 Estonian championship ahead of Thórdarson's FC Flora in the final table.

Flora were effectively forced to abandon their hopes of a third successive title after financial complications necessitated the sale of several of their leading players. Experienced Estonian internationals Urmas Kirs, Martin Reim, Andres Oper, Marek Lemsalu and Marko Kristal all

LEAGUE CHAMPIONSHIP RESULTS 1999

		1	2	3	4	5	6	7	8
1	EP Jõhvi		1-6	1-3	0-0	0-5	1-0	1-2	1-0
			0-1	1-4	0-0	1-9	0-4	0-2	0-0
2	FC Flora Tallinn	4-0		3-0	2-2	1-2	5-0	5-2	0-1
		7-1		3-1	2-1	0-3	1-1	1-1	1-1
3	FC Lantana Tallinn	0-0	3-3		1-1	0-1	1-1	1-3	2-0
		1-1	3-2		0-0	1-3	0-2	1-2	0-0
4	Lelle SK	0-0	1-0	4-2		1-1	0-3	0-1	0-2
		3-1	0-1	1-1		1-5	1-0	2-4	0-0
5	FC Levadia Maardu	6-0	0-0	3-0	5-2		2-0	2-1	+++
		xxx	3-1	4-0	3-2		1-0	4-0	3-0
6	Trans Narva	4-1	1-3	7-0	1-0	1-2		1-1	1-1
		2-0	1-1	2-0	1-0	0-0		2-0	0-1
7	Tulevik Viljandi	1-0	2-4	1-1	2-0	0-3	1-3		1-0
		14-0	1-0	3-2	3-0	0-0	3-1		0-0
8	VMK Tallinn	0-0	1-1	0-2	3-0	0-3	0-0	0-4	
		3-1	0-2	0-1	1-3	0-4	2-1	0-2	

N.B. +++ match void; awarded as away win.
xxx match void; awarded as home win.

INTERNATIONAL HONOURS

None

LEAGUE CHAMPIONSHIP FINAL TABLE 1999

			Home					Away					Total						
		Pd	W	D	L	F	A	W	D	L	F	A	W	D	L	F	A	Pt	GD
1	FC Levadia Maardu	28	12	1	1	36	6	11	3	0	41	6	23	4	1	77	12	73	65
2	Tulevik Viljandi	28	8	3	3	32	14	8	2	4	25	20	16	5	7	57	34	53	23
3	FC Flora Tallinn	28	7	4	3	35	16	6	4	4	25	17	13	8	7	60	33	47	27
4	Trans Narva	28	7	4	3	24	10	4	3	7	16	18	11	7	10	40	28	40	12
5	VMK Tallinn	28	3	3	8	10	24	4	6	4	6	9	7	9	12	16	33	30	-17
6	FC Lantana Tallinn	28	2	7	5	14	19	4	2	8	17	33	6	9	13	31	52	27	-21
7	Lelle SK	28	4	4	6	14	21	1	5	8	11	24	5	9	14	25	45	24	-20
8	EP Jõhvi	28	2	3	9	7	36	0	4	10	5	45	2	7	19	12	81	13	-69

jumped ship in mid-season to pursue their careers abroad, and that left Flora having to rely increasingly on graduates from the youth team. It was never going to be enough, and Thórdarson's last home game in charge proved symptomatic as Flora were beaten 3-0 by Levadia Maardu, the team which a few weeks earlier had relieved Flora of their championship crown.

Levadia won the title by a landslide margin. They would have gone through the season without a defeat had it not been for a technical error which cost them a statutory forfeit of their home game with mid-table VMK Tallinn. On the pitch, though, Levadia were unbeatable, and right from the start it was obvious that no other team would be able to live with them.

What made Levadia's victory so remarkable was the fact that they were appearing in Estonia's premier division for the first time. They were newcomers in name only, however, for many of their players had belonged previously to Tallinna Sadam, the runners-up the previous two seasons and the club with which Levadia had merged at the start of the year.

Levadia's coach, Sergei Ratnikov, was also a refugee from Tallinna Sadam, and he worked diligently to bring the best out of a talented squad which had been assembled thanks to the strong, ambitious funding of the club's backers. Levadia were blessed with two exceptional strikers in Toomas Krõm and Andrei Krõlov. Between them they scored 37 goals, with the former just pipping the

DOMESTIC CUP 99/00

1/8 FINALS
FC Valga 1, VMK Tallinn 5
FC Strommi Tallinn 1, Trans Narva 0
MC Tallinn 2, FC Lootus Kohtla-Järve 6
Irbis Kiviõli 1, Tulevik Viljandi 7
Vigri Tartu 0, Lelle SK 1
FC Kuressaare 2, FC Levadia Maardu 4
FC Maardu 0, FC Lantana Tallinn 1 (aet)
FC Flora Tallinn w/o EP Jõhvi

QUARTER-FINALS
Tervis Pärnu 0, VMK Tallinn 7 (Embrich 7, 85, Gorjatshov 9p, 71p, Teplovs 18, Jushka 54, 82)
VMK Tallinn 2 (Kostin 29, Kisseljov 51), Tervis Pärnu 1 (Teino 59)
(VMK Tallinn 9-1)

FC Flora Tallinn 2 (Lindpere 5, 55), FC Valga 0
FC Valga 0, FC Flora Tallinn 4
(Saharov 9, Anniste 32, Jääger 60, 89)
(FC Flora Tallinn 6-0)

Tulevik Viljandi 2 (Ustritski 14, Õun 23), FC Lootus Kohtla-Järve 1 (Marashov 50)
FC Lootus Kohtla-Järve 1 (Tomashevski 88), Tulevik Viljandi 1 (Allas 65p)
(Tulevik Viljandi 3-2)

FC Strommi Tallinn 0, FC Levadia Maardu 6 (Krõm 8, 16, 28, Bragin 88, Tshelnokov 88, Kolbassenko 89)
FC Levadia Maardu 9 (Tshelnokov 1, 11, O'Konnel-Bronin 31, 89, Olumets 38, Krõlov 50, 74, Ratnikov 58, Leitan V. 84), FC Strommi Tallinn 0
(FC Levadia Maardu 15-0)

N.B. FC Lantana Tallinn withdrew; replaced by FC Valga.

SEMI-FINALS
VMK Tallinn 1 (Jushka 24), FC Levadia Maardu 3 (Kapustin 6og, Olumets 34, Tshelnokov 62)
FC Levadia Maardu 3 (Krõlov 9, Krõm 22, Staleliunas 82), VMK Tallinn 0
(FC Levadia Maardu 6-1)

Tulevik Viljandi 2 (Allas 58p, Õun 84), FC Flora Tallinn 0
FC Flora Tallinn 1 (Jürisson 79), Tulevik Viljandi 0
(Tulevik Viljandi 2-1)

FINAL
28/05/2000, Pärnu
FC LEVADIA MAARDU 2 Olumets (65), Leetma (75)
TULEVIK VILJANDI 0
referee - Kaldma
FC LEVADIA MAARDU - Pareiko, Krasnopjorov, Prins, Vinogradov, Kolbassenko, Krõlov, Leetma, Olumets (Bragin 81), Leitan V. (Tshelnokov 57), Staleliunas, Krõm (Kirillov 87).
TULEVIK VILJANDI - Kaalma, Lemsalu, Nõmmik, Olesk, Vink (Meet 81), Sirevicius, Lelov, Allas, Anis (Vahtramäe 81), Dovydenas, Ustritski.

latter to the league's top-scorer prize by one goal - thanks to a hat-trick in the penultimate game against his old club FC Flora. As winners already of the 1999 Estonian Cup, Levadia completed a calendar year 'double' with their league triumph. They then made it three trophies in a row by retaining the Cup in 2000, beating Tulevik Viljandi 2-0 in the final with second-half goals from midfielders Indro Olumets and Liivo Leetma.

Tulevik were thus made to wait a while longer before they could inscribe a first major title into the club's roll-of-honour. Runners-up in league and Cup, they did at least have the consolation of making a swift return to Europe. They had taken a UEFA Cup place in 1999/2000 thanks to the luck of the draw in the Fair Play lottery, but, like Estonia's other three representatives - Flora, Levadia and Lantana Tallinn - Tulevik were beaten

NATIONAL TEAM APPEARANCES 99/00

Coach - Teitur THÓRDARSON; Tarmo RÜÜTLI	ARM	FAR	SCO	BOS	IRQ	UAE	TRK	GRE	FIN	THA	LUX	BLS	GEO	Cps	Gls
Toomas TOHVER (24/04/73) - FC Flora Tallinn	G							G						23	-
Raio PIIROJA (11/07/79) - FC Flora Tallinn	D	D	D	D							D	s84	M46	9	2
Sergei HOHLOV-SIMSON (22/04/72) - FC Flora Tallinn	D73	D	D	D	D	D	D39	D					s75	53	2
Erko SAVIAUK (20/10/77) - FC Flora Tallinn	D55	D90	D	s61	s80		s39	s57			D		D60	25	1
Viktor ALONEN (23/10/69) - FC Flora Tallinn	D	D		D	M80	D	D	s60			s72	M	M	66	-
Urmas KIRS (05/11/66) - KTP (FIN)	M70	M	D	D	D	D	D	D57	D	D	D			80	5
Aivar ANNISTE (18/02/80) - FC Flora Tallinn	M	M67	M	M61	s46	M86	M46	M60			M72	M	M	15	-
Marko KRISTAL (02/06/73) - FC Flora Tallinn/FC Lahti (FIN)	M	A	M	M	M84	s86	M	M	M85	M	M66			96	7
Martin REIM (14/05/71) - KTP (FIN)	M	M	M	M	M	M	M	M	M	M	M			89	12
Andres OPER (07/11/77) - AaB (DEN)	A75	A	A	A46	A45	A89	A	A	A	s46	A84	A		53	13
Indrek ZELINSKI (13/11/74) - FC Flora Tallinn/FC Lahti (FIN)	A87	A75	s46	A40	A55			s61		M	A	A	A	60	14
Janek MEET (02/05/74) - FC Flora Tallinn/Tulevik Viljandi	s55							s88	s85	s64				37	-
Kert HAAVISTU (18/01/80) - FC Flora Tallinn	s70			s84	s67	M64					D			5	-
Marek LEMSALU (24/11/72) - Strømsgodset IF (NOR)/Tulevik Viljandi	s73	s90							D	D	D	D	D	69	1
Dmitri USTRITSKI (08/05/75) - Tulevik Viljandi	s75	s75		s46				s89	A61	s82				7	1
Ivan O'KONNEL-BRONIN (10/02/73) - FC Levadia Maardu	s87	s67	A46	s74	s63	M67	s64							22	-
Mart POOM (03/02/72) - Derby County (ENG)		G	G								G	G	G	72	-
Sergei TEREHHOV (18/04/75) - FC Flora Tallinn/SK Brann (NOR)		M	M	M74	M	M88	s46	M			M66	M	M	34	4
Martin KAALMA (14/04/77) - Lelle SK/Tulevik Viljandi			G	G	G	G			G	G				9	-
Kristen VIIKMÄE (10/02/79) - FC Flora Tallinn				s40	A63	s55	s46	s57						41	3
Urmas ROOBA (08/07/78) - FC Flora Tallinn					D46		D						s60	22	1
Andrei STEPANOV (16/03/79) - Lelle SK/FC Flora Tallinn					D	D	D	D				D	D	6	-
Joel LINDPERE (05/10/81) - Lelle SK							s45	A46						2	-
Argo ARBEITER (05/12/73) - KTP (FIN)								A57	M	M82		s57		29	6
Gert OLESK (08/08/73) - Tulevik Viljandi									D	D				11	-
Raivo NÕMMIK (11/02/77) - Tulevik Viljandi									D					17	-
Teet ALLAS (02/06/77) - Tulevik Viljandi									M	D	s66	D	D75	10	-
Andre ANIS (25/05/77) - Tulevik Viljandi										M64				2	-
Aleksander SAHAROV (22/04/82) - FC Flora Tallinn											A46			1	-
Janno JÜRISSON (06/10/80) - FC Flora Tallinn											s66	M57	s46	3	-

PLAYERS OF THE SEASON

ANDRES OPER

Andres Oper made a million-dollar move from FC Flora Tallinn to reigning Danish champions AaB in the summer of 1999. He had a satisfactory first season abroad, scoring seven goals in the Danish Superliga and another in an exciting Champions' League qualifier away to Dynamo Kiev. The experience of playing regularly at a higher level undoubtedly increased the young striker's value to the Estonian national team, and he proved that by scoring eight international goals over the course of the 1999/2000 season, including six in as many games under new Estonia coach Tarmo Rüütli, two of them in an encouraging 2-2 draw away to Greece on Rüütli's début. Oper's rapid, incisive forward play also provoked three penalties over the same period, and it goes without saying that he will be Estonia's most marked man during the 2002 World Cup qualifying campaign.

MART POOM

Mart Poom is a legend in his own land. Many Estonians are agreed that the giant goalkeeper is the most influential player in the national team. When he is playing, team-mates and fans alike feel twice as confident as usual about Estonia's chances. He certainly made quite a difference when he was between the posts in 1999/2000. He played five

matches and conceded just one goal - a stoppage-time equaliser by Luxembourg. He had a blinder in the 0-0 draw against Scotland, twice denying Billy Dodds by sprawling himself in customary fashion at the onrushing striker's feet. At club level Poom (pictured below, right) also played consistently well, and although Derby County had a poor season in the Premiership, many were of the opinion that without the heroics of their Estonian 'keeper the East Midlands side could well have been relegated.

EUROPEAN CUPS 99/00

CHAMPIONS' CUP

● **FC FLORA TALLINN**
Preliminary round 1 PARTIZAN BEOGRAD (YUG)
A 0-6
 Tohver, Alonen, Hohlov-Simson, Lemsalu, Saviauk (Lepa 65), Razanauskas, Piiroja, Terehhov, Haavistu (Kristal 46), Zelinski, Viikmäe.
H 1-4 Viikmäe (52)
 Tohver, Alonen, Hohlov-Simson, Piiroja, Saviauk (Lepa 68), Terehhov (Reiska 41), Razanauskas, Anniste, Haavistu, Viikmäe, Zelinski (Kristal 35).

UEFA CUP

● **FC LANTANA TALLINN**
Qualifying round TORPEDO KUTAISI (GEO)
H 0-5
 Kisseljov (Kotenko 82), Kalimullin, Kolotsei, Voronin, Mitjunov, Tshelnokov, Dolinin, Leitan (Belov 54), Valuiski (Mirski 87), Gorjatshov, Kulakov.
A 2-4 Leitan (37), Dolinin (56)
 Kotenko, Kaimullin, Kolotsei, Voronin, Mitjunov, Tshelnokov, Dolinin, Leitan, Valuiski, Gorjatshov, Kulakov.

● **FC LEVADIA MAARDU**
Qualifying round STEAUA BUCURESTI (ROM)
A 0-3
 Pareiko, Vinogradov, Leitan, Prins, Leetma, Rõtshkov (Brattshuk 84), Kolbassenko, Krõlov, Bragin (Staleliunas 83), O'Konnel-Bronin, Krõm (Afanassov 28).
H 1-4 Olumets (29)
 Pareiko, Staleliunas, Leitan, Prins, Leetma, Rõtshkov, Kolbassenko, Olumets (Afanassov 70), Bragin (Tshurilkin 72), O'Konnel-Bronin, Krõlov (Brattshuk 80).

● **TULEVIK VILJANDI**
Qualifying round CLUB BRUGGE KV (BEL)
H 0-3
 Vessenberg, Olesk, Lell, Pari, Rooba (Sirel 62), Lelov, Dovydenas, Ustritski, Vahtramäe (Jürisson 63), Allas, Anis.
A 0-2
 Vessenberg, Olesk, Lell, Pari (Nõmmik 56), Sirel, Lelov, Dovydenas, Ustritski, Vahtramäe (Jürisson 61), Allas, Anis (Rooba 58).

comfortably home and away in their one and only tie.

A few months after their UEFA Cup exit Lantana were preparing to drop out of the domestic championship. They were not relegated but chose to decline participation in the 2000 premier division campaign through lack of finance. Lelle SK did likewise, which made a mockery of their play-off victory over first division runners-up Lootus Kohtla-Järve, who were thus promoted anyway, joining first-placed FC Kuressare and... fourth-placed FC Valga, who assumed the place made vacant by Lantana's withdrawal. EP Jõhvi, rock bottom of the top flight with just two wins from their 28 matches, also began the new millennium in a different division.

TOP SCORERS

19	Toomas KRÕM	(FC Levadia Maardu)
18	Andrei KRÕLOV	(FC Levadia Maardu)
16	Dmitri USTRITSKI	(Tulevik Viljandi)
15	Vitali LEITAN	(FC Lantana Tallinn)
14	Indrek ZELINSKI	(FC Flora Tallinn)
13	Maksim GRUZNOV	(Trans Narva)
12	Kristen VIIKMÄE	(FC Flora Tallinn)
10	Aleksandr MARASHOV	(Trans Narva)
9	Konstantin KOLBASSENKO	
	(FC Levadia Maardu)	
8	Indro OLUMETS	(FC Levadia Maardu)

NATIONAL TEAM RESULTS 99/00

18/08/99	Armenia	H	Pärnu	2-0	Kristal (79), Ustritski (90)
04/09/99	Faroe Islands (ECQ)	A	Toftir	2-0	Reim (88), Piiroja (90)
08/09/99	Scotland (ECQ)	H	Tallinn	0-0	
09/10/99	Bosnia-Herzegovina (ECQ)	H	Tallinn	1-4	Oper (4)
30/10/99	Iraq	N	Abu Dhabi	1-1	Mahmoud (27og)
01/11/99	United Arab Emirates	A	Abu Dhabi	2-2	Reim (19p), Oper (38)
03/11/99	Turkmenistan	N	Abu Dhabi	1-1	Viikmäe (47)
18/12/99	Greece	A	Trikala	2-2	Oper (17, 38)
23/02/00	Finland	N	Bangkok	2-4	Zelinski (71p), Oper (84)
25/02/00	Thailand	A	Bangkok	1-2	Reim (74p)
26/04/00	Luxembourg	A	Luxembourg	1-1	Oper (84)
04/06/00	Belarus	H	Tallinn	2-0	Oper (5, 80)
11/06/00	Georgia	H	Tallinn	1-0	Piiroja (17)

PROMOTED CLUBS 1999

SECOND DIVISION FINAL TABLE

		Pd	W	D	L	F	A	Pt	GD
1	**FC Kuressare**	28	21	4	3	92	25	67	67
2	**Lootus Kohtla-Järve**	28	21	2	5	81	33	65	48
3	Vigri Tartu	28	18	6	4	70	28	60	42
4	**FC Valga**	28	11	2	15	34	59	35	-25
5	MC Tallinn	28	9	4	15	39	73	31	-34
6	FC Maardu	28	8	6	14	47	60	30	-13
7	FC Lelle	28	5	2	21	26	75	17	-49
8	Sillamäe JK	28	5	2	21	26	62	17	-36

PROMOTION/RELEGATION PLAY-OFF
Lootus Kohtla-Järve 0, Lelle SK 3
Lelle SK 2, Lootus Kohtla-Järve 1
(Lelle SK 5-1)

N.B. Lelle SK subsequently declined promotion and Lootus Kohtla-Järve were promoted instead;
FC Valga also promoted after FC Lantana Tallinn withdrew.

CLUB DIRECTORIES

FC Kuressaare
Staadioni 2, 93815 Kuressaare
tel - (45) 33556 / fax - (45) 33546
Year of Formation - 1997
President - Priit Penu
Coach - Jan Vazhinski
Stadium - Kuressaare Linnastaadion (2,000)

FC Lootus Kohtla-Järve
Spordi 4, Kohtla-Järve
tel - (50) 36171 / fax - (33) 71217
Year of Formation - 1998
President - Sergei Dorofejev
Coach - Sergei Zamogilnõi
Stadium - Kohtla-Järve Spordikeskus (2,000)

FC Valga
Enno 15, 68204 Valga
tel - (76) 61762 / fax - (76) 61759
Year of Formation - 1997
President - Rein Randver
Coach - Ene Kralla
Stadium - Valga Linnastaadion (500)

EP JÕHVI

CLUB DIRECTORY

Jalgpalliklubi Eesti Põlevkivi Jõhvi
Jaama 10
Jõhvi EE 2045
tel - (33) 64427
fax - (33) 70054
Year of Formation - 1974
President - Väino Viilup
Secretary - Rudolf Varunov
Coach - Pavel Lukyanov
Stadium - Eesti Põlevkivi (2,000)

APPEARANCES 1999

	P	Ap	(s)	Gls
Roman ABORNEV	M	24	(1)	
Ruslan BEROV	M		(6)	
Oleg BOGDANOV	D	21		
Juri BRAIKO	A	25		2
Aleksei GALOTSHKIN	A	11	(10)	
Aleksander GROMOV	M	2		
Dmitri GULJAJENKO	D	21		
Sergei IVANOV	D	3	(5)	
Aleksandr IVARINEN	D	14	(7)	1
Artur JUREVITSH	G	3		
Andrei JÕGI	A	2		
Aleksandr KOVALJOV	G		(2)	
Alex LUIK	M	4	(8)	
Oleg LUKJANOV	A	16	(9)	1
Andrei MUSTONEN	D	23		
Dmitri PEREDKOV	D	21	(3)	2
Konstantin RUBTSOV	G	25		
Konstantin RUBTSOV	D	1		
Eduard SARAJEV	D	26		1
Andrei SHKALETA	D	20		1
Nikolai SHISHELOV	M	13		3
Vladimir TIHHON	M	21		1
Artur VARUNOV	A	1	(3)	

LEAGUE RESULTS 1999

03/04/99	Tulevik Viljandi	H	1-2	Shishelov (p)
14/04/99	Tulevik Viljandi	A	0-1	
23/04/99	Lelle SK	H	0-0	
02/05/99	FC Flora Tallinn	H	1-6	Tihhon
08/05/99	FC Lantana Tallinn	A	0-0	
16/05/99	Trans Narva	A	1-4	Shkaleta
22/05/99	VMK Tallinn	H	1-0	Shishelov (p)
30/05/99	FC Levadia Maardu	H	0-5	
13/06/99	Lelle SK	A	0-0	
19/06/99	FC Flora Tallinn	A	0-4	
30/06/99	FC Lantana Tallinn	H	1-3	Peredkov
04/07/99	Trans Narva	H	1-0	Shishelov
09/07/99	VMK Tallinn	A	0-0	
17/07/99	FC Levadia Maardu	A	0-6	
01/08/99	Tulevik Viljandi	A	0-14	
05/08/99	Lelle SK	H	0-0	
12/08/99	FC Flora Tallinn	H	0-1	
20/08/99	FC Lantana Tallinn	A	1-1	Lukjanov
29/08/99	Trans Narva	A	0-2	
05/09/99	VMK Tallinn	H	0-0	
12/09/99	FC Levadia Maardu	H	1-9	Braiko
17/09/99	Tulevik Viljandi	H	0-2	
25/09/99	Lelle SK	A	1-3	Braiko
29/09/99	FC Flora Tallinn	A	1-7	Peredkov
03/10/99	FC Lantana Tallinn	H	1-4	Sarajev
17/10/99	Trans Narva	H	0-4	
23/10/99	VMK Tallinn	A	1-3	Ivarinen
31/10/99	FC Levadia Maardu	A	0-0	(w/o; awarded as home win)

FC FLORA TALLINN

CLUB DIRECTORY

Football Club Flora Tallinn
Toomkooli 21, 10130 Tallinn
tel - (6) 311397/279940/279941
fax - (6) 418021
Year of Formation - 1990
President - Aivar Pohlak
Secretary - Anne Samarüütel
Coach - Teitur Thórdarson
Stadium - Kadriorg (6,000)

MAJOR HONOURS
League Championship - (4)
1994, 1995, 1998, 1998.
Domestic Cup - (2) 1995, 1998.

APPEARANCES 1999

	P	Ap	(s)	Gls
Viktor ALONEN	D	24	(1)	2
Aivar ANNISTE	M	17	(2)	3
Kert HAAVISTU	M	15	(2)	
Trond Inge HAUGLAND (NOR)	D	3	(3)	
Sergei HOHLOV-SIMSON	D	24		4
Enver JÄÄGER	A		(2)	
Urmas KAAL	D	3	(1)	
Taivo KASK	M	11	(5)	
Urmas KIRS	D	5	(1)	
Marko KRISTAL	M	13	(3)	1
Kert KÜTT	G	8		
Marek LEMSALU	D	8		2
Martin LEPA	D	2		
Janek MEET	D	14	(5)	
Rene MIILEN	D	2		
Priit MURUMETS	A	6	(4)	3
Andres OPER	A	8	(2)	4
Raio PIIROJA	D	10		2
Tomas RAZANAUSKAS (LIT)	M	3	(1)	
Martin REIM	M	8	(1)	3
Priit REISKA	M	3		
Urmas ROOBA	D	4	(4)	
Aleksander SAHAROV	A	5	(7)	2
Erko SAVIAUK	D	22		1
Mark SHVETS	M	4	(2)	
Maksim SMIRNOV	M	5	(5)	1
Zaur TAGI-ZADE (AZB)	M	4	(1)	
Sergei TEREHHOV	M	22		4
Tiit TIKENBERG	M		(4)	
Toomas TOHVER	G	20		
Kristen VIIKMÄE	A	15	(2)	12
Vjatsheslav ZAHOVAIKO	M		(2)	2
Indrek ZELINSKI	A	20	(5)	14

LEAGUE RESULTS 1999

04/04/99	Trans Narva	A	3-1	Zelinski 2, Oper
14/04/99	Trans Narva	H	5-0	Reim (p), Hohlov-Simson 2, Smirnov, Oper
23/04/99	FC Lantana Tallinn	H	3-0	Viikmäe 2, Reim (p)
02/05/99	EP Jõhvi	A	6-1	Zelinski 5, Lemsalu
08/05/99	Tulevik Viljandi	A	4-2	Viikmäe, Reim (p), Lemsalu, Oper
16/05/99	VMK Tallinn	H	0-1	
22/05/99	FC Levadia Maardu	A	0-0	
30/05/99	Lelle SK	H	2-2	Hohlov-Simson, Viikmäe
13/06/99	FC Lantana Tallinn	A	3-3	Anniste, Viikmäe, Hohlov-Simson
19/06/99	EP Jõhvi	H	4-0	Viikmäe 2, Oper, Alonen
01/07/99	Tulevik Viljandi	H	5-2	Zelinski 2, Terehhov 2, Alonen
05/07/99	VMK Tallinn	A	1-1	Viikmäe
09/07/99	FC Levadia Maardu	H	1-2	Piiroja
31/07/99	Trans Narva	H	1-1	Zelinski
08/08/99	FC Lantana Tallinn	H	3-1	Saharov, Murumets, Anniste
12/08/99	EP Jõhvi	A	1-0	Saviauk
22/08/99	Tulevik Viljandi	A	0-1	
29/08/99	VMK Tallinn	H	1-1	Murumets
12/09/99	Lelle SK	H	2-1	Kristal, Zelinski
17/09/99	Trans Narva	A	1-1	Piiroja
21/09/99	Lelle SK	A	0-1	
25/09/99	FC Lantana Tallinn	A	2-3	Terehhov, Zelinski
29/09/99	EP Jõhvi	H	7-1	Zelinski 2, Murumets, Anniste, Saharov, Zahovaiko 2
03/10/99	Tulevik Viljandi	H	1-1	Terehhov
13/10/99	FC Levadia Maardu	A	1-3	Viikmäe
17/10/99	VMK Tallinn	A	2-0	Viikmäe 2
23/10/99	FC Levadia Maardu	H	0-3	
31/10/99	Lelle SK	A	1-0	Viikmäe

FC LANTANA TALLINN

CLUB DIRECTORY

Football Club Lantana Tallinn
Kaupmehe 4-28
Tallinn EE 0001
tel - (2) 445549
fax - (2) 443738
Year of Formation - 1995
President - Sergei Belov
Coach - Anatoli Belov
Stadium - Viimsi (3,000)

MAJOR HONOURS
League Championship - (2) 1996, 1997.

APPEARANCES 1999

	P	Ap	(s)	Gls
Pavel APALINSKI	A	7	(5)	1
Juri ARTAMONOV	M		(1)	
Sergei BELOV	M	21		2
Vadim DOLININ	M	27		2
Oleg GORJATSHOV	M	20		1
Andrei KALIMULLIN	D	26		
Dmitri KIRILLOV	M	2	(4)	
Pavel KISSELJOV	G	18	(1)	
Oleg KOLOTSEI	D	24		
Artur KOTENKO	G	10		
Andrei KRASNOPJOROV	D	9		1
Vjatesheslav KULAKOV	D	14		
Dmitri KULIKOV	D	6		
Vitali LEITAN	A	23		15
Dmitri MARTSHENKO (LIT)	M	9	(11)	
Roman MIRSKI	A	11	(5)	2
Andrei MITJUNOV	M	23		
Aleksandr RADOMSKI	M		(1)	
Andrei TJUNIN	M	3		
Vladimir TSHELNOKOV	A	12		3
Juri TSHURILKIN	D	3		1
Vitali VALUISKI	D	23		1
Osvald VARES	D	1	(2)	
Fjodor VORONIN	D	16	(1)	2

LEAGUE RESULTS 1999

14/04/99	VMK Tallinn	H	2-0	Leitan 2
23/04/99	FC Flora Tallinn	A	0-3	
02/05/99	FC Levadia Maardu	A	0-3	
08/05/99	EP Jõhvi	H	0-0	
16/05/99	Lelle SK	A	2-4	Mirski, Krasnopjorov
22/05/99	Trans Narva	A	0-7	
30/05/99	Tulevik Viljandi	H	1-3	Tshurilkin
13/06/99	FC Flora Tallinn	H	3-3	Dolinin (p), Leitan 2
19/06/99	FC Levadia Maardu	H	0-1	
23/06/99	VMK Tallinn	A	2-0	Mirski, Belov
30/06/99	EP Jõhvi	A	3-1	Leitan 3
04/07/99	Lelle SK	H	1-1	Leitan
10/07/99	Trans Narva	H	1-1	Valuiski
17/07/99	Tulevik Viljandi	A	1-1	Apalinski
01/08/99	VMK Tallinn	H	0-0	
05/08/99	FC Flora Tallinn	A	1-3	Tshelnokov
15/08/99	FC Levadia Maardu	A	0-4	
20/08/99	EP Jõhvi	H	1-1	Tshelnokov
30/08/99	Lelle SK	A	1-1	Voronin
05/09/99	Trans Narva	A	0-2	
12/09/99	Tulevik Viljandi	H	1-2	Leitan
17/09/99	VMK Tallinn	A	1-0	Belov
25/09/99	FC Flora Tallinn	H	3-2	Leitan, Tshelnokov, Gorkatshov
29/09/99	FC Levadia Maardu	H	1-3	Leitan
03/10/99	EP Jõhvi	A	4-1	Leitan 3, Dolinin
17/10/99	Lelle SK	H	0-0	
23/10/99	Trans Narva	H	0-2	
27/10/99	Tulevik Viljandi	A	2-3	Leitan, Voronin

LELLE SK

CLUB DIRECTORY

Lelle SK
Pargi 3
Kehtna EE3505
tel - (48) 75297
fax - (48) 75536
Year of Formation - 1990
President - Janno Kaljuvee
Secretary - Edda Sirel
Coach - Zaur Tsilingarashvili
Stadium - Kehtna Football School (1,500)

APPEARANCES 1999

	P	Ap	(s)	Gls
Aivar ANNISTE	M	8		1
Simen FOSSUM (NOR)	A	8		2
Kert HAAVISTU	M	8		1
Jesper JOHANSSON (FIN)	M	21		4
Martin KAALMA	G	17		
Marek KAHR	D	21	(1)	
Dmitri KOPAREV	D	2	(1)	
Margus KORJU	A		(5)	
Märt KOSEMETS	M	22	(2)	2
Siim KÄRSON	A	6	(3)	1
Kert KÜTT	G	11		
Joel LINDPERE	A	18	(4)	5
Ott MEERITS	M	6	(7)	
Maksim MILOVIDOV	A	7	(13)	
Raio PIIROJA	D	7		2
Marko PÄRNPUU	D	20	(2)	
Taavi RÄHN	D	27		
Tarmo SAKS	A	25	(1)	6
Tomas SIREVICIUS (LIT)	M	25		1
Andrei STEPANOV	D	21		
Siim TEKKEL	M	4	(10)	
Tiit TIKENBERG	M	1	(2)	
Silver TIKS	M	10	(4)	
Andrei TIMOFEJEV	M	13	(1)	

LEAGUE RESULTS 1999

04/04/99	FC Levadia Maardu	A	2-5	Anniste (p), Saks
14/04/99	FC Levadia Maardu	H	1-1	Fossum
23/04/99	EP Jõhvi	A	0-0	
02/05/99	VMK Tallinn	A	0-3	
09/05/99	Trans Narva	H	0-3	
16/05/99	FC Lantana Tallinn	H	4-2	Fossum, Sirevicius, Piiroja, Saks
22/05/99	Tulevik Viljandi	A	0-2	
30/05/99	FC Flora Tallinn	A	2-2	Haavistu, Piiroja
13/06/99	EP Jõhvi	H	0-0	
19/06/99	VMK Tallinn	H	0-2	
30/06/99	Trans Narva	A	0-1	
04/07/99	FC Lantana Tallinn	A	1-1	Kosemets
10/07/99	Tulevik Viljandi	H	0-1	
01/08/99	FC Levadia Maardu	H	1-5	Johansson
05/08/99	EP Jõhvi	A	0-0	
10/08/99	VMK Tallinn	A	3-1	Lindpere 2, Johansson
22/08/99	Trans Narva	H	1-0	Lindpere
30/08/99	FC Lantana Tallinn	H	1-1	Saks
12/09/99	FC Flora Tallinn	A	1-2	Lindpere
21/09/99	FC Flora Tallinn	H	1-0	Saks
25/09/99	EP Jõhvi	H	3-1	Saks, Kosemets, Lindpere (p)
29/09/99	VMK Tallinn	H	0-0	
03/10/99	Trans Narva	A	0-1	
13/10/99	Tulevik Viljandi	A	0-3	
17/10/99	FC Lantana Tallinn	A	0-0	
20/10/99	FC Levadia Maardu	A	2-3	Johansson 2
23/10/99	Tulevik Viljandi	H	2-4	Saks, Kärson
27/10/99	FC Flora Tallinn	H	0-1	

FC LEVADIA MAARDU

CLUB DIRECTORY

FC Levadia Maardu
Karjääri 4
EE0030 Maardu
tel - (6) 379147
fax - (6) 319846
Year of Formation - 1999
President - Viktor Levada
Secretary - Vladimir Plesjakov
Coach - Sergei Ratnikov
Stadium - Maardu (600)

MAJOR HONOURS
League Championship - (1) 1999.
Domestic Cup - (2) 1999, 2000.

APPEARANCES 1999

	P	Ap	(s)	Gls
Andrei AFANASSOV	M	1	(3)	1
Sergei BRAGIN	M	10	(4)	6
Igor BRATSHUK	M	5	(18)	
Ilja GUSSEV	A	2	(17)	1
Vladislav IVANOV	G	5	(1)	
Pavel KAZAKOV	M		(1)	
Konstantin KOLBASSENKO	M	24	(1)	9
Andrei KRÕLOV	A	21	(2)	18
Toomas KRÕM	A	17	(1)	19
Liivo LEETMA	M	25	(1)	5
Juri LEITAN	D	26		
Ernest MARTINSONS	G	7	(1)	
Ivan O'KONNEL-BRONIN	M	23	(2)	5
Indro OLUMETS	M	24		8
Sergei PAREIKO	G	15		
Igor PRINS	D	26		
Maksim RÕTSHKOV	M	23	(1)	4
Gerol SILKIN	D		(2)	
Dalius STALELIUNAS (LIT)	D	19		
Stanislav SVETOGOR	M	2	(5)	
Eduard VINOGRADOV	D	22		1

LEAGUE RESULTS 1999

04/04/99	Lelle SK	H	5-2	O'Konnel-Bronin, Kolbassenko, Rõtshkov, Olumets 2
14/04/99	Lelle SK	A	1-1	Krõlov
23/04/99	Trans Narva	H	2-0	O'Konnel-Bronin, Krõlov
02/05/99	FC Lantana Tallinn	H	3-0	Kolbassenko, Olumets, Leetma
08/05/99	VMK Tallinn	A	3-0	Olumets, Kolbassenko (p), O'Konnel-Bronin
16/05/99	Tulevik Viljandi	A	3-0	Krõlov 2, Kolbassenko
22/05/99	FC Flora Tallinn	H	0-0	
30/05/99	EP Jõhvi	A	5-0	Vinogradov, Kolbassenko, Krõlov, Krõm, O'Konnel-Bronin
12/06/99	Trans Narva	A	2-1	Gussev, Krõm (p)
19/06/99	FC Lantana Tallinn	A	1-0	Krõm
30/06/99	VMK Tallinn	H	0-0	(w/o; awarded as away win)
05/07/99	Tulevik Viljandi	H	2-1	Krõm, Leetma
09/07/99	FC Flora Tallinn	A	2-1	Krõm, Krõlov
17/07/99	EP Jõhvi	H	6-0	Krõm 3, O'Konnel-Bronin, Krõlov, Rõtshkov
01/08/99	Lelle SK	A	5-1	Krõlov 2, Bragin 2, Afanassov
05/08/99	Trans Narva	H	1-0	Krõm (p)
15/08/99	FC Lantana Tallinn	H	4-0	Leetma, Krõlov 2, Bragin
18/08/99	VMK Tallinn	A	4-0	Bragin, Krõlov, Leetma, Kolbassenko
29/08/99	Tulevik Viljandi	A	0-0	
12/09/99	EP Jõhvi	A	9-1	Krõm 2, Krõlov 2, Olumets 2, Kolbassenko, Rõtshkov, Bragin
25/09/99	Trans Narva	A	0-0	
29/09/99	FC Lantana Tallinn	A	3-1	Krõm, Olumets, Bragin
03/10/99	VMK Tallinn	H	3-0	Krõm, Olumets, Leetma
13/10/99	FC Flora Tallinn	H	3-1	Krõm 2, Rõtshkov
17/10/99	Tulevik Viljandi	H	4-0	Krõlov 2 (1p), Kolbassenko, Krõm
20/10/99	Lelle SK	H	3-2	Krõlov 2, Kolbassenko
23/10/99	FC Flora Tallinn	A	3-0	Krõm 3
27/10/99	EP Jõhvi	H	0-0	(w/o; awarded as home win)

TRANS NARVA

CLUB DIRECTORY

Jalgpalliklubi Trans Narva
Kangelaste 45-20
Narva EE 2000
tel - (35) 43696/43975
fax - (35) 44284
Year of Formation - 1979
President - Nikolai Burdakov
Coach - Valeri Bondarenko
Stadium - Kreenholm (2,000)

APPEARANCES 1999

	P	Ap	(s)	Gls
Konstantin ANDREJEV	M		(1)	
Andrei FROLOV	M	19	(1)	1
Konstantin GOLITSÕN	M		(1)	
Maksim GRUZNOV	A	22		13
Aleksei JAGUDIN	D	24		1
Andrei JELISSEJEV	D	11	(12)	
Konstantin KARIN	M	3	(1)	
Sergei KAZAKOV	M	5	(14)	
Oleg KUROTSHKIN	D	13		
Dmitri LIPARTOV (RUS)	A	25		7
Aleksandr MARASHOV	M	23	(1)	10
Aleksandr MOLEV (RUS)	D	8		
Boris NEJOLOV	A	15	(6)	6
Jevgeni NOVIKOV	M	19	(1)	
Anton POMAZAN	A	2	(4)	
Levani PORTSHIDZE	G	1		
Aleksandr RJABTSHUN	G	9	(3)	
Denis RUMJANTSEV	M	17	(4)	1
Dmitri SHELEHHOV	D	1	(8)	
Andrei SUVOROV	M	1		
Aleksandr TARASSENKOV	M	19	(1)	
Nikolai TOSHTSHEV	M	2		1
Sergei USSOLTSEV	G	18		
Vitali VASHTSHENKO	D	26	(1)	
Viktor VJALOV	D	23	(3)	
Sergei ZAMORSKI	M	2		

LEAGUE RESULTS 1999

04/04/99	FC Flora Tallinn	H	1-3	Toshtshev
14/04/99	FC Flora Tallinn	A	0-5	
23/04/99	FC Levadia Maardu	A	0-2	
02/05/99	Tulevik Viljandi	H	1-1	Jagudin
09/05/99	Lelle SK	A	3-0	Frolov, Gruznov 2
16/05/99	EP Jõhvi	H	4-1	Marashov 2, Nejolov, Gruznov
22/05/99	FC Lantana Tallinn	H	7-0	Gruznov 4 (1p), Lipartov 2, Marashov
30/05/99	VMK Tallinn	A	0-0	
12/06/99	FC Levadia Maardu	H	1-2	Marashov (p)
16/06/99	Tulevik Viljandi	A	3-1	Lipartov 2, Gruznov
30/06/99	Lelle SK	H	1-0	Nejolov
04/07/99	EP Jõhvi	A	0-1	
10/07/99	FC Lantana Tallinn	A	1-1	Nejolov
17/07/99	VMK Tallinn	H	1-1	Marashov
31/07/99	FC Flora Tallinn	A	1-1	Gruznov (p)
05/08/99	FC Levadia Maardu	A	0-1	
22/08/99	Lelle SK	A	0-1	
29/08/99	EP Jõhvi	H	2-0	Gruznov, Marashov (p)
05/09/99	FC Lantana Tallinn	H	2-0	Gruznov, Nejolov
12/09/99	VMK Tallinn	A	1-2	Lipartov
17/09/99	FC Flora Tallinn	H	1-1	Gruznov
21/09/99	Tulevik Viljandi	H	2-0	Lipartov, Gruznov
25/09/99	FC Levadia Maardu	H	0-0	
29/09/99	Tulevik Viljandi	A	1-3	Lipartov
03/10/99	Lelle SK	H	1-0	Marashov
17/10/99	EP Jõhvi	A	4-0	Marashov 2, Nejolov, Rumjantsev
23/10/99	FC Lantana Tallinn	A	2-0	Marashov, Nejolov
27/10/99	VMK Tallinn	H	0-1	

TULEVIK VILJANDI

Jalgpalliklubi Tulevik Viljandi
Ranna pst 6
Viljandi 71003
tel - (43) 48015
fax - (43) 48016
Year of Formation - 1990
President - Dzintar Klavan
Secretary - Pille Söstra
Coach - Tarmo Rüütli
Stadium - Kalev (1,000)

APPEARANCES 1999

	P	Ap	(s)	Gls
Teet ALLAS	M	22		4
Andre ANIS	D	21	(1)	2
Marius DOVYDENAS (LIT)	A	19	(4)	7
Janno JÜRISSON	M	3	(16)	1
Alari LELL	D	14	(5)	
Marko LELOV	M	24		6
Ruslan MUSSAEV (AZB)	A	4		
Raivo NÕMMIK	D	22	(1)	
Gert OLESK	D	27		1
Mati PARI	M	18		2
Meelis ROOBA	M	17	(6)	5
Mihkel SIIM	D	2	(4)	
Jaanus SIREL	M	17	(7)	3
Ivar SOVA	D	2	(1)	
Ain TAMMUS	G	17		
Dmitri USTRITSKI	A	26		16
Vahur VAHTRAMÄE	M	25	(1)	3
Rain VESSENBERG	G	11	(1)	
Jan ÕUN	A	17	(7)	6

LEAGUE RESULTS 1999

Date	Opponent	H/A	Score	Scorers
04/04/99	EP Jõhvi	A	2-1	Lelov, Rooba
14/04/99	EP Jõhvi	H	1-0	Rooba
23/04/99	VMK Tallinn	H	1-0	Pari
02/05/99	Trans Narva	A	1-1	Ustritski
08/05/99	FC Flora Tallinn	H	2-4	Pari, Anis
16/05/99	FC Levadia Maardu	H	0-3	
22/05/99	Lelle SK	H	2-0	Sirel, Jürisson
30/05/99	FC Lantana Tallinn	A	3-1	Vahtramäe, Õun, Allas (p)
12/06/99	VMK Tallinn	A	4-0	Allas (p), Dovydenas, Ustritski, Olesk
16/06/99	Trans Narva	H	1-3	Ustritski
01/07/99	FC Flora Tallinn	A	2-5	Ustritski 2
05/07/99	FC Levadia Maardu	A	1-2	Ustritski
10/07/99	Lelle SK	A	1-0	Ustritski
17/07/99	FC Lantana Tallinn	H	1-1	Dovydenas
01/08/99	EP Jõhvi	H	14-0	Ustritski 5, Lelov 4, Dovydenas 3, Allas, Vahtramäe
05/08/99	VMK Tallinn	H	0-0	
21/08/99	FC Flora Tallinn	H	1-0	Allas (p)
29/08/99	FC Levadia Maardu	H	0-0	
12/09/99	FC Lantana Tallinn	A	2-1	Anis, Sirel
17/09/99	EP Jõhvi	A	2-0	Lelov, Õun
21/09/99	Trans Narva	A	0-2	
25/09/99	VMK Tallinn	A	2-0	Ustritski, og (Kurjanov)
29/09/99	Trans Narva	H	3-1	Rooba, Õun, Sirel
03/10/99	FC Flora Tallinn	A	1-1	Dovydenas
13/10/99	Lelle SK	H	3-0	Õun 3
17/10/99	FC Levadia Maardu	A	0-4	
23/10/99	Lelle SK	A	4-2	Ustritski 2, Rooba, Dovydenas
27/10/99	FC Lantana Tallinn	H	3-2	Ustritski, Rooba, Vahtramäe

VMK TALLINN

CLUB DIRECTORY

VMK Tallinn
Pärnu mnt 69
Tallinn EE 0001
tel - (6) 261616
fax - (6) 261622
Year of Formation - 1995
President - Vjatsheslav Smirnov
Coach - Vjatsheslav Smirnov
Stadium - Kalev (12,000)

APPEARANCES 1999

	P	Ap	(s)	Gls
Oleg ANDREJEV	G	27		
Roman DEMENTSENKO	M		(1)	
Dmitri DENISSOV	D	2	(4)	
Aleksandr DJATSHENKO	D	1		
Ilja DJORD	M		(1)	
Aleksandr DMITRIJEV	M	4	(4)	
Aleksandr EMBRICH	A	13	(1)	
Ruslan JAGUDIN	M	3	(1)	1
Aleksei KAPUSTIN	D	20		
Maksim KISSELJOV	M	28		3
Andrei KOSTIN	M	23	(1)	1
Jevgeni KURJANOV	D	26		3
Rafael KUSHNIR	M	1	(3)	
Juri LEBRET	M	1	(1)	
Denis MALOV	D	23		1
Anton MÖKOLENKO	M	21		
Anatoli NOVOZHILOV	A	12		2
Aleksandr OLERSKI	A	8		2
Anton PAITSEV	M	25	(1)	
Viktor PASSIKUTA	M	1		
Dmitri SKIPERSKI (RUS)	M	26		2
Anton SMETANIN	M		(1)	
Aleksandr SMÕKOVSKI	M	1	(2)	
Keijo TAUHANPÄÄ	A	1		
Vladimir URJUPIN	D	22		
Ruslan VAKULITSH	A	8	(4)	1

LEAGUE RESULTS 1999

14/04/99	FC Lantana Tallinn	A	0-2	
23/04/99	Tulevik Viljandi	A	0-1	
02/05/99	Lelle SK	H	3-0	Kurjanov, Olerski (p), Kostin
08/05/99	FC Levadia Maardu	H	0-3	
16/05/99	FC Flora Tallinn	A	1-0	Olerski
22/05/99	EP Jõhvi	A	0-1	
30/05/99	Trans Narva	H	0-0	
12/06/99	Tulevik Viljandi	H	0-4	
19/06/99	Lelle SK	A	2-0	Kurjanov, Skiperski
23/06/99	FC Lantana Tallinn	H	0-2	
30/06/99	FC Levadia Maardu	A	0-0	(w/o; awarded as away win)
05/07/99	FC Flora Tallinn	H	1-1	Kurjanov
09/07/99	EP Jõhvi	H	0-0	
17/07/99	Trans Narva	A	1-1	Skiperski
01/08/99	FC Lantana Tallinn	A	0-0	
05/08/99	Tulevik Viljandi	A	0-0	
10/08/99	Lelle SK	H	1-3	Kisseljov
20/08/99	FC Levadia Maardu	H	0-4	
29/08/99	FC Flora Tallinn	A	1-1	Jagudin
05/09/99	EP Jõhvi	A	0-0	
12/09/99	Trans Narva	H	2-1	Kisseljov 2
17/09/99	FC Lantana Tallinn	H	0-1	
25/09/99	Tulevik Viljandi	H	0-2	
29/09/99	Lelle SK	A	0-0	
03/10/99	FC Levadia Maardu	A	0-3	
17/10/99	FC Flora Tallinn	H	0-2	
23/10/99	EP Jõhvi	H	3-1	Novozhilov 2, Malov
27/10/99	Trans Narva	A	1-0	Vakulitsh

FAROE ISLANDS

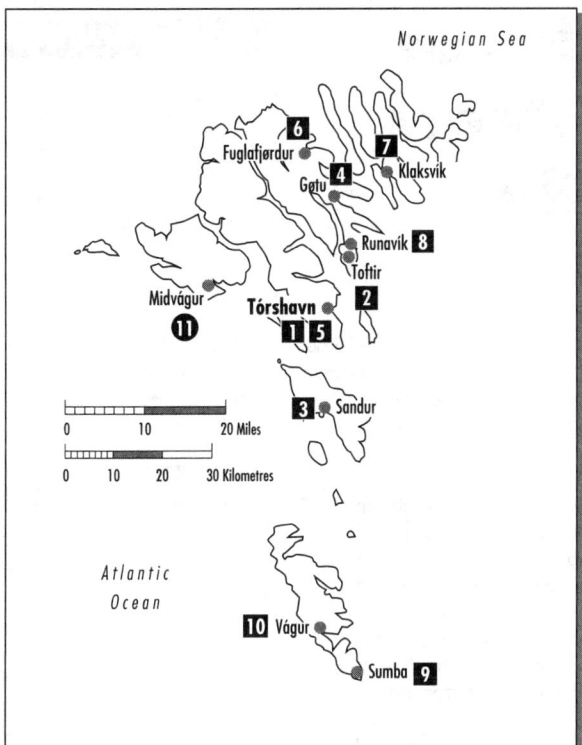

1	B36	352	7	KÍ	358
2	B68	353	8	NSÍ	359
3	B71	354	9	SUMBA	360
4	GÍ	355	10	VB	361
5	HB	356	**Promoted club**		
6	ÍF	357	11	FS VÁGAR	

NEW STADIUM OPENS IN TORSHAVN

Englishman Paris steers KÍ to the 'double'

FEDERATION DIRECTORY

Fotboltssamband Føroya
Postboks 3028, Gundadalur, 110 Torshavn

tel - 316707/457607   Year of Formation - 1979
fax - 319079   President - Torleif Sigurdsson
                         Secretary - Isak Mikladal

Stadium - Torsvøllur, Torshavn (6,000)

KÍ from Klaksvik were the team of the year in the Faroe Islands. Both of the domestic trophies ended up in their possession after a campaign in which they proved themselves to be far and away the most solid and consistent, if not the most spectacular and entertaining, of the ten First Division teams.

Coached, for one season only, by Englishman Tony Paris - he received US$10,000 for his six months' work - KÍ completed the first part of their 'double' in early July when they beat pre-match favourites B36 in the Cup final. Watched by a crowd of 2,328 spectators in the Gundadalur Stadium, KÍ ripped their opponents to shreds, winning 3-1 after dominating the match from start to finish.

KÍ's second goal was scored by striker Kurt Mørkøre, who thus took his total in the competition to a top-scoring nine. The veteran goalgrabber was also to become the club's leading marksman in the league, with 13, but his absence from the team in

the final third of the season - he left for Norway to join Sogndal - almost proved costly as KÍ were taken to the wire by their defeated Cup final opponents.

B36 recovered well from their Cup defeat to register

LEAGUE CHAMPIONSHIP RESULTS 1999

		1	2	3	4	5	6	7	8	9	10
1	B36		4-0	6-1	4-0	0-2	4-2	2-0	3-2	3-1	6-1
2	B68	1-2		2-0	2-5	1-5	1-2	2-3	0-0	3-1	0-0
3	B71	0-0	1-0		2-5	2-2	6-0	1-2	2-3	2-1	1-3
4	GÍ	2-1	3-0	2-1		1-2	2-1	2-1	4-1	7-2	3-1
5	HB	4-2	1-1	7-1	2-0		4-0	1-2	1-3	2-2	2-0
6	ÍF	1-4	2-4	3-3	1-5	0-1		0-1	1-1	2-1	1-2
7	KÍ	3-2	5-0	3-1	0-0	0-0	4-1		3-0	2-1	2-1
8	NSÍ	1-3	5-0	4-0	1-1	0-2	0-0	1-3		1-0	1-0
9	Sumba	1-6	2-3	1-1	1-1	0-3	2-2	2-3	1-1		1-0
10	VB	0-0	0-2	1-1	1-3	1-0	3-1	2-1	2-0	1-2	

LEAGUE CHAMPIONSHIP FINAL TABLE 1999

			Home					Away					Total						
		Pd	W	D	L	F	A	W	D	L	F	A	W	D	L	F	A	PT	GD
1	KÍ	18	7	2	0	22	6	6	0	3	16	13	13	2	3	38	19	41	19
2	GÍ	18	8	0	1	26	10	4	3	2	20	14	12	3	3	46	24	39	22
3	B36	18	8	0	1	32	9	4	2	3	20	13	12	2	4	52	22	38	30
4	HB	18	5	2	2	24	11	6	2	1	17	5	11	4	3	41	16	37	25
5	NSÍ	18	4	2	3	14	9	2	3	4	11	17	6	5	7	25	26	23	-1
6	VB	18	4	2	3	11	10	2	1	6	8	17	6	3	9	19	27	21	-8
7	B68	18	2	2	5	12	18	3	1	5	10	23	5	3	10	22	41	18	-19
8	B71	18	3	2	4	17	16	0	3	6	9	29	3	5	10	26	45	14	-19
9	Sumba	18	1	4	4	11	20	1	1	7	11	23	2	5	11	22	43	11	-21
10	ÍF	18	1	2	6	11	22	1	2	6	9	26	2	4	12	20	48	10	-28

NATIONAL TEAM APPEARANCES 99/00

Coach - Allan SIMONSEN	ISL	EST	LIT	CZE	FIN	ISL	LIE	Cps	Gls
Jens Martin KNUDSEN (11/06/67) - Gĺ/Ayr United (SCO)	G			G	G46	G	G	61	-
Oli JOHANNESEN (06/05/72) - AGF (DEN)	D	D	D	D		D		45	1
Jens Kristian HANSEN (03/09/71) - B36	D	D	D	D	D	D	D	34	2
Pol THORSTEINSSON (17/11/73) - B36	D	D74	D	D				19	-
Hans Frodi HANSEN (25/08/75) - HB	D	D	D	D				11	1
Samal JOENSEN (15/01/75) - Gĺ	M77	M89		M	M	s67	M76	15	-
Julian JOHNSSON (24/02/75) - Sogndal IL (NOR)	M85	M	M65	M	M	M	M	33	1
Allan MØRKØRE (22/11/71) - ÍBV (ISL)/HB	M	M	M	M	s46	D67	M54	54	1
Todi JONSSON (02/02/72) - FC København (DEN)	M	M	M	M		A	M	40	9
Uni ARGE (21/01/71) - Leiftur (ISL)/HB	A84	A89	A46		s61		s54	29	6
John PETERSEN (22/04/72) - B36	A	A		A71			A90	25	2
Frodi BENJAMINSEN (14/12/77) - B68	s77		s65		M	M76	D	5	-
Jakup a BORG (26/10/79) - B36	s84	s89	s46		A61		s54	10	-
Røgvi JACOBSEN (05/03/79) - Kĺ	s85			s71	s66	s76	s76	5	-
Jakup MIKKELSEN (14/08/70) - Herfølge BK (DEN)		G	G					12	-
Øssur HANSEN (07/01/71) - B36		s74	M	s89	s61	D	D76	39	1
Henning JARNSKOR (15/11/72) - Gĺ		s89	M84	M89	M	M	s76	34	2
Hedin a LAKJUNI (13/02/78) - Kĺ			s84		M61	s76		4	-
Johannis JOENSEN (27/11/70) - HB					D46	s46	s90	7	-
Jan DAM (07/09/68) - HB					D	D46	D	48	3
Kurt MØRKØRE (20/02/69) - Sogndal IL (NOR)					A66	A76	A54	29	3
Sunnvard JOENSEN (14/07/68) - Gĺ					s46			1	-

four victories on the trot, which brought them to within a point of Kĺ with five games left. But then the goals of prolific strike pair John Petersen and Jakup a Borg temporarily dried up and they suffered a calamitous three-match run which effectively put them out of the picture, enabling Gĺ

to become Kĺ's closest rivals. Kĺ could have sewn up the title in their penultimate match, away to B36, but the team from the capital spoiled the visitors' party by suddenly rediscovering their form and winning 2-0 in front of a huge (by local standards) 3,500 crowd. With Gĺ simultaneously

TOP SCORERS

17	Jakup a BORG (B36)
16	John PETERSEN (B36)
13	Kurt MØRKØRE (Kĺ)
12	Eli HENTZE (B71)
	Henning JARNSKOR (Gĺ)
11	Aleksandar RADOSAVLJEVIC (Gĺ)
10	Suni Fridi JOHANNESEN (HB)
	Røgvi JACOBSEN (Kĺ)
	Nebojsa VELJKOVIC (Sumba)

NATIONAL TEAM RESULTS 99/00

18/08/99	Iceland	H	Torshavn	0-1	
04/09/99	Estonia (ECQ)	H	Torshavn	0-2	
08/09/99	Lithuania (ECQ)	H	Torshavn	0-1	
09/10/99	Czech Republic (ECQ)	A	Prague	0-2	
31/01/00	Finland	N	La Manga	0-1	
04/02/00	Iceland	N	La Manga	2-3	Mørkøre K. (19), Jonsson (37)
26/04/00	Liechtenstein	A	Vaduz	1-0	Arge (71)

EUROPEAN CUPS 99/00

CHAMPIONS' CUP
● HB
Preliminary round 1 FC HAKA (FIN)
H 1-1 a Lakjuni (47)
Johannesen B., Mohr, Johannesen S.F., a Lag, Rasmussen (Højgaard 74), Nolsøe, Joensen, a Lakjuni, Danielsen (Arting 70), Dam J.H. (av Flotum 65), Hansen.
A 0-6 Johannesen B., Mohr, Olsen (Dam J. 12), a Lag, Rasmussen, Nolsøe, av Flotum, Joensen, a Lakjuni (Mortansson 49), Dam J.H. (Johannesen S.F. 46), Hansen.

UEFA CUP
● B36
Qualifying round ANKARAGÜCÜ (TUR)
A 0-1 Høgnesen E., Thorsteinsson, Sivic (Samuelsson 77), Hansen J.K., a Borg (Høgnesen C. 69), Petersen, Danielsen, Guttesen, Milankovic, Hansen Ø. (Zachariassen 80), Prior.
H 0-1 Høgnesen E., Thorsteinsson, Danielsen, Hansen J.K., Prior (Høgnesen C. 67), Guttesen, Sivic (Clementsen 82), Hansen Ø., Milankovic, a Borg, Petersen.

● KÍ
Qualifying round GRAZER AK (AUT)
H 0-5 Boyle, Pacek, Andreasen, Ryan, Bertholdsen (Nysted 81), Joensen J., Jacobsen, Wierzbicki (Klakkstein 67), Joensen A., Mørkøre, Hansen.
A 0-4 Boyle, Andreasen, Pacek, Wierzbicki, Bertholdsen, Klakkstein, Joensen J., Jacobsen, a Lakjuni, Danielsen (Baldvinsson 80), Joensen A.

INTERNATIONAL HONOURS

None

thrashing strugglers ÍF 5-1 away from home, it meant that KÍ, with a mere two-point advantage and an inferior goal difference, had to win their final fixture, at home to ÍF, to secure their first title in eight years.

With the rain pouring down and only around 600 supporters in attendance, KÍ duly got their win. In fact, they treated the hardy spectators to their biggest victory since the opening day of the season, winning 4-1. KÍ's first 'double' for 33 years was complete.

In the final table the gap between the top four teams was just four points, but while GÍ and B36 received UEFA Cup places for their season's efforts, fourth-placed HB, the 'double'-winners of the previous season, ended up with nothing more than a consolation spot in the InterToto. That was a major disappointment for the Torshavn club, but they only had themselves to blame, having consistently dropped points in unlikely places throughout the season and even allowed KÍ to come back and beat them in the semi-final of the Cup after they had won the first leg in Klaksvik.

Although they were coached by a Romanian - Ion Geolgau - HB were the only club in the league which had no foreigners in their playing squad. In total there were 26 overseas players employed on the islands during 1999. Most of them were from Eastern Europe, but B68 spiced up the local scene by acquiring four Brazilians, and KÍ's goalkeeper, Stephen Boyle, was a former United States international.

The most talked about goal scored by a foreigner during the season was the one by Sumba's Yugoslav defender Spasoje Bibercic in the final minute of the final game, away to local rivals VB. That controversial strike enabled Sumba to escape automatic relegation and send ÍF down in their place. It was their first away victory of the

DOMESTIC CUP 99/00

SECOND ROUND
(Played in Groups)
Final Positions
Group A - 1 HB 18 pts; 2 GÍ 12 pts; 3 ÍF 6 pts; 4 B71 0 pts
Groiup B - 1 VB 12 pts; 2 KÍ 12 pts; 3 B68 9 pts; 4 TB 0 pts
Group C - 1 B36 15 pts; 2 NSÍ 15 pts; 3 Sumba 3 pts; 4 LÍF 3 pts

QUARTER-FINALS
B36 2 (Sivic 61, Petersen 89),
NSÍ 1 (Jacobsen C.H. 69)

VB 3 (Holm 29, Samuelsen 32, og 33),
B68 1 (Benjaminsen 53)

KÍ 4 (a Lakjuni 30, Danielsen 33, 69, Jacobsen 42), GÍ 0

HB 10 (Mørkøre 41, 78, 83, Mortansson 44, 53, 71, og 45, a Flotum 62, Hansen 77, Johannesen S.F. 81), ÍF 0

SEMI-FINALS
B36 3 (Høgnesen C. 14, Petersen 25, a Borg 89p),
VB 1 (Eystberg 60)

VB 1 (Gaerdbø 5),
B36 1 (Petersen 16)
(B36 4-2)

KÍ 0,
HB 1 (Johannesen S.F. 19)

HB 1 (a Lakjuni 36),
KÍ 2 (Mørkøre 45, 88)
(2-2; KÍ on away goals)

FINAL
04/07/99, Torshavn
KÍ 3 Jacobsen (27), Mørkøre (50), Joensen A. (67)
B36 1 Hansen J.K. (81)
referee - Andreasen
KÍ - Boyle, Pacek, Andreassen, Hansen, Bertholdsen, Jacobsen (Niclasen 88), Wierzbicki, Joensen J., Joensen A. (Baldvinsson 88), Mørkøre, a Lakjuni.
B36 - Høgnesen E., Prior (Zachariassen 88), Thorsteinsson, Danielsen, Hansen J.K., Hansen Ø. (Høgnesen C. 88), Guttesen (Joensen 8), Sivic, Milankovic, a Borg, Petersen.

season and, with confidence duly boosted, Sumba went on to defeat LÍF in the play-offs, which meant that FS Vágar, the runaway Second Division champions, were promoted alone.

The Faroe Islands' European Championship qualifying campaign ended in unsatisfactory fashion with three defeats and no goals. The new Tørsvallur Stadium in Torshavn was inaugurated with a friendly against North Atlantic cousins Iceland, but a 0-1 defeat in that encounter set the tone for the two Euro 2000 games which followed a few weeks later at the same venue.

The concession of two late counter-attack goals brought defeat against Estonia, and there was more disappointment for the home fans four days later when Lithuania plundered a 1-0 win. Allan Simonsen's men closed their European Championship account with a 2-0 defeat in Prague, a result which enabled the Czech Republic to complete a perfect ten out of ten in the qualifying campaign.

There was a rare away win for the Faroe Islands the following spring when a goal from Uni Arge - his sixth at international level - brought a 1-0 victory over Liechtenstein. The only realistic hope Simonsen and his players will have of repeating that feat in the 2002 World Cup qualifiers is when they take on Luxembourg. The other four teams in their qualifying group - Yugoslavia, Russia, Switzerland and Slovenia - will surely be far too strong

PLAYERS OF THE SEASON

JAKUP MIKKELSEN

It is unusual for a player from the Faroe Islands to be involved with a championship-winning team in a foreign country, but national team goalkeeper Jakup Mikkelsen proved to be a worthy medal-winner during the 1999/2000 season, helping small-time club Herfølge to become the surprise champions of Denmark. Mikkelsen, who was the Faroe Islands' regular 'keeper during the Euro 2000 qualifiers, having assumed the mantle of Jens Martin Knudsen, missed only two of Herfølge's league games and was the only non-Danish player in coach John Jensen's squad. The former postman and handball-player left local club KÍ for Herfølge in 1995 but it was only after Jensen's arrival that he became a permanent fixture in the side. Now, thanks to his overseas exploits, the 30-year-old is the toast of his homeland.

for them. Still, if they can finish above Luxembourg and nick a bonus point here and there off the other teams, Simonsen and his players won't be too distressed.

PROMOTED CLUB 99/00

SECOND DIVISION FINAL TABLE

		Pd	W	D	L	F	A	Pt	GD
1	FS Vágar	18	16	0	2	78	27	48	51
2	LÍF	18	12	3	3	68	30	39	38
3	TB	18	9	2	7	59	45	29	14
4	HB II	18	8	5	5	43	37	29	6
5	Royn	18	7	3	8	30	34	24	-4
6	NSÍ II	18	7	2	9	37	45	23	-8
7	GÍ II	18	5	5	9	34	59	20	-25
8	EB/Streymur	18	4	5	9	24	43	17	-19
9	KÍ II	18	4	3	11	25	39	15	-14
10	Skala	18	3	3	12	29	68	12	-39

PROMOTION/RELEGATION PLAY-OFF
LÍF 2, Sumba 1
Sumba 5, LÍF 0
(Sumba 6-2)

CLUB DIRECTORY

FS Vágar
360 Sandavagur
tel - 333287
fax - 332335
Year of Formation - 1993
President - Alvur Samuelsen
Secretary - Jakup a Stongum
Coach - Ole Andersen (2000 - Ketutis Latoza)
Stadium - Sandavagur (1,000)

B36

CLUB DIRECTORY

Boltfelagid 36 (B 36)
Postrum 1136
110 Tórshavn
tel - 311936
fax - 318036
Year of Formation - 1936
President - Kristian a Neystabø
Secretary - Sjurdur Høsdal
Coach - Tomislav Sivic
Stadium - Gundadalur (6,000)

MAJOR HONOURS
League Championship - (6)
1936, 1948, 1950, 1959, 1962, 1997.
Domestic Cup - (1) 1991.

APPEARANCES 1999

	P	Ap	(s)	Gls
Jakup a BORG	A	17		17
Sigfridur CLEMENTSEN	A		(7)	
Arnbjørn DANIELSEN	D	17		
Jan GUTTESEN	M	15		
Jens Kristian HANSEN	D	15		2
Øssur HANSEN	M	16		4
Carl HØGNESEN	D	9	(6)	2
Egin HØGNESEN	G	10		
Djoni J. JOENSEN	D	9	(1)	2
Danjal Petur JOHANSEN	D	2	(5)	
Herbert i LON JACOBSEN	D		(1)	
Ninoslav MILANKOVIC (YUG)	D	14		2
John PETERSEN	A	17	(1)	16
Bjarni PRIOR	D	7	(3)	2
Ronnie SAMUELSEN	M	7	(7)	1
Tomislav SIVIC (YUG)	M	8	(7)	1
Pol THORSTEINSSON	D	18		
János TIMÁR (HUN)	G	5	(1)	
Trondur VATNHAMAR	G	3	(1)	
Egil ZACHARIASSEN	M	9	(5)	2

LEAGUE RESULTS 1999

25/04/99	Sumba	A	6-1	og (Bibercic S.), Høgnesen C., Petersen, Joensen, a Borg 2
30/04/99	VB	A	0-0	
09/05/99	ÍF	H	4-2	a Borg, Høgnesen C., Petersen, Sivic
16/05/99	B68	A	2-1	Petersen 2 (1p)
22/05/99	B71	H	6-1	Hansen Ø., Petersen 3, a Borg 2 (1p)
30/05/99	HB	A	2-4	a Borg 2
13/06/99	GÍ	H	4-0	a Borg, Hansen Ø., Prior, Petersen
20/06/99	KÍ	A	2-3	Samuelsen, Zachariassen
27/06/99	NSÍ	H	3-2	a Borg (p), Petersen 2
01/08/99	Sumba	H	3-1	Prior, Petersen, a Borg
08/08/99	VB	H	6-1	Joensen, Hansen Ø., Hansen J.K., a Borg 2, Zachariassen
15/08/99	ÍF	A	4-1	a Borg, Milankovic, Petersen 2
22/08/99	B68	H	4-0	Hansen J.K., a Borg, Hansen Ø., Petersen
29/08/99	B71	A	0-0	
12/09/99	HB	H	0-2	
19/09/99	GÍ	A	1-2	a Borg (p)
26/09/99	KÍ	H	2-0	Petersen, Milankovic
02/10/99	NSÍ	A	3-1	a Borg 2, Petersen

B68

Tofta Ítrottarfelag B 68
650 Toftir
tel - 448068
fax - 449050
Year of Formation - 1962
President - Niclas Davidsen
Secretary - Olavur Jensen
Coach - Bjørn Krogh (2000 - Johannes Jacobsen)
Stadium - Svangaskard (6,000)

MAJOR HONOURS
League Championship - (3) 1984, 1985, 1992.

	P	Ap	(s)	Gls
Frodi BENJAMINSEN	M	17		1
Frodi CLEMENTSEN	D	10	(1)	1
Lúcio Roberto DE OLIVEIRA (BRA)	M	4	(1)	
Jakup DJURHUUS	D	11	(6)	
Røgvi FOSDALSA	A		(1)	
Steinar HANSEN	A		(1)	
Samal Erik HENTZE	D	5	(2)	
Aksel HØJGAARD	A	5	(5)	1
Olaf HØJGAARD	M	5	(4)	
Edmund JACOBSEN	D	5		
Øssur JACOBSEN	A	9	(8)	2
Allan G. JOENSEN	G	9		
Oleif JOENSEN	D	8	(2)	
Signar JOHANNESEN	D	17		
Marlo Christiano JORGE (BRA)	M	17		2
Marcelo MARCOLINO (BRA)	A	14		8
Finn MORK	M	17		
Mannbjørn NESA	D		(1)	
Messias Martin PERREIRA (BRA)	D	15	(1)	1
Bogi PETERSEN	M		(3)	
Jan PETERSEN	M	17		4
Kristian POULSEN	D		(5)	1
Magnus E. POULSEN	G	9		
Janus THOMSEN	D	4	(3)	

25/04/99	KÍ	A	0-5	
30/04/99	NSÍ	H	0-0	
09/05/99	Sumba	A	3-2	Petersen J. 2, Jacobsen Ø.
16/05/99	B36	H	1-2	Petersen J. (p)
22/05/99	ÍF	A	4-2	Marcolino 3, og (Joensen)
30/05/99	VB	A	2-0	Marcolino 2
13/06/99	B71	H	2-0	Højgaard A., Petersen J.
20/06/99	HB	A	1-1	Marcolino
23/06/99	GÍ	H	2-5	Jorge 2
01/08/99	KÍ	H	2-3	Marcolino, Pereira
08/08/99	NSÍ	A	0-5	
15/08/99	Sumba	H	3-1	Benjaminsen, Clementsen, Marcolino
22/08/99	B36	A	0-4	
29/08/99	ÍF	H	1-2	Jacobsen Ø.
12/09/99	VB	H	0-0	
19/09/99	B71	A	0-1	
26/09/99	HB	H	1-5	Poulsen K.
02/10/99	GÍ	A	0-3	

B71

CLUB DIRECTORY

Sandoyar Ítrottarfelag B 71
210 Sandur
tel - 361655
fax - 361733/361835
Year of Formation - 1970
President - Joannes Johannesen
Secretary - Eli Hentze
Coach - Ivan Hristov
Stadium - Sandur (2,000)

MAJOR HONOURS
League Championship - (1) 1989.
Domestic Cup - (1) 1983.

APPEARANCES 1999

	P	Ap	(s)	Gls
Jonsvein BAERENTSEN	M		(3)	
Jon BREKKU	A	2	(4)	1
Hans Jørgen DJURHUUS	M	7		
Iulian FLORESCU (ROM)	M	14		3
Eli HENTZE	A	17	(1)	12
Ivan HRISTOV (BUL)	M	8	(1)	
Frankie JENSEN	D	1		
Torbjørn JENSEN	A	2	(3)	
Hendrik JUUL	G	1		
Ernst LOKJA	D	1	(1)	
Antines MAGNUSSEN	D	13	(1)	
Kari NIELSEN	M	11	(1)	
Kristian NIELSEN	M	10	(3)	1
Waldemar NOWICKI (POL)	G	16		
Ib Mohr OLSEN	D	7		
Jøgvan Jon PETERSEN	M	4		
Pall a REYNATUGVU	M	13		
Peter RITTER	D	15		2
Allan SIMONSEN	G	1		
Allan SIMONSEN	D	6	(1)	
Runi i SOYLU	M	13		5
Bergleif SOLSKER	D	9		
Kari SØRENSEN	A	11	(6)	2
Jonsvein THOMSEN	A		(1)	
Bjørn THORSTEINSSON	D	12		
Mourits VIDERO	D	4	(3)	
Kristofur VIDTFELDT	M		(1)	

LEAGUE RESULTS 1999

25/04/99	GÍ	A	1-2	Sørensen
30/04/99	KÍ	H	1-2	Nielsen Kr.
09/05/99	NSÍ	A	0-4	
16/05/99	Sumba	H	2-1	Hentze (p), Brekku
22/05/99	B36	A	1-6	i Soylu
30/05/99	ÍF	H	6-0	Ritter, Hentze 2, i Soylu, Florescu, Sørensen
13/06/99	B68	A	0-2	
20/06/99	VB	A	1-1	Florescu
27/06/99	HB	H	2-2	Hentze 2
01/08/99	GÍ	H	2-5	i Soylu 2
08/08/99	KÍ	A	1-3	Hentze
15/08/99	NSÍ	H	2-3	Hentze, Ritter
22/08/99	Sumba	A	1-1	Hentze (p)
29/08/99	B36	H	0-0	
12/09/99	ÍF	A	3-3	Hentze 2, Florescu
19/09/99	B68	H	1-0	Hentze
26/09/99	VB	H	1-3	i Soylu
02/10/99	HB	A	1-7	Hentze

GÍ

CLUB DIRECTORY

Gotu Ítrottarfelag (GÍ)
Postrum 4
510 Gotu
tel - 442024
fax - 442024
Year of Formation - 1926
President - Urd Potts
Secretary - Andrias Poulsen
Coach - Johan Nielsen
Stadium - Gotu (3,000)

MAJOR HONOURS
League Championship - (6)
1983, 1986, 1993, 1994, 1995, 1996.
Domestic Cup - (4) 1983, 1985, 1996, 1997.

APPEARANCES 1999

	P	Ap	(s)	Gls
Bartal ELIASSEN	D	17		3
Poul ENNIGARD	D	11		1
Leivur HANSEN	D	4	(8)	
Magni JACOBSEN	M	3	(4)	2
Henning JARNSKOR	M	18		12
Magni JARNSKOR	M	17		2
Pauli JARNSKOR	M	17		1
Mortan JOENSEN	G	1		
Samal JOENSEN	M	16		3
Sunvard JOENSEN	G	16		
Alvi JUSTINUSSEN	D	9	(2)	
Runi JUSTINUSSEN	D	16		
Simun Petur JUSTINUSSEN	M	1	(4)	1
Jens Martin KNUDSEN	G	1		
Joan Petur OLSEN	M	18		1
Suni OLSEN	A	15		4
Svenn OLSEN	D	2	(4)	
Hans Pauli PETERSEN	M		(1)	1
Alexander RADOSAVLJEVIC (YUG)	A	13		11
Erland TVORFOSS	A	3	(5)	1

LEAGUE RESULTS 1999

25/04/99	B71	H	2-1	Elliassen, Joensen Sa.
30/04/99	HB	A	0-2	
09/05/99	VB	H	3-1	Elliassen, Olsen Su., Tvorfoss
16/05/99	KÍ	H	2-1	Olsen J.P., Elliassen
22/05/99	NSÍ	A	1-1	og (Jacobsen)
30/05/99	Sumba	H	7-2	Joensen Sa. 2, Jarnskor H. 2, Jacobsen 2,
				Jarnskor M.
13/06/99	B36	A	0-4	
16/06/99	ÍF	H	2-1	Jarnskor H., Ennigard
23/06/99	B68	A	5-2	Radosavljevic 3, Jarnskor H. 2
01/08/99	B71	A	5-2	Radosavljevic 3, Jarnskor P., Jarnskor M.
08/08/99	HB	H	1-2	og (a Lag)
15/08/99	VB	A	3-1	Radosavljevic, og (Jacobsen), Olsen Su.
22/08/99	KÍ	A	0-0	
29/08/99	NSÍ	H	4-1	Radosavljevic 2, Jarnskor H. 2
12/09/99	Sumba	A	1-1	Jarnskor H.
19/09/99	B36	H	2-1	Olsen Su. 2
26/09/99	ÍF	A	5-1	Jarnskor H. 2 (1p), Radosavljevic,
				Justinussen S.P., Petersen
02/10/99	B68	H	3-0	Jarnskor H. 2, Radosavljevic

HB

CLUB DIRECTORY

Havnar Boltfelag (HB)
Postrum 1333
110 Tórshavn
tel - 314046/283346
fax - 318502
Year of Formation - 1904
President - Gunnar Mohr
Secretary - Hans J. Mikkelsen
Coach - Ion Geolgau
Stadium - Gundadalur (8,000)

MAJOR HONOURS

League Championship - (15) 1955, 1960, 1963,
1964, 1965, 1971, 1973, 1974, 1975, 1978,
1981, 1982, 1988, 1990, 1998.
Domestic Cup - (25) 1955, 1957, 1959, 1962,
1963, 1964, 1968, 1969, 1971, 1972, 1973,
1975, 1976, 1978, 1979, 1980, 1981, 1982,
1984, 1987, 1988, 1989, 1992, 1995, 1998.

APPEARANCES 1999

	P	Ap	(s)	Gls
Uni ARGE	A	2		6
Roi ARTING	M	4	(7)	1
Jan DAM	D	9	(1)	
John Heri DAM	M	4	(5)	1
Hallur DANIELSEN	M	14	(4)	
Hans Jørgen DJURHUUS	M	5	(1)	
Andrew av FLOTUM	A	11	(6)	5
Hans Frodi HANSEN	D	16		2
Eydun HØJGAARD	M	1	(5)	1
Jon Roi JACOBSEN	A		(2)	
Johannes JOENSEN	D	11		
Bardur JOHANNESEN	G	17		
Kaj Leo JOHANNESEN	G	1	(3)	
Suni Fridi JOHANNESEN	A	15		10
Hans a LAG	D	13		
Magnus a LAKJUNI	A	12	(1)	4
Bjarki MOHR	D	8	(4)	1
Vagnur MOHR MORTENSEN	D		(1)	
Allan MØRKØRE	M	8		5
Bardur MORTANSSON	A	1	(12)	
Runi NOLSØE	M	17		3
Jacob Eli OLSEN	D	11	(1)	
Jens Erik RASMUSSEN	M	18		1

LEAGUE RESULTS 1999

25/04/99	VB	H	2-0	Johannesen S.F., av Flotum
30/04/99	GÍ	H	2-0	Johannesen S.F., av Flotum
09/05/99	KÍ	A	0-0	
16/05/99	NSÍ	H	1-3	Mørkøre
22/05/99	Sumba	A	3-0	a Lakjuni, Johannesen S.F. (p), Højgaard
30/05/99	B36	H	4-2	Mørkøre 2, Johannesen S.F. 2
13/06/99	ÍF	A	1-0	a Lakjuni
20/06/99	B68	H	1-1	Rasmussen (p)
27/06/99	B71	A	2-2	av Flotum, Johannesen S.F.
01/08/99	VB	A	0-1	
08/08/99	GÍ	A	2-1	Johannesen S.F. (p), a Lakjuni
15/08/99	KÍ	H	1-2	av Flotum
22/08/99	NSÍ	A	2-0	a Lakjuni, Dam J.H.
29/08/99	Sumba	H	2-2	Mohr, Nolsøe
12/09/99	B36	A	2-0	Arting, og (Samuelsson)
19/09/99	ÍF	H	4-0	Johannesen S.F. 2, Hansen, Nolsøe
26/09/99	B68	A	5-1	Hansen, av Flotum, Arge 2, Mørkøre
02/10/99	B71	H	7-1	Arge 4, Johannesen S.F., Mørkøre (p), Nolsøe

ÍF

CLUB DIRECTORY

Ítrottarfelag Fuglafjardar (ÍF)
Postrum 94
530 Fuglafjørdur
tel - 444636
fax - 444636
Year of Formation - 1946
President - Roy Róin
Secretary - Unn Eldevig
Coach - Piotr Krakowski
Stadium - Fuglafjordur (3,000)

MAJOR HONOURS
League Championship - (1) 1979.

APPEARANCES 1999

	P	Ap	(s)	Gls
Sigridur ABRAHAMNSEN	D	5		
Ken BAERENDSEN	M	4	(2)	1
Robert CIESLEWICZ (POL)	A	15	(1)	2
Jakup Helgi EGHOLM	A		(2)	
Hergeir ELDEVIG	A		(2)	
Simun ELIASEN	M	8		2
Abraham HANSEN	D	4		1
Høgni HANSEN	D	6	(2)	
Jøgvan Arnfinn JACOBSEN	A		(1)	
Erling JOENSEN	G	8		
Runi JOENSEN	G	10		
Torstein JOENSEN	D	15		
Viggo JOHANNESEN	D	13	(3)	2
Chris KNIGHT (ENG)	D	7		
Bardur a LAKJUNI	A	5	(2)	3
Høgni a LAKJUNI	M		(2)	
Hjalti LUNDSBJERG	M		(1)	
Uni MORTENSEN	M	2		
Bogi NON	D	1	(2)	
Aslakur PETERSEN	M	18		2
Eydolvur PETERSEN	M	14	(1)	
Runi PETERSEN	M	7	(10)	
Tomasz PRZYBYLSKI (POL)	M	16		2
Røgvi ROIN	M	15		1
Roy ROIN	M	16		
Eydun SAMUELSEN	A	8	(3)	4
Mortan THOMSEN	M	1	(3)	

LEAGUE RESULTS 1999

25/04/99	NSÍ	A	0-0	
30/04/99	Sumba	H	2-1	Samuelsen, Przybylski
09/05/99	B36	A	2-4	Petersen A., Johannesen
16/05/99	VB	A	1-3	Cieslewicz
22/05/99	B68	H	2-4	Samuelsen, Cieslewicz
30/05/99	B71	A	0-6	
13/06/99	HB	H	0-1	
16/06/99	GÍ	A	1-2	Eliasen
27/06/99	KÍ	H	0-1	
01/08/99	NSÍ	H	1-1	Przybylski
08/08/99	Sumba	A	2-2	Roin Rog., Eliasen
15/08/99	B36	H	1-4	Samuelsen
22/08/99	VB	H	1-2	Samuelsen
29/08/99	B68	A	2-1	a Lakjuni B., Johannesen
12/09/99	B71	H	3-3	a Lakjuni B., Petersen A., Hansen A.
19/09/99	HB	A	0-4	
26/09/99	GÍ	H	1-5	a Lakjuni B.
02/10/99	KÍ	A	1-4	Baerendsen

KÍ

Klaksvíkar Ítróttarfelag (KÍ)
Postrum 204
700 Klaksvík
tel - 456184
fax - 456167
Year of Formation - 1904
President - Heri Olsen
Secretary - Arnfinn Danielsen
Coach - Tony Paris (2000 - Tomislav Sivic)
Stadium - Klaksvík (4,000)

MAJOR HONOURS
League Championship - (17) 1942, 1945, 1952,
1953, 1954, 1956, 1957, 1958, 1961, 1966,
1967, 1968, 1969, 1970, 1972, 1991, 1999.
Domestic Cup - (5)
1966, 1967, 1990, 1994, 1999.

APPEARANCES 1999

	P	Ap	(s)	Gls
Jan ANDREASEN	D	17		
Finn BALDVINSSON	D	3	(5)	
Harley BERTHOLDSEN	D	18		2
Stephen BOYLE (USA)	G	18		
Olgar DANIELSEN	A	2	(4)	1
Simun Wag HØGNESEN	M		(2)	
Røgvi JACOBSEN	A	18		11
Arhold JOENSEN	D	18		
Jan JOENSEN	M	18		
Eydun KLAKKSTEIN	M		(8)	
Hedin a LAKJUNI	A	18		6
Johan LUTZEN	D		(1)	
Kurt MØRKØRE	A	11		13
Jan Allan MÜLLER	A	6		2
Niclas NICLASEN	M	1	(6)	
Ove NYSTED	A		(2)	
Andrzej PACEK (POL)	M	18		1
Joseph PARIS (ENG)	M		(1)	
John RYAN	M	14	(1)	
Marek WIERZBICKI (POL)	M	18		1

LEAGUE RESULTS 1999

25/04/99	B68	H	5-0	Pacek, Jacobsen, Mørkøre 3
30/04/99	B71	A	2-1	Mørkøre, Danielsen
09/05/99	HB	H	0-0	
16/05/99	GÍ	A	1-2	Mørkøre
22/05/99	VB	H	2-1	Jacobsen 2
30/05/99	NSÍ	H	3-0	a Lakjuni, Mørkøre 2
13/06/99	Sumba	A	3-2	Jacobsen, Mørkøre 2
20/06/99	B36	H	3-2	a Lakjuni, Mørkøre 2
27/06/99	ÍF	A	1-0	Mørkøre
01/08/99	B68	A	3-2	a Lakjuni 2, Jacobsen
08/08/99	B71	H	3-1	a Lakjuni 2, Jacobsen
15/08/99	HB	A	2-1	Jacobsen, Mørkøre
22/08/99	GÍ	H	0-0	
29/08/99	VB	A	1-2	Bertholdsen
12/09/99	NSÍ	A	3-1	Müller 2, Jacobsen
19/09/99	Sumba	H	2-1	Jacobsen, Wierzbicki
26/09/99	B36	A	0-2	
02/10/99	ÍF	H	4-1	Bertholdsen, Jacobsen 2, og (Petersen)

NSÍ

CLUB DIRECTORY

Nes Soknar Íttrotarfelag (NSÍ)
Postrum 173
620 Runavik
tel - 448100
fax - 448566
Year of Formation - 1957
President - Samal Jakup Højgaard
Secretary - Niklaj Nielsen
Coach - Trygvi Mortensen
Stadium - Runavik (2,000)

MAJOR HONOURS
Domestic Cup - (1) 1986.

APPEARANCES 1999

	P	Ap	(s)	Gls
Milan CIMBUROVIC (YUG)	D	1		
Petur HAMMER	M		(1)	
Bergur HANSEN	M	1	(4)	
Danjal HANSEN	D	18		2
Kari HANSEN	M	12	(3)	
Mortan HANSEN	A	3	(2)	1
Oli HANSEN	A	2		
Ian HØJGAARD	A	13	(3)	6
Olavur HØJGAARD	G	1		
Christian Høgni JACOBSEN	A	9	(1)	4
Jakup Martin JACOBSEN	D	2	(1)	
Sjurdur JACOBSEN	D	18		4
Hjørleif KLEIN	M		(1)	
Arnfinn LANGAARD	D	13	(2)	
Gert LANGAARD	A	9	(2)	2
Eddie MIKKELSEN	M	12	(3)	1
Dejan MILANOVIC (YUG)	G	17		1
Brinjolvur NIELSEN	M	6	(3)	
Jann NONKLETT	M		(2)	
Ken NONKLETT	A		(1)	
Dagfinn OLSEN	D		(1)	
Helgi L. PETERSEN	M	13	(1)	2
Jonstein PETERSEN	M	17		1
Sonni L. PETERSEN	A	1	(6)	
Runi RASMUSSEN	M		(1)	
Kari SIGVARDSEN	D	16	(1)	1
Johnny SKIBENAES	D	3	(2)	
Eydstein SKIPANES	M	11	(3)	

LEAGUE RESULTS 1999

25/04/99	ÍF	H	0-0	
30/04/99	B68	A	0-0	
09/05/99	B71	H	4-0	Jacobsen C.H. 2, Jacobsen S., Sigvardsen
16/05/99	HB	A	3-1	Jacobsen C.H., Langaard G. 2
22/05/99	GÍ	H	1-1	Petersen H.L.
30/05/99	KÍ	A	0-3	
13/06/99	VB	H	1-0	Petersen H.L.
20/06/99	Sumba	H	1-0	Jacobsen C.H.
27/06/99	B36	A	2-3	Højgaard I., Milankovic (p)
01/08/99	ÍF	A	1-1	Højgaard I.
08/08/99	B68	H	5-0	Hansen D., Højgaard I. 2, Jacobsen S. (p), Petersen J.
15/08/99	B71	A	3-2	Højgaard I., Jacobsen S. (p), Hansen D.
22/08/99	HB	H	0-2	
29/08/99	GÍ	A	1-4	Jacobsen S.
12/09/99	KÍ	H	1-3	Mikkelsen
19/09/99	VB	A	0-2	
26/09/99	Sumba	A	1-1	Højgaard I.
02/10/99	B36	H	1-3	Hansen M.

SUMBA

CLUB DIRECTORY

Sumbiar Itrottarfelag (Sumba)
970 - Sumba
tel - 370213
fax - 370111
Year of Formation - 1940
President - Jacob Poulsen
Secretary - Maibritt ur Horg
Coach - Milan Cimburovic
Stadium - Sumba (7,000)

APPEARANCES 1999

	P	Ap	(s)	Gls
Nikola BIBERCIC (YUG)	A	13	(1)	1
Spasoje BIBERCIC (YUG)	D	16		1
Mortan u HORG	M	17		3
Danjal Johan JOENSEN	M	16		1
Eirikur JOENSEN	A	8	(2)	
Hallur Dam JOENSEN	M	4	(9)	1
Birgir JØRGENSEN	A	9	(8)	1
Peter JØRGENSEN (DEN)	D	15	(1)	
Leon KJAERBAEK	D		(1)	
Pall Magnar KJAERBAEK	D	18		
Marlon KJAERBO	D	2		
Sonne KJAERBO	D	7	(1)	
Jon LISBERG	D		(2)	
Runi LISBERG	G	1		
Frodi MORTENSEN	G	12		
Tryggvi NIELSEN	D	5	(2)	1
Thomas Jon NONFJALL	M		(4)	
Kristian OLSEN	M	1	(4)	
Jan POULSEN	M	11	(5)	
Anfinn THOMSEN	G	5		
Eydbjørn THOMSEN	D		(1)	
Hans Jacob THOMSEN	M	2	(7)	
René THOMSEN	M	11	(1)	3
Nebosja VELJKOVIC (YUG)	A	16		10
Bergur VINTHER	M	9		

LEAGUE RESULTS 1999

25/04/99	B36	H	1-6	Veljkovic
30/04/99	ÍF	A	1-2	Bibercic N.
09/05/99	B68	H	2-3	Veljkovic 2
16/05/99	B71	A	1-2	Veljkovic
22/05/99	HB	H	0-3	
30/05/99	GÍ	A	2-7	Veljkovic, Joensen D.J.
13/06/99	KÍ	H	2-3	Thomsen R., Jørgensen B.
20/06/99	NSÍ	A	0-1	
27/06/99	VB	H	1-0	Thomsen R.
01/08/99	B36	A	1-3	Veljkovic (p)
08/08/99	ÍF	H	2-2	Joensen H.D., Veljkovic
15/08/99	B68	A	1-3	Veljkovic (p)
22/08/99	B71	H	1-1	Nielsen
29/08/99	HB	A	2-2	Veljkovic (p), Thomsen R.
12/09/99	GÍ	H	1-1	Veljkovic
19/09/99	KÍ	A	1-2	ur Horg
26/09/99	NSÍ	H	1-1	ur Horg
02/10/99	VB	A	2-1	ur Horg, Bibercic S.

VB

CLUB DIRECTORY

VB
Postrum 134
900 Vagur
tel - 373679
fax - 373679
Year of Formation - 1905
President - Petur Ludvig
Secretary - Maria Vagfjall
Coach - Krzysztof Popczynski
Stadium - Vestri a Eidinum (3,000)

APPEARANCES 1999

	P	Ap	(s)	Gls
Olivur ABRAHAMNSEN	A		(1)	
Palli AUGUSTINUSSEN	M	14	(3)	1
Milan CULJIC (YUG)	M	16		3
Hans Pauli DAHL	D	2	(5)	
Dan DJURHUUS	M	10	(3)	2
John EYSTBERG	M	5	(2)	
Jon GAERDBO	D	9	(4)	
Elian HANSEN	D	3	(4)	1
Tordur HOLM	M	17	(1)	1
Eydun JACOBSEN	D	18		1
Magni JACOBSEN	D	18		
Bjarni JOHANSEN	G	18		
Janus KJAERBO	D	13		
Michael i LAGABO	M	9	(1)	
Magni MOHR	A	3		
Jon Pauli OLSEN	A	17		4
Krzysztof POPCZYNSKI (POL)	A	15	(1)	5
Marner RICHARD	D	5	(4)	
Petur Oli SAMUELSEN	M	6	(8)	

LEAGUE RESULTS 1999

25/04/99	HB	A	0-2	
30/04/99	B36	H	0-0	
09/05/99	GÍ	A	1-3	Olsen
16/05/99	ÍF	H	3-1	Culjic, Olsen, Hansen
22/05/99	KÍ	A	1-2	Holm
30/05/99	B68	H	0-2	
13/06/99	NSÍ	A	0-1	
20/06/99	B71	H	1-1	Popczynski
27/06/99	Sumba	A	0-1	
01/08/99	HB	H	1-0	Popczynski
08/08/99	B36	A	1-6	Djurhuus
15/08/99	GÍ	H	1-3	Culjic
22/08/99	ÍF	A	2-1	Popczynski
29/08/99	KÍ	H	2-1	Olsen, Augustinussen
12/09/99	B68	A	0-0	
19/09/99	NSÍ	H	2-0	og (Petersen J.), Popczynski (p)
26/09/99	B71	A	3-1	Djurhuus, Popczynski, Olsen
02/10/99	Sumba	H	1-2	Jacobsen E.

FINLAND

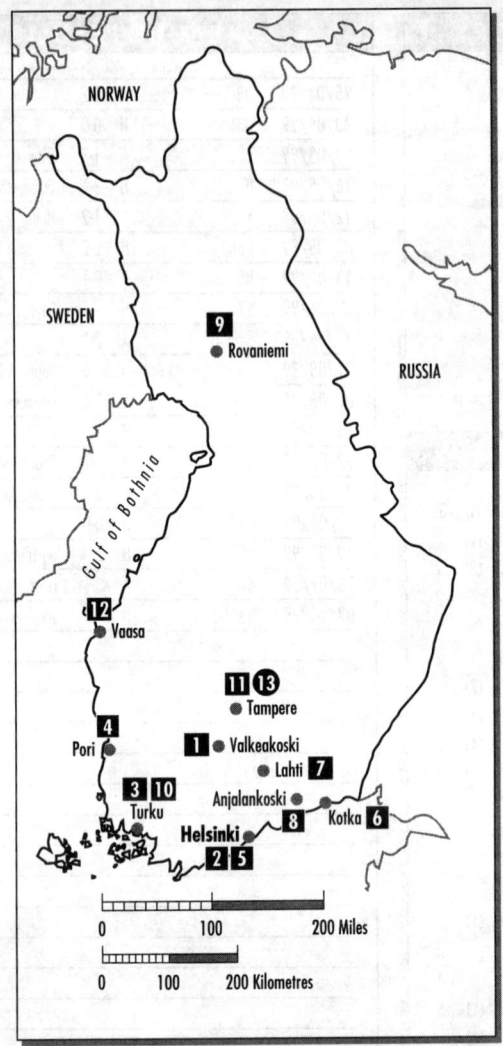

1	FC HAKA	368	8	MYPA	375
2	HJK	369	9	ROPS	376
3	FC INTER	370	10	TPS	377
4	FC JAZZ	371	11	TPV	378
5	FC JOKERIT	372	12	VPS	379
6	KTP	373	**Promoted club**		
7	FC LAHTI	374	13	**TAMPERE UNITED**	

MUURINEN LEAVES HJK FOR NATIONAL TEAM

Haka hold their nerve to retain title

FEDERATION DIRECTORY

Suomen Palloliitto
Finlands Bollförbund, Urheilukatu 1, 00251 Helsinki

tel - (09) 742151   Year of Formation - 1907
fax - (09) 74215200   President - Pekka Hämäläinen
website - www.palloliitto.fi   Secretary - Pertti Alaja

Stadium - Olympiastadion, Helsinki (40,000)

Finland may struggle more than any other European country to find the perfect shape and structure for their national championship, but although the 1999 model didn't meet with the approval of the spectators - average attendances dropped to below 2,000 for the first time since 1994 - it certainly served to produce a riveting finale.

There were two teams involved in the championship race - defending champions FC Haka and pre-season favourites HJK. For much of the season it looked as if Haka would have things all their own way. They beat HJK 1-0 in the first game of the season and went on to set a Veikkausliga record by remaining unbeaten for their first 13 matches, winning ten of them. Central to that early success was the goalscoring of Russian import Valeriy Popovich (or 'Valeri Popovits', as he was referred to locally), who contributed a dozen goals.

When the league was split into two sections after 22 matches, Haka held a three-point lead over HJK. The rest of the clubs were nowhere. With seven matches to go, the championship race involved two clubs only, and HJK were the team in form. Antti Muurinen's side had strung together five straight wins to complete the regular season, and they took that form into the play-offs. With Brazilian striker Rafael, newly re-recruited from FC Jazz, scoring freely, HJK extended their winning run to 11 games - another league record - and by the end of it, they had not only made up the gap on Haka but taken a one-point lead with just one match to go.

Their final fixture, however, was away to Haka in Valkeakoski. The league structure guaranteed that the top two teams after 22 rounds would meet on the last day, but not even the most manipulative fixture-planner could have concocted a finale with so much riding on it. It was the

LEAGUE CHAMPIONSHIP RESULTS 1999

FIRST PHASE

		1	2	3	4	5	6	7	8	9	10	11	12
1	FC Haka		1-0	1-0	1-1	2-2	4-1	4-2	4-0	0-0	5-2	3-1	2-0
2	HJK	0-1		0-1	4-1	2-1	3-1	1-1	2-0	4-0	0-0	2-0	3-0
3	FC Inter	0-1	2-7		3-0	1-0	0-0	3-1	1-2	2-2	1-2	2-0	3-1
4	FC Jazz	2-2	1-1	1-1		1-1	1-1	3-0	3-0	2-0	3-2	2-0	0-1
5	FC Jokerit	1-0	1-2	0-1	0-0		1-0	1-0	0-1	1-1	1-1	1-0	1-0
6	KTP	1-0	1-1	1-0	0-1	3-4		0-1	0-0	1-1	2-0	1-0	2-2
7	FC Lahti	0-2	2-5	3-2	2-2	0-1	0-1		1-2	1-0	1-2	1-1	2-1
8	MyPa	1-2	0-3	0-1	2-0	2-0	0-0	4-0		1-1	3-1	1-1	1-1
9	RoPS	2-3	0-1	3-1	0-0	3-0	1-2	2-2	2-1		1-0	2-2	3-2
10	TPS	1-1	0-0	0-1	1-1	1-1	0-3	1-2	2-3	4-1		2-0	2-1
11	TPV	0-3	0-1	0-0	1-3	0-5	2-0	1-2	2-2	0-2	0-1		1-3
12	VPS	0-1	0-1	0-2	1-0	1-3	3-1	2-1	0-1	0-0	0-2	3-1	

CHAMPIONSHIP PLAY-OFFS

		1	2	3	4	5	6	7	8
1	FC Haka		1-0		0-0	2-0		2-0	
2	HJK			2-1		2-1	1-0	2-1	
3	FC Inter	0-3				0-1	3-3	0-2	
4	FC Jazz		0-2	1-1			1-0		
5	FC Jokerit			1-1			1-2	1-2	4-0
6	KTP	1-3						0-0	1-1
7	MyPa	0-0			4-1				3-1
8	RoPS			0-1	0-5	2-0			

RELEGATION PLAY-OFFS

		1	2	3	4
1	FC Lahti		0-3	4-3	0-4
2	TPS	0-0		1-1	1-1
3	TPV	2-3	0-6		3-1
4	VPS	2-2	1-2	3-1	

INTERNATIONAL HONOURS

None

LEAGUE CHAMPIONSHIP FINAL TABLES 1999

FIRST PHASE

			Home					Away					Total					
		Pd	W	D	L	F	A	W	D	L	F	A	W	D	L	F	A	Pt	GD
1	FC Haka	22	8	3	0	27	9	7	2	2	16	8	15	5	2	43	17	50	26
2	HJK	22	7	2	2	21	6	7	3	1	22	8	14	5	3	43	14	47	29
3	FC Inter	22	5	2	4	18	16	5	2	4	10	9	10	4	8	28	25	34	3
4	FC Jokerit	22	5	3	3	8	6	4	3	4	18	16	9	6	7	26	22	33	4
5	MyPa	22	4	4	3	15	10	5	2	4	12	17	9	6	7	27	27	33	0
6	FC Jazz	22	5	5	1	19	9	2	5	4	9	15	7	10	5	28	24	31	4
7	KTP	22	4	4	3	12	10	3	3	5	10	15	7	7	8	22	25	28	-3
8	RoPS	22	5	3	3	19	14	1	6	4	8	16	6	9	7	27	30	27	-3
9	TPS	22	3	4	4	14	14	4	2	5	13	17	7	6	9	27	31	27	-4
10	FC Lahti	22	3	2	6	13	19	3	2	6	12	22	6	4	12	25	41	22	-16
11	VPS	22	4	1	6	10	13	2	2	7	12	20	6	3	13	22	33	21	-11
12	TPV	22	1	2	8	7	22	0	3	8	6	20	1	5	16	13	42	8	-29

PLAY-OFFS

Championship Group

			Home					Away					Total					
		Pd	W	D	L	F	A	W	D	L	F	A	W	D	L	F	A	Pt	GD
1	FC Haka	29	11	4	0	32	9	9	3	2	22	9	20	7	2	54	18	67	36
2	HJK	29	11	2	2	28	9	9	3	2	25	9	20	5	4	53	18	65	35
3	MyPa	29	6	5	3	22	12	7	3	5	17	20	13	8	8	39	32	47	7
4	FC Jokerit	29	6	4	5	15	11	5	3	6	20	20	11	7	11	35	31	40	4
5	FC Inter	29	5	3	7	21	25	6	3	5	17	12	11	6	12	38	37	39	1
6	FC Jazz	29	6	6	2	21	12	2	7	6	11	22	8	13	8	32	34	37	-2
7	KTP	29	4	6	4	14	14	4	4	7	15	21	8	10	11	29	35	34	-6
8	RoPS	29	6	3	5	21	20	1	7	7	10	26	7	10	12	31	46	31	-15

Relegation Group

			Home					Away					Total					
		Pd	W	D	L	F	A	W	D	L	F	A	W	D	L	F	A	Pt	GD
9	TPS	28	3	7	4	16	16	7	2	5	24	18	10	9	9	40	34	39	6
10	FC Lahti	28	4	2	8	17	29	4	4	6	17	26	8	6	14	34	55	30	-21
11	VPS	28	5	2	7	16	18	3	3	8	18	24	8	5	15	34	42	29	-8
12	TPV	28	2	2	10	12	32	8	0	4	11	28	2	6	20	23	60	12	-37

N.B. After 22 matches the top eight play off for the title. The bottom four play off to avoid relegation.

DOMESTIC CUP 1999

SIXTH ROUND
FinnPa 0, FC Inter 0 (aet; 3-2 on pens.)
Pyry Nokia 0, TPS 5
FC Hämeenlinna 0, FC Lahti 4
Rakuunat 1, Atlantis 0
SalPa 0, Tampere United 5
FC Honka 5, TPV 2
Kultsu 0, FC Jazz 3
FC Mikkeli 2, RiPS 1 (aet)
TP-Seinäjoki 1, RoPS 2
WTP 0, FF Jaro 3

SEVENTH ROUND
FC Honka 1, MyPa 4
FC Jazz 2, VPS 1 (aet)
FF Jaro 4, RoPS 0
TPS 2, KTP 1

FC Mikkeli 1, FC Lahti 2
Rakuunat 1, FC Jokerit 2
Tampere United 2, FC Haka 0
FinnPa 1, HJK 3

QUARTER-FINALS
FC Jokerit 2 (Lehtinen 17, Ylä-Jussila 89),
FC Lahti 1 (Marjamaa 41)
TPS 2 (Lallukka 83, Herne 101),
HJK 2 (Kuqi 33, 114) (aet; 1-3 on pens.)
FC Jazz 0, FF Jaro 2 (Borissov 23, Ekman 45)
Tampere United 1 (Lopez 63), MyPa 5 (Manso 39,
47, Multaharju 50, Malakeev 78, Lindström 86)

SEMI-FINALS
MyPa 0, FF Jaro 1 (Ekman 85)
FC Jokerit 1 (Helin 72), HJK 0

FINAL
30/10/99, Helsinki
FC JOKERIT 2 Sumiala (67, 70)
FF JARO 1 Widjeskog (45)
referee - Vuorela
FC JOKERIT - Laaksonen, Roiko, Hyryläinen, Ylä-
Jussila, Räsänen, Helin, Koskela (Paavola 66),
Rantanen, Sumiala, Lehtinen (Hiukka 77), Ristilä
(Corrigan 90).
FF JARO - Varivontshik, Lindholm (Ekman 74), Kass,
Suominen, Snellman (Zenoli 77), Widjeskog,
Koppinen, Kivilompolo, Milinkovic, Peltola (Borissov
58), Pell.

NATIONAL TEAM RESULTS 99/00

18/08/99	Belgium	A	Bruges	4-3	Wiss (32), Johansson (45, 53), Lehkosuo (63)
04/09/99	Germany (ECQ)	H	Helsinki	1-2	Salli (63)
09/10/99	Northern Ireland (ECQ)	H	Helsinki	4-1	Johansson (9), Hyypiä (63), Kolkka (72, 82)
31/01/00	Faroe Islands	N	La Manga	1-0	Sumiala (57)
02/02/00	Iceland	N	La Manga	0-1	
04/02/00	Denmark	N	La Manga	2-1	Vasara (33, 89)
20/02/00	Thailand	A	Bangkok	0-0	
23/02/00	Estonia	N	Bangkok	4-2	Kottila (12), Tuomela (14, 56), Kuqi (60)
27/02/00	Thailand	A	Bangkok	1-5	Kallio (68)
29/03/00	Wales	A	Cardiff	2-1	Litmanen (21), Blake (42og)
26/04/00	Poland	A	Poznan	0-0	

TOP SCORERS

23	Valeriy POPOVICH (FC Haka)
12	Neathan GIBSON (MyPa)
	Saku PUHAKAINEN (TPS)
11	Kai NYYSSÖNEN (FC Haka)
	Shefki KUQI (HJK)
10	Péter KOVÁCS (FC Lahti)
	RAFAEL (FC Jazz/HJK)
	Marco CASAGRANDE (TPS)

championship-winning goal five minutes before half-time.

It would have been tough luck on Haka to have been pipped at the post, having led from the front all season, but the spirit instilled in the team by English coach Keith Armstrong finally pulled them through. Popovich, who played in every game and finished up with 23 goals - almost twice as many as the next highest scorer in the league - was the undisputed star of a team that lacked any significant international profile. Only defender Janne Salli played for the Finnish national side during the season, although his impressive defensive partner Tero Penttilä later emulated him after leaving to join Scottish champions Rangers - the team who thrashed

classic scenario - the home team had to win to take the title, and the away side required only a draw.

Intrigued by the possibilities, a massive crowd of 6,406 turned up to watch. That was more than twice as many as Haka's previous best attendance. The local fans' optimism was buoyed by the knowledge that Haka had beaten HJK in their two previous encounters, and, sure enough, Haka were to make it a hat-trick of 1-0 wins, with Dutchman Martin Reynders scoring the all-important

EUROPEAN CUPS 99/00

CHAMPIONS' CUP
● **FC HAKA**
Preliminary round 1 HB (FAR)
A 1-1 Popovich (64)
Vilnrotter; Penttilä, Karjalainen, Salli, Räsänen; Ivanov, Hyökyvaara, Ruhanen, Wilson; Popovich, Niemi.
H 6-0 Salli (26), Reynders (44), Nyyssönen (47), Wilson (62), Popovich (80), Torkkeli (90)
Vilnrotter; Penttilä, Karjalainen, Salli (Hyökyvaara 54), Räsänen; Reynders (Ivanov 71), Nyyssönen (Torkkeli 61), Popovich, Savolainen; Wilson, Niemi.

Preliminary round 2 RANGERS (SCO)
H 1-4 Niemi (51)
Vilnrotter; Penttilä, Karjalainen, Räsänen, Savolainen; Ivanov (Torkkeli 55), Hyökyvaara (Okkonen 83), Reynders, Wilson; Popovich, Niemi (Nyyssönen 73).
A 0-3 Vilnrotter; Penttilä, Karjalainen, Okkonen, Räsänen (Savolainen 62); Ivanov (Nyyssönen 55), Reynders, Rantala, Wilson; Popovich, Niemi (Torkkeli 72).

UEFA CUP
● **HJK**
Qualifying round SHIRAK GYUMRI (ARM)
H 2-0 Rafael (21), Ilola (70)
Viander; Tihinen, Nylund, Saastamoinen, Kuivasto; Yeremenko (Ilola 66), Vasara, Piracaia (Turpeinen 79), Lehkosuo; Kuqi, Rafael (Uzuner 85).
A 0-1 Viander; Tihinen, Nylund, Saastamoinen, Turpeinen; Kuivasto, Yeremenko (Piracaia 61), Vasara (Jävajä 77), Lehkosuo; Kuqi, Rafael (Nybäck 89).

1st round OLYMPIQUE LYONNAIS (FRA)
H 0-1 Viander; Turpeinen, Nylund, Saastamoinen, Kuivasto; Yeremenko (Kallio 63), Vasara (Jävajä 85), Piracaia (Ilola 46), Lehkosuo; Kuqi, Rafael.
A 1-5 Lehkosuo (40)
Viander; Tihinen, Turpeinen, Nylund, Saastamoinen; Kuivasto, Ilola (Vasara 51), Lehkosuo, Kallio (Yeremenko 17); Kuqi, Rafael (Piracaia 74).

● **VPS**
Qualifying round ST. JOHNSTONE (SCO)
H 1-1 Pohja (41)
Toivonen; Kautonen, Suoste, Kokko, Jaakkola; Jalonen, Enqvist, Pohja, Kangaskorpi; Priha, Sykora (Kaijasilta 32).
A 0-2 Stringheim (Sillanpää 72); Kautonen, Kokko, Jaakkola (Nygård 84), Sivonen; Jalonen, Kangaskorpi, Enqvist, Pohja; Essandoh, Kaijasilta (Sykora 63).

Haka in the qualifying round of the Champions' League.

The national-team representation at HJK was much greater, with as many as seven players being summoned in the autumn, including nationalised Albanian Shefki Kuqi, who, with 11 goals, was the Helsinki club's leading marksman in the league. Coach Muurinen quit HJK at the end of the campaign to replace the departing Richard Møller-Nielsen as the new Finnish national team boss. He had enjoyed three excellent years at HJK, his most notable achievement being qualification for the Champions' League in 1998/99. There was no such joy for Muurinen's men in the 1999/2000 UEFA Cup. Nor

NATIONAL TEAM APPEARANCES 99/00

Coach - Richard MØLLER-NIELSEN; Antti MUURINEN	BEL	GER	NIR	FAR	ISL	DEN	THA	EST	THA	WAL	POL	Cps	Gls
Pasi LAAKSONEN (15/08/72) - FC Jokerit	G46	s46			G	G						4	-
Harri YLÖNEN (21/12/71) - SK Brann (NOR)	D	D46		D	s69	D	D		s46		D	33	1
Toni KUIVASTO (31/12/75) - HJK	D	D	D		D	s58		D				15	-
Hannu TIHINEN (01/07/76) - HJK/Viking FK (NOR)	D		D	D	D	D58				D	D	9	1
Sami YLÄ-JUSSILA (07/10/69) - FC Jokerit	D	s86										3	-
Mika LEHKOSUO (08/01/70) - HJK	M		M	M	M	s46	M	s71	M	s69	D	17	1
Jarkko WISS (17/04/72) - Lillestrøm SK (NOR)/Moss FK (NOR)	M	M	M86	M		M	M	M71	M	s65	M	27	2
Aki RIIHILAHTI (09/09/76) - Vålerenga IF (NOR)	M41	M	M86							M	s56	19	1
Joonas KOLKKA (28/09/74) - PSV (HOL)	M60		M							M	M89	27	6
Mika-Matti PAATELAINEN (03/02/67) - Hibernian (SCO)	A74		A							s46	s58	69	18
Jonatan JOHANSSON (16/08/75) - Rangers (SCO)	A	A	A									25	9
Vesa VASARA (16/08/76) - HJK	s41 /89			M63	s85	M	M70	s83	s62			7	2
Jani VIANDER (18/08/75) - HJK	s46		G	G			G		s46			7	-
Tommi KAUTONEN (24/12/71) - VPS	s60											8	-
Jarmo SAASTAMOINEN (20/09/67) - HJK	s74	D		D69	s40	D		D	D46			18	-
Shefki KUQI (10/11/76) - HJK	s89	s46		s74	A	s80	s70	A	A62			8	1
Antti NIEMI (31/05/72) - Rangers (SCO)/Heart of Midlothian (SCO)	G46										G	38	-
Sami HYYPIÄ (07/10/73) - Liverpool (ENG)	D	D								D		31	1
Janne SALLI (14/12/77) - FC Haka	D		D	s82	D40							5	1
Teemu TAINIO (27/11/79) - AJ Auxerre (FRA)	M					M61	M					6	-
Mika KOTTILA (22/09/74) - SK Brann (NOR)/Trelleborgs FF (SWE)	A				s81	A83	A			s89		9	1
Jari LITMANEN (20/02/71) - FC Barcelona (ESP)		M								M69	M89	61	15
Simo VALAKARI (28/04/73) - Motherwell (SCO)		s86								M65		14	-
Ville NYLUND (14/08/72) - HJK				D	D82		D		D			7	-
Tommi GRÖNLUND (09/12/69) - Trelleborgs FF (SWE)				M	M	M46	M	s46	M		M56	24	1
Jari NIEMI (02/02/77) - Tampere United				M63	s66	M46						3	-
Antti SUMIALA (20/02/74) - FC Jokerit				A74	s59	A	A81		A46			33	8
Petri HELIN (13/12/69) - FC Jokerit				s63	M85		s61	M			s46	14	2
Toni KALLIO (09/08/78) - HJK				s63	A66	s46		A	s46			5	1
Timo MARJAMAA (27/06/76) - FC Jokerit				M59	M		M46					3	-
Toni HUTTUNEN (12/01/73) - MyPa					D80							5	-
Tero PENTTILÄ (09/03/75) - Rangers (SCO)							D				D	2	-
Magnus BAHNE (15/03/79) - FC Inter								G	G46			2	-
Janne HIETANEN (02/06/78) - VPS								D	D46			2	-
Marko TUOMELA (03/03/72) - Tromsø IL (NOR)								D	D	s46	s89	20	2
Peter ENCKELMAN (10/03/77) - Aston Villa (ENG)									G46			1	-
Juha REINI (19/03/75) - KRC Genk (BEL)									D			12	-
Mika NURMELA (26/12/71) - SC Heerenveen (HOL)										M	M46	14	-
Mikael FORSSELL (15/03/81) - Chelsea (ENG)										A46	A58	3	-
Teuvo MOILANEN (12/12/73) - Preston North End (ENG)										s46		3	-

were they able to make a successful defence of the Finnish Cup.

The team which eliminated HJK in the semi-finals, FC Jokerit, went on to win the trophy, beating FF Jaro 2-1 in the final thanks to two goals from experienced international striker Antti Sumiala. Jokerit, in their former guise as PK-35, had been the beaten finalists a year earlier, so revenge was sweet. Particularly enthralled by the club's first trophy was multi-millionaire businessman Harry Harkimo, whose huge investment in the club appeared to be paying off. The well-known ice-hockey impresario has great ambitions for FC Jokerit and he has already fulfilled the dream of many Finnish football enthusiasts by building a new football stadium in the centre of Helsinki. The Finnair

Stadium was officially opened in the spring of 2000.

Another upwardly-mobile club, Tampere United, achieved their immediate goal of promotion to the National League, although the side coached by Harri Kampman needed a play-off victory over Atlantis before they could take the place of relegated TPV, their local rivals. Atlantis then lost a further play-off, against VPS, and with Jaro also losing out to FC Lahti in the other tie, there was just one new arrival in the 2000 Veikkausliga, which had undergone yet another revamping, having returned to the 33-match programme in which each of the 12 teams play each other three times. One day, perhaps, the Finnish league authorities will at last find a system that works and stick with it...

PROMOTED CLUB 1999

SECOND DIVISION FINAL TABLES
FIRST PHASE

NORTH		Pd	W	D	L	F	A	Pt	GD
1	**Tampere United**	**18**	**13**	**2**	**3**	**46**	**14**	**41**	**32**
2	FF Jaro	18	10	7	1	44	16	37	28
3	MuSa	18	9	5	4	29	29	32	0
4	Pyry Nokia	18	8	3	7	32	37	27	-5
5	TP-Seinäjoki	18	7	5	6	40	34	26	6
6	P-Iirot	18	6	5	7	22	23	23	-1
7	KPV-j	18	6	4	8	26	34	22	-8
8	KPT-85	18	4	6	8	24	28	18	-4
9	Närpes Kraft	18	4	4	10	21	38	16	-17
10	KajHa	18	0	5	13	9	40	5	-31

SOUTH		Pd	W	D	L	F	A	Pt	GD
1	HIK	18	10	5	3	41	31	35	10
2	Atlantis	18	8	6	4	22	17	30	5
3	FC Mikkeli	18	6	10	2	28	18	28	10
4	KuPS	18	7	5	6	29	24	26	5
5	FC Honka	18	6	6	6	28	25	24	3
6	FC HIFK	18	7	3	8	27	32	24	-5
7	RiPS	18	5	7	6	30	28	22	2
8	FinnPa	18	5	7	6	22	22	22	0
9	AC Vantaa	18	5	4	9	22	29	19	-7
10	Kultsu	18	3	3	12	15	38	12	-23

SECOND PHASE		Pd	W	D	L	F	A	Pt	GD
1	Atlantis	9	7	0	2	27	10	24	17
2	Tampere United	9	6	1	2	22	13	24	9
3	FF Jaro	9	6	1	2	19	13	22	6
4	HIK	9	2	4	3	13	14	15	-1
5	FC Honka	9	4	0	5	15	13	12	2
6	Pyry Nokia	9	3	2	4	14	14	12	0
7	KuPS	9	3	2	4	16	21	12	-5
8	MuSa	9	2	2	5	13	19	10	-6
9	TP-Seinäjoki	9	3	1	5	19	29	10	-10
10	FC Mikkeli	9	2	1	6	14	26	9	-12

N.B. The top five teams from the two First Phase Groups qualify for the Second Phase with the following bonus points: 1st place = 5 pts; 2nd = 3 pts; 3rd = 2 pts; 4th = 1 pts; 5th = 0 pts.

CLUB DIRECTORY
Tampere United
Salhojankatu 27
PL 639
331010 Tampere
tel - (03) 2554454
fax - (03) 3469140
Year of Formation - 1999
President - Jyrki Laiho
Manager - Kalevi Salonen
Coach - Harri Kampman
Stadium - Tammela (6,000)

PROMOTION PLAY-OFFS
Atlantis 0, Tampere United 2

Atlantis 2, VPS 1
VPS 2, Atlantis 0
(VPS 3-2)

FF Jaro 0, FC Lahti 0
FC Lahti 1, FF Jaro 0
(FC Lahti 1-0)

FC HAKA

CLUB DIRECTORY

FC Haka
Kirjaskatu 1, 37600 Valkeakoski
tel - (03) 5845364 / fax - (02) 04163629
Year of Formation - 1934
President - Heikki Huoviala
Manager - Erkki Salo
Coach - Keith Armstrong
Stadium - Tehtaankenttä (2,850)

MAJOR HONOURS
League Championship - (7)
1960, 1962, 1965, 1977, 1995, 1998, 1999.
Domestic Cup - (10) 1955, 1959, 1960, 1963,
1969, 1977, 1982, 1985, 1988, 1997.

APPEARANCES 1999

	P	Ap	(s)	Gls
Janne HYÖKYVAARA	M	16	(3)	1
Oleg IVANOV (RUS)	M	14	(5)	3
Lasse KARJALAINEN	M	26	(1)	1
Janne MÄKELÄ	D	8		
Jari NIEMI	A	22	(6)	3
Kimmo NURMINEN	M		(2)	
Kai NYYSSÖNEN	A	18	(9)	11
Jarkko OKKONEN	D	12	(6)	
Jaakko PASANEN	D	1	(1)	
Tero PENTTILÄ	D	28		3
Valeriy POPOVICH (RUS)	A	29		23
Jukka RANTALA	M	9	(8)	
Martin REYNDERS (HOL)	A	12	(2)	4
Jukka RUHANEN	A	19	(5)	2
Jouni RÄSÄNEN	D	27		
Janne SALLI	D	23	(1)	2
Janne SAVOLAINEN	D	2	(12)	
Tommi TORKKELI	M	6	(14)	
András VILNROTTER (HUN)	G	29		
David WILSON (ENG)	M	18	(3)	

LEAGUE RESULTS 1999

Date	Opponent		Score	Scorers
25/04/99	HJK	H	1-0	Popovich (p)
02/05/99	FC Inter	A	1-0	Penttilä
06/05/99	MyPa	H	4-0	Niemi, Popovich, Nyyssönen 2
09/05/99	FC Lahti	A	2-0	Niemi, Popovich
17/05/99	TPV	H	3-1	Popovich 2, Niemi
23/05/99	RoPS	A	3-2	Nyyssönen, Salli, Ruhanen
27/05/99	FC Jokerit	H	2-2	Popovich 2
30/05/99	VPS	A	1-0	Popovich
13/06/99	FC Jazz	H	1-1	Popovich
17/06/99	KTP	H	4-1	Penttilä, Ivanov, Popovich, Nyyssönen
20/06/99	TPS	A	1-1	Ruhanen
28/06/99	HJK	A	1-0	Nyyssönen
01/07/99	FC Lahti	H	4-2	Ivanov, Popovich 2, Nyyssönen
07/07/99	FC Jokerit	A	0-1	
11/07/99	RoPS	H	0-0	
18/07/99	TPV	A	3-0	og, Nyyssönen, Popovich
25/07/99	VPS	H	2-0	Popovich, Ivanov
01/08/99	MyPa	A	2-1	Reynders, Popovich
08/08/99	FC Jazz	A	2-2	Nyyssönen, Popovich
15/08/99	FC Inter	H	1-0	Popovich
22/08/99	TPS	H	5-2	Popovich 3, Salli, Nyyssönen
29/08/99	KTP	A	0-1	
13/09/99	FC Inter	A	3-0	Hyökyvaara, Penttilä, Popovich
18/09/99	FC Jazz	H	0-0	
23/09/99	FC Jokerit	H	2-0	Reynders, Nyyssönen
27/09/99	KTP	A	3-1	Popovich, Reynders, Nyyssönen
02/10/99	RoPS	H	2-0	Popovich, Karjalainen
13/10/99	MyPa	A	0-0	
16/10/99	HJK	H	1-0	Reynders

HJK

CLUB DIRECTORY

Helsingin Jalkapalloklubi
Mannerheimintie 19, 00250 Helsinki
tel - (09) 4774550 / fax - (09) 47745510
Year of Formation - 1907
President - Olli-Pekka Lyytikäinen
Manager - Kari Haapiainen
Coach - Antti Muurinen (2000 - Jyrki Heliskoski)
Stadium - Finnair Stadium (11,000)

MAJOR HONOURS
League Championship - (19) 1911, 1912, 1917,
1918, 1919, 1923, 1925, 1936, 1938, 1964,
1973, 1978, 1981, 1985, 1987, 1988, 1990,
1992, 1997.
Domestic Cup - (6)
1966, 1981, 1984, 1993, 1996, 1998.

APPEARANCES 1999

	P	Ap	(s)	Gls
Jari ILOLA	D	24	(3)	2
Jari JÄVÄJÄ	A	2	(10)	1
Toni KALLIO	A	2	(7)	
Tommi KOIVISTOINEN	G	2		
Peter KOPTEFF	A	3	(7)	
Toni KUIVASTO	D	28		1
Shefki KUQI	A	21	(4)	11
Mika LEHKOSUO	M	21	(1)	2
LUIZ ANTÓNIO (BRA)	A	9	(1)	6
Timo NYBÄCK	D		(4)	
Ville NYLUND	D	28		
PIRACAÍA (BRA)	M	22	(6)	3
RAFAEL Pires Vieira (BRA)	A	11		7
Juha RIIPPA	M	3	(2)	
Paulus ROIHA	A		(1)	
Janne SAARINEN	M	1	(7)	
Jarmo SAASTAMOINEN	D	24	(2)	1
Hannu TIHINEN	D	24	(3)	4
Aarno TURPEINEN	D	18	(4)	
UZUNER Sükrü (TUR)	A	8	(8)	2
Vesa VASARA	M	12	(13)	6
Jani VIANDER	G	27		
Aleksei YEREMENKO (RUS)	M	29		7

LEAGUE RESULTS 1999

25/04/99	FC Haka	A	0-1	
02/05/99	TPS	H	0-0	
06/05/99	FC Jokerit	H	2-1	Tihinen, Kuqi
09/05/99	TPV	A	1-0	Kuqi
16/05/99	MyPa	H	2-0	Kuqi, Yeremenko
24/05/99	VPS	H	3-0	Luiz António 2, Vasara
27/05/99	KTP	A	1-1	Luiz António
13/06/99	FC Inter	A	7-2	Kuivasto, Uzuner, Luiz António 2,
				Kuqi 2, Tihinen
17/06/99	FC Lahti	H	1-1	Kuqi
20/06/99	FC Jazz	A	1-1	Luiz António
23/06/99	RoPS	A	1-0	Lehkosuo
28/06/99	FC Haka	H	0-1	
01/07/99	TPV	H	2-0	Jäväjä, Yeremenko
04/07/99	MyPa	A	3-0	Uzuner, Ilola, Piracaía
11/07/99	TPS	A	0-0	
14/07/99	FC Jokerit	A	2-1	Tihinen, Yeremenko (p)
18/07/99	FC Inter	H	0-1	
25/07/99	KTP	H	3-1	Ilola, Saastamoinen, Vasara
01/08/99	FC Jazz	H	4-1	Rafael 3, Kuqi
08/08/99	VPS	A	1-0	Vasara
21/08/99	RoPS	H	4-0	Yeremenko, Vasara, Rafael, Tihinen
29/08/99	FC Lahti	A	5-2	Rafael, Yeremenko (p), Kuqi 2,
				Vasara
12/09/99	FC Jazz	A	2-0	Piracaía, Vasara
19/09/99	MyPa	H	2-1	Lehkosuo, Rafael
22/09/99	FC Inter	H	2-1	Kuqi, Yeremenko
25/09/99	RoPS	A	1-0	Yeremenko
04/10/99	FC Jokerit	H	2-1	Piracaía, Rafael
13/10/99	KTP	H	1-0	Kuqi
16/10/99	FC Haka	A	0-1	

FC INTER

CLUB DIRECTORY

FC Inter
Linnankatu 36 A1
20100 Turku
tel - (02) 2792700
fax - (02) 2792710
Year of Formation - 1993
President - Stefan Håkans
Coach - Timo Askolin
Stadium - Kupittaa (10,000)

APPEARANCES 1999

	P	Ap	(s)	Gls
Magnus BAHNE	G	25		
Tero FORSS	M	13	(4)	6
Mats GUSTAFSSON	A	5	(11)	2
Mikko HELMINEN	M	6	(3)	
Lee ISAAC (ENG)	A	3	(19)	
Joakim JENSEN (SWE)	D	21		
Kimmo KARVINEN	M	3	(6)	
Jani KEULANEN	D	17		
Mark KULMALA	M		(1)	
Janne LEHTINEN	M	20	(1)	2
Petri LEHTONEN	D	20		1
Samuli LINDELÖF	A	19	(4)	4
Jani MÄENPÄÄ	M	18	(2)	2
Janne OINAS	D	19	(2)	
Petro PUNNA	M	13	(6)	1
Marko RAJAMÄKI	A	12	(9)	2
Richard TEBERIO (SWE)	A	21	(8)	9
Jari VANHALA	A	29		8
Petri VILJANEN	G	4		
Petteri VILJANEN	D	24	(1)	
Jami WALLENIUS	D	27		

LEAGUE RESULTS 1999

25/04/99	MyPa	A	1-0	Teberio
02/05/99	FC Haka	H	0-1	
06/05/99	FC Lahti	A	2-3	Punna, Teberio
09/05/99	FC Jazz	H	3-0	Teberio 2, Vanhala
16/05/99	KTP	A	0-1	
24/05/99	TPS	A	1-0	Lindelöf
27/05/99	RoPS	H	2-2	Teberio, og
30/05/99	TPV	A	0-0	
13/06/99	HJK	H	2-7	Vanhala, Lehtonen
16/06/99	FC Jokerit	A	1-0	Mäenpää
21/06/99	VPS	H	3-1	Mäenpää, Forss, Lehtinen
30/06/99	FC Jokerit	H	1-0	Forss
04/07/99	RoPS	A	1-3	Lindelöf
08/07/99	MyPa	H	1-2	Gustafsson
11/07/99	VPS	A	2-0	Vanhala, Teberio
18/07/99	HJK	A	1-0	Vanhala
25/07/99	TPS	H	1-2	Forss (p)
01/08/99	KTP	H	0-0	
08/08/99	FC Lahti	H	3-1	Lehtinen, Gustafsson, Rajamäki
15/08/99	FC Haka	A	0-1	
23/08/99	FC Jazz	A	1-1	Vanhala
29/08/99	TPV	H	2-0	Lindelöf 2
13/09/99	FC Haka	H	0-3	
18/09/99	RoPS	A	5-0	Vanhala 3, Teberio, Forss
22/09/99	HJK	A	1-2	Forss
25/09/99	MyPa	H	0-2	
03/10/99	KTP	H	3-3	Teberio 2, Forss (p)
13/10/99	FC Jokerit	H	0-1	
16/10/99	FC Jazz	A	1-1	Rajamäki

FC JAZZ

FC Jazz
Isolinnankatu 2
28 100 Pori
tel - (02) 6331999
fax - (02) 6331244
Year of Formation - 1934
President - Arto Vitikka
Coach - Pertti Lundell
Stadium - Porin Stadion (10,000)

MAJOR HONOURS
League Championship - (2) 1993, 1996.

APPEARANCES 1999

		P	Ap	(s)	Gls
Hasan CETINKAYA (SWE)	M	28	(1)	6
Victor Hugo DUBON (SAL)	M	13	(13)	1
Rami HAKANPÄÄ	D	24		1
Jarno HEINIKANGAS	M		(5)	
Olli KANGASLAHTI	A	6	(2)	1
Peter KOPTEFF	A	10		1
Saku LAAKSONEN	A	14	(11)	4
Vesa LAMMINEN	A		(3)	
Ville LEHTINEN	M	17	(6)	1
Antal LÖRINCZ (HUN)	D	23		1
MARCO António Pogioli (BRA)	A	28		6
Sándor MATUS (HUN)	G	4		
Rami NIEMINEN	D	28		4
Jussi PELLIKKA	M	20	(4)	
RAFAEL Pires Vieira (BRA)	A	15	(1)	3
Vesa RANTANEN	D	17	(1)	
Jani RAUKKO	A	10	(9)	
Jyrki ROVIO	G	25		
Esa SALMINHEIMO	D	7	(6)	
Mauricio SOTO (CHL)	M	1	(6)	
Kim SUOMINEN	M	28		3
Teemu VIHTILÄ	M	1	(3)	

LEAGUE RESULTS 1999

25/04/99	KTP	H	1-1	Marco
02/05/99	TPV	A	3-1	Suominen, Cetinkaya, Nieminen (p)
06/05/99	RoPS	H	2-0	Hakanpää, Cetinkaya
09/05/99	FC Inter	A	0-3	
16/05/99	FC Lahti	H	3-0	Marco 2, Rafael
23/05/99	MyPa	A	0-2	
27/05/99	TPS	H	3-2	Cetinkaya, Dubon, Laaksonen
31/05/99	FC Jokerit	H	1-1	Rafael
13/06/99	FC Haka	A	1-1	Nieminen
17/06/99	VPS	A	0-1	
20/06/99	HJK	H	1-1	Laaksonen
27/06/99	MyPa	H	3-0	Laaksonen, Cetinkaya, Marco
01/07/99	KTP	A	1-0	Rafael
04/07/99	VPS	H	0-1	
12/07/99	FC Lahti	A	2-2	Laaksonen, Lörincz
18/07/99	TPS	A	1-1	Suominen
26/07/99	TPV	H	2-0	Kopteff, Marco
01/08/99	HJK	A	1-4	Marco
08/08/99	FC Haka	H	2-2	Suominen, Nieminen
12/08/99	FC Jokerit	A	0-0	
23/08/99	FC Inter	H	1-1	Kangaslahti
29/08/99	RoPS	A	0-0	
12/09/99	HJK	H	0-2	
18/09/99	FC Haka	A	0-0	
23/09/99	KTP	H	1-0	Cetinkaya
26/09/99	FC Jokerit	A	1-1	Nieminen
02/10/99	MyPa	A	1-4	Cetinkaya
13/10/99	RoPS	A	0-2	
16/10/99	FC Inter	H	1-1	Lehtinen

FC JOKERIT

CLUB DIRECTORY

FC Jokerit
Areenakuja 1
00240 Helsinki
tel - (09) 02041997
fax - (09) 0204194445
Year of Formation - 1999
President - Harry Harkimo
Manager - Mecki Kähre
Coach - Pasi Rautiainen
Stadium - Finnair Stadium (11,000)

MAJOR HONOURS
Domestic Cup - (1) 1999.

APPEARANCES 1999

	P	Ap	(s)	Gls
Martyn CORRIGAN (SCO)	M	13		
Roberto Maia FERNANDES (BRA)	M	1		
Oscar GEAGEA	M	1		
Petri HELIN	M	26	(1)	1
Matti HIUKKA	A	17	(11)	9
Erik HOLMGREN	D	10	(4)	
Pasi HYRYLÄINEN	D	15	(1)	2
Tero KOSKELA	M	14	(3)	
Pasi LAAKSONEN	G	29		
Kalle LEHTINEN	A	18	(6)	6
Mika NENONEN	M	12	(8)	1
Tommi PAAVOLA	A	17	(10)	2
Antti POHJA	M	5	(6)	
Jani PYLKÄS	M	17	(4)	
Rami RANTANEN	M	22	(3)	2
Martin REYNDERS (HOL)	A	6	(4)	3
Sami RISTILÄ	M	12	(1)	2
Ari-Pekka ROIKO	M	15	(5)	
Janne RÄSÄNEN	D	16	(1)	
Antti SUMIALA	A	13	(3)	5
Jarno TUUNAINEN	D	6	(1)	
Anssi VIREN	D	8	(6)	
Sami YLÄ-JUSSILA	D	26		2

LEAGUE RESULTS 1999

Date	Opponent	H/A	Score	Scorers
25/04/99	VPS	H	1-0	Paavola
03/05/99	FC Lahti	H	1-0	Helin
06/05/99	HJK	A	1-2	Hiukka
09/05/99	RoPS	H	1-1	Reynders
16/05/99	TPS	A	1-1	Lehtinen
23/05/99	KTP	H	1-0	Rantanen
27/05/99	FC Haka	A	2-2	Reynders 2
31/05/99	FC Jazz	A	1-1	Ylä-Jussila
13/06/99	MyPa	A	0-2	
16/06/99	FC Inter	H	0-1	
23/06/99	TPV	H	1-0	Nenonen
30/06/99	FC Inter	A	0-1	
07/07/99	FC Haka	H	1-0	Paavola
14/07/99	HJK	H	1-2	Hiukka
21/07/99	RoPS	A	0-3	
28/07/99	MyPa	H	0-1	
02/08/99	VPS	A	3-1	Hiukka 2, Rantanen
09/08/99	KTP	A	4-3	Ristilä, Hiukka 2, Hyryläinen
12/08/99	FC Jazz	H	0-0	
15/08/99	FC Lahti	A	1-0	Lehtinen
23/08/99	TPV	A	5-0	Sumiala, Lehtinen 3, Ylä-Jussila
27/08/99	TPS	H	1-1	Hiukka
11/09/99	RoPS	H	4-0	Ristilä, Hiukka, Lehtinen, Hyryläinen
20/09/99	KTP	H	1-2	Hiukka
23/09/99	FC Haka	A	0-2	
26/09/99	FC Jazz	H	1-1	Sumiala
04/10/99	HJK	A	1-2	Sumiala
13/10/99	FC Inter	A	1-0	Sumiala
16/10/99	MyPa	H	1-2	Sumiala

KTP

CLUB DIRECTORY

Kotkan TP
Puistotie 9-11, 48100 Kotka
tel - (05) 2181600
fax - (05) 2181601
Year of Formation - 1927
President - Jaakko Kilpeläinen
Manager - Jukka Vakkila
Coach - Hannu Touru
Stadium - Kotkan Urheilukeskus (4,500)

MAJOR HONOURS
League Championship - (2) 1951, 1952,
Domestic Cup - (4) 1958, 1961, 1967, 1980.

APPEARANCES 1999

	P	Ap	(s)	Gls
Argo ARBEITER (EST)	A	24	(1)	3
Aleksei GOULO (RUS)	D	29		2
Elhan HASANOV (AZB)	G	16	(2)	
Vesa HELENIUS	A		(2)	
Janne HYPPÖNEN	A	14	(4)	2
Toomas KÄLLASTE (EST)	M	25	(3)	
Janne KAURIA	M	14	(11)	
Mauri KESKITALO	A	16	(1)	5
Tommi KEVERI	M	3	(1)	
Urmas KIRS (EST)	M	16		2
Vesa LAURIKAINEN	A	8	(6)	1
Lassi LEHTONEN	D	10	(8)	
Kim LILJEQVIST	D		(9)	
Meelis LINDMAA (EST)	D	11	(5)	
Sándor MATUS (HUN)	G	4		
Janne MOILANEN	M	25		2
Tuomo PAAKKARI	D	22	(1)	
Mika PULKKINEN	A	24		5
Toni PULLI	D	13	(5)	
Antti PYNNÖNEN	G	9	(1)	
Lembit RAJALA (EST)	A	2	(1)	
Martin REIM (EST)	M	20	(1)	2
UZUNER Sükrü (TUR)	A	7	(1)	4
Petri VAINIO	D	1	(1)	
Jukka VILKKI	D	2		
Antti VÄISÄNEN	A	4	(10)	1

LEAGUE RESULTS 1999

25/04/99	FC Jazz	A	1-1	Pulkkinen (p)
02/05/99	RoPS	H	1-1	Goulo
06/05/99	TPV	H	1-0	Hyppönen
10/05/99	VPS	A	1-3	Pulkkinen (p)
16/05/99	FC Inter	H	1-0	Pulkkinen (p)
23/05/99	FC Jokerit	A	0-1	
27/05/99	HJK	H	1-1	Pulkkinen
30/05/99	MyPa	A	0-0	
14/06/99	TPS	H	2-0	Arbeiter, Laurikainen
17/06/99	FC Haka	A	1-4	Hyppönen
20/06/99	FC Lahti	A	1-0	Goulo
27/06/99	FC Lahti	H	0-1	
01/07/99	FC Jazz	H	0-1	
04/07/99	TPS	A	3-0	Arbeiter, Väisänen, Reim
12/07/99	TPV	A	0-2	
18/07/99	VPS	H	2-2	Reim, Keskitalo
25/07/99	HJK	A	1-3	Keskitalo
01/08/99	FC Inter	A	0-0	
09/08/99	FC Jokerit	H	3-4	Moilanen, Arbeiter, Kirs
15/08/99	RoPS	A	2-1	Moilanen, Pulkkinen
22/08/99	MyPa	H	0-0	
29/08/99	FC Haka	H	1-0	Keskitalo
11/09/99	MyPa	H	0-0	
20/09/99	FC Jokerit	A	2-1	Keskitalo 2
23/09/99	FC Jazz	A	0-1	
27/09/99	FC Haka	H	1-3	Kirs
03/10/99	FC Inter	A	3-3	Uzuner 3
13/10/99	HJK	A	0-1	
16/10/99	RoPS	H	1-1	Uzuner

FC LAHTI

CLUB DIRECTORY

FC Lahti
Rautatienkatu 19
15110 Lahti
tel - (03) 880810
fax - (03) 8808131
Year of Formation - 1996
President - Erkki Puolakka
Manager - Petri Tiainen
Secretary - Irmeli Rantanen
Coach - Esa Pekonen (2000 - Jari Pyykölä)
Stadium - Lahden Stadion (15,000)

APPEARANCES 1999

	P	Ap	(s)	Gls
BOLA Pereira João Batista (BRA)	D	12	(1)	1
DECO (BRA)	D	7	(3)	
Toni ETU-SEPPÄLÄ	G	11		
Mikko HARILA	A	8	(12)	
Niki HELENIUS	A	2	(6)	2
Björn HOFVENDAHL (SWE)	A	19	(5)	3
Petri JÄRVINEN	M	12	(2)	1
Jari KAASALAINEN	M	15	(1)	2
Tomi KINNUNEN	D	12	(1)	
Jarkko KOSKINEN	D	26		2
Péter KOVÁCS (HUN)	A	24	(4)	10
Tuomas KUPARINEN	A	14	(5)	1
Ismo LIUS	A	1	(1)	1
Timo MARJAMAA	D	27		5
Luciano MARTINS (BRA)	A	2	(6)	
Mika MOTTURI	D	24	(1)	
Petri PASANEN	D	25	(2)	
Esa PEKONEN	D	3		
Lasse PELTONEN	M	21	(1)	1
RODRIGO (BRA)	M	13	(2)	2
Niko SIMOLA	G	17	(2)	
Antal SIMON (HUN)	M	2	(3)	1
Ville VÄISÄNEN	A	2	(5)	
Mika VÄYRYNEN	M	9	(6)	1

LEAGUE RESULTS 1999

25/04/99	RoPS	H	1-0	Rodrigo
03/05/99	FC Jokerit	A	0-1	
06/05/99	FC Inter	H	3-2	Simon, Hofvendahl, Marjamaa
09/05/99	FC Haka	H	0-2	
16/05/99	FC Jazz	A	0-3	
23/05/99	TPV	A	2-1	Kovács, Peltonen
27/05/99	MyPa	H	1-2	Kuparinen
30/05/99	TPS	A	2-1	Kovács 2
13/06/99	VPS	H	2-1	Hofvendahl, Kaasalainen
17/06/99	HJK	A	1-1	Rodrigo
20/06/99	KTP	H	0-1	
27/06/99	KTP	A	1-0	Kovács
01/07/99	FC Haka	A	2-4	Marjamaa, Kovács
04/07/99	TPV	H	1-1	Kovács
12/07/99	FC Jazz	H	2-2	Lius, Marjamaa
19/07/99	MyPa	A	0-4	
25/07/99	RoPS	A	2-2	Kovács, og
02/08/99	TPS	H	1-2	Bola
08/08/99	FC Inter	A	1-3	Helenius
15/08/99	FC Jokerit	H	0-1	
22/08/99	VPS	A	1-2	Kovács
29/08/99	HJK	H	2-5	Järvinen, Marjamaa
11/09/99	TPS	H	0-3	
18/09/99	VPS	A	2-2	Helenius, Hofvendahl
22/09/99	TPV	H	4-3	Marjamaa, Väyrynen, Koskinen (p), Kovács
26/09/99	TPV	A	3-2	Koskinen, Kovács, Kaasalainen
02/10/99	TPS	A	0-0	
13/10/99	VPS	H	0-4	

MYPA

CLUB DIRECTORY

Myllykosken Pallo-47
Koulutie 1
46800 Anjalankoski
tel - (05) 3656686
fax - (05) 3255292
Year of Formation - 1947
President - Matti Tiihonen
Manager - Seppo Mäkinen
Coach - Juha Malinen
Stadium - Anjalankosken stadion (8,000)

MAJOR HONOURS
Domestic Cup - (2) 1992, 1995.

APPEARANCES 1999

	P	Ap	(s)	Gls
Tuomas AHO	D	5	(3)	
Neathan GIBSON (SAF)	A	24		12
Merka HAUTALA	A	4	(4)	1
Markus HEIKKINEN	D	29		1
Mika HERNESNIEMI	M	25	(1)	3
Toni HUTTUNEN	D	28		1
Janne KORHONEN	G	1		
Mikko KORHONEN	A	6	(9)	4
Arto LAUTAMATTI	A	4	(6)	
Janne LINDBERG	M	26		2
Jukka LINDSTRÖM	D	29		3
Vjacheslav MALAKEEV (RUS)	M	14	(13)	2
Marco MANSO (BRA)	M	15	(2)	2
István MITRING (HUN)	G	28		
Miika MULTAHARJU	D	19	(7)	2
Tomi PAKARINEN	D	26		1
Brent SANCHO (TRI)	D	1		
Yevgeniy SMIRNOV (RUS)	A	1	(19)	1
Sampsa TIMOSKA	D	3	(11)	
Jani UOTINEN	M	15	(4)	2
Sami VÄISÄNEN	A	16	(6)	1

LEAGUE RESULTS 1999

25/04/99	FC Inter	H	0-1	
02/05/99	VPS	A	1-0	Gibson
06/05/99	FC Haka	A	0-4	
09/05/99	TPS	H	3-1	Gibson, Hautala, Multaharju
16/05/99	HJK	A	0-2	
23/05/99	FC Jazz	H	2-0	Korhonen M., Manso
27/05/99	FC Lahti	A	2-1	Korhonen M., Hernesniemi
30/05/99	KTP	H	0-0	
13/06/99	FC Jokerit	H	2-0	Gibson, Smirnov
16/06/99	TPV	A	2-2	Malakeev, Gibson
20/06/99	RoPS	H	1-1	Gibson
27/06/99	FC Jazz	A	0-3	
01/07/99	RoPS	A	1-2	Uotinen
04/07/99	HJK	H	0-3	
08/07/99	FC Inter	A	2-1	Gibson, og
19/07/99	FC Lahti	H	4-0	Lindström, Hernesniemi, Gibson 2
28/07/99	FC Jokerit	A	1-0	Gibson
01/08/99	FC Haka	H	1-2	Heikkinen
08/08/99	TPV	H	1-1	Malakeev
15/08/99	TPS	A	3-2	Gibson 2, Väisänen
22/08/99	KTP	A	0-0	
29/08/99	VPS	H	1-1	Lindberg (p)
11/09/99	KTP	A	0-0	
19/09/99	HJK	A	1-2	Pakarinen
22/09/99	RoPS	H	3-1	Uotinen, Gibson, Lindberg
25/09/99	FC Inter	A	2-0	Manso, Lindström
02/10/99	FC Jazz	H	4-1	Lindström, Huttunen, Multaharju, Hernesniemi
13/10/99	FC Haka	H	0-0	
16/10/99	FC Jokerit	A	2-1	Korhonen M. 2

ROPS

CLUB DIRECTORY

Rovaniemen Palloseura
PL 2230
96201 Rovaniemi
tel - (016) 314977
fax - (016) 319837
Year of Formation - 1950
President - Oskari Jänkälä
Manager - Jouko Kiistala
Coach - Olavi Tammimies
Stadium - Keskuskenttä (4,000)

MAJOR HONOURS
Domestic Cup - (1) 1986.

APPEARANCES 1999

	P	Ap	(s)	Gls
Dabid CHILUFYA (ZAM)	M	27		1
George CHILUFYA (ZAM)	D	23		1
Mika HUIKARI	M	12	(8)	1
Tero KEMPPAINEN	D	26	(1)	1
Marko KOIVURANTA	D	17	(3)	
Marek KRYNSKI (POL)	A	22	(3)	6
Iiro KYLMÄNEN	D		(4)	
Tuomo KÖNÖNEN	M	13	(13)	
Mika LUMIJVÄRI	M	21	(5)	3
Mordon MALITOLI (ZAM)	D	25		3
Jani MERILÄINEN	G	29		
Ilkka MÄKELÄ	D	26	(1)	2
Jacek PERZYK (POL)	M	11	(2)	
Zeddy SAILETI (ZAM)	M	29		6
Kimmo SAVOLAINEN	A	16	(11)	4
Vesa TAURIAINEN	A	18	(4)	2
Samuli YLIASKA	A	4	(5)	1

LEAGUE RESULTS 1999

25/04/99	FC Lahti	A	0-1	
02/05/99	KTP	A	1-1	Huikari
06/05/99	FC Jazz	A	0-2	
09/05/99	FC Jokerit	A	1-1	Krynski
16/05/99	VPS	H	3-2	Tauriainen, Savolainen 2
23/05/99	FC Haka	H	2-3	Malitoli, Savolainen
27/05/99	FC Inter	A	2-2	Malitoli, Lumijväri
13/06/99	TPV	H	2-2	Krynski, Saileti
17/06/99	TPS	H	1-0	Mäkelä
20/06/99	MyPa	A	1-1	Krynski
23/06/99	HJK	H	0-1	
27/06/99	VPS	A	0-0	
01/07/99	MyPa	H	2-1	Kemppainen (p), Lumijärvi
04/07/99	FC Inter	H	3-1	Chilufya G., Saileti 2
11/07/99	FC Haka	A	0-0	
21/07/99	FC Jokerit	H	3-0	Lumijärvi, Saileti, Krynski
25/07/99	FC Lahti	H	2-2	Mäkelä, Saileti
01/08/99	TPV	A	2-0	Tauriainen, Malitoli
09/08/99	TPS	A	1-4	Krynski
15/08/99	KTP	H	1-2	Savolainen
21/08/99	HJK	A	0-4	
29/08/99	FC Jazz	H	0-0	
11/09/99	FC Jokerit	A	0-4	
18/09/99	FC Inter	H	0-5	
22/09/99	MyPa	A	1-3	Yliaska
25/09/99	HJK	H	0-1	
02/10/99	FC Haka	A	0-2	
13/10/99	FC Jazz	H	2-0	Krynski, Chilufya D.
16/10/99	KTP	A	1-1	Saileti

TPS

CLUB DIRECTORY

Turun Palloseura
PL 701
20701 Turku
tel - (02) 2500000
fax - (02) 2731130
Year of Formation - 1922
President - Jouka Narvanmaa
Coach - Seppo Miettinen
Stadium - Kupittaa (10,000)

MAJOR HONOURS
League Championship - (8) 1928, 1939, 1941,
1949, 1968, 1971, 1972, 1975.
Domestic Cup - (2) 1991, 1994.

APPEARANCES 1999

	P	Ap	(s)	Gls
Jukka BJÖRN	M		(4)	
Marco CASAGRANDE	M	23	(1)	10
Tom ENBERG	A	16	(1)	1
Mikko HARJA	D	10	(4)	
Juha HERNE	M	4	(5)	1
Petri IHONEN	D	21		
Petri JALAVA	D	6	(7)	2
Petteri KAIJASILTA	A	10	(4)	3
Juha LALLUKKA	A	11	(9)	3
Kim LEHTONEN	M	12	(7)	1
Joni MELTORANTA	A	7	(10)	3
Olli MÄLKÖNEN	A	2	(1)	1
Vesa NOPONEN	M	3	(3)	
Tommi PAATTAKAINEN	G	11		
Markus PAIJA	D	25		
Saku PUHAKAINEN	A	25		12
Tuukka SALONEN	A	2	(4)	
Mikko SIREN	D	15	(2)	
Petri SULONEN	D	23	(1)	2
Jani TUOMALA	G	17		
Juha VIRKKI	D	20	(4)	1
Mika WALLDEN	M	20	(4)	
Hans WIKBERG	M	25	(3)	

LEAGUE RESULTS 1999

25/04/99	TPV	H	2-0	Kaijasilta 2
02/05/99	HJK	A	0-0	
06/05/99	VPS	H	2-1	Puhakainen, Kaijasilta
09/05/99	MyPa	A	1-3	Casagrande
16/05/99	FC Jokerit	H	1-1	Meltoranta
24/05/99	FC Inter	H	0-1	
27/05/99	FC Jazz	A	2-3	Casagrande, Jalava
30/05/99	FC Lahti	H	1-2	Enberg
14/06/99	KTP	A	0-2	
17/06/99	RoPS	A	0-1	
20/06/99	FC Haka	H	1-1	Puhakainen
27/06/99	TPV	A	1-0	Meltoranta
01/07/99	VPS	A	2-0	Puhakainen, Casagrande
04/07/99	KTP	H	0-3	
11/07/99	HJK	H	0-0	
18/07/99	FC Jazz	H	1-1	Casagrande
25/07/99	FC Inter	A	2-1	Casagrande (p), Meltoranta
02/08/99	FC Lahti	A	2-1	Casagrande (p), Lallukka
09/08/99	RoPS	H	4-1	Puhakainen 2, Casagrande (p),
				Lallukka
15/08/99	MyPa	H	2-3	Puhakainen 2
22/08/99	FC Haka	A	2-5	Sulonen, Virkki
27/08/99	FC Jokerit	A	1-1	Puhakainen
11/09/99	FC Lahti	A	3-0	Sulonen, Lallukka, Casagrande (p)
19/09/99	TPV	H	1-1	Herne
22/09/99	VPS	H	1-1	Casagrande (p)
25/09/99	VPS	A	2-1	Casagrande, Jalava
02/10/99	FC Lahti	H	0-0	
13/10/99	TPV	A	6-0	Lehtonen, Puhakainen 4, Mälkönen

TPV

CLUB DIRECTORY

TPV
Teiskontie 1 A 7, 33540 Tampere
tel - (03) 2617214 / fax - (03) 2617241
Year of Formation - 1995
President - Jukka Gustafsson
Manager - Miika Juntunen
Coach - Jan Mak
Stadium - Tammelan Stadion (6,000)

APPEARANCES 1999

	P	Ap	(s)	Gls
Sulley ABDALLAH	M	1		
John ALLEN (WAL)	A	18		1
Dragan BAJIC (YUG)	D	21		
Vasil BANOV (BUL)	D	2		
Bertalan BICSKEI (HUN)	G	2		
Gerry CREANEY (SCO)	A	1		
Zsolt GREZSAK (HUN)	M	3		
Sergei DIMITROV (BUL)	M	1		
Marko GRANHOLM	D	28		
Sándor HALÁSZ (HUN)	G	20		
Kai HAUTAKOSKI	M		(1)	
Sasu IIVONEN	M	3	(8)	
Strati ILIEV (BUL)	A	9		7
Mikko INNANEN	M	2		
Miika JUNTUNEN	M	23		1
Jari JÄVÄJÄ	A	3		1
Toni KALLIO	A	18		6
Jokke KANGASKORPI	A	2		
Olli KANGASLAHTI	A	2		
Dave KASTELEIN (HOL)	D	7		
Jean Didi KIMA (CMR)	A	6	(2)	2
Matti KORHONEN	M		(1)	
Sampo LIND	M	1	(1)	
Meelis LINDMAA (EST)	D	1		
Dariusz MARZEC (POL)	D	7	(3)	
David MOORE (ENG)	D	19	(2)	
Graeme MORRISON (SCO)	M	7		
Nenad NONKOVIC (YUG)	M	1	(1)	
Tuomo NUOJUA	D	19	(3)	
Mikko PALO	M		(2)	
Anssi PELLIKKA	M	7	(13)	
Antti POHJA	M	1		
Jarmo POSKIPARTA	D	7	(1)	
Velibor PUDAR (YUG)	G	6		
László REPÁSI (HUN)	D	1	(1)	
Marko RIIPI	M		(1)	
Sakari SAARINEN	M	17	(8)	
Srdjan SAVICEVIC (YUG)	A	7	(1)	1
Antal SIMON (HUN)	M	18		3
Dejan SRDIC (SLO)	M	2	(3)	
Jussi TERVANIEMI	M	1	(1)	
Jarno TUUNAINEN	D	1		
Ville VÄISÄNEN	A	10		1
Grzegorz WAGNER (POL)	M	3		
Toni YLINEN	M		(1)	

LEAGUE RESULTS 1999

25/04/99	TPS	A	0-2	
02/05/99	FC Jazz	H	1-3	Kallio
06/05/99	KTP	A	0-1	
09/05/99	HJK	H	0-1	
17/05/99	FC Haka	A	1-3	Kallio
23/05/99	FC Lahti	H	1-2	Kallio
27/05/99	VPS	A	1-3	Simon
30/05/99	FC Inter	H	0-0	
13/06/99	RoPS	A	2-2	Jäväjä, Väisänen (p)
16/06/99	MyPa	H	2-2	Kallio 2
23/06/99	FC Jokerit	A	0-1	
27/06/99	TPS	H	0-1	
01/07/99	HJK	A	0-2	
04/07/99	FC Lahti	A	1-1	Simon (p)
12/07/99	KTP	H	2-0	Allen, Kallio
18/07/99	FC Haka	H	0-3	
26/07/99	FC Jazz	A	0-2	
01/08/99	RoPS	H	0-2	
08/08/99	MyPa	A	1-1	Simon
15/08/99	VPS	H	1-3	Kima
23/08/99	FC Jokerit	H	0-5	
29/08/99	FC Inter	A	0-2	
12/09/99	VPS	H	3-1	Iliev 3
19/09/99	TPS	A	1-1	Iliev
22/09/99	FC Lahti	A	3-4	Savicevic, Iliev, Kima
26/09/99	FC Lahti	H	2-3	Iliev 2
03/10/99	VPS	A	1-3	Juntunen
13/10/99	TPS	H	0-6	

VPS

CLUB DIRECTORY

Vaasan Palloseura
Hartmanninkuja 4
65100 Vaasa
tel - (06) 3620705
fax - (06) 3620706
Year of Formation - 1924
President - Jukka Niemi
Coach - Sören Cratz; Kimmo Lipponen
(2000 - Jukka Ikäläinen)
Stadium - Hietalahti (5,000)

MAJOR HONOURS
League Championship - (2) 1945, 1948.

APPEARANCES 1999

	P	Ap	(s)	Gls
Björn ENGVIST (SWE)	D	13		3
Roy ESSANDOH (SCO)	A	18	(3)	3
Mikael GÖRANSSON (SWE)	M	15		1
Jyrki HUHTAMÄKI	M		(2)	
Teemu JAAKKOLA	D	16	(3)	
Jasse JALONEN	M	17	(2)	1
Petteri KAIJASILTA	A	9		5
Juuso KANGASKORPI	A	21	(2)	
Tommi KAUTONEN	D	25		1
Christoffer KLOO	D	6		
Petri KOKKO	M	25	(1)	2
Mathias LARSSON (SWE)	A	4	(4)	1
Rami LOUKE	A	1	(8)	
Tomas NYGÅRD	D	13	(4)	3
Björn NYMAN	D	1		
Mike PELTOLA	D	16		
Antti POHJA	A	10	(2)	3
Ville PRIHA	A	18	(3)	8
Henri SILLANPÄÄ	G	8	(2)	
Arto SIVONEN	D	20	(8)	
Björn STRINGHEIM (SWE)	G	18		
Christian SUND	M	2	(8)	
Marko SUOSTE	D	19	(1)	2
Vladimir SYKORA (SVK)	M	2	(7)	
Kimmo TARKKIO	M	9	(6)	1
Panu TOIVONEN	G	2		

LEAGUE RESULTS 1999

Date	Opponent		Score	Scorers
25/04/99	FC Jokerit	A	0-1	
02/05/99	MyPa	H	0-1	
06/05/99	TPS	A	1-2	Nygård
10/05/99	KTP	H	3-1	Kokko, Priha, Essandoh
16/05/99	RoPS	A	2-3	Priha, Göransson (p)
24/05/99	HJK	A	0-3	
27/05/99	TPV	H	3-1	Priha 3
30/05/99	FC Haka	H	0-1	
13/06/99	FC Lahti	A	1-2	Kokko
17/06/99	FC Jazz	H	1-0	Larsson
21/06/99	FC Inter	A	1-3	Suoste
27/06/99	RoPS	H	0-0	
01/07/99	TPS	H	0-2	
04/07/99	FC Jazz	A	1-0	Priha
11/07/99	FC Inter	H	0-2	
18/07/99	KTP	A	2-2	Tarkkio, Priha
25/07/99	FC Haka	A	0-2	
02/08/99	FC Jokerit	H	1-3	Priha
08/08/99	HJK	H	0-1	
15/08/99	TPV	A	3-1	Suoste, Kaijasilta, Enqvist
22/08/99	FC Lahti	H	2-1	Enqvist, Jalonen
29/08/99	MyPa	A	1-1	Enqvist
12/09/99	TPV	A	1-3	Essandoh
18/09/99	FC Lahti	H	2-2	Kaijasilta 2
22/09/99	TPS	A	1-1	Pohja
25/09/99	TPS	H	1-2	Kaijasilta
03/10/99	TPV	H	3-1	Kautonen, Nygård, Kaijasilta
13/10/99	FC Lahti	A	4-0	Nygård, Essandoh, Pohja 2

FRANCE

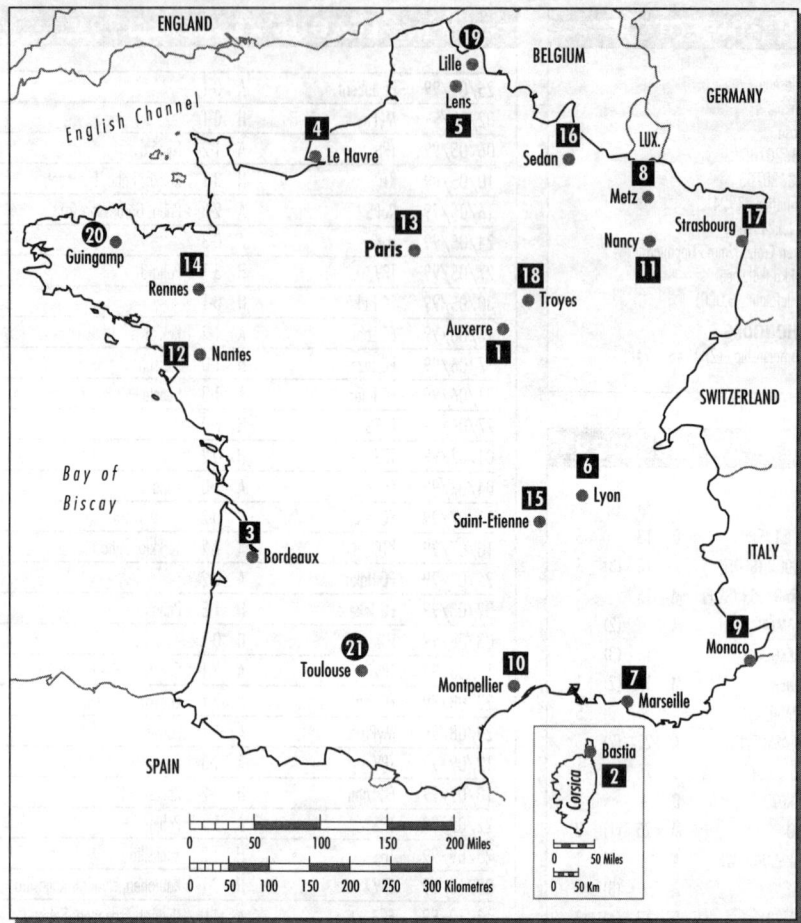

1	**AJ AUXERRE**	392	12	**FC NANTES**	403
2	**SC BASTIA**	393	13	**PARIS SAINT-GERMAIN**	404
3	**GIRONDINS DE BORDEAUX**	394	14	**STADE RENNAIS FC**	405
4	**LE HAVRE AC**	395	15	**AS SAINT-ETIENNE**	406
5	**RC LENS**	396	16	**CS SEDAN ARDENNES**	407
6	**OLYMPIQUE LYONNAIS**	397	17	**RC STRASBOURG**	408
7	**OLYMPIQUE MARSEILLE**	398	18	**A TROYES AC**	409
8	**FC METZ**	399		**Promoted clubs**	
9	**AS MONACO**	400	19	**LILLE OSC**	
10	**MONTPELLIER HSC**	401	20	**EN AVANT GUINGAMP**	
11	**AS NANCY-LORRAINE**	402	21	**TOULOUSE FC**	

AMATEURS CALAIS REACH CUP FINAL

Late late shows bring European glory

FEDERATION DIRECTORY

Fédération Française de Football
60 bis Avenue d'Iena, 75783 Paris cedex 16

tel - (1 44) 317300   Year of Formation - 1919
fax - (1 47) 208296   President - Claude Simonet
website - www.fff.fr   Secretary - Gérard Enault

Stadium - Stade de France, Saint-Denis (80,000)

France became the first reigning world champions to lift the European Championship and they did so with a team that was even better than the one which had claimed the World Cup on home soil two years.

Better, but no less lucky. While France were undeniably the most complete and most consistent of the 16 teams at Euro 2000, they certainly got all the breaks going. In each of their three knockout matches they needed a late stroke of fortune to see them through. In the quarter-final against Spain their 2-1 lead was preserved when Raúl blazed his last-minute penalty over the bar. In the semi-final against Portugal an eagle-eyed linesman spotted the hand-ball which led to Zinedine Zidane's late 'golden penalty'. And, just to prove that good as well as bad things come in threes, France saved themselves in the final with almost the last kick of the game as Sylvain Wiltord drilled his shot through the legs of an Italian defender.

France set the tone for the tournament with a mesmerising opening display against Denmark. They never quite matched the splendour of that 3-0 win in subsequent matches but the football they played was always of a very high standard, and in Zinedine Zidane they had a world-class player operating at the peak of his form.

The Juventus playmaker was the outstanding individual of the tournament, his supreme skill and vision serving to radiate confidence throughout the rest of the

LEAGUE CHAMPIONSHIP RESULTS 99/00

		1	2	3	4	5	6	7	8	9	10	11	12	13	14	15	16	17	18
1	AJ Auxerre		3-1	1-0	2-1	3-2	2-0	2-2	1-1	0-2	2-1	2-1	1-1	1-0	4-0	2-1	3-1	0-1	0-1
2	SC Bastia	2-0		1-1	1-1	2-0	3-0	0-0	0-0	1-0	1-0	1-1	2-1	1-2	4-2	4-0	1-0	3-0	5-0
3	Girondins de Bordeaux	1-0	3-2		3-0	1-2	1-3	2-1	0-0	3-2	2-0	2-1	3-0	1-1	1-0	1-2	1-1	3-0	4-0
4	Le Havre AC	0-0	2-2	3-0		1-1	0-1	0-0	1-0	1-4	2-1	0-1	0-1	3-1	0-1	1-0	2-1	0-1	2-0
5	RC Lens	2-1	4-0	3-3	4-0		4-3	0-0	1-0	1-0	1-0	0-1	1-2	3-2	1-1	0-2	0-3	3-0	0-1
6	Olympique Lyonnais	0-0	2-1	1-1	3-0	1-0		2-0	2-0	2-1	1-2	2-1	2-0	1-0	2-2	0-0	2-0	0-0	1-3
7	Olympique Marseille	0-1	1-1	0-2	2-0	1-2	0-1		1-1	4-2	0-0	2-2	1-1	4-1	1-1	3-3	3-0	4-1	1-0
8	FC Metz	3-0	1-1	2-1	3-0	0-0	0-1	2-0		1-1	2-2	2-2	2-1	1-3	0-0	1-1	1-1	0-0	3-1
9	AS Monaco	2-0	4-0	1-0	5-2	2-0	1-0	1-1	2-2		1-0	2-2	2-0	1-0	3-1	2-2	2-1	3-0	3-0
10	Montpellier HSC	2-0	1-1	2-2	0-0	1-1	2-2	3-1	0-1	2-3		1-0	3-0	0-1	1-2	0-1	1-1	1-1	2-2
11	AS Nancy-Lorraine	2-0	1-0	2-2	3-0	2-1	1-0	2-2	0-0	1-2	1-2		2-1	1-1	3-0	1-0	0-2	2-3	1-2
12	FC Nantes	3-1	1-1	0-1	1-0	0-1	6-1	0-0	1-3	0-3	3-0	2-0		0-4	3-0	0-1	1-0	3-1	3-0
13	Paris Saint-Germain	1-1	2-0	2-1	2-1	4-1	2-2	0-2	2-1	0-3	3-0	1-1	0-0		1-0	2-0	3-2	4-2	1-0
14	Stade Rennais FC	1-0	0-0	2-1	2-1	3-0	1-2	1-2	2-0	2-1	1-3	3-1	0-0	1-3		4-1	5-0	2-1	2-2
15	AS Saint-Etienne	0-0	1-1	1-2	3-3	0-2	1-1	5-1	2-0	3-1	5-4	2-1	0-2	1-1	1-0		2-3	0-1	1-0
16	CS Sedan Ardennes	1-1	2-0	0-1	0-1	0-0	2-0	2-2	0-2	2-1	2-1	3-1	0-0	1-1	2-1	3-2		2-1	2-1
17	RC Strasbourg	1-3	2-0	2-2	0-1	1-0	4-2	3-1	1-1	3-2	2-0	0-2	3-2	1-1	2-1	0-1	1-1		2-0
18	A Troyes AC	2-0	1-0	2-0	3-1	0-1	1-2	1-2	2-2	1-4	2-1	2-0	1-0	2-2	1-0	0-1	0-2	2-1	

LEAGUE CHAMPIONSHIP FINAL TABLE 99/00

		Pd	Home					Away					Total					PT	GD
			W	D	L	F	A	W	D	L	F	A	W	D	L	F	A		
1	AS Monaco	34	13	4	0	37	11	7	1	9	32	27	20	5	9	69	38	65	31
2	Paris Saint-Germain	34	11	4	2	30	17	5	6	6	24	23	16	10	8	54	40	58	14
3	Olympique Lyonnais	34	10	5	2	24	11	6	3	8	21	31	16	8	10	45	42	56	3
4	Girondins de Bordeaux	34	11	3	3	32	15	4	6	7	20	25	15	9	10	52	40	54	12
5	RC Lens	34	9	3	5	28	19	5	4	8	14	22	14	7	13	42	41	49	1
6	AS Saint-Etienne	34	7	5	5	28	23	6	4	7	18	24	13	9	12	46	47	48	-1
7	CS Sedan Ardennes	34	9	5	3	24	16	4	4	9	19	28	13	9	12	43	44	48	-1
8	AJ Auxerre	34	11	3	3	29	16	2	5	10	8	23	13	8	13	37	39	47	-2
9	RC Strasbourg	34	9	4	4	28	20	4	3	10	14	32	13	7	14	42	52	46	-10
10	SC Bastia	34	11	5	1	32	8	0	7	10	11	31	11	12	11	43	39	45	4
11	FC Metz	34	6	9	2	24	15	3	8	6	14	18	9	17	8	38	33	44	5
12	FC Nantes	34	9	2	6	27	17	3	5	9	12	23	12	7	15	39	40	43	-1
13	Stade Rennais FC	34	10	3	4	32	18	2	4	11	12	30	12	7	15	44	48	43	-4
14	A Troyes AC	34	9	2	6	23	19	4	2	11	13	33	13	4	17	36	52	43	-16
15	Olympique Marseille	34	6	7	4	28	19	3	8	6	17	26	9	15	10	45	45	42	0
16	AS Nancy-Lorraine	34	8	4	5	25	18	3	5	9	18	27	11	9	14	43	45	42	-2
17	Le Havre AC	34	7	4	6	18	15	2	3	12	12	37	9	7	18	30	52	34	-22
18	Montpellier HSC	34	4	8	5	22	19	3	2	12	17	31	7	10	17	39	50	31	-11

team. France were well-manned in every department, and they also had splendid strength in depth. It was largely the same team as the France '98 vintage. The famous back five of Fabien Barthez, Lilian Thuram, Marcel Desailly, Laurent Blanc and Bixente Lizarazu were every bit as resilient and reliable as they had been two years earlier. Didier Deschamps, the captain, who during the course of the tournament became the first French international to reach a century of caps, was his usual industrious, undemonstrative self, ably supprted by Patrick Vieira in the centre of midfield. Youri Djorkaeff maintained his impressive goalscoring record, and Zidane, well, he was Zidane, the arch-schemer, the sublime creator, the man through whom almost every productive French attack was channelled.

Zidane was of course fortunate to have in front of him two of the speediest young strikers in the game. Nicolas Anelka, one of only four changes from the World Cup squad, was to have a modest tournament, but Thierry Henry was the best striker on view. A threat at all times with his pace and direct running, he scored three goals and proved to be the final piece in the French jigsaw.

France also had two tremendous forwards in reserve. Sylvain Wiltord and David Trezeguet were the French saviours in the final, and it is fair to say that neither player will ever score a more important goal. The

Thierry Henry gave the national side the cutting edge they sought in front of goal.

manner of the victory against Italy ensured celebrations back in France that were every bit as intense and unrestrained as those of two years earlier. Within the space of a few minutes Wiltord and Trezeguet transported the French fans from deep despair to utter euphoria. It was the perfect escape to victory, a climax to ensure the wildest, most feverish outpouring of emotion.

One man who remained amazingly calm amidst the frenzy of celebration was France's Cup-winning coach, Roger Lemerre. He had been on a hiding to nothing when he succeeded Aimé Jacquet after the

NATIONAL TEAM APPEARANCES 99/00

Coach - Roger LEMERRE

Player	NIR	UKR	ARM	ISL	CRO	POL	SCO	SLO	CRO	JPN	MAR	DEN	CZE	HOL	ESP	POR	ITA	Cps	Gls
Fabien BARTHEZ (28/06/71) - AS Monaco	G	G	G			G		G	G	G		G	G		G	G	G	38	-
Lilian THURAM (01/01/72) - Parma (ITA)	D	D	D	D	D	D	D	D	D	D	D	D	D		D	D	D	62	2
Laurent BLANC (19/11/65) - Inter (ITA)	D	D	D	D		D46	D	D	D75	D		D	D		D	D	D	95	16
Marcel DESAILLY (07/09/68) - Chelsea (ENG)	D65	D	D	D	D	D	D		D	D68	D	D	D	D	D	D	D	72	2
Bixente LIZARAZU (09/12/69) - FC Bayern München (GER)	D56	D	D	D		D	D	D	D	D	D		D			D	D85	58	2
Patrick VIEIRA (23/06/76) - Arsenal (ENG)	M84	M		s90	M	s58	s60	M	M	s46	s46	M	s58	M	M90	M	M	30	-
Alain BOGHOSSIAN (27/10/70) - Parma (ITA)	M		M90	M73														22	2
Robert PIRES (29/01/73) - Olympique Marseille	M	s69		M60	s58	s71	M62	M46	M46					M		s87	s85	38	5
Johan MICOUD (24/07/73) - Girondins de Bordeaux	M			M85		s46	s46	s60			M66				M			7	-
Sylvain WILTORD (10/05/74) - Girondins de Bordeaux	A56		A66	A90		A58	s46		A	A46	s86	s82	s90	A80		s71	s57	18	6
Lilian LASLANDES (04/09/71) - Girondins de Bordeaux	A77	s52	A	A63														7	3
Vincent CANDELA (24/10/73) - Roma (ITA)	s56				D			s82					D		D	D		23	1
Laurent ROBERT (21/05/75) - Paris Saint-Germain	s56		s66															2	-
Frank LEBOEUF (22/01/68) - Chelsea (ENG)	s65						D	s46	D	s75	s68	D			D			30	3
Tony VAIRELLES (10/04/73) - Olympique Lyonnais	s77						s90	s60	s74		s62							8	1
Frédéric DEHU (01/12/72) - FC Barcelona (ESP)	s84	s72		s73														4	-
Christian KAREMBEU (03/12/70) - Real Madrid (ESP)		M	M										D	D				44	1
Didier DESCHAMPS (15/10/68) - Chelsea (ENG)	M	M	M	s85	M	M60	M62	M	M46	s66	M	M	s90		M	M	M	101	4
Youri DJORKAEFF (09/03/68) - 1.FC Kaiserslautern (GER)	M69	M	M	s46	M74	M46				s46	M61	M58	s46	s68	M		M75	67	26
Zinedine ZIDANE (23/06/72) - Juventus (ITA)		M	M72	M	M46	M		M	M82	M89	s61	M	M		M	M	M	59	16
Nicolas ANELKA (14/03/79) - Real Madrid (ESP)	A52									s76	A	A82	A54	s80	s81	A71		17	4
Bernard LAMA (07/04/63) - Paris Saint-Germain					G						G			G				43	-
David TREZEGUET (15/10/77) - AS Monaco				s63		A		s46	s46	A76		A				s105	s75	21	8
Stéphane PORATO (19/09/73) - Olympique Marseille				G														1	-
Stéphane GUIVARC'H (06/09/70) - AJ Auxerre				A46														14	1
Florian MAURICE (20/01/74) - Olympique Marseille				s46														6	1
Emmanuel PETIT (22/09/70) - Arsenal (ENG)						M58	M	s62	M46	M	s75	M	M46			M87		41	3
Ulrich RAME (19/09/72) - Girondins de Bordeaux							G											2	-
Ludovic GIULY (10/07/76) - AS Monaco						M46												1	-
Christophe DUGARRY (24/03/72) - Girondins de Bordeaux						A71	A46		s46	A86		s54	M68	M		M57		43	7
Thierry HENRY (17/08/77) - Arsenal (ENG)							A	A46	A60	s89	A75	A	A90		A81	A105	A	21	8

World Cup win, but his diligent work ensured a seamless transition. The team he guided to Euro 2000 glory was largely an inherited one but he certainly merited his fair share of the credit for France's triumph, not least in the final, when both goals were created and scored by players he had boldly introduced as substitutes.

Lemerre now has two years free of competitive pressures in which to prepare 'Les Bleus' for the World Cup defence in the Far East. He will have to make do without Blanc and Deschamps, both of whom decided that Euro 2000 would be a fitting swansong to their international careers. But the rest of the team is likely to remain intact and that should ensure that France will once again be one of the favourites in 2002. No European team has ever won the World Cup outside their own continent, but having won their first major tournament on foreign soil in Belgium and Holland, Zidane, Henry and co. will be unburdened by history as they bid for a glorious and unprecedented 'treble' in Japan and Korea.

If the present trend is maintained, France's 2002 World Cup side could well be made up entirely of expatriates. After Euro 2000, Barthez, Wiltord and Trezeguet joined fellow squad members Robert Pires and Johan Micoud in leaving France for a foreign club, with only Anelka tipping the scales in the opposite direction by quitting Real Madrid in a French-record £20m transfer to Paris Saint-Germain.

Despite his troubled year in Spain, Anelka is being hailed as the man who can reignite both PSG and the French league in general. Although average crowds in the First Division during 1999/2000 were up from 19,807 to 22,324, the French domestic game still pales in comparison to the more glamourous, affluent leagues of Italy, England and Spain. Very few top-class stars choose the homeland of the world and European champions as their preferred destination, and with France's best homegrown players now abandoning the ship, a reduction in standards is the inevitable consequence.

There was nothing sub-standard about Monaco in the 1999/2000 season. The team from the Principality may have suffered the odd upset or two in Cup competitions but in the league they were imperious. They romped to a seventh French championship title, leaving the opposition for dead in the middle section of the campaign during which they won 12 games out of 15 to storm into an unassailable lead.

It was no contest. While all of their rivals went through rough patches, Monaco kept firmly on course. They claimed big wins at important times, slamming PSG

INTERNATIONAL HONOURS

World Cup Finals appearances: 1930, 1938 (2nd round), 1954, 1958 (3rd), 1966, 1978, 1982 (4th), 1986 (3rd), 1998 (Winners)

European Championship appearances: 1960 (4th), 1964, 1968, 1984 (Winners), 1992, 1996 (semi-finals), 2000 (Winners)

European Club Competitions

Champions' Cup	Olympique Marseille (1993)
Cup-winners' Cup	Paris Saint-Germain (1996)

3-0 in the Parc des Princes at the end of September and then doing the 'double' over the bigshots from the capital with a 1-0 victory in early February. Another significant win was the one at home to Auxerre on the first day of December. Two goals from the team's clever Argentinian midfielder Marcelo Gallardo enabled Monaco to win this game in hand 2-0 and take a five-point lead at the halfway point. From then on Monaco increased their lead at a steady rate, peaking in mid-February when they went 13 points clear.

A sudden loss of form on their travels in the closing weeks delayed Monaco's coronation until round 30 when a last-minute equaliser at home to relegation strugglers Nancy made mathematically certain of their victory. The title celebrations were led by unsung coach Claude Puel, the club's former long-serving midfielder who had also won the championship as a Monaco player in both 1982 and 1988.

Monaco were an attractive team to watch. Their great strength was in attack where, well served by Gallardo, the twin strikeforce of Trezeguet and Marco Simone consistently found the net. Monaco had far and away the best attack in the league, and of the team's 69-goal total 22 were supplied by Trezeguet and 21 by Simone, with many of them entering the net in spectacular fashion. Goalkeeper Barthez was injured in mid-season but he was barely missed thanks to the capabilities of the outfield defenders, foremost among them young centre-back Philippe Christanval, who just missed out on Euro 2000, and right-back Willy Sagnol. The enterprising nature of Monaco's play even seduced the normally football-shy locals, resulting in average home gates of over 10,000.

Big-city Paris Saint-German, of course, drew many more fans than that - 43,185 on average - but the fare served up in the Parc des Princes was not as sumptuous. PSG actually lost fewer games than the champions (eight as opposed to nine) but they won less than half of their matches and that was why they trailed in seven points behind.

Even so, most PSG fans were reasonably happy with second place, which brought with it a guarantee of Champions' League participation. It was certainly a vast improvement on the previous season, when the club drifted from one crisis to another and used three different coaches. The last of that trio, Philippe Bergeroo, kept his place for the duration this time and did a fine job, especially in restoring harmony and humility to a team in which the most impressive performers were low-profile non-internationals such as Eric Rabesandratana, Pierre Ducrocq and Brazilian striker Christian. Veteran goalkeeper Bernard Lama also had a splendid farewell season for the club, while newcomers Ali Benarbia and Laurent Robert both added an extra dimension in attack, the former with his subtle passing, the latter with his ferocious long-range shooting. Robert was on fire at the end of the season, scoring five goals in as many games to help PSG into that cherished runners-up spot.

The third Champions' League place went, for the second year running, to Lyon. Bernard Lacombe's team suffered an unexpected setback at the start of the season when they were comprehensively beaten by Slovenian side Maribor in the Champions' League qualifiers. This was a major jolt to the ambitions of a club which had spent heavily on three new players - French internationals Tony Vairelles and Pierre Laigle and, for a record French fee, Brazilian striker Sonny Ânderson - and was also doing well domestically at the time.

Because of those reinforcements and the generous financial support of the club's new sponsors, Lyon were widely tipped as pre-season favourites. For much of the first half

of the season they were well in contention for that first ever championship title, but once Monaco broke clear, they were unable to give chase and their season eventually petered out amidst a welter of tawdry performances away from home, the worst of which resulted in a 4-0 defeat in Bremen and an inglorious exit from the UEFA Cup. Lyon did eventually rescue their season by finishing third, and there was a pleasant bonus for Ânderson as he claimed the top-scorer crown, but for coach Lacombe there was to be no mercy. He was sacked and replaced by the club's technical director, Jacques Santini.

Lacombe's former club Bordeaux had a poor season in defence of their title. Only two points separated them from a Champions' League place, but fourth spot was about as high as they deserved to finish at the end of a campaign in which the distraction of competing in the Champions' League took its toll. The Girondins retained their title-winning attacking trio of Wiltord, Micoud and Lilian Laslandes, but although all three players had their moments, the goals did not flow as readily as before. Bordeaux succeeded in reaching the second group phase of the Champions' League but an awful run of five games without a goal eroded their confidence and ensured that they went no further.

TOP SCORERS

23	Sonny ÂNDERSON (Olympique Lyonnais)
22	David TREZEGUET (AS Monaco)
21	Marco SIMONE (AS Monaco)
16	CHRISTIAN (Paris Saint-Germain)
	Shabani NONDA (Stade Rennais FC)
15	Tony CASCARINO (AS Nancy-Lorraine)
	ALEX DIAS (AS Saint-Etienne)
14	Stéphane GUIVARC'H (AJ Auxerre)
	Lilian LASLANDES (Girondins de Bordeaux)
13	Antoine SIBIERSKI (FC Nantes)
	Sylvain WILTORD (Girondins de Bordeaux)

NATIONAL TEAM RESULTS 99/00

18/08/99	Northern Ireland	A	Belfast	1-0	Laslandes (67)
04/09/99	Ukraine (ECQ)	A	Kiev	0-0	
08/09/99	Armenia (ECQ)	A	Yerevan	3-2	Djorkaeff (45p), Zidane (67), Laslandes (74)
09/10/99	Iceland (ECQ)	H	Saint-Denis	3-2	Dadason (17og), Djorkaeff (38),
					Trezeguet (71)
13/11/99	Croatia	H	Saint-Denis	3-0	Pires (47), Maurice (69), Vairelles (72)
23/02/00	Poland	H	Saint-Denis	1-0	Zidane (88)
29/03/00	Scotland	A	Glasgow	2-0	Wiltord (53), Henry (88)
26/04/00	Slovenia	H	Saint-Denis	3-2	Trezeguet (63, 90), Blanc (76)
28/05/00	Croatia	A	Zagreb	2-0	Pires (25), Trezeguet (70)
04/06/00	Japan	N	Casablanca	2-2	(4-2 on pens.) Zidane (60), Djorkaeff (74)
06/06/00	Morocco	A	Casablanca	5-1	Henry (26), Djorkaeff (56p), Dugarry (75),
					Anelka (84), Wiltord (90)
11/06/00	Denmark (ECF)	N	Bruges	3-0	Blanc (16), Henry (65), Wiltord (90)
16/06/00	Czech Republic (ECF)	N	Bruges	2-1	Henry (7), Djorkaeff (60)
21/06/00	Holland (ECF)	A	Amsterdam	2-3	Dugarry (8), Trezeguet (30)
25/06/00	Spain (ECF)	N	Bruges	2-1	Zidane (32), Djorkaeff (44)
28/06/00	Portugal (ECF)	N	Brussels	2-1	Henry (51), Zidane (117p)
02/07/00	Italy (ECF)	N	Rotterdam	2-1	Wiltord (90), Trezeguet (103)

EUROPEAN CUPS 99/00

CHAMPIONS' CUP
● GIRONDINS DE BORDEAUX
Champions' League

1st match SPARTA PRAHA (CZE)
A 0-0
> Ramé; Grenet, Afanou, Saveljic, Alicarte; Martins (Battles 90), Diabaté, Rouvière. Micoud; Wiltord, Laslandes.

2nd match WILLEM II (HOL)
H 3-2 Victoria (16og), Laslandes (21), Feindouno (83)
> Ramé; Grenet, Saveljic, Afanou, Bonnissel; Rouvière, Diabaté, Micoud, Martins (Battles 63); Laslandes, Wiltord (Feindouno 73).

3rd match SPARTAK MOSKVA (RUS)
H 2-1 Wiltord (9), Micoud (56)
> Ramé; Grenet, Afanou, Saveljic, Bonnissel; Martins (Battles 72), Pavon, Diabaté, Micoud; Laslandes, Wiltord (Feindouno 86).

4th match SPARTAK MOSKVA (RUS)
A 2-1 Micoud (21), Wiltord (76)
> Ramé; Grenet, Afanou, Alicarte. Bonnissel; Martins (Rouvière 76), Diabaté, Pavon, Micoud; Laslandes, Wiltord (Battles 87).

5th match SPARTA PRAHA (CZE)
H 0-0
> Ramé; Jemmali, Alicarte, Saveljic, Bonnissel; Diabaté (Battles 66), Pavon, Rouvière, Martins (Micoud 76); Laslandes, Wiltord (Zanotti 90).

6th match WILLEM II (HOL)
A 0-0
> Richert; Jemmali, Afanou, Alicarte, Bonnissel; Rouvière, Diabaté, Battles (Feindouno 68), Martins (Grenet 83); Micoud; Wiltord.

7th match VALENCIA CF (ESP)
A 0-3
> Ramé; Grenet, Saveljic, Afanou, Alicarte; Martins (Ziani 58), Pavon, Diabaté (Rouvière 86), Micoud; Laslandes, Wiltord.

8th match FIORENTINA (ITA)
H 0-0
> Ramé; Grenet, Afanou, Saveljic, Alicarte; Martins (Rouvière 84), Diabaté, Pavon, Micoud; Laslandes, Wiltord.

9th match MANCHESTER UNITED (ENG)
A 0-2
> Ramé; Grenet, Afanou, Alicarte, Bonnissel; Martins (Ziani 65), Diabaté, Pavon, Micoud; Laslandes, Wiltord.

10th match MANCHESTER UNITED (ENG)
H 1-2 Pavon (9)
> Ramé; Grenet, Saveljic, Afanou, Bonnissel; Pavon, Battles (Diabaté 9), Micoud, Ziani (Rouvière 61); Laslandes, Wiltord (Feindouno 82).

11th match VALENCIA CF (ESP)
H 1-4 Wiltord (54)
> Ramé; Grenet, Saveljic, Alicarte, Bonnissel; Pavon, Diabaté (Afanou 50), Ziani, Micoud (Rouvière 78); Wiltord, Feindouno (Colucci 63).

12th match FIORENTINA (ITA)
A 3-3 Wiltord (5), Zanotti (87), Battles (90)
> Ramé; Battles, Diabaté, Pavon, Alicarte, Bonnissel; Rouvière (Colucci 73), Micoud (Zanotti 80), Ziani (Sahnoun 59); Wiltord, Laslandes.

● OLYMPIQUE LYONNAIS
Qualifying round NK MARIBOR (SLO)
H 0-1
> Coupet; Bak, Fournier, Devaux; Malbranque, Violeau, Dhorasoo, Linarès (Kanouté 68); Ânderson, Caveglia, Vairelles.
A 0-2
> Coupet; Carteron, Bak, Fournier, Blanc (Delmotte 51); Violeau, Malbranque (Kanouté 56), Dhorasoo; Ânderson, Caveglia (Laigle 35), Vairelles.

● OLYMPIQUE MARSEILLE
Champions' League

1st match SK STURM GRAZ (AUT)
H 2-0 Pires (9), Ravanelli (33)
> Porato; Pérez, Gallas, Berizzo, Blondeau; Brando, Pires, Luccin, Dalmat (Belmadi 76); Ravanelli (Keita 88), Maurice (Diawara 82).

2nd match CROATIA ZAGREB (CRO)
A 2-1 Bakayoko (5), Pérez (77)
> Porato; Pérez, Gallas, Berizzo, Blondeau (Brando 58); Keita (Ravanelli 67), Pires, Issa, Luccin, Dalmat; Bakayoko (Diawara 86).

3rd match MANCHESTER UNITED (ENG)
A 1-2 Bakayoko (40)
> Porato; Pérez, Gallas, Fischer, Blondeau; Brando, Issa (Belmadi 82), Luccin (De la Peña 77), Dalmat; Ravanelli (Pires 62), Bakayoko.

4th match MANCHESTER UNITED (ENG)
H 1-0 Gallas (69)
> Porato; Pérez, Berizzo, Gallas, Blondeau; Issa, Brando (De la Peña 64), Pires, Luccin, Dalmat (Reina 88); Ravanelli (Maurice 74).

5th match SK STURM GRAZ (AUT)
A 2-3 Dugarry (53, 78)
> Porato; Pérez, Berizzo, Gallas, Blondeau; Pires, Issa (De la Peña 46; Dugarry 51), Luccin, Dalmat; Maurice (Reina 70), Ravanelli.

6th match CROATIA ZAGREB (CRO)
H 2-2 Bakayoko (53), Diawara (89)
> Porato; Pérez, Berizzo, Luccin, Reina; Montenegro (Dalmat 59), Brando, Belmadi, Dugarry (Pires 66); Diawara, Bakayoko (Ravanelli 78).

7th match LAZIO (ITA)
H 0-2
> Porato; Pérez (Maurice 67), Berizzo, Fischer, Gallas; Brando, Luccin, Pires, Dalmat; Dugarry, Diawara (Ravanelli 58).

8th match FEYENOORD (HOL)
A 0-3
> Porato; Berizzo (Issa 46), Gallas, Fischer, Pérez, Pires (Martin 69); Brando, Luccin, Dalmat; Maurice (Bakayoko 80), Dugarry.

9th match CHELSEA (ENG)
H 1-0 Pires (16)
> Trévisan; Blondeau, Cyprien, Luccin, Abardonado; Pires, Brando, Leroy, Dalmat; Pouget (De la Peña 72); Bakayoko (Moses 90).

EUROPEAN CUPS 99/00 (CONTINUED)

10th match CHELSEA (ENG)
A 0-1
Trévisan; Pérez (Fischer 38), Cyprien (De la Peña 66), Luccin, Abardonado, Dalmat; Pires, Brando, Leroy; Bakayoko, Pouget.

11th match LAZIO (ITA)
A 1-5   Leroy (50)
Porato; Abardonado, Luccin, Fischer (Martini 46); Martin (Bakayoko 46), Brando, Leroy, Dalmat; Pires, Pouget (Moses 61), De la Peña.

12th match FEYENOORD (HOL)
H 0-0
Porato; Fischer, Martini, Luccin, Abardonado, Reina; Leroy, Brando, Keita (Gavanon 90); De la Peña, Bakayoko (Moses 62).

UEFA CUP
● AS MONACO
1st round ST. JOHNSTONE (SCO)
H 3-0   Simone (69, 90), Trezeguet (73)
Barthez; Sagnol, Marquez, Christanval, Léonard (Legwinski 84); Da Costa, Lamouchi (Riise 56), Giuly (N'Diaye 83), Gallardo; Trezeguet, Simone.
A 3-3   Prso (9), Riise (25), Legwinski (69)
Barthez; Sagnol, Irles, Marquez, Léonard; N'Diaye (Giuly 60), Legwinski, Lamouchi (Gallardo 46), Riise; Simone (Trezeguet 46), Prso.

2nd round WIDZEW LODZ (POL)
A 1-1   Giuly (40)
Sylva; Contreras, Marquez, Christanval, Léonard; Lamouchi, Riise; N'Diaye, Giuly, Trezeguet (Djetou 78), Farnerud (Prso 55).
H 2-0   Lamouchi (50), Trezeguet (85)
Sylva; Sagnol (Contreras 78), Djetou, Christanval, Léonard; Giuly (N'Diaye 75), Lamouchi, Riise, Gallardo; Simone, Trezeguet.

3rd round AEK (GRE)
A 2-2   Giuly (26), Simone (78)
Aubry; Sagnol, Christanval, Marquez, Contreras; Giuly, Lamouchi, Djetou, Gallardo; Eloi (Prso 46; Da Costa 80), Simone.
H 1-0   Simone (32)
Barthez (Sylva 28); Sagnol, Christanval (Di Tommaso 64), Marquez, Léonard (Riise 49); Lamouchi, Da Costa, Djetou, Gallardo; Trezeguet, Simone.

4th round RCD MALLORCA (ESP)
A 1-4   Simone (2)
Barthez; Sagnol, Djetou, Marquez, Contreras; Giuly (Christanval 46), Da Costa, Lamouchi, Gallardo; Trezeguet (Diao 60), Simone (Prso 78).
H 1-0   Simone (33)
Barthez; Contreras (Riise 64), Christanval, Djetou, Léonard (Prso 84); Giuly (N'Diaye 68), Lamouchi, Da Costa, Gallardo; Trezeguet, Simone.

● FC NANTES
1st round IONIKOS (GRE)
A 3-1   Lièvre (56), Monterrubio (67, 83)
Landreau; Chanelet, Gillet, Fabbri, Savinaud (Piocelle 74), Lièvre; Carrière, Olembé, Sibierski (Piocelle 75); Da Rocha, Monterrubio (Ahamada 85).
H 1-0   Da Rocha (48)
Landreau; Lièvre (Devineau 81), Chanelet, Gillet, Olembé; Da Rocha, Carrière, Piocelle, Leroy; Sibierski, Monterrubio (Bustos 69).

2nd round INTER BRATISLAVA (SVK)
A 3-0   Sibierski (26p), Da Rocha (35), Carrière (86)
Landreau; Chanelet, Savinaud, Gillet, Lièvre; Carrière, Sibierski, Piocelle; Da Rocha, Ahamada (Leroy 84), Bustos.
H 4-0   Sibierski (49), Monterrubio (60), Devineau (74), Da Rocha (82)
Landreau; Chanelet, Savinaud, Gillet, Lièvre; Carrière (Devineau 68), Piocelle, Olembé, Sibierski (Macé 78); Da Rocha, Monterrubio (Bustos 63).

3rd round ARSENAL (ENG)
A 0-3
Landreau; Chanelet, Savinaud, Gillet, Deroff (Olembé 42); Carrière, Sibierski, Piocelle, Leroy; Ahamada (Touré 54), Monterrubio (Gope-Fenepej 70).
H 3-3   Sibierski (13, 58), Vahirua (79)
Landreau; Olembé (Lièvre 46), Savinaud, Gillet, Leroy; Touré, Carrière, Berson (Fenillat 68), Bustos; Da Rocha, Sibierski (Vahirua 77).

● MONTPELLIER HSC
1st round CRVENA ZVEZDA BEOGRAD (YUG)
A 1-0   Loko (3)
Cassard; Rodriguez, Silvestre, Decroix, Ferrier (Dos Santos 58); Serredszum, Mahouvé, Sorlin (Fugier 46), Barbosa (Maoulida 65); Loko, Ouédec.
H 2-2   Ouédec (35), Loko (52)
Cassard; Fugier, Silvestre, Decroix, Ferrier, Dos Santos (Rodriguez 78); Mahouvé (Serredszum 68), Delaye, Barbosa; Loko, Ouédec (Sorlin 70).

2nd round RC DEPORTIVO (ESP)
A 1-3   Delaye (6)
Cassard; Rodriguez, Decroix, Silvestre, Ferrier (Barbosa 58); Fugier, Mahouvé, Dos Santos, Delaye (Gourvennec 43); Ouédec, Loko (Maoulida 67).
H 0-2
Cassard; Rodriguez, Silvestre, Decroix, Ferrier; Sorlin, Mahouvé, Barbosa (Fugier 79); Gourvennec; Loko, Ouédec (Maoulida 68).

● OLYMPIQUE LYONNAIS
1st round HJK (FIN)
A 1-0   Vairelles (16)
Coupet; Carteron, Fournier, Laville, Bréchet; Violeau, Linarès, Laigle, Dhorasoo; Vairelles, Ânderson (Malbranque 72).
H 5-1   Ânderson (11), Blanc (15), Linarès (17), Vairelles (71, 86)
Coupet; Carteron, Laville, Bak, Blanc; Violeau, Linarès (Vairelles 71), Laigle (Delmotte 30), Dhorasoo; Ânderson (Kanouté 59), Caveglia.

2nd round CELTIC (SCO)
H 1-0   Blanc (64)
Coupet; Carteron, Bréchet, Laville, Blanc; Bak (Malbranque 53), Violeau, Delmotte, Dhorasoo; Ânderson, Vairelles (Caveglia 75).
A 1-0   Vairelles (17)
Coupet; Carteron, Laville, Bak, Blanc (Devaux 78); Linarès, Violeau, Delmotte; Dhorasoo (Malbranque 65); Vairelles, Ânderson (Uras 87).

3rd round SV WERDER BREMEN (GER)
H 3-0   Ânderson (13, 45), Vairelles (77)
Coupet; Carteron, Laville (Bréchet 82), Bak, Blanc; Linarès, Violeau, Dhorasoo, Delmotte; Ânderson (Kanouté 90), Vairelles (Uras 83).
A 0-4   (aet)
Coupet; Carteron, Bak, Bréchet (Malbranque 85), Blanc (Uras 62); Linarès (Kanouté 78), Violeau, Dhorasoo, Delmotte; Ânderson, Vairelles.

EUROPEAN CUPS 99/00 (CONTINUED)

● **RC LENS**

1st round MACCABI TEL-AVIV (ISR)
A 2-2 Sakho (39), Job (54)
Warmuz; Sikora, Coulibaly, Ismaël, Rool; Coridon (Lachor 82), Blanchard, Nyarko, Brunel; Job, Sakho (Bogaczyk 82).
H 2-1 Nouma (77), Delporte (80)
Warmuz; Sikora, Ismaël, Nyarko, Rool; Blanchard, Dacourt, Coridon (Sakho 56), Brunel (Delporte 68); Job, Nouma.

2nd round VITESSE (HOL)
H 4-1 Brunel (3), Nouma (17), Nyarko (75), Blanchard (87)
Warmuz; Sikora (Barul 67), Pierre-Fanfan, Ismaël, Lachor; Blanchard, Nyarko, Dacourt (Coridon 77); Rool; Nouma, Brunel (Job 90).
A 1-1 Blanchard (90)
Warmuz; Sikora, Ismaël, Pierre-Fanfan, Lachor; Blanchard, Nyarko, Dacourt, Coridon; Nouma (Bogaczyk 62), Brunel.

3rd round 1.FC KAISERSLAUTERN (GER)
H 1-2 Schjønberg (84og)
Warmuz; Sikora, Pierre-Fanfan, Ismaël, Rool; Blanchard, Nyarko, Coridon (Moreira 82), Dacourt (Job 46); Brunel; Nouma (Sakho 46).
A 4-1 Job (20, 40), Strasser (56og), Nyarko (90)
Warmuz; Sikora, Pierre-Fanfan, Ismaël, Lachor; Nyarko, Blanchard, Rool; Nouma (Coridon 83), Job, Brunel.

4th round ATLETICO MADRID (ESP)
A 2-2 Dacourt (16, 78)
Warmuz; Sikora, Pierre-Fanfan, Ismaël, Queudrue; Blanchard, Dacourt, Nyarko, Coridon, Brunel (Moreira 62); Nouma (Sakho 74).
H 4-2 Nouma (29, 53), Sakho (37), Brunel (71)
Warmuz; Sikora, Ismaël, Pierre-Fanfan, Queudrue; Blanchard, Coridon (Lachor 83), Dacourt, Brunel; Sakho (Moreira 72), Nouma (Rodriguez 86).

Quarter-final RC CELTA (ESP)
A 0-0
Warmuz; Sikora, Ismaël, Pierre-Fanfan, Queudrue (Job 87); Blanchard, Nyarko, Dacourt, Brunel (Lachor 82); Sakho (Moreira 65), Nouma.
H 2-1 Ismaël (62p), Nouma (72)
Warmuz; Coly, Pierre-Fanfan, Ismaël, Queudrue; Nyarko, Blanchard, Dacourt, Brunel; Sakho, Nouma.

Semi-final ARSENAL (ENG)
A 0-1
Warmuz; Sikora, Coly, Mawéné, Queudrue; Moreira (Sakho 79), Blanchard, Nyarko, Brunel, Coridon; Nouma.
H 1-2 Nouma (73)
Warmuz; Sikora, Pierre-Fanfan, Ismaël, Queudrue; Brunel (Moreira 59), Coridon (Rodriguez 76), Dacourt, Nyarko; Nouma (Job 89), Sakho.

Marseille, the previous season's runners-up, had a similar experience in the Champions' League. They started well and came successfully through their opening group, memorably beating holders Manchester United 1-0 at the Stade Vélodrome, but they found their level in the second phase, by which stage their season was on the brink of self-destruction.

At the end of November coach Rolland Courbis decided to resign after a bust-up with club president Yves Marchand. It proved to be a pivotal moment, because after his departure the team gradually went to pieces. Strikers Fabrizio Ravanelli and Christophe Dugarry left in mid-season, and, with Laurent Blanc having also been released, largely against his will, the previous summer, Marseille suddenly found themselves bereft of quality. They made several new signings, but the inexperience of stand-in coach Bernard Casoni aggravated the situation and before long the country's best-supported team (average home gate 51,686) were embroiled in a desperate fight against relegation.

Big wins at home to PSG and Monaco gave Marseille room to breathe but when they let in a late equaliser at home to fellow strugglers Nancy in their penultimate match, it meant that they had to get something from their final fixture, away to the season's surprise package, Sedan, to retain their Division One status. To great relief all round, they drew 2-2, which meant that they finished above Nancy only on goal difference.

Several clubs were involved in the battle to avoid 18th place on the final day, but with Nantes and Rennes both winning and Troyes securing a mutually beneficial draw with Paris Saint-Germain, it meant that Nancy's 2-0 victory over Auxerre was not enough to save them. They therefore joined pre-condemned Montpellier and Le Havre in Division Two. It was a sad farewell for veteran striker Tony Cascarino, who scored both of Nancy's goals, and for visiting coach Guy Roux, who ended his world-record 39-year spell in office with a defeat. He 'retired' to a role of general manager, with his long-time assistant Daniel Rolland taking over on the bench.

Lille, Guingamp and Toulouse all won promotion after brief spells away, but the Division Two team with most to celebrate was FC Gueugnon, who won the first major trophy in their history when they beat Paris Saint-Germain 2-0 in the League Cup final, played in front of 75,000 spectators in the Stade de France. The victory was also worth a place in Europe - another first for the village club from Burgundy.

In any other season Gueugnon's exploit would have been regarded as sensational, but their giantkilling feats were dwarfed by those of amateur club Calais in the other domestic knockout competition, the 'Coupe de France'.

Calais did not win the trophy - that honour went, for the second season running, to First Division Nantes - but the 1999/2000 competition will be forever remembered as Calais's Cup. A team of true amateurs - every player had a full-time day job - the Channel port club had a modest league season in Group A of France's CFA - the regional fourth division - but in the Cup they produced one miracle after another.

Obliged to enter at the fourth-round stage, Calais easily picked off lesser-ranked opponents Campagne-lès-Hesdin, Saint-Nicolas-lès-Arras, Marly-lès-Valenciennes and Béthune before thumping coastal rivals Dunkirk 4-0 in round eight. Then it started to get interesting as they overcame Second Division high-fliers Lille on penalties. In the next round they were again drawn against lower-grade opponents in Langon-Castets and won 3-0. Next up were Second Division Cannes, beaten by another penalty shoot-out. It looked as if the run would end when they were drawn to face top-flight Strasbourg in the quarter-finals. Not a bit of it. Calais switched the game to nearby Lens and won it 2-1.

The Stade Bollaert was again the venue in the semi-final as Calais came face to face with Bordeaux. A crowd of 38,374 witnessed a moment of history as the underdogs, led by coach Ladislas Lozano, took Bordeaux to extra-time and then beat them 3-1, becoming the first amateur club ever to reach the French Cup final.

Had Monaco won the other semi-final, at home to Nantes, Calais would have qualified for Europe. But there was another upset in the Stade Louis II as the holders won 1-0. Thus, Calais's European dream could only be realised if they triumphed in the final at the Stade de France.

Calais did everything in their power to produce the perfect happy ending to a story that by now had gripped the entire nation. They even led 1-0 at half-time thanks to a goal from Jérôme Dutitre. But the match and the fairytale was to have a tragic ending. Level just after the interval through their goalscoring midfielder Antoine Sibierski, Nantes could scarcely believe their luck when,

DOMESTIC CUP 99/00

1/32 FINALS
Stade Lavallois 0, CS Sedan Ardennes 0 (aet; 3-2 on pens.)
FC Sochaux 2, Le Havre AC 2 (aet; 2-4 on pens.)
Amiens SCF 1, AJ Auxerre 0
FC Lorient 2, Montpellier HSC 1
Stade Rennais FC 2, LB Châteauroux 0
Racing Club Paris 0, AS Monaco 1
Pacy-sur-Eure 0, FC Metz 2
Besançon RC 2, RC Lens 1
Thouars 1, AS Nancy-Lorraine 0
Grenoble 1, AS Saint-Etienne 2 (aet)
Vannes 0, A Troyes AC 1
Saint-Quentin 1, SC Bastia 0
Limoges 2, Paris Saint-Germain 4
Tours 0, Olympique Lyonnais 1 (aet)
Sefré 0, Olympique Marseille 1
Marignane 0, RC Strasbourg 1
Schiltigheim 1, Girondins de Bordeaux 3
Carcassonne 1, FC Nantes 4
Nîmes Olympique 2, Louhans-Cuiseaux 71 0
FC Gueugnon 1, US Créteil 0
Calais 1, Lille OSC 1 (aet; 7-6 on pens.)
La Roche/Yon 1, Toulouse FC 1 (aet; 4-5 on pens.)
Aurillac 0, AS Cannes 1
Mondeville 0, ASOA Valence 2
Lyon-La Duchère 1, Chamois Niortais 3
Baume-Les-Dames 1, AS Evry 1 (aet; 5-4 on pens.)
Levallois 0, Red Star 93 1
Pontivy 1, Brest 0
Porto-Vecchio 1, Vaulx 1 (aet; 4-3 on pens.)

Langon-Castets 3, US Montagnarde 0
Montceau 3, Vesoul 2 (aet)
Les Herbiers 3, Compiègne 0

1/16 FINALS
Olympique Lyonnais 1, A Troyes AC 0
Olympique Marseille 3, FC Gueugnon 4
AS Saint-Etienne 0, FC Lorient 0 (aet; 3-4 on pens.)
Besançon 2, RC Strasbourg 2 (aet; 2-4 on pens.)
Red Star 1, Le Havre AC 0
Thouars 1, AS Monaco 2
Porto-Vecchio 1, Girondins de Bordeaux 4
Saint-Quentin 1, FC Metz 3
Baume-les-Dames 0, Paris Saint-Germain 2
Les Herbiers 0, Stade Rennais FC 4
Montceau-les-Mines 0, FC Nantes 6
Amiens SCF 1, Stade Lavallois 1 (aet; 5-3 on pens.)
Chamois Niortais 0, AS Cannes 3
Nîmes Olympique 1, Toulouse FC 0
Pontivy 2, ASOA Valence 1
Calais 3, Langon-Castets 0

1/8 FINALS
Girondins de Bordeaux 1, FC Metz 0
RC Strasbourg 1, Paris Saint-Germain 0
Stade Rennais FC 3, FC Lorient 2
FC Nantes 0, FC Gueugnon 0 (aet; 5-3 on pens.)
Red Star 1, Olympique Lyonnais 2
Pontivy 0, AS Monaco 4
Nîmes Olympique 2, Amiens SCF 0
Calais 1, AS Cannes 1 (aet; 4-1 on pens.)

QUARTER-FINALS
Olympique Lyonnais 1 (Laigle 35),
AS Monaco 3 (Prso 59, Simone 78, Giuly 90)
FC Nantes 2 (Fabbri 37, Sibierski 118),
Stade Rennais FC 1 (Le Roux 79) (aet)
Girondins de Bordeaux 1 (Laslandes 47),
Nîmes Olympique 0
Calais 2 (Hogard 39, Merlen 45),
RC Strasbourg 1 (Echouafni 6)

SEMI-FINALS
Calais 3 (Jandau 99, Millien 113, Gérard 119),
Girondins de Bordeaux 1 (Laslandes 108) (aet)
AS Monaco 0, FC Nantes 1 (Da Rocha 81)

FINAL
07/05/2000, Saint-Denis
FC NANTES 2 Sibierski (49, 90p)
CALAIS 1 Dutitre (34)
referee - Colombo
FC NANTES - Landreau; Chanelet, Gillet, Fabbri, Olembé; Carrière, Berson, Devineau (Monterrubio 68), Touré (Caveglia 72); Sibierski, Da Rocha.
CALAIS - Schille; Merlen, Becque, Baron, Deswarte; Jandau, Hogard, Lefebvre (Canu 53), Vasseur; Gérard, Dutitre (Millien 53; Lestavel 90).

PLAYERS OF THE SEASON

THIERRY HENRY

Unwanted by Juventus and offloaded to Arsenal for a £10m fee, Thierry Henry developed into a goalscoring sensation at Highbury. Once he had adjusted to the special needs of the English game, the pacy youngster proved uncontainable. In the second half of the season he was the hottest, most dangerous striker in the Premiership. He ended up with 17 league goals - the same number scored the previous season by the man he replaced, compatriot Nicolas Anelka - and he also struck eight goals in Europe, including seven in Arsenal's run to the UEFA Cup final, a match in which he came very close to scoring the winning goal. His club form was successfully carried into Euro 2000, where he was France's top scorer, finding the net against Denmark, the Czech Republic and Portugal. Although he also scored three times at the 1998 World Cup, Henry's overall game has improved enormously since then and 'Les Bleus' now have a striker who can stand proud alongside the world-class performers in every other sector of the team.

DAVID TREZEGUET

"Le Roi David" proclaimed the laser lights on the Arc de Triomphe after France's dramatic Euro 2000 final victory over Italy. "King David" was David Trezeguet (pictured right), the man who scored the stupendous 'golden goal' that decided the final in France's favour and enabled them to sample European Championship glory just two years after winning the World Cup. It was Trezeguet, too, who eight months earlier had scored the all-important goal at home to Iceland that enabled 'Les Bleus' to qualify for the European finals. A supersub par excellence for his country, the young two-footed striker was one of the main men in Monaco's runaway French championship triumph, scoring 22 goals to finish second in the French First Division goal charts and, in tandem with Italian strike-partner Marco Simone, drive his team to a second title in four years. It was to be Trezeguet's final season at Monaco. In the summer he was signed by Juventus for a club-record £15m.

ZINEDINE ZIDANE

As one Frenchman arrived in Turin, there was some speculation that another might be about to depart. But Zinedine Zidane eventually scotched the

rumours by agreeing a new long-term contract that will keep him at Juventus for the best years of his career. Now 28, the brilliant Frenchman will be hard-pressed in the future to recreate the majesty of his command performance at Euro 2000, where he was the most skilful, exciting and influential footballer on view. He hit the ground running with a beautifully decorative and effective display against Denmark and was a telling contributor to the French cause on every subsequent appearance, scoring crucial goals in the knockout games against Spain (a trademark free-kick) and Portugal (a truly great penalty under pressure) and figuring prominently in France's late siege on the Italian goal in the final - even if, from an individual perspective, that was his least prominent performance of the tournament. Some critics have always maintained that he is a "poor man's Platini", but Euro 2000 showed that amidst his contemporaries Zidane is second to no one. Another European Footballer of the Year crown awaits.

with just seconds remaining, they were awarded a hugely contentious penalty after substitute Alain Caveglia had taken a theatrical dive following a challenge in the area.

Only a referee with a heart of stone could have pointed to the spot, but M. Colombo did just that. Sibierski buried the spot-kick and Nantes, for the first time in the match, were ahead. A minute or two later the final whistle sounded and the drama was at an end. For the second season in a row Nantes had won the Cup final with a hotly disputed penalty. Calais, mortified by their ill-fortune, wept in despair, but the title of 'moral champions' belonged exclusively to them - a fact acknowledged by Nantes' young skipper Mickaël Landreau, who, in a gesture of supreme sportsmanship, invited his Calais counterpart Réginald Becque to hoist the Cup aloft with him.

Calais did not return home with the trophy the next day, but they were treated to a heroes' reception nonetheless. To many, the tale of Calais and their extraordinary Cup run was every bit as deserving of its place in French footballing legend as the national team's European Championship triumph in Rotterdam a few weeks later.

PROMOTED CLUBS 99/00

SECOND DIVISION FINAL TABLE

		Pd	W	D	L	F	A	Pt	GD
1	Lille OSC	38	25	8	5	58	25	83	33
2	En Avant Guingamp	38	18	13	7	62	41	67	21
3	Toulouse FC	38	18	9	11	52	31	63	21
4	FC Sochaux	38	18	8	12	53	41	62	12
5	FC Gueugnon	38	13	17	8	47	34	56	13
6	SM Caen	38	12	17	9	50	37	53	13
7	AJ Ajaccio	38	15	8	15	37	41	53	-4
8	LB Châteauroux	38	13	13	12	44	44	52	0
	Le Mans UC 72	38	12	16	10	44	44	52	0
10	Stade Lavallois	38	12	15	11	41	40	51	1
11	OGC Nice	38	10	20	8	34	33	50	1
12	AS Cannes	38	12	12	14	33	38	48	-5
13	FC Lorient	38	12	11	15	32	39	47	-7
14	Olympique Nîmes	38	11	12	15	39	44	45	-5
15	Chamois Niortais	38	10	15	13	42	49	45	-7
16	ES Wasquehal	38	9	17	12	33	39	44	-6
17	US Créteil	38	11	11	16	36	52	44	-16
18	Amiens SCF	38	7	16	15	30	43	37	-13
19	ASOA Valence	38	6	15	17	37	54	33	-17
20	Louhans-Cuiseaux 71	38	5	9	24	32	67	24	-35

CLUB DIRECTORIES

Lille Olympique Sporting Club
Stade Grimonprez-Jooris
Allée du Petit-Paradis
59044 Lille Cedex
tel - (0320) 128292
fax - (0320) 420678
Year of Formation - 1944
President - Luc Dayan
Secretary - Xavier Thuillot
Coach - Vahid Halilhodzic
Stadium - Grimonprez-Jooris (21,000)

MAJOR HONOURS
League Championship - (2) 1946, 1954.
French Cup - (5)
1946, 1947, 1948, 1953, 1955.

En Avant Guingamp
15 boulevard Clemenceay
BP 50222
22202 Guingamp Cedex
tel - (0296) 401313
fax - (0296) 210777
Year of Formation - 1912
President - Alain Aubert
Secretary - Aimé Dagorn
Coach - Guy Lacombe
Stadium - Roudourou (18,040)

Toulouse Football Club
Stadium Municipal
Allée Gabriel-Biènes
31400 Toulouse
tel - (0561) 551111
fax - (0561) 535567
Year of Formation - 1970
President - Jacques Rubio
Sports Director - Didier Couécou
Coach - Alain Giresse
Stadium - Stadium Municipal (37,000)

AJ AUXERRE

CLUB DIRECTORY

Association de la Jeunesse Auxerroise
Stade de l'Abbé-Deschamps
Route de Vaux
89000 Auxerre
tel - (0386) 723232
fax - (0386) 522087
website - www.aja.tm.fr
Year of Formation - 1905
President - Jean-Claude Hamel
Secretary - Jean Edy
Coach - Guy Roux (00/01 - Daniel Rolland)
Stadium - Abbé-Deschamps (21,000)

MAJOR HONOURS
League Championship - (1) 1996.
French Cup - (2) 1994, 1996.

APPEARANCES 99/00

	P	Ap	(s)	Gls
Kuami AGBOH	M	23	(3)	
Eric ASSATI	D	20		
Gérald BATICLE	M	2	(3)	1
Stéphane CARNOT	M	25	(5)	1
Laurent CIECHELSKI	D	20	(2)	2
Djibril CISSE	A		(2)	
Alexandre COMISETTI (SUI)	A	12	(7)	1
Lilian COMPAN	A	2		
Fabien COOL	G	34		
Frédéric DANJOU	D	2		
Bernard DIOMEDE	A	19		3
Amdy FAYE (SEN)	M	1	(2)	
Stéphane GUIVARC'H	A	32		14
Jean-Sébastien JAURES	M	2	(6)	
Frédéric JAY	D	26	(6)	
Cyril JEUNECHAMP	M	29	(1)	
Narcisse KAPO	A	7	(8)	3
Tomasz KLOS (POL)	D	25	(1)	
Ronan LE CROM	G		(1)	
Cyrille MAGNIER	D	10	(1)	
Steve MARLET	A	33		9
Philippe MEXES	D	1	(4)	
Johan RADET	M	4	(4)	
Pedro REYES (CHL)	D	30		
Teemu TAINIO (FIN)	M	15	(10)	3

LEAGUE RESULTS 1999/2000

31/07/99	AS Nancy-Lorraine	H	2-1	Guivarc'h, Comisetti
07/08/99	FC Metz	A	0-3	
14/08/99	CS Sedan Ardennes	H	3-1	Guivarc'h, Ciechelski, Tainio
20/08/99	Paris Saint-Germain	A	1-1	Guivarc'h
28/08/99	Le Havre AC	H	2-1	Tainio, Guivarc'h
11/09/99	Olympique Lyonnais	A	0-0	
18/09/99	AS Saint-Etienne	H	2-1	Guivarc'h (p), Carnot
25/09/99	Girondins de Bordeaux	A	0-1	
03/10/99	RC Lens	H	3-2	Diomède 2, Guvarc'h
13/10/99	RC Strasbourg	A	3-1	Ciechelski, Guivarc'h, Marlet
16/10/99	SC Bastia	H	3-1	Marlet, Guivarc'h, Tainio
30/10/99	Montpellier HSC	H	2-1	Marlet, Guivarc'h
07/11/99	FC Nantes	A	1-3	Marlet
10/11/99	A Troyes AC	H	0-1	
20/11/99	Olympique Marseille	A	1-0	Marlet
27/11/99	Stade Rennais FC	A	0-1	
01/12/99	AS Monaco	A	0-2	
05/12/99	FC Metz	H	1-1	Kapo
11/12/99	CS Sedan Ardennes	A	1-1	Guivarc'h
17/12/99	Paris Saint-Germain	H	1-0	Baticle
12/01/00	Le Havre AC	A	0-0	
15/01/00	Olympique Lyonnais	H	2-0	Kapo, Marlet
26/01/00	AS Saint-Etienne	A	0-0	
01/02/00	Girondins de Bordeaux	H	1-0	Guivarc'h
05/02/00	RC Lens	A	1-2	Kapo
16/02/00	RC Strasbourg	H	0-1	
26/02/00	SC Bastia	A	0-2	
12/03/00	AS Monaco	H	0-2	
25/03/00	Montpellier HSC	A	0-2	
08/04/00	FC Nantes	H	1-1	Guivarc'h (p)
15/04/00	A Troyes AC	A	0-2	
30/04/00	Olympique Marseille	H	2-2	Marlet 2
04/05/00	Stade Rennais FC	H	4-0	Guivarc'h 2, Marlet, Diomède
13/05/00	AS Nancy-Lorraine	A	0-2	

SC BASTIA

CLUB DIRECTORY

Sporting Club de Bastia
Stade Armand-Cesari-Furiani
BP 640
20601 Bastia Cedex
tel - (0495) 300080
fax - (0495) 336774
website - www.sc-bastia.fr
Year of Formation - 1905
President - François Nicolaï
General Manager - Christian Villanova
Coach - Frédéric Antonetti
Stadium - Armand-Cesari-Furiani (10,800)

MAJOR HONOURS
French Cup - (1) 1981.

APPEARANCES 99/00

	P	Ap	(s)	Gls
Pierre-Yves ANDRE	A	26	(4)	7
Pascal BERENGUER	M		(1)	
Ali BOUMNIJEL (MAR)	G		(1)	
Zoumana CAMARA	D	24	(3)	1
Laurent CASANOVA	D	29		1
José CLAYTON (TUN)	M	4	(3)	
Christophe DEGUERVILLE	D	4	(6)	
Eric DURAND	G	31		
Cyril EBOKI-POH	A		(1)	
Paul ESSOLA (CMR)	M		(1)	
Franck JURIETTI	D	31		3
Yann LACHUER	M	31	(2)	3
Pierre LAURENT	A	5	(14)	3
Franck MATINGOU	D	6	(6)	
Frédéric MENDY	M	26	(1)	1
Patrick MOREAU	D	3	(1)	
Lilian NALIS	M	21	(7)	1
Frédéric NEE	A	30		11
Stéphane ODET	M		(2)	
Nicolas PENNETEAU	G	3		
Dan PETERSEN (DEN)	A	9	(17)	3
PRINCE Daye (LIB)	A	7	(11)	7
Morlaye SOUMAH	D	32		
Ousmane SOUMAH (GUI)	A		(4)	1
Piotr SWIERCZEWSKI (POL)	M	29	(1)	1
Patrick VALERY	D	23	(1)	

LEAGUE RESULTS 1999/2000

30/07/99	Girondins de Bordeaux	A	2-3	Née, Petersen (p)
06/08/99	RC Strasbourg	H	3-0	Casanova, Petersen, Née
14/08/99	AS Monaco	A	0-4	
22/08/99	FC Nantes	H	2-1	Laurent, Prince
28/08/99	Olympique Marseille	A	1-1	Née
11/09/99	AS Nancy-Lorraine	H	1-1	André
19/09/99	CS Sedan Ardennes	A	0-2	
25/09/99	Le Havre AC	H	1-1	Jurietti
02/10/99	AS Saint-Etienne	A	1-1	André
13/10/99	RC Lens	H	2-0	Née, Prince
16/10/99	AJ Auxerre	A	1-3	Soumah
24/10/99	Montpellier HSC	A	1-1	Prince
30/10/99	A Troyes AC	H	5-0	Lachuer, Jurietti, André, Prince, Mendy
06/11/99	Stade Rennais FC	A	0-0	
10/11/99	FC Metz	H	0-0	
19/11/99	Paris Saint-Germain	A	0-2	
28/11/99	Olympique Lyonnais	H	3-0	Lachuer, Née 2
03/12/99	RC Strasbourg	A	0-2	
12/12/99	AS Monaco	H	1-0	Camara
18/12/99	FC Nantes	A	1-1	Née
12/01/00	Olympique Marseille	H	0-0	
15/01/00	AS Nancy-Lorraine	A	0-1	
26/01/00	CS Sedan Ardennes	H	1-0	Laurent
02/02/00	Le Havre AC	A	2-2	Jurietti, Laurent
05/02/00	AS Saint-Etienne	H	4-0	Lachuer, Née 2, Swierczewski
16/02/00	RC Lens	A	0-4	
26/02/00	AJ Auxerre	H	2-0	André 2
11/03/00	Montpellier HSC	H	1-0	Prince
25/03/00	A Troyes AC	A	0-1	
08/04/00	Stade Rennais FC	H	4-2	André 2, Nalis, Née
15/04/00	FC Metz	A	1-1	Prince
30/04/00	Paris Saint-Germain	H	1-2	Petersen (p)
04/05/00	Olympique Lyonnais	A	1-2	Née
13/05/00	Girondins de Bordeaux	H	1-1	Prince

GIRONDINS DE BORDEAUX

CLUB DIRECTORY

Football Club des Girondins de Bordeaux
Rue Juliot-Curie
BP 33
33186 Le Haillan Cedex
tel - (0556) 161111
fax - (0556) 575446
website - www.girondins.com
Year of Formation - 1881
President - Jean-Louis Triaud
Secretary - Alain Deveseleer
Coach - Elie Baup
Stadium - Parc Lescure (34,088)

MAJOR HONOURS
League Championship - (5)
1950, 1984, 1985, 1987, 1999.
French Cup - (3) 1941, 1986, 1987.

APPEARANCES 99/00

	P	Ap	(s)	Gls
Kodko AFANOU	D	26	(1)	
Hervé ALICARTE	D	27		5
Laurent BATTLES	D	3	(16)	
Jérôme BONNISSEL	D	25	(1)	
Lassina DIABATE (CIV)	M	18	(6)	
Christophe DUGARRY	A	12		3
Pascal FEINDOUNO (GUI)	A		(11)	
François GRENET	D	30	(1)	
David JEMMALI	D	5	(7)	
Lilian LASLANDES	A	27	(4)	14
Sylvain LEGWINSKI	M	13		1
Corentin MARTINS	M	15	(6)	
Johan MICOUD	M	31		6
Michel PAVON	M	28		1
Ulrich RAME	G	34		
Jean-Christophe ROUVIERE	M	11	(7)	
Christophe SANCHEZ	A	3	(12)	1
Nisa SAVELJIC (YUG)	D	21		2
Sylvain WILTORD	A	27	(5)	13
Marc ZANOTTI	M	1	(6)	
Stéphane ZIANI	M	17	(3)	6

LEAGUE RESULTS 1999/2000

Date	Opponent		Score	Scorers
30/07/99	SC Bastia	H	3-2	Alicarte, Laslandes, Micoud
07/08/99	Montpellier HSC	A	2-2	Micoud, Wiltord
14/08/99	A Troyes AC	H	4-0	Ziani 2, Laslandes 2
20/08/99	Stade Rennais FC	A	1-2	Laslandes
28/08/99	FC Metz	H	0-0	
12/09/99	Paris Saint-Germain	A	1-2	Wiltord (p)
18/09/99	Olympique Lyonnais	H	1-3	Wiltord
25/09/99	AJ Auxerre	H	1-0	Laslandes
02/10/99	RC Strasbourg	A	2-2	Wiltord 2
13/10/99	AS Monaco	H	3-2	Laslandes 2, Wiltord
16/10/99	FC Nantes	A	1-0	Micoud
23/10/99	Olympique Marseille	H	2-1	Laslandes 2
30/10/99	AS Nancy-Lorraine	A	2-2	Wiltord, Sanchez
06/11/99	CS Sedan Ardennes	H	1-1	Micoud
10/11/99	Le Havre AC	A	0-3	
19/11/99	AS Saint-Etienne	H	1-2	Alicarte
28/11/99	RC Lens	A	3-3	Wiltord, Ziani 2
03/12/99	Montpellier HSC	H	2-0	Alicarte, Wiltord
11/12/99	A Troyes AC	A	0-2	
17/12/99	Stade Rennais FC	H	1-0	Wiltord
11/01/00	FC Metz	A	1-2	Wiltord
16/01/00	Paris Saint-Germain	H	1-1	Laslandes
26/01/00	Olympique Lyonnais	A	1-1	Laslandes
01/02/00	AJ Auxerre	A	0-1	
05/02/00	RC Strasbourg	H	3-0	Ziani, Micoud, Laslandes
16/02/00	AS Monaco	A	0-1	
26/02/00	FC Nantes	H	3-0	Saveljic, Legwinski, Micoud
11/03/00	Olympique Marseille	A	2-0	Dugarry, Laslandes
25/03/00	AS Nancy-Lorraine	H	2-1	Pavon, Wiltord
07/04/00	CS Sedan Ardennes	A	1-0	Dugarry
15/04/00	Le Havre AC	H	3-0	Alicarte 2 (2p), Saveljic
29/04/00	AS Saint-Etienne	A	2-1	Laslandes, Dugarry
04/05/00	RC Lens	H	1-2	Ziani
13/05/00	SC Bastia	A	1-1	Wiltord

LE HAVRE AC

CLUB DIRECTORY

Le Havre Athletic Club Football Association
32 rue de la Cavée-Verte
BP 404
76620 Le Havre
tel - (0235) 131415
fax - (0235) 131400
website - www.hac.asso.fr
Year of Formation - 1872
President - Jean-Pierre Louvel
Director - Alain Belsoeur
Coach - Francis Smerecki
(00/01 - Joël Beaujouan)
Stadium - Jules-Deschaseaux (18,000)

MAJOR HONOURS
French Cup - (1) 1959.

APPEARANCES 99/00

		P	Ap	(s)	Gls
Gustave BAHOKEN (CMR)	D			(1)	
Miladin BECANOVIC (YUG)	A		4	(6)	2
Guillaume BEUZELIN	M		20	(4)	4
Jean-Alain BOMSONG	D		22	(1)	
Mohamed Fadel BRAHAMI	A		3	(4)	
Philippe BRINQUIN	D		6	(1)	
Mohammed CAMARA (GUI)	D			(2)	
Pascal CHIMBONDA	D		1	(1)	
William CORREA	A		1		
Adnan CUSTOVIC (YUG)	A		2	(5)	1
Michaël DEBEVE	M		26	(1)	2
Eric DELOUMEAUX	D		24	(4)	
Thierry DE NEEF	M		23	(1)	1
Thomas DENIAUD	A		22	(6)	6
Hamed DIALLO (CIV)	A		7	(7)	1
Souleymane DIAWARA (SEN)	D		18	(7)	
Xavier GRAVELAINE	A		11		1
Sébastien HAMEL	G		34		
Jérémy HENIN	D		26	(1)	
Karim KERKAR (ALG)	M		12	(5)	1
Jean-Michel LESAGE	M		17	(9)	3
Mamar MAMOUNI (ALG)	D		15	(6)	2
Yazid MANSOURI	M		29		
Raphaël MICELI (BEL)	M		4	(3)	
Cyrille POUGET	A		16	(1)	4
Yann SOLOY	M			(1)	
Argemiro VEIGA (BRA)	M			(1)	
Nicolas WEBER	D		31		1

LEAGUE RESULTS 1999/2000

31/07/99	FC Nantes	A	0-1	
05/08/99	Olympique Marseille	H	0-0	
14/08/99	AS Nancy-Lorraine	A	0-3	
20/08/99	CS Sedan Ardennes	H	2-1	Deniaud, Kerkar
28/08/99	AJ Auxerre	A	1-2	De Neef
11/09/99	AS Saint-Etienne	A	3-3	Pouget, Deniaud, Weber
19/09/99	RC Lens	H	1-1	og (Sikora)
25/09/99	SC Bastia	A	1-1	Pouget
02/10/99	Montpellier HSC	H	2-1	Debève, Pouget
13/10/99	A Troyes AC	A	1-3	Deniaud
16/10/99	Stade Rennais FC	H	0-1	
24/10/99	FC Metz	A	0-3	
30/10/99	Paris Saint-Germain	H	3-1	Lesage 2, Beuzelin
07/11/99	Olympique Lyonnais	A	0-3	
10/11/99	Girondins de Bordeaux	H	3-0	Debève, Diallo, Pouget (p)
19/11/99	RC Strasbourg	A	1-0	Lesage
27/11/99	AS Monaco	H	1-4	Mamouni
03/12/99	Olympique Marseille	A	0-2	
11/12/99	AS Nancy-Lorraine	H	0-1	
12/01/00	AJ Auxerre	H	0-0	
15/01/00	AS Saint-Etienne	H	1-0	Beuzelin
19/01/00	CS Sedan Ardennes	A	1-0	Becanovic
26/01/00	RC Lens	A	0-4	
02/02/00	SC Bastia	H	2-2	Beuzelin, Gravelaine
05/02/00	Montpellier HSC	A	0-0	
16/02/00	A Troyes AC	H	2-0	Deniaud 2
26/02/00	Stade Rennais FC	A	1-2	Becanovic
11/03/00	FC Metz	H	1-0	Deniaud
25/03/00	Paris Saint-Germain	A	1-2	Mamouni
08/04/00	Olympique Lyonnais	H	0-1	
15/04/00	Girondins de Bordeaux	A	0-3	
29/04/00	RC Strasbourg	H	0-1	
04/05/00	AS Monaco	A	2-5	Beuzelin, Custovic
13/05/00	FC Nantes	H	0-1	

RC LENS

CLUB DIRECTORY

Racing Club de Lens
Stade Félix-Bollaert
BP 236
62304 Lens
tel - (0321) 692899
fax - (0321) 692884
website - www.rclens.fr
Year of Formation - 1906
President - Gervais Martel
Secretary - Louis Plet
Coach - Daniel Leclercq;
François Brisson (00/01 - Rolland Courbis)
Stadium - Félix-Bollaert (41,649)

MAJOR HONOURS
League Championship - (1) 1998.
League Cup - (1) 1999.

APPEARANCES 99/00

	P	Ap	(s)	Gls
Patrick BARUL	D	4	(5)	
Jocelyn BLANCHARD	M	27		1
Olivier BOGACZYK	A	3	(7)	1
Philippe BRUNEL	M	27	(5)	2
Sébastien CHABBERT	G	2		
Stéphane COLLET	M	2	(2)	
Ferdinand COLY	D	7	(3)	
Charles-Edouard CORIDON	M	18	(10)	2
Adama COULIBALY (MLI)	D	4	(1)	
Olivier DACOURT	M	25	(1)	2
Ludovic DELPORTE	A	1	(4)	
Valérien ISMAEL	D	30		1
Joseph-Desiré JOB (CMR)	A	15	(9)	4
Yoan LACHOR	D	19	(4)	
Youl MAWENE	D	5	(1)	
Daniel MOREIRA	M	15	(7)	4
Pascal NOUMA	A	12	(7)	8
Alex NYARKO (GHA)	M	20	(1)	1
José Karl PIERRE-FANFAN	D	25	(1)	2
Franck QUEUDRUE	D	12	(4)	1
Bruno RODRIGUEZ	A	8	(2)	1
Cyril ROOL	M	15		
Lamine SAKHO (SEN)	A	17	(6)	8
Eric SIKORA	D	29	(1)	2
Guillaume WARMUZ	G	32		

LEAGUE RESULTS 1999/2000

Date	Opponent	H/A	Score	Scorers
31/07/99	RC Strasbourg	A	0-1	
06/08/99	AS Monaco	H	1-0	Moreira
14/08/99	FC Nantes	A	1-0	Job
22/08/99	Olympique Marseille	H	0-0	
28/08/99	AS Nancy-Lorraine	A	1-2	Ismaël
11/09/99	CS Sedan Ardennes	H	0-3	
19/09/99	Le Havre AC	A	1-1	Sakho
26/09/99	AS Saint-Etienne	H	0-2	
03/10/99	AJ Auxerre	A	2-3	Blanchard, Pierre-Fanfan
13/10/99	SC Bastia	A	0-2	
16/10/99	Montpellier HSC	H	1-0	Bogaczyk
24/10/99	A Troyes AC	A	1-0	Nouma
31/10/99	Stade Rennais FC	H	1-1	Nouma
07/11/99	FC Metz	A	0-0	
10/11/99	Paris Saint-Germain	H	3-2	Job 2, Nouma
20/11/99	Olympique Lyonnais	A	0-1	
28/11/99	Girondins de Bordeaux	H	3-3	Sakho, Nyarko, Coridon
05/12/99	AS Monaco	A	0-2	
14/12/99	FC Nantes	H	1-2	Job
18/12/99	Olympique Marseille	A	2-1	og (Gallas), Queudrue
12/01/00	AS Nancy-Lorraine	H	0-1	
15/01/00	CS Sedan Ardennes	A	0-0	
26/01/00	Le Havre AC	H	4-0	Nouma, Coridon, Sikora, Pierre-Fanfan
02/02/00	AS Saint-Etienne	A	2-0	Sakho, Moreira
05/02/00	AJ Auxerre	H	2-1	Dacourt 2
16/02/00	SC Bastia	H	4-0	Sakho 2, Nouma, Brunel
26/02/00	Montpellier HSC	A	1-1	Sakho
12/03/00	A Troyes AC	H	0-1	
26/03/00	Stade Rennais FC	A	0-3	
09/04/00	FC Metz	H	1-0	Sikora
14/04/00	Paris Saint-Germain	A	1-4	Rodriguez
29/04/00	Olympique Lyonnais	H	4-3	og (Delmotte), Nouma, Sakho 2
04/05/00	Girondins de Bordeaux	A	2-1	Nouma 2
13/05/00	RC Strasbourg	H	3-0	Moreira 2, Brunel

OLYMPIQUE LYONNAIS

CLUB DIRECTORY

Olympique Lyonnais
350 avenue Jean-Jaurès
69007 Lyon
tel - (0478) 767604
fax - (0478) 720399
website - www.olympiquelyonnais.com
Year of Formation - 1950
President - Jean-Michel Aulas
Secretary - Marino Faccioli
Coach - Bernard Lacombe
(00/01 - Jacques Santini)
Stadium - Gerland (42,000)

MAJOR HONOURS
French Cup - (3) 1964, 1967, 1973.

APPEARANCES 99/00

	P	Ap	(s)	Gls
Sonny ÂNDERSON (BRA)	A	32		23
Jacek BAK (POL)	D	14	(4)	1
Serge BLANC	D	20	(4)	2
Jérémie BRECHET	D	8	(8)	
Patrice CARTERON	D	31		2
Alain CAVEGLIA	A	4	(9)	1
Grégory COUPET	G	34		
Christophe DELMOTTE	M	20	(6)	2
Jean-Christophe DEVAUX	D	4	(9)	
Vikash DHORASOO	M	32		
Hubert FOURNIER	D	17	(3)	
Sidney GOVOU	A	1	(3)	
David HELLEBUYCK	A		(1)	
Angelo HUGUES	G		(1)	
Frédéric KANOUTE	A		(13)	1
Pierre LAIGLE	M	15	(3)	2
Florent LAVILLE	D	28		
David LINARES	M	23	(5)	
Steed MALBRANQUE	M	19	(9)	3
Cédric URAS	D	10	(6)	
Tony VAIRELLES	A	31	(2)	6
Philippe VIOLEAU	M	31		1

LEAGUE RESULTS 1999/2000

31/07/99	Montpellier HSC	H	1-2	Vairelles
05/08/99	A Troyes AC	A	2-1	Vairelles 2
15/08/99	Stade Rennais FC	H	2-2	Ânderson, Carteron
20/08/99	FC Metz	A	1-0	Caveglia
29/08/99	Paris Saint-Germain	H	1-0	Ânderson (p)
11/09/99	AJ Auxerre	H	0-0	
18/09/99	Girondins de Bordeaux	A	3-1	Carteron, Ânderson 2
25/09/99	RC Strasbourg	H	0-0	
03/10/99	AS Monaco	A	0-1	
12/10/99	FC Nantes	H	2-0	Ânderson 2
15/10/99	Olympique Marseille	A	1-0	Ânderson
24/10/99	AS Nancy-Lorraine	H	2-1	Ânderson, Blanc
29/10/99	CS Sedan Ardennes	A	0-2	
07/11/99	Le Havre AC	H	3-0	Delmotte, Ânderson 2
10/11/99	AS Saint-Etienne	A	1-1	Ânderson
20/11/99	RC Lens	H	1-0	Ânderson (p)
28/11/99	SC Bastia	A	0-3	
03/12/99	A Troyes AC	H	1-3	Delmotte
11/12/99	Stade Rennais FC	A	2-1	Malbranque, Ânderson
18/12/99	FC Metz	H	2-0	Malbranque, Ânderson
11/01/00	Paris Saint-Germain	A	2-2	Ânderson, Vairelles
15/01/00	AJ Auxerre	A	0-2	
26/01/00	Girondins de Bordeaux	H	1-1	Laslandes
02/02/00	RC Strasbourg	A	2-4	Ânderson, Kanouté
06/02/00	AS Monaco	H	2-1	Ânderson, og (Sagnol)
15/02/00	FC Nantes	A	1-6	Vairelles
26/02/00	Olympique Marseille	H	2-0	Vairelles, Ânderson
12/03/00	AS Nancy-Lorraine	A	0-1	
26/03/00	CS Sedan Ardennes	H	2-0	Malbranque, Ânderson
08/04/00	Le Havre AC	A	1-0	Ânderson
14/04/00	AS Saint-Etienne	H	0-0	
29/04/00	RC Lens	A	3-4	Ânderson 2 (1p), Blanc
04/05/00	SC Bastia	H	2-1	Violeau, Laigle
13/05/00	Montpellier HSC	A	2-2	Laigle, Ânderson

OLYMPIQUE MARSEILLE

CLUB DIRECTORY

Olympique de Marseille
25 rue de Negresko, BP 124
13267 Marseille Cedex 08
tel - (0491) 765609 / fax - (0491) 760777
website - www.olympiquedemarseille.com
Year of Formation - 1899
President - Yves Marchand
Secretary - Louis Vassalucci
Coach - Rolland Courbis; Bernard Casoni
(00/01 - Abel Braga)
Stadium - Vélodrome (60,000)

MAJOR HONOURS
League Championship - (8) 1937, 1948, 1971,
1972, 1989, 1990, 1991, 1992.
French Cup - (10) 1924, 1926, 1927, 1935,
1938, 1943, 1969, 1972, 1976, 1989.
European Champions' Cup - (1) 1993.

APPEARANCES 99/00

	P	Ap	(s)	Gls
Jacques ABARDONADO	D	10	(3)	2
Ibrahima BAKAYOKO (CIV)	A	15	(8)	8
Djamel BELMADI	M	1	(8)	1
Eduardo BERIZZO (ARG)	D	13		
Patrick BLONDEAU	D	23		
Frédéric BRANDO	M	22	(4)	2
Adama COULIBALY (MLI)	D		(1)	
Jean-Pierre CYPRIEN	D	7		
DAHOU	M		(4)	
Stéphane DALMAT	M	27	(2)	1
Eric DECROIX	D	3		
Iván DE LA PEÑA (ESP)	M	5	(7)	1
Kaba DIAWARA	A	3	(12)	
Christophe DUGARRY	A	14	(1)	3
Franck DUMAS	D	12		
Yannick FISCHER	D	11	(2)	
William GALLAS	D	22		
Pierre ISSA (SAF)	D	7	(1)	
Seydou KEITA (MLI)	M	1	(5)	
Jérôme LEROY	M	11		2
Peter LUCCIN	M	27	(1)	1
Lilian MARTIN	D	1	(1)	
Richard MARTINI	D	2	(1)	
Florian MAURICE	A	12	(5)	8
Daniel MONTENEGRO (ARG)	M	2	(3)	1
Arthur MOSES (GHA)	A		(2)	
Sébastien PEREZ	D	28	(1)	2
Robert PIRES	M	32		2
Stéphane PORATO	G	29		
Cyrille POUGET	A	12		5
Fabrizio RAVANELLI (ITA)	A	13	(1)	6
Loris REINA	D	4	(2)	
Stéphane TREVISAN	G	5	(1)	

LEAGUE RESULTS 1999/2000

31/07/99	CS Sedan Ardennes	H	3-0	Bakayoko, Dugarry, Belmadi
05/08/99	Le Havre AC	A	0-0	
15/08/99	AS Saint-Etienne	H	3-3	Ravanelli, Bakayoko (p), Maurice
22/08/99	RC Lens	A	0-0	
28/08/99	SC Bastia	H	1-1	Bakayoko
11/09/99	Montpellier HSC	A	1-3	Dugarry
19/09/99	A Troyes AC	H	1-0	Ravanelli
26/09/99	Stade Rennais FC	A	2-1	Ravanelli (p), Brando
02/10/99	FC Metz	H	1-1	Ravanelli
12/10/99	Paris Saint-Germain	A	2-0	Ravanelli, Maurice
15/10/99	Olympique Lyonnais	H	0-1	
23/10/99	Girondins de Bordeaux	A	1-2	De la Peña
30/10/99	RC Strasbourg	H	4-1	Pires, Maurice, Ravanelli, Bakayoko
07/11/99	AS Monaco	A	1-1	Luccin
10/11/99	FC Nantes	H	1-1	Maurice
20/11/99	AJ Auxerre	H	0-1	
27/11/99	AS Nancy-Lorraine	A	2-2	Maurice 2
03/12/99	Le Havre AC	H	2-0	Maurice, Dugarry
12/12/99	AS Saint-Etienne	A	1-5	Dalmat
18/12/99	RC Lens	H	1-2	Montenegro
12/01/00	SC Bastia	A	0-0	
16/01/00	Montpellier HSC	H	0-0	
25/01/00	A Troyes AC	A	2-1	Pires, Pouget
02/02/00	Stade Rennais FC	H	1-1	Pouget
06/02/00	FC Metz	A	0-2	
15/02/00	Paris Saint-Germain	H	4-1	Pérez, Pouget, Abardonado, Maurice
26/02/00	Olympique Lyonnais	A	0-2	
11/03/00	Girondins de Bordeaux	H	0-2	
25/03/00	RC Strasbourg	A	1-3	Bakayoko
07/04/00	AS Monaco	H	4-2	Pouget, Bakayoko 2, Brando
15/04/00	FC Nantes	A	0-0	
30/04/00	AJ Auxerre	A	2-2	Leroy, Abardonado
04/05/00	AS Nancy-Lorraine	H	2-2	Pouget, Pérez
13/05/00	CS Sedan Ardennes	A	2-2	Leroy, Bakayoko

FC METZ

CLUB DIRECTORY

Football Club de Metz
Stade Saint-Symphorien
Nouvelle Tribune
57050 Longeville-lès-Metz
tel - (0387) 667215
fax - (0387) 561429
website - www.fcmetz.com
Year of Formation - 1932
President - Carlo Molinari
Coach - Joël Muller
Stadium - Saint-Symphorien (26,304)

MAJOR HONOURS
French Cup - (2) 1984, 1988.
League Cup - (1) 1996.

APPEARANCES 99/00

	P	Ap	(s)	Gls
Ludovic ASUAR	M	18	(6)	1
Christophe BASTIEN	M	8	(3)	2
Gérald BATICLE	A	14		5
André BIANCARELLI	G	3		
Danny BOFFIN (BEL)	M	33		4
Stéphane BORBICONI	D		(2)	
Stéphane BOULILA	A		(1)	
Christophe EGGIMANN	G		(1)	
Philippe GAILLOT	D	31	(1)	2
Nicolas GOUSSE	A	10	(13)	1
Jonathan JAGER	A	1	(1)	
Nenad JESTROVIC (YUG)	A	5	(15)	3
Sylvain KASTENDEUCH	D	33		
Lionel LETIZI	G	31		
Sylvain MARCHAL	D	3	(3)	
Frédéric MEYRIEU	M	26		4
Stéphane MORISOT	D	13		
Michele PADOVANO (ITA)	A	9		4
Pascal PIERRE	D	14	(12)	
Grégory PROMENT	M	20	(1)	
David REGIS (USA)	D	3	(4)	
Franck RIZZETTO	M	6	(8)	
Louis SAHA	A	19	(4)	4
Sébastien SCHEMMEL	D	21		1
Serhiy SKACHENKO (UKR)	A	12	(4)	4
Geoffroy TOYES	D	27		1
Gunther VAN HANDENHOVEN (BEL)	M	14	(3)	

LEAGUE RESULTS 1999/2000

31/07/99	Stade Rennais FC	H	0-0	
07/08/99	AJ Auxerre	H	3-0	Meyrieu (p), Bastien, Saha
14/08/99	Paris Saint-Germain	A	1-2	Meyrieu
20/08/99	Olympique Lyonnais	H	0-1	
28/08/99	Girondins de Bordeaux	A	0-0	
11/09/99	RC Strasbourg	H	0-0	
19/09/99	AS Monaco	A	2-2	Gaillot, Skachenko
25/09/99	FC Nantes	H	2-1	Skachenko, Boffin
02/10/99	Olympique Marseille	A	1-1	Padovano
13/10/99	AS Nancy-Lorraine	H	2-2	Padovano, Jestrovic
17/10/99	CS Sedan Ardennes	A	2-0	Goussé, Jestrovic
24/10/99	Le Havre AC	H	3-0	Asuar, Padovano (p), Boffin
30/10/99	AS Saint-Etienne	A	0-2	
07/11/99	RC Lens	H	0-0	
10/11/99	SC Bastia	A	0-0	
19/11/99	Montpellier HSC	H	2-2	Saha, Padovano (p)
27/11/99	A Troyes AC	A	2-2	Skachenko, Bastien
05/12/99	AJ Auxerre	A	1-1	Skachenko
12/12/99	Paris Saint-Germain	H	1-3	Jestrovic
18/12/99	Olympique Lyonnais	A	0-2	
11/01/00	Girondins de Bordeaux	H	2-1	Baticle, Meyrieu
15/01/00	RC Strasbourg	A	1-1	Saha
25/01/00	AS Monaco	H	1-1	Baticle
02/02/00	FC Nantes	A	3-1	Saha, Baticle, og (Carrière)
06/02/00	Olympique Marseille	H	2-0	Boffin, Baticle
16/02/00	AS Nancy-Lorraine	A	0-0	
26/02/00	CS Sedan Ardennes	H	1-1	Meyrieu (p)
11/03/00	Le Havre AC	A	0-1	
25/03/00	AS Saint-Etienne	H	1-1	Gaillot
09/04/00	RC Lens	A	0-1	
15/04/00	SC Bastia	H	1-1	Schemmel
29/04/00	Montpellier HSC	A	1-0	Boffin
04/05/00	A Troyes AC	H	3-1	og (Arpinon), Toyes, Baticle
13/05/00	Stade Rennais FC	A	0-2	

AS MONACO

CLUB DIRECTORY

Association Sportive de Monaco
7 avenue des Castelans, 98000 Monaco
tel - (37792) 057473
fax - (37792) 052454
website - www.asm-foot.mc
Year of Formation - 1924
President - Jean-Louis Campora
Secretary - Emile Rossi
Coach - Claude Puel
Stadium - Louis II (20,000)

MAJOR HONOURS
League Championship - (7)
1961, 1963, 1978, 1982, 1988, 1997, 2000.
French Cup - (5)
1960, 1963, 1980, 1985, 1991.

APPEARANCES 99/00

	P	Ap	(s)	Gls
Jean-Marc AUBRY	G	4		
Fabien BARTHEZ	G	24		
Philippe CHRISTANVAL	D	25		
Pablo CONTRERAS (CHL)	D	15	(2)	
Francisco DA COSTA (POR)	M	25	(3)	1
Salif DIAO (SEN)	M		(1)	
David DI TOMMASO	D	1	(6)	
Martin DJETOU	D	20	(2)	
Wagneau ELOI	A	2	(7)	
Pontus FARNERUD (SWE)	M	5	(10)	
Marcelo GALLARDO (ARG)	M	27	(1)	8
Ludovic GIULY	M	28	(5)	5
Bruno IRLES	D	7	(1)	
LACOMBE	M		(1)	
Sabri LAMOUCHI	M	31	(1)	3
Sylvain LEGWINSKI	M	4	(6)	
Philippe LEONARD (BEL)	D	17	(2)	2
LUZI	G	1		
Rafael MARQUEZ (MEX)	D	22	(1)	3
Moussa N'DIAYE	A	1	(12)	1
Christophe PIGNOL	D	5		
Dado PRSO	A	7	(13)	2
John Arne RIISE (NOR)	M	10	(11)	1
Julien RODRIGUEZ	D	1	(1)	
Willy SAGNOL	D	25	(1)	
Marco SIMONE (ITA)	A	34		21
Tony Mario SYLVA	G	5	(1)	
David TREZEGUET	A	28	(2)	22

LEAGUE RESULTS 1999/2000

30/07/99	AS Saint-Etienne	H	2-2	Simone, Trezeguet
06/08/99	RC Lens	A	0-1	
14/08/99	SC Bastia	H	4-0	Trezeguet 3, Giuly (p)
20/08/99	Montpellier HSC	A	3-2	Trezeguet, Simone 2
29/08/99	A Troyes AC	H	3-0	Trezeguet 2, Simone
12/09/99	Stade Rennais FC	A	1-2	Gallardo
19/09/99	FC Metz	H	2-2	N'Diaye, Trezeguet
25/09/99	Paris Saint-Germain	A	3-0	Trezeguet (p), Léonard, Giuly
03/10/99	Olympique Lyonnais	H	1-0	Gallardo
13/10/99	Girondins de Bordeaux	A	2-3	Simone 2
16/10/99	RC Strasbourg	H	3-0	Simone 2, Lamouchi
29/10/99	FC Nantes	A	3-0	Simone, Trezeguet, Giuly
07/11/99	Olympique Marseille	H	1-1	Marquez
10/11/99	AS Nancy-Lorraine	A	2-1	Simone, Da Costa
20/11/99	CS Sedan Ardennes	H	2-1	Marquez, Lamouchi
27/11/99	Le Havre AC	A	4-1	Simone 2, Lamouchi, Marquez
01/12/99	AJ Auxerre	H	2-0	Gallardo 2
05/12/99	RC Lens	H	2-0	Trezeguet 2
12/12/99	SC Bastia	A	0-1	
18/12/99	Montpellier HSC	H	1-0	Simone
12/01/00	A Troyes AC	A	4-1	Simone, Gallardo 2, Giuly
15/01/00	Stade Rennais FC	H	3-1	Trezeguet 2, Simone
25/01/00	FC Metz	A	1-1	Simone
01/02/00	Paris Saint-Germain	H	1-0	Trezeguet
06/02/00	Olympique Lyonnais	A	1-2	Trezeguet
16/02/00	Girondins de Bordeaux	H	1-0	Riise
27/02/00	RC Strasbourg	A	2-3	Trezeguet 2
12/03/00	AJ Auxerre	A	2-0	Léonard, Gallardo
26/03/00	FC Nantes	H	2-0	Prso, Giuly
09/04/00	Olympique Marseille	A	2-4	Trezeguet 2
15/04/00	AS Nancy-Lorraine	H	2-2	Simone, Prso
29/04/00	CS Sedan Ardennes	A	1-2	Simone
04/05/00	Le Havre AC	H	5-2	Simone 2, Gallardo, Trezeguet 2
13/05/00	AS Saint-Etienne	A	1-3	Simone

MONTPELLIER HSC

Montpellier Hérault Sports Club
Avenue Albert-Einstein
34000 Montpellier
tel - (0467) 104500
fax - (0467) 104506
website - www.mhscfoot.com
Year of Formation - 1974
President - Louis Nicollin
Secretary - Philippe Peybernes
Coach - Jean-Louis Gasset; Michel Mézy
Stadium - La Mosson (30,000)

MAJOR HONOURS
French Cup - (1) 1990.

APPEARANCES 99/00

	P	Ap	(s)	Gls
Pascal BAILLS	D	5	(2)	
Cédric BARBOSA	M	15	(15)	1
Grégory CARMONA	A		(3)	
Stéphane CASSARD	G	14		
Eric DECROIX	D	15		
Philippe DELAYE	M	29		6
Manuel DOS SANTOS	D	29	(1)	
Nenad DZODIC (YUG)	D	19		1
Romain FERRIER	D	15	(2)	
Pascal FUGIER	D	30	(1)	1
Frédéric GARNY	A		(6)	1
Jocelyn GOURVENNEC	M	4	(3)	
GOUVEIA (POR)	M	9		1
Eric GUEI (CIV)	A		(1)	
Mariano HERRON (ARG)	M	4	(1)	
Patrice LOKO	A	24	(2)	8
Ahmed Reda MADOUNI	A		(1)	
Marcel MAHOUVE (CMR)	M	15	(5)	2
Toifilou MAOULIDA	A	13	(16)	5
Nicolas OUEDEC	A	16	(2)	2
Reynald PEDROS	M	3	(1)	
Rudy RIOU	G	20		
Michel RODRIGUEZ	D	20	(4)	
RUI PATACA (ANG)	A	11		5
Cyril SERREDSZUM	M	13	(6)	
Franck SILVESTRE	D	31		4
Olivier SORLIN	M	20	(8)	1
Didier THIMOTHEE	A		(5)	

31/07/99	Olympique Lyonnais	A	2-1	Loko, Barbosa
07/08/99	Girondins de Bordeaux	H	2-2	Dzodic, Loko
14/08/99	RC Strasbourg	A	0-2	
20/08/99	AS Monaco	H	2-3	Sorlin, Maoulida
28/08/99	FC Nantes	A	0-3	
11/09/99	Olympique Marseille	H	3-1	Delaye 2, Ouédec
19/09/99	AS Nancy-Lorraine	A	2-1	Silvestre, Mahouvé
25/09/99	CS Sedan Ardennes	H	1-1	Loko (p)
02/10/99	Le Havre AC	A	1-2	Ouédec
13/10/99	AS Saint-Etienne	H	0-1	
16/10/99	RC Lens	A	0-1	
24/10/99	SC Bastia	H	1-1	Fugier
30/10/99	AJ Auxerre	A	1-2	Loko
07/11/99	A Troyes AC	A	1-2	Silvestre
10/11/99	Stade Rennais FC	H	1-2	Delaye
19/11/99	FC Metz	A	2-2	Loko, Delaye
27/11/99	Paris Saint-Germain	H	0-1	
03/12/99	Girondins de Bordeaux	A	0-2	
11/12/99	RC Strasbourg	H	1-1	Delaye
18/12/99	AS Monaco	A	0-1	
12/01/00	FC Nantes	H	3-0	Delaye, Mahouvé, Garny
16/01/00	Olympique Marseille	A	0-0	
26/01/00	AS Nancy-Lorraine	H	1-0	Loko
02/02/00	CS Sedan Ardennes	A	1-2	Maoulida (p)
05/02/00	Le Havre AC	H	0-0	
16/02/00	AS Saint-Etienne	A	4-5	og (Wallemme), Loko 2, Rui Pataca
26/02/00	RC Lens	H	1-1	Rui Pataca
11/03/00	SC Bastia	A	0-1	
25/03/00	AJ Auxerre	H	2-0	Rui Pataca 2
08/04/00	A Troyes AC	H	2-2	Gouveia, Maoulida
15/04/00	Stade Rennais FC	A	3-1	Maoulida, Rui Pataca, Silvestre
29/04/00	FC Metz	H	0-1	
04/05/00	Paris Saint-Germain	A	0-3	
13/05/00	Olympique Lyonnais	H	2-2	Silvestre, Maoulida

AS NANCY-LORRAINE

CLUB DIRECTORY

Association Sportive Nancy-Lorraine
BP 1117
54523 Laxou Cedex
tel - (0383) 232822
fax - (0383) 233037
website - www.asnl.net
Year of Formation - 1967
President - Jacques Rousselot
Secretary - Pascal Rivière
Coach - Laszlo Bölöni (00/01 - Francis Smerecki)
Stadium - Marcel-Picot (16,844)

MAJOR HONOURS
Domestic Cup - (1) 1978.

APPEARANCES 99/00

	P	Ap	(s)	Gls
Frédéric BIANCALANI	M	20	(8)	1
Jérôme BOTTELIN	A	7	(5)	2
Tony CASCARINO (IRL)	A	24	(6)	15
Saïd CHIBA (MAR)	M	26		1
Pablo CORREA (URU)	A	1	(13)	1
Demetrius FERREIRA (BRA)	D	30		1
Paul FISCHER	D	12	(3)	
Nicolas FLORENTIN	A		(2)	
Youssouf HADJI	A		(4)	
Vincent HOGNON	D	6		
Soufiane KONE	A	2		
Bertrand LAQUAIT	G	34		
Cédric LECLUSE	D	30		1
Fabien LEFEVRE	M	18	(9)	3
Medhi MENIRI	D	25	(3)	1
Laurent MORACCHINI	M	28		
Cédric MOURET	A	6	(2)	2
Youssef MOUSTAID	M	12	(11)	
Egutu OLISEH (NIG)	M	2	(6)	
Abdelnasser OUADAH	M	1	(3)	1
Abdeslam OUADDOU (MAR)	D	15	(1)	
Olivier RAMBO	D	30	(1)	3
Mickaël RODRIGUES	D	13	(8)	1
Samuel WIART	A	24	(4)	7
ZÉ ALCINO (BRA)	A	8	(1)	3

LEAGUE RESULTS 1999/2000

31/07/99	AJ Auxerre	A	1-2	Wiart
06/08/99	CS Sedan Ardennes	A	1-3	Cascarino
14/08/99	Le Havre AC	H	3-0	Bottelin, Biancalani, Cascarino
20/08/99	AS Saint-Etienne	A	1-2	Chiba
28/08/99	RC Lens	H	2-1	Cascarino, Wiart
11/09/99	SC Bastia	A	1-1	Ouadah
19/09/99	Montpellier HSC	H	1-2	Ferreira
25/09/99	A Troyes AC	A	0-2	
02/10/99	Stade Rennais FC	H	3-0	Cascarino 3 (1p)
13/10/99	FC Metz	A	2-2	Lefèvre, Mouret
16/10/99	Paris Saint-Germain	H	1-1	Wiart
24/10/99	Olympique Lyonnais	A	1-2	Rodriguez
30/10/99	Girondins de Bordeaux	H	2-2	Mouret, Wiart
06/11/99	RC Strasbourg	A	2-0	Wiart, Lefèvre
18/11/99	AS Monaco	H	1-2	Correa
20/11/99	FC Nantes	A	0-2	
27/11/99	Olympique Marseille	H	2-2	Cascarino 2 (1p)
03/12/99	CS Sedan Ardennes	H	0-2	
11/12/99	Le Havre AC	A	1-0	Cascarino (p)
18/12/99	AS Saint-Etienne	H	1-0	Rambo
12/01/00	RC Lens	A	1-0	Bottelin
15/01/00	SC Bastia	H	1-0	Lécluse
26/01/00	Montpellier HSC	A	0-1	
02/02/00	A Troyes AC	H	1-2	Zé Alcino
05/02/00	Stade Rennais FC	A	1-3	Zé Alcino
16/02/00	FC Metz	H	0-0	
26/02/00	Paris Saint-Germain	A	1-1	Cascarino (p)
12/03/00	Olympique Lyonnais	H	1-0	Zé Alcino
25/03/00	Girondins de Bordeaux	A	1-2	Wiart
08/04/00	RC Strasbourg	H	2-3	Cascarino 2
15/04/00	AS Monaco	A	2-2	Rambo, Lefèvre
29/04/00	FC Nantes	H	2-1	Cascarino, Rambo (p)
04/05/00	Olympique Marseille	A	2-2	Wiart, Méniri
13/05/00	AJ Auxerre	H	2-0	Cascarino 2

FC NANTES

Football Club de Nantes Atlantique
Centre Sportif José-Arribas-la Jonelière
44240 La Chappelle-sur-Erdre
tel - (0240) 372929
fax - (0240) 372921
website - www.fcna.fr
Year of Formation - 1943
President - Kléber Bobin
Director - Eric Leport
Coach - Raynald Denoueix
Stadium - La Beaujoire-Louis-Fonteneau (38,373)

MAJOR HONOURS
League Championship - (7)
1965, 1966, 1973, 1977, 1980, 1983, 1995.
French Cup - (3) 1979, 1999, 2000.

APPEARANCES 99/00

	P	Ap	(s)	Gls
Hassan AHAMADA	M	8	(9)	
Pierre ARISTOUY	A		(4)	
Mathieu BERSON	M	10	(2)	
Diego BUSTOS (ARG)	A	6	(10)	
Eric CARRIERE	M	32		5
Alain CAVEGLIA	A	8	(2)	1
Jean-Marc CHANELET	D	32		1
Frédéric DA ROCHA	A	30	(2)	6
Pascal DELHOMMEAU	D	6	(1)	
Yves DEROFF	M	3	(3)	
Charles DEVINEAU	M	16	(3)	2
Néstor FABBRI (ARG)	D	22		
Samuel FENILLAT	M	1	(2)	
Nicolas GILLET	D	20	(5)	1
Willy GRONDIN	G	1		
Mickaël LANDREAU	G	33		
Mehdi LEROY	M	7	(11)	2
Stéphane LIEVRE	D	21		
Sébastien MACE	M	1	(4)	
Mirza MESIC (BOS)	A		(1)	
Olivier MONTERRUBIO	A	15	(2)	3
Salomon OLEMBE (CMR)	M	17	(5)	2
Sébastien PIOCELLE	M	19	(2)	
Goran RUBIL (CRO)	M		(2)	
Nicolas SAVINAUD	M	28		1
Antoine SIBIERSKI	M	28		13
Patrick SUFFO (CMR)	A	1	(4)	
Alioune TOURE	A	2	(4)	1
Marama VAHIRUA	A	7	(5)	1

LEAGUE RESULTS 1999/2000

31/07/99	Le Havre AC	H	1-0	Sibierski
06/08/99	AS Saint-Etienne	A	2-0	Monterrubio, Sibierski
14/08/99	RC Lens	H	0-1	
22/08/99	SC Bastia	A	1-2	Leroy
28/08/99	Montpellier HSC	H	3-0	Sibierski, Monterrubio, Olembé
11/09/99	A Troyes AC	A	0-1	
19/09/99	Stade Rennais FC	H	3-0	Carrière 2, Sibierski
25/09/99	FC Metz	A	1-2	Monterrubio
03/10/99	Paris Saint-Germain	H	0-4	
12/10/99	Olympique Lyonnais	A	0-2	
16/10/99	Girondins de Bordeaux	H	0-1	
24/10/99	RC Strasbourg	A	2-3	Gillet, Da Rocha
29/10/99	AS Monaco	H	0-3	
07/11/99	AJ Auxerre	H	3-1	Sibierski, Olembé, Savinaud
10/11/99	Olympique Marseille	A	1-1	Sibierski
20/11/99	AS Nancy-Lorraine	H	2-0	Sibierski, Carrière
28/11/99	CS Sedan Ardennes	A	0-0	
03/12/99	AS Saint-Etienne	H	0-1	
14/12/99	RC Lens	A	2-1	Da Rocha, Caveglia
18/12/99	SC Bastia	H	1-1	Da Rocha
12/01/00	Montpellier HSC	A	0-3	
15/01/00	A Troyes AC	H	3-0	Sibierski 2 (1p), Da Rocha
26/01/00	Stade Rennais FC	A	0-0	
02/02/00	FC Metz	H	1-3	Da Rocha
05/02/00	Paris Saint-Germain	A	0-0	
15/02/00	Olympique Lyonnais	H	6-1	Da Rocha, Sibierski 2, Devineau 2, Chanelet
26/02/00	Girondins de Bordeaux	A	0-3	
11/03/00	RC Strasbourg	H	3-1	Carrière, Sibierski, Leroy
26/03/00	AS Monaco	A	0-2	
08/04/00	AJ Auxerre	A	1-1	Sibierski
15/04/00	Olympique Marseille	H	0-0	
29/04/00	AS Nancy-Lorraine	A	1-2	Carrière
04/05/00	CS Sedan Ardennes	H	1-0	Touré
13/05/00	Le Havre AC	A	1-0	Vahirua

PARIS SAINT-GERMAIN

CLUB DIRECTORY

Paris Saint-Germain Football Club
24 rue du Commandant-Guilbaud
75016 Paris
tel - (0141) 107171
fax - (0141) 107100
website - www.psg.fr
Year of Formation - 1970
President - Pierre Lescure
Secretary - Pierre Frelot
Coach - Philippe Bergeroo
Stadium - Parc des Princes (48,527)

MAJOR HONOURS
League Championship - (2) 1986, 1994.
French Cup - (5)
1982, 1983, 1993, 1995, 1998.
League Cup - (2) 1995, 1998.
European Cup-winners' Cup - (1) 1996.

APPEARANCES 99/00

	P	Ap	(s)	Gls
Fabrice ABRIEL	M		(1)	
Jimmy ALGERINO	D	19	(1)	2
Ali BENARBIA	M	27		
Bruno CAROTTI	M		(1)	
Dominique CASAGRANDE	G	1		
CÉSAR Augusto Belli (BRA)	D	10		1
CHRISTIAN Correa Dionísio (BRA)	A	27	(2)	16
Aliou CISSE (SEN)	D	21	(4)	1
Edouard CISSE	M	13	(15)	
Kaba DIAWARA	A	2	(8)	
Pierre DUCROCQ	M	33		1
Talal EL KARKOURI (MAR)	D	10		
Bernard LAMA	G	33		
Nicolas LASPALLES	D	18	(3)	
Jérôme LEROY	M	3	(4)	
Laurent LEROY	A	16	(11)	8
Michaël MADAR	A	16	(5)	8
Edwin MURATI (ALB)	M	8	(8)	
Augustine "Jay-Jay" OKOCHA (NIG)	M	22	(1)	2
Godwin OKPARA (NIG)	D	14	(1)	
Eric RABESANDRATANA	D	33		1
Laurent ROBERT	A	28		9
Bruno RODRIGUEZ	A	5		1
Igor YANOVSKIY (RUS)	D	15	(8)	2

LEAGUE RESULTS 1999/2000

31/07/99	A Troyes AC	H	1-0	og (Zavagno)
07/08/99	Stade Rennais FC	A	3-1	Robert 2, Madar (p)
14/08/99	FC Metz	H	2-1	Algerino, Okocha
20/08/99	AJ Auxerre	H	1-1	Rodriguez
29/08/99	Olympique Lyonnais	A	0-1	
12/09/99	Girondins de Bordeaux	H	2-1	Madar, Okocha
19/09/99	RC Strasbourg	A	1-1	Madar (p)
25/09/99	AS Monaco	H	0-3	
03/10/99	FC Nantes	A	4-0	Algerino, Madar, Leroy L. 2
12/10/99	Olympique Marseille	H	0-2	
16/10/99	AS Nancy-Lorraine	A	1-1	Madar
24/10/99	CS Sedan Ardennes	H	3-2	Madar, Christian, Robert
30/10/99	Le Havre AC	A	1-3	Christian
06/11/99	AS Saint-Etienne	H	2-0	Madar, Leroy L.
10/11/99	RC Lens	A	2-3	Madar, Christian (p)
19/11/99	SC Bastia	H	2-0	César, Leroy L.
27/11/99	Montpellier HSC	A	1-0	Christian
05/12/99	Stade Rennais FC	H	1-0	Cissé A.
12/12/99	FC Metz	A	3-1	Christian 3
17/12/99	AJ Auxerre	A	0-1	
11/01/00	Olympique Lyonnais	H	2-2	Christian, Robert (p)
16/01/00	Girondins de Bordeaux	A	1-1	Christian
26/01/00	RC Strasbourg	H	4-2	Christian 4
01/02/00	AS Monaco	A	0-1	
05/02/00	FC Nantes	H	0-0	
15/02/00	Olympique Marseille	A	1-4	Christian
26/02/00	AS Nancy-Lorraine	H	1-1	Rabesandratana
11/03/00	CS Sedan Ardennes	A	1-1	Christian
25/03/00	Le Havre AC	H	2-1	Yanovskiy, Leroy L.
08/04/00	AS Saint-Etienne	A	1-1	Robert
14/04/00	RC Lens	H	4-1	Leroy L. 3, Robert
30/04/00	SC Bastia	A	2-1	Robert, Yanovskiy
04/05/00	Montpellier HSC	H	3-0	Robert, og (Rodriguez), Ducrocq
13/05/00	A Troyes AC	A	2-2	Robert, Christian

STADE RENNAIS FC

Stade Rennais Football Club
111 route de Lorient
35000 Rennes
tel - (0299) 143570
fax - (0299) 143577
website - www.staderennais.com
Year of Formation - 1901
President - Pierre Blayau
General Manager - Gérard Lefillatre
Coach - Paul Le Guen
Stadium - Route de Lorient (23,625)

MAJOR HONOURS
French Cup - (2) 1965, 1971.

APPEARANCES 99/00

	P	Ap	(s)	Gls
Dominique ARRIBAGE	D	24		
Mickaël BAILLY	A		(1)	
Cédric BARDON	A	19	(8)	4
Christian BASSILA	M	15	(8)	1
Yoann BIGNE	M	22	(5)	1
Philippe BRINQUIN	D	1	(1)	
Mickaël CITONY	A		(2)	
Fabien DEBEC	G	7	(1)	
Lamine DIATTA	D	33		3
El Hadji DIOUF (SEN)	A	17	(11)	1
Jean-Luc DOGON	D	7	(3)	
Jean-Félix DOROTHEE	D		(2)	
Julien ESCUDE	D	19	(2)	
Fabrice FERNANDES	A	9	(8)	1
Franck GAVA	M	18		1
Jocelyn GOURVENNEC	M	7	(2)	
Stéphane GREGOIRE	M	33	(1)	3
Benoît LE BRIS	A	3	(3)	1
Christophe LE ROUX	M	27		6
Grégory MALICKI	G	9		
Daniel MESLIN	A		(1)	
Amadou N'DIAYE	M	9	(3)	2
Shabani NONDA (BUR)	A	29	(1)	16
Christophe REVAULT	G	18		
Anthony REVEILLERE	D	15	(1)	
David SOMMEIL	D	30		1
Cyril YAPI	A	3	(8)	

LEAGUE RESULTS 1999/2000

31/07/99	FC Metz	A	0-0	
07/08/99	Paris Saint-Germain	H	1-3	Diatta
15/08/99	Olympique Lyonnais	A	2-2	Bassila, Nonda
20/08/99	Girondins de Bordeaux	H	2-1	Diouf, og (Saveljic)
28/08/99	RC Strasbourg	A	1-2	Nonda
12/09/99	AS Monaco	H	2-1	og (Da Costa), Nonda
19/09/99	FC Nantes	A	0-3	
26/09/99	Olympique Marseille	H	1-2	Gava
02/10/99	AS Nancy-Lorraine	A	0-3	
13/10/99	CS Sedan Ardennes	H	5-0	N'Diaye, Bardon, Fernandes, Nonda, Le Roux
16/10/99	Le Havre AC	A	1-0	og (Deloumeaux)
23/10/99	AS Saint-Etienne	H	4-1	Nonda 2, Grégoire, Diatta
31/10/99	RC Lens	A	1-1	Nonda
06/11/99	SC Bastia	H	0-0	
10/11/99	Montpellier HSC	A	2-1	Nonda, Grégoire
19/11/99	A Troyes AC	H	2-2	Nonda, Grégoire
27/11/99	AJ Auxerre	H	1-0	Bardon
05/12/99	Paris Saint-Germain	A	0-1	
11/12/99	Olympique Lyonnais	H	1-2	Bardon
17/12/99	Girondins de Bordeaux	A	0-1	
12/01/00	RC Strasbourg	H	2-1	Le Roux, Bardon
15/01/00	AS Monaco	A	1-3	Le Roux
26/01/00	FC Nantes	H	0-0	
02/02/00	Olympique Marseille	A	1-1	Nonda
05/02/00	AS Nancy-Lorraine	H	3-1	Sommeil, Nonda 2
16/02/00	CS Sedan Ardennes	A	1-2	Diatta
26/02/00	Le Havre AC	H	2-1	N'Diaye, Le Bris
11/03/00	AS Saint-Etienne	A	0-1	
26/03/00	RC Lens	H	3-0	Nonda 2, Le Roux
08/04/00	SC Bastia	A	2-4	Nonda, Le Roux
15/04/00	Montpellier HSC	H	1-3	Nonda
29/04/00	A Troyes AC	A	0-1	
04/05/00	AJ Auxerre	A	0-4	
13/05/00	FC Metz	H	2-0	Bigné, Le Roux

AS SAINT-ETIENNE

CLUB DIRECTORY

Association Sportive de Saint-Etienne
Stade Geoffroy-Guichard
14 rue Paul-et-Pierre-Guichard
42028 Saint-Etienne Cedex 01
tel - (0477) 923170
fax - (0477) 923182
website - www.asse.fr
Year of Formation - 1933
President - Alain Bompard
Secretary - Didier Lacombe
Coach - Robert Nouzaret
Stadium - Geoffroy-Guichard (35,600)

MAJOR HONOURS
League Championship - (10) 1957, 1964, 1967,
1968, 1969, 1970, 1974, 1975, 1976, 1981.
Domestic Cup - (6)
1962, 1968, 1970, 1974, 1975, 1977.

APPEARANCES 99/00

	P	Ap	(s)	Gls
ALEX DIAS (BRA)	A	26	(3)	15
ALOÍSIO da Silva (BRA)	A	29		8
Jérôme ALONZO	G	25		
Romarin BILLONG (CMR)	D	6	(2)	
Fabien BOUDARENE	M	8	(15)	1
Bruno CAROTTI	M	4	(6)	1
Loïc CHAVERIAT	A		(12)	
Bertrand FAYOLLE	M	1	(1)	
Kader FERHAOUI (ALG)	M	7	(13)	
Tchiressou GUEL (CIV)	M	28		2
Patrick GUILLOU	D	2	(4)	
Stéphane HERNANDEZ	D	5	(1)	
Jérémie JANOT	G	5		
Bjørn Tore KVARME (NOR)	D	24		
Gilles LECLERC	D	4		
Francis LLACER	D	14	(5)	
Alain MASUDI	M	4		1
Lucien METTOMO (CMR)	D	26		1
Philippe MONTANIER	G	4		
Stéphane PEDRON	M	33		7
PERICARD	A	1	(1)	
Lionel POTILLON	D	30	(1)	4
Patrick REVELLES	A	10	(12)	
Julien SABLE	M	29	(3)	1
Pape SARR (SEN)	M	28	(2)	2
Nestor SUBIAT (SUI)	A	1	(7)	1
Jean-Guy WALLEMME	D	20	(1)	1

LEAGUE RESULTS 1999/2000

30/07/99	AS Monaco	A	2-2	Pédron, Aloísio
06/08/99	FC Nantes	H	0-2	
15/08/99	Olympique Marseille	A	3-3	Pédron 2, Sarr
20/08/99	AS Nancy-Lorraine	H	2-1	Alex, Aloísio
28/08/99	CS Sedan Ardennes	A	2-3	Sarr, Aloísio
11/09/99	Le Havre AC	H	3-3	Alex, Guel (p), Potillon
18/09/99	AJ Auxerre	A	1-2	Alex
26/09/99	RC Lens	A	2-0	Alex, Aloísio
02/10/99	SC Bastia	H	1-1	Alex
13/10/99	Montpellier HSC	A	1-0	Alex
16/10/99	A Troyes AC	H	1-0	Alex
23/10/99	Stade Rennais FC	A	1-4	Pédron
30/10/99	FC Metz	H	2-0	Alex, Subiat
06/11/99	Paris Saint-Germain	A	0-2	
10/11/99	Olympique Lyonnais	H	1-1	Pédron
19/11/99	Girondins de Bordeaux	A	2-1	Aloísio, Boudarène
27/11/99	RC Strasbourg	H	0-1	
03/12/99	FC Nantes	A	1-0	Aloísio
12/12/99	Olympique Marseille	H	5-1	Alex 4, Potillon
18/12/99	AS Nancy-Lorraine	A	0-1	
12/01/00	CS Sedan Ardennes	H	2-3	Pédron, Sablé
15/01/00	Le Havre AC	A	0-1	
26/01/00	AJ Auxerre	H	0-0	
02/02/00	RC Lens	H	0-2	
05/02/00	SC Bastia	A	0-4	
16/02/00	Montpellier HSC	H	5-4	Pédron, Aloísio 2 (1p), Alex, Carotti
26/02/00	A Troyes AC	A	1-0	Potillon
11/03/00	Stade Rennais FC	H	1-0	Potillon
25/03/00	FC Metz	A	1-1	Mettomo
08/04/00	Paris Saint-Germain	H	1-1	Masudi
14/04/00	Olympique Lyonnais	A	0-0	
29/04/00	Girondins de Bordeaux	H	1-2	Alex
04/05/00	RC Strasbourg	A	1-0	Alex
13/05/00	AS Monaco	H	3-1	Wallemme, og (Christanval), Guel

CS SEDAN ARDENNES

CLUB DIRECTORY

Club Sportif Sedan Ardennes
Boulevard de Lattre-de-Tassigny
08200 Sedan
tel - (0324) 270059
fax - (0324) 293110
Year of Formation - 1919
President - Michel Bérard
Secretary - Michel Bucquet
Coach - Patrick Rémy (00/01 - Alex Dupont)
Stadium - Louis-Dugauguez (17,000)

MAJOR HONOURS
Domestic Cup - (2) 1956, 1961.

APPEARANCES 99/00

	P	Ap	(s)	Gls
Madjid ADJAOUAD	M	21	(4)	
Freddy BOURGEOIS	A	2	(4)	
Fabien BRANDES	D	6	(8)	
Eddy CAPRON	D	13	(2)	
Eric CROSNIER	M	4	(12)	2
Pierre DEBLOCK	M	33	(1)	8
Oumar DIENG	D	15	(2)	
Alex DI ROCCO	A	20	(7)	8
Billal DZIRI	D	2	(11)	
Cédric ELZEARD	D	7	(3)	
Jean-Philippe FAURE	M	12	(6)	
Geir FRIGÅRD (NOR)	A	3	(10)	1
Laurent HUARD	M	24	(7)	2
Christophe JOUAULT	D	4	(4)	
Alexandre LECOMTE	A		(2)	
Cédric MIONNET	A	19	(4)	7
Jean-Louis MONTERO	D	26	(4)	
Pius N'DIEFI (CMR)	A	24	(1)	5
Dzoni NOVAK (SLO)	D	9	(2)	
Eduardo OLIVEIRA (BRA)	D	25	(2)	1
Olivier QUINT	M	32		7
Nicolas SACHY	G	34		
Luis SATORRA	D	28		
Mathieu VERSCHUERE	M	11		1

LEAGUE RESULTS 1999/2000

31/07/99	Olympique Marseille	A	0-3	
06/08/99	AS Nancy-Lorraine	H	3-1	Deblock, Mionnet, Quint
14/08/99	AJ Auxerre	A	1-3	Di Rocco
20/08/99	Le Havre AC	A	1-2	Mionnet
28/08/99	AS Saint-Etienne	H	3-2	Mionnet, N'Diefi, Quint
11/09/99	RC Lens	A	3-0	Quint (p), Deblock, Mionnet
19/09/99	SC Bastia	H	2-0	Mionnet, Deblock
25/09/99	Montpellier HSC	A	1-1	N'Diefi
02/10/99	A Troyes AC	H	2-1	Di Rocco 2
13/10/99	Stade Rennais FC	A	0-5	
17/10/99	FC Metz	H	0-2	
24/10/99	Paris Saint-Germain	A	2-3	N'Diefi, Deblock
29/10/99	Olympique Lyonnais	H	2-0	N'Diefi, Deblock
06/11/99	Girondins de Bordeaux	A	1-1	N'Diefi
09/11/99	RC Strasbourg	H	2-1	Mionnet, Di Rocco
20/11/99	AS Monaco	A	1-2	Oliveira
28/11/99	FC Nantes	H	0-0	
03/12/99	AS Nancy-Lorraine	A	2-0	Quint 2
11/12/99	AJ Auxerre	H	1-1	Crosnier
12/01/00	AS Saint-Etienne	A	3-2	Frigård, Deblock, Quint
15/01/00	RC Lens	H	0-0	
19/01/00	Le Havre AC	H	0-1	
26/01/00	SC Bastia	A	0-1	
02/02/00	Montpellier HSC	H	2-1	Di Rocco 2 (1p)
05/02/00	A Troyes AC	A	2-0	Deblock, Crosnier
16/02/00	Stade Rennais FC	H	2-1	Di Rocco, Huard
26/02/00	FC Metz	A	1-1	Quint (p)
11/03/00	Paris Saint-Germain	H	1-1	Mionnet
26/03/00	Olympique Lyonnais	A	0-2	
07/04/00	Girondins de Bordeaux	H	0-1	
15/04/00	RC Strasbourg	A	1-1	Di Rocco
29/04/00	AS Monaco	H	2-1	og (Sagnol), Deblock
04/05/00	FC Nantes	A	0-1	
13/05/00	Olympique Marseille	H	2-2	Verschuère, Huard

RC STRASBOURG

Racing Club de Strasbourg
Stade de la Meinau
12 rue d'Extenwoerth
67100 Strasbourg
tel - (0388) 445500
fax - (0388) 445501
Year of Formation - 1906
President - Patrick Proisy
Coach - Pierre Mankowski; Claude Le Roy
Stadium - Meinau (41,228)

MAJOR HONOURS
League Championship - (1) 1979.
French Cup - (2) 1951, 1966.
League Cup - (1) 1997.

APPEARANCES 99/00

	P	Ap	(s)	Gls
Gharib AMZINE (MAR)	M	5	(5)	
Mamadou BAGAYOKO (MLI)	A	9	(2)	
Gonzalo BELLOSO (ARG)	A	9	(3)	2
Teddy BERTIN	D	34		4
Habib BEYE	D	33		1
Pascal CAMADINI	M	19	(2)	2
Thierry DEBES	G	17	(1)	
Pape Malik DIOP (SEN)	D	19		
Régis DORN	M	1	(5)	1
Olivier ECHOUAFNI	M	31		9
Fabrice EHRET	M	12	(1)	4
Diego GARAY (ARG)	M	15	(7)	4
Mario HAAS (AUT)	A	10	(6)	1
Brahim HEMDANI	M	29		3
Pascal JOHANSEN	M	12	(2)	
Cédric KANTE	D		(2)	
Pegguy LUYINDULA	A	23	(7)	7
Mickaël MARSIGLIA	M	12	(6)	1
Rafik MEZRICHE	M	1	(3)	
Joseph NDO (CMR)	M	23	(2)	
Morten NIELSEN (DEN)	D	2	(7)	
Pierre NJANKA (CMR)	D	25		
Lionel ROUXEL	A	2	(4)	
Alexander VENCEL (SVK)	G	17		
David ZITELLI	A	14	(13)	1

LEAGUE RESULTS 1999/2000

31/07/99	RC Lens	H	1-0	Hemdani
06/08/99	SC Bastia	A	0-3	
14/08/99	Montpellier HSC	H	2-0	Haas, Bertin (p)
20/08/99	A Troyes AC	A	1-2	Echouafni
28/08/99	Stade Rennais FC	H	2-1	Belloso, Echouafni
11/09/99	FC Metz	A	0-0	
19/09/99	Paris Saint-Germain	H	1-1	Echouafni
25/09/99	Olympique Lyonnais	A	0-0	
02/10/99	Girondins de Bordeaux	H	2-2	Beye, Camadini
13/10/99	AJ Auxerre	H	1-3	Echouafni
16/10/99	AS Monaco	A	0-3	
24/10/99	FC Nantes	H	3-2	Belloso, Echouafni, Garay
30/10/99	Olympique Marseille	A	1-4	Garay
06/11/99	AS Nancy-Lorraine	H	0-2	
09/11/99	CS Sedan Ardennes	A	1-2	Garay
19/11/99	Le Havre AC	H	0-1	
27/11/99	AS Saint-Etienne	A	1-0	Bertin
03/12/99	SC Bastia	H	2-0	Luyindula, Marsiglia
11/12/99	Montpellier HSC	A	1-1	Ehret
12/01/00	Stade Rennais FC	A	1-2	Echouafni
15/01/00	FC Metz	H	1-1	Zitelli
19/01/00	A Troyes AC	H	2-0	Camadini, Echouafni
26/01/00	Paris Saint-Germain	A	2-4	Ehret 2
02/02/00	Olympique Lyonnais	H	4-2	Luyindula 3, og (Laville)
05/02/00	Girondins de Bordeaux	A	0-3	
16/02/00	AJ Auxerre	A	1-0	Luyindula
27/02/00	AS Monaco	H	3-2	Echouafni, Bertin, Hemdani
11/03/00	FC Nantes	A	1-3	Hemdani
25/03/00	Olympique Marseille	H	3-1	Ehret, og (Dumas), Dorn
08/04/00	AS Nancy-Lorraine	A	3-2	Luyindula 2, Bertin
15/04/00	CS Sedan Ardennes	H	1-1	Echouafni
29/04/00	Le Havre AC	A	1-0	Garay
04/05/00	AS Saint-Etienne	H	0-1	
13/05/00	RC Lens	A	0-3	

A TROYES AC

THE EUROPEAN FOOTBALL YEARBOOK 2000-2001

CLUB DIRECTORY

Association Troyes Aube Champagne (now -
Espérance Sportive Troyes Aube Champagne)
Stade de l'Aube
Avenue Robert-Schuman
BP 226
10007 Troyes Cedex
tel - (0325) 704830
fax - (0325) 704833
Year of Formation - 1986
President - Daniel Vacelet
Secretary - Jean-Marc Pellissier
Coach - Alain Perrin
Stadium - Stade de l'Aube (18,235).

APPEARANCES 99/00

	P	Ap	(s)	Gls
Frédéric ADAM	M	27	(2)	
Frédéric ARPINON	M	29	(1)	1
Seikou BERTHE (MLI)	D	9	(1)	
Samuel BOUTAL	A	24	(4)	5
Mohamed BRADJA	D	9	(2)	
Samba DIAWARA	D	3	(7)	
Sladjan DJUKIC (YUG)	A	29	(4)	10
Farid GHAZI (ALG)	A	16	(4)	5
David HAMED	D	23	(6)	1
Tony HEURTEBIS	G	31		
Nordin JBARI (BEL)	A	7	(3)	3
Richard JEZIERSKI	D	29	(1)	1
Yannick LALISSE	D	1	(2)	
Didier LANG	M	27	(4)	1
Samuel LOBE	A		(2)	1
Damlaba MENDY	A	8	(11)	2
Jérôme MONIER	M	8	(16)	1
NADE	M		(3)	
Pascal RENIER (BEL)	D	10	(2)	
Emmanuel RIVAL	M	21	(9)	
Rafik SAIFI (ALG)	M	20	(8)	4
Edouard THOMAS	D	15	(1)	
Laurent WEBER	G	3		
Luciano ZAVAGNO (ARG)	M	25	(1)	
Rudy ZEITOUN	A		(1)	

LEAGUE RESULTS 1999/2000

Date	Opponent	H/A	Score	Scorers
31/07/99	Paris Saint-Germain	A	0-1	
05/08/99	Olympique Lyonnais	H	1-2	Jezierski
14/08/99	Girondins de Bordeaux	A	0-4	
20/08/99	RC Strasbourg	H	2-1	Ghazi, Boutal
29/08/99	AS Monaco	A	0-3	
11/09/99	FC Nantes	H	1-0	Saifi
19/09/99	Olympique Marseille	A	0-1	
25/09/99	AS Nancy-Lorraine	H	2-0	Djukic, Ghazi
02/10/99	CS Sedan Ardennes	A	1-2	Ghazi
13/10/99	Le Havre AC	H	3-1	Ghazi, Arpinon, Jbari
16/10/99	AS Saint-Etienne	A	0-1	
24/10/99	RC Lens	H	0-1	
30/10/99	SC Bastia	A	0-5	
07/11/99	Montpellier HSC	H	2-1	Djukic (p), Hamed
10/11/99	AJ Auxerre	A	1-0	Boutal
19/11/99	Stade Rennais FC	A	2-2	og (Diatta), Mendy
27/11/99	FC Metz	H	2-2	Djukic, Saifi
03/12/99	Olympique Lyonnais	A	3-1	Boutal, Djukic 2
11/12/99	Girondins de Bordeaux	H	2-0	Djukic, Ghazi
12/01/00	AS Monaco	H	1-4	Saifi
15/01/00	FC Nantes	A	0-3	
19/01/00	RC Strasbourg	A	0-2	
25/01/00	Olympique Marseille	H	1-2	Monier
02/02/00	AS Nancy-Lorraine	A	2-1	Djukic (p), Mendy
05/02/00	CS Sedan Ardennes	H	0-2	
16/02/00	Le Havre AC	A	0-2	
26/02/00	AS Saint-Etienne	H	0-1	
12/03/00	RC Lens	A	1-0	Saifi
25/03/00	SC Bastia	H	1-0	Djukic
08/04/00	Montpellier HSC	A	2-2	Jbari, Lobé
15/04/00	AJ Auxerre	H	2-0	Jbari, Boutal
29/04/00	Stade Rennais FC	H	1-0	Boutal
04/05/00	FC Metz	A	1-3	Lang
13/05/00	Paris Saint-Germain	H	2-2	Djukic 2 (1p)

GEORGIA

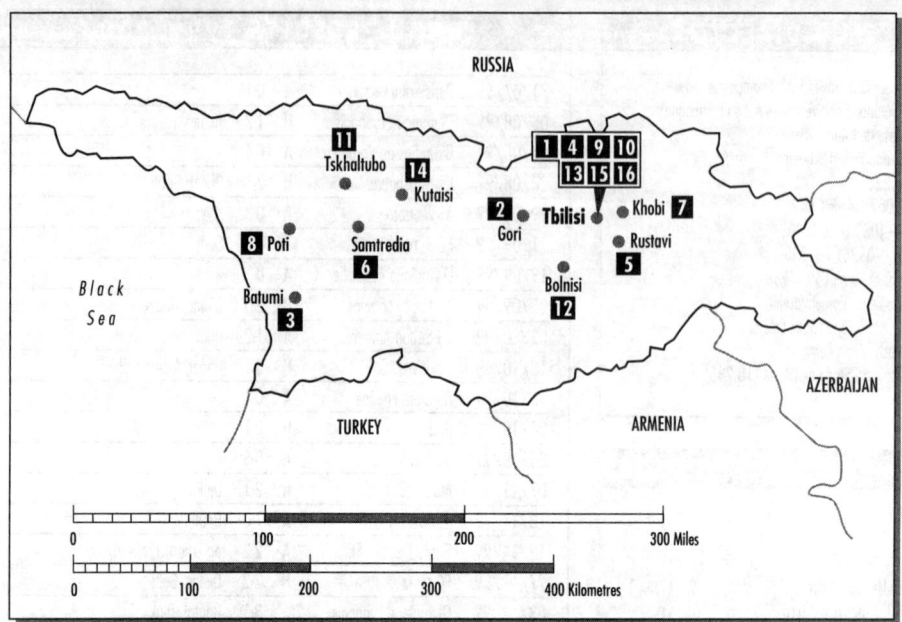

1	ARSENALI TBILISI	416	
2	DILA GORI	417	
3	DINAMO BATUMI	418	
4	DINAMO TBILISI	419	
5	GORDA RUSTAVI	420	
6	IBERIA SAMTREDIA	421	
7	KOLKHETI KHOBI	422	
8	KOLKHETI 1913 POTI	423	
9	LOKOMOTIVI TBILISI	424	
10	MERANI 91 TBILISI	425	
11	SAMGURALI TSKHALTUBO	426	
12	SIONI BOLNISI	427	
13	FC TBILISI	428	
14	TORPEDO KUTAISI	429	
15	TSU TBILISI	430	
16	VIT GEORGIA TBILISI	431	

NEW SYSTEM BRINGS NEW CHAMPIONS

Dinamo Tbilisi dethroned at long last

FEDERATION DIRECTORY

Football Federation of Georgia
5 Shota Iamanidze Str., Tbilisi 380 012

tel - (32) 960780   Year of Formation - 1990
fax - (32) 001128   President - Merab Jordania
email - gffburti@caucasus.net   Secretary - Valeri Cholaria

Stadium - Boris Paichadze, Tbilisi (75,000)

After winning the Georgian championship for ten successive years - and establishing an unprecedented European record into the bargain - Dinamo Tbilisi were finally deposed as the country's top club. It took a newly-devised league structure to bring them down - that and a crippling financial crisis forced on the club by their continual failure to make any significant impact in European competition.

Dinamo's plight was exacerbated by their inability to qualify for Europe at all in 2000/01. They could finish no higher than third place in the league and were eliminated in the semi-finals of the Cup. That amounted to a complete disaster for Georgia's most prominent club, and questions were even raised as to whether Dinamo's financial ailments might prevent them from enjoying such sustained supremacy ever again.

All seemed well at the halfway stage of the new two-tiered championship. Dinamo were clear winners of Group A, and as the points were divided by two for the second half of the season, they trailed only one club, Group B winners Torpedo Kutaisi, by a single point. However, the enforced sale of their two main strikers, Mikheil Ashvetia and Reti Aleksidze, was to have a devastating effect, and they began the spring campaign with four successive goalless draws. They never recovered. The shortage of firepower was to produce five more draws in the run-in, and although Dinamo remained undefeated in the second phase, five wins out of 14 left them too far adrift.

Torpedo, on the other hand, maintained their autumn form, collecting eight wins and four draws, which they embroidered with 37 goals. That gave them a clear five-point lead at the top of the table and a first-ever championship title. Ironically, the man behind their success, coach David Kipiani, was a former Dinamo Tbilisi idol. His new club certainly did his old one no favours when they drew their final match 0-0 with Vit Georgia. It was a result which enabled their opponents to pip Dinamo to the UEFA Cup spot based on their

LEAGUE CHAMPIONSHIP RESULTS 99/00

FIRST PHASE - GROUP A	1	2	3	4	5	6	7	8
1 Arsenali Tbilisi		0-1	2-0	0-4	2-1	0-1	1-1	1-2
2 Dinamo Batumi	1-0		1-0	4-1	0-0	4-0	2-0	0-0
3 Dinamo Tbilisi	1-1	2-1		4-0	7-1	3-0	3-2	4-1
4 Lokomotivi Tblisi	2-2	0-0	1-2		2-0	0-1	2-1	1-1
5 Samgurali Tskhaltubo	1-0	0-0	1-2	0-3		1-0	1-0	0-1
6 Sioni Bolnisi	1-0	0-0	1-3	1-0	2-0		2-2	0-0
7 FC Tbilisi	3-1	1-1	0-6	0-4	5-2	3-4		2-1
8 Vit Georgia Tbilisi	4-0	0-0	0-1	3-1	3-1	3-0	1-1	

FIRST PHASE - GROUP B	1	2	3	4	5	6	7	8
1 Dila Gori		1-2	2-0	1-0	3-0	3-2	0-5	1-1
2 Gorda Rustavi	2-0		4-0	4-1	0-1	0-0	0-2	3-1
3 Iberia Samtredia	2-1	1-0		2-1	1-0	1-1	0-3	0-1
4 Kolkheti Khobi	2-3	5-1	0-1		0-3	1-1	1-2	0-0
5 Kolkheti 1913 Poti	3-0	2-0	1-0	2-3		1-0	0-0	1-0
6 Merani 91 Tbilisi	3-1	2-1	0-0	0-0	1-2		0-1	1-1
7 Torpedo Kutaisi	2-2	1-0	5-0	0-0	4-1	3-1		3-0
8 TSU Tbilisi	0-1	1-0	1-1	4-1	3-2	0-2	0-2	

SECOND PHASE CHAMPIONSHIP GROUP	1	2	3	4	5	6	7	8
1 Dila Gori		0-1	0-3	3-0	0-2	1-0	0-4	0-2
2 Dinamo Batumi	4-0		0-0	6-0	2-0	3-0	2-1	0-1
3 Dinamo Tbilisi	6-1	0-0		2-0	1-1	3-0	1-1	0-0
4 Iberia Samtredia	2-1	0-2	0-0		1-0	0-1	0-3	0-1
5 Kolkheti 1913 Poti	3-1	1-0	0-0	1-0		5-0	2-1	2-0
6 Sioni Bolnisi	4-1	1-2	0-2	2-2	1-0		2-4	1-2
7 Torpedo Kutaisi	4-1	4-0	0-0	5-0	3-1	6-1		0-0
8 Vit Georgia Tbilisi	2-1	2-0	1-1	2-1	0-0	1-0	1-1	

RELEGATION GROUP	1	2	3	4	5	6	7	8
1 Arsenali Tbilisi		0-4	4-2	0-1	0-2	2-1	4-2	0-2
2 Gorda Rustavi	3-0		2-0	1-0	1-1	1-2	2-0	2-0
3 Kolkheti Khobi	2-1	1-4		0-7	1-2	0-2	1-2	2-4
4 Lokomotivi Tbilisi	1-0	2-1	4-1		0-0	0-0	1-1	3-0
5 Merani 91 Tbilisi	1-0	0-0	1-0	3-1		0-0	4-0	1-0
6 Samgurali Tskhaltubo	2-0	2-0	2-1	1-0	0-1		2-1	3-1
7 FC Tbilisi	2-0	1-4	3-0	0-1	0-1	0-0		0-4
8 TSU Tbilisi	2-0	1-0	7-2	0-1	2-1	1-0	2-0	

LEAGUE CHAMPIONSHIP FINAL TABLES 99/00

FIRST PHASE - GROUP A

		Pd	Home					Away					Total						
			W	D	L	F	A	W	D	L	F	A	W	D	L	F	A	Pt	GD
1	Dinamo Tbilisi	14	6	1	0	24	6	5	0	2	14	6	11	1	2	38	12	34	26
2	Dinamo Batumi	14	5	2	0	12	1	1	5	1	3	3	6	7	1	15	4	25	11
3	Vit Georgia Tbilisi	14	4	2	1	14	4	2	3	2	6	8	6	5	3	20	12	23	8
4	Sioni Bolnisi	14	3	3	1	7	5	3	0	4	6	14	6	3	5	13	19	21	-6
5	Lokomotivi Tbilisi	14	2	3	2	8	7	3	0	4	13	12	5	3	6	21	19	18	2
6	FC Tbilisi	14	3	1	3	14	19	0	3	4	7	12	3	4	7	21	31	13	-10
7	Samgurali Tskhaltubo	14	3	1	3	4	6	0	1	6	5	21	3	2	9	9	27	11	-18
8	Arsenali Tbilisi	14	2	1	4	6	10	0	2	5	4	13	2	3	9	10	23	9	-13

FIRST PHASE - GROUP B

		Pd	Home					Away					Total						
			W	D	L	F	A	W	D	L	F	A	W	D	L	F	A	Pt	GD
1	Torpedo Kutaisi	14	5	2	0	18	4	6	1	0	15	1	11	3	0	33	5	36	28
2	Kolkheti 1913 Poti	14	5	1	1	10	3	3	0	4	9	12	8	1	5	19	15	25	4
3	Dila Gori	14	4	1	2	11	10	2	1	4	8	14	6	2	6	19	24	20	-5
4	Iberia Samtredia	14	4	1	2	7	7	1	2	4	2	13	5	3	6	9	20	18	-11
5	Gorda Rustavi	14	4	1	2	13	5	1	0	6	4	13	5	1	8	17	18	16	-1
6	TSU Tbilisi	14	3	1	3	9	9	1	3	3	4	9	4	4	6	13	18	16	-5
7	Merani 91 Tbilisi	14	2	3	2	7	6	1	3	3	7	9	3	6	5	14	15	15	-1
8	Kolkheti Khobi	14	1	2	4	9	11	1	2	4	6	13	2	4	8	15	24	10	-9

SECOND PHASE
CHAMPIONSHIP GROUP

		Pd	Home					Away					Total						
			W	D	L	F	A	W	D	L	F	A	W	D	L	F	A	Pt	GD
1	Torpedo Kutaisi	14	5	2	0	22	3	3	2	2	15	8	8	4	2	37	11	46	26
2	Vit Georgia Tbilisi	14	4	3	0	9	4	4	2	1	6	3	8	5	1	15	7	41	8
3	Dinamo Tbilisi	14	3	4	0	13	3	2	5	0	6	1	5	9	0	19	4	41	15
4	Dinamo Batumi	14	5	1	1	17	2	3	1	3	5	8	8	2	4	22	10	39	12
5	Kolkheti 1913 Poti	14	6	1	0	14	2	1	2	4	4	8	7	3	4	18	10	37	8
6	Sioni Bolnisi	14	2	1	4	11	13	1	0	6	2	19	3	1	10	13	32	21	-19
7	Iberia Samtredia	14	2	1	4	3	8	0	1	6	3	21	2	2	10	6	29	17	-23
8	Dila Gori	14	2	0	5	4	12	0	0	7	6	25	2	0	12	10	37	16	-27

SECOND PHASE
RELEGATION GROUP

		Pd	Home					Away					Total						
			W	D	L	F	A	W	D	L	F	A	W	D	L	F	A	Pt	GD
9	Merani 91 Tbilisi	14	5	2	0	10	1	4	2	1	8	4	9	4	1	18	5	39	13
10	Lokomotivi Tbilisi	14	4	3	0	11	3	4	0	3	11	5	8	3	3	22	8	36	14
11	TSU Tbilisi	14	6	0	1	15	4	3	0	4	11	11	9	0	5	26	15	35	11
12	Gorda Rustavi	14	5	1	1	12	3	3	1	3	13	7	8	2	4	25	10	34	15
13	Samgurali Tskhaltubo	14	6	0	1	12	4	2	3	2	5	4	8	3	3	17	8	33	9
14	FC Tbilisi	14	2	1	4	6	10	1	1	5	6	16	3	2	9	12	26	18	-14
15	Arsenali Tbilisi	14	3	0	4	10	14	0	0	7	1	13	3	0	11	11	27	14	-16
16	Kolkheti Khobi	14	1	0	6	7	22	0	0	7	6	23	1	0	13	13	45	8	-32

N.B. After the First Phase the top eight play off for the title and the bottom eight play off against relegation. Half the points from the First Phase are carried forward.

superior record in the second phase of the championship. There were two distinct low points in Torpedo's otherwise triumphant season. The first came in September when they were annihilated in the first round of the UEFA Cup by AEK Athens. The second arrived eight months later when they were denied the 'double' after a penalty shoot-out defeat in the Cup final by Lokomotivi Tbilisi. That was a major surprise as Lokomotivi had not even made it into the championship group in the league. They too had suffered at the hands of Greek opponents in the UEFA Cup at the start of the season, losing 9-0 on aggregate to PAOK, but their mere appearance in the final ensured a return to that competition in 2000/01.

NATIONAL TEAM RESULTS 99/00

04/09/99	Slovenia (ECQ)	A	Ljubljana	1-2	Arveladze S. (56)
08/09/99	Latvia (ECQ)	H	Tbilisi	2-2	Arveladze S. (30), Kavelashvili (52)
09/10/99	Albania (ECQ)	A	Tirana	1-2	Arveladze S. (52)
02/02/00	Slovakia	N	Larnaca	2-0	Ketsbaia (83), Kavelashvili (86)
04/02/00	Romania	N	Larnaca	1-1	Ketsbaia (41)
06/02/00	Armenia	N	Limassol	2-1	Janashia Z. (7), Menteshashvili (55)
29/03/00	Israel	A	Ashkelon	1-1	Kinkladze (27)
26/04/00	Armenia	A	Yerevan	0-0	
04/06/00	Azerbaijan	A	Baku	0-0	
11/06/00	Estonia	A	Pärnu	0-1	

TOP SCORERS

25 Zurab IONANIDZE (Torpedo Kutaisi)
22 Varlan KILASONIA (Gorda Rustavi)
15 Kakhaber TSUTSUNAVA (TSU Tbilisi)
13 Giorgi KORIDZE (Vit Georgia Tbilisi)

DOMESTIC CUP 99/00

1/16 FINALS
Torpedo Kutaisi v Samegrelo Chkhorotsku 7-0; 4-0
(Torpedo Kutaisi 11-0)
Samgurali Tskhaltubo v Iberia 2 Samtredia 3-0; 3-0
(Samgurali Tskhaltubo 6-0)
Dinamo Batumi v Okeane Samtredia 2-0; 1-0
(Dinamo Batumi 3-0)
Kolkheti 1913 Poti v Shukura Kobuleti 6-0; 6-1
(Kolkheti 1913 Poti 12-1)
Iberia Samtredia v Margveti Zestafoni 1-0; 0-2
(Margveti Zestafoni 2-1)
Dila Gori v Megri Zugdidi 4-1; 0-1
(Dila Gori 4-2)
TSU Tbilisi v Metalurgi Zestafoni 1-1; 5-2
(TSU Tbilisi 6-3)
Dinamo Tbilisi v Tori Borjami 5-0; 7-0
(Dinamo Tbilisi 12-0)
Chabukiani v FC Tbilisi 0-1; 1-3
(FC Tbilisi 4-1)
Vit Georgia Tbilisi v SA Iberia Tbilisi 4-1; 2-3
(Vit Georgia Tbilisi 6-4)
Sioni Bolnisi v Zooveti Tbilisi 2-1; 0-1
(2-2; Zooveti Tbilisi on away goal)
Lokomotivi Tbilisi v Lokomotivi 2 Tbilisi 5-0; 3-1
(Lokomotivi Tbilisi 8-1)
Merani 91 Tbilisi v Tskhinvali 1-0; 1-0
(Merani 91 Tbilisi 2-0)
Arsenali Tbilisi v ShSS Akademia Tbilisi 0-0; 0-1
(ShSS Akademia Tbilisi 1-0)
Kolkheti Khobi v Guria Lanchkhuti 3-1; 0-3
(Guria Lanchkhuti 4-3)
Gorda Rustavi v Iveria Khashuri 3-0; 3-0
(Gorda Rustavi 6-0)

1/8 FINALS
ShSS Akademia Tbilisi v Torpedo Kutaisi 0-5; 0-2
(Torpedo Kutaisi 7-0)
Dinamo Tbilisi v Guria Lanchkhuti 6-0; 3-0
(Dinamo Tbilisi 9-0)
Kolkheti 1913 Poti v Merani 91 Tbilisi 1-0; 0-0
(Kolkheti 1913 Poti 1-0)
Dinamo Batumi v Gorda Rustavi 2-0; 1-1
(Dinamo Batumi 3-1)
Vit Georgia Tbilisi v TSU Tbilisi 1-1; 5-1
(Vit Georgia Tbilisi 6-2)
Dila Gori v Zooveti Tbilisi 3-0; 2-1
(Dila Gori 5-1)
Margveti Zestafoni v Samgurali Tskhaltubo 0-2; 2-2
(Samgurali Tskhaltubo 4-2)
Lokomotivi Tbilisi v FC Tbilisi 1-1; 1-0
(Lokomotivi Tbilisi 2-1)

QUARTER-FINALS
Vit Georgia Tbilisi 0, Lokomotivi Tbilisi 0
Lokomotivi Tbilisi 0, Vit Georgia Tbilisi 0
(0-0; Lokomotivi Tbilisi 3-1 on pens.)

Dinamo Batumi 3 (Mujiri 73, Machutadze 82,
Khomeriki 87), Kokheti 1913 Poti 0
Kolkheti 1913 Poti 0, Dinamo Batumi 0
(Dinamo Batumi 3-0)

Samgurali Tskhaltubo 0, Torpedo Kutaisi 0
Torpedo Kutaisi 2 (Khvadagiani 79, Megreladze 81),
Samgurali Tskhaltubo 0
(Torpedo Kutaisi 2-0)

Dinamo Tbilisi 4 (Khutsishvili 9, Tsitaishvili 21, 82,
Anchabadze 64), Dila Gori 0
Dila Gori 1 (Marekhashvili 35), Dinamo Tbilisi 4
(Sakhvadze 13, 33, 90, Rukhadze 63)
(Dinamo Tbilisi 8-1)

SEMI-FINALS
Dinamo Tbilisi 1 (Guchua 54),
Torpedo Kutaisi 1 (Megreladze 40)
Torpedo Kutaisi 0, Dinamo Tbilisi 0
(1-1; Torpedo Kutaisi on away goal)

Lokomotivi Tbilisi 2 (Kvaratskhelia 12, Jugeli 68),
Dinamo Batumi 0
Dinamo Batumi 1 (Khujadze 24), Lokomotivi Tbilisi 0
(Lokomotivi Tbilisi 2-1)

FINAL
26/05/2000, Tbilisi
LOKOMOTIVI TBILISI 0
TORPEDO KUTAISI 0
(aet; 4-2 on pens.)
referee - Kvaratskhelia
LOKOMOTIVI TBILISI - Lomaia, Balashvili, Mikadze,
Abramidze (Rusia 78), Chikhradze, Gigichaishvili,
Kvaratskhelia, Chichveishvili, Jugeli
(Ghkhaidze G. 88), Khizanishvili, Jishkariani.
TORPEDO KUTAISI - Zoidze, Ionanidze, Makhviladze
(Shekriladze 98), Kvetenadze, Gogiashvili, Janashia
(Asatiani 79), Chkhetiani, Turmanidze, Akhvlediani,
Imedadze (Megreladze 46), Khvadagiani.

Lokomotivi only staved off relegation by three points. Four teams were relegated and none promoted as the top two divisions were trimmed to just a dozen teams each for the new season.

David Kipiani's efforts with Torpedo were rewarded with his appointment as dual coach of the Georgian national team alongside ex-Latvia boss Revaz Dzodzuashvili. The twosome replaced Dutchman Johan Boskamp, whose six-month reign ended in disgrace when Georgia slumped to the bottom of their European Championship group after losing their final qualifier away to Albania. Results scarcely improved under the new regime, and despite the availability of in-form foreign-based players such as Footballer of the Year Levan Kobiashvili and Russian league top scorer Giorgi Demetradze as well as established names like Giorgi Kinkladze, Temur Ketsbaia and the Arveladze twins, there was little realistic hope of any major resurgence in time for the tough World Cup assignments against Lithuania, Italy, Romania and Hungary.

NATIONAL TEAM APPEARANCES 99/00

Coach - Johan BOSKAMP; David KIPIANI & Revaz DZODZUASHVILI	SLO	LAT	ALB	SVK	ROM	ARM	ISR	ARM	AZB	EST	Cps	Gls
David GVARAMADZE (08/11/75) - Krylya Sovetov Samara (RUS)	G	G		G	G		s46		G		14	-
Badri AKHVLEDIANI (19/10/72) - Torpedo Kutaisi	D46										2	-
Levan TSKITISHVILI (10/10/76) - SC Freiburg (GER)	D	D70									16	1
Givi DIDAVA (21/03/76) - Dinamo Tbilisi	D	D	D					s72			12	-
Kakhi KALADZE (27/02/78) - Dynamo Kyiv (UKR)	D	M	D				D				22	-
Levan KOBIASHVILI (10/07/77) - SC Freiburg (GER)	M	M	M				M		M	M	26	-
Tengiz SICHINAVA (15/05/72) - Dinamo Tbilisi	M	s70		s38	M	M22	s46	M	M	M71	9	-
Mikheil KAVELASHVILI (22/07/71) - FC Zürich (SUI)	M	A75		A89	A90	A		M		M56	34	8
Mikheil POTSKHVERIA (12/08/75) - Shakhtar Donetsk (UKR)	M										4	-
Archil ARVELADZE (22/02/73) - NAC (HOL)	A	s75	A83	M	A67	M	A81		A70	A62	26	4
Shota ARVELADZE (22/02/73) - Ajax (HOL)	A	A72	A						A86	A	35	14
Gela SHEKILADZE (14/09/70) - K Lierse SK (BEL)	s46	D	D	D29	D	s22					19	-
Mamuka TSERETELI (17/01/79) - Alania Vladikavkaz (RUS)		D									8	-
Giorgi NEMSADZE (10/05/72) - Lokomotivi Tbilisi/Dinamo Tbilisi		M	D	D	M	D	D			D	50	-
Gocha JAMARAULI (23/07/71) - FC Zürich (SUI)		M	M	M	M	M73					43	5
Giorgi DEMETRADZE (26/09/76) - Alania Vladikavkaz (RUS)/Dynamo Kyiv (UKR)		s72					A46	A		s56	13	-
Giorgi CHANTURIA (25/09/73) - Torpedo Kutaisi			G								1	-
David CHICHVEISHVILI (23/01/75) - Alania Vladikavkaz (RUS)			D								3	-
Giorgi GAKHOKIDZE (05/11/75) - Maccabi Haifa (ISR)			M								13	-
David JANASHIA (07/08/72) - Torpedo Kutaisi			s83								10	3
Levan SILAGADZE (04/08/76) - Alania Vladikavkaz (RUS)				D		D	D	D	D	D	13	-
Giorgi CHIKHRADZE (01/10/67) - Lokomotivi Tbilisi				D	D	D			D		24	-
Temur KETSBAIA (18/03/68) - Newcastle United (ENG)				M	M		M		M70	M62	41	13
Givi KVARATSKHELIA (11/05/79) - Lokomotivi Tbilisi				M38							1	-
Zaza JANASHIA (10/02/76) - Lokomotiv Moskva (RUS)				A55	s46	A46					8	4
Zurab KHIZANISHVILI (06/10/81) - Lokomotivi Tbilisi				s29	D		D	M72	D	D	7	-
Zurab MENTESHASHVILI (30/01/80) - Skonto Riga (LAT)				s55	M46	D	s73	s55			5	1
Revaz KEMOKLIDZE (13/03/79) - FC Tbilisi				s89	s67	D					3	-
Merab DZODZUASHVILI (04/11/80) - Lokomotivi Tbilisi					s90	s46					2	-
Soso GRISHIKASHVILI (31/12/72) - Dinamo Tbilisi						G	G46	G		G	9	-
Giorgi KINKLADZE (06/07/73) - Derby County (ENG)							M		M80	M71	37	7
Rati ALEKSIDZE (03/08/78) - Chelsea (ENG)							s81	M55	s80	s62	8	-
Levan MIKADZE (13/09/73) - Lokomotivi Tbilisi							D34				1	-
Sevasti TODUA (13/05/76) - Vit Georgia Tbilisi							D	D			2	-
David CHALADZE (22/01/76) - Skonto Riga (LAT)							A46			s62	3	-
Aleksandre REKHVIASHVILI (16/08/74) - Skonto Riga (LAT)							s34			s71	3	-
Zurab IONANIDZE (02/12/71) - Torpedo Kutaisi							s46				2	-
Revaz ARVELADZE (15/09/69) - Dinamo Tbilisi									s70	s71	11	1
Aleksandre IASHVILI (23/10/77) - SC Freiburg (GER)									s70		8	2
Kakhi GOGICHAISHVILI (31/10/68) - Lokomotivi Tbilisi									s86		27	1

INTERNATIONAL HONOURS

European Club Competitions
Cup-winners' Cup   Dinamo Tbilisi (1981).

EUROPEAN CUPS 99/00

CHAMPIONS' CUP
● **DINAMO TBILISI**
Preliminary round 2 ZIMBRU CHISINAU (MOL)
H 2-1 Tsitaishvili (81), Khomeriki (90)
Dhondt, Shashiashvili, Chichveishvili, Didava, Sakhvadze
(Khomeriki 72), Gigiadze, Kiknadze V., Sichinava, Aleksidze,
De Souza (Tsitaishvili 72), Ashvetia.
A 0-2
Dhondt, Khizaneishvili, Chichveishvili, Didava, Sichinava, Gigiadze V.
(Shengelia 52), Kiknadze, Aleksidze, Khomeriki, De Souza, Ashvetia
(Tsitaishvili 66).

UEFA CUP
● **LOKOMOTIVI TBILISI**
Qualifying round LINFIELD (NIR)
H 1-0 Kebadze (23)
Janelidze, Mikadze, Balashvili, Kobuladze, Chikhradze, Baramidze
(Katsiashvili 46), Barnov, Chomakhidze (Aslanadze 79), Shavgulidze
(Melkadze 77), Gogichaishvili, Kebadze.
A 1-1 Kebadze (79)
Aslanadze, Mikadze, Kobuladze, Chikhradze, Balashvili, Chomakhidze
(Katsiashvili 59), Gvelesiani, Melkadze, Baramidze, Kebadze,
Gogichaishvili.

1st round PAOK (GRE)
H 0-7
Aslanadze, Mikadze, Balashvili, Chikhradze, Kobuladze, Barnov
(Baramidze 46), Gvelesiani, Chomakhidze (Katsiashvili 76), Rusia
(Shavgulidze 51), Gogichaishvili, Kebadze.
A 0-2
Aslanadze, Balashvili, Chikhradze, Kobuladze, Bakradze, Melkadze
(Barnov 65), Mikadze, Shavgulidze (Beradze 82), Katsiashvili,
Chomakhidze (Gvelesiani 89), Kebadze.

● **TORPEDO KUTAISI**
Qualifying round FC LANTANA TALLINN (EST)
A 5-0 Khvadagiani (2), Janashia D. (32), Ionanidze (38), Chkhetiani (54),
Megreladze (65)
Chanturia, Akhvlediani, Khvadagiani, Turmanidze (Vachiberadze 80),
Shekriladze, Chkhetiani, Kvetenadze (Maisuradze V. 67), Ionanidze,
Gogiashvili, Janashia D., Megreladze (Bobokhidze 76).
H 4-2 Ionanidze (11), Megreladze (26, 29, 71)
Chanturia (Somkhishvili 85), Akhvlediani, Khvadagiani, Maisuradze V.,
Amisulashvili, Chkhetiani, Kvetenadze, Gogiashvili (Maglakelidze 67),
Ionanidze, Megreladze, Imedadze (Janashia D. 67).

1st round AEK (GRE)
H 0-1
Chanturia, Akhvlediani, Khvadagiani, Magrakelidze, Turmanidze,
Chkhetiani (Kvetenadze 82), Shekriladze, Gogiashvili (Imedadze 51),
Ionanidze, Janashia D., Megreladze (Vachiberadze 73).
A 1-6 Megreladze (73)
Chanturia, Khvadagiani, Maglakelidze, Shekriladze, Akhvlediani
(Gogiashvili 31), Turmanidze (Amisulashvili 78), Chkhetiani,
Kvetenadze (Imedadze 52), Ionanidze, Janashia D., Megreladze.

SECOND DIVISION 99/00

EAST GROUP A	Pd	W	D	L	F	A	Pt	GD
1 Tskhinvali	20	15	2	3	47	8	47	39
2 Tori Borjomi	20	15	2	3	41	14	47	27
3 Iveria Khashuri	20	14	0	6	45	20	42	25
4 SK Iberia Tbilisi	20	11	2	7	28	18	35	10
5 Meskheti Akhaltsikhe	20	9	4	7	44	36	31	8
6 Tskhumi Sokhumi	20	9	2	9	36	27	29	9
7 Gantiadi Kaspi	20	7	1	12	23	44	22	-21
8 Mretebi Tbilisi	20	5	5	10	20	37	20	-17
9 SAU Tbilisi	20	6	1	13	24	39	19	-15
10 Vardzia Aspindza	20	4	2	14	17	55	14	-38
11 Aragvi Dusheti	20	4	1	15	22	49	13	-27

EAST GROUP B	Pd	W	D	L	F	A	Pt	GD
1 Lokomotivi Tbilisi	20	14	3	3	35	16	45	19
2 Alazani Gurjaani	20	14	2	4	58	20	44	38
3 Arsenali 2 Tbilisi	20	13	4	3	43	22	43	21
4 Chabukiani	20	13	3	4	41	13	42	28
5 Zooveti Tbilisi	20	10	5	5	40	29	35	11
6 Khalibi 97 Rustavi	20	7	3	10	27	33	24	-6
7 Amirani Ochomchire	20	7	3	10	31	44	24	-13
8 Sh.SS Akademia Tbilisi	20	5	6	9	16	18	21	-2
9 Tbilisi 2	20	4	4	12	21	41	16	-20
10 Samgori Gardabani	20	3	2	15	20	55	11	-35
11 Kvareli	20	2	1	17	12	53	7	-41

WEST GROUP A	Pd	W	D	L	F	A	Pt	GD
1 Margveti Zestafoni	22	18	4	0	71	18	58	53
2 Okeane Samtredia	22	13	6	3	51	23	45	28
3 Iberia 2 Samtredia	22	12	6	4	47	26	42	21
4 Metalurgi Zestafoni	22	12	5	5	42	27	41	15
5 Interi Kutaisi	22	9	6	7	34	30	33	4
6 Dinamo Gagra	22	6	8	8	31	37	26	-6
7 Racha Ambrolauri	22	6	7	9	31	37	25	-6
8 Guria Lanchkhuti	22	7	1	14	36	45	22	-9
9 Rtsmena Kutaisi	22	5	7	10	16	29	22	-13
10 Sulori Vani	22	5	6	11	30	54	21	-24
11 Magaroeli Chiatura	22	3	6	13	28	47	15	-19
12 Meshakhte Tkibuli	22	3	4	15	24	68	13	-44

WEST GROUP B	Pd	W	D	L	F	A	Pt	GD
1 Shukura Kobuleti	22	18	2	2	66	20	56	46
2 Dinamo Zugdidi	22	16	3	3	65	21	51	44
3 Megri Zugdidi	22	16	2	4	40	17	50	23
4 Kolkheti 2 Poti	22	14	4	4	34	15	46	19
5 Laziko Zugdidi	22	12	5	5	56	24	41	32
6 Pazisi Poti	22	10	3	9	36	37	33	-1
7 Skuri Tsalenjikha	22	6	3	13	25	52	21	-27
8 Samegrelo Chkhorotsku	22	5	5	12	23	43	20	-20
9 Dinamo 2 Batumi	22	4	8	10	26	38	20	-12
10 Mertskhali Ozurgeti	22	3	7	12	20	43	16	-23
11 Chela Darcheli	22	2	4	16	19	55	10	-36
12 Bakhmaro Chokhatouri	22	2	2	18	18	63	8	-45

ARSENALI TBILISI

CLUB DIRECTORY

Arsenali Tbilisi
Chavchavadze street 53a
Tbilisi
tel - (32) 220823
Year of Formation - 1940
President - Joni Pirtskhalaishvili
Coach - David Chakhava; Mamuka Gegechkori;
Joni Janelidze; Temur Tsertsvadze
Stadium - ASC (2,000)

APPEARANCES 99/00

	P	Ap	(s)	Gls
Dimitri ABAZADZE	D	3		
Edisher ALADASHVILI	D	11		
Vepkhia AMIRIDZE	M	7		
Giorgi ARKANIA	D	1	(1)	
Guram ASPINDZELASHVILI	D	26		
Giorgi CHALADZE	D	7	(5)	
Temur CHLAIDZE	G	12		
Kakhaber DAUSHVILI	A	1		
Vakhtang GAGUA	D	7	(1)	
Boris GONCHAROV	A	13	(1)	3
Vladimer GUDUSHAURI	D	6	(1)	
Giorgi IREMASHVILI	D	22	(1)	
Akaki KAKASHVILI	A	17	(4)	6
Irakli KAPANADZE	M	11	(1)	
Guram KATSABAVA	G		(1)	
Guram KHAREBAVA	D	11	(1)	
Amiran KHMALADZE	A	13		2
Guram KHOSROSHVILI	M	17	(1)	3
Zurab KOIAVA	A	6	(3)	1
Lasha KOLBAIA	D	5		
Levan KUPARADZE	D	3	(2)	
Zviad KUPATADZE	G	16	(1)	
Temur KVIRKVELIA	A	4	(8)	
Shalva LATSABIDZE	D	5		
Mukhran MAISURADZE	M	3		
David ROBAKIDZE	M	2	(2)	
Giorgi SHUKAKIDZE	M	14		
Giorgi SULADZE	M	18	(9)	1
Irakli TARGAMADZE	A	13		2
David TARIELASHVILI	A	8	(1)	1
Gamlet TSIVTSIVADZE	A	5	(1)	1
Kakhaber TSOTADZE	D	10	(1)	
Giorgi TSOTSKOLAURI	M		(6)	
Giorgi TUGUSHI	M	11	(3)	1

LEAGUE RESULTS 1999/2000

16/08/99	Lokomotivi Tbilisi	A	2-2	Targamadze 2
21/08/99	Dinamo Tbilisi	H	2-0	Khosroshvili, Tarielashvili
29/08/99	Samgurali Tskhaltubo	A	0-1	
12/09/99	FC Tbilisi	H	1-1	Kakashvili (p)
18/09/99	Sioni Bolnisi	A	0-1	
28/09/99	Vit Georgia Tbilisi	H	1-2	Kakashvili
02/10/99	Dinamo Batumi	A	0-1	
17/10/99	Lokomotivi Tbilisi	H	0-4	
23/10/99	Dinamo Tbilisi	A	1-1	Kakashvili
30/10/99	Samgurali Tskhaltubo	H	2-1	Goncharov 2
06/11/99	FC Tbilisi	A	1-3	Goncharov
13/11/99	Sioni Bolnisi	H	0-1	
20/11/99	Vit Georgia Tbilisi	A	0-4	
28/11/99	Dinamo Batumi	H	0-1	
12/03/00	Kolkheti Khobi	A	1-2	Khosroshvili
19/03/00	TSU Tbilisi	H	0-2	
22/03/00	Gorda Rustavi	H	0-4	
26/03/00	Lokomotivi Tbilisi	A	0-1	
02/04/00	Samgurali Tskhaltubo	H	2-1	Kakashvili, Suladze
14/04/00	FC Tbilisi	H	4-2	Kakashvili 2, Tsivtsivadze, Khasroshvili
18/04/00	Merani 91 Tbilisi	A	0-1	
22/04/00	Gorda Rustavi	A	0-3	
29/04/00	Kolkheti Khobi	H	4-2	Koiava, Khmaladze 2, Tugushi
05/05/00	TSU Tbilisi	A	0-2	
13/05/00	Lokomotivi Tbilisi	H	0-1	
17/05/00	Samgurali Tskhaltubo	A	0-2	
23/05/00	FC Tbilisi	A	0-2	
31/05/00	Merani 91 Tbilisi	H	0-2	

DILA GORI

CLUB DIRECTORY

Dila Gori
David Guramishvili street 5
Gori
tel - (270) 22107
Year of Formation - 1949
President - Guram Nozadze
Coach - Merab Khutsishvili; Ivane Takadze;
Merab Kochlashvili
Stadium - Central (8,230)

APPEARANCES 99/00

	P	Ap	(s)	Gls
Vakhtang AKOPIAN	D	20	(2)	
Noe ARUTUNIAN	M	8	(11)	2
Beka CHITAIA	M	3	(2)	
Giorgi CHITAIA	D	5	(2)	
Irakli EBANDIDZE	M	4	(4)	
Erekli ELKANISHVILI	M	2	(1)	
Khvicha GAGNIDZE	D	24		
Levan GOCHASHVILI	D	23		1
Tomaz ILURIDZE	G	1		
Lasha KARELIDZE	D	3	(7)	
Revaz KHACHAPURIDZE	D	24		
Mikheil KHECHUASHVILI	M		(1)	
Zurab KHORGUASHVILI	A	12	(1)	9
Aleksi KOCHLASHVILI	M	3	(2)	
Giorgi LOMIDZE	M	26		4
David MAISURADZE	M	2	(2)	
Jimsher MAREKHASHVILI	M	7	(3)	
Roin MARGISHVILI	A	11	(1)	3
David MDIVANI	G	7	(1)	
Archil OLGESASHVILI	M	10	(7)	
Paata PEZUASHVILI	D	16	(5)	
Albert SAKVARELIDZE	A	10	(3)	
Vladimer SAMKHARADZE	D	3	(1)	
Kristepore SHATAKISHVILI	A	11		
Ramaz SOGOLASHVILI	G	20		
Saba SULTANISHVILI	A	21	(7)	6
Mikheil TAKADZE	M	12		2
Tamaz TSITSKISHVILI	M	20	(4)	1

LEAGUE RESULTS 1999/2000

15/08/99	TSU Tbilisi	H	1-1	Margishvili (p)
21/08/99	Torpedo Kutaisi	A	2-2	Takadze, Sultanishvili
29/08/99	Kolkheti 1913 Poti	H	3-0	Lomidze 2, Sultanishvili
11/09/99	Gorda Rustavi	A	0-2	
18/09/99	Kolkheti Khobi	H	1-0	og (Aianadi Zu.)
25/09/99	Iberia Samtredia	H	2-0	Sultanishvili, Arutunian
02/10/99	Merani 91 Tbilisi	A	1-3	Margishvili
17/10/99	TSU Tbilisi	A	1-0	Takadze
24/10/99	Torpedo Kutaisi	H	0-5	
30/10/99	Kolkheti 1913 Poti	A	0-3	
06/11/99	Gorda Rustavi	H	1-2	Margishvili
13/11/99	Kolkheti Khobi	A	3-2	Khorguashvili 2, Lamidze
25/11/99	Iberia Samtredia	A	1-2	Khorguashvili
28/11/99	Merani 91 Tbilisi	H	3-2	Khorguashvili 2, Tsitskishvili
04/03/00	Sioni Bolnisi	A	1-4	Khorguashvili (p)
11/03/00	Iberia Samtredia	A	1-2	Khorguashvili
20/03/00	Vit Georgia Tbilisi	A	1-2	Lomidze
26/03/00	Kolkheti 1913 Poti	A	1-3	Khorguashvili
01/04/00	Dinamo Batumi	H	0-1	
14/04/00	Torpedo Kutaisi	A	1-4	Khorguashvili
18/04/00	Dinamo Tbilisi	H	0-3	
22/04/00	Sioni Bolnisi	H	1-0	Sultanishvili
29/04/00	Iberia Samtredia	H	3-0	Sultanishvili (p), Gochashvili, Arutunian
06/05/00	Vit Georgia Tbilisi	H	0-2	
13/05/00	Kolkheti 1913 Poti	H	0-2	
17/05/00	Dinamo Batumi	A	0-4	
22/05/00	Torpedo Kutaisi	H	0-4	
30/05/00	Dinamo Tbilisi	A	1-6	Sultanishvili

DINAMO BATUMI

CLUB DIRECTORY

Dinamo Batumi
H. Barbusse street 32
Batumi
tel - (222) 72362
fax - (222) 72369
Year of Formation - 1923
President - Temur Bejanidze
Coach - Joni Karnevale
Stadium - Central (18,000)

MAJOR HONOURS
Domestic Cup - (1) 1998.

APPEARANCES 99/00

	P	Ap	(s)	Gls
Shalva APKHAZAVA	A	10	(12)	6
Zurab ARCHVADZE	D	24		
Temur CHLAIDZE	G	2		
Temur GADELIA	A	6	(5)	1
Avtandil GLONTI	M	6	(6)	1
Aleksandre KANTIDZE	M	1	(3)	
Kakhaber KATSARAVA	M	7	(4)	
Levan KHOMERIKI	A	12	(2)	8
Shalva KHUJADZE	D	17	(2)	
Kakhaber KOBIDZE	M	20	(2)	1
Gela KORIDZE	M	24	(2)	4
Paata MACHUTADZE	A	19	(4)	5
Ivane MAKHARADZE	D	15	(4)	
Malkhaz MAKHARADZE	D	25	(1)	
Zurab MINDADZE	D	19	(1)	
Amiran MUJIRI	M	23	(2)	8
Zviad PAPIDZE	D	7	(2)	
Archil ROMANADZE	M	7	(15)	1
Kakhaber SIDAMONIDZE	D	13		2
Kakha SIKHARULIDZE	M	1	(4)	
Irakli TARGAMADZE	M		(3)	
Besik TEDORADZE	M	7	(3)	
Nikoloz TOGONIDZE	G	26		
Temur TUGUSHI	M	17	(5)	
Uche UVAKVE (NIG)	A		(2)	

LEAGUE RESULTS 1999/2000

15/08/99	Dinamo Tbilisi	H	1-0	Kobidze
22/08/99	FC Tbilisi	A	1-1	Machutadze
29/08/99	Vit Georgia Tbilisi	H	0-0	
11/09/99	Lokomotivi Tbilisi	A	0-0	
18/09/99	Samgurali Tskhaltubo	H	0-0	
25/09/99	Sioni Bolnisi	A	0-0	
02/10/99	Arsenali Tbilisi	H	1-0	Mujiri
16/10/99	Dinamo Tbilisi	A	1-2	Gadelia
24/10/99	FC Tbilisi	H	2-0	Apkhazava, Machutadze
30/10/99	Vit Georgia Tbilisi	A	0-0	
07/11/99	Lokomotivi Tbilisi	H	4-1	Koridze 2, Mujiri 2
13/11/99	Samgurali Tskhaltubo	A	0-0	
20/11/99	Sioni Bolnisi	H	4-0	Apkhazava 2, Machutadze, Mujiri
28/11/99	Arsenali Tbilisi	A	1-0	Apkhazava
04/03/00	Iberia Samtredia	H	6-0	Mujiri 2, Khomeriki, Machutadze 2, Koridze
18/03/00	Dinamo Tbilisi	A	0-0	
26/03/00	Sioni Bolnisi	H	3-0	Khomeriki 2, Apkhazava
01/04/00	Dila Gori	A	1-0	Apkhazava
05/04/00	Torpedo Kutaisi	H	2-1	Mujiri, Glonti
14/04/00	Vit Georgia Tbilisi	H	0-1	
18/04/00	Kolkheti 1913 Poti	A	0-1	
23/04/00	Iberia Samtredia	A	2-0	Sidamonidze, Khomeriki
29/04/00	Torpedo Kutaisi	A	0-4	
06/05/00	Dinamo Tbilisi	H	0-0	
13/05/00	Sioni Bolnisi	A	2-1	Koridze, Sidamonidze
17/05/00	Dila Gori	H	4-0	Khomeriki 3, Mujiri (p)
23/05/00	Vit Georgia Tbilisi	A	0-2	
30/05/00	Kolkheti 1913 Poti	H	2-0	Romanadze, Khomeriki

DINAMO TBILISI

CLUB DIRECTORY

Dinamo Tbilisi
Digomi Township, 3rd Block, Tbilisi
tel - (32) 984017/237023
fax - (32) 237027
Year of Formation - 1925
President - Merab Ratiani
Coach - Otar Korgalidze; Jemal Chimakadze
Stadium - Boris Paichadze (75,000)

MAJOR HONOURS
League Championship (USSR) - (2) 1964, 1978.
League Championship - (10) 1990, 1991, 1992,
1993, 1994, 1995, 1996, 1997, 1998, 1999.
Domestic Cup (USSR) - (2) 1976, 1979.
Domestic Cup - (6)
1992, 1993, 1994, 1995, 1996, 1997.
European Cup-winners' Cup - (1) 1981.

APPEARANCES 99/00

	P	Ap	(s)	Gls
Rati ALEKSIDZE	A	14		12
Giorgi ANCHABADZE	M	17	(2)	3
Revaz ARVELADZE	M	7	(1)	4
Mikheil ASHVETIA	A	14		12
Nikoloz CHKHEIDZE	G	1	(1)	
David DATVADZE	M	6	(1)	2
Givi DIDAVA	D	26		
Danny D'HONDT (BEL)	G	9		
Giorgi GABIDAURI	M	2		
Soso GIGIADZE	M		(5)	
Vaso GIGIADZE	A	2	(6)	1
Avtandil GLONTI	M		(1)	
Soso GRISHIKASHVILI	G	18		
Valter GUCHUA	D	17	(1)	
Oleg GVELESIANI	M	2	(2)	
Paata JINCHARADZE	M	8	(10)	
Revaz KEMOKLIDZE	D	6	(3)	
Otar KHIZANEISHVILI	D	8		
Mikheil KHUTSISHVILI	A		(5)	
Giorgi KIKNADZE	M	1	(1)	
Tengiz KOBIASHVILI	D	3	(1)	
Giorgi LOMAIA	G		(1)	
Giorgi MIKADZE	A		(1)	
Mamuka MINASHVILI	A	1	(2)	
Lasha MONASELIDZE	M	5	(1)	1
Giorgi NEMSADZE	M	6		2
Tornike RUKNADZE	D	4	(4)	
Archil SAKHVADZE	D	22	(1)	1
Giorgi SHASHIASHVILI	D	12	(5)	
Murtaz SHELIA	D	1		
Giorgi SHENGELIA	A	21	(5)	3
Tengiz SICHINAVA	M	27	(1)	1
Klimenti TSITAISHVILI	A	18	(3)	9
Irakli VASHAKIDZE	D	26		1
Robert ZIRAKISHVILI	A	4	(9)	5

LEAGUE RESULTS 1999/2000

15/08/99	Dinamo Batumi	A	0-1	
21/08/99	Arsenali Tbilisi	A	0-2	
29/08/99	FC Tbilisi	H	3-2	Anchabadze, Aleksidze 2
11/09/99	Vit Georgia Tbilisi	A	1-0	Aleksidze (p)
19/09/99	Lokomotivi Tbilisi	H	4-0	Ashvetia 2, Tsitaishvili, Zirakishvili
26/09/99	Samgurali Tskhaltubo	A	2-1	Ashvetia, Aleksidze
03/10/99	Sioni Bolnisi	H	3-0	Tsitaishvili, Ashvetia, Aleksidze
16/10/99	Dinamo Batumi	H	2-1	Ashvetia, Aleksidze
23/10/99	Arsenali Tbilisi	H	1-1	Aleksidze
30/10/99	FC Tbilisi	A	6-0	Tsitaishvili, Ashvetia 4, Aleksidze
07/11/99	Vit Georgia Tbilisi	H	4-1	Tsitaishvili, Ashvetia, Aleksidze, Gigiadze V.
13/11/99	Lokomotivi Tbilisi	A	2-1	Ashvetia (p), Aleksidze
19/11/99	Samgurali Tskhaltubo	H	7-1	Tsitaishvili 2, Ashvetia, Aleksidze 2, Shengelia, Vashakidze
28/11/99	Sioni Bolnisi	A	3-1	Sichinava, Tsitaishvili, Anchabadze
04/03/00	Vit Georgia Tbilisi	H	0-0	
11/03/00	Kolkheti 1913 Poti	A	0-0	
18/03/00	Dinamo Batumi	H	0-0	
26/03/00	Torpedo Kutaisi	A	0-0	
01/04/00	Iberia Samtredia	H	2-0	Arveladze, Sakhvadze
14/04/00	Sioni Bolnisi	H	3-0	Zirakishvili, Nemsadze, Tsitaishvili
18/04/00	Dila Gori	A	3-0	Shengelia 2, Nemsadze
22/04/00	Vit Georgia Tbilisi	A	1-1	Datvadze
29/04/00	Kolkheti 1913 Poti	H	1-1	Tsitaishvili
06/05/00	Dinamo Batumi	A	0-0	
13/05/00	Torpedo Kutaisi	H	1-1	Anchabadze
17/05/00	Iberia Samtredia	A	0-0	
23/05/00	Sioni Bolnisi	A	2-0	Monaselidze, Arveladze
30/05/00	Dila Gori	H	6-1	Arveladze 2, Zirakishvili 3, Datvadze

GORDA RUSTAVI

CLUB DIRECTORY

Gorda Rustavi
Nikoladze street 5
Rustavi
tel - (235) 192741
Year of Formation - 1948
President - Valeri Kokiashvili
Coach - Iason Aladashvili
Stadium - Poladi (10,700)

APPEARANCES 99/00

	P	Ap	(s)	Gls
Kakhaber ALADASHVILI	M	13		
Lasha ALADASHVILI	A	14		4
Spartak BACHILAVA	A	5	(11)	1
Grigol BEDIASHVILI	G	14		
Pavle BEKAURI	D	18	(1)	
David BERIDZE	D	18	(2)	
Aleksabdre BUKIA	M	9	(7)	
Aleksandre BURNADZE	D	10		1
Koba CHIGUSHVILI	D	3	(1)	
Giorgi CHITAURI	M		(1)	
Mikheil GABELAIA	D	26		
Gia GONGADZE	G	1	(2)	
David INASARIDZE	A	14		4
Giorgi KHIZANISHVILI	M		(2)	
Giorgi KILASONIA	M	13		1
Varlam KILASONIA	A	22		22
Aleksandre KITEISHVILI	A	15	(8)	5
Mamuka KORIDZE	G	13		
Zurab LABADZE	M	15	(1)	1
Mamuka MELADZE	M	13		1
Khricha MCHEDLIDZE	D	18		
Giorgi MISHVELIDZE	A	17	(5)	2
Zaza PATARIDZE	M	3	(3)	
Mikheil SAKHVADZE	D	15	(6)	
Lasha SILAGADZE	D	5	(3)	
Aleksandre TELIASHVILI	M	14		
David TSIKLAURI	M		(2)	

LEAGUE RESULTS 1999/2000

16/08/99	Torpedo Kutaisi	H	0-2	
21/08/99	Kolkheti 1913 Poti	A	0-2	
29/08/99	Kolkheti Khobi	H	4-1	Aladashvili L. 2, Kiteishvili 2
11/09/99	Dila Gori	H	2-0	Kilasonia V., Inasaridze
18/09/99	Iberia Samtredia	A	0-1	
25/09/99	Merani 91 Tbilisi	H	0-0	
02/10/99	TSU Tbilisi	A	0-1	
16/10/99	Torpedo Kutaisi	A	0-1	
23/10/99	Kolkheti 1913 Poti	H	0-1	
30/10/99	Kolkheti Khobi	A	1-5	Inasaridze
06/11/99	Dila Gori	A	2-1	Aladashvili L., Kilasonia V.
13/11/99	Iberia Samtredia	H	4-0	Inasaridze, Aladashvili L., Kiteishvili, Kilasonia V.
20/11/99	Merani 91 Tbilisi	A	1-2	Kilasonia V.
28/11/99	TSU Tbilisi	H	3-1	Inasaridze, Kilasonia V. 2
12/03/00	FC Tbilisi	H	2-0	Kilasonia V. 2
19/03/00	Merani 91 Tbilisi	A	0-0	
22/03/00	Arsenali Tbilisi	A	4-0	Mishvelidze, Labadze, Kilasonia V. 2
26/03/00	Samgurali Tskhaltubo	A	0-2	
02/04/00	Kolkheti Khobi	H	2-0	Kilasonia V., Kilasonia G.
14/04/00	TSU Tbilisi	A	0-1	
18/04/00	Lokomotivi Tbilisi	H	1-0	Mishvelidze
22/04/00	Arsenali Tbilisi	H	3-0	Kilasonia V. 3
28/04/00	FC Tbilisi	A	4-1	Burnadze, Kilasonia V. 2, Meladze
06/05/00	Merani 91 Tbilisi	H	1-1	Kilasonia V.
13/05/00	Samgurali Tskhaltubo	H	1-2	Kilasonia V.
19/05/00	Kolkheti Khobi	A	4-1	Kilasonia V. 3, Bachilava
23/05/00	TSU Tbilisi	H	2-0	Kiteishvili, Kilasonia V.
31/05/00	Lokomotivi Tbilisi	A	1-2	Kiteishvili

IBERIA SAMTREDIA

CLUB DIRECTORY

Iberia Samtredia
Ketskhoveli street 87
Samtredia
tel - (211) 24988
Year of Formation - 1936
President - Nugzar Nikoleishvili
Coach - Soso Pruidze
Stadium - Erosi Manjgaladze (15,000)

APPEARANCES 99/00

	P	Ap	(s)	Gls
Giorgi ADEISHVILI	M		(2)	1
Amiran BANDZELADZE	M		(2)	
Shalva BITSADZE	D	16	(4)	
Kakha BOBOKHIDZE	M	1	(1)	
Aleksandre CHOMAKHIDZE	G	5		
Shota DARSADZE	M	2	(9)	
Gulaz DOLIDZE	G	11		
Gela GEDENIDZE	D	2	(5)	
Valeri GEGESHIDZE	D	23		3
Soso GIGIADZE	M	14		1
Vasil GIGIADZE	A	3		
Nikoloz GIORGADZE	M	6	(3)	
Bidzina IVECHIANI	A	28		4
Kakha JANASHIA	A	12	(1)	1
Malkhaz JINCHARADZE	M	27		
Giga JVANIA	D	12		
Lasha KHMALADZE	M	11	(9)	1
Giorgi KHURTSIDZE	M	7	(9)	
Givi KVELADZE	D	4		
Gela LURSMANASHVILI	D	14		1
Temur MAGLAKELIDZE	M		(1)	
Konstantine METREVELI	A	8		
Zurab METREVELI	A	17	(4)	1
Zaza MIKELTADZE	D	28		
Shalva MUMLADZE	A	23	(1)	2
David NAROUSHVILI	M		(1)	
Giga NIKOLEISHVILI	D	10		
Giorgi NOZADZE	M	5	(6)	
David ODIKADZE	M	2	(3)	
Shmogi ONIANI	M		(1)	
Levan PILIPASHVILI	A	1	(1)	
Irakli SANIKIDZE	A	4	(3)	
Robert TSOMAIA	A		(3)	
Otar VARDANIDZE	G	12		

LEAGUE RESULTS 1999/2000

14/08/99	Merani 91 Tbilisi	H	1-1	Metreveli Z.
22/08/99	TSU Tbilisi	A	1-1	Adeishvili
30/08/99	Torpedo Kutaisi	H	0-3	
11/09/99	Kolkheti 1913 Poti	A	0-1	
18/09/99	Gorda Rustavi	H	1-0	Gegeshidze (p)
25/09/99	Dila Gori	A	0-2	
02/10/99	Kolkheti Khobi	H	2-1	Ivechiani, Khmaladze
16/10/99	Merani 91 Tbilisi	A	0-0	
24/10/99	TSU Tbilisi	H	0-1	
30/10/99	Torpedo Kutaisi	A	0-5	
06/11/99	Kolkheti 1913 Poti	H	1-0	Mumladze
13/11/99	Gorda Rustavi	A	0-4	
25/11/99	Dila Gori	H	2-1	Lursmanashvili, Gegeshidze (p)
28/11/99	Kolkheti Khobi	A	1-0	Gegeshidze (p)
04/03/00	Dinamo Batumi	A	0-6	
11/03/00	Dila Gori	H	2-1	Gigiadze S., Mumladze
18/03/00	Torpedo Kutaisi	A	0-5	
26/03/00	Vit Georgia Tbilisi	H	0-1	
01/04/00	Dinamo Tbilisi	A	0-2	
14/04/00	Kolkheti 1913 Poti	H	1-0	Ivechiani
18/04/00	Sioni Bolnisi	A	2-2	Janashia, Ivechiani
22/04/00	Dinamo Batumi	H	0-2	
29/04/00	Dila Gori	A	0-3	
06/05/00	Torpedo Kutaisi	H	0-3	
13/05/00	Vit Georgia Tbilisi	A	1-2	Ivechiani
17/05/00	Dinamo Tbilisi	H	0-0	
23/05/00	Kolkheti 1913 Poti	A	0-1	
30/05/00	Sioni Bolnisi	H	0-1	

KOLKHETI KHOBI

CLUB DIRECTORY

Kolkheti Khobi
Dadiani street 49
Khobi
tel - (32) 3062/2327
Year of Formation - 1936
President - Enuki Tevzadze
Coach - Pridon Gotsiridze; Jemal Abaishvili;
Pridon Gotsiridze
Stadium - Central (12,000)

LEAGUE RESULTS 1999/2000

14/08/99	Kolkheti 1913 Poti	A	3-2	Khurtsilava, Chitaia V. 2
21/08/99	Merani 91 Tbilisi	H	1-1	Kvekveskiri
29/08/99	Gorda Rustavi	A	1-4	Danelia
12/09/99	TSU Tbilisi	H	0-0	
18/09/99	Dila Gori	A	0-1	
25/09/99	Torpedo Kutaisi	H	1-2	Chichinadze
02/10/99	Iberia Samtredia	A	1-2	Danelia
16/10/99	Kolkheti 1913 Poti	H	0-3	
23/10/99	Merani 91 Tbilisi	A	0-0	
30/10/99	Gorda Rustavi	H	5-1	Khurtsilava (p), Chichinadze 2, Chitaia V., Tkebuchava
06/11/99	TSU Tbilisi	A	1-4	Chitaia V.
13/11/99	Dila Gori	H	2-3	Toria, Chitaia V.
20/11/99	Torpedo Kutaisi	A	0-0	
28/11/99	Iberia Samtredia	H	0-1	
03/03/00	Lokomotivi Tbilisi	A	1-4	Aianadi Zu.
12/03/00	Arsenali Tbilisi	H	2-1	Odisharia 2
20/03/00	FC Tbilisi	A	0-3	
26/03/00	Merani 91 Tbilisi	H	1-2	Chitaia V.
02/04/00	Gorda Rustavi	A	0-2	
14/04/00	Samgurali Tskhaltubo	A	1-2	Bulukhia
18/04/00	TSU Tbilisi	H	2-4	Chitaia V., Aianadi Zu.
28/04/00	Lokomotivi Tbilisi	H	0-7	
29/04/00	Arsenali Tbilisi	A	2-4	Chitaia V., Bukia L.
06/05/00	FC Tbilisi	H	1-2	Chitaia V.
13/05/00	Merani 91 Tbilisi	A	0-1	
17/05/00	Gorda Rustavi	H	1-4	Chitaia V.
23/05/00	Samgurali Tskhaltubo	H	0-2	
30/05/00	TSU Tbilisi	A	2-7	Chitaia V. 2

APPEARANCES 99/00

	P	Ap	(s)	Gls
David ABAKELIA	D	3	(2)	
Zaza AIANADI	A	19		
Zurab AIANADI	D	23		2
Velodi ALANIA	D	18	(1)	
Giorgi BABUADZE	G	7		
Sulkhan BERAIA	D	2	(1)	
Lasha BUKIA	M	21	(1)	1
Manuchar BUKIA	M		(1)	
Mamuka BULUKHIA	A	7		1
Tengiz CHICHINADZE	M	20	(2)	3
David CHITAIA	M	4	(3)	
Vladimer CHITAIA	A	22	(3)	12
David DANELIA	M	3	(15)	2
Gela GEDENIDZE	M	7	(1)	
Gia GIORGADZE	M	7		
Romeo GOGITADZE	D	12	(1)	
Levan GVAZAVA	M	13	(1)	
Vladimer JAMBURIA	D	12	(5)	
Temur JGAMADZE	M		(1)	
Arsena JIKIA	M	7	(1)	
Revaz KASHIBADZE	M	10	(1)	
Kalistrate KHURTSILAVA	A	19	(2)	2
Zaza KVEKVESKIRI	D	13		1
Giorgi LATARIA	D		(3)	
Mamuka NIKABERIDZE	G	20	(1)	
Koba ODISHARIA	A	12	(2)	2
Roin ONIANI	D	11		
Manuchar TKEBUCHAVA	M	3	(4)	1
Roman TOLORDAVA	G	1		
Guram TORIA	A	7	(2)	1
Levan VARTAGAVA	M	5	(2)	

KOLKHETI 1913 POTI

Kolkheti 1913 Poti
Shevchenko street 17
Poti
tel - (293) 25814/21525
fax - (293) 22688/20630
Year of Formation - 1913
President - Jemal Inaishvili
Coach - Gia Tkebuchava
Stadium - Fazisi (7,000)

APPEARANCES 99/00

	P	Ap	(s)	Gls
Roman AKHALKATSI	A	3	(7)	1
Levan ANJAPARIDZE	D	5	(1)	
Mamuka BULUKHIA	A	2	(6)	2
Zaza BURKVADZE	M		(1)	
Giorgi CHITAIA	M	2	(5)	1
Giorgi DAVITNIDZE	D	19	(1)	1
Zavel GAGANIDZE	M	25		8
Gia GIORGADZE	M	6		
David GOGOLADZE	A	4	(2)	2
Kakhaber GOROZIA	D	22		
Eldar GVASALIA	A	16	(2)	3
Mamuka GVASALIA	G	15		
Zaza INIASHVILI	M	1		
Temur JGARKAVA	D		(3)	
Amiran KEDELASHVILI	D	14	(6)	
David KHUCHUA	A	23	(3)	4
Tamaz KIKLIASHVILI	M	23		
Mikheil KOBULADZE	D	9	(1)	3
Giorgi KRASOVSKI	M		(1)	
Gogita KUNTELIA	D	9	(2)	
Zurab KVACHAKHIA	G	13		
David KVIRKVELIA	M		(1)	
Mamuka MELADZE	M	4	(6)	
Gela PANCHULIDZE	M	13		1
Elguja PAPAVA	D	4	(4)	
Joni SHALAMBERIDZE	M	21		6
Levan SHAVGULIDZE	A	3	(8)	
Valeri TORCHINAVA	D	28		2
Gocha TRAPAIDZE	A	24	(1)	2

LEAGUE RESULTS 1999/2000

14/08/99	Kolkheti Khobi	H	2-3	Khuchua, Bulukhia
21/08/99	Gorda Rustavi	H	2-0	Trapaidze, Gogoladze
29/08/99	Dila Gori	A	0-3	
11/09/99	Iberia Samtredia	H	1-0	Torchinava (p)
18/09/99	Merani 91 Tbilisi	A	2-1	Gaganidze, Trapaidze
29/09/99	TSU Tbilisi	H	1-0	Gogoladze
03/10/99	Torpedo Kutaisi	A	1-4	Gaganidze
16/10/99	Kolkheti Khobi	A	3-0	Shalamberidze 2, Torchinava
23/10/99	Gorda Rustavi	A	1-0	Gaganidze
30/10/99	Dila Gori	H	3-0	Gvasalia E., Shalamberidze, Gaganidze
06/11/99	Iberia Samtredia	A	0-1	
13/11/99	Merani 91 Tbilisi	H	1-0	Khuchua
19/11/99	TSU Tbilisi	A	2-3	Shalamberidze (p), Bulukhia
28/11/99	Torpedo Kutaisi	H	0-0	
04/03/00	Torpedo Kutaisi	A	1-3	Kobuladze
11/03/00	Dinamo Tbilisi	H	0-0	
18/03/00	Sioni Bolnisi	A	0-1	
26/03/00	Dila Gori	H	3-1	Shalamberidze, Gaganidze, Kobuladze
01/04/00	Vit Georgia Tbilisi	A	0-0	
14/04/00	Iberia Samtredia	A	0-1	
18/04/00	Dinamo Batumi	H	1-0	Khuchua
22/04/00	Torpedo Kutaisi	H	2-1	og (Khvadagiani), Gvasalia E.
29/04/00	Dinamo Tbilisi	A	1-1	Akhalkatsi
06/05/00	Sioni Bolnisi	H	5-0	Gaganidze, Davitnidze, Gvasalia E., Kobuladze, Panchulidze
13/05/00	Dila Gori	A	2-0	Gaganidze, Chitaia
17/05/00	Vit Georgia Tbilisi	H	2-0	Gaganidze, Shalamberidze
23/05/00	Iberia Samtredia	H	1-0	Khuchua
30/05/00	Dinamo Batumi	A	0-2	

LOKOMOTIVI TBILISI

CLUB DIRECTORY

Lokomotivi Tbilisi
Vagzlis Moedani 2, Tbilisi
tel - (32) 942067
Year of Formation - 1936
President - Akaki Chkhaidze
Coach - Murtaz Khurtsilava; Temur Makhoradze;
Revaz Dzodzuashvili
Stadium - Boris Paichadze (75,000)

MAJOR HONOURS
Domestic Cup - (1) 2000.

APPEARANCES 99/00

	P	Ap	(s)	Gls
Valeri ABRAMIDZE	D	9	(1)	1
Besik AMASHUKELI	M	7		
David ASLANADZE	G	13		
David BAKRADZE	M	8	(5)	1
Giorgi BALASHVILI	D	18		
Soso BARAMIDZE	M	3	(1)	
Paata BARNOV	D	3	(4)	
Besik BERADZE	D	2		
Levan CHACHUA	D		(1)	
David CHICHVEISHVILI	D	8	(1)	
Giorgi CHIKHRADZE	D	25		1
Gia CHKHAIDZE	D	10	(1)	
Lasha CHKHAIDZE	M	1	(1)	
Shota CHOMAKHIDZE	M	12		2
Merab DZODZUASHVILI	A	6	(1)	1
Paata GAMTSEMLIDZE	M	2	(2)	
Akvsenti GILAURI	M	5	(5)	
David GODERDZISHVILI	A	8	(3)	3
Kakhi GOGICHAISHVILI	M	10		1
Evgeni GULORDAVA	M	1		
Grigol GVAZAVA	A		(3)	
Vakhtang IAGORASHVILI	M	1	(5)	
Manuchar IVARDAVA	G		(1)	
David JANELIDZE	G	4	(1)	
Ivane JUGELI	A	10	(1)	8
Genadi KATSIASHVILI	M	13	(10)	
Levan KEBADZE	A	14		9
Zurab KHIZANISHVILI	D	4	(1)	1
Tsezor KHURODZE	A	10	(1)	4
Mikheil KOBULADZE	D	14		
Givi KVARATSKHELIA	M	10		1
Giorgi LOMAIA	G	11		
Konstantine MELKADZE	M	4	(3)	
Levan MIKADZE	D	21	(2)	1
Giorgi NEMSADZE	M	2	(1)	
Giorgi NIKURADZE	G		(1)	
Roin ONIANI	D	8	(1)	
Dimitri PARAMONOV	M	2	(1)	
Mamuka RUSIA	A	24	(2)	8
Lasha SALUKVADZE	M	1		
Levan SHAVGULIDZE	A	3	(6)	
Gamlet TSIVTSIVADZE	A	1		

LEAGUE RESULTS 1999/2000

16/08/99	Arsenali Tbilisi	H	2-2	Mikadze, Rusia
21/08/99	Samgurali Tskhaltubo	H	2-0	Gogichaishvili, Rusia
30/08/99	Sioni Bolnisi	A	0-1	
11/09/99	Dinamo Batumi	H	0-0	
19/09/99	Dinamo Tbilisi	A	0-4	
03/10/99	Vit Georgia Tbilisi	A	1-3	Chomakhidze
13/10/99	FC Tbilisi	H	2-1	og (Gvelesiani), Kebadze
17/10/99	Arsenali Tbilisi	A	4-0	Rusia 2, Kebadze, Bakradze
23/10/99	Samgurali Tskhaltubo	A	3-0	Kebadze 2, Chikhradze
29/10/99	Sioni Bolnisi	H	0-1	
07/11/99	Dinamo Batumi	A	1-4	Kebadze
13/11/99	Dinamo Tbilisi	H	1-2	Kebadze
20/11/99	FC Tbilisi	A	4-0	Kebadze 2, Rusia, Chomakhidze
28/11/99	Vit Georgia Tbilisi	H	1-1	Kebadze
05/03/00	Kolkheti Khobi	H	4-1	Rusia, Khurodze 2 (1p), Dzodzuashvili
12/03/00	TSU Tbilisi	A	1-0	Goderdzishvili
19/03/00	Samgurali Tskhaltubo	H	0-0	
26/03/00	Arsenali Tbilisi	H	1-0	Goderdzishvili (p)
03/04/00	FC Tbilisi	A	1-0	Rusia
13/04/00	Merani 91 Tbilisi	H	0-0	
18/04/00	Gorda Rustavi	A	0-1	
22/04/00	Kolkheti Khobi	A	7-0	Jugeli 2, Rusia, Khurodze, Khizanishvili, Abramidze, Kvaratskhelia
29/04/00	TSU Tbilisi	H	3-0	Jugeli 3 (2p)
06/05/00	Samgurali Tskhaltubo	A	0-1	
13/05/00	Arsenali Tbilisi	A	1-0	Jugeli
17/05/00	FC Tbilisi	H	1-1	Khurodze
22/05/00	Merani 91 Tbilisi	A	1-3	Goderdzishvili
31/05/00	Gorda Rustavi	H	2-1	Jugeli 2 (2p)

MERANI 91 TBILISI

CLUB DIRECTORY

Merani 91 Tbilisi
Abastumani street 8
Tbilisi
tel - (32) 341703/340640
Year of Formation - 1991
President - David Purtseladze
Coach - Temur Chkhaidze; Sergo Gabelaia
Stadium - Sinatle (2,000)

APPEARANCES 99/00

	P	Ap	(s)	Gls
Edisher ALADASHVILI	D	13		
Bakhva AMBIDZE	M	12		3
Lasha AMBIDZE	D	13	(4)	
Levan BAJELIDZE	M	5	(4)	2
David BOLKVADZE	A	10	(1)	
Lasha CHKHAIDZE	M	5		
Malkhaz CHINCHARAULI	M	20	(6)	
Suliko DAVITASHVILI	A	18	(4)	7
Ioseb DEVIDZE	M	27		5
Gocha GUJABIDZE	D	11		
Giorgi ILURIDZE	M	8	(1)	
Shalva IVANISHVILI	D	3	(9)	
David JISHKARIANI	D	14	(4)	
Suliko KAKABADZE	A	10	(1)	3
David KARIAULI	D	17	(2)	
Guram KHAREBAVA	D	12	(1)	
Avtandil KHORKHELI	M	8		
Kakhaber KOBESASHVILI	M	9	(3)	1
Andro KOROSHINADZE	G	2		
Andro KOSHKADZE	M	1	(7)	
Giorgi KVETENADZE	M	6		2
Paata LURSMANASHVILI	D	15		1
Levan MELIKIA	A		(1)	
Koba MISHELADZE	M		(1)	
Revaz NACHKEPIA	G	26	(1)	
Dimitri PURTSELADZE	A		(1)	1
Otar ROSTIASHVILI	A	17	(6)	3
David SHOTADZE	M	1		
Levan TOLORDAVA	A	10	(7)	4
Zaza TSKIPURISHVILI	D	15	(1)	

LEAGUE RESULTS 1999/2000

14/08/99	Iberia Samtredia	A	1-1	Devidze
21/08/99	Kolkheti Khobi	A	1-1	Tolordava
30/08/99	TSU Tbilisi	H	1-1	Tolordava
11/09/99	Torpedo Kutaisi	A	1-3	Tolordava
18/09/99	Kolkheti 1913 Poti	H	1-2	Ambidze B.
25/09/99	Gorda Rustavi	A	0-0	
02/10/99	Dila Gori	H	3-1	Devidze 2, Davitashvili
16/10/99	Iberia Samtredia	H	0-0	
23/10/99	Kolkheti Khobi	H	0-0	
29/10/99	TSU Tbilisi	A	2-0	Ambidze B., Davitashvili
07/11/99	Torpedo Kutaisi	H	0-1	
13/11/99	Kolkheti 1913 Poti	A	0-1	
20/11/99	Gorda Rustavi	H	2-1	Bajelidze 2
28/11/99	Dila Gori	A	2-3	Lursmanashvili, Ambidze B. (p)
05/03/00	FC Tbilisi	A	1-0	Tolordava (p)
12/03/00	Samgurali Tskhaltubo	A	1-0	Kakabadze
19/03/00	Gorda Rustavi	H	0-0	
26/03/00	Kolkheti Khobi	A	2-1	Kvetenadze (p), Kakabadze
02/04/00	TSU Tbilisi	H	1-0	Kvetenadze (p)
13/04/00	Lokomotivi Tbilisi	A	0-0	
18/04/00	Arsenali Tbilisi	H	1-0	Rostiashvili
22/04/00	FC Tbilisi	H	4-0	Kakabadze, Davitashvili, Devidze 2
29/04/00	Samgurali Tskhaltubo	H	0-0	
06/05/00	Gorda Rustavi	A	1-1	Kobesashvili
13/05/00	Kolkheti Khobi	H	1-0	Davitashvili
17/05/00	TSU Tbilisi	A	1-2	Rostiashvili
22/05/00	Lokomotivi Tbilisi	H	3-1	Davitashvili 2, Rostiashvili
31/05/00	Arsenali Tbilisi	A	2-0	Purtseladze, Davitashvili

SAMGURALI TSKHALTUBO

CLUB DIRECTORY

Samgurali Tskhaltubo
Chavchavadze street 1
Tskhaltubo
tel - (240) 24077/23615
Year of Formation - 1945
President - Grigol Katamadze
Coach - Revaz Burkadze; Iason Bzikadze
Stadium - 26 Maisi (12,000)

APPEARANCES 99/00

	P	Ap	(s)	Gls
Shota BABUNASHVILI	M	4	(2)	
Besik BERADZE	D	9	(1)	1
Otar BOBOKHIDZE	G	11		
Tedo BODOKIA	G	3	(1)	
David CHELIDZE	D	19	(3)	
Archil CHKHABERIDZE	D	12		
Vladimer CHKONIA	A	13	(6)	
Shota DARSADZE	A	9	(3)	3
Gela DZAGNIDZE	M	14	(4)	1
Merab DZODZUASHVILI	A	9	(5)	3
Arsena GABLAIA	A		(1)	
Irakli GIORGOBIANI	M	12		1
Goderdzi GOGOLADZE	M	1	(1)	
Shalva GONGADZE	A	19		2
Givi JANELIDZE	D	3	(1)	
Ilia JAVAKHADZE	A	2	(1)	
Irakli KHACHAPURIDZE	M	11		2
Mamuka KHUNDADZE	A	9	(2)	2
Levan KOBULADZE	D	10		
Irakli KOKHREIDZE	A	6	(2)	2
Levan KOPALIANI	M	1		
Zviad KUTATELADZE	M	16	(8)	4
Revaz KVERNADZE	A	9	(4)	1
Mamuka NEBIERIDZE	D	2	(6)	
David PETRIASHVILI	A		(3)	
Zviad PKHAKADZE	M	8	(5)	
Shalva PRANGISHVILI	D	24	(1)	
Shota PUTKARADZE	A	2	(4)	
Koba SADILIANI	D	8	(3)	
Zviad STURUA	G	14		
Giorgi SUKHIASHVILI	M	24		4
Kakhaber VADACHKURIA	M		(5)	
Malkhaz VOSKANOV	D	21	(1)	
Giorgi ZURABIANI	D	3	(4)	

LEAGUE RESULTS 1999/2000

Date	Opponent	H/A	Score	Scorers
14/08/99	Vit Georgia Tbilisi	H	0-1	
21/08/99	Lokomotivi Tbilisi	A	0-2	
29/08/99	Arsenali Tbilisi	H	1-0	Khachapuridze
11/09/99	Sioni Bolnisi	H	1-0	Sukhiashvili (p)
18/09/99	Dinamo Batumi	A	0-0	
26/09/99	Dinamo Tbilisi	H	1-2	Gongadze
02/10/99	FC Tbilisi	A	2-5	Dzodzuashvili 2
16/10/99	Vit Georgia Tbilisi	A	1-3	Kokhreidze
23/10/99	Lokomotivi Tbilisi	H	0-3	
30/10/99	Arsenali Tbilisi	A	1-2	Kokhreidze
06/11/99	Sioni Bolnisi	A	0-2	
13/11/99	Dinamo Batumi	H	0-0	
19/11/99	Dinamo Tbilisi	A	1-7	Dzodzuashvili (p)
28/11/99	FC Tbilisi	H	1-0	Khachapuridze
05/03/00	TSU Tbilisi	A	0-1	
12/03/00	Merani 91 Tbilisi	H	0-1	
19/03/00	Lokomotivi Tbilisi	A	0-0	
26/03/00	Gorda Rustavi	H	2-0	Giorgobiani, Khundadze
02/04/00	Arsenali Tbilisi	A	1-2	Dzagnidze
14/04/00	Kolkheti Khobi	H	2-1	Gongadze, Beradze
18/04/00	FC Tbilisi	A	0-0	
22/04/00	TSU Tbilisi	H	3-1	Darsadze, Sukhiashvili, Kvernadze
29/04/00	Merani 91 Tbilisi	A	0-0	
06/05/00	Lokomotivi Tbilisi	H	1-0	Kutateladze
13/05/00	Gorda Rustavi	A	2-1	Kutateladze, Darsadze
17/05/00	Arsenali Tbilisi	H	2-0	Khundadze, Kutateladze
23/05/00	Kolkheti Khobi	A	2-0	Sukhiashvili (p), Kutateladze
30/05/00	FC Tbilisi	H	2-1	Sukhiashvili, Darsadze

SIONI BOLNISI

CLUB DIRECTORY

Sioni Bolnisi
Orbeliani street 106
Bolnisi
tel - (258) 22468/22500
Year of Formation - 1936
President - Giorgi Mgaloblishvili
Coach - Spartak Archvadze
Stadium - Temur Stepania (3,000)

APPEARANCES 99/00

	P	Ap	(s)	Gls
Pridon ARCHVADZE	M	1	(2)	
Archil BOKERIA	A		(5)	
Lasha CHAGELISHVILI	M		(3)	
Nugzar DALAKISHVILI	G	6	(2)	
David DATVADZE	M	14		3
Temur DIMITRISHVILI	D	22		
Zaza ELBAKIDZE	M		(5)	
Lorzenti GAGUA	M	1	(6)	
David GODERDZISHVILI	A	13		3
Kakhaber GODERDZISHVILI	D	19	(1)	
Kakha GOGOLADZE	A	14		4
Murman GOGOLADZE	M	25	(1)	1
Shalva ISIANI	A	12		5
David JAPARIDZE	M	1	(7)	
Irakli KAPANADZE	M		(4)	
Kakhaber KENCHOSHVILI	A		(2)	
Giorgi KIPSHIDZE	D	2	(1)	
Vasil MAISURADZE	D	10		
Giorgi MAZANISHVILI	M	6		
Makhare MINDIASHVILI	A		(1)	
Nikoloz MINDIASHVILI	M	24		
Bakhva MOSESHVILI	A	26		3
Mirza SAMKHARADZE	M	10	(11)	1
Temur SAMKHARADZE	M	15	(6)	
Archil SHAKIASHVILI	D	13		3
Besik SVENGELIA	M	11	(1)	1
Kakhaber SIDAMONIDZE	D	13		
David SOLOGASHVILI	M	13		
David SVANIDZE	D	14	(9)	
Vepkhia TARUGASHVILI	D	1	(2)	
Temur VOLKOV	G	22	(1)	1

LEAGUE RESULTS 1999/2000

14/08/99	FC Tbilisi	H	2-2	Moseshvili, Samkharadze M.
21/08/99	Vit Georgia Tbilisi	A	0-3	
30/08/99	Lokomotivi Tbilisi	H	1-0	Goderdzishvili D.
11/09/99	Samgurali Tskhaltubo	A	0-1	
18/09/99	Arsenali Tbilisi	H	1-0	Shakiashvili (p)
25/09/99	Dinamo Batumi	H	0-0	
03/10/99	Dinamo Tbilisi	A	0-3	
17/10/99	FC Tbilisi	A	4-3	Datvadze 2, Goderdzishvili D. 2 (1p)
23/10/99	Vit Georgia Tbilisi	H	0-0	
29/10/99	Lokomotivi Tbilisi	A	1-0	Moseshvili
06/11/99	Samgurali Tskhaltubo	H	2-0	Shakiashvili (p), Datvadze
13/11/99	Arsenali Tbilisi	A	1-0	Shakiashvili
20/11/99	Dinamo Batumi	A	0-4	
28/11/99	Dinamo Tbilisi	H	1-3	Gogoladze M.
04/03/00	Dila Gori	H	4-1	Shengelia, Gogoladze K., Isiani, Volkov (p)
11/03/00	Vit Georgia Tbilisi	A	0-1	
18/03/00	Kolkheti 1913 Poti	H	1-0	Isiani (p)
26/03/00	Dinamo Batumi	A	0-3	
01/04/00	Torpedo Kutaisi	H	2-4	Moseshvili, og (Makhviladze)
14/04/00	Dinamo Tbilisi	A	0-3	
18/04/00	Iberia Samtredia	H	2-2	Isiani (p), Gogoladze K.
22/04/00	Dila Gori	A	0-1	
29/04/00	Vit Georgia Tbilisi	H	1-2	Gogoladze K.
06/05/00	Kolkheti 1913 Poti	A	0-5	
13/05/00	Dinamo Batumi	H	1-2	Isiani
17/05/00	Torpedo Kutaisi	A	1-6	Gogoladze K.
23/05/00	Dinamo Tbilisi	H	0-2	
30/05/00	Iberia Samtredia	A	1-0	Isiani

FC TBILISI

CLUB DIRECTORY

FC Tbilisi
Khosharauli street 27, Tbilisi
tel - (32) 943290
Year of Formation - 1995
President - Malkhaz Lomtadze
Coach - Nestor Mumladze
Stadium - Boris Paichadze (75,000)

APPEARANCES 99/00

	P	Ap	(s)	Gls
Valeri ABRAMIDZE	D	13		
Lado AKHALAIA	M		(1)	
Besik AMASHUKELI	M	8	(1)	
Tornike APTSIAURI	M		(1)	
Paata BARNOV	D	9	(1)	
Zurab BATIASHVILI	G	12		
Vladimir BURDULI	M	19	(2)	2
Aleksandre CHIKHRADZE	G	10		
Aleksandre CHIVADZE	D	8	(1)	1
Vladimer DZAGNIDZE	D	3	(2)	
Kakhaber EBRALIDZE	D	1	(3)	
Tengiz ENUKIDZE	A		(1)	
Temur GADELIA	A	12		6
Valeri GAGUA	A	13	(1)	3
Boris GONCHAROV	A	7	(1)	1
Giorgi GUDUSHAURI	M	5	(1)	
Oleg GVELESIANI	M	12	(1)	
Shalva ISIANI	A	5	(3)	1
Ilia KANDELAKI	M	7	(3)	
Revaz KEMOKLIDZE	D	13		
Zurab KHIZANISHVILI	D	8	(1)	
Irakli KOKHREIDZE	M	3	(3)	
Levan KUPARADZE	M	2	(3)	
Givi KVARATSKHELIA	M	11		4
Zviad LABADZE	D	7	(1)	1
Giorgi LOLADZE	M	2	(3)	
Mamuka MACHAVAKIANI	D	13		
Tornike MAISURADZE	M		(3)	
Zurab MAMALADZE	G	6		
Ioseb MANCHARAULI	M	1	(2)	1
Konstantine MELKADZE	M	5		
Levan MELKADZE	A	12	(1)	6
Giorgi MIKADZE	A	10	(3)	5
Avtandil MUMLADZE	M	1	(1)	
Giorgi NORAKIDZE	M	3	(8)	
Zviad PAPIDZE	D	7		
Tornike RUKHADZE	D	11		1
Irakli SHENGELIA	A	17	(4)	
Tengiz SULAKVELIDZE	M	1		
David TKEBUCHAVA	M	9	(7)	
Zaza ZAMTARADZE	D	22		

LEAGUE RESULTS 1999/2000

14/08/99	Sioni Bolnisi	A	2-2	Kvaratskhelia, Isiani
22/08/99	Dinamo Batumi	H	1-1	Mikadze
29/08/99	Dinamo Tbilisi	A	2-3	Mikadze, Gagua
12/09/99	Arsenali Tbilisi	A	1-1	Rukhadze (p)
18/09/99	Vit Georgia Tbilisi	H	2-1	Melkadze L. (p), Burduli
02/10/99	Samgurali Tskhaltubo	H	5-2	Kvaratskhelia 2, Melkadze L., Mikadze 2
13/10/99	Lokomotivi Tbilisi	A	1-2	Gagua
17/10/99	Sioni Bolnisi	H	3-4	Melkadze L. 2 (1p), Mikadze (p)
24/10/99	Dinamo Batumi	A	0-2	
30/10/99	Dinamo Tbilisi	H	0-6	
06/11/99	Arsenali Tbilisi	H	3-1	Melkadze L. 2, Kvaratskhelia
14/11/99	Vit Georgia Tbilisi	A	1-1	Gagua (p)
20/11/99	Lokomotivi Tbilisi	H	0-4	
28/11/99	Samgurali Tskhaltubo	A	0-1	
05/03/00	Merani 91 Tbilisi	H	0-1	
12/03/00	Gorda Rustavi	A	0-2	
20/03/00	Kolkheti Khobi	H	3-0	Goncharov, Burduli, Godelia
26/03/00	TSU Tbilisi	A	0-2	
03/04/00	Lokomotivi Tbilisi	H	0-1	
14/04/00	Arsenali Tbilisi	A	2-4	Gadelia 2
18/04/00	Samgurali Tskhaltubo	H	0-0	
22/04/00	Merani 91 Tbilisi	A	0-4	
28/04/00	Gorda Rustavi	H	1-4	Gadelia (p)
06/05/00	Kolkheti Khobi	A	2-1	Chivadze, Mancharauli
12/05/00	TSU Tbilisi	H	0-4	
17/05/00	Lokomotivi Tbilisi	A	1-1	og (Mikadze)
23/05/00	Arsenali Tbilisi	H	2-0	Gadelia 2
31/05/00	Samgurali Tskhaltubo	A	1-2	Labadze

TORPEDO KUTAISI

CLUB DIRECTORY

Torpedo Kutaisi
Akhalgazrdobis street Mesame
Shesakhvevi 2
Kutaisi
tel - (231) 21255/20985
fax - (231) 21255
Year of Formation - 1949
President - Mikheil Korkia
Coach - David Kipiani
Stadium - Torpedo (28,800)

MAJOR HONOURS
League Championship - (1) 2000.
Domestic Cup - (1) 1999.

APPEARANCES 99/00

	P	Ap	(s)	Gls
Badri AKHVLEDIANI	D	19	(3)	2
Aleksandre AMISULASHVILI	D	3	(4)	
Malkhaz ASATIANI	M	6	(7)	3
Mikheil BOBOKHIDZE	M	4	(11)	5
Giorgi CHANTURIA	G	19		
Kakhaber CHKHETIANI	M	24	(1)	
Giorgi GOGIASHVILI	M	22	(2)	2
Gia IMEDADZE	A	3	(12)	3
Zurab IONANIDZE	A	27		25
David JANASHIA	A	27		12
Vakhtang KHVADAGIANI	D	25		3
Kakha KVETENADZE	M	23	(3)	2
Irakli MAGLAKELIDZE	D	13	(6)	
Vasil MAISURADZE	D	2	(2)	
Mikheil MAKHVILADZE	D	12	(3)	
Zaza MEDOEV	M		(2)	
Giorgi MEGRELADZE	A	21	(4)	12
Aleksandre SHEKRILADZE	D	21	(4)	
Giorgi SOMKHISHVILI	G	2		
Zviad STURUA	G	1	(1)	
Jaba TAVBERIDZE	M		(3)	
Vakhtang TURMANIDZE	D	22		
Zaza VACHIBERADZE	M	6	(7)	1
Irakli ZOIDZE	G	6		

LEAGUE RESULTS 1999/2000

16/08/99	Gorda Rustavi	A	2-0	Gogiashvili, Megreladze
21/08/99	Dila Gori	H	2-2	Gogiashvili, Imedadze
30/08/99	Iberia Samtredia	A	3-0	Imedadze, Janashia, Bobokhidze
11/09/99	Merani 91 Tbilisi	H	3-1	Ionanidze, Khvadagiani, Megreladze
25/09/99	Kolkheti Khobi	A	2-1	Ionanidze 2
03/10/99	Kolkheti 1913 Poti	H	4-1	Megreladze 2, Ionanidze 2
12/10/99	TSU Tbilisi	A	2-0	Janashia, Khvadagiani
16/10/99	Gorda Rustavi	H	1-0	Megreladze
24/10/99	Dila Gori	A	5-0	Ionanidze, Megreladze 2, Kvetenadze, Vachiberadze
30/10/99	Iberia Samtredia	H	5-0	Ionanidze 3, Janashia 2
07/11/99	Merani 91 Tbilisi	A	1-0	Ionanidze
13/11/99	TSU Tbilisi	H	3-0	Kvetenadze, Akhvlediani, Ionanidze
20/11/99	Kolkheti Khobi	H	0-0	
28/11/99	Kolkheti 1913 Poti	A	0-0	
04/03/00	Kolkheti 1913 Poti	H	3-1	Ionanidze 3 (1p)
18/03/00	Iberia Samtredia	H	5-0	Akhvlediani, Janashia, Ionanidze 2, Bobokhidze
26/03/00	Dinamo Tbilisi	H	0-0	
01/04/00	Sioni Bolnisi	A	4-2	Ionanidze 2, Megreladze, Janashia
05/04/00	Dinamo Batumi	A	1-2	Janashia
14/04/00	Dila Gori	H	4-1	Bobokhidze, Megreladze 2, Janashia
18/04/00	Vit Georgia Tbilisi	A	1-1	Ionanidze
22/04/00	Kolkheti 1913 Poti	A	1-2	Khvadagiani
29/04/00	Dinamo Batumi	H	4-0	Janashia 2, Megreladze, Ionanidze
06/05/00	Iberia Samtredia	A	3-0	Ionanidze, Janashia, Asatiani
13/05/00	Dinamo Tbilisi	A	1-1	Asatiani
17/05/00	Sioni Bolnisi	H	6-1	Bobokhidze, Asatiani, Ionanidze 3, Imedadze
22/05/00	Dila Gori	A	4-0	Bobokhidze, Ionanidze (p), Janashia, Megreladze
30/05/00	Vit Georgia Tbilisi	H	0-0	

TSU TBILISI

CLUB DIRECTORY

TSU Tbilisi
Kostava street 67
Tbilisi
tel - (32) 334301
Year of Formation - 1906
President - David Goderdzishvili
Coach - Kote Dolidze; Vladimer Khachidze;
Tengiz Katsia
Stadium - Central (Mtskheta) (3,000)

APPEARANCES 99/00

	P	Ap	(s)	Gls
Giorgi ADAMIA	A	19	(5)	8
Kahaber AKHALADZE	D	10	(5)	1
David ARCHVADZE	D	18	(5)	
Irakli BARKAIA	D	3	(1)	
Tamaz BOKERIA	A	11	(4)	
Giorgi DEKANOSIDZE	M	22	(1)	4
Kakhaber EBRALIDZE	D	14		
Malkhaz ERADZE	M	25		5
Giorgi GOTSIRIDZE	A	2	(6)	
Konstantine GUSUNAVA	G	3	(1)	
Grigol GVAZAVA	A	5	(7)	4
Paata GVIRSISHVILI	M	1		
Aleksandre INTSKIRVELI	D	13	(2)	
David JOBADZE	M	1	(5)	
Giorgi KADAGIDZE	M		(5)	
Khricho KHARTISHVILI	D	9		
Dimitri KHOMERIKI	M		(2)	
Levan KVITSIANI	D	21		
Akaki LOBJANIDZE	M	1	(5)	
Mikheil MAZIASHVILI	M	14		1
Mirza MERLANI	G	25		
Mikheil MESKHI	A	21	(2)	
Giorgi MIKADZE	A	2	(2)	
Koba NINUA	D	13		1
Beka NOZADZE	M	2	(7)	
Giorgi PARKOSADZE	M	4	(7)	
Ramaz SVANADZE	M	23	(1)	
Kakhaber TSUTSUNAVA	A	26	(1)	15

LEAGUE RESULTS 1999/2000

15/08/99	Dila Gori	A	1-1	Adamia
22/08/99	Iberia Samtredia	H	1-1	Tsutsunava
30/08/99	Merani 91 Tbilisi	A	1-1	Tsutsunava
12/09/99	Kolkheti Khobi	A	0-0	
29/09/99	Kolkheti 1913 Poti	A	0-1	
02/10/99	Gorda Rustavi	H	1-0	Gvazava
12/10/99	Torpedo Kutaisi	H	0-2	
17/10/99	Dila Gori	H	0-1	
24/10/99	Iberia Samtredia	A	1-0	Adamia
29/10/99	Merani 91 Tbilisi	H	0-2	
06/11/99	Kolkheti Khobi	H	4-1	Dekanosidze, Akhaladze, Gvazava 2
13/11/99	Torpedo Kutaisi	A	0-3	
19/11/99	Kolkheti 1913 Poti	H	3-2	Adamia 2, Ninua
28/11/99	Gorda Rustavi	A	1-3	Gvazava
05/03/00	Samgurali Tskhaltubo	H	1-0	Tsutsunava
12/03/00	Lokomotivi Tbilisi	H	0-1	
19/03/00	Arsenali Tbilisi	A	2-0	Tsutsunava, Dekanosidze
26/03/00	FC Tbilisi	H	2-0	Eradze, Adamia
02/04/00	Merani 91 Tbilisi	A	0-1	
14/04/00	Gorda Rustavi	H	1-0	Dekanosidze
18/04/00	Kolkheti Khobi	A	4-2	Dekanosidze, Eradze (p), Tsutsunava, Adamia
22/04/00	Samgurali Tskhaltubo	A	1-3	Maziashvili
29/04/00	Lokomotivi Tbilisi	A	0-3	
05/05/00	Arsenali Tbilisi	H	2-0	Tsutsunava 2
12/05/00	FC Tbilisi	A	4-0	Tsutsunava 3, Adamia
17/05/00	Merani 91 Tbilisi	H	2-1	Eradze, Adamia
23/05/00	Gorda Rustavi	A	0-2	
30/05/00	Kolkheti Khobi	H	7-2	Tsutsunava 5, Eradze 2

VIT GEORGIA TBILISI

CLUB DIRECTORY

Vit Georgia Tbilisi
Mitskevichi street 20
Tbilisi
tel - (32) 955846
fax - (32) 955846
Year of Formation - 1968
President - Guram Rukhadze
Coach - Sergo Kotrikadze
Stadium - Central (Mtskheta) (3,000)

APPEARANCES 99/00

	P	Ap	(s)	Gls
Kakhaber ALADASHVILI	M	4	(1)	
Irakli BARKAIA	D	9		
Archil BOKERIA	M	1	(3)	
Giorgi CHANKOTADZE	D	25		2
Sergo CHURADZE	G	20		
David DIGMELASHVILI	M	7	(12)	
David DOLIDZE	M	10	(6)	1
Vladimer GOCHASHVILI	A	12	(6)	4
Revaz GOTSIRIDZE	A	10	(8)	5
Zviad GVAZAVA	M	11	(9)	
Irakli KHACHAPURIDZE	M	10	(2)	
Khvicha KHARTISHVILI	D	10	(1)	1
Giorgi KIPIANI	M	24	(2)	2
Tengiz KOBIASHVILI	D	9	(3)	
Giorgi KORIDZE	A	26		13
Valeri KOTORASHVILI	M	10	(8)	1
David MAMARDASHVILI	G	8		
Mikheil MAZIASHVILI	M	5	(2)	1
Levan MELKADZE	A	3	(2)	1
David MORCHILADZE	M	1	(2)	
Jaba MUJIRI	D	20	(2)	
Lasha NOZADZE	M	28		3
Edik SAJAIA	D	24	(2)	1
Sevasti TODUA	D	21	(1)	

LEAGUE RESULTS 1999/2000

14/08/99	Samgurali Tskhaltubo	A	1-0	Koridze
21/08/99	Sioni Bolnisi	H	3-0	Chankotadze, Koridze 2
29/08/99	Dinamo Batumi	A	0-0	
11/09/99	Dinamo Tbilisi	H	0-1	
18/09/99	FC Tbilisi	A	1-2	Koridze
28/09/99	Arsenali Tbilisi	A	2-1	Gotsiridze, Koridze
03/10/99	Lokomotivi Tbilisi	H	3-1	Kipiani, Nozadze, Koridze
16/10/99	Samgurali Tskhaltubo	H	3-1	Gotsiridze 3
23/10/99	Sioni Bolnisi	A	0-0	
30/10/99	Dinamo Batumi	H	0-0	
07/11/99	Dinamo Tbilisi	A	1-4	Khartishvili
14/11/99	FC Tbilisi	H	1-1	Koridze
20/11/99	Arsenali Tbilisi	H	4 0	Sajaia, Muziushvlll, Nozadze, Dolidze
28/11/99	Lokomotivi Tbilisi	A	1-1	Koridze
04/03/00	Dinamo Tbilisi	A	0-0	
11/03/00	Sioni Bolnisi	H	1-0	Gotsiridze
18/03/00	Dila Gori	H	2-1	Koridze, Melkadze
26/03/00	Iberia Samtredia	A	1-0	Koridze
01/04/00	Kolkheti 1913 Poti	H	0-0	
14/04/00	Dinamo Batumi	A	1-0	Gochashvili
18/04/00	Torpedo Kutaisi	H	1-1	Kotorashvili
22/04/00	Dinamo Tbilisi	H	1-1	Koridze
29/04/00	Sioni Bolnisi	A	2-1	Gochashvili, Koridze
06/05/00	Dila Gori	A	2-0	Gochashvili 2
13/05/00	Iberia Samtredia	H	2-1	Nozadze, Koridze
17/05/00	Kolkheti 1913 Poti	A	0-2	
23/05/00	Dinamo Batumi	H	2-0	Kipiani, Chankotadze
30/05/00	Torpedo Kutaisi	A	0-0	

GERMANY

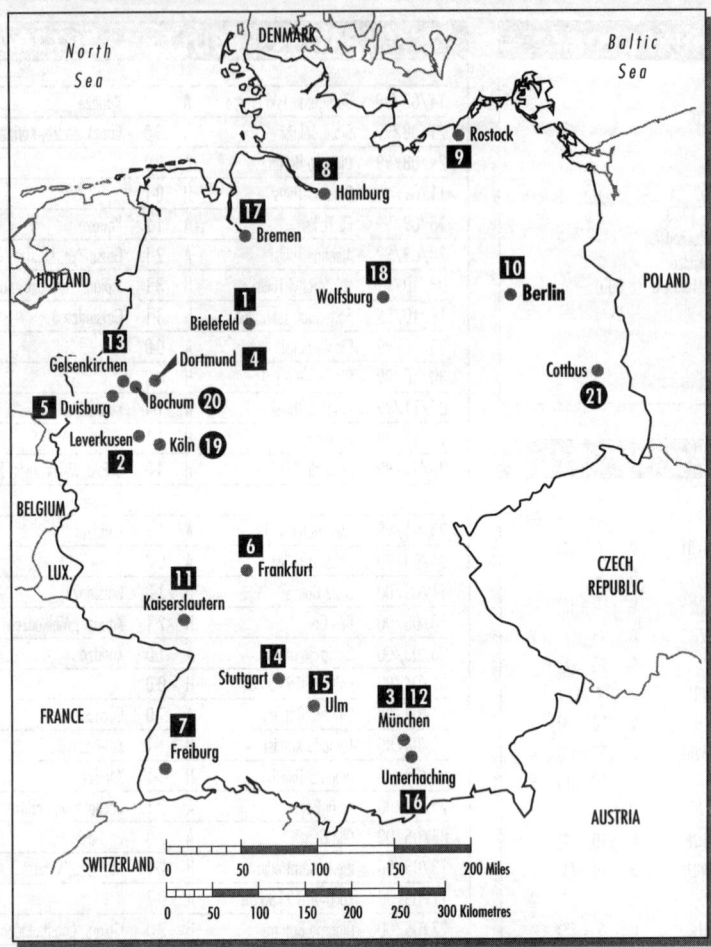

1	ARMINIA BIELEFELD	444
2	BAYER 04 LEVERKUSEN	445
3	FC BAYERN MÜNCHEN	446
4	BORUSSIA DORTMUND	447
5	MSV DUISBURG	448
6	EINTRACHT FRANKFURT	449
7	SC FREIBURG	450
8	HAMBURGER SV	451
9	FC HANSA ROSTOCK	452
10	HERTHA BSC BERLIN	453
11	1.FC KAISERSLAUTERN	454
12	TSV 1860 MÜNCHEN	455
13	FC SCHALKE 04	456
14	VFB STUTTGART	457
15	SSV ULM	458
16	SPVGG UNTERHACHING	459
17	SV WERDER BREMEN	460
18	VFL WOLFSBURG	461
Promoted clubs		
19	1.FC KÖLN	
20	VFL BOCHUM	
21	FC ENERGIE COTTBUS	

LEVERKUSEN THROW IT ALL AWAY

No escape from reality for Ribbeck's flops

FEDERATION DIRECTORY

Deutscher Fussball-Bund
Otto-Fleck-Schneise 6, Postfach 710405, 60528 Frankfurt am Main

tel - (069) 67880/1
fax - (069) 6788266
website - www.dfb.de

Year of Formation - 1900
President - Dr. Egidius Braun
Secretary - Horst R. Schmidt

It *was* safe, after all, to write off the Germans. In the run-up to Euro 2000 the temptation to dismiss the defending champions as little more than no-hopers was strong, but few dared to take the plunge for fear of being proved wrong by Germany's time-honoured ability to come good at major tournaments.

As it turned out, Germany's reputation counted for nothing. Everything that had been said and written about them was true. They really were the poorest German side in living memory. Low on quality, short on spirit and, at times, hopelessly disorganised, Erich Ribbeck's team betrayed all of their country's noble footballing traditions. In short, they were pitiful.

With just one point and one goal from their three matches, Germany's performance was their worst ever at a major championship. It took some getting used to back home, and the criticism which rained down on the coach and his players was only tempered by the low level of expectation that had accompanied the team into the tournament.

Germany were fairly fortunate to qualify for Euro 2000 in the first place, claiming their automatic ticket with an unconvincing goalless draw at home to Turkey. Had the Turks won rather than drawn their previous encounter, away to Moldova, that result in Munich would have despatched Germany into the play-offs. The Ribbeck régime was already under heavy fire following a lamentable showing at the mid-summer Confederations'

LEAGUE CHAMPIONSHIP RESULTS 99/00

		1	2	3	4	5	6	7	8	9	10	11	12	13	14	15	16	17	18
1	Arminia Bielefeld		1-2	0-3	0-2	0-1	1-1	2-1	3-0	2-2	1-1	1-2	2-2	1-2	1-2	4-1	1-0	2-2	0-0
2	Bayer 04 Leverkusen	4-1		2-0	3-1	3-0	4-1	1-1	2-2	1-1	3-1	3-1	1-1	3-2	1-0	4-1	2-1	3-2	4-1
3	FC Bayern München	2-1	4-1		1-1	4-1	4-1	6-1	2-2	4-1	3-1	2-2	1-2	4-1	0-1	4-0	1-0	3-1	5-0
4	Borussia Dortmund	1-3	1-1	0-1		2-2	1-0	1-1	0-1	3-0	4-0	0-1	1-1	1-1	1-1	1-1	1-3	1-3	2-1
5	MSV Duisburg	0-3	0-0	1-2	2-2		2-3	1-2	1-1	2-2	0-0	2-2	3-0	1-1	1-3	0-0	2-0	0-1	2-3
6	Eintracht Frankfurt	2-1	1-2	1-2	1-1	2-2		2-0	3-0	0-0	4-0	0-1	3-1	0-2	0-1	2-1	3-0	1-0	4-0
7	SC Freiburg	1-1	0-0	1-2	1-1	3-0	2-3		0-2	5-0	0-1	2-1	3-0	2-1	0-2	2-0	4-3	2-1	1-1
8	Hamburger SV	5-0	0-2	0-0	1-1	6-1	1-0	2-0		1-0	5-1	2-1	2-0	3-1	3-0	1-2	3-0	0-0	2-2
9	FC Hansa Rostock	2-1	1-1	0-3	1-0	3-1	3-1	1-1	3-3		0-1	4-2	0-0	1-0	1-4	2-1	1-1	1-1	1-1
10	Hertha BSC Berlin	2-0	0-0	1-1	0-3	2-1	1-0	0-0	2-1	5-2		0-1	1-1	2-1	1-1	3-0	2-1	1-1	0-0
11	1.FC Kaiserslautern	0-2	1-3	0-2	1-0	3-2	1-0	0-2	2-0	2-2	1-2		1-1	2-1	1-2	6-2	4-2	4-3	2-2
12	TSV 1860 München	5-0	1-2	1-0	0-3	4-1	2-0	3-1	0-0	4-3	2-1	2-1		3-3	1-1	4-1	2-1	1-0	1-2
13	FC Schalke 04	1-1	1-1	1-1	0-0	3-0	0-0	2-2	1-3	0-2	1-1	1-2	2-2		3-0	0-0	1-0	3-1	1-1
14	VfB Stuttgart	3-3	1-2	2-0	1-2	4-2	0-2	1-0	1-3	3-1	1-0	0-1	1-3	0-2		2-0	0-2	0-0	2-5
15	SSV Ulm	2-0	1-9	0-1	0-1	0-3	3-0	1-1	1-2	1-1	0-1	3-1	3-0	1-1	1-1		1-0	2-1	2-0
16	SpVgg Unterhaching	2-0	2-0	0-2	1-0	2-0	1-0	1-0	1-1	1-1	1-1	1-2	1-1	3-1	2-0	1-0		1-0	1-1
17	SV Werder Bremen	3-1	1-3	0-2	3-2	4-0	3-1	5-2	2-1	2-1	4-1	5-0	1-3	0-1	2-1	2-2	2-2		2-2
18	VfL Wolfsburg	2-0	3-1	1-1	1-0	1-0	1-0	2-1	4-4	2-0	2-3	3-2	2-1	0-0	0-2	1-2	2-2	2-7	

LEAGUE CHAMPIONSHIP FINAL TABLE 99/00

				Home				Away					Total					
		Pd	W	D	L	F	A	W	D	L	F	A	W	D	L	F	A	PT	GD
1	FC Bayern München	34	12	3	2	50	17	10	4	3	23	11	22	7	5	73	28	73	45
2	Bayer 04 Leverkusen	34	13	4	0	44	17	8	6	3	30	19	21	10	3	74	36	73	38
3	Hamburger SV	34	11	4	2	37	11	5	7	5	26	28	16	11	7	63	39	59	24
4	TSV 1860 München	34	11	3	3	36	20	3	8	6	19	28	14	11	9	55	48	53	7
5	1.FC Kaiserslautern	34	8	3	6	31	28	7	2	8	23	31	15	5	14	54	59	50	-5
6	Hertha BSC Berlin	34	8	7	2	23	14	5	4	8	16	32	13	11	10	39	46	50	-7
7	VfL Wolfsburg	34	9	4	4	29	26	3	9	5	22	32	12	13	9	51	58	49	-7
8	VfB Stuttgart	34	6	2	9	22	28	8	4	5	22	19	14	6	14	44	47	48	-3
9	SV Werder Bremen	34	10	3	4	41	25	3	5	9	24	27	13	8	13	65	52	47	13
10	SpVgg Unterhaching	34	10	5	2	22	10	2	3	12	18	32	12	8	14	40	42	44	-2
11	Borussia Dortmund	34	4	7	6	21	21	5	6	6	20	17	9	13	12	41	38	40	3
12	SC Freiburg	34	8	4	5	29	19	2	6	9	16	31	10	10	14	45	50	40	-5
13	Eintracht Frankfurt	34	9	3	5	29	14	3	2	12	13	30	12	5	17	42	44	39	-2
13	FC Schalke 04	34	4	10	3	21	17	4	5	8	21	27	8	15	11	42	44	39	-2
15	FC Hansa Rostock	34	7	7	3	25	22	1	7	9	19	38	8	14	12	44	60	38	-16
16	SSV Ulm	34	7	4	6	22	23	2	4	11	14	39	9	8	17	36	62	35	-26
17	Arminia Bielefeld	34	4	6	7	22	24	3	3	11	18	37	7	9	18	40	61	30	-21
18	MSV Duisburg	34	2	8	7	20	25	2	2	13	17	46	4	10	20	37	71	22	-34

N.B. Eintracht Frankfurt - 2 points deducted.

Cup in Mexico, where, for the second time in six months, Germany were beaten by the United States.

The counter-performances continued in the new year, with Germany suffering a real beating in Amsterdam against Holland. Even the most ardent German supporters were ready to concede that the 2-1 scoreline was immensely flattering to their team. Germany played four more warm-up games in preparation for the European Championship and they were unimpressive in all of them, even if they avoided any further defeats. An abject display at home to Switzerland would have resulted in a 0-1 defeat but for a hugely controversial late equaliser, and even tiny Liechtenstein caused the Germans problems before a late flurry of goals in the last ten minutes concealed the reality of what had gone before.

There was no hiding place and no escape route for Germany at Euro 2000, however. They just about merited a point from their first game against Romania after an opening period in which the lack of confidence and co-ordination in the German defence defied belief. Against England, Ribbeck's men had more of the ball, but with captain Oliver Bierhoff unavailable after injuring himself in training, there was no cutting edge up front and the English claimed a long-awaited victory in the clash of the dinosaurs with a single goal from Alan Shearer.

Still theoretically in with a shout of reaching the quarter-finals despite these two setbacks, Germany were offered a helping hand when Portugal, already qualified, fielded a reserve side for the final group game in Rotterdam. Ribbeck had stated repeatedly before the tournament that this was his team's most important match, but the message evidently failed to get through to his players, who succumbed without honour to a humiliating 3-0 defeat.

Ribbeck's inevitable resignation was confirmed soon after the team's return. He had seemed a reluctant national coach from day one. Never at ease with his environment and frequently at loggerheads with some of the team's most prominent players, Ribbeck quietly slid away into anonymity, branded forever as the first German coach to have concluded his time in office without winning a major trophy.

Ribbeck could hardly be blamed for the paucity of top-class talent available to him, but the general consensus was that he fell well short of maximising his resources. Perhaps his greatest folly was to persist with the ageing Lothar Matthäus. The veteran libero set a new world record of 150 international appearances in the defeat by Portugal, but the last three of those (at least) were won on reputation rather than on merit. There was even a mutiny among the

NATIONAL TEAM APPEARANCES 99/00

Coach - Erich RIBBECK	BRA	NZL	USA	FIN	NIR	TUR	NOR	HOL	CRO	SUI	CZE	LIE	ROM	ENG	POR	Cps	Gls
Jens LEHMANN (10/11/69) - Borussia Dortmund (GER)	G	G	G	G	G		G				G	G46				12	-
Lothar MATTHÄUS (21/03/61)- FC Bayern München/ New York/New Jersey MetroStars (USA)	D	D71	D	M	D	D	D	D	D	D		D30	D77	D	D	150	23
Christian WÖRNS (10/05/72) - Borussia Dortmund	D	D	D	s46	D					s35						33	-
Thomas LINKE (26/12/69) - FC Bayern München	D	D	D	D	D	D	s33	D	D	D	D	D46	D46		M	17	-
Lars RICKEN (10/07/76) - Borussia Dortmund	M	M														8	-
Michael BALLACK (26/09/76) - Bayer 04 Leverkusen	M	s71							M	M	s53	s46		s72	M46	9	-
Dariusz WOSZ (08/06/69) - Hertha BSC Berlin	M	s46	M				s46	s61	M	M46	s57	s46				16	1
Jörg HEINRICH (06/12/69) - Fiorentina (ITA)	M74	M	M41													30	2
Oliver NEUVILLE (01/05/73) - Bayer 04 Leverkusen	M79	A	A	M85	A66	A	M33	A76		s68						17	3
Michael PREETZ (17/08/67) - Hertha BSC Berlin	A71	A	A							A46						7	2
Mehmet SCHOLL (16/10/70) - FC Bayern München	A	M46		M79	M	A	A	A		M23	M46	M46	M		M	M59	29
Olaf MARSCHALL (19/03/66) - 1.FC Kaiserslautern	s71	A65														13	3
Ronald MAUL (13/02/73) - Arminia Bielefeld	s74		s76													2	-
Heiko GERBER (11/07/72) - VfB Stuttgart	s79		M76													2	-
Bernd SCHNEIDER (17/11/73) - Bayer 04 Leverkusen		M	M	s32	s66	M89										5	-
Paulo Roberto RINK (21/02/73) - Santos (BRA)/Bayer 04 Leverkusen		s65	s60						s84	s46	A	A46	A	s70	s46	11	-
Horst HELDT (09/12/69) - Eintracht Frankfurt		A60														2	-
Mustafa DOGAN (01/01/76) - Fenerbahçe (TUR)			s41		s89											2	-
Markus BABBEL (08/09/72) - FC Bayern München				D	M30	D	D68	D		D35	M46	M46		M	D	51	1
Jens NOWOTNY (11/01/74) - Bayer 04 Leverkusen				D	D46		D			D78		D	D	D	D	22	-
Jens JEREMIES (05/03/74) - FC Bayern München				M	M	M	M	M			M46			M	M78	25	1
Christian ZIEGE (01/02/72) - Middlesbrough (ENG)				M	M	M76	M		M	M88	M18	M	M46	M	M	52	8
Oliver BIERHOFF (01/05/68) - Milan (ITA)				A	A	A	A83	A	A	A	s57	A46	A			50	30
Ulf KIRSTEN (04/12/65) - Bayer 04 Leverkusen		A32					A46		A	s46		s46		A70	s69	51	21
Christian NERLINGER (21/03/73) - Borussia Dortmund		s79			s46											6	1
Thomas STRUNZ (25/04/68) - FC Bayern München					s85	s30										41	1
Marco BODE (23/07/69) - SV Werder Bremen						A	s76	M46		s18	s46	s46	s78		A	22	5
Oliver KAHN (15/06/69) - FC Bayern München						G		G	G	G			G	G	G	27	-
Dietmar HAMANN (27/08/73) - Liverpool (ENG)				M46	s46	M61	M84		s23	M53	M46	s73		M	M	27	2
Frank BAUMANN (29/10/75) - SV Werder Bremen							s68	s76								2	-
Carsten JANCKER (28/08/74) - FC Bayern München							s83			A57	s46			A	A69	9	3
Zoltan SEBESCEN (01/10/75) - VfL Wolfsburg								M46								1	-
Sebastian DEISLER (05/01/80) - Hertha BSC Berlin								s46			s46	s46	s77	M72	M	6	-
Marko REHMER (29/04/72) - Hertha BSC Berlin									M46	M68	s78	s46	s46		D	13	1
Carsten RAMELOW (20/03/74) - Bayer 04 Leverkusen									s46	D	s30					9	-
Stefan BEINLICH (13/01/72) - Bayer 04 Leverkusen									s88							4	-
Thomas HÄSSLER (30/05/66) - TSV 1860 München											M57	s46	M73		s59	101	11
Hans-Jörg BUTT (28/05/74) - Hamburger SV										s46						1	-

EUROPEAN CUPS 99/00

CHAMPIONS' CUP
● BAYER 04 LEVERKUSEN
Champions' League
1st match LAZIO (ITA)
H 1-1   Neuville (14)
Matysek, Kovac, Nowotny, Gresko (Beinlich 67), Schneider, Émerson,
Ramelow, Zé Roberto, Hejduk, Reichenberger (Róbson Ponte 81),
Neuville (Brdaric 74).

2nd match NK MARIBOR (SLO)
A 2-0   Zivkovic (82), Kirsten (90)
Matysek, Zivkovic, Nowotny (Róbson Ponte 70), Kovac, Schneider,
Ramelow, Émerson, Gresko, Beinlich, Neuville (Brdaric 82), Kirsten.

3rd match DYNAMO KYIV (UKR)
H 1-1   Kirsten (52)
Matysek, Reeb, Nowotny, Kovac, Schneider, Émerson, Ramelow, Beinlich,
Róbson Ponte (Reichenberger 85), Kirtsen, Neuville (Hejduk 46).

4th match DYNAMO KYIV (UKR)
A 2-4   Kirsten (12), Neuville (48)
Matysek, Reeb, Nowotny, Zivkovic, Schneider, Ramelow, Émerson,
Beinlich, Hejduk (Róbson Ponte 77), Kirtsen, Neuville.

5th match LAZIO (ITA)
A 1-1   Kirsten (44)
Matysek, Reeb (Hejduk 67), Nowotny, Zivkovic, Schneider, Émerson,
Ramelow, Beinlich, Gresko (Happe 26), Neuville, Kirsten (Mamic 89).

6th match NK MARIBOR (SLO)
H 0-0   Matysek, Reeb (Brdaric 46), Nowotny, Zivkovic, Hejduk, Schneider
(Hoffmann 75), Émerson, Ramelow, Beinlich, Reichenberger
(Róbson Ponte 46), Neuville.

● BORUSSIA DORTMUND
Qualifying round FK TEPLICE (CZE)
A 1-0   Nerlinger (66)
Lehmann, Wörns, Stevic, Kohler, Reuter, Nerlinger, Möller, Dedé, Ricken
(Nijhuis 90), Bobic (Barbarez 89), Ikpeba (Herrlich 76).
H 1-0   Herrlich (90)
Lehmann, Wörns, Stevic, Kohler (Nijhuis 82), Feiersinger, Nerlinger,
Möller, Herrlich, Reina (Ricken 86), Dedé, Ikpeba (Bobic 90).

Champions' League
1st match FEYENOORD (HOL)
A 1-1   Bobic (71)
Lehmann, Reuter, Evanilson, Nijhuis (Barbarez 77), Dedé, Ricken, Stevic,
Nerlinger, Reina, Bobic (Herrlich 90), Möller.

2nd match BOAVISTA FC (POR)
H 3-1   Möller (40), Bobic (52, 65)
Lehmann, Reuter, Evanilson, Kohler, Addo (Stevic 79), Ricken, Nerlinger,
Dedé, Reina (Nijhuis 88), Bobic (Herrlich 73), Möller.

3rd match ROSENBORG BK (NOR)
A 2-2   Barbarez (11), Kohler (22)
Lehmann, Reuter, Evanilson (Baumann 46), Kohler, Dedé, Stevic
(Nijhuis 74), Ricken, Nerlinger, Reina, Herrlich (Addo 69), Barbarez.

4th match ROSENBORG BK (NOR)
H 0-3   Lehmann, Reuter, Wörns (Bobic 46), Kohler, Dedé, Evanilson
(Kapetanovic 83), Ricken, Nerlinger (Addo 61), Reina, Barbarez, Möller.

5th match FEYENOORD (HOL)
H 1-1   Addo (44)
Lehmann, Reuter, Evanilson, Kohler, Dedé, Stevic, Möller, Nerlinger,
Reina, Bobic (Barbarez 74), Addo.

6th match BOAVISTA FC (POR)
A 0-1   Lehmann, Reuter, Kohler, Wörns (Barbarez 76), Ricken, Stevic, Nerlinger
(Herrlich 45), Dedé, Reina (Evanilson 61), Bobic, Addo.

● FC BAYERN MÜNCHEN
Champions' League
1st match PSV (HOL)
H 2-1   Paulo Sérgio (11, 69)
Kahn, Matthäus, Andersson, Kuffour, Strunz, Jeremies, Effenberg,
Lizarazu, Paulo Sérgio (Zickler 79), Santa Cruz (Jancker 68), Scholl
(Salihamidzic 88).

2nd match RANGERS (SCO)
A 1-1   Tarnat (90)
Wessels, Matthäus (Zickler 80), Kuffour, Linke, Jeremies, Effenberg,
Tarnat, Lizarazu (Jancker 46), Scholl, Élber, Salihamidzic.

3rd match VALENCIA CF (ESP)
H 1-1   Élber (6)
Kahn, Linke, Matthäus, Kuffour, Salihamidzic, Jeremies, Effenberg, Tarnat,
Zickler (Santa Cruz 46), Élber (Jancker 62), Scholl.

4th match VALENCIA CF (ESP)
A 1-1   Effenberg (18p)
Kahn, Kuffour, Matthäus, Linke, Babbel, Jeremies, Effenberg, Lizarazu,
Zickler (Salihamidzic 75), Élber (Jancker 81), Paulo Sérgio (Santa Cruz 90).

5th match PSV (HOL)
A 1-2   Santa Cruz (51)
Wessels, Matthäus, Andersson, Linke, Babbel, Salihamidzic (68),
Jeremies, Effenberg, Lizarazu, Zickler (Jancker 74), Élber, Paulo Sérgio
(Santa Cruz 26).

6th match RANGERS (SCO)
H 1-0   Strunz (33p)
Kahn, Babbel, Matthäus, Linke, Strunz, Fink, Effenberg (Tarnat 75),
Lizarazu, Scholl (Salihamidzic 65), Élber, Santa Cruz (Paulo Sérgio 65).

7th match ROSENBORG BK (NOR)
A 1-1   Jancker (10)
Kahn, Babbel, Andersson, Kuffour, Tarnat, Fink, Effenberg, Scholl
(Zickler 82), Paulo Sérgio (Santa Cruz 79), Jancker, Salihamidzic.

8th match DYNAMO KYIV (UKR)
H 2-1   Jancker (6), Paulo Sérgio (80)
Kahn, Matthäus, Kuffour, Linke, Babbel, Fink, Tarnat, Salihamidzic, Paulo
Sérgio (Wiesinger 90), Jancker, Santa Cruz (Zickler 75).

9th match REAL MADRID (ESP)
A 4-2   Scholl (21), Effenberg (24), Fink (39), Paulo Sérgio (66)
Kahn, Babbel (Linke 62), Matthäus, Kuffour, Salihamidzic, Fink,
Effenberg, Lizarazu, Paulo Sérgio, Élber (Santa Cruz 86), Scholl (Tarnat 86).

EUROPEAN CUPS 99/00 (CONTINUED)

10th match REAL MADRID (ESP)
H 4-1   Scholl (2), Élber (30), Zickler (79, 90)
Kahn, Matthäus (Andersson 90), Kuffour, Linke, Salihamidzic, Effenberg, Fink, Lizarazu, Paulo Sérgio, Élber (Zickler 75), Scholl (Wiesinger 88).

11th match ROSENBORG BK (NOR)
H 2-1   Scholl (10), Paulo Sérgio (39p)
Kahn, Babbel, Andersson, Kuffour, Tarnat, Fink, Jeremies, Scholl (Salihamidzic 75), Zickler, Jancker (Élber 75), Paulo Sérgio (Santa Cruz 84).

12th match DYNAMO KYIV (UKR)
A 0-2   Wessels, Kuffour, Andersson, Linke (Johansson 77), Salihamidzic, Wiesinger, Fink, Tarnat, Wojciechowski, Zickler (Di Salvio 35), Santa Cruz (Jarolim 77).

Quarter-final FC PORTO (POR)
A 1-1   Paulo Sérgio (80)
Kahn, Babbel, Kuffour, Andersson, Lizarazu, Salihamidzic (Santa Cruz 80), Jeremies, Effenberg, Scholl (Fink 87), Paulo Sérgio, Élber (Jancker 73).
H 2-1   Paulo Sérgio (14), Linke (90)
Kahn, Babbel, Andersson, Linke, Tarnat (Kuffour 81), Fink, Jeremies, Scholl, Paulo Sérgio, Élber (Jancker 90), Santa Cruz (Salihamidzic 68).

Semi-final REAL MADRID (ESP)
A 0-2   Kahn, Babbel, Jeremies, Linke, Salihamidzic (Santa Cruz 78), Fink, Tarnat (Wiesinger 46), Lizarazu, Scholl, Paulo Sérgio, Élber (Jancker 78).
H 2-1   Jancker (12), Élber (54)
Kahn, Babbel (Salihamidzic 60), Andersson, Kuffour, Lizarazu, Paulo Sérgio, Jeremies (Fink 59), Effenberg, Scholl, Élber, Jancker (Santa Cruz 79).

● HERTHA BSC BERLIN
Qualifying round ANORTHOSIS FAMAGUSTA (CYP)
H 2-0   Daei (2), Preetz (58)
Király, Herzog, Konstantinidis, Sverrisson, Wosz (Dárdai 77), Daei (Aracic 83), Rekdal (Schmidt 66), Preetz, Hartmann, Tretschok, Thom.
A 0-0   Király, Herzog, Konstantinidis, Sverrisson, Wosz (Sanneh 69), Daei (Veit 69), Dárdai, Hartmann, Tretschok, Aracic (Schmidt 90), Deisler.

Champions' League
1st match GALATASARAY (TUR)
A 2-2   Preetz (12), Wosz (13)
Király, Herzog, Helmer (Veit 17; Neuendorf 46), Schmidt, Deisler, Konstantinidis, Dárdai, Hartmann, Wosz (Thom 50), Daei, Preetz.

2nd match CHELSEA (ENG)
H 2-1   Daei (2, 70)
Király, Herzog, Van Burik, Schmidt, Sanneh (Veit 67), Deisler, Dárdai (Helmer 80), Tretschok (Michalke 12), Wosz, Daei, Preetz.

3rd match MILAN (ITA)
A 1-1   Daei (69)
Király, Helmer, Herzog, Van Burik, Schmidt, Deisler, Dárdai, Wosz, Michalke, Daei, Preetz.

4th match MILAN (ITA)
H 1-0   Wosz (41)
Király, Rekdal, Sverrisson, Helmer, Van Burik, Deisler, Dárdai (Sanneh 87), Wosz, Michalke, Daei (Aracic 70), Preetz.

5th match GALATASARAY (TUR)
H 1-4   Rekdal (35p)
Király, Rekdal (Neuendorf 82), Van Burik, Helmer (Herzog 14), Sverrisson, Deisler, Schmidt, Wosz, Michalke, Daei, Preetz (Aracic 74).

6th match CHELSEA (ENG)
A 0-2   Király, Van Burik, Helmer (Schmidt 58), Sverrisson, Rekdal, Sanneh, Deisler, Wosz (Konstantinidis 46), Michalke, Preetz, Daei (Aracic 46).

7th match FC BARCELONA (ESP)
H 1-1   Michalke (33)
Király, Rehmer (Veit 72), Van Burik, Sverrisson, Konstantinidis, Thom, Schmidt, Michalke (Herzog 87), Wosz, Daei, Preetz.

8th match FC PORTO (POR)
A 0-1   Király, Konstantinidis, Herzog, Van Burik, Rehmer (Hartmann 46), Schmidt, Michalke, Neuendorf (Thom 65), Wosz, Preetz.

9th match SPARTA PRAHA (CZE)
H 1-1   Veit (45)
Fiedler, Herzog, Van Burik, Sverrisson, Deisler, Schmidt, Wosz (Roy 88), Veit, Hartmann, Daei, Preetz.

10th match SPARTA PRAHA (CZE)
A 0-1   Fiedler, Rehmer, Rekdal, Herzog, Hartmann, Konstantinidis, Schmidt, Roy (Preetz 79), Michalke (Veit 21), Daei, Alves.

11th match FC BARCELONA (ESP)
A 1-3   Alves (7)
Király, Rehmer (Neuendorf 59), Herzog, Sverrisson, Van Burik (Wosz 57), Covic, Schmidt (Sanneh 78), Michalke, Hartmann, Preetz, Alves.

12th match FC PORTO (POR)
H 0-1   Király, Sanneh, Herzog, Van Burik (Konstantinidis 46), Sverrisson, Covic, Deisler (Dárdai 46), Michalke, Roy, Alves (Aracic 57), Daei.

UEFA CUP
● 1.FC KAISERSLAUTERN
1st round KILMARNOCK (SCO)
H 3-0   Koch H. (29), Djorkaeff (37), Marschall (39)
Reinke, Sforza, Ramzy, Koch H., Buck, Ratinho (Sobotzik 82), Hristov (Strasser 79), Wagner (Reich 71), Djorkaeff, Marschall, Pettersson.
A 2-0   Djorkaeff (22), Ramzy (29)
Reinke, Ramzy, Koch H., Schjønberg, Ratinho (Buck 46), Komljenovic, Sforza (Sobotzik 60), Strasser, Wagner, Marschall (Pettersson 60), Djorkaeff.

2nd round TOTTENHAM HOTSPUR (ENG)
A 0-1   Reinke, Ramzy, Koch H., Schjønberg, Ratinho (Buck 46), Roos (Komljenovic 74), Sforza, Strasser, Wagner (Reich 46), Marschall, Hristov.
H 2-0   Buck (89), Carr (90og)
Reinke, Ramzy (Reich 86), Koch H., Schjønberg, Buck, Ratinho, Sforza, Strasser, Hristov, Djorkaeff, Marschall (Pettersson 74).

3rd round RC LENS (FRA)
A 2-1   Sikora (31og), Wagner (37)
Reinke, Ramzy, Koch, Schjønberg, Ratinho (Pettersson 86), Roos, Hristov (Sobotzik 81), Strasser, Wagner (Reich 77), Djorkaeff, Marschall.

EUROPEAN CUPS 99/00 (CONTINUED)

H 1-4 Hristov (21)
Reinke, Ramzy (Tare 57), Koch H., Schjønberg, Buck (Roos 72), Ratinho, Sforza, Strasser (Rische 75), Wagner, Djorkaeff, Hristov.

● **BAYER 04 LEVERKUSEN**
3rd round UDINESE (ITA)
A 1-0 Ballack (76)
Matysek, Zivkovic, Hoffmann, Nowotny, Kovac, Ramelow, Émerson, Gresko, Ballack (Schneider 82), Zé Roberto (Beinlich 90), Kirsten (Mamic 90).
H 1-2 Ballack (21)
Matysek, Hoffmann, Nowotny, Kovac (Beinlich 79), Zivkovic (Schneider 46), Ramelow, Émerson, Gresko (Neuville 46), Ballack, Zé Roberto, Kirsten.

● **BORUSSIA DORTMUND**
3rd round RANGERS (SCO)
A 0-2 Lehmann, Feiersinger, Wörns, Kohler, Evanilson, Stevic, Ricken (But 73), Barbarez, Addo (Reina 46). Bobic (Herrlich 83), Möller.
H 2-0 (aet; 3-1 on pens.) Ikpeba (28), Bobic (90)
Lehmann, Wörns, Reuter, Nijuis, Ricken (Barbarez 82), Stevic (Tanko 72), But, Nerlinger, Addo, Herrlich (Bobic 61), Ikpeba.

4th round GALATASARAY (TUR)
H 0-2 Lehmann, Nijhuis, Kohler, Baumann, Evanilson (Reina 32), Stevic, Ricken, But, Dedé, Ikpeba, Bobic.
A 0-0 Lehmann, Nijhuis, Feiersinger, Kohler, Wörns, Stevic (Bugri 63), Ricken, Kapetanovic (Dedé 46), Reina (Tanko 70), Herrlich, Bobic.

● **SV WERDER BREMEN**
1st round FK BODØ/GLIMT (NOR)
A 5-0 Pizarro (11, 70), Bogdanovic (44, 55), Maximov (60)
Rost, Tjikuzu, Baumann, Júlio César, Wiedener, Frings (Maximov 46), Eilts, Wicky, Bode (Chanko 61), Pizarro, Bogdanovic (Aílton 85).
H 1-1 Aílton (76)
Brasas, Roembiak, Baumann, Júlio César, Wiedener (Chanko 46), Dabrowski, Maximov, Eilts, Bode (Herzog 61), Bogdanovic (Aílton 70), Pizarro.

2nd round VIKING FK (NOR)
H 0-0 Rost, Tjikuzu, Baumann, Júlio César, Wiedener (Bogdanovic 76), Frings (Maximov 76), Eilts (Aílton 80), Wicky, Herzog, Pizarro, Bode.
A 2-2 Wiedener (43), Herzog (63)
Rost, Fringa, Baumann, Júlio César, Wiedener, Maximov, Dabrowski, Wicky, Herzog (Seidel 79), Pizarro, Bode.

3rd round OLYMPIQUE LYONNAIS (FRA)
A 0-3 Rost, Frings, Júlio César, Baumann, Wiedener (Maximov 65), Wicky, Eilts (Dabrowski 71), Herzog, Bode, Pizarro, Aílton.
H 4-0 (aet) Bode (16), Herzog (39p), Baumann (54), Pizarro (77)
Rost, Tjikuzu, Baumann, Júlio César, Bode, Eilts, Trares, Herzog (Wiedener 90), Frings, Pizarro, Aílton.

4th round PARMA (ITA)
A 0-1 Rost, Frings, Barten, Baumann, Wiedener, Maximov, Eilts (Tjikuzu 90), Herzog, Trares, Aílton, Pizarro (Dabrowski 81).
H 3-1 Dabrowski (29), Bode (44), Aílton (66)
Rost, Frings, Barten, Baumann, Wiedener, Dabrowski, Eilts, Herzog (Bogdanovic 82), Bode (Maximov 71), Aílton (Schierenback 90), Pizarro.

Quarter-final ARSENAL (ENG)
A 0-2 Rost, Tjikuzu, Barten, Baumann, Wiedener, Frings, Dabrowski, Eilts, Herzog, Aílton (Schierenback 83), Bode.
H 2-4 Bode (41), Bogdanovic (60)
Rost, Frings, Barten, Baumann, Wiedener, Eilts (Maximov 46), Trares (Bogdanovic 46), Herzog, Bode, Pizarro, Aílton.

● **VFL WOLFSBURG**
1st round DEBRECENI VSC (HUN)
H 2-0 Akonnor (61), Juskowiak (87)
Reitmaier, O'Neil, Thomsen, Maltriz, Greiner, Nowak (Banza 53), Munteanu (Brand 73), Weiser (Dammeier 82), Akonnor, Juskowiak, Akpoborie.
A 1-2 Akpoborie (25)
Reitmaier, Greiner, O'Neill, Thomsen, Kryger, Sebescen, Ballwanz, Munteanu (Maltriz 59), Dammeier, Akpoborie (Wück 86), Juskowiak (Baumgart 82).

2nd round RODA JC (HOL)
A 0-0 Reitmaier, O'Neil, Thomsen, Kryger, Greiner, Nowak, Munteanu, Weiser, Sebescen, Juskowiak (Feldhoff 89), Akpoborie (Wück 76).
H 1-0 Akonnor (87)
Reitmaier, O'Neil, Thomsen, Kryger, Greiner, Nowak, Akonnor (Dammeier 87), Weiser, Sebescen (Banza 26; Ballwanz 90), Akpoborie, Juskowiak.

3rd round ATLETICO MADRID (ESP)
H 2-3 Juskowiak (21), Akonnor (83p)
Reitmaier, Ballwanz, O'Neil (Maltriz 57), Thomsen, Greiner, Akonnor, Nowak, Weiser, Sebescen (Wück 27), Feldhoff (Banza 70), Juskowiak.
A 1-2 Akonnor (56p)
Reitmaier, Ballwanz (Wück 50), Thomsen (Banza 46), Kryger, Biliskov, Maltriz, Nowak, Dammeier, Weiser, Akonnor, Juskowiak.

German players after the Romania game to get Matthäus dropped, but Ribbeck, loyal to the last, would have none of it.

The German FA (DFB) made immediate plans for the future by appointing Bayer Leverkusen coach Christoph Daum as the next Bundestrainer. The only problem was that he was still bound by contract to his club until June 2001.

The short-term answer, therefore, was to give the job temporarily to the Leverkusen general manager, Rudi Völler. Given that the former national team striker had no coaching experience to speak of, it seemed an odd move, especially with a crucial World Cup qualifying campaign on the immediate horizon. But, having fitted Völler out with a coaching staff that included ex-Borussia Dortmund boss Michael Skibbe, the DFB stated resolutely that the appointments would guarantee the long-term resurrection of German football.

Völler may yet prove to be a lucky talisman. Just a few days after his appointment he travelled to Switzerland for the announcement of the host nation for the 2006 World Cup, and, contrary to expectation, Germany won, beating favourites South Africa into second place by the narrowest of margins thanks to a block vote from both Europe and Asia and a controversial abstention from the representative of Oceania.

At least Germany are spared the rigours of qualifying for that event, but, considering the lack of high-class youngsters coming through - of the current crop only Sebastian Deisler, of Hertha Berlin, has the potential to be a world-beater - the qualifying roads to Japan/Korea in 2002 and Portugal in 2004 promise to be rocky and treacherous for Völler, Daum and anyone else who might follow them.

Whatever experiences lie in store for Daum in the national team hot seat, he is unlikely ever to suffer as much grief and anguish as he did on the final day of the 1999/2000 Bundesliga season when Bayer Leverkusen threw away a glorious opportunity to become German champions for the first time in their history.

Daum's team had been neck and neck with Bayern Munich at the top of the table throughout the second half of the campaign. Thanks to a run of 14 matches without defeat, 11 of which yielded the maximum three points, Leverkusen lifted themselves into a three-point lead with just one match remaining. Their mission was straight-forward: to win the title they needed to avoid defeat away to Unterhaching, the newly-promoted team from the Munich suburbs. If they lost, however, and Bayern simultaneously won at home to Werder Bremen, the silver championship plate - the so-called 'salad dish' - would remain in Munich.

It was a tense final day, but nobody honestly believed that Leverkusen would fail to get the point they required. After all, Unterhaching were a team without stars, run on a shoestring budget and housed in the Bundesliga's smallest stadium. Ultimately, though, it was all about sheer nerve and courage. Did Leverkusen have the mettle to succeed? The answer, sadly, was no.

Bayern made sure of their victory early on, scoring three times in the first 16 minutes, twice through Carsten Jancker, once through Paulo Sérgio. The matter was still in Leverkusen's hands, but after 21 minutes the gates of hell opened up when young German international midfielder Michael Ballack inadvertently put the ball into his own net. 1-0 to Unterhaching. Leverkusen had several opportunities to rectify the situation but the pressure had clearly got to the players.

The team of previous weeks would have been able to bide their time and outmanoeuvre Unterhaching with their superior quality, but on this occasion chances were snatched at, passes misplaced and errors committed, one of which enabled Unterhaching to score a second, decisive goal, from Markus Oberleitner, 18 minutes from time.

Daum, his players and the Leverkusen fans were utterly inconsolable at the final whistle. It was hard for neutrals to bear, too. Leverkusen

NATIONAL TEAM RESULTS 99/00

24/07/99	Brazil (CC)	N	Guadalajara	0-4	
28/07/99	New Zealand (CC)	N	Guadalajara	2-0	Preetz (6), Matthäus (33)
30/07/99	United States (CC)	N	Guadalajara	0-2	
04/09/99	Finland (ECQ)	A	Helsinki	2-1	Bierhoff (2, 17)
08/09/99	Northern Ireland (ECQ)	H	Dortmund	4-0	Bierhoff (2), Ziege (16, 33, 45)
09/10/99	Turkey (ECQ)	H	Munich	0-0	
14/11/99	Norway	A	Oslo	1-0	Scholl (90)
23/02/00	Holland	A	Amsterdam	1-2	Ziege (22)
29/03/00	Croatia	A	Zagreb	1-1	Rehmer (12)
26/04/00	Switzerland	H	Kaiserslautern	1-1	Kirsten (84)
03/06/00	Czech Republic	H	Nuremberg	3-2	Jancker (38), Bierhoff (63p, 90)
07/06/00	Liechtenstein	H	Freiburg	8-2	Bierhoff (1), Scholl (32), Bode (63),
					Kirsten (80, 81, 86), Jancker (83, 88)
12/06/00	Romania (ECF)	N	Liège	1-1	Scholl (29)
17/06/00	England (ECF)	N	Charleroi	0-1	
20/06/00	Portugal (ECF)	N	Rotterdam	0-3	

TOP SCORERS

19   Martin MAX (TSV 1860 München)

17   Ulf KIRSTEN (Bayer 04 Leverkusen)

14   Giovane ÉLBER (FC Bayern München)

     Ebbe SAND (FC Schalke 04)

13   Marco BODE (SV Werder Bremen)

     PAULO SÉRGIO (FC Bayern München)

12   AÍLTON (SV Werder Bremen)

     Jonathan AKPOBORIE (VfL Wolfsburg)

     Michael PREETZ (Hertha BSC Berlin)

11   Stefan BEINLICH (Bayer 04 Leverkusen)

     Youri DJORKAEFF (1.FC Kaiserslautern)

     Andrzej JUSKOWIAK (VfL Wolfsburg)

     Bruno LABBADIA (Arminia Bielefeld)

     Adel SELLIMI (SC Freiburg)

DOMESTIC CUP 99/00

SECOND ROUND
Fortuna Düsseldorf 0, SSV Ulm 2
SC Verl 0, Eintracht Frankfurt 4
1860 Rosenheim 1, FC St. Pauli 2
VfB Lübeck 0, Hannover 96 1
VfL Halle 96 1, FSV Mainz 05 2
SC Norderstedt 0, VfB Stuttgart 3
SSV Reutlingen 2, VfL Bochum 3
FC Gütersloh 0, FC Energie Cottbus 1
KFC Uerdingen 0, Tennis Borussia Berlin 4
Eintracht Trier 1, Karlsruher SC 1 (aet; 4-3 on pens.)
SV Babelsberg 1, SpVgg Unterhaching 0
FK Pirmasens 0, TSV 1860 Muunchen 3
SG Wattenscheid 09 1, 1FC Köln 7
SV Meppen 2, Kickers Offenbach 1
VFC Plauen 1, Stuttgarter Kickers 2
TuS Langerwehe 0, Chemnitzer FC 6
FC Schönberg 0, SVW Mannheim 3
FC Singen 1, SpVgg Greuther Fürth 3
1.FC Pforzheim 0, SC Freiburg 2
Dynamo Berlin 0, Arminia Bielefeld 2
SV Werder Bremen Amat. 3, Fortuna Köln 1
SpVgg Landshut 0, FC Hansa Rostock 2

THIRD ROUND
SV Babelsberg 2, SC Freiburg 4 (aet)
SVW Mannheim 3, Bayer 04 Leverkusen 2 (aet)
Hannover 96 1, Arminia Bielefeld 2

FC St. Pauli 0, SSV Ulm 2
SpVgg Greuther Fürth 1, FC Hansa Rostock 3
Stuttgarter Kickers 3, Borussia Dortmund 1
SV Werder Bremen 2, 1.FC Kaiserslautern 2
(aet; 4-3 on pens.)
1.FC Köln 2, Eintracht Frankfurt 1
SV Werder Bremen Amat. 0, VfB Stuttgart 1
Chemnitzer FC 2, VfL Wolfsburg 3
VfL Bochum 1, MSV Duisburg 1 (6-5 on pens.)
FC Energie Cottbus 2, FC Schalke 04 2
(5-4 on pens.)
SV Meppen 1, FC Bayern München 4
FSV Mainz 05 2, Hamburger SV 0
Eintracht Trier 2, TSV 1860 München 1
Tennis Borussia Berlin 2, Hertha BSC Berlin 3 (aet)

FOURTH ROUND
Eintracht Trier 0, FC Hansa Rostock 4
SC Freiburg 2, FC Energie Cottbus 0
VfB Stuttgart 4, 1.FC Köln 0
FSV Mainz 05 2, Hertha BSC Berlin 1 (aet)
SV Werder Bremen 2, SSV Ulm 1
VfL Bochum 5, VfL Wolfsburg 4
SVW Mannheim 0, FC Bayern München 3
Stuttgarter Kickers 3, Arminia Bielefeld 2 (aet)

QUARTER-FINALS
VfL Bochum 1 (Weber 63),
SV Werder Bremen 2 (Ailton 79, 88)
FC Bayern München 3 (Herzberger 18og, Jancker 63,
Santa Cruz 70), FSV Mainz 05 0
FC Hansa Rostock 2 (Arvidsson 16, 37),
VfB Stuttgart 1 (Dundee 18)
Stuttgarter Kickers 1 (Maric 39), SC Freiburg 0

SEMI-FINALS
SV Werder Bremen 2 (Dabrowski 2, Maximov 103),
Stuttgarter Kickers 1 (Özkan 82) (aet)
FC Bayern München 3 (Santa Cruz 58, 66, Kuffour 76),
FC Hansa Rostock 2 (Weilandt 75, Wibrån 82)

FINAL
06/05/2000, Berlin
FC BAYERN MÜNCHEN 3
Élber (57), Paulo Sérgio (83), Scholl (90)
SV WERDER BREMEN 0
referee - Berg
FC BAYERN MÜNCHEN - Kahn, Babbel, Andersson,
Kuffour, Tarnat, Salihamidzic, Effenberg (Fink 81),
Jeremies, Paulo Sérgio, Jancker (Santa Cruz 74),
Élber (Scholl 86).
SV WERDER BREMEN - Rost, Frings, Barten,
Baumann, Wiedener (Skripnik 14), Eilts (Flock 64),
Trares (Wicky 71), Bode, Herzog, Ailton, Pizarro.

had never had a better chance to win the Bundesliga, and the fear was that they might never get a similar opportunity in the future. So many Leverkusen players had taken their careers a step forward during the season, but the only one who obtained any tangible reward was Brazilian midfielder Émerson, voted the Bundesliga player of the season. He, together with defender Jens Nowotny and evergreen striker Ulf Kirsten, formed a sturdy backbone, and there was splendid entertainment provided by the likes of wingers Zé Roberto and Oliver Neuville, midfielder Ballack and striker Paulo Rink.

The harrowing defeat at Unterhaching was not the only major disappointment endured by Levrkusen during the season. Several months earlier they had fallen spectacularly at the first hurdle of the Champions' League after failing to win at home to Slovenian outsiders Maribor in their final match.

Leverkusen's agony meant ecstasy for Bayern Munich. Many of the Bayern players, accustomed already to success, claimed that the championship win was their sweetest triumph, if for no other reason than that it had been so unexpected. The celebrations at the sold-out

Olympiastadion were predictably manic and wild, with joy unrestrained from both players and supporters. One man unable to share in the festivities was club president Franz Beckenbauer, who was sailing the South Seas with the 2006 World Cup bidding team at the time. He later admitted that when his wife Sybille rang up to inform him of Bayern's win, he didn't believe her and took some convincing that it was true.

Ottmar Hitzfeld believed it all right. It was the charming coach's fourth Bundesliga title in five years and his second in as many attempts with Bayern. Despite the euphoria of the climax, he was honest enough to admit that his team had been fortunate to retain the title, that they had only won it because Leverkusen had handed it to them.

It was Bayern's record 16th championship victory and they ensured a perfect ending to their centenary season by winning the German Cup and thus completing their third domestic 'double' (after previous triumphs in 1969 and 1986). The Cup final in Berlin gave Bayern the opportunity to atone for their penalty shoot-out defeat a year earlier. Werder Bremen were once again their opponents, but on this occasion Bayern's class told, and three second-

PLAYERS OF THE SEASON

OLIVER KAHN
The German Footballer of the Year award for 2000 went to Bayern Munich and Germany goalkeeper Oliver Kahn, who finished well clear of his club colleague Stefan Effenberg in the annual vote. The big, blond 'keeper claimed his third Bundesliga title

in six seasons at Bayern and was the team's saviour on several occasions. His efforts alone probably earned the team as many as ten of their 73 points. A non-participant at the start of the season with a knee injury, he almost missed out on the finish after an idiot in the crowd at Freiburg threw a golf ball at him, causing a deep wound just next to his right eye. Kahn played on to the end of the game but said afterwards he felt lucky to be alive. Now firmly established as Germany's number one 'keeper - although for much of the season Erich Ribbeck claimed that he and Dortmund's Jens Lehmann were equals - Kahn will continue to be a pillar of strength to the national team through its period of transition under Rudi Völler and Christoph Daum.

ÉMERSON
Fifteen Brazilians took part in the 1999/2000 Bundesliga but Émerson Ferreira da Rosa, the all-purpose Bayer Leverkusen midfielder, was in a class of his own. Voted the Bundesliga's Player of the Season, the 24-year-old performed with a maturity way beyond his years. Not the archetypal Brazilian footballer, he shunned style for substance, fancy flair for energy and effectiveness. He was influential in almost every game, the driving force of the Leverkusen midfield. An ankle injury sustained at Rostock in round 29 threatened to end his season prematurely but he returned in time to share in the

traumatic last-day defeat at Unterhaching. That was his final game for Leverkusen because in the summer he was snapped up for £12m by Roma, a team which had long been on his trail. Everyone at Leverkusen was distraught by his departure, with coach Christoph Daum even venturing that he would take a cut in salary if it meant Émerson would stay.

MARTIN MAX
Signed in the summer of 1999 from Schalke, Martin Max enjoyed a magnificent first season with 1860 Munich. The moustachioed striker had begun to stagnate in Gelsenkirchen, but 'Lions' coach Werner Lorant quickly whipped him back into shape and, with another rejuvenated thirtysomething, Thomas Hässler, to assist him, Max not only began to enjoy his football again but also reinvented himself as a top-class goalscorer. His 19-goal total ultimately proved good enough to win him the Bundesliga top-scorer crown, and it also went some way to earning 1860 a Champions' League qualifying berth. There were many goals for him to treasure - three against his former club Schalke, the opener in the crucial 2-1 win against Hertha Berlin - but best of all was the strike which helped 1860 to a memorable 2-1 victory over Bayern Munich.

SEBASTIAN DEISLER
Sometimes the statistics do not tell the whole story. Sebastian Deisler started just 15 games in his first Bundesliga season with Hertha Berlin and scored only two goals. He also failed to find the target in eight Champions' League appearances. But those unimpressive figures did nothing to stall the hype surrounding this immensely gifted 20-year-old midfielder, who has been widely touted as the Great White Hope of German football. Injury problems delayed his national team début until the friendly against Holland in February 2000, but he was taken to the European Championship and made his first international starts there against England and Portugal. In the aftermath of Germany's wretched campaign, his promising individual displays were viewed as a beacon of light for the future. The source of the optimism is his pure natural footballing talent, which is unmatched by any other German player of his age. An excellent striker of the ball, he is also very skilful and difficult to dispossess. If he can handle the pressure, he is sure to go far.

World Cup Finals appearances: 1934 (3rd), 1938, 1954 (Winners), 1958 (4th), 1962 (qtr-finals), 1966 (runners-up), 1970 (3rd), 1974 (Winners), 1978 (2nd phase), 1982 (runners-up), 1986 (runners-up), 1990 (Winners), 1994 (qtr-finals), 1998 (qtr-finals)

European Championship appearances: 1972 (Winners), 1976 (runners-up), 1980 (Winners), 1984, 1988 (semi-finals), 1992 (runners-up), 1996 (Winners), 2000

European Club Competitions

Champions' Cup	FC Bayern München (1974, 1975, 1976)
	Hamburger SV (1983)
	Borussia Dortmund (1997)
Cup-winners' Cup	Borussia Dortmund (1966)
	FC Bayern München (1967)
	Hamburger SV (1977)
	SV Werder Bremen (1992)
UEFA Cup	Borussia Mönchengladbach (1975, 1979)
	Eintracht Frankfurt (1980)
	Bayer 04 Leverkusen (1988)
	FC Bayern München (1996)
	FC Schalke 04 (1997)
World Club Cup	FC Bayern München (1976)
	Borussia Dortmund (1997)

half goals from Giovane Élber, Paulo Sérgio and Mehmet Scholl sealed a convincing victory.

Bayern were unable, however, to gain revenge for their traumatic defeat in the 1999 Champions' League final. They did reach the semi-finals, which, given the strength of the field, was no mean feat, but their hopes of another final appearance were crushed by Real Madrid, who went through 3-2 on aggregate. It was cold comfort to Bayern that they had thrashed Real twice in the second group phase, 4-2 in the Bernabéu, 4-1 in the Olympiastadion.

Those two group games proved to be the last European matches for Lothar Matthäus, who left Bayern to join Major League Soccer outfit New York/New Jersey MetroStars in time for the start of the new season in the United States. His Bundesliga career ended with 464 appearances, the last of them a defeat at VfB Stuttgart, who, like city rivals 1860 Munich, did the 'double' over Bayern. The only other team to beat Bayern in the Bundesliga were Leverkusen, in the second match of the season.

Hitzfeld made full use of Bayern's large squad, rotating his personnel from game to game. Most of the key elements from the previous season had been retained, from Oliver Kahn in goal, Markus Babbel and Thomas Linke in defence, Jens Jeremies and Stefan Effenberg in midfield, to Jancker and Élber in attack. Paulo Sérgio, the

ex-Leverkusen forward brought back to Germany from Roma, proved to be the best of the new intake, scoring 13 goals in the league, just one fewer than his compatriot Élber. He effectively replaced the disgraced Mario Basler, sacked early in the season for his persistent flouting of club discipline.

Basler later resurfaced at Kaiserslautern, where he joined forces once again with his former coach Otto Rehhagel and helped the 'Red Devils' to a place in the UEFA Cup alongside Hertha Berlin and beaten Cup finalists Werder Bremen. All three of those teams had had moments to savour in the 1999/2000 European competitions. While Kaiserslautern staged a comeback à la Manchester United v Bayern to eliminate Tottenham Hotspur in the second round of the UEFA Cup, Bremen were eventually eliminated from the same competition by another North London side, Arsenal, but not before they had staged two astonishing second-leg comebacks at the Weserstadion to eliminate Lyon and holders Parma. Hertha beat West Londoners Chelsea and also Italian champions Milan in the first group phase of the Champions' League to reach the second phase, but they were unable to register any subsequent wins in a group containing Sparta Prague, FC Porto and Barcelona.

The two qualifying places for the 2000/01 Champions' League were claimed by Hamburg and 1860 Munich. HSV revelled in their newly refurbished Volksparkstadion and were settled in third place throughout the second half of the season. Lightweight goalpoacher Roy Präger, Croatian midfielder Niko Kovac, ex-Freiburg playmaker Rodolfo Cardoso and penalty-taking goalkeeper Hans-Jörg Butt (a perfect nine out of nine from the spot) were the best performers in a team that delivered the goods on a consistent basis until the final few weeks of the season when their prize was already secure. 1860 were even more of a surprise than Hamburg. Veteran schemer Thomas Hässler had a wonderfully resurgent season following his nightmare at Dortmund and he, together with the Bundesliga's top scorer, 19-goal Martin Max, ensured a season of refreshing success for Munich's 'other team' - although that label was hardly apt following the two victories over Bayern, the first against their city rivals for 23 years.

VfB Stuttgart had an extremely inconsistent season under coach Ralf Rangnick and they saved their worst till last, surrendering a 3-0 lead in their final game to already-relegated Arminia Bielefeld and eventually drawing a game that they needed to win to qualify for the UEFA Cup. Instead they had to seek their ticket via the summer InterToto competition, where they were joined by Wolfsburg, complete with comeback-kid Zoltan Sebescen. The 24-year-old had been plunged into the deep end when Erich Ribbeck selected him for the national side in the friendly against Holland. He had played only seven Bundesliga games prior to his selection, so it was hardly surprising that he had a nightmare against the Dutch. But with the criticism still ringing in his ears he scored a tremendous hat-trick just nine days later in a 4-4 thriller against Hamburg.

At the bottom of the table MSV Duisburg and Arminia Bielefeld were joined in the drop-zone on the final day of the season by Ulm, beaten 2-1 at Eintracht Frankfurt, while Hansa Rostock saved themselves with a 2-0 win at Schalke.

At one stage it looked as if the mighty Borussia Dortmund would take that third relegation spot. Despite a massive outlay on new players, the Bundesliga's best-supported team (average gates of 64,629 - 12,000 more than second-best Bayern) sank to unfathomable depths in the second half of the season. The sacking of coach Skibbe was supposed to help them out of their plight but it

merely aggravated it. His replacement, ex-Borussia Mönchengladbach and Real Sociedad boss Bernd Krauss, couldn't find a win from anywhere and he was dismissed after 11 fruitless attempts. This paved the way for veteran coach Udo Lattek to rescue the club from the abyss in the last five weeks of the campaign before he handed over the reins to recently retired former national team libero Matthias Sammer.

Dortmund's local rivals Schalke also had a disappointing season but there was better news for another team from the Ruhr as VfL Bochum, the eternal yo-yo club, won promotion back to the Bundesliga after just a year away. There was no way back, however, for Nuremberg or Mönchengladbach, who finished fourth and fifth, respectively. Backed by crowds of around 30,000, Cologne lifted the Second Division championship while the third promotion place was claimed, to considerable surprise, by former East German Oberliga side Energie Cottbus.

PROMOTED CLUBS 99/00

SECOND DIVISION FINAL TABLE

		Pd	W	D	L	F	A	Pt	GD
1	**1.FC Köln**	34	19	8	7	68	39	65	29
2	**VfL Bochum**	34	18	7	9	67	48	61	19
3	**FC Energie Cottbus**	34	18	4	12	62	42	58	20
4	1.FC Nürnberg	34	15	10	9	54	46	55	8
5	Borussia Mönchengladbach	34	14	12	8	60	43	54	17
6	Rot-Weiss Oberhausen	34	12	13	9	43	34	49	9
7	SpVgg Greuther Fürth	34	10	16	8	40	39	46	1
8	Alemannia Aachen	34	12	10	12	46	54	46	-8
9	FSV Mainz 05	34	11	12	11	41	42	45	-1
10	Hannover 96	34	12	8	14	56	56	44	0
11	Chemnitzer FC	34	11	10	13	42	49	43	-7
12	SV Waldhof Mannheim	34	10	12	12	50	56	42	-6
13	Tennis Borussia Berlin	34	10	10	14	42	50	40	-8
14	FC St. Pauli	34	8	15	11	37	45	39	-8
15	Stuttgarter Kickers	34	10	9	15	49	58	39	-9
16	Fortuna Köln	34	8	11	15	38	50	35	-12
17	Kickers Offenbach	34	8	11	15	35	58	35	-23
18	Karlsruher SC	34	5	12	17	35	56	27	-21

CLUB DIRECTORIES

1.FC Köln
Postfach 42 02 51, 50 896 Köln
tel - (0221) 9436430 / fax - (0221) 4301851
website - www.fc-koeln.de
Year of Formation - 1948
President - Albert Caspers
Secretary - Wolfgang Loos
Coach - Ewald Lienen
Stadium - Müngersdorfer Stadion (46,000)

MAJOR HONOURS
League Championship - (3) 1962, 1964, 1978.
Domestic Cup - (4) 1968, 1977, 1978, 1983.

VfL Bochum
Castroper Strasse 145, 44 728 Bochum
tel - (0234) 951848 / fax - (0234) 951895
website - www.vfl-bochum.de
Year of Formation - 1848
President - Werner Altegoer
Secretary - Klaus Hilpert
Coach - Ernst Middendorp; Bernhard Dietz;
Ralf Zumdick
Stadium - Ruhrstadion (33,000)

FC Energie Cottbus
Stadion der Freundschaft, 03 042 Cottbus
tel - (0355) 756950 / fax - (0355) 713026
website - www.fcenergie.de
Year of Formation - 1966
President - Dieter Krein
Secretary - Klaus Stabach
Coach - Eduard Geyer
Stadium - Stadion der Freundschaft (21,500)

ARMINIA BIELEFELD

CLUB DIRECTORY

Arminia Bielefeld
Melanchthonstrasse 2
33615 Bielefeld
tel - (0521) 966110
fax - (0521) 9661111
website - www.arminia-bielefeld.de
Year of Formation - 1905
President - Hans-Hermann Schwick
Secretary - Werner Vogt
Coach - Hermann Gerland
Stadium - Auf der Alm (22,512)

APPEARANCES 99/00

	P	Ap	(s)	Gls
Christian ALDER	M	1		
Karim BAGHERI (IRN)	M	2	(9)	1
Jörg BODE	M	17	(7)	3
Márcio BORGES (BRA)	D	2		
Jörg BÖHME	M	16	(9)	1
Marcell FENSCH	D		(1)	
Thomas GANSAUGE	M	9	(1)	
Berkant GÖKTAN (TUR)	A	3	(11)	1
Frederik GÖSSLING	G	1		
Andre HOFSCHNEIDER	M	22		
Josef IVANOVIC (CRO)	A		(1)	
Alexander KLITZPERA	D	31		
Georg KOCH	G	16		
Bruno LABBADIA	A	34		11
Ronald MAUL	M	26	(2)	1
Silvio MEISSNER	D	27		5
Zdenko MILETIC (CRO)	G	13		
Jacky PEETERS (BEL)	D	25	(4)	1
Rene RYDLEWICZ	M	17	(12)	
Michael STERNKOPF	M		(7)	
Roberto STRAAL (HOL)	D	4	(3)	
Thomas STRATOS	D	31		4
Dirk VAN DER VEN	A	22	(1)	2
Thijs WATERINK (HOL)	D	12	(9)	
Markus WEISSENBERGER (AUT)	M	32	(1)	9
Artur WICHNIAREK (POL)	M	7	(10)	
Marc ZIEGLER	G	4	(1)	

LEAGUE RESULTS 1999/2000

14/08/99	FC Schalke 04	A	1-1	Labbadia
20/08/99	Hertha BSC Berlin	H	1-1	Meissner
27/08/99	1.FC Kaiserslautern	A	2-0	Labbadia, Meissner
10/09/99	VfL Wolfsburg	H	0-0	
18/09/99	SSV Ulm	A	0-2	
26/09/99	SC Freiburg	H	2-1	Stratos, og (Hermel)
01/10/99	TSV 1860 München	A	0-5	
15/10/99	Borussia Dortmund	H	0-2	
22/10/99	FC Hansa Rostock	A	1-2	Meissner
29/10/99	Eintracht Frankfurt	H	1-1	Bagheri
07/11/99	SV Werder Bremen	H	2-2	Weissenberger 2
21/11/99	Hamburger SV	A	0-5	
27/11/99	Bayer 04 Leverkusen	H	1-2	Weissenberger
05/12/99	SpVgg Unterhaching	A	0-2	
10/12/99	MSV Duisburg	H	0-1	
14/12/99	FC Bayern München	A	1-2	Labbadia
17/12/99	VfB Stuttgart	H	1-2	Böhme
05/02/00	FC Schalke 04	H	1-2	Labbadia
08/02/00	Hertha BSC Berlin	A	0-2	
11/02/00	1.FC Kaiserslautern	H	1-2	Weissenberger
20/02/00	VfL Wolfsburg	A	0-2	
28/02/00	SSV Ulm	H	4-1	Bode 2, Weissenberger 2
03/03/00	SC Freiburg	A	1-1	Labbadia
11/03/00	TSV 1860 München	H	2-2	Labbadia 2
19/03/00	Borussia Dortmund	A	3-1	Van der Ven, Stratos, Labbadia
24/03/00	FC Hansa Rostock	H	2-2	Maul, Stratos (p)
01/04/00	Eintracht Frankfurt	A	1-2	Weissenberger
09/04/00	SV Werder Bremen	A	1-3	Bode
12/04/00	Hamburger SV	H	3-0	Labbadia, Stratos (p), Göktan
16/04/00	Bayer 04 Leverkusen	A	1-4	Meissner (p)
23/04/00	SpVgg Unterhaching	H	1-0	Weissenberger
27/04/00	MSV Duisburg	A	3-0	Van der Ven, Peeters, Labbadia
13/05/00	FC Bayern München	H	0-3	
20/05/00	VfB Stuttgart	A	3-3	Meissner, Labbadia, Weissenberger

BAYER 04 LEVERKUSEN

CLUB DIRECTORY

TSV Bayer 04 Leverkusen
Postfach 120140, 51349 Leverkusen
tel - (0214) 86600 / fax - (0214) 62709
website - www.bayer.com/sport
Year of Formation - 1904
President - Werner Wenning
Manager - Reiner Calmund
Secretary - Kuno Wack
Coach - Christoph Daum
Stadium - Ulrich-Haberland-Stadion (25,050)

MAJOR HONOURS
Domestic Cup - (1) 1993.
UEFA Cup - (1) 1988.

APPEARANCES 99/00

	P	Ap	(s)	Gls
Michael BALLACK	M	22	(1)	3
Stefan BEINLICH	M	26	(3)	11
Thomas BRDARIC	A	4	(20)	6
ÉMERSON Ferreira da Rosa (BRA)	M	29		5
Vratislav GRESKO (SVK)	D	5	(4)	
Markus HAPPE	D	7		
Dirk HEINEN	G	1	(1)	
Frankie HEJDUK (USA)	M		(6)	
Torben HOFFMANN	D	5	(8)	
Frank JURIC (AUS)	G	4		
Ulf KIRSTEN	A	27		17
Robert KOVAC (CRO)	D	27		1
Zoran MAMIC (CRO)	D	2	(5)	
Adam MATYSEK (POL)	G	29		
Oliver NEUVILLE	A	31	(2)	4
Jens NOWOTNY	D	33		1
Carsten RAMELOW	M	24	(2)	
Jörg REEB	M	10	(3)	
Thomas REICHENBERGER	A		(4)	1
Paulo Roberto RINK	M	13	(3)	10
RÓBSON PONTE (BRA)	M	11	(13)	2
Bernd SCHNEIDER	M	20	(12)	3
Jurica VRANJES	D		(2)	
ZÉ ROBERTO (BRA)	M	26	(1)	7
Boris ZIVKOVIC (CRO)	D	18	(5)	3

LEAGUE RESULTS 1999/2000

13/08/99	MSV Duisburg	A	0-0	
22/08/99	FC Bayern München	H	2-0	Kirsten, Neuville
28/08/99	VfB Stuttgart	A	2-1	Róbson Ponte, Beinlich
11/09/99	FC Schalke 04	H	3-2	Neuville, Reichenberger, Brdaric
18/09/99	Hertha BSC Berlin	A	0-0	
26/09/99	1.FC Kaiserslautern	H	3-1	Brdaric, Kirsten 2
02/10/99	VfL Wolfsburg	A	1-3	Beinlich
15/10/99	SSV Ulm	H	4-1	Zivkovic, Kirsten 2, Róbson Ponte
23/10/99	SC Freiburg	A	0-0	
30/10/99	TSV 1860 München	H	1-1	Kirsten (p)
06/11/99	Borussia Dortmund	A	1-1	Kirsten
20/11/99	FC Hansa Rostock	H	1-1	Émerson
27/11/99	Arminia Bielefeld	A	2-1	Brdaric, Zé Roberto
04/12/99	SV Werder Bremen	H	3-2	Zivkovic, Kirsten (p), Émerson
12/12/99	Hamburger SV	H	2-2	Beinlich 2
15/12/99	Eintracht Frankfurt	A	2-1	Beinlich 2
18/12/99	SpVgg Unterhaching	H	2-1	Brdaric 2
05/02/00	MSV Duisburg	H	3-0	Schneider, Beinlich 2
09/02/00	FC Bayern München	A	1-4	Ballack
12/02/00	VfB Stuttgart	H	1-0	Rink
18/02/00	FC Schalke 04	A	1-1	Rink
26/02/00	Hertha BSC Berlin	H	3-1	Kirsten, Zé Roberto, Rink
05/03/00	1.FC Kaiserslautern	A	3-1	Zé Roberto, Kirsten, Kovac
11/03/00	VfL Wolfsburg	H	4-1	Kirsten 2, Zivkovic, Beinlich
18/03/00	SSV Ulm	A	9-1	Émerson 2, Rink, Kirsten, Neuville, Zé Roberto 2, Ballack, Schneider
25/03/00	SC Freiburg	H	1-1	Émerson
01/04/00	TSV 1860 München	A	2-1	Rink, Kirsten
08/04/00	Borussia Dortmund	H	3-1	Rink 2, Brdaric
12/04/00	FC Hansa Rostock	A	1-1	Schneider
16/04/00	Arminia Bielefeld	H	4-1	Beinlich, Kirsten, Rink (p), Ballack
21/04/00	SV Werder Bremen	A	3-1	Kirsten, Rink, Zé Roberto
30/04/00	Hamburger SV	A	2-0	Zé Roberto, Nowotny
13/05/00	Eintracht Frankfurt	H	4-1	Neuville, Kirsten, Rink, Beinlich (p)
20/05/00	SpVgg Unterhaching	A	0-2	

FC BAYERN MÜNCHEN

CLUB DIRECTORY

FC Bayern München
Postfach 90 04 51, 81504 München
tel - (089) 699310 / fax - (089) 644165
website - www.fcbayern.de
Year of Formation - 1900
President - Franz Beckenbauer
Manager - Uli Hoeness
Secretary - Karl Hopfner
Coach - Ottmar Hitzfeld
Stadium - Olympiastadion (69,000)

MAJOR HONOURS
League Championship - (16) 1932, 1969, 1972,
1973, 1974, 1980, 1981, 1985, 1986, 1987,
1989, 1990, 1994, 1997, 1999, 2000.
Domestic Cup - (10) 1957, 1966, 1967, 1969,
1971, 1982, 1984, 1986, 1998, 2000.
European Champions' Cup - (3) 1974, 1975, 1976.
European Cup-winners' Cup - (1) 1967.
UEFA Cup - (1) 1996.
World Club Cup - (1) 1976.

APPEARANCES 99/00

	P	Ap	(s)	Gls
Patrik ANDERSSON (SWE)	D	11	(5)	
Markus BABBEL	D	23	(3)	1
Mario BASLER	M		(2)	
Bernd DREHER	G	5	(1)	
Stefan EFFENBERG	M	26	(1)	2
Giovane ÉLBER (BRA)	A	16	(10)	14
Thorsten FINK	M	19	(7)	
Carsten JANCKER	A	20	(3)	9
Jens JEREMIES	M	28	(2)	3
Oliver KAHN	G	27		
Samuel Osei KUFFOUR (GHA)	D	16	(2)	2
Thomas LINKE	D	26	(1)	1
Bixente LIZARAZU (FRA)	M	20	(2)	1
Lothar MATTHÄUS	D	15		1
PAULO SÉRGIO (BRA)	M	25	(3)	13
Hasan SALIHAMIDZIC (BOS)	A	27	(3)	4
Roque SANTA CRUZ (PAR)	A	14	(14)	5
Mehmet SCHOLL	M	18	(7)	6
Andrew SINKALA	D		(1)	
Thomas STRUNZ	M	6	(3)	
Michael TARNAT	M	19	(7)	1
Stefan WESSELS	G	2		
Michael WIESINGER	M	4	(9)	1
Slawomir WOJCIECHOWSKI (POL)	M	1	(2)	1
Alexander ZICKLER	A	6	(8)	7

LEAGUE RESULTS 1999/2000

14/08/99	Hamburger SV	H	2-2	Babbel, Élber
22/08/99	Bayer 04 Leverkusen	A	0-2	
28/08/99	SpVgg Unterhaching	H	1-0	Santa Cruz
11/09/99	MSV Duisburg	A	2-1	Tarnat, Linke
18/09/99	Eintracht Frankfurt	A	2-1	Élber, Kuffour
24/09/99	VfB Stuttgart	H	0-1	
02/10/99	FC Schalke 04	A	1-1	Effenberg
16/10/99	Hertha BSC Berlin	H	3-1	Élber, Paulo Sérgio 2
23/10/99	1.FC Kaiserslautern	A	2-0	Santa Cruz, Élber
30/10/99	VfL Wolfsburg	H	5-0	Élber 3, Santa Cruz, Wiesinger
06/11/99	SSV Ulm	A	1-0	Jancker
20/11/99	SC Freiburg	H	6-1	Jeremies, Matthäus, Paulo Sérgio, Jancker 2, Zickler
27/11/99	TSV 1860 München	A	0-1	
04/12/99	Borussia Dortmund	H	1-1	Jeremies
11/12/99	FC Hansa Rostock	A	3-0	Paulo Sérgio 2, Santa Cruz
14/12/99	Arminia Bielefeld	H	2-1	Salihamidzic 2 (1p)
17/12/99	SV Werder Bremen	A	2-0	Jancker, Paulo Sérgio
06/02/00	Hamburger SV	A	0-0	
09/02/00	Bayer 04 Leverkusen	H	4-1	og (Hoffmann), Effenberg, Scholl, Zickler
12/02/00	SpVgg Unterhaching	A	2-0	Paulo Sérgio, Scholl
19/02/00	MSV Duisburg	H	4-1	Paulo Sérgio, Élber, Lizarazu, Zickler
26/02/00	Eintracht Frankfurt	H	4-1	Zickler 2, Paulo Sérgio (p), Élber
04/03/00	VfB Stuttgart	A	0-2	
11/03/00	FC Schalke 04	H	4-1	Kuffour, Zickler 2, Santa Cruz
18/03/00	FC Hansa Rostock	A	1-1	Jeremies
25/03/00	1.FC Kaiserslautern	H	2-2	Élber 2
01/04/00	VfL Wolfsburg	A	1-1	Jancker
08/04/00	SSV Ulm	H	4-0	Scholl, Paulo Sérgio (p), Jancker, Wojciechowski
12/04/00	SC Freiburg	A	2-1	Jancker, Scholl (p)
15/04/00	TSV 1860 München	H	1-2	Scholl
23/04/00	Borussia Dortmund	A	1-0	Salihamidzic
29/04/00	FC Hansa Rostock	H	4-1	Paulo Sérgio 2, Élber, Scholl
13/05/00	Arminia Bielefeld	A	3-0	Salihamidzic, Élber 2
20/05/00	SV Werder Bremen	H	3-1	Jancker 2, Paulo Sérgio

BORUSSIA DORTMUND

CLUB DIRECTORY

BV 09 Borussia Dortmund
Westfalenstadion, Strobelallee, Postfach 100509
44005 Dortmund
tel - (0231) 90200 / fax - (0231) 9020105
website - www.borussia-dortmund.de
Year of Formation - 1909
President - Dr. Gerd Niebaum
Manager - Michael Meier
Secretary - Josef Schneck
Coach - Michael Skibbe; Bernd Krauss; Udo Lattek
(00/01 - Matthias Sammer)
Stadium - Westfalenstadion (68,600)

MAJOR HONOURS
League Championship - (5)
1956, 1957, 1963, 1995, 1996.
Domestic Cup - (2) 1965, 1989.
European Champions' Cup - (1) 1997.
European Cup-winners' Cup - (1) 1966.
World Club Cup - (1) 1997.

APPEARANCES 99/00

	P	Ap	(s)	Gls
Otto ADDO (GHA)	M	19	(3)	2
Sergej BARBAREZ (BOS)	M	6	(8)	2
Karsten BAUMANN	D	7	(4)	1
Fredi BOBIC	A	22	(7)	7
Francis BUGRI	M	3		
Vladimir BUT (RUS)	M	9	(10)	1
Wolfgang DE BEER	G	3	(1)	
DEDÉ (BRA)	M	24		1
EVANILSON (BRA)	M	23	(2)	
Wolfgang FEIERSINGER (AUT)	D	6	(3)	
Bashiru GAMBO (GHA)	A		(2)	
Heiko HERRLICH	A	14	(8)	6
Victor IKPEBA (NIG)	A	12	(9)	2
Sead KAPETANOVIC (BOS)	M	3	(1)	
Jürgen KOHLER	D	29	(1)	2
Jens LEHMANN	G	31		
Andreas MÖLLER	M	15	(3)	3
Christian NERLINGER	M	14	(2)	
Alfred NIJHUIS (HOL)	D	15	(5)	2
Giuseppe REINA (ITA)	A	16	(10)	5
Stefan REUTER	D	26		
Lars RICKEN	M	25	(4)	4
Miroslav STEVIC (YUG)	M	28	(2)	
Ibrahim TANKO (GHA)	A		(3)	
Christian WÖRNS	D	24	(2)	2

LEAGUE RESULTS 1999/2000

14/08/99	1.FC Kaiserslautern	A	0-1	
21/08/99	VfL Wolfsburg	H	2-1	Reina, Möller (p)
29/08/99	SSV Ulm	A	1-0	Bobic
11/09/99	SC Freiburg	H	1-1	Bobic
17/09/99	TSV 1860 München	A	3-0	Möller, og (Kurz), Bobic
25/09/99	Eintracht Frankfurt	H	1-0	Ricken
02/10/99	FC Hansa Rostock	H	3-0	Ikpeba 2, Reina
15/10/99	Arminia Bielefeld	A	2-0	Reina, Ricken
24/10/99	SV Werder Bremen	H	1-3	Ricken
30/10/99	Hamburger SV	A	1-1	Bobic
06/11/99	Bayer 04 Leverkusen	H	1-1	Addo
28/11/99	MSV Duisburg	H	2-2	Herrlich 2
01/12/99	SpVgg Unterhaching	A	0-1	
04/12/99	FC Bayern München	A	1-1	Kohler
11/12/99	VfB Stuttgart	H	1-1	Bobic
15/12/99	FC Schalke 04	A	0-0	
19/12/99	Hertha BSC Berlin	H	4-0	Nijhuis, Baumann, Bobic, Wörns
04/02/00	1.FC Kaiserslautern	H	0-1	
09/02/00	VfL Wolfsburg	A	0-1	
12/02/00	SSV Ulm	H	1-1	Herrlich
19/02/00	SC Freiburg	A	1-1	Herrlich
27/02/00	TSV 1860 München	H	1-1	Bobic
05/03/00	Eintracht Frankfurt	A	1-1	Herrlich
12/03/00	FC Hansa Rostock	A	0-1	
19/03/00	Arminia Bielefeld	H	1-3	Möller
26/03/00	SV Werder Bremen	A	2-3	Reina, But
01/04/00	Hamburger SV	H	0-1	
08/04/00	Bayer 04 Leverkusen	A	1-3	Reina
11/04/00	SpVgg Unterhaching	H	1-3	Ricken
15/04/00	MSV Duisburg	A	2-2	Addo, Wörns
23/04/00	FC Bayern München	H	0-1	
29/04/00	VfB Stuttgart	A	2-1	Kohler, Herrlich
13/05/00	FC Schalke 04	H	1-1	Nijhuis
20/05/00	Hertha BSC Berlin	A	3-0	Barbarez 2, Dedé

MSV DUISBURG

CLUB DIRECTORY

MSV Duisburg
Postfach 120438
47124 Duisburg
tel - (0203) 429240
fax - (0203) 4292444
website - www.msv-duisburg.de
Year of Formation - 1902
President - Dr. Hans Spick
Secretary - Dirk Keiper
Coach - Friedhelm Funkel; Seppo Eichkorn
(00/01 - Wolfgang Frank)
Stadium - Wedaustadion (30,160)

APPEARANCES 99/00

	P	Ap	(s)	Gls
Erik Bo ANDERSEN (DEN)	A		(1)	
Markus BEIERLE	A	27	(4)	8
Alexander BUGERA	A	3	(9)	1
Michael BÜSKENS	M	10	(2)	1
Pavel DRSEK (CZE)	D	9	(3)	1
Stefan EMMERLING	D	17	(1)	
Sercan GÜVENISIK (TUR)	A		(6)	
Tomasz HAJTO (POL)	D	21	(5)	1
Dietmar HIRSCH	M	24	(1)	3
Thomas HOERSEN	M	12	(9)	
Ralf KEIDEL	M	1	(2)	
Marijan KOVACEVIC (CRO)	D	16	(3)	3
Carsten KRÄMER	G		(1)	
Andreas MENGER	G	9	(1)	
Jörg NEUN	M	4		
Markus OSTHOFF	M	25	(1)	2
Piotr REISS (POL)	A	20	(2)	5
Martin SCHNEIDER	M	20	(3)	
Uwe SPIES	A	15	(7)	2
Gintaras STAUCE (LIT)	G	25		
Horst STEFFEN	M	3		
Stig TØFTING (DEN)	M	27	(2)	2
Andreas VOSS	M	9	(4)	1
Marcus WEDAU	M	5	(11)	
Torsten WOHLERT	D	29		1
Carsten WOLTERS	M	18	(3)	3
Michael ZEYER	M	25	(7)	3

LEAGUE RESULTS 1999/2000

Date	Opponent	H/A	Score	Scorers
13/08/99	Bayer 04 Leverkusen	H	0-0	
20/08/99	SpVgg Unterhaching	A	0-2	
29/08/99	Eintracht Frankfurt	A	2-2	Osthoff, Wolters
11/09/99	FC Bayern München	H	1-2	Osthoff
18/09/99	VfB Stuttgart	A	2-4	Hirsch, Beierle
25/09/99	FC Schalke 04	H	1-1	Hirsch
02/10/99	Hertha BSC Berlin	A	1-2	Spies
16/10/99	1.FC Kaiserslautern	H	2-2	Kovacevic (p), Beierle
24/10/99	VfL Wolfsburg	A	0-1	
30/10/99	SSV Ulm	H	0-0	
05/11/99	SC Freiburg	A	0-3	
21/11/99	TSV 1860 München	H	3-0	Reiss, Bugera, Voss
28/11/99	Borussia Dortmund	A	2-2	Tøfting, Reiss
03/12/99	FC Hansa Rostock	H	2-2	Beierle 2
10/12/99	Arminia Bielefeld	A	1-0	Kovacevic (p)
14/12/99	SV Werder Bremen	H	0-1	
18/12/99	Hamburger SV	A	1-6	Beierle
05/02/00	Bayer 04 Leverkusen	A	0-3	
09/02/00	SpVgg Unterhaching	H	2-0	Hajto, Reiss
12/02/00	Eintracht Frankfurt	H	2-3	Reiss 2
19/02/00	FC Bayern München	A	1-4	Wolters
26/02/00	VfB Stuttgart	H	1-3	Beierle
04/03/00	FC Schalke 04	A	0-3	
11/03/00	Hertha BSC Berlin	H	0-0	
18/03/00	1.FC Kaiserslautern	A	2-3	Zeyer (p), Büskens
25/03/00	VfL Wolfsburg	H	2-3	Drsek, Zeyer (p)
01/04/00	SSV Ulm	A	3-0	Beierle, Hirsch, Spies
09/04/00	SC Freiburg	H	1-2	Wohlert
12/04/00	TSV 1860 München	A	1-4	Tøfting
15/04/00	Borussia Dortmund	H	2-2	Kovacevic, Zeyer (p)
22/04/00	FC Hansa Rostock	A	1-3	Beierle
27/04/00	Arminia Bielefeld	H	0-3	
13/05/00	SV Werder Bremen	A	0-4	
20/05/00	Hamburger SV	H	1-1	Wolters

EINTRACHT FRANKFURT

CLUB DIRECTORY

Eintracht Frankfurt
Sportplatz am Riederwald, Am Erlenbruch 25
60386 Frankfurt-am-Main
tel - (01805) 7431899 / fax - (069) 42097043
website - www.eintracht-frankfurt-online.net
Year of Formation - 1899
President - Peter Fischer
Secretary - Klaus Lötzbeier
Coach - Jörg Berger; Felix Magath
Stadium - Waldstadion (61,146)

MAJOR HONOURS
League Championship - (1) 1959
Domestic Cup - (4) 1974, 1975, 1981, 1988.
UEFA Cup - (1) 1980.

APPEARANCES 99/00

	P	Ap	(s)	Gls
Uwe BINDEWALD	D	13	(7)	
Erol BULUT (TUR)	M	4	(1)	
Tibor DOMBI (HUN)	M	6	(9)	
Patrick FALK	M	5	(8)	
Jan-Åge FJØRTOFT (NOR)	A	14	(7)	5
Marco GEBHARDT	M	26	(4)	3
Rolf-Christel GUIE-MIEN (CON)	M	24	(5)	6
Dirk HEINEN	G	17		
Horst HELDT	M	23	(7)	4
Rowan HENDRICKS	D		(1)	
Petar HUBCHEV (BUL)	D	18		
Olaf JANSSEN	D	16		
Torsten KRACHT	D	32		1
Alexander KUTSCHERA	D	27	(2)	2
Michael MUTZEL	M	2	(2)	1
Oka NIKOLOV (MAC)	G	17		
Jens RASIEJEWSKI	D	17	(4)	
Thomas REICHENBERGER	M	12	(3)	1
Bachirou SALOU (TOG)	A	25	(7)	8
Uwe SCHNEIDER	D	1	(6)	
Alexander SCHUR	M	25	(1)	1
Thomas SOBOTZIK	M	11	(1)	3
Ralf WEBER	M	18		2
Christoph WESTERTHALER (AUT)	A		(4)	
Chen YANG (CHN)	A	13	(14)	4
Thomas ZAMPACH	D	8	(3)	1

LEAGUE RESULTS 1999/2000

14/08/99	SpVgg Unterhaching	H	3-0	Guié-Mien, Fjørtoft (p), Salou
21/08/99	SC Freiburg	A	3-2	Weber, Salou 2
29/08/99	MSV Duisburg	H	2-2	Salou, Guié-Mien
12/09/99	TSV 1860 München	A	0-2	
18/09/99	FC Bayern München	H	1-2	Salou
25/09/99	Borussia Dortmund	A	0-1	
01/10/99	VfB Stuttgart	H	0-1	
16/10/99	FC Hansa Rostock	A	1-3	Fjørtoft
22/10/99	FC Schalke 04	H	0-2	
29/10/99	Arminia Bielefeld	A	1-1	Guié-Mien
06/11/99	Hertha BSC Berlin	H	4-0	Guié-Mien, Weber, Fjørtoft, Heldt (p)
19/11/99	SV Werder Bremen	A	1-3	Kutschera
28/11/99	1.FC Kaiserslautern	H	0-1	
03/12/99	Hamburger SV	A	0-1	
12/12/99	VfL Wolfsburg	A	0-1	
15/12/99	Bayer 04 Leverkusen	H	1-2	Fjørtoft
18/12/99	SSV Ulm	A	0-3	
06/02/00	SpVgg Unterhaching	A	0-1	
09/02/00	SC Freiburg	H	2-0	Sobotzik, Mutzel
12/02/00	MSV Duisburg	A	3-2	Sobotzik 2, Gebhardt
19/02/00	TSV 1860 München	H	3-1	Kutschera, Heldt, Salou
26/02/00	FC Bayern München	A	1-4	Reichenberger
05/03/00	Borussia Dortmund	H	1-1	Fjørtoft
10/03/00	VfB Stuttgart	A	2-0	Yang, Gebhardt
17/03/00	FC Hansa Rostock	H	0-0	
26/03/00	FC Schalke 04	A	0-0	
01/04/00	Arminia Bielefeld	H	2-1	Zampach, Schur
08/04/00	Hertha BSC Berlin	A	0-1	
12/04/00	SV Werder Bremen	H	1-0	Heldt (p)
15/04/00	1.FC Kaiserslautern	A	0-1	
21/04/00	Hamburger SV	H	3-0	Guié-Mien 2, Yang
28/04/00	VfL Wolfsburg	H	4-0	Salou, Gebhardt, Yang 2
13/05/00	Bayer 04 Leverkusen	A	1-4	Kracht
20/05/00	SSV Ulm	H	2-1	Salou, Heldt (p)

SC FREIBURG

CLUB DIRECTORY

SC Freiburg
Schwarzwaldstrasse 193
79117 Freiburg
tel - (0761) 385510
fax - (0761) 3855150
website - www.scfreiburg.com
Year of Formation - 1904
President - Achim Stocker
Manager - Andreas Rettig
Coach - Volker Finke
Stadium - Dreisamstadion (25,000)

APPEARANCES 99/00

	P	Ap	(s)	Gls
Zoubeir BAYA (TUN)	M	23	(2)	4
Mehdi BEN SLIMANE (TUN)	A	10	(12)	4
Andreas BORNEMANN	M		(3)	
Florian BRUNS	A	11	(11)	1
Bouchaber DIARRA (MLI)	D	26	(1)	
Björn DREYER	M	4	(2)	
Richard GOLZ	G	33		
Ali Mehmet GÜNES (TUR)	M	9	(5)	2
Stefan HAMPL	A		(2)	
Lars HERMEL	D	25	(1)	
Aleksandre IASHVILI (GEO)	A	20	(2)	1
Levan KOBIASHVILI (GEO)	M	33		6
Ralf KOHL	M	8	(11)	1
Oumar KONDE (SUI)	D	19	(6)	1
Steffen KORELL	D	5	(7)	1
Stefan MÜLLER	D	18	(7)	2
Miran PAVLIN (SLO)	M		(1)	
Abder RAMDANE (EGY)	M	10	(9)	2
Timo REUS	G	1		
Daniel SCHUMANN	D	8	(4)	
Adel SELLIMI (TUN)	A	26	(1)	11
Levan TSKITISHVILI (GEO)	M	1	(2)	1
Marco WEISSHAUPT	A	23	(7)	2
Tobias WILLI	M	28	(1)	
Andreas ZEYER	M	33		4

LEAGUE RESULTS 1999/2000

Date	Opponent	H/A	Score	Scorers
15/08/99	SSV Ulm	A	1-1	og (Grauer)
21/08/99	Eintracht Frankfurt	H	2-3	Sellimi (p), Günes
28/08/99	TSV 1860 München	H	3-0	Tskitishvili, Günes, Ben Slimane
11/09/99	Borussia Dortmund	A	1-1	Baya
17/09/99	FC Hansa Rostock	H	5-0	Müller, Sellimi 3 (1p), Baya
26/09/99	Arminia Bielefeld	A	1-2	Baya
03/10/99	SV Werder Bremen	H	2-1	Zeyer, Sellimi
16/10/99	Hamburger SV	A	0-2	
23/10/99	Bayer 04 Leverkusen	H	0-0	
31/10/99	SpVgg Unterhaching	A	0-1	
05/11/99	MSV Duisburg	H	3-0	Sellimi, Zeyer, Kobiashvili
20/11/99	FC Bayern München	A	1-6	Sellimi
26/11/99	VfB Stuttgart	H	0-2	
04/12/99	FC Schalke 04	A	2-2	Sellimi (p), Bruns
11/12/99	Hertha BSC Berlin	H	0-1	
15/12/99	1.FC Kaiserslautern	A	2-0	Ramdane, Korell
18/12/99	VfL Wolfsburg	H	1-1	Sellimi
05/02/00	SSV Ulm	H	2-0	Ben Slimane 2
09/02/00	Eintracht Frankfurt	A	0-2	
13/02/00	TSV 1860 München	A	1-3	Kohl
19/02/00	Borussia Dortmund	H	1-1	Ben Slimane
25/02/00	FC Hansa Rostock	A	1-1	og (Holetschek)
03/03/00	Arminia Bielefeld	H	1-1	Müller
12/03/00	SV Werder Bremen	A	2-5	Weisshaupt, Zeyer (p)
18/03/00	Hamburger SV	H	0-2	
25/03/00	Bayer 04 Leverkusen	A	1-1	Kobiashvili
31/03/00	SpVgg Unterhaching	H	4-3	Sellimi (p), Kobiashvili, Baya, Ramdane
09/04/00	MSV Duisburg	A	2-1	Iashvili, Weisshaupt
12/04/00	FC Bayern München	H	1-2	Kobiashvili
15/04/00	VfB Stuttgart	A	0-1	
22/04/00	FC Schalke 04	H	2-1	Kobiashvili, Kondé
28/04/00	Hertha BSC Berlin	A	0-0	
13/05/00	1.FC Kaiserslautern	H	2-1	Sellimi, Kobiashvili
20/05/00	VfL Wolfsburg	A	1-2	Zeyer

HAMBURGER SV

CLUB DIRECTORY

Hamburger Sport-Verein
Sylvesterallee 7, 22525 Hamburg
tel - (040) 415501 / fax - (040) 41551060
website - www.hsv.de
Year of Formation - 1897
President - Rolf Mares
Manager - Bernd Wehmayer
Secretary - Werner Hackmann
Coach - Frank Pagelsdorf
Stadium - Volksparkstadion (55,000)

MAJOR HONOURS
League Championship - (6)
1923, 1928, 1960, 1979, 1982, 1983.
Domestic Cup - (3) 1963, 1976, 1987.
European Champions' Cup - (1) 1983.
European Cup-winners' Cup - (1) 1977.

APPEARANCES 99/00

		P	Ap	(s)	Gls
Christof BABATZ	M	2	(3)		
Hans-Jörg BUTT	G	34			9
Karsten BÄRON	A	2	(5)		
Rodolfo Esteban CARDOSO (ARG)	M	28			8
Jacek DEMBINSKI (POL)	A	2	(5)		
Thomas DOLL	M	5	(16)		
Fabian ERNST	D	7	(12)		
Andreas FISCHER	M	9	(8)		1
Dimitrios GRAMMOZIS (GRE)	M	13	(4)		1
Thomas GRAVESEN (DEN)	D	23	(3)		1
Martin GROTH	M	14	(1)		2
Vanja GRUBAC (YUG)	A		(4)		1
Vahid HASHEMIAN (IRN)	A	2	(9)		
Ingo HERTZSCH	D	31			
Bernd HOLLERBACH	M	20	(1)		2
Nico Jan HOOGMA (HOL)	D	31			3
Rasoul KHATIBI (IRN)	M		(4)		
Nico KOVAC (CRO)	M	30			8
Mehdi MAHDAVIKIA (IRN)	A	28	(1)		4
Andrej PANADIC (CRO)	D	29			1
Roy PRÄGER	A	32			9
Josip SIMUNIC (CRO)	D		(6)		
Harald SPÖRL	M		(4)		
Soner UYSAL (TUR)	A	7	(1)		1
Anthony YEBOAH (GHA)	A	24			9
Mahmut YILMAZ (TUR)	A	1	(1)		

LEAGUE RESULTS 1999/2000

14/08/99	FC Bayern München	A	2-2	Kovac, Präger
21/08/99	VfB Stuttgart	H	3-0	Cardoso, Butt 2 (2p)
27/08/99	FC Schalke 04	A	3-1	Hollerbach, Kovac, Hoogma
11/09/99	Hertha BSC Berlin	H	5-1	Hollerbach, Präger 3, Kovac
19/09/99	1.FC Kaiserslautern	A	0-2	
24/09/99	VfL Wolfsburg	H	2-2	Cardoso 2
02/10/99	SSV Ulm	A	2-1	Hoogma, Yeboah
16/10/99	SC Freiburg	H	2-0	Butt (p), Panadic
23/10/99	TSV 1860 München	A	0-0	
30/10/99	Borussia Dortmund	H	1-1	Butt (p)
05/11/99	FC Hansa Rostock	A	3-3	Butt (p), Grammozis, Grubac
21/11/99	Arminia Bielefeld	H	5-0	Yeboah 3, Präger, Fischer
28/11/99	SV Werder Bremen	A	1-2	Butt (p)
03/12/99	Eintracht Frankfurt	H	1-0	Yeboah
12/12/99	Bayer 04 Leverkusen	A	2-2	Kovac, og (Nowotny)
15/12/99	SpVgg Unterhaching	A	1-1	Mahdavikia
18/12/99	MSV Duisburg	H	6-1	Yeboah 2, og (Hajto), Butt (p), og (Hirsch), Hoogma
06/02/00	FC Bayern München	H	0-0	
09/02/00	VfB Stuttgart	A	3-1	Yeboah 2, Mahdavikia
13/02/00	FC Schalke 04	H	3-1	Kovac 2, Butt (p)
18/02/00	Hertha BSC Berlin	A	1-2	Kovac
26/02/00	1.FC Kaiserslautern	H	2-1	Präger, Butt (p)
03/03/00	VfL Wolfsburg	A	4-4	Mahdavikia 2, Cardoso 2
11/03/00	SSV Ulm	H	1-2	Gravesen
18/03/00	SC Freiburg	A	2-0	Cardoso 2
25/03/00	TSV 1860 München	H	2-0	Präger, Cardoso
01/04/00	Borussia Dortmund	A	1-0	Präger
07/04/00	FC Hansa Rostock	H	1-0	Groth
12/04/00	Arminia Bielefeld	A	0-3	
15/04/00	SV Werder Bremen	H	0-0	
21/04/00	Eintracht Frankfurt	A	0-3	
30/04/00	Bayer 04 Leverkusen	H	0-2	
13/05/00	SpVgg Unterhaching	H	3-0	Groth, Uysal, Präger
20/05/00	MSV Duisburg	A	1-1	Kovac

FC HANSA ROSTOCK

CLUB DIRECTORY

FC Hansa Rostock
Trotzenburger Weg 14, 18057 Rostock
tel - (0381) 499990 / fax - (0381) 4999970
website - www.fc-hansa-rostock.de
Year of Formation - 1965
President - Eckhardt Rehberg
Manager - Herbert Maronn
Secretary - Helmut Hergesell
Coach - Andreas Zachhuber
Stadium - Ostseestadion (24,500)

MAJOR HONOURS
League Championship (GDR) - (1) 1991.
Domestic Cup (GDR) - (1) 1991.

APPEARANCES 99/00

	P	Ap	(s)	Gls
Victor AGALI (NIG)	A	18	(4)	6
Abdelaziz AHANFOUF	A	2	(11)	
Magnus ARVIDSSON (SWE)	A	26	(7)	9
Steffen BAUMGART	M	19	(7)	4
Sven BENKEN	D	23	(1)	1
Christian BRAND	M	16	(8)	3
Matthias BREITKREUTZ	M	15	(6)	1
Perry BRÄUTIGAM	G	14	(1)	
Uwe EHLERS	D	14	(7)	
Mohamed EMARA (EGY)	M	20	(2)	
Thomas GANSAUGE	D	1	(1)	
Olaf HOLETSCHEK	D	16	(1)	1
Kreso KOVACEC	A	5	(12)	2
Timo LANGE	M	26	(1)	3
Marcus LANTZ	M	18		2
Slawomir MAJAK (POL)	M	9	(11)	
Kai OSWALD	D	16	(3)	2
Martin PIECKENHAGEN	G	20		
Abder RAMDANE (FRA)	M		(2)	
Rene SCHNEIDER	D	7	(2)	1
Ronny THIELEMANN	M	2	(5)	
Hilmar WEILANDT	D	28	(3)	
Peter WIBRÅN (SWE)	M	34		6
Radwan YASSER (EGY)	M	19	(2)	
Marco ZALLMANN	D	6	(2)	

LEAGUE RESULTS 1999/2000

15/08/99	Hertha BSC Berlin	A	2-5	Schneider, Arvidsson	
22/08/99	1.FC Kaiserslautern	H	4-2	Lange (p), og (Sforza), Agali, Arvidsson	
28/08/99	VfL Wolfsburg	A	0-2		
10/09/99	SSV Ulm	H	2-1	Oswald, Agali	
17/09/99	SC Freiburg	A	0-5		
25/09/99	TSV 1860 München	H	0-0		
02/10/99	Borussia Dortmund	A	0-3		
16/10/99	Eintracht Frankfurt	H	3-1	Brand, Holetschek, Lange (p)	
22/10/99	Arminia Bielefeld	H	2-1	Arvidsson 2	
29/10/99	SV Werder Bremen	A	1-2	Wibrån (p)	
05/11/99	Hamburger SV	H	3-3	Lange, Baumgart, Oswald	
20/11/99	Bayer 04 Leverkusen	A	1-1	Baumgart	
27/11/99	SpVgg Unterhaching	H	1-1	Baumgart	
03/12/99	MSV Duisburg	A	2-2	Baumgart, Arvidsson	
11/12/99	FC Bayern München	H	0-3		
14/12/99	VfB Stuttgart	A	1-3	Arvidsson	
19/12/99	FC Schalke 04	H	1-0	Benken	
04/02/00	Hertha BSC Berlin	H	0-1		
08/02/00	1.FC Kaiserslautern	A	2-2	Arvidsson, Agali	
12/02/00	VfL Wolfsburg	H	1-1	Brand	
20/02/00	SSV Ulm	A	1-1	Wibrån	
25/02/00	SC Freiburg	H	1-1	Wibrån	
04/03/00	TSV 1860 München	A	3-4	Arvidsson 2, Lantz	
12/03/00	Borussia Dortmund	H	1-0	og (Baumann)	
17/03/00	Eintracht Frankfurt	A	0-0		
24/03/00	Arminia Bielefeld	A	2-2	Lantz, Wibrån	
02/04/00	SV Werder Bremen	H	1-1	Wibrån	
07/04/00	Hamburger SV	A	0-1		
12/04/00	Bayer 04 Leverkusen	H	1-1	Breitkreutz	
16/04/00	SpVgg Unterhaching	A	1-1	Kovacec	
22/04/00	MSV Duisburg	H	3-1	Wibrån, Agali, Kovacec	
29/04/00	FC Bayern München	A	1-4	Agali	
13/05/00	VfB Stuttgart	H	1-4	og (Soldo)	
20/05/00	FC Schalke 04	A	2-0	Agali, Brand	

HERTHA BSC BERLIN

CLUB DIRECTORY

Hertha BSC Berlin
Hans-Braun-Strasse, Friesenhaus 2, 14053 Berlin
tel - (030) 3009280
fax - (030) 30092899
website - www.herthabsc.de
Year of Formation - 1892
President - Walter Müller
Manager - Dieter Hoeness
Secretary - Matthias Huber
Coach - Jürgen Röber
Stadium - Olympiastadion (76,243)

MAJOR HONOURS
League Championship - (2) 1930, 1931.

APPEARANCES 99/00

	P	Ap	(s)	Gls
Alex ALVES (BRA)	A	14	(1)	4
Ilija ARACIC (CRO)	A	4	(8)	1
Ante COVIC (CRO)	A	5	(1)	
Ali DAEI (IRN)	A	15	(13)	3
Pál DÁRDAI (HUN)	M	10	(5)	1
Sebastian DEISLER	M	15	(5)	2
Christian FIEDLER	G	7		
Michael HARTMANN	M	15	(1)	
Thomas HELMER	D	4	(1)	1
Hendrik HERZOG	D	15	(5)	
Gábor KIRÁLY (HUN)	G	27		
Kostas KONSTANDINIDIS (GRE)	M	18	(2)	1
Sergej MANDREKO (TAD)	M	3	(1)	
Kai MICHALKE	A	14	(4)	1
Andreas NEUENDORF	M	12	(3)	
Michael PREETZ	A	30	(2)	12
Marko REHMER	D	19		2
Kjetil REKDAL (NOR)	D	13	(1)	
Bryan ROY (HOL)	A	4	(9)	1
Anthony SANNEH (USA)	M	6	(9)	1
Andreas SCHMIDT	M	27	(5)	
Eyjólfur SVERRISSON (ISL)	D	27	(1)	1
Andreas THOM	A	5	(5)	
Rene TRETSCHOK	M	3		1
Sixten VEIT	M	8	(8)	1
Dick VAN BURIK (HOL)	D	22	(3)	
Dariusz WOSZ	M	32		5

LEAGUE RESULTS 1999/2000

15/08/99	FC Hansa Rostock	H	5-2	og (Ehlers), Daei, Wosz, Tretschok, Deisler
20/08/99	Arminia Bielefeld	A	1-1	Deisler
28/08/99	SV Werder Bremen	H	1-1	Aracic
11/09/99	Hamburger SV	A	1-5	Dárdai
18/09/99	Bayer 04 Leverkusen	H	0-0	
25/09/99	SpVgg Unterhaching	A	1-1	Helmer
02/10/99	MSV Duisburg	H	2-1	Preetz 2
16/10/99	FC Bayern München	A	1-3	Wosz
23/10/99	VfB Stuttgart	H	1-1	Wosz
30/10/99	FC Schalke 04	A	1-1	Sanneh
06/11/99	Eintracht Frankfurt	A	0-4	
20/11/99	1.FC Kaiserslautern	H	0-1	
27/11/99	VfL Wolfsburg	A	3-2	Preetz, Wosz, Michalke
04/12/99	SSV Ulm	H	3-0	Wosz, Sverrisson, Preetz
11/12/99	SC Freiburg	A	1-0	Daei
14/12/99	TSV 1860 München	H	1-1	Konstandinidis
19/12/99	Borussia Dortmund	A	0-4	
04/02/00	FC Hansa Rostock	A	1-0	Preetz
08/02/00	Arminia Bielefeld	H	2-0	Preetz 2
11/02/00	SV Werder Bremen	A	1-4	Alves
18/02/00	Hamburger SV	H	2-1	Preetz 2
26/02/00	Bayer 04 Leverkusen	A	1-3	Rehmer
04/03/00	SpVgg Unterhaching	H	2-1	Veit, Roy
11/03/00	MSV Duisburg	A	0-0	
18/03/00	FC Bayern München	H	1-1	Alves
25/03/00	VfB Stuttgart	A	0-1	
31/03/00	FC Schalke 04	H	2-1	Alves, Preetz
08/04/00	Eintracht Frankfurt	H	1-0	Preetz
11/04/00	1.FC Kaiserslautern	A	2-1	Alves, Preetz
14/04/00	VfL Wolfsburg	H	0-0	
22/04/00	SSV Ulm	A	1-0	Rehmer
28/04/00	SC Freiburg	H	0-0	
13/05/00	TSV 1860 München	A	1-2	Daei
20/05/00	Borussia Dortmund	H	0-3	

1.FC KAISERSLAUTERN

CLUB DIRECTORY

1.FC Kaiserslautern
Fritz-Walter-Stadion, 67653 Kaiserslautern
tel - (0631) 31880 / fax - (0631) 3188290
website - www.fck.de
Year of Formation - 1900
President - Robert Wieschemann
Manager - Jürgen Friedrich
Secretary - Gerhard Herzog
Coach - Otto Rehhagel
Stadium - Fritz-Walter-Stadion (41,582)

MAJOR HONOURS
League Championship - (4)
1951, 1953, 1991, 1998.
Domestic Cup - (2) 1990, 1996.

APPEARANCES 99/00

		P	Ap	(s)	Gls
Mario BASLER	M		16	(2)	1
Andreas BUCK	M		19	(7)	2
Youri DJORKAEFF (FRA)	M		24	(1)	11
Uwe GOSPODAREK	G		7	(1)	
Marian HRISTOV (BUL)	M		21	(1)	3
János HRUTKA (HUN)	D		1	(1)	
Miroslav KLOSE	D			(2)	
Georg KOCH	G		9		
Harry KOCH	D		29	(1)	6
Slobodan KOMLJENOVIC (YUG)	D		19	(4)	2
Roger LUTZ	M		1	(4)	
Olaf MARSCHALL	A		18	(7)	4
Jörgen PETTERSSON (SWE)	A		16	(9)	9
Hany RAMZY (EGY)	D		25		2
Rodrigues RATINHO (BRA)	M		22	(5)	
Marco REICH	A		7	(19)	2
Andreas REINKE	G		18		
Jürgen RISCHE	A			(5)	
Axel ROOS	D		9	(7)	
Michael SCHJØNBERG (DEN)	D		32		2
Ciriaco SFORZA (SUI)	M		27		1
Thomas SOBOTZIK	M			(3)	
Jeff STRASSER (LUX)	D		27		2
Igli TARE (ALB)	A		8	(14)	4
Martin WAGNER	M		19	(1)	1

LEAGUE RESULTS 1999/2000

14/08/99	Borussia Dortmund	H	1-0	Marschall
22/08/99	FC Hansa Rostock	A	2-4	Marschall, Djorkaeff
27/08/99	Arminia Bielefeld	H	0-2	
12/09/99	SV Werder Bremen	A	0-5	
19/09/99	Hamburger SV	H	2-0	Koch H., Marschall
26/09/99	Bayer 04 Leverkusen	A	1-3	Schjønberg (p)
03/10/99	SpVgg Unterhaching	H	4-2	Sforza, Koch H., Djorkaeff 2
16/10/99	MSV Duisburg	A	2-2	Komljenovic, Marschall
23/10/99	FC Bayern München	H	0-2	
31/10/99	VfB Stuttgart	A	1-0	Hristov
07/11/99	FC Schalke 04	H	2-1	Wagner, Djorkaeff
20/11/99	Hertha BSC Berlin	A	1-0	Strasser
28/11/99	Eintracht Frankfurt	A	1-0	Koch H.
05/12/99	VfL Wolfsburg	H	2-2	Hristov, Djorkaeff (p)
11/12/99	SSV Ulm	A	1-3	og (Bodog)
15/12/99	SC Freiburg	H	0-2	
18/12/99	TSV 1860 München	A	1-2	Djorkaeff (p)
04/02/00	Borussia Dortmund	A	1-0	Koch H.
08/02/00	FC Hansa Rostock	H	2-2	Pettersson, Komljenovic
11/02/00	Arminia Bielefeld	A	2-1	Koch H., Buck
19/02/00	SV Werder Bremen	H	4-3	Pettersson, Djorkaeff 2 (1p), Strasser
26/02/00	Hamburger SV	A	1-2	Pettersson
05/03/00	Bayer 04 Leverkusen	H	1-3	Basler
10/03/00	SpVgg Unterhaching	A	2-1	Koch H., Buck
18/03/00	MSV Duisburg	H	3-2	Djorkaeff, Ramzy, Hristov
25/03/00	FC Bayern München	A	2-2	Djorkaeff, Reich
02/04/00	VfB Stuttgart	H	1-2	Djorkaeff
08/04/00	FC Schalke 04	A	2-1	Tare, Pettersson
11/04/00	Hertha BSC Berlin	H	1-2	Pettersson
15/04/00	Eintracht Frankfurt	H	1-0	Reich
22/04/00	VfL Wolfsburg	A	2-3	Pettersson, Schjønberg (p)
29/04/00	SSV Ulm	H	6-2	Tare 3, Pettersson 2. og (Grauer)
13/05/00	SC Freiburg	A	1-2	Pettersson
20/05/00	TSV 1860 München	H	1-1	Ramzy

TSV 1860 MÜNCHEN

CLUB DIRECTORY

TSV 1860 München
Grünwalder Strasse 114, 81547 München
tel - (089) 64278560
fax - (089) 64278580
website - www.tsv1860.de
Year of Formation - 1860
President - Karl-Heinz Wildmoser
Secretary - Detlef Romeiko
Coach - Werner Lorant
Stadium - Olympiastadion (69,000)

MAJOR HONOURS
League Championship - (1) 1966.
Domestic Cup - (2) 1942, 1964.

APPEARANCES 99/00

		P	Ap	(s)	Gls
Paul AGOSTINO (AUS)	A	9	(9)	4
Daniel BORIMIROV (BUL)	M	9	(11)	2
Harald CERNY (AUT)	M	30	(2)	2
Martin CIZEK (CZE)	M	12	(7)	
Michael DINZEY (DRC)	M		(1)	
Holger GREILICH	D	15	(5)	
Daniel HOFFMANN	G	33		
Michael HOFMANN	G	1	(1)	
Thomas HÄSSLER	M	33		8
Marco KURZ	D	26		1
Martin MAX	A	29	(3)	19
Stephan PASSLACK	D	17	(7)	1
Christian PROSENIK (AUT)	M	9	(10)	1
Marcus PÜRK (AUT)	A	6	(4)	
Thomas RIEDL	M	18	(4)	1
Markus SCHROTH	A	13	(9)	3
Martin STRANZL (AUT)	D	17	(5)	
Filip TAPALOVIC (CRO)	D	15	(7)	2
Roman TYCE (CZE)	M	23	(2)	1
Gerald VANENBURG (HOL)	D	16		
Tomas VOTAVA (CZE)	D	2		
Bernhard WINKLER	A	18	(4)	3
Ned ZELIC (AUS)	D	23		2

LEAGUE RESULTS 1999/2000

Date	Opponent	H/A	Score	Scorers
14/08/99	VfL Wolfsburg	A	1-2	og (Thomsen)
21/08/99	SSV Ulm	H	4-1	Max 2, Hässler (p), Passlack
28/08/99	SC Freiburg	A	0-3	
12/09/99	Eintracht Frankfurt	H	2-0	Max, Cerny
17/09/99	Borussia Dortmund	H	0-3	
25/09/99	FC Hansa Rostock	A	0-0	
01/10/99	Arminia Bielefeld	H	5-0	Max 2 (1p), Hässler, Tyce, Agostino
16/10/99	SV Werder Bremen	A	3-1	Tapalovic, Winkler, Borimirov
23/10/99	Hamburger SV	H	0-0	
30/10/99	Bayer 04 Leverkusen	A	1-1	Winkler
06/11/99	SpVgg Unterhaching	H	2-1	Prosenik, Tapalovic
21/11/99	MSV Duisburg	A	0-3	
27/11/99	FC Bayern München	H	1-0	Riedl
04/12/99	VfB Stuttgart	A	3-1	Schroth, Zelic, Borimirov
11/12/99	FC Schalke 04	H	3-3	Hässler, Max, Cerny
14/12/99	Hertha BSC Berlin	A	1-1	Max
18/12/99	1.FC Kaiserslautern	H	2-1	Max, Hässler (p)
05/02/00	VfL Wolfsburg	H	1-2	Winkler
08/02/00	SSV Ulm	A	0-3	
13/02/00	SC Freiburg	H	3-1	Zelic, Hässler, og (Golz)
19/02/00	Eintracht Frankfurt	A	1-3	Schroth
27/02/00	Borussia Dortmund	A	1-1	Max
04/03/00	FC Hansa Rostock	H	4-3	Max 3, Hässler (p)
11/03/00	Arminia Bielefeld	A	2-2	Max, Hässler (p)
19/03/00	SV Werder Bremen	H	1-0	Kurz
25/03/00	Hamburger SV	A	0-2	
31/03/00	Bayer 04 Leverkusen	H	1-2	Schroth
07/04/00	SpVgg Unterhaching	A	1-1	Agostino
12/04/00	MSV Duisburg	H	4-1	Max 2, Agostino 2
15/04/00	FC Bayern München	A	2-1	Max, og (Jeremies)
22/04/00	VfB Stuttgart	H	1-1	Hässler
29/04/00	FC Schalke 04	A	2-2	Max 2
13/05/00	Hertha BSC Berlin	H	2-1	og (Schmidt), Max
20/05/00	1.FC Kaiserslautern	A	1-1	og (Basler)

FC SCHALKE 04

CLUB DIRECTORY

FC Schalke 04
Postfach 20 08 61, 45843 Gelsenkirchen
tel - (0209) 700870 / fax - (0209) 7008750
website - www.schalke04.de
Year of Formation - 1904
President - Gerd Rehberg
Manager - Rudi Assauer
Secretary - Peter Peters
Coach - Huub Stevens
Stadium - Parkstadion (62,004)

MAJOR HONOURS
League Championship - (7)
1934, 1935, 1937, 1939, 1940, 1942, 1958.
Domestic Cup - (2) 1937, 1972.
UEFA Cup - (1) 1997.

APPEARANCES 99/00

	P	Ap	(s)	Gls
Ünal ALPUGAN (TUR)	M	17	(9)	
Ingo ANDERBRÜGGE	M		(2)	
Gerald ASAMOAH (GHA)	A	22	(11)	4
Michael BÜSKENS	M	4	(5)	
Johan DE KOCK (HOL)	D	4		
Yves EIGENRAUCH	D	21	(2)	1
Michael GOOSSENS (BEL)	A	8	(7)	
Tamás HAJNAL (HUN)	M		(8)	
Markus HAPPE	D	15		
Oliver HELD	M	3	(15)	
Sven KMETSCH	M	21	(3)	
Radoslav LATAL (CZE)	M	17	(7)	1
Thorsten LEGAT	M	2	(2)	
Emile MPENZA (BEL)	A	15		6
Youri MULDER (HOL)	A		(3)	
Andreas MÜLLER	M	3	(3)	
Jiri NEMEC (CZE)	M	29		1
Niels OUDE KAMPHUIS (HOL)	M	24	(2)	2
Sérgio PINTO (POR)	A		(2)	
Oliver RECK	G	25		
Ebbe SAND (DEN)	A	31	(1)	14
Mathias SCHOBER	G	9	(1)	
Krisztián SZOLLAR (HUN)	D		(1)	
Olaf THON	D	23		1
Marco VAN HOOGDALEM (HOL)	D	2	(2)	
Nico VAN KERCKHOVEN (BEL)	M	16		1
Tomasz WALDOCH (POL)	D	31		1
Marc WILMOTS (BEL)	M	32		7

LEAGUE RESULTS 1999/2000

14/08/99	Arminia Bielefeld	H	1-1	Nemec
21/08/99	SV Werder Bremen	A	1-0	Asamoah
27/08/99	Hamburger SV	H	1-3	Wilmots
11/09/99	Bayer 04 Leverkusen	A	2-3	Sand, og (Gresko)
18/09/99	SpVgg Unterhaching	H	1-0	Sand
25/09/99	MSV Duisburg	A	1-1	Van Kerckhoven
02/10/99	FC Bayern München	H	1-1	Wilmots
17/10/99	VfB Stuttgart	A	2-0	Oude Kamphuis, Sand
22/10/99	Eintracht Frankfurt	A	2-0	Wilmots (p), Asamoah
30/10/99	Hertha BSC Berlin	H	1-1	Eigenrauch
07/11/99	1.FC Kaiserslautern	A	1-2	Wilmots (p)
20/11/99	VfL Wolfsburg	H	1-1	Sand
26/11/99	SSV Ulm	A	1-1	Sand
04/12/99	SC Freiburg	H	2-2	Asamoah, Wilmots (p)
11/12/99	TSV 1860 München	A	3-3	Wilmots, Sand 2
15/12/99	Borussia Dortmund	H	0-0	
19/12/99	FC Hansa Rostock	A	0-1	
05/02/00	Arminia Bielefeld	A	2-1	Sand, og (Meissner)
08/02/00	SV Werder Bremen	H	3-1	Sand 2, Mpenza
13/02/00	Hamburger SV	A	1-3	Mpenza
18/02/00	Bayer 04 Leverkusen	H	1-1	Mpenza
27/02/00	SpVgg Unterhaching	A	1-3	Wilmots
04/03/00	MSV Duisburg	H	3-0	og (Zeyer), Sand 2
11/03/00	FC Bayern München	A	1-4	Mpenza
18/03/00	VfB Stuttgart	H	3-0	Mpenza 2, Waldoch
26/03/00	Eintracht Frankfurt	H	0-0	
01/04/00	Hertha BSC Berlin	A	1-2	Sand
08/04/00	1.FC Kaiserslautern	H	1-2	Latal
11/04/00	VfL Wolfsburg	A	0-0	
14/04/00	SSV Ulm	H	0-0	
22/04/00	SC Freiburg	A	1-2	Asamoah
29/04/00	TSV 1860 München	H	2-2	Oude Kamphuis, Thon
13/05/00	Borussia Dortmund	A	1-1	Sand
20/05/00	FC Hansa Rostock	H	0-2	

VFB STUTTGART

VfB Stuttgart
Mercedesstrasse 109, 70372 Stuttgart
tel - (01805) 8325463 / fax - (0711) 5500733
website - www.vfb-stuttgart.de
Year of Formation - 1893
President - Gerhard Mayer-Vorfelder
Manager - Karl-Heinz Förster
Secretary - Ulrich Schäfer
Coach - Ralf Rangnick
Stadium - Gottlieb-Daimler-Stadion (47,000)

MAJOR HONOURS
League Championship - (4)
1950, 1952, 1984, 1992.
Domestic Cup - (3) 1954, 1958, 1997.

APPEARANCES 99/00

	P	Ap	(s)	Gls
Krasimir BALAKOV (BUL)	M	28	(2)	6
Thomas BERTHOLD	D	22	(1)	
Marcelo BORDON (BRA)	D	22	(1)	2
Bradley CARNELL (SAF)	M	13	(11)	1
Giuseppe CATIZONE	M	1	(4)	
DIDI (BRA)	A		(2)	
Kristijan DJORDJEVIC (YUG)	M	4	(5)	
Sean DUNDEE	A	20	(8)	8
Jochen ENDRESS	D	5	(15)	1
Ioan Viorel GANEA (ROM)	A	26	(3)	7
Heiko GERBER	M	28	(1)	4
Timo HILDEBRAND	G	6		
Achim HOLLERIETH	G	1		
Ahmed Sahin HOSNY (EGY)	A	1	(15)	2
Rüdiger KAUF	D	1	(1)	
Jens KELLER	D	21	(3)	
Thomas KIES	D	1	(5)	
Pavel KUKA (CZE)	A	10	(10)	1
Krisztián LISZTES (HUN)	M	23	(6)	4
Roberto PINTO (POR)	M	23	(4)	2
Sreto RISTIC (YUG)	A	1	(2)	
Thomas SCHNEIDER	D	20	(2)	
Zvonimir SOLDO (CRO)	M	31		2
Pablo THIAM (GUI)	M	33		3
Jens TODT	M	6		
Franz WOHLFAHRT (AUT)	G	27		

LEAGUE RESULTS 1999/2000

Date	Opponent	H/A	Score	Scorers
14/08/99	SV Werder Bremen	H	0-0	
21/08/99	Hamburger SV	A	0-3	
28/08/99	Bayer 04 Leverkusen	H	1-2	Soldo
11/09/99	SpVgg Unterhaching	A	0-2	
18/09/99	MSV Duisburg	H	4-2	Bordon, Ganea 2, og (Töfting)
24/09/99	FC Bayern München	A	1-0	Balakov (p)
01/10/99	Eintracht Frankfurt	A	1-0	Balakov
17/10/99	FC Schalke 04	H	0-2	
23/10/99	Hertha BSC Berlin	A	1-1	Carnell
31/10/99	1.FC Kaiserslautern	H	0-1	
06/11/99	VfL Wolfsburg	A	2-0	Gerber, Hosny
20/11/99	SSV Ulm	H	2-0	Dundee, Gerber
26/11/99	SC Freiburg	A	2-0	Lisztes, Dundee
04/12/99	TSV 1860 München	H	1-3	Thiam
11/12/99	Borussia Dortmund	A	1-1	Dundee
14/12/99	FC Hansa Rostock	H	3-1	Ganea 2, Pinto
17/12/99	Arminia Bielefeld	A	2-1	Dundee 2
05/02/00	SV Werder Bremen	A	1-2	Lisztes
09/02/00	Hamburger SV	H	1-3	Endress
12/02/00	Bayer 04 Leverkusen	A	0-1	
19/02/00	SpVgg Unterhaching	H	0-2	
26/02/00	MSV Duisburg	A	3-1	Balakov 2, Dundee
04/03/00	FC Bayern München	H	2-0	Balakov, Lisztes
10/03/00	Eintracht Frankfurt	H	0-2	
18/03/00	FC Schalke 04	A	0-3	
25/03/00	Hertha BSC Berlin	H	1-0	Dundee
02/04/00	1.FC Kaiserslautern	A	2-1	Dundee, Balakov (p)
08/04/00	VfL Wolfsburg	H	2-5	Kuka, Soldo
11/04/00	SSV Ulm	A	1-1	Bordon
15/04/00	SC Freiburg	H	1-0	Ganea
22/04/00	TSV 1860 München	A	1-1	Hosny
29/04/00	Borussia Dortmund	H	1-2	Thiam
13/05/00	FC Hansa Rostock	A	4-1	Ganea, Gerber, Lisztes, Pinto
20/05/00	Arminia Bielefeld	H	3-3	Thiam, Gerber, Ganea

SSV ULM

CLUB DIRECTORY

SSV Ulm 1846
Stadionstrasse 17
89073 Ulm
tel - (0731) 18460
fax - (0731) 1846101
website - www.ssvulm1846.de
Year of Formation - 1970
President - Florian Ebner
Secretary - Hartmut Häussler
Coach - Martin Andermatt
Stadium - Donaustadion (19,500)

APPEARANCES 99/00

	P	Ap	(s)	Gls
Tamás BÓDOG (HUN)	D	22	(1)	2
Ünal DEMIRKIRAN (TUR)	M		(2)	
Janusz GORA (POL)	M	23	(2)	3
Uwe GRAUER	D	11	(5)	
Frank KINKEL	D	10	(1)	
Marco KONRAD	D	2	(2)	
Philipp LAUX	G	34		
LEANDRO (BRA)	A	22	(3)	3
Bernd MAIER	M	23	(1)	1
Rui Manuel MARQUES (POR)	D	31	(1)	
Oliver OTTO	M	33		2
Markus PLEULER	M	9	(10)	1
Janos RADOKI	D	24	(1)	
Sascha RÖSLER	M	10	(16)	
Rainer SCHARINGER	M	18	(11)	4
Joachim STADLER	D	30	(1)	1
Dragan TRKULJA (YUG)	A	7	(13)	1
Oliver UNSÖLD	D	26	(7)	1
Evans WISE (TRI)	A	4	(5)	
Hans VAN DE HAAR (HOL)	A	22	(3)	10
David ZDRILIC (AUS)	A	13	(9)	6

LEAGUE RESULTS 1999/2000

15/08/99	SC Freiburg	H	1-1	Gora (p)
21/08/99	TSV 1860 München	A	1-4	Unsöld
29/08/99	Borussia Dortmund	H	0-1	
10/09/99	FC Hansa Rostock	A	1-2	Gora
18/09/99	Arminia Bielefeld	H	2-0	Zdrilic, Scharinger
25/09/99	SV Werder Bremen	A	2-2	Zdrilic, Van de Haar (p)
02/10/99	Hamburger SV	H	1-2	Trkulja
15/10/99	Bayer 04 Leverkusen	A	1-4	Stadler
23/10/99	SpVgg Unterhaching	H	1-0	Otto
30/10/99	MSV Duisburg	A	0-0	
06/11/99	FC Bayern München	H	0-1	
20/11/99	VfB Stuttgart	A	0-2	
26/11/99	FC Schalke 04	H	1-1	og (Sand)
04/12/99	Hertha BSC Berlin	A	0-3	
11/12/99	1.FC Kaiserslautern	H	3-1	Gora, Van de Haar, Bodog
15/12/99	VfL Wolfsburg	A	2-1	Van de Haar 2
18/12/99	Eintracht Frankfurt	H	3-0	Leandro, Scharinger, Zdrilic
05/02/00	SC Freiburg	A	0-2	
08/02/00	TSV 1860 München	H	3-0	Otto, Van de Haar, Scharinger
12/02/00	Borussia Dortmund	A	1-1	Bodog
20/02/00	FC Hansa Rostock	H	1-1	Van de Haar
28/02/00	Arminia Bielefeld	A	1-4	Pleuler
05/03/00	SV Werder Bremen	H	2-1	Van de Haar 2
11/03/00	Hamburger SV	A	2-1	Scharinger, Maier
18/03/00	Bayer 04 Leverkusen	H	1-9	Leandro
24/03/00	SpVgg Unterhaching	A	0-1	
31/03/00	MSV Duisburg	H	0-3	
08/04/00	FC Bayern München	A	0-4	
11/04/00	VfB Stuttgart	H	1-1	Leandro
14/04/00	FC Schalke 04	A	0-0	
22/04/00	Hertha BSC Berlin	H	0-1	
29/04/00	1.FC Kaiserslautern	A	2-6	Zdrilic 2
13/05/00	VfL Wolfsburg	H	2-0	Zdrilic, Van de Haar
20/05/00	Eintracht Frankfurt	A	1-2	Van de Haar

SPVGG UNTERHACHING

CLUB DIRECTORY

Spielvereinigung Unterhaching
Am Sportpark 1
82008 Unterhaching
tel - (089) 6115057
fax - (089) 6117064
website - www.spvggunterhaching.de
Year of Formation - 1925
President - Engelbert Kupka
Manager - Norbert Hartmann
Secretary - Richard Piller
Coach - Lorenz-Günter Köstner
Stadium - Sportpark (10,300)

APPEARANCES 99/00

	P	Ap	(s)	Gls
Jörg BERGEN	D	17	(2)	
Andre BREITENREITER	A	9	(10)	7
Ralf BUCHER	D	14	(7)	
Alfonso GARCIA (ESP)	A	3	(12)	1
Dennis GRASSOW	D	26		1
Marco HABER	M	26	(2)	2
Björn HERTL	M	2	(16)	
Ludwig KÖGL	M	9	(7)	1
Alberto MENDEZ (ESP)	M		(6)	
Markus OBERLEITNER	M	30	(3)	3
Altin RRAKLLI (ALB)	A	26	(6)	6
Danny SCHWARZ	M	34		2
Jan SEIFERT	D	24	(7)	2
Jochen SEITZ	A	31	(3)	5
Oliver STRAUBE	M	29	(1)	3
Alexander STREHMEL	D	25		2
Arne TAMMEN	M		(1)	
Gerhard TREMMEL	G	7		
Jürgen WITTMANN	G	27		
Peter ZEILER	M	1	(4)	
Mark ZIMMERMANN	A		(9)	
Matthias ZIMMERMANN	M	34		3

LEAGUE RESULTS 1999/2000

14/08/99	Eintracht Frankfurt	A	0-3	
20/08/99	MSV Duisburg	H	2-0	Rraklli (p), Straube
28/08/99	FC Bayern München	A	0-1	
11/09/99	VfB Stuttgart	H	2-0	Rraklli, Kögl
18/09/99	FC Schalke 04	A	0-1	
25/09/99	Hertha BSC Berlin	H	1-1	García
03/10/99	1.FC Kaiserslautern	A	2-4	Seitz 2
17/10/99	VfL Wolfsburg	H	1-1	Straube
23/10/99	SSV Ulm	A	0-1	
31/10/99	SC Freiburg	H	1-0	Rraklli (p)
06/11/99	TSV 1860 München	A	1-2	Schwarz
27/11/99	FC Hansa Rostock	A	1-1	Oberleitner
01/12/99	Borussia Dortmund	H	1-0	Rraklli (p)
05/12/99	Arminia Bielefeld	H	2-0	Strehmel, Breitenreiter (p)
10/12/99	SV Werder Bremen	A	2-2	Straube, Breitenreiter
15/12/99	Hamburger SV	H	1-1	Seitz
18/12/99	Bayer 04 Leverkusen	A	1-2	Zimmermann Mat.
06/02/00	Eintracht Frankfurt	H	1-0	Rraklli (p)
09/02/00	MSV Duisburg	A	0-2	
12/02/00	FC Bayern München	H	0-2	
19/02/00	VfB Stuttgart	A	2-0	Rraklli, Zimmermann Mat.
27/02/00	FC Schalke 04	H	3-1	Breitenreiter, Grassow, Oberleitner
04/03/00	Hertha BSC Berlin	A	1-2	Haber
10/03/00	1.FC Kaiserslautern	H	1-2	Breitenreiter
17/03/00	VfL Wolfsburg	A	2-2	Zimmermann Mat., Haber
24/03/00	SSV Ulm	H	1-0	og (Stadler)
31/03/00	SC Freiburg	A	3-4	Breitenreiter 2, Seitz
07/04/00	TSV 1860 München	H	1-1	Seifert
11/04/00	Borussia Dortmund	A	3-1	Seitz, Strehmel, Schwarz
16/04/00	FC Hansa Rostock	H	1-1	Seifert
23/04/00	Arminia Bielefeld	A	0-1	
30/04/00	SV Werder Bremen	H	1-0	Breitenreiter
13/05/00	Hamburger SV	A	0-3	
20/05/00	Bayer 04 Leverkusen	H	2-0	og (Ballack), Oberleitner

SV WERDER BREMEN

CLUB DIRECTORY

SV Werder Bremen
Am Weserstadion 7, 28205 Bremen
tel - (0180) 5937337 / fax - (0421) 493555
website - www.Werder-online.de
Year of Formation - 1899
President - Jürgen L. Born
Manager - Klaus Allofs
Secretary - Wolfgang Barkhausen
Coach - Thomas Schaaf
Stadium - Weserstadion (35,282)

MAJOR HONOURS
League Championship - (3) 1965, 1988, 1993.
Domestic Cup - (4) 1961, 1991, 1994, 1999.
European Cup-winners' Cup - (1) 1992.

APPEARANCES 99/00

		P	Ap	(s)	Gls
AÍLTON Gonçalves da Silva (BRA)	A	24	(5)	12
Mike BARTEN	D	15	(1)	
Frank BAUMANN	D	32		5
Marco BODE	A	27		13
Rade BOGDANOVIC (YUG)	A	10	(12)	4
Christoph DABROWSKI	M	10	(18)	2
Dieter EILTS	M	28	(1)	1
Dirk FLOCK	M	3	(9)	1
Dieter FREY	M		(3)	
Torsten FRINGS	A	31	(2)	3
Andreas HERZOG (AUT)	M	24	(3)	6
JÚLIO CÉSAR (BRA)	D	12		
Yuriy MAXIMOV (UKR)	M	15	(14)	3
Claudio PIZARRO (PER)	A	24	(1)	10
Lodewijk ROEMBIAK (HOL)	M	1	(1)	
Frank ROST	G	34		
Sören SEIDEL	A	3	(3)	1
Victor SKRIPNIK (UKR)	D	1	(4)	
Razundara TJIKUZU (NAM)	D	24	(1)	
Bernhard TRARES	D	18	(2)	3
Raphaël WICKY (SUI)	D	15		
Andre WIEDENER	D	23	(2)	
Pawel WOJTALA (POL)	D		(2)	

LEAGUE RESULTS 1999/2000

14/08/99	VfB Stuttgart	A	0-0	
21/08/99	FC Schalke 04	H	0-1	
28/08/99	Hertha BSC Berlin	A	1-1	Bogdanovic
12/09/99	1.FC Kaiserslautern	H	5-0	Pizarro, Bode, Bogdanovic, Frings, Dabrowski
19/09/99	VfL Wolfsburg	A	7-2	Bode 3, Aílton, Pizarro 3
25/09/99	SSV Ulm	H	2-2	Baumann, Maximov
03/10/99	SC Freiburg	A	1-2	Bogdanovic
16/10/99	TSV 1860 München	H	1-3	Herzog (p)
24/10/99	Borussia Dortmund	A	3-1	og (Lehmann), Bode, Pizarro
29/10/99	FC Hansa Rostock	H	2-1	Pizarro, Aílton
07/11/99	Arminia Bielefeld	A	2-2	Bode, Seidel
19/11/99	Eintracht Frankfurt	H	3-1	Aílton 2, Bode
28/11/99	Hamburger SV	H	2-1	Bode, Aílton
04/12/99	Bayer 04 Leverkusen	A	2-3	Pizarro, Aílton
10/12/99	SpVgg Unterhaching	H	2-2	Maximov, Aílton
14/12/99	MSV Duisburg	A	1-0	Dabrowski
17/12/99	FC Bayern München	H	0-2	
05/02/00	VfB Stuttgart	H	2-1	Trares, Herzog
08/02/00	FC Schalke 04	A	1-3	Aílton
11/02/00	Hertha BSC Berlin	H	4-1	Trares, Baumann, Eilts, Aílton
19/02/00	1.FC Kaiserslautern	A	3-4	Baumann 2, Herzog
26/02/00	VfL Wolfsburg	H	2-2	Trares, Pizarro
05/03/00	SSV Ulm	A	1-2	Aílton
12/03/00	SC Freiburg	H	5-2	Bode 2, Pizarro, Baumann, Aílton (p)
19/03/00	TSV 1860 München	A	0-1	
26/03/00	Borussia Dortmund	H	3-2	Aílton, Maximov, Bogdanovic
02/04/00	FC Hansa Rostock	A	1-1	Bode
09/04/00	Arminia Bielefeld	H	3-1	Frings 2, Herzog (p)
12/04/00	Eintracht Frankfurt	A	0-1	
15/04/00	Hamburger SV	A	0-0	
21/04/00	Bayer 04 Leverkusen	H	1-3	Flock
30/04/00	SpVgg Unterhaching	A	0-1	
13/05/00	MSV Duisburg	H	4-0	Pizarro, Bode, Herzog 2 (1p)
20/05/00	FC Bayern München	A	1-3	Bode

VFL WOLFSBURG

CLUB DIRECTORY

VfL Wolfsburg
Elsterweg 5
38446 Wolfsburg
tel - (05361) 85170
fax - (05361) 851748
website - www.vfl-wolfsburg.de
Year of Formation - 1945
President - Werner Schlimme
Manager - Peter Pander
Secretary - Klaus Fuchs
Coach - Wolfgang Wolf
Stadium - VfL-Stadion (21,600)

APPEARANCES 99/00

		P	Ap	(s)	Gls
Charles AKONNOR (GHA)	M	17	(8)	1
Jonathan AKPOBORIE (NIG)	A	17	(2)	12
Holger BALLWANZ	D	9	(7)	1
Jean-Kasongo BANZA (DRC)	A	1	(10)	2
Steffen BAUMGART	A		(1)	
Marino BILISKOV (CRO)	D	19	(1)	2
Christian BRAND	M		(1)	
Andre BREITENREITER	A		(1)	
Detlev DAMMEIER	M	8	(8)	
Nico DÄBRITZ	M	4	(7)	
Markus FELDHOFF	A	9	(9)	2
Frank GREINER	M	28	(1)	
Thomas HENGEN	A	8		1
Andrzej JUSKOWIAK (POL)	A	30	(2)	11
Waldemar KRYGER (POL)	D	31		1
Marcel MALTRITZ	M	11	(12)	
Dorinel MUNTEANU (ROM)	M	22		3
Vitus NAGORNY	A		(1)	
Krzysztof NOWAK (POL)	M	32	(1)	3
Brian O'NEIL (SCO)	D	15	(1)	1
Claus REITMAIER	G	34		
Jürgen RISCHE	M	7	(4)	4
Gerald SCHRÖDER	D		(1)	
Zoltan SEBESCEN	M	13	(4)	6
Claus THOMSEN	D	24		
Patrick WEISER	M	33		1
Christian WÜCK	A	2	(12)	

LEAGUE RESULTS 1999/2000

14/08/99	TSV 1860 München	H	2-1	Banza, Nowak
21/08/99	Borussia Dortmund	A	1-2	Akpoborie (p)
28/08/99	FC Hansa Rostock	H	2-0	Weiser, Nowak
10/09/99	Arminia Bielefeld	A	0-0	
19/09/99	SV Werder Bremen	H	2-7	Juskowiak, Akpoborie
24/09/99	Hamburger SV	A	2-2	Akpoborie 2
02/10/99	Bayer 04 Leverkusen	H	3-1	Akpoborie, Sebescen, Juskowiak
17/10/99	SpVgg Unterhaching	A	1-1	Akpoborie
24/10/99	MSV Duisburg	H	1-0	Akpoborie
30/10/99	FC Bayern München	A	0-5	
06/11/99	VfB Stuttgart	H	0-2	
20/11/99	FC Schalke 04	A	1-1	Nowak
27/11/99	Hertha BSC Berlin	H	2-3	Feldhoff, O'Neil
05/12/99	1.FC Kaiserslautern	A	2-2	Akonnor (p), Ballwanz
12/12/99	Eintracht Frankfurt	H	1-0	Biliskov
15/12/99	SSV Ulm	H	1-2	Biliskov
18/12/99	SC Freiburg	A	1-1	Juskowiak
05/02/00	TSV 1860 München	A	2-1	Juskowiak 2
09/02/00	Borussia Dortmund	H	1-0	Rische
12/02/00	FC Hansa Rostock	A	1-1	Sebescen
20/02/00	Arminia Bielefeld	H	2-0	Munteanu, Juskowiak
26/02/00	SV Werder Bremen	A	2-2	Munteanu, Hengen
03/03/00	Hamburger SV	H	4-4	Sebescen 3, Rische
11/03/00	Bayer 04 Leverkusen	A	1-4	Juskowiak
17/03/00	SpVgg Unterhaching	H	2-2	Feldhoff, Akpoborie
25/03/00	MSV Duisburg	A	3-2	Akpoborie, Juskowiak, Munteanu
01/04/00	FC Bayern München	H	1-1	Juskowiak
08/04/00	VfB Stuttgart	A	5-2	Akpoborie 3, Juskowiak, Sebescen
11/04/00	FC Schalke 04	H	0-0	
14/04/00	Hertha BSC Berlin	A	0-0	
22/04/00	1.FC Kaiserslautern	H	3-2	Banza, Rische, Kryger
28/04/00	Eintracht Frankfurt	A	0-4	
13/05/00	SSV Ulm	A	0-2	
20/05/00	SC Freiburg	H	2-1	Rische, Juskowiak

GREECE

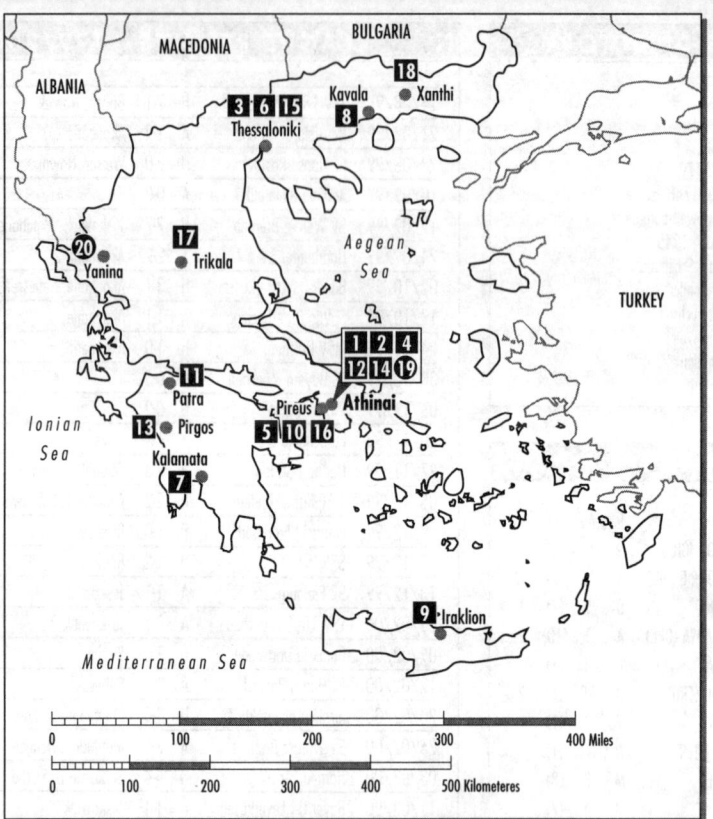

1	AEK	470	12	PANATHINAIKOS	481
2	APOLLON	471	13	PANILIAKOS	482
3	ARIS	472	14	PANIONIOS	483
4	ETHNIKOS ASTIR	473	15	PAOK	484
5	IONIKOS	474	16	PROODEFTIKI	485
6	IRAKLIS	475	17	TRIKALA	486
7	KALAMATA	476	18	XANTHI	487
8	KAVALA	477	**Promoted clubs**		
9	OFI	478	19	ATHINAIKOS	
10	OLYMPIAKOS	479	20	YANINA	
11	PANAHAIKI	480			

PANATHINAIKOS PUSH HOLDERS ALL THE WAY

Internal problems fail to halt Olympiakos

FEDERATION DIRECTORY

Elliniki Podosferiki Omospondia
Leoforos Singrou 137, Athinai 17121

tel - 9311500
fax - 9359666
website - www.epo.gr

Year of Formation - 1926
President - Konstandinos Alexandridis

Stadium - OAKA 'Spiros Louis', Athinai (74,433)

The thrill of the chase at the top of the table with the country's two heavyweights Olympiakos and Panathinaikos locked in an intense feud for the championship, made the 1999/2000 Greek season memorable in a positive sense. But, as usual, there was plenty of negative news to report, with hooliganism as rampant as ever, coaches getting the sack and a top player going on strike.

There was even a major earthquake in Athens, which forced a delay to the start of the championship and put AEK's ground permanently out of action, obliging the club to switch its home games to the stadiums of their main rivals.

As a result of this, it was perhaps unsurprising that AEK failed to make any impact on the championship race. They lost three of their first four 'home' games, including those against Panathinaikos and Olympiakos, and were never in contention after that. They did recover their form in the second half of the season, but that was only after newly-appointed Yugoslav coach Ljubisa Tumbakovic had flown the nest and been replaced by Ioanis Pathiakakis.

Remarkably, all of Greece's big three clubs finished the season under the command of Greek coaches. Only Panathinaikos had started out with one, having installed Ioanis Kirastas as a replacement for Argentinian Juan Ramón Rocha in pre-season. Olympiakos, on the other hand, went through two foreign coaches - Yugoslav Dusan Bajevic and Italian Alberto Bigon - before they decided to go with the flow and bring in Ioanis Mantzourakis from Xanthi.

To outsiders, it seemed perverse that Olympiakos should

LEAGUE CHAMPIONSHIP RESULTS 99/00

		1	2	3	4	5	6	7	8	9	10	11	12	13	14	15	16	17	18
1	AEK		3-0	2-0	2-1	5-1	3-2	6-1	3-0	1-2	0-2	3-0	1-2	1-0	0-1	2-0	3-2	2-1	4-1
2	Apollon	3-2		3-3	0-1	0-2	1-0	1-2	0-2	1-2	0-1	0-0	0-3	0-0	2-1	3-4	0-2	5-2	0-0
3	Aris	1-1	2-1		1-1	1-1	2-1	6-1	1-0	3-1	0-1	2-0	0-2	2-1	5-1	0-0	2-1	3-3	0-1
4	Ethnikos Astir	1-3	3-1	1-0		1-2	3-1	2-0	1-0	0-1	1-1	2-2	1-2	3-1	4-2	1-1	1-0	1-0	1-0
5	Ionikos	1-1	1-0	2-2	3-0		1-1	0-1	2-0	1-1	1-2	0-0	2-2	0-2	2-0	1-0	2-0	5-1	2-1
6	Iraklis	3-1	1-0	2-0	2-0	3-2		2-1	2-1	0-3	3-4	2-1	1-3	3-1	1-2	3-1	4-0	4-1	3-1
7	Kalamata	1-1	1-1	5-2	1-0	2-0	2-2		3-2	0-0	0-1	1-1	0-0	2-1	1-3	1-1	2-0	0-1	0-0
8	Kavala	0-2	1-3	1-0	2-0	0-0	3-1	0-1		0-1	0-5	0-0	1-4	2-1	3-7	1-1	2-1	4-1	1-0
9	OFI	1-2	1-0	2-1	4-1	2-0	1-1	3-2	2-2		2-1	2-2	3-4	3-2	0-2	2-0	4-3	2-0	2-1
10	Olympiakos	3-0	2-0	2-0	5-0	2-0	1-0	4-1	5-0	2-0		5-1	2-2	2-1	5-0	4-1	4-0	3-1	3-2
11	Panahaiki	1-1	1-2	1-2	2-0	1-1	0-1	1-2	3-2	3-1	0-2		1-0	2-0	1-0	1-2	2-0	3-0	1-1
12	Panathinaikos	1-0	5-0	3-0	4-0	5-0	3-0	5-0	3-0	3-2	2-0	7-1		3-1	2-1	1-1	3-1	2-0	2-1
13	Paniliakos	0-1	2-1	1-2	2-0	3-0	4-3	3-1	2-0	1-2	0-3	0-0	0-1		3-0	0-4	4-0	1-3	2-0
14	Panionios	0-2	3-1	1-3	1-0	2-0	2-2	2-0	1-1	1-4	0-1	2-1	0-4	1-2		1-1	2-1	4-1	4-0
15	PAOK	4-4	1-1	3-2	2-0	3-0	4-0	4-2	5-0	2-2	0-2	1-1	1-3	0-1	2-0		1-0	2-0	5-0
16	Proodeftiki	1-4	2-0	0-1	1-0	2-2	0-1	1-2	1-1	0-0	0-3	2-2	1-0	1-1	1-0	1-0		1-0	0-0
17	Trikala	0-1	1-0	0-1	1-2	2-2	3-3	0-2	3-1	1-1	0-2	0-1	1-3	1-1	2-3	3-5	0-0		2-1
18	Xanthi	2-2	2-0	0-0	0-0	2-1	3-0	1-0	1-0	1-1	0-1	1-0	1-3	1-0	5-0	1-2	2-1	3-0	

LEAGUE CHAMPIONSHIP FINAL TABLE 99/00

			Home				Away					Total						
		Pd	W	D	L	F	A	W	D	L	F	A	W	D	L	F	A	PT	GD
1	Olympiakos	34	16	1	0	54	9	14	1	2	32	9	30	2	2	86	18	92	68
2	Panathinaikos	34	16	1	0	54	8	12	3	2	38	16	28	4	2	92	24	88	68
3	AEK	34	13	0	4	41	16	7	6	4	28	23	20	6	8	69	39	66	30
4	OFI	34	11	3	3	36	24	7	6	4	24	20	18	9	7	60	44	63	16
5	PAOK	34	10	4	3	40	18	5	6	6	24	26	15	10	9	64	44	55	20
6	Iraklis	34	13	0	4	39	22	2	5	10	19	36	15	5	14	58	58	50	0
7	Aris	34	9	5	3	31	17	5	3	9	19	29	14	8	12	50	46	50	4
8	Panionios	34	8	3	6	27	24	6	0	11	23	39	14	3	17	50	63	45	-13
9	Kalamata	34	6	8	3	22	16	6	0	11	19	41	12	8	14	41	57	44	-16
10	Ionikos	34	8	6	3	26	14	2	5	10	14	36	10	11	13	40	50	41	-10
11	Ethnikos Astir	34	10	3	4	27	17	2	2	13	6	33	12	5	17	33	50	41	-17
12	Xanthi	34	10	4	3	26	11	1	4	12	10	32	11	8	15	36	43	41	-7
13	Paniliakos	34	9	1	7	28	21	3	3	11	16	27	12	4	18	44	48	40	-4
14	Panahaiki	34	8	3	6	24	17	1	9	7	13	30	9	12	13	37	47	39	-10
15	Kavala	34	7	3	7	21	28	1	3	13	12	38	8	6	20	33	66	30	-33
16	Proodeftiki	34	6	6	5	15	17	1	1	15	12	38	7	7	20	27	55	28	-28
17	Apollon	34	4	4	9	19	27	2	2	13	11	32	6	6	22	30	59	24	-29
18	Trikala	34	3	5	9	20	29	2	1	14	15	45	5	6	23	35	74	21	-39

N.B. Where two or more teams are level on points, classification is determined by the results of the matches between them.

need three different coaches in a season when they stormed to their fourth successive championship title in record-breaking fashion. They won 30 of their 34 matches, 22 of them without conceding a goal, and dropped a grand total of just ten points. They closed the campaign with eight straight wins, the seventh of them being good enough to secure the title at the expense of their great rivals Panathinaikos, who, showing similar consistency and stamina, had hounded them all the way.

The departure of Bajevic, who had overseen Olympiakos's three previous title wins, was not the choice of the club. The Yugoslav tendered his resignation in November. The reason he offered in public was the club's early elimination from the Champions' League, but it was obvious to everyone that he had begun to encounter major difficulties with senior officials at the club. After all, Olympiakos were still active in the UEFA Cup, and at home they led the league with six wins out of six.

Bigon, the man who had taken Maradona's Napoli to the Italian title at the start of the decade, was given the opportunity to end the 1990s in similar triumph. He made a fine start, with a 2-0 victory over AEK, but that was followed six days later by a 0-2 defeat away to Panathinaikos. It was to be the only league game in which Olympiakos failed to score all season, but it was highly

significant in that it enabled Panathinaikos to put themselves back into title contention. Many Olympiakos fans continued to hold that against Bigon in the ensuing weeks and months - despite the team's rapid recovery and a regular stream of convincing victories that kept them narrowly in front of Panathinaikos in the championship race.

The internal problems at Olympiakos were compounded by the 'Zahovic affair'. Slovenian international Zlatko Zahovic had arrived at the club from FC Porto at considerable expense during the summer, but after a couple of months he fell out with Bajevic and refused to return. This brought him a six-month ban and a £60,000 fine. In January the recalcitrant star proposed a truce, and Olympiakos decided to lift the ban and allow him to play again. The Slovenian returned with a bang, scoring a late winner against Xanthi just ten minutes after his return and then finding the net in each of the next three games as well. The peace, however, was soon broken when, in a

INTERNATIONAL HONOURS

World Cup Finals appearances: 1994
European Championship appearances: 1980

NATIONAL TEAM APPEARANCES 99/00

Coach - Vasilios DANIIL	MEX	SAL	SAL	NOR	ALB	SLO	NIG	BUL	GHA	MOL	EST	AUT	ROM	IRL	ROM	Cps	Gls
Dimitrios ELEFTHEROPOULOS (07/08/76) - Olympiakos	G67								G60						G	5	-
Dimitrios MAVROGENIDIS (23/12/76) - Olympiakos	D	D		D				s65	D	D46		D60	D65		D	17	1
Nikolaos DABIZAS (03/08/73) - Newcastle United (ENG)	D65	D77	D	D	D	D	D	D	D	s66			D	D	D73	41	-
Marinos UZUNIDIS (10/10/68) - Paniliakos	D65	D46	D	D	D		D	D	D67	s59	D	D	D	D	D	41	3
Pandeleimon KONSTANDINIDIS (16/08/75) - PAOK	M71	s46	M						s80		s64					8	-
Theodoros ZAGORAKIS (17/10/71) - Leicester City (ENG)	M	M46		M50	M46	s71	s80	M								50	-
Ilias PURSANIDIS (13/04/72) - Olympiakos	M80			D		D			s46	D46		D46	D	D	D65	29	-
Andreas NINIADIS (18/02/71) - Olympiakos	M	M46		M46	s68	s68							M46	s88	s46	12	2
Grigorios YEORGATOS (31/10/72) - Inter (ITA)	M			M	M68							M71	M77		M46	28	3
Nikolaos FRUSOS (29/04/74) - PAOK	A65	s66	s46									A				6	-
Thomas KIPARISIS (26/03/70) - Xanthi	A	A66	A46				s69	A65	A	A46	s60		A59	s58	s57	12	2
Anastasios KATSIAMBIS (30/07/73) - PAOK	s65	s46	D29		D											5	1
Ioanis PAPADIMITRIOU (15/05/76) - Xanthi	s65	s77	A				s82	s46								5	-
Paraskevas ANTZAS (18/08/76) - Olympiakos	s65	s46				D71			s67	D59						6	-
Nikolaos MIHOPOULOS (20/02/70) - PAOK	s67		G46													13	-
Emanuil DERMINTZAKIS (24/11/76) - OFI	s71		s46				s55									3	-
Yeorgios KUTSIS (10/09/73) - Aris	s80						s75	s75	s70		A46					5	-
Ilias ATMATSIDIS (24/04/69) - AEK		G46		G	G	G										47	-
Mihail KASAPIS (06/06/71) - AEK		D		D												33	-
Angelos BASINAS (03/01/76) - Panathinaikos		D46	s29				D	s83		s46	D75	D	s65	D75	s65	10	1
Andreas ZIKOS (01/06/74) - AEK		M		M	M							s46	s87	s65		10	-
Nikolaos LIMBEROPOULOS (04/08/75) - Panathinaikos		M	M	M		M	M82	s83		M	M60	M		M89	M	23	6
Andonis NIKOPOLIDIS (04/01/71) - Panathinaikos		s46	s46				G	G78		G		G	G	G		8	-
Vasilios LAKIS (10/09/76) - AEK		s46										s60		A65		3	2
Yeorgios HATZIZISIS (04/06/78) - Kavala		D60									s75					2	-
Stilianos VENETIDIS (19/11/76) - PAOK		D46				D55	D	D	D	s46	s71	s77	D	s46		10	-
Yeorgios KARANGUNIS (06/03/77) - Panathinaikos		M														1	-
Apostolos LIOLIDIS (13/08/77) - Aris		s60														2	1
Themistoklis NIKOLAIDIS (17/09/73) - AEK			A	A	A81											30	11
Stilianos YANAKOPOULOS (12/07/74) - Olympiakos			s46													11	3
Nikolaos MAHLAS (16/06/73) - Ajax (HOL)			s50	A	s81	A69	A83				A73					50	16
Yeorgios ATMANATIDIS (04/04/70) - Olympiakos			D	D			D	D46		D	D73	D		D		8	1
Vasilios TSARTAS (12/11/72) - Sevilla FC (ESP)			M	M68		M46			M65	M87	M58	M46				33	5
Yeorgios H. YEORGIADIS (08/03/72) - PAOK			s46	A	A75		A80		A	A64	A	A	A88	A		26	9
Konstandinos KONSTANDINIDIS (31/08/72)																	
- Hertha BSC Berlin (GER)			M	s64	M75						s46					25	1
Ioanis GUMAS (24/05/75) - Panathinaikos				D	D46		D66	D		s73	s75	s73				9	-
Konstandinos FRANTZESKOS (04/01/69) - PAOK				M80	M	s21	M	M	s65							38	8
Ieroklis STOLTIDIS (02/02/75) - Iraklis				M64	M83	M70	s46	s46	s73							6	-
Theofanis KATERYANAKIS (16/02/74) - Aris				s78	s60		G									3	-
Vasilios HATZIPANAGIS (26/10/54) - unattached				M21												2	-
Dimitrios MARKOS (31/01/71) - AEK				s46	M											17	1
Lambros HUTOS (12/07/79) - Roma (ITA)/Olympiakos				s46			s59									2	1
Konstandinos LUMBUTIS (10/06/79) - Aris				D46												1	-
Dimitrios NALINTZIS (25/01/76) - PAOK				s89	A57											2	-

CHAMPIONS' CUP
● **AEK**
Qualifying round AIK (SWE)

H 0-0
Atmatsidis, Petric, Zikos, Kapsis, Lakis, Kopitsis (Matjasevic 79), Savevski, Markos (Maladenis 66), Ciric, Nikolaidis, Bjekovic (Konstandinidis 76).

A 0-1
Atmatsidis, Petric, Zikos, Delas, Lakis, Markos (Matjasevic 75), Maladenis, Savevski (Konstandinidis 65), Kasapis, Ciric, Nikolaidis.

● **OLYMPIAKOS**
Champions' League
1st match REAL MADRID (ESP)

H 3-3
Giovanni (10, 64), Zahovic (67)
Eleftheropoulos, Mavrogenidis (Amponsah 46), Karataidis, Anatolakis, Ofori-Quaye, Amanatidis, Giovanni, Pursanidis, Djordjevic, Zahovic (Niniadis 85), Yanakopoulos (Gogic 59).

2nd match FC PORTO (POR)

A 0-2
Eleftheropoulos, Karataidis, Anatolakis, Amanatidis, Pursanidis, Niniadis, Zahovic (Luciano 75), Giovanni, Ofori-Quaye, Amponsah (Gogic 59), Djordjevic (Alexandris 90).

3rd match MOLDE FK (NOR)

H 3-1
Giovanni (16, 70), Luciano (77)
Eleftheropoulos, Karataidis, Anatolakis, Amanatidis, Pursanidis, Pasalis, Ofori-Quaye (Luciano 67; Antzas 77), Djordjevic, Giovanni, Zahovic, Karapialis (Gogic 60).

4th match MOLDE FK (NOR)

A 2-3
Mavrogenidis (35), Zahovic (40)
Eleftheropoulos, Mavrogenidis, Karataidis (Antzas 58), Anatolakis, Amanatidis, Pursanidis, Pasalis (Yanakopoulos 77), Giovanni, Zahovic, Djordjevic, Karapialis (Ofori-Quaye 46).

5th match REAL MADRID (ESP)

A 0-3
Eleftheropoulos, Mavrogenidis (Niniadis 75), Karataidis, Anatolakis, Amanatidis, Pursanidis, Pasalis, Zahovic, Gogic, Djordjevic, Amponsah (Yanakopoulos 60).

6th match FC PORTO (POR)

H 1-0
Yanakopoulos (55)
Eleftheropoulos, Mavrogenidis, Karataidis, Amanatidis (Gogic 46), Pasalis, Zahovic, Djordjevic, Giovanni, Ofori-Quaye (Karapialis 46), Antzas (Amponsah 78), Yanakopoulos.

UEFA CUP
● **AEK**
1st round TORPEDO KUTAISI (GEO)

A 1-0
Zikos (90)
Atmatsidis, Petric, Zikos, Delas, Lakis, Markos (Kopitsis 70), Maladenis, Kasapis, Bjekovic (Matjasevic 90), Ciric, Nikolaidis.

H 6-1
Ciric (7p), Bjekovic (21), Maladenis (24), Kopitsis (44, 88), Nikolaidis (73)
Atmatsidis, Kalintzakis, Zikos (Grétarsson 57), Delas, Savevski (Markos 66), Matjasevic, Kopitsis, Maladenis (Konstandinidis 50), Ciric, Nikolaidis, Bjekovic.

2nd round MTK HUNGÁRIA FC (HUN)

A 1-2
Ciric (61)
Atmatsidis, Kalintzakis, Zikos, Savevski (Lakis 46), Petric, Bjekovic, Maladenis (Grétarsson 26), Kopitsis, Kasapis, Ciric, Nikolaidis.

H 1-0
Ciric (75p)
Atmatsidis, Kalintzakis, Zikos, Lakis (Konstandinidis 34), Markos, Petric, Bjekovic, Kopitsis (Katsavos 81), Kasapis, Ciric, Nikolaidis.

3rd round AS MONACO (FRA)

H 2-2
Nikolaidis (45, 90)
Atmatsidis, Kapsis, Zikos, Delas, Kostenoglou, Markos (Savevski 83), Bjekovic, Maladenis, Kasapis, Ciric (Konstandinidis 83), Nikolaidis.

A 0-1
Atmatsidis, Kapsis, Zikos (Konstandinidis 75), Delas, Markos, Kostenoglou, Bjekovic, Grétarsson (Savevski 59), Kasapis, Ciric, Nikolaidis.

● **ARIS**
1st round SERVETTE FC GENEVE (SUI)

H 1-1
Mantzios (12p)
Kateryanakis, Mantzios, Lumbutis (Hristodulou 56), Koltsidas, Malous, Papadopoulos, Andrioli (Liolidis 82), Kutsis, Kizeridis (Gluscevic 46), Agathokleous, Nagoli.

A 2-1
(aet) Andrioli (37), Kizeridis (97)
Kateryanakis, Mantzios, Lumbutis, Yeorgiadis (Erak 91), Koltsidas, Malous, Papadopoulos, Andrioli, Gluscevic (Kutsis 79), Agathokleous (Kizeridis 73), Nagoli.

2nd round RC CELTA (ESP)

H 2-2
Andrioli (44), Kizeridis (68)
Kateryanakis, Mantzios, Lumbutis (Hristodulou 66), Yeorgiadis, Malous, Papadopoulos, Andrioli, Nagoli, Kizeridis, Gluscevic (Liolidis 79), Agathokleous.

A 0-2
Kateryanakis, Mantzios, Lumbutis, Koltsidas, Malous, Papadopoulos, Kizeridis (Hristodulou 72), Kutsis, Gluscevic (Liolidis 62), Agathokleous (Haristeas 88), Nagoli.

● **IONIKOS**
1st round FC NANTES (FRA)

H 1-3
Dimitriadis (90)
Strakosha, Pahaturidis (Dimitriadis 69), Deliyanis (Glauco 62), Ofridopoulos, Xanthopoulos, Haugland, Afash, Rodríguez, Kobayashi, Muchotrigo, Brewster (Alsaker 69).

A 0-1
Strakosha, Pahaturidis, Dimitriadis (Vavilis 64), Glauco (Stambulis 60), Ofridopoulos, Xanthopoulos, Girihidis, Afash, Kobayashi, Brewster, Muchotrigo (Alsaker 78).

● **OLYMPIAKOS**
3rd round JUVENTUS (ITA)

H 1-3
Yanakopoulos (14)
Eleftheropoulos, Mavrogenidis, Karataidis, Antzas, Pursanidis, Amanatidis, Niniadis, Pursaitidis (Ofori-Quaye 71), Giovanni, Yanakopoulos, Djordjevic.

A 2-1
Djordjevic (37, 80p)
Eleftheropoulos, Mavrogenidis (Yanakopoulos 46), Kostulas, Antzas, Pursanidis, Amanatidis, Pursaitidis, Pasalis, Karapialis (Niniadis 60), Djordjevic, Gogic (Alexandris 72).

subsequent match, Zahovic's response to being substituted was to verbally abuse coach Bigon. The club had had enough and suspended the player for the rest of the season.

Olympiakos did not have much luck with their expen-

EUROPEAN CUPS 99/00 (CONT.)

● **PANATHINAIKOS**
1st round HIT GORICA (SLO)
A 1-0   Limberopoulos (14)
Nikopolidis, Basinas, Olivares, Henriksen, Galetto, Gumas, Asanovic (Karangunis 84), Limberopoulos, Pflipsen (Sypniewski 71), Mykland, Warzycha (Sigurdsson 66).
H 2-0   Sigurdsson (38), Nasiopoulos (70)
Nikopolidis, Basinas, Kiasos, Henriksen, Vokolos (Gumas 66), Asanovic, Galetto (Nasiopoulos 59), Fisas, Kola, Limberopoulos (Sypniewski 76), Sigurdsson.

2nd round GRAZER AK (AUT)
A 1-2   Sypniewski (65)
Nikopolidis, Basinas, Olivares (Asanovic 85), Henriksen, Gumas, Galetto, Vokolos, Limberopoulos, Pflipsen (Kiasos 77), Karangunis (Kola 69), Sypniewski.
H 1-0   Pflipsen (90p)
Nikopolidis, Basinas, Fisas, Henriksen, Gumas, Galetto (Karangunis 73), Nasiopoulos (Warzycha 46), Limberopoulos, Pflipsen, Mykland, Sypniewski (Sigurdsson 59).

3rd round RC DEPORTIVO (ESP)
A 2-4   Warzycha (31), Galetto (67)
Nikopolidis, Basinas, Fisas, Henriksen, Gumas, Nasiopoulos, Olivares (Galetto 46), Kola, Mykland, Pflipsen (Karangunis 77), Warzycha (Sigurdsson 83).
H 1-1   Asanovic (78p)
Halkias, Basinas, Fisas, Henriksen, Gumas, Nasiopoulos (Sigurdsson 46), Olivares (Asanovic 57), Kola, Mykland, Pflipsen (Karangunis 23), Limberopoulos.

● **PAOK**
1st round LOKOMOTIVI TBILISI (GEO)
A 7-0   Yeorgiadis (17, 25), Sabry (43), Frusos (56, 62), Marangos (67), Frantzeskos (69)
Mihopoulos, Venetidis (Frantzeskos 68), Bandovic, Katsiambis, Nagbe, Frusos, Marangos (Maheridis 76), Yeorgiadis, Sabry (Vrizas 60), Dolberg, Tetradze.
H 2-0   Valencia (50), Salpingidis (87)
Kovic, Hasiotis, Maheridis (Salpingidis 62), Kulakiotis, Vrizas (Frantzeskos 62), Kafes, Valencia, Zafiriou, Karadimos, Tursunidis, Tetradze (Nagbe 62).

2nd round SL BENFICA (POR)
H 1-2   Frantzeskos (89)
Kovic, Venetidis, Frusos (Vrizas 73), Maheridis, Katsiambis, Yeorgiadis, Dolberg, Marangos, Sabry (Frantzeskos 83), Tetradze (Bandovic 54), Nagbe.
A 2-1   (aet; 4-1 on pens.) Marangos (28), Sabry (44)
Kovic, Venetidis, Maheridis, Valencia (Frusos 90), Kafes, Vrizas (Karadimos 76), Bandovic, Dolberg, Sabry (Konstandinidis 80), Marangos, Nagbe.

sive imports. Giovanni, the Brazilian striker bought from Barcelona, made a wonderful start, scoring a brace of goals in each of the team's first two home games in the Champions' League, against Real Madrid and Molde, but he was laid low with a serious knee injury soon afterwards and spent most of the season in the treatment room, returning only to indulge in the title-winning celebrations at the very end of the campaign.

PLAYERS OF THE SEASON

GRIGORIS YEORGATOS

Grigoris Yeorgatos is now back at Olympiakos but the talented Greek international had an eventful year in Italy with Inter. Early in the season he was nothing short of sensational, his brilliant left-wing surges and pin-point crosses drawing coos of admiration from fans and team-mates alike. He even got on the scoresheet twice himself, starting off a couple of routs against Lecce and Perugia in the San Siro. The shaven-headed wing-back eventually lost his place to loan signing Michele Serena but it was still a surprise when he opted to quit Inter and return to his former club after just one year. Olympiakos understandably welcomed him back with open arms - he had been the star performer in their run to the Champions' League quarter-finals in 1998/99 and had been badly missed as they dropped out of the same competition at the first group phase the following autumn.

LAMBROS HUTOS

The spelling of his name may differ from source to source, but Lambros Hutos (aka Houtos, Chutos or Choutos) gave notice during the 1999/2000 season that he could well become Greece's hottest property in the first decade of the new millennium. The youngster began the season in the youth team of Serie A giants Roma, but after he had proved his worth on several occasions in the Greek U-21 side, Olympiakos agreed to pay the Italian club £3.5m for his services. He was quickly into his stride in Piraeus, scoring six goals in his first four games and immediately becoming a favourite of the home fans as he filled the void in attack created by Giovanni's injury and Zlatko Zahovic's suspension. Shortly after his arrival he scored his first goal for the senior national team - on only his second substitute appearance - to complete a 2-0 win for Greece against Euro 2000-bound Romania in Athens.

TOP SCORERS

24	Dimitrios NALINTZIS (Panionios/PAOK)
23	Nikolaos LIMBEROPOULOS (Panathinaikos)
22	Mihail KONSTANDINOU (Iraklis)
21	Themistoklis NIKOLAIDIS (AEK)
19	Roland GOMEZ (OFI)
15	Alexios ALEXANDRIS (Olympiakos)
12	Predrag DJORDJEVIC (Olympiakos)
11	Paraskevas ZUMBULIS (Xanthi)
10	Dragan CIRIC (AEK)
	James DEBBAH (Iraklis)
	Nikolaos FRUSOS (PAOK)
	Aleksandar JOVANOVIC (Trikala)
	Jean-Jacques MISSE-MISSE (Ethnikos Astir)
	Nenad VUKCEVIC (Panahaiki)
	Krzysztof WARZYCHA (Panathinaikos)
	Stilianos YANAKOPOULOS (Olympiakos)

NATIONAL TEAM RESULTS 99/00

15/08/99	Mexico	H	Xanthi	3-2	Niniadis (21), Mavrogenidis (60), Yeorgatos (69)
18/08/99	El Salvador	H	Kavala	3-1	Limberopoulos (20, 86), Katsiambis (90)
20/08/99	El Salvador	H	Kavala	3-0	Basinas (40), Limberopoulos (50p), Liolidis (79)
04/09/99	Norway (ECQ)	A	Oslo	0-1	
06/10/99	Albania (ECQ)	H	Athens	2-0	Tsartas (1), Yeorgiadis (88)
09/10/99	Slovenia (ECQ)	A	Maribor	3-0	Tsartas (36), Yeorgiadis (42), Nikolaidis (80)
13/11/99	Nigeria	H	Kikis	2-0	Mahlas (24, 61)
17/11/99	Bulgaria	H	Kozani	1-0	Kiparisis (61)
14/12/99	Ghana	H	Salonika	1-1	Kiparisis (15)
16/12/99	Moldova	H	Larisa	2-0	Yeorgiadis (61), Frantzeskos (63)
18/12/99	Estonia	H	Trikala	2-2	Yeorgiadis (18), Limberopoulos (47p)
23/02/00	Austria	H	Kalamata	4-1	Yeorgiadis (36, 55), Uzunidis (82), Lakis (90)
29/03/00	Romania	H	Athens	2-0	Amanatidis (59), Hutos (88)
26/04/00	Republic of Ireland	A	Dublin	1-0	Lakis (16)
03/06/00	Romania	A	Bucharest	1-2	Limberopoulos (85)

With the two big stars absent, Olympiakos drew inspiration from within and played as a team. Their defence was exceptional, with the all-Greek back-line of Dimitrios Mavrogenidis, Yeorgios Anatolakis and Yeorgios Amanatidis helping goalkeeper Dimitrios Eleftheropoulos to keep a succession of shut-outs. At the other end of the field, the goals were generously shared out, with winger Alexios Alexandris and playmaker Predrag Djordjevic leading the way on 15 and 12 goals, respectively.

Olympiakos's quest for a second successive 'double' was thwarted by AEK, who beat them 4-1 on aggregate in the quarter-finals of the Cup. AEK's 3-0 victory in the second leg, played in the Olympic Stadium, was accompanied by sickening scenes of violence as Olympiakos fans went on the rampage, destroying cars belonging to the Olympiakos players and, before the match, setting fire to

DOMESTIC CUP 99/00

SECOND PHASE
Kavala 1, Panionios 2
Neapoli 2, Yanina 1
Ionikos 4, Marko 1
Paniliakos 0, Olympiakos 1
Kalamata 3, Proodeftiki 0
Nafpaktiakos Astir 1, Neapoli 0
Ethnikos Astir 3, Panionios 3 (4-5 on pens.)
Ionikos 4, Iraklis 2
OFI 3, Ayersani 0
AEK 6, Trikala 0
Olympiakos 2, PAOK 1
Aris 1, Panathinaikos 1 (4-2 on pens.)

QUARTER-FINALS
Ionikos 8 (Kobayashi 2, 79, Brewster 14, Haugland 47, 85, 89, Ofridopoulos 72, Afendulidis 90),
Nafpaktiakos Astir 0
Nafpaktiakos Astir 2 (Karayeorgos 58, Papapostolou 74), Ionikos 1 (Afendulidis 80)
(Ionikos 9-2)

Aris 0, Panionios 0
Panionios 2 (Krcmarevic 12, Ioanou 42), Aris 0
(Panionios 2-0)
Olympiakos 1 (Alexandris 74), AEK 1 (Lakis 31)
AEK 3 (Nikolaidis 25, Kopitsis 30, Petkov 48),
Olympiakos 0
(AEK 4-1)
OFI 1 (Tourment 83), Kalamata 0
Kalamata 3 (Trupkos 45, 75, Soãres 83), OFI 0
(Kalamata 3-1)

SEMI-FINALS
Kalamata 0, Ionikos 2 (Muchotrigo 84, Roberts 90)
Ionikos 4 (Xanthopoulos 9, Muchotrigo 50, Tsiavdaris 90, Afash 90), Kalamata 2 (Simons 59, Kapos 85)
(Ionikos 6-2)
AEK 4 (Nikolaidis 23p, 45, 53, Lakis 34),
Panionios 1 (Sapuntzis 86p)
Panionios 2 (Kafalis 72, Krcmarevic 90),
AEK 1 (Ciric 60)
(AEK 5-3)

FINAL
10/05/2000, Athens
AEK 3 Nikolaidis (32), Petkov (77), Maladenis (82)
IONIKOS 0
referee - Duros
AEK - Atmatsidis, Lakis, Kasapis, Delas, Kapsis, Kalintzakis (Savevski 85), Zikos, Nikolaidis, Konstandinidis (Maladenis 81), Petkov, Ciric (Karayani 70).
IONIKOS - Strakosha, Haugland, Pahaturidis (Girihidis 70), Xanthopoulos, Daraklitsas, Deliyanis, Ofridopoulos (Ledesma 70), Afash, Kobajashi (Muchotrigo 57), Roberts, Brewster.

a coach which was bringing AEK fans to the game.

AEK went on to win the Cup, beating Ionikos easily in the final. Panathinaikos's hopes of lifting that trophy were ended in sensational fashion when Aris beat them on penalties in the second round. The 'Greens' were thus left with nothing to show for a fine season other than a place in the qualifying round of the 2000/01 Champions' League. In any other year their haul of 88 points would have been enough to take the championship, but despite the contributions of 23-goal Nikolaos Limberopoulos, goalkeeper Andonios Nikopolidis and Scandinavians René Henriksen and Erik Mykland, they just didn't have quite enough to catch Olympiakos.

For the second season running Greece were entitled to four UEFA Cup places, which were taken by AEK, PAOK, OFI and - after a play-off victory over Aris - Iraklis. Play-offs were also expected to sort out a couple of the relegation places, but in the event they were not needed. The rule had been that in addition to the teams placed 17th

and 18th being relegated automatically, the teams placed between 13th and 16th place would have to play off if there was a gap of five points or less between them. But as Kavala and Proodeftiki were further adrift than that, the rule was waived and the two clubs went straight down. With the top division being reduced to 16 teams in 2000/01 (and to 14 in 2001/02), only two teams, Athinaikos and - after play-offs - Yanina, came up.

It was a busy season for the Greek national team, who played 15 matches, 12 of them friendlies. Coach Vasilios Daniil tried out 44 players and the results were pretty encouraging - 11 wins, two draws, two defeats and 30 goals. By the end of the season it looked as if Greece had a team ready and able to meet the challenge of a World Cup qualifying campaign in which they had been drawn to face Germany, England, Finland and Albania. But the proof of the pudding, as they say...

PROMOTED CLUBS 99/00

SECOND DIVISION FINAL TABLE

		Pd	W	D	L	F	A	Pt	GD
1	**Athinaikos**	**34**	**21**	**8**	**5**	**56**	**21**	**71**	**35**
2	Egaleo	34	22	4	8	60	29	70	31
3	**Yanina**	**34**	**20**	**6**	**8**	**52**	**23**	**66**	**29**
4	Panseraikos	34	19	8	7	54	27	65	27
5	Apollon Thessaloniki	34	16	9	9	54	29	57	25
6	Larisa	34	16	7	11	55	39	55	16
7	Panegialios	34	14	9	11	47	45	51	2
8	Panetolikos	34	14	8	12	43	34	50	9
9	Olympiakos Volou	34	15	5	14	46	41	50	5
10	Kalithea	34	14	7	13	41	38	49	3
11	Agios Nikolaos	34	14	7	13	44	40	49	4
12	Panelefsiniakos	34	12	9	13	50	49	45	1
13	Veria	34	12	8	14	37	40	44	-3
14	Nausa	34	11	7	16	37	52	40	-15
15	Ethnikos	34	7	8	19	53	72	29	-19
16	Ialisos	34	7	4	23	26	78	25	-52
17	Pierikos	34	4	7	23	16	62	19	-46
18	Anayenisi Karditsas	34	4	7	23	31	83	19	-52

PROMOTION PLAY-OFFS
Egaleo 2, Panseraikos 2
Yanina 3, Panseraikos 2
Egaleo 1, Yanina 1
(Yanina promoted)

CLUB DIRECTORIES

Athinaikos
Karaoil-Dimitriou 67
Athina
tel - 7645500
Year of Formation - 1917
President - Dimitrios Karangunis
Coach - Anastasios Hatziangelis
Stadium - Virona (6,000)

Yanina
N. Zerva 28-30
Yanina
tel - (0651) 27478/32639
Year of Formation - 1966
President - Manthos Kolembas
Coach - Andreas Mihalopoulos
Stadium - Zosimadon (15,000)

AEK

CLUB DIRECTORY

Athlitiki Enosi Konstantinoupoleos (AEK)
Tritis Septemvriou 144
11251 Athina
tel - 8224666/8215645
fax - 8234454
Year of Formation - 1924
President - Cornelius Sirhaus
Coach - Ljubisa Tumbakovic; Dimitrios
Karangiozopoulos; Ioanis Pathiakakis
Stadium - Nikos Goumas (33,494)

MAJOR HONOURS
League Championship - (11)
1939, 1940, 1963, 1968, 1971, 1978, 1979,
1989, 1992, 1993, 1994.
Domestic Cup - (11) 1932, 1939, 1949, 1950,
1956, 1966, 1978, 1983, 1996, 1997, 2000.

APPEARANCES 99/00

	P	Ap	(s)	Gls
Ilias ANASTASAKOS	A		(1)	
Ilias ATMATSIDIS	G	33		
Davide BELOTTI (ITA)	D		(1)	
Nenad BJEKOVIC (YUG)	A	16	(5)	5
Pablo Daniel CANTERO (ARG)	M		(1)	
Dragan CIRIC (YUG)	M	26		10
Traianos DELAS	D	19	(2)	3
Arnar GRÉTARSSON (ISL)	M	7	(7)	
Ioanis KALINTZAKIS	D	17	(6)	1
Mihail KAPSIS	D	26		2
Vaios KARAYANIS	D	11	(1)	
Mihail KASAPIS	D	13		1
Evripidis KATSAVOS	M		(10)	
Yeorgios KAVAZIS (CYP)	M		(3)	
Sotirios KONSTANDINIDIS	A	13	(12)	6
Harilaos KOPITSIS	D	24	(4)	
Nikolaos KOSTENOGLOU	D	17	(3)	
Vasilios LAKIS	M	14	(3)	3
Hristos MALADENIS	M	16	(7)	6
Dimitrios MARKOS	M	15	(14)	2
Vladimir MATJASEVIC (YUG)	D		(3)	
Hrisostomos MIHAILIDIS	G	1		
Themistoklis NIKOLAIDIS	A	32		21
Yeorgios PASIOS	A		(5)	
Milen PETKOV (BUL)	M	15		2
Goran PETRIC (YUG)	D	7		
Toni SAVEVSKI (MAC)	M	25	(6)	2
Andreas ZIKOS	M	27		1

LEAGUE RESULTS 1999/2000

20/09/99	PAOK	A	4-4	Ciric (p), Nikolaidis, og (Dolberg), Delas
26/09/99	Panathinaikos	H	1-2	Zikos
03/10/99	Ethnikos Astir	A	3-1	Ciric, Konstandinidis, Markos
17/10/99	Iraklis	H	3-2	Ciric 3 (2p)
25/10/99	Paniliakos	A	1-0	Bjekovic
31/10/99	Olympiakos	H	0-2	
06/11/99	Ionikos	A	1-1	og (Xanthopoulos)
20/11/99	Aris	H	2-0	Kapsis, og (Mantzios)
28/11/99	OFI	H	1-2	Konstandinidis
05/12/99	Xanthi	A	2-2	Markos, Konstandinidis
12/12/99	Panahaiki	H	3-0	Kapsis, Nikolaidis 2
22/12/99	Proodeftiki	A	4-1	Nikolaidis, og (Rutzieris), Bjekovic, Ciric
29/12/99	Panionios	H	0-1	
09/01/00	Apollon	A	2-3	Bjekovic, Kalintzakis
16/01/00	Kavala	H	3-0	Maladenis 3
23/01/00	Trikala	A	1-0	Ciric
31/01/00	Kalamata	A	1-1	Maladenis
06/02/00	PAOK	H	2-0	Nikolaidis 2
13/02/00	Panathinaikos	A	0-1	
20/02/00	Ethnikos Astir	H	2-1	Bjekovic, Ciric (p)
27/02/00	Iraklis	A	1-3	Savevski
05/03/00	Paniliakos	H	1-0	Ciric
12/03/00	Olympiakos	A	0-3	
19/03/00	Ionikos	H	5-1	Konstandinidis, Nikolaidis 4
24/03/00	Aris	A	1-1	Nikolaidis
01/04/00	OFI	A	2-1	Lakis, Petkov
12/04/00	Xanthi	H	4-1	Nikolaidis 2, Maladenis 2
16/04/00	Panahaiki	A	1-1	Konstandinidis
23/04/00	Proodeftiki	H	3-2	Petkov, Lakis, Nikolaidis (p)
03/05/00	Panionios	A	2-0	Nikolaidis 2
08/05/00	Apollon	H	3-0	Nikolaidis (p), Lakis, Ciric
14/05/00	Kavala	A	2-0	Nikolaidis 2
21/05/00	Trikala	H	2-1	Savevski, Delas
28/05/00	Kalamata	H	6-1	Nikolaidis 2 (2p), Kasapis, Konstandinidis, Delas, Bjekovic

APOLLON

CLUB DIRECTORY

Apollon
Antheon 45
Rizupoli
11143 Athina
tel - 2516632
fax - 2517632
Year of Formation - 1891
President - Andreas Alamanos
Coach - Hristos Arhondidis; Nikolaos Kovis;
Stefanos Gaitanos; Andreas Mihalopoulos;
Evangelos Tsingulis
Stadium - Rizoupolis (15,000)

APPEARANCES 99/00

	P	Ap	(s)	Gls
Theodoros ALEXIS	M	5	(2)	
Ilias ANASTASAKOS	A	10	(1)	3
Stojan BELAJIC (CRO)	D	26	(3)	
Guy BUELE (CMR)	M		(3)	
Zoran CIRIC (YUG)	M	7	(9)	1
Edmond DALIPI (ALB)	M	9	(2)	
Panayotis DAMVERGIS	M		(1)	
Panayotis DEDAKIS	A	4	(4)	
Yeorgios DIAMANDIS	D	8	(2)	
Indrit FORTUZI (ALB)	M	6	(23)	1
Hristos GANTZUDIS	M	13	(2)	
Mihail HATZIS	A	11	(12)	1
Spiridon HATZIS	D	29	(1)	1
Yeorgios HIMARIOS	M	1		
Konstandinos IOANOU	D	11		
Athanasios KARANIKOLAS	D	19	(3)	1
Hristos LAIOS	M	21	(1)	
Stavros LAMBRIAKOS	A	31		7
Ali Reza MANSURIAN (IRN)	M	4	(3)	1
Theofilaktos NIKOLAIDIS	D	19	(3)	
Athanasios PANGURAS	D	10	(2)	
Theodoros PAPADIMITRIOU	A	24	(2)	4
Miloje PETKOVIC (YUG)	M	19	(1)	1
Yeorgios PODARAS	M	9		
Dimitrios RUSOS	D	11	(1)	
Nikolaos SFAKIANAKIS	A	11	(8)	1
Nikolaos SKARMUTSOS	M	12	(5)	3
Tihomir TODOROV (BUL)	G	6	(4)	
Andonios VULGARIS	G	2		
Yeorgios VUREXAKIS	M	10	(4)	2
Jozef WANDZIK (POL)	G	26		

LEAGUE RESULTS 1999/2000

19/09/99	Iraklis	A	0-1	
26/09/99	Paniliakos	H	0-0	
03/10/99	Olympiakos	H	0-1	
16/10/99	Ionikos	A	0-1	
25/10/99	Aris	H	3-3	Lambriakos, Papadimitriou, og (Yanopoulos)
31/10/99	OFI	A	0-1	
07/11/99	Xanthi	H	0-0	
21/11/99	Panahaiki	A	2-1	og (Iakovou), Anastasakos
28/11/99	Proodeftiki	H	0-2	
05/12/99	Panionios	A	1-3	Anastasakos
11/12/99	Kalamata	A	1-1	Anastasakos
22/12/99	Kavala	H	0-2	
29/12/99	Trikala	A	0-1	
09/01/00	AEK	H	3-2	Lambriakos, Karanikolas, Ciric
16/01/00	PAOK	A	1-1	Fortuzi
23/01/00	Panathinaikos	H	0-3	
30/01/00	Ethnikos Astir	A	1-3	Hatzis S.
07/02/00	Iraklis	H	1-0	Lambriakos
13/02/00	Paniliakos	A	1-2	Papadimitriou
20/02/00	Olympiakos	A	0-2	
27/02/00	Ionikos	H	0-2	
05/03/00	Aris	A	1-2	Petkovic
12/03/00	OFI	H	1-2	Hatzis M.
19/03/00	Xanthi	A	0-2	
26/03/00	Panahaiki	H	0-0	
02/04/00	Proodeftiki	A	0-2	
12/04/00	Panionios	H	2-1	Lambriakos 2
16/04/00	Kalamata	H	1-2	og (Kefalas)
23/04/00	Kavala	A	3-1	Vurexakis, Sfakianakis, Mansurian
03/05/00	Trikala	H	5-2	Skarmutsos 3, Papadimitriou, Lambriakos
08/05/00	AEK	A	0-3	
13/05/00	PAOK	H	3-4	Vurexakis, Lambriakos, Papadimitriou
21/05/00	Panathinaikos	A	0-5	
28/05/00	Ethnikos Astir	H	0-1	

ARIS

CLUB DIRECTORY

Aris
Vasilisis Olgas 126
Thesaloniki
tel - (031) 862700
fax - (031) 862632
Year of Formation - 1914
President - Lakis Ioannidis
Coach - Ilija Petkovic; Ioanis Mihalitsios &
Yeorgios Semertzidis
Stadium - Harilaou (28,000)

MAJOR HONOURS
League Championship - (3) 1928, 1932, 1946.
Domestic Cup - (1) 1970.

APPEARANCES 99/00

	P	Ap	(s)	Gls
Marios AGATHOKLEOUS (CYP)	M	15	(12)	6
Paulo ANDRIOLI (BRA)	M	15	(2)	4
Theodoros DALKIDIS	M		(1)	
Predrag ERAK (CRO)	M	3	(2)	
Igor GLUSCEVIC (YUG)	A	23	(7)	8
Angelos HARISTEAS	A	10	(9)	1
Marios HRISTODULOU (CYP)	M	8	(16)	1
Merkurios KARALIOPOULOS	D	10	(2)	
Theofanis KATERYANAKIS	G	34		
Panayotis KATSIAROS	D	5	(13)	
Nikolaos KIZERIDIS	A	24	(2)	8
Yeorgios KOLTSIDAS	D	24		3
Yeorgios KUTSIS	M	24	(1)	3
Daniel Batista LIMA	A	2	(3)	
Apostolos LIOLIDIS	A	12	(9)	5
Konstandinos LUMBUTIS	M	32		1
Jozef MAJOROS (SVK)	A		(2)	
Ioanis MALOUS	D	29		1
Apostolos MANTZIOS	D	13		2
Kennedy NAGOLI (ZIM)	M	33		
Nikolaos PAPADOPOULOS	D	32		5
Dragan RADOJICIC (YUG)	M	3	(4)	1
Miroslav SAVIC (YUG)	D	9	(2)	
Yeorgios THEODORIDIS	D	3	(1)	
Oleg VERETENNIKOV (RUS)	M		(7)	
Yeorgios YEORGIADIS	D	11		
Panayotis YANOPOULOS	D		(1)	

LEAGUE RESULTS 1999/2000

20/09/99	Xanthi	A	0-0	
26/09/99	Panahaiki	H	2-0	Gluscevic, Agathokleous
04/10/99	Proodeftiki	A	1-0	Gluscevic
17/10/99	Panionios	H	5-1	Gluscevic, Koltsidas 2, Andrioli, Agathokleous
25/10/99	Apollon	A	3-3	Andrioli 2, Liolidis
31/10/99	Kavala	H	1-0	Agathokleous
08/11/99	Trikala	A	1-0	Radojicic
20/11/99	AEK	A	0-2	
28/11/99	PAOK	H	0-0	
05/12/99	Panathinaikos	A	0-3	
12/12/99	Ethnikos Astir	H	1-1	Malous
22/12/99	Iraklis	A	0-2	
30/12/99	Paniliakos	H	2-1	Kizeridis 2
09/01/00	Olympiakos	A	0-2	
17/01/00	Ionikos	H	1-1	Haristeas
23/01/00	Kalamata	H	6-1	Liolidis 3, Kutsis, Agathokleous, Gluscevic
30/01/00	OFI	A	1-2	Liolidis
06/02/00	Xanthi	H	0-1	
14/02/00	Panahaiki	A	2-1	Lumbutis, Koltsidas
20/02/00	Proodeftiki	H	2-1	Kizeridis, Papadopoulos
27/02/00	Panionios	A	3-1	Papadopoulos (p), Kutsis, Agathokleous
05/03/00	Apollon	H	2-1	Agathokleous, Gluscevic
12/03/00	Kavala	A	0-1	
19/03/00	Trikala	H	3-3	Andrioli, Kizeridis, Kutsis
25/03/00	AEK	H	1-1	Papadopoulos (p)
02/04/00	PAOK	A	2-3	og (Amponsah), Kizeridis
12/04/00	Panathinaikos	H	0-2	
16/04/00	Ethnikos Astir	A	0-1	
22/04/00	Iraklis	H	2-1	Papadopoulos (p), Gluscevic
03/05/00	Paniliakos	A	2-1	Hristodoulou, Gluscevic
08/05/00	Olympiakos	H	0-1	
14/05/00	Ionikos	A	2-2	Gluscevic, Kizeridis (p)
21/05/00	Kalamata	A	2-5	Papadopoulos, Kizeridis
28/05/00	OFI	H	3-1	Mantzios 2 (1p), Kizeridis

ETHNIKOS ASTIR

CLUB DIRECTORY

Ethnikos Astir
Ethnikis Antistasis 118
Kesariani
Athina
tel - 7238652
Year of Formation - 1927
President - Nikos Papadopoulos
Coach - Spiros Livathinos
Stadium - Kaisariadis (4,200)

APPEARANCES 99/00

	P	Ap	(s)	Gls
Stefanos BASINAS	M	30	(1)	2
Hussein BENALI (FRA)	M	27	(3)	3
Ilias BOTAITIS	A	2	(3)	
Miroslav BRADVIC (CRO)	D	1	(3)	
Dimitrios ERMILIOS	A		(3)	
Filipos FRONTZOS	D	13	(2)	1
Theodosios KIKIDAKIS	A	1	(7)	
Hristos KIURKOS	G	22		
Yeorgios KONDOPOULOS	A	27	(4)	4
Nikolaos KOSTAKIS	G	4		
Fotios LAGOS	D	29		
Branko MILOVANOVIC (YUG)	M	8	(7)	2
Jean-Jacques MISSE-MISSE (CMR)	A	25	(5)	9
Hristos PANAGULIS	D		(1)	
Dimosthenis PAPATHANASIOU	D	2	(9)	
Milan PAVLOVIC (YUG)	D	32		
Yeorgios PODARAS	M	13	(4)	
Sotirios PSARUDAKIS	M		(2)	
Youssef SALIMI (FRA)	D		(1)	
Mohamed SHAKIR (MAR)	M		(3)	
Evangelos STAVRAKOPOULOS	D		(1)	
Stjepan STOJANOVIC (YUG)	G	8		
Stanko SVITLICA (YUG)	A	1	(20)	1
Darko TESOVIC (YUG)	M	29	(3)	7
Ilias TRIANDAFILOU	D	32		
Konstandinos TSALIKIS	M	31	(2)	1
Vasilios XANTHIS	M	23	(3)	3
Dionisios YEORGOPOULOS	D	14	(13)	

LEAGUE RESULTS 1999/2000

19/09/99	Kavala	H	1-0	Kondopoulos
26/09/99	Trikala	A	2-1	Kondopoulos, Tsalikis
03/10/99	AEK	H	1-3	Xanthis
17/10/99	PAOK	A	0-2	
25/10/99	Panathinaikos	H	1-2	Svitlica
31/10/99	Kalamata	H	2-0	Missé-Missé, Benali
07/11/99	Iraklis	A	0-2	
21/11/99	Paniliakos	H	3-1	Kondopoulos, Tesovic, Benali
28/11/99	Olympiakos	A	0-5	
05/12/99	Ionikos	H	1-2	Xanthis
12/12/99	Aris	A	1-1	Frontzos
22/12/99	OFI	H	0-1	
29/12/99	Xanthi	A	0-0	
09/01/00	Panahaiki	A	0-2	
16/01/00	Proodeftiki	H	1-0	Missé-Missé
23/01/00	Panionios	A	0-1	
30/01/00	Apollon	H	3-1	Missé-Missé 3
06/02/00	Kavala	A	0-2	
13/02/00	Trikala	H	1-0	Basinas
20/02/00	AEK	A	1-2	Milovanovic
27/02/00	PAOK	H	1-1	Milovanovic
05/03/00	Panathinaikos	A	0-4	
13/03/00	Kalamata	A	0-1	
20/03/00	Iraklis	H	3-1	Benali, Missé-Missé 2
26/03/00	Paniliakos	A	0-2	
03/04/00	Olympiakos	H	1-1	Basinas
12/04/00	Ionikos	A	0-3	
16/04/00	Aris	H	1-0	Tesovic
23/04/00	OFI	A	1-4	Missé-Missé
03/05/00	Xanthi	H	1-0	Missé-Missé
07/05/00	Panahaiki	H	2-2	Tesovic 2 (1p)
14/05/00	Proodeftiki	A	0-1	
21/05/00	Panionios	H	4-2	Tesovic 2 (1p), Xanthis, Kondopoulos
28/05/00	Apollon	A	1-0	Tesovic

IONIKOS

CLUB DIRECTORY

Ionikos
Petrou Ralli 248
18451 Nikea Pireas
tel - (01) 4945000
fax - (01) 4964502
Year of Formation - 1965
President - Nikos Kanelakis
Coach - Konstandinos Polihroniou;
Sokratis Yemelos; Oleg Blokhin
Stadium - Neapolis (7,000)

APPEARANCES 99/00

	P	Ap	(s)	Gls
Mohamed AFASH (SYR)	M	31		4
Dimitrios AFENDULIDIS	A	4	(9)	1
Pål Christian ALSAKER (NOR)	A	1	(6)	
Craig BREWSTER (SCO)	A	31		8
Hristos DAGUNAKIS	M		(1)	
Yeorgios DARAKLITSAS	M	23	(3)	3
Dimitrios DELIYANIS	M	16	(6)	
Ioanis DIMITRIADIS	M	4	(1)	
Ioanis GIRIHIDIS	M	21	(6)	
António Santos GLAUCO (BRA)	M	1	(4)	
Trond Inge HAUGLAND (NOR)	D	23	(1)	
Paulo KOBAYASHI (BRA)	M	32		7
Fabian LEDESMA (ARG)	M	17	(2)	1
Baltan LEKNER (COL)	A		(3)	
Dimitrios MILONAS	M		(3)	
Dario MUCHOTRIGO (PER)	A	22	(8)	4
Sokratis OFRIDOPOULOS	D	18	(1)	2
Theodoros PAHATURIDIS	D	25	(1)	
Athanasios PANGURAS	D		(1)	
Zizi ROBERTS (LIB)	A	15		8
Martin RODRIGUEZ (PER)	M	12	(4)	
Yeorgios STAMBULIS	M	3	(10)	
Foto STRAKOSHA (ALB)	G	32		
Nikolaos TSIAVDARIS	M		(1)	
Alejandros TSOLAS	D	5	(4)	
Apostolos TSOPTSIS	D	7	(6)	
Kornelius UTEBULUZOR (NIG)	M		(4)	
Nikolaos VAVILIS	M	1	(2)	
Hrisostomos VENIAMIN	G	2	(1)	
Ioanis XANTHOPOULOS	D	28	(1)	1

LEAGUE RESULTS 1999/2000

20/09/99	Panahaiki	A	1-1	Afash
26/09/99	Proodeftiki	H	2-0	Brewster, Ofridopoulos
04/10/99	Panionios	A	0-2	
16/10/99	Apollon	H	1-0	Xanthopoulos
25/10/99	Kavala	A	0-0	
31/10/99	Trikala	A	2-2	Muchotrigo, Afash
07/11/99	AEK	H	1-1	Afash
21/11/99	PAOK	A	0-3	
28/11/99	Panathinaikos	H	2-2	Brewster, Ofridopoulos
05/12/99	Ethnikos Astir	A	2-1	Kobayashi 2
12/12/99	Iraklis	H	1-1	Brewster
22/12/99	Paniliakos	A	0-3	
29/12/99	Olympiakos	H	1-2	Muchotrigo
09/01/00	Kalamata	H	0-1	
17/01/00	Aris	A	1-1	Ledesma
23/01/00	OFI	H	1-1	Brewster
30/01/00	Xanthi	A	1-2	Daraklitsas
06/02/00	Panahaiki	H	0-0	
13/02/00	Proodeftiki	A	2-2	Roberts, Brewster
20/02/00	Panionios	H	2-0	Roberts 2
27/02/00	Apollon	A	2-0	Daraklitsas, Muchotrigo
06/03/00	Kavala	H	2-0	Roberts 2
12/03/00	Trikala	H	5-1	og (Angelopoulos), Afash,
				Kobayashi, Brewster, Muchotrigo
19/03/00	AEK	A	1-5	Roberts
26/03/00	PAOK	H	1-0	Afendulidis
02/04/00	Panathinaikos	A	0-5	
12/04/00	Ethnikos Astir	H	3-0	Daraklitsas, Kobayashi 2
16/04/00	Iraklis	A	2-3	Kobayashi, Brewster
23/04/00	Paniliakos	H	0-2	
03/05/00	Olympiakos	A	0-2	
07/05/00	Kalamata	A	0-2	
14/05/00	Aris	H	2-2	Kobayashi, Roberts
21/05/00	OFI	A	0-2	
28/05/00	Xanthi	H	2-1	Brewster, Roberts

IRAKLIS

Iraklis
Vasileos Yeorgiou 33 A
54640 Thesaloniki
tel - (031) 834300/834534
fax - (031) 836262
Year of Formation - 1908
President - Evangelos Mitilineos
Coach - Angelos Anastasiadis
Stadium - Kaftantzoglio (45,000)

MAJOR HONOURS
Domestic Cup - (1) 1976.

APPEARANCES 99/00

	P	Ap	(s)	Gls
Nikolaos ADAMIDIS	D	2	(12)	
Frank AMANKUEH (GHA)	D	5	(1)	
Nikolaos ARGIRIOU	G	20		
Panayotis BEKIARIS	A	1	(12)	
Mihail BERNEANOU	D	4	(3)	
Aleksandar BRATIC (YUG)	D	7		
James DEBBAH (LIB)	A	27	(1)	10
Panayotis DILBERIS	G	11	(4)	
Ebenezer HAGAN (GHA)	M	31		2
Dimitrios KAPETANOPOULOS	D	17	(3)	
Nekelenda-Sam KASIMBA (DRC)	M	12	(8)	
Levan KEBADZE (GEO)	A	5	(7)	3
Yeorgios KIRIAZIS	D	14	(6)	1
Mihail KONSTANDINOU (CYP)	A	29	(2)	22
Athanasios MUTSIOS	M	12	(10)	
Ilias SAPANIS	A	12	(8)	3
Kelvin SEBWE (LIB)	M	32		6
Lazaros SEMOS	D	26		1
Haralambos SOTIRIADIS	M		(5)	
Haralambos STEFANIDIS	D		(1)	
Ieroklis STOLTIDIS	M	30		5
Ilias STOYANIS	G	3		
Efstathios TAVLARIDIS	D	17	(6)	
Panayotis TSANGARIS	A		(2)	
Stavros TZIORTZIOPOULOS	D	9		
Hristos VELIS	M	16	(3)	1
Yeorgios XENIDIS	D	21	(5)	3
Ahilefs ZAFIRIOU	M	11	(1)	

LEAGUE RESULTS 1999/2000

19/09/99	Apollon	H	1-0	Sapanis
27/09/99	Kavala	A	1-3	Konstandinou (p)
03/10/99	Trikala	H	4-1	Semos, Konstandinou 2 (1p), Sebwe
17/10/99	AEK	A	2-3	Konstandinou, Sebwe
25/10/99	PAOK	H	3-1	Velis, Konstandinou 2
31/10/99	Panathinaikos	A	0-3	
07/11/99	Ethnikos Astir	H	2-0	Sapanis, Sebwe
21/11/99	Kalamata	H	2-1	Hagan, Stoltidis
28/11/99	Paniliakos	A	3-4	Stoltidis, Debbah 2
06/12/99	Olympiakos	H	3-4	Debbah 2 (1p), Xenidis
12/12/99	Ionikos	A	1-1	Sebwe
22/12/99	Aris	H	2-0	Konstandinou, Sebwe
29/12/99	OFI	A	1-1	Konstandinou
09/01/00	Xanthi	H	3-1	Konstandinou, Hagan, Debbah
16/01/00	Panahaiki	A	1-0	Debbah
23/01/00	Proodeftiki	A	1-0	Konstandinou
30/01/00	Panionios	H	1-2	Konstandinou
07/02/00	Apollon	A	0-1	
13/02/00	Kavala	H	2-1	Konstandinou (p), Stoltidis
20/02/00	Trikala	A	3-3	Kiriazis, Debbah, Stoltidis
27/02/00	AEK	H	3-1	Xenidis, Konstandinou 2 (1p)
05/03/00	PAOK	A	0-4	
12/03/00	Panathinaikos	H	1-3	Konstandinou (p)
20/03/00	Ethnikos Astir	A	1-3	Xenidis
26/03/00	Kalamata	A	2-2	Debbah, Kebadze
02/04/00	Paniliakos	H	3-1	Sapanis, Debbah, Sebwe
12/04/00	Olympiakos	A	0-1	
16/04/00	Ionikos	H	3-2	og (Xanthopoulos), Debbah, Konstandinou
22/04/00	Aris	A	1-2	Konstandinou (p)
03/05/00	OFI	H	0-3	
07/05/00	Xanthi	A	0-3	
14/05/00	Panahaiki	H	2-1	Stoltidis, Kebadze
21/05/00	Proodeftiki	H	4-0	Konstandinou 3 (1p), Kebadze
28/05/00	Panionios	A	2-2	Konstandinou 2

KALAMATA

CLUB DIRECTORY

Kalamata
Iatropoulou & Dagre 2A
24100 Kalamata
tel - (0721) 94000
fax - (0721) 93334
Year of Formation - 1967
President - Dimitrios Tsihlis
Coach - Eduardo Amorim; Vasilios Yeorgopoulos &
Anastasios Siulas
Stadium - Mesiniakou (10,000)

APPEARANCES 99/00

	P	Ap	(s)	Gls
Vasilios ALEVIZOS	D		(2)	
Mihail ALVERTIS	M	2	(4)	
Cláudio ALVES OLIVEIRA (BRA)	D	18	(4)	
Panayotis BAHRAMIS	M	15	(1)	2
Yerasimos BELEVONIS	D	21	(4)	
Vasilios BLETSAS	M	10		
Derek BOATENG (GHA)	A	10	(7)	5
Lee BULLEN (SCO)	A	2	(3)	
Carlos Luís DACROS (BRA)	M	17	(3)	3
Konstandinos DASKALAKIS	M	3	(4)	
Panayotis DRUGAS	M	27	(2)	
Aristidis GALANOPOULOS	D	11	(3)	
Geronimo HILTON (BRA)	A	22	(3)	6
Konstandinos IOANOU	D	9	(1)	
Hristos KALANTZIS	A	6	(4)	1
Efstathios KAPOS	A	3	(4)	1
Evangelos KEFALAS	D	11	(1)	1
Hristos KELPEKIS	G	15	(1)	
Dimitrios KONSTANDOPOULOS	G	2		
Vasilios KOSIFOLOGOS	M		(1)	
Evangelos KUTSURES	M	30	(1)	6
Dimitrios KUTIVAS	D	1		
Sotirios LIMBEROPOULOS	G	17		
Hristos MIKES	D	21	(3)	
Geraldo ROSA LUCINDO (BRA)	M		(1)	
Charles SAMSON (GHA)	M	13	(6)	1
Sandro SCAPIN (BRA)	D	3	(2)	
Jerry SIMONS (HOL)	A	3	(6)	1
Alexandre SOÃRES (BRA)	A	23	(3)	3
Themistoklis TZANETIS	D	20	(4)	
Thomas TRUPKOS	A	15	(9)	7
Nikolaos YEORGEAS	D	24	(4)	1

LEAGUE RESULTS 1999/2000

18/09/99	OFI	H	0-0	
26/09/99	PAOK	A	2-4	Dacros, Soãres
03/10/99	Xanthi	H	0-0	
17/10/99	Panathinaikos	A	0-5	
25/10/99	Panahaiki	H	1-1	Hilton
31/10/99	Ethnikos Astir	A	0-2	
07/11/99	Proodeftiki	H	2-0	Hilton 2
21/11/99	Iraklis	A	1-2	Hilton
28/11/99	Panionios	H	1-3	Bahramis
05/12/99	Paniliakos	A	1-3	Dacros
12/12/99	Apollon	H	1-1	Boateng
22/12/99	Olympiakos	A	1-4	Hilton
29/12/99	Kavala	H	3-2	Boateng, Kutsures, Soãres
09/01/00	Ionikos	A	1-0	Kutsures
16/01/00	Trikala	H	0-1	
23/01/00	Aris	A	1-6	Hilton
31/01/00	AEK	H	1-1	Bahramis
06/02/00	OFI	A	2-3	Kutsures, Kefalas
13/02/00	PAOK	H	1-1	Soãres
20/02/00	Xanthi	A	0-1	
27/02/00	Panathinaikos	H	0-0	
05/03/00	Panahaiki	A	2-1	Trupkos, Dacros
12/03/00	Ethnikos Astir	H	1-0	Samson
19/03/00	Proodeftiki	A	2-1	Kutsures, og (Huzuris)
26/03/00	Iraklis	H	2-2	Trupkos 2 (1p)
02/04/00	Panionios	A	0-2	
11/04/00	Paniliakos	H	2-1	og (Nusias), Kutsures
16/04/00	Apollon	A	2-1	Trupkos 2 (1p)
23/04/00	Olympiakos	H	0-1	
02/05/00	Kavala	A	1-0	Yeorgeas
07/05/00	Ionikos	H	2-0	og (Haugland), Trupkos
14/05/00	Trikala	A	2-0	Boateng, Trupkos (p)
21/05/00	Aris	H	5-2	Kalantzis, Simons, Kapos, Boateng 2
28/05/00	AEK	A	1-6	Kutsures

KAVALA

Kavala
Filikis Eterias 7
65403 Kavala
tel - (051) 225094
fax - (051) 225094
Year of Formation - 1965
President - Yeorgios Karayanis
Coach - Evangelos Vlahos; Yeorgios Parashos
Stadium - Kavala (17,000)

APPEARANCES 99/00

	P	Ap	(s)	Gls
Agapitos AMBELAS	D	24	(4)	3
Anastasios ATHANASIADIS	M	13	(9)	2
Evangelos BARDIS	D		(2)	
Ante COVIC (AUS)	G	15		
Pablo GALIANONE (URU)	M	1	(1)	
Marios HARALAMBOUS (CYP)	D	14		
Yeorgios HATZIZISIS	M	12	(16)	
Evangelos KEFALAS	D	13		2
Fotios KIPUROS	G	2		
Yeorgios KOLTSIS	D	27	(5)	1
Pandeleimon KUMBIS	A	12	(15)	6
Panayotis LOGARAS	G	17		
Ernan Rodrigo LOPEZ (URU)	A	2	(2)	
Yeorgios MALIOS	M	10	(13)	1
Yeorgios MANAFIS	D	2	(2)	
Ilias MIHELIDIS	A	5	(9)	
Haralambos MURATIDIS	M		(3)	
Weil NADJA (LIB)	A	6	(4)	
Marc OECHLER (GER)	M	15	(1)	2
Dejan PAVLOVIC (YUG)	A	17		7
Yeorgios PEGLIS	M	22	(2)	
Leszek PISZ (POL)	M	28		6
Dragan RADOJICIC (YUG)	M	10	(1)	1
Andrea SANDRI (ITA)	D	16	(7)	
Zoran SARABA (YUG)	D	23	(1)	
António da SILVA (BRA)	A		(2)	
Ifeanyi UDEZE (NIG)	M	22	(1)	
Konstandinos VAKIRTZIS	D	18		1
Dimitrios ZAVANDIAS	D	28	(2)	

LEAGUE RESULTS 1999/2000

18/09/99	Ethnikos Astir	A	0-1	
27/09/99	Iraklis	H	3-1	Pisz 2, Kumbis
03/10/99	Paniliakos	A	0-2	
15/10/99	Olympiakos	H	0-5	
25/10/99	Ionikos	H	0-0	
31/10/99	Aris	A	0-1	
07/11/99	OFI	H	0-1	
20/11/99	Xanthi	A	0-1	
28/11/99	Panahaiki	H	0-0	
05/12/99	Proodeftiki	A	1-1	Pisz
12/12/99	Panionios	H	3-7	Oechler, Ambelas, Kefalas
22/12/99	Apollon	A	2-0	Oechler, Kefalas
29/12/99	Kalamata	A	2-3	Athanasiadis, Malios
09/01/00	Trikala	H	4-1	Pisz 2, Kumbis, Athanasiadis
16/01/00	AEK	A	0-3	
23/01/00	PAOK	H	1-1	Kumbis
30/01/00	Panathinaikos	A	0-3	
06/02/00	Ethnikos Astir	H	2-0	Pavlovic, Radojicic
13/02/00	Iraklis	A	1-2	Pavlovic
19/02/00	Paniliakos	H	2-1	og (Koltzos), Pavlovic
27/02/00	Olympiakos	A	0-5	
06/03/00	Ionikos	A	0-2	
12/03/00	Aris	H	1-0	Pavlovic
19/03/00	OFI	A	2-2	Koltsis, Kumbis
26/03/00	Xanthi	H	1-0	Kumbis
02/04/00	Panahaiki	A	2-3	Ambelas, Vakirtzis
11/04/00	Proodeftiki	H	2-1	Pavlovic 2
16/04/00	Panionios	A	1-1	Kumbis
23/04/00	Apollon	H	1-3	Pavlovic
02/05/00	Kalamata	H	0-1	
07/05/00	Trikala	A	1-3	Ambelas
14/05/00	AEK	H	0-2	
21/05/00	PAOK	A	0-5	
28/05/00	Panathinaikos	H	1-4	Pisz

OFI

CLUB DIRECTORY

Omilos Filathlon Irakliou (OFI)
Ikostis Pemptis Avgoustou 18
71202 Iraklion
Kriti
tel - (081) 283920
fax - (081) 288341
Year of Formation - 1925
President - Ioannis Papamattheakis
Coach - Eugeniusz Gerard
Stadium - Irakliou (14,000)

MAJOR HONOURS
Domestic Cup - (1) 1987.

APPEARANCES 99/00

	P	Ap	(s)	Gls
Pavlos ADAMOS	D	8	(4)	
Arian BEQAJ (ALB)	G	27		
Konstandinos DEDELETAKIS	A	1		
Alexandros DEDES	M	21	(7)	
Emanuil DERMINTZAKIS	D	31		1
Angelos DINGOZIS	M	27	(2)	5
Ronald GOMEZ (CRC)	A	28		19
Michael GOTTWALD (SVK)	A		(2)	
Evangelos HOSADAS	G	7		
Nikolaos IORDANIDIS	A	4	(8)	2
Athanasios KOLITSIDAKIS	D	28	(1)	1
Ilias KOTSIOS	M	24	(2)	1
Petros MARINAKIS	M	24	(7)	7
Predrag MITIC (YUG)	A	10	(11)	5
Emanuil MITSOPOULOS	D	5	(7)	
Nikolaos NIOPLIAS	M	28		6
Yeorgios PAPAYANAKIS	M	4	(7)	
Konstandinos PAVLOPOULOS	D	20	(2)	1
Mauro da SILVA (BRA)	A	24	(5)	6
Andreas SKENTZOS	D	20	(1)	1
Alfonso SOLIS (CRC)	M	3	(7)	2
Konstandinos STAVRAKAKIS	M	21	(10)	2
Gaston TAUMENT (HOL)	M	5	(10)	
Nikolaos TZANETIS	A		(5)	
Yeorgios YEORGIADIS	D	4	(3)	

LEAGUE RESULTS 1999/2000

19/09/99	Kalamata	A	0-0	
26/09/99	Xanthi	H	2-1	Gómez 2 (1p)
03/10/99	Panahaiki	A	1-3	Gómez (p)
17/10/99	Proodeftiki	H	4-3	Gómez 2, Dingozis, Nioplias
25/10/99	Panionios	A	4-1	Gómez 2, Marinakis, Iordanidis
01/11/99	Apollon	H	1-0	Marinakis
07/11/99	Kavala	A	1-0	Gómez
21/11/99	Trikala	H	2-0	Mitic, Stavrakakis
28/11/99	AEK	A	2-1	Gómez 2
05/12/99	PAOK	H	2-0	Pavlopoulos, Nioplias
12/12/99	Panathinaikos	H	3-4	Gómez 2 (1p), Nioplias
22/12/99	Ethnikos Astir	A	1-0	Mauro
29/12/99	Iraklis	H	1-1	Iordanidis
09/01/00	Paniliakos	A	2-1	Gómez, Marinakis
16/01/00	Olympiakos	H	2-1	Nioplias, Gómez
23/01/00	Ionikos	A	1-1	Gómez
30/01/00	Aris	H	2-1	Dingozis, Gómez
06/02/00	Kalamata	H	3-2	Solis 2, Dermintzakis
13/02/00	Xanthi	A	1-1	Dingozis
20/02/00	Panahaiki	H	2-2	Mitic (p), Dingozis
27/02/00	Proodeftiki	A	0-0	
05/03/00	Panionios	H	0-2	
12/03/00	Apollon	A	2-1	Stavrakakis, Marinakis
19/03/00	Kavala	H	2-2	Mitic, Nioplias
26/03/00	Trikala	A	1-1	Skentzos
01/04/00	AEK	H	1-2	Dingozis
12/04/00	PAOK	A	2-2	Mauro 2
17/04/00	Panathinaikos	A	2-3	Marinakis, Kotsios
23/04/00	Ethnikos Astir	H	4-1	Nioplias, Marinakis 2, Gómez (p)
03/05/00	Iraklis	A	3-0	Mauro 2, Mitic
07/05/00	Paniliakos	H	3-2	Gómez 2 (1p), Mitic
14/05/00	Olympiakos	A	0-2	
21/05/00	Ionikos	H	2-0	Mauro, og (Pahaturidis)
28/05/00	Aris	A	1-3	Kolitsidakis

OLYMPIAKOS

Olympiakos
Ipsilantou 170
18535 Pireas
tel - 4297223-7
fax - 4297228
Year of Formation - 1925
President - Sokratis Kokalis
Coach - Dusan Bajevic; Alberto Bigon;
Ioanis Mantzurakis
Stadium - OAKA, 'Spiros Louis' (74,433)

MAJOR HONOURS
League Championship - (29) 1931, 1933, 1934,
1936, 1937, 1938, 1947, 1948, 1951, 1954,
1955, 1956, 1957, 1958, 1959, 1966, 1967,
1973, 1974, 1975, 1980, 1981, 1982, 1983,
1987, 1997, 1998, 1999, 2000.
Domestic Cup - (20)
1947, 1951, 1952, 1953, 1954, 1957, 1958,
1959, 1960, 1961, 1963, 1965, 1968, 1971,
1973, 1975, 1981, 1990, 1992, 1999.

	P	Ap	(s)	Gls
Alexios ALEXANDRIS	A	24	(5)	15
Yeorgios AMANATIDIS	D	29	(1)	3
Kofi AMPONSAH (GHA)	D	4	(1)	
Yeorgios ANATOLAKIS	D	24	(1)	1
Paraskevas ANTZAS	D	9	(7)	1
Predrag DJORDJEVIC (YUG)	M	30		12
Dimitrios ELEFTHEROPOULOS	G	32		
GIOVANNI da Silva Oliveira (BRA)	A	9	(5)	7
Sinisa GOGIC (CYP)	A	5	(17)	4
Lambros HUTOS	A	11	(2)	7
Dimitrios KALIKAS	A		(1)	
Vasilios KARAPIALIS	M	5	(9)	6
Kiriakos KARATAIDIS	D	16	(1)	
Athanasios KOSTULAS	D	6	(11)	
LUCIANO de Souza (BRA)	M	10	(5)	7
Dimitrios MAVROGENIDIS	D	32		
Andreas NINIADIS	M	21	(5)	3
Peter OFORI-QUAYE (GHA)	A	2	(2)	1
Petros PASALIS	M	22	(5)	
Savas PURSAITIDIS	A	11	(3)	
Ilias PURSANIDIS	M	31	(1)	
Stilianos SFAKIANAKIS	M		(2)	
Stavros TZIORTZIOPOULOS	D	6	(4)	
Kiriakos TOHOUROGLOU	G	2	(1)	
Stilianos YANAKOPOULOS	M	22	(7)	10
Zlatko ZAHOVIC (SLO)	M	11	(3)	7

18/09/99	Proodeftiki	A	3-0	Alexandris, Gogic, Yanakopoulos
26/09/99	Panionios	H	5-0	Ofori-Quaye, og (Mitsiopoulos),
				Karapialis 3
03/10/99	Apollon	A	1-0	Giovanni
17/10/99	Kavala	A	5-0	Karapialis, Yanakopoulos 2,
				Giovanni, Zahovic
25/10/99	Trikala	H	3-1	Niniadis, Karapialis, Yanakopoulos
31/10/99	AEK	A	2-0	Djordjevic (p), Giovanni
07/11/99	PAOK	H	4-1	Yanakopoulos, Niniadis,
				Amanatidis, Giovanni
21/11/99	Panathinaikos	A	0-2	
29/11/99	Ethnikos Astir	H	5-0	Djordjevic, Giovanni (p), Antzas,
				Yanakopoulos, Luciano
05/12/99	Iraklis	A	4-3	og (Velis), Yanakopoulos 2, Giovanni
12/12/99	Paniliakos	H	2-1	Alexandris 2
22/12/99	Kalamata	H	4-1	Alexandris, Djordjevic 2 (1p),
				Amanatidis
29/12/99	Ionikos	A	2-1	Djordjevic (p), Alexandris
09/01/00	Aris	H	2-0	Gogic, Djordjevic (p)
16/01/00	OFI	A	1-2	Alexandris
23/01/00	Xanthi	H	3-2	Luciano, Alexandris, Zahovic
30/01/00	Panahaiki	A	2-0	Amanataidis, Zahovic
06/02/00	Proodeftiki	H	4-0	Zahovic, Alexandris 2, Djordjevic
13/02/00	Panionios	A	1-0	Zahovic
20/02/00	Apollon	H	2-0	Alexandris, Yanakopoulos
27/02/00	Kavala	H	5-0	Hutos 2, Djordjevic (p), Zahovic,
				Alexandris
05/03/00	Trikala	A	2-0	Hutos 2
12/03/00	AEK	H	3-0	Djordjevic 2 (2p), Zahovic
19/03/00	PAOK	A	2-0	Hutos 2
26/03/00	Panathinaikos	H	2-2	Anatolakis, Alexandris
03/04/00	Ethnikos Astir	A	1-1	Alexandris
12/04/00	Iraklis	H	1-0	Luciano
16/04/00	Paniliakos	A	3-0	Niniadis, Hutos, Luciano
23/04/00	Kalamata	A	1-0	Gogic
03/05/00	Ionikos	H	2-0	Yanakopoulos, Alexandris
08/05/00	Aris	A	1-0	Djordjevic (p)
14/05/00	OFI	H	2-0	Djordjevic, Karapialis
21/05/00	Xanthi	A	1-0	Luciano
28/05/00	Panahaiki	H	5-1	Giovanni, Alexandris, Luciano 2, Gogic

PANAHAIKI

CLUB DIRECTORY

Panahaiki
Arhiepiskopou Makariou & Kitiou
Patra
tel - (061) 434542
fax - (061) 434543
Year of Formation - 1891
President - Aristidis Lukopoulos
Coach - Mojas Radonic; Nikolaos Alefandos;
Hristos Arhondidis
Stadium - Panahaikis (17,000)

APPEARANCES 99/00

	P	Ap	(s)	Gls
Yeorgios AMBADIOTAKIS	G	25		
Dimitrios BALAFAS	D	1		
Ioanis BALTIMAS	G	9		
Mauricio COPERTINO (BRA)	D	22	(2)	2
Joël EPALE (CMR)	A	9	(6)	2
Panayotis GITSIS	D	26	(7)	
Lazaros IAKOVOU (CYP)	D	5	(6)	
Dimitrios IOANOU	M	11	(9)	
Dusan JOVANOVIC (YUG)	M	26	(7)	6
Yeorgios KAPURANIS	D	2	(2)	
Konstantinos KATSURANIS	M	12	(15)	5
Konstandinos KONSTANDINIDIS	A	1	(3)	
Panayotis KORDONURIS	D	28	(3)	
Zlatko KOSTIC (YUG)	M	6	(3)	
Yeorgios KOSTIS	M	21		1
Mihail LIGNOS	D	29		
Milan MESTER (YUG)	M	20	(2)	1
Koderzi NATROSHVILI (GEO)	M	25	(3)	1
Jeronimo NAVARRO (ESP)	M	28		3
Konstantinos SOKRATOUS (CYP)	M	1	(3)	
Ilias SOLAKIS	A	26	(5)	6
Konstandinos TAXIARHIS	M	10	(4)	
Nikolaos VAVILIS	D		(4)	
Nenad VUKCEVIC (YUG)	A	15	(14)	10
Panayotis YANOPOULOS	D	16		

LEAGUE RESULTS 1999/2000

19/09/99	Ionikos	H	1-1	Vukcevic
26/09/99	Aris	A	0-2	
03/10/99	OFI	H	3-1	Copertino, Solakis, Vukcevic
17/10/99	Xanthi	A	0-1	
25/10/99	Kalamata	A	1-1	Jovanovic
31/10/99	Proodeftiki	H	2-0	Navarro, Natroshvili
07/11/99	Panionios	A	1-2	Vukcevic
21/11/99	Apollon	H	1-2	Solakis (p)
28/11/99	Kavala	A	0-0	
05/12/99	Trikala	H	3-0	Jovanovic, Mester, Vukcevic
12/12/99	AEK	A	0-3	
22/12/99	PAOK	H	1-2	Navarro (p)
29/12/99	Panathinaikos	A	1-7	Jovanovic
09/01/00	Ethnikos Astir	H	2-0	Vukcevic 2
16/01/00	Iraklis	H	0-1	
24/01/00	Paniliakos	A	0-0	
30/01/00	Olympiakos	H	0-2	
06/02/00	Ionikos	A	0-0	
14/02/00	Aris	H	1-2	Vukcevic
20/02/00	OFI	A	2-2	Jovanovic, Katsuranis
27/02/00	Xanthi	H	1-1	Solakis
05/03/00	Kalamata	H	1-2	Solakis
12/03/00	Proodeftiki	A	2-2	Vukcevic, Kostis
19/03/00	Panionios	H	1-0	Katsuranis
26/03/00	Apollon	A	0-0	
02/04/00	Kavala	H	3-2	Navarro (p), Vukcevic, Epalé
12/04/00	Trikala	A	1-0	Jovanovic
16/04/00	AEK	H	1-1	Katsuranis
23/04/00	PAOK	A	1-1	Solakis
03/05/00	Panathinaikos	H	1-0	Katsuranis
07/05/00	Ethnikos Astir	A	2-2	Copertino, Jovanovic
14/05/00	Iraklis	A	1-2	Epalé
21/05/00	Paniliakos	H	2-0	Solakis, Vukcevic
28/05/00	Olympiakos	A	1-5	Katsuranis

PANATHINAIKOS

CLUB DIRECTORY

Panathinaikos
Athlitikes Egatastasis "Peania"
Karela Peanias
19002 Attiki
tel - 6647160
fax - 6029536
Year of Formation - 1908
President - Yeorgios Vardinoyanis
Coach - Juan Ramón Rocha; Ioanis Kirastas
Stadium - OAKA 'Spiros Louis' (74,433)

MAJOR HONOURS
League Championship - (21)
1911, 1912, 1916, 1930, 1949, 1953, 1960,
1961, 1962, 1964, 1965, 1969, 1970, 1972,
1977, 1984, 1986, 1990, 1991, 1995, 1996.
Domestic Cup - (15) 1940, 1948, 1955, 1967,
1969, 1977, 1982, 1984, 1986, 1988, 1989,
1991, 1993, 1994, 1995.

APPEARANCES 99/00

	P	Ap	(s)	Gls
Yeorgios ALEXOPOULOS	A	9	(6)	
Aljosa ASANOVIC (CRO)	M	6	(13)	4
Angelos BASINAS	D	29		4
Panayotis FISAS	D	23	(1)	
Fernando GALETTO (ARG)	M	17	(4)	1
Ioanis GUMAS	A	27	(1)	7
Konstandinos HALKIAS	G	6		
René HENRIKSEN (DEN)	D	28		
Konstandinos IPIROTIS	M		(2)	
Yeorgios KARANGUNIS	M	21	(6)	8
Konstandinos KIASOS	M	12	(10)	1
Bledar KOLA (ALB)	M	22	(3)	7
Stefanos KOTSOLIS	G		(1)	
Nikolaos LIMBEROPOULOS	M	27		23
Vladan MILOJEVIC (YUG)	D	3	(6)	
Erik MYKLAND (NOR)	M	20	(2)	1
Yeorgios NASIOPOULOS	A	14	(13)	5
Andonios NIKOPOLIDIS	G	28		
Percy OLIVARES (PER)	D	14	(13)	2
Helgi SIGURDSSON (ISL)	A	13	(8)	8
Igor SYPNIEWSKI (POL)	A	12	(5)	2
Karlheinz PFLIPSEN (GER)	M	10		6
Marco VILLA (GER)	A		(2)	
Leonidas VOKOLOS	D	12	(5)	3
Krzysztof WARZYCHA (POL)	A	21	(9)	10

LEAGUE RESULTS 1999/2000

20/09/99	Trikala	H	2-0	Pflipsen (p), Gumas
26/09/99	AEK	A	2-1	Pflipsen, Asanovic
03/10/99	PAOK	H	1-1	Gumas
17/10/99	Kalamata	H	5-0	Sypniewski, Limberopoulos 2,
				Sigurdsson, Pflipsen
25/10/99	Ethnikos Astir	A	2-1	Gumas 2
31/10/99	Iraklis	H	3-0	Pflipsen, Sypniewski, Warzycha
07/11/99	Paniliakos	A	1-0	Warzycha
21/11/99	Olympiakos	H	2-0	Olivares, Warzycha
28/11/99	Ionikos	A	2-2	Pflipsen, Asanovic
05/12/99	Aris	H	3-0	Limberopoulos, Kola, Pflipsen
12/12/99	OFI	A	4-3	Kola, Limberopoulos 2, Sigurdsson
22/12/99	Xanthi	A	3-1	Limberopoulos, Karangunis, Kola
29/12/99	Panahaiki	H	7-1	Gumas, Sigurdsson 2, Limberopoulos,
				Kola, Asanovic, Karangunis
09/01/00	Proodeftiki	A	0-1	
16/01/00	Panionios	H	2-1	Mykland, Nasiopoulos
23/01/00	Apollon	A	3-0	Asanovic, Karangunis, Nasiopoulos
30/01/00	Kavala	H	3-0	Karangunis, Vokolos, Sigurdsson
06/02/00	Trikala	A	3-1	Vokolos, Limberopoulos 2
13/02/00	AEK	H	1-0	Kola
20/02/00	PAOK	A	3-1	Basinas (p), Karangunis, Warzycha
27/02/00	Kalamata	A	0-0	
05/03/00	Ethnikos Astir	H	4-0	Basinas (p), Nasiopoulos, Kola,
				Sigurdsson
12/03/00	Iraklis	A	3-1	Basinas (p), Warzycha 2
19/03/00	Paniliakos	H	3-1	Nasiopoulos, Karangunis,
				Sigurdsson
26/03/00	Olympiakos	A	2-2	Galetto, Limberopoulos
02/04/00	Ionikos	H	5-0	Karangunis 2, Limberopoulos 2,
				Kiasos
12/04/00	Aris	A	2-0	Warzycha, Limberopoulos
17/04/00	OFI	H	3-2	Warzycha 2, Sigurdsson
22/04/00	Xanthi	H	2-1	Basinas, Gumas
03/05/00	Panahaiki	A	0-1	
08/05/00	Proodeftiki	H	3-1	Kola, Limberopoulos 2
14/05/00	Panionios	A	4-0	Limberopoulos 2, Nasiopoulos,
				Olivares
21/05/00	Apollon	H	5-0	Warzycha, Limberopoulos 4
28/05/00	Kavala	A	4-1	Vokolos, Limberopoulos 2, Gumas

PANILIAKOS

CLUB DIRECTORY

Paniliakos
Ahileos 4
Pirgos
tel - (0621) 25749
fax - (0621) 25749
Year of Formation - 1958
President - Sakis Stavropoulos
Coach - Haralambos Tenes; Konstandinos Raptis;
Arie Haan
Stadium - Pirgos (10,000)

APPEARANCES 99/00

	P	Ap	(s)	Gls
Isaak ALMANIDIS	A	23	(8)	4
Bozidar BANDOVIC (YUG)	D	18	(1)	3
David DIAZ (CRC)	A	2	(12)	3
Ubiraci FERREIRA (BRA)	A	9	(8)	
Anastasios FEREKIDIS	D	31		1
Lukas GALAMELOS	M	3	(5)	1
Panayotis GONIAS	M	25	(2)	5
Yeorgios KOLTZOS	M	14	(10)	1
Sokratis KOPSAHILIS	G	8	(1)	
Evangelos KUTSOPOULOS	D		(1)	
Vladan LUKIC (YUG)	A	13	(1)	2
Xenofon MOSHOYANIS	M	20	(6)	
Konstandinos NEMBEGLERAS	M	30		2
Spiridon NUSIAS	M	26		3
César Miguel ROSALES (PER)	M	15	(10)	3
Miltiadis SAPANIS	M	5	(4)	1
Ioanis TARALIDIS	D	1	(12)	1
Anastasios TASIOPOULOS	D	32		6
Ioanis TATSIS	M	10	(1)	
Sergei TICA (BOS)	M		(2)	
Evangelos TOYAS	D	1	(8)	
Marinos UZUNIDIS	D	33		
Angelos YEORGIOU	G	26		
Panayotis ZIAKAS	A	29	(3)	7

LEAGUE RESULTS 1999/2000

19/09/99	Panionios	A	2-1	Tasiopoulos, Gonias
25/09/99	Apollon	A	0-0	
03/10/99	Kavala	H	2-0	Lukic, Rosales
17/10/99	Trikala	A	1-1	Lukic
25/10/99	AEK	H	0-1	
31/10/99	PAOK	A	1-0	Gonias
07/11/99	Panathinaikos	H	0-1	
21/11/99	Ethnikos Astir	A	1-3	Ziakas
28/11/99	Iraklis	H	4-3	Koltzos, Ziakas, Nusias, Galamelos
05/12/99	Kalamata	H	3-1	Gonias, Almanidis, Tasiopoulos
12/12/99	Olympiakos	A	1-2	Ziakas
22/12/99	Ionikos	H	3-0	Almanidis, Tasiopoulos, Ziakas
30/12/99	Aris	A	1-2	Ferekidis
09/01/00	OFI	H	1-2	Rosales
15/01/00	Xanthi	A	0-1	
24/01/00	Panahaiki	H	0-0	
30/01/00	Proodeftiki	A	1-1	Almanidis
06/02/00	Panionios	H	3-0	Gonias, Rosales, Díaz
13/02/00	Apollon	H	2-1	Bandovic, Gonias
20/02/00	Kavala	A	1-2	Tasiopoulos
27/02/00	Trikala	H	1-3	Díaz
05/03/00	AEK	A	0-1	
12/03/00	PAOK	H	0-4	
19/03/00	Panathinaikos	A	1-3	Ziakas
26/03/00	Ethnikos Astir	H	2-0	Tasiopoulos, Nusias
02/04/00	Iraklis	A	1-3	Díaz
11/04/00	Kalamata	A	1-2	Ziakas
16/04/00	Olympiakos	H	0-3	
23/04/00	Ionikos	A	2-0	og (Afash), Bandovic
03/05/00	Aris	H	1-2	Ziakas
07/05/00	OFI	A	2-3	Taralidis, Nembegleras
14/05/00	Xanthi	H	2-0	Nembegleras, Bandovic
21/05/00	Panahaiki	A	0-2	
28/05/00	Proodeftiki	H	4-0	Tasiopoulos, Almanidis, Nusias, Sapanis

PANIONIOS

THE EUROPEAN FOOTBALL YEARBOOK 2000-2001

CLUB DIRECTORY

Panionios
25is Martiou
Nea Smirni
17122 Athina
tel - 9326707
fax - 9332036
Year of Formation - 1890
President - Ahilefs Beos
Coach - Jacek Gmoch; Thomas Katsavakis;
Hristos Emvoliadis
Stadium - Neas Smirnis (15,000)

MAJOR HONOURS
Domestic Cup - (2) 1979, 1998.

APPEARANCES 99/00

	P	Ap	(s)	Gls
Paulo Rogério ALVES (BRA)	A	4	(3)	
Haralambos AMANATIDIS	D		(1)	
Thomas CHRISTIANSEN (ESP)	A	7	(5)	3
Emil EYIDI (CMR)	A	2	(6)	
Ioanis FAKIS	G	3		
Spiridon GOGOLOS	D	10	(2)	
Stilianos HASIOTIS	M	27	(1)	
Ilias IOANOU	A	5	(12)	1
Konstandinos KAFALIS	A	4	(1)	
Yeorgios KARAISARIDIS	D	7	(7)	
Jochen KIENTZ (GER)	D	13		1
Yeorgios KIURKOS	A	7	(5)	1
Miloje KLAEVIC (YUG)	D	25	(1)	1
Hristos KONDIS	M	24	(3)	
Slobodan KRCMAREVIC (YUG)	A	27	(3)	7
Juan MACEDA (ESP)	M	15	(5)	
Yeorgios MITSIOPOULOS	D	25	(1)	1
Yeorgios MUZOS	M	2	(1)	
Dimitrios NALINTZIS	A	16		13
Konstandinos PALAMARAS	D	13	(3)	
Milinko PANTIC (YUG)	M	15	(8)	4
Fotios PAPADOPOULOS	M	16	(9)	4
Evangelos PURLIOTOPOULOS	G	31		
Marcello RIBEIRO (BRA)	M	11	(4)	1
Nikolaos SAKELARIDIS	D	28	(1)	1
Andonios SAPUNTZIS	M	20	(1)	6
Denys SOKOLOVSKYI (UKR)	A	6	(5)	2
Dimitrios TANDOS	D	1	(3)	
Mihail TZIVELEKIS	M	10	(8)	1

LEAGUE RESULTS 1999/2000

18/09/99	Paniliakos	H	1-2	Papadopoulos
26/09/99	Olympiakos	A	0-5	
04/10/99	Ionikos	H	2-0	Sapuntzis, Krcmarevic
16/10/99	Aris	A	1-5	Kiurkos
25/10/99	OFI	H	1-4	og (Kotsios)
31/10/99	Xanthi	A	0-5	
07/11/99	Panahaiki	H	2-1	Nalintzis, Pantic
21/11/99	Proodeftiki	A	0-1	
28/11/99	Kalamata	A	3-1	Pantic 2, Nalintzis
05/12/99	Apollon	H	3-1	Nalintzis 3
12/12/99	Kavala	A	7-3	Nalintzis 2, Krcmarevic 2,
				Sapuntzis 3 (1p)
22/12/99	Trikala	H	4-1	Nalintzis 2, Krcmarevic, Ioanou
29/12/99	AEK	A	1-0	Nalintzis
09/01/00	PAOK	H	1-1	Nalintzis
16/01/00	Panathinaikos	A	1-2	Nalintzis
23/01/00	Ethnikos Astir	H	1-0	Tzivelekis
30/01/00	Iraklis	A	2-1	Krcmarevic, Nalintzis (p)
06/02/00	Paniliakos	A	0-3	
13/02/00	Olympiakos	H	0-1	
20/02/00	Ionikos	A	0-2	
27/02/00	Aris	H	1-3	Christiansen
05/03/00	OFI	A	2-0	Ribeiro, Sokolovskyi
12/03/00	Xanthi	H	4-0	Sokolovskyi, Papadopoulos, Pantic,
				Mitsiopoulos
19/03/00	Panahaiki	A	0-1	
26/03/00	Proodeftiki	H	2-1	og (Dangas), Christiansen
02/04/00	Kalamata	H	2-0	Kientz, Christiansen
12/04/00	Apollon	A	1-2	Sapuntzis (p)
16/04/00	Kavala	H	1-1	Sapuntzis
23/04/00	Trikala	A	3-2	Krcmarevic, Sakelaridis,
				og (Laguias)
03/05/00	AEK	H	0-2	
08/05/00	PAOK	A	0-2	
14/05/00	Panathinaikos	H	0-4	
21/05/00	Ethnikos Astir	A	2-4	Klaevic (p), Papadopoulos
28/05/00	Iraklis	H	2-2	Papadopoulos, Krcmarevic

PAOK

PAOK
Lora Margariti 13
54622 Thesaloniki
tel - (031) 238560/912362
fax - (031) 238557
Year of Formation - 1926
President - Yeorgios Batatudis
Coach - Arie Haan; Stavros Sarafis & Haralambos
Mihailidis; Dusan Bajevic
Stadium - Tumbas (40,000)

MAJOR HONOURS
League Championship - (2) 1976, 1985.
Domestic Cup - (2) 1972, 1974.

APPEARANCES 99/00

	P	Ap	(s)	Gls
Kofi AMPONSAH (GHA)	D	6	(1)	
Bozidar BANDOVIC (YUG)	D	7	(1)	
Vasilios BORBOKIS	D	19		5
Vidak BRATIC (YUG)	D	10	(1)	2
Ante COVIC (AUS)	G	4		
Christian DOLBERG (ARG)	D	7		2
Konstandinos FRANTZESKOS	M	16	(12)	4
Nikolaos FRUSOS	A	17	(8)	10
Dionisios HASIOTIS	D	21	(1)	
Pandeleimon KAFES	A	12	(14)	4
Lukas KARADIMOS	M	7	(8)	
Anastasios KATSIAMBIS	D	24	(3)	
Pandeleimon KONSTANDINIDIS	M	21	(3)	4
Yeorgios KULAKIOTIS	D	5	(4)	1
Triandafilos MAHERIDIS	M	8	(1)	
Spiridon MARANGOS	M	20	(5)	1
Nikolaos MIHOPOULOS	G	16	(1)	
Joe NAGBE (LIB)	M	17	(3)	1
Dimitrios NALINTZIS	A	16		11
Milton NUÑEZ (HON)	A	4	(6)	
Abdelsatar SABRY (EGY)	M	11	(1)	4
Grzegorz SZAMOTULSKI (POL)	G	14		
Omari TETRADZE (RUS)	M	25	(2)	
Adolfo VALENCIA (COL)	A	6	(8)	5
Stilianos VENETIDIS	D	27		
Stefanos VOSKARIDIS (CYP)	M		(2)	
Zisis VRIZAS	A	11	(13)	3
Yeorgios YEORGIADIS	M	23	(3)	5
Ahilefs ZAFIRIOU	M		(1)	

LEAGUE RESULTS 1999/2000

20/09/99	AEK	H	4-4	Marangos, Dolberg, Yeorgiadis, Valencia
26/09/99	Kalamata	H	4-2	Frantzeskos, Valencia, Sabry, Vrizas
03/10/99	Panathinaikos	A	1-1	Nagbe
17/10/99	Ethnikos Astir	H	2-0	Dolberg, Frusos
25/10/99	Iraklis	A	1-3	Frantzeskos
31/10/99	Paniliakos	H	0-1	
07/11/99	Olympiakos	A	1-4	Frantzeskos
21/11/99	Ionikos	H	3-0	Valencia 2, Sabry (p)
28/11/99	Aris	A	0-0	
05/12/99	OFI	A	0-2	
12/12/99	Xanthi	H	5-0	Frusos 2, Sabry 2 (1p), Frantzeskos
22/12/99	Panahaiki	A	2-1	Yeorgiadis, Kulakiotis
29/12/99	Proodeftiki	H	1-0	og (Rutzieris)
09/01/00	Panionios	A	1-1	Frusos
16/01/00	Apollon	H	1-1	Vrizas
23/01/00	Kavala	A	1-1	Valencia
30/01/00	Trikala	H	2-0	Vrizas (p), Frusos
06/02/00	AEK	A	0-2	
13/02/00	Kalamata	A	1-1	Bratic
20/02/00	Panathinaikos	H	1-3	Bratic
27/02/00	Ethnikos Astir	A	1-1	Nalintzis
05/03/00	Iraklis	H	4-0	Borbokis 2, Konstandinis, Nalintzis
12/03/00	Paniliakos	A	4-0	Nalintzis, Borbokis 2, Konstandinidis
19/03/00	Olympiakos	H	0-2	
26/03/00	Ionikos	A	0-1	
02/04/00	Aris	H	3-2	Nalintzis (p), Konstandinidis, Kafes
12/04/00	OFI	H	2-2	Nalintzis, og (Pavlopoulos)
17/04/00	Xanthi	A	2-1	Nalintzis (p), Yeorgiadis
23/04/00	Panahaiki	H	1-1	Yeorgiadis
04/05/00	Proodeftiki	A	0-1	
08/05/00	Panionios	H	2-0	Borbokis, Frusos
13/05/00	Apollon	A	4-3	Frusos, Kafes, Nalintzis 2
21/05/00	Kavala	H	5-0	Konstandinidis, Nalintzis 2 (1p), Kafes, Frusos
28/05/00	Trikala	A	5-3	Nalintzis, Yeorgiadis, Kafes, Frusos 2

PROODEFTIKI

Proodeftiki
Taxiarhon 49
Koridalos
18120 Pireas
tel - 4952012/5398160
fax - 4976485
Year of Formation - 1927
President - Markos Takas
Coach - Nikolaos Alefandos; Nikolaos Karulias; Athanasios Papadopoulos
Stadium - Nikeas (5,500)

APPEARANCES 99/00

	P	Ap	(s)	Gls
Haled AL JAHER (SYR)	M	25	(3)	1
Biazid AL SAID (SYR)	A	21	(8)	3
Paraskevas ANDRALAS	M	8	(18)	
Ioanis ANGELOPOULOS	D	22		1
Ioanis ARHONDULIS	A		(2)	
Sotirios BUGLAS	G	1		
Evangelos DANGAS	D	24	(2)	1
Ioanis FONDULAKIS	D	2	(3)	
Nikolaos FUSKAS	M	3	(5)	
Athanasios GONGAS	A		(2)	
Evangelos GUTIS	D	24	(1)	
Dionisios HIOTIS	G	18		
Ilias HUZURIS	D	18	(1)	
Vasilios IOANIDIS	D	21		2
Petros KARANASTASIS	G	10		
Evangelos KARASAVAS	G	5		
Yeorgios KAZANTZIS	A	14	(13)	7
Efthimios KULUHERIS	M	9	(1)	
Ahmed KURTOGLI (SYR)	M		(1)	
Oliver MAKOR (LIB)	M	22	(3)	3
Ilias NASTOPOULOS	A	6	(10)	1
Savas PANDELIDIS	D	19	(2)	
Anastasios PANDOS	D	6	(4)	
Nikolaos PILIURAS	D	14	(1)	
Petros RUTZIERIS	D	23	(1)	
Alejandro SEQUEIRA (CRC)	A	8	(3)	
Nikolaos TIMOTHEOU (CYP)	D	8		
Evangelos TOYAS	D	15		2
Sotirios TSANGAVELIS	M	2	(9)	
Kornelius UTEBULUZOR (NIG)	A		(2)	
Angelos VILANAKIS	M	15		5
Roland ZAJMI (ALB)	A	11	(2)	

LEAGUE RESULTS 1999/2000

19/09/99	Olympiakos	H	0-3	
26/09/99	Ionikos	A	0-2	
04/10/99	Aris	H	0-1	
17/10/99	OFI	A	3-4	Makor (p), Kazantzis 2
25/10/99	Xanthi	H	0-0	
31/10/99	Panahaiki	A	0-2	
07/11/99	Kalamata	A	0-2	
21/11/99	Panionios	H	1-0	Ioanidis
28/11/99	Apollon	A	2-0	Al Jaher (p), Kazantzis
05/12/99	Kavala	H	1-1	Angelopoulos
12/12/99	Trikala	A	0-0	
22/12/99	AEK	H	1-4	Kazantzis
29/12/99	PAOK	A	0-1	
09/01/00	Panathinaikos	H	1-0	Kazantzis
16/01/00	Ethnikos Astir	A	0-1	
23/01/00	Iraklis	H	0-1	
30/01/00	Paniliakos	H	1-1	Makor (p)
06/02/00	Olympiakos	A	0-4	
13/02/00	Ionikos	H	2-2	Vilanakis, Al Said
20/02/00	Aris	A	1-2	Al Said
27/02/00	OFI	H	0-0	
05/03/00	Xanthi	A	1-2	og (Karayeorgiou)
12/03/00	Panahaiki	H	2-2	Toyas, Ioanidis
19/03/00	Kalamata	H	1-2	Vilanakis
26/03/00	Panionios	A	1-2	Nastopoulos
02/04/00	Apollon	H	2-0	Kazantzis, Makor
12/04/00	Kavala	A	1-2	Vilanakis
16/04/00	Trikala	H	1-0	Vilanakis (p)
23/04/00	AEK	A	2-3	Kazantzis, Toyas
04/05/00	PAOK	H	1-0	Vilanakis
08/05/00	Panathinaikos	A	1-3	Al Said
14/05/00	Ethnikos Astir	H	1-0	Dangas
21/05/00	Iraklis	A	0-4	
28/05/00	Paniliakos	A	0-4	

TRIKALA

CLUB DIRECTORY

Trikala
Asklipiou 19
Trikala
tel - (0431) 28587/38995
fax - (0431) 24235
Year of Formation - 1963
President - Anastasios Karatzunis
Coach - Mihail Filipou; Nikolaos Gulis; Lagaras & Alexiou; Zoran Babovic
Stadium - Trikalon (18,500)

APPEARANCES 99/00

	P	Ap	(s)	Gls
Ahilefs ANGELOPOULOS	D	18	(6)	
Efthimios ANGELOPOULOS	M	22	(1)	1
Konstandinos BANDAS	D	24	(1)	1
Dimitrios BEKAS	M	3	(2)	
Dimitrios BUGAS	M	16	(2)	1
Walter CAPRILE (URU)	M	22		1
Edmond DALIPI (ALB)	M	11	(2)	
David DIAZ (CRC)	A	13	(1)	4
Ubiraci FERREIRA (BRA)	A	11	(3)	3
Anastasios GANAS	D	13	(2)	1
Ioanis HLOROS	A	22	(7)	6
Mihail IORDANIDIS	A	1		
Aleksandar JOVANOVIC (YUG)	M	20	(2)	11
Yeorgios KARAPETSAS	M	11	(1)	
Sotirios KOSTULAS	D	2	(2)	
Dimitrios KOTARAS	G	18		
Evangelos KOTSIOS	M	12	(1)	
Ahilefs LAGUIAS	D	16		
Ioanis MANIKAS	D	12	(14)	
Dimitrios MARDANIS	D	2		
Mihail MITROFANIS	D		(5)	
Vasilios MURATIDIS	M	1	(1)	
Konstandinos PAHATURIDIS	D	4	(3)	
Panayotis PAPASTERIADIS	A	3	(4)	
Hristos PRAPAS	D	3		
Athanasios PREKATES	D	16	(2)	
Anastasios SALONIDIS	M	1	(1)	
Hristos SAMARAS	D	13	(4)	
Milan SEVO (YUG)	G	9		
Periklis SPIRAKOS	A	4	(14)	
Zoran STOJNOVIC (YUG)	M	10	(2)	
Theodoros THEODOSIADIS	D	12	(4)	
Ioanis TSAKMAKIDIS	M		(2)	
Evangelos TSIUKAS	A	1	(6)	
Musa YAHAYA (NGR)	A	12	(2)	5
Konstandinos ZAFIRIS	G	5		
Anastasios ZAHOPOULOS	D	11		

LEAGUE RESULTS 1999/2000

19/09/99	Panathinaikos	A	0-2	
26/09/99	Ethnikos Astir	H	1-2	Díaz (p)
03/10/99	Iraklis	A	1-4	Díaz
17/10/99	Paniliakos	H	1-1	Ferreira
25/10/99	Olympiakos	A	1-3	Díaz (p)
31/10/99	Ionikos	H	2-2	Ferreira 2
07/11/99	Aris	H	0-1	
21/11/99	OFI	A	0-2	
28/11/99	Xanthi	H	2-1	Bandas, Díaz
05/12/99	Panahaiki	A	0-3	
12/12/99	Proodeftiki	H	0-0	
22/12/99	Panionios	A	1-4	Bugas
29/12/99	Apollon	H	1-0	Jovanovic
09/01/00	Kavala	A	1-4	Angelopoulos E.
16/01/00	Kalamata	A	1-0	Hloros
23/01/00	AEK	H	0-1	
30/01/00	PAOK	A	0-2	
06/02/00	Panathinaikos	H	1-3	Hloros
13/02/00	Ethnikos Astir	A	0-1	
20/02/00	Iraklis	H	3-3	Jovanovic, Yahaya 2
27/02/00	Paniliakos	A	3-1	Yahaya, Jovanovic 2
05/03/00	Olympiakos	H	0-2	
12/03/00	Ionikos	A	1-5	Hloros
19/03/00	Aris	A	3-3	Jovanovic, Yahaya 2
26/03/00	OFI	H	1-1	Jovanovic (p)
02/04/00	Xanthi	A	0-3	
12/04/00	Panahaiki	H	0-1	
16/04/00	Proodeftiki	A	0-1	
23/04/00	Panionios	H	2-3	Jovanovic (p), Hloros
03/05/00	Apollon	A	2-5	Ganas, Hloros
07/05/00	Kavala	H	3-1	Jovanovic 2 (1p), Hloros
14/05/00	Kalamata	H	0-2	
21/05/00	AEK	A	1-2	Caprile
28/05/00	PAOK	H	3-5	og (Katsiambis), Jovanovic 2 (1p)

XANTHI

CLUB DIRECTORY

Xanthi Skoda
Vasilisis Sofias 3
67100 Xanthi
tel - (0541) 24466/22977
fax - (0541) 25852
Year of Formation - 1967
President - Aristidis Pialoglou
Coach - Ioanis Mantzurakis; Evangelos Vlahos;
Ioanis Ispirlidis; Nikolaos Karayeorgiou
Stadium - Xanthi (12,800)

APPEARANCES 99/00

	P	Ap	(s)	Gls
Sotirios ANDONIOU	M	11	(7)	
Konstandinos ANGOS	D	1	(3)	
Ismaila BAH (SEN)	A	23	(7)	6
Vasilios BLETSAS	M	8		
Juraj BUCEK (SVK)	G	32		
Vasilios DAMIANOS	M	7	(4)	
Andonios DAMIGOS	M	1	(2)	
Nicholas DIKOUME (CMR)	A	9	(7)	1
Ioanis DIMITRIADIS	M	4	(1)	
Ousmane DIOP (SEN)	M	17	(3)	4
Dimitrios GELADARIS	D	21	(5)	
Ioakim HAVOS	M	25		
Vladimir JANOCKO (SVK)	M	11	(1)	1
Nikolaos KARAYEORGIOU	D	24		
Stefanos KARKANIS	G	1		
Prokopios KARTALIS	M	14	(7)	
Nikolaos KEHAYAS	M	27		
Thomas KIPARISIS	A	27	(2)	7
Mamadou KONATE (SEN)	M	4	(7)	2
Ali Reza MANSURIAN (IRN)	M	1	(6)	
Haralambos NIKOLAOU	D	4	(3)	
Ioanis PAPADIMITRIOU	D	13		
Hristos PATSANTZOGLOU	M	22	(1)	4
Ioanis PELTEKIDIS	D	1		
Athanasios PRITAS	A	13	(2)	
Ioanis TSAKONAKIS	G	1		
Theofanis TSUVALIDIS	D	1	(1)	
Yeorgios TURSUNIDIS	M	9	(6)	
Spiridon VALAS	D	1		
Nikolaos ZAPROPOULOS	D	12	(2)	
Dimitrios ZOGRAFAKIS	M	14	(7)	
Paraskevas ZUMBULIS	A	15	(9)	11

LEAGUE RESULTS 1999/2000

19/09/99	Aris	H	0-0	
26/09/99	OFI	A	1-2	Diop
03/10/99	Kalamata	A	0-0	
17/10/99	Panahaiki	H	1-0	Diop
25/10/99	Proodeftiki	A	0-0	
31/10/99	Panionios	H	5-0	Kiparisis, Bah 2, Konate, Diop
07/11/99	Apollon	A	0-0	
20/11/99	Kavala	H	1-0	Konate
28/11/99	Trikala	A	1-2	Bah (p)
05/12/99	AEK	H	2-2	Zumbulis 2
12/12/99	PAOK	A	0-5	
22/12/99	Panathinaikos	H	1-3	Kiparisis
29/12/99	Ethnikos Astir	H	0-0	
09/01/00	Iraklis	A	1-3	Kiparisis
16/01/00	Paniliakos	H	1-0	Bah (p)
23/01/00	Olympiakos	A	2-3	Zumbulis 2
30/01/00	Ionikos	H	2-1	Kiparisis, Zumbulis
06/02/00	Aris	A	1-0	Patsantzoglou
13/02/00	OFI	H	1-1	Kiparisis
20/02/00	Kalamata	H	1-0	Kiparisis
27/02/00	Panahaiki	A	1-1	Dikoumé
05/03/00	Proodeftiki	H	2-1	Zumbulis, Patsantzoglou
12/03/00	Panionios	A	0-4	
19/03/00	Apollon	H	2-0	Diop, Zumbulis
26/03/00	Kavala	A	0-1	
02/04/00	Trikala	H	3-0	Bah (p), Zumbulis 2
12/04/00	AEK	A	1-4	Zumbulis
17/04/00	PAOK	H	1-2	Patsantzoglou
22/04/00	Panathinaikos	A	1-2	Patsantzoglou
03/05/00	Ethnikos Astir	A	0-1	
07/05/00	Iraklis	H	3-0	Zumbulis, Janocko, Bah
14/05/00	Paniliakos	A	0-2	
21/05/00	Olympiakos	H	0-1	
28/05/00	Ionikos	A	1-2	Kiparisis

HOLLAND

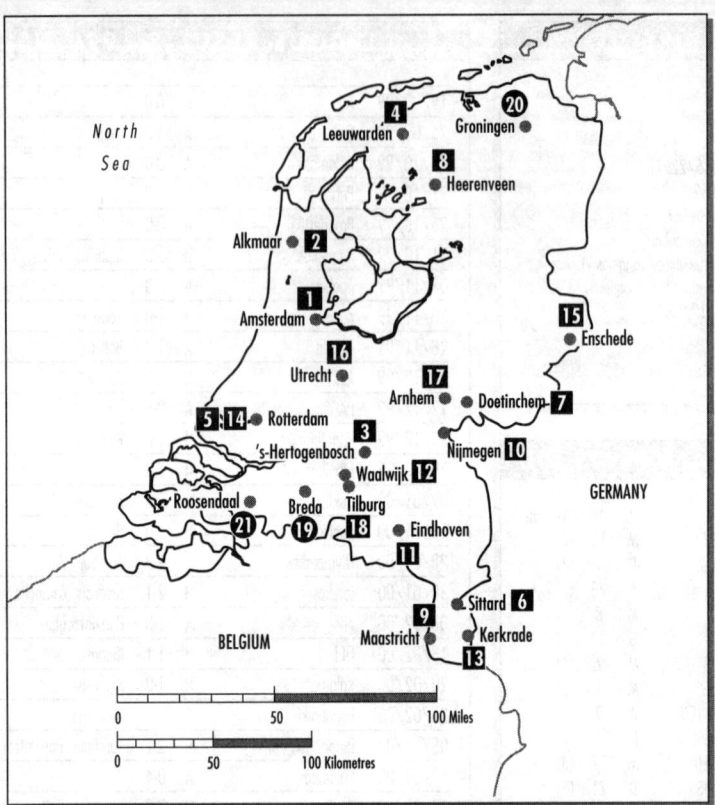

1	AJAX	498
2	AZ	499
3	FC DEN BOSCH	500
4	SC CAMBUUR LEEUWARDEN	501
5	FEYENOORD	502
6	FORTUNA SITTARD	503
7	DE GRAAFSCHAP	504
8	SC HEERENVEEN	505
9	MVV	506
10	NEC	507
11	PSV	508

12	RKC WAALWIJK	509
13	RODA JC	510
14	SPARTA	511
15	FC TWENTE	512
16	FC UTRECHT	513
17	VITESSE	514
18	WILLEM II	515
Promoted clubs		
19	NAC	
20	FC GRONINGEN	
21	RBC	

UNCHALLENGED PSV TAKE TITLE

Spot-kick agony ends another Dutch dream

FEDERATION DIRECTORY

Koninklijke Nederlandsche Voetbalbond
Woudenbergseweg 56-58, PO Box 515, 3700 AM Zeist

tel - (0343) 499211 Year of Formation - 1889
fax - (0343) 499189 President - Jeu Sprengers
  Secretary - Drs. Harry Been
Stadium - Feyenoord, Rotterdam (51,180)

Euro 2000 ended for co-hosts Holland in familiar fashion. For the fourth time in five major tournaments the Dutch were eliminated after losing a penalty shoot-out. In fact, it was worse than that because they also missed two spot-kicks during normal time in their harrowing semi-final defeat by Italy.

Clearly, the Dutch only had themselves to blame for not seizing their opportunities and making it through the final. Italy stonewalled them for two hours and Holland, despite possessing some of the most gifted attacking players in Europe and - for much of the game - one man more than their opponents, were unable to break the 'Azzurri' down. It was agony in the extreme for the orange-clad Dutch fans, who so desperately wanted their team to get their hands on the Henri Delaunay trophy. But a combination of brilliant Italian defending and predictable Dutch attacking resulted in a total stalemate. And then came the penalty shoot-out...

All over Holland people switched off their television sets. They had seen it all before and they knew what was coming. Even though Italy themselves had a wretched record of penalty-taking at major championships, the writing was clearly on the wall.

Immediately after the match Dutch coach Frank Rijkaard handed in his resignation. It was a surprise move but an honourable one. He knew he had failed to meet the fans' expectations, and the critics were not slow to remind him. Above all Rijkaard was accused of making uninspired substitutions. He brought on veteran Aron Winter (to give him his record-breaking 84th cap?), out-of-form Clarence

LEAGUE CHAMPIONSHIP RESULTS 99/00

		1	2	3	4	5	6	7	8	9	10	11	12	13	14	15	16	17	18
1	Ajax		4-1	6-1	3-1	2-2	4-1	2-1	3-2	1-0	5-2	1-3	1-2	1-2	3-2	0-1	2-0	3-1	3-1
2	AZ	1-2		2-0	4-0	0-0	2-0	2-0	0-1	2-0	1-1	0-3	4-0	1-2	4-0	2-1	0-1	0-1	2-2
3	FC Den Bosch	1-1	2-3		1-1	0-4	0-2	1-1	0-2	1-1	1-1	2-6	0-3	2-2	7-0	0-0	3-2	2-1	1-1
4	SC Cambuur Leeuwarden	0-3	2-4	1-2		2-3	0-0	1-0	0-2	2-2	0-0	0-1	2-1	2-2	0-1	1-3	4-3	1-1	0-1
5	Feyenoord	1-1	5-3	3-0	4-0		1-0	0-0	3-1	3-0	2-1	1-0	1-2	2-1	1-2	1-1	1-2	0-0	1-0
6	Fortuna Sittard	2-0	1-2	1-1	4-1	2-3		1-1	0-1	3-1	2-2	0-4	0-2	1-2	3-2	2-2	3-0	3-3	2-0
7	De Graafschap	1-1	2-5	3-0	3-1	0-1	1-0		1-1	2-1	2-2	1-2	2-0	0-0	2-3	0-0	1-2	2-2	0-2
8	SC Heerenveen	1-1	3-0	1-1	4-1	3-0	3-0	2-0		3-1	1-0	0-3	4-1	5-1	3-1	0-0	1-0	1-3	2-4
9	MVV	2-6	3-4	2-0	1-1	3-3	1-0	0-2	1-3		2-0	0-2	0-1	0-0	2-2	0-2	4-1	0-2	1-1
10	NEC	1-3	1-2	2-0	1-0	0-2	1-2	2-3	0-4	1-0		2-1	3-1	0-0	0-1	0-1	0-1	1-0	2-1
11	PSV	4-0	5-1	7-0	1-0	0-1	2-1	6-0	0-1	4-1	2-0		7-1	2-0	7-0	2-2	2-1	3-2	6-1
12	RKC Waalwijk	1-1	1-2	1-1	3-2	2-2	0-3	2-1	0-1	0-4	4-2	1-6		2-2	2-1	1-1	2-0	1-1	1-0
13	Roda JC	3-0	3-2	3-0	3-1	2-1	3-0	2-3	0-2	3-1	4-3	1-2	1-2		4-1	3-2	3-2	0-1	3-4
14	Sparta	1-2	3-6	3-2	1-2	1-3	2-3	2-1	2-1	3-0	1-0	0-2	3-1	1-2		1-1	3-0	1-1	0-2
15	FC Twente	0-0	4-1	3-2	1-0	3-3	1-0	4-0	2-0	1-2	4-2	1-3	1-0	2-1	3-2		4-2	0-0	4-0
16	FC Utrecht	3-1	3-3	2-1	1-2	3-4	2-1	2-1	2-2	2-0	1-0	1-1	4-1	1-2	3-1	1-0		2-0	1-1
17	Vitesse	3-0	0-2	1-0	1-0	3-3	2-2	3-1	3-1	6-2	5-1	1-6	2-1	2-0	2-1	4-1	3-1		3-1
18	Willem II	3-6	3-1	2-1	1-4	2-1	2-2	5-3	2-3	1-0	3-1	0-0	2-1	2-2	0-0	1-1	4-3	0-4	

LEAGUE CHAMPIONSHIP FINAL TABLE 99/00

			Home					Away					Total					
		Pd	W	D	L	F	A	W	D	L	F	A	W	D	L	F	A	PT	GD
1	PSV	34	14	1	2	60	12	13	2	2	45	12	27	3	4	105	24	84	81
2	SC Heerenveen	34	11	3	3	37	17	10	2	5	28	19	21	5	8	65	36	68	29
3	Feyenoord	34	10	4	3	30	14	8	6	3	36	28	18	10	6	66	42	64	24
4	Vitesse	34	13	2	2	44	23	5	7	5	23	20	18	9	7	67	43	63	24
5	Ajax	34	12	1	4	44	23	6	6	5	28	28	18	7	9	72	51	61	21
6	FC Twente	34	12	3	2	38	18	4	9	4	19	19	16	12	6	57	37	60	20
7	AZ	34	8	3	6	27	14	9	1	7	42	45	17	4	13	69	59	55	10
8	Roda JC	34	11	0	6	41	27	5	7	5	21	26	16	7	11	62	53	55	9
9	Willem II	34	8	5	4	33	33	5	4	8	22	32	13	9	12	55	65	48	-10
10	FC Utrecht	34	10	4	3	34	21	4	0	13	21	40	14	4	16	55	61	46	-6
11	RKC Waalwijk	34	6	6	5	24	30	6	0	11	20	37	12	6	16	44	67	42	-23
12	Fortuna Sittard	34	6	5	6	30	27	4	3	10	17	27	10	8	16	47	54	38	-7
13	Sparta	34	7	2	8	28	29	4	2	11	20	46	11	4	19	48	75	37	-27
14	De Graafschap	34	5	6	6	23	23	3	3	11	18	37	8	9	17	41	60	33	-19
15	NEC	34	7	1	9	17	22	0	5	12	18	40	7	6	21	35	62	27	-27
16	MVV	34	4	5	8	22	30	2	2	13	16	38	6	7	21	38	68	25	-30
17	SC Cambuur Leeuwarden	34	3	5	9	18	29	3	2	12	17	37	6	7	21	35	66	25	-31
18	FC Den Bosch	34	3	8	6	24	31	1	3	13	12	43	4	11	19	36	74	23	-38

Seedorf (in hope rather than expectation?) and his friend Peter van Vossen (as a final gift on his international farewell?) and none of them made any impression at all. In contrast Pierre van Hooijdonk, who had enjoyed a prolific goalscoring season with Vitesse, and Ronald de Boer, a player of craft, vision and experience, sat glued to the bench.

Not everything that was said about Rijkaard was bad. Far from it. Up until the semi-final Holland had played some excellent football. Granted, they began poorly and were incredibly lucky to beat the Czech Republic in their opening match. But after the first goal went in against Denmark, they became liberated and treated their fans to some wonderfully skilful and exciting play. They beat France 3-2 to ensure that they remained on home soil for the remainder of the tournament and then went on the rampage with a breathtaking display against Yugoslavia in the quarter-final, running up a record 6-1 scoreline

and confirming their position as the favourites to win the tournament.

But it simply wasn't to be. Those four straight wins counted for nothing against the Italians, and with five penalties missed out of six taken, Holland's dream of glory disappeared in a puff of penalty-spot chalk-dust.

Despite the disappointment of not winning the tournament, several Dutch players significantly enhanced their reputations at Euro 2000. Edgar Davids was as influential as he had been two years earlier at the World Cup. Edwin van der Sar failed to concede a single goal. Boudewijn Zenden made goals and scored them too. And Patrick Kluivert came away with a share of the Golden Boot.

It was an extraordinarily successful international season all round for the Barcelona centre-forward. He played 14 matches

Edgar Davids proved to be one of Holland's real stars during the Euro 2000 finals.

for Holland in 1999/2000 and scored 14 goals, breaking the previous record of ten set by Johnny Bosman during the 1987/88 season. Kluivert's hot streak contrasted starkly with the barren spell endured by his strike-partner Dennis Bergkamp, who ended his international career without scoring any goals at all in his final two seasons. Bergkamp, with 36 goals in 79 internationals, remains Holland's all-time leading scorer, but Kluivert, with 28 in 45, is closing fast.

One Dutchman who did set a new record was Aron Winter, whose extra-time appearance in the semi-final against Italy took him to 84 caps, one more than the total of previous record-holder Ruud Krol, who had held the honour for 21 years and 34 days.

Eight days after Rijkaard's decision to stand down from 'Oranje' the Dutch FA (KNVB) appointed Louis van Gaal as his successor on a whopping six-year contract, which will be reviewed on a two-yearly basis, after each major tournament. The appointment was a dream come true for the ex-Ajax and Barcelona boss, who had never hidden his desire to take on the job at some point in his career. Van Gaal has always set himself high standards and it is his firm intention to take Holland to victory in at least one major tournament before he retires after the

NATIONAL TEAM APPEARANCES 99/00

Coach - Frank RIJKAARD	DEN	BEL	BRA	CZE	GER	BEL	SCO	ROM	POL	CZE	DEN	FRA	YUG	ITA	Cps	Gls
Edwin VAN DER SAR (29/10/70) - Juventus (ITA)	G	G	G	G	G		G	G	G	G	G89		G65	G	51	-
Michael REIZIGER (03/05/73) - FC Barcelona (ESP)	D67	D		s75	D				D	D	D				42	1
Jaap STAM (17/07/72) - Manchester United (ENG)	D	D62		D	D	D		D46	D	D74		D	D	D	36	3
Frank DE BOER (15/05/70) - FC Barcelona (ESP)	D	D		D		D	D	D	D	D	D	D	D	D	81	9
Phillip COCU (29/10/70) - FC Barcelona (ESP)	D	D	M87	D75	M46		M	M	M	M	M			M95	46	4
Boudewijn ZENDEN (15/08/76) - FC Barcelona (ESP)	M	M	M83		M		s46	D	M46	M78	M		M80	M77	26	5
Wim JONK (12/10/66) - Sheffield Wednesday (ENG)	M														49	11
Giovanni VAN BRONCKHORST (05/02/75) - Rangers (SCO)	M	M	M	D46		s46			D	D	D			D	19	1
Jimmy Floyd HASSELBAINK (27/03/72) - Atlético Madrid (ESP)	A76				s75		A67								8	2
Patrick KLUIVERT (01/07/76) - FC Barcelona (ESP)	A	A79	A	A41	A	A	s46	A86	A62	A	A	A60	A60	A	45	28
Ruud VAN NISTELROOY (01/07/76) - PSV	A	s66	s70	s41	A75										10	1
Ronald DE BOER (15/05/70) - FC Barcelona (ESP)	s67	M	D	D75	M66				s46	s57	s61		s80		61	13
Clarence SEEDORF (01/04/76) - Real Madrid (ESP)/Inter (ITA)	s76		M	s87	M	M		M	M76	M57				s86	51	7
Edgar DAVIDS (13/03/73) - Juventus (ITA)		M			M	M80	M		s46	M	M	M	M	M	35	4
Dennis BERGKAMP (10/05/69) - Arsenal (ENG)		A66	A70	A		A46	A70	A46	A	A76	A78	A		A86	79	36
Bert KONTERMAN (14/01/71) - Feyenoord		s62	D			s56	D		s46		s74	D			11	-
Pierre VAN HOOIJDONK (29/11/69) - Vitesse		s79						s67	s86	s62					20	7
Winston BOGARDE (22/10/70) - FC Barcelona (ESP)		D					D	D56							19	-
Marc VAN HINTUM (22/06/70) - Vitesse		D	s46												7	-
Aron WINTER (01/03/67) - Ajax			M46	M			M	M46			s76	s78		s95	84	6
Jean-Paul VAN GASTEL (28/04/72) - Feyenoord		s46													5	2
Peter VAN VOSSEN (21/04/68) - Feyenoord			s83					s89	s46			s89		s77	31	9
Marc OVERMARS (29/03/73) - Arsenal (ENG)			A			A	A46	M89	s78	M61	M89		M	M	60	13
Roy MAKAAY (09/03/75) - RC Deportivo (ESP)						s66	A74	A60	s70			s60	s60		8	-
Arthur NUMAN (14/12/69) - Rangers (SCO)						s75	s80	D				D	D		40	-
Sander WESTERVELD (23/10/74) - Liverpool (ENG)						G					s89	G	s65		5	-
Paul BOSVELT (26/03/70) - Feyenoord						M	M		s76			D	D	D	6	-
Jeffrey TALAN (29/09/71) - SC Heerenveen						s74	s60								5	-
André OOIJER (11/07/74) - PSV							D	D							4	-

2006 World Cup. Those finals will, of course, be held in Germany, where the Dutch have always performed well, reaching the World Cup final in 1974 and winning Euro '88.

The first Dutch championship title of the new millennium was won by PSV. They finished streets ahead of the opposition and were confirmed as champions with three matches still to go. It was an outstanding first season at the helm for Belgian coach (and ex-PSV player) Eric Gerets. He could not have made a better start as PSV won each of their first eight league games, chalking up 40 goals in the process.

PSV were driven by their magnificent front pairing of Ruud van Nistelrooy and Luc Nilis, who between them scored 48 of the team's 105 goals. The ratio would have been even greater had Van Nistelrooy not been ruled out for the final ten matches of the season with knee-ligament damage. By then the prolific striker had knocked in 29 goals and was on the trail of the Eredivisie record of 43 set back in the 1956/57 season by another PSV player, Coen Dillen, who, like Van Nistelrooy, scored 29 goals after 24 rounds.

PSV had another poor season in the Champions' League, winning just the one group game - albeit the most important one, at home to Bayern Munich - and exiting at the end of the first stage. Of the three Dutch participants, only defending champions Feyenoord managed to reach the second group stage. In fact, the Rotterdammers played better in Europe than they did at home, with a marvellous 2-1 victory away to Lazio the undoubted highlight.

Leo Beenhakker's team managed to work themselves up for the big games, beating Ajax 3-2 to win the Super Cup and winning both league encounters against PSV, but they came unstuck far too often against the lesser sides. They even completed an astonishing hat-trick when they lost 1-3 at home to AZ in the fourth round of the Cup. PSV and Ajax also lost in the same round, which meant that the KNVB-Beker had none of the 'big three' in its quarter-final line-up for the first time since 1981.

Feyenoord's hopes of a successful title defence were undermined by internal disorder. Although the club retained the vast bulk of its championship-winning personnel, some of the team spirit was lost when key players like Jean-Paul van Gastel, Bert Konterman and Kees van Wonderen spoke out publicly against the quality of the team and the ambition of the club. Coach Beenhakker, who was due to retire at the end of the season, brought forward the date of his departure by a few weeks when the team lost two successive home games, against Sparta and Utrecht. Youth development manager Henk van Stee took over temporarily, filling the void until Fortuna Sittard's Bart van Maarwijk assumed the reins in the summer.

Ajax were also entrusted to a new coach during the close season as Co Adriaanse, a former member of Van Gaal's coaching staff during the club's halcyon period in the mid-1990s, returned from Willem II. The 1999/2000 season had been one of the worst in living memory for the Amsterdam club. They failed abysmally on all fronts and were never in contention for any trophy.

There were many problems - a long and never-ending injury list, a number of inexperienced players having to operate in unfamiliar positions, and several supposed 'stars' failing to offer more than a token effort for the cause.

NATIONAL TEAM RESULTS 99/00

18/08/99	Denmark	A	Copenhagen	0-0	
04/09/99	Belgium	H	Rotterdam	5-5	Davids (37, 43), Kluivert (45, 59, 70)
09/10/99	Brazil	H	Amsterdam	2-2	Roberto Carlos (37og), Zenden (43)
13/11/99	Czech Republic	H	Eindhoven	1-1	Stam (59)
23/02/00	Germany	H	Amsterdam	2-1	Kluivert (15), Zenden (28)
29/03/00	Belgium	A	Brussels	2-2	Kluivert (32, 81)
26/04/00	Scotland	H	Arnhem	0-0	
27/05/00	Romania	H	Amsterdam	2-1	Overmars (43), Kluivert (68)
04/06/00	Poland	N	Lausanne	3-1	De Boer F. (29), Kluivert (56, 61)
11/06/00	Czech Republic (ECF)	H	Amsterdam	1-0	De Boer F. (89p)
16/06/00	Denmark (ECF)	H	Rotterdam	3-0	Kluivert (57), De Boer R. (66), Zenden (77)
21/06/00	France (ECF)	H	Amsterdam	3-2	Kluivert (14), De Boer F. (51), Zenden (59)
25/06/00	Yugoslavia (ECF)	H	Rotterdam	6-1	Kluivert (24, 38, 54), Govedarica (51og),
					Overmars (78, 90)
29/06/00	Italy (ECF)	H	Amsterdam	0-0	(aet; 1-3 on pens.)

TOP SCORERS

29	Ruud VAN NISTELROOY (PSV)
25	Pierre VAN HOOIJDONK (Vitesse)
19	Luc NILIS (PSV)
	Arnold BRUGGINK (PSV)
	Jan VENNEGOOR OF HESSELINK (FC Twente)
18	John BOSMAN (AZ)
	Anthony LURLING (SC Heerenveen)
15	Julio Ricardo CRUZ (Feyenoord)
	Bob PEETERS (Roda JC)
	Richard KNOPPER (Ajax)

DOMESTIC CUP 99/00

SECOND ROUND
BV Veendam 3, Sparta 0
NEC 3, Spakenburg 0
FC Utrecht 2, FC Den Bosch 0
Excelsior 2, Emmen 1
Dordrecht '90 5, FC Groningen 0
Haarlem 3, AGOVV 1
Be Quick '28 2, Excesior Maassluis 0
MVV 2, Baronie 3 (aet)
Go Ahead Eagles 3, Scheveningen 1
Quick '20 1, RBC 2
Fortuna Sittard 2, Noordwijk 0
SC Cambuur Leeuwarden 0, FC Zwolle 1
FC Twente 2, Gemert 1 (aet)
Hoek 0, AZ 4
SC Heracles 3, FC Volendam 0
RKC Waalwijk 2, SC Telstar 0
ADO Den Haag 3, AFC '34 0
SC Heerenveen 2, De Graafschap 0
Eijsden 1, Helmond Sport 8
Eindhoven 2, NAC 1

THIRD ROUND
SC Heerenveen 1, NEC 2
Helmond Sport 12, Be Quick '28 1
Go Ahead Eagles 2, Baronie 1
AZ 2, SC Heracles 0
Eindhoven 4, FC Zwolle 2
RBC 2, BV Veendam 0
Excelsior 3, Fortuna Sittard 2
ADO Den Haag 1, FC Utrecht 3
Dordrecht '90 2, Haarlem 1 (aet)
RKC Waalwijk 2, FC Twente 0
byes - Feyenoord, Willem II, PSV, Ajax, Vitesse, Roda JC

FOURTH ROUND
Dordrecht '90 1, RBC 0
Feyenoord 1, AZ 3
Helmond Sport 1, Willem II 2
NEC 1, Excelsior 0
PSV 0, Vitesse 2
RKC Waalwijk 2, Eindhoven 0
Roda JC 1, Ajax 0
FC Utrecht 5, Go Ahead Eagles 3

QUARTER-FINALS
FC Utrecht 0, Roda JC 1 (Van der Luer 86)
NEC 2 (De Gier 14, Latuheru 47), Dordrecht '90 0
RKC Waalwijk 0, Vitesse 1 (Sikora 61)
Willem II 1 (Schulp 90),
AZ 2 (Opdam 36, Van den Berg 97) (asd)

SEMI-FINALS
AZ 1 (Perez 77), NEC 1 (De Gier 60)
(aet; 1-4 on pens.)
Vitesse 0, Roda JC 1 (Zafarin 105) (asd)

FINAL
21/05/2000, Rotterdam
RODA JC 2 Peeters (19), Van der Luer (90p)
NEC 0
referee - Luinge
RODA JC - Kalac, Senden, Vrede, Van Haaren, Luijpers,
Valgaeren, Van der Luer, Lawal (Van Dessel 79),
Van Houdt, Tchoutang (Doomernlk 87), Peeters
(Soetaers 70).
NEC - Roorda, Hesp, Pothuizen, De Romijn, Collen,
Koning, Janssen, Schultz (Arts 78), Latuheru, De Gier,
Renfurm.

Although Ajax celebrated their 100th birthday in style off the pitch, there was nothing much to perk up the spirits of the fans on it. Jan Wouters lost his job after the team went down at home to FC Twente in the 'centenary match' in mid-March. From the end of November onwards Ajax failed to win any matches away from home, and for the first time since the 1985/86 season they were winless in their four matches against PSV and Feyenoord. Fifth place was all they could muster, but at least that guaranteed them a place in the UEFA Cup.

The second automatic Champions' League place went, surprisingly, to Heerenveen. Like Willem II a year earlier, they ensured a Dutch provincial presence in Europe's premier competition thanks not only to the tribulations of the country's traditional powers but also to their own exceptional performances. Led, as ever, by resident coach Foppe de Haan, Heerenveen played with spirit and style, and most neutrals in Holland were delighted to see them take the coveted runners-up spot.

For the second season in a row Vitesse missed out on a Champions' League qualification spot by failing to win their last game of the campaign. It was a season of upheaval at the Arnhem club, with former superstar Ronald Koeman arriving in mid-season as the newly-appointed coach and, more significantly, long-time president Karel Aalbers being ousted from his position by the club's main sponsors, electricity company NUON. Aalbers' dismissal caused a furore among the Vitesse fans. It was he who had led the club up from the lower divisions and he who had overseen the construction of the magnificent Gelredome stadium. But in doing all this he had run up huge bills, which NUON effectively paid off by providing a massive injection of new cash in return for a dominant presence on the club board.

INTERNATIONAL HONOURS

World Cup Finals appearances: 1934, 1938, 1974 (Runners-up), 1978 (Runners-up), 1990 (2nd round), 1994 (qtr-finals), 1998 (semi-finals)

European Championship appearances: 1976 (3rd), 1980, 1988 (Winners), 1992 (semi-finals), 1996, 2000 (semi-finals)

European Club Competitions

Champions' Cup	Feyenoord (1970)
	Ajax (1971, 1972, 1973, 1995)
	PSV (1988)
Cup-winners' Cup	Ajax (1987)
UEFA Cup	Feyenoord (1974)
	PSV (1978)
	Ajax (1992)
Super Cup	Ajax (1972, 1973, 1995)
World Club Cup	Feyenoord (1970)
	Ajax (1972, 1995)

EUROPEAN CUPS 99/00

CHAMPIONS' CUP
● FEYENOORD
Champions' League
1st match BORUSSIA DORTMUND (GER)
H 1-1 Van Wonderen (68)
Dudek, Bosvelt, Van Wonderen, Konterman, Rzasa (De Visser 46),
Van Gastel, Tomasson, Paauwe, Kalou, Cruz, Van Vossen (Samardzic 82).

2nd match ROSENBORG BK (NOR)
A 2-2 Tomasson (11), Kalou (22)
Dudek, Van Gobbel, Van Wonderen, Konterman, Paauwe, Bosvelt,
Tomasson, Van Gastel, De Visser, Kalou, Cruz.

3rd match BOAVISTA FC (POR)
A 1-1 Bosvelt (62)
Dudek, Van Gobbel, Van Wonderen, Konterman, Paauwe, Bosvelt,
Van Gastel, Tomasson, De Visser, Kalou, Cruz (Van Vossen 57).

4th match BOAVISTA FC (POR)
H 1-1 Tomasson (76)
Dudek, Van Gobbel, Van Gastel, Konterman, De Visser, Bosvelt, Tomasson,
Paauwe (Somalia 70), Kalou, Cruz, Van Vossen (Samardzic 46).

5th match BORUSSIA DORTMUND (GER)
A 1-1 Van Vossen (73)
Dudek, Van Gobbel (Korneev 78), De Haan, Konterman, Rzasa, Bosvelt,
Tomasson, Paauwe (Van Vossen 58), De Visser, Somalia (Cairo 58),
Kalou.

6th match ROSENBORG BK (NOR)
H 1-0 Somalia (86)
Dudek, Van Gobbel, De Haan, Konterman, Rzasa, Van Wonderen
(Paauwe 71), Tomasson, De Visser, Kalou, Korneev (Somalia 75),
Samardzic (Van Vossen 86).

7th match CHELSEA (ENG)
A 1-3 Cruz (90)
Dudek, Van Gobbel, Van Wonderen, Konterman, De Visser, Bosvelt,
Van Gastel, Tomasson (Cruz 60), Kalou, Somalia, Van Vossen
(Samardzic 62).

8th match OLYMPIQUE MARSEILLE (FRA)
H 3-0 Cruz (72, 90), Bosvelt (83)
Dudek, Gyan, Van Wonderen, Konterman, Rzasa, Bosvelt, Van Gastel,
Paauwe, Kalou, Cruz, Van Vossen (De Visser 37).

9th match LAZIO (ITA)
A 2-1 Tomasson (78, 85)
Dudek, Van Gobbel, Konterman, De Haan, Rzasa, Bosvelt, Van Gastel
(Gyan 83), Paauwe, De Visser (Samardzic 75), Kalou (Tomasson 46),
Cruz.

10th match LAZIO (ITA)
H 0-0
Dudek, Van Gobbel, Van Wonderen, Konterman, Rzasa, Bosvelt,
Van Gastel, Paauwe (Kalou 66), De Visser, Tomasson, Cruz.

11th match CHELSEA (ENG)
H 1-3 Kalou (58)
Dudek, Van Gobbel, Konterman, Van Wonderen, Rzasa, Bosvelt,
Van Gastel, Paauwe (Kalou 46), De Visser (Samardzic 69), Cruz,
Tomasson.

12th match OLYMPIQUE MARSEILLE (FRA)
A 0-0
Dudek, Van Gobbel (Korneev 80), Konterman, Van Wonderen, Rzasa,
Bosvelt, Van Gastel (Somalia 76), Tomasson, De Visser (Van Vossen 65),
Kalou, Cruz.

● PSV
Qualifying round ZIMBRU CHISINAU (MOL)
A 0-0
Waterreus, Ooijer, Dirkx, Faber, Heintze, Stinga, Vogel (Van der Doelen 85),
Khokhlov, Bruggink (Bouma 81), Nilis (Rommedahl 87), Van Nistelrooy.
H 2-0 Nilis (79), Ooijer (88)
Waterreus, Ooijer, Dirkx, Faber, Heintze, Stinga (Rommedahl 46),
Van Bommel, Vogel, Bouma (Kolkka 69), Bruggink (Nilis 56),
Van Nistelrooy.

Champions' League
1st match FC BAYERN MÜNCHEN (GER)
A 1-2 Khokhlov (59)
Waterreus, Vogel, Dirkx (Bruggink 77), Faber, Heintze, Iwan,
Van Bommel, Nikiforov (Bouma 81), Khokhlov, Van Nistelrooy, Nilis.

2nd match VALENCIA CF (ESP)
H 1-1 Van Nistelrooy (72p)
Waterreus, Faber (Wielaert 55), Nikiforov, Dirkx, Heintze, Rommedahl
(Kolkka 74), Vogel, Stinga (Bouma 69), Khokhlov, Bruggink,
Van Nistelrooy.

3rd match RANGERS (SCO)
H 0-1
Waterreus, Wielaert, Dirkx, Nikiforov, Heintze, Rommedahl (Kolkka 63),
Van der Doelen (Bruggink 79), Stinga (Bouma 68), Khokhlov, Nilis,
Van Nistelrooy.

4th match RANGERS (SCO)
A 1-4 Van Nistelrooy (45p)
Kralj, Wielaert (Kolkka 32), Faber, Nikiforov, Heintze, Stinga
(Rommedahl 74), Van Bommel, Vogel, Khokhlov, Nilis (Bruggink 86),
Van Nistelrooy.

5th match FC BAYERN MÜNCHEN (GER)
H 2-1 Van Nistelrooy (39), Nilis (57)
Waterreus, Faber, Addo, Dirkx, Heintze, Stinga, Van Bommel, Vogel,
Kolkka (Iwan 88), Nilis (Bruggink 72), Van Nistelrooy.

6th match VALENCIA CF (ESP)
A 0-1
Waterreus, Faber (Dirkx 59), Addo, Nikiforov, Heintze, Stinga, Khokhlov,
Van Bommel, Kolkka, Nilis (Rommedahl 70), Van Nistelrooy.

● WILLEM II
1st match SPARTAK MOSKVA (RUS)
H 1-3 Arts (56)
Mampaey, Prommayon, Jaliens, Victoria, Hill, Valk (Sanou 61), Galasek,
Arts, Ceesay, Bombarda, Shukov (Schenning 90).

2nd match GIRONDINS DE BORDEAUX (FRA)
A 2-3 Abdellaoui (40), Sanou (70)
Mampaey, Jaliens, Victoria, Hill, Valk, Shukov, Galasek, Arts, Ceesay,
Bombarda (Schenning 74), Abdellaoui (Sanou 58).

EUROPEAN CUPS 99/00 (CONTINUED)

3rd match SPARTA PRAHA (CZE)
A 0-4
> Mampaey, Prommayon, Gentile (Bombarda 46), Victoria, Hill, Jaliens, Galasek, Arts, Shukov, Ceesay, Abdellaoui (Sanou 81).

4th match SPARTA PRAHA (CZE)
H 3-4 Bombarda (1), Shukov (6), Schenning (50)
> Mampaey (Van Fessem 63), Prommayon, Schenning, Victoria, Hill, Jaliens, Galasek, Landzaat, Ceesay, Bombarda (Valk 59), Shukov (Sanou 76).

5th match SPARTAK MOSKVA (RUS)
A 1-1 Sanou (63)
> Van Fessem, Prommayon, Gentile, Hill, Van Nieuwstadt, Schenning, Landzaat (Valk 84), Victoria, Ceesay, Sanou (Schulp 87), Shukov (Hermes 77).

6th match GIRONDINS DE BORDEAUX (FRA)
H 0-0
> Van Fessem, Prommayon, Gentile, Galasek, Schenning (Hill 90), Jaliens, Victoria (Valk 87), Landzaat (Ramzi 76), Ceesay, Sanou, Shukov.

UEFA CUP
● AJAX
1st round DUKLA BANSKA BYSTRICA (SVK)
H 6-1 Verlaat (25p), Reuser (26), Knopper (48), Mahlas (50, 64), Wamberto (72)
> Grim, Nieuwenberg, Verlaat (Vierklau 77), Winter (O'Brien 77), De Cler, Knopper, Reuser, Witschge, Laudrup, Mahlas, Wamberto.

A 3-1 Arveladze (47), Bobson (64), Laudrup (90)
> Grim, Vierklau (Kanu 57), Verlaat (Chivu 70), Nieuwenberg, De Cler, Reuser, O'Brien, Dani, Laudrup, Mahlas (Arveladze 33), Bobson.

2nd round HAPOEL HAIFA (ISR)
A 3-0 Mahlas (3), Knopper (12), Laudrup (56)
> Grim, Nieuwenberg, Winter, Verlaat, Chivu, O'Brien, Knopper, Witschge, Laudrup (Grønkjaer 65), Mahlas (Arveladze 46), Wamberto.

H 0-1
> Grim, Kanu, Lanzaat, Winter, Chivu, Nieuwenberg, Knopper, Witschge, Grønkjaer, Mahlas (Pique 74), Wamberto.

3rd round RCD MALLORCA (ESP)
H 0-1
> Grim, Nieuwenberg, Mokoena, Winter, O'Brien, Van Halst (De Cler 77), Knopper, Witschge, Laudrup, Wamberto (Hose 66), Grønkjaer.

A 0-2
> Grim, Nieuwenberg, Verlaat, Winter, De Cler (Kanu 46), Van Halst, Knopper (Babangida 69), Chivu, Laudrup, Mahlas (Grønkjaer 46), Wamberto.

● RODA JC
1st round SHAKHTAR DONETSK (UKR)
H 2-0 Doomernik (18), Zafarin (26)
> Kalac, Rudge, Valgaeren, Luijpers, Van Haaren, Zafarin, Doomernik, Van der Luer, Lawal, Van Houdt (Jacobs 88), Peeters (Tchoutang 72).

A 3-1 Tchoutang (28), Van der Luer (81), Van Dessel (88)
> Kalac, Rudge, Luijpers, Valgaeren, Van Haaren, Zafarin ('T Hart 75), Van der Luer, Doomernik, Lawal (Van Dessel 85), Peeters (Jacobs 89), Tchoutang.

2nd round VFL WOLFSBURG (GER)
H 0-0
> Kalac, Rudge, Vrede, Luijpers, Van Haaren, Zafarin, Van der Luer, Valgaeren, Lawal, Peeters, Tchoutang (Jacobs 82).

A 0-1
> Kalac, Rudge, Luijpers, Valgaeren, Van Haaren, Zafarin, Doomernik, Van der Luer, Lawal, Tchoutang (Vrede 85), Peeters.

● VITESSE
1st round SC BEIRA MAR (POR)
A 2-1 Van Hooijdonk (50), Grozdic (82)
> Jevric, Jochemsen, Wisgerhof, De Marchi, Van Hintum, Trustfull (Sikora 65), Kreek, Grozdic, Laros (Stefanovic 87), Janssen, Van Hooijdonk.

H 0-0
> Jevric, Jochemsen (Nanu 29), Wisgerhof (Laros 39), De Marchi, Van Hintum, Riga (Zongo 82), Grozdic, Kreek, Janssen, Van Hooijdonk, Sikora.

2nd round RC LENS (FRA)
A 1-4 Van Hooijdonk (73p)
> Jevric, Jochemsen (Collen 69), Kreek (De Marchi 53), Stefanovic, Van Hintum, Zongo, Grozdic, Janssen, Laros, Van Hooijdonk, Sikora (Riga 13).

H 1-1 Kreek (64)
> Jevric, Nanu, Kreek (De Marchi 86), Stefanovic, Van Hintum, Trustfull (Zongo 69), Grozdic, Van den Brom, Janssen (Diarra 59), Van Hooijdonk, Laros.

Vitesse knocked PSV out of the Dutch Cup with a 2-0 victory in Eindhoven shortly after Koeman's arrival but they were unable to go all the way and claim their first major trophy. In the semi-final they suffered a shock themselves when they were beaten at home by a 'golden goal' from Roda JC midfielder Davy Zafarin. A penalty shoot-out decided the other semi-final, with NEC prevailing 4-1 in the shoot-out against AZ after a 1-1 draw.

The Cup final, played, as is now customary, in Rotterdam's Feyenoord Stadium, attracted a 36,000 gate and resulted in a 2-0 victory for Roda, who thus claimed the trophy for the second time in four seasons. There was an embarrassing moment for Roda and and a worrying one for the KNVB in the team's post-final celebrations. Travelling back to Limburg on the team coach, Belgian striker Bob Peeters, who had scored the opening goal in the final with a beautiful header, held the Cup aloft through a window in the ceiling of the bus. The top of the trophy was blown off, and at first it couldn't be found. It was only a few days later that the missing part was traced and reunited with the rest of the trophy in Kerkrade.

For the first time since 1993 the maximum complement of three teams were relegated and promoted between

PLAYERS OF THE SEASON

ROY MAKAAY

You could say that Roy Makaay (pictured right) made a rather clever move when he left Tenerife to join Deportivo La Coruña in the summer of 1999. The Canary Islands club had just been relegated, and his new team were about to embark on a campaign that would end with a first-ever victory in the Spanish championship. The Dutchman was a key contributor to the Deportivo success story. He made the perfect start, scoring a wonderful hat-trick on his début against Alavés, and continued to find the net at regular intervals throughout the season, finishing up as the club's top scorer, by some distance, with 22 goals. Sharp, lively and quick off the mark, Makaay forced his way into Holland's Euro 2000 squad (ahead of another in-form Spanish-based sharpshooter, Jimmy Floyd Hasselbaink) but was only ever going to be a reserve behind the established Kluivert-Bergkamp partnership. It was a great shame, however, that he injured himself in training prior to the semi-final with Italy. He could have been just the man Holland needed to find a way through that 'Azzurri' blockade...

JAN VENNEGOOR OF HESSELINK

There are differences of opinion about the quality of the man with the longest name in Dutch professional football. Jan Vennegoor of Hesselink (he insists on the whole name) scored 19 goals for FC Twente in 1999/2000 to prove that his 21-goal haul of the previous campaign was no fluke, but while PSV showed a keenness to buy him as a replacement for long-term injury victim (and Manchester United target) Ruud van Nistelrooy, the other big clubs in Holland shied away, claiming that he was too attached to his native Enschede region to become a hit elsewhere. That, of course, was music to the ears of the Twente fans, who know just how important their goalscoring centre-forward is to the club's ambitions. Good performances for the Dutch U-21 side plus goals for Twente against PSV and Ajax provided evidence of his class, and despite the reticence of some to recognise his true value, it is obvious that the 22-year-old has a big future ahead of him.

EDGAR DAVIDS

It was a frustrating season all round for Edgar Davids. His club, Juventus, missed out on the Serie A

title on the final day of the season, and his country, Holland, threw away a golden chance of winning Euro 2000 by missing a succession of penalties in the semi-final against Italy. It was in that latter game, however, that the little power-packed midfielder in the custom-built shades demonstrated just why he is so important to the Dutch cause. While others around him were hanging their heads in desperation, he continued to drive the team on in search of the elusive goal that would put Holland in the final. It never came, of course, but it was not for the want of trying on Davids' behalf. Throughout the tournament he was Holland's most effective player, maintaining the high level of consistency which had characterised his France '98 performances. With his mentor Louis van Gaal now installed as the new Bondscoach, Davids will continue to be Holland's leading man in the qualifying campaign for Japan/Korea 2002.

the Eredivisie and Eerste Divisie. FC Den Bosch and NAC traded places automatically, and in the play-offs MVV and Cambuur Leeuwarden both finished well off the pace, enabling FC Groningen and RBC to take the other two promotion berths.

Tiny RBC, from Roosendaal in the south-west of Holland, had never reached the Eredivise before, and after finishing a mere sixth in the Eerste Divisie they were hardly expected to break that spell. But the late run of form which brought them the fourth, and last, 'period champion' prize was carried into the play-offs, where they ultimately pipped FC Zwolle by a single point.

The man chiefly responsible for RBC's rags-to-riches rise was coach Robert Maaskant, who, in sealing the team's promotion, earned himself a place in the record-books. His father, Bob Maaskant, was also once an Eredivisie coach with Go Ahead Eagles and NAC, which makes the two of them the first father-and-son pairing to have operated as coaches in Holland's top division.

PROMOTED CLUBS 99/00

FIRST DIVISION FINAL TABLE

		Pd	W	D	L	F	A	Pt	GD
1	NAC (*2)	34	27	1	6	84	36	82	48
2	FC Zwolle (*1)	34	22	8	4	90	41	74	49
3	FC Groningen (*3)	34	23	5	6	81	33	74	48
4	Excelsior	34	18	5	11	70	48	59	22
5	Emmen	34	18	4	12	53	45	58	8
6	RBC (*4)	34	17	6	11	65	49	57	16
7	SC Heracles	34	13	8	13	41	42	47	-1
8	Dordrecht '90	34	12	9	13	55	58	45	-3
9	Eindhoven	34	14	3	17	47	63	45	-16
10	Helmond Sport	34	13	3	18	45	57	42	-12
11	ADO Den Haag	34	12	6	16	37	52	42	-15
12	BV Veendam	34	10	11	13	50	61	41	-11
13	SC Telstar	34	11	4	19	44	59	37	-15
14	Go Ahead Eagles	34	9	9	16	56	58	36	-2
15	VVV	34	8	11	15	38	62	35	-24
16	Haarlem	34	9	5	20	54	72	32	-18
17	FC Volendam	34	8	7	19	40	75	31	-35
18	TOP Oss	34	8	3	23	35	74	27	-39

N.B. (*) = period champion.

PROMOTION/RELEGATION PLAY-OFFS

GROUP A FINAL TABLE		Pd	W	D	L	F	A	Pt	GD
1	FC Groningen	6	5	0	1	19	7	15	12
2	Emmen	6	2	2	2	8	10	8	-2
3	MVV	6	2	1	3	11	14	7	-3
4	SC Heracles	6	1	1	4	10	17	4	-7

GROUP B FINAL TABLE		Pd	W	D	L	F	A	Pt	GD
1	RBC	6	3	2	1	10	7	11	3
2	FC Zwolle	6	3	1	2	14	7	10	7
3	Excelsior	6	2	1	3	11	14	7	-3
4	SC Cambuur Leeuwarden	6	1	2	3	6	13	5	-7

CLUB DIRECTORIES

NAC
Postbus 3356
4800 DJ Breda
tel - (076) 5214500
fax - (076) 5211975
Year of Formation - 1912
Executive Director - Roeland Oltmans
Coach - Kees Zwamborn (00/01 - Henk ten Cate)
Stadium - FujiFilm (16,522)

MAJOR HONOURS

League Championship - (1) 1921.
Domestic Cup - (1) 1973.

FC Groningen
Postbus 1399
9701 BJ Groningen
tel - (050) 5878787
fax - (050) 3125194
Year of Formation - 1926
President - Jaap van der Linde
Executive Director - Hans Nijland
Coach - Jan van Dijk
Stadium - Oosterpark (13,000)

RBC
Postbus 280
4700 AG Roosendaal
tel - (0165) 540133
fax - (0165) 564164
Year of Formation - 1912
President - Jan Pollemans
Secretary - Joop La Lau
Director - Paul van der Kraan
Coach - Robert Maaskant
Stadium - Vast & Goed (5,000)

AJAX

CLUB DIRECTORY

Ajax
Postbus 12522, 1100 AM Amsterdam
tel - (020) 3111444 / fax - (020) 3111480
website - www.ajax.nl
Year of Formation - 1900
President - Michael van Praag
Coach - Jan Wouters; Hans Westerhof
(00/01 - Co Adriaanse)
Stadium - Amsterdam ArenA (51,324)

MAJOR HONOURS
League Championship - (27)
1918, 1919, 1931, 1932, 1934, 1937, 1939,
1947, 1957, 1960, 1966, 1967, 1968, 1970,
1972, 1973, 1977, 1979, 1980, 1982, 1983,
1985, 1990, 1994, 1995, 1996, 1998.
Domestic Cup - (14)
1917, 1943, 1961, 1967, 1970, 1971, 1972,
1979, 1983, 1986, 1987, 1993, 1998, 1999.
European Champions' Cup - (4)
1971, 1972, 1973, 1995.
European Cup-winners' Cup - (1) 1987.
UEFA Cup - (1) 1992.
European Super Cup - (3) 1972, 1973, 1995.
World Club Cup - (2) 1972, 1995.

APPEARANCES 99/00

	P	Ap	(s)	Gls
Shota ARVELADZE (GEO)	A	13	(4)	5
Tijjani BABANGIDA (NIG)	A	2	(6)	1
Kevin BOBSON	A	3		
Cristian CHIVU (ROM)	D	20	(3)	1
Tim DE CLER	D	20	(1)	
DANI (POR)	M	16	(3)	4
Fred GRIM	G	34		
Jesper GRØNKJAER (DEN)	A	24	(1)	3
Jan VAN HALST	D	19	(2)	
Pascal HEIJE	A		(2)	
Brutil HOSE	A	1	(3)	1
Pius IKEDIA (NIG)	A	1	(1)	
Christopher KANU (NIG)	D	6	(3)	
Richard KNOPPER	M	33		15
Quido LANDZAAT	M	1		
Brian LAUDRUP (DEN)	A	31		13
Nikos MAHLAS (GRE)	A	24	(1)	14
Aaron MOKOENA (SAF)	D	4	(3)	
John NIEUWENBERG	D	20	(2)	
John O'BRIEN (USA)	D	11	(5)	1
Mitchell PIQUE	D		(2)	
Martijn REUSER	A	1	(2)	
Rafael VAN DER VAART	D	1		
Frank VERLAAT	D	20	(1)	3
Ferdy VIERKLAU	D	8	(2)	
WAMBERTO (BRA)	A	4	(23)	4
Aron WINTER	M	34		3
Richard WITSCHGE	M	20		2
Abubakar YAKUBU (GHA)	M	3	(2)	

LEAGUE RESULTS 1999/2000

15/08/99	SC Heerenveen	H	3-2	Laudrup, Mahlas, Arveladze
20/08/99	MVV	A	6-2	Knopper 2, Verlaat, Witschge, Laudrup, Dani
27/08/99	SC Cambuur Leeuwarden	A	3-0	Dani, Laudrup, Wamberto
10/09/99	Feyenoord	H	2-2	Knopper, Wamberto
19/09/99	RKC Waalwijk	A	1-1	Knopper
24/09/99	Vitesse	H	3-1	Laudrup 2, Arveladze
03/10/99	Willem II	A	6-3	Knopper 2, Mahlas 2, Laudrup, Babangida
13/10/99	Fortuna Sittard	H	4-1	Wamberto, Knopper, Laudrup 2
17/10/99	NEC	A	3-1	O'Brien, Mahlas (p), Knopper
24/10/99	FC Den Bosch	H	6-1	Mahlas 3 (1p), Laudrup, Knopper, Witschge
29/10/99	Roda JC	H	1-2	Winter
07/11/99	Sparta	A	2-1	Verlaat, og (Marilia)
21/11/99	FC Utrecht	H	2-0	Winter, Grønkjaer
28/11/99	AZ	A	2-1	Knopper, Hosé
05/12/99	RKC Waalwijk	H	1-2	Wamberto
15/12/99	PSV	H	1-3	Knopper
19/12/99	De Graafschap	A	1-1	Mahlas
02/02/00	SC Heerenveen	A	1-1	Mahlas
06/02/00	SC Cambuur Leeuwarden	H	3-1	Mahlas, og (Loontjens), Laudrup
10/02/00	PSV	A	0-4	
13/02/00	Willem II	H	3-1	Mahlas, Knopper, Dani
20/02/00	De Graafschap	H	2-1	Mahlas, Dani
05/03/00	FC Twente	A	0-0	
15/03/00	Fortuna Sittard	A	0-2	
19/03/00	FC Twente	H	0-1	
26/03/00	NEC	H	5-2	Laudrup, Mahlas 2, Grønkjaer, Knopper
31/03/00	Roda JC	A	0-3	
09/04/00	Sparta	H	3-2	Arveladze, Verlaat, Laudrup (p)
16/04/00	AZ	H	4-1	Arveladze 2, Grønkjaer, Winter
19/04/00	FC Den Bosch	A	1-1	Knopper
23/04/00	Feyenoord	A	1-1	Laudrup
30/04/00	Vitesse	A	0-3	
07/05/00	MVV	H	1-0	Chivu
14/05/00	FC Utrecht	A	1-3	Knopper

AZ

AZ
Postbus 1010, 1801 KA Alkmaar
tel - (072) 5154744
fax - (072) 5158388
website - www.az-alkmaar.nl
Year of Formation - 1967
President - Dirk Scheringa
Secretary - Bert Rozemond
Technical Director - Hans van der Zee
Coach - Gerard van der Lem
Stadium - Alkmaarderhout (8,372)

MAJOR HONOURS
League Championship - (1) 1981.
Domestic Cup - (3) 1978, 1981, 1982.

APPEARANCES 99/00

	P	Ap	(s)	Gls
Peter VAN DEN BERG	D	10	(3)	
John BOSMAN	A	31		18
Elbekay BOUCHIBA (MAR)	M	8	(5)	
Dries BOUSSATTA	A	28	(1)	3
Michael BUSKERMOLEN	D	18	(2)	2
CANIGIA (BRA)	A	2	(6)	
Kenan DURMUSOGLU (TUR)	M		(2)	
Abdelkrim EL HADRIOUI (MAR)	D	29		2
Youssef FERTOUT (MAR)	A	3	(12)	4
Barry VAN GALEN	M	26	(2)	11
Ferdino HERNANDEZ	A	15	(5)	3
Erik HOMAN	M		(1)	
Max HUIBERTS	A	13	(4)	5
Patrick HUISMAN	D		(1)	
Rolf LANDERL (AUT)	A	4	(3)	1
Urvin LEE	D	28		
Olaf LINDENBERGH	D	15		
Miel MANS	M	14	(7)	
Oscar MOENS	G	33		
John MUTSAERS	A	1	(9)	1
Barry OPDAM	D	30	(4)	5
Kenneth PEREZ (DEN)	A	6	(1)	1
Fernando RICKSEN	D	29		10
Robert VAN DER WEERT	A	1	(12)	1
Robert VAN WESTEROP	G	1		
Hans VAN DER WOUDE	M	2	(7)	
Peter WIJKER	D	27	(1)	1

LEAGUE RESULTS 1999/2000

14/08/99	Fortuna Sittard	A	2-1	Van Galen 2
29/08/99	RKC Waalwijk	A	2-1	Bosman, Van Galen
10/09/99	Roda JC	H	1-2	Huiberts
15/09/99	FC Utrecht	H	0-1	
18/09/99	Willem II	A	1-3	Landerl
25/09/99	SC Cambuur Leeuwarden	A	4-2	Van Galen, Bosman 2, Boussatta
03/10/99	Feyenoord	H	0-0	
13/10/99	FC Den Bosch	A	3-2	Bosman, Van Galen 2
17/10/99	Sparta	A	6-3	Buskermolen, Van Galen, Bosman, Van der Weert, Opdam, Ricksen
22/10/99	SC Heerenveen	H	0-1	
31/10/99	PSV	H	0-3	
06/11/99	MVV	A	4-3	El Hadrioui, Huiberts, Bosman, Van Galen
19/11/99	FC Twente	H	2-1	Buskermolen (p), og (Verlinden)
28/11/99	Ajax	H	1-2	Bosman
01/12/99	De Graafschap	A	5-2	Boussatta, Bosman, Ricksen 2, Mutsaers
04/12/99	Vitesse	A	2-0	Bosman, Boussatta
10/12/99	Fortuna Sittard	H	2-0	Wijker, Opdam
18/12/99	NEC	H	1-1	Van Galen
02/02/00	FC Twente	A	1-4	Ricksen
05/02/00	SC Heerenveen	A	0-3	
09/02/00	Sparta	H	4-0	Bosman 2, Opdam, Perez
12/02/00	NEC	A	2-1	Hernandez, Fertout
22/02/00	SC Cambuur Leeuwarden	H	4-0	Huiberts, Opdam, Hernandez, Bosman
27/02/00	FC Utrecht	A	3-3	Bosman, Ricksen, Fertout
03/03/00	Willem II	H	2-2	Huiberts, Bosman
10/03/00	RKC Waalwijk	H	4-0	Ricksen, Huiberts, Fertout, Hernandez
24/03/00	FC Den Bosch	H	2-0	Fertout, Van Galen
01/04/00	PSV	A	1-5	Ricksen
07/04/00	De Graafschap	H	2-0	Bosman (p), Van Galen
16/04/00	Ajax	A	1-4	Bosman
21/04/00	MVV	H	2-0	Bosman, Ricksen
30/04/00	Feyenoord	A	3-5	El Hadrioui, Ricksen 2
07/05/00	Vitesse	H	0-1	
14/05/00	Roda JC	A	2-3	Bosman, Opdam

FC DEN BOSCH

CLUB DIRECTORY

FC Den Bosch
Victorialaan 21
5213 JG 's Hertogenbosch
tel - (073) 6464700
fax - (073) 6464709
website - www.fcdenbosch.nl
Year of Formation - 1965
President - Hans Brus
Secretary - Jos van de Wouw
Coach - Martin Koopman; Mark Wotte
Stadium - ECCO (4,900)

APPEARANCES 99/00

	P	Ap	(s)	Gls
Maikel AERTS	G	34		
Krzysztof BOCIEK (POL)	A	7	(7)	
Mark DAMEN	D	1	(1)	
Patrick DECKERS	M	27		2
Ali FATTOUCHI	M		(1)	
Patricio GRAFF (ARG)	D	11		
Cedric VAN DER GUN	A	10		
Patrick HOBBELEN	A	16	(9)	
Fred VAN DER HOORN	D	32		4
Chaly JONES	A	14	(9)	2
Harry VAN DER LAAN	A	18	(16)	8
Roel LIEFDEN	D	18	(2)	
Rafael LOSADA	A	5	(3)	
Reggi MARTINA	A		(1)	
Erik MEULENDIJK	D	5	(2)	
Mourad MGHIZRAT (MAR)	A	9		1
Jan MICHELS	M	14	(4)	3
Martin REIJNDERS	A	3	(1)	
Michel RIBEIRO (BEL)	M	1	(7)	
Mark SCHENNING	D	13		
Arnold SCHOLTEN	M	20	(1)	1
Richard STRICKER	D	10	(1)	
Peter UNEKEN	D	22		2
Roberto VERHAGEN	M	11	(10)	
Henk VOS	A	27	(3)	11
Rob WIELAERT	D	20		
Memo WILLEMS	D	21	(3)	
Christopher WREH (LIB)	A	5	(2)	2

LEAGUE RESULTS 1999/2000

13/08/99	Feyenoord	H	0-4	
21/08/99	De Graafschap	H	1-1	Michels
28/08/99	Willem II	A	1-2	Van der Laan (p)
18/09/99	MVV	H	1-1	Deckers
26/09/99	FC Utrecht	H	3-2	Deckers, Vos, Van der Laan
29/09/99	NEC	A	0-2	
02/10/99	FC Twente	A	2-3	Jones, Van der Laan (p)
13/10/99	AZ	H	2-3	Michels (p), Scholten
17/10/99	PSV	A	0-7	
24/10/99	Ajax	A	1-6	Michels
30/10/99	SC Cambuur Leeuwarden	H	1-1	Jones
07/11/99	Roda JC	A	0-3	
20/11/99	RKC Waalwijk	H	0-3	
28/11/99	FC Utrecht	A	1-2	Vos
01/12/99	SC Heerenveen	H	0-2	
04/12/99	Fortuna Sittard	A	1-1	Van der Laan
12/12/99	Vitesse	H	2-1	Van der Laan 2
15/12/99	Sparta	A	2-3	Vos 2
26/01/00	Vitesse	A	0-1	
06/02/00	PSV	H	2-6	Wreh 2
09/02/00	MVV	A	0-2	
13/02/00	FC Twente	H	0-0	
19/02/00	Roda JC	H	2-2	Uneken, Van der Hoorn
05/03/00	De Graafschap	A	0-3	
11/03/00	Feyenoord	A	0-3	
24/03/00	AZ	A	0-2	
31/03/00	Willem II	H	1-1	Vos
08/04/00	SC Cambuur Leeuwarden	A	2-1	Vos 2
16/04/00	NEC	H	1-1	Van der Laan (p)
19/04/00	Ajax	H	1-1	Uneken
23/04/00	RKC Waalwijk	A	1-1	Van der Hoorn
30/04/00	Fortuna Sittard	H	0-2	
07/05/00	SC Heerenveen	A	1-1	Mghizrat
14/05/00	Sparta	H	7-0	Vos 4, Van der Hoorn 2, Van der Laan

SC CAMBUUR LEEUWARDEN

CLUB DIRECTORY

SC Cambuur Leeuwarden
Postbus 547
8901 BH Leeuwarden
tel - (058) 2963300
fax - (058) 2963399
website - www.cambuur.nl
Year of Formation - 1964
President - Wyzte Adema
Executive Director - Herman Juckers
Coach - Gert Kruys
Stadium - Cambuur (10,000)

APPEARANCES 99/00

	P	Ap	(s)	Gls
Johan ABMA	D	22	(1)	1
Rob ALFLEN	M	25	(1)	
Frank BERGHUIS	A		(2)	
Gregg BERHALTER (USA)	D	28		
Kenan DURMUSOGLO (TUR)	M	14	(1)	
Richard ELZINGA	D	3		
Maickel FERRIER	D	27	(1)	1
Kenneth GOUDMIJN	A	15	(13)	2
Sandor VAN DER HEIDE	M	20	(7)	7
Reinder HENDRIKS	D	7		
Rob HILBERS	G	4		
Yevgeniy LEVCHENKO (UKR)	M	20	(5)	
Robert LOONTJENS	D	19	(5)	1
Rudy MANN	A		(5)	
Danny MULLER	A	2	(5)	
Robin NELISSE	A	34		12
Jan ROELOFSEN	D	1	(2)	
Wim DE RON	G	30		
Peter DE ROO	M	4		
Mischa ROOK	M	7	(11)	2
Dennis SCHARRENBURG	M	19	(5)	2
Twan SCHEEPERS	A	1	(9)	
Erik TAMMER	A	7	(2)	1
Leonard VAN UTRECHT	A	31	(2)	4
Davy VELTMAN	M		(1)	
Dominik VERGOOSSEN	D	20	(2)	1
Geert-Jelle DE VRIES	D	4	(1)	
Raymond DE WAARD	A	10	(13)	1

LEAGUE RESULTS 1999/2000

14/08/99	Vitesse	H	1-1	Nelisse
22/08/99	Feyenoord	A	0-4	
27/08/99	Ajax	H	0-3	
11/09/99	MVV	A	1-1	Goudmijn
17/09/99	FC Twente	H	1-3	Nelisse
25/09/99	AZ	H	2-4	Van der Heide, Nelisse
02/10/99	Fortuna Sittard	A	1-4	Van der Heide (p)
12/10/99	Willem II	H	0-1	
16/10/99	Vitesse	A	0-1	
23/10/99	De Graafschap	H	1-0	Scharrenburg
30/10/99	FC Den Bosch	A	1-1	De Waard
07/11/99	RKC Waalwijk	A	2-3	Nelisse 2
21/11/99	PSV	H	0-1	
26/11/99	SC Heerenveen	A	1-4	Van der Heide
01/12/99	FC Utrecht	H	4-3	Vergoossen, Van der Heide, Nelisse, Van Utrecht
05/12/99	NEC	A	0-1	
29/01/00	De Graafschap	A	1-3	Van der Heide
02/02/00	NEC	H	0-0	
06/02/00	Ajax	A	1-3	Scharrenburg
12/02/00	Fortuna Sittard	H	0-0	
15/02/00	Sparta	H	0-1	
22/02/00	AZ	A	0-4	
29/02/00	Roda JC	A	1-3	Goudmijn
04/03/00	MVV	H	2-2	Nelisse, Loontjens
11/03/00	FC Twente	A	0-1	
17/03/00	Feyenoord	H	2-3	Van Utrecht, Nelisse
25/03/00	Roda JC	H	2-2	Van Utrecht, Tammer
02/04/00	FC Utrecht	A	2-1	Van Utrecht, Nelisse (p)
08/04/00	FC Den Bosch	H	1-2	Ferrier
16/04/00	PSV	A	0-1	
22/04/00	Sparta	A	2-1	Rook, Nelisse
30/04/00	SC Heerenveen	H	0-2	
07/05/00	Willem II	A	4-1	Nelisse 2, Rook, Van der Heide
14/05/00	RKC Waalwijk	H	2-1	Abma, Van der Heide

FEYENOORD

CLUB DIRECTORY

Feyenoord
Olympiaweg 50, 3077 AL Rotterdam
tel - (010) 2926888
fax - (010) 4325819
website - www.feyenoord.nl
Year of Formation - 1908
President - Jorien van den Herik
Manager - Hans Hagelstein
Coach - Leo Beenhakker; Henk van Stee
(00/01 - Bert van Marwijk)
Stadium - Feyenoord (51,180)

MAJOR HONOURS
League Championship - (14)
1924, 1928, 1936, 1938, 1940, 1961, 1962,
1965, 1969, 1971, 1974, 1984, 1993, 1999.
Domestic Cup - (10) 1930, 1935, 1965, 1969,
1980, 1984, 1991, 1992, 1994, 1995.
European Champions' Cup - (1) 1970.
UEFA Cup - (1) 1974.
World Club Cup - (1) 1970.

APPEARANCES 99/00

	P	Ap	(s)	Gls
Paul BOSVELT	M	31	(1)	8
Ellery CAIRO	A	4	(15)	3
Julio Ricardo CRUZ (ARG)	A	26	(4)	15
Rene VAN DIEREN	D		(1)	
Jerzy DUDEK (POL)	G	34		
Jean-Paul VAN GASTEL	M	16	(6)	1
Ulrich VAN GOBBEL	D	22		
Christian GYAN (GHA)	D	9		
Ferry DE HAAN	D	11	(5)	
Bonaventure KALOU (CIV)	A	25	(4)	7
Bert KONTERMAN	D	33		3
Igor KORNEEV (RUS)	M	7	(8)	6
Steve OLFERS	D		(1)	
Patrick PAAUWE	M	22	(6)	2
Tomasz RZASA (POL)	D	30	(1)	1
Radoslav SAMARDZIC (YUG)	A	10	(4)	1
SOMALIA (BRA)	A	1	(11)	2
TININHO (BRA)	A	1	(2)	
Jon Dahl TOMASSON (DEN)	A	28		10
Jan DE VISSER	M	21	(5)	2
Peter VAN VOSSEN	A	19	(7)	4
Kees VAN WONDEREN	D	24	(4)	1

LEAGUE RESULTS 1999/2000

13/08/99	FC Den Bosch	A	4-0	Cruz 3 (1p), Tomasson
22/08/99	SC Cambuur Leeuwarden	H	4-0	Korneev, Cairo, Kalou 2
28/08/99	SC Heerenveen	H	3-1	Cruz, Kalou, Van Vossen
10/09/99	Ajax	A	2-2	Bosvelt, Kalou
18/09/99	Fortuna Sittard	H	1-0	Van Wonderen
26/09/99	RKC Waalwijk	H	1-2	Tomasson
03/10/99	AZ	A	0-0	
12/10/99	Vitesse	H	0-0	
15/10/99	Roda JC	A	1-2	Tomasson
24/10/99	NEC	H	2-1	Konterman, Bosvelt
07/11/99	FC Twente	A	3-3	Rzasa, Kalou, Somalia
19/11/99	MVV	A	3-3	Korneev 2 (1p), Somalia
28/11/99	PSV	H	1-0	Van Gastel (p)
01/12/99	Willem II	H	1-0	Kalou
04/12/99	Sparta	A	3-1	Cruz 2, Kalou
16/12/99	De Graafschap	H	0-0	
19/12/99	FC Utrecht	A	4-3	Bosvelt, De Visser 2, Cruz
03/02/00	PSV	A	1-0	Paauwe
06/02/00	Roda JC	H	2-1	Tomasson, Cairo
09/02/00	Fortuna Sittard	A	3-2	Bosvelt, Cairo, Cruz
13/02/00	Vitesse	A	3-3	Paauwe, Tomasson, Konterman
20/02/00	Willem II	A	1-2	Bosvelt
26/02/00	MVV	H	3-0	Tomasson, Cruz (p), Korneev
05/03/00	SC Heerenveen	A	0-3	
11/03/00	FC Den Bosch	H	3-0	Cruz, Tomasson 2
17/03/00	SC Cambuur Leeuwarden	A	3-2	Cruz, Van Vossen, Bosvelt
26/03/00	Sparta	H	1-2	Tomasson
02/04/00	RKC Waalwijk	A	2-2	Bosvelt, Samardzic
09/04/00	FC Utrecht	H	1-2	Cruz (p)
16/04/00	De Graafschap	A	1-0	Cruz
23/04/00	Ajax	H	1-1	Bosvelt
30/04/00	AZ	H	5-3	Tomasson, Korneev, Cruz, Van Vossen 2
07/05/00	NEC	A	2-0	Konterman, Cruz
14/05/00	FC Twente	H	1-1	Korneev

FORTUNA SITTARD

CLUB DIRECTORY

Fortuna Sittard
Postbus 36
6130 AA Sittard
tel - (046) 4113100
fax - (046) 4113199
website - www.fortuna-sittard.nl
Year of Formation - 1968
President - Juul Coenen
Secretary - Wil Dols
Technical Director - Jacques Opgenoord
Coach - Bert van Marwijk (00/01 - Henk Duut)
Stadium - Wagner + Partners (12,261)

APPEARANCES 99/00

	P	Ap	(s)	Gls
Samir AMARI (MAR)	A		(1)	
Matthew AMOAH (BFA)	A	15		10
Joos VAN BARNEVELD	M	5		
Brenny EVERS	M	4	(12)	
Dennis GERRITSEN	A	27	(3)	10
François GESTHUIZEN	M	12	(11)	1
Ronald HAMMING	A	19	(9)	7
Marco HEERING	A	11	(3)	2
Edwin HERMANS	D	34		
Kevin HOFLAND	D	24		
Wim KIEKENS (BEL)	D	22	(3)	1
Ruud KOOL	M	27		3
Dennis KRIJGSMAN	A	11	(7)	2
Rolf LANDERL (AUT)	A	22		2
Cosmin MARIS (ROM)	A		(8)	
Jaromir PACIOREK (CZE)	M	14	(2)	2
Robert ROEST	D	27		2
Remco VAN DER SCHAAF	M	14		1
Roy SCHULPEN	D		(2)	
Georges TYCHON	A		(8)	
Joost VOLMER	M	31	(1)	4
Andy WRIGHT (ENG)	M		(6)	
Dorel ZEGREAN (ROM)	D	21	(2)	
Arno VAN ZWAM	G	34		

LEAGUE RESULTS 1999/2000

14/08/99	AZ	H	1-2	Paciorek
21/08/99	Willem II	A	2-2	Kool, Gerritsen
28/08/99	PSV	A	1-2	Paciorek
11/09/99	RKC Waalwijk	H	0-2	
18/09/99	Feyenoord	A	0-1	
25/09/99	Roda JC	A	0-3	
02/10/99	SC Cambuur Leeuwarden	H	4-1	Volmer, Hamming 3
13/10/99	Ajax	A	1-4	Hamming
16/10/99	SC Heerenveen	H	0-1	
23/10/99	Sparta	H	3-2	Kiekens, Hamming, Volmer
31/10/99	MVV	A	0-1	
05/11/99	FC Utrecht	A	1-2	Landerl
20/11/99	De Graafschap	H	1-1	Gesthuizen
27/11/99	NEC	H	2-2	Landerl, Kool (p)
01/12/99	FC Twente	A	0-1	
04/12/99	FC Den Bosch	H	1-1	Kool
10/12/99	AZ	A	0-2	
18/12/99	Vitesse	H	3-3	Hamming 2, Volmer
06/02/00	RKC Waalwijk	A	3-0	Gerritsen, Volmer, Amoah
09/02/00	Feyenoord	H	2-3	Roest (p), Krijgsman
12/02/00	SC Cambuur Leeuwarden	A	0-0	
18/02/00	FC Twente	H	2-2	Amoah, Gerritsen
26/02/00	Willem II	H	2-0	Gerritsen, Van der Schaaf
10/03/00	NEC	A	2-1	Amoah, Roest
15/03/00	Ajax	H	2-0	Amoah 2
19/03/00	Sparta	A	3-2	Gerritsen, Amoah 2
24/03/00	MVV	H	3-1	Gerritsen 2, Amoah
01/04/00	De Graafschap	A	0-1	
07/04/00	PSV	H	0-4	
15/04/00	SC Heerenveen	A	0-3	
21/04/00	FC Utrecht	H	3-0	Heering, Gerritsen, Amoah
30/04/00	FC Den Bosch	A	2-0	Heering, Gerritsen
07/05/00	Roda JC	H	1-2	Amoah
14/05/00	Vitesse	A	2-2	Gerritsen, Krijgsman

DE GRAAFSCHAP

CLUB DIRECTORY

De Graafschap
Postbus 249
7000 AE Doetinchem
tel - (0314) 368450
fax - (0314) 368451
website - www.graafschap.nl
Year of Formation - 1954
President - vacant
Secretary - Cor Huntelaar
Coach - Frans Thijssen; Massimo Morales;
Rob MacDonald
Stadium - De Vijverberg (10,900)

APPEARANCES 99/00

	P	Ap	(s)	Gls
Patrick AX	A	14	(2)	5
Milan BERCK-BEELENKAMP	D	9	(5)	
Harald BERENDSEN	D	3		
Martijn BESSELINK	G	4	(2)	
Rene BOT	D	12		
Hazem EMAM (EGY)	A	18	(7)	2
Purrel FRANKEL	D	24	(2)	
Robert FUCHS	M	15		5
Abdul Rahman ISSAH (GHA)	D	5	(2)	2
Olaf LINDENBERGH	D	16	(1)	2
Eli LOUHENAPESSY	M		(2)	
Martijn MEERDINK	M	25	(4)	5
Michal NEHODA (CZE)	A	2	(1)	
Michel NOK	D	22	(1)	
Ron OLYSLAGER	G	30		
Erik REDEKER	D	11	(6)	
Richard ROELOFSEN	A	6	(3)	1
Sonny SILOOY	D	10	(7)	
Arno SPLINTER	D	5	(4)	
Komi TCHANGAI (TOG)	D	16	(5)	
Zico TUMBA (CON)	A	18	(3)	6
Dennis DEN TURK	M	26	(3)	1
Rody TURPIJN	A	14	(8)	1
Ville VÄISÄNEN (FIN)	A	8	(8)	1
Eric VISCAAL	A	31	(1)	10
Jan VREMAN	D	30		

LEAGUE RESULTS 1999/2000

14/08/99	Roda JC	H	0-0	
21/08/99	FC Den Bosch	A	1-1	Tumba
12/09/99	PSV	H	1-2	Roelofsen
15/09/99	Sparta	A	1-2	Viscaal
19/09/99	FC Utrecht	A	1-2	Issah
26/09/99	NEC	H	2-2	Meerdink, Viscaal
02/10/99	RKC Waalwijk	A	1-2	Meerdink
10/10/99	MVV	H	2-1	Viscaal, Issah
17/10/99	FC Twente	H	0-0	
23/10/99	SC Cambuur Leeuwarden	A	0-1	
27/10/99	SC Heerenveen	A	0-2	
06/11/99	Willem II	H	0-2	
20/11/99	Fortuna Sittard	A	1-1	Viscaal
28/11/99	Vitesse	H	2-2	Emam 2
01/12/99	AZ	H	2-5	Meerdink, Lindenbergh (p)
11/12/99	Roda JC	A	3-2	Tumba 2, Lindenbergh
16/12/99	Feyenoord	A	0-0	
19/12/99	Ajax	H	1-1	Tumba
29/01/00	SC Cambuur Leeuwarden	H	3-1	Fuchs 2, Tumba
02/02/00	Vitesse	A	1-3	Tumba
05/02/00	NEC	A	3-2	Turpijn, Fuchs, Ax
13/02/00	FC Utrecht	H	1-2	Viscaal
20/02/00	Ajax	A	1-2	Väisänen
05/03/00	FC Den Bosch	H	3-0	Fuchs 2, Viscaal
11/03/00	MVV	A	2-0	Ax, Viscaal
18/03/00	PSV	A	0-6	
25/03/00	RKC Waalwijk	H	2-0	Ax, Meerdink
01/04/00	Fortuna Sittard	H	1-0	Den Turk
07/04/00	AZ	A	0-2	
16/04/00	Feyenoord	H	0-1	
22/04/00	Willem II	A	3-5	Viscaal 2, Meerdink
30/04/00	Sparta	H	2-3	Ax 2
07/05/00	FC Twente	A	0-4	
14/05/00	SC Heerenveen	H	1-1	Viscaal

SC HEERENVEEN

CLUB DIRECTORY

SC Heerenveen
Postbus 513
8440 AM Heerenveen
tel - (0513) 612100
fax - (0513) 615061
website - www.sc-heerenveen.nl
Year of Formation - 1920
President - Riemer van der Velde
Managerial Director - Tjisse Wallendal
Coach - Foppe de Haan
Stadium - Abe Lenstra (14,000)

APPEARANCES 99/00

	P	Ap	(s)	Gls
Romano DENNEBOOM	A	11	(6)	4
Barry DITEWIG	G	5		
Emanuel EBIEDE (NIG)	M		(4)	
Jesper HAKANSSON (DEN)	M	6	(2)	2
Johan HANSMA	D	29		1
Ties HELDENS	D		(1)	
Thomas HOLM (NOR)	M	11	(4)	
Max HOUTTUIN	M	2	(6)	
Harris HUIZINGH	A	23	(3)	3
Daniel JENSEN (DEN)	A	22	(7)	4
Alan JEPSEN (DEN)	M	5	(5)	
Tieme KLOMPE	D	23	(1)	
Mile KRSTEV (MAC)	D		(4)	
Anthony LURLING	A	27	(5)	18
Dumitru MITRITA (ROM)	D	27		1
Dennis DE NOOIJER	A		(1)	
Gerard DE NOOIJER	D	14	(8)	4
Mika NURMELA (FIN)	A	32	(2)	8
Godfrey NWANKPA (NIG)	D	1	(2)	
Boudewijn PAHLPLATZ	A	12	(7)	2
Valeriy POPOVICH (RUS)	A	15	(3)	6
Mika PULKKINEN (FIN)	M		(5)	
Arek RADOMSKI (POL)	M	27		2
Radoslav SAMARDZIC (YUG)	A	2		1
Jeffrey TALAN	A	23	(1)	9
Ivan TZVETKOV (BUL)	M		(5)	
Ronnie VENEMA	D	28	(2)	
Hans VONK (SAF)	G	29		

LEAGUE RESULTS 1999/2000

15/08/99	Ajax	A	2-3	Talan, Hakansson
21/08/99	Sparta	H	3-1	Talan, Samardzic, Hakansson
28/08/99	Feyenoord	A	1-3	Nurmela
11/09/99	Willem II	H	2-4	Denneboom, De Nooijer G.
19/09/99	Roda JC	A	2-0	Huizingh, Talan
25/09/99	FC Twente	H	0-0	
01/10/99	MVV	A	3-1	Talan, Lurling 2
13/10/99	FC Utrecht	H	1-0	Denneboom
16/10/99	Fortuna Sittard	A	1-0	Radomski
22/10/99	AZ	A	1-0	Denneboom
27/10/99	De Graafschap	H	2-0	Jensen, Pahlplatz
03/11/99	NEC	A	4-0	Radomski, Nurmela, Denneboom, Lurling
20/11/99	Vitesse	H	1-3	Jensen
26/11/99	SC Cambuur Leeuwarden	H	4-1	Lurling, De Nooijer G., Jensen, Nurmela
01/12/99	FC Den Bosch	A	2-0	Nurmela, Pahlplatz
15/12/99	RKC Waalwijk	H	4-1	Popovich, Lurling 3
18/12/99	PSV	A	1-0	Lurling
29/01/00	Sparta	A	1-2	Talan
02/02/00	Ajax	H	1-1	Lurling
05/02/00	AZ	H	3-0	Talan, Popovich, Lurling
13/02/00	PSV	H	0-3	
20/02/00	FC Utrecht	A	2-2	Talan 2
27/02/00	FC Twente	A	0-2	
05/03/00	Feyenoord	H	3-0	Hansma, Lurling, Nurmela
11/03/00	Willem II	A	3-2	Lurling 2, Talan
18/03/00	MVV	H	3-1	Nurmela, Lurling 2
25/03/00	Vitesse	A	1-3	Jensen
31/03/00	NEC	H	1-0	Lurling (p)
09/04/00	RKC Waalwijk	A	1-0	Huizingh
15/04/00	Fortuna Sittard	H	3-0	Lurling, Nurmela, De Nooijer G.
22/04/00	Roda JC	H	5-1	Popovich 2, Lurling, Mitrita, De Nooijer G.
30/04/00	SC Cambuur Leeuwarden	A	2-0	Popovich, Nurmela
07/05/00	FC Den Bosch	H	1-1	Popovich
14/05/00	De Graafschap	A	1-1	Huizingh

MVV

CLUB DIRECTORY

MVV
Postbus 4444
6202 ZV Maastricht
tel - (043) 3525757
fax - (043) 3525758
website - www.mvv.nl
Year of Formation - 1902
President - Alfons Cremers
Secretary - Sietze Fennema
Manager - Ron Weijzen
Coach - Wim Koevermans
Stadium - De Geusselt (10,000)

APPEARANCES 99/00

	P	Ap	(s)	Gls
Roberto BLANQUEZ (BEL)	A		(2)	
Dave VAN BOGAERT	D	18	(1)	
Thomas CAERS (BEL)	D	25	(1)	4
Ralph VAN DOOREN	A		(2)	
EMERSON (BRA)	A	22	(2)	7
Rodney FALIX	D	18	(1)	1
Johan GUDJÓNSSON (ISL)	A	20		5
Davey HEYMANS (BEL)	A	2	(5)	
Dave HOLLANDERS	A	2	(8)	1
Jerry DE JONG	M	29		
Roel JANSSEN	D	7	(5)	1
Yvo JOORDENS	M	9	(1)	
Husseyin KARAPINAR (BEL)	A	2	(8)	
Bobby KOCISKI (SWE)	M	13	(9)	1
Edik KORCHAGIN (BLS)	A	14	(3)	2
Stijn MEERT (BEL)	A	11		
Pim MOONEN	D	10	(3)	
John MUTSAERS	A	11	(2)	1
Rob NUYTS (BEL)	M		(2)	
Kenneth PEREZ (DEN)	A	13		6
Rick PLUM	D	14		
Patrick RONDAGS (BEL)	G	1	(1)	
Theo SNELDERS	G	27		
Hans SPILLMANN	G	6		
Wasiu TAIWO (NIG)	M	23	(8)	5
Igor TOMASIC (CRO)	D	14	(3)	1
Jack VAESSEN	M	25	(2)	
Michel VONK	D	19	(2)	
Anton VRIESDE	D	5		
Robert VAN DER WEERT	A	14	(1)	3

LEAGUE RESULTS 1999/2000

14/08/99	PSV	A	1-4	Janssen
20/08/99	Ajax	H	2-6	Emerson, Perez
28/08/99	Vitesse	A	2-6	Kociski, Caers
11/09/99	SC Cambuur Leeuwarden	H	1-1	Taiwo
18/09/99	FC Den Bosch	A	1-1	Perez
26/09/99	Sparta	A	0-3	
01/10/99	SC Heerenveen	H	1-3	Perez
10/10/99	De Graafschap	A	1-2	Perez
16/10/99	FC Utrecht	H	4-1	Emerson 3, Taiwo
23/10/99	Willem II	A	0-1	
31/10/99	Fortuna Sittard	H	1-0	Caers
06/11/99	AZ	H	3-4	Emerson, Falix, Perez
19/11/99	Feyenoord	H	3-3	Taiwo, Perez, Korchagin
30/11/99	Roda JC	A	1-3	Taiwo
04/12/99	FC Twente	H	0-2	
12/12/99	RKC Waalwijk	A	4-0	Caers, Van der Weert 2, Gudjónsson
15/12/99	NEC	A	0-1	
21/12/99	PSV	H	0-2	
01/02/00	Roda JC	H	0-0	
04/02/00	FC Utrecht	A	0-2	
09/02/00	FC Den Bosch	H	2-0	Korchagin (p), Caers
19/02/00	Sparta	H	2-2	Taiwo, Emerson
26/02/00	Feyenoord	A	0-3	
04/03/00	SC Cambuur Leeuwarden	A	2-2	Gudjónsson 2
11/03/00	De Graafschap	H	0-2	
18/03/00	SC Heerenveen	A	1-3	Gudjónsson
24/03/00	Fortuna Sittard	A	1-3	Mutsaers
01/04/00	Vitesse	H	0-2	
08/04/00	FC Twente	A	2-1	Gudjónsson, Van der Weert
15/04/00	RKC Waalwijk	H	0-1	
21/04/00	AZ	A	0-2	
30/04/00	NEC	H	2-0	Tomasic, Emerson
07/05/00	Ajax	A	0-1	
14/05/00	Willem II	H	1-1	Hollanders

NEC

CLUB DIRECTORY

NEC
Stadionplein 1, Postbus 6562
6503 GB Nijmegen
tel - (024) 3590360
fax - (024) 3567475
website - www.nec-nijmegen.nl
Year of Formation - 1900
President - Hans van Delft
Secretary - Eric Oomen
Technical Manager - Leen Looijen
Coach - Jimmy Calderwood; Ron de Groot
(00/01 - Johan Neeskens)
Stadium - De Goffert (12,500)

APPEARANCES 99/00

	P	Ap	(s)	Gls
Arno ARTS	M	11		1
Maarten ATMODIKORO	D	20		
Pieter COLLEN (BEL)	D	12		
Adilson DOS SANTOS	A	2	(15)	
Jack DE GIER	A	30		9
Richard GOULOOZE	D	17	(3)	
Roy GROOTAERT	D	4	(3)	
Peter HENDRIKS	D		(3)	
Danny HESP	D	27		3
Anton JANSSEN	M	22	(1)	4
Marcel KONING	M	22		1
Bart LATUHERU	A	28		
Jeffrey LEIWAKABESSY	D	2	(3)	
Luuk MAES	D	3		
Pavel MIKHALEVICH (BLS)	M		(2)	
Mark OOSTERHOF	D	7	(6)	2
Patrick POTHUIZEN	D	28		4
Cor PREIN	A		(1)	
Peter VAN PUTTEN	M	9	(1)	2
Maikel RENFURM	A	24	(1)	7
Hennie DE ROMIJN	D	24	(1)	
Bas ROORDA	G	34		
Youssef ROSSI (MAR)	D	4		
Rene VAN RIJSWIJK	A	21	(10)	
Marchanno SCHULTZ	M	23	(6)	2

LEAGUE RESULTS 1999/2000

15/08/99	FC Utrecht	A	0-1	
21/08/99	FC Twente	A	2-4	Pothuizen 2
28/08/99	Roda JC	A	3-4	Van Putten, De Gier, Pothuizen
26/09/99	De Graafschap	A	2-2	Renfurm, De Gier
29/09/99	FC Den Bosch	H	2-0	Schultz, De Gier
03/10/99	Vitesse	A	1-5	Hesp
13/10/99	FC Twente	H	0-1	
17/10/99	Ajax	H	1-3	Renfurm
24/10/99	Feyenoord	A	1-2	Renfurm
27/10/99	RKC Waalwijk	A	2-4	Van Putten, Renfurm
03/11/99	SC Heerenveen	H	0-4	
07/11/99	PSV	H	2-1	De Gier, Janssen
19/11/99	Sparta	H	0-1	
27/11/99	Fortuna Sittard	A	2-2	De Gier, Janssen
05/12/99	SC Cambuur Leeuwarden	H	1-0	Janssen (p)
15/12/99	MVV	H	1-0	De Gier
18/12/99	AZ	A	1-1	Oosterhof
02/02/00	SC Cambuur Leeuwarden	A	0-0	
05/02/00	De Graafschap	H	2-3	Oosterhof, Renfurm
09/02/00	Willem II	A	1-3	Schultz
12/02/00	AZ	H	1-2	Hesp
19/02/00	RKC Waalwijk	H	3-1	Pothuizen, Koning, Renfurm
27/02/00	Sparta	A	0-1	
05/03/00	FC Utrecht	H	0-1	
10/03/00	Fortuna Sittard	H	1-2	Renfurm
17/03/00	Willem II	H	2-1	Hesp, Arts
26/03/00	Ajax	A	2-5	De Gier 2
31/03/00	SC Heerenveen	A	0-1	
07/04/00	Roda JC	H	0-0	
16/04/00	FC Den Bosch	A	1-1	Janssen
23/04/00	Vitesse	H	1-0	De Gier
30/04/00	MVV	A	0-2	
07/05/00	Feyenoord	H	0-2	
14/05/00	PSV	A	0-2	

PSV

CLUB DIRECTORY

PSV
Frederiklaan 10 A, 5616 NH Eindhoven
tel - (040) 2505501
fax - (040) 2505696
website - www.psv.nl
Year of Formation - 1913
President - Harry van Raay
Coach - Eric Gerets
Stadium - Philips (33,500)

MAJOR HONOURS
League Championship - (15) 1929, 1935, 1951,
1963, 1975, 1976, 1978, 1986, 1987, 1988,
1989, 1991, 1992, 1997, 2000.
Domestic Cup - (7)
1950, 1974, 1976, 1988, 1989, 1990, 1996.
European Champions' Cup - (1) 1988.
UEFA Cup - (1) 1978.

APPEARANCES 99/00

		P	Ap	(s)	Gls
Eric ADDO (GHA)	D	6			
Björn BECKER	M		(1)		
Kaspar BOGELUND (DEN)	M		(3)		
Wilfred BOUMA	A	24	(3)	9	
Arnold BRUGGINK	A	19	(11)	19	
Mark VAN BOMMEL	M	33		6	
Jürgen DIRKX	D	12	(1)	2	
Björn VAN DER DOELEN	M	9	(12)	1	
Ernest FABER	D	17		1	
Jan HEINTZE (DEN)	D	28		1	
Tomasz IWAN (POL)	M	2	(10)		
Dmitriy KHOKHLOV (RUS)	M	7	(6)	3	
Joonas KOLKKA (FIN)	M	16	(16)	5	
Ivica KRALJ (YUG)	G	4			
Patrick LODEWIJKS	G		(1)		
Yuriy NIKIFOROV (RUS)	D	24	(5)	3	
Luc NILIS (BEL)	A	25	(1)	19	
Ruud VAN NISTELROOY	A	23		29	
André OOIJER	D	16	(2)	1	
Johan PATER	A		(1)		
Dennis ROMMEDAHL (DEN)	A	14	(9)		
Andrei SKERLA (LIT)	D		(2)		
Ovidiu STINGA (ROM)	M	13	(5)	1	
Stan VALCKX	D		(1)		
Johann VOGEL (SUI)	M	31		2	
Ronald WATERREUS	G	30			
Chris VAN DER WEERDEN	D	15	(4)	1	
Rob WIELAERT	D	6			

LEAGUE RESULTS 1999/2000

14/08/99	MVV	H	4-1	Van Bommel, Van Nistelrooy 3
22/08/99	Vitesse	A	6-1	Bruggink 2, Faber, Van Nistelrooy 2 (1p), Khokhlov
28/08/99	Fortuna Sittard	H	2-1	Nilis, Bruggink
12/09/99	De Graafschap	A	2-1	Khokhlov, Nilis
25/09/99	Willem II	H	6-1	og (Gentile), Nikiforov, Vogel, Van Nistelrooy 3 (1p)
02/10/99	Sparta	H	7-0	Van Bommel, Van Nistelrooy 3 (1p), Nilis, Khokhlov, Kolkka
13/10/99	RKC Waalwijk	A	6-1	Nilis 3, Van Nistelrooy 2, Kolkka
17/10/99	FC Den Bosch	H	7-0	Van Nistelrooy 2 (1p), Nilis 2, Bruggink 2, Van der Doelen
23/10/99	FC Twente	H	2-2	Van Nistelrooy, Kolkka
31/10/99	AZ	A	3-0	Van Nistelrooy 2, Bruggink
07/11/99	NEC	A	1-2	Van Nistelrooy
21/11/99	SC Cambuur Leeuwarden	A	1-0	Dirkx
28/11/99	Feyenoord	A	0-1	
04/12/99	Roda JC	H	2-0	Nilis, Bouma
12/12/99	FC Utrecht	A	1-1	Bouma
15/12/99	Ajax	A	3-1	Van Nistelrooy 3
18/12/99	SC Heerenveen	H	0-1	
21/12/99	MVV	A	2-0	Van Bommel, Dirkx
03/02/00	Feyenoord	H	0-1	
06/02/00	FC Den Bosch	A	6-2	Nilis 2, Van Nistelrooy, Nikiforov, Bruggink 2
10/02/00	Ajax	H	4-0	Van Bommel, Van Nistelrooy 3 (1p)
13/02/00	SC Heerenveen	A	3-0	Nilis, Van Nistelrooy, Kolkka
19/02/00	Vitesse	H	3-2	Van Nistelrooy, Bouma, Bruggink
25/02/00	Roda JC	A	2-1	Van Nistelrooy, Bruggink
12/03/00	FC Utrecht	H	2-1	Bouma 2
18/03/00	De Graafschap	H	6-0	Bruggink 4, Nilis, Bouma
24/03/00	Willem II	A	0-0	
01/04/00	AZ	H	5-1	Bruggink, Stinga, og (Lindenbergh), Bouma, Kolkka
07/04/00	Fortuna Sittard	A	4-0	Bruggink, Nilis 3
16/04/00	SC Cambuur Leeuwarden	H	1-0	Van Bommel
21/04/00	FC Twente	A	3-1	Bruggink 3
30/04/00	RKC Waalwijk	H	7-1	Nikiforov, Van Bommel, Ooijer, Nilis, Vogel, Van der Weerden, Heintze
07/05/00	Sparta	A	2-0	Nilis, Bouma
14/05/00	NEC	H	2-0	Nilis (p), Bouma

RKC WAALWIJK

CLUB DIRECTORY

RKC Waalwijk
Postbus 4
5140 AA Waalwijk
tel - (0416) 334356
fax - (0416) 342310
website - www.rkcwaalwijk.nl
Year of Formation - 1940
President - Jan Snoeren
Secretary - Jan Gerrits
General Manager - Henk van Delft
Coach - Martin Jol
Stadium - Mandemakers (6,100)

APPEARANCES 99/00

	P	Ap	(s)	Gls
Richard BEEKINK	A		(5)	
Tim CORNELISSE	D	32		1
Yuri CORNELISSE	A	21	(11)	8
Garry DE GRAEF (BEL)	M	30	(2)	4
Rob VAN DIJK	G	34		
Dejan GOVEDARICA (YUG)	M	29		1
Ron HEESAKKERS	A	18	(15)	3
Rick HOOGENDORP	A	18		9
Darije KALEZIC (BOS)	D	15	(7)	
Roberto LANCKOHR	M	31	(3)	5
Tom VAN DER LEEGTE	M	27	(1)	3
Ad LEEMANS	D	1		
David NASCIMENTO (POR)	D	30		1
Emmanuel NWAKIRE (NIG)	D	8	(3)	1
Dennis VAN DER PENNEN	M	2	(5)	
Yuriy PETROV (RUS)	A	8	(12)	3
Maarten SCHOPS (BEL)	M	21	(5)	3
Wout VAN STEENVELDT	M		(7)	
Virgilio TEIXEIRA (POR)	D	17		
Carlos VAN WANROOY	D	32		2
Michel VAN ZUNDERT	M		(2)	

LEAGUE RESULTS 1999/2000

15/08/99	FC Twente	H	1-1	Hoogendorp
21/08/99	Roda JC	A	2-1	Schops, Hoogendorp
29/08/99	AZ	H	1-2	Heesakkers
11/09/99	Fortuna Sittard	A	2-0	Hoogendorp, Cornelisse Y.
19/09/99	Ajax	H	1-1	Lanckohr
26/09/99	Feyenoord	A	2-1	Cornelisse Y. 2
02/10/99	De Graafschap	H	2-1	De Graef, Hoogendorp
13/10/99	PSV	H	1-6	Hoogendorp
16/10/99	Willem II	A	1-2	Schops
24/10/99	FC Utrecht	A	1-4	Lanckohr
27/10/99	NEC	H	4-2	Hoogendorp 2 (1p), Van Wanrooy, De Graef
07/11/99	SC Cambuur Leeuwarden	H	3-2	Lanckohr, Van der Leegte, Schops
20/11/99	FC Den Bosch	A	3-0	Hoogendorp, Cornelisse Y. 2
28/11/99	Sparta	H	2-1	Lanckohr, Heesakkers
01/12/99	Vitesse	A	1-2	Hoogendorp
05/12/99	Ajax	A	2-1	Govedarica, Cornelisse T.
12/12/99	MVV	H	0-4	
15/12/99	SC Heerenveen	A	1-4	Cornelisse Y.
02/02/00	Willem II	H	1-0	Petrov
06/02/00	Fortuna Sittard	H	0-3	
09/02/00	FC Twente	A	0-1	
19/02/00	NEC	A	1-3	Van der Leegte
27/02/00	Vitesse	H	1-1	Petrov
05/03/00	Sparta	A	1-3	Van der Leegte
10/03/00	AZ	A	0-4	
19/03/00	Roda JC	H	2-2	De Graef, Nascimento
25/03/00	De Graafschap	A	0-2	
02/04/00	Feyenoord	H	2-2	Van Wanrooy, Cornelisse Y.
09/04/00	SC Heerenveen	H	0-1	
15/04/00	MVV	A	1-0	Nwakire
23/04/00	FC Den Bosch	H	1-1	Heesakkers
30/04/00	PSV	A	1-7	Petrov
07/05/00	FC Utrecht	H	2-0	De Graef, Cornelisse Y.
14/05/00	SC Cambuur Leeuwarden	A	1-2	Lanckohr (p)

RODA JC

CLUB DIRECTORY

Roda JC
Postbus 1156
6460 BD Kerkrade
tel - (045) 6317000
fax - (045) 6317100
website - www.rodajc.nl
Year of Formation - 1962
President - Theo Pickée
Secretary - Jo Ploum
Coach - Sef Vergoossen
Stadium - Parkstad Limburg (20,000)

MAJOR HONOURS
Domestic Cup - (2) 1997, 2000.

APPEARANCES 99/00

	P	Ap	(s)	Gls
Gregory DELWARTE (BEL)	G	4		
Arno DOOMERNIK	M	25	(5)	6
Ramon VAN HAAREN	D	33		
Stephan 'T HART	D		(6)	
Bas JACOBS	A		(10)	1
Zeljko KALAC (AUS)	G	30		
Garba LAWAL (NIG)	M	27	(1)	3
Eric VAN DER LUER	M	33		3
Mark LUIJPERS	D	34		4
Marc NYGAARD (DEN)	M	2		
Bob PEETERS (BEL)	A	28	(2)	15
Paolo RAMORA (ITA)	A	1	(3)	
Humphrey RUDGE	D	20	(7)	2
Ger SENDEN	D	19	(2)	
Tom SOETAERS (BEL)	A	1	(7)	
Samuel Bernard TCHOUTANG (CMR)	A	22	(3)	7
Gábor TORMA (HUN)	A	2	(2)	2
Joos VALGAEREN (BEL)	D	27	(3)	5
Kevin VAN DESSEL (BEL)	M	7	(16)	1
Peter VAN HOUDT (BEL)	A	21	(5)	5
Regilio VREDE	D	11	(6)	1
Davy ZAFARIN	M	27	(5)	6

LEAGUE RESULTS 1999/2000

14/08/99	De Graafschap	A	0-0	
21/08/99	RKC Waalwijk	H	1-2	Zafarin
28/08/99	NEC	H	4-3	Torma 2 (2p), Van der Luer, Peeters
10/09/99	AZ	A	2-1	Doomernik, Zafarin
19/09/99	SC Heerenveen	H	0-2	
25/09/99	Fortuna Sittard	H	3-0	Valgaeren, Tchoutang, Peeters
03/10/99	FC Utrecht	A	2-1	Peeters (p), Jacobs
11/10/99	Sparta	A	2-1	Peeters, Luijpers
15/10/99	Feyenoord	H	2-1	Zafarin, Doomernik
24/10/99	Vitesse	H	0-1	
29/10/99	Ajax	A	2-1	Peeters, Luijpers
07/11/99	FC Den Bosch	H	3-0	Van der Luer, Peeters 2
20/11/99	Willem II	A	2-2	Peeters, Van der Luer
30/11/99	MVV	H	3-1	Tchoutang, Zafarin, Lawal
04/12/99	PSV	A	0-2	
11/12/99	De Graafschap	H	2-3	Peeters, Valgaeren
18/12/99	FC Twente	A	1-2	Tchoutang
01/02/00	MVV	A	0-0	
06/02/00	Feyenoord	A	1-2	Van Dessel
10/02/00	FC Utrecht	H	3-2	Peeters 2, Doomernik
19/02/00	FC Den Bosch	A	2-2	Zafarin, Peeters
25/02/00	PSV	H	1-2	Valgaeren
29/02/00	SC Cambuur Leeuwarden	H	3-1	Tchoutang, Luijpers, Lawal
03/03/00	Vitesse	A	0-2	
11/03/00	Sparta	H	4-1	og (Van der Meer), Tchoutang, Van Houdt 2
19/03/00	RKC Waalwijk	A	2-2	Vrede, Doomernik
25/03/00	SC Cambuur Leeuwarden	A	2-2	Doomernik, Luijpers
31/03/00	Ajax	H	3-0	Doomernik, Peeters, Tchoutang
07/04/00	NEC	A	0-0	
15/04/00	Willem II	H	3-4	Peeters (p), Rudge, Zafarin
22/04/00	SC Heerenveen	A	1-5	Peeters
28/04/00	FC Twente	H	3-2	Rudge, Tchoutang, Van Houdt
07/05/00	Fortuna Sittard	A	2-1	Valgaeren, Lawal
14/05/00	AZ	H	3-2	Van Houdt 2, Valgaeren

SPARTA

CLUB DIRECTORY

Sparta Rotterdam
Postbus 1802, 3000 BV Rotterdam
tel - (010) 8909210
fax - (010) 8909225
website - www.sparta-rotterdam.nl
Year of Formation - 1888
President -Cor Van Rijn
Secretary - Peter Haubrich
Manager - Charles van der Steene
Coach - Jan Everse; Dolf Roks
Stadium - ENECO (11,000)

MAJOR HONOURS
League Championship - (6)
1909, 1911, 1912, 1913, 1915, 1959.
Domestic Cup - (3) 1958, 1962, 1966.

APPEARANCES 99/00

	P	Ap	(s)	Gls
Houssin BEZZAI (MAR)	D	16	(4)	
Nourdin BOUKHARI (MAR)	A	17		5
Alex VAN DUIJVENBODE	D	1		
John DEN DUNNEN	A	7	(6)	1
Nixon DIAS	M	2		
Ali EL KHATTABI (MAR)	A	23	(4)	11
Richard ELZINGA	D	25		
Steve GOOSSEN	D	28		
Silvan INIA	A	16	(13)	5
Kew JALIENS	D	2		1
Roland JANSEN	G	9		
Yurtcan KAYIS (TUR)	M	10	(2)	
Frank KOOIMAN	G	25		
Michel LANGERAK	M	29		2
Antoine VAN DER LINDEN	D	8	(3)	
Bram MARBUS	A	30	(1)	6
MARÍLIA (BRA)	D	26	(1)	1
Dave VAN DER MEER	D	22	(2)	1
Dave MENDES (CVD)	M	3	(1)	
Mourad MGHIZRAT (MAR)	A		(6)	1
Patrick MOLENDIJK	M		(3)	
Anders NIELSEN (DEN)	M	32		10
Mark NOORLANDER	D	6	(2)	
Roy STROEVE	A	1	(18)	
Erik TAMMER	A	2	(7)	
Arnoud TOET	G		(1)	
Fuat USTA (TUR)	M	9		2
Romeo WOUDEN	A		(1)	
Sieme ZIJM	M	25	(6)	3

LEAGUE RESULTS 1999/2000

12/08/99	Willem II	H	0-2	
21/08/99	SC Heerenveen	A	1-3	Jaliens
12/09/99	FC Utrecht	H	3-0	Marbus 2, El Khattabi
15/09/99	De Graafschap	H	2-1	Inia 2
19/09/99	Vitesse	A	1-2	Usta
26/09/99	MVV	H	3-0	Usta, Den Dunnen, Marília
02/10/99	PSV	A	0-7	
11/10/99	Roda JC	H	1-2	Zijm
17/10/99	AZ	H	3-6	Inia 2, Nielsen
23/10/99	Fortuna Sittard	A	2-3	El Khattabi 2
27/10/99	FC Twente	A	2-3	El Khattabi, Mghizrat
07/11/99	Ajax	H	1-2	El Khattabi (p)
19/11/99	NEC	A	1-0	El Khattabi
28/11/99	RKC Waalwijk	A	1-2	Nielsen
04/12/99	Feyenoord	H	1-3	Langerak
15/12/99	FC Den Bosch	H	3-2	El Khattabi, Langerak, Nielsen
18/12/99	Willem II	A	0-0	
29/01/00	SC Heerenveen	H	2-1	Nielsen, Boukhari
05/02/00	Vitesse	H	1-1	og (Grozdic)
09/02/00	AZ	A	0-4	
15/02/00	SC Cambuur Leeuwarden	A	1-0	El Khattabi
19/02/00	MVV	A	2-2	Nielsen, Marbus
27/02/00	NEC	H	1-0	Nielsen
05/03/00	RKC Waalwijk	H	3-1	Van der Meer, El Khattabi, Marbus
11/03/00	Roda JC	A	1-4	Nielsen
19/03/00	Fortuna Sittard	H	2-3	El Khattabi, Inia
26/03/00	Feyenoord	A	2-1	Nielsen, Boukhari
02/04/00	FC Twente	H	1-1	Nielsen
09/04/00	Ajax	A	2-3	Nielsen, Marbus
14/04/00	FC Utrecht	A	1-3	Marbus
22/04/00	SC Cambuur Leeuwarden	H	1-2	Boukhari
30/04/00	De Graafschap	A	3-2	Zijm 2, El Khattabi
07/05/00	PSV	H	0-2	
14/05/00	FC Den Bosch	A	0-7	

FC TWENTE

CLUB DIRECTORY

FC Twente
Colosseum 65
7521 PP Enschede
tel - (053) 8525525
fax - (053) 8525555
website - www.fctwente.nl
Year of Formation - 1965
President - Herman Wessels
Executive Manager - Ben van Dijk
Technical Manager - Theo Vonk
Coach - Hans Meyer; Fred Rutten
Stadium - Arke (13,500)

MAJOR HONOURS
Domestic Cup - (1) 1977.

APPEARANCES 99/00

	P	Ap	(s)	Gls
Berthil TER AVEST	M	33		5
Sander BOSCHKER	G	34		
Scott BOOTH (SCO)	A	27	(4)	8
Sjors BRUGGE	M		(1)	
Simon CZIOMMER (GER)	M		(3)	
Chris DE WITTE (BEL)	A	28	(5)	5
Spira GRUJIC (YUG)	D	34		1
Erik TEN HAG	D	30		2
Jeroen HEUBACH	D	17	(7)	1
Edwin HILGERINK	D	6	(5)	
Nick HOEKSTRA	A		(7)	
Thijs HOUWING	A		(1)	1
Dennis HULSHOFF	D	24	(1)	
André KARNEBEEK	D	29	(1)	1
Arjan VAN DER LAAN	M	31		6
Andy VAN DER MEYDE	A	13	(19)	2
Rahim OUEDRAOGO (BFA)	D	6	(14)	
Frédéric PEIREMANS (BEL)	D	20	(3)	5
Jörg SOBIECH (GER)	D	4		
Jan VENNEGOOR OF HESSELINK	A	34		19
Jan VERLINDEN (BEL)	D	3	(8)	
Pascal DE VRIES	M	1	(7)	

LEAGUE RESULTS 1999/2000

15/08/99	RKC Waalwijk	A	1-1	Karnebeek
21/08/99	NEC	H	4-2	Ten Hag, Vennegoor of Hesselink 3
29/08/99	FC Utrecht	A	0-1	
11/09/99	Vitesse	H	0-0	
17/09/99	SC Cambuur Leeuwarden	A	3-1	Van der Laan (p), De Witte, Vennegoor of Hesselink
25/09/99	SC Heerenveen	A	0-0	
02/10/99	FC Den Bosch	H	3-2	De Witte, Heubach, Van der Laan (p)
13/10/99	NEC	A	1-0	Vennegoor of Hesselink
17/10/99	De Graafschap	A	0-0	
23/10/99	PSV	A	2-2	Booth 2
27/10/99	Sparta	H	3-2	Vennegoor of Hesselink 2, Peiremans
07/11/99	Feyenoord	H	3-3	og (De Haan), Peiremans 2
19/11/99	AZ	A	1-2	Van der Laan (p)
27/11/99	Willem II	H	4-0	Ten Hag, Peiremans, Vennegoor of Hesselink, Van der Laan
01/12/99	Fortuna Sittard	H	1-0	Booth
04/12/99	MVV	A	2-0	Vennegoor of Hesselink, Van der Meyde
18/12/99	Roda JC	H	2-1	Van der Laan, Vennegoor of Hesselink
02/02/00	AZ	H	4-1	Grujic, Peiremans, De Witte, Vennegoor of Hesselink
05/02/00	Willem II	A	1-1	Ter Avest
09/02/00	RKC Waalwijk	H	1-0	Vennegoor of Hesselink
13/02/00	FC Den Bosch	A	0-0	
18/02/00	Fortuna Sittard	A	2-2	Vennegoor of Hesselink, Ter Avest
27/02/00	SC Heerenveen	H	2-0	De Witte, Ter Avest
05/03/00	Ajax	H	0-0	
11/03/00	SC Cambuur Leeuwarden	H	1-0	De Witte
19/03/00	Ajax	A	1-0	Vennegoor of Hesselink
26/03/00	FC Utrecht	H	4-2	Ter Avest, Houwing, Vennegoor of Hesselink, Van der Meyde
02/04/00	Sparta	A	1-1	Booth
08/04/00	MVV	H	1-2	Ter Avest
15/04/00	Vitesse	A	1-4	Vennegoor of Hesselink
21/04/00	PSV	H	1-3	Vennegoor of Hesselink
28/04/00	Roda JC	A	2-3	Van der Laan, Booth
07/05/00	De Graafschap	H	4-0	Vennegoor of Hesselink 2, Booth 2
14/05/00	Feyenoord	A	1-1	Booth

FC UTRECHT

CLUB DIRECTORY

FC Utrecht
Herculesplein 331, 3584 AA Utrecht
tel - (030) 2512521
fax - (030) 2540374
website - www.fc-utrecht.nl
Year of Formation - 1970
President - Hans Herremans
Secretary - Albert van Santbrink
Technical Director - Han Berger
Coach - Mark Wotte; Frans Adelaar
Stadium - Nieuw Galgewaard (14,000)

MAJOR HONOURS
Domestic Cup - (1) 1985.

APPEARANCES 99/00

	P	Ap	(s)	Gls
Ruud BERGER	A	1	(5)	
Pascal BOSSCHAART	D	30		
Rodney CAIRO	A	12	(13)	2
Marinus DIJKHUIZEN	A	22	(5)	4
Jamie FORRESTER (ENG)	A		(1)	
Mitchell VAN DER GAAG	D	30	(2)	7
Alfons GROENENDIJK	M	19	(3)	5
Donny DE GROOT	A		(2)	
Jean-Paul DE JONG	M	11	(6)	
John DE JONG	A	20	(4)	5
Sander KELLER	D	1		
Dirk KUIJT	A	12	(20)	6
Theo LUCIUS	M	28	(4)	3
Didier MARTEL (FRA)	A	31		8
Azubuike OLISEH (NIG)	M	20	(3)	1
Stefan POSTMA	G	1	(1)	
Reinier ROBBEMOND	M	27	(4)	5
Henny VAN SCHOONHOVEN	D	5	(4)	
Alje SCHUT	D	1	(3)	
Etienne SHEW-ATJON	D	4	(2)	
Karim TOUZANI (MAR)	M	7	(1)	1
Tom VAN MOL (BEL)	M	3		1
Stijn VREVEN (BEL)	D	29		1
Harald WAPENAAR	G	33		
Jordy ZUIDAM	M	1	(11)	
Patrick ZWAANSWJK	D	26		3

LEAGUE RESULTS 1999/2000

15/08/99	NEC	H	1-0	Van der Gaag
29/08/99	FC Twente	H	1-0	Van Mol
12/09/99	Sparta	A	0-3	
15/09/99	AZ	A	1-0	Lucius
19/09/99	De Graafschap	H	2-1	Vreven, Kuijt
26/09/99	FC Den Bosch	A	2-3	Martel (p), Van der Gaag
03/10/99	Roda JC	H	1-2	Martel
13/10/99	SC Heerenveen	A	0-1	
16/10/99	MVV	A	1-4	Martel
24/10/99	RKC Waalwijk	H	4-1	Van der Gaag, De Jong Jo. 2 (1p), Zwaanswjk
31/10/99	Vitesse	A	1-3	Lucius
05/11/99	Fortuna Sittard	H	2-1	Groenendijk, og (Kiekens)
21/11/99	Ajax	A	0-2	
28/11/99	FC Den Bosch	H	2-1	Groenendijk, Dijkhuizen
01/12/99	SC Cambuur Leeuwarden	A	3-4	De Jong Jo., Martel, Van der Gaag
05/12/99	Willem II	A	3-4	Martel (p), Robbemond, Cairo
12/12/99	PSV	H	1-1	Zwaanswjk
19/12/99	Feyenoord	H	3-4	Zwaanswjk, Dijkhuizen, De Jong Jo.
04/02/00	MVV	H	2-0	Robbemond, Cairo
10/02/00	Roda JC	A	2-3	De Jong Jo., Dijkhuizen
13/02/00	De Graafschap	A	2-1	Martel, Lucius
20/02/00	SC Heerenveen	H	2-2	Robbemond 2 (1p)
27/02/00	AZ	H	3-3	Groenendijk 2, Van der Gaag
05/03/00	NEC	A	1-0	Kuijt
12/03/00	PSV	A	1-2	Van der Gaag
19/03/00	Vitesse	H	2-0	og (De Marchi), Kuijt
26/03/00	FC Twente	A	2-4	Martel 2
02/04/00	SC Cambuur Leeuwarden	H	1-2	Kuijt
09/04/00	Feyenoord	A	2-1	Groenendijk, Kuijt
14/04/00	Sparta	H	3-1	Dijkhuizen, Kuijt, Robbemond (p)
21/04/00	Fortuna Sittard	A	0-3	
30/04/00	Willem II	H	1-1	Oliseh
07/05/00	RKC Waalwijk	A	0-2	
14/05/00	Ajax	H	3-1	Touzani, Van der Gaag, og (Hosé)

VITESSE

CLUB DIRECTORY

Vitesse
Postbus 366
6800 AJ Arnhem
tel - (026) 8807321
fax - (026) 8807009
website - www.vitesseworld.nl
Year of Formation - 1892
President - Jos Vaessen
Technical Co-ordinator - Rein Papenburg
General Director - Hans Schreudering
Coach - Herbert Neumann; Edward Sturing &
Jan Jongbloed; Ronald Koeman
Stadium - Gelredome (26,600)

APPEARANCES 99/00

	P	Ap	(s)	Gls
Kristof AELBRECHT (BEL)	A		(2)	
Matthew AMOAH (GHA)	A		(7)	1
John VAN DEN BROM	M	21	(3)	6
Dejan CUROVIC (YUG)	A		(10)	1
Marco DE MARCHI (ITA)	D	17	(3)	2
Mahamadou DIARRA (MLI)	M	9	(7)	2
Carlos FORTES	A	10	(4)	
Nenad GROZDIC (YUG)	M	20	(9)	1
Kostas HANIOTAKIS (GRE)	G		(1)	
Marc VAN HINTUM	D	31		1
Pierre VAN HOOIJDONK	A	28	(1)	25
Theo JANSSEN	M	9	(8)	
Dragoslav JEVRIC (YUG)	G	34		
Arco JOCHEMSEN	M	19	(4)	2
Michel KREEK	M	31		4
Louis LAROS	M	32		5
Rahamat MUSTAPHA	A	3	(4)	
Stefan NANU (ROM)	D	17	(5)	1
Remco VAN DER SCHAAF	D	2	(2)	
Victor SIKORA	A	24	(4)	8
Dejan STEFANOVIC (YUG)	D	13	(1)	
Orlando TRUSTFULL	M	11	(1)	1
John VELDMAN	D	16	(1)	
Peter WISGERHOF	D	7	(8)	
Mamadou ZONGO (BFA)	A	20	(3)	5

LEAGUE RESULTS 1999/2000

14/08/99	SC Cambuur Leeuwarden	A	1-1	Van Hooijdonk
22/08/99	PSV	H	1-6	Van Hooijdonk
28/08/99	MVV	H	6-2	Sikora, Van Hooijdonk 3 (1p), Van Hintum, Van den Brom
11/09/99	FC Twente	A	0-0	
19/09/99	Sparta	H	2-1	Sikora, Van Hooijdonk (p)
24/09/99	Ajax	A	1-3	Van Hooijdonk
03/10/99	NEC	H	5-1	Van Hooijdonk 3, Sikora, Amoah
12/10/99	Feyenoord	A	0-0	
16/10/99	SC Cambuur Leeuwarden	H	1-0	De Marchi
24/10/99	Roda JC	A	1-0	Van Hooijdonk
31/10/99	FC Utrecht	H	3-1	De Marchi, Van Hooijdonk 2
20/11/99	SC Heerenveen	A	3-1	Van den Brom, Grozdic, Laros
28/11/99	De Graafschap	A	2-2	Van den Brom, Van Hooijdonk
01/12/99	RKC Waalwijk	H	2-1	Zongo 2
04/12/99	AZ	H	0-2	
12/12/99	FC Den Bosch	A	1-2	Van Hooijdonk
15/12/99	Willem II	H	3-1	Van Hooijdonk 2 (1p), Zongo
18/12/99	Fortuna Sittard	A	3-3	Sikora 2, Kreek
26/01/00	FC Den Bosch	H	1-0	Van Hooijdonk
02/02/00	De Graafschap	H	3-1	Jochemsen, Laros, Diarra
05/02/00	Sparta	A	1-1	Sikora
13/02/00	Feyenoord	H	3-3	Van Hooijdonk 2 (1p), Diarra
19/02/00	PSV	A	2-3	Van den Brom, Zongo
27/02/00	RKC Waalwijk	A	1-1	Van Hooijdonk (p)
03/03/00	Roda JC	H	2-0	Kreek, Sikora
19/03/00	FC Utrecht	A	0-2	
25/03/00	SC Heerenveen	H	3-1	Kreek, Trustfull, Laros (p)
01/04/00	MVV	A	2-0	Jochemsen, Sikora
08/04/00	Willem II	A	4-0	Kreek, Van den Brom, Laros 2
15/04/00	FC Twente	H	4-1	Van Hooijdonk, og (Grujic), Zongo, og (Ter Avest)
23/04/00	NEC	A	0-1	
30/04/00	Ajax	H	3-0	Van Hooijdonk 2, Van den Brom
07/05/00	AZ	A	1-0	Van Hooijdonk
14/05/00	Fortuna Sittard	H	2-2	Nanu, Curovic

WILLEM II

THE EUROPEAN FOOTBALL YEARBOOK 2000-2001

CLUB DIRECTORY

Willem II
Postbus 235, 5000 AE Tilburg
tel - (013) 5490590
fax - (013) 5490500
website - www.willem-ii.nl
Year of Formation - 1896
President - Jan Vullings
Secretary - Mark Willems
Director of Football - Martin van Geel
Coach - Co Adriaanse; Hans Verel
(00/01 - Hans Westerhof)
Stadium - Willem II (14,700)

MAJOR HONOURS
League Championship - (3) 1916, 1952, 1955.
Domestic Cup - (2) 1944, 1963.

APPEARANCES 99/00

	P	Ap	(s)	Gls
Yassine ABDELLAOUI (MAR)	A	14	(1)	2
Arno ARTS	M	19		5
Mariano BOMBARDA (ARG)	A	15	(2)	11
Tom CALUWE (BEL)	M	12	(2)	1
Jatto CEESAY (GAM)	A	19	(6)	2
Geert DE VLIEGER (BEL)	G	16		
Jim VAN FESSEM	G	8	(1)	
Tomas GALASEK (CZE)	M	31		3
Marco GENTILE	D	20		
Reinder HENDRIKS	D		(1)	
Erwin HERMES	A		(1)	
Richard VAN DER HEIJDEN	A	4	(3)	1
Delano HILL	D	27	(3)	
Kew JALIENS	D	16	(6)	
Danny LANDZAAT	M	18	(7)	3
Kris MAMPAEY (BEL)	G	9		
Joris MATHIJSEN	D	7		
Casper NELIS	G	1		
Jos VAN NIEUWSTADT	D	4	(2)	
Geoffrey PROMMAYON (THA)	D	24	(2)	1
Adil RAMZI (MAR)	A	12	(5)	7
Ousmane SANOU (BFA)	A	9	(12)	6
Mark SCHENNING	D	2	(10)	
Dennis SCHULP	A	4	(11)	2
Tarik SEKTIOUI (MAR)	A	2	(6)	2
Dmitriy SHUKOV (RUS)	M	34		5
Marcel VALK	M	17	(3)	
Guy VELDEMAN (BEL)	D		(1)	
Raymond VICTORIA	D	29	(3)	2
Nuelson WAU	D	1		

LEAGUE RESULTS 1999/2000

Date	Opponent		Score	Scorers
12/08/99	Sparta	A	2-0	Ceesay, Bombarda
21/08/99	Fortuna Sittard	H	2-2	Bombarda 2
28/08/99	FC Den Bosch	H	2-1	Arts (p), Victoria
11/09/99	SC Heerenveen	A	4-2	Victoria, Bombarda, Sanou 2
18/09/99	AZ	H	3-1	Ceesay, Arts, Sanou
25/09/99	PSV	A	1-6	Arts
03/10/99	Ajax	H	3-6	Bombarda, Sanou, Galasek
12/10/99	SC Cambuur Leeuwarden	A	1-0	Bombarda
16/10/99	RKC Waalwijk	H	2-1	Landzaat, Bombarda
23/10/99	MVV	H	1-0	Sanou
06/11/99	De Graafschap	A	2-0	Bombarda, Arts
20/11/99	Roda JC	H	2-2	Shukov, Arts (p)
27/11/99	FC Twente	A	0-4	
01/12/99	Feyenoord	A	0-1	
05/12/99	FC Utrecht	H	4-3	Bombarda 3, Galasek
15/12/99	Vitesse	A	1-3	Sanou
18/12/99	Sparta	H	0-0	
02/02/00	RKC Waalwijk	A	0-1	
05/02/00	FC Twente	H	1-1	Schulp
09/02/00	NEC	H	3-1	og (De Romijn), Shukov, Ramzi
13/02/00	Ajax	A	1-3	Abdellaoui (p)
20/02/00	Feyenoord	H	2-1	Abdellaoui, Prommayon
26/02/00	Fortuna Sittard	A	0-2	
03/03/00	AZ	A	2-2	Shukov, Ramzi
11/03/00	SC Heerenveen	H	2-3	Sektioui 2 (1p)
17/03/00	NEC	A	1-2	Ramzi
24/03/00	PSV	H	0-0	
31/03/00	FC Den Bosch	A	1-1	Schulp
08/04/00	Vitesse	H	0-4	
15/04/00	Roda JC	A	4-3	Ramzi 2, Galasek, Landzaat (p)
22/04/00	De Graafschap	H	5-3	Van der Heijden, Shukov 2, Landzaat (p), Caluwe
30/04/00	FC Utrecht	A	1-1	Ramzi
07/05/00	SC Cambuur Leeuwarden	H	1-4	Ramzi
14/05/00	MVV	A	1-1	og (Tomasic)

HUNGARY

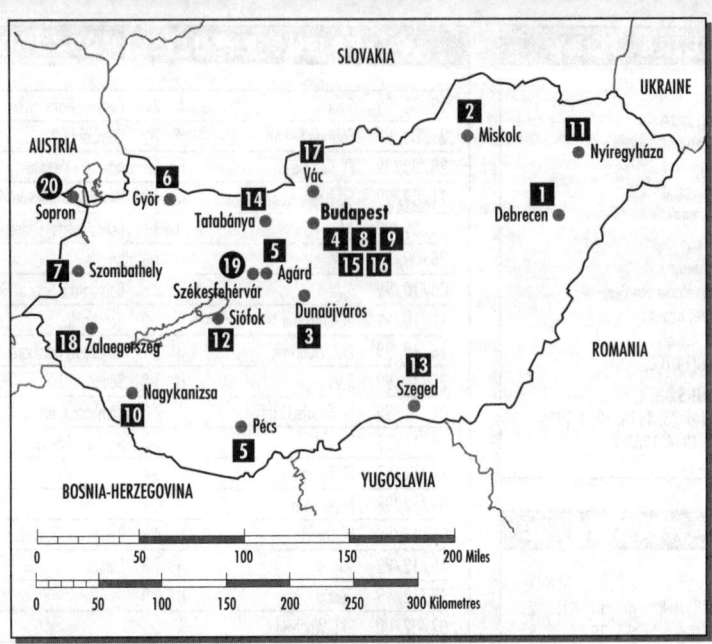

DUNAFERR TAKE FIRST TITLE IN GRAND STYLE

Survival the key as four clubs bite the dust

FEDERATION DIRECTORY

Magyar Labdarúgó Szövetség
Népstadion Toronyépület, Istvánmezei út 1-3, 1146 Budapest

tel - (1) 2220343   Year of Formation - 1901
fax - (1) 2220324   President - Imre Bozóky
website - www.mlsz.hu   Secretary - Sándor Berzi

Stadium - Népstadion, Budapest (60,000)

Which teams will finish the championship? That was the ongoing question that hogged the headlines during the 1999/2000 season in Hungary.

The financial plight of the country's top-division clubs intensified to the extent that by the end of the campaign as many as four of the 18 teams which began the inaugural Professional National Championship (PNB) had either been forced out of business or driven underground to the lower leagues.

Gázszer FC were the first to fall. This small club from the lakeside town of Agárd was essentially the private plaything of owner László Németh, and when he realised that he could not continue to sponsor the club on his own, there was nothing left for him to do other than dissolve it. Ironically, this occurred after Gázszer had enjoyed their best half-season in the top flight, taking 19 points from their first seven games. By some juridicial magic Second Division club Pécsi MFC bought the right to compete in the PNB as Gázszer's replacement. They not only took on Gázszer's points total but also had the option to take on all of their players. In the event, they signed up just three of them.

Szeged LC also went to the wall after a series of misfortunes. Controversially promoted the previous summer, Szeged never looked likely to stay the course. Barely eight games into the season they were already onto their fourth different coach. One of those had been the club's young president, Kálmán Nagylaki, who had no previous experience in the job whatsoever. It was he who accelerated the club's demise by falling out with potential sponsors

LEAGUE CHAMPIONSHIP RESULTS 99/00

		1	2	3	4	5	6	7	8	9	10	11	12	13	14	15	16	17
1	Debreceni VSC		2-0	2-1	3-0	1-1	1-0	1-1	1-1	3-1	3-0	2-0	1-0	1-3	2-3	4-2	4-1	2-2
2	Diósgyöri FC	0-1		0-3	0-0	1-2	2-0	1-1	1-3	0-2	1-1	2-2	0-0	1-2	4-1	1-1	1-1	2-1
3	Dunaferr SE	3-2	6-0		1-0	3-1	1-0	2-1	2-0	1-1	2-1	2-0	3-0	2-0	4-0	1-0	7-0	4-0
4	Ferencváros	0-1	2-0	2-2		4-1	2-2	6-2	1-0	1-0	3-0	4-0	1-2	0-1	0-0	1-2	8-0	1-1
5	Gázszer FC/Pécsi MFC	2-0	2-2	1-2	3-2		1-1	1-2	1-2	0-1	1-0	3-0	1-1	2-2	1-4	3-2	0-0	2-2
6	Györi ETO FC	1-1	1-0	2-4	2-1	0-1		4-1	4-0	2-3	4-0	4-0	1-1	0-1	3-1	2-0	1-1	0-0
7	Haladás-Milos	3-1	1-0	0-1	0-2	1-3	0-3		1-2	0-4	2-0	1-1	0-1	1-1	3-0	1-2	2-3	0-1
8	Kispest-Honvéd FC	1-0	2-0	2-2	2-3	0-0	0-3	2-0		0-2	0-0	0-1	1-1	0-0	1-1	0-4	5-1	1-0
9	MTK Hungária FC	1-2	3-1	1-4	2-3	1-1	4-0	2-2	4-0		3-1	2-0	2-1	3-1	1-0	0-0	3-0	3-1
10	Nagykanizsa	1-1	2-1	0-1	0-2	1-1	2-0	1-1	0-1	1-1		1-0	1-0	0-0	1-1	1-2	3-1	0-0
11	Nyírség-Spartacus FC	2-1	2-0	1-1	3-0	1-1	2-1	1-0	1-0	0-0	2-0		3-0	1-1	2-1	0-2	2-2	0-0
12	Siófok	4-1	0-2	1-1	2-4	0-1	0-1	2-4	1-0	2-2	2-0	0-3		1-3	1-0	0-1	1-0	1-1
13	Lombard FC Tatabánya	1-1	2-1	3-3	2-1	0-0	1-1	1-1	0-0	0-4	1-0	2-1	2-1		0-2	2-0	1-0	2-1
14	Újpest FC	2-2	5-0	0-3	2-2	1-2	1-1	0-0	0-0	1-1	3-1	4-0	2-0	0-1		4-1	1-0	1-1
15	Vasas DH	2-0	2-0	0-2	3-3	4-0	1-0	2-0	2-0	1-2	1-4	4-0	4-0	3-0	3-0		3-0	1-0
16	Vác FC-Zollner	0-5	0-2	1-1	0-2	1-2	1-4	2-4	0-1	0-5	3-4	0-1	1-0	1-1	0-4	1-3		1-3
17	Zalahús ZTE FC	2-0	0-0	1-4	0-0	5-0	2-1	0-1	2-0	0-0	0-0	1-0	4-0	1-1	1-1	0-0	1-2	

LEAGUE CHAMPIONSHIP FINAL TABLE 99/00

			Home					Away					Total					
		Pd	W	D	L	F	A	W	D	L	F	A	W	D	L	F	A	PT	GD
1	Dunaferr SE	32	15	1	0	44	6	9	6	1	35	17	24	7	1	79	23	79	56
2	MTK Hungária FC	32	10	3	3	35	16	8	6	2	29	12	18	9	5	64	28	63	36
3	Vasas DH	32	12	1	3	36	11	7	3	6	22	21	19	4	9	58	32	61	26
4	Lombard FC Tatabánya	32	8	6	2	20	17	6	7	3	17	17	14	13	5	37	34	55	3
5	Ferencváros	32	8	4	4	36	14	6	4	6	25	25	14	8	10	61	39	50	22
6	Debreceni VSC	32	10	4	2	33	16	4	4	8	19	25	14	8	10	52	41	50	11
7	Gázszer FC/Pécsi MFC	32	5	6	5	24	23	6	6	4	17	24	11	12	9	41	47	45	-6
8	Györi ETO FC	32	8	4	4	34	15	4	4	8	18	21	12	8	12	52	36	44	16
9	Nyírség-Spartacus FC	32	9	6	1	23	10	3	2	11	9	32	12	8	12	32	42	44	-10
10	Újpest FC	32	6	7	3	27	15	4	4	8	19	27	10	11	11	46	42	41	4
11	Zalahús ZTE FC	32	6	7	3	20	10	2	8	6	14	21	8	15	9	34	31	39	3
12	Kispest-Honvéd FC	32	5	6	5	17	18	5	3	8	10	21	10	9	13	27	39	39	-12
13	Haladás-Milos	32	4	2	10	16	25	4	6	6	21	28	8	8	16	37	53	32	-16
14	Nagykanizsa	32	5	7	4	15	13	2	3	11	12	31	7	10	15	27	44	31	-17
15	Siófok	32	5	3	8	18	24	2	4	10	8	27	7	7	18	26	51	25	-25
16	Diósgyöri FC	32	3	7	6	17	21	2	2	12	9	35	5	9	18	26	56	24	-30
17	Vác FC-Zollner	32	1	2	13	12	42	2	4	10	12	43	3	6	23	24	85	15	-61

N.B. Szeged LC withdrew; Siófok - 3 points deducted.

from Yugoslavia, an act which effectively switched off the club's life-support system. Nagylaki tried to keep the club afloat, but when they had to cancel four successive fixtures in the early spring, the FA had no option but to eject them from the league and annul the results of all their previous fixtures.

Siófok, Diósgyör and Vác played on but all three were on the brink of joining Gázszer and Szeged. Siófok did not travel to Nyíregyháza in the autumn as a result of a strike from the players, who had received no pay since the start of the season. The FA deducted three points from Siófok's total and announced that the spring re-match

would have to be staged in Nyíregyháza. Cash-strapped Vác practically lined up their youth side in the spring, using a grand total of 43 players. Their failure to provide financial guarantees for the 2000/01 season meant that rather than going down into the First Division (NB1) they were relegated to the next level down. As for Diósgyör, one of the best supported clubs in the country, they ceased to exist altogether. Ordered by a civil court to pay a settlement fee of 60 million florints (around £150,000) to ex-coach Barnabás Tornyi for unfair dismissal, they could not find the money and were subsequently taken into receivership. A crowd invasion from disillusioned fans forced the

TOP SCORERS

22 Attila TÖKÖLI (Dunaferr SE)
19 Péter HORVÁTH (Ferencváros)
18 Mihály TÓTH (Ferencváros)
14 Gávor ZAVADSZKY (Dunaferr SE)
13 Béla ILLÉS (MTK Hungária FC)
 Péter KABÁT (Vasas DH)
 Krisztián KENESEI (MTK Hungária FC)
11 Gyula HORVÁTH (Nagykanizsa/
 Kispest-Honvéd FC)
 Norbert TÓTH (Újpest FC)
10 Danut FRUNZA (Diósgyöri FC)
 Zsombor KEREKES (Nagykanizsa/
 Debcereni VSC)
 Zoltán KOVÁCS (Újpest FC)

NATIONAL TEAM RESULTS 99/00

18/08/99	Moldova	H	Budapest	1-1	Sebök V. (39)
04/09/99	Liechtenstein (ECQ)	A	Vaduz	0-0	
08/09/99	Azerbaijan (ECQ)	H	Budapest	3-0	Sebök V. (28), Egressy (51), Sowunmi (55)
09/10/99	Portugal (ECQ)	A	Lisbon	0-3	
23/02/00	Australia	H	Budapest	0-3	
29/03/00	Poland	H	Debrecen	0-0	
26/04/00	Northern Ireland	A	Belfast	1-0	Horváth (61)
31/05/00	Saudi Arabia	H	Györ	2-2	Horváth (18, 79)
03/06/00	Israel	H	Budapest	2-1	Illés (46), Horváth (51)

NATIONAL TEAM APPEARANCES 99/00

Coach - Bertalan BICSKEI	MOL	LIE	AZB	POR	AUS	POL	NIR	SAU	ISR	Cps	Gls
Szabolcs SÁFÁR (20/08/74) - SV Salzburg (AUT)	G									12	-
Vilmos SEBŐK (13/06/73) - Bristol City (ENG)/SVW Mannheim (GER)	D	D	D		D71	D	D	D	D	33	7
György KORSÓS (22/08/76) - SK Sturm Graz (AUT)	D	D	D	D				s57	s78	s65	17	1
János HRUTKA (26/10/74) - 1.FC Kaiserslautern (GER)	D		D		D	D	D	D	D	22	3
Tamás SZEKERES (18/09/72) - KAA Gent (BEL)	D83									5	-
Pál DÁRDAI (16/03/76) - Hertha BSC Berlin (GER)	M	M		s25			M46	M		14	1
István PISONT (16/05/70) - Hapoel Tel-Aviv (ISR)	M		M25							31	1
Ottó VINCZE (29/08/74) - SVW Mannheim (GER)	M67				M	s90				5	-
Tibor DOMBI (11/11/73) - Eintracht Frankfurt (GER)	A	A60			s58					27	1
Ferenc HORVÁTH (06/05/73) - KRC Genk (BEL)	A46	A76	s74	A76			A89	A	A90	20	6
Attila KORSÓS (25/12/71) - SV Salzburg (AUT)	A									6	1
Thomas SOWUNWI (25/07/78) - Vasas DH	s46	s60	A89	A82						4	1
Béla KOVÁCS (30/03/77) - Ferencváros	s67									1	-
Ákos FÜZI (24/03/78) - Ferencváros	s83		s89							2	-
Gábor KIRÁLY (01/04/76) - Hertha BSC Berlin (GER)		G	G	G		G	G	G	G	19	-
János MÁTYUS (20/12/74) - Ferencváros/FC Energie Cottbus (GER)		D	D	D	D	D	D			20	-
Gábor HALMAI (07/01/72) - MTK Hungária FC		M	M	M		M	s46		M	50	4
Béla ILLÉS (27/04/68) - MTK Hungária FC		M	M			M	M		M	55	13
Gábor EGRESSY (11/02/74) - MTK Hungária FC		A	A	A					s80	18	1
Miklós FEHÉR (10/07/79) - FC Porto (POR)/SC Salgueiros (POR)		A46						s66	A80	10	1
Miklós LENDVAI (07/04/75) - KFC Verbroedering Geel (BEL)		s46	M	M	M	M90	M	M	M46	9	-
Miklós HERCZEG (26/03/74) - Győri ETO FC		s76	A74	s76			s78			11	-
Attila DRAGÓNER (15/11/74) - Fortuna Köln (GER)				D	s71			D	D	9	-
Pál LAKOS (21/01/74) - Ferencváros				D						3	-
Zoltán KOVÁCS (24/09/73) - Újpest FC				s82						13	2
Gábor BABOS (24/10/74) - MTK Hungária FC					G					6	-
Tamás BÓDOG (27/09/70) - SSV Ulm (GER)					D					1	-
Gábor BUKRÁN (16/12/75) - Walsall (ENG)					M					1	-
Gábor ZAVADSZKY (10/09/74) - Dunaferr SE					A58					1	-
László KLAUSZ (24/06/71) - SVW Mannheim (GER)					A					27	6
Tamás NAGY (06/06/76) - Dunaferr SE					A					2	-
Csaba FEHÉR (02/09/75) - KFC Verbroedering Geel (BEL)						D	M	M78	M65	11	-
Károly ERŐS (20/12/71) - MTK Hungária FC						M				1	-
Krisztián LISZTES (02/06/76) - VfB Stuttgart (GER)						M79		M	s46	14	-
Attila TÖKÖLI (14/05/76) - Dunaferr SE						A46				1	-
Tamás SÁNDOR (20/06/74) - Beitar Jerusalem (ISR)						s46				11	-
Krisztián KENESEI (07/01/77) - MTK Hungária FC						s79				1	-
Zoltán PETŐ (19/09/74) - Debreceni VSC							M57	M		2	-
Sándor PREISINGER (11/12/73) - KFC Verbroedering Geel (BEL)								A78	A66	s90	5	-
István HAMAR (06/10/70) - Beitar Jerusalem (ISR)								s89		A90	17	4
Miklós SALAMON (30/11/74) - Dunaferr SE									s90	1	-

DOMESTIC CUP 99/00

THIRD ROUND

Baktalórántháza 1, Kispest-Honvéd FC 3
MTK Hungária FC 2, Gázszer FC 0
Bodajk 0, Újpest FC 3
Celldömölk 0, Siófok 2
Csepel SC 0, Dunaferr SE 3
Debreceni VSC 2, BKV Előre 1
Fót 1, Diósgyőri FC 0
Kaposfüred 2, Jászberény 2 (aet; 7-6 on pens.)
Kazincbarcika 1, Vác FC-Zollner 3
Pápai LC 0, FC Eger 1
Peasztó 2, Vasas DH 3
Szeged LC 0, BVSC 1
Tápiószentmárton 2, III. Kerület FC 1
Videoton FCF 0, Veszprém 1
Zalahús ZTE FC 0, Ferencváros 1
Győri ETO FC 1, Haladás-Milos 0

FOURTH ROUND

Győri ETO FC 0, MTK Hungária FC 1
FC Eger 1, Vác FC-Zollner 2
Kaposfüred 4, Tápiószentmárton 5
Veszprém 0, Debreceni VSC 3
BVSC 3, Fót 0
Dunaferr SE 3, Siófok 0
Vasas DH 4, Ferencváros 1
Kispest-Honvéd FC 0, Újpest FC 1

QUARTER-FINALS

MTK Hungária FC 1 (Illés 69), Dunaferr SE 0
Tápiószentmárton 2 (Simon 33p, Gulácsi 54),
Vác FC-Zollner 1 (Rusvaya 14)
Debreceni VSC 3 (Goian 70p, Kerekes 96,
Siklósi 105), BVSC 1 (Vincze G. 74) (aet)
Újpest FC 1 (Kovács Z. 24),
Vasas DH 2 (Galaschek 9, Simek 52)

SEMI-FINALS

MTK Hungária FC 4 (Gusatu 6, 79, Madar 28,
Kuttor 83), Debreceni VSC 0
Tápiószentmárton 1 (Simon 26p),
Vasas DH 4 (Kabát 23, 47, Tiber 53, 71)

FINAL

03/05/2000, Budapest
MTK HUNGÁRIA FC 3 Tóth (49og), Szilveszter
(56og), Kenesei (76)
VASAS DH 1 Szilveszter (12)
referee - Hajdó
MTK HUNGÁRIA FC - Babos; Kuttor, Szamosi, Komlósi,
Elek; Halmai; Buzsáky (Madar 46), Erős, Illés;
Kenesei (Ilea 84), Gusatu (Egressy 74).
VASAS DH - Kövesfalvi; Juhár; Tóth, László; Mónos,
Zováth, Szili (Simek 81), Aranyos (Bekő 46);
Szilveszter (Tiber 78); Kabát, Sowunmi.

abandonment of their final fixture, at home to Dunaferr. The club was then amalgamated with Borsodi Volán, although it is under the latter's name that they now compete in the third division.

The positive vibrations of the season were provided almost exclusively by Dunaferr, who won the championship for the first time and in a manner that almost defied belief. Sponsored by the Danube Iron Works ("Duna" means Danube; "Ferr" comes from the Latin word "ferrum", meaning iron), the club from Dunaújváros lost just one

match all season - their very first, against Debrecen. After that they tore through the opposition like a tornado. Already on top at the winter break, Dunaferr put together a sensational run in the spring, winning every game bar one (a 2-2 draw at Ferencváros) and extending their final winning margin to a formidable 16 points.

Dunaferr became only the fourth provincial side to take the Hungarian title (after Nagyvárdi AC in 1944, Rába ETO in 1982 and '83, and Vác in 1994). Most of their players were from a rural background, with just three from

PLAYERS OF THE SEASON

ATTILA TÖKÖLI

Prior to the 1999/2000 season Attila Tököli had scored just 23 goals in his 92 First Division appearances. But, like his club Dunaferr, he underwent a miraculous transformation and actually doubled that total in one season alone. Official statistics show that his top-scoring haul was 22 goals, but in fact he scored 25. His hat-trick in a 9-0 victory over Szeged was subsequently expunged from the records following Szeged's wthdrawal. Either way, the 24-year-old striker had a tremendous season and was honoured for his important contribution to Dunaferr's championship win by being named as Hungary's Players' Player of the Year. The Pécs-born striker also made his national team début in a friendly against Poland.

FERENCH HORVÁTH

Unable to command a regular place in his Belgian club Genk - he was a disappointed substitute in their Cup final triumph over Standard Liège, against whom he had scored a hat-trick in the league - Ferenc Horváth nevertheless proved himself to be the first-choice striker in Bertalan Bicskei's Hungarian national side. The ex-Videoton and Ferencváros striker scored four goals in three games during the spring to gave his country a glimmer of hope for the forthcoming World Cup qualifiers against Italy, Lithuania, Romania and Georgia. A sturdy striker with a good turn of pace, Horváth left Genk in the summer for German Bundesliga newcomers Energie Cottbus, where, for a club record fee, he joined forces with his Hungarian international team-mates Mátyus, Sebők and Szekeres.

EUROPEAN CUPS 99/00

CHAMPIONS' CUP
● **MTK HUNGÁRIA FC**
Preliminary round 2 ÍBV (ISL)
A 2-0   Halmai (18), Preisinger (73)
Babos; Fehér, Komlósi, Kuttor, Szamosi; Erös (Balaskó 46), Halmai, Illés (Preisinger 66); Kenesei (Buzsáky 76), Ilea, Madar.
H 3-1   Ilea (4), Kuttor (25), Illés (41)
Babos; Fehér (Balaskó 36), Komlósi, Kuttor, Szamosi; Erös, Halmai (Elek 75), Illés; Kenesei, Ilea (Preisinger 63), Madar.

Qualifying round CROATIA ZAGREB (CRO)
A 0-0
Babos; Lörincz; Fehér (Kenesei 54), Komlósi, Kuttor, Szamosi; Erös, Halmai, Illés; Ilea (Preisinger 61), Egressy (Helder 46).
H 0-2
Babos; Lörincz; Komlósi, Kuttor; Fehér (Kovács 82), Erös, Illés, Szamosi; Madar, Ilea (Egressy 46), Helder (Preisinger 77).

UEFA CUP
● **DEBRECENI VSC**
1st round VFL WOLFSBURG (GER)
A 0-2
Fekete; Goian; Bodnár, Petö; Böör; Vadicska, Sándor, Bagoly, Szatmári; Sabo (Ulveczki 73), Csoltan (Bajzát 66).
H 2-1   Sabo (54, 90)
Fekete; Goian; Bernáth, Petö; Vadicska, Sándor, Bagoly, Szatmári (Dobos 70); Sabo, Siklósi (Madar 85), Ulveczki.

● **FERENCVAROS**
Qualifying round CONSTRUCTORUL CHISINAU (MOL)
H 3-1   Horváth (36), Füzi (42), Kovács (73)
Szücs L.; Lakos (Nagy 46); Mátyus, Lilik, Szücs M. (Zöld 65); Kriston, Bárányos (Kulcsár 38), Kovács, Füzi; Fülöp, Horváth.
A 1-1   Horváth (38)
Szücs L.; Lakos; Szücs M., Mátyus; Kriston, Bárányos, Lászka, Kovács (Schultz 85); Füzi; Kulcsár (Tóth 75), Horváth (Selimi 90).

1st round FK TEPLICE (CZE)
A 1-3   Tóth (15)
Szücs L.; Lakos; Kriston, Mátyus; Szücs M., Bárányos, Kovács (Kulcsár 46), Füzi, Nagy; Horváth, Tóth.
H 1-1   Mátyus (57p)
Szücs L.; Lakos; Szücs M. (Kulcsár 46), Mátyus; Kriston, Bárányos, Kovács, Füzi, Nagy; Tóth, Horváth.

● **MTK HUNGÁRIA FC**
1st round FENERBAHÇE (TUR)
H 0-0
Babos; Fehér, Kuttor, Szamosi, Kovács (Farkas 76); Erös, Halmai (Buzsáky 62); Illés; Madar, Kenesei (Ilea 79), Egressy.
A 2-0   Kenesei (55, 63)
Babos; Fehér, Kuttor, Szamosi, Elek (Kovács 50); Komlósi; Erös, Madar, Halmai, Kenesei (Preisinger 73), Egressy (Farkas 84).

2nd round AEK (GRE)
H 2-1   Egressy (20), Erös (34)
Babos; Fehér, Kuttor, Szamosi, Kovács (Elek 86); Komlósi, Halmai, Erös; Madar (Balaskó 84), Kenesei (Preisinger 73), Egressy.
A 0-1
Babos; Fehér, Kuttor, Szamosi, Kovács (Farkas 79); Erös, Halmai, Komlósi; Madar, Kenesei (Illés 64), Egressy.

● **ÚJPEST FC**
Qualifying round VOJVODINA NOVI SAD (YUG)
A 0-4
Bíró; Némedi; Kovács B., Kiskapusi, Tamási, Szlezák; Csillag, Zimmermann (Szélesi 46); Tóth; Kopunovic, Kovács Z. (Terjék 69).
H 1-1   Kovács Z. (56)
Bíró; Szlezák (Kerényi 26); Tamási, Kiskapusi; Babos, Zimmermann (Szélesi 84), Csillag, Löw; Tokody; Terjék (Szabó 78), Kovács Z..

Budapest (Miklós Salamon, Ferenc Lengyel and Ferenc Kóczián). Most of their key men had been bought from Ferencváros (Igor Nichenko, Gábor Zavadszky) or, at the start of the season, from main rivals and defending champions MTK (Balázs Rabóczki, Zoltán Molnár, Ferenc Orosz).

Dunaferr also got their coach from MTK. Sándor Egervári, who had guided the Budapest side to their run-away 1998/99 championship triumph, was dismissed by MTK supremo Gábor Várszegi, who believed that under him his team did not play sufficiently attractive football. Várszegi had frequent cause to regret his decision during the season as Egervári made history by becoming the first coach to win successive Hungarian titles with different clubs. The match which effectively sealed the title for Dunaferr tasted especially sweet for Egervári as he led his team to a brilliant 4-1 win away to MTK - by popular

consensus, Dunaferr's most impressive and comprehensive performance of the season.

MTK had to settle for a distant runners-up spot in the league, but they performed well in other competitions, eliminating Fenerbahçe from the UEFA Cup (after going close against Croatia Zagreb in the Champions' League qualifiers) and winning the Hungarian Cup for the third time in four seasons. They knocked out Dunaferr in the quarter-finals, hammered holders Debrecen 4-0 in the semis and came from behind to beat Vasas 3-1 in the final, helped on their way by two own-goals. The triumphant MTK coach was expensively-hired Dutchman Henk ten Cate but he left in the summer, to be replaced by Gábor Pölöskei.

Vasas, whose third place in the league and runners-up spot in the Cup amounted to a successful season in most people's eyes, surprisingly got rid of their coach, András

Left: Hungary's György Korsós executes a perfect sliding tackle to dispossess Portugal's João Pinto in the Euro 2000 Group Seven qualifier.

century of goals and points en route to winning the NB1 and were joined in the new-look 16-team top division (split into two groups of eight) by Matáv Sopron.

Of Bertalan Bicskei's national team there was little to report, other than that they played better at the end of the season - thanks mainly to centre-forward Ferenc Horváth and goalkeeper Gábor Kiraly - than at the start, when a goalless draw against Liechtenstein added to the lengthening catalogue of embarrassments experienced in recent times by the less than mighty Magyars.

Komjári, and replaced him with ex-national team boss György Mezey. There was much ado on the coaching front at Ferencváros, with president József Torgyán hiring and firing on a grand scale until he opted to bring in János Csank at the end of the season. Csank, who was considered the main enemy of the Fradi fans when he coached Vác in the mid-1990s, before later becoming the national coach, earned his move to Budapest's biggest club by leading Videoton to an immediate promotion back to the PNB. The team from Székesfehérvár accumulated a

INTERNATIONAL HONOURS

World Cup Finals appearances: 1934 (2nd round), 1938 (Runners-up), 1954 (Runners-up), 1958, 1962 (qtr-finals), 1966 (qtr-finals), 1978, 1982, 1986

European Championship appearances: 1964 (3rd), 1968, 1972 (4th)

European Club Competitions
Fairs' Cup   Ferencváros (1965)

PROMOTED CLUBS 99/00

SECOND DIVISION FINAL TABLE

		Pd	W	D	L	F	A	Pt	GD
1	**Videoton FCF**	38	32	5	1	104	19	101	85
2	**Matáv Sopron**	38	24	6	8	83	28	78	55
3	BKV Elöre	38	19	9	10	59	32	66	27
4	Kecskeméti FC	38	20	6	12	60	39	66	21
5	Kaposvár	38	18	11	9	47	33	65	14
6	Békéscsaba	38	18	10	10	53	37	64	16
7	Cegléd	38	17	8	13	68	57	59	11
8	Szolnok	38	18	5	15	65	69	59	-4
9	Dunakeszi	38	16	10	12	59	53	58	6
10	III. Kerület FC	38	15	10	13	57	59	55	-2
11	Százhalombatta	38	15	9	14	59	48	54	11
12	Tiszaújváros	38	14	10	14	51	47	52	4
13	BVSC	38	13	12	13	50	44	51	6
14	Komló	38	13	10	15	52	56	49	-4
15	Hajdúszoboszló	38	12	6	20	51	91	42	-40
16	REAC	38	11	3	24	42	79	36	-37
17	Diego FC Dabas	38	8	9	21	48	75	33	-27
18	Demecser FC	38	6	12	20	40	70	30	-30
19	Komáromi FC	38	7	6	25	47	106	27	-59
20	Csepel SC	38	3	5	30	25	78	14	-53

CLUB DIRECTORIES

Videoton FC Fehérvár
Csíkvári u.10
8000 Székesfehérvár
tel - (22) 379493
fax - (22) 379493
Year of Formation - 1941
Chairman - István Szigli
Coach - János Csank
(00/01 - Ferenc Csongrádi)
Stadium - Sóstói (19,000)

Matáv Compaq Sopron
Káposztás u.1
9400 Sopron
tel - (99) 310990/353495/353939
fax - (99) 310990
Year of Formation - 1923
Chairman - Tibor Klement
Coach - Antal Róth
(00/01 - István Reszeli Soós)
Stadium - Sopron (10,000)

DEBRECENI VSC

CLUB DIRECTORY

Debreceni VSC
Oláh Gábor u. 5
4028 Debrecen
tel - (52) 340816
fax - (52) 340817
email - dvscrt@matavnet.hu
Year of Formation - 1902
Chairman - Balázs Makray jr.
Coach - Lajos Garamvölgyi
(00/01 - András Komjáti)
Stadium - Nagyerdei (10,200)

MAJOR HONOURS
Domestic Cup - (1) 1999.

APPEARANCES 99/00

	P	Ap	(s)	Gls
Gábor BAGOLY	M	23		7
Péter BAJZÁT	A	4	(16)	3
János BALOGH	G		(1)	
Csaba BERNÁTH	D	10	(15)	
László BODNÁR	D	27		3
Zoltán BÖÖR	M	26		4
Cornel CASOLTAN (ROM)	A	8	(1)	
Attila DOBOS	M	1	(10)	
Tibor DOMBI	A	9		1
Róbert FEKETE	G	22		
Zsolt FÓRIÁN	M		(1)	
Livius GOIAN (ROM)	D	28		1
Zsombor KEREKES (YUG)	A	12	(3)	8
Norbert KOVÁCS	M	5	(3)	
Zoltán PETÖ	D	15		
Radu SABO (ROM)	M	24	(3)	7
Csaba SÁNDOR	D	22	(1)	
Csaba SIKLÓSI	M	21	(9)	6
János SZABÓ	M		(1)	
Csaba SZATMÁRI	M	30		3
Gábro TÉGLÁSI	G	10		
György TURJÁN	D	2	(2)	
Zoltán ULVECZKI	M	16	(10)	1
Zsolt VADICSKA	M	30		4
Richárd VÁRSZEGI	A		(8)	2
Krisztián ZAHORECZ	D	7		

LEAGUE RESULTS 1999/2000

07/08/99	Dunaferr SE	H	2-1	Goian, Siklósi
14/08/99	Nyírség-Spartacus FC	A	1-2	Böör
21/08/99	Diósgyöri FC	H	2-0	Sabo, Bajzát
28/08/99	Györi ETO FC	H	1-0	Sabo (p)
11/09/99	Újpest FC	A	2-2	Bagoly 2
19/09/99	Lombard FC Tatabánya	H	1-3	Bagoly
24/09/99	Nagykanizsa	A	1-1	Siklósi
03/10/99	Siófok	H	1-0	Vadicska
16/10/99	Ferencváros	A	1-0	Szatmári
22/10/99	Kispest-Honvéd FC	H	1-1	Vadicska
06/11/99	Haladás-Milos	H	1-1	Bagoly
12/11/99	Vasas DH	A	0-2	
27/11/99	Zalahús ZTE FC	A	0-2	
01/12/99	Gázszer FC	H	1-1	Ulveczki
04/12/99	Vác FC-Zollner	H	4-1	Bagoly, Vadicska, Bodnár,
				og (Kádár)
10/12/99	MTK Hungária FC	A	2-1	Siklósi, Bodnár
26/02/00	Dunaferr SE	A	2-3	Vadicska, Siklósi
04/03/00	Nyírség-Spartacus FC	H	2-0	Bajzát, Böör
08/03/00	Diósgyöri FC	A	1-0	Sabo
11/03/00	Györi ETO FC	A	1-1	Kerekes
17/03/00	Újpest FC	H	2-3	Sabo, Böör
25/03/00	Lombard FC Tatabánya	A	1-1	Kerekes
01/04/00	Nagykanizsa	H	3-0	Kerekes 3
05/04/00	Siófok	A	1-4	Bagoly
08/04/00	Ferencváros	H	3-0	Bagoly, Siklósi, Bajzát
14/04/00	Kispest-Honvéd FC	A	0-1	
29/04/00	Haladás-Milos	A	1-3	Siklósi
06/05/00	Vasas DH	H	4-2	Szatmári, Bodnár, Várszegi 2
13/05/00	Pécsi MFC	A	0-2	
17/05/00	Zalahús ZTE FC	H	2-2	Kerekes 2
20/05/00	Vác FC-Zollner	A	5-0	Siklósi, Szatmári, Sabo 2, Dombi
27/05/00	MTK Hungária FC	H	3-1	Sabo, Böör, Kerekes

DIÓSGYÖRI FC

CLUB DIRECTORY

Diósgyöri FC (now merged with Borsodi Volán)
Andrássy u. 61
3533 Miskolc
tel - (46) 379451
fax - (46) 379552
Year of Formation - 1910
Chairman - Zoltán Kövy
Coach - Miklós Temesvári; Zoltán Varga
Stadium - Diósgyöri (28,000)

MAJOR HONOURS
Domestic Cup - (2) 1977, 1980.

APPEARANCES 99/00

		P	Ap	(s)	Gls
Ákos	BARVA	A	3	(7)	1
Relu	BULIGA	A	7	(4)	
Vladimir	CIRIC (YUG)	G	1		
Ferenc	CUPIK	A	6	(8)	
Béla	DUKON	M	5	(7)	
Vladan	FILIPOVIC (YUG)	A	23	(2)	2
Danut	FRUNZA	A	23	(2)	10
Remus	GANEA (ROM)	M	4	(1)	
Roland	HARNÓCZ	M	29	(2)	
Szabolcs	HERCZKU	M	8	(2)	
Balázs	HOMPOTH	D	18	(2)	
István	KÁKÓCZKI	A	22	(3)	
Ibrahim	KOMI (SUD)	A	3	(4)	1
Péter	KONYHA	A	13	(5)	1
Tibor	KOVÁCS	D	10		
Frantisek	KUNZO (SVK)	M	22	(1)	3
Ákos	LIPPAI	M	17	(5)	1
László	LIPTÁK	M	19	(3)	
Zoltán	NAGY	G	31		
Zsolt	PÁLING	M	9	(1)	
Nenad	POZDER (YUG)	D	15	(1)	
Sorin	RADU (ROM)	A	12	(3)	4
Mircea	RAICAN (ROM)	M	11	(4)	1
Csaba	SZAKOS	D	23	(3)	
György	TAKÁCS	D	2	(2)	1
Viktor	TAKÁCS	M	6	(3)	
Marian	TIMKO (SVK)	D	8		1
Vilmos	VANCZÁK	M		(1)	
Zoltán	VARGA	M		(2)	
Zoltán	VITELKI	M	2	(8)	

LEAGUE RESULTS 1999/2000

07/08/99	Nyírség-Spartacus FC	h	2-2	Frunza 2
14/08/99	Györi ETO FC	A	0-4	
21/08/99	Debreceni VSC	A	0-2	
29/08/99	Újpest FC	H	4-1	Frunza 2, Radu, Komi
11/09/99	Lombard FC Tatabánya	A	1-2	Kunzo
18/09/99	Nagykanizsa	H	1-1	Timko
25/09/99	Siófok	A	2-0	Kunzo, Raican
03/10/99	Ferencváros	H	0-0	
15/10/99	Kispest-Honvéd FC	A	0-2	
30/10/99	Haladás-Milos	A	0-1	
06/11/99	Vasas DH	H	1-1	Frunza
15/11/99	Gázszer FC	A	2-2	Konyha, Frunza
27/11/99	Vác FC-Zollner	A	2-0	Kunzo, Frunza
04/12/99	MTK Hungária FC	H	0-2	
08/12/99	Zalahús ZTE FC	H	2-1	Filipovic, Frunza
11/12/99	Dunaferr SE	A	0-6	
26/02/00	Nyírség-Spartacus FC	A	0-2	
04/03/00	Györi ETO FC	H	2-0	Frunza, Radu (p)
08/03/00	Debreceni VSC	H	0-1	
11/03/00	Újpest FC	A	0-5	
18/03/00	Lombard FC Tatabánya	H	1-2	Radu
25/03/00	Nagykanizsa	A	1-2	Radu
01/04/00	Siófok	H	0-0	
05/04/00	Ferencváros	A	0-2	
09/04/00	Kispest-Honvéd FC	H	1-3	Filipovic (p)
22/04/00	Haladás-Milos	H	1-1	Frunza
29/04/00	Vasas DH	A	0-2	
06/05/00	Pécsi MFC	H	1-2	Barva
13/05/00	Zalahús ZTE FC	A	0-0	
17/05/00	Vác FC-Zollner	H	1-1	Lippai
20/05/00	MTK Hungária FC	A	1-3	Takács G.
27/05/00	Dunaferr SE	H	0-3	(w/o)

DUNAFERR SE

CLUB DIRECTORY

Dunaferr SE
Eszperantó út 4
2400 Dunaújváros
tel - (25) 411255
fax - (25) 583266
Year of Formation - 1951
Chairman - dr. József Szabó
Coach - Sándor Egervári
Stadium - Dunaferr (11,600)

MAJOR HONOURS
League Championship - (1) 2000.

APPEARANCES 99/00

	P	Ap	(s)	Gls
László BITA	G	1	(1)	
László CSEKE	D		(5)	
László ÉGER	D	30		
Antal JÄKL	M	27		2
György KISS	D	27		1
Ferenc KÓCZIÁN	D	12	(6)	
László KOMÓDI	M	10	(16)	1
Ferenc LENGYEL	M	27	(3)	5
Dejan MILOVANOVIC (YUG)	D	1	(3)	1
Zoltán MOLNÁR	D	29		2
Tamás NAGY	A	9	(16)	4
Igor NICHENKO (UKR)	A	11	(9)	8
Balázs NIKOLOV	D		(6)	
Oleg MOZGOVOI (RUS)	M		(7)	
Ferenc OROSZ	A	22	(2)	7
Balázs RABÓCZKI	G	31		
Henrik RÓSA	M	24	(3)	3
Miklós SALAMON	D	32		1
Attila TÖKÖLI	A	27	(5)	22
Gábor ZAVADSZKY	M	32		14

LEAGUE RESULTS 1999/2000

07/08/99	Debreceni VSC	A	1-2	Nichenko
15/08/99	Újpest FC	H	4-0	Nichenko, Rósa, Zavadszky 2
21/08/99	Lombard FC Tatabánya	A	3-3	Orosz, Nichenko, Milovanovic
28/08/99	Nagykanizsa	H	2-1	Tököli, Nichenko
11/09/99	Siófok	A	1-1	Orosz
19/09/99	Ferencváros	H	1-0	Tököli
24/09/99	Kispest-Honvéd FC	A	2-2	Tököli, og (Medgyesi)
16/10/99	Haladás-Milos	A	1-0	og (Bodor)
23/10/99	Vasas DH	H	1-0	Zavadszky
30/10/99	Gázszer FC	A	2-1	Tököli 2
06/11/99	Zalahús ZTE FC	H	4-0	Zavadszky 3, Lengyel (p)
13/11/99	Vác FC-Zollner	A	1-1	Lengyel (p)
20/11/99	MTK Hungária FC	H	1-1	Lengyel
29/11/99	Györi ETO FC	A	4-2	Tököli 2, Nagy, Nichenko
04/12/99	Nyírség-Spartacus FC	A	1-1	Komódi
11/12/99	Diósgyöri FC	H	6-0	Tököli 3, Zavadszky, Nagy, Jäkl (p)
26/02/00	Debreceni VSC	H	3-2	Tököli 2, Salamon
03/03/00	Újpest FC	A	3-0	(w/o)
08/03/00	Lombard FC Tatabánya	H	2-0	Zavadszky, Tököli
12/03/00	Nagykanizsa	A	1-0	Orosz
18/03/00	Siófok	H	3-0	Tököli 2, Orosz
25/03/00	Ferencváros	A	2-2	Molnár, Tököli
01/04/00	Kispest-Honvéd FC	H	2-0	Jäkl, Kiss
08/04/00	Haladás-Milos	H	2-1	Tököli, Rósa
14/04/00	Vasas DH	A	2-0	Molnár, Zavadszky
22/04/00	Pécsi MFC	H	3-1	Zavadszky, Nagy, Nichenko
29/04/00	Zalahús ZTE FC	A	4-1	Tököli, Lengyel, Zavadszky 2
06/05/00	Vác FC-Zollner	H	7-0	Rósa, Tököli 2, Zavadszky, Orosz, Nagy, Nichenko
13/05/00	MTK Hungária FC	A	4-1	Zavadszky, Orosz 2, Nichenko
17/05/00	Györi ETO FC	H	1-0	Tököli
20/05/00	Nyírség-Spartacus FC	H	2-0	Tököli, Lengyel
27/05/00	Diósgyöri FC	A	3-0	(w/o)

FERENCVÁROS

CLUB DIRECTORY

Ferencvárosi Torna Club
Üllöi út 129, 1091 Budapest IX
tel - (1) 2156025/2153856/2153698
fax - (1) 2153698
website - www.FTC.hu
email - FRADI.center@Euroweb.hu
Year of Formation - 1899
Chairman - dr. Jószef Torgyán
Coach - József Mucha; Stanko Poklepovic
(00/01 - János Csank)
Stadium - Üllöi út (18,100)

MAJOR HONOURS
League Championship - (26)
1903, 1905, 1907, 1909, 1910, 1911, 1912,
1913, 1926, 1927, 1928, 1932, 1934, 1938,
1940, 1941, 1949, 1963, 1964, 1967, 1968,
1976, 1981, 1992, 1995, 1996.
Domestic Cup - (18) 1913, 1922, 1927, 1928,
1933, 1935, 1942, 1943, 1944, 1958, 1972,
1974, 1976, 1978, 1991, 1993, 1994, 1995.
Fairs' Cup - (1) 1965.

APPEARANCES 99/00

		P	Ap	(s)	Gls
Tibor BARANYAI	M	1	(1)		
Zsolt BÁRÁNYOS	M	30			8
Tamás BÓCZ	M	2	(2)		
Zoltán BÜKSZEGI	A	4	(3)		
Dragan CRNOMARKOVIC (YUG)	D	12	(2)		
László CSÁKVÁRI	M		(1)		
Norbert CSOKNAI (SVK)	D	14			
Csaba FÖLDVÁRI	M	7	(2)		1
Zoltán FÜLÖP	A		(4)		
Ákos FÜZI	M	26			1
István GAJDA	A		(2)		1
Gábor GYEPES	M		(2)		
Tibor HALGAS	M	4	(4)		
Péter HORVÁTH	A	32			19
Zoltán JAGODICS	M	6	(1)		
Attila KRISTON	D	19			1
Béla KOVÁCS	M	13	(2)		2
Sándor KULCSÁR	A	2	(8)		1
Pál LAKOS	D	25			
Balázs LÁSZKA	M	6	(4)		1
Pál LILIK	M	8	(9)		
János MÁTYUS	D	10			1
Norbert NAGY	M	27	(1)		
Kornél ROB	A	1	(5)		1
György SALLAI	M		(1)		
Levente SCHULZ	M	5	(6)		
Tamás SOMORJAI	M		(1)		
Lajos SZŰCS	G	32			
Mihály SZŰCS	D	20			
Zoltán VÁCZI	M	5	(3)		2
Gábor VÉN	A	13	(2)		2
Mihály TÓTH	A	28	(1)		18
Zoltán ZÖLD	M		(1)		

LEAGUE RESULTS 1999/2000

06/08/99	Vasas DH	H	1-2	Kovács
15/08/99	Gázszer FC	A	2-3	Lászka, Tóth
21/08/99	Zalahús ZTE FC	H	1-1	Kulcsár
29/08/99	Vác FC-Zollner	A	2-0	Kovács, Bárányos
11/09/99	MTK Hungária FC	H	1-0	Tóth
19/09/99	Dunaferr SE	A	0-1	
25/09/99	Nyírség-Spartacus FC	H	4-0	Tóth, Horváth 2, Mátyus (p)
03/10/99	Diósgyöri FC	A	0-0	
16/10/99	Debreceni VSC	H	0-1	
25/10/99	Újpest FC	A	2-2	Horváth 2
30/10/99	Lombard FC Tatabánya	H	0-1	
07/11/99	Nagykanizsa	A	2-0	Horváth, Bárányos
13/11/99	Siófok	H	1-2	Horváth
20/11/99	Györi ETO FC	H	2-2	Horváth, og (Vayer)
11/12/99	Haladás-Milos	A	2-0	Horváth, Tóth
18/12/99	Kispest-Honvéd FC	A	3-2	Horváth, Tóth 2
28/02/00	Vasas DH	A	3-3	Vén 2, Tóth
04/03/00	Pécsi MFC	H	4-1	Tóth 2, Bárányos, Horváth
08/03/00	Zalahús ZTE FC	A	0-0	
11/03/00	Vác FC-Zollner	H	8-0	Horváth 2, Tóth 2, Bárányos, Váczi, Földvári, og (Koller)
18/03/00	MTK Hungária FC	A	3-2	Bárányos, Füzi, Tóth
25/03/00	Dunaferr SE	H	2-2	Tóth 2
01/04/00	Nyírség-Spartacus FC	A	0-3	
05/04/00	Diósgyöri FC	H	2-0	Rob, Váczi
08/04/00	Debreceni VSC	A	0-3	
15/04/00	Újpest FC	H	0-0	
21/04/00	Lombard FC Tatabánya	A	1-2	Horváth
29/04/00	Nagykanizsa	H	3-0	Bárányos, Tóth 2
06/05/00	Siófok	A	4-2	Horváth 3 (2p), Tóth
12/05/00	Györi ETO FC	A	1-2	Bárányos
17/05/00	Kispest-Honvéd FC	H	1-0	Horváth
27/05/00	Haladás-Milos	H	6-2	Horváth 2, Tóth, Bárányos, Kriston, Gajda

GÁZSZER FC/PÉCSI MFC

CLUB DIRECTORY

Pécsi Mecsek FC
(replaced Gázszer FC in mid-season)
Stadion u.2, 7633 Pécs
tel - (72) 552880 / fax - (72) 552881
Year of Formation - 1950
Chairman - dr. László Toller
Coach - Ferenc Csongrádi (with Gázszer FC);
Gábor Szapor
Stadium - PMFC (16,200)

MAJOR HONOURS
Domestic Cup - (1) 1990.

APPEARANCES 99/00

	P	Ap	(s)	Gls
Gábor ÁRKI	M	14		2
Balázs BEKÖ	M	3	(3)	1
Balázs BERDÓ	M	3	(2)	
Béla BÍRÓ	G	1		
András DIENES	D	15		
Josip DULIC (YUG)	M	15		1
Zsolt DVÉRI	M	14		1
Balázs FÓNAI	M	5	(2)	1
Gábor FÖLDES	A	16		3
Tibor FÖLDVÁRI (ROM)	D	12	(2)	
Péter GÁLFFY	A	12	(3)	2
Zoltán GERA	M	14	(1)	4
Árpád GÖGH (SVK)	D	11	(1)	2
Ernö KARDOS	M	5	(4)	
Péter KIRÁLY	A	14	(5)	5
Goran KOLARIC (YUG)	M		(2)	
Oleg KOROL (BLS)	D	11		1
Róbert KOVÁCSEVICS	M	4		
István KÖVESFALVI	G	15		
Gábor KUTAS	D	4		1
Levente LANTOS	M	8	(1)	1
Antal LÖRINCZ	D	4	(1)	
Zoltán LUKÁCS	A	10	(4)	4
Viktor MAKRITSKYI (UKR)	D	3	(1)	
Sándor MATUS	G	12		
Norbert NÉMETH	M	8	(1)	
Pál POPOVICS	M	3	(16)	
Dragan PUSKAS (YUG)	M	13	(3)	5
Zsolt RUSKO	A	6	(4)	
János SALACZ	M	15		
Szabolcs SCHINDLER	D	15		2
Péter SIMEK	M	3	(8)	
János SIPOS	M	13	(2)	
Csaba SÓLYOM	G	4		
Zoltán SZABÓ	M	3	(6)	
Csaba SZALAI	D	13		1
Zsolt SZEKERES	M	1	(2)	
Péter SZÖKE	M	2	(3)	
Gábor TOLDI	A	13	(2)	2
Endre VARGA	M	7	(4)	1
Ernö VARGA	M	8		

LEAGUE RESULTS 1999/2000

07/08/99	Siófok	A	1-0	Földes
15/08/99	Ferencváros	H	3-2	Gögh, Lukács, Árki
20/08/99	Kispest-Honvéd FC	A	0-0	
11/09/99	Haladás-Milos	A	3-1	Földes, Lukács, Gögh
18/09/99	Vasas DH	H	3-2	Lukács, Bekö, og (László)
24/09/99	Györi ETO FC	A	1-0	Árki
02/10/99	Zalahús ZTE FC	A	0-5	
16/10/99	Vác FC-Zollner	H	0-0	
25/10/99	MTK Hungária FC	A	1-1	Schindler
30/10/99	Dunaferr SE	H	1-2	Lukács
06/11/99	Nyírség-Spartacus FC	A	1-1	Földes
15/11/99	Diósgyöri FC	H	2-2	Schindler, Dvéri
01/12/99	Debreceni VSC	A	1-1	Szalai
04/12/99	Lombard FC Tatabánya	A	0-0	
13/12/99	Nagykanizsa	H	1-0	Dulic
17/12/99	Újpest FC	H	1-4	Korol
26/02/00	Siófok	H	1-1	Puskas
04/03/00	Ferencváros	A	1-4	Puskas
07/03/00	Kispest-Honvéd FC	H	1-2	Puskas
18/03/00	Haladás-Milos	H	1-2	Varga
25/03/00	Vasas DH	A	0-4	
01/04/00	Györi ETO FC	H	1-1	Gera
05/04/00	Zalahús ZTE FC	H	2-2	Gálffy, Toldi
08/04/00	Vác FC-Zollner	A	2-1	Puskas, Gera
15/04/00	MTK Hungária FC	H	0-1	
22/04/00	Dunaferr SE	A	1-3	Puskas
29/04/00	Nyírség-Spartacus FC	H	3-0	Gera, Király 2
06/05/00	Diósgyöri FC	A	2-1	Király, Gálffy
13/05/00	Debreceni VSC	H	2-0	Fónai, Király
17/05/00	Újpest FC	A	2-1	Toldi, Király
20/05/00	Lombard FC Tatabánya	H	2-2	Kutas, Lantos
27/05/00	Nagykanizsa	A	1-1	Gera

GYÖRI ETO FC

CLUB DIRECTORY

Györi ETO FC
Nagysándor József u. 31
9027 Györ
tel - (96) 312433/314424
fax - (96) 312498
website - www.datanet.hu/eto
email - etofc@mail.datanet.hu
Year of Formation - 1904
Chairman - János Borbényi
Coach - Károly Gergely; József Garami
Stadium - Györi (25,398)

MAJOR HONOURS
League Championship - (3) 1963 (autumn),
1982, 1983.
Domestic Cup - (4) 1965, 1966, 1967, 1979.

APPEARANCES 99/00

	P	Ap	(s)	Gls
Mihály BALLA	A	3	(6)	4
Endre BAJUSZ (YUG)	D	10	(2)	1
Attila BAUMGARTNER	A	14	(4)	3
Zsolt BOGNÁR	D	15	(1)	
Attila BÖJTE	D	20	(1)	
Ákos CSISZÁR	D	24		6
Gábor ERÖS	A	14	(8)	5
István FERENCZI	A	13	(1)	3
Attila GOLLOVITZER	M		(2)	
János GYÖRI	M	29	(1)	1
Miklós HEGYI	M		(2)	
Miklós HERCZEG	A	27	(1)	9
Sándor KÁROLYI	M		(1)	
László KISER	M	13	(1)	1
Radovan MARKOVIC (YUG)	A	7	(6)	2
Mihály MRACSKÓ	M	14	(1)	1
Kornél NAGY	G	1		
László NAGY	M	14	(12)	2
Zsolt POSZA	G	31		
Dénes RÓSA	M	8		1
Claudiu SALAGEAN	D	16	(4)	1
Zsolt SEBÖK	G		(1)	
Tamás SEGOVITS	M		(2)	
Péter STARK	D	11		1
Péter SÜTÖRI	A	1	(2)	
János SZARVAS	A	1	(9)	1
Gyula TERENY	D	4		1
Zoltán VASAS	D	22	(2)	
Gábor VAYER	A	20	(11)	7
Csaba VÁMOSI	D	20	(1)	

LEAGUE RESULTS 1999/2000

14/08/99	Diósgyöri FC	H	4-0	Vayer, Herczeg, Szarvas, Csiszár
21/08/99	Haladás-Milos	H	4-1	Markovic 2, Rósa, Csiszár (p)
28/08/99	Debreceni VSC	A	0-1	
10/09/99	Vasas DH	H	2-0	Herczeg, Györi
17/09/99	Újpest FC	A	1-1	Salagean
24/09/99	Gázszer FC	H	0-1	
02/10/99	Lombard FC Tatabánya	A	1-1	Csiszár
16/10/99	Zalahús ZTE FC	H	0-0	
24/10/99	Nagykanizsa	A	0-2	
30/10/99	Vác FC-Zollner	H	1-1	Stark
08/11/99	Siófok	A	1-0	Kiser
13/11/99	MTK Hungária FC	H	2-3	Vayer, Nagy L.
20/11/99	Ferencváros	A	2-2	Herczeg, Vayer
29/11/99	Dunaferr SE	H	2-4	Tereny, og (Zavadszky)
04/12/99	Kispest-Honvéd FC	A	3-0	Csiszár, Erös 2
11/12/99	Nyírség-Spartacus FC	H	4-0	Herczeg 2, Bajusz, Erös
04/03/00	Diósgyöri FC	A	0-2	
07/03/00	Haladás-Milos	A	3-0	Csiszár, Ferenczi, Erös
11/03/00	Debreceni VSC	H	1-1	Vayer
18/03/00	Vasas DH	A	0-1	
24/03/00	Újpest FC	H	3-1	Csiszár, Herczeg, Vayer
01/04/00	Pécsi MFC	A	1-1	Ferenczi
05/04/00	Lombard FC Tatabánya	H	0-1	
08/04/00	Zalahús ZTE FC	A	1-2	Erös
15/04/00	Nagykanizsa	H	4-0	Herczeg, Ferenczi, Baumgartner, Nagy L.
22/04/00	Vác FC-Zollner	A	4-1	Baumgartner, Balla 3 (1p)
29/04/00	Siófok	H	1-1	Baumgartner
07/05/00	MTK Hungária FC	A	0-4	
12/05/00	Ferencváros	H	2-1	Vayer, Balla
17/05/00	Dunaferr SE	A	0-1	
20/05/00	Kispest-Honvéd FC	H	4-0	Herczeg 2, Vayer, og (Téger)
27/05/00	Nyírség-Spartacus FC	A	1-2	Mracskó

HALADÁS-MILOS

CLUB DIRECTORY

Haladás-Milos (now - Haladás)
Rohonczi út 3
9700 Szombathely
tel - (94) 311494
fax - (94) 311494
website - www.haladas.hu
Year of Formation - 1919
Chairman - Zsolt Szegner
Coach - Géza Vincze
Stadium - Haladás (18,000)

APPEARANCES 99/00

	P	Ap	(s)	Gls
Péter BALASSA	D	29		5
István BALOGH	A	15	(7)	4
István BODOR (ROM)	A	24	(1)	4
Csaba BORBÉLY (ROM)	M	10	(14)	2
Marian DINI (ROM)	A	2	(1)	
Gábor GYÖRVÁRI	M		(6)	
Péter HALMOSI	A	24	(2)	2
András HORVÁTH	D	30		3
András KAJ	M	17	(3)	2
Kornél KURUCSAI	G	10	(1)	
Sorin MARGINEAN (ROM)	A	17	(3)	3
Csaba NAGY	M	21	(1)	1
Gábor NAGY	D	15	(2)	
László NÉMETHY	M	7	(6)	1
Gábor NEZPÁL	M	1	(3)	
Olivér PUSZTAI	D	7	(1)	
Ciprian ROSCA	A	12	(10)	1
Barnabás SÁTORI	A	5	(1)	
Ákos SEPER	D		(2)	
Zoltán SIMON	D	29		
Norbert SIPOS	M	5	(6)	
Csaba SOMFALVI	M	24		5
Flavius STEREAN (ROM)	D	3		
Béla TAKÁCS	D	11	(5)	
Tamás TAKÁCS	G	10		
Péter TÓTH	M	12	(3)	
Zoltán VARGA	G	12		
Gábor ZSIRAI	M		(8)	

LEAGUE RESULTS 1999/2000

06/08/99	Kispest-Honvéd FC	A	0-2	
21/08/99	Györi ETO FC	A	1-4	Somfalvi
28/08/99	Vasas DH	A	0-2	
11/09/99	Gázszer FC	H	1-3	Halmosi
18/09/99	Zalahús ZTE FC	A	1-0	Marginean
25/09/99	Vác FC-Zollner	H	2-3	Marginean, Somfalvi
03/10/99	MTK Hungária FC	A	2-2	Nagy C., Bodor
16/10/99	Dunaferr SE	H	0-1	
23/10/99	Nyírség-Spartacus FC	A	0-1	
30/10/99	Diósgyöri FC	H	1-0	Horváth
06/11/99	Debreceni VSC	A	1-1	Rosca
13/11/99	Újpest FC	H	3-0	(w/o)
27/11/99	Nagykanizsa	H	2-0	Balassa, Balogh
04/12/99	Siófok	A	4-2	Balogh 2, Marginean, Balassa
08/12/99	Lombard FC Tatabánya	A	1-1	Borbély
11/12/99	Ferencváros	H	0-2	
26/02/00	Kispest-Honvéd FC	H	1-2	Kaj
07/03/00	Györi ETO FC	H	0-3	
10/03/00	Vasas DH	H	1-2	Balassa
18/03/00	Pécsi MFC	A	2-1	Balassa, Horváth
25/03/00	Zalahús ZTE FC	H	0-1	
31/03/00	Vác FC-Zollner	A	4-2	Bodor, Halmosi, Somfalvi 2 (1p)
04/04/00	MTK Hungária FC	H	0-4	
08/04/00	Dunaferr SE	A	1-2	Somfalvi
15/04/00	Nyírség-Spartacus FC	H	1-1	Horváth
22/04/00	Diósgyöri FC	A	1-1	Kaj
29/04/00	Debreceni VSC	H	3-1	Bodor, Balogh, Borbély
05/05/00	Újpest FC	A	0-0	
13/05/00	Lombard FC Tatabánya	H	1-1	og (Szabó)
17/05/00	Nagykanizsa	A	1-1	Némethy
20/05/00	Siófok	H	0-1	
27/05/00	Ferencváros	A	2-6	Balassa, Bodor

KISPEST-HONVÉD FC

CLUB DIRECTORY

Kispest-Honvéd Fútball Club
Újtemetö u. 1-3, 1194 Budapest XIX
tel - (1) 2807240/2829789
fax - (1) 2829791
Year of Formation - 1909
Chairman - Sándor Varga
Coach - Imre Komora; István Reszeli-Soós
(00/01 - Barnabás Tornyi)
Stadium - József Bozsik (15,000)

MAJOR HONOURS
League Championship - (13) 1950, 1950
(autumn), 1952, 1954, 1955, 1980, 1984,
1985, 1986, 1988, 1989, 1991, 1993.
Domestic Cup - (5)
1926, 1964, 1985, 1989, 1996.

APPEARANCES 99/00

	P	Ap	(s)	Gls
Zoltán BÁNFÖLDI	M	3	(5)	
István BORGULYA	A	13		1
József CSÁBI	D	10	(2)	
Béla DOMOKOS	M	5	(4)	
János DUBECZ	M	20		
István FARAGÓ	A	15		6
András FARKAS	M	4	(3)	
Csaba FEHÉR (ROM)	A	8	(14)	
Krisztián FÜZI	M	15	(9)	1
Zoltán HERCEGFALVI	A	2	(11)	1
Gyula HORVÁTH	A	16		6
Gábor HUNGLER	D	11		1
Róbert LÓCZI	M	3	(3)	
Antal LÖRINCZ	D	14	(1)	
László MEDGYESI	D	30		2
Norbert NÉMETH	M		(1)	
Zoltán PINTÉR	M	6	(12)	1
Attila PIROSKA (ROM)	M	21	(2)	
Attila PLÓKAI	D	7	(2)	1
Attila SZABÓ	M	9	(3)	
Tibor SZABÓ (YUG)	M	23	(6)	1
János SZEKERES	D	22	(1)	
Zsolt SZEKERES	M	3	(2)	
István SZEKÉR	D	14		2
István TÉGER (ROM)	D	30		
Sándor TORGHELLE	A	1	(6)	
József TÓTH	G	1		
Zoltán VÁCZI	M	5		1
Ádám VEZÉR	G	31		
László WUKOVICS	A	10	(1)	2

LEAGUE RESULTS 1999/2000

06/08/99	Haladás-Milos	H	2-0	Füzi, Váczi
13/08/99	Vasas DH	A	0-2	
21/08/99	Gázszer FC	H	0-0	
27/08/99	Zalahús ZTE FC	A	0-2	
10/09/99	Vác FC-Zollner	H	5-1	Szekér, Wukovics 2, Szabó T., Hercegfalvi
20/09/99	MTK Hungária FC	A	0-4	
24/09/99	Dunaferr SE	H	2-2	Medgyesi 2
02/10/99	Nyírség-Spartacus FC	A	0-1	
15/10/99	Diósgyöri FC	H	2-0	Hungler, og (Frunza)
22/10/99	Debreceni VSC	A	1-1	Szekér
29/10/99	Újpest FC	H	1-1	Borgulya
06/11/99	Lombard FC Tatabánya	A	0-0	
12/11/99	Nagykanizsa	H	0-0	
04/12/99	Györi ETO FC	H	0-3	
08/12/99	Siófok	A	0-1	
18/12/99	Ferencváros	H	2-3	Plókai, Pintér
26/02/00	Haladás-Milos	A	2-1	Horváth 2
03/03/00	Vasas DH	H	0-4	
07/03/00	Pécsi MFC	A	2-1	Faragó, Horváth
11/03/00	Zalahús ZTE FC	H	1-0	Faragó
18/03/00	Vác FC-Zollner	A	1-0	Horváth
24/03/00	MTK Hungária FC	H	0-2	
01/04/00	Dunaferr SE	A	0-2	
04/04/00	Nyírség-Spartacus FC	H	0-1	
09/04/00	Diósgyöri FC	A	3-1	Faragó 2, Horváth
14/04/00	Debreceni VSC	H	1-0	Faragó
21/04/00	Újpest FC	A	0-0	
28/04/00	Lombard FC Tatabánya	H	0-0	
07/05/00	Nagykanizsa	A	1-0	Horváth
12/05/00	Siófok	H	1-1	Faragó
17/05/00	Ferencváros	A	0-1	
20/05/00	Györi ETO FC	A	0-4	

MTK HUNGÁRIA FC

CLUB DIRECTORY

MTK Hungária FC
Salgótarjáni út 12-14, 1087 Budapest
tel - (1) 3030590/3030592/3336758
fax - (1) 3338368
website - www.mtk.hu
Year of Formation - 1888
Chairman - Gábor Várszegi
Coach - Henk ten Cate (00/01 - Gábor Pölöskei)
Stadium - Hungária úti (10,702)

MAJOR HONOURS
League Championship - (21)
1904, 1908, 1914, 1917, 1918, 1919, 1920,
1921, 1922, 1923, 1924, 1925, 1929, 1936,
1937, 1951, 1953, 1958, 1987, 1997, 1999.
Domestic Cup - (12)
1910, 1911, 1912, 1914, 1923, 1925, 1932,
1952, 1968, 1997, 1998, 2000.

APPEARANCES 99/00

	P	Ap	(s)	Gls
Gábor BABOS	G	30		1
Iván BALASKÓ	M	3	(5)	
Ákos BUZSÁKY	M	2	(4)	1
Péter CVITKOVICS	A		(1)	
Gábor EGRESSY	A	14	(12)	6
Norbert ELEK	D	20	(5)	1
Károly ERÖS	M	28		3
Viktor FARKAS	D	2		
Csaba FEHÉR	D	14		1
Radu GUSATU (ROM)	A	13	(1)	8
Gábor HALMAI	M	28	(1)	3
Glenn HELDER (HOL)	A	3	(1)	
Csaba HORVÁTH	M		(4)	
Nicolae ILEA (ROM)	A	4	(6)	3
Béla ILLÉS	M	26	(1)	13
Roland JUHÁSZ	M		(2)	
Krisztián KENESEI	A	23	(6)	13
Péter KINCSES	A	2	(3)	1
Ádám KOMLÓSI	D	23	(5)	
Henrik KOVÁCS	M	7	(5)	
József KOZMA	A		(3)	
Attila KUTTOR	D	29	(1)	
Almeida de LEANDRO (BRA)	M	1	(1)	
Csaba MADAR	M	29	(2)	2
Sándor PREISINGER	A	2	(4)	2
Ádám RÉDEI	G	2	(1)	
Szabolcs SCHINDLER	M	7	(3)	1
Tamás SZAMOSI	D	30		
Péter VÖRÖS	M	10	(5)	1

LEAGUE RESULTS 1999/2000

14/08/99	Lombard FC Tatabánya	H	3-0	Ilea, Halmai, Illés
20/08/99	Nagykanizsa	A	1-1	Illés
28/08/99	Siófok	H	2-1	Egressy, Ilea
11/09/99	Ferencváros	A	0-1	
20/09/99	Kispest-Honvéd FC	H	4-0	Kenesei 3, Halmai
03/10/99	Haladás-Milos	H	2-2	Kenesei (p), Fehér
16/10/99	Vasas DH	A	2-1	Halmai, Preisinger
25/10/99	Gázszer FC	H	1-1	Erös
29/10/99	Zalahús ZTE FC	A	0-0	
06/11/99	Vác FC-Zollner	H	3-0	Kenesei 2, Preisinger
13/11/99	Györi ETO FC	A	3-2	Illés 2, Vörös
20/11/99	Dunaferr SE	A	1-1	Egressy
27/11/99	Nyírség-Spartacus FC	H	2-0	Egressy, Kenesei
30/11/99	Újpest FC	A	1-1	Illés
04/12/99	Diósgyöri FC	A	2-0	Illés, Madar
10/12/99	Debreceni VSC	H	1-2	Kenesei
26/02/00	Újpest FC	H	1-0	Gusatu
04/03/00	Lombard FC Tatabánya	A	4-0	Madar, Egressy 2, Gusatu
08/03/00	Nagykanizsa	H	3-1	Kenesei, Gusatu, Elek
11/03/00	Siófok	A	2-2	Kenesei, Illés
18/03/00	Ferencváros	H	2-3	Illés 2
24/03/00	Kispest-Honvéd FC	A	2-0	Erös, Schindler
04/04/00	Haladás-Milos	A	4-0	Gusatu 2, Illés, Kenesei
07/04/00	Vasas DH	H	0-0	
15/04/00	Pécsi MFC	A	1-0	Illés
21/04/00	Zalahús ZTE FC	H	3-1	Buzsáky, Kenesei (p), Gusatu
29/04/00	Vác FC-Zollner	A	5-0	Erös, og (Krajecz), og (Trukker), og (Fejéregyházi), Ilea
07/05/00	Györi ETO FC	H	4-0	Gusatu, Egressy, Kenesei, Babos (p)
13/05/00	Dunaferr SE	H	1-4	Gusatu
17/05/00	Nyírség-Spartacus FC	A	0-0	
20/05/00	Diósgyöri FC	H	3-1	Szamosi, Illés, Kincses
27/05/00	Debreceni VSC	A	1-3	Illés

NAGYKANIZSA

CLUB DIRECTORY

Nagykanizsa FC
Zárda u. 16
8800 Nagykanizsa
tel - (93) 312066
Year of Formation - 1945
Chairman - János Grabant
Coach - Ferenc Keszei; Lajos Németh
(00/01 - István Mihalecz)
Stadium - Városi (10,000)

APPEARANCES 99/00

	P	Ap	(s)	Gls
Sabahudin AGIC (BOS)	D	32		1
Catalin AZOITEI (ROM)	A	7	(1)	1
Attila BALOGH	M	2	(7)	
Dragan CRNOMARKOVIC (YUG)	D	16		1
József FARKAS	M	24	(2)	1
Csaba GELENCSÉR	G	10		
Ugochukwu GORDIAN (NIG)	A	18	(6)	2
Viktor HIMICS	M		(1)	
Csaba HORVÁTH	A		(5)	1
Gergely HORVÁTH	M		(2)	
Gyula HORVÁTH	A	13	(1)	5
Zoltán HORVÁTH	M	7	(3)	1
Szabolcs KENÉZ	D	6		
Zsombor KEREKES (YUG)	A	13	(2)	2
István KISS	M	2	(7)	
László KÓNYA	M	19	(1)	
László KOVÁCS	M	11	(10)	
Zoltán KOVÁCS	G	6	(1)	
Árpád KOVÁCSEVICS	G	16		
István LUKÁCS	M		(1)	
Dejan MARINKOVIC (YUG)	M	9	(4)	1
Lajos MIKLER	D	15		
Róbert PÁLFI	D	29	(1)	
Gergely PANGHY	D	9	(1)	1
Gábor PAPP	A	1	(4)	1
László PONGRÁCZ	M		(2)	
Lajos POPOVICS	M	14		2
Géza PULAI	M	2	(5)	
Tibor PURT	M	5	(2)	
László SVÉLECZ	M	13	(8)	1
Zoltán SZABÓ	A	12	(1)	4
Csaba SZALAI	D	14		1
Csaba SZÖCZE	M	8	(7)	
László VISNOVICS	D	4	(7)	
Krisztián ZAHORECZ	D	15		1

LEAGUE RESULTS 1999/2000

08/08/99	Zalahús ZTE FC	H	0-0	
14/08/99	Vác FC-Zollner	A	4-3	Horváth G. 2, Horváth Z., Panghy
20/08/99	MTK Hungária FC	H	1-1	Horváth G.
28/08/99	Dunaferr SE	A	1-2	Horváth G.
12/09/99	Nyírség-Spartacus FC	H	1-0	Horváth G.
18/09/99	Diósgyöri FC	A	1-1	Zahorecz
24/09/99	Debreceni VSC	H	1-1	Kerekes
01/10/99	Újpest FC	A	1-3	Svélecz
17/10/99	Lombard FC Tatabánya	H	0-0	
24/10/99	Györi ETO FC	H	2-0	Crnomarkovic, Marinkovic
30/10/99	Siófok	A	0-2	
07/11/99	Ferencváros	H	0-2	
12/11/99	Kispest-Honvéd FC	A	0-0	
27/11/99	Haladás-Milos	A	0-2	
05/12/99	Vasas DH	H	1-2	Kerekes
13/12/99	Gázszer FC	A	0-1	
26/02/00	Zalahús ZTE FC	A	0-0	
05/03/00	Vác FC-Zollner	H	3-1	Azoitei, Szabó, Szalai
08/03/00	MTK Hungária FC	A	1-3	Popovics
12/03/00	Dunaferr SE	H	0-1	
18/03/00	Nyírség-Spartacus FC	A	0-2	
25/03/00	Diósgyöri FC	H	2-1	Agic, Papp
01/04/00	Debreceni VSC	A	0-3	
05/04/00	Újpest FC	H	1-1	Horváth C.
08/04/00	Lombard FC Tatabánya	A	0-1	
15/04/00	Györi ETO FC	A	0-4	
23/04/00	Siófok	H	1-0	Szabó
29/04/00	Ferencváros	A	0-3	
07/05/00	Kispest-Honvéd FC	H	0-1	
17/05/00	Haladás-Milos	H	1-1	Gordian
20/05/00	Vasas DH	A	4-1	Gordian, Szabó, Farkas, Popovics
27/05/00	Pécsi MFC	H	1-1	Szabó

NYÍRSÉG-SPARTACUS FC

CLUB DIRECTORY

Nyírség-Spartacus FC
Sóstói út 24/A
4400 Nyíregyháza
tel - (42) 402618
fax - (42) 403182
Year of Formation - 1928
Chairman - László Zákány
Coach - Tibor Öze
Stadium - Sóstói (18,000)

APPEARANCES 99/00

	P	Ap	(s)	Gls
Gusztáv ÁCS	D	29		1
Gyula BESSENYEI	M	8	(10)	
Miklós BARANYI	A	15	(4)	1
Zoltán BALOGH	D	1	(1)	
Danco CELESKI (MAC)	G	25		
Ruslan CHERNYENKO (UKR)	A	20	(6)	7
Ferenc DICAN (ROM)	M	24	(1)	2
Béla DOMOKOS	M	8	(1)	
Máté GERLICZKI	M	9	(6)	
Bertalan GÖNCZ	M	10	(8)	
Decebel GRADINARIU (ROM)	M	1	(3)	
Anasztáz KARKUSZ	M	29	(1)	2
István KOCSIS	M	7	(8)	1
József KONDORA	M	22	(5)	2
István LAKATOS	M		(1)	
Gábor LENKEI	D	1	(3)	
Sándor LŐRINCZ	M		(1)	
Sándor NAGY	D	27	(1)	3
János NOVÁK	A	26	(1)	4
Róbert RÁCZ	G	6		
Attila SZABÓ	M	13	(1)	2
Zoltán SZATKE	D	30		3
Attila SZÉCSI	A		(19)	
Mihály TURÓCZI	M	30		

LEAGUE RESULTS 1999/2000

07/08/99	Diósgyöri FC	A	2-2	Novák, Szabó
14/08/99	Debreceni VSC	H	2-1	Szabó, Dican
21/08/99	Újpest FC	A	0-4	
28/08/99	Lombard FC Tatabánya	H	1-1	Kondora
12/09/99	Nagykanizsa	A	0-1	
18/09/99	Siófok	H	3-0	(w/o)
25/09/99	Ferencváros	A	0-4	
02/10/99	Kispest-Honvéd FC	H	1-0	Baranyi
23/10/99	Haladás-Milos	H	1-0	Karkusz
01/11/99	Vasas DH	A	0-4	
06/11/99	Gázszer FC	H	1-1	Nagy
13/11/99	Zalahús ZTE FC	A	0-1	
20/11/99	Vác FC-Zollner	H	2-2	Chernyenko, Nagy
27/11/99	MTK Hungária FC	A	0-2	
04/12/99	Dunaferr SE	H	1-1	Ács
11/12/99	Győri ETO FC	A	0-4	
26/02/00	Diósgyöri FC	H	2-0	Kondora, Karkusz
04/03/00	Debreceni VSC	A	0-2	
08/03/00	Újpest FC	H	2-1	Chernyenko (p), Szatke
11/03/00	Lombard FC Tatabánya	A	1-2	Novák
18/03/00	Nagykanizsa	H	2-0	Szatke, Chernyenko
25/03/00	Siófok	A	3-0	Nagy, Dican, Chernyenko
01/04/00	Ferencváros	H	3-0	Chernyenko 2, og (Lakos)
04/04/00	Kispest-Honvéd FC	A	1-0	Chernyenko
15/04/00	Haladás-Milos	A	1-1	Szatke
22/04/00	Vasas DH	H	0-2	
29/04/00	Pécsi MFC	A	0-3	
06/05/00	Zalahús ZTE FC	H	0-0	
12/05/00	Vác FC-Zollner	A	1-0	Novák
17/05/00	MTK Hungária FC	H	0-0	
20/05/00	Dunaferr SE	A	0-2	
27/05/00	Győri ETO FC	H	2-1	Kocsis, Novák (p)

SIÓFOK

CLUB DIRECTORY

Siófoki Bányász
Révész Géza u. 1, 8600 Siófok
tel - (84) 3122443 / fax - (84) 3122443
Year of Formation - 1921
Chairman - László Lukácsik
Coach - László Borbély; József Mészáros;
Gyula Bozai; József Mészáros; Bálint Tóth
(00/01 - László Strausz)
Stadium - Bányász (12,000)

MAJOR HONOURS
Domestic Cup - (1) 1984.

APPEARANCES 99/00

	P	Ap	(s)	Gls
Ádám BABOS	D	13	(1)	1
Csaba BAKÓ	M		(1)	
Péter BALOGH	M		(2)	
Miroslav BÉDI (SVK)	M	20	(2)	
Zoltán BÉVÁRDI	D		(1)	
Tamás BIMBÓ	D	21		
Imre BÍRÓ	G	28		
Norbert CSERNYÁNSZKI	G	1		
Norbert CSOKNAY (SVK)	D	11	(1)	
Ernő CZAKÓ	M	2		
Gábor FÖLDES	A	12	(3)	5
István FÖLDES	M	6	(2)	1
Balázs GOSZTONYI	M	2		
Róbert GRÓSZ	M	21	(4)	
Viktor HANÁK	D	29	(2)	1
JERSON da Silva (BRA)	M	8	(4)	
Tamás JUHÁSZ	D	28		
Béla KOVÁCS	M	23	(3)	3
László KOVÁCS	M		(1)	
Sándor KULCSÁR	A	15		6
György KUN	M	3	(4)	
Zoltán LUKÁCS	A	1	(11)	1
Árpád MESTER	M	1		
József ÖRDÖG	A	8	(3)	1
András PERGER	D	1		
Krisztián PEST	A	12		3
Roland PEST	A	5	(3)	
Tibor SALLAI	M	20	(2)	
Attila SÁNTA	M	2	(3)	
Krisztián SOÓS	M	15	(7)	1
Csaba SZABADI	D	17	(4)	
Szabolcs SZEGLETES	M	2	(3)	
Tamás VARGA	G	2	(1)	
Lumvutu ZABUNDU (CON)	A	12	(9)	3

LEAGUE RESULTS 1999/2000

07/08/99	Gázszer FC	H	0-1	
14/08/99	Zalahús ZTE FC	A	0-4	
21/08/99	Vác FC-Zollner	H	1-0	Ördög
28/08/99	MTK Hungária FC	A	1-2	Pest K.
11/09/99	Dunaferr SE	H	1-1	Pest K.
18/09/99	Nyírség-Spartacus FC	A	0-3	(w/o)
25/09/99	Diósgyöri FC	H	0-2	
03/10/99	Debreceni VSC	A	0-1	
18/10/99	Újpest FC	H	1-0	Hanák
23/10/99	Lombard FC Tatabánya	A	1-2	Zabundu
30/10/99	Nagykanizsa	H	2-0	Zabundu, Kovács B. (p)
08/11/99	Györi ETO FC	H	0-1	
13/11/99	Ferencváros	A	2-1	Pest K., Kovács B. (p)
04/12/99	Haladás-Milos	H	2-4	Kovács B., Soós
08/12/99	Kispest-Honvéd FC	H	1-0	Földes I.
11/12/99	Vasas DH	A	0-4	
26/02/00	Pécsi MFC	A	1-1	Kulcsár
04/03/00	Zalahús ZTE FC	H	1-1	Kulcsar
08/03/00	Vác FC-Zollner	A	0-1	
11/03/00	MTK Hungária FC	H	2-2	Kulcsár 2
18/03/00	Dunaferr SE	A	0-3	
25/03/00	Nyírség-Spartacus FC	H	0-3	
01/04/00	Diósgyöri FC	A	0-0	
04/05/00	Debreceni VSC	H	4-1	Földes G. 3, Lukács
08/04/00	Újpest FC	A	0-2	
15/04/00	Lombard FC Tatabánya	H	1-3	Zabundu
23/04/00	Nagykanizsa	A	0-1	
29/04/00	Györi ETO FC	A	1-1	Kulcsár (p)
06/05/00	Ferencváros	H	2-4	Babos, Földes G.
12/05/00	Kispest-Honvéd FC	A	1-1	Földes G.
20/05/00	Haladás-Milos	A	1-0	Kulcsár (p)
27/05/00	Vasas DH	H	0-1	

SZEGED LC

CLUB DIRECTORY

Szeged Labdarúgó Club (now defunct)
Etelka sor 3
6723 Szeged
tel - (62) 420712
Year of Formation - 1929
Chairman - Kálmán Nagylaki
Coach - Ferenc Ebedli; László Strausz;
Kálmán Nagylaki; József Linka
Stadium - Városi (20,000)

APPEARANCES 99/00

	P	Ap	(s)	Gls
Zsolt BENCZE	M	4	(3)	
Budimir BASIC (YUG)	M	8	(1)	1
Csaba CSÚRI	A		(1)	
Csaba DOBÓ	G	3		
István FARAGÓ	A	14		6
Dejan GODOR (YUG)	M		(1)	
Szabolcs HERCZKU	M	13	(2)	
Zoltán KENESEI	A	14		1
András KURUCSAI	M	6	(1)	
Leaszló MAJOR	M	5		
Nenad MARKOVIC (YUG)	G	10		
Lajos MIKLER	D	15		1
Tibor NAGYPÁL	D	6	(5)	
Norbert NÉMETH	D	14	(5)	
Lóránt OLÁH	M	5	(2)	
Szabolcs PALÁGYI	D	6		
Lajos POPOVICS	D	11		
Krisztián SZÉNÁS	G		(1)	
Ákos SZULYOVSZKI	G	4		
György TURJÁN	M	9		
Szabolcs UDVARI	M	10	(4)	1
Flórián URBÁN	D	11		
Vyacheslav YEREMEYEV (RUS)	M	11		3
Péter VÖRÖS	M	8		

LEAGUE RESULTS 1999/2000

07/08/99	Györi ETO FC	H	1-1	Faragó
14/08/99	Haladás-Milos	A	1-2	Faragó
21/08/99	Vasas DH	H	0-2	
28/08/99	Gázszer FC	A	1-4	Faragó
11/09/99	Zalahús ZTE FC	H	1-0	Yeremeyev
18/09/99	Vác FC-Zollner	A	1-1	Faragó
25/09/99	MTK Hungária FC	H	1-2	Mikler
02/10/99	Dunaferr SE	A	0-9	
16/10/99	Nyírség-Spartacus FC	H	2-1	Kenesei, Udvari
23/10/99	Diósgyöri FC	A	0-0	
30/10/99	Debreceni VSC	H	0-4	
05/11/99	Újpest FC	A	0-1	
13/11/99	Lombard FC Tatabánya	H	1-4	Faragó
27/11/99	Siófok	H	1-1	Yeremeyev
01/12/99	Nagykanizsa	A	2-1	Faragó, Yeremeyev
04/12/99	Ferencváros	A	0-4	
11/12/99	Kispest-Honvéd FC	H	1-1	Basic

N.B. All the above matches subsequently deemed null and void.

LOMBARD FC TATABÁNYA

CLUB DIRECTORY

Lombard FC Tatabánya
Lónyai u. 18/a
1093 Budapest
tel - (06) 12175622/12175483
fax - (06) 12171772
Year of Formation - 1910
Chairman - Péter Bíró
Coach - József Kiprich
Stadium - Városi, Tatabánya (15,500)

APPEARANCES 99/00

	P	Ap	(s)	Gls
Máriusz ANDAI	M	1	(1)	
László ARANY	M	4	(4)	
Gábor ÁRKI	M	13		1
Tamás BALOGH	G	5		
Zsolt DULI	M		(1)	
Zsolt FÜZESI	A	2	(6)	1
Károly GELEI	G	27		
Fabrízio GONÇALVES (BRA)	M	13	(1)	2
Vendel HORNYÁK	D	16	(2)	4
József KIPRICH	A	19	(6)	5
Béla KISS (SVK)	M	18	(7)	4
Attila KOVÁCS	M	17	(8)	4
István KOZMA	M	8	(3)	
Attila LETENYEI	M	11	(5)	
MAURO Sérgio (BRA)	M	3	(1)	
Géza MÉSZÖLY	D	30		1
Sándor NAGY	A	26	(2)	7
Tamás PETRES	A		(6)	
Zoltán SÜVEGES	M	21	(5)	1
Souleymane SYLAL (GUI)	M		(1)	
József SZALMA	D	26		1
Viktor SZABÓ	D	26	(1)	
István SZENTJOBBI	M	5	(3)	
Zsolt SZOBOSZLAI	M		(11)	
Roland TÜSKE	M	14	(6)	
László VARGA	D	1	(2)	
István VINCZE	A	11	(2)	6
Attila VIRÁGH	D	20		
Vyacheslav YEREMEYEV (RUS)	M	6	(2)	
Gyula ZSIVÓCZKY	M	9	(5)	

LEAGUE RESULTS 1999/2000

07/08/99	Vác FC-Zollner	H	1-0	Süveges
14/08/99	MTK Hungária FC	A	0-3	
21/08/99	Dunaferr SE	H	3-3	Kovács, Kiprich, Nagy
28/08/99	Nyírség-Spartacus FC	A	1-1	Nagy
11/09/99	Diósgyőri FC	H	2-1	Kiprich (p), Kiss
19/09/99	Debreceni VSC	A	3-1	Kiss 2, Nagy
25/09/99	Újpest FC	H	0-2	
02/10/99	Győri ETO FC	H	1-1	Kovács (p)
17/10/99	Nagykanizsa	A	0-0	
23/10/99	Siófok	H	2-1	Nagy, Kiprich
30/10/99	Ferencváros	A	1-0	Kiss
06/11/99	Kispest-Honvéd FC	H	0-0	
27/11/99	Vasas DH	A	0-3	
01/12/99	Haladás-Milos	H	1-1	Füzesi
04/12/99	Gázszer FC	H	0-0	
11/12/99	Zalahús ZTE FC	A	1-1	Mészöly
26/02/00	Vác FC-Zollner	A	1-1	Hornyák
04/03/00	MTK Hungária FC	H	0-4	
08/03/00	Dunaferr SE	A	0-2	
11/03/00	Nyírség-Spartacus FC	H	2-1	Gonçalves, Kiprich
18/03/00	Diósgyőri FC	A	2-1	Nagy, Szalma
25/03/00	Debreceni VSC	H	1-1	Gonçalves
01/04/00	Újpest FC	A	1-0	Vincze
05/04/00	Győri ETO FC	A	1-0	Vincze
08/04/00	Nagykanizsa	H	1-0	Vincze
15/04/00	Siófok	A	3-1	Hornyák, Kovács, Kiprich
21/04/00	Ferencváros	H	2-1	Vincze, Hornyák
28/04/00	Kispest-Honvéd FC	A	0-0	
13/05/00	Haladás-Milos	A	1-1	Árki
17/05/00	Vasas DH	H	2-0	Nagy, Kovács
20/05/00	Pécsi MFC	A	2-2	Hornyák, Vincze
27/05/00	Zalahús ZTE FC	H	2-1	Nagy, Vincze

ÚJPEST FC

CLUB DIRECTORY

Újpest FC
Megyeri út 13, 1044 Budapest
tel - (1) 2310088 / fax - (1) 2310089
website - www.ujpestfc.hu
Year of Formation - 1885
Chairmen - dr. György Köteles, dr. Gábor Deák &
Ferenc Lukács
Coach - Róbert Glázer; Péter Várhidi
(00/01 - István Kisteleki)
Stadium - Megyeri út (30,000)

MAJOR HONOURS
League Championship - (20)
1930, 1931, 1933, 1935, 1939, 1945, 1946,
1947, 1960, 1969, 1970, 1971, 1972, 1973,
1974, 1975, 1978, 1979, 1990, 1998.
Domestic Cup - (7)
1969, 1970, 1975, 1982, 1983, 1987, 1992.

APPEARANCES 99/00

	P	Ap	(s)	Gls
Ádám BABOS	D	10	(1)	
Gábor BARDI	G	2	(1)	
Szabolcs BÍRÓ	G	30		
Krisztián CSILLAG	M	12	(11)	3
Csaba CSORDÁS	A		(3)	
Zsolt DVÉRI	M	13		
Sándor JENEI	M	11		1
Norbert KERÉNYI	D	10	(3)	
Balázs KISKAPUSI	D	25		1
Goran KOPUNOVIC (YUG)	A	11	(12)	2
Balázs KOVÁCS	M	15	(4)	
Péter KOVÁCS	D	3	(1)	
Zoltán KOVÁCS	A	29		10
István KOZMA	D	7		
Zsolt LÖW	D	29	(1)	
Norbert NÉMEDI	M	1		
Tamás PETÖ	M	21		2
Zoltán SZABÓ	M		(3)	
Zoltán SZÉLESI	M	9	(3)	
Zoltán SZLEZÁK	D	27		
Zoltán TAMÁSI	D	22		3
Lajos TERJÉK	A	10	(8)	5
Tibor TOKODY	A	7	(8)	2
Norbert TÓTH	M	25		11
Róbert WALTNER	A	7	(6)	3
Tamás WEISZ	M		(1)	
György VÉBER	M	4	(2)	
Tamás ZIMMERMANN	M	12	(4)	2

LEAGUE RESULTS 1999/2000

15/08/99	Dunaferr SE	A	0-4	
21/08/99	Nyírség-Spartacus FC	H	4-0	Tóth 2, Zimmermann, og (Ács)
29/08/99	Diósgyöri FC	A	1-4	Tamási
10/09/99	Debreceni VSC	H	2-2	Tamási, Tokody
17/09/99	Györi ETO FC	H	1-1	Kopunovic (p)
25/09/99	Lombard FC Tatabánya	A	2-0	Kovács Z. 2
01/10/99	Nagykanizsa	H	3-1	Tamási, Kopunovic (p), Terjék
18/10/99	Siófok	A	0-1	
25/10/99	Ferencváros	H	2-2	Terjék, Tóth
29/10/99	Kispest-Honvéd FC	A	1-1	Kovács Z.
13/11/99	Haladás-Milos	A	0-3	
30/11/99	MTK Hungária FC	H	1-1	Terjék
03/12/99	Zalahús ZTE FC	H	1-1	Tóth (p)
08/12/99	Vasas DH	H	4-1	Kovács Z., Tóth 2, Zimmermann
11/12/99	Vác FC-Zollner	A	4-0	Csillag 2, Terjék, Tóth (p)
17/12/99	Gázszer FC	A	4-1	Kiskapusi, Terjék, Tóth, Tokody
26/02/00	MTK Hungária FC	A	0-1	
03/03/00	Dunaferr SE	H	0-3	(w/o)
08/03/00	Nyírség-Spartacus FC	A	1-2	Petö
11/03/00	Diósgyöri FC	H	5-0	Kovács Z. 2, Tóth, Waltner,
				Petö (p)
17/03/00	Debreceni VSC	A	3-2	Kovács Z., Tóth, Waltner
24/03/00	Györi ETO FC	A	1-3	Waltner
01/04/00	Lombard FC Tatabánya	H	0-1	
05/04/00	Nagykanizsa	A	1-1	Tóth
08/04/00	Siófok	H	2-0	Kovács Z. 2
15/04/00	Ferencváros	A	0-0	
21/04/00	Kispest-Honvéd FC	H	0-0	
05/05/00	Haladás-Milos	H	0-0	
12/05/00	Vasas DH	A	0-3	
17/05/00	Pécsi MFC	H	1-2	Jenei
20/05/00	Zalahús ZTE FC	A	1-1	Kovács Z.
27/05/00	Vác FC-Zollner	H	1-0	Csillag

VASAS DH

CLUB DIRECTORY

Vasas Danubius Hotels
Fáy u. 58
1139 Budapest XIII
tel - (1) 3296073/3294074
fax - (1) 3296073
Year of Formation - 1911
Chairman - András Gyalog
Coach - András Komjáti
(00/01 - dr. György Mezey)
Stadium - Fáy útcai (18,000)

MAJOR HONOURS
League Championship - (6)
1957, 1961, 1962, 1965, 1966, 1977.
Domestic Cup - (4) 1955, 1973, 1981, 1986.

APPEARANCES 99/00

	P	Ap	(s)	Gls
Imre ARANYOS	M	28		4
Balázs BEKÖ	M	6	(4)	1
László FARKASHÁZY	M	12	(8)	
Péter GALASCHEK	M	24	(4)	7
Csaba HERCZEG	D	7	(2)	1
Tamás JUHÁR	D	31		3
Péter KABÁT	A	27	(2)	13
István KÖVESFALVI	G	15		
András LÁSZLÓ	D	28		1
Tamás MÓNOS	M	19	(3)	
Krisztián NYERGES	A		(6)	
Zoltán PÁL	A	1	(6)	
Balázs SALLAI	M		(3)	
Péter SIMEK	M	6	(4)	
Thomas SOWUNMI	A	20	(10)	6
Attila SZILI	M	21	(7)	8
Ferenc SZILVESZTER	M	18	(9)	7
Krisztián TIBER	A	19	(7)	6
András TÓTH	D	25		
Zoltán VÉGH	G	17		
János ZOVÁTH	M	28		

LEAGUE RESULTS 1999/2000

06/08/99	Ferencváros	A	2-1	Galaschek, Juhár (p)
13/08/99	Kispest-Honvéd FC	H	2-0	Kabát, Juhár (p)
28/08/99	Haladás-Milos	H	2-0	Szili, Kabát
10/09/99	Györi ETO FC	A	0-2	
18/09/99	Gázszer FC	A	2-3	Sowunmi, Aranyos
25/09/99	Zalahús ZTE FC	H	1-0	Szili
02/10/99	Vác FC-Zollner	A	3-1	Tiber, Kabát, Sowunmi
16/10/99	MTK Hungária FC	H	1-2	Sowunmi
23/10/99	Dunaferr SE	A	0-1	
01/11/99	Nyírség-Spartacus FC	H	4-0	Sowunmi, Juhár, Szilveszter, Galaschek
06/11/99	Diósgyöri FC	A	1-1	Galaschek
12/11/99	Debreceni VSC	H	2-0	Szilveszter, Szili
26/11/99	Lombard FC Tatabánya	H	3-0	Szili, Aranyos, Szilveszter
05/12/99	Nagykanizsa	A	2-1	Szili, Tiber
08/12/99	Újpest FC	A	1-4	Szili
11/12/99	Siófok	H	4-0	Galaschek 2 (1p), Sowunmi, Szilveszter
28/02/00	Ferencváros	H	3-3	Galaschek 2, Tiber
03/03/00	Kispest-Honvéd FC	A	4-0	Kabát, Szilveszter, Tiber 2
10/03/00	Haladás-Milos	A	2-1	Kabát, og (Balassa)
18/03/00	Györi ETO FC	H	1-0	Tiber
25/03/00	Pécsi MFC	H	4-0	Aranyos, Kabát 2, László
31/03/00	Zalahús ZTE FC	A	0-0	
04/04/00	Vác FC-Zollner	H	3-0	Aranyos, Kabát 2
07/04/00	MTK Hungária FC	A	0-0	
14/04/00	Dunaferr SE	H	0-2	
22/04/00	Nyírség-Spartacus FC	A	2-0	Szili, Herczeg
29/04/00	Diósgyöri FC	H	2-0	Szilveszter, Sowunmi
06/05/00	Debreceni VSC	A	2-4	Kabát, Bekö
12/05/00	Újpest FC	H	3-0	Szilveszter, Szili, Kabát
17/05/00	Lombard FC Tatabánya	A	0-2	
20/05/00	Nagykanizsa	H	1-4	Kabát
27/05/00	Siófok	A	1-0	Kabát

VÁC FC-ZOLLNER

CLUB DIRECTORY

Vác FC-Zollner (now - Vác FC)
Stadion u. 2, 2600 Vác
tel - (27) 314795 / fax - (27) 314324
Year of Formation - 1889
Chairman - László Hovanyecz
Coach - Károly Kis; János Adi; Sándor Gujdar
(00/01 - Sándor Haász)
Stadium - Városi (12,000)

MAJOR HONOURS
League Championship - (1) 1994.

APPEARANCES 99/00

	P	Ap	(s)	Gls
László ALMÁSI	D		(1)	
Csaba ANDRÁSSY (ROM)	A	14	(9)	1
Tibor BÁBIK	M	12	(1)	
Norbert BÁRÁNY	M	1	(2)	
József BODA	D	11	(1)	
István BUCSI	M	3	(5)	
Attila BURZI	D	13	(3)	1
Tamás FEJÉREGYHÁZI	M	11	(1)	
Antal FÜLE	A	9	(1)	1
András GASPARIK	A	8	(7)	2
Ádám GREFF	D	4	(4)	
Gábor GULYÁS	A	1	(2)	
Attila HADÁR	A	1	(3)	
Norbert HAJDÚ	M	5	(4)	
István HÁMORI	G	11		
József HAVRÁN	A	10	(3)	2
Gergely HIRT	M	9	(1)	
Zoltán IVITZ	A	8	(7)	1
István KASZA	M	14		2
Tamás KÁDÁR	D	13	(1)	
Attila KIRÁLY	M	1		
Ákos KOLLER	D	11		2
Roland KOSZORA	D	9		
Péter KOVÁCS	D	16		1
Balázs KRAJECZ	G	4	(1)	
Tibor NAGY	M	25	(1)	2
József NYIKOS	M	2		
Attila PRUKKER	M	1	(5)	
Árpád RÁKI	M	4	(1)	
Kornél ROB	A	10	(5)	5
János ROMANEK	M	6	(1)	
Gergely RUSVAY	A	3	(2)	
István SIPEKI	M	4	(10)	
Krisztián SOMOGYI	D	12		
Zoltán SOVÁB	M	12	(1)	
Csaba SZABÓ	G	5		
Dániel SZÁSZ	M	3	(2)	
Imre SZOBOSZLAI	M	5	(1)	
László SZŰCS	M	15	(1)	
Árpád TELEK	G	12		
Gábor VÉN	M	16		2
Zoltán VITELKI	M	5	(3)	
Csaba VOJTEKOVSZKI	M	13	(1)	1

LEAGUE RESULTS 1999/2000

07/08/99	Lombard FC Tatabánya	A	0-1	
14/08/99	Nagykanizsa	H	3-4	Kasza, Rob 2
21/08/99	Siófok	A	0-1	
29/08/99	Ferencváros	H	0-2	
10/09/99	Kispest-Honvéd FC	A	1-5	Rob
25/09/99	Haladás-Milos	A	3-2	Füle, Kasza, Vén
02/10/99	Vasas DH	H	1-3	Nagy
16/10/99	Gázszer FC	A	0-0	
23/10/99	Zalahús ZTE FC	H	1-3	Vén
30/10/99	Györi ETO FC	A	1-1	Rob
06/11/99	MTK Hungária FC	A	0-3	
13/11/99	Dunaferr SE	H	1-1	Ivitz
20/11/99	Nyírség-Spartacus FC	A	2-2	Rob, Kovács
27/11/99	Diósgyöri FC	H	0-2	
04/12/99	Debreceni VSC	A	1-4	Vojtekovszki
11/12/99	Újpest FC	H	0-4	
26/02/00	Lombard FC Tatabánya	H	1-1	Gasparik
05/03/00	Nagykanizsa	A	1-3	Koller
08/03/00	Siófok	H	1-0	Koller (p)
11/03/00	Ferencváros	A	0-8	
18/03/00	Kispest-Honvéd FC	H	0-1	
31/03/00	Haladás-Milos	H	2-4	Nagy, Gasparik
04/04/00	Vasas DH	A	0-3	
08/04/00	Pécsi MFC	H	1-2	Andrássy
15/04/00	Zalahús ZTE FC	A	2-1	Koller (p), Havrán
22/04/00	Györi ETO FC	H	1-4	Havrán
29/04/00	MTK Hungária FC	H	0-5	
06/05/00	Dunaferr SE	A	0-7	
12/05/00	Nyírség-Spartacus FC	H	0-1	
17/05/00	Diósgyöri FC	A	1-1	Burzi
20/05/00	Debreceni VSC	H	0-5	
27/05/00	Újpest FC	A	0-1	

ZALAHÚS ZTE FC

CLUB DIRECTORY

Zalahús Zalaegerszegi TE FC
Október 6. tér 16
8900 Zalaegerszeg
tel - (92) 314090
Year of Formation - 1920
Chairman - József Lang
Coach - Barnabás Tornyi; Zoltán Leskó;
László Disztl (00/01 - Róbert Glázer)
Stadium - Városi (20,000)

APPEARANCES 99/00

	P	Ap	(s)	Gls
László ARANY	M	7	(2)	
Ferenc BABATI	A	11	(10)	
Csaba BALOG	M	31		2
Péter BENCZE	A	1	(1)	
Liviu BONCHIS (ROM)	M	28	(2)	1
Gregor BUNC (SLO)	M	1	(5)	
Zsolt CSÓKA	D	21	(3)	
István FERENCZI	A	9	(3)	5
Attila FILÓ	D	25	(1)	4
László GAÁL	M	12	(4)	
Zoltán GYÖRI	M	11	(9)	1
Gergely KOCSÁRDI	D	29		2
Gábor MAGYARI	M		(5)	
Lajos NAGY	M	29	(1)	1
Julius NOTA (SVK)	G	1		
Ferenc RÓTH	A	7	(2)	1
József SEBÖK	A	25	(1)	6
László STRASSER	D	12	(5)	1
Csaba SZABÓ	A	16	(11)	3
Zsolt SZABÓ I	D	21	(2)	
Zsolt SZABÓ II	M	20		4
Csaba SZÖCZE	M	1	(4)	
Péter SZÖKE	M	3	(7)	1
Tamás VARGA	M		(1)	
Géza VLASZÁK	G	31		

LEAGUE RESULTS 1999/2000

08/08/99	Nagykanizsa	A	0-0	
14/08/99	Siófok	H	4-0	Filó, Sebök, Nagy, Ferenczi
21/08/99	Ferencváros	A	1-1	Sebök
27/08/99	Kispest-Honvéd FC	H	2-0	Szabó Z. II (p), Ferenczi
18/09/99	Haladás-Milos	H	0-1	
25/09/99	Vasas DH	A	0-1	
02/10/99	Gázszer FC	H	5-0	Szabó C., Ferenczi 2, Filó 2
16/10/99	Györi ETO FC	A	0-0	
23/10/99	Vác FC-Zollner	A	3-1	Szabó Z. II, Bonchis, Sebök
29/10/99	MTK Hungária FC	H	0-0	
06/11/99	Dunaferr SE	A	0-4	
13/11/99	Nyírség-Spartacus FC	H	1-0	og (Ács)
27/11/99	Debreceni VSC	H	2-0	Ferenczi, Kocsárdi
03/12/99	Újpest FC	A	1-1	Strasser
08/12/99	Diósgyöri FC	A	1-2	Sebök
11/12/99	Lombard FC Tatabánya	H	1-1	Szabó Z. II (p)
26/02/00	Nagykanizsa	H	0-0	
04/03/00	Siófok	A	1-1	Györi
08/03/00	Ferencváros	H	0-0	
11/03/00	Kispest-Honvéd FC	A	0-1	
25/03/00	Haladás-Milos	A	1-0	Balog
31/03/00	Vasas DH	H	0-0	
05/04/00	Pécsi MFC	A	2-2	Szabó C., Balog
08/04/00	Györi ETO FC	H	2-1	Filó, Róth
15/04/00	Vác FC-Zollner	H	1-2	Sebök (p)
21/04/00	MTK Hungária FC	A	1-3	Szabó Z. II (p)
29/04/00	Dunaferr SE	H	1-4	Sebök
06/05/00	Nyírség-Spartacus FC	A	0-0	
13/05/00	Diósgyöri FC	H	0-0	
17/05/00	Debreceni VSC	A	2-2	Szabó C., Kocsárdi
20/05/00	Újpest FC	H	1-1	og (Kovács B.)
27/05/00	Lombard FC Tatabánya	A	1-2	Szöke

ICELAND

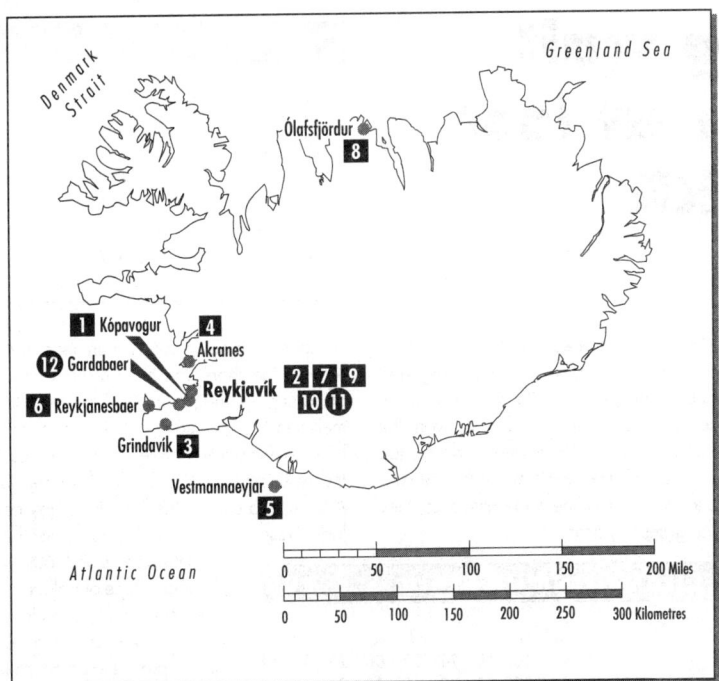

Greenland Sea

Denmark Strait

Ólafsfjördur ● **8**

1 Kópavogur   **4** Akranes

12 Gardabaer

2 7 9
10 11

6 Reykjanesbaer   Reykjavík

Grindavík **3**

Vestmannaeyjar ●
5

Atlantic Ocean

| 0 | 50 | 100 | 150 | 200 Miles |

| 0 | 50 | 100 | 150 | 200 | 250 | 300 Kilometres |

FRANCE GIVEN FRIGHT IN PARIS

Long wait over at last for KR

FEDERATION DIRECTORY

The Football Association of Iceland
Laugardalur, PO Box 8511, 128 Reykjavík

tel - 510 2900   Year of Formation - 1947
fax - 568 9793   President - Eggert Magnússon
website - www.toto.is   Secretary - Geir Thorsteinsson
email - ksi@toto.is

Stadium - Laugardalsvöllur, Reykjavík (7,000)

Iceland's biggest and best supported club, KR of Reykjavík, finally achieved in their centenary year what they had been threatening, but narrowly failing, to do for years. The Black-and-Whites from the capital had not won the Icelandic championship since 1968 and had finished runners-up five times during the 1990s. But in the last year of the decade, and the 100th of the club's existence, they at last opened the gates to paradise.

Coached by ex-national team legend Atli Edvaldsson, KR won the championship, finishing seven points ahead of defending champions ÍBV, the team that had broken their hearts a year earlier in the final match of the season. KR provided a fitting finale to a momentous year by adding the Icelandic Cup, beating ÍA of Akranes 3-1 in the final. And, just to add to the birthday party celebrations, KR ladies also won their own 'double' for the first time.

In the 1950s and '60s KR had been the dominant force of Icelandic football, but so often since then, especially over the past decade, the pressure to repeat those past glories proved to be an intolerable burden. In 1999, though, everything finally fell into place. Under the shrewd guidance of Edvaldsson KR played some outstanding football, losing just one match, away to ÍBV

LEAGUE CHAMPIONSHIP RESULTS 1999

		1	2	3	4	5	6	7	8	9	10
1	Breidablik		1-1	4-1	1-3	1-0	2-1	0-3	0-0	2-0	1-1
2	Fram	2-2		1-3	0-0	0-2	2-0	0-2	2-0	2-2	3-2
3	Grindavík	1-0	1-1		2-2	1-2	2-0	1-3	0-1	3-1	2-2
4	ÍA	2-3	1-0	1-0		1-1	2-2	0-2	0-0	0-1	1-1
5	ÍBV	2-1	1-1	2-1	2-0		1-0	2-1	5-0	2-2	3-0
6	Keflavík	2-1	2-1	2-3	2-0	1-1		1-3	2-2	4-4	3-2
7	KR	0-0	3-1	2-1	1-0	3-0	3-2		1-1	5-1	4-1
8	Leiftur	2-2	3-3	2-1	1-4	0-3	1-0	1-1		0-0	1-0
9	Valur	2-1	2-1	2-1	1-2	0-0	2-3	1-2	2-4		1-1
10	Víkingur	1-0	0-2	1-1	1-2	1-2	2-1	0-4	0-3	5-4	

INTERNATIONAL HONOURS

None

LEAGUE CHAMPIONSHIP FINAL TABLE 1999

			Home					Away					Total						
		Pd	W	D	L	F	A	W	D	L	F	A	W	D	L	F	A	PT	GD
1	KR	18	7	2	0	22	7	7	1	1	21	6	14	3	1	43	13	45	30
2	ÍBV	18	7	2	0	20	6	4	3	2	11	8	11	5	2	31	14	38	17
3	Leiftur	18	3	4	2	11	14	3	4	2	11	12	6	8	4	22	26	26	-4
4	ÍA	18	2	4	3	8	10	4	2	3	13	11	6	6	6	21	21	24	0
5	Breidablik	18	4	3	2	12	10	1	3	5	10	14	5	6	7	22	24	21	-2
6	Grindavík	18	3	3	3	13	12	2	1	6	12	17	5	4	9	25	29	19	-4
7	Fram	18	3	3	3	12	13	1	4	4	11	14	4	7	7	23	27	19	-4
8	Keflavík	18	4	3	2	19	17	1	1	7	9	17	5	4	9	28	34	19	-6
9	Valur	18	3	2	4	13	15	1	4	4	15	23	4	6	8	28	38	18	-10
10	Víkingur	18	3	1	5	11	19	0	4	5	10	19	3	5	10	21	38	14	-17

DOMESTIC CUP 1999

FOURTH ROUND
Keflavík 1, ÍBV 3
Thróttur R. 0, Víkingur R. 1
Breidablik 1, ÍR 0
FH 0, Stjarnan 4
KR 4, Fylkir 3
Valur 3, Vídir 1
Sindri 2, Haukar 0
Fram u-23 0, ÍA 3

QUARTER-FINALS
Víkingur R. 0, ÍA 5 (Thórdarson 6, 57, Högnason 25,
Matijane 55, Hauksson R. 86)
Sindri 0, ÍBV 3 (Jóhannesson S. 34, Helgason 68,
Sigurdsson 82)
Stjarnan 1 (Winnie 65og), KR 3 (Júlíusson 24,
Benediktsson 48, Daníelsson 55)
Breidablik 2 (Pétursson 32, Baldvinsson 37), Valur 0

SEMI-FINALS
KR 3 (Gunnlaugsson 45, 64, Benediktsson 88), Breidablik 0
ÍA 3 (Haraldsson P. 29, Hardarson 59, Reynisson 77), ÍBV 0

FINAL
26/09/99, Reykjavík
KR 3 Hinriksson (62), Daníelsson (66), Gunnlaugsson (83)
ÍA 1 Thórdarson (71)
referee - Bergmann
KR - Finnbogason; Jónsson S., Egilsson, Winnie, Thorsteinsson;
Júlíusson (Sigurgeirsson 83), Hinriksson (Jónsson Th. 69), Gíslason,
Daníelsson; Gunnlaugsson (Sigurdsson 87), Benediktsson.
ÍA - Gunnarsson; Haraldsson S., Leósson, Jónsson, Haraldsson P.;
Valgeirsson (Hauksson R. 83), Hardarson, Gíslason H. (Gíslason J.
72), Högnason, Reynisson; Thórdarson.

early in the season. Even the loss of three strikers - Andri Sigthórsson and Einar Thór Birgison to long-term injuries and Björn Jakobsen to a Norwegian club - failed to knock them out of their stride.

The crunch game came in round 15 when KR reaped their revenge on ÍBV for the previous season's last-game tearjerker by trouncing them 3-0 in front of a crowd of more than 5,000. This enabled them to open up a five-point lead, and with victories in each of their last three matches, KR cruised home, sealing the long-awaited title in round 17 with a 4-0 away win against Víkingur in the Laugardalsvöllur. Two of the goals were scored by Icelandic international Bjarki Gunnlaugsson, who had returned home for the domestic season and finished up as KR's top scorer with 11 goals.

KR and ÍBV had things pretty much to themselves in the league, with all the other teams flirting with relegation at some stage. Ultimately it was Leiftur who clinched third place in front of a disappointing ÍA, who found goals particularly hard to come by. Newcomers Breidablik did well to finish fifth but it was only in the penultimate round that they, along with Keflavík, saved themselves from relegation. The other four teams were all taken to the final game, and the tension was heightened by the fact that they had to play against each other. Late goals decided

both matches, with Grindavík beating Valur 3-1 and Fram gaining a 3-2 victory over Víkingur. Thus Valur and Víkingur were relegated. It was a particularly traumatic experience for Valur, who found themselves outside the top division for the first time in their history.

In European competition, the only victory achieved by an Icelandic club was ÍBV's 3-1 aggregate triumph against Albania's Tirana. KR went excruciatingly close to dumping Kilmarnock out of the UEFA Cup. 1-0 winners in Reykjavík, Iceland's team of the year were within seconds of going through when the Scottish Premier League side were awarded a disputed penalty. They equalised and then added a winner in extra-time to leave KR and their fans gnashing and wailing at the injustice of it all.

Iceland's national team were one of the surprise packets in the Euro 2000 qualifying campaign. With two matches to go, they were still in the heat of an intriguing four-way battle with France, Russia and Ukraine. A 0-1 defeat at home to Ukraine proved to be a massive disappointment but Iceland still had a marginal chance of reaching the play-offs... if they could beat the world champions in the Stade de France. The match proved to be one of the most memorable in Iceland's history. Looking dead and buried at half-time, Gudjón Thórdarson's spirited band of exiles dramatically came back from 0-2

TOP SCORERS

12	Steingrímur JÓHANNESSON (ÍBV)
11	Bjarki GUNNLAUGSSON (KR)
10	Grétar HJARTARSON (Grindavík)
	Kristján BROOKS (Keflavík)
9	Sigurbjörn HREIDARSSON (Valur)
	Gudmundur BENEDIKTSSON (KR)
8	Alexandre SANTOS (Leiftur)
	Uni ARGE (Leiftur)
6	Hreidar BJARNASON (Breidablik)
	Kristinn LÁRUSSON (Valur)

NATIONAL TEAM RESULTS 99/00

18/08/99	Faroe Islands	A	Torshavn	1-0	Gudjónsson Th. (3p)
04/09/99	Andorra (ECQ)	H	Reykjavík	3-0	Gudjónsson Th. (28), Hreidarsson (32), Gudjohnsen (90)
08/09/99	Ukraine (ECQ)	H	Reykjavík	0-1	
09/10/99	France (ECQ)	A	Saint-Denis	2-3	Sverrisson E. (47), Gunnarsson (56)
31/01/00	Norway	N	La Manga	0-0	
02/02/00	Finland	N	La Manga	1-0	Dadason (45)
04/02/00	Faroe Islands	N	La Manga	3-2	Dadason (40p, 57p), Gunnlaugsson (66)

down to draw level. The thousand-odd travelling fans were going wild, but a third French goal, from David Trezeguet, eventually silenced them.

Iceland ended up in fourth place but were entitled to feel extremely proud of their achievement.

The game in Paris was Gudjón Thórdarson's last match.

NATIONAL TEAM APPEARANCES 99/00

Coach -Gudjón THÓRDARSON; Atli EDVALDSSON	FAR	AND	UKR	FRA	NOR	FIN	FAR	Cps	Gls
Birkir KRISTINSSON (15/08/64) - ÍBV/SC Austria Lustenau (AUT)	G63	G	G	G		G	G46	67	-
Steinar ADOLFSSON (25/01/70) - Kongsvinger IL (NOR)	D							14	1
Pétur MARTEINSSON (14/07/73) - Stabaek IF (ENG)	D40		D	D80	D	D		15	-
Lárus Orri SIGURDSSON (04/06/73) - Stoke City (ENG)/West Bromwich Albion (ENG)	D	D29	D	D				31	2
Audun HELGASON (18/06/74) - Viking FK (NOR)	M36	D	D	D	D		D	16	1
Helgi KOLVIDSSON (13/09/71) - 1.FSV Mainz 05 (GER)	M		M58	s80	M	M	D	21	-
Thórdur GUDJÓNSSON (14/10/73) - KRC Genk (BEL)	M	M	M	M		M		36	9
Rúnar KRISTINSSON (05/06/69) - Lillestrøm SK (NOR)	M		M	M	M	M	M	82	3
Hermann HREIDARSSON (11/07/74) - Brentford (ENG)/Wimbledon (ENG)	M	D	D	D	D	D		29	1
Heidar HELGUSON (22/08/77) - Lillestrøm SK (NOR)/Watford (ENG)	A70	s57	s58	s65	A46	A		9	-
Ríkhardur DADASON (26/04/72) - Viking FK (NOR)	A	A75	A72	A54	A74	A79	A80	31	9
Sigursteinn GÍSLASON (25/06/68) - KR	s36							22	-
Tryggvi GUDMUNDSSON (30/07/74) - Tromsø IL (NOR)	s40	M			M46	s82	A	15	3
Árni Gautur ARASON (07/05/75) - Rosenborg BK (NOR)	s63				G		s46	6	-
Helgi SIGURDSSON (17/09/74) - Panathinaikos (GRE)	s70	A57		A65				30	4
Siggi JÓNSSON (27/09/66) - Dundee United (SCO)		D	D84					65	3
Bjarni GUDJÓNSSON (26/02/79) - KRC Genk (BEL)		M						7	1
Brynjar GUNNARSSON (16/10/75) - Örgryte IS (SWE)		M	M	M				21	3
Arnar Thór VIDARSSON (15/03/78) - KSC Lokeren (BEL)		s29	s84			D	D	5	-
Eidur Smári GUDJOHNSEN (15/09/78) - Bolton Wanderers (ENG)		s75	s72	s54				4	1
Eyjólfur SVERRISSON (30/08/68) - Hertha BSC Berlin (GER)				D				52	6
Indridi SIGURDSSON (12/10/81) - Lillestrøm SK (NOR)					D55		s31	2	-
Sigurdur Örn JÓNSSON (30/07/73) - KR					M	s83	s74	6	-
Einar Thór DANÍELSSON (19/01/70) - KR/Stoke City (ENG)					s46		M31	18	1
Thórhallur HINRIKSSON (10/09/76) - KR					s46		D	2	-
Bjarni THORSTEINSSON (31/08/76) - KR					s55			1	-
Sigthór JÚLÍUSSON (27/04/75) - KR					s74			1	-
Sverrir SVERRISSON (31/12/69) - Fylkir						D	s84	13	-
Bjarki GUNNLAUGSSON (06/03/73) - Preston North End (ENG)						M83	M84	27	7
Haukur Ingi GUDNASON (08/09/78) - Liverpool (ENG)						s79	s80	3	-
						/82			
Ólafur Örn BJARNASON (15/05/75) - Malmö FF (SWE)							M74	3	-

PLAYER OF THE SEASON

EYJÓLFUR SVERRISSON

Eyjólfur Sverrisson captained Iceland in their famous 3-2 defeat by France in October 1999 and he marked the occasion by scoring with a 30-yard thunderbolt that began Iceland's sensational comeback. That strike was proof, if any were needed, that this former striker had not lost the appetite for goalscoring which earned him a transfer from Icelandic Second Division side Tindastóll to German club Stuttgart in 1990. Sverrisson won German and

Turkish titles, respectively, with Stuttgart and Besiktas before joining Hertha Berlin, where he has developed into one of the most assured and respected centre-backs in the Bundesliga. His strong character and fighting spirit helped to carry Hertha through to the second group phase of the 1999/2000 Champions' League and he was far from overawed in the company of big-name strikers such as Shevchenko, Kluivert, Jardel and Zola who all crossed his path.

EUROPEAN CUPS 99/00

CHAMPIONS' CUP
● ÍBV

Preliminary round 1 SK TIRANA (ALB)

H 1-0 Jóhannesson S. (45)
Kristinsson; Bjarklind, Stefánsson, Miljkovic, Antonsson; Helgason (Möller 79), Ingimarsson, Bragason; Mørkøre (Aleksic 62), Jóhannesson S., Sigurdsson.

A 2-1 Jóhannesson S. (32), Sigurdsson (45)
Kristinsson; Helgason, Stefánsson, Miljkovic, Jóhannesson H.; Mørkøre (Grétarsson 80), Ingimarsson, Bragason, Aleksic (Bjarklind 25), Sigurdsson (Vidarsson 73); Jóhannesson S..

Preliminary round 2 MTK HUNGÁRIA FC (HUN)

H 0-2 Kristinsson; Bjarklind, Stefánsson, Miljkovic, Jóhannesson H.; Aleksic, Ingimarsson, Bragason; Mørkøre, Jóhannesson S. (Helgason 60), Sigurdsson.

A 1-3 Bjarklind (89)
Kristinsson; Helgason, Stefánsson, Miljkovic, Jóhannesson H.; Ingimarsson (Antonsson 58), Bragason (Vidarsson 74), Aleksic; Bjarklind, Jóhannesson S. (Möller 68), Mørkøre.

UEFA CUP
● KR

Qualifying round KILMARNOCK (SCO)

H 1-0 Hinriksson (87)
Finnbogason; Jónsson S.Ö., Winnie, Egilsson, Thorsteinsson; Júlíusson (Birgisson 70), Hinriksson, Gíslason, Daníelsson; Benediktsson, Gunnlaugsson.

A 0-2 (aet)
Finnbogason; Jónsson S.Ö., Winnie, Egilsson, Thorsteinsson; Júlíusson (Jónsson Th. 46), Hinriksson, Gíslason, Daníelsson; Benediktsson (Birgisson 64), Gunnlaugsson (Sigurdsson 82).

● LEIFTUR

Qualifying round RSC ANDERLECHT (BEL)

A 1-6 De Boeck (25og)
Knudsen; De Macedo, Birgisson, Gíslason, Gunnarsson, Peltonen (Gudbjörnsson 66); Heimisson, Da Silva, Gudmundsson (Helgason 71), Forrest; Arge (Santos 75).

H 0-3 Knudsen; De Macedo, Birgisson, Tryggvason, Gunnarsson; Helgason (Gudmundsson 69), Forrest, Gudbjörnsson, Gíslason, Peltonen (Da Silva 75); Arge (Santos 80).

He resigned to take charge of Stoke City, the English Second Division club owned by a consortium of Icelandic businessmen. His place was taken by KR's 'double'-winning coach Atli Edvaldsson, whose first three matches, at the Scandinavian winter-getaway tournament in southern Spain, resulted in a draw and two victories to maintain the team's upward momentum.

The stock of the Icelandic footballer is constantly on the rise. Many expatriate players did their country proud during the 1999/2000 season. Eyjólfur Sverrisson (Hertha Berlin) and Árni Gautur Arason (Rosenborg) played important roles in the Champions' League; Lillestrøm's Runar Kristinsson - now Iceland's most-capped international - was voted Player of the Year in Norway; Heidar Helguson made a fine start in the English Premiership with Watford, scoring goals against Liverpool (on his début), Arsenal and Manchester United; Eidur Gudjohnsen scored 22 goals for Bolton to earn himself a £4m transfer to Chelsea; Thórdur Gudjónsson scored twice in the Belgian Cup final to help Genk to a 4-1 victory over Standard Liège.

The sheer number of Icelandic players currently earning their living in mainland Europe - 50-plus and rising - is quite remarkable, bearing in mind that the country is populated by just 270,000 inhabitants - the equivalent of around three and a half capacity crowds at the Stade de France.

PROMOTED CLUBS 1999

SECOND DIVISION FINAL TABLE

		Pd	W	D	L	F	A	Pt	GD
1	Fylkir	18	15	0	3	46	20	45	26
2	Stjarnan	18	9	2	7	35	31	29	4
3	FH	18	8	4	6	41	31	28	10
4	ÍR	18	8	2	8	46	35	26	11
5	Dalvík	18	7	5	6	27	35	26	-8
6	KA	18	6	5	7	24	24	23	0
7	Skallagrímur	18	7	2	9	36	38	23	-2
8	Thróttur R.	18	6	3	9	27	29	21	-2
9	Vidir	18	6	3	9	30	44	21	-14
10	KVA	18	4	2	12	28	53	14	-25

CLUB DIRECTORIES

Íthróttafélagid Fylkir
Fylkisvegur 6, 110 Reykjavík
tel - (587) 7020 / fax - (567) 6091
e-mail - kndfylkis@isholf.is
Website - www.fylkir.is
Year of Formation - 1967
President - Kolbeinn Finnsson
Secretary - Kjartan Daníelsson
Coach - Ólafur Thórdarson
(2000 - Bjarni Jóhansson)
Stadium - Fylkisvöllur (1,000)

Ungmennafélagid Stjarnan
Ásgardur, 210 Gardabaer
tel - (565) 6860 / fax - (565) 1714
e-mail - stjarnanknd@mmedia.is
Website - www.toto.is/felog/stjarnan/
Year of Formation - 1960
President - Sigmundur Hermundsson
Secretary - Gunnar Gudmundsson
Coach - Goran Kristófer Micic
Stadium - Stjörnuvöllur (1,000)

BREIDABLIK

CLUB DIRECTORY

Ungmennafélagid Breidablik
Smárinn
Dalsmári 5
200 Kópavogur
tel - 564 2699
fax - 554 0050
website - www.breidablik.is
email - knattspyrna@breidablik.is
Year of Formation - 1950
President - Sverrir Hauksson
Secretary - Halldór Thorsteinsson
Coach - Sigurdur Grétarsson
Stadium - Kópavogsvöllur (1,500)

APPEARANCES 1999

		P	Ap	(s)	Gls
Ásgeir BALDURS	D	16			
Marel J. BALDVINSSON	A	9		(1)	3
Hreidar BJARNASON	M	18			6
Hördur BJARNASON	M			(1)	
Che BUNCE (NZL)	D	12			1
Kjartan EINARSSON	M	16			1
Gudmundur Páll GÍSLASON	M	7		(5)	1
Sigurdur GRÉTARSSON	D	12			1
Gudmundur K. GUDMUNDSSON	M	7		(8)	
Gudmundur Örn GUDMUNDSSON	D	11		(1)	
Árni K. GUNNARSSON	M	1		(4)	
Magnús Páll GUNNARSSON	D			(1)	
Thór HAUKSSON	D			(2)	
Jón Thórir JÓNSSON	D			(1)	
Pétur JÓNSSON	D	1		(4)	
Atli KNÚTSSON	G	18			
Atli KRISTJÁNSSON	A	3		(4)	
Hjalti KRISTJÁNSSON	D	17			
Ottó Karl OTTÓSSON	M			(3)	
Bjarki PÉTURSSON	A	11		(2)	1
Salih Heimir PORCA	M	12			5
Kristján Óli SIGURDSSON	M			(2)	
Ívar SIGURJÓNSSON	A	9		(5)	2
Hákon SVERRISSON	M	18			1

LEAGUE RESULTS 1999

20/05/99	Valur	H	2-0	Bjarnason, Baldvinsson
24/05/99	Grindavík	A	0-1	
27/05/99	Fram	H	1-1	Baldvinsson
01/06/99	ÍBV	H	1-0	Pétursson
12/06/99	KR	A	0-0	
20/06/99	Víkingur	H	1-1	Sverrisson
24/06/99	Keflavík	A	1-2	Porca (p)
15/07/99	Leiftur	A	2-2	Porca, Bjarnason
21/07/99	Valur	A	1-2	Porca (p)
29/07/99	Grindavík	H	4-1	Porca 2 (1p), Sigurjónsson, Baldvinsson
10/08/99	Fram	A	2-2	Sigurjónsson, Bjarnason
15/08/99	ÍBV	A	1-2	Gíslason
18/08/99	ÍA	H	1-3	Grétarsson (p)
21/08/99	KR	H	0-3	
27/08/99	Víkingur	A	0-1	
31/08/99	Keflavík	H	2-1	Bunce, Bjarnason
11/09/99	ÍA	A	3-2	Bjarnason 2, Einarsson
18/09/99	Leiftur	H	0-0	

FRAM

CLUB DIRECTORY

Knattspyrnufélagid Fram
Safamyri 28, 108 Reykjavík
tel - 533 5600 / fax - 533 5610
website - www.fram.is
email - grimur@fram.is
Year of Formation - 1908
President - Thurídur Gudnadóttir
Secretary - Bjarni Hákonarson
Coach - Ásgeir Elíasson
(2000 - Gudmundur Torfason)
Stadium - Laugardalsvöllur (7,000)

MAJOR HONOURS
League Championship - (18)
1913, 1914, 1915, 1916, 1917, 1918, 1921,
1922, 1923, 1925, 1939, 1946, 1947, 1962,
1972, 1986, 1988, 1990.
Domestic Cup - (7) 1970, 1973, 1979, 1980,
1985, 1987, 1989.

APPEARANCES 1999

	P	Ap	(s)	Gls
Arngrímur ARNARSON	A	1	(2)	
Ásmundur ARNARSSON	M	12	(6)	1
Rúnar ÁGÚSTSSON	D	2	(1)	
Albert ÁSVALDSSON	D	2		
Hilmar BJÖRNSSON	A	12		2
Saint Paul EDEH (NIG)	A		(1)	
Steinar Thór GUDGEIRSSON	M	17		1
Saevar GUDJÓNSSON	D	9	(1)	
Ágúst GYLFASON	M	18		5
Ásgeir HALLDÓRSSON	D	15		1
Haukur Snaer HAUKSSON	A	1	(5)	
Halldór HILMISSON	M	2	(6)	1
Elvar Ingi JÓNSSON	M		(1)	
Ívar JÓNSSON	M	3	(4)	1
Freyr KARLSSON	M	7	(3)	
Baldur KNÚTSSON	M	3		
Anton Björn MARKÚSSON	M	14		2
Marcel OERLEMANS (HOL)	A	14		5
Andri Fannar OTTÓSSON	A		(1)	
Sigurvin ÓLAFSSON	M	8	(1)	1
Ólafur PÉTURSSON	G	13		
Saevar PÉTURSSON	D	14	(2)	1
Valdimar K. SIGURDSSON	A	6	(4)	
Eggert STEFÁNSSON	D		(2)	
Jón Thórir SVEINSSON	M	16		
Fridrik THORSTEINSSON	G	5		
Höskuldur THÓRHALLSSON	A	4	(7)	2

LEAGUE RESULTS 1999

20/05/99	Grindavík	A	1-1	Halldórsson
24/05/99	Keflavík	H	2-0	Gylfason 2
27/05/99	Breidablik	A	1-1	Jónsson Í.
31/05/99	ÍA	H	0-0	
12/06/99	ÍBV	A	1-1	Oerlemans
20/06/99	Leiftur	H	2-0	Thórhallsson, Björnsson
24/06/99	KR	A	1-3	Pétursson S.
05/07/99	Valur	H	2-2	Gylfason (p), Oerlemans
14/07/99	Víkingur	A	2-0	Björnsson, Gylfason (p)
22/07/99	Grindavík	H	1-3	Ólafsson
29/07/99	Keflavík	A	1-2	Hilmisson
10/08/99	Breidablik	H	2-2	Oerlemans, Gudgeirsson
15/08/99	ÍA	A	0-1	
22/08/99	ÍBV	H	0-2	
29/08/99	Leiftur	A	3-3	Gylfason, Arnarsson Á., Thórhallsson
01/09/99	KR	H	0-2	
11/09/99	Valur	A	1-2	Oerlemans
18/09/99	Víkingur	H	3-2	Markússon 2, Oerlemans

GRINDAVÍK

THE EUROPEAN FOOTBALL YEARBOOK 2000-2001

CLUB DIRECTORY

Ungmennafélag Grindavíkur
Austurvegur 3
240 Grindavík
tel - 426 8605
fax - 426 7605
Year of Formation - 1963
President - Jónas Thórhallsson
Secretary - Ingvar Gudjónsson
Coach - Milan Stefán Jankovic
Stadium - Grindavíkurvöllur (1,000)

APPEARANCES 1999

	P	Ap	(s)	Gls
Jóhann H. ADALGEIRSSON	M	2	(6)	
Gudjón ÁSMUNDSSON	D	18		1
Árni Stefán BJÖRNSSON	A		(1)	
Sigurbjörn DAGBJARTSSON	M	1	(1)	
Óli Stefán FLÓVENTSSON	D	17		2
Leifur GUDJÓNSSON	A		(2)	
Sveinn Ari GUDJÓNSSON	D	5	(3)	
Jón Fannar GUDMUNDSSON	M	1	(1)	
Hjálmar HALLGRÍMSSON	M	10	(4)	1
Vignir HELGASON	M	4	(5)	
Grétar HJARTARSON	A	17		10
Ólafur INGÓLFSSON	A	11	(7)	2
Ray Anthony JÓNSSON	A		(2)	
Sinisa KEKIC (YUG)	M	16		3
Alistair McMILLAN (SCO)	M	8	(3)	1
Paul McSHANE (SCO)	M	11	(2)	
Duro MIJUSKOVIC (YUG)	M	15	(3)	1
Scott RAMSEY (SCO)	M	14	(2)	2
Albert SAEVARSSON	G	18		
Björn SKÚLASON	D	12	(1)	
Stevo VORKAPIC (YUG)	D	18		2

LEAGUE RESULTS 1999

20/05/99	Fram	H	1-1	Hjartarson
24/05/99	Breidablik	H	1-0	Hjartarson
27/05/99	ÍBV	A	1-2	Kekic
01/06/99	KR	H	1-3	Mijuskovic
13/06/99	Víkingur	A	1-1	Hjartarson
20/06/99	Keflavík	H	2-0	McMillan, Kekic
23/06/99	ÍA	A	0-1	
04/07/99	Leiftur	H	0-1	
15/07/99	Valur	A	1-2	Flóventsson
22/07/99	Fram	A	3-1	Hjartarson, Kekic, Ramsey
29/07/99	Breidablik	A	1-4	Hjartarson
08/08/99	ÍBV	H	1-2	Hjartarson
15/08/99	KR	A	1-2	Hjartarson
21/08/99	Víkingur	H	2-2	Hjartarson (p), Hallgrímsson
28/08/99	Keflavík	A	3-2	Hjartarson 2, Ramsey
01/09/99	ÍA	H	2-2	Vorkapic, Ingólfsson
11/09/99	Leiftur	A	1-2	Flóventsson
18/09/99	Valur	H	3-1	Ásmundsson, Vorkapic, Ingólfsson

ÍA

Knattspyrnufélag ÍA
Jadarsbakkar, 300 Akranes
tel - 431 3311 / fax - 431 3012
website - www.aknes.is/ia
email - kfia@aknet.is
Year of Formation - 1946
President - Smári Gudjónsson
Secretary - Kristján Thorvaldz
Coach - Logi Ólafsson; Ólafur Thórdarson
Stadium - Akranesvöllur (3,000)

MAJOR HONOURS
League Championship - (17) 1951, 1953, 1954,
1957, 1958, 1960, 1970, 1974, 1975, 1977,
1983, 1984, 1992, 1993, 1994, 1995, 1996.
Domestic Cup - (7) 1978, 1982, 1983, 1984,
1986, 1993, 1996.

APPEARANCES 1999

	P	Ap	(s)	Gls
Baldur ADALSTEINSSON	A	1	(7)	
Ragnar ÁRNASON	M	2	(5)	
Freyr BJARNASON	D	2	(2)	
Baldur Theyr BRAGASON	G	1		
Sigurdur R. EYJÓLFSSON	A	4		1
Hálfdán GÍSLASON	A	1		
Jóhannes GÍSLASON	M	2	(3)	
Heimir GUDJÓNSSON	M	17		
Ólafur Thór GUNNARSSON	G	17		
Pálmi HARALDSSON	M	18		
Sturlaugur HARALDSSON	D	16	(1)	1
Jóhannes HARDARSON	M	16		1
Jón Thór HAUKSSON	M		(2)	
Ragnar HAUKSSON	A	8	(7)	4
Alexander HÖGNASON	D	15		2
Kristján JÓHANSSON	D	5	(4)	
Gunnlaugur JÓNSSON	D	16		
Reynir LEÓSSON	D	17		
Kenneth MATIJANE (SAF)	A	11		4
Kári Steinn REYNISSON	M	18		4
Stefán Thór THÓRDARSON	A	7		4
Unnar Örn VALGEIRSSON	M	4	(9)	

LEAGUE RESULTS 1999

18/05/99	KR	A	0-1	
24/05/99	Víkingur	H	1-1	Eyjólfsson
27/05/99	Keflavík	A	0-2	
31/05/99	Fram	A	0-0	
12/06/99	Leiftur	H	0-0	
23/06/99	Grindavík	H	1-0	Hauksson R.
16/07/99	ÍBV	H	1-1	Matijane
22/07/99	KR	H	0-2	
26/07/99	Valur	A	2-1	Högnason, Matijane
29/07/99	Víkingur	A	2-1	Reynisson, Matijane
08/08/99	Keflavík	H	2-2	Haraldsson S. (p), Thórdarson
15/08/99	Fram	H	1-0	Hardarson
18/08/99	Breidablik	A	3-1	Thórdarson 2 (1p), Matijane
21/08/99	Leiftur	A	4-1	Reynisson 2, Hauksson R. 2
29/08/99	Valur	H	0-1	
01/09/99	Grindavík	A	2-2	Hauksson R., Thórdarson (p)
11/09/99	Breidablik	H	2-3	Reynisson, Högnason (p)
18/09/99	ÍBV	A	0-2	

ÍBV

CLUB DIRECTORY

ÍBV - Íthróttafélag
Tysheimild v/Hásteinsvöll, 900 Vestmannaeyjar
tel - 481 2608 / fax - 481 1260
website - eyjar.is/ibv/fotbolti
email - ibvfc@eyjar.is
Year of Formation - 1945
President - Ásmundur Fridriksson
Secretary - Thorsteinn Gunnarsson
Coach - Bjarni Jóhansson
(2000 - Kristinn Rúnar Jónsson)
Stadium - Hásteinsvöllur (1,500)

MAJOR HONOURS
League Championship - (3) 1979, 1997, 1998.
Domestic Cup - (4) 1968, 1972, 1981, 1998.

APPEARANCES 1999

	P	Ap	(s)	Gls
Goran ALEKSIC (YUG)	M	9	(2)	2
Kjartan ANTONSSON	D	10	(4)	
Ívar BJARKLIND	D	18		2
Baldur BRAGASON	M	14		
Sindri GRÉTARSSON	A		(3)	
Kristinn G. GUDMUNDSSON	G		(1)	
Kristinn HAFLIDASON	M		(2)	
Gudni Rúnar HELGASON	M	16	(1)	3
Ívar INGIMARSSON	M	18		4
Hjalti JÓHANNESSON	D	11	(5)	
Steingrímur JÓHANNESSON	A	18		12
Hjalti JÓNSSON	M		(3)	
Birkir KRISTINSSON	G	18		
Zoran MILJKOVIC (YUG)	D	16		
Jóhann Georg MÖLLER	A	3	(11)	1
Allan MØRKØRE (FAR)	M	9	(5)	1
Ingi SIGURDSSON	A	17		3
Rútur SNORRASON	M	3	(3)	1
Hlynur STEFÁNSSON	D	16		2
Gunnar H. THORVALDSSON	A		(1)	
Bjarni Geir VIDARSSON	A	2	(5)	

LEAGUE RESULTS 1999

20/05/99	Leiftur	H	5-0	Jóhannesson S. 4 (1p), Snorrason
24/05/99	Valur	A	0-0	
27/05/99	Grindavík	H	2-1	Jóhannesson S. 2
01/06/99	Breidablik	A	0-1	
12/06/99	Fram	H	1-1	Sigurdsson
19/06/99	KR	H	2-1	Stefánsson, Ingimarsson
25/06/99	Víkingur	A	2-1	Helgason 2
04/07/99	Keflavík	H	1-0	Ingimarsson
16/07/99	ÍA	A	1-1	Jóhannesson S. (p)
25/07/99	Leiftur	A	3-0	Möller, Sigurdsson, Bjarklind
08/08/99	Grindavík	A	2-1	Jóhannesson S., Stefánsson
15/08/99	Breidablik	H	2-1	Aleksic, Helgason
22/08/99	Fram	A	2-0	Ingimarsson, Bjarklind
25/08/99	Valur	H	2-2	Sigurdsson, Aleksic
28/08/99	KR	A	0-3	
01/09/99	Víkingur	H	3-0	Jóhannesson S. 2 (1p), Mørkøre
11/09/99	Keflavík	A	1-1	Jóhannesson S.
18/09/99	ÍA	H	2-0	Jóhannesson S., Ingimarsson

KEFLAVÍK

CLUB DIRECTORY

Keflavík-Ungmenna-og Íthróttafélag
Hringbraut 108, 230 Reykjanesbaer
tel - 421 5188 / fax - 421 4137
website - web.ok.is/keflavik
email - kef-fc@ok.is
Year of Formation - 1929
President - Rúnar Arnarson
Secretary - Steinbjörn Logason
Coaches - Gunnar Oddsson & Sigurdur Björgvinsson;
Kjartan Másson (2000 - Páll Gudlaugsson)
Stadium - Keflavíkurvöllur (2,000)

MAJOR HONOURS
League Championship - (4)
1964, 1969, 1971, 1973.
Domestic Cup - (2) 1975, 1997.

APPEARANCES 1999

	P	Ap	(s)	Gls
Jóhann BENEDIKTSSON	D	2	(4)	
Georg BIRGISSON	M	1	(1)	
Kristján BROOKS	A	17	(1)	10
Gudmundur BRYNJARSSON	D	1		
Karl FINNBOGASON	D	9		1
Hjörtur FJELDSTED	D	9	(1)	
Daníel FRÍMANNSSON	M	1		
Kristinn GUDBRANDSSON	D	14		
Bjarki F. GUDMUNDSSON	G	18		
Haraldur GUDMUNDSSON	M		(1)	
Gestur GYLFASON	D	16		
Eysteinn HAUKSSON	M	17	(1)	4
Vilberg JÓNASSON	A		(4)	
Snorri Már JÓNSSON	D	7	(2)	
Thórarinn KRISTJÁNSSON	A	14	(3)	5
Zoran Daniel LJUBICIC	M	13	(4)	2
Gardar NEWMAN	D	8		
Gudmundur ODDSSON	D	4	(1)	
Gunnar ODDSSON	M	18		3
Róbert SIGURDSSON	M	4	(7)	
Rútur SNORRASON	M	2	(6)	1
Ragnar STEINARSSON	M	14	(1)	1
Adolf SVEINSSON	A	2	(1)	
Marko TANASIC (YUG)	M	7	(3)	1
Magnús THORSTEINSSON	A		(2)	

LEAGUE RESULTS 1999

20/05/99	Víkingur	A	1-2	Ljubicic
24/05/99	Fram	A	0-2	
27/05/99	ÍA	H	2-0	Hauksson, Brooks
01/06/99	Leiftur	A	0-1	
12/06/99	Valur	H	4-4	Brooks 2, Tanasic, Finnbogason
20/06/99	Grindavík	A	0-2	
24/06/99	Breidablik	H	2-1	Brooks 2
04/07/99	ÍBV	A	0-1	
15/07/99	KR	H	1-3	Hauksson (p)
22/07/99	Víkingur	H	3-2	Kristjánsson, Steinarsson, Hauksson
29/07/99	Fram	H	2-1	Brooks (p), Oddsson Gun.
08/08/99	ÍA	A	2-2	Oddsson Gun., Kristjánsson
15/08/99	Leiftur	H	2-2	Ljubicic, Kristjánsson
22/08/99	Valur	A	3-2	Oddsson Gun., Kristjánsson, Brooks
28/08/99	Grindavík	H	2-3	Hauksson, Brooks (p)
31/08/99	Breidablik	A	1-2	Snorrason
11/09/99	ÍBV	H	1-1	Brooks
18/09/99	KR	A	2-3	Kristjánsson, Brooks

KR

CLUB DIRECTORY

Knattspyrnufélag Reykjavíkur
Frostaskjól 2, 107 Reykjavík
tel - 511 5515 / fax - 511 5517
website - www.kr.is
email - kr@itn.is
Year of Formation - 1899
President - Gudjón Gudmundsson
Secretary - Magnús Orri Schram
Coach - Atli Edvaldsson (2000 - Pétur Pétursson)
Stadium - KR-völlur (2,500)

MAJOR HONOURS
League Championship - (21) 1912, 1919, 1926,
1927, 1928, 1929, 1931, 1932, 1934, 1941,
1948, 1949, 1950, 1952, 1955, 1959, 1961,
1963, 1965, 1968, 1999.
Domestic Cup - (10) 1960, 1961, 1962, 1963,
1964, 1966, 1967, 1994, 1995, 1999.

APPEARANCES 1999

	P	Ap	(s)	Gls
Egill ATLASON	M		(1)	
Gudmundur BENEDIKTSSON	A	18		9
Einar Örn BIRGISSON	A	1	(5)	2
Einar Thór DANÍELSSON	M	14	(1)	1
Thormódur EGILSSON	D	18		
Kristján FINNBOGASON	G	17		
Sigursteinn GÍSLASON	M	16		1
Nökvvi GUNNARSSON	A		(1)	
Bjarki GUNNLAUGSSON	A	16		11
Gunnleifur GUNNLEIFSSON	G	1		
Thórhallur HINRIKSSON	M	14	(2)	2
Edilon HREINSSON	D	1	(1)	
Björn JAKOBSSON	A	2	(1)	1
Sigurdur Örn JÓNSSON	D	18		
Thorsteinn JÓNSSON	M	2	(4)	
Sigthór JÚLÍUSSON	M	17		4
Árni Ingi PJETURSSON	M		(2)	1
Andri SIGTHÓRSSON	A	5		3
Indridi SIGURDSSON	D	9	(7)	
Arnar Jón SIGURGEIRSSON	M	1	(13)	2
Bjarni THORSTEINSSON	D	12	(3)	1
Jóhann THÓRHALLSSON	A		(2)	
Björgvin VILHJÁLMSSON	A		(2)	
David WINNIE (SCO)	D	16		1

LEAGUE RESULTS 1999

18/05/99	ÍA	H	1-0	Júlíusson
27/05/99	Valur	H	5-1	Sigthórsson 2, Gunnlaugsson, Júlíusson,
				Gíslason
01/06/99	Grindavík	A	3-1	og (McMillan), Benediktsson, Sigthórsson
12/06/99	Breidablik	H	0-0	
19/06/99	ÍBV	A	1-2	Júlíusson
24/06/99	Fram	H	3-1	Daníelsson, Benediktsson, Gunnlaugsson
27/06/99	Leiftur	A	1-1	Hinriksson
04/07/99	Víkingur	H	4-1	Birgisson 2, Jakobsson, Gunnlaugsson
15/07/99	Keflavík	A	3-1	Gunnlaugsson 2, Benediktsson (p)
22/07/99	ÍA	A	2-0	Benediktsson, Gunnlaugsson
28/07/99	Leiftur	H	1-1	Benediktsson (p)
08/08/99	Valur	A	2-1	Gunnlaugsson, Thorsteinsson
15/08/99	Grindavík	H	2-1	Winnie, Gunnlaugsson
21/08/99	Breidablik	A	3-0	Benediktsson, Daníelsson, Gunnlaugsson
28/08/99	ÍBV	H	3-0	Júlíusson, Daníelsson, Benediktsson (p)
01/09/99	Fram	A	2-0	Sigurgeirsson, Benediktsson
11/09/99	Víkingur	A	4-0	Gunnlaugsson 2, Benediktsson (p),
				Hinriksson
18/09/99	Keflavík	H	3-2	Daníelsson, Sigurgeirsson, Pjetursson

LEIFTUR

CLUB DIRECTORY

Íthróttafélagid Leiftur
Aegisgata
625 Ólafsfjördur
tel - 466 2655
fax - 466 2665
Year of Formation - 1931
President - Thorsteinn Thorvaldsson
Secretary - Thorsteinn Ásgeirsson
Coach - Páll Gudlaugsson
(2000 - Jens Martin Knudsen)
Stadium - Ólafsfjardarvöllur (1,000)

APPEARANCES 1999

	P	Ap	(s)	Gls
Albert ARASON	D	2	(2)	
Uni ARGE (FAR)	A	17		8
Hlynur BIRGISSON	D	15		
Gordon FORREST (SCO)	M	13	(3)	
Páll V. GÍSLASON	D	18		1
Thorvaldur GUDBJÖRNSSON	D	11	(7)	
Páll GUDMUNDSSON	M	14	(1)	1
Steinn V. GUNNARSSON	D	18		
Heidar GUNNÓLFSSON	A		(6)	
Ingi Hrannar HEIMISSON	M	8	(5)	
Örlygur HELGASON	M	4	(8)	
Paul KINNAIRD (SCO)	M	1		
Jens Martin KNUDSEN (FAR)	G	18		
Brian KRISTENSEN (DEN)	M	1		
Sérgio de MACEDO (BRA)	D	17		
Max PELTONEN (FIN)	D	13	(1)	
Alexandre SANTOS (BRA)	A	13	(4)	8
Alexandre da SILVA (BRA)	M	11	(2)	3
Júlíus TRYGGVASON	D	4	(1)	

LEAGUE RESULTS 1999

20/05/99	ÍBV	A	0-5	
29/05/99	Víkingur	A	3-0	Santos 2, Arge
01/06/99	Keflavík	H	1-0	Santos
12/06/99	ÍA	A	0-0	
20/06/99	Fram	A	0-2	
24/06/99	Valur	H	0-0	
27/06/99	KR	H	1-1	Arge
04/07/99	Grindavík	A	1-0	Silva
15/07/99	Breidablik	H	2-2	Arge 2
25/07/99	ÍBV	H	0-3	
28/07/99	KR	A	1-1	Silva
07/08/99	Víkingur	H	1-0	Santos
15/08/99	Keflavík	A	2-2	Santos 2
21/08/99	ÍA	H	1-4	Arge
29/08/99	Fram	H	3-3	Gíslason, Arge (p), Silva
01/09/99	Valur	A	4-2	Arge 2, Santos, og (Stefánsson)
11/09/99	Grindavík	H	2-1	Gudmundsson, Santos
18/09/99	Breidablik	A	0-0	

VALUR

CLUB DIRECTORY

Knattspyrnufélagid Valur
Hlidarendi v/Laufásveg, 105 Reykjavík
tel - 562 3730 / fax - 562 3734
website - www.valur.is
email - valur@valur.is
Year of Formation - 1911
President - Grímur Saemundsen
Secretary - Hafsteinn Lárusson
Coach - Kristinn Björnsson; Ingi Björn Albertsson
(2000 - Ejub Purisevic)
Stadium - Hlidarendi (2,000)

MAJOR HONOURS
League Championship - (19) 1930, 1933, 1935,
1936, 1937, 1938, 1940, 1942, 1943, 1944,
1945, 1956, 1966, 1967, 1976, 1978, 1980,
1985, 1987.
Domestic Cup - (8) 1965, 1974, 1976, 1977,
1988, 1990, 1991, 1992.

APPEARANCES 1999

	P	Ap	(s)	Gls
Jón Thór ANDRÉSSON	A		(2)	
Dadi ÁRNASON	M	4	(1)	
Sindri BJARNASON	D	6	(3)	
Gudmundur BRYNJÓLFSSON	M	16	(1)	1
Izudin Dadi DERVIC	D	9	(1)	
Grímur GARDARSSON	D	2	(2)	
Arnór GUDJOHNSEN	M	14		5
Matthías GUDMUNDSSON	M	7	(6)	2
Hjörvar HAFLIDASON	G	18		
Sigurbjörn HREIDARSSON	M	17		9
Ólafur H. INGASON	A	14	(3)	3
Ingólfur R. INGÓLFSSON	M		(1)	
Lúdvik JÓNASSON	D	9		
Helgi M. JÓNSSON	D	6	(2)	
Ólafur V. JÚLÍUSSON	A		(3)	
Kristinn LÁRUSSON	M	18		6
Hördur Már MAGNÚSSON	D	12	(4)	
Ólafur K. ÓLAFS	G		(1)	
Stefán M. ÓMARSSON	D	4		
Jón Th. STEFÁNSSON	A	16		1
Ólafur STÍGSSON	M	5	(2)	
Adolf SVEINSSON	A	6	(2)	1
Sigurdur S. THORSTEINSSON	D	9	(1)	
Einar Páll TÓMASSON	D	6	(1)	

LEAGUE RESULTS 1999

20/05/99	Breidablik	A	0-2	
24/05/99	ÍBV	H	0-0	
27/05/99	KR	A	1-5	Lárusson
01/06/99	Víkingur	H	1-1	Hreidarsson (p)
12/06/99	Keflavík	A	4-4	Gudjohnsen 2, Stefánsson, Hreidarsson (p)
24/06/99	Leiftur	A	0-0	
05/07/99	Fram	A	2-2	Gudjohnsen, Lárusson
15/07/99	Grindavík	H	2-1	Hreidarsson (p), Ingason
21/07/99	Breidablik	H	2-1	Ingason, Hreidarsson (p)
26/07/99	ÍA	H	1-2	Gudmundsson
08/08/99	KR	H	1-2	Brynjólfsson
16/08/99	Víkingur	A	4-5	Hreidarsson 3 (2p), Ingason
22/08/99	Keflavík	H	2-3	Sveinsson, Gudjohnsen
25/08/99	ÍBV	A	2-2	Hreidarsson 2 (2p)
29/08/99	ÍA	A	1-0	Lárusson
01/09/99	Leiftur	H	2-4	Gudmundsson, Lárusson
11/09/99	Fram	H	2-1	Gudjohnsen, Lárusson
18/09/99	Grindavík	A	1-3	Lárusson

VÍKINGUR

THE EUROPEAN FOOTBALL YEARBOOK 2000-2001

CLUB DIRECTORY

Knattspyrnufélagid Víkingur
Víkin, Tradarland 1, 108 Reykjavík
tel - 568 7755 / fax - 588 7845
website - www.vikingur.is
email - halli@toto.is
Year of Formation - 1908
President - Gudmundur H. Pétursson
Secretary - Haraldur Haraldsson
Coach - Lúkas Kostic
Stadium - Laugardalsvöllur (7,000)

MAJOR HONOURS
League Championship - (5)
1920, 1924, 1981, 1982, 1991.
Domestic Cup - (1) 1971

APPEARANCES 1999

	P	Ap	(s)	Gls
Sumarlidi ÁRNASON	A	15	(2)	5
Finnur BJARNASON	M		(1)	
Tryggvi BJÖRNSSON	D	2	(1)	
Sváfnir GÍSLASON	A	4	(5)	1
Daníel HAFLIDASON	A	3	(4)	2
Bjarni HALL	M	15	(1)	3
Arnar HALLSSON	D	15		
Sigurdur Elí HARALDSSON	D	2	(2)	
Daníel HJALTASON	M	4	(5)	
Lárus HULDARSSON	M	17		1
Gordon HUNTER (SCO)	D	10		
Arnar Hrafn JÓHANSSON	A	6	(4)	1
Hólmsteinn JÓNASSON	M	12	(2)	
Júlíus KRISTJÁNSSON	D		(1)	
Colin McKEE (SCO)	M	5	(3)	
Gunnar S. MAGNÚSSON	G	16		
Jón Grétar ÓLAFSSON	A	10	(3)	4
Thorri ÓLAFSSON	D	17		
Sigurdur ÓMARSSON	M		(1)	
Alan PRENTICE (SCO)	M	7	(4)	1
Ögmundur RÚNARSSON	G	2		
Sigurdur SIGHVATSSON	D	9	(1)	
Thrándur SIGURDSSON	D	13	(5)	2
Haukur Armin ÚLFARSSON	M	9		
Valur Adolf ÚLFARSSON	D	5	(8)	

LEAGUE RESULTS 1999

20/05/99	Keflavík	H	2-1	Árnason 2
24/05/99	ÍA	A	1-1	Huldarsson
29/05/99	Leiftur	H	0-3	
01/06/99	Valur	A	1-1	Jóhansson
13/06/99	Grindavík	H	1-1	Árnason (p)
20/06/99	Breidablik	A	1-1	Árnason
25/06/99	ÍBV	H	1-2	Sigurdsson
04/07/99	KR	A	1-4	Hall
14/07/99	Fram	H	0-2	
22/07/99	Keflavík	A	2-3	Gíslason, Sigurdsson
29/07/99	ÍA	H	1-2	Árnason
07/08/99	Leiftur	A	0-1	
16/08/99	Valur	H	5-4	Haflidason 2, Ólnfsson J. 2, og (Thorsteinsson)
21/08/99	Grindavík	A	2-2	Ólafsson J. 2
27/08/99	Breidablik	H	1-0	Hall
01/09/99	ÍBV	A	0-3	
11/09/99	KR	H	0-4	
18/09/99	Fram	A	2-3	Prentice (p), Hall

ISRAEL

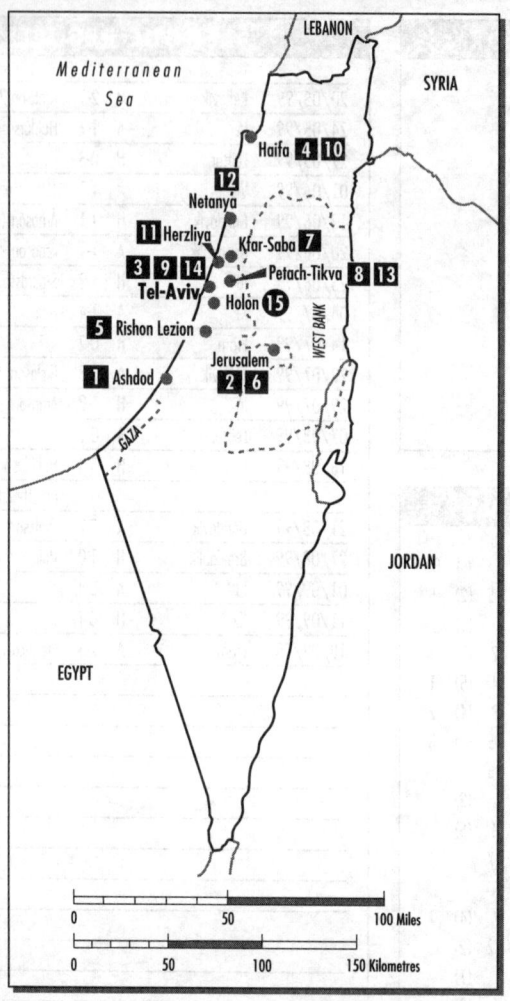

1	MS ASHDOD	562
2	BEITAR JERUSALEM	563
3	BNEI YEHUDA	564
4	HAPOEL HAIFA	565
5	HAPOEL IRONY RISHON LEZION	566
6	HAPOEL JERUSALEM	567
7	HAPOEL KFAR-SABA	568
8	HAPOEL PETACH-TIKVA	569

9	HAPOEL TEL-AVIV	570
10	MACCABI HAIFA	571
11	MACCABI HERZLIYA	572
12	MACCABI NETANYA	573
13	MACCABI PETACH-TIKVA	574
14	MACCABI TEL-AVIV	575
Promoted club		
15	ZAFRIRIM HOLON	

NATIONAL TEAM CAUGHT UP IN SLEAZE STORM

Kashtan leads Hapoel Tel-Aviv to the 'double'

FEDERATION DIRECTORY

Israel Football Association
Ramat-Gan Stadium, 299 Aba Hilell Street, Ramat-Gan, P.O. Box 3591

tel - (03) 6171503/6171504   Year of Formation - 1928
fax - (03) 5702044   President - Gavri Levi
    Secretary - Jacob Erel

Stadium - Ramat-Gan, Tel-Aviv (43,000)

1999/2000 was a perfect season for Hapoel Tel-Aviv. They won both the championship and the Cup to complete their first post-war 'double' and did so under the command of Israel's most successful coach, Dror Kashtan, who became the first man to lead two different Israeli teams to the 'double', having already achieved the feat four years earlier with local rivals Maccabi Tel-Aviv.

Kashtan, newly arrived from Beitar Jerusalem, turned a team of youngsters and veterans into a formidable force.

Of the old brigade, much travelled 35-year-old Shalom Tikva had only a peripheral role, but Hungarian midfielder István Pisont, back in Israel after a spell in Germany, proved to be every bit as influential as he had been previously at Beitar Jerusalem. Israeli international striker Ronen Harazi was another big hit, returning from Turkey to score 17 goals - despite missing several matches through injury.

The young element also excelled, with Pini Balili, Omri Affek and Salim Toema all emerging from nowhere to play prominent roles while striker Kfir Udi made such progress that he was called up to the Israeli national team, scoring on his début against Russia.

The one blemish on Hapoel Tel-Aviv's season came at the end of the match which secured the title. Drawing 1-1 at Bnei Yehuda with just 25 seconds remaining, all hell suddenly broke loose as around a thousand Hapoel supporters swarmed onto the pitch, causing the game to be abandoned. It was a case of history repeating itself, because precisely the same thing had happened a year earlier when Hapoel Haifa took the title. Although referee Amit Klein insisted that the game was not over, there was no way it could be restarted because the invading fans had destroyed the goalposts.

LEAGUE CHAMPIONSHIP RESULTS 99/00

	1	2	3	4	5	6	7	8	9	10	11	12	13	14
1 MS Ashdod		1-1	1-0	0-0	4-2	3-0	3-2	0-2	1-2	0-0	0-1	0-2	0-1	1-0
						2-0	1-1	2-2	0-0		1-0		3-2	2-4
2 Beitar Jerusalem	3-1		1-1	3-3	2-0	2-0	1-1	1-1	2-0	1-1	1-1	4-2	3-1	0-1
	1-1		2-1		1-4	1-1				3-1		2-3	1-1	
3 Bnei Yehuda	1-1	2-1		0-2	1-3	2-0	1-1	2-4	2-1	0-2	3-1	1-1	0-2	0-0
	0-1				1-1			2-1	1-1		1-0		1-0	
4 Hapoel Haifa	3-0	1-1	1-1		2-0	3-2	3-0	2-2	0-0	0-0	4-0	2-1	1-0	2-4
	0-0	0-0	5-0		1-1	3-0				0-4		1-1		
5 Hapoel Irony Rishon Lezion	0-0	1-4	1-0	0-0		2-2	2-2	1-1	1-3	0-7	3-1	1-0	0-1	0-0
	0-2					2-1	2-1	1-2		0-1		1-0		
6 Hapoel Jerusalem	0-1	0-2	0-1	1-1	1-1		2-1	0-1	0-1	1-3	1-4	1-3	0-2	0-1
		2-2		3-1			2-1				1-2	0-4		2-4
7 Hapoel Kfar-Saba	1-1	1-2	4-1	0-3	2-0	1-0		1-3	0-1	1-1	0-0	0-0	2-2	0-3
	1-1	1-1		0-0						1-0		1-1		2-2
8 Hapoel Petach-Tikva	4-2	3-0	4-0	0-2	1-0	3-1	2-1		0-1	2-5	1-0	1-0	0-1	2-1
	2-1		3-1		4-1	0-1			0-3		8-1			2-2
9 Hapoel Tel-Aviv	4-2	4-1	1-0	1-0	1-2	3-0	5-1	2-0		0-0	4-0	3-0	2-1	1-1
	2-1		3-1		3-0	1-0				1-1	2-0			2-1
10 Maccabi Haifa	0-0	0-2	3-1	3-2	4-1	1-2	1-0	2-0	1-0		3-0	1-1	5-1	1-2
	2-0		1-1		0-0	6-0		4-1			7-0	1-2		
11 Maccabi Herzliya	1-1	1-2	4-0	0-0	0-0	1-2	0-2	1-3	0-5	2-5		1-0	0-4	3-1
	0-0			1-1				0-2		2-4		0-0		0-4
12 Maccabi Netanya	0-6	2-3	1-1	1-2	2-4	2-1	4-1	1-2	2-5	1-3	0-3		0-1	3-1
	3-1	4-1		2-2			2-4	1-1					2-1	
13 Maccabi Petach-Tikva	3-1	3-0	1-1	2-1	0-0	0-2	3-2	1-2	1-5	1-2	1-0	0-0		2-1
	0-0					3-1	1-0	2-4	1-0		0-1			0-1
14 Maccabi Tel-Aviv	1-2	1-3	3-1	0-0	4-0	1-1	0-1	0-1	2-0	0-1	3-0	0-0	1-2	
	4-1	1-2	1-0	5-1		3-0					2-1			

LEAGUE CHAMPIONSHIP FINAL TABLE 99/00

			Home					Away					Total					
		Pd	W	D	L	F	A	W	D	L	F	A	W	D	L	F	A	PT	GD
1	Hapoel Tel-Aviv	39	16	3	1	45	12	10	4	5	31	16	26	7	6	76	28	85	48
2	Maccabi Haifa	39	12	4	4	46	16	10	6	3	40	19	22	10	7	86	35	76	51
3	Hapoel Petach-Tikva	39	13	1	6	42	24	10	4	5	35	28	23	5	11	77	52	74	25
4	Maccabi Petach-Tikva	39	9	4	7	25	24	9	2	8	25	23	18	6	15	50	47	60	3
5	Beitar Jerusalem	39	8	9	3	35	25	7	5	7	26	29	15	14	10	61	54	59	7
6	Maccabi Tel-Aviv	39	9	3	7	32	17	9	5	6	34	25	18	8	13	66	42	58	24
7	Hapoel Haifa	39	9	9	2	34	17	4	9	6	19	19	13	18	8	53	36	57	17
8	MS Ashdod	39	8	6	6	25	22	5	7	7	23	27	13	13	13	48	49	52	-1
9	Hapoel Irony Rishon Lezion	39	6	6	7	18	28	4	7	9	23	37	10	13	16	41	65	43	-24
10	Maccabi Netanya	39	6	3	10	33	43	4	8	8	20	28	10	11	18	53	71	41	-18
11	Bnei Yehuda	39	7	6	6	21	23	2	7	11	16	41	9	13	17	37	64	40	-27
12	Hapoel Kfar-Saba	39	4	10	5	19	22	4	4	12	21	34	8	14	17	40	56	38	-16
13	Maccabi Herzliya	39	3	6	10	17	36	6	2	12	16	37	9	8	22	33	73	35	-40
14	Hapoel Jerusalem	39	3	3	13	17	36	3	3	14	16	46	6	6	27	33	82	24	-49

N.B. Maccabi Tel-Aviv - 4 points deducted.

Bnei Yehuda, who were fighting against relegation - they eventually stayed up by the skin of their teeth - demanded to be awarded the match by default, but the Israeli FA allowed the result to stand. Hapoel Tel-Aviv celebrated four days later by winning the Cup for the second season in succession. In 1999 they had triumphed by beating Beitar Jerusalem in the final on penalties and it was exactly the same story this time, with Hapoel eventually prevailing in a shoot-out after a thrilling finish to both the 90 minutes and extra-time.

Maccabi Haifa and Hapoel Petach-Tikva were the only serious challengers to the eventual champions. Maccabi secured the runners-up spot but only after they had fired their coach for the third season in a row. Eli Cohen was the victim, paying the price for a shock home defeat against Maccabi Petach-Tikva. The club had been shaken by an incident earlier in the campaign when the team's star player, Yossi Benayoun, refused to be substituted in a match against Hapoel Haifa. The incident sparked a war of words between Benayoun and coach Cohen, which led to the integrity of both men being called into question. While Cohen ultimately got the sack, Benayoun received only a slap on the wrists from the club but was deliberately left out of the national side as a punishment for his misbehaviour.

Hapoel Petach-Tikva, inspired by a quartet of Croatian imports, played some high-quality football but, rather like Maccabi Haifa, they petered out dramatically in the run-in, which led to the dismissal of coach Nir Levin... and his subsequent replacement, for the 2000/01 season, by Eli Cohen.

Defending champions Hapoel Haifa put up a decent

NATIONAL TEAM RESULTS 99/00

18/08/99	Slovakia	A	Bratislava	0-1	
05/09/99	Cyprus (ECQ)	A	Limassol	2-3	Badir (33), Benayoun (82)
08/09/99	San Marino (ECQ)	H	Tel-Aviv	8-0	Benayoun (25, 46, 70), Mizrahi (38), Revivo (40, 69), Sivilia (83), Abuksis (89)
10/10/99	Spain (ECQ)	A	Albacete	0-3	
13/11/99	Denmark (ECQ)	H	Tel-Aviv	0-5	
17/11/99	Denmark (ECQ)	A	Copenhagen	0-3	
23/02/00	Russia	H	Haifa	4-1	Badir (3, 36), Udi (17), Nimni (86)
29/03/00	Georgia	H	Ashkelon	1-1	Berkovic (86)
26/04/00	Czech Republic	A	Prague	1-4	Berkovic (81)
03/06/00	Hungary	A	Budapest	1-2	Balili (90)

TOP SCORERS

27	Assi TUBI (Maccabi Petach-Tikva)
21	Serghei CLESCENCO (Maccabi Haifa)
19	Yossi BENAYOUN (Maccabi Haifa)
18	Rafi COHEN (Maccabi Haifa)
17	Ronen HARAZI (Hapoel Tel-Aviv)
	Kobi REFUA (Bnei Yehuda)
14	Eli ABARBNEL (Hapoel Petach-Tikva)
	Amir TURGEMAN (Hapoel Haifa)
	Itzhak ZOHAR (Maccabi Herzliya/ Maccabi Netanya)
13	Niv TAL (Hapoel Petach-Tikva)
	Nissan KAPETA (Hapoel Irony Rishon Lezion)
	Victor PAÇO (Beitar Jerusalem)

NATIONAL TEAM APPEARANCES 99/00

Coach - Shlomo SHARF; Richard MØLLER-NIELSEN	SVK	CYP	SMR	ESP	DEN	DEN	RUS	GEO	CZE	HUN	Cps	Gls
Nir DAVIDOVICH (17/12/76) - Maccabi Haifa	G77	G	G								16	-
Alon HARAZI (13/02/71) - Maccabi Haifa	D	D	D		D	D	D46	D86			65	1
Arik BENADO (05/12/73) - Maccabi Haifa	D	D	D65	D50	D		D	D	D	D	45	-
Amir SHELACH (11/07/70) - Hapoel Haifa	D	D64		D		D	D	D	D10	D	75	-
Najwan GHRAYEB (30/01/74) - Aston Villa (ENG)	D70	D							M		18	4
Yossi ABUKSIS (10/09/70) - Beitar Jerusalem	M46	M55	s61		M37						17	2
Alon HAZAN (11/09/67) - MS Ashdod	M46	D	D	M81	D	D					71	5
Eyal BERKOVIC (02/04/72) - Celtic (SCO)	M73	M16		M67	M	M		M	M	M	62	8
Tal BANIN (07/03/71) - Brescia (ITA)	M73	M		M	M76	M	M		M53		62	11
Haim REVIVO (22/02/72) - RC Celta (ESP)	M	A	A	M	M			M	M74		48	10
Alon MIZRAHI (22/11/71) - OGC Nice (FRA)	A70	A	A46								29	13
Ran BEN SHIMON (08/11/70) - Hapoel Haifa	s46 /54				D37						34	-
Walid BADIR (12/03/74) - Wimbledon (ENG)	s46	s16				s43	M	M	A	s53	23	4
Offer TALKER (22/04/73) - Hapoel Haifa	s54		D			D	D	D	D59	D46	10	-
David AMSALEM (04/09/71) - Hapoel Haifa	s70		D	D	D	D43					31	-
Nir SIVILIA (26/05/73) - Hapoel Haifa/Beitar Jerusalem	s70	s64	s46					s24			13	1
Avi TIKVA (28/06/76) - Grasshopper-Club Zürich (SUI)	s73		M61						s74	M79	11	1
Jan TELESNIKOV (11/02/72) - Dundee United (SCO)	s73		M	s81	s76	s28	s46			M79	20	4
Eran SHAIZINGER (03/12/76) - Maccabi Netanya	s77										3	-
Yossi BENAYOUN (06/06/80) - Maccabi Haifa		s55	M	s67	s37	M72					7	4
Alon HALFON (07/02/73) - Hapoel Haifa		s65	s50				s46	s86			4	-
Dudu AUAT (17/10/77) - Hapoel Haifa					G	G					2	-
Shimon GERSHON (06/10/77) - Hapoel Tel-Aviv					D		s72		D		5	-
Idan TAL (13/09/75) - Hapoel Tel-Aviv					M	s37	M28	M46	M	M	17	1
Amir TURGEMAN (05/10/72) - Hapoel Haifa				A	A	A	s66				11	2
Shavit ELIMELECH (07/09/71) - Hapoel Tel-Aviv					G						2	-
Rafi COHEN (28/11/70) - Hapoel Petach-Tikva							G46	G46		G	43	-
Adoram KEISSY (17/06/72) - Maccabi Haifa							D	D	s10	D	9	-
Avi NIMNI (26/04/72) - Derby County (ENG)/Maccabi Tel-Aviv							M		s53	M	47	9
Kfir UDI (28/08/79) - Hapoel Tel-Aviv							A66	A24			2	1
Itzhak KORENFAIN (24/09/71) - Beitar Jerusalem							s46	s46	G		6	-
Ilan BAKHAR (17/05/75) - Hapoel Tel-Aviv									s59	s46	2	-
Eyal ALMOSNINO (01/03/76) - MS Ashdod										M53	1	-
Yaniv KATAN (27/01/81) - Maccabi Haifa										A	1	-
Dedi BEN DAYAN (27/11/78) - Maccabi Tel-Aviv										s79	1	-
Pini BALILI (18/06/79) - Hapoel Tel-Aviv										s79	1	1

showing in Europe, knocking Besiktas out of the Champions' League and then beating Ajax 1-0 in the Amsterdam ArenA in the UEFA Cup, but at home they were a pale shadow of their former selves. New signings Offer Shitrit and Nir Sivilia flopped and left, and with president Robi Shapira refusing to spend any more money, the club dropped to sixth place, with coach Eli Gutman departing after three years.

Maccabi Tel-Aviv also had a poor season in the league, with coach Avraham Grant coming in for some terrible criticism from the Maccabi fans. The team were up against it from the start after being handed a four-point penalty following the revelation that one of their players, Kfir Edry, had tested positive for doping. He was banned for six games, while the club's fitness coach was suspended for a whole year.

Maccabi Tel-Aviv appointed Shlomo Sharf as their new coach for the 2000/01 season. He had ended his eight-year spell in charge of the Israeli national team the previous November following the 8-0 rout by Denmark in the Euro 2000 play-offs. The humiliation of the result was bad enough - Israel, after all, had gone into the first leg in the Ramat-Gan with genuine aspirations of reaching their first major finals in 30 years - but even the 0-5 defeat in their

EUROPEAN CUPS 99/00

CHAMPIONS' CUP
● **HAPOEL HAIFA**
Preliminary round 2 BESIKTAS (TUR)
A 1-1 Rosso (76)
 Aouate; Ben Shimon, Halfon, Shelach, Talker, Amsalem; Zeytuni, Ulyanov, Milanko (Ben Margi 87); Rosso, Sivilia (Turgeman 61).
H 0-0
 Auat; Ben Shimon, Shelach, Halfon, Talker, Amsalem; Zeytuni (Ben Margi 77), Ulyanov, Milanko; Rosso, Sivilia (Turgeman 59; Nissim 90).

Qualifying round VALENCIA CF (ESP)
H 0-2
 Auat; Talker, Ben Shimon, Shelach, Halfon, Amsalem; Zeytuni, Ulyanov, Milanko (Nissim 70), Rosso; Sivilia (Turgeman 71).
A 0-2
 Auat; Talker, Shelach, Halfon, Azoulay (Ben Margi 67), Amsalem; Ulyanov, Milanko, Rosso; Turgeman (Leibovitz 73), Sivilia (Nissim 57).

UEFA CUP
● **HAPOEL HAIFA**
1st round CLUB BRUGGE KV (BEL)
H 3-1 Turgeman (18, 32), Sivilia (44)
 Auat; Talker, Halfon, Shelach, Amsalem; Zeytuni, Atar (Azoulay 73), Milanko, Rosso; Turgeman (Ben Magri 77), Sivilia (Nissim 57).
A 2-4 Rosso (18), Turgeman (78)
 Auat; Talker, Halfon, Shelach, Amsalem; Zeytuni (Atar 55), Ulyanov, Milanko, Rosso; Turgeman (Azoulay 81), Sivilia (Nissim 68).

2nd round AJAX (HOL)
H 0-3
 Auat; Talker (Azoulay 72), Halfon, Shelach, Amsalem; Zeytuni, Milanko, Atar (Ben Shimon 60), Rosso; Turgeman, Nissim (Sivilia 70).
A 1-0 Rosso (58p)
 Auat; Talker, Ben Shimon, Halfon, Shelach, Amsalem; Ulyanov, Milanko, Rosso, Nissim (Zeytuni 73); Turgeman.

● **HAPOEL TEL-AVIV**
Qualifying round FK YEREVAN (ARM)
A 2-0 Harazi (55, 58)
 Elimelech; Bachar, Gershon, Ohaion, Antebi; Rupnik, Pisont, Racunica (Tikva 72), Ben Ami, Toema (Cimerotic 59); Harazi (Udi 77).
H 2-1 Pisont (82), Antebi (90)
 Elimelech; Bachar, Gershon, Ohaion, Antebi; Toema (Cimerotic 63), Pisont, Udi, Tikva, Racunica (Hilel 52); Harazi (Balili 76).

1st round CELTIC (SCO)
A 0-2
 Elimelech; Bachar, Gershon, Ohaion, Antebi; Rupnik, Pisont, Udi, Toema (Cohen 71), Cimerotic; Harazi (Tikva 53).
H 0-1
 Elimelech; Cohen (Baleli 80), Gershon, Ohaion, Antebi; Rupnik, Bachar (Elkayam 73), Racunica, Pisont, Toema (Harazi 46); Cimerotic.

● **MACCABI TEL-AVIV**
Qualifying round ZALGIRIS KAUNAS (LIT)
H 3-1 Kubica (13, 33), Bassis (69)
 Ubarov; Halfon, Emenalo, Brumer, Ben Dayan; Kosolapov, Wedzynski, Edri (Haim 79; Offir 90), Tzarfati (Luz 73); Bassis, Kubica.
A 1-2 Bassis (86)
 Ubarov; Offir (Halfon 56), Brumer, Emenalo, Ben Dayan; Kosolapov, Tzarfati, Wedzynski (Luz 64), Edri (Haim 70); Bassis, Kubica.

1st round RC LENS (FRA)
H 2-2 Kubica (44), Ben Dayan (85)
 Shtrauber; Halfon, Brumer, Balbul, Ben Dayan; Kosolapov, Wedzynski, Luz (Tzarfati 73), Edri, Bassis (Popov 83); Kubica.
A 1-2 Bassis (24)
 Shtrauber; Halfon, Brumer, Balbul, Emenalo (Popov 83); Ben Dayan, Kosolapov, Wedzynski (Luz 86), Edri; Bassis, Kubica.

PLAYER OF THE SEASON

SHAVIT ELIMELECH
Billed as the Footballer of the Year in just about every Israeli sports publication, Hapoel Tel-Aviv goalkeeper Shavit Elimelech earned the commendations thanks to his season-long excellence, which peaked when he saved four penalty-kicks in Hapoel's Cup final victory over Beitar Jerusalem. The 29-year-old 'keeper was the player most responsible for his club's excellent defensive record - just 28 goals conceded in the marathon 39-match Premier League campaign. Formerly with city rivals Maccabi Tel-Aviv, Elimelech had a spell with Hapoel Irony Rishon Lezion before joining Hapoel in 1998. He won his second international cap in the second leg of the Euro 2000 play-off against Denmark but was surprisingly snubbed by new national team coach Richard Møller-Nielsen.

home stadium was relegated to secondary importance by the shock revelations that emerged in one Israeli newspaper on the morning of the second leg in Copenhagen.

A story in "Maariv" reported that several Israeli players had spent the night before the first match getting drunk in the company of prostitutes. This caused a national scandal and became front-page news in every paper for days afterwards. The players denied any involvement, but, even so, the FA launched two separate investigations. One of them failed to provide evidence of any wrongdoing while the other, without mentioning names, revealed that four players had indeed been seen with call-girls but not on the night before the match, as had originally been reported.

The nation demanded the naming and shaming of the four guilty players but the FA decided to close ranks and

INTERNATIONAL HONOURS

World Cup Finals appearances: 1970

DOMESTIC CUP 99/00

1/16 FINALS
MS Ashdod 0, Maccabi Petach-Tikva 2
Beitar Jerusalem 2, Hapoel Jerusalem 0
Hapoel Haifa 2, Hapoel Irony Rishon Lezion 0
Hapoel Ashkelon 1, Maccabi Ashkelon 0
Hapoel Kfar-Saba 2, Irony Ramat Hasharon 0
Irony Dimona 0, Maccabi Netanya 3
Hapoel Beit Sh'an 1, Maccabi Herzliya 2
Zafririm Holon 1, Hakoach Ramat-Gan 0
Hapoel Nazeret Ilit 0, Maccabi Kfar-Kana 2
Maccabi Ahi Nazeret 2, Hapoel Ramat-Gan 0
Beitar Tel-Aviv 1, Hapoel Sachnin 1
(aet; 4-2 on pens.)
Hapoel Beer Sheva 3, Maccabi Kiriat-Gat 1
Hapoel Petach-Tikva 2, Maccabi Haifa 2
(aet; 2-3 on pens.)
Beitar Beer Sheva 1, Bnei Yehuda 0
Maccabi Aco 1, Hapoel Tel-Aviv 2
Hapoel Hod Hasharon 0, Maccabi Tel-Aviv 7

1/8 FINALS
Hapoel Tel-Aviv 2, Maccabi Tel-Aviv 0
Hapoel Haifa 2, Maccabi Haifa 2 (aet; 5-6 on pens.)
Beitar Tel-Aviv 2, Maccabi Ahi Nazeret 1
Maccabi Netanya 3, Maccabi Herzliya 0
Maccabi Kfar-Kana 1, Hapoel Kfar-Saba 3
Maccabi Petach-Tikva 2, Zafririm Holon 1
Hapoel Ashkelon 1, Hapoel Beer Sheva 2
Beitar Beer Sheva 1, Beitar Jerusalem 1
(aet; 6-7 on pens.)

QUARTER-FINALS
Hapoel Beer Sheva 0, Hapoel Tel-Aviv 2
Hapoel Kfar-Saba 1, Maccabi Petach-Tikva 1
(aet; 3-2 on pens.)
Maccabi Netanya 3, Beitar Jerusalem 3
(aet; 8-9 on pens.)
Maccabi Haifa 4, Beitar Tel-Aviv 0

SEMI-FINALS
Beitar Jerusalem 3 (Hamar 14, Mizrahi 41,
Paço 57), Hapoel Kfar-Saba 2 (Emola 78, 83)
Maccabi Haifa 0, Hapoel Tel-Aviv 0
(aet; 1-3 on pens.)

FINAL
17/05/2000, Tel-Aviv
HAPOEL TEL-AVIV 2 Racunica (86), Toema (114)
BEITAR JERUSALEM 2 Paço (90, 117)
(aet; 4-2 on pens.)
referee - Levi
HAPOEL TEL-AVIV - Elimelech; Bachar, Gershon, Cohen
(Tikva 101), Antebi; Onyshchenko, Ben Ami,
Racunica, Affek (Ohaion 88), Toema; Balili
(Volnerman 91).
BEITAR JERUSALEM - Korenfain; Deree G., Tretyak,
Cahila (Peretz 117), Ganon; Deree R., Abuksis,
Sándor, Hamar; Sivilia (Paço 70), Mizrahi.

in the end nobody was found guilty or publicly exposed. The players' only obligation was to sign a public apology declaring that they were sorry and promised to behave in a more dignified manner in the future. Everybody signed except for captain Tal Banin, who refused, claiming that to do so would prejudice his innocence.

When, three months later, the Israeli players reconvened, they had a new coach, Richard Møller-Nielsen. The former Denmark and Finland manager got off to a great start with a 4-1 win against Russia but after defeats in the Czech Republic and Hungary he became the target of

some strong criticism, with the players and press alike accusing him of favouring the long-ball game to the detriment of the team's more natural short-passing style. Some insiders even claimed that the new man's preferences had provoked a dressing-room revolt - not the best way for the team to prepare for the forthcoming World Cup qualifying campaign.

PROMOTED CLUB 99/00

SECOND DIVISION FINAL TABLE

		Pd	W	D	L	F	A	Pt	GD
1	**Zafririm Holon**	36	19	9	8	57	33	66	24
2	Maccabi Kiriat-Gat	36	18	8	10	52	28	62	24
3	Maccabi Ako	36	17	8	11	58	46	59	12
4	Bnei Sachnin	36	13	11	12	51	49	50	2
5	Beitar Beer Sheva	36	14	6	16	39	43	48	-4
6	Hakoah Ramat-Gan	36	13	7	16	54	61	46	-7
7	Hapoel Beer Sheva	36	11	12	13	38	35	44	3
8	Hapoel Beit Sh'an	36	11	9	16	45	59	42	-14
9	Maccabi Ahi Nazeret	36	10	11	15	41	56	41	-15
10	Hapoel Ashkelon	36	9	9	18	32	57	34	-25

N.B. Hapoel Beer Sheva - 1 point deducted
     Hapoel Ashkelon - 2 points deducted

CLUB DIRECTORY
Zafririm Holon
Halochamim St. 1
P.O. Box 146
Holon 58101
tel - (03) 5059926
fax - (03) 5038666
Year of Formation - 1972
Chairman - Shtern Haluba
Secretary - Toby Malach
Coach - Guy Levi (00/01 - Nir Levin)
Stadium - Zafririm (3,500)

MS ASHDOD

CLUB DIRECTORY

MS Ashdod
Ester H'Malka St. 5
PO Box 3536
Ashdod 77130
tel - (08) 8643434
fax - (08) 8643434
website - http://surf.to/ashdod
Year of Formation - 1999
Chairman - Gilad Trodler
Secretary - Idan Brolfan
Coach - Nissim Bachar; Miro Ben Shimon
Stadium - Municipal (7,980)

APPEARANCES 99/00

		P	Ap	(s)	Gls
Asher ALFASI	M	5		(6)	
Eyal ALMOSNINO	M	29			1
Sharon AMAR	M	3		(2)	1
Yaniv BEN ISHAY	G	3		(1)	
Ilan BOUARON	D	12			1
Miro COHEN	D	20			
Baruch DAGO	M	36			9
Amir ELKARIF	D	25		(2)	
Hanan FADIDA	M	3		(23)	2
Gal FIBACH	D	28		(5)	
Alon HAZAN	M	31		(2)	9
Gadi HAZUT	D	11			
Juraj KAKAS (SVK)	G	36			
Valeriy KOROLENCHUK (UKR)	A	3		(6)	1
Miroslav NEMEC (SVK)	A	13		(3)	4
Elek NYILAS (HUN)	M	35		(2)	7
Yossi OFFIR	M	8		(8)	
Alan OSAMO (CMR)	M	3		(2)	1
Adir SHARABI	M	19		(8)	2
Yair SIMHON	A			(2)	
Mico SMILJANIC (YUG)	D	38			
Nir SOHER	D	24		(7)	
Main SVETOZAY (YUG)	A	11		(1)	2
Avi TADESA	M	1			1
Adir TUBUL	D	8		(6)	
Shahar ZEITUN	D			(3)	
Igal ZRIHAN	A	23		(12)	7

LEAGUE RESULTS 1999/2000

14/08/99	Maccabi Netanya	A	6-0	Zrihan, Osamo, Hazan (p), Dago, Nyilas 2
20/08/99	Hapoel Irony Rishon Lezion	A	1-1	Hazan (p)
30/08/99	Maccabi Tel-Aviv	H	1-0	Nyilas
21/09/99	Hapoel Haifa	A	0-3	
25/09/99	Beitar Jerusalem	H	1-1	Sharabi
02/10/99	Hapoel Irony Rishon Lezion	A	0-0	
16/10/99	Hapoel Petach-Tikva	H	0-2	
23/10/99	Bnei Yehuda	A	1-1	Korolenchuk
01/11/99	Hapoel Tel-Aviv	H	1-2	Zrihan
06/11/99	Maccabi Haifa	A	0-0	
20/11/99	Maccabi Herzliya	A	1-1	Fadida
27/11/99	Maccabi Petach-Tikva	H	0-1	
04/12/99	Maccabi Netanya	H	0-2	
07/12/99	Hapoel Jerusalem	H	3-0	Nyilas, Sharabi, Amar
11/12/99	Hapoel Kfar-Saba	H	3-2	Hazan (p), Nemec, Nyilas (p)
18/12/99	Maccabi Tel-Aviv	A	2-1	Nemec, Dago
25/12/99	Hapoel Haifa	H	0-0	
01/01/00	Beitar Jerusalem	A	1-3	Hazan (p)
08/01/00	Hapoel Irony Rishon Lezion	H	4-2	Hazan, Nemec, Dago, Fadida
15/01/00	Hapoel Petach-Tikva	A	2-4	Hazan (p), Almosnino
22/01/00	Bnei Yehuda	H	1-0	Zrihan
29/01/00	Hapoel Tel-Aviv	A	2-4	Nemec, Zrihan
05/02/00	Maccabi Haifa	H	0-0	
12/02/00	Hapoel Jerusalem	A	1-0	Hazan
19/02/00	Maccabi Herzliya	H	0-1	
26/02/00	Maccabi Petach-Tikva	A	1-3	Zrihan
04/03/00	Maccabi Tel-Aviv	H	2-4	Dago 2
11/03/00	Hapoel Irony Rishon Lezion	A	2-0	Dago 2
18/03/00	Hapoel Kfar-Saba	H	1-1	Hazan (p)
25/03/00	Bnei Yehuda	A	1-0	Hazan (p)
01/04/00	Maccabi Herzliya	H	1-0	Zrihan
10/04/00	Maccabi Netanya	A	1-3	Nyilas
15/04/00	Hapoel Tel-Aviv	H	0-0	
22/04/00	Maccabi Haifa	A	0-2	
29/04/00	Hapoel Petach-Tikva	H	2-2	Zrihan, Svetozar
06/05/00	Beitar Jerusalem	A	1-1	Dago
13/05/00	Maccabi Petach-Tikva	H	3-2	Nyilas, Dago, Bouaron
20/05/00	Hapoel Haifa	A	0-0	
27/05/00	Hapoel Jerusalem	H	2-0	Svetozar, Tadesa

BEITAR JERUSALEM

CLUB DIRECTORY

Beitar Jerusalem
Even Shmoel St. 13/3, Jerusalem 93715
tel - (02) 867771/385444
fax - (02) 323117
website - http://beitar-jerusalem.org.il
Year of Formation - 1939
Chairman - Moshe Dadash
Secretary - Avraham Levi
Coach - Eli Ohana (00/01 - Eli Gutman)
Stadium - "Teddi" Malcha (21,000)

MAJOR HONOURS
League Championship - (4)
1987, 1993, 1997, 1998.
Domestic Cup - (5)
1976, 1979, 1985, 1986, 1989.

APPEARANCES 99/00

	P	Ap	(s)	Gls
Alon ABRAMOVICH	D	1		
Yossi ABUKSIS	M	32		6
Rehuven ATAR	M	14	(2)	5
Tommer AZOULAY	M	1		
Ehud CAHILA	D	32	(1)	
Golan DEREE	D	31	(6)	
Raanan DEREE	D	20	(9)	1
Asi DOMB	D	21	(7)	3
Kobi GANON	D	27	(3)	2
Guy GRIF	G	1		
Matti HAJAJ	M		(2)	
István HAMAR (HUN)	M	36	(2)	6
Itzhak KORENFAIN	G	38		
Shmuel LEVI	D	10	(4)	1
Alon MIZRAHI	A	17	(4)	9
Eitan MIZRAHI	M		(2)	
Victor PAÇO (ALB)	A	30	(9)	13
Eli PERATZ	D		(9)	
David PERETZ	D	2	(4)	
Danut PERJA (ROM)	D	21	(5)	
Nir REICHMAN	M		(1)	
Tamás SÁNDOR (HUN)	M	33	(2)	6
Offer SHITRIT	A	4	(2)	1
Ronen SHWAIG	A		(2)	
Haim SILVAS	M	1	(1)	
Nir SIVILIA	A	14	(11)	4
Jan TELESNIKOV	M	1		
Valentin THEODORIKA	M		(1)	
Serhiy TRETYAK (UKR)	D	39		
Elad YAACOBI	A	3	(6)	1
Tzion ZAKEN	M		(1)	

LEAGUE RESULTS 1999/2000

14/08/99	Hapoel Jerusalem	A	2-0	og (Saric), Paço
21/08/99	Maccabi Herzliya	H	1-1	Paço
28/08/99	Maccabi Petach-Tikva	A	0-3	
18/09/99	Maccabi Netanya	H	4-2	Sándor, Deree G., Shitrit, Domb
25/09/99	MS Ashdod	A	1-1	Yaacobi
04/10/99	Maccabi Tel-Aviv	H	0-1	
16/10/99	Hapoel Haifa	A	1-1	Abuksis (p)
22/10/99	Hapoel Kfar-Saba	A	2-1	Paço, Sándor
29/10/99	Hapoel Irony Rishon Lezion	H	2-0	Levi, Paço
06/11/99	Hapoel Petach-Tikva	A	0-3	
22/11/99	Hapoel Tel-Aviv	A	1-4	Atar
27/11/99	Maccabi Haifa	H	1-1	Domb
04/12/99	Hapoel Jerusalem	H	2-0	Hamar, Paço
07/12/99	Bnei Yehuda	H	1-1	Abuksis
11/12/99	Maccabi Herzliya	A	2-1	Ganon, Atar
18/12/99	Maccabi Petach-Tikva	H	3-1	Sándor, Domb, Atar
25/12/99	Maccabi Netanya	A	3-2	Paço, Sándor, Atar
01/01/00	MS Ashdod	H	3-1	Paço 2, Hamar
08/01/00	Maccabi Tel-Aviv	A	3-1	Hamar 2, Abuksis
15/01/00	Hapoel Haifa	H	3-3	Paço 2, Atar
22/01/00	Hapoel Kfar-Saba	H	1-1	Mizrahi A.
29/01/00	Hapoel Irony Rishon Lezion	A	4-1	Mizrahi A., og (Daouda), Sándor, Hamar
05/02/00	Hapoel Petach-Tikva	H	1-1	Abuksis (p)
12/02/00	Bnei Yehuda	A	1-2	og (Shwager)
21/02/00	Hapoel Tel-Aviv	H	2-0	Sándor, Sivilia
28/02/00	Maccabi Haifa	A	2-0	Abuksis (p), Paço
06/03/00	Bnei Yehuda	H	2-1	Ganon, Sivilia
11/03/00	Maccabi Herzliya	A	0-0	
18/03/00	Maccabi Netanya	H	2-3	Abuksis (p), Mizrahi A.
25/03/00	Hapoel Tel-Aviv	A	1-2	Sivilia
01/04/00	Maccabi Haifa	H	3-1	Mizrahi A. 3
08/04/00	Hapoel Petach-Tikva	A	1-2	Sivilia
15/04/00	Hapoel Jerusalem	H	1-1	Mizrahi A.
22/04/00	Maccabi Petach-Tikva	H	1-1	Paço
29/04/00	Beitar Jerusalem	A	0-0	
06/05/00	MS Ashdod	H	1-1	Mizrahi A.
13/05/00	Maccabi Tel-Aviv	A	1-4	Hamar
20/05/00	Hapoel Irony Rishon Lezion	H	1-4	Paço
27/05/00	Hapoel Kfar-Saba	A	1-1	Mizrahi A. (p)

BNEI YEHUDA

CLUB DIRECTORY

Bnei Yehuda
Kabir St. 10, Shchonat Htikva
PO Box 19069, Tel-Aviv 61190
tel - (03) 395444 / fax - (03) 5377877
website - http://members.iol.co.it/maor
Year of Formation - 1935
Chairman - Haim Barzilay
Secretary - Manache Isasharov
Manager - Giora Shpigel
Coach - Giora Shpigel; Yehushua Faygenbaum
(00/01 - Eli Ohana)
Stadium - Shchonat Htikva (8,000)

MAJOR HONOURS
League Championship - (1) 1990.
Domestic Cup - (2) 1968, 1981.

APPEARANCES 99/00

	P	Ap	(s)	Gls
Yossi ABUKSIS	M	1	(1)	
Guy ALFIA	D	2	(4)	
Rotem ASSRAF	M	3		
Yaron AVIHAIL	D	34	(1)	
Dan BARKOLIN	M	3	(1)	
Miroslav BICENIC (CRO)	M	10	(3)	
Yaniv CHICHIAN	M	8	(8)	1
Franck DIYA (FRA)	D	1	(1)	
Ronen FAYGENBAUM	D	22		
Jean-Betis FERRAND (FRA)	D	9	(2)	
Gal GEVA	M	2	(4)	
Steve GURI (FRA)	A	11	(3)	4
Oz HADARI	D	2	(1)	
Shay HESS	G	32		
Beni KOZOSHVILI	D	31	(2)	
Mario KRALJ (CRO)	M	38		
Offer LEVI	D	24	(1)	
Dudi LIBERMAN	M	17	(18)	1
Yossi MADAR	M	27	(5)	6
Hanoch MERARO	M	2	(4)	
Sahar MIZRAHI	M	18	(15)	2
Sergei NEIMAN (RUS)	D	3	(1)	
Kobi REFUA	A	38		17
Motti SASON	M	25	(5)	
Hezi SHIRAZI	A	15	(10)	5
Ilan SHWAGER	M	20	(2)	
Yair SIMHON	A	13	(4)	1
Aharon SITON	M	9	(6)	
Oren SMAMA	M	1		
Nduka UGABADE (NIG)	M	1	(4)	
Yaniv WHABA	G	7		

LEAGUE RESULTS 1999/2000

14/08/99	Hapoel Kfar-Saba	H	1-1	Chichian
23/08/99	Hapoel Tel-Aviv	H	2-1	Madar, Mizrahi
28/08/99	Maccabi Haifa	A	1-3	Refua
18/09/99	Hapoel Jerusalem	H	2-0	Refua, Liberman
25/09/99	Maccabi Herzliya	A	0-4	
02/10/99	Maccabi Petach-Tikva	H	0-2	
15/10/99	Maccabi Netanya	A	1-1	Madar
23/10/99	MS Ashdod	H	1-1	Refua
30/10/99	Maccabi Tel-Aviv	A	1-3	Mizrahi
08/11/99	Hapoel Haifa	H	0-2	
20/11/99	Hapoel Irony Rishon Lezion	H	1-3	Madar (p)
27/11/99	Hapoel Petach-Tikva	A	0-4	
04/12/99	Hapoel Kfar-Saba	A	1-4	Refua
07/12/99	Beitar Jerusalem	A	1-1	Refua
11/12/99	Hapoel Tel-Aviv	A	0-1	
20/12/99	Maccabi Haifa	H	0-2	
25/12/99	Hapoel Jerusalem	A	1-0	Refua
01/01/00	Maccabi Herzliya	H	3-1	Refua 3
08/01/00	Maccabi Petach-Tikva	A	1-1	Simhon
15/01/00	Maccabi Netanya	H	1-1	Madar
22/01/00	MS Ashdod	A	0-1	
29/01/00	Maccabi Tel-Aviv	H	0-0	
04/02/00	Hapoel Haifa	A	1-1	Guri
12/02/00	Beitar Jerusalem	H	2-1	Guri 2
19/02/00	Hapoel Irony Rishon Lezion	A	0-1	
26/02/00	Hapoel Petach-Tikva	H	2-4	Guri, Refua
06/03/00	Beitar Jerusalem	A	1-2	Madar
11/03/00	Maccabi Petach-Tikva	H	1-0	Refua
20/03/00	Hapoel Haifa	A	0-5	
25/03/00	MS Ashdod	H	0-1	
01/04/00	Maccabi Tel-Aviv	A	2-1	Refua 2
08/04/00	Hapoel Irony Rishon Lezion	H	1-1	Refua
15/04/00	Hapoel Kfar-Saba	A	1-1	Refua
22/04/00	Hapoel Jerusalem	A	2-2	Shirazi 2
29/04/00	Maccabi Herzliya	H	1-0	Refua
06/05/00	Maccabi Netanya	A	1-4	Refua
13/05/00	Hapoel Tel-Aviv	H	1-1	Shirazi
20/05/00	Maccabi Haifa	A	1-1	Madar
27/05/00	Hapoel Petach-Tikva	H	2-1	Shirazi 2

HAPOEL HAIFA

CLUB DIRECTORY

Hapoel Haifa
Hatzvi Blvd. 29
Merkaz Carmel
Haifa 35355
tel - (04) 8361177
fax - (04) 8373881
website - http://hapoel-haifa.org.il
Year of Formation - 1921
Chairman - Robi Shapira
Secretary - Avi Kaufman
Coach - Eli Gutman
Stadium - Kiriat Eliezer (17,000)

MAJOR HONOURS
League Championship - (1) 1999.
Domestic Cup - (3) 1963, 1966, 1974.

APPEARANCES 99/00

	P	Ap	(s)	Gls
David AMSALEM	D	35	(1)	2
Rehuven ATAR	M	4	(1)	2
Dudu AUAT	G	39		
Rami AZIZ	D	9	(11)	
Ami AZOULAY	D	8	(2)	
Hay BEN LULU	D	1		
Meir BEN MARGI	M	4	(15)	
Ran BEN SHIMON	D	23	(4)	3
Yossi DORA	D	1		
Alon HALFON	D	33	(1)	2
Emil KASTIEL	M	9	(3)	
Kfir LEIBOVIC	M	5	(10)	
Goran MILANKO (BOS)	M	28	(4)	3
Oren NISSIM	A	12	(21)	2
Giovanni ROSSO (CRO)	M	35	(1)	8
Amir SHELACH	D	26	(1)	
Offer SHITRIT	A	8	(4)	2
Nir SIVILIA	A	6	(2)	2
Ilan TAL	M	8	(5)	4
Offer TALKER	D	36		7
Eyal TARTASKY	M	4	(10)	
Tzahi TUBI	A		(3)	
Amir TURGEMAN	A	36		14
Dmitriy ULYANOV (RUS)	M	25	(3)	1
Eyal WOLF	M		(3)	
Oren ZEYTUNI	M	34	(2)	1

LEAGUE RESULTS 1999/2000

14/08/99	Maccabi Herzliya	A	0-0	
21/08/99	Maccabi Petach-Tikva	H	1-0	Nissim
29/08/99	Maccabi Netanya	A	2-1	Talker, Sivilia
21/09/99	MS Ashdod	H	3-0	Atar, Milanko, Nissim
25/09/99	Maccabi Tel-Aviv	A	0-0	
04/10/99	Hapoel Kfar-Saba	A	3-0	Turgeman, Sivilia (p), Rosso
16/10/99	Beitar Jerusalem	H	1-1	Atar
24/10/99	Hapoel Irony Rishon Lezion	A	0-0	
30/10/99	Hapoel Petach-Tikva	H	2-2	Turgeman 2
08/11/99	Bnei Yehuda	A	2-0	Milanko, Talker
22/11/99	Maccabi Haifa	A	2-3	Turgeman (p), Milanko
27/11/99	Hapoel Jerusalem	H	3-2	Turgeman 2, Amsalem
04/12/99	Maccabi Herzliya	H	4-0	Rosso (p), Shitrit, Zeytuni, Turgeman
07/12/99	Hapoel Tel-Aviv	H	0-0	
11/12/99	Maccabi Petach-Tikva	A	1-2	Ben Shimon
18/12/99	Maccabi Netanya	H	2-1	Turgeman 2
25/12/99	MS Ashdod	A	0-0	
03/01/00	Maccabi Tel-Aviv	H	2-4	Rosso (p), Turgeman
08/01/00	Hapoel Kfar-Saba	H	3-0	Turgeman, Talker, Shitrit
15/01/00	Beitar Jerusalem	A	3-3	Halfon, Rosso 2
22/01/00	Hapoel Irony Rishon Lezion	H	2-0	Ben Shimon, Turgeman
29/01/00	Hapoel Petach-Tikva	A	2-0	Talker 2
04/02/00	Bnei Yehuda	H	1-1	Ben Shimon
12/02/00	Hapoel Tel-Aviv	A	0-1	
19/02/00	Maccabi Haifa	H	0-0	
26/02/00	Hapoel Jerusalem	A	1-1	Halfon
02/03/00	Hapoel Irony Rishon Lezion	H	1-1	Turgeman
11/03/00	Hapoel Kfar-Saba	A	0-0	
20/03/00	Bnei Yehuda	H	5-0	Amsalem, Tal, Ulyanov, Rosso, Talker
25/03/00	Maccabi Herzliya	A	1-1	Tal
01/04/00	Maccabi Netanya	H	1-1	Rosso
08/04/00	Hapoel Tel-Aviv	A	1-3	Rosso
15/04/00	Maccabi Haifa	H	0-4	
22/04/00	Hapoel Petach-Tikva	A	1-3	Turgeman
29/04/00	Beitar Jerusalem	H	0-0	
06/05/00	Maccabi Petach-Tikva	A	0-0	
13/05/00	Hapoel Jerusalem	H	3-0	Tal 2, Talker
20/05/00	MS Ashdod	H	0-0	
27/05/00	Maccabi Tel-Aviv	A	0-1	

HAPOEL IRONY RISHON LEZION

CLUB DIRECTORY

Hapoel Irony Rishon Lezion
Perets St. 4
Rishon-Lezion 75209
tel - (03) 9641919
fax - (03) 9666760
Year of Formation - 1940
Chairman - Lior Shachar
Coach - Elisha Levi; Rami Levi
Stadium - New Municipal (7,000)

APPEARANCES 99/00

	P	Ap	(s)	Gls
Elisha ABAS	D	2	(1)	
Dani ALBERT	D	38		1
Shlomi BEN HAMO	G	2		
Shlomi BEN HAMO	M		(1)	
Alon BRUMER	M	14	(3)	2
Possini DAOUDA (NIG)	D	31	(1)	
Arik HANGALI	M		(2)	
Rami GLAM	D	14	(5)	
Udi KABUDI	A	33	(4)	5
Nissan KAPETA	A	39		13
Itay KOREN	D	11		
Nenad MARKICEVIC (CRO)	M	14	(6)	1
Gábor MÁRTON (HUN)	M	11	(2)	2
Sharon MARZIANO	M	23	(4)	
Amir NUSBAUM	M	11	(16)	2
Roni OHANA	A		(2)	
Patrick OVIE (NIG)	D	35		1
Avi PITUSI	M	33	(1)	4
Orn ROTEM	D	22	(2)	
Moshe SABAG	A	26	(8)	3
Assaf SHEMESH	D	1	(2)	
Nir SHIKVA	A	6	(19)	3
Sagie SHTRAUS	G	23		
Idan SHUM	M	20	(5)	1
Maor SINAI	D	1	(8)	
Gennadiy TUMILOVICH (BLS)	G	14		
Konstantin VOZNYUK (UKR)	A	5	(7)	2

LEAGUE RESULTS 1999/2000

14/08/99	Maccabi Haifa	A	1-4	Shikva
21/08/99	Hapoel Jerusalem	H	2-2	Shikva, Sabag
28/08/99	Maccabi Herzliya	A	0-0	
18/09/99	Maccabi Petach-Tikva	H	0-1	
24/09/99	Maccabi Netanya	A	4-2	Markicevic, Kapeta 3
02/10/99	MS Ashdod	H	0-0	
16/10/99	Maccabi Tel-Aviv	A	0-4	
24/10/99	Hapoel Haifa	H	0-0	
29/10/99	Beitar Jerusalem	A	0-2	
06/11/99	Hapoel Kfar-Saba	A	0-2	
20/11/99	Bnei Yehuda	A	3-1	Shum, Brumer 2
29/11/99	Hapoel Tel-Aviv	H	1-3	Albert
04/12/99	Maccabi Haifa	H	0-7	
07/12/99	Hapoel Petach-Tikva	H	1-1	Pitusi
11/12/99	Hapoel Jerusalem	A	1-1	Nusbaum
18/12/99	Maccabi Herzliya	H	3-1	Nusbaum, Kapeta, Sabag
28/12/99	Maccabi Petach-Tikva	A	0-0	
01/01/00	Maccabi Netanya	H	1-0	Sabag
08/01/00	MS Ashdod	A	2-4	Kapeta, Shikva
15/01/00	Maccabi Tel-Aviv	H	0-0	
22/01/00	Hapoel Haifa	A	0-2	
29/01/00	Beitar Jerusalem	H	1-4	Kabudi
05/02/00	Hapoel Kfar-Saba	H	2-2	og (Khokhov), Kapeta
12/02/00	Hapoel Petach-Tikva	A	0-1	
19/02/00	Bnei Yehuda	H	1-0	Kapeta
26/02/00	Hapoel Tel-Aviv	A	2-1	Kapeta, Márton
04/03/00	Hapoel Haifa	A	1-1	Ovie
11/03/00	MS Ashdod	H	0-2	
18/03/00	Maccabi Tel-Aviv	A	1-5	Kabudi (p)
25/03/00	Hapoel Jerusalem	A	1-3	Pitusi
01/04/00	Hapoel Kfar-Saba	H	2-1	Kapeta, Kabudi
08/04/00	Bnei Yehuda	A	1-1	Kabudi
15/04/00	Maccabi Herzliya	H	0-1	
22/04/00	Maccabi Netanya	A	2-2	Voznyuk, Kapeta
29/04/00	Hapoel Tel-Aviv	H	1-2	Kapeta
06/05/00	Maccabi Haifa	A	0-0	
13/05/00	Hapoel Petach-Tikva	H	2-1	Kapeta 2
20/05/00	Beitar Jerusalem	A	4-1	Pitusi 2, Kabudi, Márton
27/05/00	Maccabi Petach-Tikva	H	1-0	Voznyuk

HAPOEL JERUSALEM

CLUB DIRECTORY

Hapoel Jerusalem
Emek Refaym St. 64, Jerusalem 93142
tel - (02) 6511877
fax - (02) 5611881
Year of Formation - 1953
Chairman - Yossi Sassi
Secretary - Victor Yona
Manager - Mishel Dayan
Coach - Elias Levi
Stadium - "Teddi" Malcha (21,000)

MAJOR HONOURS
Domestic Cup - (1) 1973.

APPEARANCES 99/00

	P	Ap	(s)	Gls
Shadi ABU DIB	D	10	(2)	
Shay AHARON	A	23	(14)	7
Salman AMAR	D	31		
Eyal AVRAHAMI	M	19	(3)	1
Yaniv AVRAHAMI	M	1	(3)	
Dudu DAHAN	D	33	(2)	2
Shlomi DANINO	M	19	(2)	2
Shimi DAVIDIAN	D	28	(1)	
Oren DAYAN	M	2	(11)	1
Ran DZILOVSKY	M	3	(3)	
Offir EZU	M	13	(10)	1
Nir GAON	D	1	(2)	
Amir GOLA	M	22	(1)	
Golan HERMON	D	19	(2)	
Dudi HUDIDA	M	4	(3)	
Igoris KIRILOVAS (LIT)	M	25	(4)	1
Gil LEVI	M	6	(13)	
Hanan LEVI	D	2	(6)	1
Motti MENACHEM	A	34	(2)	5
Mario MESTROVIC (CRO)	M	13		
Vitaliy MINTENKO (UKR)	A	9	(1)	3
Motti MIZRAHI	G	2		
Alberto NEVADA (ARG)	M	7	(1)	1
Tomer NIRON	A	1		
Denys POTNYK (UKR)	D	16		
Nir REICHMAN	M	3	(6)	1
Senad REPUH (BOS)	A	14	(2)	
Dan ROMAN	M	1	(6)	
Mahmud SALMAN	M	2	(2)	
Aleksandar SARIC (YUG)	G	37		
Arik SASSON	D	3	(1)	1
Ronen SHWAIG	A	11	(4)	6
Yuriy SOLOVYENKO (UKR)	D	15		
SULTAN	M		(1)	

LEAGUE RESULTS 1999/2000

14/08/99	Beitar Jerusalem	H	0-2	
21/08/99	Hapoel Irony Rishon Lezion	A	2-2	Mintenko 2
28/08/99	Hapoel Petach-Tikva	H	0-1	
18/09/99	Bnei Yehuda	A	0-2	
24/09/99	Hapoel Tel-Aviv	H	0-1	
02/10/99	Maccabi Haifa	A	2-1	Sasson, Danino (p)
16/10/99	Hapoel Kfar-Saba	H	2-1	Mintenko, Aharon
22/10/99	Maccabi Herzliya	H	1-4	Aharon
30/10/99	Maccabi Petach-Tikva	A	2-0	Dahan, Dayan
06/11/99	Maccabi Netanya	H	1-3	Aharon
20/11/99	Maccabi Tel-Aviv	H	0-1	
27/11/99	Hapoel Haifa	A	2-3	Avrahami E., Kirilovas
04/12/99	Beitar Jerusalem	A	0-2	
07/12/99	MS Ashdod	A	0-3	
11/12/99	Hapoel Irony Rishon Lezion	H	1-1	Nevada
18/12/99	Hapoel Petach-Tikva	A	1-3	Aharon
25/12/99	Bnei Yehuda	H	0-1	
01/01/00	Hapoel Tel-Aviv	A	0-3	
10/01/00	Maccabi Haifa	H	1-3	Menachem
15/01/00	Hapoel Kfar-Saba	A	0-1	
21/01/00	Maccabi Herzliya	A	2-1	Menachem, Aharon
29/01/00	Maccabi Petach-Tikva	H	0-2	
05/02/00	Maccabi Netanya	A	1-2	Danino (p)
12/02/00	MS Ashdod	H	0-1	
19/02/00	Maccabi Tel-Aviv	A	1-1	Menachem
26/02/00	Hapoel Haifa	H	1-1	Menachem
04/03/00	Hapoel Tel-Aviv	A	0-3	
10/03/00	Maccabi Tel-Aviv	H	2-4	Menachem, Aharon
18/03/00	Maccabi Haifa	A	0-6	
25/03/00	Hapoel Irony Rishon Lezion	H	3-1	Reichman, Ezu, Shwaig
01/04/00	Hapoel Petach-Tikva	A	1-4	Shwaig
08/04/00	Hapoel Kfar-Saba	H	2-1	Shwaig 2
15/04/00	Beitar Jerusalem	A	1-1	Aharon
22/04/00	Bnei Yehuda	H	2-2	Dahan, Levi H.
29/04/00	Maccabi Petach-Tikva	A	1-3	Shwaig
06/05/00	Maccabi Herzliya	H	1-2	Shwaig
13/05/00	Hapoel Haifa	A	0-3	
20/05/00	Maccabi Netanya	H	0-4	
27/05/00	MS Ashdod	A	0-2	

HAPOEL KFAR-SABA

CLUB DIRECTORY

Hapoel Kfar-Saba
Ben Yehuda St. 102
PO Box 2156
Kfar-Saba
tel - (09) 7653307
fax - (09) 7676818
Year of Formation - 1928
Chairman - Eli Tabib
Secretary - Gabi Twilli
Coach - Eyal Lahman; Avi Cohen; Elisha Levi
Stadium - Irony Kfar-Saba (5,900)

MAJOR HONOURS
League Championship - (1) 1982.
Domestic Cup - (3) 1975, 1980, 1990.

APPEARANCES 99/00

	P	Ap	(s)	Gls
Yaniv ABERGIL	A	36	(3)	12
Remi ABU LABAN	M	1	(12)	2
Yossi ALFIA	M		(2)	
Tamir BEN HAIM	D	28	(3)	
BEACHA	M		(1)	
Oren COCHVI	M		(5)	
Eyal COHEN	M		(4)	
Shlomi DANINO	M	3	(7)	2
Giorgi DARASELIA (GEO)	A	38		8
Ibrahim DURO (BOS)	M	6	(5)	
Tomer ELIAHU	D	5	(1)	
Kobi GANON	D	3		
Patrick IMOLA (NIG)	D	7	(4)	3
Avigdor ITZHAK	M	20	(6)	
Mohamad KAHABA	D	20	(2)	
Jaroslav KENTOS (SVK)	D	26		1
Sergei KHOKHOV (RUS)	D	3		1
Offir KOPEL	M	30	(2)	1
Krisztián KVASZ (HUN)	M	1	(4)	
Alon MAYA	D	25		
MEIROVIC	D	1		
Tamir NETZER	D	13	(4)	
Ami ROZENBERG	G	1		
Natan SAKURI	D	22	(7)	
Avi SANDOR	M	4	(16)	
Gabi SAPIR	D	14	(2)	
Tomer SHEM TOV	D	19	(9)	
Shaul SMADGA	G	38		
József SOMOGYI (HUN)	M	32	(3)	2
Ohad TZOR	M	13	(8)	1
Ayegbeni YAKUBU (NIG)	A	20	(3)	6

LEAGUE RESULTS 1999/2000

Date	Opponent		Score	Scorers
14/08/99	Bnei Yehuda	A	1-1	Daraselia
20/08/99	MS Ashdod	H	1-1	Abergil
28/08/99	Hapoel Tel-Aviv	A	1-5	Abergil
21/09/99	Maccabi Tel-Aviv	H	0-3	
25/09/99	Maccabi Haifa	A	0-1	
04/10/99	Hapoel Haifa	H	0-3	
16/10/99	Hapoel Jerusalem	A	1-2	og (Salman)
22/10/99	Beitar Jerusalem	H	1-2	Abergil (p)
30/10/99	Maccabi Herzliya	A	2-0	Tzor, Abergil
06/11/99	Hapoel Irony Rishon Lezion	H	2-0	Kentos, Kopel
20/11/99	Hapoel Petach-Tikva	H	1-3	Yakubu
27/11/99	Maccabi Netanya	A	1-4	Abergil
04/12/99	Bnei Yehuda	H	4-1	Abergil 2, Daraselia, Abu Laban
07/12/99	Maccabi Petach-Tikva	A	2-3	Daraselia, Abu Laban
11/12/99	MS Ashdod	A	2-3	Yakubu, Daraselia
18/12/99	Hapoel Tel-Aviv	H	0-1	
25/12/99	Maccabi Tel-Aviv	A	1-0	Abergil
01/01/00	Maccabi Haifa	H	1-1	Yakubu
08/01/00	Hapoel Haifa	A	0-3	
15/01/00	Hapoel Jerusalem	H	1-0	Yakubu
22/01/00	Beitar Jerusalem	A	1-1	Daraselia
28/01/00	Maccabi Herzliya	H	0-0	
05/02/00	Hapoel Irony Rishon Lezion	A	2-2	Yakubu, Khokhov
11/02/00	Maccabi Petach-Tikva	H	2-2	Yakubu, Imola
19/02/00	Hapoel Petach-Tikva	A	1-2	Daraselia
25/02/00	Maccabi Netanya	H	0-0	
03/03/00	Maccabi Petach-Tikva	A	0-1	
11/03/00	Hapoel Haifa	H	0-0	
18/03/00	MS Ashdod	A	1-1	Imola
24/03/00	Maccabi Tel-Aviv	H	2-2	Imola, Daraselia
01/04/00	Hapoel Irony Rishon Lezion	A	1-2	Abergil
08/04/00	Hapoel Jerusalem	A	1-2	Abergil
15/04/00	Bnei Yehuda	H	1-1	Danino
22/04/00	Maccabi Herzliya	A	2-0	Danino, Somogyi
29/04/00	Maccabi Netanya	H	1-1	Daraselia
06/05/00	Hapoel Tel-Aviv	A	0-1	
13/05/00	Maccabi Haifa	H	1-0	Somogyi
20/05/00	Hapoel Petach-Tikva	A	1-0	Abergil (p)
27/05/00	Beitar Jerusalem	H	1-1	Abergil

HAPOEL PETACH-TIKVA

CLUB DIRECTORY

Hapoel Petach-Tikva
Gissin St. 9
PO Box 2108
Petach-Tikva 49120
tel - (03) 9218358
fax - (03) 9248353
Year of Formation - 1930
Chairman - Dani Levi
Secretary - Tamir Fridman
Coach - Nir Levin (00/01 - Eli Cohen)
Stadium - Petach-Tikva (12,250)

MAJOR HONOURS
League Championship - (6) 1955, 1959, 1960,
1961, 1962, 1963.
Domestic Cup - (2) 1957, 1992.

APPEARANCES 99/00

	P	Ap	(s)	Gls
Remi AAMAR	D	8	(5)	
Eli ABARBNEL	M	31		14
Eyal ABRAMOV	G		(1)	
Danijel BOGDAN (CRO)	D	38		
Ilan BUARON	D	17		
Ivan BULAT (CRO)	M	22	(7)	4
Rafi COHEN	G	39		
Miroslav DJOKIC (YUG)	A	4	(6)	
Dudu FADLON	D	6	(4)	
Krunoslav GREGORIC (CRO)	D	30		
Manor HASSAN	M	28	(4)	8
Yaniv HERMASH	D	6	(7)	
Idan HILEL	A	9	(21)	3
Motti KAKUN	A	11	(1)	7
Yaniv LUZON	M		(11)	1
Alon MAYA	D	2	(2)	
Jasmin MUJDZA (BOS)	D	11		
Borimir PERKOVIC (CRO)	M	37		12
Yossi ROZEN	M	13	(20)	3
Guy SHAMIR	M	29	(2)	5
Yair SIMHON	A	5	(1)	
Niv TAL	A	30	(9)	13
Adrian UNGUR (ROM)	A	3		2
Avi YEHIEL	D	27		
Michael ZANDBERG	M	23	(13)	3

LEAGUE RESULTS 1999/2000

15/08/99	Hapoel Petach-Tikva	A	0-2	
21/08/99	Maccabi Haifa	H	2-5	Abarbnel, Ungur
28/08/99	Hapoel Jerusalem	A	1-0	Ungur
18/09/99	Maccabi Herzliya	H	1-0	Abarbnel
25/09/99	Maccabi Petach-Tikva	A	2-1	Tal, Shamir
02/10/99	Maccabi Netanya	H	1-0	Bulat
16/10/99	MS Ashdod	A	2-0	Bulat 2
25/10/99	Maccabi Tel-Aviv	H	2-1	Perkovic 2
30/10/99	Hapoel Haifa	A	2-2	Tal, Hassan
06/11/99	Beitar Jerusalem	H	3-0	Abarbnel 2 (1p), Hilel
20/11/99	Hapoel Kfar-Saba	A	3-1	Shamir, Abarbnel, Perkovic
27/11/99	Bnei Yehuda	H	4-0	Abarbnel, Perkovic 2, Hassan
04/12/99	Hapoel Tel-Aviv	H	0-1	
07/12/99	Hapoel Irony Rishon Lezion	A	1-1	Tal
13/12/99	Maccabi Haifa	A	0-2	
18/12/99	Hapoel Jerusalem	H	3-1	Hilel, Perkovic 2
25/12/99	Maccabi Herzliya	A	3-1	og (Koratzky), Abarbnel 2
01/01/00	Maccabi Petach-Tikva	H	0-1	
08/01/00	Maccabi Netanya	A	2-1	Shamir, Perkovic
15/01/00	MS Ashdod	H	4-2	Hassan, Zandberg 2, Tal
22/01/00	Maccabi Tel-Aviv	A	1-0	Abarbnel
29/01/00	Hapoel Haifa	H	0-2	
07/02/00	Beitar Jerusalem	A	1-1	Perkovic
12/02/00	Hapoel Irony Rishon Lezion	H	1-0	Abarbnel (p)
19/02/00	Hapoel Kfar-Saba	H	2-1	Tal 2
26/02/00	Bnei Yehuda	A	4-2	Abarbnel 2 (1p), Hassan, Kakun
04/03/00	Maccabi Herzliya	H	8-1	Hassan, Kakun 2, Abarbnel, Zandberg, Tal, Perkovic, Shamir
11/03/00	Maccabi Netanya	A	4-2	Abarbnel, Rozen, Tal, Bulat
18/03/00	Hapoel Tel-Aviv	H	0-3	
27/03/00	Maccabi Haifa	A	1-4	Abarbnel (p)
01/04/00	Hapoel Jerusalem	H	4-1	Kakun 2 (1p), Tal, Rozen
08/04/00	Beitar Jerusalem	H	2-1	Hassan, Shamir
15/04/00	Maccabi Petach-Tikva	A	4-2	Tal 2, Perkovic, Kakun
22/04/00	Hapoel Haifa	H	3-1	Hassan, Hilel, Tal
29/04/00	MS Ashdod	A	2-2	Hassan, Tal
06/05/00	Maccabi Tel-Aviv	H	2-2	Rozen (p), Perkovic
13/05/00	Hapoel Irony Rishon Lezion	A	1-2	Luzon
20/05/00	Hapoel Kfar-Saba	H	0-1	
27/05/00	Bnei Yehuda	A	1-2	Kakun

HAPOEL TEL-AVIV

CLUB DIRECTORY

Hapoel Tel-Aviv
Ha'tchia St. 1
PO Box 8402
Tel-Aviv -Jaffa 61084
tel - (03) 6827711
fax - (03) 6827722
website - http://hapoelta.euro-ball.com
Year of Formation - 1919
Chairman - Moti Orenstein
Secretary - Arie Hershkovich
Coach - Dror Kashtan
Stadium - Bloomfield (17,500)

MAJOR HONOURS
League Championship - (13)
1934, 1935, 1936, 1938, 1940, 1943, 1957,
1966, 1969, 1981, 1986, 1988, 2000.
Domestic Cup - (9) 1928, 1934, 1937, 1938,
1940, 1960, 1972, 1999, 2000.

APPEARANCES 99/00

	P	Ap	(s)	Gls
Omri AFFEK	A	17	(6)	3
Igal ANTEBI	D	37	(1)	1
Ilan BACHAR	D	36	(1)	2
Pini BALILI	A	15	(16)	12
Eyal BEN AMI	D	2	(4)	
Sebastjan CIMEROTIC (SLO)	M	19	(10)	7
Israel COHEN	D	24	(6)	
Shavit ELIMELECH	G	37		
Edi ELKAYAM	D		(2)	
Shimon GERSHON	D	37		7
Ronen HARAZI	A	24	(3)	17
Yaacov HILEL	D	9	(12)	
Ziv KAVEDA	M	1	(3)	
Motti OHAION	D	21	(2)	1
Denys ONYSHCHENKO (UKR)	M	13		1
István PISONT (HUN)	M	36		6
Dean RACUNICA (CRO)	M	33	(4)	2
Nir RAHMIN	G	2		
Davor RUPNIK (CRO)	M	20	(8)	
Shalom TIKVA	M	1	(16)	1
Salim TOEMA	M	21	(10)	7
Kfir UDI	A	24	(3)	6
Aviv VOLNERMAN	A		(2)	

LEAGUE RESULTS 1999/2000

15/08/99	Hapoel Petach-Tikva	H	2-0	og (Bulat), Udi
23/08/99	Bnei Yehuda	A	1-2	Harazi
29/08/99	Hapoel Kfar-Saba	H	5-1	Cimerotic 2, Toema, Ohaion, Udi
18/09/99	Maccabi Haifa	H	0-0	
25/09/99	Hapoel Jerusalem	A	1-0	Udi
04/10/99	Maccabi Herzliya	H	4-0	Pisont, Harazi, Cimerotic, Gershon
16/10/99	Maccabi Petach-Tikva	A	5-1	Gershon 2 (2p), Harazi, Pisont, Balili
23/10/99	Maccabi Netanya	H	3-0	Bachar, Gershon, Harazi
01/11/99	MS Ashdod	A	2-1	Balili, og (Smiljanic)
08/11/99	Maccabi Tel-Aviv	H	1-1	Harazi
20/11/99	Beitar Jerusalem	H	4-1	Cimerotic 2, Gershon (p), Pisont
29/11/99	Hapoel Irony Rishon Lezion	A	3-1	Balili, Tikva, Cimerotic
04/12/99	Hapoel Petach-Tikva	A	1-0	Harazi
07/12/99	Hapoel Haifa	A	0-0	
11/12/99	Bnei Yehuda	H	1-0	Gershon
17/12/99	Hapoel Kfar-Saba	A	1-0	Antebi
27/12/99	Maccabi Haifa	A	0-1	
01/01/00	Hapoel Jerusalem	H	3-0	Harazi, Toema, Bachar
08/01/00	Maccabi Herzliya	A	5-0	Harazi 3, Toema, Udi
17/01/00	Maccabi Petach-Tikva	H	2-1	Harazi 2
22/01/00	Maccabi Netanya	A	5-2	og (Vranjes), Harazi 2, Toema, Cimerotic
29/01/00	MS Ashdod	H	4-2	Toema, Affek, Balili 2
07/02/00	Maccabi Tel-Aviv	A	0-2	
14/02/00	Hapoel Haifa	H	1-0	Pisont
21/02/00	Beitar Jerusalem	A	0-2	
26/02/00	Hapoel Irony Rishon Lezion	H	1-2	Harazi
04/03/00	Hapoel Jerusalem	H	3-0	Toema, Balili, Harazi
13/03/00	Maccabi Haifa	H	1-1	Onyshchenko
18/03/00	Hapoel Petach-Tikva	A	3-0	Udi, Affek, Balili
25/03/00	Beitar Jerusalem	H	2-1	Udi, Balili
01/04/00	Maccabi Petach-Tikva	A	0-1	
08/04/00	Hapoel Haifa	H	3-1	Harazi, Gershon (p), Racunica
15/04/00	MS Ashdod	A	0-0	
22/04/00	Maccabi Tel-Aviv	H	2-1	Pisont, Toema
29/04/00	Hapoel Irony Rishon Lezion	A	2-1	Balili 2
06/05/00	Hapoel Kfar-Saba	H	1-0	Balili
13/05/00	Bnei Yehuda	A	1-1	Affek
20/05/00	Hapoel Tel-Aviv	H	2-0	Racunica, Pisont
27/05/00	Maccabi Netanya	A	1-1	Balili

MACCABI HAIFA

CLUB DIRECTORY

Maccabi Haifa
Heinrich Heina St. 14
Haifa 34485
tel - (04) 8380620
fax - (04) 8371540
website - http://www.maccabi-haifa.nana.co.il
Year of Formation - 1919
Chairman - Ya'acov Shahar
Secretary - Lulu Yaron
Manager - Eli Cohen
Coach - Roni Levi (00/01 - Avraham Grant)
Stadium - Kiriat Eliezer (17,000)

MAJOR HONOURS
League Championship - (5)
1984, 1985, 1989, 1991, 1994.
Domestic Cup - (5)
1962, 1991, 1993, 1995, 1998.

APPEARANCES 99/00

		P	Ap	(s)	Gls
Rehuven ATAR	M	8	(5)		2
Arik BENADO	D	36			1
Yossi BENAYOUN	M	38	(1)		19
Jerzy BRZECZEK (POL)	M	34	(1)		9
Serghei CLESCENCO (MOL)	A	38			21
Rafi COHEN	A	23	(13)		18
Nir DAVIDOVICH	G	23			
Yaron ELKAYAM	M	2	(2)		
Giorgi GAKHOKIDZE (GEO)	M	25	(7)		1
Camal GAVRIN	D		(1)		
Alon HARAZI	D	30	(1)		1
Vasiliy IVANOV (RUS)	D	33	(3)		2
Avishay JANO	D	32	(3)		4
Yaniv KATAN	M	21	(15)		3
Adoram KEISSY	D	35			2
Assi KELMAN	M		(6)		
Itay KOREN	D	1	(7)		
Guy MELAMED	M		(6)		
Radoslaw MICHALSKI (POL)	M	10	(1)		2
Shuki NAGAR	D	9	(20)		1
Avi PERETZ	G	16			
Amos SASSI	D		(1)		
Shlomi SIMAN TOV	M		(1)		
Raimondas ZUTAUTAS (LIT)	M	15	(2)		

LEAGUE RESULTS 1999/2000

14/08/99	Hapoel Irony Rishon Lezion	H	4-1	Clescenco, Harazi, Cohen, Jano (p)
21/08/99	Hapoel Petach-Tikva	A	5-2	Brzeczek, Clescenco 4
28/08/99	Bnei Yehuda	H	3-1	Katan, Clescenco, Benayoun
21/09/99	Hapoel Tel-Aviv	A	0-0	
25/09/99	Hapoel Kfar-Saba	H	1-0	Cohen
02/10/99	Hapoel Jerusalem	H	1-2	Clescenco
18/10/99	Maccabi Herzliya	A	5-2	Brzeczek, Cohen 2, Clescenco, Ivanov
23/10/99	Maccabi Petach-Tikva	H	5-1	Cohen, Benayoun, Clescenco,
				Brzeczek, Katan (p)
30/10/99	Maccabi Netanya	A	3-1	Cohen 2, Benayoun
06/11/99	MS Ashdod	H	0-0	
22/11/99	Hapoel Haifa	H	3-2	Benayoun 2, Cohen
27/11/99	Beitar Jerusalem	A	1-1	Gakhokidze
04/12/99	Hapoel Irony Rishon Lezion	A	7-0	Benayoun 2, Cohen 3, Brzeczek,
				Clescenco
08/12/99	Maccabi Tel-Aviv	A	1-0	Brzeczek
13/12/99	Hapoel Petach-Tikva	H	2-0	Benayoun, Brzeczek
20/12/99	Bnei Yehuda	A	2-0	Nagar, Benayoun
27/12/99	Hapoel Tel-Aviv	H	1-0	Clescenco
01/01/00	Hapoel Kfar-Saba	A	1-1	Clescenco
10/01/00	Hapoel Jerusalem	A	3-1	Brzeczek 2 (1p), Benayoun
15/01/00	Maccabi Herzliya	H	3-0	Cohen, Benayoun 2
24/01/00	Maccabi Petach-Tikva	A	2-1	Cohen, Clescenco
29/01/00	Maccabi Netanya	H	1-1	Cohen
05/02/00	MS Ashdod	A	0-0	
12/02/00	Maccabi Tel-Aviv	H	1-2	Jano (p)
19/02/00	Hapoel Haifa	A	0-0	
28/02/00	Beitar Jerusalem	H	0-2	
04/03/00	Maccabi Netanya	H	7-0	Benayoun 3, Keissy, Atar, Clescenco 2
13/03/00	Hapoel Tel-Aviv	A	1-1	Cohen
18/03/00	Hapoel Jerusalem	H	6-0	Ivanov, Cohen 2, Keissy, Clescenco 2
27/03/00	Hapoel Petach-Tikva	H	4-1	Benado, Clescenco, Jano (p),
				Benayoun
01/04/00	Beitar Jerusalem	A	1-3	Brzeczek
10/04/00	Maccabi Petach-Tikva	H	1-2	Cohen
15/04/00	Hapoel Haifa	A	4-0	Michalski 2, Clescenco, Atar
22/04/00	MS Ashdod	H	2-0	Clescenco, Jano
29/04/00	Maccabi Tel-Aviv	A	0-3	
06/05/00	Hapoel Irony Rishon Lezion	H	0-0	
13/05/00	Hapoel Kfar-Saba	A	0-1	
20/05/00	Bnei Yehuda	H	1-1	Katan
27/05/00	Maccabi Herzliya	A	4-2	Benayoun 3, Clescenco

MACCABI HERZLIYA

CLUB DIRECTORY

Maccabi Herzliya
Porzai Hadereech St. 2/10
Herzliya 46101
tel - (09) 5974774
fax - (09) 9509865
Year of Formation - 1926
Chairman - Ariel Shaynman
Secretary - Shimon Mesika
Coach - Yehushua Faygenbaum; Nissim Bachar;
Eli Driks; Avi Cohen
Stadium - Irony Herzliya (8,200)

APPEARANCES 99/00

	P	Ap	(s)	Gls
Shay ABUKSIS	A	1		2
Eitan ARBEL	D	23	(2)	
Lior ASULIN	A	21	(9)	3
Avi AZOULAY	M	27	(1)	
Ronen BADASH	M	11	(8)	4
Josko BILIC (CRO)	D	15		
Alex BREMCHER	D	17	(4)	
Eliko COHEN	M	2	(1)	
Meir COHEN	G	16		
Shahar COHEN	M	9		1
Eli DRIKS	A	3	(2)	1
Ronen FAYGENBAUM	D	10		
Oren GABAY	M		(2)	
Guy GAT	M	15	(2)	
Danny GRIEVES (ENG)	M	7	(2)	
Meni KALIMIAN	M		(9)	
Yaacov KORATZKY	D	32	(3)	
Moshe LEVI	D		(4)	
Shmuel LEVI	D	1	(1)	
Robert MARUSIC (SLO)	M	19	(16)	2
Guy MISHAL	M	5	(2)	
Eitan MIZRAHI	D	15	(1)	1
Ismet MUNISHI (BOS)	M	9	(1)	
Oleh NADUDA (UKR)	M	31	(4)	1
Guy NACHMAN	D	15	(1)	
Ron NACHMAN	D	8	(3)	
Alon OFFIR	M	22	(2)	2
Oren ROTEM	D	16	(4)	
István SALLÓI (HUN)	M	27	(6)	9
Guy SALOMON	G	4		
Kobi SHALO	G	19		
Aleksandr SHIGALOV (RUS)	D	6		
Santos SIERO (BRA)	A	9	(7)	2
Itzhak ZOHAR	M	14	(3)	3

LEAGUE RESULTS 1999/2000

14/08/99	Hapoel Haifa	H	0-0	
21/08/99	Beitar Jerusalem	A	1-1	Sallói
28/08/99	Hapoel Irony Rishon Lezion	H	0-0	
18/09/99	Hapoel Petach-Tikva	A	0-1	
25/09/99	Bnei Yehuda	H	4-0	Sallói 3, Driks
04/10/99	Hapoel Tel-Aviv	A	0-4	
18/10/99	Maccabi Haifa	H	2-5	Marusic, Sallói
22/10/99	Hapoel Jerusalem	A	4-1	Zohar 2, og (Abu Dib), Asulin
30/10/99	Hapoel Kfar-Saba	H	0-2	
06/11/99	Maccabi Petach-Tikva	H	0-4	
20/11/99	MS Ashdod	H	1-1	Sallói
27/11/99	Maccabi Tel-Aviv	A	0-3	
04/12/99	Hapoel Haifa	A	0-4	
07/12/99	Maccabi Netanya	A	3-0	Asulin, Zohar, Sallói
11/12/99	Beitar Jerusalem	H	1-2	Marusic
18/12/99	Hapoel Irony Rishon Lezion	A	1-3	Siero
25/12/99	Hapoel Petach-Tikva	H	1-3	Asulin
01/01/00	Bnei Yehuda	A	1-3	Sallói
08/01/00	Hapoel Tel-Aviv	H	0-5	
15/01/00	Maccabi Haifa	A	0-3	
21/01/00	Hapoel Jerusalem	H	1-2	Badash
28/01/00	Hapoel Kfar-Saba	A	0-0	
05/02/00	Maccabi Petach-Tikva	A	0-1	
12/02/00	Maccabi Netanya	H	1-0	Badash
19/02/00	MS Ashdod	A	1-0	Badash
26/02/00	Maccabi Tel-Aviv	H	3-1	Sallói, Mizrahi, Offir
04/03/00	Hapoel Petach-Tikva	A	1-8	Naduda
11/03/00	Beitar Jerusalem	H	0-0	
18/03/00	Maccabi Petach-Tikva	A	1-0	Offir
25/03/00	Hapoel Haifa	H	1-1	Badash
01/04/00	MS Ashdod	A	0-1	
10/04/00	Maccabi Tel-Aviv	H	0-4	
15/04/00	Hapoel Irony Rishon Lezion	A	1-0	Siero
22/04/00	Hapoel Kfar-Saba	H	0-2	
29/04/00	Bnei Yehuda	A	0-1	
06/05/00	Hapoel Jerusalem	A	2-1	Cohen S., Asulin
13/05/00	Maccabi Netanya	H	0-0	
20/05/00	Hapoel Tel-Aviv	A	0-2	
27/05/00	Maccabi Haifa	H	2-4	Abuksis 2

MACCABI NETANYA

CLUB DIRECTORY

Maccabi Netanya
Milhemet Sheshet H'yamim St. 34
PO Box 2242
Netanya
tel - (09) 8620503
fax - (09) 8620503
website - http://members.tripod.com/~mnetanya
Year of Formation - 1942
Chairman - Itzhak Tshuva
Secretary - Kobi Baladev
Manager - Uri Malmilian
Coach - Motti Iwanir; Rami Levi; Gideon Damti
Stadium - Maccabi Netanya (6,500)

MAJOR HONOURS
League Championship - (5)
1971, 1974, 1978, 1980, 1983.
Domestic Cup - (1) 1978.

APPEARANCES 99/00

	P	Ap	(s)	Gls
Ronen BADASH	A	2	(12)	
László CZÉH (HUN)	M	14	(14)	5
Shlomi DAHAN	M	22	(11)	3
Daniel DUMITRESCU (ROM)	M	2	(1)	
Moshe GLAM	D	26		2
Ferenc HÁMORI (HUN)	M	9	(7)	
Shay HOLTZMAN	A	5	(2)	2
Wissam ISMI	A	7	(15)	1
Lior LARIDO	D	6	(2)	
Yossi MALKA	D	13	(1)	1
Amos NAHYSSI	D	15	(5)	
Shimon PAHIMA	G	2		
Darko RAIC-SUDAR (CRO)	M	38		6
Daniel ROZBAN	D	1		
Kalimi SABAN	D	29	(5)	1
Amos SASI	D	7	(4)	
Eran SHAIZINGER	G	37		
Moshe SHAPIRA	D	1		
Guy SHARABI	D	17	(1)	
Offer SHITRIT	A	13	(2)	2
Noam SHOHAM	M	9	(3)	
Viorel TANASE (ROM)	M	27	(3)	5
Kfir TZUKOL	M		(2)	
Uri UZAN	D	21	(5)	
Liron VILNER	A	21	(10)	9
Stjepan VRANJES (CRO)	D	34	(1)	1
Itzhak ZOHAR	M	17	(1)	11
Israel ZWITY	M	33	(2)	2

LEAGUE RESULTS 1999/2000

14/08/99	MS Ashdod	H	0-6	
21/08/99	Maccabi Tel-Aviv	A	0-0	
29/08/99	Hapoel Haifa	H	1-2	Ismi
18/09/99	Beitar Jerusalem	A	2-4	Dahan, Holtzman (p)
25/09/99	Hapoel Irony Rishon Lezion	H	2-4	Dahan, Holtzman
02/10/99	Hapoel Petach-Tikva	A	0-1	
15/10/99	Bnei Yehuda	H	1-1	Raic-Sudar
23/10/99	Hapoel Tel-Aviv	A	0-3	
30/10/99	Maccabi Haifa	H	1-3	Tanase
06/11/99	Hapoel Jerusalem	A	3-1	Zwity 2, Czéh
20/11/99	Maccabi Petach-Tikva	A	0-0	
27/11/99	Hapoel Kfar-Saba	H	4-1	Vilner, Czéh, Tanase, Dahan
04/12/99	MS Ashdod	A	2-0	Czéh 2 (1p)
07/12/99	Maccabi Herzliya	H	0-3	
13/12/99	Maccabi Tel-Aviv	H	3-1	Glam, Vilner 2
18/12/99	Hapoel Haifa	A	1-2	og (Halfon)
25/12/99	Beitar Jerusalem	H	2-3	Vilner, Vranjes
01/01/00	Hapoel Irony Rishon Lezion	A	0-1	
08/01/00	Hapoel Petach-Tikva	H	1-2	Vilner
15/01/00	Bnei Yehuda	A	1-1	Raic-Sudar
22/01/00	Hapoel Tel-Aviv	H	2-5	Malka, Vilner (p)
29/01/00	Maccabi Haifa	A	1-1	Vilner
05/02/00	Hapoel Jerusalem	H	2-1	Tanase, Zohar
12/02/00	Maccabi Herzliya	A	0-1	
18/02/00	Maccabi Petach-Tikva	H	0-1	
25/02/00	Hapoel Kfar-Saba	A	0-0	
04/03/00	Maccabi Haifa	A	0-7	
11/03/00	Hapoel Petach-Tikva	H	2-4	Czéh, Vilner
18/03/00	Beitar Jerusalem	A	3-2	Raic-Sudar 2, Zohar
24/03/00	Maccabi Petach-Tikva	H	2-1	Zohar 2
01/04/00	Hapoel Haifa	A	1-1	Saban
08/04/00	MS Ashdod	H	3-1	Shitrit, Zohar, Tanase
15/04/00	Maccabi Tel-Aviv	A	1-2	Tanase
22/04/00	Hapoel Irony Rishon Lezion	H	2-2	Shitrit, og (Eliaho)
29/04/00	Hapoel Kfar-Saba	A	1-1	Zohar
06/05/00	Bnei Yehuda	H	4-1	Zohar 3 (1p), Glam
13/05/00	Maccabi Herzliya	A	0-0	
20/05/00	Hapoel Jerusalem	A	4-0	Raic-Sudar 2, Vilner, Zohar
27/05/00	Hapoel Tel-Aviv	H	1-1	Zohar

MACCABI PETACH-TIKVA

CLUB DIRECTORY

Maccabi Petach-Tikva
Finstein Corner of Ben Dror St.
PO Box 67
Petach-Tikva
tel - (03) 934879
fax - (03) 9347560
Year of Formation - 1912
Chairman - Avi Luzon
Secretary - Dov Lahav
Coach - Yossi Mizrahi
Stadium - Petach-Tikva (12,250)

MAJOR HONOURS
Domestic Cup - (2) 1935, 1952.

APPEARANCES 99/00

	P	Ap	(s)	Gls
Guy AGIV	D	1	(2)	
Ismael AMAR	D	37		1
Ihor BABENKO (UKR)	A		(1)	
Wahab BARACAT	D	6	(5)	
Rajib BARANSI	A	11	(7)	1
Tomer BEN YOUSEF	D	20	(11)	
Erez BIALA	M	2	(7)	
Assaf DAGAI	M	5	(8)	
Sami DANIEL	M	30	(4)	1
Adrian ELIAT (ALB)	D	16	(1)	2
Denés ESZENYI (HUN)	A		(7)	
Martin GARGIC (SLO)	M	6		
Ehud GORESH	G	1		
Shay HOLTZMAN	A	15	(6)	7
Guy ITZHAK	M	26	(7)	5
Eran LEVI	D	1	(3)	
David LIANI	M	5		
Yetav LUZON	M		(2)	
Murad MAGOMEDOV (AZB)	D	31		
Idan MALIHI	M	34	(4)	2
Golan MALOL	G	38		
Assi MASHIACH	M		(1)	
Shabi MIRA	M		(2)	
Uzi OHAION	M	4	(5)	
Kfir PARTIELI	D	20	(2)	1
Tzahi PRIENTA	D	1	(1)	
Tzahi SHMARIAHO	M	21	(13)	3
Dragan TADIC (CRO)	M	26	(8)	
Assi TUBI	A	39		27
Sharon TZOFIN	D	33		

LEAGUE RESULTS 1999/2000

15/08/99	Maccabi Tel-Aviv	H	2-1	Baransi, Tubi
21/08/99	Hapoel Haifa	A	0-1	
28/08/99	Beitar Jerusalem	H	3-0	Tubi 3
18/09/99	Hapoel Irony Rishon Lezion	A	1-0	Tubi
25/09/99	Hapoel Petach-Tikva	H	1-2	Tubi
02/10/99	Bnei Yehuda	A	2-0	Itzhak, Tubi
16/10/99	Hapoel Tel-Aviv	H	1-5	Itzhak
23/10/99	Maccabi Haifa	A	1-5	Tubi
30/10/99	Hapoel Jerusalem	H	0-2	
06/11/99	Maccabi Herzliya	A	4-0	Tubi 3, Shmariaho
20/11/99	Maccabi Netanya	H	0-0	
27/11/99	MS Ashdod	A	1-0	Tubi
04/12/99	Maccabi Tel-Aviv	A	2-1	Holtzman 2
07/12/99	Hapoel Kfar-Saba	H	3-2	Holtzman 2, Tubi
11/12/99	Hapoel Haifa	H	2-1	Holtzman, Tubi
18/12/99	Beitar Jerusalem	A	1-3	Tubi
28/12/99	Hapoel Irony Rishon Lezion	H	0-0	
01/01/00	Hapoel Petach-Tikva	A	1-0	Itzhak
08/01/00	Bnei Yehuda	H	1-1	Tubi
17/01/00	Hapoel Tel-Aviv	A	1-2	Tubi
24/01/00	Maccabi Haifa	H	1-2	Amar
29/01/00	Hapoel Jerusalem	A	2-0	Partieli, Tubi
07/02/00	Maccabi Herzliya	H	1-0	Tubi (p)
11/02/00	Hapoel Kfar-Saba	A	2-2	Eliat, Itzhak
18/02/00	Maccabi Netanya	A	1-0	Shmariaho
26/02/00	MS Ashdod	H	3-1	Tubi 2, Itzhak
03/03/00	Hapoel Kfar-Saba	H	1-0	Malihi
11/03/00	Bnei Yehuda	A	0-1	
18/03/00	Maccabi Herzliya	H	0-1	
24/03/00	Maccabi Netanya	A	1-2	Tubi
01/04/00	Hapoel Tel-Aviv	H	1-0	Daniel
08/04/00	Maccabi Haifa	A	2-1	Malihi, Tubi
15/04/00	Hapoel Petach-Tikva	H	2-4	Shmariaho, Holtzman
22/04/00	Beitar Jerusalem	A	1-1	Tubi
29/04/00	Hapoel Jerusalem	H	3-1	Tubi 2, Holtzman
06/05/00	Hapoel Haifa	H	0-0	
13/05/00	MS Ashdod	A	2-3	Tubi, Eliat
20/05/00	Maccabi Tel-Aviv	H	0-1	
27/05/00	Hapoel Irony Rishon Lezion	A	0-1	

MACCABI TEL-AVIV

CLUB DIRECTORY

Maccabi Tel-Aviv
Maccabi St. 4, Tel-Aviv 63293
tel - (03) 5250712
fax - (03) 5288503
website - http://www.netking.com/maccabi
Year of Formation - 1910
Chairman - Loni Herzikovich
Secretary - Shimon Korek
Coach - Avraham Grant (00/01 - Shlomo Sharf)
Stadium - Ramat-Gan (43,000)

MAJOR HONOURS
League Championship - (18)
1937, 1939, 1941, 1947, 1949, 1950, 1951,
1952, 1954, 1956, 1968, 1970, 1972, 1977,
1979, 1992, 1995, 1996.
Domestic Cup - (19)
1929, 1930, 1933, 1941, 1946, 1947, 1954,
1955, 1958, 1959, 1964, 1965, 1967, 1970,
1977, 1987, 1988, 1994, 1996.

APPEARANCES 99/00

	P	Ap	(s)	Gls
Dudu AVRAHAM	M		(1)	
Marco BALBUL	D	28	(1)	
Liron BASSIS	A	27	(4)	5
Dedi BEN DAYAN	D	37		11
Eli BITON	A	1	(13)	
Gadi BRUMER	D	31	(1)	1
Kfir EDRY	M	30	(3)	5
Michael EMENALO (NIG)	D	19	(2)	
Roni GAFNI	D	1	(3)	
Offir HAIM	M	7	(17)	3
Felix HALFON	D	35		3
Jefri ISHAY	D	3	(1)	
Aleksei KOSOLAPOV (RUS)	M	32	(1)	2
Andrzej KUBICA (POL)	A	24	(2)	8
Oleksandr KUSYRIN (UKR)	A	9	(8)	4
Meni LEVI	M	1	(3)	
Ben LUZ	M	25	(5)	1
Avi NIMNI	M	11	(1)	8
Alon OFFIR	M	2	(2)	
Dimitriy POPOV (RUS)	M	1	(3)	
David REVIVO	A	14	(3)	1
Eyal SHEN	M		(1)	
Liran SHTRAUBER	G	24		
Avi STRUL	D		(1)	
Guy TZARFATI	M	20	(13)	9
Aleksandr UVAROV (RUS)	G	15	(2)	
Grzegorz WEDZYNSKI (POL)	M	32	(5)	5

LEAGUE RESULTS 1999/2000

15/08/99	Maccabi Petach-Tikva	A	1-2	Kubica
21/08/99	Maccabi Netanya	H	0-0	
30/08/99	MS Ashdod	A	0-1	
21/09/99	Hapoel Kfar-Saba	A	3-0	Kubica, Wedzynski, Ben Dayan
25/09/99	Hapoel Haifa	H	0-0	
04/10/99	Beitar Jerusalem	A	1-0	Edry
16/10/99	Hapoel Irony Rishon Lezion	H	4-0	Kubica, Bassis 2, Tzarfati
25/10/99	Hapoel Petach-Tikva	A	1-2	Tzarfati
30/10/99	Bnei Yehuda	H	3-1	Ben-Dayan 2, Tzarfati (p)
08/11/99	Hapoel Tel-Aviv	A	1-1	Wedzynski
20/11/99	Hapoel Jerusalem	A	1-0	Kubica
27/11/99	Maccabi Horzliya	H	3-0	Edry, Tzarfati, Ben Dayan
04/12/99	Maccabi Petach-Tikva	H	1-2	Kubica (p)
08/12/99	Maccabi Haifa	H	0-1	
11/12/99	Maccabi Netanya	A	1-3	Tzarfati
18/12/99	MS Ashdod	H	1-2	Wedzynski
25/12/99	Hapoel Kfar-Saba	H	0-1	
03/01/00	Hapoel Haifa	A	4-2	Wedzynski, Ben Dayan, Kubica 2
08/01/00	Beitar Jerusalem	H	1-3	Tzarfati
15/01/00	Hapoel Irony Rishon Lezion	A	0-0	
22/01/00	Hapoel Petach-Tikva	H	0-1	
29/01/00	Bnei Yehuda	A	0-0	
07/02/00	Hapoel Tel-Aviv	H	2-0	Kubica, Kosolapov
12/02/00	Maccabi Haifa	A	2-1	Ben Dayan, Kosolapov (p)
19/02/00	Hapoel Jerusalem	H	1-1	Wedzynski
26/02/00	Maccabi Herzliya	A	1-3	Halfon (p)
04/03/00	MS Ashdod	A	4-2	Edry, Ben Dayan 2, Luz
10/03/00	Hapoel Jerusalem	A	4-2	Revivo, Bassis, Nimni, Halfon (p)
18/03/00	Hapoel Irony Rishon Lezion	H	5-1	Nimni 2 (1p), Edry, Kusyrin, Tzarfati
24/03/00	Hapoel Kfar-Saba	A	2-2	Nimni (p), Tzarfati
01/04/00	Bnei Yehuda	H	1-2	Nimni
10/04/00	Maccabi Herzliya	A	4-0	Nimni, Ben Dayan, Bassis, Kusyrin
15/04/00	Maccabi Netanya	H	2-1	Haim, Kusyrin
22/04/00	Hapoel Tel-Aviv	A	1-2	Kusyrin
29/04/00	Maccabi Haifa	H	3-0	Halfon, Tzarfati, Nimni
06/05/00	Hapoel Petach-Tikva	A	2-2	Bassis, Edry
13/05/00	Beitar Jerusalem	H	4-1	Ben Dayan 2, Nimni, Brumer
20/05/00	Maccabi Petach-Tikva	H	1-0	Haim
27/05/00	Hapoel Haifa	H	1-0	Haim

ITALY

1	**BARI**	588	**13**	**REGGINA**	600
2	**BOLOGNA**	589	**14**	**ROMA**	601
3	**CAGLIARI**	590	**15**	**TORINO**	602
4	**FIORENTINA**	591	**16**	**UDINESE**	603
5	**INTER**	592	**17**	**VENEZIA**	604
6	**JUVENTUS**	593	**18**	**VERONA**	605
7	**LAZIO**	594	**Promoted clubs**		
8	**LECCE**	595	**19**	**VICENZA**	
9	**MILAN**	596	**20**	**ATALANTA**	
10	**PARMA**	597	**21**	**BRESCIA**	
11	**PERUGIA**	598	**22**	**NAPOLI**	
12	**PIACENZA**	599			

COLOUR INDEX

Plate 2

NATIONAL FEDERATIONS

FIRST KIT   **ALBANIA**   SECOND KIT

FIRST KIT   **ANDORRA**   SECOND KIT

FIRST KIT   **ARMENIA**   SECOND KIT

FIRST KIT   **AUSTRIA**   SECOND KIT

Plate 3

NATIONAL FEDERATIONS

FIRST KIT   **AZERBAIJAN**   SECOND KIT

FIRST KIT   **BELARUS**   SECOND KIT

FIRST KIT   **BELGIUM**   SECOND KIT

FIRST KIT   **BOSNIA-HERZEGOVINA**   SECOND KIT

Plate 4

NATIONAL FEDERATIONS

FIRST KIT   **BULGARIA**   SECOND KIT

FIRST KIT   **CROATIA**   SECOND KIT

FIRST KIT   **CYPRUS**   SECOND KIT

FIRST KIT   **CZECH REPUBLIC**   SECOND KIT

Plate 5

NATIONAL FEDERATIONS

FIRST KIT   **DENMARK**   SECOND KIT

FIRST KIT   **ENGLAND**   SECOND KIT

FIRST KIT   **ESTONIA**   SECOND KIT

FIRST KIT   **FAROE ISLANDS**   SECOND KIT

Plate 6

NATIONAL FEDERATIONS

FIRST KIT   **FINLAND**   SECOND KIT

FIRST KIT   **FRANCE**   SECOND KIT

FIRST KIT   **GEORGIA**   SECOND KIT

FIRST KIT   **GERMANY**   SECOND KIT

Plate 7

NATIONAL FEDERATIONS

FIRST KIT   GREECE   SECOND KIT

FIRST KIT   HOLLAND   SECOND KIT

FIRST KIT   HUNGARY   SECOND KIT

FIRST KIT   ICELAND   SECOND KIT

Plate 8

NATIONAL FEDERATIONS

FIRST KIT

ISRAEL

SECOND KIT

FIRST KIT

ITALY

SECOND KIT

FIRST KIT

LATVIA

SECOND KIT

FIRST KIT

LIECHTENSTEIN

SECOND KIT

Plate 9

NATIONAL FEDERATIONS

FIRST KIT   **LITHUANIA**   SECOND KIT

FIRST KIT   **LUXEMBOURG**   SECOND KIT

FIRST KIT   **MACEDONIA**   SECOND KIT

FIRST KIT   **MALTA**   SECOND KIT

Plate 10

NATIONAL FEDERATIONS

FIRST KIT

MOLDOVA

SECOND KIT

FIRST KIT

NORTHERN IRELAND

SECOND KIT

FIRST KIT

NORWAY

SECOND KIT

FIRST KIT

POLAND

SECOND KIT

Plate 11

NATIONAL FEDERATIONS

FIRST KIT

PORTUGAL

SECOND KIT

FIRST KIT

REPUBLIC OF IRELAND

SECOND KIT

FIRST KIT

ROMANIA

SECOND KIT

FIRST KIT

RUSSIA

SECOND KIT

Plate 12

NATIONAL FEDERATIONS

FIRST KIT   **SAN MARINO**   SECOND KIT

FIRST KIT   **SCOTLAND**   SECOND KIT

FIRST KIT   **SLOVAKIA**   SECOND KIT

FIRST KIT   **SLOVENIA**   SECOND KIT

Plate 13

NATIONAL FEDERATIONS

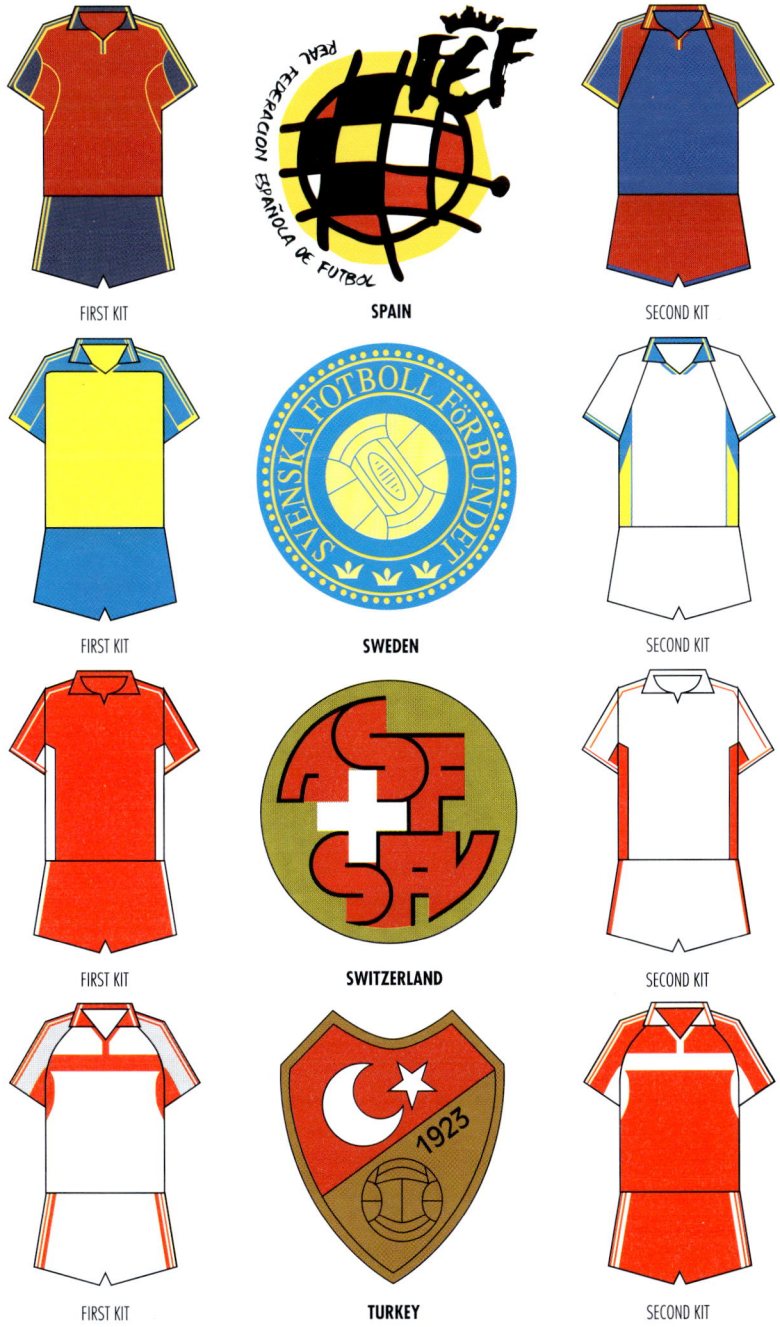

FIRST KIT   SPAIN   SECOND KIT

FIRST KIT   SWEDEN   SECOND KIT

FIRST KIT   SWITZERLAND   SECOND KIT

FIRST KIT   TURKEY   SECOND KIT

Plate 14

NATIONAL FEDERATIONS

FIRST KIT	**UKRAINE**	SECOND KIT
FIRST KIT	**WALES**	SECOND KIT
FIRST KIT	**YUGOSLAVIA**	SECOND KIT

Plate 16

AUSTRIA

FK AUSTRIA WIEN SW BREGENZ GRAZER AK LASK LINZ

SC AUSTRIA LUSTENAU SK RAPID WIEN SV RIED

SV SALZBURG SK STURM GRAZ FC TIROL INNSBRUCK

VFB ADMIRA MÖDLING

Plate 17

AUSTRIA

FK AUSTRIA WIEN

SW BREGENZ

GRAZER AK

LASK LINZ

SC AUSTRIA LUSTENAU

SK RAPID WIEN

SV RIED

SV SALZBURG

SK STURM GRAZ

FC TIROL INNSBRUCK

VFB ADMIRA MÖDLING

Plate 18

BELGIUM

RSC ANDERLECHT

KSK BEVEREN

CLUB BRUGGE KV

RSC CHARLEROI

KSC EENDRACHT AALST

R EXCELSIOR MOUSCRON

KRC GENK

KAA GENT

GERMINAL BEERSCHOT ANTWERPEN

KRC HARELBEKE

K LIERSE SK

KSC LOKEREN

KFC LOMMELSE SK

KV MECHELEN

K ST.-TRUIDENSE VV

R STANDARD LIEGE

KFC VERBROEDERING GEEL

KVC WESTERLO

ROYAL ANTWERP FC

RAA LA LOUVIERE

Plate 19

BELGIUM

RSC ANDERLECHT

KSK BEVEREN

CLUB BRUGGE KV

RSC CHARLEROI

KSC EENDRACHT AALST

R EXCELSIOR MOUSCRON

KRC GENK

KAA GENT

GERMINAL BEERSCHOT ANTWERPEN

KRC HARELBEKE

K LIERSE SK

KSC LOKEREN

KFC LOMMELSE SK

KV MECHELEN

K ST.-TRUIDENSE VV

R STANDARD LIEGE

KFC VERBROEDERING GEEL

KVC WESTERLO

ROYAL ANTWERP FC

RAA LA LOUVIERE

Plate 20

BULGARIA

BELASITSA PETRICH

BOTEV PLOVDIV

CHERNOMORETS BOURGAS

CSKA SOFIA

DOBRUDZHA DOBRICH

LEVSKI SOFIA

LOKOMOTIV SOFIA

LOVECH

MINIOR PERNIK

NEFTOCHIMIK BOURGAS

OLYMPIC-BEROE STARA ZAGORA

PIRIN BLAGOEVGRAD

SHUMEN

SLAVIA SOFIA

SPARTAK VARNA

VELBAZHD KIUSTENDIL

CHERNO MORE VARNA

ISKAR-HEBAR PAZARDZHIK

Plate 21

BULGARIA

BELASITSA PETRICH

BOTEV PLOVDIV

CHERNOMORETS BOURGAS

CSKA SOFIA

DOBRUDZHA DOBRICH

LEVSKI SOFIA

LOKOMOTIV SOFIA

LOVECH

MINIOR PERNIK

NEFTOCHIMIK BOURGAS

OLYMPIC-BEROE STARA ZAGORA

PIRIN BLAGOEVGRAD

SHUMEN

SLAVIA SOFIA

SPARTAK VARNA

VELBAZHD KIUSTENDIL

CHERNO MORE VARNA

ISKAR-HEBAR PAZARDZHIK

Plate 22

CROATIA

CIBALIA VINKOVCI   DINAMO ZAGREB   HAJDUK SPLIT   HRVATSKI DRAGOVOLJAC ZAGREB

ISTRA PULA   OSIJEK   RIJEKA   SIBENIK

SLAVEN BELUPO KOPRIVNICA   VARTEKS VARAZDIN   ZAGREB   VUKOVAR '91

MARSONIA SLAVONSKI BROD   CAKOVEC

Plate 23

CROATIA

CIBALIA VINKOVCI

DINAMO ZAGREB

HAJDUK SPLIT

HRVATSKI DRAGOVOLJAC ZAGREB

ISTRA PULA

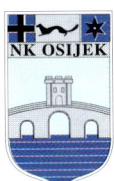

OSIJEK

RIJEKA

SIBENIK

SLAVEN BELUPO KOPRIVNICA

VARTEKS VARAZDIN

VUKOVAR '91

ZAGREB

MARSONIA SLAVONSKI BROD

CAKOVEC

Plate 24

CYPRUS

AEK LARNACA

AEL LIMASSOL

ALKI LARNACA

ANAGENNISIS DHERYNIA

ANORTHOSIS FAMAGUSTA

APOEL NICOSIA

APOLLON LIMASSOL

APOP PAPHOS

ETHNIKOS AKHNA

ETHNIKOS ASHIA

NEA SALAMINA FAMAGUSTA

OLYMPIAKOS NICOSIA

OMONIA NICOSIA

PARALIMNI

DIGHENIS MORPHOU

ARIS LIMASSOL

DOXA KATOKOPIA

Plate 25

CYPRUS

AEK LARNACA

AEL LIMASSOL

ALKI LARNACA

ANAGENNISIS DHERYNIA

ANORTHOSIS FAMAGUSTA

APOEL NICOSIA

APOLLON LIMASSOL

APOP PAPHOS

ETHNIKOS AKHNA

ETHNIKOS ASHIA

NEA SALAMINA FAMAGUSTA

OLYMPIAKOS NICOSIA

OMONIA NICOSIA

PARALIMNI

DIGHENIS MORPHOU

ARIS LIMASSOL

DOXA KATOKOPIA

Plate 26

CZECH REPUBLIC

BANIK OSTRAVA

BOBY BRNO

BOHEMIANS PRAHA

SK CESKE BUDEJOVICE

CHMEL BLSANY

DUKLA PRIBRAM

SK HRADEC KRALOVE

FK JABLONEC 97

PETRA DRNOVICE

SFC OPAVA

SIGMA OLOMOUC

SLAVIA PRAHA

SLOVAN LIBEREC

SPARTA PRAHA

FK TEPLICE

VIKTORIA ZIZKOV

SYNOT STARE MESTO

VIKTORIA PLZEN

Plate 27

CZECH REPUBLIC

BANIK OSTRAVA

BOBY BRNO

BOHEMIANS PRAHA

SK CESKE BUDEJOVICE

FK CHMEL BLSANY

DUKLA PRIBRAM

SK HRADEC KRALOVE

FK JABLONEC 97

PETRA DRNOVICE

SFC OPAVA

SIGMA OLOMOUC

SLAVIA PRAHA

SLOVAN LIBEREC

SPARTA PRAHA

FK TEPLICE

VIKTORIA ZIZKOV

SYNOT STARE MESTO

VIKTORIA PLZEN

Plate 28

DENMARK

AAB	AB	AGF	BRØNDBY IF
ESBJERG FB	HERFØLGE BK	FC KØBENHAVN	LYNGBY FC
OB	SILKEBORG IF	VEJLE BK	VIBORG FF
FC MIDTJYLLAND	HADERSLEV FK		

Plate 29

DENMARK

AAB

AB

AGF

BRØNDBY IF

ESBJERG FB

HERFØLGE BK

FC KØBENHAVN

LYNGBY FC

OB

SILKEBORG IF

VEJLE BK

VIBORG FF

FC MIDTJYLLAND

HADERSLEV FK

Plate 30

ENGLAND

ARSENAL

ASTON VILLA

BRADFORD CITY

CHELSEA

COVENTRY CITY

DERBY COUNTY

EVERTON

LEEDS UNITED

LEICESTER CITY

LIVERPOOL

MANCHESTER UNITED

MIDDLESBROUGH

NEWCASTLE UNITED

SHEFFIELD WEDNESDAY

SOUTHAMPTON

SUNDERLAND

TOTTENHAM HOTSPUR

WATFORD

WEST HAM UNITED

WIMBLEDON

CHARLTON ATHLETIC

MANCHESTER CITY

IPSWICH TOWN

Plate 31

ENGLAND

ARSENAL

ASTON VILLA

BRADFORD CITY

CHELSEA

COVENTRY CITY

DERBY COUNTY

EVERTON

LEEDS UNITED

LEICESTER CITY

LIVERPOOL

MANCHESTER UNITED

MIDDLESBROUGH

NEWCASTLE UNITED

SHEFFIELD WEDNESDAY

SOUTHAMPTON

SUNDERLAND

TOTTENHAM HOTSPUR

WATFORD

WEST HAM UNITED

WIMBLEDON

CHARLTON ATHLETIC

MANCHESTER CITY

IPSWICH TOWN

Plate 32

FINLAND

FC HAKA   HJK   FC INTER   FC JAZZ

FC JOKERIT   KTP   FC LAHTI   MYPA

ROPS   TPS   TPV   VPS

TAMPERE UNITED

Plate 33

FINLAND

FC HAKA

HJK

FC INTER

FC JAZZ

FC JOKERIT

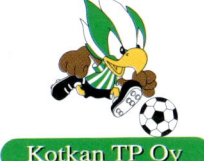

KTP

FC LAHTI

MYPA

ROPS

TPS

TPV

VPS

TAMPERE UNITED

Plate 34

FRANCE

AJ AUXERRE

SC BASTIA

GIRONDINS DE BORDEAUX

LE HAVRE AC

RC LENS

OLYMPIQUE LYONNAIS

OLYMPIQUE MARSEILLE

FC METZ

AS MONACO

MONTPELLIER HSC

AS NANCY-LORRAINE

FC NANTES

PARIS SAINT-GERMAIN

STADE RENNES FC

AS SAINT-ETIENNE

CS SEDAN ARDENNES

RC STRASBOURG

A TROYES AC

LILLE OSC

EN AVANT GUINGAMP

TOULOUSE FC

Plate 35

FRANCE

AJ AUXERRE

SC BASTIA

GIRONDINS DE BORDEAUX

LE HAVRE AC

RC LENS

OLYMPIQUE LYONNAIS

OLYMPIQUE MARSEILLE

FC METZ

AS MONACO

MONTPELLIER HSC

AS NANCY-LORRAINE

FC NANTES

PARIS SAINT-GERMAIN

STADE RENNAIS FC

AS SAINT-ETIENNE

CS SEDAN ARDENNES

RC STRASBOURG

A TROYES AC

LILLE OSC

EN AVANT GUINGAMP

TOULOUSE FC

Plate 36

GEORGIA

ARSENALI TBILISI

DILA GORI

DINAMO BATUMI

DINAMO TBILISI

GORDA RUSTAVI

IBERIA SAMTREDIA

KOLKHETI KHOBI

KOLKHETI 1913 POTI

LOKOMOTIVI TBILISI

MERANI 91 TBILISI

SAMGURALI TSKHALTUBO

SIONI BOLNISI

FC TBILISI

TORPEDO KUTAIS!

TSU TBILISI

VIT GEORGIA TBILISI

Plate 37

GEORGIA

ARSENALI TBILISI

DILA GORI

DINAMO BATUMI

DINAMO TBILISI

GORDA RUSTAVI

IBERIA SAMTREDIA

KOLKHETI KHOBI

KOLKHETI 1913 POTI

LOKOMOTIVI TBILISI

MERANI 91 TBILISI

SAMGURALI TSKHALTUBO

SIONI BOLNISI

FC TBILISI

TORPEDO KUTAISI

TSU TBILISI

VIT GEORGIA TBILISI

Plate 38

GERMANY

ARMINIA BIELEFELD

BAYER 04 LEVERKUSEN

FC BAYERN MÜNCHEN

BORUSSIA DORTMUND

MSV DUISBURG

EINTRACHT FRANKFURT

SC FREIBURG

HAMBURGER SV

FC HANSA ROSTOCK

HERTHA BSC BERLIN

1.FC KAISERSLAUTERN

TSV 1860 MÜNCHEN

FC SCHALKE 04

VFB STUTTGART

SSV ULM

SPVGG UNTERHACHING

SV WERDER BREMEN

VFL WOLFSBURG

1.FC KÖLN

VFL BOCHUM

FC ENERGIE COTTBUS

Plate 39

GERMANY

ARMINIA BIELEFELD

BAYER 04 LEVERKUSEN

FC BAYERN MÜNCHEN

BORUSSIA DORTMUND

MSV DUISBURG

EINTRACHT FRANKFURT

SC FREIBURG

HAMBURGER SV

FC HANSA ROSTOCK

HERTHA BSC BERLIN

1.FC KAISERSLAUTERN

TSV 1860 MÜNCHEN

FC SCHALKE 04

VFB STUTTGART

SSV ULM

SPVGG UNTERHACHING

SV WERDER BREMEN

VFL WOLFSBURG

1.FC KÖLN

VFL BOCHUM

FC ENERGIE COTTBUS

Plate 40

GREECE

AEK   APOLLON   ARIS   ETHNIKOS ASTIR   IONIKOS

IRAKLIS   KALAMATA   KAVALA   OFI   OLYMPIAKOS

PANAHAIKI   PANATHINAIKOS   PANILIAKOS   PANIONIOS

PAOK   PROODEFTIKI   TRIKALA   XANTHI

ATHINAIKOS   YANINA

Plate 41

GREECE

AEK

APOLLON

ARIS

ETHNIKOS ASTIR

IONIKOS

IRAKLIS

KALAMATA

KAVALA

OFI

OLYMPIAKOS

PANAHAIKI

PANATHINAIKOS

PANILIAKOS

PANIONIOS

PAOK

PROODEFTIKI

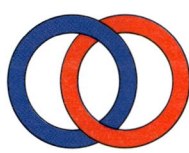
TRIKALA

XANTHI

ATHINAIKOS

YANINA

Plate 42

HOLLAND

AJAX

AZ

FC DEN BOSCH

SC CAMBUUR LEEUWARDEN

FEYENOORD

FORTUNA SITTARD

DE GRAAFSCHAP

SC HEERENVEEN

MVV

NEC

PSV

RKC WAALWIJK

RODA JC

SPARTA

FC TWENTE

FC UTRECHT

VITESSE

WILLEM II

NAC

FC GRONINGEN

RBC

Plate 43

HOLLAND

AJAX

AZ

FC DEN BOSCH

SC CAMBUUR LEEUWARDEN

FEYENOORD

FORTUNA SITTARD

DE GRAAFSCHAP

SC HEERENVEEN

MVV

NEC

PSV

RKC WAALWIJK

RODA JC

SPARTA

FC TWENTE

FC UTRECHT

VITESSE

WILLEM II

NAC

FC GRONINGEN

RBC

Plate 44

HUNGARY

DEBRECENI VSC

DIÓSGYÖRI FC

DUNAFERR SE

FERENCVÁROS

GÁZSZER FC

GYÖRI ETO FC

HALADÁS-MILOS

KISPEST-HONVÉD FC

MTK HUNGÁRIA FC

NAGYKANIZSA

NYÍRSÉG-SPARTACUS FC

SIÓFOK

SZEGED LC

LOMBARD FC TATABÁNYA

ÚJPEST FC

VASAS DH

VÁC FC-ZOLLNER

ZALAHÚS ZTE FC

VIDEOTON FCF

MÁTAV SOPRON

Plate 45

HUNGARY

DEBRECENI VSC

DIÓSGYŐRI FC

DUNAFERR SE

FERENCVÁROS

GÁZSZER FC

GYŐRI ETO FC

HALADÁS-MILOS

KISPEST-HONVÉD FC

MTK HUNGÁRIA FC

NAGYKANIZSA

NYÍRSÉG-SPARTACUS FC

SIÓFOK

SZEGED LC

LOMBARD FC TATABÁNYA

ÚJPEST FC

VASAS DH

VÁC FC-ZOLLNER

ZALAHÚS ZTE FC

VIDEOTON FCF

MÁTAV SOPRON

Plate 46

ICELAND

BREIDABLIK   FRAM   GRINDAVÍK   ÍA

ÍBV   KEFLAVÍK   KR

LEIFTUR   VALUR   VÍKINGUR

FYLKIR   STJARNAN

Plate 47

ICELAND

BREIDABLIK

FRAM

GRINDAVÍK

ÍA

ÍBV

KEFLAVÍK

KR

LEIFTUR

VALUR

VÍKINGUR

FYLKIR

STJARNAN

Plate 48

ISRAEL

MS ASHDOD

BEITAR JERUSALEM

BNEI YEHUDA

HAPOEL HAIFA

HAPOEL IRONY RISHON LEZION

HAPOEL JERUSALEM

HAPOEL KFAR-SABA

HAPOEL PETACH-TIKVA

HAPOEL TEL-AVIV

MACCABI HAIFA

MACCABI HERZLIYA

MACCABI NETANYA

MACCABI PETACH-TIKVA

MACCABI TEL-AVIV

ZAFRIRIM HOLON

Plate 49

ISRAEL

MS ASHDOD

BEITAR JERUSALEM

BNEI YEHUDA

HAPOEL HAIFA

HAPOEL IRONY RISHON LEZION

HAPOEL JERUSALEM

HAPOEL KFAR-SABA

HAPOEL PETACH-TIKVA

HAPOEL TEL-AVIV

MACCABI HAIFA

MACCABI HERZLIYA

MACCABI NETANYA

MACCABI PETACH-TIKVA

MACCABI TEL-AVIV

ZAFRIRIM HOLON

Plate 50

ITALY

BARI BOLOGNA CAGLIARI FIORENTINA INTER

JUVENTUS LAZIO LECCE MILAN PARMA

PERUGIA PIACENZA REGGINA ROMA

TORINO UDINESE VENEZIA VERONA

VICENZA ATALANTA BRESCIA NAPOLI

Plate 51

ITALY

BARI

BOLOGNA

CAGLIARI

FIORENTINA

INTER

JUVENTUS

LAZIO

LECCE

MILAN

PARMA

PERUGIA

PIACENZA

REGGINA

ROMA

TORINO

UDINESE

VENEZIA

VERONA

VICENZA

ATALANTA

BRESCIA

NAPOLI

Plate 52

LATVIA

DINABURG DAUGAVPILS

METALURGS LIEPAYA

POLICE FK RIGA

FK REZEKNE

FK RIGA

SKONTO RIGA

FK VALMIERA

FK VENTSPILS

LU DAUGAVA RIGA

DINABURG DAUGAVPILS

METALURGS LIEPAYA

POLICE FK RIGA

FK REZEKNE

FK RIGA

SKONTO RIGA

FK VALMIERA

FK VENTSPILS

LU DAUGAVA RIGA

Plate 53

LIECHTENSTEIN

FC BALZERS

USV ESCHEN-MAUREN

FC RUGGELL

FC SCHAAN

FC TRIESEN

FC TRIESENBERG

FC VADUZ

LITHUANIA

ATLANTAS KLAIPEDA

BANGA GARGZDAI

EKRANAS PANEVEZYS

INKARAS KAUNAS

KAREDA SIAULIAI

NEVEZIS KEDAINIAI

ZALGIRIS KAUNAS

ZALGIRIS VILNIUS

Plate 54

LUXEMBOURG

ARIS BONNEVOIE

AVENIR BEGGEN

F91 DUDELANGE

CS GREVENMACHER

CS HOBSCHEID

JEUNESSE ESCH

FC MONDERCANGE

US RUMELANGE

FC SCHIFFLANGE 95

SPORTING MERTZIG

UNION LUXEMBOURG

FC WILTZ 71

ETZELLA ETTELBRUCK

FC RODANGE 91

Plate 55

LUXEMBOURG

ARIS BONNEVOIE

AVENIR BEGGEN

F91 DUDELANGE

CS GREVENMACHER

CS HOBSCHEID

JEUNESSE ESCH

FC MONDERCANGE

US RUMELANGE

FC SCHIFFLANGE 95

SPORTING MERTZIG

UNION LUXEMBOURG

FC WILTZ 71

ETZELLA ETTELLBRUCK

FC RODANGE 91

Plate 56

MALTA

BIRKIRKARA   FLORIANA   GOZO   HIBERNIANS

NAXXAR LIONS   PIETA HOTSPURS   RABAT AJAX

SLIEMA WANDERERS   VALLETTA   ZURRIEQ

HAMRUN SPARTANS   XGHAJRA TORNADOES

Plate 57

MALTA

BIRKIRKARA

FLORIANA

GOZO

HIBERNIANS

NAXXAR LIONS

PIETA HOTSPURS

RABAT AJAX

SLIEMA WANDERERS

VALLETTA

ZURRIEQ

HAMRUN SPARTANS

XGHAJRA TORNADOES

Plate 58

NORTHERN IRELAND

BALLYMENA UNITED   CLIFTONVILLE   COLERAINE   CRUSADERS

GLENAVON   GLENTORAN   LINFIELD   LISBURN DISTILLERY

NEWRY TOWN   PORTADOWN   OMAGH TOWN

Plate 59

NORTHERN IRELAND

BALLYMENA UNITED

CLIFTONVILLE

COLERAINE

CRUSADERS

GLENAVON

GLENTORAN

LINFIELD

LISBURN DISTILLERY

NEWRY TOWN

PORTADOWN

OMAGH TOWN

Plate 60

NORWAY

FK BODØ/GLIMT

SK BRANN

KONGSVINGER IL

LILLESTRØM SK

MOLDE FK

MOSS FK

ODD GRENLAND

ROSENBORG BK

SKEID

STABAEK IF

STRØMSGODSET IF

TROMSØ IL

VIKING FK

VÅLERENGA IF

FK HAUGESUND

BRYNE FK

IK START

Plate 61

NORWAY

FK BODØ/GLIMT

SK BRANN

KONGSVINGER IL

LILLESTRØM SK

MOLDE FK

MOSS FK

ODD GRENLAND

ROSENBORG BK

SKEID

STABAEK IF

STRØMSGODSET IF

TROMSØ IL

VIKING FK

VÅLERENGA IF

FK HAUGESUND

BRYNE FK

IK START

Plate 62

POLAND

AMICA WRONKI

GORNIK ZABRZE

GROCLIN DYSKOBOLIA GRODZISK

LECH POZNAN

LEGIA WARSZAWA

LKS LODZ

ODRA WODZISLAW

PETRO PLOCK

POGON SZCZECIN

POLONIA WARSZAWA

RUCH CHORZOW

RUCH RADZIONKOW

STOMIL OLSZTYN

WIDZEW LODZ

WISLA KRAKOW

ZAGLEBIE LUBIN

SLASK WROCLAW

GKS KATOWICE

Plate 63

POLAND

AMICA WRONKI

GORNIK ZABRZE

GROCLIN DYSKOBOLIA GRODZISK

LECH POZNAN

LEGIA WARSZAWA

LKS LODZ

ODRA WODZISLAW

PETRO PLOCK

POGON SZCZECIN

POLONIA WARSZAWA

RUCH CHORZOW

RUCH RADZIONKOW

STOMIL OLSZTYN

WIDZEW LODZ

WISLA KRAKOW

ZAGLEBIE LUBIN

SLASK WROCLAW

GKS KATOWICE

Plate 64

PORTUGAL

FC ALVERCA

CF OS BELENENSES

SL BENFICA

BOAVISTA FC

SC BRAGA

SC CAMPOMAIORENSE

CF ESTRELA AMADORA

SC FARENSE

GIL VICENTE FC

CS MARÍTIMO

FC PORTO

RIO AVE FC

SC SALGUEIROS

CD SANTA CLARA

SPORTING CP

UNIÃO LEIRIA

VITÓRIA GUIMARÃES

VITÓRIA SETÚBAL

FC PAÇOS FERREIRA

SC BEIRA MAR

DESPORTIVO AVES

Plate 65

PORTUGAL

FC ALVERCA

CF OS BELENENSES

SL BENFICA

BOAVISTA FC

SC BRAGA

SC CAMPOMAIORENSE

CF ESTRELA AMADORA

SC FARENSE

GIL VICENTE FC

CS MARÍTIMO

FC PORTO

RIO AVE FC

SC SALGUEIROS

CD SANTA CLARA

SPORTING CP

UNIÃO LEIRIA

VITÓRIA GUIMARÃES

VITÓRIA SETÚBAL

FC PAÇOS FERREIRA

SC BEIRA MAR

DESPORTIVO AVES

Plate 66

REPUBLIC OF IRELAND

BOHEMIANS   CORK CITY   DERRY CITY   DROGHEDA UNITED

FINN HARPS   GALWAY UNITED   ST. PATRICK'S ATHLETIC   SHAMROCK ROVERS

SHELBOURNE   SLIGO ROVERS   UCD   WATERFORD UNITED

BRAY WANDERERS   LONGFORD TOWN   KILKENNY CITY

Plate 67

REPUBLIC OF IRELAND

BOHEMIANS

CORK CITY

DERRY CITY

DROGHEDA UNITED

FINN HARPS

GALWAY UNITED

ST. PATRICK'S ATHLETIC

SHAMROCK ROVERS

SHELBOURNE

SLIGO ROVERS

UCD

WATERFORD UNITED

BRAY WANDERERS

LONGFORD TOWN

KILKENNY CITY

Plate 68

ROMANIA

FC ARGES DACIA PITESTI

ASTRA PLOIESTI

FCM BACAU

FC BRASOV

CEAHLAUL PIATRA NEAMT

DINAMO BUCURESTI

FC EXTENSIV CRAIOVA

FC FARUL CONSTANTA

GLORIA BISTRITA

FC NATIONAL BUCURESTI

FC ONESTI

OTELUL GALATI

PETROLUL PLOIESTI

RAPID BUCURESTI

CSM RESITA

ROCAR BUCURESTI

STEAUA BUCURESTI

UNIVERSITATEA CRAIOVA

FORESTA FALTICENI

GAZ METAN MEDIAS

Plate 69

ROMANIA

FC ARGES DACIA PITESTI

ASTRA PLOIESTI

FCM BACAU

FC BRASOV

CEAHLAUL PIATRA NEAMT

DINAMO BUCURESTI

FC EXTENSIV CRAIOVA

FC FARUL CONSTANTA

GLORIA BISTRITA

FC NATIONAL BUCURESTI

FC ONESTI

OTELUL GALATI

PETROLUL PLOIESTI

RAPID BUCURESTI

CSM RESITA

ROCAR BUCURESTI

STEAUA BUCURESTI

UNIVERSITATEA CRAIOVA

FORESTA FALTICENI

GAZ METAN MEDIAS

Plate 70

RUSSIA

ALANIA VLADIKAVKAZ   CHERNOMORETS NOVOROSSIISK   CSKA MOSKVA   DINAMO MOSKVA   KRYLYA SOVETOV SAMARA

LOKOMOTIV MOSKVA   LOKOMOTIV NIZHNIY NOVGOROD   ROSTSELMASH ROSTOV-NA-DONU   ROTOR VOLGOGRAD   SATURN RAMONSKOE

SHINNIK YAROSLAVL   SPARTAK MOSKVA   TORPEDO MOSKVA   URALAN ELISTA

ZENIT SANKT-PETERBURG   ZHEMCHUZHINA SOCHI   ANZHI MAKHACHKALA   FAKEL VORONEZH

Plate 71

RUSSIA

ALANIA VLADIKAVKAZ

CHERNOMORETS NOVOROSSIISK

CSKA MOSKVA

DINAMO MOSKVA

KRYLYA SOVETOV SAMARA

LOKOMOTIV MOSKVA

LOKOMOTIV NIZHNIY NOVGOROD

ROSTSELMASH ROSTOV-NA-DONU

ROTOR VOLGOGRAD

SATURN RAMONSKOE

SHINNIK YAROSLAVL

SPARTAK MOSKVA

TORPEDO MOSKVA

URALAN ELISTA

ZENIT SANKT-PETERBURG

ZHEMCHUZHINA SOCHI

ANZHI MAKHACHKALA

FAKEL VORONEZH

Plate 72

SCOTLAND

ABERDEEN

CELTIC

DUNDEE

DUNDEE UNITED

HEART OF MIDLOTHIAN

HIBERNIAN

KILMARNOCK

MOTHERWELL

RANGERS

ST. JOHNSTONE

DUNFERMLINE ATHLETIC

ST. MIRREN

Plate 73

SCOTLAND

ABERDEEN

CELTIC

DUNDEE

DUNDEE UNITED

HEART OF MIDLOTHIAN

HIBERNIAN

KILMARNOCK

MOTHERWELL

RANGERS

ST. JOHNSTONE

DUNFERMLINE ATHLETIC

ST. MIRREN

Plate 74

SLOVAKIA

ARTMEDIA PETRZALKA

BANIK PRIEVIDZA

DAC DUNAJSKA STREDA

ZTS DUBNICA

DUKLA BANSKA BYSTRICA

HFC HUMENNE

INTER BRATISLAVA

VTJ KOBA SENEC

1.FC KOSICE

FC NITRA

OZETA DUKLA TRENCIN

SCP RUZOMBEROK

SLOVAN BRATISLAVA

SPARTAK TRNAVA

TATRAN PRESOV

MSK ZILINA

MATADOR PUCHOV

Plate 75

SLOVAKIA

ARTMEDIA PETRZALKA

BANÍK PRIEVIDZA

DAC DUNAJSKA STREDA

ZTS DUBNICA

DUKLA BANSKA BYSTRICA

HFC HUMENNE

INTER BRATISLAVA

VTJ KOBA SENEC

1.FC KOSICE

FC NITRA

OZETA DUKLA TRENCIN

SCP RUZOMBEROK

SLOVAN BRATISLAVA

SPARTAK TRNAVA

TATRAN PRESOV

MSK ZILINA

MATADOR PUCHOV

Plate 76

SLOVENIA

NK DOMZALE NK DRAVOGRAD FEROTERM POHORJE HIT GORICA

KOROTAN PREVALJE NK MARIBOR MURA MURSKA SOBOTA POTROSNIK BELTINCI

PRIMORJE AJDOVSCINA PUBLIKUM CELJE RUDAR VELENJE SCT OLIMPIJA LJUBLJANA

NK KOPER TABOR SEZANA

Plate 77

SLOVENIA

NK DOMZALE

NK DRAVOGRAD

FEROTERM POHORJE

HIT GORICA

KOROTAN PREVALJE

NK MARIBOR

MURA MURSKA SOBOTA

POTROSNIK BELTINCI

PRIMORJE AJDOVSCINA

PUBLIKUM CELJE

RUDAR VELENJE

SCT OLIMPIJA LJUBLJANA

NK KOPER

TABOR SEZANA

Plate 78

SPAIN

DEPORTIVO ALAVES

ATHLETIC BILBAO

ATLETICO MADRID

FC BARCELONA

REAL BETIS

RC CELTA

RC DEPORTIVO

RCD ESPANYOL

MALAGA CF

RCD MALLORCA

CD NUMANCIA

REAL OVIEDO

RACING SANTANDER

RAYO VALLECANO

REAL MADRID

REAL SOCIEDAD

SEVILLA FC

VALENCIA CF

REAL VALLADOLID

REAL ZARAGOZA

UD LAS PALMAS

CA OSASUNA

VILLARREAL CF

Plate 79

SPAIN

DEPORTIVO ALAVES

ATHLETIC BILBAO

ATLETICO MADRID

FC BARCELONA

REAL BETIS

RC CELTA

RC DEPORTIVO

RCD ESPANYOL

MALAGA CF

RCD MALLORCA

CD NUMANCIA

REAL OVIEDO

RACING SANTANDER

RAYO VALLECANO

REAL MADRID

REAL SOCIEDAD

SEVILLA FC

VALENCIA CF

REAL VALLADOLID

REAL ZARAGOZA

UD LAS PALMAS

CA OSASUNA

VILLARREAL CF

Plate 80

SWEDEN

AIK

DJURGÅRDENS IF

IF ELFSBORG

IFK GÖTEBORG

HALMSTADS BK

HAMMARBY IF

HELSINGBORGS IF

KALMAR FF

MALMÖ FF

IFK NORRKÖPING

TRELLEBORGS FF

VÄSTRA FRÖLUNDA IF

ÖREBRO SK

ÖRGRYTE IS

GIF SUNDSVALL

BK HÄCKEN

GAIS

Plate 81

SWEDEN

AIK

DJURGÅRDENS IF

IF ELFSBORG

IFK GÖTEBORG

HALMSTADS BK

HAMMARBY IF

HELSINGBORGS IF

KALMAR FF

MALMÖ FF

IFK NORRKÖPING

TRELLEBORGS FF

VÄSTRA FRÖLUNDA IF

ÖREBRO SK

ÖRGRYTE IS

GIF SUNDSVALL

BK HÄCKEN

GAIS

Plate 82

SWITZERLAND

FC AARAU

FC BASEL

SR DELEMONT

GRASSHOPPER-CLUB ZÜRICH

LAUSANNE-SPORTS

FC LUGANO

FC LUZERN

NEUCHATEL XAMAX FC

FC ST. GALLEN

SERVETTE FC GENEVE

YVERDON-SPORTS

FC ZÜRICH

FC SION

Plate 83

SWITZERLAND

FC AARAU

FC BASEL

SR DELEMONT

GRASSHOPPER-CLUB ZÜRICH

LAUSANNE-SPORTS

FC LUGANO

FC LUZERN

NEUCHATEL XAMAX FC

FC ST. GALLEN

SERVETTE FC GENEVE

YVERDON-SPORTS

FC ZÜRICH

FC SION

Plate 84

TURKEY

ADANASPOR

ALTAY

ANKARAGÜCÜ

ANTALYASPOR

BESIKTAS

BURSASPOR

DENZILISPOR

ERZURUMSPOR

FENERBAHÇE

GALATASARAY

GAZIANTEPSPOR

GENÇLERBIRLIGI

GÖZTEPE

ISTANBULSPOR

KOCAELISPOR

SAMSUNSPOR

TRABZONSPOR

VANSPOR

YIMPAS YOZGATSPOR

SIIRT JETPA

ÇAYKUR RIZESPOR

Plate 85

TURKEY

ADANASPOR

ALTAY

ANKARAGÜCÜ

ANTALYASPOR

BESIKTAS

BURSASPOR

DENIZLISPOR

ERZURUMSPOR

FENERBAHÇE

GALATASARAY

GAZIANTEPSPOR

GENÇLERBIRLIGI

GÖZTEPE

ISTANBULSPOR

KOCAELISPOR

SAMSUNSPOR

TRABZONSPOR

VANSPOR

YIMPAS YOZGATSPOR

SIIRT JETPA

ÇAYKUR RIZESPOR

Plate 86

UKRAINE

CHORNOMORETS ODESA

CSCA KYIV

DNIPRO DNIPROPETROVSK

DYNAMO KYIV

KARPATY LVIV

KRYVBAS KRYVYI RIH

METALIST KHARKIV

METALURG DONETSK

METALURG MARIUPOL

METALURG ZAPORIZHZHYA

NYVA TERNOPIL

PRYKARPATTYA IVANO-FRANKIVSK

SHAKHTAR DONETSK

TAVRIYA SIMFEROPOL

VORSKLA POLTAVA

ZIRKA KIROVOHRAD

STAL ALCHEVSK

Plate 87

UKRAINE

CHORNOMORETS ODESA

CSCA KYIV

DNIPRO DNIPROPETROVSK

DYNAMO KYIV

KARPATY LYIV

KRYVBAS KRYVYI RIH

METALIST KHARKIV

METALURG DONETSK

METALURG MARIUPOL

METALURG ZAPORIZHZHYA

NYVA TERNOPIL

PRYKARPATTYA IVANO-FRANKIVSK

SHAKHTAR DONETSK

TAVRIYA SIMFEROPOL

VORSKLA POLTAVA

ZIRKA KIROVOHRAD

STAL ALCHEVSK

Plate 88

WALES

ABERYSTWYTH TOWN   AFAN LIDO   BANGOR CITY   BARRY TOWN   CAERNARFON TOWN

CAERSWS   CARMARTHEN TOWN   CONNAH'S QUAY NOMADS   CONWY UNITED   CWMBRAN TOWN

FLEXSYS CEFN DRUIDS   HAVERFORDWEST COUNTY   INTER CARDIFF   LLANELLI

NEWTOWN   RHAYADER TOWN   RHYL   TOTAL NETWORK SOLUTIONS

PORT TALBOT ATHLETIC   OSWESTRY TOWN

Plate 89

WALES

ABERYSTWYTH TOWN

AFAN LIDO

BANGOR CITY

BARRY TOWN

CAERNARFON TOWN

CAERSWS

CARMARTHEN TOWN

CONNAH'S QUAY NOMADS

CONWY UNITED

CWMBRAN TOWN

FLEXSYS CEFN DRUIDS

HAVERFORDWEST COUNTY

INTER CARDIFF

LLANELLI

NEWTOWN

RHAYADER TOWN

RHYL

TOTAL NETWORK SOLUTIONS

PORT TALBOT ATHLETIC

OSWESTRY TOWN

Plate 90

ALBANIA

APOLONIA FIER

BYLIS BALLSH

DINAMO TIRANË

ELBASANI

FLAMURTARI VLORË

LUSHNJA

PARTIZANI TIRANË

SHKUMBINI PEQIN

SHQIPONJA GJIROKASTËR

SKËNDERBEU KORÇË

TEUTA DURRËS

SK TIRANA

TOMORI BERAT

VLLAZNIA SHKODËR

BESLIDHJA LEZHË

BESA KAVAJË

Plate 91

ANDORRA • ARMENIA • AZERBAIJAN

ANDORRA
CE PRINCIPAT

ANDORRA
CONSTELACIO ESPORTIVA

ARMENIA
ARARAT YEREVAN

ARMENIA
EREBUNI YEREVAN

AZERBAIJAN
KAPAZ GANJA

AZERBAIJAN
NEFTCHI BAKU

AZERBAIJAN
SHAMKIR

AZERBAIJAN
SHIRAK GYUMRI

AZERBAIJAN
TURAN TOVUZ

AZERBAIJAN
VILASH MASALLI

BELARUS

FC BATE BORISOV

BELSHINA BOBRUISK

DINAMO BREST

DINAMO MINSK

DNEPR-TRANSMASH MOGILEV

FC GOMEL

LOKOMOTIV-96 VITEBSK

FC MOLODECHNO

NAFTAN-DEVON NOVOPOLOTSK

NEMAN-BELKARD GRODNO

SHAKHTER SOLIGORSK

SLAVIYA MOZYR

TORPEDO-MAZ MINSK

TORPEDO-KADINO MOGILEV

KOMMUNALNIK SLONIM

Plate 92

BOSNIA-HERZEGOVINA

BORAC BANJA LUKA

BOSNA VISOKO

BUDUCNOST BANOVICI

CELIK ZENICA

GRADINA SREBRNICA

ISKRA BUGOJNO

JEDINSTVO BIHAC

LUKAVAC

POSUSJE

RUDAR KAKANJ

SARAJEVO

SLOBODA TUZLA

VELEZ MOSTAR

ZELJEZNICAR SARAJEVO

Plate 93

ESTONIA

JALGPALLIKLUBI
EESTI PÕLEVKIVI
EP JÕHVI

FC FLORA TALLINN

FC LANTANA TALLINN

LELLE SK

FC LEVADIA MAARDU

TRANS NARVA

TULEVIK VILJANDI

VMK TALLINN

FC KURESSAARE

FAROE ISLANDS

B36

B68

B71

GÍ

HB

ÍF

KÍ

NSÍ

SUMBA

VB

FS VÁGAR
FS VÁGAR

Plate 94

MACEDONIA

BOREC MHK VELES

CEMENTARNICA 55 SKOPJE

MAKEDONIJA GP SKOPJE

PELISTER BITOLA

PROBEDA PRILEP

SASA MAKEDONSKA KAMENICA

SILEKS KRATOVO

SLOGA JUGOMAGNAT SKOPJE

VARDAR SKOPJE

MOLDOVA

FC AGRO CHISINAU

CONSTRUCTORUL CHISINAU

OLIMPIA BALTI

SERIF TIRASPOL

TILIGUL TIRASPOL

ZIMBRU CHISINAU

Plate 95

SAN MARINO

CAILUNGO

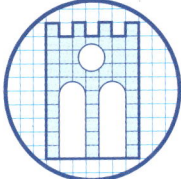

COSMOS

DOGANA

DOMAGNANO

FAETANO

FIORITA

FOLGORE

JUVENES

LIBERTAS

MONTEVITO

MURATA

PENNAROSSA

SAN GIOVANNI

TRE FIORI

TRE PENNE

VIRTUS

Plate 96

YUGOSLAVIA

BORAC CACAK

BUDUCNOST PODGORICA

CRVENA ZVEZDA BEOGRAD

CUKARICKI BEOGRAD

HAJDUK BEOGRAD

HAJDUK KULA

MILICIONAR BEOGRAD

MOGREN BUDVA

OBILIC BEOGRAD

OFK BEOGRAD

PARTIZAN BEOGRAD

PROLETER ZRENJANIN

RAD BEOGRAD

RADNICKI KRAGUJEVAC

RADNICKI NIS

SARTID SMEDEREVO

SPARTAK SUBOTICA

SUTJESKA NIKSIC

VOJVODINA NOVI SAD

ZELEZNIK BEOGRAD

FK ZEMUN

CENTENARY 'DOUBLE' FOR LAZIO

'Azzurri' adventure ends in agony

FEDERATION DIRECTORY

Federazione Italiana Giuoco Calcio
Via Gregorio Allegri 14, CP 2450, 00198 Roma

tel - (06) 84911
fax - (06) 84912239
website - www.lega-calcio.it/

Year of Formation - 1898
President - Luciano Nizzola
Secretary - Guglielmo Petrosino

So near yet so far. Italy were literally seconds away from winning Euro 2000. The final was 94 minutes old when Sylvain Wiltord brought screams of horror from Italian fans everywhere by scoring France's equalising goal. It was a truly sickening moment for the 'Azzurri' and they could not recover from it. David Trezeguet's booming left-foot strike 13 minutes into extra-time ensured that it was France, not Italy, who would lift the first major international football prize of the 21st century.

The feeling in the Italian camp afterwards was one of utter despair. The country had not won a significant international trophy since the 1982 World Cup. To come so very close and then be denied by almost the last kick of the game was a stomach-wrenching experience. Italy had had the European title in their grasp yet somehow they had let it slip. What made it even harder to take was that they

had played so well and were arguably the better team on the night.

Outside Italy, there were many who rejoiced in their defeat. While the 'Azzurri' had played with considerable flair and adventure against France, the memory of their semi-final triumph over Holland was still fresh. That was a game which Dino Zoff's team won in the old-fashioned Italian style, getting everybody behind the ball and stifling the creativity out of their opponents to the detriment of the overall spectacle. Although Italy had the excuse that they were down to ten men for the majority of the game, it was evident even before Gianluca Zambrotta's 34th-minute red card that they were playing predominantly for penalties.

In view of Italy's poor record in penalty shoot-outs, that might have been construed as a very risky strategy, but ultimately, thanks to Holland's profligacy from the spot

LEAGUE CHAMPIONSHIP RESULTS 99/00

		1	2	3	4	5	6	7	8	9	10	11	12	13	14	15	16	17	18
1	Bari		1-1	1-0	1-0	2-1	1-1	0-0	3-1	1-1	0-1	0-2	3-2	1-1	0-0	1-1	1-1	3-0	1-1
2	Bologna	1-0		1-0	0-0	3-0	0-2	2-3	2-0	2-3	1-0	2-1	0-0	0-1	1-0	0-0	2-1	1-1	0-0
3	Cagliari	2-3	2-2		1-1	0-2	0-1	0-0	0-0	0-0	2-3	2-1	3-0	0-1	1-0	1-1	0-3	1-1	0-1
4	Fiorentina	1-0	2-2	2-0		2-1	1-1	3-3	3-0	2-1	0-2	1-0	2-1	1-0	1-3	1-1	1-1	3-0	4-1
5	Inter	3-0	1-1	2-1	0-4		1-2	1-1	6-0	1-2	5-1	5-0	2-1	1-1	2-1	1-1	3-0	3-0	3-0
6	Juventus	2-0	2-0	1-1	1-0	1-0		0-1	1-0	3-1	1-0	3-0	1-0	1-1	2-1	3-2	4-1	1-0	1-0
7	Lazio	3-1	3-1	2-1	2-0	2-2	0-0		4-2	4-4	0-0	1-0	2-0	3-0	2-1	3-0	2-1	3-2	4-0
8	Lecce	1-0	1-1	2-1	0-0	1-0	2-0	0-1		2-2	0-0	0-1	0-1	2-1	0-0	2-1	1-0	2-1	2-1
9	Milan	4-1	4-0	2-2	1-1	1-2	2-0	2-1	2-2		2-1	3-1	1-0	2-2	2-2	2-0	4-0	3-0	3-3
10	Parma	2-1	1-1	3-1	0-4	1-1	1-1	1-2	4-1	1-0		1-2	1-0	3-0	2-0	4-1	0-0	3-1	3-0
11	Perugia	1-2	3-2	3-0	1-2	1-2	1-0	0-2	2-2	0-3	1-1		2-0	2-1	2-2	1-0	0-5	2-1	0-0
12	Piacenza	2-1	0-0	1-1	2-0	1-3	0-2	0-2	1-1	0-1	1-2	0-0		0-0	1-1	0-2	0-1	2-2	1-0
13	Reggina	1-0	1-0	1-1	2-2	0-1	0-2	0-0	2-1	1-2	2-2	1-1	1-0		0-4	2-1	0-0	1-0	1-1
14	Roma	3-1	2-0	2-2	4-0	0-0	0-1	4-1	3-2	1-1	0-0	3-1	2-1	0-2		1-0	1-1	5-0	3-1
15	Torino	3-1	2-1	1-1	1-0	0-1	0-0	2-4	1-2	2-2	2-2	0-1	2-1	2-1	1-1		0-1	2-1	0-3
16	Udinese	5-1	2-1	5-2	1-1	3-0	1-1	0-3	2-1	1-2	0-1	2-1	3-0	3-2	0-2	0-0		5-2	3-3
17	Venezia	0-1	0-1	3-0	2-1	1-0	0-4	2-0	0-0	1-0	0-2	1-2	0-0	2-0	1-3	2-2	1-1		2-2
18	Verona	0-1	0-0	2-0	2-2	1-2	2-0	1-0	2-0	0-0	4-3	2-0	1-0	1-1	2-2	0-1	2-2	1-0	

LEAGUE CHAMPIONSHIP FINAL TABLE 99/00

		Pd	Home					Away					Total					PT	GD
			W	D	L	F	A	W	D	L	F	A	W	D	L	F	A		
1	Lazio	34	13	4	0	40	15	8	5	4	24	18	21	9	4	64	33	72	31
2	Juventus	34	14	2	1	28	8	7	6	4	18	12	21	8	5	46	20	71	26
3	Milan	34	10	6	1	40	18	6	7	4	25	22	16	13	5	65	40	61	25
4	Inter	34	10	4	3	40	16	7	3	7	18	20	17	7	10	58	36	58	22
5	Parma	34	10	4	3	31	16	6	6	5	21	21	16	10	8	52	37	58	15
6	Roma	34	10	5	2	34	14	4	7	6	23	20	14	12	8	57	34	54	23
7	Fiorentina	34	10	5	2	30	17	3	7	7	18	21	13	12	9	48	38	51	10
8	Udinese	34	9	4	4	36	23	4	7	6	19	22	13	11	10	55	45	50	10
9	Verona	34	8	6	3	23	14	2	7	8	17	31	10	13	11	40	45	43	-5
10	Perugia	34	7	4	6	22	25	5	2	10	14	27	12	6	16	36	52	42	-16
11	Bologna	34	8	5	4	18	12	1	8	8	14	27	9	13	12	32	39	40	-7
12	Reggina	34	6	7	4	16	18	3	6	8	15	24	9	13	12	31	42	40	-11
13	Lecce	34	9	5	3	18	11	1	5	11	15	38	10	10	14	33	49	40	-16
14	Bari	34	6	9	2	20	14	4	0	13	14	34	10	9	15	34	48	39	-14
15	Torino	34	6	5	6	21	23	2	7	8	14	24	8	12	14	35	47	36	-12
16	Venezia	34	6	5	6	18	19	0	3	14	12	41	6	8	20	30	60	26	-30
17	Cagliari	34	3	7	7	15	20	0	6	11	14	34	3	13	18	29	54	22	-25
18	Piacenza	34	3	7	7	12	19	1	2	14	7	26	4	9	21	19	45	21	-26

during regular play and Italy's own masterful, thou-shalt-not-pass defending, the gamble paid off.

The negativity of Italy's performance against the Dutch - heightened by the Italian players' excessive fouling, time-wasting and diving - was depressing from a neutral perspective because they had played so well in their four previous games, winning every one of them, against Turkey, Belgium, Sweden and Romania. Rather fortunate in the manner of their opening victory over the Turks - a penalty that should not have been awarded - they were nevertheless the better team in that match and the three which followed. Italy played pretty much the same way in each match, blocking all routes to their own goal while posing constant danger in the other half of the field with their sharp, speedy counter-attacks. It was that modus operandi which almost won them the final.

Italy were unable to dictate the flow and rhythm of the game like the French and the Dutch did, but the tactics employed by Dino Zoff were shrewd and effective and geared to suit the team's strengths. The most impressive Italian players at Euro 2000 were those charged with defensive responsibilities. Francesco Toldo was the best goalkeeper at the tournament bar none, while Alessandro Nesta and Fabio Cannavaro both enhanced their already formidable reputations as two of the world's outstanding young defenders. Paolo Maldini, the captain and new record cap-holder, also had a fine tournament and, as at the 1994 World Cup, a particularly great final. There was particular sorrow for him after Italy's defeat as another

golden opportunity to crown his glorious career with a first international trophy vanished before his eyes.

The villain of the final was Alessandro Del Piero, who missed two wonderful opportunities to add to Marco Delvecchio's classic opening goal and put Italy in the clear. He, like club colleague Filippo Inzaghi, had a generally disappointing time in attack, where the 'Azzurri' would clearly have benefitted from the thrust and power of the injured Christian Vieri. Roma's Francesco Totti, however, proved to be one of the revelations of the tournament, scoring two goals and generally illuminating the Italian attack with his incisive through-balls, several of which even unhinged the famous French back-four in the final.

Going into the tournament, Italy were said to have major personnel probems in midfield, but the experience of Demetrio Albertini and Antonio Conte gave the 'Azzurri' a very solid base in that sector of the field, and newcomer Stefano Fiore looked every inch the classic Italian playmaker. He scored the most picturesque of Italy's nine goals with his brilliant first-time strike against Belgium. It was his first international goal on only his sixth appearance for the 'Azzurri'.

Coach Zoff, who had been widely criticised in the lead-up to the tournament - which, with four defeats in seven games, was hardly surprising - emerged from the tournament with his reputation soundly restored. However, one man who had not run out of ammunition to fire at him was Silvio Berlusconi. The Milan president came out with all sorts of inane and unjustified rhetoric in the wake of the final defeat, and this upset Zoff so much that he decided to quit. The Italian FA did their best to persuade him to change his mind, but Zoff was adamant. It seemed a bizarre and totally inappropriate exit, but Zoff had clearly had enough of the pressures of the job and Berlusconi's broadside was a convenient pretext for him to leave with his honour and integrity intact.

A Euro 2000 triumph would have sealed an impressive 'double' for Italian football as a few weeks earlier Marco

NATIONAL TEAM APPEARANCES 99/00

Coach - Dino ZOFF	DEN	BLS	BEL	SWE	ESP	POR	NOR	TUR	BEL	SWE	ROM	HOL	FRA	Cps	Gls
Gianluigi BUFFON (28/01/78) - Parma	G	G	G	G	G		G56							15	-
Christian PANUCCI (12/04/73) - Inter	D	D	D46	s64										21	1
Alessandro NESTA (19/03/76) - Lazio	D	D		D		D	D87	D	D	s42	D	D	D	31	-
Fabio CANNAVARO (13/09/73) - Parma	D	D	D	D	D	D	D77	D	D	s50	D	D	D	41	-
Giuseppe PANCARO (26/08/71) - Lazio	D			s74										4	-
Diego FUSER (11/11/68) - Parma	M		M71		M46									25	3
Dino BAGGIO (24/07/71) - Parma	M46		M											60	7
Demetrio ALBERTINI (23/08/71) - Milan	M		M			M46	M	M	M		M	M77	M	72	2
Eusebio DI FRANCESCO (08/09/69) - Roma	M70			M46		s76								13	1
Filippo INZAGHI (09/08/73) - Juventus	A	A	A68	s60	A46	A	A77	A	A77		A	A66		25	8
Christian VIERI (12/07/73) - Inter	A77	A81	A60											20	10
Giuliano GIANNICHEDDA (21/09/74) - Udinese	s46													3	-
Antonio CONTE (31/07/69) - Juventus	s70	M				M76	M28	M	M		M55			20	2
Francesco TOTTI (27/09/76) - Roma	s77		A78	s46	s46	s46	A	A82	A64		A74	s82	M	18	3
Paolo MALDINI (26/06/68) - Milan		D			D		D	D	M	D42	M46	M	M	111	7
Francesco MORIERO (31/03/69) - Inter		M												8	2
Luigi DI BIAGIO (03/06/71) - Inter		M			M46	s46 /89				M	s55	M	M65	19	2
Gianluca ZAMBROTTA (19/02/77) - Juventus		M		s46	M	M	M	M		M	M			10	-
Alessandro DEL PIERO (09/11/74) - Juventus	s81	A	s46	A46		s46	s74	s64	A	s74	A		s52	36	11
Ciro FERRARA (11/02/67) - Juventus		D	D75	D		s77				D				49	-
Paolo VANOLI (12/08/72) - Parma		M				s89								2	1
Mark IULIANO (12/08/73) - Juventus				s46	s75		D	s87	s61	D	D50	D	D	11	1
Vincenzo MONTELLA (18/06/74) - Roma		s68	A46			s77				A			s85	6	-
Gianluca PESSOTTO (11/08/70) - Juventus		s71	D	M74	M90		M	M61		M	s46	s77	M	20	-
Tomas LOCATELLI (09/06/76) - Udinese		s78	s80											2	-
Alessio TACCHINARDI (23/07/75) - Juventus				M80	s46									3	-
Massimo AMBROSINI (29/05/77) - Milan				M46	M60	s90	s28		s83	M			s65	8	-
Stefano FIORE (17/04/72) - Udinese				M64	M60	M	M46	M74	M83	s64	M	M82	M52	10	1
Gennaro GATTUSO (09/01/78) - Milan				s46	s60									2	-
Marco DELVECCHIO (07/04/73) - Roma				s46	A46				s77			s66	A85	7	1
Simone INZAGHI (05/04/76) - Lazio					s60									1	-
Francesco TOLDO (12/02/71) - Fiorentina						G	s56	G	G	G	G	G	G	14	-
Angelo DI LIVIO (26/07/66) - Fiorentina								s82		M64				29	-
Paolo NEGRO (16/04/72) - Lazio											M			8	-

EUROPEAN CUPS 99/00

CHAMPIONS' CUP
● **FIORENTINA**
Qualifying round WIDZEW LODZ (POL)
H 3-1 Adani (17), Cois (57), Rui Costa (90)
Toldo; Repka, Padalino, Adani; Di Livio (Bressan 52), Cois, Rui Costa,
Heinrich; Chiesa, Batistuta (Balbo 7), Mijatovic,
A 2-0 Chiesa (39), Cois (66)
Toldo; Repka, Padalino, Pierini; Di Livio, Cois (Okon 70), Amoroso,
Rui Costa (Firicano 85), Heinrich; Chiesa (Balbo 73), Mijatovic.

Champions' League
1st match ARSENAL (ENG)
H 0-0
Toldo; Repka, Padalino, Pierini (Adani 84); Di Livio, Cois, Rui Costa,
Heinrich; Chiesa, Batistuta, Mijatovic.

2nd match FC BARCELONA (ESP)
A 2-4 Batistuta (50), Chiesa (79)
Toldo; Padalino, Adani, Repka, Heinrich; Di Livio, Cois, Rui Costa, Amoroso
(Chiesa 55); Mijatovic (Balbo 86), Batistuta (Amor 76).

3rd match AIK (SWE)
A 0-0
Toldo; Repka, Padalino, Pierini; Di Livio (Bressan 61), Cois (Rossitto 90),
Rui Costa, Heinrich; Chiesa, Batistuta, Mijatovic (Balbo 72).

4th match AIK (SWE)
H 3-0 Batistuta (5), Chiesa (36), Balbo 86)
Toldo; Repka, Firicano, Pierini; Di Livio, Cois (Okon 71), Rui Costa,
Heinrich; Chiesa (Balbo 82), Batistuta, Mijatovic (Amoroso 53).

5th match ARSENAL (ENG)
A 1-0 Batistuta (75)
Toldo; Pierini, Firicano, Repka; Di Livio, Rossitto, Cois (Adani 46), Heinrich;
Rui Costa; Chiesa, Batistuta.

6th match FC BARCELONA (ESP)
H 3-3 Bressan (14), Balbo (56, 69)
Toldo; Heinrich, Pierini, Firicano, Adani; Bressan, Di Livio, Rossitto;
Rui Costa; Balbo, Chiesa (Okon 34).

7th match MANCHESTER UNITED (ENG)
H 2-0 Batistuta (24), Balbo (51)
Toldo; Repka, Firicano, Pierini (Adani 79); Torricelli, Cois, Di Livio
(Rossitto 67), Heinrich; Rui Costa; Batistuta, Balbo (Bressan 79).

8th match GIRONDINS DE BORDEAUX (FRA)
A 0-0
Toldo; Repka, Firicano, Pierini; Torricelli, Di Livio, Amoroso (Rossitto 70),
Heinrich; Rui Costa; Chiesa (Bressan 71), Balbo.

9th match VALENCIA CF (ESP)
H 1-0 Mijatovic (20p)
Toldo; Repka, Adani, Pierini (Tarozzi 80); Torricelli, Cois (Amoroso 83),
Di Livio (Rossitto 72), Heinrich; Rui Costa; Batistuta, Mijatovic.

10th match VALENCIA CF (ESP)
A 0-2
Taglialatela; Torricelli (Tarozzi 77), Repka, Adani, Pierini, Heinrich
(Amoroso 53); Cois, Rui Costa, Di Livio; Batistuta, Mijatovic (Balbo 57).

11th match MANCHESTER UNITED (ENG)
A 1-3 Batistuta (16)
Toldo; Repka, Adani, Pierini; Torricelli (Tarozzi 76), Rossitto, Di Livio
(Amoroso 76), Heinrich; Rui Costa; Batistuta, Mijatovic (Chiesa 63).

12th match GIRONDINS DE BORDEAUX (FRA)
H 3-3 Chiesa (47p), Batistuta (60), Rui Costa (64)
Toldo; Repka, Firicano, Pierini; Bressan (Amoroso 83), Di Livio, Cois
(Okon 73), Torricelli; Rui Costa; Batistuta (Balbo 80), Chiesa.

● **LAZIO**
Champions' League
1st match BAYER 04 LEVERKUSEN (GER)
A 1-1 Mihajlovic (18)
Marchegiani; Negro, Nesta, Mihajlovic, Pancaro; Lombardo, Almeyda, Verón
(Simeone 51), Stankovic, Mancini (Nedved 76); Boksic (Salas 81).

2nd match DYNAMO KYIV (UKR)
H 2-1 Negro (70), Salas (72)
Ballotta; Negro, Nesta, Mihajlovic, Favalli; Stankovic (Salas 52), Verón
(Lombardo 80), Almeyda, Nedved; Boksic, Mancini (Simeone 74).

3rd match NK MARIBOR (SLO)
H 4-0 Inzaghi (60), Sérgio Conceição (62), Salas (70, 77)
Marchegiani; Negro, Nesta, Mihajlovic (Almeyda 72), Pancaro; Lombardo
(Verón 67), Stankovic (Salas 46), Sensini, Sérgio Conceição; Inzaghi,
Mancini.

4th match NK MARIBOR (SLO)
A 4-0 Mihajlovic (36), Inzaghi (50, 73), Stankovic (62)
Ballotta; Pancaro, Nesta (Fernando Couto 18), Mihajlovic, Favalli;
Sérgio Conceição (Marcolin 75), Stankovic, Simeone, Sensini, Nedved
(Gottardi 70); Inzaghi.

5th match BAYER 04 LEVERKUSEN (GER)
H 1-1 Nedved (1)
Marchegiani; Pancaro, Fernando Couto, Mihajlovic, Favalli;
Sérgio Conceição (Stankovic 76), Verón (Simeone 89), Almeyda, Nedved;
Salas, Boksic (Inzaghi 58).

6th match DYNAMO KYIV (UKR)
A 1-0 Mamedov (17og)
Ballotta; Gottardi, Negro, Fernando Couto, Pancaro; Stankovic (Pinzi 64),
Simeone, Sensini, Marcolin; Inzaghi, Mancini.

7th match OLYMPIQUE MARSEILLE (FRA)
A 2-0 Stankovic (64), Sérgio Conceição (77)
Marchegiani; Pancaro, Nesta, Mihajlovic, Favalli; Sérgio Conceição,
Stankovic, Sensini, Nedved (Almeyda 81), Mancini (Verón 73); Salas
(Boksic 79).

8th match CHELSEA (ENG)
H 0-0
Marchegiani; Gottardi, Nesta, Fernando Couto, Favalli; Lombardo
(Boksic 68), Verón, Simeone, Nedved; Mancini (Sérgio Conceição 79),
Inzaghi (Salas 46).

9th match FEYENOORD (HOL)
H 1-2 Verón (37)
Marchegiani; Lombardo, Fernando Couto, Mihajlovic (Negro 40), Gottardi;
Simeone, Sensini, Mancini, Verón (Nedved 69); Inzaghi (Stankovic 60),
Boksic.

EUROPEAN CUPS 99/00 (CONTINUED)

10th match FEYENOORD (HOL)
A 0-0

Marchegiani; Negro, Nesta, Mihajlovic, Pancaro; Sérgio Conceição, Sensini, Verón, Nedved; Salas, Mancini (Inzaghi 67).

11th match OLYMPIQUE MARSEILLE (FRA)
H 5-1   Inzaghi (17, 37, 38, 71), Boksic (82)

Marchegiani; Negro, Nesta, Mihajlovic (Fernando Couto 60), Pancaro (Gottardi 73); Sérgio Conceição, Stankovic (Sensini 68), Simeone, Nedved; Inzaghi, Boksic.

12th match CHELSEA (ENG)
A 2-1   Inzaghi (54), Mihajlovic (66)

Marchegiani; Negro, Fernando Couto, Mihajlovic, Pancaro; Stankovic (Boksic 46), Almeyda, Verón, Simeone, Nedved; Inzaghi (Salas 68; Gottardi 88).

Quarter-final VALENCIA CF (ESP)
A 2-5   Inzaghi (28), Salas (87)

Ballotta; Gottardi, Negro, Mihajlovic, Pancaro; Stankovic (Sérgio Conceição 62), Almeyda, Simeone (Salas 76), Nedved; Verón; Inzaghi (Boksic 68).

H 1-0   Verón (52)

Marchegiani; Negro, Nesta, Mihajlovic, Pancaro (Mancini 76); Sérgio Conceição, Almeyda (Simeone 84), Verón, Nedved (Inzaghi 46); Salas, Boksic.

● MILAN
1st match CHELSEA (ENG)
A 0-0

Abbiati; Costacurta, Ayala, Maldini; Helveg, Albertini, Gattuso, Guglielminpietro; Leonardo (Giusti 83), Bierhoff, Shevchenko.

2nd match GALATASARAY (TUR)
H 2-1   Leonardo (44), Shevchenko (45)

Abbiati; Costacurta (N'Gotty 83), Ayala, Maldini; Helveg, Albertini, Gattuso, Serginho; Leonardo (Giunti 69), Bierhoff, Shevchenko (Ganz 88).

3rd match HERTHA BSC BERLIN (GER)
H 1-1   Bierhoff (74)

Abbiati; Costacurta, Ayala, Maldini; Helveg (Guglielminpietro 57), Albertini (Giunti 75), Gattuso, Serginho; Leonardo, Bierhoff, Shevchenko.

4th match HERTHA BSC BERLIN (GER)
A 0-1

Abbiati; Sala, Costacurta (Ayala 46), Maldini; Guglielminpietro, Albertini, Ambrosini (Giunti 64), Serginho (Orlandini 75); Leonardo; Bierhoff, Shevchenko.

5th match CHELSEA (ENG)
H 1-1   Bierhoff (74)

Abbiati; Costacurta, Ayala, Maldini; Guglielminpietro, Ambrosini, Gattuso, Serginho (Orlandini 86); Leonardo (Boban 56); Bierhoff, Shevchenko.

6th match GALATASARAY (TUR)
A 2-3   Weah (20), Giunti (51)

Abbiati; N'Gotty, Ayala, Maldini; Helveg, Albertini, Gattuso, Guglielminpietro (Serginho 56); Giunti (Bierhoff 87); Weah (Boban 83), Shevchenko.

● PARMA
Qualifying round RANGERS (SCO)
A 0-2

Buffon; Sartor, Thuram, Cannavaro F.; Serena, Baggio (Fuser 60), Walem, Boghossian, Vanoli; Ortega (Torrisi 83), Di Vaio (Stanic 86).

H 1-0   Walem (67)

Buffon; Lassissi, Torrisi, Thuram; Fuser, Baggio, Boghossian (Walem 63), Vanoli (Serena 77); Ortega; Crespo, Di Vaio (Stanic 63).

UEFA CUP
● BOLOGNA
1st round ZENIT SANKT-PETERBURG (RUS)
A 3-0   Ventola (38), Signori (69, 90p)

Pagliuca; Falcone (Lucic 88), Paganin, Bia, Tarantino; Binotto (Eriberto 46), Ingesson, Zé Elias, Nervo; Ventola (Sanchez 49), Signori.

H 2-2   Fontolan (38), Cipriani (75)

Pagliuca; Falcone, Bia, Boselli, Tarantino (Lucic 60); Eriberto, Ingesson, Zé Elias, Fontolan (Signori 46); Cipriani, Binotto (Ferrari 55).

2nd round RSC ANDERLECHT (BEL)
A 1-2   Signori (90)

Pagliuca; Falcone, Boselli, Bia, Tarantino; Fontolan, Paramatti (Eriberto 83), Zé Elias (Paganin 35), Nervo; Ventola, Signori.

H 3-0   Crasson (45og), De Boeck (51og), Nervo (90)

Pagliuca; Paramatti, Paganin, Bia, Tarantino; Eriberto (Falcone 79), Ingesson, Zé Elias (Wome 71), Nervo; Ventola (Cipriani 89), Signori.

3rd round GALATASARAY (TUR)
H 1-1   Signori (67)

Pagliuca; Falcone, Bia, Paganin, Tarantino; Nervo, Ingesson, Zé Elias (Wome 44), Paramatti; Ventola (Cipriani 88), Signori (Eriberto 76).

A 1-2   Ventola (8)

Pagliuca; Falcone (Fontolan 46), Bia, Paganin; Nervo (Zé Elias 82), Ingesson, Paramatti, Wome, Tarantino; Ventola (Cipriani 62), Signori.

● JUVENTUS
1st round OMONIA NICOSIA (CYP)
A 5-2   Inzaghi (3, 17), Kovacevic (22), Esnáider (25), Del Piero (83)

Van der Sar; Birindelli, Montero, Tudor; Zambrotta, Tacchinardi, Davids, Bachini; Esnáider (Conte 65); Kovacevic, Inzaghi (Del Piero 46).

H 5-0   Kovacevic (21, 47, 87), Tacchinardi (55), Conte (90)

Rampulla; Birindelli, Tudor, Mirkovic; Bachini, Conte, Tacchinardi (Zambrotta 80), Pessotto; Esnáider (Zidane 72); Kovacevic, Del Piero (Inzaghi 72).

2nd round LEVSKI SOFIA (BUL)
A 3-1   Oliseh (23), Kovacevic (52, 89)

Van der Sar; Birindelli, Montero, Tudor; Bachini, Conte, Oliseh, Pessotto; Zidane; Esnáider (Zambrotta 74), Kovacevic.

H 1-1   Kovacevic (79)

Van der Sar; Mirkovic, Tudor (Montero 53), Iuliano, Pessotto; Birindelli (Zidane 63), Oliseh, Davids (Tacchinardi 46), Zambrotta; Kovacevic, Fonseca.

3rd round OLYMPIAKOS (GRE)
A 3-1   Tudor (27), Kovacevic (67), Inzaghi (87)

Rampulla; Ferrara (Montero 69), Tudor, Mirkovic; Pessotto, Tacchinardi, Davids, Oliseh, Bachini (Birindelli 76); Kovacevic, Del Piero (Inzaghi 63).

H 1-2   Kovacevic (2)

Rampulla; Ferrara, Tudor, Mirkovic; Birindelli, Oliseh, Tacchinardi (Pessotto 46), Bachini (Zambrotta 74); Esnáider; Kovacevic, Del Piero (Montero 62).

EUROPEAN CUPS 99/00 (CONTINUED)

4th round RC CELTA (ESP)
H 1-0 Kovacevic (50)
Van der Sar; Mirkovic, Montero, Iuliano; Birindelli (Zambrotta 57), Tacchinardi, Oliseh (Pessotto 69), Bachini (Del Piero 46); Davids; Inzaghi, Kovacevic.

A 0-4
Van der Sar; Birindelli (Iuliano 63), Ferrara (Tudor 80), Montero, Mirkovic; Conte, Tacchinardi, Davids, Zambrotta (Zidane 63); Kovacevic, Del Piero.

● PARMA
1st round KRYVBAS KRYVYI RIH (UKR)
H 3-2 Di Vaio (13, 20), Baggio (67)
Buffon; Thuram, Torrisi, Cannavaro F.; Fuser, Breda (Sartor 75), Baggio, Serena (Benarrivo 54); Stanic (Amoroso 61), Di Vaio, Ortega.

A 3-0 Boghossian (38), Crespo (40), Di Vaio (67)
Buffon; Sartor, Thuram, Cannavaro F.; Serena, Boghossian (Breda 84), Walem, Baggio (Maini 46); Vanoli, Crespo, Di Vaio (Montaño 71).

2nd round HELSINGBORGS IF (SWE)
H 1-0 Cannavaro F. (44)
Buffon; Thuram, Torrisi, Cannavaro F.; Serena (Benarrivo 68), Boghossian (Breda 76), Maini, Vanoli; Ortega (Walem 81), Stanic, Di Vaio.

A 3-1 Di Vaio (11, 42, 43)
Buffon; Sartor, Thuram, Cannavaro F.; Serena, Boghossian (Breda 59), Walem, Baggio (Longo 82), Benarrivo; Stanic, Di Vaio (Montaño 52).

3rd round SK STURM GRAZ (AUT)
H 2-1 Di Vaio (16), Stanic (62)
Buffon; Lassissi, Torrisi, Thuram; Breda, Longo (Sartor 57), Baggio (Cannavaro F. 61), Walem, Montaño (Ortega 77); Stanic, Di Vaio.

A 3-3 (aet) Stanic (5, 110), Crespo (120)
Guardalben (Micillo 75); Thuram, Torrisi, Cannavaro F.; Serena, Boghossian, Walem, Baggio (Breda 70), Vanoli; Stanic, Di Vaio (Crespo 46).

4th round SV WERDER BREMEN (GER)
H 1-0 Crespo (5)
Buffon; Sartor, Thuram, Cannavaro F.; Fuser, Paulo Sousa, Baggio, Vanoli; Ortega (Breda 82), Crespo, Stanic (Di Vaio 90)

A 1-3 Stanic (32)
Buffon; Sartor, Thuram, Cannavaro F.; Fuser (Benarrivo 72), Paulo Sousa (Di Vaio 69), Baggio, Vanoli; Ortega (Dabo 46), Crespo, Stanic.

● ROMA
1st round VITÓRIA SETÚBAL (POR)
H 7-0 Aldair (12), Montella (14, 73), Alenichev (16, 54, 76), Macros Assunção (40)
Antonioli; Rinaldi, Aldair, Zago; Cafú, Tommasi (Di Francesco 46), Marcos Assunção, Alenichev, Candela (Gurenko 46); Montella (Fábio Júnior 74), Delvecchio.

A 0-1
Antonioli; Rinaldi, Aldair, Zago; Gurenko, Di Francesco, Marcos Assunção (Zanetti 60), Candela; Alenichev; Fábio Júnior, Delvecchio (Hutos 75).

2nd round IFK GÖTEBORG (SWE)

A 2-0 Montella (37, 52)
Antonioli; Zago, Aldair, Rinaldi; Cafú (Gurenko 76), Tommasi, Marcos Assunção, Di Francesco, Candela; Montella (Alenichev 62), Fábio Júnior.

H 1-0 Fábio Júnior (88)
Antonioli; Rinaldi, Aldair, Zago; Gurenko (Tommasi 77), Zanetti, Marcos Assunção, Di Francesco, Candela; Montella (Totti 55), Fábio Júnior.

3rd round NEWCASTLE UNITED (ENG)
H 1-0 Totti (51p)
Antonioli; Rinaldi, Aldair, Zago; Cafú, Di Francesco, Marcos Assunção, Candela; Totti; Montella, Delvecchio.

A 0-0
Antonioli; Zago, Aldair, Mangone; Cafú, Tommasi, Marcos Assunção, Candela; Totti; Montella (Di Francesco 61), Delvecchio.

4th round LEEDS UNITED (ENG)
H 0-0
Antonioli; Zago, Aldair, Mangone; Cafú, Nakata, Tommasi, Candela; Montella, Delvecchio, Totti.

A 0-1
Antonioli; Zago, Aldair, Mangone; Rinaldi, Tommasi, Nakata (Di Francesco 76), Candela; Totti; Montella, Delvecchio.

● UDINESE
1st round AAB (DEN)
H 1-0 Sottil (9)
Turci; Sottil, Gargo, Bertotto; Genaux, Giannichedda, Fiore, Jørgensen (Van der Vegt 73); Locatelli (Sosa 73); Poggi (Warley 81), Muzzi.

A 2-1 Muzzi (52), Locatelli (90)
Turci; Gargo, Zanchi, Bertotto (Sottil 7); Bisgaard, Giannichedda, Fiore, Jørgensen (Locatelli 83); Poggi, Margiotta (Genaux 70), Muzzi.

2nd round LEGIA WARSZAWA (POL)
H 1-0 Sosa (29)
Turci; Sottil (Van der Vegt 81), Gargo, Bertotto; Genaux, Giannichedda, Fiore, Jørgensen (Locatelli 89); Poggi, Sosa (Zanchi 70), Muzzi.

A 1-1 Sosa (41)
Turci; Sottil, Zanchi, Bertotto; Genaux, Giannichedda, Van der Vegt (Locatelli 74), Jørgensen; Fiore; Sosa (Toledo 85), Poggi (Margiotta 87).

3rd round BAYER 04 LEVERKUSEN (GER)
H 0-1
Turci; Zanchi, Sottil, Bertotto; Genaux, Giannichedda (Pineda 59), Fiore, Jørgensen (Toledo 35); Locatelli; Sosa (Muzzi 71), Poggi.

A 2-1 Margiotta (9, 18)
De Sanctis; Zanchi, Sottil, Bertotto; Genaux, Gargo, Fiore, Jørgensen (Esposito 89); Locatelli (Bisgaard 81); Muzzi (Manfredini 86), Margiotta.

4th round SLAVIA PRAHA (CZE)
A 0-1
Turci; Zamboni, Zanchi, Gargo; Jørgensen, Giannichedda, Fiore, Manfredini (Appiah 83); Locatelli (Alberto 70); Sosa (Margiotta 79), Muzzi.

H 2-1 Fiore (23), Sosa (51)
De Sanctis; Gargo, Sottil (Zanchi 25), Bertotto; Fiore, Giannichedda, Van der Vegt (Alberto 58), Jørgensen; Locatelli; Margiotta (Sosa 51), Muzzi.

Tardelli's Under-21 side had been victorious in their own European Championship, beating the Czech Republic 2-1 in the final thanks to two goals from playmaker Andrea Pirlo. The success of the national selections was extremely opportune given the poor season that Italian teams had just been through in the European club competitions.

It was Serie A's worst collective performance for years. No fewer than eight clubs were engaged in either the

Champions' League or the UEFA Cup but there were to be no trophy-winners or beaten finalists. In fact, the best Italy could manage was one quarter-finalist, Lazio in the Champions' League, and even they lost face when they went out after a 5-2 thrashing in Valencia. The same Spanish side had earlier accounted for Fiorentina, in the second group phase, whereas reigning Italian champions Milan were bundled unceremoniously out of Europe's premier club tournament after just six first-round matches, only one of which they won.

Parma were unable to reach the Champions' League proper after losing in the qualifying round to Rangers, and they were to become one of four Italian sides who crashed out of the UEFA Cup at the fourth-round stage in March, leaving Italy without a quarter-finalist for the first time since 1984. Udinese, Roma and Juventus all joined the holders on the scrapheap, with Juve suffering one of the most humiliating defeats in their proud European history when they went down 4-0 in north-west Spain to Celta Vigo, having conceded a goal after 30 seconds and had two players sent off in the first half.

Juve's European exit was particularly surprising because at the time they were firing on all cylinders in Serie A and looked to be heading inexorably towards their 26th 'scudetto'. Only Lazio were within catching distance, but when Juve beat city rivals Torino 3-2 to claim their sixth successive league victory, their lead had stretched to nine points and the championship appeared to be a formality.

Within a week, however, that lead was cut to six when Juve lost 2-0 away to Milan - their first Serie A defeat in 23 matches - and Lazio won their own local derby, beating Roma 2-1. The crunch fixture took place on the evening of Saturday, April 1 when Lazio visited the Stadio delle Alpi. It was the classic six-pointer. If Juve won, the championship would practically be theirs; if Lazio were the victors, they would be right back in the thick of the title race. It was a closely-contested affair, but the all-important winning goal went to Lazio, headed home midway through the second half by Argentinian midfielder Diego Simeone.

The heat was now on Juventus but they responded well, winning each of their next three fixtures - 2-0 at Bologna, 2-1 at Inter and 1-0 at home to Fiorentina - while Lazio dropped a further two points back after conceding a last-minute equaliser in a 3-3 draw at Fiorentina. Again, Juventus appeared to be in the clear. But on the day they might have clinched the title, they were well beaten by in-form Verona, for whom striker Fabrizio Cammarata scored twice in a handsome 2-0 win. Lazio, 3-2 winners at home to Venezia, were back in it, but they needed Juventus to falter again.

In round 33, Lazio almost had their title hopes destroyed by old boy Giuseppe Signori but they came from behind to win 3-2 at Bologna. Meanwhile, in Turin, Alessandro Del Piero's long-awaited first league goal of the season from open play appeared to have given Juventus a priceless 1-0 victory against Parma. In the very last minute, however, Parma won a corner and defender Fabio Cannavaro headed the ball into the net...only to have the broad smile wiped off his face when the referee ruled out the goal for what he deemed to have been a push by the Italian international. It was a hugely controversial decision and one which inevitably received the full televisual replay analysis, which in turn could find absolutely nothing wrong with the goal.

Parma were aggrieved, but Lazio were enraged. They claimed that the incident had scarred the championship and that, not for the first time, Juventus were being unfairly assisted by biased referees. The Lazio fans took their anger to the streets, causing a riot outside the Italian FA offices in Rome.

Of course, the title race was not yet over. Juventus were

INTERNATIONAL HONOURS

World Cup Finals appearances, 1934 (Winners), 1938 (Winners), 1950, 1954, 1962, 1966, 1970 (Runners-up), 1974, 1978 (4th), 1982 (Winners), 1986 (2nd round), 1990 (3rd), 1994 (Runners-up), 1998 (qtr-finals)

European Championship appearances: 1968 (Winners), 1972, 1980 (4th), 1988 (semi-finals), 1996, 2000 (runners-up)

European Club Competitions

Champions' Cup	Milan (1963, 1969, 1989, 1990, 1994)
	Inter (1964, 1965)
	Juventus (1985, 1996)
Cup-winners' Cup	Fiorentina (1961)
	Milan (1968, 1973)
	Juventus (1984)
	Sampdoria (1990)
	Parma (1993)
	Lazio (1999)
Fairs' Cup	Roma (1961)
UEFA Cup	Juventus (1977, 1990, 1993)
	Napoli (1989)
	Inter (1991, 1994, 1998)
	Parma (1995, 1999)
Super Cup	Juventus (1985)
	Milan (1989, 1990, 1995)
	Parma (1994)
	Lazio (1999)
World Club Cup	Inter (1964, 1965)
	Milan (1969, 1989, 1990)
	Juventus (1985)

DOMESTIC CUP 99/00

SECOND ROUND

Sampdoria 0, Bologna 2; Bologna 2, Sampdoria 0
(Bologna 4-0)

Cagliari 3, Genoa 1; Genoa 1, Cagliari 4
(Cagliari 7-2)

Pescara 0, Venezia 0; Venezia 1, Pescara 0
(Venezia 1-0)

Napoli 1, Bari 0; Bari 1, Napoli 1
(Napoli 2-1)

Reggina 0, Piacenza 0; Piacenza 2, Reggina 0
(Piacenza 2-0)

Ravenna 2, Verona 1; Verona 1, Ravenna 2
(Ravenna 4-2)

Ternana 1, Perugia 2; Perugia 1, Ternana 1
(Perugia 3-2)

Atalanta 3, Torino 1; Torino 2, Atalanta 1
(Atalanta 4-3)

THIRD ROUND

Inter 2, Bologna 1; Bologna 1, Inter 3
(Inter 5-2)

Ravenna 1, Lazio 1; Lazio 4, Ravenna 1
(Lazio 5-2)

Cagliari 1, Parma 0; Parma 2, Cagliari 2
(Cagliari 3-2)

Napoli 1, Juventus 3; Juventus 1, Napoli 0
(Juventus 4-1)

Perugia 1, Fiorentina 0; Fiorentina 2, Perugia 0
(Fiorentina 2-1)

Roma 0, Piacenza 1; Piacenza 0, Roma 3 (aet)
(Roma 3-1)

Venezia 3, Udinese 0; Udinese 2, Venezia 0
(Venezia 3-2)

Atalanta 3, Milan 2; Milan 3, Atalanta 0
(Milan 5-2)

QUARTER-FINALS

Milan 2 (Shevchenko 43, 55),
Inter 3 (Vieri 29, Mutu 54, Seedorf 68)

Inter 1 (Baggio 37), Milan 1 (Shevchenko 35)
(Inter 4-3)

Roma 0, Cagliari 1 (Oliveira 24)

Cagliari 1 (O'Neill 80), Roma 0
(Cagliari 2-0)

Juventus 3 (Zidane 12, Conte 30, Kovacevic 43),
Lazio 2 (Ravanelli 52p, Mancini 80)

Lazio 2 (Boksic 54, Simeone 80),
Juventus 1 (Del Piero 73)
(4-4; Lazio on away goals)

Venezia 0, Fiorentina 0

Fiorentina 1 (Adani 63), Venezia 1 (Berg 84)
(1-1; Venezia on away goal)

SEMI-FINALS

Cagliari 1 (Modesto 56),
Inter 3 (Mutu 48, Vieri 60, 90)

Inter 1 (Zamorano 11),
Cagliari 2 (Sulcis 21, Corradi 27)
(Inter 4-3)

Lazio 5
(Mancini 14, 24, Mihajlovic 28p, 49p, Ravanelli 89),
Venezia 0

Venezia 2 (Valtolina 52, Negro 89og),
Lazio 2 (Inzaghi 1, 72)
(Lazio 7-2)

FINAL
11/04/2000, Rome
LAZIO 2 Nedved (39), Simone (51)
INTER 1 Seedorf (8)
referees - Trentalange/Pellegrino
LAZIO - Ballotta; Gottardi, Fernando Couto,
Mihajlovic, Pancaro; Sérgio Conceição, Sensini,
Stankovic (Mancini 53), Simeone (Almeyda 80),
Nedved; Inzaghi (Salas 76).
INTER - Peruzzi; Panucci, Blanc, Córdoba; Moriero
(Di Biagio 46), Zanetti, Seedorf, Cauet, Serena;
Baggio (Zamorano 58), Mutu (Ronaldo 58).

18/05/2000, Milan
INTER 0
LAZIO 0
referees - Paparesta/Rosetti
INTER - Peruzzi; Serena (Georgatos 67), Córdoba,
Blanc, Domoraud; Zanetti, Di Biagio, Cauet, Seedorf;
Baggio (Recoba 61), Zamorano (Vieri 46).
LAZIO - Ballotta; Pancaro (Fernando Couto 87),
Nesta, Negro, Favalli; Sérgio Conceição, Sensini,
Verón, Simeone, Mancini (Ravanelli 46); Inzaghi
(Salas 46).

(LAZIO 2-1)

two points ahead but there was still one last match to play. Remarkably, the scenario was almost identical to the one 12 months earlier when Lazio were battling for the 'scudetto' with Milan. Yet again the Rome side's final game was at home (to Reggina) while their challengers concluded their campaign in Perugia. The only difference this time was that Lazio were two points, rather than one, behind their rivals. This meant that if Lazio won their match - which everyone agreed was a dead cert - there were three possible outcomes depending on the result in Perugia. If Juve won, they would be champions; if Juve lost, the title would be Lazio's; if Juve drew, Serie A would have its first championship play-off for 36 years.

The situation was simple, but nobody could possibly have foreseen the complicated drama that was about to unfold. At half-time, Lazio were comfortably ahead against Reggina thanks to two penalties converted by Simone Inzaghi and Juan Sebastián Verón. In Perugia it was

goalless. A play-off beckoned. But then, during the half-time interval, a fierce flash-storm broke out in Perugia. Torrential rain cascaded down from the dark clouds and within a few minutes transformed the pitch in the Renato Curi Stadium into a giant puddle. The waterlogged surface was evidently unplayable. On any other day the match would have been abandoned, but because of the significance of the situation, it was decided to wait and allow the pitch to dry out.

Eventually the game resumed 80 minutes later than scheduled, by which time Lazio had duly secured their three points against Reggina, winning 3-0. Nobody left the Stadio Olimpico, however. The Lazio fans remained in their thousands awaiting the outcome from Perugia. Within five minutes pandemonium broke out when the news filtered through that Perugia had gone ahead, Alessandro Calori seizing on an error from Juve skipper Antonio Conte to score. Juve were now a point behind

Lazio. They had to find a goal. But although they dominated the rest of the game, they just couldn't make the breakthrough. When Pippo Inzaghi blasted a golden opportunity over the bar in the final moments, it proved to be Juventus's last chance.

The title thus belonged to Lazio. They had won it by a point, having been behind for 13 weeks and a full nine points adrift just two months earlier. It was an extraordinary comeback and the perfect way for the Rome club to celebrate its centenary year.

Most non-partisan fans were delighted to see Lazio crowned as champions at last. They had waited 26 long years for their second 'scudetto', and in taking the title they had finally released the Juventus/Milan stranglehold that had lasted for eight seasons. Lazio played the most attractive football in the league, but they also dug in when they had to. Their run of seven wins and one draw from the last eight games showed that they had great resolve and character as well as huge talent. Sven Göran Eriksson, who at times had seemed alone in believing in Lazio's destiny, proved himself to be a superb coach and leader, and he was fulsomely praised as such by Lazio's owner and paymaster Sergio Cragnotti, whose passion for the club was clear for all to see when he broke down in tears of joy on hearing the confirmation of Juventus's defeat in Perugia.

On the playing side, Lazio had a brilliant and inspirational captain in local boy Alessandro Nesta, but there were others who shared his top billing, notably the Argentinians Verón and Simeone, Yugoslav free-kick expert Sinisa Mihajlovic and Czech midfield powerhouse Pavel Nedved.

Lazio's splendid season was augmented with another trophy when they beat Inter over two legs to win the Coppa Italia, thus securing an historic league and Cup 'double'. Simeone, a goalscorer in each of the team's last four league fixtures as well as in the head-to-head with Juventus in Turin, was also the matchwinner in the Cup final, which Lazio won 2-1 on aggregate to condemn Inter to their 11th consecutive season without a domestic prize.

Inter's season was rescued from total oblivion when they subsequently beat Parma 3-1 in a play-off for the fourth and final Champions' League place, but all in all it was a campaign best forgotten by the 'Nerazzurri' fans. Marcello Lippi, the former trophy-hoarding coach of Juventus, had been expected to work similar wonders at Inter. But the club's lavish spending bore only minimal dividends. Christian Vieri cost the club a world-record fee when he joined in the close season from Lazio, but he started less than half of Inter's Serie A matches and was persistently troubled by a thigh injury. Only once did Inter's dream strike partnership of Vieri and Ronaldo kick-off a Serie A match together. The Brazilian sustained a knee injury in a 6-0 victory over Lecce in November but came back too quickly and suffered horrific ligament damage to the same knee when he returned for the first leg of the Coppa Italia final in Rome.

Milan, on the other hand, obtained regular five-star service from their ace striker. Andriy Shevchenko, a new arrival from Dynamo Kiev, had a wonderful first season and ended it with the title of 'capocannoniere' thanks to his tally of 24 goals. It was a fantastic performance from the Ukrainian, but other than him there were few satisfactions in a Milan team that never genuinely threatened to make a successful defence of the 'scudetto' and were paralysed by their shock early exit from Europe, when they ceded participation in both the Champions' League and the UEFA Cup after giving away two late goals to Galatasaray in Istanbul.

NATIONAL TEAM RESULTS 99/00

08/09/99	Denmark (ECQ)	H	Naples	2-3	Fuser (10), Vieri (34)
09/10/99	Belarus (ECQ)	A	Minsk	0-0	
13/11/99	Belgium	H	Lecce	1-3	Vanoli (26)
23/02/00	Sweden	H	Palermo	1-0	Del Piero (79p)
29/03/00	Spain	A	Barcelona	0-2	
26/04/00	Portugal	H	Reggio di Calabria	2-0	Iuliano (75), Totti (88)
03/06/00	Norway	A	Oslo	0-1	
11/06/00	Turkey (ECF)	N	Arnhem	2-1	Conte (52), Inzaghi F. (70p)
14/06/00	Belgium (ECF)	A	Brussels	2-0	Totti (6), Fiore (66)
19/06/00	Sweden (ECF)	N	Eindhoven	2-1	Di Biagio (39), Del Piero (88)
24/06/00	Romania (ECF)	N	Brussels	2-0	Totti (34), Inzaghi F. (43)
29/06/00	Holland (ECF)	A	Amsterdam	0-0	(aet, 3-1 on pens.)
02/07/00	France (ECF)	N	Rotterdam	1-2	Delvecchio (56)

TOP SCORERS

24	Andriy SHEVCHENKO (Milan)
23	Gabriel BATISTUTA (Fiorentina)
22	Hernán CRESPO (Parma)
18	Vincenzo MONTELLA (Roma)
	Marco FERRANTE (Torino)
15	Giuseppe SIGNORI (Bologna)
	Filippo INZAGHI (Juventus)
	Cristiano LUCARELLI (Lecce)
13	Christian VIERI (Inter)

PLAYERS OF THE SEASON

HERNAN CRESPO

His club, Parma, had a season which veered between the ridiculous and the sublime, but through good times and bad Hernán Crespo (pictured right) continued to find the net. He was the one constant for Parma during a campaign which never quite reached the heights their fans expected. Crespo was desperately disappointed to miss out on the Champions' League but he did not let that bother him. A run of 11 goals in 12 games from the Argentinian ace lifted Parma from the relegation total into title contention, and he saved his best till last with a stunning last-minute equaliser at home to Juventus after Parma had been reduced to nine men. Crespo ended the season on 22 goals - his best total in four Serie A campaigns - and would have finished ahead of his great rival and compatriot Gabriel Batistuta but for the latter's hat-trick on his farewell appearance for Fiorentina. Crespo, too, switched clubs in the summer, joining the growing Argentinian clan in the Italian capital by signing for Lazio in a then world-record £36.5m transfer.

FRANCESCO TOLDO

When Italy's first-choice goalkeeper Gianluigi Buffon injured his hand in a friendly against Norway and had to be withdrawn from the Euro 2000 squad, the 'Azzurri' fans had little to fear. They knew that in Francesco Toldo their team had a perfect replace-ment. The giant Fiorentina 'keeper had enjoyed a brilliant season at club level, especially in the Champions' League, where he made several breath-taking saves - the best of them against Arsenal at Wembley - to help the 'Viola' to the brink of the quarter-finals. At Euro 2000 he was nothing short of sensational, proving himself to be the scourge of both co-hosts. Man of the match for Italy in the group game against Belgium, he had the game of his life in the semi-final against Holland, saving no fewer than three penalties. Another excellent display in the final against France confirmed his status as the tournament's outstanding goalkeeper.

ALESSANDRO NESTA

If Toldo was Euro 2000's number one 'keeper, then the prize for the best defender surely belonged to Alessandro Nesta. The 24-year-old was security personified, holding Italy's back-three together with strength and style and demonstrating the kind of natural authority and command that marks him out as an obvious candidate for the future captaincy of his country. Nesta is already the skipper of his hometown club Lazio, and it was with immense pride and satisfaction that he led the team to an historic Serie A/Coppa Italia 'double' in their cente-nary year. He was the bulwark of the Lazio defence, his anticipation and speed of recovery frequently coming to the team's rescue when it seemed as if the back-four's lack of natural pace might be exposed. Nesta's former tempestuous nature was seldom in evidence, although he did lose his cool early in the season when arch-rivals Roma ran the Lazio defence ragged with four goals in the first half. It was a rare off-day for Nesta, who subsequently took some fearful stick from the Roma fans. By the end of the season, though, it was he who had the last laugh.

At least Milan made it back into the Champions' League. Parma, Fiorentina and Roma all missed out, having made entry to that competition their fixed goal for the season. Parma had Hernán Crespo to thank for lifting them up the table after a bad start, while Fiorentina were once again indebted to Gabriel Batistuta for their UEFA Cup qualification. Both of those Argentinian goal-machines were on their way to new clubs at the end of the season, with Crespo joining champions Lazio and Batistuta ending his long association with the 'Viola' by moving to Roma - a team that was hardly short of forwards, what with Italian international trio Delvecchio, Totti and Montella already on the books and showing no inclination to leave.

Fiorentina also bade farewell to Giovanni Trapattoni, who finally fulfilled a lifelong ambition by becoming Italy's new national team manager. After Dino Zoff's impressive performance at Euro 2000, the most decorated Italian club coach of them all knows that he will have a tough act to follow.

PROMOTED CLUBS 99/00

SECOND DIVISION FINAL TABLE

		Pd	W	D	L	F	A	Pt	GD
1	**Vicenza**	**38**	**20**	**7**	**11**	**69**	**45**	**67**	**24**
2	**Atalanta**	**38**	**17**	**12**	**9**	**51**	**34**	**63**	**17**
3	**Brescia**	**38**	**16**	**15**	**7**	**54**	**38**	**63**	**16**
4	**Napoli**	**38**	**17**	**12**	**9**	**55**	**44**	**63**	**11**
5	Sampdoria	38	17	11	10	45	40	62	5
6	Genoa	38	16	9	13	51	42	57	9
7	Salernitana	38	14	10	14	55	61	52	-6
8	Treviso	38	13	12	13	56	48	51	8
9	Empoli	38	13	12	13	42	52	51	-10
10	Ternana	38	11	16	11	45	47	49	-2
11	Ravenna	38	11	15	12	41	39	48	2
12	Cosenza	38	11	51	12	36	41	48	-5
13	Pescara	38	10	17	11	62	55	47	7
14	Monza	38	9	20	9	45	46	47	-1
15	Chievo	38	11	14	13	48	53	47	-5
16	Cesena	38	8	21	9	47	45	45	2
17	Pistoiese	38	13	10	15	39	43	45	-4
18	Alzano	38	10	12	16	39	51	42	-12
19	Savoia	38	6	11	21	36	62	29	-26
20	Fermana	38	6	11	21	36	66	29	-30

N.B. Pistoiese - 4 points deducted

Società Sportiva Calcio Napoli
Via Vicinale Paradiso, 80126 Napoli
tel - (081) 7661701 / fax - (081) 7662763
website - www.calcionapoli.it
Year of Formation - 1926
President - Federico Scalingi
Secretary - Alberto Vallefuoco
Coach - Walter Novellino (00/01 - Zdenek Zeman)
Stadium - San Paolo (78,210)

MAJOR HONOURS
League Championship - (2) 1987, 1990.
Domestic Cup - (3) 1962, 1976, 1987.
UEFA Cup - (1) 1989.

CLUB DIRECTORIES

Vicenza Calcio
Via Schio 21, 36100 Vicenza
tel - (0444) 505044 / fax - (0444) 544764
website - www.keycom/it/vicenzacalcio
Year of Formation - 1902
President - Aronne Miola
Secretary - Fabio Rizzitelli
Coach - Edoardo Reja
Stadium - Romeo Menti (20,920)

MAJOR HONOURS
Domestic Cup - (1) 1997.

Atalanta Bergamasca Calcio
Via Pitentino 14/a, 24124 Bergamo
tel - (035) 242555 / fax - (035) 239677
website - www.atalanta.it
Year of Formation - 1899
President - Ivan Ruggeri
Secretary - Carlo Valenti
Coach - Giovanni Vavassori
Stadium - Atleti Azzurri d'Italia (26,724)

MAJOR HONOURS
Domestic Cup - (1) 1963.

Brescia Calcio
Via Bazoli, 25127 Brescia
tel - (030) 2410751/ fax - (030) 2410787
website - www.legacalcio.it/ita/bres
Year of Formation - 1911
President - Luigi Corioni
Secretary - Alberto Bonometti
Coach - Nedo Sonetti (00/01 - Carlo Mazzone)
Stadium - Mario Rigamonti (25,000)

BARI

CLUB DIRECTORY

Associazione Sportiva Bari
Strada Torrebella
70124 Bari
tel - (080) 5055099
fax - (080) 5055164
website - www.asbari.it
Year of Formation - 1908
President - Vincenzo Matarrese
General Manager - Carlo Regalia
Secretary - Pietro Doronzo
Coach - Eugenio Fascetti
Stadium - San Nicola (58,270)

APPEARANCES 99/00

	P	Ap	(s)	Gls
Daniel ANDERSSON (SWE)	M	32		5
Antonio BELLAVISTA	M	9	(5)	
Antonio CASSANO	A	14	(7)	3
Mattia COLLAUTO	M	26		
Pascual DE GREGORIO (CHL)	A	4	(4)	
Alessandro DEL GROSSO	D	25	(5)	
Gaetano DE ROSA	D	26	(1)	
Hugo ENYINNAYA (NIG)	A	4	(8)	2
Matteo FERRARI	D	15	(11)	
Luigi GARZYA	D	22	(2)	
Rodolfo GIORGETTI	M		(12)	
Attilio GREGORI	G		(2)	
Duccio INNOCENTI	D	27	(1)	4
Michael MADSEN (DEN)	D	5	(1)	
Francesco MANCINI	G	34		
Michele MARCOLINI	M	25	(2)	2
Diego MARKIC (ARG)	M	12	(6)	
Phil MASINGA (SAF)	A	11		1
Rachid NEQROUZ (MAR)	D	19	(1)	3
Davide OLIVARES	M	4	(12)	1
Yksel OSMANOVSKI (SWE)	A	22	(2)	7
Simone PERROTTA	M	24	(7)	1
Gionatha SPINESI	A	14	(9)	5

LEAGUE RESULTS 1999/2000

29/08/99	Fiorentina	A	0-1	
11/09/99	Lazio	H	0-0	
18/09/99	Milan	H	1-1	Osmanovski
26/09/99	Verona	A	1-0	Osmanovski
03/10/99	Udinese	H	1-1	Innocenti
17/10/99	Torino	A	1-3	Innocenti
24/10/99	Juventus	H	1-1	Spinesi
31/10/99	Parma	A	1-2	Innocenti
06/11/99	Perugia	A	2-1	Andersson, Masinga
21/11/99	Reggina	H	1-1	Andersson (p)
28/11/99	Cagliari	A	3-2	Osmanovski 2, Olivares
05/12/99	Piacenza	H	3-2	Marcolini, Neqrouz 2
11/12/99	Lecce	A	0-1	
18/12/99	Inter	H	2-1	Enyinnaya, Cassano
06/01/00	Roma	A	1-3	Cassano
09/01/00	Venezia	H	3-0	Perrotta, Enyinnaya, Andersson (p)
15/01/00	Bologna	A	0-1	
23/01/00	Fiorentina	H	1-0	Spinesi
30/01/00	Lazio	A	1-3	Spinesi
06/02/00	Milan	A	1-4	Spinesi
12/02/00	Verona	H	1-1	Neqrouz
20/02/00	Udinese	A	1-5	Marcolini
27/02/00	Torino	H	1-1	Osmanovski
05/03/00	Juventus	A	0-2	
12/03/00	Parma	H	0-1	
19/03/00	Perugia	H	0-2	
25/03/00	Reggina	A	0-1	
02/04/00	Cagliari	H	1-0	Andersson (p)
09/04/00	Piacenza	A	1-2	Andersson
16/04/00	Lecce	H	3-1	Spinesi, Osmanovski, Cassano
22/04/00	Inter	A	0-3	
30/04/00	Roma	H	0-0	
07/05/00	Venezia	A	1-0	Innocenti
14/05/00	Bologna	H	1-1	Osmanovski

BOLOGNA

Bologna 1909 Football Club
Via Casteldebole 10
40132 Bologna
tel - (051) 6111111
fax - (051) 6111122
website - www.bolognafc.it
Year of Formation - 1909
President - Giuseppe Gazzoni Frascara
Secretary - Renato Cipollini
Coach - Sergio Buso; Francesco Guidolin
Stadium - Renato Dall'Ara (40,572)

MAJOR HONOURS
League Championship - (7)
1925, 1929, 1936, 1937, 1939, 1941, 1964.
Domestic Cup - (2) 1970, 1974.

APPEARANCES 99/00

	P	Ap	(s)	Gls
Kennet ANDERSSON (SWE)	A	25	(3)	7
Giovanni BIA	D	24	(2)	1
Jonatan BINOTTO	M	6	(6)	
Nicola BOSELLI	D	7	(2)	
Alessandro DAL CANTO	D	17		
ERIBERTO da Silva (BRA)	M	4	(10)	1
Giulio FALCONE	D	21	(4)	
Davide FONTOLAN	A	6	(9)	1
Alessandro GAMBERINI	D	2	(2)	
Roberto GORETTI	M	5	(2)	
Klas INGESSON (SWE)	M	32	(2)	1
Igor KOLYVANOV (RUS)	A	2	(6)	
Teddy LUCIC (SWE)	D	1		
Giancarlo MAROCCHI	M	23		
Carlo NERVO	M	29	(3)	1
Paolo ORLANDONI	G	2	(1)	
Massimo PAGANIN	D	19	(2)	
Gianluca PAGLIUCA	G	32		
Michele PARAMATTI	D	27	(1)	3
Giovanni PIACENTINI	M	10	(9)	
Christophe SANCHEZ (FRA)	A	2	(1)	
Giuseppe SIGNORI	A	30	(1)	15
Massimo TARANTINO	M	16		
Max TONETTO	M	7	(4)	
Nicola VENTOLA	A	6	(8)	
Pierre Nlend WOME (CMR)	D	9	(5)	1
José Marcelo ZÉ ELIAS (BRA)	M	10	(9)	

LEAGUE RESULTS 1999/2000

28/08/99	Torino	H	0-0	
12/09/99	Parma	A	1-1	Signori
19/09/99	Reggina	H	0-1	
25/09/99	Milan	A	0-4	
03/10/99	Lecce	H	2-0	Fontolan, Signori
17/10/99	Piacenza	A	0-0	
24/10/99	Verona	H	0-0	
30/10/99	Venezia	A	1-0	og (Bilica)
07/11/99	Inter	H	3-0	Andersson 2, Signori
20/11/99	Udinese	A	1-2	Paramatti
27/11/99	Fiorentina	H	0-0	
04/12/99	Juventus	A	0-2	
12/12/99	Roma	H	1-0	Signori
19/12/99	Perugia	A	2-3	Wome, Signori
06/01/00	Cagliari	H	1-0	Andersson
09/01/00	Lazio	A	1-3	Andersson
15/01/00	Bari	H	1-0	Signori
23/01/00	Torino	A	1-2	Signori
30/01/00	Parma	H	1-0	Bia
06/02/00	Reggina	A	0-1	
12/02/00	Milan	H	2-3	Ingesson, Eriberto
20/02/00	Lecce	A	1-1	Signori
27/02/00	Piacenza	H	0-0	
05/03/00	Verona	A	0-0	
11/03/00	Venezia	H	1-1	Andersson
18/03/00	Inter	A	1-1	Paramatti
25/03/00	Udinese	H	2-1	Signori, Nervo
01/04/00	Fiorentina	A	2-2	Signori, Andersson
09/04/00	Juventus	H	0-2	
16/04/00	Roma	A	0-2	
22/04/00	Perugia	H	2-1	Signori, Andersson
30/04/00	Cagliari	A	2-2	Paramatti, Signori
07/05/00	Lazio	H	2-3	Signori 2
14/05/00	Bari	A	1-1	Signori (p)

CAGLIARI

CLUB DIRECTORY

Cagliari Calcio
Viale La Plaia 15
09123 Cagliari
tel - (070) 604201
fax - (070) 454082
website - www.cagliaricalcio.it
Year of Formation - 1920
President - Massimo Cellino
Secretary - Sergio Loviselli
Coach - Oscar Washington Tabarez; Renzo Ulivieri
(00/01 - Gianfranco Bellotto)
Stadium - Sant'Elia (43,177)

MAJOR HONOURS
League Championship - (1) 1970.

APPEARANCES 99/00

	P	Ap	(s)	Gls
Nélson ABEIJON (URU)	M	4	(2)	
Raffaele AMETRANO	M	8	(3)	
Daniele BERRETTA	M	32		6
Stefano BIANCONI	D	5	(3)	
Davide CARRUS	M	2	(5)	
Gianni CAVEZZI	M		(6)	
Daniele CONTI	M	4	(5)	1
Bernardo CORRADI	A	3	(17)	
Tiziano DE PATRE	M	26	(1)	1
Nicola DILISO	D	12	(5)	
Maurizio FRANZONE	G	2		
Gianluca GRASSADONIA	D	9		
Diego LOPEZ (URU)	D	29		
Fabio MACELLARI	D	31		2
Jason MAYELE (FRA)	M	24	(2)	1
Patrick MBOMA (CMR)	A	24	(3)	8
Emiliano MELIS	M	5	(6)	
François MODESTO (FRA)	D	11	(11)	
Domenico MORFEO	A	4	(1)	1
Luís OLIVEIRA (BEL)	A	22	(2)	4
Fabian O'NEILL (URU)	M	21		2
Alessio SCARPI	G	32		
David SUAZO (HON)	A	4	(9)	1
Giovanni SULCIS	D	7	(3)	1
Matteo VILLA	D	29		
Jonathan ZEBINA (FRA)	D	24	(2)	

LEAGUE RESULTS 1999/2000

30/08/99	Lazio	A	1-2	O'Neill
12/09/99	Juventus	H	0-1	
18/09/99	Perugia	A	0-3	
26/09/99	Venezia	H	1-1	Berretta
02/10/99	Torino	H	1-1	Mboma
17/10/99	Milan	A	2-2	Morfeo, Berretta
24/10/99	Udinese	H	0-3	
31/10/99	Roma	A	2-2	Oliveira, Mboma (p)
06/11/99	Fiorentina	H	1-1	Mboma (p)
21/11/99	Parma	A	1-3	Mboma
28/11/99	Bari	H	2-3	Macellari, Berretta
05/12/99	Verona	A	0-2	
12/12/99	Reggina	A	1-1	Mayelé
19/12/99	Lecce	H	0-0	
06/01/00	Bologna	A	0-1	
09/01/00	Piacenza	H	3-0	Oliveira, Mboma 2
16/01/00	Inter	A	1-2	Oliveira
22/01/00	Lazio	H	0-0	
30/01/00	Juventus	A	1-1	Sulcis
05/02/00	Perugia	H	2-1	Berretta 2
13/02/00	Venezia	A	0-3	
20/02/00	Torino	A	1-1	O'Neill (p)
27/02/00	Milan	H	0-0	
04/03/00	Udinese	A	2-5	Oliveira, Macellari
12/03/00	Roma	H	1-0	Mboma
18/03/00	Fiorentina	A	0-2	
25/03/00	Parma	H	2-3	Berretta, De Patre
02/04/00	Bari	A	0-1	
09/04/00	Verona	H	0-1	
16/04/00	Reggina	H	0-1	
22/04/00	Lecce	A	1-2	Conti
30/04/00	Bologna	H	2-2	Mboma, og (Dal Canto)
07/05/00	Piacenza	A	1-1	Suazo
14/05/00	Inter	H	0-2	

FIORENTINA

CLUB DIRECTORY

Associazione Calcio Fiorentina
Piazza Girolamo Savonarola 6
50132 Firenze
tel - (055) 50721
fax - (055) 579556
website - www.acfiorentina.it
Year of Formation - 1926
President - Vittorio Cecchi Gori
General Manager - Giancarlo Antognoni
Secretary - Raffaele Righetti
Coach - Giovanni Trapattoni (00/01 - Fatih Terim)
Stadium - Artemio Franchi (47,282)

MAJOR HONOURS
League Championship - (2) 1956, 1969.
Domestic Cup - (5)
1940, 1961, 1966, 1975, 1996.
European Cup-winners' Cup - (1) 1961.

APPEARANCES 99/00

	P	Ap	(s)	Gls
Daniele ADANI	D	23	(4)	1
Guillermo AMOR (ESP)	M	2	(6)	
Christian AMOROSO	M	15	(8)	
Abel BALBO (ARG)	A	9	(10)	3
Gabriel BATISTUTA (ARG)	A	30		23
Mauro BRESSAN	M	6	(14)	1
Enrico CHIESA	A	24		7
Sandro COIS	M	20	(3)	
Angelo DI LIVIO	M	30		1
Aldo FIRICANO	D	19	(1)	1
Jörg HEINRICH (GER)	M	24		2
Predrag MIJATOVIC (YUG)	A	12	(4)	2
Paul OKON (AUS)	M	3	(8)	
Luís OLIVEIRA (BEL)	A		(1)	
Pasquale PADALINO	D	7	(1)	
Alessandro PIERINI	D	26	(2)	1
Tomas REPKA (CZE)	D	26	(3)	
Fabio ROSSITTO	M	12	(14)	
RUI COSTA (POR)	M	29	(1)	4
Riccardo TADDEI	M		(2)	
Andrea TAROZZI	D	8	(10)	1
Francesco TOLDO	G	34		
Moreno TORRICELLI	D	14	(1)	
Georgios VAKOUFTSIS (GRE)	A	1	(1)	

LEAGUE RESULTS 1999/2000

29/08/99	Bari	H	1-0	Chiesa
11/09/99	Reggina	A	2-2	Firicano, Heinrich
19/09/99	Verona	H	4-1	Batistuta 3, Chiesa
26/09/99	Udinese	A	1-1	Batistuta
03/10/99	Roma	H	1-3	Batistuta
16/10/99	Parma	H	0-2	
24/10/99	Piacenza	A	0-2	
30/10/99	Torino	H	1-1	Balbo
06/11/99	Cagliari	A	1-1	og (Grassadonia)
20/11/99	Perugia	H	1-0	Pierini
27/11/99	Bologna	A	0-0	
05/12/99	Milan	H	2-1	Batistuta, Heinrich
12/12/99	Lazio	A	0-2	
19/12/99	Juventus	H	1-1	Batistuta
06/01/00	Lecce	A	0-0	
09/01/00	Inter	H	2-1	Batistuta, Adani
15/01/00	Venezia	A	1-2	Batistuta
23/01/00	Bari	A	0-1	
30/01/00	Reggina	H	1-0	Batistuta
06/02/00	Verona	A	2-2	Batistuta, Rui Costa
13/02/00	Udinese	H	1-1	Batistuta
19/02/00	Roma	A	0-4	
26/02/00	Parma	A	4-0	Balbo, Rui Costa 2, Mijatovic
04/03/00	Piacenza	H	2-1	Balbo, Rui Costa
12/03/00	Torino	A	0-1	
18/03/00	Cagliari	H	2-0	Batistuta, Mijatovic
25/03/00	Perugia	A	2-1	Batistuta, Chiesa
01/04/00	Bologna	H	2-2	Batistuta 2
09/04/00	Milan	A	1-1	Di Livio
15/04/00	Lazio	H	3-3	Batistuta 2, Chiesa
22/04/00	Juventus	A	0-1	
30/04/00	Lecce	H	3-0	Tarozzi, Chiesa, Batistuta
07/05/00	Inter	A	4-0	Chiesa 2, Batistuta, Bressan
14/05/00	Venezia	H	3-0	Batistuta 3

INTER

CLUB DIRECTORY

Internazionale Milano Football Club
Via Durini 24, 20122 Milano
tel - (02) 77151
fax - (02) 781514
website - www.inter.it
Year of Formation - 1908
President - Massimo Moratti
Secretary - Luciano Cucchia
Coach - Marcello Lippi
Stadium - Giuseppe Meazza (85,700)

MAJOR HONOURS

League Championship - (13) 1910, 1920, 1930,
1938, 1940, 1953, 1954, 1963, 1965, 1966,
1971, 1980, 1989.
Domestic Cup - (3) 1939, 1978, 1982.
European Champions' Cup - (2) 1964, 1965.
UEFA Cup - (3) 1991, 1994, 1998.
World Club Cup - (2) 1964, 1965.

APPEARANCES 99/00

	P	Ap	(s)	Gls
Roberto BAGGIO	A	7	(11)	4
Laurent BLANC (FRA)	D	34		3
Benoît CAUET (FRA)	M	20	(9)	1
Francesco COLONNESE	D	2	(5)	
Iván CORDOBA (COL)	D	19		
Ousmane DABO (FRA)	M	3	(5)	
Luigi DI BIAGIO	M	23	(6)	2
Cyril DOMORAUD (FRA)	D	2	(4)	
Fabrizio FERRON	G	1	(3)	
Salvatore FRESI	D	8	(1)	
Grigoris GEORGATOS (GRE)	M	24	(4)	2
Vladimir JUGOVIC (YUG)	M	14	(3)	2
Francesco MORIERO	M	10	(7)	2
Adrian MUTU (ROM)	A	3	(7)	
Christian PANUCCI	D	26		1
PAULO SOUSA (POR)	M	8	(2)	
Angelo PERUZZI	G	33		
Alvaro RECOBA (URU)	A	17	(10)	10
RONALDO				
Luiz Nazário de Lima (BRA)	A	5	(2)	3
Nello RUSSO	A		(1)	1
Clarence SEEDORF (HOL)	M	19	(1)	3
Michele SERENA	M	5	(5)	
Dario SIMIC (CRO)	D	19		1
Christian VIERI	A	16	(3)	13
Iván ZAMORANO (CHL)	A	22	(8)	7
Javier ZANETTI (ARG)	M	34		1

LEAGUE RESULTS 1999/2000

Date	Opponent	H/A	Score	Scorers
29/08/99	Verona	H	3-0	Vieri 3
12/09/99	Roma	A	0-0	
19/09/99	Parma	H	5-1	Zamorano 2, Vieri, Moriero, og (Thuram)
26/09/99	Torino	A	1-0	Vieri
02/10/99	Piacenza	H	2-1	Panucci, Ronaldo
17/10/99	Venezia	A	0-1	
23/10/99	Milan	H	1-2	Ronaldo (p)
30/10/99	Lazio	H	1-1	Zamorano
07/11/99	Bologna	A	0-3	
21/11/99	Lecce	H	6-0	Georgatos, Zanetti, Jugovic, Zamorano, Ronaldo (p), Recoba
28/11/99	Reggina	A	1-0	Recoba
05/12/99	Udinese	H	3-0	Recoba, Vieri, Russo
12/12/99	Juventus	A	0-1	
18/12/99	Bari	A	1-2	Vieri
06/01/00	Perugia	H	5-0	Georgatos, Seedorf, Vieri, Jugovic, og (Hilário)
09/01/00	Fiorentina	A	1-2	Recoba
16/01/00	Cagliari	H	2-1	Simic, Moriero
23/01/00	Verona	A	2-1	Recoba, Baggio
29/01/00	Roma	H	2-1	Vieri, Baggio
06/02/00	Parma	A	1-1	Vieri
13/02/00	Torino	H	1-1	Vieri
20/02/00	Piacenza	A	3-1	Blanc 2, Vieri
27/02/00	Venezia	H	3-0	Vieri, Zamorano, Recoba
05/03/00	Milan	A	2-1	Zamorano, Di Biagio
11/03/00	Lazio	A	2-2	Recoba, Di Biagio
18/03/00	Bologna	H	1-1	Recoba
25/03/00	Lecce	A	0-1	
02/04/00	Reggina	H	1-1	Recoba
08/04/00	Udinese	A	0-3	
16/04/00	Juventus	H	1-2	Seedorf
22/04/00	Bari	H	3-0	Cauet, Blanc, Baggio
30/04/00	Perugia	A	2-1	Seedorf, Recoba
07/05/00	Fiorentina	H	0-4	
14/05/00	Cagliari	A	2-0	Baggio (p), Zamorano

JUVENTUS

CLUB DIRECTORY

Juventus Football Club
Piazza Crimea 7, 10147 Torino
tel - (011) 65631 / fax - (011) 6604134
website - www.juventus.it
Year of Formation - 1897
President - Vittorio Chiusano
General Manager - Luciano Moggi
Coach - Carlo Ancelotti
Stadium - Delle Alpi (69,041)

MAJOR HONOURS
League Championship - (25)
1905, 1926, 1931, 1932, 1933, 1934, 1935,
1950, 1952, 1958, 1960, 1961, 1967, 1972,
1973, 1975, 1977, 1978, 1981, 1982, 1984,
1986, 1995, 1997, 1998.
Domestic Cup - (9) 1938, 1942, 1959, 1960,
1965, 1979, 1983, 1990, 1995.
European Champions' Cup - (2) 1985, 1996.
European Cup-winners' Cup - (1) 1984.
UEFA Cup - (3) 1977, 1990, 1993.
European Super Cup - (2) 1984, 1997.
World Club Cup - (2) 1985, 1996.

APPEARANCES 99/00

	P	Ap	(s)	Gls
Jonathan BIACHINI	M	2	(4)	
Alessandro BIRINDELLI	D	4	(18)	
Antonio CONTE	M	28		4
Edgar DAVIDS (HOL)	M	27		1
Alessandro DEL PIERO	A	34		9
Juan Eduardo ESNAIDER (ARG)	A	1	(5)	
Ciro FERRARA	D	31		1
Filippo INZAGHI	A	32	(1)	15
Mark IULIANO	D	32		
Darko KOVACEVIC (YUG)	A	3	(23)	6
Enzo MARESCA	M		(1)	
Zoran MIRKOVIC (YUG)	D	1	(7)	
Paolo MONTERO (URU)	D	28		
Sunday OLISEH (NIG)	M	2	(6)	
Gianluca PESSOTTO	M	25	(5)	1
Michelangelo RAMPULLA	G	2	(1)	
Alessio TACCHINARDI	M	27	(3)	
Igor TUDOR (CRO)	D	7	(10)	1
Edwin VAN DER SAR (HOL)	G	32		
Gianluca ZAMBROTTA	M	24	(8)	1
Zinedine ZIDANE (FRA)	M	32		4

LEAGUE RESULTS 1999/2000

29/08/99	Reggina	H	1-1	Inzaghi
12/09/99	Cagliari	A	1-0	Conte
19/09/99	Udinese	H	4-1	Del Piero (p), Inzaghi 2 (1p),
				Zambrotta
25/09/99	Lecce	A	0-2	
03/10/99	Venezia	H	1-0	Conte
17/10/99	Roma	A	1-0	Zidane
24/10/99	Bari	A	1-1	Pessotto
31/10/99	Piacenza	H	1-0	Del Piero (p)
07/11/99	Torino	A	0-0	
21/11/99	Milan	H	3-1	Conte, Inzaghi, Kovacevic
28/11/99	Lazio	A	0-0	
04/12/99	Bologna	H	2-0	Inzaghi 2
12/12/99	Inter	H	1-0	Inzaghi
19/12/99	Fiorentina	A	1-1	Tudor
06/01/00	Verona	H	1-0	Inzaghi
09/01/00	Parma	A	1-1	Del Piero (p)
16/01/00	Perugia	H	3-0	Del Piero (p), Zidane, Kovacevic
23/01/00	Reggina	A	2-0	Kovacevic, Zidane
30/01/00	Cagliari	H	1-1	Inzaghi
05/02/00	Udinese	A	1-1	Ferrara
13/02/00	Lecce	H	1-0	Zidane
20/02/00	Venezia	A	4-0	Del Piero (p), Inzaghi 3
27/02/00	Roma	H	2-1	Davids, Inzaghi
05/03/00	Bari	H	2-0	Conte, Del Piero (p)
12/03/00	Piacenza	A	2-0	Inzaghi 2
19/03/00	Torino	H	3-2	og (Brambilla), og (Lentini),
				Del Piero (p)
24/03/00	Milan	A	0-2	
01/04/00	Lazio	H	0-1	
09/04/00	Bologna	A	2-0	Kovacevic, og (Paganin)
16/04/00	Inter	A	2-1	Kovacevic 2
22/04/00	Fiorentina	H	1-0	Del Piero (p)
30/04/00	Verona	A	0-2	
07/05/00	Parma	H	1-0	Del Piero
14/05/00	Perugia	A	0-1	

LAZIO

CLUB DIRECTORY

Società Sportiva Lazio
Via di Santa Cornelia 14
00060 Formello (Roma)
tel - (06) 9040601
fax - (06) 9040022
website - www.sslazio.it
Year of Formation - 1900
President - Sergio Cragnotti
General Manager - Nello Governato
Secretary - Gabriella Grassi
Coach - Sven Göran Eriksson
Stadium - Olimpico (82,566)

MAJOR HONOURS
League Championship - (2) 1974, 2000.
Domestic Cup - (3) 1958, 1998, 2000.
European Cup-winners' Cup - (1) 1999.

APPEARANCES 99/00

	P	Ap	(s)	Gls
Matias ALMEYDA (ARG)	M	15	(4)	1
Kennet ANDERSSON (SWE)	A		(2)	
Marco BALLOTTA	G	6	(3)	
Alen BOKSIC (CRO)	A	15	(4)	4
Giuseppe FAVALLI	D	16	(2)	
FERNANDO COUTO (POR)	D	10	(4)	
Guerino GOTTARDI	D	4	(1)	
Simone INZAGHI	A	10	(12)	7
Attilio LOMBARDO	M	3	(7)	1
Roberto MANCINI	A	8	(12)	
Luca MARCHEGIANI	G	28		
Sinisa MIHAJLOVIC (YUG)	D	26		6
Pavel NEDVED (CZE)	M	28		5
Paolo NEGRO	D	25	(1)	2
Alessandro NESTA	D	28		
Giuseppe PANCARO	D	26	(2)	3
Fabrizio RAVANELLI	A	5	(11)	2
Marcelo SALAS (CHL)	A	26	(2)	11
Néstor SENSINI (ARG)	M	15	(8)	1
SÉRGIO CONCEIÇÃO (POR)	M	22	(8)	2
Diego SIMEONE (ARG)	M	15	(13)	5
Dejan STANKOVIC (YUG)	M	12	(4)	3
Juan Sebastián VERÓN (ARG)	M	31		8

LEAGUE RESULTS 1999/2000

Date	Opponent		Score	Scorers
30/08/99	Cagliari	H	2-1	Verón, Inzaghi
11/09/99	Bari	A	0-0	
19/09/99	Torino	H	3-0	Verón (p), Inzaghi, Salas
26/09/99	Parma	A	2-1	og (Boghossian), Almeyda
03/10/99	Milan	H	4-4	Verón, og (Abbiati), Salas 2
16/10/99	Udinese	A	3-0	Verón, Boksic, Mihajlovic
24/10/99	Lecce	H	4-2	Pancaro, Stankovic 2, Inzaghi
30/10/99	Inter	A	1-1	Pancaro
07/11/99	Verona	H	4-0	Verón, Salas, Negro, Boksic
21/11/99	Roma	A	1-4	Mihajlovic (p)
28/11/99	Juventus	H	0-0	
04/12/99	Perugia	A	2-0	Salas, Sérgio Conceição
12/12/99	Fiorentina	H	2-0	Boksic, Stankovic
19/12/99	Piacenza	H	2-0	Salas, Mihajlovic
05/01/00	Venezia	A	0-2	
09/01/00	Bologna	H	3-1	Salas, Nedved, Ravanelli
16/01/00	Reggina	A	0-0	
22/01/00	Cagliari	A	0-0	
30/01/00	Bari	H	3-1	Mihajlovic (p), Salas, Nedved
06/02/00	Torino	A	4-2	Sensini, Mihajlovic (p), Ravanelli, Salas
13/02/00	Parma	H	0-0	
20/02/00	Milan	A	1-2	Inzaghi
26/02/00	Udinese	H	2-1	Negro, Salas
05/03/00	Lecce	A	1-0	Nedved
11/03/00	Inter	H	2-2	Inzaghi, Pancaro
19/03/00	Verona	A	0-1	
25/03/00	Roma	H	2-1	Nedved, Verón
01/04/00	Juventus	A	1-0	Simeone
09/04/00	Perugia	H	1-0	Lombardo
15/04/00	Fiorentina	A	3-3	Nedved, Boksic, Mihajlovic (p)
22/04/00	Piacenza	A	2-0	Simeone, Verón
30/04/00	Venezia	H	3-2	Simeone, Inzaghi, og (Maniero)
07/05/00	Bologna	A	3-2	Sérgio Conceição, Simeone, Salas
14/05/00	Reggina	H	3-0	Inzaghi (p), Verón (p), Simeone

LECCE

Union Sportiva Lecce
Via Templari 11
73100 Lecce
tel - (0832) 240211
fax - (0832) 243171
website - www.uslecce.it
Year of Formation - 1908
President - Mario Maroni
Secretary - Roberto Zanzi
Coach - Alberto Cavasin
Stadium - Via del Mare (36,285)

APPEARANCES 99/00

	P	Ap	(s)	Gls
Ivan AIARDI	G		(1)	
David BALLERI	D	32		
Emiliano BILIOTTI	A	6	(13)	
Claudio BONOMI	M	8	(16)	3
Jorge CASANOVA	M	1		
Antonio CHIMENTI	G	33		
Giacomo CIPRIANI	A	1	(7)	
Gianluca COLONNELLO	D	14	(13)	
Alessandro CONTICCHIO	M	32	(1)	4
Domenico DI CARLO	M		(4)	
JUAREZ de Souza (BRA)	D	32	(1)	
Francisco LIMA (BRA)	M	32		1
Massimo LOTTI	G	1		
Cristiano LUCARELLI	A	29	(1)	15
Francesco MARINO	A	6	(10)	
Riccardo MASPERO	M		(1)	
Angelo PARADISO	M	2	(1)	
Luigi PIANGERELLI	M	24	(5)	
Matteo PIVOTTO	D	20	(7)	1
Mirko SADOTTI	D		(2)	
Alberto SAVINO	D	31		1
David SESA (SUI)	A	27	(2)	7
Martino TRAVERSA	D	11	(10)	
William VIALI	D	32		1

Date	Opponent	H/A	Score	Scorers
29/08/99	Milan	H	2-2	Savino, Lucarelli
12/09/99	Verona	A	0-2	
19/09/99	Piacenza	A	1-1	Lucarelli
25/09/99	Juventus	H	2-0	Lima, Conticchio
03/10/99	Bologna	A	0-2	
17/10/99	Reggina	H	2-1	Sesa (p), Bonomi
24/10/99	Lazio	A	2-4	Lucarelli 2
31/10/99	Perugia	H	0-1	
07/11/99	Udinese	H	1-0	Lucarelli
21/11/99	Inter	A	0-6	
28/11/99	Venezia	H	2-1	Lucarelli, Vanoli
05/12/99	Roma	A	2-3	Sesa, Pivotto
11/12/99	Bari	H	1-0	Conticchio
19/12/99	Cagliari	A	0-0	
06/01/00	Fiorentina	H	0-0	
09/01/00	Torino	A	2-1	Lucarelli 2
16/01/00	Parma	H	0-0	
23/01/00	Milan	A	2-2	Lucarelli 2
30/01/00	Verona	H	2-1	Lucarelli (p), Conticchio
06/02/00	Piacenza	H	0-1	
13/02/00	Juventus	A	0-1	
20/02/00	Bologna	H	1-1	Lucarelli
27/02/00	Reggina	A	1-2	Lucarelli (p)
05/03/00	Lazio	H	0-1	
12/03/00	Perugia	A	2-2	Sesa, Lucarelli (p)
19/03/00	Udinese	A	1-2	Sesa
25/03/00	Inter	H	1-0	Sesa
02/04/00	Venezia	A	0-0	
09/04/00	Roma	H	0-0	
16/04/00	Bari	A	1-3	Sesa (p)
22/04/00	Cagliari	H	2-1	Bonomi 2
30/04/00	Fiorentina	A	0-3	
07/05/00	Torino	H	2-1	Sesa, Conticchio
14/05/00	Parma	A	1-4	Lucarelli

MILAN

CLUB DIRECTORY

Milan Associazione Calcio
Via Filippo Turati 3, 20121 Milano
tel - (02) 62281 / fax - (02) 6598876
website - www.acmilan.com
Year of Formation - 1899
President - Silvio Berlusconi
General Manager - Adriano Galliani
Coach - Alberto Zaccheroni
Stadium - Giuseppe Meazza (85,700)

MAJOR HONOURS
League Championship - (16) 1901, 1906, 1907,
1951, 1955, 1957, 1959, 1962, 1968, 1979,
1988, 1992, 1993, 1994, 1996, 1999.
Domestic Cup - (4) 1967, 1972, 1973, 1977.
European Champions' Cup - (5)
1963, 1969, 1989, 1990, 1994.
European Cup-winners' Cup - (2) 1968, 1973.
European Super Cup - (3) 1989, 1990, 1995.
World Club Cup - (3) 1969, 1989, 1990.

APPEARANCES 99/00

		P	Ap	(s)	Gls
Christian ABBIATI		G	29		
Demetrio ALBERTINI		M	23	(3)	1
Mohammed ALIYU-DATI (NIG)		A		(1)	
Massimo AMBROSINI		M	25	(4)	2
Roberto AYALA (ARG)		D	9	(4)	
Oliver BIERHOFF (GER)		A	28	(2)	12
Zvonimir BOBAN (CRO)		M	11	(6)	6
José Antonio CHAMOT (ARG)		D	13		
Alessandro COSTACURTA		D	27		
Diego DE ASCENTIS		M	14	(5)	
Maurizio GANZ		A		(1)	1
Gennaro GATTUSO		M	16	(6)	1
Federico GIUNTI		M	11	(13)	
Andrés GUGLIELMINPIETRO (ARG)		M	19	(4)	1
Thomas HELVEG (DEN)		M	17	(10)	
JOSE MARI (ESP)		A	6	(9)	1
LEONARDO					
Nascimento de Araújo (BRA)		M	11	(9)	4
Paolo MALDINI		D	27		1
Bruno NGOTTY (FRA)		D	7	(2)	
Pierluigi ORLANDINI		M	1	(1)	1
Sebastiano ROSSI		G	5		
Luigi SALA		D	16	(4)	
SERGINHO					
Cláudio dos Santos (BRA)		M	18	(6)	2
Andriy SHEVCHENKO (UKR)		A	30	(2)	24
George WEAH (LIB)		A	8	(2)	4
Taribo WEST (NIG)		D	3	(1)	1

LEAGUE RESULTS 1999/2000

29/08/99	Lecce	A	2-2	Weah, Shevchenko
12/09/99	Perugia	H	3-1	Bierhoff, Shevchenko, Leonardo
18/09/99	Bari	A	1-1	Serginho
25/09/99	Bologna	H	4-0	Weah, Leonardo, Bierhoff (p), Ganz
03/10/99	Lazio	A	4-4	og (Mihajlovic), Shevchenko 3 (1p)
17/10/99	Cagliari	H	2-2	Shevchenko (p), Bierhoff
23/10/99	Inter	A	2-1	Shevchenko, Weah
31/10/99	Verona	A	0-0	
07/11/99	Venezia	H	3-0	Bierhoff, Weah, Orlandini
21/11/99	Juventus	A	1-3	og (Zidane)
28/11/99	Parma	H	2-1	Boban 2
05/12/99	Fiorentina	A	1-2	Bierhoff
11/12/99	Torino	H	2-0	Bierhoff, Shevchenko (p)
19/12/99	Reggina	H	2-2	Shevchenko 2
06/01/00	Piacenza	A	1-0	Bierhoff
09/01/00	Roma	H	2-2	Bierhoff, José Mari
16/01/00	Udinese	A	2-1	Boban, Shevchenko
23/01/00	Lecce	H	2-2	Maldini, Bierhoff
30/01/00	Perugia	A	3-0	Shevchenko 3
06/02/00	Bari	H	4-1	Boban, Serginho, Bierhoff, Shevchenko
12/02/00	Bologna	A	3-2	Gattuso, Shevchenko, Bierhoff
20/02/00	Lazio	H	2-1	Boban 2 (1p)
27/02/00	Cagliari	A	0-0	
05/03/00	Inter	H	1-2	Shevchenko (p)
12/03/00	Verona	H	3-3	Albertini, Shevchenko 2 (1p)
19/03/00	Venezia	A	0-1	
24/03/00	Juventus	H	2-0	Shevchenko 2 (1p)
02/04/00	Parma	A	0-1	
09/04/00	Fiorentina	H	1-1	Leonardo
16/04/00	Torino	A	2-2	Ambrosini, Guglielminpietro
22/04/00	Reggina	A	2-1	og (Vargas), Shevchenko
30/04/00	Piacenza	H	1-0	Ambrosini
07/05/00	Roma	A	1-1	Shevchenko (p)
14/05/00	Udinese	H	4-0	Bierhoff, Shevchenko (p), West, Leonardo

PARMA

CLUB DIRECTORY

Parma Associazione Calcio
Viale Partigiani d'Italia 1
43100 Parma
tel - (0521) 505111
fax - (0521) 505100
website - www.acparma.it
Year of Formation - 1913
President - Stefano Tanzi
Secretary - Renzo Ongaro
Coach - Alberto Malesani
Stadium - Ennio Tardini (29,149)

MAJOR HONOURS
Domestic Cup - (2) 1992, 1999.
European Cup-winners' Cup - (1) 1993.
UEFA Cup - (2) 1995, 1999.
European Super Cup - (1) 1994.

APPEARANCES 99/00

	P	Ap	(s)	Gls
Márcio AMOROSO (BRA)	A	14	(2)	4
Dino BAGGIO	M	23	(1)	
Antonio BENARRIVO	D	16	(2)	
Alain BOGHOSSIAN (FRA)	M	11		3
Jorge BOLAÑO (COL)	M	7	(3)	
Roberto BREDA	M	5	(11)	
Gianluigi BUFFON	G	32		
Fabio CANNAVARO	D	31		2
Paolo CANNAVARO	D		(1)	
Hernán CRESPO (ARG)	A	34		22
Ousmane DABO (FRA)	M	15	(1)	
Marco DI VAIO	A	12	(11)	7
Diego FUSER	M	28		3
Matteo GUARDALBEN	G	1		
Saliou LASSISSI (FRA)	D	11	(3)	
Raffaele LONGO	M	4	(5)	
Giampiero MAINI	M		(6)	
Davide MICILLO	G	1		
Ariel ORTEGA (ARG)	M	16	(2)	3
PAULO SOUSA (POR)	M	7	(1)	
Manuele SACCANI	M		(1)	
Luigi SARTOR	D	15	(1)	
Michele SERENA	D	10	(5)	
Mario STANIC (CRO)	M	11	(12)	5
Lilian THURAM (FRA)	D	33		
Stefano TORRISI	D	5		1
Paolo VANOLI	M	24	(5)	
Johan WALEM (BEL)	M	8	(16)	

LEAGUE RESULTS 1999/2000

29/08/99	Perugia	A	1-1	Stanic
12/09/99	Bologna	H	1-1	og (Ingesson)
19/09/99	Inter	A	1-5	Crespo
26/09/99	Lazio	H	1-2	Boghossian
03/10/99	Verona	H	3-0	Amoroso, Ortega, Crespo
16/10/99	Fiorentina	A	2-0	Di Vaio, Boghossian
24/10/99	Reggina	A	2-2	Crespo 2
31/10/99	Bari	H	2-1	Cannavaro F., Di Vaio
07/11/99	Piacenza	A	2-1	Crespo, Boghossian
21/11/99	Cagliari	H	3-1	Crespo (p), Di Vaio 2
28/11/99	Milan	A	1-2	Crespo
05/12/99	Torino	H	4-1	Crespo 2, Ortega, og (Cruz)
12/12/99	Venezia	A	2-0	Cannavaro F., Crespo
19/12/99	Roma	H	2-0	Crespo, Torrisi
06/01/00	Udinese	A	1-0	Di Vaio
09/01/00	Juventus	H	1-1	Crespo
16/01/00	Lecce	A	0-0	
23/01/00	Perugia	H	1-2	Ortega
30/01/00	Bologna	A	0-1	
06/02/00	Inter	H	1-1	Crespo (p)
13/02/00	Lazio	A	0-0	
20/02/00	Verona	A	3-4	Stanic, Fuser, Crespo
26/02/00	Fiorentina	H	0-4	
05/03/00	Reggina	H	3-0	Fuser, Crespo 2 (1p)
12/03/00	Bari	A	1-0	Amoroso
19/03/00	Piacenza	H	1-0	Crespo (p)
25/03/00	Cagliari	A	3-2	Fuser, Amoroso, Stanic
02/04/00	Milan	H	1-0	Crespo
08/04/00	Torino	A	2-2	Crespo, Amoroso
16/04/00	Venezia	H	3-1	Crespo 2, Di Vaio
22/04/00	Roma	A	0-0	
30/04/00	Udinese	H	0-0	
07/05/00	Juventus	A	0-1	
14/05/00	Lecce	H	4-1	Di Vaio, Stanic 2, Crespo (p)

PERUGIA

CLUB DIRECTORY

Perugia Calcio
Via Cortonese
Località Pian di Massiano
06125 Perugia
tel - (075) 5006641
fax - (075) 5051616
website - www.perugiacalcio.it
Year of Formation - 1905
President - Luciano Gaucci
Secretary - Ilvano Ercoli
Coach - Carlo Mazzone (00/01 - Serse Cosmi)
Stadium - Renato Curi (26,524)

APPEARANCES 99/00

	P	Ap	(s)	Gls
Dmitriy ALENICHEV (RUS)	M	12	(3)	
Nicola AMORUSO	A	22	(3)	11
Ibrahim BA (FRA)	M	13	(3)	1
Pierpaolo BISOLI	M	21	(11)	
Alessandro CALORI	D	33		5
Sergio CAMPOLO	M	2	(7)	
Massimiliano CAPPIOLI	M	4	(9)	2
Daniele DAINO	D	7	(1)	
Massimiliano ESPOSITO	A	19	(8)	1
Stefano GUIDONI	A	1	(1)	
HILÁRIO (POR)	D	16	(4)	
Marco MATERAZZI	D	21		3
Andrea MAZZANTINI	G	33		
Alessandro MELLI	A	17	(8)	1
Mauro MILANESE	D	25		
Salvatore MONACO	D	6	(2)	
Hidetoshi NAKATA (JPN)	M	15		2
Renato OLIVE	M	27	(1)	6
Angelo PAGOTTO	G	1	(1)	
Milan RAPAJC (CRO)	A	25	(3)	2
Roberto RIPA	D	19	(3)	1
Claudio RIVALTA	D	7	(9)	
Sean SOGLIANO	D	2	(6)	
Andrea SUSSI	D	4	(3)	
Héctor TAPIA (CHL)	A		(4)	
Giovanni TEDESCO	M	22	(4)	

LEAGUE RESULTS 1999/2000

29/08/99	Parma	H	1-1	Olive
12/09/99	Milan	A	1-3	Materazzi
18/09/99	Cagliari	H	3-0	Nakata, Materazzi, Melli
26/09/99	Roma	A	1-3	Olive
03/10/99	Reggina	H	2-1	og (Stovini), Nakata (p)
17/10/99	Verona	A	0-2	
23/10/99	Venezia	H	2-1	Amoruso 2
31/10/99	Lecce	A	1-0	Olive
06/11/99	Bari	H	1-2	Ba
20/11/99	Fiorentina	A	0-1	
28/11/99	Torino	A	1-0	Calori
04/12/99	Lazio	H	0-2	
12/12/99	Piacenza	A	0-0	
19/12/99	Bologna	H	3-2	Calori, Amoruso, Ripa
06/01/00	Inter	A	0-5	
09/01/00	Udinese	H	0-5	
16/01/00	Juventus	A	0-3	
23/01/00	Parma	A	2-1	Calori, Olive
30/01/00	Milan	H	0-3	
05/02/00	Cagliari	A	1-2	Amoruso (p)
13/02/00	Roma	H	2-2	Olive 2
19/02/00	Reggina	A	1-1	Esposito
27/02/00	Verona	H	0-0	
05/03/00	Venezia	A	2-1	Amoruso, Cappioli
12/03/00	Lecce	H	2-2	Calori, Cappioli
19/03/00	Bari	A	2-0	Amoruso 2 (1p)
25/03/00	Fiorentina	H	1-2	Rapajc
02/04/00	Torino	H	1-0	Amoruso
09/04/00	Lazio	A	0-1	
16/04/00	Piacenza	H	2-0	Materazzi, Rapajc
22/04/00	Bologna	A	1-2	Amoruso
30/04/00	Inter	H	1-2	Amoruso
07/05/00	Udinese	A	1-2	Amoruso
14/05/00	Juventus	H	1-0	Calori

PIACENZA

CLUB DIRECTORY

Piacenza Football Club
Via Gorra 25
29100 Piacenza
tel - (0523) 757010
fax - (0523) 453405
website - www.piacenzacalcio.it
Year of Formation - 1919
President - Fabrizio Garilli
General Manager - Gian Pietro Marchetti
Secretary - Paolo Armenia
Coach - Luigi Simoni; Maurizio Braghin;
Daniele Bernazzani (00/01 - Walter Novellino)
Stadium - Leonardo Garilli (21,608)

APPEARANCES 99/00

	P	Ap	(s)	Gls
Renato BUSO	M	7	(5)	
Giordano CAINI	D		(1)	
Paolo CRISTALLINI	M	26	(2)	1
Daniele DELLI CARRI	D	19	(2)	1
Arturo DI NAPOLI	A	8	(10)	4
Davide DIONIGI	A	10	(4)	3
Luigi FORLINI	A		(2)	
Carmine GAUTIERI	A	17	(6)	1
Alberto GILARDINO	A	12	(5)	3
Gianluca LAMACCHI	D	20	(5)	
Alessandro LUCARELLI	D	25	(1)	
Andrea MACCAGNI	D	1	(1)	
Giampaolo MANIGHETTI	D	23	(2)	
Alessandro MAZZOLA	M	21		
Stefano MORRONE	M	16	(7)	
Michele NICOLETTI	G	2		
Giampietro PIOVANI	A	10	(10)	2
Cleto POLONIA	D	27		
Massimo RASTELLI	A	20	(2)	1
Ruggiero RIZZITELLI	A	11	(10)	
Flavio ROMA	G	32		
Stefano SACCHETTI	D	22	(1)	
Matteo SAVIONI	D		(1)	
Francesco STATUTO	M	9	(3)	
Giovanni STROPPA	M	7	(6)	1
Andrea TAGLIAFERRI	M	7	(6)	
Pietro VIERCHOWOD	D	21	(1)	
Francesco ZITOLO	M	1	(2)	

LEAGUE RESULTS 1999/2000

29/08/99	Roma	H	1-1	Stroppa
11/09/99	Udinese	A	0-3	
19/09/99	Lecce	H	1-1	Dionigi
26/09/99	Reggina	A	0-1	
02/10/99	Inter	A	1-2	Dionigi (p)
17/10/99	Bologna	H	0-0	
24/10/99	Fiorentina	H	2-0	Cristallini, Di Napoli (p)
31/10/99	Juventus	A	0-1	
07/11/99	Parma	H	1-2	Di Napoli (p)
21/11/99	Venezia	A	0-0	
27/11/99	Verona	H	1-0	Di Napoli (p)
05/12/99	Bari	A	2-3	og (Neqrouz), Dionigi
12/12/99	Perugia	H	0-0	
19/12/99	Lazio	A	0-2	
06/01/00	Milan	H	0-1	
09/01/00	Cagliari	A	0-3	
16/01/00	Torino	H	0-2	
22/01/00	Roma	A	1-2	Piovani
29/01/00	Udinese	H	0-1	
06/02/00	Lecce	A	1-0	Rastelli
13/02/00	Reggina	H	0-0	
20/02/00	Inter	H	1-3	Delli Carri
27/02/00	Bologna	A	0-0	
04/03/00	Fiorentina	A	1-2	Di Napoli
12/03/00	Juventus	H	0-2	
19/03/00	Parma	A	0-1	
25/03/00	Venezia	H	2-2	Gilardino, Piovani
02/04/00	Verona	A	0-1	
09/04/00	Bari	H	2-1	Gilardino, Gautieri
16/04/00	Perugia	A	0-2	
22/04/00	Lazio	H	0-2	
30/04/00	Milan	A	0-1	
07/05/00	Cagliari	H	1-1	og (Villa)
14/05/00	Torino	A	1-2	Gilardino

REGGINA

CLUB DIRECTORY

Reggina Calcio
Via Tommaso Gulli 1
89127 Reggio Calabria
tel - (0965) 811555
fax - (0965) 526343
website - www.regginacalcio.it
Year of Formation - 1914
President - Pasquale Foti
Secretary - Franco Iacopino
Coach - Franco Colomba
Stadium - Oreste Granillo (28,020)

APPEARANCES 99/00

	P	Ap	(s)	Gls
Roberto BARONIO	M	30	(1)	3
Emanuele BELARDI	G	3	(1)	
Andrea BERNINI	M	15	(8)	
Erion BOGDANI (ALB)	A	7	(3)	2
Ezio BREVI	M	26	(2)	
Massimo CAMPO	A		(1)	
Bruno CIRILLO	D	31	(1)	2
Francesco COZZA	M	9	(8)	2
Serge DIE (CIV)	M		(4)	
Paolo FOGLIO	D	13	(2)	
Simone GIACCHETTA	D	30		1
Alessandro IANNUZZI	A		(3)	
Mohamed KALLON (SRL)	A	28	(2)	11
Tonino MARTINO	M	5	(4)	
Giovanni MORABITO	D	30		
Paolo ORLANDONI	G	13		
Joseph Dayo OSHADOGAN	D	11	(7)	
Andrea PIRLO	M	19	(9)	6
Maurizio POLI	M		(6)	
Davide POSSANZINI	A	24	(7)	3
Nenad PRALIJA (CRO)	M	16	(7)	
Enrique REGGI (ARG)	A	6	(16)	1
Wladimiro SBAGLIA	D		(1)	
Lorenzo STOVINI	D	34		
Massimo TAIBI	G	18		
Jorge VARGAS (CHL)	D	6	(4)	
Salvatore VICARI	M		(2)	

LEAGUE RESULTS 1999/2000

29/08/99	Juventus	A	1-1	Kallon
11/09/99	Fiorentina	H	2-2	Kallon (p), Reggi
19/09/99	Bologna	A	1-0	Possanzini
26/09/99	Piacenza	H	1-0	Cirillo
03/10/99	Perugia	A	1-2	Giacchetta
17/10/99	Lecce	A	1-2	Baronio (p)
24/10/99	Parma	H	2-2	Baronio, Pirlo
31/10/99	Udinese	A	2-3	Kallon, Possanzini
07/11/99	Roma	H	0-4	
21/11/99	Bari	A	1-1	Kallon
28/11/99	Inter	H	0-1	
05/12/99	Venezia	A	0-2	
12/12/99	Cagliari	H	1-1	Kallon
19/12/99	Milan	A	2-2	Pirlo, Kallon
06/01/00	Torino	H	2-1	Kallon 2 (1p)
09/01/00	Verona	A	1-1	Pirlo
16/01/00	Lazio	H	0-0	
23/01/00	Juventus	H	0-2	
30/01/00	Fiorentina	A	0-1	
06/02/00	Bologna	H	1-0	Pirlo
13/02/00	Piacenza	A	0-0	
19/02/00	Perugia	H	1-1	Baronio
27/02/00	Lecce	H	2-1	Pirlo, Kallon (p)
05/03/00	Parma	A	0-3	
12/03/00	Udinese	H	0-0	
19/03/00	Roma	A	2-0	Cozza, Cirillo
25/03/00	Bari	H	1-0	Kallon
02/04/00	Inter	A	1-1	Possanzini
09/04/00	Venezia	H	1-0	Bogdani
16/04/00	Cagliari	A	1-0	Cozza
22/04/00	Milan	H	1-2	Pirlo
30/04/00	Torino	A	1-2	Kallon (p)
07/05/00	Verona	H	1-1	Bogdani
14/05/00	Lazio	A	0-3	

ROMA

Associazione Sportiva Roma
Via di Trigoria km. 3.600
00128 Roma
tel - (06) 5060200
fax - (06) 5061736
website - www.asromacalcio.it
Year of Formation - 1927
President - Franco Sensi
Coach - Fabio Capello
Stadium - Olimpico (82,566)

MAJOR HONOURS
League Championship - (2) 1942, 1983.
Domestic Cup - (7)
1964, 1969, 1980, 1981, 1984, 1986, 1991.
Fairs' Cup - (1) 1961.

APPEARANCES 99/00

	P	Ap	(s)	Gls
ALDAIR dos Santos (BRA)	D	34		1
Dmitriy ALENICHEV (RUS)	M	3	(4)	1
Francesco ANTONIOLI	G	30		
Gustavo BARTELT (ARG)	A		(3)	
Manuele BLASI	M	1	(4)	
Marcos CAFÚ (BRA)	D	28		2
Vincent CANDELA (FRA)	D	26		2
Lambros CHOUTOS (GRE)	A		(2)	
Marco DELVECCHIO	A	27	(1)	12
Eusebio DI FRANCESCO	M	24	(6)	2
EDNÍLSON (BRA)	M		(1)	
FÁBIO JÚNIOR (BRA)	A	1	(8)	1
Carmine GAUTIERI	M		(1)	
Sergei GURENKO (BLS)	D	1	(4)	
Cristiano LUPATELLI	G	4		
Amedeo MANGONE	D	25		
MARCOS ASSUNÇÃO (BRA)	M	20	(1)	1
Vincenzo MONTELLA	A	30	(1)	18
Hidetoshi NAKATA (JPN)	M	15		2
Paolo POGGI	A	4	(7)	
Alessandro RINALDI	D	18	(5)	
Ivan TOMIC (YUG)	M		(1)	
Damiano TOMMASI	M	25	(8)	2
Francesco TOTTI	A	27		7
António Carlos ZAGO (BRA)	D	25	(2)	1
Cristiano ZANETTI	M	6	(5)	

LEAGUE RESULTS 1999/2000

29/08/99	Piacenza	A	1-1	Totti (p)
12/09/99	Inter	H	0-0	
19/09/99	Venezia	A	3-1	Delvecchio 2, Alenichev
26/09/99	Perugia	H	3-1	Montella, Marcos Assunção, Totti (p)
03/10/99	Fiorentina	A	3-1	Cafú 2, Tommasi
17/10/99	Juventus	H	0-1	
24/10/99	Torino	A	1-1	Di Francesco
31/10/99	Cagliari	H	2-2	Montella, Delvecchio
07/11/99	Reggina	A	4-0	og (Oshadogan), Montella,
				Fábio Júnior, Totti (p)
21/11/99	Lazio	H	4-1	Delvecchio 2, Montella 2
28/11/99	Udinese	A	2-0	Delvecchio 2
05/12/99	Lecce	H	3-2	Totti, Candela, og (Pivotto)
12/12/99	Bologna	A	0-1	
19/12/99	Parma	A	0-2	
06/01/00	Bari	H	3-1	Montella 3 (1p)
09/01/00	Milan	A	2-2	Delvecchio, Montella
16/01/00	Verona	H	3-1	Montella, og (Apolloni), Totti
22/01/00	Piacenza	H	2-1	Di Francesco, Totti
29/01/00	Inter	A	1-2	Aldair
06/02/00	Venezia	H	5-0	Candela, Delvecchio 2, Montella,
				og (Ngotty)
13/02/00	Perugia	A	2-2	Nakata, Montella (p)
19/02/00	Fiorentina	H	4-0	Montella 3, og (Firicano)
27/02/00	Juventus	A	1-2	Delvecchio
05/03/00	Torino	H	1-0	Delvecchio
12/03/00	Cagliari	A	0-1	
19/03/00	Reggina	H	0-2	
25/03/00	Lazio	A	1-2	Montella
02/04/00	Udinese	H	1-1	Nakata
09/04/00	Lecce	A	0-0	
16/04/00	Bologna	H	2-0	Montella (p), Totti (p)
22/04/00	Parma	H	0-0	
30/04/00	Bari	A	0-0	
07/05/00	Milan	H	1-1	Zago
14/05/00	Verona	A	2-2	Tommasi, Montella

TORINO

Torino Calcio
Via Maria Vittoria 1, 10123 Torino
tel - (011) 5623941 / fax - (011) 5622018
website - www.toro.it
Year of Formation - 1906
President - Attilio Romero
Secretary - Federico Bonetto
Coach - Emiliano Mondonico
(00/01 - Luigi Simoni)
Stadium - Delle Alpi (69,041)

MAJOR HONOURS
League Championship - (7)
1927, 1943, 1946, 1947, 1948, 1949, 1976.
Domestic Cup - (5)
1936, 1943, 1968, 1971, 1993.

APPEARANCES 99/00

		P	Ap	(s)	Gls
Edoardo	ARTISTICO	A	2	(6)	2
Antonino	ASTA	M	5	(3)	
Mauro	BONOMI	D	29		
Massimo	BRAMBILLA	M	26	(2)	
Luca	BUCCI	G	32		
Emanuele	CALAIO	A		(7)	1
Francesco	COCO	D	15	(6)	
Massimo	CRIPPA	M		(3)	
André	CRUZ (BRA)	D	13		1
Marco	CUDINI	D	1	(5)	
Djibril	DIAWARA (FRA)	M	13	(1)	
Alejandro	ESCALONA	D		(3)	
Marco	FERRANTE	A	30		18
Massimo	FICCADENTI	M	6	(5)	
Abdulla	FUSSEINI (GHA)	M		(1)	
Fabio	GALANTE	D	20	(3)	2
Alessandro	GRANDONI	D	15	(2)	1
Ilija	IVIC (YUG)	A	10	(9)	
Krunoslav	JURCIC (CRO)	M	10		
Gianluigi	LENTINI	M	20	(4)	
Roberto	MALTAGLIATI	D	18	(3)	
Jacopo	MARIANI	D		(1)	
Gustavo	MENDEZ (URU)	M	23		1
Lorenzo	MINOTTI	D		(1)	
Luigi	PANARELLI	D	1	(2)	
Luca	PASTINE	G	2		
Fabio	PECCHIA	M	15	(7)	1
André Luciano	PINGA (BRA)	A	5	(2)	2
Fabio	QUAGLIARELLA	A		(1)	
Alessio	SCARCHILLI	M	14		2
Gennaro	SCARLATO	A	2	(3)	
Andrea	SILENZI	A	7	(4)	2
Vincenzo	SOMMESE	M	25	(4)	2
Fabio	TRICARICO	M	15	(11)	

LEAGUE RESULTS 1999/2000

28/08/99	Bologna	A	0-0	
12/09/99	Venezia	H	2-1	Ferrante, Artistico
19/09/99	Lazio	A	0-3	
26/09/99	Inter	H	0-1	
02/10/99	Cagliari	A	1-1	Ferrante (p)
17/10/99	Bari	H	3-1	Silenzi, Ferrante (p), Scarchilli
24/10/99	Roma	H	1-1	Scarchilli
30/10/99	Fiorentina	A	1-1	Sommese
07/11/99	Juventus	H	0-0	
21/11/99	Verona	A	1-0	Artistico
28/11/99	Perugia	H	0-1	
05/12/99	Parma	A	1-4	Cruz
12/12/99	Milan	A	0-2	
19/12/99	Udinese	H	0-1	
06/01/00	Reggina	A	1-2	Calaiò
09/01/00	Lecce	H	1-2	Ferrante (p)
16/01/00	Piacenza	A	2-0	Ferrante, Pecchia
23/01/00	Bologna	H	2-1	Ferrante 2
30/01/00	Venezia	A	2-2	Grandoni, Ferrante
06/02/00	Lazio	H	2-4	Ferrante (p), Galante
13/02/00	Inter	A	1-1	Mendez
20/02/00	Cagliari	H	1-1	Ferrante
27/02/00	Bari	A	1-1	Ferrante
05/03/00	Roma	A	0-1	
12/03/00	Fiorentina	H	1-0	Ferrante
19/03/00	Juventus	A	2-3	Ferrante 2 (2p)
25/03/00	Verona	H	0-3	
02/04/00	Perugia	A	0-1	
08/04/00	Parma	H	2-2	Sommese, Silenzi
16/04/00	Milan	H	2-2	Pinga 2
22/04/00	Udinese	A	0-0	
30/04/00	Reggina	H	2-1	Galante, Ferrante
07/05/00	Lecce	A	1-2	Ferrante (p)
14/05/00	Piacenza	H	2-1	Ferrante 2 (1p)

UDINESE

CLUB DIRECTORY

Udinese Calcio
Via A. Candolini 2
33100 Udine
tel - (0432) 544911
fax - (0432) 544933
website - www.udinese.it
Year of Formation - 1896
President - Giovanni Caratozzolo
Secretary - Sigfrido Marcatti
Coach - Luigi De Canio
Stadium - Friuli (41,825)

APPEARANCES 99/00

	P	Ap	(s)	Gls
ALBERTO (BRA)	D	5	(9)	
Stephen APPIAH (GHA)	M	2	(2)	
Valerio BERTOTTO	D	30		
Morten BISGAARD (DEN)	M	14	(6)	1
Abdoulaje CAMARA (MLI)	D		(2)	
Morgan DE SANCTIS	G	6	(1)	
Mauro ESPOSITO	A		(6)	
Stefano FIORE	M	33		9
Mohammed GARGO (GHA)	M	19		
Régis GENAUX (BEL)	D	15	(2)	
Giuliano GIANNICHEDDA	M	29		1
Martin JØRGENSEN (DEN)	M	26	(4)	7
JORGINHO (BRA)	M	1	(2)	
Tomas LOCATELLI	M	15	(8)	2
Thomas MANFREDINI	D	10	(4)	1
Massimo MARGIOTTA	A	8	(5)	2
Roberto MUZZI	A	27	(2)	12
Mauricio PINEDA (ARG)	D		(2)	
David PIZARRO (CHL)	M	1	(4)	
Paolo POGGI	A	10	(4)	3
Roberto Carlos SOSA (ARG)	A	21	(9)	6
Andrea SOTTIL	D	29		5
Délio César TOLEDO (PAR)	D	1	(1)	
Luigi TURCI	G	28		
Henry VAN DER VEGT (HOL)	M	17	(5)	1
WARLEY Silva dos Santos (BRA)	A	4	(11)	3
Marco ZAMBONI	D	2	(2)	
Marco ZANCHI	D	21	(2)	

LEAGUE RESULTS 1999/2000

29/08/99	Venezia	A	1-1	Muzzi
11/09/99	Piacenza	H	3-0	Poggi (p), Locatelli, Muzzi
19/09/99	Juventus	A	1-4	Bisgaard
26/09/99	Fiorentina	H	1-1	Fiore
03/10/99	Bari	A	1-1	Warley
16/10/99	Lazio	H	0-3	
24/10/99	Cagliari	A	3-0	Van der Vegt, Muzzi 2
31/10/99	Reggina	H	3-2	Poggi 2, Fiore
07/11/99	Lecce	A	0-1	
20/11/99	Bologna	H	2-1	Sottil, Muzzi
28/11/99	Roma	H	0-2	
05/12/99	Inter	A	0-3	
12/12/99	Verona	H	3-3	Muzzi, og (Franceschetti), Sottil
19/12/99	Torino	A	1-0	Jørgensen
06/01/00	Parma	H	0-1	
09/01/00	Perugia	A	5-0	Sottil, og (Calori), Manfredini, Fiore, Jørgensen
16/01/00	Milan	H	1-2	Muzzi
23/01/00	Venezia	H	5-2	Fiore, Sottil, Muzzi 2, Jørgensen
29/01/00	Piacenza	A	1-0	Muzzi
05/02/00	Juventus	H	1-1	Jørgensen
13/02/00	Fiorentina	A	1-1	Jørgensen
20/02/00	Bari	H	5-1	Giannichedda, Fiore, Sosa, Sottil, Jørgensen
26/02/00	Lazio	A	1-2	Locatelli
04/03/00	Cagliari	H	5-2	Margiotta, Jørgensen, Fiore 2 (1p), Muzzi
12/03/00	Reggina	A	0-0	
19/03/00	Lecce	H	2-1	Sosa, Warley
25/03/00	Bologna	A	1-2	Muzzi
02/04/00	Roma	A	1-1	Sosa
08/04/00	Inter	H	3-0	Sosa 3
15/04/00	Verona	A	2-2	Fiore 2
22/04/00	Torino	H	0-0	
30/04/00	Parma	A	0-0	
07/05/00	Perugia	H	2-1	Warley, Margiotta
14/05/00	Milan	A	0-4	

VENEZIA

CLUB DIRECTORY

AC Venezia
Via Ceccherini 19
30174 Venezia - Mestre
tel - (041) 2380711
fax - (041) 950104
website - www.veneziacalcio.it
Year of Formation - 1907
President - Maurizio Zamparini
Secretary - Stefano Bazzacco
Coach - Luciano Spalletti; Giuseppe Materazzi;
Luciano Spalletti; Francesco Oddo
(00/01 - Claudio Cesare Prandelli)
Stadium - Pierluigi Penzo (13,511)

APPEARANCES 99/00

	P	Ap	(s)	Gls
Francesco BENUSSI	G	7		
Runar BERG (NOR)	M	18	(10)	2
Stefano BETTARINI	D	18	(2)	
Fábio BILICA (BRA)	D	18		
Massimo BORGOBELLO	A	2	(4)	
Emanuele BRIOSCHI	D	17	(3)	
Igor BUDAN (CRO)	A	5	(11)	2
Giuseppe CARDONE	D	18	(1)	
Daniele CARNASCIALI	D	7	(5)	
Fabrizio CASAZZA	G	11	(3)	
Francesco CIULLO	A		(2)	
Alessandro DAL CANTO	D	8	(2)	
Maurizio GANZ	A	16	(3)	8
Ciro GINESTRA	A	2	(4)	
Giuseppe IACHINI	M	15	(1)	
Robert IBERTSBERGER (AUT)	M	2	(2)	
Michael KONSEL (AUT)	G	15		
Gianluca LUPPI	D	21	(1)	
Rubén MALDONADO (PAR)	D	9	(1)	
Filippo MANIERO	A	28	(2)	9
Nicola MARANGON	D	1	(7)	
Salvatore MICELI	M	1		
Hiroshi NANAMI (JPN)	M	13	(11)	1
Bruno NGOTTY (FRA)	D	16		
Pierluigi ORLANDINI	M	6	(4)	1
Simone PAVAN	D	8	(8)	
Francesco PEDONE	M	26	(2)	1
Dejan PETKOVIC (YUG)	A	12	(1)	1
Tomislav RUKAVINA (CRO)	M	3		
Massimo TAIBI	G	1		
Fabian VALTOLINA	A	25	(6)	4
Sergio VOLPI	M	25		1

LEAGUE RESULTS 1999/2000

29/08/99	Udinese	H	1-1	Maniero
12/09/99	Torino	A	1-2	Valtolina
19/09/99	Roma	H	1-3	Petkovic
26/09/99	Cagliari	A	1-1	Valtolina
03/10/99	Juventus	A	0-1	
17/10/99	Inter	H	1-0	Maniero
23/10/99	Perugia	A	1-2	Maniero
30/10/99	Bologna	H	0-1	
07/11/99	Milan	A	0-3	
21/11/99	Piacenza	H	0-0	
28/11/99	Lecce	A	1-2	Valtolina
05/12/99	Reggina	H	2-0	Maniero 2
12/12/99	Parma	H	0-2	
18/12/99	Verona	A	0-1	
05/01/00	Lazio	H	2-0	Ganz, Maniero
09/01/00	Bari	A	0-3	
16/01/00	Fiorentina	H	2-1	Volpi, Maniero
23/01/00	Udinese	A	2-5	Ganz, Nanami
30/01/00	Torino	H	2-2	Ganz (p), Berg
06/02/00	Roma	A	0-5	
13/02/00	Cagliari	H	3-0	Ganz 2 (1p), Orlandini
20/02/00	Juventus	H	0-4	
27/02/00	Inter	A	0-3	
05/03/00	Perugia	H	1-2	Maniero
11/03/00	Bologna	A	1-1	Ganz
19/03/00	Milan	H	1-0	Maniero
25/03/00	Piacenza	A	2-2	Valtolina, Berg
02/04/00	Lecce	H	0-0	
09/04/00	Reggina	A	0-1	
16/04/00	Parma	A	1-3	Budan
22/04/00	Verona	H	2-2	Budan, Ganz
30/04/00	Lazio	A	2-3	Pedone, Ganz
07/05/00	Bari	H	0-1	
14/05/00	Fiorentina	A	0-3	

VERONA

CLUB DIRECTORY

Hellas Verona Football Club
Piazzale Olimpia-Cancello E
37138 Verona
tel - (045) 577555
fax - (045) 568665
website - www.hellasverona.it
Year of Formation - 1903
President - Giambattista Pastorello
Secretary - Enzo Bertolini
Coach - Claudio Cesare Prandelli
(00/01 - Attilio Perotti)
Stadium - Nuovo Bentegodi (44,092)

MAJOR HONOURS
League Championship - (1) 1985.

APPEARANCES 99/00

	P	Ap	(s)	Gls
ADAILTON Martins (BRA)	A	17	(11)	7
Alfredo AGLIETTI	A	10	(2)	2
Giuseppe ANASTASI	D		(1)	
Luigi APOLLONI	D	28		2
Graziano BATTISTINI	G	5	(1)	
Cristian BROCCHI	M	26	(1)	2
Fabrizio CAMMARATA	A	20	(8)	9
Leonardo COLUCCI	M	29	(2)	2
Michele COSSATO	A	2	(6)	
Aimo DIANA	D	20	(5)	
Gianluca FALSINI	D	29	(2)	1
Giancarlo FILIPPINI	M	17	(5)	
Marco FRANCESCHETTI	M	19	(2)	
Sébastien FREY (FRA)	G	29	(1)	
Marco GIANDEBIAGGI	M	11	(2)	
Natale GONNELLA	D	4		
Vincenzo ITALIANO	M	8	(4)	
Martin LAURSEN (DEN)	D	16	(3)	2
Antonio MARASCO	M	32		1
Martino MELIS	M	26	(6)	3
Luca MEZZANO	D	4		
Domenico MORFEO	A	10		5
Alessandro ROMANO	M	1		
Emiliano SALVETTI	M	8	(18)	2
Anthony SERIC (CRO)	D	2	(8)	
Robert SPEHAR (CRO)	A	1	(2)	
Tonci ZILIC (CRO)	D		(1)	

LEAGUE RESULTS 1999/2000

29/08/99	Inter	A	0-3	
12/09/99	Lecce	H	2-0	Marasco, Aglietti
19/09/99	Fiorentina	A	1-4	Melis
26/09/99	Bari	H	0-1	
03/10/99	Parma	A	0-3	
17/10/99	Perugia	H	2-0	Cammarata, og (Calori)
24/10/99	Bologna	A	0-0	
31/10/99	Milan	H	0-0	
07/11/99	Lazio	A	0-4	
21/11/99	Torino	H	0-1	
27/11/99	Piacenza	A	0-1	
05/12/99	Cagliari	H	2-0	Aglietti, Adailton
12/12/99	Udinese	A	3-3	og (Sottil), Adailton 2
18/12/99	Venezia	H	1-0	Adailton (p)
06/01/00	Juventus	A	0-1	
09/01/00	Reggina	H	1-1	Adailton (p)
16/01/00	Roma	A	1-3	Salvetti
23/01/00	Inter	H	1-2	Laursen
30/01/00	Lecce	A	1-2	Colucci
06/02/00	Fiorentina	H	2-2	Morfeo 2
12/02/00	Bari	A	1-1	Morfeo
20/02/00	Parma	H	4-3	Brocchi, Morfeo, Colucci, Melis
27/02/00	Perugia	A	0-0	
05/03/00	Bologna	H	0-0	
12/03/00	Milan	A	3-3	Apolloni, Laursen, Cammarata
19/03/00	Lazio	H	1-0	Morfeo
25/03/00	Torino	A	3-0	Melis, Cammarata 2
02/04/00	Piacenza	H	1-0	Brocchi
09/04/00	Cagliari	A	1-0	Falsini
15/04/00	Udinese	H	2-2	Apolloni, Cammarata
22/04/00	Venezia	A	2-2	Adailton, Salvetti
30/04/00	Juventus	H	2-0	Cammarata 2
07/05/00	Reggina	A	1-1	Cammarata
14/05/00	Roma	H	2-2	Adailton, Cammarata

LATVIA

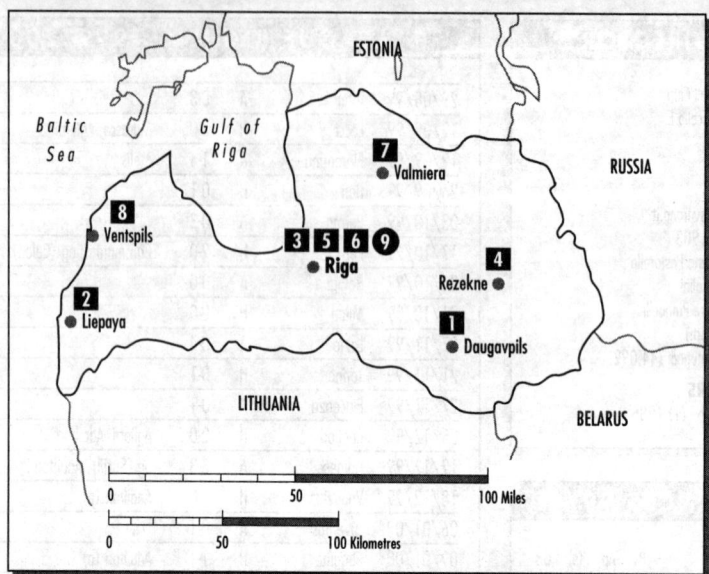

1	DINABURG DAUGAVPILS	612
2	METALURGS LIEPAYA	613
3	POLICE FK RIGA	614
4	FK REZEKNE	615
5	FK RIGA	616

6	SKONTO RIGA	617
7	FK VALMIERA	618
8	FK VENTSPILS	619
Promoted club		
9	LU DAUGAVA RIGA	

ENGLISH CONNECTIONS ON THE INCREASE

Eighth straight title for super Skonto

FEDERATION DIRECTORY

Latvijas Futbola Federacija
1 Augsiela, LV-1009 Riga

tel - (2) 292988
fax - 7828331
email - futbols@latnet.lv

Year of Formation - 1921
President - Guntis Indricksons
Secretary - Janis Mezhetsky

Stadium - Daugava, Riga (5,800)

One day, perhaps, the Latvian national championship will be won by a club other than Skonto Riga, but that looks unlikely to happen for the foreseeable future. Ever since the country earned the right to its own UEFA-recognised domestic league, only one club has been crowned as champions, and such is Skonto's continued predominance that the quest for a potential rival remains, for now at least, a forlorn task.

The club's eighth successive title was, as ever, something of a formality. Skonto lost far more matches than usual - five in total, including two at home - yet there was never any serious threat to their supremacy. When they did lose, the tendency was for them to compensate by going on a long winning run. This happened after their opening-day defeat to FK Ventspils, when a nine-game winning sequence ensued, and again after a defeat at Dinaburg Daugavpils, which was countered with eight victories in succession.

Led once again by resident coach Alexander Starkov, Skonto were a potent combination of Latvian internationals and imports from other ex-Soviet states. Of the latter, two Georgians in particular excelled. Midfielder Alexander Rekhviashvili was appointed as club captain at the start of the season and he enjoyed by far the best of his four seasons in the Latvian capital, becoming the most influential midfielder in the championship. David Chaladze also made a sparkling contribution on his return to the club, becoming the team's top scorer with 16 goals, a total boosted by a double hat-trick in Skonto's 12-0 away win over newly-promoted Police FK - the only time the champions reached double figures during the season.

There were sterling contributions also from young guns Vladimir Kolesnichenko and Andrey Rubins as well as senior team-members Vitaly Astafyev and Imants Bleidelis, both of whom elected to join English clubs once the season had ended, with Astafyev - the new record cap-holder of Latvia, after making his 64th appearance in February against Romania - moving to Bristol Rovers, and Bleidelis joining his national team colleague Marian Pahars at Southampton.

Pahars was a worthy winner of the 1999 Latvian Footballer of the Year award after making such an impressive start to his professional career in the English Premiership. Whether he becomes the trailblazer for his fellow countrymen remains to be seen, but he certainly benefitted from the excellent schooling he received during his time at Skonto.

LEAGUE CHAMPIONSHIP RESULTS 1999

#		1	2	3	4	5	6	7	8
1	Dinaburg Daugavpils		0-0	1-1	2-0	2-0	1-0	0-0	1-0
			0-1	2-1	6-1	0-1	1-5	1-3	0-2
2	Metalurgs Liepaya	3-0		4-1	6-0	3-2	2-3	3-0	3-1
		6-1		7-0	5-1	1-2	1-0	2-0	2-1
3	Police FK Riga	0-4	0-5		5-1	2-1	0-9	0-1	0-2
		0-5	1-3		1-1	3-0	0-12	1-1	2-8
4	FK Rezekne	1-2	0-4	0-1		0-0	0-2	0-3	0-2
		0-1	0-1	2-0		1-3	0-5	1-3	0-1
5	FK Riga	0-0	1-5	0-0	2-0		1-3	3-1	0-1
		0-1	1-0	5-0	5-0		0-4	0-0	2-4
6	Skonto Riga	1-0	3-2	2-0	2-1	1-0		5-0	3-1
		4-0	3-0	5-0	8-0	1-2		3-0	0-2
7	FK Valmiera	0-4	1-1	1-1	4-0	2-3	0-1		0-3
		1-0	0-2	2-3	4-0	3-0	0-1		2-1
8	FK Ventspils	0-0	2-0	5-2	5-1	2-1	1-0	3-0	
		1-2	1-1	4-0	7-1	2-0	0-2	0-1	

INTERNATIONAL HONOURS

None

LEAGUE CHAMPIONSHIP FINAL TABLE 1999

			Home					Away					Total						
		Pd	W	D	L	F	A	W	D	L	F	A	W	D	L	F	A	PT	GD
1	Skonto Riga	28	12	0	2	41	8	11	0	3	47	7	23	0	5	88	15	69	73
2	Metalurgs Liepaya	28	12	0	2	48	12	7	3	4	25	13	19	3	6	73	25	60	48
3	FK Ventspils	28	9	2	3	33	11	9	0	5	29	15	18	2	8	62	26	56	36
4	Dinaburg Daugavpils	28	6	3	5	17	15	7	2	5	20	17	13	5	10	37	32	44	5
5	FK Valmiera	28	5	2	7	20	20	5	3	6	13	22	10	5	13	33	42	35	-9
6	FK Riga	28	5	3	6	20	19	5	1	8	15	23	10	4	14	35	42	34	-7
7	Police FK Riga	28	3	2	9	15	53	2	3	9	10	40	5	5	18	25	93	20	-68
8	FK Rezekne	28	1	1	12	5	28	0	1	13	7	62	1	2	25	12	90	5	-78

Pahars has proved to be the perfect ambassador for Latvian football, but its growing stature is not solely down to him. Skonto are improving as an international force almost on an annual basis. In 1999/2000 they went three rounds of the Champions' League qualifying campaign before losing out to English heavyweights Chelsea.

An easy win over Jeunesse Esch - in which striker Mikhail Mikholap scored a record six goals, including five in the home leg - was followed by a very impressive 5-4 aggregate win over Romanian champions Rapid Bucharest. Even Chelsea were put to the test, with the first leg at Stamford Bridge remaining goalless until 15 minutes from time when Gianluca Vialli's team finally broke loose.

Skonto also gave Polish side Widzew Lodz a good run for their money in the UEFA Cup, and the following winter Latvia's finest again put up a top-class display in the indoor CIS Cup, finishing third but coming away with the 'moral champions' tag after their 5-0 annihilation of Dynamo Kiev (including four goals from the outstanding Kolesnichenko) and a 2-1 win over hosts Spartak Moscow.

Skonto Riga were joined in the 2000/01 European club competitions by Metalurgs Liepaya and FK Ventspils. Metalurgs were the runners-up in both league and Cup, with the latter title being secured by Skonto some six months after their league triumph thanks to a convincing, trouble-free 4-1 victory in the final at the Daugava stadium. On the losing side was Metalurgs striker Victor Dobretsov, who in 1999 had been crowned the league's top scorer for the second season running.

Ventspils, an emerging force, were thrashed by Metalurgs in the Cup semi-finals but in the league they twice beat Skonto and also demonstrated some international prowess by overcoming the previous season's European Cup-winners' Cup quarter-finalists Vålerenga in the InterToto competition.

Relegation was as much a formality as the championship race, with FK Rezekne, the team rescued at the eleventh hour in each of the previous two campaigns, dropping out of the élite with just five points. Their place in the 2000 championship was taken by

TOP SCORERS

22 Victor DOBRETSOV (Metalurgs Liepaya)
18 Victor VORONKOV (FK Ventspils)
16 David CHALADZE (Skonto Riga)
14 Mikhail MIKHOLAP (Skonto Riga)
13 Vladimir KOLESNICHENKO (Skonto Riga)
12 Vladislav BEZBORODOV (FK Ventspils)
11 Yevgeny VDOVENKO (FK Ventspils)
9 Vitaly ASTAFYEV (Skonto Riga)
8 Saulius ATMANAVICIUS (Metalurgs Liepaya)
  Rolands BOULDERS (Metalurgs Liepaya)
  Stanislav DUBROVIN (Dinaburg Daugavpils)

NATIONAL TEAM RESULTS 99/00

04/09/99	Albania (ECQ)	A	Tirana	3-3	Astafyev (21, 63), Shtolcers (70)
08/09/99	Georgia (ECQ)	A	Tbilisi	2-2	Bleidelis (62), Stepanov (90)
09/10/99	Norway (ECQ)	H	Riga	1-2	Pahars (53)
02/02/00	Romania	N	Paphos	0-2	
04/02/00	Slovakia	N	Paphos	1-3	Shtolcers (84)
06/02/00	Lithuania	N	Larnaca	1-2	Peltsis (4)
26/04/00	Lithuania	A	Kaunas	1-2	Peltsis (12)
03/06/00	Finland	H	Riga	1-0	Peltsis (59)

NATIONAL TEAM APPEARANCES 99/00

Coach - Gary JOHNSON	ALB	GEO	NOR	ROM	SVK	LIT	LIT	FIN	Cps	Gls
Alexander KOLINKO (18/06/75) - Skonto Riga	G	G	G	G		G	G	G	13	-
Igor N. STEPANOV (21/01/76) - Skonto Riga	D	D	D80			D46	D		35	2
Mikhail ZEMLINSKY (21/12/69) - Skonto Riga	D	D	D	D		D	D		62	6
Valentin LOBANYOV (23/10/71) - Shinnik Yaroslavl (RUS)/Skonto Riga	D	D	D	s80	D	D	D	D	30	1
Victor LUKASHEVICH (17/03/72) - FK Ventspils	D		D82	D	s54	D			17	-
Valery IVANOV (23/02/70) - Shinnik Yaroslavl (RUS)	M60	M	M	M				M	62	1
Imants BLEIDELIS (16/08/75) - Skonto Riga/Southampton (ENG)	M	M	M	M			M	M	43	5
Vitaliy ASTAFYEV (03/04/71) - Skonto Riga/Bristol Rovers (ENG)	M82		M	M82			M	M	66	9
Andrey RUBINS (26/11/78) - Skonto Riga	M	M	M	M58	M	M46	M	M	14	-
Andrey SHTOLCERS (07/07/74) - Shakhtar Donetsk (UKR)	A85	A74	A	A	s68		A71	A46	43	5
Mikhail MIKHOLAP (24/08/74) - Skonto Riga	A								8	-
Oleg BLAGONADEZHDIN (16/05/73) - Skonto Riga	s60		D					s56	34	1
Vladimir BABICHEV (22/04/68) - Skonto Riga	s82	s59							51	4
Rolands BOULDERS (12/03/65) - Metalurgs Liepaya	s85	s83							33	3
Yury LAIZANS (06/01/79) - Skonto Riga		D83	s82	D	M	M	M	D	23	-
Alexander ISAKOV (16/09/73) - Lokomotiv Nizhniy Novgorod (RUS)		M59							14	-
Marian PAHARS (05/08/76) - Southampton (ENG)		A	A	A				A	38	9
Alexey SHARANDO (01/01/64) - FK Riga		s74							24	2
Nickolay POLYAKOV (02/07/75) - Police FK Riga				s58	D	M	D	D56	12	-
Renars VUTSANS (04/11/76) - Skonto Riga				s82	M68	M	s62		4	-
Andris VANIN (30/04/80) - FK Ventspils					G				1	-
Igor KORABLYOV (23/11/74) - FK Riga					D	D			6	-
Alexey PASHIN (12/07/79) - Skonto Riga					D				1	-
Genady SOLONITSIN (03/01/80) - Metalurgs Liepaya					M54	s46			2	-
Vladimir KOLESNICHENKO (04/05/80) - Skonto Riga					A	A	s71		7	-
Maris VERPAKOVSKY (15/10/79) - Metalurgs Liepaya					A				3	1
Eriks PELTSIS (25/06/78) - LG Cheetahs (KOR)						A	A62	s46	3	3
Artur ZAKRESHEVSKY (07/08/71) - Metalurgs Liepaya							s46		30	-

LU Daugave Riga, who won the Second Division by a veritable landslide, winning 24 of their 28 matches and drawing the others.

The heavily Skonto-influenced Latvian national team predictably failed to claim their place in the European Championship play-offs, although overall there was plenty of satisfaction to be gained from the ten-match campaign, which was concluded by two eventful draws in Albania and Georgia and an unlucky home defeat against group winners Norway.

The team underwent quite a transformation in the summer of 1999 when Georgian coach Revaz Dzodzuashvili suddenly announced that he was leaving to take charge of Saudi Arabian club Al-Ittihad. His replacement was an Englishman, but not one of any great repute. Gary Johnson, whose modest employment beforehand had been as the director of youth development at Watford, was drafted in by the Latvian FA and appointed as the head coach to work in liaison with Skonto boss Starkov.

EUROPEAN CUPS 99/00

CHAMPIONS' CUP
● SKONTO RIGA
Preliminary round 1 JEUNESSE ESCH (LUX)
A 2-0 Astafyev (67), Mikholap (73)
Kolinko, Laizans, Zemlinsky, Tereskinas, Blagonadezhdin (Olshansky 82), Bleidelis, Rekhviashvili, Rubins (Korgalidze 78), Astafyev, Mikholap, Chaladze (Kolesnichenko 78).
H 8-0 Bleidelis (38, 50), Mikholap (40, 54, 61, 84p, 90p), Kolesnichenko (77)
Kolinko, Laizans, Zemlinsky, Silagadze (Tereskinas 46), Blagonadezhdin (Stepanov 63), Bleidelis, Rekhviashvili (Melnik 72), Rubins, Astafyev, Mikholap, Kolesnichenko.

Preliminary round 2 RAPID BUCURESTI (ROM)
A 3-3 Chaladze (4, 33), Astafyev (60)
Kolinko, Laizans, Zemlinsky, Tereskinas (Menteshashvili 76), Blagonadezhdin, Bleidelis, Rekhviashvili, Rubins, Astafyev, Mikholap, Chaladze (Silagadze 57).
H 2-1 Laizans (77), Rubins (87)
Kolinko, Laizans, Zemlinsky, Silagadze, Blagonadezhdin (Menteshashvili 69), Bleidelis, Rekhviashvili, Rubins, Astafyev, Mikholap, Chaladze (Tereskinas 80).

Qualifying round CHELSEA (ENG)
A 0-3
Kolinko, Laizans, Silagadze, Zemlinsky, Tereskinas, Bleidelis, Rekhviashvili, Rubins, Astafyev, Mikholap (Menteshashvili 78), Chaladze (Blagonadezhdin 40).
H 0-0
Kolinko, Laizans (Kolesnichenko 88), Silagadze, Zemlinsky, Blagonadezhdin, Bleidelis (Menteshashvili 76), Rekhviashvili, Rubins, Astafyev, Mikholap, Chaladze (Babichev 63).

UEFA CUP
● FK RIGA
Qualifying round HELSINGBORGS IF (SWE)
H 0-0
Karavayev, Pumpa, Korablyov, Sprogis, Jakeliunas, Sharando, Kurbatov (Platonov 73), Gaigalas, Aksyonov (Molotkov 46), Tkachouk (Vutsans 63), Kitto.
A 0-5
Karavayev, Pumpa (Nesterenko 55), Korablyov, Sprogis, Jakeliunas, Sharando, Kurbatov (Aksyonov 46), Gaigalas, Vutsans, Tkachouk (Molotkov 46), Kitto.

● METALURGS LIEPAYA
Qualifying round LECH POZNAN (POL)
H 3-2 Boulders (36), Verpakovsky (53), Dragun (62)
Bryaunis, Rinkus (Dragun 26), Zirnis (Verpakovsky 46), Zakreshevsky, Yuiko, Vaineikis, Dobretsov (Lobanov 64), Boulders, Makarenko, Atmanavicius, Solonitsin.
A 1-3 Boulders (87)
Bryaunis, Magdishauskas, Zirnis, Zakreshevsky, Yuiko (Dragun 23), Vaineikis, Dobretsov (Verpakovsky 71), Boulders, Makarenko (Osichenko 46), Atmanavicius, Solonitsin.

● SKONTO RIGA
1st round WIDZEW LODZ (POL)
H 1-0 Astafyev (31)
Kolinko, Laizans, Silagadze, Zemlinsky, Blagonadezhdin (Babichev 88), Bleidelis, Rekhviashvili, Rubins, Astafyev, Mikholap, Chaladze (Menteshashvili 79).
A 0-2
Kolinko, Laizans (Babichev 73), Silagadze, Stepanov (Menteshashvili 44; Kolesnichenko 81), Blagonadezhdin, Bleidelis, Zemlinsky, Rekhviashvili, Rubins, Astafyev, Chaladze.

DOMESTIC CUP 99/00

FIRST ROUND
Skonto Riga 11, Fortuna Ogre 0
LU Daugava Riga 1, VRS LUP Malnava Ludza 0
FK Rezekne 0, Dinaburg Daugavpils 2
Police FK Riga 2, Zibens/Zemessardze Daugavpils 1
Bergu Bulls Riga 0, Metalurgs Liepaya 6
FK Riga 5, Viola Yelgava 1
FK Tsesis 0, FK Ventspils 12
FK Valmiera 2, Ostas Policija 0

QUARTER-FINALS
LU Daugava Riga 0, Skonto Riga 7
(Sukharev 4og, Rekhviashvili 21, Rubins 24, Zemlinsky 40p, Kolesnichenko 61, Chaladze 72, 90)
Dinaburg Daugavpils 2 (Dubrovin 33, Stratil 45), Police FK Riga 1 (Rizhevsky 74)
Metalurgs Liepaya 1 (Zakreshevsky 82), FK Riga 0

FK Ventspils 7 (Bezborodov 12, 67, 89p, Boulders 19, 33, Panfyorov 31, Agafonov 70), FK Valmiera 0

SEMI-FINALS
Dinaburg Daugavpils 1 (Loginov 87), Skonto Riga 4 (Chaladze 21, Rubins 33, 52, Korgalidze 68)
Skonto Riga 4 (Samusevas 14, 42, Buda 63, Blagonadezhdin 88), Dinaburg Daugavpils 0 (Skonto Riga 8-1)

Metalurgs Liepaya 6 (Zakreshevsky 8, 10, Vaineikis 36, 61, Verpakovsky 43, Dobretsov 57), FK Ventspils 2 (Boulders 15, Panfyorov 30)
FK Ventspils 1 (Bezborodov 45p), Metalurgs Liepaya 4 (Karlsons 8, Lobanov 31, 36, 75)
(Metalurgs Liepaya 10-3)

FINAL
27/05/2000, Riga
SKONTO RIGA 4 Rubins (8, 63), Kolesnichenko (33), Stradinsh (52og)
METALURGS LIEPAYA 1 Verpakovsky (83)
referee - Sipailo
SKONTO RIGA - Kolinko, Stepanov, Laizans, Lobanyov, Samusevas, Menteshashvili (Korgalidze 67), Rekhviashvili, Buitkus (Tereskinas 76), Rubins, Kolesnichenko (Blagonadezhdin 75), Chaladze.
METALURGS LIEPAYA - Malishev, Rinkus (Zutautas 46), Zakreshevsky, Ivanov, Kamzyuk, Vaineikis, Dobretsov, Lobanov (Verpakovsky 46), Stradinsh, Atmanavicius, Solonitsin (Dragun 52).

Johnson oversaw the end of the European Championship campaign and then took his team to a mid-winter tournament in Cyprus, where they lost all three matches. The poor run continued with a 2-1 defeat by Lithuania in the opening 2000 Baltic Cup fixture, but in June, at long last, the Englishman broke his duck with a 1-0 victory over Finland in Riga.

The matchwinner against the Finns was youngster Eriks Peltsis, a striker based in South Korea who had also found the target in each of the previous two matches, both against Lithuania. With three goals in his first three internationals, the 21-year-old had made quite an impact. The prospect of Peltsis and Pahars playing up front together, with new in-form Spartak Moscow signing Andrey Shtolcers as first reserve, served to whet the appetite for the World Cup qualifiers, although most Latvian fans were well aware that their team would have to suprass themselves several times over in order to give Peltsis the opportunity to play international football in his adopted country in the summer of 2002.

PLAYER OF THE SEASON

ANDREY RUBINS

The replacement for Southampton-bound Marian Pahars at Skonto Riga, Andrey Rubins is destined to become the next Latvian player to make it big abroad. The talented 21-year-old, who has already tried his hand briefly in Sweden, enjoyed a full and rewarding season of domestic and international activity with both Skonto and the Latvian national side in 1999 and there was a hint of even better to come on both fronts during the first six months of 2000, notably with his match-winning, two-goal display in the Latvian Cup final and an excellent performance for his country in a friendly against Finland. A very quick and techni-cally skilled left-sided midfielder, Rubins has been invited for trials by both Spartak Moscow and Arsenal. His future, he hopes, will be in the English Premiership.

PROMOTED CLUB 1999

FIRST DIVISION FINAL TABLE

		Pd	W	D	L	F	A	Pt	GD
1	LU Daugava Riga	28	24	4	0	104	16	76	88
2	LBB-Mido Riga	28	18	3	7	85	54	54	31
3	Zibens-Zemessardze Daugavpils	28	15	6	7	56	52	51	4
4	Skonto/metals-Rinar Riga	28	12	6	10	49	30	42	19
5	Auda Riga	28	7	6	15	31	51	27	-20
6	Yauniba Daugavpils	28	7	4	17	25	59	25	-34
7	Tselinieks Ilukste	28	6	5	17	28	59	23	-31
8	FK Saldus	28	4	4	20	18	75	16	-57

N.B. LBB-Mido Riga - 3 points deducted

CLUB DIRECTORY

LU Daugava Riga
Kuldigas Str. 39, 1083 Riga
tel - 7601917
fax - 7601922
Year of Formation - 1995
President - Janis Melbardis
Secretary - Stanislav Androsov
Coach - Igor Klyosov
Stadium - LU (5,000)

DINABURG DAUGAVPILS

CLUB DIRECTORY

Dinaburg Daugavpils
Rigas str. 42-3
5400 Daugavpils
tel - (54) 39235
fax - (54) 39235
Year of Formation - 1996
President - Oleg Gavrilov
Secretary - Ilze Stalidzane
Coach - Vladimir Bodrov; Roman Grigorchouk
Stadium - Tseltnieks (3,000)

APPEARANCES 1999

	P	Ap	(s)	Gls
Edgar BURLAKOV	M	23	(1)	1
Orest DOROSH (UKR)	M	13		1
Stanislav DUBROVIN (RUS)	A	19	(5)	8
Vladimir DZUBANOV (RUS)	A	9		4
Alexander FEDOTOV	M	25	(1)	6
Vadim FYODOROV	G		(1)	
Roman GRIGORCHOUK (UKR)	A	14	(6)	6
Alexander ISAKOV	D	12		
Alexander IVANOV	D	11		
Kirill KURBATOV (RUS)	M	4	(3)	1
Zhanis KUROV	A	1	(2)	2
Alexey LEONOV (RUS)	A	1	(1)	
Genady LISITSIN (RUS)	M	2		
Sergey LOGINOV (RUS)	M	10		1
Andrey MELDERS	M	1	(1)	
Dmitriy NALIVAIKO	M	23	(2)	
Vitaly PINYASKIN (RUS)	M	22	(2)	
Yurgis PUCHINSKY	M	22	(2)	1
Igor REUTOV (RUS)	M	4		
Genady ROGOV	M	10	(5)	
Pyotr RUSAK (UKR)	A	7		
Oleg SELIVANOV	D	5	(9)	
Yury SHULYATITSKY (UKR)	A	5	(1)	
Victor SPOLE	G	28		
Alexey VOLOSANOV	M	6	(14)	3
Andrey ZHUROMSKY	M	4	(2)	
Mikhail ZIZILEV	M	27		2

LEAGUE RESULTS 1999

10/04/99	FK Riga	A	0-0	
17/04/99	Metalurgs Liepaya	A	0-3	
21/04/99	FK Valmiera	H	0-0	
02/05/99	Skonto Riga	A	0-1	
08/05/99	FK Rezekne	H	2-0	Kurbatov (p), Zizilev
15/05/99	FK Ventspils	A	0-0	
22/05/99	Police FK Riga	H	1-1	Dubrovin
30/05/99	FK Riga	H	2-0	Zizilev, Dzubanov
15/06/99	FK Valmiera	A	4-0	Dzubanov 3, Dubrovin
20/06/99	Metalurgs Liepaya	H	0-0	
01/07/99	Skonto Riga	H	1-0	Grigorchouk
07/07/99	FK Rezekne	A	2-1	Volosanov, Grigorchouk
16/07/99	FK Ventspils	H	1-0	og (Ivanov)
25/07/99	Police FK Riga	A	4-0	Dubrovin 3, Loginov
31/07/99	FK Riga	A	1-0	Grigorchouk
05/08/99	Metalurgs Liepaya	A	1-6	Dorosh
14/08/99	FK Valmiera	H	1-3	Grigorchouk
20/08/99	Skonto Riga	A	0-4	
28/08/99	FK Rezekne	H	6-1	Fedotov 2 (1p), Burlakov, Dubrovin, Grigorchouk 2
12/09/99	FK Ventspils	A	2-1	Fedotov, Dubrovin
19/09/99	Police FK Riga	H	2-1	Fedotov, Dubrovin
25/09/99	FK Riga	H	0-1	
02/10/99	Metalurgs Liepaya	H	0-1	
13/10/99	FK Valmiera	A	0-1	
17/10/99	Skonto Riga	H	1-5	Volosanov
24/10/99	FK Rezekne	A	1-0	Fedotov
30/10/99	FK Ventspils	H	0-2	
06/11/99	Police FK Riga	A	5-0	Kurov 2, Volosanov, Fedotov, Puchinsky

METALURGS LIEPAYA

CLUB DIRECTORY

Metalurgs Liepaya
Brivibas str. 93
3401 Liepaya
tel - (34) 55212
fax - 2580313
Year of Formation - 1996
President - Sergey Zakharyin
Secretary - Alexander Rogoza
Coach - Yury Popkov
Stadium - Daugava Liepaya (6,000)

APPEARANCES 1999

	P	Ap	(s)	Gls
Saulius ATMANAVICIUS (LIT)	D	25		8
Rolands BOULDERS	A	21	(4)	8
Algimantas BRYAUNIS (LIT)	G	18		
Victor DOBRETSOV	A	18	(2)	22
Vladimir DRAGUN	M	22	(3)	6
Girts KARLSONS	A	3	(7)	2
Alexander LASHKO	M		(3)	
Andrey LOBANOV (BLS)	A	10	(10)	5
Darius MAGDISHAUSKAS (LIT)	D	20	(2)	1
Dmitry MAKARENKO (BLS)	M	13	(2)	1
Vladimir MALISHEV (BLS)	G	10		
Pavel MIKHADYUK	M	2	(1)	
Andrey OSICHENKO	D	13	(3)	
Janis RINKUS	M	13	(8)	1
Oleg RUDENKO	M	14	(5)	
Genady SOLONITSIN	M	18	(4)	5
Rolandas VAINEIKIS (LIT)	M	26	(1)	5
Maris VERPAKOVSKY	A	5	(12)	5
Victor YUIKO (BLS)	M	10	(8)	
Artur ZAKRESHEVSKY	M	21	(2)	1
Dzintars ZIRNIS	D	26	(1)	3

LEAGUE RESULTS 1999

10/04/99	FK Rezekne	A	4-0	Dobretsov, Vaineikis 2, Dragun
17/04/99	Dinaburg Daugavpils	H	3-0	Dobretsov 3
21/04/99	FK Ventspils	A	0-2	
01/05/99	FK Valmiera	H	3-0	Karlsons, Atmanavicius (p), Dragun
08/05/99	Police FK Riga	A	5-0	Dobretsov 2, Verpakovsky 2, Vaineikis
15/05/99	Skonto Riga	H	2-3	Boulders, Atmanavicius (p)
22/05/99	FK Riga	A	5-1	Dragun, Zirnis, Dobretsov 3
30/05/99	FK Rezekne	H	6-0	Verpakovsky 2, Dobretsov 3 (1p), Atmanavicius (p)
15/06/99	FK Ventspils	H	3-1	Dobretsov 2, Atmanavicius (p)
20/06/99	Dinaburg Daugavpils	A	0-0	
01/07/99	FK Valmiera	A	1-1	Dobretsov
05/07/99	Skonto Riga	A	2-3	Verpakovsky, Dragun
08/07/99	Police FK Riga	H	4-1	Makarenko, Dobretsov, Dragun, Boulders
20/07/99	FK Ventspils	A	1-1	Dobretsov
24/07/99	FK Riga	H	3-2	Karlsons, Boulders, Lobanov
31/07/99	FK Rezekne	A	1-0	Dobretsov
05/08/99	Dinaburg Daugavpils	H	6-1	Boulders, Solonitsin 2, Dragun, Lobanov, Atmanavicius
19/08/99	FK Valmiera	H	2-0	Boulders, Dobretsov
29/08/99	Police FK Riga	A	3-1	Zirnis 2, Dobretsov
19/09/99	FK Riga	A	0-1	
25/09/99	FK Rezekne	H	5-1	Atmanavicius 2 (1p), Boulders, Vaineikis 2
02/10/99	Dinaburg Daugavpils	A	1-0	Zakreshevsky
13/10/99	FK Ventspils	H	2-1	Solonitsin, Atmanavicius (p)
17/10/99	FK Valmiera	A	2-0	Lobanov, Magdishauskas
21/10/99	Skonto Riga	H	1-0	Lobanov
24/10/99	Police FK Riga	H	7-0	Boulders 2, Lobanov, Solonitsin 2, Rinkus, Dobretsov
30/10/99	Skonto Riga	A	0-3	
06/11/99	FK Riga	H	1-2	Dobretsov

POLICE FK RIGA

CLUB DIRECTORY

Police FK Riga
Gauyas Str. 17/19
1026 Riga
tel - 7219875
fax - 7371763
Year of Formation - 1996
President - Roman Potanin
Secretary - Vladimir Zhuk
Coach - Georgy Gusarenko
Stadium - Daugava (5,800)

APPEARANCES 1999

	P	Ap	(s)	Gls
Yury ADAMOVICH	D	23	(2)	2
Oleg ALEXEYENKO	D	1		
Georgs ATVARS	G	17		
Oleg BORSCHEVSKY	M	2	(1)	
Rikhards BUTKUS	M	20	(4)	3
Ediys DANILOV	A	22	(3)	2
Stanislav GEIKIN	M	1	(4)	
Alexander GLAZOV	D	9		1
Yurgis KAZMIN	M	21	(5)	3
Marek KERE	A	15	(2)	4
Aldis KUKSHA	D	22	(3)	
Janis LAGZDINSH	A	8	(1)	1
Raimonds LAIZANS	G	11		
Vsevolod LIDAKS	D	10		
Mikhail LISYAKOV	D	10		
Valery MARTINKEVICH	M	6	(1)	
Oleg POPOV	D		(3)	
Yevgeny ROMANOV	D	17	(6)	
Vitaly RYABININ	A	11		2
Artur SALNA	D	2	(6)	
Artur SHKETOV	M	23		3
Alberts SHVANS	D	28		
Vadim SINITSIN	D	10	(2)	1
Vladislav SKORODIKHIN	M	12	(2)	
Alexey SOSNIN	M	1	(5)	
Sergey TARASOV	A	6	(2)	
Vladimir VERBITSKY	A		(3)	
Vladislav ZABLOTSKY	G		(1)	

LEAGUE RESULTS 1999

10/04/99	FK Valmiera	H	0-1	
17/04/99	Skonto Riga	A	0-2	
21/04/99	FK Rezekne	H	5-1	Shketov 2, Kere 2, Sinitsin
01/05/99	FK Ventspils	A	2-5	Glazov, Kazmin
08/05/99	Metalurgs Liepaya	H	0-5	
15/05/99	FK Riga	H	2-1	Kere, Adamovich
22/05/99	Dinaburg Daugavpils	A	1-1	Ryabinin
28/05/99	FK Valmiera	A	1-1	Kazmin
15/06/99	FK Rezekne	A	1-0	Ryabinin (p)
20/06/99	Skonto Riga	H	0-9	
08/07/99	Metalurgs Liepaya	A	1-4	Kere (p)
15/07/99	FK Riga	A	0-0	
25/07/99	Dinaburg Daugavpils	H	0-4	
31/07/99	FK Valmiera	H	1-1	Lagzdinsh
07/08/99	Skonto Riga	A	0-5	
11/08/99	FK Ventspils	H	0-2	
14/08/99	FK Rezekne	H	1-1	Shketov
21/08/99	FK Ventspils	A	0-4	
29/08/99	Metalurgs Liepaya	H	1-3	Kazmin
12/09/99	FK Riga	H	3-0	(w/o; original result 0-2)
19/09/99	Dinaburg Daugavpils	A	1-2	Danilov
25/09/99	FK Valmiera	A	3-2	Danilov, Butkus, Adamovich
03/10/99	Skonto Riga	H	0-12	
07/10/99	FK Rezekne	A	0-2	
18/10/99	FK Ventspils	H	2-8	Butkus 2 (2p)
24/10/99	Metalurgs Liepaya	A	0-7	
29/10/99	FK Riga	A	0-5	
06/11/99	Dinaburg Daugavpils	H	0-5	

FK REZEKNE

CLUB DIRECTORY

FK Rezekne
18. Novembra str. 39
4600 Rezekne
tel - (46) 22055
fax - (46) 22055
Year of Formation - 1992
President - Vasily Alekseyev
Secretary - Peteris Tukishs
Coach - Alexander Dorofeyev
Stadium - Town Stadium (3,000)

APPEARANCES 1999

	P	Ap	(s)	Gls
Artur BASTRIKIN	M	4	(4)	
Vadim BEKERIS	M	9	(3)	
Aigars BONDARS	G	4		
Igor DERBAKOV	M	15	(5)	
Valery GRABUSTS	M		(1)	
Andris GRUZDE	G	23		
Vycheslav IZMAILOV	M	7	(1)	
Yuris KANEPE	M		(1)	
Valery KIRILLOV	M	25		2
Anatoly KLYUYEV	D	26	(1)	1
Nickolay KOCHERIGIN	A	26	(2)	4
Alexander KUCHEROV	M		(3)	
Dainis LAIZANS	D	16	(7)	
Maris LESCHINSKY	D		(3)	
Zhanis LESCHINSKY	M	3	(8)	
Vadim LOGINS	D	8	(8)	
Victor MIVRINIEKS	M	6	(3)	
Ilya NIKITIN	M		(11)	
Sergey POGODIN	D	13		
Aivars POZNYAK	A	19	(3)	
Alexander PUSHKASH	A	6	(4)	
Eduard PUTRA	M	17	(6)	1
Ilmars RANCANS	M		(1)	
Vitaly SHANDOV	G	1	(2)	
Alen SHEIN	M	26		1
Andris SHMAUKSTELIS	D	3		
Alexey VISHNYAKOV	D		(1)	
Vitaly VOSKANS	M	26		3
Alexey YEGOROV	D	25		
Victor ZAKHAROV	M		(2)	

LEAGUE RESULTS 1999

10/04/99	Metalurgs Liepaya	H	0-4	
17/04/99	FK Ventspils	H	0-2	
21/04/99	Police FK Riga	A	1-5	Kocherigin
01/05/99	FK Riga	H	0-0	
08/05/99	Dinaburg Daugavpils	A	0-2	
15/05/99	FK Valmiera	H	0-3	
22/05/99	Skonto Riga	H	0-2	
30/05/99	Metalurgs Liepaya	A	0-6	
15/06/99	Police FK Riga	H	0-1	
23/06/99	FK Ventspils	A	1-5	Voskans
01/07/99	FK Riga	A	0-2	
07/07/99	Dinaburg Daugavpils	H	1-2	Kocherigin
12/07/99	FK Valmiera	A	0-4	
24/07/99	Skonto Riga	A	1-2	Voskans (p)
31/07/99	Metalurgs Liepaya	H	0-1	
07/08/99	FK Ventspils	H	0-1	
14/08/99	Police FK Riga	A	1-1	Shein
22/08/99	FK Riga	H	1-3	Kocherigin
28/08/99	Dinaburg Daugavpils	A	1-6	Klyuyev
12/09/99	FK Valmiera	H	1-3	Putra
19/09/99	Skonto Riga	A	0-8	
25/09/99	Metalurgs Liepaya	A	1-5	Kirillov
02/10/99	FK Ventspils	A	1-7	Kocherigin (p)
07/10/99	Police FK Riga	H	2-0	Kirillov, Voskans
17/10/99	FK Riga	A	0-5	
24/10/99	Dinaburg Daugavpils	H	0-1	
30/10/99	FK Valmiera	A	0-4	
06/11/99	Skonto Riga	H	0-5	

FK RIGA

CLUB DIRECTORY

FK Riga
Kalpaka bulv. 12
1050 Riga
tel - 7225269
fax - 7242890
Year of Formation - 1999
President - Leonid Loginov
Secretary - Janis Skredelis
Coach - Janis Gilis
Stadium - LU (5,000)

MAJOR HONOURS
Domestic Cup - (1) 1999.

APPEARANCES 1999

	P	Ap	(s)	Gls
Igor AKSYONOV (RUS)	A	17	(2)	5
Arunas BALSEVICIUS (LIT)	A	10	(4)	4
Edmundas GAIGALAS (LIT)	M	10		
Erik GRIGYAN	G	7	(1)	
Arturas JAKELIUNAS (LIT)	M	22		4
Yury KARASHAUSKAS	A	12	(1)	2
Oleg KARAVAYEV	G	21	(1)	
Stanislas KITTO (EST)	M	21	(1)	4
Igor KORABLYOV	D	27		
Alexander KOZLOV	M	3	(13)	
Kirill KURBATOV (RUS)	M	15		
Yury MOLOTKOV	A	19	(7)	7
Vladislav NESTERENKO	D	16	(4)	
Roman PLATONOV	M	3	(12)	
Andrey PUMPA	D	24	(2)	
Alexey SEMYONOV	M	1	(5)	
Alexey SHARANDO	M	23		5
Dzintars SPROGIS	D	24		1
Alexander TKACHOUK (RUS)	M	10	(2)	
Yevgeny VASYUKOV	D	8	(12)	
Renars VUTSANS	A	15	(11)	4

LEAGUE RESULTS 1999

10/04/99	Dinaburg Daugavpils	H	0-0	
17/04/99	FK Valmiera	A	3-2	Molotkov, Jakeliunas, Aksyonov
21/04/99	Skonto Riga	H	1-3	Molotkov
01/05/99	FK Rezekne	A	0-0	
08/05/99	FK Ventspils	H	0-1	
15/05/99	Police FK Riga	A	1-2	Karashauskas
22/05/99	Metalurgs Liepaya	H	1-5	Balsevicius
30/05/99	Dinaburg Daugavpils	A	0-2	
15/06/99	Skonto Riga	A	0-1	
20/06/99	FK Valmiera	H	3-1	Sharando, Sprogis, Karashauskas
01/07/99	FK Rezekne	H	2-0	Sharando 2
07/07/99	FK Ventspils	H	2-4	Molotkov (p), Vutsans
15/07/99	Police FK Riga	H	0-0	
24/07/99	Metalurgs Liepaya	A	2-3	Kitto, Molotkov
31/07/99	Dinaburg Daugavpils	H	0-1	
07/08/99	FK Valmiera	A	0-3	
16/08/99	Skonto Riga	H	0-4	
22/08/99	FK Rezekne	A	3-1	Molotkov, Kitto 2
30/08/99	FK Ventspils	A	1-2	Vutsans
12/09/99	Police FK Riga	A	0-3	(w/o; original result 2-0 Jakeliunas, Aksyonov)
19/09/99	Metalurgs Liepaya	H	1-0	Vutsans
25/09/99	Dinaburg Daugavpils	A	1-0	Jakeliunas
02/10/99	FK Valmiera	H	0-0	
13/10/99	Skonto Riga	A	2-1	Vutsans, Aksyonov
17/10/99	FK Rezekne	H	5-0	Aksyonov 2 (1p), Molotkov, Kitto, Sharando
24/10/99	FK Ventspils	A	0-2	
29/10/99	Police FK Riga	H	5-0	Balsevicius 2, Sharando, Jakeliunas, Molotkov
06/11/99	Metalurgs Liepaya	A	2-1	og (Zirnis), Balsevicius

SKONTO RIGA

CLUB DIRECTORY

Skonto Riga
Elizabetes str. 75, 1050 Riga
tel - 7282669   fax - 7284390
email - sball@mail.eunet.lv
Year of Formation - 1991
President - Guntis Indricksons
Secretary - Genady Karavayev
Coach - Alexander Starkov
Stadium - Daugava (5,800)

MAJOR HONOURS
League Championship - (8) 1992, 1993, 1994,
1995, 1996, 1997, 1998, 1999.
Domestic Cup - (5)
1992, 1995, 1997, 1998, 2000.

APPEARANCES 1999

	P	Ap	(s)	Gls
Vitaly ASTAFYEV	M	16	(2)	9
Vladimir BABICHEV	A	6	(5)	1
Roman BEZZUBOV	A		(2)	
Oleg BLAGONADEZHDIN	D	20	(3)	
Imants BLEIDELIS	M	15	(4)	4
David CHALADZE (GEO)	A	14	(1)	16
Armaz DZHELADZE (GEO)	A	2	(3)	
Vladimir KOLESNICHENKO	A	20	(5)	13
Alexander KOLINKO	G	18		
Levan KORGALIDZE (GEO)	M	4	(9)	1
Yury LAIZANS	D	25	(2)	3
Vladimir MELNIK (UKR)	M	3	(10)	3
Zurab MENTESASHVILI (GEO)	M	7	(10)	1
Mikhail MIKHOLAP	A	20		14
Victor MOROZ	A		(1)	
Victor OLSHANSKY (LIT)	D	10	(10)	
Andrey PIEDELS	G	10		
Alexander REKHVIASHVILI (GEO)	M	24		1
Andrey RUBINS	M	23	(2)	6
Levan SILAGADZE (GEO)	D	20		
Sergey SOLOVYEV (RUS)	A	4	(2)	1
Igor N. STEPANOV	D	16	(4)	4
Andreyus TERESKINAS (LIT)	D	16	(2)	1
Sergey YERMOLENKO (BLS)	D		(2)	
Mikhail ZEMLINSKY	D	15	(1)	7

LEAGUE RESULTS 1999

10/04/99	FK Ventspils	A	0-1	
17/04/99	Police FK Riga	H	2-0	Mikholap, Astafyev
21/04/99	FK Riga	A	3-1	Rubins, Astafyev, Mikholap
02/05/99	Dinaburg Daugavpils	H	1-0	Mikholap
09/05/99	FK Valmiera	A	1-0	Rubins
15/05/99	Metalurgs Liepaya	A	3-2	Kolesnichenko 2, Zemlinsky (p)
22/05/99	FK Rezekne	A	2-0	Mikholap, Solovyev
30/05/99	FK Ventspils	H	3-1	Bleidelis, Astafyev, Kolesnichenko
15/06/99	FK Riga	H	1-0	Laizans
20/06/99	Police FK Riga	A	9-0	Mentesashvili, Rubins,
				Zemlinsky 3 (3p), Mikholap,
				Laizans, Bleidelis, Kolesnichenko
01/07/99	Dinaburg Daugavpils	A	0-1	
05/07/99	Metalurgs Liepaya	H	3-2	Mikholap, Bleidelis, Astafyev
08/07/99	FK Valmiera	H	5-0	Chaladze 2, Mikholap 3 (2p)
24/07/99	FK Rezekne	H	2-1	Rubins, Melnik
07/08/99	Police FK Riga	H	5-0	Mikholap 2 (1p), Bleidelis,
				Chaladze, og (Shvans)
16/08/99	FK Riga	A	4-0	Chaladze 2, Mikholap, Rubins
20/08/99	Dinaburg Daugavpils	H	4-0	Zemlinsky (p), og (Burlakov),
				Chaladze, Astafyev
29/08/99	FK Valmiera	A	1-0	Tereskinas
19/09/99	FK Rezekne	H	8-0	Mikholap 2, Kolesnichenko 3,
				Melnik, Korgalidze, Babichev
23/09/99	FK Ventspils	H	0-2	
03/10/99	Police FK Riga	A	12-0	Stepanov 2, Chaladze 6,
				og (Kuksha), Kolesnichenko 3 (1p)
13/10/99	FK Riga	H	1-2	Stepanov
17/10/99	Dinaburg Daugavpils	A	5-1	Astafyev, Chaladze,
				Zemlinsky 2 (2p), Stepanov
21/10/99	Metalurgs Liepaya	A	0-1	
24/10/99	FK Valmiera	H	3-0	Kolesnichenko 3
30/10/99	Metalurgs Liepaya	H	3-0	Astafyev 2, Chaladze
03/11/99	FK Ventspils	A	2-0	Astafyev, Chaladze
06/11/99	FK Rezekne	A	5-0	Chaladze, Laizans, Rekhviashvili,
				Melnik, Rubins

FK VALMIERA

CLUB DIRECTORY

FK Valmiera
Stacijas str. 22
4201 Valmiera
tel - (42) 21468
fax - (7) 894216
Year of Formation - 1995
President - Imants Saulitis
Secretary - Valery Barkov
Coach - Vladimir Serbin
Stadium - J. Dalinsha Stadium (2,000)

APPEARANCES 1999

	P	Ap	(s)	Gls
Alexander ATAMAN	M	2	(12)	1
Victor BASKAKOV	M	13	(1)	1
Gatis ERGLIS	D	26		2
Igor GARNIER	D	23		
Ivo KALNINSH	G	5	(1)	
Boris KOROTKEVICH	A	26	(1)	4
Rolands KRAGLIKS	D	21	(3)	
Andrey KRASOVSKY	M	2	(8)	
Eduard KUDRYASHOV	A	21	(1)	4
Vsevolod LIDAKS	D	14		
Agnis MEZHGAILIS	M	1	(11)	
Nickolay OZOLS	M		(1)	1
Vitas RIMKUS	A	16	(4)	3
Denis ROMANOV	G	23		
Dzintars SAVALNIEKS	M	21		3
Roman SIDOROV	M	13	(12)	3
Maris SMIRNOV	M	19	(3)	1
Victor TERENTYEV	M	25	(3)	4
Andrey TROITSKY	M	15		
Janis ZUYEV	M		(10)	1
Modris ZUYEV	A	22	(1)	5

LEAGUE RESULTS 1999

Date	Opponent		Score	
10/04/99	Police FK Riga	A	1-0	Terentyev
17/04/99	FK Riga	H	2-3	Terentyev 2
21/04/99	Dinaburg Daugavpils	A	0-0	
01/05/99	Metalurgs Liepaya	A	0-3	
09/05/99	Skonto Riga	H	0-1	
15/05/99	FK Rezekne	A	3-0	Sidorov, Savalnieks, Rimkus
22/05/99	FK Ventspils	H	0-3	
28/05/99	Police FK Riga	H	1-1	Sidorov
15/06/99	Dinaburg Daugavpils	H	0-4	
20/06/99	FK Riga	A	1-3	Kudryashov
01/07/99	Metalurgs Liepaya	H	1-1	Savalnieks
08/07/99	Skonto Riga	A	0-5	
12/07/99	FK Rezekne	H	4-0	Zuyev M. 3, Ozols
24/07/99	FK Ventspils	A	0-3	
31/07/99	Police FK Riga	A	1-1	Korotkevich
07/08/99	FK Riga	H	3-0	Erglis (p), Rimkus 2
14/08/99	Dinaburg Daugavpils	A	3-1	Baskakov, Zuyev M., Korotkevich
19/08/99	Metalurgs Liepaya	A	0-2	
29/08/99	Skonto Riga	H	0-1	
12/09/99	FK Rezekne	A	3-1	Kudryashov, Erglis, Sidorov
19/09/99	FK Ventspils	H	2-1	Korotkevich, Terentyev
25/09/99	Police FK Riga	H	2-3	Smirnov, Zuyev J.
02/10/99	FK Riga	A	0-0	
13/10/99	Dinaburg Daugavpils	H	1-0	Kudryashov
17/10/99	Metalurgs Liepaya	H	0-2	
24/10/99	Skonto Riga	A	0-3	
30/10/99	FK Rezekne	H	4-0	Korotkevich, Zuyev M., Kudryashov, Ataman
06/11/99	FK Ventspils	A	1-0	Savalnieks

FK VENTSPILS

CLUB DIRECTORY

FK Ventspils
Dzintaru Str. 20a
3602 Ventspils
tel - (36) 81354
fax - (36) 80380
Year of Formation - 1997
President - Oleg Stepanov
Secretary - Mikhail Kopcha
Coach - Boris Sinitsin
Stadium - Daugava Ventspils (5,000)

APPEARANCES 1999

	P	Ap	(s)	Gls
Vladislav BASKOV (RUS)	M	13	(2)	1
Mikhail BESCHASTNYKH (RUS)	M	5	(4)	1
Vladislav BEZBORODOV (RUS)	A	17		12
Valery BOROVKOV	M		(1)	
Mindaugas CEPAS (LIT)	M	2	(8)	1
Sergey DIGULYOV	G	3		
Sergey IVANOV	M	17	(4)	
Mindaugas KAIRIS (LIT)	A	1		
Edgar KVASHNIN	D	17	(3)	
Andrey LAPSA	D	17	(2)	
Victor LUKASHEVICH	D	22		1
Vladlen OSIPIOV	M	1	(4)	
Sergey POGODIN	M		(1)	
Nickolay POLYAKOV	M	11	(8)	3
Gintaras RIMKUS (LIT)	M	11	(11)	2
Vyacheslav RUDAKOV (RUS)	M	21	(2)	3
Vadim SINITSIN	D	15		
Igor V. STEPANOV	M	23	(2)	1
Andris VANIN	G	25		
Yevgeny VDOVENKO (RUS)	M	22	(3)	11
Victor VORONKOV (RUS)	M	25	(1)	18
Vladimir ZHAVORONKOV	A	9	(13)	6
Alexander ZHIZHMANOV	D	20	(1)	1
Andrius ZUTA (LIT)	M	11	(6)	1

LEAGUE RESULTS 1999

10/04/99	Skonto Riga	H	1-0	Voronkov
17/04/99	FK Rezekne	A	2-0	Voronkov (p), Polyakov
21/04/99	Metalurgs Liepaya	H	2-0	Voronkov, Polyakov
01/05/99	Police FK Riga	H	5-2	Vdovenko 2, Polyakov, Voronkov, Zuta
08/05/99	FK Riga	A	1-0	Voronkov
15/05/99	Dinaburg Daugavpils	H	0-0	
22/05/99	FK Valmiera	A	3-0	Voronkov, Vdovenko, Rudakov
30/05/99	Skonto Riga	A	1-3	Voronkov
15/06/99	Metalurgs Liepaya	A	1-3	Voronkov
23/06/99	FK Rezekne	H	5-1	Vdovenko 2, Stepanov, Beschastnykh (p), Zhavoronkov
07/07/99	FK Riga	A	4-2	Bezborodov, Vdovenko, Zhavoronkov 2
16/07/99	Dinaburg Daugavpils	A	0-1	
20/07/99	Metalurgs Liepaya	H	1-1	Bezborodov
24/07/99	FK Valmiera	H	3-0	Voronkov (p), Vdovenko, Rudakov
07/08/99	FK Rezekne	A	1-0	Baskov
11/08/99	Police FK Riga	A	2-0	Bezborodov, Voronkov
21/08/99	Police FK Riga	H	4-0	Voronkov 2, Vdovenko, Bezborodov
30/08/99	FK Riga	H	2-1	Bezborodov, Zhavoronkov
12/09/99	Dinaburg Daugavpils	H	1-2	Voronkov
19/09/99	FK Valmiera	A	1-2	Bezborodov (p)
23/09/99	Skonto Riga	A	2-0	Voronkov, Bezborodov
02/10/99	FK Rezekne	H	7-1	Vdovenko, Lukashevich, Bezborodov 2, Voronkov 2, Zhavoronkov
13/10/99	Metalurgs Liepaya	A	1-2	Rimkus
18/10/99	Police FK Riga	A	8-2	Vdovenko 2, Rudakov, Zhizhmanov, Cepas, Voronkov 2, Zhavoronkov
24/10/99	FK Riga	H	2-0	Bezborodov 2
30/10/99	Dinaburg Daugavpils	A	2-0	Rimkus, Bezborodov
03/11/99	Skonto Riga	H	0-2	
06/11/99	FK Valmiera	H	0-1	

LIECHTENSTEIN

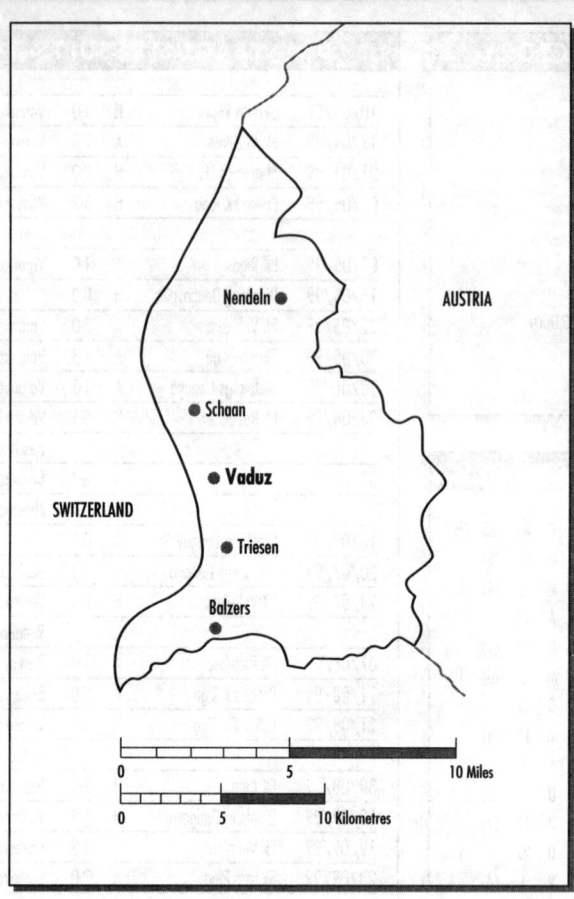

CUP HAT-TRICK FOR FC VADUZ

Level after an hour... then fitness tells

FEDERATION DIRECTORY

Liechtensteiner Fussball-Verband
Malbuner Haus, Altenbach 11, Postfach 165, 9490 Vaduz

tel - (75) 2374747	Year of Formation - 1933
fax - (75) 2374748	President - Otto Biedermann
website - www.sportsnet.li.lfv	Secretary - Sonja Lins

Stadium - Rheinpark, Vaduz (3,548)

The Liechtenstein national team, still under the command of German-born Ralf Loose, came close to a sensational result in their final outing of the 1999/2000 season. They had not scored a goal in their previous eight internationals - a run stretching back 20 months to their historic Euro 2000 qualifying victory over Azerbaijan - but against Germany, who invited them over to Freiburg for some pre-European Championship target practice, they not only found the net twice but also gave their hosts an almighty fright.

Although they went 1-0 down after just 52 seconds, Liechtenstein refused to buckle. Martin Stocklasa, of just-crowned Swiss Cup winners FC Zürich, pounced on an error from German warhorse Lothar Matthäus and equalised after 17 minutes. It was a stunner for the 25,000-strong crowd in the Dreisamstadion but there was more of the same to come. After Mehmet Scholl had given the Germans the half-time lead with a lucky deflected shot, Liechtenstein, amazingly, equalised once again, with midfielder Christoph Frick netting his first international goal amidst understandable euphoria in the Liechtenstein camp.

After the pride, though, came the fall. Germany quickly retook the lead and in the last ten minutes, with lack of fitness becoming a major problem for the visiting part-timers, Erich Ribbeck's team added five more goals to give a thoroughly misleading look to the final scoreline.

Those last ten minutes soured what had otherwise been a relatively satisfying season for Loose and his players. Considerable pleasure was gained from the first of the five matches, at home to Hungary in September, when Liechtenstein emerged valiantly with a goalless draw - thanks mainly to the brilliance of their 17-year-old goalkeeper, Peter Jehle. It was only the third competitive match in which Liechtenstein had avoided defeat.

The campaign ended with two further defeats, 0-2 in Slovakia and then 0-3 at home to Romania in a game their opponents needed to win in order to top the qualifying group. The countdown to the World Cup qualifiers - and a group containing Spain, Israel, Bosnia-Herzegovina and neighbouring Austria - began with a lacklustre 0-1 home defeat by the Faroe Islands, but the players certainly bucked their ideas up for the Germany game that followed... at least they did for 80 minutes of it.

The German influence on Liechtenstein football grew with the appointment of former Bayern Munich and Borussia Dortmund striker Jürgen Wegmann as the new player-coach of FC Vaduz. The 36-year-old ex-Bundesliga professional's first task was to lead Vaduz into Europe. For the first time ever Liechtenstein had a representative in the UEFA Cup, and Cup holders Vaduz made a decent fist of their

EUROPEAN CUPS 99/00

UEFA CUP
● **FC VADUZ**
Qualifying round FK BODØ/GLIMT (NOR)
A 0-1
    Crespo, Hefti, Kubli, Koch, Bossi, Hasler, Stocklasa (Hafner 78), Stilz, Moitzi (Telser 56), Wegmann, Polverino (Fischer 64).
H 1-2   Wegmann (38)
    Crespo, Hefti, Kubli, Koch, Bossi (Telser 79), Hasler, Hafner (Fischer 60), Stilz, Polverino (Schmid 70), Wegmann, Moitzi.

NATIONAL TEAM RESULTS 99/00

18/08/99	Bosnia-Herzegovina	H	Vaduz	0-0	
04/09/99	Hungary (ECQ)	H	Vaduz	0-0	
08/09/99	Slovakia (ECQ)	A	Bratislava	0-2	
09/10/99	Romania (ECQ)	H	Vaduz	0-3	
26/04/00	Faroe Islands	H	Vaduz	0-1	
07/06/00	Germany	A	Freiburg	2-8	Stocklasa Ma. (17), Frick C. (56)

qualifying-round tie with Norwegian side FK Bodø/Glimt, losing only 1-0 away and coming within seven minutes of an honourable draw in the return leg, which they eventually lost 2-1 in front of around 500 spectators in the new Rheinpark Stadium.

For Vaduz's next major appointment at their new home, the Liechtenstein Cup final, which took place some nine months later, the attendance was up to 1,150. It was a repeat scenario of the 1999 final, with Vaduz bidding to defend their title against FC Balzers, but whereas the game 12 months earlier had been a thriller, resolved 3-2 in Vaduz's favour, the 2000 version became a one-sided rout.

Vaduz claimed their 29th Cup win (out of 55 tournaments) with a simple victory - despite the absence through injury of Wegmann and national team midfielder Michael Stocklasa. In command from as early as the seventh minute, when Daniele Polverino opened the scoring with his seventh Cup final goal in three seasons, Vaduz went further ahead just before half-time with captain Daniel Hasler's converted penalty after Lithuanian import Vaidotas Slekys was fouled by national team libero Harry Zech. It was already all over, but Vaduz treated their fans to an exhibition in the final 20 minutes, knocking in four more goals - headers from Roman Hafner and Hasler, a precise shot from ex-Balzers midfielder Martin Telser and a direct free-kick from Slekys. The 6-0 final scoreline meant that Vaduz had gone through the competition without conceding a

goal while scoring 31 themselves... in three games! The bulk of those goals came in the quarter-final when Wegmann's men put FC Triesen's second team to the sword in merciless fashion, romping home 22-0.

NATIONAL TEAM APPEARANCES 99/00

Coach - Ralf LOOSE	BOS	HUN	SVK	ROM	FAR	GER	Cps	Gls
Peter JEHLE (22/01/82) - FC Schaan	G	G	G	G	G	G	11	-
Harry ZECH (25/02/69) - FC Balzers	D	D	D	D	D	D	29	1
Daniel HASLER (18/05/74) - FC Vaduz	D	D	D		D	D	33	1
Patrik HEFTI (19/11/69) - FC Vaduz	D	D		D	D	D	25	
Frédéric GIGON (03/02/73) - Stade Lausanne (SUI)	D90	D	D57		D79	D79	6	
Jürgen OSPELT (16/01/74) - FC Vaduz	M	M	M	M	D82	M	26	
Martin STOCKLASA (29/05/79) - FC Zürich (SUI)	M	M	M	M	M83	M	18	1
Martin TELSER (16/10/78) - FC Vaduz	M	M60	M	M69	M	M	20	1
Michael STOCKLASA (02/12/80) - FC Vaduz	M79	M		M		M	12	
Christoph FRICK (28/08/74) - FC Balzers	M			M89		M	19	1
Mario FRICK (07/09/74) - FC Zürich (SUI)	A	A90	A12	A	A	A	29	2
Christof RITTER (18/01/81) - FC Winterthur (SUI)	s79	s60	D	D	s79	s79	14	
Thomas HANSELMANN (21/04/76) - FC Balzers	s90						23	
Thomas BECK (21/02/78) - FC Vaduz		A83	A	A	A69	A70	9	
Herbert BICKER (01/11/75) - FC Schaan		s83		s69	s82	s90	13	
Matthias BECK (05/10/81) - FC St. Gallen (SUI)		s90	s57	M	s83		7	
Ronny BÜCHEL (19/03/82) - FC Vaduz		s12		s69	s70	5		
		/57			/90			
Albert WOHLWEND (06/11/79) - FC Rorschach (SUI)		s57	s89				7	

DOMESTIC CUP 99/00

FIRST ROUND
FC Triesen II 3, FC Schaan Azzurri 3
(aet; 4-3 on pens.)
FC Balzers II 2, FC Triesenberg 1
FC Triesenberg II 0, FC Balzers 9
FC Triesen 1, FC Vaduz II 1 (aet; 2-1 on pens.)
FC Vaduz III 3, FC Ruggell 0
FC USV Eschen/Mauren II 0, FC Schaan 3
FC Ruggell 2, FC USV Eschen/Mauren (aet)
bye - FC Vaduz

QUARTER-FINALS
FC Triesen II 0, FC Vaduz 22
FC Vaduz III 0, FC Balzers 2
FC Triesen 2, FC USV Eschen/Mauren 1
FC Balzers II 1, FC Schaan 2

SEMI-FINALS
FC Schaan 2, FC Balzers 2 (aet; 7-8 on pens.)
FC Triesen 0, FC Vaduz 3

FINAL
10/05/2000, Vaduz
FC VADUZ 6 Polverino (7), Hasler (43p, 79),
Hafner (72), Telser (75), Slekys (85)
FC BALZERS 0
referee - Schluchter (SUI)
FC VADUZ - Crespo; Bossi; Hefti, Koch (Keel 75); Ospelt,
Hasler, Telser, Hafner, Slekys; Beck
(Fischer 54), Polverino (Schmid 70).
FC BALZERS - Nüesch; Zech; Heinzle, Hanselmann; Alge
(Risch 20), Frick C., Benz, Foser C. (Stocker Hu. 81),
Stocker He. (Cortese 46); Foser P., Frick D..

INTERNATIONAL HONOURS

None

LITHUANIA

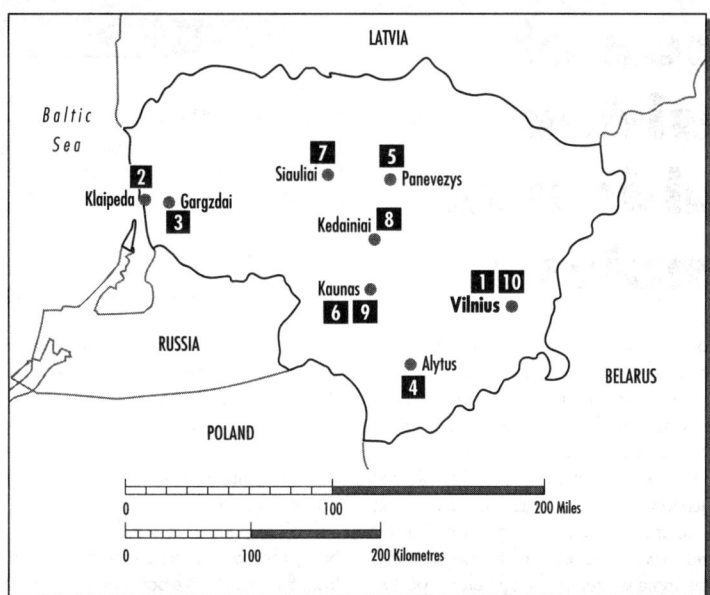

ZALGIRIS VILNIUS PLAY SECOND FIDDLE AGAIN

Season of transition heralds new champions

FEDERATION DIRECTORY

Lietuvos Futbolo Federacija
Seimyniskiu 15, 2051 Vilnius

tel - (2) 723654
fax - (2) 723651
website - www.lsff.lt
email - lsff@lsff.lt

Year of Formation - 1922
President - Vytautas Zimnickas
Secretary - Robertas Mackevicius

Stadium - Zalgiris, Vilnius (13,000)

Lithuania has now aligned itself with the rest of the Baltic region and introduced a domestic football calendar that runs from spring to autumn. As part of the transition, a brief mini-league was staged in the second half of 1999, with 18 matchdays squeezed into a four-month timespan.

Although the usual rewards of a championship title and European qualification were up for grabs, the competition did not exactly capture the public's imagination. Interest was minimal, and so was the quality of the football, with lots of low-scoring matches being played before spartan crowds.

There was some excitement at the top of the table, however, with Zalgiris Kaunas and defending champions Zalgiris Vilnius waging an intriguing battle for the title. Both teams lost their opening match but recovered to put together lengthy unbeaten runs, which were still intact by the time the two rivals came face to face twice in three weeks in the third quarter of the campaign.

The first meeting, in Vilnius, resulted in a goalless draw, but when Kaunas won the return fixture 1-0, thanks to a goal from defender Ignas Dedura, it catapulted them into an almost unassailable position - four points clear with a game in hand. That was the pivotal moment of the season, and from there on in the team from Lithuania's second city held their nerve to complete the first championship triumph in the club's history.

As is the trend in Lithuania, the champions actually ended the season with a different name from the one with which they had started it. In the beginning they were FBK Kaunas, but at the end of August they were renamed Zalgiris Kaunas. This was the decision of a rich Kaunas-born, Moscow-based businessman who took the name from the local basketball team, whom he had just led to victory in that sport's equivalent of the European Champions' League.

As well as the name change, Zalgiris Kaunas were also provided with a new coach - ex-Soviet Union international defender Andrey Bal - as well as a number of players from abroad, something of a rare luxury for the Lithuanian domestic game.

Although the foreigners did their bit, the championship victory was essentially a home-made triumph. The team's most dangerous forward was 22-year-old striker Audrius Ksanavaicius, who was duly voted as the official player of the season, while the main man in defence was veteran libero Raimondas Vainoras, a long-time member of the Lithuanian national side.

Zalgiris Kaunas were destined, however, to be a one-season wonder as their backer withdrew his interest at the end of the season and the club reverted to their former name of FBK Kaunas. They did go out with a bang, though, treating the home fans to a 6-0 victory in their final game, in which Belarus international forward Sergei Gerasimets - the best-known of the foreign contingent - scored twice.

Kaunas's victims in that game were Banga Gargzdai, but they recovered sufficiently from the mauling to preserve their top-flight status with an 8-1 demolition of

LEAGUE CHAMPIONSHIP RESULTS 1999

		1	2	3	4	5	6	7	8	9	10
1	Ardena Vilnius		0-2	1-1	0-2	0-0	1-3	0-2	0-1	0-3	0-3
2	Atlantas Klaipeda	0-0		2-2	5-0	1-2	3-2	3-2	3-1	2-2	1-1
3	Banga Gargzdai	xxx	1-2		2-1	0-2	0-1	0-4	1-1	0-3	1-3
4	Dainava Alytus	1-3	1-2	2-2		0-4	0-2	0-4	0-0	0-1	0-0
5	Ekranas Panevezys	1-0	1-2	1-1	4-1		0-0	1-0	0-0	0-0	0-0
6	Inkaras Kaunas	1-3	1-1	2-0	4-0	1-1		1-0	1-0	1-4	1-1
7	Kareda Siauliai	1-0	0-0	3-0	3-0	0-3	1-1		3-1	2-4	0-1
8	Nevezis Kedainiai	1-1	0-4	1-1	2-0	1-1	0-2	0-2		0-2	0-1
9	Zalgiris Kaunas	0-0	3-1	6-0	2-1	2-0	1-0	2-2	0-1		1-0
10	Zalgiris Vilnius	4-1	5-0	5-0	4-0	2-1	2-1	1-2	0-0	0-0	

LEAGUE CHAMPIONSHIP FINAL TABLE 1999

			Home				Away				Total						
		Pd	W	D	L	F	A	W	D	L	F	A	W	D	L	F	A	PT	GD
1	Zalgiris Kaunas	18	6	2	1	17	5	6	3	0	19	5	12	5	1	36	10	41	26
2	Zalgiris Vilnius	18	6	2	1	23	5	4	4	1	10	4	10	6	2	33	9	36	24
3	Atlantas Klaipeda	18	4	4	1	20	12	5	2	2	14	12	9	6	3	34	24	33	10
4	Kareda Siauliai	18	4	2	3	13	10	5	1	3	18	8	9	3	6	31	18	30	13
5	Ekranas Panevezys	18	3	5	1	8	4	4	3	2	14	7	7	8	3	22	11	29	11
6	Inkaras Kaunas	18	4	3	2	13	10	4	2	3	12	8	8	5	5	25	18	29	7
7	Nevezis Kedainiai	18	1	3	5	5	14	2	4	3	5	8	3	7	8	10	22	16	-12
8	Banga Gargzdai	18	2	1	6	5	17	0	5	4	7	23	2	6	10	12	40	12	-28
9	Ardena Vilnius	18	0	2	7	2	17	2	3	4	8	9	2	5	11	10	26	11	-16
10	Dainava Alytus	18	0	3	6	4	18	1	0	8	5	26	1	3	14	9	44	6	-35

Tauras Taurage in the promotion/relegation play-off. The other play-off proved to be a much closer contest, with Ardena (ex-Lokomotyvas) Vilnius also staying up, but only on the away-goals rule after two draws with Gelezinis Vilkas Vilnius.

Gelezinis Vilkas were entitled to feel hard done by in their quest for promotion. They had finished level on points with Second Division 'champions' Kauno Jegeriai but had lost out on automatic promotion in a penalty shoot-out. Then came the away-goals loss to Ardena, but that was

not all. Kauno Jegeriai subsequently declined their hard-won promotion, which meant that the First Division's bottom club, Dainava Alytus - rather than Gelezinis Vilkas - were allowed to take the tenth and last top-flight place for the fully-fledged 2000 season.

The first trophy-winners of the new millennium in Lithuania were Ekranas Panevezys, who won the Cup for the second time in three years, beating hapless Zalgiris Vilnius 1-0 in the final with a second-half penalty from defender Mindaugas Gardzijauskas. Ekranas's victory

EUROPEAN CUPS 99/00

CHAMPIONS' CUP
● ZALGIRIS VILNIUS
Preliminary round 1 TSEMENT ARARAT (ARM)

H 2-0   Stesko I. (45), Stesko A. (87)
Dilys, Sorokinas, Buzmakovas, Radzius (Grudzinskas 69) Novikovas, Joksas (Barevicius 79), Stesko I., Stesko A., Vasiliauskas, Saulenas (Karcemarskas 72), Poskus.

A 3-0   Novikovas (7), Joksas (31), Vasiliauskas (65)
Dilys, Sorokinas, Radzius, Novikovas, Buzmakovas, Grudzinskas, Stesko I., Stesko A., Joksas (Puotkalis 73), Vasiliauskas (Juska 78), Poskus (Barevicius 68).

Preliminary round 2 DYNAMO KYIV (UKR)

A 0-2
Dilys, Sorokinas, Radzius (Juska 81), Novikovas, Buzmakovas, Grudzinskas, Stesko I., Stesko A., Joksas (Saulenas 75), Vasiliauskas (Barevicius 67), Poskus.

H 0-1
Dilys, Sorokinas, Sobolis, Novikovas, Buzmakovas, Sanajevas, Stesko I., Stesko A., Joksas (Saulenas 46), Vasiliauskas (Puotkalis 78), Poskus.

UEFA CUP
● KAREDA SIAULIAI
Qualifying round SCT OLIMPIJA LJUBLJANA (SLO)

A 1-1   Fomenka (68)
Martinkenas, Barasa, Zudys, Kancelskis, Lunskis, Graziunas, Danilicevas (Pocius 81), Gedgaudas, Juodeikis, Zalys (Upstas 89), Fomenka.

H 2-2   Fomenka (67, 70)
Martinkenas, Barasa, Zudys, Kancelskis, Lunskis, Graziunas (Upstas 74), Danilicevas, Gedgaudas, Juodeikis (Jakimavicius 85), Zalys (Maciulevicius 57), Fomenka.

● FBK KAUNAS
Qualifying round MACCABI TEL-AVIV (ISR)

A 1-3   Papeckys (19)
Skrupskis, Vainoras, Zutautas, Dedura, Pacevicius, Stradins, Papeckys, Bezykornovas (Slekys 81), Petrenka, Ksanavicius (Prokhorenkov 57), Trakys (Rudzionis 71).

H 2-1   Pacevicius (29, 48)
Skrupskis, Vainoras, Zutautas, Dedura, Pacevicius, Stradins, Bezykornovas (Rudzionis 85), Petrenka, Ksanavicius, Prokhorenkov (Velicka 87), Trakys (Slekys 80).

NATIONAL TEAM APPEARANCES 99/00

Coach - Kestutis LATOZA; Robertas TAUTKUS; Stasys STANKUS	NOR	CZE	FAR	SCO	CYP	MOL	LAT	LAT	ARM	Cps	Gls
Pavelas LEUSAS (15/09/78) - Zalgiris Vilnius	G			G						7	-
Sergejus NOVIKOVAS (05/05/72) - Zalgiris Vilnius	D									5	-
Arturas SOBOLIS (24/11/80) - Zalgiris Vilnius	D									1	-
Vidas ALUNDERIS (27/03/79) - Zalgiris Vilnius	D									1	-
Nerijus RADZIUS (27/08/76) - Zalgiris Vilnius	D									4	-
Andrius JOKSAS (12/01/79) - Zalgiris Vilnius/Krybvas Kryvyi Rih (UKR)	M							s89		4	-
Zydrunas GRUDZINSKAS (08/07/75) - Zalgiris Vilnius	M									8	-
Egidijus JUSKA (12/03/75) - Zalgiris Vilnius	M85									1	-
Nerijus VASILIAUSKAS (20/06/77) - Zalgiris Vilnius	M76									3	1
Giedrius BAREVICIUS (09/08/76) - Zalgiris Vilnius	M66									3	-
Robertas POSKUS (05/05/79) - Zalgiris Vilnius/Widzew Lodz (POL)	A								s85	2	-
Andrius PUOTKALIS (06/10/80) - Zalgiris Vilnius	s66									1	-
Dainius SAULENAS (13/03/79) - Zalgiris Vilnius	s76									3	-
Rolandas KARCEMARSKAS (07/09/80) - Zalgiris Vilnius	s85									2	-
Gintaras STAUCE (24/12/69) - MSV Duisburg (GER)		G	G79							45	-
Darius ZUTAUTAS (30/09/78) - Alania Vladikavkaz (RUS)		D	D	D					D	12	-
Andrius TERESKINAS (10/07/70) - Skonto Riga (LAT)		D	D	D64	s43		D			56	3
Tomas ZVIRGZDAUSKAS (18/03/75) - Polonia Warszawa (POL)		D	D	D	D	D	D46	s46		17	-
Deividas SEMBERAS (02/08/78) - Dinamo Moskva (RUS)	D56	M		D78	M46				D	17	-
Donatas VENCEVICIUS (28/11/73) - FC København (DEN)	M	M	s54	M20	s46	M	M78	s60		19	-
									/74		
Tomas RAZANAUSKAS (07/01/76) - Malmö FF (SWE)	M	M77	M							11	3
Aidas PREIKSAITIS (15/07/70) - Stomil Olsztyn (POL)	M80	A88								35	3
Saulius MIKALAJUNAS (06/09/72) - Uralan Elista (RUS)	M	M	M				M	M		22	1
Valdas IVANAUSKAS (31/07/66) - SV Wilhelmshaven (GER)	A38									26	8
Edgaras JANKAUSKAS (12/03/75) - Club Brugge KV (BEL)/Real Sociedad (ESP)	A							A	A	21	4
Tomas RAMELIS (28/05/71) - Stomil Olsztyn (POL)	s38	A								15	5
Andrius SKERLA (29/04/77) - PSV (HOL)	s56	s77	D					D	D85	23	-
Tomas DANILEVICIUS (18/07/78)											
- SV Ingelmunster (BEL)/Lausanne-Sports (SUI)	s80	s88						A	A60	5	-
Marius SKINDERIS (13/10/74) - GKS Belchatow (POL)			D	D	D	D	s66	D46	D	15	-
Gytis PADIMANSKAS (13/05/72) - Nevezis Kedainiai			s79							1	-
Irmantas STUMBRYS (30/05/72) - Torpedo-ZIL Moskva (RUS)				M54						37	2
Vidas DANCENKA (02/08/73) - Uralan Elista (RUS)				M54				s61	s74	4	1
Grazvydas MIKULENAS (16/12/73) - Croatia Zagreb (CRO)				A						11	1
Darius MACIULEVICIUS (06/11/73) - Kareda Siauliai/Hakoah Ramat-Gan (ISR)				s54				M89	M	25	8
Arturas FOMENKA (14/02/77)											
- Kareda Siauliai/Spartak Moskva (RUS)/Rostselmash Rostov-na-Donu (RUS)				s64	A	A	A		s65	9	4
Marius POSKUS (07/08/70) - FBK Kaunas					G	G	G	G	G	16	-
Dainius GLEVECKAS (05/03/77) - Shakhtar Donetsk (UKR)					D	D	D	D		16	-
Vitalijus DANILICEVAS (31/10/70) - FBK Kaunas					M59	M46	s46			3	-
Aurelijus SKARBALIUS (12/05/73) - Brøndby IF (DEN)					M	M	M66			42	5
Raimondas ZUTAUTAS (04/09/72) - Maccabi Haifa (ISR)					M43					24	-
Orestas BUITKUS (11/04/75) - Skonto Riga (LAT)					M70	M	s43	M	M	20	4
Audrius KSANAVICIUS (28/01/77) - FBK Kaunas					s20	A	M43			8	-
Todas GRAZIUNAS (18/04/78) - Spartak Moskva (RUS)/Rostselmash Rostov-na-Donu (RUS)					s59	s46	D	D61		5	-
Rolandas DZIAUKSTAS (01/04/78) - Dynamo Kyiv (UKR)					s70	D	D			4	-
Ignas DEDURA (01/06/78) - FBK Kaunas					s78					4	-
Valdas TRAKYS (20/03/79) - Torpedo Moskva (RUS)							A75	s78		3	1
Rimantas ZVINGILAS (03/09/73) - Torpedo Moskva (RUS)							s75		A65	23	3

DOMESTIC CUP 99/00

1/16 FINALS
Kauno Jegeriai 0, Kareda Siauliai 1
Dainava Alytus 1, Ekranas Panevezys 3 (aet)
Atletas Kaunas 0, Inkaras Kaunas 5
Tauras Taurage 1, Atlantas Klaipeda 6
Lietava Jonava 1, Zalgiris Vilnius 4
Polonija Vilnius 1, Nevezis Kedainiai 10
Ardena Vilnius 2, Banga Gargzdai 3
Zalgiris II Vilnius 0, FBK Kaunas 5

QUARTER-FINALS
Ekrana Panevezys 2 (Steckis 27, Banevicius 70),
Atlantas Klaipeda 2 (Suika 35, 77)
Atlantas Klaipeda 0, Ekranas Panevezys 2
(Stankevicius 54, Gardzijauskas 82)
(Ekranas Panevezys 4-2)
Zalgiris Vilnius 1 (Vasiliauskas 12),
Nevezis Kedainiai 1 (Silajevas 82)
Nevezis Kedainiai 0,
Zalgiris Vilnius 2 (Lemezis 77, 88)
(Zalgiris Vilnius 3-1)

FBK Kaunas 2 (Ksanavicius 27, Rudzionis 83),
Inkaras Kaunas 2 (Vaskunas 44, Sivinskis 57)
Inkaras Kaunas 0, FBK Kauans 0
(2-2; Inkaras Kaunas on away goals)
Kareda Siauliai 4 (Danilicevas 33, Zalys 54,
Gedgaudas 73, Upstas 90), Banga Gargzdai 0
Banga Gargzdai 0,
Kareda Siauliai 3 (Pocius 9, 73, Fomenka 83)
(Kareda Siauliai 7-0)

SEMI-FINALS
Atletas-Inkaras Kaunas 0, Ekrana Panevezys 2
(Cesnauskis 76, Varnas 80)
Ekranas Panevezys 3 (Stankevicius 15, 37,
Varnas 85), Atletas-Inkaras Kaunas 0
(Ekranas Panevezys 5-0)
Kareda Kaunas 1 (Kunevicius 40), Zalgiris Vilnius 1
(Karcemarskas 58p)
Zalgiris Vilnius 3 (Novikovas 55, Osipovich 83,
Saulenas 89), Kareda Kaunas 0
(Zalgiris Vilnius 4-1)

FINAL
20/05/2000, Marijampole
EKRANAS PANEVEZYS 1 Gardzijauskas (59p)
ZALGIRIS VILNIUS 0
referee - Miliauskas
EKRANAS PANEVEZYS - Skrupskis, Petrukaitis,
Banevicius, Urbonas (Sasnauskas 67), Stankevicius,
Gardzijauskas, Zeniauskas (Vileniskis 46), Kucys,
Savenas (Kavaliauskas 77), Cesnauskis, Varnas.
ZALGIRIS VILNIUS - Dilys, Sorokinas, Novikovas
(Alunderis 5), Veikutis, Radzius, Ringys (Zurza 76),
Lemezis (Yakushev 80), Shilo, Barevicius, Osipovich,
Saulenas.

---

ensured their own UEFA Cup qualification while at the same time scuppering the hopes of Atlantas Klaipeda, who had finished third in the league and been forced to wait six months to know if it would be good enough to bring them European football for the first time. Had Zalgiris won the Cup, that third European spot would indeed have been theirs.

There was little for Lithuanian fans to crow about on the international front in 1999/2000. Interest in European club competitions was ended at the qualifying-round stage, and the national team went from one poor performance to another, starting with a 0-4 defeat in Vilnius by the Czech Republic in the Euro 2000 qualifying campaign and

ending with a shocking 1-2 friendly defeat by Armenia nine months later in Kaunas. The only bright spots were a couple of back-to-back 2-1 victories over neighbours Latvia, both of them secured with late winning goals after their opponents had led at half-time.

The national side went through three different coaches during the season, with Kestutis Latoza being relieved of his duties in the early autumn and replaced by Robertas Tautkus, who in turn packed his bags in mid-winter to make way for 52-year-old Stasys Stankus, the assistant coach to the previous three incumbents.

Perhaps more significantly, there was also a change at the head of the Lithuanian FA (LFF), with the unpopular

TOP SCORERS

10	Nerijus VASILIAUSKAS (Zalgiris Vilnius)	
9	Ricardas BENIUSIS (Inkaras Kaunas)	
8	Arunas SUIKA (Atlantas Klaipeda)	
	Arturas FOMENKA (Kareda Siauliai)	
7	Vidas KAUSPADAS (Inkaras Kaunas)	
6	Aivaras LAURISAS (Atlantas Klaipeda)	
	Dainius ZERNYS (Atlantas Klaipeda)	
	Audrius KSANAVICIUS (Zalgiris Kaunas)	
	Andrius PUOTKALIS (Zalgiris Vilnius)	

NATIONAL TEAM RESULTS 99/00

18/08/99	Norway	A	Oslo	0-1	
04/09/99	Czech Republic (ECQ)	H	Vilnius	0-4	
08/09/99	Faroe Islands (ECQ)	A	Torshavn	1-0	Ramelis (55)
09/10/99	Scotland (ECQ)	A	Glasgow	0-3	
02/02/00	Cyprus	A	Limassol	1-2	Fomenka (86)
04/02/00	Moldova	N	Larnaca	1-2	Fomenka (78)
06/02/00	Latvia	N	Larnaca	2-1	Trakys (54), Fomenka (89)
26/04/00	Latvia	H	Kaunas	2-1	Dancenka (64), Maciulevicius (87)
03/06/00	Armenia	H	Kaunas	1-2	Jankauskas (23)

autocrat Vytautas Dirmeikis finally bowing to pressure and resigning from his post as LFF president. The position was filled temporarily by Vytautas Zimnickas pending full-scale presidential elections in October...

PLAYER OF THE SEASON

SAULIUS MIKALAJUNAS

Lithuania will have their work cut out to plunder many points from a World Cup qualifying group that contains Romania, Italy, Hungary and Georgia. Much will depend on the form of their foreign-based luminaries, one of whom is 28-year-old midfield playmaker Saulius Mikalajunas, a former double champion of Lithuania with Kareda Siauliai who now plays his club football in Russia. He played from the start in all but the first of Lithuania's Euro 2000 qualifiers and also had an impressive début season in the Russian Premier League for Uralan Elista, lifting the club to mid-table after an awful start. Voted Lithuanian Player of the Year for 1999, Mikalajunas is a tricky schemer in the mould of German veteran Thomas Hässler - small, industrious, creative and always prepared to let fly from distance.

SECOND DIVISION FINAL TABLE 1999

		Pd	W	D	L	F	A	Pt	GD
1	Kauno Jegeriai	14	11	3	0	30	5	36	25
2	Gelezinis Vilkas Vilnius	14	12	0	2	39	13	36	26
3	Tauras Taurage	14	9	3	2	23	10	30	13
4	Pieno Cechas Kalvarija	14	8	3	3	31	16	27	15
5	Interas Visaginas	14	7	5	2	20	12	26	8
6	Laisve Silute	14	6	4	4	17	13	22	4
7	Lietava Jonava	14	5	3	6	21	19	18	2
8	Zerutis Radviliskis	14	5	0	9	13	23	15	-10
9	Vienybe Ukmerge	14	3	5	6	19	27	14	-8
10	Zalgiris II Vilnius	14	4	2	8	16	16	14	0
11	Anyksciai	14	3	4	7	9	25	13	-16
12	Babrungas Plunge	14	3	4	7	10	18	13	-8
13	Atletas Kaunas	14	3	3	8	17	29	12	-12
14	Savinge Kaisiadorys	14	3	3	8	15	28	12	-13
15	Klevas Siauliai	14	0	4	10	10	36	4	-26

PROMOTION PLAY-OFF

Kauno Jegeriai 0, Gelezinis Vilkas Vilnius 0 (aet; 4-2 on pens.)
N.B. Kauno Jegeriai subsequently declined promotion.

PROMOTION/RELEGATION PLAY-OFFS

Tauras Taurage 0, Banga Gargzdai 3
Banga Gargzdai 5, Tauras Taurage 1
(Banga Gargzdai 8-1)

Gelezinis Vilkas Vilnius 1, Ardena Vilnius 1
Ardena Vilnius 0, Gelezinis Vilkas Vilnius 0
(1-1; Ardena Vilnius on away goal)

ARDENA VILNIUS

CLUB DIRECTORY

Ardena Vilnius (now - Polonija Vilnius)
Zolyno 29
2040 Vilnius
tel - (2) 341494
fax - (2) 344187
Year of Formation - 1951
President - Janusas Loputis
Coach - Saulius Sirmelis
Stadium - Vingis (3,000)

APPEARANCES 1999

	P	Ap	(s)	Gls
Vidas ALUNDERIS	D	15		1
Darius ARTIMOVAS	A	9	(1)	
Andrius BRAZAUSKAS	A	16		2
Gediminas BUTRIMAVICIUS	M	16	(1)	2
Mindaugas GRIGALEVICIUS	A	1	(13)	
Mantas GRYBAUSKAS	D	10	(2)	
Egidijus JUSKA	A	6		1
Marius KIZYS	M	7	(3)	
Virmantas LEMEZIS	M	9		1
Andzejus MAKSIMOVICIUS	M	6	(1)	
Mindaugas MAKSVYTIS	G	6	(1)	
Mindaugas PONOMARIOVAS	M		(1)	
Mindaugas PUODZIUNAS	M	11	(5)	
Audrius RAMONAS	G	11	(1)	
Arunas SILALE	D	15		
Gintas SIRMELIS	M	4		
Gediminas STAKNEVICIUS	D	10	(2)	
Audrius TOLIS	D	12	(1)	
Anatoliy YAKUSHEV (RUS)	M	8	(6)	
Mindaugas ZURZA	M	15		3

LEAGUE RESULTS 1999

09/07/99	Atlantas Klaipeda	H	0-2	
17/07/99	Kareda Siauliai	A	0-1	
24/07/99	Zalgiris Vilnius	A	1-4	Butrimavicius
28/07/99	Banga Gargzdai	H	1-1	Alunderis
07/08/99	Nevezis Kedainiai	H	0-1	
14/08/99	Ekranas Panevezys	A	0-1	
21/08/99	Dainava Alytus	H	0-2	
28/08/99	Inkaras Kaunas	A	3-1	Lemezis, Zurza, Brazauskas
11/09/99	Zalgiris Vilnius	H	0-3	
19/09/99	Atlantas Klaipeda	A	0-0	
22/09/99	Zalgiris Kaunas	A	0-0	
25/09/99	Kareda Siauliai	H	0-2	
03/10/99	Banga Gargzdai	A	0-0	(awarded as home win)
13/10/99	Ekranas Panevezys	H	0-0	
16/10/99	Zalgiris Kaunas	H	0-3	
30/10/99	Dainava Alytus	A	3-1	Zurza 2, Brazauskas
03/11/99	Nevezis Kedainiai	A	1-1	Butrimavicius
06/11/99	Inkaras Kaunas	H	1-3	Juska

ATLANTAS KLAIPEDA

CLUB DIRECTORY

FK Atlantas Klaipeda
Sportininku 46
5813 Klaipeda
tel - (6) 312449
fax - (6) 312449
email - scarus@takas.lt
Year of Formation - 1960
President - Aidas Rudys
Secretary - Arunas Suika
Coach - Vaclovas Lekevicius
Stadium - Zalgiris (10,000)

APPEARANCES 1999

	P	Ap	(s)	Gls
Rokas BLINSTRUBAS	M		(4)	
Valerijs BOROVKOVS (LAT)	M	5		
Kestutis DEVEIKA	D	8	(5)	
Edmundas GAIGALAS	D	3		
Mindaugas KAIRYS	D	16		1
Gediminas KONTAUTAS	M	14	(3)	
Aivaras LAURISAS	A	11		6
Edvinas LUKOSEVICIUS	D		(2)	
Romualdas MACIULEVICIUS	D	16		1
Andrius MAZALIAUSKAS	M	5	(1)	
Andrius PETREIKIS	M	8	(3)	1
Robertas RINGYS	M	11	(5)	3
Arunas SUIKA	A	14	(1)	8
Antanas TAUTVYDAS	A	4	(11)	5
Darius TETENSKAS	M		(7)	
Liudvikas VALIUS	G	18		
Aleksandras VESELJEVAS	A	13	(5)	3
Dainius ZERNYS	M	17		6
Tomas ZIUKAS	D	17		
Egidijus ZUKAUSKAS	D	18		
Algirdas ZUPERKA	M		(1)	

LEAGUE RESULTS 1999

05/07/99	Inkaras Kaunas	A	1-1	Zernys
09/07/99	Ardena Vilnius	A	2-0	Zernys, Ringys
17/07/99	Banga Gargzdai	H	2-2	Zernys 2 (1p)
28/07/99	Nevezis Kedainiai	A	4-0	Suika 2, Zernys, Maciulevicius
01/08/99	Dainava Alytus	H	5-0	Ringys, Suika, Tautvydas, Veseljevas, Kairys
08/08/99	Zalgiris Vilnius	A	0-5	
20/08/99	Zalgiris Kaunas	A	1-3	Zernys
28/08/99	Ekranas Panevezys	H	1-2	Laurisas
11/09/99	Inkaras Kaunas	H	3-2	Suika, Laurisas 2
19/09/99	Ardena Vilnius	H	0-0	
23/09/99	Banga Gargzdai	A	2-1	Veseljevas, Tautvydas
03/10/99	Nevezis Kedainiai	H	3-1	Tautvydas, Petreikis, Suika
13/10/99	Kareda Siauliai	H	3-2	Laurisas, Suika, Tautvydas
16/10/99	Dainava Alytus	A	2-1	Laurisas, Tautvydas
27/10/99	Zalgiris Vilnius	H	1-1	Laurisas
30/10/99	Zalgiris Kaunas	H	2-2	Veseljevas, Ringys
04/11/99	Kareda Siauliai	A	0-0	
06/11/99	Ekranas Panevezys	A	2-1	Suika 2

BANGA GARGZDAI

CLUB DIRECTORY

Banga Gargzdai
Kranto 5
5840 Gargzdai
tel - (6) 452505
fax - (6) 452647
Year of Formation - 1957
President - Antanas Blinstrubas
Secretary - Antanas Blinstrubas
Coach - Vaidas Liutikas
Stadium - Gargzdai (2,000)

APPEARANCES 1999

	P	Ap	(s)	Gls
Zenonas ATUTIS	D	7	(2)	
Saulius DRASUTIS	M	13	(1)	1
Egidijus GRUDYS	D	11	(1)	
Rimvydas GRUDYS	M	5	(2)	
Igoris GURJANOVAS	A	6	(7)	3
Saulius JOKUMAITIS	D	15	(1)	
tadas KARINAUSKAS	A	7	(6)	2
Rimas LUKOSIUS	G		(1)	
Andrius MIKALAUSKAS	D		(1)	
Kestutis NAZAROVAS	M	16	(1)	3
Romas PETKEVICIUS	M	16		
Giedrius RATKUS	D		(2)	
Petras RAUKTYS	M	11		
Rimas RUDYS	M	17		
Genadijus SAMSONIKAS	M	6	(6)	
Mindaugas SIMKUS	A	8	(7)	3
Tomas TAMOSAUSKAS	M	1	(4)	
Raimondas VENSKUS	G	17		
Mindaugas VIJEIKIS	M	16	(1)	
Romas VOLUNGEVICIUS	D	15		

LEAGUE RESULTS 1999

06/07/99	Ekranas Panevezys	A	1-1	Karinauskas
10/07/99	Inkaras Kaunas	H	0-1	
17/07/99	Atlantas Klaipeda	A	2-2	Karinauskas, Simkus
28/07/99	Ardena Vilnius	A	1-1	Gurjanovas
01/08/99	Nevezis Kedainiai	H	1-1	Simkus
06/08/99	Dainava Alytus	A	2-2	Nazarovas 2 (1p)
16/08/99	Zalgiris Vilnius	H	1-3	Nazarovas
20/08/99	Kareda Siauliai	A	0-3	
29/08/99	Zalgiris Kaunas	H	0-3	
11/09/99	Ekranas Panevezys	H	0-2	
18/09/99	Inkaras Kaunas	A	0-2	
23/09/99	Atlantas Klaipeda	H	1-2	Gurjanovas
03/10/99	Ardena Vilnius	H	0-0	(awarded as home win)
16/10/99	Nevezis Kedainiai	A	1-1	Simkus
20/10/99	Dainava Alytus	H	2-1	Drasutis, Gurjanovas
24/10/99	Zalgiris Vilnius	A	0-5	
30/10/99	Kareda Siauliai	H	0-4	
06/11/99	Zalgiris Kaunas	A	0-6	

DAINAVA ALYTUS

CLUB DIRECTORY

Dainava Alytus
Birutes 5
4580 Alytus
tel - (35) 35968
fax - (35) 53541
Year of Formation - 1943
President - Anatolijus Kacalapas
Secretary - Aidas Kalimavicius
Coach - Rimas Kochanauskas
Stadium - Alytus (2,000)

APPEARANCES 1999

	P	Ap	(s)	Gls
Eugenijus BALIONIS	D	7	(1)	
Kestutis BALKEVICIUS	M	18		1
Irmantas BARTKEVICIUS	M	1	(1)	
Martynas BIRZINIS	M	17	(1)	2
Saulius GRISKEVICIUS	M	2	(5)	
Ricardas JANKAUSKAS	D	18		
Aivaras KADIJAUSKAS	M	1	(2)	
Aidas KALIMAVICIUS	M	2	(5)	
Andrius KAMANDAUSKAS	D	2	(2)	
Zydrunas KARCEMARSKAS	G	3	(1)	
Andrius KOCHANAUSKAS	A	10	(5)	1
Saulius LAIBINIS	A	18		2
Zilvinas MARCIULIONIS	A	5		
Kestutis MIGLINAS	M		(1)	
Arturas MIKNEVICIUS	A	11	(7)	1
Virgis MIKNEVICIUS	M	17		2
Aurimas MINIAUSKAS	M	17		
Ricardas PADEGIMAS	M	13		
Gintaras PAKETURAS	M	7	(6)	
Audrius PASKEVICIUS	G	15		
Vaidas POCEVICIUS	D	14	(2)	

LEAGUE RESULTS 1999

06/07/99	Kareda Siauliai	A	0-3	
10/07/99	Zalgiris Kaunas	H	0-1	
17/07/99	Ekranas Panevezys	A	1-4	Miknevicius V.
28/07/99	Inkaras Kaunas	H	0-2	
01/08/99	Atlantas Klaipeda	A	0-5	
06/08/99	Banga Gargzdai	H	2-2	Kochanauskas, Balkevicius
14/08/99	Nevezis Kedainiai	A	0-2	
21/08/99	Ardena Vilnius	A	2-0	Miknevicius A. (p), Laibinis
28/08/99	Zalgiris Vilnius	H	0-0	
11/09/99	Kareda Siauliai	H	0-4	
19/09/99	Zalgiris Kaunas	A	1-2	Birzinis
25/09/99	Ekranas Panevezys	H	0-4	
02/10/99	Inkaras Kaunas	A	0-4	
16/10/99	Atlantas Klaipeda	H	1-2	Miknevicius V.
20/10/99	Banga Gargzdai	A	1-2	Birzinis
24/10/99	Nevezis Kedainiai	H	0-0	
30/10/99	Ardena Vilnius	H	1-3	Laibinis
06/11/99	Zalgiris Vilnius	A	0-4	

EKRANAS PANEVEZYS

FK Ekranas Panevezys
Elektronikos 1
5319 Panevezys
tel - (5) 435545
fax - (5) 435515
website - www.omnitel.net/fk-ekranas
email - fk_ekranas@post.omnitel.net
Year of Formation - 1963
President - Valdemaras Steinas
Secretary - Valdemaras Steinas
Coach - Virginijus Liubsys
Stadium - Aukstaitija (10,000)

MAJOR HONOURS
League Championship - (1) 1993.
Domestic Cup - (2) 1998, 2000.

	P	Ap	(s)	Gls
Gerdas ALEKSA	M	1	(3)	
Audrius BANEVICIUS	A	17		3
Marius BUTENAS	M	1	(1)	
Deividas CESNAUSKIS	A	16		2
Mindaugas GARDZIJAUSKAS	D	17		5
Vitalijus KAVALIAUSKAS	A		(4)	1
Aurimas KUCYS	M	13	(3)	1
Povilas LUKSYS	A	12	(6)	
Raimondas PETRUKAITIS	D	16	(1)	
Nerijus SASNAUSKAS	D	8	(4)	
Irmantas SATAS	G	18		
Mantas SAVENAS	A	7	(8)	1
Marius STANKEVICIUS	D	18		1
Romas STECKIS	D	13	(4)	1
Egidijus VARNAS	A	14	(4)	5
Raimondas VILENISKIS	M	17		2
Erikas ZABURAS	G		(1)	
Kestutis ZENIAUSKAS	M	10	(8)	

Date	Opponent	H/A	Score	Scorers
06/07/99	Banga Gargzdai	H	1-1	Vileniskis
10/07/99	Nevezis Kedainiai	A	1-1	Stankevicius
17/07/99	Dainava Alytus	H	4-1	Gardzijauskas (p), Cesnauskis, Kucys, Varnas
01/08/99	Kareda Siauliai	H	1-0	Gardzijauskas
14/08/99	Ardena Vilnius	H	1-0	Gardzijauskas (p)
22/08/99	Inkaras Kaunas	H	0-0	
28/08/99	Atlantas Klaipeda	A	2-1	Banevicius, Steckis
11/09/99	Banga Gargzdai	A	2-0	Banevicius, Cesnauskis
19/09/99	Nevezis Kedainiai	H	0-0	
22/09/99	Zalgiris Vilnius	A	1-2	Vileniskis
25/09/99	Dainava Alytus	A	4-0	Varnas 2, Savenas, Gardzijauskas
03/10/99	Zalgiris Vilnius	H	0-0	
13/10/99	Ardena Vilnius	A	0-0	
16/10/99	Kareda Siauliai	A	3-0	Varnas, Gardzijauskas, Kavaliauskas
27/10/99	Zalgiris Kaunas	A	0-2	
30/10/99	Inkaras Kaunas	A	1-1	Varnas
03/11/99	Zalgiris Kaunas	H	0-0	
06/11/99	Atlantas Klaipeda	H	1-2	Banevicius

INKARAS KAUNAS

CLUB DIRECTORY

FK Inkaras Kaunas (now - Atletas-Inkaras Kaunas)
Ausros 42, 3005 Kaunas
tel - (7) 730650
fax - (7) 730773
Year of Formation - 1937
President - Kastytis Klimas
Secretary - Viaceslavas Novikovas
Coach - Igoris Pankratjevas
Stadium - Inkaras (4,000)

MAJOR HONOURS
League Championship - (2) 1995, 1996.
Domestic Cup - (1) 1995.

APPEARANCES 1999

	P	Ap	(s)	Gls
Rimvydas BAKUS	M	18		
Ricardas BENIUSIS	A	9	(5)	9
Saulius BUTKUS	M	14		1
Vitoldas CEPAUSKAS	D	17		
Rimantas CEPOVAS	M	4	(6)	
Audrius JUODEIKIS	M	9	(4)	1
Vidas KAUSPADAS	A	17		7
Marekas KRUKOVSKIS	M	14	(4)	2
Marius KURSEVICIUS	A	10	(5)	1
Ramunas MERKELIS	G	18		
Arunas MIKA	D	4	(2)	
Povilas POZERSKIS	M	3	(2)	
Kestutis RUDZIONIS	M	4		2
Vidas SAVICKAS	M	8		
Arturas SIRKA	D	16	(1)	
Andzejus SIVINSKIS	M	13	(4)	
Raimondas STATKEVICIUS	D		(1)	
Darius URBELIONIS	M	11	(3)	2
Vytautas VASKUNAS	M	9	(4)	

LEAGUE RESULTS 1999

05/07/99	Atlantas Klaipeda	H	1-1	Krukovskis
10/07/99	Banga Gargzdai	A	1-0	Rudzionis
16/07/99	Nevezis Kedainiai	H	1-0	Kauspadas
28/07/99	Dainava Alytus	A	2-0	Rudzionis, Butkus
06/08/99	Kareda Siauliai	A	1-1	Urbelionis
12/08/99	Zalgiris Vilnius	H	1-1	Beniusis
16/08/99	Zalgiris Kaunas	H	1-4	Kauspadas
22/08/99	Ekranas Panevezys	A	0-0	
28/08/99	Ardena Vilnius	H	1-3	Kauspadas (p)
11/09/99	Atlantas Klaipeda	A	2-3	Kauspadas 2
18/09/99	Banga Gargzdai	H	2-0	Beniusis 2
25/09/99	Nevezis Kedainiai	A	2-0	Kauspadas, Beniusis
02/10/99	Dainava Alytus	H	4-0	Beniusis 3, Kursevicius
16/10/99	Zalgiris Vilnius	A	1-2	Beniusis
20/10/99	Kareda Siauliai	H	1-0	Krukovskis
24/10/99	Zalgiris Kaunas	A	0-1	
30/10/99	Ekranas Panevezys	H	1-1	Juodeikis
06/11/99	Ardena Vilnius	A	3-1	Urbelionis, Kauspadas, Beniusis

KAREDA SIAULIAI

CLUB DIRECTORY

FK Kareda Siauliai (now - Kareda Kaunas)
Donelaicio 60
3000 Kaunas
tel - (7) 208729
fax - (7) 202888
Year of Formation - 1954
President - Mindaugas Neoras
Secretary - Mindaugas Neoras
Coach - Valdemaras Martinkenas
(2000 - Kazimieras Brickus)
Stadium - Kariuomenes (1,000)

MAJOR HONOURS
League Championship - (2) 1997, 1998.
Domestic Cup - (2) 1996, 1999.

APPEARANCES 1999

	P	Ap	(s)	Gls
Nerijus BARASA	D	15	(2)	
Deimantas BICKA	M	2		1
Vitalijus DANILICEVAS	M	16		
Arturas FOMENKA	A	17		8
Andrius GEDGAUDAS	M	15	(1)	4
Tadas GRAZIUNAS	D	16		
Jonas JAKIMAVICIUS	D		(1)	
Gintaras JUODEIKIS	M	15	(1)	3
Tomas KANCELSKIS	D	14		2
Tomas KAVOLIS	M	1	(7)	
Eduardas KURSKIS	G	9	(1)	
Edvinas LUKOSEVICIUS	D	3	(2)	
Deividas LUNSKIS	D	15	(2)	
Darius MACIULEVICIUS	M	6	(2)	3
Valdemaras MARTINKENAS	G	9		
Remigijus POCIUS	A	12	(3)	4
Igoris STUKALINAS	M		(1)	
Andrius UPSTAS	M	12	(4)	2
Robertas ZALYS	A	11	(7)	2
Zilvinas ZUDYS	D	10		

LEAGUE RESULTS 1999

06/07/99	Dainava Alytus	H	3-0	Zalys, Upstas, Kancelskis
10/07/99	Zalgiris Vilnius	A	2-1	Bicka, Gedgaudas
17/07/99	Ardena Vilnius	H	1-0	Zalys
28/07/99	Zalgiris Kaunas	H	2-4	Gedgaudas, Fomenka
01/08/99	Ekranas Panevezys	A	0-1	
06/08/99	Inkaras Kaunas	H	1-1	Fomenka
20/08/99	Banga Gargzdai	H	3-0	Gedgaudas, Upstas, Kancelskis (p)
11/09/99	Dainava Alytus	A	4-0	Juodeikis 2, Maciulevicius, Fomenka
19/09/99	Zalgiris Vilnius	H	0-1	
22/09/99	Nevezis Kedainiai	A	2-0	Pocius, Fomenka
25/09/99	Ardena Vilnius	A	2-0	Pocius, Fomenka
03/10/99	Zalgiris Kaunas	A	2-2	Maciulevicius 2
13/10/99	Atlantas Klaipeda	A	2-3	Juodeikis, og (Valius)
16/10/99	Ekranas Panevezys	H	0-3	
20/10/99	Inkaras Kaunas	A	0-1	
30/10/99	Banga Gargzdai	A	4-0	Pocius 2, Fomenka 2
04/11/99	Atlantas Klaipeda	H	0-0	
06/11/99	Nevezis Kedainiai	H	3-1	Fomenka, og (Sakalys), Gedgaudas

NEVEZIS KEDAINIAI

CLUB DIRECTORY

Nevezis Kedainiai
Jaugelio-Telegos 2
5030 Kedainiai
tel - (57) 50669
fax - (57) 53537
Year of Formation - 1946
President - Juozas Baniota
Secretary - Vygantas Jodenis
Coach - Romas Juknevicius
Stadium - Kedainiai (3,000)

APPEARANCES 1999

	P	Ap	(s)	Gls
Vidas ADOMAITIS	M	8	(7)	
Evaldas BABENSKAS	A	2	(7)	
Aidas BLAZYS	A	1	(1)	
Darius BUTKUS	D	15		
Zilvinas CENYS	M	14	(2)	2
Zygimantas CEPULIS	A	4	(13)	1
Vygintas GODELIS	A		(4)	1
Arturas JANUSKEVICIUS	D	12	(1)	1
Laisvunas JONAVICIUS	M		(3)	
Martynas JUKNEVICIUS	M	15		
Dainius JUODIS	M	17		1
Romas KIULKIS	G	3		
Gytis PADIMANSKAS	G	15		
Edvinas SAKALYS	D	17		
Mantas SAMUSIOVAS	D	11		
Tomas SENDZIKAS	D	13		1
Robertas SILAJEVAS	M	18		1
Renaldas SKREBUTENAS	D		(4)	
Kestutis SRUOGIS	M	15	(2)	1
Vaidas STRUMECKAS	D	17		
Rolandas TUTORIUS	M	1	(4)	

LEAGUE RESULTS 1999

06/07/99	FBK Kaunas	A	1-0	Cepulis
10/07/99	Ekranas Panevezys	H	1-1	Cenys
16/07/99	Inkaras Kaunas	A	0-1	
28/07/99	Atlantas Klaipeda	H	0-4	
01/08/99	Banga Gargzdai	A	1-1	Januskevicius
07/08/99	Ardena Vilnius	A	1-0	Sruogis
14/08/99	Dainava Alytus	H	2-0	Cenys, Juodis
22/08/99	Zalgiris Vilnius	A	0-0	
11/09/99	Zalgiris Kaunas	H	0-2	
19/09/99	Ekranas Panevezys	A	0-0	
22/09/99	Kareda Siauliai	H	0-2	
25/09/99	Inkaras Kaunas	H	0-2	
03/10/99	Atlantas Klaipeda	A	1-3	Godelis
16/10/99	Banga Gargzdai	H	1-1	Silajevas
24/10/99	Dainava Alytus	A	0-0	
30/10/99	Zalgiris Vilnius	H	0-1	
03/11/99	Ardena Vilnius	H	1-1	Sendzikas (p)
06/11/99	Kareda Siauliai	A	1-3	og (Barasa)

ZALGIRIS KAUNAS

CLUB DIRECTORY

Zalgiris Kaunas (now - FBK Kaunas)
Raudondvario pl 93
3024 Kaunas
tel - (7) 360322
fax - (7) 360323
website - www.fbk.lt
email - info@fbk.lt
Year of Formation - 1960
President - Vidas Damalakas
Secretary - Romualdas Kontrimas
Coach - Senderis Girsovicius; Andrey Bal
(2000 - Senderis Girsovicius)
Stadium - Dariaus ir Gireno (12,000)

MAJOR HONOURS
League Championship - (1) 1999 (autumn).

APPEARANCES 1999

		P	Ap	(s)	Gls
Marius BEZYKORNOVAS	M	14	(4)	5
Martynas CIKAS	M	3	(4)	1
Ignas DEDURA	D	17		5
Sergei GERASIMETS (BLS)	M	5		2
Igoris KIRILOVAS	M	1	(1)	1
Denis KLEBANOV (RUS)	M		(1)	
Audrius KSANAVICIUS	A	16	(1)	6
Arunas MIKA	D	5	(1)	
Mindaugas PACEVICIUS	M	17	(1)	
tadas PAPECKYS	D	18		1
Vadimas PETRENKA	M	16		4
Aleksandr PROKHORENKOV (RUS)	A	9	(4)	3
Arturas RAMOSKA	G	8		
Kestutis RUDZIONIS	M	4	(8)	2
Arvydas SKRUPSKIS	G	8	(1)	
Audrius SLEKYS	A	4	(6)	1
Modestas STONYS	G	1		
Aleksandr STRADINS (LAT)	D	2	(7)	
Dainius SULIAUSKAS	D	10		1
Valdas TRAKYS	A	12	(2)	4
Raimondas VAINORAS	D	17		
Audrius VELICKA	A	5	(5)	
Irakli ZOIDZE (GEO)	G	1		
Giedrius ZUTAUTAS	D	5	(4)	

LEAGUE RESULTS 1999

06/07/99	Nevezis Kedainiai	H	0-1	
10/07/99	Dainava Alytus	A	1-0	Kirilovas
28/07/99	Kareda Siauliai	A	4-2	Ksanavicius, Trakys 2, Slekys
16/08/99	Inkaras Kaunas	A	4-1	Ksanavicius 2, Papeckys, Prokhorenkov
20/08/99	Atlantas Klaipeda	H	3-1	Suliauskas, Bezykornovas 2 (1p)
29/08/99	Banga Gargzdai	A	3-0	Petrenka, Rudzionis, Cikas
11/09/99	Nevezis Kedainiai	A	2-0	Bezykornovas 2 (2p)
19/09/99	Dainava Alytus	H	2-1	Trakys, Dedura
22/09/99	Ardena Vilnius	H	0-0	
25/09/99	Zalgiris Vilnius	A	0-0	
03/10/99	Kareda Siauliai	H	2-2	Petrenka, Dedura
13/10/99	Zalgiris Vilnius	H	1-0	Dedura
16/10/99	Ardena Vilnius	A	3-0	Ksanavicius, Trakys, Dedura
24/10/99	Inkaras Kaunas	H	1-0	Dedura
27/10/99	Ekranas Panevezys	H	2-0	Ksanavicius, Prokhorenkov
30/10/99	Atlantas Klaipeda	A	2-2	Rudzionis, Petrenka (p)
03/11/99	Ekranas Panevezys	A	0-0	
06/11/99	Banga Gargzdai	H	6-0	Petrenka (p), Gerasimets 2 (1p), Bezykornovas, Prokhorenkov, Ksanavicius

ZALGIRIS VILNIUS

CLUB DIRECTORY

FK Zalgiris Vilnius
Zolyno 29
2040 Vilnius
tel - (2) 341494
fax - (2) 344187
Year of Formation - 1947
President - Janusas Loputis
Secretary - Ala Dipskaja
Coach - Kestutis Latoza; Eugenijus Riabovas
Stadium - Zalgiris (13,000)

MAJOR HONOURS
League Championship - (3) 1991, 1992, 1999.
Domestic Cup - (4) 1991, 1993, 1994, 1997.

APPEARANCES 1999

	P	Ap	(s)	Gls
Giedrius BAREVICIUS	M	4	(6)	2
Vladimiras BUZMAKOVAS	D	17		
Audrius DILYS	G	3		
Zydrunas GRUDZINSKAS	D	12	(2)	
Andrius JOKSAS	D	15	(1)	
Egidijus JUSKA	A	2	(1)	
Rolandas KARCEMARSKAS	A	10	(3)	5
Virmantas LEMEZIS	M	8	(1)	
Pavelas LEUSAS	G	15		
Sergejus NOVIKOVAS	D	17		1
Robertas POSKUS	A	7	(1)	5
Andrius PUOTKALIS	A	8	(5)	6
Nerijus RADZIUS	D	12	(1)	
Darius SANAJEVAS	D	2	(1)	
Dainius SAULENAS	A	4	(10)	1
Arturas SOBOLIS	D	3	(4)	
Andrejus SOROKINAS	D	13		
Arturas STESKO	M	12	(2)	2
Igoris STESKO	M	13	(1)	1
Nerijus VASILIAUSKAS	A	14	(3)	10
Audrius VEIKUTIS	D	5	(2)	
Irmantas ZELMIKAS	D	2		

LEAGUE RESULTS 1999

10/07/99	Kareda Siauliai	H	1-2	Vasiliauskas
24/07/99	Ardena Vilnius	H	4-1	Vasiliauskas, Stesko A., Barevicius, Stesko I.
08/08/99	Atlantas Klaipeda	H	5-0	Vasiliauskas 2, Poskus 3
12/08/99	Inkaras Kaunas	A	1-1	Vasiliauskas
16/08/99	Banga Gargzdai	A	3-1	Poskus 2, Barevicius
22/08/99	Nevezis Kedainiai	H	0-0	
28/08/99	Dainava Alytus	A	0-0	
11/09/99	Ardena Vilnius	A	3-0	Puotkalis, Vasiliauskas, Karcemarskas
19/09/99	Kareda Siauliai	A	1-0	Stesko A.
22/09/99	Ekranas Panevezys	H	2-1	Vasiliauskas, Novikovas
25/09/99	Zalgiris Kaunas	H	0-0	
03/10/99	Ekranas Panevezys	A	0-0	
13/10/99	Zalgiris Kaunas	A	0-1	
16/10/99	Inkaras Kaunas	H	2-1	Karcemarskas, Puotkalis
24/10/99	Banga Gargzdai	H	5-0	Puotkalis 2, Karcemarskas 2, Vasiliauskas
27/10/99	Atlantas Klaipeda	A	1-1	Saulenas
30/10/99	Nevezis Kedainiai	A	1-0	Puotkalis
06/11/99	Dainava Alytus	H	4-0	Vasiliauskas 2, Puotkalis, Karcemarskas

LUXEMBOURG

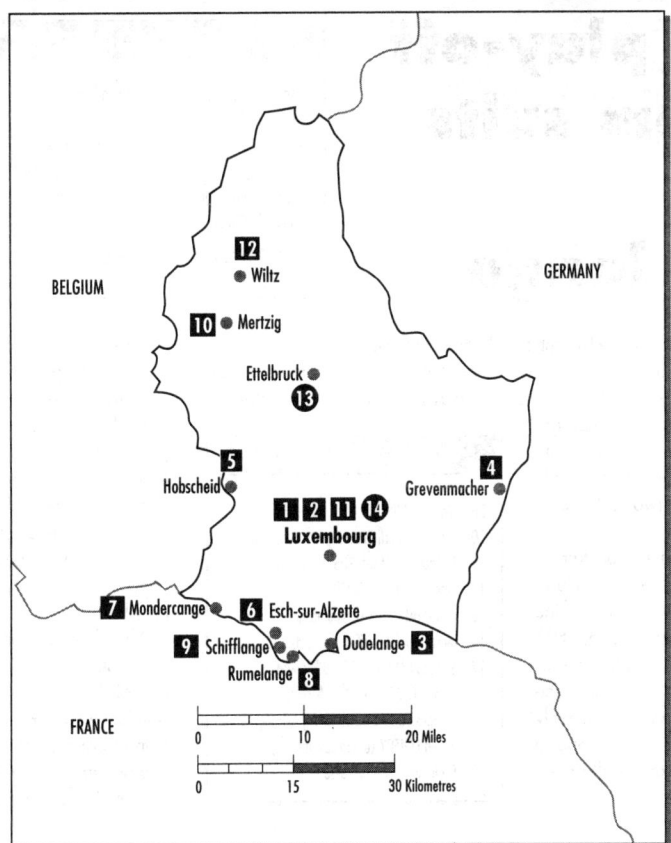

CUP CONSOLATION FOR JEUNESSE ESCH

New play-off system suits F91 Dudelange

FEDERATION DIRECTORY

Fédération Luxembourgeoise de Football
50 rue de Strasbourg, 2560 Luxembourg

tel - 488665-1   Year of Formation - 1908
fax - 400201   President - Henri Roemer
website - www.football.lu   Secretary - Joël Wolff
email - flf@pt.lu

Stadium - Josy Barthel, Luxembourg (8,250)

There was a new look to the Luxembourg National Division in 1999/2000. In order to drum up more excitement, the league authorities decided to add a series of play-offs onto the regular 22-match campaign, with the top four teams closing ranks to contest the title and the other eight being split into two relegation groups.

The plan, however, backfired. Not through any inherent structural flaws, but simply because one of the teams in the top group, F91 Dudelange, proved vastly superior to the others, romping home to the first title in their history with unseemly haste thanks to five wins and a draw in those extra half-dozen fixtures.

It was in the fifth of those matches, a 4-2 victory over outgoing champions Jeunesse Esch, that Dudelange sealed their historic triumph. It was quite an achievement for a club which had been formed just nine years earlier (from a merger of CS Alliance, CS Stade and US Dudelange) and which, even after finishing the regular season in second place, on goal difference, had been generally regarded as the outsiders for the play-offs.

It had been decided during the winter break that that the club's coaching duo of Angelo Fiorucci and Damon Damiani would be replaced at the end of the season by national team record cap-holder Carlo Weis, from Avenir Beggen, but any dressing-room unrest

TOP SCORERS

26	Marcel CHRISTOPHE (FC Mondercange)
20	Frédéric CICCHIRILLO (Sporting Mertzig)
19	Philippe DILLMANN (US Rumelange)
17	Franco IOVINO (FC Wiltz 71)
16	Daniel HUSS (CS Grevenmacher)
14	Marc DELAZZER (CS Hobscheid)
12	Stefano FANELLI (F91 Dudelange)
	Ahmed EL AOUAD (CS Hobscheid)
	Georges TSAPANOS (Sporting Mertzig)
11	Benoît LAHERY (Union Luxembourg)
10	Paolo AMODIO (Jeunesse Esch)

LEAGUE CHAMPIONSHIP RESULTS 99/00

First Phase

		1	2	3	4	5	6	7	8	9	10	11	12
1	Aris Bonnevoie		0-1	0-2	1-1	0-4	0-2	2-4	2-3	4-3	1-2	0-2	0-1
2	Avenir Beggen	4-0		1-1	1-2	0-1	1-0	0-0	2-1	2-0	2-0	1-1	2-0
3	F91 Dudelange	3-0	1-1		1-1	2-1	1-1	3-0	1-0	3-0	2-2	0-2	3-1
4	CS Grevenmacher	3-0	3-1	2-2		1-1	0-0	4-0	4-0	2-1	2-0	0-3	2-2
5	CS Hobscheid	7-1	1-3	1-2	0-3		1-1	2-1	4-1	2-1	1-1	1-0	0-0
6	Jeunesse Esch	2-0	2-1	0-0	1-2	2-1		2-2	2-1	3-1	2-3	1-1	2-1
7	FC Mondercange	6-0	0-2	4-2	0-3	3-0	2-3		4-2	4-2	1-3	1-1	1-2
8	US Rumelange	1-0	0-2	1-1	1-0	0-4	2-2	3-0		2-1	1-1	3-0	3-2
9	FC Schifflange 95	3-0	1-2	1-0	1-1	1-3	0-2	0-1	1-2		1-0	1-1	2-2
10	Sporting Mertzig	4-2	3-0	1-2	1-0	1-0	1-2	0-0	4-0	1-0		0-1	5-1
11	Union Luxembourg	1-1	2-1	0-2	1-1	0-0	2-1	3-0	1-1	2-3	3-0		1-1
12	FC Wiltz 71	5-0	0-2	0-2	0-5	2-0	3-3	6-1	0-0	0-0	1-2	4-1	

Championship Group	1	2	3	4
1 Avenir Beggen		2-3	0-2	2-2
2 F91 Dudelange	5-1		1-1	4-2
3 CS Grevenmacher	0-1	2-3		0-2
4 Jeunesse Esch	5-1	1-2	2-2	

Relegation Group A	1	2	3	4
1 CS Hobscheid		3-0	2-1	4-2
2 FC Schifflange 95	2-0		2-1	3-1
3 Sporting Mertzig	10-3	4-5		0-3
4 FC Wiltz 71	2-4	0-2	3-1	

Relegation Group B	1	2	3	4
1 Aris Bonnevoie		3-2	2-1	3-2
2 FC Mondercange	5-1		6-1	1-1
3 US Rumelange	4-2	0-1		2-1
4 Union Luxembourg	1-2	0-3	0-0	

LEAGUE CHAMPIONSHIP FINAL TABLES 99/00

First Phase		Pd	Home W	D	L	F	A	Away W	D	L	F	A	Total W	D	L	F	A	Pt	GD
1	CS Grevenmacher	22	6	4	1	23	10	5	4	2	19	8	11	8	3	42	18	41	24
2	F91 Dudelange	22	6	4	1	20	9	5	4	2	16	11	11	8	3	36	20	41	16
3	Avenir Beggen	22	6	3	2	16	6	6	1	4	16	13	12	4	6	32	19	40	13
4	Jeunesse Esch	22	6	3	2	19	13	4	5	2	17	13	10	8	4	36	26	38	10
5	Sporting Mertzig	22	7	1	3	21	8	4	3	4	14	17	11	4	7	35	25	37	10
6	Union Luxembourg	22	4	5	2	16	11	4	4	3	13	12	8	9	5	29	23	33	6
7	CS Hobscheid	22	5	3	3	20	14	4	2	5	15	12	9	5	8	35	26	32	9
8	US Rumelange	22	6	3	2	17	13	2	2	7	11	25	8	5	9	28	38	29	-10
9	FC Wiltz 71	22	4	3	4	21	16	2	4	5	13	21	6	7	9	34	37	25	-3
10	FC Mondercange	22	5	1	5	26	20	2	3	6	9	25	7	4	11	35	45	25	-10
11	FC Schifflange 95	22	3	3	5	12	14	1	1	9	12	25	4	4	14	24	39	16	-15
12	Aris Bonnevoie	22	1	1	9	10	25	0	1	10	4	39	1	2	19	14	64	5	-50

Play-offs Championship Group		Pd	Home W	D	L	F	A	Away W	D	L	F	A	Total W	D	L	F	A	Pt	GD
1	F91 Dudelange	28	8	5	1	30	13	8	4	2	24	16	16	9	3	54	29	57	25
2	CS Grevenmacher	28	6	4	4	25	16	6	6	2	24	11	12	10	6	49	27	46	22
3	Jeunesse Esch	28	7	4	3	27	18	5	6	3	23	19	12	10	6	50	37	46	13
4	Avenir Beggen	28	6	4	4	20	13	7	1	6	19	23	13	5	10	39	36	44	3

Relegation Group A		Pd	W	D	L	F	A	W	D	L	F	A	W	D	L	F	A	Pt	GD
1	CS Hobscheid	28	8	3	3	29	17	5	2	7	22	26	13	5	10	51	43	44	8
2	Sporting Mertzig	28	8	1	5	35	19	4	3	7	17	24	12	4	12	52	43	40	9
3	FC Wiltz 71	28	5	3	6	26	23	3	4	7	19	28	8	7	13	45	51	31	-6
4	FC Schifflange 95	28	6	3	5	19	16	3	1	10	19	32	9	4	15	38	48	31	-10

Relegation Group B		Pd	W	D	L	F	A	W	D	L	F	A	W	D	L	F	A	Pt	GD
1	FC Mondercange	28	7	2	5	38	23	4	3	7	15	28	11	5	12	53	51	38	2
2	US Rumelange	28	8	3	3	23	17	2	3	9	13	33	10	6	12	36	50	36	-14
3	Union Luxembourg	28	4	6	4	17	16	4	5	5	17	18	8	11	9	34	34	35	0
4	Aris Bonnevoie	28	4	1	9	18	30	1	1	12	9	49	5	2	21	27	79	17	-52

this decision might have caused was rarely evident as the team got to grips with their title challenge in impressive fashion, losing just one of their 17 league games after the turn of the year. Players and management stayed focussed even after a shock exit from the Cup, and with key players like strikers Florim Alijaj and Stefano Fanelli, skipper Marco Morgante and ex-national team goalkeeper Paul Koch all coming strong at the end, Dudelange proved themselves to be more than worthy champions.

Grevenmacher, the eternal bridesmaids, rolled home in a distant second place. Had the old 22-match system been retained, they would have been champions for the first time. But, as it was, they buckled once again under the pressure of being leaders. Three home defeats in succession during the play-offs soon unravelled their challenge.

Jeunesse Esch, the champions in each of the previous five seasons, also surrendered in meek fashion, losing both play-off games to Dudelange. They struggled to adapt to life under their new French coach Eric Brusco, who had replaced serial title-winner Alex Pecqueur at the start of the campaign and promptly led the club to their heaviest-ever defeat in Europe - 0-8 away to Skonto Riga. Jeunesse's season was rescued by a successful defence of

NATIONAL TEAM RESULTS 99/00

04/09/99	England (ECQ)	A	Wembley	0-6	
08/09/99	Sweden (ECQ)	H	Luxembourg	0-1	
10/10/99	Bulgaria (ECQ)	A	Sofia	0-3	
23/02/00	Northern Ireland	H	Luxembourg	1-3	Cardoni (41)
26/04/00	Estonia	H	Luxembourg	1-1	Vanek (90)
07/06/00	Spain	H	Luxembourg	0-1	

EUROPEAN CUPS 99/00

CHAMPIONS' CUP
● JEUNESSE ESCH
Preliminary round 1 SKONTO RIGA (LAT)
H 0-2
  Van Rijswijck, Lamborelle, Schauls, Meylender (Wagner 77), Schaack, Borbiconi, Divoy (Pace 73), Kurtz, Cardoni, Amodio, Morocutti (Braun 55).
A 0-8
  Felgen, Thill, Schaack, Lamborelle, Schauls (Laruell 24), Wagner, Divoy (Sabotic 55), Kurtz (Pace 63), Amodio, Cardoni, Braun.

UEFA CUP
● F91 DUDELANGE
Qualifying round HAJDUK SPLIT (CRO)
A 0-5
  Koch, Kaba, Galli, Funck, Gomes, Ubaldini, Ganser (Barnabo 67), Cangini, Alijaj (Kabongo 53), Morgante (Ngindon 72), Balenga.
H 1-1 Kabongo (49)
  Koch, Posing (Balenga 56), Galli, Kaba, Ubaldini, Gomes, Funck, Barnabo (Morgante 77), Fanelli (Alijaj 68), Kabongo, Cangini.

● FC MONDERCANGE
Qualifying round DINAMO BUCURESTI (ROM)
H 2-6 Christophe (38), Neves (90)
  Scherer, Fogel, Minault, Ferrassini (Neves 69), Sorcinelli, Makoumbou, Deville, De Sousa, Biver (Schiltz 84), Christophe, Yagoub (Braun 69).
A 0-7
  Schaber, Ferrassini (Sorcinelli 46; Sannipoli 76), Fogel, Minault, Deville, Makoumbou, Biver, De Sousa, Neves, Braun (Yagoub 46), Christophe.

the Luxembourg Cup. The final was virtually a remake of the previous season's encounter, with FC Mondercange once again playing the role of outplayed outsiders in a heavy defeat. It was a wonderful day in particular for Jeunesse's long-serving captain, libero Marc Lamborelle, who helped himself to a hat-trick in the 4-1 win.

Paul Philipp's national team continued their gradual rejuventaion process, with younger elements such as Manou Schauls, Daniel Huss and goalkeeper Alija Besic all being introduced during the course of the season. With Marc Birsens retiring, the next most-capped international, Jeff Saibene, of second division side Swift Hesperange, was appointed as the new skipper. He, together with play-maker Manuel Cardoni, Bundesliga pro Jeff Strasser and the domestic league's leading marksman Marcel Christophe, will have the responsibility of steering Luxembourg through a tough World Cup qualifying ordeal. Despite an encouraging warm-up game at home to Spain, Philipp's men will have difficulty avoiding a repeat of the Euro 2000 campaign, which, as expected, brought nothing but defeats.

INTERNATIONAL HONOURS

European Championship: 1964

DOMESTIC CUP 99/00

SECOND ROUND
FC Victoria Rosport 4, FC Minerva Lintgen 2
Titus Lamadelaine 0, Union Luxembourg 3
FC Bastendorf 0, Swift Hesperange 10
AS Hosingen 0, CS Grevenmacher 5
Union Sportive Schouweiler 0, Etzella Ettelbruck 2
US Feulen 0, Spora Luxembourg 3
Résidence Walferdange 0, Young Boys Diekirch 5
Sporting Beckerich 0, SC Tétange 2
Atert Bissen 2, Progrès Niedercorn 6
Jeunesse Junglinster 0, FC Mondercange 2
FC Beles 0, Jeunesse Esch 3
Orania Vianden 0, CS Pétange 3
US Bous 1, US Rumelange 3
Union Mertert/Wasserbillig 0, Koeppchen Wormeldange 3
AS Luxembourg 0, FC Wiltz 4
Red Star Merl/Belair 0, FC Schifflange 1
US Rambrouch 0, CS Hollerich 4
US Sandweiler 0, FC Rodange 6
Avenir Flaxweiler 0, Avenir Beggen 11
AS Differdange 1, CS Hobscheid 3 (aet)
Racing Heiderscheid/Eschdorf 1, FC Hamm 2
Tricolore Gasperich 5, RM 86 Luxembourg 3 (after pens.)
Olympique Eischen 5, Etoile Sportive Clemency 4 (after pens.)
FC Lorentzweiler 1, Daring Echternach 2
US Reisdorf 4, AS Wincrange 1
US Folschette 0, Blue Boys Mühlenbach 5
Racing Troisvierges 4, Old Boys Consdorf 1
Red Boys Differdange 2, Green Boys Harlange/Tarchamps 3
Berdenia Berbourg 2, AS Pratzerthal 3
Sporting-Club Ell 0, F91 Dudelange 8
FC Perlé 0, UN Kuachjéng 6

1/16 FINALS
Etzella Ettelbruck 1, Spora Luxembourg 2
SC Tétange 0, FC Rodange 5
Daring Echternach 0, Union Luxembourg 3
AS Pratzerthal 2, Sporting Mertzig 14
Koeppchen Wormeldange 0, FC Wiltz 1
Olympique Eischen 0, Jeunesse Esch 5
Blue Boys Mühlenbach 1, FC Schifflange 0
FC Victoria Rosport 1, Avenir Beggen 2
Green Boys Harlange/Tarchamps 2, CS Hollerich 3 (aet)
Racing Troisvierges 5, UN Kuachjéng 4 (after pens.)
US Reisdorf 3, Progrès Niedercorn 2
FC Hamm 0, CS Grevenmacher 1
CS Hobscheid 8, US Rumelange 2 (aet)
Swift Hesperange 3, Young Boys Diekirch 4 (after pens.)
CS Pétange 0, F91 Dudelange 2
Tricolore Gasperich 1, FC Mondercange 6

1/8 FINALS
FC Rodange 5, US Reisdorf 1
Racing Troisvierges 2, Young Boys Diekirch 3
F91 Dudelange 3, Blue Boys Mühlenbach 5 (after pens.)
Sporting Mertzig 2, CS Hobscheid 0
Jeunesse Esch 6, FC Wiltz 0
Avenir Beggen 0, CS Grevenmacher 1

Union Luxembourg 4, FC Mondercange 5 (after pens.)
CS Hollerich 1, Spora Luxembourg 4

QUARTER-FINALS
Spora Luxembourg 0, Jeunesse Esch 1 (Lamborelle 89)
FC Rodange 1 (Tinant 61p),
FC Mondercange 2 (Christophe 30, De Sousa 79)
Young Boys Diekirch 0,
CS Grevenmacher 1 (Schneider 78)
Blue Boys Mühlenbach 0, Sporting Mertzig 6 (Cicchirillo 19, 56, 57 p, 84, Nekaa 46, Breckler 82)

SEMI-FINALS
Jeunesse Esch 2 (Divoy 65, Amodio 74),
CS Grevenmacher 1 (Alverdi 88)
Sporting Mertzig 0, FC Mondercange 3
(Christophe 56, De Sousa 61, Schiltz 70)

FINAL
26/05/2000, Luxembourg
JEUNESSE ESCH 4 Lamborelle (16, 27p, 71), Morocutti (86)
FC MONDERCANGE 1 Christophe (84)
referee - Gross
JEUNESSE ESCH - Felgen, Lamborelle, Schaack, Schauls, Thill (Kurtz 81), Sabotic, Meylender (Wagner 78), Cardoni, Scuto, Neis (Morocutti 83), Amodio.
FC MONDERCANGE - Scherer, Schiltz, Minault (Sannipoli 81), Sorcinelli, Ferrassini (Yagoub 55), Fogel, Deville, Neves, Biver (Braun E. 76), De Sousa, Christophe.

NATIONAL TEAM APPEARANCES 99/00

Coach - Paul PHILIPP	ENG	SWE	BUL	NIR	EST	ESP	Cps	Gls
Philippe FELGEN (08/10/75) - Jeunesse Esch	G	G	G				8	-
Marc BIRSENS (17/09/66) - Union Luxembourg	D	D	D	M6			54	1
Nico FUNCK (17/10/72) - F91 Dudelange	D	D					10	-
Manou SCHAULS (13/02/72) - Jeunesse Esch	D	D	D			D	4	-
Ralph FERRON (13/05/72) - Etzella Ettelbruck	D					D	18	-
Jean VANEK (19/01/69) - Avenir Beggen	M	D	D	D	D	D	31	2
Patrick POSING (09/09/71) - F91 Dudelange	M82	M	M58		s56		15	-
Jeff SAIBENE (13/09/68) - Swift Hesperange	M	M87	M	M	D	D	52	-
Sacha SCHNEIDER (23/06/72) - CS Grevenmacher	M46	M46		M46	M46	M	9	-
Dany THEIS (11/09/67) - Spora Luxembourg	M	s72	s70				28	-
Marcel CHRISTOPHE (19/08/74) - FC Mondercange	A62	A	A	s46	s46	A73	13	1
Christian ALVERDI (05/11/73) - CS Grevenmacher	s46	M72	M70	s6			8	-
Mikhail ZARITSKI (03/10/73) - Ayos Nikolaos (GRE)	s62	s46	A	s60		s73	9	-
Frank DEVILLE (12/08/70) - FC Mondercange	s82		s58	M			27	-
Jeff STRASSER (05/10/74) - 1.FC Kaiserslautern (GER)		D	D	D	M	M	30	-
Luc HOLTZ (14/06/69) - Etzella Ettelbruck		s87	s86	M75	M	M88	37	1
Manuel CARDONI (22/09/72) - Jeunesse Esch			M86	M	M	M	37	3
Alija BESIC (30/03/75) - Union Luxembourg				G	G	G	3	-
Roland SCHAACK (07/07/73) - Jeunesse Esch				D	D		2	-
Gordon BRAUN (25/05/77) - Jeunesse Esch				A60	s78		5	-
Daniel HUSS (08/10/79) - CS Grevenmacher				s75	A78		2	-
Claude REITER (02/07/81) - Union Luxembourg					D		1	-
René PETERS (15/06/81) - R Standard Liège (BEL)					M56	s88	2	-
Laurent DEVILLE (24/11/67) - Union Luxembourg						D	9	-

PROMOTED CLUBS 99/00

SECOND DIVISION FINAL TABLE

		Pd	W	D	L	F	A	Pt	GD
1	Etzella Ettelbruck	26	20	3	3	79	24	63	55
2	FC Rodange 91	26	19	3	4	61	24	60	37
3	Young Boys Diekirch	26	19	2	5	59	21	59	38
4	Swift Hesperange	26	14	5	7	53	32	47	21
5	Spora Luxembourg	26	13	6	7	50	35	45	15
6	Koeppchen Wormeldange	26	9	8	9	45	41	35	4
7	CS Pétange	26	8	8	10	40	39	32	1
8	FC Hamm 37	26	8	8	10	42	52	32	-10
9	CS Hollerich	26	9	4	13	40	45	31	-5
10	Progrès Niedercorn	26	8	4	14	38	48	28	-10
11	UN Khäerjhéng 97	26	5	9	12	34	66	24	-32
12	Fola Esch	26	4	6	16	25	62	18	-37
13	SC Tétange	26	2	10	14	22	62	16	-40
14	RM 86 Luxembourg	26	2	8	16	24	61	14	-37

CLUB DIRECTORIES

FC Etzella Ettelbruck
BP 183, 9002 Ettelbruck
tel - 817674
fax - 818209
Year of Formation - 1917
President - Jean-Pierre Gauthier
Secretary - Jean Goetzinger
Coach - Luc Holtz
Stadium - Deich (5,000)

FC Rodange 91
177 rue du Clopp, 4810 Rodange
tel - 500427
fax - 505190
Year of Formation - 1991
President - Romain Rosenfeld
Secretary - Jean Hoffmann
Coach - Daniel Alverdi
Stadium - Jos Philippart (4,000)

ARIS BONNEVOIE

CLUB DIRECTORY

FC Aris Bonnevoie
14 rue des Prés, 2349 Luxembourg
tel - 485998
fax - 408922
Year of Formation - 1922
President - Laurent Mosar
Secretary - André Friedrich
Coach - Jean-Claude Wagener; Maurice Spitoni
Stadium - Camille Polfer (3,500)

MAJOR HONOURS
League Championship - (3) 1964, 1966, 1972.
Domestic Cup - (1) 1967.

APPEARANCES 99/00

	P	Ap	(s)	Gls
Carlo ANTONICELLI	M	6	(5)	
Alain BOJKOVSKI	M		(2)	
Marc CHAUSSY	D	23	(1)	2
Claude CONTER	M	18	(5)	4
João CRUZ (POR)	A	5	(2)	
David EYSCHEN	D	13	(9)	
Sydney FERREIRA (BRA)	D	22	(1)	1
Norbert HOOR (GER)	D	22		
Alain HOSCHEID	A	15	(1)	1
José JIMENEZ	M	10	(3)	1
Wolf-Peter KLOHE (GER)	M		(4)	
Patrick LEOGRANDE	D	13	(6)	
Frank LESSURE	D	22		5
Tomasz LIGENZA (POL)	M	7	(13)	
António LOPES (POR)	A	3	(2)	
Luc MISCHO	A	25		7
Adis OMEROVIC	A	19	(5)	1
Franklin PEREIRA	M	13	(6)	4
Roby REILAND	M	5	(1)	
Marc REUTER	G	28		
Marc SCHODER	D	16	(3)	
Haxhe SHALA (YUG)	M	23	(2)	1
Luís Filipe SOARES (POR)	M		(3)	

LEAGUE RESULTS 1999/2000

18/08/99	CS Grevenmacher	H	1-1	Chaussy
22/08/99	Sporting Mertzig	A	2-4	Shala, Mischo
19/09/99	Jeunesse Esch	H	0-2	
22/09/99	Avenir Beggen	A	0-4	
26/09/99	Union Luxembourg	H	0-2	
24/10/99	US Rumelange	H	2-3	Conter, Ferreira
31/10/99	FC Wiltz 71	A	0-5	
07/11/99	CS Hobscheid	H	0-4	
14/11/99	FC Mondercange	A	0-6	
21/11/99	FC Schifflange 95	H	4-3	Mischo, Jimenez, Omerovic, Pereira
28/11/99	F91 Dudelange	A	0-3	
13/02/00	CS Grevenmacher	A	0-3	
19/02/00	Jeunesse Esch	A	0-2	
27/02/00	Avenir Beggen	H	0-1	
04/03/00	Union Luxembourg	A	1-1	Lessure
12/03/00	US Rumelange	A	0-1	
19/03/00	FC Wiltz 71	H	0-1	
22/03/00	Sporting Mertzig	H	1-2	Pereira
26/03/00	CS Hobscheid	A	1-7	Lessure (p)
02/04/00	FC Mondercange	H	2-4	Mischo, Lessure (p)
09/04/00	FC Schifflange 95	A	0-3	
16/04/00	F91 Dudelange	H	0-2	
29/04/00	Union Luxembourg	H	3-2	Lessure 2, Conter
03/05/00	FC Mondercange	A	1-5	Conter
07/05/00	US Rumelange	H	2-1	Mischo, Chaussy (p)
14/05/00	Union Luxembourg	A	2-1	Pereira 2
18/05/00	FC Mondercange	H	3-2	Mischo, Conter, Hoscheid
21/05/00	US Rumelange	A	2-4	Mischo 2

AVENIR BEGGEN

CLUB DIRECTORY

FC Avenir Beggen
BP 25, 7201 Walferdange
tel - 787186 / fax - 787060
Year of Formation - 1915
President - Théo Mersch
Secretary - Marc Peters
Coach - Carlo Weis (00/01 - Vinicio Monacelli)
Stadium - Henri Dunant (5,500)

MAJOR HONOURS
League Championship - (6)
1969, 1982, 1984, 1986, 1993, 1994.
Domestic Cup - (6)
1983, 1984, 1987, 1992, 1993, 1994.

APPEARANCES 99/00

	P	Ap	(s)	Gls
Christophe BOULARD (FRA)	M	13		
Serge CARDONI	D	15	(7)	
Cláudio DA LUZ (POR)	A		(8)	
Lionel DA SILVA	D	12	(3)	1
Eric DELOBEL (FRA)	M	23	(1)	5
Jean-Philippe FACQUES (FRA)	D	28		1
Frank GOERGEN	D	5	(9)	
Alberto GOMES	D	1	(2)	
Kevin HARTERT	G	13		
Jérôme HELLER	A		(1)	
Kiuda KIVUNGHE (BEL)	A	12	(4)	7
Nico KONSBRÜCK	G	15		
Frédéric LARICCIA (FRA)	D	26		1
José LLAMAS	A	16	(7)	6
Gabriel LOPES (POR)	M	13	(8)	3
Aldino MEDINA (POR)	A	14		7
André MERGEN	M	9	(9)	1
Grégory MOLITOR	M	20	(1)	
Claude OTTELE	D	20	(1)	
Jean VANEK	D	26		6
Carlo WEIS	D	14		1
Hervé WETZ (FRA)	M	13		

LEAGUE RESULTS 1999/2000

18/08/99	Sporting Mertzig	H	2-0	Kivunghe 2
22/08/99	Jeunesse Esch	A	1-2	Llamas
22/09/99	Aris Bonnevoie	H	4-0	Vanek 2, Llamas, Kivunghe
26/09/99	US Rumelange	A	2-0	Kivunghe, Mergen
20/10/99	Union Luxembourg	H	1-1	Lopes
24/10/99	FC Wiltz 71	H	2-0	Kivunghe 2
31/10/99	CS Hobscheid	A	3-1	Delobel, Llamas, Kivunghe
07/11/99	FC Mondercange	H	0-0	
14/11/99	FC Schifflange 95	A	2-1	Vanek (p), Llamas
21/11/99	F91 Dudelange	H	1-1	Lopes
27/11/99	CS Grevenmacher	A	1-3	Llamas
13/02/00	Sporting Mertzig	A	0-3	
19/02/00	Union Luxembourg	A	1-2	Lariccia
27/02/00	Aris Bonnevoie	A	1-0	Weis
04/03/00	US Rumelange	H	2-1	Vanek, Medina
12/03/00	FC Wiltz 71	A	2-0	Medina, Delobel
19/03/00	CS Hobscheid	H	0-1	
22/03/00	Jeunesse Esch	H	1-0	Facques
26/03/00	FC Mondercange	A	2-0	Medina, Da Silva
02/04/00	FC Schifflange 95	H	2-0	Medina, Lopes
09/04/00	F91 Dudelange	A	1-1	Medina
16/04/00	CS Grevenmacher	H	1-2	Delobel
30/04/00	Jeunesse Esch	H	2-2	Delobel, Vanek
03/05/00	CS Grevenmacher	A	1-0	Medina
07/05/00	F91 Dudelange	A	1-5	Medina
13/05/00	Jeunesse Esch	A	1-5	Delobel
18/05/00	CS Grevenmacher	H	0-2	
21/05/00	F91 Dudelange	H	2-3	Llamas, Vanek (p)

F91 DUDELANGE

CLUB DIRECTORY

F91 Dudelange
BP 287
3403 Dudelange
tel - 514267
fax - 516269
Year of Formation - 1991
President - Romain Schumacher
Secretary - Théo Fellerich
Coach - Angelo Fiorucci & Damon Damiani
Stadium - Jos Nosbaum (5,300)

MAJOR HONOURS
Leaguue Championship - (1) 2000.

APPEARANCES 99/00

	P	Ap	(s)	Gls
Florim ALIJAJ (YUG)	A	21	(6)	7
Henri BALENGA (DRC)	A	4	(3)	1
Cosimo BARNABO	A	18	(9)	6
Christian BERCHEM	M		(1)	
David CANGINI (FRA)	M	24		2
Rico CARDONI	M	2	(3)	
Mauro CASTELLANI	G		(1)	
Stefano FANELLI	A	15	(5)	12
Nico FUNCK	D	12	(12)	1
Marco GALLI (FRA)	D	24		
Claude GANSER	M	14	(8)	1
Manuel GOMES (FRA)	D	21	(2)	
Michael KABA (FRA)	D	25	(1)	
Evariste KABONGO (BEL)	A	26	(1)	7
Paul KOCH	G	28		
Marco MORGANTE (FRA)	M	26		6
Caliste NGNINDON (FRA)	D		(4)	
Gilles PARASCH	M	2	(14)	
Patrick POSING	D	25		7
Jérôme RAUS	D		(3)	
Patrick UBALDINI (FRA)	D	21	(1)	2
Luc WEYLAND	D		(6)	

LEAGUE RESULTS 1999/2000

18/08/99	US Rumelange	A	1-1	Kabongo
22/08/99	FC Wiltz 71	H	3-1	og (Kharoubi), Balenga, Barnabo
19/09/99	CS Hobscheid	A	2-1	Barnabo, Fanelli
22/09/99	FC Mondercange	H	3-0	Cangini, Posing, Morgante
26/09/99	FC Schifflange 95	A	0-1	
24/10/99	Union Luxembourg	H	0-2	
31/10/99	CS Grevenmacher	H	1-1	Morgante (p)
07/11/99	Sporting Mertzig	A	2-1	Posing, Morgante
14/11/99	Jeunesse Esch	H	1-1	Posing
21/11/99	Avenir Beggen	A	1-1	Ubaldini
28/11/99	Aris Bonnevoie	H	3-0	Fanelli 2, Ubaldini
13/02/00	US Rumelange	H	1-0	Kabongo
19/02/00	CS Hobscheid	H	2-1	Fanelli, Barnabo
27/02/00	FC Mondercange	A	2-4	Fanelli 2
04/03/00	FC Schifflange 95	H	3-0	Kabongo, Fanelli, Posing
12/03/00	Union Luxembourg	A	2-0	Alijaj, Kabongo
19/03/00	CS Grevenmacher	A	2-2	Kabongo, Ganser
22/03/00	FC Wiltz 71	A	2-0	Barnabo, Posing
26/03/00	Sporting Mertzig	H	2-2	Barnabo, Funck
02/04/00	Jeunesse Esch	A	0-0	
09/04/00	Avenir Beggen	H	1-1	Morgante
16/04/00	Aris Bonnevoie	A	2-0	Kabongo, Alijaj
30/04/00	CS Grevenmacher	H	1-1	Alijaj
03/05/00	Jeunesse Esch	A	2-1	Posing, Alijaj
07/05/00	Avenir Beggen	H	5-1	Alijaj 2, Morgante 2, Fanelli
14/05/00	CS Grevenmacher	A	3-2	Fanelli 2, Cangini
17/05/00	Jeunesse Esch	H	4-2	Fanelli 2, Alijaj, Kabongo
21/05/00	Avenir Beggen	A	3-2	Posing, og (Lariccia), Barnabo

CS GREVENMACHER

CLUB DIRECTORY

Club Sportif Grevenmacher
3 rue de la Congrégation
1352 Luxembourg
tel - 4782636
fax - 466212
Year of Formation - 1909
President - Jos Ronk
Secretary - Norry Stoltz
Coach - Michel Clement; Joé Hansen
(00/01 - Carlo Weis)
Stadium - Op Flohr (4,500)

MAJOR HONOURS
Domestic Cup - (2) 1995, 1998.

APPEARANCES 99/00

	P	Ap	(s)	Gls
Christian ALVERDI	M	22		2
Lidio ALVES SILVA (POR)	A		(9)	
Tom BAMBERG	M		(2)	
Steve BIRTZ	M	14	(14)	
Frank BUSCHMANN (GER)	D	20		1
Massimo DORMIO	M		(4)	
Claude DUBLIN	M	21	(1)	
Guy ENTRINGER	M	1	(4)	
Bernhard HEINZ (GER)	D	19	(2)	1
Daniel HUSS	A	27		16
Jonathan JOUBERT (FRA)	G	27		
Mario MENDOZA (ARG)	M	28		2
Laurent OLINGER	G	1	(1)	
Thierry PAUK (FRA)	D	23		1
Benoît POUJADE (FRA)	M	8	(2)	
Jan RASTODER	M		(1)	
Marcico RODRIGUES (BEL)	A	22	(1)	9
Sacha SCHNEIDER	M	27		7
Erik SCHRÖDER (GER)	D	10	(6)	
Damian STOKLOSA (GER)	D	17	(3)	2
Serge THILL	A	14	(6)	6
Jadranko ZELENIKA (CRO)	D	7	(11)	

LEAGUE RESULTS 1999/2000

18/08/99	Aris Bonnevoie	A	1-1	Huss
22/08/99	US Rumelange	H	4-0	Thill, Alverdi, Schneider, Huss
18/09/99	FC Wiltz 71	A	5-0	Huss 2, Rodrigues, Thill, Alverdi
22/09/99	CS Hobscheid	H	1-1	Rodrigues
26/09/99	FC Mondercange	A	3-0	Schneider 2, Rodrigues
24/10/99	FC Schifflange 95	H	2-1	Huss, Schneider
31/10/99	F91 Dudelange	A	1-1	Huss
07/11/99	Union Luxembourg	H	0-3	
14/11/99	Sporting Mertzig	H	2-0	Mendoza, Huss
21/11/99	Jeunesse Esch	A	2-1	Rodrigues 2
28/11/99	Avenir Beggen	H	3-1	Huss, Buschmann, Pauk
13/02/00	Aris Bonnevoie	H	3-0	Rodrigues, og (Ferreira), Thill
19/02/00	FC Wiltz 71	H	2-2	Rodrigues, Schneider (p)
27/02/00	CS Hobscheid	A	3-0	Huss 3
04/03/00	FC Mondercange	H	4-0	Schneider, Rodrigues, Huss, Thill
12/03/00	FC Schifflange 95	A	1-1	Thill
19/03/00	F91 Dudelange	H	2-2	Huss, Heinz
22/03/00	US Rumelange	A	0-1	
26/03/00	Union Luxembourg	A	1-1	Thill
01/04/00	Sporting Mertzig	A	0-1	
09/04/00	Jeunesse Esch	H	0-0	
16/04/00	Avenir Beggen	A	2-1	Schneider, Huss
30/04/00	F91 Dudelange	A	1-1	Huss
03/05/00	Avenir Beggen	H	0-1	
07/05/00	Jeunesse Esch	H	0-2	
14/05/00	F91 Dudelange	H	2-3	Stoklosa 2
18/05/00	Avenir Beggen	A	2-0	og (Delobel), Mendoza
21/05/00	Jeunesse Esch	A	2-2	Huss, Rodrigues

CS HOBSCHEID

CLUB DIRECTORY

CS Hobscheid
4 op Eechelter
8366 Hagen
tel - 397540
fax - 390130
Year of Formation - 1932
President - Camille Stockreiser
Secretary - François Kalmes
Coach - Nico Leider
Stadium - Koericherberg (2,400)

APPEARANCES 99/00

	P	Ap	(s)	Gls
Prparin BAFTIJARI (YUG)	D	2	(9)	
Vidak BEJATOVIC (YUG)	D	25	(1)	1
Claude BIVER	D		(8)	
Rhida BOUKHAROUBA (BEL)	M	25		3
Manuel CHANTRE (FRA)	M	20	(5)	
Marc DELAZZER (FRA)	A	21	(2)	14
Boubacar DIALLO (BEL)	D	19	(1)	1
Pascal DOUANE (FRA)	M	6	(1)	1
Ahmed EL AOUAD (MAR)	A	25		12
Alain EVEN	D	28		
Joé FLICK	G	28		
Patrick KARGER	M		(1)	
Enver KELMENDI (YUG)	D	27		3
Claude KOHL	M	23		2
Pierre MANZANGALA (BUR)	D	28		3
Mario MUGE (FRA)	M		(2)	
Timotheo RABICO (POR)	M		(4)	
Patrick SCHMIT	M	1	(4)	
Patrick WELTER	A	1	(4)	
Steve WELTER	A	6	(12)	3
Ahmed ZERROUKI (MAR)	M	23	(2)	8

LEAGUE RESULTS 1999/2000

17/08/99	FC Mondercange	H	2-1	Zerrouki, Delazzer
22/08/99	FC Schifflange 95	A	3-1	Delazzer 2, Zerrouki
19/09/99	F91 Dudelange	H	1-2	El Aouad
22/09/99	CS Grevenmacher	A	1-1	Kelmendi
26/09/99	Sporting Mertzig	H	1-1	Zerrouki
24/10/99	Jeunesse Esch	A	1-2	Zerrouki
31/10/99	Avenir Beggen	H	1-3	Zerrouki
07/11/99	Aris Bonnevoie	A	4-0	Kelmendi 2, Zerrouki, Diallo
14/11/99	US Rumelange	H	4-1	Delazzer 2, El Aouad 2
21/11/99	FC Wiltz 71	A	0-2	
28/11/99	Union Luxembourg	A	0-0	
12/02/00	FC Mondercange	A	0-3	
19/02/00	F91 Dudelange	A	1-2	El Aouad
27/02/00	CS Grevenmacher	H	0-3	
04/03/00	Sporting Mertzig	A	0-1	
12/03/00	Jeunesse Esch	H	1-1	Delazzer
19/03/00	Avenir Beggen	A	1-0	Manzangala
22/03/00	FC Schifflange 95	H	2-1	Kohl, El Aouad
26/03/00	Aris Bonnevoie	H	7-1	Delazzer 3, Boukharouba, Manzangala, Zerrouki, Welter S.
02/04/00	US Rumelange	A	4-0	Delazzer 3, El Aouad
09/04/00	FC Wiltz 71	H	0-0	
16/04/00	Union Luxembourg	H	1-0	Manzangala
29/04/00	FC Wiltz 71	H	4-2	Bejatovic, Kohl, Welter S., Boukharouba
03/05/00	FC Schifflange 95	A	0-2	
07/05/00	Sporting Mertzig	A	3-10	El Aouad 2, Douana
14/05/00	FC Wiltz 71	A	4-2	El Aouad 2, Delazzer 2
18/05/00	FC Schifflange 95	H	3-0	El Aouad 2, Boukharouba
21/05/00	Sporting Mertzig	H	2-1	Zerrouki, Welter S.

JEUNESSE ESCH

CLUB DIRECTORY

AS La Jeunesse d'Esch
BP 45, 4001 Esch-sur-Alzette
tel - 574130 / fax - 543297
Year of Formation - 1907
President - Jean-Pierre Barboni
Secretary - John Fries
Coach - Eric Brusco
Stadium - De la Frontière (7,500)

MAJOR HONOURS
League Championship - (26)
1921, 1937, 1951, 1954, 1958, 1959, 1960,
1963, 1967, 1968, 1970, 1973, 1974, 1975,
1976, 1977, 1980, 1983, 1985, 1987, 1988,
1995, 1996, 1997, 1998, 1999.
Domestic Cup - (12)
1935, 1937, 1946, 1954, 1973, 1974, 1976,
1981, 1988, 1997, 1999, 2000.

APPEARANCES 99/00

	P	Ap	(s)	Gls
Paolo AMODIO	A	24	(1)	10
David BORBICONI (FRA)	M	21		1
Gordon BRAUN	A	15	(5)	4
Manuel CARDONI	M	25		6
Yves DIVOY (BEL)	M	12	(4)	2
Philippe FELGEN	G	17		
Claude KURTZ (FRA)	M	15	(2)	1
Marc LAMBORELLE	D	28		1
Ludovic LARUELL (FRA)	M	15	(6)	2
Claude MEYLENDER	M	19	(3)	3
Patrick MOROCUTTI	A	8	(9)	5
Ludovic NEIS (FRA)	M	15	(8)	9
Carlo PACE	A	7	(9)	
Jérôme PEIFFER	M		(1)	
Ernad SABOTIC (YUG)	A	12	(5)	2
Roland SCHAACK	D	20	(1)	
Manuel SCHAULS	D	12	(1)	2
Denis SCUTO	M	2	(1)	
Johny THILL	D	11	(4)	
John VAN RIJSWIJCK	G	11		
Jean WAGNER	D	19	(4)	

LEAGUE RESULTS 1999/2000

18/08/99	Union Luxembourg	H	1-1	Cardoni
22/08/99	Avenir Beggen	H	2-1	Cardoni, Borbiconi
18/09/99	Aris Bonnevoie	A	2-0	Laruell, Morocutti
22/09/99	US Rumelange	H	2-1	Morocutti 2
26/09/99	FC Wiltz 71	A	3-3	Amodio, Morocutti, Laruell
24/10/99	CS Hobscheid	H	2-1	Morocutti, Braun
31/10/99	FC Mondercange	A	3-2	Amodio 3
07/11/99	FC Schifflange 95	H	3-1	Meylender, Amodio 2
14/11/99	F91 Dudelange	A	1-1	Kurtz
21/11/99	CS Grevenmacher	H	1-2	Lamborelle (p)
28/11/99	Sporting Mertzig	A	2-1	Neis, Sabotic
13/02/00	Union Luxembourg	A	1-2	Cardoni
19/02/00	Aris Bonnevoie	H	2-0	Neis, Amodio
27/02/00	US Rumelange	A	2-2	Cardoni, Braun
04/03/00	FC Wiltz 71	H	2-1	Braun, Neis
12/03/00	CS Hobscheid	A	1-1	Braun
19/03/00	FC Mondercange	H	2-2	Divoy, Meylender
22/03/00	Avenir Beggen	A	0-1	
26/03/00	FC Schifflange 95	A	2-0	Divoy, Cardoni
02/04/00	F91 Dudelange	H	0-0	
09/04/00	CS Grevenmacher	A	0-0	
16/04/00	Sporting Mertzig	H	2-3	Sabotic, Amodio
30/04/00	Avenir Beggen	A	2-2	og (Vanek), Neis
03/05/00	F91 Dudelange	H	1-2	Amodio
07/05/00	CS Grevenmacher	A	2-0	Neis, Schauls
13/05/00	Avenir Beggen	H	5-1	Schauls, Neis 2, Amodio, Meylender
17/05/00	F91 Dudelange	A	2-4	Cardoni, og (Posing)
21/05/00	CS Grevenmacher	H	2-2	Neis 2

FC MONDERCANGE

CLUB DIRECTORY

FC Mondercange
110 Grand-rue
3927 Mondercange
tel - 551375
fax - 559010
Year of Formation - 1933
President - Jean Cazzaro
Secretary - Liane Galasso
Coach - Vinicio Monacelli; Jean-Marie Nürenberg
Stadium - Nouveau Stade (4,500)

APPEARANCES 99/00

	P	Ap	(s)	Gls
Alain BERNARD	M		(3)	
Luc BIVER	M	26	(1)	4
Eric BRAUN	A	13	(15)	3
Marcel CHRISTOPHE	A	25	(2)	26
Dinis DE SOUSA	M	26		7
Frank DEVILLE	M	24	(2)	1
Marc ERBETTA	G		(2)	
Daniel FERRASSINI (FRA)	D	24	(1)	1
Jean-Charles FOGEL (FRA)	D	26	(1)	
David LOHEI	D		(1)	
Serge MAKOUMBOU (FRA)	M	11	(14)	1
Hervé MINAULT (FRA)	D	17		
Arthur NEVES (FRA)	A	23	(5)	2
Patrick ROMITELLI	A		(4)	
Daniel SANNIPOLI	D	14	(2)	1
Fernand SCHABER	G	2		
Sébastien SCHERER (FRA)	G	26		
Ralph SCHILTZ	M	12	(3)	1
Mike SCHUMACHER	D		(2)	
Toni SORCINELLI	D	21	(2)	
Abdel Aziz YAGOUB (FRA)	A	18	(9)	6

LEAGUE RESULTS 1999/2000

17/08/99	CS Hobscheid	A	1-2	Makoumbou
22/08/99	Union Luxembourg	A	0-3	
18/09/99	FC Schifflange 95	H	4-2	Biver 2, De Sousa, Christophe (p)
22/09/99	F91 Dudelange	A	0-3	
26/09/99	CS Grevenmacher	H	0-3	
24/10/99	Sporting Mertzig	A	0-0	
31/10/99	Jeunesse Esch	H	2-3	Biver, Neves
07/11/99	Avenir Beggen	A	0-0	
14/11/99	Aris Bonnevoie	H	6-0	Braun, Neves, Deville, De Sousa,
				Sannipoli, Ferrassini
21/11/99	US Rumelange	A	0-3	
28/11/99	FC Wiltz 71	H	1-2	Christophe
12/02/00	CS Hobscheid	H	3-0	De Sousa 2, Christophe
19/02/00	FC Schifflange 95	A	1-0	Christophe
27/02/00	F91 Dudelange	H	4-2	Christophe 2, Biver, De Sousa
04/03/00	CS Grevenmacher	A	0-4	
11/03/00	Sporting Mertzig	H	1-3	Braun
19/03/00	Jeunesse Esch	A	2-2	Schiltz, Christophe
22/03/00	Union Luxembourg	H	1-1	Christophe
26/03/00	Avenir Beggen	H	0-2	
02/04/00	Aris Bonnevoie	A	4-2	Christophe 2, Yagoub 2
09/04/00	US Rumelange	H	4-2	Yagoub 2, Christophe (p), De Sousa
16/04/00	FC Wiltz 71	A	1-6	Yagoub
30/04/00	US Rumelange	A	1-0	Christophe
03/05/00	Aris Bonnevoie	H	5-1	Christophe 4, Braun
06/05/00	Union Luxembourg	A	3-0	Christophe 2, Yagoub
14/05/00	US Rumelange	H	6-1	Christophe 5, De Sousa
18/05/00	Aris Bonnevoie	A	2-3	Christophe 2
21/05/00	Union Luxembourg	H	1-1	Christophe (p)

US RUMELANGE

CLUB DIRECTORY

Union Sportive Rumelange
BP 3
3701 Rumelange
tel - 567382
fax - 567984
Year of Formation - 1908
President - René Minelli
Secretary - Fernand Oswald
Coach - Gérard Jeitz
Stadium - Municipal (3,500)

MAJOR HONOURS
Domestic Cup - (2) 1968, 1974.

APPEARANCES 99/00

	P	Ap	(s)	Gls
David COGNOLI (FRA)	M	3		
Serge DA COSTA	A	27	(1)	4
Cyril DALSTEIN (FRA)	M	27		2
Walter DI CARLO	G	16	(1)	
Philippe DILLMANN (FRA)	A	26	(1)	19
Thierry DI PALMA	M		(1)	
Gérard JEITZ	M		(3)	
Yves JUCHEMES	D	10	(4)	
Frédéric LAMBINET (FRA)	M	23		2
Reinaldo PEREIRA	D	7	(14)	
Franck PETITFRERE (FRA)	M		(3)	
Sven PHILIPPI	D	2	(4)	
Irfan RAMCILOVIC	M		(1)	
Aris RAMDEDOVIC	M		(1)	
Kim ROHMANN	G	1		
Sascha ROHMANN	M	26	(2)	
Albert RUBIO (FRA)	M	20		
Jean-François SALERNO (FRA)	D	28		
Daniel SANTOS	A		(10)	
Miguel SANTOS	M	16		
Dzemal SKENDEROVIC	M	12	(9)	1
Dzevib SKENDEROVIC	M		(7)	
Anthony SOMMEN (FRA)	D	23	(1)	
Fabio TOMASSINI	G	11		
Mauro VAGLI (FRA)	A	10		3
Sylvain WAWRZYNOWICZ (FRA)	D	20		4

LEAGUE RESULTS 1999/2000

18/08/99	F91 Dudelange	H	1-1	Dillmann
22/08/99	CS Grevenmacher	A	0-4	
19/09/99	Sporting Mertzig	H	1-1	Dillmann
22/09/99	Jeunesse Esch	A	1-2	Dillmann (p)
26/09/99	Avenir Beggen	H	0-2	
24/10/99	Aris Bonnevoie	A	3-2	Wawrzynowicz, Lambinet, Dillmann
31/10/99	Union Luxembourg	A	1-1	Da Costa
07/11/99	FC Wiltz 71	H	3-2	Dillmann 2, Wawrzynowicz
14/11/99	CS Hobscheid	A	1-4	Da Costa
21/11/99	FC Mondercange	H	3-0	Dillmann 2, Vagli
28/11/99	FC Schifflange 95	A	2-1	Vagli, Dillmann (p)
13/02/00	F91 Dudelange	A	0-1	
19/02/00	Sporting Mertzig	A	0-4	
27/02/00	Jeunesse Esch	H	2-2	Wawrzynowicz, Dillmann
04/03/00	Avenir Beggen	A	1-2	Dillmann
12/03/00	Aris Bonnevoie	H	1-0	Wawrzynowicz
19/03/00	Union Luxembourg	H	3-0	Dillmann 3
22/03/00	CS Grevenmacher	H	1-0	Dillmann
26/03/00	FC Wiltz 71	A	0-0	
02/04/00	CS Hobscheid	H	0-4	
09/04/00	FC Mondercange	A	2-4	Dalstein 2
16/04/00	FC Schifflange 95	H	2-1	Lambinet, Skenderovic Dzem.
30/04/00	FC Mondercange	H	0-1	
03/05/00	Union Luxembourg	A	0-0	
07/05/00	Aris Bonnevoie	A	1-2	og (Schoder)
14/05/00	FC Mondercange	A	1-6	Vagli
18/05/00	Union Luxembourg	H	2-1	Dillmann 2
21/05/00	Aris Bonnevoie	H	4-2	Da Costa 2, Dillmann 2

FC SCHIFFLANGE 95

CLUB DIRECTORY

FC Schifflange 95
BP 46
3801 Schifflange
tel - 548366
fax - 549744
Year of Formation - 1995
President - Osvaldo Costantini
Secretary - Nico Hansen
Coach - Augusto Dias Martins
(00/01 - Francesco Controguerra)
Stadium - Rue Denis Netgen (3,500)

APPEARANCES 99/00

	P	Ap	(s)	Gls
Philippe CHRISMOUSSE (FRA)	G	28		
Gilberto CORREIA LOPES (POR)	D		(1)	
Renato DA SILVA (POR)	D	24		2
José DALOIA (FRA)	M	7	(3)	
Mike DEL BON	D	14	(7)	
Augusto DIAS MARTINS (POR)	M		(2)	
Paul DIAS MARTINS (POR)	D	19	(4)	1
Eduardo DINIS OLIVEIRA (POR)	M	11	(7)	3
Luc DUARTE	M	3	(10)	
Jean-Paul FARRAJOTA (POR)	D	27		1
Cédric FULAT (FRA)	M	21	(2)	4
Malik HANEL (FRA)	M	6	(7)	1
Paul HUNNEWALD	D	21	(1)	
Marcelo MACHADO (POR)	A	2	(3)	
Sauro MARINELLI	A	5	(1)	1
Davide MATOS (POR)	D	19	(1)	
Telmo MATOS (POR)	D	25		5
Rafik MEDINI (FRA)	A	15		5
Marc MEYERS	A	3	(8)	1
Fahrudin PJANIC (YUG)	M	15		4
Augusto RIVAS CRUZ (POR)	M	2		
Álvaro SILVA DA CRUZ (POR)	M	13	(8)	4
Steve THEODOR	D	9	(8)	
Tanguy WENDLING (FRA)	A	19	(5)	6

LEAGUE RESULTS 1999/2000

18/08/99	FC Wiltz 71	A	0-0	
22/08/99	CS Hobscheid	H	1-3	Pjanic (p)
18/09/99	FC Mondercange	A	2-4	Matos T., Silva Da Cruz
22/09/99	Union Luxembourg	A	3-2	Farrajota, Wendling, Silva Da Cruz
26/09/99	F91 Dudelange	H	1-0	Wendling
24/10/99	CS Grevenmacher	A	1-2	Pjanic
31/10/99	Sporting Mertzig	H	1-0	Da Silva
07/11/99	Jeunesse Esch	A	1-3	Fulat
14/11/99	Avenir Beggen	H	1-2	Marinelli
21/11/99	Aris Bonnevoie	A	3-4	Pjanic 2, Dinis Oliveira
28/11/99	US Rumelange	H	1-2	Silva Da Cruz
13/02/00	FC Wiltz 71	H	2-2	Matos T., Dinis Oliveira
19/02/00	FC Mondercange	H	0-1	
27/02/00	Union Luxembourg	H	1-1	Dias Martins P.
04/03/00	F91 Dudelange	A	0-3	
12/03/00	CS Grevenmacher	H	1-1	Matos T.
19/03/00	Sporting Mertzig	A	0-1	
22/03/00	CS Hobscheid	A	1-2	Meyers
26/03/00	Jeunesse Esch	H	0-2	
02/04/00	Avenir Beggen	A	0-2	
09/04/00	Aris Bonnevoie	H	3-0	Fulat, Silva Da Cruz, Medini
16/04/00	US Rumelange	A	1-2	Wendling
30/04/00	Sporting Mertzig	A	5-4	Medini 2, Matos T., Fulat, Wendling
03/05/00	CS Hobscheid	H	2-0	Matos T., Medini
07/05/00	FC Wiltz 71	H	3-1	Medini, Dinis Oliveira, Hanel
14/05/00	Sporting Mertzig	H	2-1	Fulat, Wendling
18/05/00	CS Hobscheid	A	0-3	
21/05/00	FC Wiltz 71	A	2-0	Wendling, Da Silva

SPORTING MERTZIG

CLUB DIRECTORY

FC Sporting Mertzig
2 rue du Lavoir
9189 Vichten
tel - 889039
fax - 889176
Year of Formation - 1961
President - Norbert Gremling
Secretary - Claude Decker
Coach - Jean Fiedler
Stadium - An de Burwiesen (2,800)

APPEARANCES 99/00

	P	Ap	(s)	Gls
Walter ANTUNEZ (ARG)	M	9	(4)	1
Malik BADJI (BEL)	D	25	(1)	
Abdel BERRIH (FRA)	M	21	(3)	5
Yves BOSSERS	G	8		
Eric BRECKLER (FRA)	M	16	(11)	3
Frédéric CICCHIRILLO (FRA)	A	28		20
Max CLEES	D		(5)	
Claude DIEDERICH	D		(2)	
Laurent ERLINGER (FRA)	M	12	(4)	1
Mário MACHADO (POR)	A	9	(2)	
Claude MAUSEN	G	1		
Jaba MOREIRA (POR)	D	15	(7)	
Kalambay MUTOMBO (DRC)	D	25	(1)	3
Omar NEKAA (BEL)	A	8	(10)	4
Albert POLO (FRA)	G	19		
Sébastien REMY (FRA)	M	23	(1)	1
Laurent ROCHETTE (BEL)	D	23		1
Christian SAVINO	A		(1)	
Paul SIEBENALER	M	1	(5)	
Spencer TAVARES (POR)	M	12	(6)	1
Manuel TEIXEIRA (POR)	M	1		
Laurent THILL (FRA)	D	23	(1)	
Georges TSAPANOS (BEL)	A	15	(11)	12
Philippe VALTELHAS (POR)	D		(2)	
Antoine WELLENREITER (FRA)	D	14	(1)	

LEAGUE RESULTS 1999/2000

18/08/99	Avenir Beggen	A	0-2	
22/08/99	Aris Bonnevoie	H	4-2	Tsapanos 3, Breckler
19/09/99	US Rumelange	A	1-1	Cicchirillo (p)
22/09/99	FC Wiltz 71	H	5-1	Cicchirillo 3, Antunez, Tsapanos
26/09/99	CS Hobscheid	A	1-1	Mutombo
24/10/99	FC Mondercange	H	0-0	
31/10/99	FC Schifflange 95	A	0-1	
07/11/99	F91 Dudelange	H	1-2	Mutombo
14/11/99	CS Grevenmacher	A	0-2	
21/11/99	Union Luxembourg	H	0-1	
28/11/99	Jeunesse Esch	H	1-2	Berrih
13/02/00	Avenir Beggen	H	3-0	Berrih, Nekaa, Tsapanos
19/02/00	US Rumelange	H	4-0	Tsapanos 2, Cicchirillo, Nekaa
27/02/00	FC Wiltz 71	A	2-1	Cicchirillo 2 (1p)
04/03/00	CS Hobscheid	H	1-0	Mutombo
11/03/00	FC Mondercange	A	3-1	Cicchirillo 2, Remy
19/03/00	FC Schifflange 95	H	1-0	Nekaa
22/03/00	Aris Bonnevoie	A	2-1	Berrih, Cicchirillo
26/03/00	F91 Dudelange	A	2-2	Nekaa, Cicchirillo
01/04/00	CS Grevenmacher	H	1-0	Cicchirillo
09/04/00	Union Luxembourg	A	0-3	
16/04/00	Jeunesse Esch	A	3-2	Tsapanos, Rochette, Erlinger
30/04/00	FC Schifflange 95	H	4-5	Cicchirillo 2, Tsapanos 2
03/05/00	FC Wiltz 71	A	1-3	Cicchirillo
07/05/00	CS Hobscheid	H	10-3	Tavares, Cicchirillo 4 (1p),
				Tsapanos, Breckler 2, Berrih 2
14/05/00	FC Schifflange 95	A	1-2	Cicchirillo (p)
18/05/00	FC Wiltz 71	H	0-3	
21/05/00	CS Hobscheid	A	1-2	Tsapanos

UNION LUXEMBOURG

CLUB DIRECTORY

Union Sportive Luxembourg
BP 1614, 1016 Luxembourg
tel - 4383498 / fax - 404747
Year of Formation - 1908
President - Rolphe Reding
Secretary - Kurt Zikes
Coach - Gilbert Neumann; Fernand Braun (00/01 -
Romain Delhalt)
Stadium - Achille Hammerel (6,000)

MAJOR HONOURS
League Championship - (11)
1912, 1914, 1915, 1916, 1917, 1927, 1962,
1971, 1990, 1991, 1992.
Domestic Cup - (10) 1947, 1959, 1963, 1964,
1969, 1970, 1986, 1989, 1991, 1996.

APPEARANCES 99/00

	P	Ap	(s)	Gls
Eugène AFRIKA	D	23	(4)	2
Samuel BLANC	A	1		
Daniel BERNARD	A	6	(6)	
Alija BESIC	G	26		
Marc BIRSENS	D	3		
Ronny BONVINI	M	9	(10)	
Sébastien COGNART (BEL)	M	21	(5)	3
Luciano CRAPA (BEL)	M	16		2
Laurent DEVILLE	D	20	(2)	
Georges FERNANDES	A	9	(8)	4
Pierre GRISIUS	D	14	(1)	2
Fernando GUTIERREZ (ARG)	D	19	(1)	
Steve KOENIG	M	1	(4)	
Yves KOLLWELTER	M	1	(2)	
Marc KUNEN	M	1	(2)	
Benoît LAHERY (FRA)	M	26		11
José MADIMBA (POR)	M		(1)	
Victor MESTRE	D	24		2
Manuel MOROCUTTI	A		(4)	
Francy NANA MBAKOP (FRA)	A	1	(3)	
Laurent PELLEGRINO (FRA)	D	24		
Claude POURCHAUX (FRA)	G	1	(1)	
Claude REITER	D	23		
Arnaud SZYMANSKI (FRA)	A	14	(7)	4
Paulino TAVARES	M	6	(4)	
Luc THIMMESCH	M	18	(9)	3
Olivier UNSEN	G	1	(1)	

LEAGUE RESULTS 1999/2000

18/08/99	Jeunesse Esch	A	1-1	Szymanski
22/08/99	FC Mondercange	H	3-0	Thimmesch, Szymanski, Cognart
22/09/99	FC Schifflange 95	H	2-3	Cognart, Szymanski
26/09/99	Aris Bonnevoie	A	2-0	Lahéry, Szymanski
20/10/99	Avenir Beggen	A	1-1	Grisius
24/10/99	F91 Dudelange	A	2-0	Lahéry 2
31/10/99	US Rumelange	H	1-1	Thimmesch
07/11/99	CS Grevenmacher	A	3-0	Mestre, Afrika, Grisius
14/11/99	FC Wiltz 71	H	1-1	Pellegrino
21/11/99	Sporting Mertzig	A	1-0	Mestre
28/11/99	CS Hobscheid	H	0-0	
13/02/00	Jeunesse Esch	H	2-1	Lahéry (p), Cognart (p)
19/02/00	Avenir Beggen	H	2-1	Fernandes, Crapa
27/02/00	FC Schifflange 95	A	1-1	Lahéry
04/03/00	Aris Bonnevoie	H	1-1	Lahéry
12/03/00	F91 Dudelange	H	0-2	
19/03/00	US Rumelange	A	0-3	
22/03/00	FC Mondercange	A	1-1	Lahéry
26/03/00	CS Grevenmacher	H	1-1	Thimmesch
02/04/00	FC Wiltz 71	A	1-4	Lahéry
09/04/00	Sporting Mertzig	H	3-0	Lahéry 2, Crapa
16/04/00	CS Hobscheid	A	0-1	
29/04/00	Aris Bonnevoie	A	2-3	Lahéry, Fernandes
03/05/00	US Rumelange	H	0-0	
06/05/00	FC Mondercange	H	0-3	
14/05/00	Aris Bonnevoie	H	1-2	Afrika
18/05/00	US Rumelange	A	1-2	Fernandes
21/05/00	FC Mondercange	A	1-1	Fernandes

FC WILTZ 71

CLUB DIRECTORY

FC Wiltz 71
BP 47
9501 Wiltz
tel - 949343
fax - 957391
Year of Formation - 1971
President - John Shinn
Secretary - Jean-Claude Thines
Coach - Albert Adams
(00/01 - Jacques Dodemont)
Stadium - Getzt, Niederwiltz (3,000)

APPEARANCES 99/00

		P	Ap	(s)	Gls
Mohammed AMDA (FRA)	A	9	(12)	3
Emmanuel ANDRIEN (BEL)	G	8	(1)	
Mike CZEKANOWICZ	D	19	(2)	3
Marc ESCHETTE	A		(9)	
Patrick FLICK	M	1	(7)	
Marc GIRA	M	12	(6)	2
Franco IOVINO (BEL)	A	20	(6)	17
Mustapha KHAROUBI (FRA)	M	24		9
David MALANNEE (BEL)	G	20		
Luc MELCHIOR	D	15	(1)	
Asmir MUJKIC	D	1		
Mario MUJKIC	D	1		
Nunzio OLIVIERI (BEL)	M	10		1
Didier PANZOKOU (BEL)	D	24		
Alain PAULY	D	5	(4)	
João PEREIRA	M	22	(2)	4
Thierry ROUYR (BEL)	M	28		
Tom SCHAACK	M	18	(3)	
Dany SCHAMMEL	D	8	(6)	
Chris SPOGEN	A	13	(5)	3
Dan SPOGEN	M	3	(2)	
Pedro TEIXEIRA (POR)	M	23	(2)	1
Maurice VAN HAM (HOL)	M	24		2

LEAGUE RESULTS 1999/2000

18/08/99	FC Schifflange 95	H	0-0	
22/08/99	F91 Dudelange	A	1-3	Iovino
18/09/99	CS Grevenmacher	H	0-5	
22/09/99	Sporting Mertzig	A	1-5	Kharoubi (p)
26/09/99	Jeunesse Esch	H	3-3	Amda, Kharoubi (p), Czekanowicz
24/10/99	Avenir Beggen	A	0-2	
31/10/99	Aris Bonnevoie	H	5-0	Iovino 2, Amda, Spogen C., Olivieri
07/11/99	US Rumelange	A	2-3	Iovino 2
14/11/99	Union Luxembourg	A	1-1	Kharoubi
21/11/99	CS Hobscheid	H	2-0	Iovino 2
28/11/99	FC Mondercange	A	2-1	Spogen C., Iovino
13/02/00	FC Schifflange 95	A	2-2	Van Ham, Kharoubi (p)
19/02/00	CS Grevenmacher	A	2-2	Kharoubi, Iovino
27/02/00	Sporting Mertzig	H	1-2	Iovino
04/03/00	Jeunesse Esch	A	1-2	Spogen C.
12/03/00	Avenir Beggen	H	0-2	
19/03/00	Aris Bonnevoie	A	1-0	Kharoubi
22/03/00	F91 Dudelange	H	0-2	
26/03/00	US Rumelange	H	0-0	
02/04/00	Union Luxembourg	H	4-1	Iovino 2, Kharoubi, Pereira
09/04/00	CS Hobscheid	A	0-0	
16/04/00	FC Mondercange	H	6-1	Kharoubi 2, Iovino 2, Czekanowicz, Gira
29/04/00	CS Hobscheid	A	2-4	Amda, Iovino (p)
03/05/00	Sporting Mertzig	H	3-1	Czekanowicz, Iovino 2
07/05/00	FC Schifflange 95	A	1-3	Van Ham
14/05/00	CS Hobscheid	H	2-4	Pereira 2
18/05/00	Sporting Mertzig	A	3-0	Gira, Teixeira, Pereira
21/05/00	FC Schifflange 95	H	0-2	

MACEDONIA

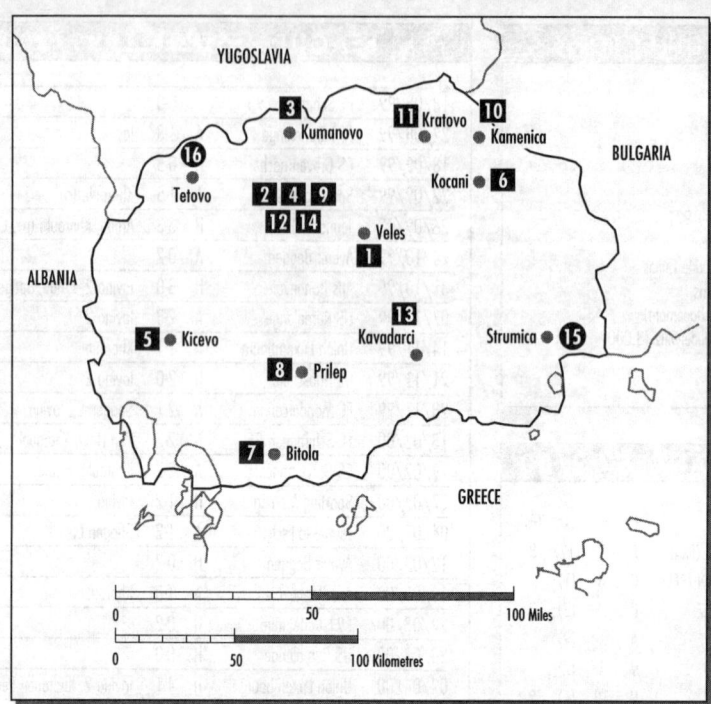

1	BOREC MHK VELES	661
2	CEMENTARNICA 55 SKOPJE	662
3	FK KUMANOVO	663
4	MAKEDONIJA GP SKOPJE	664
5	NAPREDOK KICEVO	665
6	OSOGOVO KOCANI	666
7	PELISTER BITOLA	667
8	POBEDA PRILEP	668
9	RABOTNICKI KOMETAL SKOPJE	669
10	SASA MAKEDONSKA KAMENICA	670
11	SILEKS KRATOVO	671
12	SLOGA JUGOMAGNAT SKOPJE	672
13	TIKVES KAVADARCI	673
14	VARDAR SKOPJE	674
Promoted clubs		
15	BELASICA STRUMICA	
16	SKENDIJA HB TETOVO	

VARDAR PLUMB THE DEPTHS

Sloga Jugomagnat secure the 'double'

FEDERATION DIRECTORY

Macedonian Football Union
8-ma Udarna Brigada 31a, 1000 Skopje

tel - (91) 229042
fax - (91) 235448

Year of Formation - 1909
President - Lambe Arnaudov
Secretary - Nikola Bosalevski

Stadium - Gradski, Skopje (22,000)

For the second season running the Macedonian national championship was dominated by Sloga Jugomagnat Skopje. In fact, their superiority over the rest of the teams was even more pronounced than before. They took the championship by a nine-point victory margin and also won the Cup, thrashing league runners-up Pobeda Prilep 6-0 in the final... played in Prilep.

As with every previous season, the leading club at the halfway stage went on to lift the title. After 13 matches Sloga Jugomagnat were undefeated and four points clear. They stretched their unbeaten run to 23 matches (33 including the previous season's games) and confirmed themselves as champions in the last of those games - a 6-1 victory over Tikves Kavadarci, which was their biggest league win of the campaign.

When Sloga Jugomagnat were finally beaten, a week later, the defeat was emphatic - 4-0 by former champions Sileks Kratovo - but also academic. Gjore Jovanovski's team were evidently saving themselves for the Cup final six days later. It paid off, because they produced their best performance of the season against Pobeda, ramming in five second-half goals, three of them from the league's top scorer Ardzend Beciri.

While Beciri was undoubtedly the team's leading attraction, there were others who had a large say in Sloga Jugomagnat's convincing 'double' triumph. Skipper Nedzmedin Memedi was the driving force in midfield, Saso Zdravevski held things together in defence, and goalkeeper Jane Nikolovski achieved the remarkable feat of going 1111 minutes without conceding a goal at home in the Cair stadium.

The Cup final thrashing was a painful sting in the tail for Pobeda at the end of a season in which they proved to be worthy runners-up, helped along by their Brazilian import Zilson. Third-placed Rabotnicki Kometal Skopje were even more of a surprise. They had only reached the top flight two years earlier yet did enough to join Pobeda in the 2000/01 UEFA Cup.

Macedonia's most popular team, Vardar Skopje, had a disastrous season on all fronts. Annihilated 9-0 on aggregate by Legia Warsaw in the UEFA Cup qualifying round, they fared little better on the domestic scene. They won only seven of their 26 matches and slumped to 10th place. At one stage the club's financial crisis forced the players to go on strike, but by the end of the season they had recovered sufficiently to buy several new players, three of them from champions Sloga Jugomagnat including veteran international Memedi.

LEAGUE CHAMPIONSHIP RESULTS 99/00

		1	2	3	4	5	6	7	8	9	10	11	12	13	14
1	Borec MHK Veles		0-0	2-2	1-0	2-2	4-1	1-2	2-0	1-0	2-1	1-2	0-3	5-1	1-1
2	Cementarnica 55 Skopje	3-1		1-0	2-1	2-0	4-0	3-2	0-0	0-1	1-0	3-1	2-2	1-1	2-0
3	FK Kumanovo	0-3	0-0		0-1	2-2	3-1	1-2	0-2	0-2	1-2	2-0	0-2	0-3	0-8
4	Makedonija GP Skopje	0-0	0-2	4-1		1-0	2-0	1-2	3-1	0-1	2-1	0-0	0-0	3-2	3-1
5	Napredok Kicevo	3-0	0-1	10-0	0-1		1-1	3-3	0-8	1-0	2-0	0-3	0-0	1-1	2-2
6	Osogovo Kocani	2-1	1-4	3-0	2-2	3-1		1-2	0-0	2-0	1-1	2-1	0-2	4-1	1-0
7	Pelister Bitola	3-0	5-1	4-0	2-0	4-1	3-1		2-2	1-0	3-1	3-0	0-2	1-0	1-1
8	Pobeda Prilep	2-0	3-1	6-1	1-0	1-0	2-1	2-0		3-4	4-0	2-0	1-1	4-0	5-2
9	Rabotnicki Kometal Skopje	1-0	3-0	4-0	3-0	4-0	3-1	0-0	1-0		0-2	2-1	0-3	2-1	2-1
10	Sasa Makedonska Kamenica	0-1	1-0	5-1	0-1	1-0	1-1	1-1	1-4			1-1	0-2	1-0	0-2
11	Sileks Kratovo	6-0	2-1	2-0	1-1	1-0	4-2	2-0	2-2	2-2	0-0		4-0	5-0	2-1
12	Sloga Jugomagnat Skopje	4-0	3-1	1-0	2-2	4-0	3-0	1-0	0-0	4-0	3-0	1-0		6-1	2-0
13	Tikves Kavadarci	2-1	1-4	3-2	2-1	0-0	5-3	2-0	1-3	2-0	0-1	3-1	1-3		2-0
14	Vardar Skopje	1-1	1-4	4-0	1-0	3-1	3-0	3-2	1-2	0-2	0-0	0-0	1-1	2-2	

LEAGUE CHAMPIONSHIP FINAL TABLE 99/00

			Home				Away				Total					
		Pd	W	D	L	F	A	W	D	L	F	A	W	D	L	F	A	PT	GD
1	Sloga Jugomagnat Skopje	26	11	2	0	34	4	7	5	1	21	9	18	7	1	55	13	61	42
2	Pobeda Prilep	26	11	1	1	36	10	4	6	3	21	13	15	7	4	57	23	52	34
3	Rabotnicki Kometal Skopje	26	10	1	2	25	9	6	1	6	16	17	16	2	8	41	26	50	15
4	Pelister Bitola	26	10	2	1	32	9	4	3	6	16	21	14	5	7	48	30	47	18
5	Cementarnica 55 Skopje	26	9	3	1	24	9	5	2	6	19	20	14	5	7	43	29	47	14
6	Sileks Kratovo	26	9	4	0	33	9	2	3	8	10	20	11	7	8	43	29	40	14
7	Makedonija GP Skopje	26	7	3	3	19	11	3	3	7	10	17	10	6	10	29	28	36	1
8	Tikves Kavadarci	26	8	1	4	24	19	1	3	9	13	35	9	4	13	37	54	31	-17
9	Borec MHK Veles	26	6	4	3	22	15	2	2	9	8	27	8	6	12	30	42	30	-12
10	Vardar Skopje	26	5	5	3	20	15	2	3	8	19	23	7	8	11	39	38	29	1
11	Sasa Makedonska Kamenica	26	4	4	5	13	15	3	3	7	9	19	7	7	12	22	34	28	-12
12	Osogovo Kocani	26	7	3	3	22	15	0	2	11	12	38	7	5	14	34	53	26	-19
13	Napredok Kicevo	26	4	5	4	23	20	0	3	10	7	28	4	8	14	30	48	20	-18
14	FK Kumanovo	26	2	2	9	9	28	0	1	12	7	49	2	3	21	16	77	9	-61

EUROPEAN CUPS 99/00

CHAMPIONS' CUP
● **SLOGA JUGOMAGNAT SKOPJE**
Preliminary round 1 KAPAZ GANJA (AZB)
H 1-0 Memedi (66)
Jovcev, Colakovic, Omeragic, Zdravevski, Abazi, Arif (Fetai 58), Memedi, Blazevski (Miserdovski 58), Beganovic, Mustafi (Presilski 75), Beciri.
A 1-2 Arif (34)
Jovcev, Colakovic, Omeragic, Zdravevski, Abazi, Arif, Memedi, Blazevski (Fetai 85), Beganovic, Mustafi (Presilski 80), Beciri (Miserdovski 46).

Preliminary round 2 BRØNDBY IF (DEN)
H 0-1
Jovcev, Colakovic, Omeragic, Zdravevski, Abazi, Miserdovski (Fetai 62), Memedi, Beganovic (Presilski 75), Mustafi (Blazevski 62), Arif, Beciri.
A 0-1
Jovcev, Colakovic, Omeragic, Zdravevski, Abazi, Miserdovski, Memedi, Beganovic (Presilski 70), Mustafi (Blazevski 60), Arif (Fetai 62), Beciri.

UEFA CUP
● **SILEKS KRATOVO**
Qualifying round SHAKHTAR DONETSK (UKR)
A 1-3 Gokic (90)
Ugrenovic, Ignatov, Lilic (Spasovski 90), Mitrevski, Gosev (Tanusev 67), Stojkov, Gokic, Kovrlija, Simovski, Ivanov, Gosevski (Trajcev 46).
H 2-1 Ignatov (19p), Simovski (74)
Ugrenovic, Ignatov, Gosevski (Ivanov 78), Lilic (Trajcev 63), Novakov, Mitrevski, Gosev (Tanusev 46), Stojanov, Gokic, Kovrlija, Simovski.

● **VARDAR SKOPJE**
Qualifying round LEGIA WARSZAWA (POL)
H 0-5
Zekir, Ljusev, Stojanov, Vasevski, Markoski, Krstev, Petreski, Saciri, Nacevski (Simonovski 46), Demir (Janevski 53), Trajcov (Georgievski 58).
A 0-4
Zekir, Jovanoski, Ljusev, Stojanov, Markoski, Vasevski, Nacevski, Trajcov, Demir (Eftimov 75), Janevski (Georgievski 62), Krstev.

NATIONAL TEAM RESULTS 99/00

05/09/99	Yugoslavia (ECQ)	A	Belgrade	1-3	Ciric (65p)
08/09/99	Yugoslavia (ECQ)	H	Skopje	2-4	Saciri (61), Ciric (87)
09/10/99	Republic of Ireland (ECQ)	H	Skopje	1-1	Stavrevski (90)
23/02/00	Yugoslavia	H	Skopje	1-2	Karanfilovski (78)
29/03/00	Bosnia-Herzegovina	A	Zenica	0-1	
26/04/00	Albania	H	Prilep	1-0	Serafimovski (35)
05/06/00	South Korea	A	Teheran	1-2	Saciri (90)
07/06/00	Iran	A	Teheran	1-3	Hristov (5)

TOP SCORERS

19 Ardzend BECIRI (Sloga Jugomagnat Skopje)
16 Dejan RISTOVSKI (Cementarnica 55 Skopje)
13 Nikolce ZDRAVEVSKI (Pobeda Prilep)
    Dejvi GLAVEVSKI (Pelister Bitola)
12 Antonio TASEV (Tikves Kavadarci)

INTERNATIONAL HONOURS

None

Sileks Kratovo also underperformed. Some put this down to the fact that the Sileks company president, Ljubisav Ivanov, had been replaced at the head of the Macedonian FA. His successor was Lambe Arnaudov, the country's deputy minister of agriculture.

The Macedonian national team also had a new man in charge, with Dragan Kanatlarovski replacing Gjoko Hadzievski for the final stages of the Euro 2000

qualifying campaign. Two defeats by Yugoslavia in the new coach's first two matches did not bode well, but an unwanted hat-trick was avoided when defender Goran Stavrevski powered in an equalising header in the last seconds of the final qualifier at home to the Republic of Ireland. The goal had far more significance for the Irish than the Macedonians, who, as expected, finished fourth in the group.

NATIONAL TEAM APPEARANCES 99/00

Coach - Goko HADZIEVSKI; Dragan KANATLAROVSKI	YUG	YUG	IRL	YUG	BOS	ALB	KOR	IRN	Cps	Gls
Petar MILOSEVSKI (06/12/73) - Trabzonspor (TUR)	G	G		s60				G83	16	-
Goran STAVREVSKI (02/01/74) - Zagreb (CRO)	D	D	D	D	D	D	D	D	15	1
Zoran JOVANOVSKI (21/08/72) - Helsingborgs IF (SWE)	D46	D	D77						24	-
Goran LAZAREVSKI (17/12/74) - Pobeda Prilep	D	D		M63	s70	s68	s59	M61	15	-
Boban BABUNSKI (05/05/68) - CD Logroñés (ESP)	D	D	D	D60	D		D56	D	23	1
Toni SAVEVSKI (08/07/64) - AEK (GRE)	M	M46	M						7	-
Dragan VESELINOVSKI (11/08/68) - Makedonija GP Skopje	M	M40							13	-
Toni MICEVSKI (20/01/70) - Pelister Bitola	M50	M40			M65	M89			35	3
Georgi HRISTOV (30/01/76) - Barnsley (ENG)	A	A	A	A63	A	A68	A70	A65	34	10
Sasa CIRIC (11/01/68) - Tennis Borussia Berlin (GER)	A75	A		A46	A	s68			21	7
Artim SACIRI (23/09/73) - Tennis Borussia Berlin (GER)	A	A		A75	A	A78	A	A	29	5
Nedzmedin MEMEDI (20/03/66) - Sloga Jugomagnat Skopje	s46		s77	s46			s56	s46	32	2
Zarko SERAFIMOVSKI (13/02/71) - Makedonija GP Skopje	s50	s40		M	M89	M	M	M	23	2
Marjan GERASIMOVSKI (12/03/74) - Partizan Beograd (YUG)	s75	s46	D	D46	s65				6	-
Dzevdet SAINOVSKI (08/06/73) - Hannover 96 (GER)		s40	M						20	2
Antonio FILEVSKI (23/06/66) - Zeleznik Beograd (YUG)			G		G46	s52	G		6	-
Goce SEDLOSKI (10/04/74) - Dinamo Zagreb (CRO)			D		D	D	D	D	25	-
Goran STANIC (18/09/74) - UE Lleida (ESP)			D70						1	-
Milan STOJANOSKI (16/09/73) - Partizan Beograd (YUG)			M56	M	D70	D68			16	1
Ardzend BECIRI (30/04/75) - Sloga Jugomagnat Skopje			s56	s63		s36	A80	s65	6	-
Srjan ZAHARIEVSKI (12/09/73) - VfB Stuttgart (GER)			s70						21	3
Orhej NIKOLOV (24/05/74) - Eintracht Frankfurt (GER)				G60	s46	G52			4	-
Igor Sasa NIKOLOVSKI (16/07/73) - Tranbzonspor (TUR)				D		D	D	D46	33	1
Blaze GEORGIESKI (01/12/75) - Crvena zvezda Beograd (YUG)				s46	s55	M36			3	-
Rade KARANFILOVSKI (03/07/68) - Pobeda Prilep				s60	M55	M	M59		5	1
Zoran MISERDOVSKI (05/05/75) - Sloga Jugomagnat Skopje				s63		s89		s53	4	-
Robert PETROV (02/06/78) - Pobeda Prilep				s75					1	-
Saso ZDRAVESKI (11/08/73) - Sloga Jugomagnat Skopje					s89	s78	D77		3	-
Arben NEHU (27/02/72) - KSK Beveren (BEL)							s70	A53	2	-
Mile KRSTEV (01/05/79) - SC Heerenveen (HOL)							s77	M	3	-
Dejan RISTOVSKI (01/08/73) - Cementarnica 55 Skopje							s80	s61	2	-
Goce GRUJOSKI (20/08/74) - Pobeda Prilep								s83	1	-

DOMESTIC CUP 99/00

QUARTER-FINALS

Sileks Kratovo v Sloga Jugomagnat Skopje 0-1; 1-3 (Sloga Jugomagnat Skopje 4-1)
Rabotnicki Kometal Skopje v FCU 1-1; 2-1 (Rabotnicki Kometal Skopje 3-2)
Makedonija GP Skopje v Pobeda Prilep 0-0; 2-3 (Pobeda Prilep 3-2)
Pelister Bitola v Vardar Skopje 1-0; 2-1 (Pelister Bitolj 3-1)

SEMI-FINALS

Rabotnicki Kometal Skopje v Sloga Jugomagnat Skopje 1-1; 1-3
(Sloga Jugomagnat Skopje 4-2)
Pelister Bitola v Pobeda Prilep 2-2; 1-2 (Pobeda Prilep 4-3)

FINAL

20/05/2000, Prilep
POBEDA PRILEP 0 SLOGA JUGOMAGNAT SKOPJE 6
Miserdovski (42), Beciri (55, 65, 74), Mustafi (70), Presilski (82)
referee - Bungurov
SLOGA JUGOMAGNAT SKOPJE - Nikolovski, Ramadan, Colakovic, Mustafi
(Banduliev 82), Zdravevski, Abazi, Miserdovski, Memedi, Maznov (Bajram 76),
Beganovic (Presilski 74), Beciri.
POBEDA PRILEP - Grujoski, Stefanov (Meglenski 79), Risteski, Nikolaevski
(Todoroski 60), Lazarevski, Nacev, Jilson, Karanfilovski, Zdravevski, Naumoski,
Dinic (Dimitievic 46).

PROMOTED CLUBS 99/00

SECOND DIVISION FINAL TABLES

EAST		Pd	W	D	L	F	A	Pt	GD
1	**Belasica Strumica**	**30**	**27**	**0**	**3**	**116**	**18**	**81**	**98**
2	Sloga Vinica	30	20	2	8	81	27	62	54
3	Baskimi Kumanovo	30	18	3	9	79	34	57	45
4	Bregalnica Delcevo	30	17	4	9	64	48	55	16
5	Jaka Radovis	30	16	7	7	53	43	55	10
6	Males Berovo	30	16	4	10	52	34	52	18
7	Vardar Negotino	30	16	2	12	62	50	50	12
8	Tiverija Strumica	30	15	2	13	38	49	47	-11
9	Bregalnica Stip	30	13	6	11	62	32	45	30
10	Metalurg Veles	30	13	5	12	47	43	44	4
11	Udarnik Pirava	30	12	2	16	31	52	38	-21
12	Kozuf Gevgelija	30	9	2	19	51	83	29	-32
13	Dojransko Ezero Dojran	30	8	3	19	23	67	27	-44
14	FC Belo Brdo	30	7	3	20	35	74	24	-39
15	Ovce Pole Sveti Nikole	30	4	3	23	27	96	15	-69
16	Karpos Kumanovo	30	4	2	24	32	103	14	-71

WEST		Pd	W	D	L	F	A	Pt	GD
1	**Skendija HB Tetovo**	**34**	**24**	**5**	**5**	**96**	**21**	**77**	**75**
2	Karaorman Struga	34	22	4	8	78	42	70	36
3	Teteks Tetovo	34	21	5	8	87	34	68	53
4	FC Ohrid	34	21	3	10	91	43	66	48
5	FC Novaci	34	21	3	10	77	30	66	47
6	Jugohrom Jegunovce	34	21	3	10	76	59	66	17
7	Alumina Skopje	34	20	5	9	102	46	65	56
8	Skendija Aracinovo	34	20	4	10	94	38	64	56
9	Butel Skopje	34	19	4	11	50	38	61	12
10	Madzari Solidarnost Skopje	34	16	3	15	79	57	51	22
11	FC Voska	34	16	2	16	53	61	50	-8
12	FC Skopje	34	14	2	18	63	57	44	6
13	Korab Debar	34	13	1	20	45	81	40	-36
14	Balkan Skopje	34	10	2	22	46	76	32	-30
15	FC Bitola	34	5	5	24	35	62	20	-27
16	Prespa Resen	34	6	2	26	38	122	20	-84
17	FC Gostivar	34	5	1	28	33	154	16	-121
18	FC Velesta	34	4	2	28	33	155	14	-122

CLUB DIRECTORIES

FC Belasica Strumica
Leninova b.b.
92 400 Strumica
tel - (902) 21211
fax - (902) 31123
Year of Formation - 1922
President - Vanco Takovski
Director - Bobi Todorov
Coach - Ilija Matenicarov
Stadium - Gradski (5,000)

FC Skendija HB Tetovo
Butik Emona TC Lovec
94 000 Tetovo
tel - (94) 32308
fax - (94) 32308
Year of Formation - 1960
President - Sinan Idrizi
Coach - Zoran Smilevski
Stadium - Gradski (10,000)

BOREC MHK VELES

CLUB DIRECTORY

FK Borec MHK
Gradski stadion bb
93 000 Veles
tel - (93) 31587
fax - (93) 31249
Year of Formation - 1926
President - Risto Jordanov
Secretary - Risto Temelkov
Coach - Trajce Kovacev
Stadium - Gradski (5,000)

APPEARANCES 99/00

	P	Ap	(s)	Gls
Angel ANASTASOV	M	5		
Ilija ATANASOV	M		(2)	
Ilco BOROV	M	8		3
Goko CVETKOVSKI	M		(1)	
Todorce DAVCEVSKI	D	24		
Igor DIMITRIEVSKI	M	1	(2)	
Igor DIMOVSKI	D	1	(2)	
Risto DORIEV	D	22		1
Ivica GLIGOROVSKI	A	23	(1)	4
Vladislav GROZDANOVIC (YUG)	M	16	(2)	2
Igor ILIEVSKI	D	3	(5)	
Toni ILKOVSKI	M		(2)	
Ace JAVASEV	D	9		1
Marjan JOVANOVSKI	A	9	(1)	2
Darko KADINSKI	D	9	(1)	
Goran KRSTEV	M	5	(2)	
Srgjan KRSTIC (YUG)	A	19	(3)	7
Pance KUMBEV	M	23		2
Aco LEVKOV	M	1		
Dimce MANEVSKI	D	6		
Ivan MARKOV	A		(2)	
Dejan MARKOVSKI	G	1		
Pero NASTEV	D	2		
Zoran PAUNOV	G	23		
Sasa PETROVIC	A	11		2
Nako STOEV	D	5		
Saso STOILJKOVIC (YUG)	M	1	(2)	
Ile STOJANOV	G	2		
Ivan STOJANOVIC	A		(1)	
Zafir STOJMANOV	D	22		1
Marjan SOTIROV	M	20	(1)	1
Angel TEMELKOV	M	2	(7)	1
Dimce TODOROVSKI	D	1	(4)	
Dragan TOMOVSKI	M		(1)	
Jovan VASILEV	A	12	(4)	

LEAGUE RESULTS 1999/2000

15/08/99	Osogovo Kocani	A	1-2	Krstic
22/08/99	Napredok Kicevo	H	2-2	Krstic, Borov
29/08/99	Cementarnica 55 Skopje	A	1-3	Krstic
12/09/99	FK Kumanovo	A	3-0	(w/o)
19/09/99	Vardar Skopje	H	1-1	Borov
26/09/99	Sloga Jugomagnat Skopje	A	0-4	
03/10/99	Pobeda Prilep	H	2-0	Borov, Krstic
17/10/99	Tikves Kavadarci	A	1-2	Petrovic
24/10/99	Sileks Kratovo	H	1-2	Krstic
31/10/99	Makedonija GP Skopje	A	0-0	
07/11/99	Rabotnicki Kometal Skopje	H	1-0	Petrovic
14/11/99	Pelister Bitola	A	0-3	
21/11/99	Sasa Makedonska Skopje	H	2-1	Gligorovski 2
05/03/00	Osogovo Kocani	H	4-1	Kumbev, Jovanovski, Grozdanovic (p), Krstic
12/03/00	Napredok Kicevo	A	0-3	
19/03/00	Cementarnica 55 Skopje	H	0-0	
26/03/00	FK Kumanovo	H	2-2	Krstic, Javasev
02/04/00	Vardar Skopje	A	1-1	Temelkov
09/04/00	Sloga Jugomagnat Skopje	H	0-3	
16/04/00	Pobeda Prilep	A	0-2	
23/04/00	Tikves Kavadarci	H	5-1	Gligorovski, Sotirov, Grozdanovic (p), Stojmanov, Jovanovski
30/04/00	Sileks Kratovo	A	0-6	
07/05/00	Makedonija GP Skopje	H	1-0	Gligorovski
14/05/00	Rabotnicki Kometal Skopje	A	0-1	
24/05/00	Pelister Bitola	H	1-2	Kumbev
28/05/00	Sasa Makedonska Skopje	A	1-0	Doriev

CEMENTARNICA 55 SKOPJE

CLUB DIRECTORY

FK Cementarnica 55
Prvomajska bb
91 000 Skopje
tel - (91) 421083
fax - (91) 163871
Year of Formation - 1955
President - Miroslav Georgievski
Secretary - Goce Jovanovic
Coach - Alekso Mackov
Stadium - Cementarnica (2,500)

APPEARANCES 99/00

	P	Ap	(s)	Gls
Aleksandar ANCEVSKI	M	3	(4)	
Igor ANGELOVSKI	A	23		
Dejan AVRAMOVIC	D	1	(1)	
Zvonko BUCKOV	D		(3)	
Dejan CVETKOVSKI	M	12	(11)	2
Dejan DIMITROVSKI	M	24		3
Igor DIMOV	G	11		
Ilco GJORGJIOSKI	M	6		1
Vlatko GROZDANOVSKI	M	1	(7)	
Goran HRISTOVSKI	M	24		
Toni JAKIMOVSKI	M	22		2
Gjorgji JOVANOVSKI	G	3		
Ljupco KMETOVSKI	G	12		
Miroslav LAZAREVSKI	M	10	(1)	
Igor MILEVSKI	D	11	(7)	1
Dejan RISTOVSKI	A	26		16
Zanko SAVOV	A	24		10
Vlatko SETINOV	M	2	(5)	2
Vlatko SPASOVSKI	M	5	(2)	1
Svetozar STANKOVSKI	D	3	(1)	
Dragan STEFANOVSKI	M	19		
Dragan TRENOVSKI	M	7	(1)	
Goran TRPKOVSKI	A	15	(9)	5
Aleksandar VASOVSKI	D	22		

LEAGUE RESULTS 1999/2000

15/08/99	Napredok Kicevo	A	1-0	Ristovski
22/08/99	FK Kumanovo	A	0-0	
29/08/99	Borec MHK Veles	H	3-1	Ristovski, Trpkovski, Cvetkovski
12/09/99	Vardar Skopje	A	4-1	Trpkovski, Jakimovski, Savov (p), Milevski
19/09/99	Sloga Jugomagnat Skopje	H	2-2	Ristovski, Dimitrovski
26/09/99	Pobeda Prilep	A	1-3	Ristovski
03/10/99	Tikves Kavadarci	H	1-1	Savov (p)
17/10/99	Sileks Kratovo	A	1-2	Jakimovski
24/10/99	Makedonija GP Skopje	H	2-1	Ristovski, Setinov
31/10/99	Rabotnicki Kometal Skopje	A	0-3	
07/11/99	Pelister Bitola	H	3-2	Ristovski, Savov, Dimitrovski
14/11/99	Sasa Makedonska Skopje	A	0-1	
21/11/99	Osogovo Kocani	H	4-0	Ristovski 2, Savov, Setinov
05/03/00	Napredok Kicevo	H	2-0	Savov 2
12/03/00	FK Kumanovo	H	1-0	Trpkovski
19/03/00	Borec MHK Veles	A	0-0	
26/03/00	Vardar Skopje	H	2-0	Trpkovski, Spasovski
02/04/00	Sloga Jugomagnat Skopje	A	1-3	Dimitrovski
09/04/00	Pobeda Prilep	H	0-0	
16/04/00	Tikves Kavadarci	A	4-1	Ristovski 3, Savov
23/04/00	Sileks Kratovo	H	3-1	Ristovski 3
30/04/00	Makedonija GP Skopje	A	2-0	Savov, Gjorgjioski
07/05/00	Rabotnicki Kometal Skopje	H	0-1	
14/05/00	Pelister Bitola	A	1-5	Savov
24/05/00	Sasa Makedonska Skopje	H	1-0	Trpkovski
28/05/00	Osogovo Kocani	A	4-1	Ristovski 2, Cvetkovski, Savov

FK KUMANOVO

FK Kumanovo
Gradski stadion bb, Kumanovo
tel - (901) 25020 / fax - (901) 411344
Year of Formation - 1930
President - Vlado Matevski
Secretary - Momcilo Trendafilov
Coach - Erkan Jusuf; Miroslav Jakovljevic
Stadium - Gradski (7,000)

APPEARANCES 99/00

	P	Ap	(s)	Gls
Goran ALEKSOV	D	10		1
Arse ANDOVSKI	D	12		
Arse ANGELEVSKI	G	2		
Ivan ANTIC	M	2		
BASKIM	M		(1)	
Jovce BIZIMOVSKI	D	12		
Petar DIMESKI	M		(2)	
Aleksandar CVETKOVSKI	M	11	(4)	1
Nenad CVETKOVSKI	M	10		
Jovce DZIPUNOV	A	1	(1)	
Ljupco DENKOVSKI	D		(4)	
Goran GEORGIEVSKI	D	14		
Goran GIEVSKI	M		(1)	
Goko HRISTOVSKI	M	2		
Bekam IBRAHIMI	M	8	(1)	
Pero JACEV	D		(1)	
Zoran JOVANOVSKI	D	3	(2)	
Pero JOVCEVSKI	M		(2)	
Toni KOLEV	D	8		
Toni KOMNENOV	D	8		
Aleksandar KOWANOWSKI	M	4		
Mile KUPANOV	G	4	(1)	
Vlatko KUPANOV	M	6	(1)	
LIMANI	D	1	(3)	
Zoran MANEV	A	6	(1)	
Zoran MARKOVSKI	G	14		
Igor MITREVSKI	D	3	(4)	1
Igor NESKOVSKI	D	9		
Saso PETKOVSKI	A	5		2
Zoran PETKOVSKI	M	9		4
Zoran RISTIC	G	6		
Artim SACIROV	M	7		1
Grozde SPASOVSKI	M	6		
Predrag STANOJEVIC	M	18		
Kire STERJOV	M	7		
Milan STOJCEVSKI	M	3		
Toni STOSIC	M		(10)	
Todor TERZIEV	D	11		
Dejan TRAJKOVSKI	D	4	(5)	
Ilija TRAJKOVSKI	A	4		
Bobi VUCEVSKI	M	8	(2)	1
Boban ZLATANOVSKI	M	11	(3)	
Dejan ZIKOVSKI	A	8	(3)	5

LEAGUE RESULTS 1999/2000

15/08/99	Sileks Kratovo	A	0-2	
22/08/99	Cementarnica 55 Skopje	H	0-0	
29/08/99	Makedonija GP Skopje	A	1-4	Mitrevski
12/09/99	Borec MHK Veles	H	0-3	
19/09/99	Rabotnicki Kometal Skopje	A	0-4	
26/09/99	Vardar Skopje	H	0-8	
03/10/99	Pelister Bitola	A	0-4	
17/10/99	Sloga Jugomagnat Skopje	H	0-2	
24/10/99	Sasa Makedonska Skopje	A	1-5	Sacirov
31/10/99	Pobeda Prilep	H	0-2	
07/11/99	Osogovo Kocani	A	0-3	
14/11/99	Tikves Kavadarci	H	0-3	
21/11/99	Napredok Kicevo	A	0-10	
05/03/00	Sileks Kratovo	H	2-0	Petkovski S., Zikovski
12/03/00	Cementarnica 55 Skopje	A	0-1	
19/03/00	Makedonija GP Skopje	H	0-1	
26/03/00	Borec MHK Veles	A	2-2	Petkovski S., Petkovski Z.
02/04/00	Rabotnicki Kometal Skopje	H	0-2	
09/04/00	Vardar Skopje	A	0-4	
16/04/00	Pelister Bitola	H	1-2	Zikovski
23/04/00	Sloga Jugomagnat Skopje	A	0-1	
30/04/00	Sasa Makedonska Skopje	H	1-2	Vucevski
07/05/00	Pobeda Prilep	A	1-6	Aleksov
14/05/00	Osogovo Kocani	H	3-1	Petkovski Z., Cvetkovski A., Zikovski
24/05/00	Tikves Kavadarci	A	2-3	Petkovski Z. 2
28/05/00	Napredok Kicevo	H	2-2	Zikovski 2

MAKEDONIJA GP SKOPJE

CLUB DIRECTORY

FK Makedonija Gjorce Petrov
Mice Kozar st. Gjorce Petrov, 91 000 Skopje
tel - (91) 344444 / fax - (91) 228534
Year of Formation - 1932
President - Darko Pancev
Secretary - Trajce Todorovski
Coach - Kiril Dojcinovski; Slobodan Goracinov;
Vujadin Stanojkovic
Stadium - Gjorce Petrov (2,500)

APPEARANCES 99/00

	P	Ap	(s)	Gls
Vlatko ANDONOVSKI	M	18	(2)	2
Stojan ANGELOV	M	1	(2)	
Nikola AVRAMOVSKI	M	6		
Ilija BOEV	D	2	(4)	
Vasko BOZINOVSKI	M	16	(2)	1
Jesus BRAGA (BRA)	D	7		
Valentin CELESKI	A	4	(6)	3
Ljupco DIMITKOVSKI	M	1	(1)	
Arantes EDSON (BRA)	M		(1)	
Dejan GEORGIEVSKI	D	1	(2)	
Goran GEORGIEVSKI	D	3		
Krste GEORGIEVSKI	M	1		
Gjoko ILIOSKI	D	22	(1)	
Todor IVANOVSKI	D	12	(1)	1
Boban JANCEVSKI	A	12	(1)	5
Vladimir KOLEV	D	8	(2)	
Dragan KOSTADINOVSKI	M		(3)	
Blagoja MILEVSKI	D	25		1
Goce MARKOSKI	M	14	(1)	2
Ivica OROZOVSKI	M	3	(4)	
Mario PETKOV (BUL)	A	9		4
Zoran RISTEVSKI	G	17		
RISTOV	A	1		1
Zarko SERAFIMOVSKI	M	20		4
Dejan SPALJEVIC	G	6		
Vlatko SPASOVSKI	A	4	(5)	
Petre STOILOV	D	2		
Zoran STOJANOVIC (YUG)	G	3		
Dalibor STOJKOVIC	M	22	(2)	3
Boris STOJMENOV	M	2		
Jovan STOJMENOVSKI	D	5		
Saso TODOROVSKI	M	10	(7)	1
Martin TRAJCEV	M	1	(2)	
Denis TRAJKOVSKI	M	8	(2)	
Dragan VESELINOVSKI	M	20		

LEAGUE RESULTS 1999/2000

15/08/99	Tikves Kavadarci	H	3-2	Milevski, Ristov, Andonovski
22/08/99	Sileks Kratovo	A	1-1	Jancevski
29/08/99	FK Kumanovo	H	4-1	Jancevski 3, Stojkovic
12/09/99	Rabotnicki Kometal Skopje	H	0-1	
19/09/99	Pelister Bitola	A	0-2	
26/09/99	Sasa Makedonska Skopje	H	2-1	Bozinovski, Celeski
03/10/99	Osogovo Kocani	A	2-2	Todorovski, Jancevski
17/10/99	Napredok Kicevo	H	1-0	Stojkovic
24/10/99	Cementarnica 55 Skopje	A	1-2	og (Vasovski)
31/10/99	Borec MHK Veles	H	0-0	
07/11/99	Vardar Skopje	A	0-1	
14/11/99	Sloga Jugomagnat Skopje	H	0-0	
21/11/99	Pobeda Prilep	A	0-1	
05/03/00	Tikves Kavadarci	A	1-2	Stojkovic
12/03/00	Sileks Kratovo	H	0-0	
19/03/00	FK Kumanovo	A	1-0	Petkov
26/03/00	Rabotnicki Kometal Skopje	A	0-3	
02/04/00	Pelister Bitola	H	1-2	Ivanovski
09/04/00	Sasa Makedonska Skopje	A	1-0	Markoski
16/04/00	Osogovo Kocani	H	2-0	Serafimovski, Celeski
23/04/00	Napredok Kicevo	A	1-0	Serafimovski
30/04/00	Cementarnica 55 Skopje	H	0-2	
07/05/00	Borec MHK Veles	A	0-1	
14/05/00	Vardar Skopje	H	3-1	Celeski, Serafimovski, Markoski
24/05/00	Sloga Jugomagnat Skopje	A	2-2	Petkov, Andonovski
28/05/00	Pobeda Prilep	H	3-1	Petkov 2, Serafimovski (p)

NAPREDOK KICEVO

CLUB DIRECTORY

FK Napredok
Aleksandar Makedonski bb
95 000 Kicevo
tel - (95) 32643
fax - (95) 32480
Year of Formation - 1924
President - Ljubomir Despotovski
Secretary - Ruse Sekulovski
Coach - Ilija Dimoski; Ivan Manakovski
Stadium - Gradski (5,000)

APPEARANCES 99/00

	P	Ap	(s)	Gls
Elvir ALABESOVSKI	M	1	(2)	
Klaudemir ALVEZ (BRA)	M	14	(3)	2
Boris ANGELESKI	A	19	(3)	2
Dejan AVRAMOVIC	D	24		2
Fadilj BALAZI	M	2		
Igor DAMJANOVSKI	D	4	(1)	1
Blagoja DIMOVSKI	D	12	(5)	1
Boban DUJKOVIC	A	19		
Robert ENDEKOVSKI	M	20	(2)	1
Fernandez JEFERSON (BRA)	A	13	(5)	2
Miki JONOSKI	G	9		
Jovan JOVANOVSKI	D	2	(10)	
Dragan MATEVSKI	D	18	(1)	2
Vlatko MICEVSKI	A	25		8
Stanislav MICKOVSKI (YUG)	A	13	(4)	3
Goran MILOVANOVSKI	M	4	(4)	
Goran NAJDESKI	G	8		
Goran NAJDEVSKI	D	7		2
Ivica PAVICIC	D	5		
Robert PEJOVSKI	D	18	(2)	
Zoran POPPANEV	M	17		1
Ilija SEFEDINOVSKI	M	1	(1)	
Zoran STOJANOVIC (YUG)	G	9		
Jovan TANEV	D	3	(1)	1
Vanco TRAJANOV	M	15		2
Zoran TRAJKOVSKI	M	1	(2)	
Ilija TRPEVSKI	M	2	(1)	
Stojan ZAFIROVSKI	M	1	(3)	

LEAGUE RESULTS 1999/2000

15/08/99	Cementarnica 55 Skopje	H	0-1	
22/08/99	Borec MHK Veles	A	2-2	Micevski, Tanev
29/08/99	Vardar Skopje	H	2-2	Angelevski, Matevski
12/09/99	Sloga Jugomagnat Skopje	A	0-4	
19/09/99	Pobeda Prilep	H	0-8	
26/09/99	Tikves Kavadarci	A	0-0	
03/10/99	Sileks Kratovo	H	0-3	
17/10/99	Makedonija GP Skopje	A	0-1	
24/10/99	Rabotnicki Kometal Skopje	H	1-0	Trajanov
31/10/99	Pelister Bitola	A	1-4	Micevski
07/11/99	Sasa Makedonska Skopje	H	2-0	Jeferson, Micevski (p)
14/11/99	Osogovo Kocani	A	1-3	Mickovski
21/11/99	FK Kumanovo	H	10-0	Alvez 2, Micevski 2, Mickovski 2, Poppanev, Dimovski, Matevski, Trajanov
05/03/00	Cementarnica 55 Skopje	A	0-2	
12/03/00	Borec MHK Veles	H	3-0	Avramovic, Najdeski, Angeleski
19/03/00	Vardar Skopje	A	1-3	Micevski
26/03/00	Sloga Jugomagnat Skopje	H	0-0	
02/04/00	Pobeda Prilep	A	0-1	
09/04/00	Tikves Kavadarci	H	1-1	Micevski
16/04/00	Sileks Kratovo	A	0-1	
23/04/00	Makedonija GP Skopje	H	0-1	
30/04/00	Rabotnicki Kometal Skopje	A	0-4	
07/05/00	Pelister Bitola	H	3-3	Najdeski, Avramovic, Jeferson
14/05/00	Sasa Makedonska Skopje	A	0-1	
24/05/00	Osogovo Kocani	H	1-1	Endekovski
28/05/00	FK Kumanovo	A	2-2	Damjanovski, Micevski

OSOGOVO KOCANI

CLUB DIRECTORY

FK Osogovo
Lazar Andonov B.B.
Kocani
tel - (903) 25793
fax - (903) 25793
Year of Formation - 1924
President - Vanco Karanfilov
Director - Valentin Nikolov
Coach - Ljupco Serafimov (00/01 - Ilija Dimoski)
Stadium - Nikola Mantov (4,000)

APPEARANCES 99/00

	P	Ap	(s)	Gls
Toni ANGELOV	M	1		
Sasko ATANASOV	M	9	(8)	3
Igorco DANEV	G	3		
Blasko GEORGIEV	A	18	(1)	
Goran GEORGIEV	M	7		5
Borce GEORGIEVSKI	M	4	(1)	
Blage GERASIMOV	A	3	(7)	
Borce GICEV	D	8		
Dobrinko ILIEVSKI	D	10		1
Todor IVANOVSKI	A	1		1
Stevco JANEV	D	17	(5)	3
Vlatko JANEV	G	20		
Simo JORDANOV	D	1	(2)	
Saso JOVANOV	D	22		
Vlatko JOVANOVSKI	M	20	(2)	1
Jordan MANOV	D	21		3
Stojce MILOSEVSKI	D	4		
Sreten MILOSOSKI	M	24		5
Mite MITEV	M		(1)	
Igor NAUMOV	M	2		
Pero NIKOLOV	M	7		
Ivan PAPAROV	G	3		
Mario PETKOV	A	11		7
Risto PETKOV	M	11		
Igor RANGELOV	M	6		2
Aleksandar SOKOLOV	M	13	(5)	2
Eftim STOJANOV	D	1	(4)	
Pero STOJANOVSKI	M	12		1
Igor TEMELKOV	A	1	(7)	
Zoran TODOROV	M	5	(7)	
Risto TRAJANOV	D	21	(1)	

LEAGUE RESULTS 1999/2000

15/08/99	Borek MHK Skopje	H	2-1	Atanasov 2
22/08/99	Vardar Skopje	A	0-3	
29/08/99	Sloga Jugomagnat Skopje	H	0-2	
12/09/99	Pobeda Prilep	A	1-2	Georgiev
19/09/99	Tikves Kavadarci	H	4-1	Sokolov 2, Georgiev, Petkov M.
26/09/99	Sileks Kratovo	A	2-4	Petkov M., Rangelov
03/10/99	Makedonija GP Skopje	H	2-2	Petkov M., Georgiev
17/10/99	Rabotnicki Kometal Skopje	A	1-3	Milososki
24/10/99	Pelister Bitola	H	1-2	Rangelov
31/10/99	Sasa Makedonska Skopje	A	1-1	Georgiev
07/11/99	FK Kumanovo	H	3-0	Petkov M. 2, Atanasov
14/11/99	Napredok Kicevo	H	3-1	Petkov M. 2, Manov
21/11/99	Cementarnica 55 Skopje	A	0-4	
05/03/00	Borec MHK Veles	A	1-4	Manov
12/03/00	Vardar Skopje	H	1-0	Janev S.
19/03/00	Sloga Jugomagnat Skopje	A	0-3	
26/03/00	Pobeda Prilep	H	0-0	
02/04/00	Tikves Kavadarci	A	3-5	Milososki, Ivanovski, Georgiev
09/04/00	Sileks Kratovo	H	2-1	Jovanovski, Manov
16/04/00	Makedonija GP Skopje	A	0-2	
23/04/00	Rabotnicki Kometal Skopje	H	2-0	Milososki 2
30/04/00	Pelister Bitola	A	1-3	Milososki
07/05/00	Sasa Makedonska Skopje	H	1-1	Stojanovski
14/05/00	FK Kumanovo	A	1-3	Ilievski
24/05/00	Napredok Kicevo	A	1-1	Janev S.
28/05/00	Cementarnica 55 Skopje	H	1-4	Janev S.

PELISTER BITOLA

CLUB DIRECTORY

FK Pelister
Gradski stadion "Tumbe Kafe" bb
97 000 Bitola
tel - (97) 222785
fax - (97) 222785
Year of Formation - 1945
President - Goran Nevenovski
Secretary - Pece Josifovski
Coach - Nedzat Husein; Kiril Dojcinovski
Stadium - Tumbe Kafe (6,000)

APPEARANCES 99/00

	P	Ap	(s)	Gls
Zlatko CVETANOSKI	D		(1)	
Pece CVETKOVSKI	M	5	(4)	
Dejan DEMJANSKI	M	19		
Mile DIMOV	D	18	(1)	
Ilir ELMAZOVSKI	D	22	(1)	1
Dejvi GLAVEVSKI	A	24		13
Kire GROZDANOV	D	12	(9)	1
Predrag JANCIC (YUG)	D	17	(1)	1
Sinisa JOVANOVSKI	D	7		
Dimitar KAPINKOVSKI	M	25		1
Zlatko KITEVSKI	M		(1)	
Goran KOLEV	M		(1)	
Toni MICEVSKI	M	24	(1)	11
Zoran MICEVSKI	G	21		
Gorazd MIHAJLOV	A	2	(5)	
Miroslav MILOSEVIC	M	2	(3)	
Saso NAUMOVSKI	D	1	(1)	
Goran PASOVSKI	G	3		
Saso PETROVSKI	G	2		
Blagojce RUTEVSKI	M	4	(8)	
Pece SIVEVSKI	M	15	(9)	6
Slobodan SPASOV	D	11	(2)	
Igor STAMENOVSKI	M	6	(1)	
Kire STERJOV	A	4	(6)	4
Zoran STERJOVSKI	D	18	(3)	2
Nikola STISNIOVSKI	M	11	(6)	6
Igor TALEVSKI	D	1	(1)	
Viktor TRENEVSKI	M	12		2

LEAGUE RESULTS 1999/2000

15/08/99	Sloga Jugomagnat Skopje	H	0-2	
22/08/99	Pobeda Prilep	A	0-2	
29/08/99	Tikves Kavadarci	H	1-0	Sterjov
12/09/99	Sileks Kratovo	A	0-2	
19/09/99	Makedonija GP Skopje	H	2-0	Micevski T., Glavevski
26/09/99	Rabotnicki Kometal Skopje	A	0-0	
03/10/99	FK Kumanovo	H	4-0	Elmazovski, Micevski T., Stisnioski, Glavevski
17/10/99	Sasa Makedonska Skopje	H	3-1	Stisnioski 2, Sivevski
24/10/99	Osogovo Kocani	A	2-1	Micevski T. 2
31/10/99	Napredok Kicevo	H	4-1	Glavevski 3, Micevski T.
07/11/99	Cementarnica 55 Skopje	A	2-3	Kapinkovski, Glavevski
14/11/99	Borec MHK Veles	H	3-0	Glavevski 2, Micevski T.
21/11/99	Vardar Skopje	A	2-3	Glavevski, Sivevski
05/03/00	Sloga Jugomagnat Skopje	A	0-1	
12/03/00	Pobeda Prilep	H	2-2	Sivevski, Jancic
19/03/00	Tikves Kavadarci	A	0-2	
26/03/00	Sileks Kratovo	H	3-0	Sterjov 2, Trenevski
02/04/00	Makedonija GP Skopje	A	2-1	Sterjov (p), Micevski T.
09/04/00	Rabotnicki Kometal Skopje	H	1-0	Sterjovski
16/04/00	FK Kumanovo	A	2-1	Glavevski 2
23/04/00	Sasa Makedonska Skopje	A	1-1	Sivevski
30/04/00	Osogovo Kocani	H	3-1	Micevski T., Stisnioski, Sivevski
07/05/00	Napredok Kicevo	A	3-3	Trenevski, Micevski T., Sterjovski
14/05/00	Cementarnica 55 Skopje	H	5-1	Micevski T. 2, Stisnioski, Sivevski, Glavevski
24/05/00	Borec MHK Veles	A	2-1	Grozdanov, Glavevski
28/05/00	Vardar Skopje	H	1-1	Stisnioski

POBEDA PRILEP

CLUB DIRECTORY

FK Pobeda
Mosa Pijade st
Gradski Stadion Goce Delcev
98 000 Prilep
tel - (98) 254555
fax - (98) 21173
Year of Formation - 1941
President - Haralampie Hadji Risteski
Secretary - Trajce Madzovski
Coach - Dragan Kanatlarovski; Krume Mitrikeski
(00/01 - Nikola Ilievski)
Stadium - Goce Delcev (10,000)

APPEARANCES 99/00

	P	Ap	(s)	Gls
Bojan DAMESKI	D		(3)	
Dejan DAMESKI	G	1	(1)	
Dejan DIMITRIEVIC (YUG)	D	19		
Darko DINIC (YUG)	A	6	(5)	3
Goce GRUJOSKI	G	25		
Goran JANCEVSKI	M	1		
Rade KARANFILOVSKI	M	21		3
Goran LAZAREVSKI	M	26		1
Toni MEGLENSKI	A	3	(7)	
Vanco MICEVSKI	A	24	(1)	9
Blagojce NACEV	D	8		2
Toni NAUMOVSKI	M	25		9
Igor NIKOLAEVSKI	D	15	(3)	
Igor PANOV	M	3	(6)	2
Oliver PATOVSKI	G		(1)	
Robert PETROV	D	12	(3)	
Pance RISTESKI	M	22	(4)	1
Vasko STEFANOV	D	11	(12)	2
Nebojsa STOJKOVIC (YUG)	D	12		1
Trajce STOJKOSKI	A	5	(8)	
Goranco TODOROVSKI	M	5	(5)	2
Jesu da Silva ZILSON (BRA)	M	22	(2)	9
Nikolce ZDRAVEVSKI	M	20	(1)	13

LEAGUE RESULTS 1999/2000

15/08/99	Rabotnicki Kometal Skopje	A	0-1	
22/08/99	Pelister Bitola	H	2-0	Zdravevski, Naumoski
29/08/99	Sasa Makedonska Skopje	A	1-1	Zilson
12/09/99	Osogovo Kocani	H	2-1	Karanfiloski, Panov
19/09/99	Napredok Kicevo	A	8-0	Zilson 3, Zdravevski 3, Karanfiloski, Panov
26/09/99	Cementarnica 55 Skopje	H	3-1	Naumoski, Zdravevski, Lazarevski
03/10/99	Borec MHK Veles	A	0-2	
17/10/99	Vardar Skopje	H	5-2	Zilson 3, Karanfiloski, Naumoski
24/10/99	Sloga Jugomagnat Skopje	A	0-0	
31/10/99	FK Kumanovo	A	2-0	Zdravevski, Naumoski
07/11/99	Tikves Kavadarci	H	4-0	Zdravevski 2, Micevski 2
14/11/99	Sileks Kratovo	A	2-2	Stojkovic, Micevski
21/11/99	Makedonija GP Skopje	H	1-0	Naumoski
05/03/00	Rabotnicki Kometal Skopje	H	3-4	Zdravevski 2, Risteski
12/03/00	Pelister Bitola	A	2-2	Micevski, Nacev
19/03/00	Sasa Makedonska Skopje	H	4-0	Dinic, Naumoski, Nacev, Micevski
26/03/00	Osogovo Kocani	A	0-0	
02/04/00	Napredok Kicevo	H	1-0	Todorovski
09/04/00	Cementarnica 55 Skopje	A	0-0	
16/04/00	Borec MHK Veles	H	2-0	Todorovski, Naumoski (p)
23/04/00	Vardar Skopje	A	2-1	Zdravevski, Naumoski
30/04/00	Sloga Jugomagnat Skopje	H	1-1	Naumoski
07/05/00	FK Kumanovo	H	6-1	Micevski 3, Dinic 2, Stefanov
14/05/00	Tikves Kavadarci	A	3-1	Zdravevski 2, Micevski
24/05/00	Sileks Kratovo	H	2-0	Zilson, Stefanov
28/05/00	Makedonija GP Skopje	A	1-3	Zilson

RABOTNICKI KOMETAL SKOPJE

CLUB DIRECTORY

FK Rabotnicki Kometal
Gradski Park bb
91 000 Skopje
tel - (91) 234044
fax - (91) 234044
Year of Formation - 1937
President - Zoran Nikolovski
Secretary - Stojce Trajceski
Coach - Mirsad Jonuz
Stadium - Gradski (22,000)

LEAGUE RESULTS 1999/2000

15/08/99	Pobeda Prilep	H	1-0	Markovski
22/08/99	Tikves Kavadarci	A	0-2	
29/08/99	Sileks Kratovo	H	2-1	Lazarevski, Markovski
12/09/99	Makedonija GP Skopje	A	1-0	Milosevski
19/09/99	FK Kumanovo	H	4-0	Todorovski, Lazarevski,
				Nedelkovski, Bozinovski
26/09/99	Pelister Bitola	H	0-0	
03/10/99	Sasa Makedonska Skopje	A	4-1	Markovski, Srbovski, Lazarevski,
				Milosevski
17/10/99	Osogovo Kocani	H	3-1	Srbovski, Bozinovski, Markovski
24/10/99	Napredok Kicevo	A	0-1	
31/10/99	Cementarnica 55 Skopje	H	3-0	Lazarevski 2, Milosevski
07/11/99	Borec MHK Veles	A	0-1	
14/11/99	Vardar Skopje	H	2-1	Milosevski, Lazarevski
21/11/99	Sloga Jugomagnat Skopje	A	0-4	
05/03/00	Pobeda Prilep	A	4-3	Nedeljkovic, Despotovski,
				Milosevski, Nedelkovski
12/03/00	Tikves Kavadarci	H	2-1	Nedelkovski, Janevski
19/03/00	Sileks Kratovo	A	2-2	Nedeljkovic, Janevski (p)
26/03/00	Makedonija GP Skopje	H	3-0	Vasevski, Milosevski, Despotovski
02/04/00	FK Kumanovo	A	2-0	og (Bizimovski), Milosevski
09/04/00	Pelister Bitola	A	0-1	
16/04/00	Sasa Makedonska Skopje	H	0-2	
23/04/00	Osogovo Kocani	A	0-2	
30/04/00	Napredok Kicevo	H	4-0	Boskovski 2, Janevski, Nedeljkovic
07/05/00	Cementarnica 55 Skopje	A	1-0	Milosevski
14/05/00	Borec MHK Veles	H	1-0	Boskovski
24/05/00	Vardar Skopje	A	2-0	Markovski, Vasevski
28/05/00	Sloga Jugomagnat Skopje	H	0-3	

APPEARANCES 99/00

		P	Ap	(s)	Gls
Aleksandar ALCINOV	G			(1)	
Marjan ANDREVSKI	D		24		
Ljupco BLAZEVSKI	M			(4)	
Zoran BOSKOVSKI	A		6	(3)	3
Zoran BOZINOVSKI	M		13		2
Vladimir DESPOTOVSKI	D		23		2
Bojan DIMEVSKI	D		2	(8)	
Dejan GEORGIEVSKI	D		13		
Krste GEORGIEVSKI	M		6	(5)	
Goran JANEVSKI	M		12		3
Gogo JOVCEV	G		15		
Ljupco KMETOVSKI	G		11		
Dejan KUSKINSKI	A			(3)	
Miroslav LAZAREVSKI	M		12		6
Marko MARKOVSKI	A		22	(4)	5
Marjan MITKOV	M			(1)	
Zoran MIHAJLOVSKI	M			(1)	
Saso MILOSEVSKI	A		25		8
Dusko NEDELJKOVIC	A		2	(14)	3
Pavel NEDELKOVSKI	M		19	(3)	3
Srdjan OBRADOVIC (YUG)	D		1	(2)	
Riste PETKOV	D		6		
Cane SLAVEVSKI	A			(3)	
Vlatko SPASOVSKI	M			(1)	
Dragan SRBOVSKI	M		22	(2)	2
Dragan TEVDOVSKI	M		19	(5)	
Zoran TODOROVSKI	M		13		1
Dragan TREVOVSKI	D		12		
Zoran VASEVSKI	D		8	(2)	2

SASA MAKEDONSKA KAMENICA

CLUB DIRECTORY

FK Sasa
Marsal Tito st 4
Makedonska Kamenica
tel - (903) 431417
fax - (903) 431417
Year of Formation - 1968
President - Vide Velinovski
Secretary - Mile Postolovski
Coach - Danco Samokovliski
Stadium - Gradski (3,000)

APPEARANCES 99/00

	P	Ap	(s)	Gls
Toni ANASTASOVSKI	M	19	(2)	2
Angel ANGELOV (BUL)	D	10		
Aleksandar CVETINOV	M		(1)	
Goce DANEV	A	11	(10)	1
Juli DIMITROV (BUL)	A	20	(2)	2
Viktor EFTIMOV	D	12	(2)	
Dinko GARGANCEV (BUL)	M	14		
Trifun GEORGIEV (BUL)	D	13	(3)	
Dinko GICEV	M	2	(2)	
Lastimir IGNATOV	D	1	(4)	
Ilija ILIEVSKI	M	10		1
Ljupco IVANOVSKI	D	17		1
Ile JAKIMOV	D	23		1
Ace JAVASEV	D	11		1
Kirco JOVANOVSKI	D	9	(5)	1
Mile JOVANOVSKI	M	6	(1)	2
Draganco MILENKOVSKI	A	18	(4)	4
Zoran MILOSEVSKI	D	8	(1)	
Vlatko MLADENOVSKI	M	4	(1)	
Stevce PETKOVSKI	D	12		
Vlatko SETINOV	A	3	(7)	1
Nako STOEV	D	1	(2)	1
Aleksandar STOJANOVSKI	M	4		1
Zoran SUMANOV	M	8	(2)	
Kire TEMCEV	M	24		3
Bobi TENEV	G	26		

LEAGUE RESULTS 1999/2000

15/08/99	Vardar Skopje	H	0-2	
22/08/99	Sloga Jugomagnat Skopje	A	0-3	
29/08/99	Pobeda Prilep	H	1-1	Danevski
12/09/99	Tikves Kavadarci	A	1-0	Milenkovski
19/09/99	Sileks Kratovo	H	1-1	Jakimov
26/09/99	Sasa Makedonska Skopje	A	1-2	Milenkovski
03/10/99	Rabotnicki Kometal Skopje	H	1-4	Jovanovski K.
17/10/99	Pelister Bitola	A	1-3	Stojanovski (p)
24/10/99	FK Kumanovo	H	5-1	Jovanovski M. 2, Javasev, Milenkovski, Temcev
31/10/99	Osogovo Kocani	H	1-1	Ilievski
07/11/99	Napredok Kicevo	A	0-2	
14/11/99	Cementarnica 55 Skopje	H	1-0	Ivanovski
21/11/99	Borec MHK Veles	A	1-2	Temcev
05/03/00	Vardar Skopje	A	0-0	
12/03/00	Sloga Jugomagnat Skopje	H	0-2	
19/03/00	Pobeda Prilep	A	0-4	
26/03/00	Tikves Kavadarci	H	1-0	Anastasovski
02/04/00	Sileks Kratovo	A	0-0	
09/04/00	Makedonija GP Skopje	H	0-1	
16/04/00	Rabotnicki Kometal Skopje	A	2-0	Dimitrov, Temcev
23/04/00	Pelister Bitola	H	1-1	Anastasovski
30/04/00	FK Kumanovo	A	2-1	Milenkovski, Stoev
07/05/00	Osogovo Kocani	A	1-1	Setinov
14/05/00	Napredok Kicevo	H	1-0	Dimitrov
24/05/00	Cementarnica 55 Skopje	A	0-1	
28/05/00	Borec MHK Veles	H	0-1	

SILEKS KRATOVO

CLUB DIRECTORY

FK Sileks
Gradski Stadion st. bb, Kratovo
tel - (901) 481830
fax - (901) 481830
Year of Formation - 1965
President - Vlasto Savevski
Secretary - Dobre Ivanov
Coach - Lazar Plackov; Zoran Mitevski
Stadium - RIK (3,000)

MAJOR HONOURS
League Championship - (3) 1996, 1997, 1998.
Domestic Cup - (2) 1994, 1997.

APPEARANCES 99/00

	P	Ap	(s)	Gls
Zoran ALEKSANDROVIC	M	6	(4)	
Toni ANGELOV	M	9		5
Dime ANGELOVSKI	D	1		
Goranco GEORGIEV	A	12		2
Miroslav GJOKIC	A	7		8
Nikola GJOSEVSKI	D	23		4
Vlatko GOSEV	M	7	(1)	1
Stojan IGNJATOV	A	22		5
Davor IGNJATOVSKI	M		(4)	1
Dragan IVANOV	A	5	(3)	2
Aleksandar KONJANOVSKI	D	17		1
Bosko KOVRLIJA (YUG)	M	8		1
Zoran KULIC	A	17	(2)	3
Zoran LILIC	D	9		
Igor MITREVSKI	D	23		
Vlatko NOVAKOV	D	17		
Borce POSTOLOV	A		(6)	
Ljupco SIMOVSKI	A	16	(3)	3
Dimitar SPASOVSKI	A	7	(8)	6
Dragance STEFANOV	G	2		
Aleksandar STOJANOV	D	17	(4)	
Nikolce TANUSEV	D	18	(3)	
Stefan TOLEVSKI	M	3	(4)	
Jovica TRAJCEV	A	14	(7)	1
Kire TRAJCEV	G	1		
Dragan UGRENOVC (YUG)	G	23		
Goran ZDRAVKOV	D	2	(1)	

LEAGUE RESULTS 1999/2000

15/08/99	FK Kumanovo	H	2-0	Gjosevski, Ignjatov
22/08/99	Makedonija GP Skopje	H	1-1	Gosev (p)
29/08/99	Rabotnicki Kometal Skopje	A	1-2	Ivanov
12/09/99	Pelister Bitola	H	2-0	Gjokic, Ignjatov
19/09/99	Sasa Makedonska Skopje	A	1-1	Kovrlija
26/09/99	Osogovo Kocani	H	4-2	Gjokic 3, Spasovski
03/10/99	Napredok Kicevo	A	3-0	Angelov 3
17/10/99	Cementarnica 55 Skopje	H	2-1	Ivanov, Gjokic
24/10/99	Borec MHK Veles	A	2-1	Trajcev J., Gjokic
31/10/99	Vardar Skopje	H	2-1	Gjokic 2
07/11/99	Sloga Jugomagnat Skopje	A	0-1	
14/11/99	Pobeda Prilep	H	2-2	Angelov, Gjosevski
21/11/99	Tikves Kavadarci	A	1-3	Angelov
05/03/00	FK Kumanovo	A	0-2	
12/03/00	Makedonija GP Skopje	A	0-0	
19/03/00	Rabotnicki Kometal Skopje	H	2-2	Gjosevski 2
26/03/00	Pelister Bitola	A	0-3	
02/04/00	Sasa Makedonska Skopje	H	0-0	
09/04/00	Osogovo Kocani	A	1-2	Kulic
16/04/00	Napredok Kicevo	H	1-0	Simovski
23/04/00	Cementarnica 55 Skopje	A	1-3	Konjanovski
30/04/00	Borec MHK Veles	H	6-0	Simovski 2, Spasovski 2, Ignjatov, Ignjatovski
07/05/00	Vardar Skopje	A	0-0	
14/05/00	Sloga Jugomagnat Skopje	H	4-0	Spasovski 2, Kulic 2
24/05/00	Pobeda Prilep	A	0-2	
28/05/00	Tikves Kavadarci	H	5-0	Georgiev 2, Ignjatov 2, Spasovski

SLOGA JUGOMAGNAT SKOPJE

CLUB DIRECTORY

FK Sloga Jugomagnat
Kemal Sejfula st. bb, 91 000 Skopje
tel - (91) 614772 / fax - (91) 616694
website - www.sloga-jugomagnat.com.mk
Year of Formation - 1927
President - Rafet Muminovic
Secretary - Ramadan Topojani
Coach - Gjore Jovanovski
Stadium - Cair (4,500)

MAJOR HONOURS
League Championship - (2) 1999, 2000.
Domestic Cup - (2) 1996, 2000.

APPEARANCES 99/00

	P	Ap	(s)	Gls
Arsim ABAZI	D	22		1
Refik ARIF	M	18		4
Oljaj BAJRAM	M	20	(2)	1
Toni BANDULIEV	M	2	(2)	
Ardzend BECIRI	A	20	(1)	19
Feim BEGANOVIC	M	15	(2)	4
Esad COLAKOVIC	D	20		
Bojan DIMITRIEVSKI	A	3	(3)	
Toni DZOLEV	M	1	(1)	
Haris FAKIC	M		(2)	
Gasi FETAI	M		(6)	4
Goran JOVANOVSKI	D	11		1
Goran MAZNOV	A	4	(4)	1
Nedzmedin MEMEDI	M	17		
Zoran MISERDOVSKI	A	21	(1)	10
Nebi MUSTAFI	M	18	(3)	5
Jane NIKOLOVSKI	G	24		
Masar OMERAGIC	M		(1)	
Bruno PRESILSKI	M	6	(9)	1
Zekirija RAMADAN	D	12	(4)	3
Gasi RAMADANI	A	2	(7)	
Saso ZDRAVEVSKI	D	21	(1)	1
Suat ZENDELI	G	2		

LEAGUE RESULTS 1999/2000

15/08/99	Pelister Bitolj	A	2-0	Beciri, Miserdovski
22/08/99	Sasa Makedonska Skopje	H	3-0	Miserdovski, Beganovic, Mustafi
29/08/99	Osogovo Kocani	A	2-0	Abazi, Beciri
12/09/99	Napredok Kicevo	H	4-0	Beciri 2, Miserdovski, Fetai
19/09/99	Cementarnica 55 Skopje	A	2-2	Beciri, Fetai
26/09/99	Borec MHK Veles	H	4-0	Beciri 2, Arif, Fetai
03/10/99	Vardar Skopje	A	1-1	Miserdovski
17/10/99	FK Kumanovo	A	2-0	Ramadan, Fetai
24/10/99	Pobeda Prilep	H	0-0	
31/10/99	Tikves Kavadarci	A	3-1	Miserdovski, Ramadan, Beciri
07/11/99	Sileks Kratovo	H	1-0	Arif
14/11/99	Makedonija GP Skopje	A	0-0	
21/11/99	Rabotnicki Kometal Skopje	H	4-0	Beciri 2, Beganovic, Bajram
05/03/00	Pelister Bitola	H	1-0	Beganovic
12/03/00	Sasa Makedonska Skopje	A	2-0	Beganovic, Zdravevski (p)
19/03/00	Osogovo Kocani	H	3-0	Mustafi, Beciri 2
26/03/00	Napredok Kicevo	A	0-0	
02/04/00	Cementarnica 55 Skopje	H	3-1	Ramadan, Miserdovski, Mustafi
09/04/00	Borec MHK Veles	A	3-0	Arif 2, Beciri (p)
16/04/00	Vardar Skopje	H	2-0	Beciri, Maznov
23/04/00	FK Kumanovo	H	1-0	Miserdovski
30/04/00	Pobeda Prilep	A	1-1	Beciri
07/05/00	Tikves Kavadarci	H	6-1	Beciri 3, Miserdovski 2, Jovanoski
14/05/00	Sileks Kratovo	A	0-4	
24/05/00	Makedonija GP Skopje	H	2-2	Presilski, Mustafi
28/05/00	Rabotnicki Kometal Skopje	A	3-0	Miserdovski, Beciri, Mustafi

TIKVES KAVADARCI

CLUB DIRECTORY

FK Tikves
ul. Disanska 2
93 000 Kavadarci
tel - (93) 410 521
fax - (93) 410521
Year of Formation - 1926
President - Cvetko Kabranov
Secretary - Sasko Tasev
Coach - Blagoja Kitanovski; Trajce Kocevski
Stadium - Gradski (3,000)

APPEARANCES 99/00

	P	Ap	(s)	Gls
Toni ANGELOV	M	11		3
Dragan DIMITROVSKI	A	18		10
Mario DIMOV	D	3		
Saso DIMOV	D	14	(1)	
Blagoja DONEV	M	9	(9)	
Enrike Masiel FLÁVIO (BRA)	M		(3)	
Dejan GEORGIEVSKI	M	1	(1)	
Kiro GORGIEV	M	12	(5)	2
Mitko ILIEV	D	12		
Jovan IVANOV	D	7		
Pane IVANOV	D		(1)	
Petre IVANOVSKI	D	17	(2)	
Vanco KOSTOV	D	7		1
Laze KUZMANOV	G	1		
Ilija MILENKOVSKI	M	2	(5)	
Mile MILEV	A	3	(1)	
Mateja MIRKOV	G	5		
Ivan MITREV	M	1		
Zoran MITREV	A	18	(3)	6
Petar MITREV	M	20		1
Zlatko NIKOLOV	D	11	(7)	1
Vito PEREIRA (BRA)	M	2		
Igor STOJANOV	D	19	(1)	
Antonio TASEV	A	18		12
Sasko TRAJKOV	M	16	(2)	
Milan TOSIC (YUG)	G	9		
Goce TOLEVSKI	M	6	(3)	1
Milan TRENCEVSKI	G	11	(1)	
Nenad VUCKOVSKI	A	3	(3)	
Aleksandar VELEVSKI	D	7	(2)	

LEAGUE RESULTS 1999/2000

15/08/99	Makedonja Asiba Skopje	A	2-3	Tasev, Mitrev Z.
22/08/99	Rabotnicki Kometal Skopje	H	2-0	Tasev 2
29/08/99	Pelister Bitola	A	0-1	
12/09/99	Sasa Makedonska Skopje	H	0-1	
19/09/99	Osogovo Kocani	A	1-4	Mitrev Z.
26/09/99	Napredok Kicevo	H	0-0	
03/10/99	Cementarnica 55 Skopje	A	1-1	Mitrev Z. (p)
17/10/99	Borec MHK Veles	H	2-1	Nikolov Z., Tasev
24/10/99	Vardar Skopje	A	2-2	Tasev 2
31/10/99	Sloga Jugomagnat Skopje	H	1-3	Tasev
07/11/99	Pobeda Prilep	A	0-4	
14/11/99	FK Kumanovo	A	3-0	Gorgiev, Tasev, Mitrev Z.
21/11/99	Sileks Kratovo	H	3-1	Dimitrovski 2, Tasev
05/03/00	Makedonija GP Skopje	H	2-1	Dimitrovski 2
12/03/00	Rabotnicki Kometal Skopje	A	1-2	Tasev (p)
19/03/00	Pelister Bitola	H	2-0	Mitrev P., Tasev
26/03/00	Sasa Makedonska Skopje	A	0-1	
02/04/00	Osogovo Kocani	H	5-3	Dimitrovski 2, Gorgiev, Angelov, Tolevski
09/04/00	Napredok Kicevo	A	1-1	Mitrev Z.
16/04/00	Cementarnica 55 Skopje	H	1-4	Dimitrovski
23/04/00	Borec MHK Veles	A	1-5	Kostov
30/04/00	Vardar Skopje	H	2-0	Dimitrovski 2
07/05/00	Sloga Jugomagnat Skopje	A	1-6	Tasev (p)
14/05/00	Pobeda Prilep	H	1-3	Mitrev Z.
24/05/00	FK Kumanovo	H	3-2	Angelov 2 (1p), Dimitrovski
28/05/00	Sileks Kratovo	A	0-5	

VARDAR SKOPJE

CLUB DIRECTORY

FK Vardar
Kej 13 Noemvri bb, 91 000 Skopje
tel - (91) 114782 / fax - (91) 115639
website - http://members.tripod.com/fcvardar/
Year of Formation - 1947
President - Aleksandar Trpevski
Secretary - Miso Majstorovic
Coach - Koco Dimitrovski; Vangel Simev;
Dragi Setinov; Petar Gruevski
Stadium - Gradski (22,000)

MAJOR HONOURS
League Championship (Yugoslavia) - (1) 1987.
League Championship - (3) 1993, 1994, 1995.
Domestic Cup (Yugoslavia) - (1) 1961.
Domestic Cup - (4) 1993, 1995, 1998, 1999.

APPEARANCES 99/00

	P	Ap	(s)	Gls
Nikola ANGELESKI	D		(1)	
Milan ARSOVSKI	D		(2)	
Nikola AVRAMOVSKI	M	8		
Ace BAJEVSKI	A	10	(6)	2
Marjan BELCEV	M	7		
Ilco BOROV	M	2	(1)	
Bobi BOZINOVSKI	D	7	(1)	
Erol DEMIR	D	9		2
Toni EFTIMOV	A	3	(3)	4
Slavco GEORGIEVSKI	M	12	(7)	2
Stole GORGIEV	D	4	(3)	
Daniel GOSEVSKI	D		(2)	
Bobi GRNCAROV	D	2	(4)	
Davor IGNATOVSKI	M	2	(6)	
Milan ILIEVSKI	D	2	(3)	
Tose IVANOV	D	1	(1)	
Saso JANEV	D	9		
Goran JANEVSKI	M	2		
Goran JOVANOSKI	D	11		
Ivica JOVANOVSKI	M	11	(1)	2
Saso KARADZOV	D	2	(2)	1
Darko KOSTOV	D	5		
Zarko KOSTOVSKI	M		(1)	
Saso KRSTEV	A	21	(1)	5
Nenad LAZAREVSKI	D		(1)	
Vlatko LJUSEV	D	15		
Goce MARKOSKI	M	6		
Srecko MISAJLOVSKI	M	1	(1)	
Dragan NACEVSKI	A	12	(5)	2
Igor NIKOLOVSKI	D	5	(1)	
Altin NUHI	D		(1)	
Edi NUREDINOSKI	G		(1)	
Masar OMERAGIC	M	3		
Goran PETRESKI	A	18	(3)	10
Sasa PETROVIC	A	1	(2)	
Artim SACIRI	A	9		2
Nenad SIMONOVSKI	D		(1)	
Vojo SIMONOVSKI	D	7	(4)	
Mirko SPASESKI	D	7		1
Igorce STOJANOV	D	20		
Darko STOJMENOV	D	2	(5)	
Vance TRAJCOV	A	19		6
Aleksandar VASEVSKI	D	5		
Muarem ZEKIR	G	23		
Igor ZLATANOVIC	G	3	(1)	

LEAGUE RESULTS 1999/2000

15/08/99	Sasa Makedonska Skopje	A	2-0	Eftimov, Trajcov
22/08/99	Osogovo Kocani	H	3-0	Petreski 2, Eftimov
29/08/99	Napredok Kicevo	A	2-2	Petreski, Eftimov
12/09/99	Cementarnica 55 Skopje	H	1-4	Trajcov
19/09/99	Borec MHK Veles	A	1-1	Trajcov
26/09/99	FK Kumanovo	A	8-0	Krstev 2, Petreski 3, Saciri, Trajcov, Nacevski
03/10/99	Sloga Jugomagnat Skopje	H	1-1	Nacevski
17/10/99	Pobeda Prilep	A	2-5	Georgievski, Petreski
24/10/99	Tikves Kavadarci	H	2-2	Trajcov, Bajevski
31/10/99	Sileks Kratovo	A	1-2	Bajevski
07/11/99	Makedonija GP Skopje	H	1-0	Demir
14/11/99	Rabotnicki Kometal Skopje	A	1-2	Demir
21/11/99	Pelister Bitola	H	3-2	Petreski, Saciri (p), Krstev
05/03/00	Sasa Makedonska Skopje	H	0-0	
12/03/00	Osogovo Kocani	A	0-1	
19/03/00	Napredok Kicevo	H	3-1	Karadzov, Petreski 2
26/03/00	Cementarnica 55 Skopje	A	0-2	
02/04/00	Borec MHK Veles	H	1-1	Jovanovski
09/04/00	FK Kumanovo	H	4-0	Trajcov (p), Krstev, Jovanovski, Georgievski
16/04/00	Sloga Jugomagnat Skopje	A	0-2	
23/04/00	Pobeda Prilep	H	1-2	Spaseski (p)
30/04/00	Tikves Kavadarci	A	0-2	
07/05/00	Sileks Kratovo	H	0-0	
14/05/00	Makedonija GP Skopje	A	1-3	Eftimov
24/05/00	Rabotnicki Kometal Skopje	H	0-2	
28/05/00	Pelister Bitola	A	1-1	Krstev

MALTA

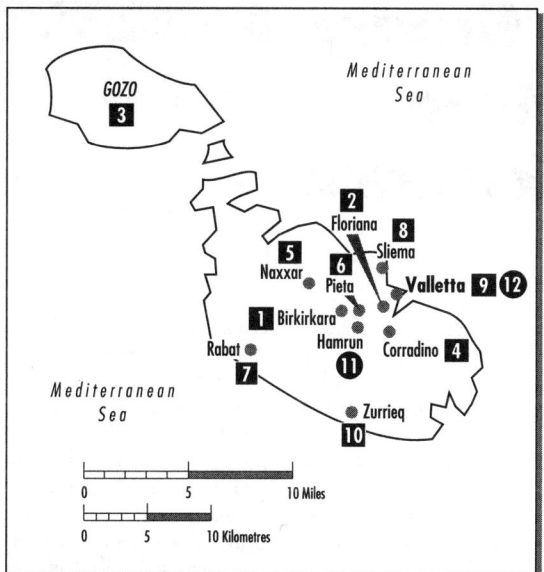

1	BIRKIRKARA	680
2	FLORIANA	681
3	GOZO	682
4	HIBERNIANS	683
5	NAXXAR LIONS	684
6	PIETA HOTSPURS	685
7	RABAT AJAX	686

8	SLIEMA WANDERERS	687
9	VALLETTA	688
10	ZURRIEQ	689
Promoted clubs		
11	HAMRUN SPARTANS	
12	XGHAJRA TORNADOES	

CENTENARY CELEBRATIONS FOR MFA

Dream finally comes true for Birkirkara

FEDERATION DIRECTORY

Malta Football Association
280 St. Paul's Street, Valletta, VLT 07

tel - 222697/232581   Year of Formation - 1900
fax - 245136   President - Joseph Mifsud
website - www.mfa.com.mt   Secretary - Joseph A. Sacco

Stadium - National, Ta' Qali (18,000)

Bridesmaids no more. After three successive years as runners-up, Birkirkara finally made it onto the top podium, winning the Maltese championship for the first time. It was the perfect way for the club to celebrate its 50th anniversary.

The Maltese Premier Division had a new format in 1999/2000. Instead of the previous three-round system, the ten clubs played each other home and away before being split into two play-off groups, with the top six contesting the championship and the bottom four trying to stave off relegation.

By the end of the first phase Birkirkara had a clear lead, seven points ahead of defending champions Valletta and 13 ahead of the third-placed team, Floriana. But with points being halved at this stage (as in Switzerland), the gap was reduced accordingly, and when Birkirkara surprisingly lost their first two play-off fixtures, against sixth-placed Hibernians and fifth-placed Pieta Hotspurs, it looked as if nerves were going to get the better of them once again. Valletta had joined them at the top of the table, and the pressure was well and truly on.

Birkirkara claimed a crucial victory in their next match, 2-0 against Sliema Wanderers, but the really vital win came two weeks later when they overcame Valletta 2-1. The match had everything, including an extraordinary climax. 1-0 up at half-time, Birkirkara lost defender Michael Spiteri to a red card. Shortly afterwards Valletta's Stefan Giglio missed a penalty, but then, in the final minute, Valletta skipper Kristian Laferla equalised with a lucky deflected shot. But Birkirkara were not to be denied, and they stole the points in sensational fashion with a last-minute penalty, midfielder Ivan Zammit coolly despatching the spot-kick after striker Chucks Nwoko had been brought down.

Once again Birkirkara had shown their mettle when it mattered. During the 'regular season' they had taken four points from their two encounters with Valletta, and now they had made it seven from three. It was the pivotal result of the season, because from there on in Birkirkara were in command. They won each of their next three games, sewing up the title with a 2-0 victory over Sliema Wanders - their fourth win out of four against the team that would ultimately pip a fading Valletta to the runners-up spot.

LEAGUE CHAMPIONSHIP FINAL TABLES 99/00

FIRST PHASE		Pd	W	D	L	F	A	Pt	GD	
1	Birkirkara	18	15	2	1	39	9	47	30	(24)
2	Valletta	18	13	1	4	58	22	40	36	(20)
3	Floriana	18	11	1	6	35	24	34	11	(17)
4	Sliema Wanderers	18	10	3	5	41	23	33	18	(17)
5	Pieta Hotspurs	18	7	5	6	33	36	26	-3	(13)
6	Hibernians	18	5	7	6	28	25	22	3	(11)
7	Naxxar Lions	18	4	4	10	27	40	16	-13	(8)
8	Gozo	18	3	5	10	14	29	14	-15	(7)
9	Zurrieq	18	3	3	12	20	55	12	-35	(6)
10	Rabat Ajax	18	2	3	13	19	51	9	-32	(5)

N.B. Figures in brackets indicate points carried forward to the Second Phase.

SECOND PHASE									
Championship Pool		Pd	W	D	L	F	A	Pt	GD
1	Birkirkara	28	22	3	3	61	14	46	47
2	Sliema Wanderers	28	17	4	7	62	36	39	26
3	Valletta	28	18	2	8	75	36	36	39
4	Floriana	28	14	2	12	50	44	27	6
5	Pieta Hotspurs	28	10	5	13	45	57	22	-12
6	Hibernians	28	8	7	13	37	48	20	-11
Relegation Pool		Pd	W	D	L	F	A	Pt	GD
7	Naxxar Lions	24	8	5	11	44	49	21	-5
8	Rabat Ajax	24	5	6	13	34	62	17	-28
9	Gozo	24	4	7	13	22	39	12	-17
10	Zurrieq	24	4	3	17	32	77	9	-45

DOMESTIC CUP 99/00

FIRST ROUND
Lija Athletics 1, Zurrieq 0
Floriana 2, Gzira United 0
Rabat Ajax 2, Mosta 2 (aet; 4-2 on pens.)
Marsa 0, Gozo 3
Hamrun Spartans 2, St. Patrick 0
Pieta Hotspurs 2, Tarxien Rainbows 0
Xghajra Tornadoes 2, St. Andrews 1
Zebbug Rangers 2, Naxxar Lions 3 (aet)

SECOND ROUND
Floriana 2, Naxxar Lions 1
Pieta Hotspurs 1, Rabat Ajax 1 (aet; 1-3 on pens.)
Lija Athletics 2, Gozo 4
Hamrun Spartans 2, Xghajra Tornadoes 1

QUARTER-FINALS
Sliema Wanderers 6 (Mifsud 13, 44, 67, 73, Farrugia 14, Busuttil 47),
Gozo 1 (Elkiate 82)

Valletta 5 (Agius G. 9, 89, Veselji 23, 41, Radak 46),
Floriana 4 (Galea 13, 90, Zaitsev 29, Mattocks 42)
Hibernians 2 (Cohen 95, Mifsud 110), Hamrun Spartans 1 (Zammit 105) (aet)
Birkirkara 2 (Brincat 63, 78), Rabat Ajax 1 (Petrovic 30)

SEMI-FINALS
Valletta 2 (Agius G. 26, Radak 62p),
Sliema Wanderers 3 (Mifsud 19, Turner 23p, Antic 78)
Birkirkara 3 (Eminyan 76, 86, Zammit 90), Hibernians 0

FINAL
18/05/2000, Ta' Qali
SLIEMA WANDERERS 4 Bonnici M.A. (10), Mifsud (36, 41), Busuttil (75)
BIRKIRKARA 1 Grima (74og)
referee - Darmanin
SLIEMA WANDERERS - Barry, Bonnici M.A., Gregory (Camilleri 84), Zammit Fava,
Antic, Dimech, Turner, Busuttil, Mifsud, Ogbodo (Farrugia 81), Grima (Galea 90).
BIRKIRKARA - Savic, Eminyan (Braunovic 33), Bencini, Spiteri, Pintac, Zammit,
Cutajar, Brincat, Nwoko, Mamo (Galea 46), Magri Overand (Suda 68).

Birkirkara's final figures made impressive reading. They had lost just three matches and conceded a miserly 14 goals - an average of one every other game. Valletta and Sliema both outscored them, but it was the Birkirkara defence, underpinned by the team's three Yugoslav imports - goalkeeper Robert Savic and stoppers Drasko Braunovic and Djordje Pintac - that provided the foundation for the club's historic triumph. Birkirkara had also had a Yugoslav coach at the start of the season, but Vlado Pejovic was dimissed after a 7-0 hammering by Lyngby in the UEFA Cup and replaced by Bulgarian Atanas Marinov. Of the local players, veteran Maltese international midfielder Joe Brincat and top scorer Michael Galea both contributed a great deal, while naturalised Nigerian Nwoko did enough to earn himself regular selection for the Maltese national side.

Birkirkara had the opportunity to supplement their hard-won championship title with a first-ever victory in the FA Trophy. They reached the final with victories over Rabat Ajax and Hibernian, but Sliema Wanderers finally gained revenge for all their league defeats by destroying Birkirkara 4-1 to take the Cup for the 18th time, thus equalling the record number of wins set by Floriana. Sliema then repeated the feat in the Super Cup, beating Birkirkara 3-0.

There were no surprises in the league relegation pool, with the two newly-promoted sides, Zurrieq and Gozo, both going down.

As expected, Hamrun Spartans also came straight back from the First Division, finishing on top despite a two-point deduction. They were accompanied into the top flight by Xghajra Tornadoes.

TOP SCORERS

21	Michael MIFSUD (Sliema Wanderers)
17	Gilbert AGIUS (Valletta)
	Stefan GIGLIO (Valletta)
15	Nenad VESELJI (Valletta)
	Nikolai KIRILOV (Zurrieq)
14	Michael GALEA (Birkirkara)
	Rufin OBA (Floriana)
	Orosko ANONAM (Naxxar Lions)

INTERNATIONAL HONOURS

None

NATIONAL TEAM RESULTS 99/00

21/08/99	Croatia (ECQ)	A	Zagreb	1-2	Carabott (61)
08/09/99	Republic of Ireland (ECQ)	H	Ta' Qali	2-3	Said (62), Carabott (68p)
24/11/99	Lebanon	A	Beirut	0-0	
15/12/99	Lebanon	H	Ta' Qali	1-0	Carabott (80p)
20/01/00	Qatar	H	Ta' Qali	2-0	Carabott (40p), Busuttil (47)
06/02/00	Azerbaijan	H	Ta' Qali	3-0	Buttigieg (32), Agius (53, 90p)
08/02/00	Andorra	H	Ta' Qali	1-1	Mallia (15)
10/02/00	Albania	H	Ta' Qali	0-1	
28/03/00	Northern Ireland	H	Ta' Qali	0-3	
29/05/00	South Africa	H	Ta' Qali	0-1	
03/06/00	England	H	Ta' Qali	1-2	Carabott (27p)

It was a big season for the Malta Football Association, which, as one of Europe's oldest national football federations, celebrated its 100th birthday in 2000. One of the highlights of the centenary festivities was the visit of England to the Ta' Qali at the beginning of June. It was the national team's final fixture of a busy season and they came so close to ending it on a real high. In the final minute of a game in which Malta fielded 22 players David Carabott missed a penalty that would have given the home side a precious 2-2 draw.

Some months earlier Malta also put up a very respectable showing in their final Euro 2000 qualifier, at home to the Republic of Ireland. It was the team's fervent desire to end the campaign by winning their first point, but, having come back from 0-2 to 2-2, they lost the game to a late winner from Irish defender Steve Staunton.

Malta made a bright start to their centenary year when they beat Qatar 2-0 and Azerbaijan 3-0 in their first two matches. When added to the controversial 1-0 victory achieved against Lebanon in the last match of 1999 - the game was actually abandoned in the 88th minute after

NATIONAL TEAM APPEARANCES 99/00

Coach - Josef ILIC	CRO	IRL	LBN	LBN	QTR	AZB	AND	ALB	NIR	SAF	ENG	Cps	Gls
Ernest BARRY (01/07/67) - Sliema Wanderers	G	G	G		G	G	G	G	G46	G	G90	18	-
Brian SAID (15/05/73) - Floriana	D	D						D	D		D77	19	1
Silvio VELLA (08/02/67) - Hibernians	D	s29						D58			D41	90	1
Darren DEBONO (09/01/74) - Valletta	D	D	D	D		D	D	D	D	D	D33	36	-
David CARABOTT (18/06/68) - Hibernians	D	D	D	D	D				M	D	M90	91	9
David CAMILLERI (21/08/74) - Sliema Wanderers	M	M	M67								s33	59	1
Carmel BUSUTTIL (29/02/64) - Sliema Wanderers	M77	M	M62		M59	M72	M62	M	M62	M77	M46	103	23
Nicky SALIBA (26/08/66) - Valletta	M	M										65	4
Joe BRINCAT (05/03/70) - Birkirkara	M		M46	M55	M59					M54	A82	84	5
Chucks NWOKO (21/11/78) - Birkirkara	M90	A	A90	A77		A		A66	A75	A46	s46	18	-
Gilbert AGIUS (21/02/74) - Valletta	A83	A67	A46		A73	A	s62	A	A46	s46	A60	53	4
Digger OKONKWO (30/08/77) - Naxxar Lions	s77		s90		s68				s46		s77	5	-
Stefan SULTANA (18/07/68) - Hibernians	s83											33	4
Adrian MIFSUD (11/12/74) - Rabat Ajax	s90				s59			s66	s46			7	-
Jeffrey CHETCUTI (22/04/74) - Valletta		D23		s46	D	D	D	D	D		s55	41	-
John BUTTIGIEG (05/10/63) - Valletta		D29	D	D46	D68	D	D	D	D46	D	D55	95	1
Richard BUHAGIAR (17/03/72) - Floriana		s23										54	-
Daniel THEWMA (29/06/71) - Valletta		s67	D	D	s46	D	D	D46		D	s41	10	-
Antoine ZAHRA (08/03/79) - Birkirkara			A	A								26	1
Jonathan HOLLAND (15/07/78) - Floriana			s46	M	M	M	M74			s77	s82	8	-
George MALLIA (10/10/78) - Floriana			s46	s77	A	s72	A46		s75		s60	7	1
Nenad VESELJI (03/02/71) - Valletta			s62	A46			A		s62		s87	5	-
Stefan GIGLIO (26/02/79) - Valletta			s67	M	M46	M61	s46	s46				12	-
Mario MUSCAT (18/08/76) - Hibernians				G					s46		s90	19	-
Michael GALEA (01/02/79) - Birkirkara				s46			A					2	-
Massimo GRIMA (05/07/79) - Sliema Wanderers				s55	D	D46						4	-
Edward AZZOPARDI (13/12/77) - Valletta					s59	s61			s58	s88		5	-
Adrian CIANTAR (09/08/78) - Hibernians					s73		s74	s66	M46		s90	5	-
Noel TURNER (09/12/74) - Sliema Wanderers						s46	D	M66	s46	M88	M87	36	1
Michael MIFSUD (17/04/81) - Sliema Wanderers								A		A		2	-
Luke DIMECH (11/01/77) - Sliema Wanderers										D	s77	3	-
Dybril SYLLA - Gozo										s54		1	-
Michael SPITERI (25/02/69) - Birkirkara											D77	17	1

EUROPEAN CUPS 99/00

CHAMPIONS' CUP
● VALLETTA
Preliminary round 1 BARRY TOWN (WAL)
A 0-0
  Cini, Giglio, Chetcuti, Radak, Debono, Buttigieg, Agius G.
  (Azzopardi 89), Saliba, Veselji (Camilleri 75), Ivanov, Thewma.
H 3-2 Agius G. (41, 45), Chetcuti (56)
  Cini, Giglio, Chetcuti, Radak, Debono,Buttigieg, Agius G., Saliba
  (Azzopardi 84), Veselji (Laferla 69), Ivanov (Camilleri 58), Thewma.

Preliminary round 2 SK RAPID WIEN (AUT)
A 0-3
  Cini, Giglio, Chetcuti, Radak, Debono, Buttigieg (Laferla 25), Agius G.,
  Saliba (Agius J. 90), Veselji (Camilleri 71), Ivanov, Thewma.
H 0-2
  Cini (Sullivan 72), Giglio (Debono 79), Chetcuti, Radak, Thewma,
  Camilleri, Agius G., Saliba, Veselji, Ivanov (Laferla 40), Azzopardi.

UEFA CUP
● BIRKIRKARA
Qualifying round LYNGBY FC (DEN)
A 0-7
  Savic, Pintac, Magri Overand (Spiteri M. 35), Zammit, Cutajar (Galea 46),
  Matanovic, Zahra, Brincat, Bencini (Suda 78), Nwoko, Eminyan.
H 0-0
  Savic, Bencini, Matanovic, Pintac, Magri Overand, Zammit (Zahra 68),
  Suda (Sammut 78), Brincat, Galea (Spiteri O. 90), Nwoko, Eminyan.

● SLIEMA WANDERERS
Qualifying round FC ZÜRICH (SUI)
H 0-3
  Barry, Ciantar, Antic, Eguavon, Bergodi, Dimech, Policano (Zammit Fava
  72), Busuttil (Debono 88), Ogbodo, Camilleri, Grima (Bonnici M.A. 57).
A 0-1
  Barry, Ciantar, Antic, Eguavon (Grima 53), Bergodi, Dimech, Policano
  (Bonnici M.A. 75), Busuttil, Ogbodo (Mifsud 56), Camilleri, Bonnici K..

PLAYER OF THE SEASON

MICHAEL MIFSUD
Michael Mifsud was the name on every Maltese
football fan's lips during the 1999/2000 season.
The Sliema Wanderers teenager was in awesome
goalscoring form throughout the campaign. He
was the Premier League's leading marksman on 21
goals and added another ten in other competitions
(including a brace in the Wanderers' Cup final win
over Birkirkara) to finish up with a grand total of
31. A hugely exciting talent, he was rewarded with
his first senior international cap - while still only 18
- against Albania in the Rothmans International
Tournament in February and played again later in
the season against South Africa. He missed the
prestige friendly with England because he was on
trial with German club Borussia Mönchengladbach,
where he left a very favourable impression, scoring
three goals in two games.

chaos broke out on the pitch between brawling players -
Malta found themselves celebrating the rare feat of
winning three matches in a row.

The third of the victories, against Azerbaijan, was
also memorable for being the 100th international match
played by Carmel Busuttil. The veteran Sliema Wanderers
midfielder reached the magic figure just a few weeks
before his 36th birthday. His first cap had come a remarkable 18 years earlier. He also took his haul of international
goals to 23 in the previous win, against Qatar.

While there are several other Maltese players who seem
set to join Busuttil in the 100-cap club - John Buttigieg,
David Carabott and Silvio Vella all ended the season in
the nineties - it is inconceivable that anyone will ever break
his goalscoring record. Carabott, with his five international
goals scored during the season, took his total to nine,
putting him a distant second to Busuttil in the all-time
classification.

PROMOTED CLUBS 99/00

FIRST DIVISION FINAL TABLE

		Pd	W	D	L	F	A	Pt	GD
1	Hamrun Spartans	18	13	5	0	39	15	42	24
2	Xghajra Tornadoes	18	10	5	3	38	15	35	23
3	Lija Athletics	18	9	3	6	26	22	30	4
4	St. Andrews	18	8	4	6	31	26	28	5
5	Tarxien Rainbows	18	8	2	8	31	27	26	4
6	Marsa	18	7	2	9	24	26	23	-2
7	Mosta	18	6	4	8	23	24	22	-1
8	St. Patrick	18	6	4	8	19	33	22	-14
9	Gzira United	18	4	6	8	14	24	18	-10
10	Zebbug Rangers	18	0	3	15	11	44	3	-33

N.B. Hamrun Spartans - 2 points deducted

CLUB DIRECTORIES

Hamrun Spartans FC
42 Dun Nerik Cordina Street,
Hamrun
tel - 241682 / fax - 251482
Year of Formation - 1907
President - Gejtu Debattista
Secretary - Stephen Saliba
Coach - Andy Weavill
Stadium - Victor Tedesco (6,000)

Xghajra Tornadoes FC
Church Street, Xghajra, Zabbar
tel - 692710
Year of Formation - 1985
President - Joe Mizzi
Secretary - Lawrence Lia
Coach - Bobby Gyorev
Stadium - National, Ta' Qali
(18.000)

MAJOR HONOURS
League Championship - (7)
1914, 1918, 1947, 1983,
1987, 1988, 1991.
Domestic Cup - (6) 1983, 1984,
1987, 1988, 1989, 1992.

BIRKIRKARA

CLUB DIRECTORY

Birkirkara FC
Old Church Street
Birkirkara
tel - 447005
fax - 489214
Year of Formation - 1950
President - Victor Zammit
Secretary - Joe Brincat
Coach - Vlado Pejovic; Atanas Marinov
Stadium - National, Ta' Qali (18,000)

MAJOR HONOURS
League Championship - (1) 2000.

APPEARANCES 99/00

	P	Ap	(s)	Gls
Graham BENCINI	D	25		
Drasko BRAUNOVIC (YUG)	D	24	(1)	2
Roderick BRIFFA	D	3	(2)	
Joe BRINCAT	M	18	(3)	10
Michael CUTAJAR	A	19	(2)	8
Andy EMINYAN	M	5	(3)	
Michael GALEA	A	25	(2)	14
Jonathan MAGRI OVERAND	D	11	(11)	
Carlo MAMO	D	21	(3)	
Clint MICALLEF	M		(4)	
Marco MUSCAT	D		(1)	
Chucks NWOKO	A	22		7
Djordje PINTAC (YUG)	D	26		1
Darren PISANI	M	1		
Simon SAMMUT	A	12	(11)	1
Robert SAVIC (YUG)	G	27		
Charles SCIBBERAS	G	1	(2)	
Kenneth SCICLUNA	D		(5)	
Michael SPITERI	D	23	(1)	4
Oliver SPITERI	M	10	(4)	
Hubert SUDA	A	6	(6)	2
Alan TABONE	D	1	(3)	
Antoine ZAHRA	A	11	(7)	2
Ivan ZAMMIT	M	17	(3)	8

LEAGUE RESULTS 1999/2000

29/08/99	Floriana	2-1	Galea, Zahra
01/09/99	Zurrieq	4-1	Pintac, Zahra (p), Braunovic, Sammut
12/09/99	Sliema Wanderers	2-1	Galea, Brincat
17/09/99	Hibernians	0-0	
25/09/99	Pieta Hotspurs	3-1	Brincat 2, Galea
03/10/99	Naxxar Lions	5-1	Braunovic, Spiteri M., Brincat 2 (1p), Nwoko
10/10/99	Gozo	0-1	
17/10/99	Rabat Ajax	2-0	Galea, Suda (p)
22/10/99	Valletta	2-0	Galea, Cutajar
15/11/99	Zurrieq	2-0	Galea 2
20/11/99	Floriana	1-0	Brincat
04/12/99	Sliema Wanderers	1-0	Galea
18/12/99	Pieta Hotspurs	1-0	Nwoko
21/12/99	Hibernians	2-0	Galea, Brincat
03/01/00	Naxxar Lions	5-2	Galea 2 (1p), Spiteri M., Zammit, Cutajar
17/01/00	Gozo	2-0	Zammit, Cutajar
23/01/00	Rabat Ajax	4-0	Cutajar 2, Zammit, Suda
30/01/00	Valletta	1-1	Zammit
19/02/00	Hibernians	0-1	
26/02/00	Pieta Hotspurs	0-1	
04/03/00	Sliema Wanderers	2-0	Nwoko, Cutajar
11/03/00	Floriana	3-0	Nwoko, Zammit (p), Galea
19/03/00	Valletta	2-1	Brincat, Zammit (p)
01/04/00	Hibernians	2-0	Cutajar, Galea
08/04/00	Pieta Hotspurs	5-0	Spiteri M., Nwoko 2, Cutajar, og (Azzopardi)
16/04/00	Sliema Wanderers	2-0	Nwoko, og (Grima)
24/04/00	Floriana	1-1	Spiteri M.
30/04/00	Valletta	5-1	Zammit 2 (1p), Galea, Brincat 2

FLORIANA

CLUB DIRECTORY

Floriana FC
28 St. Anne Street, Floriana VLT 15
tel - 447151 / fax - 496482
Year of Formation - 1894
President - Dennis Burke
Secretary - Charles Micallef
Coach - Mark Miller & Traiko Sokolov
Stadium - National, Ta' Qali (18,000)

MAJOR HONOURS
League Championship - (25)
1910, 1912, 1913, 1921, 1922, 1925, 1927,
1928, 1929, 1931, 1935, 1937, 1950, 1951,
1952, 1953, 1955, 1958, 1962, 1968, 1970,
1973, 1975, 1977, 1993.
Domestic Cup - (18) 1938, 1945, 1947, 1949,
1950, 1953, 1954, 1955, 1957, 1958, 1961,
1966, 1967, 1972, 1976, 1981, 1993, 1994.

APPEARANCES 99/00

	P	Ap	(s)	Gls
Nicholas BALDACHINO	M		(3)	
Etienne BARBARA	M	11	(6)	
Glen BARRY	A	7	(7)	
Richard BUHAGIAR	A	8	(5)	3
Albert BUSUTTIL	A	17	(2)	3
William CAMENZULI	D	24		1
Mathew CAMILLERI	G	19		
Mario CARUANA	D	16	(1)	
Dennis CAUCHI	D	14	(1)	
Clifton CIANTAR	D		(4)	
FORMOSA	M	1		
Mark GALEA	A	13	(7)	8
Justin HABER	G	9		
Jonathan HOLLAND	M	24		4
George MALLIA	A	16		2
Claude MATTOCKS	M	16	(6)	3
James NAVARRO	D	12	(4)	
Rufin OBA (CON)	A	21	(3)	14
Brian SAID	D	10	(2)	1
Charles SCIBBERAS	M	12	(8)	2
SULLIVAN	M		(1)	
Ivan VASILEV (BUL)	D	19	(2)	1
Kim WRIGHT	M	4	(1)	
Antoine ZAHRA	M	12	(9)	3
Todor ZAITSEV (BUL)	M	23	(3)	5

LEAGUE RESULTS 1999/2000

24/08/99	Naxxar Lions	2-0	Oba, Sciberras
29/08/99	Birkirkara	1-2	Buhagiar
12/09/99	Gozo	5-1	Holland 2, Busuttil, Buhagiar, Oba
19/09/99	Sliema Wanderers	1-2	Oba
25/09/99	Rabat Ajax	4-3	Sciberras, Zaitsev, Oba, Vasilev
01/10/99	Hibernians	1-0	Oba
09/10/99	Valletta	3-1	Zaitsev, Oba, Zahra
16/10/99	Pieta Hotspurs	2-3	Oba (p), Galea
23/10/99	Zurrieq	3-2	Galea 2, Oba (p)
15/11/99	Naxxar Lions	0-3	
20/11/99	Birkirkara	0-1	
04/12/99	Rabat Ajax	4-1	Mattocks 2, Galea 2
09/12/99	Gozo	1-0	Zaitsev
21/12/99	Sliema Wanderers	1-0	Holland
02/01/00	Hibernians	2-0	Galea 2
15/01/00	Valletta	1-2	Zahra
23/01/00	Pieta Hotspurs	2-2	Zaitsev, Mattocks
30/01/00	Zurrieq	2-1	Mallia, Holland
20/02/00	Pieta Hotspurs	2-0	Oba (p), Mallia
26/02/00	Valletta	0-3	
05/03/00	Hibernians	1-2	Buhagiar
11/03/00	Birkirkara	0-3	
19/03/00	Sliema Wanderers	4-5	Busuttil, Oba 2 (1p), Zaitsev
02/04/00	Pieta Hotspurs	3-2	Oba (p), Zahra, Said
09/04/00	Valletta	0-2	
16/04/00	Hibernians	3-0	Busuttil, Oba, Camenzuli
24/04/00	Birkirkara	1-1	Galea
29/04/00	Sliema Wanderers	1-2	Oba (p)

GOZO

CLUB DIRECTORY

Gozo FC
Gozo Football Association
Gozo Stadium
Imgarr Street
Xewkija, Gozo
tel - 558124
fax - 559448
Year of Formation - 1936
President - Joe Micallef
Secretary - Joe Camilleri
Coach - Alfred Cardona
Stadium - Gozo Stadium (6,000)

APPEARANCES 99/00

	P	Ap	(s)	Gls
Sammy ATTARD	G	7		
BORG	D	1	(1)	
Mark BUTTIGIEG	M	20		
Chris CAMILLERI	M	15	(3)	1
David CLUETT	G	17		
Miguel CORBOLAN (ARG)	A	6	(2)	
Martin CREMONA	M	19		1
Chris DEBRINCAT	D	15	(2)	
Ventislav DIMITROV (BUL)	D	2	(11)	
Mustafa ELKIATE	D	6	(8)	2
Saviour FARRUGIA	D	5	(13)	
Dione LAUTIER	A	6	(10)	4
Velibor MATANOVIC (YUG)	D	20		5
Brian MEILAQ	M	9	(7)	
Reuben MERCIECA	M	3		
Benneth NJOKU (NIG)	D	22		2
Igor STEFANOVIC (YUG)	A	24		5
Dybril SYLLA	M	9		
Angel TERZYSKI	M	19		1
Mahjoub TOUALI (MAR)	A	12	(3)	1
Giovann VELLA	D	11	(4)	
Jonathan XUEREB	G		(1)	
Joe ZARB	M	16		

LEAGUE RESULTS 1999/2000

29/08/99	Naxxar Lions	1-2	Matanovic (p)
12/09/99	Floriana	1-5	Lautier
18/09/99	Rabat Ajax	1-1	Matanovic (p)
21/09/99	Pieta Hotspurs	0-0	
26/09/99	Valletta	0-2	
03/10/99	Zurrieq	1-1	Matanovic (p)
10/10/99	Birkirkara	1-0	Stefanovic
17/10/99	Sliema Wanderers	1-2	Lautier
24/10/99	Hibernians	1-3	Stefanovic
14/11/99	Pieta Hotspurs	3-2	Njoku, Cremona, Elkiate
01/12/99	Naxxar Lions	0-0	
09/12/99	Floriana	0-1	
13/12/99	Rabat Ajax	1-2	Lautier
19/12/99	Valletta	0-1	
03/01/00	Zurrieq	1-0	Touali
17/01/00	Birkirkara	0-2	
29/01/00	Sliema Wanderers	1-4	Camilleri
15/02/00	Hibernians	1-1	Njoku
20/02/00	Naxxar Lions	0-1	
12/03/00	Rabat Ajax	0-0	
01/04/00	Zurrieq	3-1	Stefanovic 2, Matanovic (p)
08/04/00	Naxxar Lions	1-3	Stefanovic
22/04/00	Rabat Ajax	1-1	Lautier
29/04/00	Zurrieq	3-4	Matanovic (p), Elkiate, Terzyski

HIBERNIANS

Hibernians FC
PO Box 22, Paola
tel - 677764 / fax - 677764
Year of Formation - 1932
President - Anthony Bezzina
Secretary - Savior Cachia
Coach - Robert Gatt
Stadium - Hibernians Ground, Corradino (8,000)

MAJOR HONOURS
League Championship - (8) 1961, 1967, 1969,
1979, 1981, 1982, 1994, 1995.
Domestic Cup - (6)
1962, 1970, 1971, 1980, 1982, 1998.

APPEARANCES 99/00

	P	Ap	(s)	Gls
Kenneth ABELA	A	12	(10)	3
Darren ATTARD	A		(3)	
Lawrence ATTARD	D	13	(2)	
Roderick BALDACHINO	D	26		2
Martin BORG	M	7	(12)	
David CARABOTT	A	22	(1)	5
Albert CARUANA	M	1	(1)	
Ndubisi CHUKUNYERE (NIG)	A	12	(6)	5
Adrian CIANTAR	A	24	(2)	1
Andrew COHEN	A	2	(5)	1
Daniel COSAITIS	A		(1)	
Victor EGERE (NIG)	A	16	(1)	6
Rainier FARRUGIA	G	4	(1)	
Paul GRAHAM (ENG)	M		(1)	
Claude MANGION	M	2		
Essien MBONG (NIG)	M	26		2
Adrian MIFSUD	A	12	(1)	3
Mario MUSCAT	G	24		
Michael PORTELLI	M		(1)	
Charles SCERRI	M	4	(1)	1
Roderick SPITERI	M	1	(1)	
Wilfred SPITERI	D	9	(3)	
Stefan SULTANA	A	16	(6)	6
Trevor THOMAS	A		(1)	
Malcolm TIRCHETT	A		(1)	
Silvio VELLA	D	22	(1)	
Roger WALKER (ENG)	D	22		1
Aaron XUEREB	D	27		
Simon ZERAFA	A	4	(2)	

LEAGUE RESULTS 1999/2000

24/08/99	Rabat Ajax	3-0	Sultana 2, Mbong
28/08/99	Valletta	3-2	Baldachino 2, Chukunyere
12/09/99	Zurrieq	1-2	Scerri
17/09/99	Birkirkara	0-0	
26/09/99	Sliema Wanderers	3-3	Carabott 2, Sultana
01/10/99	Floriana	0-1	
10/10/99	Pieta Hotspurs	2-2	Sultana (p), Abela
17/10/99	Naxxar Lions	0-0	
24/10/99	Gozo	3-1	Egere 3
14/11/99	Rabat Ajax	3-0	Sultana (p), Carabott (p), Abela
27/11/99	Valletta	0-2	
05/12/99	Zurrieq	1-2	Egere
18/12/99	Sliema Wanderers	1-1	Ciantar
21/12/99	Birkirkara	0-2	
02/01/00	Floriana	0-2	
17/01/00	Pieta Hotspurs	4-1	Chukunyere 2, Mifsud, Egere (p)
29/01/00	Naxxar Lions	3-3	Abela, Chukunyere, og (Muscat)
15/02/00	Gozo	1-1	Sultana
19/02/00	Birkirkara	1-0	Mifsud
27/02/00	Sliema Wanderers	1-2	Egere (p)
05/03/00	Floriana	2-1	Walker, Mifsud
11/03/00	Valletta	1-2	Mbong
18/03/00	Pieta Hotspurs	0-4	
01/04/00	Birkirkara	0-2	
09/04/00	Sliema Wanderers	2-5	Carabott (p), Chukunyere
16/04/00	Floriana	0-3	
23/04/00	Valletta	2-1	Cohen, Carabott (p)
28/04/00	Pieta Hotspurs	0-3	

NAXXAR LIONS

CLUB DIRECTORY

Naxxar Lions FC
29/30 Victory Square
Naxxar NXR 03
tel - 411974
fax - 336578
Year of Formation - 1920
President - Michael Zammit Tabona
Secretary - Franco Vella
Coach - Terenzio Polverini; Simon Lane
Stadium - National, Ta' Qali (18,000)

APPEARANCES 99/00

	P	Ap	(s)	Gls
Orosko ANONAM (NIG)	A	19		14
Victor BELLIA	A	16	(1)	1
Stephen BONAVIA	M	1	(4)	
Andrea BONNICI	M	9	(3)	
Omar BORG	G	2		
Matthew CALASCIONE	A	21		4
Kevin CASSAR	A	1		
Ridha DARDOURI (TUN)	A	14	(7)	6
Reuben DEBONO	G	9	(1)	
Andy EZENWATA (NIG)	M		(1)	
FENECH	M	2		
Sandro GAMBIN	M	10		
Mark MARLOW	M	18	(5)	4
Franklyn MUSCAT	A	5	(2)	
Simon MUSCAT	A	4	(6)	
Peter OHAKA (NIG)	M	2	(3)	1
Gordon OHEAGBU (NIG)	M	1		
Chris OKOH (NIG)	D	20		1
Digger OKONKWO (NIG)	D	19	(1)	1
Chris ORETAN (NIG)	A	22		8
Matthew REED (ENG)	G	11		
Joe SANT FOURNIER	M	20		2
Kevin SCHEMBRI	D	4	(4)	
Paul SIXSMITH	M	22	(1)	1
Carmel SPITERI	D	6	(7)	
Michael WOODS	D	4	(3)	
Andrew XUEREB	G	2		

LEAGUE RESULTS 1999/2000

24/08/99	Floriana	0-2	
29/08/99	Gozo	2-1	Oretan, Sant Fournier
11/09/99	Rabat Ajax	3-2	Anonam, Marlow, Oretan
19/09/99	Valletta	2-4	Marlow (p), Ohaka
26/09/99	Zurrieq	2-2	Anonam, Okoh
03/10/99	Birkirkara	1-5	Oretan
10/10/99	Sliema Wanderers	0-3	
17/10/99	Hibernians	0-0	
23/10/99	Pieta Hotspurs	0-1	
15/11/99	Floriana	3-0	Anonam 2, og (Camenzuli)
01/12/99	Gozo	0-0	
08/12/99	Rabat Ajax	2-3	Anonam 2
11/12/99	Valletta	0-3	
19/12/99	Zurrieq	3-0	Anonam 2, Dardouri
03/01/00	Birkirkara	2-5	Anonam 2
23/01/00	Sliema Wanderers	2-3	Anonam 2
29/01/00	Hibernians	3-3	Anonam, Oretan, Okonkwo
13/02/00	Pieta Hotspurs	2-3	Oretan 2
20/02/00	Gozo	1-0	Dardouri
05/03/00	Zurrieq	2-0	Oretan, Sant Fournier
18/03/00	Rabat Ajax	3-3	Anonam, Oretan, Marlow (p)
08/04/00	Gozo	3-1	Calascione, Bellia, Marlow (p)
23/04/00	Zurrieq	6-2	Dardouri 4, Calascione 2
28/04/00	Rabat Ajax	2-3	Sixsmith, Calascione

PIETA HOTSPURS

CLUB DIRECTORY

Pieta Hotspurs FC
Our Lady of Sorrows Street
Pieta
tel - 231336
fax - 234150
Year of Formation - 1932
President - Edward Schembri
Secretary - Mario Mallia
Coach - George Deanov
Stadium - National, Ta' Qali (18,000)

APPEARANCES 99/00

	P	Ap	(s)	Gls
Sacho ANGELOV (BUL)	D	22		
Pierre AQUILINA	D	20	(4)	
Louis AZZOPARDI	D	10	(6)	
Julian BUHAGIAR	A		(1)	
Joe CAMILLERI	M	17	(3)	3
CAMILLERI	A		(1)	
Sergio CAPPITTA (ITA)	A		(1)	
Saviour DARMANIN	G	23	(1)	
Martin DEANOV (BUL)	M	23	(1)	3
Jesmond DELIA	D	24	(1)	2
Kevin FARRUGIA	D	3		
Carmel FORMOSA	A	15	(10)	3
Anthony GALEA	A	9	(8)	2
Malcolm LICARI	A	26		12
Edmond LUFI (ALB)	M	21	(1)	11
Kevin MAMO	A	24	(2)	
Etienne MERCIECA	G	4	(1)	
Marian METLAROV (BUL)	A	12		3
Clive MIZZI	M	6	(3)	1
Slavcho PAVLOV (BUL)	A	4		
Gianluca PORCARELLI (ITA)	G	1	(1)	
Eric SALIBA	D	16	(5)	1
Massimo SCHEMBRI	D	9	(5)	
Ullo TINDARO (ITA)	D	3		1
Ivan WOODS	M	16	(2)	3

LEAGUE RESULTS 1999/2000

28/08/99	Rabat Ajax	2-1	Tindaro, Lufi
11/09/99	Valletta	3-5	Lufi (p), Mizzi, Licari
18/09/99	Zurrieq	2-1	Licari, Lufi (p)
21/09/99	Gozo	0-0	
25/09/99	Birkirkara	1-3	Lufi (p)
02/10/99	Sliema Wanderers	0-0	
10/10/99	Hibernians	2-2	Saliba, Licari
16/10/99	Floriana	3-2	Licari, Lufi (p), Camilleri J.
23/10/99	Naxxar Lions	1-0	Camilleri J.
14/11/99	Gozo	2-3	Licari, Formosa
21/11/99	Rabat Ajax	2-2	Lufi (p), Licari
05/12/99	Valletta	2-5	Metlarov, Licari
11/12/99	Zurrieq	4-1	Lufi 2 (2p), Licari, Woods
18/12/99	Birkirkara	0-1	
03/01/00	Sliema Wanderers	3-2	Lufi, Delia, Metlarov
17/01/00	Hibernians	1-4	Camilleri J.
23/01/00	Floriana	2-2	Lufi (p), Deanov
13/02/00	Naxxar Lions	3-2	Deanov, Licari 2
20/02/00	Floriana	0-2	
26/02/00	Birkirkara	1-0	Licari
04/03/00	Valletta	0-2	
12/03/00	Sliema Wanderers	0-2	
18/03/00	Hibernians	4-0	Lufi, Metlarov, Formosa, Licari
02/04/00	Floriana	2-3	Formosa, Galea
08/04/00	Birkirkara	0-5	
15/04/00	Valletta	2-4	Deanov, Delia (p)
22/04/00	Sliema Wanderers	0-3	
28/04/00	Hibernians	3-0	Woods 2, Galea

RABAT AJAX

CLUB DIRECTORY

Rabat Ajax FC
Civic Centre, Parish Square,
Rabat RBT 05
tel - 454244/455847
Year of Formation - 1930
President - Noel Farrugia
Secretary - Mario Grima
Coach - Ziya Yildiz
Stadium - National, Ta' Qali (18,000)

MAJOR HONOURS
League Championship - (2) 1985, 1986.
Domestic Cup - (1) 1986.

APPEARANCES 99/00

	P	Ap	(s)	Gls
Roderick ASCIAK	A	24		7
Jonathan BEZZINA	M	1		
Angelo BORG	M		(3)	
Charles BORG	D	7	(7)	
William BORG	A	14	(6)	5
Rodney CAMILLERI	D	21	(1)	
Cedric CARUANA	D	21		6
Michael FARRUGIA	D	13	(1)	1
Keith FENECH	M	21		
Donovan FRIGGIERI	M	15	(3)	
Joe GALEA	D	19	(2)	3
Keith MICALLEF	A		(3)	
Michael MICALLEF	A	14	(6)	5
Adrian MIFSUD	A	11		1
Chris MUSCAT	A		(2)	
Vesko PETROVIC (YUG)	D	16	(3)	1
Joe Craig SCHEMBRI	D	11	(7)	2
Stoian SIMEONOV (BUL)	G	24		
Zija YILDIZ (BOS)	D	23		3
Jeffrey ZAMMIT	M	9	(3)	

LEAGUE RESULTS 1999/2000

24/08/99	Hibernians	0-3	
28/08/99	Pieta Hotspurs	1-2	Yildiz
11/09/99	Naxxar Lions	2-3	Schembri, Borg W.
18/09/99	Gozo	1-1	Schembri
25/09/99	Floriana	3-4	Caruana, Asciak, Galea
02/10/99	Valletta	0-9	
09/10/99	Zurrieq	1-1	Borg W.
17/10/99	Birkirkara	0-2	
24/10/99	Sliema Wanderers	1-3	Yildiz
14/11/99	Hibernians	0-3	
21/11/99	Pieta Hotspurs	2-2	Asciak 2
04/12/99	Floriana	1-4	Farrugia
08/12/99	Naxxar Lions	3-2	Caruana, Mifsud, Borg W.
13/12/99	Gozo	2-1	Asciak, Borg W.
02/01/00	Valletta	1-2	Micallef M.
15/01/00	Zurrieq	1-3	Galea
23/01/00	Birkirkara	0-4	
13/02/00	Sliema Wanderers	0-2	
27/02/00	Zurrieq	5-3	Micallef M., Petrovic, Asciak, Yildiz, Galea
12/03/00	Gozo	0-0	
18/03/00	Naxxar Lions	3-3	Caruana 2 (1p), Micallef M.
15/04/00	Zurrieq	3-2	Micallef M., Caruana, Asciak
22/04/00	Gozo	1-1	Caruana
28/04/00	Naxxar Lions	3-2	Asciak, Micallef M., Borg W.

SLIEMA WANDERERS

CLUB DIRECTORY

Sliema Wanderers FC
PO Box 7, Sliema
tel - 332033/346981/319426
fax - 320219/377739
Year of Formation - 1909
President - Robert Arrigo
Secretary - Olvin Mangion
Coach - Augustine Eguavon; Vlado Pejovic
Stadium - National, Ta' Qali (18,000)

MAJOR HONOURS
League Championship - (23) 1920, 1923, 1924,
1926, 1930, 1933, 1934, 1936, 1938, 1939,
1940, 1949, 1954, 1956, 1957, 1964, 1965,
1966, 1971, 1972, 1976, 1989, 1996.
Domestic Cup - (18) 1935, 1936, 1937, 1940,
1946, 1948, 1951, 1952, 1956, 1959, 1963,
1965, 1968, 1969, 1974, 1979, 1990, 2000.

APPEARANCES 99/00

	P	Ap	(s)	Gls
Zoran ANTIC (YUG)	D	22	(1)	2
Ernest BARRY	G	28		
Cristiano BERGODI (ITA)	D	18		1
Karl BONNICI	M	17	(5)	1
Mark Anthony BONNICI	M	13	(10)	1
Pablo BUGEJA	G		(1)	
Carmel BUSUTTIL	M	22		7
David CAMILLERI	A	11	(2)	5
Ian CIANTAR	D	20	(2)	
Anatole DEBONO	A	4	(11)	6
Luke DIMECH	D	10	(1)	1
Augustine EGUAVON (NIG)	D	1		
Joe FARRUGIA	M	9	(8)	2
Lino GALEA	D	20	(5)	1
Martin GREGORY	M	8	(7)	2
Massimo GRIMA	D	24	(1)	6
Michael MIFSUD	A	24	(4)	21
Uwa OGBODO (NIG)	A	20	(3)	3
Kevin SAMMUT	M		(11)	
Trevor TEMPLEMAN	A		(2)	
Noel TURNER	M	13		2
Brendan ZAMMIT	D		(1)	
Sandro ZAMMIT FAVA	D	24	(1)	

LEAGUE RESULTS 1999/2000

29/08/99	Zurrieq	5-0	Busuttil, Bonnici M.A., Dimech, Camilleri, Debono
01/09/99	Valletta	2-1	Camilleri, Busuttil
12/09/99	Birkirkara	1-2	Grima
19/09/99	Floriana	2-1	Busuttil, Grima
26/09/99	Hibernians	3-3	Camilleri 2, Antic
02/10/99	Pieta Hotspurs	0-0	
10/10/99	Naxxar Lions	3-0	Mifsud 3
17/10/99	Gozo	2-1	Bergodi, Grima
24/10/99	Rabat Ajax	3-1	Mifsud 2, Camilleri
20/11/99	Valletta	1-3	Grima
27/11/99	Zurrieq	7-2	Mifsud 3, Debono 3, Ogbodo
04/12/99	Birkirkara	0-1	
18/12/99	Hibernians	1-1	Mifsud
21/12/99	Floriana	0-1	
03/01/00	Pieta Hotspurs	2-3	Ogbodo, Gregory
23/01/00	Naxxar Lions	3-2	Farrugia, Gregory, Debono
29/01/00	Gozo	4-1	Debono, Farrugia, Busuttil, Antic
13/02/00	Rabat Ajax	2-0	Mifsud 2
19/02/00	Valletta	0-0	
27/02/00	Hibernians	2-1	Mifsud, Busuttil
04/03/00	Birkirkara	0-2	
12/03/00	Pieta Hotspurs	2-0	Mifsud 2
19/03/00	Floriana	5-4	Mifsud 3, Busuttil, Bonnici K.
02/04/00	Valletta	2-1	Busuttil, Mifsud
09/04/00	Hibernians	5-2	Grima, Turner, Mifsud 2, og (Vella)
16/04/00	Birkirkara	0-2	
22/04/00	Pieta Hotspurs	3-0	Ogbodo, Grima, Mifsud
29/04/00	Floriana	2-1	Galea, Turner (p)

VALLETTA

CLUB DIRECTORY

Valletta FC
126 St. Lucia Street, Valletta
tel - 224939 / fax - 230803
Year of Formation - 1904
President - Joe Caruana Curran
Secretary - Benny Pace
Coach - Krasimir Manolov
Stadium - National, Ta' Qali (18,000)
MAJOR HONOURS
League Championship - (17) 1915, 1932, 1945,
1946, 1948, 1959, 1960, 1963, 1974, 1978,
1980, 1984, 1990, 1992, 1997, 1998, 1999.
Domestic Cup - (10) 1960, 1964, 1975, 1977,
1978, 1991, 1995, 1996, 1997, 1999.

APPEARANCES 99/00

	P	Ap	(s)	Gls
Gilbert AGIUS	M	23	(1)	17
Jeremy AGIUS	A		(4)	
Jerome AGIUS	M		(1)	
Edward AZZOPARDI	D	14	(10)	2
John BUTTIGIEG	M	23	(1)	2
Joe CAMILLERI	D		(2)	
Jeffrey CHETCUTI	D	20	(1)	
Reggie CINI	G	19		
Darren DEBONO	D	23	(2)	
Rene FORACE	M	7	(9)	
Stefan GIGLIO	M	22	(1)	17
Lee GRIMA	D		(1)	
Alexander IVANOV (BUL)	M	8	(1)	1
Kristian LAFERLA	A	23	(1)	5
Clive MIZZI	D	9	(8)	
Pavel MRAZ (CZE)	A	13		5
Sinisa RADAK (YUG)	A	27	(1)	2
Antoine SACCO	A		(8)	1
Nicky SALIBA	M	7		1
Sean SULLIVAN	G	9	(3)	
Justin TELLUS	M	14	(7)	
Daniel THEWMA	A	21	(3)	7
Nenad VESELJI	A	25	(1)	15
Ivan WOODS	A		(7)	
Joe ZARB	M	1	(1)	

LEAGUE RESULTS 1999/2000

Date	Opponent	Score	Scorers
28/08/99	Hibernians	2-3	Laferla, Ivanov
01/09/99	Sliema Wanderers	1-2	Veselji
11/09/99	Pieta Hotspurs	5-3	Veselji 3, Thewma, Agius G.
19/09/99	Naxxar Lions	4-2	Agius G. 2, Veselji, Thewma
26/09/99	Gozo	2-0	Agius G., Veselji
02/10/99	Rabat Ajax	9-0	Agius G. 4, Giglio 2, Thewma 2, Azzopardi
09/10/99	Floriana	1-3	Giglio
16/10/99	Zurrieq	9-1	Veselji 3, Giglio 2, Saliba, Radak, Thewma, Agius G.
22/10/99	Birkirkara	0-2	
20/11/99	Sliema Wanderers	3-1	Laferla 2, Agius G.
27/11/99	Hibernians	2-0	Agius G. 2
05/12/99	Pieta Hotspurs	5-2	Giglio 2, Veselji 2, Agius G.
11/12/99	Naxxar Lions	3-0	Giglio 2 (1p), Agius G.
19/12/99	Gozo	1-0	Giglio (p)
02/01/00	Rabat Ajax	2-1	Mraz 2
15/01/00	Floriana	2-1	Thewma, Agius G.
23/01/00	Zurrieq	6-0	Mraz 2 (1p), Azzopardi, Radak, Veselji (p), Sacco
30/01/00	Birkirkara	1-1	Mraz
19/02/00	Sliema Wanderers	0-0	
26/02/00	Floriana	3-0	Giglio 2 (1p), Laferla
04/03/00	Pieta Hotspurs	2-0	Veselji, Giglio (p)
11/03/00	Hibernians	2-1	Thewma, Giglio
19/03/00	Birkirkara	1-2	Laferla
02/04/00	Sliema Wanderers	1-2	Veselji
09/04/00	Floriana	2-0	Giglio (p), Agius G.
15/04/00	Pieta Hotspurs	4-2	Giglio 2, Buttigieg, Agius G.
23/04/00	Hibernians	1-2	Buttigieg
30/04/00	Birkirkara	1-5	Veselji

ZURRIEQ

Zurrieq FC
30 Main Street, Zurrieq
tel - 640642
Year of Formation - 1949
President - Savior Farrugia
Secretary - Alfred Damato
Coach - Lawrence Borg; Vincent Carbonaro
Stadium - National, Ta' Qali (18,000)

MAJOR HONOURS
Domestic Cup - (1) 1985.

APPEARANCES 99/00

	P	Ap	(s)	Gls
Jean Pierre ABDILLA	M	2	(1)	
Darren BELLIZZI	D	8		
BEZZINA	M	1	(1)	
Tyron BONNICI	A		(7)	
Franklin BORG	D	18		
Anton BRIFFA	D		(1)	
Gordon CAMENZULI	A	9	(8)	
Neil CAMILLERI	A	10	(3)	
Tonio CARUANA	M	1		
Carmel FARRUGIA	M		(2)	
Colin FARRUGIA	A		(1)	
Franky FARRUGIA	G	1		
Jeffrey FARRUGIA	D	9	(1)	
Marco FARRUGIA	G	21		1
Franco FRANCALANZA	D	21		
Dami IRIELE	M	7		
Nikolai KIRILOV (BUL)	A	20		15
Gordon NAUDI	M	4	(4)	
Beppe PACE	A	18	(4)	
Kevin POLIDANO	M	3	(7)	
Franco PORTELLI	G	1		
Fethi RAMA (ALB)	M	10		
Saviour SACCO	M	7	(4)	
Jason SALIBA	D	3	(11)	
SALIBA	D	1		
Carmel SAMMUT	G	1	(1)	
Aldo SCARDINO	D	3		
Keith SEYCHELL	A		(2)	
Nikola SLAVCHEV (BUL)	A	16		5
Mark SULTANA	M	21		4
Ibrahim TARAK	A	1	(1)	
Graham UNAH (NIG)	M	7		
Josef VASSALLO	D	1		
Stephen WELLMAN	A	16	(16)	6
Edmond ZAMMIT	D	23		

LEAGUE RESULTS 1999/2000

29/08/99	Sliema Wanderers	0-5	
01/09/99	Birkirkara	1-4	Wellman
12/09/99	Hibernians	2-1	Wellman, Kirilov (p)
18/09/99	Pieta Hotspurs	1-2	Kirilov (p)
26/09/99	Naxxar Lions	2-2	Kirilov, Farrugia M.
03/10/99	Gozo	1-1	Kirilov
09/10/99	Rabat Ajax	1-1	og (Camilleri)
16/10/99	Valletta	1-9	Kirilov (p)
23/10/99	Floriana	2-3	Kirilov 2
15/11/99	Birkirkara	0-2	
27/11/99	Sliema Wanderers	2-7	Kirilov, Slavchev
05/12/99	Hibernians	2-1	Slavchev (p), Sultana
11/12/99	Pieta Hotspurs	1-4	Slavchev (p)
19/12/99	Naxxar Lions	0-3	
03/01/00	Gozo	0-1	
15/01/00	Rabat Ajax	3-1	Wellman 2, Sultana
23/01/00	Valletta	0-6	
30/01/00	Floriana	1-2	Wellman
27/02/00	Rabat Ajax	3-5	Wellman, Kirilov, Slavchev (p)
05/03/00	Naxxar Lions	0-2	
01/04/00	Gozo	1-3	Slavchev (p)
15/04/00	Rabat Ajax	2-3	Sultana, Kirilov
23/04/00	Naxxar Lions	2-6	Kirilov 2
29/04/00	Gozo	4-3	Sultana, Kirilov 3 (1p)

MOLDOVA

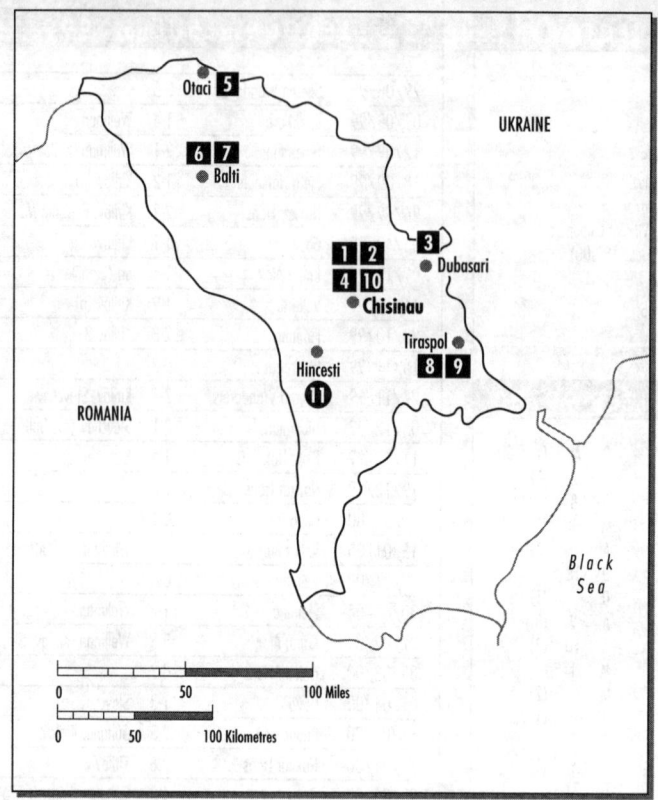

1	FC AGRO CHISINAU	695
2	CONSTRUCTORUL CHISINAU	696
3	ENERGHETIC DUBASARI	697
4	MOLDOVA-GAZ CHISINAU	698
5	NISTRU-UNISPORT OTACI	699
6	OLIMPIA BALTI	700

7	ROMA BALTI	701
8	SERIF TIRASPOL	702
9	TILIGUL TIRASPOL	703
10	ZIMBRU CHISINAU	704
Promoted club		
11	HAIDUCUL HINCESTI	

ENCOURAGING RESULTS IN EUROPE

Zimbru's title again as Serif falter

FEDERATION DIRECTORY

Federatia Moldoveneasca de Futbol
str. Tricolorului 39, 2012 Chisinau

tel - (22) 247875
fax - (22) 247890
website - www.iatp.md/fmf

Year of Formation - 1990
President - Pavel Ciobanu
Secretary - Nicolae Cebotari

Stadium - Republican (22,500)

The annual ritual of Zimbru Chisinau claiming the Moldovan championship was under serious threat in 1999/2000. For years the country's second city of Tiraspol had been striving to find a team that could take the title away from the capital, and the dream almost came true as Serif, picking up where Tiligul had left off in previous years, ran Zimbru extremely close. In the end there was only one point in it, but, as usual, it was Zimbru who finished first and their provincial challengers who had to settle for the runners-up spot.

The pattern was familiar, with Zimbru coming on strong in the closing weeks of the campaign to catch and overtake their challengers. At the mid-season break Serif held a four-point lead. They remained in first place through a busy spring period despite dropping unexpected points in three successive home games. The key fixture took place six rounds from the end of the marathon 36-match campaign when Serif entertained Zimbru at home.

Serif went into the match with a one-point advantage. Honours were even from the previous three meetings, with a win apiece and one draw, but when the defending champions raced into a 2-0 lead at half-time, Serif's title hopes looked dead and buried. After the interval, however, they stormed back, scoring three goals in six minutes to claim a hugely significant victory.

But even that four-point cushion with five games left proved insufficient. While Zimbru went on to win every subsequent match, including a controversial 2-1 win at Constructorul, Serif blew their chances with a shock 2-1 defeat at Olimpia on matchday 34. It was a game Serif should have won. 1-0 up as

LEAGUE CHAMPIONSHIP RESULTS 99/00

		1	2	3	4	5	6	7	8	9	10
1	FC Agro Chisinau		2-5	3-1	0-2	0-2	0-0	2-1	1-1	1-0	1-2
			0-1	2-0	2-1	2-1	0-2	4-1	1-3	2-0	0-2
2	Constructorul Chisinau	0-0		4-1	0-0	1-0	2-0	1-0	1-0	3-0	1-1
		3-1		3-1	1-0	2-1	1-0	7-1	2-2	0-0	1-2
3	Energhetic Dubasari	1-0	0-2		1-3	1-5	0-1	2-1	0-6	0-0	1-2
		0-2	1-4		0-3	0-4	0-1	0-1	0-1	0-3	0-2
4	Moldova-Gaz Chisinau	1-1	0-2	2-0		0-2	1-2	1-1	2-3	0-0	1-1
		2-0	1-1	4-1		1-1	1-2	0-1	0-2	0-0	0-1
5	Nistru Unisport	0-0	1-0	2-0	3-0		2-2	1-0	0-2	4-2	2-1
		1-1	0-0	5-0	1-0		3-0	2-0	1-2	0-0	0-1
6	Olimpia Balti	1-3	1-0	2-0	1-2	2-3		4-1	1-2	1-3	0-3
		0-0	0-0	4-0	0-2	2-2		0-1	2-1	3-2	2-5
7	Roma Balti	1-1	1-0	3-0	1-4	2-1	0-2		1-2	0-2	0-3
		1-1	2-3	2-1	1-1	0-1	1-1		0-3	0-0	+++
8	Serif Tiraspol	5-1	1-0	4-0	3-0	0-0	2-1	6-0		2-1	2-0
		1-0	0-0	8-0	3-1	1-1	0-1	1-0		2-0	3-2
9	Tiligul Tiraspol	4-0	1-1	1-1	1-0	0-0	1-1	1-0	1-0		0-2
		1-1	1-0	4-0	0-1	1-0	1-0	2-1	0-2		1-1
10	Zimbru Chisinau	6-1	1-0	2-0	6-0	0-0	3-0	1-2	3-0	1-1	
		3-0	0-0	4-0	3-0	2-1	3-0	5-0	1-1	3-0	

+++ - match void; awarded as away win.

INTERNATIONAL HONOURS

None

TOP SCORERS

20 Serghei ROGACIOV (Serif Tiraspol)

15 Vladimir PUSTOVIT (Moldova-Gaz Chisinau/ Constructorul Chisinau)
   Victor BERCO (Zimbru Chisinau)

14 Vladimir DOVGHII (Constructorul Chisinau)
   Iurie MITEREV (Zimbru Chisinau)

12 Serghei POGREBAN (Tiligul Tiraspol)
   David MUDJIRI (Serif Tiraspol)
   Alexander BERCO (Nistru Unisport Otaci)

11 Viorel FRUNZE (FC Agro Chisinau)

LEAGUE CHAMPIONSHIP FINAL TABLE 99/00

				Home				Away					Total						
		Pd	W	D	L	F	A	W	D	L	F	A	W	D	L	F	A	PT	GD
1	Zimbru Chisinau	36	13	4	1	47	6	12	3	3	31	15	25	7	4	78	21	82	57
2	Serif Tiraspol	36	14	3	1	44	8	11	3	4	33	17	25	6	5	77	25	81	52
3	Constructorul Chisinau	36	12	5	1	33	10	6	6	6	19	13	18	11	7	52	23	65	29
4	Nistru-Unisport Otaci	36	10	5	3	28	11	6	6	6	25	17	16	11	9	53	28	59	25
5	Tiligul Tiraspol	36	9	6	3	21	11	3	7	8	14	22	12	13	11	35	33	49	2
6	Olimpia Balti	36	6	3	9	26	30	7	4	7	16	21	13	7	16	42	51	46	-9
7	FC Agro Chisinau	36	8	2	8	23	25	2	8	8	13	31	10	10	16	36	56	40	-20
8	Moldova-Gaz Chisinau	36	3	7	8	17	21	7	2	9	20	27	10	9	17	37	48	39	-11
9	Roma Balti	36	4	5	9	16	26	4	1	13	12	40	8	6	22	28	66	30	-38
10	Energhetic Dubasari	36	2	1	15	7	41	0	1	17	6	59	2	2	32	13	100	8	-87

early as the sixth minute, they missed several chances to increase that lead and were made to pay when their hosts equalised from the penalty spot 13 minutes from time. That was not the end of it either, because Olimpia went on to claim all three points with a winning goal seven minutes from time.

Ironically, it was on the same ground, a week later, that Zimbru clinched the championship, hammering Olimpia 5-2 to take their eighth title in nine years.

The only other team to win the Moldovan championship were Constructorul (in 1996/97) and they carved another entry into their roll of honour by winning the Moldovan Cup. The final against Zimbru was a heated affair decided by a winning goal in the final seconds from Evghenie Boicenco. By the time Constructorul were presented with the trophy, the Zimbru players had all left the stadium in a huff. A touch more respect would have been appreciated, especially as Constructorul dedicated their victory to late president Valerii Rotaru, who had been shot dead by the Moldovan mafia a few months earlier.

Earlier in the season Zimbru had demonstrated that they were able competitors in European competition, reaching the third qualifying round of the Champions' League before going down with a fight to Dutch side PSV. They thrashed St. Patrick's Athletic 10-0 on aggregate before also overcoming Dinamo Tbilisi. Against both PSV and (in

DOMESTIC CUP 99/00

1/8 FINALS
Energhetic Dubasari v Olimpia Balti 0-2; 2-5
(Olimpia Balti 7-2)
Constructorul Chisinau v Intersport Chisinau 9-1; 1-0
(Constructorul Chisinau 10-1)
Moldova Gaz Chisinau v FC Chitcani 7-1; 4-1
(Moldova Gaz Chisinau 11-2)
Cimentul Ribnita v Serif Tiraspol 0-3; 1-9
(Serif Tiraspol 12-1)
Petrocub Spicul Sarata Galbena v Zimbru Chisinau 1-2; 0-4
(Zimbru Chisinau 6-1)
Unisport II Chisinau v Roma Balti 1-1; 1-0
(Unisport II Chisinau 2-1)
FC Agro Chisinau v Nistru Unisport Otaci 1-1; 0-0
(1-1; Nistru Unisport Otaci on away goal)
Tiligul Tiraspol v Haiduc Sporting Hincesti 1-2; 2-0
(Tiligul Tiraspol 3-2)

QUARTER-FINALS
Constructorul Chisinau 3 (Pustovit 70, Dovghii 75, 86p), Olimpia Balti 0

Olimpia Balti 2 (Pernai 47, Savinov 75),
Constructorul Chisinau 0
(Constructorul Chisinau 3-2)
Moldova-Gaz Chisinau 0, Serif Tiraspol 0
Serif Tiraspol 1 (Colbasciuc 38og),
Moldova-Gaz Chisinau 1
(1-1; Moldova-Gaz Chisinau on away goal)
Zimbru Chisinau 10 (Dodul 1, Miterev 15, 52, 81, 84, 88, Gusila 42, Gavriliuc 71, Butelschi 75, 90),
Unisport II Chisinau 0
Unisport II Chisinau v Zimbru Chisinau void
(Zimbru Chisinau 10-0)
Nistru Unisport Otaci 1 (Popescu 2), Tiligul Tiraspol 0
Tiligul Tiraspol 1 (Lungu 67og),
Nistru Unisport Otaci 2 (Revenco 12, Grosev 80)
(Nistru Unisport Otaci 3-1)

SEMI-FINALS
Nistru Unisport Otaci 0, Zimbru Chisinau 3
(Tropanet 43, Ghilazev 50, Berco 53)
Zimbru Chisinau 1 (Miterev 45),

Nistru Unisport Otaci 1 (Leala 78)
(Zimbru Chisinau 4-1)
Moldova-Gaz Chisinau 1 (Cojusea 84),
Constructorul Chisinau 2 (Osipenco 45p, 63)
Constructorul Chisinau 4 (Comlionoc 39, 68,
Pusca 60, Boicenco 75), Moldova-Gaz Chisinau 0
(Constructorul Chisinau 6-1)

FINAL
24/05/2000. Chisinau
CONSTRUCTORUL CHISINAU 1 Boicenco (90)
ZIMBRU CHISINAU 0
referee - Antonov
CONSTRUCTORUL CHISINAU - Dinov, Pogorelov,
Tabanov, Pusca, Mincev, Boicenco, Mirza, Osipenco,
Comlionoc, Pustovit (Druta 71), Dovghii (Platon 86).
ZIMBRU CHISINAU - Romanenco, Cebotari, Kulic,
Telesnenco, Ghilazev, Catinsus, Berco, Boret
(Dodul 67), Tropanet (Butelschi 73), Rusnac,
Miterev (Gusila 66).

the UEFA Cup) Tottenham Hotspur they were unable to score but they did register creditable goalless draws at home.

The Moldovan national team rounded off their Euro 2000 qualifying campaign by holding Turkey 1-1 in Chisinau - a result which brought glee to defending champions Germany. It was Moldova's fourth draw of the competition and might even have been a first win had they not succumbed again to their habit of failing to defend a lead.

The scorer of Moldova's third-minute goal, Sergiu Epureanu, was crowned the country's Footballer of the Year for 1999. He had a good season in Turkey with Samsunspor but the man who finished runner-up in the

NATIONAL TEAM RESULTS 99/00

18/08/99	Hungary	A	Budapest	1-1	Clescenco (66)
08/09/99	Turkey (ECQ)	H	Chisinau	1-1	Epureanu (3)
16/12/99	Greece	A	Larisa	0-2	
02/02/00	Armenia	N	Larnaca	1-2	Popovici (70)
04/02/00	Lithuania	N	Larnaca	2-1	Rogaciov (14, 75)
06/02/00	Slovakia	N	Larnaca	2-0	Testimitanu (77p),
					Popovici (81)
26/04/00	San Marino	A	Serravalle	1-0	Clescenco (49)
04/06/00	Russia	H	Chisinau	0-1	

NATIONAL TEAM APPEARANCES 99/00

Coach - Ivan DANILIANT; Alexandru MATIURA	HUN	TUR	GRE	ARM	LIT	SVK	SMR	RUS	Cps	Gls
Serghei DINOV (23/04/69) - Constructorul Chisinau	G	G	G46	G		G	G		14	-
Oleg FISTICAN (02/02/75) - Zimbru Chisinau	D	D	D		s46	D87			27	-
Alexandru GUZUN (29/09/66) - SK Mykolaiv (UKR)/FC Agro Chisinau	D	D78	D		s68	D46			18	1
Sergiu EPUREANU (12/09/76) - Zimbru Chisinau/Samsunspor (TUR)	D	M					M	M79	25	2
Oleg SISCHIN (07/01/75) - CSKA Moskva (RUS)	D	s78		M	M68		M70	M46	21	-
Serghei STRONENCO (22/02/67) - Tiligul Tiraspol	M	M		M	M	s46	M88		38	-
Igor OPREA (05/10/69) - Zimbru Chisinau	M70	M	M46				M60	M	33	4
Vladimir GAIDAMASCIUC (11/06/71) - Serif Tiraspol	M	M46						s50	36	1
Gheorghe STRATULAT (13/12/76) - Dnipro Dnipropetrovsk (UKR)	M61	s46	s46						11	1
Vadim BORET (05/09/76) - Zimbru Chisinau	A	A	A62	s65	M	M	s75		7	-
Serghei CLESCENCO (20/05/72) - Maccabi Haifa (ISR)	A89	A82	A				A	A	40	8
Iurie OSIPENCO (06/07/74) - Constructorul Chisinau	s61	M	M71	M65	s46	M89	M46	M50	9	-
Serghei BELOUS (21/11/71) - Tiligul Tiraspol	s70		M						26	1
Serghei KIRILOV (05/06/73) - Nistru-Unisport Chisinau	s89	s82							12	-
Radu REBEJA (08/06/73) - Uralan Elista (RUS)		D		D	D	D46	D	D67	37	1
Valeriu CATANSUS (27/04/78) - Zimbru Chisinau		D	M46	M46	M85			s46	5	-
Alexandru COVALENCO (07/07/78) - Tiligul Tiraspol		D	D	D	s87	D	D		6	-
Iurie MITEREV (28/02/75) - Zimbru Chisinau		M46	s60	A76	A				25	7
Denis ROMANENCO (18/11/74) - Zimbru Chisinau		s46		G					14	-
Serghei ROGACIOV (20/05/77) - Serif Tiraspol		s46	A60	A	A		s79		14	2
Veaceslav LUNGU (19/04/77) - FK Cherkasy (UKR)		s62	s46	s82	s46				4	-
Veaceslav RUSNAC (27/08/75) - Zimbru Chisinau		s71	D60	s76					3	-
Ion TESTIMITANU (27/04/74) - Bristol City (ENG)			D		D	D75	D		29	5
Alexandru POPOVICI (09/04/77) - Torpedo ZIL (RUS)			M	M82	M	s60			17	3
Vladimir TANURCOV (27/11/77) - Serif Tiraspol			s60	D46	s89				3	-
Iurie PRIGANIUC (23/10/78) - Tiligul Tiraspol						s85	s46		2	-
Alexandru CURTIANU (11/02/74) - Zenit Sankt-Peterburg (RUS)						M	M		30	2
Ghenadie PUSCA (22/04/75) - Constructorul Chisinau						s70			4	-
Lilian POPESCU (15/11/73) - Nistru-Unisport Otaci						s88	s67		5	-
Evgeni HMARUC (13/06/77) - Tiligul Tiraspol							G		1	-
Adrian SOSNOVSCHI (13/06/77) - Spartak Moskva (RUS)							D		2	-

poll, striker Serghei Clescenco, proved to be an even better ambassador for Moldovan football, scoring 21 goals in the Israeli league for Maccabi Haifa. Clescenco also became his country's all-time top scorer, with eight goals, when he netted the winner in an April 2000 friendly against San Marino. By then Moldova were under the command of a new coach, with Alexandr Matiura having stepped up from the Under-21s to replace Ivan Daniliant at the end of the European Championship campaign.

EUROPEAN CUPS 99/00

CHAMPIONS' CUP
● ZIMBRU CHISINAU
Preliminary round 1 ST. PATRICK'S ATHLETIC (IRL)
A 5-0   Berco (30, 43), Epureanu (36, 84), Boret (71)
Romanenco, Dodul (Butelski 90), Kulik, Boret, Telesnenco, Catansus, Gilazev, Oprea, Tropanet, Epureanu, Berco (Ribacov 78).
H 5-0   Tropanet (25, 40), Boret (31, 75), Oprea (83p)
Romanenco, Dodul, Kulik, Boret, Telesnenco, Catansus, Ghilazev, Oprea, Epureanu (Gavriliuc 81), Tropanet (Butelski 73), Berco (Miterev 58).

Preliminary round 2 DINAMO TBILISI (GEO)
A 1-2   Berco (68)
Romanenco, Dodul, Kulik, Boret, Telesnenco, Catansus, Ghilazev, Oprea, Epureanu (Ribacov 85), Tropanet (Butelski 74), Berco.
H 2-0   Dodul (24), Epureanu (90)
Romanenco, Dodul (Robu 46), Kulik, Boret, Telesnenco, Catansus, Ghilazev, Oprea, Tropanet, Epureanu, Berco (Ribacov 86).

Qualifying round PSV (HOL)
H 0-0   Romanenco, Dodul (Miterev 70), Kulik, Boret, Telesnenco, Catansus, Ghizalev, Oprea (Fistican 89), Tropanet (Robu 78), Epureanu, Berco.
A 0-2   Romanenco, Dodul (Robu 69), Kulik, Boret, Telesnenco, Catansus, Ghizalev, Oprea, Tropanet (Ribakov 86), Epureanu, Berco (Miterev 46).

UEFA CUP
● CONSTRUCTORUL CHISINAU
Qualifying round FERENCVÁROS (HUN)
A 1-3   Comlionoc (78)
Dinov, Pogorelov, Mincev, Podgaetchi (Boicenco 58), Zabolotnii, Mirza, Truhanov, Osipenco, Comlionoc, Druta (Scrupschi 76), Platon.
H 1-1   Zabolotnii (40)
Dinov, Pogorelov, Mincev, Podgaetchi (Comlionoc 62; Ostap 85), Zabolotnii, Mirza, Osipenco, Druta, Dovghii, Truhanov (Boicenco 46), Tabanov.

● SERIF TIRASPOL
Qualifying round SIGMA OLOMOUC (CZE)
H 1-1   Mudjiri (10)
Perhun, Revazishvili, Talpa, Okoronkwo, Tarhnishvili, Stukalinas, Bicica (Gaidamasciuc 71), Tanurcov (Aliuta 85), Poroshin, Mudjiri (Ivanov S. 61), Rogaciov.
A 0-0   Perhun, Revazishvili, Talpa, Okoronkwo, Tarhnishvili, Tanurcov, Rogaciov, Aliuta (Ivanov S. 80), Stukalinas (Mudjiri 77), Bicica, Anyamkegh (Hutsishvili 71).

● ZIMBRU CHISINAU
1st round TOTTENHAM HOTSPUR (ENG)
A 0-3   Romanenco, Kulik, Telesnenco, Catansus, Ghizalev, Oprea, Miterev (Gusila 83), Epureanu, Dodul (Robu 46), Boret, Tropanet (Fistican 46).
H 0-0   Romanenco, Telesnenco, Catansus, Ghizalev, Oprea, Miterev, Epureanu (Robu 83), Dodu (Kulik 75), Boret, Tropanet, Berco (Gusila 86).

PROMOTED CLUB 99/00

SECOND DIVISION FINAL TABLE

		Pd	W	D	L	F	A	Pt	GD
1	Serif II Tiraspol	26	19	4	3	53	16	61	+37
2	**Haiducul Sporting Hincesti**	**26**	**18**	**5**	**3**	**44**	**21**	**59**	**+23**
3	Petrocub Spicul Sarata Galbena	26	15	5	6	49	21	50	+28
4	Intersport Chisinau	26	14	6	6	42	20	48	+22
5	Cimentul Ribnita	26	13	3	10	32	34	42	-2
6	Venita Lipcani	26	10	7	9	37	32	37	+5
7	Zimbru II Chisinau	26	9	8	9	37	25	35	+12
8	Dinamo-Stimold Bender	26	10	3	13	27	36	33	-9
9	ULIM Chisinau	26	7	8	11	27	34	29	-7
10	Unisport II Chisinau	26	7	7	12	28	40	28	-12
11	Maiak Chirsova	26	7	4	15	26	46	25	-20
12	Raut Orhei	26	6	6	14	23	49	24	-26
13	Dumbrava Cojusna	26	7	2	17	26	47	23	-21
14	Victoria CSA Chisinau	26	5	2	19	23	53	17	-30

N.B. Serif II Tiraspol ineligible for promotion.

CLUB DIRECTORY
Haiducul Sporting Hincesti
(now - Haiducul-Sporting-USM Chisinau)
Str. Cosmonautilor 6
Off. 24
2005 Chisinau
tel - (2) 233493
fax - (2) 242206
President - Tudor Leanca
Secretary - Victor Cascaval
Coach - Ilie Carp (00/01 - Victor Zemlianoi)
Stadium - Dinamo (5,000)

FC AGRO CHISINAU

CLUB DIRECTORY

FC Agro Chisinau
str. Miron Costin 7
camera 801
277001 Chisinau
tel - (2) 438130
Year of Formation - 1990
President - Ion Taranu
Coach - Vladimir Vusatii
Stadium - Speia (12,000)

APPEARANCES 99/00

	P	Ap	(s)	Gls
Vitalie ANTONOV	D	16		
Vasile ARLET	D	16		
Serghei BARAN	M	14	(17)	6
Ruslan BARBUROS	A	4	(7)	2
Oleg BELAN	M	22	(6)	2
Sergiu BOTNARI	M	1	(1)	
Alexandru BUDANOV	D	15		
Veaceslav BUGNEAC	M	10	(6)	3
Valeriu CATANA	D	1		
Boris CEBOTARI	M	17		4
Vitalie CULIBABA	D	12		1
Viorel FRUNZE	A	24	(11)	11
Eugen GILCA	M	9	(2)	
Vlad GOIAN	M	21	(3)	
Lilian GOLBAN	A	10	(3)	
Victor GRAUR	A		(3)	
Alexandru GUZUN	D	5		
Gheorghe HAREA	A	2		
Veaceslav JIGAILOV	G	1		
Dumitru MARTUN	D	17	(10)	1
Ghenadie MILCEV	M	31	(4)	
Anatol MOCANOV	D	24	(3)	
Vladimir MURA	G	31		
Ruslan NAVODARSKI	M	8	(7)	
Ion PASECINIC	M	6	(4)	
Marcel RESETCO	A	18		3
Ruslan ROIC	D	17		
Iurie ROMANIUC	M	15	(3)	1
Ruslan SCRELEA	M		(3)	
Vladimir SLAVINSCHI	G	4	(1)	
Vadim SOSNOVSCHI	M		(2)	
Alexandru SIROCOV	M	2	(5)	
Oleg SOIMU	M	11		
Vasile TOLOCONNICOV	D	11		1
Serghei VACARIUC	D	1	(1)	

LEAGUE RESULTS 1999/2000

31/07/99	Constructorul Chisinau	A	0-0	
07/08/99	Tiligul Tiraspol	H	1-0	Belan
14/08/99	Olimpia Balti	A	3-1	Resetco 2, Cebotari
22/08/99	Energhetic Dubasari	H	3-1	Frunze, Culibaba, Baran
29/08/99	Nistru-Unisport Otaci	H	0-2	
12/09/99	Moldova-Gaz Chisinau	A	1-1	Frunze
18/09/99	Serif Tiraspol	H	1-1	Cebotari
22/09/99	Roma Balti	A	1-1	Baran
26/09/99	Zimbru Chisinau	A	1-6	Baran
02/10/99	Constructorul Chisinau	H	2-5	Cebotari (p), Resetco
06/10/99	Zimbru Chisinau	H	1-2	Toloconnicov
10/10/99	Tiligul Tiraspol	A	0-4	
16/10/99	Olimpia Balti	H	0-0	
24/10/99	Energhetic Dubasari	A	0-1	
30/10/99	Nistru-Unisport Otaci	A	0-0	
07/11/99	Moldova-Gaz Chisinau	H	0-2	
13/11/99	Serif Tiraspol	A	1-5	Cebotari
21/11/99	Roma Balti	H	2-1	Belan, Romaniuc
11/03/00	Zimbru Chisinau	H	0-2	
19/03/00	Constructorul Chisinau	A	1-3	Frunze
25/03/00	Tiligul Tiraspol	H	2-0	Frunze, Bugneac
02/04/00	Olimpia Balti	A	0-0	
09/04/00	Energhetic Dubasari	H	2-0	Martun, Frunze
12/04/00	Nistru-Unisport Otaci	H	2-1	og (Podgaetchi), Frunze
16/04/00	Moldova-Gaz Chisinau	A	0-2	
23/04/00	Serif Tiraspol	H	1-3	Baran
29/04/00	Roma Balti	A	1-1	Baran
06/05/00	Zimbru Chisinau	A	0-3	
10/05/00	Constructorul Chisinau	H	0-1	
14/05/00	Tiligul Tiraspol	A	1-1	Bugneac
20/05/00	Olimpia Balti	H	0-2	
28/05/00	Energhetic Dubasari	A	2-0	Frunze, Barburos
31/05/00	Nistru-Unisport Otaci	A	1-1	Frunze
07/06/00	Moldova-Gaz Chisinau	H	2-1	Frunze 2
11/06/00	Serif Tiraspol	A	0-1	
14/06/00	Roma Balti	H	4-1	Baran, Frunze, Bugneac, Barburos

CONSTRUCTORUL CHISINAU

CLUB DIRECTORY

FC Constructorul-93 Chisinau
str. Tudor Vladimirescu 18, 277001 Chisinau
tel - (2) 439176 / fax - (2) 439756
Year of Formation - 1993
President - Larisa Rotari
Coach - Ion Caras (00/01 - Vlad Tinkler)
Stadium - Republican (18,500)

MAJOR HONOURS
Leagu Championship - (1) 1997.
Domestic Cup - (2) 1996, 2000.

APPEARANCES 99/00

	P	Ap	(s)	Gls
Adrian BOGDAN	G	12		
Evghenie BOICENCO	M	26	(3)	5
BURLACA	M		(1)	
Iulian BURSUC	M		(9)	
CARAMAN	D	1		
Victor COLOMEET	A	3	(2)	1
Victor COMLIONOC	M	26	(3)	7
Serghei DINOV	G	16	(2)	
Andrei DONICI	D	3	(9)	
Vladimir DOVGHII (UKR)	A	30	(2)	14
Aurel DRUTA	A	22	(12)	2
Claudiu FRUMOACA (ROM)	A	8	(2)	4
Gheorghe HAREA	M	2		
Denis LOZINSCHI	M	1	(1)	
MASTALER	M		(1)	
Nicolae MINCEV	D	30		
Iurie MIRZA	M	32		1
NINICU	M		(1)	
Ruslan NOVODARSKI	M		(1)	
Eric OCOCO	M		(2)	
Iurie OSIPENCO	M	33	(1)	5
Anatol OSTAP	M	5	(17)	1
Iurie PLATON	M	12	(11)	1
Anatoli PODGAETCHI	D	4		
Valeriu POGORELOV	D	27	(1)	1
Vladimir PUSTOVIT	A	10	(1)	4
Ghenadie PUSCA	D	16		4
Iuri ROSSIP	M	3	(7)	
SAVA	A		(1)	
Alexandru SCRUPSCHI	M	3	(7)	
SECRIERU	D	1		
Ivan TABANOV	D	25	(1)	
TAMASCOV	A	1		
Anatol TCACIUC (UKR)	G	8	(1)	
Dumitru TRICOLICI	D	7	(7)	
Konstantin TRUHANOV (UKR)	A	6	(2)	
Ivan ZABOLOTNII	M	23	(6)	1

LEAGUE RESULTS 1999/2000

24/07/99	Olimpia Balti	A	0-1	
31/07/99	FC Agro Chisinau	H	0-0	
06/08/99	Nistru-Unisport Otaci	A	0-1	
21/08/99	Serif Tiraspol	A	0-1	
31/08/99	Roma Balti	H	1-0	Dovghii (p)
12/09/99	Zimbru Chisinau	A	0-1	
18/09/99	Energhetic Dubasari	A	2-0	Dovghii (p), Boicenco
22/09/99	Tiligul Tiraspol	H	3-0	Pogorelov, Dovghii, Zabolotnii
25/09/99	Olimpia Balti	H	2-0	Dovghii 2 (1p)
02/10/99	FC Agro Chisinau	A	5-2	Frumoaca 2, Dovghii 2 (1p), Ostap
06/10/99	Moldova-Gaz Chisinau	H	0-0	
10/10/99	Nistru-Unisport Otaci	H	1-0	Dovghii
16/10/99	Moldova-Gaz Chisinau	A	2-0	Frumoaca, Platon
24/10/99	Serif Tiraspol	H	1-0	Dovghii (p)
30/10/99	Roma Balti	A	0-1	
07/11/99	Zimbru Chisinau	H	1-1	Frumoaca
13/11/99	Energhetic Dubasari	H	4-1	Comlionoc 3, Osipenco
21/11/99	Tiligul Tiraspol	A	1-1	Boicenco
11/03/00	Olimpia Balti	A	0-0	
19/03/00	FC Agro Chisinau	H	3-1	Pusca, Osipenco, Pustovit
25/03/00	Nistru-Unisport Otaci	A	0-0	
02/04/00	Moldova-Gaz Chisinau	H	1-0	Pusca
09/04/00	Serif Tiraspol	A	0-0	
12/04/00	Roma Balti	H	7-1	Pusca, Dovghii, Pustovit 2, Osipenco 2 (1p), Druta
16/04/00	Zimbru Chisinau	A	0-0	
23/04/00	Energhetic Dubasari	A	4-1	Pustovit, Osipenco (p), Dovghii, Comlionoc
29/04/00	Tiligul Tiraspol	H	0-0	
06/05/00	Olimpia Balti	H	1-0	Boicenco
10/05/00	FC Agro Chisinau	A	1-0	Boicenco
14/05/00	Nistru-Unisport Otaci	H	2-1	Comlionoc 2
19/05/00	Moldova-Gaz Chisinau	A	1-1	Comlionoc
28/05/00	Serif Tiraspol	H	2-2	Boicenco, Pusca
31/05/00	Roma Balti	A	3-2	Colomeet, Mirza, Dovghii
07/06/00	Zimbru Chisinau	H	1-2	og (Cebotari)
11/06/00	Energhetic Dubasari	H	3-1	Dovghii 2, Druta
14/06/00	Tiligul Tiraspol	A	0-1	

ENERGHETIC DUBASARI

CLUB DIRECTORY

Energhetic Dubasari
str. Dzerjinschi 50
4500 Dubasari
tel - (245) 35077
fax - (245) 36999
President - Veaceslav Finaghin
Coach - Anatol Grigorenco
Stadium - Gorodskoi (5,000)

APPEARANCES 99/00

	P	Ap	(s)	Gls
Mihail AKBAS	M	18		
Ruslan BARBAROS	A	14	(3)	3
Eduard BASIUL	A	12		
Serghei BASIUL	D	11	(2)	
Vitalie BASIUL	D	4	(13)	
Serghei BATIN	G	1	(1)	
Serghei BESLEAGA	M	22	(3)	
Veaceslav BUGNEAC	A	12	(1)	2
Alexandru CHIORU	D	8		
Andrei CONDRATIEV	M	9	(6)	
Oleg CONDROV	M	4	(10)	2
CRAVET	A		(3)	
Alexandru CRIVOI	G	7	(4)	
CURLAT	M	3	(5)	
Ivan DIRUL	D	30	(2)	
Alexandru GLUHU	M		(8)	
Vlad GOIAN	M	10		
Gheorghi GOLOVATCHI	M	16		3
Alexandru GOREACEV	M	6	(8)	
Alexandru GRIGORENCO	A	13	(6)	
Serghei GRIGORENCO	A	10	(3)	1
Alexandru KIRILOV	G	11		
Denis MELNICOV	M	11		
Alexandru MITITEL	D	30	(1)	
Anatol MINZU	D	2		
Vitalie MORARI	G	17		
NEGARA	D	2	(5)	
Vladislav POCATILO	M	22	(12)	1
Alexandru SCICOTA	M	11	(1)	
Vlad SOHIREV	M	12	(3)	
Serghei TRUHANOV	M	8		
Serghei TVERDOHLEB	D	34		
Serghei VACARIUC	D	10		
Iakob ZALEVSCHI	M	12	(3)	1
Alexandru ZELENIUC	D	4	(1)	

LEAGUE RESULTS 1999/2000

24/07/99	Tiligul Tiraspol	A	1-1	Zalevschi
31/07/99	Serif Tiraspol	H	0-6	
07/08/99	Olimpia Balti	A	0-2	
14/08/99	Roma Balti	H	2-1	Barbaros, Golovatchi
22/08/99	FC Agro Chisinau	A	1-3	Bugneac (p)
31/08/99	Zimbru Chisinau	H	1-2	Golovatchi
12/09/99	Nistru-Unisport Otaci	A	0-2	
18/09/99	Constructorul Chisinau	H	0-2	
22/09/99	Moldova-Gaz Chisinau	A	0-2	
26/09/99	Tiligul Tiraspol	H	0-0	
02/10/99	Serif Tiraspol	A	0-4	
10/10/99	Olimpia Balti	H	0-1	
16/10/99	Roma Balti	A	0-3	
24/10/99	FC Agro Chisinau	H	1-0	Golovatchi
30/10/99	Zimbru Chisinau	A	0-2	
13/11/99	Constructorul Chisinau	A	1-4	Barbaros
21/11/99	Moldova-Gaz Chisinau	H	1-3	Bugneac
25/11/99	Nistru-Unisport Otaci	H	1-5	Barbaros
11/03/00	Tiligul Tiraspol	A	0-4	
19/03/00	Serif Tiraspol	H	0-1	
25/03/00	Olimpia Balti	A	0-4	
02/04/00	Roma Balti	H	0-1	
09/04/00	FC Agro Chisinau	A	0-2	
12/04/00	Zimbru Chisinau	H	0-2	(w/o)
16/04/00	Nistru-Unisport Otaci	A	0-5	
23/04/00	Constructorul Chisinau	H	1-4	Condrov
29/04/00	Moldova-Gaz Chisinau	A	1-4	Pocatilo
06/05/00	Tiligul Tiraspol	H	0-3	
10/05/00	Serif Tiraspol	A	0-8	
14/05/00	Olimpia Balti	H	0-1	
20/05/00	Roma Balti	A	1-2	Condrov
28/05/00	FC Agro Chisinau	H	0-2	
31/05/00	Zimbru Chisinau	A	0-4	
07/06/00	Nistru-Unisport Otaci	H	0-4	
11/06/00	Constructorul Chisinau	A	1-3	Grigorenco S.
14/06/00	Moldova-Gaz Chisinau	H	0-3	

MOLDOVA-GAZ CHISINAU

CLUB DIRECTORY

FC Moldova-Gaz Chisinau
str. Albisoara 38, Chisinau
tel - (2) 578122
President - Mihai Lesnic
Coach - Vitalii Galat
Stadium - INCFS (3,000)

APPEARANCES 99/00

	P	Ap	(s)	Gls
Maxim ANDRONIC	M		(1)	
Ghenadie ANGHEL	M	15		2
Cristinel BADALUTA (ROM)	A	9	(6)	
Ghenadie BOTGROS	M	4	(7)	
Emil CARAS	D	31		
CARETNIK	M	9	(1)	
V. CIGOREANU	A	2	(7)	1
Lilian CODA	M	20	(6)	
Mihail COJUSEA	M	12	(5)	1
Vladimir COLBASIUC	D	27	(3)	
Sergiu CONDREA	D	26	(3)	
Alexandru CRIVOI	G		(1)	
CRIVOI	A	1		
Igor CUCIUC	M	1	(2)	
Oleg FLENTEA	M	29	(2)	
Alin GEORGESCU	A	14		2
Igor GHEORGHIES	A		(8)	1
Eugen GILCA	M	10		
Lilian GOLBAN	A	10	(2)	
Veaceslav JIGAILOV	G	4		
Alexei JMURCO	G	32	(1)	
Iuri LISENCO	A	3	(5)	
Evgheni MAIOROV	M	3	(8)	1
Andrei MARTIN	M	23	(6)	1
Andrei MIRON	A	6	(9)	5
NALIVAICO	M	9	(1)	
Serghei NANI	D	5	(1)	
Aurel NELIPOVSCHI	D	12	(2)	3
Roman ONICA	D	6	(4)	
Ion PASECINIC	D	10	(3)	1
Serghei PAVLENCO	M	16		2
Vladimir PUSTOVIT	A	16		11
Aurel REVENCO	M	1	(3)	
RODIONOV	A	1	(2)	
Vladimir SOHIREV	A	6	(8)	5
Iaroslav SUBBOTIN	A		(2)	
Anatol TAMBUR	M	13	(3)	1
Viorel TUDORAN (ROM)	D	1		
Eduard VALUTA	D	8	(8)	
VASILIAN	D	1		

LEAGUE RESULTS 1999/2000

24/07/99	Serif Tiraspol	H	2-3	Martin, Pustovit
31/07/99	Roma Balti	A	4-1	Pavlenco, Gheorghies, Pasecinic, Pustovit
14/08/99	Zimbru Chisinau	H	1-1	Pustovit
22/08/99	Tiligul Tiraspol	H	0-0	
29/08/99	Olimpia Balti	A	2-1	Pavlenco, Maiorov
12/09/99	FC Agro Chisinau	H	1-1	Pustovit (p)
18/09/99	Nistru-Unisport Otaci	A	0-3	
22/09/99	Energhetic Dubasari	H	2-0	Pustovit 2
26/09/99	Serif Tiraspol	A	0-3	
02/10/99	Roma Balti	H	1-1	Pustovit
06/10/99	Constructorul Chisinau	A	0-0	
10/10/99	Zimbru Chisinau	A	0-6	
16/10/99	Constructorul Chisinau	H	0-2	
24/10/99	Tiligul Tiraspol	A	0-1	
30/10/99	Olimpia Balti	H	1-2	Tambur
07/11/99	FC Agro Chisinau	A	2-0	Pustovit 2
13/11/99	Nistru-Unisport Otaci	H	0-2	
21/11/99	Energhetic Dubasari	A	3-1	Pustovit 2, Anghel
11/03/00	Serif Tiraspol	H	0-2	
19/03/00	Roma Balti	A	1-1	Nelipovschi
25/03/00	Zimbru Chisinau	H	0-1	
02/04/00	Constructorul Chisinau	A	0-1	
09/04/00	Tiligul Tiraspol	H	0-0	
12/04/00	Olimpia Balti	A	2-0	Georgescu, Nelipovschi
16/04/00	FC Agro Chisinau	H	2-0	Nelipovschi, Sohirev
23/04/00	Nistru-Unisport Otaci	A	0-1	
29/04/00	Energhetic Dubasari	H	4-1	Sohirev, Georgescu, Miron 2
06/05/00	Serif Tiraspol	A	1-3	Miron
10/05/00	Roma Balti	H	0-1	
14/05/00	Zimbru Chisinau	A	0-3	
19/05/00	Constructorul Chisinau	H	1-1	Cigoreanu
28/05/00	Tiligul Tiraspol	A	1-0	Sohirev
31/05/00	Olimpia Balti	H	1-2	Cojusea
07/06/00	FC Agro Chisinau	A	1-2	Anghel
11/06/00	Nistru-Unisport Otaci	H	1-1	Miron
14/06/00	Energhetic Dubasari	A	3-0	Sohirev 2, Miron

NISTRU-UNISPORT OTACI

CLUB DIRECTORY

FC Nistru-Unisport Otaci
str. S. Lazo 14
Otaci
tel - (271) 24965
fax - (271) 24965
President - Vasile Traghira
Coach - Anatoliy Murahovski; Valeri Krohan;
Nicolae Bunea (00/01 - Ion Caras)
Stadium - Calaraseuca (1,000)

APPEARANCES 99/00

	P	Ap	(s)	Gls
Ghenadie ANGHEL	A	2	(1)	
Dumitru ARABADJI (UKR)	M	10		
Eugen BEZUBKO	A	7		
Alexandru BLAJCO	A	17	(1)	12
Anatol BOROVICOV	G	27	(2)	
Vladimir CRIVENCO	D	29	(3)	
Vitalie DINTU	G	9	(2)	
Vladislav GAVRILIUC	D	5	(1)	1
Iurie GROSEV	M	18	(14)	3
Serghei KIRILOV	D	17		9
Nicolae KOPISTEANSKI (UKR)	D	26	(7)	
A. KOVGAN	A	2	(1)	
I. KOVGAN	M		(1)	
Serghei LASCENCOV (UKR)	D	27	(3)	
Alexandru LEALA (BRA)	M	18	(5)	7
Maxim LIPSIUK	M		(1)	
Vitalie LUNGU	D	8	(19)	1
Valentin LUPASCU	D	35		1
Alexandru MALITCHI	M	20	(8)	2
Aurel NELIPOVSKI	A	5	(7)	
Anatol PODGAETCHI	M	24	(1)	1
Lilian POPESCU	M	26	(2)	6
Veaceslav REVENCO	M	23	(7)	7
Vitalie ROJCOVOI	A	1	(6)	
Andrei STROENCO	M	15		
Anatol SABLEVSCHI	M	5	(12)	
Igor SUMILO	A	13	(3)	1
Alexandru TCACIUC (UKR)	M	7	(10)	

LEAGUE RESULTS 1999/2000

24/07/99	Roma Balti	H	1-0	Kirilov
06/08/99	Constructorul Chisinau	H	1-0	Popescu
14/08/99	Tiligul Tiraspol	A	0-0	
22/08/99	Olimpia Balti	H	2-2	Kirilov, og (Dolinta)
29/08/99	FC Agro Chisinau	A	2-0	Kirilov (p), Popescu
12/09/99	Energhetic Dubasari	H	2-0	Revenco, Malitchi
18/09/99	Moldova-Gaz Chisinau	H	3-0	Revenco 2, Popescu
22/09/99	Serif Tiraspol	A	0-0	
26/09/99	Roma Balti	A	1-2	Leala
03/10/99	Zimbru Chisinau	H	2-1	Malitchi, Kirilov
10/10/99	Constructorul Chisinau	A	0-1	
24/10/99	Olimpia Balti	A	3-2	Revenco 3
27/10/99	Zimbru Chisinau	A	0-0	
30/10/99	FC Agro Chisinau	H	0-0	
13/11/99	Moldova-Gaz Chisinau	A	2-0	Leala, Kirilov
17/11/99	Tiligul Tiraspol	H	4-2	Leala, Lungu, Kirilov 2
21/11/99	Serif Tiraspol	H	0-2	
25/11/99	Energhetic Dubasari	A	5-1	Kirilov 2, Revenco, Leala, Popescu
11/03/00	Roma Balti	H	2-0	Blajco, Popescu
19/03/00	Zimbru Chisinau	A	1-2	og (Ghilazev)
25/03/00	Constructorul Chisinau	H	0-0	
02/04/00	Tiligul Tiraspol	A	0-1	
09/04/00	Olimpia Balti	H	3-0	Popescu, Blajco 2
12/04/00	FC Agro Chisinau	A	1-2	Blajco
16/04/00	Energhetic Dubasari	H	5-0	Blajco 3 (1p), Leala, Sumilo
23/04/00	Moldova-Gaz Chisinau	H	1-0	Leala
29/04/00	Serif Tiraspol	A	1-1	Leala
06/05/00	Roma Balti	A	1-0	Blajco
10/05/00	Zimbru Chisinau	H	0-1	
14/05/00	Constructorul Chisinau	A	1-2	Grosev
19/05/00	Tiligul Tiraspol	H	0-0	
28/05/00	Olimpia Balti	A	2-2	Blajco, Gavriliuc
31/05/00	FC Agro Chisinau	H	1-1	Grosev
07/06/00	Energhetic Dubasari	A	4-0	Blajco 3, Podgaetchi
11/06/00	Moldova-Gaz Chisinau	A	1-1	Lupascu
14/06/00	Serif Tiraspol	H	1-2	Grosev

OLIMPIA BALTI

CLUB DIRECTORY

FC Olimpia Balti
str. Kiev 155
279200 Balti
tel - (231) 20314
fax - (231) 22378
President - Boris Bucicovski
Coach - Vladimir Oleanschi
Stadium - Municipal (7,000)

APPEARANCES 99/00

	P	Ap	(s)	Gls
Dumitru ARABADJI (UKR)	M	17		
Oleg BOBU	D	28	(2)	1
Grigore BOGHIU	M	8	(23)	
Andrei BURCOVSCHI	M	34		1
Valeriu CERES	D	36		
Ion CHISTOL	G		(1)	
COVTONIUC	A	2	(3)	1
Vadim CROHAN (UKR)	A	9		3
Serghei DERENIOV	G	18		
Ion DOLINTA	M	7		
Alexandru GOLOVACIUC	M		(9)	
Nicolae LAHMAI	D	32	(1)	
Andrei LEVCO	M		(1)	
Denis LITFIN	M		(4)	
Igor LUCICOV	M	1	(3)	
Evghenie MAIOROV	M	1	(1)	
MOROSANU	M		(4)	
Vladimir NEAMTU	M	4	(9)	
Oleg NICOLAICIUC	G	18	(2)	
Alexandru PATROMAN	A	29	(6)	3
Ruslan PERNAI	M	35		3
Serghei PISNIC	M	15	(2)	2
Veaceslav RUSNAC	D	16	(1)	3
Iurie SAVINOV	D	17		2
Oleg SOIMU	A	11	(2)	6
Anatol STAVILA	M	17	(1)	7
Vladimir TARANU	A	24	(9)	3
Vadim TATURIN	M	17		5

LEAGUE RESULTS 1999/2000

24/07/99	Constructorul Chisinau	H	1-0	og (Podgaetchi)
31/07/99	Tiligul Tiraspol	A	1-1	Patroman
07/08/99	Energhetic Dubasari	H	2-0	Taranu, Patroman
14/08/99	FC Agro Chisinau	H	1-3	Taturin
22/08/99	Nistru-Unisport Otaci	A	2-2	Rusnac, og (Lascenkov)
29/08/99	Moldova-Gaz Chisinau	H	1-2	Rusnac
11/09/99	Serif Tiraspol	A	1-2	Soimu
18/09/99	Roma Balti	H	4-1	Taturin 2 (1p), Pernai, Soimu
22/09/99	Zimbru Chisinau	A	0-3	
25/09/99	Constructorul Chisinau	A	0-2	
02/10/99	Tiligul Tiraspol	H	1-3	Taranu
10/10/99	Energhetic Dubasari	A	1-0	Bobu
16/10/99	FC Agro Chisinau	A	0-0	
24/10/99	Nistru-Unisport Otaci	H	2-3	Soimu, Taturin (p)
30/10/99	Moldova-Gaz Chisinau	A	2-1	Soimu 2
07/11/99	Serif Tiraspol	H	1-2	Rusnac
13/11/99	Roma Balti	A	2-0	Soimu, Tatarin
21/11/99	Zimbru Chisinau	H	0-3	
11/03/00	Constructorul Chisinau	H	0-0	
19/03/00	Tiligul Tiraspol	A	0-1	
25/03/00	Energhetic Dubasari	H	4-0	Stavila 2, Savinov, Pisnic
02/04/00	FC Agro Chisinau	H	0-0	
09/04/00	Nistru-Unisport Otaci	A	0-3	
12/04/00	Moldova-Gaz Chisinau	H	0-2	
16/04/00	Serif Tiraspol	A	1-0	Covtoniuc
23/04/00	Roma Balti	H	0-1	
29/04/00	Zimbru Chisinau	A	0-3	
06/05/00	Constructorul Chisinau	A	0-1	
10/05/00	Tiligul Tiraspol	H	3-2	Crohan (p), Stavila, Patroman
14/05/00	Energhetic Dubasari	A	1-0	Stavila
20/05/00	FC Agro Chisinau	A	2-0	Burcovschi, Pernai
28/05/00	Nistru-Unisport Otaci	H	2-2	Stavila, Pisnic
31/05/00	Moldova-Gaz Chisinau	A	2-1	Pernai, Crohan
07/06/00	Serif Tiraspol	H	2-1	Crohan (p), Stavila
11/06/00	Roma Balti	A	1-1	Stavila
14/06/00	Zimbru Chisinau	H	2-5	Savinov, Taranu

ROMA BALTI

CLUB DIRECTORY

FC Roma Balti
str. Moscovei 17
Balti
tel - (231) 25551
Year of Formation - 1995
President - Nicolae Rotari
Coach - Valeri Crohan; Anatoliy Murahovski;
Mihail Zastavski; Vladimir Lukianov
Stadium - Tineretea (6,000)

APPEARANCES 99/00

	P	Ap	(s)	Gls
Andrei ALBU	G	12		
Dumitru ARALCHIN	D	2	(1)	
Nicolae BODNAR	M		(3)	
Veaceslav BRADULEAC	M		(5)	
Evghenie CARABULEA	A	8	(7)	
Veaceslav CARDAS	M		(2)	
CEPOI	M		(1)	
Dumitru COCIAN	M		(3)	
Vadim CROHAN (UKR)	M	2	(2)	
Serghei DARII	A	35		6
Vladimir GHENAITIS	M	21	(5)	2
Serghei GIRLA	G		(1)	
Igor GLUSOC (UKR)	D	28	(1)	1
Oleg GREBENICOV	D	33	(2)	
Andrei GRINER (UKR)	D	22		1
Serghei GVOZDI (UKR)	D	2	(1)	
Vasili HRIPLIVII	M		(4)	
Andrei IATIN (UKR)	M	28	(1)	4
Igor ISTRATI	D	7	(15)	
Maxim KIZILOV (RUS)	D	16		
Nicolae LIZUN (UKR)	M	24	(5)	2
Vitalie MEREUTA	M		(1)	
Igor MIHAESCU	A	29		9
Oleg OBOROC	D	29	(6)	1
Serghei PLAMADEALA	M	31	(1)	
Alexandru REZNIC	G	15	(2)	
Dumitru SAMBUR	D		(1)	
Serghei SAPOGOVSCHI	M	7	(12)	1
Andrei SCALETCHI	M	16	(10)	1
Gabriel TUDORACHE (ROM)	G	8		
Alexandru USATII	D	10	(7)	

LEAGUE RESULTS 1999/2000

24/07/99	Nistru-Unisport Otaci	A	0-1	
31/07/99	Moldova-Gaz Chisinau	H	1-4	Darii
06/08/99	Serif Tiraspol	A	0-6	
14/08/99	Energhetic Dubasari	A	1-2	Oboroc
21/08/99	Zimbru Chisinau	H	0-3	
31/08/99	Constructorul Chisinau	A	0-1	
12/09/99	Tiligul Tiraspol	H	0-2	
18/09/99	Olimpia Balti	A	1-4	Mihaescu (p)
22/09/99	FC Agro Chisinau	H	1-1	Iatin
25/09/99	Nistru-Unisport Otaci	H	2-1	Mihaescu (p), Darii
02/10/99	Moldova-Gaz Chisinau	A	1-1	Ghenaitis
10/10/99	Serif Tiraspol	H	1-2	Mihaescu
16/10/99	Energhetic Dubasari	H	3-0	Glusoc, Iatin 2
24/10/99	Zimbru Chisinau	A	2-1	Ghenaitis, Darii
30/10/99	Constructorul Chisinau	H	1-0	Scaletchi
07/11/99	Tiligul Tiraspol	A	0-1	
13/11/99	Olimpia Balti	H	0-2	
21/11/99	FC Agro Chisinau	A	1-2	Darii
11/03/00	Nistru-Unisport Otaci	A	0-2	
19/03/00	Moldova-Gaz Chisinau	H	1-1	Griner
25/03/00	Serif Tiraspol	A	0-1	
02/04/00	Energhetic Dubasari	A	1-0	Mihaescu
09/04/00	Zimbru Chisinau	H	0-0	(w/o; 0-1 abandoned; awarded as away win)
12/04/00	Constructorul Chisinau	A	1-7	Lizun
16/04/00	Tiligul Tiraspol	H	0-0	
23/04/00	Olimpia Balti	A	1-0	Iatin
29/04/00	FC Agro Chisinau	H	1-1	Mihaescu
06/05/00	Nistru-Unisport Otaci	H	0-1	
10/05/00	Moldova-Gaz Chisinau	A	1-0	Darii
14/05/00	Serif Tiraspol	H	0-3	
20/05/00	Energhetic Dubasari	H	2-1	Mihaescu (p), Sapogovschi
28/05/00	Zimbru Chisinau	A	0-5	
31/05/00	Constructorul Chisinau	H	2-3	Mihaescu 2 (1p)
07/06/00	Tiligul Tiraspol	A	1-2	Lizun
11/06/00	Olimpia Balti	H	1-1	Darii
14/06/00	FC Agro Chisinau	A	1-4	Mihaescu

SERIF TIRASPOL

CLUB DIRECTORY

Serif Tiraspol
str. Sevcenko 81
Tiraspol
tel - (233) 32230/31312
fax - (233) 32276
Year of Formation - 1996
President - Victor Gusan
Coach - Vladimir Zemleanoi
(00/01 - Ivan Daniliant)
Stadium - Gorodskoi (9,000)

MAJOR HONOURS
Domestic Cup - (1) 1999.

APPEARANCES 99/00

	P	Ap	(s)	Gls
Marian ALIUTA (ROM)	M	11	(7)	1
Edward ANYAMKEGH (NIG)	M	7	(18)	8
Vasili ARLET	D	2		
Victor BARISEV	D	9	(9)	3
Deimantas BICICA (LIT)	M	33	(3)	5
Alexandru BUDANOV	M		(1)	
Serghei DODU	D	1	(3)	
Vladimir GAIDAMASCIUC	M	12	(7)	1
Mihail HUTSISHVILI	A	1	(5)	1
Oleg ICHIM	D	1		
Evgheni IVANOV	G	2	(1)	
Stanislav IVANOV	M	28	(5)	6
Alexandru LAPACI	M	9	(11)	1
Alexandru MELENCIUC	G	5		
David MUJIRI (GEO)	A	28	(6)	12
Andrei NESTERUC	M	1		
Issak OKORONKWO (NIG)	D	31	(1)	1
Evghenie PATULA	A	1	(6)	
Serghei PERHUN (UKR)	G	29		
Tamaz PERTIA (GEO)	M	4	(8)	
Andrei POROSIN (UKR)	M	18	(9)	9
Gheorghe REVAZISHVILI (GEO)	M	10	(6)	
Serghei ROGACIOV	A	33	(1)	20
Iuri ROMANIUC	M	1		
Serhiy SHMATOVALENKO (UKR)	D	10	(1)	
Vadim SOLODKI	M	2	(2)	1
Igoris STUKALINAS (LIT)	M	33	(1)	5
Radu TALPA	D	26	(2)	
Vladimir TANURCOV	M	13	(13)	1
Vaja TARHNISHVILI (GEO)	D	34		1
Mihail TOKADZE	M	1		

LEAGUE RESULTS 1999/2000

Date	Opponent		Score	Scorers
24/07/99	Moldova-Gaz Chisinau	A	3-2	Porosin 2, Hutsishvili
31/07/99	Energhetic Dubasari	A	6-0	Stukalinas, Mujiri, Porosin, Rogaciov 3 (1p)
06/08/99	Roma Balti	H	6-0	Porosin, Rogaciov 3, Mujiri 2
21/08/99	Constructorul Chisinau	H	1-0	Tanurcov
31/08/99	Tiligul Tiraspol	A	0-1	
11/09/99	Olimpia Balti	H	2-1	Anyamkegh, Bicica
18/09/99	FC Agro Chisinau	A	1-1	Rogaciov
22/09/99	Nistru-Unisport Otaci	H	0-0	
26/09/99	Moldova-Gaz Chisinau	H	3-0	og (Condrea), Bicica, Solodki
02/10/99	Energhetic Dubasari	H	4-0	Anyamkegh, Rogaciov 2, Stukalinas
10/10/99	Roma Balti	A	2-1	Bicica, Rogaciov
16/10/99	Zimbru Chisinau	H	2-0	Stukalinas, Rogaciov (p)
24/10/99	Constructorul Chisinau	A	0-1	
30/10/99	Tiligul Tiraspol	H	2-1	Porosin, Rogaciov (p)
07/11/99	Olimpia Balti	A	2-1	Rogaciov, Aliuta
13/11/99	FC Agro Chisinau	H	5-1	Mujiri 2, Anyamkegh 2, Porosin (p)
17/11/99	Zimbru Chisinau	A	0-3	
21/11/99	Nistru-Unisport Otaci	A	2-0	Porosin, Ivanov S.
11/03/00	Moldova-Gaz Chisinau	A	2-0	Ivanov S., Mujiri
19/03/00	Energhetic Dubasari	A	1-0	Mujiri
25/03/00	Roma Balti	H	1-0	Rogaciov
02/04/00	Zimbru Chisinau	A	1-1	Mujiri
09/04/00	Constructorul Chisinau	H	0-0	
12/04/00	Tiligul Tiraspol	A	2-0	Ivanov S. 2
16/04/00	Olimpia Balti	H	0-1	
23/04/00	FC Agro Chisinau	A	3-1	Porosin, Rogaciov, Lapaci
29/04/00	Nistru-Unisport Otaci	H	1-1	Bicica
06/05/00	Moldova-Gaz Chisinau	H	3-1	Anyamkegh, Mujiri, Rogaciov
10/05/00	Energhetic Dubasari	H	8-0	Tarhnishvili, Anyamkegh 2, Rogaciov 3 (1p), Gaidamasciuc, Porosin
14/05/00	Roma Balti	A	3-0	Mujiri, Ivanov S., Barisev
19/05/00	Zimbru Chisinau	H	3-2	Stukalinas, Rogaciov, Barisev
28/05/00	Constructorul Chisinau	A	2-2	Okoronkwo, Mujiri (p)
31/05/00	Tiligul Tiraspol	H	2-0	Barisev, Ivanov S.
07/06/00	Olimpia Balti	A	1-2	Mujiri
11/06/00	FC Agro Chisinau	H	1-0	Bicica
14/06/00	Nistru-Unisport Otaci	A	2-1	Anyamkegh, Stukalinas (p)

TILIGUL TIRASPOL

CLUB DIRECTORY

FC Tiligul Tiraspol
str. Sverdlov 46, ap.1, 278000 Tiraspol
tel - (233) 61195
fax - (233) 51020
President - Grigori Corzun
Coach - Alexandru Spiridon; Alexandru Golocolosov;
Evghenie Sincarenco
Stadium - Gorodskoi (9,000)

MAJOR HONOURS
Domestic Cup - (3) 1993, 1994, 1995.

APPEARANCES 99/00

	P	Ap	(s)	Gls
Serghei BELOUS	M	18		1
Vitalie CARMAC	G	5		
Vladimir CIUBCO	M	3	(13)	1
Oleg CIUPAC	A	16		1
Serghei COVALCIUC	D	23	(8)	
Alexandru COVALENECO	D	34		
Serghei CUCEAREVENCO	M	13	(4)	
GEORGIEV	M	3	(14)	1
Vitalie GLAVCEV	M	7	(12)	
Evgheni GORDIENCO	A	21	(3)	
Eduard GROSU	D	31	(1)	1
Evghenie HMARUC	G	30		
Ruslan HODOS (UKR)	D	1	(2)	
Valentin IVANENCO	M	15	(1)	1
Vadim KIRILOV	M	10	(16)	6
Igori LISTVIN	D	2	(1)	
Anatol LUCHIANCICOV	D	1	(1)	
MAKASER	D	1	(3)	
Alexandru MELNIC	M	3	(4)	
Alecsandr MURAHOVSKI	M		(5)	
PINCIUC	A	4		
Sergiu POGREBAN	A	31	(4)	12
Iurie PRIGANIUC	D	36		3
SICIOV	M	4	(2)	
Serghei STROENCO	M	32		2
SVET	M		(2)	
TOFAN	M		(5)	
Serghei TRUHANOV	M	2	(5)	
Veaceslav TRUHANOV (UKR)	M	21	(10)	1
Evghenie TUCANOV	G	1	(1)	
Andrei ZAVORATNIUC (UKR)	M	28		5

LEAGUE RESULTS 1999/2000

24/07/99	Energhetic Dubasari	H	1-1	Priganiuc
31/07/99	Olimpia Balti	H	1-1	Belous
07/08/99	FC Agro Chisinau	A	0-1	
14/08/99	Nistru-Unisport Otaci	H	0-0	
21/08/99	Moldova-Gaz Chisinau	A	0-0	
31/08/99	Serif Tiraspol	H	1-0	Ciubco
12/09/99	Roma Balti	A	2-0	Zavaratniuc, Pogreban
22/09/99	Constructorul Chisinau	A	0-3	
26/09/99	Energhetic Dubasari	A	0-0	
02/10/99	Olimpia Balti	A	3-1	Ciupac, Truhanov V., Priganiuc
10/10/99	FC Agro Chisinau	H	4-0	Stroenco (p), Zavaratniuc, Pogreban 2
24/10/99	Moldova-Gaz Chisinau	H	1-0	Zavaratniuc
30/10/99	Serif Tiraspol	A	1-2	Pogreban
07/11/99	Roma Balti	H	1-0	Pogreban
13/11/99	Zimbru Chisinau	A	1-1	Pogreban
17/11/00	Nistru-Unisport Otaci	A	2-4	Zavaratniuc, Georgiev
21/11/99	Constructorul Chisinau	H	1-1	Pogreban
25/11/99	Zimbru Chisinau	H	0-2	
11/03/00	Energhetic Dubasari	H	4-0	Pogreban, Kirilov 3
19/03/00	Olimpia Balti	H	1-0	Pogreban
25/03/00	FC Agro Chisinau	A	0-2	
02/04/00	Nistru-Unisport Otaci	H	1-0	Pogreban
09/04/00	Moldova-Gaz Chisinau	A	0-0	
12/04/00	Serif Tiraspol	H	0-2	
16/04/00	Roma Balti	A	0-0	
23/04/00	Zimbru Chisinau	H	1-1	Zavaratniuc
29/04/00	Constructorul Chisinau	A	0-0	
06/05/00	Energhetic Dubasari	A	3-0	Priganiuc, Pogreban, Kirilov
10/05/00	Olimpia Balti	A	2-3	Ivanenco, Stroenco
14/05/00	FC Agro Chisinau	H	1-1	Grosu
20/05/00	Nistru-Unisport Otaci	A	0-0	
28/05/00	Moldova-Gaz Chisinau	H	0-1	
31/05/00	Serif Tiraspol	A	0-2	
07/06/00	Roma Balti	H	2-1	Kirilov, Pogreban
11/06/00	Zimbru Chisinau	A	0-3	
14/06/00	Constructorul Chisinau	H	1-0	Kirilov

ZIMBRU CHISINAU

CLUB DIRECTORY

FC Zimbru Chisinau
str. Butuclui 1
277060 Chisinau
tel - (2) 766481
fax - (2) 762753
President - Nicolae Ciornâi
Coach - Semion Altman
(00/01 - Alexandru Spiridon)
Stadium - FC Zimbru (3,000)

MAJOR HONOURS
League Championship - (8) 1992, 1993, 1994,
1995, 1996, 1998, 1999, 2000.
Domestic Cup - (2) 1997, 1998.

APPEARANCES 99/00

	P	Ap	(s)	Gls
Victor BERCO	A	28	(5)	15
Vadim BORET	D	32	(1)	6
Serghei BUTELSCHI	A	11	(14)	3
Valeriu CATINSUS	M	26	(4)	7
Boris CEBOTARI	D	15		2
Serghei DODUL	M	15	(6)	1
Sergiu EPUREANU	A	8	(5)	3
Oleg FISTICAN	D	10		
Vlad GAVRILIUC	M	3	(7)	2
Ruslan GHILAZEV (UKR)	M	29		3
Alexandru GRAB	A	11	(9)	
Dumitru GUSILA	A	9	(17)	8
Grigol GVAZAVA (GEO)	M	2	(8)	
Konstantin KULIK (UKR)	D	27	(4)	7
Iurie MITEREV	M	20	(6)	15
Ghenadie OLEXICI	D	1	(7)	
Igor OPREA	M	27		
Vlad ROBU	D	16	(1)	1
Denis ROMENENCO	G	35		
Veaceslav RUSNAC	A	9	(4)	
Andrei TELESNENCO (UKR)	D	35		1
Boris TROPANET	M	16	(5)	
Serghei ZGURA (UKR)	M		(5)	1

LEAGUE RESULTS 1999/2000

14/08/99	Moldova-Gaz Chisinau	A	1-1	Gusila
21/08/99	Roma Balti	A	3-0	Robu, Miterev 2
31/08/99	Energhetic Dubasari	A	2-1	Epureanu, Ghilazev
12/09/99	Constructorul Chisinau	H	1-0	Miterev
22/09/99	Olimpia Balti	H	3-0	Epureanu, Miterev, Boret
26/09/99	FC Agro Chisinau	H	6-1	Boret, Miterev, Butelschi, Telesnenco, Berco, Gusila
03/10/99	Nistru-Unisport Otaci	A	1-2	Ghilazev
06/10/99	FC Agro Chisinau	A	2-1	Miterev, Kulik
10/10/99	Moldova-Gaz Chisinau	H	6-0	Gusila, Berco 2, Gavriliuc 2, Catinsus
16/10/99	Serif Tiraspol	A	0-2	
24/10/99	Roma Balti	H	1-2	Berco
27/10/99	Nistru-Unisport Otaci	H	0-0	
30/10/99	Energhetic Dubasari	H	2-0	Catinsus, Boret
07/11/99	Constructorul Chisinau	A	1-1	Gusila
13/11/99	Tiligul Tiraspol	H	1-1	Epureanu
17/11/99	Serif Tiraspol	H	3-0	Butelschi, Berco 2
21/11/99	Olimpia Balti	A	3-0	Miterev 2, Gusila
25/11/99	Tiligul Tiraspol	A	2-0	Catinsus, Gusila
11/03/00	FC Agro Chisinau	A	2-0	Catinsus 2
19/03/00	Nistru-Unisport Otaci	H	2-1	Miterev, Butelschi
25/03/00	Moldova-Gaz Chisinau	A	1-0	Catinsus
02/04/00	Serif Tiraspol	H	1-1	Cebotari
09/04/00	Roma Balti	A	0-0	(w/o; 1-0 Gusila abandoned; awarded as away win)
12/04/00	Energhetic Dubasari	A	2-0	(w/o)
16/04/00	Constructorul Chisinau	H	0-0	
23/04/00	Tiligul Tiraspol	A	1-1	Boret
29/04/00	Olimpia Balti	H	3-0	og (Ceres), Dodul, Kulik
06/05/00	FC Agro Chisinau	H	3-0	Berco, Kulik 2 (1p)
10/05/00	Nistru-Unisport Otaci	A	1-0	Kulik
14/05/00	Moldova-Gaz Chisinau	H	3-0	og (Coda), Berco 2
19/05/00	Serif Tiraspol	A	2-3	Cebotari, Berco
28/05/00	Roma Balti	H	5-0	Miterev 2, Berco 2, Ghilazev
31/05/00	Energhetic Dubasari	H	4-0	Boret, Catinsus, Miterev, Zgura (p)
07/06/00	Constructorul Chisinau	A	2-1	Miterev, Kulik (p)
11/06/00	Tiligul Tiraspol	H	3-0	Boret, Miterev, Gusila
14/06/00	Olimpia Balti	A	5-2	Kulik, Miterev, Berco 3

NORTHERN IRELAND

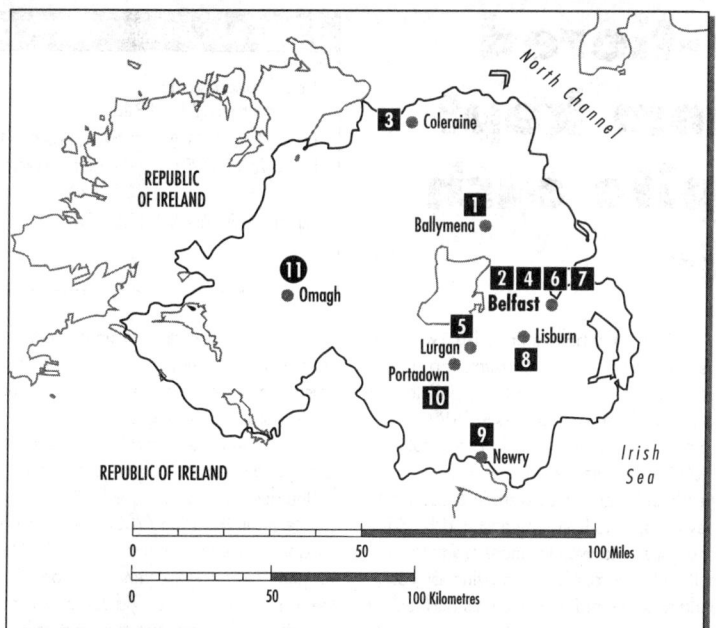

1	BALLYMENA UNITED	710
2	CLIFTONVILLE	711
3	COLERAINE	712
4	CRUSADERS	713
5	GLENAVON	714
6	GLENTORAN	715

7	LINFIELD	716
8	LISBURN DISTILLERY	717
9	NEWRY TOWN	718
10	PORTADOWN	719
Promoted club		
11	OMAGH TOWN	

McMENEMY OUT, McILROY IN

Two-tiered system kept despite cash crisis

FEDERATION DIRECTORY

The Irish Football Association
20 Windsor Avenue, Belfast BT9 6EE

tel - (01232) 669458/9   Year of Formation - 1880
fax - (01232) 667620   President - Jim Boyce
                            Secretary - David I. Bowen

Stadium - Windsor Park, Belfast (28,500)

Northern Irish domestic football is in crisis, with the majority of the 20 senior clubs encountering major financial difficulties. Even Belfast's 'Big Two', Linfield and Glentoran, who shared the major trophies in 1999/2000, are feeling the pinch, having each been forced to cut their wage bill by £100,000 for the new season.

The days when Irish League clubs were in a position to splash out money on players from England and Scotland appear to be long gone, and even the more recent trend of buying from south of the border is now proving too costly. Dwindling attendances, dilapidated stadiums and lack of sponsors and investors are all contributory factors to the decline.

Unfortunately, the Irish League authorities seem oblivious to the problems that face them. There is a widespread consensus within the Province that the current league structure of two ten-club divisions needs to be reorganised, the reason being that fans are not attracted by the prospect of teams meeting each other four times a season. Yet, in July, an extraordinary meeting of the Irish League decided, in their wisdom, to maintain the status quo for another two seasons, prompting accusations from some quarters that this would be the death of Irish League football.

Interest in the 1999/2000 championship was reduced by Linfield's unchallenged romp to the title. Their first Irish League crown for six years was practically sewn up by the turn of the year. David Jeffrey's team put together a magnificent 25-game unbeaten run which lasted from early September to the beginning of March, and by the end of the campaign they had built up a huge lead of 18 points. Ironically, they sealed their triumph with a defeat, but as nearest challengers Glentoran were simultaneously beaten by Lisburn Distillery as Linfield went down 2-1 in Coleraine, it meant Northern Ireland's record champions celebrated April Fool's Day with their 42nd national title - the second-highest total of any European club, behind Scottish 'cousins' Rangers.

The most intriguing contest was the three-way battle for second place and a guaranteed UEFA Cup spot. Coleraine, Glenavon and Glentoran all had their chances, but in the end it was Coleraine who prevailed, clinching the place by the narrowest of goal-difference margins from Glenavon after all three contenders won on the final Saturday. Coleraine's success was primarily attributable to manager Marty Quinn, who took over at the Showgrounds in October following the resignation of Kenny Shiels. At the time Coleraine were languishing two places off the bottom, having lost each of their three opening games and won only two of their first 11.

Glentoran claimed the second UEFA Cup spot by winning the Irish Cup. The previous season's champions were never consistent enough to defend

LEAGUE CHAMPIONSHIP RESULTS 99/00

		1	2	3	4	5	6	7	8	9	10
1	Ballymena United		2-1	0-0	1-1	0-3	0-0	1-3	1-1	2-2	1-1
			2-2	2-2	2-2	2-0	2-1	0-1	2-1	0-0	2-4
2	Cliftonville	1-1		1-4	1-1	1-2	1-2	0-1	0-0	3-2	1-2
		3-2		0-0	1-1	1-1	2-2	2-3	0-2	0-2	2-0
3	Coleraine	1-1	1-1		1-2	1-1	1-2	0-1	3-0	2-0	4-1
		1-0	0-1		4-2	2-0	1-2	2-1	3-0	4-1	4-0
4	Crusaders	3-0	1-1	1-3		3-1	1-0	1-1	1-2	1-0	2-4
		2-2	1-1	0-2		0-4	2-2	0-4	2-0	1-0	0-1
5	Glenavon	0-0	0-1	0-1	2-1		3-3	0-0	2-0	2-1	3-1
		2-0	4-0	0-0	1-0		3-3	3-0	1-2	3-0	1-1
6	Glentoran	3-1	1-1	3-2	2-0	1-2		1-0	3-1	0-3	5-3
		3-2	3-0	2-0	1-2	2-1		1-1	2-0	2-1	1-0
7	Linfield	3-0	3-1	3-1	0-0	1-0	2-0		3-2	3-1	3-1
		3-2	1-2	3-0	0-0	1-1	1-2		1-0	3-2	2-1
8	Lisburn Distillery	3-4	0-1	1-3	2-2	1-1	2-0	1-2		0-1	2-1
		2-1	1-0	1-2	0-1	1-2	1-0	1-4		2-3	2-1
9	Newry Town	3-1	3-1	3-0	1-1	0-1	1-0	0-3	2-1		1-1
		2-2	3-2	0-1	2-0	0-2	3-4	0-3	1-1		0-1
10	Portadown	2-2	2-2	3-6	2-1	1-3	1-0	1-1	4-1	0-0	
		0-2	3-0	3-2	4-2	2-0	4-0	0-2	3-2	5-0	

LEAGUE CHAMPIONSHIP FINAL TABLE 99/00

			Home					Away					Total					
		Pd	W	D	L	F	A	W	D	L	F	A	W	D	L	F	A	PT	GD
1	Linfield	36	13	3	2	36	16	11	4	3	31	14	24	7	5	67	30	79	37
2	Coleraine	36	10	3	5	35	16	8	4	6	29	26	18	7	11	64	42	61	22
3	Glenavon	36	9	6	3	30	14	8	4	6	25	20	17	10	9	55	34	61	21
4	Glentoran	36	13	2	3	36	20	5	5	8	23	31	18	7	11	59	51	61	8
5	Portadown	36	10	4	4	40	26	5	3	10	24	36	15	7	14	64	62	52	2
6	Newry Town	36	7	4	7	25	25	4	3	11	19	33	11	7	18	44	58	40	-14
7	Crusaders	36	6	5	7	22	28	3	8	7	19	27	9	13	14	41	55	40	-14
8	Ballymena United	36	4	10	4	22	25	2	6	10	23	37	6	16	14	45	62	34	-17
9	Cliftonville	36	3	7	8	20	28	4	6	8	18	31	7	13	16	38	59	34	-21
10	Lisburn Distillery	36	6	2	10	23	29	3	3	12	16	34	9	5	22	39	63	32	-24

their league title, but they successfully retained the Gold Cup and the County Antrim Shield and completed a hat-trick of knockout trophies by beating Portadown 1-0 in the end-of-season showpiece at Windsor Park. Roy Coyle's men had reached the final with a stirring and dramatic 3-2 victory over Linfield in the previous round.

The other semi-final was won by Portadown in a replayed match against Coleraine. The inevitable matchwinner was Portadown's prolific striker Vinny Arkins, who achieved a milestone in the league by scoring 29 goals to become the Irish League's top marksman for the third season in a row - the first hat-trick of its type since Coleraine's legendary Des Dickson did likewise in the early 1970s.

At the bottom of the table Lisburn Distillery were relegated after just one season in the top flight. For the second summer in a row they swapped places with Omagh Town, who were convincing winners of the First Division. Another repeat of the previous year was Cliftonville's play-off victory over Ards, which enabled the 1998 champions to retain their Premier League status.

Northern Ireland's national team sank to a new low under the so-called 'Dream Team' of Lawrie McMenemy and his high-profile assistants Joe Jordan and Pat Jennings. Heavy defeats in the last three Euro 2000 qualifying games against Turkey, Germany

PLAYER OF THE SEASON

GERRY TAGGART

When Gerry Taggart stepped out to earn his 46th Northern Ireland cap in the friendly against Hungary in April 2000, it ended a spell of almost two years in the international wilderness for the strapping, left-footed centre-back. He had been an outcast during Lawrie McMenemy's period in office but Sammy McIlroy was quick to recall him. There would have been an immediate comeback against Luxembourg but for the fact that Taggart was playing for Leicester City at Wembley in the English League Cup final a few days later - a game his team won, 2-1 against Tranmere, to bring him the first significant silverware of his career. Signed on a free transfer from Bolton, Taggart had a marvellous second season at Filbert Street - both as a defender and a goalscorer - and was duly voted Player of the Year by the Leicester supporters.

TOP SCORERS

29 Vinny ARKINS (Portadown)
20 Tony GRANT (Glenavon)
   Glenn HUNTER (Ballymena United)
16 Stuart ELLIOTT (Glentoran)
15 Darren LARMOUR (Linfield)
14 Chris MORGAN (Linfield)
13 Tommy McCALLION (Cliftonville)

NATIONAL TEAM RESULTS 99/00

18/08/99	France	H	Belfast	0-1	
04/09/99	Turkey (ECQ)	H	Belfast	0-3	
08/09/99	Germany (ECQ)	A	Dortmund	0-4	
09/10/99	Finland (ECQ)	A	Helsinki	1-4	Whitley Je. (59)
23/02/00	Luxembourg	A	Luxembourg	3-1	Healy (21, 48), Quinn (87)
28/03/00	Malta	A	Ta' Qali	3-0	Hughes M. (13p), Quinn (16), Healy (41)
26/04/00	Hungary	H	Belfast	0-1	

EUROPEAN CUPS 99/00

CHAMPIONS' CUP
● **GLENTORAN**
Preliminary round 1 LOVECH (BUL)
A 0-3

Gough, Nixon, Kennedy, Walker, Ferguson, Leeman, McCann (Young 46), Hamill, Elliott (Finlay 85), Batey, McBride (Rainey 73).

H 0-2

Gough, Nixon (Livingstone 34), Kennedy, Walker, Ferguson, Leeman (Finlay 87), McCann, Hamill, Rainey 74), Elliott, Batey, Young.

UEFA CUP
● **LINFIELD**
Qualifying round LOKOMOTIVI TBILISI (GEO)

A 0-1

Robinson, McDonald, Easton, Kelly, Murphy, Beatty, Larmour, Gorman, Callaghan, Marks, Bailie

H 1-1 Larmour (67)

Mathers, McDonald (Rogan 85), Easton (McMullan 65), Kelly, Murphy, Morgan (Semple 90), Larmour, Beatty, Callaghan, Marks, Bailie.

● **PORTADOWN**
Qualifying round CSKA SOFIA (BUL)
H 0-3

Dalton, McKeown, Davidson, Byrne (Quigley 75), Strain, Major, Clarke, Dunne, Arkins, Campbell R., Millar.

A 0-5

Dalton, McKeown, Davidson, Quigley, Strain, Major, Clarke, Dunne, Hill (O'Hara 85), Arkins, Irwin.

NATIONAL TEAM APPEARANCES 99/00

Manager - Lawrie McMENEMY; Sammy McILROY	FRA	TUR	GER	FIN	LUX	MLT	HUN	Cps	Gls
Maik TAYLOR (04/09/71) - Fulham (ENG)	G46	G	G	G	s75	s85	G	11	-
Aaron HUGHES (08/11/79) - Newcastle United (ENG)	D	D			D		D	12	-
Mark WILLIAMS (28/09/70) - Watford (ENG)	D	D	D	D	D65	D	s57	11	-
Barry HUNTER (18/11/68) - Reading (ENG)	D	D						15	1
Kevin HORLOCK (01/11/72) - Manchester City (ENG)	D	D	D			s77		21	-
Jon McCARTHY (18/08/70) - Birmingham City (ENG)	M	M63	M	M				16	-
Steve LOMAS (18/01/74) - West Ham United (ENG)	M	M	M		M	M		35	2
Neil LENNON (25/06/71) - Leicester City (ENG)	M	M	M46	M		M	M	33	2
Peter KENNEDY (10/09/73) - Watford (ENG)	M73	M	M	M				6	-
Michael HUGHES (02/08/71) - Wimbledon (ENG)	M	M	M	M74	s78	M77	M	54	4
Iain DOWIE (09/01/65) - Queens Park Rangers (ENG)	A55	A73	A46					59	12
Tommy WRIGHT (29/08/63) - Manchester City (ENG)	s46							31	-
James QUINN (15/12/74) - West Bromwich Albion (ENG)	s55	s73	s46	A68	A88	A70		21	3
Keith GILLESPIE (18/02/75) - Blackburn Rovers (ENG)	s73	s63	s46		M89	M62	M76	32	1
Ian NOLAN (09/07/70) - Sheffield Wednesday (ENG)			D	D	D	D	D	12	-
Steve MORROW (02/07/70) - Queens Park Rangers (ENG)			D	D				39	1
Iain JENKINS (24/11/72) - Dundee United (SCO)				D79				6	-
Jeff WHITLEY (28/01/79) - Manchester City (ENG)				M				4	1
Adrian COOTE (30/09/78) - Norwich City (ENG)				s68	s88	s70	s57	6	-
Damien JOHNSON (18/11/78) - Blackburn Rovers (ENG)				s74	M78	s62	s73	5	-
Jim WHITLEY (14/04/75) - Manchester City (ENG)				s79				3	-
Roy CARROLL (30/09/77) - Wigan Athletic (ENG)					G75	G85		4	-
Danny GRIFFIN (10/08/77) - St. Johnstone (SCO)					D90	D	D73	12	1
Jim MAGILTON (06/05/79) - Ipswich Town (ENG)					M75			40	5
David HEALY (05/08/79) - Manchester United (ENG)					A	A	A	3	3
Colin MURDOCK (02/07/75) - Preston North End (ENG)					s65	D46	s76	3	-
Danny SONNER (09/01/72) - Sheffield Wednesday (ENG)					s75	s46	M85	6	-
Steve ROBINSON (10/12/74) - Bournemouth (ENG)					s89		s85	5	-
Pat McGIBBON (06/09/73) - Wigan Athletic (ENG)					s90			7	-
Gerry TAGGART (18/10/70) - Leicester City (ENG)							D57	46	7
Andy KIRK (29/05/79) - Heart of Midlothian (SCO)							A57	1	-

DOMESTIC CUP 99/00

FIFTH ROUND
Ballinamallard United 1, Killyleagh Youth Club 2
Banbridge Town 3, East Belfast 2
Bangor 3, Carrick Rangers 0
Brantwood 2, Bessbrook United 3
Cliftonville 3, Portstewart 0
Coleraine 7, Comber Recreation 0
Dungannon Swifts 0, Ards 0
(replay) Ards 0, Dungannon Swifts 1
Glenavon 0, Newry Town 1
Glentoran 3, Crusaders 0
Institute 1, RUC 2
Larne 1, Portadown 5
Limavady United 0, Armagh City 2
Linfield 3, FC Enkalon 1
Lisburn Distillery 2, Omagh Town 1
Loughgall 0, Ballymena United 1
Tobermore United 4, Ballyclare Comrades 2

SIXTH ROUND
Armagh City 2, Glentoran 2
(replay) Glentoran 4, Armagh City 0
Bangor 3, Coleraine 3
(replay) Coleraine 8, Bangor 3
Ballymena United 2, Bessbrook United 1
Dungannon Swifts 4, Tobermore United 0
Linfield 1, Killyleagh Youth Club 0
Lisburn Distillery 3, RUC 0
Newry Town 3, Banbridge Town 0
Portadown 1, Cliftonville 0

QUARTER-FINALS
Coleraine 1 (Devine 90), Ballymena United 0
Linfield 2 (Larmour 32, Ferguson 64p),
Dungannon Swifts 2 (Moore 31, Houston 46)
(replay) Dungannon Swifts 1 (Montgomery 77p),
Linfield 2 (Kelly 36, Ferguson 118) (aet)
Lisburn Distillery 0, Portadown 2 (Larkin 40, Atkins 84)

Newry Town 1 (Fitzgerald 90),
Glentoran 3 (Young 35, McCann 45, Reddish 52og)

SEMI-FINALS
Portadown 0, Coleraine 0
(replay) Portadown 1 (Arkins 58), Coleraine 0
Linfield 2 (Larmour 34, Murphy 90),
Glentoran 3 (Hamill 45, Elliott 51, Armstrong 90)

FINAL
06/05/2000, Belfast
GLENTORAN 1 Gilzean (59)
PORTADOWN 0
referee - Ferry
GLENTORAN - Gough, Nixon, Kennedy, Dickson,
McCombe, Young, McCann, Hamill, Russell
(Gilzean 54), Batey, Elliott.
PORTADOWN - Dalton, Brown, O'Hara, Byrne,
Strain, Major, Larkin, Clarke, Sheridan, Arkins, Hill
(Davidson 65).

and Finland left McMenemy with little option but to decline the IFA's extraordinarily generous offer of an extension to his contract. Jordan and Jennings swiftly followed him out, as did U-21 boss Chris Nicholl. The IFA had hoped to lure Leicester City's Martin O'Neill on a part-time basis, but he declined so the job was offered, full-time, to another member of the country's great early '80s side, Sammy McIlroy. The former midfielder, who collected 88 caps in his 15-year international career, chose Jim Harvey, the one-time Arsenal midfielder, as his right-hand man.

McIlroy won his first two internationals, although anything less would have been deemed a failure given that their opponents were Luxembourg and Malta. The most encour-

INTERNATIONAL HONOURS

World Cup Finals appearances: 1958 (qtr-finals), 1982 (2nd round), 1986

aging feature of these games was the unearthing of a goal-scoring striker - something the team had been lacking for so long. Young Manchester United reserve David Healy scored twice on his début against Luxembourg and once more against Malta. They did lose at home to Hungary in April but even after just three matches it was obvious that McIlroy had instilled back into the players some of the passion that was lacking during the previous régime.

PROMOTED CLUB 99/00

FIRST DIVISION FINAL TABLE

		Pd	W	D	L	F	A	Pt	GD
1	**Omagh Town**	36	20	10	6	65	35	70	30
2	Ards	36	16	16	4	65	36	64	29
3	Limavady United	36	17	9	10	54	42	60	12
4	Bangor	36	16	9	11	60	49	57	11
5	Larne	36	15	9	12	56	53	54	3
6	Institute	36	14	9	13	59	53	51	6
7	Armagh City	36	10	10	16	50	61	40	-11
8	Dungannon Swifts	36	9	8	19	43	62	35	-19
9	Carrick Rangers	36	8	10	18	45	64	34	-19
10	Ballyclare Comrades	36	8	4	24	39	81	28	-42

PROMOTION/RELEGATION PLAY-OFF
Ards 0, Cliftonville 2   Cliftonville 1, Ards 0
(Cliftonville 3-0)

CLUB DIRECTORY

Omagh Town FC
St. Julians Road, Mullaghmore, Omagh
tel - (028) 256242927
fax - (028) 256242927
Year of Formation - 1964
Chairman - N. Hunter
Secretary - Pat McGlinchey
Manager - Roy McCreadie
Stadium - St. Julians Road (8,000)

BALLYMENA UNITED

CLUB DIRECTORY

Ballymena United FC
The Showgrounds
Warden Street
Ballymena
tel - (028) 25652049
fax - (028) 25659490
website - www.ballymenaunited.co.uk
Year of Formation - 1928
Chairman - Robert Cupples
Secretary - William Bell
Manager - Nigel Best
The Showgrounds (8,000)

MAJOR HONOURS
Domestic Cup - (6)
1929, 1940, 1958, 1981, 1984, 1989.

APPEARANCES 99/00

	P	Ap	(s)	Gls
Jason ALLEN	D	22	(3)	
Noel ANDERSON	A		(1)	
Geoff BEGGS	A		(2)	
Nigel BOYD	D	11	(3)	
David CALDERWOOD	M	5	(7)	1
Paul CALLAGHAN	G	6		
Mark CARLISLE	D	21	(3)	
Ricky CULBERTSON	D	9	(1)	1
Scott DRUMMOND	A	20	(11)	2
Gareth FULTON	D	20		
Gerry FLYNN	D	26	(2)	1
John GREGG	M	17	(1)	2
Glenn HUNTER	A	33	(2)	20
Philip KNELL	M	18	(7)	7
Kieran LOUGHRAN	M	3	(2)	
John McCONNELL	D	32		
Declan McGREEVY	M		(5)	1
Ray McGUINNESS	D	12	(4)	
Paul MUIR	D	5	(1)	
Ollie MULLAN	D	5		
Kevin O'HAGAN	D	2	(1)	
Dermot O'NEILL (IRL)	G	29		
Darren PARKER	D	16	(4)	1
Barry PATTON (IRL)	A	20	(3)	5
Paul RICE	G	1		
Andy SWALWELL (ENG)	M	20	(5)	2
Terry TENNYSON	M	15	(8)	
Barry TUMILTY	M	25		
Ian WILKINS (ENG)	D	3		

LEAGUE RESULTS 1999/2000

14/08/99	Glenavon	A	0-0	
21/08/99	Lisburn Distillery	H	1-1	Hunter
28/08/99	Cliftonville	A	1-1	McGreevy
31/08/99	Coleraine	H	0-0	
07/09/99	Newry Town	A	1-3	Hunter
11/09/99	Linfield	A	0-3	
18/09/99	Glentoran	H	0-0	
25/09/99	Crusaders	H	1-1	Drummond
02/10/99	Portadown	A	2-2	Parker, Hunter (p)
09/10/99	Glenavon	H	0-3	
16/10/99	Lisburn Distillery	A	4-3	Hunter 3 (1p), Gregg
23/10/99	Cliftonville	H	2-1	Culbertson, Knell
30/10/99	Coleraine	A	1-1	Calderwood
06/11/99	Newry Town	H	2-2	Gregg, Knell
12/11/99	Linfield	H	1-3	Swalwell
20/11/99	Glentoran	A	1-3	Patton
27/11/99	Crusaders	A	0-3	
04/12/99	Portadown	H	1-1	Flynn (p)
11/12/99	Newry Town	A	2-2	Knell, Hunter
18/12/99	Crusaders	H	2-2	Knell, Hunter
27/12/99	Coleraine	H	2-2	Knell, og (Stewart)
03/01/00	Linfield	A	2-3	Drummond, Hunter (p)
08/01/00	Glenavon	H	2-0	Swalwell, Hunter
29/01/00	Cliftonville	A	2-3	Patton, Hunter
05/02/00	Glentoran	A	2-3	Hunter 2
12/02/00	Portadown	H	2-4	Hunter, Patton
26/02/00	Newry Town	H	0-0	
04/03/00	Crusaders	A	2-2	Hunter 2
18/03/00	Coleraine	A	0-1	
25/03/00	Linfield	H	0-1	
28/03/00	Lisburn Distillery	H	2-1	Hunter 2
01/04/00	Glenavon	A	0-2	
15/04/00	Lisburn Distillery	A	1-2	og (Henry)
18/04/00	Glentoran	H	2-1	Knell, Hunter
22/04/00	Cliftonville	H	2-2	Patton 2
29/04/00	Portadown	A	2-0	Hunter, Knell

CLIFTONVILLE

CLUB DIRECTORY

Cliftonville FC
Solitude, Cliftonville Street, Belfast BT14 6LP
tel - (028) 90754628
fax - (028) 90729011
website - www.cliftonville.com
Year of Formation - 1879
Chairman - Hugh McCartan
Secretary - John Duffy
Manager - Marty Quinn; Laurence Stitt
Stadium - Solitude (17,000)

MAJOR HONOURS
League Championship - (3) 1906, 1910, 1998.
Domestic Cup - (8) 1883, 1888, 1897, 1900, 1901, 1907, 1909, 1979.

APPEARANCES 99/00

	P	Ap	(s)	Gls
John CAMPBELL	A	1	(1)	
Michael COLLINS	M	27		2
Damian DAVEY	D	1		
Conor DEVINE	A	2	(2)	
Brian DONAGHEY	M	13	(12)	1
Michael DONNELLY	M	28		
Gerry FLYNN	D	4	(2)	
Innes GRAY	A		(1)	
Simon GRIBBEN	A	17	(10)	4
Liam HARTLEY	G	9		
Brian JOHNSTON	M	1	(3)	
Tommy McCALLION	M	29	(4)	13
Ryan McCLUSKEY	A		(2)	
Ciaran McLAUGHLIN	G	24		
Larry McMAHON	D	25	(6)	
Mark McMENAMIN	M	10	(2)	
Shane MULHOLLAND	M	23	(1)	5
Keith MULVENNA	M	33		1
Peter MURRAY	M	24	(3)	3
Alan O'CONNOR	A	5	(3)	
Barry ROONEY	M	7	(1)	1
Chris SCANNELL	A	19	(11)	6
Ronan SCANNELL	D	25		
Stephen SCULLION	G	2		
Stephen SMALL	D	29	(2)	
Paul SNODDEN	G	1		
Martin TABB	D	17	(2)	
Jody TOLAN	A	10	(8)	
Gavin TREANOR	A	5		
Kevin TRUEMAN	D	1		
Peter WITHNELL	A	4		

LEAGUE RESULTS 1999/2000

14/08/99	Newry Town	H	3-2	Mulholland 2, Scannell C.
21/08/99	Portadown	A	2-2	Donaghey, Scannell C.
28/08/99	Ballymena United	H	1-1	Scannell C.
31/08/99	Crusaders	A	1-1	Scannell C.
07/09/99	Glentoran	A	1-1	Gribben
11/09/99	Lisburn Distillery	H	0-0	
18/09/99	Glenavon	H	1-2	Collins
25/09/99	Coleraine	A	1-1	Mulholland
02/10/99	Linfield	H	0-1	
09/10/99	Newry Town	A	1-3	McCallion
16/10/99	Portadown	H	1-2	Mulholland
23/10/99	Ballymena United	A	1-2	McCallion
30/10/99	Crusaders	H	1-1	Scannell C.
06/11/99	Glentoran	H	1-2	McCallion
13/11/99	Lisburn Distillery	A	1-0	McCallion (p)
20/11/99	Glenavon	A	1-0	McCallion
27/11/99	Coleraine	H	1-4	Murray
04/12/99	Linfield	A	1-3	McCallion
11/12/99	Glenavon	H	1-1	McCallion
18/12/99	Portadown	H	2-0	Gribben, McCallion
27/12/99	Crusaders	H	1-1	Gribben
03/01/00	Coleraine	A	1-0	Mulholland
08/01/00	Newry Town	A	2-3	McCallion, Collins
29/01/00	Ballymena United	H	3-2	McCallion 3 (1p)
05/02/00	Lisburn Distillery	A	0-1	
12/02/00	Glentoran	H	2-2	Scannell C., og (Russell)
26/02/00	Glenavon	A	0-4	
04/03/00	Portadown	A	0-3	
18/03/00	Crusaders	A	1-1	McCallion
25/03/00	Coleraine	H	0-0	
28/03/00	Linfield	H	2-3	Murray, O'Connor
01/04/00	Newry Town	H	0-2	
15/04/00	Linfield	A	2-1	Murray, Mulvenna
22/04/00	Ballymena United	A	2-2	Gribben, Rooney
24/04/00	Lisburn Distillery	H	0-2	
29/04/00	Glentoran	A	0-3	

COLERAINE

CLUB DIRECTORY

Coleraine FC
The Showgrounds
Ballycastle Road
Coleraine
tel - (028) 70353655
fax - (028) 703320932
website - www.coleraine-fc.freeserve.co.uk
Year of Formation - 1927
Chairman - Sammy Lyle
Secretary - Freddie Monahan
Manager - Kenny Shiels; Marty Quinn
Stadium - The Showgrounds (8,000)

MAJOR HONOURS
League Championship - (1) 1974.
Domestic Cup - (4) 1965, 1972, 1975, 1977.

APPEARANCES 99/00

	P	Ap	(s)	Gls
Carl CHILLINGSWORTH (ENG)	A	30	(5)	11
Stuart CLANACHAN	D	34	(1)	
Gary DALLAS	M	1	(3)	
John DEVINE	D	34		10
Paul GASTON	D	19	(8)	
Joe GRAY	M	19	(4)	3
Kevin KEEGAN	A	10	(13)	3
Russell KERR	A	3	(2)	2
Dessie LOUGHERY	A	24	(6)	7
Conor LYNCH	D	1	(2)	
Pat McALLISTER	M	26	(3)	2
Oliver McAULEY	D	32		2
Marty McCANN	M	22	(10)	4
Damian McDONALD	D	1		
Michael McHUGH (IRL)	A	13	(4)	9
Kevin McKEOWN (SCO)	G	29		
Ross MURRAY	G	7		
Mark PICKING	M	22	(11)	6
Andy ROBERTSON (SCO)	A	1		
Michael SMYTH	D	36		4
Alfie STEWART	D	28	(2)	
Paul STOKES	A	4	(6)	

LEAGUE RESULTS 1999/2000

14/08/99	Glentoran	H	1-2	Chillingsworth
21/08/99	Linfield	A	1-3	Picking
27/08/99	Crusaders	H	1-2	Chillingsworth
31/08/99	Ballymena United	A	0-0	
07/09/99	Glenavon	H	1-1	Gray
11/09/99	Portadown	H	4-1	og (McKeown), McCann, Picking, McAuley
18/09/99	Newry Town	A	0-3	
25/09/99	Cliftonville	H	1-1	Devine (p)
02/10/99	Lisburn Distillery	A	3-1	Loughery 2, Picking
09/10/99	Glentoran	A	2-3	McHugh, McCann
16/10/99	Linfield	H	0-1	
23/10/99	Crusaders	A	3-1	Chillingsworth, McHugh 2
30/10/99	Ballymena United	H	1-1	McHugh
06/11/99	Glenavon	A	1-0	Devine (p)
13/11/99	Portadown	A	6-3	Keegan 2, Devine 2 (1p), Picking, Loughery
20/11/99	Newry Town	H	2-0	Smyth, Chillingsworth
27/11/99	Cliftonville	A	4-1	Devine, McAuley, McHugh, Chillingsworth
04/12/99	Lisburn Distillery	H	3-0	Chillingsworth, Devine, McHugh
11/12/99	Crusaders	A	2-0	Smyth, Chillingsworth
18/12/99	Lisburn Distillery	H	3-0	Smyth, McAllister, McCann
27/12/99	Ballymena United	A	2-2	Chillingsworth (p), McCann
03/01/00	Cliftonville	H	0-1	
08/01/00	Linfield	A	0-3	
15/01/00	Glenavon	H	2-0	Picking, Loughery
29/01/00	Glentoran	A	0-2	
05/02/00	Portadown	A	2-3	Gray, Loughery
12/02/00	Newry Town	H	4-1	McAllister, Smyth, Devine (p), Chillingsworth
26/02/00	Crusaders	H	4-2	Gray, Devine (p), Chillingsworth, McHugh
04/03/00	Lisburn Distillery	A	2-1	McHugh 2
18/03/00	Ballymena United	H	1-0	Keegan
25/03/00	Cliftonville	A	0-0	
01/04/00	Linfield	H	2-1	Devine 2 (1p)
15/04/00	Glenavon	A	0-0	
22/04/00	Glentoran	H	1-2	Loughery
24/04/00	Portadown	H	4-0	Kerr, Loughery, Picking, Chillingsworth
29/04/00	Newry Town	A	1-0	Kerr

CRUSADERS

THE EUROPEAN FOOTBALL YEARBOOK 2000-2001

CLUB DIRECTORY

Crusaders FC
Seaview
Shore Road
Belfast BT15 3PL
tel - (028) 90370777
fax - (028) 90771049
website -
www.geocities.com/Colosseum/Pressbox/9420
Year of Formation - 1898
Chairman - Jim Semple
Secretary - Harry Davison
Manager - Martin Murray (00/01 - Gary McCartney)
Stadium - Seaview (9,000)

MAJOR HONOURS
League Championship - (4)
1973, 1976, 1995, 1997.
Domestic Cup - (2) 1967, 1968.

APPEARANCES 99/00

	P	Ap	(s)	Gls
Stuart BYRNE (IRL)	M	7	(1)	1
Keith DALLAS	D	3		
Michael DEEGAN (IRL)	M	11		2
Ciaran DONAGHY	D	28	(2)	
Ciaran DONNELLY (IRL)	D		(1)	
Graham DOYLE (IRL)	M	7		1
Glenn DUNLOP	D	34		
Paul DWYER	M	3		
David FAIRCLOUGH (IRL)	D	4	(6)	
Peter GILGUNN	D	1	(6)	1
Ian HILL (IRL)	D	33	(1)	
Darren LOCKHART	M	24	(1)	3
Declan McGREEVY	M	8		
Crawford McRAE	A	29		11
Noel MONAGHAN	D		(1)	
Damian MOONEY	A	6	(18)	
Paul MUIR	M	15	(2)	1
Peter MURRAY (IRL)	D	34		1
Maurice O'DRISCOLL (IRL)	M	3		
David O'HARE	G	35		
Mark O'NEILL (IRL)	M	7		1
Pat O'TOOLE (IRL)	M	26	(2)	
Martin REILLY (IRL)	A	36		11
John ROSBOTHAM	G	1		
Trevor SMITH (SCO)	A	13	(3)	7
Glen WADE	M	23	(8)	1
David WILLIAMSON	M	5		

LEAGUE RESULTS 1999/2000

21/08/99	Newry Town	A	1-1	Byrne (p)
27/08/99	Coleraine	A	2-1	Reilly, Smith
31/08/99	Cliftonville	H	1-1	Lockhart
07/09/99	Portadown	A	1-2	Lockhart
11/09/99	Glentoran	H	1-0	Smith (p)
18/09/99	Lisburn Distillery	A	2-2	Smith 2 (1p)
21/09/99	Linfield	H	1-1	Reilly, Smith
25/09/99	Ballymena United	A	1-1	McRae
02/10/99	Glenavon	H	3-1	O'Neill, McRae, Smith (p)
09/10/99	Linfield	A	0-0	
16/10/99	Newry Town	H	1-0	Smith (p)
23/10/99	Coleraine	H	1-3	Reilly
30/10/99	Cliftonville	A	1-1	McRae
06/11/99	Portadown	H	2-4	Wade, McRae
13/11/99	Glentoran	A	0-2	
20/11/99	Lisburn Distillery	H	1-2	Gilgunn
27/11/99	Ballymena United	H	3-0	McRae, Doyle, Reilly
04/12/99	Glenavon	A	1-2	Deegan
11/12/99	Coleraine	H	0-2	
18/12/99	Ballymena United	A	2-2	Reilly, McRae
27/12/99	Cliftonville	A	1-1	Reilly
03/01/00	Newry Town	H	1-0	McRae
08/01/00	Portadown	A	2-4	og (Clarke), Deegan
15/01/00	Glentoran	H	2-2	Reilly 2
29/01/00	Lisburn Distillery	A	1-0	McRae
05/02/00	Glenavon	H	0-4	
12/02/00	Linfield	A	0-0	
26/02/00	Coleraine	A	2-4	McRae, Reilly
04/03/00	Ballymena United	H	2-2	Murray, Muir
18/03/00	Cliftonville	H	1-1	McRae
25/03/00	Newry Town	A	0-2	
01/04/00	Portadown	H	0-1	
15/04/00	Glentoran	A	2-1	Reilly, McRae
22/04/00	Lisburn Distillery	H	2-0	Lockhart, Reilly
24/04/00	Glenavon	A	0-1	
29/04/00	Linfield	H	0-4	

GLENAVON

CLUB DIRECTORY

Glenavon FC
Mourneview Park
Lurgan BT66 8EW
tel - (028) 38322472
fax - (028) 38327694
website - www.glenavonfc.com
Year of Formation - 1889
Chairman - Adrian Teer
Secretary - T.R. Kerr
Manager - Roy Walker (00/01 - Colin Malone)
Stadium - Mourneview Park (15,000)

MAJOR HONOURS
League Championship - (3) 1952, 1957, 1960.
Domestic Cup - (5)
1957, 1959, 1961, 1992, 1997.

APPEARANCES 99/00

		P	Ap	(s)	Gls
Brian ADAIR	D	5	(5)		
Stuart ADDIS	G	23			
Gavin ARTHUR	A	34	(1)	11	
Stephen BAXTER	A	18	(2)	3	
Aaron CALLAGHAN (IRL)	D	17		2	
Lee DOHERTY	M	27		1	
Alan DORNAN	D	31			
Ryan EVANS	A	8	(11)		
Jim GARDINER	A		(1)		
Mark GLENDINNING	D	29		5	
Mark GRAHAM	M	18	(1)	1	
Tony GRANT (IRL)	A	36		20	
Sam HAUGHEY	A		(6)		
Mark McCANN	M	17	(6)	6	
Mark McMENEMY	M	2	(2)		
Aidan McVEIGH	A	2	(1)		
Philip MATTHEWS	G	13			
Philip MITCHELL	M	3	(3)		
Darren MURPHY	M	20	(7)		
Donal O'BRIEN (IRL)	M	25	(6)	4	
Alan O'CONNOR (IRL)	A	4	(7)		
Darragh PEDEN	D		(1)		
Colin RUSSELL	D	27	(4)	1	
Gary SMYTH	D	9		1	
Jeff SPIERS	D	28	(3)		

LEAGUE RESULTS 1999/2000

14/08/99	Ballymena United	H	0-0	
21/08/99	Glentoran	A	2-1	O'Brien, Grant
31/08/99	Portadown	A	3-1	Grant 2, O'Brien
07/09/99	Coleraine	A	1-1	Arthur
11/09/99	Newry Town	H	2-1	Grant, Smyth
18/09/99	Cliftonville	A	2-1	O'Brien, Arthur
25/09/99	Lisburn Distillery	H	2-0	Arthur, Glendinning
02/10/99	Crusaders	A	1-3	Baxter
05/10/99	Linfield	H	0-0	
09/10/99	Ballymena United	A	3-0	Grant, O'Brien, Arthur
16/10/99	Glentoran	H	3-3	Grant 3
23/10/99	Linfield	A	0-1	
30/10/99	Portadown	H	3-1	Russell, Glendinning, McCann
06/11/99	Coleraine	H	0-1	
12/11/99	Newry Town	A	1-0	Baxter
20/11/99	Cliftonville	H	0-1	
27/11/99	Lisburn Distillery	A	1-1	Arthur (p)
04/12/99	Crusaders	H	2-1	McCann, Grant
11/12/99	Cliftonville	A	1-1	McCann
18/12/99	Linfield	A	1-1	Arthur
27/12/99	Portadown	A	0-2	
03/01/00	Glentoran	H	3-3	Grant, McCann, Arthur
08/01/00	Ballymena United	A	0-2	
15/01/00	Coleraine	A	0-2	
29/01/00	Newry Town	H	3-0	Baxter, Grant, Arthur
05/02/00	Crusaders	A	4-0	Glendinning, Arthur 2, Grant
12/02/00	Lisburn Distillery	H	1-2	Grant
26/02/00	Cliftonville	H	4-0	McCann, Grant, Glendinning, Doherty
04/03/00	Linfield	H	3-0	Callaghan, Graham, Grant
18/03/00	Portadown	H	1-1	Grant
25/03/00	Glentoran	A	1-2	Grant
01/04/00	Ballymena United	H	2-0	Grant, McCann
15/04/00	Coleraine	H	0-0	
22/04/00	Newry Town	A	2-0	Callaghan, Glendinning
24/04/00	Crusaders	H	1-0	Grant
29/04/00	Lisburn Distillery	A	2-1	Grant, Arthur

GLENTORAN

CLUB DIRECTORY

Glentoran FC
The Oval
Mersey Street
Belfast BT4 1FG
tel - (028) 90457670
fax - (028) 90732956
website - www.glentoran.com
Year of Formation - 1882
Chairman - Ted Brownlee
Secretary - Tom Cairns
Manager - Roy Coyle
Stadium - The Oval (30,000)

MAJOR HONOURS

League Championship - (20)
1894, 1897, 1905, 1912, 1913, 1921, 1925,
1931, 1951, 1953, 1964, 1967, 1968, 1970,
1972, 1977, 1981, 1988, 1992, 1999.
Domestic Cup - (18) 1914, 1917, 1921, 1932,
1933, 1935, 1951, 1966, 1973, 1983, 1985,
1986, 1987, 1988, 1990, 1996, 1998, 2000.

APPEARANCES 99/00

	P	Ap	(s)	Gls
Neil ARMSTRONG	G	5		
Sean ARMSTRONG	A		(6)	1
Pete BATEY (ENG)	M	21	(2)	1
Hugh DICKSON	D	4	(1)	
Stuart ELLIOTT	M	32	(2)	16
Michael FERGUSON	D	14	(3)	
Darren FINLAY	M	6	(2)	
Ian GILZEAN (SCO)	A	16	(9)	6
Alan GOUGH (IRL)	G	31		
Michael HALLIDAY	M	2		
Rory HAMILL	A	30	(4)	3
Liam KELLY (IRL)	A	3	(4)	1
John KENNEDY	D	28		4
Paul LEEMAN	D	22	(1)	1
Stevie LIVINGSTONE	A	2		
Tim McCANN	M	25	(8)	4
Ally McCOMBE	D	36		2
Colin NIXON	D	31	(2)	
David RAINEY	A	13	(17)	4
Brian RUSSELL	A	23	(6)	6
Chris WALKER	D	19	(1)	
Scott YOUNG (SCO)	M	33	(2)	9

LEAGUE RESULTS 1999/2000

14/08/99	Coleraine	A	2-1	Kelly, Elliott
21/08/99	Glenavon	H	1-2	Elliott
28/08/99	Lisburn Distillery	A	0-2	
31/08/99	Linfield	H	1-0	Elliott
07/09/99	Cliftonville	H	1-1	Leeman
11/09/99	Crusaders	A	0-1	
18/09/99	Ballymena United	A	0-0	
25/09/99	Portadown	H	5-3	McCann 2, Russell, Kennedy, Young
02/10/99	Newry Town	A	0-1	
09/10/99	Coleraine	H	3-2	Rainey 2, Elliott
16/10/99	Glenavon	A	3-3	McCombe, Kennedy, Elliott
23/10/99	Lisburn Distillery	H	3-1	Kennedy, Elliott, McCann
30/10/99	Linfield	A	0-2	
06/11/99	Cliftonville	A	2-1	Elliott, Gilzean
13/11/99	Crusaders	H	2-0	Elliott, Young
20/11/99	Ballymena United	H	3-1	Young, Russell, Gilzean
27/11/99	Portadown	A	0-1	
04/12/99	Newry Town	H	0-3	
11/12/99	Portadown	A	0-4	
18/12/99	Newry Town	H	2-1	Young (p), Russell
27/12/99	Linfield	H	1-1	McCombe
03/01/00	Glenavon	A	3-3	McCann, Gilzean, Kenendy
08/01/00	Lisburn Distillery	H	2-0	Gilzean, Elliott
15/01/00	Crusaders	A	2-2	Young, Elliott
29/01/00	Coleraine	H	2-0	og (Smyth), Elliott
05/02/00	Ballymena United	H	3-2	Elliott, Young 2 (1p)
12/02/00	Cliftonville	A	2-2	Gilzean, Russell
26/02/00	Portadown	H	1-0	Elliott
03/03/00	Newry Town	A	4-3	Hamill, Young, Russell 2
18/03/00	Linfield	A	2-1	Hamill, Rainey
25/03/00	Glenavon	H	2-1	Rainey, Elliott
01/04/00	Lisburn Distillery	A	0-1	
15/04/00	Crusaders	H	1-2	Batey
18/04/00	Ballymena United	A	1-2	Elliott
22/04/00	Coleraine	A	2-1	Gilzean, Young
29/04/00	Cliftonville	H	3-0	Elliott, Hamill, Armstrong

LINFIELD

CLUB DIRECTORY

Linfield FC
Windsor Park, Donegal Ave, Belfast BT12 6LW
tel - (028) 90244198 / fax - (028) 90244691
website - www.linfieldfc.co.uk
Year of Formation - 1886
Chairman - Billy McCoubrey
Secretary - Derek Brooks
Manager - David Jeffrey
Stadium - Windsor Park (28,500)

MAJOR HONOURS
League Championship - (43) 1891, 1892, 1893,
1895, 1898, 1902, 1904, 1907, 1908, 1909,
1911, 1914, 1922, 1923, 1930, 1932, 1934,
1935, 1949, 1950, 1954, 1955, 1956, 1959,
1961, 1962, 1966, 1969, 1971, 1975, 1978,
1979, 1980, 1982, 1983, 1984, 1985, 1986,
1987, 1989, 1993, 1994, 2000.
Domestic Cup - (35)
1891, 1892, 1893, 1895, 1898, 1899, 1902,
1904, 1912, 1913, 1915, 1916, 1919, 1922,
1923, 1930, 1931, 1934, 1936, 1939, 1942,
1945, 1946, 1948, 1950, 1953, 1960, 1962,
1963, 1970, 1978, 1980, 1982, 1994, 1995.

APPEARANCES 99/00

	P	Ap	(s)	Gls
Noel BAILIE	M	31		
Stephen BEATTY	M	29		4
Stuart CALLAGHAN (SCO)	M	26	(7)	5
Gary CHISHOLM	A	2	(3)	
Stephen COLLIER	D	19	(2)	
John EASTON	D	16		
Glenn FERGUSON	A	13	(6)	8
Tony GORMAN (IRL)	M	33	(1)	5
Norman KELLY	M	14	(8)	1
David LARMOUR	A	29	(7)	15
Ian McCOOSH	M	5	(10)	3
Craig McCRACKEN	A	1	(1)	
Tommy McDONALD	D	18		
John McGRATH	M		(2)	
Ryan McLAUGHLIN	D	7		1
Trevor McMULLAN	D		(3)	
Pat McSHANE	D	23	(1)	
Jamie MARKS	M	29	(2)	5
Paul MATHERS (SCO)	G	31		
Chris MORGAN	A	30	(5)	14
William MURPHY	D	32		3
Robert ROBINSON	G	5		
Philip ROGAN	M		(7)	
Johnny SHAW	D	1	(1)	
Ian YOUNG	D	2	(1)	

LEAGUE RESULTS 1999/2000

21/08/99	Coleraine	H	3-1	Morgan, Larmour, Gorman
31/08/99	Glentoran	A	0-1	
07/09/99	Lisburn Distillery	H	3-2	Beatty, Morgan, Callaghan
11/09/99	Ballymena United	H	3-0	Morgan, Beatty, Kelly
18/09/99	Portadown	A	1-1	og (Dalton)
21/09/99	Crusaders	A	1-1	Larmour
25/09/99	Newry Town	H	3-1	Morgan, Gorman, Larmour
02/10/99	Cliftonville	A	1-0	Larmour
05/10/99	Glenavon	A	0-0	
09/10/99	Crusaders	H	0-0	
16/10/99	Coleraine	A	1-0	Morgan
23/10/99	Glenavon	H	1-0	Morgan
30/10/99	Glentoran	H	2-0	Murphy, Marks
06/11/99	Lisburn Distillery	A	2-1	Morgan 2
12/11/99	Ballymena United	A	3-1	Morgan, Gorman, Beatty
20/11/99	Portadown	H	3-1	Larmour, McLaughlin, Marks
27/11/99	Newry Town	A	3-0	Larmour 2 (1p), Morgan
04/12/99	Cliftonville	H	3-1	Larmour 2, Ferguson
11/12/99	Lisburn Distillery	A	4-1	Ferguson 2 (1p), Callaghan, McCoosh
18/12/99	Glenavon	H	1-1	Callaghan
27/12/99	Glentoran	A	1-1	Gorman
03/01/00	Ballymena United	H	3-2	Beatty, Ferguson, og (Boyd)
08/01/00	Coleraine	H	3-0	Marks 2, Larmour
29/01/00	Portadown	H	2-1	McCoosh, og (Strain)
05/02/00	Newry Town	A	3-0	Marks, McCoosh, Larmour
12/02/00	Crusaders	H	0-0	
26/02/00	Lisburn Distillery	H	1-0	Morgan
04/03/00	Glenavon	A	0-3	
18/03/00	Glentoran	H	1-2	Ferguson
25/03/00	Ballymena United	A	1-0	Larmour
28/03/00	Cliftonville	A	3-2	Ferguson, Murphy, Morgan
01/04/00	Coleraine	A	1-2	Ferguson (p)
12/04/00	Newry Town	H	3-2	Ferguson, Morgan, Larmour
15/04/00	Cliftonville	H	1-2	Murphy
22/04/00	Portadown	A	2-0	Larmour, Gorman
29/04/00	Crusaders	A	4-0	Callaghan 2, Larmour, Morgan

LISBURN DISTILLERY

CLUB DIRECTORY

Lisburn Distillery
New Grosvenor Stadium
Ballyskeagh, Lambeg, Lisburn
tel - (028) 90301148
website - www.bigfoot.com/~distilleryfc/
Year of Formation - 1879
Chairman - Thomas Allen
Secretary - Fred Robinson
Manager - Paul Kirk
Stadium - New Grosvenor (14,000)

MAJOR HONOURS
League Championship - (6)
1896, 1899, 1901, 1903, 1906, 1963.
Domestic Cup - (12)
1884, 1885, 1886, 1889, 1894, 1896, 1903,
1905, 1910, 1925, 1956, 1971.

APPEARANCES 99/00

	P	Ap	(s)	Gls
Darren ARMOUR	A	24	(3)	11
Graeme ARTHUR	A	16	(2)	3
Kevin BATES (ENG)	A	21	(6)	6
Johnny CLAPHAM	A	7	(6)	2
Gary CLIFFORD	D	26	(8)	
Declan COOLEY	A		(1)	
Chris COFFEY	M	17	(1)	
Peter CROTHERS	D	12		
Michael CROWE	M	11	(4)	1
Chris DEEGAN	D	32	(3)	2
Darren FINLAY	M	14	(2)	3
Eddie HILL	M	4	(2)	1
Ross HEGAN	D	22	(2)	
David HENRY	G	21		
Robbie HORN (SCO)	A	8		1
Stephen JOHNSTON	D	3	(3)	
Paul McBRIDE	D	18	(3)	
Jim McCLOSKEY	M	25	(5)	3
Michael McDERMOTT	D	9	(2)	
Jim McDONAGH	A	5	(2)	
Phil McDONAGH	A	1	(6)	
Andy McDONALD	G	14		
Tim McILROY	M		(1)	
Tony McSHANE	M	18	(7)	1
John MARTIN	M	19	(2)	1
Alan MURPHY	D	16	(1)	1
Glenn MURRAY	D	15	(3)	
Jim PAVIS	M		(2)	
Keith PERCY	M	4		
Paul PRENTER	A	6	(5)	1
Barry REID	D	7	(2)	
Paul RICE	G	1		
Mark STERLING	A		(1)	

LEAGUE RESULTS 1999/2000

14/08/99	Portadown	H	2-1	McCloskey, Clapham
21/08/99	Ballymena United	A	1-1	Crowe
28/08/99	Glentoran	H	2-0	Armour, og (Nixon)
31/08/99	Newry Town	H	0-1	
07/09/99	Linfield	A	2-3	McCloskey, Armour (p)
11/09/99	Cliftonville	A	0-0	
18/09/99	Crusaders	H	2-2	Armour 2
25/09/99	Glenavon	A	0-2	
02/10/99	Coleraine	H	1-3	Armour
09/10/99	Portadown	A	1-4	Armour
16/10/99	Ballymena United	H	3-4	McCloskey, Armour, Clapham
23/10/99	Glentoran	A	1-3	Deegan
30/10/99	Newry Town	A	1-2	Hill
06/11/99	Linfield	H	1-2	Bates
13/11/99	Cliftonville	H	0-1	
20/11/99	Crusaders	A	2-1	Bates, Horn
27/11/99	Glenavon	H	1-1	Armour
04/12/99	Coleraine	A	0-3	
11/12/99	Linfield	H	1-4	Murphy
18/12/99	Coleraine	A	0-3	
27/12/99	Newry Town	A	1-1	Deegan
03/01/00	Portadown	H	2-1	og (Dalton), Finlay
08/01/00	Glentoran	A	0-2	
29/01/00	Crusaders	H	0-1	
05/02/00	Cliftonville	H	1-0	McShane
12/02/00	Glenavon	A	2-1	Finlay, Bates
26/02/00	Linfield	A	0-1	
04/03/00	Coleraine	H	1-2	Bates
18/03/00	Newry Town	H	2-3	Bates, Armour
25/03/00	Portadown	A	2-3	Prenter, Arthur
28/03/00	Ballymena United	A	1-2	Arthur
01/04/00	Glentoran	H	1-0	Arthur
15/04/00	Ballymena United	H	2-1	Martin, Armour (p)
22/04/00	Crusaders	A	0-2	
24/04/00	Cliftonville	A	2-0	Armour, Finlay
29/04/00	Glenavon	H	1-2	Bates

NEWRY TOWN

CLUB DIRECTORY

Newry Town FC
The Showgrounds, Newry
tel - (028) 30252581
Year of Formation - 1923
Chairman - Joe Rice
Secretary - Eamon Cole
Manager - Trevor Anderson (00/01 - Alfie Wylie)
Stadium - The Showgrounds (5,000)

APPEARANCES 99/00

	P	Ap	(s)	Gls
John BLACK	D		(1)	
Patrick BURNS	D		(1)	
Raymond CAMPBELL	M	23		2
Mark CARTWRIGHT (ENG)	G	5		
Robert CASEY	M	13		4
John CONNOLLY (IRL)	G	24		
Jonathan COWAN	D	16	(4)	
John DRAKE	D	6		
Paul DONEGAN	D	1		
Ciaran FEEHAN	A	15	(5)	1
Dean FITZGERALD (IRL)	M	34	(1)	2
Peter GILGUNN	D	7		
Dessie GORMAN (IRL)	A	9	(4)	3
Alan HALL	D	16	(2)	
John HOOKS	D	13		1
Carl HUGHES	M	1	(7)	
Seamus KANE	D	25	(1)	1
Neil KING	M	1		1
Adrian LARKIN	M	4		2
John McDONNELL (IRL)	D	27	(4)	2
Kevin McKEOWN (SCO)	G	1		
Stuart McLEAN (SCO)	D	27		2
Michael McMANUS	D	1		
Kieran McPARLAND	D		(1)	
John MAGUIRE	A	12	(5)	4
Sean MALLON	M	5	(1)	
Chris MURPHY	A	10	(11)	
Pat O'HARE	D	2		
John O'LOUGHLIN (IRL)	A	9		3
Shane REDDISH (IRL)	M	30		2
Stephen RODGERS	M	3		
Mark RUTHERFORD (ENG)	A	23	(1)	6
Tony SCAPPATICCI	D	6	(1)	
Alex SPACKMAN	G	6		
Ben TREANOR	A	8	(6)	4
Felix VALENTINE	A		(1)	
Brian VAUGH	M	1	(1)	
Pat WALL	A	6	(1)	1
Peter WITHNELL	A	6	(1)	1

LEAGUE RESULTS 1999/2000

Date	Opponent		Score	Scorers
14/08/99	Cliftonville	A	2-3	Gorman, McLean
21/08/99	Crusaders	H	1-1	og (Smith)
28/08/99	Portadown	H	1-1	Rutherford
31/08/99	Lisburn Distillery	A	1-0	Larkin
07/09/99	Ballymena United	H	3-1	Rutherford, og (Culbertson), Larkin (p)
11/09/99	Glenavon	A	1-2	Reddish
18/09/99	Coleraine	H	3-0	Rutherford (p), Reddish, Treanor
25/09/99	Linfield	A	1-3	Treanor
02/10/99	Glentoran	H	1-0	Rutherford
09/10/99	Cliftonville	H	3-1	Rutherford, Gorman, Fitzgerald
16/10/99	Crusaders	A	0-1	
23/10/99	Portadown	A	0-0	
30/10/99	Lisburn Distillery	H	2-1	Casey, Treanor
06/11/99	Ballymena United	A	2-2	Campbell, Treanor
12/11/99	Glenavon	H	0-1	
20/11/99	Coleraine	A	0-2	
27/11/99	Linfield	H	0-3	
04/12/99	Glentoran	A	3-0	Rutherford, Feehan, Casey
11/12/99	Ballymena United	H	2-2	McDonnell, Campbell
18/12/99	Glentoran	A	1-2	Kane
27/12/99	Lisburn Distillery	H	1-1	Gorman
03/01/00	Crusaders	A	0-1	
08/01/00	Cliftonville	H	3-2	McLean, Casey 2
15/01/00	Portadown	H	0-1	
29/01/00	Glenavon	A	0-3	
05/02/00	Linfield	H	0-3	
12/02/00	Coleraine	A	1-4	Maguire
26/02/00	Ballymena United	A	0-0	
03/04/00	Glentoran	H	3-4	O'Loughlin, Maguire, Hooks
18/03/00	Lisburn Distillery	A	3-2	Withnell, Fitzgerald, Wall
25/03/00	Crusaders	H	2-0	McDonnell, Maguire
01/04/00	Cliftonville	A	2-0	O'Loughlin 2
12/04/00	Linfield	A	2-3	Maguire, King
15/04/00	Portadown	A	0-5	
22/04/00	Glenavon	H	0-2	
29/04/00	Coleraine	H	0-1	

PORTADOWN

CLUB DIRECTORY

Portadown FC
Shamrock Park
Brownstown Road
Portadown
tel - (028) 38332726
fax - (028) 38332726
website - www.btinternet.com/~portadownfc
Year of Formation - 1924
Chairman - Roy McMahon
Secretary - Lewis Singleton
Manager - Ronnie McFall
Stadium - Shamrock Park (15,000)

MAJOR HONOURS

League Championship - (3) 1990, 1991, 1996.
Domestic Cup - (2) 1991, 1999.

APPEARANCES 99/00

	P	Ap	(s)	Gls
Vinny ARKINS (IRL)	A	34		29
Chris BOYLE	M	1	(3)	
Kenny BROWN (ENG)	D	9		
Raymond BYRNE	M	31	(1)	2
Raymond CAMPBELL	M	2		
Stephen CAMPBELL	A		(5)	1
Richard CLARKE	M	27	(10)	3
Tim DALTON (IRL)	G	29		
Greg DAVIDSON	D	15	(1)	
Liam DUNNE (IRL)	M	15	(4)	2
Derek FERGUSON (SCO)	M	6		1
Sean FRIARS	M	2		
Rory GALLAGHER	D	7	(2)	1
Glen HARBINSON	M		(1)	
Dwyer HILL	A	17	(8)	6
David IRWIN	M	13	(10)	3
Michael KEENAN	G	6		
Adrian LARKIN	M	29		6
Brian McGINTY (SCO)	M	8		1
Philip McKEOWN	D	15	(1)	
Philip MAJOR	D	24		2
Paul MILLAR	A	1		
Keith O'HARA	D	20	(4)	
Nigel QUIGLEY	M	18	(6)	1
Ross PREECE	G	1		
Tony SHERIDAN (IRL)	A	33		4
Gareth SPROULE	M	1	(8)	1
Brian STRAIN	D	26	(1)	
Jonathan TOPLEY	A	6	(2)	
Chris TRAYNOR	A		(1)	

LEAGUE RESULTS 1999/2000

14/08/99	Lisburn Distillery	A	1-2	Irwin
21/08/99	Cliftonville	H	2-2	Arkins 2
28/08/99	Newry Town	A	1-1	Arkins
31/08/99	Glenavon	H	1-3	Arkins
07/09/99	Crusaders	H	2-1	Arkins, Ferguson
11/09/99	Coleraine	A	1-4	Larkin
18/09/99	Linfield	H	1-1	Dunne
25/09/99	Glentoran	A	3-5	Quigley, Arkins 2 (1p)
02/10/99	Ballymena United	H	2-2	Arkins (p), Irwin
09/10/99	Lisburn Distillery	H	4-1	Larkin, Arkins 3 (1p)
16/10/99	Cliftonville	A	2-1	Arkins 2
23/10/99	Newry Town	H	0-0	
30/10/99	Glenavon	A	1-3	Dunne
06/11/99	Crusaders	A	4-2	Arkins, Hill, Clarke, Sproule
12/11/99	Coleraine	H	3-6	Hill, Arkins 2
20/11/99	Linfield	A	1-3	Larkin
27/11/99	Glentoran	H	1-0	Arkins
04/12/99	Ballymena United	A	1-1	Clarke
11/12/99	Glentoran	H	4-0	Hill, Larkin, Sheridan, Arkins (p)
18/12/99	Cliftonville	A	0-2	
27/12/99	Glenavon	H	2-0	Byrne, Sheridan
03/01/00	Lisburn Distillery	A	1-2	Arkins
08/01/00	Crusaders	H	4-2	og (Dunlop), Arkins, Clarke, Sheridan
15/01/00	Newry Town	A	1-0	Arkins
29/01/00	Linfield	A	1-2	Arkins
05/02/00	Coleraine	H	3-2	Byrne, Arkins, Major
12/02/00	Ballymena United	A	4-2	McGinty, Arkins 2, Campbell S.
26/02/00	Glentoran	A	0-1	
04/03/00	Cliftonville	H	3-0	Arkins, Irwin, Larkin
18/03/00	Glenavon	A	1-1	Arkins
25/03/00	Lisburn Distillery	H	3-2	Gallagher, Hill 2
01/04/00	Crusaders	A	1-0	Major
15/04/00	Newry Town	H	5-0	Arkins 2 (1p), Sheridan, Hill, Larkin
22/04/00	Linfield	H	0-2	
24/04/00	Coleraine	A	0-4	
29/04/00	Ballymena United	H	0-2	

NORWAY

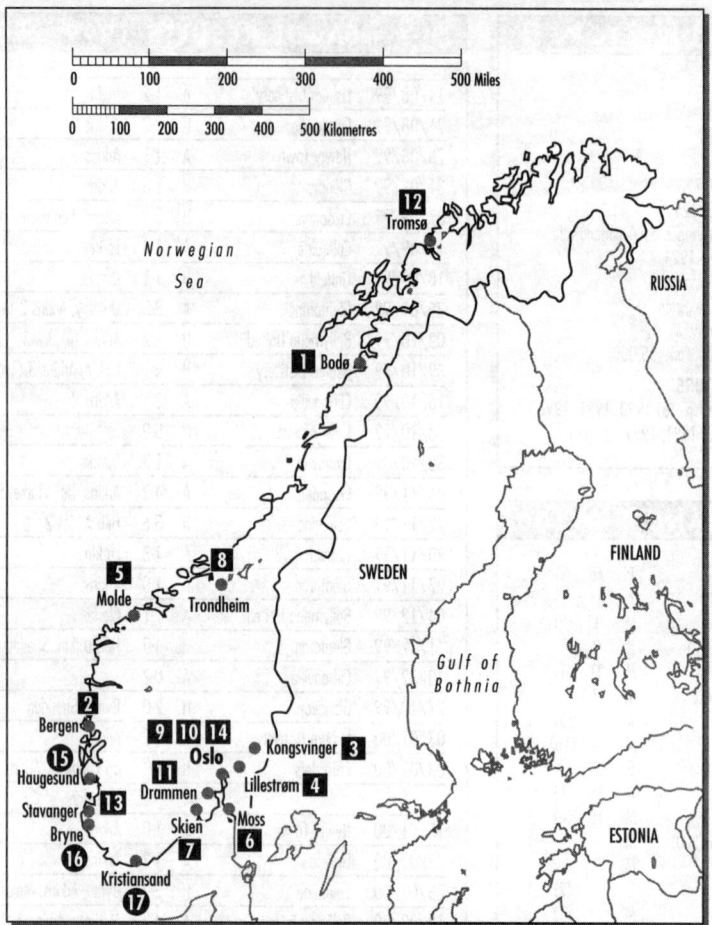

1	FK BODØ/GLIMT	728
2	SK BRANN	729
3	KONGSVINGER IL	730
4	LILLESTRØM SK	731
5	MOLDE FK	732
6	MOSS FK	733
7	ODD GRENLAND	734
8	ROSENBORG BK	735
9	SKEID	736
10	STABAEK IF	737
11	STRØMSGODSET IF	738
12	TROMSØ IL	739
13	VIKING FK	740
14	VÅLERENGA IF	741
Promoted clubs		
15	FK HAUGESUND	
16	BRYNE FK	
17	IK START	

'DOUBLE' DELIGHT AGAIN FOR ROSENBORG

Negative Norwegians fail to shine in Euro 2000

FEDERATION DIRECTORY

Norges Fotballforbund
Postboks 3823, Ullevål Hageby, 0805

tel - (21) 029300   Year of Formation - 1902
fax - (21) 029301   Chairman - Per Ravn Omdal
website - www.fotball.no   Secretary - Karen Espelund
email - nff@fotball.no

Stadium - Ullevaal , Oslo (22,500)

The manner of Norway's departure from Euro 2000 was cruel in the extreme, but very few neutrals were prepared to shed a tear for them. They were arguably the dullest, most negative team at the tournament, and only their own fans were truly sorry to see them go.

Coach Nils Johan Semb and his players failed to capture the mood of the competition. Their tactics were predictable and unenterprising, and it was no coincidence that they were involved in three of the most unappealing matches of the first round.

It could possibly be argued that Norway's approach was conditioned by their 1-0 victory over Spain in the opening game. The Norwegians' favoured strategy of absorb-and-counter proved successful in that match, and that was the reason they stuck with it. An alternative view was that they only knew how to play the one way and were ultimately made to pay for their lack of flexibility.

Whichever way you looked at it, Norway were woeful against both Yugoslavia and Slovenia. They would have

earned a draw had they not spurned a late chance against the Yugoslavs but it would not have been deserved. And against Slovenia the Norwegians barely created a decent opening in a match which they needed to win to guarantee their passage into the next round.

Even so, four points a goal balance of 1-1 would have been enough had Spain not staged their miraculous stoppage-time comeback against Yugoslavia. That was the hardest thing for the Norwegian fans and players to stomach. But for those two late goals in Bruges, Norway's first appearance in the European Championship would have been considered a success, but, as it was, the team suddenly became a target of vilification, not just from the purists but also from within their own support.

Coach Semb had agreed before the tournament that he would be quitting the post in the summer of 2002, but there were those in Norway who suggested that it might be a good idea if he brought forward the date of his departure by a couple of years. He did concur with the masses that a change in the team's approach was necessary, with more variation having to be added to their play, but he also reminded everybody how Norway had stylishly qualified for Euro 2000, winning every one of their five away fixtures - albeit in a fairly tame group.

The only Norwegian player who left a positive impression in Belgium and Holland was long-serving midfielder Erik Mykland - a bundle of energy from first minute to last - although from a defensive point of view goalkeeper Thomas Myhre

LEAGUE CHAMPIONSHIP RESULTS 1999

		1	2	3	4	5	6	7	8	9	10	11	12	13	14
1	FK Bodø/Glimt		1-3	2-0	1-2	3-1	4-0	4-0	2-4	4-2	4-0	3-1	1-3	3-3	1-1
2	SK Brann	0-2		5-4	1-3	0-1	1-0	3-0	2-1	0-1	2-3	2-2	3-1	1-0	2-1
3	Kongsvinger IL	2-1	0-2		1-1	2-3	1-0	1-0	0-1	1-2	1-3	2-4	3-1	1-3	4-0
4	Lillestrøm SK	3-0	2-0	6-2		0-1	1-0	1-2	3-2	2-1	1-2	4-2	1-2	4-1	4-1
5	Molde FK	2-1	1-3	3-2	2-0		3-1	1-0	0-2	3-0	0-0	3-0	4-0	3-4	4-3
6	Moss FK	4-1	0-2	3-0	1-3	0-1		1-0	1-4	5-0	2-0	2-5	2-4	0-2	1-0
7	Odd Grenland	4-2	3-1	3-1	0-2	0-0	1-0		0-0	2-1	3-2	2-2	2-1	1-3	0-3
8	Rosenborg BK	6-1	2-3	4-1	4-0	2-1	5-0	3-5		3-0	2-1	3-1	2-2	3-2	4-2
9	Skeid	1-3	1-2	0-1	4-4	3-5	0-6	3-1	1-7		1-3	4-0	2-1	3-2	0-2
10	Stabaek IF	3-2	2-3	1-1	1-6	4-2	3-1	2-5	2-0	5-0		2-1	1-1	3-1	3-0
11	Strømsgodset IF	0-1	1-2	2-1	1-1	0-2	2-5	3-5	1-3	3-1	4-3		3-6	1-0	0-3
12	Tromsø IL	5-1	5-0	4-1	4-1	1-2	1-1	5-0	2-1	8-2	3-3	3-2		1-3	2-2
13	Viking FK	3-3	2-0	3-0	2-4	4-1	1-1	1-2	0-2	0-1	2-3	3-2	2-1		2-0
14	Vålerenga IF	1-1	1-2	2-1	3-1	2-0	1-2	2-1	0-5	2-2	1-3	2-3	1-3	4-2	

LEAGUE CHAMPIONSHIP FINAL TABLE 1999

			Home				Away				Total						
		Pd	W	D	L	F	A	W	D	L	F	A	W	D	L	F	A	PT	GD
1	Rosenborg BK	26	10	1	2	43	19	8	1	4	32	14	18	2	6	75	33	56	42
2	Molde FK	26	9	1	3	29	16	7	1	5	20	21	16	2	8	49	37	50	12
3	SK Brann	26	7	1	5	22	19	9	0	4	23	21	16	1	9	45	40	49	5
4	Lillestrøm SK	26	9	0	4	32	16	6	3	4	28	25	15	3	8	60	41	48	19
5	Stabaek IF	26	8	2	3	32	23	6	2	5	26	26	14	4	8	58	49	46	9
6	Tromsø IL	26	8	3	2	44	19	5	2	6	26	27	13	5	8	70	46	44	24
7	Odd Grenland	26	7	3	3	21	18	5	0	8	21	30	12	3	11	42	48	39	-6
8	Viking FK	26	6	2	5	25	20	5	1	7	26	28	11	3	12	51	48	36	3
9	FK Bodø/Glimt	26	7	2	4	33	20	3	2	8	19	34	10	4	12	52	54	34	-2
10	Moss FK	26	6	0	7	22	22	3	2	8	17	24	9	2	15	39	46	29	-7
11	Vålerenga IF	26	5	2	6	22	26	3	2	8	18	27	8	4	14	40	53	28	-13
12	Strømsgodset IF	26	4	1	8	21	33	3	2	8	25	35	7	3	16	46	68	24	-22
13	Skeid	26	4	1	8	23	37	3	1	9	13	38	7	2	17	36	75	23	-39
14	Kongsvinger IL	26	5	1	7	19	21	1	1	11	15	38	6	2	18	34	59	20	-25

and centre-back Bjørn Otto Bragstad both lived up to their reputations. Not so the attacking triumvirate of Steffen Iversen, Tore André Flo and Ole Gunnar Solskjaer, who managed just one goal between them - and that the product of a defensive howler by Spain's goalkeeper.

Norway's transformation from all-conquering qualifiers to vanquished finalists maintained a reversal of fortunes for Norwegian football that had begun earlier in the year when Rosenborg lost four Champions' League matches in as many weeks to drop like a stone out of a competition which they had graced with their presence during the autumn. The

sacking of ex-national team boss Egil Olsen at Norwegian-owned English Premiership club Wimbledon - and their subsequent relegation - completed an unhappy start to the new millennium for Norwegian football and its image abroad.

TOP SCORERS

23	Rune LANGE (Tromsø IL)
21	Andreas LUND (Molde FK)
18	Jostein FLO (Strømsgodset IF)
17	John CAREW (Vålerenga IF/Rosenborg BK)
	Rikhardur DADASON (Viking FK)
16	Bengt SAETERNES (FK Bodø/Glimt)
	Heidar HELGUSON (Lillestrøm SK)
15	Sigurd RUSHFELDT (Rosenborg BK)
14	Tore André DAHLUM (Rosenborg BK)
	Helgi SIGURDSSON (Stabaek IF)
	Petter BELSVIK (Stabaek IF)

NATIONAL TEAM RESULTS 99/00

18/08/99	Lithuania	H	Oslo	1-0	Lund (87)
04/09/99	Greece (ECQ)	H	Oslo	1-0	Leonhardsen (35)
08/09/99	Slovenia (ECQ)	H	Oslo	4-0	Istenic (16og), Iversen (18),
					Solskjaer (30), Leonhardsen (68)
09/10/99	Latvia (ECQ)	A	Riga	2-1	Solskjaer (52), Flo (86)
14/11/99	Germany	H	Oslo	0-1	
31/01/00	Iceland	N	La Manga	0-0	
02/02/00	Denmark	N	La Manga	4-2	Berg H. (50, 89), Lund (54, 90)
04/02/00	Sweden	N	La Manga	1-1	Carew (83)
23/02/00	Turkey	A	Istanbul	2-0	Riise (38), Strand (78)
29/03/00	Switzerland	A	Lugano	2-2	Solbakken (32), Skammelsrud (73p)
26/04/00	Belgium	H	Oslo	0-2	
27/05/00	Slovakia	H	Oslo	2-0	Solskjaer (21p), Iversen (85)
03/06/00	Italy	H	Oslo	1-0	Carew (52)
13/06/00	Spain (ECF)	N	Rotterdam	1-0	Iversen (66)
18/06/00	Yugoslavia (ECF)	N	Liège	0-1	
21/06/00	Slovenia (ECF)	N	Arnhem	0-0	

NATIONAL TEAM APPEARANCES 99/00

Coach - Nils Johan SEMB	LIT	GRE	SLO	LAT	GER	ISL	DEN	SWE	TUR	SUI	BEL	SVK	ITA	ESP	YUG	SLO	Cps	Gls
Frode OLSEN (12/10/67) - Stabaek IF/Sevilla FC (ESP)	G46	G	G	G	G		G		G		s46						14	-
Vegard HEGGEM (13/07/75) - Liverpool (ENG)	D46	D	D	D	D			D46			D66	D68		D	D35		20	1
Henning BERG (01/09/69) - Manchester United (ENG)	D	D	D	D		D	D		D	D	D	D		D59			72	8
Erik HOFTUN (03/03/69) - Rosenborg BK	D	D	D	D	D			s46	D								22	-
André BERGDØLMO (13/10/71) - Rosenborg BK	D	D	D	D	D		D	D43	D	D	D	D	D	D	D	D	27	-
Steffen IVERSEN (10/11/76) - Tottenham Hotspur (ENG)	M	M	M	M46	M33				M85	M	s66		M90	M71	M		18	6
Erik MYKLAND (21/07/71) - Panathinaikos (GRE)	M	M	M	M80	M74				M	M	M66		M	M	M	M	75	2
Øyvind LEONHARDSEN (17/08/70) - Tottenham Hotspur (ENG)	M	M74	M	M	M74												66	16
Bent SKAMMELSRUD (18/05/66) - Rosenborg BK	M66	M	M78	M	M74		M	M	M				M	M	M		37	6
Ole Gunnar SOLSKJAER (26/02/73) - Manchester United (ENG)	M	M69	M79	M89	s33				M	A46	M	M	M	M	M	M	34	14
Tore André FLO (15/06/73) - Chelsea (ENG)	A	A	A89	A	A			A	A	s46	A	A80	A70	A		A	51	21
Espen BAARDSEN (07/12/77) - Tottenham Hotspur (ENG)	s46				G												4	-
Gunnar HALLE (11/08/65) - Bradford City (ENG)	s46																64	5
Andreas LUND (07/05/75) - Molde FK	s66		s89	s46	s74	s73	s44	A83									8	4
Petter RUDI (17/09/73) - Sheffield Wednesday (ENG)		s69															27	3
Vidar RISETH (21/04/72) - Celtic (SCO)			s74	s79	s89		D	s52		s43		s82	s66	s80	s90		27	2
Jan Derek SØRENSEN (28/12/71) - Rosenborg BK				s78		M74	M	M44		s85	s61						6	-
Ståle SOLBAKKEN (27/02/68) - AaB (DEN)				s80	s74	M	M	s90	s87	M62	s77	M90			M		58	9
Trond ANDERSEN (06/01/75) - Wimbledon (ENG)						D	D	D52		s46	D	D		s60			8	-
Roar STRAND (02/02/70) - Rosenborg BK				s74	s80	M	M	M87	s62		s58	s65		s76	s82		26	4
Kjetil REKDAL (06/11/68) - Hertha BSC Berlin (GER)				s74				M		M82	s90						83	17
Claus LUNDEKVAM (22/02/73) - Southampton (ENG)						D											8	-
Ørjan BERG (20/08/68) - Rosenborg BK						M		M90									19	1
John Arne RIISE (24/09/80) - AS Monaco (FRA)						M80	M83		M83		M61	s77	s90				6	1
Ole Martin ÅRST (19/07/74) - KAA Gent (BEL)						M80		M81									2	-
John CAREW (05/09/79) - Rosenborg BK						A73	A	M	M		M77	M77	M90	s70	s71	M61	16	3
Jostein FLO (03/10/64) - Strømsgodset IF						s80		s83									53	11
Bjørn Otto BRAGSTAD (05/01/71) - Rosenborg BK						D	D	D46		D	D	D	D	D		14	-
Raymond KVISVIK (08/11/74) - SK Brann						s83											1	-
Morten BAKKE (16/12/68) - Molde FK						G											1	-
Mike KJØLØ (26/10/71) - Stabaek IF						D											1	-
Roger NILSEN (08/08/69) - Molde FK						D											32	3
Jan Frode NORNES (08/01/73) - Odd Grenland						s81											1	-
Eirik BAKKE (13/09/77) - Leeds United (ENG)							s83		M58	M65	M	M76	s61				8	-
															/82			
Thomas MYHRE (16/10/73) - Everton (ENG)/Birmingham City (ENG)								G	G	G46	G	G	G	G	13	-
Dan EGGEN (13/01/70) - Deportivo Alavés (ESP)										D60	s59	D		D	D	21	2
Stig Inge BJØRNEBYE (11/12/69) - Brøndby IF										s68		s35		D		73	1

EUROPEAN CUPS 99/00

CHAMPIONS' CUP
● MOLDE FK
Preliminary round 2 CSKA MOSKVA (RUS)
A 0-2
    Bakke; Strande (Singsaas 87), Andersen, Tessem, Fostervold; Sundgot
    (Santos 82), Olsen, Fjørtoft, Berg Hestad, Mork; Lund.
H 4-0 Tessem (47), Berg Hestad (65), Hoseth (67, 81)
    Bakke; Strande (Santos 79), Andersen, Lydersen, Fostervold; Olsen
    (Hoseth 46), Fjørtoft, Berg Hestad; Tessem, Lund, Mork (Sundgot 74).

Qualifying round RCD MALLORCA (ESP)
H 0-0
    Bakke; Strande, Tessem, Lydersen (Santos 46), Fostervold; Berg Hestad,
    Fjørtoft, Hoseth; Olsen, Lund, Mork (Sundgot 60).
A 1-1 Lund (85p)
    Bakke; Santos, Tessem, Lydersen, Fostervold; Olsen, Berg Hestad, Fjørtoft,
    Hoseth (Singsaas 85), Mork (Sundgot 70); Lund.

Champions' League
1st match FC PORTO (POR)
H 0-1
    Bakke; Strande, Tessem, Fostervold, Santos; Berg Hestad, Fjørtoft
    (Sundgot 87), Hoseth; Olsen, Lund, Mork (Schei Lindbaek 46).

2nd match REAL MADRID (ESP)
A 1-4 Schei Lindbaek (80)
    Bakke; Strande, Lydersen (Singsaas 85), Tessem, Fostervold; Olsen,
    Fjørtoft, Berg Hestad; Schei Lindbaek (Sundgot 89), Lund, Hoseth
    (Mork 66).

3rd match OLYMPIAKOS (GRE)
A 1-3 Lund (58)
    Bakke; Strande (Santos 72), Lydersen, Tessem, Fostervold; Olsen, Fjørtoft,
    Berg Hestad; Sundgot (Hoseth 74), Lund, Mork (Schei Lindbaek 54).

4th match OLYMPIAKOS (GRE)
H 3-2 Lund (54, 59), Berg Hestad (74)
    Bakke; Strande (Santos 72), Lydersen, Tessem, Fostervold; Olsen, Fjørtoft,
    Berg Hestad; Sundgot (Hoseth 74), Lund, Mork (Schei Lindbaek 54).

5th match FC PORTO (POR)
A 1-3 Berg Hestad (82)
    Bakke; Santos, Singsaas, Lydersen, Fostervold; Olsen, Fjørtoft,
    Berg Hestad; Tessem, Lund, Hoseth (Mork 88).

6th match REAL MADRID (ESP)
H 0-1
    Bakke; Strande, Singsaas, Lydersen, Fostervold (Santos 46); Olsen,
    Fjørtoft, Berg Hestad; Tessem (Mork 87), Lund, Hoseth
    (Schei Lindbaek 62).

● ROSENBORG BK
Champions' League
1st match BOAVISTA FC (POR)
A 3-0 Sørensen (9), Berg Ø. (44), Strand R. (73)
    Jamtfall; Johnsen, Bragstad, Hoftun, Bergdølmo; Strand R.
    (Winsnes F. 89), Skammelsrud, Berg Ø.; Sørensen (Dahlum 82), Carew,
    Jakobsen.

2nd match FEYENOORD (HOL)
H 2-2 Carew (21, 24)
    Jamtfall; Johnsen (Winsnes F. 65), Bragstad, Hoftun, Bergdølmo;
    Strand R., Skammelsrud, Berg Ø.; Sørensen, Carew, Jakobsen
    (Dahlum 59).

3rd match BORUSSIA DORTMUND (GER)
H 2-2 Sørensen (35), Carew (68)
    Jamtfall; Basma (Winsnes F. 25), Bragstad, Hoftun, Bergdølmo; Strand R.,
    Skammelsrud, Berg Ø.; Sørensen, Carew, Jakobsen (Dahlum 63).

4th match BORUSSIA DORTMUND (GER)
A 3-0 Sørensen (17, 58), Winsnes F. (70)
    Jamtfall; Strand R., Bragstad, Hoftun, Bergdølmo; Winsnes F.,
    Skammelsrud, Berg Ø.; Sørensen, Carew, Jakobsen.

5th match BOAVISTA FC (POR)
H 2-0 Berg Ø. (61), Dahlum (66)
    Jamtfall; Strand R., Bragstad, Hoftun, Bergdølmo; Winsnes F.,
    Skammelsrud, Berg Ø. (Johnsen 89); Sørensen, Carew, Jakobsen
    (Dahlum 58).

6th match FEYENOORD (HOL)
A 0-1
    Jamtfall; Strand R., Bragstad, Hoftun, Bergdølmo; Winsnes F.,
    Skammelsrud, Berg Ø.; Sørensen, Carew, Jakobsen (Dahlum 62).

7th match FC BAYERN MÜNCHEN (GER)
H 1-1 Skammelsrud (47)
    Jamtfall; Basma, Bragstad, Hoftun, Bergdølmo; Winsnes F. (Dahlum 70),
    Skammelsrud, Berg Ø.; Sørensen, Carew, Strand R..

8th match REAL MADRID (ESP)
A 1-3 Carew (47)
    Jamtfall; Basma, Johnsen, Hoftun, Bergdølmo; Strand R. (Aarøy 90),
    Skammelsrud, Berg Ø.; Sørensen, Carew, Jakobsen (Winsnes F. 51).

9th match DYNAMO KYIV (UKR)
A 1-2 Jakobsen (48)
    Arason; Basma, Bragstad, Hoftun, Bergdølmo; Strand R. (Storflor 46;
    Johnsen 90), Skammelsrud, Berg Ø.; Winsnes F., Carew, Jakobsen.

10th match DYNAMO KYIV (UKR)
H 1-2 Berg Ø. (38)
    Arason; Basma, Bragstad, Hoftun, Johnsen; Strand R. (Storvik 79),
    Skammelsrud, Berg Ø.; Sørensen, Carew, Jakobsen (Knutsen 79).

11th match FC BAYERN MÜNCHEN (GER)
A 1-2 Carew (64)
    Arason; Basma, Bragstad, Johnsen, Bergdølmo; Strand R. (Winsnes F. 82),
    Skammelsrud, Berg Ø.; Sørensen, Carew, Knutsen (Jakobsen 72).

12th match REAL MADRID (ESP)
H 0-1
    Arason; Basma, Hoftun, Johnsen, Bergdølmo; Strand R., Skammelsrud,
    Berg Ø.; Sørensen, Carew, Jakobsen (Knutsen 70).

EUROPEAN CUPS 99/00 (CONTINUED)

UEFA CUP

● FK BODØ/GLIMT
Qualifying round FC VADUZ (LIE)
H 1-0 Staurvik (27)
Guttulsrød; Mikalsen, Steen, Staurvik, Evjen; Robertson, Hansen A., Berg A. (Sakariassen 80); Bjørkan, Saeternes (Eriksen 30), Bergersen.
A 2-1 Saeternes (29, 83)
Horn; Mikalsen, Steen, Staurvik, Evjen (Breivik 88); Hansen A., Robertson (Hansen C. 76), Berg A. (Ludvigsen 85); Bjørkan, Saeternes, Bergersen.

1st round SV WERDER BREMEN (GER)
H 0-5
Horn; Breivik, Steen, Staurvik, Evjen; Berg C. (Mikalsen 67), Robertson (Hansen C. 67), Berg A. (Eriksen 81); Bjørkan, Saeternes, Bergersen.
A 1-1 Staurvik (76)
Guttulsrød; Breivik, Steen, Staurvik, Evjen; Hansen A., Robertson, Berg A. (Ludvigsen 82), Bjørkan (Berg C. 90), Bergersen; Saeternes (Eriksen 82).

● STABAEK IF
1st round RC DEPORTIVO (ESP)
H 1-0 Finstad (57)
Olsen F.; Holter, Skistad, Flem, Stenersen; Andresen (Stenvoll 80), Svindal Larsen (Marteinsson 14), Linderoth, Kolle (Ackon 80); Finstad, Belsvik.
A 0-2
Olsen F.; Holter, Skistad, Flem, Stenersen (Svensson 79); Andresen, Linderoth, Marteinsson (Stenvoll 69), Kolle (Ackon 65); Finstad, Belsvik.

● VIKING FK
Qualifying round CE PRINCIPAT (AND)
H 7-0 Lunde Aarsheim (5), Svensson (17, 48), Dadason (40, 72, 82), Nygaard (64)
Bø (Snørteland 80); Helgason, Eike Hansen, Solberg, Espevoll (Kristensen 62); Lunde Aarsheim, Svensson, Nygaard; Sanne, Dadason, Berland (Berre 62).
A 11-0 Dadason (37, 42), Berre (43, 61, 75), Berland (44, 45), Sanne (64, 65, 67), Mathiassen (83)
Bø; Nygaard (Dahl 46), Eike Hansen (Knudsen 65), Espevoll, Pereira; Kristensen, Lunde Aarsheim, Sanne; Berre, Dadason, Berland (Mathiassen 46).

1st round SPORTING CP (POR)
H 3-0 Svensson (57), Berre (70), Espevoll (78p)
Bø; Helgason, Eike Hansen, Espevoll, Pereira; Lunde Aarsheim, Svensson, Nygaard (Knudsen 79); Berre (Sanne 75), Dadason, Berland (Kristensen 86).
A 0-1
Bø; Helgason, Eike Hansen, Espevoll, Pereira; Berre (Knudsen 60), Lunde Aarsheim (Mathiassen 72), Svensson, Nygaard, Berland (Sanne 53); Dadason.

2nd round SV WERDER BREMEN (GER)
A 0-0
Bø; Helgason, Eike Hansen (Dahl 82), Espevoll, Pereira; Lunde Aarsheim, Svensson, Nygaard; Berre (Aase 85), Dadason, Berland (Sanne 76).
H 2-2 Berland (3), Dadason (84)
Bø; Dahl, Helgason, Espevoll, Pereira (Mathiassen 89); Lunde Aarsheim, Svensson, Nygaard (Sanne 60); Berre, Dadason, Berland (Aase 46).

The picture had been very different as the 20th century drew to a close, particularly for Rosenborg, who not only won their opening Champions' League group, hammering 1997 winners Borussia Dortmund 3-0 in the Westfalenstadion en route, but also maintained their total supremacy in the domestic game by winning their eighth successive Tippeliga title and the sixth 'double' in their history. It was a triumphant return for coach Nils Arne Eggen, who had taken a year off in 1998 but who seemed as if he had never been away as he steered Rosenborg to yet more silverware and European success.

Trondheim's finest were able to deal with the twin challenges of domestic and European competition, and although they occasionally looked vulnerable in the league, that eighth consecutive title was never seriously in doubt. They did lose six matches, but two of those came after the championship had been won, by which stage Eggen had chosen to rest some of his key players for the more testing engagements in Europe.

Rosenborg effectively sealed the title with a burst of four straight wins in August. It was at this time that Rosenborg welcomed into their squad much talked-about striker John

Carew. The young giant was lured from Vålerenga for a record Norwegian domestic fee, ostensibly to replace Sigurd Rushfeldt, who had just left for Spain. Carew justified his fee by scoring ten goals in only eight appearances, and he was also to make quite an impression in the Champions' League with goals against Dortmund, Feyenoord, Real Madrid and Bayern Munich.

Fellow striker Jan Derek Sørensen also found the target regularly in all competitions, and it was his brace which enabled Rosenborg to complete the domestic 'double' with a 2-0 victory in the Cup final against Brann, a team which had done their own 'double' over Rosenborg in the league. As ever, the Cup final was a sell-out, with a crowd of 25,296 packing the Ullevaal. That was the largest crowd for any domestic game during the season. The best in the league had been 19,514 for Rosenborg's 3-1 home win

INTERNATIONAL HONOURS

World Cup Finals appearances: 1938, 1994, 1998 (2nd round)
European Championship appearances: 2000

DOMESTIC CUP 1999

SECOND ROUND
Mosjøen 0, FK Bodø/Glimt 2
Fana 0, SK Brann 2
Åsane 1, FK Haugesund 4
Ørsta 3, IL Hødd 1
Manglerud/Star 2, Kongsvinger IL 3 (aet)
Faaberg 0, Lillestrøm SK 1
Moss FK 3, Runar 0
Odd Grenland 1, Sandefjord 0
Mercantile 0, Skeid 1 (aet)
Abildsø 0, Stabaek IF 3
Strømsgodset IF 4, Tollnes 0
Tromsø IL 3, Skjervøy 1
Vard-Haugesund 0, Viking FK 2
Nybergsund 0, Vålerenga IF 2
Sola 2, Bryne 4
Verdal 0, Byåsen 1
Clausenengen 0, Strindheim 1
Kjelsås IL 3, Sprint/Jeløy 0
Liv/Fossekallen Hønefoss 0, Fredrikstad FK 5
Mo 2, Lofoten 1
Ørn Horten 0, SFK Lyn 1
Raufoss IL 7, Årvoll 0
Vigør 1, IK Start 6
Alta 3, Skarp 2
Os 4, Fyllingen 3
Ålgård 0, Vidar 0 (aet; 4-3 on pens.)
Narvik 6, Finnsnes 1
Grei 0, Ullern 1
Gjøvik/Lyn 2, Hamarkameratene 1

Florø 0, Sogndal 3
Molde FK 6, Sunndal 0
Rosenborg BK 5, Ranheim 0

THIRD ROUND
Narvik 1, Rosenborg BK 9
FK Bodø/Glimt 9, Mo 0
SK Brann 3, Ørsta 1
Kongsvinger IL 1, Bryne FK 0
Lillestrøm SK 3, Os Turn 0
Byåsen IL 1, Moss FK 2
Strindheim IL 1, Molde FK 3
Ullern 0, Odd Grenland 2
Skeid 3, Raufoss IL 4
Stabaek IF 6, Gjøvik/Lyn 1
FK Haugesund 5, Strømsgodset IF 1
Alta 1, Tromsø IL 6
Viking FK 5, Ålgård FK 0
Fredrikstad FK 0, Vålerenga IF 3
Sogndal IL 0, Kjelsås IL 2
SFK Lyn 2, IK Start 1 (aet)

FOURTH ROUND
Kjelsås IL 2, Molde FK 3
FK Bodø/Glimt 2, SFK Lyn 4 (aet)
Vålerenga IF 1, SK Brann 3
Raufoss IL 2, Kongsvinger IL 1
Lillestrøm SK 3, FK Haugesund 1
Rosenborg BK 4, Moss FK 1
Odd Grenland 2, Viking FK 1
Tromsø IL 2, Stabaek IF 1

QUARTER-FINALS
SK Brann 3 (Kvisvik 8p, Guntveit 68, 78),
Odd Grenland 2 (Fevang 49, Johnsen F. 75)
Tromsø IL 5 (Hafstad 9, Lange Ru. 39, 68p,
Fermann 77, Gudmundsson 88), Raufoss IL 0
SFK Lyn 1 (Kaasa 75),
Rosenborg BK 2 (Jakobsen 47, Johnsen 65)
Molde FK 3 (Lund 59, Olsen 73, Sundgot 79),
Lillestrøm SK 0

SEMI-FINALS
Rosenborg BK 2 (Johnsen 36, Berg Ø. 56),
Tromsø IL 1 (Lange Ru. 23)
Molde FK 3 (Lund 65, 71, Schei Lindbaek 73),
SK Brann 4 (Kvisvik 6, 64, Helstad 90, Ludvigsen 110)
(aet)

FINAL
30/10/99, Oslo
ROSENBORG BK 2 Sørensen (49, 56)
SK BRANN 0
referee - Øvrebø
ROSENBORG BK - Jamtfall (Arason 90); Strand R.,
Bragstad, Hoftun, Bergdølmo; Winsnes F.,
Skammelsrud, Berg Ø. (Johnsen 90); Sørensen,
Carew, Jakobsen (Dahlum 69).
SK BRANN - Kihlstedt; Brendesaether, Ludvigsen,
Moen, Ylönen (Mjelde 90); Guntveit, Helland,
Pedersen, Samuelsson, Kvisvik; Helstad (Karadas 88).

PLAYERS OF THE SEASON

EIRIK BAKKE

Eirik Bakke added his name to the lengthy list of Norwegian imports in the English Premiership when he joined Leeds United from Sogndal IL for £1m in the summer of 1999. Already a Norwegian international at the time, little was made of the transfer in England, but it was not too long before the tigerish young midfielder claimed a regular place in David O'Leary's exciting young team and began to catch the eye. A natural replacement for the injured David Batty, he was particularly outstanding in the FA Cup, where he scored four goals in three matches, but he also played a significant part in helping the Yorkshire club into the semi-finals of the UEFA Cup and third place in the Premiership. Recognition for his consistency came with a place in Norway's Euro 2000 team, where he was preferred to former stalwarts Kjetil Rekdal and Ståle Solbakken as well as another promising young gun, Monaco's John Arne Riise.

JAN DEREK SØRENSEN

Had he not been injured and therefore unavailable, Jan Derek Sørensen would almost certainly have been selected for Norway's Euro 2000 squad. The pacy winger-cum-striker was the revelation of the 1999 season, masterminding Rosenborg's all-conquering march to glory with important goals in every competition. His was the winning strike in the 2-1 victory over Molde that effectively sealed the championship triumph and he also struck both goals in the Cup final against Brann. In Europe, he opened Rosenborg's account with the first goal in a 3-0 win at Boavista and then added three more in the two games against Borussia Dortmund, including two in the famous 3-0 win at the Westfalenstadion that propelled the Norwegian champions to the top of the group and into the next round.

against Strømsgodset in mid-May. Rosenborg's average gate was 13,359, with only Brann (10,398) accompanying them past the five-figure barrier.

Molde FK, backed by an average of 7,163 fans, finished as runners-up to Rosenborg for the second year running. They claimed that prize with a last-day victory over Lillestrøm, but, unlike the previous year, it did not carry with it a ticket into the qualifying round of the Champions' League. That was a pity for Molde, because they had done the 'impossible' and reached the Champions' League proper a couple of months earlier, sensationally beating both CSKA Moscow and Mallorca to take their place at the top table of European football alongside Real Madrid, FC Porto and Olympiakos. Erik Bragstad's unsung team were never likely to survive for long in such exalted company, but they did at least win one match, beating Olympiakos 3-2 thanks to two goals from their prolific striker Andreas

Lund - second only in the Tippeliga top-scorer listings to Tromsø IL's Rune Lange.

Viking FK, who possessed the official Tippeliga Player of the Year in Swedish midfielder Magnus Svensson (he narrowly denied Rosenborg skipper Erik Hoftun a hat-trick of wins), also made waves in Europe by eliminating Portuguese club Sporting from the UEFA Cup first round and then going close against Werder Bremen a few weeks later. It was a respectable way for the Stavanger club to finish off its centenary season, although there had been little for the supporters to get their teeth into on the domestic front, where they finished a lowly eighth in the league.

Skeid and Kongsvinger, the two worst-supported teams in the top division, were relegated automatically and subseqently joined by Strømsgodset, beaten at home in the play-offs by IK Start, who thus returned to the Tippeliga with two other familiar names, Haugesund and Bryne.

PROMOTED CLUBS 1999

FIRST DIVISION FINAL TABLE

		Pd	W	D	L	F	A	Pt	GD
1	FK Haugesund	26	16	4	6	61	32	52	29
2	Bryne FK	26	14	7	5	43	33	49	10
3	IK Start	26	13	8	5	42	31	47	11
4	SFK Lyn	26	11	9	6	54	30	42	24
5	Sogndal IL	26	12	6	8	38	32	42	6
6	Kjelsås IL	26	11	8	7	33	28	41	5
7	Eik-Tønsberg	26	10	7	9	39	39	37	0
8	Liv/Fossekallen Hønefoss	26	10	5	11	43	42	35	1
9	Raufoss IL	26	8	8	10	35	36	32	-1
10	Byåsen IL	26	9	6	11	37	32	30	5
11	Lofoten	26	8	6	12	38	47	30	-9
12	Skjetten SK	26	8	5	13	29	43	29	-14
13	IL Hødd	26	5	6	15	34	51	21	-17
14	Clausenengen FK	26	4	1	21	24	74	13	-50

PROMOTION/RELEGATION PLAY-OFF
IK Start 2, Strømsgodset IF 2
Strømsgodset IF 0, IK Start 1
(IK Start 3-2)

CLUB DIRECTORIES

Fotballklubben Haugesund
Postboks 406, 5501 Haugesund
tel - (52) 714238 / fax - (52) 717645
website - www.fk-haugesund.no
email - post@fk-haugesund.no
Year of Formation - 1993
Chairman - Ingolf Steensnaes
Coach - Åge Steen
Stadium - Haugesund (12,000)

Bryne Fotballklubb
Postboks 257, 4341 Bryne
tel - (51) 777700 / fax - (51) 777701
website - www.brynefk.no
email - bryne.fk@rl.telia.no
Year of Formation - 1926
Chairman - Svein Bergstad
Coach - Kenneth Rosén
Stadium - Bryne (10,500)
MAJOR HONOURS
Domestic Cup - (1) 1987.

Idrettsklubben Start
Postboks 1533 Volhalla, 4688 Kristiansand
tel - (38) 106666 / fax - (38) 097535
website - www.start.no
email - adm@start.no
Year of Formation - 1905
Chairman - Svein B. Sødal
Coach - Jan Halvor Halvorsen
Stadium - Kristiansand stadion (15,000)
MAJOR HONOURS
League Championship - (2) 1978, 1980.

FK BODØ/GLIMT

CLUB DIRECTORY

Fotballklubben Bodø/Glimt
Postboks 179, 8001 Bodø
tel - (75) 545500
fax - (75) 545510
website - www.glimt.no
email - bg@glimt.no
Year of Formation - 1916
Chairman - Harald Hansen
Coach - Dag Opjordsmoen
Stadium - Aspmyra (13,000)

MAJOR HONOURS
Domestic Cup - (2) 1975, 1993.

APPEARANCES 1999

	P	Ap	(s)	Gls
Arild BERG	M	15	(3)	4
Christian BERG	M	11	(5)	1
Ørjan BERG	M	17		
Tommy BERGERSEN	A	23	(2)	9
Aasmund BJØRKAN	A	26		8
Thomas BREIVIK	D	8	(7)	
Eivind ERIKSEN	A	11	(12)	3
Andreas EVJEN	D	25		
Clas-André GUTTULSRØD	G	19	(1)	
André HANSEN	M	11	(3)	1
Cato HANSEN	D	11	(8)	
Trond Vidar HANSEN	A		(4)	
Tor Egil HORN	G	7		
Trond Fredrik LUDVIGSEN	A	1	(8)	3
Thor MIKALSEN	D	19		
Lee ROBERTSON (SCO)	M	12	(3)	
Håvard SAKARIASSEN	A		(2)	
Odd Karl STANGNES	D		(1)	
Tom Kåre STAURVIK	D	22	(4)	5
Christian STEEN	D	26		1
Bengt SAETERNES	A	22	(3)	16

LEAGUE RESULTS 1999

10/04/99	Vålerenga IF	A	1-1	Eriksen
18/04/99	Strømsgodset IF	H	3-1	Staurvik, Saeternes 2
23/04/99	Molde FK	A	1-2	Eriksen
02/05/99	SK Brann	H	1-3	Ludvigsen
08/05/99	Rosenborg BK	A	1-6	Bergersen
13/05/99	Viking FK	H	3-3	Saeternes, Eriksen, Bjørkan
16/05/99	Stabaek IF	A	2-3	Bjørkan, Saeternes
24/05/99	Odd Grenland	H	4-0	Bergersen (p), Bjørkan, Berg C., Saeternes
09/06/99	Moss FK	A	1-4	og (Trondsen)
13/06/99	Lillestrøm SK	H	1-2	Bergersen (p)
16/06/99	Tromsø IL	A	1-5	Bergersen
20/06/99	Kongsvinger IL	H	2-0	Bergersen (p), Saeternes
27/06/99	Skeid	A	3-1	Saeternes, Bjørkan, Berg A.
04/07/99	Vålerenga IF	H	1-1	Saeternes
11/07/99	Strømsgodset IF	A	1-0	Saeternes
25/07/99	Molde FK	H	3-1	Bergersen, Bjørkan, Hansen A.
01/08/99	SK Brann	A	2-0	Saeternes, Berg A.
08/08/99	Rosenborg BK	H	2-4	Berg A., Bergersen (p)
15/08/99	Viking FK	A	3-3	Bjørkan 2, Steen
22/08/99	Stabaek IF	H	4-0	Staurvik, Saeternes, Bjørkan, Bergersen (p)
29/08/99	Odd Grenland	A	2-4	Saeternes, Staurvik
12/09/99	Moss FK	H	4-0	Saeternes 2, Staurvik, Bergersen
19/09/99	Lillestrøm SK	A	0-3	
03/10/99	Tromsø IL	H	1-3	Staurvik
17/10/99	Kongsvinger IL	A	1-2	Berg A.
23/10/99	Skeid	H	4-2	Ludvigsen 2, Saeternes 2

SK BRANN

CLUB DIRECTORY

Sportsklubben Brann
Postboks 161, Minde, 5826 Bergen
tel - (55) 598500 / fax - (55) 598525
website - www.brann.no
email - jlarsen@brann.no
Year of Formation - 1908
Chairman - Harald Andersen
Manager - Arne Møller
Coach - Harald Aabrekk (2000 - Teitur Thórdarson)
Stadium - Brann (19,000)

MAJOR HONOURS
League Championship - (2) 1962, 1963
Domestic Cup - (5)
1923, 1925, 1972, 1976, 1982.

APPEARANCES 1999

	P	Ap	(s)	Gls
Vidar BAHUS	G	1	(1)	
Geirmund BRENDESAETHER	D	22	(3)	
Cato GUNTVEIT	M	26		1
Erlend HANSTVEIT	D	6	(5)	
Roger HELLAND	M	11	(9)	3
Thorstein HELSTAD	A	16	(5)	8
Azar KARADAS	A		(6)	
Magnus KIHLSTEDT (SWE)	G	24		
Mika KOTTILA (FIN)	A	7	(6)	1
Raymond KVISVIK	M	18	(5)	4
Per Ove LUDVIGSEN	D	21	(2)	3
Kjetil LØVVIK	A	10	(2)	10
Mons Ivar MJELDE	A	10	(5)	3
Arne Vidar MOEN	D	24		2
Kjell OLSEN	G	1		
Stefan PALDAN (SWE)	D	9		1
Jan Ove PEDERSEN	M	23	(1)	6
Svante SAMUELSSON (SWE)	M	25		
Egil ULFSTEIN	D	5	(5)	1
Harri YLÖNEN (FIN)	D	26		1
Alex VALENCIA	M		(1)	
Roy WASSBERG	D	1	(2)	

LEAGUE RESULTS 1999

11/04/99	Lillestrøm SK	H	1-3	Helstad
18/04/99	Tromsø IL	A	0-5	
23/04/99	Kongsvinger IL	H	5-4	Mjelde 2 (1p), Ylönen, Løvvik,
				Pedersen
02/05/99	FK Bodø/Glimt	A	3-1	Pedersen, Paldan, Løvvik
09/05/99	Vålerenga IF	H	2-1	Mjelde (p), Løvvik
13/05/99	Strømsgodset IF	A	2-1	Moen, Pedersen
16/05/99	Molde FK	H	0-1	
24/05/99	Skeid	H	0-1	
13/06/99	Viking FK	H	1-0	Kvisvik
17/06/99	Stabaek IF	A	3-2	og (Flem), Løvvik, Helstad
20/06/99	Odd Grenland	H	3-0	Helland, Løvvik 2
27/06/99	Moss FK	A	2-0	Løvvik 2
07/07/99	Rosenborg BK	A	3-2	Løvvik 2, Helstad
22/07/99	Lillestrøm SK	A	0-2	
25/07/99	Kongsvinger IL	A	2-0	Ludvigsen, Kottila
01/08/99	FK Bodø/Glimt	H	0-2	
08/08/99	Vålerenga IF	A	2-1	Helstad, Kvisvik (p)
15/08/99	Strømsgodset IF	H	2-2	Ludvigsen, Pedersen
22/08/99	Molde FK	A	3-1	Gintveit, Moen, Helland
25/08/99	Tromsø IL	H	3-1	Ulfstein, Helland, Kvisvik
29/08/99	Skeid	A	2-1	Helstad 2
11/09/99	Rosenborg BK	H	2-1	Pedersen, Kvisvik
18/09/99	Viking FK	A	0-2	
13/10/99	Stabaek IF	H	2-3	Ludvigsen, Helstad
17/10/99	Odd Grenland	A	1-3	Helstad
23/10/99	Moss FK	H	1-0	Pedersen (p)

KONGSVINGER IL

CLUB DIRECTORY

Kongsvinger Idrettslag Toppfotball
Postboks 682
2204 Kongsvinger
tel - (62) 888510
fax - (62) 888511
website - www.kil.no
email - kilpost@kil.no
Year of Formation - 1892
Chairman - Petter Norstrøm
Coach - Per Brogeland (2000 - Hans Knutsen)
Stadium - Gjemselund (6,000)

APPEARANCES 1999

	P	Ap	(s)	Gls
Steinar Dagur ADOLFSSON (ISL)	D	19		1
Abdul-Karim AHMED (GHA)	M	9	(5)	
Andreas ALM (SWE)	M	25		10
Filip APELSTAV (SWE)	D	11	(1)	
Kristian BERG	A		(2)	
Trym BERGMAN	M	22		4
Eirik DYBENDAL	M	18	(6)	8
Vidar EVENSEN	D	24	(1)	2
Caleb FRANCIS	M	22	(3)	2
Marius GULLERUD	M	12	(10)	4
Pål HÅPNES	D	21		
Rune BUER JOHANSEN	M	12	(1)	2
Julian JOHNSSON (FAR)	M	4	(2)	
Jørn KARLSRUD	M	22		
Odd Harald KONTERUD	A	4	(2)	
Ole Arvid PETTERSEN LANGNES	G	24		
Johan Martin LIANES	G	2	(1)	
Ole Einar MARTINSEN	D	16	(3)	
Karl Erik RIMFELDT	D	2	(1)	
Ståle RØNNINGEN	D	4	(2)	
Harald Martin SOLBERG	A	3	(7)	
Harald STORMOEN	M	2	(5)	
Sven Eirik SAETRE	M	3	(6)	1
Stefán THÓRDARSON (ISL)	A	5	(1)	

LEAGUE RESULTS 1999

Date	Opponent	H/A	Score	Scorers
11/04/99	Strømsgodset IF	A	1-2	Alm (p)
18/04/99	Molde FK	H	2-3	Adolfsson, Bergman
23/04/99	SK Brann	A	4-5	Dybendal 2, Bergman, Alm (p)
02/05/99	Rosenborg BK	H	0-1	
09/05/99	Viking FK	A	0-3	
13/05/99	Stabaek IF	H	1-3	Alm
16/05/99	Odd Grenland	A	1-3	Evensen
24/05/99	Moss FK	H	1-0	Dybendal
13/06/99	Tromsø IL	H	3-1	Dybendal 2, Buer Johansen
16/06/99	Skeid	A	1-0	Dybendal
20/06/99	FK Bodø/Glimt	A	0-2	
04/07/99	Strømsgodset IF	H	2-4	Bergman, Alm
07/07/99	Lillestrøm SK	A	2-6	Saetre, Francis (p)
11/07/99	Molde FK	A	2-3	Alm 2
25/07/99	SK Brann	H	0-2	
30/07/99	Rosenborg BK	A	1-4	Francis
04/08/99	Vålerenga IF	H	4-0	Gullerud, Evensen, Bergman, Alm
08/08/99	Viking FK	H	1-3	Alm (p)
15/08/99	Stabaek IF	A	1-1	Gullerud
22/08/99	Odd Grenland	H	1-0	Alm
29/08/99	Moss FK	A	0-3	
12/09/99	Lillestrøm SK	H	1-1	Dybendal
19/09/99	Tromsø IL	A	1-4	Buer Johansen
03/10/99	Skeid	H	1-2	Dybendal
17/10/99	FK Bodø/Glimt	H	2-1	Gullerud 2
23/10/99	Vålerenga IF	A	1-2	Alm

LILLESTRØM SK

Lillestrøm Sportsklubb
Postboks 196, 2001 Lillestrøm
tel - (63) 805662 / fax - (63) 805670
website - www.lsk.no
email - lsk@lsk.no
Year of Formation - 1917
Chairman - Frank Grønlund
Coach - Arne Erlandsen
Stadium - Åråsen (12,000)

MAJOR HONOURS
League Championship (5)
1959, 1976, 1977, 1986, 1989.
Domestic Cup - (4)
1977, 1978, 1981, 1985.

APPEARANCES 1999

	P	Ap	(s)	Gls
Emille BARON (SAF)	G	15		
Stian BERGET	M	5	(2)	1
Tommy BERNTSEN	D	25		8
Torgeir BJARMANN	D	26		5
Trond BJØRNSEN	M	1	(4)	
Mamadou DIALLO (SEN)	A	3		
Sveinung FJELDSTAD	A	1	(4)	1
Torjus HANSÉN	D	20		
Tore HOLM	A	3	(8)	2
Heidar HELGUSON (ISL)	A	25		16
Magnus KIHLBERG (SWE)	M	9		
Runar KRISTINSSON (ISL)	M	24		7
Per Magne MISUND	G	10	(1)	
Kjetil NILSEN	M		(5)	
Runar NORMANN	M	15	(1)	3
Kenneth NYSAETHER	A	3	(7)	
Ivar RØNNINGEN	G	1	(1)	
Leif Gunnar SMERUD	M	9	(5)	2
Rune STAKKELAND	M		(5)	
Pål STRAND	M	24		2
Arild SUNDGOT	A	21		7
Espen SØGÅRD	M		(1)	
Stian THOMASSEN	D	2	(3)	
Peter WERNI	D	24		
Jarkko WISS (FIN)	M	16		4
Olav ZANETTI	D	4		

LEAGUE RESULTS 1999

11/04/99	SK Brann	A	3-1	Sundgot 2, Kristinsson
17/04/99	Rosenborg BK	H	3-2	Sundgot, Strand, Bjarmann
23/04/99	Viking FK	A	4-2	Bjarmann, Berntsen, Helguson, Kristinsson
02/05/99	Stabaek IF	H	1-2	Helguson
09/05/99	Odd Grenland	A	2-0	Berntsen, Helguson
13/05/99	Moss FK	H	1-0	Kristinsson (p)
16/05/99	Skeid	A	4-4	Sundgot, Helguson, Berntsen (p), Normann
24/05/99	Tromsø IL	A	1-4	Helguson
13/06/99	FK Bodø/Glimt	A	2-1	Bjarmann, Smerud
16/06/99	Vålerenga IF	H	4-1	Helguson 2, Sundgot, Strand
19/06/99	Strømsgodset IF	A	1-1	og (Strøm)
27/06/99	Molde FK	H	0-1	
07/07/99	Kongsvinger IL	H	6-2	Bjarmann, Helguson 2, Berntsen 2 (1p), Normann
11/07/99	Rosenborg BK	A	0-4	
22/07/99	SK Brann	H	2-0	Sundgot, Kristinsson
25/07/99	Viking FK	H	4-1	Kristinsson, Helguson 2, Normann
01/08/99	Stabaek IF	A	6-1	Helguson 4, Smerud, Holm
08/08/99	Odd Grenland	H	1-2	Wiss
15/08/99	Moss FK	A	3-1	og (Trondsen), Wiss, Holm
22/08/99	Skeid	H	2-1	Fjeldstad, Berntsen (p)
29/08/99	Tromsø IL	H	1-2	Helguson
12/09/99	Kongsvinger IL	A	1-1	Berntsen (p)
19/09/99	FK Bodø/Glimt	H	3-0	Berntsen (p), Kristinsson 2
03/10/99	Vålerenga IF	A	1-3	Berget
17/10/99	Strømsgodset IF	H	4-2	Wiss 2 (1p), Sundgot, Bjarmann
23/10/99	Molde FK	A	0-2	

MOLDE FK

CLUB DIRECTORY

Molde Fotballklubb
Julsundveien 14, 6412 Molde
tel - (71) 202500
fax - (71) 202501
website - www.moldefk.no
email - mfk@moldefk.no
Year of Formation - 1911
Chairman - Einar Sekkeseter
Coach - Erik Brakstad
Stadium - Nye Molde (13,400)

MAJOR HONOURS
Domestic Cup - (1) 1994.

APPEARANCES 1999

	P	Ap	(s)	Gls
Trond ANDERSEN	D	17		1
Morten BAKKE	G	26		
Svein Tore BRANDSHAUG	M		(3)	
Karl Oskar FJØRTOFT	M	25		1
Knut Anders FOSTERVOLD	D	24		2
Anders HASSELGÅRD	A	7		
Daniel BERG HESTAD	M	25		4
Magne HOSETH	M	10	(4)	2
Bernt HULSKER	A		(2)	
André SCHEI LINDBAEK	A	3	(2)	1
Andreas LUND	A	24		21
Pål LYDERSEN	D	14		1
Thomas MORK	A	9	(15)	1
Odd Inge OLSEN	M	26		4
Torgeir RAMSLI RUUD	M		(1)	
Freddy dos SANTOS	D	15	(6)	
Dennis SCHILLER (SWE)	D	1	(3)	
Petter Christian SINGSAAS	D	8	(4)	1
Trond STRANDE	D	19	(2)	
Ole Bjørn SUNDGOT	A	7	(13)	2
Jo TESSEM	A	26		6
Jarkko WISS (FIN)	M		(3)	

LEAGUE RESULTS 1999

10/04/99	Tromsø IL	H	4-0	Lund 2, Fostervold, Olsen
18/04/99	Kongsvinger IL	A	3-2	og (Rønningen), Lund 2
23/04/99	FK Bodø/Glimt	H	2-1	Lund (p), Berg Hestad
03/05/99	Vålerenga IF	A	0-2	
09/05/99	Strømsgodset IF	H	3-0	Fostervold, Tessem 2
13/05/99	Skeid	H	3-0	Tessem, Lund, Fjørtoft
16/05/99	SK Brann	A	1-0	Lund
24/05/99	Rosenborg BK	H	0-2	
12/06/99	Stabaek IF	H	0-0	
16/06/99	Odd Grenland	A	0-0	
20/06/99	Moss FK	H	3-1	Lund 3
27/06/99	Lillestrøm SK	A	1-0	Lund (p)
03/07/99	Tromsø IL	A	2-1	Lund (p), Andersen
07/07/99	Viking FK	A	1-4	Olsen
11/07/99	Kongsvinger IL	H	3-2	Lund, Olsen, Berg Hestad
25/07/99	FK Bodø/Glimt	A	1-3	Tessem
01/08/99	Vålerenga IF	H	4-3	Sundgot, Berg Hestad, Lydersen (p), Tessem
08/08/99	Strømsgodset IF	A	2-0	Hoseth, Lund
15/08/99	Skeid	A	5-3	Sundgot, Lund, og (Sveen), Tessem, Mork
22/08/99	SK Brann	H	1-3	Olsen
29/08/99	Rosenborg BK	A	1-2	Hoseth
12/09/99	Viking FK	H	3-4	Lund 2, Berg Hestad
18/09/99	Stabaek IF	A	2-4	Lund 2 (1p)
13/10/99	Odd Grenland	H	1-0	Singsaas
17/10/99	Moss FK	A	1-0	Lund
23/10/99	Lillestrøm SK	H	2-0	Lund, Schei Lindbaek

MOSS FK

CLUB DIRECTORY

Moss Fotballklubb
Postboks 47, 1501 Moss
tel - (69) 243970 / fax - (69) 256650
website - www.mossfk.no
email - mfk@mossfk.no
Year of Formation - 1906
Chairman - Per A. Bakke
Coach - Knut Thorbjørn Eggen
Stadium - Melløs (9,000)

MAJOR HONOURS
League Championship - (1) 1987.
Domestic Cup - (1) 1983.

APPEARANCES 1999

	P	Ap	(s)	Gls
Magnus AMUNDSEN	M	1	(1)	
Leif Erik ANDERSEN	D	1	(10)	
Dagfinn ENERLY	A	21		7
Lars HABBERSTAD	M		(1)	
Rino André HANSEN	G	17		
Joakim HERMANSEN	A		(8)	
Carsten JOHANSEN	D	19	(3)	2
Geir JOHANSEN	D	10	(2)	
Christian JOHNSEN	A	14	(8)	5
Anders JULIUSSEN	M	13	(3)	
Gard KRISTIANSEN	M	25		1
Kenneth LØVLIEN	A	2	(1)	
Thomas MEYER HANSSEN	D		(1)	
Thomas MICHELSEN	M	1	(2)	
Jerry MÅNSSON (SWE)	A	13	(8)	5
Kjell OLOFSSON (SWE)	A	18		3
Jan Tore OPHAUG	M	14		2
Hans PALMQVIST (SWE)	D	23	(2)	2
Christian PETERSEN	A	5	(15)	
Jørgen PETTERSEN	A		(1)	
Hans Erik RAMBERG	M	15	(7)	3
Thomas SANDEM	G	9		
Sander SOLBERG	M	3		
Tommy SYLTE	M	21		6
Rune TANGEN	D	7	(1)	
Tor TRONDSEN	D	24		2
Johan Petter WINSNES	D	10		

LEAGUE RESULTS 1999

11/04/99	Rosenborg BK	A	0-5	
18/04/99	Viking FK	H	0-2	
23/04/99	Stabaek IF	A	1-3	Johnsen
02/05/99	Odd Grenland	H	1-0	Enerly
09/05/99	Skeid	A	6-0	Palmqvist 2, Månsson 2, Sylte (p), Ramberg
13/05/99	Lillestrøm SK	A	0-1	
16/05/99	Tromsø IL	H	2-4	Sylte, Månsson
24/05/99	Kongsvinger IL	A	0-1	
09/06/99	FK Bodø/Glimt	H	4-1	Sylte, Enerly, Ophaug, Trondsen
13/06/99	Vålerenga IF	A	2-1	Enerly, Månsson
16/06/99	Strømsgodset IF	H	2-5	Månsson, Johansen C.
20/06/99	Molde FK	A	1-3	Ophaug
27/06/99	SK Brann	H	0-7	
04/07/99	Rosenborg BK	H	1-4	Sylte
11/07/99	Viking FK	A	1-1	Johnsen C.
25/07/99	Stabaek IF	H	2-0	Kristiansen, Johnsen
01/08/99	Odd Grenland	A	0-1	
08/08/99	Skeid	H	5-0	Enerly 2, og (Noppi), Johnsen, Ramberg
15/08/99	Lillestrøm SK	H	1-3	Enerly
22/08/99	Tromsø IL	A	1-1	Johnsen
29/08/99	Kongsvinger IL	H	3-0	Sylte (p), Johnsen, Olofsson
12/09/99	FK Bodø/Glimt	A	0-4	
19/09/99	Vålerenga IF	H	1-0	Trondsen
03/10/99	Strømsgodset IF	A	5-2	Sylte, Enerly, Olofsson 2, Ramberg
17/10/99	Molde FK	H	0-1	
23/10/99	SK Brann	A	0-1	

ODD GRENLAND

CLUB DIRECTORY

Odd Grenland
Postboks 1605 Falkum, 3705 Skien
tel - (35) 900150 / fax - (35) 900159
website - www.oddgrenland.no
email - info@oddgrenland.no
Year of Formation - 1894
Chairman - Erik Holmberg
Coach - Tom Nordlie (2000 - Arne Sandstø)
Stadium - Odd (10,000)

MAJOR HONOURS
Domestic Cup - (11) 1903, 1904, 1905, 1906,
1913, 1915, 1919, 1922, 1924, 1926, 1931.

APPEARANCES 1999

	P	Ap	(s)	Gls
Alexander AAS	D	26		1
Christian FLINDT BJERG (DEN)	M	23	(3)	5
Bård BORGERSEN	D	19	(3)	5
Svein Roger DAHLEN	G	5	(1)	
Ronny DEILA	D	25		2
Morten FEVANG	M	22	(2)	2
Tom HAMMERBORG	M		(1)	
Espen HOFF	A	1	(6)	1
Erik HOLTAN	G	21		
Tom Helge JACOBSEN	A	2	(12)	1
Frode JOHNSEN	A	25		9
Tor Gunnar JOHNSEN	A	20	(2)	3
Sami MAHLIO (FIN)	M	13	(7)	1
Jan Frode NORNES	D	24		
Erik PEDERSEN	M	7	(3)	1
Anders RAMBEKK	D	9	(10)	
Torgeir RUGTVEDT	D		(4)	
Thomas RØED	A	22	(4)	9
Arne SANDSTØ	M	18		1
Tor Arne SANNERHOLT	A	4	(7)	
Jørn Marius THERKELSEN	M		(1)	

LEAGUE RESULTS 1999

11/04/99	Viking FK	A	2-1	Johnsen F., Flindt Bjerg
18/04/99	Stabaek IF	H	3-2	Røed, Fevang, Johnsen T.G.
23/04/99	Skeid	H	2-1	Røed, Johnsen T.G.
02/05/99	Moss FK	A	0-1	
09/05/99	Lillestrøm SK	H	0-2	
13/05/99	Tromsø IL	A	0-5	
16/05/99	Kongsvinger IL	H	3-1	Deila, Flindt Bjerg, Johnsen F.
24/05/99	FK Bodø/Glimt	A	0-4	
09/06/99	Vålerenga IF	H	0-3	
13/06/99	Strømsgodset IF	A	5-3	Deila, Røed, Flindt Bjerg 2, Johnsen F.
16/06/99	Molde FK	H	0-0	
20/06/99	SK Brann	A	0-3	
26/06/99	Rosenborg BK	H	0-0	
04/07/99	Viking FK	H	1-3	og (Dadason)
11/07/99	Stabaek IF	A	5-2	Jacobsen, Johnsen F., Flindt Bjerg (p), Borgersen, Sandstø
25/07/99	Skeid	A	1-3	Borgersen
01/08/99	Moss FK	H	1-0	Røed
08/08/99	Lillestrøm SK	A	2-1	Mahlio, Røed
15/08/99	Tromsø IL	H	2-1	Aas, Røed
22/08/99	Kongsvinger IL	A	0-1	
29/08/99	FK Bodø/Glimt	H	4-2	Borgersen 2, Johnsen F. 2
12/09/99	Vålerenga IF	A	1-2	Johnsen F.
19/09/99	Strømsgodset IF	H	2-2	Pedersen, Røed
13/10/99	Molde FK	A	0-1	
17/10/99	SK Brann	H	3-1	Johnsen F., Røed 2
24/10/99	Rosenborg BK	A	5-3	Fevang, Johnsen F., Johnsen T.G., Borgersen, Hoff

ROSENBORG BK

Rosenborg Ballklub
7492 Trondheim
tel - (73) 822100 / fax - (73) 944070
website - www.rbk.no
email - info@rbk.no
Year of Formation - 1917
Chairman - Knut Skoglund
President - Rune Bratseth
General Manager - Nils Skutle
Coach - Nils Arne Eggen
Stadium - Lerkendal (25,000)

MAJOR HONOURS
League Championship - (14) 1967, 1969, 1971,
1985, 1988, 1990, 1992, 1993, 1994, 1995,
1996, 1997, 1998, 1999.
Domestic Cup - (8) 1960, 1964, 1971, 1988,
1990, 1992, 1995, 1999.

	P	Ap	(s)	Gls
Tor Hogne AARØY	A		(1)	
Paal Christian ALSAKER	A		(4)	
Arni Gautur ARASON (ISL)	G	6		
Christer BASMA	D	22		1
Runar BERG	M	17	(1)	3
Ørjan BERG	M	4	(1)	
André BERGDØLMO	D	25		
Bjørn Otto BRAGSTAD	D	25		1
John CAREW	A	7	(1)	10
Tore André "Totto" DAHLUM	A	19	(5)	14
Espen EDVARDSEN	A		(2)	
Børge HERNES	A	1	(13)	1
Erik HOFTUN	D	26		1
John Ivar "Mini" JAKOBSEN	A	11	(10)	2
Jørn JAMTFALL	G	20		
Bent Inge JOHNSEN	A	7	(7)	5
Morten PEDERSEN	D		(2)	
Sigurd RUSHFELDT	A	15		15
Ole Johan SINGSDAL	D	2		
Bent SKAMMELSRUD	M	25		6
Mads Kristian SKJAERVOLD	M	1		
Øyvind STORFLOR	A		(4)	
Lasse STRAND	D	2		
Roar STRAND	M	10	(3)	3
Jan-Derek SØRENSEN	A	22	(1)	11
Arne WINSNES	A		(1)	
Fredrik WINSNES	M	19	(7)	

11/04/99	Moss FK	H	5-0	Rushfeldt 3, Sørensen, Dahlum
17/04/99	Lillestrøm SK	A	2-3	og (Helguson), Skammelsrud (p)
23/04/99	Tromsø IL	H	2-2	Strand R., Jakobsen
02/05/99	Kongsvinger IL	A	1-0	Dahlum
08/05/99	FK Bodø/Glimt	H	6-1	Bragstad, Dahlum 3, Rushfeldt, Hernes
12/05/99	Vålerenga IF	A	5-0	Sørensen 2, Rushfeldt 2, Dahlum
16/05/99	Strømsgodset IF	H	3-1	Dahlum, Berg R., Sørensen
24/05/99	Molde FK	A	2-0	Rushfeldt 2
13/06/99	Skeid	H	3-0	og (Vaaler), Rushfeldt 2 (1p)
16/06/99	Viking FK	A	2-0	Rushfeldt, Sørensen
20/06/99	Stabaek IF	H	2-1	Rushfeldt 2
26/06/99	Odd Grenland	A	0-0	
04/07/99	Moss FK	A	4-1	Sørensen, Johnsen, Rushfeldt 2
07/07/99	SK Brann	H	2-3	Berg R. 2
11/07/99	Lillestrøm SK	H	4-0	Sørensen 2, Skammelsrud, Dahlum
25/07/99	Tromsø IL	A	1-2	Johnsen
30/07/99	Kongsvinger IL	H	4-1	Sørensen 2, Dahlum 2
08/08/99	FK Bodø/Glimt	A	4-2	Dahlum, Johnsen, Skammelsrud 2 (1p)
15/08/99	Vålerenga IF	H	4-2	Strand R., Johnsen, Dahlum,
				Skammelsrud (p)
22/08/99	Strømsgodset IF	A	3-1	Basma, Carew 2
29/08/99	Molde FK	H	2-1	Hoftun, Sørensen
11/09/99	SK Brann	A	1-2	Carew
19/09/99	Skeid	A	7-1	Carew 4, Jakobsen, Strand R., Dahlum
03/10/99	Viking FK	H	3-2	Carew 2, Skamelsrud (p)
16/10/99	Stabaek IF	A	0-2	
24/10/99	Odd Grenland	H	3-5	Carew, Johnsen, Dahlum

SKEID

CLUB DIRECTORY

Skeid
Postboks 5, Grefsen, 0409 Oslo
tel - (22) 222882 / fax - (22) 222963
website - www.skeid.no
email - skeid@oslonett.no
Year of Formation - 1915
Chairman - Anders Hornslien
Coach - Bengt Eriksen
Stadium - Voldsløkka (4,000)

MAJOR HONOURS
League Championship - (1) 1966.
Domestic Cup - (8) 1947, 1954, 1955, 1956, 1958, 1963, 1965, 1974.

APPEARANCES 1999

	P	Ap	(s)	Gls
Ståle ANDERSEN	M	22	(1)	
Bjørn BAKKEN	D	7	(2)	
Stein Petter EIDAL	D	18	(4)	1
Jan FJELLER	D	11	(4)	3
Espen GRINA	A	3	(9)	2
Knut Helge HAGEN	M	26		
Petter HALVORSEN	A	23	(1)	4
Jørgen ISNES	M	1	(1)	
Marius JOHANNESSEN	M	1	(5)	
Ole Martin JOHANSEN	M	20	(4)	3
André SCHEI LINDBAEK	A	20		12
Ronny LØVLIEN	D	23		
Erik NOPPI	D	24		2
Iver SLETTEN	A	10	(9)	2
Lennart STEFFENSEN	M	26		3
Alexander SVEEN	D	8	(1)	2
André ULLA	G		(1)	
Roger VAALER	G	26		
Yngvar ÅNENSEN	M	17	(4)	2

LEAGUE RESULTS 1999

11/04/99	Stabaek IF	A	0-5	
19/04/99	Vålerenga IF	H	0-2	
23/04/99	Odd Grenland	A	1-2	Schei Lindbaek
02/05/99	Strømsgodset IF	H	4-0	Steffensen, Halvorsen, Schei Lindbaek 2
09/05/99	Moss FK	H	0-6	
13/05/99	Molde FK	A	0-3	
16/05/99	Lillestrøm SK	H	4-4	Schei Lindbaek 3, Grina
24/05/99	SK Brann	A	1-0	Noppi
09/06/99	Tromsø IL	H	2-1	Schei Lindbaek 2
13/06/99	Rosenborg BK	A	0-3	
16/06/99	Kongsvinger IL	H	0-1	
20/06/99	Viking FK	A	1-0	Sletten
27/06/99	FK Bodø/Glimt	H	1-3	Fjeller (p)
04/07/99	Stabaek IF	H	1-3	Eidal
11/07/99	Vålerenga IF	A	2-2	Schei Lindbaek 2
25/07/99	Odd Grenland	H	3-1	Halvorsen 2, Schei Lindbaek
01/08/99	Strømsgodset IF	A	1-3	Steffensen
08/08/99	Moss FK	A	0-5	
15/08/99	Molde FK	H	3-5	Grina, Schei Lindbaek, Noppi
22/08/99	Lillestrøm SK	A	1-2	Ånensen
29/08/99	SK Brann	H	1-2	Fjeller (p)
12/09/99	Tromsø IL	A	2-8	Sletten, Fjeller (p)
19/09/99	Rosenborg BK	H	1-7	Sveen
03/10/99	Kongsvinger IL	A	2-1	Johansen, Halvorsen
17/10/99	Viking FK	H	3-2	Ånensen, Johansen, Steffensen
23/10/99	FK Bodø/Glimt	A	2-4	Sveen, Johansen

STABAEK IF

CLUB DIRECTORY

Stabaek Idrettsforening
Postboks 103, 1341 Bekkestua
tel - (67) 121212
fax - (67) 582610
website - www.stabak.no
email - sfotball@online.no
Year of Formation - 1912
Chairman - Erik Loe
Coach - Anders Linderoth
Stadium - Nadderud (10,000)

MAJOR HONOURS
Domestic Cup - (1) 1998.

APPEARANCES 1999

	P	Ap	(s)	Gls
Richard ACKON (GHA)	M	10	(4)	
Martin ANDRESEN	M	22		8
Petter BELSVIK	A	14	(2)	14
Thomas FINSTAD	A	9	(7)	3
André FLEM	D	21	(3)	4
David HANSSEN	M	3	(8)	2
Andraes HAUGER	M		(2)	
Christian HOLTER	D	18	(3)	1
Jesper JANSSON (SWE)	M	5	(2)	1
Axel KOLLE	M	18	(4)	3
Tommy SVINDAL LARSEN	M	19	(2)	3
Tobias LINDEROTH (SWE)	M	23		3
Pétur MARTEINSSON (ISL)	D	14	(4)	
Christian MICHELSEN	A	7	(9)	
Frode OLSEN	G	25		
Inge André OLSEN	D	4		
Anders ROTEVATN	G	1		
Helgi SIGURDSSON (ISL)	A	18		14
John Arvid SKISTAD	D	25		
Tommy STENERSEN	D	20	(3)	
Tom STENVOLL	D	9	(6)	
Niclas SVENSSON (SWE)	D	1	(2)	

LEAGUE RESULTS 1999

11/04/99	Skeid	H	5-0	og (Eidal), Belsvik (p), Svindal Larsen, Sigurdsson, Andresen
18/04/99	Odd Grenland	A	2-3	Andresen, Flem
23/04/99	Moss FK	H	3-1	Flem, Belsvik (p), Sigurdsson
02/05/99	Lillestrøm SK	A	2-1	Sigurdsson, og (Sundgot)
09/05/99	Tromsø IL	H	1-1	Andresen
13/05/99	Kongsvinger IL	A	3-1	Sigurdsson, Andresen 2
16/05/99	FK Bodø/Glimt	H	3-2	Linderoth, Jansson, Sigurdsson
24/05/99	Vålerenga IF	A	3-1	Kolle, Sigurdsson 2
12/06/99	Molde FK	A	0-0	
17/06/99	SK Brann	H	2-3	Sigurdsson, Belsvik
20/06/99	Rosenborg BK	A	1-2	Finstad
27/06/99	Viking FK	H	3-1	Sigurdsson, Belsvik, Linderoth
04/07/99	Skeid	A	3-1	Sigurdsson (p), Andresen, Kolle
07/07/99	Strømsgodset IF	H	2-1	Sigurdsson 2 (1p)
11/07/99	Odd Grenland	H	2-5	Andresen, Sigurdsson (p)
25/07/99	Moss FK	A	0-2	
01/08/99	Lillestrøm SK	H	1-6	Sigurdsson
08/08/99	Tromsø IL	A	3-3	Finstad, Svindal Larsen, Holter
15/08/99	Kongsvinger IL	H	1-1	Linderoth
22/08/99	FK Bodø/Glimt	A	0-4	
29/08/99	Vålerenga IF	H	3-0	Belsvik 2, Kolle
11/09/99	Strømsgodset IF	A	3-4	Finstad, Svindal Larsen, Andresen
18/09/99	Molde FK	H	4-2	Belsvik 2 (1p), Hanssen, Flem
13/10/99	SK Brann	A	3-2	Belsvik 3
16/10/99	Rosenborg BK	H	2-0	Flem, Belsvik
24/10/99	Viking FK	A	3-2	Belsvik 2 (1p), Hanssen

STRØMSGODSET IF

CLUB DIRECTORY

Strømsgodset Idrettsforening
Fotballgruppa
Postboks 4140
3005 Drammen
tel - (32) 265770
fax - (32) 830175
website - www.godset.no
email - godset@godset.no
Year of Formation - 1907
Chairman - Runar Hannevold
Coach - Jens Martin Støten (2000 - Arne Dokken)
Stadium - Marienlyst (12,000)

MAJOR HONOURS
League Championship - (1) 1970.
Domestic Cup - (4) 1969, 1970, 1973, 1991.

APPEARANCES 1999

	P	Ap	(s)	Gls
Pål Henning ALBERTSEN	G	1		
Kent BERGERSEN	M	7	(1)	4
Jostein FLO	A	25		18
Christer GEORGE	A	12	(12)	3
Stefán GÍSLASON (ISL)	M	10	(8)	
Valur GÍSLASON (ISL)	D	11	(5)	
Lars GRANÅS	M	21	(3)	1
Erik HAGEN	D	16		
Rune HAGEN	A	19	(7)	3
Glenn Arne HANSEN	G	25		
Lars MYHRE HJELMESETH	M		(1)	
Tommy JAHNSEN	M		(2)	
Erland JOHNSEN	D		(4)	
Kenneth KARLSEN	D	19		2
Kim KRISTIANSEN	M		(1)	
Marek LEMSALU (EST)	D	7	(1)	
Anders MICHELSEN	D	18	(3)	
Ousman NYAN	M	18		2
Benny OLSEN	M		(2)	
Lasse OLSEN	A	24	(2)	7
Christer PEDERSEN	M		(3)	
Vegard STRØM	D	19		
Thomas WAEHLER	D	14	(1)	1
Hans Erik ØDEGAARD	M	20	(5)	2

LEAGUE RESULTS 1999

11/04/99	Kongsvinger IL	H	2-1	Flo 2 (1p)
18/04/99	FK Bodø/Glimt	A	1-3	Flo
23/04/99	Vålerenga IF	H	0-3	
02/05/99	Skeid	A	0-4	
09/05/99	Molde FK	A	0-3	
13/05/99	SK Brann	H	1-2	Flo (p)
16/05/99	Rosenborg BK	A	1-3	og (Bragstad)
24/05/99	Viking FK	H	1-0	Flo
13/06/99	Odd Grenland	H	3-5	Flo (p), Hagen R., Bergersen
16/06/99	Moss FK	A	5-2	Flo, Bergersen 2, Hagen R., Olsen L.
19/06/99	Lillestrøm SK	H	1-1	Ødegaard
27/06/99	Tromsø IL	A	2-3	Olsen L. 2
04/07/99	Kongsvinger IL	A	4-2	Flo 2 (1p), Bergersen, Karlsen
07/07/99	Stabaek IF	A	1-2	George
11/07/99	FK Bodø/Glimt	H	0-1	
25/07/99	Vålerenga IF	A	3-2	Hagen R., Granås, Flo
01/08/99	Skeid	H	3-1	Flo 2, Olsen L.
08/08/99	Molde FK	H	0-2	
15/08/99	SK Brann	A	2-2	Karlsen, George
22/08/99	Rosenborg BK	H	1-3	Nyan
29/08/99	Viking FK	A	2-3	Flo 2 (1p)
11/09/99	Stabaek IF	H	4-3	Waehler, Flo 2, Nyan
19/09/99	Odd Grenland	A	2-2	Ødegaard, og (Deila)
03/10/99	Moss FK	H	2-5	Flo, og (Trondsen)
17/10/99	Lillestrøm SK	A	2-4	Olsen L., George
23/10/99	Tromsø IL	H	3-6	Flo (p), Olsen L. 2

TROMSØ IL

Tromsø Idrettslag
Postboks 5
9251 Tromsø
tel - (77) 602600
fax - (77) 602601
website - www.til.no
email - post@til.no
Year of Formation - 1920
Chairman - Gunnar Wilhelmsen
Manager - Tore Rismo
Coach - Terje Skarsfjord
Stadium - Alfheim (11,000)

MAJOR HONOURS
Domestic Cup - (2) 1986, 1996.

APPEARANCES 1999

	P	Ap	(s)	Gls
Robin BERNTSEN	D	22		
Knut BORCH	G	5	(1)	
Jan Egil BREKKE	D	2	(15)	
Leif Arne BREKKE	A		(1)	
Roar CHRISTENSEN	M	23		3
Frode FERMANN	A	10	(10)	4
Tryggvi GUDMUNDSSON (ISL)	A	26		13
Thomas HAFSTAD	M	19	(4)	8
Gaute UGELSTAD HELSTRUP	M	11	(5)	1
Bjørn JOHANSEN	M	25		6
Ståle JOHANSEN	D	2	(2)	
Svein Morten JOHANSEN	D	25	(1)	2
Morten KRAEMER	D	24		1
Roger LANGE	D	21	(2)	1
Rune LANGE	A	26		23
Ole Andreas NILSEN	D	2	(7)	
Andreas OTTOSSON (SWE)	M	16	(6)	6
Olav RÅSTAD	M	4	(11)	1
Marko TUOMELA (FIN)	D	2	(2)	
Thomas TØLLEFSEN	G	21		

LEAGUE RESULTS 1999

10/04/99	Molde FK	A	0-4	
18/04/99	SK Brann	H	5-0	Lange Ru., Gudmundsson, Ottosson 2, Christensen
23/04/99	Rosenborg BK	A	2-2	Ottosson, Lange Ru.
02/05/99	Viking FK	H	1-3	Ottosson
09/05/99	Stabaek IF	A	1-1	Ottosson
13/05/99	Odd Grenland	H	5-0	Ugelstad Helstrup, Lange Ru., Christensen, Ottosson, og (Deila)
16/05/99	Moss FK	A	4-2	Lange Ru. 2, Gudmundsson, Hafstad
24/05/99	Lillestrøm SK	H	4-1	Johansen B., Lange Ru. (p), Gudmundsson 2
09/06/99	Skeid	A	1-2	Lange Ru.
13/06/99	Kongsvinger IL	A	1-3	Johansen B.
16/06/99	FK Bodø/Glimt	H	5-1	Johansen B., Hafstad, Lange Ru. 2, Gudmundsson
27/06/99	Strømsgodset IF	H	3-2	Gudmundsson 2, Lange Ru.
03/07/99	Molde FK	H	1-2	Johansen B.
07/07/99	Vålerenga IF	A	3-1	Fermann, Gudmundsson, Råstad
25/07/99	Rosenborg BK	H	2-1	Hafstad, Lange Ru.
01/08/99	Viking FK	A	1-2	Lange Ru. (p)
08/08/99	Stabaek IF	H	3-3	Fermann, Lange Ru. 2
15/08/99	Odd Grenland	A	1-2	Gudmundsson
22/08/99	Moss FK	H	1-1	Lange Ru.
25/08/99	SK Brann	A	1-3	Fermann
29/08/99	Lillestrøm SK	A	2-1	Gudmundsson, Fermann
12/09/99	Skeid	H	8-2	Hafstad 2, Gudmundsson, Johansen B. 2, Lange Ru., Johansen S.M., Lange Ro.
19/09/99	Kongsvinger IL	H	4-1	Christensen, Gudmundsson, Lange Ru. 2
03/10/99	FK Bodø/Glimt	A	3-1	Hafstad, Lange Ru. 2
17/10/99	Vålerenga IF	H	2-2	Johansen S.M., Lange Ru. (p)
23/10/99	Strømsgodset IF	A	6-3	Hafstad 2, Lange Ru. 2, Kraemer, Gudmundsson (p)

VIKING FK

CLUB DIRECTORY

Viking Fotballklubb
Postboks 4051 Tasta
4092 Stavanger
tel - (51) 840080
fax - (51) 840081
email - viking@viking-fk.no
Year of Formation - 1899
Chairman - Inge Valen
Coach - Poul Erik Andreassen (2000 - Benny
Lennartsson)
Stadium - Stavanger (17,000)

MAJOR HONOURS
League Championship - (8) 1958, 1972, 1973,
1974, 1975, 1979, 1982, 1991.
Domestic Cup - (4) 1953, 1959, 1979, 1989.

APPEARANCES 1999

	P	Ap	(s)	Gls
Bjarte LUNDE AARSHEIM	M	20	(1)	1
Gunnar AASE	A	9	(3)	2
Bjørn BERLAND	A	18	(4)	10
Morten BERRE	A	9	(4)	6
Helge BJØNSAAS	D	4	(5)	
Lars Gaute BØ	G	26		
Ríkhardur DADASON (ISL)	A	19	(2)	17
Bjørn DAHL	D	6	(8)	
Odd Arne ESPEVOLL	D	15	(1)	1
Frode EIKE HANSEN	D	21	(1)	1
Audun HELGASON (ISL)	D	25		1
Patrick HOLTET	M		(1)	
Martin KNUDSEN	D	13	(6)	1
Ronny KRISTENSEN	M	12	(9)	
Idar MATHIASSEN	A	6	(13)	2
Trygve NYGAARD	M	19	(2)	2
Thomas PEREIRA	D	9	(6)	
Tom SANNE	A	20	(4)	3
Thomas SOLBERG	D	9	(2)	1
Magnus SVENSSON (SWE)	M	26		3
Jørgen TENGESDAL	A		(1)	

LEAGUE RESULTS 1999

11/04/99	Odd Grenland	H	1-2	Berre
18/04/99	Moss FK	A	2-0	Berre, Aase
23/04/99	Lillestrøm SK	H	2-4	Dadason 2
02/05/99	Tromsø IL	A	3-1	Aase, Sanne, Svensson
09/05/99	Kongsvinger IL	H	3-0	Mathiassen, Nygaard, Berland
13/05/99	FK Bodø/Glimt	A	3-3	Sanne, Helgason, Berland
16/05/99	Vålerenga IF	H	2-0	Sanne, Dadason
24/05/99	Strømsgodset IF	A	0-1	
13/06/99	SK Brann	A	0-1	
16/06/99	Rosenborg BK	H	0-2	
20/06/99	Skeid	H	0-1	
27/06/99	Stabaek IF	A	1-3	Dadason
04/07/99	Odd Grenland	A	3-1	Dadason 2 (1p), Berland
07/07/99	Molde FK	H	4-1	Berland 2, Dadason, Eike Hansen
11/07/99	Moss FK	H	1-1	Svensson
25/07/99	Lillestrøm SK	A	1-4	Berland
01/08/99	Tromsø IL	H	2-1	Svensson, Solberg
08/08/99	Kongsvinger IL	A	3-1	Berland, Dadason 2 (1p)
15/08/99	FK Bodø/Glimt	H	3-3	Nygaard, Dadason, Berland
22/08/99	Vålerenga IF	A	2-4	Dadason, Lunde Aarsheim
29/08/99	Strømsgodset IF	H	3-2	Dadason, Berre, Mathiassen
12/09/99	Molde FK	A	4-3	Berland 2, Dadason, Knudsen
18/09/99	SK Brann	H	2-0	Berre, Dadason
03/10/99	Rosenborg BK	A	2-3	Dadason, Berre
17/10/99	Skeid	A	2-3	Espevoll (p), Dadason
24/10/99	Stabaek IF	H	2-3	Berre, Dadason

VÅLERENGA IF

CLUB DIRECTORY

Vålerenga Idrettsforening Fotball
Postboks 6064 Etterstad, 0601 Oslo
tel - (22) 880480 / fax - (22) 880491
website - www.vpn.no
email - sentralbord@vif.no
Year of Formation - 1913
Chairman - Morten Grødahl
Coach - Egil Olsen & Lars Tjaernås; Knut Ljøberg
(2000 - Tom Nordlie)
Stadium - Bislett (20,000)

MAJOR HONOURS
League Championship - (4)
1965, 1981, 1983, 1984.
Domestic Cup - (2) 1980, 1997.

APPEARANCES 1999

	P	Ap	(s)	Gls
Thomas BERNTSEN	D	4	(4)	
Øyvind BOLTHOF	G	26		
John CAREW	A	14	(1)	7
Mamadou DIALLO (SEN)	A	7		4
Ronny DØHLI	D	17		
Christer ELLEFSEN	D		(1)	
Knut Henry HARALDSEN	D	26		
Espen HAUG	M	3	(3)	1
Børge HERNES	A	7	(3)	1
Tom Henning HOVI	M	24		1
Pa Modou KAH	D		(1)	
Kent KARLSEN	D	5	(3)	
Fredrik KJØLNER	D	25		
Juro KUVICEK	A		(4)	
Bjørn Arild LEVERNES	M	17	(7)	2
Espen MUSAEUS	A	4	(14)	4
Morten PEDERSEN	D	9		
Aki RIIHILAHTI (FIN)	M	23	(2)	5
Dag RIISNAES	M	25		2
Kamal SAALITI	A		(1)	
Pascal SIMPSON (SWE)	A	19		8
Fredrik THORSEN	M	7	(14)	2
Hai Ngoc TRAN	D	1		
Bjørn VILJUGREIN	M		(1)	
Joachim WALLTIN	M	20		2
Jon Eirik ØDEGAARD	M	3	(13)	

LEAGUE RESULTS 1999

Date	Opponent	H/A	Score	Scorers
10/04/99	FK Bodø/Glimt	H	1-1	Simpson (p)
19/04/99	Skeid	A	2-0	Haug, Musaeus
23/04/99	Strømsgodset IF	A	3-0	Musaeus, og (Ødegaard), Carew
03/05/99	Molde FK	H	2-0	Levernes, Simpson
09/05/99	SK Brann	A	1-2	Simpson
12/05/99	Rosenborg BK	H	0-5	
16/05/99	Viking FK	A	0-2	
24/05/99	Stabaek IF	H	1-3	Carew
09/06/99	Odd Grenland	A	3-0	Carew 2, Levernes
13/06/99	Moss FK	H	1-2	Simpson
16/06/99	Lillestrøm SK	A	1-4	Carew
04/07/99	FK Bodø/Glimt	A	1-1	Riisnaes
07/07/99	Tromsø IL	H	1-3	Carew
11/07/99	Skeid	H	2-2	Simpson, Carew
25/07/99	Strømsgodset IF	H	2-3	Riihilahti, Thorsen
01/08/99	Molde FK	A	3-4	Musaeus, Wallltin, Thorsen
04/08/99	Kongsvinger IL	A	0-4	
08/08/99	SK Brann	H	1-2	Riihilahti
15/08/99	Rosenborg BK	A	2-4	Diallo, Riihilahti (p)
22/08/99	Viking FK	H	4-2	Diallo, Simpson, Hernes, Musaeus
29/08/99	Stabaek IF	A	0-3	
12/09/99	Odd Grenland	H	2-1	Riihilahti (p), Riisnaes
19/09/99	Moss FK	A	0-1	
03/10/99	Lillestrøm SK	H	3-1	Hovi, Diallo 2
17/10/99	Tromsø IL	A	2-2	Walltin, Simpson
23/10/99	Kongsvinger IL	H	2-1	Simpson, Riihilahti

POLAND

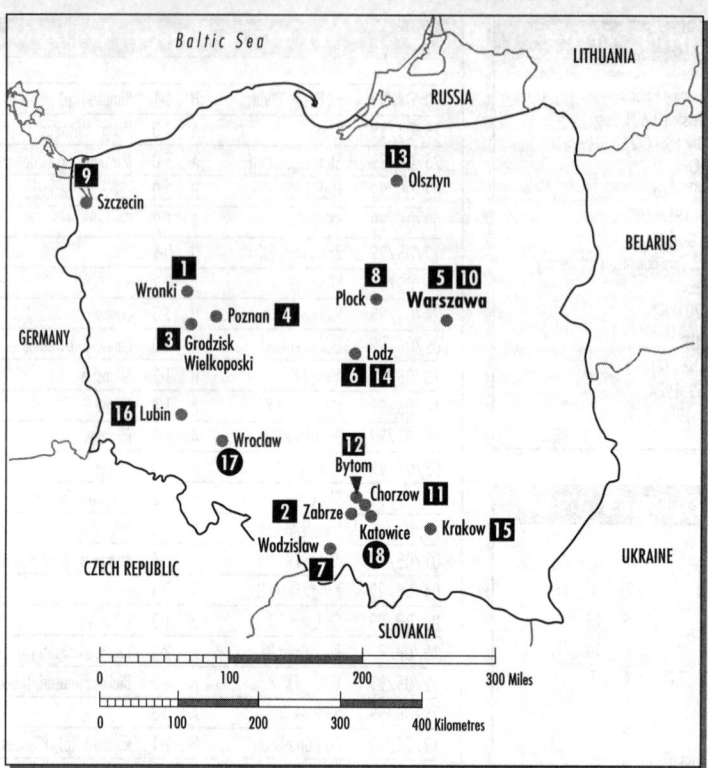

1	**AMICA WRONKI**	749
2	**GORNIK ZABRZE**	750
3	**GROCLIN DYSKOBOLIA GRODZISK**	751
4	**LECH POZNAN**	752
5	**LEGIA WARSZAWA**	753
6	**LKS LODZ**	754
7	**ODRA WODZISLAW**	755
8	**PETRO PLOCK**	756
9	**POGON SZCZECIN**	757
10	**POLONIA WARSZAWA**	758

11	**RUCH CHORZOW**	759
12	**RUCH RADZIONKOW**	760
13	**STOMIL OLSZTYN**	761
14	**WIDZEW LODZ**	762
15	**WISLA KRAKOW**	763
16	**ZAGLEBIE LUBIN**	764
Promoted clubs		
17	**SLASK WROCLAW**	
18	**GKS KATOWICE**	

CUP HAT-TRICK FOR AMICA WRONKI

Polonia power their way to the top

FEDERATION DIRECTORY

Polski Zwiazek Pilki Noznej
Miodowa 1, 00-080 Warszawa

tel - (022) 8271211   Year of Formation - 1919
fax - (022) 8270704   President - Michal Listkiewicz
                             Secretary - Zdzislaw Krecina

Stadium - Slaski, Chorzow (35,000)

Against all odds and expectations the first Polish championship of the new millennium was won by Polonia Warsaw. The little-known club from the capital, which had not held the title for 54 years, were convincing winners. Inspired by their coach, one-time Celtic, Reading and Poland full-back Dariusz Wdowczyk, Polonia comfortably held off the challenge of the much more fancied trio of Wisla Krakow, Legia Warsaw and Ruch Chorzow and even crowned their magnificent season by beating local rivals Legia in the final of the newly reintroduced League Cup to claim a remarkable 'double'.

Placed fifth the previous season, some 27 points behind champions Wisla, Polonia benefitted from some very wise moves in the transfer market. This was fundamentally the work of the club's sports director Jerzy Engel, who left the club in mid-season to become Poland's national team coach. Before he departed, he reinforced an already promising team with the purchase of players such as Maciej Bykowski, Tomasz Kielbowicz and Tomasz Wieszczycki. The dvidends were immediate, with Polonia taking over at the top of the table in the second round after the winter break and reeling off six straight wins, all of them without conceding a goal.

That fabulous run was halted by a 2-2 draw at previous leaders Ruch Chorzow, but when Polonia followed that minor setback with three more victories, they were effectively in the clear. A first defeat in the spring, 2-1 at Zaglebie Lubin, merely delayed the inevitable, and there was immense satisfaction for the club's fans when Polonia clinched the title in round 28 with a sumptuous 3-0 victory away to...Legia.

For much of the season Polonia came in for some harsh criticism for their hard, uncompromising style of play. They were not the most spectator-friendly of teams but they certainly knew how to roll their sleeves up and work for their victories. And thanks to coach Wdowczyk the players were always hyper-motivated - a quality which had become alien to many Polish teams. Polonia also bene-

LEAGUE CHAMPIONSHIP RESULTS 99/00

		1	2	3	4	5	6	7	8	9	10	11	12	13	14	15	16
1	Amica Wronki		3-2	0-1	1-0	1-2	2-1	1-0	2-1	2-2	5-0	1-4	1-1	1-1	2-0	0-0	1-1
2	Gornik Zabrze	1-3		1-2	4-0	2-2	3-1	0-2	4-1	2-2	0-1	1-2	5-0	1-0	0-1	1-0	0-0
3	Groclin Dyskobolia Grodzisk	1-1	0-2		1-2	1-0	2-1	0-1	3-1	1-2	0-1	0-3	2-1	3-2	1-0	1-2	1-0
4	Lech Poznan	2-1	1-1	0-0		1-2	1-1	0-1	1-0	1-1	1-3	1-2	3-1	1-2	3-5	4-1	2-0
5	Legia Warszawa	2-0	0-0	5-0	1-1		0-0	1-1	1-0	5-1	0-3	3-1	4-2	4-0	2-1	0-2	2-2
6	LKS Lodz	3-0	2-2	1-0	1-0	1-1		1-0	1-2	4-3	0-2	2-2	1-0	1-1	2-3	0-2	4-2
7	Odra Wodzislaw	0-2	3-3	0-2	4-0	0-2	2-0		1-2	1-0	3-1	2-2	0-0	3-1	2-0	0-3	1-1
8	Petro Plock	0-0	1-0	1-1	2-1	3-1	2-0	0-1		3-1	2-1	0-0	1-3	1-1	0-0	1-1	2-1
9	Pogon Szczecin	0-3	0-1	1-0	4-3	2-4	0-0	0-0	2-1		0-2	1-1	4-0	3-0	2-3	3-3	1-0
10	Polonia Warszawa	4-0	1-0	1-0	5-0	1-1	1-0	4-1	2-0	4-0		0-2	4-1	2-0	1-0	2-1	1-1
11	Ruch Chorzow	1-1	2-1	4-1	2-0	0-1	3-0	3-1	3-1	2-2	2-2		2-1	3-0	4-1	1-1	0-2
12	Ruch Radzionkow	0-3	1-0	2-0	4-1	1-1	1-0	2-1	2-1	1-0	0-2	1-2		0-1	4-1	4-1	1-0
13	Stomil Olsztyn	1-1	1-0	5-2	1-1	1-0	1-0	2-1	2-2	1-1	0-0	0-0	1-0		2-2	1-1	1-1
14	Widzew Lodz	3-2	1-1	2-3	2-2	3-2	2-0	1-1	4-3	1-2	1-1	1-0	2-1	2-2		3-4	2-1
15	Wisla Krakow	1-1	6-3	3-0	2-0	1-1	1-0	3-1	3-1	1-1	2-3	4-0	2-0	4-2	3-1		4-0
16	Zaglebie Lubin	2-2	2-1	1-0	2-1	2-3	1-0	1-0	5-0	3-1	2-1	0-0	3-3	2-0	1-0	3-2	

LEAGUE CHAMPIONSHIP FINAL TABLE 99/00

				Home				Away					Total						
		Pd	W	D	L	F	A	W	D	L	F	A	W	D	L	F	A	PT	GD
1	Polonia Warszawa	30	12	2	1	33	7	8	3	4	23	18	20	5	5	56	25	65	31
2	Wisla Krakow	30	11	3	1	40	14	5	5	5	24	24	16	8	6	64	38	56	26
3	Ruch Chorzow	30	9	4	2	32	15	6	6	3	21	17	15	10	5	53	32	55	21
4	Legia Warszawa	30	8	5	2	30	14	6	5	4	23	20	14	10	6	53	34	52	19
5	Zaglebie Lubin	30	11	3	1	30	14	1	6	8	12	23	12	9	9	42	37	45	5
6	Amica Wronki	30	7	5	3	23	16	4	6	5	20	21	11	11	8	43	37	44	6
7	Widzew Lodz	30	7	5	3	30	25	4	2	9	18	29	11	7	12	48	54	40	-6
8	Odra Wodzislaw	30	6	4	5	22	19	4	3	8	12	19	10	7	13	34	38	37	-4
9	Stomil Olsztyn	30	6	9	0	20	12	2	4	9	13	31	8	13	9	33	43	37	-10
10	Ruch Radzionkow	30	10	1	4	24	14	1	3	11	14	35	11	4	15	38	49	37	-11
11	Groclin Dyskobolia Grodzisk	30	7	1	7	17	19	4	2	9	12	27	11	3	16	29	46	36	-17
12	Pogon Szczecin	30	6	4	5	23	21	2	6	7	19	32	8	10	12	42	53	34	-11
13	Petro Plock	30	7	6	2	19	12	2	1	12	16	36	9	7	14	35	48	34	-13
14	Gornik Zabrze	30	6	3	6	25	17	2	5	8	17	24	8	8	14	42	41	32	1
15	LKS Lodz	30	7	4	4	24	20	0	3	12	4	22	7	7	16	28	42	28	-14
16	Lech Poznan	30	5	4	6	22	21	1	3	11	12	36	6	7	17	34	57	25	-23

fitted from the strength in depth of their squad. Although there were no superstars in the team, the champions possessed at least two players of the same calibre in every position, which made them resistant to injuries and suspensions. Despite the criticism there could be no doubt whatsoever about the team's credentials as championship-winners. They won far more games (20) than any other team and finished nine points clear.

Wisla Krakow's hopes of a successful title defence were effectively dashed the moment that Franciszek Smuda, the best coach in the country, walked out after just eight matches. Smuda had become disaffected with the club's transfer policies and decided to depart in the wake of Wisla's 2-3 home defeat by Polonia in mid-September. Wisla subsequently became very instable, with no fewer than four additional

TOP SCORERS

19 Adam KOMPALA (Gornik Zabrze)
17 Tomasz FRANKOWSKI (Wisla Krakow)
16 Sylwester CZERESZEWSKI (Legia Warszawa)
14 Krzysztof BIZACKI (Ruch Chorzow)
13 Mariusz NOSAL (Petro Plock)
12 Emmanuel OLISADEBE (Polonia Warszawa)
    Maciej ZURAWSKI (Lech Poznan/Wisla Krakow)
11 Pawel KRYSZALOWICZ (Amica Wronki)
    Piotr WLODARCZYK (Ruch Chorzow)
10 Piotr GIERCZAK (Gornik Zabrze)
    Rafal PAWLAK (Widzew Lodz)
    Lukasz SOSIN (Odra Wodzislaw)

coaches - Jerzy Kowalik, Marek Kusto, Wojciech Lazarek and Adam Nawalka - being employed during the remainder of the season. A strong finish, made possible by the goals of top scorer Tomasz Frankowski, enabled Wisla to claim second place, but the season had been one to forget for several of the team's highly-rated players, notably Maciej Zurawski, Grzegorz Kaliciak and Krzysztof Bukalski, who missed almost the entire season through injury.

Ruch Chorzow joined Wisla Krakow in the 2000/01 UEFA Cup by finishing third. One of Poland's oldest clubs had hoped to celebrate their 80th birthday with a 15th title, and at the halfway mark they led the way, two points ahead of Polonia, thanks to shrewd management of modest resources by coach Edward Lorens. The mid-season signings of Robert Gorski and Mariusz Srutwa were expected to strengthen the Blues' challenge, but the team faded badly after the restart, with players allegedly lacking motivation over the delayed payment of their wages.

There were no financial probems at Legia Warsaw,

NATIONAL TEAM RESULTS 99/00

18/08/99	Spain	H	Warsaw	1-2	Hajto (7)
08/09/99	England (ECQ)	H	Warsaw	0-0	
09/10/99	Sweden (ECQ)	A	Solna	0-2	
26/01/00	Spain	A	Cartagena	0-3	
23/02/00	France	A	Saint-Denis	0-1	
29/03/00	Hungary	A	Debrecen	0-0	
26/04/00	Finland	H	Poznan	0-0	
04/06/00	Holland	N	Lausanne	1-3	Kryszalowicz (38)

INTERNATIONAL HONOURS

World Cup Finals appearances: 1938, 1974 (3rd), 1978 (2nd phase), 1982 (3rd), 1986 (2nd round)

NATIONAL TEAM APPEARANCES 99/00

Coach - Janusz WOJCIK; Jerzy ENGEL	ESP	ENG	SWE	ESP	FRA	HUN	FIN	HOL	Cps	Gls
Adam MATYSEK (19/07/68) - Bayer 04 Leverkusen (GER)	G52	G	G				G		29	-
Tomasz WALDOCH (10/05/71) - FC Schalke 04 (GER)	D	D	D		D	D	D	D	58	2
Jacek ZIELINSKI (10/10/67) - Legia Warszawa	D	D	D	D		s62		s76	39	1
Tomasz HAJTO (16/10/72) - MSV Duisburg (GER)	D	M	M		s65				28	4
Dariusz ADAMCZUK (21/10/69) - Rangers (SCO)	M87								11	1
Rafal SIADACZKA (21/02/72) - FK Austria Wien (AUT)	M	D	M						17	2
Krzysztof NOWAK (29/05/75) - VfL Wolfsburg (GER)	M81	M	s73						10	1
Tomasz IWAN (12/06/71) - PSV (HOL)	M	M		M	M73	s46	M	M	30	4
Piotr SWIERCZEWSKI (08/04/72) - SC Bastia (FRA)	M	s60	M88		M	M46	M	M86	48	1
Miroslaw TRZECIAK (11/04/68) - CA Osasuna (ESP)	A67	A60	A						22	8
Artur WICHNIAREK (28/02/77) - Widzew Lodz	A87		s88						7	2
Jerzy DUDEK (23/03/73) - Feyenoord (HOL)	s52				G	G		G	5	-
Radoslaw KALUZNY (02/02/74) - Wisla Krakow	s67					s78			15	3
Ryszard CZERWIEC (28/02/68) - Wisla Krakow	s81			M84					28	-
Tomasz KLOS (07/03/73) - AJ Auxerre (FRA)	s87	D89	D		D	D	D	D76	19	1
Piotr WLODARCZYK (04/05/77) - Ruch Chorzow	s87								1	-
Radoslaw MICHALSKI (21/09/69) - Widzew Lodz/Maccabi Haifa (ISR)		M	M	M			M46		28	-
Radoslaw GILEWICZ (08/05/71) - FC Tirol Innsbruck (AUT)		A64		A75		A	s46	s46	7	-
Andrzej JUSKOWIAK (03/11/70) - VfL Wolfsburg (GER)		s64	A81						34	13
Jacek BAK (24/03/73) - Olympique Lyonnais (FRA)		s89			D	D62		D	27	1
Sylwester CZERESZEWSKI (04/10/71) - Legia Warszawa			M73						23	4
Pawel KRYSZALOWICZ (26/06/74) - Amica Wronki			s81	A53	s57		A71	A82	5	1
Radoslaw MAJDAN (10/05/72) - Pogon Szczecin			G						1	-
Marek ZAJAC (17/09/73) - Wisla Krakow			D60						1	-
Michal ZEWLAKOW (22/04/76) - R Excelsior Mouscron (BEL)			D	D65	D	D	D		6	-
Jacek KRZYNOWEK (15/05/76) - 1.FC Nürnberg (GER)			M66	M90	M78	s46			5	-
Slawomir MAJAK (12/01/69) - FC Hansa Rostock (GER)			M						22	-
Maciej ZURAWSKI (12/09/76) - Wisla Krakow			s53			s71			6	-
Arkadiusz KALISZAN (13/11/72) - Polonia Warszawa			s60						1	-
Pawel KACZOROWSKI (22/03/74) - Lech Poznan			s66			s79			2	-
Krzysztof BIZACKI (07/04/73) - Ruch Chorzow			s75		s59				2	-
Marcin BASZCZYNSKI (07/06/77) - Ruch Chorzow			s84						1	-
Bartosz KARWAN (13/01/76) - Legia Warszawa				M	M	M79			4	-
Piotr REISS (20/06/72) - MSV Duisburg (GER)				A82	A59				4	1
Marcin ZEWLAKOW (22/04/76) - R Excelsior Mouscron (BEL)				A57		A46	A46		3	-
Tomasz WIESZCZYCKI (21/12/71) - Polonia Warszawa				s73					11	3
Tomasz RZASA (11/03/73) - Feyenoord (HOL)				s82	s59		M79		4	1
Tomasz KIELBOWICZ (21/02/76) - Polonia Warszawa				s90			s79		2	-
Tomasz ZDEBEL (25/03/73) - K Lierse SK (BEL)					M59		s66		2	-
Mariusz KUKIELKA (07/11/76) - Amica Wronki						D			3	-
Maciej MURAWSKI (20/02/74) - Legia Warszawa							D66		2	-
Tomasz FRANKOWSKI (16/08/74) - Wisla Krakow							s82		3	-
Mariusz PAWLAK (19/01/72) - Polonia Warszawa							s86		1	-

who continued to benefit from the generous patronage of their South Korean sponsors Daewoo. It was they who pilfered Franciszek Smuda after his departure from Wisla and everybody fully expected them to win the championship, especially after the mid-season recruitment drive which saw the arrival of four Polish internationals - Pawel Wojtala from Hamburg, Rafal Siadaczka from Austria

Vienna, and Tomasz Lapinski and Marek Citko from hard-up Widzew Lodz. But Legia were never able to make up the ground on Polonia and a terrible closing run of five defeats in eight games ultimately left them without even the consolation of a European place.

Zaglebie Lubin, in contrast, were happy with their fifth place. Having adopted a mainly defensive approach

EUROPEAN CUPS 99/00

CHAMPIONS' CUP
● WIDZEW LODZ
Preliminary round 2 LITEKS LOVECH (BUL)

A 1-4 Wichniarek (89p)
Olszewski, Pawlak, Lapinski, Bogusz (Terlecki 82), Stolarczyk, Gula, Michalski, Gesior, Kielbowicz, Citko (Zajac 69), Wichniarek.

H 4-1 (aet; 3-2 on pens.) Gesior (15), Wichniarek (52, 62), Michalski (74)
Olszewski, Bogusz, Lapinski, Stolarczyk, Pawlak (Zajac 59), Gesior, Michalski, Kaczmarczyk (Gula 85), Kielbowicz, Citko (Terlecki 58), Wichniarek.

Qualifying round FIORENTINA (ITA)

A 1-3 Adani (74og)
Olszewski, Pawlak, Lapinski, Michalski, Stolarczyk, Gesior, Terlecki (Gula 61), Kaczmarczyk, Kielbowicz (Dudek 86), Citko (Zajac 70), Wichniarek.

H 0-2 Matuszek, Pawlak, Terlecki, Bogusz, Gula (Szymkowiak 63), Michalski, Gesior (Dudek 80), Kaczmarczyk, Kielbowicz, Citko, Wichniarek (Zajac 78).

UEFA CUP
● AMICA WRONKI
1st round BRØNDBY IF (DEN)

H 2-0 Dawidowski (23), Bosacki (70)
Strozynski, Siara, Kukielka, Bosacki, Przerada, Bieniuk (Dubiela 82), Jackiewicz, Sokolowski, Koscielniak, Kryszalowicz (Krol 88), Dawidowski.

A 3-4 Kryszalowicz (53, 68), Kukielka (65p)
Strozynski, Bosacki, Kukielka, Siara, Przerada (Peczak 46), Bieniuk, Sokolowski, Jackiewicz, Koscielniak (Sobocinski 62), Kryszalowicz, Dawidowski (Dubiela 82).

2nd round ATLÉTICO MADRID (ESP)

A 0-1 Strozynski (Michniewicz 58), Siara, Kukielka, Bajor, Bosacki, Peczak, Sokolowski (Bieniuk 46), Jackiewicz, Sobocinski, Kryszalowicz, Dawidowski (Kalu 65).

H 1-4 Jackiewicz (34)
Strozynski, Bosacki, Kukielka, Siara, Sobocinski (Dubiela 65), Peczak, Jackiewicz, Bajor, Dawidowski (Sokolowski 46), Kryszalowicz, Kalu (Krol 64).

● LECH POZNAN
Qualifying round METALURGS LIEPAYA (LAT)

A 2-3 Zurawski (23), Najewski (59)
Kokoszanek, Drajer, Urbaniak, Augustyniak, Kaczorowski, Scherfchen, Golinski, Salnica (Pastuszka 58), Najewski, Mackiewicz (Nnorom 71), Zurawski.

H 3-1 Golinski (55), Kubicki (72), Mackiewicz (79)
Kokoszanek, Glowacki, Urbaniak, Drajer, Pastuszka, Scherfchen, Piskula (Najewski 46), Kubicki, Golinski (Augustyniak 73), Nnorom (Mackiewicz 53), Zurawski.

1st round IFK GÖTEBORG (SWE)

H 1-2 Zurawski (44p)
Kokoszanek, Drajer (Augustyniak 73), Glowacki, Bocian, Nnorom, Scherfchen, Pastuszka, Piskula (Urbaniak 88), Gruber, Zurawski, Mackiewicz.

A 0-0 Kokoszanek, Bocian, Glowacki, Drajer, Scherfchen (Najewski 57), Piskula, Urbaniak, Gruber (Mackiewicz 69), Golinski (Nnorom 77), Zurawski, Kubicki.

● LEGIA WARSZAWA
Qualifying round VARDAR SKOPJE (MAC)

A 5-0 Mieciel (8), Czereszewski (19), Srutwa (58, 74), Wroblewski (66)
Szamotulski, Mosor, Zielinski, Bednarz (Rutka 70), Czereszewski, Murawski (Jarzebowski 81), Magiera, Sokolowski, Sawicki (Srutwa 56), Mieciel, Wroblewski.

H 4-0 Czereszewski (5), Karwan (16), Sokolowski (53), Mieciel (77)
Szamotulski, Mosor, Zielinski, Bednarz (Nowak 83), Sokolowski, Murawski, Magiera (Jarzebowski 75), Czereszewski, Wiechowski (Rutka 46), Karwan, Mieciel.

1st round ANORTHOSIS FAMAGUSTA (CYP)

A 0-1 Szamotulski, Bednarz, Nowak, Mosor, Czereszewski, Magiera, Murawski, Majewski (Piekarski 74), Wroblewski (Sokolowski 59), Mieciel, Karwan.

H 2-0 Mieciel (48), Czereszewski (68)
Szamotulski, Mosor, Zielinski, Murawski, Bednarz, Karwan, Majewski, Piekarski (Srutwa 79), Sokolowski, Czereszewski, Mieciel (Wroblewski 90).

2nd round UDINESE (ITA)

A 0-1 Szamotulski, Mosor, Zielinski, Murawski, Bednarz (Wiechowski 82), Karwan, Majewski, Czereszewski, Sokolowski, Wroblewski (Srutwa 79), Mieciel (Magiera 90).

H 1-1 Czereszewski (11)
Szamotulski, Mosor, Zielinski, Murawski, Bednarz (Sawicki 83), Karwan, Majewski, Mieciel, Sokolowski, Srutwa (Wroblewski 64), Czereszewski.

● WIDZEW LODZ
1st round SKONTO RIGA (LAT)

A 0-1 Matuszek, Pawlak (Gula 27), Michalski, Bogusz, Terlecki, Szymkowiak, Citko, Gesior, Kielbowicz, Zajac (Kaczmarczyk 84), Wichniarek (Hinc 90).

H 2-0 Wichniarek (1), Gesior (43)
Matuszek, Bogusz, Lapinski, Stolarczyk, Szymkowiak (Pawlak 70), Gesior, Michalski, Terlecki, Kielbowicz, Citko (Kaczmarczyk 89), Wichniarek (Gula 89).

2nd round AS MONACO (FRA)

H 1-1 Wichniarek (6p)
Matuszek, Bogusz, Terlecki, Stolarczyk, Gula, Michalski, Gesior, Szymkowiak, Pawlak (Kielbowicz 71), Citko (Stasiak 78), Wichniarek.

A 0-2 Matuszek, Pawlak, Terlecki, Stolarczyk, Gula, Gesior, Michalski, Kaczmarczyk (Citko 70), Kielbowicz, Szymkowiak, Zajac.

DOMESTIC CUP 99/00

1/16 FINALS
Inkopax Wroclaw 0, Pomerania Police 2
Wawel Krakow 1, Gornik Zabrze 3
Stomil Olsztyn 1, Odra Wodzislaw 1 (aet; 2-4 on pens.)
GKS Belchatow 2, Zaglebie Lubin 1
RKS Radomsko 1, Korona Kielce 0
Odra Szczecin 1, Lech Poznan 2
Lechia Gdansk 0, Wisla Krakow 2
Slask Wroclaw 0, Widzew Lodz 1
Rakow Czestochowa 0, Petro Plock 2
KP Konin 1, Legia Warszawa 2
Hutnik Krakow 2, Polonia Warszawa 2
(aet; 4-5 on pens.)
Tloki Gorzyce 1, KS Myszkow 1 (aet; 2-4 on pens.)
GKS Katowice 0, LKS Lodz 2
Jagiellonka Nieszawa 1, Stal Stalowa Wola 2 (aet)
Ruch Chorzow 2, Pogon Szczecin 0
Amica Wronki 2, Ruch Radzionkow 1 (aet)

1/8 FINALS
Petro Plock 0, Polonia Warszawa 2
Odra Wodzislaw 0, Legia Warszawa 2
Stal Stalowa Wola 2, Wisla Krakow 2 (aet; 3-5 on pens.)
RKS Radomsko 1, Gornik Zabrze 1 (aet; 5-4 on pens.)
KS Myszkow 1, Widzew Lodz 3
Ruch Chorzow 1, GKS Belchatow 2 (aet)
Pomerania Police 3, Lech Poznan 2 (aet)
Amica Wronki 2, LKS Lodz 1 (aet)

QUARTER-FINALS
Polonia Warszawa 1 (Zvirzdauskas 86),
Pomerania Police 0
Pomerania Police 0, Polonia Warszawa 1 (Mikulenas 26)
(Polonia Warszawa 2-0)
Legia Warszawa 3 (Mieciel 41, 47, Karwan 76),
Amica Wronki 2 (Krol 20, 86)
Amica Wronki 3 (Kryszalowicz 35, 48, Andraszak
73), Legia Warszawa 2 (Czereszewski 57, 86) (aet)
(5-5; Amica Wronki 3-1 on pens.)
GKS Belchatow 1 (Florek 62), Wisla Krakow 0
Wisla Krakow 2 (Pater 41, Kaluzny 80),
GKS Belchatow 0
(Wisla Krakow 2-1)
Widzew Lodz 3 (Poskus 17, Gula 31, Szymkowiak
90), RKS Radomsko 1 (Jelonkowski 67)
RKS Radomsko 2 (Jelonkowski 29, Stocki 90),
Widzew Lodz 0
(3-3; RKS Radomsko on away goal)

SEMI-FINALS
Wisla Krakow 2 (Moskalewicz 40, Zurawski 90p),
Polonia Warszawa 1 (Bartczak 74)
Polonia Warszawa 0,
Wisla Krakow 2 (Frankowski 45, Zurawski 88)
(Wisla Krakow 4-1)
Amica Wronki 5 (Krol 38, 47, 90, Kryszalowicz 42,
Sokolowski 45), RKS Radomsko 3 (Jelonkowski 5,
Kowalczyk R. 14, Nowak M. 53)
RKS Radomsko 0, Amica Wronki 1 (Krol 89)
(Amica Wronki 6-3)

FINAL
06/06/2000, Krakow
WISLA KRAKOW 2 Frankowski (44, 77)
AMICA WRONKI 2 Sobocinski (25), Sokolowski (65)
referee - Wojcik
WISLA KRAKOW - Sarnat, Zajac M., Lekki (Pater 78),
Wegrzyn, Kosowski, Moskal, Kaluzny, Czerwiec
(Zurawski 68), Kulawik (Kaliciak 78), Moskalewicz,
Frankowski.
AMICA WRONKI - Strozynski, Wodkiewicz (Bosacki
46), Bajor, Peczek, Sokolowski, Bieniuk, Jackiewicz,
Bilinski (Siara 80), Zienczuk, Sobocinski,
Kryszalowicz (Krol 59).

09/06/2000, Wronki
AMICA WRONKI 3 Bilinski (8), Zienczuk (45),
Sobocinski (84)
WISLA KRAKOW 0
referee - Mikulski
AMICA WRONKI - Strozynski (Michniewicz 35),
Wodkiewicz, Bajor, Peczek (Siara 65), Sokolowski,
Bosacki, Bilinski, Zienczuk (Dawidowski 87),
Kryszalowicz, Sobocinski, Krol.
WISLA KRAKOW - Sarnat, Zajac M., Glowncki,
Kaluzny, Wegrzyn, Moskal, Moskalewicz, Kulawik
(Kaliciak 46), Kosowski (Pater 81), Brasilia
(Zurawski 46), Frankowski.

(AMICA WRONKI 5-2)

during the autumn, they transformed themselves into a team of free-flowing flair in the spring, beating each of the top three in successive weeks and more than doubling their goal output in the second half of the season. The chief contributor to this improved strike-rate was Jerzy Podbrozny, the ex-Lech Poznan and Legia Warsaw hitman who returned to Poland in mid-season after spells in Spain and the United States.

In sixth place were the ever-improving, albeit inconsistent, Amica Wronki. For the third season running the unsung westerners won the Polish Cup. It was an extra-ordinary achievement for a team that had never previously won a thing. Coached by ex-national team stopper Stefan Majewski, Amica overcame bigger hurdles than in the previous two seasons, beating Legia on penalties after two thrilling quarter-final ties and then hammering Wisla 5-2 on aggregate in the two-legged final.

Other than Amica's continued Cup exploits, the biggest surprise was the extraordinary end-of-season resurgence of newly-promoted Groclin Dyskobolia Grodzisk. Seemingly doomed to the drop after a calamitous autumn, during which they claimed a total of only five points, they

PLAYER OF THE SEASON

JERZY DUDEK
When Jerzy Dudek left his homeland for Dutch giants Feyenoord in 1996, he was a virtual unknown, having played just 15 games in the Polish First Division for (now defunct) Sokol Tychy. For the last three seasons, however, he has not missed a single Eredivisie match for the Rotterdam club and at the end of the 1999/2000 campaign he was voted as the Player of the Season by Holland's biggest daily newspaper, "De Telegraaf". He particular excelled in the Champions' League and it was his consistency in that competition that prompted new Polish national team boss Jerzy Engel to promote him ahead of another in-form goalkeeping exile, Bayer Leverkusen's Adam Matysek. The two 'keepers are well matched, but while Matysek is the more experienced at international level, Dudek has the long-term advantage of being, at 27, five years younger.

came back from the dead by winning nine matches in a row in the final third of the campaign to escape relegation.

There was no way out, however, for LKS Lodz and Lech Poznan, neither of whom had been tipped for the drop at the start of the campaign. LKS, the 1998 champions, suffered from the systematic departure of their leading players, while once-mighty Lech, who began the season in the UEFA Cup, also had the heart ripped out of the team due to financial difficulties. LKS and Lech were replaced in the top division by two equally well-known clubs, GKS Katowice and Slask Wroclaw, both of whom accumulated more than 100 points en route to promotion from Division Two.

It was another disappointing season on the international front for Polish teams. Wisla Krakow were banned from competing in the Champions' League but their replacements Widzew Lodz fell predictably in the qualifying round to Fiorentina, having staged a marvellous comeback to beat Bulgaria's Liteks Lovech on penalties. In fairness, every Polish representative got past at least one round in the UEFA Cup before going out to discernibly stronger opposition.

There was a miserable end to the Polish national team's European Championship qualifying campaign. Having achieved the inevitable home draw with England, they needed just a point from their final match away to already-qualified Sweden to reach the play-offs. But a poor performance resulted in a deserved 2-0 defeat and that proved to be the end of Janusz Wojcik's reign.

47-year-old Jerzy Engel was handed the job in his stead - after Legia Warsaw refused to release Franciszek Smuda - and he had a truly awful start. Poland's goal-scoring stalemate, which began with the 0-0 draw against England, extended through Engel's first four matches - two defeats and two draws - before at last Pawel Kryszalowicz, the skilful, pacy Amica Wronki striker who had been the star performer of the domestic season, ended the drought with a goal in the final international of the season, a 3-1 defeat by Holland in Lausanne.

By the summer the dearth of quality available to Engel resulted in the naturalisation of Nigerian striker Emmanuel Olisadebe - the top scorer of champions Polonia Warsaw. He was seen as a direct replacement for Andrzej Juskowiak, who had controversially put into words what many had secretly felt about the Polish team in a highly critical German newspaper article - for which he duly received harsh disciplinary action from the Polish FA.

PROMOTED CLUBS 99/00

SECOND DIVISION FINAL TABLE

		Pd	W	D	L	F	A	Pt	GD
1	**Slask Wroclaw**	**46**	**31**	**10**	**5**	**91**	**30**	**103**	**61**
2	**GKS Katowice**	**46**	**30**	**12**	**4**	**67**	**26**	**102**	**41**
3	Gornik Leczna	46	30	7	9	85	37	97	48
4	GKS Belchatow	46	27	14	5	71	22	95	49
5	Wlokniarz Kietrz	46	21	11	14	64	45	74	19
6	RKS Radomsko	46	20	9	17	70	50	69	20
7	Ceramika Opoczno	46	20	9	17	65	46	69	19
8	Odra Opole	46	19	11	16	48	48	68	0
9	Polar Wroclaw	46	19	10	17	63	59	67	4
10	Stal Stalowa Wola	46	18	12	16	53	65	66	-12
11	Polonia Bytom	46	18	9	19	44	43	63	1
12	KSZO Ostrowiec	46	17	12	17	50	45	63	5
13	Swit Nowy Dwor	46	16	13	17	63	60	61	3
14	Lechia Gdansk	46	16	13	17	55	63	61	-8
15	KP Myszkow	46	17	9	20	64	65	60	-1
16	Hetman Zamosc	46	16	12	18	54	56	60	-2
17	Hutnik Krakow	46	15	13	18	54	54	58	0
18	Siarka Tarnobrzeg	46	13	14	19	49	70	53	-21
19	Grunwald Ruda Slaska	46	13	9	24	54	68	48	-14
20	Jeziorak Ilawa	46	12	12	22	31	49	48	-18
21	Odra Szczecin	46	10	15	21	32	66	45	-34
22	Rakow Czestochowa	46	11	7	28	49	80	40	-31
23	Korona Kielce	46	7	8	31	29	106	29	-77
24	KP Konin	46	5	11	30	26	78	26	-52

CLUB DIRECTORIES

Slask Wroclaw
Ul. Oporowska 62
53-434 Wroclaw
tel - (071) 3613342
Year of Formation - 1977
President - Ryszard Sobiesiak
Secretary - Waldemar Prusik
Coach - Wojciech Lazarek; Jan Calinski
Stadium - Slask (15,000)

MAJOR HONOURS
League Championship - (1) 1977.
Domestic Cup - (1) 1987.

Gorniczy Klub Sportowy Katowice
Ul. Bukowa 1
40-145 Katowice
tel - (032) 2546321/2501757
fax - (032) 25011956
Year of Formation - 1964
President - Stanislaw Wilk
Coach - Marek Koniarek; Pawel Kowalski
Stadium - GKS (10,000)

MAJOR HONOURS
Domestic Cup - (3) 1986, 1991, 1993.

AMICA WRONKI

CLUB DIRECTORY

Klub Sportowy Amica Wronki
ul. Lesna 15a, 64-510 Wronki
tel - (067) 2540724
fax - (067) 2540724
website - www.amica.com.pl
Year of Formation - 1992
President - Wojciech Kaszynski
Secretary - Marek Pogorzelczyk
Coach - Stefan Majewski
Stadium - Amica (6,000)

MAJOR HONOURS
Domestic Cup - (3) 1998, 1999, 2000.

APPEARANCES 99/00

		P	Ap	(s)	Gls
Rafal ANDRASZAK	M	5	(4)	1
Marek BAJOR	D	13	(2)	
Jaroslaw BIENIUK	D	13	(8)	
Radoslaw BILINSKI	M	5	(1)	
Bartosz BOSACKI	D	22		
Tomasz DAWIDOWSKI	M	7	(9)	5
Piotr DUBIELA	M	11	(3)	1
Dariusz DUDKA	D	1	(1)	
Dariusz JACKIEWICZ	M	27		4
Maxwell KALU (NIG)	A	10	(8)	1
Bartlomiej KONIECZNY	M		(1)	
Dmitriy KOSAKOV (UKR)	A	5	(2)	1
Ireneusz KOSCIELNIAK	D	8	(4)	
Grzegorz KROL	A	11	(7)	5
Pawel KRYSZALOWICZ	A	22	(5)	11
Mariusz KUKIELKA	D	20	(1)	4
Tomasz LEWANDOWSKI	M	4	(3)	
Czeslaw MICHNIEWICZ	G	3		
Konstantin PANIN (UKR)	A	2	(3)	1
Pawel PECZAK	M	11	(2)	1
Krzysztof PISKULA	M	8	(5)	1
Andrzej PRZERADA	M	1	(3)	
Miroslaw SIARA	D	26		
Remigiusz SOBOCINSKI	M	16	(9)	4
Tomasz SOKOLOWSKI	M	21	(4)	3
Jaroslaw STROZYNSKI	G	27		
Grzegorz WODKIEWICZ	M	17	(1)	
Marek ZIENCZUK	M	14		

LEAGUE RESULTS 1999/2000

17/07/99	Gornik Zabrze	H	3-2	Dawidowski (p), Sokolowski, Kryszalowicz
24/07/99	Zaglebie Lubin	A	2-2	Kryszalowicz, Kukielka
31/07/99	Lech Poznan	H	1-0	Sokolowski
06/08/99	Legia Warszawa	H	1-2	Dawidowski
14/08/99	Odra Wodzislaw	A	2-0	Sokolowski, Kryszalowicz
21/08/99	Petro Plock	H	2-1	Kryszalowicz, Kukielka
29/08/99	Widzew Lodz	A	2-3	Dawidowski 2 (1p)
11/09/99	Ruch Radzionkow	H	1-1	Dawidowski (p)
19/09/99	Groclin Dyskobolia Grodzisk	A	1-1	Dubiela
25/09/99	Pogon Szczecin	H	2-2	Kosakov, Jackiewicz
03/10/99	Stomil Olsztyn	A	1-1	Peczak
16/10/99	Polonia Warszawa	H	5-0	Jackiewicz, Kryszalowicz, Kukielka (p), Krol, Panin
24/10/99	Ruch Chorzow	A	1-1	Kukielka
30/10/99	Wisla Krakow	H	0-0	
07/11/99	LKS Lodz	A	0-3	
04/03/00	Gornik Zabrze	A	3-1	Jackiewicz, Krol 2
12/03/00	Zaglebie Lubin	H	1-1	Jackiewicz
15/03/00	Lech Poznan	A	1-2	Kryszalowicz
18/03/00	Legia Warszawa	A	0-2	
25/03/00	Odra Wodzislaw	H	1-0	Kryszalowicz
01/04/00	Petro Plock	A	0-0	
07/04/00	Widzew Lodz	H	2-0	Sobocinski, Krol
15/04/00	Ruch Radzionkow	A	3-0	Andraszak, Kryszalowicz 2
22/04/00	Groclin Dyskobolia Grodzisk	H	0-1	
29/04/00	Pogon Szczecin	A	3-0	Kryszalowicz 2, Sobocinski
07/05/00	Stomil Olsztyn	H	1-1	Krol
14/05/00	Polonia Warszawa	A	0-4	
19/05/00	Ruch Chorzow	H	1-4	Kalu
24/05/00	Wisla Krakow	A	1-1	Sobocinski
28/05/00	LKS Lodz	H	2-1	Piskula (p), Sobocinski

GORNIK ZABRZE

CLUB DIRECTORY

SSA Gornik Zabrze
Ul. Roosevelta 81, 41-800 Zabrze
tel - (032) 2714926/2710941
fax - (032) 2710530
Year of Formation - 1948
President - Stanislaw Ploskon
Secretary - Stanislaw Oslizlo
Coach - Jan Zurek; Jozef Dankowski;
Marcin Bochynek; Mieczyslaw Broniszewski
Stadium - Gornik (20,000)

MAJOR HONOURS
League Championship - (14) 1957, 1959, 1961,
1963, 1964, 1965, 1966, 1967, 1971, 1972,
1985, 1986, 1987, 1988.
Domestic Cup - (6)
1965, 1968, 1969, 1970, 1971, 1972.

APPEARANCES 99/00

	P	Ap	(s)	Gls
Andrzej BLEDZEWSKI	G	29		
Grzegorz BONK	M	28	(1)	4
Marcin BROSZ	M	12	(7)	
Dariusz DZWIGALA	M	15		
Daniel GACEK	A	9	(8)	
Piotr GIERCZAK	M	27	(2)	10
Shingayi KAONDERA (ZIM)	A	8	(14)	1
Rafal KOCYBA	M	5	(7)	
Robert KOLASA	D	29		2
Daniel KOLODZIEJSKI	M		(2)	
Adam KOMPALA	M	30		19
Kamil KOSOWSKI	M	10		
Maciej KRZETOWSKI	D	11		
Grzegorz LEKKI	D	15		
Dariusz MARZEC	M	3	(4)	1
Arkadiusz MATEJKO	M		(5)	
Tomasz PRASNAL	M	18	(7)	
Michal PROBIERZ	M	30		1
Piotr ROCKI	A	19	(4)	2
Tomasz SOBCZAK	A		(1)	
Rafal SZWED	M	5	(1)	2
Miroslaw WARZECHA	G	1		
Jacek WISNIEWSKI	D	23		
Mariusz WLOKA	D	1	(1)	
Stanislaw WROBEL	A	2	(21)	

LEAGUE RESULTS 1999/2000

17/07/99	Amica Wronki	A	2-3	Kompala 2
24/07/99	Legia Warszawa	H	2-2	Rocki, Kolasa
31/07/99	Odra Wodzislaw	A	3-3	Kompala 2, Rocki
07/08/99	Petro Plock	H	4-1	Probierz, Kaondera, Kompala 2 (1p)
15/08/99	Widzew Lodz	A	1-1	Gierczak
21/08/99	Ruch Radzionkow	H	5-0	Gierczak 3, Bonk 2
28/08/99	Groclin Dyskobolia Grodzisk	A	2-0	Kompala 2
12/09/99	Pogon Szczecin	H	2-2	Bonk, Kompala
18/09/99	Stomil Olsztyn	A	0-1	
25/09/99	Polonia Warszawa	H	0-1	
02/10/99	Ruch Chorzow	A	1-2	Bonk
16/10/99	Wisla Krakow	H	1-0	Kompala
23/10/99	LKS Lodz	A	2-2	Gierczak 2
30/10/99	Lech Poznan	A	1-1	Gierczak
05/11/99	Zaglebie Lubin	H	0-0	
04/03/00	Amica Wronki	H	1-3	Kompala (p)
11/03/00	Legia Warszawa	A	0-0	
15/03/00	Odra Wodzislaw	H	0-2	
18/03/00	Petro Plock	A	0-1	
25/03/00	Widzew Lodz	H	0-1	
01/04/00	Ruch Radzionkow	A	0-1	
08/04/00	Groclin Dyskobolia Grodzisk	H	1-2	Kompala (p)
15/04/00	Pogon Szczecin	A	1-0	Szwed
22/04/00	Stomil Olsztyn	H	1-0	Szwed
29/04/00	Polonia Warszawa	A	0-1	
06/05/00	Ruch Chorzow	H	1-2	Kompala (p)
14/05/00	Wisla Krakow	A	3-6	Kompala 2 (2p), Gierczak
20/05/00	LKS Lodz	H	3-1	Gierczak, Kompala 2
24/05/00	Lech Poznan	H	4-0	Kolasa, Gierczak, Kompala 2 (1p)
28/05/00	Zaglebie Lubin	A	1-2	Marzec

GROCLIN DYSKOBOLIA GRODZISK

CLUB DIRECTORY

Klub Sportowy Groclin Dyskobolia Grodzisk
Wielkopolski, Ul. Sportowa 2
64-065 Grodzisk Wielopolski
tel - (061) 4446019 / fax - (061) 4446020
Year of Formation - 1922
President - Ryszard Kaczmarek
Secretary - Stanislaw Bamber
Coach - Marcin Bochynek; Jan Stempczak;
Janusz Bialek
Stadium - Dyskobolia (6,000)

APPEARANCES 99/00

	P	Ap	(s)	Gls
Jaroslaw ARASZKIEWICZ	M	7	(7)	2
Przemyslaw BERESZYNSKI	D	14	(2)	
Piotr BIELAK	A	5	(1)	1
Douda CAMARA (GUI)	D	6	(6)	
Maciej HANCZEWSKI	M	4	(2)	
Andrzej JANECZEK	M	16	(7)	
JULCIMAR				
Conceição de Souza (BRA)	D		(3)	
Krzysztof JUTRZENKA	M		(5)	
Jacek KACPRZAK	M	15		5
Marcin KLACZKA	M	18	(2)	
Krzysztof KLOSINSKI	A	14	(1)	6
Dmitriy KOSAKOV (UKR)	A	1	(4)	2
Krzysztof KOTOROWSKI	G	30		
Igor KOZIOL	D	21		
Zbigniew KROLIK	M		(3)	
Adam KRYGER	M	6	(1)	
Mariusz LEWANDOWSKI	D	12	(2)	
Maciej MALINOWSKI	M	8	(3)	
Zbigniew MALACHOWSKI	D	3		
Grzegorz MATLAK	M	9	(2)	1
Tomasz MOLEWSKI	M	3	(2)	
Grzegorz MOTYKA	M	13	(1)	2
Benedykt NOCON	D	2		
Maciej NUCKOWSKI	A	9	(2)	1
Piotr PIECHNIAK	M	14		1
Wojciech POCHYLSKI	D	1	(6)	
Bogdan PRUSEK	M	29	(1)	3
Mariusz ROSIAK	A	5	(3)	
Tomasz RYBARCZYK	M	23	(3)	2
Roman SKORUPA	M	6	(1)	
Jan SPYCHALSKI	M	2	(9)	
Rafal WITKOWSKI	D	25	(2)	2
Dariusz WOJCIECHOWSKI	A	7	(5)	
Krzysztof ZAGORSKI	M	2	(2)	1

LEAGUE RESULTS 1999/2000

17/07/99	Pogon Szczecin	H	1-2	Prusek
24/07/99	Stomil Olsztyn	A	2-5	Matlak, Rybarczyk
31/07/99	Polonia Warszawa	H	0-1	
07/08/99	Ruch Chorzow	A	1-4	Zagorski
14/08/99	Wisla Krakow	H	1-2	Motyka
21/08/99	LKS Lodz	A	0-1	
28/08/99	Gornik Zabrze	H	0-2	
11/09/99	Zaglebie Lubin	A	0-1	
19/09/99	Amica Wronki	H	1-1	Bielak
26/09/99	Legia Warszawa	A	0-5	
02/10/99	Odra Wodzislaw	H	0-1	
16/10/99	Petro Plock	A	1-1	Prusek
24/10/99	Widzew Lodz	H	1-0	Motyka (p)
30/10/99	Ruch Radzionkow	A	0-2	
07/11/99	Lech Poznan	H	1-2	Araszkiewicz
05/03/00	Pogon Szczecin	A	0-1	
11/03/00	Stomil Olsztyn	H	3-2	Klosinski, Witkowski 2
15/03/00	Polonia Warszawa	A	0-1	
18/03/00	Ruch Chorzow	H	0-3	
25/03/00	Wisla Krakow	A	0-3	
01/04/00	LKS Lodz	H	2-1	Nuckowski, Klosinski
08/04/00	Gornik Zabrze	A	2-1	Prusek, Klosinski
16/04/00	Zaglebie Lubin	H	1-0	Kacprzak
22/04/00	Amica Wronki	A	1-0	Rybarczyk
30/04/00	Legia Warszawa	H	1-0	Kacprzak
06/05/00	Odra Wodzislaw	A	2-0	Kacprzak, Klosinski
14/05/00	Petro Plock	H	3-1	Kacprzak, Kosakov, Piechniak
20/05/00	Widzew Lodz	A	3-2	Klosinski 2, Araszkiewicz
24/05/00	Ruch Radzionkow	H	2-1	Kosakov, Kacprzak
28/05/00	Lech Poznan	A	0-0	

LECH POZNAN

CLUB DIRECTORY

Wielkopolski Klub Pilkarski Lech Poznan
Ul. Bulgarska 5/7, 60-320 Poznan
tel - (061) 8673061 / fax - (061) 8672661
website - www.lech.poznan.pl
Year of Formation - 1922
President - Stanislaw Butka
Secretary - Bogdan Niemczyk
Coach - Adam Topolski; Marian Kurowski;
Zbigniew Franiak; Wojciech Wasikiewicz
Stadium - Lech (15,000)

MAJOR HONOURS
League Championship - (5)
1983, 1984, 1990, 1992, 1993.
Domestic Cup - (3) 1982, 1984, 1988.

APPEARANCES 99/00

	P	Ap	(s)	Gls
Tomasz AUGUSTYNIAK	D	21	(3)	
Tomasz BEKAS	D		(1)	
Pawel BOCIAN	D	17	(1)	1
Marcin DRAJER	M	23	(1)	
Arkadiusz GLOWACKI	D	13		
Michal GOLINSKI	M	5	(13)	
Aleksandar GRUBER (YUG)	M	4	(3)	
Krzysztof JABLONSKI	M		(1)	
Pawel KACZOROWSKI	M	22		1
Piotr KASPERSKI	M	9	(4)	
Michal KOKOSZANEK	G	24	(1)	
Jacek KUBICKI	M	8	(4)	3
Jaroslaw MACKIEWICZ	A	24	(3)	7
Grzegorz MATLAK	D	13		
Tomasz MATUSZCZAK	D		(1)	
Maciej MIELCARZ	G	1		
Tomasz NAJEWSKI	M	12	(9)	
Justin Chidi NNOROM (NIG)	M	6	(10)	1
Maciej PASTUSZKA	M	5	(1)	
Krzysztof PISKULA	M	13		4
Marcin ROSLON	D	2	(1)	
Maciej SCHERFCHEN	M	27		1
Dariusz SOLNICA	M	3	(4)	
Piotr SOLTYSIAK	D		(1)	
Slawomir SUCHOMSKI	M	20	(1)	7
Marek SZEMONSKI	A	8		1
Bartosz SLUSARSKI	A	1	(11)	2
Slawomir TWARDYGROSZ	M	4	(6)	
Norbert TYRAJSKI	G	5	(1)	
Przemyslaw URBANIAK	D	26		
Leszek ZAWADZKI	D	6	(6)	
Maciej ZURAWSKI	A	8	(1)	6

LEAGUE RESULTS 1999/2000

17/07/99	Zaglebie Lubin	A	1-2	Zurawski (p)
24/07/99	Pogon Szczecin	H	1-1	Zurawski
31/07/99	Amica Wronki	A	0-1	
07/08/99	Stomil Olsztyn	H	1-2	Zurawski
15/08/99	Legia Warszawa	A	1-1	Nnorom
21/08/99	Polonia Warszawa	H	1-3	Scherfchen
29/08/99	Odra Wodzislaw	A	0-4	
12/09/99	Ruch Chorzow	H	1-2	Piskula (p)
19/09/99	Petro Plock	A	1-2	Zurawski (p)
26/09/99	Wisla Krakow	H	4-1	Zurawski 2, Piskula, Kubicki
03/10/99	Widzew Lodz	A	2-2	Mackiewicz, Piskula
16/10/99	LKS Lodz	H	1-1	Kubicki
23/10/99	Ruch Radzionkow	A	1-4	Suchomski
30/10/99	Gornik Zabrze	H	1-1	Kubicki
07/11/99	Groclin Dyskobolia Grodzisk	A	2-1	Kaczorowski, Piskula
05/03/00	Zaglebie Lubin	H	2-0	Suchomski 2
11/03/00	Pogon Szczecin	A	3-4	Mackiewicz, Slusarski, Suchomski (p)
15/03/00	Amica Wronki	H	2-1	Suchomski (p), Slusarski
18/03/00	Stomil Olsztyn	A	1-1	Bocian
25/03/00	Legia Warszawa	H	1-2	Suchomski (p)
01/04/00	Polonia Warszawa	A	0-5	
08/04/00	Odra Wodzislaw	H	0-1	
15/04/00	Ruch Chorzow	A	0-2	
29/04/00	Wisla Krakow	A	0-2	
06/05/00	Widzew Lodz	H	3-5	Mackiewicz, Szemonski, Suchomski (p)
10/05/00	Petro Plock	H	1-0	Mackiewicz
13/05/00	LKS Lodz	A	0-1	
20/05/00	Ruch Radzionkow	H	3-1	Mackiewicz 3
24/05/00	Gornik Zabrze	A	0-4	
28/05/00	Groclin Dyskobolia Grodzisk	H	0-0	

LEGIA WARSZAWA

CLUB DIRECTORY

ASPN Legia Daewoo Warszawa
Ul. Lazienkowska 3, 00-449 Warszawa
tel - (022) 6210896/6281360
fax - (022) 6218261
website - www.legia.com.pl
Year of Formation - 1916
President - Marek Pietruszka
Secretary - Wladyslaw Stachurski
Coach - Dariusz Kubicki; Franciszek Smuda
Stadium - Wojska Polskiego (15,000)

MAJOR HONOURS
League Championship - (6)
1955, 1956, 1969, 1970, 1994, 1995.
Domestic Cup - (12)
1955, 1956, 1964, 1966, 1973, 1980, 1981,
1989, 1990, 1994, 1995, 1997.

APPEARANCES 99/00

	P	Ap	(s)	Gls
Jacek BEDNARZ	M	24	(2)	3
Marek CITKO	A	9	(2)	1
Sylwester CZERESZEWSKI	M	30		16
Rafal DEBINSKI	M		(2)	
Maciej JANIAK	M		(3)	
Tomasz JARZEBOWSKI	M	4	(2)	1
Bartosz KARWAN	M	26		6
Igor KOZIOL	D	2		
Tomasz LAPINSKI	D	1		
Jacek MAGIERA	M		(10)	1
Adam MAJEWSKI	M	28		2
Tomasz MAZURKIEWICZ	M	3	(7)	
Marcin MIECIEL	A	30		8
Piotr MOSOR	D	13		1
Maciej MURAWSKI	M	27	(1)	
Sebastian NOWAK	D	2		
Mariusz PIEKARSKI	M	7	(4)	1
Zbigniew ROBAKIEWICZ	G	15		
Slawomir RUTKA	D	3		
Maciej SAWICKI	A	3	(5)	1
Rafal SIADACZKA	D	15		1
Pawel SKRZYPEK	M	1	(5)	
Tomasz SOKOLOWSKI	M	25	(2)	4
Dariusz SOLNICA	M		(1)	
Grzegorz SZAMOTULSKI	G	15		
Mariusz SRUTWA	A	4	(6)	3
Sergiusz WIECHOWSKI	M	1	(5)	
Pawel WOJTALA	D	1		
Radoslaw WROBLEWSKI	M	13	(12)	
Jacek ZIELINSKI	D	28		1

LEAGUE RESULTS 1999/2000

Date	Opponent		Score	Scorers
16/07/99	LKS Lodz	H	0-0	
24/07/99	Gornik Zabrze	A	2-2	Karwan, Sawicki
31/07/99	Zaglebie Lubin	H	2-2	Mosor, Czereszewski (p)
06/08/99	Amica Wronki	A	2-1	Czereszewski (p), Mieciel
15/08/99	Lech Poznan	H	1-1	Zielinski
21/08/99	Odra Wodzislaw	H	1-1	Sokolowski
29/08/99	Petro Plock	A	1-3	Magiera
11/09/99	Widzew Lodz	H	2-1	Mieciel, Czereszewski
19/09/99	Ruch Radzionkow	A	1-1	Karwan
26/09/99	Groclin Dyskobolia Grodzisk	H	5-0	Czereszewski 3 (1p), Karwan, Bednarz
03/10/99	Pogon Szczecin	A	4-2	Bednarz, Majewski, Czereszewski 2 (1p)
16/10/99	Stomil Olsztyn	H	4-0	og (Kucharski), Czereszewski, Mieciel, Srutwa
24/10/99	Polonia Warszawa	A	1-1	Mieciel
30/10/99	Ruch Chorzow	H	3-1	Czereszewski, Srutwa 2
07/11/99	Wisla Krakow	A	1-1	Mieciel
04/03/00	LKS Lodz	A	1-1	Sokolowski
11/03/00	Gornik Zabrze	H	0-0	
15/03/00	Zaglebie Lubin	A	3-2	Mieciel, og (Majka), Citko
18/03/00	Amica Wronki	H	2-0	Czereszewski 2
25/03/00	Lech Poznan	A	2-1	Karwan, og (Golinski)
01/04/00	Odra Wodzislaw	A	2-0	Siadaczka, Bednarz
08/04/00	Petro Plock	H	1-0	Mieciel
15/04/00	Widzew Lodz	A	2-3	Czereszewski, Mieciel
22/04/00	Ruch Radzionkow	H	4-2	Jarzebowski, Majewski, Czereszewski, Karwan
30/04/00	Groclin Dyskobolia Grodzisk	A	0-1	
07/05/00	Pogon Szczecin	H	5-1	Karwan, Sokolowski 2, Czereszewski (p), Piekarski
13/05/00	Stomil Olsztyn	A	0-1	
20/05/00	Polonia Warszawa	H	0-3	
24/05/00	Ruch Chorzow	A	1-0	Czereszewski
28/05/00	Wisla Krakow	H	0-2	

LKS LODZ

CLUB DIRECTORY

LKS-Ptak Lodz
Ul. Unii 2, 94-020 Lodz
tel - (042) 6860668/6863745
fax - (042) 6881313
website - www.ptak.com.pl
Year of Formation - 1908
President - Antoni Ptak
Secretary - Witold Bendkowski
Coach - Ryszard Polak; Boguslaw Pietrzak
Stadium - LKS (30,000)

MAJOR HONOURS
League Championship - (2) 1958, 1998.
Domestic Cup - (1) 1957.

APPEARANCES 99/00

		P	Ap	(s)	Gls
Pawel ABBOTT	A			(8)	
Leandro Santos BATATA (BRA)	D	21			1
Jaroslaw DZIEDZIC	D	19			
Eddy Lord DOMBRAYE (NIG)	A	5		(5)	
Robert GORSKI	M	13			2
Rafal GRZELAK	M	15			1
Austin HAMLET (NIG)	A	26		(4)	3
Ariel JAKUBOWSKI	M	20		(9)	
Artur KOSCIUK	D	26			1
Grzegorz KRYSIAK	D	5		(5)	
Marcin KRYSINSKI	D	7		(1)	1
Andrzej KRZYSZTALOWICZ	G	13		(1)	
Tomasz LENART	D	13		(4)	
Michal LABEDZKI	M	15		(7)	
Lukasz MADEJ	M	9		(6)	2
Pawel MAGDON	M	2		(2)	
Radoslaw MATUSIAK	A			(4)	
Roberto Claudio MILAR (URU)	M	11		(1)	2
Darlington OMODIAGBE (NIG)	M	6			
Michal OSINSKI	M	2		(4)	
Jacek PASZULEWICZ	D	11			2
Marek SAGANOWSKI	A	22		(2)	6
Michal SLAWUTA	G	10			
Sebastian TOMASIAK	A	3		(7)	
Daniel TRESCINSKI	D	5		(9)	
Tomasz WIESZCZYCKI	M	15			3
Zbigniew WYCISZKIEWICZ	M	27		(1)	4
Boguslaw WYPARLO	G	7			
Dzidoslaw ZUBEREK	A	2		(5)	

LEAGUE RESULTS 1999/2000

16/07/99	Legia Warszawa	A	0-0	
24/07/99	Odra Wodzislaw	H	1-0	Hamlet
31/07/99	Petro Plock	A	0-2	
14/08/99	Ruch Radzionkow	A	0-1	
21/08/99	Groclin Dyskobolia Grodzisk	H	1-0	Saganowski (p)
28/08/99	Pogon Szczecin	A	0-0	
11/09/99	Stomil Olsztyn	H	1-1	Gorski
18/09/99	Polonia Warszawa	A	0-1	
25/09/99	Ruch Chorzow	H	2-2	Hamlet, Gorski
02/10/99	Wisla Krakow	A	0-1	
16/10/99	Lech Poznan	A	1-1	Paszulewicz
23/10/99	Gornik Zabrze	H	2-2	Paszulewicz, Wieszczycki
27/10/99	Widzew Lodz	H	2-3	Wyciszkiewicz, Wieszczycki
31/10/99	Zaglebie Lubin	A	0-1	
07/11/99	Amica Wronki	H	3-0	Wyciszkiewicz, Wieszczycki, Batata
04/03/00	Legia Warszawa	H	1-1	Wyciszkiewicz
12/03/00	Odra Wodzislaw	A	0-2	
15/03/00	Petro Plock	H	1-2	Hamlet
19/03/00	Widzew Lodz	A	0-2	
25/03/00	Ruch Radzionkow	H	1-0	Saganowski
01/04/00	Groclin Dyskobolia Grodzisk	A	1-2	Milar
08/04/00	Pogon Szczecin	H	4-3	Madej, Grzelak, Kosciuk, Saganowski
15/04/00	Stomil Olsztyn	A	0-1	
22/04/00	Polonia Warszawa	H	0-2	
29/04/00	Ruch Chorzow	A	0-3	
06/05/00	Wisla Krakow	H	0-2	
13/05/00	Lech Poznan	H	1-0	Saganowski
20/05/00	Gornik Zabrze	A	1-3	Krysinski
24/05/00	Zaglebie Lubin	H	4-2	Madej, Saganowski 2, Wyciszkiewicz
28/05/00	Amica Wronki	A	1-2	Milar

ODRA WODZISLAW

CLUB DIRECTORY

Miejski Klub Sportowy Odra Wodzislaw
Ul. Boguminska 8
44-300 Wodzislaw Slaski
tel - (036) 4551394
fax - (036) 4554435
Year of Formation - 1922
President - Ireneusz Serwotka
Secretary - Edward Socha
Coach - Jerzy Wyrobek
Stadium - Odra (8,000)

APPEARANCES 99/00

	P	Ap	(s)	Gls
Pawel ADAMCZYK	M	30		
Arkadiusz BALUSZYNSKI	A	5	(12)	
Marcin BEDNAREK	A	1	(1)	
Michal CHALBINSKI	A	13	(2)	6
Adam JACHIMOWICZ	M		(3)	
Piotr JEGOR	D	19	(1)	3
Arkadiusz KAMPKA	M	3	(6)	
Dariusz KLODA	G	4		
Grzegorz KOLISZ	M	9	(11)	
Marek KOLEK	D	4	(3)	
Adam KUCZ	A	9		
Piotr KUS	M	4	(2)	
Jakub LISEK	M	2	(5)	
Marcin MALINOWSKI	M	28		1
Wojciech MALOCHA	A	4	(2)	
Jacek MATYJA	D	22	(1)	2
Marcin PAWLOWSKI	M	1	(5)	
Przemyslaw PLUTA	M	19	(3)	1
Maciej POLAK	G	4		
Rafal POLICHT	A	7	(9)	
Pawel SIBIK	M	28	(1)	5
Bartlomiej SOCHA	A		(2)	1
Lukasz SOSIN	A	21	(6)	10
Piotr SOWISZ	D	13		
Marcin STANIEK	D		(1)	
Miroslaw STANIEK	D	20	(2)	2
Ryszard STANIEK	M	7	(3)	
Adam SMIGIELSKI	M	1	(3)	
Adam SWITALA	M	4		
Grzegorz TOMALA	G	22		
Jan WOS	A	26		2

LEAGUE RESULTS 1999/2000

18/07/99	Wisla Krakow	H	0-3	
24/07/99	LKS Lodz	A	0-1	
31/07/99	Gornik Zabrze	H	3-3	Matyja, Jegor, Sosin
07/08/99	Zaglebie Lubin	A	0-1	
14/08/99	Amica Wronki	H	0-2	
21/08/99	Legia Warszawa	A	1-1	Pluta
29/08/99	Lech Poznan	H	4-0	Jegor (p), Staniek Mi., Sosin 2
11/09/99	Petro Plock	H	1-2	Matyja
19/09/99	Widzew Lodz	A	1-1	Sosin
25/09/99	Ruch Radzionkow	H	0-0	
02/10/99	Groclin Dyskobolia Grodzisk	A	1-0	Sosin
16/10/99	Pogon Szczecin	H	1-0	og (Faltynski)
23/10/99	Stomil Olsztyn	A	1-2	Sosin (p)
30/10/99	Polonia Warszawa	H	3-1	Jegor, Wos 2
06/11/99	Ruch Chorzow	A	1-3	Sosin
04/03/00	Wisla Krakow	A	1-3	Sosin
12/03/00	LKS Lodz	H	2-0	Sibik (p), Chalbinski
15/03/00	Gornik Zabrze	A	2-0	Sosin, Sibik
18/03/00	Zaglebie Lubin	H	1-1	Sibik
25/03/00	Amica Wronki	A	0-1	
01/04/00	Legia Warszawa	H	0-2	
08/04/00	Lech Poznan	A	1-0	Sibik
15/04/00	Petro Plock	A	1-0	Staniek Mi.
22/04/00	Widzew Lodz	H	2-0	Chalbinski, Socha
29/04/00	Ruch Radzionkow	A	1-2	Chalbinski
06/05/00	Groclin Dyskobolia Grodzisk	H	0-2	
13/05/00	Pogon Szczecin	A	0-0	
20/05/00	Stomil Olsztyn	H	3-1	Chalbinski 2, Sosin
24/05/00	Polonia Warszawa	A	1-4	Chalbinski
28/05/00	Ruch Chorzow	H	2-2	Malinowski, Sibik

PETRO PLOCK

CLUB DIRECTORY

Sportowa Spolka Akcyjna Petro Plock
Ul. Lukasiewicza 34, 09-400 Plock
tel - (024) 2622555/2624638
fax - (024) 3655220
Year of Formation - 1947
President - Krzysztof Gawlowski
Secretary - Szczepan Targowski
Coach - Jerzy Kasalik; Adam Topolski;
Albin Mikulski
Stadium - Petro (12,800)

APPEARANCES 99/00

	P	Ap	(s)	Gls
Waldemar ADAMCZYK	A	11	(1)	4
Artur ADAMUS	M	3	(4)	
Mieczyslaw AGAFON	M	16	(3)	3
Ahmed ALIYU (NIG)	M	1	(1)	
Mike APPLE (USA)	M		(1)	
Dondu AVAA (NIG)	A	3	(3)	
Eduard BOLTRUSHEVICH (BLS)	D	4		
Miroslaw BUDKA	M	11	(2)	1
Sekou DRAME (GUI)	M	3	(4)	
Justin EVANS (USA)	M	4		1
Marcin FLOREK	A		(2)	
Vahan GEVORYAN (ARM)	D	10	(7)	3
Artur KAPELA	M	2	(10)	
Vladimir KLIMOVICH (BLS)	D		(1)	
Jaroslaw KRUPSKI	G	17		
Wojciech LOBODZINSKI	M		(3)	
Krzysztof MAJDA	M	15	(5)	
Pawel MIASZKIEWICZ	M	15	(2)	3
Miroslaw MILEWSKI	D	2	(2)	
Mike MOUZIE (NIG)	D	15		
Mariusz NOSAL	A	24	(1)	13
Eneka Abor OBEIDILE (NIG)	A	4		1
Maciej PASTUSZKA	M	13	(2)	
Jacek POPEK	M	14	(7)	
Marcin ROGALSKI	D	4	(2)	
Dariusz ROMUZGA	M	26		1
Artur SEJUD	G	10	(1)	
Radoslaw SOBOLEWSKI	D	25	(3)	1
Piotr SOCZEWKA	M	12	(4)	
Ikemefuna Ozuah SUDY (NIG)	D	8		
Kamil SZARNECKI	M	9	(8)	3
Andrzej SZYSZKO	G	3		
Sebastian TOMASIAK	M		(3)	
Robert WILK	M	25		1
Marek WITKOWSKI	M	2	(3)	
Jerzy WOJNECKI	D	19	(2)	

LEAGUE RESULTS 1999/2000

17/07/99	Ruch Chorzow	H	0-0	
25/07/99	Wisla Krakow	A	1-3	Agafon
31/07/99	LKS Lodz	H	2-0	Miaszkiewicz, Nosal
07/08/99	Gornik Zabrze	A	1-4	Wilk
14/08/99	Zaglebie Lubin	H	2-1	Adamczyk 2 (1p)
21/08/99	Amica Wronki	A	1-2	Romuzga
29/08/99	Legia Warszawa	H	3-1	Miaszkiewicz, Nosal, Agafon
11/09/99	Odra Wodzislaw	A	2-1	Miaszkiewicz, Adamczyk
19/09/99	Lech Poznan	H	2-1	Agafon, Adamczyk
25/09/99	Widzew Lodz	H	0-0	
02/10/99	Ruch Radzionkow	A	1-2	Nosal
16/10/99	Groclin Dyskobolia Grodzisk	H	1-1	Evans
23/10/99	Pogon Szczecin	A	1-2	Nosal (p)
30/10/99	Stomil Olsztyn	H	1-1	Nosal (p)
06/11/99	Polonia Warszawa	A	0-2	
04/03/00	Ruch Chorzow	A	1-3	Gevoryan
12/03/00	Wisla Krakow	H	1-1	Szarnecki
15/03/00	LKS Lodz	A	2-1	Sobolewski, Gevoryan
18/03/00	Gornik Zabrze	H	1-0	Nosal
26/03/00	Zaglebie Lubin	A	0-5	
01/04/00	Amica Wronki	H	0-0	
08/04/00	Legia Warszawa	A	0-1	
15/04/00	Odra Wodzislaw	H	0-1	
07/05/00	Ruch Radzionkow	H	1-3	Nosal
10/05/00	Lech Poznan	A	0-1	
14/05/00	Groclin Dyskobolia Grodzisk	A	1-3	Budka
17/05/00	Widzew Lodz	A	3-4	Nosal 2 (1p), Obeidile
20/05/00	Pogon Szczecin	H	3-1	Szarnecki, Nosal 2 (1p)
24/05/00	Stomil Olsztyn	A	2-2	Nosal (p), Szarnecki
28/05/00	Polonia Warszawa	H	2-1	Gevoryan, Nosal

POGON SZCZECIN

CLUB DIRECTORY

Morski Klub Sportowy Pogon Szczecin
Ul. Karlowicza 28
71-102 Szczecin
tel - (091) 4878658
fax - (091) 4878658
Year of Formation - 1948
President - Sabri Bekdas
Secretary - Artur Korneluk
Coach - Albin Mikulski; Mariusz Kuras
Stadium - Pogon (17,500)

APPEARANCES 99/00

	P	Ap	(s)	Gls
Rafal ANDRUSZKO	M	5	(3)	2
Artur BLAZEJEWSKI	M	5	(4)	
Artur BUGAJ	A	17	(5)	1
Ferdinand CHIFON (CMR)	M	22	(1)	3
Jaroslaw CHWASTEK	D	6	(5)	
Maciej DOLEGA	A	1	(8)	
Pawel DRUMLAK	M	23		4
Robert DYMKOWSKI	A	27		8
Dariusz DZWIGALA	M	14		4
Maciej FALTYNSKI	M	10	(11)	1
Dariusz FORNALAK	M	25		4
Janusz GALUSZKA	D	21		
Rafal HUEBSCHER	M		(1)	
Piotr JACYNA	D	6	(6)	
Maciej KACZOROWSKI	A		(10)	
Bartosz LAWA	M	6	(12)	3
Radoslaw MAJDAN	G	29		
Rafal PIOTROWSKI	M	26	(3)	4
Leszek POKLADOWSKI	M	25	(2)	2
Ryszard REMIEN	M	14	(2)	1
Andrzej RYCAK	M		(2)	
Serhiy SHIPOVSKIY (UKR)	G	1		
Robert SIKORSKI	M	10	(8)	
Dariusz SZUBERT	M	15	(2)	5
Marek WALBURG	D	22		

LEAGUE RESULTS 1999/2000

17/07/99	Groclin Dyskobolia Grodzisk	A	2-1	Dymkowski, Fornalak (p)
24/07/99	Lech Poznan	A	1-1	Dymkowski
31/07/99	Stomil Olsztyn	H	3-0	Piotrowski, Dymkowski (p), Pokladowski
07/08/99	Polonia Warszawa	A	0-4	
14/08/99	Ruch Chorzow	H	1-1	Dymkowski
22/08/99	Wisla Krakow	A	1-1	Piotrowski
28/08/99	LKS Lodz	H	0-0	
12/09/99	Gornik Zabrze	A	2-2	Bugaj, Fornalak (p)
18/09/99	Zaglebie Lubin	H	1-0	Lawa
25/09/99	Amica Wronki	A	2-2	Dymkowski, Remien
03/10/99	Legia Warszawa	H	2-4	Drumlak, Chifon
16/10/99	Odra Wodzislaw	A	0-1	
23/10/99	Petro Plock	H	2-1	Fornalak (p), Drumlak
30/10/99	Widzew Lodz	A	2-1	Szubert 2
06/11/99	Ruch Radzionkow	H	4-0	Piotrowski, Szubert, Pokladowski, Lawa
05/03/00	Groclin Dyskobolia Grodzisk	H	1-0	Szubert
11/03/00	Lech Poznan	H	4-3	Chifon, Lawa, Dymkowski, Fornalak (p)
15/03/00	Stomil Olsztyn	A	1-1	Dzwigala
18/03/00	Polonia Warszawa	H	0-2	
25/03/00	Ruch Chorzow	A	2-2	Piotrowski, Szubert
01/04/00	Wisla Krakow	H	3-3	Dymkowski, Drumlak, Faltynski
08/04/00	LKS Lodz	A	3-4	Dzwigala 2, Chifon
15/04/00	Gornik Zabrze	H	0-1	
21/04/00	Zaglebie Lubin	A	1-3	Dymkowski
29/04/00	Amica Wronki	H	0-3	
07/05/00	Legia Warszawa	A	1-5	Drumlak
13/05/00	Odra Wodzislaw	H	0-0	
20/05/00	Petro Plock	A	1-3	Andruszko
24/05/00	Widzew Lodz	H	2-3	Dzwigala (p), Andruszko
28/05/00	Ruch Radzionkow	A	0-1	

POLONIA WARSZAWA

CLUB DIRECTORY

Klub Piłkarski Polonia Warszawa SSA
Ul. Konwiktorska 6
00-206 Warszawa
tel - (022) 6351399/6351401
fax - (022) 6351637
Year of Formation - 1911
President - Krzysztof Mencel
Secretary - Marek Ruszkiewicz
Coach - Dariusz Wdowczyk
Stadium - Polonia (10,000)

MAJOR HONOURS
League Championship - (2) 1946, 2000.

APPEARANCES 99/00

	P	Ap	(s)	Gls
Mladen ALEJBEG (CRO)	M		(5)	
Mateusz BARTCZAK	M	15	(9)	1
Arkadiusz BAK	M	20	(2)	4
Przemyslaw BOLDT	D	12	(4)	
Maciej BYKOWSKI	A	15		1
Tomasz CIESIELSKI	D	18	(2)	1
Jacek DABROWSKI	M	14	(3)	1
Piotr DZIEWICKI	M	12	(9)	2
Emmanuel EKWUEME (NIG)	M	23	(3)	1
Igor GOLASZEWSKI	M	22	(6)	7
Arkadiusz KALISZAN	M	20	(3)	1
Tomasz KIELBOWICZ	M	15		5
Marcin KUS	D		(1)	
Mariusz LIBERDA	G	14	(1)	
Mariusz MALINOWSKI	D	5	(8)	
Jaroslaw MAZURKIEWICZ	M	3	(11)	1
Grazvydas MIKULENAS (LIT)	A	3	(4)	2
Tomasz MOSKAL	A	9	(9)	4
Emmanuel OLISADEBE (NIG)	A	23	(1)	12
Jacek PASZULEWICZ	D	10		
Mariusz PAWLAK	D	27	(1)	2
Maciej SZCZESNY	G	16	(1)	
Mariusz UNIERZYSKI	D		(2)	
Donatas VENCEVICIUS (LIT)	M	1		
Marcin WACHOWICZ	A		(1)	
Tomasz WIESZCZYCKI	M	13		6
Lukasz WOZNIAK	A		(1)	
Tomas ZVIRGZDAUSKAS (LIT)	D	20	(1)	

LEAGUE RESULTS 1999/2000

21/07/99	Widzew Lodz	A	1-1	Dabrowski
31/07/99	Groclin Dyskobolia Grodzisk	A	1-0	Moskal
07/08/99	Pogon Szczecin	H	4-0	Olisadebe 2, Moskal, Golaszewski
14/08/99	Stomil Olsztyn	A	0-0	
21/08/99	Lech Poznan	A	3-1	Pawlak, og (Mielcarz), Golaszewski
25/08/99	Ruch Radzionkow	H	4-1	Moskal 2 (1p), Olisadebe 2
28/08/99	Ruch Chorzow	H	0-2	
12/09/99	Wisla Krakow	A	3-2	Golaszewski, Olisadebe, Dziewicki
18/09/99	LKS Lodz	H	1-0	Golaszewski
25/09/99	Gornik Zabrze	A	1-0	Ekwueme
02/10/99	Zaglebie Lubin	H	1-1	og (Lewandowski)
16/10/99	Amica Wronki	A	0-5	
24/10/99	Legia Warszawa	H	1-1	Bak (p)
30/10/99	Odra Wodzislaw	A	1-3	Dziewicki
06/11/99	Petro Plock	H	2-0	Kaliszan, Mazurkiewicz
05/03/00	Widzew Lodz	H	1-0	Kielbowicz
11/03/00	Ruch Radzionkow	A	2-0	Olisadebe, Kielbowicz
15/03/00	Groclin Dyskobolia Grodzisk	H	1-0	Bak
18/03/00	Pogon Szczecin	A	2-0	Mikulenas, Bak
25/03/00	Stomil Olsztyn	H	2-0	Wieszczycki 2 (1p)
01/04/00	Lech Poznan	H	5-0	Wieszczycki 2, Olisadebe 2, Ciesielski
08/04/00	Ruch Chorzow	A	2-2	og (Szuflita), og (Baszczynski)
16/04/00	Wisla Krakow	H	2-1	Bartczak, Kielbowicz
22/04/00	LKS Lodz	A	2-0	Olisadebe, Golaszewski
29/04/00	Gornik Zabrze	H	1-0	Bak
06/05/00	Zaglebie Lubin	A	1-2	Wieszczycki
14/05/00	Amica Wronki	H	4-0	Golaszewski, Olisadebe 2, Kielbowicz
20/05/00	Legia Warszawa	A	3-0	Olisadebe, Wieszczycki, Bykowski
24/05/00	Odra Wodzislaw	H	4-1	og (Matyja), Pawlak, Kielbowicz, Mikulenas
28/05/00	Petro Plock	A	1-2	Golaszewski

RUCH CHORZOW

CLUB DIRECTORY

Klub Sportowy Ruch Chorzow
Ul. Cicha 6, 41-500 Chorzow
tel - (032) 2462012/2461040
fax - (032) 2461714
website - www.ruch-chorzow.com.pl
Year of Formation - 1920
President - Krystian Rogala
Secretary - Jacek Blok
Coach - Edward Lorens
Stadium - Ruch (20,000)

MAJOR HONOURS
League Championship - (14)
1933, 1934, 1935, 1936, 1938, 1951, 1952,
1953, 1960, 1968, 1974, 1975, 1979, 1989.
Domestic Cup - (3) 1951, 1974, 1996.

APPEARANCES 99/00

	P	Ap	(s)	Gls
Dawid BARTOS	D	1	(1)	
Marcin BASZCZYNSKI	D	24		1
Krzysztof BIZACKI	A	30		14
Daniel DUBICKI	M	5	(5)	
Mamia DZIKIJA (GEO)	M	8	(6)	
Marcin FOLGA	A		(8)	1
Damian GORAWSKI	A	4	(13)	1
Robert GORSKI	M	12		
Bartlomiej JAMROZ	M	29		6
Mariusz JENDRYCZKO	D	2	(1)	
Rafal KWIECINSKI	M	12	(1)	3
Piotr LECH	G	1		
Michal LORENS	M		(12)	
Mariusz MASTERNAK	D	25		
Marek MATUSZEK	G	2	(2)	
Maciej MIZIA	M	23	(1)	4
Marcin MOLEK	M	4	(1)	
Tomasz MOSKALA	A		(2)	
Slawomir PALUCH	A	21	(2)	5
Jaroslaw POTOK	M	3	(2)	1
Krzysztof SMOLINSKI	D	2	(1)	
Lukasz SURMA	M	29		2
Tomasz SZUFLITA	D	9	(1)	
Rafal SZWED	M	2	(6)	
Mariusz SRUTWA	A	6	(5)	3
Jakub WIERZCHOWSKI	G	27		
Marek WLECIALOWSKI	D	25		
Piotr WLODARCZYK	A	24	(2)	11

LEAGUE RESULTS 1999/2000

17/07/99	Petro Plock	A	0-0	
24/07/99	Widzew Lodz	H	4-1	Wlodarczyk 2, Bizacki 2
31/07/99	Ruch Radzionkow	A	2-1	Potok, Jamroz
07/08/99	Groclin Dyskobolia Grodzisk	H	4-1	Bizacki, og (Malachowski), Mizia (p), Gorawski
14/08/99	Pogon Szczecin	A	1-1	Wlodarczyk
22/08/99	Stomil Olsztyn	H	3-0	Jamroz, Paluch, Kwiecinski
28/08/99	Polonia Warszawa	A	2-0	Mizia 2
12/09/99	Lech Poznan	A	2-1	Paluch, Bizacki
18/09/99	Wisla Krakow	H	1-1	Bizacki
25/09/99	LKS Lodz	A	2-2	Jamroz, Surma
02/10/99	Gornik Zabrze	H	2-1	Kwiecinski, Wlodarczyk
17/10/99	Zaglebie Lubin	A	0-0	
24/10/99	Amica Wronki	H	1-1	Wlodarczyk
30/10/99	Legia Warszawa	A	1-3	Kwiecinski
06/11/99	Odra Wodzislaw	H	3-1	Bizacki 2 (2p), Folga
04/03/00	Petro Plock	H	3-1	Jamroz, Bizacki 2 (1p)
12/03/00	Widzew Lodz	A	0-1	
15/03/00	Ruch Radzionkow	H	2-1	Jamroz, Srutwa (p)
18/03/00	Groclin Dyskobolia Grodzisk	A	3-0	Srutwa, Bizacki 2
25/03/00	Pogon Szczecin	H	2-2	Wlodarczyk, Jamroz
01/04/00	Stomil Olsztyn	A	0-0	
08/04/00	Polonia Warszawa	H	2-2	Bizacki 2
15/04/00	Lech Poznan	H	2-0	Wlodarczyk 2
24/04/00	Wisla Krakow	A	0-4	
29/04/00	LKS Lodz	H	3-0	Mizia, Bizacki, Baszczynski
06/05/00	Gornik Zabrze	A	2-1	Srutwa, Paluch
13/05/00	Zaglebie Lubin	H	0-2	
19/05/00	Amica Wronki	A	4-1	Paluch, Wlodarczyk 3
24/05/00	Legia Warszawa	H	0-1	
28/05/00	Odra Wodzislaw	A	2-2	Surma, Paluch

RUCH RADZIONKOW

CLUB DIRECTORY

GKS Ruch Radzionkow
Ul. Narutowicza 11
41-933 Bytom
tel - (032) 2890011 ext.5140
fax - (032) 2893261
Year of Formation - 1919
President - Pawel Bomba
Secretary - Konrad Holewa
Coach - Gothard Kokott; Piotr Piekarczyk
Stadium - Ruch (10,000)

APPEARANCES 99/00

	P	Ap	(s)	Gls
Adam BANAS	A		(1)	
Roman CEGIELKA	A	2	(15)	
Tomasz FORNALIK	M	18	(3)	1
Damian GALEJA	M	3	(3)	
Tomasz GROSMANI	D	6	(11)	1
Wojciech GRZYB	M	25	(3)	5
Marian JANOSZKA	M	12	(1)	4
Hubert JAROMIN	M	1	(1)	
Rafal JAROSZ	A	26	(1)	8
Krystian KAMPA	D	1	(1)	
Dariusz KLYTTA	G	25		
Krzysztof KOKOSZKA	M		(1)	
Krzysztof MARKOWSKI	M	2	(3)	1
Wojciech MYSZOR	M	25		3
Andrzej MYSLIWIEC	M	9		
Piotr NIKODEM	A	5	(7)	1
Rafal OPRZONDEK	D	26	(2)	1
Robert SIERKA	M	29		6
Tomasz SOBCZAK	A	10	(16)	1
Marek SZYMINSKI	D	27		
Andrzej URBANCZYK	G	5		
Ireneusz WALUS	A		(1)	
Bartlomiej WILK	M	24	(2)	
Andrzej WROBLEWSKI	D	7	(1)	
Czeslaw WRZESNIEWSKI	D	24		
Marcin WUJEK	D	1	(7)	
Jozef ZYMANCZYK	A	17	(9)	5

LEAGUE RESULTS 1999/2000

17/07/99	Stomil Olsztyn	H	0-1	
31/07/99	Ruch Chorzow	H	1-2	Janoszka
06/08/99	Wisla Krakow	A	0-2	
14/08/99	LKS Lodz	H	1-0	Oprzondek
21/08/99	Gornik Zabrze	A	0-5	
25/08/99	Polonia Warszawa	A	1-4	Sierka
28/08/99	Zaglebie Lubin	H	1-0	Janoszka
11/09/99	Amica Wronki	A	1-1	Jarosz
19/09/99	Legia Warszawa	H	1-1	Grosmani
25/09/99	Odra Wodzislaw	A	0-0	
02/10/99	Petro Plock	H	2-1	Myszor 2
17/10/99	Widzew Lodz	A	1-2	Janoszka
23/10/99	Lech Poznan	H	4-1	Janoszka, Jarosz, Grzyb 2
30/10/99	Groclin Dyskobolia Grodzisk	H	2-0	Myszor, Sierka
06/11/99	Pogon Szczecin	A	0-4	
04/03/00	Stomil Olsztyn	A	0-1	
11/03/00	Polonia Warszawa	H	0-2	
15/03/00	Ruch Chorzow	A	1-2	Jarosz
18/03/00	Wisla Krakow	H	4-1	Nikodem, Grzyb, Sierka, Zymanczyk
25/03/00	LKS Lodz	A	0-1	
01/04/00	Gornik Zabrze	H	1-0	Sierka
09/04/00	Zaglebie Lubin	A	3-3	Jarosz 2, Markowski
15/04/00	Amica Wronki	H	0-3	
22/04/00	Legia Warszawa	A	2-4	Jarosz 2
29/04/00	Odra Wodzislaw	H	2-1	Zymanczyk 2
07/05/00	Petro Plock	A	3-1	Zymanczyk, og (Popek), Grzyb
13/05/00	Widzew Lodz	H	4-1	Grzyb, Jarosz, Sierka 2
20/05/00	Lech Poznan	A	1-3	Sobczak
24/05/00	Groclin Dyskobolia Grodzisk	A	1-2	Zymanczyk
28/05/00	Pogon Szczecin	H	1-0	Fornalik

STOMIL OLSZTYN

CLUB DIRECTORY

Miejski Olsztynski Klub Sportowy Stomil Olsztyn
Ul. Pilsudskiego 69a
10-596 Olsztyn
tel - (089) 5333160
fax - (089) 5336133
website - www.moks-stomil.com.pl
Year of Formation - 1945
President - Ryszard Sosnowicz
Secretary - Leszek Dudzik
Coach - Boguslaw Kaczmarek
Stadium - Stomil (18,000)

APPEARANCES 99/00

	P	Ap	(s)	Gls
Jaroslaw BAKO	G	3		
Andrzej BIEDRZYCKI	D	30		
Maciej BYKOWSKI	A	15		3
Jacek GABRUSEWICZ	A		(3)	
Lukasz GIERMASINSKI	M		(3)	
Lukasz GORSZKOW	M	28		
Pawel HOLC	M	25	(2)	5
Andrzej JANKOWSKI	M	9	(4)	
Artur JANUSZEWSKI	D	28		1
Bartosz JURKOWSKI	D	28		7
Rafal KACZOR	G	1		
Michal KATEK	A		(7)	
Cezary KUCHARSKI	A	23	(3)	8
Marek KWIATKOWSKI	M		(7)	
Wojciech LOBODZINSKI	A		(1)	
Krzysztof MACIEJCZUK	M		(1)	
Zbigniew MALKOWSKI	G	26		
Slawomir MATUK	M	19	(2)	
Piotr MATYS	A	14	(8)	1
Piotr NAJEWSKI	A	5	(3)	
Piotr ORLINSKI	M	4	(13)	
Aidas PREIKSAITIS (LIT)	M	10		1
Tomasz RADZIWON	M	6	(10)	
Tomas RAMELIS (LIT)	A	3	(11)	3
Marcin ROGALSKI	D		(2)	
Michal STOLARZ	M	5		
Marcin SZULIK	M	29		3
Marcin WINCEL	M		(3)	
Piotr ZAJACZKOWSKI	M	19	(2)	1

LEAGUE RESULTS 1999/2000

17/07/99	Ruch Radzionkow	A	1-0	Bykowski
24/07/99	Groclin Dyskobolia Grodzisk	H	5-2	Jurkowski (p), Preiksaitis, Holc,
				Ramelis 2
31/07/99	Pogon Szczecin	A	0-3	
07/08/99	Lech Poznan	A	2-1	Bykowski, Kucharski
14/08/99	Polonia Warszawa	H	0-0	
22/08/99	Ruch Chorzow	A	0-3	
28/08/99	Wisla Krakow	H	1-1	Jurkowski (p)
11/09/99	LKS Lodz	A	1-1	Jurkowski (p)
18/09/99	Gornik Zabrze	H	1-0	Bykowski
25/09/99	Zaglebie Lubin	A	0-2	
03/10/99	Amica Wronki	H	1-1	Szulik
16/10/99	Legia Warszawa	A	0-4	
23/10/99	Odra Wodzislaw	H	2-1	Ramelis, Januszewski
30/10/99	Petro Plock	A	1-1	Jurkowski (p)
07/11/99	Widzew Lodz	H	2-2	Kucharski 2
04/03/00	Ruch Radzionkow	H	1-0	Jurkowski (p)
11/03/00	Groclin Dyskobolia Grodzisk	A	2-3	Szulik, Kucharski
15/03/00	Pogon Szczecin	H	1-1	Holc
18/03/00	Lech Poznan	H	1-1	Holc
25/03/00	Polonia Warszawa	A	0-2	
01/04/00	Ruch Chorzow	H	0-0	
08/04/00	Wisla Krakow	A	2-4	Zajaczkowski, Jurkowski (p)
15/04/00	LKS Lodz	H	1-0	Holc
22/04/00	Gornik Zabrze	A	0-1	
29/04/00	Zaglebie Lubin	H	1-1	Kucharski
07/05/00	Amica Wronki	A	1-1	Kucharski
13/05/00	Legia Warszawa	H	1-0	Matys
20/05/00	Odra Wodzislaw	A	1-3	Holc
24/05/00	Petro Plock	H	2-2	Szulik, Jurkowski (p)
28/05/00	Widzew Lodz	A	2-2	Kucharski 2

WIDZEW LODZ

CLUB DIRECTORY

Sekcja Pilki Noznej Widzew Lodz
Ul. Pilsudskiego 138, 92-230 Lodz
tel - (042) 6747218 / fax - (042) 6740175
Year of Formation - 1910
President - Andrzej Pawelec
Secretary - Andrzej Wojciechowski
Coach - Marek Dziuba; Grzegorz Lato; Orest
Lenczyk; Andrzej Pyrdol; Jan Zurek
Stadium - Widzew (20,000)

MAJOR HONOURS
League Championship - (4)
1981, 1982, 1996, 1997.
Domestic Cup - (1) 1985.

APPEARANCES 99/00

	P	Ap	(s)	Gls
Daniel BOGUSZ	D	25		3
Marek CITKO	A	11	(3)	
Dariusz DUDEK	D		(4)	
Andrius GEDGAUDAS (LIT)	M	2	(6)	
Dariusz GESIOR	M	28	(1)	8
Slawomir GULA	M	22	(4)	4
Bartosz HINC	M		(5)	
Rafal KACZMARCZYK	M	23	(2)	1
Tomasz KIELBOWICZ	M	14	(1)	2
Tomasz LAPINSKI	D	6		
Jacek MAGIERA	M	10	(4)	1
Lukasz MASLOWSKI	A		(3)	1
Marek MATUSZEK	G	10	(1)	
Radoslaw MICHALSKI	M	14		1
Andriy MIKHALCHUK (UKR)	M	2		
Piotr MOSOR	D	10	(1)	
Slawomir OLSZEWSKI	G	13		
Rafal PAWLAK	D	27	(2)	10
Szymon PINKOWSKI	A		(5)	
Robertas POSKUS (LIT)	A	9	(3)	5
Szymon RUTKA	D	3	(7)	
Michal STASIAK	D	3	(3)	
Arturas STESKO (LIT)	M	3	(9)	1
Igoris STESKO (LIT)	M	2	(1)	
Maciej STOLARCZYK	D	22		
Miroslaw SZYMKOWIAK	M	21	(3)	
Maciej TERLECKI	M	11	(2)	
Artur WICHNIAREK	A	12	(1)	6
Sergiusz WIECHOWSKI	M	1	(1)	
Andrzej WOZNIAK	G	7		
Marcin ZAJAC	M	19	(8)	5

LEAGUE RESULTS 1999/2000

21/07/99	Polonia Warszawa	H	1-1	Michalski
24/07/99	Ruch Chorzow	A	1-4	Gesior
31/07/99	Wisla Krakow	H	3-4	Gesior, Wichniarek 2 (1p)
15/08/99	Gornik Zabrze	H	1-1	Pawlak
21/08/99	Zaglebie Lubin	A	0-1	
29/08/99	Amica Wronki	H	3-2	Bogusz, Wichniarek 2 (2p)
11/09/99	Legia Warszawa	A	1-2	Zajac
19/09/99	Odra Wodzislaw	H	1-1	Gesior
25/09/99	Petro Plock	A	0-0	
03/10/99	Lech Poznan	H	2-2	Gula, Wichniarek
17/10/99	Ruch Radzionkow	H	2-1	Gesior, Wichniarek
24/10/99	Groclin Dyskobolia Grodzisk	A	0-1	
27/10/99	LKS Lodz	A	3-2	Kielbowicz 2, Zajac
30/10/99	Pogon Szczecin	H	1-2	Maslowski
07/11/99	Stomil Olsztyn	A	2-2	Bogusz, Gula
05/03/00	Polonia Warszawa	A	0-1	
12/03/00	Ruch Chorzow	H	1-0	Pawlak
15/03/00	Wisla Krakow	A	1-3	Poskus
19/03/00	LKS Lodz	H	2-0	Poskus 2
25/03/00	Gornik Zabrze	A	1-0	Pawlak
01/04/00	Zaglebie Lubin	H	2-1	Pawlak 2 (1p)
07/04/00	Amica Wronki	A	0-2	
15/04/00	Legia Warszawa	H	3-2	Zajac 2, Gesior
22/04/00	Odra Wodzislaw	A	0-2	
06/05/00	Lech Poznan	A	5-3	Bogusz, Pawlak 2, Gula 2
13/05/00	Ruch Radzionkow	A	1-4	Poskus
17/05/00	Petro Plock	H	4-3	Magiera, Kaczmarczyk, Gesior, Stesko A.
20/05/00	Groclin Dyskobolia Grodzisk	H	2-3	Pawlak 2
24/05/00	Pogon Szczecin	A	3-2	Gesior, Poskus, Pawlak
28/05/00	Stomil Olsztyn	H	2-2	Zajac, Gesior

WISLA KRAKOW

CLUB DIRECTORY

ASPN Wisla Krakow
Ul. Reymonta 22, 30-059 Krakow
tel - (012) 6377120 / fax - (012) 6307692
website - www.wisla.krakow.pl
Year of Formation - 1906
President - Stanislaw Zietek
Secretary - Zdzislaw Kapka
Coach - Franciszek Smuda; Jerzy Kowalik;
Marek Kusto; Wojciech Lazarek; Adam Nawalka
Stadium - Wisla (15,000)

MAJOR HONOURS
League Championship - (6)
1927, 1928, 1949, 1950, 1978, 1999.
Domestic Cup - (2) 1926, 1967.

APPEARANCES 99/00

	P	Ap	(s)	Gls
Cristiano de Souza				
BRASÍLIA (BRA)	A	9	(14)	2
Krzysztof BUKALSKI	M		(1)	
Ryszard CZERWIEC	M	21	(5)	2
Valdeci José da Silva DECI (BRA)	D		(2)	
Daniel DUBICKI	M		(4)	
Tomasz FRANKOWSKI	A	23	(3)	17
Arkadiusz GLOWACKI	D	5	(1)	2
Kelechi Zeal IHEANACHO (NIG)	A	1	(3)	
Mariusz JOP	D	4	(9)	2
Grzegorz KALICIAK	M	7	(8)	
radoslaw KALUZNY	D	27		4
Kamil KOSOWSKI	M	14	(5)	1
Tomasz KULAWIK	M	27	(1)	3
Grzegorz LEKKI	D	12		
Kazimierz MOSKAL	M	12	(5)	2
Olgierd MOSKALEWICZ	A	24	(4)	7
Grzegorz NICINSKI	A	1	(6)	
Slawomir PALUCH	A	4		2
Grzegorz PATER	M	25	(3)	2
Adam PIEKUTOWSKI	G	6		
Artur SARNAT	G	24		
Ibrahim SUNDAY (NIG)	M	3	(2)	
Pawel WEINAR	M		(2)	
Kazimierz WEGRZYN	D	25		4
Karol WOJCIK	A		(1)	
Bogdan ZAJAC	D	13		
Marek ZAJAC	D	27	(1)	6
Maciej ZURAWSKI	A	16	(4)	6

LEAGUE RESULTS 1999/2000

18/07/99	Odra Wodzislaw	A	3-0	Frankowski, Czerwiec, Paluch
25/07/99	Petro Plock	H	3-1	Frankowski, Moskalewicz, Paluch
31/07/99	Widzew Lodz	A	4-3	Zajac M., Moskalewicz, Frankowski 2
06/08/99	Ruch Radzionkow	H	2-0	Zajac M., Frankowski
14/08/99	Groclin Dyskobolia Grodzisk	A	2-1	Moskalewicz, Zajac M.
22/08/99	Pogon Szczecin	H	1-1	Moskalewicz
28/08/99	Stomil Olsztyn	A	1-1	Jop
12/09/99	Polonia Warszawa	H	2-3	Wegrzyn, Moskalewicz
18/09/99	Ruch Chorzow	A	1-1	Pater
26/09/99	Lech Poznan	A	1-4	Frankowski
02/10/99	LKS Lodz	H	1-0	Czerwiec
16/10/99	Gornik Zabrze	A	0-1	
24/10/99	Zaglebie Lubin	H	4-0	Brasília, Moskal, Kulawik, Jop
30/10/99	Amica Wronki	A	0-0	
07/11/99	Legia Warszawa	H	1-1	Kaluzny
04/03/00	Odra Wodzislaw	H	3-1	Frankowski, Zurawski, Pater
12/03/00	Petro Plock	A	1-1	Frankowski
15/03/00	Widzew Lodz	H	3-1	Frankowski, Zajac, Zurawski
18/03/00	Ruch Radzionkow	A	1-4	og (Grzyb)
25/03/00	Groclin Dyskobolia Grodzisk	H	3-0	Wegrzyn, Brasília, Zajac M.
01/04/00	Pogon Szczecin	A	3-3	Moskalewicz, Kaluzny, Frankowski
08/04/00	Stomil Olsztyn	H	4-2	Moskalewicz, Kaluzny, Zurawski 2
16/04/00	Polonia Warszawa	A	1-2	og (Bak)
22/04/00	Ruch Chorzow	H	4-0	Wegrzyn 2, Zurawski (p), Kulawik
29/04/00	Lech Poznan	H	2-0	Kulawik, Zajac M.
06/05/00	LKS Lodz	A	2-0	Moskal, Glowacki
14/05/00	Gornik Zabrze	H	6-3	Frankowski 4, Glowacki, Zurawski
20/05/00	Zaglebie Lubin	A	2-3	Frankowski, Kosowski
24/05/00	Amica Wronki	H	1-1	Kaluzny
28/05/00	Legia Warszawa	A	2-0	Frankowski 2

ZAGLEBIE LUBIN

CLUB DIRECTORY

Miedzyzakladowy Klub Sportowy Zaglebie Lubin
Ul. Marii Sklodowskiej-Curie 98
59-301 Lubin
tel - (076) 8478550
fax - (076) 8478565
Year of Formation - 1946
President - Jacek Kordela
Secretary - Michal Lulek
Coach - Miroslaw Jablonski
Stadium - Zaglebie (32,000)

MAJOR HONOURS
League Championship - (1) 1991.

APPEARANCES 99/00

	P	Ap	(s)	Gls
Marcin ADAMSKI	M	20	(1)	
Robert BUBNOWICZ	D	17		1
Edward CECOT	D	4		
Daniel DUBICKI	M	11	(2)	5
Wojciech GORSKI	M	2	(2)	
Zbigniew GRZYBOWSKI	M	25	(2)	4
Radoslaw JASINSKI	A	16	(4)	2
Krzysztof KAZIMIERCZAK	M		(2)	
Jedrzej KEDZIORA	G	5	(1)	
Arkadiusz KLIMEK	A	5	(3)	3
Krzysztof KLOSINSKI	M		(4)	
Ireneusz KOWALSKI	M	17	(9)	2
Jaroslaw KRZYZANOWSKI	M	18	(6)	
Mariusz LEWANDOWSKI	D	1	(2)	
Boguslaw LIZAK	M		(7)	1
Rafal MAJKA	M	23	(5)	3
Jacek MANUSZEWSKI	M	23	(5)	3
Robert MIODUSZEWSKI	G	25		
Moses MOLONGO (CMR)	A	7	(3)	2
Emil NOWAKOWSKI	M		(3)	
Maciej NUCKOWSKI	M	9	(6)	2
Wojciech OLSZOWIAK	M		(3)	
Pawel PASIK	M	9	(12)	2
Pawel PIOTROWSKI	M	2	(2)	
Jerzy PODBROZNY	A	13		7
Piotr PRZERYWACZ	D	26	(1)	
Jakub PUCHALSKI	M	4		
Andrzej SZCZYPKOWSKI	M	21		
Dariusz ZURAW	D	27	(1)	5

LEAGUE RESULTS 1999/2000

17/07/99	Lech Poznan	H	2-1	Molongo, Grzybowski
24/07/99	Amica Wronki	H	2-2	Kowalski, Molongo
31/07/99	Legia Warszawa	A	2-2	Nuckowski, Jasinski (p)
07/08/99	Odra Wodzislaw	H	1-0	Bubnowicz
14/08/99	Petro Plock	A	1-2	Pasik
21/08/99	Widzew Lodz	H	1-0	Jasinski
28/08/99	Ruch Radzionkow	A	0-1	
11/09/99	Groclin Dyskobolia Grodzisk	H	1-0	Majka
18/09/99	Pogon Szczecin	A	0-1	
25/09/99	Stomil Olsztyn	H	2-0	Nuckowski, Zuraw
02/10/99	Polonia Warszawa	A	1-1	Manuszewski
17/10/99	Ruch Chorzow	H	0-0	
24/10/99	Wisla Krakow	A	0-4	
31/10/99	LKS Lodz	H	1-0	Manuszewski
05/11/99	Gornik Zabrze	A	0-0	
05/03/00	Lech Poznan	A	0-2	
12/03/00	Amica Wronki	A	1-1	Podbrozny (p)
15/03/00	Legia Warszawa	H	2-3	Dubicki, Kowalski
18/03/00	Odra Wodzislaw	A	1-1	Dubicki
26/03/00	Petro Plock	H	5-0	Majka, Dubicki, Podbrozny 2, Zuraw
01/04/00	Widzew Lodz	A	1-2	Dubicki
09/04/00	Ruch Radzionkow	H	3-3	Grzybowski, Podbrozny 2
16/04/00	Groclin Dyskobolia Grodzisk	A	0-1	
21/04/00	Pogon Szczecin	H	3-1	Dubicki, Zuraw 2
29/04/00	Stomil Olsztyn	A	1-1	Manuszewski
06/05/00	Polonia Warszawa	H	2-1	Grzybowski, Pasik
13/05/00	Ruch Chorzow	A	2-0	Klimek, Lizak
20/05/00	Wisla Krakow	H	3-2	Klimek, Podbrozny (p), Grzybowski
24/05/00	LKS Lodz	A	2-4	Zuraw, Majka
28/05/00	Gornik Zabrze	H	2-1	Klimek, Podbrozny

PORTUGAL

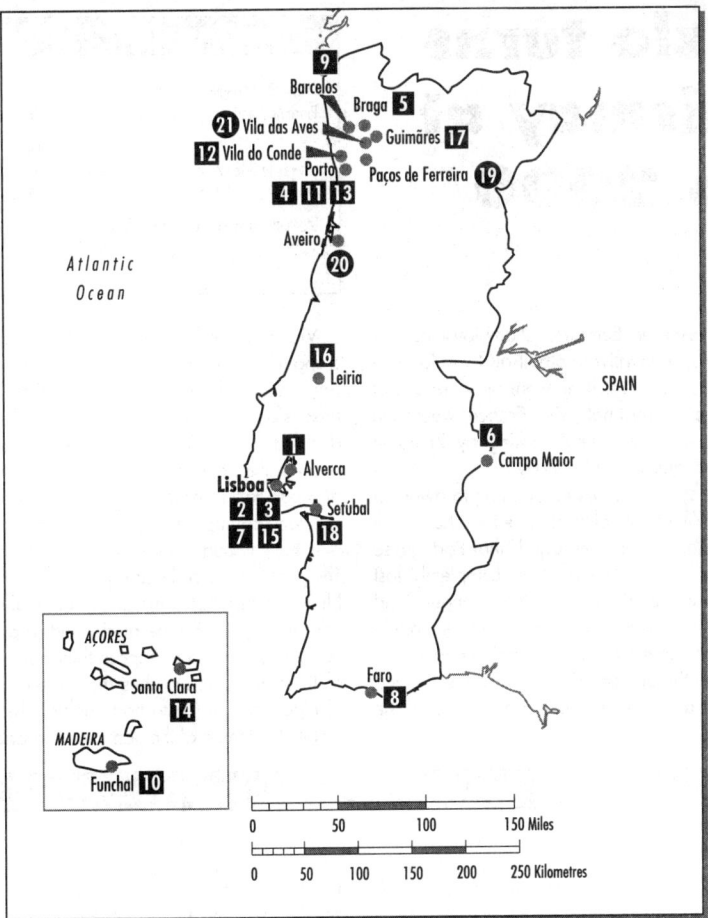

LONG WAIT OVER FOR SPORTING

Dazzle turns to dismay at Euro 2000

FEDERATION DIRECTORY

Federação Portuguesa de Futebol
Praça de Alegria 25, Caixa postal 21 100, 1128 Lisboa Codex

tel - (21) 3428207   Year of Formation - 1914
fax - (21) 3467231   President - Gilberto Madail
website - www.fpf.pt   Secretary - António Sequeira

Stadium - National, Lisboa (51,000)

Portugal had an excellent European Championship. They played attractive, innovative football and would have made worthy winners. Yet it all went up in smoke at the end of their semi-final with France when the 'golden generation' were sent packing by Zinedine Zidane's hugely controversial penalty.

The decision by the Slovakian linesman to award a penalty in the 27th minute of extra-time for a hand-ball by full-back Abel Xavier enraged the Portuguese players so much that some of them completely lost their professional cool. Whilst their anger and frustration was understandable - they were on the brink, possibly, of reaching the first major final in Portuguese football history - the unfettered fury which they vented at the officials was extremely unpleasant and over the top.

Video replays showed that the decision to award a spot-kick was in fact correct, although at the time, in fairness, it did seem very harsh. Either way, it was an unsatisfactory way for such an important match to be decided. The irony was that Abel Xavier might so easily have been the hero, rather than the villain, half an hour earlier had his 90th-minute header not been spectacularly tipped over by Fabien Barthez.

In truth, Portugal were not at their best in the semi-final. The goal they scored was a piece of individual magic by Nuno Gomes that came almost out of the blue. Denied time and space by the disciplined, organised French, Portugal struggled to impose their authority. In all four of their previous matches the masterful midfield play of Figo and Rui Costa had enabled the Portuguese to dictate the tempo of the game, and invariably they were

LEAGUE CHAMPIONSHIP RESULTS 99/00

		1	2	3	4	5	6	7	8	9	10	11	12	13	14	15	16	17	18
1	FC Alverca		1-1	3-1	1-0	3-2	1-0	0-1	0-1	4-2	1-1	1-1	3-1	2-0	0-1	2-1	0-0	2-1	0-1
2	CF Os Belenenses	4-2		0-0	1-1	0-3	2-2	1-1	1-1	1-1	1-1	0-0	2-1	2-1	3-1	0-1	1-0	2-0	0-1
3	SL Benfica	3-2	2-3		1-1	2-1	2-0	2-0	6-2	3-0	2-1	1-0	1-0	1-0	1-0	0-0	3-2	3-0	3-0
4	Boavista FC	2-0	1-0	1-1		2-2	2-1	1-2	2-1	2-0	0-2	1-1	2-0	2-1	2-1	0-1	0-1	2-0	1-0
5	SC Braga	3-1	0-0	3-2	1-0		4-1	0-1	1-0	0-0	1-2	0-1	0-1	2-0	3-1	0-2	0-2	2-4	3-0
6	SC Campomaiorense	0-0	2-1	2-4	0-1	2-4		2-1	1-0	0-0	1-0	1-0	1-1	0-1	1-0	0-2	2-0	2-1	0-1
7	CF Estrela Amadora	3-0	0-3	3-0	1-2	3-3	3-0		1-1	0-1	1-1	0-2	1-0	1-0	0-0	0-0	1-1	2-2	3-0
8	SC Farense	1-2	2-1	0-1	0-2	1-1	2-2	1-1		0-3	1-0	3-3	4-0	3-2	2-2	0-3	2-1	2-1	0-0
9	Gil Vicente FC	2-2	1-1	0-2	1-3	0-0	3-0	2-2	4-0		5-1	2-1	4-0	2-0	3-1	1-1	2-0	1-0	2-0
10	CS Marítimo	3-0	0-0	0-0	1-1	1-0	1-0	2-2	3-0	1-0		2-1	5-2	0-1	0-0	0-2	0-0	1-1	1-0
11	FC Porto	0-0	2-1	2-0	1-0	3-0	2-0	2-1	5-0	2-0	3-2		4-1	2-0	1-0	3-0	4-2	2-1	4-1
12	Rio Ave FC	2-0	3-0	1-1	2-1	2-0	1-0	0-1	1-1	3-1	0-2	2-2		4-1	0-5	1-2	0-0	1-1	1-1
13	SC Salgueiros	0-2	0-0	1-2	1-3	1-1	2-1	1-1	0-0	1-2	1-0	0-4	1-1		2-0	0-4	3-0	0-1	1-0
14	CD Santa Clara	4-3	1-0	0-3	0-1	1-2	2-2	1-1	1-2	0-0	0-0	0-2	1-0	0-0		2-2	1-1	3-2	2-1
15	Sporting CP	1-1	1-0	0-1	2-0	2-0	1-0	1-1	3-1	1-1	4-2	2-0	2-1	2-0	4-1		2-0	1-0	2-1
16	União Leiria	3-0	1-0	2-1	0-0	3-0	1-2	1-1	2-0	1-1	0-1	0-1	0-0	1-4	3-2	1-1		1-0	0-0
17	Vitória Guimarães	1-0	4-2	2-1	2-0	1-0	4-1	1-0	3-0	1-0	1-3	1-1	2-1	2-2	2-1	1-2	0-1		4-0
18	Vitória Setúbal	1-0	0-2	1-2	2-1	0-2	1-2	1-0	1-1	0-1	4-2	1-4	2-0	1-2	1-0	1-2	0-0	1-1	

LEAGUE CHAMPIONSHIP FINAL TABLE 99/00

		Pd	Home W	D	L	F	A	Away W	D	L	F	A	Total W	D	L	F	A	PT	GD
1	Sporting CP	34	13	3	1	31	10	10	5	2	26	12	23	8	3	57	22	77	35
2	FC Porto	34	16	1	0	42	9	6	6	5	24	17	22	7	5	66	26	73	40
3	SL Benfica	34	14	2	1	36	12	7	4	6	22	21	21	6	7	58	33	69	25
4	Boavista FC	34	10	3	4	23	14	6	4	7	17	17	16	7	11	40	31	55	9
5	Gil Vicente FC	34	10	5	2	35	14	4	6	7	13	20	14	11	9	48	34	53	14
6	CS Marítimo	34	8	7	2	21	10	5	4	8	21	26	13	11	10	42	36	50	6
7	Vitória Guimarães	34	12	2	3	32	15	2	4	11	16	28	14	6	14	48	43	48	5
8	CF Estrela Amadora	34	6	7	4	23	16	4	8	5	17	19	10	15	9	40	35	45	5
9	SC Braga	34	8	2	7	23	18	4	5	8	21	27	12	7	15	44	45	43	-1
10	União Leiria	34	7	6	4	20	14	3	6	8	11	21	10	12	12	31	35	42	-4
11	FC Alverca	34	9	4	4	24	15	2	4	11	15	33	11	8	15	39	48	41	-9
12	CF Os Belenenses	34	6	8	3	21	17	3	5	9	15	21	9	13	12	36	38	40	-2
13	SC Campomaiorense	34	8	3	6	17	17	2	3	12	14	34	10	6	18	31	51	36	-20
14	SC Farense	34	6	6	5	24	25	2	5	10	11	35	8	11	15	35	60	35	-25
15	SC Salgueiros	34	5	5	7	15	22	4	2	11	15	27	9	7	18	30	49	34	-19
16	Vitória Setúbal	34	6	3	8	18	22	3	3	11	7	27	9	6	19	25	49	33	-24
17	Rio Ave FC	34	7	6	4	24	19	1	3	13	10	35	8	9	17	34	54	33	-20
18	CD Santa Clara	34	5	7	5	19	22	2	3	12	16	28	7	10	17	35	50	31	-15

N.B. Where two or more teams are level on points, classification is determined by the results of the matches between them.

a joy to watch. England, Germany and Turkey were all well beaten, and although Romania proved a touch more resilient, even they ended up on the losing side when Costinha headed in the winner deep into stoppage-time. The comeback from 0-2 down against England, spiced with three glorious goals, was arguably Portugal's most accomplished performance but the 3-0 win against Germany, fashioned by a superb hat-trick from Sérgio Conceição, was the most impressive result - especially as coach Humberto Coelho fielded a near-reserve side. The quarter-final, against Turkey, was something of a rout, and the meagre 2-0

TOP SCORERS

38	Mário JARDEL (FC Porto)
22	Alberto ACOSTA (Sporting CP)
21	GAÚCHO I (CF Estrela Amadora)
18	NUNO GOMES (SL Benfica)
16	BRANDÃO (Vitória Guimarães)
13	TOEDTLI (CS Marítimo)
12	HUGO HENRIQUE (Rio Ave FC)
11	Lucian MARINESCU (SC Farense)
	WHELLITON (Boavista FC)
10	MANICHE (SL Benfica)
	ODAIR (SC Braga)
	EDMILSON (Vitória Guimarães)

NATIONAL TEAM RESULTS 99/00

18/08/99	Andorra	H	Lisbon	4-0	Rui Costa (18), João Pinto (36), Figo (45), Pauleta (68)
04/09/99	Azerbaijan (ECQ)	A	Baku	1-1	Figo (90)
08/09/99	Romania (ECQ)	A	Bucharest	1-1	Figo (45)
09/10/99	Hungary (ECQ)	H	Lisbon	3-0	Rui Costa (14p), João Pinto (16), Abel Xavier (57)
23/02/00	Belgium	A	Charleroi	1-1	Sá Pinto (80)
29/03/00	Denmark	H	Leiria	2-1	Rui Costa (41p), Figo (50)
26/04/00	Italy	A	Reggio di Calabria	0-2	
02/06/00	Wales	H	Chaves	3-0	Figo (21), Sá Pinto (44), Capucho (66)
12/06/00	England (ECF)	N	Eindhoven	3-2	Figo (22), João Pinto (38), Nuno Gomes (60)
17/06/00	Romania (ECF)	N	Arnhem	1-0	Costinha (90)
20/06/00	Germany (ECF)	N	Rotterdam	3-0	Sérgio Conceição (35, 54, 71)
24/06/00	Turkey (ECF)	N	Amsterdam	2-0	Nuno Gomes (44, 56)
28/06/00	France (ECF)	N	Brussels	1-2	Nuno Gomes (19)

EUROPEAN CUPS 99/00

CHAMPIONS' CUP
● BOAVISTA FC
Qualifying round BRØNDBY IF (DEN)
A 2-1 Mário Silva (24), Moreira (73)
Andem, Paulo Sousa, Litos, Pedro Emanuel, Mário Silva (Moreira 63), Rui Bento, Luís Manuel (Emanuel 45), Timofte, Jorge Couto, Ahinful (Gilmar 74), Quevedo.
H 4-2 (aet) Litos (12), Ahinful (99, 109), Rui Bento (116)
Andem, Paulo Sousa, Litos, Pedro Emanuel, Mário Silva, Rui Bento, Luís Manuel, Timofte (Jorge Silva 70), Moreira (Jorge Couto 54), Gilmar (Whelliton 81), Ahinful.

Champions' League
1st match ROSENBORG BK (NOR)
H 0-3
Andem, Paulo Sousa, Litos, Pedro Emanuel, Mário Silva, Luís Manuel (Emanuel 46), Rui Bento, Timofte (Formoso 9), Jorge Couto, Ahinful, Gilmar (Whelliton 54).

2nd match BORUSSIA DORTMUND (GER)
A 1-3 Rui Bento (45)
Andem, Paulo Sousa, Litos, Pedro Emanuel, Mário Silva, Jorge Silva, Rui Bento, Luís Manuel (Formoso 44), César, Ahinful (Gilmar 71), Rogério.

3rd match FEYENOORD (HOL)
H 1-1 Mário Silva (85)
Andem, Paulo Sousa, Litos, Pedro Emanuel, Mário Silva, Rui Bento, Jorge Silva, Jorge Couto, Emanuel (Formoso 77), Ahinful (Douala 66), César (Gilmar 46).

4th match FEYENOORD (HOL)
A 1-1 Timofte (82p)
Ricardo Pereira, Paulo Sousa, Litos, Jorge Silva, Pedro Emanuel, Rui Bento, Timofte (Rogério 89), Luís Manuel (Sérgio 74), Emanuel, Jorge Couto, Ahinful (Martelinho 74).

5th match ROSENBORG BK (NOR)
A 0-2
Ricardo Pereira, Paulo Sousa, Rui Bento, Pedro Emanuel, Litos, Timofte, Luís Manuel (Ahinful 71), Jorge Silva, Nilton, Jorge Couto, Whelliton (Gilmar 83).

6th match BORUSSIA DORTMUND (GER)
H 1-0 Pedro Emanuel (16)
Ricardo Pereira, Paulo Sousa, Litos, Jorge Silva, Pedro Emanuel, Sérgio Carvalho, Nilton, Emanuel, Luís Manuel (Carlos Alberto 90), Douala (Ricardo Silva 68), Whelliton (Rogério 61).

● FC PORTO
Champions' League
1st match MOLDE FK (NOR)
A 1-0 Deco (88)
Vítor Baía, Jorge Costa, Argel, Peixe (Paulinho Santos 81), Secretário, Drulovic (Aloísio 88), Deco, Capucho (Alessandro 53), Esquerdinha, Chainho, Jardel.

2nd match OLYMPIAKOS (GRE)
H 2-0 Esquerdinha (6), Jardel (46)
Vítor Baía, Secretário, Jorge Costa, Argel, Esquerdinha, Peixe, Deco (Aloísio 88), Chainho (Rui Barros 75), Capucho (Alessandro 61), Drulovic, Jardel.

3rd match REAL MADRID (ESP)
A 1-3 Jardel (28)
Vítor Baía, Secretário, Jorge Costa, Argel, Esquerdinha, Peixe, Chainho (Rubens Júnior 57), Capucho (Alessandro 50; Féher 87), Deco, Drulovic, Jardel.

4th match REAL MADRID (ESP)
H 2-1 Jardel (12, 34)
Vítor Baía, Jorge Costa, Rubens Júnior (Drulovic 35), Argel (Aloísio 74), Secretário, Peixe, Esquerdinha, Chainho, Deco, Capucho (Paulinho Santos 71), Jardel.

5th match MOLDE FK (NOR)
H 3-1 Deco (1, 28), Jardel (58)
Vítor Baía, Secretário, Jorge Costa, Aloísio, Esquerdinha, Peixe, Deco (Alessandro 28), Chainho (Ricardo Sousa 69), Drulovic, Capucho, Jardel (Domingos 75).

6th match OLYMPIAKOS (GRE)
A 0-1
Hilário, Rubens Júnior, Aloísio, Secretário, Ricardo Silva, Ricardo Sousa (Féher 62), Rodolfo (Chainho 62), Alessandro, Paulinho Santos, Drulovic, Romeu (Duda 71).

7th match SPARTA PRAHA (CZE)
A 2-0 Drulovic (76), Jardel (83)
Vítor Baía, Secretário, Aloísio, Jorge Costa, Esquerdinha, Paulinho Santos, Chainho (Domingos 88), Deco, Rubens Júnior (Drulovic 72), Capucho, Jardel (Argel 86).

8th match HERTHA BSC BERLIN (GER)
H 1-0 Drulovic (77)
Vítor Baía (Hilário 73), Secretário, Jorge Costa, Aloísio, Esquerdinha, Paulinho Santos, Deco, Chainho, Rubens Júnior (Drulovic 55), Capucho, Jardel (Ricardo Silva 90).

9th match FC BARCELONA (ESP)
A 2-4 Jardel (4, 79)
Hilário, Secretário, Aloísio, Peixe (Alessandro 73), Esquerdinha, Jorge Costa, Rui Barros (Domingos 38), Chainho, Capucho (Clayton 73), Drulovic, Jardel.

10th match FC BARCELONA (ESP)
H 0-2
Hilario, Secretário, Aloísio, Ricardo Silva, Esquerdinha, Paulinho Santos (Clayton 64), Peixe (Chainho 45), Rubens Júnior (Domingos 43), Drulovic, Capucho, Jardel.

11th match SPARTA PRAHA (CZE)
H 2-2 Jorge Costa (16), Capucho (64)
Vítor Baía, Jorge Costa, Secretário, Esquerdinha, Ricardo Silva, Domingos (Paulinho Santos 88), Drulovic, Chainho (Peixe 52), Capucho (Rui Barros 81), Deco, Jardel.

12th match HERTHA BSC BERLIN (GER)
A 1-0 Clayton (70)
Vítor Baía, Jorge Costa, Aloísio, Secretário, Esquerdinha, Drulovic (Clayton 68), Jardel, Chainho, Paulinho Santos, Capucho (Alessandro 76), Deco (Peixe 89).

EUROPEAN CUPS 99/00 (CONTINUED)

Quarter-final FC BAYERN MÜNCHEN (GER)
H 1-1 Jardel (46)
Hilário, Nélson, Jorge Costa, Aloísio, Esquerdinha, Paulinho Santos, Deco, Chainho (Domingos 83), Capucho (Clayton 72), Jardel, Drulovic.
A 1-2 Jardel (89)
Hilário, Nélson, Jorge Costa, Aloísio, Esquerdinha, Paulinho Santos, Chainho (Rui Barros 43; Domingos 76), Deco (Clayton 60), Drulovic, Capucho, Jardel.

UEFA CUP

● **SC BEIRA MAR**
1st round VITESSE (HOL)
H 1-2 Fary (41)
Palatsi, Gila, Lobão, Cristiano, Fernando Aguiar, Fary, Marques (João Paulo 84), Fusco, Paulo Sérgio (Rui Dolores 67), Vítor Silva, Konadu (Óscar 79).
A 0-0
Palatsi, Gila, Lobão, Cristiano, Fernando Aguiar, João Paulo (Óscar 71; Marques 90), Fary (Rui Dolores 71), Fusco, Paulo Sérgio, Vítor Silva, Konadu.

● **SL BENFICA**
1st round DINAMO BUCURESTI (ROM)
H 0-1
Enke, Tahar (Sérgio Nunes 44), Paulo Madeira, Ronaldo, Rojas, Calado, Chano (Maniche 66), Bruno Basto (Tote 66), Poborsky, João Pinto, Nuno Gomes.
A 2-0 Maniche (24), Chano (71)
Enke, Okunowo, Paulo Madeira, Ronaldo, Rojas, Poborsky (Chano 70), Calado, Kandaurov (Sérgio Nunes 60), Maniche, João Pinto, Nuno Gomes (Bruno Basto 87).

2nd round PAOK (GRE)
A 2-1 Nuno Gomes (67), Ronaldo (89)
Enke, Okunowo (Andrade 46), Paulo Madeira, Ronaldo, Sérgio Nunes, Calado, Kandaurov, Poborsky (Bruno Basto 46), Maniche, João Pinto (Chano 64), Nuno Gomes.

H 1-2 (aet; 4-1 on pens.) Kandaurov (25)
Enke, Andrade (Tahar 85), Paulo Madeira, Ronaldo, Rojas, Calado, Kandaurov, Poborsky (Chano 72), João Pinto, Nuno Gomes, Bruno Basto (Maniche 62).

3rd round RC CELTA (ESP)
A 0-7
Enke, Andrade, Paulo Madeira, Ronaldo, Rojas (Bruno Basto 54), Calado (Chano 63), Poborsky, Maniche, Kandaurov (Tahar 45), João Pinto, Nuno Gomes.
H 1-1 Cáceres (79og)
Enke, Andrade, José Soares, Sérgio Carvalho, Rojas, Poborsky (Maniche 57), Calado (Porfírio 46), Chano, Marco Freitas, Cadete (Tote 69), Luís Carlos.

● **SPORTING CP**
1st round VIKING FK (NOR)
A 0-3
Schmeichel, Quiroga, Beto, Marcos, Vinicius (Rui Jorge 17), Delfim, Duscher, Toñito, Pedro Barbosa (Hanuch 58), Ayew, Edmilson (Acosta 75).
H 1-0 Ayew (75p)
Schmeichel, Saber, Beto, Marcos, Quim Berto, Delfim, Duscher, Toñito (Yordanov 35), Edmilson (Hanuch 61), Pedro Barbosa (Acosta 70), Ayew.

● **VITÓRIA SETÚBAL**
1st round ROMA (ITA)
A 0-7
Marco Tábuas, Paulo Filipe, Quim, Mário Loja, Pedro Henriques, Hélio, Mamede, Frechaut (Pedro Mendes 75), Semedo (Chipenda 46), Sérgio João (Maki 46), Chiquinho Conde.
H 1-0 Maki (77)
Brassard, Paulo Filipe, Mário Loja, Quim, Pedro Henriques, Frechaut, Mamede, Hélio, Jorge Matos (Maki 62), Marco Ferreira, Chiquinho Conde.

---

scoreline did scant justice to the massive superiority of a team playing at the peak of their form... except in front of goal.

Portugal's chief strength was the technical excellence of their midfielders, chief among them the wonderful Figo, who lived up to all the pre-tournament hype, and then some. The defence also performed well, with Fernando Couto and Jorge Costa forming a solid, unflappable central pairing and Vítor Baía putting his injury worries behind him in goal. Up front, Portugal finally found a goalscorer worthy of the name in Nuno Gomes, whose four goals were all of a high calibre and all hugely significant within the context of the match.

Praise was also merited by coach Humberto who played to the team's individual strengths by opting for a customised 4-2-3-1 formation, which provided for security in defence as well as the freedom for his creative players to express themselves in attack. It was a surprise

and a disappointment that Humberto announced his decision to resign after the team's chaotic semi-final exit. He was clearly emotionally troubled by the manner of his team's elimination and made a spot decision, but no amount of subsequent encouragement and sympathy could persuade him to go back on his word.

Appointed in his stead was António Oliveira, the man who led Portugal to the quarter-finals of Euro '96. His mission now is to take the team to the finals of the World Cup for the first time in 16 years. It would be unthinkable for Portugal's 'golden generation' to miss out entirely on the World Cup experience, but this is their last chance to rectify that. The final bow for Figo, Rui Costa, Fernando Couto, João Pinto and the rest will probably come in 2004 when Portugal host the next European Championship finals. But by then the team will undoubtedly need to have welcomed in some fresh faces if they are to remain as competitive as they were in the Low Countries. A side full of thirtysomethings never won anything...

The national team still seek to end their World Cup jinx, but one other hoodoo was finally quashed in 1999/2000 when Sporting, of Lisbon, were crowned champions of Portugal for the first time in 18 long years.

The frustration endured for so long by Sporting's large and loyal support ended at last on Sunday, May 14, 2000 when the team won their last match of the season 4-0 at Salgueiros. Sporting went into the match with a one-point lead over FC Porto, the champions for the previous five years, and they made sure of their triumph in convincing style, even if it was two minutes into the second half before the first of those four goals went in.

Sporting might have wrapped up the title a week earlier. The setting had been perfect - a home game against arch-foes Benfica, with victory required to end all the seasons of misery and clinch the championship. But a packed Alvalade stadium was to suffer one more night of immense frustration as Benfica stole the game with an 89th-minute winner. That slip-up meant that the Portuguese title was to be decided on the final weekend for the first time in 20 years. Mercifully, Sporting did not blow it again, but even if they had lost at Salgueiros, it would not have mattered because Porto went down 2-1 at Gil Vicente anyway.

It had been an intriguing season, with all of the country's 'big three' harbouring genuine title hopes at one stage or another. It was Benfica who made the best start. Newly coached by German Jupp Heynckes, the man who

NATIONAL TEAM APPEARANCES 99/00

Coach - HUMBERTO COELHO	AND	AZB	ROM	HUN	BEL	DEN	ITA	WAL	ENG	ROM	GER	TUR	FRA	Cps	Gls
VÍTOR BAÍA (15/10/69) - FC Porto	G46	G	G	G				G	G	G		G	G	74	-
SECRETÁRIO (12/05/70) - FC Porto	D	D		D46	D		D59				D			31	1
PAULO MADEIRA (06/09/70) - SL Benfica	D66	D	D	D										24	3
JORGE COSTA (04/10/71) - FC Porto	D70				D		D	D	D	D	D	D	D	32	-
DIMAS (16/02/69) - Fenerbahçe (TUR)	D	D	D	D	D80	D	D	D68	D	D	D		D91	39	-
FIGO (04/11/72) - FC Barcelona (ESP)	M46	M	M	M	M84	M63	M	M59	M	M		M	M	65	15
PAULO BENTO (20/06/69) - Real Oviedo (ESP)	M	M30	M	s84	M13		M89	M	M	M		M	s60	26	-
PAULO SOUSA (30/08/70) - Inter (ITA)	M46	M67	M69	M			M				M71	s46		46	-
RUI COSTA (29/03/72) - Fiorentina (ITA)	M	M	M	M84	M63	M75	M70	M	M84	M87		M87	M76	56	18
JOÃO PINTO (19/08/71) - SL Benfica	A54	A	A80	A89	A57	s63	s70	A77	M75	M56		M	s76	62	19
SÁ PINTO (10/10/72) - Real Sociedad (ESP)	A60	A46	A	s89	s63	s46	s59	A62		s56		A	s74	40	9
QUIM (13/11/75) - SC Braga	s46						G				s89			3	-
SÉRGIO CONCEIÇÃO (15/11/74) - Lazio (ITA)	s46	s46	s69	M	s57	M89	M	s46	s75	s56	M	D	M	29	5
PAULETA (28/04/73) - RC Deportivo (ESP)	s46	s30	s80	A		s46	A59	s77			A66			14	3
CAPUCHO (21/02/72) - FC Porto	s54	s67			s84		s59	s90			M	s87		17	2
NUNO GOMES (05/07/76) - SL Benfica	s60				A	A46	s89	s62	A90	A56	s66	A74	A	17	4
BETO (03/05/76) - Sporting CP	s66				s13	D		s84			D			8	-
LITOS (25/02/74) - Boavista FC	s70													2	-
FERNANDO COUTO (02/08/69) - Lazio (ITA)		D	D		D70	D	D	D	D	D	D	D	D	68	6
RUI BENTO (14/01/72) - Boavista FC		D		D										5	-
ABEL XAVIER (30/11/72) - Everton (ENG)					s46		D	D	D				D	15	2
PEDRO ESPINHA (25/09/65) - Vitória Guimarães					G	G					G89			5	-
VIDIGAL (15/03/73) - Sporting CP					M	M	M46	M	M		s71		M60	7	-
DANI (02/11/76) - Ajax (HOL)					s70	s46								9	-
RUI JORGE (27/03/73) - Sporting CP					s80	s89	s68				D		s91	7	-
COSTINHA (01/12/74) - AS Monaco (FRA)						s75			s59	s87	M	M46	M	7	1

PLAYERS OF THE SEASON

FIGO
Luís Filipe Madeira Caeiro, aka Figo (pictured above), is now the world's most expensive footballer. His shock £37m move from Barcelona to Real Madrid during the summer eclipsed the fee paid by Lazio to Parma for Hernán Crespo a couple of weeks earlier. It is impossible to evaluate whether a footballer is worth such an exorbitant fee but the depth of the dismay felt by the Barça fans at the loss of their captain to the

arch-enemy proved that some players are considered priceless. Figo won no prizes in his last season at the Nou Camp but on an individual level he was consistently outstanding, and he carried that form through to Euro 2000, where, other than France's Zinedine Zidane, he was the most dazzling and exciting player on view. The term 'world-class' is frequently over-used but it certainly applies to this exquisitely talented midfield maestro.

NUNO GOMES
Portugal's hunt for a "new Eusébio" could be over at last. 24-year-old Nuno Gomes (pictured right) proved at Euro 2000 that he has a taste for the big time and can score goals from anywhere. He found the net once against England, twice against Turkey and once again in the semi-

final against France to become the competiton's third-ranked marksman behind Patrick Kluivert and Savo Milosevic. Pretty impressive stuff, really, given that he hadn't scored an international goal prior to the tournament and would not have started the opening game against England but for the unavailability of his rivals, the injured Sá Pinto and the suspended Pauleta. An excellent season for Benfica - he was an ever-present in the league, scoring 18 goals - gave him his chance, and he took it brilliantly. The reward for his Euro 2000 displays came with a transfer bid from Fiorentina, who happily shelled out a club record £11.9m to bring him in as the replacement centre-forward for Roma-bound legend Gabriel Batistuta.

led Real Madrid to Champions' League glory in 1998 before getting the sack, Benfica drew their opening game and then won six in a row, all without conceding a goal. But a first defeat, at Alverca, was soon followed by another one, 0-2 at FC Porto, and then, just to prove that disasters go in threes, Benfica were totally annihilated by Celta Vigo in the UEFA Cup. The 7-0 defeat in the first leg of the third-round tie was the heaviest in the club's history and led to all sorts of

recriminations, both internal and external. Benfica were never the same after that, and their woeful away form during the remainder of the season, when they kept on conceding goals in the final minutes, completely undermined their challenge.

Sporting, by contrast, struggled to get into gear in the early stages. They, too, had brought in a new foreign coach, Italian Giuseppe Materazzi, but his stay was cut short after only a few weeks following a disastrous first-round defeat by Norwegian part-timers Viking in the UEFA Cup. Sporting called in out-of-work former club captain Augusto Inácio to take over, and he too had an edgy start. Like Benfica, Sporting lost successive away games to Alverca and FC Porto, and it looked for all the world as if their title hopes had gone.

But while leaders Benfica began to toil, Sporting suddenly found form, rattling off six straight victories in the run-up to Christmas and putting themselves firmly back in contention. The purple patch on the field coincided - or was governed by - a restructuring of personnel in the Sporting boardroom. In December, Sporting found the money to buy in four new foreign players - Mbo Mpenza, André Cruz, César Prates and Robert Spehar. Apart from the latter, who was injured immediately after his arrival, the new intake were to have a tremendous influence on the quality and consistency of Sporting's performances in the second half of the season.

From the end of January, with Benfica on an irreversible decline, the race was on between Sporting and FC Porto. It was neck and neck for several weeks, with the defending champions just staying in front by the odd point or two. But Porto's Champions' League exertions - they had reached the second group phase and were performing well - were to eventually take their toll when the two sides came face to face in the Alvalade for the biggest match of the season. It had become traditional in the recent past for Porto to win this fixture, but two first-half goals from veterans André Cruz - a lovely free-kick - and Alberto Acosta - after a defensive howler by Portuguese international Secretário - gave Sporting a priceless win. Not only that, but it also put them on top of the table for the first time in the season.

Sporting's lead was extended to four points a fortnight later when Porto lost to a late goal away to Benfica, and that was still the advantage they carried into their

DOMESTIC CUP 99/00

FOURTH ROUND
SL Benfica 1, CD Torres Novas 0
SC Braga 2, CS Marítimo 1
SC Farense 3, CF Os Belenenses 1
Gil Vicente FC 3, Leça FC 2
Portimonense SC 1, Rio Ave FC 4
CD Ribeiro Brava 0, FC Porto 4
Vitória Setúbal 2, UD Vilafranquense 1 (aet)
SC Salgueiros 1, SC Lusitânia 0
FC Famalicão 1, CD Santa Clara 2
CF Estrela Amadora 2, CSD Câmara de Lobos 0
CF Canelas 0, Sporting CP 1
União Leiria 3, Anadia FC 0
SC Campomaiorense 2, Benfica Castelo Branco 1
Imortal DC 1, SC Beira Mar 0
FC Penafiel 0, Naval 1. de Maio 1 (aet)
Varzim SC 1, SC Covilhã 1 (aet)
(replay) SC Covilhã 1, Varzim SC 0
FC Felgueiras 2, Leixões SC 1
SC Freamunde 1, FC Infesta 2
FC Barreirense 2, Moreirense FC 2 (aet)
(replay) Moreirense FC 2, FC Barreirense 0
FC Paços Ferreira 0, SC Dragões Sandinenses 1
Académica Coimbra 6, CD Alcains 1
AD Fafe 2, CF União Madeira 0
FC Vizela 3, AD Guarda 1
Vilanovense FC 2, Louletano DC 1
Casa Pia AC 2, GD Estoril-Praia 1
Amora FC 1, AD Potomosense 1
(replay) AD Potomosense 2, Amora FC 2
(aet; 5-4 on pens.)
USC Paredes 3, EFC Vendas Novas 1
Vitória Guimarães 1, FC Maia 0
FC Alverca 1, Boavista FC 2 (aet)

FIFTH ROUND
SC Dragões Sandinenses 2, Vilanovense FC 0
FC Vizela 2, AD Fafe 2 (aet)
(replay) AD Fafe 2, FC Vizela 2 (aet; 5-4 on pens.)
SC Farense 2, CF Estrela Amadora 3
Boavista FC 8, USC Paredes 2
SC Covilhã 0, Rio Ave FC 2
Vitória Guimarães 3, Casa Pia AC 0
FC Infesta 1, Naval 1. de Maio 1 (aet)
(replay) Naval 1. de Maio 2, FC Infesta 1
Moreirense FC 3, CD Santa Clara 2
Imortal DC 0, FC Felgueiras 0 (aet)
(replay) FC Felgueiras 3, Imortal DC 0
SL Benfica 7, Amora FC 0
Académica Coimbra 2, Vitória Setúbal 1
SC Salgueiros 2, SC Campomaiorense 0
Sporting CP 1, União Leiria 0
FC Porto 4, SC Braga 1

1/8 FINALS
Vitória Guimarães 3, Gil Vicente FC 0
SC Salgueiros 1, AD Fafe 2 (aet)
CF Estrela Amadora 1, SC Dragões Sandinenses 2
Académica Coimbra 0, Moreirense FC 1 (aet)
Rio Ave FC 0, Naval 1. de Maio 0 (aet)
(replay) Naval 1. de Maio 2, Rio Ave FC 3
Boavista FC 2, FC Felgueiras 1
SL Benfica 1, Sporting CP 3
bye - FC Porto

QUARTER-FINALS
Sporting CP 3, SC Dragões Sandinenses 0
FC Porto 3, AD Fafe 0
Vitória Guimarães 0, Moreirense FC 1
Rio Ave FC 1, Boavista FC 0

SEMI-FINALS
Moreirense FC 0, Sporting CP 1 (Ayew 54)
FC Porto 3 (Domingos 18, Jardel 29, Ricardo Silva 30), Rio Ave FC 0

FINAL
21/05/2000, Lisbon
SPORTING CP 1 Hilário (57og)
FC PORTO 1 Jardel (3)
(aet)
referee - António Costa
SPORTING CP - Schmeichel; Rui Jorge (Quiroga 67), Saber, Cruz, Beto; Vidigal, Duscher, De Franceschi (Toñito 87), Pedro Barbosa (Mpenza 68); Acosta, Ayew.
FC PORTO - Hilário; Secretário, Ricardo Silva, Aloísio, Esquerdinha; Rubens Júnior (Clayton 46), Chainho, Paulinho Santos (Rui Barros 36); Capucho, Jardel (Alessandro 105), Drulovic.

(replay)
25/05/2000, Lisbon
FC PORTO 2 Clayton (49), Deco (75)
SPORTING CP 0
referee - Lucílio Baptista
FC PORTO - Vítor Baía; Secretário, Jorge Costa, Aloísio, Esquerdinha; Deco (Domingos 89), Chainho, Drulovic; Capucho (Alessandro 89), Jardel, Clayton (Rui Barros 77).
SPORTING CP - Schmeichel; Saber, Cruz (Quiroga 42), Beto, Rui Jorge; Pedro Barbosa (Toñito 67), Duscher, Vidigal, Edmilson (De Franceschi 69); Ayew, Mpenza.

INTERNATIONAL HONOURS

World Cup Finals appearances: 1966 (3rd), 1986

European Championship appearances: 1960, 1984 (semi-finals), 1996, 2000 (semi-finals)

European Club Competitions

Champions' Cup	SL Benfica (1961, 1962)
	FC Porto (1987)
Cup-winners' Cup	Sporting CP (1964)
Super Cup	FC Porto (1987)
World Club Cup	FC Porto (1987)

penultimate fixture - the fateful Lisbon derby in the Alvalade.

Heroes abounded in Sporting's championship-winning side. Acosta, the previously unsung Argentinian, netted 22 goals to finish second in the top-scorer listings. Full-back Rui Jorge was the most consistent defender in the league. Vidigal provided power, security and energy in midfield. And in goal the Great Dane himself,

Peter Schmeichel, proved to be just as talismanic and influential for Sporting as he had been when he joined Manchester United eight years earlier.

Porto gained a modicum of revenge over Sporting when they won the Portuguese Cup final. They needed a replay to do it, winning 2-0 after a 1-1 draw. The second match proved to be the farewell appearance for the remarkable Jardel, whose goal ratio in four years at FC Porto ended at over one per game. In the league he scored an amazing 130 goals in 125 matches, winning the Golden Boot every season, and his contribution to Porto's run to the Champions' League quarter-finals was 10 goals, making him the joint-top scorer of the competition.

Jardel's departure to Galatasaray leaves a huge void at the apex of the Porto attack. Sporting, on the other hand, seem well set to maintain their progress, having brought in several established internationals during the summer, including João Pinto, controversially sacked by Benfica despite his long and loyal service, the latter years as club captain.

PROMOTED CLUBS 99/00

SECOND DIVISION FINAL TABLE

		Pd	W	D	L	F	A	Pt	GD
1	FC Paços Ferreira	34	19	8	7	56	31	65	25
2	SC Beira Mar	34	18	11	5	54	30	65	24
3	Desportivo Aves	34	18	7	9	33	24	61	9
4	Varzim SC	34	17	9	8	53	33	60	20
5	Académica Coimbra	34	16	9	9	55	37	57	18
6	FC Penafiel	34	14	14	6	52	33	56	19
7	FC Felgueiras	34	14	9	11	42	36	51	6
8	União Lamas	34	14	4	16	39	50	46	-11
9	SC Freamunde	34	11	12	11	42	37	45	5
10	SC Espinho	34	13	6	15	51	48	45	3
11	Leça FC	34	13	6	15	41	49	45	-8
12	GD Chaves	34	11	11	12	46	45	44	1
13	Naval 1. de Maio	34	11	9	14	53	55	42	-2
14	FC Maia	34	11	9	14	35	44	42	-9
15	Imortal DC	34	8	9	17	43	64	33	-21
16	Moreirense FC	34	6	11	17	29	49	29	-20
17	AD Esposende	34	8	4	22	31	65	28	-34
18	SC Covilhã	34	5	10	19	23	48	25	-25

CLUB DIRECTORIES

Futebol Clube Paços de Ferreira
Praça D. Luís,
4590 Paços de Ferreira
tel - (055) 965230 / fax - (055) 965230
President - Hernâni Silva
Coach - Henrique Calisto
Stadium - Mata Real (15,000)

Sport Clube Beira-Mar
Estádio Mário Duarte, 3800 Aveiro
tel - (034) 242282 / fax - (034) 421309
website - www.uebe.pt/beiramar/
Year of Formation - 1922
President - Mano Nunes
Coach - António Sousa
Stadium - Mário Duarte (20,000)

MAJOR HONOURS
Domestic Cup - (1) 1999.

Clube Desportivo das Aves
Lugar do Longal,
4780 Vila das Aves
tel - (052) 941816 / fax - (052) 873267
Year of Formation - 1930
President - António José Freitas
Coach - Neca
Stadium - Desportivo das Aves (12,500)

FC ALVERCA

CLUB DIRECTORY

Futebol Clube de Alverca
Rua Coronel Henrique Nova
Apartado 53
2615 Alverca
tel - (21) 9580956
fax - (21) 9580412
Year of Formation - 1939
President - Luís Filipe Vieira
Coach - José Romão
(00/01 - Jesualdo Ferreira)
Stadium - Complexo Desportivo (20,000)

APPEARANCES 99/00

	P	Ap	(s)	Gls
ABEL SILVA	D	8	(1)	
ALHANDRA	M	2		
ANDERSON (BRA)	A	15	(10)	5
BERNARDO (ANG)	M	11	(3)	
CAJU (BRA)	A	17		7
CAPUCHO	A	4	(1)	1
DIOGO	D	22	(2)	1
DUDA (BRA)	M	10	(5)	5
FILIPE AZEVEDO	A	10	(7)	
GASPAR	D	25	(1)	1
GILBER (BRA)	D		(2)	
HUGO COSTA	D	23	(2)	1
JAMIR (BRA)	M	18	(1)	1
Vasiliy KULKOV (RUS)	M	14	(5)	
MARCO CANEIRA	D	15	(1)	
Nikola MILINKOVIC (YUG)	M	24	(4)	6
Iván MINER (ESP)	M	4	(13)	
NÉLSON MORAIS	D	12	(1)	
NUNO ASSIS	A	5	(14)	
Sergei OVCHINNIKOV (RUS)	G	27		
PAULO COSTA	A	5	(10)	1
PAULO SANTOS	G	7	(1)	
PEDRINHO	M	1		
PEDRO MANTORRAS	M		(1)	
PEDRO MANUEL (ANG)	M		(4)	
RAMIRES	M	17	(3)	4
RUI BORGES	M	27	(6)	5
SOUSA	D	24		
VERÍSSIMO	D	27		1

LEAGUE RESULTS 1999/2000

22/08/99	SC Braga	H	3-2	Caju 2, Milinkovic
28/08/99	FC Porto	A	0-0	
13/09/99	SC Campomaiorense	H	1-0	Milinkovic (p)
19/09/99	CF Os Belenenses	A	2-4	Caju 2
26/09/99	União Leiria	H	0-0	
02/10/99	Vitória Guimarães	A	0-1	
17/10/99	Sporting CP	H	2-1	Rui Borges, Anderson
24/10/99	CS Marítimo	A	0-3	
31/10/99	SL Benfica	H	3-1	Milinkovic (p), Anderson 2
07/11/99	SC Salgueiros	A	2-0	Caju 2
21/11/99	CD Santa Clara	H	0-1	
28/11/99	Vitória Setúbal	A	0-1	
04/12/99	SC Farense	H	0-1	
11/12/99	CF Estrela Amadora	A	0-3	
19/12/99	Gil Vicente FC	H	4-2	Milinkovic, Anderson, Capucho, Caju
09/01/00	Boavista FC	A	0-2	
16/01/00	Rio Ave FC	H	3-1	Ramires, Anderson, Paulo Costa
23/01/00	SC Braga	A	1-3	Milinkovic (p)
30/01/00	FC Porto	H	1-1	Ramires
05/02/00	SC Campomaiorense	A	0-0	
13/02/00	CF Os Belenenses	H	1-1	Ramires
20/02/00	União Leiria	A	0-3	
27/02/00	Vitória Guimarães	H	2-1	Rui Borges, Gaspar
04/03/00	Sporting CP	A	1-1	Hugo Costa
12/03/00	CS Marítimo	H	1-1	Milinkovic
19/03/00	SL Benfica	A	2-3	Duda 2
26/03/00	SC Salgueiros	H	2-0	Diogo, Duda
01/04/00	CD Santa Clara	A	3-4	Rui Borges 2, Duda
09/04/00	Vitória Setúbal	H	0-1	
14/04/00	SC Farense	A	2-1	Ramires, Duda
22/04/00	CF Estrela Amadora	H	0-1	
30/04/00	Gil Vicente FC	A	2-2	Jamir, Veríssimo
07/05/00	Boavista FC	H	1-0	Rui Borges
14/05/00	Rio Ave FC	A	0-2	

CF OS BELENENSES

Clube de Futebol "Os Belenenses"
Avenida do Restelo, 1400 Lisboa
tel - (21) 3010461
fax - (21) 3016525
Year of Formation - 1919
President - Sequeira Nunes
Coach - Vítor Oliveira (00/01 - Marinho Peres)
Stadium - Restelo (42,000)

MAJOR HONOURS
League Championship - (1) 1946.
Domestic Cup - (6)
1927, 1929, 1933, 1942, 1960, 1989.

APPEARANCES 99/00

	P	Ap	(s)	Gls
BALTASAR	M	3	(16)	
BOTELHO	G	9		
CABRAL (ANG)	D	28		2
CAFU	M		(14)	
Haruna DODA (NIG)	A	9	(15)	1
FERNANDO MENDES	A	21	(1)	2
FILGUEIRA (BRA)	D	28		4
FRANKLIM (ANG)	M	19	(1)	1
GOUVEIA	M	18		1
JOÃO PAULO BRITO	A	19	(12)	2
JOSÉ CARLOS	D	22		3
LITO (ANG)	D	25	(3)	1
LUÍS FERREIRA	G	1		
LUÍS NUNES	A		(3)	1
MARCO AURÉLIO (BRA)	G	24	(1)	
NECA	M	3	(6)	
NILSON (BRA)	D	9	(3)	
PEDRO ESTRELA	M	6	(5)	
RENATO	A	9	(9)	
RUI DUARTE	M	4	(4)	
RUI GREGÓRIO	M	1	(2)	1
RUI PATACA (ANG)	A	19		6
Jesús SEBA (ESP)	M	33		8
TUCK	M	31		1
WILSON (ANG)	D	33		

LEAGUE RESULTS 1999/2000

22/08/99	CF Estrela Amadora	A	3-0	og (Lazaro), Cabral, Rui Pataca
29/08/99	Gil Vicente FC	H	1-1	Fernando Mendes
10/09/99	Boavista FC	A	0-1	
19/09/99	FC Alverca	H	4-2	José Carlos 2, Seba, Cabral
26/09/99	SC Braga	A	0-0	
04/10/99	FC Porto	H	0-0	
17/10/99	SC Campomaiorense	A	1-2	Rui Pataca
24/10/99	Rio Ave FC	H	2-1	Gouveia, Rui Pataca
31/10/99	União Leiria	H	1-0	Seba
05/11/99	Vitória Guimarães	A	2-4	Rui Pataca, Seba
21/11/99	Sporting CP	H	0-1	
26/11/99	CS Marítimo	A	0-0	
04/12/99	SL Benfica	H	0-0	
12/12/99	SC Salgueiros	A	0-0	
19/12/99	CD Santa Clara	H	3-1	Seba 2, Rui Pataca
08/01/00	Vitória Setúbal	A	2-0	João Paulo Brito, Seba
16/01/00	SC Farense	H	1-1	João Paulo Brito
21/01/00	CF Estrela Amadora	H	1-1	Tuck (p)
30/01/00	Gil Vicente FC	A	1-1	Rui Pataca
04/02/00	Boavista FC	H	1-1	og (Mário Silva)
13/02/00	FC Alverca	A	1-1	Filgueira
18/02/00	SC Braga	H	0-3	
26/02/00	FC Porto	A	1-2	Lito
06/03/00	SC Campomaiorense	H	2-2	Franklim, Filgueira
12/03/00	Rio Ave FC	A	0-3	
19/03/00	União Leiria	A	0-1	
25/03/00	Vitória Guimarães	H	2-0	Filgueira, Seba
02/04/00	Sporting CP	A	0-1	
09/04/00	CS Marítimo	H	1-1	Doda
16/04/00	SL Benfica	A	3-2	Fernando Mendes, Filgueira, Rui Gregório
22/04/00	SC Salgueiros	H	2-1	Seba, Luís Nunes
30/04/00	CD Santa Clara	A	0-1	
06/05/00	Vitória Setúbal	H	0-1	
14/05/00	SC Farense	A	1-2	José Carlos

SL BENFICA

CLUB DIRECTORY

Sport Lisboa e Benfica
Avenida General Norton de Matos, 1500 Lisboa
tel - (21) 7266129 / fax - (21) 7264761
website - www.slbenfica.pt
Year of Formation - 1904
President - João Vale e Azevedo
Coach - Jupp Heynckes
Stadium - Luz (77,844)

MAJOR HONOURS
League Championship - (30) 1936, 1937, 1938,
1942, 1943, 1945, 1950, 1955, 1957, 1960,
1961, 1963, 1964, 1965, 1967, 1968, 1969,
1971, 1972, 1973, 1975, 1976, 1977, 1981,
1983, 1984, 1987, 1989, 1991, 1994.
Domestic Cup - (26)
1930, 1931, 1935, 1940, 1943, 1944, 1949,
1951, 1952, 1953, 1955, 1957, 1959, 1962,
1964, 1969, 1970, 1972, 1980, 1981, 1983,
1985, 1986, 1987, 1993, 1996.
European Champions' Cup - (2) 1961, 1962.

APPEARANCES 99/00

	P	Ap	(s)	Gls
ANDRADE	D	9	(2)	
Carlos BOSSIO (ARG)	G	8		
BRUNO BASTO	D	25	(2)	
CALADO	M	25	(3)	2
Sebastián CHANO (ESP)	M	7	(26)	
Robert ENKE (GER)	G	26		
JOÃO PINTO	M	26	(3)	3
JOÃO TOMAS	A	2	(7)	2
JORGE CADETE	A		(3)	
JORGE RIBEIRO	D	1		
JOSÉ SOARES	D	1		
Serhiy KANDAUROV (UKR)	M	30	(1)	6
LUÍS CARLOS	M	4	(3)	
Triandafilos MAHERIDIS (GRE)	D	11	(3)	
MANICHE	M	18	(10)	10
MARCO FREITAS	M	1		
MAWETE JÚNIOR	A		(3)	
NUNO GOMES	A	33	(1)	18
Samuel OKUNOWO (NIG)	D	9		1
PAULO MADEIRA	D	32		1
Karel POBORSKY (CZE)	M	25	(4)	5
PORFÍRIO	A	1	(2)	
Ricardo ROJAS (ARG)	D	21	(2)	
RONALDO (BRA)	D	26	(1)	1
Abdelsatar SABRY (EGY)	A	11	(2)	5
SÉRGIO NUNES	D	12	(5)	2
TAHAR El Khalej (MAR)	D	2	(2)	
Jorge López TOTE (ESP)	A	1	(6)	
Christian URIBE (CHL)	M	7	(4)	1

LEAGUE RESULTS 1999/2000

22/08/99	Rio Ave FC	A	1-1	Sérgio Nunes
29/08/99	SC Salgueiros	H	1-0	Nuno Gomes
12/09/99	CD Santa Clara	A	3-0	Maniche, Kandaurov, Nuno Gomes
20/09/99	Vitória Setúbal	H	3-0	Kandaurov (p), Maniche, Nuno Gomes
25/09/99	SC Farense	A	1-0	Nuno Gomes
04/10/99	CF Estrela Amadora	H	2-0	Okunowo, Ronaldo (p)
17/10/99	Gil Vicente FC	A	2-0	Maniche, Calado
24/10/99	Boavista FC	H	1-1	João Pinto
31/10/99	FC Alverca	A	1-3	Nuno Gomes
08/11/99	SC Braga	H	2-1	Nuno Gomes, Kandaurov
20/11/99	FC Porto	A	0-2	
29/11/99	SC Campomaiorense	H	2-0	Paulo Madeira, Maniche
04/12/99	CF Os Belenenses	A	0-0	
13/12/99	União Leiria	H	3-2	Nuno Gomes, Kandaurov, Maniche
19/12/99	Vitória Guimarães	A	1-2	Nuno Gomes
09/01/00	Sporting CP	H	0-0	
15/01/00	CS Marítimo	A	0-0	
23/01/00	Rio Ave FC	H	1-0	Nuno Gomes
30/01/00	SC Salgueiros	A	2-1	Poborsky, Nuno Gomes
06/02/00	CD Santa Clara	H	1-0	Nuno Gomes
14/02/00	Vitória Setúbal	A	2-1	Poborsky, Maniche
20/02/00	SC Farense	H	6-2	Maniche 3, Nuno Gomes 2, Poborsky
27/02/00	CF Estrela Amadora	A	0-3	
04/03/00	Gil Vicente FC	H	3-0	Nuno Gomes 2, og (Carlos)
12/03/00	Boavista FC	A	1-1	Kandaurov
19/03/00	FC Alverca	H	3-2	Sabry, Uribe (p), João Tomas
25/03/00	SC Braga	A	2-3	Sabry (p), Nuno Gomes
01/04/00	FC Porto	H	1-0	Sabry
08/04/00	SC Campomaiorense	A	4-2	Sabry, João Pinto, Poborsky, Calado
16/04/00	CF Os Belenenses	H	2-3	João Tomas, Maniche
21/04/00	União Leiria	A	1-2	Nuno Gomes
30/04/00	Vitória Guimarães	H	3-0	Poborsky, João Pinto, Nuno Gomes
06/05/00	Sporting CP	A	1-0	Sabry
14/05/00	CS Marítimo	H	2-1	Sérgio Nunes, Kandaurov

BOAVISTA FC

Boavista Futebol Clube
Rua O Primeiro de Janeiro
4100 Porto
tel - (22) 6071000
fax - (22) 6071031
Year of Formation - 1903
President - João Loureiro
Coach - Jaime Pacheco
Stadium - Bessa (23,000)

MAJOR HONOURS
Domestic Cup - (5)
1975, 1976, 1979, 1992, 1997.

APPEARANCES 99/00

	P	Ap	(s)	Gls
William ANDEM (CMR)	G	24	(1)	
Augustine AHINFUL (GHA)	A	8	(2)	1
CARLOS ALBERTO (BRA)	D	3		
CÉSAR Atienza (ESP)	A	2	(1)	
DEMÉTRIOS (BRA)	A	5	(7)	5
Rudolph DOUALA (CMR)	A	8	(6)	1
EMANUEL	M	20	(7)	2
ERIVAN	A		(1)	
FORMOSO	M	1	(2)	
GILMAR (BRA)	A	13	(5)	3
JORGE COUTO	A	20	(2)	1
JORGE SILVA	D	16	(7)	
LITOS	D	30		4
LUÍS MANUEL	M	18	(2)	1
MÁRIO SILVA	D	26		
MARTELINHO	M	6	(13)	
MOREIRA	A	8	(9)	1
NÍLTON	D	5	(7)	
PAULO SOUSA	D	16		
PEDRO COSTA	D	5		
PEDRO EMANUEL	D	32		
PEDRO MARTINS	M	2		
William QUEVEDO (FRA)	M	1		
RICARDO SILVA	M	1		
RICARDO PEREIRA	G	10		
ROGÉRIO (BRA)	A	13	(6)	4
RUI BENTO	M	30	(1)	1
Erwin SÁNCHEZ (BOL)	M	17	(1)	3
SÉRGIO CARVALHO	D	11	(2)	
Ion TIMOFTE (ROM)	M	8	(8)	
WHELLITON (BRA)	A	15	(8)	11

LEAGUE RESULTS 1999/2000

21/08/99	FC Porto	H	1-1	Ahinful
29/08/99	SC Campomaiorense	A	1-0	Emanuel
10/09/99	CF Os Belenenses	H	1-0	Gilmar
19/09/99	União Leiria	A	0-0	
26/09/99	Vitória Guimarães	H	2-0	Luís Manuel, Douala
04/10/99	Sporting CP	A	0-2	
17/10/99	CS Marítimo	H	0-2	
24/10/99	SL Benfica	A	1-1	Whelliton
30/10/99	SC Salgueiros	H	2-1	Litos, Rogério (p)
08/11/99	CD Santa Clara	A	1-0	Whelliton
20/11/99	Vitória Setúbal	H	1-0	Whelliton (p)
29/11/99	SC Farense	A	2-0	Gilmar, Emanuel
04/12/99	CF Estrela Amadora	H	1-2	og (Raúl Oliveira)
11/12/99	Gil Vicente FC	A	3-1	Gilmar, Whelliton 2
19/12/99	Rio Ave FC	A	1-2	Whelliton
09/01/00	FC Alverca	H	2-0	Sánchez, Whelliton
16/01/00	SC Braga	A	0-1	
23/01/00	FC Porto	A	0-1	
29/01/00	SC Campomaiorense	H	2-1	Moreira, Litos
04/02/00	CF Os Belenenses	A	1-1	Demétrios
12/02/00	União Leiria	H	0-1	
20/02/00	Vitória Guimarães	A	0-2	
28/02/00	Sporting CP	H	0-1	
03/03/00	CS Marítimo	A	1-1	Rui Bento
12/03/00	SL Benfica	H	1-1	Litos
18/03/00	SC Salgueiros	A	3-1	Whelliton 2, og (André)
26/03/00	CD Santa Clara	H	2-1	Whelliton, Rogério
31/03/00	Vitória Setúbal	A	1-2	Demétrios
10/04/00	SC Farense	H	2-1	Rogério, Demétrios
17/04/00	CF Estrela Amadora	A	2-1	Jorge Couto, Demétrios
22/04/00	Gil Vicente FC	H	2-0	Sánchez 2
29/04/00	Rio Ave FC	H	2-0	Rogério, Whelliton
07/05/00	FC Alverca	A	0-1	
14/05/00	SC Braga	H	2-2	Demétrios, Litos

SC BRAGA

CLUB DIRECTORY

Sporting Clube de Braga
Parque da Ponte
4700 Braga
tel - (253) 610591
fax - (253) 611686
website - www.scbraga.pt
Year of Formation - 1921
President - João Gomes de Oliveira
Coach - Manuel Cajuda
Stadium - 1o de Maio (40,000)

MAJOR HONOURS
Domestic Cup - (2) 1966, 1992.

APPEARANCES 99/00

	P	Ap	(s)	Gls
ARTUR JORGE	M	23	(2)	1
BARROSO	M	30		6
BRUNO	M	6	(1)	
CABRAL	D	1	(1)	
CASTANHEIRA	M	20	(9)	1
Evariste DIBO (CIV)	M	13	(5)	1
HENRIQUE	M		(1)	
HUGO CAJUDA	M		(2)	
IDALÉCIO	D	18	(6)	
JEAN PAULISTA (BRA)	A	2	(4)	
JORDÃO (ANG)	M	17	(5)	
JOSÉ NUNO AZEVEDO	D	26	(2)	1
LINO (ANG)	D	17	(2)	
LUÍS FILIPE	M	18	(1)	5
LUÍS MIGUEL (ANG)	D	13	(9)	
MAGUINHO	D	3		
MOZER	M	11	(2)	
NUNO CAVALEIRO	A	3	(7)	
NUNO HENRIQUE	A		(1)	
Theodore NZUENGUEMA (GAB)	A		(3)	
ODAIR (BRA)	D	33		10
PEDRO LAVOURA (VEN)	M	30	(1)	2
QUIM	G	34		
SILVA (BRA)	A	16	(9)	5
TAILSON	A	14	(3)	5
TIAGO	A	10	(8)	1
TONI (CVD)	A	16	(9)	6

LEAGUE RESULTS 1999/2000

22/08/99	FC Alverca	A	2-3	Toni, Odair
29/08/99	Rio Ave FC	H	0-1	
11/09/99	FC Porto	H	0-1	
19/09/99	SC Campomaiorense	A	4-2	Pedro Lavoura, Silva, Barroso, Castanheira
26/09/99	CF Os Belenenses	H	0-0	
03/10/99	União Leiria	A	0-3	
17/10/99	Vitória Guimarães	H	2-4	Barroso (p), Toni
23/10/99	Sporting CP	A	0-2	
31/10/99	CS Marítimo	H	1-2	Silva
08/11/99	SL Benfica	A	1-2	Toni
21/11/99	SC Salgueiros	H	2-0	Toni, Barroso
28/11/99	CD Santa Clara	A	2-1	Odair, Silva
05/12/99	Vitória Setúbal	H	3-0	Toni, Odair (p), Dibo
12/12/99	SC Farense	A	1-1	Toni
17/12/99	CF Estrela Amadora	H	0-1	
09/01/00	Gil Vicente FC	A	0-0	
16/01/00	Boavista FC	H	1-0	Odair
23/01/00	FC Alverca	H	3-1	Odair, Barroso, Tailson
30/01/00	Rio Ave FC	A	0-2	
05/02/00	FC Porto	A	0-3	
13/02/00	SC Campomaiorense	H	4-1	Tailson, Odair, Luís Filipe, Silva
18/02/00	CF Os Belenenses	A	3-0	Odair, Luís Filipe, Barroso
25/02/00	União Leiria	H	0-2	
04/03/00	Vitória Guimarães	A	0-1	
10/03/00	Sporting CP	H	0-2	
17/03/00	CS Marítimo	A	0-1	
25/03/00	SL Benfica	H	3-2	Tailson, José Nuno Azevedo, Odair
02/04/00	SC Salgueiros	A	1-1	Barroso
09/04/00	CD Santa Clara	H	3-1	Tailson, Odair, Luís Filipe
16/04/00	Vitória Setúbal	A	2-0	Odair, Tiago
22/04/00	SC Farense	H	1-0	Tailson
28/04/00	CF Estrela Amadora	A	3-3	Silva, Pedro Lavoura, Artur Jorge
07/05/00	Gil Vicente FC	H	0-0	
14/05/00	Boavista FC	A	2-2	Luís Filipe 2

SC CAMPOMAIORENSE

CLUB DIRECTORY

Sporting Clube Campomaiorense
Rua Vasco Sardinha 10
7370 Campo Maior
tel - (268) 699310
fax - (268) 686385
Year of Formation - 1926
President - João Nabeiro
Coach - Carlos Manuel
Stadium - Capitão César Correia (10,000)

APPEARANCES 99/00

	P	Ap	(s)	Gls
ABÍLIO	M	30		5
ARLEY ALVAREZ (BRA)	D	2	(2)	
BEKE (BRA)	D	29		3
BRUNO MENDES	D	14	(6)	
CAU (CVD)	M	26	(2)	2
CONSTANTINO	A	8	(8)	3
DEMÉTRIOS (BRA)	A	5	(3)	
HÉLDER GARCIA	A		(8)	
HUGO CUNHA	M	20	(5)	2
JORGE RIBEIRO	A	3	(1)	
JORGINHO	A	13	(9)	2
JOSÉ SOARES	D	14		1
LAELSON	M	29	(1)	5
MARCO SILVA	M		(1)	
MÁRIO JORGE (ANG)	M	27	(1)	
MICKEY	A	13	(13)	2
NÉLSON	A		(2)	
PAULO SÉRGIO	G	29		
POEJO	M	23	(6)	1
Dragoslav POLEKSIC (YUG)	G	5		
RENÉ RIVAS (BRA)	D	7	(1)	1
ROGÉRIO MATIAS	D	32	(1)	1
SANDRO	M		(1)	
SOUSA (ANG)	M	2	(2)	
TORRÃO	D	30	(1)	
WALDO Antonio (ESP)	M	2	(9)	
WELLINGTON (BRA)	A	11	(13)	3

LEAGUE RESULTS 1999/2000

22/08/99	Gil Vicente FC	A	0-3	
29/08/99	Boavista FC	H	0-1	
13/09/99	FC Alverca	A	0-1	
19/09/99	SC Braga	H	2-4	Wellington, Rogério Matias (p)
24/09/99	FC Porto	A	0-2	
02/10/99	Rio Ave FC	H	1-1	Abílio
17/10/99	CF Os Belenenses	H	2-1	René Rivas, Laelson
24/10/99	União Leiria	A	2-1	Abílio, Laelson
29/10/99	Vitória Guimarães	H	2-1	Laelson, Abílio
06/11/99	Sporting CP	A	0-1	
21/11/99	CS Marítimo	H	1-0	Beke
29/11/99	SL Benfica	A	0-2	
05/12/99	SC Salgueiros	H	0-1	
12/12/99	CD Santa Clara	A	2-2	Cau, Wellington
19/12/99	Vitória Setúbal	H	0-1	
08/01/00	SC Farense	A	2-2	Mickey, Laelson
16/01/00	CF Estrela Amadora	H	2-1	José Soares, Abílio
22/01/00	Gil Vicente FC	H	0-0	
29/01/00	Boavista FC	A	1-2	Jorginho
05/02/00	FC Alverca	H	0-0	
13/02/00	SC Braga	A	1-4	Beke
19/02/00	FC Porto	H	1-0	Laelson
27/02/00	Rio Ave FC	A	0-1	
06/03/00	CF Os Belenenses	A	2-2	Constantino, Wellington
12/03/00	União Leiria	H	2-0	Beke, Constantino
19/03/00	Vitória Guimarães	A	1-4	Jorginho
24/03/00	Sporting CP	H	0-2	
02/04/00	CS Marítimo	A	0-1	
08/04/00	SL Benfica	H	2-4	Hugo Cunha, Abílio (p)
16/04/00	SC Salgueiros	A	1-2	Mickey
22/04/00	CD Santa Clara	H	1-0	Constantino
30/04/00	Vitória Setúbal	A	2-1	Hugo Cunha, Poejo
07/05/00	SC Farense	H	1-0	Cau
14/05/00	CF Estrela Amadora	A	0-3	

CF ESTRELA AMADORA

CLUB DIRECTORY

Clube de Futebol Estrela da Amadora
Rua Gomes Freire 27
Apartado 9077
2700 Amadora
tel - (21) 4999110
fax - (21) 4999288
Year of Formation - 1932
President - José María Salvado
Coach - Jorge Jesus (00/01 - Quinita)
Stadium - José Gomes (25,000)

MAJOR HONOURS
Domestic Cup - (1) 1990.

APPEARANCES 99/00

	P	Ap	(s)	Gls
GAÚCHO I (BRA)	A	31		21
GAÚCHO II (BRA)	M	27	(5)	
GILBERTO (BRA)	A	3	(14)	3
HÉLDER QUENTAL (ANG)	M		(2)	
JOÃO PIRES	M	1	(1)	
JORGE ANDRADE	D	31		
JOSÉ CARLOS	D	10	(10)	1
KENEDY	M	21	(4)	1
LÁZARO (ANG)	A	29		4
LEAL	D	14	(3)	1
Leo LEWIS (TRI)	A	12	(7)	
LUÍS VASCO	G	6		
MIGUEL	M	17	(11)	
PEDRO SIMÕES	M	17	(6)	
RAUL OLIVEIRA	D	28	(1)	4
REBELO	D	11		
RUI NEVES	D	29	(1)	1
SERGINHO (BRA)	A	8	(9)	1
SÉRGIO MARQUÊS	M	10	(3)	
STÊNIO (BRA)	A		(5)	
TIAGO	G	28	(1)	
VERONA (BRA)	M	18	(8)	2
VÍTOR VIEIRA	A	23	(6)	

LEAGUE RESULTS 1999/2000

22/08/99	CF Os Belenenses	H	0-3	
29/08/99	União Leiria	A	1-1	Gaúcho I
12/09/99	Vitória Guimarães	H	2-2	Serginho, Raul Oliveira
20/09/99	Sporting CP	A	1-1	Gaúcho I
26/09/99	CS Marítimo	H	1-1	Gilberto
04/10/99	SL Benfica	A	0-2	
17/10/99	SC Salgueiros	H	1-0	José Carlos
24/10/99	CD Santa Clara	A	1-1	Gaúcho I
01/11/99	Vitória Setúbal	H	3-0	Gaúcho I 2, Lazaro
07/11/99	SC Farense	A	1-1	og (Miguel Serôdio)
21/11/99	Rio Ave FC	A	1-0	Gaúcho I (p)
28/11/99	Gil Vicente FC	H	0-1	
05/12/99	Boavista FC	A	2-1	Gaúcho I 2
11/12/99	FC Alverca	H	3-0	Lazaro 2, Raul Oliveira
17/12/99	SC Braga	A	1-0	Gaúcho I
08/01/00	FC Porto	H	0-2	
16/01/00	SC Campomaiorense	A	1-2	Gaúcho I
21/01/00	CF Os Belenenses	A	1-1	Gaúcho I
30/01/00	União Leiria	H	1-1	Lazaro
06/02/00	Vitória Guimarães	A	0-1	
13/02/00	Sporting CP	H	0-0	
20/02/00	CS Marítimo	A	2-2	Gaúcho I 2
27/02/00	SL Benfica	H	3-0	Gaúcho I 2, Kenedy
04/03/00	SC Salgueiros	A	1-1	Gaúcho I
13/03/00	CD Santa Clara	H	0-0	
19/03/00	Vitória Setúbal	A	0-1	
26/03/00	SC Farense	H	1-1	Verona
02/04/00	Rio Ave FC	H	1-0	Raul Oliveira
09/04/00	Gil Vicente FC	A	2-2	Gaúcho I 2
17/04/00	Boavista FC	H	1-2	Verona
22/04/00	FC Alverca	A	1-0	Gilberto
28/04/00	SC Braga	H	3-3	Leal, Gilberto, Raul Oliveira
07/05/00	FC Porto	A	1-2	Gaúcho I
14/05/00	SC Campomaiorense	H	3-0	Rui Neves, Gaúcho I 2 (2p)

SC FARENSE

CLUB DIRECTORY

Sporting Clube Farense
Praça de Tânger
8000 Faro
tel - (289) 804859
fax - (289) 802754
Year of Formation - 1910
President - João Pedro Carvalho
Coach - João Alves; Horácio Vaqueiro; João Portela;
Ismael Diaz (00/01 - Manuel Balela)
Stadium - São Luís (15,000)

APPEARANCES 99/00

	P	Ap	(s)	Gls
Nail BESIROVIC (YUG)	M	9	(2)	
Darko BUTOROVIC (CRO)	D	1		
CANDEIAS	G	25		
CARLOS COSTA	M	34		1
CARLOS FERNANDES	M	26	(2)	
CAVACO	M	16	(2)	
DIEB	A	1	(3)	1
DIEGO	A		(3)	
DINO	D	12	(2)	
EUGÉNIO	D	9	(2)	
EVERSON (BRA)	A	6	(8)	3
FÁBIO	M	1	(3)	
Ilshat FAIZULIN (RUS)	A	1	(5)	
Diego FERREIRA (PAR)	A	1		
Redouane HAJRY (MAR)	M	12	(9)	1
HASSAN Nader (MAR)	A	23	(4)	7
KING (BRA)	D	9	(3)	
LUNARI	M	3	(8)	2
MARCO NUNO	A	15	(13)	1
Lucian MARINESCU (ROM)	A	27		11
MIGUEL MOTA	M	13	(3)	
MIGUEL ROSA	G	3		
MIGUEL SERÔDIO	D	15	(3)	
Zoran MIJANOVIC (YUG)	G	6		
NUNO CAMPOS	M	13	(2)	
PAULO FERREIRA	M	12	(2)	2
PAULO SÉRGIO (BRA)	D	27	(2)	1
QUINZINHO	A	5	(1)	1
TULIPA	A	8	(11)	
VÍTOR MANUEL	M	21	(2)	
ZÉ TÓ	M	20	(3)	4

LEAGUE RESULTS 1999/2000

22/08/99	União Leiria	H	2-1	Hassan. Dieb
27/08/99	Vitória Guimarães	A	0-3	
12/09/99	Sporting CP	H	0-3	
19/09/99	CS Marítimo	A	0-3	
25/09/99	SL Benfica	H	0-1	
03/10/99	SC Salgueiros	A	0-0	
17/10/99	CD Santa Clara	H	2-2	Everson, Marinescu
22/10/99	Vitória Setúbal	A	1-1	Everson
31/10/99	Rio Ave FC	A	1-1	Hassan
07/11/99	CF Estrela Amadora	H	1-1	Marinescu (p)
21/11/99	Gil Vicente FC	A	0-4	
29/11/99	Boavista FC	H	0-2	
04/12/99	FC Alverca	A	1-0	Marinescu (p)
12/12/99	SC Braga	H	1-1	Marinescu (p)
20/12/99	FC Porto	A	0-5	
08/01/00	SC Campomaiorense	H	2-2	Marinescu, Carlos Costa
16/01/00	CF Os Belenenses	A	1-1	Hassan
23/01/00	União Leiria	A	0-2	
29/01/00	Vitória Guimarães	H	2-1	Marinescu, Paulo Sérgio
05/02/00	Sporting CP	A	1-3	Quinzinho
13/02/00	CS Marítimo	H	1-0	Marinescu (p)
20/02/00	SL Benfica	A	2-6	Paulo Ferreira, Hassan
27/02/00	SC Salgueiros	H	3-2	Marinescu (p), Hassan, Lunari
04/03/00	CD Santa Clara	A	2-1	Paulo Ferreira, Hassan
12/03/00	Vitória Setúbal	H	0-0	
19/03/00	Rio Ave FC	H	4-0	Zé Tó 2, Marinescu, Lunari
26/03/00	CF Estrela Amadora	A	1-1	Hajry
03/04/00	Gil Vicente FC	H	0-3	
10/04/00	Boavista FC	A	1-2	Zé Tó
14/04/00	FC Alverca	H	1-2	Zé Tó
22/04/00	SC Braga	A	0-1	
29/04/00	FC Porto	H	3-3	Marinescu 2, Everson
07/05/00	SC Campomaiorense	A	0-1	
14/05/00	CF Os Belenenses	H	2-1	Marco Nuno, Hassan

GIL VICENTE FC

CLUB DIRECTORY

Gil Vicente Futebol Clube
Rua D. Diogo Pinheiro 25
4750 Barcelos
tel - (253) 811523
fax - (253) 823102
Year of Formation - 1924
President - João Miranda Magalhães
Coach - Álvaro Magalhães
Stadium - Adelino Ribeiro Novo (8,000)

APPEARANCES 99/00

	P	Ap	(s)	Gls
ANDRÉ	M	4	(10)	
AURI (BRA)	D	31		2
BESSA	D	24		
CARLITOS	M	21	(9)	6
CARLOS	D	31		
CASQUILHA	M	32		3
Ovidiu CUC (ROM)	A	6	(21)	3
FANGUEIRO	A	29	(2)	7
GUGA (BRA)	A	20	(5)	8
JAIMINHO	A		(6)	1
LEMOS (BRA)	M	8	(8)	1
MARQUINHOS	M	1	(1)	
MATIAS	M	10	(1)	
PALECAS	G	1		
PAULO JORGE (ANG)	G	32		
PAULO LOPES	G		(1)	
PEDRO SANTOS (VEN)	M	22		4
PETIT	M	29	(1)	4
RICARDO NASCIMENTO	A	20	(5)	5
RONDINHA (BRA)	A	1	(4)	
Peter RUFAI (NIG)	G	1		
RUI GUERREIRO	D	10	(6)	
SÉRGIO LOMBA (ANG)	D	32		2
TAVARES (GBU)	M	6	(10)	2
XANDI (BRA)	M		(1)	
ZÉ NANDO	M	3	(1)	

LEAGUE RESULTS 1999/2000

22/08/99	SC Campomaiorense	H	3-0	Guga, Ricardo Nascimento, Jaiminho
29/08/99	CF Os Belenenses	A	1-1	Ricardo Nascimento (p)
12/09/99	União Leiria	H	2-0	Ricardo Nascimento 2 (1p)
19/09/99	Vitória Guimarães	A	0-1	
25/09/99	Sporting CP	H	1-1	Fangueiro
03/10/99	CS Marítimo	A	0-1	
17/10/99	SL Benfica	H	0-2	
24/10/99	SC Salgueiros	A	2-1	Pedro Santos, Casquilha
31/10/99	CD Santa Clara	H	3-1	Petit, Sérgio Lomba, Tavares
07/11/99	Vitória Setúbal	A	1-0	Fangueiro
21/11/99	SC Farense	H	4-0	Ricardo Nascimento (p), Carlitos 2, Cuc
28/11/99	CF Estrela Amadora	A	1-0	Guga
05/12/99	Rio Ave FC	A	1-3	Petit (p)
11/12/99	Boavista FC	H	1-3	Cuc
19/12/99	FC Alverca	A	2-4	Casquilha, Guga (p)
09/01/00	SC Braga	H	0-0	
17/01/00	FC Porto	A	0-2	
22/01/00	SC Campomaiorense	A	0-0	
30/01/00	CF Os Belenenses	H	1-1	Petit
06/02/00	União Leiria	A	1-1	Pedro Santos
13/02/00	Vitória Guimarães	H	1-0	Casquilha
19/02/00	Sporting CP	A	1-1	Carlitos
27/02/00	CS Marítimo	H	5-1	Guga, Pedro Santos 2, Cuc, Fangueiro
04/03/00	SL Benfica	A	0-3	
12/03/00	SC Salgueiros	H	2-0	Carlitos, Fangueiro
19/03/00	CD Santa Clara	A	0-0	
26/03/00	Vitória Setúbal	H	2-0	Tavares, Carlitos (p)
03/04/00	SC Farense	A	3-0	Auri, Fangueiro, Guga
09/04/00	CF Estrela Amadora	H	2-2	Sérgio Lomba, Auri
16/04/00	Rio Ave FC	H	4-0	Guga, Petit, Fangueiro 2
22/04/00	Boavista FC	A	0-2	
30/04/00	FC Alverca	H	2-2	Guga 2
07/05/00	SC Braga	A	0-0	
14/05/00	FC Porto	H	2-1	Lemos, Carlitos

CS MARÍTIMO

CLUB DIRECTORY

Clube Sport Marítimo
Rua D. Carlos I 17
9050 Funchal
tel - (291) 205000
fax - (291) 222939
website - www.scmaritimo-madeira.pt
Year of Formation - 1910
President - Carlos Pereira
Coach - Nelo Vingada
Stadium - Barreiros (33,000)

MAJOR HONOURS
Domestic Cup - (1) 1926.

APPEARANCES 99/00

	P	Ap	(s)	Gls
ALBERTINO	M	30	(2)	1
Patrick ASSELMAN (BEL)	M		(1)	
BRUNO	M	30	(3)	
CARLOS JORGE	D	6	(9)	1
DANI DIAZ (ESP)	M	8	(11)	
EUSÉBIO	D	31		
Ilian ILIEV (BUL)	M	32		4
JOÃO PINTO	A	5	(9)	2
JOEL	M	2	(1)	1
Predrag JOKANOVIC (YUG)	M	22	(5)	4
JORGE SOARES	D	33		2
LINO (GBU)	A	12	(6)	1
MÁRCIO ABREU	M		(1)	
MARIANO	M	30	(1)	3
NÉLSON (ANG)	G	2	(1)	
NUNO AFONSO	D	7	(2)	
PEDRO MOUTINHO	M		(1)	
Rubén PIAGGIO (ARG)	A	4	(10)	1
RONALDO	M		(4)	
RUI ÓSCAR	D	22	(2)	1
Ion SBURLEA (ROM)	D	3		
Musa SHANNON (USA)	A		(3)	2
Axel SMEETS (BEL)	D	3	(13)	1
Marius SUMUDICA (ROM)	A	24	(4)	4
Mariano TOEDTLI (ARG)	A	29	(2)	13
TONI (GBU)	A		(1)	
Yves VAN DER STRAETEN (BEL)	G	32		
ZECA	M	7		1

LEAGUE RESULTS 1999/2000

22/08/99	SC Salgueiros	A	0-1	
29/08/99	CD Santa Clara	H	0-0	
12/09/99	Vitória Setúbal	A	2-4	Zeca, Toedtli
19/09/99	SC Farense	H	3-0	Sumudica, Toedtli, Jokanovic
26/09/99	CF Estrela Amadora	A	1-1	Toedtli
03/10/99	Gil Vicente FC	H	1-0	Toedtli
17/10/99	Boavista FC	A	2-0	Toedtli 2
24/10/99	FC Alverca	H	3-0	Toedtli, Sumudica 2 (1p)
31/10/99	SC Braga	A	2-1	Toedtli, Sumudica
08/11/99	FC Porto	H	2-1	Albertino, Rui Óscar
21/11/99	SC Campomaiorense	A	0-1	
26/11/99	CF Os Belenenses	H	0-0	
05/12/99	União Leiria	A	1-0	Toedtli
10/12/99	Vitória Guimarães	H	1-1	Piaggio
18/12/99	Sporting CP	A	2-4	Toedtli, Mariano
08/01/00	Rio Ave FC	A	2-0	Mariano, Jokanovic
15/01/00	SL Benfica	H	0-0	
23/01/00	SC Salgueiros	H	0-1	
30/01/00	CD Santa Clara	A	0-0	
05/02/00	Vitória Setúbal	H	1-0	Jokanovic (p)
13/02/00	SC Farense	A	0-1	
20/02/00	CF Estrela Amadora	H	2-2	Toedtli, Jorge Soares
27/02/00	Gil Vicente FC	A	1-5	Toedtli
03/03/00	Boavista FC	H	1-1	Jokanovic (p)
12/03/00	FC Alverca	A	1-1	Mariano
17/03/00	SC Braga	H	1-0	Iliev
25/03/00	FC Porto	A	2-3	Iliev, Toedtli
02/04/00	SC Campomaiorense	H	1-0	Iliev
09/04/00	CF Os Belenenses	A	1-1	João Pinto
16/04/00	União Leiria	H	0-0	
24/04/00	Vitória Guimarães	A	3-1	Iliev, Lino, Carlos Jorge
30/04/00	Sporting CP	H	0-2	
07/05/00	Rio Ave FC	H	5-2	Jorge Soares, Smeets, Joel, Shannon 2
14/05/00	SL Benfica	A	1-2	João Pinto

FC PORTO

CLUB DIRECTORY

Futebol Clube do Porto
Estádio das Antas
Avenida Fernão de Magalhães, 4300 Porto
tel - (22) 5570500 / fax - (22) 5070522
website - fcporto.pt
Year of Formation - 1893
President - Jorge Nuno Pinto da Costa
Coach - Fernando Santos
Stadium - Antas (76,000)

MAJOR HONOURS
League Championship - (18)
1935, 1939, 1940, 1956, 1959, 1978, 1979,
1985, 1986, 1988, 1990, 1992, 1993, 1995,
1996, 1997, 1998, 1999.
Domestic Cup - (14)
1922, 1925, 1932, 1937, 1956, 1958, 1968,
1977, 1984, 1988, 1991, 1994, 1998, 2000.
European Champions' Cup - (1) 1987.
European Super Cup - (1) 1987.
World Club Cup - (1) 1987.

APPEARANCES 99/00

		P	Ap	(s)	Gls
ALESANDRO (BRA)	A	9	(11)	1
ALOÍSIO (BRA)	D	29	(1)	
ARGEL (BRA)	D	5		1
CAJU	M	2		
CAPUCHO	A	31	(1)	6
CHAINHO	M	25	(3)	1
CLAYTON (BRA)	A	4	(14)	
DECO (BRA)	M	21	(2)	1
DOMINGOS	A	8	(13)	6
Ljubinko DRULOVIC (YUG)	M	23	(10)	4
DUDA (BRA)	D	1		
ESQUERDINHA (BRA)	D	25		1
Miklós FEHÉR (HUN)	A		(5)	1
FOLHA	A	3	(1)	
HILÁRIO	G	19		
Mário JARDEL (BRA)	A	31	(1)	38
JOÃO MANUEL PINTO	D	1	(2)	
JORGE COSTA	D	31		1
NÉLSON	D	8	(2)	
PAULINHO SANTOS	D	26	(2)	
PEIXE	D	13	(8)	
RICARDO SILVA	D	2	(1)	1
RICARDO SOUSA	M		(1)	
RODOLFO	M	1	(2)	
ROMEU	A	1	(7)	
RUBENS JÚNIOR (BRA)	D	15	(3)	1
RUI BARROS	M	2	(6)	2
SECRETÁRIO	D	23		
VÍTOR BAÍA	G	15		

LEAGUE RESULTS 1999/2000

21/08/99	Boavista FC	A	1-1	Jardel
28/08/99	FC Alverca	H	0-0	
11/09/99	SC Braga	A	1-0	Jardel (p)
19/09/99	Rio Ave FC	H	4-1	Jardel 3, Rui Barros
24/09/99	SC Campomaiorense	H	2-0	Jardel, Fehér
04/10/99	CF Os Belenenses	A	0-0	
17/10/99	União Leiria	H	4-2	Argel, Capucho, Jardel (p), Deco
23/10/99	Vitória Guimarães	A	1-1	Ricardo Silva
30/10/99	Sporting CP	H	3-0	Chainho, Jardel 2
08/11/99	CS Marítimo	A	1-2	Jardel
20/11/99	SL Benfica	H	2-0	Capucho, Jardel
28/11/99	SC Salgueiros	A	4-0	Jardel 3 (1p), Drulovic
03/12/99	CD Santa Clara	H	1-0	Jardel
13/12/99	Vitória Setúbal	A	4-1	Jardel 3 (1p), Rubens Júnior
20/12/99	SC Farense	H	5-0	Esquerdinha, Jardel 3, Capucho
08/01/00	CF Estrela Amadora	A	2-0	Jardel 2
17/01/00	Gil Vicente FC	H	2-0	Jardel 2 (1p)
23/01/00	Boavista FC	H	1-0	Alessandro
30/01/00	FC Alverca	A	1-1	Jorge Costa
05/02/00	SC Braga	H	3-0	Capucho, Jardel 2
13/02/00	Rio Ave FC	A	2-2	Domingos 2
19/02/00	SC Campomaiorense	A	0-1	
26/02/00	CF Os Belenenses	H	2-1	Drulovic, Domingos
04/03/00	União Leiria	A	1-0	Domingos
11/03/00	Vitória Guimarães	H	2-1	Domingos, Jardel
18/03/00	Sporting CP	A	0-2	
25/03/00	CS Marítimo	H	3-2	Jardel 2, Capucho
01/04/00	SL Benfica	A	0-1	
09/04/00	SC Salgueiros	H	2-0	Rui Barros, Jardel
15/04/00	CD Santa Clara	A	2-0	Capucho, Jardel
22/04/00	Vitória Setúbal	H	4-1	Domingos, Jardel 3 (1p)
29/04/00	SC Farense	A	3-3	Jardel 2 (1p), Drulovic
07/05/00	CF Estrela Amadora	H	2-1	Jardel, og (Rebelo)
14/05/00	Gil Vicente FC	A	1-2	Drulovic

RIO AVE FC

CLUB DIRECTORY

Rio Ave Futebol Clube
Estádio do Rio Ave FC
4480 Vila do Conde
tel - (252) 640590
fax - (252) 640599
Year of Formation - 1939
President - Paulo Carvalho
Coach - Carlos Brito
(00/01 - Vítor Oliveira)
Stadium - Rio Ave (12,500)

APPEARANCES 99/00

	P	Ap	(s)	Gls
ALÉRCIO (BRA)	M	22	(3)	2
ANDRÉ JACARÉ (BRA)	A	8	(5)	
ARMANDO (MOZ)	D	29		1
ARTUR JORGE VICENTE (CVD)	A	21	(5)	3
CHICABALA	A	2	(4)	1
COSTA	M	14	(4)	
GAMA	A	15	(17)	4
HUGO HENRIQUE (BRA)	A	31	(2)	12
JADER (BRA)	M	3	(3)	
JORGE	D	10	(1)	1
LUÍS COENTRÃO	M	13	(6)	3
MARTINS	D	11	(1)	
Fabio MERELES (PAR)	M	23	(3)	1
MIGUELITO	M	1	(11)	1
NIQUINHA (BRA)	M	30	(3)	2
NITO	D	31		
PAULO LIMA PEREIRA	M	9	(9)	
PEU (BRA)	D	26	(1)	2
ROCHINHA	M	1	(3)	
SANDRO (BRA)	M	24	(3)	
SÉRGIO CHINA (BRA)	M	16	(12)	1
TÓ LUÍS	G	30		
TÓ ZÉ	G	4		

LEAGUE RESULTS 1999/2000

22/08/99	SL Benfica	H	1-1	Hugo Henrique
29/08/99	SC Braga	A	1-0	Armando
12/09/99	SC Salgueiros	H	4-1	Hugo Henrique 3, Gama
19/09/99	FC Porto	A	1-4	Artur Jorge Vicente
26/09/99	CD Santa Clara	H	0-5	
02/10/99	SC Campomaiorense	A	1-1	Hugo Henrique
17/10/99	Vitória Setúbal	H	1-1	Chicabala
24/10/99	CF Os Belenenses	A	1-2	Hugo Henrique
31/10/99	SC Farense	H	1-1	Peu
07/11/99	União Leiria	A	0-0	
21/11/99	CF Estrela Amadora	H	0-1	
28/11/99	Vitória Guimarães	A	1-2	Hugo Henrique
05/12/99	Gil Vicente FC	H	3-1	Peu, Alércio, Gama
12/12/99	Sporting CP	A	1-2	Niquinha
19/12/99	Boavista FC	H	2-1	Hugo Henrique, Luís Coentrão
08/01/00	CS Marítimo	H	0-2	
16/01/00	FC Alverca	A	1-3	Artur Jorge Vicente
23/01/00	SL Benfica	A	0-1	
30/01/00	SC Braga	H	2-0	Artur Jorge Vicente, Jorge
06/02/00	SC Salgueiros	A	1-1	Hugo Henrique
13/02/00	FC Porto	H	2-2	Hugo Henrique 2
19/02/00	CD Santa Clara	A	0-1	
27/02/00	SC Campomaiorense	H	1-0	Miguelito
04/03/00	Vitória Setúbal	A	0-2	
12/03/00	CF Os Belenenses	H	3-0	Mereles, Luís Coentrão 2
19/03/00	SC Farense	A	0-4	
26/03/00	União Leiria	H	0-0	
02/04/00	CF Estrela Amadora	A	0-1	
07/04/00	Vitória Guimarães	H	1-1	Hugo Henrique
16/04/00	Gil Vicente FC	A	0-4	
21/04/00	Sporting CP	H	1-2	Alércio
29/04/00	Boavista FC	A	0-2	
07/05/00	CS Marítimo	A	2-5	Niquinha, Gama
14/05/00	FC Alverca	H	2-0	Gama, Sérgio China

SC SALGUEIROS

CLUB DIRECTORY

Sport Comércio e Salgueiros
Rua Álvares Cabral 366
4050 Porto
tel - (22) 2000004
fax - (22) 2008397
website - sportcsalgueiros.cjb.net
Year of Formation - 1911
President - José António Linhares
Coach - Dito; Vítor Manuel
Stadium - Vidal Pinheiro (11,000)

APPEARANCES 99/00

	P	Ap	(s)	Gls
ADEMIR (BRA)	D	2		
ANDRÉ (ANG)	M	24	(2)	
BASÍLIO ALMEIDA	A	29	(1)	4
CÂNDIDO COSTA	M	5	(4)	
CARLOS FERREIRA	M	20		1
EDU (BRA)	M	15	(5)	2
Miklós FEHÉR (HUN)	A	12	(2)	5
FERNANDO ALMEIDA (BRA)	A	2	(9)	
FILIPE CÂNDIDO	A		(3)	
JOÃO PEDRO	A	9	(23)	3
JORGE SILVA	G	34		
MARCO CLÁUDIO	M		(3)	
NÉLSON	D	24	(1)	1
NEVES	D	25	(2)	
Basarab PANDURU (ROM)	M	1	(6)	1
PAQUITO (BRA)	A	14	(6)	4
PAULINHO	D	23		
PEDRO REIS	D	29	(2)	1
PEDROSA	D	20	(2)	
RAMOS	A	2	(14)	3
RENATO (BRA)	M	20	(6)	4
RICARDO FERNANDES	D	23		
RUI FERREIRA	M	31	(2)	
TONINHO CRUZ	M	10	(6)	

LEAGUE RESULTS 1999/2000

22/08/99	CS Marítimo	H	1-0	Edu
29/08/99	SL Benfica	A	0-1	
12/09/99	Rio Ave FC	A	1-4	Paquito
19/09/99	CD Santa Clara	H	2-0	Renato (p), Ramos
26/09/99	Vitória Setúbal	A	2-1	Basílio Almeida, og (Quim)
03/10/99	SC Farense	H	0-0	
17/10/99	CF Estrela Amadora	A	0-1	
24/10/99	Gil Vicente FC	H	1-2	Paquito
30/10/99	Boavista FC	A	1-2	Edu
07/11/99	FC Alverca	H	0-2	
21/11/99	SC Braga	A	0-2	
28/11/99	FC Porto	H	0-4	
05/12/99	SC Campomaiorense	A	1-0	Basílio Almeida
12/12/99	CF Os Belenenses	H	0-0	
19/12/99	União Leiria	A	4-1	Renato 2 (1p), Nélson, Fehér
07/01/00	Vitória Guimarães	H	0-1	
10/01/00	Sporting CP	A	0-2	
23/01/00	CS Marítimo	A	1-0	João Pedro
30/01/00	SL Benfica	H	1-2	Basílio Almeida
06/02/00	Rio Ave FC	H	1-1	Renato
12/02/00	CD Santa Clara	A	0-0	
20/02/00	Vitória Setúbal	H	1-0	Carlos Ferreira
27/02/00	SC Farense	A	2-3	Pedro Reis, Fehér
04/03/00	CF Estrela Amadora	H	1-1	Panduru (p)
12/03/00	Gil Vicente FC	A	0-2	
18/03/00	Boavista FC	H	1-3	Paquito
26/03/00	FC Alverca	A	0-2	
02/04/00	SC Braga	H	1-1	Basílio Almeida
09/04/00	FC Porto	A	0-2	
16/04/00	SC Campomaiorense	H	2-1	Fehér, João Pedro
22/04/00	CF Os Belenenses	A	1-2	Fehér
30/04/00	União Leiria	H	3-0	Fehér (p), Paquito, João Pedro
05/05/00	Vitória Guimarães	A	2-2	Ramos 2
14/05/00	Sporting CP	H	0-4	

CD SANTA CLARA

CLUB DIRECTORY

Clube Desportivo Santa Clara
Rua Comandante Jaime de Sousa no. 21
9500 Ponta Delgada
tel - (296) 283191
fax - (296) 629044
Year of Formation - 1921
President - Paulino Pavão
Coach - Manuel Fernandes
Stadium - São Miguel (20,000)

APPEARANCES 99/00

	P	Ap	(s)	Gls
ADIR	G	18		
AMARAL (MOZ)	M	3	(10)	1
BARRIGANA	M	15	(7)	
CLÁUDIO ABREU (ANG)	M	19	(2)	
CLAYTON (BRA)	A	12		8
DÁRIO	A	1		
Mustapha EL IDRISSI (FRA)	A	7	(11)	3
EURICO	D	4	(4)	
FERNANDO (ANG)	G	4	(1)	
FIGUEIREDO (ANG)	M	31		2
FORMOSO	M	10	(6)	
GAMBOA	A	18	(6)	3
GEORGE (BRA)	A	29	(3)	7
LUÍS CARLOS (BRA)	M	6	(1)	
LUÍS MIGUEL	M	17	(2)	
MADUREIRA	G	12		
MICAEL	M	10	(2)	
MOLEIRO	M		(1)	
PATACAS	D	22	(1)	1
PEDRO MARTINS	M	18	(1)	
PORTELA	M	15	(4)	1
Dmitriy PROKOPENKO (RUS)	A	15	(11)	6
RENÉ RIVAS (BRA)	D	7	(2)	
RICARDO SOUSA	M	11	(6)	2
SANDRO	M	12		1
SÉRGIO ABREU (BRA)	M	29		
SÉRGIO GAMEIRO	M	1	(9)	
SÉRGIO PEDRO (ANG)	M		(2)	
TELMO (BRA)	M	28		
WANDERLEY (BRA)	A		(5)	

LEAGUE RESULTS 1999/2000

21/08/99	Sporting CP	H	2-2	Gamboa 2
29/08/99	CS Marítimo	A	0-0	
12/09/99	SL Benfica	H	0-3	
19/09/99	SC Salgueiros	A	0-2	
26/09/99	Rio Ave FC	A	5-0	George 2, Clayton 3 (1p)
05/10/99	Vitória Setúbal	H	2-1	Clayton 2 (1p)
17/10/99	SC Farense	A	2-2	Patacas, Clayton
24/10/99	CF Estrela Amadora	H	1-1	Portela
31/10/99	Gil Vicente FC	A	1-3	Clayton (p)
08/11/99	Boavista FC	H	0-1	
21/11/99	FC Alverca	A	1-0	George
28/11/99	SC Braga	H	1-2	Clayton
03/12/99	FC Porto	A	0-1	
12/12/99	SC Campomaiorense	H	2-2	George, Prokopenko
19/12/99	CF Os Belenenses	A	1-3	Prokopenko
08/01/00	União Leiria	H	1-1	El Idrissi
16/01/00	Vitória Guimarães	A	1-2	George
22/01/00	Sporting CP	A	1-4	Figueiredo
30/01/00	CS Marítimo	H	0-0	
06/02/00	SL Benfica	A	0-1	
12/02/00	SC Salgueiros	H	0-0	
19/02/00	Rio Ave FC	H	1-0	George
27/02/00	Vitória Setúbal	A	0-1	
04/03/00	SC Farense	H	1-2	Prokopenko
13/03/00	CF Estrela Amadora	A	0-0	
19/03/00	Gil Vicente FC	H	0-0	
26/03/00	Boavista FC	A	1-2	El Idrissi
01/04/00	FC Alverca	H	4-3	Ricardo Sousa 2, George,
				Prokopenko (p)
09/04/00	SC Braga	A	1-3	Sandro
15/04/00	FC Porto	H	0-2	
22/04/00	SC Campomaiorense	A	0-1	
30/04/00	CF Os Belenenses	H	1-0	Prokopenko
07/05/00	União Leiria	A	2-3	Figueiredo (p), Gamboa
14/05/00	Vitória Guimarães	H	3-2	Prokopenko, El Idrissi, Amaral

SPORTING CP

CLUB DIRECTORY

Sporting Clube de Portugal
Rua Francisco Stromp 10-A, 1700 Lisboa
tel - (21) 7589021 / fax - (21) 7599391
website - www.scp.pt
Year of Formation - 1906
President - José Roquette
Coach - Giuseppe Materazzi; Augusto Inácio
Stadium - José Alvalade (52,411)

MAJOR HONOURS
League Championship - (17) 1941, 1944, 1947,
1948, 1949, 1951, 1952, 1953, 1954, 1958,
1962, 1966, 1970, 1974, 1980, 1982, 2000.
Domestic Cup - (16) 1923, 1934, 1936, 1938,
1941, 1945, 1946, 1948, 1954, 1963, 1971,
1973, 1974, 1978, 1982, 1995.
European Cup-winners' Cup - (1) 1964.

APPEARANCES 99/00

	P	Ap	(s)	Gls
Alberto ACOSTA (ARG)	A	31	(2)	22
AFONSO MARTINS	M	2		
AYEW Kwame (GHA)	A	13	(13)	7
BETO	D	28		2
BINO	M	3	(8)	
CÉSAR PRATES (BRA)	D	13	(1)	1
André CRUZ (BRA)	D	18		4
Ivone DE FRANCESCHI (ITA)	M	20	(5)	3
DELFIM	M	17		3
Aldo DUSCHER (ARG)	M	28		3
EDMILSON (BRA)	A	14	(6)	2
Mauricio HANUCH (ARG)	A	3	(8)	
Petar KRPAN (CRO)	A		(2)	
Marco ALMEIDA	D		(1)	
MARCOS (BRA)	D	5		
Mbo MPENZA (BEL)	A	13	(4)	3
NÉLSON	G	6		
PEDRO BARBOSA	M	28	(3)	2
QUIM BERTO	D	3	(1)	
Facundo QUIROGA (ARG)	D	12	(1)	
António ROBAINA (ESP)	M		(3)	
RUI JORGE	D	33	(1)	2
Abdelilah SABER (MAR)	D	17	(1)	
Peter SCHMEICHEL (DEN)	G	28		
TOÑITO (ESP)	M	3	(24)	
VIDIGAL	M	29	(3)	1
VINICIUS (BRA)	D	3	(1)	
Juan Francisco VIVEROS (CHL)	M	3		
Ivailo YORDANOV (BUL)	A	1	(10)	1

LEAGUE RESULTS 1999/2000

21/08/99	CD Santa Clara	A	2-2	Edmilson, Acosta
30/08/99	Vitória Setúbal	H	2-1	Ayew, Beto
12/09/99	SC Farense	A	3-0	Ayew, Rui Jorge, Delfim
20/09/99	CF Estrela Amadora	H	1-1	Acosta
25/09/99	Gil Vicente FC	A	1-1	Delfim
04/10/99	Boavista FC	H	2-0	Delfim, Acosta (p)
17/10/99	FC Alverca	A	1-2	Rui Jorge
23/10/99	SC Braga	H	2-0	Yordanov, De Franceschi
30/10/99	FC Porto	A	0-3	
06/11/99	SC Campomaiorense	H	1-0	Vidigal
21/11/99	CF Os Belenenses	A	1-0	Acosta
27/11/99	União Leiria	H	2-0	Acosta 2
04/12/99	Vitória Guimarães	A	2-1	Duscher, og (Evaldo)
12/12/99	Rio Ave FC	H	2-1	Ayew, De Franceschi
18/12/99	CS Marítimo	H	4-2	Ayew, De Franceschi, Duscher, Acosta
09/01/00	SL Benfica	A	0-0	
16/01/00	SC Salgueiros	H	2-0	Acosta 2 (1p)
22/01/00	CD Santa Clara	H	4-1	Acosta, Mpenza 2, Pedro Barbosa
31/01/00	Vitória Setúbal	A	2-1	Mpenza, Acosta
05/02/00	SC Farense	H	3-1	Acosta 2, Beto
13/02/00	CF Estrela Amadora	A	0-0	
19/02/00	Gil Vicente FC	H	1-1	Acosta (p)
28/02/00	Boavista FC	A	1-0	Pedro Barbosa
04/03/00	FC Alverca	H	1-1	Edmilson
10/03/00	SC Braga	A	2-0	Ayew, César Prates
18/03/00	FC Porto	H	2-0	Cruz, Acosta
24/03/00	SC Campomaiorense	A	2-0	Acosta 2 (1p)
02/04/00	CF Os Belenenses	H	1-0	Acosta
07/04/00	União Leiria	A	1-1	Cruz
17/04/00	Vitória Guimarães	H	1-0	Acosta
21/04/00	Rio Ave FC	A	2-1	Ayew, Acosta
30/04/00	CS Marítimo	A	2-0	Acosta 2 (1p)
06/05/00	SL Benfica	H	0-1	
14/05/00	SC Salgueiros	A	4-0	Cruz 2, Ayew, Duscher

UNIÃO LEIRIA

CLUB DIRECTORY

União Desportiva de Leiria
Estádio Municipal Dr. Magalhães Pessoa
Arrabalde D'Aquem
2400 Leiria
tel - (244) 823532
fax - (244) 827987
Year of Formation - 1966
President - João Bartolomeu
Coach - Mário Reis; Manuel José
Stadium - Municipal Magalhães Pessoa (25,000)

APPEARANCES 99/00

	P	Ap	(s)	Gls
ALFREDO BÓIA	D	6	(4)	
BAPTISTA	G	26	(1)	
BILRO	D	33		1
CHIQUINHO	A		(5)	
DERLEI (BRA)	A	16	(10)	8
DINDA (BRA)	A	20	(10)	4
Emmanuel DUAH (GHA)	M	33	(1)	7
Mark EDUSEI (GHA)	M	8	(4)	
HERIVELTO (BRA)	M	4	(2)	
HUGO	M		(1)	
JOÃO MANUEL	M	30	(1)	1
Petar KRPAN (CRO)	A	18	(1)	2
LEÃO	M	31		2
LUÍS VOUZELA	A	30		1
MARÇAL	D	15	(4)	
MARCELINO	M	4	(12)	1
NUNO VALENTE	D	26	(2)	
PAULO ALVES	A	3	(16)	2
PAULO DUARTE	D	24	(1)	1
PAULO VIDA	A		(1)	
REINALDO	A		(2)	
RENATO	D	32		
ROCHINHA	D	4		
ZEZINHO (CVD)	M	3	(8)	
Miroslav ZITNJAK (CRO)	G	8		

LEAGUE RESULTS 1999/2000

22/08/99	SC Farense	A	1-2	Derlei
29/08/99	CF Estrela Amadora	H	1-1	Derlei
12/09/99	Gil Vicente FC	A	0-2	
19/09/99	Boavista FC	H	0-0	
26/09/99	FC Alverca	A	0-0	
03/10/99	SC Braga	H	3-0	Derlei, Duah, Luís Vouzela
17/10/99	FC Porto	A	2-4	og (Rubens Júnior), Duah
24/10/99	SC Campomaiorense	H	1-2	Bilro (p)
31/10/99	CF Os Belenenses	A	0-1	
07/11/99	Rio Ave FC	H	0-0	
21/11/99	Vitória Guimarães	H	1-0	Duah
27/11/99	Sporting CP	A	0-2	
05/12/99	CS Marítimo	H	0-1	
13/12/99	SL Benfica	A	2-3	Duah 2
19/12/99	SC Salgueiros	H	1-4	Leão
08/01/00	CD Santa Clara	A	1-1	João Manuel
16/01/00	Vitória Setúbal	H	0-0	
23/01/00	SC Farense	H	2-0	Leão, Duah
30/01/00	CF Estrela Amadora	A	1-1	Marcelino
06/02/00	Gil Vicente FC	H	1-1	Derlei
12/02/00	Boavista FC	A	1-0	Duah
20/02/00	FC Alverca	H	3-0	Dinda, Derlei 2
25/02/00	SC Braga	A	2-0	Krpan 2
04/03/00	FC Porto	H	0-1	
12/03/00	SC Campomaiorense	A	0-2	
19/03/00	CF Os Belenenses	H	1-0	Dinda
26/03/00	Rio Ave FC	A	0-0	
02/04/00	Vitória Guimarães	A	1-0	Paulo Duarte
07/04/00	Sporting CP	H	1-1	Paulo Alves
16/04/00	CS Marítimo	A	0-0	
21/04/00	SL Benfica	H	2-1	Paulo Alves, Dinda
30/04/00	SC Salgueiros	A	0-3	
07/05/00	CD Santa Clara	H	3-2	Derlei 2, Dinda
14/05/00	Vitória Setúbal	A	0-0	

VITÓRIA GUIMARÃES

CLUB DIRECTORY

Vitória Sport Clube
Rua D. João 1 83
4800 Guimarães
tel - (253) 432570
fax - (253) 432573
website - www.vitoriasc.pt
Year of Formation - 1922
President - António Pimenta Machado
Coach - Quinito; António Ribeiro
(00/01 - Paulo Autuori)
Stadium - D. Afonso Henriques (33,000)

APPEARANCES 99/00

	P	Ap	(s)	Gls
ALEXANDRE (BRA)	D	12	(1)	
BRANDÃO (BRA)	A	23	(9)	16
BRUNO SOUSA	M		(1)	
CARLOS ALVAREZ Pérez (ESP)	M	14	(2)	
EDMILSON (BRA)	A	30	(1)	10
EVALDO (GBU)	D	24		
EVANDO	A		(5)	
FEIJÃO	A	2		1
FERNANDO MEIRA	D	30		2
FLÁVIO	D	2		
FONSECA (MOZ)	D	4		
GERALDO (BRA)	A	5	(20)	2
JAIRSON (STO)	A	7	(13)	3
KIPULU	D	5		
LIMA	A	1	(2)	
LIXA (CVD)	A	3	(1)	
MÁRCIO THEODORO (BRA)	D	25		1
NANDINHO	A	21	(9)	
PAIVA	M	28		
PAULO GOMES	M	5		
PEDRO ESPINHA	G	33		
PEDRO MENDES	M	9	(3)	1
PRETO	M	6	(5)	1
REGO	M	5	(8)	1
RIVA (BRA)	A	18	(13)	8
RUIVO	D	2		
Fredrik SÖDERSTRÖM (SWE)	M	33		1
TITO	D	26		
VÍTOR NUNO	G	1		

LEAGUE RESULTS 1999/2000

20/08/99	Vitória Setúbal	A	1-1	Edmilson
27/08/99	SC Farense	H	3-0	Edmilson 2, Rego
12/09/99	CF Estrela Amadora	A	2-2	Edmilson, Riva
19/09/99	Gil Vicente FC	H	1-0	Fernando Meira
26/09/99	Boavista FC	A	0-2	
02/10/99	FC Alverca	H	1-0	Brandão (p)
17/10/99	SC Braga	A	4-2	og (Odair), Brandão 2 (1p), Pedro Mendes
23/10/99	FC Porto	H	1-1	Geraldo
29/10/99	SC Campomaiorense	A	1-2	Söderström
05/11/99	CF Os Belenenses	H	4-2	Edmilson 3, Brandão (p)
21/11/99	União Leiria	A	0-1	
28/11/99	Rio Ave FC	H	2-1	Jairson, Brandão
04/12/99	Sporting CP	H	1-2	Brandão
10/12/99	CS Marítimo	A	1-1	Riva
19/12/99	SL Benfica	H	2-1	Brandão, Riva
07/01/00	SC Salgueiros	A	1-0	Geraldo
16/01/00	CD Santa Clara	H	2-1	Fernando Meira, Brandão
22/01/00	Vitória Setúbal	H	4-0	Brandão 2, Riva 2
29/01/00	SC Farense	A	1-2	Brandão
06/02/00	CF Estrela Amadora	H	1-0	Brandão
13/02/00	Gil Vicente FC	A	0-1	
20/02/00	Boavista FC	H	2-0	Preto, Riva
27/02/00	FC Alverca	A	1-2	Edmilson
04/03/00	SC Braga	H	1-0	Brandão
11/03/00	FC Porto	A	1-2	Edmilson
19/03/00	SC Campomaiorense	H	4-1	Brandão, Riva, Edmilson, Jairson
25/03/00	CF Os Belenenses	A	0-2	
02/04/00	União Leiria	H	0-1	
07/04/00	Rio Ave FC	A	1-1	Márcio Theodoro
17/04/00	Sporting CP	A	0-1	
24/04/00	CS Marítimo	H	1-3	Brandão
30/04/00	SL Benfica	A	0-3	
05/05/00	SC Salgueiros	H	2-2	Feijão, Brandão
14/05/00	CD Santa Clara	A	2-3	Jairson, Riva (p)

VITÓRIA SETÚBAL

CLUB DIRECTORY

Vitória Futebol Clube
Palácio Salema
Rua do Bocage 4
2901 Setúbal
tel - (265) 526959
fax - (265) 221746
Year of Formation - 1910
President - Jorge Gois
Coach - Carlos Cardoso; Rui Águas
Stadium - Bonfim (35,000)

MAJOR HONOURS
Domestic Cup - (2) 1965, 1967.

APPEARANCES 99/00

	P	Ap	(s)	Gls
BRASSARD	G	10	(1)	
CARLOS MANUEL	M	11	(2)	1
CATARINO	M		(9)	
CHIPENDA	M	7	(8)	
CHIQUINHO CONDE (MOZ)	A	28	(2)	7
FRECHAUT	M	14	(3)	1
HÉLIO	M	30	(1)	3
HERIVELTO (BRA)	A	1	(5)	
JORGE MATOS	A	11	(7)	
JORGE RIBEIRO	M	1		
JOSÉ RUI	D	2		
Henry Makinwa "MAKI" (NIG)	A	21	(4)	2
MAMEDE	M	32		1
MANUEL DO CARMO	M	1		
MARCO FERREIRA	A	14	(6)	
MARCO TÁBUAS	G	24		
MÁRIO LOJA	D	22		
MEYONG	A	5	(4)	2
NÉLSON SILVA	D	11	(4)	
PAULO FILIPE	D	19	(1)	1
PEDRO HENRIQUES	D	21	(1)	1
PEDRO MENDES	M	1	(8)	
QUIM	D	28	(2)	
RICARDO CARVALHO	D	25		2
RICARDO ESTEVES	A	13	(1)	
RUI CARLOS	M	2	(3)	
RUI GOMES	A		(7)	1
SEMEDO	D	15	(3)	1
SÉRGIO JOÃO	A	5	(2)	2

LEAGUE RESULTS 1999/2000

20/08/99	Vitória Guimarães	H	1-1	Sérgio João
30/08/99	Sporting CP	A	1-2	Pedro Henriques
12/09/99	CS Marítimo	H	4-2	Paulo Filipe, Chiquinho Conde,
				Sérgio João, Semedo
20/09/99	SL Benfica	A	0-3	
26/09/99	SC Salgueiros	H	1-2	Rui Gomes
05/10/99	CD Santa Clara	A	1-2	Hélio
17/10/99	Rio Ave FC	A	1-1	Hélio
22/10/99	SC Farense	H	1-1	Chiquinho Conde
01/11/99	CF Estrela Amadora	A	0-3	
07/11/99	Gil Vicente FC	H	0-1	
20/11/99	Boavista FC	A	0-1	
28/11/99	FC Alverca	H	1-0	Carlos Manuel
05/12/99	SC Braga	A	0-3	
13/12/99	FC Porto	H	1-4	Frechaut
19/12/99	SC Campomaiorense	A	1-0	Ricardo Carvalho
08/01/00	CF Os Belenenses	H	0-2	
16/01/00	União Leiria	A	0-0	
22/01/00	Vitória Guimarães	A	0-4	
31/01/00	Sporting CP	H	1-2	Maki
05/02/00	CS Marítimo	A	0-1	
14/02/00	SL Benfica	H	1-2	Chiquinho Conde
20/02/00	SC Salgueiros	A	0-1	
27/02/00	CD Santa Clara	H	1-0	Maki
04/03/00	Rio Ave FC	H	2-0	Chiquinho Conde 2 (1p)
12/03/00	SC Farense	A	0-0	
19/03/00	CF Estrela Amadora	H	1-0	Meyong
26/03/00	Gil Vicente FC	A	0-2	
31/03/00	Boavista FC	H	2-1	Mamede, Hélio (p)
09/04/00	FC Alverca	A	1-0	Maki
16/04/00	SC Braga	H	0-2	
22/04/00	FC Porto	A	1-4	Meyong
30/04/00	SC Campomaiorense	H	1-2	Chiquinho Conde
06/05/00	CF Os Belenenses	A	1-0	Ricardo Carvalho
14/05/00	União Leiria	H	0-0	

REPUBLIC OF IRELAND

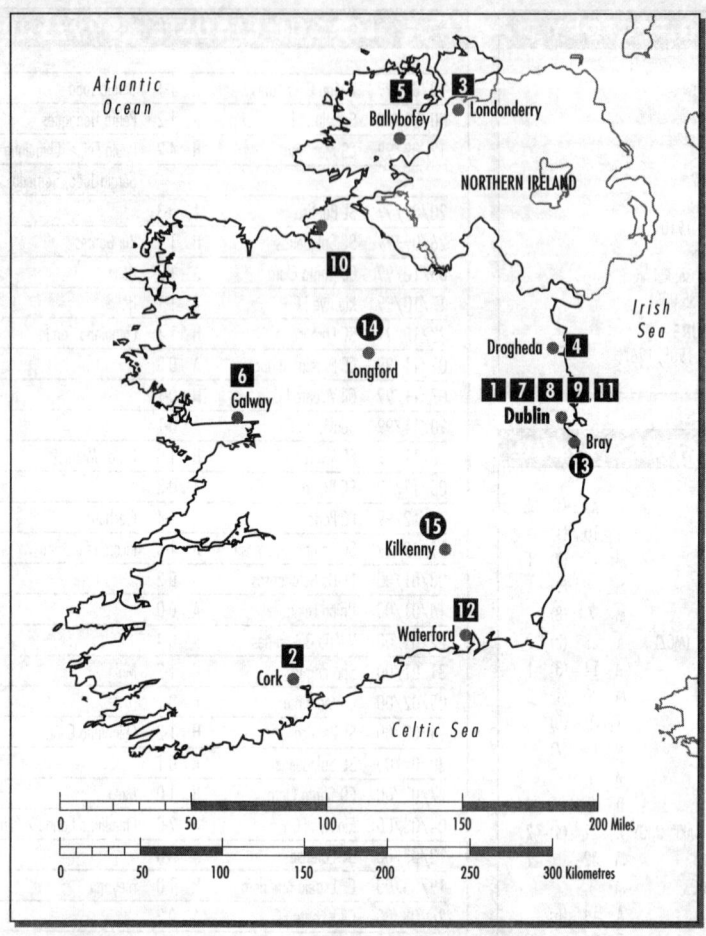

1	BOHEMIANS	798	9	SHELBOURNE	806
2	CORK CITY	799	10	SLIGO ROVERS	807
3	DERRY CITY	800	11	UCD	808
4	DROGHEDA UNITED	801	12	WATERFORD UNITED	809
5	FINN HARPS	802	**Promoted clubs**		
6	GALWAY UNITED	803	13	BRAY WANDERERS	
7	ST. PATRICK'S ATHLETIC	804	14	LONGFORD TOWN	
8	SHAMROCK ROVERS	805	15	KILKENNY CITY	

PLAY-OFF JINX STRIKES AGAIN

Shelbourne sweep all before them

FEDERATION DIRECTORY

The Football Association of Ireland
80 Merrion Square, Dublin 2

tel - (01) 6766864
fax - (01) 6610931
website - www.fai.ie

Year of Formation - 1921
Chairman - Michael Hyland
Secretary - Donal Crowther

Stadium - Lansdowne Road, Dublin (48,000)

The Dublin Reds of Shelbourne won the Irish league and Cup 'double' for the first time. Their first championship win since 1992 was never really in doubt following a coruscating start, during which they strung together 20 games without defeat.

Shelbourne rarely took their opponents to the cleaners, but they did have the extraordinary knack of squeezing out significant victories by the odd goal. Seven of the 12 victories they posted during that opening run were by one goal to nil. They upped their goal-rate towards the end of the season, but even the team's leading individual marksman, the ever-prolific Stephen Geoghegan, finished some distance behind the league's top scorer, 20-goal Pat Morley of Cork City.

Shelbourne ended the season unbeaten at their Tolka Park home and with a clear 11-point gap between themselves and runners-up Cork. Manager Dermot Keely claimed a distinguished hat-trick, having also taken Shamrock Rovers (1987) and Dundalk (1995) to the title. The leadership on the field came predominantly from centre-back Pat Scully and midfielder Pat Fenlon, both of whom played with magnificent consistency all season.

The team's major 'find' was young midfielder Richie Baker, who created and scored an abundance of crucial goals.

Once again, the final of the FAI Cup went to a replay. For the first time ever, the end-of-season showpiece was contested between Ireland's two oldest clubs, Shelbourne and Bohemians. The first game, at Shels' Tolka Park, ended goalless, but the replay, at Bohs' Dalymount Park, was decided by a solitary goal from Fenlon, which capped a memorable year for the diminutive midfielder and an historic one for his club.

Bohemians' runners-up spot in the Cup was enough to earn the club a return to Europe. They also finished third in the league, which was a considerable improvement on the previous season, when they retained their Premier Division status only after surviving a relegation play-off. Cork

LEAGUE CHAMPIONSHIP RESULTS 99/00

		1	2	3	4	5	6	7	8	9	10	11	12
1	Bohemians		3-0 / 0-0	3-0	2-1	1-0	1-3	0-0 / 0-1	1-3 / 0-0	0-1 / 1-1	3-2 / 4-1	1-0 / 1-2	0-2
2	Cork City	1-1 / 2-1		0-0	3-0 / 3-1	2-0	3-0	1-0 / 1-1	2-0	1-2	0-1 / 0-0	1-0 / 1-1	0-0
3	Derry City	0-0	1-0 / 1-4		0-2 / 2-1	2-0	2-0	0-3	1-0	1-0 / 0-0	1-3 / 0-0	0-2 / 2-0	3-0 / 1-1
4	Drogheda United	0-2 / 0-3	0-0	1-2		3-2 / 0-2	3-1	1-2 / 0-3	0-4 / 0-0	0-0	1-1	0-1 / 0-5	1-1 / 1-0
5	Finn Harps	0-1 / 0-0	1-2 / 1-1	1-1 / 1-2	0-0		1-2	1-1	1-0	0-1 / 2-3	2-1 / 2-1	0-0	4-0
6	Galway United	1-2 / 0-1	1-4 / 0-2	0-2 / 2-1	1-1 / 2-2	1-3 / 0-4		1-2 / 1-0	0-3	0-0	5-0	2-1	0-0
7	St. Patrick's Athletic	1-3	2-0 / 1-1	1-2	1-0 / 1-0	2-1	3-0		1-1 / 0-0	1-1 / 1-2	3-2	0-0	1-0 / 0-0
8	Shamrock Rovers	0-1	1-3 / 1-2	3-0	4-1	3-1 / 3-3	2-1 / 0-0	2-1		1-1 / 2-1	4-1 / 4-2	0-0	1-0 / 1-2
9	Shelbourne	1-0 / 4-0	3-2 / 2-2	2-0 / 0-0	1-0	1-1 / 1-1	1-1	1-0	3-0		1-0 / 2-1	0-0	1-0
10	Sligo Rovers	0-0	0-5	2-0	1-1 / 0-0	1-1	1-0 / 1-1	0-1 / 2-2	3-5	2-4 / 0-4		1-2 / 0-1	1-0
11	UCD	0-2	2-2	1-0	3-0	1-0 / 1-1	0-2 / 1-1	2-2 / 2-1	3-0 / 1-1	0-2	1-1		2-2 / 2-1
12	Waterford United	0-2 / 0-0	1-3 / 2-2	2-2	1-0	2-3 / 1-0	1-2 / 0-0	3-1	0-0	0-0	1-0 / 0-2	0-2 / 1-0	

LEAGUE CHAMPIONSHIP FINAL TABLE 99/00

			Home					Away					Total					
		Pd	W	D	L	F	A	W	D	L	F	A	W	D	L	F	A	PT	GD
1	Shelbourne	33	10	6	0	24	8	9	6	2	25	12	19	12	2	49	20	69	29
2	Cork City	33	8	6	2	21	8	8	4	5	32	24	16	10	7	53	32	58	21
3	Bohemians	33	7	4	6	21	17	9	5	2	19	6	16	9	8	40	23	57	17
4	UCD	33	6	7	3	22	18	7	5	5	18	11	13	12	8	40	29	51	11
5	Shamrock Rovers	33	9	4	4	32	20	4	7	5	17	16	13	11	9	49	36	50	13
6	St. Patrick's Athletic	33	7	6	3	19	13	6	5	6	21	18	13	11	9	40	31	50	9
7	Derry City	33	8	4	5	17	16	4	6	6	15	22	12	10	11	32	38	46	-6
8	Finn Harps	33	4	6	6	17	16	4	4	9	22	25	8	10	15	39	41	34	-2
9	Galway United	33	4	4	9	17	28	4	6	6	15	21	8	10	15	32	49	34	-17
10	Waterford United	33	5	6	6	15	19	2	6	8	9	19	7	12	14	24	38	33	-14
11	Sligo Rovers	33	3	6	7	15	27	2	4	11	16	33	5	10	18	31	60	25	-29
12	Drogheda United	33	3	5	9	11	29	1	6	9	10	24	4	11	18	21	53	23	-32

finished second in the league to join Bohemians in the UEFA Cup but lost long-serving manager Dave Barry at the season's end. The Intertoto spot went surprisingly to UCD. The unexpected death of club guru Dr. Tony O'Neill inspired the Students, and Martin Moran's appointment as manager was the spark they needed to reach their highest league position of all time.

There was great disapppintment for two other Dublin sides, Shamrock Rovers and St. Patrick's Athletic. The former, still without a permanent home following the demise of Milltown in 1987, based themselves at Morton Athletics Stadium. Their inconsistency condemned them to a place in mid-table. St. Pat's, the defending champions, never recovered from the abject humiliation of being destroyed 10-0 on aggregate by the modest Moldovans of Zimbru Chisinau in the preliminary round of the Champions' League. They parted company with title-winning boss Liam Buckley in

mid-season, with former manager Pat Dolan once again taking over.

St. Pats' capitulation to the Moldovan champions raised new questions about the standard of the League of Ireland. However, Cork City did at least salvage some pride when they beat former winners IFK Gothenburg 1-0 at home in the UEFA Cup qualifying round (with Morley the inevitable match-winner), but, sadly, they had already lost the first leg 3-0 in Sweden so went out together with Bray Wanderers, crushed home and away by Swiss side Grasshopper.

Bray may have started the season badly but they ended it by winning promotion back to the Premier Division after

TOP SCORERS

- 20 Pat MORLEY (Cork City)
- 12 James MULLIGAN (Finn Harps)
- Stephen GEOGHEGAN (Shelbourne)
- 11 Padraig MORAN (Sligo Rovers)
- 9 Glen CROWE (Bohemians)
- 8 Liam COYLE (Derry City)
- Ciaran MARTYN (UCD)
- John CAULFIELD (Cork City)

NATIONAL TEAM RESULTS 99/00

01/09/99	Yugoslavia (ECQ)	H	Dublin	2-1	Keane Rob. (53), Kennedy (69)
04/09/99	Croatia (ECQ)	A	Zagreb	0-1	
08/09/99	Malta (ECQ)	A	Ta' Qali	3-2	Keane Rob. (13), Breen (21), Staunton (73)
09/10/99	Macedonia (ECQ)	A	Skopje	1-1	Quinn N. (18)
13/11/99	Turkey (ECQ)	H	Dublin	1-1	Keane Rob. (79)
17/11/99	Turkey (ECQ)	A	Bursa	0-0	
23/02/00	Czech Republic	H	Dublin	3-2	Rada (16og), Harte (43), Keane Rob. (87)
26/04/00	Greece	H	Dublin	0-1	
30/05/00	Scotland	H	Dublin	1-2	Kennedy (2)
04/06/00	Mexico	N	Chicago	2-2	Dunne (60), Foley (71)
06/06/00	United States	A	Foxboro	1-1	Foley (31)
11/06/00	South Africa	N	New Jersey	2-1	McPhail (43), Quinn N. (69)

just one season away. Two other teams went up with them - Longford Town, who were promoted automatically, and Kilkenny City, who beat Waterford United home and away in the play-offs.

'Play-off' is fast becoming a dirty word in Ireland. For the third major tournament running, the Republic of Ireland failed to qualify by the back-door route. Holland had beaten them at Anfield in the Euro '96 tie-breaker, Belgium had done likewise over two legs en route to France '98, and to complete an unwanted hat-trick, Turkey broke Irish hearts again to deprive Mick McCarthy's team of a place at Euro 2000.

NATIONAL TEAM APPEARANCES 99/00

Manager - Mick McCARTHY	YUG	CRO	MLT	MAC	TUR	TUR	CZE	GRE	SCO	MEX	USA	SAF	Cps	Gls
Alan KELLY (11/08/68) - Blackburn Rovers (ENG)	G	G	G	G	G61		G		G		G		30	-
Denis IRWIN (31/10/65) - Manchester United (ENG)	D66			D	D	D							56	4
Ken CUNNINGHAM (28/06/71) - Wimbledon (ENG)	D	D	D	D	D	D	D	D					31	-
Gary BREEN (12/12/73) - Coventry City (ENG)	D	D	D75	D	D	D		D	D77	D	D	D	31	4
Steve STAUNTON (19/01/69) - Liverpool (ENG)	D	D	D	D		s83	D						84	6
Mark KENNEDY (15/05/76) - Manchester City (ENG)	M		M55	M85			M46		M61	M	s72	s44	30	4
Roy KEANE (10/08/71) - Manchester United (ENG)	M69				M	M	M						46	5
Mark KINSELLA (12/08/72) - Charlton Athletic (ENG)	M	M	M	M		M	M	M					16	-
Kevin KILBANE (01/02/77) -														
West Bromwich Albion (ENG)/Sunderland (ENG)	M	s57	M66		M	M	M83	M	D	s41	M	s42	16	-
Niall QUINN (06/10/66) - Sunderland (ENG)	A78	s83	A	A78		A	A		A77	A	s72	A76	79	20
Robbie KEANE (08/07/80) - Coventry City (ENG)	A		A	A66	A		A90	A	A	A46		s46	18	6
Stephen CARR (29/08/76) - Tottenham Hotspur (ENG)	s66	D	D		D	D4			D	D	D	D	12	-
Lee CARSLEY (28/02/74) - Blackburn Rovers (ENG)	s69	M	M		M								15	-
Tony CASCARINO (01/09/62) - AS Nancy-Lorraine (FRA)	s78	A83		s78	A75	s81							88	19
Gary KELLY (09/07/74) - Leeds United (ENG)		M73		M			D						31	1
Alan McLOUGHLIN (20/04/67) - Portsmouth (ENG)		M	s55	M									41	2
Damien DUFF (02/03/79) - Blackburn Rovers (ENG)		M57	s66		s53	s78			s61				14	-
Ian HARTE (31/08/77) - Leeds United (ENG)		s73	s75				D						22	3
Keith O'NEILL (16/02/76) - Middlesbrough (ENG)				s66									13	4
Matt HOLLAND (11/04/74) - Ipswich Town (ENG)				s85					M	M	M		4	-
Rory DELAP (06/07/76) - Derby County (ENG)					M53	M		s33					6	-
Dean KIELY (10/10/70) - Charlton Athletic (ENG)					s61	G		s46		G			4	-
David CONNOLLY (06/06/77) - Excelsior (HOL)					s75	A78	s90	A54					22	7
Jeff KENNA (27/08/70) - Blackburn Rovers (ENG)					s4	/81							27	-
Paul BUTLER (02/11/72) - Sunderland (ENG)							D46						1	-
Phil BABB (30/11/70) - Liverpool (ENG)							s46		D	s82	D	D	34	-
Jason McATEER (18/06/71) - Blackburn Rovers (ENG)							s46		M	M	s37	M44	35	1
Shay GIVEN (20/04/76) - Newcastle United (ENG)							G46					G	25	-
Richard DUNNE (21/09/79) - Everton (ENG)							D	s77	D82				3	1
Barry QUINN (09/05/79) - Coventry City (ENG)							M33		M41	s88	s85		4	-
Steve FINNAN (20/04/76) - Fulham (ENG)							M71	M					2	-
Alan MAHON (04/04/78) - Tranmere Rovers (ENG)							s54				M42		2	-
Gary DOHERTY (31/01/80) - Tottenham Hotspur (ENG)							s71		A72	s76			3	-
Stephen McPHAIL (09/12/79) - Leeds United (ENG)								M61		M37	M85		3	1
Terry PHELAN (16/03/67) - Fulham (ENG)								s61	D	D	D		42	-
Dominic FOLEY (07/07/76) - Watford (ENG)								s77	s46	A88	A46		4	2
Gareth FARRELLY (28/08/75) - Bolton Wanderers (ENG)										M72			6	-

In truth, the Irish should have made certain of automatic qualification. Although they were in a tough group, alongside Croatia and Yugoslavia, they won all their matches at Lansdowne Road and were within 12 seconds of topping the group when they conceded a last-gasp equaliser to Macedonia in their final game. It was heartbreaking stuff but it was not as if McCarthy's men had not been warned. A month or so earlier they had also conceded a crucial stoppage-time goal, in a 1-0 defeat away to Croatia.

The horror-shows in Zagreb and Skopje plunged Ireland into the play-offs. When Robbie Keane gave his team the lead late on in the home leg, Euro 2000 beckoned. But a stupidly conceded penalty soon afterwards allowed Turkey to equalise. Ireland were prepared for a daunting second leg in Bursa but it was the loss of Robbie Keane, who foolishly picked up a second yellow card in the first leg, that made their task so difficult. They needed a goal to qualify but without their young front man their goal threat was minimal. Stand-in goalkeeper Dean Kiely played well to keep the Turksih attack at bay but Ireland's failure to score spelt elimination on away goals.

The match in Bursa marked a record-breaking 88th and last international appearance for veteran striker Tony Cascarino. He will not forget the game in a hurry

EUROPEAN CUPS 99/00

CHAMPIONS' CUP
● ST. PATRICK'S ATHLETIC
Preliminary round 1 ZIMBRU CHISINAU (MOL)
H 0-5
> Wood. McGuinness, Campbell, Hawkins, Croly, Gormley, Osam (Harte 61), Russell (Hallows 46), Burke, Molloy, Gilzean (Devereux 83).

A 0-5
> Wood, Croly, Byrne (Campbell 46), McGuinness, Hawkins, Gormley, Russell (Osam 46), Harte, Devereux, Morgan, Molloy.

UEFA CUP
● BRAY WANDERERS
Qualifying round GRASSHOPPER-CLUB ZÜRICH (SUI)
A 0-4
> Walsh, Tresson, Farrell, Kenny, Doohan, Keogh (Tierney 86), Byrne, Lynch (Brien 46), O'Brien, Fox, Connolly (O'Connor 59).

H 0-4
> Walsh, Tresson, McKeever (O'Connor 77), Doohan, Farrell, Kenny (Larkin 70), Tierney, Smyth (Power 70), Byrne, Fox, O'Brien.

● CORK CITY
Qualifying round IFK GÖTEBORG (SWE)
A 0-3
> Mooney, Napier, Cronin, Hill, Daly, Freyne (Caulfield 71), Cahill, Flanagan, Herrick, Morley (Dobbs 71), O'Brien C..

H 1-0 Morley (30)
> Mooney, Napier, Cronin, Hill, Daly, Freyne, Cahill (O'Halloran 72), Flanagan, O'Brien L., Morley (Dobbs 70), O'Brien C..

DOMESTIC CUP 99/00

FIRST ROUND
Athlone Town 4, Limerick 1
Clonmel Town 1, Rockmount 1
(replay) Rockmount 1, Clonmel Town 3
Cobh Ramblers 0, Bohemians 1
Derry City 1, Bray Wanderers 1
(replay) Bray Wanderers 2, Derry City 1
Drogheda United 0, Bangor Celtic 1
Fairview Rangers 0, College Corinthians 0
(replay) College Corinthians 1, Fairview Rangers 3 (aet)
Finn Harps 2, Home Farm Fingal 0
Galway United 1, St. Patrick's Athletic 1
(replay) St. Patrick's Athletic 2, Galway United 3 (aet)
Kilkenny City 1, Dundalk 1
(replay) Dundalk 1, Kilkenny City 1 (aet; 2-3 on pens.)
Longford Town 2, Waterford United 2
(replay) Waterford United 0, Longford Town 1
Monaghan United 0, UCD 4
St. Francis 0, Shelbourne 1
St. Mochtais 3, Evergreen 1
Shamrock Rovers 1, Cork City 1
(replay) Cork City 3, Shamrock Rovers 1
Sligo Rovers 0, Bluebell United 1
Swilly Rovers 5, Parkvilla 0

SECOND ROUND
Athlone Town 0, Galway United 0

(replay) Galway United 1, Athlone Town 1
(aet; 4-2 on pens.)
Bangor Celtic 2, Shelbourne 3
Bohemians 3, UCD 3
(replay) UCD 0, Bohemians 3
Clonmel Town 1, Bluebell United 1
(replay) Bluebell United 2, Clonmel Town 0
Cork City 0, Kilkenny City 2
Fairview Rangers 0, Bray Wanderers 2
Longford Town 2, Finn Harps 2
(replay) Finn Harps 7, Longford Town 1
Swilly Rovers 1, St. Mochtais 2

QUARTER-FINALS
Bluebell United 0, Shelbourne 0

(replay) Shelbourne 2 (Keddy 30, McCarthy 67),
Bluebell United 1 (McGovern 35)
Bohemians 2 (Kelly 62, 75), St. Mochtais 0
Finn Harps 1 (Turner 69),
Galway United 3 (Keane 20, Keogh 41, Lavine 68)
Kilkenny City 0,
Bray Wanderers 2 (Byrne 9, Tresson 57)

SEMI-FINALS
Bohemians 2 (Hunt 6, Kelly 71),
Bray Wanderers 1 (Tresson 30)

Galway United 0,
Shelbourne 2 (Keddy 46, Baker D. 63)

FINAL
30/04/2000, Dublin (Tolka Park)
BOHEMIANS 0
SHELBOURNE 0
referee - Stacey
BOHEMIANS - Dempsey Mi., O'Connor T., Brunton, Hunt (Doyle 61), Maher, John, Byrne (Kelly 56), Caffrey, Swan (Crowe 82), O'Connor G., Dempsey Ma..
SHELBOURNE - Williams, Heary, Geoghegan D., McCarthy, Scully, Baker D., Doolin, Geoghegan S., Fenlon, Keddy, Baker R..

(replay)
05/05/2000, Dublin (Dalymount Park)
SHELBOURNE 1 Fenlon (39)
BOHEMIANS 0
referee - Stacey
SHELBOURNE - Williams, Heary, Geoghegan D., McCarthy, Scully, Baker D., Doolin (Campbell 90), Geoghegan S., Fenlon, Keddy, Baker R..
BOHEMIANS - Dempsey Mi., O'Connor T., Brunton (Doyle 87), Hunt, Maher, John, Byrne (Swan 51), Caffrey, Kelly (Crowe 63), O'Connor G., Dempsey Ma..

as he was assaulted by Turkish players and fans after the final whistle and subsequently suspended!

Manager McCarthy was subjected to some rare press criticism in the wake of Ireland's failure but there was never any serious threat to his position. He saw out the season with a series of friendlies that produced a mixture of good and bad performances. A decimated squad travelled to America in June for the US Cup and returned unbeaten with two draws and a victory. They would rather, of course, have made the shorter trip to Belgium and Holland to compete in the European Championship, but the games against Mexico, the USA and South Africa did serve the useful purpose of restoring camaraderie and confidence before the two big opening World Cup qualifiers in the early autumn away to Holland and Portugal.

INTERNATIONAL HONOURS

World Cup Finals appearances: 1990 (qtr-finals), 1994 (2nd round)
European Championship appearances: 1964, 1988

PLAYER OF THE SEASON

NIALL QUINN

Two more of the famous Boys in Green from the Jack Charlton era decided to quit the Republic of Ireland team in 1999/2000. But while Tony Cascarino and Denis Irwin have called it a day, Niall Quinn continues to soldier on, despite his 34 years. The gentle giant had quite a season, both for club and country. In the English Premiership he formed a lethal 'little and large' attacking duo with Kevin Phillips at Sunderland, helping the newly-promoted club to finish as high as seventh. And for Ireland he managed to equal the all-time scoring record previously held alone by Frank Stapleton. His landmark 20th goal came in the final match of the season and proved to be the winning goal in a 2-1 victory over South Africa. With 79 caps, he also looks set to surpass Cascarino's record total and - who knows? - perhaps go on to become Ireland's first centurion.

PROMOTED CLUBS 99/00

FIRST DIVISION FINAL TABLE

		Pd	W	D	L	F	A	Pt	GD
1	**Bray Wanderers**	36	21	9	6	69	38	72	31
2	**Longford Town**	36	21	7	8	71	40	70	31
3	**Kilkenny City**	36	20	7	9	65	34	67	31
4	Dundalk	36	20	6	10	50	31	66	19
5	Cobh Ramblers	36	14	8	14	52	59	50	-7
6	Athlone Town	36	8	14	14	31	42	38	-11
7	Home Farm Fingal	36	8	11	17	43	60	35	-17
8	Fingal St. Francis	36	6	15	15	28	54	33	-26
9	Monaghan United	36	6	12	18	46	73	30	-27
10	Limerick	36	6	11	19	36	60	29	-24

PROMOTION/RELEGATION PLAY-OFF
Kilkenny City 1, Waterford United 0
Waterford United 0, Kilkenny City 1
(Kilkenny City 2-0)

CLUB DIRECTORIES

Bray Wanderers FC
Carlisle Grounds, Bray, Co. Wicklow
tel - (01) 2828214 / fax - (01) 2861685
Year of Formation - 1942
Chairman - Philip Hannigan
Secretary - John O'Brien
Manager - Pat Devlin
Stadium - Carlisle Grounds (6,500)

MAJOR HONOURS
Domestic Cup - (2) 1990, 1999.

Longford Town FC
Mullogher, Strokestown Road, Longford
tel - (043) 41637 / fax - (043) 46955
Year of Formation - 1924
Chairman - Michael Cox
Secretary - Una Glancy
Manager - Stephen Kenny
Stadium - Strokestown Road (8,750)

Kilkenny City FC
Buckley Park, Derdimus, Callan Road, Kilkenny
tel - (056) 51888 / fax - (056) 51888
Year of Formation - 1966
Chairman - Tom Cantwell
Secretary - Jim Rhatigan
Manager - Pat Byrne; Paul Power
(00/01 - Pat Byrne)
Stadium - Buckley Park (6,850)

BOHEMIANS

CLUB DIRECTORY

Bohemian FC
Dalymount Park, Phibsborough, Dublin 7
tel - (01) 8680923/8681022/8682880
fax - (01) 8681022
Year of Formation - 1890
Chairman - Felim O'Reilly
Secretary - Gerry Cuffe
Manager - Roddy Collins
Stadium - Dalymount Park (14,700)

MAJOR HONOURS
League Championship - (7)
1924, 1928, 1930, 1934, 1936, 1975, 1978.
Domestic Cup - (5)
1928, 1935, 1970, 1976, 1992.

APPEARANCES 99/00

		P	Ap	(s)	Gls
Robbie BRUNTON	D	17	(1)	
Paul BYRNE	M	24	(8)	7
Stephen CAFFREY	D	30	(2)	2
Michael CRAWFORD (STK)	M		(2)	
Glen CROWE	A	26	(4)	9
Mark DEMPSEY	M	20	(1)	
Michael DEMPSEY	G	14		
Graham DOYLE	M	4	(1)	
Jamie HARRIS (WAL)	A	21	(3)	4
Austin HUGGINS (TRI)	M	3	(1)	
Kevin HUNT (ENG)	M	28	(1)	1
Avery JOHN (TRI)	M	20	(1)	
Ray KELLY	A	13	(7)	1
Jordan LANCASTER	M		(1)	
Graham LAWLOR	A		(4)	
Shaun MAHER	D	28		1
Eoin MULLEN	D	23	(2)	
Gareth O'CONNOR	A	19	(3)	4
Tony O'CONNOR	D	24	(3)	2
Maurice O'DRISCOLL	D	7	(2)	
Graham O'HANLON	M	8	(3)	1
Wayne RUSSELL (WAL)	G	19		
Derek SWAN	A	8	(21)	6
Pascal VAUDEQUIN (FRA)	D	6	(1)	
David WILLIAMSON (ENG)	M		(1)	
Tony WITTER (ENG)	D	1	(1)	

LEAGUE RESULTS 1999/2000

13/08/99	Waterford United	A	2-0	Harris, Crowe
20/08/99	Shelbourne	H	0-1	
03/09/99	Drogheda United	A	2-0	O'Connor T., Byrne
10/09/99	Derry City	H	3-0	Crowe, Byrne, Harris
19/09/99	Shamrock Rovers	H	1-3	Crowe
24/09/99	Galway United	A	2-1	Crowe, Byrne
01/10/99	St. Patrick's Athletic	H	0-0	
10/10/99	Cork City	A	1-1	O'Connor T.
17/10/99	UCD	A	2-0	Crowe, og (Kavanagh)
23/10/99	Finn Harps	A	1-0	Caffrey
31/10/99	Sligo Rovers	H	3-2	Crowe, Swan, Hunt
05/11/99	Waterford United	H	0-2	
12/11/99	Shelbourne	A	0-1	
19/11/99	Drogheda United	H	2-1	Harris, Caffrey
27/11/99	Derry City	A	0-0	
05/12/99	Shamrock Rovers	A	1-0	og (Purdy)
12/12/99	Galway United	H	1-3	O'Connor G.
17/12/99	St. Patrick's Athletic	A	3-1	Crowe, O'Hanlon, Swan
27/12/99	Cork City	H	3-0	Crowe, Harris, Swan
02/01/00	UCD	H	1-0	Maher
14/01/00	Finn Harps	H	1-0	Swan
22/01/00	Sligo Rovers	A	0-0	
28/01/00	Waterford United	A	0-0	
11/02/00	Shelbourne	H	1-1	Byrne (p)
18/02/00	Drogheda United	A	3-0	Kelly, O'Connor G., Swan
25/02/00	Derry City	H	0-0	
10/03/00	Shamrock Rovers	H	0-0	
18/03/00	Galway United	A	1-0	Crowe
24/03/00	St. Patrick's Athletic	H	0-1	
07/04/00	UCD	H	1-2	O'Connor G.
12/04/00	Cork City	A	1-2	Swan
18/04/00	Finn Harps	A	0-0	
23/04/00	Sligo Rovers	H	4-1	Byrne 3 (1p), O'Connor G.

CORK CITY

CLUB DIRECTORY

Cork City FC
Turners Cross Stadium
Curragh Road, Turners Cross, Cork
tel - (021) 311526 / fax - (021) 503628
Year of Formation - 1984
Chairman - Terry Dunne
Secretary - Jim Murphy
Manager - Dave Barry (00/01 - Derek Mountfield)
Stadium - Turners Cross (10,850)

MAJOR HONOURS
League Championship - (1) 1993.
Domestic Cup - (1) 1998.

APPEARANCES 99/00

		P	Ap	(s)	Gls
Anthony BUCKLEY	M	1	(3)		1
Ollie CAHILL	M	33			1
John CAULFIELD	A	11	(18)		8
John COTTER	M	7	(5)		2
Derek COUGHLAN	D	16	(1)		1
Gareth CRONIN	D	29			
Declan DALY	D	29			
Gerald DOBBS (ENG)	A	7	(6)		
Kelvin FLANAGAN	M	9	(4)		1
Patsy FREYNE	M	19	(3)		1
Johnny GLYNN	A	1	(13)		2
Phil HARRINGTON (WAL)	G	14			
Noel HARTIGAN	A	2	(6)		
Mark HERRICK	M	27			3
Dave HILL (ENG)	D	21	(2)		
Noel MOONEY	G	19			
Pat MORLEY	A	33			20
Stephen NAPIER	D	23	(3)		
Colin O'BRIEN	M	23	(7)		5
Liam O'BRIEN	M	25	(2)		4
Greg O'HALLORAN	D	14	(3)		2

LEAGUE RESULTS 1999/2000

14/08/99	Finn Harps	A	2-1	Morley, Cotter
21/08/99	Sligo Rovers	H	0-1	
03/09/99	Galway United	A	4-1	Cahill (p), Morley, O'Brien C., Freyne
11/09/99	St. Patrick's Athletic	H	1-0	O'Halloran
17/09/99	Shelbourne	A	2-3	Morley, Caulfield
01/10/99	Waterford United	A	3-1	O'Brien L. 2, Morley
10/10/99	Bohemians	H	1-1	Morley
13/10/99	UCD	H	1-0	Morley
17/10/99	Shamrock Rovers	A	3-1	Herrick, Caulfield, Morley
24/10/99	Drogheda United	H	3-0	Caulfield, Morley 2
31/10/99	Derry City	A	0-1	
07/11/99	Finn Harps	H	2-0	og (Vaudequin), Glynn
14/11/99	Sligo Rovers	A	5-0	Caulfield, O'Brien C. 3, Morley
21/11/99	Galway United	H	3-0	Flanagan (p), Morley, Glynn
26/11/99	St. Patrick's Athletic	A	0-2	
05/12/99	Shelbourne	H	1-2	Caulfield
12/12/99	UCD	A	2-2	Morley, Caulfield
19/12/99	Waterford United	H	0-0	
27/12/99	Bohemians	A	0-3	
02/01/00	Shamrock Rovers	H	2-0	Buckley, Morley
16/01/00	Drogheda United	A	0-0	
23/01/00	Derry City	H	0-0	
29/01/00	Finn Harps	A	1-1	Caulfield
13/02/00	Sligo Rovers	H	0-0	
27/02/00	St. Patrick's Athletic	H	1-1	O'Brien C.
10/03/00	Shelbourne	A	0-4	
14/03/00	Galway United	A	2-0	Herrick, Morley
18/03/00	UCD	H	1-1	Morley
24/03/00	Waterford United	A	2-2	Morley, Herrick
09/04/00	Shamrock Rovers	A	2-1	Cotter, Morley
12/04/00	Bohemians	H	2-1	O'Halloran, Morley (p)
16/04/00	Drogheda United	H	3-1	O'Brien L., Coughlan, Caulfield
23/04/00	Derry City	A	4-1	O'Brien L., og (Hargan), Morley 2

DERRY CITY

CLUB DIRECTORY

Derry City FC
12 Queen Street, Londonderry BT48 7EF,
Northern Ireland
tel - (01504) 281333
fax - (01504) 281334
Year of Formation - 1928
Chairman - vacant
Secretary - Eamon McCourt
Manager - Kevin Mahon
Stadium - Brandywell (7,500)

MAJOR HONOURS
League Championship - (2) 1989, 1997.
Domestic Cup - (2) 1989, 1995.

APPEARANCES 99/00

	P	Ap	(s)	Gls
Gary BECKETT (NIR)	M	27	(1)	4
Liam COYLE (NIR)	A	23	(1)	8
Paul CURRAN (NIR)	D	3	(1)	1
Eamonn DOHERTY (NIR)	D	28		2
Shaun GALLAGHER (NIR)	M	6	(5)	1
Billy GARNON (NIR)	A		(1)	
Floyd GILMOUR (NIR)	A	1	(4)	
Sean HARGAN (NIR)	D	27		2
Paul HEGARTY	M	26	(2)	
Peter HUTTON (NIR)	D	31		
Darren KELLY (NIR)	D	29	(1)	
Eddie McCALLION (NIR)	D	32		
Darren McCAUL (NIR)	A	12	(18)	4
Darren McCREADY (NIR)	M	11	(4)	1
Damien McGINLEY (NIR)	A		(1)	
Michael McHUGH (NIR)	A	3	(1)	
Johnny McIVOR (NIR)	M	21	(6)	4
Paddy McLAUGHLIN (NIR)	M	11	(7)	
Patrick McLAUGHLIN (NIR)	M	1	(2)	
Andy MORAN (ENG)	A	19	(6)	1
David PLATT (NIR)	G	32		
Vill POWELL (ENG)	A	1		
James QUIGLEY (NIR)	M	11	(4)	1
Perry TAYLOR (ENG)	A	7	(4)	3
Ciaran WILKINSON (NIR)	G	1		

LEAGUE RESULTS 1999/2000

13/08/99	St. Patrick's Athletic	A	2-1	Beckett 2
22/08/99	Waterford United	H	3-0	Coyle, Gallagher, Quigley
05/09/99	Shamrock Rovers	H	1-0	McCaul
10/09/99	Bohemians	A	0-3	
19/09/99	Drogheda United	H	0-2	
25/09/99	Finn Harps	A	1-1	McIvor
08/10/99	Galway United	A	2-0	McIvor, McCaul
17/10/99	Sligo Rovers	H	1-3	Curran
22/10/99	Shelbourne	A	0-2	
24/10/99	UCD	H	0-2	
31/10/99	Cork City	H	1-0	McIvor
07/11/99	St. Patrick's Athletic	H	0-3	
14/11/99	Waterford United	A	2-2	Hargan, Moran
21/11/99	Shamrock Rovers	A	0-3	
27/11/99	Bohemians	H	0-0	
05/12/99	Drogheda United	A	2-1	Doherty, McCaul
19/12/99	UCD	A	0-1	
21/12/99	Finn Harps	H	2-0	McCready, Beckett
26/12/99	Galway United	H	2-0	Coyle 2
03/01/00	Sligo Rovers	A	0-2	
16/01/00	Shelbourne	H	1-0	Coyle
23/01/00	Cork City	A	0-0	
28/01/00	St. Patrick's Athletic	A	1-1	Coyle
13/02/00	Waterford United	H	1-1	Coyle
19/02/00	Shamrock Rovers	H	0-0	
25/02/00	Bohemians	A	0-0	
12/03/00	Drogheda United	H	2-1	McIvor, McCaul
18/03/00	Finn Harps	A	2-1	Coyle, Taylor
26/03/00	UCD	H	2-0	Taylor, Beckett
08/04/00	Sligo Rovers	H	0-0	
11/04/00	Galway United	A	1-2	Hargan
16/04/00	Shelbourne	A	2-2	Doherty, Coyle
23/04/00	Cork City	H	1-4	Taylor

DROGHEDA UNITED

CLUB DIRECTORY

Drogheda United FC
United Park
Windmill Road, Drogheda, Co. Louth
tel - (041) 9830190
fax - (041) 9830195
Year of Formation - 1919
Chairman - John Little
Secretary - Gerry Kelly
Manager - Martin Lawlor; Eddie May
(00/01 - Harry McCue)
Stadium - United Park (6,000)

APPEARANCES 99/00

	P	Ap	(s)	Gls
Martin BEGGS	D	1	(1)	
Gerry BOYLE	D	20	(4)	
John BUTLER	M	14	(7)	2
Gareth BYRNE	G	30		
Mark BYRNE	M	16	(6)	5
Fergal COLEMAN	A	17	(2)	3
Gary CRONIN	D	4	(5)	
Andy ESTELL (ENG)	A		(1)	
Wayne FITZELL	M	2	(2)	
Colm FOLEY	D	11	(1)	
Bobby HANNON	M	1	(2)	
James IMPEY (ENG)	D	21	(1)	
Mickey McCANN	A	3	(19)	
Peter McDONALD (SCO)	D	18		
Tom McNULTY (SCO)	M	7		
Damien MAHER	D	33		1
Alan MURPHY	D	30		1
Colm MURPHY	M	26	(4)	
David NUGENT	A	1		
Greg O'DOWD	M	29		2
Darren O'KEEFFE	M	25		4
Justin O'NEILL	G	3	(2)	
John POWELL (HOL)	A	3		
Mark REVINS	A	13	(5)	1
Christian ROBERTS (WAL)	M	6		
Stephen ROCHE	M	4	(4)	1
Derek SHEVLIN	D	2	(3)	
Dai THOMAS (WAL)	A	4		1
Derek THORNTON	A	14		
Ray WALLACE (ENG)	M	5		

LEAGUE RESULTS 1999/2000

13/08/99	Shamrock Rovers	H	0-4	
20/08/99	Galway United	A	1-1	Maher
03/09/99	Bohemians	H	0-2	
11/09/99	Sligo Rovers	A	1-1	Byrne M.
19/09/99	Derry City	A	2-0	O'Keeffe, Coleman
24/09/99	Waterford United	H	1-1	Revins
01/10/99	Finn Harps	H	3-2	O'Dowd, O'Keeffe, Roche
08/10/99	Shelbourne	A	0-1	
15/10/99	St. Patrick's Athletic	H	1-2	Butler
24/10/99	Cork City	A	0-3	
29/10/99	UCD	H	0-1	
07/11/99	Shamrock Rovers	A	1-4	Byrne M.
12/11/99	Galway United	H	3-1	Byrne M. 3
19/11/99	Bohemians	A	1-2	Murphy A.
26/11/99	Sligo Rovers	H	1-1	Coleman
05/12/99	Derry City	H	1-2	Coleman
10/12/99	Waterford United	A	0-1	
18/12/99	Finn Harps	A	0-0	
26/12/99	Shelbourne	H	0-0	
02/01/00	St. Patrick's Athletic	A	0-1	
16/01/00	Cork City	H	0-0	
21/01/00	UCD	A	0-3	
30/01/00	Shamrock Rovers	H	0-0	
13/02/00	Galway United	A	2-2	Thomas, O'Keeffe
18/02/00	Bohemians	H	0-3	
27/02/00	Sligo Rovers	A	0-0	
12/03/00	Derry City	A	1-2	O'Keeffe
19/03/00	Waterford United	H	1-0	O'Dowd
24/03/00	Finn Harps	H	0-2	
04/04/00	Shelbourne	A	0-0	
07/04/00	St. Patrick's Athletic	H	0-3	
16/04/00	Cork City	A	1-3	Butler
23/04/00	UCD	H	0-5	

FINN HARPS

CLUB DIRECTORY

Finn Harps FC
Finn Park
Ballybofey, Co. Donegal
tel - (074) 32635/30070
fax - (074) 30075
Year of Formation - 1954
Chairman - Conor Boyce
Secretary - Martin Hannigan
Manager - Charlie McGeever; Gavin Dykes
Stadium - Finn Park (8,400)

MAJOR HONOURS
Domestic Cup - (1) 1974.

APPEARANCES 99/00

	P	Ap	(s)	Gls
Niall BONNER	M		(1)	
Declan BOYLE	D	31		1
John Paul BOYLE	D	3		
Shane BRADLEY	D	8		1
Gavin CULLEN	G	9		
Kevin DOCHERTY (SCO)	A	1		
Gavin DYKES	D	26	(2)	
Stephen GRANT	A	1		
Fergal HARKIN	M	30	(3)	7
Mark HUTCHISON (SCO)	D	17	(1)	
Johnny KENNY	M	25	(2)	3
Jason LYDIATE (ENG)	M	2		
Gerard McGRANAGHAN	M	2	(2)	
Paddy McGRENAGHAN	M	24	(9)	1
Kevin McHUGH	A	4	(14)	2
Brian McKENNA	G	24		
Brendan McLAUGHLIN	D	1	(1)	
Alistair McMILLAN (SCO)	M	5	(1)	
Jonathan MINNOCK	D	30	(1)	4
Tom MOHAN (NIR)	M	20	(3)	
James MULLIGAN	A	26	(1)	12
Declan PERKINS	A		(1)	
Trevor SCANLON	D	8	(4)	
Eamonn SHERIDAN	A	2	(5)	
Jonathan SPEAK (NIR)	A	16	(8)	4
Dom TIERNEY	M	21	(2)	
Mike TURNER (ENG)	A	11		4
Pascal VAUDEQUIN (FRA)	D	16	(1)	

LEAGUE RESULTS 1999/2000

14/08/99	Cork City	H	1-2	McHugh
22/08/99	Shamrock Rovers	A	1-3	Harkin
03/09/99	St. Patrick's Athletic	A	1-2	Harkin
11/09/99	Shelbourne	H	0-1	
17/09/99	UCD	A	0-1	
25/09/99	Derry City	H	1-1	Mulligan
01/10/99	Drogheda United	A	2-3	Mulligan 2 (1p)
08/10/99	Sligo Rovers	H	2-1	Speak, Mulligan
15/10/99	Galway United	A	3-1	Speak 2, Mulligan
23/10/99	Bohemians	H	0-1	
31/10/99	Waterford United	A	3-2	Mulligan 2, Boyle D.
07/11/99	Cork City	A	0-2	
12/11/99	Shamrock Rovers	H	1-0	Speak
20/11/99	St. Patrick's Athletic	H	1-1	Harkin
25/11/99	Shelbourne	A	1-1	Kenny
04/12/99	UCD	H	0-0	
18/12/99	Drogheda United	H	0-0	
21/12/99	Derry City	A	0-2	
27/12/99	Sligo Rovers	A	1-1	Harkin (p)
03/01/00	Galway United	H	1-2	McHugh
14/01/00	Bohemians	A	0-1	
22/01/00	Waterford United	H	4-0	Harkin 2 (1p), Turner, Mulligan
29/01/00	Cork City	H	1-1	Minnock
13/02/00	Shamrock Rovers	A	3-3	Mulligan, Minnock, McGreneghan
18/02/00	St. Patrick's Athletic	A	0-1	
26/02/00	Shelbourne	H	2-3	Turner, Minnock
12/03/00	UCD	A	1-1	Bradley
18/03/00	Derry City	H	1-2	Harkin
24/03/00	Drogheda United	A	2-0	Mulligan, Turner
01/04/00	Sligo Rovers	H	2-1	Mulligan 2
07/04/00	Galway United	A	4-0	Turner, Minnock, Kenny 2
18/04/00	Bohemians	H	0-0	
23/04/00	Waterford United	A	0-1	

GALWAY UNITED

CLUB DIRECTORY

Galway United FC
Terryland Park
Dyke Road, Galway
tel - (091) 561000
fax - (091) 568866
Year of Formation - 1937
Chairman - Gerry Gray
Secretary - John Byrne
Manager - Don O'Riordan
Stadium - Terryland Park (6,580)

MAJOR HONOURS
Domestic Cup - (1) 1991.

APPEARANCES 99/00

	P	Ap	(s)	Gls
Billy CLERY	D	23	(4)	6
Fergal COLEMAN	A	8	(2)	
Adrian CREGG	M	9	(6)	1
Aubrey DOLAN	M	25	(1)	
Michael DONNELLAN	M	1	(7)	
Nick FLOWERS (ENG)	G	1	(1)	
Kieran FOLEY	D	30	(1)	4
David FORDE	G	5		
David GOLDBEY	A	7	(5)	2
Gareth GORMAN	M	19	(8)	2
Eddie HICKEY	G	27	(1)	
Jason KABIA (ENG)	A	4	(1)	1
Mike KEANE	M	12	(3)	
Ollie KEOGH	M	12	(6)	5
Conor KILLEEN	A	1	(7)	
Jonathan KING	A	2		
Eric LAVINE (BAR)	A	28	(3)	5
Sean MALEE	D	11	(6)	
Scott MORGAN (ENG)	D	24		
Alan MURPHY	M		(1)	
Ollie NEARY	M	23	(3)	1
Brendan O'CONNOR	M	15	(3)	
Alan O'DONNELL	A	5	(1)	
Neil OGDEN (ENG)	M	10	(5)	1
Mathias O'MALLEY	A	2	(1)	
Mick QUIRKE	D	16	(2)	
Darragh SHERIDAN	M	29		1
Paul THORNTON	A	1	(4)	
Luther WATSON (BAR)	D	13	(1)	1

LEAGUE RESULTS 1999/2000

13/08/99	Shelbourne	A	1-1	Keogh
20/08/99	Drogheda United	H	1-1	Keogh
03/09/99	Cork City	H	1-4	Clery
12/09/99	UCD	A	2-0	Clery (p), Cregg
17/09/99	Waterford United	A	2-1	Neary, Gorman
24/09/99	Bohemians	H	1-2	Clery
03/10/99	Shamrock Rovers	A	1-2	Clery (p)
08/10/99	Derry City	H	0-2	
15/10/99	Finn Harps	H	1-3	Keogh
23/10/99	Sligo Rovers	A	0-1	
29/10/99	St. Patrick's Athletic	H	1-2	Watson
05/11/99	Shelbourne	H	0-0	
12/11/99	Drogheda United	A	1-3	Kabia
21/11/99	Cork City	A	0-3	
26/11/99	UCD	H	2-1	Lavine, Keogh
05/12/99	Waterford United	H	0-0	
12/12/99	Bohemians	A	3-1	Foley 3
17/12/99	Shamrock Rovers	H	0-3	
26/12/99	Derry City	A	0-2	
03/01/00	Finn Harps	A	2-1	Lavine, Foley
14/01/00	Sligo Rovers	H	5-0	Clery, Lavine 2, og, Ogden
21/01/00	St. Patrick's Athletic	A	0-3	
28/01/00	Shelbourne	A	1-1	og (McCarthy)
13/02/00	Drogheda United	H	2-2	Sheridan, Lavine
27/02/00	UCD	A	1-1	Keogh
10/03/00	Waterford United	A	0-0	
14/03/00	Cork City	H	0-2	
18/03/00	Bohemians	H	0-1	
26/03/00	Shamrock Rovers	A	0-0	
07/04/00	Finn Harps	H	0-4	
11/04/00	Derry City	H	2-1	Goldbey, Gorman
16/04/00	Sligo Rovers	A	1-1	Goldbey
23/04/00	St. Patrick's Athletic	H	1-0	Clery

ST. PATRICK'S ATHLETIC

CLUB DIRECTORY

St. Patrick's Athletic FC
Stadium of Light, Richmond Park,
125 Emmett Road, Inchicore, Dublin 8
tel - (01) 4546332 / fax - (01) 4546211
Year of Formation - 1929
Chairman - Tim O'Flaherty
Secretary - Phil Mooney
Manager - Liam Buckley; Pat Dolan
Stadium - Richmond Park (5,800)

MAJOR HONOURS
League Championship - (7)
1952, 1955, 1956, 1990, 1996, 1998, 1999.
Domestic Cup - (2) 1959, 1961.

APPEARANCES 99/00

	P	Ap	(s)	Gls
Donal BROUGHAN	D	13	(4)	
Willie BURKE	D	11	(1)	
Des BYRNE	D	6	(5)	
Aaron CALLAGHAN	D	4		
Paul CAMPBELL	D	1		
Trevor CROLY	D	21	(5)	1
Robbie DEVEREUX (ENG)	M	1	(3)	
Paul DONNELLY	M	5		
Keith DOYLE	D	22	(1)	
Padraig DREW	A	5	(3)	
Ian GILZEAN (SCO)	A	4		3
Eddie GORMLEY	M	20	(5)	3
Marcus HALLOWS (ENG)	A	22	(6)	7
Shane HARTE	M	8	(8)	1
Colin HAWKINS	D	27		2
Liam KELLY	A	2	(9)	
Packie LYNCH	D	27		2
Ger McCARTHY	A	8	(5)	1
Robbie McGUINNESS	A	2	(2)	2
Stephen McGUINNESS	D	22	(2)	1
Alan McNEVIN	A	15	(8)	5
Trevor MOLLOY	A	27	(2)	7
Thomas MORGAN	M	3	(2)	
Paul OSAM	M	13	(1)	
Barry PRENDERVILLE	D	14	(1)	
Martin RUSSELL	M	27	(1)	2
Trevor WOOD (NIR)	G	33		

LEAGUE RESULTS 1999/2000

13/08/99	Derry City	H	1-2	Gilzean
20/08/99	UCD	A	2-2	Gilzean 2
03/09/99	Finn Harps	H	2-1	Gormley (p), Russell
11/09/99	Cork City	A	0-1	
18/09/99	Sligo Rovers	A	1-0	Hallows
24/09/99	Shelbourne	H	1-1	og (McCarthy)
01/10/99	Bohemians	A	0-0	
08/10/99	Waterford United	H	1-0	Russell
15/10/99	Drogheda United	A	2-1	Hallows, McNevin
24/10/99	Shamrock Rovers	H	1-1	Hallows
29/10/99	Galway United	A	2-1	McNevin, Harte
07/11/99	Derry City	A	3-0	Molloy, Hallows, McNevin
12/11/99	UCD	H	0-0	
20/11/99	Finn Harps	A	1-1	McGuinness R.
26/11/99	Cork City	H	2-0	Molloy, McNevin
03/12/99	Sligo Rovers	H	3-2	McGuinness S., Molloy (p), Croly
10/12/99	Shelbourne	A	0-1	
17/12/99	Bohemians	H	1-3	Hawkins
27/12/99	Waterford United	A	1-3	Hallows
02/01/00	Drogheda United	H	1-0	Lynch
16/01/00	Shamrock Rovers	A	1-2	og (Brazil)
21/01/00	Galway United	H	3-0	Hallows, Hawkins, og (Gorman)
28/01/00	Derry City	H	1-1	Molloy (p)
13/02/00	UCD	A	1-2	Gormley (p)
18/02/00	Finn Harps	H	1-0	Hallows
27/02/00	Cork City	A	1-1	Molloy
12/03/00	Sligo Rovers	A	2-2	Lynch, Molloy (p)
17/03/00	Shelbourne	H	1-2	McNevin
24/03/00	Bohemians	A	1-0	Gormley (p)
31/03/00	Waterford United	H	0-0	
07/04/00	Drogheda United	A	3-0	Molloy, McCarthy, McGuinness R.
16/04/00	Shamrock Rovers	H	0-0	
23/04/00	Galway United	A	0-1	

SHAMROCK ROVERS

CLUB DIRECTORY

Shamrock Rovers FC
A3 Parkway Business Centre
Ballymount, Dublin 24
tel - (01) 4604105 / fax - (01) 4604660
Year of Formation - 1901
Chairman - Joe Colwell
Secretary - Joe Colwell
Manager - Damien Richardson
Stadium - Morton Stadium (10,000)

MAJOR HONOURS
League Championship - (15) 1923, 1925, 1927,
1932, 1938, 1939, 1954, 1957, 1959, 1964,
1984, 1985, 1986, 1987, 1994.
Domestic Cup - (24) 1925, 1929, 1930, 1931,
1932, 1933, 1936, 1940, 1944, 1945, 1948,
1955, 1956, 1962, 1964, 1965, 1966, 1967,
1968, 1969, 1978, 1985, 1986, 1987.

APPEARANCES 99/00

		P	Ap	(s)	Gls
Gino BRAZIL	D	19	(4)		
Matt BRITTON	D	21	(5)		
Brian BYRNE	M	20	(5)	6	
Jason COLWELL	M	28	(4)	2	
Tony COUSINS	A	10	(7)	2	
Paul CROWLEY	M	2	(10)	3	
Pat DEANS	D		(2)		
Tommy DUNNE	D	31			
Declan FITZGERALD	D		(1)		
Sean FRANCIS	A	21		7	
Stuart HOLT	M		(1)		
Robbie HORGAN	G	13	(2)		
Shane JACKSON	D	12	(2)	1	
Marc KENNY	M	25	(2)		
Graham LAWLOR	A	20		6	
Ray McLOUGHLIN	M	1	(1)		
Brendan MARKEY	A		(1)		
Tony O'DOWD	G	20			
Terry PALMER	D	29		4	
Richie PURDY	M	23	(3)	6	
Shane ROBINSON	M	19	(10)	3	
Anthony STEWART	M	4	(9)		
Derek TRACEY	M	18	(2)	1	
Billy WOODS	M	27		7	

LEAGUE RESULTS 1999/2000

13/08/99	Drogheda United	A	4-0	Jackson, Robinson, Francis, Palmer
22/08/99	Finn Harps	H	3-1	og (Lydiate), Cousins, Tracey
05/09/99	Derry City	A	0-1	
12/09/99	Waterford United	H	1-0	Woods
19/09/99	Bohemians	A	3-1	Purdy 2, Robinson
26/09/99	Sligo Rovers	H	4-1	Colwell, Woods, Cousins, Crowley
03/10/99	Galway United	H	2-1	Purdy 2
08/10/99	UCD	A	0-3	
17/10/99	Cork City	H	1-3	Woods (p)
24/10/99	St. Patrick's Athletic	A	1-1	Lawlor
30/10/99	Shelbourne	H	1-1	Byrne
07/11/99	Drogheda United	H	4-1	Woods 3, Francis
12/11/99	Finn Harps	A	0-1	
21/11/99	Derry City	H	3-0	Lawlor 2, Palmer
26/11/99	Waterford United	A	0-0	
05/12/99	Bohemians	H	0-1	
11/12/99	Sligo Rovers	A	5-3	Colwell, Lawlor, Purdy, Robinson, Francis
17/12/99	Galway United	A	3-0	Byrne, Francis 2
02/01/00	Cork City	A	0-2	
16/01/00	St. Patrick's Athletic	H	2-1	Francis, Woods
21/01/00	Shelbourne	A	0-3	
23/01/00	UCD	H	0-0	
30/01/00	Drogheda United	A	0-0	
13/02/00	Finn Harps	H	3-3	Francis, Byrne, Purdy
19/02/00	Derry City	A	0-0	
27/02/00	Waterford United	H	1-2	Crowley
10/03/00	Bohemians	A	0-0	
19/03/00	Sligo Rovers	H	4-2	Palmer 2, Lawlor 2
26/03/00	Galway United	H	0-0	
02/04/00	UCD	A	1-1	Byrne
09/04/00	Cork City	H	1-2	Crowley
16/04/00	St. Patrick's Athletic	A	0-0	
23/04/00	Shelbourne	H	2-1	Byrne 2

SHELBOURNE

CLUB DIRECTORY

Shelbourne FC
Tolka Park, Richmond Road, Dublin 3
tel - (01) 8375536/8375754/8368781
fax - (01) 8375588
Year of Formation - 1895
Chairman - Gary Browne
Secretary - Ollie Byrne
Manager - Dermot Keely
Stadium - Tolka Park (10,000)

MAJOR HONOURS
League Championship - (9) 1926, 1929, 1931,
1944, 1947, 1953, 1962, 1992, 2000.
Domestic Cup - (7)
1939, 1960, 1963, 1993, 1996, 1997, 2000.

APPEARANCES 99/00

	P	Ap	(s)	Gls
Dessie BAKER	M	27	(3)	4
Richie BAKER	M	30	(1)	7
Barry BURKE	M		(1)	
Tommy BYRNE	M	3	(5)	
Dave CAMPBELL	D	10	(13)	1
Shane CAREW	D		(1)	
Paul DOOLIN	M	23	(4)	1
Pat FENLON	M	33		6
Declan GEOGHEGAN	D	25	(1)	
Stephen GEOGHEGAN	A	30		12
Garry HAYLOCK (ENG)	A	13	(6)	3
Eoin HEARY	D	33		
Mark HUTCHINSON (SCO)	D	7	(1)	
James KEDDY	M	23		6
Ben KELLY	M		(1)	
Tony McCARTHY	D	33		1
Neil OGDEN (ENG)	M	4	(1)	
Danny O'LEARY	G	1	(1)	
John POWELL (HOL)	A	1	(6)	2
Pat SCULLY	D	31		4
Carel VAN DER VELDEN (HOL)	M	4	(13)	1
Steve WILLIAMS (WAL)	G	32		

LEAGUE RESULTS 1999/2000

13/08/99	Galway United	H	1-1	Fenlon
20/08/99	Bohemians	A	1-0	Geoghegan S.
03/09/99	UCD	H	0-0	
11/09/99	Finn Harps	A	1-0	Geoghegan S.
17/09/99	Cork City	H	3-2	Baker R., Geoghegan S., Haylock
24/09/99	St. Patrick's Athletic	A	1-1	Van der Velden
02/10/99	Sligo Rovers	A	4-2	Powell 2, og (Boswell), Baker R.
08/10/99	Drogheda United	H	1-0	Campbell
15/10/99	Waterford United	A	0-0	
22/10/99	Derry City	H	2-0	Scully, Haylock
30/10/99	Shamrock Rovers	A	1-1	Scully
05/11/99	Galway United	A	0-0	
12/11/99	Bohemians	H	1-0	Baker D.
19/11/99	UCD	A	2-0	Keddy, Haylock
25/11/99	Finn Harps	H	1-1	Fenlon
05/12/99	Cork City	A	2-1	Baker R., Geoghegan S.
10/12/99	St. Patrick's Athletic	H	1-0	Geoghegan S. (p)
17/12/99	Sligo Rovers	H	1-0	Fenlon
26/12/99	Drogheda United	A	0-0	
03/01/00	Waterford United	H	1-0	Scully
16/01/00	Derry City	A	0-1	
21/01/00	Shamrock Rovers	H	3-0	Baker R., Doolin, Baker D.
28/01/00	Galway United	H	1-1	Keddy
11/02/00	Bohemians	A	1-1	Geoghegan S.
18/02/00	UCD	H	2-1	Baker R., Fenlon
26/02/00	Finn Harps	A	3-2	Fenlon, Geoghegan S., Scully
10/03/00	Cork City	H	4-0	Fenlon, Geoghegan S., Keddy, Baker R.
17/03/00	St. Patrick's Athletic	A	2-1	Geoghegan S. (p), McCarthy
26/03/00	Sligo Rovers	A	4-0	Baker D., Geoghegan S. (p), Keddy 2
04/04/00	Drogheda United	H	0-0	
07/04/00	Waterford United	A	2-0	Geoghegan S., Baker R.
14/04/00	Derry City	H	2-2	Geoghegan S., Keddy
23/04/00	Shamrock Rovers	A	1-2	Baker D.

SLIGO ROVERS

CLUB DIRECTORY

Sligo Rovers FC
PO Box 275, The Showgrounds, Sligo
tel - (071) 71212
fax - (071) 71331
Year of Formation - 1928
Chairman - Ray Gallagher
Secretary - Mary McGowan
Manager - Jim McInally; Tommy Cassidy
Stadium - The Showgrounds (7,000)

MAJOR HONOURS

League Championship - (2) 1937, 1977
Domestic Cup - (2) 1983, 1994.

APPEARANCES 99/00

	P	Ap	(s)	Gls
Steve BIRKS (ENG)	D	19	(2)	1
Paul BONNAR (SCO)	D	19	(1)	2
Matt BOSWELL (ENG)	G	11	(1)	
Nick BROUJOS (USA)	G	22		
Tommy BYRNE	M	8		
Packie CALLAGHAN	D		(4)	
Wesley CHARLES (STV)	D	24	(1)	
Paddy CONLON	M		(1)	
Jonathan DAVEY	M	14	(1)	
Khalib EL KHAFILI (MAR)	A	6	(10)	
Billy FINDLAY (SCO)	M	5		
Sean FLANNERY	A	14		5
Keith GILROY	M	15	(5)	1
Dale GRAY (SCO)	D	5	(1)	3
Alan HENRY	D	1		
Damien KENNEDY	D	9	(2)	
Declan LYNCH	M		(2)	
Ian LYNCH	D	21	(2)	
Keith LYNCH	A	1	(2)	1
Andrew McCANN	M		(3)	
Jim McINALLY (SCO)	D	13		
Ross McLYNN	D	14		
Lee MARSHALL	M	15	(11)	
Padraig MORAN	A	26	(2)	11
Donagh OATES	A	2	(13)	1
Conor O'GRADY	M	30		1
Ian ROSSITER	D	26		
Glen SHANNON	A	26	(4)	3
Jim SHERIDAN	D	15		1
David WILLIAMSON (ENG)	M	2		

LEAGUE RESULTS 1999/2000

14/08/99	UCD	H	1-2	Moran
21/08/99	Cork City	A	1-0	Moran
03/09/99	Waterford United	A	0-1	
11/09/99	Drogheda United	H	1-1	Shannon
18/09/99	St. Patrick's Athletic	H	0-1	
26/09/99	Shamrock Rovers	A	1-4	Gilroy
02/10/99	Shelbourne	H	2-4	Shannon, Moran (p)
08/10/99	Finn Harps	A	1-2	Birks
17/10/99	Derry City	A	3-1	Moran 3
23/10/99	Galway United	H	1-0	Sheridan
31/10/99	Bohemians	A	2-3	Gray, Moran
05/11/99	UCD	A	1-1	Moran
14/11/99	Cork City	H	0-5	
20/11/99	Waterford United	H	1-0	Gray
26/11/99	Drogheda United	A	1-1	Bonnar
03/12/99	St. Patrick's Athletic	A	2-3	Flannery, og (Harte)
11/12/99	Shamrock Rovers	H	3-5	Moran 3
17/12/99	Shelbourne	A	0-1	
27/12/99	Finn Harps	H	1-1	Gray
03/01/00	Derry City	H	2-0	Flannery, Bonnar
14/01/00	Galway United	A	0-5	
22/01/00	Bohemians	H	0-0	
29/01/00	UCD	H	0-1	
13/02/00	Cork City	A	0-0	
18/02/00	Waterford United	A	0-1	
27/02/00	Drogheda United	H	0-0	
12/03/00	St. Patrick's Athletic	H	2-2	O'Grady, Flannery
19/03/00	Shamrock Rovers	A	2-4	Shannon, Flannery
26/03/00	Shelbourne	H	0-4	
01/04/00	Finn Harps	A	1-2	Flannery (p)
08/04/00	Derry City	A	0-0	
16/04/00	Galway United	H	1-1	Oates
23/04/00	Bohemians	A	1-4	Lynch K.

UCD

CLUB DIRECTORY

University College Dublin AFC
Room 203, UCD Sports Complex,
Belfield, Dublin 4
tel - (01) 7062183
fax - (01) 2698099
Year of Formation - 1895
Chairman - Gerry Horkan
Secretary - Brendan Dillon
Manager - Theo Dunne; Martin Moran
Stadium - Belfield Park (4,500)

MAJOR HONOURS
Domestic Cup - (1) 1984.

APPEARANCES 99/00

	P	Ap	(s)	Gls
Eoin BENNIS	M	23	(5)	3
Clive DELANEY	D	28	(1)	1
Robert DUNNE	M	4	(6)	1
Glen FITZPATRICK	A	3	(11)	
Peter HANRAHAN	M	10	(4)	3
Ciaran KAVANAGH	M	31		1
Ken KILMURRAY	A	15	(10)	4
Aidan LYNCH	D	26		3
Robert McAULEY	D	13	(2)	1
Tony McDONNELL	D	14	(1)	
Karl McGETTRICK	M		(1)	
Eamon McLAUGHLIN	D	22	(2)	
Alan McNALLY	M	1	(2)	
Alan MAHON	D	32		
John MARTIN	M	19	(2)	2
Ciaran MARTYN	M	31	(1)	8
Brian MOONEY	M	26	(1)	2
Andy NOONAN	M	4	(3)	
Mick O'BYRNE	A	20	(1)	7
Mick O'DONNELL	A	4	(2)	2
Barry RYAN	G	33		
Darragh RYAN	M	3		
James TIMMONS	M	1	(2)	

LEAGUE RESULTS 1999/2000

14/08/99	Sligo Rovers	A	2-1	Lynch, O'Byrne (p)
20/08/99	St. Patrick's Athletic	H	2-2	Martyn, Mooney
03/09/99	Shelbourne	A	0-0	
12/09/99	Galway United	H	0-2	
17/09/99	Finn Harps	H	1-0	Martyn (p)
08/10/99	Shamrock Rovers	H	3-0	Hanrahan, Bennis 2
13/10/99	Cork City	A	0-1	
17/10/99	Bohemians	H	0-2	
22/10/99	Waterford United	H	2-2	Kilmurray, Lynch
24/10/99	Derry City	A	2-0	Martyn, Kilmurray
29/10/99	Drogheda United	A	1-0	Martyn
05/11/99	Sligo Rovers	H	1-1	Lynch
12/11/99	St. Patrick's Athletic	A	0-0	
19/11/99	Shelbourne	H	0-2	
26/11/99	Galway United	A	1-2	O'Byrne
04/12/99	Finn Harps	A	0-0	
12/12/99	Cork City	H	2-2	Bennis, Martyn
19/12/99	Derry City	H	1-0	O'Byrne
02/01/00	Bohemians	A	0-1	
16/01/00	Waterford United	A	2-0	og (Whittle), Hanrahan
21/01/00	Drogheda United	H	3-0	Hanrahan, Martin, Mooney
23/01/00	Shamrock Rovers	A	0-0	
29/01/00	Sligo Rovers	A	1-0	O'Byrne
13/02/00	St. Patrick's Athletic	H	2-1	Martin, og (Wood)
18/02/00	Shelbourne	A	1-2	O'Byrne
27/02/00	Galway United	H	1-1	Martyn
12/03/00	Finn Harps	H	1-1	Martyn (p)
18/03/00	Cork City	A	1-1	McAuley
26/03/00	Derry City	A	0-2	
02/04/00	Shamrock Rovers	H	1-1	O'Donnell
07/04/00	Bohemians	A	2-1	Kilmurray, O'Byrne
16/04/00	Waterford United	H	2-1	Delaney, Martyn
23/04/00	Drogheda United	A	5-0	Kavanagh, Kilmurray, Dunne, O'Byrne, O'Donnell

WATERFORD UNITED

CLUB DIRECTORY

Waterford United FC
15 Parnell Street
Waterford
tel - (051) 853222
fax - (051) 853226
Year of Formation - 1982
Chairman - Michael Finnegan
Secretary - John Delaney
Manager - Mike Flanagan (00/01 - Paul Power)
Stadium - Regional Sports Centre (8,250)

APPEARANCES 99/00

	P	Ap	(s)	Gls
Michael DEVINE	G	33		
Lee DOHERTY	D	2		
Brian FLOOD	M	1	(2)	
John FROST	D	26	(2)	
Karl GANNON	A	24	(2)	4
Stephen GRANT	M	12	(3)	4
Robbie GRIFFIN	M	25	(4)	3
Christian HYSLOP (ENG)	D	8		
Dominic IORFA (NIG)	A	5	(6)	2
Jason KABIA (ENG)	A	3	(1)	
Alan KIRBY	M	32		2
Derek McGRATH	M	20	(7)	3
Tim McGRATH	D	24	(1)	
Brendan MARKEY	A	14	(6)	3
Kevin O'BRIEN	D	7	(5)	1
Alan REYNOLDS	M	18	(1)	
Sean RIORDAN	D	29		
Dave SMITH	D	32		
Jered STIRLING (SCO)	M	23	(2)	2
David WHITTLE	D	18	(1)	
Barry WOOD (SCO)	A	7	(12)	

LEAGUE RESULTS 1999/2000

13/08/99	Bohemians	H	0-2	
22/08/99	Derry City	A	0-3	
03/09/99	Sligo Rovers	H	1-0	McGrath D. (p)
12/09/99	Shamrock Rovers	A	0-1	
17/09/99	Galway United	H	1-2	Stirling
24/09/99	Drogheda United	A	1-1	Kirby
01/10/99	Cork City	H	1-3	Griffin
08/10/99	St. Patrick's Athletic	A	0-1	
15/10/99	Shelbourne	H	0-0	
22/10/99	UCD	A	2-2	Gannon, Iorfa
31/10/99	Finn Harps	H	2-3	Iorfa, O'Brien
05/11/99	Bohemians	A	2-0	Stirling, Gannon
14/11/99	Derry City	H	2-2	Grant 2
20/11/99	Sligo Rovers	A	0-1	
26/11/99	Shamrock Rovers	H	0-0	
05/12/99	Galway United	A	0-0	
10/12/99	Drogheda United	H	1-0	Grant
19/12/99	Cork City	A	0-0	
27/12/99	St. Patrick's Athletic	H	3-1	Markey 3
03/01/00	Shelbourne	A	0-1	
16/01/00	UCD	H	0-2	
22/01/00	Finn Harps	A	0-4	
28/01/00	Bohemians	H	0-0	
13/02/00	Derry City	A	1-1	Gannon
18/02/00	Sligo Rovers	H	1-0	McGrath D. (p)
27/02/00	Shamrock Rovers	A	2-1	Grant, Griffin
10/03/00	Galway United	H	0-0	
19/03/00	Drogheda United	A	0-1	
24/03/00	Cork City	H	2-2	McGrath D., Kirby
31/03/00	St. Patrick's Athletic	A	0-0	
07/04/00	Shelbourne	H	0-2	
16/04/00	UCD	A	1-2	Gannon
23/04/00	Finn Harps	H	1-0	Griffin

ROMANIA

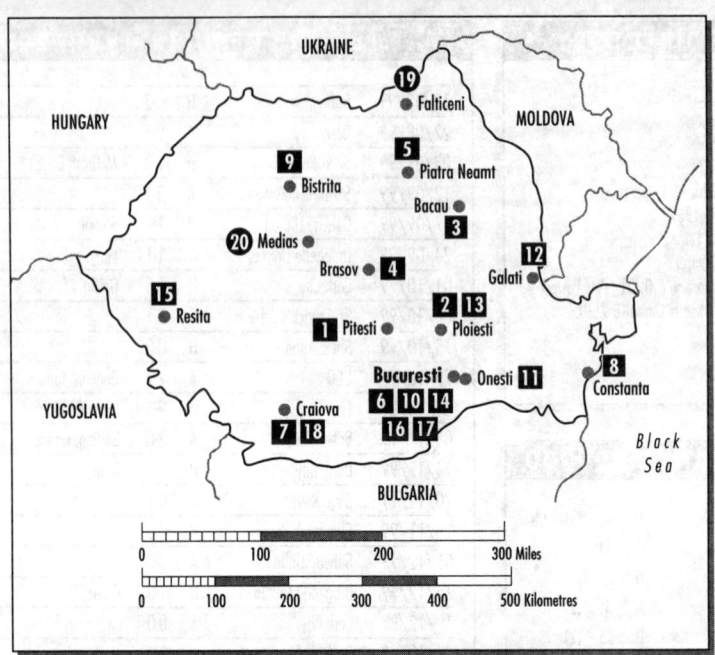

1	FC ARGES DACIA PITESTI	818
2	ASTRA PLOIESTI	819
3	FCM BACAU	820
4	FC BRASOV	821
5	CEAHLAUL PIATRA NEAMT	822
6	DINAMO BUCURESTI	823
7	FC EXTENSIV CRAIOVA	824
8	FC FARUL CONSTANTA	825
9	GLORIA BISTRITA	826
10	FC NATIONAL BUCURESTI	827
11	FC ONESTI	828

12	OTELUL GALATI	829
13	PETROLUL PLOIESTI	830
14	RAPID BUCURESTI	831
15	CSM RESITA	832
16	ROCAR BUCURESTI	833
17	STEAUA BUCURESTI	834
18	UNIVERSITATEA CRAIOVA	835
Promoted clubs		
19	FORESTA FALTICENI	
20	GAZ METAN MEDIAS	

DINAMO SCOOP DOMESTIC SPOILS

Life after Hagi is no empty dream

FEDERATION DIRECTORY

Federatia Româna de Fotbal
Bdul Poligrafiei Nr.3, Sector 1, Bucuresti

tel - (01) 2229993   Year of Formation - 1909
fax - (01) 3126337   President - Mircea Sandu
website - www.frf.pcnet.ro Secretary - Adalbert Kassai

Stadium - Lia Manoliu, Bucuresti (70,000)

Romania's third appearance at the European Championship finals proved much more memorable than the previous two. They surpassed expectations by qualifying from a tough first-round group containing England, Germany and Portugal to reach the quarter-finals, and although they could go no further when confronted by the might of Italy, much pride and satisfaction was gleaned from the way in which Emeric Ienei's team performed in Belgium and Holland.

The crux of Romania's tournament was the do-or-die encounter against England in Charleroi. Having drawn 1-1 to Germany and lost to a last-minute goal against Portugal - a complete reversal, that, of Romania's crucial 1-0 victory over the Portuguese in Oporto during the qualifying campaign - the only way Romania could remain in the competition was with a win against Kevin Keegan's team, and even that was no guarantee should Germany win their final game against already-qualified Portugal by a greater margin.

At kick-off the die appeared to be cast against the Romanians, especially as their talisman, Gheorghe Hagi, was missing through suspension. But what transpired over the next 90 minutes proved beyond doubt that the side could not only live without their illustrious skipper but actually perform more potently as a team without him.

Although Romania only won the game with a late penalty, gifted to them by England defender Phil Neville's woeful tackle on Viorel Moldovan, they thoroughly deserved their 3-2 victory. It was the first match Romania had ever won at the European Championship finals and

LEAGUE CHAMPIONSHIP RESULTS 99/00

		1	2	3	4	5	6	7	8	9	10	11	12	13	14	15	16	17	18
1	FC Arges Dacia Pitesti		1-1	1-1	1-0	1-1	2-3	2-0	2-1	2-0	3-1	2-0	3-0	1-0	0-1	1-1	3-1	4-0	2-0
2	Astra Ploiesti	0-1		1-0	1-1	0-1	1-2	1-1	3-2	2-1	1-1	5-0	1-1	2-0	2-3	2-1	3-1	1-0	2-0
3	FCM Bacau	1-0	1-2		1-0	2-0	0-3	1-0	1-1	3-2	1-1	3-0	1-0	3-0	0-0	1-0	1-0	2-1	3-0
4	FC Brasov	2-1	2-0	1-1		3-1	4-3	2-1	3-2	4-2	3-1	5-1	3-0	0-1	2-0	4-0	4-0	1-2	0-1
5	Ceahlaul Piatra Neamt	1-0	4-0	3-1	2-1		2-2	3-1	2-1	1-0	3-2	6-0	3-2	2-0	0-3	4-2	2-0	0-2	1-1
6	Dinamo Bucuresti	4-0	2-1	2-1	3-1	1-1		3-0	4-0	5-0	1-0	7-1	3-2	4-1	2-1	2-1	3-0	3-2	5-2
7	FC Extensiv Craiova	2-1	0-1	0-2	0-1	0-0	0-1		1-3	1-2	1-2	0-0	3-0	0-0	1-2	1-0	2-1	0-3	2-3
8	FC Farul Constanta	1-0	1-1	3-0	0-0	1-0	0-2	1-0		2-1	2-0	3-1	1-1	2-1	1-1	3-1	0-1	2-1	2-0
9	Gloria Bistrita	2-0	2-0	2-0	2-0	5-4	1-0	1-0	2-1		1-0	2-0	2-3	4-0	1-2	2-0	2-1	4-0	1-0
10	FC National Bucuresti	4-1	1-0	2-2	2-0	5-1	1-3	2-0	6-0	3-1		3-0	1-1	4-1	2-3	5-1	2-0	3-0	1-0
11	FC Onesti	1-2	1-0	1-0	3-2	1-1	2-4	3-2	2-1	3-2	1-0		0-3	5-1	2-5	2-1	1-5	1-3	0-0
12	Otelul Galati	1-2	0-1	3-1	1-0	3-0	5-3	8-2	1-0	0-0	2-0	2-1		3-2	2-0	1-2	2-1	4-5	1-0
13	Petrolul Ploiesti	1-1	1-0	1-0	1-0	1-0	1-2	2-0	0-0	1-2	1-0	4-1	2-1		4-2	4-2	4-1	5-1	0-0
14	Rapid Bucuresti	1-0	1-1	2-1	2-1	1-2	4-0	4-2	0-0	2-1	3-2	3-1	2-1	2-0		4-0	1-1	2-2	3-1
15	CSM Resita	0-0	2-5	1-2	3-1	1-3	0-6	0-0	1-1	1-1	1-0	6-1	1-2	2-2	0-1		0-1	2-0	0-0
16	Rocar Bucuresti	0-3	2-1	3-0	1-0	2-0	1-2	3-1	2-1	5-1	3-2	2-1	5-1	3-2	0-1	4-0		1-2	2-2
17	Steaua Bucuresti	0-1	4-1	1-0	2-2	3-0	1-1	5-2	1-0	2-1	2-3	3-0	2-1	1-4	1-3	5-0	2-1		1-0
18	Universitatea Craiova	3-1	0-0	2-3	1-0	0-2	1-2	3-0	3-0	3-1	2-0	1-0	4-0	5-1	2-0	2-2	2-1	1-2	

LEAGUE CHAMPIONSHIP FINAL TABLE 99/00

			Home				Away				Total					
		Pd	W	D	L	F	A	W	D	L	F	A	W	D	L	F	A	PT	GD
1	Dinamo Bucuresti	34	16	1	0	54	14	11	2	4	39	26	27	3	4	93	40	84	53
2	Rapid Bucuresti	34	12	4	1	37	16	10	2	5	28	22	22	6	6	65	38	72	27
3	Steaua Bucuresti	34	11	2	4	36	20	7	1	9	26	36	18	3	13	62	56	57	6
4	Ceahlaul Piatra Neamt	34	13	2	2	39	18	4	4	9	17	30	17	6	11	56	48	57	8
5	FC Arges Dacia Pitesti	34	11	4	2	31	11	5	2	10	14	24	16	6	12	45	35	54	10
6	Gloria Bistrita	34	15	0	2	36	11	2	2	13	18	38	17	2	15	54	49	53	5
7	FCM Bacau	34	12	3	2	25	11	3	3	11	15	29	15	6	13	40	39	51	1
8	Otelul Galati	34	12	1	4	39	20	3	3	11	20	35	15	4	15	59	55	49	4
9	FC National Bucuresti	34	13	2	2	47	14	2	2	13	14	30	15	4	15	61	44	49	17
10	Astra Ploiesti	34	9	4	4	28	16	4	4	9	15	25	13	8	13	43	41	47	2
11	Petrolul Ploiesti	34	12	3	2	33	13	2	2	13	15	42	14	5	15	48	55	47	-7
12	Rocar Bucuresti	34	12	1	4	36	18	3	1	13	16	34	15	2	17	52	52	47	0
13	Universitatea Craiova	34	11	2	4	35	15	2	5	10	10	26	13	7	14	45	41	46	4
14	FC Brasov	34	13	1	3	43	17	1	3	13	10	26	14	4	16	53	43	46	10
15	FC Farul Constanta	34	11	4	2	25	11	1	4	12	13	34	12	8	14	38	45	44	-7
16	FC Onesti	34	9	2	6	29	32	0	1	16	8	60	9	3	22	37	92	30	-55
17	CSM Resita	34	4	6	7	21	26	1	2	14	14	47	5	8	21	35	73	23	-38
18	FC Extensiv Craiova	34	4	3	10	14	22	0	2	15	12	44	4	5	25	26	66	17	-40

N.B. Where two or more teams are level on points, classification is determined by the results of the matches between them.

it was also arguably the best performance the team had produced since the heavenly heights of the 1994 World Cup.

Youngsters Christian Chivu and Adrian Mutu were truly inspirational, and for long periods Romania gave England the runaround. The lead the English carried into the half-time interval was a travesty of justice, and once Dorinel Munteanu had brought the scores level again soon after the interval, there was only one team in it. Ioan Ganea's nerveless penalty-kick ensured that the right team won the game.

Sadly, the legacy of that historic win was an injury to veteran libero Gheorge Popescu and second yellow cards for three key players - Dan Petrescu, Adrian Ilie and Cosmin Contra. A revamped team, including the restored Hagi, did as well as they could against Italy in the quarter-final, but after a promising beginning they were eventually worn down and never looked likely to come back from a 0-2 deficit, particularly after Hagi had stupidly got himself sent off for two yellow-card offences within the space of three minutes.

It was a shameful and undignified way for the maestro to exit the international scene on the occasion of his 125th appearance. Indeed, he had been lucky to escape a straight red card for the first of his offences - a horror-tackle on Antonio Conte which put the Italian in hospital. The second card, shown to him for an exaggerated fall in the penalty area, served as a form of delayed retribution.

Another man bowing out at the end of the tournament was coach Ienei. He had confirmed himself at Euro 2000 as Romania's most successful coach - it was he who had steered the team into the uncharted waters of the World Cup second round a decade earlier - and was expected to see the remainder of his contract through to 2002. But after only half a year in the job he chose to leave, with Ladislau Bölöni, the coach of relegated French club Nancy, being elected to replace him.

The man who had taken Romania successfully through the Euro 2000 qualifiers, Victor Piturca, had been sacked shortly afterwards following a row with some of the team's senior players, foremost among them Hagi. Piturca claimed unfair dismissal, and, with a record of nine wins,

INTERNATIONAL HONOURS

World Cup Finals appearances: 1930, 1934, 1938, 1970, 1990 (2nd round), 1994 (qtr-finals), 1998 (2nd round)

European Championship appearances: 1960, 1972, 1984, 1996, 2000 (qtr-finals)

European Club Competitions

Champions' Cup	Steaua Bucuresti (1986)
Super Cup	Steaua Bucuresti (1986)

EUROPEAN CUPS 99/00

CHAMPIONS' CUP
● RAPID BUCURESTI
Preliminary round 2 SKONTO RIGA (LAT)
H 3-3 Barbu (15), Schumacher (53), Mutica (72)
Lobont; Andone (Bundea 35), Stanciu, Rednic, Iencsi, Bolohan (Mutica 46); Maldarasanu, Lupu, Schumacher; Raducan, Barbu (Dascalescu 65).
A 1-2 Raducan (33)
Lobont; Stanciu, Rednic, Mutica; Sabau (Bolohan 76), Maldarasanu (Schumacher 80), Lupu, Raducan, Iencsi; Radu, Barbu.

UEFA CUP
● DINAMO BUCURESTI
Qualifying round FC MONDERCANGE (LUX)
A 6-2 Lupescu (21p), Petre F. (28), Mihalcea (49), Mutu (51, 78), Niculae (80)
Preda; Ciobotariu, Nastase, Florea; Petre F., Lupescu (Kirita 55), Haldan, Iftodi (Dobre 76); Mihalcea (Niculae 67), Vladoiu, Mutu.
H 7-0 Mutu (8p, 19), Niculae (23, 29, 74), Fogel (71og), Petre T. (89)
Fouhami; Petre T., Ciobotariu (Lazar 60), Mihali, Dobre (Utfineant 86); Iftodi (Petre F. 46), Kirita, Timofte; Mihalcea, Niculae, Mutu.

1st round SL BENFICA (POR)
A 1-0 Nastase (34)
Preda; Petre F. (Petre T. 87), Ciobotariu, Nastase, Florea; Haldan, Lupescu, Iftodi (Niculae 64); Mihalcea (Kirita 82), Vladoiu.
H 0-2
Preda; Petre F., Ciobotariu, Nastase, Florea; Kirita, Lupescu, Haldan; Mutu (Timofte 88), Vladoiu (Iftodi 77), Niculae.

● STEAUA BUCURESTI
Qualifying round FC LEVADIA MAARDU (EST)
H 3-0 Ilie (40, 89), Ciocoiu (79)
Ritli; Reghecampf, Duro, Belodedici (Zotinca 31), Iordache (Bordeanu 74); Trica, Baciu, Lacatus, Lutu; Danciulescu (Ciocoiu 18), Ilie.
A 4-1 Reghecampf (53), Rosu (69, 80), Ilie (84)
Tudor, Reghecampf, Miu, Belodedici, Iordache (Bordeanu 81); Lutu (Lincar 58), Duro, Lacatus, Trica (Rosu 51); Ilie, Ciocoiu.

1st round LASK LINZ (AUT)
H 2-0 Ciocoiu (63), Danciulescu (82)
Ritli; Reghecampf, Miu, Baciu, Bordeanu, Lutu (Lacatus 73), Lincar, Trica (Danciulescu 51), Rosu; Ciocoiu (Luca 81), Ilie.
A 3-2 Bordeanu (7), Ilie (30), Duro (61)
Tudor, Reghecampf, Miu, Baciu, Bordeanu; Lincar, Duro (Trica 67), Danciulescu, Rosu (Lutu 76); Ilie (Luca 80), Ciocoiu.

2nd round WEST HAM UNITED (ENG)
H 2-0 Rosu (39), Ilie (57)
Ritli; Reghecampf, Miu, Baciu, Bordeanu; Danciulescu (Lutu 86), Duro, Lincar, Rosu; Ilie (Luca 79), Ciocoiu (Ogararu 89).
A 0-0
Ritli; Reghecampf, Miu, Baciu, Duro, Bordeanu; Danciulescu (Trica 69); Lincar (Lacatus 84); Rosu; Ilie, Ciocoiu (Lutu 88).

3rd round SLAVIA PRAHA (CZE)
A 1-4 Lutu (82)
Ritli; Reghecampf, Duro, Baciu, Miu, Bordeanu; Danciulescu (Lutu 51), Lincar (Lacatus 69), Rosu; Ciocoiu, Ilie.
H 1-1 Ciocoiu (45)
Ritli; Reghecampf, Duro, Baciu, Miu, Bordeanu (Lacatus 83); Danciulescu (Lutu 53), Lincar, Rosu; Ilie, Ciocoiu.

---

six draws and just one defeat, he had a point. But there was no way back and he promptly took over Ienei's former post as the head coach at Steaua Bucharest.

Ienei had endured a wretched autumn with Steaua, and Piturca was unable to arrest the club's side, which left them without a place in Europe for the first time in 16 years. Paradoxically, Steaua had been Romania's only worthwhile European performers in 1999/2000. While champions Rapid were embarrassingly bundled out of the Champions' League by Skonto Riga at the second preliminary round stage and Dinamo Bucharest exited the UEFA Cup in the first round after being unable to defend a fine first-leg win in Lisbon against Benfica, Steaua came through four rounds of the UEFA Cup, gaining a prestige victory over English side West Ham before losing heavily to Slavia Prague.

Steaua's miserable year at home paved the way for traditional rivals Dinamo to reclaim the high ground and win the Romanian championship for the first time in eight years. Dinamo's joy was accentuated by the fact that they clinched the title with a 3-2 victory over Steaua. It was the first derby win for Dinamo in nine seasons and could not have come at a more appropriate time. A 70th-minute winner from striker Adrian Mihalcea, following earlier goals from midfielders Florentin Petre and Ioan Lupescu, not only brought the long, unhappy sequence of adverse results against Steaua to an end but also made mathematically certain of Dinamo's 15th national title.

Dinamo had been champions-in-waiting for several weeks. Their intentions were plain right from the start of the season when they won each of their opening nine matches to take a commanding lead at the top of the table. By the winter break they held a comprehensive 11-point advantage, which left lone pursuers Rapid hoping only for a miracle in the second half of the season.

Rapid were given some encouragement when Dinamo's top scorer, Adrian Mutu, was sold during the winter to Italian giants Inter, with another high-scoring forward, Ion Vladoiu, departing soon afterwards for Germany. But there was no let-up whatsoever in Dinamo's victory march

DOMESTIC CUP 99/00

1/16 FINALS
Hondor Agigea 1, Rapid Bucuresti 1
(aet; 3-4 on pens.)
West Petrom Arad 0, Steaua Bucuresti 1
AS Curtea de Arges 0, FC National Bucuresti 3
Inter Petrila 1, Astra Ploiesti 3
Vrancart Adjud 0, CSM Resita 1
Telecom Arad 1, Universitatea Craiova 3
Petrolul Berca 3, FC Farul Constanta 2 (aet)
FC Brasov 4, FC Onesti 1
Tractorul Brasov 1, Dinamo Bucuresti 4
Cimentul Fieni 1, Otelul Galati 2 (aet)
Metalul Filipestii de Padure 0, Petrolul Ploiesti 1
Ceahlaul Piatra Neamt 4, Extensiv Craiova 1
NC Foresta Suceava 1, FC Arges Pitesti 2 (aet)
Progresul Somcuta Mare 0, FCM Bacau 1 (aet)
Otelul Stei 0, Rocar Bucuresti 3
Pandurii Targu Jiu 1, Gloria Bistrita 2 (aet)

1/8 FINALS
Rapid Bucuresti 1, Gloria Bistrita 0
FCM Bacau 1, Cheahlaul Piatra Neamt 0
Universitatea Craiova 1, Steaua Bucuresti 0

FC National Bucuresti 4, FC Brasov 2
Petrolul Berca 0, Petrolul Ploiesti 2
Dinamo Bucuresti 3, Rocar Bucuresti 1
Otelul Galati 2, Astra Ploiesti 1 (aet)
FC Arges Pitesti 1, CSM Resita 3

QUARTER-FINALS
Dinamo Bucuresti 3 (Mihalcea 20, Mutu 50, 89p),
FC National Bucuresti 2 (Savu M. 15, Carabas 48)
Rapid Bucuresti 2 (Voicu 55, Maier 95),
FCM Bacau 1 (Petcu 61) (aet)
Universitatea Craiova 1 (Niculescu 63),
Petrolul Ploiesti 0
CSM Resita 1 (Ciocoi 39),
Otelul Galati 2 (Tofan 76, Ion V. 86).

SEMI-FINALS
Otelul Galati 0,
Dinamo Bucuresti 2 (Dragan 28, Mihalcea 85)
Dinamo Bucuresti 3 (Petre 19, 53, Niculae 63),
Otelul Galati 1 (Gurita 44)
(Dinamo Bucuresti 5-1)

Universitatea Craiova 2 (Stoican 39, Vochin 73),
Rapid Bucuresti 0
Rapid Bucuresti 2 (Radu 31, Maldarasanu 71),
Universitatea Craiova 1 (Barcauan 52)
(Universitatea Craiova 3-2)

FINAL
14/05/2000, Bucharest
DINAMO BUCURESTI 2 Niculae (31p), Haldan (88)
UNIVERSITATEA CRAIOVA 0
referee - Corpodean
DINAMO BUCURESTI - Preda; Kirita, Nastase, Mihali,
Florea; Petre (Buta 89), Haldan, Lupescu, Iftodi;
Mihalcea (Mara 70), Niculae.
UNIVERSITATEA CRAIOVA - Prunea; Dragomir
(Grigorie 57), Batranu, Papura (Vancea 69), Stoican:
Sava, Cristescu, Vigariu (Neagoe 84), Frasineanu;
Niculescu, Barcauan.

---

after the resumption. Six successive victories gave them an even bigger lead, and although Rapid delayed the inevitable by thumping Dinamo 4-0, the long-awaited victory over Steaua closed the book on the title race one week later.

Coach Cornel Dinu was the mastermind behind Dinamo's success, which was completed with a 'double'-clinching victory in the Romanian Cup (2-0 v Universitatea Craiova in the final). His team were a productive amalgam of experience and youth. The former was epitomised by ex-national team stalwarts such as Gheorghe Mihali, Daniel Iftodi, Stefan Preda and the aforementioned Lupescu and Vladoiu, while the latter came in the budding shape of Mutu and his highly effective replacement, 19-year-old Marius Niculae.

TOP SCORERS

20	Marian SAVU (FC National Bucuresti)
18	Adrian MUTU (Dinamo Bucuresti)
16	Marian IVAN (FC Brasov)
	Claudiu NICULESCU (Universitatea Craiova)
14	Florin PETCU (FCM Bacau)
	Ionel DANCIULESCU (Steaua Bucuresti)
13	Adrian MIHALCEA (Dinamo Bucuresti)
	Laurentiu ROSU (Steaua Bucuresti)
12	Marius NICULAE (Dinamo Bucuresti)
	Ion VLADOIU (Dinamo Bucuresti)

NATIONAL TEAM RESULTS 99/00

18/08/99	Cyprus	A	Limassol	2-2	Lupescu (45p), Filipescu (81)
04/09/99	Slovakia (ECQ)	A	Bratislava	5-1	Ilie (6), Hagi (30), Ciobotariu (66), Moldovan (88, 90)
08/09/99	Portugal (ECQ)	H	Bucharest	1-1	Ilie (37)
09/10/99	Liechtenstein (ECQ)	A	Vaduz	3-0	Rosu (25), Ganea (65, 74)
02/02/00	Latvia	N	Paphos	2-0	Rosu (18), Niculae (69)
04/02/00	Georgia	N	Larnaca	1-1	Haldan (81) (aet; 4-3 on pens.)
06/02/00	Cyprus	A	Nicosia	2-3	Mara (16), Stoica (55)
29/03/00	Greece	A	Athens	0-2	
26/04/00	Cyprus	H	Constanta	2-0	Mutu (58), Ganea (81p)
27/05/00	Holland	A	Amsterdam	1-2	Moldovan (70)
03/06/00	Greece	H	Bucharest	2-1	Ciobotariu (7), Petre (79)
12/06/00	Germany (ECF)	N	Liège	1-1	Moldovan (5)
17/06/00	Portugal (ECF)	N	Arnhem	0-1	
20/06/00	England (ECF)	N	Charleroi	3-2	Chivu (22), Munteanu (48), Ganea (88p)
24/06/00	Italy (ECF)	N	Brussels	0-2	

NATIONAL TEAM APPEARANCES 99/00

Coach - Victor PITURCA; Emeric IENEI	CYP	SVK	POR	LIE	LAT	GEO	CYP	GRE	CYP	HOL	GRE	GER	POR	ENG	ITA	Cps	Gls
Bogdan STELEA (05/12/67) - UD Salamanca (ESP)	G	G	G	G				G78	G78			G	G	G	G	69	-
Dan PETRESCU (22/12/67) - Chelsea (ENG)	D86	D	D46	D				M75		D46	D	M69	M64	M		92	12
Stefan NANU (08/09/68) - Vitesse (HOL)	D84		s46	D						D46						7	-
Gheorghe POPESCU (09/10/67) - Galatasaray (TUR)	D	D	D	D					D	D	D80	D	D	D32		101	15
Iulian FILIPESCU (29/03/74) - Real Betis (ESP)	D89	D	D					D	s70	D58	D	D	D	D	D	38	1
Ioan Ovidiu SABAU (12/02/68) - Rapid Bucuresti	M74	M82	M													52	8
Ioan LUPESCU (09/12/68) - Dinamo Bucuresti	M	s76	s67	s75	D		D					M	s84		s68	73	6
Dorinel MUNTEANU (25/06/68) - VfL Wolfsburg (GER)	M	M	M					M65	M46	s46	M74	M	M	M	M	90	11
Constantin GALCA (08/03/72) - RCD Espanyol (ESP)	M80	M	M	M75							M60	M	M	M68	M68	58	4
Viorel MOLDOVAN (08/08/72) - Fenerbahçe (TUR)	A34	s58	A67	A61				A57	A66	A73	s46	A84	A69	A	A54	52	21
Ioan Viorel GANEA (10/08/73) - VfB Stuttgart (GER)	A	A58	s86	s61					s57	s66	s73	A46	s69	s74	s54	16	8
Bogdan LOBONT (18/01/78) - Rapid Bucuresti/Ajax (HOL)	s34					G		s78	s78	G	G85					11	-
Florentin PETRE (15/01/76) - Dinamo Bucuresti	s74			M	M77	s56	M80	s75		s70	s65		s64		M	20	2
Ion VLADOIU (05/11/68) - Dinamo Bucuresti	s80															27	2
Cristian CHIVU (15/10/80) - Universitatea Craiova/Ajax (HOL)	s84								s46	D	s74	D	D	D	D	8	1
Vladimir STOICAN (24/11/76) - Universitatea Craiova	s86															1	-
Liviu CIOBOTARIU (26/03/71) - Dinamo Bucuresti	s89	D	D	D				D	D	D	D	D			D	25	2
Gheorghe HAGI (05/02/65) - Galatasaray (TUR)		M76	M	M77				M	M	M	M75	M			M	125	34
Adrian ILIE (20/04/74) - Valencia CF (ESP)		A	A86	A								A69	A	A78	A74	37	11
Ovidiu STINGA (05/12/72) - PSV (HOL)		s82		s77												24	-
Laurentiu ROSU (26/10/75) - Steaua Bucuresti			M	M90	M59	M85	s65	s46		s69			s78	s68		16	3
Florin PRUNEA (08/08/68) - Universitatea Craiova					G	G						s85				38	-
Florentin DUMITRU (25/05/77) - Astra Ploiesti					D	D	D73									3	-
Florin BATRANU (19/03/71) - Universitatea Craiova					D	D										8	-
Iulian CRIVAC (04/07/76) - Rapid Bucuresti					D	D56										2	-
Catalin HALDAN (03/02/76) - Dinamo Bucuresti					M	M	M	M80	s57		s60					8	1
Adrian MIHALCEA (24/05/76) - Dinamo Bucuresti					M87	A56	s67	s65								10	-
Marius MALDARASANU (19/04/75) - Rapid Bucuresti					M	M80	s80			M70						4	-
Marius NICULAE (16/05/81) - Dinamo Bucuresti					A	A59	A67									3	1
Dorel MUTICA (14/03/73) - Rapid Bucuresti					s77	D	D									3	-
Bogdan MARA (29/09/77) - FC Arges Dacia Pitesti					s87	s59	A67									3	1
Pompiliu STOICA (10/09/76) - Astra Ploiesti					s90	s56	D	s80								4	1
Mugur BOLOHAN (28/05/76) - Rapid Bucuresti						D	D									3	-
Radu NICULESCU (02/03/75) - FC National Bucuresti						s59	s67									15	2
Narcis RADUCAN (23/09/74) - Rapid Bucuresti						s80										1	-
Cornel BUTA (01/11/77) - Dinamo Bucuresti							s73									1	-
Valentin NASTASE (04/10/74) - Dinamo Bucuresti							s85	D								3	-
Cosmin CONTRA (15/12/75) - Deportivo Alavés (ESP)								D	D	s58		s69	D	D		15	-
Adrian MUTU (08/01/79) - Inter (ITA)								A65	A	A	A65	s75		M	A	7	1
Erik LINCAR (16/10/78) - Steaua Bucuresti								M57	M							3	-
Stelian CARABAS (02/10/74) - Steaua Bucuresti								M70								1	-
Miodrag BELODEDICI (20/05/64) - Steaua Bucuresti										s80				s32	D	52	5

PLAYERS OF THE SEASON

CRISTIAN CHIVU

Cristian Chivu's transfer from Universitatea Craiova to Ajax in the summer of 1999 made very few waves either in Romania or Holland. But a year later the 19-year-old left-back had become one of the most talked-about footballers in both countries. He was one of the major revelations of Euro 2000, especially after his superb performance against England, which

included the game's opening goal. Some called it a fluke but Chivu (pictured below) preferred to believe that the ball had been blown into the net from on high by his recently deceased father. The youngster owes his father more than that goal. Mircea Chivu was his first coach at hometown club CSM Resita and the man who put him on the road to superstardom. Much is now expected of the newly-billed "Maldini of the Carpathians" as he sets out to confirm his budding progress, both with Ajax and Romania.

ADRIAN MUTU

Another prominent member of Romania's young generation, Adrian Mutu enjoyed a spectacular rise during the 1999/2000 season. In the autumn he was in sensational goalscoring form for Dinamo Bucharest, scoring 18 goals in as many games to give his club an unassailable lead in the Romanian championship race. Such prolific form inevitably attracted the attention of foreign scouts, and before anyone else could act, the big-spending Italians of Inter despatched a cheque for $2m to Bucharest to bring Mutu to the San Siro. Inevitably, he struggled to work his way into a team already overladen with superstars, but he began to play regularly for his country and at Euro 2000 he was selected to replace suspended playmaker Gheorghe Hagi for the crunch game against England - a challenge he rose to in magnificent fashion. Another fine performance followed against Italy, and suddenly a new Romanian star - complete with film-star looks - was born. Mutu should have a better opportunity to impress Serie A audiences in 2000/01, having been sold on by Inter to Verona.

Rapid lacked the overall strength of Dinamo and were unable to make a decent fist of their title defence. The sale of several important players from their championship-winning campaign - Ganea, Nanu, Sumudica, Pancu - made life very difficult for coach Mircea Lucescu. Two early-season blows rocked the team's confidence. The first was the early Champions' League exit, but much greater trauma was to follow in Rapid's opening league match of the season, against Astra Ploiesti - not because of the result, a 1-1 draw, but because of the fatal injury incurred by Astra's débutant midfielder, 24-year-old Stefan Vrabioru. Shortly after entering the field in the 57th minute as a substitute, Vrabioru collided heavily with Rapid's Mugur Bolohan. A few minutes later he collapsed and lost consciousness. He was transported to hospital but the doctors were unable to revive him and he died the same day.

Lucescu was to leave Rapid at the end of season and become the new coach of UEFA Cup winners Galatasaray. He took Gavril Balint as his assistant, thus adding to an already strong Romanian connection at the Istanbul club, with Hagi and Popescu already long established on the playing staff.

Hagi's first club, Farul Constanta, decided to name their stadium after the Black Sea resort's most famous son, but it brought them no added fortune, because at the end of the season they joined the already pre-condemned three-some of Extensiv Craiova, CSM Resita and FC Onesti in the relegation zone.

Had they won their final match, away to Onesti, they would have survived, but for once there was no cheap trade-off and Farul were beaten 2-1, which enabled FC Brasov to stay up instead.

Once again, the championship was tarnished with repeated claims of corruption and match-fixing. It was suggested that several teams in the lower half of the table made deals with others to guarantee one home win each, at three points apiece, rather than risk the less rewarding prospect of two draws. But the Romanian FA (FRF) came up with their stock excuse, "we have no proof", and so nothing was done by way of prevention or punishment.

One FRF decision which did receive favourable press was the reduction of the top division from 18 to 16 teams for the 2000/01 season. The four relegated clubs were thus replaced by just two newcomers, Foresta Falticeni and Gaz Metan Medias, each of whom won their respective 'B' division by a comfortable distance.

PROMOTED CLUBS 99/00

SECOND DIVISION FINAL TABLE

SERIA I		Pd	W	D	L	F	A	Pt	GD
1	**Foresta Falticeni**	**34**	**24**	**5**	**5**	**76**	**28**	**77**	**48**
2	AS Midia Navodari	34	20	6	8	64	28	66	36
3	Sportul Studentesc Bucuresti	34	17	8	9	59	35	59	24
4	Dacia Pitesti	34	16	6	12	53	47	54	6
5	Tractorul Brasov	34	16	4	14	44	41	52	3
6	Metrom Brasov	34	15	7	12	38	32	52	6
7	Callatis Mangalia	34	16	4	14	41	41	52	0
8	Laminorul Roman	34	16	4	14	60	48	52	12
9	Politehnica Iasi	34	16	2	16	49	45	50	4
10	Poiana Campina	34	15	4	15	51	44	49	7
11	Cimentul Fieni	34	14	7	13	34	37	49	-3
12	Juventus Bucuresti	34	13	9	12	45	39	48	6
13	Diplomatic Focsani	34	13	8	13	37	37	47	0
14	Precizia Sacele	34	12	11	11	38	34	47	4
15	Petrolul Moinesti	34	13	6	15	30	40	45	-10
16	Dunarea Galati	34	11	4	19	31	63	37	-32
17	Chindia Targoviste	34	4	4	26	23	83	16	-60
18	Gloria Buzau	34	3	5	26	21	72	14	-51

SERIA II		Pd	W	D	L	F	A	Pt	GD
1	**Gaz Metan Medias**	**34**	**21**	**6**	**7**	**53**	**22**	**69**	**31**
2	ARO Campulung	34	18	4	12	49	35	58	14
3	Corvinul Hunedoara	34	16	6	12	51	33	54	18
4	Jiul Petrosani	34	16	5	13	41	38	53	3
5	Olimpia Satu Mare	34	15	8	11	54	32	53	22
6	UT Arad	34	16	4	14	49	39	52	10
7	Apulum Alba Iulia	34	15	7	12	50	40	52	10
8	UM Timisoara	34	13	10	11	61	45	49	16
9	FC Inter Sibiu	34	14	6	14	39	43	48	-4
10	Flacara Rm. Valcea	34	13	9	12	45	41	48	4
11	FC Drobeta Turnu Severin	34	17	3	14	49	61	48	-12
12	Electro Bere Craiova	34	15	3	16	48	53	48	-5
13	ASA Tirgu Mures	34	13	7	14	45	38	46	7
14	FC Bihor Oradea	34	12	10	12	34	45	46	-11
15	Politehnica Timisoara	34	12	6	16	50	54	42	-4
16	Chimica Tarnaveni	34	12	5	17	36	51	41	-15
17	Universitatea Cluj	34	6	6	22	30	76	24	-46
18	Minerul Motru	34	6	5	23	28	66	23	-38

N.B. FC Drobeta Turnu Severin - 3 points deducted.

CLUB DIRECTORIES

FC Foresta Falticeni
B-dul 1 Decembrie 1918 nr.7
5800 Suceava
tel - (030) 216145
Year of Formation - 1954
President - Eugen Hutu
Coach - Marin Barbu
Stadium - Areni, Suceava (12,000)

Gaz Metan Medias
Piata Regele Ferdinand 12
Medias
tel - (069) 814623
fax - (069) 814623
Year of Formation - 1945
President - Ilie Vlad
Coach - Jean Gavrila
Stadium - Gaz Metan (3,500)

FC ARGES DACIA PITESTI

CLUB DIRECTORY

FC Arges Dacia Pitesti
str. Armand Calinescu 15
0300 Pitesti
tel - (048) 632842
Year of Formation - 1953
President - Constantin Stroe
Coach - Mihai Zamfir; Florin Halagian;
Mihai Zamfir; Andrei Speriatu; Marian Bondrea
Stadium - Trivale (16,000)

MAJOR HONOURS
League Championship - (2) 1972, 1979.

APPEARANCES 99/00

	P	Ap	(s)	Gls
Cristian BALASA	M	31		6
Vasile BARDES	M	17		4
Marius Ion BILASCO	A	2	(3)	
Laurentiu Adrian BOGOI	D	18	(2)	
Cristian Nicolae BRATU	A	8	(7)	1
Augustin Eduard CHIRITA	M	13	(16)	2
Paul Constantin CODREA	M	16	(5)	1
Danut Dumitru COMAN	G	4	(1)	
Claudiu Mircea CORNACI	D	8	(6)	
Gabriel CRACIUN	D	1		
Cornel CRISTESCU	M	4	(2)	
Iulian CRIVAC	D	19		2
Ioan Cristian DANCIA	D	12		
Marius DITA	D	1	(2)	
Nicolae DITA	D	30	(1)	3
Cristian Valeriu FERARU	M	4	(8)	
Remus Ion GALMENCEA	D	23		3
Attila GHINDA	A	18	(3)	6
Bogdan Ion MARA	A	14	(10)	5
Daniel Emil MOGOSANU	D	28		
Adrian Constantin NEAGA	M	14	(8)	6
Cristinel Adrian NEDELEA	M		(4)	
Constantin PANA	M	9	(2)	2
Mihai PARLOG	M	3	(3)	
Marius Adrian RADU	D	17	(7)	
Daniel Eugen REDNIC	M	5	(1)	
Danut SOMCHERECHI	A	6	(4)	1
Daniel Eduard STANCIU	G	5		
Dragos STROE	D	8		
Ciprian TANASA	A	1	(1)	
Florin Alexandru TENE	G	13		
Bogdan Arges VINTILA	G	11		

LEAGUE RESULTS 1999/2000

23/07/99	FC Extensiv Craiova	A	1-2	Balasa (p)
01/08/99	Petrolul Ploiesti	H	1-0	Dita
04/08/99	Rocar Bucuresti	A	3-0	(w/o)
07/08/99	FC Brasov	H	1-0	Balasa
14/08/99	Rapid Bucuresti	A	0-1	
20/08/99	FC National Bucuresti	H	3-1	Galmencea, Bardes, Chirita
28/08/99	FC Onesti	A	2-1	Ghinda, Mara
11/09/99	FC Farul Constanta	H	2-1	Balasa, Mara
18/09/99	CSM Resita	A	0-0	
25/09/99	Universitatea Craiova	H	2-0	Balasa (p), Galmencea
02/10/99	Astra Ploiesti	A	1-0	Balasa (p)
16/10/99	FCM Bacau	H	1-1	Bardes
23/10/99	Ceahlaul Piatra Neamt	A	0-1	
30/10/99	Dinamo Bucuresti	A	0-4	
05/11/99	Otelul Galati	A	2-1	Ghinda 2
13/11/99	Gloria Bistrita	H	2-0	Mara 2
20/11/99	FC Extensiv Craiova	H	2-0	Bardes, Crivac
27/11/99	Petrolul Ploiesti	A	1-1	Bardes
04/12/99	Rocar Bucuresti	H	3-1	Galmencea, Mara, Neaga
13/12/99	Steaua Bucuresti	H	4-0	Codrea, Pana 2, Crivac
03/03/00	FC Brasov	A	1-2	Neaga
11/03/00	Rapid Bucuresti	H	0-1	
19/03/00	FC National Bucuresti	A	1-4	Neaga
22/03/00	FC Onesti	H	2-0	Balasa, Neaga
25/03/00	FC Farul Constanta	A	0-1	
01/04/00	CSM Resita	H	1-1	Neaga (p)
05/04/00	Universitatea Craiova	A	1-3	Somcherechi
08/04/00	Astra Ploiesti	H	1-1	Dita
15/04/00	FCM Bacau	A	0-1	
22/04/00	Ceahlaul Piatra Neamt	H	1-1	Bratu
29/04/00	Steaua Bucuresti	A	1-0	Dita
03/05/00	Dinamo Bucuresti	H	2-3	Ghinda 2
06/05/00	Otelul Galati	H	3-0	Ghinda, Neaga, Chirita
10/05/00	Gloria Bistrita	A	0-2	

ASTRA PLOIESTI

CLUB DIRECTORY

Astra Ploiesti
B-ul. Petrolistului 59
2000 Ploiesti
tel - (044) 198012
fax - (044) 144842
Year of Formation - 1934
President - Ion Niculae
Coach - Vasile Simionas; Costica Stefanescu
(00/01 - Ion Marin)
Stadium - Astra (10,000)

APPEARANCES 99/00

	P	Ap	(s)	Gls
Eugen Daniel BASTON	A	6	(9)	3
Constantin BARSAN	A	18	(8)	3
Claudiu BATRANU	M		(4)	
Florin Valentin BERARU	M	1	(6)	
Marius BRATU	G	10		
Costin CARAMAN	A	2	(3)	
Mircea CIOREA	M	30	(3)	11
Emil Gavril DANCUS	M	24		
Florentin DUMITRU	D	25	(1)	
Marin DUNA	A	12	(1)	1
Daniel DUNAREANU	A	14	(4)	1
Ionel FULGA	M	2		
Robert ILYES	M	32		6
Florian Dan LACUSTA	D	20		
Cornel MIHART	M	3	(15)	1
Daniel MOVILA	M	10	(14)	2
Catalin Emanuel MULTESCU	G	23		
Octavian NICOLA	M		(1)	
Bogdan Gheorghe NICOLAE	D	26	(2)	1
Ioan Daniel PETROIESC	D	28	(1)	1
Florin Flavius POGACEAN	M	12	(7)	1
Florin PRUNEA	G	1		
Gheorghe ROHAT	D	25	(2)	4
Ketlas SAID (MAR)	M		(1)	
Valentin SANDRU	M		(1)	
Ionut Cristian SAVU	A	25	(5)	5
Pompilu Sorin STOICA	M	23	(1)	2
Vasile VOINEA	M	2	(2)	
Stefan VRABIORU	M		(1)	
Bogdan Mihaita VRAJITOAREA	A		(1)	

LEAGUE RESULTS 1999/2000

24/07/99	Rapid Bucuresti	A	1-1	Rohat
04/08/99	FC Onesti	A	0-1	
07/08/99	FC Farul Constanta	H	3-2	Nicolae, Petroiesc, Ciorea
14/08/99	CSM Resita	A	5-2	Savu, Ciorea 2 (1p), Mihart, Movila
22/08/99	Universitatea Craiova	H	2-0	Rohat, Ciorea (p)
29/08/99	Dinamo Bucuresti	H	1-2	Savu
11/09/99	FCM Bacau	A	2-1	Ilyes, Ciorea (p)
17/09/99	Ceahlaul Piatra Neamt	H	0-1	
24/09/99	Steaua Bucuresti	A	1-4	Ciorea (p)
02/10/99	FC Arges Dacia Pitesti	H	0-1	
16/10/99	Otelul Galati	A	1-0	Rohat
23/10/99	Gloria Bistrita	H	2-1	Ciorea, Baston
27/10/99	FC Extensiv Craiova	A	1-0	Baston
31/10/99	Petrolul Ploiesti	H	2-0	Barsan, Stoica
03/11/99	FC National Bucuresti	H	1-1	Ciorea (p)
06/11/99	Rocar Bucuresti	A	1-2	Dunareanu
13/11/99	FC Brasov	H	1-1	Ciorea
21/11/99	Rapid Bucuresti	H	2-3	Ilyes, Barsan
27/11/99	FC National Bucuresti	A	0-1	
04/12/99	FC Onesti	H	5-0	Baston, og (Masati), Ciorea 2 (1p), Savu
04/03/00	FC Farul Constanta	A	1-1	Rohat
11/03/00	CSM Resita	H	2-1	Stoica, Ilyes
18/03/00	Universitatea Craiova	A	0-0	
22/03/00	Dinamo Bucuresti	A	1-2	Barsan
25/03/00	FCM Bacau	H	1-0	Ilyes
01/04/00	Ceahlaul Piatra Neamt	A	0-4	
05/04/00	Steaua Bucuresti	H	1-0	Pogacean
08/04/00	FC Arges Dacia Pitesti	A	1-1	Duna
15/04/00	Otelul Galati	H	1-1	Savu
22/04/00	Gloria Bistrita	A	0-2	
29/04/00	FC Extensiv Craiova	H	1-1	Ilyes
03/05/00	Petrolul Ploiesti	A	0-1	
06/05/00	Rocar Bucuresti	H	3-1	Movila, Ilyes, Savu
10/05/00	FC Brasov	A	0-2	

FCM BACAU

CLUB DIRECTORY

FCM Bacau
str. Pictor Aman 94
5500 Bacau
tel (034) 141922
Year of Formation - 1950
President - Gheorghe Chivorchian
Coach - Florin Halagian; Gheorghe Poenaru
Stadium - Nicolae Paduraru (25,000)

APPEARANCES 99/00

		P	Ap	(s)	Gls
Florin ANTON	G	8	(1)		
Stefan APOSTOL	M	25	(1)		
Alexandru Cristian AXINTE	M	17	(11)	3	
Daniel Jean BOGDAN	G	26			
Dan Vasile BOLFA	D	24	(3)	1	
Ionel Giani CAPUSA	M	14	(8)	2	
Radu Eduard CIOBANU	D	14			
Gheorghe Ciprian CIURLEA	D	2	(3)		
Sorin CONDURACHE	M	1	(4)		
Florin GANEA	D	19	(14)	2	
Florin GANTZ	M		(1)		
Marius GIREADA	D	30		1	
Danut MUNTEANU	D	22	(5)		
Vlad MUNTEANU	M	17	(7)	4	
Florin PAVEL	M	26	(3)		
Florin Lucian PETCU	A	28	(3)	14	
S. PETCU	D		(1)		
Cristian Daniel POPOVICI	D	18	(5)	1	
Ovidiu Vasile ROTARIU	D	18	(9)	1	
Ionica SEREA	A	26	(6)	5	
Ioan Ovidiu STRATULAT	D		(1)		
Ionel Sorin TROFIN	M	27	(5)	1	
Aurelian Ioan ZLATI	M	12	(9)	4	

LEAGUE RESULTS 1999/2000

24/07/99	FC Brasov	A	1-1	Petcu
31/07/99	Rapid Bucuresti	H	0-0	
03/08/99	FC National Bucuresti	A	2-2	Petcu 2 (1p)
07/08/99	FC Onesti	H	3-0	Munteanu, Petcu, Ganea
14/08/99	FC Farul Constanta	A	0-3	
21/08/99	CSM Resita	H	1-0	Petcu (p)
27/08/99	Universitatea Craiova	A	3-2	Serea, Petcu, Ganea
11/09/99	Astra Ploiesti	H	1-2	Popovici
25/09/99	Ceahlaul Piatra Neamt	A	1-3	Capusa
02/10/99	Steaua Bucuresti	H	2-1	og (Danciulescu), Gireada
16/10/99	FC Arges Dacia Pitesti	A	1-1	Capusa
23/10/99	Otelul Galati	H	1-0	Trofin
27/10/99	Gloria Bistrita	A	0-2	
30/10/99	FC Extensiv Craiova	H	1-0	Axinte
03/11/99	Dinamo Bucuresti	H	0-3	
06/11/99	Petrolul Ploiesti	A	0-1	
14/11/99	Rocar Bucuresti	H	1-0	Petcu (p)
20/11/99	FC Brasov	H	1-0	Petcu (p)
28/11/99	Rapid Bucuresti	A	1-2	Munteanu
03/12/00	FC National Bucuresti	H	1-1	Petcu
04/03/00	FC Onesti	A	0-1	
11/03/00	FC Farul Constanta	H	1-1	Axinte
17/03/00	CSM Resita	A	2-1	Serea, Zlati
22/03/00	Universitatea Craiova	H	3-0	Petcu 2, Zlati
25/03/00	Astra Ploiesti	A	0-1	
02/04/00	Dinamo Bucuresti	A	1-2	Munteanu
05/04/00	Ceahlaul Piatra Neamt	H	2-0	Serea, Zlati
09/04/00	Steaua Bucuresti	A	0-1	
15/04/00	FC Arges Dacia Pitesti	H	1-0	Axinte
21/04/00	Otelul Galati	A	1-3	Serea
29/04/00	Gloria Bistrita	H	3-2	Petcu 2, Rotariu
03/05/00	FC Extensiv Craiova	A	2-0	Munteanu, Serea
06/05/00	Petrolul Ploiesti	H	3-0	Bolfa, Petcu, Zlati
10/05/00	Rocar Bucuresti	A	0-3	

FC BRASOV

CLUB DIRECTORY

Fotbal Club Brasov
str. Mihai Viteazul 168
2200 Brasov
tel - (068) 116033
Year of Formation - 1937
President - Ion Nicolae
Coach - Ioan Andonie; Adrian Harlab;
Florin Halagian; Adrian Harlab
(00/01 - Gabriel Stan)
Stadium - Tineretului (12,500)

APPEARANCES 99/00

	P	Ap	(s)	Gls
Iuliu Paris ANDRASI	D	7	(5)	
Florin Adrian ANGHEL	M	3	(14)	4
Lucian BICA	D	13		
Cosmin BODEA	D	5	(1)	
Mugurel Mihai BUGA	M	25	(2)	4
Cornel BUTA	D	19		4
Remus George CIOLANEL	A		(1)	
Octavian COCAN	M	20	(3)	2
Constantin CONSTANTINESOU	A		(1)	
Florin CONSTANTINOVICI	M	13		1
Alexandru COZMA	A	17	(10)	11
Dragos CRISTEAN	A	4	(6)	
Vasile ELCA	D	21	(2)	
Marian GHEORGHE	M	1	(4)	
Aurel GHINDARU	D	32		
Vasile GHINDARU	M	12	(7)	
Tiberiu GHIOANE	M	1		
Ioan Gabriel GNANDT	M	8	(14)	3
Daniel Ionut ISAILA	D	30	(1)	2
Marian IVAN	A	32		16
Gabriel KAJCSA	G	14		
Daniel Stefan LICA	D		(1)	
Razvan LUCESCU	G	13		
Gheorghe LUPU	D		(1)	
Marian MANOLE	A	3	(1)	1
Endre Istvan MATYAS	G	6		
Ionel Marin MAUTA	D	31	(1)	2
Flavius Lucian MOLDOVAN	D	1		
Constantin PANA	M	9	(1)	1
Tinel Tanase PETRE	D	8	(2)	1
Valentin Octavian SUCIU	M	2	(4)	
Radu TURDEAN	G	1	(1)	
Cristian Marius VASC	M	23	(1)	1
Attila VAJDA	M		(1)	

LEAGUE RESULTS 1999/2000

24/07/99	FCM Bacau	H	1-1	Ivan
30/07/99	Ceahlaul Piatra Neamt	A	1-2	Buta
04/08/99	Steaua Bucuresti	H	1-2	Gnandt
07/08/99	FC Arges Dacia Pitesti	A	0-1	
13/08/99	Otelul Galati	H	3-0	Ivan 2 (1p), Manole
21/08/99	Gloria Bistrita	A	0-2	
28/08/99	FC Extensiv Craiova	H	2-1	Ivan, Vasc
11/09/99	Petrolul Ploiesti	A	0-1	
17/09/99	Rocar Bucuresti	H	4-0	Cozma 2, Buga, Gnandt
25/09/99	Dinamo Bucuresti	A	1-3	Buta
02/10/99	Rapid Bucuresti	A	1-2	Ivan
15/10/99	FC National Bucuresti	H	3-1	Cozma 2, Cocan
23/10/99	FC Onesti	A	2-3	Cozma, Cocan
27/10/99	FC Farul Constanta	H	3-2	Cozma, Buta, Isaila
30/10/99	CSM Resita	A	1-3	Ivan (p)
06/11/99	Universitatea Craiova	H	0-1	
13/11/99	Astra Ploiesti	A	1-1	Mauta
20/11/99	FCM Bacau	A	0-1	
26/11/99	Ceahlaul Piatra Neamt	H	3-1	Ivan, Cozma, Buta
04/12/99	Steaua Bucuresti	A	2-2	Ivan 2 (1p)
03/03/00	FC Arges Dacia Pitesti	H	2-1	Ivan 2 (1p)
10/03/00	Otelul Galati	A	0-1	
18/03/00	Gloria Bistrita	H	4-2	Pana, Buga 2, Anghel
22/03/00	FC Extensiv Craiova	A	1-0	Anghel
25/03/00	Petrolul Ploiesti	H	0-1	
01/04/00	Rocar Bucuresti	A	0-1	
05/04/00	Dinamo Bucuresti	H	4-3	Ivan 2, Buga, Cozma
08/04/00	Rapid Bucuresti	H	2-0	Petre, Cozma
14/04/00	FC National Bucuresti	A	0-2	
22/04/00	FC Onesti	H	5-1	Ivan 3, Cozma 2
29/04/00	FC Farul Constanta	A	0-0	
03/05/00	CSM Resita	H	4-0	Mauta, Anghel, Isaila, Gnandt
06/05/00	Universitatea Craiova	A	0-1	
10/05/00	Astra Ploiesti	H	2-0	Constantinovici, Anghel

CEAHLAUL PIATRA NEAMT

CLUB DIRECTORY

Ceahlaul Piatra Neamt
Str. Eroilor 18
5600 Piatra Neamt
tel - (033) 612702
Year of Formation - 1919
President - Gheorghe Stefan
Technical Director - Mircea Nedelcu
Coach - Viorel Hizo
Stadium - Ceahlaul (15,000)

APPEARANCES 99/00

	P	Ap	(s)	Gls
Angelo Dumitru ALISTAR	D	28	(1)	1
Eugen Catalin ANGHEL	G	11	(1)	
Cristinel ATOMULESEI	D	3	(2)	
Vasile Valentin AVADANEI	D	3	(2)	
Vasile Florin AXINIA	A	22	(3)	4
Adrian BALDOVIN	D	17	(3)	3
Dumitru BOTEZ	M	28		3
Codrut Stefan DOMSA	D	16	(11)	
Constantin ENACHE	M	15	(4)	
Leo Florian GROZAVU	D	31		7
Ion Lavi HRIB	A	11	(2)	9
Constantin Ionut ILIE	M	30		7
Mihai Dan IONESCU	M	18	(5)	2
Radu Gabriel LEFTER	G	23		
Ovidiu MARC	M	28	(1)	7
Mihai NEMTANU	A	16	(15)	6
Gheorghe Florin NOHAI	D	2	(1)	
Danut PERJA	D	7		2
Iordache Marian PURICA	D	10	(7)	1
Gabriel RADULESCU	D	2		
Daniel SCANTEIE	A	14	(7)	2
Adrian Constantin SOLOMON	M	14	(19)	
Tiberiu SERBAN	M	5	(8)	
Tudor SERBAN	M		(1)	
Tudorel Cristian SOIMARU	D	20	(6)	2

LEAGUE RESULTS 1999/2000

30/07/99	FC Brasov	H	2-1	Ilie, Perja
07/08/99	FC National Bucuresti	H	3-2	Ionescu, Grozavu (p), Alistar
14/08/99	FC Onesti	A	1-1	Marc
18/08/99	Rocar Bucuresti	A	0-2	
21/08/99	FC Farul Constanta	H	2-1	Scanteie, Purica
28/08/99	CSM Resita	A	3-1	Baldovin, Grozavu 2 (1p)
12/09/99	Universitatea Craiova	H	1-1	Perja
17/09/99	Astra Ploiesti	A	1-0	Ionescu
25/09/99	FCM Bacau	H	3-1	Botez, Axinia, Nemtanu
03/10/99	Dinamo Bucuresti	H	2-2	Marc, Botez
15/10/99	Steaua Bucuresti	A	0-3	
23/10/99	FC Arges Dacia Pitesti	H	1-0	Ilie
26/10/99	Otelul Galati	A	0-3	
30/10/99	Gloria Bistrita	H	1-0	Marc
03/11/99	Rapid Bucuresti	A	2-1	Baldovin, Axinia
06/11/99	FC Extensiv Craiova	A	0-0	
14/11/99	Petrolul Ploiesti	H	2-0	Ilie, Grozavu (p)
20/11/99	Rocar Bucuresti	H	2-0	Baldovin, Nemtanu
26/11/99	FC Brasov	A	1-3	Ilie
04/12/99	Rapid Bucuresti	H	0-3	
05/03/00	FC National Bucuresti	A	1-5	Hrib
11/03/00	FC Onesti	H	6-0	Marc 2, Grozavu (p), Ilie, Axinia, Hrib
18/03/00	FC Farul Constanta	A	0-1	
22/03/00	CSM Resita	H	4-2	Hrib 3, Grozavu
25/03/00	Universitatea Craiova	A	2-0	Grozavu, Axinia
01/04/00	Astra Ploiesti	H	4-0	Soimaru, Ilie, Hrib 2
05/04/00	FCM Bacau	A	0-2	
08/04/00	Dinamo Bucuresti	A	1-1	Soimaru
16/04/00	Steaua Bucuresti	H	0-2	
22/04/00	FC Arges Dacia Pitesti	A	1-1	Botez
28/04/00	Otelul Galati	H	3-2	Scanteie, Nemtanu 2
03/05/00	Gloria Bistrita	A	4-5	Hrib, Ilie, Nemtanu 2 (1p)
06/05/00	FC Extensiv Craiova	H	3-1	Hrib, Marc 2
10/05/00	Petrolul Ploiesti	A	0-1	

DINAMO BUCURESTI

CLUB DIRECTORY

FC Dinamo Bucuresti
Calea Floreasca 22, 71401 Bucuresti
tel - (01) 2103519 / fax - (01) 2103519
Year of Formation - 1948
President - Mircea Stoenescu
Coach - Cornel Dinu
Stadium - Dinamo (18,000)

MAJOR HONOURS
League Championship - (15) 1955, 1962, 1963,
1964, 1965, 1971, 1973, 1975, 1977, 1982,
1983, 1984, 1990, 1992, 2000.
Domestic Cup - (8) 1959, 1964, 1968, 1982,
1984, 1986, 1990, 2000.

APPEARANCES 99/00

	P	Ap	(s)	Gls
Bogdan Aurelian ALDEA	A	1	(9)	1
Alexandru BALTOI	A	1	(1)	1
Cornel BUTA	D	7	(2)	3
Florin CERNAT	M	4	(6)	
Liviu CIOBOTARIU	D	9		
Cristian CONSTANTIN	M	1		
Marius Mihai COPORAN	M	2	(7)	
Serban CRISTESCU	D	1		
Cornel DOBRE	D	1	(3)	
Claudiu DRAGAN	A	5	(6)	5
Daniel FLOREA	D	25		
Khalid FOUHAMI (MAR)	G	4		
Catalin George HALDAN	M	29		1
Daniel IFTODI	M	29		4
Sorin IODI	D	2		
Adrian IORDACHE	D	1		
Giani Stelian KIRITA	D	22	(10)	3
Ioan Angelo LUPESCU	M	29		6
Bogdan Ion MARA	A	6	(2)	2
Adrian Dumitru MIHALCEA	A	27	(2)	13
Gheorghe MIHALI	D	20	(1)	3
Adrian MUTU	A	18		18
Valentin Vasile NASTASE	D	26		
Marius Constantin NICULAE	A	17	(10)	12
Ionel Laurentiu OPRICEANA	D	1		
Razvan PADURETU	M		(1)	
Florentin PETRE	M	19		7
Tinel Tanase PETRE	D	12	(6)	
Madalin POPA	D		(1)	
Gabriel POPESCU	M	6	(3)	
Stefan Gabriel PREDA	G	30		
Constantin STAN	A		(1)	
Iosif Ovidiu TALVAN	D	3	(6)	
Daniel TIMOFTE	A		(6)	
Marian VATAVU	D	1	(1)	
Cristian Nicolae VLAD	M	5	(7)	1
Ion VLADOIU	A	10	(2)	12

LEAGUE RESULTS 1999/2000

25/07/99	FC Farul Constanta	A	2-0	Mutu, Iftodi
31/07/99	Gloria Bistrita	H	5-0	Petre, Vladoiu 3, Mutu
04/08/99	CSM Resita	A	6-0	Vladoiu 2 (1p), Iftodi 2, Petre, Mutu
08/08/99	FC Extensiv Craiova	H	3-0	Mutu, Lupescu 2
15/08/99	Universitatea Craiova	A	2-1	Mihalcea, Niculae
22/08/99	Petrolul Ploiesti	H	4-1	Vladoiu 3, Niculae
29/08/99	Astra Ploiesti	A	2-1	Niculae, Vladoiu
11/09/99	Rocar Bucuresti	H	3-0	Vladoiu (p), Niculae, og (Serban)
25/09/99	FC Brasov	H	3-1	Mutu, Vladoiu 2
03/10/99	Ceahlaul Piatra Neamt	A	2-2	Mutu 2
17/10/99	Rapid Bucuresti	H	2-1	Mihali, Mutu
24/10/99	Steaua Bucuresti	A	1-1	Mutu
27/10/99	FC National Bucuresti	A	3-1	Mihalcea 2, Lupescu (p)
30/10/99	FC Arges Dacia Pitesti	H	4-0	Mutu 3 (2p), Mihalcea
03/11/99	FCM Bacau	A	3-0	Mutu, Mihalcea, Niculae
07/11/99	FC Onesti	A	4-2	Mihalcea, Mutu 2, Petre
14/11/99	Otelul Galati	H	3-2	Mihalcea, Mihali, Mutu
20/11/99	FC Farul Constanta	H	4-0	Mutu 2 (2p), Lupescu, Mihalcea
27/11/99	Gloria Bistrita	A	0-1	
04/12/99	CSM Resita	H	2-1	Niculae, Mihalcea
04/03/00	FC Extensiv Craiova	A	1-0	Lupescu (p)
12/03/00	Universitatea Craiova	H	5-2	Dragan 2, Petre 2, Mihalcea
18/03/00	Petrolul Ploiesti	A	2-1	Kirita, Vlad (p)
22/03/00	Astra Ploiesti	H	2-1	Kirita, Petre
25/03/00	Rocar Bucuresti	A	2-1	Mihali, Dragan
02/04/00	FCM Bacau	H	2-1	Niculae 2
05/04/00	FC Brasov	A	3-4	Niculae, Kirita, Haldan
08/04/00	Ceahlaul Piatra Neamt	H	1-1	Mihalcea
15/04/00	Rapid Bucuresti	A	0-4	
22/04/00	Steaua Bucuresti	H	3-2	Petre, Lupescu, Mihalcea
29/04/00	FC National Bucuresti	H	1-0	Aldea
03/05/00	FC Arges Dacia Pitesti	A	3-2	Niculae 2 (1p), Dragan
06/05/00	FC Onesti	H	7-1	Mara, Niculae, Mihalcea, Iftodi, Buta 3
10/05/00	Otelul Galati	A	3-5	Mara, Dragan, Baltoi

FC EXTENSIV CRAIOVA

CLUB DIRECTORY

FC Extensiv Craiova
Calea Dunarii
1100 Craiova
tel - (051) 414762
Year of Formation - 1949
President - Nicolae Mihailescu
Coach - Sorin Cartu
Stadium - Extensiv (15,000)

APPEARANCES 99/00

	P	Ap	(s)	Gls
Gheorghe BITA	D	7	(8)	
Ionut BUCA	A	6	(7)	1
Daniel COJAN	D		(2)	
Valentin Ion DAVID	G	9		
Vasile Florin FABIAN	M	6	(10)	
Robert GHINDEANU	A	5	(5)	
Gabriel GHITA	D	9	(2)	
Radu Mugur GUSATU	A	7	(1)	
Vasile JELER	D	1		
Arpad Alin LACZKO	M	27	(2)	
Victor Claudiu LEPADATU	M	14		3
Valeriu Iulian MIEILA	D	27	(1)	
Florinel Cristi MIREA	D	23	(1)	1
Vasile NAGY MARE	G	4		
Alexandru Marius NEGRILA	D	10	(2)	
Catalin Marian NITA	A		(2)	
Catalin NITU	M		(3)	
Mihai PANC	M	8	(5)	1
Daniel PARASCHIV	D	25	(1)	
Lucian Ferentz POPESCU	A	11	(4)	3
Ioan Dorin RADOI	M	27	(4)	1
Mirel RADOI	D	14		
Claudiu Nicu RADUCANU	A	16	(3)	5
Catalin Marius RISTEA	A	14	(7)	3
Iosif ROTARIU	M	20		2
Marcel Ilie RUS	M	1	(2)	
Daniel Petrisior SIMA	D	8	(5)	
Costin Florin SOAVA	M	17		3
Pavel SOLA	M	14	(12)	1
Florin Mihai STIRBULESCU	A	6	(4)	
Gheorghe STOIANOV	G	19	(1)	
Nicolae ZANFIR	D	17		
Daniel ZDRANCA	G	2		

LEAGUE RESULTS 1999/2000

23/07/99	FC Arges Dacia Pitesti	H	2-1	Raducanu, Popescu
31/07/99	Otelul Galati	A	2-8	Raducanu, Rotariu (p)
04/08/99	Gloria Bistrita	H	1-2	og (Velcea)
08/08/99	Dinamo Bucuresti	A	0-3	
14/08/99	Petrolul Ploiesti	A	0-2	
21/08/99	Rocar Bucuresti	H	2-1	Raducanu, Soava (p)
28/08/99	FC Brasov	A	1-2	Rotariu
11/09/99	Rapid Bucuresti	H	1-2	og (Stanciu)
18/09/99	FC National Bucuresti	A	0-2	
25/09/99	FC Onesti	H	0-0	
02/10/99	FC Farul Constanta	A	0-1	
16/10/99	CSM Resita	H	1-0	Soava
23/10/99	Universitatea Craiova	A	0-3	
27/10/99	Astra Ploiesti	H	0-1	
30/10/99	FCM Bacau	A	0-1	
06/11/99	Ceahlaul Piatra Neamt	H	0-0	
13/11/99	Steaua Bucuresti	A	2-5	Soava, Raducanu (p)
20/11/99	FC Arges Dacia Pitesti	A	0-2	
27/11/99	Otelul Galati	H	3-0	Popescu 2, Raducanu
04/12/99	Gloria Bistrita	A	0-1	
04/03/00	Dinamo Bucuresti	H	0-1	
11/03/00	Petrolul Ploiesti	H	0-0	
18/03/00	Rocar Bucuresti	A	1-3	Ristea
22/03/00	FC Brasov	H	0-1	
25/03/00	Rapid Bucuresti	A	2-4	Radoi, Sola
01/04/00	FC National Bucuresti	H	1-2	Lepadatu
05/04/00	FC Onesti	A	2-3	Buca, Lepadatu
08/04/00	FC Farul Constanta	H	1-3	Panc
15/04/00	CSM Resita	A	0-0	
22/04/00	Universitatea Craiova	H	2-3	Ristea, Mirea
29/04/00	Astra Ploiesti	A	1-1	Lepadatu (p)
03/05/00	FCM Bacau	H	0-2	
06/05/00	Ceahlaul Piatra Neamt	A	1-3	Ristea
10/05/00	Steaua Bucuresti	H	0-3	

FC FARUL CONSTANTA

CLUB DIRECTORY

FC Farul Constanta
str. Primaverii 2
8700 Constanta
tel - (041) 616142
fax - (041) 644827
Year of Formation - 1949
President - Jean Garabet
Coach - Gabriel Zahiu; Vasile Simionas
Stadium - Gheorghe Hagi (24,000)

APPEARANCES 99/00

	P	Ap	(s)	Gls
Cristian Marcel ABALUTA	M	27	(1)	1
Ionut BADESCU	M	30	(2)	
Lucian BALABAN	M		(1)	
Gheorghe BARBU	D	12	(1)	2
Ion BARBU	D	13		
Gheorghe BUTOIU	A	15	(3)	2
Petru CHIRATCU	A	4	(17)	5
Cosmin CHIREA	M	4	(2)	1
Ioan Lucian COVRIG	G	14		
Vasile CRISTOCEA	M	7	(9)	
Cristian DICU	M	2	(4)	
Cosmin DRAGULIN	A	20	(9)	2
Catalin GHERBEZAN	D	6		
Giani Marius GORGA	M	2	(4)	
Daniel Petru HUZA	D	16	(1)	4
Alexandru ILIUCIUC	G	14		
Daniel Florin JILAVU	A	4	(3)	2
Sorin MOCANU	D	1		
Eugen Gheorghe NAE	G	6		
Victor NAICU	D	16		1
Cristian Eugen NEGRU	A	30	(2)	7
Alin Gabriel NICOLA	M		(2)	
Fanel Daniel NIIA	M	1	(3)	
Norbert Sorin NITA	D	29	(1)	
Cristian Ionel PETCU	D	11	(1)	1
Valeriu RACHITA	D	3		
Iulian Vasile ROSOAGA	M	5	(8)	
Florin SARARU	D	8	(8)	
Mircea Valerica STAN	D	23	(3)	
Mihai STERE	M	26	(3)	5
Iulian Teodor STEFAN	M		(5)	
Grigorie TUDOR	M	25	(1)	5
Razvan TARLEA	D		(1)	

LEAGUE RESULTS 1999/2000

25/07/99	Dinamo Bucuresti	H	0-2	
31/07/99	CSM Resita	A	1-1	Negru
04/08/99	Universitatea Craiova	H	2-0	Petcu, Dragulin
07/08/99	Astra Ploiesti	A	2-3	Stere (p), Chiratcu
14/08/99	FCM Bacau	H	3-0	Stere (p), Butoiu, Negru
21/08/99	Ceahlaul Piatra Neamt	A	1-2	Naicu
29/08/99	Steaua Bucuresti	H	2-1	Chiratcu (p), Tudor
11/09/99	FC Arges Dacia Pitesti	A	1-2	Tudor
18/09/99	Otelul Galati	H	1-1	Stere
25/09/99	Gloria Bistrita	A	1-2	Butoiu
02/10/99	FC Extensiv Craiova	H	1-0	Stere
16/10/99	Petrolul Ploiesti	A	0-0	
23/10/99	Rocar Bucuresti	H	0-1	
27/10/99	FC Brasov	A	2-3	Negru, Chiratcu (p)
30/10/99	Rapid Bucuresti	H	1-1	Huza (p)
06/11/99	FC National Bucuresti	A	0-6	
12/11/99	FC Onesti	H	3-1	Negru, Huza, Chiratcu
20/11/99	Dinamo Bucuresti	A	0-4	
27/11/99	CSM Resita	H	3-1	Tudor, Huza 2
04/12/99	Universitatea Craiova	A	0-3	
04/03/00	Astra Ploiesti	H	1-1	Chiratcu (p)
11/03/00	FCM Bacau	A	1-1	Negru
18/03/00	Ceahlaul Piatra Neamt	H	1-0	Tudor
22/03/00	Steaua Bucuresti	A	0-1	
25/03/00	FC Arges Dacia Pitesti	H	1-0	Tudor
31/03/00	Otelul Galati	A	0-1	
05/04/00	Gloria Bistrita	H	2-1	Negru (p), Jilavu
08/04/00	FC Extensiv Craiova	A	3-1	Barbu (p), Negru, Jilavu
15/04/00	Petrolul Ploiesti	H	2-1	Stere, Chirea
22/04/00	Rocar Bucuresti	A	0-2	
29/04/00	FC Brasov	H	0-0	
03/05/00	Rapid Bucuresti	A	0-0	
06/05/00	FC National Bucuresti	H	2-0	Barbu (p), Dragulin
10/05/00	FC Onesti	A	1-2	Abaluta

GLORIA BISTRITA

CLUB DIRECTORY

Gloria Bistrita
str. Parcului 3
4400 Bistrita
tel - (063) 212998
fax - (063) 217437
Year of Formation - 1922
President - Jean Padureanu
Coach - Constantin Carstea
Stadium - Gloria (12,000)

APPEARANCES 99/00

	P	Ap	(s)	Gls
Marian ALEXANDRU	A	9	(18)	5
Costel CAMPEANU	G	33		
Ion Romica CEAUSU	M	21	(1)	1
Ambrozie Cristian COROIAN	M	15	(3)	2
Sergiu Ioan COSTIN	M		(3)	
Florin Cristian DAN	M		(1)	
Emil Gavril DANCUS	M	5		1
Sorin IODI	D	12	(2)	
Valentin IVAN	M		(1)	
Vasile Ilie JULA	D	17	(2)	
Danut MATEI	A	11	(8)	3
Sergiu Sebastian MANDREAN	D	17	(5)	1
Daniel MIF	M	6	(2)	2
Alin Ilie MINTEUAN	M	28		5
Ioan MISZTI	D	33		10
Lucian NAN	D	22	(4)	
Petru Rodin NEGREA	M	9	(7)	
Ioan Vasile OANA	A	12	(4)	6
Florin Flavius POGACEAN	M	1	(2)	
Vasile Nicolae POPA	D	26		3
Marius PREDATU	A	7	(9)	3
Lucian SANMARTEAN	M	4	(5)	
Valer SASARMAN	D	32		1
Ovidiu Gheorghe SUCIU	G		(2)	
Cristian Dorin TUDOR	A	2	(1)	
Cristian TURCU	A	20	(10)	7
Petru TARCAS	G	1		
Valentin VELCEA	M	31		3

LEAGUE RESULTS 1999/2000

24/07/99	Otelul Galati	H	2-3	Predatu, Matei
31/07/99	Dinamo Bucuresti	A	0-5	
04/08/99	FC Extensiv Craiova	A	2-1	og (Radoi), Predatu
07/08/99	Petrolul Ploiesti	H	4-0	Turcu 2, Velcea, Matei
14/08/99	Rocar Bucuresti	A	1-3	Dancus
21/08/99	FC Brasov	H	2-0	Predatu, Sasarman
28/08/99	Rapid Bucuresti	A	1-2	Turcu
10/09/99	FC National Bucuresti	H	1-0	Matei
18/09/99	FC Onesti	A	2-3	Oana, Miszti (p)
25/09/99	FC Farul Constanta	H	2-1	Mif (p), Alexandru
02/10/99	CSM Resita	A	1-1	Minteuan
16/10/99	Universitatea Craiova	H	1-0	Popa
23/10/99	Astra Ploiesti	A	1-2	Alexandru
27/10/99	FCM Bacau	H	2-0	Oana, Mif
30/10/99	Ceahlaul Piatra Neamt	A	0-1	
10/11/99	Steaua Bucuresti	H	4-0	Velcea, Minteuan, Alexandru, Miszti
13/11/99	FC Arges Dacia Pitesti	A	0-2	
20/11/99	Otelul Galati	A	0-0	
27/11/99	Dinamo Bucuresti	H	1-0	Minteuan
04/12/99	FC Extensiv Craiova	H	1-0	Miszti
04/03/00	Petrolul Ploiesti	A	2-1	Miszti (p), Oana
11/03/00	Rocar Bucuresti	H	2-1	Miszti (p), Popa
18/03/00	FC Brasov	A	2-4	Turcu, Alexandru
22/03/00	Rapid Bucuresti	H	1-2	Turcu
26/03/00	FC National Bucuresti	A	1-3	Oana
01/04/00	FC Onesti	H	2-0	Oana, Mandrean
05/04/00	FC Farul Constanta	A	1-2	Minteuan
08/04/00	CSM Resita	H	2-0	Popa, Oana
15/04/00	Universitatea Craiova	A	1-3	Turcu
22/04/00	Astra Ploiesti	H	2-0	Ceausu, Miszti (p)
29/04/00	FCM Bacau	A	2-3	Miszti, Alexandru
03/05/00	Ceahlaul Piatra Neamt	H	5-4	Miszti 2 (2p), Minteuan, Velcea, Coroian
07/05/00	Steaua Bucuresti	A	1-2	Coroian
10/05/00	FC Arges Dacia Pitesti	H	2-0	Miszti (p), Turcu

FC NATIONAL BUCURESTI

CLUB DIRECTORY

FC National Bucuresti
str. Dr. Lister 37
76209 Bucuresti
tel - (01) 4106606
Year of Formation - 1946
President - Gino Iorgulescu
Coach - Mihai Stoichita
(00/01 - Marius Lacatus)
Stadium - Cotroceni (16,000)

MAJOR HONOURS
Domestic Cup - (1) 1960.

APPEARANCES 99/00

	P	Ap	(s)	Gls
Marius AXINCIUC	M	22		3
Alin Gheorghe BANCEU	M	3	(9)	
Stelian CARABAS	M	18		3
Gabriel Gheorghe CARAMARIN	A	12	(10)	
Boris CEKA (ALB)	M		(6)	
Gigel COMAN	M	8	(13)	1
Tiberiu Cristian CURT	D	20	(7)	2
Viorel DINU	M		(2)	
Marin DUNA	A	16		3
Adrian FALUB	D	31		
Ion Lavi HRIB	A	4	(9)	
Sabin ILIE	A	11		8
Marius Sandu IORDACHE	M	13		
Marius Mihai LACATUS	A	12		
Nicolae Catalin LITA	M	31		8
Razvan LUCESCU	G	8	(1)	
Petre MARIN	D	32		1
Adrian MATEI	D	21		
Slavisa MITROVIC (BOS)	A	1	(7)	
Cristian MUNTEANU	G	9		
Marius NAE	M		(2)	
Radu Horia NICULESCU	A	23		8
Adrian OLAH	D	6	(2)	
Constantin Razvan PAUNESCU	M		(7)	
Ovidiu PETRE	D	1	(2)	
Adrian Ion PIGULEA	M	6	(20)	4
Marius Viorel POPA	G		(1)	
Milen RADUKANOV (BUL)	D	16		
Marian SAVU	A	32	(1)	20
Ion SBURLEA	D	1		
Bogdan Arges VINTILA	G	17		

LEAGUE RESULTS 1999/2000

24/07/99	Universitatea Craiova	H	1-0	Pigulea
03/08/99	FCM Bacau	H	2-2	Carabas, Niculescu
07/08/99	Ceahlaul Piatra Neamt	A	2-3	Savu, Pigulea
15/08/99	Steaua Bucuresti	H	3-0	Carabas, Savu, Axinciuc
20/08/99	FC Arges Dacia Pitesti	A	1-3	Axinciuc
28/08/99	Otelul Galati	H	1-1	Niculescu
10/09/99	Gloria Bistrita	A	0-1	
18/09/99	FC Extensiv Craiova	H	2-0	Carabas, Duna
25/09/99	Petrolul Ploiesti	A	0-1	
02/10/99	Rocar Bucuresti	H	2-0	Duna, Marin
15/10/99	FC Brasov	A	1-3	Duna (p)
23/10/99	Rapid Bucuresti	H	2-3	Axinciuc, Savu
27/10/99	Dinamo Bucuresti	H	1-3	Pigulea
30/10/99	FC Onesti	A	0-1	
03/11/99	Astra Ploiesti	A	1-1	Curt
06/11/99	FC Farul Constanta	H	6-0	Savu 2, Lita 2, Pigulea, Curt
14/11/99	CSM Resita	A	0-1	
19/11/99	Universitatea Craiova	A	0-2	
27/11/99	Astra Ploiesti	H	1-0	Niculescu
03/12/99	FCM Bacau	A	1-1	Niculescu
05/03/00	Ceahlaul Piatra Neamt	H	5-1	Ilie 2, Niculescu, Savu, Coman
12/03/00	Steaua Bucuresti	A	3-2	Lita 2, Ilie
19/03/00	FC Arges Dacia Pitesti	H	4-1	Niculescu 2, Savu 2
22/03/00	Otelul Galati	A	0-2	
26/03/00	Gloria Bistrita	H	3-1	Lita, Savu 2
01/04/00	FC Extensiv Craiova	A	2-1	Ilie 2
05/04/00	Petrolul Ploiesti	H	4-1	Savu 2, Niculescu, Lita
09/04/00	Rocar Bucuresti	A	1-2	Savu
14/04/00	FC Brasov	H	2-0	Ilie, Savu
22/04/00	Rapid Bucuresti	A	2-3	Ilie, Savu
29/04/00	Dinamo Bucuresti	A	0-1	
03/05/00	FC Onesti	H	3-0	Lita, Ilie, Savu
06/05/00	FC Farul Constanta	A	0-2	
10/05/00	CSM Resita	H	5-1	Savu 4, Lita

FC ONESTI

CLUB DIRECTORY

FC Onesti
str. Victor Babes 3b
5450 Onesti
Year of Formation - 1994
President - Nicolae Puiu
Coach - Toader Stet; Alexandru Moldovan
Stadium - FC Onesti (10,000)

APPEARANCES 99/00

	P	Ap	(s)	Gls
Viorel AVADANEI	D	1		
Marius Ioan BILASCO	A	15	(4)	2
Constantin Adrian BLID	G	17		
Radu CHIOREANU	M	6	(4)	
Dumitru CHIRIAC	D	11	(3)	
Aristica CIOABA	M	19		
Ionut CIOBANU	M		(5)	
Danut COPACEL	M	2	(3)	
Dorin CRISTACHE	A	6	(3)	2
Ionut DRAGOMIRESCU	D	3	(3)	
Mihai FLORIA	G	5	(1)	
Giani Marius GORGA	M	25		7
Mircea ILIE	M	9	(4)	4
Ionel IRIZA	A	25	(1)	8
Vasile JERCALAU	D	33		3
Victor Claudiu LEPADATU	M	1	(3)	
Bogdan MANDRIC	G	12	(1)	
Altin MASATI (ALB)	D	15	(8)	1
Constantin Stelian MUNTEANU	D	25	(1)	2
Daniel MUNTEANU	D	8	(1)	
Florin MUNTEANU	M	22	(5)	1
Marian Nicu NICULITA	D	15	(5)	
Ioan Cristian OROS	M	22	(4)	
Narcis Ionel PANDURU	D		(4)	
Ionel Antonel PARVU	M	12	(1)	2
Arpad PETER	G		(2)	
Daniel SABOU	D	30	(1)	
Remus Daniel SAFTA	A	6	(9)	1
Marius SITARU	A	1	(1)	
Dumitru STIRBU	D	11		
Dragos STROE	M	6	(7)	1
Anghel Cristian TANASE	M	9	(4)	1
Nicolae Adrian VELICIOIU	A	2	(5)	

LEAGUE RESULTS 1999/2000

24/07/99	CSM Resita	H	2-1	Gorga, Jercalau (p)
31/07/99	Universitatea Craiova	A	0-1	
04/08/99	Astra Ploiesti	H	1-0	Gorga
07/08/99	FCM Bacau	A	0-3	
14/08/99	Ceahlaul Piatra Neamt	H	1-1	og (Serban)
21/08/99	Steaua Bucuresti	A	0-3	
28/08/99	FC Arges Dacia Pitesti	H	1-2	Bilasco
11/09/99	Otelul Galati	A	1-2	Bilasco
18/09/99	Gloria Bistrita	H	3-2	Iriza, Gorga, Munteanu C.
25/09/99	FC Extensiv Craiova	A	0-0	
02/10/99	Petrolul Ploiesti	H	5-1	Gorga 2, Jercalau, Iriza 2
16/10/99	Rocar Bucuresti	A	1-5	Gorga
23/10/99	FC Brasov	H	3-2	og (Kajcsa), Iriza, Gorga
27/10/99	Rapid Bucuresti	A	1-3	Tanase
30/10/99	FC National Bucuresti	H	1-0	Iriza
07/11/99	Dinamo Bucuresti	H	2-4	Safta, Iriza (p)
12/11/99	FC Farul Constanta	A	1-3	Jercalau
20/11/99	CSM Resita	A	1-6	Stroe
27/11/99	Universitatea Craiova	H	0-0	
04/12/99	Astra Ploiesti	A	0-5	
04/03/00	FCM Bacau	H	1-0	Munteanu F.
11/03/00	Ceahlaul Piatra Neamt	A	0-6	
18/03/00	Steaua Bucuresti	H	1-3	Cristache
22/03/00	FC Arges Dacia Pitesti	A	0-2	
25/03/00	Otelul Galati	H	0-3	
01/04/00	Gloria Bistrita	A	0-2	
05/04/00	FC Extensiv Craiova	H	3-2	Ilie 2, Iriza
08/04/00	Petrolul Ploiesti	A	1-4	Ilie
15/04/00	Rocar Bucuresti	H	1-5	Masati
22/04/00	FC Brasov	A	1-5	Munteanu C.
29/04/00	Rapid Bucuresti	H	2-5	Iriza, Parvu
03/05/00	FC National Bucuresti	A	0-3	
06/05/00	Dinamo Bucuresti	A	1-7	Ilie
10/05/00	FC Farul Constanta	H	2-1	Parvu, Cristache

OTELUL GALATI

CLUB DIRECTORY

Otelul Galati
str. Milcov 25
6200 Galati
tel - (036) 452321
fax (036) 462150
Year of Formation - 1964
President - Mihai Stoica
Coach - Dumitru Dumitriu
(00/01 - Aurel Ticleanu)
Stadaium - Otelul (13,500)

APPEARANCES 99/00

	P	Ap	(s)	Gls
Bogdan Ioan ANDONE	A	12		3
Dorin ARCANU	G	8		
Dorel Marin BALINT	D	30		1
Daniel Eugen BASTINA	M	30	(1)	3
Stelian BORDEIANU	G	14	(1)	
Gabriel BOSTINA	M	27	(6)	1
Florin CERNAT	M	17	(1)	3
Sorin GHIONEA	D	3	(2)	1
Mihai GURITA	A	13	(14)	3
Sorin Florin HARAGA	D	12	(3)	1
Marius HUMELNICU	M	1	(1)	
Viorel ION	A	22		4
Costin MALES	M	21	(6)	7
Dragos Mihail MIHALACHE	A	19	(1)	7
Costel Ciprian MOZACU	M	10	(11)	3
Cristian Marius MUNTEANU	G	12		
Leonard Ion NEMTANU	D	30		1
Robert Ionel NITA	A	1	(11)	3
Danut Stelian OPREA	A	21	(7)	6
Tudorel PELIN	D	15	(4)	
Emil SPIREA	M	16	(9)	1
Claudiu STAN	M	2	(9)	1
Viorel TANASE	A	8		3
Catalin TOFAN	D	26		4
Adrian TOMA	A	2	(5)	1
Danut VOICILA	M	2	(7)	1

LEAGUE RESULTS 1999/2000

24/07/99	Gloria Bistrita	A	3-2	Tanase, Mihalache, Tofan (p)
31/07/99	FC Extensiv Craiova	H	8-2	Bastina, Tanase, Oprea 2,
				og (Stirbulescu), Mihalache 2, Nita
04/08/99	Petrolul Ploiesti	A	1-2	Tanase
07/08/99	Rocar Bucuresti	H	2-1	Mihalache 2
13/08/99	FC Brasov	A	0-3	
21/08/99	Rapid Bucuresti	H	2-0	Males, Gurita
28/08/99	FC National Bucuresti	A	1-1	Oprea
11/09/99	FC Onesti	H	2-1	Nita, Cernat
18/09/99	FC Farul Constanta	A	1-1	Haraga
25/09/99	CSM Resita	H	1-2	Stan
01/10/99	Universitatea Craiova	A	0-4	
16/10/99	Astra Ploiesti	H	0-1	
23/10/99	FCM Bacau	A	0-1	
26/10/99	Ceahlaul Piatra Neamt	H	3-0	Mihalache, Tofan, Cernat
30/10/99	Steaua Bucuresti	A	1-2	Mihalache
05/11/99	FC Arges Dacia Pitesti	H	1-2	Bastina
14/11/99	Dinamo Bucuresti	A	2-3	Bastina, Ion
20/11/99	Gloria Bistrita	H	0-0	
27/11/99	FC Extensiv Craiova	A	0-3	
05/12/99	Petrolul Ploiesti	H	3-2	Males (p), Cernat, Nita
04/03/00	Rocar Bucuresti	A	2-3	Ion, Oprea
10/03/00	FC Brasov	H	1-0	Males (p)
18/03/00	Rapid Bucuresti	A	1-2	Oprea
22/03/00	FC National Bucuresti	H	2-0	Ion, Males
25/03/00	FC Onesti	A	3-0	Gurita, Tofan 2
31/03/00	FC Farul Constanta	H	1-0	Balint
05/04/00	CSM Resita	A	2-1	Andone, Ion
08/04/00	Universitatea Craiova	H	1-0	Nemtanu
15/04/00	Astra Ploiesti	A	1-1	Mozacu
21/04/00	FCM Bacau	H	3-1	Andone, Oprea, Toma
28/04/00	Ceahlaul Piatra Neamt	A	2-3	Gurita, Mozacu
03/05/00	Steaua Bucuresti	H	4-5	Ghionea, Andone, Males, Bostina
06/05/00	FC Arges Dacia Pitesti	A	0-3	
10/05/00	Dinamo Bucuresti	H	5-3	Males 2, Spirea, Voicila, Mozacu

PETROLUL PLOIESTI

CLUB DIRECTORY

Petrolul Ploiesti
str. Stadionului 26
2000 Ploiesti
tel - (044) 112258
Year of Formation - 1952
Director - Florin Bercea
Coach - Virgil Dridea
(00/01 - Victor Rosca)
Stadium - Petrolul (18,000)

MAJOR HONOURS
League Championship - (3) 1958, 1959, 1966.
Domestic Cup - (2) 1963, 1995.

APPEARANCES 99/00

	P	Ap	(s)	Gls
Taulant BAKIU (ALB)	D	2	(2)	
Dragos Ionut BUCUR	A	1	(4)	
Cornel CERNEA	G	1		
Nicolae CONSTANTIN	A	9		4
Laurentiu Dumitru COSTACHE	M	1	(13)	
Daniel Stefan COSTESCU	A	29	(3)	9
Cristian CRACIUN	M	28	(2)	5
Marian GHEORGHE	M	1	(1)	
Orlando Ion GHEORGHE	A	13	(6)	3
Catalin GRIGORE	G	11		
Octavian GRIGORE	D	34		2
Mihai Iulian ILIE	G	2		
Marius Ionut IRIMESCU	M	20	(7)	3
Florin MANEA	M		(4)	
Giani Liviu NEGOITA	D	31		2
Nana Falemi N'GASSAN (CMR)	D	11		
Victor Mihai OANCEA	D	26	(1)	
Bogdan Mihai ONUT	D	32		5
Florin PANCOVICI	M	9	(14)	3
Florin Cristian PARVU	M	32		7
Leonat PERLOSHI (ALB)	A	7	(3)	
Florentin RADULESCU	G	20		
Marin ROSU	M	21	(2)	
Romeo Constantin STAN	D		(5)	
Adrian Orlin TOADER	A	1	(1)	
Marius Dinu TODORAN	M	9	(10)	
Eusebiu Iulian TUDOR	M	1	(12)	
Cristian Nicolae VLAD	M	15	(1)	2
Vasile VOINEA	D	7	(6)	2

LEAGUE RESULTS 1999/2000

24/07/99	Steaua Bucuresti	H	5-1	Vlad, Onut (p), Costescu, Constantin, Parvu
01/08/99	FC Arges Dacia Pitesti	A	0-1	
04/08/99	Otelul Galati	H	2-1	Irimescu, Vlad
07/08/99	Gloria Bistrita	A	0-4	
14/08/99	FC Extensiv Craiova	H	2-0	Constantin, Gheorghe O.
22/08/99	Dinamo Bucuresti	A	1-4	Constantin
28/08/99	Rocar Bucuresti	A	1-2	Constantin
11/09/99	FC Brasov	H	1-0	Craciun
18/09/99	Rapid Bucuresti	A	0-2	
25/09/99	FC National Bucuresti	H	1-0	Costescu
02/10/99	FC Onesti	A	1-5	Gheorghe O.
16/10/99	FC Farul Constanta	H	0-0	
22/10/99	CSM Resita	A	2-2	Craciun, Costescu
27/10/99	Universitatea Craiova	H	0-0	
31/10/99	Astra Ploiesti	A	0-2	
06/11/99	FCM Bacau	H	1-0	Craciun
14/11/99	Ceahlaul Piatra Neamt	A	0-2	
20/11/99	Steaua Bucuresti	A	4-1	Costescu 2, Negoita, og (Duro)
27/11/99	FC Arges Dacia Pitesti	H	1-1	Parvu
05/12/99	Otelul Galati	A	2-3	Gheorghe O., Parvu
04/03/00	Gloria Bistrita	H	1-2	Voinea
11/03/00	FC Extensiv Craiova	A	0-0	
18/03/00	Dinamo Bucuresti	H	1-2	Costescu
22/03/00	Rocar Bucuresti	H	4-1	Onut 2, Costescu, Parvu
25/03/00	FC Brasov	A	1-0	Onut (p)
01/04/00	Rapid Bucuresti	H	4-2	Grigore, Costescu, Irimescu, Pancovici
05/04/00	FC National Bucuresti	A	1-4	Craciun
08/04/00	FC Onesti	H	4-1	Pancovici, Craciun, Voinea, Onut
15/04/00	FC Farul Constanta	A	1-2	Pavcovici
22/04/00	CSM Resita	H	4-2	Parvu 2, Grigore, Negoita
29/04/00	Universitatea Craiova	A	1-5	Parvu
03/05/00	Astra Ploiesti	H	1-0	Costescu
06/05/00	FCM Bacau	A	0-3	
10/05/00	Ceahlaul Piatra Neamt	H	1-0	Irimescu (p)

RAPID BUCURESTI

CLUB DIRECTORY

Rapid Bucuresti
Calea Giulesti 18, 78254 Bucuresti
tel - (01) 6170301
fax - (01) 2203215
Year of Formation - 1923
President - George Copos
Coach - Mircea Lucescu
(00/01 - Anghel Iordanescu)
Stadium - Rapid (18,000)

MAJOR HONOURS
League Championship - (2) 1967, 1999.
Domestic Cup - (10) 1935, 1937, 1938, 1939, 1940, 1941, 1942, 1972, 1975, 1998.

APPEARANCES 99/00

	P	Ap	(s)	Gls
Bogdan ANDONE	D	2	(3)	
Tiberiu Gabriel BALAN	M	1	(8)	1
Constantin BARBU	A	3		1
Mugur Cristian BOLOHAN	D	19	(3)	3
Marius BRATU	G	4		
Zeno Marius BUNDEA	M		(3)	
Daniel CHIRITA	D	16	(9)	3
Nicolae CONSTANTIN	A	12		4
Iulian CRIVAC	D	8		
Mihai Valentin DASCALESCU	A	14	(7)	7
Tiberiu GHIOANE	M	2	(3)	
Mihai Adrian IENCSI	D	21	(5)	5
Sergei KIRILOV	A		(1)	
Bogdan Ionut LOBONT	G	16		
LUIS Fabiano				
Lima dos Santos (BRA)	M		(1)	
Danut LUPU	M	21	(1)	5
Ovidiu MAIER	A	2	(9)	
Marius Constantin MALDARASANU	M	30	(1)	6
Silviu MARGARITESCU	M	5	(6)	
Endre Istvan MATYAS	G	1		
Dorel MUTICA	D	26	(3)	6
Sergiu Marian RADU	A	26	(4)	11
Narcis Claudiu RADUCAN	M	15	(1)	
Florentin RADULESCU	G	13		
Razvan Dinca RAT	A	10	(10)	1
Mircea REDNIC	D	26		1
Ioan Ovidiu SABAU	M	21		1
Constantin SCHUMACHER	M	18	(11)	6
Nicolae STANCIU	D	27	(3)	2
Dumitru TARTAU	A	4	(1)	
Ionut VOICU	D	11	(4)	1

LEAGUE RESULTS 1999/2000

24/07/99	Astra Ploiesti	H	1-1	Rednic
31/07/99	FCM Bacau	A	0-0	
07/08/99	Steaua Bucuresti	A	3-1	Radu, Iencsi (p), Barbu
14/08/99	FC Arges Dacia Pitesti	H	1-0	Schumacher
21/08/99	Otelul Galati	A	0-2	
28/08/99	Gloria Bistrita	H	2-1	Radu, Mutica
10/09/99	FC Extensiv Craiova	A	2-1	Iencsi (p), Sabau
18/09/99	Petrolul Ploiesti	H	2-0	Mutica, Radu
26/09/99	Rocar Bucuresti	A	1-0	Radu
02/10/99	FC Brasov	H	2-1	Radu, Lupu
17/10/99	Dinamo Bucuresti	A	1-2	Maldarasanu
23/10/99	FC National Bucuresti	A	3-2	Chirita, og (Falub), Bolohan
27/10/99	FC Onesti	H	3-1	Lupu, Radu, Rat
30/10/99	FC Farul Constanta	A	1-1	Lupu (p)
03/11/99	Ceahlaul Piatra Neamt	H	1-2	Mutica
06/11/99	CSM Resita	H	4-0	Bolohan, Mutica, Voicu, Maldarasanu
14/11/99	Universitatea Craiova	A	0-2	
21/11/99	Astra Ploiesti	A	3-2	Maldarasanu 2, Dascalescu
28/11/99	FCM Bacau	H	2-1	Constantin, Maldarasanu
04/12/99	Ceahlaul Piatra Neamt	A	3-0	Bolohan, Stanciu, Radu
05/03/00	Steaua Bucuresti	H	2-2	Schumacher, Constantin
11/03/00	FC Arges Dacia Pitesti	A	1-0	Dascalescu
18/03/00	Otelul Galati	H	2-1	Iencsi (p), Dascalescu
22/03/00	Gloria Bistrita	A	2-1	Mutica, Radu
25/03/00	FC Extensiv Craiova	H	4-2	Iencsi, Dascalescu 2, Schumacher
01/04/00	Petrolul Ploiesti	A	2-4	Lupu (p), Schumacher
05/04/00	Rocar Bucuresti	H	1-1	Stanciu
08/04/00	FC Brasov	A	0-2	
15/04/00	Dinamo Bucuresti	H	4-0	Lupu (p), Iencsi (p), Radu 2
22/04/00	FC National Bucuresti	H	3-2	Chirita 2, Balan
29/04/00	FC Onesti	A	5-2	Constantin, Schumacher 2, Dascalescu 2
03/05/00	FC Farul Constanta	H	0-0	
06/05/00	CSM Resita	A	1-0	Maldarasanu
10/05/00	Universitatea Craiova	H	3-1	Constantin, Mutica, Radu

CSM RESITA

CLUB DIRECTORY

CSM Resita
str. Valea Domanului 1
1700 Resita
tel - (055) 210052
Year of Formation - 1926
President - Marius Popescu
Coach - Gabriel Stan; Viorel Visan; Dan Firiteanu;
Viorel Visan
Stadium - Mircea Chivu (12,500)

APPEARANCES 99/00

	P	Ap	(s)	Gls
Mihai Virgil ANTAL	A	2	(4)	1
Lucian Daniel BADALUTA	D	2	(1)	
Claudiu BALACI	A	3	(2)	
Mircea Liviu BATRANU	D	1		
Alexandru Cristian BERCSENYI	A	3	(4)	
Bogdan Calin BOEREAN	D	8	(1)	
Ovidiu BREHUI	M	6		
Ion Florin CALUGARITA	D	18	(1)	
Florin Daniel CAPRARIU	D	22	(5)	
Ionel CAZANGIU	D	6		
Vasile Sansiro CIOCOI	M	13	(4)	
Ion Valentin CIUCUR	M	17	(10)	3
Virgil Ciprian DIANU	M	21	(4)	1
Leontin DOANA	M	28	(4)	3
Lucian Mihail DOBRE	D	31		
Ion IBRIC	D	10	(6)	
Alexandru KOVACS	M	3	(1)	
Daniel LUPASCU	A	1	(8)	1
Catalin Raducan NECULA	D	24		
Constantin Doru NICA	M	25	(3)	6
Adrian Alexandru PAUNA	M	1		
Alexandru PELICI	D	4		
Gabriel PERSA	A	7	(6)	1
Marius Nicolae PRISECEANU	M	5	(2)	1
David RADU	D	2		
Marius SASU	A	9	(2)	2
Alin Mircea SAVU	M	9	(6)	
Mircea STANCIU	A	25	(2)	12
Mihaita Gabriel SZEKELY	M	16	(4)	
Iosif SZIJJ	A	12	(8)	3
Gabriel Alexandru TELEKI	D	1	(1)	
Aurel Florea TUDOR	M		(5)	
Robert Emil TUFISI	G	26		
Andrei URAI	G	8		
Dorin Bogdan ZOTINCA	D	5	(1)	1

LEAGUE RESULTS 1999/2000

24/07/99	FC Onesti	A	1-2	Szijj
31/07/99	FC Farul Constanta	H	1-1	Szijj
04/08/99	Dinamo Bucuresti	H	0-6	
07/08/99	Universitatea Craiova	A	2-2	Stanciu, Priseceanu
14/08/99	Astra Ploiesti	H	2-5	Zotinca, Antal
21/08/99	FCM Bacau	A	0-1	
28/08/99	Ceahlaul Piatra Neamt	H	1-3	Szijj
10/09/99	Steaua Bucuresti	A	0-5	
18/09/99	FC Arges Dacia Pitesti	H	0-0	
25/09/99	Otelul Galati	A	2-1	Nica, Stanciu
02/10/99	Gloria Bistrita	H	1-1	Nica
16/10/99	FC Extensiv Craiova	A	0-1	
22/10/99	Petrolul Ploiesti	H	2-2	Sasu, Nica
27/10/99	Rocar Bucuresti	A	0-4	
30/10/99	FC Brasov	H	3-1	Sasu, Nica, Stanciu
06/11/99	Rapid Bucuresti	A	0-4	
17/11/99	FC National Bucuresti	H	1-0	Stanciu
20/11/99	FC Onesti	H	6-1	Stanciu 2 (1p), Dianu, Doana, Nica, Ciucur
27/11/99	FC Farul Constanta	A	1-3	Stanciu (p)
04/12/99	Dinamo Bucuresti	A	1-2	Lupascu
04/03/00	Universitatea Craiova	H	0-0	
11/03/00	Astra Ploiesti	A	1-2	Nica (p)
17/03/00	FCM Bacau	H	1-2	Doana
22/03/00	Ceahlaul Piatra Neamt	A	2-4	Stanciu 2
26/03/00	Steaua Bucuresti	H	2-0	Stanciu (p), Persa
01/04/00	FC Arges Dacia Pitesti	A	1-1	Ciucur (p)
05/04/00	Otelul Galati	H	1-2	Ciucur
08/04/00	Gloria Bistrita	A	0-2	
15/04/00	FC Extensiv Craiova	H	0-0	
22/04/00	Petrolul Ploiesti	A	2-4	Stanciu 2
29/04/00	Rocar Bucuresti	H	0-1	
03/05/00	FC Brasov	A	0-4	
06/05/00	Rapid Bucuresti	H	0-1	
10/05/00	FC National Bucuresti	A	1-5	Doana

ROCAR BUCURESTI

CLUB DIRECTORY

Rocar Bucuresti
str. Ostrov 3
75308 Bucuresti
tel - (01) 3128506
Year of Formation - 1953
President - Gheorghe Netoiu
Coach - Silviu Dumitrescu; Florin Marin
(00/01 - Dumitru Dumitriu)
Stadium - Rocar (8,000)

APPEARANCES 99/00

	P	Ap	(s)	Gls
Dan ALEXA	M	2	(10)	
Dorin ARCANU	G	6		
Adrian BALDOVIN	D	9		
Romulus BUIA	A		(6)	
Augustin Aurel CALIN	M	25	(1)	6
Catalin Petre CRACIUNESCU	D	12	(4)	
Cornel CRISTESCU	D	11	(4)	
Ciprian DANCIU	M	26	(1)	8
Cezar Alexandru DINU	M	19	(1)	1
Cornel DOBRE	D	13		3
Victoras IACOB	M		(9)	2
Laurentiu LICA	M	4	(6)	3
Gabriel MARGARIT	M	16	(1)	
Mircea MINESCU	D	18	(9)	
Marius Dan MITU	D	30	(2)	10
Victor NAICU	D	11	(1)	
Cristinel Adrian NEDELEA	M	10		
Marian NICULITA	D	8		
Daniel Fanel NIIA	D	20	(2)	1
Viorel OAJDEA	M		(1)	
Mircea Vasile OPREA	M		(6)	2
Adrian Dragos PITU	A	27	(3)	8
Daniel Eugen REDNIC	M	9		
Eusebiu Adrian STATE	A	5	(5)	
Ionel SERBAN	D	18	(4)	3
Iosif Ovidiu TALVAN	D		(2)	
Alexandru Florin TENE	G	10		
Daniel Ovidiu TUDOR	G	17	(1)	
Cristinel Florin TERMURE	D	12	(2)	
Constantin Irinel VOICU	D	10	(5)	
Bogdan Mihaita VRAJITOAREA	A	15	(6)	4

LEAGUE RESULTS 1999/2000

31/07/99	Steaua Bucuresti	A	1-2	Dinu
04/08/99	FC Arges Dacia Pitesti	H	0-3	
07/08/99	Otelul Galati	A	1-2	Lica
14/08/99	Gloria Bistrita	H	3-1	Calin 2, Oprea
18/08/99	Ceahlaul Piatra Neamt	H	2-0	Pitu, Danciu
21/08/99	FC Extensiv Craiova	A	1-2	Lica
28/08/99	Petrolul Ploiesti	H	2-1	Serban (p), Oprea
11/09/99	Dinamo Bucuresti	A	0-3	
17/09/99	FC Brasov	A	0-4	
26/09/99	Rapid Bucuresti	H	0-1	
02/10/99	FC National Bucuresti	A	0-2	
16/10/99	FC Onesti	H	5-1	Pitu 2, Mitu, Serban 2
23/10/99	FC Farul Constanta	A	1-0	Mitu
27/10/99	CSM Resita	H	4-0	Pitu 2, og (Calugarita), Lica
30/10/99	Universitatea Craiova	A	1-2	Pitu
06/11/99	Astra Ploiesti	H	2-1	Calin, Niia
14/11/99	FCM Bacau	A	0-1	
20/11/99	Ceahlaul Piatra Neamt	A	0-2	
04/12/99	FC Arges Dacia Pitesti	A	1-3	Danciu
04/03/00	Otelul Galati	H	3-2	Pitu, Calin, Iacob
11/03/00	Gloria Bistrita	A	1-2	Calin
18/03/00	FC Extensiv Craiova	H	3-1	Mitu 2, Vrajitoarea
22/03/00	Petrolul Ploiesti	A	1-4	Danciu
25/03/00	Dinamo Bucuresti	H	1-2	Calin
01/04/00	FC Brasov	H	1-0	Danciu
05/04/00	Rapid Bucuresti	A	1-1	Vrajitoarea
09/04/00	FC National Bucuresti	H	2-1	Vrajitoarea, Mitu
12/04/00	Steaua Bucuresti	H	1-2	Danciu (p)
15/04/00	FC Onesti	A	5-1	Mitu 2, Dobre 2, Vrajitoarea
22/04/00	FC Farul Constanta	H	2-0	Dobre, Iacob
29/04/00	CSM Resita	A	1-0	Pitu
03/05/00	Universitatea Craiova	H	2-2	Mitu 2
06/05/00	Astra Ploiesti	A	1-3	Danciu
10/05/00	FCM Bacau	H	3-0	Mitu, Danciu 2 (1p)

STEAUA BUCURESTI

CLUB DIRECTORY

Steaua Bucuresti
bulevardul Ghencea 35, 76803 Bucuresti
tel - (01) 4102182 / fax - (01) 4100179
Year of Formation - 1947
President - Viorel Paunescu
Coach - Emeric Ienei; Victor Piturca
Stadium - Ghencea (28,000)

MAJOR HONOURS
League Championship - (20)
1951, 1952, 1953, 1956, 1960, 1961, 1968,
1976, 1978, 1985, 1986, 1987, 1988, 1989,
1993, 1994, 1995, 1996, 1997, 1998.
Domestic Cup - (21)
1949, 1950, 1951, 1952, 1955, 1962, 1966,
1967, 1969, 1970, 1971, 1976, 1979, 1985,
1987, 1988, 1989, 1992, 1996, 1997, 1999.
European Champions' Cup - (1) 1986.
European Super Cup - (1) 1986.

APPEARANCES 99/00

	P	Ap	(s)	Gls
Marius Achim BACIU	D	28	(1)	
Miodrag BELODEDICI	D	19	(1)	
Valeriu Ionut BORDEANU	D	23	(4)	1
Stelian CARABAS	M	12		2
Elton CENO (ALB)	M	1	(3)	
Radu CHIOREAN	M	1	(1)	
Cristian CIOCOIU	A	26	(7)	11
Ionel Daniel DANCIULESCU	A	25	(5)	14
Florentin DUMITRU	D	7		1
Albert DURO (ALB)	M	17	(2)	
Mihaita GHEORGHE	M		(1)	
Miroslav Matea GIUCHICHI	A		(1)	
Dumitru HOTOBOC	G	3	(2)	
Sabin ILIE	A	15		3
Marius Sandu IORDACHE	M	8	(1)	1
Marius LACATUS	A	5	(1)	
Erik Augustin LINCAR	M	23	(2)	
Marius LUCA	A	1	(8)	3
Tiberiu Adrian LUNG	G	5	(1)	
Ion Ionut LUTU	M	11	(8)	3
Iulian Ilie MIU	D	25		
Eugen Gheorghe NAE	G	3		
Nana Falemi N'GASSAN (CMR)	M	7	(6)	
Robert Ionel NITA	M		(5)	
Zoran NOVAKOVIC (BOS)	A	1	(5)	
George OGARARU	D	3	(4)	
Ioan Sorin PARASCHIV	M	1		
Daniel Claudiu PRODAN	D	1		
Claudiu Nicu RADUCANU	A	8	(6)	5
Laurentiu Aurelian REGHECAMPF	D	22		2
Zoltan RITLI	G	5		
Laurentiu Dumitru ROSU	M	26		13
Stefan STOICA	M	1	(2)	
Eugen TRICA	M	20	(9)	3
Martin Gheorghe TUDOR	G	18		
Alexandru ZOTINCA	M	3	(2)	

LEAGUE RESULTS 1999/2000

24/07/99	Petrolul Ploiesti	A	1-5	Rosu
31/07/99	Rocar Bucuresti	H	2-1	Ilie (p), Danciulescu
04/08/99	FC Brasov	A	2-1	Iordache, Danciulescu
07/08/99	Rapid Bucuresti	H	1-3	Lutu
15/08/99	FC National Bucuresti	A	0-3	
21/08/99	FC Onesti	H	3-0	Reghecampf 2 (1p), Trica
29/08/99	FC Farul Constanta	A	1-2	Ilie
10/09/99	CSM Resita	H	5-0	Rosu 2, Ciocoiu 2, Luca
19/09/99	Universitatea Craiova	A	2-1	Danciulescu, Ciocoiu
24/09/99	Astra Ploiesti	H	4-1	Rosu 2, Ciocoiu, Danciulescu
02/10/99	FCM Bacau	A	1-2	Lutu
15/10/99	Ceahlaul Piatra Neamt	H	3-0	Luca 2, Rosu
24/10/99	Dinamo Bucuresti	H	1-1	Rosu
30/10/99	Otelul Galati	H	2-1	Ilie, Ciocoiu
10/11/99	Gloria Bistrita	A	0-4	
13/11/99	FC Extensiv Craiova	H	5-2	Danciulescu 3, Ciocoiu, Lutu
18/11/99	Petrolul Ploiesti	H	1-4	Rosu
04/12/99	FC Brasov	H	2-2	Ciocoiu, Rosu
13/12/99	FC Arges Dacia Pitesti	A	0-4	
05/03/00	Rapid Bucuresti	A	2-2	Carabas, Trica
12/03/00	FC National Bucuresti	H	2-3	Rosu, Danciulescu
19/03/00	FC Onesti	A	3-1	Carabas, Danciulescu, Trica
22/03/00	FC Farul Constanta	H	1-0	Ciocoiu
26/03/00	CSM Resita	A	0-2	
02/04/00	Universitatea Craiova	H	1-0	Rosu
05/04/00	Astra Ploiesti	A	0-1	
09/04/00	FCM Bacau	H	1-0	Danciulescu
12/04/00	Rocar Bucuresti	A	2-1	Ciocoiu, Bordeanu
16/04/00	Ceahlaul Piatra Neamt	A	2-0	Danciulescu, Ciocoiu
22/04/00	Dinamo Bucuresti	A	2-3	Ciocoiu, Danciulescu
29/04/00	FC Arges Dacia Pitesti	H	0-1	
03/05/00	Otelul Galati	A	5-4	Raducanu 3, Rosu 2
07/05/00	Gloria Bistrita	H	2-1	Danciulescu, Dumitru
10/05/00	FC Extensiv Craiova	A	3-0	Raducanu 2, Danciulescu

UNIVERSITATEA CRAIOVA

CLUB DIRECTORY

Universitatea Craiova
str. Libertatii 9, 1100 Craiova
tel - (051) 132480 / fax - (051) 115067
Year of Formation - 1948
President - George Ilinca
Coach - Marian Bondrea; Emil Sandoi
(00/01 - Florin Marin)
Stadium - Central (40,000)

MAJOR HONOURS
League Championship - (4)
1974, 1980, 1981, 1991.
Domestic Cup - (7)
1977, 1978, 1981, 1983, 1991, 1993, 1994.

APPEARANCES 99/00

	P	Ap	(s)	Gls
Cosmin BARCAOAN	A	17	(15)	2
Florin Ionel BATRANU	D	23		2
Catalin Elian BELDEANU	M	1	(2)	
Cristian CHIVU	D	6		
Silvian CRISTESCU	M	24	(1)	4
Viorel DOMOCOS	A	13	(8)	
Ionut Daniel DRAGOMIR	D	25	(1)	1
Gabriel DUMITRU	M	5	(10)	
Danut Cornel FRASINEANU	M	27	(1)	2
Stefan Costel GRIGORIE	M	7	(8)	2
Florin Nicolae IORGA	A	4	(4)	2
Tiberiu Adrian LUNG	G	7		
Casian Vasile MICLAUS	D	8	(1)	
Narcis Lucian MOHORA	D	2	(1)	
Eugen NEAGOE	A	16	(5)	3
Cristian NEAMTU	G	1		
Alin Gabriel NICOLA	D	2	(6)	
Claudiu Iulian NICULESCU	A	25	(1)	16
Gabriel OPREA	D		(1)	
Corneliu PAPURA	D	28		1
Marian PACLESAN	M	8		
Florin PRUNEA	G	24		
Ionut ROTARU	M	1	(1)	
Marius SAVA	M	24	(4)	7
Flavius Vladimir STOICAN	D	26		
Costin Florin SOAVA	D	7	(5)	
George Daniel SERBAN	D	1		
Paul STEFANESCU	G	2		
Cosmin Cristian URSU	D	8	(3)	
Lucian TILIHOI	M		(1)	
Robert Dumitru VANCEA	D	2	(4)	
Alin Stefan VIGARIU	A	2	(10)	2
Gabriel VOCHIN	D	28	(1)	
Mircea VOICU	M		(1)	

LEAGUE RESULTS 1999/2000

24/07/99	FC National Bucuresti	A	0-1	
31/07/99	FC Onesti	H	1-0	Neagoe (p)
04/08/99	FC Farul Constanta	A	0-2	
07/08/99	CSM Resita	H	2-2	Sava, Iorga
15/08/99	Dinamo Bucuresti	H	1-2	Niculescu (p)
22/08/99	Astra Ploiesti	A	0-2	
27/08/99	FCM Bacau	H	2-3	Sava, Iorga
12/09/99	Ceahlaul Piatra Neamt	A	1-1	Sava
19/09/99	Steaua Bucuresti	H	1-2	Niculescu
25/09/99	FC Arges Dacia Pitesti	A	0-2	
01/10/99	Otelul Galati	H	4-0	Cristescu 2, Niculescu 2
16/10/99	Gloria Bistrita	A	0-1	
23/10/99	FC Extensiv Craiova	H	3-0	Sava (p), Niculescu 2
27/10/99	Petrolul Ploiesti	A	0-0	
30/10/99	Rocar Bucuresti	H	2-1	Papura, Sava (p)
06/11/99	FC Brasov	A	1-0	Frasineanu
14/11/99	Rapid Bucuresti	H	2-0	Sava (p), Niculescu
19/11/99	FC National Bucuresti	H	2-0	Niculescu, Batranu
27/11/99	FC Onesti	A	0-0	
04/12/99	FC Farul Constanta	H	3-0	Niculescu, Cristescu, Vigariu
04/03/00	CSM Resita	A	0-0	
12/03/00	Dinamo Bucuresti	A	2-5	Neagoe 2
18/03/00	Astra Ploiesti	H	0-0	
22/03/00	FCM Bacau	A	0-3	
25/03/00	Ceahlaul Piatra Neamt	H	0-2	
02/04/00	Steaua Bucuresti	A	0-1	
05/04/00	FC Arges Dacia Pitesti	H	3-1	Dragomir, Batranu, Frasineanu
08/04/00	Otelul Galati	A	0-1	
15/04/00	Gloria Bistrita	H	3-1	Niculescu 2, Grigorie
22/04/00	FC Extensiv Craiova	A	3-2	Niculescu 2 (1p), Cristescu
29/04/00	Petrolul Ploiesti	H	5-1	Niculescu 3, Barcauan, Sava
03/05/00	Rocar Bucuresti	A	2-2	Barcauan, Grigorie
06/05/00	FC Brasov	H	1-0	og (Bodea)
10/05/00	Rapid Bucuresti	A	1-3	Vigariu

RUSSIA

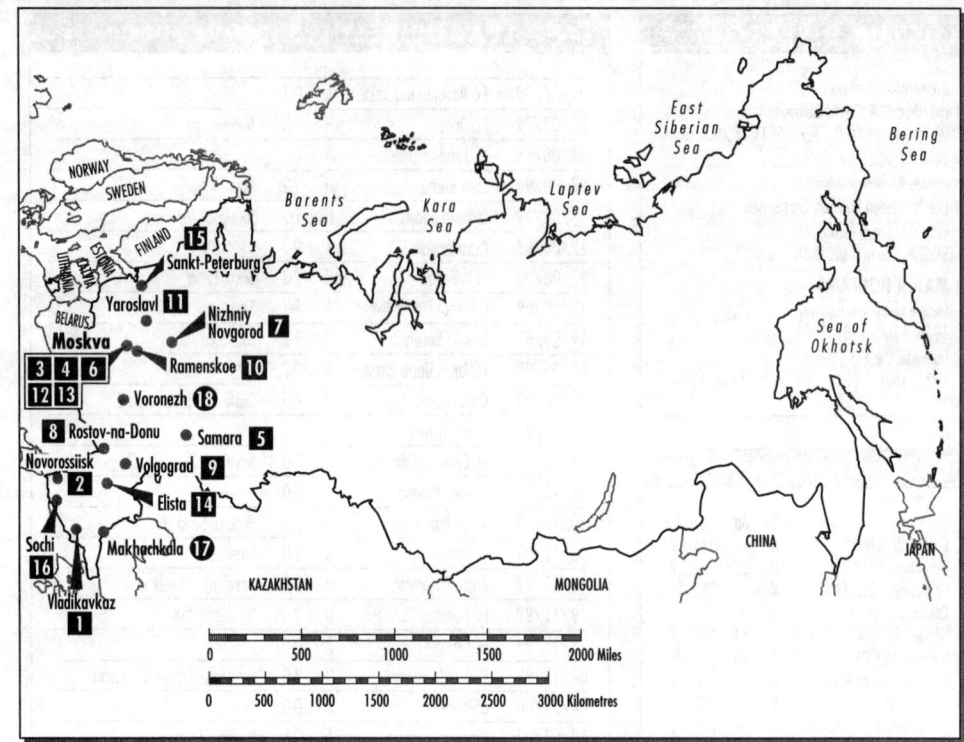

1	ALANIA VLADIKAVKAZ	843
2	CHERNOMORETS NOVOROSSIISK	844
3	CSKA MOSKVA	845
4	DINAMO MOSKVA	846
5	KRYLYA SOVETOV SAMARA	847
6	LOKOMOTIV MOSKVA	848
7	LOKOMOTIV NIZHNIY NOVGOROD	849
8	ROSTSELMASH ROSTOV-NA-DONU	850
9	ROTOR VOLGOGRAD	851
10	SATURN RAMENSKOE	852
11	SHINNIK YAROSLAVL	853
12	SPARTAK MOSKVA	854
13	TORPEDO MOSKVA	855
14	URALAN ELISTA	856
15	ZENIT SANKT-PETERBURG	857
16	ZHEMCHUZHINA SOCHI	858
Promoted clubs		
17	ANZHI MAKHACHKALA	
18	FAKEL VORONEZH	

AUTUMN OF DISCONTENT IN EUROPE

Filimonov error delivers mortal blow

FEDERATION DIRECTORY

Russian Football Union
Luzhnetskaja Naberezhnaja 8, 119 270 Moskva

tel - (095) 2010834   Year of Formation - 1991
fax - (095) 2011303   President - Dr. Vyacheslav Koloskov
website - www.feesmg-football.ru   Secretary - Vladimir Radionov

Stadium - Luzhniki, Moskva (96,000)

The autumn of 1999 was a depressing period for Russian football. While the clubs dropped like flies in the Champions' League and the UEFA Cup, the national team suffered a gut-wrenching elimination from the European Championship.

Russian goalkeeper Aleksandr Filimonov may yet go on to achieve great things in his football career, but no Russian fan will ever forgive or forget the elementary error he made with three minutes remaining of Russia's all-important final Euro 2000 qualifier at home to Ukraine. With Russia leading 1-0 thanks to Valeriy Karpin's 75th minute free-kick and the 80,000 crowd in the Luzhniki stadium poised to celebrate a remarkable qualification as group winners, Filimonov completely misjudged an inswinging free-kick from Ukrainian superstar Andriy Shevchenko and succeeded merely in carrying the ball backwards and dropping it over the line.

All of a sudden the Luzhniki had the atmosphere of a morgue. Throughout the country there was widespread dismay. With France beating Iceland in Paris, Filimonov's howler meant that Russia had gone from automatic qualification to immediate elimination. With just three minutes left there was no way back. The final whistle had the sound of a death-knell for Russian football. It was the second time in a row that the national team had failed to qualify for a major tournament.

What made it so hard to stomach was that Filimonov's one moment of madness had unravelled all the hard work achieved by the team following the re-appointment of Oleg Romantsev as coach ten months earlier. Defeats in each of their first three qualifying matches - under previous incumbent Anatoliy Byshovets - had put the Russians in an almost impossible position from which to qualify, but with Romantsev back in the saddle the team won each of their

LEAGUE CHAMPIONSHIP RESULTS 1999

		1	2	3	4	5	6	7	8	9	10	11	12	13	14	15	16
1	Alania Vladikavkaz		3-1	0-1	5-1	1-1	0-2	5-2	3-1	3-0	2-0	3-1	0-1	6-1	4-2	2-2	2-2
2	Chernomorets Novorossiisk	1-0		2-1	2-1	1-1	1-4	0-1	1-0	1-1	1-1	1-1	1-1	1-2	0-0	1-0	3-0
3	CSKA Moskva	4-1	5-2		4-1	1-1	1-0	3-1	2-0	5-1	1-0	5-0	0-4	0-0	2-0	2-2	3-0
4	Dinamo Moskva	0-0	0-1	1-0		3-3	2-4	2-1	4-0	2-1	0-0	3-1	1-1	1-1	1-0	0-1	3-0
5	Krylya Sovetov Samara	0-3	1-1	1-1	1-2		1-2	3-0	0-0	0-1	2-0	4-2	3-1	1-2	0-1	3-2	4-2
6	Lokomotiv Moskva	4-1	2-1	1-0	2-1	2-0		3-1	3-0	5-1	3-0	4-1	0-3	1-2	1-0	1-1	1-1
7	Lokomotiv Nizhniy Novgorod	2-1	3-2	0-2	1-3	3-0	0-0		0-0	1-1	0-1	1-0	2-4	0-1	1-2	1-0	2-1
8	Rostselmash Rostov-na-Donu	4-2	1-0	1-3	1-3	2-1	1-1	1-0		1-1	4-1	0-0	0-3	0-0	2-0	2-1	2-1
9	Rotor Volgograd	0-2	5-2	1-1	1-2	2-1	1-0	2-3	0-1		1-1	2-0	3-3	0-2	3-1	2-2	0-0
10	Saturn Ramenskoe	0-1	3-0	2-3	3-3	2-0	1-1	1-1	1-1	1-0		0-0	0-3	2-2	2-0	1-0	3-0
11	Shinnik Yaroslavl	1-1	1-0	0-0	3-1	1-2	2-4	0-1	0-3	2-0	0-0		1-2	1-0	1-0	0-0	0-0
12	Spartak Moskva	3-0	2-0	1-0	2-2	3-0	3-0	2-2	1-0	4-1	3-1	4-1		0-1	3-0	4-1	4-0
13	Torpedo Moskva	1-1	3-1	2-2	0-1	3-1	2-4	3-2	1-2	2-1	0-2	0-0	0-0		3-1	1-0	1-0
14	Uralan Elista	3-0	3-1	1-1	1-0	2-1	0-1	3-0	2-1	0-1	2-0	1-0	0-1	1-1		0-0	1-1
15	Zenit Sankt-Peterburg	2-2	1-1	1-1	0-0	3-1	1-2	1-0	1-0	1-1	2-1	2-1	1-2	0-0	2-0		3-1
16	Zhemchuzhina Sochi	2-0	2-0	2-2	1-0	0-2	1-4	1-1	1-1	2-2	2-0	1-0	3-7	1-1	0-0	1-3	

LEAGUE CHAMPIONSHIP FINAL TABLE 1999

		Pd	Home					Away					Total					PT	GD
			W	D	L	F	A	W	D	L	F	A	W	D	L	F	A		
1	Spartak Moskva	30	12	2	1	39	9	10	4	1	36	15	22	6	2	75	24	72	51
2	Lokomotiv Moskva	30	11	2	2	33	13	9	3	3	29	17	20	5	5	62	30	65	32
3	CSKA Moskva	30	11	3	1	38	13	4	7	4	18	16	15	10	5	56	29	55	27
4	Torpedo Moskva	30	7	4	4	22	18	6	7	2	16	15	13	11	6	38	33	50	5
5	Dinamo Moskva	30	7	5	3	23	14	5	3	7	21	27	12	8	10	44	41	44	3
6	Alania Vladikavkaz	30	9	3	3	39	18	3	4	8	15	27	12	7	11	54	45	43	9
7	Rostselmash Rostov-na-Donu	30	8	4	3	22	17	3	4	8	10	20	11	8	11	32	37	41	-5
8	Zenit Sankt-Peterburg	30	7	6	2	21	13	2	6	7	15	21	9	12	9	36	34	39	2
9	Uralan Elista	30	8	4	3	20	9	2	2	11	7	25	10	6	14	27	34	36	-7
10	Saturn Ramenskoe	30	6	6	3	22	15	2	4	9	8	23	8	10	12	30	38	34	-8
11	Lokomotiv Nizhniy Novgorod	30	6	3	6	17	18	3	3	9	16	30	9	6	15	33	48	33	-15
12	Krylya Sovetov Samara	30	6	3	6	24	20	2	4	9	15	29	8	7	15	39	49	31	-10
13	Rotor Volgograd	30	5	5	5	23	21	2	5	8	13	30	7	10	13	36	51	31	-15
14	Chernomorets Novorossiisk	30	6	6	3	17	14	1	2	12	13	35	7	8	15	30	49	29	-19
15	Zhemchuzhina Sochi	30	5	6	4	20	23	0	5	10	9	32	5	11	14	29	55	26	-26
16	Shinnik Yaroslavl	30	5	5	5	13	14	0	4	11	8	31	5	9	16	21	45	24	-24

PLAYERS OF THE SEASON

ALEKSEI SMERTIN

Born in the icy cold Siberian town of Barnaul, 25-year-old Aleksei Smertin can now bask in the more appealing climate of France's Atlantic coast following his summer transfer from Lokomotiv Moscow to Bordeaux. Voted Russia's Footballer of the Year for 1999, Smertin was rewarded for his commanding displays in midfield for Lokomotiv and in defence for the Russian national team. At the beginning of that year he was a largely unheralded figure, having completed only one season of top-flight football with Uralan Elista. But at Lokomotiv he made such rapid and ceaseless progress that he soon became a fixture in Russia's European Championship team. Although his preference would have been to move to an English club (he is a dedicated fan of British rock music), he was delighted to agree terms with Bordeaux and continue his career in France - despite the appeal of staying with Lokomotiv a few months longer and trying to help the club to a first Russian title.

STANISLAV CHERCHESOV

Veteran goalkeeper Stanislav Cherchesov had a season to remember with FC Tirol Innsbruck. His fifth year at the Alpine club brought him an Austrian championship winner's medal, and nobody deserved it more. The burly 'keeper played in all 36 of Tirol's league matches and kept clean sheets in over half of them. News of his spectacular form spread back to the motherland, and when Spartak Moscow's Aleksandr Filimonov became persona non grata after his disastrous error in the decisive Euro 2000 qualifier against Ukraine, Cherchesov was recalled, at 36, to the national team for the February 2000 friendly against Israel. Sadly, though, he conceded four goals in a heavy defeat and was discarded for the next game against the United States, during which Lokomotiv's Ruslan Nigmatullin staked a strong claim for permanent selection with a brilliant début display.

NATIONAL TEAM RESULTS 99/00

18/08/99	Belarus	A	Minsk	2-0	Beschastnykh (40), Panov (47)
04/09/99	Armenia (ECQ)	H	Moscow	2-0	Beschastnykh (8p), Karpin (70)
08/09/99	Andorra (ECQ)	A	Andorra La Vella	2-1	Onopko (23, 57)
09/10/99	Ukraine (ECQ)	H	Moscow	1-1	Karpin (75)
23/02/00	Israel	A	Haifa	1-4	Beschastnykh (59p)
26/04/00	United States	H	Moscow	2-0	Titov (63), Karpin (90)
31/05/00	Slovakia	H	Moscow	1-1	Beschastnykh (60)
04/06/00	Moldova	A	Chisinau	1-0	Buznikin (15)

TOP SCORERS

21 Giorgi DEMETRADZE (Alania Vladikavkaz)
19 Andrei TIKHONOV (Spartak Moskva)
14 Vladimir KULIK (CSKA Moskva)
Dmitriy LOSKOV (Lokomotiv Moskva)
Oleg TERYOKHIN (Dinamo Moskva)
13 Arsen AVAKOV (Lokomotiv Nizhniy Novgorod)
12 Vyacheslav KAMOLTSEV (Torpedo Moskva)
Sergei SEMAK (CSKA Moskva)
Oleg VERETENNIKOV (Rotor Volgograd)
Yegor TITOV (Spartak Moskva)

next six matches, including a momentous 3-2 triumph against the world champions in the Stade de France.

But the draw against Ukraine rendered all that had gone before utterly meaningless. Russian football had to go back to the drawing board and start again from scratch in preparation for the 2002 World Cup qualifiers.

When the first game in the new year ended in a 4-1 defeat by Israel, Romantsev offered to resign. But a show of support from his players persuaded him to change his mind. Three further low-key friendlies in the spring, against the United States, Slovakia and Moldova, were used primarily for experimentation, but although the results were healthy enough, there was little for the Russian fans to get excited about ahead of the World Cup campaign. The

game at home to Slovakia was arranged only after the controversial cancellation of a fixture against England at Wembley. To rub salt into Russian wounds, the FA then chose to play Ukraine instead. How the mighty had fallen...

The depression was made deeper by the Russian Under-21 team's failure to reach their own European finals - and, by extension, the Olympic Games. At club level, too, results in Europe were extremely poor. CSKA Moscow failed even to get past the second preliminary round in the Champions' League, beaten by Norwegian side Molde FK; Cup holders Zenit St. Petersburg crashed heavily in the first round of the UEFA Cup to Bologna; and Lokomotiv Moscow were destroyed home and away in the second

DOMESTIC CUP 99/00

1/16 FINALS
Amkap Perm 2, Rotor Vologograd 2
(aet; 4-5 on pens.)
Spartak-Chukotka Moskva 1,
Lokomotiv Nizhniy Novgorod 0
Spartak Nalchik 4, Zhemchuzhina Sochi 0
Anzhi Makhachkala 3, Torpedo Moskva 1
Sokol Saratov 1, Shinnik Yaroslavl 0
Fakel Voronezh 3, Rostselmash Rostov-na-Donu 2
(aet)
Mosenergo Moskva 0, Dinamo Moskva 0
(aet; 5-6 on pens.)
Lokomotiv Sankt-Peterburg 1, Lokomotiv Moskva 5
Arsenal Tula 1, Saturn Ramenskoe 3
Dinamo Stavropol 2, Chernomorets Novorossiisk 1
(aet)
Gazovik-Gazprom Izhevsk 2, Zenit Sankt-Peterburg 1
Lokomotiv Chita 0, Uralan Elista 1
Metallurg Lipetsk 1, Alania Vladikavkaz 0
Tom Tomsk 0, CSKA Moskva 5
Baltika Kaliningrad 2, Krylya Sovetov Samara 0
Lada-Toliatti-Vaz Toliatti 0, Spartak Moskva 2

1/8 FINALS
Metallurg Lipetsk 4, Dinamo Stavropol 0
Anzhi Makhachkala 2, Gazovik-Gazprom Izhevsk 0
Rotor Volgograd 0, Saturn Ramenskoe 1
Uralan Elista 3, Fakel Voronezh 0
Lokomotiv Moskva 2, Baltika Kaliningrad 1
Dinamo Moskva 1, Spartak Nalchik 0 (aet)
CSKA Moskva 3, Spartak-Chukotka Moskva 0
Sokol Saratov 0, Spartak Moskva 1 (aet)

QUARTER-FINALS
Spartak Moskva 1 (Buznikin 60), Saturn Ramenskoe 0
Metallurg Lipetsk 1 (Vekovischev 2), Lokomotiv
Moskva 2 (Loskov 53p, Teryokhin 66)
Anzhi Makhachkala 1 (Oskolov og), CSKA Moskva 1
(Bychkov) (aet; 3-5 on pens.)
Uralan Elista 1 (Avalyan), Dinamo Moskva 0

SEMI-FINALS
Uralan Elista 1 (Jefferson 57), Lokomotiv Moskva 4
(Tsymbalar 7, Loskov 92, 103, 112) (aet)
CSKA Moskva 3 (Kulik 21, 59, Varlamov 41),
Spartak Moskva 1 (Titov 36)

FINAL
21/05/2000, Moscow
LOKOMOTIV MOSKVA 3 Yevseyev (41), Bulykin
(96), Tsymbalar (113)
CSKA MOSKVA 2 Semak (31), Kornaukhov (120)
(aet)
referee - Levnikov
LOKOMOTIV MOSKVA - Nigmatullin, Cherevchenko,
Chugainov, Nizhegorodov, Solomatin (Drozdov 46),
Yevseyev, Sennikov (Kharlachyov 41), Tsymbalar,
Loskov, Teryokhin, Bulykin (Pashinin 97).
CSKA MOSKVA - Okroshidze, Varlamov, Minko,
Bokov, Kornaukhov, Yevsikov, Filippenkov (Yenin
86), Shishkin (Geraschenko 62), Skripchenko
(Khomukha 46), Semak, Kulik.

round of the same competition by Leeds. As for standard-bearers Spartak Moscow, they qualified comfortably for the Champions' League thanks to two impressive displays against Yugoslav champions Partizan Belgrade, but in the group phase they were unable to profit from a victorious start - 3-1 away to Dutch side Willem II, including a hat-trick from midfielder Andrei Tikhonov - and won no further games. The failure to register at least one home win against Sparta Prague, Bordeaux and Willem II left Spartak in a hopeless position, and in the end they were grateful for the lifeline that enabled them, as the third-placed team, to switch over to the UEFA Cup.

But their sojourn in that competition was to last just one round. Forced against their will to play their home leg against Leeds United in Sofia, a week later than scheduled, because of unplayable conditions in Moscow, Spartak came from behind to win that first leg 2-1 but were beaten in the return by a late goal from South African defender Lucas Radebe, which eliminated them on the away-goals rule.

By the time Spartak's European involvement came to a close, they were already safely qualified for the following season's Champions' League, having comfortably won their fourth Russian championship in a row and their

NATIONAL TEAM APPEARANCES 99/00

Coach - Oleg ROMANTSEV	BLS	ARM	AND	UKR	ISR	USA	SVK	MOL	Cps	Gls
Aleksandr FILIMONOV (15/10/73) - Spartak Moskva	G	G	G	G			G		13	-
Dmitriy KHLESTOV (21/01/71) - Spartak Moskva	D	D	D	D	D	D	D	D	43	-
Aleksei SMERTIN (01/05/75) - Lokomotiv Moskva	D	D	D	D	D	D			12	-
Igor YANOVSKIY (03/08/74) - Paris Saint-Germain (FRA)	D70	s73	s61		D46				26	1
Viktor ONOPKO (14/10/69) - Real Oviedo (ESP)	M	M	D	D	D	s46	D	D59	76	6
Dmitriy KHOKHLOV (22/12/75) - PSV (HOL)/Real Sociedad (ESP)	M	M	M65	M	M65	M46	M46	s56	22	-
Valeriy KARPIN (02/02/69) - RC Celta (ESP)	M46	M	M	M		M			52	16
Yegor TITOV (29/05/76) - Spartak Moskva	M77	M80	M	M	M46	M	M	M	14	2
Andrei TIKHONOV (16/10/70) - Spartak Moskva	M82	M73	M	M61	M46	s46	M72	M77	29	1
Vladimir BESCHASTNYKH (01/04/74) - Racing Santander (ESP)	A	A	A46	s61	s46	A	A	A56	46	16
Aleksandr PANOV (21/09/75) - Zenit Sankt-Peterburg	A63	A78	s46	A76	A46	s60	s46	s56	13	3
Dmitriy ALENICHEV (20/10/72) - Roma (ITA)/Perugia (ITA)	s46	M	M61	M	M	M46			28	4
Sergei SEMAK (27/02/75) - CSKA Moskva	s63	s80		s76	M	A60	s46	s56	19	-
Vladimir BUT (24/09/77) - Borussia Dortmund (GER)	s70				s65				2	-
Viktor BULATOV (22/01/72) - Spartak Moskva	s77							M56	5	-
Yuriy DROZDOV (16/01/72) - Lokomotiv Moskva	s82			D			s69	s59	5	-
Aleksandr SHIRKO (24/11/76) - Spartak Moskva		s78	A		s46				4	-
Artyom BEZRODNYI (10/02/79) - Spartak Moskva			s65						1	-
Stanislav CHERCHESOV (02/09/63) - FC Tirol Innsbruck (AUT)					G				39	-
Igor CHUGAINOV (06/04/70) - Lokomotiv Moskva					s46				16	-
Omari TETRADZE (13/10/69) - PAOK (GRE)					s46				31	1
Ruslan NIGMATULLIN (07/10/74) - Lokomotiv Moskva						G		G	2	-
Maxim DEMENKO (21/03/76) - Zenit Sankt-Peterburg						D	D69		2	-
Andrei SOLOMATIN (09/09/75) - Lokomotiv Moskva						D			2	-
Gennadiy NIZHEGORODOV (07/06/77) - Lokomotiv Moskva							D	D	2	-
Rolan GUSEV (17/09/77) - Dinamo Moskva							M	M	2	-
Maxim BUZNIKIN (01/03/77) - Spartak Moskva							A46	A56	2	1
Dmitriy LOSKOV (13/02/74) - Lokomotiv Moskva							s72	s77	2	-
Yevgeniy BUSHMANOV (02/11/71) - Spartak Moskva								D	7	-

seventh out of a possible eight. Spartak had just one challenger, Lokomotiv Moscow, but Oleg Romantsev's side were always out in front and never seriously looked likely to drop their guard low enough to allow their city rivals to bring them down. Spartak won each of the two direct confrontations 3-0, and the second of them, in mid-October, proved to be a fitting occasion for them to make mathematically certain of the title.

Driven on by their goalscoring midfielders Titov and Tikhonov, Spartak were also well served in other depart-

EUROPEAN CUPS 99/00

CHAMPIONS' CUP
● CSKA MOSKVA
Preliminary round 2 MOLDE FK (NOR)

H 2-0   Sischin (7), Khomukha (85)
Goncharov, Minko, Varlamov, Bokov, Semak, Kornaukhov, Khomukha, Sischin, Holly (Tsaplin 80), Kulik, Filippenkov (Gutalj 61).

A 0-4
Goncharov, Minko, Varlamov, Bokov, Semak, Kornaukhov, Khomukha (Gutalj 78), Sischin (Filippenkov 46), Holly, Kulik, Aksenov.

● SPARTAK MOSKVA
Qualifying round PARTIZAN BEOGRAD (YUG)

H 2-0   Shirko (37), Tikhonov (73)
Filimonov, Kovtun, Khlestov, Bushmanov, Bulatov, Titov, Kechinov, Tikhonov, Parfyonov, Shirko, Robson,

A 3-1   Shirko (20, 46), Titov (85p)
Filimonov, Kovtun, Khlestov, Bushmanov, Baranov, Bulatov, Titov, Tikhonov (Bezrodnyi 23), Parfyonov, Shirko (Tsymbalar 87), Robson.

Champions' League
1st match WILLEM II (HOL)

A 3-1   Tikhonov (27p, 37, 53p)
Filimonov, Parfyonov, Khlestov, Bushmanov, Kovtun, Baranov, Titov (Yevseyev 71), Bezrodnyi, Tikhonov, Kechinov (Tsymbalar 46), Robson.

2nd match SPARTA PRAHA (CZE)

H 1-1   Bezrodnyi (73)
Filimonov, Parfyonov, Khlestov, Bushmanov, Kovtun, Baranov (Kechinov 63), Titov, Bulatov (Bezrodnyi 70), Tikhonov, Tsymbalar (Shirko 56), Robson.

3rd match GIRONDINS DE BORDEAUX (FRA)

A 1-2   Bezrodnyi (64)
Filimonov, Parfyonov, Bushmanov, Khlestov, Yevseyev, Baranov (Kechinov 55), Bulatov (Tsymbalar 46), Tikhonov, Titov, Shirko, Bezrodnyi.

4th match GIRONDINS DE BORDEAUX (FRA)

H 1-2   Tikhonov (55p)
Filimonov, Bushmanov, Parfyonov, Khlestov, Kovtun, Baranov (Kechinov 55), Bulatov, Tikhonov, Shirko, Titov, Bezrodnyi.

5th match WILLEM II (HOL)

H 1-1   Bezrodnyi (25)
Filimonov, Bushmanov, Parfyonov, Khlestov, Kovtun, Baranov (Yevseyev 46), Bulatov (Kechinov 58), Tikhonov, Shirko, Titov, Bezrodnyi.

6th match SPARTA PRAHA (CZE)

A 2-5   Bulatov (34), Bezrodnyi (45)
Filimonov, Bushmanov, Khlestov, Ananko, Parfyonov, Bulatov, Titov, Tikhonov, Bezrodnyi, Shirko (Melyoshin 73), Robson (Baranov 53).

UEFA CUP
● LOKOMOTIV MOSKVA
Qualifying round FC BATE BORISOV (BLS)

A 7-1   Janashia (6, 34, 60), Loskov (24), Sarkisyan (55), Bulykin (73, 86)
Nigmatullin, Chrevchenko, Lavrik, Kharlachyov, Hovhannisyan (Drozdov 46), Chugainov, Smertin (Maminov 60), Pashinin, Janashia, Loskov (Bulykin 46), Sarkisyan.

H 5-0   Chugainov (17), Loskov (23), Smertin (36), Kharlachyov (66, 75)
Polyakov, Arifulin, Drozdov, Lavrik, Solomatin (Pachinin 46), Chugainov, Smertin (Kharlachyov 46), Sarkisyan, Maminov, Loskov, Bulykin (Pimenov 46).

1st round LYNGBY FC (DEN)

A 2-1   Chugainov (13), Bulykin (37)
Nigmatullin, Arifulin (Solomatin 82), Drozdov (Maminov 46), Kharlachyov, Hovhannisyan (Cherevchenko 65), Chugainov, Smertin, Sarkisyan, Pashinin, Loskov, Bulykin.

H 3-0   Kharlachyov (20), Drozdov (43), Janashia (44)
Nigmatullin, Arifulin, Drozdov, Kharlachyov, Cherevchenko, Chugainov, Smertin (Solomatin 62), Pashinin, Janashia (Maminov 70), Loskov (Semenenko 46), Sarkisyan.

2nd round LEEDS UNITED (ENG)

A 1-4   Loskov (80)
Nigmatullin, Arifulin, Drozdov, Kharlachyov, Lavrik, Chugainov, Smertin, Pashinin (Hovhannisyan 66), Janashia (Bulykin 39), Loskov, Sarkisyan (Maminov 76).

H 0-3
Nigmatullin, Arifulin, Lavrik, Pashinin (Kharlachyov 46), Hovhannisyan (Semenenko 76), Chugainov, Smertin, Solomatin, Bulykin (Pimenov 74), Loskov, Sarkisyan.

● SPARTAK MOSKVA
3rd round LEEDS UNITED (ENG)

H 2-1   Shirko (38), Robson (65)
Filimonov, Kovtun, Khlestov, Bushmanov, Parfyonov, Bulatov, Baranov, Bezrodnyi, Titov, Shirko, Robson.

A 0-1
Filimonov (Smetanin 34), Parfyonov, Khlestov, Bushmanov, Yevseyev, Bulatov, Baranov, Robson, Titov, Shirko, Tikhonov.

● ZENIT SANKT-PETERBURG
1st round BOLOGNA (ITA)

H 0-3
Berezovski, Davydov, Lepyukhin, Hovsepyan, Babiy (Petukhov 73), Vernidub, Kobelev, Gorshkov (Maksimyuk 54), Popovich (Curtianu 57), Ugarov, Panov.

A 2-2   Panov (35), Kondrashov (89)
Berezovski, Davydov, Kondrashov, Hovsepyan, Igonin, Vernidub, Curtianu, Maksimyuk (Babiy 73), Petukhov (Kobelev 73), Ugarov, Panov (Popovich 82).

ments, notably in the closing weeks of the campaign by Brazilian striker Robson, who proved to be one of the more exotic and exciting imports in the Russian league.

Spartak's title celebrations had to be put on hold when coach Romantsev suffered a heart-attack and was taken to hospital. The chain-smoking workaholic was not out of action for long, however, and by the start of the following season he was still carrying out his joint functions for club and country.

Lokomotiv, who finished as the clear runners-up to Spartak in the league, made bold plans to reinforce their challenge for the 2000 campaign by buying in several new players, including Dinamo Moscow hotshot Oleg Teryokhin and Vadim Yevseyev and Iliya Tsymbalar from Spartak. The investment brought immediate dividends when the new-look team won the Russian Cup, beating city rivals CSKA 3-2 after extra-time in a riveting, incident-packed final, with Yevseyev and Tsymbalar both getting their names on the scoresheet. It was Lokomotiv's fourth Cup final appearance in five seasons and their third victory.

By finishing as runners-up in the league, Lokomotiv earned the right to a place in the Champions' League qualifying round. Their Cup win also freed another UEFA

INTERNATIONAL HONOURS

World Cup Finals appearances: 1994.

European Championship appearances:1996.

Cup place, which was gratefully accepted by Alania Vladikavkaz, who thus joined the three Muscovites, CSKA, Torpedo and Dinamo, in a four-strong Russian challenge. Vladikavkaz, the only club to have denied Spartak a clean sweep of Russian titles, set another milestone in the 1999 season when their Georgian striker Giorgi Demetradze became the first foreigner to win the league's top-scorer crown. He scored 21 goals before quitting at the end of the season to join Dynamo Kiev.

Torpedo were the most improved team in the country, lifting themselves from 11th in 1998 to fourth in 1999. They were the only team to take four points off champions Spartak and possessed arguably the most clear-thinking, forward-looking coach in Vitaliy Shevchenko - a prominent candidate for the national team job if and when the indefatigable Romantsev ever decides to call it a day.

PROMOTED CLUBS 1999

SECOND DIVISION FINAL TABLE

		Pd	W	D	L	F	A	Pt	GD
1	**Anzhi Makhachkala**	42	26	8	8	55	20	86	35
2	**Fakel Voronezh**	42	26	7	9	65	31	85	34
3	Sokol Saratov	42	25	7	10	74	39	82	35
3	Torpedo-ZIL Moskva	42	23	13	6	67	27	82	40
5	Baltika Kaliningrad	42	22	8	12	60	37	74	23
6	Amkar Perm	42	20	10	12	65	49	70	16
7	Rubin Kazan	42	18	12	12	56	49	66	7
8	Gazovik-Gazprom Izhevsk	42	20	4	18	50	47	64	3
9	Arsenal Tula	42	19	7	16	61	51	64	10
10	Lokomotiv Chita	42	19	5	18	48	50	62	-2
11	Kristall Saratov	42	17	7	18	44	49	58	-5
12	Tomy Tomsk	42	17	7	18	48	54	58	-6
13	Spartak Nalchik	42	17	5	20	49	61	56	-12
14	Metallurg Krasnoyarsk	42	14	12	16	38	43	54	-5
15	Metallurg Lipetsk	42	15	8	19	51	53	53	-2
16	Lokomotiv Sankt-Peterburg	42	14	9	19	35	51	51	-16
17	Volgar-Gazprom Astrakhan	42	14	8	20	41	49	50	-8
18	FK Tyumen	42	13	9	20	43	59	48	-16
19	Torpedo-Victoria Nizhniy Novgorod	42	11	10	21	47	67	43	-20
20	Lada-Simbirsk Dimitrovgrad	42	12	4	26	37	69	40	-32
21	Dinamo Stavropol	42	10	9	23	31	50	39	-19
22	Spartak-Orekhovo Orekhovo-Zuyevo	42	2	7	33	25	85	13	-60

CLUB DIRECTORIES

Anzhi Makhachkala
Zmirova str. 5
367 012 Makhachkala
tel - (8722) 678494
fax - (8722) 678520
Year of Formation - 1992
President - Khizri Shikhsaidov
Coach - Gadzhi Gadzhiev
Stadium - Trud (10,000)

Fakel Voronezh
Truda prospekt 28
394 061 Voronezh
tel - (0732) 166771/345645
fax - (0732) 166771
website - www.facel.vrn.ru
Year of Formation - 1954
President - Yuriy Batyshev
Secretary - Andrei Nikolshev
Coach - Valeriy Nenenko
Stadium - Centralnyi (30,000)

ALANIA VLADIKAVKAZ

CLUB DIRECTORY

Alania Vladikavkaz
Shmulevicha Str. 6
362 007 Vladikavkaz
tel - (8672) 758146/538548/530340
fax - (8672) 748806
website - www.fcalania.cjb.net
Year of Formation - 1921
General Manager - Batraz Bitarov
Secretary - Aleksandr Stelmakh
Coach - Valeriy Gazzayev
(2000 - Vladimir Gutsaev)
Stadium - Spartak (38,000)

MAJOR HONOURS
League Championship - (1) 1995.

APPEARANCES 1999

	P	Ap	(s)	Gls
Alan AGAYEV	D	14	(6)	
Ara AKOPYAN (ARM)	A		(4)	
Elio BATISTA (BRA)	M	10	(4)	1
Jambulat BAZAYEV	M	13	(9)	1
Aleksandr CHAIKA (BLS)	M	29		1
David CHICHVEISHVILI (GEO)	D	6	(1)	
Giorgi CHKHAIDZE (GEO)	D	4	(5)	
Giorgi DEMETRADZE (GEO)	A	28	(1)	21
Eduardo Moreira "EDU" (BRA)	A	13	(11)	4
Andrei FYODOROV (UZB)	D	13	(1)	1
JEFFERSON Alesandre Batista (BRA)	A	9	(2)	1
Anatoliy KANISCHEV	A	8	(3)	2
Mirdzhalol KASYMOV (UZB)	M	7	(4)	2
Zaur KHAPOV	G	23		
Oleg KORNIENKO	D	4	(6)	
Konstantin KOVALENKO	A	1	(2)	
German KUTARBA	D	16	(1)	3
Veniamin MANDRYKIN	G	7		
Artur PAGAYEV	D	12	(2)	
PAULO EMÍLIO Borges (BRA)	M	12	(12)	4
Alan SAKIEV	A		(1)	
Igor TARLOVSKIY (BLS)	D	16	(7)	4
Bakhva TEDEYEV	M	25		3
Zaur TEDEYEV	M		(1)	
Mamuka TSERETELI (GEO)	D	20		1
Darius ZUTAUTAS (LIT)	D	27	(1)	1
Raimondas ZUTAUTAS (LIT)	M	13		1

LEAGUE RESULTS 1999

03/04/99	Spartak Moskva	H	0-1	
11/04/99	CSKA Moskva	H	0-1	
17/04/99	Rotor Volgograd	A	2-0	Jefferson, Demetradze
25/04/99	Rostselmash Rostov-na-Donu	H	3-1	Tedeyev B., Kanischev 2
02/05/99	Torpedo Moskva	A	1-1	Tedeyev B.
09/05/99	Lokomotiv Nizhniy Novgorod	H	5-2	Demetradze 2 (1p), Fyodorov, Kutarba (p), Tsereteli
15/05/99	Saturn Ramenskoe	A	1-0	Edu
22/05/99	Zhemchuzhina Sochi	H	2-2	Paulo Emílio, Demetradze (p)
29/05/99	Lokomotiv Moskva	A	1-4	Zutautas R.
13/06/99	Dinamo Moskva	H	5-1	Tarlovskiy, Demetradze 2 (1p), Kutarba, Paulo Emílio
19/06/99	Krylya Sovetov Samara	A	3-0	Zutautas D., Demetradze (p), Tedeyev B.
23/06/99	Chernomorets Novorossiisk	A	0-1	
27/06/99	Uralan Elista	H	4-2	Demetradze 3 (2p), Kutarba
03/07/99	Shinnik Yaroslavl	A	1-1	Demetradze (p)
07/07/99	Zenit Sankt-Peterburg	H	2-2	Demetradze 2 (1p)
14/07/99	CSKA Moskva	A	1-4	Demetradze
21/07/99	Rotor Volgograd	H	3-0	(w/o)
04/08/99	Torpedo Moskva	H	6-1	Edu 2, Tarlovskiy, Bazayev, Demetradze 2 (1p)
14/08/99	Lokomotiv Nizhniy Novgorod	A	1-2	Demetradze
21/08/99	Saturn Ramenskoe	H	2-0	Edu, Demetradze
28/08/99	Zhemchuzhina Sochi	A	0-2	
11/09/99	Lokomotiv Moskva	H	0-2	
18/09/99	Dinamo Moskva	A	0-0	
25/09/99	Krylya Sovetov Samara	H	1-1	Paulo Emílio
28/09/99	Rostselmash Rostov-na-Donu	A	2-4	Batista, Chaika
02/10/99	Chernomorets Novorossiisk	H	3-1	Kasymov, Paulo Emílio, Demetradze
16/10/99	Uralan Elista	A	0-3	
23/10/99	Shinnik Yaroslavl	H	3-1	Demetradze 2, Tarlovskiy
30/10/99	Zenit Sankt-Peterburg	A	2-2	Tarlovskiy, Kasymov
08/11/99	Spartak Moskva	A	0-3	

CHERNOMORETS NOVOROSSIISK

CLUB DIRECTORY

Chernomorets Novorossiisk
Sovetov Str. 55
353 900 Novorossiisk
tel - (8617) 252191
fax - (8617) 254329
website - www.chat.ru/chernomorets
Year of Formation - 1960
President - Valeriy Prokhorenko
General Manager - Viktor Ivasyev
Coach - Sergei Butenko; Vladimir Fedotov
(2000 - Anatoliy Baidachnyi)
Stadium - Trud (13,500)

APPEARANCES 1999

	P	Ap	(s)	Gls
Eduard BAKAYEV	A	5	(6)	
Konstantin BELKOV	M	5	(2)	
Lev BEREZNER	M	16	(3)	2
Albert DOGUZOV	M	28		4
Eduard DYOMIN	D	17	(1)	1
Hans Eric EKUNGA (CMR)	M	7	(4)	1
Vyacheslav GERASHCHENKO (BLS)	M	17	(1)	4
Konstantin GORDIYUK (BLS)	D	14	(3)	2
Vladimir ISAKOV	D	10	(1)	
Konstantin KAMNEV (UKR)	A	24	(1)	5
Tokam Bruno KOAGNE (CMR)	M		(1)	
Eduard KURDYUMOV (KAZ)	M	3	(9)	
Aleksei KUTSENKO	A	12		3
Sergei LAPSHIN	M	3	(1)	
Oleg LEPIK	D		(2)	
Ivan LEVENETS	G	2		
Maxym LEVYTSKYI (UKR)	G	14		
Eduard MAMOTOV (UZB)	D	14	(3)	
Lev MAYOROV (AZB)	M	25	(3)	1
Anatoliy MOROZOV	M	25	(2)	
Andrei NIKOLAYEV	M		(5)	
Yevgeniy POLOVINA	A	1	(2)	
Denis POPOV	A	2	(11)	2
Stanislav RUDENKO	G	7		
Maxim SHEVCHENKO (KAZ)	M		(7)	
Andrei SHKURIN	D	4		
Aleksandr SHUTOV	A	11	(1)	
Badri SPANDERASHVILI (GEO)	M	22	(4)	2
Jerry Christian TCHUJSE (CMR)	D	5		
Igor USMINSKIY	G	7		
Anatoliy VANZHULA	M	5	(8)	
Vladimir ZAYARNYI (UKR)	D	12		3
Andrei ZHIROV	D	13		

LEAGUE RESULTS 1999

03/04/99	Shinnik Yaroslavl	A	0-1	
11/04/99	Saturn Ramenskoe	H	1-1	Dyomin
17/04/99	Zenit Sankt-Peterburg	A	1-1	Ekunga
25/04/99	Zhemchuzhina Sochi	H	3-0	Doguzov (p), Mayorov, Berezner
02/05/99	Spartak Moskva	A	0-2	
09/05/99	Lokomotiv Moskva	H	1-4	Gerashchenko
15/05/99	CSKA Moskva	A	2-5	Berezner, Gerashchenko
22/05/99	Dinamo Moskva	H	2-1	Kamnev, Doguzov
29/05/99	Rotor Volgograd	A	2-5	Doguzov 2 (2p)
13/06/99	Krylya Sovetov Samara	H	1-1	Kamnev
19/06/99	Rostselmash Rostov-na-Donu	A	0-1	
23/06/99	Alania Vladikavkaz	H	1-0	Spanderashvili
27/06/99	Torpedo Moskva	A	1-3	Gordiyuk
03/07/99	Uralan Elista	H	0-0	
07/07/99	Lokomotiv Nizhniy Novgorod	H	0-1	
14/07/99	Saturn Ramenskoe	A	0-3	
21/07/99	Zenit Sankt-Peterburg	H	1-0	Popov
28/07/99	Zhemchuzhina Sochi	A	0-2	
04/08/99	Spartak Moskva	H	1-1	Kamnev
15/08/99	Lokomotiv Moskva	A	1-2	Kamnev
21/08/99	CSKA Moskva	H	2-1	Kutsenko 2
28/08/99	Dinamo Moskva	A	1-0	Gerashchenko
11/09/99	Rotor Volgograd	H	1-1	Kutsenko
18/09/99	Krylya Sovetov Samara	A	1-1	Gordiyuk
25/09/99	Rostselmash Rostov-na-Donu	H	1-0	Zayarnyi (p)
02/10/99	Alania Vladikavkaz	A	1-3	Zayarnyi
16/10/99	Torpedo Moskva	H	1-2	Kamnev
23/10/99	Uralan Elista	A	1-3	Zayarnyi
30/10/99	Lokomotiv Nizhniy Novgorod	A	2-3	Gerashchenko, Popov
08/11/99	Shinnik Yaroslavl	H	1-1	Spanderashvili

CSKA MOSKVA

CLUB DIRECTORY

Centralnyi Sportivnyi Klub Armyi (CSKA) Moskva
Leningradskiy prospekt 39 A
125 167 Moskva
tel - (095) 2137329
fax - (095) 2132809
website - www.cska.ru
Year of Formation - 1923
President - Shakhridiy Dadakhanov
Secretary - Sergei Khorev
Coach - Oleg Dolmatov
Stadium - CSKA (10,000)

MAJOR HONOURS
League Championship (USSR) - (7)
1946, 1947, 1948, 1950, 1951, 1970, 1991.
Domestic Cup (USSR) - (5)
1945, 1948, 1951, 1955, 1991.

APPEARANCES 1999

	P	Ap	(s)	Gls
Magomed ADIEV (AZB)	A	1	(3)	
Igor AKSYONOV	D	9	(7)	
Maxim BOKOV	D	28		1
Aleksandr BORODKIN	M	4	(9)	
Sergei FILIPPENKOV	M	23	(6)	6
Dmitriy GONCHAROV	G	18		
Aleksandr GRISHIN	D	9	(3)	
Goran GUTALJ (BOS)	A	1	(1)	1
Marek HOLLY (SVK)	M	13	(1)	1
Dmitriy KHOMUKHA (TRK)	M	28	(2)	8
Oleg KORNAUKHOV	D	26		
Artyom KOVALENKO	M		(1)	
Andrei KRASNOPJOROV (EST)	M	1		
Vladimir KULIK	A	29	(1)	14
Aleksandr LEBEDEV	M		(1)	
Valeriy MINKO	D	28		1
Viktor NAVOCHENKO	M	6	(7)	
Maxim NIZOVTSEV	M	1	(1)	
Andrei NOVOSADOV	G	12		
Denis PERVUSHIN	D	1	(3)	
Ante PESIC (CRO)	D	2	(2)	
Sergei RODIN	A	1	(1)	
Aleksei SAVELYEV	M	10	(14)	2
Sergei SEMAK	M	29		12
Oleg SISCHIN (MOL)	M	13	(2)	3
Aleksandr SUCHKOV	A	1	(1)	
Andrei TSAPLIN	M	13	(12)	
Yevgeniy VARLAMOV	D	21		5
Denis YEVSIKOV	D	2	(1)	

LEAGUE RESULTS 1999

03/04/99	Krylya Sovetov Samara	H	1-1	Kulik
11/04/99	Alania Vladikavkaz	A	1-0	Khomukha (p)
17/04/99	Uralan Elista	H	2-0	Khomukha (p), Semak
25/04/99	Shinnik Yaroslavl	A	0-0	
02/05/99	Zenit Sankt-Peterburg	H	2-2	Kulik 2
09/05/99	Spartak Moskva	A	0-1	
15/05/99	Chernomorets Novorossiisk	H	5-2	Semak 3, Varlamov, Filippenkov
22/05/99	Rotor Volgograd	H	5-1	Varlamov 2, Semak, Filippenkov 2
29/05/99	Rostselmash Rostov-na-Donu	A	3-1	Varlamov, Minko, Semak
13/06/99	Torpedo Moskva	H	0-0	
19/06/99	Lokomotiv Nizhniy Novgorod	A	2-0	Khomukha, Savelyev
23/06/99	Saturn Ramenskoe	H	1-0	Filippenkov
27/06/99	Zhemchuzhina Sochi	A	2-2	Filippenkov, Savelyev
03/07/99	Lokomotiv Moskva	H	1-0	Sischin
07/07/99	Dinamo Moskva	A	0-1	
11/07/99	Zenit Sankt-Peterburg	A	1-1	Khomukha (p)
14/07/99	Alania Vladikavkaz	H	4-1	Kulik, Khomukha 2 (1p), Semak
18/07/99	Shinnik Yaroslavl	H	5-0	Khomukha, Gutalj, Kulik, Semak 2
21/07/99	Uralan Elista	A	1-1	Kulik
15/08/99	Spartak Moskva	H	0-4	
21/08/99	Chernomorets Novorossiisk	A	1-2	Khomukha (p)
28/08/99	Rotor Volgograd	A	1-1	Kulik
11/09/99	Rostselmash Rostov-na-Donu	H	2-0	Semak, Kulik
18/09/99	Torpedo Moskva	A	2-2	Varlamov, Semak
25/09/99	Lokomotiv Nizhniy Novgorod	H	3-1	Kulik 2, Sischin
02/10/99	Saturn Ramenskoe	A	3-2	Kulik, og (Lyapkin), Semak
16/10/99	Zhemchuzhina Sochi	H	3-0	Kulik 2, Filippenkov
24/10/99	Lokomotiv Moskva	A	0-1	
30/10/99	Dinamo Moskva	H	4-1	Sischin, Bokov, og (Golovskoi), Kulik
08/11/99	Krylya Sovetov Samara	A	1-1	Holly

DINAMO MOSKVA

CLUB DIRECTORY

Dinamo Moskva
Leningradskiy prospekt 36
125 167 Moskva
tel - (095) 2128432/2145463
fax - (095) 2138305
website - www.aha.ru/-turbopr/
Year of Formation - 1923
President - Nikolai Tolstykh
Secretary - Sergei Nikulin
Coach - Georgiy Yartsev; Aleksei Petrushin
(2000 - Valeriy Gazzayev)
Stadium - Dinamo (36,880)

MAJOR HONOURS
League Championship (USSR) - (11)
1936, 1937, 1940, 1945, 1949, 1954, 1955,
1957, 1959, 1963, 1976.
Domestic Cup - (1) 1995.
Domestic Cup (USSR) - (6)
1937, 1953, 1967, 1970, 1977, 1984.

APPEARANCES 1999

	P	Ap	(s)	Gls
Sergei ARTYOMOV	A		(1)	
Ansar AYUPOV	M	8		
Andrei BULATOV	D	13	(2)	
Konstantin GOLOVSKOI	M	24	(1)	7
Sergei GRISHIN	M	20	(4)	1
Rolan GUSEV	M	30		5
Lucky ISIBOR (NIG)	A	2	(10)	
Roman KAGAZEZHEV	A		(1)	
Denis KLYUYEV	M	27		3
Dmitriy KRAMARENKO (AZB)	G	9	(1)	
Aleksandr KULCHIY (BLS)	M	8	(8)	
Yuriy KUZNETSOV	M	1	(1)	
Aleksandr MAKAROV	A		(4)	
Andrei OSTROVSKIY (BLS)	D	24		1
Nikolai PISAREV	A	8	(8)	4
Yevgeniy PLOTNIKOV	G	20		
Aleksandr POPOVICI (MOL)	A		(1)	
Vladislav RADIMOV	M	22		2
Maxim ROMASHCHENKO (BLS)	A	17	(9)	5
Andrei SAMORUKOV	G	1		
Deyvidas SEMBERAS (LIT)	D	20	(4)	
Sergei SHTANYUK (BLS)	D	1	(1)	
Oleg TERYOKHIN	A	28		14
Aleksandr TOCHILIN	D	25	(1)	
Erik YAKHIMOVICH (BLS)	D	22	(1)	1

LEAGUE RESULTS 1999

03/04/99	Rotor Volgograd	A	2-1	Gusev, Teryokhin
11/04/99	Rostselmash Rostov-na-Donu	H	4-0	Romashchenko 2, Gusev, Pisarev
17/04/99	Torpedo Moskva	A	1-0	Teryokhin (p)
25/04/99	Lokomotiv Nizhniy Novgorod	H	2-1	og (Urbanek), Romashchenko
02/05/99	Saturn Ramenskoe	A	3-3	Golovskoi, Romashchenko 2
09/05/99	Zhemchuzhina Sochi	H	3-0	Radimov 2, Teryokhin
15/05/99	Lokomotiv Moskva	A	1-2	Ostrovskiy
22/05/99	Chernomorets Novorossiisk	A	1-2	Pisarev
29/05/99	Krylya Sovetov Samara	H	3-3	Pisarev, Teryokhin 2
13/06/99	Alania Vladikavkaz	A	1-5	Teryokhin
19/06/99	Uralan Elista	H	1-0	Teryokhin
23/06/99	Shinnik Yaroslavl	A	1-3	Gusev
27/06/99	Zenit Sankt-Peterburg	H	0-1	
03/07/99	Spartak Moskva	A	2-2	Golovskoi, Gusev
07/07/99	CSKA Moskva	H	1-0	Teryokhin
14/07/99	Rostselmash Rostov-na-Donu	A	3-1	Golovskoi 2, Teryokhin
21/07/99	Torpedo Moskva	H	1-1	Golovskoi
28/07/99	Lokomotiv Nizhniy Novgorod	A	3-1	Teryokhin, Grishin, Gusev
04/08/99	Saturn Ramenskoe	H	0-0	
14/08/99	Zhemchuzhina Sochi	A	0-1	
21/08/99	Lokomotiv Moskva	H	2-4	Teryokhin, Golovskoi (p)
28/08/99	Chernomorets Novorossiisk	H	0-1	
11/09/99	Krylya Sovetov Samara	A	2-1	Klyuyev, Yakhimovich
18/09/99	Alania Vladikavkaz	H	0-0	
25/09/99	Uralan Elista	A	0-1	
02/10/99	Shinnik Yaroslavl	H	3-1	Klyuyev, Teryokhin 2
16/10/99	Zenit Sankt-Peterburg	A	0-0	
23/10/99	Spartak Moskva	H	1-1	Golovskoi (p)
30/10/99	CSKA Moskva	A	1-4	Teryokhin
08/11/99	Rotor Volgograd	H	2-1	Klyuyev, Pisarev

KRYLYA SOVETOV SAMARA

CLUB DIRECTORY

Krylya Sovetov Samara
Shushenskaya Str. 50A
443 011 Samara
tel - (8462) 354778/355441
fax - (8462) 351633
Year of Formation - 1943
President - Aleksandr Morozov
Secretary - Anatoliy Bytkin
Coach - Aleksandr Tarkhanov
Stadium - Metallurg (38,800)

APPEARANCES 1999

		P	Ap	(s)	Gls
Vasile COSELEV (MOL)	G	13			
Aleksandr GERASIMOV	M	1		(1)	
David GVARAMADZE (GEO)	G	11		(1)	
Sergei IGNASHEVICH	D	6			1
Yevgeniy IVANOV	M	8		(1)	1
JORGINHO Rodrigues (BRA)	A	1		(4)	
Konstantin KAYNOV	M	11			4
Andrei KONOVALOV	A	8			
Sergei KULICHENKO	A			(1)	
Vasiliy KULKOV	D	5		(2)	
Serhiy LUSHCHAN (UZB)	D	24		(1)	2
Ramiz MAMEDOV	D	13		(1)	1
Karapet MIKAELYAN (ARM)	A	22		(5)	8
Sergei MITIN	M	3		(5)	
Artur MKRCHYAN (ARM)	D	8		(7)	
Aleksandr NIKULIN	M			(2)	
Tigran PETROSYAN (ARM)	M	19		(2)	2
Zurab POPKHADZE (GEO)	D	24		(1)	2
Vitaliy ROZGON	D			(1)	
Vitaliy SAFRONOV	A	17			5
Yuriy SAK (UKR)	D	28			
Sergei SHISHKIN	D	12		(2)	1
Serhiy SHMATOVALENKO (UKR)	D	6		(1)	
Vasiliy SLOBODKO	G	6			
Oleg SYOMIN	D	22		(4)	1
Dmitriy TETERIN	M	21		(5)	5
Zurab TSIKLAURI	A	13		(14)	5
Aleksandr TSYGANKOV	M	23		(1)	
Alexander VRHOVAC (SVK)	A			(6)	
Robert YEVDOKIMOV	M	5		(10)	

LEAGUE RESULTS 1999

03/04/99	CSKA Moskva	A	1-1	Tsiklauri
07/04/99	Spartak Moskva	A	0-3	
11/04/99	Rotor Volgograd	H	0-1	
17/04/99	Rostselmash Rostov-na-Donu	A	1-2	Safronov
25/04/99	Torpedo Moskva	H	1-2	Mikaelyan
02/05/99	Lokomotiv Nizhniy Novgorod	A	0-3	
09/05/99	Saturn Ramenskoe	H	2-0	Lushchan, Safronov (p)
15/05/99	Zhemchuzhina Sochi	A	2-0	Safronov, Teterin
22/05/99	Lokomotiv Moskva	H	1-2	Teterin
29/05/99	Dinamo Moskva	A	3-3	Teterin, Mamedov, Mikaelyan
13/06/99	Chernomorets Novorossiisk	A	1-1	Shishkin
19/06/99	Alania Vladikavkaz	H	0-3	
23/06/99	Uralan Elista	A	1-2	Safronov (p)
27/06/99	Shinnik Yaroslavl	H	4-2	Safronov (p), Popkhadze (p),
				Mikaelyan, Tsiklauri
03/07/99	Zenit Sankt-Peterburg	A	1-3	Petrosyan
07/07/99	Spartak Moskva	H	3-1	Mikaelyan, og (Bulatov),
				Tsiklauri
14/07/99	Rotor Volgograd	A	1-2	Lushchan
21/07/99	Rostselmash Rostov-na-Donu	H	0-0	
28/07/99	Torpedo Moskva	A	1-3	Popkhadze (p)
04/08/99	Lokomotiv Nizhniy Novgorod	H	3-0	Mikaelyan, Syomin, Ivanov
14/08/99	Saturn Ramenskoe	A	0-2	
21/08/99	Zhemchuzhina Sochi	H	4-2	Mikaelyan, Kaynov 2, Tsiklauri
28/08/99	Lokomotiv Moskva	A	0-2	
11/09/99	Dinamo Moskva	H	1-2	Petrosyan
18/09/99	Chernomorets Novorossiisk	H	1-1	Mikaelyan (p)
25/09/99	Alania Vladikavkaz	A	1-1	Ignashevich
02/10/99	Uralan Elista	H	0-1	
16/10/99	Shinnik Yaroslavl	A	2-1	Mikaelyan, Teterin
23/10/99	Zenit Sankt-Peterburg	H	3-2	Tsiklauri, Teterin, Kaynov
08/11/99	CSKA Moskva	H	1-1	Kaynov

LOKOMOTIV MOSKVA

CLUB DIRECTORY

Lokomotiv Moskva
B. Cherkizovskaya Str. 125A
107 553 Moskva
tel - (095) 1619704/1619090
fax - (095) 1619977
Year of Formation - 1936
President - Valeriy Filatov
Secretary - Vladimir Korotkov
Coach - Yuriy Syomin
Stadium - Lokomotiv (24,000)

MAJOR HONOURS
Domestic Cup - (3) 1996, 1997, 2000.
Domestic Cup (USSR) - (2) 1936, 1957.

APPEARANCES 1999

		P	Ap	(s)	Gls
Aleksei ARIFULLIN	D	13	(3)		
Aleksandr BORODYUK	A	1			
Dmitriy BULYKIN	A	13	(13)		8
Igor CHEREVCHENKO (TAD)	D	20			2
Igor CHUGAINOV	D	29			4
Yuriy DROZDOV	M	16	(5)		
Sergei GURENKO (BLS)	D	5	(1)		2
Sarkis HOVHANNISYAN (ARM)	D	15	(2)		2
Zaza JANASHIA (GEO)	A	19	(1)		6
Yevgeniy KHARLACHYOV	M	24	(3)		9
Andrei LAVRIK (BLS)	D	25	(1)		
Dmitriy LOSKOV	M	28			14
Vladimir MAMINOV	M	6	(15)		3
Sergei NERETIN	M		(3)		
Ruslan NIGMATULIN	G	29			
Oleg PASHININ	D	24	(1)		1
Ruslan PIMENOV	A	1	(3)		1
Aleksei POLYAKOV	G	1			
Nikolai RYNDYUK (BLS)	A		(4)		
Albert SARKISYAN (ARM)	M	24	(2)		4
Semyon SEMENENKO	D	2	(4)		
Aleksei SMERTIN	M	29			6
Andrei SOLOMATIN	D	6	(7)		

LEAGUE RESULTS 1999

03/04/99	Rostselmash Rostov-na-Donu	A	1-1	Kharlachyov
12/04/99	Torpedo Moskva	H	1-2	Gurenko
17/04/99	Lokomotiv Nizhniy Novgorod	A	0-0	
26/04/99	Saturn Ramenskoe	H	3-0	Chugainov, Bulykin 2
02/05/99	Zhemchuzhina Sochi	A	4-1	Gurenko, Sarkisyan 2, Hovhannisyan
09/05/99	Chernomorets Novorossiisk	A	4-1	Loskov 2, Kharlachyov, Bulykin
15/05/99	Dinamo Moskva	H	2-1	Kharlachyov, Smertin
22/05/99	Krylya Sovetov Samara	A	2-1	Janashia 2
29/05/99	Alania Vladikavkaz	H	4-1	Bulykin, Loskov, Sarkisyan, Chugainov
13/06/99	Uralan Elista	A	1-0	Loskov
19/06/99	Shinnik Yaroslavl	H	4-1	Loskov 2, Chugainov, Maminov
23/06/99	Zenit Sankt-Peterburg	A	2-1	Smertin, Bulykin
27/06/99	Spartak Moskva	H	0-3	
03/07/99	CSKA Moskva	A	0-1	
07/07/99	Rotor Volgograd	H	5-1	Loskov, Sarkisyan, Janashia, Pashinin, Bulykin
14/07/99	Torpedo Moskva	A	4-2	Loskov (p), Janashia, Hovhannisyan, Bulykin
21/07/99	Lokomotiv Nizhniy Novgorod	H	3-1	Smertin, Janashia 2
28/07/99	Saturn Ramenskoe	A	1-1	Kharlachyov
04/08/99	Zhemchuzhina Sochi	H	1-1	Kharlachyov
15/08/99	Chernomorets Novorossiisk	H	2-1	Loskov, Smertin
21/08/99	Dinamo Moskva	A	4-2	Smertin, Bulykin, Loskov 2
29/08/99	Krylya Sovetov Samara	H	2-0	Smertin, Kharlachyov
11/09/99	Alania Vladikavkaz	A	2-0	Kharlachyov, Loskov
19/09/99	Uralan Elista	H	1-0	Cherevchenko
25/09/99	Shinnik Yaroslavl	A	4-2	Kharlachyov 2, Loskov, Maminov
03/10/99	Zenit Sankt-Peterburg	H	1-1	Cherevchenko
16/10/99	Spartak Moskva	A	0-3	
24/10/99	CSKA Moskva	H	1-0	Chugainov
30/10/99	Rotor Volgograd	A	0-1	
08/11/99	Rostselmash Rostov-na-Donu	H	3-0	Loskov, Maminov, Pimenov

LOKOMOTIV NIZHNIY NOVGOROD

CLUB DIRECTORY

Lokomotiv Nizhniy Novgorod
Balaklavskiy per. 1
603 010 Nizhniy Novgorod
tel - (8312) 488053
fax - (8312) 422321
Year of Formation - 1987
President - Valeriy Ovchinnikov
Secretary - Nikolai Kozin
Coach - Valeriy Ovchinnikov
Stadium - Lokomotiv (20,400)

APPEARANCES 1999

	P	Ap	(s)	Gls
Arsen AVAKOV (TAD)	A	28		13
Pyotr BYSTROV	M	12	(6)	1
Anzor DZHAMIKOV	M	23	(4)	1
Oleg GARIN	A		(4)	
Aleksei GERASIMOV	M		(3)	
Gocha GOGRICHIANI (GEO)	A	7	(6)	3
Igor GORELOV	A	14	(1)	
Darius GVILDIS (LIT)	D	12	(2)	
Richard HÖGER (SVK)	M	6	(1)	1
Marek HOLLY (SVK)	M	15		2
Aleksandr ISAKOV (LAT)	M	10		
Nikolai KASHENTSEV	A	4	(9)	
Serhiy KRUKOVETS (UKR)	D	24	(1)	1
Dmitriy KUZNETSOV	D	25		4
Aleksandr LIPKO	D	8	(4)	1
Oleg MASLENNIKOV	G	4	(1)	
Gennadiy NIZHEGORODOV	D	19	(5)	
Artur PETROSYAN (ARM)	M	5	(1)	
Aleksandr SAYUN	M	5	(2)	
Valeriy SHANTALOSOV (BLS)	G	26		
Andrei TALALAYEV	A		(1)	
Vladimir TATARCHUK	M	14	(5)	1
Karel URBANEK (CZE)	D	18	(3)	
Dmitriy VLASOV	M	25	(1)	
Dmitriy VYAZMIKIN	M	26	(2)	5
Tamazi YENIK	M		(3)	

LEAGUE RESULTS 1999

03/04/99	Saturn Ramenskoe	H	0-1	
11/04/99	Zhemchuzhina Sochi	A	1-1	Avakov
17/04/99	Lokomotiv Moskva	H	0-0	
25/04/99	Dinamo Moskva	A	1-2	Avakov
02/05/99	Krylya Sovetov Samara	H	3-0	Dzhamikhov, Krukovets, Avakov
09/05/99	Alania Vladikavkaz	A	2-5	Höger, Holly
15/05/99	Uralan Elista	H	1-2	Kuznetsov (p)
22/05/99	Shinnik Yaroslavl	A	1-0	Holly
29/05/99	Zenit Sankt-Peterburg	H	1-0	Avakov
13/06/99	Spartak Moskva	A	2-2	Vyazmikin 2
19/06/99	CSKA Moskva	H	0-2	
23/06/99	Rotor Volgograd	A	3-2	Kuznetsov 2 (1p), Avakov
27/06/99	Rostselmash Rostov-na-Donu	H	0-0	
03/07/99	Torpedo Moskva	A	2-3	Vyazmikin, Bystrov
07/07/99	Lokomotiv Nizhniy Novgorod	A	1-0	Avakov
14/07/99	Zhemchuzhina Sochi	H	2-1	Avakov, Gogrichiani
21/07/99	Lokomotiv Moskva	A	1-3	Avakov
28/07/99	Dinamo Moskva	H	1-3	Avakov
04/08/99	Krylya Sovetov Samara	A	0-3	
14/08/99	Alania Vladikavkaz	H	2-1	Avakov, Lipko
21/08/99	Uralan Elista	A	0-3	
28/08/99	Shinnik Yaroslavl	H	1-0	Avakov
11/09/99	Zenit Sankt-Peterburg	A	0-1	
18/09/99	Spartak Moskva	H	2-4	Avakov, Vyazmikin
25/09/99	CSKA Moskva	A	1-3	Vyazmikin
02/10/99	Rotor Volgograd	H	1-1	Avakov
16/10/99	Rostselmash Rostov-na-Donu	A	0-1	
23/10/99	Torpedo Moskva	H	0-1	
30/10/99	Chernomorets Novorossiisk	H	3-2	Kuznetsov, Gogrichiani 2
08/11/99	Saturn Ramenskoe	A	1-1	Tatarchuk

ROSTSELMASH ROSTOV-NA-DONU

CLUB DIRECTORY

Rostselmash Rostov-na-Donu
Pervoi Konnoi Armii Str. 6A
344 077 Rostov-na-Donu
tel - (8632) 527947
fax - (8632) 519539
website - www.rsm.io.ru
Year of Formation - 1930
President - Viktor Usachyov
General Manager - Vasiliy Maznev
Coach - Sergei Andreyev
Stadium - Rostselmash (15,600)

APPEARANCES 1999

	P	Ap	(s)	Gls
Igor BAKHTIN	M	2	(5)	
Anatoliy BESSMERTNYI (UKR)	D	24	(1)	1
Yuriy BOROVSKOI	D	15	(8)	2
Aslan DATDEYEV	M	5	(1)	
Vladislav DUYUN (UKR)	M	19	(7)	3
Yuriy DYADYUK	M	6	(4)	
Aleksei GUSCHIN	D	28		
Igor KHANKEYEV	M	26	(3)	5
Dmitriy KIRICHENKO	A	22	(6)	6
Sergei KOLOTOVKIN	D	28	(1)	1
Vladimir KOMAROV	M		(1)	
Mikhail KUPRIYANOV	D	23	(5)	2
Igor KUTEPOV (UKR)	G	12		
Sergei MASLOV	A	1	(7)	
Volodymyr MATSYGURA (UKR)	D	16	(10)	2
Yuriy MATVEYEV	A	23	(3)	2
Oleg PESTRYAKOV (UKR)	M	26	(4)	7
Vladislav PRUDIUS (UKR)	M	16	(9)	
Anton ROGOCHIY	D		(2)	
Oleg SANKO	M	5	(3)	
Vladimir SAVCHENKO (UKR)	G	18		
Valentin SLYUSAR (UKR)	M		(1)	
Gennadiy STYOPUSHKIN	D	15	(4)	
Bohdan YESYP (UKR)	M		(1)	

LEAGUE RESULTS 1999

03/04/99	Lokomotiv Moskva	H	1-1	Kirichenko
11/04/99	Dinamo Moskva	A	0-4	
17/04/99	Krylya Sovetov Samara	H	2-1	Matveyev, Pestryakov
25/04/99	Alania Vladikavkaz	A	1-3	og (Zutautas)
02/05/99	Uralan Elista	H	2-0	Kolotovkin, Bessmertnyi
09/05/99	Shinnik Yaroslavl	A	3-0	Kirichenko, Pestryakov 2
15/05/99	Zenit Sankt-Peterburg	H	2-1	Khankeyev 2
22/05/99	Spartak Moskva	A	0-1	
29/05/99	CSKA Moskva	H	1-3	Khankeyev
13/06/99	Rotor Volgograd	A	1-0	Duyun
19/06/99	Chernomorets Novorossiisk	H	1-0	Matveyev
23/06/99	Torpedo Moskva	H	0-0	
27/06/99	Lokomotiv Nizhniy Novgorod	A	0-0	
30/06/99	Saturn Ramenskoe	H	4-1	Khankeyev (p), Pestryakov 2, Matsygura
07/07/99	Zhemchuzhina Sochi	A	1-1	Matsygura
14/07/99	Dinamo Moskva	H	1-3	Kupriyanov
21/07/99	Krylya Sovetov Samara	A	0-0	
14/08/99	Shinnik Yaroslavl	H	0-0	
21/08/99	Zenit Sankt-Peterburg	A	0-1	
24/08/99	Uralan Elista	A	1-2	Borovskoi
29/08/99	Spartak Moskva	H	0-3	
11/09/99	CSKA Moskva	A	0-2	
18/09/99	Rotor Volgograd	H	1-1	Duyun
25/09/99	Chernomorets Novorossiisk	A	0-1	
28/09/99	Alania Vladikavkaz	H	4-2	Pestryakov 2, Kirichenko 2
02/10/99	Torpedo Moskva	A	2-1	Borovskoi, Kirichenko
16/10/99	Lokomotiv Nizhniy Novgorod	H	1-0	Kirichenko
23/10/99	Saturn Ramenskoe	A	1-1	Duyun
30/10/99	Zhemchuzhina Sochi	H	2-1	Kupriyanov, Khankeyev
08/11/99	Lokomotiv Moskva	A	0-3	

ROTOR VOLGOGRAD

CLUB DIRECTORY

Rotor Volgograd
Prospekt Lenina 76
400 005 Volgograd
tel - (8442) 340053
fax - (8442) 341507
website - www.rotor-volgograd.ru
Year of Formation - 1933
President - Vladimir Goryunov
Secretary - Rokhus Shokh
Coach - Viktor Prokopenko
(2000 - Georgiy Yartsev)
Stadium - Centralnyi (40,000)

APPEARANCES 1999

	P	Ap	(s)	Gls
Vitaliy ABRAMOV	M	18	(6)	3
Aleksandr BERKETOV	M	27	(1)	
Maxim BONDARENKO	M		(1)	
Iliya BORODIN	A	2	(7)	
Albert BORZENKOV	D	23	(3)	1
Andrei CHICHKIN	G	10		
Andrei DUROV	D	1		
Sergei KOPNIN	D	6	(10)	
Andrei KRIVOV	M	12	(4)	1
Denis MATIOLA	D	13	(1)	
Mikhail MYSIN	M		(3)	
Vladimir NIDERGAUS	A	7	(2)	
Nikolai OLENIKOV	D	23	(6)	1
Mikhail OSINOV	M	27	(1)	3
Aleksandr SHMARKO	D	23		
Vladimir SMIRNOV	M	22	(7)	
Maxim TISCHCHENKO (UKR)	M	9	(10)	3
Oleg VERETENNIKOV	M	30		12
Valeriy YESIPOV	M	18	(3)	6
Platon ZAKHARCHUK (UKR)	G	20		
Aleksandr ZERNOV	A	9	(2)	
Denis ZUBKO	A	30		6

LEAGUE RESULTS 1999

03/04/99	Dinamo Moskva	H	1-2	Veretennikov
11/04/99	Krylya Sovetov Samara	A	1-0	Yesipov
17/04/99	Alania Vladikavkaz	H	0-2	
25/04/99	Uralan Elista	A	1-0	Abramov
02/05/99	Shinnik Yaroslavl	H	2-0	Veretennikov 2 (1p)
09/05/99	Zenit Sankt-Peterburg	A	1-1	Veretennikov
15/05/99	Spartak Moskva	H	3-3	Veretennikov, Zubko, Abramov
22/05/99	CSKA Moskva	A	1-5	Yesipov
29/05/99	Chernomorets Novorossiisk	H	5-2	Veretennikov, Zubko, Yesipov, Tishchenko 2 (1p)
13/06/99	Rostselmash Rostov-na-Donu	H	0-1	
19/06/99	Torpedo Moskva	A	1-2	Veretennikov
23/06/99	Lokomotiv Nizhniy Novgorod	H	2-3	Veretennikov, Osinov
27/06/99	Saturn Ramenskoe	A	0-1	
03/07/99	Zhemchuzhina Sochi	H	0-0	
07/07/99	Lokomotiv Moskva	A	1-5	Zubko
11/07/99	Spartak Moskva	A	1-4	Zubko
14/07/99	Krylya Sovetov Samara	H	2-1	Veretennikov, Borzenkov
21/07/99	Alania Vladikavkaz	A	0-3	(w/o)
28/07/99	Uralan Elista	H	3-1	Osinov (p), Yesipov, Zubko
04/08/99	Shinnik Yaroslavl	A	0-2	
14/08/99	Zenit Sankt-Peterburg	H	2-2	Krivov, Osinov (p)
28/08/99	CSKA Moskva	H	1-1	Veretennikov
11/09/99	Chernomorets Novorossiisk	A	1-1	Veretennikov
18/09/99	Rostselmash Rostov-na-Donu	A	1-1	Olenikov
25/09/99	Torpedo Moskva	H	0-2	
02/10/99	Lokomotiv Nizhniy Novgorod	A	1-1	Tishchenko
16/10/99	Saturn Ramenskoe	H	1-1	Veretennikov
23/10/99	Zhemchuzhina Sochi	A	2-2	Yesipov 2
30/10/99	Lokomotiv Moskva	H	1-0	Zubko
08/11/99	Dinamo Moskva	A	1-2	Abramov

SATURN RAMENSKOE

CLUB DIRECTORY

Saturn Ramenskoe
Gorodskoi park
Moskovskaya obl.
140103 Ramenskoe,
tel - (246) 34474/31216
fax - (246) 34474
website - www.saturn-fc.ru
Year of Formation - 1958
President - Nikolai Burlinov
Secretary - Sergei Tryapkin
Coach - Sergei Pavlov
Stadium - Saturn (9,000)

APPEARANCES 1999

	P	Ap	(s)	Gls
Andrei AFANASEV	D	23	(2)	
Vladimir BAKSHEEV	M	4	(3)	
Maxim BUZNIKIN	A	11	(2)	3
Dmitriy CHESNOKOV	A	3	(11)	
Valeriy CHIZHOV	G	13		
Igor GAVRILIN	A	19	(9)	7
Aleksandr GRYAZIN	M	21	(2)	3
Iliya KAZAKOV	G	2	(1)	
Vladimir KURAEV	D	23	(2)	
Dmitriy LYAPKIN	D	16	(1)	
Aleksei MEDVEDEV	M	8	(18)	6
Igor MENSHCHIKOV	M	26	(2)	4
Aleksei MOROZOV	M	8	(1)	
Oleg MOROZOV	D	27		
Sergei NATALUSHKO	A	8		3
Andrei SAMORUKOV	G	15		
Dmitriy SHIRSHAKOV	D	11	(4)	
Yevgeniy SMERTIN	D	27	(1)	
Oleg SOLOVYOV	M	15	(12)	2
Adrian SOSNOVSCHI (MOL)	D	14	(1)	1
Dmitriy VARFOLOMEYEV	A	15	(3)	1
Sergei VARFOLOMEYEV	M		(1)	
Aleksandr ZHIDKOV	M	21	(5)	

LEAGUE RESULTS 1999

03/04/99	Lokomotiv Nizhniy Novgorod	A	1-0	Gavrilin
11/04/99	Chernomorets Novorossiisk	A	1-1	Medvedev
17/04/99	Zhemchuzhina Sochi	H	3-0	Natalushko 3
26/04/99	Lokomotiv Moskva	A	0-3	
02/05/99	Dinamo Moskva	H	3-3	Gavrilin, Menshchikov, Medvedev
05/05/99	Spartak Moskva	A	1-3	Medvedev
09/05/99	Krylya Sovetov Samara	A	0-2	
15/05/99	Alania Vladikavkaz	H	0-1	
22/05/99	Uralan Elista	A	0-2	
29/05/99	Shinnik Yaroslavl	H	0-0	
13/06/99	Zenit Sankt-Peterburg	A	1-2	Gavrilin
19/06/99	Spartak Moskva	H	0-3	
23/06/99	CSKA Moskva	A	0-1	
27/06/99	Rotor Volgograd	H	1-0	Gavrilin
30/06/99	Rostselmash Rostov-na-Donu	A	1-4	Gryazin
07/07/99	Torpedo Moskva	H	2-2	Menshchikov, Buznikin
14/07/99	Chernomorets Novorossiisk	H	3-0	Gryazin, Sosnovschi, Medvedev
21/07/99	Zhemchuzhina Sochi	A	0-2	
28/07/99	Lokomotiv Moskva	H	1-1	Buznikin
04/08/99	Dinamo Moskva	A	0-0	
14/08/99	Krylya Sovetov Samara	H	2-0	Gryazin, Menshchikov (p)
21/08/99	Alania Vladikavkaz	A	0-2	
28/08/99	Uralan Elista	H	2-0	Solovyov, Gavrilin
11/09/99	Shinnik Yaroslavl	A	0-0	
19/09/99	Zenit Sankt-Peterburg	H	1-0	Solovyov
02/10/99	CSKA Moskva	H	2-3	Menshchikov, Medvedev
16/10/99	Rotor Volgograd	A	1-1	Varfolomeyev D.
23/10/99	Rostselmash Rostov-na-Donu	H	1-1	Gavrilin
30/10/99	Torpedo Moskva	A	2-0	Gavrilin, Buznikin
08/11/99	Lokomotiv Nizhniy Novgorod	H	1-1	Medvedev

SHINNIK YAROSLAVL

CLUB DIRECTORY

Shinnik Yaroslavl
Ploschad Truda
Stadion Shinnik
150 040 Yaroslavl
tel - (0852) 720626/720576
fax - (0852) 720626
Year of Formation - 1957
President - Valeriy Frolov
Coach - Aleksandr Averyanov; Benjaminas
Zelkevicius; Aleksandr Pobegalov;
Aleksandr Averyanov
Stadium - Shinnik (24,000)

APPEARANCES 1999

	P	Ap	(s)	Gls
Garnik AVALYAN (ARM)	A	7	(3)	
Aleksei BOBROV	M	11	(1)	
Dmitriy BORISOV	M		(1)	
Aleksei BYCHKOV	A	28	(1)	7
Vasiliy CHERNITSYN	G	1	(1)	
Andrei GALIYANOV	M	4	(9)	
Aleksandr GUTEYEV	G	23		
Valery IVANOV (LAT)	D	21		1
Yevgeniy KALESHIN	M	5	(4)	
Aleksei KAZALOV	M	26	(1)	
Dmitriy KLABUKOV	D	1	(3)	
Valeriy KLEIMYONOV	G	6		
Nikolai KOVARDAYEV	A	8	(8)	2
Sergei LEBEDEV (UZB)	M	2	(1)	
Valentin LOBANYOV (LAT)	D	22	(1)	2
Mohamed Anas MAKHLUF (SYR)	A		(4)	
Marat MAKHMUTOV	D	28		
Damian MILITARU (ROM)	M	6		
Mukhsin MUKHAMADIYEV	A	10	(1)	1
Andrei NOVGORODOV	D	24		1
Andrei REZANTSEV	D	17	(2)	
Albert SCHERBAKOV	D	11	(4)	
Dmitriy SKOBLYAKOV	M	1	(7)	
Serhiy SNYTKO (UKR)	M	25		2
Vladislav TERNAVSKIY	D	2		
Fyodor TUVIN	M	7	(8)	1
Artyom YENIN	A	30		4
Dmitriy ZHDANOV	M	4	(7)	
Aleksandr ZINOVIEV	M		(1)	

LEAGUE RESULTS 1999

03/04/99	Chernomorets Novorossiisk	H	1-0	Kovardayev
11/04/99	Zenit Sankt-Peterburg	H	0-0	
17/04/99	Spartak Moskva	A	1-4	Bychkov
25/04/99	CSKA Moskva	H	0-0	
02/05/99	Rotor Volgograd	A	0-2	
09/05/99	Rostselmash Rostov-na-Donu	H	0-3	
15/05/99	Torpedo Moskva	A	0-0	
22/05/99	Lokomotiv Nizhniy Novgorod	H	0-1	
29/05/99	Saturn Ramenskoe	A	0-0	
13/06/99	Zhemchuzhina Sochi	H	0-0	
19/06/99	Lokomotiv Moskva	A	1-4	Bychkov
23/06/99	Dinamo Moskva	H	3-1	Yenin, Lobanyov, Bychkov
27/06/99	Krylya Sovetov Samara	A	2-4	Lobanyov, Bychkov
03/07/99	Alania Vladikavkaz	H	1-1	Novgorodov (p)
07/07/99	Uralan Elista	A	0-1	
14/07/99	Zenit Sankt-Peterburg	A	1-2	Snytko
18/07/99	CSKA Moskva	A	0-5	
21/07/99	Spartak Moskva	H	1-2	Bychkov
04/08/99	Rotor Volgograd	H	2-0	Bychkov, Yenin
14/08/99	Rostselmash Rostov-na-Donu	A	0-0	
21/08/99	Torpedo Moskva	H	1-0	Bychkov
28/08/99	Lokomotiv Nizhniy Novgorod	A	0-1	
11/09/99	Saturn Ramenskoe	H	0-0	
18/09/99	Zhemchuzhina Sochi	A	0-1	
25/09/99	Lokomotiv Moskva	H	2-4	Ivanov, Mukhamadiyev
02/10/99	Dinamo Moskva	A	1-3	Snytko
16/10/99	Krylya Sovetov Samara	H	1-2	Yenin
23/10/99	Alania Vladikavkaz	A	1-3	Kovardayev
30/10/99	Uralan Elista	H	1-0	Yenin
08/11/99	Chernomorets Novorossiisk	A	1-1	Tuvin

SPARTAK MOSKVA

CLUB DIRECTORY

Spartak Moskva
1-st Koptelskiy per. 18 str. 2
129 010 Moskva
tel - (095) 2088736/2088749
fax - (095) 9752385
website - www.spartak.com
Year of Formation - 1922
President - Oleg Romantsev
General Manager - Yuriy Zavarzin
Secretary - Valeriy Zilyayev
Coach - Oleg Romantsev
Stadium - Luzhniki (84,745)

MAJOR HONOURS
League Championship - (7)
1992, 1993, 1994, 1996, 1997, 1998, 1999.
League Championship (USSR) - (12)
1936, 1938, 1939, 1952, 1953, 1956, 1958,
1962, 1969, 1979, 1987, 1989.
Domestic Cup - (2) 1994, 1998.
Domestic Cup (USSR) - (10) 1938, 1939, 1946,
1947, 1950, 1958, 1963, 1965, 1971, 1992.

APPEARANCES 1999

	P	Ap	(s)	Gls
Dmitriy ANANKO	D	7		
Vasiliy BARANOV (BLS)	M	18	(6)	4
Artyom BEZRODNYI	M	8	(11)	5
Viktor BULATOV	M	28	(1)	3
Yevgeniy BUSHMANOV	D	8	(1)	
Maxim BUZNIKIN	A		(6)	1
EVERTON Penice Romuald (BRA)	M		(2)	
Aleksandr FILIMONOV	G	28		
Anatoliy KANISCHEV	A		(1)	
Valeriy KECHINOV	M	20	(6)	4
Dmitriy KHLESTOV	D	27		1
Yuriy KOVTUN	D	26		2
Aleksei MELYOSHIN	M	1	(1)	
Eduard MOR (UKR)	D	22	(1)	
Dmitriy PARFYONOV (UKR)	D	12	(5)	
Luís ROBSON Pereira (BRA)	A	12	(8)	7
Aleksandr SHIRKO	A	26	(1)	9
Andrei SMETANIN	G	2	(3)	
Andrei TIKHONOV	M	29		19
Yegor TITOV	M	29		12
Iliya TSYMBALAR	M	7	(4)	2
Vadim YEVSEYEV	D	4	(7)	1
Sergei YURAN	A	16	(2)	3
Aleksei ZLYDNEV	M		(2)	

LEAGUE RESULTS 1999

03/04/99	Alania Vladikavkaz	A	1-0	Tikhonov
07/04/99	Krylya Sovetov Samara	H	3-0	Bezrodnyi 2, Tikhonov
11/04/99	Uralan Elista	A	1-0	Baranov
17/04/99	Shinnik Yaroslavl	H	4-1	Tikhonov (p), Kechinov, Yuran, Shirko
21/04/99	Torpedo Moskva	H	0-1	
25/04/99	Zenit Sankt-Peterburg	A	2-1	Tikhonov 2
02/05/99	Chernomorets Novorossiisk	H	2-0	Titov, Kechinov
05/05/99	Saturn Ramenskoe	H	3-1	Bezrodnyi, Tikhonov (p), Buznikin
09/05/99	CSKA Moskva	H	1-0	Shirko
15/05/99	Rotor Volgograd	A	3-3	Shirko 2, Tikhonov (p)
22/05/99	Rostselmash Rostov-na-Donu	H	1-0	Shirko
29/05/99	Torpedo Moskva	A	0-0	
13/06/99	Lokomotiv Nizhniy Novgorod	H	2-2	Yuran, Bulatov
19/06/99	Saturn Ramenskoe	A	3-0	Titov 2, Tikhonov
23/06/99	Zhemchuzhina Sochi	H	4-0	Tikhonov, Baranov, Yuran, Kechinov
27/06/99	Lokomotiv Moskva	A	3-0	Tikhonov, Tsymbalar, og (Cherevchenko)
03/07/99	Dinamo Moskva	H	2-2	Tikhonov, Yevseyev
07/07/99	Krylya Sovetov Samara	A	1-3	Tikhonov (p)
11/07/99	Rotor Volgograd	H	4-1	og (Berketov), Tikhonov 2, Titov
14/07/99	Uralan Elista	H	3-0	Bulatov, Kovtun, Titov
21/07/99	Shinnik Yaroslavl	A	2-1	Khlestov, Tikhonov
28/07/99	Zenit Sankt-Peterburg	H	4-1	Bulatov, Tikhonov (p), Shirko, Titov
04/08/99	Chernomorets Novorossiisk	A	1-1	Shirko
15/08/99	CSKA Moskva	A	4-0	Baranov, Titov, Bezrodnyi 2
29/08/99	Rostselmash Rostov-na-Donu	A	3-0	Robson 2, Titov
18/09/99	Lokomotiv Nizhniy Novgorod	A	4-2	Robson, Titov 2, Tsymbalar
03/10/99	Zhemchuzhina Sochi	A	7-3	Shirko 2, Robson 3, Tikhonov, Titov
16/10/99	Lokomotiv Moskva	H	3-0	Tikhonov, Kovtun, Robson
23/10/99	Dinamo Moskva	A	1-1	Titov
08/11/99	Alania Vladikavkaz	H	3-0	Tikhonov, Kechinov, Baranov

TORPEDO MOSKVA

CLUB DIRECTORY

Torpedo Moskva
Luzhnetskaya Naberezhnaya 24
119 048 Moskva
tel - (095) 2011310/2011238
fax - (095) 2460105
Year of Formation - 1924
President - Pavel Borodin
Secretary - Yuriy Mishin
Coach - Vitaliy Shevchenko
Stadium - Luzhniki (84,745)

MAJOR HONOURS
League Championship (USSR) - (3)
1960, 1965, 1976.
Domestic Cup - (1) 1993.
Domestic Cup (USSR) - (6)
1949, 1952, 1960, 1968, 1972, 1986.

APPEARANCES 1999

	P	Ap	(s)	Gls
Aleksandr AVERIYANOV	M	1	(15)	
Sergei BURCHENKOV	M	3	(8)	
Vyacheslav DAYEV	D	30		5
Mihai DRAGUS (ROM)	A	6	(9)	1
Yevgeniy DURNEV	A	19		5
Andrei GASHKIN	M	24	(1)	1
Aleksandr IGNATIEV	M	8	(4)	
Vyacheslav KAMOLTSEV	A	23	(7)	12
Vladimir KAZAKOV	M	26		
Yevgeniy KORNYUKHIN	G	22		
Vladimir LEONCHENKO	M	5	(8)	
Vitaliy LITVINOV	D	19	(2)	2
Aleksandr LUKHVICH (BLS)	D	28		2
Andrei MALAI	D	28		
Radislav ORLOVSKIY (BLS)	D	28	(2)	1
Andrei PANFYOROV	D	1	(1)	
Andrei SAPUGA (UKR)	D	9	(6)	
Igor SEMSHOV	M	18	(10)	3
Pavlo SHKAPENKO (UKR)	M	13	(3)	4
Serhiy SIMONENKO (UKR)	M		(4)	1
Serhiy SKACHENKO (UKR)	A	11	(1)	1
Valeriy VOROBYOV (UKR)	G	8		

LEAGUE RESULTS 1999

03/04/99	Zhemchuzhina Sochi	H	1-0	Kamoltsev
11/04/99	Lokomotiv Moskva	A	2-1	Semshov, Lukhvich
17/04/99	Dinamo Moskva	H	0-1	
21/04/99	Spartak Moskva	A	1-0	Durnev (p)
25/04/99	Krylya Sovetov Samara	A	2-1	Dayev 2
02/05/99	Alania Vladikavkaz	H	1-1	Skachenko
09/05/99	Uralan Elista	A	1-1	Orlovskiy
15/05/99	Shinnik Yaroslavl	H	0-0	
22/05/99	Zenit Sankt-Peterburg	A	0-0	
29/05/99	Spartak Moskva	H	0-0	
13/06/99	CSKA Moskva	A	0-0	
19/06/99	Rotor Volgograd	H	2-1	Kamoltsev 2
23/06/99	Rostselmash Rostov-na-Donu	A	0-0	
27/06/99	Chernomorets Novorossiisk	H	3-1	Kamoltsev 2, Lukhvich
03/07/99	Lokomotiv Nizhniy Novgorod	H	3-2	Semshov, Dayev, Durnev
07/07/99	Saturn Ramenskoe	A	2-2	Dayev, Durnev
14/07/99	Lokomotiv Moskva	H	2-4	Durnev, Dayev
21/07/99	Dinamo Moskva	A	1-1	Shkapenko
28/07/99	Krylya Sovetov Samara	H	3-1	Kamoltsev, Litvinov, Durnev
04/08/99	Alania Vladikavkaz	A	1-6	Kamoltsev
14/08/99	Uralan Elista	H	3-1	Kamoltsev, Shkapenko 2 (1p)
21/08/99	Shinnik Yaroslavl	A	0-1	
28/08/99	Zenit Sankt-Peterburg	H	1-0	Litvinov
18/09/99	CSKA Moskva	H	2-2	Kamoltsev, Gashkin
25/09/99	Rotor Volgograd	A	2-0	Kamoltsev, Semshov
02/10/99	Rostselmash Rostov-na-Donu	H	1-2	Shkapenko (p)
16/10/99	Chernomorets Novorossiisk	A	2-1	Dragus, Kamoltsev
23/10/99	Lokomotiv Nizhniy Novgorod	A	1-0	Kamoltsev
30/10/99	Saturn Ramenskoe	H	0-2	
08/11/99	Zhemchuzhina Sochi	A	1-1	Simonenko

URALAN ELISTA

CLUB DIRECTORY

Uralan Elista
Lenina str. 218
358004 Elista
tel - (84722) 20946/20920
fax - (84722) 20920
website - www.uralan.ru
Year of Formation - 1958
President - Nikolai Shovgurov
Secretary - Valeriy Zuvakov
Coach - Pavel Yakovenko; Yevgeniy Skrinnikov;
Yevgeniy Kucherevskyi; Aleksandr Averyanov
Stadium - Uralan (10,000)

APPEARANCES 1999

	P	Ap	(s)	Gls
Yuriy AKSYONOV	M	11	(1)	1
Dmitriy ALEKSEEV	G	23		
Garnik AVALYAN (ARM)	A	13	(1)	4
Vidas DANCENKA (LIT)	A	19	(6)	2
Oleg GARIN	A	8	(3)	1
Dmitriy IVANOV	A	21	(1)	3
JEFFERSON Alesandre Batista (BRA)	A	1		1
Aleksei KOZLOV	D	28		
Igor LAGOIDA (UKR)	M	7	(16)	
Mikhail LUNIN	M	1		
Taras LUTSENKO (UKR)	G	7		
Vitalie MAEVICI (MOL)	D	5		
Saulius MIKALAJUNAS (LIT)	M	28		6
Yevgeniy OVSHINOV	M		(1)	
Radu REBEJA (MOL)	D	21	(4)	
Aleksandr SAYUN (UZB)	D	4	(2)	
Sergei SHISHKIN	D	7	(2)	
Pavlo SHKAPENKO (UKR)	A		(1)	
Yuriy SHUKANOV (BLS)	A	23	(3)	1
Oleg TERESCHENKO	D	24	(3)	
Akhrik TSVEIBA	D	19	(1)	1
Dmitriy TUTICHENKO (UKR)	M	23	(2)	2
Vyacheslav VISHNEVSKIY	A	3	(12)	2
Artur VOSKANYAN (ARM)	M	12	(6)	2
Vasiliy YABLONSKIY	M		(9)	
Sergei YEGOROV (KAZ)	M	5	(8)	
Mikhail ZHARINOV	D	17	(2)	

LEAGUE RESULTS 1999

03/04/99	Zenit Sankt-Peterburg	A	0-2	
11/04/99	Spartak Moskva	H	0-1	
17/04/99	CSKA Moskva	A	0-2	
25/04/99	Rotor Volgograd	H	0-1	
02/05/99	Rostselmash Rostov-na-Donu	A	0-2	
09/05/99	Torpedo Moskva	H	1-1	Mikalajunas
15/05/99	Lokomotiv Nizhniy Novgorod	A	2-1	Ivanov, Vishnevskiy
22/05/99	Saturn Ramenskoe	H	2-0	og (Afanasyev), Aksyonov
29/05/99	Zhemchuzhina Sochi	A	0-0	
13/06/99	Lokomotiv Moskva	H	0-1	
19/06/99	Dinamo Moskva	A	0-1	
23/06/99	Krylya Sovetov Samara	H	2-1	Dancenka, Ivanov (p)
27/06/99	Alania Vladikavkaz	A	2-4	Tsveiba, Voskanyan
03/07/99	Chernomorets Novorossiisk	A	0-0	
07/07/99	Shinnik Yaroslavl	H	1-0	Vishnevskiy
14/07/99	Spartak Moskva	A	0-3	
21/07/99	CSKA Moskva	H	1-1	Jefferson
28/07/99	Rotor Volgograd	A	1-3	Avalyan
14/08/99	Torpedo Moskva	A	1-3	Mikalajunas
21/08/99	Lokomotiv Nizhniy Novgorod	H	3-0	Mikalajunas 2, Avalyan
24/08/99	Rostselmash Rostov-na-Donu	H	2-1	Ivanov, Mikalajunas
28/08/99	Saturn Ramenskoe	A	0-2	
11/09/99	Zhemchuzhina Sochi	H	1-1	Shukanov
19/09/99	Lokomotiv Moskva	A	0-1	
25/09/99	Dinamo Moskva	H	1-0	Dancenka
02/10/99	Krylya Sovetov Samara	A	1-0	Voskanyan
16/10/99	Alania Vladikavkaz	H	3-0	Avalyan, Tutichenko, Mikalajunas
23/10/99	Chernomorets Novorossiisk	H	3-1	Tutichenko, Avalyan, Garin
30/10/99	Shinnik Yaroslavl	A	0-1	
08/11/99	Zenit Sankt-Peterburg	H	0-0	

ZENIT SANKT-PETERBURG

CLUB DIRECTORY

Zenit Sankt-Peterburg
Nekrasova Str. 3/5
191 104 Sankt Peterburg
tel - (812) 2750330
fax - (812) 2750333
www.fc-zenit.ru
Year of Formation - 1931
President - Vitaliy Mutko
Secretary - Vyacheslav Melnikov
Coach - Anatoliy Davydov
Stadium - Petrovskiy (20,000)

MAJOR HONOURS
League Championship (USSR) - (1) 1984.
Domestic Cup - (1) 1999.
Domestic Cup (USSR) - (1) 1944.

APPEARANCES 1999

	P	Ap	(s)	Gls
Aleksandr BABIY (UKR)	D	18	(4)	4
Roman BEREZOVSKI (ARM)	G	23		
Aleksandr CURTIANU (MOL)	M	5	(10)	4
Dmitriy DAVYDOV	D	19		
Sergei GERASIMETS (BLS)	A		(4)	
Boris GOROVOI (BLS)	A	4	(5)	
Aleksandr GORSHKOV	M	28	(1)	3
Sarkis HOVSEPYAN (ARM)	D	28		2
Aleksei IGONIN	D	17	(1)	
Andrei KOBELEV	M	20	(4)	1
Andrei KONDRASHOV	D	16	(2)	
Konstantin LEPYOKHIN	D	26	(1)	1
Roman MAKSIMYUK (UKR)	M	16	(3)	2
Vyacheslav MALAFEYEV	G	7	(1)	
Sergei OSIPOV	M	1	(17)	1
Aleksandr PANOV	A	26	(3)	5
Aleksandr PETUKHOV	A	3	(12)	4
Gennadiy POPOVICH (UKR)	A	23	(4)	7
Denis UGAROV	M	16	(7)	
Yuriy VERNIDUB (UKR)	D	28		1
Igor ZAZULIN	M	6	(7)	1

LEAGUE RESULTS 1999

Date	Opponent	H/A	Score	Scorers
03/04/99	Uralan Elista	H	2-0	Osipov, Gorshkov
11/04/99	Shinnik Yaroslavl	A	0-0	
17/04/99	Chernomorets Novorossiisk	H	1-1	Popovich
25/04/99	Spartak Moskva	H	1-2	Vernidub
02/05/99	CSKA Moskva	A	2-2	Panov, Popovich
09/05/99	Rotor Volgograd	H	1-1	Zazulin
15/05/99	Rostselmash Rostov-na-Donu	A	1-2	Panov
22/05/99	Torpedo Moskva	H	0-0	
29/05/99	Lokomotiv Nizhniy Novgorod	A	0-1	
13/06/99	Saturn Ramenskoe	H	2-1	Popovich, Babiy
19/06/99	Zhemchuzhina Sochi	A	3-1	Gorshkov 2, Babiy
23/06/99	Lokomotiv Moskva	H	1-2	Babiy (p)
27/06/99	Dinamo Moskva	A	1-0	Popovich
03/07/99	Krylya Sovetov Samara	H	3-1	Curtianu, Popovich, Babiy (p)
07/07/99	Alania Vladikavkaz	A	2-2	Maximyuk, Kobelev
11/07/99	CSKA Moskva	H	1-1	Panov
14/07/99	Shinnik Yaroslavl	H	2-1	Maximyuk, Petukhov
21/07/99	Chernomorets Novorossiisk	A	0-1	
28/09/99	Spartak Moskva	A	1-4	Panov
14/08/99	Rotor Volgograd	A	2-2	Panov, Lepyokhin
21/08/99	Rostselmash Rostov-na-Donu	H	1-0	Curtianu
28/08/99	Torpedo Moskva	A	0-1	
11/09/99	Lokomotiv Nizhniy Novgorod	H	1-0	Popovich
19/09/99	Saturn Ramenskoe	A	0-1	
25/09/99	Zhemchuzhina Sochi	H	3-1	Petukhov 2, Hovsepyan
03/10/99	Lokomotiv Moskva	A	1-1	Petukhov
16/10/99	Dinamo Moskva	H	0-0	
23/10/99	Krylya Sovetov Samara	A	2-3	Hovsepyan, Curtianu
30/10/99	Alania Vladikavkaz	H	2-2	Curtianu, Popovich
08/11/99	Uralan Elista	A	0-0	

ZHEMCHUZHINA SOCHI

CLUB DIRECTORY

Zhemchuzhina Sochi
Vinogradnaya Str. 43
354 008 Sochi
tel - (8622) 933398/933392
fax - (8622) 933398
Year of Formation - 1990
President - Nikolai Karpov
General Manager - Karp Nachariyan
Secretary - Vram Kakosiyan
Coach - Anatoliy Baidachnyi; Gennadiy Afanasyev;
Viktor Antichovich
Stadium - Centralnyi (12,500)

APPEARANCES 1999

	P	Ap	(s)	Gls
Stanislav BONDAREV	M	25	(2)	1
Gennadiy BONDARUK	D	23		1
Maxim DEMENKO	D	17		5
Konstantin DYMARCHUK (UKR)	D		(3)	
Giorgi GOGIASHVILI (GEO)	M	8	(1)	
Gocha GOGRICHIANI (GEO)	A	5	(5)	2
Dmitriy GRADILENKO	D	8		
Gizo JELADZE (GEO)	M	5	(7)	
Manuk KAKOSYAN (ARM)	A	23	(6)	1
Artashes KALAIDZHYAN (ARM)	M	18	(6)	3
Lyubomir KANTONISTOV	M	9	(14)	
Pyotr KHRUSTOVSKIY	A	12	(2)	3
Konstantin KOVALENKO (BLS)	M	14	(1)	5
Artur KUZNETSOV	M	6	(4)	
Leonid LAZARIDI	D		(1)	
Konstantin LEDOVSKIKH	G	11	(2)	
Rustam MUSTAFIN	D	16		1
Anatoliy OPREA (UKR)	D	7	(3)	
Eduard PARTSIKYAN	M	6	(5)	
Vadim SOKOLOV	M	27		1
Ruslan SUANOV	A	10	(11)	1
Tengiz TARBA	M	10	(2)	
Gennadiy TUMILOVICH (BLS)	G	19		
Aleksandr YESHCHENKO	D	13		2
Eduard ZATSEPIN	A	15	(10)	3
Vladimir ZHURAVEL (BLS)	D	23		

LEAGUE RESULTS 1999

03/04/99	Torpedo Moskva	A	0-1	
11/04/99	Lokomotiv Nizhniy Novgorod	H	1-1	Gogrichiani
17/04/99	Saturn Ramenskoe	A	0-3	
25/04/99	Chernomorets Novorossiisk	A	0-3	
02/05/99	Lokomotiv Moskva	H	1-4	Yeshchenko (p)
09/05/99	Dinamo Moskva	A	0-3	
15/05/99	Krylya Sovetov Samara	H	0-2	
22/05/99	Alania Vladikavkaz	A	2-2	Suanov, Kalaidzhyan
29/05/99	Uralan Elista	H	0-0	
13/06/99	Shinnik Yaroslavl	A	0-0	
19/06/99	Zenit Sankt-Peterburg	H	1-3	Yeshchenko (p)
23/06/99	Spartak Moskva	A	0-4	
27/06/99	CSKA Moskva	H	2-2	Kalaidzhyan, Gogrichiani
03/07/99	Rotor Volgograd	A	0-0	
07/07/99	Rostselmash Rostov-na-Donu	H	1-1	Zatsepin
14/07/99	Lokomotiv Nizhniy Novgorod	A	1-2	Kovalenko
21/07/99	Saturn Ramenskoe	H	2-0	Zatsepin, Kovalenko
28/07/99	Chernomorets Novorossiisk	H	2-0	Kakosyan, Kovalenko
04/08/99	Lokomotiv Moskva	A	1-1	Demenko
14/08/99	Dinamo Moskva	H	1-0	Kovalenko
21/08/99	Krylya Sovetov Samara	A	2-4	Sokolov, Demenko
28/08/99	Alania Vladikavkaz	H	2-0	Kovalenko, Bondaruk
11/09/99	Uralan Elista	A	1-1	Bondarev
18/09/99	Shinnik Yaroslavl	H	1-0	Demenko
25/09/99	Zenit Sankt-Peterburg	A	1-3	Kalaidzhyan
03/10/99	Spartak Moskva	H	3-7	Demenko, Zatsepin, Mustafin
16/10/99	CSKA Moskva	A	0-3	
23/10/99	Rotor Volgograd	H	2-2	Demenko, Khrustovskiy
30/10/99	Rostselmash Rostov-na-Donu	A	1-2	Khrustovskiy
08/11/99	Torpedo Moskva	H	1-1	Khrustovskiy

SAN MARINO

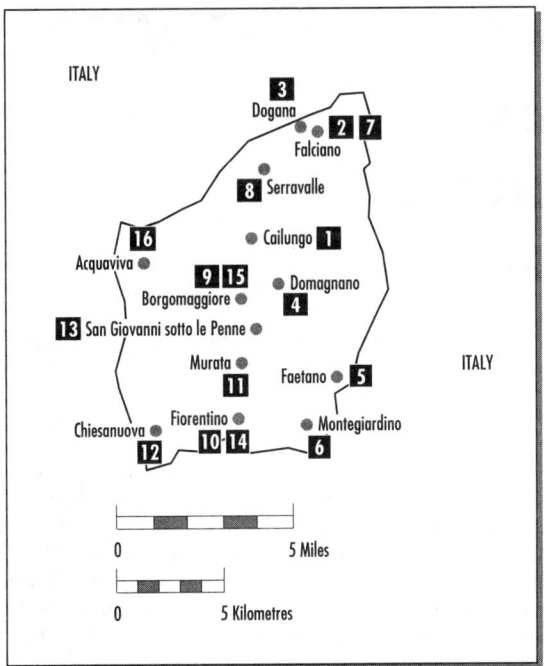

1	CAILUNGO	863	9	LIBERTAS	871
2	COSMOS	864	10	MONTEVITO	872
3	DOGANA	865	11	MURATA	873
4	DOMAGNANO	866	12	PENNAROSSA	874
5	FAETANO	867	13	SAN GIOVANNI	875
6	FIORITA	868	14	TRE FIORI	876
7	FOLGORE	869	15	TRE PENNE	877
8	JUVENES	870	16	VIRTUS	878

NO WINS IN 50 FOR NATIONAL TEAM

Europe beckons first-timers Folgore

FEDERATION DIRECTORY

Federazione Sammarinese Giuoco Calcio
Via Campo dei Giudei 14, 47031 Rep. San Marino

tel - 990515 Year of Formation - 1931
fax - 992348 President - Giorgio Crescentini
  Secretary - Luciano Casadei

Stadium - Olimpico, Serravalle (5,000)

Being proclaimed the champions of San Marino meant more than ever before in 1999/2000. For the first time the country decided to join the other 50 UEFA-affiliated nations and apply for inclusion in the European club competitions.

Like Andorra, San Marino were only entitled to one place to start with - and that was in the UEFA Cup rather than the Champions' League. It was predominantly the lure of some extra revenue that persuaded the San Marino FA to alter their stance and allow their teams to participate, but from a purely sporting perspective, the European carrot certainly added a touch of additional intrigue to the race for the title.

Ultimately San Marino had a worthy first European entrant in Folgore, the team which had won the championship in 1997 and 1998 only to be denied a hat-trick in the 1999 play-off final by Faetano. In 2000 they were back at the top of the tree, completing their third triumph in four years with a 3-1 victory over Domagnano in the championship final, played before a crowd of around 1,150 in the Serravalle stadium.

It was Folgore's third successive league win over Domagnano. They had beaten them 4-1 during the 'regular season' and 3-1 in the fourth round of the play-offs. It was a fitting final as both teams had finished on top of their respective first-phase groups, advancing with Cailungo, Virtus, Tre Fiori and Libertas.

Tre Penne were nowhere in the league but they came on very strong in the end-of-season Coppa Titano, a competition made even more complicated by a new set

LEAGUE CHAMPIONSHIP RESULTS 99/00

GROUP A		1	2	3	4	5	6	7	8	9	10	11	12	13	14	15	16
1	Cailungo		1-0	5-0	0-1	3-1	1-1	4-2	0-3		2-1	1-0	2-1				2-2
2	Cosmos	0-0		4-0	4-2	4-0	0-0	4-0	0-2	0-0		0-0		0-0			1-2
3	Fiorita	1-0	1-6		2-3	0-2	1-2	0-1	1-4				0-1		2-3	0-3	1-1
4	Folgore	0-1	0-0	2-1		5-0	7-0	7-1	1-0			3-3			2-1	1-0	3-1
5	Juvenes	0-3	1-1	2-3	1-3		1-1	2-5	0-4	3-0	0-8			2-3	1-1		
6	Pennarossa	1-2	0-4	1-0	2-1	2-1		3-1	2-2			0-1		1-3	2-0	2-0	
7	Tre Penne	2-6	3-5	2-2	1-1	3-3	4-3		2-5	3-1	1-3		2-0	2-1			
8	Virtus	1-3	0-1	1-1	2-1	4-0	1-2	3-2		0-0	2-1		2-2			2-0	
GROUP B		9	10	11	12	13	14	15	16	1	2	3	4	5	6	7	8
9	Dogana		0-2	1-1	1-2	1-0	1-3	1-0	3-2	0-1		1-1	1-2	2-1			
10	Domagnano	1-2		3-2	1-1	5-0	2-1	4-1	2-2	1-1	1-0	1-4		2-2			
11	Faetano	3-1	1-1		1-2	3-1	0-2	0-0	2-1			4-0		3-0		1-0	1-2
12	Libertas	0-1	1-1	2-1		1-2	4-3	3-1	0-1		0-2	0-1	3-2	2-0			
13	Montevito	2-1	0-6	0-0	2-3		2-3	0-1	0-4	0-0		1-0	2-3				0-2
14	Murata	4-1	2-6	1-2	1-1	3-6		3-2	2-3	3-1	1-1					1-0	3-3
15	San Giovanni	0-0	1-5	0-0	1-3	3-0	1-4		2-2	1-2	0-2			2-2	0-2		
16	Tre Fiori	1-1	1-2	4-1	6-3	4-2	6-3	6-2						0-0	3-2	3-0	1-2

of rules which enabled Domagnano to reach the third phase after a 6-1 defeat and then ultimately pay for it when Folgore went through to the final instead of them despite an inferior goal difference. Tre Penne denied Folgore the 'double' by beating them 3-1 after extra-time. Their Cup-clinching goal was scored by Davide Gualtieri, the international striker who scored San Marino's most famous goal, against England in a World Cup qualifier.

The San Marino national team played just two games during the season, losing them both. Wallopped 8-0 by Israel in their final Euro 2000 qualifier, Gian Paolo Mazza's side then warmed up for the World Cup campaign with a 0-1 home defeat against Moldova. That was San Marino's 50th international, and the team's record since their first match, against Canada in March 1986, does not make happy reading: no wins, two draws, 48 defeats, six goals for, 215 against.

Things can only get better... or is that being a touch optimistic?

INTERNATIONAL HONOURS

None

LEAGUE CHAMPIONSHIP FINAL TABLES 99/00

GROUP A

		Pd		Home					Away					Total				
		Pd	W	D	L	F	A	W	D	L	F	A	W	D	L	F	A	Pt	GD
1	Folgore	22	8	2	1	31	8	7	1	3	22	16	15	3	4	53	24	48	29
2	Cailungo	22	7	2	2	21	12	7	2	2	19	9	14	4	4	40	21	46	19
3	Virtus	22	5	3	3	18	13	8	2	1	29	11	13	5	4	47	24	44	23
4	Cosmos	22	4	5	2	17	6	6	4	1	23	8	10	9	3	40	14	39	26
5	Pennarossa	22	6	1	4	16	15	2	4	5	14	24	8	5	9	30	39	29	-9
6	Tre Penne	22	4	3	4	25	30	3	0	8	14	28	7	3	12	39	58	24	-19
7	Juvenes	22	1	3	7	13	32	1	3	7	11	29	2	6	14	24	61	12	-37
8	Fiorita	22	1	1	9	9	26	1	3	7	8	24	2	4	16	17	50	10	-33

GROUP B

		Pd		Home					Away					Total				
		Pd	W	D	L	F	A	W	D	L	F	A	W	D	L	F	A	Pt	GD
1	Domagnano	22	5	4	2	23	16	7	2	2	36	11	12	6	4	59	27	42	32
2	Tre Fiori	22	7	2	2	35	18	4	4	3	21	18	11	6	5	56	36	39	20
3	Libertas	22	5	1	5	16	15	5	3	3	19	19	10	4	8	35	34	34	1
4	Faetano	22	6	2	3	19	10	2	5	4	11	15	8	7	7	30	25	31	5
5	Murata	22	4	3	4	24	26	5	1	5	24	23	9	4	9	48	49	31	-1
6	Dogana	22	4	2	5	12	15	2	4	5	8	17	6	6	10	20	32	24	-12
7	Montevito	22	2	2	7	9	23	4	1	6	18	25	6	3	13	27	48	21	-21
8	San Giovanni	22	1	4	6	11	22	2	1	8	10	22	3	5	14	21	44	14	-23

N.B. The top three teams in each group play off for the title.

CHAMPIONSHIP PLAY-OFFS
FIRST ROUND
Tre Fiori 3, Virtus 1
Cailungo 3, Libertas 0

SECOND ROUND
Domagnano 0, Cailugo 0 (aet; 5-4 on pens.)
Folgore 0, Tre Fiori 0 (aet; 5-3 on pens.)

THIRD ROUND
Virtus 3, Cailungo 3 (aet; 4-2 on pens.)
Tre Fiori 2, Libertas 1 (aet)
(Cailungo and Libertas eliminated)

FOURTH ROUND
Folgore 3, Domagnano 1
Virtus 2, Tre Fiori 1
(Tre Fiori eliminated)

SEMI-FINAL
Domagnano 1, Virtus 0
(Virtus eliminated)

FINAL
05/05/2000, Serravalle
FOLGORE 3 Della Torre (7), Zanotti (53, 90)
DOMAGNANO 1 Zucchi (18)

DOMESTIC CUP 99/00

FIRST ROUND
GROUP A
Cosmos 2, Dogana 2
Tre Penne 2, Virtus 1
Cosmos 5, Libertas 0
San Giovanni 0, Domagnano 2
Cosmos 2, Fiorita 0
San Giovanni 1, Cailungo 6

Tre Penne 3, San Giovanni 1
Montevito 1, Cosmos 6
Tre Penne 6, Montevito 1
Cosmos 1, San Giovanni 0
Cosmos 2, Tre Penne 1
Montevito 4, San Giovanni 1
(Cosmos and Tre Penne qualify)

GROUP B
Fiorita 2, Libertas 0
Folgore 2, Montevito 1
Fiorita 2, Dogana 3
Cailungo 1, Faetano 3
Folgore 0, Tre Fiori 0
Virtus 3, Juvenes 1

Folgore 0, Cailungo 0
Virtus 0, Fiorita 0
Virtus 1, Folgore 1
Fiorita 0, Cailungo 1
Folgore 5, Fiorita 0
Virtus 2, Cailungo 1
(Folgore, Virtus and Cailungo qualify)

GROUP C
Domagnano 0, Cailungo 0
Tre Fiori 3, Murata 5
Juvenes 0, Tre Penne 4
Tre Fiori 4, Montevito 3
Domagnano 1, Faetano 0
Libertas 2, Dogana 2

Juvenes 1, Domagnano 3
Libertas 1, Tre Fiori 2
Libertas 1, Domagnano 1
Tre Fiori 7, Juvenes 0
Libertas 6, Juvenes 2
Domagnano 1, Tre Fiori 1
(Domagnano and Tre Fiori qualify)

GROUP D
Faetano 6, San Giovanni 1
Pennarossa 3, Juvenes 3
Murata 0, Folgore 3
Pennarossa 1, Virtus 2
Pennarossa 2, Tre Penne 2
Murata 3, Montevito 0

Pennarossa 4, Dogana 0
Faetano 4, Murata 0
Murata 1, Pennarossa 3
Faetano 4, Dogana 2
Faetano 1, Pennarossa 0
Murata 3, Dogana 2
(Faetano, Murata and Pennarossa qualify)

SECOND ROUND
Folgore 3, Murata 2
Tre Fiori 4, Cailungo 1
Faetano 6, Domagnano 1
Cosmos 7, Pennarossa 2
Tre Penne 4, Virtus 2

N.B. Domagnano qualify as losing team with best first-round record

THIRD ROUND
GROUP A
Tre Penne 2, Tre Fiori 0
Cosmos 4, Tre Fiori 1
Tre Penne 2, Cosmos 0
(Tre Penne qualify)

GROUP B
Domagnano 3, Folgore 3
Folgore 2, Faetano 1
Domagnano 4, Faetano 2
(Folgore qualify)

FINAL
28/06/2000, Serravalle
TRE PENNE 3 Gobbi (30), Cecchi (93), Gualtieri (118)
FOLGORE 1 Giovagnoli (54)
(aet)

NATIONAL TEAM APPEARANCES 99/00

Coach - Gian Paolo MAZZA	ISR	MOL	Cps	Gls
Federico GASPERONI (10/09/76) - CBR Pietracuta (ITA)	G	G	15	-
Marco TOMASSONI (22/02/80) - Villa Verucchio (ITA)	D		1	-
Mirco GENNARI (29/03/66) - Almas Ponte Rimini (ITA)/Juvenes (ITA)	D	D	34	-
Simone BACCIOCCHI (22/01/77) - Torre Pedrera (ITA)	D72	s79	6	-
Fabrizio PELLICCIONI (13/10/76) - Folgore	D		1	-
Simone DELLA BALDA (02/12/72) - Tre Penne/Olimpia Macerata Feltria (ITA)	M	D	5	-
Bryan GASPERONI (26/09/74) - CBR Pietracuta (ITA)	M	M79	14	-
Ermanno ZONZINI (01/04/74) - San Giovanni Marignano (ITA)/Juvenes (ITA)	M	M	6	-
Nicola BACIOCCHI (16/12/71) - Domagnano	M57	s86	32	1
Paolo MONTAGNA (28/05/76) - Juvenes (ITA)	A80	A72	20	-
Andy SELVA (23/05/76) - Catanzaro (ITA)/Tivoli (ITA)	A	A	7	1
Roberto SELVA (02/01/81) - San Marino (ITA)	s57		2	-
Pier Domenico DELLA VALLE (04/05/70) - Rivazzurra (ITA)	s72		19	1
Marco DE LUIGI (21/03/78) - CBR Pietracuta (ITA)	s80	s65	2	-
Mauro MARANI (09/03/75) - Juvenes (ITA)		D	7	-
Ivan MATTEONI (21/08/70) - CBR Pietracuta (ITA)		D	29	-
Pier Angelo MANZAROLI (25/03/69) - Pennarossa		M86	32	-
Luciano MULARONI (31/08/71) - CBR Pietracuta (ITA)		M65	5	-
Cristian SELVA (05/07/77) - Juvenes (ITA)		s72	1	-

TOP SCORERS

17 Gian Carlo CARNEVALI (Libertas)
16 Andrea FIORE (Tre Fiori)
   Khalid ZABOUL (Tre Fiori)
15 Paride RENZI (Virtus)
14 Marco GASPERI (Domagnano)
   Andrea PIERINI (Domagnano)
13 Andrea TOSI (Cailungo)
   Matteo MAZZA (Folgore)

NATIONAL TEAM RESULTS 99/00

08/09/99	Israel (ECQ)	A	Tel-Aviv	0-8
26/04/00	Moldova	H	Serravalle	0-1

CAILUNGO

CLUB DIRECTORY

Società Polisportiva Cailungo
Via cà del Lunghi 11
47031 Cailungo
tel - 902413
Year of Formation - 1974
President - Paolo Rondelli
Secretary - Daniele Forcellini
Coach - Gilberto Rossi
Stadium - Fonte dell' Ovo (500)

APPEARANCES 99/00

	P	Ap	(s)	Gls
Claudio BIANCHI	M		(1)	
Gianluca BOLLINI	M	19		
Massimo BOLLINI	D		(1)	
Sebastiano BOLLINI	M		(2)	
Michael BRUSCHI	A	2	(2)	
Filippo CASADEI	D		(1)	
Fabrizio CENNI	D		(3)	
Mirko CONTI	M	5	(3)	
Rossano CONTI	D	3	(2)	
Stefano DE LUIGI	A	15		9
John ERCOLANI	D	20		
Daniele FORCELLINI	D	2		
Marino GASPERONI	G	1	(1)	
Gianluca GERLONI (ITA)	M	18		2
Claudio GUERRA	G	21		
Riccardo MAESTRINI (ITA)	D	1	(4)	
Marco MORRI (ITA)	D	13	(3)	
Davide PELLANDRA	M		(3)	
Thomas ROMANI (ITA)	M	17		5
Luca RONDELLI	D		(5)	
Daniele ROSSI (ITA)	D	20		
Davide SCHIARATURA	A	20		7
Gilberto SERRA	D		(4)	
Giovanni STEFANELLI	D	5	(3)	
Paolo SUCCI	M	20		
Serafino TERENZI	A		(2)	
Adriano TOSI (ITA)	D	20		3
Andrea TOSI (ITA)	A	20		13
Gabriele VENTURINI	M		(3)	

LEAGUE RESULTS 1999/2000

11/09/99	Folgore	H	0-1	
18/09/99	Cosmos	A	0-0	
23/09/99	Juvenes	A	3-0	Tosi Ad., De Luigi 2
02/10/99	Virtus	H	0-3	
09/10/99	Pennarossa	H	1-1	De Luigi
16/10/99	Fiorita	A	0-1	
23/10/99	Tre Penne	A	6-2	Tosi An. (p), De Luigi, Schiaratura 3, Tosi Ad.
30/10/99	Tre Fiori	H	2-2	og (Matteoni M.), De Luigi
06/11/99	Montevito	A	0-0	
13/11/99	San Giovanni	A	2-1	Tosi An. 2
20/11/99	Libertas	H	2-1	Tosi Ad., Romani
27/11/99	Dogana	A	1-0	Schiaratura
04/12/99	Domagnano	H	2-1	Tosi An., Romani
11/12/99	Faetano	H	1-0	Gerloni
19/02/00	Murata	A	1-3	Tosi An.
26/02/00	Folgore	A	1-0	Romani
04/03/00	Cosmos	H	1-0	Schiaratura
11/03/00	Juvenes	H	3-1	Tosi An. 2 (1p), Romani
18/03/00	Virtus	A	3-1	Schiaratura, Tosi An., De Luigi
25/03/00	Pennarossa	A	2-1	Schiaratura, Romani
28/03/00	Fiorita	H	5-0	Gerloni, Tosi An. 3, De Luigi
01/04/00	Fiorita	H	4-2	Tosi An. 2, De Luigi 2

COSMOS

CLUB DIRECTORY

Società Polisportiva Cosmos
Strada del Bargello 36
47031 Falciano
tel - 996392
Year of Formation - 1979
President - Adelmiro Bartolini
Secretary - Stefano Bevitori
Coach - Bruno Albani
Stadium - Falciano (500)

MAJOR HONOURS
League Championship - (2) 1980, 1981.
Domestic Cup - (2) 1995, 1999.

APPEARANCES 99/00

	P	Ap	(s)	Gls
Fabrizio ALBANI	M	4	(4)	
Matteo ALBANI	D	13	(1)	1
Marco BENEDETTINI	M	21		10
Daniele BERTI	A	15	(2)	2
Alessandro BEVITORI	M	9	(4)	
Stefano BORGHINI (ITA)	M	1	(6)	
Agostino BUCCI	M	2	(2)	
Maurizio CECCOLI	D	1	(8)	
Emanuel CELLI	D	15	(1)	
Marco CONTI	D	4	(5)	1
Daniele DONATI	G	4		
Francesco DONINI (ITA)	M	2	(3)	
Adriano FORCELLINI	A	1	(6)	1
Agostino LEARDINI	D	14		
Mirco MANZAROLI	M	12	(2)	4
Luca NANNI	A	17		
Waldes PASOLINI	D	17		6
Giampiero PASQUALI	D		(4)	
Giovanni PODAVINI (ITA)	D	3	(1)	
Marco PROTTI (ITA)	A	7	(3)	4
Giulio RICCI (ITA)	G	18		
Jonny ROSSI	M	17		
Dario SARTORI (ARG)	A	13	(1)	6
Cristian SENSOLI (ITA)	M	22		2
Silvano ZONZINI	M	10	(4)	2

LEAGUE RESULTS 1999/2000

Date	Opponent	H/A	Score	Scorers
11/09/99	Juvenes	A	1-1	Pasolini (p)
18/09/99	Cailungo	H	0-0	
25/09/99	Pennarossa	A	4-0	Protti, Benedettini, Zonzini, Forcellini
02/10/99	Fiorita	H	4-0	Manzaroli, Benedettini 2, Albani M.
09/10/99	Tre Penne	H	4-0	Benedettini 2, Zonzini, Protti
16/10/99	Folgore	H	4-2	Protti, Benedettini 3 (2p)
23/10/99	Virtus	A	1-0	Pasolini
30/10/99	Montevito	H	0-0	
06/11/99	Dogana	H	0-0	
13/11/99	Tre Fiori	H	1-2	Pasolini
20/11/99	San Giovanni	A	2-0	Pasolini, Sartori
27/11/99	Faetano	H	0-0	
04/12/99	Murata	A	1-1	Protti
11/12/99	Libertas	A	2-0	Sartori 2
19/02/00	Domagnano	A	1-1	Pasolini
26/02/00	Juvenes	H	4-0	og (Tamagnini), Manzaroli 2, Berti
04/03/00	Cailungo	A	0-1	
11/03/00	Pennarossa	H	0-0	
18/03/00	Fiorita	A	6-1	Sartori 2, Benedettini 2, Manzaroli, Sensoli
25/03/00	Tre Penne	A	5-3	Pasolini, Sartori, Sensoli, Berti, Conti
28/03/00	Folgore	A	0-0	
01/04/00	Virtus	H	0-2	

DOGANA

Gruppo Sportiva Dogana
CP 21, 47031 Dogana
tel - 905156
Year of Formation - 1970
President - Massimo Morri
Secretary - Raul Bianchi
Coach - Flavio Varchetta
Stadium - Dogana (500)

MAJOR HONOURS
League Championship - (2) 1977, 1979.

APPEARANCES 99/00

	P	Ap	(s)	Gls
Claudio BABBONI	D	15	(2)	
Cristian BAGLI	A	8		2
Natalino BERNARDI	D	1	(4)	
Thomas BERTI	M	14	(3)	2
Roberto BORASCO (ITA)	D	21		1
Gian Luca CELLI	A	6	(3)	2
Gian Carlo FALCONE	A	12	(3)	
Daniele FIACCONI	M	16	(2)	
FOSCHI	G	13		
Loriano FRISONI	M	10	(4)	
Leonardo GASPERONI	D	2	(3)	
Michele GIACOBBI	D	17	(1)	
Cristian GIARDI	D	15		2
Andrea GUALANDI	D	2	(2)	
Gabriele LOTTI	M	16	(2)	1
Federico MAZZA	D		(4)	
Francesco MAZZA	M		(3)	
Leonardo MUCCIOLI	M	6	(3)	
Davide PARI	G	8		
Alessandro PROTTI	M	3	(4)	
Roberto RASCHI	A		(2)	
Marco RENZI (ITA)	M	1	(4)	
ROSONI	G	1		
Alessandro ROSSI	M	14	(1)	
Danilo ROSSI (ITA)	D		(3)	
Francesco SELVA	M		(1)	
Nicola SELVA	A	3	(2)	
Massimo VAGNETTI	D	18		
Flavio VARCHETTA (ITA)	A	20		9

LEAGUE RESULTS 1999/2000

11/09/99	Montevito	A	1-2	Varchetta
18/09/99	Tre Fiori	H	3-2	Varchetta, og (Matteoni I.), Lotti
25/09/99	Murata	A	1-4	Bagli
02/10/99	Faetano	H	1-1	Celli
09/10/99	Domagnano	A	2-1	Varchetta (p), Borasco
16/10/99	San Giovanni	H	1-0	Celli
23/10/99	Libertas	H	1-2	Varchetta
30/10/99	Juvenes	A	0-3	
06/11/99	Cosmos	A	0-0	
13/11/99	Tre Penne	A	1-3	Varchetta
20/11/99	Pennarossa	H	2-1	Giardi, Varchetta
27/11/99	Cailungo	H	0-1	
04/12/99	Virtus	A	0-0	
11/12/99	Fiorita	H	1-1	Giardi
19/02/00	Folgore	H	1-2	Varchetta (p)
26/02/00	Montevito	H	1-0	Berti
04/03/00	Tre Fiori	A	1-1	Bagli (p)
11/03/00	Murata	H	1-3	Berti
18/03/00	Faetano	A	1-3	Varchetta
25/03/00	Domagnano	H	0-2	
28/03/00	San Giovanni	A	0-0	
01/04/00	Libertas	A	1-0	Varchetta

DOMAGNANO

CLUB DIRECTORY

Società Polisportiva Domagnano
Via Cà Giannino 1, 47031 Domagnano
tel - 902059
Year of Formation - 1966
President - Corrado Maiani
Secretary - Andrea Felici
Coach - Primo Moretti
Stadium - Domagnano (500)

MAJOR HONOURS
League Championship - (2) 1972, 1989.
Domestic Cup - (4) 1988, 1990, 1992, 1996.

APPEARANCES 99/00

	P	Ap	(s)	Gls
Daniele BACIOCCHI	D	17		
Nicola BACIOCCHI	M	15		5
Stefano BIORDI	M	1	(3)	
Silvano BOLLINI	D	5	(4)	
Henry BUCCI	A		(3)	
Samuele BUGLI	G	17		
Nicola CANCELLI (ITA)	A	2	(3)	
Larry CAPICCHIONI	D	22		
Stefano CAPICCHIONI	D	2	(4)	2
Federico DONATI	M	17	(1)	1
Fabio FELICI	M	2	(4)	
Marco GASPERI	A	13	(4)	14
GENTLINI (ITA)	G	5		
Michele GIACOBBI	A	3	(4)	
Paolo GIACOBBI	D	13	(2)	
Michel KOUFAL (CZE)	M	5		2
Secondo LAZZARI	D		(1)	
Massimo MARANI	D		(1)	
Marco MULARONI	M	18		12
PAGANI	D	1	(2)	
PAGNETTI	D	15	(2)	
Loris PALMIERI	M	3	(2)	
Pietro PAOLINI	D	3	(2)	
Alessandro PASOLINI	M	3	(1)	
Oscar PASOLINI	M	15	(1)	
Marco PAZZINI	A	3	(2)	
Andrea PIERINI (ITA)	A	19		14
Massimo ROSSI	M	12	(2)	1
Gian Luca UGOLINI	M		(2)	
Enea ZUCCHI	A	11		5

LEAGUE RESULTS 1999/2000

11/09/99	Tre Fiori	A	2-1	Pierini 2
18/09/99	Libertas	H	1-1	Capicchioni S.
25/09/99	San Giovanni	H	4-1	og (Marinelli), Mularoni, Pierini, Gasperi
02/10/99	Murata	A	6-2	Mularoni 2, Gasperi 2, Koufal, Pierini
09/10/99	Dogana	H	1-2	Koufal
16/10/99	Montevito	H	5-0	Zucchi 2, Gasperi, Baciocchi N. 2
23/10/99	Faetano	A	1-1	Pierini
30/10/99	Pennarossa	H	2-2	Zucchi, Mularoni
06/11/99	Fiorita	H	1-0	Mularoni
13/11/99	Folgore	H	1-4	Mularoni
20/11/99	Virtus	A	1-2	Zucchi
27/11/99	Juvenes	A	8-0	Pierini 4, Baciocchi N., Pagnetti, Gasperi 2
04/12/99	Cailungo	A	1-2	Baciocchi N.
11/12/99	Tre Penne	A	3-1	Mularoni, Capicchioni S., Pierini
19/02/00	Cosmos	H	1-1	Pierini
26/02/00	Tre Fiori	H	2-2	Zucchi, Gasperi
04/03/00	Libertas	A	1-1	Pagnetti
11/03/00	San Giovanni	A	5-1	Rossi, Baciocchi N., Gasperi 2, Pierini
18/03/00	Murata	H	2-1	Mularoni 2
25/03/00	Dogana	A	2-0	Gasperi, Mularoni
28/03/00	Montevito	A	6-0	Gasperi 3, Mularoni 2, Donati
01/04/00	Faetano	H	3-2	Pierini 2, Gasperi

FAETANO

CLUB DIRECTORY

Società Calcio Faetano
Piazza del Massaro 2
47031 Faetano
tel - 996057
Year of Formation - 1962
President - Fabio Gasperoni
Secretary - Riccardo Gasperoni
Coach - Berto Carlino
Stadium - Faetano (500)

MAJOR HONOURS
League Championship - (3) 1986, 1991, 1999.
Domestic Cup - (3) 1993, 1994, 1998.

APPEARANCES 99/00

	P	Ap	(s)	Gls
Ettore BEDETTI	G	4	(1)	
Alex BUGLI	A		(3)	
Alessandro CASADEI	M	10	(1)	
Fulvio CASADEI	M	10	(2)	2
Luciano CONTI	M	3	(4)	
Marco CONTI	D	14	(1)	
Paolo CONTI	D	1	(2)	
Stefano CONTI	M	10	(1)	1
Agostino DALL'OLMO	M	14	(2)	
Pier Domenico DELLA VALLE	M	15		1
Pier Paolo DONATI	M	15		1
Marco GASPERONI	A	7	(1)	
Maurizio GASPERONI	D	1	(4)	
Riccardo GASPERONI	D	11	(1)	
Massimiliano GIANNI	A	7	(2)	2
Paolo GIULIANELLI	A	2	(3)	1
Filippo MENGHI	M	9	(4)	5
Federico MORONI	D	18		3
Michele MORONI	A	5	(1)	
Paolo MORONI	M		(6)	
Stefano MUCCIOLI	G	18		
Denis MULARONI	A	12		3
Manuel MULARONI	D	4	(6)	1
Luca RICCARDI	A	15		5
Silvio RICCARDI	D	15	(1)	
Luigi RINALDI	D	1	(5)	
Michele RINALDI	M	21		4

LEAGUE RESULTS 1999/2000

11/09/99	San Giovanni	A	0-0	
18/09/99	Montevito	H	3-1	Rinaldi 2, Gianni
25/09/99	Tre Fiori	A	1-4	og (Benedettini)
02/10/99	Dogana	A	1-1	Rinaldi (p)
09/10/99	Murata	H	0-2	
16/10/99	Libertas	A	1-2	Della Valle
23/10/99	Domagnano	H	1-1	Riccardi L.
30/10/99	Tre Penne	H	1-0	Riccardi L.
06/11/99	Folgore	A	3-3	Menghi, Mularoni D. 2
13/11/99	Virtus	H	1-2	Moroni F.
20/11/99	Fiorita	H	4-0	Donati, Riccardi L., Casadei F., Moroni F.
27/11/99	Cosmos	A	0-0	
04/12/99	Pennarossa	A	1-0	Menghi
11/12/99	Cailungo	A	0-1	
19/02/00	Juvenes	H	3-0	Moroni F., Giulianelli, Menghi
26/02/00	San Giovanni	H	0-0	
04/03/00	Montevito	A	0-0	
11/03/00	Tre Fiori	H	2-1	Mularoni M., Riccardi L.
18/03/00	Dogana	H	3-1	Mularoni D., Riccardi L., Menghi
25/03/00	Murata	A	2-1	Rinaldi, Casadei F.
28/03/00	Libertas	H	1-2	Gianni
01/04/00	Domagnano	A	2-3	Conti S. (p), Menghi

FIORITA

CLUB DIRECTORY

Società Polisportiva La Fiorita
Via del Dragone 17
47031 Montegiardino
tel - 996202
Year of Formation - 1967
President - Luciano Zanotti
Secretary - Mauro Rinaldi
Coach - Stefano Rosati
Stadium - Montegiardino (200)

MAJOR HONOURS
League Championship - (2) 1987, 1990.
Domestic Cup - (1) 1986.

APPEARANCES 99/00

	P	Ap	(s)	Gls
Julian ALYAJ (ALB)	M	18	(1)	1
Cristian BERARDI	A	7	(4)	
Davide BERNARDI	M	16	(3)	
Alain BOLLINI	A		(3)	
Nicola CANAREZZA (ITA)	M	8	(2)	2
Michele DELLA VALLE	A	1	(1)	
Marcello FABBRI	G	3		
Lorenzo FORCELLINI	M	3	(6)	
Federico FRANCINI	M	17		
Elia GORINI	M	1		
Alain MANCINI	M	5		
Denis MANZI	M		(4)	
MARRO (ITA)	D	10		
Franco MEZZANOTTE	M	20		
Marco MONTALI	D	11	(2)	1
Lorenzo MORETTI	A		(2)	
Antonio MULARONI	D	3	(3)	
Riccardo MULARONI	A	2	(4)	
Carlo MURACCINI	A	1	(2)	
Ivan MURACCINI	A	3	(2)	
Roberto PELLANDRA	D	6	(2)	
Costantino RENZI (ITA)	D	5		
Marco RIGHI	D	20		
Matteo SAMMARITANI	M	20		2
L. ZAFFERANI	A	1	(1)	
Mario ZAFFERANI	D	7	(5)	1
Alex ZANOTTI	G	19		
Manuel ZANOTTI	D	6	(4)	
Marco ZANOTTI	A	4	(3)	
Paolo ZANOTTI	D	6	(6)	
Sebastiano ZAVALLONI (ITA)	A	19		9

LEAGUE RESULTS 1999/2000

11/09/99	Tre Penne	H	0-1	
18/09/99	Pennarossa	A	0-1	
25/09/99	Virtus	H	1-4	Zavalloni
02/10/99	Cosmos	A	0-4	
09/10/99	Juvenes	H	0-2	
16/10/99	Cailungo	H	1-0	og (Stefanelli)
23/10/99	Folgore	A	1-2	Montali
30/10/99	San Giovanni	H	0-3	
06/11/99	Domagnano	A	0-1	
13/11/99	Murata	H	2-3	Zavalloni, Canarezza
20/11/99	Faetano	A	0-4	
27/11/99	Libertas	H	0-1	
04/12/99	Montevito	A	0-1	
11/12/99	Dogana	A	1-1	Canarezza
19/02/00	Tre Fiori	H	1-1	Zavalloni
26/02/00	Tre Penne	A	2-2	Zavalloni, Alyaj
04/03/00	Pennarossa	H	1-2	Zavalloni (p)
11/03/00	Virtus	A	1-1	Zavalloni
18/03/00	Cosmos	H	1-6	Zafferani M.
25/03/00	Juvenes	A	3-2	Sammaritani 2, Zavalloni
28/03/00	Cailungo	A	0-5	
01/04/00	Folgore	H	2-3	Zavalloni 2

FOLGORE

CLUB DIRECTORY

Società Sportiva Folgore
Strada La Zanetta 10
47031 Falciano
tel - 908088
Year of Formation - 1972
President - Francesco Prosperini
Secretary - Renato Cappelini
Coach - Oriano Bustelli
Stadium - Falciano (500)

MAJOR HONOURS
League Championship - (3) 1997, 1998, 2000.

APPEARANCES 99/00

	P	Ap	(s)	Gls
William BALLABENE (ITA)	M		(1)	
Gabriele BARTOLETTI	M	16		
Cristian BERNARDINI (ITA)	A	5	(3)	1
Augusto BIANCHI	M	10	(1)	
Simone BIANCHI	M	18		6
David BOLOGNA	A	8	(4)	1
Filippo BRUSCHI	A		(3)	
Stefano CIACCI	G	21		
Claudio CORBELLI	M	11	(2)	
Alessandro DELLA TORRE	D	20		2
Alessandro DELLA VALLE	M		(3)	
Andrea DURELLI	A	19	(1)	8
Luigi FERRANTE (ITA)	D		(6)	
Christian GASPERONI	M	1	(3)	
Ferdinando GASPERONI	D	5	(5)	
Cristian GIARDI	D		(3)	
Graziano GIOVAGNOLI	M	2	(5)	
Michele GIOVAGNOLI	A	5	(3)	
Matteo MAZZA	A	12	(2)	13
Fabrizio PELLICCIONI	D	17		
Federico PELLICCIONI	D	19		6
Enrico PROSPERINI (ITA)	A		(6)	
Matteo RIGHI	G	1	(1)	
Leonardo ROSSI	D	13	(2)	
Alessandro SARTINI	M	7	(4)	3
Harry SELVA	A		(4)	2
Anselmo SENSOLI	G		(1)	
Francesco UGOLINI	M	16		2
Alessandro ZANOTTI	A	10		7
Loris ZANOTTI	A	6		2

LEAGUE RESULTS 1999/2000

11/09/99	Cailungo	A	1-0	Mazza
18/09/99	Juvenes	H	5-0	Mazza 2, Zanotti L., Durelli, Selva
25/09/99	Tre Penne	A	1-1	Mazza
02/10/99	Pennarossa	H	7-0	Bologna, Mazza, Durelli, Selva, Sartini 2, Pelliccioni Fe.
09/10/99	Virtus	A	1-2	Della Torre (p)
16/10/99	Cosmos	A	2-4	Zanotti A., Mazza
23/10/99	Fiorita	H	2-1	Sartini, Mazza
30/10/99	Libertas	A	1-0	Zanotti A.
06/11/99	Faetano	H	3-3	Durelli 2, Zanotti A.
13/11/99	Domagnano	A	4-1	Durelli (p), Pelliccioni Fe., Bianchi S., Mazza
20/11/99	Montevito	A	3-2	Ugolini, Bianchi S., Pelliccioni Fe.
27/11/99	Murata	H	2-1	Durelli, Pelliccioni Fe.
04/12/99	Tre Fiori	H	3-1	Della Torre, Zanotti A., Mazza
11/12/99	San Giovanni	H	1-0	Zanotti L.
19/02/00	Dogana	A	2-1	Bianchi S., Ugolini
26/02/00	Cailungo	H	0-1	
04/03/00	Juvenes	A	3-1	Pelliccioni Fe., Zanotti A., Bianchi S.
11/03/00	Tre Penne	H	7-1	Zanotti A. 2, Pelliccioni Fe., Bianchi S., Mazza 2, Durelli
18/03/00	Pennarossa	A	1-2	Mazza
25/03/00	Virtus	H	1-0	Mazza
28/03/00	Cosmos	H	0-0	
01/04/00	Fiorita	A	3-2	Durelli (p), Bernardini, Bianchi S.

JUVENES

CLUB DIRECTORY

Società Sportiva Juvenes
Via Balducci
47031 Serravalle
tel - 900336
Year of Formation - 1953
President - Bruno Passerini
Secretary - Luigi Zafferani
Coach - Danilo Forcellini
Stadium - Domagnano (500)

MAJOR HONOURS
League Championship - (5)
1965, 1968, 1976, 1978, 1984.

APPEARANCES 99/00

	P	Ap	(s)	Gls
Gian Luigi BALDUCCI	M	21		
Stefano BORGHINI	A	7	(5)	
Manuel CAPICCHIONI	M	14	(3)	3
Andrea CASADEI	D	9	(4)	
Cristian CASADEI	G	13		
Daniele CASADEI	G	9	(1)	
Gian Luca COLA (ITA)	D	4	(3)	3
Alessandro CONTI	D	7	(3)	
Enzo CONTI	M		(2)	
Massimiliano CONTI	D	15	(1)	
Salvatore DEL TITO	D	10	(1)	
Fabio FERRARINI	M	11	(5)	1
Claudio FORCELLINI	D		(2)	
Loriano FRISONI	M	14	(1)	
Athos GASPERONI	M	6		
Rolando GASPERONI	M	14	(2)	2
Roberto GIORGETTI	A		(3)	
Gian Luca LAZZARI	D	8	(1)	2
Danilo MAIANI	A	2	(1)	
Mirco MANCINELLA	A	7		4
Gian Luca METALLI	M	15		2
Marco MORRI	M	14	(2)	1
Stefano MORRI	A	2	(2)	2
Ivan PAZZINI	M	10	(1)	
PERACCINI	A		(2)	
Claudio PEVERANI	M		(4)	
Roberto SARTI	A	17	(1)	4
Filippo SBERLATI	A	2	(5)	
Massimo TAMAGNINI	M	11	(1)	

LEAGUE RESULTS 1999/2000

11/09/99	Cosmos	H	1-1	Mancinella (p)
18/09/99	Folgore	A	0-5	
25/09/99	Cailungo	H	0-3	
02/10/99	Tre Penne	A	3-3	Morri S., Metalli, Cola
09/10/99	Fiorita	A	2-0	Sarti, Metalli
16/10/99	Virtus	H	0-4	
23/10/99	Pennarossa	A	1-2	Morri M.
30/10/99	Dogana	H	3-0	Sarti, Gasperoni R. 2
06/11/99	San Giovanni	A	2-2	Mancinella, Lazzari
13/11/99	Montevito	H	2-3	Sarti, Ferrarini
20/11/99	Tre Fiori	A	0-0	
27/11/99	Domagnano	H	0-8	
04/12/99	Libertas	A	2-3	Mancinella, Lazzari
11/12/99	Murata	H	1-1	Mancinella
19/02/00	Faetano	A	0-3	
26/02/00	Cosmos	A	0-4	
04/03/00	Folgore	H	1-3	Capicchioni
11/03/00	Cailungo	A	1-3	Morri S.
18/03/00	Tre Penne	H	2-5	Capicchioni 2
25/03/00	Fiorita	H	2-3	Cola, Sarti
28/03/00	Virtus	A	0-4	
01/04/00	Pennarossa	H	1-1	Cola

LIBERTAS

CLUB DIRECTORY

Società Polisportiva Libertas
Via 28 Luglio 1/B, 47031 Borgomaggiore
tel - 906472
Year of Formation - 1928
President - Paride Andreoli
Secretary - Stefano Biordi
Coach - Roberto Marcucci
Stadium - Fonte dell'Ovo (500)

MAJOR HONOURS
League Championship - (7)
1937, 1950, 1954, 1958, 1959, 1961, 1996.
Domestic Cup - (3) 1987, 1989, 1991.

APPEARANCES 99/00

	P	Ap	(s)	Gls
Franco AGARICI	M	19		3
Sandro AGARICI	D	7	(10)	1
Stefano BIORDI	D	16		
Luca BONIFAZI	M	4	(11)	1
Gian Carlo CARNEVALI (ITA)	A	20		17
CARRARA	A		(3)	
Federico CAVALLI	M	3	(8)	1
Michele CECCOLI	G	4		
Fulvio EVARISTI	A	1	(7)	
Federico FOSCOLI (ITA)	G	1		
Fabio FRANCINI	M	20		5
Franco FRANCIOSI	A	3	(3)	
Massimo GHIOTTI	M	16		1
Luca MORONI	D	16		
Federico ROSSI (ITA)	D	12	(4)	1
Floriano SPERINDIO (ITA)	G	1		
Floriano SPERINDIO (ITA)	A	13	(6)	1
Daniele TOCCACELI	M	22		2
Davide TOCCACELI	M	1	(9)	1
Ivan TOCCACELI	D	16		
Valerio TOCCACELI	M	14		1
Andrea VANNUCCI	M	17		
Matteo VENERUCCI	G	16		

LEAGUE RESULTS 1999/2000

11/09/99	Murata	A	1-1	Bonifazi
18/09/99	Domagnano	A	1-1	Carnevali
25/09/99	Montevito	H	1-2	Carnevali
02/10/99	Tre Fiori	A	3-6	Carnevali 3
09/10/99	San Giovanni	A	3-1	Agarici F. (p), Agarici S., Toccaceli V.
16/10/99	Faetano	H	2-1	Carnevali, Francini
23/10/99	Dogana	A	2-1	Sperindio, Cavalli
30/10/99	Folgore	H	0-1	
06/11/99	Virtus	A	2-2	Carnevali 2
13/11/99	Pennarossa	H	2-0	Carnevali, Toccaceli Dan.
20/11/99	Cailungo	A	1-2	Agarici F.
27/11/99	Fiorita	A	1-0	Francini
04/12/99	Juvenes	H	3-2	Carnevali 2, Francini (p)
11/12/99	Cosmos	H	0-2	
19/02/00	Tre Penne	A	0-2	
26/02/00	Murata	H	4-3	Ghiotti, Carnevali 2, Agarici F.
04/03/00	Domagnano	H	1-1	Francini
11/03/00	Montevito	A	3-2	Francini, Carnevali 2
18/03/00	Tre Fiori	H	0-1	
25/03/00	San Giovanni	H	3-1	Toccaceli Dav., Carnevali, Rossi
28/03/00	Faetano	A	2-1	Toccaceli Dan., Carnevali
01/04/00	Dogana	H	0-1	

MONTEVITO

CLUB DIRECTORY

Società Sportiva Montevito
Via La Rena 19, 47031 Fiorentino
tel - 888208
Year of Formation - 1974
President - Silvio Fabbri
Secretary - Mimmo Protti
Coach - Federico Rossini
Stadium - Fiorentino (2,000)

MAJOR HONOURS
League Championship - (1) 1992.

APPEARANCES 99/00

	P	Ap	(s)	Gls
Pier Angelo AMATI	M	12		
Denis AMICI	M		(5)	
Diego BALDACCI	M	13		
Loris BALDACCI (ITA)	M	1	(3)	
Manuel BERARDI	M		(2)	1
Daniele BONCI (ITA)	M	16		
Gianni BONELLI	D		(2)	
Giacomo CASADEI	M	8	(4)	
Maurizio CASALI	D	11		
Davide CECCHETTI	M	20		
Gian Luca CECCHETTI	M		(5)	
Giorgio CESARINI	A	9	(5)	4
Mauro COMANDUCCI (ITA)	M	19		6
Denis FABBRI	M	1	(3)	
Daniel FRANCESCONI	A	1	(3)	
Leo Marino FRANCIONI	D	13		1
Andrea GASPERONI	A		(2)	1
Fabio GIARDI	M	15		
Roberto GUERRA	D	15		
Federico MARZI	A		(4)	
Cristian MONALDI	D	3	(3)	
Alberto MONTANARI	G	7		
Yuri PEDINI	A	3	(3)	
Gian Luca PESARESI	A	2		
Mimmo PROTTI	M		(5)	
Antonio RAMBERTI (ITA)	G	15		
Antonio RAMBERTI (ITA)	A	1		
Stefano RIDOLFI	M	1		1
Gustavo ROSSINI (ARG)	A	14		7
Cristian ROSTI	A	1	(3)	
Armando SCHIANO	D	7	(3)	1
Massimiliano SENTINI (ITA)	M	14		
Ivan UGOLINI	A	6	(3)	
Massimo ZANOTTI	A	1	(2)	2
Filippo ZAVOLI	M	12		3
Paolo ZONZINI	D	1	(4)	

LEAGUE RESULTS 1999/2000

11/09/99	Dogana	H	2-1	Rossini, Francioni
18/09/99	Faetano	A	1-3	Zavoli
25/09/99	Libertas	A	2-1	Comanducci (p), Zavoli
02/10/99	San Giovanni	H	0-1	
09/10/99	Tre Fiori	H	0-4	
16/10/99	Domagnano	A	0-5	
23/10/99	Murata	H	2-3	Rossini, Gasperoni
30/10/99	Cosmos	A	0-0	
06/11/99	Cailungo	H	0-0	
13/11/99	Juvenes	A	3-2	Rossini, Cesarini, Ridolfi
20/11/99	Folgore	H	2-3	Cesarini, Comanducci (p)
27/11/99	Tre Penne	A	1-2	Comanducci
04/12/99	Fiorita	H	1-0	Rossini
11/12/99	Pennarossa	A	3-1	Cesarini 2, Rossini
19/02/00	Virtus	H	0-2	
26/02/00	Dogana	A	0-1	
04/03/00	Faetano	H	0-0	
11/03/00	Libertas	H	2-3	Rossini 2
18/03/00	San Giovanni	A	0-3	
25/03/00	Tre Fiori	A	2-4	Schiano, Comanducci (p)
28/03/00	Domagnano	H	0-6	
01/04/00	Murata	A	6-3	Zavoli, Zanotti 2, Berardi, Comanducci 2

MURATA

CLUB DIRECTORY

Società Sportiva Murata
Via del Serrone
47031 Murata
tel - 997440
Year of Formation - 1966
President - Libero Casadei
Secretary - Giancarlo Simoncini
Coach - Duilio Felici
Stadium - Acquaviva (1,000)

MAJOR HONOURS
Domestic Cup - (1) 1997.

APPEARANCES 99/00

	P	Ap	(s)	Gls
Luca ALBANI	D	16		
Alberto ALBERTINI (ITA)	D	22		2
Michele BACCHIOCCHI	D	11	(4)	
Pier Angelo BATTISTINI	D	2	(3)	
Sebastiano BOLLINI	D		(3)	
Denis CASADEI	A	2	(3)	
Giacomo CASADEI	A	10	(4)	1
Federico CAVAGNA	D	10	(2)	2
Agostino CORBELLI	D	8		4
Giuliano CORBELLI	D	2		
Roberto FAZZARDI	D	17	(3)	1
Daniel FRANCESCONI	G		(1)	
Diego GASPERONI	A	16		12
Denis GIANNINI	D	16		
Oriano LAZZARETTI	A	16		12
Lorenzo MANCHISI (ITA)	M	20		1
Luigi NICOLINI	D	10	(4)	1
Denis OTTAVIANI	A	4	(4)	3
Nicola PELLICCIONI	D	2	(5)	
PETRETI (ROM)	M	3	(3)	
Raffaele RICCI (ITA)	A	9	(4)	2
Marco SACCANI (ITA)	M	21		3
Marco SCHIAVI (ITA)	G	1	(1)	
Marco SCHIAVI (ITA)	A	1	(4)	2
Michele SERRA	M	1	(4)	
Jader VAGNINI	M	1	(10)	
Denis VENERUCCI	G	21		

LEAGUE RESULTS 1999/2000

11/09/99	Libertas	H	1-1	Lazzaretti
18/09/99	San Giovanni	A	4-1	Lazzaretti, Corbelli A. 2 (1p), Ottaviani
25/09/99	Dogana	H	4-1	Gasperoni 2 (1p), Corbelli A. 2 (1p)
02/10/99	Domagnano	H	2-6	Lazzaretti 2
09/10/99	Faetano	A	2-0	Lazzaretti 2
16/10/99	Tre Fiori	A	3-6	Ricci, Lazzaretti, og (Capicchioni)
23/10/99	Montevito	A	3-2	Ricci, Lazzaretti, Gasperoni
30/10/99	Virtus	H	3-3	Gasperoni 3 (1p)
06/11/99	Pennarossa	A	0-2	
13/11/99	Fiorita	A	3-2	Gasperoni (p), Cavagna, Lazzaretti
20/11/99	Tre Penne	H	1-0	Schiavi
27/11/99	Folgore	A	1-2	Cavagna
04/12/99	Cosmos	H	1-1	Lazzaretti
11/12/99	Juvenes	A	1-1	Casadei G.
19/02/00	Cailungo	H	3-1	Saccani, Gasperoni (p), Ottaviani
26/02/00	Libertas	A	3-4	Saccani, Gasperoni, Schiavi
04/03/00	San Giovanni	H	3-2	Albertini, Fazzardi, Gasperoni
11/03/00	Dogana	A	3-1	og (Varchetta), Nicolini, Gasperoni
18/03/00	Domagnano	A	1-2	Saccani
25/03/00	Faetano	H	1-2	Lazzaretti
28/03/00	Tre Fiori	H	2-3	Ottaviani, Manchisi
01/04/00	Montevito	H	3-6	Lazzaretti, Albertini, Gasperoni

PENNAROSSA

CLUB DIRECTORY

Società Sportiva Pennarossa
Piazza Salvatore Conti
47031 Chiesanuova
tel - 3010395
Year of Formation - 1968
President - Massimo Barbieri
Secretary - Marino Rosti
Coach - Riccardo Pancotti
Stadium - Chiesanuova (500)

APPEARANCES 99/00

		P	Ap	(s)	Gls
William ALBERTINI	M	13	(3)		1
Simone BERGANTINI	M	16	(2)		
Ivan BONCI	M	6	(5)		1
Vincenzo BOSCHI	D	7	(4)		
Gian Luca CESARINI	G	1			
Maurizio CHIARUZZI	D		(3)		
CIACCI (ITA)	A	2	(4)		
Ligor COBO (ALB)	M	16	(2)		3
Matteo COMANDINI	M	14			
Enrico ESPOSITO	D	2			1
Gilberto FELICI	M	18			
Davide FRANCIONI	A		(3)		
Luca FRANCIONI	M		(5)		
Gabriele FRISONI	G	20			
Gian Luca GUALTIERI	A	20			12
Andrea GUERRA	D	10	(4)		
Andrea LIVIDINI	A		(4)		
Pier Angelo MANZAROLI	M	9			2
Mauro MARANI	D	1	(4)		
Paolo MARIOTTI	M	12			3
Alessandro MELONI	D	3	(3)		
Paolo NANNI	M	12			
Alessandro PANCOTTI	A	15			7
Stefano SAMMARITANI	G	1	(1)		
Nicola SATALINO (ITA)	D	19			
Davide SELVA	D	8			
Tiziano SELVA	D	8			
Emanuele SEMPRINI (ITA)	M	7	(3)		
Massimiliano VANDI	D	2	(6)		

LEAGUE RESULTS 1999/2000

11/09/99	Virtus	A	2-1	Gualtieri 2
18/09/99	Fiorita	H	1-0	Albertini
25/09/99	Cosmos	H	0-4	
02/10/99	Folgore	A	0-7	
09/10/99	Cailungo	A	1-1	Cobo
16/10/99	Tre Penne	H	3-1	Pancotti, Manzaroli (p), Gualtieri
23/10/99	Juvenes	H	2-1	Gualtieri, Mariotti
30/10/99	Domagnano	A	2-2	Gualtieri, Manzaroli
06/11/99	Murata	H	2-0	Cobo, Bonci
13/11/99	Libertas	A	0-2	
20/11/99	Dogana	A	1-2	Pancotti
27/11/99	Tre Fiori	A	2-3	Pancotti 2
04/12/99	Faetano	H	0-1	
11/12/99	Montevito	H	1-3	Gualtieri
19/02/00	San Giovanni	H	2-0	Gualtieri 2
26/02/00	Virtus	H	2-2	Pancotti 2
04/03/00	Fiorita	A	2-1	Pancotti, Cobo
11/03/00	Cosmos	A	0-0	
18/03/00	Folgore	H	2-1	Gualtieri, Mariotti
25/03/00	Cailungo	H	1-2	Gualtieri
28/03/00	Tre Penne	A	3-4	Esposito, Mariotti, Gualtieri (p)
01/04/00	Juvenes	A	1-1	Gualtieri (p)

SAN GIOVANNI

CLUB DIRECTORY

Società Sportiva San Giovanni
Strada San Gianno
47031 San Giovanni
tel - 906715
Year of Formation - 1948
President - Valerio Zanotti
Secretary - Walter Santi
Coach - Paolo Marinelli
Stadium - Chiesanuova (500)

APPEARANCES 99/00

	P	Ap	(s)	Gls
Luca ALBANI	D	5	(1)	
Fabrizio BINDI	D	14		
BURLACCHI	M	6	(2)	1
Riccardo CEPPARI	M	11	(3)	3
Cristian COLONNA (ITA)	M	15		4
Luca CONTI	M	3	(4)	
Fabrizio COSTANTINI	M	17	(1)	
Achille FABBRI	D	7	(4)	2
Alessandro FABBRI	D	17		2
FABRIZI	D	1	(1)	
Angelo FAMIGLIETTI (ITA)	A	5	(2)	1
Giuseppe FELICITÀ (ITA)	G	15		
Gabriel FRANCINI	A	1	(4)	
Fabrizio FRANCIONI	D	8	(7)	
Antonio LACALÀ	A	7	(4)	
LOMBARDI (ITA)	G	1		
LOMBARDI (ITA)	D	12		1
Giovanni LONFERNINI	A	7		2
Denis MANZI	D	4	(7)	
Paolo MARINELLI	M	2	(5)	1
Stefano MARINELLI	D	11		1
Fabio MINI	D	18		1
Nicola PARENTI	G	6		
Cornel PETRE (ARG)	A		(5)	
Emanuele SANTI	M	19		
Loris VALENTINI	D	14		1
Yazar YAZICI (TUR)	A	11		1
Luca ZANOTTI	M	5	(5)	

LEAGUE RESULTS 1999/2000

11/09/99	Faetano	H	0-0	
18/09/99	Murata	H	1-4	Fabbri Ac.
25/09/99	Domagnano	A	1-4	Valentini
02/10/99	Montevito	A	1-0	Fabbri Ac.
09/10/99	Libertas	H	1-3	Yazici
16/10/99	Dogana	A	0-1	
23/10/99	Tre Fiori	H	2-2	Lonfernini, Marinelli S.
30/10/99	Fiorita	A	3-0	Colonna 2, Lonfernini
06/11/99	Juvenes	H	2-2	Marinelli P., Colonna
13/11/99	Cailungo	H	1-2	Fabbri Al.
20/11/99	Cosmos	H	0-2	
27/11/99	Virtus	A	0-2	
04/12/99	Tre Penne	H	0-2	
11/12/99	Folgore	A	0-1	
19/02/00	Pennarossa	A	0-2	
26/02/00	Faetano	A	0-0	
04/03/00	Murata	A	2-3	Famiglietti, Ceppari
11/03/00	Domagnano	H	1-5	Colonna (p)
18/03/00	Montevito	H	3-0	Burlacchi, Ceppari, Mini
25/03/00	Libertas	A	1-3	Fabbri Al.
28/03/00	Dogana	H	0-0	
01/04/00	Tre Fiori	A	2-6	Ceppari, Lombardi

TRE FIORI

CLUB DIRECTORY

Società Polisportiva Tre Fiori
Via 21 Settembre 93
47031 Fiorentino
tel - 878026
Year of Formation - 1949
President - Marino Casali
Secretary - Mauro Amici
Coach - Giorgio Leoni
Stadium - Fiorentino (2,000)

MAJOR HONOURS
League Championship - (9) 1966, 1971, 1974, 1975, 1985, 1988, 1993, 1994, 1995.

APPEARANCES 99/00

		P	Ap	(s)	Gls
Roberto BENEDETTINI	D	8	(4)	4
Nicola CANAREZZA (ITA)	M	10	(2)	
Matteo CANINI	D		(6)	
Gabriele CAPICCHIONI	M	16		
Alfredo CECCHETTI	M	8		1
Davide CECCHETTI	D	8		2
Daniele CHIARUZZI	G	1	(1)	
Massimo DOLCINI	M	6	(5)	1
Marcello FABBRI (ITA)	G	1	(1)	
Alessandro FAETANINI	M	13		1
Andrea FIORE (ITA)	A	20		16
Michele LEONI	D	3	(5)	
Alessandro LISI (ITA)	M		(6)	
Ivan LISI (ITA)	A	14		5
Nicola MANZARI	G	6		
Andrea MARIOTTI	G	3		
Ivan MATTEONI	M	17		2
Jader MATTEONI	M	17		3
Manuel MATTEONI	D	10		
Giorgio MIGANI	D	15		
PARA	A		(7)	
Diego PEDINI	M	2	(6)	
Marco PELLICCIONI	G	11		
Luigi RAGANINI	A	2	(5)	
Marco RIGHI	D	4	(6)	1
Mario RONCI	M	10		3
Khalid ZABOUL (MAR)	A	17		16
Massimo ZANOTTI	D	2	(6)	
Matteo ZAVOLI	D	18		

LEAGUE RESULTS 1999/2000

11/09/99	Domagnano	H	1-2	Matteoni J.
18/09/99	Dogana	A	2-3	Matteoni J., Fiore
25/09/99	Faetano	H	4-1	Fiore 3, Zaboul
02/10/99	Libertas	H	6-3	Lisi I. 2, Zaboul 2, Fiore, Benedettini
09/10/99	Montevito	A	4-0	Zaboul 2, Fiore 2
16/10/99	Murata	H	6-3	Matteoni I., Fiore, Zaboul 3, Benedettini
23/10/99	San Giovanni	A	2-2	Lisi I., Benedettini
30/10/99	Cailungo	A	2-2	Matteoni I., Lisi I.
06/11/99	Tre Penne	H	3-0	Cecchetti D., Zaboul 2
13/11/99	Cosmos	A	2-1	Fiore, Zaboul
20/11/99	Juvenes	H	0-0	
27/11/99	Pennarossa	H	3-2	Fiore (p), Benedettini, Righi
04/12/99	Folgore	A	1-3	Cecchetti D.
11/12/99	Virtus	H	1-2	Fiore
19/02/00	Fiorita	A	1-1	Zaboul
26/02/00	Domagnano	A	2-2	Zaboul, Fiore
04/03/00	Dogana	H	1-1	Lisi I.
11/03/00	Faetano	A	1-2	Zaboul
18/03/00	Libertas	A	1-0	Fiore
25/03/00	Montevito	H	4-2	Faetanini, Fiore, Cecchetti A., Ronci
28/03/00	Murata	A	3-2	Ronci, Zaboul, Fiore
01/04/00	San Giovanni	H	6-2	Fiore, Ronci, Zaboul, og (Costantini), Dolcini, Matteoni J.

TRE PENNE

CLUB DIRECTORY

Società Polisportiva Tre Penne
Via Ugo Bassi 13, 47031 Borgo Maggiore
tel - 906699 / fax - 903758
Year of Formation - 1956
President - Andrea Della Balda
Secretary - Franco Santi
Coach - Alessandro Giaquinto
Stadium - Fonte Dell'Ovo (500)

MAJOR HONOURS
League Championship - (4)
1967, 1970, 1982, 1983.
Domestic Cup - (1) 2000.

APPEARANCES 99/00

		P	Ap	(s)	Gls
Luigi BELISARDI	G	6			
Luigi BELISARDI	A	2	(6)	2	
Massimiliano BERTI	M		(5)		
Lorenzo BOLLINI	D	20		2	
Aldo CAPICCHIONI	M	20		8	
Gabriele CAPICCHIONI	A		(3)	1	
Marco CAPICCHIONI	M	8	(4)	4	
CECCHI	M	6	(3)	5	
CECCOLI	D	1	(4)		
Manuel DE ANGELI	G	4	(1)		
Danilo DE BIAGI	M		(5)		
Franco DELLA BALDA	M	1	(3)		
Simone DELLA BALDA	M	13		1	
Sergio DEL BIANCO (ITA)	G	2	(1)		
Sergio DEL BIANCO (ITA)	M	4	(5)		
FABBRI	A	1	(2)		
GHIOTTI	M	1	(1)		
Alessandro GIAQUINTO (ITA)	M	15			
Loris GOBBI	A		(4)		
Paolo GOBBI	M	9	(1)		
Andrea GUALTIERI	M	17			
Davide GUALTIERI	A	15		9	
MANCINI	A	2	(5)		
Paolo NANNI	M	13			
PAESINI	D	5	(1)		
Fabio PIERGIOVANNI	M	8	(3)		
Tommaso ROSSINI	G	8			
Reves SALVATORI	M	16		4	
Emiliano SANTI	M	4	(3)		
Franco SANTI	M	6	(2)	3	
TEODORANI	G	2			
Serafino TERENZI	D	13			
Paolo VALENTINI	M	5	(1)		
Gian Luigi ZANOTTI	D	15			

LEAGUE RESULTS 1999/2000

11/09/99	Fiorita	A	1-0	Santi F. (p)
18/09/99	Virtus	H	2-5	Salvatori, Gualtieri D.
25/09/99	Folgore	H	1-1	Della Balda S.
02/10/99	Juvenes	H	3-3	Capicchioni M. 2, Capicchioni A.
09/10/99	Cosmos	A	0-4	
16/10/99	Pennarossa	A	1-3	Belisardi
23/10/99	Cailungo	H	2-6	Gualtieri D. 2
30/10/99	Faetano	A	0-1	
06/11/99	Tre Fiori	A	0-3	
13/11/99	Dogana	H	3-1	Cecchi, Capicchioni A., Salvatori
20/11/99	Murata	A	0-1	
27/11/99	Montevito	H	2-1	Salvatori, Capicchioni A.
04/12/99	San Giovanni	A	2-0	Belisardi, Capicchioni A.
11/12/99	Domagnano	H	1-3	Cecchi
19/02/00	Libertas	H	2-0	Santi F. 2 (1p)
26/02/00	Fiorita	H	2-2	Gualtieri D., Capicchioni A.
04/03/00	Virtus	A	2-3	Gualtieri D., Capicchioni A.
11/03/00	Folgore	A	1-7	Capicchioni A.
18/03/00	Juvenes	A	5-2	Salvatori, Capicchioni M., Capicchioni A., Gualtieri D., Bollini
25/03/00	Cosmos	H	3-5	Gualtieri D. 2, Capicchioni G.
28/03/00	Pennarossa	H	4-3	Cecchi 3, Bollini
01/04/00	Cailungo	A	2-4	Capicchioni M., Gualtieri D.

VIRTUS

CLUB DIRECTORY

Società Sportiva Virtus
Via Il Gualdaria
47031 Acquaviva
tel - 999249
Year of Formation - 1960
President - Maurizo Ghiotti
Secretary - Pier Domenico Giulianelli
Coach - Pietro Rossi
Stadium - Acquaviva (1,000)

APPEARANCES 99/00

	P	Ap	(s)	Gls
Carlo BALSIMELLI	D	20		2
Fabio BASCHETTI (ITA)	A	15		5
BELLANISTA	G	21		
Davide BOLLINI	D		(3)	
Corrado CASADEI	D		(2)	
Maurizio CECCOLI	M		(6)	
CRESCENTINI	D	4	(2)	
Irish DE BIAGI	A	3	(4)	
Orazio DELLA VALLE	D	14		
Cristian DONATI	M		(4)	
Giuseppe FRANCIONI	M	5	(6)	
Bryan GASPERONI	D	1		1
Paolo GATTI	D	10		1
Massimo GAZZI	D	12		4
Tiziano GIACOBBI	M		(7)	
Giuliano GIANNI	A		(5)	
Samuele GIANNINI	A	19		8
Fabio GIARDI	D	1	(3)	
Flavio GUIDI (ITA)	M	14		2
Fabrizio MUCCIOLI	A	1	(5)	
Enrico NICOLINI	G	1		
Luigi NICOLINI	M	4	(5)	
Andrea RAFFELLI	M	17		4
Paolo RASCHI	D	22		
Paride RENZI	A	16		15
Cristian ROSSI	G		(1)	
Pietro ROSSI	D		(1)	
Davide SAMMARITANI	D	15		
Vladimiro SELVA	D	1	(6)	
Enea SILVAGNI	M	8	(4)	
Andrea UGOLINI	A	2		3
Moris VALENTINI	A		(2)	
Damiano VANNUCCI	A	2		
Evert ZAVOLI	M	14		1

LEAGUE RESULTS 1999/2000

11/09/99	Pennarossa	H	1-2	Renzi
18/09/99	Tre Penne	A	5-2	Giannini, Gazzi, Baschetti, Zavoli, Renzi
25/09/99	Fiorita	A	4-1	Giannini, Renzi 3 (1p)
02/10/99	Cailungo	A	3-0	Renzi, Raffelli, Guidi
09/10/99	Folgore	H	2-1	Gatti, Gazzi (p)
16/10/99	Juvenes	A	4-0	Baschetti 2, Raffelli, Gazzi
23/10/99	Cosmos	H	0-1	
30/10/99	Murata	A	3-3	Renzi 2, Raffelli
06/11/99	Libertas	H	2-2	Renzi, Baschetti
13/11/99	Faetano	A	2-1	Renzi, Gasperoni
20/11/99	Domagnano	H	2-1	og (Donati F.), Giannini
27/11/99	San Giovanni	H	2-0	Balsimelli, Gazzi
04/12/99	Dogana	H	0-0	
11/12/99	Tre Fiori	A	2-1	Renzi (p), Guidi
19/02/00	Montevito	A	2-0	Baschetti, Renzi
26/02/00	Pennarossa	A	2-2	Renzi 2 (1p)
04/03/00	Tre Penne	H	3-2	Balsimelli, Giannini, Renzi
11/03/00	Fiorita	H	1-1	Giannini
18/03/00	Cailungo	H	1-3	Raffelli
25/03/00	Folgore	A	0-1	
28/03/00	Juvenes	H	4-0	Giannini 2 (2p), Ugolini 2
01/04/00	Cosmos	A	2-0	Ugolini, Giannini

SCOTLAND

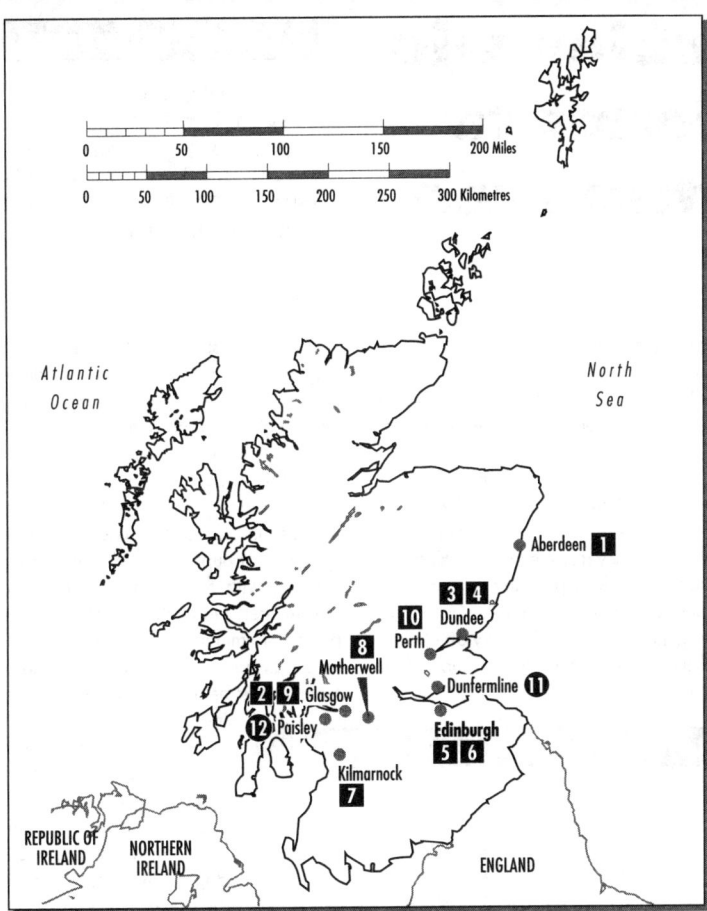

1	**ABERDEEN**	886		8	**MOTHERWELL**	893
2	**CELTIC**	887		9	**RANGERS**	894
3	**DUNDEE**	888		10	**ST. JOHNSTONE**	895
4	**DUNDEE UNITED**	889		**Promoted club**		
5	**HEART OF MIDLOTHIAN**	890		11	**DUNFERMLINE ATHLETIC**	
6	**HIBERNIAN**	891		12	**ST. MIRREN**	
7	**KILMARNOCK**	892				

TOO EASY FOR RUNAWAY RANGERS

Wembley win conforms to Scottish type

FEDERATION DIRECTORY

The Scottish Football Association
6 Park Gardens, Glasgow G3 7YE

tel - (0141) 3326372 Year of Formation - 1873
fax - (0141) 3327559 Chairman - John McGinn
website - www.scottishfa.co.uk Secretary - David Taylor

Stadium - Hampden Park, Glasgow (52,670)

Scotland are the masters when it comes to glorious failure. The manner in which Craig Brown's team missed out on qualification for Euro 2000 might have been pre-scripted. The old "Braveheart" headlines were dredged up for the umpteenth time as Scotland came to Wembley with nothing to lose and beat the Auld Enemy 1-0.

Unfortunately, they had lost the first leg of the play-off 2-0 at Hampden five days earlier, so, great victory though it was - and how they deserved it, outwitting, out-manoeuvring and thoroughly outplaying their opponents - it counted for absolutely nothing. A bit like the 3-2 win over Holland at Argentina '78, the 3-0 victory over the CIS at Euro '92, all those honourable World Cup defeats against Brazil, etc. etc.

It was the first time that Craig Brown had failed to take his team successfully through a qualifying tournament. But the manner of the elimination, the way in which he thoughtfully and skilfully deployed his resouces at Wembley, ensured that he would remain in place for the 2002 World Cup qualifying campaign.

The play-offs were all that Scotland could ever hope for after the Czech Republic had run away with their qualifying group, and they claimed their place in some comfort, with three wins and a draw in their final four fixtures. No matter that the win which sealed their place - an immensely fortunate 1-0 victory over Bosnia-Herzegovina at Ibrox - was achieved with one of the team's worst performances in years. Scotland did what they had to.

Against England at Hampden, in the first leg of the so-called "Battle of Britain", the Scots paid the price for missed chances and were shown how to finish by England's Paul Scholes, who scored twice to send a dagger into Scottish hearts. Then came the re-match at Wembley and the historic headed goal from English-born Don Hutchison that carried the Scots to the brink of the promised land...but not, of course, all the way. That would have been so terribly un-Scottish. But how they made the English suffer!

Scotland proved at Wembley they are not just a team of strong spirit and sound organisation. They also have talented individuals. Neil McCann, who set up Hutchison's goal, had an excellent game, as did the three midfielders Barry Ferguson, John Collins and Craig Burley. Collins was to announce his international retirement after the match, but without him Scotland put up another couple of impressive away

LEAGUE CHAMPIONSHIP RESULTS 99/00

		1	2	3	4	5	6	7	8	9	10
1	Aberdeen		0-5	0-2	1-2	3-1	2-2	2-2	1-1	1-5	0-3
			0-6	0-1	3-1	1-2	4-0	5-1	2-1	1-1	2-1
2	Celtic	7-0		6-2	4-1	4-0	4-0	5-1	0-1	1-1	3-0
		5-1		2-2	2-0	2-3	1-1	4-2	4-0	0-1	4-1
3	Dundee	1-3	1-2		0-2	1-0	3-4	0-0	0-1	2-3	1-2
		0-2	0-3		3-0	0-0	1-0	1-2	4-1	1-7	1-1
4	Dundee United	3-1	2-1	2-1		0-2	3-1	0-0	0-2	0-4	1-0
		1-1	0-1	1-0		0-1	0-0	2-2	1-2	0-2	0-1
5	Heart of Midlothian	3-0	1-2	4-0	3-0		0-3	2-2	1-1	0-4	1-1
		3-0	1-0	2-0	1-2		2-1	0-0	0-0	1-2	0-0
6	Hibernian	2-0	0-2	5-2	3-2	1-1		0-3	2-2	0-1	0-1
		1-0	2-1	1-2	1-0	3-1		2-2	2-2	2-2	3-3
7	Kilmarnock	2-0	0-1	0-2	1-1	2-2	0-2		0-1	1-1	1-2
		1-0	1-1	2-2	1-0	0-1	1-0		0-2	0-2	3-2
8	Motherwell	5-6	3-2	0-2	2-2	2-1	2-2	0-4		1-5	1-0
		1-0	1-1	0-3	1-3	0-2	2-0	2-0		2-0	2-1
9	Rangers	3-0	4-2	1-2	4-1	1-0	2-0	2-1	4-1		3-1
		5-0	4-0	3-0	3-0	1-0	5-2	1-0	6-2		0-0
10	St. Johnstone	1-1	1-2	0-1	0-1	1-4	1-1	2-0	1-1	1-1	
		2-1	0-0	2-1	2-0	0-1	1-0	0-0	1-1	0-2	

LEAGUE CHAMPIONSHIP FINAL TABLE 99/00

			Home				Away					Total						
		Pd	W	D	L	F	A	W	D	L	F	A	W	D	L	F	A	PT	GD
1	Rangers	36	16	1	1	52	12	12	5	1	44	14	28	6	2	96	26	90	70
2	Celtic	36	12	3	3	58	17	9	3	6	32	21	21	6	9	90	38	69	52
3	Heart of Midlothian	36	7	6	5	25	18	8	3	7	22	22	15	9	12	47	40	54	7
4	Motherwell	36	8	3	7	27	34	6	7	5	22	29	14	10	12	49	63	52	-14
5	St. Johnstone	36	5	7	6	16	18	5	5	8	20	26	10	12	14	36	44	42	-8
6	Hibernian	36	7	6	5	30	27	3	5	10	19	34	10	11	15	49	61	41	-12
7	Dundee	36	4	3	11	20	33	8	2	8	25	31	12	5	19	45	64	41	-19
8	Dundee United	36	6	4	8	16	22	5	2	11	18	35	11	6	19	34	57	39	-23
9	Kilmarnock	36	5	5	8	16	22	3	8	7	22	30	8	13	15	38	52	37	-14
10	Aberdeen	36	6	4	8	28	37	3	2	13	16	46	9	6	21	44	83	33	-39

performances the following spring, drawing 0-0 in Holland and beating the Republic of Ireland 2-1 in Dublin.

Scotland's 'nearly-men' tag was borrowed for the season by the country's top club, Rangers, who were knocked out of both European club competitions by the slenderest of margins, having threatened to make 1999/2000 their most productive season in Europe for several years.

The Ibrox club boosted their overseas image considerably when they eliminated the Italians of Parma in the Champions' League qualifying round. Parma had beaten Rangers en route to lifting the UEFA Cup the previous season, but this time the Scottish champions successfully preserved their first-leg advantage and came through 2-1 on aggregate to reach the Champions' League proper.

Drawn in an extremely difficult group alongside Bayern Munich, Valencia and PSV, Dick Advocaat's multi-national team started badly but home and away wins over PSV put them right back in contention. They travelled to Munich for their final group game needing only a draw to reach the second phase, but it was to be a

totally luckless evening for Scotland's finest. Several times they struck the frame of the goal but the ball just wouldn't cross the line, and they eventually lost the game to a first-half penalty, which goalkeeper Stefan Klos almost saved. Just to rub salt in Rangers' wounds, their new star striker Michael Mols suffered a severe injury during the match and did not play again all season.

Third place in the group allowed Rangers to switch over to the UEFA Cup. Once again they were drawn against German opposition, but having built up a handsome 2-0 first-leg lead against Borussia Dortmund, they unaccountably surrendered the tie in the Westfalenstadion. With the tie seemingly won, they conceded an 'equalising' goal in the third minute of stoppage time, then missed an unmissable chance through McCann ten minutes into the extra period before losing on penalties after failing to convert three spot-kicks out of four.

European success is everything these days to Rangers, and the defeats by Bayern and Dortmund left a huge void in the club's season. At the time of their European exit they

TOP SCORERS

25	Mark VIDUKA (Celtic)
19	Billy DODDS (Dundee United/Rangers)
17	Jörg ALBERTZ (Rangers)
16	Rod WALLACE (Rangers)
13	Willie FALCONER (Dundee United)
	Gary McSWEGAN (Heart of Midlothian)
11	Mark BURCHILL (Celtic)
	Kenny MILLER (Hibernian)
	John SPENCER (Motherwell)
10	Nathan LOWNDES (St. Johnstone)

NATIONAL TEAM RESULTS 99/00

04/09/99	Bosnia-Herzegovina (ECQ)	A	Sarajevo	2-1	Hutchison (13), Dodds (45)
08/09/99	Estonia (ECQ)	A	Tallinn	0-0	
05/10/99	Bosnia-Herzegovina (ECQ)	H	Glasgow	1-0	Collins (26p)
09/10/99	Lithuania (ECQ)	H	Glasgow	3-0	Hutchison (48), McSwegan (50), Cameron (88)
13/11/99	England (ECQ)	H	Glasgow	0-2	
17/11/99	England (ECQ)	A	Wembley	1-0	Hutchison (38)
29/02/00	France	H	Glasgow	0-2	
26/04/00	Holland	A	Arnhem	0-0	
30/05/00	Republic of Ireland	A	Dublin	2-1	Hutchison (17), Ferguson (30)

already had the Scottish championship virtually wrapped up. Yet another flawed challenge from arch-rivals Celtic had enabled Rangers to turn the championship race into a one-club procession. Eight wins in as many games at the very start of the campaign put Rangers on the right road, and they never left it. Victories came thick and fast all season long, and the three Old Firm clashes with Celtic yielded ten points, with the 4-0 annihilation at Ibrox at the end of March killing off the last remnants of any challenge from the green half of Glasgow.

Rangers added to their 49th championship a 29th Scottish Cup triumph, which in turn completed a 16th 'double'. The Cup win, which took them to within one of Celtic's record total, came just as easily as the Premier League triumph. Rangers won every match without recourse to a replay. They beat Hearts 4-1 in the quarter-final and Ayr United 7-0 in the semi before crushing Aberdeen 4-0 in a final that was decided early on when Aberdeen's veteran 'keeper Jim Leighton suffered a serious injury in the early minutes of what was supposed to be his farewell appearance. The Dons had no substitute 'keeper on the bench and were eventually pummelled into submission by the champions, who scored four goals in a 15-minute purple patch either side of the half-time interval.

Aberdeen's season was full of peaks and troughs, with more of the latter than the former. The club had been anticipating a bright new start when they appointed Danish coach Ebbe Skovdahl from Brøndby. But he suffered a nightmare start as the team lost every one of their first six league games without scoring a goal. It was match number ten before they finally won - a bizarre

NATIONAL TEAM APPEARANCES 99/00

Coach - Craig BROWN	BOS	EST	BOS	LIT	ENG	ENG	FRA	HOL	IRL	Cps	Gls
Neil SULLIVAN (24/02/70) - Wimbledon (ENG)	G	G	G		G	G	G	G	G	16	-
David WEIR (10/05/70) - Everton (ENG)	D	D	D	D	D	D		D		20	-
Colin HENDRY (07/12/65) - Rangers/Coventry City (ENG)	D	D	D37		D	D	D			45	1
Colin CALDERWOOD (20/01/65) - Aston Villa (ENG)	D46		s37							36	1
David HOPKIN (21/08/70) - Leeds United (ENG)	M		M							7	2
Craig BURLEY (24/09/71) - Celtic/Derby County (ENG)	M	M	M	M46	M	M		M46	M	38	3
Barry FERGUSON (02/02/78) - Rangers	M69	s65			M	M	M		M84	7	1
John COLLINS (31/01/68) - Everton (ENG)	M	M	M		M	M				58	12
Neil McCANN (11/08/74) - Rangers	M	s54				A74	s46	M	M90	8	-
Don HUTCHISON (09/05/71) - Everton (ENG)	A	A		M	M	A	M	A	A	10	5
Billy DODDS (05/02/69) - Dundee United/Rangers	A	A	A90	s79	A	A	A	A	A46	18	4
Christian DAILLY (23/10/73) - Blackburn Rovers (ENG)	s46	D	D	D	D	D	D	D85	D	23	1
Ian DURRANT (29/10/66) - Kilmarnock	s69	M65						s46	s89	20	-
Allan JOHNSTON (14/12/73) - Sunderland (ENG)/Bolton Wanderers (ENG)		M54					s68		s75	9	2
Callum DAVIDSON (26/06/76) - Blackburn Rovers (ENG)		M	M	M		M	M			12	-
Paul LAMBERT (07/08/69) - Celtic		M	M					M	M75	24	-
Kevin GALLACHER (23/11/66) - Newcastle United (ENG)			A80	s83	A83		A79		s46	48	8
Mark BURCHILL (18/08/80) - Celtic			s80	A79	s83	s74	s79	s67		6	-
Gary McSWEGAN (24/09/70) - Heart of Midlothian			s90	A83						2	1
Jonathan GOULD (18/07/68) - Celtic					G					1	-
Brian O'NEIL (06/09/72) - VfL Wolfsburg (GER)					D			s85	D	5	-
Paul RITCHIE (21/08/75) - Heart of Midlothian/Bolton Wanderers (ENG)					M	M	D46	D		6	1
Colin CAMERON (23/10/72) - Heart of Midlothian				s46			M46		s84	5	1
Paul TELFER (21/10/71) - Coventry City (ENG)							M68			1	-
Steven PRESSLEY (11/10/73) - Heart of Midlothian							s46		s90	2	-
Matt ELLIOTT (01/11/68) - Leicester City (ENG)								D	D	9	-
Jackie McNAMARA (24/10/73) - Celtic								M67		10	-
Gary NAYSMITH (16/11/78) - Heart of Midlothian									M89	1	-

EUROPEAN CUPS 99/00

CHAMPIONS' CUP
● RANGERS
Preliminary round 2 FC HAKA (FIN)
A 4-1 Amoruso (17), Mols (26, 41), Moore (86)
Klos, Adamczuk, Moore, Amoruso, Numan, Reyna (Nicholson 34),
Ferguson B., Van Bronckhorst (Albertz 69), McCann, Mols, Wallace
(Johansson 69).
H 3-0 Wallace (15), Johansson (28), Amato (66)
Klos, Adamczuk, Moore, Amoruso, Numan (Vidmar 39), Ferguson B.
(Nicholson 71), Albertz, Van Bronckhorst, Wallace, Mols (Amato 46),
Johansson.

Qualifying round PARMA (ITA)
H 2-0 Vidmar (33), Reyna (76)
Klos, Porrini, Moore, Amoruso, Vidmar (Albertz 55), Reyna, Ferguson B.,
Van Bronckhorst, McCann, Mols, Wallace.
A 0-1
Charbonnier, Porrini, Moore, Amoruso, Vidmar, Adamczuk (Hendry 83),
Reyna, Ferguson B. (Albertz 73), Van Bronckhorst, Mols, Wallace
(McCann 60).

Champions' League
1st match VALENCIA CF (ESP)
A 0-2
Charbonnier, Porrini (Kanchelskis 71), Amoruso, Moore, Vidmar, Reyna,
Ferguson B., Van Bronckhorst (Johansson 84), McCann (Albertz 46),
Amato, Mols.

2nd match FC BAYERN MÜNCHEN (GER)
H 1-1 Albertz (22)
Charbonnier, Porrini, Amoruso, Moore, Numan, Reyna, Ferguson B., Albertz,
Van Bronckhorst, Mols (Hendry 84), Johansson (McCann 90).

3rd match PSV (HOL)
A 1-0 Albertz (84)
Charbonnier, Porrini, Amoruso, Moore, Numan, Reyna (Albertz 23),
Ferguson B., Van Bronckhorst, McCann, Wallace, Mols.

4th match PSV (HOL)
H 4-1 Amoruso (19), Mols (34, 80), McCann (56)
Klos, Porrini, Amoruso, Moore, Vidmar, Ferguson B., McInnes,
Van Bronckhorst, McCann (Albertz 71), Mols (Johansson 81), Wallace
(Kanchelskis 88).

5th match VALENCIA CF (ESP)
H 1-2 Moore (60)
Klos, Porrini, Amoruso, Moore, Vidmar (Albertz 61), Ferguson B., McInnes
(Kanchelskis 38), Van Bronckhorst, McCann, Mols, Wallace (Johansson 75).

6th match FC BAYERN MÜNCHEN (GER)
A 0-1
Klos, Porrini, Amoruso, Moore, Numan (McCann 71), Reyna, Ferguson B.,
Albertz, Van Bronckhorst, Mols (Johansson 29), Wallace (Amato 79).

UEFA CUP
● CELTIC
Qualifying round CWMBRAN TOWN (WAL)
A 6-0 Berkovic (2), Tébily (19), Larsson (32, 59), Viduka (49), Brattbakk (84)
Gould, Riseth, Stubbs, Tébily, Mahé, Burley, Berkovic, Lambert, Petta
(Blinker 46), Larsson (Johnson 81), Viduka (Brattbakk 81).
H 4-0 Brattbakk (8), Smith (60), Mjällby (65), Johnson (88)
Kharin, Healy, Riseth, Stubbs, McKinlay, Petta (Johnson 70), Wieghorst
(Smith 46), Mjällby, Blinker, Burchill, Brattbakk.

1st round HAPOEL TEL-AVIV (ISR)
H 2-0 Larsson (24, 49p)
Gould, McNamara, Stubbs, Tébily, Mahé, Moravcik, Lambert, Burley, Petta
(Blinker 85), Larsson, Burchill.
A 1-0 Larsson (60)
Gould, Riseth, Stubbs, Tébily, Petrov (Wieghorst 60), McNamara, Burley,
Lambert, Moravcik (Blinker 63), Viduka (Berkovic 70), Larsson.

2nd round OLYMPIQUE LYONNAIS (FRA)
A 0-1
Gould, McNamara, Stubbs, Tébily, Riseth, Burley, Lambert, Mjällby, Moravcik
(Petta 64), Larsson (Burchill 9), Viduka.
H 0-1
Gould, McNamara, Stubbs, Tébily, Riseth, Berkovic, Lambert, Burley,
Moravcik (Blinker 80), Viduka, Burchill.

● KILMARNOCK
Qualifying round KR (ISL)
A 0-1
Meldrum, McPherson, Jeffrey (Wright 85), McGowne, Innes, Reilly, Holt,
Mitchell, Dindeleux, Roberts (Vareille 61), Hay.
H 2-0 (aet) Wright (90p), Bagan (92)
Meldrum, MacPherson, Henry (Bagan 80), Holt, Lauchlan, Baker, Dindeleux,
Durrant, Mahood (Vareille 46), McCoist (Jeffrey 67), Wright.

1st round 1.FC KAISERSLAUTERN (GER)
A 0-3
Meldrum, MacPherson, McGowne, Holt, Lauchlan, Durrant (Reilly 75),
Mahood, Baker, Bagan, Mitchell (Burke 60), Vareille (Jeffrey 70).
H 0-2
Meldrum, MacPherson, Baker, McGowne, Innes, Dindeleux, Durrant, Holt,
Vareille (Jeffrey 60), Reilly, McCoist (Mitchell 65).

● RANGERS
3rd round BORUSSIA DORTMUND (GER)
H 2-0 Kohler (18og), Wallace (44)
Myhre, Adamczuk, Moore, Vidmar, Numan, Reyna (Kanchelskis 85),
Ferguson B., Albertz, Van Bronckhorst, Wallace (McCann 67), Amato
(Johansson 46).
A 0-2 (aet; 3-1 on pens.)
Myhre, Adamczuk (Kanchelskis 90), Amoruso, Moore, Numan, Ferguson B.,
Reyna, Albertz (Durie 46), Van Bronckhorst, McCann, Wallace (Vidmar 89).

● ST. JOHNSTONE
Qualifying round VPS (FIN)
A 1-1 Lowndes (76)
Main, McQuillan, Bollan, Dasovic, Weir, Dods, Simão (Grant 54), O'Neil,
McAnespie, McMahon (Lowndes 70), Kane.
H 2-0 Simão (87, 90)
Main, McQuillan, Weir, Dods, Bollan, O'Neil, Kane, Dasovic, McMahon,
McAnespie (Grant 55), Lowndes (Simão 81).

1st round AS MONACO (FRA)
A 0-3
Main, McQuillan, Bollan, McAnespie, Weir, Griffin, Simão (McCluskey 79),
O'Neil, Thomas (Lowndes 63), O'Halloran, Kane.
H 3-3 Léonard (5og), Dasovic (35), O'Neil (76)
Main, McQuillan, Griffin, Kernaghan, Bollan, Dasovic, Kane (McAnespie 60),
O'Halloran (Grant 80), O'Neil, Simão, Lowndes (O'Boyle 80).

DOMESTIC CUP 99/00

THIRD ROUND
Albion Rovers 1, Partick Thistle 2
Clyde 3, Raith Rovers 1
Clydebank 1, Stirling Albion 0
Dundee 0, Ayr United 0
(replay) Ayr United 1, Dundee 1 (aet; 7-6 on pens.)
Falkirk 3, Peterhead 1
Heart of Midlothian 3, Stenhousemuir 2
Hibernian 4, Dunfermline Athletic 1
Queen of the South 0, Livingston 7
St. Mirren 1, Aberdeen 1
(replay) Aberdeen 2, St. Mirren 0
Stranraer 1, Berwick Rangers 2
Dundee United 4, Airdrieonians 1
Greenock Morton 1, Brechin City 1
(replay) Brechin City 0, Greenock Morton 0
(aet; 3-4 on pens.)
St. Johnstone 0, Rangers 2
Arbroath 1, Motherwell 1
(replay) Motherwell 2, Arbroath 0
Kilmarnock 0, Alloa Athletic 0
(replay) Alloa Athletic 1, Kilmarnock 0
Celtic 1, Inverness Caledonian Thistle 3

FOURTH ROUND
Alloa Athletic 2, Dundee United 2
(replay) Dundee United 4, Alloa Athletic 0
Berwick Rangers 0, Falkirk 0
(replay) Falkirk 3, Berwick Rangers 0
Clyde 0, Heart of Midlothian 2
Greenock Morton 0, Rangers 1
Hibernian 1, Clydebank 1
(replay) Clydebank 0, Hibernian 3
Partick Thistle 2, Livingston 1
Inverness Caledonian Thistle 1, Aberdeen 1
(replay) Aberdeen 1, Inverness Caledonian Thistle 0
Motherwell 3, Ayr United 4

QUARTER-FINALS
Ayr United 2 (Duffy 25, Tarrant 50), Partick Thistle 0
Hibernian 3 (Latapy 25, 43p, McGinlay 90),
Falkirk 1 (Lawrie 32)
Dundee United 0, Aberdeen 1 (Jess 83)
Rangers 4 (Ferguson B. 12, Numan 17, Amoruso 69,
Dodds 79p),
Heart of Midlothian 1 (Cameron 34p)

SEMI-FINALS
Ayr United 0, Rangers 7 (Rozental 18, 89,
Kanchelskis 27, Wallace 41, Dodds 66, 72, 86)
Hibernian 1 (Latapy 56),
Aberdeen 2 (Stavrum 64, Dow 68)

FINAL
27/05/2000, Glasgow (Hampden)
RANGERS 4 Van Bronckhorst (35), Vidmar (47),
Dodds (49), Albertz (51)
ABERDEEN 0
referee - McCluskey
RANGERS - Klos, Reyna, Moore (Porrini 71), Vidmar,
Numan, Kanchelskis, Ferguson B., Van Bronckhorst
(Tugay 73), Albertz, Dodds, Wallace (McCann 66).
ABERDEEN - Leighton (Winters 71), Whyte, Solberg,
Anderson (Belabed 40), McAllister, Dow, Bernard,
Rowson, Guntveit, Jess, Stavrum (Zerouali 68).

PLAYERS OF THE SEASON

BARRY FERGUSON

Barry Ferguson is that rare and precious commodity - a locally-born footballer who is an automatic selection for Rangers. These days it is common to find more Italians, Germans and South Americans in the Rangers line-up than Scotsmen. But Ferguson is no shrinking violet and has worked hard to get where he is, forcing his way through the Ibrox ranks with a succession of impressive performances to claim near-permanent residence in Dick Advocaat's first-choice XI. A midfielder of immense promise, the 22-year-old became a regular for Scotland during the 1999/2000 season and was a strong candidate for man of the match in the 1-0 victory over England at Wembley, where his clever distribution and coolness under pressure were extremely impressive. Ferguson's sustained excellence for both club and country earned him the Scottish Writers' Footballer of the Year award for 2000, ample consolation for having just missed out on the Players' equivalent, which went to Celtic's Australian striker Mark Viduka, the Scottish Premier League's top scorer with 25 goals.

DON HUTCHISON

Very much a journeyman professional for much of his career, Gateshead-born Don Hutchison hogged the headlines on both sides of the Border when he scored the winning goal for his adopted Scotland against his native England in the Euro 2000 play-off showdown at Wembley. That was just one of four international goals the tall, abrasive midfielder-cum-striker scored in 1999/2000, the others also helping Scotland to victories - against Bosnia-Herzegovina, Lithuania and the Republic of Ireland. His début international goal had come the season before in a 1-0 win away to Germany, so he clearly specialises in scoring meaningful goals. Hutchison also had a creditable season at club level with Everton, although in the summer the Merseysiders agreed to a £2.25m transfer bid from Sunderland, which enabled the 29-year-old to return to his native North-East.

6-5 victory away to Motherwell - but the Dons were never able to claw themselves clear of bottom place.

As the tenth-placed club, Aberdeen should have entered a three-way play-off with the second and third-placed teams in the First Division in order to preserve their Premier League status, but as Falkirk's ground did not not conform with Premier League requirements, Aberdeen were spared. In the Cups, Skovdahl's men were transformed. They reached both finals, even eliminating Rangers en route to the League Cup final, which they lost 2-0 to Celtic.

The League Cup victory was cold comfort to Celtic fans in a season that they would gladly erase from the memory. The appointment of inexperienced ex-English international winger John Barnes as the team's head coach, with former Celtic idol Kenny Dalglish as 'director of football', always seemed a suspect choice. The team began the season reasonably well, but they soon fell behind Rangers and never looked likely to make up the deficit.

There were a succession of low points for the fans to contend with. Exiting the UEFA Cup at the second-round stage was bad enough, but in doing so the team lost the services of their best player, Swedish striker Henrik Larsson, who suffered a terrible double leg fracture during the first game away to Lyon. Then there were the three Old Firm defeats - two at Ibrox, one at Parkhead. Above all, though, there was the humiliating Scottish Cup defeat at home to Inverness Caledonian Thistle. Celtic were beaten 3-1 by the First Division side on a night that many Celtic

INTERNATIONAL HONOURS

World Cup Finals appearances: 1954, 1958, 1974, 1978, 1982, 1986, 1990, 1998

European Championship appearances: 1992, 1996

European Club Competitions
Champions' Cup	Celtic (1967)
Cup-winners' Cup	Rangers (1972)
	Aberdeen (1983)
Super Cup	Aberdeen (1983)

supporters regarded as one of the blackest in the club's 113-year history.

The fall-out resulted in the inevitable sacking of Barnes, who was replaced, temporarily, by Dalglish. It made little difference to the team's fortunes, and in any case there was not much left for Celtic to play for. They were already certain of securing second place. For the final few weeks of the season the main topic of interest at the club was who would be appointed to take charge for the 2000/01 season. At the end of May, the Celtic faithful got their answer when the club proudly unveiled Martin O'Neill as their new manager. The Ulsterman had worked wonders in England with Leicester City, and his credentials, added to a Catholic background, made him a highly popular choice. If anyone could bring an end to Rangers' supremacy, then O'Neill would be the man. At least that was the fervent hope in the East End of Glasgow...

PROMOTED CLUBS 99/00

FIRST DIVISION FINAL TABLE

		Pd	W	D	L	F	A	Pt	GD
1	**St. Mirren**	36	23	7	6	75	39	76	36
2	**Dunfermline Athletic**	36	20	11	5	66	33	71	33
3	Falkirk	36	20	8	8	67	40	68	27
4	Livingston	36	19	7	10	60	45	64	15
5	Raith Rovers	36	17	8	11	55	40	59	15
6	Inverness Caledonian Thistle	36	13	10	13	60	55	49	5
7	Ayr United	36	10	8	18	42	52	38	-10
8	Greenock Morton	36	10	6	20	45	61	36	-16
9	Airdrieonians	36	7	8	21	29	69	29	-40
10	Clydebank	36	1	7	28	17	82	10	-65

CLUB DIRECTORIES

Dunfermline Athletic FC
East End Park, Halbeath Road, Dunfermline
Fife KY12 7RB
tel - (01383) 724295 / fax - (01383) 723468
Year of Formation - 1885
Chairman - C.R. Woodrow
Manager - Jim Calderwood
Stadium - East End Park (12,509)

MAJOR HONOURS
Scottish Cup - (2) 1961, 1968.

St. Mirren FC
St. Mirren Park, Love Street, Paisley PA3 2EJ
tel - (0141) 8892558 / fax - (0141) 8486444
Year of Formation - 1877
Chairman - S.G. Gilmour
Managaer - Tom Hendrie
Stadium - St. Mirren Park (10,866)

MAJOR HONOURS
Scottish Cup - (3) 1926, 1959, 1987.

ABERDEEN

THE EUROPEAN FOOTBALL YEARBOOK 2000-2001

CLUB DIRECTORY

Aberdeen FC
Pittodrie Stadium, Pittodrie Street
Aberdeen AB24 5QH
tel - (01224) 650400 / fax - (01224) 644173
website - www.afc.co.uk
email - talkback@thedons.co.uk
Year of Formation - 1903
Chairman - Stewart Milne
Secretary - Richard A.M. Ramsay
Manager - Ebbe Skovdahl
Stadium - Pittodrie Stadium (22,199)

MAJOR HONOURS
League Championship - (4)
1955, 1980, 1984, 1985.
Scottish Cup - (7)
1947, 1970, 1982, 1983, 1984, 1986, 1990.
League Cup - (5)
1956, 1977, 1986, 1990, 1996.
European Cup-winners' Cup - (1) 1983
European Super Cup - (1) 1983.

APPEARANCES 99/00

	P	Ap	(s)	Gls
Russell ANDERSON	D	34		1
Rachid BELABED (MAR)	M	6	(15)	1
Paul BERNARD	M	24	(1)	4
Baldur BETT (ISL)	A		(1)	
Jamie BUCHAN	D	5	(3)	
Chris CLARK	A		(2)	
Juan COBIAN (ARG)	D	2	(1)	
Andy DOW	M	35		5
Ryan ESSON	G	1		
Ricky GILLIES	M	3	(7)	1
Cato GUNTVEIT (NOR)	M	20		3
Jim HAMILTON	A	3	(4)	
Michael HART	M	2	(1)	
Eoin JESS	A	25	(1)	5
Ilian KIRIAKOV (BUL)	M	6	(2)	
Jim LEIGHTON	G	26		
David LILLEY	D	14	(3)	
Jamie McALLISTER	D	29	(5)	
Phil McGUIRE	M		(3)	
Darren MACKIE	A	2	(2)	
Andreas MAYER (GER)	M	20	(1)	
Nigel PEPPER (ENG)	D	4		
Mark PERRY	D	10	(8)	
Dave PREECE (ENG)	G	9	(1)	
David ROWSON	M	2	(3)	1
Kevin RUTKIEWICZ	M	1	(9)	
Gary SMITH	D	6		
Thomas SOLBERG (NOR)	D	26		4
Arild STAVRUM (NOR)	A	22		9
Derek WHYTE	D	19	(1)	
Robbie WINTERS	A	23	(10)	7
Dennis WYNESS	M	1	(2)	
Darren YOUNG	D	1	(2)	
Derek YOUNG	M	9	(5)	
Hicham ZEROUALI (MAR)	A	6	(8)	3

LEAGUE RESULTS 1999/2000

Date	Opponent	H/A	Score	Scorers
01/08/99	Celtic	H	0-5	
07/08/99	Kilmarnock	A	0-2	
14/08/99	Dundee	H	0-2	
22/08/99	Heart of Midlothian	A	0-3	
29/08/99	St. Johnstone	H	0-3	
11/09/99	Rangers	A	0-3	
18/09/99	Dundee United	H	1-2	Dow
02/10/99	Hibernian	H	2-2	Jess, Gillies
16/10/99	Celtic	A	0-7	
20/10/99	Motherwell	A	6-5	Dow, Winters 3, Jess, Bernard
23/10/99	Kilmarnock	H	2-2	Bernard 2
30/10/99	Rangers	H	1-5	Solberg (p)
06/11/99	Dundee United	A	1-3	Solberg (p)
21/11/99	St. Johnstone	A	1-1	Dow
27/11/99	Hibernian	A	0-2	
08/12/99	Heart of Midlothian	H	3-1	Jess, Stavrum, Guntveit
11/12/99	Celtic	H	0-6	
27/12/99	Dundee United	H	3-1	Zerouali, Belabed, Stavrum (p)
22/01/00	Rangers	A	0-5	
26/01/00	Motherwell	H	1-1	Zerouali
05/02/00	St. Johnstone	H	2-1	Stavrum (p), Winters
23/02/00	Dundee	A	3-1	Dow, Stavrum, Bernard
26/02/00	Hibernian	H	4-0	Stavrum 2, Guntveit, Anderson
04/03/00	Motherwell	A	0-1	
22/03/00	Heart of Midlothian	A	0-3	
25/03/00	Dundee United	A	1-1	Stavrum
01/04/00	Rangers	H	1-1	Guntveit
12/04/00	Kilmarnock	A	0-1	
15/04/00	Heart of Midlothian	H	1-2	Stavrum
18/04/00	Dundee	H	0-1	
22/04/00	Motherwell	H	2-1	Dow, Solberg
29/04/00	Hibernian	A	0-1	
02/05/00	St. Johnstone	A	1-2	Winters
06/05/00	Celtic	A	1-5	Winters
14/05/00	Kilmarnock	H	5-1	Zerouali, Rowson, Jess, Solberg (p), Winters
21/05/00	Dundee	A	2-0	Stavrum, Jess

CELTIC

Celtic FC
Celtic Park, Glasgow G40 3RE
tel - (0141) 5562611 / fax - (0141) 5518106
website - www.celticfc.co.uk
Year of Formation - 1887
Chief Executive - Allan McDonald
Manager - John Barnes; Kenny Dalglish
(00/01 - Martin O'Neill)
Stadium - Celtic Park (60,506)

MAJOR HONOURS
League Championship - (36) 1893, 1894, 1896,
1898, 1905, 1906, 1907, 1908, 1909, 1910,
1914, 1915, 1916, 1917, 1919, 1922, 1926,
1936, 1938, 1954, 1966, 1967, 1968, 1969,
1970, 1971, 1972, 1973, 1974, 1977, 1979,
1981, 1982, 1986, 1988, 1998.
Scottish Cup - (30) 1892, 1899, 1900, 1904,
1907, 1908, 1911, 1912, 1914, 1923, 1925,
1927, 1931, 1933, 1937, 1951, 1954, 1965,
1967, 1969, 1971, 1972, 1974, 1975, 1977,
1980, 1985, 1988, 1989, 1995.
League Cup - (11) 1957, 1958, 1966, 1967,
1968, 1969, 1970, 1975, 1983, 1997, 1999.
European Champions' Cup - (1) 1967.

	P	Ap	(s)	Gls
Eyal BERKOVIC (ISR)	M	27	(1)	9
Regi BLINKER (HOL)	A	10	(7)	4
Tom BOYD (D)	D	10		
Harald BRATTBAKK (NOR)	A		(2)	
Mark BURCHILL (A)	A	12	(16)	11
Craig BURLEY	M	6	(2)	1
John CONVERY (NIR)	D		(1)	
Stephen CRAINEY	D	5	(4)	
Fernando DE ORNELAS (POR)	D		(4)	
Mark FOTHERINGHAM	M	1	(1)	
James GOODWIN (IRL)	D	1		
Jonathan GOULD	G	28	(1)	
Colin HEALY (IRL)	M	8	(2)	1
Tommy JOHNSON (ENG)	A	7	(3)	9
John KENNEDY	M	1	(4)	
Stewart KERR	G	4		
Dmitriy KHARIN (RUS)	G	4		
Paul LAMBERT	M	25		1
Henrik LARSSON (SWE)	A	8	(1)	7
Simon LYNCH	A	1	(1)	1
Ryan McCANN	A	1		
Brian McCOLLIGAN	D	1		
Jackie McNAMARA	M	23		
Stéphane MAHE (FRA)	D	19		4
Liam MILLER (IRL)	D		(1)	
Johan MJÄLLBY (SWE)	D	26	(4)	2
Lubomir MORAVCIK (SVK)	M	29	(1)	8
Stilian PETROV (BUL)	M	20	(6)	1
Bobby PETTA (HOL)	M	2	(10)	
RAFAEL Scheidt (BRA)	D	1	(2)	
Vidar RISETH (NOR)	D	28		
Paul SHIELDS	M		(1)	
Alan STUBBS (ENG)	D	23		
Olivier TEBILY (CIV)	D	19	(4)	
Mark VIDUKA (AUS)	A	28		25
Morten WIEGHORST (DEN)	D	14	(3)	3
Ian WRIGHT (ENG)	A	4	(4)	3

01/08/99	Aberdeen	A	5-0	Larsson 2 (1p), Viduka 2, Burchill
07/08/99	St. Johnstone	H	3-0	Mjällby, Viduka, Wieghorst
15/08/99	Dundee United	A	1-2	Berkovic
21/08/99	Dundee	A	2-1	Mahé, Larsson
29/08/99	Heart of Midlothian	H	4-0	Viduka, Larsson, Berkovic 2
12/09/99	Kilmarnock	A	1-0	Burchill
25/09/99	Hibernian	A	2-0	Viduka 2
16/10/99	Aberdeen	H	7-0	Berkovic, Larsson 3, Viduka 3
24/10/99	St. Johnstone	A	2-1	Burchill, Wieghorst
27/10/99	Motherwell	H	0-1	
30/10/99	Kilmarnock	H	5-1	Viduka 3, Wright, Burley
07/11/99	Rangers	A	2-4	Berkovic 2
20/11/99	Heart of Midlothian	A	2-1	Wright, Moravcik
28/11/99	Motherwell	A	2-3	Berkovic, Viduka (p)
04/12/99	Hibernian	H	4-0	Viduka (p), Moravcik 2, Wieghorst
11/12/99	Aberdeen	A	6-0	Lambert, Mahé, Moravcik, Viduka,
				Blinker, Wright
18/12/99	Dundee United	H	4-1	Blinker, Viduka, Moravcik, Burchill
27/12/99	Rangers	H	1-1	Viduka
23/01/00	Kilmarnock	A	1-1	Viduka
05/02/00	Heart of Midlothian	H	2-3	Moravcik, Viduka
12/02/00	Dundee	A	3-0	Mjällby, Viduka, Healy
01/03/00	Dundee	H	6-2	Johnson 3, Viduka 2 (1p), Petrov
05/03/00	Hibernian	A	1-2	Viduka
08/03/00	Rangers	H	0-1	
11/03/00	St. Johnstone	H	4-1	Burchill 2, Viduka 2
26/03/00	Rangers	A	0-4	
02/04/00	Kilmarnock	H	4-2	Johnson, Blinker, Berkovic, Burchill
05/04/00	Motherwell	H	4-0	Johnson 2, Berkovic, Blinker
08/04/00	Heart of Midlothian	A	0-1	
15/04/00	Dundee	H	2-2	Mahé, Burchill
22/04/00	Hibernian	H	1-1	Mahé
29/04/00	Motherwell	A	1-1	Burchill
02/05/00	Dundee United	A	1-0	Burchill
06/05/00	Aberdeen	H	5-1	Johnson 3, Moravcik 2
13/05/00	St. Johnstone	A	0-0	
21/05/00	Dundee United	H	2-0	Lynch, Burchill

DUNDEE

CLUB DIRECTORY

Dundee FC
Dens Park Stadium
Sandeman Street
Dundee, DD3 7JY
tel - (01382) 889966
fax - (01382) 832284
email - dfc@dundeefc.co.uk
Year of Formation - 1893
Chairman - Jim Marr
Chief Executive - Peter Marr
Manager - Jocky Scott (00/01 - Ivano Bonetti)
Stadium - Dens Park (12,371)

MAJOR HONOURS
League Championship - (1) 1962
Scottish Cup - (1) 1910.
League Cup - (3) 1952, 1953, 1974.

APPEARANCES 99/00

	P	Ap	(s)	Gls
Eddie ANNAND	A	18	(9)	4
Javiez ARTERO LOPEZ (ARG)	M	6	(3)	1
Nicky BANGER (ENG)	A	2	(4)	
Graham BAYNE	A	3	(10)	1
Patrizio BILLIO (ITA)	M	16	(1)	1
Stephen BOYAK	A	32	(4)	1
Tommy COYNE (IRL)	A		(1)	
Robert DOUGLAS	G	35		
John ELLIOTT	A		(1)	
Willie FALCONER	A	31		13
Jim GRADY	A	18	(13)	6
Craig IRELAND	D	14		1
James LANGFIELD	G	1		
LUNA (BRA)	A	5	(4)	3
Shaun McSKIMMING	M	20	(2)	2
Lee MADDISON (ENG)	D	19	(1)	
Roberto MATUTE (ESP)	A	1	(4)	
Willie MILLER	D	10	(2)	
Gavin RAE	D	35		4
Robert RAESIDE	D	1		
Hugh ROBERTSON	D	15	(8)	2
Lee SHARP	D	11	(3)	1
Mark SLATER	D		(1)	
Barry SMITH	D	32		
Steven TWEED	D	34		2
Frank VAN EIJS (HOL)	D	14	(2)	
Lee WILKIE	D	21	(3)	
Michael YATES	A	2	(3)	1

LEAGUE RESULTS 1999/2000

31/07/99	Dundee United	A	1-2	Falconer
08/08/99	Hibernian	H	3-4	og (Lovering), McSkimming, Annand (p)
14/08/99	Aberdeen	A	2-0	Falconer 2
21/08/99	Celtic	H	1-2	Sharp
28/08/99	Motherwell	A	2-0	Annand, Falconer
11/09/99	Heart of Midlothian	A	0-4	
19/09/99	St. Johnstone	H	1-2	Yates
25/09/99	Kilmarnock	A	2-0	Boyack, Rae
02/10/99	Rangers	H	2-3	McSkimming, Falconer
17/10/99	Dundee United	H	0-2	
23/10/99	Hibernian	A	2-5	Falconer 2
30/10/99	Heart of Midlothian	H	1-0	Tweed
06/11/99	St. Johnstone	A	1-0	Annand
20/11/99	Motherwell	H	0-1	
28/11/99	Rangers	A	2-1	Ireland, Rae
12/12/99	Dundee United	A	0-1	
27/12/99	St. Johnstone	H	1-1	Falconer
22/01/00	Heart of Midlothian	A	0-2	
26/01/00	Kilmarnock	H	0-0	
05/02/00	Motherwell	A	3-0	Robertson, Rae, Grady (p)
12/02/00	Celtic	H	0-3	
23/02/00	Aberdeen	H	1-3	Bayne
27/02/00	Rangers	H	1-7	Tweed
01/03/00	Celtic	A	2-6	Robertson, Grady
04/03/00	Kilmarnock	A	2-2	Annand, Grady
21/03/00	Hibernian	A	2-1	Falconer 2
25/03/00	St. Johnstone	A	1-2	Falconer
01/04/00	Heart of Midlothian	H	0-0	
08/04/00	Motherwell	H	4-1	Grady 2, Billio (p), Luna
15/04/00	Celtic	A	2-2	Luna, og (Gould)
18/04/00	Aberdeen	A	1-0	Artero López
22/04/00	Kilmarnock	H	1-2	Luna
30/04/00	Rangers	A	0-3	
06/05/00	Dundee United	H	3-0	Falconer 2, Grady
14/05/00	Hibernian	H	1-0	Rae
21/05/00	Aberdeen	H	0-2	

DUNDEE UNITED

CLUB DIRECTORY

Dundee United FC
Tannadice Park, Tannadice Street
Dundee DD3 7JW
tel - (01382) 833166 / fax - (01382) 889398
email - dundee.united.fc@cableinet.co.uk
Year of Formation - 1909
Chairman - Jim McLean
Secretary - Miss Priti Trivedi
Manager - Paul Stuurock
Stadium - Tannadice Park (14,209)

MAJOR HONOURS
League Championship - (1) 1983.
Scottish Cup - (1) 1994.
League Cup - (2) 1980, 1981.

APPEARANCES 99/00

	P	Ap	(s)	Gls
Raphael BOVE	D		(1)	
David BYRNE (IRL)	M		(1)	
Alan COMBE	G	35		
Hugh DAVIDSON	A	17	(6)	
Jason DE VOS (CAN)	D	35		2
Jean-Pierre DELAUNAY (FRA)	D	1		
Billy DODDS	A	15		9
Craig EASTON	M	22	(10)	1
Joaquim FERRAZ (POR)	A	15	(13)	6
Paul GALLACHER	G	1		
Jim HAMILTON	A	8	(5)	1
David HANNAH	M	33		6
Iain JENKINS (NIR)	D	1		
Leigh JENKINSON (ENG)	A	1	(3)	
Siggi JÓNSSON (ISL)	M	14		
Stephen McCONALOGUE	A	9	(7)	
David McCRACKEN	D	2		
Scott McCULLOCH	D	10	(5)	
John McQUILLAN	D	11		
Maurice MALPAS	D	8	(4)	
Alex MATHIE	A	10	(2)	3
Sean O'CONNOR (IRL)	M	1		
David PARTRIDGE (ENG)	D	29		
Bernard PASCUAL (FRA)	D	30	(2)	
Jim PATERSON	M	8		1
Darren PATTERSON (NIR)	D	6		
Antoine PREGET (FRA)	D	3	(1)	
Magnus SKÖLDMARK (SWE)	A	7	(4)	1
Tony SMITH	M	4	(3)	
Jan TELESNIKOV (ISR)	M	22	(3)	3
Steven THOMPSON	A	16	(11)	1
Anastasios VENETIS (GRE)	M	12	(5)	
David WORRELL (IRL)	D	10	(3)	

LEAGUE RESULTS 1999/2000

31/07/99	Dundee	H	2-1	Sköldmark, Ferraz
07/08/99	Motherwell	A	2-2	Dodds, Ferraz
15/08/99	Celtic	H	2-1	Easton, Dodds
21/08/99	Rangers	A	1-4	De Vos
29/08/99	Kilmarnock	H	0-0	
11/09/99	Hibernian	H	3-1	Telesnikov, Hannah, Dodds (p)
18/09/99	Aberdeen	A	2-1	Hannah, Dodds
25/09/99	Heart of Midlothian	H	0-2	
17/10/99	Dundee	A	2-0	Dodds, Thompson
23/10/99	Motherwell	H	0-2	
27/10/99	St. Johnstone	A	1-0	Dodds
31/10/99	Hibernian	A	2-3	Dodds, Telesnikov
06/11/99	Aberdeen	H	3-1	Dodds 2, Paterson
20/11/99	Kilmarnock	A	1-1	Hannah
27/11/99	St. Johnstone	H	1-0	Telesnikov
05/12/99	Heart of Midlothian	A	0-3	
12/12/99	Dundee	H	1-0	Ferraz
18/12/99	Celtic	A	1-4	Ferraz
27/12/99	Aberdeen	A	1-3	Hannah
22/01/00	Hibernian	H	0-0	
02/02/00	Rangers	H	0-4	
26/02/00	St. Johnstone	A	0-2	
04/03/00	Heart of Midlothian	H	0-1	
15/03/00	Kilmarnock	H	2-2	Hannah, Ferraz
25/03/00	Aberdeen	H	1-1	Ferraz
01/04/00	Hibernian	A	0-1	
04/04/00	Rangers	A	0-3	
08/04/00	Kilmarnock	A	0-1	
15/04/00	Rangers	H	0-2	
19/04/00	Motherwell	A	3-1	Mathie, Hannah, De Vos
22/04/00	Heart of Midlothian	A	2-1	Mathie 2
29/04/00	St. Johnstone	H	0-1	
02/05/00	Celtic	H	0-1	
06/05/00	Dundee	A	0-3	
13/05/00	Motherwell	H	1-2	Hamilton (p)
21/05/00	Celtic	A	0-2	

HEART OF MIDLOTHIAN

CLUB DIRECTORY

Heart of Midlothian FC
Tynecastle Park
Gorgie Road
Edinburgh EH11 2NL
tel - (0131) 2007200
fax - (0131) 2007222
website - www.heartsfc.co.uk
Year of Formation - 1874
Chairman - Douglas Smith
Chief Executive - Christopher P. Robinson
Manager - Jim Jefferies
Stadium - Tynecastle Park (18,000)

MAJOR HONOURS
League Championship - (4)
1895, 1897, 1958, 1960.
Scottish Cup - (6)
1891, 1896, 1901, 1906, 1956, 1998.
League Cup - (4) 1955, 1959, 1960, 1963.

APPEARANCES 99/00

	P	Ap	(s)	Gls
Stéphane ADAM (FRA)	A	18	(7)	4
Colin CAMERON	M	31	(1)	8
Thomas FLÖGEL (AUT)	M	28	(1)	1
Steve FULTON	M	16	(10)	1
Alasdair GRAHAM	A		(1)	
Darren JACKSON	A	31	(4)	6
Kevin JAMES	D	8	(2)	
JUANJO Carricondo Pérez (ESP)	A	2	(13)	3
Andy KIRK (NIR)	A	1	(3)	
Fabien LECLERCQ (FRA)	D	8	(2)	
Gary LOCKE	D	9	(3)	
Roddy McKENZIE	G	3	(2)	
Rob McKINNON	D	3		
Gary McSWEGAN	A	23	(7)	13
Lee MAKEL (ENG)	M	11	(6)	
Kenny MILNE	D		(1)	
Grant MURRAY	D	15	(5)	
Gary NAYSMITH	D	34	(1)	1
Antti NIEMI (FIN)	G	17		
Gordan PETRIC (YUG)	D	17	(1)	
Steven PRESSLEY	D	36		
José QUITONGO (ANG)	A		(1)	
Paul RITCHIE	D	14		1
Gilles ROUSSET (FRA)	G	16		
Scott SEVERIN	A	18	(5)	2
Fitzroy SIMPSON (JAM)	M	7	(4)	
Robert TOMASCHEK (SVK)	M	13	(1)	
Gary WALES	A	17	(8)	6

LEAGUE RESULTS 1999/2000

31/07/99	St. Johnstone	A	4-1	McSwegan, Flögel, og (Dodds), Cameron
07/08/99	Rangers	H	0-4	
14/08/99	Hibernian	A	1-1	McSwegan
22/08/99	Aberdeen	H	3-0	McSwegan 3
29/08/99	Celtic	A	0-4	
11/09/99	Dundee	H	4-0	Adam, Jackson, Cameron, Severin
25/09/99	Dundee United	A	2-0	Adam 2
16/10/99	St. Johnstone	H	1-1	McSwegan
27/10/99	Kilmarnock	H	2-2	Cameron, Juanjo
30/10/99	Dundee	A	0-1	
06/11/99	Motherwell	H	1-1	McSwegan
20/11/99	Celtic	H	1-2	Cameron
23/11/99	Motherwell	A	1-2	McSwegan
27/11/99	Kilmarnock	A	2-2	McSwegan, Ritchie
05/12/99	Dundee United	H	3-0	Juanjo, Jackson, Adam
08/12/99	Aberdeen	A	1-3	Severin
19/12/99	Hibernian	H	0-3	
22/12/99	Rangers	A	0-1	
22/01/00	Dundee	H	2-0	Wales, Jackson
05/02/00	Celtic	A	3-2	Cameron 2 (1p), Naysmith
26/02/00	Kilmarnock	H	0-0	
01/03/00	Motherwell	A	2-0	Jackson, Wales
04/03/00	Dundee United	A	1-0	Cameron (p)
15/03/00	St. Johnstone	A	1-0	McSwegan
18/03/00	Hibernian	A	1-3	Jackson
22/03/00	Aberdeen	H	3-0	Cameron, Wales, Fulton
25/03/00	Motherwell	H	0-0	
01/04/00	Dundee	A	0-0	
08/04/00	Celtic	H	1-0	McSwegan
12/04/00	Rangers	H	1-2	McSwegan
15/04/00	Aberdeen	A	2-1	Wales, Jackson
22/04/00	Dundee United	H	1-2	Wales
29/04/00	Kilmarnock	A	1-0	Wales
06/05/00	St. Johnstone	H	0-0	
13/05/00	Rangers	A	0-1	
21/05/00	Hibernian	H	2-1	Juanjo, McSwegan

HIBERNIAN

CLUB DIRECTORY

Hibernian FC
Easter Road Stadium
Albion Road
Edinburgh EH7 5QG
tel - (0131) 6612159
fax - (0131) 6596488/6521907
website - www.hibs.co.uk
Year of Formation - 1875
Chairman - Malcolm McPherson
Secretary - Mary Anne McAdam
Manager - Alex McLeish
Stadium - Easter Road (16,032)

MAJOR HONOURS
League Championship - (4)
1903, 1948, 1951, 1952.
Scottish Cup - (2) 1887, 1902.
League Cup - (2) 1973, 1992.

APPEARANCES 99/00

		P	Ap	(s)	Gls
Scott BANNERMAN	M			(1)	
Grant BREBNER	M		27	(1)	
Nick COLGAN (IRL)	G		24		
Derek COLLINS	D		23	(1)	
Steve CRAWFORD	A		1	(2)	
Mark DEMPSIE	D		7	(1)	
Shaun DENNIS	D		23	(1)	
Ólafur GOTTSKÁLKSSON (ISL)	G		12		
Paul HARTLEY	A		14	(10)	1
Fabrice HENRY (FRA)	M		6	(3)	
John HUGHES	D		20		
Matthias JACK (GER)	D		20	(2)	1
Earl JEAN (STL)	A			(5)	
Russell LATAPY (TRI)	M		28	(4)	9
Dirk LEHMANN (GER)	A		18	(12)	7
Stuart LOVELL (AUS)	M		19	(7)	1
Paul LOVERING	D		9	(1)	
Pat McGINLAY	M		22	(9)	3
Martin McINTOSH	D		9		
Tom McMANUS	D		1	(1)	
Kenny MILLER	A		23	(8)	11
Ian MURRAY	M		8	(1)	
Mika-Matti PAATELAINEN (FIN)	A		25	(6)	9
Alan REID	M			(1)	
Michael RENWICK	D		11	(2)	
Franck SAUZEE (FRA)	M		24	(1)	5
Justin SKINNER (ENG)	M		1	(1)	
Tom SMITH	D		21		

LEAGUE RESULTS 1999/2000

31/07/99	Motherwell	H	2-2	Lehmann 2
08/08/99	Dundee	A	4-3	Lehmann, Sauzée 2, Miller
14/08/99	Heart of Midlothian	H	1-1	Latapy (p)
21/08/99	St. Johnstone	A	1-1	og (McAnespie)
28/08/99	Rangers	H	0-1	
11/09/99	Dundee United	A	1-3	Latapy
19/09/99	Kilmarnock	H	0-3	
25/09/99	Celtic	H	0-2	
02/10/99	Aberdeen	A	2-2	Paatelainen, Jack
16/10/99	Motherwell	A	2-2	Latapy (p), Paatelainen
23/10/99	Dundee	H	5-2	Miller, Latapy 2, Sauzée, Lehmann
31/10/99	Dundee United	H	3-2	og (De Vos), Latapy 2 (1p)
06/11/99	Kilmarnock	A	2-0	Miller 2
20/11/99	Rangers	A	0-2	
24/11/99	St. Johnstone	H	0-1	
27/11/99	Aberdeen	H	2-0	McGinlay, Paatelainen
04/12/99	Celtic	A	0-4	
11/12/99	Motherwell	H	2-2	Paatelainen, McGinlay
19/12/99	Heart of Midlothian	A	3-0	Lehmann, Sauzée, Miller
27/12/99	Kilmarnock	H	2-2	Paatelainen, Miller
22/01/00	Dundee United	A	0-0	
06/02/00	Rangers	H	2-2	Miller 2
22/02/00	St. Johnstone	A	0-1	
26/02/00	Aberdeen	A	0-4	
05/03/00	Celtic	H	2-1	McGinlay, Miller
18/03/00	Heart of Midlothian	H	3-1	Latapy, Sauzée, Paatelainen
21/03/00	Dundee	H	1-2	Paatelainen
25/03/00	Kilmarnock	A	0-1	
01/04/00	Dundee United	H	1-0	Hartley
15/04/00	St. Johnstone	H	3-3	Latapy, Paatelainen, Lehmann
22/04/00	Celtic	A	1-1	Lovell
29/04/00	Aberdeen	H	1-0	Miller
03/05/00	Rangers	A	2-5	Miller, Lehmann
06/05/00	Motherwell	A	0-2	
14/05/00	Dundee	A	0-1	
21/05/00	Heart of Midlothian	A	1-2	Paatelainen

KILMARNOCK

CLUB DIRECTORY

Kilmarnock FC
Rugby Park, Rugby Road
Kilmarnock KA1 2DP
tel - (01563) 525184
fax - (01563) 522181
website - www.kilmarnockfc.co.uk
email - kfc@sol.co.uk
Year of Formation - 1869
Chairman - William Costley
Secretary - Kevin D. Collins
Manager - Bobby Wiliamson
Stadium - Rugby Park (18,128)

MAJOR HONOURS
League Championship - (1) 1965.
Scottish Cup - (3) 1920, 1929, 1997.

APPEARANCES 99/00

	P	Ap	(s)	Gls
Samassi ABOU (FRA)	A	5	(5)	
David BAGAN	M	2	(1)	
Martin BAKER	D	11		
Darren BEESLEY (ENG)	M	1	(1)	
Max BURKE	A	3	(6)	
Peter CANERO	D	6	(5)	
Christophe COCARD (FRA)	A	24	(1)	8
Stuart DAVIDSON	M		(2)	
Frédéric DINDELEUX (FRA)	D	28		1
Ian DURRANT	M	32		4
James FOWLER	M	1	(4)	
Garry HAY	D	8	(2)	2
John HENRY	M	1		
Sean HESSEY (ENG)	D	7	(4)	
Gary HOLT	M	35		
Chris INNES	D	5		
Michael JEFFREY (ENG)	N	10	(8)	2
Jim LAUCHLAN	D	29		2
Ally McCOIST	A	5	(4)	1
Gary McCUTCHEON	M		(2)	
Kevin McGOWNE	D	9		
Tosh McKINLAY	D	14	(1)	
Gus MacPHERSON	D	30		1
Alan MAHOOD	M	6	(12)	1
Gordon MARSHALL	G	14		
Colin MELDRUM	G	18		
Ally MITCHELL	A	22	(4)	2
Mark REILLY	M	28	(1)	3
Mark ROBERTS	A	2		
Andy SMITH	A	11	(4)	2
Jérôme VAREILLE (FRA)	M	13	(10)	3
Michael WATT	G	4		
Paul WRIGHT	A	12	(4)	5

LEAGUE RESULTS 1999/2000

31/07/99	Rangers	A	1-2	Mitchell
07/08/99	Aberdeen	H	2-0	May 2
15/08/99	St. Johnstone	A	0-2	
21/08/99	Motherwell	H	0-1	
29/08/99	Dundee United	A	0-0	
12/09/99	Celtic	H	0-1	
19/09/99	Hibernian	A	3-0	Reilly, Jeffrey, McCoist (p)
25/09/99	Dundee	H	0-2	
16/10/99	Rangers	H	1-1	Jeffrey
23/10/99	Aberdeen	A	2-2	Cocard, Mitchell
27/10/99	Heart of Midlothian	A	2-2	MacPherson, Cocard
30/10/99	Celtic	A	1-5	Cocard
06/11/99	Hibernian	H	0-2	
20/11/99	Dundee United	H	1-1	Cocard (p)
27/11/99	Heart of Midlothian	H	2-2	Mahood, Reilly
11/12/99	Rangers	A	0-1	
18/12/99	St. Johnstone	H	1-2	Wright
27/12/99	Hibernian	A	2-2	Smith, Cocard (p)
23/01/00	Celtic	H	1-1	Reilly
26/01/00	Dundee	A	0-0	
12/02/00	Motherwell	H	0-2	
22/02/00	Motherwell	A	4-0	Cocard 2, Vareille 2
26/02/00	Heart of Midlothian	A	0-0	
04/03/00	Dundee	H	2-2	Durrant, Dindeleux
15/03/00	Dundee United	A	2-2	Durrant 2
18/03/00	St. Johnstone	A	0-0	
25/03/00	Hibernian	H	1-0	Vareille
02/04/00	Celtic	A	2-4	Wright, Lauchlan
08/04/00	Dundee United	H	1-0	og (McQuillan)
12/04/00	Aberdeen	H	1-0	Wright
16/04/00	Motherwell	A	0-2	
22/04/00	Dundee	A	2-1	Wright 2 (1p)
29/04/00	Heart of Midlothian	H	0-1	
07/05/00	Rangers	H	0-2	
14/05/00	Kilmarnock	A	1-5	Lauchlan
21/05/00	St. Johnstone	H	3-2	Durrant, Smith, Cocard

MOTHERWELL

THE EUROPEAN FOOTBALL YEARBOOK 2000-2001

CLUB DIRECTORY

Motherwell FC
Fir Park Stadium
Motherwell ML1 2QN
tel - (01698) 333333
fax - (01698) 338001
Year of Formation - 1886
Chairman - John Boyle
Secretary - Alisdair Barron
Manager - Billy Davies
Stadium - Fir Park (13,742)

MAJOR HONOURS
League Championship - (1) 1932.
Scottish Cup - (2) 1952, 1991.
League Cup - (1) 1951.

APPEARANCES 99/00

	P	Ap	(s)	Gls
Derek ADAMS	M	15	(2)	1
Ged BRANNAN (ENG)	M	33		5
Martin CORRIGAN	D	18	(1)	1
Stephen CRAIGAN (NIR)	D	3	(2)	
Sasa CURCIC (YUG)	M	3	(3)	
John DAVIES	M	7	(1)	
Greig DENHAM	D	6		
Michel DOESBURG (HOL)	D	17	(2)	
Don GOODMAN (ENG)	A	25	(4)	7
Andy GORAM	G	22		
Stephen HALLIDAY (ENG)	A	1	(4)	
Steven HAMMELL	D	3	(1)	
Paul HARVEY	A	6	(7)	
Benito KEMBLE	D	25		1
Lee McCULLOCH	A	28	(1)	9
Jamie McGOWAN	D	10	(3)	
Stephen McMILLAN	D	31		3
Rob MATTHAEI (HOL)	D	2	(1)	
Pat NEVIN	M	6	(22)	2
Stephen NICHOLAS	M	2	(19)	1
Douglas RAMSAY	M		(2)	
John SPENCER	A	25	(3)	11
Greg STRONG	D	10		
Shaun TEALE (ENG)	D	16		2
Tony THOMAS (ENG)	M	6		
Derek TOWNSLEY (ENG)	M	16	(9)	1
Kevin TWADDLE	M	18	(7)	5
Simo VALAKARI (FIN)	M	28	(2)	
Stephen WOODS	G	14	(1)	

LEAGUE RESULTS 1999/2000

31/07/99	Hibernian	A	2-2	Nevin, Nicholas
07/08/99	Dundee United	H	2-2	McCulloch 2
15/08/99	Rangers	A	1-4	McCulloch
21/08/99	Kilmarnock	A	1-0	Adams
28/08/99	Dundee	H	0-2	
11/09/99	St. Johnstone	A	1-1	Spencer
16/10/99	Hibernian	H	2-2	McCulloch, McMillan
20/10/99	Aberdeen	H	5-6	Spencer 3, Goodman, Teale (p)
23/10/99	Dundee United	A	2-0	Spencer, Teale (p)
27/10/99	Celtic	A	1-0	Twaddle
30/10/99	St. Johnstone	H	1-0	Twaddle
06/11/99	Heart of Midlothian	A	1-1	Spencer
20/11/99	Dundee	A	1-0	McCulloch
23/11/99	Heart of Midlothian	H	2-1	McCulloch, Nevin
28/11/99	Celtic	H	3-2	Brannan, Townsley, Goodman
11/12/99	Hibernian	A	2-2	Spencer 2
18/12/99	Rangers	H	1-5	Goodman
22/01/00	St. Johnstone	A	1-1	McMillan
26/01/00	Aberdeen	A	1-1	Spencer
05/02/00	Dundee	H	0-3	
12/02/00	Kilmarnock	A	2-0	Spencer, McMillan
22/02/00	Kilmarnock	H	0-4	
01/03/00	Heart of Midlothian	H	0-2	
04/03/00	Aberdeen	H	1-0	Goodman
18/03/00	Rangers	A	2-6	Kemble, McCulloch
25/03/00	Heart of Midlothian	A	0-0	
01/04/00	St. Johnstone	H	2-1	Brannan (p), Corrigan
05/04/00	Celtic	A	0-4	
08/04/00	Dundee	A	1-4	Goodman
16/04/00	Kilmarnock	H	2-0	Brannan, McCulloch
19/04/00	Dundee United	H	1-3	McCulloch
22/04/00	Aberdeen	A	1-2	Brannan (p)
29/04/00	Celtic	H	1-1	Brannan
06/05/00	Hibernian	H	2-0	Twaddle 2
13/05/00	Dundee United	A	2-1	Goodman 2
21/05/00	Rangers	H	2-0	Twaddle, Spencer

RANGERS

CLUB DIRECTORY

Rangers FC
Ibrox Stadium, 150 Edmiston Drive, Glasgow G51 2XD
tel - (0141) 5808500 / fax - (0141) 5808504
website - www.rangers.co.uk
Year of Formation - 1872
Chairman - David E. Murray
Secretary - R. Campbell Ogilvie
Manager - Dick Advocaat
Stadium - Ibrox Stadium (50,467)

MAJOR HONOURS
League Championship - (49)
1891, 1899, 1900, 1901, 1902, 1911, 1912,
1913, 1918, 1920, 1921, 1923, 1924, 1925,
1927, 1928, 1929, 1930, 1931, 1933, 1934,
1935, 1937, 1939, 1947, 1949, 1950, 1953,
1956, 1957, 1959, 1961, 1963, 1964, 1975,
1976, 1978, 1987, 1989, 1990, 1991, 1992,
1993, 1994, 1995, 1996, 1997, 1999, 2000.
Scottish Cup - (29) 1894, 1897, 1898, 1903,
1928, 1930, 1932, 1934, 1935, 1936, 1948,
1949, 1950, 1953, 1960, 1962, 1963, 1964,
1966, 1973, 1976, 1978, 1979, 1981, 1992,
1993, 1996, 1999, 2000.
League Cup - (21)
1947, 1949, 1961, 1962, 1964, 1965, 1971,
1976, 1978, 1979, 1982, 1984, 1985, 1987,
1988, 1989, 1991, 1993, 1994, 1997, 1999.
European Cup-winners' Cup - (1) 1972.

APPEARANCES 99/00

		P	Ap	(s)	Gls
Dariusz ADAMCZYK (POL)	D	5	(5)		
Jörg ALBERTZ (GER)	M	30	(5)	17	
Gabriel AMATO (ARG)	A	4	(4)	3	
Lorenzo AMORUSO (ITA)	D	30		2	
Mark BROWN	G	1			
Lionel CHARBONNIER (FRA)	G	7			
Billy DODDS	A	16	(2)	10	
Gordon DURIE	A	1	(6)		
Barry FERGUSON	M	31		4	
Ian FERGUSON	M		(2)		
Jimmy GIBSON	M		(1)		
Colin HENDRY	D	1	(1)		
Stephen HUGHES	M		(1)		
Jonatan JOHANSSON (FIN)	A	8	(8)	6	
Andrei KANCHELSKIS (RUS)	M	25	(3)	4	
Stefan KLOS (GER)	G	24			
Neil McCANN	M	12	(18)	3	
Derek McINNES	M		(1)		
Robert MALCOLM	D	1	(2)		
Michael MOLS (HOL)	A	9		9	
Craig MOORE (AUS)	D	22		1	
Thomas MYHRE (NOR)	G	3			
Barry NICHOLSON	D		(2)		
Antti NIEMI (FIN)	G	1			
Arthur NUMAN (HOL)	D	29	(1)	1	
Tero PENTTILA (FIN)	D	3			
Sergio PORRINI (ITA)	D	11	(1)		
Claudio REYNA (USA)	M	25	(4)	5	
Maurice ROSS	D		(1)		
Sebastian ROZENTAL (CHL)	A	6	(5)	3	
TUGAY Kerimoglu (TUR)	M	9	(7)	1	
Giovanni VAN BRONCKHORST (HOL)	M	27		4	
Tony VIDMAR (AUS)	D	21	(6)	6	
Rod WALLACE (ENG)	A	25	(3)	16	
Scott WILSON	D	9			

LEAGUE RESULTS 1999/2000

31/07/99	Kilmarnock	H	2-1	Wallace, Reyna
07/08/99	Heart of Midlothian	A	4-0	Reyna 2, Mols, Albertz
15/08/99	Motherwell	H	4-1	Mols 4
21/08/99	Dundee United	H	4-1	Reyna, Van Bronckhorst, Wallace, Vidmar
28/08/99	Hibernian	A	1-0	Johansson
11/09/99	Aberdeen	H	3-0	Mols 2, Albertz
25/09/99	St. Johnstone	H	3-1	Albertz 2 (1p), Mols
02/10/99	Dundee	A	3-2	Kanchelskis, Wallace, Amato
16/10/99	Kilmarnock	A	1-1	Van Bronckhorst
30/10/99	Aberdeen	A	5-1	Johansson 3, Mols, Amato
07/11/99	Celtic	H	4-2	Johansson, Albertz (p), Amoruso, Amato
20/11/99	Hibernian	H	2-0	Johansson, Albertz
28/11/99	Dundee	H	1-2	Wallace
11/12/99	Kilmarnock	H	1-0	Albertz
18/12/99	Motherwell	A	5-1	Kanchelskis 2, Amoruso, Dodds 2
22/12/99	Heart of Midlothian	H	1-0	Albertz
27/12/99	Celtic	A	1-1	Dodds
22/01/00	Aberdeen	H	5-0	Moore, Van Bronckhorst, Numan, Wallace, Ferguson B.
02/02/00	Dundee United	A	4-0	Vidmar 2, Wallace, McCann
06/02/00	Hibernian	A	2-2	Wallace, McCann
15/02/00	St. Johnstone	A	1-1	Vidmar
27/02/00	Dundee	A	7-1	Wallace 3, Vidmar 2, Albertz, Rozental
04/03/00	St. Johnstone	H	0-0	
08/03/00	Celtic	A	1-0	Wallace
18/03/00	Motherwell	H	6-2	Wallace 3, Rozental (p), Albertz, Tugay (p)
26/03/00	Celtic	H	4-0	Albertz 2, Kanchelskis, Van Bronckhorst
01/04/00	Aberdeen	A	1-1	Ferguson B.
04/04/00	Dundee United	H	3-0	Albertz, Dodds, Wallace
12/04/00	Heart of Midlothian	A	2-1	Wallace, Dodds
15/04/00	Dundee United	A	2-0	Ferguson B., Albertz
23/04/00	St. Johnstone	A	2-0	Dodds 2
30/04/00	Dundee	H	3-0	Dodds, McCann, Rozental
03/05/00	Hibernian	H	5-2	Ferguson B., Dodds, og (Dennis), Albertz 2 (1p)
07/05/00	Kilmarnock	A	2-0	Reyna, Albertz
13/05/00	Heart of Midlothian	H	1-0	Dodds
21/05/00	Motherwell	A	0-2	

ST. JOHNSTONE

CLUB DIRECTORY

St. Johnstone FC
McDiarmid Park
Crieff Road
Perth
PH1 2SJ
tel - (01738) 459090
fax - (01738) 625771
website - www.stjohnstonefc.co.uk
Year of Formation - 1884
Chairman - Geoffrey S. Brown
Secretary - Stewart Duff
Manager - Sandy Clark
Stadium - McDiarmid Park (10,673)

APPEARANCES 99/00

	P	Ap	(s)	Gls
Garry BOLLAN	D	34		2
Paddy CONNOLLY	A	9	(2)	1
Chris CONWAY	D		(1)	
Nick DASOVIC (CAN)	D	13		
Darren DODS	D	22		2
Allan FERGUSON	G	3		
Stephen FRAIL	D	9		
Roddy GRANT	A	1	(2)	
Danny GRIFFIN (NIR)	D	26	(3)	1
Graeme JONES	A	15	(4)	3
Paul KANE	M	33	(1)	1
Martin LAUCHLAN	M		(5)	
Nathan LOWNDES (ENG)	A	16	(9)	10
Kieran McANESPIE	M	14	(5)	1
John Paul McBRIDE	A	18	(1)	1
Stuart McCLUSKEY	M	5	(1)	
Gerry McMAHON (NIR)	M	9	(10)	
John McQUILLAN	D	18		1
Alan MAIN	G	21		
Marc MILLAR	A	3	(5)	2
George O'BOYLE (NIR)	A	4	(4)	
Keith O'HALLORAN	M	31	(1)	1
John O'NEIL	A	31	(2)	3
Keigan PARKER	A	6	(4)	2
Stephen ROBERTSON	G	12	(1)	
Craig RUSSELL (ENG)	A	1		1
Miguel SIMÃO (POR)	A	6	(11)	1
Kevin THOMAS	A	5	(7)	2
Jim WEIR	D	31		1

LEAGUE RESULTS 1999/2000

31/07/99	Heart of Midlothian	H	1-4	McQuillan
07/08/99	Celtic	A	0-3	
15/08/99	Kilmarnock	H	2-0	Bollan, Lowndes
21/08/99	Hibernian	H	1-1	Lowndes
29/08/99	Aberdeen	A	3-0	Thomas, Weir, Lowndes
11/09/99	Motherwell	H	1-1	Thomas
19/09/99	Dundee	A	2-1	Lowndes 2
25/09/99	Rangers	A	1-3	Simão
16/10/99	Heart of Midlothian	A	1-1	Lowndes
24/10/99	Celtic	H	1-2	Lowndes
27/10/99	Dundee United	H	0-1	
30/10/99	Motherwell	A	0-1	
06/11/99	Dundee	H	0-1	
21/11/99	Aberdeen	H	1-1	Jones
24/11/99	Hibernian	A	1-0	Jones
27/11/99	Dundee United	A	0-1	
18/12/99	Kilmarnock	A	2-1	McBride, O'Neil
27/12/99	Dundee	A	1-1	Lowndes
22/01/00	Motherwell	H	1-1	Jones
05/02/00	Aberdeen	A	1-2	O'Neil
15/02/00	Rangers	H	1-1	Lowndes
22/02/00	Hibernian	H	1-0	O'Halloran (p)
26/02/00	Dundee United	H	2-0	Griffin, Lowndes
04/03/00	Rangers	A	0-0	
11/03/00	Celtic	A	1-4	Connolly
15/03/00	Heart of Midlothian	H	0-1	
18/03/00	Kilmarnock	H	0-0	
25/03/00	Dundee	H	2-1	Bollan, Miller
01/04/00	Motherwell	A	1-2	Russell
15/04/00	Hibernian	A	3-3	O'Neill, McAnespie, Parker
23/04/00	Rangers	H	0-2	
29/04/00	Dundee United	A	1-0	Dods
02/05/00	Aberdeen	H	2-1	Dods, Kane
06/05/00	Heart of Midlothian	A	0-0	
13/05/00	Celtic	H	0-0	
21/05/00	Kilmarnock	A	2-3	Millar, Parker

SLOVAKIA

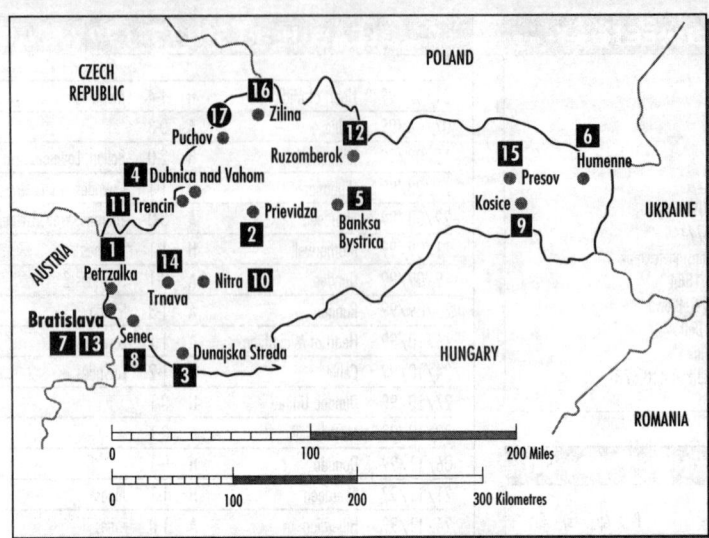

#			#		
1	ARTMEDIA PETRZALKA	902	10	FC NITRA	911
2	BANIK PRIEVIDZA	903	11	OZETA DUKLA TRENCIN	912
3	DAC DUNAJSKA STREDA	904	12	SCP RUZOMBEROK	913
4	ZTS DUBNICA	905	13	SLOVAN BRATISLAVA	914
5	DUKLA BANSKA BYSTRICA	906	14	SPARTAK TRNAVA	915
6	HFC HUMENNE	907	15	TATRAN PRESOV	916
7	INTER BRATISLAVA	908	16	MSK ZILINA	917
8	VTJ KOBA SENEC	909	**Promoted club**		
9	1.FC KOSICE	910	17	MATADOR PUCHOV	

UNDER-21S REACH OLYMPIC GAMES

Inter's late spurt brings 'double' glory

FEDERATION DIRECTORY

Slovensky Futbalovy Zvaz
Junácka 6, 835 80 Bratislava

tel - (07) 49249151   Year of Formation - 1990
fax - (07) 49249554   President - Frantisek Laurinec
                          Secretary - Ladislaw Veselsky

Stadium - Tehelne pole, Bratislava (30,087)

The seventh season of the Slovakian "Superliga" was unique in that almost half of the teams who competed in it were relegated. It was agreed before the start by representatives of the First Division clubs and an FA committee that the league would be reduced from 16 clubs to just ten in one fell swoop, which meant as many as seven teams being relegated and just one promoted.

The move was ordained primarily for financial reasons, although its objective was to attempt to raise the standard of the football in the country's top division. 16 clubs had long been considered an overburdensome number. Virtually every football club in Slovakia is hard up for cash, and there are simply not enough quality players to go around. It was significant that in the 1999/2000 season four clubs in the so-called 'professional' league - Dunajska Streda, Senec, Humenne and Prievidza - had no players under professional contract.

The reduction to ten clubs is expected to lead to massively improved attendance figures. The average per game in 1999/2000 was down to a mere 3,037, meaning that some 100,000 spectators had been lost in comparison to the previous year.

The league was wound up in some haste in order to accommodate the European U-21 championship finals, the hosting rights of which had been granted to Slovakia. One team had no problem with that whatsoever. Inter Bratislava, who had not won a major title for 41 years - when, as Red Star Bratislava, they won the old Czechoslovakian championship - ran into a formidable streak of form in the closing weeks of the campaign to win both the league and the Cup, pipping 1.FC Kosice into second place in both competitions.

Inter's success was a reward for the club's perseverance with coach Jozef Bubenko. He had been appointed in 1996 and under his modest but active leadership Inter had steadily improved each year. After finishing fourth, third and second in Bubenko's first three years, it was logical that they would climb to the top of the tree in 1999/2000.

Bubenko was assisted by a very supportive board of

LEAGUE CHAMPIONSHIP RESULTS 99/00

		1	2	3	4	5	6	7	8	9	10	11	12	13	14	15	16
1	Artmedia Petrzalka		3-1	2-0	4-1	3-1	2-2	0-1	2-0	0-4	1-2	0-0	1-0	1-3	2-1	3-1	2-1
2	Banik Prievidza	4-3		0-2	3-0	1-3	1-0	1-3	1-4	1-3	2-1	0-2	0-2	1-1	0-1	1-5	1-0
3	DAC Dunajska Streda	1-1	5-1		1-2	2-2	4-0	0-0	2-2	0-2	1-0	0-0	1-0	0-3	0-0	1-2	0-1
4	ZTS Dubnica	0-0	0-1	0-0		1-0	5-0	0-1	0-1	2-0	5-0	0-0	0-0	0-3	1-0	1-0	1-4
5	Dukla Banska Bystrica	1-2	1-0	1-2	0-1		1-1	0-2	1-0	2-1	1-2	1-0	0-1	0-1	1-2	1-2	3-2
6	HFC Humenne	2-0	1-1	1-0	0-1	2-0		1-1	1-0	2-2	3-1	0-1	2-1	3-3	1-0	2-0	3-1
7	Inter Bratislava	1-0	7-0	1-0	3-0	3-0	6-0		2-0	2-1	3-0	1-1	2-3	1-1	0-0	2-0	2-0
8	VTJ KOBA Senec	3-2	1-1	0-0	3-0	1-0	1-0	0-5		3-1	2-1	1-1	2-0	0-1	0-0	2-2	0-0
9	1.FC Kosice	3-2	3-2	2-1	2-1	3-1	1-0	3-1	2-1		3-1	4-0	2-1	0-2	0-0	3-0	2-0
10	FC Nitra	2-0	2-1	2-0	1-1	2-3	1-0	1-3	2-0	1-1		0-1	0-0	1-0	0-1	0-1	0-2
11	Ozeta Dukla Trencin	2-0	2-0	2-0	2-0	5-2	4-1	1-3	2-2	0-0	1-1		2-0	1-0	1-2	2-0	3-0
12	SCP Ruzomberok	2-2	1-1	1-0	1-0	1-0	1-1	1-1	1-0	0-2	3-0	3-1		1-0	1-0	1-0	2-0
13	Slovan Bratislava	0-1	5-1	4-0	1-1	2-1	2-0	1-1	1-1	1-2	1-0	3-0	2-0		3-0	6-0	0-0
14	Spartak Trnava	4-2	2-0	3-0	1-1	4-0	1-0	0-2	2-2	1-0	1-0	2-0	1-0	0-0		4-1	4-1
15	Tatran Presov	3-0	4-2	1-1	1-0	3-0	1-0	0-3	1-0	2-1	2-0	2-1	1-1	1-1	1-0		1-1
16	MSK Zilina	2-2	4-0	6-0	2-0	1-0	0-2	1-2	2-1	1-4	1-0	1-0	2-0	0-1	1-1	2-0	

LEAGUE CHAMPIONSHIP FINAL TABLE 99/00

		Pd	Home W	D	L	F	A	Away W	D	L	F	A	Total W	D	L	F	A	PT	GD
1	Inter Bratislava	30	11	3	1	36	6	10	4	1	29	10	21	7	2	65	16	70	49
2	1.FC Kosice	30	13	1	1	33	13	6	3	6	24	18	19	4	7	57	31	61	26
3	Slovan Bratislava	30	9	4	2	32	8	7	5	3	20	10	16	9	5	52	18	57	34
4	Spartak Trnava	30	11	3	1	30	9	4	5	6	8	12	15	8	7	38	21	53	17
5	Ozeta Dukla Trencin	30	10	3	2	30	11	3	5	7	18	18	13	8	9	38	29	47	9
6	Tatran Presov	30	10	4	1	24	11	4	1	10	14	31	14	5	11	38	42	47	-4
7	SCP Ruzomberok	30	10	4	1	20	8	3	3	9	9	18	13	7	10	29	26	46	3
8	MSK Zilina	30	9	2	4	26	13	3	3	9	13	24	12	5	13	39	37	41	2
9	Artmedia Petrzalka	30	9	2	4	26	18	2	4	9	17	30	11	6	13	43	48	39	-5
10	VTJ KOBA Senec	30	7	6	2	19	14	2	4	9	14	22	9	10	11	33	36	37	-3
11	ZTS Dubnica	30	6	4	5	16	10	3	3	9	9	25	9	7	14	25	35	34	-10
12	HFC Humenne	30	9	4	2	24	12	1	3	11	7	31	10	7	13	31	43	34	-12
13	FC Nitra	30	6	3	6	15	14	2	1	12	9	30	8	4	18	24	44	28	-20
14	DAC Dunajska Streda	30	4	6	5	18	16	2	3	10	6	26	6	9	15	24	42	27	-18
15	Dukla Banska Bystrica	30	5	1	9	14	19	2	1	12	13	34	7	2	21	27	53	23	-26
16	Banik Prievidza	30	5	1	9	17	30	1	3	11	12	41	6	4	20	29	71	22	-42

N.B. HFC Humenne - 3 points deducted.

directors, who generally backed up all of his decisions and allowed him the time and the resources to achieve his goals. The relative financial stability of the club ensured an atmosphere of calm, and this was reflected when the team went out to play.

Things did not look too good initially when Inter lost their opening game at home to Ruzomberok and managed just one win in their first four matches. But once they got into their stride with a 2-1 win at home to Kosice, they became very difficult to stop. They led at halfway by two points, but when Kosice gained a revenge win at the end of March to end Inter's 18-match unbeaten run, the positions were suddenly reversed.

It was then, though, that Bubenko's men went into overdrive and sped clear. Their last ten fixtures yielded a maxi-

mum 30 points and a remarkable goal balance of 34-3.

A hat-trick for striker Szilard Nemeth in the final match, a 6-0 win against Humenne, enabled him to take the league top scorer crown, and Inter's final victory margin was a comprehensive nine points. Further evidence of the club's revival under Bubenko was the number of Inter players represented in the national selections. Aside from Szilard Nemeth, there were five others who played for the Slovakian senior team during the season - goalkeeper Miroslav Hyll, defenders Roman Kratochvil and Marian Suchancok, and midfielders Attila Pinte and Peter Nemeth - as well as another three who played for the successful U-21 side - defender Marian Cisovsky, midfielder Juraj Czinege and striker Peter Babnic.

Kosice made a valiant effort to deny Inter, but the pace

DOMESTIC CUP 99/00

1/8 FINALS
DAC Dunajska Streda 4, HFC Humenne 0
VTJ KOBA Senec 2, SCP Ruzomberok 0
Tatran Presov 0, Inter Bratislava 2
ZTS Dubnica 1, NCHZ Novaky 2
FC Nitra 1, Dukla Banska Bystrica 1 (6-7 on pens.)
Trans Licartovce 0, Artmedia Petrzalka 1
1.FC Kosice 3, Ozeta Dukla Trencin 1
Spartak Trnava 2, Matador Puchov 0

QUARTER-FINALS
1.FC Kosice v Artmedia Petrzalka 1-1; 2-1
(1.FC Kosice 3-2)
Inter Bratislava v NCHZ Novaky 1-0; 4-2
(Inter Bratislava 5-2)

VTJ KOBA Senec v Spartak Trnava 0-2; 1-3
(Spartak Trnava 5-1)
Dukla Banska Bystrica v DAC Dunajska Streda 0-0; 2-1
(Dukla Banska Bystrica 2-1)

SEMI-FINALS
Inter Bratislava 2 (Kratochvil 40, 62),
Spartak Trnava 1 (Bukovic 50)
Spartak Trnava 0, Inter Bratislava 1 (Lalik 36)
(Inter Bratislava 3-1)
1.FC Kosice 1 (Semenik 17),
Dukla Banska Bystrica 0
Dukla Banska Bystrica 1 (Faktor 89),
1.FC Kosice 1 (Zatek 53)
(1.FC Kosice 2-1)

FINAL
08/05/2000, Presov
INTER BRATISLAVA 1 Nemeth S. (38)
1.FC KOSICE 1 Kozak (50)
(aet; 4-2 on pens.)
referee - Gadosi
INTER BRATISLAVA - Hyll; Kratochvil, Chrenko, Suchancok, Sevela; Pinte, Czinege (Cisovsky 87), Nemeth P. (Lalik 38), Hornyak; Nemeth S., Babnic (Kreici 62).
1.FC KOSICE - Seman; Zatek, Zabavnik (Onofrej 46); Hanc; Lyubarskyi, Kral, Dzurik, Kozak (Zvara 64), Jambor; Oravec (Semenik 46), Kozlej.

the champions set in the final furlongs was too much for Ladislav Molnar's team. Their frustration was compounded by defeat in the Cup final, which Inter won in a penalty shoot-out after a 1-1 draw in Presov watched by only 3,150 spectators.

Defending champions Slovan Bratislava had a very

NATIONAL TEAM APPEARANCES 99/00

Coach - Jozef ADAMEC	ISR	ROM	LIE	AZB	PER	COL	GUA	CRC	BUL	AUS	CHL	GER	SAU	NOR	RUS	JPN	BOL	Cps	Gls
Kamil SUSKO (06/11/74) - Spartak Trnava	G		G	G		G		G	G	G	G	G46	G46	G		G	G	15	-
Jaroslav HRABAL (08/09/74) - Spartak Trnava	D	s74	s42		D	D	D90	D	D	D	D	D	D					12	1
Stanislav VARGA (08/10/72) - Slovan Bratislava	D	D	D	D		D	D	D				D	D	D	D	D	D	29	-
Jozef VALACHOVIC (12/07/75) - Ozeta Dukla Trencin	D	D	D		M84	M	D		D	D	M		s66	D	M	D	D83	17	-
Roman KRATOCHVIL (24/06/74) - Inter Bratislava	D	D74	D						D						D		D	11	1
Attila PINTE (06/06/71) - Inter Bratislava	M77			s84									s88	s59		M	M	16	-
Peter NEMETH (14/09/72) - Inter Bratislava	M84	M	s61	M								s69	M71	s85	M	M	M	12	-
Robert TOMASCHEK (25/08/72) - Slovan Bratislava/Heart of Midlothian (SCO)	M											M			s76			45	3
Vladimir LABANT (08/06/74) - Sparta Praha (CZE)	M84	M	M	M84														8	2
Martin FABUS (11/11/76) - Sigma Olomouc (CZE)/Ozeta Dukla Trencin	A90	A81	A61	A			s61			A89	A69			s71	A63	s90	A75	21	5
Jozef MAJOROS (19/03/70) - Slovan Bratislava	A68																	23	5
Marek UJLAKY (26/03/74) - Spartak Trnava	s68	s81	M	M		A	A	M		M	M43			s66	s33	M59		34	2
Vladimir KOZUCH (15/10/75) - Tatran Presov/Slovan Liberec (CZE)	s77		s76	s90	A	A		A62	A61	s43	A60	s69	A	A71	s63	A90	s75	18	3
Marian SUCHANCOK (13/07/71) - Inter Bratislava	s84			D														3	-
Vladimir LEITNER (28/06/74) - Spartak Trnava	s84			M68				M	M	M	s83	s89	D69	s66	M	D	M	13	1
Marian ZEMAN (07/07/74) - Vitesse (HOL)	s90			s86														24	2
Miroslav KÖNIG (01/06/72) - Slovan Bratislava/Grasshopper-Club Zürich (SUI)		G			G		G					s46						18	-
Miroslav KARHAN (21/06/76) - Real Betis (ESP)	D	D	M86										D	M	D			36	1
Igor BALIS (05/01/70) - Spartak Trnava	M68	M							M	D	M					D	M90	35	1
Vladimir JANOCKO (02/12/76) - 1.FC Kosice		M	M42	M90	M84	M61	M60	s55	M83	s60	s69	s71			M63			12	-
Szilard NEMETH (08/08/78) - Inter Bratislava		A	A76															15	3
Tibor JANCULA (16/06/69) - Slovan Bratislava	s68								A	A								27	9
Peter DZURIK (29/12/68) - 1.FC Kosice				D					M	M	M	M			D85	M	M65	19	1
Ivan KOZAK (18/06/70) - Tennis Borussia Berlin (GER)				D														33	-
Milan TIMKO (28/11/72) - Slovan Bratislava				D	D46				D	D	D	D	D66	D	D	D	D	20	1
Tibor ZATEK (14/06/71) - 1.FC Kosice				D		M	M		M90	s81					s61	s65		14	-
Martin KONECNY (25/12/72) - Ozeta Dukla Trencin					D	M	s60	M										6	-
Jozef KOZLEJ (08/07/73) - 1.FC Kosice					A46		s60	A55										17	1
Karol SCHULZ (18/06/74) - Artmedia Petrzalka					s46	D	s90	D										4	-
Marian DIRNBACH (13/09/79) - Ozeta Dukla Trencin					s46	s61		s62										3	-
Ondrej SMELKO (21/09/67) - Ozeta Dukla Trencin					s68	M		M		M	M							5	1
Robert HANKO (28/12/76) - Ozeta Dukla Trencin					s84	M79	M60											3	-
Peter SUCHY (18/01/76) - ZTS Dubnica					s84	s79												2	-
Frantisek HADVIGER (13/07/76) - ZTS Dubnica							D		s90	D						s83		4	-
Vladislav ZVARA (11/12/71) - 1.FC Kosice									M	M	M81							30	-
Samuel SLOVAK (17/10/75) - CD Tenerife (ESP)												M69	A	M88	s63			13	-
Ljubomir MORAVCIK (22/06/65) - Celtic (SCO)												M	M66	M33				35	6
Igor DEMO (18/09/75) - Borussia Mönchengladbach (GER)												M						4	-
Peter DUBOVSKY (07/05/72) - Real Oviedo (ESP)													M66	M	M76			33	12
Miroslav HYLL (20/09/73) - Inter Bratislava													s46					2	-
Juraj BUCEK (15/07/73) - Xanthi (GRE)														G				1	-
Erik JEZIK (16/10/76) - Slovan Bratislava																M61	s90	2	-

NATIONAL TEAM RESULTS 99/00

18/08/99	Israel	H	Bratislava	1-0	Fabus (80)
04/09/99	Romania (ECQ)	H	Bratislava	1-5	Labant (22)
08/09/99	Liechtenstein (ECQ)	H	Dubnica	2-0	Nemeth S. (4), Karhan (56)
09/10/99	Azerbaijan (ECQ)	A	Baku	1-0	Labant (70)
17/11/99	Peru	A	Lima	1-2	Kozuch (21)
20/11/99	Colombia	A	Bogotá	0-1	
23/11/99	Guatemala	A	Guatemala City	1-0	Hrabal (76)
25/11/99	Costa Rica	A	Alajuela	0-4	
09/02/00	Bulgaria	N	Valparaíso	0-1	
12/02/00	Australia	N	Valparaíso	0-0	
15/02/00	Chile	A	Valparaíso	2-0	Balis (5), Smelko (17)
25/04/00	Germany B	H	Presov	4-1	Slovak (33), Leitner (68), Kozuch (79), Nemeth P. (90)
24/05/00	Saudi Arabia	H	Nitra	1-1	Kozuch (37)
27/05/00	Norway	A	Oslo	0-2	
31/05/00	Russia	A	Moscow	1-1	Fabus (25)
11/06/00	Japan	A	Sendai	1-1	Dzurik (7)
14/06/00	Bolivia	A	Saga	2-0	Kratochvil (22), Fabus (45)

TOP SCORERS

- 16 Szilard NEMETH (Inter Bratislava)
- 15 Ruslan LYUBARSKYI (1.FC Kosice)
- 14 Tomas MEDVED (Artmedia Petrzalka)
- 12 Marek MINTAL (MSK Zilina)
- 10 Fábio Luís GOMES (Spartak Trnava)
- 9 Jozef URBLIK (Banik Prievidza)
  - Marian LALIK (Inter Bratislava)
  - Julius SIMON (Artmedia Petrzalka/ DAC Dunajska Streda)
  - Stanislav VARGA (Slovan Bratislava)
  - Jozef KOZLEJ (1.FC Kosice)

INTERNATIONAL HONOURS

European Club Competitions
Cup-winners' Cup Slovan Bratislava (1969)

EUROPEAN CUPS 99/00

CHAMPIONS' CUP
● SLOVAN BRATISLAVA
Preliminary round 2 ANORTHOSIS FAMAGUSTA (CYP)
A 1-2 Hrncar (51)
König; Pecko, Timko, Varga, Hornyak; Hrncar, Tomaschek, Skrtel, Fabula; Jancula (Kriss 88), Majoros (Meszaros 75).
H 1-1 Timko (60)
König; Pecko, Timko, Varga, Sobona; Hrncar, Tomaschek, Kriss (Sedlak 46), Skrtel (Fabula 46); Jancula, Majoros (Meszaros 74).

UEFA CUP
● DUKLA BANSKA BYSTRICA
1st round AJAX (HOL)
A 1-6 Verlaat (14og)
Juracka; Karasek, Bartos (Strba 77), Laurinc, Kentos; Strelec, Helbich, Faktor, Bubenko (Malatinsky 46); Kovac, Pancik.
H 1-3 Malatinsky (44)
Juracka; Karasek, Bartos, Laurinc, Kentos; Strelec, Helbich, Faktor, Malatinsky; Strba, Pancik.

● INTER BRATISLAVA
Qualifying round BYLIS BALLSH (ALB)
H 3-1 Gerich (16), Kratochvil (28), Pernis (75)
Hyll; Cisovsky, Suchancok, Sevela; Kratochvil, Kusalik, Nemeth P., Lalik, Gerich; Tomovcik (Pernis 71), Babnic.
A 2-0 Nemeth S. (34, 64)
Hyll; Kratochvil, Chrenko, Suchancok, Sevela; Pinte, Kusalik (Babnic 80), Nemeth P., Lalik (Czinege 71); Gerich, Nemeth S. (Pernis 65).

1st round SK RAPID WIEN (AUT)
H 1-0 Lalik (45)
Hyll; Kratochvil, Chrenko, Suchancok, Sevela; Czinege, Nemeth P., Lalik (Cisovsky 78), Gerich (Kusalik 37); Nemeth S. (Pernis 90), Babnic.

A 2-1 Suchancok (45), Babnic (64)
Hyll; Kratochvil, Chrenko, Suchancok, Sevela; Czinege, Nemeth P., Lalik (Cisovsky 84), Gerich; Nemeth S. (Kusalik 76), Babnic (Pernis 90).

2nd round FC NANTES (FRA)
H 0-3
Hyll; Kratochvil, Chrenko, Suchancok, Sevela (Lalik 46); Pinte, Czinege (Kusalik 46), Nemeth P., Babnic; Gerich, Nemeth S. (Pernis 46).
A 0-4
Hyll; Kratochvil, Chrenko, Suchancok, Sevela; Czinege, Nemeth P., Lalik (Kusalik 62), Gerich; Nemeth S. (Pernis 81), Babnic (Pinte 71).

● SPARTAK TRNAVA
Qualifying round VLLAZNIA SHKODËR (ALB)
A 1-1 Leitner (29)
Susko; Hrabal, Poljovka, Horky, Leitner; Talda (Balis 56), Kostka, Ujlaky, Formanko; Bukovic, Gomes (Bugar 75).
H 2-0 Ujlaky (58, 89)
Susko; Poljovka, Hrabal, Horky, Leitner; Talda (Balis 57), Kostka (Fall 78), Ujlaky, Formanko, Timko; Gomes (Pavlik 46).

1st round GRAZER AK (AUT)
A 0-3
Susko; Fall, Hrabal, Horky, Leitner; Balis, Kostka, Ujlaky, Formanko (Talda 75); Timko, Gomes (Dian 81).
H 2-1 Muzlay (45, 70)
Susko; Fall, Hrabal, Horky, Leitner; Balis, Kostka, Ujlaky, Formanko; Muzlay, Gomes.

JURAJ CZINEGE

It seems that Slovakian football might have at last found a possible long-term successor to veteran schemer Ljubomir Moravcik. 23-year-old Juraj Czinege captained the Slovakian U-21 team to fourth place in the European Championship and demonstrated in that tournament that he is a player of skill, vision and considerable authority. An important member of Inter Bratislava's championship-winning team, he is an all-round midfielder who can use both feet and is always available to help out in defence even though his main attribute is providing an accurate service for the front players. Czinege is particularly popular with the press as he always has an honest answer to even the trickiest of questions. Thoughtful, talented and mature, he should go far.

erratic season. It got off to a catastrophic start when they were beaten by Cypriot club Anorthosis in the Champions' League preliminaries. That was a defeat which ate deep into the club's crippling finances and throughout the autumn Slovan were in a complete mess, both on and off the field. By the halfway juncture they were stuck in tenth place - the relegation zone - and seemed to be heading for oblivion. But the new year heralded an amazing turnaround. Slovan started as they meant to go on by hammering Tatran Presov 6-0 and with victories coming thick and fast, they hauled themselves all the way up to third place, which brought with it a ticket to the UEFA Cup. Slovan's record during the spring was 12 wins and three draws - even better than that of champions and city rivals Inter.

The Slovakian national team, still coached by Jozef Adamec, had a very busy season, making two trips to Latin America and another to the Far East as they counted down to the World Cup qualifying tournament. With the Under-21 side finishing fourth in their European Championship and therefore qualifying for the Olympic football tournament in Sydney, there was even more work to do for the FA's travel agents.

Having been drawn in a relatively weak World Cup group - Sweden, Turkey, Macedonia, Azerbaijan and Moldova are the other group members - Slovakia must feel that they have a half-decent chance of making the play-offs. Tragically, though, the team will have to launch their bid without the talents of playmaker Peter Dubovsky, who was killed in a freak accident while on holiday in Thailand.

Dubovsky, who once played for Real Madrid, will be a great loss. His absence puts greater pressure on the team's other exported stars such as Celtic's Lubo Moravcik, Sunderland new boy Stanislav Varga and the Czech-based duo of Vladimir Kozuch and Vladimir Labant to impose their authority in the important matches. And then there are the U-21 graduates, who will have had a taste of the big time in Sydney and are sure to be hungry for more...

SECOND DIVISION FINAL TABLE

		Pd	W	D	L	F	A	Pt	GD
1	**Matador Puchov**	34	25	4	5	71	19	79	52
2	NCHZ Novaky	34	24	5	5	67	19	77	48
3	Zeleziarne Podbrezova	34	23	5	6	62	30	74	32
4	Steel Trans Licartovce	34	17	10	7	69	39	61	30
5	FC Rimavska Sobota	34	18	6	10	65	41	60	24
6	BSK Bardejov	34	17	6	11	48	32	57	16
7	SKP Devin	34	17	5	12	50	31	56	19
8	SH Senica	34	15	8	11	61	55	53	6
9	ZSNP Ziar nad Hronom	34	14	6	14	47	42	48	5
10	Slovan Bratislava B	34	15	3	16	38	43	48	-5
11	Slovan Levice	34	15	3	16	34	43	48	-9
12	Inter Bratislava B	34	10	10	14	39	43	40	-4
13	Tesla Stropkov	34	10	9	15	31	45	39	-14
14	FKM Nove Zamky	34	10	7	17	28	46	37	-18
15	Duslo Sala	34	9	5	20	30	55	32	-25
16	PFK Piestany	34	9	4	21	29	62	31	-33
17	Lokomotiva Kosice	34	4	6	24	25	76	18	-51
18	Spisska Nova Ves	34	1	4	29	12	85	7	-73

CLUB DIRECTORIES

SK Matador
Sportovcov 3
020 01 Puchov
tel - (0825) 631761
fax - (0825) 632952
Year of Formation - 1920
President - Vlastimil Samanek
Secretary - Pavol Holescak
Coach - Jozef Suran
Stadium - Matador (8,000)

ARTMEDIA PETRZALKA

CLUB DIRECTORY

FC Artmedia Petrzalka
Krasovskeho 1
851 01 Bratislava
tel - (07) 62250043/62250115
fax - (07) 62250043
Year of Formation - 1898
President - Vladimir Bajan
Secretary - Vladimir Weiss
Coach - Vladimir Weiss
Stadium - Za starym mostom (10,000)

APPEARANCES 99/00

	P	Ap	(s)	Gls
Martin BALIAK	D	15	(7)	1
Jan BELICA	G	1		
Juraj COBEJ	G	5		
Ondrej DEBNAR	D	22	(1)	1
Ondrej DESIATNIK	M	5	(5)	
Juraj ERÖS	M	5	(4)	
Miroslav FILIPKO	G	24		
Robert FORMANKO	M	12	(2)	
Erik HRNCAR	M	21	(5)	4
Martin KARNAS	D	12	(4)	
Michal KUBALA	A	20	(5)	
Martin KUNA	D	18	(4)	3
Stefan MAIXNER	A	18	(1)	4
Jozef MAJOROS	M	4	(8)	
Tomas MEDVED	A	28	(2)	14
Jozef OLEJNIK	D		(1)	
Lubomir ORABINEC	M	15	(4)	
Karol SCHULZ	D	21	(2)	1
Julius SIMON	M	11	(1)	3
Milan STRELEC	A	3	(5)	
Milan SUKAL	A	5	(8)	
Milos TOMAS	D	23	(3)	3
Radovan VASIK	A	13	(7)	8
Vladimir WEISS	M	1	(2)	
Tomas ZARECKY	M	19	(1)	
Ivan ZIGA	M	9	(5)	

LEAGUE RESULTS 1999/2000

Date	Opponent	H/A	Score	Scorers
23/07/99	DAC Dunajska Streda	A	1-1	Hrncar
31/07/99	Inter Bratislava	H	0-1	
07/08/99	FC Nitra	A	0-2	
15/08/99	ZTS Dubnica	H	4-1	Maixner 2, Medved, Hrncar
20/08/99	VTJ KOBA Senec	A	2-3	Medved, og (Zemlik)
29/08/99	HFC Humenne	H	2-2	Medved, Kuna
11/09/99	SCP Ruzomberok	A	2-2	Medved 2
18/09/99	Ozeta Dukla Trencin	A	0-2	
26/09/99	Spartak Trnava	H	2-1	Maixner, Hrncar (p)
02/10/99	Slovan Bratislava	A	1-0	Baliak
17/10/99	1.FC Kosice	H	0-4	
23/10/99	Banik Prievidza	A	3-4	Vasik 2, Hrncar
31/10/99	MSK Zilina	H	2-1	Kuna, Schulz (p)
06/11/99	Tatran Presov	A	0-3	
09/11/99	Dukla Banska Bystrica	H	3-1	Medved, Maixner, Vasik
11/03/00	DAC Dunajska Streda	H	2-0	Kuna, Simon
14/03/00	Inter Bratislava	A	0-1	
19/03/00	FC Nitra	H	1-2	Simon (p)
25/03/00	ZTS Dubnica	A	0-0	
28/03/00	VTJ KOBA Senec	H	2-0	Vasik, Medved
01/04/00	HFC Humenne	A	0-2	
08/04/00	SCP Ruzomberok	H	1-0	Simon
11/04/00	Ozeta Dukla Trencin	H	0-0	
15/04/00	Spartak Trnava	A	2-4	Vasik, Medved
23/04/00	Slovan Bratislava	H	1-3	Vasik
29/04/00	1.FC Kosice	A	2-3	Medved 2
02/05/00	Banik Prievidza	H	3-1	Tomas, Vasik, Medved (p)
11/05/00	MSK Zilina	A	2-2	Medved, Debnar
14/05/00	Tatran Presov	H	3-1	Tomas 2, Medved
17/05/00	Dukla Banska Bystrica	A	2-1	Medved, Vasik

BANIK PRIEVIDZA

CLUB DIRECTORY

FK Banik Prievidza
Sportova 37
971 01 Prievidza
tel - (0862) 5422858
fax - (0862) 5425692
Year of Formation - 1919
President - Jaroslav Vido
Secretary - Milan Kusnir
Coach - Vladimir Goffa
Stadium - Banik (10,000)

APPEARANCES 99/00

	P	Ap	(s)	Gls
Branislav BENKO	G	11		
Jozef BILIK	A	9	(8)	
Peter CERGE	A		(4)	
Juraj FURKA	G	3		
Juraj HALASKA	D	15	(1)	
Norbert HOKSA	D	12	(1)	
Marek HOLMIK	M	27	(1)	7
Stanislav HORNAK	D	12		2
Jan HULENI	M		(3)	
Jozef JELSIC	A	11	(1)	3
Milan KRSKO	D		(1)	
Milos KRSKO	D	9		
Pavol KUBOVICH	M		(6)	
Vladimir MAJSNIAR	A	12	(3)	
Adrian MASAROVIC	A	12	(1)	
Marek MECIAR	M	11	(3)	
Marek MICHALICKA	M	6	(5)	
Branislav OBZERA	A	18	(7)	
Stefan ONDRAS	D	14	(1)	
Juraj ORCO	D		(1)	
Miroslav ORSULA	M	9	(3)	1
Miroslav PAPRANEC	M	26	(2)	2
Milan PASTVA	M	17	(11)	3
Anton PAVLICEK	M		(1)	
Martin PETRAS	D	27	(1)	2
Miroslav POLIACEK	M	2	(2)	
Peter RICHTER	A		(5)	
Peter RYBAR	M	3	(3)	
Martin SEDLACEK	G	7		
Robert STOFAN	M	9	(3)	
Marek SVEC	A	2	(1)	
Marcel SVRCEK	D	6	(3)	
Jozef URBLIK	A	27	(1)	9
Ivan VANO	G	9		
Jan ZEMLIK (CZE)	A	4	(1)	
Tomas ZIMANYI	M		(2)	

LEAGUE RESULTS 1999/2000

24/07/99	Ozeta Dukla Trencin	H	0-2	
31/07/99	MSK Zilina	H	1-0	Urblik
07/08/99	Tatran Presov	A	2-4	Urblik (p), Papranec
14/08/99	Dukla Banska Bystrica	H	1-3	Jelsic
21/08/99	DAC Dunajska Streda	A	1-5	Urblik (p)
29/08/99	Inter Bratislava	H	1-3	Urblik
10/09/99	FC Nitra	A	1-2	Urblik
18/09/99	ZTS Dubnica	H	3-0	Jelsic, Holmik, Urblik
25/09/99	VTJ KOBA Senec	A	1-1	Urblik
02/10/99	HFC Humenne	H	1-0	Jelsic
16/10/99	SCP Ruzomberok	A	1-1	Orsula
23/10/99	Artmedia Petrzalka	H	4-3	Pastva 2, Petras, Hornak
30/10/99	Spartak Trnava	A	0-2	
05/11/99	Slovan Bratislava	H	1-1	Hornak
09/11/99	1.FC Kosice	A	2-3	Holmik 2
11/03/00	Ozeta Dukla Trencin	A	0-2	
14/03/00	MSK Zilina	A	0-4	
18/03/00	Tatran Presov	H	1-5	Holmik
25/03/00	Dukla Banska Bystrica	A	0-1	
28/03/00	DAC Dunajska Streda	H	0-2	
01/04/00	Inter Bratislava	A	0-7	
08/04/00	FC Nitra	H	2-1	Holmik 2
11/04/00	ZTS Dubnica	A	1-0	Urblik
15/04/00	VTJ KOBA Senec	H	1-4	Urblik
22/04/00	HFC Humenne	A	1-1	Papranec
29/04/00	SCP Ruzomberok	H	0-2	
02/05/00	Artmedia Petrzalka	A	1-3	Petras
11/05/00	Spartak Trnava	H	0-1	
14/05/00	Slovan Bratislava	A	1-5	Holmik
17/05/00	1.FC Kosice	H	1-3	Pastva

DAC DUNAJSKA STREDA

CLUB DIRECTORY

FK DAC
Sportova 18, 929 01 Dunajska Streda
tel - (0709) 5526874/5515430
fax - (0709) 5525660/5526621
Year of Formation - 1904
President - Imrich Santa
Secretary - Zoltan Csoka
Coach - Viliam Ilko; Ladislav Kuna
Stadium - DAC (16,410)

MAJOR HONOURS
Domestic Cup (Czechoslovakia) - (1) 1987.
Domestic Cup - (1) 1987.

APPEARANCES 99/00

		P	Ap	(s)	Gls
Vojtech BALLA	M	13			1
Radoslav BARAN	M	3	(1)		1
Balazs BORBELY	M	19	(6)		
Kornel CSICSAY	A		(7)		
Attila DOMIK	D	29			1
Juraj ERÖS	M	10	(2)		1
Stanislav FISAN	G	18			
Arpad GÖGH	M	1			
Roman GREGUSKA	M	29	(1)		1
Jan KAPKO	D	15	(8)		
Oleh KOROL (UKR)	D	13			1
Zdenko KRSTENANSKY	D	5	(2)		
Rudolf MATTA	D	22	(2)		
Zoltan MESZAROS	M	1	(5)		
Miroslav NEMEC	A	7	(1)		2
Jozef NEMETH	M		(7)		
Krisztian NEMETH	D	20			
Jozef OLEJNIK	D	13			
Mikulas RADVANYI	A	24	(4)		6
János ROMANEK (HUN)	M	6	(7)		
Peter SANTA	G	12			
Julius SIMON	M	14			6
Ladislav SUCHANEK	A	23	(4)		4
Tibor SZABAN	D	6	(2)		
Erik SZEIF	M	4	(6)		
Tomas URBAN	M	9	(2)		
Dezider VARGA	M	3	(3)		
Roman ZIMA	A	11	(3)		

LEAGUE RESULTS 1999/2000

23/07/99	Artmedia Petrzalka	H	1-1	Domik
31/07/99	Spartak Trnava	A	0-3	
07/08/99	Slovan Bratislava	H	0-3	
14/08/99	1.FC Kosice	A	1-2	Baran
21/08/99	Banik Prievidza	H	5-1	Simon 3 (1p), Balla, Radvanyi
28/08/99	MSK Zilina	A	0-6	
11/09/99	Tatran Presov	H	1-2	Nemec
19/09/99	Dukla Banska Bystrica	A	2-1	Erös, Radvanyi
25/09/99	Ozeta Dukla Trencin	H	0-0	
03/10/99	Inter Bratislava	H	0-0	
16/10/99	FC Nitra	A	0-2	
23/10/99	ZTS Dubnica	H	1-2	Nemec
30/10/99	VTJ KOBA Senec	A	0-0	
06/11/99	HFC Humenne	H	4-0	Simon 3, Radvanyi
09/11/99	SCP Ruzomberok	A	0-1	
11/03/00	Artmedia Petrzalka	A	0-2	
14/03/00	Spartak Trnava	H	0-0	
18/03/00	Slovan Bratislava	A	0-4	
25/03/00	1.FC Kosice	H	0-2	
28/03/00	Banik Prievidza	A	2-0	Suchanek 2
01/04/00	MSK Zilina	H	0-1	
08/04/00	Tatran Presov	A	1-1	Greguska
11/04/00	Dukla Banska Bystrica	H	2-2	Radvanyi (p), Suchanek
15/04/00	Ozeta Dukla Trencin	A	0-2	
22/04/00	Inter Bratislava	A	0-1	
29/04/00	FC Nitra	H	1-0	Korol
02/05/00	ZTS Dubnica	A	0-0	
11/05/00	VTJ KOBA Senec	H	2-2	Radvanyi 2 (2p)
14/05/00	HFC Humenne	A	0-1	
17/05/00	SCP Ruzomberok	H	1-0	Suchanek

ZTS DUBNICA

CLUB DIRECTORY

FK ZTS Dubnica
Sportovcov 655
018 41 Dubnica nad Vahom
tel - (0827) 4420025
fax - (0827) 4420033
Year of Formation - 1926
President - Ing. Ivan Nemeckay
Manager - Jaroslav Schroner
Coach - Anton Dragun; Peter Gergely;
Jozef Jankech
Stadium - ZTS (8,000)

APPEARANCES 99/00

	P	Ap	(s)	Gls
Eugen BARI	A	23	(2)	2
Igor DRAZIK	M		(1)	
Viktor DYAK (UKR)	A	11	(4)	2
Frantisek HADVIGER	D	28		
Michal HANEK	D	21	(4)	2
Rastislav HEVESSY	D		(1)	
Alexander HOMER	D	29		3
Erik JENES	M		(7)	
Michal KANTOR	M	1	(3)	
Peter KISKA	M	2	(2)	
Pavol KOVAC	G	30		
Peter MASAROVIC	A	11	(7)	4
Branislav MRAZ	D	21	(2)	
Peter NEMECKAY	A	16	(13)	3
Lubos NOSICKY	M	18	(5)	1
Tomas POLACH (CZE)	M	24		1
Vladimir ROZNIK	A	2	(4)	
Pavol STRAKA	A	7	(9)	3
Anton SUCHY	M	24	(3)	1
Peter SUCHY	A	1	(3)	
Andrej SUPKA	M	28	(1)	
Jan SVIKRUHA	M	10	(8)	1
Stanislav TURZA	D	22	(6)	2
Jozef VALACHOVIC	A		(2)	
Marian ZIMEN	M	1	(1)	

LEAGUE RESULTS 1999/2000

24/07/99	VTJ KOBA Senec	H	0-1	
20/07/99	HFC Humenne	A	1-0	Suchy A.
07/08/99	SCP Ruzomberok	H	0-0	
15/08/99	Artmedia Petrzalka	A	1-4	Dyak
21/08/99	Spartak Trnava	H	1-0	Svikruha
28/08/99	Slovan Bratislava	A	1-1	Hanek
11/09/99	1.FC Kosice	H	2-0	Bari, Turza
18/09/99	Banik Prievidza	A	0-3	
24/09/99	MSK Zilina	H	1-4	Homer (p)
02/10/99	Tatran Presov	A	0-1	
16/10/99	Dukla Banska Bystrica	H	1-0	Nemeckay
23/10/99	DAC Dunajska Streda	A	2-1	Homer 2 (1p)
30/10/99	Inter Bratislava	H	0-1	
06/11/99	FC Nitra	A	1-1	Dyak
09/11/99	Ozeta Dukla Trencin	H	0-0	
11/03/00	VTJ KOBA Senec	A	0-3	
14/03/00	HFC Humenne	H	5-0	Masarovic 2, Turza, Polach, Nemeckay
18/03/00	SCP Ruzomberok	A	0-1	
25/03/00	Artmedia Petrzalka	H	0-0	
28/03/00	Spartak Trnava	A	1-1	Masarovic (p)
01/04/00	Slovan Bratislava	H	0-3	
08/04/00	1.FC Kosice	A	1-2	Nosicky
11/04/00	Banik Prievidza	H	0-1	
15/04/00	MSK Zilina	A	0-2	
22/04/00	Tatran Presov	H	1-0	Straka
29/04/00	Dukla Banska Bystrica	A	1-0	Straka
02/05/00	DAC Dunajska Streda	H	0-0	
11/05/00	Inter Bratislava	A	0-3	
14/05/00	FC Nitra	H	5-0	Bari, Masarovic, Hanek, Straka, Nemeckay
17/05/00	Ozeta Dukla Trencin	A	0-2	

DUKLA BANSKA BYSTRICA

CLUB DIRECTORY

FK Dukla
Stiavnicky, Stadion SNP na Stiavnickach
974 01 Banska Bystrica
tel - (088) 4230444   fax - (088) 4138176
Year of Formation - 1965
President - Jozef Venglos jnr.
Secretary - Karol Ihring
Coach - Milos Targas; Anton Dragun; Igor Novak
Stadium - SNP na Stiavnickach (11,500)

MAJOR HONOURS
Domestic Cup - (1) 1981.

APPEARANCES 99/00

	P	Ap	(s)	Gls
Ivan BARTOS	D	8	(1)	
Daniel BENKOVSKY	M	2	(1)	
Peter BOROS	G	14		
Marek BUBENKO	A	5	(6)	1
Peter CVIRIK	A	17	(1)	1
Lubomir FAKTOR	M	19	(2)	5
Tibor GOLJAN	M	3	(5)	1
Vladimir HELBICH	M	13		
Lubomir HOROCHONIC	M	14		2
Peter HRUBINA	M	1	(1)	
Marcel JELENCIK	M	9		
Norbert JURACKA	G	10	(1)	
Dusan KAPRAL	A	2	(2)	
Stefan KARASEK	D	18		1
Jaroslav KENTOS	D	8		
Maros KLIMPL	M	6	(2)	1
Martin KOLENIK	M	8	(3)	2
Patrik KONUSIK	D	13		
Ondrej KOSTUR	A	14	(10)	2
Marian KOVAC	A	16	(4)	1
Tomas KOZAR	M	4	(8)	
Martin LAURINC	M	24	(3)	1
Juraj LESTAK	D	3	(2)	
Peter LUPTAK	A		(3)	1
Milan MALATINSKY	M	4	(2)	
Stefan MIHALIK	D	9		
Sasho Iliev MIKHAILOV (BUL)	A	1	(5)	
Michal PANCIK	M	13	(1)	1
Viktor PECOVSKY	A		(3)	
Peter PINTER	M	3	(6)	
Richard RUBINT	D	6	(1)	
João Luís SILVEIRA (BRA)	A	11		3
Roman STRBA	A	16	(4)	3
Marian STRELEC	M	11	(1)	
Igor VODECKY	A	2	(6)	
Richard ZAJAC	G	6		
Mario ZAVATERNIK	D	17		1

LEAGUE RESULTS 1999/2000

24/07/99	Spartak Trnava	H	1-2	Kovac
31/07/99	Slovan Bratislava	A	1-2	Pancik
07/08/99	1.FC Kosice	H	2-1	Faktor 2
14/08/99	Banik Prievidza	A	3-1	Luptak, Faktor, Cvirik
21/08/99	MSK Zilina	H	3-2	Faktor (p), Bubenko, Kostur
28/08/99	Tatran Presov	A	0-3	
11/09/99	Ozeta Dukla Trencin	H	1-0	Faktor
19/09/99	DAC Dunajska Streda	H	1-2	Kostur
26/09/99	Inter Bratislava	A	0-3	
03/10/99	FC Nitra	H	1-2	Klimpl
16/10/99	ZTS Dubnica	A	0-1	
23/10/99	VTJ KOBA Senec	H	1-0	Laurinc
30/10/99	HFC Humenne	A	0-2	
06/11/99	SCP Ruzomberok	H	0-1	
09/11/99	Artmedia Petrzalka	A	1-3	Karasek
11/03/00	Spartak Trnava	A	0-4	
14/03/00	Slovan Bratislava	H	0-1	
18/03/00	1.FC Kosice	A	1-3	Strba
25/03/00	Banik Prievidza	H	1-0	Strba
28/03/00	MSK Zilina	A	0-1	
01/04/00	Tatran Presov	H	1-2	Horochonic (p)
08/04/00	Ozeta Dukla Trencin	A	2-5	Silveira, Zavaternik
11/04/00	DAC Dunajska Streda	A	2-2	Horochonic (p), Silveira
15/04/00	Inter Bratislava	H	0-2	
22/04/00	FC Nitra	A	3-2	Goljan, Silveira, Kolenik
29/04/00	ZTS Dubnica	H	0-1	
02/05/00	VTJ KOBA Senec	A	0-1	
11/05/00	HFC Humenne	H	1-1	Kolenik
14/05/00	SCP Ruzomberok	A	0-1	
17/05/00	Artmedia Petrzalka	H	1-2	Strba

HFC HUMENNE

CLUB DIRECTORY

HFC Humenne
Chemlonska 1
066 01 Humenne
tel - (0933) 62696
fax - (0933) 64643
Year of Formation - 1903
President - Dusan Kapral
Secretary - Jozef Matta
Coach - Vladimir Gombar; Vladimir Sivy
Stadium - Chemlon (18,000)

MAJOR HONOURS
Domestic Cup - (1) 1996.

APPEARANCES 99/00

	P	Ap	(s)	Gls
Jozef ALUSIK	A		(1)	
Norbert BELAN	G	1	(1)	
Michal CERNEGA	A	16	(10)	3
Martin CERNOCH	A	15		2
Jan FECENKO	M		(1)	
Miroslav HAJDUCKO	M	13	(2)	1
Miroslav JANTEK	D	29		2
Dalibor KARNAY	M		(7)	1
Igor KASANA	M	18		1
Ruslan KIRPIKOV (UKR)	M	1	(1)	
Miroslav KOZAK	A	5	(8)	
Marcel LOJ	M	14		
Marek LUKAC	A	25	(3)	5
Peter MARINIC	D	6	(4)	
Gabriel MELNIK	A		(1)	
Lubomir MICAK	M	4		
Peter MURINCAK	M	30		4
Patrik MYCIO	M	10	(2)	
Jan PETRAS	M	4	(2)	
Ivo PILIP	G	29		
Peter SAMO	D	5	(6)	
Miroslav SECEN	D	29		1
Radoslav SIMKO	M	15	(6)	1
Dusan SNINSKY	M	26	(1)	8
Jaroslav SOVIC	D	20	(1)	1
Peter SUKOVSKY	D	15	(1)	

LEAGUE RESULTS 1999/2000

24/07/99	FC Nitra	A	0-1	
30/07/99	ZTS Dubnica	H	0-1	
07/08/99	VTJ KOBA Senec	A	0-1	
14/08/99	Ozeta Dukla Trencin	A	1-4	Sninsky
21/08/99	SCP Ruzomberok	H	2-1	Sninsky, Lukac
29/08/99	Artmedia Petrzalka	A	2-2	Hajducko, Cernega
11/09/99	Spartak Trnava	H	1-0	Secen
18/09/99	Slovan Bratislava	A	0-2	
25/09/99	1.FC Kosice	H	2-2	Lukac, Cernega
02/10/99	Banik Prievidza	A	0-1	
16/10/99	MSK Zilina	H	3-1	Sovic, Sninsky, Karnay
23/10/99	Tatran Presov	A	0-1	
30/10/99	Dukla Banska Bystrica	H	2-0	Cernega, Kasana
06/11/99	DAC Dunajska Streda	A	0-4	
21/11/99	Inter Bratislava	H	1-1	Murincak
11/03/00	FC Nitra	H	3-1	Sninsky, Jantek, Lukac
14/03/00	ZTS Dubnica	A	0-5	
18/03/00	VTJ KOBA Senec	H	1-0	Sninsky
25/03/00	Ozeta Dukla Trencin	H	0-1	
28/03/00	SCP Ruzomberok	A	1-1	Murincak
01/04/00	Artmedia Petrzalka	H	2-0	Cernoch, Lukac
08/04/00	Spartak Trnava	A	0-1	
11/04/00	Slovan Bratislava	H	3-3	og (Pecko), Sninsky 2
15/04/00	1.FC Kosice	A	0-1	
22/04/00	Banik Prievidza	H	1-1	Murincak
29/04/00	MSK Zilina	A	2-0	Jantek (p), Sninsky
02/05/00	Tatran Presov	H	2-0	Lukac, Murincak
11/05/00	Dukla Banska Bystrica	A	1-1	Cernoch
14/05/00	DAC Dunajska Streda	H	1-0	Simko
17/05/00	Inter Bratislava	A	0-6	

INTER BRATISLAVA

CLUB DIRECTORY

ASK Inter Slovnaft Bratislava
Vajnorska 100, 832 04 Bratislava
tel - (07) 44371007
fax - (07) 44451341
Year of Formation - 1940
President - Ing. Juraj Oblozinsky
Secretary - Rudolf Jancek
Coach - Jozef Bubenko
Stadium - Inter (15,000)

MAJOR HONOURS
League Championship (Czechoslovakia) - (1)
1959.
League Championship - (1) 2000.
Domestic Cup - (3) 1984, 1995, 2000.

APPEARANCES 99/00

	P	Ap	(s)	Gls
Peter BABNIC	A	25	(3)	8
Peter BARTALSKY	G	1		
Jan CHRENKO	D	23	(4)	
Marian CISOVSKY	D	5	(7)	
Juraj CZINEGE	M	20	(4)	6
Jozef GASPAR	D	9	(2)	
Tomas GERICH	M	25	(2)	3
Zsolt HORNYAK	D	21	(1)	
Miroslav HYLL	G	29		
Roman KRATOCHVIL	D	29		6
Marek KREJCI	A	4	(6)	1
Milan KUSALIK	M	5	(9)	1
Marian LALIK	M	21	(6)	9
Tomas MASARYK	M		(1)	
Peter NEMETH	M	26	(2)	3
Szilard NEMETH	A	23	(3)	16
Lubos PERNIS	A	2	(13)	4
Attila PINTE	M	18	(9)	4
Martin SEVELA	D	17	(4)	1
Marian SUCHANCOK	D	26		1
Rastislav TOMOVCIK	A	1	(9)	
Ladislav VENCEL	M		(1)	

LEAGUE RESULTS 1999/2000

24/07/99	SCP Ruzomberok	H	2-3	Babnic, Kratochvil (p)
31/07/99	Artmedia Petrzalka	A	1-0	Gerich
07/08/99	Spartak Trnava	H	0-0	
15/08/99	Slovan Bratislava	A	1-1	Lalik
21/08/99	1.FC Kosice	H	2-1	Kratochvil (p), Sevela
29/08/99	Banik Prievidza	A	3-1	Nemeth S. 2, Pernis
11/09/99	MSK Zilina	H	2-0	Kratochvil, Nemeth S.
19/09/99	Tatran Presov	A	3-0	Nemeth P., Nemeth S., Babnic
26/09/99	Dukla Banska Bystrica	H	3-0	Kratochvil, Nemeth S. 2
03/10/99	DAC Dunajska Streda	A	0-0	
16/10/99	Ozeta Dukla Trencin	H	1-1	Pernis
24/10/99	FC Nitra	H	3-0	Nemeth S., Babnic, Czinege
30/10/99	ZTS Dubnica	A	1-0	Lalik
08/11/99	VTJ KOBA Senec	H	2-0	Kusalik, Babnic
21/11/99	HFC Humenne	A	1-1	Kratochvil
11/03/00	SCP Ruzomberok	A	1-1	Czinege
14/03/00	Artmedia Petrzalka	H	1-0	Lalik
17/03/00	Spartak Trnava	A	2-0	Czinege, Krejci
24/03/00	Slovan Bratislava	H	1-1	Nemeth S.
28/03/00	1.FC Kosice	A	1-3	Nemeth P.
01/04/00	Banik Prievidza	H	7-0	Pernis 2, Nemeth S. 2, Gerich (p), Lalik, Nemeth P.
07/04/00	MSK Zilina	A	2-1	Lalik, Czinege
11/04/00	Tatran Presov	H	2-0	Lalik, og (Chovan)
15/04/00	Dukla Banska Bystrica	A	2-0	Suchancok, Lalik
22/04/00	DAC Dunajska Streda	H	1-0	Kratochvil (p)
29/04/00	Ozeta Dukla Trencin	A	3-1	Babnic 2, Nemeth S.
02/05/00	FC Nitra	A	3-1	og (Datko), Lalik, Pinte
11/05/00	ZTS Dubnica	H	3-0	Babnic, Nemeth S., Pinte
14/05/00	VTJ KOBA Senec	A	5-0	Lalik, Gerich, Babnic, Nemeth S., Czinege
17/05/00	HFC Humenne	H	6-0	Nemeth S. 3, Pinte 2, Czinege

VTJ KOBA SENEC

CLUB DIRECTORY

FK VTJ Koba Senec
Rybarska 29
903 01 Senec
tel - (07) 4527242/4527241
fax - (07) 45927242
Year of Formation - 1991
President - Daniel Bartko
Secretary - Stanislav Krajc
Coach - Ladislav Jurkemik
Stadium - Senec (6,500)

APPEARANCES 99/00

	P	Ap	(s)	Gls
Peter ANDREJCO	M	1	(1)	
Daniel BARTKO	A		(1)	
Jozef CELKO	D		(2)	
Ondrej DESIATNIK	M	5	(8)	
Marek FIGLAR	M	1	(1)	
Jan FILAK	D	25	(1)	
Martin GAJDOS	M	26	(1)	2
Daniel GOGA	M	5	(5)	1
Jaroslav HALAHIJA	M	6	(5)	
Ales HELLEBRAND (CZE)	D	14		
Martin JANCULA	D	15	(3)	3
Marcel JELENCIK	A	7		
Pavol KAMESCH	G	26		
Daniel KASPRIK (CZE)	A	11	(1)	3
Jozef KESZÖCZE	A	6	(7)	1
Jan KOZIAK	A	1	(9)	
Oskar LANCZ	M	19		1
Milos LIPOVSKY	D	5	(7)	
Martin LUKAC	M	14		
Tomas NOVOTNY	D	9		1
Kamil PAPUGA	M	3		
Jaroslav PASZKO	A		(3)	
Pavol PIATKA	A	13		5
Rastislav SENDECKY	D	3	(3)	
Gabriel SIKORJAK	A	24	(5)	3
Marian SÜTTÖ	M	15		2
Martin SVEJNOHA (CZE)	M	12		1
Robert TOMKO	A	6	(6)	3
Richard TRUTZ	D	9	(1)	
Lubomir VNUK	M	3	(5)	
Patrik VOLF	M	26	(2)	2
Marek VOMACKA (CZE)	M	2	(5)	1
Miroslav VRABEL	G	4		
Jan ZEMLIK	A	13	(2)	3
Roman ZIMA	A	1	(5)	1

LEAGUE RESULTS 1999/2000

24/07/99	ZTS Dubnica	A	1-0	Zemlik
31/07/99	Ozeta Dukla Trencin	A	2-2	Zima, Keszöcze
07/08/99	HFC Humenne	H	1-0	Tomko
14/08/99	SCP Ruzomberok	A	0-1	
20/08/99	Artmedia Petrzalka	H	3-2	Süttö, Novotny, Zemlik
29/08/99	Spartak Trnava	A	2-2	Zemlik, Goga
11/09/99	Slovan Bratislava	H	0-1	
17/09/99	1.FC Kosice	A	1-2	Volf
25/09/99	Banik Prievidza	H	1-1	Tomko
02/10/99	MSK Zilina	A	1-2	Jancula
16/10/99	Tatran Presov	H	2-2	Tomko, Lancz
23/10/99	Dukla Banska Bystrica	A	0-1	
30/10/99	DAC Dunajska Streda	H	0-0	
02/11/99	FC Nitra	H	2-1	Svejnoha, Süttö
08/11/99	Inter Bratislava	A	0-2	
11/03/00	ZTS Dubnica	H	3-0	Gajdos, Piatka, Vomacka
14/03/00	Ozeta Dukla Trencin	H	1-1	Piatka
18/03/00	HFC Humenne	A	0-1	
25/03/00	SCP Ruzomberok	H	2-0	Kasprik, Volf
28/03/00	Artmedia Petrzalka	A	0-2	
01/04/00	Spartak Trnava	H	0-0	
08/04/00	Slovan Bratislava	A	1-1	Jancula
11/04/00	1.FC Kosice	H	3-1	Kasprik, Sikorjak (p), Jancula
15/04/00	Banik Prievidza	A	4-1	Piatka 2 (1p), Sikorjak 2
22/04/00	MSK Zilina	H	0-0	
29/04/00	Tatran Presov	A	0-1	
02/05/00	Dukla Banska Bystrica	H	1-0	Kasprik
11/05/00	DAC Dunajska Streda	A	2-2	Gajdos, Piatka
14/05/00	Inter Bratislava	H	0-5	
17/05/00	FC Nitra	A	0-2	

1.FC KOSICE

CLUB DIRECTORY

1.FC Kosice
Alejova 2, 040 11 Kosice
tel - (095) 6424871/6224253/436956
fax - (095) 6444871/436956
Year of Formation - 1992
President - Julius Rezes
Secretary - Vladimir Varga
Coach - Jan Kozak; Ladislav Molnar
Stadium - Lokomotiva Kosice (10,000)

MAJOR HONOURS
League Championship - (2) 1997, 1998.
Domestic Cup (Czechoslovakia) - (1) 1993.
Domestic Cup - (3) 1973, 1980, 1993.

APPEARANCES 99/00

	P	Ap	(s)	Gls
Rastislav BELICAK	A		(1)	
Juraj BENO	A		(1)	
Kamil CONTOFALSKY	G	8	(1)	
Peter DZURIK	D	27	(1)	3
Frantisek HANC	D	25	(1)	1
Martin HLOUSEK	M		(1)	
Milan JAMBOR	D	16	(4)	
Vladimir JANOCKO	M	15		2
Jan KOZAK	M	9	(1)	6
Jozef KOZLEJ	A	27	(2)	9
Radoslav KRAL	D	27		5
Tomas LIBIC	M	5	(2)	
Ruslan LYUBARSKYI (UKR)	A	27		15
Robert NOVAK	M		(7)	
Ladislav ONOFREJ	M	12	(10)	
Tomas ORAVEC	A	4	(16)	2
Miroslav SEMAN	G	22		
Robert SEMENIK	D	14	(1)	3
Peter SLICHO	A	2	(6)	
Marek SPILAR	D	25		3
Dusan TOTH	D	8		1
Rudolf URBAN	M	2	(17)	2
Radoslav ZABAVNIK	M	1	(5)	
Tibor ZATEK	D	30		
Vladislav ZVARA	M	24	(3)	4

LEAGUE RESULTS 1999/2000

24/07/99	MSK Zilina	A	4-1	Janocko (p), Lyubarskyi, Urban, Dzurik
01/08/99	Tatran Presov	H	3-0	Lyubarskyi 2 (1p), Toth
07/08/99	Dukla Banska Bystrica	A	1-2	Kral
14/08/99	DAC Dunajska Streda	H	2-1	Janocko (p), Dzurik
21/08/99	Inter Bratislava	A	1-2	Zvara
28/08/99	FC Nitra	H	3-1	Dzurik, Kral, Hanc
11/09/99	ZTS Dubnica	A	0-2	
17/09/99	VTJ KOBA Senec	H	2-1	Kral, Lyubarskyi
25/09/99	HFC Humenne	A	2-2	Kozlej, Zvara
01/10/99	SCP Ruzomberok	H	2-1	Kozlej, Lyubarskyi (p)
17/10/99	Artmedia Petrzalka	A	4-0	Lyubarskyi 2, Kozlej, Zvara
22/10/99	Spartak Trnava	H	0-0	
29/10/99	Slovan Bratislava	A	2-1	og (Skrtel), Kozlej
06/11/99	Ozeta Dukla Trencin	A	0-0	
09/11/99	Banik Prievidza	H	3-2	Kozlej, Urban, Spilar
10/03/00	MSK Zilina	H	2-0	Kozlej, Lyubarskyi
14/03/00	Tatran Presov	A	1-2	Kozlej
18/03/00	Dukla Banska Bystrica	H	3-1	Lyubarskyi 2, Kozak
25/03/00	DAC Dunajska Streda	A	2-0	Kozak, Kozlej
28/03/00	Inter Bratislava	H	3-1	Spilar, Lyubarskyi, Kozak
31/03/00	FC Nitra	A	1-1	Kral
08/04/00	ZTS Dubnica	H	2-1	Kozak, Semenik
11/04/00	VTJ KOBA Senec	A	1-3	Kozak (p)
15/04/00	HFC Humenne	H	1-0	Zvara (p)
21/04/00	SCP Ruzomberok	A	2-0	Kozlej, Spilar
29/04/00	Artmedia Petrzalka	H	3-2	Semenik, Kral, Kozak
02/05/00	Spartak Trnava	A	0-1	
11/05/00	Slovan Bratislava	H	0-2	
14/05/00	Ozeta Dukla Trencin	H	4-0	Lyubarskyi 2, Semenik, Oravec
17/05/00	Banik Prievidza	A	3-1	Lyubarskyi 2, Oravec

FC NITRA

CLUB DIRECTORY

FC Nitra
Jeseskeho 4
949 01 Nitra
tel - (087) 513255/510112
fax - (087) 414958
Year of Formation - 1919
President - Ing. Jan Kovarcik
Secretary - Gustav Antalik
Coach - Jozef Prochotsky; Jan Gregus
Stadium - Pod Zoborom (11,384)

APPEARANCES 99/00

	P	Ap	(s)	Gls
Marek BAKOS	A		(1)	
Henrich BENCIK	A	27	(1)	1
Patrik BREZINA	G	2	(1)	
Marian DATKO	D	18	(1)	
Marian DIRNBACH	A	14		1
Jozef DOJCAN	M	11		
Juraj DOVICOVIC	M	26	(2)	3
Ivan HODUR	M	28	(2)	3
Stefan HOK	A	1	(12)	
Eduard HRNCAR	D	27		2
Jozef JELSIC	A	8	(6)	4
Robert JEZ	A	21	(5)	4
Tomas KOMPAS	D	2		
Marek KOSTOLANI	M	1	(1)	
Mikulas LÖRINC	A		(3)	
Miroslav LÖRINC	M	9		
Slavomir LUKAC	D	17	(4)	
Jan MUCHA	G	11		
Peter OREMUS	M	10	(8)	
Rastislav ÖLVECKY	A	4	(9)	
Marcel PAVLIK	M	28		1
Jozef RYBNIKAR	M	17	(3)	2
Stefan SENECKY	G	17		
Martin SEVCIK	D	21	(3)	3
Jan STAJER	A		(3)	
Martin STANCEK	A		(7)	
Robert VOJVODA	D	10		
Juraj VONDRA	M		(1)	

LEAGUE RESULTS 1999/2000

24/07/99	HFC Humenne	H	1-0	Hodur
31/07/99	SCP Ruzomberok	A	0-3	
07/08/99	Artmedia Petrzalka	H	2-0	Jez, Dovicovic
15/08/99	Spartak Trnava	A	0-1	
21/08/99	Slovan Bratislava	H	1-0	Bencik
28/08/99	1.FC Kosice	A	1-3	Hodur
10/09/99	Banik Prievidza	H	2-1	Rybnikar, Sevcik
18/09/99	MSK Zilina	A	0-1	
25/09/99	Tatran Presov	H	0-1	
03/10/99	Dukla Banska Bystrica	A	2-1	Sevcik, Jez
16/10/99	DAC Dunajska Streda	H	2-0	Hrncar, Hodur
24/10/99	Inter Bratislava	A	0-3	
30/10/99	Ozeta Dukla Trencin	H	0-1	
02/11/99	VTJ KOBA Senec	A	1-2	Sevcik
06/11/99	ZTS Dubnica	H	1-1	Dovicovic
11/03/00	HFC Humenne	A	1-3	Jelsic
14/03/00	SCP Ruzomberok	H	0-0	
19/03/00	Artmedia Petrzalka	A	2-1	Jelsic, Pavlik
25/03/00	Spartak Trnava	H	0-1	
28/03/00	Slovan Bratislava	A	0-1	
31/03/00	1.FC Kosice	H	1-1	Jelsic
08/04/00	Banik Prievidza	A	1-2	Jez
11/04/00	MSK Zilina	H	0-2	
15/04/00	Tatran Presov	A	0-2	
22/04/00	Dukla Banska Bystrica	H	2-3	Dirnbach, Dovicovic
29/04/00	DAC Dunajska Streda	A	0-1	
02/05/00	Inter Bratislava	H	1-3	Rybnikar
11/05/00	Ozeta Dukla Trencin	A	1-1	Jelsic
14/05/00	ZTS Dubnica	A	0-5	
17/05/00	VTJ KOBA Senec	H	2-0	Hrncar, Jez

OZETA DUKLA TRENCIN

CLUB DIRECTORY

FK Ozeta Dukla Trencin
Mladeznicka 1
911 01 Trencin
tel - (0831) 523302/7441137
fax - (0831) 7441137
Year of Formation - 1992
President - Pavol Hozlar
Secretary - Miroslav Karas
Coach - Robert Paldan
Stadium - Na Sihoti (12,000)

APPEARANCES 99/00

	P	Ap	(s)	Gls
Juraj ANCIC	A		(8)	1
Vladimir CIFRANIC	D	8	(9)	
Marian DIRNBACH	A	14	(1)	4
Martin FABUS	A	15		4
Jozef FRIGA	D	3	(2)	
Petr GOTTWALD (CZE)	M	11	(1)	5
Robert HANKO	M	28	(1)	
Stanislav HORNAK	M	8		
Miroslav HORVATOVIC	M	21	(1)	
Roman HRNCAR	D	25		
Karol KISEL	M	11	(2)	1
Martin KONECNY	D	25	(3)	1
Jan KOZIAK	M	1	(2)	
Milos KRSKO	M	13	(4)	2
Alojz KULLA	M	18	(9)	
Martin LIPCAK	G	28		
Lubomir MATI	A	2	(3)	
Damir MATIJASEVIC (CRO)	A	5	(3)	2
Ivo MÜLLER (CZE)	M	11	(1)	
Ondrej ONDROVIC	M	11	(13)	2
Andrej PORAZIK	A	21	(4)	6
Vladimir ROZNIK	A	2	(6)	
Jozef RYBNIKAR	A		(2)	
Frantisek SMAK	G	2	(1)	
Ondrej SMELKO	D	19	(3)	1
Jozef VALACHOVIC	D	28		7

LEAGUE RESULTS 1999/2000

24/07/99	Banik Prievidza	A	2-0	Porazik, Matijasevic
31/07/99	VTJ KOBA Senec	H	2-2	Matijasevic, Dirnbach
07/08/99	MSK Zilina	A	0-1	
14/08/99	HFC Humenne	H	4-1	Porazik, og (Secen), Dirnbach, Valachovic
21/08/99	Tatran Presov	A	1-2	Dirnbach
27/08/99	SCP Ruzomberok	H	2-0	Porazik, Ancic
11/09/99	Dukla Banska Bystrica	A	0-1	
18/09/99	Artmedia Petrzalka	H	2-0	Dirnbach, Valachovic
25/09/99	DAC Dunajska Streda	A	0-0	
03/10/99	Spartak Trnava	H	1-2	Valachovic (p)
16/10/99	Inter Bratislava	A	1-1	Ondrovic
23/10/99	Slovan Bratislava	H	1-0	Porazik
30/10/99	FC Nitra	A	1-0	Kisel
06/11/99	1.FC Kosice	H	0-0	
09/11/99	ZTS Dubnica	A	0-0	
11/03/00	Banik Prievidza	H	2-0	Valachovic, Fabus
14/03/00	VTJ KOBA Senec	A	1-1	Smelko
18/03/00	MSK Zilina	H	3-0	Porazik, Krsko, Konecny
25/03/00	HFC Humenne	A	1-0	Fabus
28/03/00	Tatran Presov	H	2-0	Gottwald, Fabus
08/04/00	Dukla Banska Bystrica	H	5-2	Gottwald 2, Valachovic, Krsko, og (Karasek)
11/04/00	Artmedia Petrzalka	A	0-0	
15/04/00	DAC Dunajska Streda	H	2-0	Gottwald, Valachovic
18/04/00	SCP Ruzomberok	A	1-3	Ondrovic
22/04/00	Spartak Trnava	A	0-2	
29/04/00	Inter Bratislava	H	1-3	Gottwald
02/05/00	Slovan Bratislava	A	0-3	
11/05/00	FC Nitra	H	1-1	Porazik
14/05/00	1.FC Kosice	A	0-4	
17/05/00	ZTS Dubnica	H	2-0	Valachovic, Fabus

SCP RUZOMBEROK

CLUB DIRECTORY

FK SCP Ruzomberok
Zilinska cesta 21
034 01 Ruzomberok
tel - (0848) 323589/322506
fax - (0848) 323589
Year of Formation - 1906
President - Milan Bezak
Secretary - Vendelin Kniha
Coach - Igor Novak; Miroslav Gerhat; Milan Bagin;
Miroslav Mentel
Stadium - SCP (9,000)

APPEARANCES 99/00

	P	Ap	(s)	Gls
Mario ADAMCIK	A	4	(7)	1
Juraj BAKOS	A		(2)	
Daniel BEZAK	D	4	(2)	
Jaroslav CHLEBEK	D	9	(11)	
Csaba CSANYI	M	21	(2)	
Stanislav DURIS	M	20		
Robert HAZUCHA	A	21	(3)	6
Vladimir HELBICH	M	11	(1)	1
Ales HELLEBRAND (CZE)	M	14	(1)	2
Lubomir HOROCHONIC	A	4		
Vladimir HUTKA	M	14	(6)	1
Viliam HYRAVY	M	23	(3)	7
Jaroslav JOSEFIK (CZE)	M		(3)	
Maros KLIMPL	D	13	(1)	
Gabriel MAJOROS	M	1	(7)	
Jan MELICHERCIK	M	15	(5)	
Frantisek MIKULAS	D	28		1
Juraj MINTAL	D	15		
Eduard MYDLIAR	A	19	(3)	4
Peter RATAJ	D	16		2
Jan SAFRANKO	A	27	(2)	
Remus SAFTA (ROM)	M	2	(4)	
Miroslav SVARNY	A	3	(4)	
Ivan TRABALIK	G	30		
Martin VYSKOC	A	16	(7)	4

LEAGUE RESULTS 1999/2000

24/07/99	Inter Bratislava	A	3-2	Hyravy 2 (1p), Hazucha
31/07/99	FC Nitra	H	3-0	Hazucha, Hyravy, Mydliar
07/08/99	ZTS Dubnica	A	0-0	
14/08/99	VTJ KOBA Senec	H	1-0	Mydliar
21/08/99	HFC Humenne	A	1-2	Hyravy
27/08/99	Ozeta Dukla Trencin	A	0-2	
11/09/99	Artmedia Petrzalka	H	2-2	Rataj, Hyravy (p)
19/09/99	Spartak Trnava	A	0-1	
25/09/99	Slovan Bratislava	H	1-0	Hazucha
01/10/99	1.FC Kosice	A	1-2	Hyravy (p)
16/10/99	Banik Prievidza	H	1-1	Hazucha
23/10/99	MSK Zilina	A	0-2	
30/10/99	Tatran Presov	H	1-0	Vyskoc
06/11/99	Dukla Banska Bystrica	A	1-0	Rataj
09/11/99	DAC Dunajska Streda	H	1-0	Vyskoc
11/03/00	Inter Bratislava	H	1-1	Mikulas
14/03/00	FC Nitra	A	0-0	
18/03/00	ZTS Dubnica	H	1-0	Hazucha
25/03/00	VTJ KOBA Senec	A	0-2	
28/03/00	HFC Humenne	H	1-1	Hazucha
08/04/00	Artmedia Petrzalka	A	0-1	
11/04/00	Spartak Trnava	H	1-0	Adamcik
15/04/00	Slovan Bratislava	A	0-2	
18/04/00	Ozeta Dukla Trencin	H	3-1	Hyravy, Hellebrand, Vyskoc
21/04/00	1.FC Kosice	H	0-2	
29/04/00	Banik Prievidza	A	2-0	Hellebrand, Vyskoc
02/05/00	MSK Zilina	H	2-0	Mydliar 2
11/05/00	Tatran Presov	A	1-1	Helbich
14/05/00	Dukla Banska Bystrica	H	1-0	Hutka
17/05/00	DAC Dunajska Streda	A	0-1	

SLOVAN BRATISLAVA

CLUB DIRECTORY

SK Slovan Bratislava
Junacka 2, 831 04 Bratislava
tel - (07) 44373034/44372777
fax - (07) 44373-14
Year of Formation - 1919
President - Ludovit Zlocha
Secretary - Mikulas Tarci
Coach - Stanislav Griga; Stanislav Jarabek
Stadium - Tehelne pole (30,087)

MAJOR HONOURS
League Championship (Czechoslovakia) - (8)
1949, 1950, 1951, 1955, 1970, 1974, 1975,
1992.
League Championship - (4)
1994, 1995, 1996, 1999.
Domestic Cup (Czechoslovakia) - (5)
1962, 1963, 1968, 1974, 1982.
Domestic Cup - (10) 1970, 1972, 1974, 1976,
1982, 1983, 1989, 1994, 1997, 1999.
European Cup-winners' Cup - (1) 1969.

APPEARANCES 99/00

	P	Ap	(s)	Gls
Tomas BERNADY	G	10		
Martin BIELIK	D		(1)	
Serhiy BORISENKO (UKR)	A	2	(5)	1
Juraj COBEJ	G	5		
Marek FABULA	M	11	(4)	2
Branislav FODREK	M		(3)	
Arpad GÖGH	M	3	(12)	1
Norbert HRNCAR	M	29		4
Martin JANCULA	D	1	(3)	
Tibor JANCULA	A	14	(7)	4
Erik JEZIK	M	15		2
Frantisek KALMAN	M		(1)	
Ladislav KOZMER	D	1	(1)	1
Miroslav KÖNIG	G	15		
Miroslav KRISS	A	18	(6)	2
Jozef MAJOROS	A	6	(2)	1
Lubomir MESZAROS	A	24	(4)	7
Pavol MIKULEC	M	5	(7)	
Tomas NOVOTNY	D		(3)	
Michal PANCIK	M	14		5
Ladislav PECKO	M	29		1
Maros PUCHNER	D	2	(1)	
Pavol SEDLAK	M	27		4
Milos SOBONA	D	25	(2)	2
Roman SKRTEL	M	10	(2)	1
Milan TIMKO	D	23		2
Robert TOMASCHEK	M	5		
Stanislav VARGA	D	28		9
Robert VITTEK	A	5	(9)	2
Lubomir VNUK	M	3	(5)	

LEAGUE RESULTS 1999/2000

23/07/99	Tatran Presov	A	1-1	Timko
31/07/99	Dukla Banska Bystrica	H	2-1	Skrtel, Fabula
07/08/99	DAC Dunajska Streda	A	3-0	Meszaros, Borisenko, Hrncar
15/08/99	Inter Bratislava	H	1-1	Majoros
21/08/99	FC Nitra	A	0-1	
28/08/99	ZTS Dubnica	H	1-1	Sedlak
11/09/99	VTJ KOBA Senec	A	1-0	Fabula
18/09/99	HFC Humenne	H	2-0	Jancula T., Varga (p)
25/09/99	SCP Ruzomberok	A	0-1	
02/10/99	Artmedia Petrzalka	H	0-1	
15/10/99	Spartak Trnava	A	0-0	
23/10/99	Ozeta Dukla Trencin	A	0-1	
29/10/99	1.FC Kosice	H	1-2	Sedlak
05/11/99	Banik Prievidza	A	1-1	Kozmer
09/11/99	MSK Zilina	H	0-0	
11/03/00	Tatran Presov	H	6-0	Varga 2 (1p), Kriss, Hrncar, Timko, Pancik
14/03/00	Dukla Banska Bystrica	A	1-0	Jezik
18/03/00	DAC Dunajska Streda	H	4-0	Sedlak, Varga (p), Pancik, Gögh
24/03/00	Inter Bratislava	A	1-1	Varga (p)
28/03/00	FC Nitra	H	1-0	Pancik
01/04/00	ZTS Dubnica	A	3-0	Jancula T., Pecko, Hrncar
08/04/00	VTJ KOBA Senec	H	1-1	Sobona
11/04/00	HFC Humenne	A	3-3	Varga 2, Meszaros
15/04/00	SCP Ruzomberok	H	2-0	Hrncar, Pancik
23/04/00	Artmedia Petrzalka	A	3-1	Varga (p), Jezik, Sobona
28/04/00	Spartak Trnava	H	3-0	Meszaros, Kriss, Vittek
02/05/00	Ozeta Dukla Trencin	H	3-0	og (Valachovic), Meszaros, Vittek
11/05/00	1.FC Kosice	A	2-0	Varga, Meszaros
14/05/00	Banik Prievidza	H	5-1	Meszaros 2, Jancula T., Pancik, Sedlak
17/05/00	MSK Zilina	A	1-0	Jancula T.

SPARTAK TRNAVA

CLUB DIRECTORY

FC Spartak Trnava
Sportova 1, 917 60 Trnava
tel - (0805) 5503805
fax - (0805) 5503806
Year of Formation - 1923
President - Jozef Bachraty
Secretary - Stefan Batalik
Coach - Anton Janos
Stadium - Anton Malatinsky (18,500)

MAJOR HONOURS
League Championship (Czechoslovakia) - (5)
1968, 1969, 1971, 1972, 1973.
Domestic Cup (Czechoslovakia) - (4)
1967, 1971, 1975, 1986.
Domestic Cup - (5)
1971, 1975, 1986, 1991, 1998.

APPEARANCES 99/00

	P	Ap	(s)	Gls
Igor BALIS	M	20	(4)	
Vojtech BALLA	M	16		1
Dusan BESTVINA	D	8		
Peter BUGAR	A	6	(6)	
Nikola BUKOVIC	M	2	(16)	1
Peter CERNAK	A	13	(2)	4
Michal DIAN	M	5	(10)	
Souleymane FALL (SEN)	D	21	(2)	1
Robert FORMANKO	M	9	(4)	1
Michal GASPARIK	A	1	(2)	
Fábio Luís GOMES (BRA)	A	22	(4)	10
Marcel HORKY	M	22	(3)	
Jaroslav HRABAL	D	27		2
Ivan JEDINAK	M		(2)	
Rastislav KOSTKA	M	12	(3)	1
Vladimir LEITNER	D	26	(1)	
Jozef MUZLAY	A	13	(6)	2
Jozef PAVLIK	M	13	(7)	1
Martin POLJOVKA	D	7		
Kamil SUSKO	G	30		
Lubomir TALDA	M	20	(2)	4
Jaroslav TIMKO	A	14		2
Marek UJLAKY	M	23	(3)	8

LEAGUE RESULTS 1999/2000

24/07/99	Dukla Banska Bystrica	A	2-1	Gomes, Ujlaky
31/07/99	DAC Dunajska Streda	H	3-0	Timko 2, Kostka
07/08/99	Inter Bratislava	A	0-0	
15/08/99	FC Nitra	H	1-0	Formanko
21/08/99	ZTS Dubnica	A	0-1	
29/08/99	VTJ KOBA Senec	H	2-2	Gomes, Fall
11/09/99	HFC Humenne	A	0-1	
19/09/99	SCP Ruzomberok	H	1-0	Ujlaky
26/09/99	Artmedia Petrzalka	A	1-2	Talda
03/10/99	Ozeta Dukla Trencin	A	2-1	Gomes 2
15/10/99	Slovan Bratislava	H	0-0	
22/10/99	1.FC Kosice	A	0-0	
30/10/99	Banik Prievidza	H	2-0	Gomes 2 (1p)
06/11/99	MSK Zilina	A	1-1	Ujlaky
09/11/99	Tatran Presov	H	4-1	Talda 2, Gomes 2
11/03/00	Dukla Banska Bystrica	H	4-0	Gomes 2, Ujlaky, Cernak
14/03/00	DAC Dunajska Streda	A	0-0	
17/03/00	Inter Bratislava	H	0-2	
25/03/00	FC Nitra	A	1-0	Pavlik
28/03/00	ZTS Dubnica	H	1-1	Ujlaky (p)
01/04/00	VTJ KOBA Senec	A	0-0	
08/04/00	HFC Humenne	H	1-0	Cernak
11/04/00	SCP Ruzomberok	A	0-1	
15/04/00	Artmedia Petrzalka	H	4-2	Muzlay 2, Hrabal, Talda
22/04/00	Ozeta Dukla Trencin	H	2-0	Hrabal, Ujlaky
28/04/00	Slovan Bratislava	A	0-3	
02/05/00	1.FC Kosice	H	1-0	Ujlaky
11/05/00	Banik Prievidza	A	1-0	Cernak
14/05/00	MSK Zilina	H	4-1	Cernak, Balla, Bukovic, Ujlaky
17/05/00	Tatran Presov	A	0-1	

TATRAN PRESOV

CLUB DIRECTORY

FC Tatran Presov
Capajevova 47
080 01 Presov
tel - (091) 732566
fax - (091) 733553
Year of Formation - 1898
President - Vladislav Sabol
Secretary - Jozef Matuscin
Coach - Mikulas Komanicky
Stadium - Tatran (14,000)

APPEARANCES 99/00

	P	Ap	(s)	Gls
Marian ADAM	A	5	(4)	3
Vladimir BEDNAR	M	5	(6)	
Vladimir CHOVAN	M	7	(4)	1
Jan DIC	M		(1)	
Rastislav DORD	D	23	(1)	
Miroslav DROBNAK	D	22	(5)	4
Andrej FILIP	M	27		1
Peter HLINKA	D	24		1
Peter HRICKO	M		(1)	
Lubomir JACKO	A		(2)	
Martin JAKUBKO	M		(1)	
Patrik KAMINSKY	A		(4)	
Zsolt KIANEK	M	20	(3)	3
Radovan KOCUREK	M	18	(6)	1
Karol KOVALIK	A	5	(3)	
Vladimir KOZUCH	A	15		8
Ladislav KUBALIK	M	1		
Julius LELKES	M	9	(5)	2
Milos LENGYEL	M	25	(3)	1
Tomas MARTAUS	M	12	(9)	2
Marek PETRUS	D	13		3
Pavol PIATKA	A	2	(6)	
Gejza PULEN	G	17		
Marek SEMAN	D	21	(2)	
Richard SOBOTA	M	1		
Anton SOLTIS	A	20		5
Vladimir STAS	A	1	(7)	
Martin TRANCIK	G	1		
Richard TRUTZ	D		(1)	
Martin URBAN	D	14		
Jozef VALKUCAK	M	5		3
Serhiy ZAYCHEV (UKR)	D	5	(3)	
Daniel ZITKA (CZE)	G	12		

LEAGUE RESULTS 1999/2000

23/07/99	Slovan Bratislava	H	1-1	Soltis
01/08/99	1.FC Kosice	A	0-3	
07/08/99	Banik Prievidza	H	4-2	Valkucak 2 (1p), Kianek, Kocurek
14/08/99	MSK Zilina	A	0-2	
21/08/99	Ozeta Dukla Trencin	H	2-1	Valkucak (p), Kozuch
28/08/99	Dukla Banska Bystrica	H	3-0	Martaus, Kozuch, Soltis
11/09/99	DAC Dunajska Streda	A	2-1	Kozuch, Martaus
19/09/99	Inter Bratislava	H	0-3	
25/09/99	FC Nitra	A	1-0	Kianek
02/10/99	ZTS Dubnica	H	1-0	Kozuch
16/10/99	VTJ KOBA Senec	A	2-2	Kozuch 2
23/10/99	HFC Humenne	H	1-0	Filip
30/10/99	SCP Ruzomberok	A	0-1	
06/11/99	Artmedia Petrzalka	H	3-0	Drobnak 2, Kozuch
09/11/99	Spartak Trnava	A	1-4	Kozuch
11/03/00	Slovan Bratislava	A	0-6	
14/03/00	1.FC Kosice	H	2-1	Drobnak, Chovan
18/03/00	Banik Prievidza	A	5-1	Lelkes 2, Soltis, Drobnak, Kianek
25/03/00	MSK Zilina	H	1-1	Petrus
28/03/00	Ozeta Dukla Trencin	A	0-2	
01/04/00	Dukla Banska Bystrica	A	2-1	Soltis 2
08/04/00	DAC Dunajska Streda	H	1-1	Adam
11/04/00	Inter Bratislava	A	0-2	
15/04/00	FC Nitra	H	2-0	Adam 2
22/04/00	ZTS Dubnica	A	0-1	
29/04/00	VTJ KOBA Senec	H	1-0	Hlinka
02/05/00	HFC Humenne	A	0-2	
11/05/00	SCP Ruzomberok	H	1-1	Petrus
14/05/00	Artmedia Petrzalka	A	1-3	Petrus
17/05/00	Spartak Trnava	H	1-0	Lengyel

MSK ZILINA

CLUB DIRECTORY

MSK Zilina
Sportova 9
010 01 Zilina
tel - (089) 622280/621884
fax - (089) 623464
Year of Formation - 1908
President - Jan Slota
Secretary - Karol Belanik
Coach - Jozef Barmos
Stadium - Pod Dubnom (12,000)

APPEARANCES 99/00

	P	Ap	(s)	Gls
Mario ADAMCIK	A	14		4
Stefan ADAMUS	D		(2)	
Miroslav BARCIK	M	29	(1)	4
Lubos BOHUNSKY	G	7	(1)	
Michal DRAHNO	D	11	(1)	
Petr DROZD (CZE)	D	29		2
Martin DURICA	M	2	(1)	
Tomas DURICA	M	22	(2)	2
Michal FILO	M	13		
Tibor GOLJAN	A		(1)	
Peter HLUSKO	D	25	(1)	
Peter HOLEC	G	23		
Ivan JURIK	M	18	(4)	1
Marina KEKELY	M	1	(4)	
Viliam KOPECKY	M	11	(8)	
Lubomir KOSTOLANSKY	A	1	(2)	1
Igor KUREK	A	3	(4)	
Fedor KURINCAK	D		(1)	
Branislav KUZMA	M	1	(4)	
Branislav LABANT	M	2	(4)	1
Marek MINTAL	M	28	(1)	12
Vladimir ONDRAS	D	24	(3)	3
Milan PAVLIK	D	1	(2)	
Miroslav PIKUS	A	7	(17)	2
Lubos REITER	A	14	(7)	2
Martin RYBON	M	1	(1)	
Juraj STALMASEK	M		(1)	
Petr STRNADEL (CZE)	A	13	(2)	1
Jaroslav TRHANCIK	M	4		
Slavomir ZATEK	D	26	(1)	3

LEAGUE RESULTS 1999/2000

24/07/99	1.FC Kosice	H	1-4	Zatek
31/07/99	Banik Prievidza	A	0-1	
07/08/99	Ozeta Dukla Trencin	H	1-0	Adamcik
14/08/99	Tatran Presov	H	2-0	Mintal 2 (1p)
21/08/99	Dukla Banska Bystrica	A	2-3	Mintal, Drozd
28/08/99	DAC Dunajska Streda	H	6-0	Adamcik 2, Mintal, Zatek, Reiter, Barcik
11/09/99	Inter Bratislava	A	0-2	
18/09/99	FC Nitra	H	1-0	Barcik
24/09/99	ZTS Dubnica	A	4-1	Pikus, Mintal, Adamcik, Ondras
02/10/99	VTJ KOBA Senec	H	2-1	Zatek, Kostolansky
16/10/99	HFC Humenne	A	1-3	Jurik
23/10/99	SCP Ruzomberok	H	2-0	Mintal, Barcik
31/10/99	Artmedia Petrzalka	A	1-2	Barcik
06/11/99	Spartak Trnava	H	1-1	Mintal
09/11/99	Slovan Bratislava	A	0-0	
10/03/00	1.FC Kosice	A	0-2	
14/03/00	Banik Prievidza	H	4-0	Ondras, Mintal, Durica T. (p), Labant
18/03/00	Ozeta Dukla Trencin	A	0-3	
25/03/00	Tatran Presov	A	1-1	Ondras
28/03/00	Dukla Banska Bystrica	H	1-0	Mintal
01/04/00	DAC Dunajska Streda	A	1-0	Mintal
07/04/00	Inter Bratislava	H	1-2	Durica T.
11/04/00	FC Nitra	A	2-0	Strnadel, Mintal
15/04/00	ZTS Dubnica	H	2-0	Drozd, Pikus
22/04/00	VTJ KOBA Senec	A	0-0	
29/04/00	HFC Humenne	H	0-2	
02/05/00	SCP Ruzomberok	A	0-2	
11/05/00	Artmedia Petrzalka	H	2-2	og (Orabinec), Reiter
14/05/00	Spartak Trnava	A	1-4	Mintal
17/05/00	Slovan Bratislava	H	0-1	

SLOVENIA

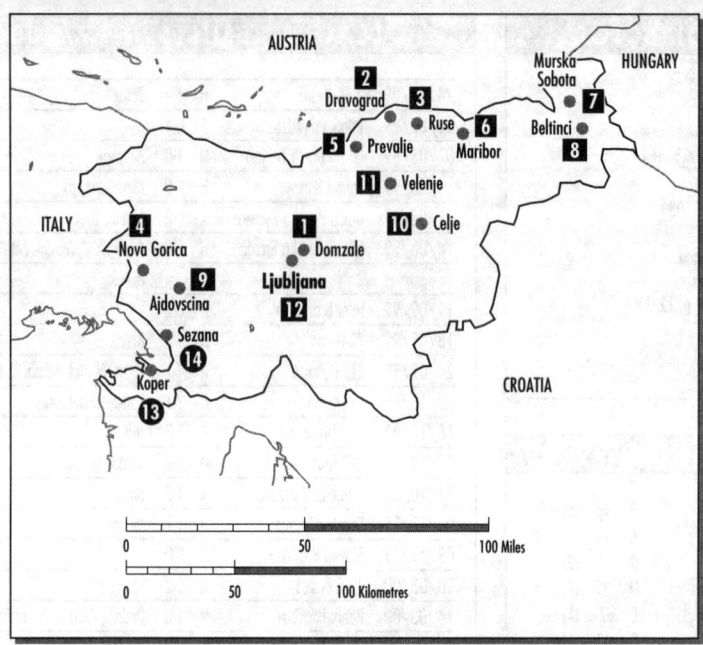

1	NK DOMZALE	925	9	PRIMORJE AJDOVSCINA	933
2	NK DRAVOGRAD	926	10	PUBLIKUM CELJE	934
3	FEROTERM POHORJE	927	11	RUDAR VELENJE	935
4	HIT GORICA	928	12	SCT OLIMPIJA LJUBLJANA	936
5	KOROTAN PREVALJE	929	**Promoted clubs**		
6	NK MARIBOR	930	13	NK KOPER	
7	MURA MURSKA SOBOTA	931	14	TABOR SEZANA	
8	POTROSNIK BELTINCI	932			

FOUR IN A ROW FOR MARIBOR

Katanec's braves put Slovenia on the map

FEDERATION DIRECTORY

Nogometna Zveza Slovenija
Cerinova 4, P.P.33986, 1101 Ljubljana

tel - (061) 5300400   Year of Formation - 1920
fax - (061) 5300410   President - Rudolf Zavrl
website - www.nzs.si   Secretary - Dane Jost

Stadium - Bezigrad, Ljubljana (18,000)

Slovenian football has come of age. The national team's highly respectable performance at Euro 2000, for which they were totally unexpected qualifiers, not only drew admirers from around Europe and beyond but also helped to put this relatively new and modestly populated country on the map.

Slovenia may have finished bottom of their first-round group in the Low Countries, but they picked up two points - which was two more than most pundits had predicted.

Those who glibly wrote them off before the tournament had clearly not seen the impressive way in which Srecko Katanec's side had accounted for much-fancied Ukraine in the play-offs.

Of all the four play-off ties, Slovenia v Ukraine appeared to be the most one-sided, but the Slovenians turned the form book upside down with two highly accomplished performances. Despite being behind in both games, the men in green and white had the resolve and the talent to come back and secure their qualification. A 2-1 victory in Ljubljana, made possible by Zlatko Zahovic's ninth goal of the qualifying competition and an unbelievable 40-yard lob from substitute Milenko Acimovic six minutes from time, gave Slovenia half a chance for the return in Kiev, and on a snowbound pitch, which made proper football virtually impossible, Katanec's braves dug in and were rewarded with Miran Pavlin's equalising goal, which gave Slovenia a 3-2 aggregate win and ensured the country's historic first participation at a major finals.

Katanec and his players were transformed overnight into national heroes. Qualification was way beyond the expectations of a country which in the previous qualifying competition, for France '98, had taken a solitary point from their eight games. Katanec, the former Yugoslav international who spent much of his career in European football's fast lane with

LEAGUE CHAMPIONSHIP RESULTS 99/00

		1	2	3	4	5	6	7	8	9	10	11	12
1	NK Domzale		1-1	2-1	0-2	1-1	1-4	1-0	4-1	3-1	5-0	0-3	2-0
				6-1		3-2		0-0				0-0	1-2
2	NK Dravograd	2-4		2-1	2-4	0-2	1-3	2-1	2-0	0-0	1-1	3-1	0-4
		2-1			1-1		0-3		3-1	2-4			
3	Feroterm Pohorje	1-2	1-3		0-0	3-5	2-1	0-1	2-1	0-0	0-0	1-3	0-3
		1-0				0-1		2-2				2-3	1-4
4	HIT Gorica	2-0	1-1	5-0		2-0	2-1	2-1	2-0	5-0	1-0	0-1	2-1
		2-0		1-0		2-1	1-3				4-0		3-0
5	Korotan Prevalje	2-2	1-2	4-0	0-1		2-4	1-1	2-1	3-1	1-1	1-0	3-2
		1-2						3-0	1-2	0-1	2-1	2-0	
6	NK Maribor	3-2	2-0	5-0	4-0	0-0		3-1	5-1	2-2	2-1	4-1	0-0
		1-0		3-1		3-0					4-0	2-1	2-0
7	Mura Murska Sobota	3-1	2-2	2-0	2-0	0-2	2-2		1-0	1-1	1-3	0-3	3-0
		2-3		1-2		1-3			6-0	2-1			
8	Potrosnik Beltinci	1-1	1-1	1-0	0-0	1-3	0-2	0-3		0-5	0-0	1-2	0-5
		0-4		2-3	0-3	0-6				2-0			
9	Primorje Ajdovscina	5-1	1-0	1-0	1-0	2-2	1-3	1-0	2-2		2-2	2-1	6-0
		2-2		0-0	2-1		2-2				2-2		3-2
10	Publikum Celje	3-0	0-0	1-1	3-3	2-1	1-2	3-2	2-0	3-1		0-0	3-0
		0-0	2-2	5-1				2-1	7-0				
11	Rudar Velenje	1-0	2-0	1-0	3-0	2-2	2-2	1-2	1-0	2-1	1-1		0-1
		1-1		2-1				2-1	2-0	3-0	0-2		
12	SCT Olimpija Ljubljana	2-0	4-2	3-1	4-0	1-5	2-4	2-1	5-0	1-3	3-0	1-2	
		0-1				0-2		5-1	3-3		2-2	2-2	

LEAGUE CHAMPIONSHIP FINAL TABLE 99/00

		Pd		Home					Away					Total					
			W	D	L	F	A	W	D	L	F	A	W	D	L	F	A	PT	GD
1	NK Maribor	33	14	3	0	45	10	11	3	2	45	20	25	6	2	90	30	81	60
2	HIT Gorica	33	14	1	2	37	9	5	4	7	18	25	19	5	9	55	34	62	21
3	Rudar Velenje	33	10	4	3	26	14	7	3	6	23	21	17	7	9	49	35	58	14
4	Korotan Prevalje	33	8	3	6	29	21	7	4	5	29	22	15	7	11	58	43	52	15
5	Primorje Ajdovscina	33	9	7	1	35	20	4	4	8	21	29	13	11	9	56	49	50	7
6	Publikum Celje	33	9	6	1	37	14	2	8	7	16	31	11	14	8	53	45	47	8
7	SCT Olimpija Ljubljana	33	8	3	6	40	29	6	1	9	24	29	14	4	15	64	58	46	6
8	NK Dravograd	33	6	3	7	23	31	5	7	5	21	23	11	10	12	44	54	43	-10
9	NK Domzale	33	8	4	4	30	19	3	4	10	20	32	11	8	14	50	51	41	-1
10	Mura Murska Sobota	33	7	3	6	29	23	3	3	11	18	30	10	6	17	47	53	36	-6
11	Feroterm Pohorje	33	3	4	9	16	29	1	2	14	10	44	4	6	23	26	73	18	-47
12	Potrosnik Beltinci	33	2	4	10	9	38	1	2	14	12	50	3	6	24	21	88	15	-67

DOMESTIC CUP 99/00

FIRST ROUND
Zivila Triglav 0, NK Maribor 4
Drava 1, Primorje Ajdovscina 4
Aluminij 0, SCT Olimpija Ljubljana 2
Brda 0, Publikum Celje 2
Ilirska Bistrica 0, NK Domzale 2
Zeleznicar 1, Potrosnik Beltinci 1 (4-3 on pens.)
Tabor Jadran 0, Feroterm Phorje 1
Mura Murska Sobota 2, Rudar Velenje 0
Ivancna gorica 0, Korotan Prevalje 1
Tromejnik 0, HIT Gorica 9
Britaf 2, Factor 1
Crensovci 5, Paloma sega 0
Beltrans 3, Lesce 0 (w/o)
Elan 3, Esotech smartno 1
Idrija 0, Odranci 1
Koper 4, Sentjur 1

SECOND ROUND
Elan 2, Odranci 0
Beltrans 0, Korotan Prevalje 8
Britof 0, Publikum Celje 6
Koper 0, HIT Gorica 3
Zeleznicar 2, Mura Murska Sobota 3
SCT Olimpija Ljubljana 5, Feroterm Pohorje 1
NK Domzale 0, Primorje Ajdovscina 2
Crensovci 0, NK Maribor 8

QUARTER-FINAL
NK Maribor 3 (Sankovic 25og, Bozgo 75, 83),
Publikum Celje 2 (Stancar 47, Sumilikovski 70)

Publikum Celje 0, NK Maribor 2 (Balajic 8, Seslar 52)
(NK Maribor 5-2)
Mura Murska Sobota 1 (Cifer 24),
SCT Olimpija Ljubljana 2 (Kosic 65, Puc 90)
SCT Olimpija Ljubljana 4 (Ekmecic 21, 50,
Kmetec 45, 80),
Mura Murska Sobota 1 (Denio 9)
(SCT Olimpija Ljubljana 6-2)

HIT Gorica 5
(Zlogar 25, 29, Vulic 52, 75, Znidercic 71),
Elan 2 (Lucic T. 3, 46)
Elan 2 (Zagar 59, Plevnik 90),
HIT Gorica 0
(HIT Gorica 5-4)

Primorje Ajdovscina 0, Korotan Prevalje 2 (Tiganj 27, 45)
Korotan Prevalje 1 (Jolic 87), Primorje Ajdovscina 0
(Korotan Prevalje 3-0)

SEMI-FINALS
SCT Olimpija Ljubljana 2 (Osterc 20, Kosic 59),
HIT Gorica 1 (Gunjac 33)
HIT Gorica 1 (Alomerovic 82p),
SCT Olimpija Ljubljana 1 (Zulic 43)
(SCT Olimpija Ljubljana 3-2)

NK Maribor 3 (Ekmecic 3, 9, 88),
Korotan Prevalje 1 (Breznik 84)
Korotan Prevalje 3 (Kamberovic 40, 41,
Poglajen 84), NK Maribor 0
(Korotan Prevalje 4-3)

FINAL
10/05/2000, Prevalje
KOROTAN PREVALJE 2 Tiganj (44, 53)
SCT OLIMPIJA LJUBLJANA 1 Kosic (43)
referee - Borosak
KOROTAN PREVALJE - Sraga, Boskovic, Silo, Breznik,
Barun (Pirc 46), Plesec, Svab, Vuksanovic, Tosevski,
Begic (Usnik 62), Tiganj (Poglajen 75).
SCT OLIMPIJA LJUBLJANA - Pejkovic, Zulic, Fridl,
Mirtic, Miskic (Pokorn 85), Kujovic, Agic (Jurkovic
78), Kosic, Zezelj, Osterc (Moro 64), Kmetec.

17/05/2000, Ljubljana
SCT OLIMPIJA LJUBLJANA 2
Kujovic (44), Kmetec (65)
KOROTAN PREVALJE 0
referee - Zirnstein
SCT OLIMPIJA LJUBLJANA - Pejkovic, Zulic, Fridl
(Zezelj 87), Pokorn, Kujovic, Agic (Mirtic 65), Kosic,
Jukic, Dasovic, Osterc (Deisinger 80), Kmetec.
KOROTAN PREVALJE - Sraga, Boskovic, Silo (Zec 89),
Breznik (Poglajen 65), Barun, Pirc, Plesec, Svab,
Tosevski (Kamberovic 49), Begic, Tiganj.

(SCT OLIMPIJA LJUBLJANA 3-2)

NATIONAL TEAM APPEARANCES 99/00

Coach - Srecko KATANEC	ALB	GEO	NOR	GRE	UKR	UKR	UAE	OMN	FRA	SAU	YUG	ESP	NOR	Cps	Gls
Mladen DABANOVIC (13/09/71) - KSC Lokeren (BEL)	G		s46		G	G		G46	G	G46	G	G	G	14	-
Darko MILANIC (18/12/67) - SK Sturm Graz (AUT)	D69			D75	D	D46	s31	D	D	D	D68			42	-
Marinko GALIC (22/04/70) - NK Maribor	D	D		D		D	D	D31	s70	D46	D		D83	53	-
Aleksander KNAVS (05/12/75) - FC Tirol Innsbruck (AUT)	D	D	D		D		D60		D	s46		s68	D	23	1
Mladen RUDONJA (26/07/71) - K St.-Truidense VV (BEL)	M	M	M	M	M	M	M	M46	M	M72	M	M	M	40	-
Dzoni NOVAK (04/09/69) - Le Havre AC (FRA)/															
CS Sedan-Ardennes (FRA)	M90	M	M	M	M	M	M	s46	M87	M75	M	M	M	51	2
Ales CEH (07/04/68) - Grazer AK (AUT)	M	M	M	M	M	M	M60	s46	M	M	M	M	M	54	1
Miran PAVLIN (08/10/71) - SC Freiburg (GER)/															
Karlsruher SC (GER)	M	M	M		M	M	M	M46	M63	M57	M74	M82	M	27	3
Zlatko ZAHOVIC (01/02/71) - Olympiakos (GRE)	M	M90	M		M	M	M46	M	M	M	M	M	M	49	25
Milan OSTERC (04/07/75) - Hércules CF (ESP)/															
SCT Olimpija Ljubljana	A	A46	A81	s60	s75	s79	A	A46	s58	s72	s78	s46	s86	23	5
Saso UDOVIC (13/12/68) - LASK Linz (AUT)	A46	A75	A39	A46	A46	A56	s46	s46	A58	A46	A64	A46		39	15
Milenko ACIMOVIC (15/02/77) - Crvena zvezda Beograd (YUG)	s46	s46	s81	M	s46	s56	s46	M		s46	s64	s82	s83	23	5
Zeljko MILINOVIC (12/10/69) - LASK Linz (AUT)	s69	D	D		D	D	s46	D	D	D	D	D	D	19	1
Rudi ISTENIC (10/01/71) - KFC Uerdingen 05 (GER)	s90	s90	M				s60	M						16	-
Marko SIMEUNOVIC (06/12/67) - NK Maribor		G	G46	G			G	s46		s46				26	-
Amir KARIC (31/12/73) - NK Maribor		s75	s39	s46	M	M79	M46	s67	M70	s46	M78	M	M	27	1
Edo BAJREKTAREVIC (15/01/70) - SCT Olimpija Ljubljana				D										1	-
Muamer VUGDALIC (25/08/77) - NK Maribor				D86										1	-
Simon SESLAR (05/04/74) - NK Maribor				M										7	-
Ante SIMUNDZA (28/09/71) - NK Maribor				A60										3	-
Robert ENGLARO (25/08/69) - Atalanta (ITA)				s86										38	-
Spasoje BULAJIC (24/11/75) - 1.FC Köln (GER)							s60	D						8	1
Saso GAJSER (11/02/74) - KAA Gent (BEL)								M67	s87	s75				6	1
Zoran PAVLOVIC (27/06/76) - Dinamo Zagreb (CRO)										s63	s57	s74		5	-
Ermin SILJAK (11/05/73) - Servette FC Genève (SUI)										A46			A86	20	4

Stuttgart and Sampdoria, was the man responsible for the team's metamorphosis. Appointed to the post at the age of just 35 on July 1, 1998, his accomplishments over the past two years have earned him the well-deserved reputation as the saviour of Slovenian football.

Katanec cut an impressive figure at Euro 2000, and the same could be said for many of his players. The classy Zahovic, who had had a troubled year in Greece with Olympiakos, maintained his extraordinary scoring record, netting two goals in the dramatic 3-3 draw against Yugoslavia and another in the 2-1 defeat by Spain. He was ably supported by the flair of Miran Pavlin and the industry of Ales Ceh, while left wing-back Amir Karic provided some

of the most dangerous crosses in the whole tournament.

Of course there was profound regret among the Slovenian fans that the team could not hold onto their amazing 3-0 lead against ten-man Yugoslavia in the opening match, but for an hour Zahovic and co. held a huge worldwide television audience spellbound by their intricate, skilful team-play. They also gave Spain quite a fright in the next match, and although that defeat left them with only a slim chance of making progress when they took on Norway in their final group game, it was Slovenia who created the better chances in a rather dull goalless draw.

Slovenia went home early, as predicted, but they had every reason to hold their heads up high. Katanec had

NATIONAL TEAM RESULTS 99/00

Date	Opponent	H/A/N	Venue	Score	Scorers
18/08/99	Albania (ECQ)	H	Ljubljana	2-0	Zahovic (49), Osterc (80)
04/09/99	Georgia (ECQ)	H	Ljubljana	2-1	Acimovic (48), Zahovic (80)
08/09/99	Norway (ECQ)	A	Oslo	0-4	
09/10/99	Greece (ECQ)	H	Maribor	0-3	
13/11/99	Ukraine (ECQ)	H	Ljubljana	2-1	Zahovic (53), Acimovic (84)
17/11/99	Ukraine (ECQ)	A	Kiev	1-1	Pavlin (79)
19/02/00	United Arab Emirates	N	Muscat	1-1	Udovic (82)
23/02/00	Oman	A	Muscat	4-0	Pavlin (15), Zahovic (32), Udovic (57), Acimovic (65p)
26/04/00	France	A	Saint-Denis	2-3	Milinovic (3), Udovic (10)
03/06/00	Saudi Arabia	H	Ljubljana	2-0	Zahovic (16), Acimovic (46)
13/06/00	Yugoslavia (ECF)	N	Charleroi	3-3	Zahovic (23, 57), Pavlin (52)
18/06/00	Spain (ECF)	N	Amsterdam	1-2	Zahovic (59)
21/06/00	Norway (ECF)	N	Arnhem	0-0	

TOP SCORERS

24	Kliton BOZGO (NK Maribor)
23	Oskar DROBNE (NK Domzale)
17	Uros BARUT (Primorje Ajdovscina)
16	Marko KMETEC (SCT Olimpija Ljubljana)
14	Aljosa SIVKO (NK Dravograd)
13	Tonci ZLOGAR (HIT Gorica)
12	Andrej GORSEK (Publikum Celje)
11	Dejan DJURANOVIC (NK Maribor)
	Vanja STARCEVIC (Primorje Ajdovscina)
	Aleksandar RADOSAVLJEVIC (Publikum Celje)

INTERNATIONAL HONOURS

European Championship appearances: 2000.

PLAYERS OF THE SEASON

MIRAN PAVLIN

It was Miran Pavlin (below) who scored the most important goal in Slovenia's football history. It came 11 minutes from the end of the Euro 2000 play-off second leg against Ukraine in Kiev. It was no picture-book goal but its significance was enormous. Zlatko Zahovic took a free-kick, it deflected off the wall to Mladen Rudonja, whose shot was re-directed into the net by Pavlin. It was a moment to savour for the tall, left-footed midfielder, whose club career had got bogged down after an ill-fated move from

Freiburg to German Sercond Division strugglers Karlsruhe. But an impressive performance at Euro 2000 - notably in the opener against Yugoslavia, when he scored again, with a tremendous header - enabled him to choose his next club from a host of intriguing possibilities, and he decided to join Zahovic's old team FC Porto.

UROS BARUT

20-year-old Uros Barut was the young revelation of the domestic season in Slovenia. Although his club, Primorje Ajdovscina, had a fair-to-middling season, he consistently earned headlines for himself with his scoring of spectacular goals. His overall total for the season was 17, which placed him third in the league listings, behind Maribor's Kliton Bozgo and Domzale's Oskar Drobne, but, impressively, his haul included three goals against champions Maribor and five against Cup winners Olimpija. Clearly a man for the big occasion, Barut is blessed with exceptional pace, which makes him a potent threat on the counter-attack. Difficult to dispossess, he is also elusive and sharp to react to goalscoring opportunities. He has not yet been called up for the senior national team, but if his 1999/2000 form is maintained, it will become impossible for Srecko Katanec to leave him out.

proved himself on the big stage, and his well-balanced, settled team - nine players started all three games, and only 16 of the 22-man squad were used - demonstrated that they could continue to be a force in the 2002 World Cup qualifying campaign, despite the handicap of being seeded fourth in a group containing, among others, Russia, Switzerland and - once again - Yugoslavia.

The national team were not the only source of pride for Slovenian followers during the season. Maribor, the country's leading club, reached the UEFA Champions' League with stunning victories over Belgian champions Genk and big-spending Lyon of France, and they even caused a major upset in their opening group match when

they won 1-0 away to the previous season's semi-finalists Dynamo Kiev. Maribor soon found their place once they came across Lazio, but roused themselves sufficiently for the final game in Leverkusen, which they drew 0-0 to send the Germans out of the competition.

Maribor were able to enjoy themselves in Europe and still deliver the goods at home. They began the season in devastating form, crushing every opponent they encountered to string together nine successive victories, scoring 32 goals in the process. Bojan Prasnikar's side were firmly on course for a fourth successive Slovenian title, but there then followed a mid-season mini-crisis, and when Maribor were unceremoniously dumped out of the Cup

EUROPEAN CUPS 99/00

CHAMPIONS' CUP
● **NK MARIBOR**
Preliminary round 2 KRC GENK (BEL)
H 5-1 Balajic (24), Galic (62), Karic (69p), Simundza (76), Djuranovic (90)
Simeunovic, Galic, Seslar, Zidan, Karic (Vugdalic 80), Filipovic (Simundza 54), Çipi, Balajic, Djuranovic, Bozgo, Sarkezi.
A 0-3 Simeunovic, Galic, Sarkezi, Çipi, Zidan, Karic, Balajic (Filipovic 65), Djuranovic, Seslar (Vugdalic 53), Bozgo, Simundza (Pregelj 80).

Qualifying round OLYMPIQUE LYONNAIS (FRA)
A 1-0 Filipovic (88)
Simeunovic; Galic, Vugdalic, Sarkezi, Seslar, Djuranovic, Balajic (Pregelj 80), Filekovic, Zidan, Simundza (Filipovic 66), Bozgo.
H 2-0 Simundza (24), Balajic (45)
Simeunovic, Vugdalic (Filekovic 73), Seslar, Zidan, Simundza (Filipovic 90), Çipi, Balajic (Karic 49), Djuranovic, Galic, Bozgo, Sarkezi.

Champions' League
1st match DYNAMO KYIV (UKR)
A 1-0 Simundza (73)
Simeunovic, Seslar, Zidan, Karic, Simundza (Filipovic 82), Çipi, Balajic (Vugdalic 64), Djuranovic, Galic, Bozgo (Pregelj 90), Sarkezi.

2nd match BAYER 04 LEVERKUSEN (GER)
H 0-2
Simeunovic, Vugdalic, Seslar, Zidan, Simundza, Çipi, Balajic (Dragusha 85), Filekovic (Pregelj 52), Djuranovic, Galic, Bozgo.

3rd match LAZIO (ITA)
A 0-4
Simeunovic, Vugdalic, Seslar, Zidan (Pregelj 81), Simundza (Sarkezi 46), Çipi, Balajic, Karic, Djuranovic, Galic, Bozgo (Filipovic 68).

4th match LAZIO (ITA)
H 0-4
Simeunovic, Vugdalic, Seslar (Dragusha 84), Zidan, Simundza (Pregelj 80), Balajic, Karic, Djuranovic, Galic, Bozgo (Filipovic 61), Sarkezi.

5th match DYNAMO KYIV (UKR)
H 1-2 Balajic (50)
Gresak, Vugdalic, Seslar, Zidan, Simundza, Filipovic (Pregelj 69), Balajic (Bozgo 61), Karic, Djuranovic, Sarkezi (Filekovic 86), Çipi.

6th match BAYER 04 LEVERKUSEN (GER)
A 0-0
Gresak, Vugdalic, Seslar, Zidan, Simundza (Bozgo 55), Balajic (Dragusha 90), Djuranovic, Galic, Filipovic (Filekovic 90), Sarkezi, Karic.

UEFA CUP
● **HIT GORICA**
Qualifying round INTER CARDIFF (WAL)
H 2-0 Mitrakovic (74p), Zlogar (83)
Mavric, Ribaric, Moleffe (Drobne 26), Srebrnic, Alomerovic, Becaj, Mitrakovic, Zlogar, Halili, Vulic (Znidercic 56), Ipavec.
A 0-1 Mavric, Ribaric, Moleffe, Srebrnic, Alomerovic, Becaj, Mitrakovic, Zlogar, Halili, Vulic, Ipavec (Znidercic 30).

1st round PANATHINAIKOS (GRE)
H 0-1 Mavric, Ribaric, Gunjac, Srebrnic, Alomerovic, Sculac D., Becaj, Mitrakovic (Kovacevic N. 86), Zlogar, Halili (Vulic 70), Drobne (Debenjak 65).
A 0-2 Mavric, Ribaric, Gunjac, Srebrnic (Kapic 60), Alomerovic, Sculac D., Becaj, Zlogar, Halili (Vulic 77), Debenjak, Ipavec (Mitrakovic 56).

● **SCT OLIMPIJA LJUBLJANA**
Qualifying round KAREDA SIAULIAI (LIT)
H 1-1 Moro (27)
Pejkovic, Zulic, Bajrektarevic, Jukic, Kosic, Agic, Zezelj, Ceh, Fridl, Ekmecic (Kmetec 68), Moro.
A 2-2 Moro (21), Kmetec (87)
Pejkovic, Kosic, Ceh, Agic (Kmetec 80), Zulic, Bajrektarevic, Jukic, Fridl, Moro (Mirtic 88), Zezelj (Puc 85), Ekmecic.

1st round RSC ANDERLECHT (BEL)
A 1-3 Ekmecic (54)
Pejkovic, Bajrektarevic, Zulic, Jukic, Kosic, Ceh, Agic, Zezelj (Kmetec 70), Fridl (Trgo 87), Moro (Mirtic 62), Ekmecic.
H 0-3 Pejkovic, Bajrektarevic (Deisinger 87), Jukic, Kosic, Ceh, Agic, Zezelj (Kmetec 63), Fridl, Trgo (Kujovic 80), Moro, Ekmecic.

by Koroton - they lost 3-0 in Prevalje after winning the first leg 3-1 - Prasnikar decided that it was time for him to go and offered his resignation.

There were a number of applicants for the vacant position, but in the end the club directors decided to promote from within and offered the job to Prasnikar's assistant, ex-player Matjaz Kek. It proved to be a truly inspired choice, for the team suddenly rediscovered the flamboyant, all-conquering form of the start of the season and put together another irresistible sequence of victories. Fortified by two mid-season signings from Olimpija Ljubljana - Ismet Ekmecic and Nastja Ceh - and the prolific goalscoring of the league's leading marksman - Albanian Kliton Bozgo - Maribor left the rest of the field for dead and reeled off 15 wins and one draw in their last 16 matches. Three of the team's star players - goalkeeper Marko Simeunovic, defender Marinko Galic and wing-back Karic - were rewarded with places in Slovenia's Euro 2000 squad, with the latter two starting all three matches in the Low Countries.

Olimpija Ljubljana had been on Maribor's tail at the mid-point of the season, but they faded away woefully in the spring, dropping all the way down to seventh place - their lowest position to date. They did gain some consolation by winning the Cup, beating Maribor's conquerors Korotan 3-2 in the two-legged final. That win secured a European place, which was one of the reasons why Prasnikar, the man who had won two Slovenian titles

with the club, decided to return as coach for the new season.

HIT Gorica ensured that Slovenia's European representation in 2000/01 would be unchanged from the previous season by clinching the runners-up spot in the league for the second year running. Gorica hovered close to the top of the table throughout

Maribor's Amir Karic.

the campaign and eventually held off a determined challenge from Rudar Velenje, coached by ex-Yugoslavia international Branko Oblak, to finish second. Gorica's top player was young attacking midfielder Anton 'Tonci' Zlogar, who did enough to earn a late call-up to the Euro 2000 squad.

The fight to avoid relegation turned out to be as cut and dried as the race for the title. Potrosnik Beltinci and newly-promoted Feroterm Pohorje were isolated early on and never looked like making up the ground. Between them they managed just seven wins all season. The situation at the top of the Second Division was equally straightforward, with yo-yo club NK Koper and previously unheralded Tabor Sezana finishing some distance ahead of the rest to claim the two promotion places.

PROMOTED CLUBS 99/00

SECOND DIVISION FINAL TABLE

		Pd	W	D	L	F	A	Pt	GD
1	**Koper**	30	22	6	2	76	21	72	55
2	**Tabor Sezana**	30	21	6	3	64	13	69	51
3	Esotech Smartno	30	18	5	7	57	39	59	18
4	Aluminij	30	16	7	7	62	32	55	30
5	Zeleznicar Maribor	30	16	5	9	47	32	53	15
6	Zagorje	30	14	6	10	53	35	48	18
7	Elan	30	14	5	11	43	35	47	8
8	Ivancna gorica	30	14	3	13	52	47	45	5
9	Triglav	30	11	5	14	37	42	38	-5
10	Jadran sepic	30	9	10	11	34	37	37	-3
11	Nafta	30	9	7	14	34	49	34	-15
12	Sentjur	30	7	9	14	29	52	30	-23
13	Drava	30	7	8	15	34	47	29	-13
14	Crensovci	30	6	5	19	31	82	23	-51
15	Montavar Rogoza	30	5	5	20	25	68	20	-43
16	Avtoplus Korte	30	2	6	22	17	64	12	-47

CLUB DIRECTORIES

NK Koper
Ljubljanska c.2, 6000 Koper
tel - (066) 32222 / fax - (066) 33033
Year of Formation - 1920
President - Bogomir Baraga
Secretary - Valter Valencic
Coach - Branko Zupan
Stadium - SCR Bonifika (10,000)

MAJOR HONOURS
League Championship - (2) 1985, 1988.
Domestic Cup - (1) 1991.

NK Tabor
Kosovelova 4b, 7210 Sezana
tel - (067) 344290 / fax - (067) 344290
Year of Formation - 1923
President - Anton Zobec
Secretary - Albin Spacal
Coach - Marjan Kovacic
Stadium - Mestni (3,000)

NK DOMZALE

CLUB DIRECTORY

NK Domzale
Kopaliska 4
1230 Domzale
tel - (061) 710373
fax - (061) 722031
President - Stane Orazem
Secretary - Ivan Ledenko
Coach - Mihajlo Petrovic
Stadium - Domzale (2,000)

APPEARANCES 99/00

	P	Ap	(s)	Gls
Bostjan AVGUSTIN	D		(1)	
Darko BIRJUKOV (BOS)	M	9	(3)	
Sinisa BRKIC	D	20	(2)	1
Marjan CVIJANOVIC	M	18	(1)	
Oskar DROBNE	A	22		23
Janez HRIBAR	M	29		2
Branko JERSIN	M	6	(5)	2
Kaja KALINIC (CRO)	D	19	(1)	1
Vlado KARADZIC	G	14	(1)	
Darko KARAPETROVIC	M	10	(3)	1
Martin KLESNIK	G	2		
Saso KOSTIC	M	2	(7)	
Marko KUNSTELJ	D		(2)	
Danilo KUSAR	D	16	(2)	1
Robert LAH	M		(1)	
Damir MARETIC (CRO)	D	16		
Armando MLINAR (CRO)	M	15		3
Janez MRAK	A	8	(7)	2
Vladimir PETRIC (YUG)	M	3		
Ismir PINTOL (BOS)	G	13		
Milos POPIVODA	G	4		
Nenad PROTEGA	M	18	(3)	6
Bosko RADIC (CRO)	M	4	(1)	
Andrej RAZDRH	D	3	(2)	
Dejan STEFANOVIC	M	28		
Alen SULEJMANI	M	31	(1)	1
Agron SALJA	M	23	(1)	3
Blaz SKOF	D	26		1
Mihael VONCINA	A	1		
Marko ZAVRSAN	D	2	(5)	
Igor ZINIC	A	1	(21)	3

LEAGUE RESULTS 1999/2000

02/08/99	NK Maribor	H	1-4	Protega
08/08/99	Primorje Ajdovscina	A	1-5	Mrak
15/08/99	Mura Murska Sobota	H	1-0	Protega
22/08/99	Rudar Velenje	H	0-3	
29/08/99	Korotan Prevalje	A	2-2	Mrak, Kusar
12/09/99	Feroterm Pohorje	H	2-1	Hribar, Zinic
19/09/99	Potrosnik Beltinci	A	1-1	Protega
26/09/99	HIT Gorica	H	0-2	
03/10/99	SCT Olimpija Ljubljana	A	0-2	
17/10/99	Publikum Celje	H	5-0	Drobne 3, Protega, Salja
24/10/99	NK Dravograd	A	4-2	Drobne 2, Skof, Salja
31/10/99	NK Maribor	A	2-3	Drobne 2
03/11/99	Primorje Ajdovscina	H	3-1	Drobne 2 (1p), Kalinic
07/11/99	Rudar Velenje	A	0-1	
14/11/99	Mura Murska Sobota	A	1-3	Brkic
21/11/99	Korotan Prevalje	H	1-1	Salja
27/02/00	Feroterm Pohorje	A	2-1	Mlinar, Drobne
05/03/00	Potrosnik Beltinci	H	4-1	Mlinar 2, Drobne, Karapetrovic
12/03/00	HIT Gorica	A	0-2	
19/03/00	SCT Olimpija Ljubljana	H	2-0	Drobne 2
22/03/00	Publikum Celje	A	0-3	
26/03/00	NK Dravograd	H	1-1	Drobne
02/04/00	HIT Gorica	A	0-2	
05/04/00	Rudar Velenje	H	0-0	
09/04/00	NK Maribor	A	0-1	
12/04/00	Mura Murska Sobota	H	0-0	
16/04/00	Publikum Celje	A	0-0	
22/04/00	NK Dravograd	A	1-2	Drobne
30/04/00	Feroterm Pohorje	H	6-1	Sulejmani, Hribar, Protega 2, Jersin, Zinic
03/05/00	Potrosnik Beltinci	A	4-0	Drobne 3, Zinic
07/05/00	SCT Olimpija Ljubljana	H	1-2	Drobne (p)
14/05/00	Primorje Ajdovscina	A	2-2	Drobne 2
21/05/00	Korotan Prevalje	H	3-2	Drobne 2 (1p), Jersin

NK DRAVOGRAD

CLUB DIRECTORY

NK Dravograd
Trg 4. julija 7
2370 Dravograd
tel - (0602) 84431
fax - (0602) 84431
Year of Formation - 1948
President - Rihard Versovnik
Coach - Marjan Pusnik (00/01 - Drago Kostanjsek)
Stadium - NK Dravograd (1,000)

APPEARANCES 99/00

	P	Ap	(s)	Gls
Nedzad BOTONJIC	G	24		
Branko BOZIC	D	12		
Mitja BRULC	M	22	(8)	2
Milan CAVNIK	D	29	(1)	3
Gjergji DEMA (ALB)	D	21	(1)	
Ehad GOGA (YUG)	M	11	(1)	2
Grega HELBL	D	28		
Peter HROVAT	G	9	(2)	
Jaka JAKOPIC	M	5	(13)	1
Ilija KITIC	A	13	(3)	2
Robert KOREN	M	30	(1)	2
Robert KRASOVEC	A	1	(11)	
Erion MEHILLI (ALB)	M	23		1
Iztok PIPENBAHER	A	3	(8)	
Miha PITAMIC	A	27	(1)	4
Borut PUSNIK	M	1	(6)	
Matej REBOL	D		(8)	
Goran SENTIC	D		(1)	
Aljosa SIVKO	A	20	(10)	14
Matej SNOFL	D	31		
Tadej STEHARNIK	D		(5)	
Bostjan STURM	M	3	(7)	
Stanislav TOT (CRO)	M	16		4
Matej VIDOVIC	M		(2)	
Samo VIDOVIC	A	29	(1)	9
Igor VORIH	M	3	(2)	
Borut VRHNJAK	D	2	(1)	

LEAGUE RESULTS 1999/2000

02/08/99	Rudar Velenje	A	0-2	
08/08/99	Korotan Prevalje	A	2-1	Koren, Cavnik
15/08/99	Feroterm Pohorje	A	3-1	Vidovic S., Pitamic, Koren
22/08/99	Potrosnik Beltinci	H	2-0	Vidovic S., Cavnik (p)
29/08/99	HIT Gorica	A	1-1	Sivko
12/09/99	SCT Olimpija Ljubljana	H	0-4	
19/09/99	Publikum Celje	A	0-0	
26/09/99	Mura Murska Sobota	A	2-2	Goga 2
03/10/99	NK Maribor	H	1-3	Vidovic S.
17/10/99	Primorje Ajdovscina	A	0-1	
24/10/99	NK Domzale	H	2-4	Vidovic S. (p), Sivko
31/10/99	Rudar Velenje	H	3-1	Sivko 2, Brulc
03/11/99	Korotan Prevalje	H	0-2	
07/11/99	Feroterm Pohorje	H	2-1	Mehilli, Vidovic S.
14/11/99	Potrosnik Beltinci	A	1-1	Sivko
21/11/99	HIT Gorica	H	2-4	Vidovic S. 2
27/02/00	SCT Olimpija Ljubljana	A	2-4	Sivko, Kitic
05/03/00	Publikum Celje	H	1-1	Pitamic
12/03/00	Mura Murska Sobota	H	2-1	Cavnik, Sivko
19/03/00	NK Maribor	A	0-2	
22/03/00	Primorje Ajdovscina	H	0-0	
26/03/00	NK Domzale	A	1-1	Sivko
02/04/00	Korotan Prevalje	A	2-1	Vidovic S., Sivko
05/04/00	HIT Gorica	H	1-1	Pitamic
09/04/00	Rudar Velenje	A	1-1	Brulc
12/04/00	NK Maribor	H	0-3	
16/04/00	Mura Murska Sobota	A	3-2	Tot 2, Sivko
22/04/00	NK Domzale	H	2-1	Tot, Vidovic S.
30/04/00	Publikum Celje	A	2-2	Jakopic, Sivko
03/05/00	Feroterm Pohorje	A	0-1	
07/05/00	Potrosnik Beltinci	H	3-1	Sivko 2, Kitic
14/05/00	SCT Olimpija Ljubljana	A	1-0	Tot
21/05/00	Primorje Ajdovscina	H	2-4	Sivko, Pitamic (p)

FEROTERM POHORJE

NK Feroterm Pohorje
Stadionska 15
2342 Ruse
tel - (062) 660188
fax - (062) 671353
Year of Formation - 1956
President - Peter Lamut
Secretary - Stanislav Ozim
Coach - Jozef Hadler; Marijan Bloudek
Stadium - Ruse (2,000)

APPEARANCES 99/00

	P	Ap	(s)	Gls
Peter BINKOVSKI	M	9		
Ingemar BLOUDEK	M	18	(1)	1
CRESNAR	M		(2)	
Darko DALJEVIC	M		(4)	
Bojan DOBAJ	D	7	(5)	
Rade DOBRIJEVIC (CRO)	D	8	(10)	
Crtomir GOJKOVIC	M	7	(3)	
Bostjan GRIZOLD	A	22		5
Oliver HAFNER	M	7	(1)	
Damjan JANZEKOVIC	D	18	(3)	
Simon KREPEK	A	14	(15)	1
Mitja LAMUT	D	6	(15)	1
Boris LJUTICA (YUG)	M	23	(3)	1
Matjaz MAJCEN	A	30	(1)	5
Ales MAJCENOVIC	D	25		3
Andrej MUZLOVIC	M		(7)	
Jure NABERNIK	D	9	(2)	
Benjamin PREDNIK	D	27		
Rajko PRELEC	G	27		
Marko PUNGARTNIK	G	6		
Bostjan RATKOVIC	M	14		1
Rok SVENSEK	D	20	(3)	
Danijel SIREC	A	17		3
Nikola SOJIC (YUG)	M	11		1
STORGELT	M	1	(4)	
Igor VORIH	M	17	(1)	3
ZAGOREC	M		(1)	
Mladen ZIMET	D	20	(2)	1

LEAGUE RESULTS 1999/2000

02/08/99	SCT Olimpija Ljubljana	H	0-3	
08/08/99	Publikum Celje	A	1-1	Lamut
15/08/99	NK Dravograd	H	1-3	Majcen
22/08/99	NK Maribor	A	0-5	
29/08/99	Primorje Ajdovscina	H	0-0	
12/09/99	NK Domzale	A	1-2	Bloudek
19/09/99	Rudar Velenje	H	1-3	Majcenovic
26/09/99	Korotan Prevalje	A	0-4	
03/10/99	Mura Murska Sobota	H	0-1	
17/10/99	Potrosnik Beltinci	H	2-1	Grizold 2
24/10/99	HIT Gorica	A	0-5	
31/10/99	SCT Olimpija Ljubljana	A	1-3	Vorih
03/11/99	Publikum Celje	H	0-0	
07/11/99	NK Dravograd	A	1-2	Majcenovic
14/11/99	NK Maribor	H	2-1	Majcen, Vorih (p)
21/11/99	Primorje Ajdovscina	A	0-1	
27/02/00	NK Domzale	H	1-2	Sojic
05/03/00	Rudar Velenje	A	0-1	
12/03/00	Korotan Prevalje	H	3-5	Vorih, Ljutica, Majcen
19/03/00	Mura Murska Sobota	A	0-2	
22/03/00	Potrosnik Beltinci	A	0-1	
26/03/00	HIT Gorica	H	0-0	
02/04/00	Primorje Ajdovscina	A	0-0	
05/04/00	Korotan Prevalje	H	0-1	
09/04/00	HIT Gorica	A	0-1	
12/04/00	Rudar Velenje	H	2-3	Grizold, Zimet
16/04/00	NK Maribor	A	1-3	Ratkovic
22/04/00	Mura Murska Sobota	H	2-2	Sirec 2
30/04/00	NK Domzale	A	1-6	Krepek
03/05/00	NK Dravograd	H	1-0	Majcen
07/05/00	Publikum Celje	A	1-5	Sirec
14/05/00	Potrosnik Beltinci	A	3-2	Majcen, Majcenovic, Grizold
21/05/00	SCT Olimpija Ljubljana	H	1-4	Grizold

HIT GORICA

CLUB DIRECTORY

NK HIT Gorica
Baazoviska 4, p.p.95
5001 Nova Gorica
tel - (065) 22458
fax - (065) 22458
Year of Formation - 1938
President - Danilo Likar
Secretary - Josip Koradin
Coach - Nedzad Verlasevic; Edin Osmanovic
Stadium - Nova Gorica (5,000)

MAJOR HONOURS
League Championship - (1) 1996.

APPEARANCES 99/00

	P	Ap	(s)	Gls
Fahrudin ALOMEROVIC (BOS)	D	27		
Vili BECAJ	M	27	(2)	7
Husein BEGANOVIC (MAC)	D	4	(1)	
Erik CIRKVENCIC	M		(3)	
Florijan DEBENJAK	A	24	(6)	
Oskar DROBNE	A		(3)	
Edmond GUNJAC	D	28		
Goran GUTALJ (YUG)	A	11	(3)	4
Mahir HALILI (ALB)	A	11	(3)	3
Patrik IPAVEC	A	23	(6)	7
Adem KAPIC	A	1	(1)	
Roni KLANCIC	M		(2)	
Ales KOKOT	M	4	(2)	
Mladen KOVACEVIC	A	1	(4)	1
Nebojsa KOVACEVIC	M	7	(12)	
Borut MAVRIC	G	16		
Matej MAVRIC	D		(4)	
Zeljko MITRAKOVIC	D	9	(4)	3
Thabang MOLEFE (SAF)	D		(5)	
Mitja PIRIH	G	17	(1)	
Alen RESCIC	A	2	(7)	2
Elvis RIBARIC	M	27		2
Adnan SARAJLIC (BOS)	A	2	(2)	1
Miran SREBRNIC	M	31		3
Alen SCULAC	D	27	(1)	1
Marko VOGRIC	M	8	(15)	
Ivica VULIC	A	24	(8)	8
Simon ZIVEC	D	1	(9)	
Tonci ZLOGAR	M	31	(1)	13
Tomaz ZNIDERCIC	A		(7)	

LEAGUE RESULTS 1999/2000

02/08/99	Potrosnik Beltinci	A	0-0	
08/08/99	Mura Murska Sobota	A	0-2	
15/08/99	SCT Olimpija Ljubljana	H	2-1	Ipavec, Vulic
22/08/99	Publikum Celje	A	3-3	Halili 2, Mitrakovic
29/08/99	NK Dravograd	H	1-1	Vulic
12/09/99	NK Maribor	A	0-4	
19/09/99	Primorje Ajdovscina	H	5-0	Becaj 2, Vulic, Srebrnic, Halili
26/09/99	NK Domzale	A	2-0	Becaj (p), Zlogar
03/10/99	Rudar Velenje	H	0-1	
17/10/99	Korotan Prevalje	A	1-0	Zlogar
24/10/99	Feroterm Pohorje	H	5-0	Zlogar 2, Vulic 2, Ribaric
31/10/99	Potrosnik Beltinci	H	2-0	Zlogar, Ipavec
03/11/99	Mura Murska Sobota	H	2-1	Ipavec, Becaj (p)
07/11/99	SCT Olimpija Ljubljana	A	0-4	
14/11/99	Publikum Celje	H	1-0	Kovacevic M.
21/11/99	NK Dravograd	A	4-2	Mitrakovic 2, Ipavec, Becaj
27/02/00	NK Maribor	H	2-1	Becaj (p), Gutalj
05/03/00	Primorje Ajdovscina	A	0-1	
12/03/00	NK Domzale	H	2-0	Ipavec, Zlogar
19/03/00	Rudar Velenje	A	0-3	
22/03/00	Korotan Prevalje	H	2-0	Gutalj, Rescic
26/03/00	Feroterm Pohorje	A	0-0	
02/04/00	NK Domzale	H	2-0	Sculac, Zlogar
05/04/00	NK Dravograd	A	1-1	Zlogar
09/04/00	Feroterm Pohorje	H	1-0	Rescic
12/04/00	Potrosnik Beltinci	A	3-0	Gutalj, Vulic, Zlogar
16/04/00	SCT Olimpija Ljubljana	H	3-0	Zlogar 2, Becaj
22/04/00	Primorje Ajdovscina	A	1-2	Ipavec
30/04/00	Korotan Prevalje	H	2-1	Ribaric, Zlogar
03/05/00	Publikum Celje	H	4-0	Zlogar, Vulic, Ipavec, Sarajlic
07/05/00	Rudar Velenje	A	1-2	Srebrnic
14/05/00	NK Maribor	H	1-3	Vulic
21/05/00	Mura Murska Sobota	A	2-1	Gutalj, Srebrnic

KOROTAN PREVALJE

CLUB DIRECTORY

NK Korotan
Ugasle peci 1
2391 Prevalje
tel - (0602) 33556
fax - (0602) 33556
Year of Formation - 1933
President - dr. Matic Tasic
Secretary - Saso Puc
Coach - Toni Tomazic (00/01 - Dinko Vrabac)
Stadium - Korotan (5,000)

APPEARANCES 99/00

	P	Ap	(s)	Gls
Marko BARUN	M	24	(3)	
Osman BEGIC	A	15	(10)	1
Igor BENEDEJCIC	M	1		
Milan BOSKOVIC (YUG)	M	16		
Peter BREZNIK	D	22	(2)	7
Bostjan DAMIS	M	9	(4)	
Goran JOLIC	M	16		8
Faik KAMBEROVIC (BOS)	A	8	(1)	5
Dusan KORDEZ	G	1		
Matjaz LAKOVNIK	M		(2)	
Goran MARKOVIC (BOS)	M	2	(1)	1
Armando MLINAR (CRO)	M	7		
Simon PIRC	D	6	(5)	
Roman PLESEC	M	26	(1)	5
Zoran POGLAJEN	A	6	(7)	4
PUSNIK	M		(1)	
Bostjan RATKOVIC	D	14	(7)	
Ilir SILO (ALB)	D	22	(1)	1
Robert SRAGA	G	32		
Mladen STOJANOVIC	M	4	(16)	3
Andrej STRUNA	A	19	(9)	6
Kristjan SVAB	D	29		
Senad TIGANJ	A	11	(7)	3
Nenad TOSEVSKI	M	18	(3)	1
Anton USNIK	M	11	(1)	2
Zikica VUKSANOVIC	D	28		2
Robert ZEC	M	14	(10)	7
Adnan ZILDZEVIC (BOS)	M	2	(9)	2

LEAGUE RESULTS 1999/2000

Date	Opponent	H/A	Score	Scorers
02/08/99	Publikum Celje	H	1-1	Struna
08/08/99	NK Dravograd	H	1-2	Breznik
15/08/99	NK Maribor	H	2-4	Zildzevic, Jolic
22/08/99	Primorje Ajdovscina	A	2-2	Markovic, Struna
29/08/99	NK Domzale	H	2-2	Jolic, Tiganj
12/09/99	Rudar Velenje	A	2-2	Struna, Tosevski
19/09/99	Mura Murska Sobota	H	1-1	Breznik
26/09/99	Feroterm Pohorje	H	4-0	Zec 2, Struna, Jolic
03/10/99	Potrosnik Beltinci	A	3-1	Breznik, Zildzevic, Jolic
17/10/99	HIT Gorica	H	0-1	
24/10/99	SCT Olimpija Ljubljana	A	5-1	Zec 2, Jolic, Struna, Stojanovic
31/10/99	Publikum Celje	A	1-2	Stojanovic
03/11/99	NK Dravograd	A	2-0	Breznik, Jolic
07/11/99	Primorje Ajdovscina	H	3-1	Jolic 2, Zec
14/11/99	NK Domzale	A	1-1	Breznik
21/11/99	NK Maribor	A	0-0	
27/02/00	Rudar Velenje	H	1-0	Kamberovic
05/03/00	Mura Murska Sobota	A	2-0	Kamberovic 2
12/03/00	Feroterm Pohorje	A	5-3	Breznik 2, Begic, Plesec, Poglajen
19/03/00	Potrosnik Beltinci	H	2-1	Kamberovic, Vuksanovic
22/03/00	HIT Gorica	A	0-2	
26/03/00	SCT Olimpija Ljubljana	H	3-2	Zec 2, Silo
02/04/00	NK Dravograd	H	1-2	Usnik
05/04/00	Feroterm Pohorje	A	1-0	Kamberovic
09/04/00	Potrosnik Beltinci	H	1-2	Stojanovic
12/04/00	SCT Olimpija Ljubljana	A	2-0	Plesec 2
16/04/00	Primorje Ajdovscina	H	0-1	
22/04/00	Publikum Celje	H	2-1	Vuksanovic, Poglajen
30/04/00	HIT Gorica	A	1-2	Plesec
03/05/00	Rudar Velenje	H	2-0	Tiganj 2
07/05/00	NK Maribor	A	0-3	
14/05/00	Mura Murska Sobota	H	3-0	Poglajen 2, Usnik
21/05/00	NK Domzale	A	2-3	Struna, Plesec (p)

NK MARIBOR

CLUB DIRECTORY

NK Maribor
Mladinska 29, 2000 Maribor
tel - (062) 224645/28534
fax - (062) 28534/212986
Year of Formation - 1958
President - Joze Jagodnik
Secretary - Zeljko Fundak
Coach - Bojan Prasnikar; Matjaz Kek
Stadium - Ljudski vrt (15,000)

MAJOR HONOURS
League Championship - (9) 1961, 1976, 1982,
1984, 1986, 1997, 1998, 1999, 2000.
Domestic Cup - (17) 1965, 1966, 1968, 1973,
1974, 1978, 1980, 1982, 1984, 1986, 1987,
1989, 1990, 1992, 1994, 1997, 1999.

APPEARANCES 99/00

	P	Ap	(s)	Gls
Stipe BALAJIC (CRO)	M	18	(2)	6
Kliton BOZGO (ALB)	A	27	(4)	24
Fabijan CIPOT	M		(10)	2
Geri ÇIPI (ALB)	D	22	(3)	1
Nastja CEH	M	14	(3)	5
Dejan DJURANOVIC	M	31	(1)	11
Mehmet DRAGUSHA (YUG)	M	5	(5)	2
Ismet EKMECIC (BOS)	A	7	(4)	5
Suad FILEKOVIC	D	19	(6)	
Dalibor FILIPOVIC (CRO)	A	12	(9)	7
Marinko GALIC	D	24		2
Luka GRESAK	G	12	(1)	
Ales KACICNIK	M	13	(2)	1
Amir KARIC	M	24	(1)	3
Matej MILJATOVIC	M		(2)	
Tomaz MURKO	G		(1)	
Damir PEKIC	A	5	(4)	1
Martin PREGELJ	M	10	(10)	
Simon SESLAR	M	26	(4)	1
Marko SIMEUNOVIC	G	21		
Marinko SARKEZI	D	13	(1)	
Ante SIMUNDZA	A	17	(10)	9
Jovica VICO (CRO)	A	2	(1)	
Muamer VUGDALIC	D	24	(3)	5
Gregor ZIDAN	M	17	(5)	4

LEAGUE RESULTS 1999/2000

02/08/99	NK Domzale	A	4-1	Djuranovic 2, Bozgo, Dragusha
08/08/99	Rudar Velenje	H	4-1	Simundza, Karic, Bozgo, Djuranovic
15/08/99	Korotan Prevalje	A	4-2	Vugdalic 2, Filipovic, Galic
22/08/99	Feroterm Pohorje	H	5-0	Zidan 2 (1p), Bozgo 2, Seslar
29/08/99	Potrosnik Beltinci	A	2-0	Pekic, Djuranovic
12/09/99	HIT Gorica	H	4-0	Bozgo, Simundza, Balajic, Djuranovic
19/09/99	SCT Olimpija Ljubljana	A	4-2	Çipi, Bozgo, Simundza, Zidan (p)
26/09/99	Publikum Celje	H	2-1	Vugdalic, Bozgo
03/10/99	NK Dravograd	A	3-1	Balajic 2, Bozgo
17/10/99	Mura Murska Sobota	A	2-2	Simundza, Galic
24/10/99	Primorje Ajdovscina	H	2-2	Dragusha, Simundza
31/10/99	NK Domzale	H	3-2	Filipovic 3 (1p)
03/11/99	Rudar Velenje	A	2-2	Filipovic, Simundza
07/11/99	Feroterm Pohorje	A	1-2	Filipovic
14/11/99	Potrosnik Beltinci	H	5-1	Bozgo 4 (1p), Simundza
21/11/99	Korotan Prevalje	H	0-0	
27/02/00	HIT Gorica	A	1-2	Ekmecic
05/03/00	SCT Olimpija Ljubljana	H	0-0	
12/03/00	Publikum Celje	A	2-1	Bozgo, Zidan (p)
19/03/00	NK Dravograd	H	2-0	Balajic 2
22/03/00	Mura Murska Sobota	H	3-1	Ceh, Bozgo, Kacicnik
26/03/00	Primorje Ajdovscina	A	3-1	Djuranovic 2, Ceh
02/04/00	Publikum Celje	H	4-0	Ekmecic, Vugdalic, Simundza, og (Blatnik)
05/04/00	Mura Murska Sobota	A	3-1	Djuranovic, Ceh, Bozgo
09/04/00	NK Domzale	H	1-0	Ekmecic
12/04/00	NK Dravograd	A	3-0	Ceh, Ekmecic, Bozgo
16/04/00	Feroterm Pohorje	H	3-1	Bozgo 2, Vugdalic
22/04/00	Potrosnik Beltinci	A	6-0	Bozgo, Simundza, Cipot 2, Karic, Filipovic
30/04/00	SCT Olimpija Ljubljana	H	2-0	Karic, Djuranovic
03/05/00	Primorje Ajdovscina	A	2-2	Ceh (p), Djuranovic
07/05/00	Korotan Prevalje	H	3-0	Bozgo 3
14/05/00	HIT Gorica	A	3-1	Bozgo, Balajic, Ekmecic
21/05/00	Rudar Velenje	H	2-1	Djuranovic, Bozgo

MURA MURSKA SOBOTA

CLUB DIRECTORY

NK Mura
Kopaliska 45, 9000 Murska Sobota
tel - (069) 32701 / fax - (069) 32701
Year of Formation - 1946
President - Milan Moerec
Secretary - Joze Filo
Coach - Milovan Tarbuk; Milan Koblencer
(00/01 - Zlatko Kranjcar)
Stadium - Fazanerija (5,000)

MAJOR HONOURS
League Championship - (1) 1970.
Domestic Cup - (1) 1995.

APPEARANCES 99/00

	P	Ap	(s)	Gls
Ales BAGOLA	D	3	(4)	
Adamo BARANJA	M	8	(2)	
Ivan BENKO	D	1	(3)	
Senad BRKIC (YUG)	M		(1)	
CELCAR	A	1	(2)	
Franc CIFER	D	28		4
Fabijan CIPOT	M	14		6
Mederios DENIO (BRA)	A	8		2
Marjan DOMINKO	A	25	(1)	4
Simon DVORSAK	M	25	(3)	8
Roman FAJDIGA	D		(3)	
Matej FRAS	M	2	(9)	
Ales GABOR	M	25	(2)	1
GOSTAN	M	2	(2)	
Safet HADZIC	D	2		
KAMNIK	G	1		
Ales KOLOSA	D	3	(1)	1
Ales LUK	G	2		
Saso LUKIC	D	22		2
Alan MESARIC	M	28	(4)	3
MOREC	M		(1)	
Ismet MUNISHI (YUG)	M	7		
Dejan NEMEC	G	29		
Saso NOVAK	M	3	(4)	
Damjan OSLAJ	D	32		2
Robert PETROVIC	A	7	(13)	1
Marko PIMA (YUG)	D	14	(3)	1
Igor PREININGER	D	2	(3)	
Goran RISTIC	M	21	(10)	3
SABOTIN	M	1		
Stefan SKAPER	A	3	(2)	1
SNUKER	M		(1)	
Nikola TALABER	G	1	(1)	
Sebastjan VOGRINCIC	M	26	(2)	6
Davor ZILAVEC	M	1		
Sebastjan ZILAVEC	M	16	(9)	

LEAGUE RESULTS 1999/2000

Date	Opponent		Score	Scorers
02/08/99	Primorje Ajdovscina	A	0-1	
08/08/99	HIT Gorica	H	2-0	Mesaric 2
15/08/99	NK Domzale	A	0-1	
22/08/99	SCT Olimpija Ljubljana	H	3-0	Cifer 2 (1p), Cipot
29/08/99	Rudar Velenje	A	2-1	Skaper, Ristic
12/09/99	Publikum Celje	H	1-3	Oslaj
19/09/99	Korotan Prevalje	A	1-1	Dominko
26/09/99	NK Dravograd	H	2-2	Vogrincic, Ristic
03/10/99	Feroterm Pohorje	A	1-0	Cipot
17/10/99	NK Maribor	H	2-2	Cipot 2
24/10/99	Potrosnik Beltinci	A	3-0	Cifer 2 (2p), Cipot
31/10/99	Primorje Ajdovscina	H	1-1	Pima (p)
03/11/99	HIT Gorica	A	1-2	Dvorsak
07/11/99	NK Domzale	H	3-1	Cipot, Denio, Ristic
14/11/99	Rudar Velenje	H	0-3	
21/11/99	SCT Olimpija Ljubljana	A	1-2	Lukic
27/02/00	Publikum Celje	A	2-3	Dvorsak, Vogrincic
05/03/00	Korotan Prevalje	H	0-2	
12/03/00	NK Dravograd	A	1-2	Vogrincic
19/03/00	Feroterm Pohorje	H	2-0	Denio, Lukic
22/03/00	NK Maribor	A	1-3	og (Karic)
26/03/00	Potrosnik Beltinci	H	1-0	Oslaj
02/04/00	Rudar Velenje	A	1-2	Dvorsak
05/04/00	NK Maribor	H	1-3	Dvorsak
09/04/00	Publikum Celje	A	1-2	Dvorsak (p)
12/04/00	NK Domzale	A	0-0	
16/04/00	NK Dravograd	H	2-3	Dvorsak (p), Petrovic
22/04/00	Feroterm Pohorje	A	2-2	Dvorsak (p), Dominko
30/04/00	Potrosnik Beltinci	H	6-0	Mesaric, Dominko, Vogrincic 3, og (Antolin)
03/05/00	SCT Olimpija Ljubljana	A	1-5	Kolosa
07/05/00	Primorje Ajdovscina	H	2-1	Dvorsak, Gabor
14/05/00	Korotan Prevalje	A	0-3	
21/05/00	HIT Gorica	H	1-2	Dominko

POTROSNIK BELTINCI

CLUB DIRECTORY

NK Potrosnik
Sportni park Beltinci, 9231 Beltinci
tel - (069) 41444 / fax - (069) 41444
Year of Formation - 1970
President - Valentin Erjavec
Secretary - Janez Breznik
Coach - Nikola Skrbic; Vojislav Simeunovic;
Ivan Markovic; Nikola Skrbic
Stadium - Beltinci (4,000)

APPEARANCES 99/00

	P	Ap	(s)	Gls
David ADJEJI (GHA)	A	18		3
Denis ALILOVIC (CRO)	M	2	(1)	
Cveto ANTOLIN	M	16	(5)	3
Simon BARANJA	D	6	(2)	
Igor BEDO	A	7	(2)	
Mihael BUKOVEC	D	25	(3)	
Zdravko CENER	M	24	(3)	
Bogdan CRNKO	M	1		
DUH	M		(1)	
ERJAVEC	M	3	(2)	
Mitja ERNISA	D	13		
Safet HADZIC	D	2		
Danilo HORVAT	D	1	(1)	
Matej HORVAT	M	10	(3)	
KAVAS	M	14	(2)	
Edin KENDIC	M	6	(3)	
Ilija KITIC	A	2		
Joze KOKAS	M	18	(2)	
Dejan KRSLIN	A	1	(1)	
Stanko KUZMA	G	21		
Bojan MERTUK	D		(4)	
Saso NOVAK	D	15	(1)	
Robert PEVNIK	M	7		
POPESCU (ROM)	A	15		6
Vukasin RISTIC (YUG)	A	3	(2)	
Dejan SLANA	M	4	(2)	
Predrag STOJILJKOVIC (YUG)	A	2	(1)	
Danijel SIREC	A	4	(5)	
Matej SKAFAR	M	15	(4)	5
Bostjan TRATNJEK	D	26		1
Simon ULEN	D	30		
Dario UTROSA	A	2	(6)	1
VIRAG	M		(2)	
Aleksandr VOROBJOV (RUS)	M	6		
Danijel ZLATAR	D	16	(1)	
Milan ZORICA (YUG)	M	15		2
Andrej ZVER	M		(4)	
Kristijan ZVER	G	12	(1)	
Mario ZVER	A	1	(2)	

LEAGUE RESULTS 1999/2000

02/08/99	HIT Gorica	H	0-0	
08/08/99	SCT Olimpija Ljubljana	A	0-5	
15/08/99	Publikum Celje	H	0-0	
22/08/99	NK Dravograd	A	0-2	
29/08/99	NK Maribor	H	0-2	
12/09/99	Primorje Ajdovscina	A	2-2	Utrosa, Adjeji
19/09/99	NK Domzale	H	1-1	Popescu
26/09/99	Rudar Velenje	A	0-1	
03/10/99	Korotan Prevalje	H	1-3	Popescu (p)
17/10/99	Feroterm Pohorje	A	1-2	Popescu
24/10/99	Mura Murska Sobota	H	0-3	
31/10/99	HIT Gorica	A	0-2	
03/11/99	SCT Olimpija Ljubljana	H	0-5	
07/11/99	Publikum Celje	A	0-2	
14/11/99	NK Dravograd	H	1-1	Popescu (p)
21/11/99	NK Maribor	A	1-5	Popescu
27/02/00	Primorje Ajdovscina	H	0-5	
05/03/00	NK Domzale	A	1-4	Zorica
12/03/00	Rudar Velenje	H	1-2	Zorica
19/03/00	Korotan Prevalje	A	1-2	Antolin
22/03/00	Feroterm Pohorje	H	1-0	Adjeji
26/03/00	Mura Murska Sobota	A	0-1	
02/04/00	SCT Olimpija Ljubljana	A	3-3	Skafar 2, Antolin
05/04/00	Primorje Ajdovscina	H	2-0	Tratnjek, Skafar
09/04/00	Korotan Prevalje	A	2-1	Antolin, Adjeji
12/04/00	HIT Gorica	H	0-3	
16/04/00	Rudar Velenje	A	0-2	
22/04/00	NK Maribor	H	0-6	
30/04/00	Mura Murska Sobota	A	0-6	
03/05/00	NK Domzale	H	0-4	
07/05/00	NK Dravograd	A	1-3	Skafar
14/05/00	Feroterm Pohorje	H	2-3	Skafar, Popescu
21/05/00	Publikum Celje	A	0-7	

PRIMORJE AJDOVSCINA

CLUB DIRECTORY

NK Primorje
Gregorciceva 44, p.p. 3, 5270 Ajdovscina
tel - (065) 61042
fax - (065) 61042
Year of Formation - 1924
President - Dusan Crnigoj
Secretary - Miran Lulik
Coach - Ivan Marjon; Borivoje Lucic; Nermin
Hadjiahmetovic (00/01 - Ivica Matkovic)
Stadium - Primorje (5,000)

MAJOR HONOURS
Domestic Cup - (1) 1976.

APPEARANCES 99/00

	P	Ap	(s)	Gls
Uros BARUT	A	32		17
Admir BEGIC	D	10	(2)	2
Luka BUSINELLO (CRO)	D	9		
Jernej CERNIGOJ	M	4	(2)	
Nermin FATIC (BOS)	D	12	(2)	1
Simon GREGORIC	M	23	(1)	3
Jasmin HURIC (BOS)	D	19		
Ales KODELJA	M	10	(7)	1
Andrej KOMAC	D	20	(7)	
Erik KRZISNIK	D	14	(2)	1
Matej MAVRIC	D	2	(1)	
Matej MLAKAR	M	9	(15)	1
Alen MUJANOVIC	A	5	(7)	1
Sefik MULAHMETOVIC (YUG)	M	31		2
Janez PATE	M	23	(2)	8
Goran RELJIC	D	23	(4)	
Uros RUTAR	G	4	(3)	
Ramiz SMAJLOVIC	A		(7)	1
Goran STAMENOV	M	1	(2)	
Vanja STARCEVIC	A	17	(9)	11
Janez STRAJNAR	G	29		
Almir TANJIC	D	6	(1)	
Luka VIDMAR	D	7	(4)	
Goran VINCETIC (CRO)	M	29	(1)	3
Marko VOGRIC	A	12	(3)	3
Igor ZOBEC	M	12	(5)	1

LEAGUE RESULTS 1999/2000

02/08/99	Mura Murska Sobota	H	1-0	Pate (p)
08/08/99	NK Domzale	H	5-1	Begic 2, Mulahmetovic, Mujanovic, Starcevic
15/08/99	Rudar Velenje	A	1-2	Barut
22/08/99	Korotan Prevalje	H	2-2	Krzisnik, Zobec
29/08/99	Feroterm Pohorje	A	0-0	
12/09/99	Potrosnik Beltinci	H	2-2	Gregoric, Barut
19/09/99	HIT Gorica	A	0-5	
26/09/99	SCT Olimpija Ljubljana	H	6-0	Barut 3, Starcevic 3
03/10/99	Publikum Celje	A	1-3	Smajlovic
17/10/99	NK Dravograd	H	1-0	Mulahmetovic
24/10/99	NK Maribor	A	2-2	Barut 2
31/10/99	Mura Murska Sobota	A	1-1	Vincetic
03/11/99	NK Domzale	A	1-3	Starcevic
07/11/99	Rudar Velenje	H	2-1	Pate, Barut
14/11/99	Korotan Prevalje	A	1-3	Barut
21/11/99	Feroterm Pohorje	H	1-0	Pate
27/02/00	Potrosnik Beltinci	A	5-0	Barut 2, Kodelja, Starcevic (p), Vincetic
05/03/00	HIT Gorica	H	1-0	Starcevic
12/03/00	SCT Olimpija Ljubljana	A	3-1	Starcevic, Vincetic, Barut
19/03/00	Publikum Celje	H	2-2	Starcevic (p), Mlakar
22/03/00	NK Dravograd	A	0-0	
26/03/00	NK Maribor	H	1-3	Fatic
02/04/00	Feroterm Pohorje	H	0-0	
05/04/00	Potrosnik Beltinci	A	0-2	
09/04/00	SCT Olimpija Ljubljana	H	3-2	Pate 2, Barut
12/04/00	Publikum Celje	H	2-2	Pate, Vogric
16/04/00	Korotan Prevalje	A	1-0	Barut
22/04/00	HIT Gorica	H	2-1	Pate 2
30/04/00	Rudar Velenje	A	0-3	
03/05/00	NK Maribor	H	2-2	Barut, Vogric
07/05/00	Mura Murska Sobota	A	1-2	Barut
14/05/00	NK Domzale	H	2-2	Vogric, Starcevic
21/05/00	NK Dravograd	A	4-2	Gregoric 2, Starcevic, Barut

PUBLIKUM CELJE

CLUB DIRECTORY

NK Publikum
Cesta na grad 12, 63 000 Celje
tel - (063) 482250/482252
fax - (063) 482251
Year of Formation - 1946
President - Marjan Vengust
Secretary - Darko Zickar
Coach - Nikola Ilijevski; Dragan Grbavac
(00/01 - Marjan Pusnik)
Stadium - Skalna klet (5,000)

MAJOR HONOURS
League Championship - (1) 1964.
Domestic Cup - (1) 1964.

APPEARANCES 99/00

	P	Ap	(s)	Gls
Dragan ANGELOVSKI (MAC)	M	2	(2)	
Matej BERANIC	M	15	(1)	2
Dominik BERSNJAK	M	14	(14)	4
Gregor BLATNIK	D	25		
Oliver BOGATINOV	A	12	(3)	5
BOJOVIC	M		(1)	
Panco GEORGIJEVSKI (MAC)	M	11		3
Miran GOBEC	D		(1)	
Sebastjan GOBEC	M	25	(1)	3
Uros GORENEK	M	13	(6)	
Andrej GORSEK	A	29	(1)	12
Bostjan HODZAR	M	1	(11)	2
Andrej JOZEF	M	8	(6)	
Ales KACICNIK	M	15		2
Mladen KOLJIC	A		(4)	
Marko KRIZANIC	M	2	(4)	1
Marko KRIZNIK	D	18	(5)	1
Marko MITIC	M	24	(2)	1
Amel MUJCINOVIC (BOS)	G	31		
Denis PERSE	D	1	(2)	
Aleksandar RADOSAVLJEVIC	M	32		11
Damjan ROMIH	M	27	(3)	1
ROZMAN	M		(1)	
Goran SANKOVIC	D	13	(1)	1
Aleksander SELIGA	G	2	(1)	
Danijel SIREC	A	2	(2)	
SOSTAR	A		(4)	
Matjaz STANCAR	M	24	(3)	2
Velice SUMULIKOVSKI (MAC)	M	15	(6)	2
Nenad ULAGA	D	2	(6)	
Brane VODOPIVEC	M		(1)	
Adnan ZILDZEVIC (BOS)	M		(3)	

LEAGUE RESULTS 1999/2000

02/08/99	Korotan Prevalje	A	1-1	Radosavljevic
08/08/99	Feroterm Pohorje	H	1-1	Gorsek (p)
15/08/99	Potrosnik Beltinci	A	0-0	
22/08/99	HIT Gorica	H	3-3	Radosavljevic 2, Hodzar
29/08/99	SCT Olimpija Ljubljana	A	0-3	
12/09/99	Mura Murska Sobota	A	3-1	Sankovic, Georgijevski, Gorsek
19/09/99	NK Dravograd	H	0-0	
26/09/99	NK Maribor	A	1-2	Bersnjak
03/10/99	Primorje Ajdovscina	H	3-1	Georgijevski, Kacicnik, Sumulikovski
17/10/99	NK Domzale	A	0-5	
24/10/99	Rudar Velenje	H	0-0	
31/10/99	Korotan Prevalje	H	2-1	Gorsek, Gobec
03/11/99	SCT Olimpija Ljubljana	H	3-0	Bersnjak, Georgijevski, Radosavljevic
07/11/99	Feroterm Pohorje	A	0-0	
14/11/99	Potrosnik Beltinci	H	2-0	Hodzar, Kacicnik
21/11/99	HIT Gorica	A	0-1	
27/02/00	Mura Murska Sobota	H	3-2	Gorsek 2, Kriznik
05/03/00	NK Dravograd	A	1-1	Stancar (p)
12/03/00	NK Maribor	H	1-2	Krizanic
19/03/00	Primorje Ajdovscina	A	2-2	Beranic, Stancar (p)
22/03/00	NK Domzale	H	3-0	Sumulikovski, Radosavljevic, Bogatinov
26/03/00	Rudar Velenje	A	1-1	Bogatinov
02/04/00	NK Maribor	A	0-4	
05/04/00	SCT Olimpija Ljubljana	A	2-2	Bogatinov, Gorsek
09/04/00	Mura Murska Sobota	H	2-1	Boigatinov, Gobec
12/04/00	Primorje Ajdovscina	A	2-2	Romih, Radosavljevic
16/04/00	NK Domzale	H	0-0	
22/04/00	Korotan Prevalje	A	1-2	Gorsek
30/04/00	NK Dravograd	H	2-2	Radosavljevic, Gorsek
03/05/00	HIT Gorica	A	0-4	
07/05/00	Feroterm Pohorje	H	5-1	Gorsek 2, Radosavljevic 2, Bersnjak
14/05/00	Rudar Velenje	A	2-0	Gobec, Mitic
21/05/00	Potrosnik Beltinci	H	7-0	Gorsek 2, Beranic, Bogatinov, Radosavljevic 2, Bersnjak

RUDAR VELENJE

CLUB DIRECTORY

NK Rudar
Cesta ob jezeru 7, p.p.54, 3320 Velenje
tel - (063) 856656
fax - (063) 866181
Year of Formation - 1948
President - Miran Lah
Secretary - Bojan Ograjensek
Coach - Branko Oblak (00/01 - Toni Tomazic)
Stadium - Ob jezeru (7,000)

MAJOR HONOURS
League Championship - (2) 1977, 1991.
Domestic Cup - (1) 1998.

APPEARANCES 99/00

	P	Ap	(s)	Gls
Samir BALAGIC	D	11	(1)	
Peter BINKOVSKI	M	10		
Zlatko CERIMOVIC	D	5	(1)	
Damjan GAJSER	M	27		8
Miha GOLOB	M	26	(3)	1
Goran GRANIC (CRO)	D	30		2
Anton GROBELSEK	M	3	(6)	
Mitja HONIK	M		(1)	
Jernej JAVORNIK	M		(8)	2
Slavko JAVORNIK	D	1	(2)	
Alfred JERMANIS	M	13	(1)	4
Damjan JESENICNIK	M	8	(9)	
Goran JOLIC	M	10		2
Marko KRIZANIC	M		(6)	
Dino LALIC	G	30		
Klemen LAVRIC	A	26	(4)	8
Darko MILANOVIC	M	1		
Robert OBLAK	M	26		2
Niko PODVINSKI	M	21	(2)	5
Zeljko SPASOJEVIC	M	12	(3)	1
Ednan SOFTIC	D		(3)	
Almir SULEJMANOVIC	M	15	(4)	2
Janko SRIBAR	G	3	(2)	
Peter SUMNIK	A	19	(4)	3
Ales TURK	M	11	(3)	
Zivojin VIDOJEVIC (YUG)	A	28	(1)	8
Marko VOGRIC	A	6	(5)	
Bostjan ZEMLJIC	D	21	(1)	1

LEAGUE RESULTS 1999/2000

02/08/99	NK Dravograd	H	2-0	Vidojevic, Gajser
08/08/99	NK Maribor	A	1-4	Podvinski
15/08/99	Primorje Ajdovscina	H	2-1	Vidojevic, Jermanis
22/08/99	NK Domzale	A	3-0	Vidojevic, Lavric, Jermanis
29/08/99	Mura Murska Sobota	H	1-2	Vidojevic
12/09/99	Korotan Prevalje	H	2-2	Zemljic, Jermanis
19/09/99	Feroterm Pohorje	A	3-1	Jermanis, Golob, Podvinski
26/09/99	Potrosnik Beltinci	H	1-0	Granic
03/10/99	HIT Gorica	A	1-0	Granic
17/10/99	SCT Olimpija Ljubljana	H	0-1	
24/10/99	Publikum Celje	A	0-0	
31/10/99	NK Dravograd	A	1-3	Oblak
03/11/99	NK Maribor	H	2-2	Vidojevic, Gajser
07/11/99	Primorje Ajdovscina	A	1-2	Lavric
14/11/99	NK Domzale	H	1-0	Gajser
21/11/99	Mura Murska Sobota	A	3-0	Gajser 2, Lavric
27/02/00	Korotan Prevalje	A	0-1	
05/03/00	Feroterm Pohorje	H	1-0	Lavric
12/03/00	Potrosnik Beltinci	A	2-1	Gajser, Jolic
19/03/00	HIT Gorica	H	3-0	Lavric, Oblak, Gajser
22/03/00	SCT Olimpija Ljubljana	A	2-1	Sumnik, Lavric
26/03/00	Publikum Celje	H	1-1	Jolic
02/04/00	Mura Murska Sobota	H	2-1	Vidojevic, Lavric
05/04/00	NK Domzale	A	0-0	
09/04/00	NK Dravograd	H	1-1	Sumnik
12/04/00	Feroterm Pohorje	A	3-2	Sulejmanovic, Podvinski, Spasojevic
16/04/00	Potrosnik Beltinci	H	2-0	Sulejmanovic, Gajser
22/04/00	SCT Olimpija Ljubljana	A	2-2	Sumnik, Javornik J.
30/04/00	Primorje Ajdovscina	H	3-0	Vidojevic, Lavric, Javornik J.
03/05/00	Korotan Prevalje	A	0-2	
07/05/00	HIT Gorica	H	2-1	Podvinski, Vidojevic
14/05/00	Publikum Celje	H	0-2	
21/05/00	NK Maribor	A	1-2	Podvinski

SCT OLIMPIJA LJUBLJANA

CLUB DIRECTORY

NK SCT Olimpija (now - NK Olimpija)
Vodovodna 20, p.p.2620, 1001 Ljubljana
tel - (061) 348397 / fax - (061) 341847
Year of Formation - 1911
President - Ivan Zidar
General Manager - Miro Gavez
Secretary - Olga Cucek
Coach - Jedinko Perica; Milovan Tarbuk
(00/01 - Bojan Prasnikar)
Stadium - Bezigrad (18,000)

MAJOR HONOURS

League Championship - (8) 1947, 1952, 1962,
1987, 1992, 1993, 1994, 1995.
Domestic Cup - (18) 1953, 1954, 1955, 1956,
1958, 1962, 1963, 1969, 1970, 1971, 1972,
1976, 1977, 1981, 1988, 1993, 1996, 2000.

APPEARANCES 99/00

	P	Ap	(s)	Gls
Amir AGIC	M	22	(4)	
Edi BAJREKTAREVIC	D	15	(1)	1
Milan BOSKOVIC (YUG)	M	8		1
Rok CIRAR	D	13	(8)	1
Edis CAUSEVIC	M		(9)	
Nastja CEH	M	12	(1)	2
Goran DASOVIC (CRO)	M	14	(2)	1
Bogomir DEISINGER	D		(10)	
Ismet EKMECIC (BOS)	A	15		5
Franci FRIDL	D	24		
Dejan GRABIC	M		(1)	
Jasmin HANDANOVIC	G	1		
Sinisa JUKIC (CRO)	M	24		1
Jaksa JURKOVIC (CRO)	A	2	(7)	
Marko KMETEC	A	23	(1)	16
Dusan KOSIC	D	32		6
Selvad KUJOVIC	M	15	(13)	3
Gregor MIRTIC	D	9	(6)	
Goran MISKIC	M	6	(2)	
Issah MORO (GHA)	A	8	(4)	8
Milan OSTERC	A	16		6
Nihad PEJKOVIC	G	26		3
Jalen POKORN	M	7	(6)	
Blaz PUC	A	1	(7)	3
Ziga STARIC	D	2	(1)	
Miha SPORAR	D	9	(5)	2
Sani TRGO	M	2		
Dalibor VARKAS	G	6	(1)	
Samir ZULIC	D	22		
Drazen ZEZELJ	A	29	(2)	5

LEAGUE RESULTS 1999/2000

02/08/99	Feroterm Pohorje	A	3-0	Moro 3
08/08/99	Potrosnik Beltinci	H	5-0	Moro 2, Pejkovic (p), Ekmecic, Ceh
15/08/99	HIT Gorica	A	1-2	Kosic
22/08/99	Mura Murska Sobota	A	0-3	
29/08/99	Publikum Celje	H	3-0	Ceh, Ekmecic, Jukic
12/09/99	NK Dravograd	A	4-0	Kmetec 2, Zezelj, Ekmecic
19/09/99	NK Maribor	H	2-4	Moro 2
26/09/99	Primorje Ajdovscina	A	0-6	
03/10/99	NK Domzale	H	2-0	Ekmecic, Kujovic
17/10/99	Rudar Velenje	A	1-0	Kosic
24/10/99	Korotan Prevalje	H	1-5	Kujovic
31/10/99	Feroterm Pohorje	H	3-1	Kmetec 2, Ekmecic
03/11/99	Publikum Celje	A	0-3	
07/11/99	Potrosnik Beltinci	A	5-0	Puc 2, Bajrektarevic, Kmetec, Moro
14/11/99	HIT Gorica	H	4-0	Kmetec 2, Kosic, Boskovic
21/11/99	Mura Murska Sobota	H	2-1	Kmetec 2
27/02/00	NK Dravograd	H	4-2	Osterc, Zezelj, Kmetec, Dasovic
05/03/00	NK Maribor	A	0-0	
12/03/00	Primorje Ajdovscina	H	1-3	Kosic
19/03/00	NK Domzale	A	0-2	
22/03/00	Rudar Velenje	H	1-2	Kujovic
26/03/00	Korotan Prevalje	A	2-3	Zezelj, Kosic
02/04/00	Potrosnik Beltinci	H	3-3	Kmetec 2 (1p), Kosic
05/04/00	Publikum Celje	H	2-2	Sporar, Kmetec
09/04/00	Primorje Ajdovscina	A	2-3	Osterc 2
12/04/00	Korotan Prevalje	H	0-2	
16/04/00	HIT Gorica	A	0-3	
22/04/00	Rudar Velenje	H	2-2	Pejkovic (p), Sporar
30/04/00	NK Maribor	A	0-2	
03/05/00	Mura Murska Sobota	H	5-1	Osterc 3, Kmetec 2
07/05/00	NK Domzale	A	2-1	Pejkovic (p), Kmetec
14/05/00	NK Dravograd	H	0-1	
21/05/00	Feroterm Pohorje	A	4-1	Zezelj 2, Puc, Cirar

SPAIN

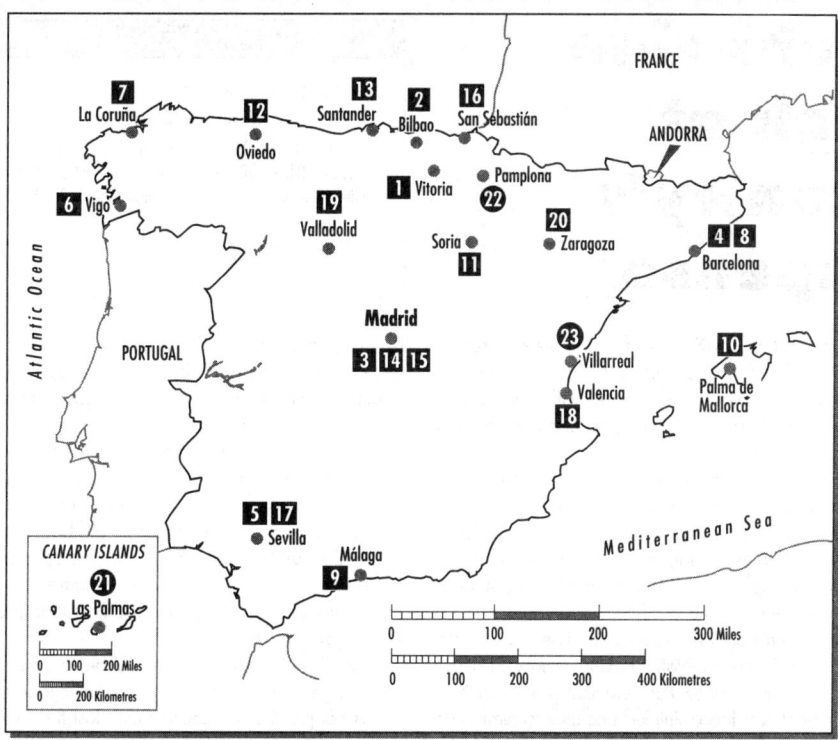

1	**DEPORTIVO ALAVES**	949		13	**RACING SANTANDER**	961
2	**ATHLETIC BILBAO**	950		14	**RAYO VALLECANO**	962
3	**ATLETICO MADRID**	951		15	**REAL MADRID**	963
4	**FC BARCELONA**	952		16	**REAL SOCIEDAD**	964
5	**REAL BETIS**	953		17	**SEVILLA FC**	965
6	**RC CELTA**	954		18	**VALENCIA CF**	966
7	**RC DEPORTIVO**	955		19	**REAL VALLADOLID**	967
8	**RCD ESPANYOL**	956		20	**REAL ZARAGOZA**	968
9	**MALAGA CF**	957		**Promoted clubs**		
10	**RCD MALLORCA**	958		21	**UD LAS PALMAS**	
11	**CD NUMANCIA**	959		22	**CA OSASUNA**	
12	**REAL OVIEDO**	960		23	**VILLARREAL CF**	

FIESTA IN THE CHAMPIONS' LEAGUE

Clubs ride high at country's expense

FEDERATION DIRECTORY

Real Federación Española de Fútbol
Calle Alberto Bosch 13, 28014 Madrid

tel - (914) 201362/203321   Year of Formation - 1913
fax - (914) 204294/203304   President - Angel María Villar
website - www.sportec.com/rfef   Manager - Gerardo González Otero

The best traditions of Spanish football were observed during the 1999/2000 season as the country's leading clubs collectively conquered Europe while the national team once again failed to live up to expectations at a major tournament.

All three of the Spanish clubs which participated in the UEFA Champions' League - Barcelona, Real Madrid and Valencia - succeeded in reaching the semi-finals. There was an all-Spanish final, too, with Real eventually collecting the trophy for the second time in three seasons and a record eighth time in all.

If only Spain's national team could rise to such lofty heights. The European Nations' Cup victory of 1964 remains their only significant achievement. Since then there has only ever been disappointment and underachievement. Euro 2000 was the latest chapter in a long-running story.

Shortlisted among the favourites in Belgium and Holland, José Antonio Camacho's side were entitled to feel confident. They had blitzed their way through the qualifying competition, amassing 42 goals in their eight matches, with superstar striker Raúl bagging 11 of them for himself to become the tournament's leading individual marksman. Camacho had emerged as a liberating force, freeing the team from the constraints imposed by the previous régime. In truth, the goals did begin to dry up during the build-up to the European Championship, but the success of Spain's clubs in the Champions' League merely added strength to the argument that 2000 was finally going to be Spain's year.

It took just 90 minutes for the bubble to burst. Spain's opening game with Norway was an unmitigated disaster. It was not just that Camacho's men lost the match. The manner of the defeat rekindled memories of the drab goalless draw against Paraguay at the 1998 World Cup when

LEAGUE CHAMPIONSHIP RESULTS 99/00

		1	2	3	4	5	6	7	8	9	10	11	12	13	14	15	16	17	18	19	20
1	Deportivo Alavés	–	1-2	2-0	2-1	2-0	1-0	2-1	0-0	2-1	2-2	2-2	1-0	2-1	0-1	1-3	2-1	0-0	0-1	1-0	0-2
2	Athletic Bilbao	2-1	–	4-2	0-4	1-0	1-0	2-3	2-1	2-2	1-1	2-1	1-1	2-2	1-2	2-2	1-1	1-1	1-0	1-0	2-2
3	Atlético Madrid	1-0	1-2	–	0-3	0-0	1-2	1-3	1-1	2-2	1-0	2-2	5-0	2-0	0-2	1-1	1-1	1-1	1-2	3-1	2-2
4	FC Barcelona	0-1	4-0	2-1	–	4-1	2-2	2-1	3-0	1-2	0-3	4-0	3-2	1-0	0-2	2-2	3-1	2-0	3-0	4-0	2-0
5	Real Betis	0-1	2-1	2-1	2-1	–	0-0	0-0	2-5	0-0	1-0	1-2	1-0	2-2	1-1	0-2	1-0	1-1	1-0	0-1	2-1
6	RC Celta	1-1	1-1	0-1	0-2	5-1	–	2-1	2-1	2-4	1-0	0-0	5-3	2-0	0-1	1-0	4-1	2-1	0-0	1-1	2-1
7	RC Deportivo	4-1	2-0	4-1	2-1	2-0	1-0	–	2-0	4-1	2-1	0-2	3-1	0-3	3-2	5-2	2-0	5-2	2-0	2-0	2-2
8	RCD Espanyol	2-3	0-0	3-1	1-1	3-0	3-0	0-0	–	0-2	1-2	3-1	2-1	1-0	5-1	0-2	0-0	2-2	3-2	1-1	1-1
9	Málaga CF	0-1	3-4	2-3	1-2	3-0	0-1	1-0	1-0	–	0-0	3-1	4-0	0-0	2-0	1-1	0-0	3-0	1-1	0-0	0-0
10	RCD Mallorca	2-0	2-1	1-2	3-2	4-0	1-0	2-2	1-3	2-1	–	3-0	1-1	2-1	1-2	2-1	3-1	1-0	0-0	2-0	1-1
11	CD Numancia	0-0	1-1	3-0	3-3	1-2	3-1	1-0	2-0	1-1	3-1	–	1-1	2-1	3-1	0-0	1-2	2-0	1-2	1-0	1-2
12	Real Oviedo	1-0	1-0	2-2	3-0	1-1	1-0	0-1	1-0	2-2	0-0	1-0	–	1-2	2-0	1-1	0-1	4-2	0-0	1-1	1-0
13	Racing Santander	0-0	2-2	2-1	1-2	1-1	3-0	0-0	2-2	2-3	1-1	1-1	3-1	–	1-1	1-1	0-0	2-2	1-1	1-1	1-2
14	Rayo Vallecano	0-1	1-2	1-1	1-1	1-3	1-0	2-0	2-1	4-1	2-1	0-0	1-2	1-2	–	2-3	2-0	1-3	4-1	0-1	0-1
15	Real Madrid	0-1	3-1	1-3	3-0	2-1	1-0	1-1	2-1	1-0	2-1	4-1	2-2	2-4	0-0	–	1-1	3-1	2-3	0-1	1-5
16	Real Sociedad	1-1	4-1	4-1	0-0	1-0	0-2	0-1	1-0	2-2	2-1	2-1	0-0	2-5	2-1	1-1	–	1-1	0-0	3-0	2-1
17	Sevilla FC	2-2	0-0	2-1	3-2	3-0	0-1	1-3	1-2	0-0	0-4	4-0	2-3	1-0	2-3	1-1	2-2	–	1-2	0-1	0-0
18	Valencia CF	0-2	2-0	2-0	3-1	3-1	1-1	2-0	1-2	2-2	1-0	4-0	6-2	1-2	3-1	1-1	4-0	2-0	–	0-0	2-1
19	Real Valladolid	1-1	1-0	1-0	0-2	0-3	1-3	4-1	1-0	4-2	2-1	2-0	2-1	1-1	0-1	2-0	2-1	0-0	1-1	–	1-1
20	Real Zaragoza	2-1	0-0	1-1	0-0	1-0	2-1	2-1	1-1	3-2	3-0	3-3	4-0	4-1	1-1	0-1	0-0	2-0	2-1	4-2	–

LEAGUE CHAMPIONSHIP FINAL TABLE 99/00

		Pd	Home					Away					Total					PT	GD
			W	D	L	F	A	W	D	L	F	A	W	D	L	F	A		
1	RC Deportivo	38	16	1	2	47	19	5	5	9	19	25	21	6	11	66	44	69	22
2	FC Barcelona	38	13	2	4	42	18	6	5	8	28	28	19	7	12	70	46	64	24
3	Valencia CF	38	12	4	3	40	16	6	6	7	19	23	18	10	10	59	39	64	20
4	Real Zaragoza	38	11	7	1	36	17	5	8	6	24	23	16	15	7	60	40	63	20
5	Real Madrid	38	9	4	6	31	27	7	10	2	27	21	16	14	8	58	48	62	10
6	Deportivo Alavés	38	10	4	5	23	18	7	6	6	18	19	17	10	11	41	37	61	4
7	RC Celta	38	10	5	4	31	20	5	3	11	14	23	15	8	15	45	43	53	2
8	Real Valladolid	38	11	3	5	26	20	3	8	8	10	24	14	11	13	36	44	53	-8
9	Rayo Vallecano	38	8	3	8	28	24	7	4	8	23	29	15	7	16	51	53	52	-2
10	RCD Mallorca	38	11	4	4	33	20	3	5	11	19	25	14	9	15	52	45	51	7
11	Athletic Bilbao	38	8	8	3	29	26	4	6	9	18	31	12	14	12	47	57	50	-10
12	Málaga CF	38	7	7	5	25	14	4	8	7	30	36	11	15	12	55	50	48	5
13	Real Sociedad	38	9	7	3	28	19	2	7	10	14	30	11	14	13	42	49	47	-7
14	RCD Espanyol	38	8	7	4	31	20	4	4	11	20	28	12	11	15	51	48	47	3
15	Racing Santander	38	3	13	3	25	22	7	3	9	27	28	10	16	12	52	50	46	2
16	Real Oviedo	38	9	7	3	23	13	2	5	12	21	47	11	12	15	44	60	45	-16
17	CD Numancia	38	9	6	4	30	18	2	6	11	17	41	11	12	15	47	59	45	-12
18	Real Betis	38	8	6	5	19	18	3	3	13	14	38	11	9	18	33	56	42	-23
19	Atlético Madrid	38	5	8	6	26	25	4	3	12	22	39	9	11	18	48	64	38	-16
20	Sevilla FC	38	5	6	8	25	27	0	7	12	17	40	5	13	20	42	67	28	-25

N.B. Where two or more teams are level on points, classification is determined by the results of the matches between them.

Spain, frustrated by a tight, well-organised, combative defence, lacked the skill or the richness of imagination to break it down. It didn't help that Raúl was not fit, nor that his in-form Real Madrid strike-partner Fernando Morientes had been left at home. The omission from the starting line-up of Valencia's man of the moment Gaizka Mendieta also hindered the Spanish cause. When he was belatedly introduced, Spain improved, but the damage had already been done when a rash error of judgment from goalkeeper Molina gifted the Norwegians a goal.

With Mendieta on from the start, Spain recovered to beat Slovenia 2-1 in their next game, but again it was an unconvincing performance. The situation before the final match with Yugoslavia in Bruges was that Spain needed a win to guarantee their progress to the next round. Three times they went behind, and with the clock on 93 minutes and the scoreline at 3-2 to Yugoslavia, Spain were virtually dead and buried. But then...the miracle fightback. A debatable penalty was converted by Mendieta to make it 3-3. And then, just seconds before the final whistle, striker Alfonso squeezed a superb left-foot shot inside the far post to send Spain and their supporters into raptures.

The prize for this astonishing great escape was first place in the group and a quarter-final encounter with France. Again Bruges was the venue, and again the match was compelling from start to finish. But this time Spain were unable to capitalise on their good fortune. For the second match running defender Abelardo went down in the area and was rewarded with a controversial last-gasp penalty, but on this occasion, with France leading 2-1, a bedraggled Raúl whacked his shot over the bar. Crucially, regular penalty-taker Mendieta had already been substituted.

And so another group of Spanish glory-hunters returned home with nothing other than dented pride and a few tarnished reputations. Camacho was the first in the firing line, mainly through his selection errors, but he was not held sufficiently culpable for his job to be under threat. After all, he had been hailed as a national messiah only a few weeks earlier.

Despite the general disappointment a number of players emerged from the tournament with credit. Mendieta and Guardiola were consistently productive in midfield, and there were memorable contributions - albeit in patches - from Alfonso, Etxeberria and Munitis. The ease with which the latter outplayed Lilian Thuram, one of the world's best defenders, in the quarter-final made him one of the few genuinely exciting newcomers in a tournament chiefly dominated by established stars.

Spain may struggle when they get to major tournaments but they remain experts at qualifying for them, and they should have little difficulty in reaching their seventh successive World Cup, having been drawn in a straight-forward group that reacquaints them with Austria and Israel, two teams they defeated convincingly both home and away en route to Euro 2000.

On the club front Spain will find the 1999/2000

season an extremely hard act to follow. It was a year in which the country replaced Italy as Europe's dominant football nation. The collective exploits in the Champions' League were phenomenal. The extended involvement of Real Madrid, Valencia and Barcelona was studded with several stunning highlights - Real romping into a 3-0 lead against holders Manchester United at Old Trafford, Valencia crushing Lazio 5-2 in the Mestalla, Barça storming back from the dead against Chelsea in the Nou Camp - and it was no fluke that each of the trio went as far as they did.

Perhaps the least spectacular advance was that of Real, the eventual winners. Beaten by Porto in the first round, they were twice mauled by Bayern Munich in the second group

phase. But they survived to gain their revenge on the Germans in the semi-finals and then, like all true champions, saved their very best performance of the entire competition for the final, when they demolished Valencia 3-0.

Although the end was glorious, Real's season for the most part was fractured and unsettling. Victory in Europe was achieved at the expense of a poor domestic campaign. In the autumn Real were an embarrassment in the league. They went eight matches without a win and only stopped the rot with a last-minute winner away to local rivals Rayo Vallecano, who had had the audacity to lead the table in the early weeks. There were problems galore. One of them was resolved when coach John Toshack was given the sack, allowing club loyalist Vicente

NATIONAL TEAM APPEARANCES 99/00

Coach - José Antonio CAMACHO	POL	AUT	CYP	ISR	BRA	ARG	POL	CRO	ITA	SWE	LUX	NOR	SLO	YUG	FRA	Cps	Gls
Santiago CAÑIZARES (18/12/69) - Valencia CF	G74	G	G78						s46		G60		G	G	G	26	-
Miguel Angel "MICHEL" SALGADO (22/10/75) - Real Madrid	D	D	D	D	D					D		D	D	D46	D	17	-
Francisco Jémez "PACO" (18/04/70) - Real Zaragoza	D	D		D	D	D	D	s46	D	D		D		D64	D	16	-
CESAR Martín (02/04/77) - RC Deportivo	D		D	s24												3	2
Agustín ARANZABAL (15/03/73) - Real Sociedad	D		D			D	D	D	D73	D	s78	D	D		D	21	-
Joseba ETXEBERRIA (05/09/77) - Athletic Bilbao	M71	M80	M46	M	M67	s46	M46	A82	M63	M46	s60	M71	M	s22	s72	30	7
Vicente ENGONGA (20/10/65) - RCD Mallorca	M	s72			s67		s65	M	s81	s63	M		s88			14	1
Francisco Javier FARINOS (29/03/78) - Valencia CF	M46															1	-
LUIS ENRIQUE Martínez (08/05/70) - FC Barcelona	M46	M	M60	M	M82	M46	M	M63								51	12
RAUL González (27/06/77) - Real Madrid	A	A	A	A	A85	A46	A		A77			A	A	A	A	35	17
Fernando MORIENTES (05/04/76) - Real Madrid	A62	A87		A77	A67	s73										12	9
Gaizka MENDIETA (27/03/74) - Valencia CF	s46	s80	s60	s69	s82	M73	s46	s46		s46	M60	s71	M	M	M56	17	4
Juan Carlos VALERON (17/06/75) - Atlético Madrid	s46	M72			M67	s67	M75	M	M81	M63	M60	M79	M88			14	-
Pedro Manuel MUNITIS (19/06/75) - Racing Santander	s62		s46		s67	s46			s77	s46	A			s46	M72	12	2
Julen GUERRERO (07/01/74) - Athletic Bilbao	s71	s87	M	M69		M67										38	13
José Francisco MOLINA (08/08/70) - Atlético Madrid	s74				G	G	G83	G	G46	G63		G				9	-
Fernando Ruiz HIERRO (23/03/68) - Real Madrid		D	D	D24			D	D46		D46	s60	D	D			73	23
Sergio Barjuán "SERGI" (28/12/71) - FC Barcelona		D	D	D					s46	D78			D			47	1
Josep GUARDIOLA (18/01/71) - FC Barcelona	M	M	M	M		M	M65		M77	M			M	M80	M	39	5
Ismael URZAIZ (07/10/71) - Athletic Bilbao		A	s77	s67	s22	A68	A77	A46	A46		A	s70	s64	s56		20	8
Antonio Jiménez "TONI" (12/10/70) - Atlético Madrid		s78	G													3	-
ABELARDO Fernández (19/03/70) - FC Barcelona				D			D	D		D		D	D	D	D	48	3
ALFONSO Pérez (26/09/72) - Real Betis				s85	A22			s46	A63		A	s71	A70	A	A	38	11
Albert FERRER (06/06/70) - Chelsea (ENG)					D											36	-
Miguel Angel NADAL (28/07/66) - RCD Mallorca					D											47	2
Juan VELASCO (17/05/77) - RC Celta						D	D	D		D						4	-
Salvador Ballesta "SALVA" (25/05/75) - Racing Santander						s68	s77									2	-
LUIS CEMBRANOS Martínez (06/06/72) - Rayo Vallecano						s75										1	-
Juan Manuel García "JUANMI" (09/03/71) - Real Zaragoza						s83										1	-
Francisco Javier González "FRAN" (14/07/69) - RC Deportivo							M46	M	M46	M60	M71		M22			16	2
VICTOR Manuel Fernández (17/04/74) - Real Valladolid							s63									1	-
Enrique Fernández ROMERO (23/06/77) - RC Deportivo							s82									1	-
Francisco Joaquín Pérez RUFETE (20/11/70) - CD Málaga									s63							1	-
Juan Francisco García "JUANFRAN" (15/07/76) - RC Celta									s73							1	-
Iván HELGUERA (28/03/75) - Real Madrid									s77	s46	D	s79	s80	M	M77	10	-
Iker CASILLAS (20/05/81) - Real Madrid										s63	s60					2	-
GERARD López (12/03/79) - Valencia CF										s63	s60				s77	3	-

del Bosque to rise from the club's junior section and take his place in the hot seat. But the troubles caused by the difficult adjustment of record signing Nicolas Anelka lingered on and on and reached crisis point in the spring when the errant Frenchman missed training and was subsequently suspended for 45 days. Only when he agreed to lose face publicly and admit the error of his ways was his re-integration permitted.

Another problem was the club's lack of a top-class goalkeeper following a long-term injury to German import Bodo Illgner. It was Toshack's utterances on this subject which led to his dismissal, but in fact it was not a problem at all because teenager Iker Casillas came in and had a quite magnificent season, which concluded with his well-earned selection for Spain's Euro 2000 squad.

Real represented Europe in the new Club World Championship in Brazil in mid-season, and the break clearly refreshed them, because shortly after they returned they lifted themselves all the way from 17th place back into the title frame. But a woeful end to the domestic campaign, with home defeats following one after another against Racing Santander, Alavés and Valladolid, ensured that they would not be champions of Spain as well as Europe. In fact, it was only by beating Valencia in the Stade de France that Real ensured their presence in the 2000/01 Champions' League.

Valencia were bitterly disappointed to fare so badly in Paris. But, then again, most of their best Champions' League displays had been reserved for their home stadium. Of the nine teams they faced in the Mestalla, only two - Bayern Munich and Manchester United - avoided defeat. Lazio and Barcelona were both crushed there, in the quarter-finals and semi-finals, respectively, and it was with those two brilliant performances that Valencia alerted the whole Continent to the strength in depth of the Spanish game.

The likes of Claudio López, Kily González, Mendieta, Gerard and Farinós all benefitted hugely from the input of the club's Argentinian coach Héctor Cúper. The former Mallorca boss arrived with a reputation for safety-first, defensive play, and when Valencia lost their four opening league fixtures, it looked as if he was heading for an early dismissal. Things could only get better and they did, rapidly. Impressive victories over Rangers in the Champions' League and Real Madrid in La Liga enabled Cúper to turn the corner, and from then

INTERNATIONAL HONOURS

World Cup Finals appearances: 1934, 1950 (4th), 1962, 1966, 1978, 1982 (2nd phase), 1986 (qtr-finals), 1990 (2nd round), 1994 (qtr-finals), 1998

European Championship appearances: 1964 (Winners), 1968, 1976, 1980, 1984 (runners-up), 1988, 1996 (qtr-finals), 2000 (qtr-finals)

European Club Competitions

Champions' Cup	Real Madrid (1956, 1957, 1958, 1959, 1960, 1966, 1998, 2000)
	FC Barcelona (1992)
Cup-winners' Cup	Atlético Madrid (1962)
	FC Barcelona (1979, 1982, 1989, 1997)
	Valencia CF (1980)
	Real Zaragoza (1995)
Fairs' Cup	FC Barcelona (1958, 1960, 1966)
	Valencia CF (1962, 1963)
	Real Zaragoza (1964)
UEFA Cup	Real Madrid (1985, 1986)
Super Cup	Valencia CF (1981)
	FC Barcelona (1992, 1998)
World Club Cup	Real Madrid (1960, 1998)
	Atlético Madrid (1974)

TOP SCORERS

27 SALVA Ballesta (Racing Santander)
24 CATANHA (Málaga CF)
 Jimmy Floyd HASSELBAINK (Atlético Madrid)
23 Savo MILOSEVIC (Real Zaragoza)
22 Roy MAKAAY (RC Deportivo)
19 DIEGO TRISTAN (RCD Mallorca)
17 RAUL González (Real Madrid)
15 Patrick KLUIVERT (FC Barcelona)
13 Gaizka MENDIETA (Valencia CF)
 VICTOR Manuel Fernández (Real Valladolid)
12 JUAN CARLOS Gómez (Sevilla FC)
 Fernando MORIENTES (Real Madrid)
 RIVALDO (FC Barcelona)

NATIONAL TEAM RESULTS 99/00

18/08/99	Poland	A	Warsaw	2-1	Morientes (55), Munitis (67)
04/09/99	Austria (ECQ)	A	Vienna	3-1	Raúl (22), Hierro (55), Luis Enrique (87)
08/09/99	Cyprus (ECQ)	H	Badajoz	8-0	Urzaiz (20, 25, 38), Guerrero (33, 42, 57), César (82), Hierro (89)
10/10/99	Israel (ECQ)	H	Albacete	3-0	Morientes (30), César (37), Raúl (21)
13/11/99	Brazil	H	Vigo	0-0	
17/11/99	Argentina	H	Seville	0-2	
26/01/00	Poland	H	Cartagena	3-0	Raúl (15), Urzaiz (53, 56)
23/02/00	Croatia	A	Split	0-0	
29/03/00	Italy	H	Barcelona	2-0	Alfonso (61), Abelardo (80)
03/06/00	Sweden	A	Gothenburg	1-1	Guardiola (42p)
07/06/00	Luxembourg	A	Luxembourg	1-0	Mendieta (2)
13/06/00	Norway (ECF)	N	Rotterdam	0-1	
18/06/00	Slovenia (ECF)	N	Amsterdam	2-1	Raúl (4), Etxeberria (60)
21/06/00	Yugoslavia (ECF)	N	Bruges	4-3	Alfonso (38, 90), Munitis (51), Mendieta (90p)
25/06/00	France (ECF)	N	Bruges	1-2	Mendieta (38p)

DOMESTIC CUP 99/00

SECOND ROUND
Barakaldo CF v Villarreal CF 0-0; 0-1
(Villarreal CF 1-0)
RC Deportivo v Málaga CF 1-0; 1-2
(2-2; RC Deportivo on away goal)
Athletic Bilbao v Rayo Vallecano 0-1; 0-0
(Rayo Vallecano 1-0)
Sporting Gijón v RC Celta 0-3; 2-4
(RC Celta 7-2)
CA Osasuna v Valencia CF 3-0; 0-2
(CA Osasuna 3-2)
CD Logroñés v Real Oviedo 3-2; 1-2
(4-4; Real Oviedo on away goals)
Real Unión Irún v Deportivo Alavés 1-0; 1-2
(2-2; Real Unión Irún on away goal)
UE Lleida v SD Eibar 0-0; 1-1
(1-1; UE Lleida on away goal)
CD Ourense v RCD Mallorca 2-2; 2-1
(CD Ourense 4-3)
Real Zaragoza v Racing Santander 2-1; 4-1
(Real Zaragoza 6-2)
Albacete Balompié v RCD Espanyol 0-0; 0-2
(RCD Espanyol 2-0)
Mérida CP v Real Betis 1-0; 1-0
(Mérida CP 2-0)
Polideportivo Almería v FC Barcelona 0-0; 0-2
(FC Barcelona 2-0)
UD Las Palmas v Atlético Madrid 2-2; 0-1
(Atlético Madrid 3-2)
CD Tenerife v SD Compostela 2-2; 0-2
(SD Compostela 4-2)
bye - Real Madrid

1/8 FINALS
Real Zaragoza v Real Madrid 0-0; 0-2
(Real Madrid 2-0)
Real Unión Irún v Atlético Madrid 0-3; 0-2
(Atlético Madrid 5-0)
CA Osasuna v RC Deportivo 1-0; 1-0
(CA Osasuna 2-0)
UE Lleida v Rayo Vallecano 2-3; 1-3
(Rayo Vallecano 6-3)
RCD Espanyol v RC Celta 2-1; 1-0
(RCD Espanyol 3-1)
Mérida CP v Real Oviedo 1-0; 0-0
(Mérida CP 1-0)
SD Compostela v Villarreal CF 3-0; 0-3
(3-3; SD Compostela on pens.)
CD Ourense v FC Barcelona 1-2; 0-0
(FC Barcelona 2-1)

QUARTER-FINALS
Real Madrid 1 (Zárate 52), Mérida CP 0
Mérida CP 2 (Illgner 40og, Prieto 117),
Real Madrid 1 (Zárate 112) (aet)
(2-2; Real Madrid on away goal)
Atlético Madrid 0, Rayo Vallecano 0
Rayo Vallecano 2 (Míchel Carrilero 26, 50),
Atlético Madrid 2 (Hasselbaink 2, Baraja 89)
(2-2; Atlético Madrid on away goals)
RCD Espanyol 5 (Galca 3p, 45, 48,
Toni Velamazán 22, Arteaga 82),
SD Compostela 1 (Sion 85)
SD Compostela 1 (Gudelj 73p), RCD Espanyol 0
(RCD Espanyol 5-2)

CA Osasuna 0, FC Barcelona 4 (Luis Enrique 36, 61,
Dani 74, Kluivert 89)
FC Barcelona 2 (Litmanen 2, Dani 68), CA Osasuna 0
(FC Barcelona 6-0)

SEMI-FINALS
Real Madrid 0, RCD Espanyol 0
RCD Espanyol 1 (Posse 29), Real Madrid 0
(RCD Espanyol 1-0)
Atlético Madrid 3 (Hasselbaink 29, Baraja 46,
Hugo Leal 52), FC Barcelona 0
FC Barcelona v Atlético Madrid void
(Atlético Madrid 3-0)

FINAL
27/05/2000, Valencia
RCD ESPANYOL 2 Tamudo (3), Sergio (85)
ATLETICO MADRID 1 Hasselbaink (90)
referee - López Nieto (ESP)
RCD ESPANYOL - Cavallero; Cristóbal, Nando,
Pochettino, Roger; Toni Velamazán, Sergio, Galca,
Arteaga; Posse (Rotchen 78), Tamudo (Serrano 71).
ATLETICO MADRID - Toni Jiménez; Aguilera (Solari
77), Gaspar, Santi, Gamarra (Luque 53), Capdevila;
Valerón, Hugo Leal, Baraja; Kiko, Hasselbaink.

---

on his stock rose repeatedly, culminating in the unforgettable victories against Lazio and Barça.

Barcelona might have known that Valencia would bar their route to Champions' League glory. They had long suffered a complex against the team from down the Mediterranean coast, and Claudio López had developed a habit of becoming their chief excutioner, so it was doubly fitting that the Argentinian should score the 90th-minute goal in the first leg of the semi-final that gave Valencia a 4-1 win, thereby rendering the Catalans' task virtually impossible for the re-match in the Nou Camp.

Louis van Gaal's side had come back from 3-1 down against Chelsea in the previous round, but they exhibited no such powers of recovery against Valencia and were extremely lucky to win the second leg, having been distinctly second best once again. That defeat proved a major let-down for the Barcelona supporters because for most of the competition their team had been the most impressive on show. With world-class superstars Figo and Rivaldo working their magic on a regular basis, Barça

came through both of their groups unbeaten, averaging three goals a game.

Like Real Madrid, Barcelona's efforts in Europe had an adverse effect when it came to administering their domestic duties. Leaders early on, they went through a really rough period in November - the month of the club's centenary - losing four matches in a row. Never again did they return to the top of the table, and only once - in March, after a 3-0 beating by Real Madrid - did they put together a run of form capable of lifting them back into serious contention.

The Champions' League defeat by Valencia knocked the stuffing out of them, and with players flagging through fatigue, Barcelona's season gradually petered out, leaving them with nothing to show for nine months of intense combat on three fronts. Semi-finalists in the Champions' League, they also reached that stage of the Copa del Rey before refusing to play the second leg of their tie with Atlético Madrid, the official reason being that their squad had been almost totally denuded by international call-ups. The unofficial reason for the boycott was that Barça had

PLAYERS OF THE SEASON

GAIZKA MENDIETA

Valencia's blond skipper confirmed in 1999/2000 the vast potential he had hinted at the previous season. A long hard campaign for club and country yielded a steady string of brilliant performances from the classy midfielder. His profile raised by the Champions' League, which he embellished with five goals, including two marvellous strikes at Ibrox and the Nou Camp, he enhanced it even further at Euro 2000 where he was one of Spain's most effective and imaginative players. It was thanks to him that Spain gained their victories over Slovenia and Yugoslavia, but when his country needed him most, to take the last-minute penalty against France in the quarter-final, he was not there. Coach Camacho had substituted him. Who knows what might have become of Spain's Euro 2000 adventure had he, rather than Raúl, stepped up to take that vital spot-kick?...

SALVA

There was strong competition for the 'Pichichi' award in 1999/2000. Yugoslavia's Milosevic, Brazil's Catanha, Holland's Makaay and Hasselbaink all kept chipping away on behalf of La Liga's foreign legion, but ultimately the prize went to a Spaniard - and a fairly unknown Spaniard at that. Salvador Ballesta, aka Salva, was regarded as no more than a journeyman striker at the start of the season, but the Racing Santander hitman soon got people to notice him, scoring six goals in his first four games and then another seven in two games the following month. He went through a barren spell during February and March but returned with a vengeance in the final weeks to lift his final total to 27 goals - the best in the division. Called up by national team boss Camacho for a couple of friendlies, he was later discarded, with his Racing team-mate Pedro Munitis travelling to Euro 2000 instead of him. The big shock came at the end of the season when, with several clubs to choose from, he

opted to move to Atlético Madrid, who had just been relegated to the Second Division.

HELGUERA

A pre-season signing from Espanyol, Iván Helguera (below) was one of the less hyped of Real Madrid's many new arrivals, but while the likes of McManaman, Baljic and Anelka blew more cold than hot, he was a picture of consistency. His chief contribution was to plug the gap in the defence vacated by the injured Fernando Hierro - a task he performed with great style, providing the extra security which allowed Fernando Redondo to indulge in the more creative aspects of his play. Like Hierro, Helguera can flit seamlessly between defence and midfield. An excellent tackler and distributor, the 25-year-old demonstrated both in the Champions' League and at Euro 2000 that he has a very bright future ahead of him both at club and international level.

been well beaten in the first leg and saw the domestic Cup as an unwanted distraction. Barcelona could do no better than finish second in the league. They had been the favourites to win all three competitions but ended up with nothing. That was the trigger for long-serving president Josep Lluis Núñez to throw in the towel and call for new elections. Without the support of a president who had

always backed him, Van Gaal decided that it was time for him to leave as well. Although he had surrounded himself with his fellow countrymen, the haughty Dutchman never felt completely at home at the Nou Camp. He was unable to bond with the fans, and a fall-out during the season with World and European Footballer of the Year Rivaldo did nothing to enhance his popularity.

EUROPEAN CUPS 99/00

CHAMPIONS' CUP
● FC BARCELONA
Champions' League
1st match AIK (SWE)
A 2-1 Abelardo (85), Dani (90)
Hesp, De Boer R., De Boer F., Bogarde (Abelardo 26), Sergi, Litmanen, Xavi (Gabri 77), Cocu, Figo, Kluivert (Dani 74), Rivaldo.

2nd match FIORENTINA (ITA)
H 4-2 Figo (7), Luis Enrique (10), Rivaldo (67p, 69)
Hesp, De Boer R., Reiziger, Bogarde, Sergi, Luis Enrique, Guardiola (Xavi 79), Cocu (Zenden 75), Figo, Kluivert (Dani 60), Rivaldo.

3rd match ARSENAL (ENG)
H 1-1 Luis Enrique (16)
Hesp, Reiziger (De Boer R. 70), De Boer F., Bogarde, Sergi, Luis Enrique (Litmanen 76), Guardiola, Cocu, Figo, Dani, Rivaldo.

4th match ARSENAL (ENG)
A 4-2 Rivaldo (13p), Luis Enrique (15), Figo (55), Cocu (69)
Arnau, Reiziger, Abelardo, Bogarde, Sergi, Luis Enrique (Gabri 69), Guardiola (Déhu 90), Cocu (Zenden 90), Figo, Kluivert, Rivaldo.

5th match AIK (SWE)
H 5-0 Kluivert (14, 33), Zenden (42), Gabri (53), Déhu (56)
Arnau, Puyol (Nano 46), Abelardo (Reiziger 80), Déhu, Zenden, Litmanen (Mario 46), Xavi, Gabri, Simão, Kluivert, De Boer R..

6th match FIORENTINA (ITA)
A 3-3 Figo (19), Rivaldo (43, 73)
Arnau, De Boer R. (Puyol 46), Déhu, Bogarde, Zenden, Luis Enrique, Guardiola (Xavi 46), Cocu, Figo, Kluivert, Rivaldo.

7th match HERTHA BSC BERLIN (GER)
A 1-1 Luis Enrique (13)
Hesp, Reiziger, Déhu, De Boer F., Zenden, Luis Enrique, Guardiola, Cocu, Figo, Kluivert (Dani 71), De Boer R. (Simão 68).

8th match SPARTA PRAHA (CZE)
H 5-0 Kluivert (44, 70), Luis Enrique (45, 76), Guardiola (60)
Arnau, Reiziger (Xavi 83), Déhu, De Boer F., Zenden, Luis Enrique (De Boer R. 74), Guardiola, Cocu, Figo (De Boer R. 85), Kluivert, Rivaldo.

9th match FC PORTO (POR)
H 4-2 Rivaldo (15, 87), De Boer F. (22), Kluivert (44)
Hesp, Puyol (Reiziger 46), Abelardo, De Boer F., Zenden (Déhu 51), Luis Enrique, Guardiola, Cocu, Figo (De Boer R. 85), Kluivert, Rivaldo.

10th match FC PORTO (POR)
A 2-0 Abelardo (38), Rivaldo (58)
Hesp, Puyol, Abelardo, De Boer F., Bogarde, De Boer R., Guardiola, Cocu (Gabri 46), Figo (Xavi 90), Kluivert, Rivaldo (Dani 74).

11th match HERTHA BSC BERLIN (GER)
H 3-1 Xavi (10), Gabri (49), Kluivert (82)
Hesp, Puyol, Abelardo (Déhu 53), De Boer F., Bogarde, De Boer R. (Litmanen 70), Xavi, Gabri, Figo (Simão 46), Kluivert, Rivaldo.

12th match SPARTA PRAHA (CZE)
A 2-1 Gabri (52, 88)
Hesp, Reiziger, Déhu, De Boer F., Bogarde, Gabri, Guardiola (Xavi 90), Cocu (Litmanen 74), Simão, Dani, Rivaldo (De Boer R. 46).

Quarter-final CHELSEA (ENG)
A 1-3 Figo (62)
Hesp, Puyol (Litmanen 46), Abelardo, De Boer F., Bogarde, Gabri, Xavi, Cocu, Figo, Kluivert (Dani 70), Rivaldo.

H 5-1 (aet) Rivaldo (23, 97p), Figo (44), Dani (83), Kluivert (104)
Hesp, Reiziger (Sergi 105), De Boer F., Puyol (Abelardo 84), Gabri, Guardiola, Cocu, Rivaldo, Figo, Kluivert, Zenden (Dani 71).

Semi-final VALENCIA CF (ESP)
A 1-4 Pellegrino (27og)
Hesp, Puyol (Bogarde 46), De Boer F., Reiziger, Gabri, Guardiola, Rivaldo, Cocu, Dani (Litmanen 59), Kluivert, Zenden (Simão 74).

H 2-1 De Boer F. (77), Cocu (90)
Hesp, Reiziger, Abelardo (Litmanen 76), De Boer F., Cocu, Xavi, Guardiola (Sergi 68), Zenden (Simão 61), Rivaldo, Figo, Kluivert.

● RCD MALLORCA
Qualifying round MOLDE FK (NOR)
A 0-0
Burgos, Olaizola, Niño, Siviero, Soler M., Lauren, Engonga, Ibagaza (Serrizuela 83), Stankovic, Quinteros (Gabrich 65), Carlos (Djokac 78).

H 1-1 Stankovic (22p)
Franco, Olaizola, Niño, Siviero, Soler M., Lauren, Engonga (Diego Tristán 85), Ibagaza, Stankovic, Carlos (Soler F. 78), Quinteros (Gabrich 68).

● REAL MADRID
Champions' League
1st match OLYMPIAKOS (GRE)
A 3-3 Sávio (24), Roberto Carlos (32), Raúl (80)
Casillas, Michel Salgado, Hierro (Helguera 60), Júlio César, Roberto Carlos, Geremi, Redondo (Guti 72), McManaman, Raúl, Sávio, Morientes.

2nd match MOLDE FK (NOR)
H 4-1 Morientes (27), Sávio (60, 69p), Guti (81)
Casillas, Michel Salgado, Iván Campo, Júlio César, Roberto Carlos, Helguera, Redondo, McManaman (Baljic 64), Morientes, Sávio (Eto'o 74), Anelka (Guti 55).

3rd match FC PORTO (POR)
H 3-1 Morientes (23), Helguera (37), Hierro (68p)
Bizzarri, Michel Salgado, Hierro, Júlio César, Roberto Carlos, Helguera (Sanchis 84), Redondo, McManaman (Seedorf 57), Raúl, Sávio (Eto'o 90), Morientes.

4th match FC PORTO (POR)
A 1-2 Peixe (68og)
Illgner, Michel Salgado, Hierro, Iván Campo, Roberto Carlos, Geremi (Guti 66), Redondo, Raúl, Sávio, Anelka (Seedorf 48), Morientes.

5th match OLYMPIAKOS (GRE)
H 3-0 Raúl (21), Morientes (64), Roberto Carlos (83)
Bizarri, Geremi (Michel Salgado 62), Hierro (Iván Campo 42), Júlio César, Roberto Carlos, Helguera, Redondo, Seedorf, Raúl, Guti (McManaman 71), Morientes.

6th match MOLDE FK (NOR)
A 1-0 Karembeu (43)
Bizarri, Michel Salgado, Júlio César, Iván Campo, Karanka, Roberto Carlos, Karembeu, Helguera, Sanchis, Seedorf, Aranda (Eto'o 55).

EUROPEAN CUPS 99/00 (CONTINUED)

7th match DYNAMO KYIV (UKR)
A 2-1   Morientes (17), Raúl (48)
Bizarri, Míchel Salgado (Iván Campo 27), Karembeu, Júlio César, Roberto Carlos, Seedorf (Karanka 90), Helguera, Guti, Sávio (Sanchis 67), Raúl, Morientes.

8th match ROSENBORG BK (NOR)
H 3-1   Raúl (18), Sávio (84), Roberto Carlos (90)
Casillas, Karembeu, Hierro, Karanka, Roberto Carlos, Helguera, Redondo, Guti (Seedorf 63; Anelka 90), Sávio, Raúl, Morientes (Júlio César 88).

9th match FC BAYERN MÜNCHEN (GER)
H 2-4   Morientes (26), Raúl (47)
Casillas, Míchel Salgado, Hierro, Karanka, Roberto Carlos, Geremi, Redondo, Guti (McManaman 60), Raúl, Morientes (Ognjenovic 78), Anelka.

10th match FC BAYERN MÜNCHEN (GER)
A 1-4   Helguera (69)
Casillas, Míchel Salgado, Hierro, Karanka (Anelka 69), Roberto Carlos, Geremi (McManaman 63), Redondo, Helguera, Guti, Raúl, Morientes (Iván Campo 84).

11th match DYNAMO KYIV (UKR)
H 2-2   Raúl (13p), Roberto Carlos (71)
Casillas, Míchel Salgado, Hierro, Karanka, Roberto Carlos, Geremi (Helguera 80), Redondo, McManaman (Meca 60), Guti, Raúl, Morientes.

12th match ROSENBORG BK (NOR)
A 1-0   Raúl (3)
Casillas, Míchel Salgado, Iván Campo, Hierro (Karanka 46), Roberto Carlos, McManaman, Helguera, Redondo, Guti, Raúl, Aganzo (Baljic 55; Karembeu 85).

Quarter-final MANCHESTER UNITED (ENG)
H 0-0   Casillas, Míchel Salgado, Iván Campo, Karanka, Roberto Carlos, McManaman, Helguera, Redondo, Sávio (Baljic 75), Morientes (Ognjenovic 85), Raúl.
A 3-2   Keane (20og), Raúl (50, 52)
Casillas, Míchel Salgado, Iván Campo, Karanka, Roberto Carlos, McManaman (Júlio César 90), Helguera, Redondo, Sávio (Geremi 65), Morientes (Anelka 73), Raúl.

Semi-final FC BAYERN MÜNCHEN (GER)
H 2-0   Anelka (4), Jeremies (33og)
Casillas, Míchel Salgado, Iván Campo, Helguera, Karanka, Roberto Carlos, McManaman, Redondo, Raúl, Morientes (Sávio 61), Anelka (Baljic 80).
A 1-2   Anelka (31)
Casillas, Geremi, Iván Campo, Helguera, Júlio César, Roberto Carlos, McManaman (Baljic 90), Redondo, Raúl, Anelka (Sanchis 89), Sávio (Karembeu 81).

Final VALENCIA CF (ESP)
3-0   Morientes (39), McManaman (67), Raúl (75)
Casillas, Míchel Salgado (Hierro 84), Iván Campo, Helguera, Karanka, Roberto Carlos, McManaman, Redondo, Raúl, Anelka (Sanchis 79), Morientes (Sávio 71).

● **VALENCIA CF**
Qualifying round HAPOEL HAIFA (ISR)
A 2-0   López (68), Farinós (75)
Cañizares, Angloma, Björklund, Djukic, Fagiani, Angulo, Albelda, Farinós (Gerard 80), Mendieta, López, Ilie (Sánchez 65).

H 2-0   Sánchez (59, 65)
Cañizares, Angloma, Björklund, Djukic, Fagiani, Angulo, Albelda, Farinós (Gerard 69), Mendieta, López (Kily González 84), Sánchez.

Champions' League
1st match RANGERS (SCO)
H 2-0   Moore (56og), Kily González (73)
Cañizares, Angloma, Björklund, Pellegrino, Carboni, Mendieta, Albelda, Gerard, Kily González, López (Ilie 70), Sánchez (Angulo 80).

2nd match PSV (HOL)
A 1-1   López (4)
Cañizares, Angloma, Björklund, Pellegrino, Carboni, Mendieta, Albelda, Gerard, Kily González, López (Oscar 90), Sánchez (Angulo 73).

3rd match FC BAYERN MÜNCHEN (GER)
A 1-1   Gerard (79)
Palop, Angloma, Björklund, Pellegrino, Carboni, Mendieta (Angulo 86), Albelda, Gerard, Kily González (Farinós 84), López, Sánchez (Ilie 61).

4TH match FC BAYERN MÜNCHEN (GER)
H 1-1   Ilie (11)
Palop, Angulo, Björklund (Djukic 19), Pellegrino, Carboni, Mendieta (Farinós 65), Albelda, Gerard, Kily González (Oscar 86), Ilie, López.

5th match RANGERS (SCO)
A 2-1   Mendieta (35), López (45)
Palop, Angulo, Djukic, Pellegrino, Carboni, Mendieta (Soria 80), Albelda, Gerard, Kily González (Farinós 67), Ilie (Sánchez 60), López.

6th match PSV (HOL)
H 1-0   López (70)
Palop, Angulo, Pellegrino, Djukic, Carboni, Mendieta, Farinós, Gerard, Kily González, López (Oscar 76).

7th match GIRONDINS DE BORDEAUX (FRA)
H 3-0   Farinós (60), Ilie (69), Kily González (90)
Palop, Angloma, Pellegrino, Djukic, Carboni, Farinós (Angulo 79), Mendieta, Gerard, Kily González, Ilie (Albelda 75), López (Sánchez 90).

8th match MANCHESTER UNITED (ENG)
A 0-3   Palop, Angloma, Björklund, Djukic, Pellegrino, Carboni, Mendieta, Milla, Farinós, Oscar (Sánchez 68), López (Vlaovic 85).

9th match FIORENTINA (ITA)
A 0-1   Cañizares, Angloma, Djukic, Pellegrino, Carboni, Farinós, Milla (Angulo 26), Gerard, Kily González, López, Ilie (Sánchez 80).

10th match FIORENTINA (ITA)
H 2-0   Ilie (35), Mendieta (90p)
Cañizares, Angloma, Djukic, Pellegrino, Carboni, Mendieta, Gerard, Farinós, Kily González (Angulo 90), López, Ilie (Oscar 75).

11th match GIRONDINS DE BORDEAUX (FRA)
A 4-1   Djukic (41), Mendieta (48p), Kily González (72), Sánchez (90)
Cañizares, Angloma, Djukic, Pellegrino, Carboni, Mendieta (Björklund 55), Gerard, Farinós, Kily González (Oscar 85), Sánchez, Ilie (Angulo 73).

12th match MANCHESTER UNITED (ENG)
H 0-0   Cañizares, Angloma, Djukic, Pellegrino, Carboni, Angulo, Farinós, Gerard, Kily González, López, Sánchez (Ilie 70).

EUROPEAN CUPS 99/00 (CONTINUED)

Quarter-final LAZIO (ITA)

H 5-2   Angulo (2), Gerard (4, 40, 79), López (90)
Cañizares, Angloma, Djukic, Pellegrino, Carboni, Angulo, Farinós, Gerard, Kily González, López, Sánchez (Oscar 81).

A 0-1   Cañizares, Angloma, Djukic, Pellegrino, Björklund, Mendieta (Albelda 60), Farinós, Gerard, Kily González, Angulo (Oscar 81), López.

Semi-final FC BARCELONA (ESP)

H 4-1   Angulo (9, 42), Mendieta (45p), López (90)
Cañizares, Angloma, Djukic, Pellegrino, Carboni, Mendieta, Gerard (Sánchez 83), Farinós, Kily González, Abgulo (Albelda 77), López.

A 1-2   Mendieta (70)
Cañizares, Angloma (Gerardo 86), Djukic, Pellegrino, Carboni, Mendieta, Farinós (Sánchez 90), Gerard, Kily González (Albelda 73), Angulo, López.

Final REAL MADRID (ESP)

0-3
Cañizares, Angloma, Djukic, Pellegrino, Gerardo (Ilie 68), Mendieta, Farinós, Gerard, Kily González, Angulo, López.

UEFA CUP
● **ATLETICO MADRID**
1st round ANKARAGÜCÜ (TUR)

H 3-0   Gamarra (41), Hasselbaink (46), Paunovic (59)
Molina, Gaspar (Paunovic 46), Gamarra, Chamot, Aguilera, Bejbl (Solari 46), Baraja, Capdevila, Valerón, Correa, Hasselbaink (Pablo García 84).

A 0-1   Molina, Pilipauskas, Chamot, Gustavo, Toni, Hugo Leal (Aguilera 90), Lardín, Bejbl, Roberto (Pablo García 78), Solari (Santi 59), Correa.

2nd round AMICA WRONKI (POL)

H 1-0   Baraja (86)
Molina, Gamarra, Santi, Chamot, Aguilera (Baraja 46), Bejbl, Valerón, Capdevila, Solari (Hugo Leal 83), Hasselbaink, José Mari (Correa 46).

A 4-1   Hasselbaink (30), Capdevila (44), Baraja (51), Correa (84)
Molina, Gaspar, Chamot, Gamarra, Capdevila, José Mari, Bejbl, Baraja (Valerón 70), Solari (Aguilera 59), Correa, Hasselbaink (Paunovic 83).

3rd round VFL WOLFSBURG (GER)

A 3-2   Aguilera (6, 58), Hasselbaink (37)
Molina, Gaspar, Santi, Gustavo, Toni, Aguilera, Bejbl, Baraja (Valerón 76), Solari (Roberto 84), José Mari, Hasselbaink (Correa 86).

H 2-1   Hasselbaink (4), Correa (86)
Molina, Gaspar (Chamot 75), Santi, Gamarra, Gustavo, Paunovic, Bejbl (Hugo Leal 46), Baraja, Solari, Correa, Hasselbaink (Pilipauskas 46).

4th round RC LENS (FRA)

H 2-2   Hasselbaink (24, 79)
Molina, Aguilera, Santi, Ayala, Gamarra, Capdevila (Toni Muñoz 85), Hugo Leal, Bejbl (Baraja 34), Valerón, Kiko, Hasselbaink.

A 2-4   Hasselbaink (45), Kiko (64)
Molina, Aguilera, Gamarra, Ayala, Capdevila, Njegus, Bejbl, Valerón (Hugo Leal 81), Solari (Kiko 46), Roberto (Correa 68), Hasselbaink.

● **RC CELTA**
1st round LAUSANNE-SPORTS (SUI)

A 2-3   Revivo (61), Karpin (67p)
Dutruel, Velasco, Cáceres, Djorovic, Juanfran, Makelele, Celades (Giovanella 68), Karpin, Revivo, López (Kaviedes 61), McCarthy (Mostovoi 85).

H 4-0   McCarthy (11, 85, 89), Mostovoi (76)
Dutruel, Velasco (Sergio 46), Cáceres, Djorovic, Juanfran, Makelele, Giovanella, López (Mostovoi 61), Karpin, Revivo (Tomás 79), McCarthy.

2nd round ARIS (GRE)

A 2-2   Karpin (41, 42)
Dutruel, Velasco, Cáceres, Djorovic, Juanfran, Makelele, Giovanella, Karpin (Celades 89), Mostovoi (López 81), Tomás (Sergio 68), McCarthy.

H 2-0   Djorovic (66), Turdó (90)
Dutruel, Velasco, Cáceres, Djorovic, Juanfran, Makelele, Celades, Karpin (Tomás 89), Mostovoi, Revivo (López 60), McCarthy (Turdó 60).

3rd round SL BENFICA (POR)

H 7-0   Karpin (19p, 53), Makelele (29), Turdó (39, 50), Juanfran (42), Mostovoi (60)
Dutruel, Velasco, Cáceres, Djorovic, Juanfran (Coria 66), Makelele, Giovanella, Karpin, Mostovoi (Tomás 75), López, Turdó (McCarthy 57).

A 1-1   McCarthy (19)
Pinto, Coria, Cáceres, Sergio, Juanfran (Adriano 63), Mazinho, Celades, Karpin (Kaviedes 46), Revivo, Tomás, McCarthy (Jonathan 75).

4th round JUVENTUS (ITA)

A 0-1   Pinto, Celades, Cáceres, Sergio, Juanfran, Karpin, Makelele, López, Mostovoi, Revivo (Tomás 75), McCarthy.

H 4-0   Makelele (1), Birindelli (30og), McCarthy (46, 69)
Pinto, Celades, Cáceres, Sergio, Juanfran, Makelele, Giovanella, Karpin, Mostovoi (Revivo 58), López (Tomás 78), McCarthy (Mazinho 80).

Quarter-final RC LENS (FRA)

H 0-0   Pinto, Celades, Cáceres, Sergio, Juanfran, Makelele, Giovanella (Velasco 63), Karpin, Revivo (Hoogendorp 63), López, McCarthy.

A 1-2   Revivo (55)
Pinto, Velasco, Cáceres, Sergio, Juanfran, Makelele, Giovanella, Karpin, Revivo, López (Hoogendorp 74), McCarthy.

● **RC DEPORTIVO**
1st round STABAEK IF (NOR)

A 0-1   Songo'o, Manuel Pablo, Naybet, César, Romero, Víctor (Iván 85), Jokanovic (Fernando 62), Mauro Silva, Djalminha, Pauleta, Makaay (Turu Flores 75).

H 2-0   Jokanovic (37), Flávio Conceição (62)
Songo'o, Manuel Pablo, César, Naybet, Romero, Víctor (Scaloni 68), Mauro Silva, Jokanovic (Flávio Conceição 46), Djalminha, Makaay (Pauleta 77), Turu Flores.

2nd round MONTPELLIER HSC (FRA)

H 3-1   Pauleta (17), Djalminha (50p), Makaay (53)
Songo'o, Manuel Pablo, Naybet, Donato, Romero, Makaay, Mauro Silva, Jokanovic, Djalminha (Scaloni 87), Víctor (Fernando 67), Pauleta (Turu Flores 58).

A 2-0   Makaay (45), Pauleta (83)
Songo'o, Manuel Pablo, Naybet, Donato, Romero, Mauro Silva, Jokanovic, Víctor (Scaloni 75), Djalminha (Flávio Conceição 80), Fernando, Makaay (Pauleta 60).

3rd round PANATHINAIKOS (GRE)

H 4-2   Olivares (7og), Pauleta (12), Djalminha (14), Donato (30)
Songo'o, Scaloni, Donato, Naybet, Romero, Mauro Silva (Jaime 46), Flávio Conceição, Makaay, Djalminha, Fernando (Fran 74), Pauleta (Bassir 33).

EUROPEAN CUPS 99/00 (CONTINUED)

A 1-1   Makaay (90)
> Songo'o, Manuel Pablo, Donato, Naybet, Romero, Flávio Conceição (Jaime 78), Mauro Silva, Víctor, Djalminha (Manel 86), Fernando (Fran 65), Makaay.

4th round ARSENAL (ENG)
A 1-5   Djalminha (54p)
> Songo'o, Manuel Pablo, Donato, Naybet, Romero, Mauro Silva, Jokanovic (Víctor 52), Flávio Conceição, Djalminha, Turu Flores (Fernando 66), Makaay (Pauleta 75).

H 2-1   Víctor (69), Iván (90)
> Kouba, Scaloni, Ramis, Naybet, Manel, Makaay (Víctor 57), Jaime (Fran 63), Mauro Silva, Fernando (Iván 79), Pauleta, Turu Flores.

● RCD MALLORCA
1st round SIGMA OLOMOUC (CZE)
A 3-1   Engonga (11), Diego Tristán (51), Stankovic (75)
> Burgos, Olaizola, Nadal, Siviero, Soler M., Lauren (Serrizuela 35), Engonga, Ibagaza, Stankovic (Carreras 83), Diego Tristán (Armando 73), Carlos.

H 0-0
> Burgos, Olaizola, Nadal, Siviero, Soler M., Armando, Engonga, Ibagaza (Serrizuela 72), Carreras, Carlos (Diego Tristán 62), Djokaj (Quinteros 62).

2nd round FK TEPLICE (CZE)
A 2-1   Diego Tristán (26, 31)
> Burgos, Olaizola, Nadal, Siviero, Soler M., Lauren, Soler F. (Carreras 75), Serrizuela, Stankovic, Diego Tristán, Quinteros (Ibagaza 61).

H 3-0   Nadal (30), Stankovic (58), Niño (68)
> Franco, Armando, Niño, Nadal, Soler M., Lauren (Carreras 69), Engonga, Stankovic (David 69), Ibagaza, Djokaj (Diego Tristán 46), Biagini.

3rd round AJAX (HOL)
A 1-0   Diego Tristán (34)
> Burgos, Olaizola, Nadal, Siviero, Soler M., Lauren, Engonga, Soler F., Stankovic (Carreras 78), Biagini (Carlos 72), Diego Tristán.

H 2-0   Soler F. (3), Biagini (70)
> Franco, Olaizola, Nadal, Siviero, Soler M., Lauren, Engonga, Soler F., Carreras (Djokaj 78), Diego Tristán (Quinteros 90), Biagini (Ibagaza 85).

4th round AS MONACO (FRA)
H 4-1   Stankovic (42, 53p, 63p), Diego Tristán (90)
> Franco, Olaizola, Siviero, Nadal, Soler M., Lauren, Engonga, Soler F., Stankovic (Carreras 90), Carlos (Ibagaza 71), Diego Tristán.

A 0-1
> Franco, Olaizola, Nadal, Siviero, Soler M., Armando, Engonga (Niño 71), Soler F., Lauren, Carlos (Ibagaza 70), Diego Tristán (Carreras 88).

Quarter-final GALATASARAY (TUR)
H 1-4   Lauren (78)
> Franco, Olaizola (Armando 60), Nadal, Siviero, Soler M., Lauren, Engonga, Soler F. (Ibagaza 60), Stankovic, Carlos (Novo 88), Diego Tristán.

A 1-2   Carlos (62)
> Franco, Armando, Nadal, Siviero, Carreras, Novo (Djokaj 70), Robles, Romerito, Serrizuela, Carlos (Diego Tristán 63), Ibagaza (Stankovic 70).

Maybe if Van Gaal had succeeded in his bid for a hat-trick of Spanish league titles, it would all have been different. But while Barcelona, Valencia and Real were galavanting around Europe, the domestic crown was snatched, for the very first time, by Deporivo La Coruña.

The Galicians led the way from the late autumn onwards and were never dethroned. Yet time and again Javier Irureta's team gave the chasing pack the opportunity to close in - which, in turn, they persistently failed to take. Eight points clear in mid-December after a crucial 1-0 home win over regional rivals Celta Vigo, Deportivo were repeatedly found wanting on their travels, taking just one point from their next six away fixtures and continuing to struggle even after they had stopped the rot with a 3-1 victory in Seville.

The routine became familiar. Deportivo would follow every away defeat with a home win. Under normal circumstances this would have been no more than mid-table form, but because the other challengers had bigger fish to fry in Europe and because Deportivo always had a lead to play with, they got away with it. In fairness, they were ruthlessly efficient at home. Eight successive victories from January through to April enabled them to keep their noses in front, and only once during that sequence was the margin of victory less than two goals.

Panic set in when Deportivo were finally held in the Riazor, 2-2 by Zaragoza, in their penultimate home fixture, and memories of the club's infamous failure to win the 1993/94 championship (when they missed a penalty in the last minute of the final match) came flooding back. But a draw in Santander and a last-day 2-0 victory at home to Espanyol (who might or might not have been saving themselves for the Spanish Cup final) saw them safely home.

It had been a rare old struggle, but Deportivo had done it, and the coastal town of La Coruña went predictably ballistic in its celebration of the club's unprecedented achievement. They were the first team from outside the twin power-bases of Madrid and Barcelona to win the Spanish title in 16 years, and nobody in La Coruña cared two hoots that they had become champions despite running up 11 defeats. There were many heroes. Dutchman Roy Makaay proved an inspired signing and scored 22 goals, while behind him the Brazilian triumvirate of Mauro Silva, Flávio Conceição and Djalminha all made telling contributions. Veteran Jacques Songo'o was a dedicated and occasionally spectacular performer in goal, even foregoing his country's African Nations' Cup triumph to be with Deportivo at their time of need. And then there was the captain, Fran, a local boy made good who returned from injury to ensure that the painful memories of six years earlier would be banished forever.

It was a tremendous season for Spanish coaches. As well as the victorious Vicente del Bosque (Champions' League) and Javier Irureta (Spanish championship), Paco Flores got his hands on an important piece of silverware when his team Espanyol beat Atlético Madrid to win the Spanish Cup. Barcelona's 'other team' had won the competition twice before but not for 60 years, so there was immense jubilation in the blue-and-white camp after the 2-1 victory over Atlético in the Mestalla. A team devoid of stars, Espanyol triumphed without their most prominent individual, Paraguayan World Cup winger Miguel Angel Benítez, who suffered a career-threatening knee injury a few months earlier.

Atlético's second successive Cup final defeat was hard for their fans to take but it paled into insignificance compared to the sense of despair brought on by the club's shock relegation to the Second Division. Atlético were in a dishevelled state throughout the season. New Italian coach Claudio Ranieri went the same way as his compatriot Arrigo Sacchi 12 months earlier, and with president Jesús Gil serving time for fraud and the club's day-to-day dealings in the hands of the judiciary, it was virtually impossible for the players to concentrate fully on their main objective of winning football matches. Imported Dutchman Jimmy Floyd Hasselbaink did his valiant best with goals galore in every competition, but even that wasn't enough to save Atlético from their first relegation in 66 years.

There was another shock at the bottom as the two Seville clubs, Betis and Sevilla, went down with Atlético. No love was lost between these two arch-rivals and there were even claims made by Betis that Sevilla deliberately lost at home to relegation rivals Oviedo in order to worsen Betis's plight.

It was a season of surprises all round. Nobody could have foreseen, for example, that Alavés would be the pick of the Basque clubs, let alone that they would do the 'double' over Barcelona, finish as high as sixth and qualify for the UEFA Cup. Zaragoza also flew surprisingly high. With Yugoslav striker Savo Milosevic leading from the front, they finished fourth and would have taken the last Champions' League place but for the UEFA rule that forbids any country from entering more than four teams. Real Madrid's victory over Valencia in Paris thus demoted Txetxu Rojo's team to the UEFA Cup - a blow to Zaragoza but a boost perhaps to Spanish chances of a repeat performance in 2000/01. A four-strong Spanish armada of Real, Barcelona, Valencia and Deportivo might once again take some stopping...

PROMOTED CLUBS 99/00

SECOND DIVISION FINAL TABLE

		Pd	W	D	L	F	A	Pt	GD
1	**UD Las Palmas**	42	20	12	10	60	41	72	19
2	**CA Osasuna**	42	20	7	15	50	36	67	14
3	**Villarreal CF**	42	18	12	12	61	46	66	15
4	UD Salamanca	42	18	12	12	54	43	66	11
5	UE Lleida	42	18	9	15	66	52	63	14
6	CP Mérida	42	16	15	11	41	34	63	7
7	Levante UD	42	16	13	13	55	52	61	3
8	CF Extremadura	42	16	13	13	49	47	61	2
9	Sporting Gijón	42	17	9	16	54	48	60	6
10	Albacete Balompié	42	15	14	13	51	53	59	-2
11	SD Eibar	42	14	15	13	48	49	57	-1
12	Córdoba CF	42	15	12	15	46	49	57	-3
13	CD Leganés	42	14	14	14	39	47	56	-8
14	CD Tenerife	42	14	13	15	50	48	55	2
15	Elche CF	42	12	17	13	48	58	53	-10
16	CD Badajoz	42	9	24	9	38	39	51	-1
17	Atlético Madrid/B	42	13	11	18	43	57	50	-14
18	SD Compostela	42	10	19	13	50	53	49	-3
19	Getafe CF	42	13	9	20	39	51	48	-12
20	CD Logroñés	42	11	13	18	52	56	46	-4
21	RC Recreativo	42	12	9	21	40	54	45	-14
22	CD Toledo	42	10	10	22	34	55	40	-21

CLUB DIRECTORIES

Unión Deportiva Las Palmas
Pío XII 29
35005 Las Palmas de Gran Canaria (Canarias)
tel - (928) 241342 / fax - (928) 246714
Year of Formation - 1949
President - Fernando Arencibia
Manager - Sabino López
Coach - Sergei Kresic
Stadium - Insular (22,000)

Club Atlético Osasuna
Plaza del Castillo 30 bajo
31001 Pamplona (Navarra)
tel - (948) 152636 / fax - (948) 224714
Year of Formation - 1920
President - Javier Miranda Martínez
Manager - Angel Luis Vizcay
Coach - Miguel Angel Lotina
Stadium - El Sadar (20,000)

Villarreal Club de Fútbol
Plaza Mayor 2, 12540 Villarreal (Castellón)
tel - (964) 522714 / fax - (964) 520337
Year of Formation - 1923
President - Fernando Roig Alfonso
Manager - Manuel Llorca Maset
Coach - Joaquín Caparrós; Francisco García "Paquito"
Stadium - El Madrigal (12,000)

DEPORTIVO ALAVES

Deportivo Alavés
Paseo Cervantes s/n
01007 Vitoria
tel - (945) 131018
fax - (945) 232532
Year of Formation - 1921
President - Gonzalo Antón Sanjuán
Manager - Juan Carlos Rodríguez
Coach - José Manuel Esnal "Mané"
Stadium - Mendizorroza (19,900)

APPEARANCES 99/00

	P	Ap	(s)	Gls
Mauricio ASTUDILLO (ARG)	M	27	(2)	4
Jorge AZKOITIA	M	7	(14)	3
Ibón BEGOÑA	M	17	(6)	
Ignacio BERRUET	D	3	(2)	
Cosmin CONTRA (ROM)	D	33		2
Hermes DESIO (ARG)	M	35		1
Dan EGGEN (NOR)	D	8	(3)	
Raúl GAÑAN	M	2	(6)	
Jesús HERRERA	D		(1)	
Martin HERRERA (ARG)	G	38		
Manuel Romás "JOSETE"	D	4	(1)	
Antonio KARMONA	D	35		1
Meho KODRO (BOS)	A	25	(5)	5
MAGNO Mocelin (BRA)	A	15	(16)	3
Angel MORALES	M	22	(5)	2
Javier "JAVI" MORENO	A	20	(17)	7
PABLO Gómez	M	34		1
Joan "NAN" RIBERA	M	21	(8)	2
Asier SALCEDO	M		(5)	
Julio SALINAS	A	6	(22)	8
Oscar TELLEZ	D	33		1
Víctor TORRES MESTRE	D	33		

LEAGUE RESULTS 1999/2000

22/08/99	RC Deportivo	A	1-4	Morales
29/08/99	Málaga CF	H	2-1	Salinas 2
11/09/99	Valencia CF	A	2-0	Magno, Astudillo
18/09/99	FC Barcelona	H	2-1	Astudillo, Nan Ribera
26/09/99	Real Oviedo	A	0-1	
03/10/99	Sevilla FC	H	0-0	
12/10/99	Atlético Madrid	A	0-1	
17/10/99	Rayo Vallecano	H	0-1	
24/10/99	Real Sociedad	A	1-1	Astudillo
31/10/99	RC Celta	H	1-0	Salinas
07/11/99	Real Zaragoza	A	1-2	Kodro
28/11/99	RCD Espanyol	A	3-2	Magno, Contra, Javi Moreno
05/12/99	RCD Mallorca	H	2-2	Kodro, Javi Moreno
08/12/99	Racing Santander	H	2-1	Karmona, Salinas (p)
12/12/99	Real Betis	H	2-0	Kodro, Javi Moreno
18/12/99	Real Valladolid	A	1-1	Contra
21/12/99	Real Madrid	H	1-3	Morales
05/01/00	CD Numancia	A	0-0	
09/01/00	Athletic Bilbao	H	1-2	Salinas (p)
16/01/00	RC Deportivo	H	2-1	Salinas (p), Javi Moreno
23/01/00	Málaga CF	A	1-0	Azkoitia
30/01/00	Valencia CF	H	0-1	
06/02/00	FC Barcelona	A	1-0	Nan Ribera
13/02/00	Real Oviedo	H	1-0	Desio
20/02/00	Sevilla FC	A	2-2	Kodro (p), Astudillo
27/02/00	Atlético Madrid	H	2-0	Magno, og (Bejbl)
05/03/00	Rayo Vallecano	A	1-0	Téllez
12/03/00	Real Sociedad	H	2-1	Javi Moreno 2
19/03/00	RC Celta	A	1-1	Javi Moreno
25/03/00	Real Zaragoza	H	0-2	
02/04/00	Racing Santander	A	0-0	
09/04/00	RCD Espanyol	H	0-0	
16/04/00	RCD Mallorca	A	0-2	
23/04/00	Real Betis	A	1-0	Kodro (p)
30/04/00	Real Valladolid	H	1-0	Salinas
06/05/00	Real Madrid	A	1-0	Azkoitia
14/05/00	CD Numancia	H	2-2	Pablo, Azkoitia
19/05/00	Athletic Bilbao	A	1-2	Salinas

ATHLETIC BILBAO

CLUB DIRECTORY

Athletic Club
Alameda Mazarredo 23, 48009 Bilbao
tel - (944) 240877 / fax - (944) 233324
website - www.athletic-club.es
Year of Formation - 1898
President - José María Arrate
Manager - Fernando Lamikiz
Coach - Luis Fernandez (00/01 - José Francisco Rojo)
Stadium - San Mamés (46,223)

MAJOR HONOURS
League Championship - (8) 1930, 1931, 1934, 1936, 1943, 1956, 1983, 1984.
Domestic Cup - (23) 1903, 1904, 1910, 1911, 1914, 1915, 1916, 1921, 1923, 1930, 1931, 1932, 1933, 1943, 1944, 1945, 1950, 1955, 1956, 1958, 1969, 1973, 1984.

APPEARANCES 99/00

	P	Ap	(s)	Gls
Bittor ALKIZA	M	26	(1)	
Rafael ALKORTA	D	24		1
Eduardo ALONSO	M	10	(13)	
David ASENSIO	M	1		
David CARANCA	D		(2)	
CARLOS GARCIA	D	23	(4)	4
Imanol ETXEBERRIA	G	26		
Joseba ETXEBERRIA	A	33	(2)	11
Unai EXPOSITO	A	1	(1)	
Santiago EZQUERRO	A	23	(6)	6
FELIPE Guréndez	D	31	(3)	
Francisco FERREIRA	D	23	(2)	1
Javier GONZALEZ	D	5	(17)	
Julen GUERRERO	M	28	(4)	6
Andoni IMAZ	M	5	(8)	
"JOSE MARI" García	M	10	(2)	1
Jesús LACRUZ	D	28	(2)	4
Ignaio LAFUENTE	G	12	(2)	
Iñigo LARRAINZAR	D	13	(1)	1
Aitor LARRAZABAL	D	23	(4)	4
Mikel LASA	D	3		
Roberto RIOS	D	2	(4)	
Arturo Igorioín "SIVORI"	A	2	(11)	
Roberto Martínez "TIKO"	D	8	(9)	1
Josu URRUTIA	M	27	(2)	
Ismael URZAIZ	A	22	(11)	5
Oscar VALES	M	5		
Francisco Javier YESTE	M	4	(2)	

LEAGUE RESULTS 1999/2000

21/08/99	Real Betis	H	1-0	Etxeberria J.
29/08/99	Real Valladolid	A	0-1	
12/09/99	Real Madrid	H	2-2	Guerrero, og (Geremi)
19/09/99	CD Numancia	A	1-1	Urzaiz
26/09/99	RCD Mallorca	A	1-2	Etxeberria J.
03/10/99	RC Deportivo	H	2-3	José Mari, Ezquerro
12/10/99	Málaga CF	A	4-3	Alkorta, Lacruz 2, Etxeberria J.
16/10/99	Valencia CF	H	1-0	Urzaiz
23/10/99	FC Barcelona	A	0-4	
31/10/99	Real Oviedo	H	1-1	Ezquerro
07/11/99	Sevilla FC	A	0-0	
20/11/99	Atlético Madrid	H	4-2	Etxeberria J., Guerrero, Carlos García, Ezquerro (p)
28/11/99	Rayo Vallecano	A	2-1	Guerrero, Larrazábal
04/12/99	Real Sociedad	H	1-1	Etxeberria J.
12/12/99	RC Celta	A	1-1	Ezquerro
19/12/99	Real Zaragoza	H	2-2	Ezquerro, Lacruz
22/12/99	Racing Santander	A	2-2	Etxeberria J., Guerrero
05/01/00	RCD Espanyol	H	2-1	Larrainzar, Larrazábal (p)
09/01/00	Deportivo Alavés	A	2-1	Etxeberria J., Larrazábal (p)
16/01/00	Real Betis	A	1-2	Larrazábal (p)
23/01/00	Real Valladolid	H	1-0	Carlos García
30/01/00	Real Madrid	A	1-3	Etxeberria J.
07/02/00	CD Numancia	H	2-1	Urzaiz, Carlos García
12/02/00	RCD Mallorca	H	1-1	Ferreira
19/02/00	RC Deportivo	A	0-2	
27/02/00	Málaga CF	H	2-2	Urzaiz, Tiko
04/03/00	Valencia CF	A	0-2	
11/03/00	FC Barcelona	H	0-4	
19/03/00	Real Oviedo	A	0-1	
25/03/00	Sevilla FC	H	1-1	Etxeberria J.
02/04/00	Atlético Madrid	A	2-1	Etxeberria J., Guerrero
09/04/00	Rayo Vallecano	H	1-2	Ezquerro
16/04/00	Real Sociedad	A	1-4	og (Pikabea)
23/04/00	RC Celta	H	1-0	Urzaiz
30/04/00	Real Zaragoza	A	0-0	
07/05/00	Racing Santander	H	2-2	Lacruz, Etxeberria J.
14/05/00	RCD Espanyol	A	0-0	
19/05/00	Deportivo Alavés	H	2-1	Guerrero, Carlos García

ATLETICO MADRID

Club Atlético de Madrid
Paseo Virgen del Puerto 67, 28005 Madrid
tel - (913) 664707 / fax - (913) 641722
website - www.at-madrid.es
Year of Formation - 1903
President - Jesús Gil y Gil
Manager - Miguel Angel Gil Marín
Coach - Claudio Ranieri; Radomir Antic;
Fernando Zambrano
Stadium - Vicente Calderón (57,500)

MAJOR HONOURS
League Championship - (9) 1940, 1941, 1950,
1951, 1966, 1970, 1973, 1977, 1996.
Domestic Cup - (9) 1960, 1961, 1965, 1972,
1976, 1985, 1991, 1992, 1996.
European Cup-winners' Cup - (1) 1962.
World Club Cup - (1) 1974.

APPEARANCES 99/00

		P	Ap	(s)	Gls
Carlos AGUILERA	D	25	(4)		1
Celso AYALA (PAR)	D	9			1
Rubén BARAJA	M	17	(9)		3
Radek BEJBL (CZE)	M	28	(3)		
Juan CAPDEVILA	D	31			2
José Antonio CHAMOT (ARG)	D	12			
Fernando Edgardo CORREA (URU)	A	8	(12)		1
Carlos Alberto GAMARRA (PAR)	D	32			
GASPAR Gálvez	D	25	(2)		
GUSTAVO de la Parra	D	4			
Jimmy Floyd HASSELBAINK (HOL)	A	34			24
HUGO LEAL (POR)	M	16	(7)		1
"JOSE MARI" Romero	A	11	(1)		2
Francisco Narváez "KIKO"	A	17	(3)		
Jordi LARDIN	M	2	(5)		
Juan Manuel LOPEZ	D		(2)		
José Juan LUQUE	M	2	(4)		
Oscar Alcides MENA (ARG)	D	2	(4)		
José Francisco MOLINA	G	31			
Zoran NJEGUS (YUG)	D	4	(7)		
Veljko PAUNOVIC (YUG)	M	6	(11)		2
Eduardo PILIPAUSKAS (URU)	D	4			
ROBERTO Fresnodoso	M	3	(12)		1
"SANTI" Denia	D	25	(3)		
Santiago Hernán SOLARI (ARG)	M	28	(6)		6
"TONI" Jiménez	G	7			
"TONI" Muñoz	D	5	(2)		
Juan Carlos VALERON	M	26	(9)		4
Giorgio VENTURIN (ITA)	D	4	(2)		

LEAGUE RESULTS 1999/2000

22/08/99	Rayo Vallecano	H	0-2	
28/08/99	Real Sociedad	A	1-4	Solari
12/09/99	RC Celta	H	1-2	Valerón
19/09/99	Real Zaragoza	A	1-1	Hasselbaink
26/09/99	Racing Santander	H	2-0	Hasselbaink, Baraja
03/10/99	RCD Espanyol	A	1-3	Hasselbaink
12/10/99	Deportivo Alavés	H	1-0	Hasselbaink
17/10/99	Real Betis	A	1-2	Solari
24/10/99	Real Valladolid	H	3-1	Capdevila, Solari, Hasselbaink
30/10/99	Real Madrid	A	3-1	Hasselbaink 2, José Mari
07/11/99	CD Numancia	H	2-2	Baraja, Hasselbaink
20/11/99	Athletic Bilbao	A	2-4	Hasselbaink (p), Paunovic
28/11/99	RC Deportivo	H	1-3	Baraja
05/12/99	Málaga CF	A	3-2	Hasselbaink 2, José Mari
12/12/99	Valencia CF	H	1-2	Hasselbaink
19/12/99	FC Barcelona	A	1-2	Hasselbaink (p)
22/12/99	Real Oviedo	H	5-0	Valerón, Ayala, Hasselbaink 2, Correa
05/01/00	Sevilla FC	A	1-2	Hasselbaink
09/01/00	RCD Mallorca	H	1-0	Hasselbaink (p)
15/01/00	Rayo Vallecano	A	1-1	Aguilera
23/01/00	Real Sociedad	H	1-1	Hasselbaink
29/01/00	RC Celta	A	1-0	Valerón
06/02/00	Real Zaragoza	H	2-2	Hasselbaink 2 (1p)
13/02/00	Racing Santander	A	1-2	Roberto
20/02/00	RCD Espanyol	H	1-1	Hasselbaink
27/02/00	Deportivo Alavés	A	0-2	
05/03/00	Real Betis	H	0-0	
12/03/00	Real Valladolid	A	0-1	
18/03/00	Real Madrid	H	1-1	Solari
25/03/00	CD Numancia	A	0-3	
02/04/00	Athletic Bilbao	H	1-2	Hasselbaink
08/04/00	RC Deportivo	A	1-4	Hasselbaink
16/04/00	Málaga CF	H	2-2	Valerón, Solari
22/04/00	Valencia CF	A	0-2	
29/04/00	FC Barcelona	H	0-3	
07/05/00	Real Oviedo	A	2-2	Capdevila, Hasselbaink
13/05/00	Sevilla FC	H	1-1	Hugo Leal
19/05/00	RCD Mallorca	A	2-1	Paunovic, Solari

FC BARCELONA

CLUB DIRECTORY

Fútbol Club Barcelona
Arístides Maillol s/n, 08028 Barcelona
tel - (934) 963600 / fax - (934) 112219
website - www.fcbarcelona.es
Year of Formation - 1899
President - Joan Gaspart
Manager - Josep Maria Antràs
Coach - Louis van Gaal (00/01 - Lorenzo Serra Ferrer)
Stadium - Camp Nou (98,600)

MAJOR HONOURS
League Championship - (16) 1929, 1945, 1948,
1949, 1952, 1953, 1959, 1960, 1974, 1985,
1991, 1992, 1993, 1994, 1998, 1999.
Domestic Cup - (24) 1910, 1912, 1913, 1920,
1922, 1925, 1926, 1928, 1942, 1951, 1952,
1953, 1957, 1959, 1963, 1968, 1971, 1978,
1981, 1983, 1988, 1990, 1997, 1998.
European Champions' Cup - (1) 1992.
European Cup-winners' Cup - (4)
1979, 1982, 1989, 1997.
Fairs' Cup - (3) 1958, 1960, 1966.
European Super Cup - (2) 1992, 1998.

APPEARANCES 99/00

	P	Ap	(s)	Gls
ABELARDO Fernández	D	25		1
Francesc ARNAU	G	16		
Winston BOGARDE (HOL)	D	14	(7)	2
Phillip COCU (HOL)	M	34	(1)	6
"DANI" García	A	15	(12)	11
Frank DE BOER (HOL)	D	20	(2)	
Ronald DE BOER (HOL)	D	10	(10)	1
Frédéric DEHU (FRA)	D	9	(2)	
Luís Madeira "FIGO" (POR)	M	32		9
"GABRI" García	M	10	(7)	2
Josep GUARDIOLA	M	22	(3)	
Ruud HESP (HOL)	G	22		
Patrick KLUIVERT (HOL)	A	24	(2)	15
Jari LITMANEN (FIN)	M	14	(7)	3
LUIS ENRIQUE Martínez	M	15	(4)	3
Fernando Macedo "NANO"	A		(1)	
Carlos PUYOL	D	18	(6)	
Michael REIZIGER (HOL)	D	29		
RIVALDO Vítor Borba Ferreira (BRA)	M	30	(1)	12
Sergio SANTAMARIA	D		(1)	
SERGI Barjuán	D	14	(5)	1
SIMÃO Pedro Sabrosa (POR)	M	9	(12)	1
"XAVI" Hernández	M	15	(9)	
Boudewijn ZENDEN (HOL)	M	21	(8)	2

LEAGUE RESULTS 1999/2000

Date	Opponent		Score	Scorers
22/08/99	Real Zaragoza	H	2-0	Figo, Dani
29/08/99	Racing Santander	A	2-1	Rivaldo, Cocu
11/09/99	RCD Espanyol	H	3-0	Rivaldo 2, Kluivert
18/09/99	Deportivo Alavés	A	1-2	Dani
25/09/99	Real Betis	H	4-1	Dani 3, Luis Enrique
02/10/99	Real Valladolid	A	2-0	Kluivert, Rivaldo
13/10/99	Real Madrid	H	2-2	Rivaldo, Figo
16/10/99	CD Numancia	A	3-3	Figo, Litmanen, Dani
23/10/99	Athletic Bilbao	H	4-0	Cocu, Rivaldo, Figo (p), Dani
30/10/99	RC Deportivo	A	1-2	Rivaldo
07/11/99	Málaga CF	H	1-2	Bogarde
20/11/99	Valencia CF	A	1-3	Zenden
28/11/99	RCD Mallorca	A	2-3	Kluivert 2
04/12/99	Real Oviedo	H	3-2	Cocu 2, Kluivert
11/12/99	Sevilla FC	A	2-3	Dani, Luis Enrique
19/12/99	Atlético Madrid	H	2-1	Luis Enrique, Zenden
22/12/99	Rayo Vallecano	A	1-1	Simão
05/01/00	Real Sociedad	H	3-1	Figo 2, Litmanen
09/01/00	RC Celta	A	2-0	Figo, Rivaldo
16/01/00	Real Zaragoza	A	0-0	
23/01/00	Racing Santander	H	1-0	Rivaldo
29/01/00	RCD Espanyol	A	1-1	Kluivert
06/02/00	Deportivo Alavés	H	0-1	
13/02/00	Real Betis	A	1-2	Kluivert
20/02/00	Real Valladolid	H	4-0	De Boer R., og (Heinze), Rivaldo 2
26/02/00	Real Madrid	A	0-3	
04/03/00	CD Numancia	H	4-0	Gabri, Dani 2, Figo
11/03/00	Athletic Bilbao	A	4-0	Cocu 2, Kluivert, Figo
18/03/00	RC Deportivo	H	2-1	Kluivert, Rivaldo
25/03/00	Málaga CF	A	2-1	Abelardo, Kluivert (p)
02/04/00	Valencia CF	H	3-0	Bogarde, Kluivert 2
09/04/00	RCD Mallorca	H	0-3	
15/04/00	Real Oviedo	A	0-3	
22/04/00	Sevilla FC	H	2-0	Kluivert, Litmanen
29/04/00	Atlético Madrid	A	3-0	Sergi, Dani, Gabri
06/05/00	Rayo Vallecano	H	0-2	
14/05/00	Real Sociedad	A	0-0	
19/05/00	RC Celta	H	2-2	Kluivert 2 (1p)

REAL BETIS

CLUB DIRECTORY

Real Betis Balompié
Avenida de Heliópolis s/n, 41012 Sevilla
tel - (954) 610340 / fax - (954) 614774
website - www.realbetisbalompie.es
Year of Formation - 1907
President - Manuel Ruiz de Lopera
Manager - José Antonio González Flores
Coach - Carlos Timoteo Griguol; Guus Hiddink;
Faruk Hadzibegic
Stadium - Manuel Ruiz de Lopera (52,500)

MAJOR HONOURS
League Championship - (1) 1935.
Domestic Cup - (1) 1977.

APPEARANCES 99/00

	P	Ap	(s)	Gls
ALEXIS Trujillo	M	18	(7)	
ALFONSO Pérez	A	32	(2)	9
BENJAMIN Zarandona	M	12	(14)	
Joaquín BORNES	D	19	(2)	
Juan José CAÑAS	D	8	(4)	1
Sebastián CROSA (ARG)	D	27	(1)	
Angel Manuel CUELLAR	A	6	(7)	
DENILSON de Oliveira (BRA)	A	29	(3)	4
Iulian FILIPESCU (ROM)	D	35	(1)	1
FINIDI George (NIG)	M	24		8
José GALVEZ	A	6	(17)	1
Antonio Alvarez "ITO"	M	13	(6)	3
JUAN JESUS Cabrera	D	1	(2)	
Miroslav KARHAN (SVK)	D	28	(5)	2
LUIS Fernández	D	17	(4)	
Juan MERINO	D	25	(3)	
Oliverio Alvarez "OLI"	A	16	(8)	1
Jorge OTERO	D	21		
Antonio PRATS	G	37		2
David RIVAS	D	15	(1)	1
Sebastián Ariel ROMERO (ARG)	M	15	(8)	
Roberto SOLOZABAL	D		(1)	
Joaquín Enrique VALERIO	G	1		
Risto VIDAKOVIC (BOS)	D	13		

LEAGUE RESULTS 1999/2000

21/08/99	Athletic Bilbao	A	0-1	
29/08/99	RC Deportivo	H	0-0	
12/09/99	Málaga CF	A	0-3	
18/09/99	Valencia CF	H	1-0	Oli
25/09/99	FC Barcelona	A	1-4	Karhan
03/10/99	Real Oviedo	H	1-0	Finidi
12/10/99	Sevilla FC	A	0-3	
17/10/99	Atlético Madrid	H	2-1	Prats, Finidi
24/10/99	Rayo Vallecano	A	3-1	Alfonso 2 (1p), Denilson
31/10/99	Real Sociedad	H	1-0	Finidi
07/11/99	RC Celta	A	1-5	Alfonso
21/11/99	Real Zaragoza	H	2-0	Finidi 2 (1p)
28/11/99	Racing Santander	A	1-1	Karhan
05/12/99	RCD Espanyol	H	2-5	Alfonso, Denilson
12/12/99	Deportivo Alavés	A	0-2	
19/12/99	RCD Mallorca	H	1-0	Finidi
22/12/99	Real Valladolid	H	0-1	
09/01/00	CD Numancia	H	1-2	Alfonso
16/01/00	Athletic Bilbao	H	2-1	Ito 2
22/01/00	RC Deportivo	A	0-2	
26/01/00	Real Madrid	A	1-2	Prats
30/01/00	Málaga CF	H	0-0	
05/02/00	Valencia CF	A	1-3	Filipescu
13/02/00	FC Barcelona	H	2-1	Ito, Alfonso
20/02/00	Real Oviedo	A	1-1	Alfonso
27/02/00	Sevilla FC	H	1-1	Denilson (p)
05/03/00	Atlético Madrid	A	0-0	
11/03/00	Rayo Vallecano	H	1-1	Finidi
19/03/00	Real Sociedad	A	0-1	
26/03/00	RC Celta	H	0-0	
02/04/00	Real Zaragoza	A	0-1	
09/04/00	Racing Santander	H	2-2	Alfonso 2 (2p)
16/04/00	RCD Espanyol	A	0-3	
23/04/00	Deportivo Alavés	H	0-1	
30/04/00	RCD Mallorca	A	0-4	
07/05/00	Real Valladolid	A	3-0	Gálvez, Denilson, Finidi
14/05/00	Real Madrid	H	0-2	
20/05/00	CD Numancia	A	2-1	Cañas, Rivas

RC CELTA

CLUB DIRECTORY

Real Club Celta de Vigo
Avenida de Balaídos s/n
36210 Vigo (Pontevedra)
tel - (986) 213230
fax - (986) 292040
Year of Formation - 1923
President - Horacio Gómez Araújo
Coach - Víctor Fernández
Stadium - Balaídos (31,800)

APPEARANCES 99/00

	P	Ap	(s)	Gls
ADRIANO Teixeira (BRA)	D	1	(1)	
Djamel BELMADI (FRA)	D	3	(7)	
Iago BOUZON	A		(2)	
BRUNO CAIRES (POR)	M		(2)	
Fernando Gabriel CACERES (ARG)	D	35		1
Albert CELADES	M	19	(5)	1
Pablo COIRA	D	3	(4)	
Goran DJOROVIC (YUG)	D	23		1
Richard DUTRUEL (FRA)	G	19		
Everton GIOVANELLA (BRA)	M	28	(6)	
Rick HOOGENDORP (HOL)	A	3	(4)	
"JUANFRAN" García	D	27		2
Valeriy KARPIN (RUS)	M	33	(1)	6
Iván KAVIEDES (ECU)	M		(5)	
Gustavo LOPEZ (ARG)	M	27	(5)	6
Claude MAKELELE (FRA)	M	33	(1)	1
Iomar Nascimento "MAZINHO" (BRA)	M	1	(5)	
Benni McCARTHY (SAF)	A	25	(6)	8
José María MENA	M		(3)	
Aleksandr MOSTOVOI (RUS)	A	22	(4)	6
José Manuel PINTO	G	19		
Haim REVIVO (ISR)	A	18	(9)	2
SERGIO Fernández	D	25	(2)	1
TOMAS Hervás	D	5	(16)	1
Mario Héctor TURDO (ARG)	A	12	(13)	7
Juan VELASCO	D	28	(1)	1
Nelson VIVAS (ARG)	D	9	(4)	

LEAGUE RESULTS 1999/2000

22/08/99	Real Oviedo	A	0-1	
29/08/99	Sevilla FC	H	2-1	McCarthy, Makelele
12/09/99	Atlético Madrid	A	2-1	Karpin (p), Juanfran
19/09/99	Rayo Vallecano	H	0-1	
25/09/99	Real Sociedad	A	2-0	Mostovoi, Karpin
03/10/99	RCD Mallorca	H	1-0	Karpin
13/10/99	Real Zaragoza	H	2-1	Cáceres, Mostovoi
16/10/99	Racing Santander	A	0-3	
24/10/99	RCD Espanyol	H	2-1	López, Juanfran
31/10/99	Deportivo Alavés	A	0-1	
07/11/99	Real Betis	H	5-1	López, Turdó 2, Mostovoi, Karpin
21/11/99	Real Valladolid	A	3-1	Djorovic, Karpin, McCarthy
28/11/99	Real Madrid	H	1-0	Celades
05/12/99	CD Numancia	A	1-3	Mostovoi
12/12/99	Athletic Bilbao	H	1-1	Turdó
18/12/99	RC Deportivo	A	0-1	
22/12/99	Málaga CF	H	2-4	Karpin (p), Revivo
04/01/00	Valencia CF	A	1-1	Velasco
09/01/00	FC Barcelona	H	0-2	
16/01/00	Real Oviedo	H	5-3	Turdó 3, Mostovoi, Revivo
23/01/00	Sevilla FC	A	1-0	McCarthy
29/01/00	Atlético Madrid	H	0-1	
06/02/00	Rayo Vallecano	A	0-1	
13/02/00	Real Sociedad	H	4-1	og (Fuentes), Sergio, López 2
20/02/00	RCD Mallorca	A	0-1	
27/02/00	Real Zaragoza	A	1-2	McCarthy
05/03/00	Racing Santander	H	2-0	McCarthy, Mostovoi
12/03/00	RCD Espanyol	A	0-3	
19/03/00	Deportivo Alavés	H	1-1	McCarthy
26/03/00	Real Betis	A	0-0	
02/04/00	Real Valladolid	H	1-1	McCarthy
09/04/00	Real Madrid	A	0-1	
16/04/00	CD Numancia	H	0-0	
22/04/00	Athletic Bilbao	A	0-1	
30/04/00	RC Deportivo	H	2-1	McCarthy, López
07/05/00	Málaga CF	A	1-0	López
14/05/00	Valencia CF	H	0-0	
19/05/00	FC Barcelona	A	2-2	Tomás, Turdó

RC DEPORTIVO

CLUB DIRECTORY

Real Club Deportivo de La Coruña
Plaza de Pontevedra 19, 15003 La Coruña
tel - (981) 259500 / fax - (981) 265919
website - www.canaldeportivo.com
Year of Formation - 1906
President - Augusto Joaquín César Lendoiro
Manager - Manuel Montiel Duque
Coach - Javier Iruretagoyena
Stadium - Riazor (35,600)

MAJOR HONOURS
League Championship - (1) 2000.
Domestic Cup - (1) 1995.

APPEARANCES 99/00

	P	Ap	(s)	Gls
CESAR Martín	D	10	(1)	1
"DJALMINHA" Feitoza (BRA)	M	29	(2)	10
DONATO Gama da Silva	D	27	(2)	3
FERNANDO Sánchez	M	3	(16)	
FLÁVIO da CONCEIÇÃO (BRA)	M	25	(2)	4
"FRAN" González	M	16	(6)	1
IVAN PEREZ	A		(3)	
JAIME Sánchez	M	7	(14)	
Slavisa JOKANOVIC (YUG)	M	20	(3)	2
Petr KOUBA (CZE)	G	2		
Roy MAKAAY (HOL)	A	34	(2)	22
"MANEL" Menéndez	M	1	(5)	
MANUEL PABLO García	D	33	(4)	
MAURO da SILVA (BRA)	M	33		
Noureddine NAYBET (MAR)	D	25		
Pedro Carreiro "PAULETA" (POR)	A	12	(18)	8
Luis Miguel RAMIS	D	2	(1)	
Enrique Fernández ROMERO	D	32	(2)	1
Lionel Sebastián SCALONI (ARG)	D	4	(10)	
Gabriel Francisco SCHURRER (ARG)	D	18	(1)	
Jacques SONGO'O (CMR)	G	36		
José Oscar "TURU" FLORES (ARG)	A	15	(19)	8
VICTOR Sánchez	M	34	(3)	4

LEAGUE RESULTS 1999/2000

22/08/99	Deportivo Alavés	H	4-1	Makaay 3, Djalminha
29/08/99	Real Betis	A	0-0	
11/09/99	Real Valladolid	H	2-0	Makaay, Djalminha (p)
18/09/99	Real Madrid	A	1-1	Djalminha
26/09/99	CD Numancia	H	0-2	
03/10/99	Athletic Bilbao	A	3-2	Pauleta, Flávio Conceição, Víctor
12/10/99	RCD Mallorca	A	2-2	Pauleta 2
16/10/99	Málaga CF	H	4-1	Donato, Djalminha 2, Víctor
23/10/99	Valencia CF	A	0-2	
30/10/99	FC Barcelona	H	2-1	Makaay 2
07/11/99	Real Oviedo	A	1-0	Djalminha (p)
21/11/99	Sevilla FC	H	5-2	Djalminha, Pauleta 3 (1p), Romero
28/11/99	Atlético Madrid	A	3-1	Makaay 2, Víctor
05/12/99	Rayo Vallecano	H	3-2	Makaay, Turu Flores, Pauleta
12/12/99	Real Sociedad	A	1-0	og (Guerrero)
18/12/99	RC Celta	H	1-0	Turu Flores
22/12/99	Real Zaragoza	A	1-2	Turu Flores
05/01/00	Racing Santander	H	0-3	
08/01/00	RCD Espanyol	A	0-0	
16/01/00	Deportivo Alavés	A	1-2	Makaay
22/01/00	Real Betis	H	2-0	Pauleta, Makaay
30/01/00	Real Valladolid	A	1-4	Turu Flores (p)
06/02/00	Real Madrid	H	5-2	Makaay, Djalminha, Víctor, Turu Flores 2
13/02/00	CD Numancia	A	0-1	
19/02/00	Athletic Bilbao	H	2-0	Flávio Conceição, og (Ferreira)
27/02/00	RCD Mallorca	H	2-1	Makaay, Djalminha
05/03/00	Málaga CF	A	0-1	
12/03/00	Valencia CF	H	2-0	Fran, Flávio Conceição
18/03/00	FC Barcelona	A	1-2	Flávio Conceição
26/03/00	Real Oviedo	H	3-1	Makaay 2, Donato
02/04/00	Sevilla FC	A	3-1	Jokanovic 2, Makaay
08/04/00	Atlético Madrid	H	4-1	Turu Flores, Makaay 3
16/04/00	Rayo Vallecano	A	0-2	
23/04/00	Real Sociedad	H	2-0	Makaay, César
30/04/00	RC Celta	A	1-2	Turu Flores
07/05/00	Real Zaragoza	H	2-2	Makaay, Djalminha
14/05/00	Racing Santander	A	0-0	
19/05/00	RCD Espanyol	H	2-0	Donato, Makaay

RCD ESPANYOL

CLUB DIRECTORY

Reial Club Deportiu Espanyol de Barcelona
Paseo Olímpico 17-19, 08038 Barcelona
tel - (934) 248800
fax - (934) 254552
website - www.rcd-espanyol.com
Year of Formation - 1900
President - Daniel Sánchez Llibre
Manager - Enric Mas
Coach - Miguel Angel Brindisi; Francisco Flores
Stadium - Montjuïc (56,000)

MAJOR HONOURS
Domestic Cup - (3) 1929, 1940, 2000.

APPEARANCES 99/00

	P	Ap	(s)	Gls
Moisés García "ARTEAGA"	M	34	(3)	4
Miguel Angel BENITEZ (PAR)	A	20	(3)	7
Branko BRNOVIC (YUG)	D		(1)	
Carlos David CASARTELLI (ARG)	M		(5)	
David CATALA	A		(1)	
Pablo Oscar CAVALLERO (ARG)	G	26		
Sergio CORINO	D	2	(2)	
CRISTOBAL Parralo	D	37		
DAVID García	M		(1)	
Enrique DE LUCAS	A	19	(11)	4
Iván DIAZ	D	1		
Constantin GALCA (ROM)	M	32		6
Sergio GONZALEZ	M	30	(3)	
Alberto LOPO	D	6	(1)	
"MANEL" Martínez	M	1	(12)	2
Balázs MOLNÁR (HUN)	M	1	(3)	
Juan Luis MORA	G	12	(1)	
"NANDO" Muñoz	D	20	(2)	1
Mauro Esteban NAVAS (ARG)	M	27	(6)	
Mauricio POCHETTINO (ARG)	D	29		1
Martin POSSE (ARG)	A	15	(11)	3
ROGER García	M	18	(12)	4
Pablo Oscar ROTCHEN (ARG)	D	14	(2)	1
César Elías SANTIS (CHL)	D		(1)	
Manuel SERRANO	A	6	(17)	3
Antonio SOLDEVILLA	D	6	(1)	
Raúl TAMUDO	A	30	(4)	10
Adelio César TOLEDO (PAR)	M	4		
"TONI" VELAMAZAN	M	28	(6)	5

LEAGUE RESULTS 1999/2000

22/08/99	Málaga CF	A	0-1	
29/08/99	Valencia CF	H	3-2	Benítez, De Lucas, Martín Posse
11/09/99	FC Barcelona	A	0-3	
18/09/99	Real Oviedo	H	2-1	Tamudo, Benítez
26/09/99	Sevilla FC	A	2-1	Galca (p), Benítez
03/10/99	Atlético Madrid	H	3-1	Tamudo, Benítez, Rotchen
13/10/99	Rayo Vallecano	A	1-2	Toni Velamazán
17/10/99	Real Sociedad	H	0-0	
24/10/99	RC Celta	A	1-2	De Lucas
31/10/99	Real Zaragoza	H	1-1	Pochettino
07/11/99	Racing Santander	A	2-2	De Lucas (p), Arteaga
21/11/99	RCD Mallorca	H	1-2	Roger
28/11/99	Deportivo Alavés	H	2-3	Toni Velamazán, Roger
05/12/99	Real Betis	A	5-2	Tamudo, Toni Velamazán, Galca 2 (1p), De Lucas (p)
12/12/99	Real Valladolid	H	1-1	Galca (p)
18/12/99	Real Madrid	A	1-2	Benítez
22/12/99	CD Numancia	H	3-1	Toni Velamazán, Serrano 2
05/01/00	Athletic Bilbao	A	1-2	Serrano
08/01/00	RC Deportivo	H	0-0	
16/01/00	Málaga CF	H	0-2	
23/01/00	Valencia CF	A	2-1	Benítez, Arteaga
29/01/00	FC Barcelona	H	1-1	Benítez
06/02/00	Real Oviedo	A	0-1	
13/02/00	Sevilla FC	H	2-2	Tamudo 2
20/02/00	Atlético Madrid	A	1-1	Tamudo
27/02/00	Rayo Vallecano	H	5-1	Tamudo, Posse 2, Arteaga, Galca
05/03/00	Real Sociedad	A	0-1	
12/03/00	RC Celta	H	3-0	Tamudo 2, Roger (p)
19/03/00	Real Zaragoza	A	1-1	Arteaga
25/03/00	Racing Santander	H	1-0	Toni Velamazán
02/04/00	RCD Mallorca	A	3-1	Galca (p), Roger, Manel
09/04/00	Deportivo Alavés	A	0-0	
16/04/00	Real Betis	H	3-0	Tamudo, Nando, Manel
22/04/00	Real Valladolid	A	0-1	
29/04/00	Real Madrid	H	0-2	
06/05/00	CD Numancia	A	0-2	
14/05/00	Athletic Bilbao	H	0-0	
19/05/00	RC Deportivo	A	0-2	

MALAGA CF

CLUB DIRECTORY

Málaga Club de Fútbol
Paseo de Martiricos s/n
29011 Málaga
tel - (952) 614210
fax - (952) 613737
Year of Formation - 1994
President - Fernando Puche
Coach - Joaquín Peiró
Stadium - La Rosaleda (37,000)

APPEARANCES 99/00

	P	Ap	(s)	Gls
Joaquin AGOSTINHO (POR)	M	18	(8)	1
Sebastián Fernández "BASTI"	A		(2)	
Francisco Javier López BRAVO	D	27		
Miguel Angel BURREZO	A		(1)	
Henrique Guedes				
"CATANHA" (BRA)	A	33		24
Pedro CONTRERAS	G	37		
Gonzalo DE LOS SANTOS (URU)	M	36		4
EDGAR de Carvalho (POR)	M	27		5
GENILSON Alves (BRA)	M		(3)	
Raúl IZNATA	D	3	(2)	
Domingo LARRAINZAR	D	32	(1)	1
Alberto LUQUE	M	5	(18)	3
José María MOVILLA	M	34	(1)	2
Kiki MUSAMPA (HOL)	M	2	(11)	2
"RAFA" González	G	1		
Roberto ROJAS	D	32		
Miguel Angel ROTETA	D	8	(8)	
Francisco Manuel RUANO	M	14	(10)	
Joaquín Pérez RUFETE	M	28	(3)	5
"SANDRO" Sierra	M	7	(21)	
Fernando SANZ	D	21	(5)	
Dario SILVA (URU)	M	16	(7)	4
Vicente VALCARCE	D	37		3
Ariel Silvio ZARATE (ARG)	A		(1)	

LEAGUE RESULTS 1999/2000

22/08/99	RCD Espanyol	H	1-0	Catanha
29/08/99	Deportivo Alavés	A	1-2	Catanha
12/09/99	Real Betis	H	3-0	Valcarce, De los Santos, Catanha
18/09/99	Real Valladolid	A	2-4	Catanha, De los Santos
25/09/99	Real Madrid	H	1-1	Larraínzar
02/10/99	CD Numancia	A	1-1	Edgar
12/10/99	Athletic Bilbao	H	3-4	Edgar, Catanha 2 (1p)
16/10/99	RC Deportivo	A	1-4	Catanha (p)
24/10/99	RCD Mallorca	A	1-2	De los Santos
30/10/99	Valencia CF	H	1-1	Edgar
07/11/99	FC Barcelona	A	2-1	Agostinho, Valcarce
21/11/99	Real Oviedo	H	4-0	Catanha 3, Movilla
27/11/99	Sevilla FC	A	0-0	
05/12/99	Atlético Madrid	H	2-3	Luque 2
12/12/99	Rayo Vallecano	A	1-4	Catanha
19/12/99	Real Sociedad	H	0-0	
22/12/99	RC Celta	A	4-2	Catanha 3, Rufete
05/01/00	Real Zaragoza	H	0-0	
09/01/00	Racing Santander	A	3-2	Valcarce, Edgar, Catanha
16/01/00	RCD Espanyol	A	2-0	Silva, Rufete
23/01/00	Deportivo Alavés	H	0-1	
30/01/00	Real Betis	A	0-0	
06/02/00	Real Valladolid	H	0-0	
12/02/00	Real Madrid	A	0-1	
20/02/00	CD Numancia	H	3-1	Catanha, De los Santos, Edgar
27/02/00	Athletic Bilbao	A	2-2	Silva, Movilla (p)
05/03/00	RC Deportivo	H	1-0	Silva
12/03/00	RCD Mallorca	H	0-0	
18/03/00	Valencia CF	A	2-2	Catanha 2 (1p)
25/03/00	FC Barcelona	H	1-2	Catanha
02/04/00	Real Oviedo	A	2-2	Catanha 2
09/04/00	Sevilla FC	H	3-0	Catanha, Rufete, Luque
16/04/00	Atlético Madrid	A	2-2	Rufete, Catanha
22/04/00	Rayo Vallecano	H	2-0	Silva, Musampa
30/04/00	Real Sociedad	A	2-2	Catanha, Musampa
07/05/00	RC Celta	H	0-1	
14/05/00	Real Zaragoza	A	2-3	Rufete, og (Paco)
20/05/00	Racing Santander	H	0-0	

RCD MALLORCA

CLUB DIRECTORY

Real Club Deportivo Mallorca
Plaza de Barcelona 15
07011 Palma de Mallorca
tel - (971) 220020
fax - (971) 452351
website - www.rcdmallorca.es
Year of Formation - 1916
President - Guillermo Reynés
Coach - Mario Carlos Gómez; Fernando Vázquez
(00/01 - Luis Aragonés)
Stadium - San Moix (26,500)

APPEARANCES 99/00

	P	Ap	(s)	Gls
ARMANDO Alvarez	D	9	(8)	1
Leonardo BIAGINI (ARG)	A	5	(3)	1
Germán Adrián BURGOS (ARG)	G	10		
CARLOS Domínguez	A	18	(11)	9
Luis CARRERAS	M	9	(12)	3
Jorge CORDERO	D		(1)	
DAVID Castedo	D	7	(1)	1
DIEGO TRISTAN	A	31	(4)	19
Ardian DJOKAJ (YUG)	A	1	(5)	
Vicente ENGONGA	M	31		
Samuel ETO'O (CMR)	A	9	(4)	6
Leonardo FRANCO	G	28	(2)	
Iván César GABRICH (ARG)	A		(5)	
Daniel González GÜIZA	D		(1)	
Ariel Miguel IBAGAZA (ARG)	M	19	(12)	1
LAUREN Bisama				
Etame Mayer (CMR)	M	30		3
José Luis MARTI	M		(1)	
Miguel Angel NADAL	D	29	(2)	
Fernando NIÑO	D	13	(4)	
Alvaro NOVO	M	3	(3)	
Javier OLAIZOLA	D	37		
Jorge QUINTEROS (ARG)	M	4	(6)	2
Julián ROBLES	A		(1)	
Antonio Ruiz "ROMERITO"	A	2	(1)	1
Francisco SANZ	M		(1)	
Juan José SERRIZUELA (ARG)	M	12	(7)	
Gustavo SIVIERO (ARG)	D	29		
Francisco SOLER	M	27	(5)	
Miguel SOLER	D	31	(1)	
Jovan STANKOVIC (YUG)	M	24		4

LEAGUE RESULTS 1999/2000

21/08/99	Real Madrid	H	1-2	Carlos
29/08/99	Rayo Vallecano	A	1-2	Carreras
12/09/99	CD Numancia	H	3-0	Stankovic (p), Carlos, Diego Tristán
19/09/99	Real Sociedad	A	1-2	Diego Tristán
26/09/99	Athletic Bilbao	H	2-1	Carlos, Diego Tristán (p)
03/10/99	RC Celta	A	0-1	
12/10/99	RC Deportivo	H	2-2	Quinteros, Diego Tristán (p)
17/10/99	Real Zaragoza	A	0-3	
24/10/99	Málaga CF	H	2-1	Lauren, Quinteros
31/10/99	Racing Santander	A	1-1	Stankovic
07/11/99	Valencia CF	H	1-0	Diego Tristán
21/11/99	RCD Espanyol	A	2-1	Stankovic, Biagini
28/11/99	FC Barcelona	H	3-2	Diego Tristán 2 (1p), Stankovic
05/12/99	Deportivo Alavés	A	2-2	Diego Tristán 2
12/12/99	Real Oviedo	H	1-1	Diego Tristán
19/12/99	Real Betis	A	0-1	
22/12/99	Sevilla FC	H	3-1	og (Prieto), Carreras, Ibagaza
05/01/00	Real Valladolid	H	0-0	
09/01/00	Atlético Madrid	A	0-1	
17/01/00	Real Madrid	A	1-2	Romerito
23/01/00	Rayo Vallecano	H	2-1	David Castedo, Diego Tristán (p)
30/01/00	CD Numancia	A	1-3	Diego Tristán
06/02/00	Real Sociedad	H	2-1	Carlos, Armando
12/02/00	Athletic Bilbao	A	1-1	Diego Tristán
20/02/00	RC Celta	H	1-0	Diego Tristán
27/02/00	RC Deportivo	A	1-2	Diego Tristán
05/03/00	Real Zaragoza	H	1-1	Carlos
12/03/00	Málaga CF	A	0-0	
19/03/00	Racing Santander	H	1-2	Diego Tristán
25/03/00	Valencia CF	A	0-1	
02/04/00	RCD Espanyol	H	1-3	Eto'o
09/04/00	FC Barcelona	A	3-0	Eto'o 2, Carreras
16/04/00	Deportivo Alavés	H	2-0	Lauren, Carlos
23/04/00	Real Oviedo	A	0-0	
30/04/00	Real Betis	H	4-0	Lauren, Diego Tristán, Eto'o 2
07/05/00	Sevilla FC	A	4-0	Diego Tristán 2, Carlos 2
14/05/00	Real Valladolid	A	1-2	Carlos
19/05/00	Atlético Madrid	H	1-2	Eto'o

CD NUMANCIA

Club Deportivo Numancia
Av. Mariano Vicent 16
42003 Soria
tel - (975) 227303
fax - (975) 224081
website - www.cdnumancia.com
Year of Formation - 1945
President - Francisco Rubio Garcés
Manager - Felipe Martínez Lago
Coach - Andoni Goikoetxea
(00/01 - Francisco Herrera)
Stadium - Los Pajaritos (10,000)

APPEARANCES 99/00

	P	Ap	(s)	Gls
Constantin BARBU (ROM)	M	24	(10)	6
Alberto BELSUE	D	18	(2)	
Francisco José CASTAÑO	D	30	(4)	4
Jorge Luis DELGADO (URU)	A	7	(6)	5
Juan ELEDER	D	3	(1)	
"IÑAQUI" Hurtado	D	15	(9)	
Diego JAUME (URU)	M	21	(3)	
José Luis MORALES	M		(12)	3
Alejandro MORAN	M	14	(6)	2
Fabrice MOREAU (CMR)	M	3	(6)	
Juan Ramón López MUÑIZ	D	36		
Raúl MUÑOZ (CHL)	M	3	(1)	
Domingo NAGORE	M	37		1
Alvaro Adrián NUÑEZ	G	37		
OCTAVIO Viñals	D	34		1
Pedro Rafael OJEDA (ARG)	A	30	(3)	3
José Rojo "PACHETA"	M	32		7
Jorge PEREZ	M		(10)	
Gabriel POPESCU (ROM)	M	7		1
Alberto RIVERA	M	7	(22)	1
Iván ROCHA (BRA)	D	28		1
RUBEN NAVARRO	A	18	(4)	10
Miguel Angel SORIA	D	12	(2)	1
Vicente Blasco "TITO"	D	1	(4)	
Roberto URROZ	G	1		

LEAGUE RESULTS 1999/2000

22/08/99	Real Valladolid	H	1-0	Rubén Navarro
29/08/99	Real Madrid	A	1-4	Moran
12/09/99	RCD Mallorca	A	0-3	
19/09/99	Athletic Bilbao	H	1-1	Pacheta
26/09/99	RC Deportivo	A	2-0	Popescu, Morales
02/10/99	Málaga CF	H	1-1	Morales
13/10/99	Valencia CF	A	0-4	
16/10/99	FC Barcelona	H	3-3	Ojeda (p), Rubén Navarro, Pacheta
24/10/99	Real Oviedo	A	0-1	
31/10/99	Sevilla FC	H	2-0	Rubén Navarro, Morán
07/11/99	Atlético Madrid	A	2-2	Castaño, Nagore
21/11/99	Rayo Vallecano	H	3-1	Rubén Navarro, Morales, Castaño
28/11/99	Real Sociedad	A	1-2	Castaño (p)
05/12/99	RC Celta	H	3-1	og (Cáceres), Rubén Navarro, Octavio
12/12/99	Real Zaragoza	A	3-3	Rubén Navarro 2, Barbu
19/12/99	Racing Santander	H	2-1	Pacheta, Barbu
22/12/99	RCD Espanyol	A	1-3	Rubén Navarro
05/01/00	Deportivo Alavés	H	0-0	
09/01/00	Real Betis	A	2-1	Barbu (p), Ojeda
16/01/00	Real Valladolid	A	0-2	
23/01/00	Real Madrid	H	0-0	
30/01/00	RCD Mallorca	H	3-1	Pacheta 2, Castaño (p)
07/02/00	Athletic Bilbao	A	1-2	Pacheta
13/02/00	RC Deportivo	H	1-0	Pacheta
20/02/00	Málaga CF	A	1-3	Rivera
26/02/00	Valencia CF	H	1-2	Soria
04/03/00	FC Barcelona	A	0-4	
12/03/00	Real Oviedo	H	1-1	Delgado
19/03/00	Sevilla FC	A	0-4	
25/03/00	Atlético Madrid	H	3-0	Delgado 2, Barbu
02/04/00	Rayo Vallecano	A	0-0	
09/04/00	Real Sociedad	H	1-2	Delgado
16/04/00	RC Celta	A	0-0	
22/04/00	Real Zaragoza	H	1-2	Rocha (p)
30/04/00	Racing Santander	A	1-1	Rubén Navarro
06/05/00	RCD Espanyol	H	2-0	Barbu, Ojeda
14/05/00	Deportivo Alavés	A	2-2	Barbu, Rubén Navarro
20/05/00	Real Betis	H	1-2	Delgado

REAL OVIEDO

CLUB DIRECTORY

Real Oviedo Club de Fútbol
Palacio Valdés 9
33002 Oviedo (Asturias)
tel - (985) 212897
fax - (985) 224058
Year of Formation - 1926
President - Eugenio Prieto Alvarez
Manager - Félix Ortega
Coach - Luis Aragonés
(00/01 - Radomir Antic)
Stadium - Carlos Tartiere (23,500)

APPEARANCES 99/00

	P	Ap	(s)	Gls
Oscar ALVAREZ	D		(3)	
Daniel AMIEVA	M	4	(11)	1
Iván ANIA	M	4	(9)	1
Ricardo González BANGO	M	8	(3)	3
BORIS González	D	34	(1)	1
Gert CLAESSENS (BEL)	M	3	(5)	
Mateo CORBO (URU)	D	3	(3)	
Frédéric DANJOU (FRA)	D	31	(3)	2
Julio César DELY VALDES (PAN)	A	34		11
Peter DUBOVSKY (SVK)	M	18	(1)	2
Xabier ESKURZA	D	22	(5)	
ESTEBAN Andrés	G	38		
FÁBIO PINTO (BRA)	A	1	(13)	
Juan Antonio GONZALEZ (URU)	A	3	(13)	2
IVAN IGLESIAS	M	7	(16)	2
JAIME Fernández	M	1	(9)	1
KEITA Idrissa (NIG)	M	17		
Roberto LOSADA	M	34	(1)	6
Peter MØLLER (DEN)	A		(1)	
Albert NADJ (YUG)	D	13	(3)	
Viktor ONOPKO (RUS)	D	31		2
PAULO BENTO (POR)	M	36		3
Roberto Fabián POMPEI (ARG)	M	36	(1)	4
Franck RABARIVONY (FRA)	D	28	(4)	
RUBEN Suárez	M	12	(6)	3

LEAGUE RESULTS 1999/2000

22/08/99	RC Celta	H	1-0	Danjou
29/08/99	Real Zaragoza	A	0-4	
12/09/99	Racing Santander	H	1-2	Dely Valdés
18/09/99	RCD Espanyol	A	1-2	Dely Valdés
26/09/99	Deportivo Alavés	H	1-0	Losada
03/10/99	Real Betis	A	0-1	
13/10/99	Real Valladolid	H	1-1	Dely Valdés
16/10/99	Real Madrid	A	2-2	Paulo Bento, Pompei
24/10/99	CD Numancia	H	1-0	Losada
31/10/99	Athletic Bilbao	A	1-1	Dubovsky
07/11/99	RC Deportivo	H	0-1	
21/11/99	Málaga CF	A	0-4	
28/11/99	Valencia CF	H	0-0	
04/12/99	FC Barcelona	A	2-3	Losada, González
12/12/99	RCD Mallorca	A	1-1	Dely Valdés
19/12/99	Sevilla FC	H	4-2	Onopko, Iván Iglesias, Dely Valdés, Jaime
22/12/99	Atlético Madrid	A	0-5	
05/01/00	Rayo Vallecano	H	2-0	Losada, Iván Iglesias
09/01/00	Real Sociedad	A	0-0	
16/01/00	RC Celta	A	3-5	Dely Valdés 2, Bango
23/01/00	Real Zaragoza	H	1-0	Dely Valdés (p)
30/01/00	Racing Santander	A	1-3	Amieva
06/02/00	RCD Espanyol	H	1-0	Rubén
13/02/00	Deportivo Alavés	A	0-1	
20/02/00	Real Betis	H	1-1	Rubén
27/02/00	Real Valladolid	A	1-2	Bango
04/03/00	Real Madrid	H	1-1	González
12/03/00	CD Numancia	A	1-1	Dely Valdés
19/03/00	Athletic Bilbao	H	1-0	Bango
26/03/00	RC Deportivo	A	1-3	Danjou
02/04/00	Málaga CF	H	2-2	Boris, Rubén
09/04/00	Valencia CF	A	2-6	Onopko, Pompei
15/04/00	FC Barcelona	H	3-0	Dely Valdés 2, Pompei
23/04/00	RCD Mallorca	H	0-0	
30/04/00	Sevilla FC	A	3-2	Paulo Bento, Pompei, Losada
07/05/00	Atlético Madrid	H	2-2	Losada, Paulo Bento (p)
14/05/00	Rayo Vallecano	A	2-1	Dubovsky, Ania
20/05/00	Real Sociedad	H	0-1	

RACING SANTANDER

CLUB DIRECTORY

Real Racing Club de Santander
Paseo de Pereda 28
39004 Santander
tel - (942) 282828
fax - (942) 283038
website - www.realracingclub.es
Year of Formation - 1913
President - Miguel Angel Díaz Díaz
Manager - Miguel Sánchez
Coach - Gustavo Benítez
(00/01 - Andoni Goikoetxea)
Stadium - El Sardinero (25,000)

APPEARANCES 99/00

	P	Ap	(s)	Gls
José Emilio AMAVISCA	M	32		2
Claudio David ARZENO (ARG)	D	28	(2)	2
Vladimir BESCHASTNYKH (RUS)	A	3	(21)	1
Pablo CASAR	D		(1)	
José María CEBALLOS	G	21		
José María Alonso "CHEMA"	D	12	(6)	
Gonzalo COLSA	M	16	(2)	
Marcelo Fabián ESPINA (ARG)	M	36		2
ISMAEL Ruiz	M	13	(7)	1
Erwin LEMMENS (BEL)	G	17		
Javier MANJARIN	M	23	(8)	2
Olof MELLBERG (SWE)	D	37		
Fernando MORAN	D	1	(3)	
Pedro Manuel MUNITIS	A	35		6
Francisco Enrique "NERU"	D	17	(9)	
Daniel ROIZ	G		(2)	
Sigurd RUSHFELDT (NOR)	A	3	(22)	2
"SALVA" Ballesta	A	36		27
Sergei SHUSTIKOV (RUS)	D	3	(8)	
José María Suárez "SIETES"	D	31	(1)	
Washington TAIS (URU)	D	20	(2)	1
David VILLABONA	M	4	(1)	
Angel VIVAR DORADO	M	30	(2)	6

LEAGUE RESULTS 1999/2000

21/08/99	Valencia CF	A	2-1	Salva 2 (1p)
29/08/99	FC Barcelona	H	1-2	Salva (p)
12/09/99	Real Oviedo	A	2-1	Salva 2 (1p)
19/09/99	Sevilla FC	H	2-2	Salva (p), Munitis
26/09/99	Atlético Madrid	A	0-2	
03/10/99	Rayo Vallecano	H	1-1	Beschastnykh
13/10/99	Real Sociedad	A	5-2	Munitis, Salva 4
16/10/99	RC Celta	H	3-0	Salva 3
24/10/99	Real Zaragoza	A	1-4	Tais
31/10/99	RCD Mallorca	H	1-1	Amavisca (p)
07/11/99	RCD Espanyol	H	2-2	Arzeno, Salva
28/11/99	Real Betis	H	1-1	Vivar Dorado
05/12/99	Real Valladolid	A	0-1	
08/12/99	Deportivo Alavés	A	1-2	Salva
12/12/99	Real Madrid	H	1-1	Vivar Dorado
19/12/99	CD Numancia	A	1-2	Rushfeldt
22/12/99	Athletic Bilbao	H	2-2	Salva (p), Amavisca
05/01/00	RC Deportivo	A	3-0	Salva 2, Munitis
09/01/00	Málaga CF	H	2-3	Salva 2 (1p)
16/01/00	Valencia CF	H	1-1	Salva (p)
23/01/00	FC Barcelona	A	0-1	
30/01/00	Real Oviedo	H	3-1	Munitis, Vivar Dorado, Espina
06/02/00	Sevilla FC	A	0-1	
13/02/00	Atlético Madrid	H	2-1	Vivar Dorado 2
20/02/00	Rayo Vallecano	A	2-1	Ismael, Arzeno
27/02/00	Real Sociedad	H	0-0	
05/03/00	RC Celta	A	0-2	
12/03/00	Real Zaragoza	H	1-2	Munitis
19/03/00	RCD Mallorca	A	2-1	Manjarín, Munitis
25/03/00	RCD Espanyol	A	0-1	
02/04/00	Deportivo Alavés	H	0-0	
09/04/00	Real Betis	A	2-2	Salva (p), Rushfeldt
16/04/00	Real Valladolid	H	1-1	Salva
22/04/00	Real Madrid	A	4-2	Manjarín, Vivar Dorado, Salva 2 (1p)
30/04/00	CD Numancia	H	1-1	Salva
07/05/00	Athletic Bilbao	A	2-2	Espina, Salva (p)
14/05/00	RC Deportivo	H	0-0	
20/05/00	Málaga CF	A	0-0	

RAYO VALLECANO

CLUB DIRECTORY

Rayo Vallecano de Madrid
Avda Payaso Fofó s/n
28018 Madrid
tel - (914) 782253
fax - (914) 771754
website - www.rayovallecano.es
Year of Formation - 1924
President - María Teresa Rivero Sánchez
Manager - Félix Uceda
Coach - Juan de la Cruz Ramos
Stadium - María Teresa Rivero Sánchez (15,500)

APPEARANCES 99/00

	P	Ap	(s)	Gls
Angel Luis ALCAZAR	D	36		
Iván AMAYA	D	15	(6)	1
Juan Antonio Pérez "BOLO"	A	28	(4)	10
Daniel BOUZAS	A		(1)	
Manuel CANABAL	A	21	(12)	11
David CLOTET	D	15	(5)	1
Jesús Diego COTA	D	35	(1)	
Mark DRAPER (ENG)	M	1	(3)	
Eduardo ESTIBARIZ	M	20	(3)	1
Jordi FERRON	D	24	(11)	7
GILMAR Jorge dos Santos (BRA)	M	1	(1)	
HÉLDER Martino Rodrigues (ANG)	D	22	(5)	1
Jean-François HERNANDEZ (FRA)	D	33		4
Kasey KELLER (USA)	G	28		
Carlos LLORENS	M	34	(1)	4
Julen LOPETEGUI	G	10		
LUIS CEMBRANOS	M	30	(5)	4
Martín Roberto MANDRA (ARG)	D		(2)	
"MICHEL" Sánchez	M	16	(13)	5
"MICHEL" Carrilero	A	9	(14)	1
Gerhard POSCHNER (GER)	M	25	(2)	
"QUINZINHO" da Silva (POR)	M		(1)	
Pablo SANZ	D	14	(13)	
Dave VAN DEN BERGH (HOL)	M	1	(8)	

LEAGUE RESULTS 1999/2000

22/08/99	Atlético Madrid	A	2-0	Hernández, Ferrón
29/08/99	RCD Mallorca	H	2-1	Luis Cembranos, Canabal
12/09/99	Real Sociedad	H	2-1	Ferrón, Míchel Sánchez
19/09/99	RC Celta	A	1-0	Bolo
26/09/99	Real Zaragoza	H	0-1	
03/10/99	Racing Santander	A	1-1	Bolo
13/10/99	RCD Espanyol	H	2-1	Hernández, Canabal
17/10/99	Deportivo Alavés	A	1-0	Bolo
24/10/99	Real Betis	H	1-3	Luis Cembranos
31/10/99	Real Valladolid	A	2-1	Ferrón, Llorens
06/11/99	Real Madrid	H	2-3	Ferrón, Canabal
21/11/99	CD Numancia	A	1-3	Canabal
28/11/99	Athletic Bilbao	H	1-2	Estibariz
05/12/99	RC Deportivo	A	2-3	Bolo, Hélder
12/12/99	Málaga CF	H	4-1	Bolo, Hernández, Llorens, Canabal
19/12/99	Valencia CF	A	1-3	Luis Cembranos
22/12/99	FC Barcelona	H	1-1	Luis Cembranos
05/01/00	Real Oviedo	A	0-2	
09/01/00	Sevilla FC	H	2-0	Clotet, Bolo
15/01/00	Atlético Madrid	H	1-1	Llorens (p)
23/01/00	RCD Mallorca	A	1-2	Canabal
30/01/00	Real Sociedad	A	1-2	Ferrón
06/02/00	RC Celta	H	1-0	Ferrón
13/02/00	Real Zaragoza	A	1-1	Míchel Carrilero
20/02/00	Racing Santander	H	1-2	Míchel Sánchez
27/02/00	RCD Espanyol	A	1-5	Canabal
05/03/00	Deportivo Alavés	H	0-1	
11/03/00	Real Betis	A	1-1	Míchel Sánchez
18/03/00	Real Valladolid	H	4-1	Amaya, Canabal 2, og (Peña)
25/03/00	Real Madrid	A	0-0	
02/04/00	CD Numancia	H	0-0	
09/04/00	Athletic Bilbao	A	2-1	Míchel Sánchez, Llorens (p)
16/04/00	RC Deportivo	H	2-0	Míchel Sánchez (p), Ferrón
22/04/00	Málaga CF	A	0-2	
29/04/00	Valencia CF	H	1-3	Bolo
06/05/00	FC Barcelona	A	2-0	Bolo 2
14/05/00	Real Oviedo	H	1-2	Canabal
19/05/00	Sevilla FC	A	3-2	Canabal, Bolo, Hernández

REAL MADRID

Real Madrid Club de Fútbol
Concha Espina 1, 28036 Madrid
tel - (913) 984300 / fax - (913) 440695
website - www.realmadrid.es
Year of Formation - 1902
President - Florentino Pérez
Coach - John Toshack; Vicente Del Bosque
Stadium - Santiago Bernabéu (106,500)

MAJOR HONOURS
League Championship - (27)
1932, 1933, 1954, 1955, 1957, 1958, 1961,
1962, 1963, 1964, 1965, 1967, 1968, 1969,
1972, 1975, 1976, 1978, 1979, 1980, 1986,
1987, 1988, 1989, 1990, 1995, 1997.
Domestic Cup - (17) 1905, 1906, 1907, 1908,
1917, 1934, 1936, 1946, 1947, 1962, 1970,
1974, 1975, 1980, 1982, 1989, 1993.
European Champions' Cup - (8) 1956, 1957,
1958, 1959, 1960, 1966, 1998, 2000.
UEFA Cup - (2) 1985, 1986.
World Club Cup - (2) 1960, 1998.

APPEARANCES 99/00

	P	Ap	(s)	Gls
David AGANZO	M		(4)	
Nicolas ANELKA (FRA)	A	12	(7)	2
Elvir BALJIC (BOS)	M	3	(8)	1
Albano BIZZARRI (ARG)	G	7		
Iker CASILLAS	G	26	(1)	
Javier DORADO	D	1	(1)	
Samuel ETO'O (CMR)	A		(2)	
FERNANDO Fernández	M	1		
GEREMI Njitap (CMR)	D	15	(5)	
José María Gutiérrez "GUTI"	M	21	(7)	6
Iván HELGUERA	D	27	(6)	
Fernando Ruiz HIERRO	D	19	(1)	5
Bodo ILLGNER (GER)	G	5		
IVAN CAMPO	D	17	(3)	
JÚLIO CÉSAR Santos (BRA)	D	20	(1)	
Aitor KARANKA	D	19	(3)	
Christian KAREMBEU (FRA)	M	10	(5)	
Steve McMANAMAN (ENG)	M	19	(9)	3
José Manuel MECA	M	1	(9)	1
MICHEL SALGADO	D	28	(1)	
Fernando MORIENTES	A	28	(1)	12
Perica OGNJENOVIC (YUG)	M	3	(8)	
RAUL González	A	32	(2)	17
Fernando REDONDO (ARG)	M	30		
ROBERTO CARLOS da Silva (BRA)	D	35		4
Manuel SANCHIS	D	5	(9)	
SÁVIO Bortolini (BRA)	A	23	(2)	4
Clarence SEEDORF (HOL)	M	8	(2)	
Rolando David ZARATE (ARG)	A	3	(3)	1

LEAGUE RESULTS 1999/2000

21/08/99	RCD Mallorca	A	2-1	Morientes, Raúl
29/08/99	CD Numancia	H	4-1	og (Rocha), Sávio, McManaman, Hierro (p)
12/09/99	Athletic Bilbao	A	2-2	McManaman, Guti
18/09/99	RC Deportivo	H	1-1	Raúl
25/09/99	Málaga CF	A	1-1	og (Rufete)
03/10/99	Valencia CF	H	2-3	Morientes 2
13/10/99	FC Barcelona	A	2-2	Raúl 2
16/10/99	Real Oviedo	H	2-2	Morientes, Sávio
23/10/99	Sevilla FC	A	1-1	Raúl
30/10/99	Atlético Madrid	H	1-3	Morientes
06/11/99	Rayo Vallecano	A	3-2	Morientes, Hierro (p), Raúl
21/11/99	Real Sociedad	H	1-1	Sávio
28/11/99	RC Celta	A	0-1	
04/12/99	Real Zaragoza	H	1-5	Raúl
12/12/99	Racing Santander	A	1-1	Raúl
18/12/99	RCD Espanyol	H	2-1	Raúl, Hierro
21/12/99	Deportivo Alavés	A	3-1	Hierro, Guti, Raúl
17/01/00	RCD Mallorca	H	2-1	Raúl, Roberto Carlos
23/01/00	CD Numancia	A	0-0	
26/01/00	Real Betis	H	2-1	Guti, Morientes
30/01/00	Athletic Bilbao	H	3-1	Guti, Morientes, Raúl
06/02/00	RC Deportivo	A	2-5	Morientes, Hierro
12/02/00	Málaga CF	H	1-0	Zárate
15/02/00	Real Valladolid	H	1-0	Meca
20/02/00	Valencia CF	A	1-1	Guti
26/02/00	FC Barcelona	H	3-0	Roberto Carlos, Anelka, Morientes
04/03/00	Real Oviedo	A	1-1	Raúl
11/03/00	Sevilla FC	H	3-1	Raúl, Guti, Morientes
18/03/00	Atlético Madrid	A	1-1	Morientes
25/03/00	Rayo Vallecano	H	0-0	
01/04/00	Real Sociedad	A	1-1	Sávio
09/04/00	RC Celta	H	1-0	Raúl
15/04/00	Real Zaragoza	A	1-0	Raúl (p)
22/04/00	Racing Santander	H	2-4	Roberto Carlos, McManaman
29/04/00	RCD Espanyol	A	2-0	Baljic, Raúl (p)
06/05/00	Deportivo Alavés	H	0-1	
14/05/00	Real Betis	A	2-0	Roberto Carlos, Anelka
19/05/00	Real Valladolid	H	0-1	

REAL SOCIEDAD

CLUB DIRECTORY

Real Sociedad de Fútbol
Paseo de Anoeta 1, 20014 San Sebastián
tel - (943) 462833 / fax - (943) 458941
website - www.real-sociedad.com
Year of Formation - 1909
President - Luis Uranga Otaegui
Manager - Iñaki Otegi Arbelaiz
Coach - Bernd Krauss; Javier Clemente
Stadium - Anoeta (32,000)

MAJOR HONOURS
League Championship - (2) 1981, 1982.
Domestic Cup - (2) 1909, 1987.

APPEARANCES 99/00

	P	Ap	(s)	Gls
Mutiu ADEPOJU (NIG)	M	9	(4)	
ALBERTO López	G	37		
Aitor ALDEONDO	A		(14)	1
Iker ALVAREZ	G	1	(2)	
Mikel ANTIA	D	6	(8)	1
Mikel ARANBURU	A	22	(5)	3
Agustín ARANZABAL	D	31		1
José Javier BARKERO	M	2	(4)	1
Víctor Manuel BONILLA (COL)	A	11	(8)	3
Sergio CORINO	D	9		
Oscar DE PAULA	A	19	(15)	9
Francisco Javier DE PEDRO	M	23	(4)	3
Miguel Angel FUENTES	D	20	(1)	
Juan GOMEZ (ARG)	M	25	(6)	
Félix GUERRERO	D	13	(1)	1
Zuhaitz GURRUTXAGA	D	16		
Iñigo IDIAKEZ	M	18	(9)	4
Edgaras JANKAUSKAS (LIT)	A	15		4
Igor JAUREGI	D	2	(3)	
Dmitriy KHOKHLOV (RUS)	M	21		3
Dietmar KÜHBAUER (AUT)	M	4	(8)	
Joseba LLORENTE	M	1	(7)	1
Aitor LOPEZ REKARTE	D	26	(5)	1
"LOREN" Juarros	D	30		1
José Antonio PIKABEA	D	25	(1)	2
Ricardo Manuel SÁ PINTO (POR)	A	32	(2)	2

LEAGUE RESULTS 1999/2000

22/08/99	Sevilla FC	A	2-2	De Pedro 2 (1p)
28/08/99	Atlético Madrid	H	4-1	De Paula 2, Bonilla 2
12/09/99	Rayo Vallecano	A	1-2	Idiakez
19/09/99	RCD Mallorca	H	2-1	Idiakez, Aldeondo
25/09/99	RC Celta	H	0-2	
03/10/99	Real Zaragoza	A	0-2	
13/10/99	Racing Santander	H	2-5	Bonilla, Antía
17/10/99	RCD Espanyol	A	0-0	
24/10/99	Deportivo Alavés	H	1-1	López Rekarte
31/10/99	Real Betis	A	0-1	
07/11/99	Real Valladolid	H	3-0	De Pedro, Sá Pinto, De Paula
21/11/99	Real Madrid	A	1-1	Pikabea
28/11/99	CD Numancia	H	2-1	De Paula, Llorente
04/12/99	Athletic Bilbao	A	1-1	Aranburu
12/12/99	RC Deportivo	H	0-1	
19/12/99	Málaga CF	A	0-0	
22/12/99	Valencia CF	H	0-0	
05/01/00	FC Barcelona	A	1-3	og (Guardiola)
09/01/00	Real Oviedo	H	0-0	
16/01/00	Sevilla FC	H	1-1	Guerrero
23/01/00	Atlético Madrid	A	1-1	Jankauskas
30/01/00	Rayo Vallecano	H	2-1	Jankauskas, De Paula
06/02/00	RCD Mallorca	A	1-2	Aranburu
13/02/00	RC Celta	A	1-4	De Paula
20/02/00	Real Zaragoza	H	2-1	Aranburu. Loren
27/02/00	Racing Santander	A	0-0	
05/03/00	RCD Espanyol	H	1-0	Jankauskas
12/03/00	Deportivo Alavés	A	1-2	Khokhlov
19/03/00	Real Betis	H	1-0	Jankauskas
25/03/00	Real Valladolid	A	1-2	Sá Pinto
01/04/00	Real Madrid	H	1-1	De Paula
09/04/00	CD Numancia	A	2-1	Idiakez 2
16/04/00	Athletic Bilbao	H	4-1	Aranzábal, Khokhlov, De Paula 2
23/04/00	RC Deportivo	A	0-2	
30/04/00	Málaga CF	H	2-2	Khokhlov, Pikabea
06/05/00	Valencia CF	A	0-4	
14/05/00	FC Barcelona	H	0-0	
20/05/00	Real Oviedo	A	1-0	Barkero

SEVILLA FC

CLUB DIRECTORY

Sevilla Fútbol Club
Estadio Sánchez Pizjuán
Avda Eduardo Dato s/n, 41005 Sevilla
tel - (954) 535353 / fax - (954) 536061
website - www.sevillafc.es
Year of Formation - 1905
President - Rafael Carrión
Manager - Herminio Menéndez
Coach - Marcos Alonso; Juan Carlos Alvarez
Stadium - Sánchez Pizjuán (55,000)

MAJOR HONOURS
League Championship - (1) 1946.
Domestic Cup - (3) 1935, 1939, 1948.

APPEARANCES 99/00

	P	Ap	(s)	Gls
ALFREDO Santaelena	D	1		
ANGEL Rodríguez	D	17	(8)	
Orlando Lemos "BAKERO" (POR)	M		(1)	
Sebastián Manuel CORONA	D	1		
FRANCISCO Lama	M	24	(2)	
GERMAN Rojas	D	3	(1)	
HECTOR Berenguel	D	28	(3)	
Mirsad HIBIC (BOS)	D	29		
"JESULI" Mora	A	15	(16)	3
JESUS Heredia	G		(1)	
JUAN CARLOS Gómez	A	30	(4)	12
Ivan JURIC (CRO)	M	10	(2)	2
"LOREN" del Pino	A	7	(7)	2
Carlos MARCHENA	D	33		
MARCOS Antonio García	D		(1)	
Francisco MIJE	M	3		
Gabriel MOYA	M	2	(8)	1
"NANDO" Martínez	D	30		
Nicolás OLIVERA (URU)	A	9	(9)	2
Frode OLSEN (NOR)	G	18		
Marcelo OTERO (URU)	A	13	(9)	1
Inti PODESTA (URU)	M	8	(2)	
José Miguel PRIETO	D	14	(3)	
José María QUEVEDO	M	24	(1)	3
Gerardo RABAJDA (URU)	G	2		
José Antonio REYES	A		(1)	
Julián Villena SORIANO	D		(2)	
TABARE Abayuba Silva (URU)	M	21	(4)	
Vasilios TSARTAS (GRE)	M	30	(3)	10
Juan José VALENCIA	G	18		
VICTOR Salas	M	9	(10)	1
Marcelo ZALAYETA (URU)	A	19	(9)	5

LEAGUE RESULTS 1999/2000

22/08/99	Real Sociedad	H	2-2	Juan Carlos, Tsartas
29/08/99	RC Celta	A	1-2	Tsartas
12/09/99	Real Zaragoza	H	0-0	
19/09/99	Racing Santander	A	2-2	Tsartas, Olivera
26/09/99	RCD Espanyol	H	1-2	Juan Carlos
03/10/99	Deportivo Alavés	A	0-0	
12/10/99	Real Betis	H	3-0	Quevedo, Juan Carlos, Loren
17/10/99	Real Valladolid	A	1-2	Otero
23/10/99	Real Madrid	H	1-1	Tsartas
31/10/99	CD Numancia	A	0-2	
07/11/99	Athletic Bilbao	H	0-0	
21/11/99	RC Deportivo	A	2-5	Moya, Tsartas (p)
27/11/99	Málaga CF	H	0-0	
04/12/99	Valencia CF	A	0-2	
11/12/99	FC Barcelona	H	3-2	Juan Carlos 2, Víctor
19/12/99	Real Oviedo	A	2-4	Juan Carlos 2
22/12/99	RCD Mallorca	A	1-3	Zalayeta
05/01/00	Atlético Madrid	H	2-1	Juan Carlos, Zalayeta
09/01/00	Rayo Vallecano	A	0-2	
16/01/00	Real Sociedad	A	1-1	Quevedo
23/01/00	RC Celta	H	0-1	
30/01/00	Real Zaragoza	A	1-2	Tsartas
06/02/00	Racing Santander	H	1-0	Zalayeta
13/02/00	RCD Espanyol	A	2-2	Tsartas 2 (2p)
20/02/00	Deportivo Alavés	H	2-2	Juan Carlos, Zalayeta
27/02/00	Real Betis	A	1-1	Tsartas (p)
05/03/00	Real Valladolid	H	0-1	
11/03/00	Real Madrid	A	1-3	Juan Carlos
19/03/00	CD Numancia	H	4-0	Zalayeta, Juric, Jesuli, Quevedo
25/03/00	Athletic Bilbao	A	1-1	Juan Carlos
02/04/00	RC Deportivo	H	1-3	Juan Carlos
09/04/00	Málaga CF	A	0-3	
15/04/00	Valencia CF	H	1-2	Jesuli
22/04/00	FC Barcelona	A	0-2	
30/04/00	Real Oviedo	H	2-3	Loren, Olivera
07/05/00	RCD Mallorca	H	0-4	
13/05/00	Atlético Madrid	A	1-1	Tsartas
19/05/00	Rayo Vallecano	H	2-3	Jesuli, Juric

VALENCIA CF

CLUB DIRECTORY

Valencia Club de Fútbol
Avda de Aragón 33, 46010 Valencia
tel - (963) 372626 / fax - (963) 611235
website - www.valenciacf.es
Year of Formation - 1919
President - Pedro Cortés
Manager - Manuel Llorente Martín
Coach - Héctor Cúper
Stadium - Mestalla (55,000)

MAJOR HONOURS
League Championship - (4)
1942, 1944, 1947, 1971.
Domestic Cup - (6)
1941, 1949, 1954, 1967, 1979, 1999.
European Cup-winners' Cup - (1) 1980.
Fairs' Cup - (2) 1962, 1963.
European Super Cup - (1) 1980.

APPEARANCES 99/00

	P	Ap	(s)	Gls
David ALBELDA	M	14	(7)	
Jocelyn ANGLOMA (FRA)	D	30		1
Miguel Angel ANGULO	M	19	(10)	5
Joachim BKÖRKLUND (SWE)	D	14	(9)	
Santiago CAÑIZARES	G	23		
Amedeo CARBONI (ITA)	D	27	(1)	1
Miroslav DJUKIC (YUG)	D	33		
Daniel FAGIANI (ARG)	D	5	(3)	
Francisco Javier FARINOS	M	25	(9)	5
GERARD López	M	32	(1)	4
GERARDO García	D	5	(5)	
Adrian ILIE (ROM)	A	15	(7)	5
Cristián "KILY" GONZALEZ (ARG)	M	28	(3)	2
Claudio LOPEZ (ARG)	A	32	(2)	11
Gaizka MENDIETA	M	31	(2)	13
Luis MILLA	M	9	(3)	
OSCAR García	M	3	(17)	4
Andrés PALOP	G	15		
Mauricio PELLEGRINO (ARG)	D	33		1
Alain ROCHE (FRA)	D	1	(1)	
Juan SANCHEZ	A	23	(9)	5
Denis SERBAN (ROM)	M		(1)	
Miguel Angel SORIA	D	1	(2)	
Goran VLAOVIC (CRO)	A		(4)	

LEAGUE RESULTS 1999/2000

21/08/99	Racing Santander	H	1-2	Mendieta (p)
29/08/99	RCD Espanyol	A	2-3	Mendieta (p), Sánchez
11/09/99	Deportivo Alavés	H	0-2	
18/09/99	Real Betis	A	0-1	
25/09/99	Real Valladolid	H	0-0	
03/10/99	Real Madrid	A	3-2	Mendieta (p), Gerard, López
13/10/99	CD Numancia	H	4-0	Ilie 2, Farinós, Oscar
16/10/99	Athletic Bilbao	A	0-1	
23/10/99	RC Deportivo	H	2-0	Kily González, Gerard
30/10/99	Málaga CF	A	1-1	López
07/11/99	RCD Mallorca	A	0-1	
20/11/99	FC Barcelona	H	3-1	López, Ilie, Gerard
28/11/99	Real Oviedo	A	0-0	
04/12/99	Sevilla FC	H	2-0	Sánchez, López
12/12/99	Atlético Madrid	A	2-1	Mendieta, Sánchez
19/12/99	Rayo Vallecano	H	3-1	Sánchez 2, Mendieta
22/12/99	Real Sociedad	A	0-0	
04/01/00	RC Celta	H	1-1	Gerard
09/01/00	Real Zaragoza	A	2-4	Mendieta 2 (1p)
16/01/00	Racing Santander	A	1-1	Mendieta (p)
23/01/00	RCD Espanyol	H	1-2	Kily González
30/01/00	Deportivo Alavés	A	1-0	Farinós (p)
05/02/00	Real Betis	H	3-1	Ilie, Mendieta (p), Farinós
12/02/00	Real Valladolid	A	0-0	
20/02/00	Real Madrid	H	1-1	Ilie
26/02/00	CD Numancia	A	2-1	Mendieta, López
04/03/00	Athletic Bilbao	H	2-0	Oscar, López
12/03/00	RC Deportivo	A	0-2	
18/03/00	Málaga CF	H	2-2	Angulo 2
25/03/00	RCD Mallorca	H	1-0	Angloma
02/04/00	FC Barcelona	A	0-3	
09/04/00	Real Oviedo	H	6-2	López 2, og (Danjou), Angulo, Farinós (p), Oscar
15/04/00	Sevilla FC	A	2-1	Mendieta, og (Zalayeta)
22/04/00	Atlético Madrid	H	2-0	López, Angulo
29/04/00	Rayo Vallecano	A	3-1	Farinós, Mendieta, Oscar
06/05/00	Real Sociedad	H	4-0	Angulo, López, Carboni, Mendieta
14/05/00	RC Celta	A	0-0	
19/05/00	Real Zaragoza	H	2-1	Pellegrino, López

REAL VALLADOLID

CLUB DIRECTORY

Real Valladolid
Avenida Mundial 82, s/n
47014 Valladolid
tel - (983) 360342
fax - (983) 372164
website - www.realvalladolid.es
Year of Formation - 1928
President - Marcos Fernández Fermoselle
Manager - Carlos Palacios Aparicio
Coach - Gregorio Manzano
(00/01 - Pacho Ferraro)
Stadium - José Zorrilla (31,000)

APPEARANCES 99/00

	P	Ap	(s)	Gls
ALBERTO López	A	11	(16)	2
ARILSON Gilberto da Costa (BRA)	D	2	(3)	
José Luis Pérez CAMINERO	M	14	(9)	4
"CHEMA" José Manuel Jiménez	D	11	(9)	
Edwin Arturo CONGO (COL)	M	5	(7)	1
EUSEBIO Sacristán	M	9	(19)	1
José Antonio GARCIA CALVO	D	33		1
Luis GARCIA	A		(6)	
Gabriel Iván HEINZE (ARG)	D	16	(2)	
Dragan ISAILOVIC (YUG)	M		(7)	
Javier "JAVI" JIMENEZ	M	12		2
Shoji JO (JPN)	A	12	(3)	2
Harold LOZANO (COL)	D	20		
Alberto MARCOS	D	37		
Luis MARQUEZ	D	5	(6)	1
ORLANDO Gutiérrez	D	2		
José Manuel PEÑA (BOL)	D	34		
Alen PETERNAC (CRO)	A	5	(6)	
RICARDO López	G	2	(1)	
RODRIGO Fabri (BRA)	M	29		8
César SANCHEZ	G	36		
José Luis SANTAMARIA	D	31		
Manuel TENA	D	1	(2)	
Javier TORRES GOMEZ	D	25		
Jesús Angel TURIEL	M	14	(6)	
VICTOR Manuel Fernández	M	34		13
Juan VIZCAINO	M	18	(6)	

LEAGUE RESULTS 1999/2000

22/08/99	CD Numancia	A	0-1	
29/08/99	Athletic Bilbao	H	1-0	Víctor
11/09/99	RC Deportivo	A	0-2	
18/09/99	Málaga CF	H	4-2	og (Roteta), Rodrigo, Víctor 2
25/09/99	Valencia CF	A	0-0	
02/10/99	FC Barcelona	H	0-2	
13/10/99	Real Oviedo	A	1-1	Rodrigo (p)
17/10/99	Sevilla FC	H	2-1	Congo, Víctor
24/10/99	Atlético Madrid	A	1-3	Víctor
31/10/99	Rayo Vallecano	H	1-2	Víctor
07/11/99	Real Sociedad	A	0-3	
21/11/99	RC Celta	H	1-3	Rodrigo
28/11/99	Real Zaragoza	A	1-1	Víctor
05/12/99	Racing Santander	H	1-0	Rodrigo
12/12/99	RCD Espanyol	A	1-1	Rodrigo
18/12/99	Deportivo Alavés	H	1-1	Rodrigo
22/12/99	Real Betis	A	1-0	Caminero
05/01/00	RCD Mallorca	A	0-0	
16/01/00	CD Numancia	H	2-0	Rodrigo, Víctor
23/01/00	Athletic Bilbao	A	0-1	
30/01/00	RC Deportivo	H	4-1	Caminero, Víctor 3
06/02/00	Málaga CF	A	0-0	
12/02/00	Valencia CF	H	0-0	
15/02/00	Real Madrid	H	0-1	
20/02/00	FC Barcelona	A	0-4	
27/02/00	Real Oviedo	H	2-1	Jo 2
05/03/00	Sevilla FC	A	1-0	Márquez
12/03/00	Atlético Madrid	H	1-0	Javi Jiménez
18/03/00	Rayo Vallecano	A	1-4	Javi Jiménez
25/03/00	Real Sociedad	H	2-1	Alberto, García Calvo
02/04/00	RC Celta	A	1-1	Caminero
09/04/00	Real Zaragoza	H	1-1	Víctor (p)
16/04/00	Racing Santander	A	1-1	Alberto
22/04/00	RCD Espanyol	H	1-0	Rodrigo (p)
30/04/00	Deportivo Alavés	A	0-1	
07/05/00	Real Betis	H	0-3	
14/05/00	RCD Mallorca	H	2-1	Caminero, Eusebio
19/05/00	Real Madrid	A	1-0	Víctor

REAL ZARAGOZA

CLUB DIRECTORY

Real Zaragoza
Luis Bermejo 3, 50009 Zaragoza
tel - (976) 567777
fax - (976) 568863
Year of Formation - 1932
President - Alfonso Solans Solans
Manager - Javier Paricio Agüeras
Coach - José Francisco Rojo
(00/01 - Juan Manuel Lillo)
Stadium - La Romareda (34,741)

MAJOR HONOURS
Domestic Cup - (4) 1964, 1966, 1986, 1994.
European Cup-winners' Cup - (1) 1995.
Fairs' Cup - (1) 1964.

APPEARANCES 99/00

		P	Ap	(s)	Gls
Roberto Miguel ACUÑA (ARG)	D	29	(2)	5
Xavier AGUADO	D	29		2
Santiago ARAGON	M	29	(4)	1
Luis Carlos CUARTERO	D	10	(9)	
Ander GARITANO	M	23	(7)	4
Luis HELGUERA	D	10	(6)	
Paulo Roberto JAMELLI (BRA)	M	8	(7)	1
JOSE IGNACIO Sáenz	M	5	(11)	
"JUANELE" Castaño	M	29	(5)	8
"JUANMI" García	G	37		
César LAINEZ	G	1	(1)	
Marco LANNA (ITA)	D	17	(2)	
MARCOS VALES	M	14	(10)	2
Jorge Daniel MARTINEZ (ARG)	A		(1)	
Savo MILOSEVIC (YUG)	A	37		23
PABLO Javier Díaz	D	27		
Francisco Jémez "PACO"	D	34		
Vladislav RADIMOV (RUS)	M	8	(2)	1
Jesús Angel SOLANA	D	5	(3)	
Gary SUNDGREN (SWE)	D	28		
Martín VELLISCA	M	29	(5)	3
Jorge González "YORDI"	A	9	(14)	9

LEAGUE RESULTS 1999/2000

22/08/99	FC Barcelona	A	0-2	
29/08/99	Real Oviedo	H	4-0	Jamelli, Vellisca, Milosevic 2
12/09/99	Sevilla FC	A	0-0	
19/09/99	Atlético Madrid	H	1-1	Milosevic
26/09/99	Rayo Vallecano	A	1-0	Milosevic
03/10/99	Real Sociedad	H	2-0	Aragón, Milosevic
13/10/99	RC Celta	A	1-2	Milosevic
17/10/99	RCD Mallorca	H	3-0	Milosevic 2 (1p), Acuña
24/10/99	Racing Santander	H	4-1	Milosevic 3, Juanele
31/10/99	RCD Espanyol	A	1-1	Acuña
07/11/99	Deportivo Alavés	H	2-1	Milosevic 2
21/11/99	Real Betis	A	0-2	
28/11/99	Real Valladolid	H	1-1	Milosevic
04/12/99	Real Madrid	A	5-1	Milosevic 2, Juanele 2, Garitano
12/12/99	CD Numancia	H	3-3	Yordi 2, Vellisca
19/12/99	Athletic Bilbao	A	2-2	Vellisca, Milosevic (p)
22/12/99	RC Deportivo	H	2-1	Milosevic 2
05/01/00	Málaga CF	A	0-0	
09/01/00	Valencia CF	H	4-2	Juanele 2, Milosevic, Radimov
16/01/00	FC Barcelona	H	0-0	
23/01/00	Real Oviedo	A	0-1	
30/01/00	Sevilla FC	H	2-1	Juanele, Aguado
06/02/00	Atlético Madrid	A	2-2	Yordi, Garitano
13/02/00	Rayo Vallecano	H	1-1	Yordi
20/02/00	Real Sociedad	A	1-2	Garitano (p)
27/02/00	RC Celta	H	2-1	Acuña, Milosevic
05/03/00	RCD Mallorca	A	1-1	Garitano (p)
12/03/00	Racing Santander	A	2-1	Yordi 2
19/03/00	RCD Espanyol	H	1-1	Juanele
25/03/00	Deportivo Alavés	A	2-0	Acuña 2
02/04/00	Real Betis	H	1-0	Yordi
09/04/00	Real Valladolid	A	1-1	Marcos Vales
15/04/00	Real Madrid	H	0-1	
23/04/00	CD Numancia	A	2-1	og (Rocha), Yordi
30/04/00	Athletic Bilbao	H	0-0	
07/05/00	RC Deportivo	A	2-2	Juanele, Aguado
14/05/00	Málaga CF	H	3-2	Marcos Vales, Yordi, Milosevic
19/05/00	Valencia CF	A	1-2	Milosevic

SWEDEN

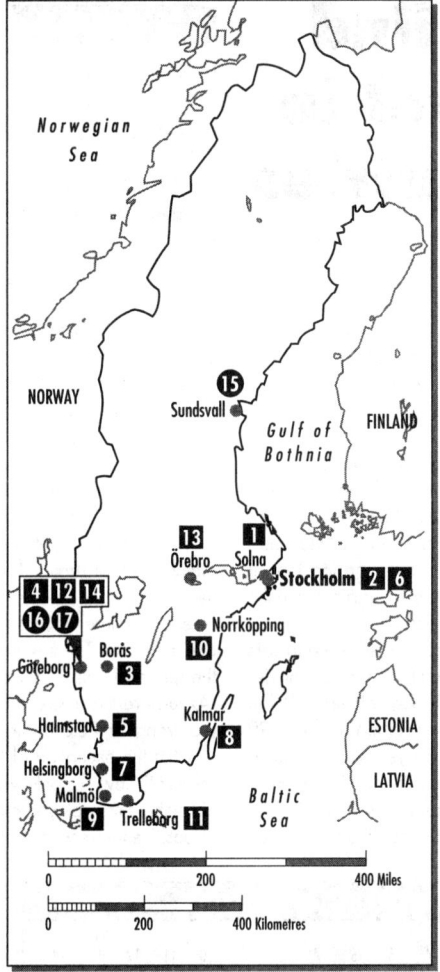

1	AIK	976	10	IFK NORRKÖPING	985
2	DJURGÅRDENS IF	977	11	TRELLEBORGS FF	986
3	IF ELFSBORG	978	12	VÄSTRA FRÖLUNDA IF	987
4	IFK GÖTEBORG	979	13	ÖREBRO SK	988
5	HALMSTADS BK	980	14	ÖRGRYTE IS	989
6	HAMMARBY IF	981	**Promoted clubs**		
7	HELSINGBORGS IF	982	15	GIF SUNDSVALL	
8	KALMAR FF	983	16	BK HÄCKEN	
9	MALMÖ FF	984	17	GAIS	

HELSINGBORG TURN TABLES ON AIK

Swedes find their level in Low Countries

FEDERATION DIRECTORY

Svenska Fotbollförbundet
P.O. Box 1216, 171 23 Solna

tel - (08) 7350900
fax - (08) 275147
website - www.svenskfotboll.se

Year of Formation - 1904
President - Lars-Åke Lagrell
Secretary - Sune Hellströmer

Stadium - Råsunda Stadion, Solna (36,800)

Sweden achieved their first qualification for the European Championship in grand style, dropping just two points and conceding a single goal along the way. But it was a very different story when they had to step up a gear at the finals themselves.

The near-flawless qualifying campaign was something for the Swedes to be proud of, but it could not fully mask the shortage of genuine top-quality players in the team. The pre-Euro 2000 consensus was that all of the side's prominent individuals would have to be on top form if Sweden were to keep their heads above water, but in the event very few did themselves justice.

The task of joint coaches Tommy Söderberg and Lars Lagerbäck was significantly hindered by the serious injuries sustained by two of the team's key players. Stefan Schwarz, crowned Sweden's Player of the Year for 1999 on the basis of his outstanding displays during the qualifying campaign, injured his Achilles tendon in a friendly against Austria and was ruled out of the finals. Henrik Larsson, the team's top scorer in the qualifiers with three goals, broke his leg in October 1999 and missed the rest of the season with his club Celtic. A miraculous recovery enabled him to be selected for Euro 2000, and although he played, he was clearly a long way short of full fitness.

Sweden's defence, so miserly during the qualifiers, came unstuck in the opening match against Belgium. A succession of uncharacteristic howlers at the back helped to hand victory to the co-hosts in the tournament's opening game. And although there was a clean sheet in the next match, against Turkey, for which the joint-coaches rang the changes in every department bar goalkeeper, Sweden's failure to score themselves left them on the brink of elimination. There was still a chance they could reach the quarter-finals if they beat Italy, but even though the 'Azzurri' rested several first-choice players, they were still too strong for the Scandinavians and won the game 2-1.

With the exception of the Celtic duo of Larsson and Johan Mjällby - the only two Swedes to find the net - it was difficult to find a player in a yellow shirt who left any kind of positive impression on the tournament.

The stalwarts of the past, like Joachim Björklund, Niclas Alexandersson and the two Anderssons, Patrik and Kennet, had the air of has-beens, and young gun Fredrik Ljungberg fell well below expectations, even manufacturing the miss of the tournament in the game against Italy.

The future is not necessarily bleak for the Swedes, however. They have been handed a very easy World Cup qualifying group, in which only Turkey appear to be serious rivals for the auto-

LEAGUE CHAMPIONSHIP RESULTS 1999

		1	2	3	4	5	6	7	8	9	10	11	12	13	14
1	AIK		3-1	3-0	2-0	0-1	2-0	2-1	4-0	3-0	2-0	3-0	1-0	1-1	1-1
2	Djurgårdens IF	0-0		1-2	2-0	0-2	1-0	2-4	0-3	4-1	3-0	2-2	1-1	0-1	0-3
3	IF Elfsborg	2-2	2-1		0-1	1-4	3-0	1-1	3-0	5-2	2-1	1-2	2-3	3-1	1-2
4	IFK Göteborg	1-0	0-0	2-0		1-1	2-2	0-1	2-0	1-0	2-3	1-0	1-0	0-1	1-0
5	Halmstads BK	1-0	4-1	3-0	4-0		3-1	4-0	1-0	2-1	1-1	2-2	1-2	5-1	0-0
6	Hammarby IF	0-2	2-1	2-1	2-1	1-0		2-1	2-2	0-1	3-0	4-0	1-2	2-1	0-0
7	Helsingborgs IF	0-2	4-1	1-1	3-1	1-0	2-0		3-0	1-0	0-1	5-3	1-0	2-1	2-0
8	Kalmar FF	1-3	0-0	0-1	0-1	2-0	4-1	0-2		1-0	1-1	3-2	3-1	2-0	2-2
9	Malmö FF	2-1	2-0	4-2	1-1	0-1	2-0	0-4	0-1		0-0	1-2	2-1	3-1	1-1
10	IFK Norrköping	0-1	1-1	1-1	3-0	4-0	3-2	1-0	4-2	5-1		2-5	2-1	1-0	0-2
11	Trelleborgs FF	1-0	2-2	1-2	3-1	1-1	2-2	2-3	1-0	3-1	0-4		1-0	2-1	0-0
12	Västra Frölunda IF	0-1	1-1	4-4	1-2	0-0	1-1	0-0	2-0	2-1	1-1	2-1		2-0	2-1
13	Örebro SK	0-2	1-1	1-0	1-2	1-2	3-1	0-1	2-0	2-0	2-1	1-0	0-1		0-1
14	Örgryte IS	1-1	0-1	5-1	2-2	1-0	2-1	0-1	3-0	4-4	3-1	2-0	4-0	1-1	

LEAGUE CHAMPIONSHIP FINAL TABLE 1999

		Pd	Home					Away					Total					
			W	D	L	F	A	W	D	L	F	A	W	D	L	F	A	PT	GD
1	Helsingborgs IF	26	10	1	2	25	10	7	2	4	19	14	17	3	6	44	24	54	20
2	AIK	26	10	2	1	27	5	6	3	4	15	9	16	5	5	42	14	53	28
3	Halmstads BK	26	9	3	1	31	9	5	3	5	12	13	14	6	6	43	22	48	21
4	Örgryte IS	26	7	4	2	28	13	4	6	3	13	10	11	10	5	41	23	43	18
5	IFK Norrköping	26	8	2	3	27	16	3	4	6	14	20	11	6	9	41	36	39	5
6	IFK Göteborg	26	7	3	3	15	9	4	2	7	12	24	11	5	10	27	33	38	-6
7	Västra Frölunda IF	26	5	6	2	18	13	4	1	8	12	20	9	7	10	30	33	34	-3
8	Trelleborgs FF	26	6	4	3	19	17	3	2	8	20	30	9	6	11	39	47	33	-8
9	IF Elfsborg	26	6	2	5	26	20	3	3	7	15	28	9	5	12	41	48	32	-7
10	Hammarby IF	26	8	2	3	21	12	0	3	10	11	30	8	5	13	32	42	29	-10
11	Kalmar FF	26	6	3	4	19	14	2	1	10	8	27	8	4	14	27	41	28	-14
12	Örebro SK	26	6	1	6	14	12	2	2	9	10	24	8	3	15	24	36	27	-12
13	Malmö FF	26	6	3	4	18	15	1	1	11	12	33	7	4	15	30	48	25	-18
14	Djurgårdens IF	26	4	3	6	16	19	1	6	6	11	22	5	9	12	27	41	24	-14

matic qualifying place. Even with a team not too dissimilar from the one which failed at Euro 2000, Sweden should be strong enough to make it two successful qualifications out of two.

The national team's fortunes in the European Championship were echoed almost exactly by those of AIK in the Champions' League. The 1998 Swedish champions came through their two qualifying rounds, against Dnepr-Transmash Mogilev and AEK Athens, without conceding a goal, but there the party ended. In the Champions' League proper AIK were swamped by the extra quality and professionalism of Barcelona, Fiorentina and Arsenal.

In fairness, the Stockholmers were extremely unlucky not to get anything out of their first two matches, at home to Barça and away to Arsenal, but two late goals conceded in each game left them without

reward. In the end the only point they picked up from their six matches was from a 0-0 draw at home to Fiorentina.

Sweden's other two European representatives, Helsingborg and IFK Gothenburg, also found themselves outclassed when they exited the UEFA Cup at the hands of Italians clubs Parma and Roma, respectively.

Helsingborg had a ready-made excuse for their 1-3 home defeat by Parma. They were still hung over from the euphoria of winning the Swedish championship five days earlier. A priceless 1-0 victory away to Gothenburg on the final day of the Allsvenskan season had sealed the club's first national title in 58 years.

A huge crowd - by Swedish standards - of 15,322 had

TOP SCORERS

15 Marcus ALLBÄCK (Örgryte IS)
13 Henrik BERTILSSON (Halmstads BK)
11 Arild STAVRUM (Helsingborgs IF)
  Mats LILIENBERG (Malmö FF)
10 Christer MATTIASSON (AIK)
9 Michael HANSSON (Trelleborgs FF)
  Jonas WALLERSTEDT (IFK Norrköping)
8 Gustaf ANDERSSON (Västra Frölunda IF)
  Pär EKSTRÖM (Örebro SK)
  Magnus POWELL (Helsingborgs IF)
  Sharbel TOUMA (Djurgårdens IF)

NATIONAL TEAM RESULTS 99/00

18/08/99	Austria	H	Malmö	0-0	
04/09/99	Bulgaria (ECQ)	H	Solna	1-0	Alexandersson (65)
08/09/99	Luxembourg (ECQ)	A	Luxembourg	1-0	Alexandersson (39)
09/10/99	Poland (ECQ)	H	Solna	2-0	Andersson K. (64), Larsson (90)
27/11/99	South Africa	A	Pretoria	0-1	
31/01/00	Denmark	N	La Manga	1-0	Allbäck (22)
04/02/00	Norway	N	La Manga	1-0	Andersson Anders (87p)
23/02/00	Italy	A	Palermo	0-1	
29/03/00	Austria	A	Graz	1-1	Pettersson (86)
26/04/00	Denmark	A	Copenhagen	1-0	Pettersson (39)
03/06/00	Spain	H	Gothenburg	1-1	Nilsson (76p)
10/06/00	Belgium (ECF)	A	Brussels	1-2	Mjällby (53)
15/06/00	Turkey (ECF)	N	Eindhoven	0-0	
19/06/00	Italy (ECF)	N	Eindhoven	1-2	Larsson (77)

NATIONAL TEAM APPEARANCES 99/00

Coaches - Tommy SÖDERBERG & Lars LAGERBÄCK	AUT	BUL	LUX	POL	SAF	DEN	NOR	ITA	AUT	DEN	ESP	BEL	TUR	ITA	Cps	Gls
Magnus HEDMAN (19/03/73) - Coventry City (ENG)	G46	G	G	G			G			G46	G	G	G	G	26	-
Tomas GUSTAFSSON (07/05/73) - AIK/Coventry City (ENG)	D				D			D46			s90			D75	5	-
Johan MJÄLLBY (09/02/71) - Celtic (SCO)	D	M	D	M				s46	M	M	M	M	M	M56	22	3
Teddy LUCIC (15/04/73) - Bologna (ITA)/AIK	D		D			D	D72			s56		s46	D		31	-
Pontus KÅMARK (05/04/69) - AIK	D46	D		D	D	D	s46		D	s46					53	-
										/56						
Niclas ALEXANDERSSON (29/12/71) - Sheffield Wednesday (ENG)	M46	s63	M	M				M		M	M68	M	M62	s52	45	5
Magnus SVENSSON (10/03/69) -																
Viking FK (NOR)/Brøndby IF (DEN)	M46	s83	M46		M	M	M		M				s78	M52	14	-
Daniel ANDERSSON (28/08/77) - Bari (ITA)	M	M						M	s44	M73	M	M70		s56	21	-
Yksel OSMANOVSKI (24/02/77) - Bari (ITA)	M								s66	s70			A		8	2
Kennet ANDERSSON (06/10/67) - Lazio (ITA)/Bologna (ITA)	A	A	A	A				A46		A84	A66	A	A46	s75	79	31
Henrik LARSSON (20/09/71) - Celtic (SCO)	A46	A	A	A						s66	s50	A78	A		50	11
Magnus KIHLSTEDT (29/02/72) - SK Brann (NOR)	s46			G46					s46						6	-
Michael SVENSSON (25/11/75) - Halmstads BK	s46					D									2	-
Fredrik LJUNGBERG (16/04/77) - Arsenal (ENG)	s46	M63		M83						M	M	M	M	17	2
Jörgen PETTERSSON (29/09/75) - 1.FC Kaiserslautern (GER)	s46							A	A	A46	A66	A50	s46		26	7
Håkan MILD (14/06/71) - IFK Göteborg	s46	M83	M	s83	M	M56			M	s68			M	M	61	6
Roland NILSSON (27/11/63) - Helsingborgs IF		D	D	D46	D	D74	D46		D	D46	D90	D46			112	2
Patrik ANDERSSON (18/08/71) - FC Bayern München (GER)		D	D	D				D	D46	D	D	D		D	79	2
Joachim BJÖRKLUND (15/03/71) - Valencia CF (ESP)		D		D				D		D	D	D	D	D	75	-
Stefan SCHWARZ (18/04/69) - Sunderland (ENG)		M81		M				M46	M44						66	6
Pär ZETTERBERG (14/10/70) - RSC Anderlecht (BEL)		s46													30	6
Gary SUNDGREN (25/10/67) - Real Zaragoza (ESP)			s81	s46				D		D46	D46		D		31	1
Andreas JACOBSSON (06/10/72) - Helsingborgs IF					D										10	-
Daniel TJERNSTRÖM (19/02/74) - AIK					M59										5	-
Andreas ANDERSSON (10/04/74) - AIK					M	M	A		s46	s84					28	5
Mattias JONSSON (16/01/74) - Helsingborgs IF					A88	A89	M80	s76	s57						15	1
Marcus ALLBÄCK (05/07/73) - Örgryte IS					A79	A83	A87			s46					4	1
Mattias ASPER (20/03/74) - AIK					s46				G						2	-
Tobias LINDEROTH (21/04/79) - Stabaek IF (NOR)					s59	s83	s80								3	-
Jonas WALLERSTEDT (18/03/78) - IFK Norrköping					s79	s89	s78								3	-
Anders SVENSSON (17/07/76) - IF Elfsborg					s88	s56	M78								3	-
Eddie GUSTAFSSON (31/01/77) - IFK Norrköping					G										1	-
Kléber SAARENPÄÄ (14/12/75) - IFK Norrköping					D	D									2	-
Anders ANDERSSON (15/03/74) - AaB (DEN)						M	M	M76	M	s73			s62		15	2
Christoffer ANDERSSON (22/10/78) - Helsingborgs IF					s74										1	-
Dime JANKULOVSKI (18/06/77) - Västra Frölunda IF						G									1	-
Karl CORNELIUSSON (17/11/76) - AIK						s72									1	-
Michael HANSSON (22/01/72) - Helsingborgs IF						s87									1	-
Magnus ARVIDSSON (12/02/73) - FC Hansa Rostock (GER)								s46	A57						2	-
Olof MELLBERG (03/09/77) - Racing Santander (ESP)								s46	D	s46	s46	D	D	D	7	-

EUROPEAN CUPS 99/00

CHAMPIONS' CUP

● AIK

Preliminary round 2 DNEPR-TRANSMASH MOGILEV (BLS)

A 1-0 Tjernström (89)
Asper, Kjølø, Kåmark, Brundin, Gustafsson, Andersson O.
(Corneliusson 64), Nordin (Ljung 82), Lagerlöf, Tjernström, Åslund,
Novakovic.

H 2-0 Corneliusson (54), Gustafsson (77)
Asper, Kjølø, Kåmark, Brundin, Gustafsson, Corneliusson
(Andersson O. 75), Nordin, Lagerlöf, Tjernström, Åslund (Mattiasson 46),
Novakovic (Ljung 86).

Qualifying round AEK (GRE)

A 0-0
Asper, Kjølø (Ljung 69), Kåmark, Brundin, Gustafsson, Lagerlöf, Nordin,
Andersson O., Tjernström, Andersson A. (Åslund 62), Novakovic
(Hoch 90).

H 1-0 Novakovic (57)
Asper, Kjølø (Ljung 88), Kåmark, Brundin, Gustafsson, Corneliusson
(Mattiasson 50), Nordin, Lagerlöf, Tjernström, Andersson A., Novakovic
(Andersson O. 78).

Champions' League

1st match FC BARCELONA (ESP)

H 1-2 Novakovic (72)
Asper, Kjølø, Ljung, Brundin, Kåmark (Corneliusson 86), Nordin, Lagerlöf,
Andersson O., Tjernström (Bergh 74), Novakovic (Mattiasson 85),
Andersson A..

2nd match ARSENAL (ENG)

A 1-3 Nordin (53)
Asper, Kåmark (Kjølø 46), Ljung, Brundin, Gustafsson, Lagerlöf, Nordin,
Andersson O., Tjernström, Andersson A. (Corneliusson 88), Novakovic
(Åslund 82).

3rd match FIORENTINA (ITA)

H 0-0
Asper, Kjølø, Ljung, Brundin, Gustafsson, Tjernström, Nordin, Andersson O.
(Corneliusson 55), Lagerlöf, Novakovic, Andersson A..

4th match FIORENTINA (ITA)

A 0-3
Asper, Kjølø, Ljung, Brundin, Gustafsson, Lagerlöf (Corneliusson 58),
Nordin, Andersson O., Tjernström, Mattiasson (Johansson 72),
Novakovic (Hoch 46).

5th match FC BARCELONA (ESP)

A 0-5
Asper, Kjølø, Ljung, Brundin, Kåmark, Corneliusson, Nordin
(Andersson A. 46), Gustafsson, Tjernström (Lagerlöf 75), Hoch
(Mattiasson 46), Novakovic.

6th match ARSENAL (ENG)

H 2-3 Andersson A. (41, 68)
Asper (Baxter 71), Kjølø, Lagerlöf, Kåmark, Gustafsson, Corneliusson
(Åslund 71), Nordin, Andersson O., Tjernström, Novakovic, Andersson A..

UEFA CUP

● HELSINGBORGS IF

Qualifying round FK RIGA (LAT)

A 0-0
Andersson S., Nilsson O., Nilsson R., Jansson, Prica (Johansen 73),
Wahlstedt (Powell 58), Jonsson, Markstedt, Lindström, Andersson C.,
Stavrum (Bakkerud 46).

H 5-0 Andersson C. (4), Jonsson (16), Powell (43), Prica (66), Bakkerud (84)
Andersson S., Nilsson O., Nilsson R., Jakobsson, Jansson, Powell
(Bakkerud 46), Jonsson, Markstedt, Prica (Wahlstedt 73), Andersson C.,
Stavrum (Johansen 57).

1st round KARPATY LVIV (UKR)

H 1-1 Jonsson (85)
Andersson S., Nilsson O., Jacobsson, Jovanovski, Andersson C., Bakkerud
(Powell 65), Jansson, Wahlstedt (Nilsson R. 46), Stavrum, Johansen
(Prica 46), Jonsson.

A 1-1 (aet; 2-4 on pens.) Jonsson (90)
Andersson S., Nilsson R., Jacobsson, Nilsson O., Andersson C., Bakkerud
(Markstedt 81), Jansson, Jonsson, Stavrum, Prica (Wahlstedt 81),
Johansen (Powell 31).

2nd round PARMA (ITA)

A 0-1
Andersson S., Nilsson R., Nilsson O., Jakobsson, Andersson C., Prica
(Wahlstedt 67), Johansen (Bakkerud 68), Jansson, Jonsson, Powell,
Stavrum.

H 1-3 Stavrum (86)
Andersson S., Nilsson R., Nilsson O., Jakobsson, Andersson C., Bakkerud
(Prica 46; Ljung 68), Johansen, Jansson, Powell, Stavrum, Wahlstedt.

● IFK GÖTEBORG

Qualifying round CORK CITY (IRL)

H 3-0 Andersson P. (36), Karlsson P. (74, 87)
Andersson B., Pedersen, Anegrund, Nilsson, Landberg, Persson, Mild,
Erlingmark, Karlsson P., Andersson P., Hermansson (Tetteh 61).

A 0-1
Andersson B., Nilsson, Anegrund, Erlingmark, Landberg, Høiland, Mild,
Henriksson, Karlsson P., Andersson P. (Hermansson 86), Tetteh
(Svensson 88).

1st round LECH POZNAN (POL)

A 2-1 Andersson P. (27), Mild (83)
Andersson B., Høiland, Nilsson, Erlingmark, Landberg, Henriksson, Mild,
Karlsson P. (Svensson 86), Lundén, Andersson P., Tetteh (Hermansson 81).

H 0-0
Andersson B., Pedersen, Nilsson, Erlingmark, Landberg, Høiland, Mild,
Henriksson, Karlsson P., Andersson P., Tetteh.

2nd round ROMA (ITA)

H 0-2
Andersson B., Pedersen, Erlingmark, Nilsson, Landberg, Høiland, Svensson
(Hermansson 80), Henriksson, Karlsson P., Tetteh, Andersson P.
(Lundén 61).

A 0-1
Andersson B., Pedersen, Erlingmark, Nilsson, Svensson (Karlsson C. 85),
Lundén, Mild, Henriksson, Anegrund, Tetteh (Hermansson 68), Andersson P.

DOMESTIC CUP 99/00

QUARTER-FINALS
GIF Sundsvall 0, AIK 1
Örgryte IS 3, Åtvidabergs FF 0
IFK Göteborg 1, Lira Luleå BK 0
Gunnilse IS 1, IF Sylvia 0

SEMI-FINALS
IFK Göteborg 2 (Andersson G. 15, Mild 48),
Örgryte IS 2 (Allbäck 13, 73) (aet; 6-7 on pens.)

Gunnilse IS 0, AIK 2 (Lucic 55, Hoch 67)

FINAL
25/05/2000, Solna
AIK 0
ÖRGRYTE IS 2 Allbäck (30, 54)
referee - Sundell
AIK - Asper, Corneliusson, Lucic, Brundin, Kibeke
(Casserly 57), Bergh, Lagerlöf, Andersson O.,
Tjernström (Thylander 81), Alm, Hoch (Mattiasson 61).
ÖRGRYTE IS - Perstedt, Owusu, Anegrund, Sjöstedt,
Tomaz, Kuhn (Lohm 89), Johannesson, Källander
(Lindqvist 81), Ulander, Allbäck (Johansson 87),
Karlsson.

01/06/2000, Gothenburg
ÖRGRYTE IS 0
AIK 1 Mattiasson (85)
referee - Sundell
ÖRGRYTE IS - Perstedt, Nilsson, Anegrund, Sjöstedt,
Tomaz, Kuhn (Lindqvist 89), Johannesson, Källander,
Ulander, Allbäck, Karlsson (Löfgren 71).
AIK - Asper, Corneliusson, Lucic, Brundin, Kibeke,
Bergh, Lagerlöf, Andersson O., Tjernström, Alm, Hoch
(Mattiasson 61).

(ÖRGRYTE IS 2-1)

attended the game, and Helsingborg's large contingent of travelling supporters were given a day to remember as Norwegian striker Arild Stavrum netted the all-important winning goal midway through the second half to keep Helsingborg a point clear of defending champions AIK on top of the table.

A year earlier Helsingborg had lost their final game in Gothenburg - against BK Häcken - to hand the title to AIK, but this time they made no mistake. Helsingborg had come from four points behind AIK to nick the title with victories in each of their last five games.

Goal-hero Stavrum left the club to join Aberdeen at the end of the season, and he was accompanied out by his fellow Norwegian, coach Åge Hareide, who made the short trip across the Øresund strait to become the new boss of Danish side Brøndby. He, in turn, was replaced by Nanne Bergstrand, who arrived from Kalmar FF.

Kalmar had just been relegated to the First Division after a play-off defeat by GAIS, who, in joining automatically promoted BK Häcken, took the number of Gothenburg-based clubs in the 2000 Allsvenskan up to an unprecedented five. One of that quintet, Örgryte, made it an even happier start to the new millennium for the country's second city by winning the Swedish Cup.

Örgryte had won 14 championships in the (mostly distant) past but had never previously won the 'Svenska Cupen'. They faced a formidable final opponent in the shape of AIK, three-time winners in the previous four years, but a 2-0 first-leg victory in Solna, courtesy of a brace from the Allsvenskan's leading marksman Marcus Allbäck, gave them a clear advantage and they held on to that a week later despite undergoing a very nervous last five minutes.

AIK thus had to settle for second place in both league and Cup. They were the best-supported club in the Allsvenskan, averaging crowds of 13,521 (only Hammarby on 11,917 and Helsingborg on 10,583 joined them in five figures), although that paled into insignificance when compared with the 30,000-plus attendances they drew to the Råsunda stadium for each of their three

INTERNATIONAL HONOURS

World Cup Finals appearances: 1934 (2nd round), 1938 (4th), 1950 (3rd), 1958 (runners-up), 1970, 1974 (2nd phase), 1978, 1990, 1994 (3rd)

European Championship appearances: 1964, 1992 (semi-finals), 2000

European Club Competitions
UEFA Cup   IFK Göteborg (1982, 1987)

PLAYER OF THE SEASON

PÄR ZETTERBERG
It will remain an unsolved mystery forever, but many Swedish fans will continue to pose the question: how would Sweden have fared at Euro 2000 if Pär Zetterberg had been there to pull the strings in midfield? The brilliant schemer would have been the perfect replacement for injured Stefan Schwarz, but he had already burned his bridges with the national team, saying that he would not play for Sweden again as long as Tommy Söderberg remained as coach. The decision

was doubly detrimental - to Sweden, obviously, but also to himself, for he would have been performing on familiar territory, having spent the previous ten years in Belgium. Zetterberg was also in prime form, having helped Anderlecht to their first Belgian title in five years. An ever-present, he scored 14 goals in his 34 appearances and was unrivalled as the best midfielder in the country. In the summer the Swede caused dismay among the Anderlecht fans when he sealed a lucrative transfer to Greek champions Olympiakos.

Champions' League games. The biggest Allsvenskan attendance of the season - 28,054 - was for AIK's derby game with Djurgårdens IF in mid-June. There would be no repeat of that fixture in 2000, however, for Djurgården finished bottom of the table and were relegated.

Joining them and Kalmar were... Malmö FF, the country's one-time record champions, whose 63-year presence in the top flight ended after a season marked by awful performances away from home and a never-ending list of injury casualties.

PROMOTED CLUBS 1999

FIRST DIVISION FINAL TABLES

NORTH		Pd	W	D	L	F	A	Pt	GD
1	**GIF Sundsvall**	**26**	**13**	**9**	**4**	**65**	**32**	**48**	**33**
2	Assyriska FF Södertälje	26	14	5	7	44	25	47	19
3	IF Sylvia	26	15	2	9	47	33	47	14
4	Enköpings SK FK	26	13	6	7	40	26	45	14
5	IK Brage	26	12	3	11	33	26	39	7
6	Västerås SK FK	26	10	7	9	32	24	37	8
7	Umeå FC	26	9	9	8	32	28	36	4
8	Gefle IF	26	10	6	10	32	38	36	-6
9	Degerfors IF	26	9	8	9	34	36	35	-2
10	IF Brommapojkarna	26	9	4	13	31	42	31	-11
11	Nacka FF	26	8	7	11	28	39	31	-11
12	Lira Luleå BK	26	8	4	14	31	45	28	-14
13	IK Sirius FK	26	6	7	13	27	52	25	-25
14	Spårvägens FF	26	6	3	17	18	48	21	-30

SOUTH		Pd	W	D	L	F	A	Pt	GD
1	**BK Häcken**	**26**	**15**	**6**	**5**	**62**	**28**	**51**	**34**
2	**GAIS**	**26**	**14**	**7**	**5**	**35**	**27**	**49**	**8**
3	Mjällby AIF	26	15	2	9	51	33	47	18
4	Panos Ljungskile SK	26	13	7	6	38	26	46	12
5	Landskrona BoIS	26	12	9	5	52	30	45	22
6	Gunnilse IS	26	12	6	8	39	30	42	9
7	Åtvidabergs FF	26	11	8	7	38	32	41	6
8	Östers IF	26	11	6	9	32	30	39	2
9	Kristiansunds FF	26	9	4	13	34	46	31	-12
10	IK Kongahälla	26	7	7	12	31	40	28	-9
11	Husqvarna FF	26	8	3	15	32	50	27	-18
12	Fakenbergs FF	26	8	2	16	36	59	26	-23
13	Motala AIF FK	26	7	2	17	28	47	23	-19
14	Stenungsunds IF	26	4	3	19	28	58	15	-30

PROMOTION/RELEGATION PLAY-OFFS

Assyriska FF Södertälje 1, Örebro SK 1
Örebro SK 2, Assyriska FF Södertälje 1 (aet)
(Örebro SK 3-2)

GAIS 2, Kalmar FF 1
Kalmar FF 1, GAIS 1
(GAIS 3-2)

CLUB DIRECTORIES

GIF Sundsvall
Box 311
851 05 Sundsvall
tel - (060) 126037
fax - (060) 175592
website - gifsundsvall,se
email - gif-sundsvall@swipnet.se
Year of Formation - 1903
President - Johan Sterner
Secretary - Walter Rönnmark
Coach - Anders Grönhagen
Stadium - Idrottsparken (9,000)

Bollklubben Häcken
Box 22051
400 72 Göteborg
tel - (031) 510233
fax - (031) 238389
website - www.hacken.o.se
email - kansli@hacken.o.se
Year of Formation - 1940
President - Åke Nilsson
Secretary - Tomas Ohlsson
Coach - Kjell Pettersson
Stadium - Rambergsvallen (7,000)

GAIS
Box 52016
400 16 Göteborg
tel - (031) 403690
fax - (031) 406685
website - www.gais.se
email - gais.kansli@goteborg.utfors.se
Year of Formation - 1894
President - Stefan Gustavsson
Secretary - Gunnar Hejde
Coach - Lennart Ottordahl
Stadium - Gamla Ullevi (18,000)

AIK

CLUB DIRECTORY

Allmänna Idrottsklubben
Box 1408, 171 27 Solna
tel - (08) 7359600 / fax - (08) 7359679
website - www.aik.se
email - fotboll@aik.se
Year of Formation - 1891
President - Sune Hellströmer
Secretary - Lars Pettersson
Coach - Stuart Baxter
Stadium - Råsunda Stadion (36,800)

MAJOR HONOURS
League Championship - (10) 1900, 1901, 1911,
1914, 1916, 1923, 1932, 1937, 1992, 1998.
Domestic Cup - (7)
1949, 1950, 1976, 1985, 1996, 1997, 1999.

APPEARANCES 1999

		P	Ap	(s)	Gls
Andreas ANDERSSON	A	6	(2)	2
Ola ANDERSSON	M	8	(7)	1
Mattias ASPER	G	26		
Marcus BENGTSSON	M		(1)	
Hans BERGH	M	8	(4)	
Michael BRUNDIN	D	26		
Karl CORNELIUSSON	D	10	(10)	3
Patrick ENGLUND	D	7		
Tomas GUSTAFSSON	D	24		1
Daniel HOCH	A	1	(8)	2
Andreas JOHANSSON	M	7	(5)	1
Mike KJØLØ (NOR)	D	24		2
Pontus KÅMARK	D	7	(2)	
Thomas LAGERLÖF	M	21	(4)	4
David LJUNG	D	19	(4)	
Christer MATTIASSON	A	19	(6)	10
Krister NORDIN	M	22		3
Nebojsa NOVAKOVIC (YUG)	A	21		7
Marino RAHMBERG	A	3	(6)	
Daniel TJERNSTRÖM	M	22	(3)	4
Martin ÅSLUND	M	5	(9)	1

LEAGUE RESULTS 1999

12/04/99	Örebro SK	H	1-1	Johansson
20/04/99	Malmö FF	A	1-2	Novakovic
25/04/99	Kalmar FF	H	4-0	Lagerlöf 2, Kjølø, Tjernström
04/05/99	Hammarby IF	A	2-0	Novakovic, Mattiasson
10/05/99	Helsingborgs IF	H	2-1	Nordin, Mattiasson
17/05/99	Trelleborgs FF	A	0-1	
24/05/99	Örgryte IS	H	1-1	Tjernström
30/05/99	Halmstads BK	A	0-1	
08/06/99	IFK Göteborg	H	2-0	Novakovic (p), Mattiasson
14/06/99	Djurgårdens IF	H	3-1	Novakovic 2 (1p), Nordin
21/06/99	IF Elfsborg	A	2-2	Mattiasson 2
28/06/99	IFK Norrköping	A	1-0	Andersson O.
05/07/99	Västra Frölunda IF	A	1-0	Hoch
19/07/99	IFK Norrköping	H	2-0	og (Ström), Mattiasson
31/07/99	IF Elfsborg	H	3-0	Mattiasson, Corneliusson, Kjølø
07/08/99	Trelleborgs FF	H	3-0	Åslund, Corneliusson, Hoch
15/08/99	Helsingborgs IF	A	2-0	Corneliusson, Lagerlöf
21/08/99	Västra Frölunda IF	H	1-0	Mattiasson
30/08/99	Djurgårdens IF	A	0-0	
11/09/99	IFK Göteborg	A	0-1	
18/09/99	Hammarby IF	H	2-0	Novakovic, Mattiasson
25/09/99	Kalmar FF	A	3-1	Novakovic, Mattiasson, Tjernström
03/10/99	Halmstads BK	H	0-1	
16/10/99	Örgryte IS	A	1-1	Lagerlöf
23/10/99	Malmö FF	H	3-0	Tjernström, Andersson A., Gustafsson
30/10/99	Örebro SK	A	2-0	Andersson A., Nordin

DJURGÅRDENS IF

CLUB DIRECTORY

Djurgårdens Idrettsförening
Klocktornet, Olympiastadion, 114 33 Stockholm
tel - (08) 54515800 / fax - (08) 54515801
website - www.dif.se
email - dif.fotboll@dif.se
Year of Formation - 1891
President - Bo Lundquist
Secretary - Dan Svanell
Coach - Michael Andersson; Sören Åkeby
Stadium - Olympiastadion (14,500)

MAJOR HONOURS
League Championship - (8) 1912, 1915, 1917, 1920, 1955, 1959, 1964, 1966.
Domestic Cup - (1) 1990.

APPEARANCES 1999

		P	Ap	(s)	Gls
Stefan ALVÉN	D		24		
Bo Braastrup ANDERSEN (DEN)	G		11		
Michael BORGQVIST	M		20	(2)	1
Patricio CISTERNAS	D		12	(2)	
Fredrik DAHLSTRÖM	A		18	(4)	3
Patrik ERIKSSON-OHLSSON	D		18	(2)	
Pierre GALLO	D		19	(2)	1
Christian GRÖNING	M			(1)	
Richard HENRIKSSON	D		1		
Markus KARLSSON	M		12	(8)	
Jones KUSI-ASARE	A		4	(11)	1
Magnus LINDBLAD	G		8	(1)	
Martin LOSSMAN	G		7		
Lucas NILSSON	A		17	(8)	4
Magnus PEHRSSON	M		20	(3)	1
Jon PERSSON	M		8	(3)	1
Nicklas RASCK	M		22	(1)	2
Joel RIDDEZ	M		7	(11)	
Magnus SAMUELSSON	D		18		
Zoran STOJCEVSKI	M		2	(10)	1
Sharbel TOUMA	A		24		8
Samuel WOWOAH	A		14	(2)	3

LEAGUE RESULTS 1999

Date	Opponent	H/A	Score	Scorers
11/04/99	IFK Norrköping	H	3-0	Rasck, Dahlström, Nilsson
22/04/99	IFK Göteborg	A	0-0	
25/04/99	Helsingborgs IF	A	1-4	Kusi-Asare
03/05/99	Trelleborgs FF	H	2-2	Nilsson, Borgqvist
10/05/99	Västra Frölunda IF	A	1-1	Nilsson
17/05/99	Örgryte IS	H	0-3	
24/05/99	Kalmar FF	H	0-3	
31/05/99	Hammarby IF	H	1-0	Touma
09/06/99	IF Elfsborg	A	1-2	Touma (p)
14/06/99	AIK	A	1-3	Dahlström
17/06/99	Halmstads BK	A	1-4	Gallo (p)
29/06/99	Malmö FF	H	4-1	Persson, Touma 2, Stojcevski
05/07/99	Örebro SK	H	0-1	
11/07/99	Malmö FF	A	0-2	
03/08/99	Halmstads BK	H	0-2	
09/08/99	Örgryte IS	A	1-0	Wowoah
15/08/99	Västra Frölunda IF	H	1-1	Wowoah
23/08/99	Örebro SK	A	1-1	Touma
30/08/99	AIK	H	0-0	
13/09/99	IF Elfsborg	H	1-2	Pehrsson
19/09/99	Trelleborgs FF	A	2-2	og (Olsson), Touma
25/09/99	Helsingborgs IF	H	2-4	Nilsson, Wowoah
04/10/99	Hammarby IF	A	1-2	Dahlström
18/10/99	Kalmar FF	A	0-0	
24/10/99	IFK Göteborg	H	2-0	Touma, Rasck
30/10/99	IFK Norrköping	A	1-1	Touma (p)

IF ELFSBORG

CLUB DIRECTORY

Idrottsföreningen Elfsborg
Skaraborgsvägen 55, 506 30 Borås
tel - (033) 139191 / fax - (033) 129191
website - www.elfsborg.se
email - info@elfsborg.se
Year of Formation - 1904
President - Sture Svensson
Secretary - Rolf Eriksson
Coach - Karl-Gunnar Björklund; Bengt-Arne Strömberg
Stadium - Ryavallen (19,400)

MAJOR HONOURS
League Championship - (4)
1936, 1939, 1940, 1961.

APPEARANCES 1999

		P	Ap	(s)	Gls
Joakim ALEXANDERSSON	D	24	(1)		2
Stefan ANDREASSON	M	5			
Kristoffer ARVHAGE	D	17	(2)		1
Jesper BENGTSSON	M	22	(1)		
Fredrik BERGLUND	A	15	(10)		7
Anders BOGSJÖ	G	25			
Lars-Gunnar CARLSTRAND	A	17	(5)		5
Mikael GÖRANSSON	M	3	(2)		
Haraldur INGÓLFSSON (ISL)	M	13	(9)		5
Nicklas JOHANSSON	G	1	(2)		
Andreas KLARSTRÖM	M	3	(11)		2
Marko KRISTAL (EST)	M		(4)		
Mikael MARTINSSON	A	20	(2)		5
Joacim MODIGH	D	3	(1)		
Stefan MOGREN	D	20	(2)		2
Andreas NICKLASSON	M	10	(9)		3
Kjetil Ruthford PEDERSEN (NOR)	D	24			1
Niclas PETERSMO	M		(1)		
Johan SJÖBERG	D	14			
Martin STRÖMBERG	M	10	(1)		1
Anders SVENSSON	M	19	(1)		3
Daniel UNG	D	13			
Jorgen WÄLEMARK	A	8	(11)		4

LEAGUE RESULTS 1999

12/04/99	Kalmar FF	H	3-0	Carlstrand, Martinsson, Wälemark
25/04/99	Hammarby IF	H	3-0	Ncklasson, Ingólfsson, Berglund
03/05/99	IFK Göteborg	A	0-2	
10/05/99	Trelleborgs FF	H	1-2	Berglund
16/05/99	IFK Norrköping	A	1-1	Pedersen
19/05/99	Örebro SK	A	0-1	
24/05/99	Halmstads BK	H	1-4	Mogren
30/05/99	Malmö FF	A	2-4	Carlstrand, Wälemark
09/06/99	Djurgårdens IF	H	2-1	Martinsson (p), Klarström
15/06/99	Helsingborgs IF	A	1-1	Carlstrand
21/06/99	AIK	H	2-2	Svensson, Mogren
28/06/99	Västra Frölunda IF	H	2-3	Nicklasson, Berglund
01/07/99	Örgryte IS	A	1-5	Berglund
19/07/99	Västra Frölunda IF	A	4-4	Martinsson 2, Nicklasson, Arvhage
31/07/99	AIK	A	0-3	
09/08/99	IFK Norrköping	H	2-1	Wälemark, Klarström
19/08/99	Trelleborgs FF	A	2-1	Ingólfsson, Wälemark
22/08/99	Örgryte IS	H	1-2	Martinsson (p)
30/08/99	Helsingborgs IF	H	1-1	Svensson
13/09/99	Djurgårdens IF	A	2-1	Carlstrand, Alexandersson
20/09/99	IFK Göteborg	H	0-1	
27/09/99	Hammarby IF	A	1-2	Berglund
04/10/99	Malmö FF	H	5-2	Strömberg, Carlstrand, Ingólfsson 2 (1p), Svensson
17/10/99	Halmstads BK	A	0-3	
24/10/99	Örebro SK	H	3-1	Berglund 2, Ingólfsson
30/10/99	Kalmar FF	A	1-0	Alexandersson

IFK GÖTEBORG

CLUB DIRECTORY

Idrottsföreningen Kamraterna Göteborg
Alfreds Gärdes Väg, 416 55 Göteborg
tel - (031) 7037300 / fax - (031) 404121
website - www.ifkgoteborg.se
Year of Formation - 1904
President - Gunnar Larsson
Secretary - Ronny Sjölund
Coach - Reine Almqvist; Stefan Lundin
Stadium - Gamla Ullevi (18,000)

MAJOR HONOURS
League Championship - (17) 1908, 1910, 1918,
1935, 1942, 1958, 1969, 1982, 1983, 1984,
1987, 1990, 1991, 1993, 1994, 1995, 1996.
Domestic Cup - (4) 1979, 1982, 1983, 1991.
UEFA Cup - (2) 1982, 1987.

APPEARANCES 1999

	P	Ap	(s)	Gls
Bengt ANDERSSON	G	26		
Patric ANDERSSON	A	15	(6)	7
Johan ANEGRUND	D	19	(2)	1
Stefan BÄRLIN	M	12	(3)	
Magnus ERLINGMARK	M	26		1
Sebastian HENRIKSSON	M	17	(7)	3
Andreas HERMANSSON	A	12	(8)	2
Jon Inge HØILAND (NOR)	D	22		
Christian KARLSSON	D	3		
Pär KARLSSON	M	21	(4)	1
Stefan LANDBERG	D	21		
Jonas LUNDÉN	A	5	(14)	1
Håkan MILD	M	20	(1)	
Erik NEVLAND (NOR)	A		(4)	
Mikael NILSSON	D	17	(3)	
Steinar PEDERSEN (NOR)	D	24		1
Joakim PERSSON	M	11	(4)	2
Jimmy SVENSSON	M	3	(5)	
Emmanuel TETTEH (GHA)	A	12	(1)	7

LEAGUE RESULTS 1999

10/04/99	Helsingborgs IF	A	1-3	Hermansson
22/04/99	Djurgårdens IF	H	0-0	
25/04/99	Trelleborgs FF	A	1-3	Erlingmark
03/05/99	IF Elfsborg	H	2-0	Persson, Pedersen
11/05/99	Örgryte IS	A	2-2	Karlsson P., Lundén
17/05/99	Halmstads BK	H	1-1	Andersson P.
24/05/99	Hammarby IF	H	2-2	Andersson P., Anegrund
31/05/99	IFK Norrköping	A	0-3	
08/06/99	AIK	A	0-2	
14/06/99	Västra Frölunda IF	H	1-0	Hermansson
22/06/99	Malmö FF	A	1-1	Persson
30/06/99	Örebro SK	H	0-1	
04/07/99	Kalmar FF	A	1-0	Henriksson (p)
28/07/99	Örebro SK	A	2-1	Tetteh 2
02/08/99	Malmö FF	H	1-0	Andersson P.
08/08/99	Halmstads BK	A	0-4	
15/08/99	Örgryte IS	H	1-0	Andersson P.
22/08/99	Kalmar FF	H	2-0	Tetteh, Henriksson (p)
30/08/99	Västra Frölunda IF	A	2-1	Andersson P. 2
11/09/99	AIK	H	1-0	Tetteh
20/09/99	IF Elfsborg	A	1-0	Tetteh
26/09/99	Trelleborgs FF	H	2-1	og (Svensson), Tetteh
04/10/99	IFK Norrköping	H	2-3	Henriksson, Tetteh
18/10/99	Hammarby IF	A	1-2	Andersson P.
24/10/99	Djurgårdens IF	A	0-2	
30/10/99	Helsingborgs IF	H	0-1	

HALMSTADS BK

CLUB DIRECTORY

Halmstads Bollklubb
Box 223, 301 06 Halmstad
tel - (035) 171880 / fax - (035) 103436
website - www.halmstadsbk.se
email - info@halmstadsbk.se
Year of Formation - 1914
President - Stig Nilsson
Director - Mikael Kaller
Coach - Tom Prahl
Stadium - Örjans Vall (17,000)

MAJOR HONOURS
League Championship - (3) 1976, 1979, 1997.
Domestic Cup - (1) 1995.

APPEARANCES 1999

	P	Ap	(s)	Gls
Daniel ALEXANDERSSON	A	1	(7)	1
Fredrik ANDERSSON	D	19	(2)	
Robert ANDERSSON	A	18	(3)	6
Torbjörn ARVIDSSON	M	17	(2)	
Jeffrey AUBYNN	A	6	(8)	1
Henrik BERTILSSON	A	23	(2)	13
Joel BORGSTRAND	D	4	(1)	2
Björn CARLSSON	M	7	(7)	2
Joel CEDERGREN	M		(3)	
Fredrik GUSTAFSSON	M	9		
Mikael GUSTAVSSON	D	26		2
Petter HANSSON	D	24	(1)	3
Mattias HED	M	2	(4)	
Tommy JÖNSSON	D	24	(1)	1
Peter LENNARTSSON	M	21	(4)	1
Stefan SELAKOVIC (BOS)	A	20	(5)	7
Håkan SVENSSON	G	26		
Michael SVENSSON	D	19	(2)	
Stefan VENNBERG	M	20	(3)	3

LEAGUE RESULTS 1999

11/04/99	Örgryte IS	A	0-1	
22/04/99	Västra Frölunda IF	H	1-2	Gustavsson
25/04/99	IFK Norrköping	H	1-1	Bertilsson
02/05/99	Malmö FF	A	1-0	og (Persson)
09/05/99	Hammarby IF	H	3-1	Selakovic, Lennartsson, Bertilsson
17/05/99	IFK Göteborg	A	1-1	Bertilsson
24/05/99	IF Elfsborg	A	4-1	Aubynn, Bertilsson, Selakovic, Alexandersson
30/05/99	AIK	H	1-0	Andersson R.
09/06/99	Örebro SK	H	5-1	Bertilsson 3, Andersson R., Vennberg
13/06/99	Kalmar FF	A	0-2	
17/06/99	Djurgårdens IF	H	4-1	Andersson R., Bertilsson, Gustavsson, Vennberg
23/06/99	Helsingborgs IF	A	0-1	
30/06/99	Trelleborgs FF	A	1-1	Vennberg
11/07/99	Helsingborgs IF	H	4-0	Andersson R. 2, Borgstrand, Carlsson
03/08/99	Djurgårdens IF	A	2-0	Bertilsson, Selakovic
08/08/99	IFK Göteborg	H	4-0	Selakovic 2, Borgstrand, Hansson
15/08/99	Hammarby IF	A	0-1	
23/08/99	Trelleborgs FF	H	2-2	Jonsson, Selakovic
29/08/99	Kalmar FF	H	1-0	Bertilsson
13/09/99	Örebro SK	A	2-1	Bertilsson 2
19/09/99	Malmö FF	H	2-1	Hansson, Carlsson
27/09/99	IFK Norrköping	A	0-4	
03/10/99	AIK	A	1-0	Andersson R.
17/10/99	IF Elfsborg	H	3-0	Hansson, Bertilsson (p), Selakovic
24/10/99	Västra Frölunda IF	A	0-0	
30/10/99	Örgryte IS	H	0-0	

HAMMARBY IF

CLUB DIRECTORY

Hammarby Idrottsförening
Box 200 6
104 60 Stockholm
tel - (08) 6413592
fax - (08) 4629320
website - www.hammarby-if.se/fotboll
email - hammarbyfotboll@swipnet.se
Year of Formation - 1897
President - Göran Paulsson
Secretary - Tomas Andersson
Coach - Rolf Zetterlund; Sören Cratz
Stadium - Söderstadion (10,011)

APPEARANCES 1999

	P	Ap	(s)	Gls
Johan ANDERSSON	D	24		
Mikael ANDERSSON	M	22	(4)	3
Patrik ANDERSSON	A	17	(7)	7
Kennedy BAKIRCIOGLU	A	22	(3)	2
Hans BERGGREN	A	24	(1)	6
Filip BERGMAN	D	8	(5)	
Andreas BILD	M	8	(3)	
Lars ERIKSSON	G	22		
Kaj ESKELINEN	M	19	(5)	3
Hans ESKILSSON	D	22	(2)	2
Christer FURSTH	M	20	(4)	3
Jens GUSTAFSON	M	13	(11)	1
Mikael HELLSTRÖM	D	26		
Thomas HÖGLUND	G	3	(1)	
Nicklas JOHANSSON	G	1		
Mats LARSSON	D	2	(3)	
Cesar PACHA	A	2	(5)	
Roger SANDBERG	D	9		
Mate SESTAN (CRO)	A	6	(5)	4
Suleyman SLEYMAN	D		(3)	
Jonas STARK	D	16	(4)	1
Christian ZEILOTH	A		(4)	

LEAGUE RESULTS 1999

11/04/99	Trelleborgs FF	A	2-2	Eskelinen (p), Andersson P.
21/04/99	Helsingborgs IF	H	2-1	Andersson P., Berggren
25/04/99	IF Elfsborg	A	0-3	
04/05/99	AIK	H	0-2	
09/05/99	Halmstads BK	A	1-3	Berggren
18/05/99	Malmö FF	H	0-1	
24/05/99	IFK Göteborg	A	2-2	Berggren, Fursth
31/05/99	Djurgårdens IF	A	0-1	
08/06/99	Västra Frölunda IF	A	1-1	Fursth
13/06/99	Örgryte IS	H	0-0	
16/06/99	Örebro SK	A	1-3	Eskelinen
23/06/99	Kalmar FF	H	2-2	Andersson P., Andersson M.
01/07/99	IFK Norrköping	H	3-0	Andersson M., Bakircioglu, Berggren
14/07/99	Kalmar FF	A	1-4	Andersson P.
02/08/99	Örebro SK	H	2-1	Eskilsson, Eskelinen
09/08/99	Malmö FF	A	0-2	
15/08/99	Halmstads BK	H	1-0	Berggren
23/08/99	IFK Norrköping	A	2-3	Andersson P., Gustafson
29/08/99	Örgryte IS	A	1-2	Sestan
13/09/99	Västra Frölunda IF	H	1-2	Sestan
18/09/99	AIK	A	0-2	
27/09/99	IF Elfsborg	H	2-1	Andersson P. 2
04/10/99	Djurgårdens IF	H	2-1	Eskilsson, Andersson M.
18/10/99	IFK Göteborg	H	2-1	Stark, Berggren
24/10/99	Helsingborgs IF	A	0-2	
30/10/99	Trelleborgs FF	H	4-0	Fursth, Sestan 2, Bakircioglu

HELSINGBORGS IF

CLUB DIRECTORY

Helsingborgs Idrottsförening
Box 2074, 250 02 Helsingborg
tel - (042) 377000 / fax - (042) 377027
website - www.hif.se
email - info@hif.se
Year of Formation - 1907
President - Claes Johansson
Secretary - Jerker Swanstein
Coach - Åge Hareide (2000 - Nanne Bergstrand)
Stadium - Olympia (17,000)

MAJOR HONOURS
League Championship - (6)
1929, 1930, 1933, 1934, 1941, 1999.
Domestic Cup - (2) 1941, 1998.

APPEARANCES 1999

	P	Ap	(s)	Gls
Christoffer ANDERSSON	D	18	(7)	
Sven ANDERSSON	G	26		
Lars BAKKERUD	M	11	(2)	1
Erik EDMAN	D	12		1
Andreas JACOBSSON	D	24	(1)	
Ulrik JANSSON	M	13	(2)	
Stig JOHANSEN (NOR)	A	15	(7)	3
Mattias JONSSON	A	24		5
Zoran JOVANOVSKI (MAC)	D	1	(6)	
Marcus LANTZ	M	12		1
Marcus LINDBERG	D	1		
Mattias LINDSTRÖM	M	6	(4)	1
Per-Ola LJUNG	D	7	(3)	
Peter MARKSTEDT	D	3	(6)	
Ola NILSSON	D	24		
Roland NILSSON	D	19		2
Magnus POWELL	A	20	(4)	8
Rade PRICA	A	12	(5)	6
Arild STAVRUM (NOR)	A	23	(3)	11
Kenneth STORVIK (NOR)	M	12		2
Erik WAHLSTEDT	A	3	(15)	3

LEAGUE RESULTS 1999

10/04/99	IFK Göteborg	H	3-1	Wahlstedt, Stavrum, Storvik
21/04/99	Hammarby IF	A	1-2	Stavrum
25/04/99	Djurgårdens IF	H	4-1	Stavrum 2, Powell, Lindström
03/05/99	IFK Norrköping	A	0-1	
10/05/99	AIK	A	1-2	Jonsson
17/05/99	Västra Frölunda IF	H	1-0	Edman
24/05/99	Örebro SK	H	2-1	Johansen, Jonsson
30/05/99	Kalmar FF	A	2-0	Powell, Stavrum
10/06/99	Trelleborgs FF	A	3-2	Storvik, Powell 2
15/06/99	IF Elfsborg	H	1-1	Lantz
20/06/99	Örgryte IS	A	1-0	Johansen
23/06/99	Halmstads BK	H	1-0	Powell
06/07/99	Malmö FF	A	4-0	Jonsson, Stavrum, Prica, Wahlstedt
11/07/99	Halmstads BK	A	0-4	
02/08/99	Örgryte IS	H	2-0	Jonsson, Prica
07/08/99	Västra Frölunda IF	A	0-0	
15/08/99	AIK	H	0-2	
21/08/99	Malmö FF	H	1-0	Stavrum
30/08/99	IF Elfsborg	A	1-1	Jonsson
11/09/99	Trelleborgs FF	H	5-3	Stavrum 2, Prica 2, Johansen
20/09/99	IFK Norrköping	H	0-1	
25/09/99	Djurgårdens IF	A	4-2	Stavrum, Prica 2, Bakkerud
04/10/99	Kalmar FF	H	3-0	Powell 3
12/10/99	Örebro SK	A	1-0	Nilsson R. (p)
24/10/99	Hammarby IF	H	2-0	Nilsson R. (p), Wahlstedt
30/10/99	IFK Göteborg	A	1-0	Stavrum

KALMAR FF

Kalmar FF
Box 122, 391 22 Kalmar
tel - (0480) 411477 / fax - (0480) 88720
website - www.kalmarff.nu/
email - kalmar.ff@telia.com
Year of Formation - 1910
President - Ronny Nilsson
Secretary - Irene Hermansson
Coach - Nanne Bergstrand (2000 - Simon Hunt)
Stadium - Fredriksskans (10,000)

MAJOR HONOURS
Domestic Cup - (2) 1981, 1987.

	P	Ap	(s)	Gls
Marcus ANDREASSON	D	7		
Kjell CARLSSON	D	5	(5)	
Tobias CARLSSON	D	17		
Jonas GUNNARSSON	M	8	(12)	
Andreas GUSTAVSSON	M		(2)	
Daniel HOLM	M	11	(10)	2
Johan JAENSSON	D	9	(4)	
Lasse JOHANSSON	M	26		4
Niklas KALDNER	D	22	(2)	1
Andreas KLING	M		(2)	
Håkan LINDQVIST	M	23	(3)	1
Christian NILSSON	D	13		
Dennis NILSSON	D	24	(1)	
Jens NILSSON	A	17	(7)	3
Johan PAULSSON	M	15	(11)	7
Christer PERSSON	M	15	(10)	1
Henrik RYDSTRÖM	M	25		
Andreas THOMSSON	A	23	(2)	7
Petter WASTÅ	G	26		

12/04/99	IF Elfsborg	A	0-3	
18/04/99	Trelleborgs FF	H	3-2	Thomsson, Persson, og (Olsson)
25/04/99	AIK	A	0-4	
02/05/99	Västra Frölunda IF	H	3-1	Johansson, Thomsson, Paulsson
09/05/99	Malmö FF	A	1-0	Holm
16/05/99	Örebro SK	H	2-0	Thomsson, Johansson
24/05/99	Djurgårdens IF	A	3-0	Nilsson J. 3
30/05/99	Helsingborgs IF	H	0-2	
09/06/99	Örgryte IS	A	0-3	
13/06/99	Halmstads BK	H	2-0	Thomsson, Paulsson
20/06/99	IFK Norrköping	H	1-1	Johansson (p)
23/06/99	Hammarby IF	A	2-2	Thomsson, Kaldner
04/07/99	IFK Göteborg	H	0-1	
14/07/99	Hammarby IF	H	4-1	Johansson, Thomsson, Paulsson 2
01/08/99	IFK Norrköping	A	2-4	Paulsson 2
08/08/99	Örebro SK	A	0-2	
15/08/99	Malmö FF	H	1-0	Paulsson
22/08/99	IFK Göteborg	A	0-2	
29/08/99	Halmstads BK	A	0-1	
12/09/99	Örgryte IS	H	2-2	Holm, Lindqvist
19/09/99	Västra Frölunda IF	A	0-2	
25/09/99	AIK	H	1-3	Thomsson
04/10/99	Helsingborgs IF	A	0-3	
18/10/99	Djurgårdens IF	H	0-0	
24/10/99	Trelleborgs FF	A	0-1	
30/10/99	IF Elfsborg	H	0-1	

MALMÖ FF

CLUB DIRECTORY

Malmö Fotbollförening
Box 19067, 200 73 Malmö
tel - (040) 326600 / fax - (040) 326601
website - www.mff.se
email - info@malmoff.com
Year of Formation - 1910
President - Bengt Madsen
Secretary - Bo Malmquist
Coach - Roland Andersson
(2000 - Michael Andersson)
Stadium - Malmö IP (7,000)

MAJOR HONOURS
League Championship - (14)
1944, 1949, 1950, 1951, 1953, 1965, 1967,
1970, 1971, 1974, 1975, 1977, 1986, 1988.
Domestic Cup - (14)
1944, 1946, 1947, 1951, 1953, 1967, 1973,
1974, 1975, 1977, 1980, 1984, 1986, 1989.

APPEARANCES 1999

	P	Ap	(s)	Gls
Christian BANK	M	1		
Ólafur Örn BJARNASON (ISL)	M	13	(1)	1
Jonnie FEDEL	G	12		
Tony FLYGARE	A		(7)	
Niklas GUDMUNDSSON	A	18	(1)	1
Zlatan IBRAHIMOVIC	M		(6)	1
Niklas KINDVALL	A	16	(2)	1
Martin LARSSON	M	1		
Mats LILIENBERG	A	21	(3)	11
Hans MATTISSON	M	24		1
Jens NORDSTRÖM	M	9	(6)	
Jörgen OHLSSON	D	26		1
Dejan PAVLOVIC (YUG)	A	19	(1)	5
Olof PERSSON	D	26		4
Tomas RAZANAUSKAS (LIT)	M	8	(1)	
Mikael ROTH	D	23		
Milan SIMEUNOVIC (SLO)	G	2		
Sverrir SVERRISSON (ISL)	M	4	(2)	1
Jimmy TAMANDI	M	5	(1)	
Brune TAVELL	M	19	(4)	2
Mattias THYLANDER	D	7		
Ola TIDMAN	G	12	(2)	
Goran TRPEVSKI	M	1	(2)	
Markus VAAPLI	D	14	(2)	
Jonas WIRMOLA	D	5		

LEAGUE RESULTS 1999

12/04/99	Västra Frölunda IF	A	1-2	Lilienberg
20/04/99	AIK	H	2-1	Pavlovic 2 (1p)
24/04/99	Örgryte IS	A	4-4	Lilienberg 3, Persson
02/05/99	Halmstads BK	H	0-1	
09/05/99	Kalmar FF	H	0-1	
18/05/99	Hammarby IF	A	1-0	Persson
24/05/99	Trelleborgs FF	A	1-3	Gudmundsson
30/05/99	IF Elfsborg	H	4-2	Pavlovic, Tavell 2, og (Svensson)
09/06/99	IFK Norrköping	H	0-0	
13/06/99	Örebro SK	A	0-2	
22/06/99	IFK Göteborg	H	1-1	Pavlovic (p)
29/06/99	Djurgårdens IF	A	1-4	Ohlsson
06/07/99	Helsingborgs IF	H	0-4	
11/07/99	Djurgårdens IF	H	2-0	Kindvall, Mattisson
02/08/99	IFK Göteborg	A	0-1	
09/08/99	Hammarby IF	H	2-0	Bjarnason, Pavlovic
15/08/99	Kalmar FF	A	0-1	
21/08/99	Helsingborgs IF	A	0-1	
30/08/99	Örebro SK	H	3-1	Persson, Lilienberg 2
13/09/99	IFK Norrköping	A	1-5	Lilienberg
19/09/99	Halmstads BK	A	1-2	Lilienberg
27/09/99	Örgryte IS	H	1-1	Lilienberg
04/10/99	IF Elfsborg	A	2-5	Sverrisson, Lilienberg
18/10/99	Trelleborgs FF	H	1-2	Lilienberg
23/10/99	AIK	A	0-3	
30/10/99	Västra Frölunda IF	H	2-1	Ibrahimovic, Persson

IFK NORRKÖPING

Idrottsföreningen Kamraterna Norrköping
Box 12067, 600 12 Norrköping
tel - (011) 215500 / fax - (011) 215515
website - ifknorrkoping.e.se
email - ifk@ifknorrkoping.e.se
Year of Formation - 1897
President - Björn Ahlberg
Coach - Olle Nordin
Stadium - Norrköpings Idrottspark (20,000)

MAJOR HONOURS
League Championship - (12)
1943, 1945, 1946, 1947, 1948, 1952, 1956,
1957, 1960, 1962, 1963, 1989.
Domestic Cup - (6)
1943, 1945, 1969, 1988, 1992, 1994.

	P	Ap	(s)	Gls
Pär ANDERSSON	M	11	(7)	5
Kristian BERGSTRÖM	M	26		4
Fredrik BILD	D	26		
Jonas BJURSTRÖM	M	12	(6)	
Mikael BLOMBERG	D	21	(1)	2
Simon DOGAN	D		(1)	
Mattias FLODSTRÖM	A	10	(10)	5
Matthias FLORÉN	D	26		2
Peter FYHR	A	11	(3)	3
Mathias GRAVEM (NOR)	A	6	(11)	2
Eddie GUSTAFSSON	G	8		
Mikael HANSSON	D	21		1
Jan JANSSON	M		(4)	
Thor André OLSEN (NOR)	G	6		
Thomas OLSSON	M	22	(2)	6
Klebér SAARENPÄÄ	D	25		
Mikael STRÖM	D	4	(11)	
Andreas THOMAS	A	1	(2)	
Thórdur THÓRDARSON (ISL)	G	12	(1)	
Jonas WALLERSTEDT	M	24	(2)	9
Matias ÖSTBERG	M	12	(5)	1
Alexander ÖSTLUND	M	2	(9)	1

11/04/99	Djurgårdens IF	A	0-3	
18/04/99	Örgryte IS	H	0-2	
25/04/99	Halmstads BK	A	1-1	Olsson
03/05/99	Helsingborgs IF	H	1-0	Andersson
09/05/99	Örebro SK	A	1-2	Fyhr
16/05/99	IF Elfsborg	H	1-1	Gravem
23/05/99	Västra Frölunda IF	A	1-1	Fyhr
31/05/99	IFK Göteborg	H	3-0	Wallerstedt, Flodström, Fyhr
09/06/99	Malmö FF	A	0-0	
14/06/99	Trelleborgs FF	H	2-5	Olsson, Flodström
20/06/99	Kalmar FF	A	1-1	Florén
28/06/99	AIK	H	0-1	
01/07/99	Hammarby IF	A	0-3	
19/07/99	AIK	A	0-2	
01/08/99	Kalmar FF	H	4-2	Andersson 2 (1p), Wallerstedt 2
09/08/99	IF Elfsborg	A	1-2	Olsson
15/08/99	Örebro SK	H	1-0	Andersson
23/08/99	Hammarby IF	H	3-2	Andersson, Hansson, Olsson
29/08/99	Trelleborgs FF	A	4-0	Wallerstedt, Olsson, Östberg, Bergström
13/09/99	Malmö FF	H	5-1	Florén, Wallerstedt 2, Bergström, Östlund
20/09/99	Helsingborgs IF	A	1-0	Blomberg
27/09/99	Halmstads BK	H	4-0	Flodström 3, Bergström
04/10/99	IFK Göteborg	A	3-2	Wallerstedt 2, Olsson
18/10/99	Västra Frölunda IF	H	2-1	Wallerstedt, Bergström
24/10/99	Örgryte IS	A	1-3	Blomberg
30/10/99	Djurgårdens IF	H	1-1	Gravem

TRELLEBORGS FF

CLUB DIRECTORY

Trelleborgs Fotbollsförening
Hejderidaregatan 2
231 44 Trelleborg
tel - (0410) 13190
fax - (0410) 13125
website - www.tff.m.se
email - info@tff.m.se
Year of Formation - 1926
President - Bo Forsén
Secretary - Bengt Cederberg
Coach - Alf Westerberg
Stadium - Vångavallen (10,000)

APPEARANCES 1999

	P	Ap	(s)	Gls
Peter ABELSSON	D	19	(3)	1
Daniel ANDERSSON	G	15		
Johan ANDERSSON	A	6	(4)	2
Martin ANDERSSON	M	4	(1)	
Peter ANDERSSON	M	5	(10)	
Magnus ARVIDSSON	A	11		5
Lee BOYLAN (ENG)	A	2	(3)	
Mikael DANIELSSON	D	18	(1)	2
Jörgen ERIKSSON	D	24		
Anders FRIBERG	D	20	(2)	1
Tommi GRÖNLUND (FIN)	M	24		3
Michael HANSSON	M	26		9
Andreas ISAKSSON	G	11		
Mattias KRONVALL	D	21	(1)	1
Patrik LARSSON	D	7		
Thomas MAGNUSSON	D	1	(4)	
Håkan NILSSON	D	6	(4)	
Jonas NILSSON	M	25		6
Patrik OLSSON	A	18	(3)	6
Markus PERSSON	A	1	(3)	1
Petter SOLLI (NOR)	D	2	(5)	
Jens SVENSSON	M	11	(4)	
Jörgen SVENSSON	A	3	(15)	1
Patrik SVENSSON	M	6	(4)	

LEAGUE RESULTS 1999

11/04/99	Hammarby IF	H	2-2	Olsson, Arvidsson
18/04/99	Kalmar FF	A	2-3	Grönlund, Persson
25/04/99	IFK Göteborg	H	3-1	Friberg (p), Hansson, Arvidsson
03/05/99	Djurgårdens IF	A	2-2	Nilsson J., Arvidsson
10/05/99	IF Elfsborg	A	2-1	Olsson 2
17/05/99	AIK	H	1-0	Nilsson J.
24/05/99	Malmö FF	H	3-1	Hansson, Danielsson, Abelsson
31/05/99	Örebro SK	A	0-1	
10/06/99	Helsingborgs IF	H	2-3	Arvidsson, Danielsson
14/06/99	IFK Norrköping	A	5-2	Nilsson J., Arvidsson, Kronvall,
				Hansson, Svensson
21/06/99	Västra Frölunda IF	A	1-2	Hansson
27/06/99	Örgryte IS	H	0-0	
30/06/99	Halmstads BK	H	1-1	Hansson
18/07/99	Örgryte IS	A	0-2	
01/08/99	Västra Frölunda IF	H	1-0	Olsson
07/08/99	AIK	A	0-3	
19/08/99	IF Elfsborg	H	1-2	Nilsson J.
23/08/99	Halmstads BK	A	2-2	Grönlund, Andersson J.
29/08/99	IFK Norrköping	H	0-4	
11/09/99	Helsingborgs IF	A	3-5	Hansson, Olsson 2
19/09/99	Djurgårdens IF	H	2-2	Grönlund, Hansson
26/09/99	IFK Göteborg	A	1-2	Hansson
03/10/99	Örebro SK	H	2-1	Nilsson J. 2 (1p)
18/10/99	Malmö FF	A	2-1	og (Sverrisson), Hansson
24/10/99	Kalmar FF	H	1-0	Andersson J.
30/10/99	Hammarby IF	A	0-4	

VÄSTRA FRÖLUNDA IF

CLUB DIRECTORY

Västra Frölunda Idrettsförening
Box 213
421 23 Västra Frölunda
tel - (031) 452660
fax - (031) 492080
website - www.vfif.o.se
email - info@vfif.o.se
Year of Formation - 1930
President - Benno Lindblom
Secretary - Leif Turefeldt
Coach - Torbjörn Nilsson (2000 - Stig Fredriksson)
Stadium - Ruddalens Idrottsplats (5,000)

APPEARANCES 1999

	P	Ap	(s)	Gls
Gustaf ANDERSSON	A	24		8
Robert BENGTSSON	D	25	(1)	2
Karl BERGDAHL	D		(1)	
Hans BLOMQVIST	M	2		
Mikael BJÖRKQVIST	D	26		3
Magnus DAHLQVIST	D	21		
Mats HEDÉN	D	20	(1)	
Dime JANKULOVSKI	G	24		
Niclas JOHANSSON	M	7	(10)	
Ola JOHANSSON	M	6	(4)	
Magnus LARSSON	M		(4)	
Björn LUNDBERG	M	16	(6)	1
Christian LUNDSTRÖM	A	22	(2)	7
Peter NILSSON	A		(12)	1
Joakim PALMERÉN	M	2	(8)	
Tomas ROSENQVIST	A	25		3
Klas RUBENDAHL	M	17		1
Mikael SANDKLEF	M	25		2
Anildo SPENCER	D	12	(3)	
Robert TRANBERG	G	2		
Ville VILJANEN	M	10	(10)	2

LEAGUE RESULTS 1999

12/04/99	Malmö FF	H	2-1	Viljanen, Rubendahl
22/04/99	Halmstads BK	A	2-1	Rosenkvist, Lundström
25/04/99	Örebro SK	H	2-0	Lundström, Andersson
02/05/99	Kalmar FF	A	1-3	Bengtsson
10/05/99	Djurgårdens IF	H	1-1	Björkvist
17/05/99	Helsingborgs IF	A	0-1	
23/05/99	IFK Norrköping	H	1-1	Lundström
31/05/99	Örgryte IS	A	0-4	
08/06/99	Hammarby IF	H	1-1	Andersson
14/06/99	IFK Göteborg	A	0-1	
21/06/99	Trelleborgs FF	H	2-1	Sandklef, Lundström
28/06/99	IF Elfsborg	A	3-2	Andersson 3
05/07/99	AIK	H	0-1	
19/07/99	IF Elfsborg	H	4-4	Lundstrom, Sandklef, Björkvist, Rosenkvist
01/08/99	Trelleborgs FF	A	0-1	
07/08/99	Helsingborgs IF	H	0-0	
15/08/99	Djurgårdens IF	A	1-1	Andersson
21/08/99	AIK	A	0-1	
30/08/99	IFK Göteborg	H	1-2	Lundström
13/09/99	Hammarby IF	A	2-1	Andersson, Lundström
19/09/99	Kalmar FF	H	2-0	Bengtsson, Rosenkvist
27/09/99	Örebro SK	A	1-0	Nilsson
04/10/99	Örgryte IS	H	2-1	Lundberg, Andersson
18/10/99	IFK Norrköping	A	1-2	Björkvist
24/10/99	Halmstads BK	H	0-0	
30/10/99	Malmö FF	A	1-2	Viljanen

ÖREBRO SK

CLUB DIRECTORY

Örebro Sportklubb
Eyragatan 1
702 25 Örebro
tel - (019) 167300
fax - (019) 167319
website - www.nerikes.se/osk
email - fotboll@orebro-sk.se
Year of Formation - 1908
President - Jan-Erik Westerlund
Secretary - Ola Ström
Coach - Sven Dahlkvist (2000 - Mats Jingblad)
Stadium - Eyravallen (10,700)

APPEARANCES 1999

	P	Ap	(s)	Gls
Gustaf ANDERSSON	D	7	(6)	
Per ANDERSSON	M		(1)	
Thomas ANDERSSON	D	25		2
Patrik ANTTONEN	A		(7)	
Einar BREKKAN	A	12	(6)	1
Pär EKSTRÖM	A	22		8
Per GAWELIN	M	6		
Niklas GUSTAFSON	D	20		
Asbjörn HELGELAND	M	21	(2)	1
Fredrik JANSSON	D	13	(1)	
Anders KARLSSON	G	26		
Peter KARLSSON	D	26		2
Jon LUNDBLAD	A		(5)	2
Fredrik NORDBACK (FIN)	M	2	(7)	1
Jonas PELGANDER	M	25		
Mathias PERSSON	A	1	(3)	
Mats RUBARTH	A	10	(6)	2
Mikael STEEN	M	24		
Tommy STÅHL	D	4		
Johan WALLINDER	A	17	(7)	2
Salar YASIN	A		(5)	
Lars ZETTERLUND	M	25		3

LEAGUE RESULTS 1999

12/04/99	AIK	A	1-1	Wallinder
25/04/99	Västra Frölunda IF	A	0-2	
03/05/99	Örgryte IS	H	0-1	
09/05/99	IFK Norrköping	H	2-1	Ekström, Zetterlund
16/05/99	Kalmar FF	A	0-2	
19/05/99	IF Elfsborg	H	1-0	Karlsson P.
24/05/99	Helsingborgs IF	A	1-2	Ekström
31/05/99	Trelleborgs FF	H	1-0	Ekström
09/06/99	Halmstads BK	A	1-5	Rubarth
13/06/99	Malmö FF	H	2-0	Zetterlund, Ekström
16/06/99	Hammarby IF	H	3-1	Brekkan, Rubarth, Lundblad
30/06/99	IFK Göteborg	A	1-0	Andersson T.
05/07/99	Djurgårdens IF	A	1-0	Helgeland
28/07/99	IFK Göteborg	H	1-2	Ekström
02/08/99	Hammarby IF	A	1-2	Ekström
08/08/99	Kalmar FF	H	2-0	Ekström, Wallinder
15/08/99	IFK Norrköping	A	0-1	
23/08/99	Djurgårdens IF	H	1-1	Ekström
30/08/99	Malmö FF	A	1-3	Zetterlund
13/09/99	Halmstads BK	H	1-2	Karlsson P.
20/09/99	Örgryte IS	A	1-1	Nordback
27/09/99	Västra Frölunda IF	H	0-1	
03/10/99	Trelleborgs FF	A	1-2	Andersson T.
12/10/99	Helsingborgs IF	H	0-1	
24/10/99	IF Elfsborg	A	1-3	Lundblad
30/10/99	AIK	H	0-2	

ÖRGRYTE IS

CLUB DIRECTORY

Örgryte Idrottssällskap
Box 52025, 400 25 Göteborg
tel - (031) 879310 / fax - (031) 879547
website - www.ois.se
email - webmaster@ois.o.se
Year of Formation - 1887
President - Benny Rosén
Secretary - Stefan Allbäck
Coach - Erik Hamrén
Stadium - Gamla Ullevi (18,000)

MAJOR HONOURS
League Championship - (14)
1896, 1897, 1898, 1899, 1902, 1904, 1905,
1906, 1907, 1909, 1913, 1926, 1928, 1985.
Domestic Cup - (1) 2000.

APPEARANCES 1999

	P	Ap	(s)	Gls
Marcus ALLBÄCK	A	26		15
Johan ELMANDER	A	7	(11)	2
Brynjar GUNNARSSON (ISL)	D	24		1
Christian HEMBERG	A		(9)	1
Markus JOHANNESSON	D	23	(2)	3
Erik JOHANSSON	A	12	(7)	4
Joachim KARLSSON	A	20	(1)	6
Allan KUHN (DEN)	M	23	(2)	2
Magnus KÄLLANDER	M	25		2
Roger LINDQVIST	D	3	(6)	
Daniel LOHM	M	1	(2)	1
Niklas LÖFGREN	A		(1)	
Morgan NILSSON	D	23	(1)	
Mike OWUSU	D		(1)	
Thomas PERSTEDT	G	15		
Anders PRYTZ	D	6		
Freddie ROTH	G	11	(1)	
Patrik SANDSTRÖM	M	8	(10)	
Niclas SJÖSTEDT	D	23	(2)	2
Walter TOMAZ Júnior (BRA)	D	21		1
Martin VIANDER	M	15	(4)	1

LEAGUE RESULTS 1999

11/04/99	Halmstads BK	H	1-0	Allbäck
16/04/99	IFK Norrköping	A	2-0	Lohm, Johansson
24/04/99	Malmö FF	H	4-4	Allbäck, Karlsson 3
03/05/99	Örebro SK	A	1-0	Gunnarsson
11/05/99	IFK Göteborg	H	2-2	Johansson, Källander
17/05/99	Djurgårdens IF	A	3-0	Johannesson (p), Allbäck, Johansson
24/05/99	AIK	A	1-1	Karlsson
31/05/99	Västra Frölunda IF	H	4-0	Tomaz, Allbäck, Kuhn, Hemberg
09/06/99	Kalmar FF	H	3-0	Allbäck, Kuhn, Karlsson
13/06/99	Hammarby IF	A	0-0	
20/06/99	Helsingborgs IF	H	0-1	
27/06/99	Trelleborgs FF	A	0-0	
01/07/99	IF Elfsborg	H	5-1	Allbäck 2, Sjöstedt, Elmander, Källander
18/07/99	Trelleborgs FF	H	2-0	Johannesson (p), Karlsson
02/08/99	Helsingborgs IF	A	0-2	
09/08/99	Djurgårdens IF	H	0-1	
15/08/99	IFK Göteborg	A	0-1	
22/08/99	IF Elfsborg	A	2-1	Allbäck 2
29/08/99	Hammarby IF	H	2-1	Allbäck 2
12/09/99	Kalmar FF	A	2-2	Allbäck 2
20/09/99	Örebro SK	H	1-1	Johannesson
27/09/99	Malmö FF	A	1-1	Allbäck
04/10/99	Västra Frölunda IF	A	1-2	Ulander
16/10/99	AIK	H	1-1	Elmander
24/10/99	IFK Norrköping	H	3-1	Allbäck, Sjöstedt, Johansson
30/10/99	Halmstads BK	A	0-0	

SWITZERLAND

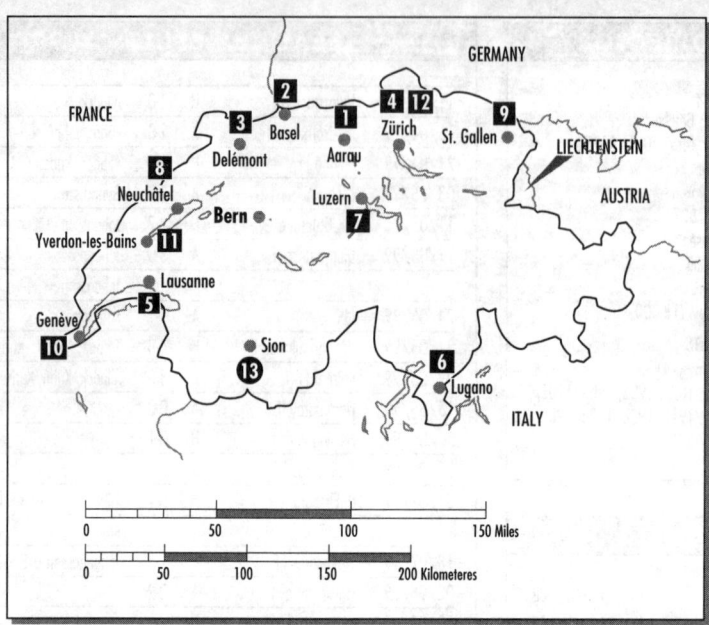

1	**FC AARAU**	997	8	**NEUCHATEL XAMAX FC**	1004
2	**FC BASEL**	998	9	**FC ST. GALLEN**	1005
3	**SR DELEMONT**	999	10	**SERVETTE FC GENEVE**	1006
4	**GRASSHOPPER-CLUB ZÜRICH**	1000	11	**YVERDON-SPORTS**	1007
5	**LAUSANNE-SPORTS**	1001	12	**FC ZÜRICH**	1008
6	**FC LUGANO**	1002	**Promoted club**		
7	**FC LUZERN**	1003	13	**FC SION**	

GRESS GOES BUT WINS THE CUP

St. Gallen tip the formbook upside down

FEDERATION DIRECTORY

Schweizerischer Fussballverband
Haus des Fussballs, Postfach, 3000 Bern 15

tel - (031) 9508111   Year of Formation - 1895
fax - (031) 9508181   President - Marcel Mathier
website - www.fussballverband.ch   Secretary - Peter Gilliéron

Stadium - Wankdorf, Bern (28,000)

1999/2000 was a season in which very little ran to form in Switzerland. Shocks and surprises abounded, none more so than the remarkable championship triumph of unheralded FC St. Gallen, a club whose only previous Swiss title had come several generations earlier in 1904.

Most pre-season predictions had St. Gallen down as relegation strugglers with little chance of surviving the halfway cut. But in coach Marcel Koller, who had arrived from Second Division outfit FC Wil during the course of the previous campaign, St. Gallen had a leader who had experienced the high life as a player - including seven championships and five Cup wins for Grasshopper plus 57 international caps for Switzerland - and was determined to scale the same peaks in his new profession.

Koller's powers of motivation and confidence reinforcement turned a largely unsung group of players into a cohesive force. They made a tremendous start, winning their first three games without conceding a goal, and that form was maintained throughout the season. Leaders by eight points at the end of the first phase, St. Gallen opened up an even bigger gap in the spring. Their consistency was relentless, and at times they were strong enough to rip the opposition to shreds, most memorably when they destroyed FC Luzern 7-1 at the beginning of April.

When Koller took over, St. Gallen possessed just one Swiss international, defender Marco Zwyssig. But during the course of the season he was joined in the national team squad by team-mates Jörg Stiel, Marc Zellweger, Sascha Müller and Giuseppe Mazzarelli. Two of the foreign players Koller had brought with him from FC Wil - Brazilian playmaker Jairo and goalscoring Ghanaian Charles Amoah - also excelled, particularly during the 15-match, six-month unbeaten run that carried St. Gallen beyond the reach of their pursuers and enabled them to clinch the championship as early as four rounds from the end. Remarkably, only one St. Gallen player had ever played European football before, and that was veteran keeper Stiel...all of 12 years earlier.

Two other underdogs, Yverdon and Luzern, also achieved far more than was expected them. Yverdon, coached by ex-Swiss

LEAGUE CHAMPIONSHIP RESULTS 99/00

AUTUMN (FIRST PHASE)	1	2	3	4	5	6	7	8	9	10	11	12
1 FC Aarau		1-3	4-2	2-1	1-3	0-2	1-0	4-1	1-0	3-2	1-1	1-1
2 FC Basel	2-1		3-0	1-1	3-3	1-0	2-0	1-1	4-1	0-0	1-2	0-0
3 SR Delémont	4-2	2-2		2-1	1-1	1-0	0-1	2-2	0-3	1-3	1-3	2-2
4 Grasshopper-Club Zürich	4-0	1-1	4-0		1-1	2-1	2-0	4-0	2-2	4-2	0-0	2-1
5 Lausanne-Sports	3-1	1-0	3-0	3-3		2-0	2-1	0-2	0-1	0-1	2-2	2-0
6 FC Lugano	4-1	1-1	1-2	1-5	1-1		1-1	2-1	1-1	3-0	2-2	1-1
7 FC Luzern	2-1	3-0	2-0	2-0	2-1	3-0		1-1	2-2	2-4	4-1	0-1
8 Neuchâtel Xamax FC	1-1	1-2	2-0	0-1	1-2	3-1	3-1		2-2	3-2	1-1	3-0
9 FC St. Gallen	4-1	1-1	2-1	2-1	2-2	2-1	2-0	2-1		2-0	3-2	3-0
10 Servette FC Genève	1-1	1-1	1-1	2-1	0-1	1-3	1-0	2-4	2-1		3-1	3-0
11 Yverdon-Sports	1-1	0-1	3-1	2-0	0-0	1-0	3-0	0-0	0-1	2-1		1-1
12 FC Zürich	0-1	0-1	3-1	0-0	2-2	2-1	1-1	2-1	1-3	2-0	1-0	

SPRING (FINAL ROUND)	1	2	3	4	5	6	7	8
1 FC Basel		2-2	0-3	0-0	1-1	3-1	1-0	2-0
2 Grasshopper-Club Zürich	3-0		1-1	0-2	1-3	4-4	2-3	4-1
3 Lausanne-Sports	0-0	3-1		3-1	2-1	1-3	2-1	2-0
4 FC Luzern	3-2	0-1	1-0		1-2	1-2	1-1	2-1
5 Neuchâtel Xamax FC	1-2	1-3	1-2	3-1		0-3	2-2	7-2
6 FC St. Gallen	1-1	1-1	1-0	7-1	3-0		0-0	4-1
7 Servette FC Genève	1-1	1-3	1-3	6-0	3-3	1-2		2-0
8 Yverdon-Sports	0-1	4-4	1-0	2-3	3-0	0-1	1-3	

LEAGUE CHAMPIONSHIP FINAL TABLES 99/00

AUTUMN (FIRST PHASE)		Home					Away					Total						
		Pd	W	D	L	F	A	W	D	L	F	A	W	D	L	F	A	Pt	GD
1	FC St. Gallen	22	9	2	0	25	10	4	4	3	17	15	13	6	3	42	25	45	17
2	FC Basel	22	5	5	1	18	9	4	5	2	13	12	9	10	3	31	21	37	10
3	Lausanne-Sports	22	6	2	3	18	11	3	7	1	17	14	9	9	4	35	25	36	10
4	Grasshopper-Club Zürich	22	7	4	0	26	8	2	3	6	14	17	9	7	6	40	25	34	15
5	Yverdon -Sports	22	5	4	2	13	6	2	5	4	15	19	7	9	6	28	25	30	3
6	Neuchâtel Xamax FC	22	5	3	3	20	13	2	4	5	14	20	7	7	8	34	33	28	1
7	FC Luzern	22	7	2	2	23	11	1	2	8	5	18	8	4	10	28	29	28	-1
8	Servette FC Genève	22	5	3	3	17	14	3	1	7	15	22	8	4	10	32	36	28	-4
9	FC Aarau	22	6	2	3	19	16	1	3	7	11	26	7	5	10	30	42	26	-12
10	FC Zürich	22	5	3	3	14	11	1	5	5	7	18	6	8	8	21	29	26	-8
11	FC Lugano	22	3	6	2	18	16	2	0	9	9	18	5	6	11	27	34	21	-7
12	SR Delémont	22	3	4	4	16	20	1	1	9	8	28	4	5	13	24	48	17	-24

SPRING (FINAL ROUND)		Home					Away					Total						
		Pd	W	D	L	F	A	W	D	L	F	A	W	D	L	F	A	Pt	GD
1	FC St. Gallen	14	4	3	0	17	4	5	1	1	16	10	9	4	1	33	14	54	19
2	Lausanne-Sports	14	5	1	1	13	7	3	1	3	9	6	8	2	4	22	13	44	9
3	FC Basel	14	3	3	1	9	7	2	3	2	7	9	5	6	3	16	16	40	0
4	Grasshopper-Club Zürich	14	2	2	3	15	14	3	3	1	15	12	5	5	4	30	26	37	4
5	FC Luzern	14	3	1	3	9	9	2	1	4	8	21	5	2	7	17	30	31	-13
6	Servette FC Genève	14	2	2	3	15	12	2	3	2	10	9	4	5	5	25	21	31	4
7	Neuchâtel Xamax FC	14	2	1	4	15	15	2	2	3	10	14	4	3	7	25	29	29	-4
8	Yverdon-Sports	14	2	1	4	11	12	0	0	7	5	23	2	1	11	16	35	22	-19

N.B. After 22 matches the top eight play off for the title, taking half their points total. The bottom four enter a promotion/relegation play-off group with the top two from the Second Division. In the Final Round, when teams are level on points, classification is determined by the position of the teams at the end of the First Phase.

international Lucien Favre, caused a sensation by qualifying for the play-offs, while Luzern, under the command of another Switzerland old boy, Andy Egli, did even better, finishing fifth, thanks in the main to the perfect fusion of their forward line, with star of tomorrow Alex Frei linking up superbly alongside on-loan veteran Kubilay Türkyilmaz.

By contrast, the two traditional giants of Swiss football, Servette and Grasshopper, suffered a season of drastic underachievement which ended with both of them missing out on a place in Europe.

Servette, the defending champions, sacked their title-winning coach Gérard Castella after a bleak spell which saw the Geneva club perform embarrassingly badly in Europe and suffer a succession of unexpected defeats in the league. On-field troubles were exacerbated by rumblings in the boardroom, with French backers Canal+ preparing to end their interest, only to stay in place after a proposed buy-out belatedly fell through. Servette just scraped into the play-offs under their new French coach René Exbrayat but they were never in a position to win anything more than self-respect.

Grasshopper also ended up with nothing at the end of a season in which they had used three coaches, including high-profile Englishman Roy Hodgson, the man who had become a Swiss national hero in the mid-1990s by qualifying the national side for both World Cup '94 and Euro '96. Armed with the biggest budget ever made available to a Swiss club, Grasshopper were the clear favourites for the championship. They even managed to secure the services of top-class Swiss international striker Stéphane Chapuisat from Borussia Dortmund. But the Hodgson/Chapuisat 'dream team' never functioned to its full potential, and by the end of the season the coach had been dismissed (after a 0-2 home defeat by Luzern) and the star player was in the treatment room nursing a bad injury (sustained in a 3-1 win at Neuchâtel).

The three clubs which qualified alongside champions St. Gallen for the 2000/01 European competitions were Lausanne, Basel and FC Zürich.

Lausanne, cleverly coached by Pierre-André Schurmann, finished runners-up in both league and Cup. Six wins in their last seven NLA matches took them four points clear of Christian Gross's Basel, but they were

NATIONAL TEAM APPEARANCES 99/00

Coach - Gilbert GRESS; Hans-Peter ZAUGG	CZE	DEN	BLS	WAL	OMN	UAE	NOR	GER	Cps	Gls
Stefan HUBER (14/06/66) - Grasshopper-Club Zürich	G46	G	G						16	-
Marc HODEL (06/11/70) - Grasshopper-Club Zürich	D	D	D	D	D	s46			13	1
Sébastien JEANNERET (12/12/73) - Servette FC Genève	D52	D		M	D			D	s89	17	-
Stefan WOLF (31/01/71) - Servette FC Genève	D		s78						14	-
Raphaël WICKY (26/04/77) - SV Werder Bremen (GER)	D	D89	D						27	-
Régis ROTHENBÜHLER (11/10/70) - Neuchâtel Xamax FC	D77								18	-
Ciriaco SFORZA (02/03/70) - 1.FC Kaiserslautern (GER)	M	M	M			M	M46	M	69	6
Johann VOGEL (08/03/77) - PSV (HOL)	M77	M	M	M			M	M	34	1
Fabio CELESTINI (31/10/75) - Lausanne-Sports	M								6	-
Stéphane CHAPUISAT (28/06/69) - Grasshopper-Club Zürich	A86	A	A63				A		78	18
Alexandre COMISETTI (21/07/73) - AJ Auxerre (FRA)	A68		s63	s66	s71	M			20	3
Andreas HILFIKER (11/02/69) - Tennis Borussia Berlin (GER)	s46								8	-
Marco ZWYSSIG (24/10/71) - FC St. Gallen	s52								5	-
Sascha MÜLLER (28/02/70) - FC St. Gallen	s68	s77			s71	s77			4	-
Boris SMILJANIC (28/09/76) - Grasshopper-Club Zürich	s77								1	-
Thomas WYSS (29/08/66) - FC Luzern	s77	s89		s70	M				11	-
Alexandre REY (22/09/72) - Servette FC Genève	s86		A66		A77	A86	A68	s70	11	2
Franco DI JORIO (22/09/73) - FC Zürich		M60	M	M					9	-
Patrick MÜLLER (17/12/76) - Grasshopper-Club Zürich		D	D78				D	D	15	1
Patrick BÜHLMANN (16/08/71) - Servette FC Genève/Lausanne-Sports		M	A71	A	M71	s88	M78	M82	12	1
David SESA (10/07/73) - Lecce (ITA)		A77	s71	M			M	A	25	1
Kubilay TÜRKYILMAZ (04/03/67) - FC Luzern		s60	A						58	27
Stéphane HENCHOZ (07/09/74) - Liverpool (ENG)			D	D		D	D		41	-
Pascal ZUBERBÜHLER (08/01/71) - FC Basel			G	G			G	G	9	-
Bernt HAAS (08/04/78) - Grasshopper-Club Zürich			D		D			D	9	1
Christophe JAQUET (02/04/76) - Yverdon-Sports				D70	D	D			3	-
Sébastien FOURNIER (27/06/71) - Servette FC Genève					D	D88			26	2
Andres GERBER (26/04/73) - Lausanne-Sports					M71	M46	s78	s82	4	-
Mario CANTALUPPI (11/04/74) - FC Basel					M	M77	s46	M89	10	3
Léonard THURRE (09/09/77) - Servette FC Genève					A	A			2	-
Hakan YAKIN (22/02/77) - Grasshopper-Club Zürich					s77	s86	s68	A70	4	2
Marco PASCOLO (09/05/66) - FC Zürich						G			46	-
Giuseppe MAZZARELLI (14/08/72) - FC St. Gallen							D	D	3	-
Murat YAKIN (15/09/74) - FC Basel								D	20	3

unable to repeat that form in the Swiss Cup final. Bidding to win the trophy for the third year running, Lausanne were beaten in Berne on penalties after an exciting 2-2 draw with FC Zürich. Lausanne missed all three of their spotkicks - Christophe Ohrel, Oscar Londono and Sven Christ were the culprits - whereas FC Zürich scored all three of theirs - thanks to Urs Fischer, Philippe Douglas and Mikheil Kavelashvili.

The Cup win rescued FC Zürich from a season of anonymity. They would have qualified for the champion-ship play-offs but for a very costly administrative error by coach Raimondo Ponte in the final first-phase fixture against Neuchâtel Xamax. He fielded one foreign player too many and the team thus forfeited a game they had drawn 1-1 with a 0-3 scoreline, which meant that they, rather than Xamax, dropped into the promotion/relegation group. Ponte eventually lost his job - after nearly nine years' service - and was replaced by Gilbert Gress, who had been dismissed himself four months earlier from his position as Switzerland's national team coach. Gress made

DOMESTIC CUP 99/00

FIFTH ROUND
FC Mendrisio 1, FC Basel 5
Altstetten Zürich 0, FC Luagno 2
FC Granges 0, Lausanne-Sports 4
Etoile Carouge FC 3, SR Delémont 0
FC Solothurn 2, Neuchâtel Xamax FC 3
FC Chiasso 1, FC St. Gallen 4
FC Wil 1, FC Zürich 2
Freienbach 1, Grasshopper-Club Zürich 2
FC Baden 0, FC Luzern 3
FC Winterthur 1, FC Aarau 3
Martigny-Sports 1, Servette FC Genève 4
FC Sion 4, Yverdon-Sports 2
FC Fribourg 2, BSC Young Boys Bern 1
Serrières Neuchâtel 1, FC Thun 2
Malcantone Agno 1, AC Bellinzona 3
Horgen 1, YF Juventus Zürich 0

1/8 FINALS
Etoile-Carouge FC 0, FC Zürich 1
Horgen 1, FC Luzern 2
AC Bellinzona 0, Lausanne-Sports 4
FC Sion 1, FC St. Gallen 3 (aet)
Neuchâtel Xamax FC 0, FC Lugano 4
FC Basel 1, Grasshopper-Club Zürich 1
(aet; 5-4 on pens.)
FC Fribourg 0, FC Thun 3
FC Aarau 1, Servette FC Genève 3

QUARTER-FINALS
FC Thun 1 (Okpala 55),
FC Zürich 2 (Tsawa 1, Ndlovu 117) (aet)
FC Lugano 1 (Gimenez 41), FC St. Gallen 0
FC Luzern 3 (Branca 30, Frei 53, Joller 57),
Servette FC Genève 2 (Rey 78, Wolf 90)
Lausanne-Sports 3 (Kuzba 32, Gerber 34, 88),
FC Basel 2 (Koumantarakis 50, N'Tiamoah 76)

SEMI-FINALS
FC Zürich 7 (Bartlett 17, 79, 94, Frick 98,
Del Signore 107p, Jamarauli 113, Chassot 116),
FC Luzern 2 (Frei 7, Gian 78) (aet)
Lausanne-Sports 3 (Kuzba 8, 21, 60),
FC Lugano 2 (Gaspoz 79, Rothenbühler 81)

FINAL
28/05/2000, Berne
FC ZÜRICH 2 Jamarauli (77), Bartlett (95)
LAUSANNE-SPORTS 2 Danilevicius (36), Gerber (105)
(aet; 3-0 on pens.)
referee - Bertolini
FC ZÜRICH - Pascolo, Fischer; Tsawa, Djordjevic; Pallas
(Chassot 46), Del Signore (Douglas 57), Jamarauli,
Quentin, Frick (Kavelashvili 63); Bartlett, Giannini.
LAUSANNE-SPORTS - Rapo; Londono, Puce, Christ,
Hänzi; Ohrel, Rehn, Celestini, Gerber (Simon 114);
Mazzoni, Danilevicius (Horjak 76)

quite an impact, notably when his team beat Luzern 7-2 after extra-time in the Cup semi-final and then, again, with the victory over Lausanne in the final.

Gress's contract with the national team was prematurely terminated following Switzerland's failure to qualify for Euro 2000. They only just missed out on the play-offs, finishing on the same number of points as Denmark, but were left to rue the match at home to the Danes early in the campaign when they had conceded a stoppage-time equaliser. Denmark's shock 3-2 win in Italy rendered Switzerland's back-to-back victories over Belarus and Wales meaningless, but those wins did at least enable Gress to balance the books before his departure, with his final record reading six wins, six draws and six defeats.

It was long-time national team assistant coach Hans-Peter Zaugg who was seconded into filling the vacancy. He was very popular with the majority of the players, but

the Swiss FA insisted that he lacked the experience for the top job and after some deliberation plumped for Argentinian Enzo Trossero as the next permanent coach.

The one glitch was that Trossero was not available to take over until the summer; he was still under contract at his Argentinian club Independiente. This meant that Zaugg was retained to oversee the two friendlies in the spring against Norway and Germany. In the latter game, played in Kaiserslautern, the Swiss came excruciatingly close to victory only to be denied by a dreadful refereeing error which allowed Germany's late equaliser to stand despite a clear foul in the build-up to the goal. The Swedish official later apologised to Swiss officials for his error after viewing the incident on video tape.

Trossero was a controversial choice. When

NATIONAL TEAM RESULTS 99/00

18/08/99	Czech Republic	A	Drnovice	0-3	
04/09/99	Denmark (ECQ)	A	Copenhagen	1-2	Türkyilmaz (80)
08/09/99	Belarus (ECQ)	H	Lausanne	2-0	Türkyilmaz (68, 87p)
09/10/99	Wales (ECQ)	A	Wrexham	2-0	Rey (16), Bühlmann (60)
19/02/00	Oman	A	Muscat	4-1	Cantaluppi (17, 67), Rey (38), Yakin H. (89)
23/02/00	United Arab Emirates	N	Muscat	0-1	
29/03/00	Norway	H	Lugano	2-2	Chapuisat (55), Cantaluppi (74)
26/04/00	Germany	A	Kaiserslautern	1-1	Yakin H. (35)

TOP SCORERS

25   Charles AMOAH (FC St. Gallen)
21   Rainer BIELI (Neuchâtel Xamax FC)
16   Efan EKOKU (Grasshopper-Club Zürich)
14   Alexandre REY (Servette FC Genève)
13   Alex FREI (FC Luzern)
      George KOUMANTARAKIS (FC Basel)
      Marcin KUZBA (Lausanne-Sports)
12   Henri CAMARA (Neuchâtel Xamax FC)
11   Stéphane CHAPUISAT (Grasshopper-Club Zürich)
10   Hakan YAKIN (Grasshopper-Club Zürich)
      Javier MAZZONI (Lausanne-Sports)
      Rumen IVANOV (FC Aarau)

EUROPEAN CUPS 99/00

CHAMPIONS' CUP
● SERVETTE FC GENEVE
Qualifying round SK STURM GRAZ (AUT)
A 1-2 Lonfat (45)
       Pédat (Margairaz 40); Jeanneret, Wolf, Juarez; Ouadja (Varela 73),
       Durix, Lonfat, Bühlmann; Rey (Thurre 53), Vurens, Petrov.
H 2-2 Juarez (50), Thurre (90)
       Pédat; Jeanneret (Ouadja 76), Wolf, Juarez; Vurens (Petrov 67),
       El Brazi, Durix, Bühlmann; Varela (Melunovic 81); Rey, Thurre.

UEFA CUP
● FC ZÜRICH
Qualifying round SLIEMA WANDERERS (MLT)
A 3-0 Kavelashvili (36), Bartlett (80), Kebe (90)
       Pascolo; Castillo, Andreoli, Fischer, Quentin (Stocklosa 89); Giannini
       (Kebe 83), Jamarauli, Sant'Anna; Frick, Bartlett, Kavelashvili
       (Douglas 81).
H 1-0 Kebe (70)
       Pascolo; Chassot, Castillo, Fischer, Quentin; Kavelashvili, Kebe, Sant'Anna,
       Frick (Douglas 30); Bartlett (Stocklosa 53), Jamarauli (Jodice 75).

1st round K LIERSE SK (BEL)
H 1-0 Jamarauli (29)
       Pascolo; Sant'Anna, Stocklosa, Djordjevic (Andreoli 69), Quentin; Chassot
       (Akale 77), Eydelie, Frick, Jamarauli; Kavelashvili (Del Signore 64),
       Bartlett.
A 4-3 Jamarauli (2), Frick (59), Eydelie (88), Daems (90og)
       Pascolo; Giannini (Frick 53), Stocklosa, Fischer (Malacarne 69), Quentin;
       Kebe, Eydelie, Sant'Anna, Del Signore; Jamarauli (Kavelashvili 81);
       Bartlett.

2nd round NEWCASTLE UNITED (ENG)
H 1-2 Castillo (68)
       Pascolo; Castillo, Stocklosa, Djordjevic, Kebe (Douglas 65); Frick (Akale
       76), Eydelie, Sant'Anna, Chassot (Del Signore 65); Kavelashvili, Bartlett.
A 1-3 Jamarauli (16)
       Pascolo; Giannini (Castillo 71), Stocklosa, Djordjevic, Quentin;
       Kavelashvili, Kebe (Chassot 46), Eydelie, Sant'Anna, Jamarauli; Bartlett
       (Frick 46).

● GRASSHOPPER-CLUB ZÜRICH
Qualifying round BRAY WANDERERS (IRL)
H 4-0 Chapuisat (30, 63), Isabella (78, 85)
       Huber; Zanni, Haas, Gren, Smiljanic; Sermeter (Cabañas 80), Hodel,
       Tikva (Løvvik 64), Magro; Yakin (Isabella 74), Chapuisat.
A 4-0 Tikva (6, 39), De Napoli (53), Muff (65)
       Huber; Zanni, De Nicola, Gren, Smiljanic (Schwegler 69); Isabella
       (Sermeter 67), Tikva (Muff 63), Hodel; Cabañas, Magro, De Napoli.

1st round AB (DEN)
A 2-0 Bjur (50og), Ekoku (82)
       Huber; Zanni, Haas, Gren, Smiljanic; Cabañas, Hodel, Tararache, Yakin
       (Isabella 83); Chapuisat (De Napoli 87), Ekoku.
H 1-1 Magro (79)
       Huber; Haas, Hodel, Gren, Smiljanic; Magro, Cabañas, Tararache; Yakin
       (Tikva 66), Ekoku (Isabella 84), Chapuisat (Løvvik 82).

2nd round SLAVIA PRAHA (CZE)
A 1-3 Yakin (23)
       Walker; Haas, Hodel, Gren, Yakin; Tikva (Müller 63), Cabañas, Tararache,
       Sermeter (De Napoli 76); Ekoku, Chapuisat.
H 1-0 Yakin (76)
       Walker; Haas, De Nicola, Hodel, Yakin; Cabañas (Obiorah 70), Müller,
       Tararache, Sermeter (Huber 72); Ekoku (Tikva 90), Chapuisat.

● LAUSANNE-SPORTS
1st round RC CELTA (ESP)
H 3-2 Kuzba (20), Mazzoni (22, 58)
       Rapo; Karlen, Puce, Magnin, Hänzi; Ohrel, Londono, Rehn (Pizzinat 75);
       Diogo (Christ 68); Kuzba (Gerber 82), Mazzoni.
A 0-4
       Rapo; Ohrel, Puce, Iglesias (Shahgeldyan 61), Hänzi; Celestini
       (Pizzinat 87), Rehn, Londono, Diogo (Gerber 46); Kuzba, Mazzoni.

● SERVETTE FC GENEVE
1st round ARIS (GRE)
A 1-1 Petrov (88)
       Pédat; Ouadja, Wolf, Vanetta, Jeanneret; Potocianu (Bah 80), Lonfat
       (El Brazi 72), Veiga; Varela, Rey (Petrov 67), Bühlmann.
H 1-2 (aet) Lonfat (35)
       Pédat; Jeanneret, Wolf, El Brazi, Bühlmann; Varela (Vanetta 46), Durix
       (Petrov 91), Lonfat, Veiga (Vurens 68); Thurre, Rey.

he won the title with Sion in 1992, he earned himself a reputation for his defensive style of play. He also speaks very little German and is not fully conversant in French or Italian, either. Furthermore, his most recent experience in Switzerland was a negative one - he was sacked on the eve of the 1999/2000 campaign by Lugano, having fallen out with the club's bankrolling Italian millionaire Pietro Belardelli.

Lugano were to have a bad season all round but they did secure their return to the NLA by topping the promotion/relegation group in the spring. Close behind them were Trossero's other ex-club, Sion, who returned to the top flight after a year away. They were the only team promoted and took the place of Delémont, who, unlike Lugano, FC Zürich and Aarau, failed to make an instant return to the élite.

INTERNATIONAL HONOURS

World Cup Finals appearances: 1934, 1938 (2nd round), 1950,
1954 (qtr-finals), 1962, 1966, 1994 (2nd round)

European Championship appearances: 1996

PLAYERS OF THE SEASON

GIUSEPPE MAZZARELLI

A former youth star of Swiss football, Giuseppe Mazzarelli cast off his rebellious image to reach full maturity in 1999/2000. He was the defensive lynchpin of a St. Gallen side that won the Swiss championship. Previous unhappy experiences at FC Zürich, Manchester City, Grasshopper and Young Boys Berne were forgotten as the 28-year-old responded with wisdom and responsibility to the instructions of St. Gallen coach Marcel Koller and delivered far and away the most productive season of his career. A central stopper for his club, he was selected for the national team by interim coach Hans-Peter Zaugg in the left-back role and performed commendably against both Norway and Germany. Although he seemed set to stay at St. Gallen, Mazzarelli decided to move to Italy. The only problem was that he signed contracts for two clubs, Ancona and Bari. It was a mess of his own making, but FIFA intervened and allowed him to continue his career in Serie A with Bari.

CHARLES AMOAH

Another key member of St. Gallen's championship-winning team, Charles Amoah emerged from nowhere to become the NLA's top marksman, scoring 25 goals in his 34 appearances. In fairness, he was not a complete revelation as he had topped the NLB charts the previous season, with FC Wil, but prior to that the Ghanaian striker's experiences in his adopted country had been wholly negative. Small and stocky, he has the look of a boxer but the speed of an Olympic athlete. Like many Africans who come to Switzerland, he has taken a while to overcome the problems of the winter climate. Proof of his adaptation, however, was evident in early 2000 when he refused to return home to play for Ghana at the African Nations' Cup, preferring to concentrate on his preparation for the season's resumption in Switzerland. His reward for that loyalty came a few months later when he collected a championship winner's medal.

PROMOTED CLUB 99/00

SECOND DIVISION FINAL TABLE

		Pd	W	D	L	F	A	Pt	GD
1	AC Bellinzona	22	13	5	4	43	17	44	26
2	**FC Sion**	22	12	4	6	41	21	40	20
3	FC Thun	22	10	8	4	34	24	38	10
4	FC Baden	22	10	7	5	32	20	37	12
5	SC Kriens	22	10	7	5	37	28	37	9
6	Etoile Carouge FC	22	9	8	5	24	18	35	6
7	FC Winterthur	22	9	3	10	30	33	30	-3
8	FC Wil	22	8	5	9	40	41	29	-1
9	FC Solothurn	22	7	2	13	29	37	23	-8
10	BSC Young Boys Bern	22	5	6	11	31	45	21	-14
11	Stade Nyonnais	22	5	3	14	30	53	18	-23
12	FC Schaffhausen	22	2	6	14	16	50	12	-34

PROMOTION/RELEGATION PLAY-OFFS FINAL TABLE 99/00

		Pd	W	D	L	F	A	Pt	GD
1	FC Lugano	14	8	4	2	26	18	28	8
2	FC Sion	14	7	3	4	28	19	24	9
3	FC Zürich	14	7	3	4	17	12	24	5
4	FC Aarau	14	6	4	4	23	16	22	7
5	AC Bellinzona	14	4	8	2	21	14	20	7
6	FC Thun	14	4	4	6	17	18	16	-1
7	SR Delémont	14	4	2	8	18	29	14	-11
8	FC Baden	14	1	2	11	7	31	5	-24

CLUB DIRECTORY

FC Sion
38 rue des Echutes
1950 Sion
tel - (027) 2037172/3
fax - (027) 2037174
Year of Formation - 1909
President - Gilbert Kadji
Secretary - Eddy Hudanski
Coach - Roberto Morini; Henri Stambouli
Stadium - Tourbillon (19,526)

MAJOR HONOURS

League Championship - (2) 1992, 1997.
Domestic Cup - (9) 1965, 1974, 1980, 1982, 1986, 1991, 1995, 1996, 1997.

FC AARAU

CLUB DIRECTORY

FC Aarau
Postfach 2738
5001 Aarau
tel - (062) 8232922
fax - (062) 8232924
Year of Formation - 1902
President - Ernst Lämmli
Secretaries - Rolf Suter & Fredy Strasser
Coach - Jochen Dries; Rolf Fringer
Stadium - Brügglifeld (13,200)

MAJOR HONOURS
League Championship - (3) 1912, 1914, 1993.
Domestic Cup - (1) 1985.

APPEARANCES 99/00

	P	Ap	(s)	Gls
Petar ALEKSANDROV (BUL)	A	3	(8)	2
David BADER	D	6	(3)	
Roberto BALDASSARRI	M	21		2
Olivier BAUDRY (FRA)	D	13	(1)	
Ivan BENITO	G	22		
Chris BONGO (CIV)	A		(4)	
Mario EGGIMANN	D		(1)	
Lucio ESPOSITO	A		(5)	
Marcel HELDMANN	M	22		2
Rumen IVANOV (BUL)	A	20		10
Jean-Pierre LA PLACA	A	3	(12)	
Frédéric PAGE	D	17	(4)	2
Mirko PAVLICEVIC (CRO)	D	20	(1)	1
Ivan PREVITALI	M	9	(2)	
Remo SENN	M	2	(4)	
Dariusz SKRZYPCZAK (POL)	M	18	(1)	1
Beat STUDER	D	12		
Daniel TARONE	M	12	(1)	1
André WIEDERKEHR	M	20		2
Slawomir WOJCIECHOWSKI (POL)	A	22		6

LEAGUE RESULTS 1999/2000

07/07/99	Neuchâtel Xamax FC	A	1-1	Aleksandrov
13/07/99	Yverdon-Sports	H	1-1	Ivanov (p)
17/07/99	Grasshopper-Club Zürich	A	0-4	
21/07/99	FC St. Gallen	H	1-0	Ivanov
24/07/99	SR Delémont	A	2-4	Aleksandrov, Page
01/08/99	Servette FC Genève	H	3-2	Ivanov 2, Baldassarri
07/08/99	FC Luzern	A	1-2	Wojciechowski
14/08/99	Lausanne-Sports	H	1-3	Ivanov (p)
21/08/99	FC Zürich	A	1-0	Wiederkehr
28/08/99	FC Lugano	A	1-4	Page
11/09/99	FC Basel	H	1-3	Wojciechowski
18/09/99	Neuchâtel Xamax FC	H	4-1	Ivanov 2, Heldmann, Wojciechowski
26/09/99	Yverdon-Sports	A	1-1	Ivanov
03/10/99	Grasshopper-Club Zürich	H	2-1	Ivanov, Tarone
16/10/99	FC St. Gallen	A	1-4	Ivanov (p)
24/10/99	SR Delémont	H	4-2	og (Romano), Wojciechowski, Pavlicevic, Baldassarri
30/10/99	Servette FC Genève	A	1-1	Wojciechowski
07/11/99	FC Luzern	H	1-0	Heldmann
20/11/99	Lausanne-Sports	A	1-3	Wojciechowski
28/11/99	FC Zürich	H	1-1	Wiederkehr
05/12/99	FC Lugano	H	0-2	
12/12/99	FC Basel	A	1-2	Skrzypczak

FC BASEL

CLUB DIRECTORY

FC Basel 1893
Postfach 260
4028 Basel
tel - (061) 3133666
fax - (061) 3133633
Year of Formation - 1893
President - René C. Jäggi
Coach - Christian Gross
Stadium - Schützenmatte (11,400)

MAJOR HONOURS
League Championship - (8) 1953, 1967, 1969,
1970, 1972, 1973, 1977, 1980.
Domestic Cup - (5)
1933, 1947, 1963, 1967, 1975.

APPEARANCES 99/00

	P	Ap	(s)	Gls
Sébastien BARBERIS	M	28	(3)	2
Luís CALAPES (POR)	D	6	(1)	
Mario CANTALUPPI	M	30		3
Massimo CECCARONI	D	29		
Philippe CRAVERO	D	29		2
Çetin GÜNER (TUR)	A	5	(16)	
Urs GÜNTENSPERGER	A	3	(2)	
Thomas HÄBERLI	M	2	(7)	
Benjamin HUGGEL	M	34		4
Raphäel KEHRLI	M	15	(9)	
Ivan KNEZ (ARG)	D	32		1
George KOUMANTARAKIS (SAF)	A	31	(1)	13
Oliver KREUZER (GER)	D	30		9
Edmond N'TIAMOAH (FRA)	A	3	(9)	
Marco PEREZ (ESP)	M	1	(4)	
Alexandre QUENNOZ	D	6	(2)	
Aleksandr RICHKOV (RUS)	M		(1)	
Attila SAHIN (TUR)	D		(3)	
Nenad SAVIC	M	29	(3)	3
Agent SAWU (ZIM)	A	2	(6)	
Didier THOLOT (FRA)	A	30	(1)	8
Marco TSCHOPP	A	3	(18)	1
Murat YAKIN	D	12		1
Pascal ZUBERBÜHLER	G	36		

LEAGUE RESULTS 1999/2000

07/07/99	FC Lugano	A	1-1	Kreuzer
14/07/99	Neuchâtel Xamax FC	H	1-1	Tholot
21/07/99	Grasshopper-Club Zürich	H	1-1	Cravero
31/07/99	SR Delémont	H	3-0	Tholot 2, Kreuzer
05/08/99	Servette FC Genève	A	1-1	Koumantarakis
10/08/99	Yverdon-Sports	A	1-0	Tholot
15/08/99	FC Luzern	H	2-0	Koumantarakis, Huggel
21/08/99	Lausanne-Sports	A	0-1	
24/08/99	FC St. Gallen	A	1-1	Knez
29/08/99	FC Zürich	H	0-0	
11/09/99	FC Aarau	A	3-1	Huggel, Cantaluppi, Savic
18/09/99	FC Lugano	H	1-0	Barberis
23/09/99	Neuchâtel Xamax FC	A	2-1	Tholot, Tschopp
02/10/99	Yverdon-Sports	H	1-2	Koumantarakis
17/10/99	Grasshopper-Club Zürich	A	1-1	Kreuzer
24/10/99	FC St. Gallen	H	4-1	Koumantarakis 3, Kreuzer
31/10/99	SR Delémont	A	2-2	Huggel, Kreuzer
07/11/99	Servette FC Genève	H	0-0	
21/11/99	FC Luzern	A	0-3	
27/11/99	Lausanne-Sports	H	3-3	Cravero, Koumantarakis, Kreuzer (p)
05/12/99	FC Zürich	A	1-0	Koumantarakis
12/12/99	FC Aarau	H	2-1	Cantaluppi, Kreuzer (p)
12/03/00	Lausanne-Sports	A	0-0	
19/03/00	Grasshopper-Club Zürich	H	2-2	Savic, Cantaluppi
26/03/00	FC Luzern	A	2-3	Koumantarakis, Kreuzer
01/04/00	Servette FC Genève	H	1-0	Koumantarakis
07/04/00	FC St. Gallen	A	1-1	Barberis
15/04/00	Yverdon-Sports	H	2-0	Koumantarakis, Kreuzer (p)
22/04/00	Neuchâtel Xamax FC	H	1-1	Huggel
29/04/00	Neuchâtel Xamax FC	A	2-1	Koumantarakis, Yakin (p)
07/05/00	Yverdon-Sports	A	1-0	Koumantarakis
12/05/00	FC St. Gallen	H	3-1	Tholot 2, Savic
21/05/00	Servette FC Genève	A	1-1	Tholot
27/05/00	FC Luzern	H	0-0	
02/06/00	Grasshopper-Club Zürich	A	0-3	
07/06/00	Lausanne-Sports	H	0-3	

SR DELEMONT

CLUB DIRECTORY

Sports Réunis Delémont
Case postale 951
2800 Delémont 1
tel - (032) 4220633
fax - (032) 4231851
Year of Formation - 1909
President - Pierre Willemin
Secretary - Christian Mathez
Coach - Heinz Hermann
Stadium - La Blancherie (6,000)

APPEARANCES 99/00

	P	Ap	(s)	Gls
Thierry BALLY	G	2		
David BLANCHARD	A		(3)	
Hoang-Doc BUI	M	17	(2)	2
Vareiro DA SILVA (BRA)	M		(2)	
Pape DIAW (SEN)	A		(2)	
Samuel DRAKOPOULOS (GRE)	A	16	(6)	4
Vincent DUCOMMUN	G	6		
Fábio de Souza FABINHO (BRA)	A	21		6
Francis FROIDEVAUX	D	17	(1)	
Luca GABRIELE	M	3	(8)	
Lulzim HUSHI (ALB)	D	19	(1)	1
David INGUSCIO	G	14		
Fernando ITAMAR (BRA)	M	12	(2)	1
Frédéric KLOETZLI	D	18	(1)	
Sebastián LANDRO (ARG)	M	2	(2)	
Vannak MANN	M		(1)	
Yoshika MATSUBARA (JPN)	A	3	(3)	
Kader MEKHRAF	M		(1)	
Erickson NAHIMANA (BUR)	A	4	(4)	4
Adam NDLOVU (ZIM)	A	9		3
Aleksandr RICHKOV (RUS)	M	6	(1)	1
Umberto ROMANO (ITA)	D	21		1
Harlington SHERENI (ZIM)	D	5	(1)	
Simão TANIELTON (BRA)	D	14	(3)	
Johan THEUBET	A		(4)	
Olivier THOMMEN	M	20		1
Alain VERNIER	D	13	(5)	

LEAGUE RESULTS 1999/2000

07/07/99	Servette FC Genève	H	1-3	Nahimana
10/07/99	FC Luzern	A	0-2	
17/07/99	Lausanne-Sports	H	1-1	Drakopoulos
21/07/99	FC Zürich	A	1-3	Ndlovu
24/07/99	FC Aarau	H	4-2	Fabinho 2, Drakopoulos, Ndlovu
31/07/99	FC Basel	A	0-3	
07/08/99	Neuchâtel Xamax FC	H	2-2	Nahimana, Itamar
14/08/99	Yverdon-Sports	A	1-3	Bui
22/08/99	Grasshopper-Club Zürich	H	2-1	Nahimana 2
28/08/99	FC St. Gallen	A	1-2	Ndlovu
12/09/99	FC Lugano	H	1-0	Drakopoulos
19/09/99	Servette FC Genève	A	1-1	Thommen
26/09/99	FC Luzern	H	0-1	
04/10/99	Lausanne-Sports	A	0-3	
17/10/99	FC Zürich	H	2-2	Fabinho, Drakopoulos
24/10/99	FC Aarau	A	2-4	Bui, Romano
31/10/99	FC Basel	H	2-2	Fabinho, Richkov (p)
06/11/99	Neuchâtel Xamax FC	A	0-2	
21/11/99	Yverdon-Sports	H	1-3	Fabinho
28/11/99	Grasshopper-Club Zürich	A	0-4	
05/12/99	FC St. Gallen	H	0-3	
12/12/99	FC Lugano	A	2-1	Hushi, Fabinho

GRASSHOPPER-CLUB ZÜRICH

CLUB DIRECTORY

Grasshopper-Club Zürich
Fussball-Sektion, Postfach 217, 8037 Zürich
tel - (01) 4474646 / fax - (01) 4474690
Year of Formation - 1886
President - Dr. Peter Widmer
Secretary - Georges Perego
Coach - Roger Hegi; Roy Hodgson; Piet Hamberg
(00/01) - Hans-Peter Zaugg
Stadium - Hardturm (20,079)

MAJOR HONOURS
League Championship - (25)
1898, 1900, 1901, 1905, 1921, 1927, 1928,
1931, 1937, 1939, 1942, 1943, 1945, 1952,
1956, 1971, 1978, 1982, 1983, 1984, 1990,
1991, 1995, 1996, 1998.
Domestic Cup - (18) 1926, 1927, 1932, 1934,
1937, 1938, 1940, 1941, 1942, 1943, 1946,
1952, 1956, 1983, 1988, 1989. 1990, 1994.

APPEARANCES 99/00

	P	Ap	(s)	Gls
Patrick BAUMANN	M	1	(1)	
Bruno BERNER	D	2	(3)	1
Ricardo CABAÑAS (ESP)	M	30	(1)	7
Stéphane CHAPUISAT	A	21		11
Luis CRAYTON (LIB)	G	3		
Patrick DE NAPOLI	A	8	(3)	1
Luca DE NICOLA	D	3	(4)	
Efan EKOKU (NIG)	A	21		16
Antonio ESPOSITO	M	7	(1)	1
Mats GREN (SWE)	D	20		
Bernt HAAS	D	27	(2)	1
Marc HODEL	D	26		2
Stephan HUBER	G	18		
Patrick ISABELLA	M	10	(4)	
Kim JAGGY	D			(1)
Miroslav KÖNIG (SVK)	G	8		
Kjetil LØVVIK (NOR)	A	2	(4)	1
Tosh McKINLAY (SCO)	D	4		
Feliciano MAGRO (ITA)	M	13	(4)	1
Andy MUFF	A	3	(4)	4
Patrick MÜLLER	M	23	(1)	1
Blaise N'KUFO	A	3	(2)	2
James OBIORAH	A	1	(11)	
Mladen PETRIC	A		(2)	
Roland SCHWEGLER	D	3	(1)	
Gürkan SERMETER (TUR)	M	15	(13)	2
Boris SMILJANIC	D	24	(2)	1
Mihai TARARACHE (ROM)	M	29	(2)	2
Avi TIKVA (ISR)	A	14	(11)	4
Philipp WALKER	G	7	(1)	
Hakan YAKIN	M	25	(4)	10
Reto ZANNI	D	12	(9)	
Marian ZEMAN (SVK)	D	13		1

LEAGUE RESULTS 1999/2000

07/07/99	Lausanne-Sports	H	1-1	Cabañas
11/07/99	FC Zürich	A	0-0	
17/07/99	FC Aarau	H	4-0	Yakin 2, Hodel, Cabañas
21/07/99	FC Basel	A	1-1	De Napoli
24/07/99	Neuchâtel Xamax FC	H	4-0	Chapuisat 2, Yakin, Løvvik
31/07/99	Yverdon-Sports	A	0-2	
08/08/99	FC Lugano	H	2-1	Hodel, Yakin
15/08/99	FC St. Gallen	H	2-2	Yakin, Magro
22/08/99	SR Delémont	A	1-2	Tikva
29/08/99	Servette FC Genève	H	4-2	Ekoku 2, Cabañas, Chapuisat (p)
12/09/99	FC Luzern	A	0-2	
20/09/99	Lausanne-Sports	A	3-3	Yakin, Ekoku 2
25/09/99	FC Zürich	H	2-1	Smiljanic, Chapuisat
03/10/99	FC Aarau	A	1-2	Ekoku
17/10/99	FC Basel	H	1-1	Ekoku
24/10/99	Neuchâtel Xamax FC	A	1-0	Chapuisat
31/10/99	Yverdon-Sports	H	0-0	
07/11/99	FC Lugano	A	5-1	Ekoku 2, Chapuisat, Yakin 2
23/11/99	FC St. Gallen	A	1-2	Sermeter
28/11/99	SR Delémont	H	4-0	Chapuisat 2 (2p), Ekoku 2
05/12/99	Servette FC Genève	A	1-2	Ekoku
12/12/99	FC Luzern	H	2-0	Zeman, Ekoku
10/03/00	FC St. Gallen	H	4-4	Yakin, Chapuisat, Haas, Cabañas
19/03/00	FC Basel	A	2-2	Tikva, Chapuisat (p)
26/03/00	Yverdon-Sports	H	4-1	Tararache, Ekoku, Chapuisat, Muff
01/04/00	Neuchâtel Xamax FC	A	3-1	Ekoku, Muff, Cabañas
09/04/00	Lausanne-Sports	H	1-1	Cabañas
16/04/00	FC Luzern	A	1-0	N'Kufo
22/04/00	Servette FC Genève	H	2-3	N'Kufo, Sermeter
29/04/00	Servette FC Genève	A	3-1	Tikva, og (Devaux), Ekoku
07/05/00	FC Luzern	H	0-2	
14/05/00	Lausanne-Sports	A	1-3	Ekoku
20/05/00	Neuchâtel Xamax FC	H	1-3	Tikva
27/05/00	Yverdon-Sports	A	4-4	Cabañas, Yakin, Muff, Müller
02/06/00	FC Basel	H	3-0	Esposito, Berner, Muff
07/06/00	FC St. Gallen	A	1-1	Tararache

LAUSANNE-SPORTS

CLUB DIRECTORY

Lausanne-Sports
Case postale 175
1018 Lausanne 18
tel - (021) 6461341
fax - (021) 6461359
Year of Formation - 1896
President - Waldemar Kita
Secretary - Christian Lariepe
Coach - Pierre-André Schurmann
Stadium - Stade Olympique La Pontaise (16,000)

MAJOR HONOURS
League Championship - (7)
1913, 1932, 1935, 1936, 1944, 1951, 1965.
Domestic Cup - (9) 1935, 1939, 1944, 1950,
1962, 1964, 1981, 1998, 1999.

APPEARANCES 99/00

	P	Ap	(s)	Gls
Patrick BÜHLMANN	M	8	(5)	1
Fabio CELESTINI	M	20	(2)	3
Sven CHRIST	D	20	(9)	
Tomas DANILEVICIUS (LIT)	A	2	(5)	
Paulo DIOGO (POR)	M	20		1
Andres GERBER	M	27	(6)	7
Stéphane GOBET	D	1		
Vagner GOMES	M		(1)	
Erich HÄNZI	D	28	(1)	
Cédric HORJAK (FRA)	M	4	(12)	
Ricardo IGLESIAS (ESP)	D	2	(4)	
Jean-Philippe KARLEN	D	13	(9)	1
Marcin KUZBA (POL)	A	30	(3)	13
Oscar LONDONO (FRA)	M	31	(3)	6
Yevhen LUTSENKO (UKR)	M		(14)	
Eduardo MAGNIN (ARG)	D	17	(2)	
Javier MAZZONI (ARG)	A	34		10
Serge MOBWETE	A		(2)	
Christophe OHREL	D	32	(1)	1
Lionel PIZZINAT	M	5	(13)	
Daniel PUCE (ITA)	D	28		2
Eric RAPO	G	35		
Stefan REHN (SWE)	M	35		8
Armen SHAHGELDYAN (ARM)	A	2	(9)	2
Christophe SIMON	A	1	(5)	
Pascal ZETZMANN	G	1	(1)	

LEAGUE RESULTS 1999/2000

07/07/99	Grasshopper-Club Zürich	A	1-1	Shahgeldyan
10/07/99	FC St. Gallen	H	0-1	
17/07/99	SR Delémont	A	1-1	Rehn
21/07/99	Servette FC Genève	H	0-1	
25/07/99	FC Luzern	A	1-2	Mazzoni
31/07/99	FC Lugano	A	1-1	Rehn
07/08/99	FC Zürich	H	2-0	Kuzba 2
14/08/99	FC Aarau	A	3-1	Kuzba 2, Rehn
21/08/99	FC Basel	H	1-0	Mazzoni
28/08/99	Neuchâtel Xamax FC	A	2-1	Mazzoni, Celestini
11/09/99	Yverdon-Sports	H	2-2	og (Diogo), Puce
20/09/99	Grasshopper-Club Zürich	H	3-3	Kuzba, Gerber, Mazzoni
25/09/99	FC St. Gallen	A	2-2	Londono, Shahgeldyan
04/10/99	SR Delémont	H	3-0	Kuzba, Karlen, Mazzoni
16/10/99	Servette FC Genève	A	1-0	Puce
23/10/99	FC Luzern	H	2-1	Gerber, Mazzoni
30/10/99	FC Lugano	H	2-0	Londono, Kuzba
07/11/99	FC Zürich	A	2-2	Mazzoni, Londono
20/11/99	FC Aarau	H	3-1	Rehn, Kuzba 2
27/11/99	FC Basel	A	3-3	Gerber, Rehn, Diogo (p)
05/12/99	Neuchâtel Xamax FC	H	0-2	
12/12/99	Yverdon-Sports	A	0-0	
12/03/00	FC Basel	H	0-0	
17/03/00	FC St. Gallen	A	0-1	
25/03/00	Neuchâtel Xamax FC	H	2-1	Rehn, Bühlmann
02/04/00	Yverdon-Sports	A	0-1	
09/04/00	Grasshopper-Club Zürich	A	1-1	Londono (p)
15/04/00	Servette FC Genève	H	2-1	Gerber, og (Wolf)
22/04/00	FC Luzern	A	0-1	
29/04/00	FC Luzern	H	3-1	Londono (p), Gerber, Mazzoni
06/05/00	Servette FC Genève	A	3-1	Gerber, Rehn, Ohrel
14/05/00	Grasshopper-Club Zürich	H	3-1	Mazzoni 2, Rehn
20/05/00	Yverdon-Sports	H	2-0	Celestini, Kuzba
23/05/00	Neuchâtel Xamax FC	A	2-1	Celestini, Kuzba
02/06/00	FC St. Gallen	H	1-3	Kuzba
07/06/00	FC Basel	A	3-0	Londono (p), Gerber, Kuzba

FC LUGANO

CLUB DIRECTORY

FC Lugano
CP 4136
6904 Lugano
tel - (091) 9409040
fax - (091) 9409055
Year of Formation - 1908
President - Helios Jermini
Secretary - Ivan Degli Espositi
Coach - Giuliano Sonzogni; Andrea Ortelli &
Roberto Gatti; Roberto Morinini
Stadium - Cornaredo (15,000)

MAJOR HONOURS
League Championship - (3) 1938, 1941, 1949.
Domestic Cup - (3) 1931, 1968, 1993.

APPEARANCES 99/00

		P	Ap	(s)	Gls
Ghislain AKASSOU (CIV)	D	2	(3)	1
Eddy BAREA (ESP)	D	9	(2)	
Sergio BASTIDA (BOL)	M	8	(3)	4
Erol BEKIROVSKI (SWE)	M	6	(2)	1
Markus BRUNNER	D	14	(1)	1
Fabrizio BULLO	M	6	(4)	
Marc EMMERS (BEL)	D	6		
Walter FERNANDEZ	D	21		1
Alain GASPOZ	M		(2)	
Christian GIMENEZ (ARG)	A	4	(3)	2
Michaël HOY (FRA)	M	12	(3)	2
Erich HÜRZELER	G	2		
Mohamed Abdel KADER (TOG)	A	5	(3)	
Massimo LOMBARDO	M	9	(3)	
Joël MAGNIN	A	10	(4)	4
Ludovico MORESI	M	10	(3)	1
René MORF	D	16	(2)	
Blaise NKUFO	A	9	(1)	4
Ronald O'BRIEN (IRL)	D	2	(3)	
Stefano RAZZETTI (ITA)	G	19		
Julio Hernán ROSSI (ARG)	A	13	(4)	3
Dario ROTA	M	22		
Jero SHAKPOKE (NIG)	D	5	(1)	1
Bruno SUTTER	M	9	(7)	
Eric TABORDA (FRA)	M	17	(1)	
Romano THOMA	M	5	(2)	
Germano VAILATI	G	1	(1)	

LEAGUE RESULTS 1999/2000

07/07/99	FC Basel	H	1-1	Magnin
10/07/99	Servette FC Genève	A	3-1	Hoy, Nkufo, Magnin
17/07/99	Neuchâtel Xamax FC	A	1-3	Magnin
21/07/99	FC Luzern	H	1-1	Magnin
24/07/99	Yverdon-Sports	A	0-1	
31/07/99	Lausanne-Sports	H	1-1	Nkufo (p)
08/08/99	Grasshopper-Club Zürich	A	1-2	Shakpoke
15/08/99	FC Zürich	H	1-1	og (Castillo)
21/08/99	FC St. Gallen	A	1-2	Nkufo
28/08/99	FC Aarau	H	4-1	Akassou, Bastida 2, Hoy
12/09/99	SR Delémont	A	0-1	
18/09/99	FC Basel	A	0-1	
25/09/99	Servette FC Genève	H	3-0	Nkufo, Rossi, Bekirovski
01/10/99	Neuchâtel Xamax FC	H	2-1	Brunner, Fernandez (p)
17/10/99	FC Luzern	A	0-3	
24/10/99	Yverdon-Sports	H	2-2	Moresi, og (Peço)
30/10/99	Lausanne-Sports	A	0-2	
07/11/99	Grasshopper-Club Zürich	H	1-5	Rossi
21/11/99	FC Zürich	A	1-2	Rossi
28/11/99	FC St. Gallen	H	1-1	Gimenez
05/12/99	FC Aarau	A	2-0	Gimenez, Bastida
12/12/99	SR Delémont	H	1-2	Bastida

FC LUZERN

CLUB DIRECTORY

FC Luzern
Kauffmannweg 7, Postfach 2918, 6002 Luzern
tel - (041) 2102041
fax - (041) 2102141
Year of Formation - 1901
President - Albert Koller
Secretary - Martin Müller
Coach - Andy Egli
Stadium - Allmend (25,300)

MAJOR HONOURS
League Championship - (1) 1989.
Domestic Cup - (2) 1960, 1992.

APPEARANCES 99/00

	P	Ap	(s)	Gls
AMARILDO Ferreira (BRA)	D	2	(2)	
Melchior ARNOLD (USA)	D	31	(1)	
Stephan BLUNSCHI	D	5		
Marco BRANCA (ITA)	A	8	(1)	2
Paolo COLLAVITI	G	3		
Satilanis DILAVER (TUR)	D	12	(6)	1
Abdel EL BOUZIDI (MAR)	A	9	(15)	2
Silvio ENRIQUE (URU)	M	4	(3)	
Patrick FOLETTI	G	32		
Alex FREI	A	28	(4)	13
Dias Dantas GIAN (BRA)	M	20	(1)	3
Selver HODZIC	D	3	(5)	
Simon HOFER	M	1	(1)	
Raphaele IZZO (ITA)	D	4	(2)	
Daniel JOLLER	M	25		1
Marco KOTTMANN	M	3	(10)	
Sébastien LIPAWSKY	M	4	(16)	
Denis LOVRIC	D		(1)	
Badile LUBAMBA	D	32		
Olivier MARIC	D	2	(1)	
Maximiliano MAX (BRA)	D	11	(1)	1
Remo MEYER	D	22		1
Marcelo SANDER (BRA)	M	17	(3)	4
Siradji SANI (NGR)	M	3	(3)	
Massimo SCARAFELLI	A		(1)	
Slobodan SCEPANOVIC (YUG)	A	1	(6)	
Guido SCHNARWILER	G	1	(1)	
Patrick SCHNARWILER	D	11	(3)	1
SILVIO Gonçalves (BRA)	D		(2)	
Christoph SPYCHER	M	29	(3)	
Oliver TONELLI	M		(1)	
Igor TRNINIC	D	26	(1)	
Kubilay TÜRKYILMAZ	A	14		6
Thomas WYSS	M	33		9

LEAGUE RESULTS 1999/2000

07/07/99	FC St. Gallen	A	0-2	
10/07/99	SR Delémont	H	2-0	Frei, Sander
17/07/99	Servette FC Genève	A	0-1	
21/07/99	FC Lugano	A	1-1	Gian
25/07/99	Lausanne-Sports	H	2-1	Frei, El Bouzidi
31/07/99	FC Zürich	A	1-1	Gian
07/08/99	FC Aarau	H	2-1	Gian, Türkyilmaz
15/08/99	FC Basel	A	0-2	
21/08/99	Neuchâtel Xamax FC	H	1-1	Türkyilmaz
28/08/99	Yverdon-Sports	A	0-3	
12/09/99	Grasshopper-Club Zürich	H	2-0	Wyss (p), Joller
19/09/99	FC St. Gallen	H	2-2	og (Zellweger), Wyss
26/09/99	SR Delémont	A	1-0	Sander
03/10/99	Servette FC Genève	H	2-4	Türkyilmaz, Max
17/10/99	FC Lugano	H	3-0	Meyer, Türkyilmaz, Wyss (p)
23/10/99	Lausanne-Sports	A	1-2	Wyss
30/10/99	FC Zürich	H	0-1	
07/11/99	FC Aarau	A	0-1	
21/11/99	FC Basel	H	3-0	Frei 2, Türkyilmaz
27/11/99	Neuchâtel Xamax FC	A	1-3	Frei
05/12/99	Yverdon-Sports	H	4-1	Frei 3, Türkyilmaz
12/12/99	Grasshopper-Club Zürich	A	0-2	
12/03/00	Neuchâtel Xamax FC	H	1-2	Frei
19/03/00	Yverdon-Sports	A	3-2	Frei 2, El Bouzidi
26/03/00	FC Basel	H	3-2	Sander, Frei, Branca
02/04/00	FC St. Gallen	A	1-7	Frei
08/04/00	Servette FC Genève	A	0-6	
16/04/00	Grasshopper-Club Zürich	H	0-1	
22/04/00	Lausanne-Sports	H	1-0	Wyss
29/04/00	Lausanne-Sports	A	1-3	Sander
07/05/00	Grasshopper-Club Zürich	A	2-0	Dilaver, Branca
13/05/00	Servette FC Genève	H	1-1	Wyss
19/05/00	FC St. Gallen	H	1-2	Wyss
27/05/00	FC Basel	A	0-0	
03/06/00	Yverdon-Sports	H	2-1	Wyss 2 (1p)
07/06/00	Neuchâtel Xamax FC	A	1-3	Schnarwiler P. (p)

NEUCHATEL XAMAX FC

CLUB DIRECTORY

Neuchâtel Xamax FC
Boîte postale 78
2000 Neuchâtel 8 Monruz
tel - (038) 7254428
fax - (038) 7242128
Year of Formation - 1970
President - Gilbert Facchinetti
Secretary - Michel Favre
Coach - Alain Geiger
Stadium - La Maladière (20,000)

MAJOR HONOURS
League Championship - (2) 1987, 1988.

APPEARANCES 99/00

	P	Ap	(s)	Gls
Rainer BIELI	A	31	(4)	21
Hervé BOCHUZ (FRA)	D	1	(1)	
Samir BOUGHANEM (FRA)	M	20	(2)	
Manuel BUEHLER	M	3	(5)	
Henri CAMARA (SEN)	A	20		12
Dino CARRACIOLO (ITA)	M		(8)	
Massimo COLOMBA (ITA)	G	5	(1)	
Florent DELAY	G	31		
Maxime DROZ-PORTNER	D	1	(2)	
Didier GIGON	M	23	(5)	1
Jérôme GYGER	D	1	(2)	
Stefan KELLER	D	28	(4)	1
Patrick KOCH	M	24	(5)	5
Ahmed KOSHARY (EGY)	A	1		
Vladimir MARTINOVIC (YUG)	D	19	(5)	3
Abdel Ahmed MONEIM (EGY)	A		(5)	
Lionel MORET	D	5	(5)	
Seyni N'DIAYE (SEN)	A	5		1
Pascal OPPLIGER	D		(1)	
Richard PERRET	A	14	(18)	5
Benjamin ROOS	M		(1)	
André ROQUE	M		(1)	
Sébastien SANSONI (FRA)	D	18	(3)	
Tarek SEKTIOUI (MAR)	M	5	(4)	
David SENE (FRA)	D	34		1
Augustine SIMO (CMR)	M	32		2
Julien STAUFFER	D	12	(8)	
Mostafa TAREK (EGY)	M	5	(2)	1
Charles WITTL (GHA)	M	24	(1)	1
Sébastien ZAMBAZ	M	34		2

LEAGUE RESULTS 1999/2000

07/07/99	FC Aarau	H	1-1	N'Diaye
14/07/99	FC Basel	A	1-1	Bieli
17/07/99	FC Lugano	H	3-1	Simo, Perret, Gigon
21/07/99	Yverdon-Sports	H	1-1	Sène
24/07/99	Grasshopper-Club Zürich	A	0-4	
31/07/99	FC St. Gallen	H	2-2	Perret, og (Tsawa)
07/08/99	SR Delémont	A	2-2	Bieli 2
14/08/99	Servette FC Genève	H	3-2	Keller, Zambaz, Koch
21/08/99	FC Luzern	AA	1-1	Koch
28/08/99	Lausanne-Sports	H	1-2	Bieli
11/09/99	FC Zürich	A	1-2	Bieli
18/09/99	FC Aarau	A	1-4	Bieli
23/09/99	FC Basel	H	1-2	Bieli
01/10/99	FC Lugano	A	1-2	Tarek
17/10/99	Yverdon-Sports	A	0-0	
24/10/99	Grasshopper-Club Zürich	H	0-1	
31/10/99	FC St. Gallen	A	1-2	Bieli
06/11/99	SR Delémont	H	2-0	Koch, Perret
20/11/99	Servette FC Genève	A	4-2	Bieli 2, Camara, Martinovic (p)
27/11/99	FC Luzern	H	3-1	Camara 2, Wittl
05/12/99	Lausanne-Sports	A	2-0	Camara, Bieli
12/12/99	FC Zürich	H	3-0	(w/o; original result 1-1 Bieli)
12/03/00	FC Luzern	A	2-1	Camara, Bieli
18/03/00	Servette FC Genève	H	2-2	Koch, Camara
25/03/00	Lausanne-Sports	A	1-2	Bieli
01/04/00	Grasshopper-Club Zürich	H	1-3	Perret
09/04/00	Yverdon-Sports	A	0-3	
15/04/00	FC St. Gallen	H	0-3	
22/04/00	FC Basel	A	1-1	Bieli
29/04/00	FC Basel	H	1-2	Bieli (p)
07/05/00	FC St. Gallen	A	0-3	
13/05/00	Yverdon-Sports	H	7-2	Camara 3, Bieli 2, Koch, Perret
20/05/00	Grasshopper-Club Zürich	A	3-1	Camara 2, Zambaz
23/05/00	Lausanne-Sports	H	1-2	Martinovic (p)
03/06/00	Servette FC Genève	A	3-3	Camara, Bieli, Simo
07/06/00	FC Luzern	H	3-1	Martinovic, Bieli 2 (1p)

FC ST. GALLEN

CLUB DIRECTORY

FC St. Gallen
Postfach 14
9009 St. Gallen
tel - (071) 2456765
fax - (071) 2454671
Year of Formation - 1879
President - Thomas Müller
Secretary - Peter Stadelmann
Coach - Marcel Koller
Stadium - Espenmoos (13,700)

MAJOR HONOURS
League Championship - (2) 1904, 2000.
Domestic Cup - (1) 1969.

APPEARANCES 99/00

	P	Ap	(s)	Gls
Thomas ALDER	G	1		
Charles AMOAH (GHA)	A	34		25
Sergio COLACINO (ITA)	M	13	(7)	
Giorgio CONTINI	A	18	(16)	9
Ivan DAL SANTO	D	31	(2)	1
Valdir DAMÁSIO (BRA)	A		(4)	
Adrian EUGSTER	M	9	(15)	1
Ionel GANE (ROM)	A	16	(12)	9
GUIDO Alves Neto Pereira (BRA)	M	11		1
Wilco HELLINGA (HOL)	M	17	(1)	1
Daniel IMHOF	M	6	(5)	
Luiz Filho JAIRO (BRA)	M	33		8
Giuseppe MAZZARELLI	D	31		3
Philipp MEYER	D	2	(1)	
Sascha MÜLLER	M	26	(5)	5
Valemirino da Souza NERI (BRA)	A		(3)	
Dino PINELLI (ITA)	D	10	(2)	2
Jörg STIEL	G	35		
Pascal THÜLER	M	17	(9)	3
Enzo TODISCO	A		(1)	
Dorjee TSAWA	D	6	(4)	
Patrick WINKLER	M	15	(10)	
Marc ZELLWEGER	D	33		3
Marco ZWYSSIG	D	32	(1)	2

LEAGUE RESULTS 1999/2000

07/07/99	FC Luzern	H	2-0	Jairo (p), Amoah
10/07/99	Lausanne-Sports	A	1-0	Amoah
18/07/99	FC Zürich	H	3-0	Jairo, Müller, Hellinga
21/07/99	FC Aarau	A	0-1	
31/07/99	Neuchâtel Xamax FC	A	2-2	Amoah 2
07/08/99	Yverdon-Sports	H	3-2	Gane, Amoah 2
15/08/99	Grasshopper-Club Zürich	A	2-2	Müller, Dal Santo
21/08/99	FC Lugano	H	2-1	Müller, Amoah (p)
24/08/99	FC Basel	H	1-1	Amoah
28/08/99	SR Delémont	H	2-1	Thüler, Amoah
11/09/99	Servette FC Genève	A	1-2	Gane
19/09/99	FC Luzern	A	2-2	Amoah, Müller
25/09/99	Lausanne-Sports	H	2-2	Jairo, Thüler
03/10/99	FC Zürich	A	3-1	Thüler, Contini, Jairo
16/10/99	FC Aarau	H	4-1	og (Page), Amoah, Contini, Jairo
24/10/99	FC Basel	A	1-4	Amoah
31/10/99	Neuchâtel Xamax FC	H	2-1	Pinelli, Gane
06/11/99	Yverdon-Sports	A	1-0	Amoah
23/11/99	Grasshopper-Club Zürich	H	2-1	Contini, Amoah
28/11/99	FC Lugano	A	1-1	Pinelli
05/12/99	SR Delémont	A	3-0	Amoah 2, Contini
12/12/99	Servette FC Genève	H	2-0	Contini, Zellweger
10/03/00	Grasshopper-Club Zürich	A	4-4	Amoah 2, Gane, Jairo
17/03/00	Lausanne-Sports	H	1-0	Mazzarelli
25/03/00	Servette FC Genève	A	2-1	Amoah, Gane
02/04/00	FC Luzern	H	7-1	Guido, Jairo, Zwyssig, Amoah 2, Gane, Zellweger
07/04/00	FC Basel	H	1-1	Gane
15/04/00	Neuchâtel Xamax FC	A	3-0	Jairo, Gane, Eugster
22/04/00	Yverdon-Sports	A	1-0	Contini
30/04/00	Yverdon-Sports	H	4-1	Zwyssig, Contini, Mazzarelli 2
07/05/00	Neuchâtel Xamax FC	H	3-0	Contini, Amoah 2
12/05/00	FC Basel	A	1-3	Amoah
19/05/00	FC Luzern	A	2-1	Müller, Zellweger
26/05/00	Servette FC Genève	H	0-0	
02/06/00	Lausanne-Sports	A	3-1	Contini, Gane, og (Puce)
07/06/00	Grasshopper-Club Zürich	H	1-1	Amoah

SERVETTE FC GENEVE

CLUB DIRECTORY

Servette FC Genève
Case postale 431, 1219 Châtelaine (Genève)
tel - (022) 9495949 / fax - (022) 9495939
Year of Formation - 1890
President - Christian Hervé
Secretary - Patrick Trotignon
Coach - Gérard Castella; Bosko Djurovski; René
Exbrayat (00/01 - Lucien Favre)
Stadium - Les Charmilles (11,078)

MAJOR HONOURS
League Championship - (17) 1907, 1918, 1922,
1925, 1926, 1930, 1933, 1934, 1940, 1946,
1950, 1961, 1962, 1979, 1985, 1994, 1999.
Domestic Cup - (6)
1928, 1949, 1971, 1978, 1979, 1984.

APPEARANCES 99/00

	P	Ap	(s)	Gls
Thierno BAH	M	5	(9)	1
Adel BOUTOUBBA (FRA)	M		(2)	
Patrick BÜHLMANN	M	20	(1)	
Christophe DEVAUD (FRA)	D	11		
Paulo DIOGO (POR)	M	5	(1)	1
Emanuele DI ZENZO	M	2	(5)	
Franck DURIX (FRA)	M	13	(2)	1
Faouzi EL BRAZI (MAR)	D	18	(2)	
Sébastien FOURNIER	M	6		
Sébastien JEANNERET	M	29	(1)	
JUAREZ de Souza (BRA)	D	8		
Johann LONFAT	M	29	(1)	5
Fabien MARGAIRAZ	G	4		
Elvir MELUNOVIC	M	11	(8)	1
Alban NORIEGA	M		(2)	
Lanjame OUAJDA (TOG)	M	13	(2)	
Diego PARRA	M		(1)	
Eric PEDAT	M	29		
Martin PETROV (BUL)	A	23	(8)	9
Lionel PIZZINAT	M	7	(1)	
Dan POTOCIANU (ROM)	D	3	(9)	1
Alexandre REY	A	29	(2)	14
Sébastien ROTH	G	3		
Ermin SILJAK (SLO)	A	6	(4)	4
Léonard THURRE	A	18	(4)	7
Olivier TRANCHET	M		(1)	
Matteo VANETTA	D	24	(4)	
Carlos VARELA (ESP)	A	24	(4)	5
Argemiro VEIGA (BRA)	M	9	(1)	
Edwin VURENS (HOL)	M	12	(11)	4
Roger WAGNER	A		(1)	
Stefan WOLF	D	35		4

LEAGUE RESULTS 1999/2000

07/07/99	SR Delémont	A	3-1	Petrov 3
10/07/99	FC Lugano	H	1-3	Thurre
17/07/99	FC Luzern	H	1-0	Wolf
21/07/99	Lausanne-Sports	A	1-0	Vurens
24/07/99	FC Zürich	H	3-0	Wolf, Durix, Petrov
01/08/99	FC Aarau	A	2-3	Thurre, Varela
05/08/99	FC Basel	H	1-1	Thurre
14/08/99	Neuchâtel Xamax FC	A	2-3	Lonfat, Thurre
20/08/99	Yverdon-Sports	H	3-1	Varela, Melunovic, Rey
29/08/99	Grasshopper-Club Zürich	A	2-4	Thurre, Rey
11/09/99	FC St. Gallen	H	2-1	Wolf, Rey (p)
19/09/99	SR Delémont	H	1-1	Petrov
25/09/99	FC Lugano	A	0-3	
03/10/99	FC Luzern	A	4-2	Thurre 2, Rey, Potocianu
16/10/99	Lausanne-Sports	H	0-1	
24/10/99	FC Zürich	A	0-2	
30/10/99	FC Aarau	H	1-1	Wolf
07/11/99	FC Basel	A	0-0	
20/11/99	Neuchâtel Xamax FC	H	2-4	Vurens, Petrov
28/11/99	Yverdon-Sports	A	1-2	Rey
05/12/99	Grasshopper-Club Zürich	H	2-1	Lonfat, Rey
12/12/99	FC St. Gallen	A	0-2	
11/03/00	Yverdon-Sports	H	2-0	Rey, Petrov
18/03/00	Neuchâtel Xamax FC	A	2-2	Bah, Lonfat
25/03/00	FC St. Gallen	H	1-2	Varela
01/04/00	FC Basel	A	0-1	
08/04/00	FC Luzern	H	6-0	Diogo (p), Lonfat, Varela, Rey, Vurens 2
15/04/00	Lausanne-Sports	A	1-2	Rey
22/04/00	Grasshopper-Club Zürich	A	3-2	Siljak 2, Petrov
29/04/00	Grasshopper-Club Zürich	H	1-3	Siljak
06/05/00	Lausanne-Sports	H	1-3	Rey
13/05/00	FC Luzern	A	1-1	Rey
21/05/00	FC Basel	H	1-1	Siljak
26/05/00	FC St. Gallen	A	0-0	
03/06/00	Neuchâtel Xamax FC	H	3-3	Lonfat, Rey 2 (1p)
07/06/00	Yverdon-Sports	A	3-1	Varela, Petrov, Rey

YVERDON-SPORTS

FC Yverdon-Sports
Case postale 564
1401 Yverdon-les-Bains
tel - (024) 4252610
fax - (024) 4361243
Year of Formation - 1897
President - Paul-André Cornu
Secretary - Stéphane Cornu
Coach - Lucien Favre; Philippe Perret
Stadium - Stade Municipal (7,900)

APPEARANCES 99/00

	P	Ap	(s)	Gls
Robson Vicente Gonçalves ABEDI	M	4	(7)	
ADÃOZINHO Elvino Amadeo (BRA)	M	17	(4)	5
Albino BENCIVENGA (ITA)	A	6	(9)	1
Olivier BIAGGI	D	31		2
CAVALHO da Silva (BRA)	M	7	(6)	2
Mirsad DEDIC (BOS)	G	2		
Steve DEVOLZ	D	11		
Victor DIOGO (POR)	D	35		1
Thierry EBE	A		(1)	
ENILTON Menezes (BRA)	M	15	(3)	4
Daniel FASEL	D	8	(2)	
Loïc FAVRE	M	2	(5)	
Alain FLÜCKIGER	G	32		
Roman FRIEDLI	M	31	(1)	
Christophe JAQUET	D	30		
Pascal JENNY	M	32	(2)	4
Abdel JINANI (MAR)	A	4	(2)	
Gilson dos Santos Júnior JUNINHO	D	4		
LEANDRO Fonseca (BRA)	A	15		6
Ludovic MAGNIN	D	34	(1)	2
Gregory MATTHEY	G	2		
Cleumides NENZÃO (BRA)	A	4	(4)	1
Jerren NIXON (TRI)	A	5	(4)	1
Arjan PEÇO (ALB)	M	31	(3)	
Boniface RENATUS	A		(3)	
Pascal RENFER	A	10	(20)	6
Alain ROCHAT	D	2	(1)	
Jean-Michel TCHOUGA (CMR)	A	22	(4)	9

LEAGUE RESULTS 1999/2000

07/07/99	FC Zürich	H	1-1	Renfer
13/07/99	FC Aarau	A	1-1	Leandro
21/07/99	Neuchâtel Xamax FC	A	1-1	Adãozinho
24/07/99	FC Lugano	H	1-0	Leandro
31/07/99	Grasshopper-Club Zürich	H	2-0	Leandro, Adãozinho
07/08/99	FC St. Gallen	A	2-3	Biaggi 2
10/08/99	FC Basel	H	0-1	
14/08/99	SR Delémont	H	3-1	Leandro 2, Adãozinho
20/08/99	Servette FC Genève	A	1-3	Enilton
28/08/99	FC Luzern	H	3-0	Enilton, Adãozinho, Leandro (p)
11/09/99	Lausanne-Sports	A	2-2	Enilton, Jenny
20/09/99	FC Zürich	A	0-1	
26/09/99	FC Aarau	H	1-1	Enilton
02/10/99	FC Basel	A	2-1	Tchouga 2
17/10/99	Neuchâtel Xamax FC	H	0-0	
24/10/99	FC Lugano	A	2-2	Tchouga 2
31/10/99	Grasshopper-Club Zürich	A	0-0	
06/11/99	FC St. Gallen	H	0-1	
21/11/99	SR Delémont	A	3-1	Tchouga, Jenny, Renfer
28/11/99	Servette FC Genève	H	2-1	Nenzão, Jenny
05/12/99	FC Luzern	A	1-4	Adãozinho
12/12/99	Lausanne-Sports	H	0-0	
11/03/00	Servette FC Genève	A	0-2	
19/03/00	FC Luzern	H	2-3	Renfer, Jenny
26/03/00	Grasshopper-Club Zürich	A	1-4	Magnin
02/04/00	Lausanne-Sports	H	1-0	Tchouga
09/04/00	Neuchâtel Xamax FC	H	3-0	Cavalho 2, Renfer (p)
15/04/00	FC Basel	A	0-2	
22/04/00	FC St. Gallen	H	0-1	
30/04/00	FC St. Gallen	A	1-4	Renfer
07/05/00	FC Basel	H	0-1	
13/05/00	Neuchâtel Xamax FC	A	2-7	Bencivenga, Tchouga
20/05/00	Lausanne-Sports	A	0-2	
27/05/00	Grasshopper-Club Zürich	H	4-4	Nixon, Tchouga 2, Diogo
03/06/00	FC Luzern	A	1-2	Renfer
07/06/00	Servette FC Genève	H	1-3	Magnin

FC ZÜRICH

CLUB DIRECTORY

FC Zürich
Postfach
8021 Zürich
tel - (01) 4927474
fax - (01) 4910759
Year of Formation - 1896
President - Sven Hotz
Secretary - Erich Schmid
Coach - Raimondo Ponte; Gilbert Gress
Stadium - Letzigrund (23,500)

MAJOR HONOURS
League Championship - (9) 1902, 1924, 1963,
1966, 1968, 1974, 1975, 1976, 1981.
Domestic Cup - (6)
1966, 1970, 1972, 1973, 1976, 2000.

APPEARANCES 99/00

	P	Ap	(s)	Gls
Christian ANDREOLI	D	13	(2)	
Shaun BARTLETT (SAF)	A	20		2
Pascal CASTILLO	M	14	(3)	
Frédéric CHASSOT	A	5	(8)	1
Giorgio DEL SIGNORE (ITA)	M	3		
Aleksandar DJORDJEVIC (YUG)	D	3		
Philippe DOUGLAS	M	5	(10)	2
Jean-Jacques EYDELIE (FRA)	M	10	(1)	
Urs FISCHER	D	17		
Mario FRICK (LIE)	A	15	(4)	4
Alain GASPOZ	M	5	(1)	1
Mauro GIANNINI (ITA)	M	10	(7)	1
Daniel GYGAX	D	1	(1)	
Luca IODICE (ITA)	D		(2)	
Gocha JAMARAULI (GEO)	M	22		4
Akale KANGA (CIV)	A		(2)	
Mikhail KAVELASHVILI (GEO)	M	10	(1)	1
Saidou KEBE (SEN)	D	12	(6)	1
Francisco LIMA (BRA)	M	2		1
Diango MALACARNE (ITA)	D	1		
Mirsad MIJADINOSKI	M		(1)	
Adam NDLOVU (ZIM)	A	3	(4)	1
David PALLAS	M		(1)	
Marco PASCOLO	G	21		
Yvan QUENTIN	D	18	(2)	
César SANT'ANNA (BRA)	M	17	(2)	
Martin STOCKLASA (LIE)	D	14	(3)	
Christian TROMBINI (ITA)	G	1		

LEAGUE RESULTS 1999/2000

07/07/99	Yverdon-Sports	A	1-1	Lima
11/07/99	Grasshopper-Club Zürich	H	0-0	
18/07/99	FC St. Gallen	A	0-3	
21/07/99	SR Delémont	H	3-1	Jamarauli, Frick, Bartlett
24/07/99	Servette FC Genève	A	0-3	
31/07/99	FC Luzern	H	1-1	Frick
07/08/99	Lausanne-Sports	A	0-2	
15/08/99	FC Lugano	A	1-1	Jamarauli
21/08/99	FC Aarau	H	0-1	
29/08/99	FC Basel	A	0-0	
11/09/99	Neuchâtel Xamax FC	H	2-1	Jamarauli, og (Moret)
20/09/99	Yverdon-Sports	H	1-0	Chassot
25/09/99	Grasshopper-Club Zürich	A	1-2	og (Sien)
03/10/99	FC St. Gallen	H	1-3	Ndlovu
17/10/99	SR Delémont	A	2-2	Frick 2
24/10/99	Servette FC Genève	H	2-0	Bartlett, Douglas
30/10/99	FC Luzern	A	1-0	Giannini
07/11/99	Lausanne-Sports	H	2-2	Jamarauli, Douglas
21/11/99	FC Lugano	H	2-1	Gaspoz, Kebe
28/11/99	FC Aarau	A	1-1	Kavelashvili
05/12/99	FC Basel	H	0-1	
12/12/99	Neuchâtel Xamax FC	A	0-3	(w/o; original result 1-1 Fischer)

TURKEY

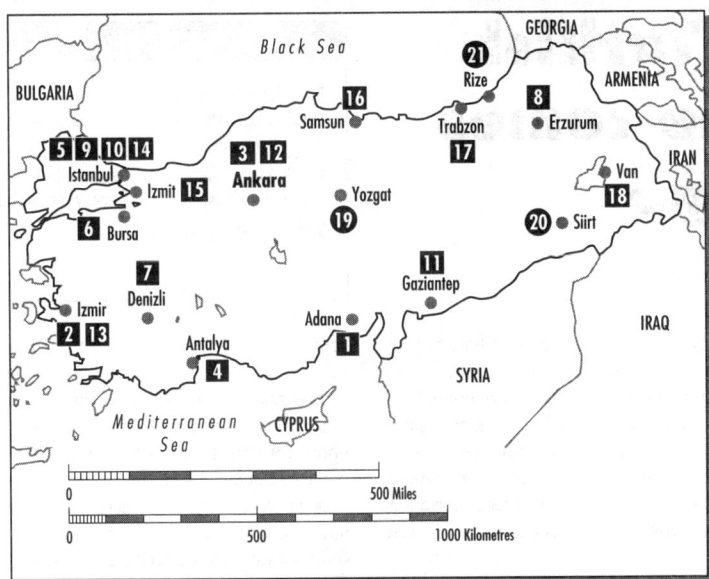

1	ADANASPOR	1017
2	ALTAY	1018
3	ANKARAGÜCÜ	1019
4	ANTALYASPOR	1020
5	BESIKTAS	1021
6	BURSASPOR	1022
7	DENIZLISPOR	1023
8	ERZURUMSPOR	1024
9	FENERBAHÇE	1025
10	GALATASARAY	1026
11	GAZIANTEPSPOR	1027

12	GENÇLERBIRLIGI	1028
13	GÖZTEPE	1029
14	ISTANBULSPOR	1030
15	KOCAELISPOR	1031
16	SAMSUNSPOR	1032
17	TRABZONSPOR	1033
18	VANSPOR	1034

Promoted clubs

19	YIMPAS YOZGATSPOR
20	SIIRT JETPA
21	ÇAYKUR RIZESPOR

UNIQUE 'TREBLE' FOR GALATASARAY

The Turkish game comes of age

FEDERATION DIRECTORY

Türkiye Futbol Federasyonu
Konaklar Mahallesi Ihlamurlu Sokak 9, 80620, 4.Levent, Istanbul

tel - (212) 2827020
fax - (212) 2827008
website - www.tff.org.tr

Stadium - Inönu, Istanbul (45,000)

Year of Formation - 1923
President - Haluk Ulusoy
Secretary - Ata Aksu

It was a season of on-field success and off-field tragedy for Turkish football. Galatasaray became the first Turkish club to win a European trophy, and the national team surpassed all expectations by reaching the quarter-finals of Euro 2000. But celebrations of these achievements were overshadowed by widespread violence on the streets, which included the fatal stabbing of two Leeds United fans on the eve of Galatasaray's UEFA Cup semi-final first leg in Istanbul.

The season began under a huge cloud. A colossal earthquake hit the north-west of the country, killing thousands of people. This forced a month-long suspension of the domestic championship and almost led to the withdrawal of First Division club Kocaelispor, whose home stadium had been partially destroyed. Football was something of an irrelevance at this desperate time, but eventually normal service was resumed.

The nation was certainly cheered up by Turkey's successful qualification for the European Championship finals. Mustafa Denizli's team came extremely close to automatic qualification. They had much the better of their final game in Munich against group leaders Germany but missed three gilt-edged chances early on. Even then, the 0-0 final scoreline would have been good enough to take the place reserved for the best runners-up had Portugal not scored three goals without reply in another group game against Hungary - precisely the margin of victory required to pip Turkey on goal difference.

No matter, Turkey were still in the play-offs, and they were to come through their two-legged tie with

LEAGUE CHAMPIONSHIP RESULTS 99/00

#	Team	1	2	3	4	5	6	7	8	9	10	11	12	13	14	15	16	17	18
1	Adanaspor		1-0	2-2	1-2	1-3	1-1	3-2	2-0	1-3	3-4	3-0	1-2	2-0	2-1	3-0	0-1	1-2	2-0
2	Altay	2-1		0-0	2-0	2-2	1-2	1-0	3-0	2-3	1-0	1-3	0-2	0-0	0-0	0-1	2-1	3-1	2-0
3	Ankaragücü	0-0	3-0		1-3	2-3	2-1	3-1	1-0	1-1	0-2	1-1	0-0	1-2	2-2	3-2	1-2	1-1	1-0
4	Antalyaspor	2-2	3-1	0-0		2-2	1-1	2-2	1-2	2-3	1-3	0-0	2-1	1-0	0-3	3-0	0-1	0-2	4-1
5	Besiktas	0-1	3-0	3-1	4-0		5-1	1-1	2-0	1-3	1-1	1-0	4-0	2-1	3-0	1-0	4-0	1-1	2-1
6	Bursaspor	3-1	1-4	3-1	4-2	0-1		4-1	4-2	2-1	0-0	0-1	2-5	1-2	1-0	2-0	2-2	2-3	3-2
7	Denizlispor	4-2	2-1	1-1	4-0	0-2	1-3		2-1	1-1	2-4	1-0	1-3	2-0	3-1	3-1	4-1	0-2	1-0
8	Erzurumspor	4-1	0-0	2-1	4-0	1-4	4-1	0-1		1-5	0-0	1-1	1-1	0-0	0-0	3-3	1-0	2-1	2-0
9	Fenerbahçe	2-4	3-1	1-1	1-0	2-1	2-2	2-1	2-0		1-2	0-0	1-3	2-3	1-0	1-1	1-0	2-1	3-0
10	Galatasaray	4-0	3-1	5-0	2-0	1-0	6-2	6-2	4-1	0-1		1-2	6-0	2-0	1-1	5-0	3-1	2-0	2-1
11	Gaziantepspor	1-1	1-0	2-2	1-2	0-0	1-0	0-0	6-0	5-1	0-1		2-1	2-1	1-0	1-0	5-2	3-0	1-3
12	Gençlerbirligi	5-2	0-0	1-2	4-1	1-0	1-0	3-1	5-0	2-2	1-1	0-1		1-0	1-1		0-4	1-0	0-1
13	Göztepe	0-1	0-1	2-0	1-2	2-4	0-1	2-4	1-4	0-0	0-2	0-1	3-2		2-0	0-0	1-2	1-1	2-1
14	Istanbulspor	3-2	1-0	2-6	0-0	0-2	1-0	1-1	1-1	1-4	0-0	1-1	3-1	3-0		4-1	0-1	5-1	0-0
15	Kocaelispor	0-0	2-1	4-1	1-1	1-2	3-2	1-0	4-0	1-1	1-2	1-2	0-0	2-1			0-4	1-0	6-1
16	Samsunspor	2-1	1-0	2-0	0-1	0-2	1-0	6-2	2-1	1-1	0-1	0-2	1-2	4-0	5-1			0-0	5-1
17	Trabzonspor	0-1	2-1	3-1	2-0	1-2	2-0	1-1	2-0	2-0	1-2	0-0	1-2	2-0	1-1	1-0	3-2		4-2
18	Vanspor	0-2	1-1	2-3	2-4	0-6	3-1	2-3	0-2	1-2	1-3	1-2	2-5	1-0	1-1	5-0	0-0	2-2	

LEAGUE CHAMPIONSHIP FINAL TABLE 99/00

			Home				Away					Total						
		Pd	W	D	L	F	A	W	D	L	F	A	W	D	L	F	A	PT	GD
1	Galatasaray	34	13	2	2	49	10	11	5	1	28	13	24	7	3	77	23	79	54
2	Besiktas	34	12	3	2	38	11	11	3	3	36	16	23	6	5	74	27	75	47
3	Gaziantepspor	34	9	5	3	32	15	8	6	3	17	12	17	11	6	49	27	62	22
4	Fenerbahçe	34	9	4	4	27	20	8	6	3	32	24	17	10	7	59	44	61	15
5	Gençlerbirligi	34	8	5	4	27	17	8	3	6	30	30	16	8	10	57	47	56	10
6	Trabzonspor	34	10	3	4	28	15	5	5	7	19	26	15	8	11	47	41	53	6
7	Samsunspor	34	10	2	5	31	15	6	2	9	20	28	16	4	14	51	43	52	8
8	Denizlispor	34	10	2	5	32	23	3	6	8	23	34	13	8	13	55	57	47	-2
9	Adanaspor	34	8	2	7	29	23	5	4	8	22	32	13	6	15	51	55	45	-4
10	Bursaspor	34	9	2	6	34	28	3	4	10	17	35	12	6	16	51	63	42	-12
11	Antalyaspor	34	5	6	6	24	24	6	2	9	18	34	11	8	15	42	58	41	-16
12	Kocaelispor	34	9	4	4	30	18	2	3	12	14	40	11	7	16	44	58	40	-14
13	Ankaragücü	34	6	6	5	23	21	3	6	8	22	35	9	12	13	45	56	39	-11
14	Erzurumspor	34	7	7	3	26	19	3	1	13	14	42	10	8	16	40	61	38	-21
15	Istanbulspor	34	7	6	4	26	21	1	7	9	12	22	8	13	13	38	43	37	-5
16	Altay	34	8	4	5	22	16	2	3	12	12	27	10	7	17	34	43	37	-9
17	Göztepe	34	4	3	10	17	26	3	2	12	9	28	7	5	22	26	54	26	-28
18	Vanspor	34	3	4	10	24	37	1	2	14	14	41	4	6	24	38	78	18	-40

the Republic of Ireland successfully, albeit by virtue of the away-goals rule and an excellent goalkeeping performance by Rüstü Reçber in Dublin.

Turkey had suffered a total whitewash at Euro '96, but they seemed better prepared this time around, even if coach Denizli drew criticism for organising just one bona fide international friendly in the run-up to the tournament. Turkey played modestly in their opening game against Italy and deserved to lose, although the penalty which condemned them was extremely harsh. The critics were at Denizli's throat again after the game, accusing him of favouring players from Fenerbahçe (his destination after the finals) over those from just-crowned UEFA Cup winners Galatasaray.

A new-look team struggled to a dull, lifeless 0-0 draw against Sweden, but even Turkey's first point at the European finals seemed insufficient to bring realistic hope of progression into the quarter-finals. The final group game was against Belgium, in Brussels. For half an hour Turkey were overrun, but fine defending, notably from Rüstü and classy centre-back Alpay, kept them in the hunt, and then, just before half-time, completely against the run of play, the previously discreet Hakan Sükür seized on an error of judgment by Belgian 'keeper Filip De Wilde and scored. Turkey needed a win to have any chance of going through, but they had to defend for their lives in the second half against a continuous Belgian onslaught. Just

when it seemed as if they might crack, a quick counter-attack resulted in Hakan blasting home his second goal of the evening. Turkey, against all odds, were through.

The Turks celebrated an historic qualification, but they were to meet their match in the quarter-finals, against Portugal. The course of the game was coloured by Alpay's contentious dismissal after half an hour, and when Arif missed a penalty on the stroke of half-time - just after Portugal had opened the scoring - Turkey's dream was over. The second half was all Portugal, and the 2-0 final scoreline greatly flattered the losers.

Denizli and his players returned home to a warm reception, but the big party had come the previous month in the wake of Galatasaray's historic victory in the UEFA Cup.

The penalty shoot-out victory over Arsenal in Copenhagen completed a perfect season for Fatih Terim's side. They had already won the Turkish championship and

INTERNATIONAL HONOURS

World Cup Finals appearances: 1954

European Championship appearances: 1996, 2000 (qtr-finals)

European Club Competitions
UEFA Cup   Galatasaray (2000)

Cup, and the UEFA Cup triumph enabled Galatasaray's 1999/2000 team to be billed as the greatest Turkish club side of all time.

Galatasaray's journey to Copenhagen was a long and complex one. Like Arsenal, they began their European campaign in the Champions' League but were 'demoted' after finishing third in their group. Not that the Turkish champions felt like second-class citizens after they had staged a dramatic late comeback to eliminate Milan 3-2 in their final game.

That miraculous Champions' League win in the Ali Sami Yen stadium was to be followed by a succession of superb performances away from home in the UEFA Cup. After

eliminating another Serie A side, Bologna, Gala produced two brilliant displays in Dortmund and Mallorca to reach the semi-finals. The tie with Leeds was blackened by the horrific murders in Istanbul but on the field Galatasaray went about their business with ruthless efficiency, winning the first leg 2-0 and then closing out the tie with an early penalty at Elland Road - a game from which travelling Turkish fans had understandably been barred.

And so to Copenhagen for the biggest match in the history of Turkish club football. Once again, sadly, the occasion was ruined by street violence between Turkish and English thugs. On the pitch there was little to choose between the two sides. Galatasaray had marginally the

NATIONAL TEAM APPEARANCES 99/00

Coach - MUSTAFA Denizli	NIR	MOL	GER	IRL	IRL	NOR	ITA	SWE	BEL	POR	Cps	Gls
RÜSTÜ Reçber (10/05/73) - Fenerbahçe	G	G	G	G	G38		G	G	G	G	46	-
ALI EREN Beserler (25/10/75) - Besiktas	D	D	D	D	D						6	-
OGÜN Temizkanoglu (06/10/69) - Fenerbahçe	D	D	D	D	D	D69	D	D59	D	D84	64	5
ALPAY Özalan (29/05/73) - Fenerbahçe	D	D	D	D	D		D	D	D	D	49	1
TAYFUN Korkut (02/04/74) - Fenerbahçe	M		M	M	M46	M	M	s44	M	M	27	-
TAYFUR Havutçu (23/04/70) - Besiktas	M	M	M85	M	M	M	M		s37	M	25	5
SERGEN Yalçin (05/10/72) - Fenerbahçe/Galatasaray	M89	M88	M	M85	M	M53	M81	s57		s84	32	5
TUGAY Kerimoglu (24/08/70) - Galatasaray/Rangers (SCO)	M	s46		s67		M68		s76	s59	M37	59	2
ABDULLAH Ercan (08/12/71) - Fenerbahçe	M75		M69	D	M	M	M		M		54	-
ARIF Erdem (02/01/72) - Galatasaray	A79	A	s72	s46	A84	A75	s81	A	A87	A62	38	6
HAKAN Sükür (01/09/71) - Galatasaray	A	A	A	A	A	A46	A	A	A	A	56	28
HAKAN Ünsal (14/05/73) - Galatasaray	s75	M		M67				M		M	15	-
OKAN Buruk (19/10/73) - Galatasaray	s79	M46	M72		M	s53	M88	M	M77	M62	14	1
ÜMIT Karan (01/10/76) - Gençlerbirligi	s89					s75					2	-
FATIH Akyel (26/12/77) - Galatasaray		M46	D		s46	D	D	D	D	D	18	-
AYHAN Akman (23/02/77) - Besiktas		s46				s53					6	-
ÜMIT Davala (30/07/73) - Galatasaray		s88		M46	s84	D53	M76	M44			8	-
ERGÜN Penbe (17/05/72) - Galatasaray		s69					s88		s77	M	6	-
OKTAY Derelioglu (17/12/75) - Gaziantepspor		s85								s62	14	8
MERT Korkmaz (16/08/71) - Gaziantepspor			s85								5	-
ENGIN Ipekoglu (07/06/71) - Fenerbahçe				s38							32	-
FEVZI Tuncay (14/09/77) - Besiktas						G83					1	-
AHMET Dursun (25/01/78) - Besiktas						s46					1	-
EMRE Belözoglu (07/09/80) - Galatasaray						s68					1	-
RAMAZAN Tunç (17/09/75) - Gaziantepspor						s69					1	-
METIN Aktas (01/08/77) - Trabzonspor						s83					1	-
SUAT Kaya (26/08/67) - Galatasaray								M	M	s62	10	1
Muzzy IZZET (31/10/74) - Leicester City (ENG)							M57				1	-
OSMAN Özköylü (26/08/71) - Trabzonspor									s87		12	-

EUROPEAN CUPS 99/00

CHAMPIONS' CUP

● **BESIKTAS**

Preliminary round 2 HAPOEL HAIFA (ISR)

H 1-1 Ayhan (90)
Shorunmu, Ali Eren (Sellami 42), Rahim, Schäfer, Yasin, Ayhan, Mehmet (Atilla 73), Tayfur, Mutlu, Nihat (Ahmet 63), Ertugrul.

A 0-0 Shorunmu, Sellami, Rahim, Ali Eren (Ertugrul 46), Atilla, Yasin, Ayhan, Tayfur, Mutlu (Ersen 70), Ahmet, Nihat (Mehmet 46).

● **GALATASARAY**

Qualifying round SK RAPID WIEN (AUT)

A 3-0 Hakan Ünsal (34), Fatih (38), Hagi (90)
Taffarel, Fatih, Popescu, Capone, Hakan Ünsal, Okan (Ergün 75), Ümit, Suat, Emre (Ahmet 82), Hagi, Hakan Sükür (Arif 79).

H 1-0 Okan (53)
Taffarel, Fatih, Capone, Popescu, Hakan Ünsal, Okan, Ümit (Tugay 63), Suat, Emre (Saffet 79), Hakan Sükür (Arif 29), Hagi.

Champions' League

1st match HERTHA BSC BERLIN (GER)

H 2-2 Hakan Sükür (23), Hagi (86p)
Taffarel, Ümit, Popescu, Capone, Hakan Ünsal, Okan (Fatih 46), Bruno (Tugay 46), Suat, Hagi, Hakan Sükür, Arif (Márcio 67).

2nd match MILAN (ITA)

A 1-2 Ümit (50)
Tafafrel, Fatih (Ergün 49), Popescu, Capone, Hakan Ünsal, Ümit, Suat, Hagi (Arif 46), Bruno (Okan 46), Ahmet, Hakan Sükür.

3rd match CHELSEA (ENG)

A 0-1 Taffarel, Fatih, Capone, Popescu, Hakan Ünsal, Okan (Emre 72), Ümit, Hagi (Hasan 73), Ergün, Hakan Sükür, Arif (Mehmet Bolukbasi 34).

4th match CHELSEA (ENG)

H 0-5 Mehmet Bolukbasi, Fatih (Ümit 46), Popescu, Capone, Hakan Ünsal, Okan, Emre, Tugay, Hagi (Hasan 46), Hakan Sükür (Saffet 65), Arif.

5th match HERTHA BSC BERLIN (GER)

A 4-1 Hakan Sükür (48, 66), Tugay (81), Okan (90)
Taffarel, Fatih (Ergün 46), Popescu, Capone, Ahmet, Okan, Suat, Emre, Hasan (Tugay 72), Arif (Emrah 86), Hakan Sükür.

6th match MILAN (ITA)

H 3-2 Capone (27), Hakan Sükür (86), Ümit (90p)
Taffarel, Capone, Popescu (Ergün 70), Ahmet, Okan, Ümit, Hagi (Hasan 66), Emre, Hakan Ünsal, Hakan Sükür, Arif (Márcio 72).

UEFA CUP

● **ANKARAGÜCÜ**

Qualifying round B36 (FAR)

H 1-0 Ünal (15)
Özkan, Hakan Kutlu, Gökmen Baris, Faruk, Mkhalele (Ümit 73), Baidoo, Ünal, Fatih, Ramazan, Birol (Sapula 87), Hakan Keles (Gökmen Yildiran 55).

A 1-0 Hakan Keles (81)
Özkan, Hakan Kutlu, Gökmen Baris, Faruk, Ümit, Fatih, Yilmaz, Ünal, Mkhalele, Hakan Keles (Sami 88), Birol.

1st round ATLETICO MADRID (ESP)

A 0-3 Özkan, Hakan Kutlu, Yilmaz, Faruk, Ümit, Baidoo, Fatih, Gökmen Baris (Birol 62), Mbele (Gökmen Yildiran 65), Mkhalele, Hakan Keles (Ndeki 73).

H 1-0 Birol (85)
Özkan, Hakan Kutlu, Yilmaz, Faruk, Ümit, Fatih (Gökmen Baris 63), Ünal, Baidoo, Ramazan (Sami 65), Birol, Hakan Keles (Gökmen Yildiran 89).

● **FENERBAHÇE**

1st round MTK HUNGÁRIA FC (HUN)

A 0-0 Rüstü, Johnson, Ogün, Alpay, Erkan, Moshoeu (Mustafa 62), Sergen, Murat Yakin, Tayfun, Preko, Moldovan (Aygün 85).

H 0-2 Rüstü, Mustafa, Saffet, Alpay, Tayfun, Johnson (Murat Yakin 61), Sergen, Moshoeu, Abdullah, Moldovan, Bolic.

● **GALATASARAY**

3rd round BOLOGNA (ITA)

A 1-1 Hakan Sükür (82)
Taffarel, Capone, Popescu, Ahmet, Hakan Ünsal, Ümit (Saffet 90), Emre, Suat, Hasan (Fatih 84), Hagi (Ergün 55), Hakan Sükür.

H 2-1 Hasan (5), Ümit (29)
Taffarel, Capone, Popescu, Ahmet (Tugay 71), Fatih, Ümit, Emre, Suat, Okan (Alper 90), Hasan (Bülent 88), Hakan Sükür.

4th round BORUSSIA DORTMUND (GER)

A 2-0 Hakan Sükür (32), Hagi (45)
Taffarel, Ümit, Bülent, Capone, Ergün, Okan (Hasan 83), Emre, Suat, Hagi (Ahmet 86), Arif (Márcio 87), Hakan Sükür.

H 0-0 Taffarel, Capone, Bülent, Popescu, Ergün, Ümit, Suat (Ahmet 86), Emre, Hagi (Márcio 88), Arif (Hasan 82), Hakan Sükür.

Quarter-final RCD MALLORCA (ESP)

A 4-1 Arif (44), Emre (48), Hakan Sükür (59), Okan (65)
Taffarel, Capone, Bülent, Capone, Ergün, Okan (Ahmet 89), Suat, Hagi (Hasan 82), Emre, Arif, Hakan Sükür (Márcio 86).

H 2-1 Capone (34), Hakan Sükür (46)
Taffarel, Capone, Fatih, Bülent, Ergün, Okan (Mehmet Yozgatli 78), Ahmet, Hagi, Hasan, Arif (Hakan Ünsal 67), Hakan Sükür (Márcio 86).

Semi-final LEEDS UNITED (ENG)

H 2-0 Hakan Sükür (12), Capone (44)
Taffarel, Capone, Bülent, Popescu, Ergün, Okan (Hakan Ünsal 62), Suat, Emre, Hagi (Ahmet 89), Arif (Hasan 79), Hakan Sükür.

A 2-2 Hagi (5p), Hakan Sükür (42)
Taffarel, Capone, Bülent, Popescu, Ergün, Okan (Hasan 87), Suat (Ahmet 80), Emre, Hagi, Hakan Sükür, Arif (Hakan Ünsal 46).

Final ARSENAL (ENG)

0-0 (aet; 4-1 on pens.)
Taffarel, Capone, Bülent, Popescu, Ergün, Okan (Hakan Ünsal 83), Suat (Ahmet 94), Hagi, Ümit, Hakan Sükür, Arif (Hasan 95).

DOMESTIC CUP 99/00

THIRD ROUND
Pendikspor 2, Fenerbahçe 1
Adanaspor 1, Samsunspor 2
Siirt Jet-Pa 1, Altay 1 (Altay on pens.)
Erzurumspor 4, Denizlispor 1
Elazigspor 0, Gaziantepspor 5
Vanspor 1, Kartalspor 0
Trabzonspor 3, Göztepe 1
Kayserispor 1, Bursaspor 2
Karabükspor 0, Kocaelispor 4
Antalyaspor 2, Yimzat Yozgatspor 0
Y. Nazillispor 1, Gençlerbirligi 1
(Y. Nazillispor on pens.)
Istanbulspor 2, Konyaspor Endustri 0
Çaykur Rizespor 2, Ankaragücü 2
(Ankaragücü on pens.)
Çanakkale Dardanelspor 1, Besiktas 0
Galatasaray 5, BS Bld Ankara 1

FOURTH ROUND
Bursaspor 3, Vanspor 0
Çanakkale Dardanelspor 2, Pendikspor 0

Y. Nazillispor 0, Erzurumspor 0
(Y. Nazillispor on pens.)
Bakirköyspor 0, Antalyaspor 2
Istanbulspor 1, Ankaragücü 2
Gaziantepspor 1, Altayspor 1
(Gaziantepspor on pens.)
Kocaelispor 0, Trabzonspor 2
Galatasaray 2, Samsunspor 1

QUARTER-FINALS
Ankaragücü 7 (Faruk 5, Saffet 41, 76, Hakan Keles
65, Tarik 71, 90, Hakan Kutlu 75), Y. Nazillispor 0
Antalyaspor 3 (Fazli 25, Mustafa 47, Gueye 90),
Çanakkale Dardanelspor 1 (Ufuk 12)
Bursaspor 1 (Tolunay 77), Gaziantepspor 0
Trabzonspor 1 (Vugrinec 14),
Galatasaray 2 (Sergen 67, 72)

SEMI-FINALS
Antalyaspor 2 (Zafer 52, Fazili 73), Bursaspor 0
Ankaragücü 0, Galatasaray 2 (Okan 32, Hasan 89)

FINAL
03/05/2000, Diyarbakir
GALATASARAY 5
Ümit (14), Márcio (74), Hakan Ünsal (100),
Mehmet Yozgatli (112), Hakan Sükür (114)
ANTALYASPOR 3
Mustafa (40), Zafer (72), Kamil (95)
(aet)
referee - Metin Tokat
GALATASARAY - Kerem, Capone, Popescu (Mehmet
Yozgatli 97), Ahmet, Hakan Ünsal, Okan, Ümit, Hagi
(Hasan 91), Ergün, Arif (Márcio 46), Hakan Sükür.
ANTALYASPOR - Adnan, Ginchev, Burhan, Nuri, Music,
Kamil, Zafer, Mustafa, Senol (Ahmet 91), Dursun
(Gaudino 68), Fazli (Gueye 64).

better of a dull, uneventful 90 minutes of normal time, but after Gheorghe Hagi idiotically earned himself a red card for swinging a punch, Arsenal created numerous chances to claim the all-important 'golden goal'. But Brazilian goalkeeper Cláudio Taffarel would not be beaten and Galatasary held on for penalties. The shoot-out was no contest. Galatasary took four spot-kicks and scored the lot, while Arsenal converted just one of three. It was up to Romanian veteran Gheorghe Popescu - once of Arsenal's London rivals Tottenham - to deliver the fatal blow, and he smashed his shot low into the corner to take Galatasaray - and Turkish football - to the promised land.

The UEFA Cup final provided a fitting occasion for the farewell of charismatic coach Fatih Terim, whose fabulous four years at the club had brought seven major trophies, including championship triumphs in every season. That portfolio was impressive enough to earn him a lucrative one-year contract at Italian club Fiorentina, where his mission was to replace the legendary Giovanni Trapattoni.

The fourth of Fatih Terim's league victories was never really in serious doubt. Although Gala were beaten at home on the opening day, they recovered to win their next five games and remain unbeaten for the next 24, dropping just six points in the process. This put them well clear at the top of the table, and although they got the

TOP SCORERS

30	SERKAN Aykut (Samsunspor)
21	AHMET Dursun (Besiktas)
20	FAZLI Ulusal (Antalyaspor)
18	Viorel MOLDOVAN (Fenerbahçe)
	ÜMIT Karan (Gençlerbirligi)
16	CAFER Aydin (Ankaragücü)
	OKTAY Derelioglu (Gaziantepspor)
14	ERTUGRUL Saglam (Besiktas)
	OKAN Yilmaz (Bursaspor)
	HAKAN Sükür (Galatasaray)

NATIONAL TEAM RESULTS 99/00

04/09/99	Northern Ireland (ECQ)	A	Belfast	3-0	Arif (45, 46, 49)
08/09/99	Moldova (ECQ)	A	Chisinau	1-1	Tayfur (76)
09/10/99	Germany (ECQ)	A	Munich	0-0	
13/11/99	Republic of Ireland (ECQ)	A	Dublin	1-1	Tayfur (83p)
17/11/99	Republic of Ireland (ECQ)	H	Bursa	0-0	
23/02/00	Norway	H	Istanbul	0-2	
11/06/00	Italy (ECF)	N	Arnhem	1-2	Okan (61)
15/06/00	Sweden (ECF)	N	Eindhoven	0-0	
19/06/00	Belgium (ECF)	A	Brussels	2-0	Hakan Sükür (45, 70)
24/06/00	Portugal (ECF)	N	Amsterdam	0-2	

jitters near the end as Besiktas mounted a late challenge, they had enough points in the bag to edge home the weekend before the UEFA Cup final.

The first leg of the domestic 'double' came 11 days earlier when Galatasaray won an extraordinary Cup final against underdogs Antalyaspor in Diyarbakir. The match finished 2-2 in normal time, and if the 'golden goal' rule had been in force, the underdogs would have won. But Antalyaspor's advantage lasted only five minutes and in the second extra period Galatasaray took command, with the inevitable Hakan Sükür scoring the last and decisive goal in a memorable 5-3 win.

The latter stages of the Cup were conspicuous by the absence of Besiktas and Fenerbahçe, both of whom had been eliminated humiliatingly in the third round by lower-division teams.

It was Fenerbahçe's 2-1 defeat by the 'unknowns' of Pendikspor that summed up a thoroughly forgettable season for the Yellow-and-Blues. They had been expected to mount a serious challenge to Galatasaray after a summer spending spree that brought in Turkish internationals Alpay, Abdullah and Ogün as well as the talented African trio of Yaw Preko, Samuel Johnson and Souleymane Oulare. But whereas Gala had a settled playing and coaching staff, Fener had too many individuals pulling in different directions.

New coach Ridvan Dilmen resigned after a shock first-round UEFA Cup defeat by Hungarian side MTK. He was replaced by the strict disciplinarian Zdenek Zeman,

Hakan Sükür netted the final goal in a memorable Turkish Cup final.

PLAYERS OF THE SEASON

CLÁUDIO TAFFAREL

Supporter surveys suggest that the most popular player in the Turkish league is not a Turk but a Brazilian. Cláudio Taffarel, the veteran goalkeeper of Galatasaray, endeared himself to all and sundry during the 1999/2000 season. A colourful and jovial character both on and off the pitch, he is also an exceptional 'keeper - which probably explains why Brazil have employed him between the posts in each of the last three World Cups. He was a fundamental contributor to Gala's remarkable 'treble' triumph and became an adopted hero of the Turkish people after his brilliance in extra-time of the UEFA Cup final against Arsenal. His importance to the team was spelt out when he was sent off in the Champions' League at Chelsea and missed the return match in Istanbul - a game in which, without their charismatic last line of defence, Galatasaray were hammered 5-0.

SERKAN AYKUT

Hakan Sükür remains out on his own as the number one Turkish striker - it could hardly be any other way after his ten European goals in 1999/2000 were followed by those two decisive strikes against Belgium at Euro 2000 - but the big centre-forward for once had to surrender his position at the head of the Turkish First Division goal charts. That honour went instead to the previously anonymous Serkan Aykut, who, despite playing for modest Samsunspor, struck 30 goals - well over half of his team's total. A small and lively forward in the mould of ex-Turkish legend Tanju Çolak, Serkan deserved a place in Turkey's Euro 2000 squad but Mustafa Denizli remained aloof to his charms. At 25 he still has time to make a name for himself at international level. He gets goals from everywhere, including free-kicks and technically perfect headers, and is too talented to be written off as a mere one-season wonder.

but his attempts to impose his trademark 4-3-3 formation floundered, especially after Swiss international Murat Yakin decided to return home following the earthquake disaster. Then there was the case of Sergen Yalçin. Brilliant in the Euro 2000 qualifiers with Turkey, he couldn't get on with Zeman and moved to Galatasaray, where he was to make even less of an impression.

Zeman's frustrations boiled over after the Cup defeat and he resigned. Assistant boss Turhan Sofuoglu assumed the reins for the remainder of the season and had the satisfaction of leading Fenerbahçe to victories in all of the derby games, including the one against Galatasaray, which was decided by a deflected Johnson free-kick. Turhan knew all along, however, that Mustafa Denizli would be arriving at the end of the season - albeit to a club that failed to qualify for Europe.

Besiktas also had problems on the coaching front. German boss Karlheinz Feldkamp quit due to ill health early in the season and was replaced by ex-German international Hans-Peter Briegel. A team of few stars - only midfielder Tayfur was active at Euro 2000 - Besiktas came

to life after the turn of the year with a storming run of 12 consecutive victories. They were just one short of a league record before the sequence was halted by Galatasaray in the crunch game of the season. 1-0 up and heading for a crucial win, Besiktas were stunned by a late equaliser following a dreadful error by goalkeeper Fevzi, who allowed a backpass to roll under his feet and into the net. The 1-1 draw effectively killed Besiktas's title challenge, although it was the only point they earned from any of the big derby games throughout the season.

In the spring Besiktas appointed a new president, with the young and energetic Serdar Bilgili ending Süleyman Seba's 16-year reign. One of the new man's first acts was to replace Briegel with ex-Parma and Borussia Dortmund coach Nevio Scala - a man who had turned down rivals Fenerbahçe earlier in the season.

That meant that Istanbul's 'big three' all began the 2000/01 season with new coaches - Scala at Besiktas, Denizli at Fenerbahçe and, replacing Fatih Terim at Galatasaray, the highly-rated Romanian, Mircea Lucescu.

PROMOTED CLUBS 99/00

PROMOTION GROUP

		Pd	W	D	L	F	A	Pt	GD
1	**Yimpas Yozgatspor**	**18**	**10**	**3**	**5**	**35**	**31**	**33**	**14**
2	**Siirt Jetpa**	**18**	**9**	**6**	**3**	**36**	**23**	**33**	**13**
3	**Çaykur Rizespor**	**18**	**10**	**2**	**6**	**27**	**23**	**32**	**4**
4	Diyarbakirspor	18	9	3	6	27	24	30	3
5	Konyaspor	18	9	3	6	25	22	30	3
6	Çanakkale Dardanelspor	18	8	4	6	31	19	28	12
7	Endustrispor	18	3	8	7	15	27	17	-12
8	Kayserispor	18	4	4	10	25	37	16	-12
9	Sariyer	18	3	7	8	21	33	16	-12
10	Izmirspor	18	3	4	11	26	39	13	-13

PROMOTION PLAY-OFFS
N.B. Teams 3-5 in Promotion Group join the five Second Division group winners after the second phase.

QUARTER-FINALS
Konyaspor 3, BB Ankaraspor 1
Çaykur Rizespor 6, Gaziantep Belediyespor 2
Diyarbakirspor 3, Agrispor 1
Aydinspor 5, Karabükspor 1

SEMI-FINALS
Çaykur Rizespor 4, Aydinspor 1
Diyarbakirspor 0, Konyaspor 0 (8-7 on pens.)

FINAL
Çaykur Rizespor 2, Diyarbakirspor 0

CLUB DIRECTORIES

Yimpas Yozgatspor Kulübü
Adnan Menderes Bulvari No: 190/21
Yozgat
tel - (354) 2121805
fax - (354) 2125558
Year of Formation - 1959
President - Mehmet Yilmaz
Coach - Hüseyin Kalpar

Siirt Jetpa Kulübü
Köy Hizmetleri Il Mudurlugu Sösyal
Tesisleri-Siirt
tel - (484) 2242856
fax - (484) 2243195
Year of Formation - 1969
President - Fadil Akgündüz
Coach - Sakip Özberk

Çaykur Rizespor Kulübü
Mehmet Cengiz Sösyal Tesisleri
Taslidere-Rize
tel - (464) 2121012
fax - (464) 2141911
President - Mehmet Cengiz
Coach - Rasim Kara

ADANASPOR

CLUB DIRECTORY

Adanaspor Kulübü
Kenan Evren Bulvari 1873
Sokak No:2
Adana
tel - (322) 2340486
fax - (322) 2340486
Year of Formation - 1954
President - Hakan Uzan
Coach - Nejat Biyedic; Hikmet Karaman
(00/01 - Hikmet Karaman)
Stadium - 5 Ocak (30,000)

APPEARANCES 99/00

	P	Ap	(s)	Gls
AHMET Özen	M		(10)	
ALI ASIM Balkaya	A	22	(9)	7
ALTAN Aksoy	A	22	(6)	9
ATAKAN Sancarbarlaz	M	26	(1)	2
ATILLA Kucuktaka	G	6		
BÜLENT Selvü	M	2	(4)	
Alban BUSHI (ALB)	A	24	(5)	10
CAFER Aydin	A	4	(1)	3
CENK Isler	A	15	(7)	10
ENGIN Özdemir	M	16	(2)	3
ERBIL Uzel	D	11	(4)	
ERCAN Yoruk	M	14	(5)	
HAYATI Köse	D	30		
IBRAHIM Köseoglu	M	10	(9)	1
KAYA	M		(1)	1
KORAY Ergin	M	1		
KORHAN Ataasik	M	1	(2)	
Ivan KIRILOV (BUL)	D	21		
OGUZ Çetin	M	32	(1)	3
OKAN Babahasan	M	2	(1)	
SAVAS Kaya	M	14	(7)	
SENOL Yavas	D	8		
SERKAN Bekiroglu	D	21	(5)	
Olivier SURAY (BEL)	M	4	(2)	
VOLKAN Bekiroglu	M	32	(1)	1
VOLKAN Özturk	M	5	(7)	
YAVUZ Erayadin	G	4	(1)	
Zlatomir ZAGORCIC (BUL)	D	3		
Zdravko ZDRAVKOV (BUL)	G	24		

LEAGUE RESULTS 1999/2000

08/08/99	Trabzonspor	H	1-2	Oguz
15/08/99	Ankaragücü	A	0-0	
12/09/99	Samsunspor	A	1-2	Cafer
17/09/99	Galatasaray	H	3-4	Ali Asim, Cafer 2
26/09/99	Antalyaspor	A	2-2	Volkan Bekiroglu, Cenk (p)
17/10/99	Bursaspor	H	1-1	Cenk
24/10/99	Göztepe	A	1-0	Oguz
30/10/99	Fenerbahçe	H	1-3	Cenk
21/11/99	Erzurumspor	A	1-4	Bushi
27/11/99	Gençlerbirligi	H	1-2	Engin (p)
04/12/99	Besiktas	A	1-0	Ali
10/12/99	Denizlispor	H	3-2	Bushi 3
19/12/99	Vanspor	A	2-0	Altan 2
25/12/99	Kocaelispor	H	3-0	Atakan, Altan, Engin (p)
08/01/00	Altay	A	1-2	Atakan
16/01/00	Istanbulspor	H	2-1	Bushi 2
22/01/00	Gaziantepspor	A	1-1	Bushi
28/01/00	Trabzonspor	A	1-0	Altan
06/02/00	Ankaragücü	H	2-2	Cenk, Bushi
12/02/00	Samsunspor	H	0-1	
20/02/00	Galatasaray	A	0-4	
26/02/00	Antalyaspor	H	1-2	og (Ginchev)
05/03/00	Bursaspor	A	1-3	Altan (p)
12/03/00	Göztepe	H	2-0	Ali Asim 2
17/03/00	Fenerbahçe	A	4-2	Cenk 2, Ali Asim, Altan
25/03/00	Erzurumspor	H	2-0	Cenk 2
01/04/00	Gençlerbirligi	A	2-5	Bushi, Cenk
08/04/00	Besiktas	H	1-3	Ali Asim
15/04/00	Denizlispor	A	2-4	Cenk, Oguz
22/04/00	Vanspor	H	2-0	Ali Asim, Altan
29/04/00	Kocaelispor	A	0-0	
07/05/00	Altay	H	1-0	Altan
12/05/00	Istanbulspor	A	2-3	Ibrahim, Bushi
20/05/00	Gaziantepspor	H	3-0	Engin, Altan, Kaya

ALTAY

CLUB DIRECTORY

Altay Spor Kulübü
Sehitlar Caddesi, Alsancak Stadi C Blok
Alsancak-Izmir
tel - (232) 4210626
fax - (232) 4215668
Year of Formation - 1914
President - Nafiz Zorlu
Coach - Ümit Kayihan; Celal Bolgen; Turgut Ucar;
Zafer Bilgetay
Stadium - Alsancak (20,000)

MAJOR HONOURS
Domestic Cup - (2) 1967, 1980.

APPEARANCES 99/00

	P	Ap	(s)	Gls
BAYRAM Bektas	A	8		3
Senad BRKIC (BOS)	A	4		1
CELALETTIN Kocak	M	2	(3)	
EMRE Gusar	D	14	(3)	1
Ilshat FAIZULIN (RUS)	A	5		
FARUK Namdar	A	4	(7)	1
Sead HALILOVIC (BOS)	M	13	(5)	
Kenan HASAGIC (BOS)	G	2	(1)	
HASAN Özer	A	30		12
HAYDAR Koç	M	2	(7)	
ILHAN Akgül	M	11	(6)	
KENAN Arayici	D	30		1
KENAN Yelek	D	14	(5)	
Norman MAPEZA (ZIM)	D	25	(1)	1
MURAT Alacayir	M	4	(3)	
MUSLUM Can	M	16	(3)	1
NECATI Ates	M	1	(8)	
NIHAT Tumkaya	G	32		
ORHAN Üstündag	D	23		2
Muhammed OSSAMA (EGY)	A	1	(2)	
ÖZKAN Koçtürk	M	5	(9)	3
SERKAN Dökme	M	27	(5)	1
SERKAN Karababa	M	14	(3)	1
SINAN Ertan	A	17	(13)	3
Olivier SURAY (BEL)	M	7		
TAHIR Karapinar	M	28	(1)	
TELAT Özden	M	20	(4)	3
YAKUP Sertkaya	M	15	(8)	

LEAGUE RESULTS 1999/2000

Date	Opponent	H/A	Score	Scorers
08/08/99	Bursaspor	A	4-1	Brkic, Hasan 2, Kenan Arayici
13/08/99	Göztepe	H	0-0	
12/09/99	Fenerbahçe	A	1-3	Bayram
19/09/99	Erzurumspor	H	3-0	Sinan, Bayram, Telat
26/09/99	Gençlerbirligi	A	0-0	
17/10/99	Besiktas	H	2-2	Bayram, Telat
24/10/99	Denizlispor	A	1-2	Mapeza (p)
31/10/99	Vanspor	H	2-0	Serkan Dökme, Hasan
21/11/99	Kocaelispor	H	0-1	
28/11/99	Samsunspor	H	2-1	Hasan, Orhan
05/12/99	Istanbulspor	H	0-0	
12/12/99	Gaziantepspor	A	0-1	
19/12/99	Trabzonspor	H	3-1	Hasan 2, Özkan
25/12/99	Ankaragücü	A	0-3	
08/01/00	Adanaspor	H	2-1	Hasan, Faruk
15/01/00	Galatasaray	A	1-3	Emre
23/01/00	Antalyaspor	H	2-0	Sinan, Orhan
30/01/00	Bursaspor	H	1-2	Hasan
06/02/00	Göztepe	A	1-0	Hasan
12/02/00	Fenerbahçe	H	2-3	Serkan Karababa, Özkan
20/02/00	Erzurumspor	A	0-0	
27/02/00	Gençlerbirligi	H	0-2	
03/03/00	Besiktas	A	0-3	
11/03/00	Denizlispor	H	1-0	Hasan
19/03/00	Vanspor	A	1-1	Sinan
26/03/00	Kocaelispor	A	1-2	Hasan
02/04/00	Samsunspor	A	0-1	
08/04/00	Istanbulspor	A	0-1	
15/04/00	Gaziantepspor	H	1-3	Muslum
22/04/00	Trabzonspor	A	1-2	Özkan
29/04/00	Ankaragücü	H	0-0	
07/05/00	Adanaspor	A	0-1	
12/05/00	Galatasaray	H	1-0	Telat
21/05/00	Antalyaspor	A	1-3	Hasan

ANKARAGÜCÜ

CLUB DIRECTORY

Makina Kimya Endüstrisi Ankaragücü Kulübü
Sosyal Tesisleri, GMK Bulvari, Tandogan-Ankara
tel - (312) 2220175
fax - (312) 2312772
Year of Formation - 1910
President - Cemal Aydin
Secretary - Zülküf Aker
Coach - Tinaz Tirpan; Hayati Söydas; Gheorghe
Multescu; Ümit Kayihan (00/01 - Ersun Yanal)
Stadium - 19 Mayis (24,000)

MAJOR HONOURS
Domestic Cup - (2) 1972, 1981.

APPEARANCES 99/00

		P	Ap	(s)	Gls
ADEM Dursun	A	4	(8)		
ADNAN Erkan	G	19	(2)		
Stephen BAIDOO (GHA)	M	23		4	
BIROL Alsancak	A	6	(7)		
CAFER Aydin	A	15	(2)	13	
FARUK Sarman	D	25	(1)	1	
FATIH Sezer	M	7	(1)		
FUAT Kirimca	M	2	(1)		
GÖKMEN Baris	D	30	(1)		
GÖKMEN Yildiran	A	1	(6)		
HAKAN Keles	A	22	(10)	6	
HAKAN Kutlu	D	21	(6)		
Ohene KENNEDY (GHA)	A	11	(8)	4	
Emile MBELE (DRC)	M	3			
Helman MKHALELE (SAF)	M	24	(3)		
Joseph NDEKI (SAF)	A	2	(2)		
Dumisa NGOBE (SAF)	M	10	(2)		
OSMAN Coskan	M		(3)		
ÖZKAN Karsli	G	8	(1)		
Valeriu RACHITA (ROM)	D	5			
RAMAZAN Özalp	M	22	(2)		
SAFFET Akyüz	A	10	(3)	4	
SAMI Kökten	M		(5)		
Godfrey SAPULA (SAF)	A	1	(1)		
TAREK Mustafa (EGY)	M	8	(7)		
TARIK Dasgün	M	21	(1)	8	
ÜMIT Hatipoglu	M	5	(2)		
ÜNAL Karaman	M	20		4	
YASIN Çelik	M	18	(4)		
YILMAZ Özen	D	23	(6)		
ZAFER Özgültekin	G	7	(1)		
ZAFER Uysal	M	1	(1)		

LEAGUE RESULTS 1999/2000

07/08/99	Samsunspor	A	0-2	
15/08/99	Adanaspor	H	0-0	
11/09/99	Galatasaray	A	0-5	
19/09/99	Antalyaspor	H	1-3	Baidoo
26/09/99	Bursaspor	A	1-3	Hakan Keles
16/10/99	Göztepe	H	1-2	Ünal
24/10/99	Fenerbahçe	A	1-1	Ünal
30/10/99	Erzurumspor	H	1-0	Baidoo
21/11/99	Gençlerbirligi	A	2-1	Cafer 2
26/11/99	Besiktas	H	2-3	Cafer 2
05/12/99	Denizlispor	A	1-1	Kenendy
12/12/99	Vanspor	H	1-0	Tarik
18/12/99	Kocaelispor	H	3-2	Kennedy 2, Cafer
25/12/99	Altay	H	3-0	Cafer 2 (1p), Faruk
09/01/00	Istanbulspor	A	6-2	Baidoo, Ünal, Cafer 3, Kennedy
15/01/00	Gaziantepspor	H	1-1	og (Mehmet)
23/01/00	Trabzonspor	A	1-3	Hakan Keles
29/01/00	Samsunspor	H	1-2	Tarik
06/02/00	Adanaspor	A	2-2	Saffet, Hakan Keles
13/02/00	Galatasaray	H	0-2	
20/02/00	Antalyaspor	A	0-0	
26/02/00	Bursaspor	H	2-1	Saffet 2
05/03/00	Göztepe	A	0-2	
11/03/00	Fenerbahçe	H	1-1	Hakan Keles
18/03/00	Erzurumspor	A	1-2	Saffet
26/03/00	Gençlerbirligi	H	0-0	
02/04/00	Besiktas	A	1-3	Ünal
09/04/00	Denizlispor	H	3-1	Tarik 2, Hakan Keles
16/04/00	Vanspor	A	3-2	Cafer 2, Tarik
23/04/00	Kocaelispor	A	1-4	Cafer
29/04/00	Altay	A	0-0	
07/05/00	Istanbulspor	H	2-2	Tarik, Hakan Keles
12/05/00	Gaziantepspor	A	2-2	Tarik 2
21/05/00	Trabzonspor	H	1-1	Baidoo

ANTALYASPOR

CLUB DIRECTORY

Antalyaspor Kulübü
Kiliç Arslan Mahallesi Park Sokak No:12
Antalya
tel - (242) 2478062
fax - (242) 2474760
Year of Formation - 1966
President - Ünal Öger
Coach - Rüdiger Abramczik; Metin Ünal
Stadium - Atatürk (12,000)

APPEARANCES 99/00

	P	Ap	(s)	Gls
ADNAN Karahan	G	34		
AHMET Sönmez	M	11	(8)	
BURHAN Saatcioglu	D	27		
DURSUN Karaman	M	12	(5)	1
FARUK Karaca	A	1	(10)	
FAZLI Ulusal	A	31		20
Maurizio GAUDINO (GER)	M	17	(10)	1
Gocho GINCHEV (BUL)	D	29		2
Adama GUEYE (SEN)	A	2	(8)	
KAMIL Çakar	M	24	(7)	4
MEHMET Toprak	M		(6)	
MUHAMMED Akyayci	A	7	(4)	
Vedin MUSIC (BOS)	M	17	(13)	
MUSTAFA Gürsel	M	30	(3)	1
NURI Kamburoglu	D	30	(1)	
OLGUN Karamanoglu	A	6	(8)	4
Dirk SCHUSTER (GER)	M	29		
SENOL Yavas	M	20		3
TOPRAK Kirtoglu	M	1	(3)	
UGUR Yasan	M	14	(8)	2
ZAFER Demiray	M	32		3

LEAGUE RESULTS 1999/2000

08/08/99	Istanbulspor	H	0-3	(w/o; original result 1-0 Olgun)
15/08/99	Gaziantepspor	A	2-1	Zafer, Olgun
10/09/99	Trabzonspor	H	0-2	
19/09/99	Ankaragücü	A	3-1	Zafer, Fazli, Olgun
26/09/99	Adanaspor	H	2-2	Ginchev, Olgun
15/10/99	Galatasaray	A	0-2	
24/10/99	Samsunspor	A	1-0	Fazli
31/10/99	Bursaspor	H	1-1	Gaudino
20/11/99	Göztepe	A	2-1	Dursun, Fazli
27/11/99	Fenerbahçe	H	2-3	Fazli 2
05/12/99	Erzurumspor	A	0-4	
12/12/99	Gençlerbirligi	H	2-1	og (Metin), Fazli
19/12/99	Besiktas	A	0-4	
25/12/99	Denizlispor	H	2-2	Fazli, Kamil
09/01/00	Vanspor	A	4-2	og (Murat Duman), Senol 2, Zafer
15/01/00	Kocaelispor	H	3-0	Kamil, Fazli, Mustafa
23/01/00	Altay	A	0-2	
29/01/00	Istanbulspor	A	0-0	
06/02/00	Gaziantepspor	H	0-0	
12/02/00	Trabzonspor	A	0-2	
20/02/00	Ankaragücü	H	0-0	
26/02/00	Adanaspor	A	2-1	Ugur, Senol
05/03/00	Galatasaray	H	1-3	Kamil
12/03/00	Samsunspor	H	0-1	
18/03/00	Bursaspor	A	2-4	Ugur, Fazli (p)
26/03/00	Göztepe	H	1-0	Fazli
01/04/00	Fenerbahçe	A	0-1	
09/04/00	Erzurumspor	H	1-2	Fazli
15/04/00	Gençlerbirligi	A	1-4	Fazli
22/04/00	Besiktas	H	2-2	Ginchev, Fazli
29/04/00	Denizlispor	A	0-4	
07/05/00	Vanspor	H	4-1	Fazli 4 (2p)
12/05/00	Kocaelispor	A	1-1	Fazli
21/05/00	Altay	H	3-1	Fazli 2, Kamil

BESIKTAS

CLUB DIRECTORY

Besiktas Jimnastik Kulübü
Akaretler Spor Caddesi No: 92, Besiktas-Istanbul
tel - (212) 2278790 / fax - (212) 2588194
Year of Formation - 1903
President - Serdar Bilgili
Secretary - Fahrettin Curoglu
Coach - Karlheinz Feldkamp; Hans-Peter Briegel
(00/01 - Nevio Scala)
Stadium - BJK Inönü (45,000)

MAJOR HONOURS
League Championship - (9) 1960, 1966, 1967,
1982, 1986, 1990, 1991, 1992, 1995.
Domestic Cup - (5)
1975, 1989, 1990, 1994, 1998.

APPEARANCES 99/00

		P	Ap	(s)	Gls
AHMET Dursun	A	29	(1)	21
ALI EREN Beserler	D	6	(1)	
ATILLA Birlik	M	3	(3)	
AYHAN Akman	M	19	(6)	7
BAYRAM Bektas	A	10	(10)	1
ERSEN Martin	A	5	(13)	2
ERTUGRUL Saglam	A	22	(3)	14
FEVZI Tuncay	G	24		
Sead HALILAGIC (BOS)	D	25		1
Thomas HENGEN (GER)	D	6		
ILHAN Sahin	M	1	(10)	
MEHMET Özdilek	M	32	(1)	11
Markus MÜNCH (GER)	M	33		4
MURAT Alacayir	M	5	(8)	1
MUTLU Topçu	M		(6)	
NIHAT Kahveci	A	22	(10)	7
RAHIM Zafer	D	26	(3)	
Oliver SCHÄFER (GER)	D	28		
SAVAS Kaya	M		(2)	
Jamal SELLAMI (MAR)	D	15	(3)	
Ike SHORUNMU (NIG)	G	10		
TAYFUR Havutçu	M	32		3
TUNC Kip	M		(2)	
YASIN Sülün	M	21	(9)	

LEAGUE RESULTS 1999/2000

07/08/99	Gençlerbirligi	A	0-1	
15/08/99	Samsunspor	H	4-0	Ahmet 3, Münch
12/09/99	Denizlispor	H	1-1	Ertugrul
19/09/99	Vanspor	A	6-0	Ahmet 2, Nihat 2, Mehmet, og (Birol)
25/09/99	Kocaelispor	H	1-0	Ertugrul
17/10/99	Altay	A	2-2	Ahmet, Mehmet
23/10/99	Istanbulspor	H	3-0	Nihat, Ertugrul, Mehmet
31/10/99	Gaziantepspor	A	0-0	
21/11/99	Trabzonspor	H	1-1	Ahmet
26/11/99	Ankaragücü	A	3-2	Ahmet 2, Ersen
04/12/99	Adanaspor	H	0-1	
12/12/99	Galatasaray	A	0-1	
19/12/99	Antalyaspor	H	4-0	Münch, Ertugrul 2, Mehmet
24/12/99	Bursaspor	A	1-0	Ahmet
07/01/00	Göztepe	H	2-1	Tayfur, Ertugrul
16/01/00	Fenerbahçe	A	1-2	Ayhan
23/01/00	Erzurumspor	H	2-0	Ahmet, Mehmet
29/01/00	Gençlerbirligi	H	4-0	Mehmet, Ahmet, Halilagic, Ertugrul
04/02/00	Samsunspor	A	2-0	Ertugrul, Nihat
11/02/00	Denizlispor	A	2-0	Mehmet, Ersen
18/02/00	Vanspor	H	2-1	Bayram, Ahmet
26/02/00	Kocaelispor	A	2-1	Ahmet 2
03/03/00	Altay	H	3-0	Ahmet (p), Ertugrul, Nihat
12/03/00	Istanbulspor	A	2-0	Ayhan, Ertugrul (p)
18/03/00	Gaziantepspor	H	1-0	Mehmet
25/03/00	Trabzonspor	A	2-1	Ahmet, Ertugrul
02/04/00	Ankaragücü	H	3-1	Ertugrul 2, Ahmet
08/04/00	Adanaspor	A	3-1	Ertugrul, og (Serkan), Ayhan
14/04/00	Galatasaray	H	1-1	Mehmet
22/04/00	Antalyaspor	A	2-2	Mehmet, Ayhan
28/04/00	Bursaspor	H	5-1	Tayfur, Ayhan 2, Münch (p), Murat
06/05/00	Göztepe	A	4-2	Ahmet (p), Mehmet, Tayfur, Ayhan
14/05/00	Fenerbahçe	H	1-3	Münch (p)
21/05/00	Erzurumspor	A	4-1	Ahmet 2, Nihat 2

BURSASPOR

CLUB DIRECTORY

Bursaspor Kulübü
Vakıfköy Tesisleri, Vakıfköy-Bursa
tel - (224) 3664883
fax - (224) 3664995
Year of Formation - 1963
President - Erdogan Bilenser
Secretary - Osman Yilmaz
Coach - Kemal Batmaz; Yilmaz Vural
(00/01 - Jörg Berger)
Stadium - Atatürk (24,000)

MAJOR HONOURS
Domestic Cup - (1) 1986.

APPEARANCES 99/00

	P	Ap	(s)	Gls
ADNAN Ilgin	D		(2)	
DENIZ Kolgu	M	30		4
Muhammed EL BADRAOUI (MAR)	A	5		3
ENDER Alkan	M	23	(6)	3
ERKAN Özbey	D	31		
FATIH Sen	M	1		
MESUT Ünal	D	1		
MURAT Alkan	G	4	(2)	
MURAT Sözkesen	A	27	(6)	11
MUSTAFA Gönden	M	19	(7)	1
OKAN Yilmaz	A	20	(5)	14
ÖMER Kilic	D	24	(1)	
Senad REPUH (BOS)	A	2	(2)	
Ibrahim SAMIR (EGY)	D	20		1
SENOL Karagöl	G	28		
SERDAR Kulbilge	G	2		
SERKAN Damla	M	5	(13)	1
SINAN Yesil	M	5	(14)	1
TAHIR Alagöz	D	14	(6)	2
TANER Gülleri	A		(1)	
TAYFUN Seven	M	13	(4)	1
Emmanuel TETTEH (GHA)	A	4	(7)	3
TOLUNAY Kafkas	M	23	(1)	1
TURAN Sen	D	9	(1)	
UFUK Talay (AUS)	M	9	(15)	1
ÜNAL Sari	M	27	(1)	1
Mirza VARESANOVIC (BOS)	M	27		2
Noureddine ZIYATI (MAR)	M	1	(7)	1

LEAGUE RESULTS 1999/2000

08/08/99	Altay	H	1-4	Murat Sözkesen
14/08/99	Istanbulspor	A	0-1	
12/09/99	Gaziantepspor	H	0-1	
18/09/99	Trabzonspor	A	0-2	
26/09/99	Ankaragücü	H	3-1	Ziyati, Murat Sözkesen, Sinan
17/10/99	Adanaspor	A	1-1	Ender
22/10/99	Galatasaray	H	0-0	
31/10/99	Antalyaspor	A	1-1	Murat Sözkesen
21/11/99	Samsunspor	A	0-1	
28/11/99	Göztepe	H	1-2	Samir (p)
05/12/99	Fenerbahçe	A	2-2	El Badraoui, Murat Sözkesen
12/12/99	Erzurumspor	H	4-2	Murat Sözkesen, El Badraoui 2, Ender
19/12/99	Gençlerbirligi	A	0-1	
24/12/99	Besiktas	H	0-1	
08/01/00	Denizlispor	A	3-1	Tolunay, Tahir, Okan
15/01/00	Vanspor	H	3-2	Okan, Deniz, Tahir
23/01/00	Kocaelispor	A	2-3	Deniz (p), Okan
30/01/00	Altay	A	2-1	Mustafa, Varesanovic
05/02/00	Istanbulspor	H	1-0	Murat Sözkesen
12/02/00	Gaziantepspor	A	1-1	Ufuk
20/02/00	Trabzonspor	H	2-3	Deniz, Serkan
26/02/00	Ankaragücü	A	1-2	Okan
05/03/00	Adanaspor	H	3-1	Okan, Murat Sözkesen, Ender
12/03/00	Galatasaray	A	0-6	
18/03/00	Antalyaspor	H	4-2	Tayfun (p), Okan 2, Varesanovic
25/03/00	Samsunspor	H	2-2	Okan, Tetteh
01/04/00	Göztepe	A	1-0	Okan
07/04/00	Fenerbahçe	H	2-1	Okan, Tetteh
16/04/00	Erzurumspor	A	1-4	Okan
22/04/00	Gençlerbirligi	H	2-5	Tetteh, Deniz
28/04/00	Besiktas	A	1-5	Okan
06/05/00	Denizlispor	H	4-1	Murat Sözkesen, Okan 2, Ünal
12/05/00	Vanspor	A	1-3	Murat Sözkesen
21/05/00	Kocaelispor	H	2-0	Murat Sözkesen

DENIZLISPOR

Denizlispor Kulübü
Lise Caddesi
Subay Gazinosu Karpisi
Denizli
tel - (258) 2620721
fax - (258) 2620721
Year of Formation - 1966
President - Ali Marim
Coach - Ersun Yanal; Tevfik Lav
Stadium - Denizli Sehir (15,000)

	P	Ap	(s)	Gls
ALATTIN Gülerce	M	8	(6)	
ALI Isik	A	5	(15)	2
ALI Tandogan	M	30	(2)	3
AYDIN Gencer	G	3		
AYDIN Tuna	M		(1)	
BÜLENT Akin	M	30		1
Doncho DONEV (BUL)	A	18	(9)	5
Hasan EL SAKA (EGY)	D	27		3
ENGIN Sentürk	M	5	(15)	2
Ilco GJORGIOSKI (MAC)	M	4	(2)	
Adama GUEYE (SEN)	A	5	(4)	3
HASAN Sermet	M	11	(5)	
KEMAL Sönmez	D	26		
LEVENT Kartop	A	9	(7)	
MOHAMMED ALI Kurtulus	M	16	(7)	5
SALIH Yildiz	D	2	(1)	
SERDAL Böyraz	M	3	(4)	
SERKAN Görgeç	M	18	(9)	2
SEYFETTIN Kurtulmus	M		(1)	
SÜLEYMAN Küçük	G	31		
Mohamed SYLLA (GUI)	D	9	(1)	
ÜMIT Bozkurt	D	32		4
VEYSEL Cihan	A	26	(5)	8
Mohammed YOUSSEF (EGY)	M	24	(3)	6
YUSUF Simsek	M	32		11

08/08/99	Erzurumspor	A	1-0	Gueye
15/08/99	Gençlerbirligi	H	1-3	Gueye
12/09/99	Besiktas	A	1-1	Gueye
19/09/99	Samsunspor	H	4-1	Engin, Youssef 2 (1p), Veysel
26/09/99	Vanspor	H	1-0	Veysel
17/10/99	Kocaelispor	H	3-1	Donev, Youssef, Yusuf
24/10/99	Altay	H	2-1	Youssef, Veysel
31/10/99	Istanbulspor	A	1-1	Serkan
19/11/99	Gaziantepspor	H	1-0	Bülent
28/11/99	Trabzonspor	A	1-1	Engin
05/12/99	Ankaragücü	H	1-1	Donev
10/12/99	Adanaspor	A	2-3	Mohammed Ali, Yusuf
18/12/99	Galatasaray	H	2-4	Youssef, Veysel
25/12/99	Antalyaspor	A	2-2	El Saka, Ali Tandogan
08/01/00	Bursaspor	H	1-3	Yusuf
16/01/00	Göztepe	A	4-2	Mohammed Ali 2, Ali Isik, Yusuf
21/01/00	Fenerbahçe	H	1-1	Ümit
30/01/00	Erzurumspor	H	2-1	Yusuf 2 (1p)
05/02/00	Gençlerbirligi	A	1-3	Ali Isik
11/02/00	Besiktas	H	0-2	
19/02/00	Samsunspor	A	2-6	Yusuf (p), Veysel
27/02/00	Vanspor	A	3-2	Ümit 2, Yusuf
04/03/00	Kocaelispor	A	0-1	
11/03/00	Altay	A	0-1	
19/03/00	Istanbulspor	H	3-1	Veysel, Yusuf 2
24/03/00	Gaziantepspor	A	0-0	
31/03/00	Trabzonspor	H	0-2	
09/04/00	Ankaragücü	A	1-3	Ali Tandogan
15/04/00	Adanaspor	H	4-2	El Saka 2, Donev, Youssef
23/04/00	Galatasaray	A	2-2	Donev, Mohammed Ali
29/04/00	Antalyaspor	H	4-0	Donev, Ümit, Mohammed Ali, Veysel
06/05/00	Bursaspor	A	1-4	Ali Tandogan
13/05/00	Göztepe	H	2-0	Yusuf, Veysel
20/05/00	Fenerbahçe	A	1-2	Serkan

ERZURUMSPOR

CLUB DIRECTORY

Erzurumspor
Havaalani Yolu Üzeri
Tesisleri
Erzurum
tel - (0442) 2183464
fax - (0442) 2349690
Year of Formation - 1968
President - Cemal Polat
Coach - Sadi Tekelioglu; Necdet Gümüsenek;
Ruslan Abdullayev
Stadium - Cemal Gürsel (17,500)

APPEARANCES 99/00

	P	Ap	(s)	Gls
ABDÜLKADIR Saksak	M	11	(2)	
ALI Yilmaz	A	15	(11)	1
ALI RIZA Salci	D	14	(2)	
ALPARSLAN Tuce	M	19	(6)	2
ALTAY Can	M	15		1
ALTAY Dagdelen	G	10	(2)	
Serhiy BEZHENAR (UKR)	D	32		
BURAK Gök	M	3		
COSKUN Birdal	A	15		6
Sasa DELAIN (CON)	A	8	(7)	
ERGIN Yücetas	M	20	(2)	1
EYÜP Saka	D	8	(2)	
Adnan GUSO (BOS)	G	24		
KURSAT Karakas	M	22	(1)	
Alexander LÖBE (GER)	A	25	(1)	8
Enes MESANOVIC (BOS)	M	17	(11)	3
MUTLU Dervisoglu	A	9	(13)	5
MUZAFFER Bilazer	M	23	(9)	7
ÖMER Erdogan	D	31	(1)	2
SELÇUK Beyaz	M	12	(5)	2
SERKAN Güney	M	3	(2)	
SONER Neliker	M	14	(4)	
TANER Aykut	M		(2)	
ZAFER Demir	M	24	(6)	1

LEAGUE RESULTS 1999/2000

08/08/99	Denizlispor	H	0-1	
15/08/99	Vanspor	A	2-0	Altay Can, Mesanovic
12/09/99	Kocaelispor	H	3-3	Coskun 2, Mutlu
19/09/99	Altay	A	0-3	
26/09/99	Istanbulspor	H	0-0	
17/10/99	Gaziantepspor	A	0-6	
24/10/99	Trabzonspor	H	2-1	Alparslan, Coskun
30/10/99	Ankaragücü	A	0-1	
21/11/99	Adanaspor	H	4-1	Coskun (p), Löbe 2, Muzaffer
28/11/99	Galatasaray	A	1-4	Zafer
05/12/99	Antalyaspor	H	4-0	Muzaffer, Coskun 2, Löbe
12/12/99	Bursaspor	A	2-4	Löbe, Ergin
19/12/99	Göztepe	H	0-0	
25/12/99	Fenerbahçe	A	0-2	
08/01/00	Samsunspor	H	1-0	Mutlu
16/01/00	Gençlerbirligi	H	1-1	Mutlu
23/01/00	Besiktas	A	0-2	
30/01/00	Denizlispor	A	1-2	Mesanovic
06/02/00	Vanspor	H	2-0	Alparslan, Selçuk
12/02/00	Kocaelispor	A	0-4	
20/02/00	Altay	H	0-0	
27/02/00	Istanbulspor	A	1-1	Mesanovic
04/03/00	Gaziantepspor	H	1-1	Selçuk
10/03/00	Trabzonspor	A	0-2	
18/03/00	Ankaragücü	H	2-1	Muzaffer 2
25/03/00	Adanaspor	A	0-2	
01/04/00	Galatasaray	H	0-0	
09/04/00	Antalyaspor	A	2-1	Löbe, Ali
16/04/00	Bursaspor	H	4-1	Löbe, Ömer, Mutlu 2
23/04/00	Göztepe	A	4-1	og (Burhanettin), Ömer, Muzaffer, Löbe
30/04/00	Fenerbahçe	H	1-5	Muzaffer
07/05/00	Samsunspor	A	1-2	Löbe
12/05/00	Gençlerbirligi	A	0-5	
21/05/00	Besiktas	H	1-4	Muzaffer

FENERBAHÇE

CLUB DIRECTORY

Fenerbahçe Spor Kulübü
Dereagzi Tesisleri, Samandira-Istanbul
tel - (216) 3450940 / fax - (216) 3483060
Year of Formation - 1907
President - Aziz Yildirim
Coach - Ridvan Dilmen; Zdenek Zeman; Turhan
Sofuoglu (00/01 - Mustafa Denizli)
Stadium - Fenerbahçe Sükrü Saracoglu (30,000)

MAJOR HONOURS
League Championship - (13)
1959, 1961, 1964, 1965, 1968, 1970, 1974,
1975, 1978, 1983, 1985, 1989, 1996.
Domestic Cup - (4) 1968, 1974, 1979, 1983.

APPEARANCES 99/00

	P	Ap	(s)	Gls
ABDULLAH Ercan	M	29		1
ALPAY Özalan	D	29		3
AYGÜN Taskiran	A	1	(3)	
Elvir BOLIC (BOS)	A	16	(4)	11
Manuel DIMAS (POR)	M	1		
EFE Inanc	M		(2)	
ENGIN Ipekoglu	G	5	(2)	
ERKAN Sözeri	M	4	(7)	
FARUK Yigit	A	1	(1)	
GÖKHAN	A	1	(6)	1
GÜVENC Özkan	M		(6)	
Samuel JOHNSON (GHA)	M	23		4
KEMALETTIN Sentürk	M	10	(3)	
MEHMET Ayaz	M	1	(2)	
METIN Diyadin	M	19	(3)	
Viorel MOLDOVAN (ROM)	A	26		18
John MOSHOEU (SAF)	M	18	(3)	2
MURAT Sahin	G		(1)	
MUSTAFA Dogan (GER)	D	22		
OGÜN Temizkanoglu	D	27	(1)	2
ÖGUZ Daglaroglu	G	4		
OMER Karabacak	M	6		
Souleyman OULARE (GUI)	A	11		5
Yaw PREKO (GHA)	A	16	(6)	7
RÜSTÜ Reçber	G	25		
SAFFET Akbas	D	7	(3)	
SERGEN Yalçin	M	6	(3)	1
SERKAN Özsoy	D	17	(7)	1
TAYFUN Korkut	M	33		1
TUFAN Apayadin	M	4	(5)	
UCHE Okechukwu (NIG)	D	10	(1)	
Murat YAKIN (SUI)	M	2	(1)	

LEAGUE RESULTS 1999/2000

08/08/99	Vanspor	H	3-0	Alpay, Bolic 2
14/08/99	Kocaelispor	H	1-1	Sergen
12/09/99	Altay	H	3-1	Johnson 2, Serkan
19/09/99	Istanbulspor	A	4-1	Oulare, Moldovan, Preko 2
26/09/99	Gaziantepspor	H	0-0	
16/10/99	Trabzonspor	A	0-2	
24/10/99	Ankaragücü	H	1-1	Bolic
30/10/99	Adanaspor	A	3-1	Moldovan 3 (1p)
27/11/99	Antalyaspor	A	3-2	Preko 2, Bolic (p)
05/12/99	Bursaspor	H	2-2	Bolic, Moldovan
11/12/99	Göztepe	A	0-0	
17/12/99	Samsunspor	A	1-1	Bolic
22/12/99	Galatasaray	H	1-2	Moldovan
25/12/99	Erzurumspor	H	2-0	Bolic (p), Moldovan
08/01/00	Gençlerbirligi	A	2-2	Moldovan, Bolic (p)
16/01/00	Besiktas	H	2-1	Moldovan, Bolic
21/01/00	Denizlispor	A	1-1	Moldovan
28/01/00	Vanspor	A	2-1	Bolic (p), Ogün
05/02/00	Kocaelispor	A	1-1	Bolic
12/02/00	Altay	A	3-2	Abdullah, Preko, Ogün
19/02/00	Istanbulspor	H	1-0	Tayfun
27/02/00	Gaziantepspor	A	1-5	Moldovan (p)
04/03/00	Trabzonspor	H	2-1	Oulare, Moldovan
11/03/99	Ankaragücü	A	1-1	Moldovan
17/03/00	Adanaspor	H	2-4	Alpay, Johnson
26/03/00	Galatasaray	A	1-0	Johnson
01/04/00	Antalyaspor	H	1-0	Oulare
07/04/00	Bursaspor	A	1-2	Alpay
16/04/00	Göztepe	H	2-3	Moldovan 2
21/04/00	Samsunspor	H	1-0	Moldovan
30/04/00	Erzurumspor	A	5-1	Oulare 2, Moshoeu, og (Eyüp),
				og (Ali Riza)
05/05/00	Gençlerbirligi	H.	1-3	Moldovan
14/05/00	Besiktas	A	3-1	Preko 2, Moldovan
20/05/00	Denizlispor	H	2-1	Moshoeu, Gökhan

GALATASARAY

CLUB DIRECTORY

Galatasaray Spor Kulübü
Metin Oktay Tesisleri, Florya-Istanbul
tel - (212) 6630090
fax - (212) 5740424/2511212
Year of Formation - 1905
President - Faruk Süren
Coach - Fatih Terim (00/01 - Mircea Lucescu)
Stadium - Ali Sami Yen (40,000)

MAJOR HONOURS
League Championship - (14)
1962, 1963, 1969, 1971, 1972, 1973, 1987,
1988, 1993, 1994, 1997, 1998, 1999, 2000.
Domestic Cup - (13)
1963, 1964, 1965, 1966, 1973, 1976, 1982,
1985, 1991, 1993, 1996, 1999, 2000.
UEFA Cup - (1) 2000.

APPEARANCES 99/00

	P	Ap	(s)	Gls
AHMET Yildirim	M	10	(7)	2
ALPER Tezcan	M		(1)	
ARIF Erdem	A	16	(5)	7
BÜLENT Korkmaz	D	14	(8)	
Carlos CAPONE (BRA)	D	25		3
EMRAH Eren	M	1	(9)	
EMRE Belözoglu	M	24		5
ERGÜN Penbe	M	24	(4)	1
FATIH Akyel	D	11	(6)	
Gheorghe HAGI (ROM)	M	17	(2)	12
HAKAN Sükür	A	32		14
HAKAN Ünsal	M	12	(4)	1
HASAN Sas	A	15	(10)	3
KEREM Inan	G	1		
MÁRCIO dos Santos (BRA)	A	12	(12)	9
MEHMET Bolukbasi	G	3	(2)	
MEHMET Yozgatli	A	1	(8)	
OKAN Buruk	M	28		8
OSMAN Coskun	M	1		
Gheorghe POPESCU (ROM)	D	24		2
SAFFET Akyüz	A	2	(7)	
SERGEN Yalçin	M	12	(6)	4
SUAT Kaya	M	26	(2)	1
Cláudio TAFFAREL (BRA)	G	30		
TUGAY Kerimoglu	M	6	(4)	1
ÜMIT Davala	M	27	(1)	
VEDAT Inceefe	D		(1)	

LEAGUE RESULTS 1999/2000

06/08/99	Gaziantepspor	H	1-2	Hagi
15/08/99	Trabzonspor	A	2-1	Emre, Hagi
11/09/99	Ankaragücü	H	5-0	Hagi 2, Capone, Arif, Márcio
17/09/99	Adanaspor	A	4-3	Tugay, Hakan Sükür 2, Ahmet
24/09/99	Samsunspor	A	1-0	Hagi (p)
15/10/99	Antalyaspor	H	2-0	Arif, Capone
22/10/99	Bursaspor	A	0-0	
29/10/99	Göztepe	H	2-0	Popescu (p), Hakan Sükür
28/11/99	Erzurumspor	H	4-1	Okan 2, Emre, Hakan Sükür (p)
03/12/99	Gençlerbirligi	A	1-1	Hakan Sükür
12/12/99	Besiktas	H	1-0	Okan
18/12/99	Denizlispor	A	4-2	Okan, Márcio, Hasan, Emre
22/12/99	Fenerbahçe	A	2-1	Hasan, Márcio
26/12/99	Vanspor	H	2-1	Okan, Arif
09/01/00	Kocaelispor	A	2-1	Hagi, Okan
15/01/00	Altay	H	3-1	Hagi, Capone, Emre
23/01/00	Istanbulspor	A	0-0	
30/01/00	Gaziantepspor	A	1-0	Hakan Sükür
06/02/00	Trabzonspor	H	2-0	Okan, Hakan Sükür
13/02/00	Ankaragücü	A	2-0	Hagi, og (Yasin)
20/02/00	Adanaspor	H	4-0	Hakan Sükür 2, Popescu, Arif
25/02/00	Samsunspor	H	3-1	Hakan Sükür, Sergen, Suat
05/03/00	Antalyaspor	A	3-1	Hakan Sükür, Arif 2
12/03/00	Bursaspor	H	6-0	Márcio 2, Hakan Sükür (p), Sergen, Ergün, Ahmet
19/03/00	Göztepe	A	2-0	Sergen, Hagi
26/03/00	Fenerbahçe	H	0-1	
01/04/00	Erzurumspor	A	0-0	
09/04/00	Gençlerbirligi	H	6-0	og (Ümit Özat), Hasan, Arif, Emre, Hagi, Hakan Sükür
14/04/00	Besiktas	A	1-1	og (Halilagic)
23/04/00	Denizlispor	H	2-2	Hagi, Márcio
29/04/00	Vanspor	A	3-1	Hagi, Sergen, Márcio
07/05/00	Kocaelispor	H	5-0	Okan, Márcio 2, Hakan Sükür, Hakan Ünsal
12/05/00	Altay	A	0-1	
21/05/00	Istanbulspor	H	1-1	og (Recep)

GAZIANTEPSPOR

CLUB DIRECTORY

Gaziantepspor Kulübü
Subarcu Caddesi No: 2
Gaziantep
tel - (342) 2311259
fax - (342) 2308420
Year of Formation - 1969
President - Celal Dogan
Secretary - Naci Topcuoglu
Coach - Hüseyin Kalpar; Sakip Özberk
(00/01 - Erdogan Arica)
Stadium - Kamil Ocak (20,000)

APPEARANCES 99/00

	P	Ap	(s)	Gls
ALI IBRAHIM (GHA)	A	13		1
ALMIR Fraga (BRA)	A	5	(9)	2
BÜLENT Bal	D		(1)	
Saloiu DIALLO (GUI)	G	2		
ENGIN Hossoy	M	4	(5)	
ERHAN Albayrak	M	31		5
ERHAN Namli	M	25	(5)	1
EROL Kapusuz	A		(3)	
Robert ESHUN (GHA)	A	8	(4)	1
HAKAN Bayraktar	M	30		
HALIT Koprulu	M		(7)	
HASAN Gultang	G	2		
HASAN Ugur	A	8	(14)	
HASAN Yigit	M	33		1
IBRAHIM Üzülmez	M	31	(1)	2
ILYAS Kahraman	M	5	(8)	2
Desiré M'BONABUCYA (RWA)	A	20	(5)	9
MEHMET Polat	D	31		3
MERT Korkmaz	D	25		1
MURAT Salar	M		(6)	
MUSTAFA Özdenk	D	1		
MUSTAFA Sahintürk	A	12	(1)	3
MUTTALIP Kandemir	D		(1)	
NIYAZI Güney	A	2	(10)	
OKTAY Derelioglu	A	18	(2)	16
ÖMER Çatkiç	G	30		
RAMAZAN Tunc	D	29		2
Mohamed SYLLA (GUI)	D	9	(4)	

LEAGUE RESULTS 1999/2000

06/08/99	Galatasaray	A	2-1	M'Bonabucya 2
15/08/99	Antalyaspor	H	1-2	Ibrahim
12/09/99	Bursaspor	A	1-0	Ramazan
19/09/99	Göztepe	H	2-1	Ersun, Erhan Namli
26/09/99	Fenerbahçe	A	0-0	
17/10/99	Erzurumspor	H	6-0	Ramazan, M'Bonabucya 4, Mehmet
24/10/99	Gençlerbirligi	A	1-0	M'Bonabucya
31/10/99	Besiktas	H	0-0	
19/11/99	Denizlispor	A	0-1	
28/11/99	Vanspor	H	1-3	Oktay
05/12/99	Kocaelispor	H	1-0	Ali Ibrahim
12/12/99	Altay	H	1-0	Hasan Yigit
19/12/99	Istanbulspor	A	1-1	Mehmet
26/12/99	Samsunspor	H	5-2	Mehmet, Oktay 3 (1p), M'Bonabucya
09/01/00	Trabzonspor	A	0-0	
15/01/00	Ankaragücü	A	1-1	Oktay
22/01/00	Adanaspor	H	1-1	Mert
30/01/00	Galatasaray	H	0-1	
06/02/00	Antalyaspor	A	0-0	
12/02/00	Bursaspor	H	1-1	Oktay (p)
19/02/00	Gaziantepspor	A	1-0	Mustafa Sahintürk
27/02/00	Fenerbahçe	H	5-1	Oktay 4, Ibrahim
04/03/00	Erzurumspor	A	1-1	Oktay
11/03/00	Gençlerbirligi	H	2-1	Erhan Albayrak, Almir
18/03/00	Besiktas	A	0-1	
24/03/00	Denizlispor	H	0-0	
01/04/00	Vanspor	A	2-1	Mustafa Sahintürk, Erhan Albayrak
08/04/00	Kocaelispor	A	2-1	Mustafa Sahintürk, Erhan Albayrak
15/04/00	Altay	A	3-1	M'Bonabucya, Ilyas 2 (1p)
23/04/00	Istanbulspor	H	1-0	Oktay
30/04/00	Samsunspor	A	2-0	Oktay, Almir
06/05/00	Trabzonspor	H	3-0	Oktay 2 (1p), Erhan Albayrak
12/05/00	Ankaragücü	H	2-2	Oktay, Erhan Albayrak
20/05/00	Adanaspor	A	0-3	

GENÇLERBIRLIGI

CLUB DIRECTORY

Gençlerbirligi Spor Kulübü
Gazi Mustafa Kemal Bulvari 75/B
06570 Maltepe-Ankara
tel - (312) 2295852
fax - (312) 2212280
Year of Formation - 1923
President - Ilhan Cavcav
Coach - Karol Pecze; Samet Aybaba
Stadium - 19 Mayis (25,000)

MAJOR HONOURS
Domestic Cup - (1) 1987.

APPEARANCES 99/00

	P	Ap	(s)	Gls
Lahcen ABRAMI (MAR)	M	12		
AYKUT Karan	A		(1)	
BEYHAN Sumer	D	1	(6)	
FERDI Tatli	M	13	(7)	1
GÖKHAN	A		(2)	1
HAKAN Biçici	M	10	(4)	2
HAKAN Demir	M	23	(6)	2
HASAN Sönmez	G	20		
ILKER Dalçiçek	M	10	(12)	
ISMAIL Dogan	D	26	(1)	1
ISMAIL Gulduren	D	22	(2)	
André KONA (DRC)	A	18	(1)	12
Hamid MARAKSHI (ALG)	A	3	(1)	1
MEHMET Simsek	M	16	(4)	1
METIN Akçevre	G	13	(1)	2
Dumisa NGOBE (SAF)	M	6	(7)	
NIHAT Bastürk	M	26	(5)	4
ÖMER Topraktepe	D	3	(6)	
Alfred PHIRI (SAF)	M	31	(1)	5
Christian SCHANDALL (AUT)	A	2	(11)	2
Robert SEMENIK (SVK)	A	1	(2)	
SERDAR Samatyali	M		(4)	
Marcelo SOUZA (BRA)	M	12	(4)	1
TOLGA Dogantez	D	33		1
ÜMIT Karan	A	33		18
ÜMIT Özat	D	33		2
UTKU Yilmaz	M		(1)	
YALÇIN Demir	M		(2)	
Zlatko YANKOV (BUL)	M	6	(3)	
YÜKSEL Sariyar	M		(7)	
ZIYA Aydin	G	1		

LEAGUE RESULTS 1999/2000

07/08/99	Besiktas	H	1-0	Ümit Karan
15/08/99	Denizlispor	A	3-1	Ümit Karan 2, Metin (p)
12/09/99	Vanspor	H	1-1	Hakan Bicici
18/09/99	Kocaelispor	H	0-4	
26/09/99	Altay	H	0-0	
17/10/99	Istanbulspor	A	1-3	Marakshi
24/10/99	Gaziantepspor	H	0-1	
31/10/99	Trabzonspor	A	2-1	Metin (p), Phiri
21/11/99	Ankaragücü	H	1-2	Schandall
27/11/99	Adanaspor	A	2-1	Hakan Bicici, Ferdi
03/12/99	Galatasaray	H	1-1	Phiri
12/12/99	Antalyaspor	A	1-2	Ümit Karan
19/12/99	Bursaspor	H	1-0	Phiri
26/12/00	Göztepe	A	2-3	Schandall, Ümit Karan
08/01/00	Fenerbahçe	H	2-2	Kona, Ümit Karan
16/01/00	Erzurumspor	A	1-1	Ismail Dogan
23/01/00	Samsunspor	H	1-0	Hakan Demir
29/01/00	Besiktas	A	0-4	
05/02/00	Denizlispor	H	3-1	Ümit Karan 2, Kona
12/02/00	Vanspor	A	5-2	Ümit Karan 2, Kona, Nihat, og (Serkan Bensöl)
19/02/00	Kocaelispor	A	0-0	
27/02/00	Altay	A	2-0	Ümit Karan, Kona (p)
04/03/00	Istanbulspor	H	1-1	Kona
11/03/00	Gaziantepspor	A	1-2	Ümit Karan
19/03/00	Trabzonspor	H	0-1	
26/03/00	Ankaragücü	A	0-0	
01/04/00	Adanaspor	H	5-2	Ümit Karan, Ümit Özat, Mehmet, Phiri, Kona (p)
09/04/00	Galatasaray	A	0-6	
15/04/00	Antalyaspor	H	4-1	Phiri, Ümit Karan, Hakan Demir, Tolga
22/04/00	Bursaspor	A	5-2	Nihat 2, Ümit Karan 2, Kona
30/04/00	Göztepe	H	1-0	Kona (p)
05/05/00	Fenerbahçe	A	3-1	Ümit Özat, Ümit Karan, Kona
12/05/00	Erzurumspor	H	5-0	Nihat, Kona 2, Souza, Gökhan
19/05/00	Samsunspor	A	2-1	Kona, Ümit Karan

GÖZTEPE

Göztepe Kulübü
Ankara Asfalti Sirgeli Kavsagi No:3
Yeni Asir Gazetesi Bornova, Izmir
tel - (232) 4418814 / fax - (232) 2477370
Year of Formation - 1925
President - Aydin Bilgin
Coach - Jozef Jarabinsky; Celal Kibrizli; Ali Caglar
Stadium - Atatürk (80,000)

APPEARANCES 99/00

	P	Ap	(s)	Gls
ABDULLAH Col	D	4	(1)	
AKIN Dagdelen	G	1	(1)	
Emilio ALDAMA (PAR)	D	24	(1)	
ALI Köse	M	1	(1)	
ATILLA Sahin	M	23	(2)	1
BÜLENT Ataman	G	13		
BÜLENT Uçüncü	M	18	(8)	5
BÜLENT Uygun	A	5	(5)	
BÜNYAMIN	A		(4)	
BURAK Akdis	A	13	(8)	
BURAK Atasoy	M	4	(5)	1
BURHANETTIN Kaymak	D	28	(2)	
CEM	A	1	(5)	
EMRAH Ünsal	M		(1)	
EMRE Dogru	D	6	(2)	
Reda ERAYAHI (EGY)	M	6	(3)	
Eber FERNANDEZ (BRA)	A	3	(4)	
IBRAHIM Özer	A	1	(3)	
Richard KINGSTON (GHA)	G	19		
KUBILAY Toptas	M	2	(3)	
KURAL Altintas	D	2	(2)	
KURTHAN Yilmaz	A	24	(3)	6
Zdrahal LUDEK (CZE)	A	8		1
MEHMET Önür	M	12	(3)	
MUAMMER Sürmeli	D	13		
Pollen NDLANYA (SAF)	A	3	(1)	1
OLGAY	D	4		
REMZI Acet	M	31	(2)	6
ROGÉRIO de Mello (BRA)	M	1	(3)	
SALIH Akkaya	M	15	(5)	2
SERTAN Gürüz	M	24	(3)	
SEVKET Dürül	D	21		1
TANER Savut	M	13	(6)	
TARIK Akin	M	16	(8)	1
TAYFUN Yungul	M	12		
TUNAY	M	2		
ÜMIT Özisik	G	1		
VURAL	M		(1)	

LEAGUE RESULTS 1999/2000

08/08/99	Kocaelispor	H	0-0	
13/08/99	Altay	A	0-0	
12/09/99	Istanbulspor	H	2-0	Remzi, Ndlanya
19/09/99	Gaziantepspor	A	1-2	Salih
26/09/99	Trabzonspor	H	1-1	Kurthan (p)
16/10/99	Ankaragücü	A	2-1	Kurthan, Remzi
24/10/99	Adanaspor	H	0-1	
29/10/99	Galatasaray	A	0-2	
20/11/99	Antalyaspor	H	1-2	Remzi
28/11/99	Bursaspor	A	2-1	Remzi, Kurthan
05/12/99	Samsunspor	A	0-4	
11/12/99	Fenerbahçe	H	0-0	
19/12/99	Erzurumspor	A	0-0	
26/12/99	Gençlerbirligi	H	3-2	Salih, Ludek, Tarik
07/01/00	Besiktas	A	1-2	Attila
16/01/00	Denizlispor	H	2-4	Remzi, Sevket
29/01/00	Kocaelispor	A	0-2	
02/02/00	Vanspor	A	0-1	
06/02/00	Altay	H	0-1	
13/02/00	Istanbulspor	A	0-3	
19/02/00	Gaziantepspor	H	0-1	
26/02/00	Trabzonspor	A	0-2	
05/03/00	Ankaragücü	H	2-0	Kurthan 2
12/03/00	Adanaspor	A	0-2	
19/03/00	Galatasaray	H	0-2	
26/03/00	Antalyaspor	A	0-1	
01/04/00	Bursaspor	H	0-1	
08/04/00	Samsunspor	H	1-2	Kurthan (p)
16/04/00	Fenerbahçe	A	3-2	Remzi, Burak Atasoy, Bülent Uçüncü
23/04/00	Erzurumspor	H	1-4	Bülent Uçüncü
30/04/00	Gençlerbirligi	A	0-1	
06/05/00	Besiktas	H	2-4	og (Rahim), Bülent Uçüncü
13/05/00	Denizlispor	A	0-2	
20/05/00	Vanspor	H	2-1	Bülent Uçüncü 2

ISTANBULSPOR

CLUB DIRECTORY

Istanbulspor Kulübü
Basin Ekspres Yolu Star Sokak No: 2
Ikitelli-Istanbul
tel - (212) 6979840
fax - (212) 6979840
Year of Formation - 1926
President - Tayfun Gündogar
Coach -Ziya Dogan; Aykut Kocaman
Stadium - Bayrampasa (15,000)

APPEARANCES 99/00

	P	Ap	(s)	Gls
AHMET Arslanagiz	M		(2)	
ATILLA Günes	A	1	(4)	
AYDIN Kaldirim	M	1	(3)	
AYKUT Kocaman	A	5	(14)	5
BRUNO Quadros (BRA)	M	4	(5)	
BÜLENT Duman	M	6	(5)	
Enes DEMIROVIC (BOS)	M	17	(4)	
EMRE Asik	D	26		6
ENGIN Özdemir	M	4	(1)	1
FUAT Buruk	M	29	(1)	
GÖKHAN Keskin	D	6	(1)	
GÖKHAN Sakar	M		(2)	
GÜVEN Kocabal	M	9	(7)	
HAKAN Dursun	D	2	(4)	
Sead HALILAGIC (BOS)	D	8		
HALUK Güngör	G	34		
ILKAN Aksöy	M	18	(2)	1
MEHMET Ogut	A	2		
MITHAT Yavas	A	28	(3)	6
MURAT Erdogan	M	12	(8)	1
NIYAZI Hüseyinoglu	D	13	(5)	
Ivailo PETKOV (BUL)	M	31		
RECEP Çetin	D	16	(1)	
Alioum SAIDOU (MAR)	M	16	(7)	1
Jonah SAWIEH (LIB)	A	10	(5)	3
SERTAN Eser	A	26	(1)	9
TIMUR Yanyali	D	18	(3)	
VEDAT Inceefe	D	10		
ZEKI Önatli	D	22	(2)	

LEAGUE RESULTS 1999/2000

08/08/99	Antalyaspor	A	3-0	(w/o; original result 0-1)
14/08/99	Bursaspor	H	1-0	Aykut (p)
12/09/99	Göztepe	A	0-2	
19/09/99	Fenerbahçe	H	1-4	Engin
26/09/99	Erzurumspor	A	0-0	
17/10/99	Gençlerbligi	H	3-1	Sertan 2, Mithat
23/10/99	Besiktas	A	0-3	
31/10/99	Denizlispor	H	1-1	Sertan
21/11/99	Vanspor	A	1-1	Mithat
28/11/99	Kocaelispor	H	4-1	Sertan, Sawieh, og (Stark), Mithat (p)
05/12/99	Altay	A	0-0	
11/12/99	Samsunspor	H	0-1	
19/12/99	Gaziantepspor	H	1-1	Sertan
26/12/99	Trabzonspor	A	1-1	Ilkan
09/01/00	Ankaragücü	H	2-6	Mithat, Emre
16/01/00	Adanaspor	A	1-2	Aykut
23/01/00	Galatasaray	H	0-0	
29/01/00	Antalyaspor	H	0-0	
05/02/00	Bursaspor	A	0-1	
13/02/00	Göztepe	H	3-0	Emre, Sawieh 2
19/02/00	Fenerbahçe	A	0-1	
27/02/00	Erzurumspor	H	1-1	Sertan
04/03/00	Gençlerbligi	A	1-1	Saidou
12/03/00	Besiktas	H	0-2	
19/03/00	Denizlispor	A	1-3	og (El Saka)
25/03/00	Vanspor	H	0-0	
02/04/00	Kocaelispor	A	1-2	Sertan
08/04/00	Altay	H	1-0	Sertan
16/04/00	Samsunspor	A	0-1	
23/04/00	Gaziantepspor	A	0-1	
29/04/00	Trabzonspor	H	5-1	Sertan, Emre, Aykut 3
07/05/00	Ankaragücü	A	2-2	Mithat, Murat
12/05/00	Adanaspor	H	3-2	Emre 3
21/05/00	Galatasaray	A	1-1	Mithat

KOCAELISPOR

CLUB DIRECTORY

Kocaelispor Kulübü
Ankara Caddesi 396
Dostluk Ishani No: 53 Kat: 7
Izmit
tel - (262) 3215969
fax - (262) 3246467
Year of Formation - 1966
President - Sefa Sirmen
Coach - Güvenç Kurtar
Stadium - Ismetpasa (20,000)

MAJOR HONOURS
Domestic Cup - (1) 1997.

APPEARANCES 99/00

	P	Ap	(s)	Gls
Medhat ABDEL HADY (EGY)	D	9	(3)	
AHMET Arslaner	D	17	(1)	
ALI Mumcu	A		(11)	
BÜLENT Taner	A	3	(4)	
CEM SINAN Vergul	M	19	(3)	1
CENKER Dirlik	A	4	(7)	2
CIHAN Haspolatli	M	14	(15)	
Roman DABROWSKI (POL)	A	30	(1)	13
ENGIN Öztonga	M	22	(6)	1
ERGIN Altay	G	1		
EVREN Turhan	M		(1)	
HALIL IBRAHIM Kara	M	12	(5)	
Ahmed HASSAN (EGY)	M	20		3
ILKER Yagcioglu	M	14	(2)	1
Vyacheslav KAMOLTSEV (RUS)	A	11	(2)	3
MERT Korkmaz	D	6		
METIN Mert	G	9	(1)	
Misko MIRKOVIC (YUG)	D	34		3
MURAT Çolak	M		(1)	
MURAT Sahim	D	1		
Samir MURATOVIC (BOS)	A	3	(2)	
NURI Çolak	M	24	(2)	1
ORHAN Ak	D	18	(3)	
ORHAN Kaynak	A	10	(5)	3
OSMAN Çakir	D	10	(7)	
SABAN Serin	D		(1)	
Jonah SAWIEH (LIB)	A	5		1
SERDAR Topraktepe	M	27	(2)	9
SONER Boz	M	12	(9)	1
Péter STARK (HUN)	D	2		
Dumitriu STINGACIU (ROM)	G	24		
TARIK Dasgun	M	6	(1)	
ZEKI Önatli	D	7		

LEAGUE RESULTS 1999/2000

08/08/99	Göztepe	A	0-0	
14/08/99	Fenerbahçe	A	1-1	Dabrowski (p)
12/09/99	Erzurumspor	A	3-3	Sawieh, Ilker, Orhan Kaynak
18/09/99	Gençlerbirligi	A	4-0	Serdar, Orhan Kaynak,
				Dabrowski 2 (1p)
25/09/99	Besiktas	A	0-1	
17/10/99	Denizlispor	A	1-3	Dabrowski
24/10/99	Vanspor	A	0-5	
31/10/99	Samsunspor	A	1-5	Cenker
21/11/99	Altay	A	1-0	Orhan Kaynak
28/11/99	Istanbulspor	A	1-4	Dabrowski (p)
05/12/99	Gaziantepspor	A	0-1	
12/12/99	Trabzonspor	A	0-1	
18/12/99	Ankaragücü	A	2-3	Cenker, Soner
25/12/99	Adanaspor	A	0-3	
09/01/00	Galatasaray	H	1-2	Dabrowski
15/01/00	Antalyaspor	A	0-3	
23/01/00	Bursaspor	H	3-2	Serdar 2, Dabrowski
29/01/00	Göztepe	H	2-0	Kamoltsev, Dabrowski
05/02/00	Fenerbahçe	H	1-1	Cem Sinan
12/02/00	Erzurumspor	H	4-0	Kamoltsev, Serdar, Mirkovic,
				Dabrowski
19/02/00	Gençlerbirligi	H	0-0	
26/02/00	Besiktas	H	1-2	Kamoltsev
04/03/00	Denizlispor	H	1-0	Hassan (p)
11/03/00	Vanspor	H	6-1	Serdar 2, Mirkovic, Dabrowski 2, Nuri
18/03/00	Samsunspor	H	0-4	
26/03/00	Altay	H	2-1	Serdar, og (Kenan)
02/04/00	Istanbulspor	H	2-1	Engin Öztonga, Serdar
08/04/00	Gaziantepspor	H	1-2	Hassan (p)
15/04/00	Trabzonspor	H	1-0	og (Nikolovski)
23/04/00	Ankaragücü	H	4-1	Mirkovic, Dabrowski 2 (1p), Serdar
29/04/00	Adanaspor	H	0-0	
07/05/00	Galatasaray	A	0-5	
12/05/00	Antalyaspor	H	1-1	Hassan (p)
21/05/00	Bursaspor	A	0-2	

SAMSUNSPOR

CLUB DIRECTORY

Samsunspor Kulübü
Nuri Asan Tesisleri
Garajlar Karsisi
Samsun
tel - (362) 2383696
fax - (362) 2383788
Year of Formation - 1965
President - Ismail Uyanik
Coach - Erdogan Arica (00/01 - Bülent Ünder)
Stadium - 19 Mayis (20,000)

APPEARANCES 99/00

	P	Ap	(s)	Gls
ADNAN Güngör	M	5	(9)	
ALI Akdeniz	M	30		
AZAD Akin	M		(1)	
Alioum BOUKAR (CMR)	G	6		
CELIL Sagir	M	6	(2)	
Sergiu EPUREANU (MOL)	M	23	(1)	2
ERCAN Kologlu	D	27		1
ERMAN Güracar	D	32		1
FURKAN	M	1	(2)	
GÖKSEL Gencer	G	28		
GÜNGÖR Öztürk	D	23	(7)	1
HAKKI Hocaoglu	M		(12)	
ILHAN Mansiz	A	28	(3)	10
IMDAT Arslan	D	33	(1)	
ISMET Tasdemir	M	20	(11)	3
Giorgi KIKNADZE (GEO)	M		(1)	
KÜRSAT Demir	G		(1)	
LEVENT Yilmaz	M	1	(4)	
MEHMET Nas	M	32		
MURAT Ismailoglu	M	2	(14)	1
SERKAN Aykut	A	33		30
TÜMER Metin	M	21	(2)	2
UGUR Dagdelen	A	1	(6)	
VURAL Korkmaz	M	22	(8)	

LEAGUE RESULTS 1999/2000

Date	Opponent	H/A	Score	Scorers
07/08/99	Ankaragücü	H	2-0	Serkan 2 (1p)
15/08/99	Besiktas	A	0-4	
12/09/99	Adanaspor	H	2-1	Serkan, Tümer
19/09/99	Denizlispor	A	1-4	Ilhan
24/09/99	Galatasaray	H	0-1	
17/10/99	Vanspor	A	0-0	
24/10/99	Antalyaspor	H	0-1	
31/10/99	Kocaelispor	H	5-1	Serkan 3, Ilhan, Ismet
21/11/99	Bursaspor	H	1-0	Serkan
28/11/99	Altay	A	1-2	Serkan
05/12/99	Göztepe	H	4-0	Epureanu, Serkan (p), Erman, Murat
11/12/99	Istanbulspor	A	1-0	Serkan
17/12/99	Fenerbahçe	H	1-1	Serkan
26/12/99	Gaziantepspor	A	2-5	Serkan 2
08/01/00	Erzurumspor	A	0-1	
14/01/00	Trabzonspor	H	0-0	
23/01/00	Gençlerbirligi	A	0-1	
29/01/00	Ankaragücü	A	2-1	Serkan, Tümer
04/02/00	Besiktas	H	0-2	
12/02/00	Adanaspor	A	1-0	Ilhan
19/02/00	Denizlispor	H	6-2	Ercan, Ilhan 2, Epureanu, Serkan 2 (1p)
25/02/00	Galatasaray	A	1-3	Ismet
05/03/00	Vanspor	H	5-1	Serkan 4, Ilhan
12/03/00	Antalyaspor	A	1-0	Serkan
18/03/00	Kocaelispor	A	4-0	Serkan 3, Ilhan
25/03/00	Bursaspor	A	2-2	Ismet, Serkan
02/04/00	Altay	H	1-0	Serkan (p)
08/04/00	Göztepe	A	2-1	Serkan, Ilhan
16/04/00	Istanbulspor	H	1-0	Serkan (p)
21/04/00	Fenerbahçe	A	0-1	
30/04/00	Gaziantepspor	H	0-2	
07/05/00	Erzurumspor	H	2-1	Ilhan, Serkan
13/05/00	Trabzonspor	A	2-3	Güngör, Ilhan
19/05/00	Gençlerbirligi	H	1-2	Serkan

TRABZONSPOR

CLUB DIRECTORY

Trabzonspor Kulübü
Mehmet Ali Yilmaz Tesisleri, Trabzon
tel - (462) 3266796 / fax - (462) 3265767
Year of Formation - 1967
President - Mehmet Ali Yilmaz
Coach - Ahmet Suat Özyazici; Giray Bulak
Stadium - Avni Aker (30,000)

MAJOR HONOURS
League Championship - (6)
1976, 1977, 1979, 1980, 1981, 1984.
Domestic Cup - (5)
1977, 1978, 1984, 1992, 1995.

APPEARANCES 99/00

	P	Ap	(s)	Gls
ABDÜLKADIR Demirci	M	22	(2)	9
BÜLENT Uygun	M		(2)	
CEM Beceren	D	3	(1)	
ERMAN Özgur	M	23	(7)	3
EROL Bülüt	M	21	(1)	
FATIH Tekke	A	16	(5)	2
GÖKDENIZ Karadeniz	M	6	(4)	
HAMI Mandirali	A	24	(5)	13
HUSEYIN Cimsir	M	8	(6)	
MACIT Güven	D	7	(5)	
MEHMET Ipek	M	7	(7)	
METIN Aktas	G	24		
Petar MILOSEVSKI (MAC)	G	10	(1)	
MURAT Bolukbas	A	2	(7)	2
NESIM Özgür	M	22		1
Igor Sasa NIKOLOVSKI (MAC)	D	18		
OKAN Çebi	M	3		
OKAN Özke	D	18		
OLIVEIRA da Costa (BRA)	A	8	(3)	1
ORHAN Çikrikçi	M	25	(4)	2
OSMAN Özköylü	D	26		4
SELAHATTIN Özbir	A	5	(13)	1
SELIM Özer	D	18	(6)	
TAMER Tuna	M	26		3
TANSEL Baser (AUS)	D	1	(2)	
Emmanuel TETTEH (GHA)	A	3		
Davor VUGRINEC (CRO)	A	23	(4)	5
YUSUF TOKAC	M	5	(3)	

LEAGUE RESULTS 1999/2000

08/08/99	Adanaspor	A	2-1	Erman 2
15/08/99	Galatasaray	H	1-2	Hami (p)
10/09/99	Antalyaspor	A	2-0	Vugrinec, Hami
18/09/99	Bursaspor	H	2-0	Oliveira, Hami (p)
26/09/99	Göztepe	A	1-1	Vugrinec
16/10/99	Fenerbahçe	H	2-0	Osman, Vugrinec
24/10/99	Erzurumspor	A	1-2	Vugrinec
31/10/99	Gençlerbirligi	H	1-2	Hami
21/11/99	Besiktas	A	1-1	Selahattin
28/11/99	Denizlispor	H	1-1	Hami (p)
05/12/99	Vanspor	A	2-2	Orhan, Murat
12/12/99	Kocaelispor	H	1-0	Hami
19/12/99	Altay	A	1-3	Abdülkadir
26/12/99	Istanbulspor	H	1-1	Abdülkadir
09/01/00	Gazlantepspor	H	0-0	
14/01/00	Samsunspor	A	0-0	
23/01/00	Ankaragücü	H	3-1	Taner, Nesim, Abdülkadir
28/01/00	Adanaspor	H	0-1	
06/02/00	Galatasaray	A	0-2	
12/02/00	Antalyaspor	H	2-0	Fatih, Hami
20/02/00	Bursaspor	A	3-2	Hami 2 (1p), Osman
26/02/00	Göztepe	H	2-0	Hami, Orhan
04/03/00	Fenerbahçe	A	1-2	Osman
10/03/00	Erzurumspor	H	2-0	Erman, Tamer
19/03/00	Gençlerbirligi	A	1-0	Abdülkadir
25/03/00	Besiktas	H	1-2	Abdülkadir
31/03/00	Denizlispor	A	2-0	Hami, Abdülkadir
09/04/00	Vanspor	H	4-2	Fatih, Abdülkadir 2, Hami
15/04/00	Kocaelispor	A	0-1	
22/04/00	Altay	H	2-1	og (Serkan Karababa), Osman
29/04/00	Istanbulspor	A	1-5	Murat
06/05/00	Gaziantepspor	A	0-3	
13/05/00	Samsunspor	H	3-2	Tamer, Vugrinec, Abdülkadir
21/05/00	Ankaragücü	A	1-1	Hami

VANSPOR

CLUB DIRECTORY

Vanspor Kulübü
Iskele Caddesi, Çevik Kuvvet Arkasi, Van
tel - (432) 2231474 / fax - (432) 2233495
Year of Formation - 1974
President - Feridun Irak
Coach - Samet Aybaba; Nevzat Sipal; Ilyas Tüfeçki;
Murat Simsek
Stadium - Vali Mahmut Yilbas (10,000)

APPEARANCES 99/00

	P	Ap	(s)	Gls
AHMET	M	9		1
ALI Ravci	A	10	(11)	
AMIR Alibaz	M		(2)	
ATILLA Metin	D		(2)	
BIROL	D	13		
BÜLENT Yenihayat	D	10	(2)	1
CEM Kosanoglu	M	17	(7)	1
Fernand COULIBALY (MLI)	A	14	(5)	9
ERBAY Bertiz	D	3	(1)	
ERCÜMENT Sahin	A	6	(5)	3
ERSOY Öz	D	3	(2)	1
FARUK Akilli	G	4		
FELIX (CMR)	D	1		
FURKAN Sükürcü	D	11		
HAKAN Caliskan	G	21		
ISMAIL	A	10	(1)	
KUBILAY Toptas	A	5		1
MEHMET Deliorman	M	16	(14)	3
MEHMET Kaplan	A		(1)	
MEVLÜT Can	M	25	(3)	2
MUAMMER	D	8		1
MURAT Deniz	A	4	(2)	
MURAT Duman	D	5	(4)	
MURAT Yigiter	G	9	(1)	
MUSA Ulutas	M		(1)	
MUSTAFA Bayat	M	22	(4)	
MUTLU Sezer	M	25	(2)	4
OKAN Çebi	M	3	(2)	
OLIVEIRA da Costa (BRA)	A	2		
ÖZGÜR Kaymaz	M	9	(3)	1
SERKAN Bensöl	M	25	(1)	
SERKAN Turhan	A	10	(2)	3
SEYIT CEM	A	3	(4)	4
Mohammed SYLLA (SRL)	D	22	(2)	2
Emmanuel TETTEH (GHA)	A	1		
TANSEL Baser (AUS)	D	3	(1)	
TARIK	D	3		
TURAN Bilge	M	19	(4)	
YAHYA Ünal	M	17	(3)	1
Zlatko YANKOV (BUL)	M	6		

LEAGUE RESULTS 1999/2000

08/08/99	Fenerbahçe	A	0-3	
15/08/99	Erzurumspor	H	0-2	
12/09/99	Gençlerbirligi	A	1-1	Mevlüt
19/09/99	Besiktas	H	0-6	
26/09/99	Denizlispor	A	0-1	
17/10/99	Samsunspor	H	0-0	
24/10/99	Kocaelispor	H	5-0	Mehmet Deliorman, Sylla, Coulibaly 2, Özgür
31/10/99	Altay	A	0-2	
21/11/99	Istanbulspor	H	1-1	Coulibaly
28/11/99	Gaziantepspor	A	3-1	Coulibaly 2 (1p), Ahmet
05/12/99	Trabzonspor	H	2-2	Sylla, Ercüment
12/12/99	Ankaragücü	A	0-1	
19/12/99	Adanaspor	H	0-2	
26/12/99	Galatasaray	A	1-2	Kubilay
09/01/00	Antalyaspor	H	2-4	Ercüment 2
15/01/00	Bursaspor	A	2-3	Mehmet Deliorman, Cem
28/01/00	Fenerbahçe	H	1-2	Muammer
02/02/00	Göztepe	H	1-0	Mutlu (p)
06/02/00	Erzurumspor	A	0-2	
12/02/00	Gençlerbirligi	H	2-5	Mutlu (p), Yahya
18/02/00	Besiktas	A	1-2	Mutlu
27/02/00	Denizlispor	H	2-3	Coulibaly, Mutlu (p)
05/03/00	Samsunspor	A	1-5	Serkan Turhan
11/03/00	Kocaelispor	A	1-6	Serkan Turhan
19/03/00	Altay	H	1-1	Bülent
25/03/00	Istanbulspor	A	0-0	
01/04/00	Gaziantepspor	H	1-2	Seyit Cem
09/04/00	Trabzonspor	A	2-4	Seyit Cem 2
16/04/00	Ankaragücü	H	2-3	Serkan Turhan, Seyit Cem
22/04/00	Adanaspor	A	0-2	
29/04/00	Galatasaray	H	1-3	Coulibaly
07/05/00	Antalyaspor	A	1-4	Mevlüt (p)
12/05/00	Bursaspor	H	3-1	Coulibaly 2, Ersoy
20/05/00	Göztepe	A	1-2	Mehmet Deliorman

UKRAINE

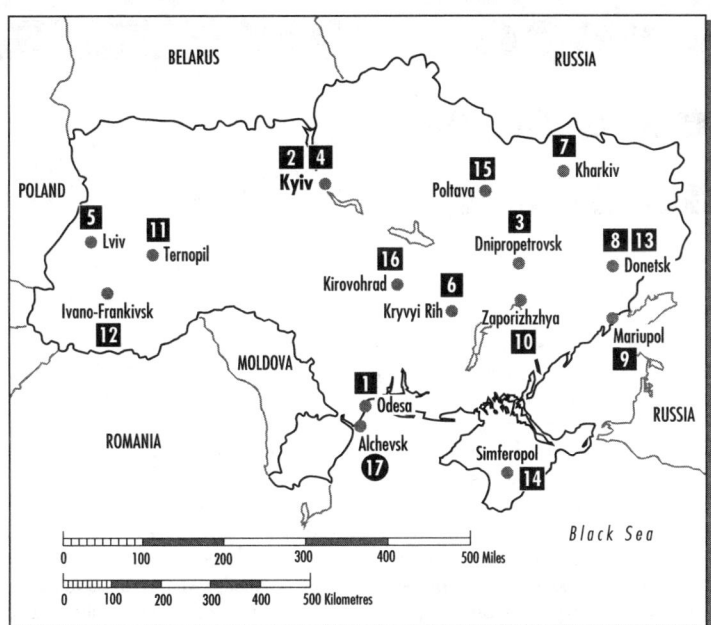

1	**CHORNOMORETS ODESA**	1042
2	**CSCA KYIV**	1043
3	**DNIPRO DNIPROPETROVSK**	1044
4	**DYNAMO KYIV**	1045
5	**KARPATY LVIV**	1046
6	**KRYVBAS KRYVYI RIH**	1047
7	**METALIST KHARKIV**	1048
8	**METALURG DONETSK**	1049
9	**METALURG MARIUPOL**	1050
10	**METALURG ZAPORIZHZHYA**	1051
11	**NYVA TERNOPIL**	1052
12	**PRYKARPATTYA IVANO-FRANKIVSK**	1053
13	**SHAKHTAR DONETSK**	1054
14	**TAVRIYA SIMFEROPOL**	1055
15	**VORSKLA POLTAVA**	1056
16	**ZIRKA KIROVOHRAD**	1057
	Promoted club	
17	**STAL ALCHEVSK**	

HIGH AND MIGHTY DYNAMO RULE AGAIN

Euro 2000 hopes buried in the snow

FEDERATION DIRECTORY

Football Federation of Ukraine
vul. Ulyanovykh 1, 02023 Kyiv

tel - (044) 2528474/2528457/   Year of Formation - 1991
2528700/2528935   President - Hryhoriy Surkis
fax - (044) 2528404/2529493   Secretary - Anatoliy Popov
website - www.ffu.org.ua

Stadium - National Sport Komplex Olimpiyskyi , Kyiv (83,160)

A traumatic tale of the unexpected ended Ukraine's bid to participate in the finals of a major international tournament for the first time. When they were drawn against Slovenia in the Euro 2000 play-offs, the odds seemed heavily stacked in Ukraine's favour. But Jozsef Szabo and his players clearly underestimated what their opponents had to offer and were beaten fair and square over the two legs.

It was a crying shame, of course, that the European Championship finals were played without the presence of Andriy Shevchenko, arguably the most dangerous striker in world football. It was his late free-kick in Moscow - aided and abetted by the Russian goalkeeper - which had enabled Ukraine to qualify for the play-offs at the expense of their geographical rivals. And when he found the target again with a brilliant left-foot shot to put his team 1-0 up against Slovenia in Ljubljana, Ukraine looked poised for a place in the finals. But then over-caution set in, and in a nightmare second half Slovenia scored twice and Ukraine had two players sent off.

The second leg, in Kiev, was played in farcical conditions, with snow and mud making proper football virtually impossible. Yet a stroke of good fortune saw Ukraine take the lead from a Serhiy Rebrov penalty. Again, Szabo's men were in the driving seat, but once more they allowed their grip to slip and Slovenia came back to equalise with the decisive goal of the tie.

The recriminations began the second after the final whistle and lasted for weeks on end thereafter. It was the second tournament in a row in which the Ukrainians had been eliminated in a play-off, and the nationwide depression was tinged with considerable anger and resentment. Coach Szabo decided to jump before he was pushed, which opened the door for one of two great

LEAGUE CHAMPIONSHIP RESULTS 99/00

		1	2	3	4	5	6	7	8	9	10	11	12	13	14	15	16
1	Chornomorets Odesa		2-0	+++	2-2	0-0	2-0	0-1	0-1	3-4	1-0	1-0	0-0	0-3	1-2	1-1	1-0
2	CSCA Kyiv	3-0		3-0	0-3	2-3	1-2	0-1	1-0	1-1	1-0	0-0	2-1	1-0	3-0	1-1	3-0
3	Dnipro Dnipropetrovsk	1-1	2-1		0-2	1-1	1-0	1-0	0-1	1-0	0-2	1-1	1-1	1-2	1-0	2-1	2-0
4	Dynamo Kyiv	4-1	3-1	4-0		3-0	2-1	2-1	1-0	6-1	2-0	4-1	6-0	2-1	2-0	3-0	3-0
5	Karpaty Lviv	5-0	1-0	4-0	2-3		1-0	1-1	1-1	3-1	1-0	0-1	0-1	1-0	0-1	3-1	3-0
6	Kryvbas Kryvyi Rih	2-0	2-1	2-2	1-1	2-1		2-0	0-0	2-1	1-0	5-1	3-0	1-0	2-1	4-0	3-1
7	Metalist Kharkiv	1-1	2-0	2-1	0-5	1-0	1-1		2-1	2-0	0-0	5-2	2-0	0-1	2-1	2-1	4-0
8	Metalurg Donetsk	4-0	0-0	5-1	0-4	2-1	0-0	1-1		2-1	2-1	3-2	4-1	2-3	0-0	2-3	2-0
9	Metalurg Mariupol	5-0	2-1	3-2	2-3	1-0	0-2	3-1	4-1		1-1	2-1	2-0	1-2	4-1	2-1	3-0
10	Metalurg Zaporizhzhya	2-0	2-2	6-1	0-3	3-1	1-2	1-1	1-1	2-1		4-0	2-2	1-0	3-2	3-1	2-0
11	Nyva Ternopil	3-1	2-2	1-1	0-1	1-2	3-3	2-1	3-0	2-1	0-3		3-1	1-1	1-1	1-1	3-0
12	Prykarpattya Ivano-Frankivsk	1-0	0-0	1-1	1-2	3-1	1-3	2-1	1-1	3-0	1-0	2-1		0-2	0-2	0-1	4-2
13	Shakhtar Donetsk	0-1	3-0	2-0	0-0	4-0	3-1	3-1	2-0	3-0	4-0	5-0	1-0		2-0	0-0	1-0
14	Tavriya Simferopol	1-1	1-2	1-1	1-3	4-1	2-4	2-2	1-1	1-0	1-2	1-1	1-0	0-3		0-3	2-0
15	Vorskla Poltava	4-0	2-0	4-0	1-2	1-0	3-0	3-1	0-0	1-1	3-0	4-2	2-0	0-3	4-0		1-1
16	Zirka Kirovohrad	0-0	0-0	1-1	1-4	0-2	0-3	2-2	0-2	1-2	1-1	1-1	1-1	1-1	2-6	2-2	

N.B. +++ - match void; awarded as away win.

LEAGUE CHAMPIONSHIP FINAL TABLE 99/00

			Home					Away					Total					
		Pd	W	D	L	F	A	W	D	L	F	A	W	D	L	F	A	PT	GD
1	Dynamo Kyiv	30	15	0	0	47	7	12	3	0	38	11	27	3	0	85	18	84	67
2	Shakhtar Donetsk	30	12	2	1	33	3	9	1	5	27	13	21	3	6	60	16	66	44
3	Kryvbas Kryvyi Rih	30	12	3	0	32	9	6	3	6	22	21	18	6	6	54	30	60	24
4	Vorskla Poltava	30	10	3	2	33	10	4	4	7	17	24	14	7	9	50	34	49	16
5	Metalist Kharkiv	30	10	3	2	26	14	2	5	8	15	25	12	8	10	41	39	44	2
6	Metalurg Zaporizhzhya	30	9	4	2	33	17	3	4	8	10	18	12	8	10	43	35	44	8
7	Metalurg Donetsk	30	8	4	3	29	18	3	6	6	10	17	11	10	9	39	35	43	4
8	Metalurg Mariupol	30	11	1	3	35	15	2	2	11	14	33	13	3	14	49	48	42	1
9	Karpaty Lviv	30	9	2	4	26	10	3	2	10	13	28	12	4	14	39	38	40	1
10	CSCA Kyiv	30	8	3	4	22	12	1	5	9	9	24	9	8	13	31	36	35	-5
11	Dnipro Dnipropetrovsk	30	7	4	4	15	13	1	5	9	11	39	8	9	13	26	52	33	-26
12	Nyva Ternopil	30	6	6	3	26	19	1	4	10	14	38	7	10	13	40	57	31	-17
13	Tavriya Simferopol	30	4	5	6	19	24	3	3	9	13	27	7	8	15	32	51	29	-19
14	Prykarpattya Ivano-Frankivsk	30	6	4	5	19	17	1	4	10	8	30	7	8	15	27	47	29	-20
15	Chornomorets Odesa	30	5	4	6	14	14	1	4	10	6	36	6	8	16	20	50	26	-30
16	Zirka Kirovohrad	30	0	8	7	12	29	0	1	14	4	37	0	9	21	16	66	9	-50

N.B. Where two or more teams are level on points, classification is determined by the results of the matches between them.

Ukrainian footballing icons to take over. Oleh Blokhin, the former European Footballer of the Year, and Valeriy Lobanovskyi, the Dynamo Kiev supremo and ex-USSR national coach, were both touted as likely successors, but it was the latter who had the more impressive CV, and although he was suffering from ill health, Lobanovskyi eventually persuaded to sign a two-year contract which would take him through to the end of the 2002 World Cup qualifying campaign.

Lobanovskyi was in no rush to make the commitment. He knew he was a wanted man, so, before signing, he ensured that certain conditions were met with regard to his plans for the further development of Ukrainian football. Lobanovskyi had two matches during the spring in which to get his team ready for World Cup combat but he was unable to attend the second of them, against England at Wembley,

after being deemed too ill to travel. It could be that his appointed assistants, Leonid Buryak and Vladimir Veremeyev, will play an important role in team affairs during the World Cup qualifying campaign.

Lobanovskyi's day job, as coach to Dynamo Kiev, continues to provide plenty of foreign travel. In 1999/2000 Dynamo played 16 European matches and reached the second group phase of the Champions'

INTERNATIONAL HONOURS

European Club Competitions
Cup-winners' Cup   Dynamo Kyiv (1975, 1986)
Super Cup   Dynamo Kyiv (1975)

TOP SCORERS

20 Maxim SHATSKIKH (Dynamo Kyiv)
19 Ivan HETSKO (Karpaty Lviv/
   Kryvbas Kryvyi Rih)
18 Serhiy REBROV (Dynamo Kyiv)
15 Andriy VOROBEI (Shakhtar Donetsk)
12 Avtandil KAPANADZE (Nyva Ternopil)
   Hennadiy ZUBOV (Shakhtar Donetsk)
   Kostyantyn BABYCH (Metalurg Mariupol)

NATIONAL TEAM RESULTS 99/00

18/08/99	Bulgaria	H	Kiev	1-1	Rebrov (83p)
04/09/99	France (ECQ)	H	Kiev	0-0	
08/09/99	Iceland (ECQ)	A	Reykjavik	1-0	Rebrov (43p)
09/10/99	Russia (ECQ)	A	Moscow	1-1	Shevchenko (87)
13/11/99	Slovenia (ECQ)	A	Ljubljana	1-2	Shevchenko (33)
17/11/99	Slovenia (ECQ)	H	Kiev	1-1	Rebrov (67p)
26/04/00	Bulgaria	A	Sofia	1-0	Shevchenko (55)
31/05/00	England	A	Wembley	0-2	

League, narrowly failing to make the knockout stages for the third season running.

The departure of superstar Shevchenko to Milan inevitably had an adverse bearing on Dynamo's chances of survival, but the team showed commendable powers of resilience throughout their stay in the competition. As in the previous season, they made bad starts in each of the two group phases. Having qualified at the expense of Zalgiris Vilnius and AaB, the latter by virtue of a last-minute 'winner' from Shevchenko-replacement Maxim Shatskikh, Dynamo completely messed up their Champions' League opener, losing 0-1 at home to outsiders Maribor. Ultimately, however, they would be grateful to the Slovenians for holding Bayer Leverkusen 0-0 in their final game and enabling Kiev to progress at the Germans' expense.

NATIONAL TEAM APPEARANCES 99/00

Coach - Jozsef SZABO; Valeriy LYOBANOVSKYI	BUL	FRA	ISL	RUS	SLO	SLO	BUL	ENG	Cps	Gls
Olexandr SHOVKOVSKYI (02/01/75) - Dynamo Kyiv	G63	G	G	G	G	G	G		26	-
Yuriy DMITRULIN (10/02/75) - Dynamo Kyiv	D	D46	D	D76	D	D	D46	D	23	1
Vladyslav VASHCHUK (02/01/75) - Dynamo Kyiv	D	D	D	D	D	D	D	D	28	1
Olexandr HOLOVKO (06/01/72) - Dynamo Kyiv	D	D	D	D	D	D	D	D	36	-
Volodymyr MYKYTYN (28/04/70) - Shakhtar Donetsk	M62	s46	s79	s42					13	-
Andriy GUSIN (11/12/72) - Dynamo Kyiv	M65	M79		M	M		s46	M	24	4
Yuriy MAXIMOV (08/12/68) - SV Werder Bremen (GER)	M	M66	M	M76					23	5
Serhiy KOVALEV (22/11/71) - Shakhtar Donetsk	M46			s76		s46	M46		10	1
Vitaliy KOSOVSKYI (11/08/73) - Dynamo Kyiv	M46	M	M		M	M73			24	2
Olexandr PALYANYTSYA (29/02/72) - Kryvbas Kryvyi Rih	A46								2	-
Serhiy REBROV (03/06/74) - Dynamo Kyiv	A	A	A	A	A	A	s46	A	36	12
Eduard TSYKHMEISTRUK (24/06/73) - CSCA Kyiv	s46	s79	s66						7	-
Serhiy POPOV (22/04/71) - Shakhtar Donetsk	s46	D	D		D	s73		D71	32	4
Roman MAXYMYUK (14/06/74) - Zenit Sankt-Peterburg (RUS)/Dynamo Kyiv	s46						s62		4	-
Olexandr KIRYUKHIN (01/10/74) - Dynamo Kyiv	s62								2	-
Valeriy VOROBYOV (14/01/70) - Torpedo Moskva (RUS)	s63								6	-
Serhiy KONOVALOV (01/03/72) - Dynamo Kyiv	s65	s66	M66						18	3
Oleh LUZHNYI (05/08/68) - Arsenal (ENG)		D	D79	D		D	s46	D	35	-
Andriy SHEVCHENKO (29/09/76) - Milan (ITA)		A	A	A	A	A	A70	A	29	9
Serhiy MIZIN (25/09/72) - Karpaty Lviv/Kryvbas Kryvyi Rih					M		M46		6	-
Serhiy SKACHENKO (18/11/72) - FC Metz (FRA)				A42		A58			15	3
Hennadiy MOROZ (27/03/75) - Kryvbas Kryvyi Rih				s76		s58	A46	s64	4	-
Dmytro PARFENOV (11/09/74) - Spartak Moskva (RUS)					D				6	-
Serhiy KANDAUROV (02/12/72) - SL Benfica (POR)					M57	M46		M64	3	-
Vasyl KARDASH (14/01/73) - Dynamo Kyiv					s57				9	-
Serhiy FEDOROV (18/02/75) - Dynamo Kyiv						D			1	-
Mykhailo STAROSTYAK (13/10/73) - Shakhtar Donetsk							D46		6	-
Anatoliy TYMOSHCHUK (30/03/79) - Shakhtar Donetsk							D62	D	2	-
Hennadiy ZUBOV (12/09/77) - Shakhtar Donetsk							M46		8	-
Dmytro MYKHAILENKO (11/07/73) - Dynamo Kyiv							s46		22	2
Andriy NESMACHNYI (28/02/79) - Dynamo Kyiv							s46		1	-
Ihor KOSTYUK (14/07/75) - Dynamo Kyiv							s46		1	-
Serhiy KORMILTSEV (23/01/74) - Dynamo Kyiv							s70		1	-
Vyacheslav KERNOZENKO (04/06/76) - Dynamo Kyiv								G85	1	-
Andriy VOROBEI (29/11/78) - Shakhtar Donetsk								s71	1	-
Maxym LEVYTSKYI (26/11/72) - Chernomorets Novorossiisk (RUS)								s85	1	-

Successive defeats by Real Madrid and Bayern Munich (their two opponents in the previous season's knockout stages) gave Dynamo much to contemplate during the winter break, but on the resumption they roared back into form, winning three and drawing one of their remaining four fixtures. However, although that gave them three points more than in the first group phase, this time it was not enough.

As ever, Kiev sought consolation for their European exit by collecting another domestic title. The perennial champions made it eight wins in a row and they did so in the face of negligible resistance, cantering to the championship with an 18-point winning margin over runners-up Shakhtar Donetsk.

It was a domestic season bordering on perfection for Lobanovskyi's men. Their 30 matches brought 27 victories and three draws. They won all 15 home fixtures, found the net in every game bar one - a goalless draw away to Shakhtar - and scored at a rate of almost three goals per match. Newcomer Shatskikh, an Uzbekistani international, proved his worth by netting 20 goals to claim the league's top-scorer crown. Close behind was team leader Serhiy Rebrov, who scored 18 league goals to complement the ten he registered in Europe - and this despite misisng a third of the fixtures.

During the second half of the season the Kiev attack was augmented by the arrival of Georgian international Giorgi Demetradze, signed for a fee of £3m from Russian club Alania Vladikavkaz. He joined a lengthening list of foreigners on the Kiev books, one of whom, Belarus inter-

national Alexandr Khatskevich, was responsible for completing a hat-trick of domestic 'doubles' for Dynamo when he scored the only goal in the Cup final victory over Kryvbas Kryvyi Rih.

PLAYER OF THE SEASON

ANDRIY SHEVCHENKO

The European Championship finals took place without the Continent's number one striker. Ukraine's shock defeat by Slovenia in the qualifying play-off meant that Andriy Shevchenko was unable to demonstrate his formidable talent on the big stage. Some might say that Euro 2000 needed Shevchenko more than the other way round. After all, the 24-year-old striker had proved his world-class talent beyond doubt during a magnificent début season in Italy with Milan, in which he added considerable value to his large transfer fee by becoming the Serie A top scorer with 24 goals, beating Argentinian duo Batistuta and Crespo into second and third place, respectively. A clear winner of the 1999 Ukrainian Footballer of the Year award, he was also voted third in the European Footballer of the Year poll. Pace, balance, finishing power, two good feet - Shevchenko has the lot. Ukrainian fans are not alone in hoping that he gets the chance to grace the World Cup finals with his skills in 2002.

DOMESTIC CUP 99/00

1/16 FINALS
FC Lviv 4, Metalurg Mariupol 0
SK Kherson 1, Chornomorets Odesa 0
Volyn Lutsk 1, Dnipro Dnipropetrovsk 3
Yavir-Sumykrasnopillya 1, Tavriya Simferopol 2
Naftovyk Okhtyrka 0, Metalurg Zaporizhzhya 2
Stal Alchevsk 0, CSKA Kyiv 2
Polissya Zhytomyr 2, Vorskla Poltava 5
Metalurg Nikopol 1, Zirka Kirovohrad 1
(aet; 1-3 on pens.)
FC Vynnytsya 2, Metalist Kharkiv 2
(aet; 4-2 on pens.)
Borysfen Boryspil 0, Prykarpattya Ivano-Frankivsk 0
(aet; 3-1 on pens.)
SK Mykolaiv 1, Shakhtar Donetsk 2
Obolon-PPO Kyiv 0, Nyva Ternopil 1
FC Cherkasy 1, Karpaty Lviv 2
Poligraftekhnika Olexandriya 0, Kryvbas Kryvyi Rih 1
Zakarpattya Uzhgorod 1, Metalurg Donetsk 2

1/8 FINALS
CSKA Kyiv 2, Vorskla Poltava 1
Zirka Kirovohrad 2, FC Vynnytsya 0
Shakhtar Donetsk 5, Borysfen Boryspil 0
FC Lviv 1, Dnipro Dnipropetrovsk 0
Metalurg Donetsk 2, Kryvbas Kryvyi Rih 3
Metalurg Zaporizhzhya 3, Tavriya Simferopol 0
Dynamo Kyiv 4, SK Kherson 0
Nyva Ternopil 1, Karpaty Lviv 2 (aet)

QUARTER-FINALS
Kryvbas Kryvyi Rih 1 (Palyanytsya 18), CSKA Kyiv 0
Zirka Kirovohrad 0, Shakhtar Donetsk 0
(aet; 6-5 on pens.)
Metalurg Zaporizhzhya 3 (Polvavets 28p, Cherevan 38, Spivak 80), Karpaty Lviv 0
FC Lviv 1 (Lapko 74), Dynamo Kyiv 4 (Gusin 12, Rebrov 34p, Belkevich 56, Shatskikh 89)

SEMI-FINALS
Kryvbas Kryvyi Rih 2 (Hetsko 44, Palyanytsya 59), Zirka Kirovohrad 1 (Kislov 24)
Dynamo Kyiv 6 (Rebrov 9, Shatskikh 18, 89, Belkevich 60, Demetradze 66p, 82), Metalurg Zaporizhzhya 1 (Smirnov 61)

FINAL
27/05/2000, Kiev
DYNAMO KYIV 1 Khatskevich (44)
KRYVBAS KRYVYI RIH 0
referee - Onufer
DYNAMO KYIV - Kernozenko, Mamedov
(Yashkin 57), Holovko, Vashchuk, Dmitrulin,
Khatskevich, Gusin, Belkevich, Kaladze, Shatskikh
(Demetradze 73), Rebrov.
KRYVBAS KRYVYI RIH - Lavrentsov, Yezerskyi
(Platonov 88), Monakhov, Granovskyi, Zotov,
Simakov (Joksas 88), Mizin, Hetsko, Palyanytsya
(Rymshin 73), Moroz, Ponomarenko.

EUROPEAN CUPS 99/00

CHAMPIONS' CUP
● **DYNAMO KYIV**
Preliminary round 2 ZALGIRIS VILNIUS (LIT)
H 2-0   Shatskikh (38, 78)
Shovkovskyi, Kormiltsev (Serebryannikov 56), Gerasimenko, Holovko, Vashchuk, Dmitrulin, Kaladze, Gusin, Yashkin, Shatskikh, Rebrov.
A 1-0   Rebrov (35)
Shovkovskyi, Kiryujhin (Fedorov 59), Gerasimenko, Holovko, Vashchuk, Dmitrulin, Kaladze, Gusin, Yashkin (Kormiltsev 80), Shatskikh (Serebryannikov 67), Rebrov.

Qualifying round AAB (DEN)
A 2-1   Rebrov (13), Shatskikh (40)
Shovkovskyi, Kardash (Konovalov 62), Gerasimenko, Holovko, Vashchuk, Dmitrulin, Kaladze, Gusin, Yashkin, Shatskikh, Rebrov.
H 2-2   Gusin (74), Shatskikh (90)
Shovkovskyi, Gusin, Gerasimenko (Kormiltsev 60), Holovko, Vashchuk, Dmitrulin, Kaladze, Kosovskyi, Yashkin, Shatskikh, Rebrov.

Champions' League
1st match NK MARIBOR (SLO)
H 0-1
Shovkovskyi, Kormiltsev (Fedorov 60), Gerasimenko (Konovalov 70), Holovko, Vashchuk, Dmitrulin, Kaladze, Gusin, Kosovskyi, Shatskikh (Venhlynskyi 66), Rebrov.

2nd match LAZIO (ITA)
A 1-2   Rebrov (67p)
Shovkovskyi, Kormiltsev (Kosovskyi 46), Gerasimenko (Konovalov 46), Holovko, Vashchuk, Dmitrulin, Kaladze, Gusin, Fedorov, Shatskikh (Venhlynskyi 83), Rebrov.

3rd match BAYER 04 LEVERKUSEN (GER)
A 1-1   Gusin (71)
Shovkovskyi, Mamedov (Fedorov 81), Konovalov (Gerasimenko 58), Holovko, Vashchuk, Dmitrulin (Kormiltsev 74), Kaladze, Gusin, Kosovskyi, Shatskikh, Rebrov.

4th match BAYER 04 LEVERKUSEN (GER)
H 4-2   Kosovskyi (4), Shatskikh (36), Holovko (61), Vashchuk (89)
Shovkovskyi, Mamedov, Gerasimenko (Belkevich 46), Holovko, Vashchuk, Dmitrulin (Yashkin 59), Kaladze, Gusin, Kosovskyi, Shatskikh, Rebrov.

5th match NK MARIBOR (SLO)
A 2-1   Rebrov (37, 84p)
Shovkovskyi, Mamedov, Yashkin (Belkevich 6), Holovko, Vashchuk, Dmitrulin, Kaladze, Gusin, Kosovskyi, Shatskikh, Rebrov.

6th match LAZIO (ITA)
H 0-1
Shovkovskyi, Mamedov, Fedorov (Shatskikh 46), Holovko, Vashchuk, Dmitrulin, Kaladze, Gusin, Kosovskyi, Belkevich, Rebrov.

7th match REAL MADRID (ESP)
H 1-2   Rebrov (85p)
Shovkovskyi, Mamedov, Khatskevich, Holovko, Vashchuk, Dmitrulin, Yashkin, Gusin, Belkevich, Konovalov (Shatskikh 46), Rebrov.

8th match FC BAYERN MÜNCHEN (GER)
A 1-2   Rebrov (50)
Shovkovskyi, Kardash, Khatskevich (Gerasimenko 48), Holovko, Vashchuk, Dmitrulin, Kaladze, Gusin, Belkevich, Yashkin (Venhlynskyi 46), Rebrov.

9th match ROSENBORG BK (NOR)
H 2-1   Khatskevich (10), Rebrov (29)
Shovkovskyi, Mamedov (Fedorov 86), Gerasimenko, Holovko, Khatskevich, Nesmachnyi, Kaladze, Gusin, Belkevich, Demetradze (Shatskikh 87), Rebrov.

10th match ROSENBORG BK (NOR)
A 2-1   Rebrov (32, 67)
Shovkovskyi, Mamedov, Gerasimenko, Fedorov, Khatskevich, Nesmachnyi (Kormiltsev 67), Kaladze, Gusin, Belkevich, Shatskikh (Demetradze 46), Rebrov.

11th match REAL MADRID (ESP)
A 2-2   Khatskevich (42), Hierro (56og)
Shovkovskyi, Mamedov, Gerasimenko, Holovko, Khatskevich, Nesmachnyi, Belkevich, Gusin, Demetradze, Shatskikh (Kardash 46), Rebrov (Kostyuk 77).

12th match FC BAYERN MÜNCHEN (GER)
H 2-0   Kaladze (34), Demetradze (71)
Shovkovskyi, Mamedov, Gerasimenko, Holovko, Khatskevich (Kardash 85), Nesmachnyi (Yashkin 35), Kaladze, Gusin, Belkevich, Demetradze, Rebrov.

UEFA CUP
● **KARPATY LVIV**
1st round HELSINGBORGS IF (SWE)
A 1-1   Hetsko (17)
Strontsitskyi, Vilchynskyi, Tanasyuk, Yevtushok, Pavlyukh, Kovalets (Sharan 76), Mizin, Nazarov, Khoma, Vovchuk (Lutsyshyn 81), Hetsko.
H 1-1   (aet; 2-4 on pens.) Hetsko (90)
Strontsitskyi, Vilchynskyi (Yevhlevskyi 58; Vovchuk 115), Tanasyuk, Yevtushok, Pavlyukh, Kovalets, Mizin, Nazarov, Khoma, Pokladok (Semochko 98), Hetsko.

● **KRYVBAS KRYVYI RIH**
Qualifying round SHAMKIR (AZB)
H 3-0   Ponomarenko (8), Palyanytsya (66), Moroz (80)
Lavrentsov, Anishchenko, Doroshenko, Granovskyi, Zotov, Simakov, Platonov (Yakymenko 56), Rymshyn (Monarev 31), Palyanytsya, Moroz, Ponomarenko.
A 2-0   Simakov (24, 70)
Lavrentsov, Anishchenko, Doroshenko, Granovskyi, Zotov, Simakov, Platonov (Kriulin 77), Datsenko, Palyanytsya (Monarev 58), Moroz, Ponomarenko (Rymshyn 69).

1st round PARMA (ITA)
A 2-3   Palyanytsya (5), Monarev (74)
Lavrentsov, Anishchenko, Doroshenko, Granovskyi, Zotov, Simakov, Platonov , Kriulin, Palyanytsya (Monarev 71), Yakymenko (Yaskov 60), Ponomarenko (Rymshyn 84).
H 0-3
Lavrentsov, Anishchenko, Doroshenko, Granovskyi, Zotov, Simakov, Platonov (Yakymenko 64), Monarev (Kriulin 26), Palyanytsya (Rymshyn 66), Moroz, Ponomarenko.

EUROPEAN CUPS 99/00 (CONT.)

● **SHAKHTAR DONETSK**
Qualifying round SILEKS KRATOVO (MAC)
H 3-1 Seleznev (60), Shtolcers (80, 89)
Virt, Starostyak, Koval (Tymoshchuk 59), Kotov, Benio, Zubov
(Bakharev 65), Popov, Seleznev, Orbu, Matveyev (Mykytyn 81),
Shtolcers.

A 1-2 Seleznev (22)
Virt, Starostyak, Chyzhevskyi, Tymoshchuk, Benio, Koval, Popov,
Seleznev, Kovalev (Shelayev 88), Bakharev (Orbu 50), Shtolcers
(Matveyev 77).

1st round RODA JC (HOL)
A 0-2
Virt, Starostyak, Bakharev (Zubov 67), Nahornyak, Benio, Mykytyn,
Popov, Seleznev, Kovalev, Kriventsov, Shtolcers (Vorobei 58).

H 1-3 Benio (32)
Virt, Starostyak, Kotov, Nahornyak (Potskhveria 67), Benio, Kovalev,
Popov, Seleznev, Orbu, Vorobei, Shtolcers (Zubov 55).

For much of the season it looked as if Kryvbas would finish as runners-up in the league as well. The ambitious and financially-stable club surpassed themselves in the early part of the season, even giving holders Parma a fright in the UEFA Cup, but despite the arrival in mid-season of Karpaty Lviv hot-shot Ivan Hetsko, they were unable to recover ground lost in the autumn and three successive away defeats in the closing weeks, the first of them to rivals Shakhtar, condemned them to third spot.

Second place was a worthwhile prize because it carried with it a passport into the Champions' League. Shakhtar seized it thanks to a brilliant run of form in the spring, in which they won all but two of their matches, losing only to Dynamo Kiev. During the autumn Shakhtar's challenge had been undone by controversial Russian coach Anatoliy Byshovets. He tinkered with the personnel and tactics far too much for his, and the team's, own good and was duly dismissed. The improvement in the climate at the club after his departure was wholly evident from the team's results.

There was no turning back, however, for Zirka Kirovohrad, who ended their 30-match campaign without a single victory. With the top division being reduced in number to a more manageable 14 clubs, Zirka were joined in relegation by two other teams, Chornomorets Odesa and Prykarpattya Ivano-Frankivsk. Chornomorets paid the price for changing players like socks, while Prykarpattya were unable to extend the stay of execution which they had earned by way of an unexpected play-off 12 months earlier.

Only one team, Stal Alchevsk, came up, but they were not the Second Division champions. That title went to Dynamo Kiev's second team - further proof, if any were needed, that one club, and one club only, rules supreme in Ukrainian football.

PROMOTED CLUB 99/00

SECOND DIVISION FINAL TABLE

		Pd	W	D	L	F	A	Pt	GD
1	Dynamo-2 Kyiv	34	22	7	5	75	21	73	54
2	**Stal Alchevsk**	**34**	**21**	**7**	**6**	**58**	**36**	**70**	**22**
3	FC Cherkasy	34	17	8	9	48	34	59	14
4	Shakhtar-2 Donetsk	34	16	8	10	47	38	56	9
5	CSCA-2 Kyiv	34	16	6	12	38	26	54	12
6	SC Mykolaiv	34	15	7	12	40	38	52	2
7	FC Lviv	34	12	12	9	34	31	51	3
8	Poligraftekhnika Olexandriya	34	13	10	11	34	34	49	0
9	Yavir-Sumy Sumy	34	14	6	14	42	45	48	-3
10	Volyn Lutsk	34	13	9	12	42	41	48	1
11	FC Vynnytsya	34	14	6	14	29	39	48	-10
12	Metalurg Nikopol	34	14	6	14	31	34	48	-3
13	Zakarpattya Uzhgorod	34	14	6	14	36	49	48	-13
14	Naftovyk Okhtyrka	34	13	5	16	42	51	44	-9
15	Polissya Zhytomyr	34	11	7	16	36	51	40	-15
16	Obolon-PPO Kyiv	34	5	12	17	23	52	27	-29
17	Chornomorets-2 Odesa	34	6	5	23	25	49	23	-24
18	Torpedo Zaporizhzhya	34	5	1	28	21	32	16	-11

CLUB DIRECTORY

Stal Alchevsk
vul. Leningradska 41, 94200 Alchevsk
tel - (06442) 23487/25256
fax - (06442) 23487/29831
Year of Formation - 1935
President - Anatoliy Volobuyev
Secretary - Irnya Yermolenko
Coach - Anatoliy Volobuyev
Stadium - Stal (12,000)

CHORNOMORETS ODESA

CLUB DIRECTORY

Chornomorets Odesa
Central Stadium, Shevchenko Park, 65014 Odesa
tel - (0482) 684894/406224/226580
fax - (0482) 449878/680415
Year of Formation - 1958
President - Leonid Klimov
Secretary - Oleh Taraday
Coach - Olexandr Golokolosov; Anatoliy Azarenkov
Stadium - Central (43,000)

MAJOR HONOURS
Domestic Cup - (2) 1992, 1994.

APPEARANCES 99/00

	P	Ap	(s)	Gls
Serhiy ARTEMENKO	D	24	(2)	1
Eduard BAGIROV	D	3		
Olexandr BONDARENKO	D	3		
Yuriy BUKEL	D	16		
Serhiy BULYGIN	D	7	(2)	
Andriy CHERNOV	M	14	(1)	
Anatoliy CHISTOV	G	11	(3)	
Serhiy DRANYTSKYI	A	11		3
Ovik GALSTYAN	A	1	(6)	1
Olexandr GOLOKOLOSOV	A	9	(1)	
Timerlan GUSEINOV	A	15	(8)	1
Volodymyr IIAPON	M	12	(12)	
Viktor HRYSHKO	G	11		
Olexandr HUMENYUK	G	7		
Dmytro KARYAKA	M	15	(3)	1
Hennadiy KHROL	M	12	(1)	
Vitaliy KOLESNYCHENKO	M	25		
Ivan KORPONAI	A	1	(3)	
Serhiy KOSTYUK	M	7	(3)	
Serhiy KOVRYZHKIN	M	1	(2)	
Dmytro KRISANOV	M	9	(6)	
Vyacheslav MATYUSHENKO	M	5		1
Oleh MOCHULYAK	M	23	(6)	5
Vasyl MOKAN	M	18	(4)	1
Volodymyr POLISHCHUK	D	4		
Serhiy PONOMARENKO	A		(1)	1
Ruslan ROMANCHUK	M	5		1
Vitaliy RUDENKO	G	1		
Yuriy SAK	D	14		
Olexandr SOBKOVYCH	M	5	(1)	
Olexandr SPITSYN	D	11	(2)	
Vasyl STEZHKOVYI	D	1	(3)	
Eduard STOYANOV	A		(1)	1
Vyacheslav SUKHOLMINOV	M		(2)	
Vyacheslav TERESHCHENKO	A	9	(5)	3
Ruslan VASYLKIV	M		(2)	
Anatoliy VORONA	A		(1)	
Mykola VTVYTSKYI	M		(4)	
Vasyl YATSURAK	D	5	(1)	
Andrei YEROKHIN (BLS)	D	15		

LEAGUE RESULTS 1999/2000

12/07/99	Metalurg Mariupol	A	0-5	
16/07/99	Nyva Ternopil	H	1-0	Matyushenko
20/07/99	CSCA Kyiv	A	0-3	
24/07/99	Metalist Kharkiv	H	0-1	
01/08/99	Karpaty Lviv	A	0-5	
07/08/99	Dynamo Kyiv	A	1-4	Mokan
15/08/99	Metalurg Donetsk	H	0-1	
21/08/99	Zirka Kirovohrad	A	0-0	
29/08/99	Tavriya Simferopol	H	1-2	Mochulyak
25/09/99	Dnipro Dnipropetrovsk	A	1-1	Artemenko
16/10/99	Vorskla Poltava	A	0-4	
24/10/99	Metalurg Zaporizhzhya	H	1-0	Mochulyak
28/10/99	Kryvbas Kryvyi Rih	H	2-0	Mochulyak (p), Stoyanov
02/11/99	Shakhtar Donetsk	A	1-0	Karyaka
07/11/99	Prykarpattya Ivano-Frankivsk	H	0-0	
18/03/00	Prykarpattya Ivano-Frankivsk	A	0-1	
25/03/00	Shakhtar Donetsk	H	0-3	
02/04/00	Metalurg Zaporizhzhya	A	0-2	
08/04/00	Vorskla Poltava	H	1-1	Guseinov
16/04/00	Kryvbas Kryvyi Rih	A	0-2	
22/04/00	Dnipro Dnipropetrovsk	H	0-0	(awarded as away win; original result 2-2 Yerokhin, Dranytskyi)
29/04/00	Tavriya Simferopol	A	1-1	Mochulyak
06/05/00	Zirka Kirovohrad	H	1-0	Galstyan
14/05/00	Metalurg Donetsk	A	0-4	
21/05/00	Dynamo Kyiv	H	2-2	Dranytskyi 2
26/05/00	Karpaty Lviv	H	0-0	
04/06/00	Metalist Kharkiv	A	1-1	Tereshchenko
08/06/00	CSCA Kyiv	H	2-0	Tereshchenko 2
16/06/00	Nyva Ternopil	A	1-3	Romanchuk
20/06/00	Metalurg Mariupol	H	3-4	Mochulyak, Dranytskyi, Ponomarenko

CSCA KYIV

CLUB DIRECTORY

CSCA Kyiv
vul. Pushkinska 42/4
01004 Kyiv
tel - (044)
2454337/2454319/2253262/4619661
fax - (044) 2454337/4619661
website - www.pnn.@ukrpost.net
Year of Formation - 1996
President - Andriy Artemenko
Secretary - Anatoliy Linnyk
Coach - Volodymyr Bessonov
Stadium - CSK ZSU (12,000)

APPEARANCES 99/00

	P	Ap	(s)	Gls
Andriy ANNENKOV	D	24		2
Viktor AREFIYEV	A	2	(8)	
Roman BAIRASHEVSKYI	G		(1)	
Anatoliy BALATSKYI	D	4	(3)	
Vitaliy BALYTSKYI	D	24		
Pavlo BLAZHAYEV	G	1		
Vitaliy DARASELIA (GEO)	M	2	(4)	
Yuriy KALITVINTSEV	M	10		1
Andriy KARYAKA	M	3	(7)	3
Dmytro KORENEV	M		(1)	
Ruslan KOSTYSHYN	A	24	(3)	2
Viktor LEONENKO	A	1		
Vitaliy LEVCHENKO (TAD)	D	27	(1)	1
Roman MONAREV	A		(5)	1
Viktor MOROZ	M	2	(2)	
Volodymyr MUSOLITIN	A	18	(7)	5
Olexandr OLEXIYENKO	A	1	(2)	
Olexiy OLIYNYK	M	9	(14)	1
Roman PAKHOLYUK	A	1	(6)	
Borys POLYAKOV	D	13		
Oleh POLYARUSH	M	4	(1)	
Vitaliy REVA	G	29		
Serhiy REVUT	D	4	(1)	
Serhiy SELEZNEV	M	11	(3)	1
Dmytro SEMCHUK	D	13		
Pavlo SKOROPAD	D	15	(1)	1
Serhiy TKACHENKO	D	14		
Eduard TSYKHMEISTRUK	M	27		5
Viktor ULYANYTSKYI	D	13	(2)	
Olexandr YEVTUSHOK	D	11		1
Serhiy ZAKARLYUKA	M	23	(2)	7

LEAGUE RESULTS 1999/2000

Date	Opponent		Score	Scorers
12/07/99	Metalist Kharkiv	H	0-1	
16/07/99	Karpaty Lviv	A	0-1	
20/07/99	Chornomorets Odesa	H	3-0	Zakarlyuka, Tsykhmeistruk, Karyaka
24/07/99	Metalurg Donetsk	A	0-0	
01/08/99	Zirka Kirovohrad	H	3-0	Zakarlyuka 2 (1p), Karyaka
07/08/99	Tavriya Simferopol	A	2-1	Tsykhmeistruk, Musolitin
21/08/99	Kryvbas Kryvyi Rih	A	1-2	Annenkov
29/08/99	Vorskla Poltava	H	1-1	Oliynyk
25/09/99	Metalurg Zaporizhzhya	A	2-2	Tsykhmeistruk, Karyaka
16/10/99	Prykarpattya Ivano-Frankivsk	A	0-0	
20/10/99	Dnipro Dnipropetrovsk	A	1-2	Skoropad
24/10/99	Metalurg Mariupol	H	1-1	Musolitin
28/10/99	Shakhtar Donetsk	H	1-0	Musolitin
01/11/99	Nyva Ternopil	A	2-2	Musolitin (p), Annenkov
07/11/99	Dynamo Kyiv	H	0-3	
18/03/00	Dynamo Kyiv	A	1-3	Zakarlyuka
25/03/00	Nyva Ternopil	H	0-0	
02/04/00	Metalurg Mariupol	A	0-2	
08/04/00	Prykarpattya Ivano-Frankivsk	H	2-1	Seleznev, Kostyshyn
16/04/00	Shakhtar Donetsk	A	0-3	
22/04/00	Metalurg Zaporizhzhya	H	1-0	Zakarlyuka (p)
29/04/00	Vorskla Poltava	A	0-2	
06/05/00	Kryvbas Kryvyi Rih	H	1-2	Zakarlyuka
14/05/00	Dnipro Dnipropetrovsk	H	3-0	Kalitvintsev, Zakarlyuka, Monarev
21/05/00	Tavriya Simferopol	H	3-0	Kostyshyn, Tsykhmeistruk 2
26/05/00	Zirka Kirovohrad	A	0-0	
04/06/00	Metalurg Donetsk	H	1-0	Levchenko
08/06/00	Chornomorets Odesa	A	0-2	
16/06/00	Karpaty Lviv	H	2-3	Yevtushok, Musolitin
20/06/00	Metalist Kharkiv	A	0-2	

DNIPRO DNIPROPETROVSK

CLUB DIRECTORY

Dnipro Dnipropetrovsk
vul. Bilshovytska 1, 49105 Dnipropetrovsk
tel - (0562) 342988/342989
fax - (0562) 342990
website - www.fcdnipro.dp.ua
Year of Formation - 1962
President - Yuriy Alexeyev
Secretary - Volodymyr Proch
Coach - Leonid Koltun; Mykola Fedorenko
Stadium - Meteor (30,352)

MAJOR HONOURS
League Championship (USSR) - (2)1983, 1988.
Domestic Cup (USSR) - (1) 1989.

APPEARANCES 99/00

	P	Ap	(s)	Gls
Olexandr BABYCH	D	1	(1)	
Vitaliy BELIKOV	D	8	(3)	
Serhiy BERBAT	D		(1)	
Denys FILIMONOV	M		(5)	
Alexandru GUZUN (MOL)	D	2		
Volodymyr HERASHCHENKO	D	9		
Oleh HRYTSAI	A	3	(3)	
Olexandr HRYTSAI	D	13	(1)	
Maxym KALYNYCHENKO	M	4	(2)	
Ihor KHOMENKO	D	14	(5)	
Dmytro KONDRATOVYCH	M		(1)	
Serhiy KOSILOV	M	19	(5)	1
Hennadiy KOZAR	D	1		
Artem KUSLIY	G	5		
Anatoliy MATKEVYCH	M	2	(8)	
Andriy MATVEYEV	A		(4)	
Serhiy MATYUKHIN	M	21		4
Mykola MEDIN	G	6		
Yevhen MYKULA	D		(1)	
Serhiy NAZARENKO	M	15	(3)	2
Denys ONYSHCHENKO	M	1	(2)	
Olexandr PINENKO	D		(1)	
Olexandr POKLONSKYI	D	14		1
Hennadiy PRYKHODKO	D	14		
Olexiy RACHYBA	M	1	(2)	
Ruslan ROTAN	M	6	(3)	
Olexandr SAVENCHUK	M	9	(6)	1
Bohdan SHERSHUN	D	15	(2)	
Serhiy SHEVTSOV	A	24	(2)	3
Yuriy SLABYSHEV	A	16	(5)	4
Maxym STARTSEV	G	19		
Gheorghe STRATULAT (MOL)	M	5	(2)	
Alexandru SUHAREV (MOL)	A	3	(4)	1
Vitaliy TARASENKO	A	2	(1)	1
Olexiy TELYATNIKOV	A	4	(1)	
Serhiy VALYAYEV	A	24	(2)	2
Serhiy ZADOROZHNYI	D	26		4
Andriy ZUBCHENKO	M	24	(3)	2

LEAGUE RESULTS 1999/2000

12/07/99	Vorskla Poltava	A	0-4	
16/07/99	Metalurg Zaporizhzhya	H	0-2	
20/07/99	Shakhtar Donetsk	A	0-2	
24/07/99	Prykarpattya Ivano-Frankivsk	H	1-1	Shevtsov
01/08/99	Metalurg Mariupol	A	2-3	Valyayev, Savenchuk
07/08/99	Nyva Ternopil	H	1-1	Poklonskyi
21/08/99	Metalist Kharkiv	H	1-0	Shevtsov
29/08/99	Karpaty Lviv	A	0-4	
25/09/99	Chornomorets Odesa	H	1-1	Slabyshev
03/10/99	Metalurg Donetsk	A	1-5	Slabyshev
16/10/99	Zirka Kirovohrad	H	2-0	Kosilov, Valyayev
20/10/99	CSCA Kyiv	H	2-1	Zubchenko, Nazarenko
24/10/99	Tavriya Simferopol	A	1-1	Slabyshev
30/10/99	Dynamo Kyiv	A	0-4	
07/11/99	Kryvbas Kryvyi Rih	H	1-0	Slabyshev
18/03/00	Kryvbas Kryvyi Rih	A	2-2	Matyukhin, Zubchenko
26/03/00	Dynamo Kyiv	H	0-2	
03/04/00	Tavriya Simferopol	H	1-0	Suharev
08/04/00	Zirka Kirovohrad	A	1-1	Zadorozhnyi (p)
16/04/00	Metalurg Donetsk	H	0-1	
22/04/00	Chornomorets Odesa	A	0-0	awarded as away win; original result 2-2 Valyayev, Matyukhin)
06/05/00	Metalist Kharkiv	A	1-2	Matyukhin
10/05/00	Karpaty Lviv	H	1-1	Nazarenko
14/05/00	CSCA Kyiv	A	0-3	
21/05/00	Nyva Ternopil	A	1-1	Zadorozhnyi
26/05/00	Metalurg Mariupol	H	1-0	Zadorozhnyi
04/06/00	Prykarpattya Ivano-Frankivsk	A	1-1	Matyukhin
08/06/00	Shakhtar Donetsk	H	1-2	Tarasenko
16/06/00	Metalurg Zaporizhzhya	A	1-6	Matyukhin
20/06/00	Vorskla Poltava	H	2-1	Shevtsov, Zadorozhnyi (p)

DYNAMO KYIV

CLUB DIRECTORY

Dynamo Kyiv
vul. Hrushevskoho 3, 01001 Kyiv
tel - (044) 2280209/2284533/2283438/
2295637
fax - (044) 2284135/2284407
website - www.fcdynamo.kiev.ua
Year of Formation - 1927
President - vacant
Secretary - Serhiy Polkhovskyi
Coach - Valeriy Lobanovskyi
Stadium - National Sport Komplex Olimpiyskyi
(83,160)

MAJOR HONOURS
League Championship (USSR) - (13) 1961, 1966,
1967, 1968, 1971, 1974, 1975, 1977, 1980,
1981, 1985, 1986, 1990.
League Championship - (8) 1993, 1994, 1995,
1996, 1997, 1998, 1999, 2000.
Domestic Cup (USSR) - (9) 1954, 1964, 1966,
1974, 1978, 1982, 1985, 1987, 1990.
Domestic Cup - (5) 1993, 1996, 1998, 1999, 2000.
European Cup-winners' Cup - (2) 1975, 1986.
European Super Cup - (1) 1975.

APPEARANCES 99/00

	P	Ap	(s)	Gls
Valentin BELKEVICH (BLS)	M	15	(5)	6
Giorgi DEMETRADZE (GEO)	A	10	(4)	8
Yuriy DMITRULIN	D	19	(1)	
Serhiy FEDOROV	D	8	(3)	2
Alexei GERASIMENKO (RUS)	M	14	(1)	
Andriy GUSIN	M	25	(2)	5
Olexandr Borysovych HOLOVKO	D	21	(1)	
Kakhi KALADZE (GEO)	D	25		1
Vasyl KARDASH	M	8	(5)	1
Vyacheslav KERNOZENKO	G	15		
Alexandr KHATSKEVICH (BLS)	M	11	(4)	4
Olexandr KIRYUKHIN	D	3	(2)	
Serhiy KONOVALOV	M	4	(6)	4
Serhiy KORMILTSEV	M	9	(9)	
Vitaliy KOSOVSKYI	M	7		3
Ihor KOSTYUK	M	2	(3)	
Olexandr KOSYRIN	A	2		1
Ramiz MAMEDOV (RUS)	D	13		
Roman MAXYMYUK	M	2	(5)	
Dmytro MYKHAILENKO	M	6	(4)	5
Andriy NESMACHNYI	D	14	(2)	
Olexandr RADCHENKO	D	1		
Serhiy REBROV	A	18	(2)	18
Serhiy SEREBRYANNIKOV	A	3	(2)	1
Maxim SHATSKIKH (UZB)	A	16	(9)	20
Olexandr SHOVKOVSKYI	G	15		
Yuriy TSELYKH	M		(1)	
Vladyslav VASHCHUK	D	20		1
Oleh VENHLYNSKYI	A	5	(1)	1
Artem YASHKIN	M	14	(5)	3
Volodymyr YEZERSKYI	D	5		

LEAGUE RESULTS 1999/2000

12/07/99	Kryvbas Kryvyi Rih	A	1-1	Rebrov (p)
16/07/99	Metalist Kharkiv	H	2-1	Serebryannikov, Rebrov
20/07/99	Vorskla Poltava	A	2-1	Kaladze, Gusin
24/07/99	Karpaty Lviv	H	3-0	Rebrov 3
07/08/99	Chornomorets Odesa	H	4-1	Rebrov 3 (1p), Shatskikh
21/08/99	Metalurg Donetsk	H	1-0	Rebrov (p)
25/09/99	Zirka Kirovohrad	H	3-0	Shatskikh, Gusin, Kosovskyi
03/10/99	Metalurg Mariupol	A	3-2	Kosovskyi (p), Konovalov, Vashchuk
15/10/99	Tavriya Simferopol	H	2-0	Shatskikh, Belkevich
23/10/99	Nyva Ternopil	A	1-0	Shatskikh
30/10/99	Dnipro Dnipropetrovsk	H	4-0	Venhlynskyi, Konovalov 2 (1p), Kosyrin
07/11/99	CSCA Kyiv	A	3-0	Fedorov, Kosovskyi, Shatskikh
21/11/99	Metalurg Zaporizhzhya	H	2-0	Yashkin, Konovalov
29/11/99	Shakhtar Donetsk	A	0-0	
03/12/99	Prykarpattya Ivano-Frankivsk	H	6-0	Belkevich 2, Shatskikh, Rebrov 3
18/03/00	CSCA Kyiv	H	3-1	Belkevich, Fedorov, Khatskevich
26/03/00	Dnipro Dnipropetrovsk	A	2-0	Khatskevich, Shatskikh
02/04/00	Nyva Ternopil	H	4-1	Yashkin, Rebrov (p), Demetradze 2
08/04/00	Tavriya Simferopol	A	3-1	Demetradze, Yashkin, Rebrov
16/04/00	Metalurg Mariupol	H	6-1	og (Rusanovskyi), Rebrov 2 (1p), Gusin, Demetradze 2
22/04/00	Zirka Kirovohrad	A	4-1	Mykhailenko 3, Shatskikh
29/04/00	Prykarpattya Ivano-Frankivsk	A	2-1	Gusin, Belkevich
06/05/00	Metalurg Donetsk	A	4-0	Gusin, Shatskikh, Rebrov 2
14/05/00	Shakhtar Donetsk	H	2-1	Khatskevich, Belkevich
21/05/00	Chornomorets Odesa	A	2-2	Shatskikh 2
04/06/00	Karpaty Lviv	A	3-2	Shatskikh 2, Demetradze
08/06/00	Vorskla Poltava	H	3-0	Shatskikh 3 (1p)
12/06/00	Metalurg Zaporizhzhya	A	3-0	Mykhailenko, Shatskikh 2
16/06/00	Metalist Kharkiv	A	5-0	Mykhailenko, Shatskikh 2, Demetradze, Kardash
20/06/00	Kryvbas Kryvyi Rih	H	2-1	Khatskevich, Demetradze

KARPATY LVIV

CLUB DIRECTORY

Karpaty Lviv
Av. Adam Mickewicz 6/7, 79005 Lviv
tel - (0322) 971011/724972/727744/705876
fax - (0322) 724072
website - www.lviv.ua/pfc-karpaty
email - karpaty@wertep.com
Year of Formation - 1963
President - Leonid Tkachuk
Secretary - Yuriy Nazarkevych
Coach - Lev Brovarskyi
Stadium - Ukraina (28,058)

MAJOR HONOURS
Domestic Cup (USSR) - (1) 1969.

APPEARANCES 99/00

	P	Ap	(s)	Gls
Serhiy DANYLOVSKYI	D	2	(5)	
Andriy DONETS	D		(1)	
Ivan HETSKO	A	13		10
Taras KABANOV	A	5	(8)	
Yaroslav KHOMA	M	24		1
Serhiy KOVALETS	M	15	(6)	2
Ihor LUCHKEVYCH	M	8	(1)	1
Mykhailo LUTSYSHYN	M	15	(8)	2
Ihor MAKOVEI	A	8	(3)	3
Serhiy MIZIN	M	14		5
Yevhen NAZAROV	M	29		2
Pavlo ONYSKO	A		(1)	
Ivan PAVLYUKH	D	20	(3)	1
Andriy POKLADOK	A	28	(1)	5
Dmytro SEMOCHKO	A	2	(3)	2
Volodymyr SHARAN	M	7	(3)	2
Vitaliy SHUKATKA	M	3		
Bohdan STRONTSITSKYI	G	28		
Serhiy TANASYUK	D	20	(5)	2
Andriy TLUMAK	G	2		
Roman TOLOCHKO	M	12	(6)	1
Oleh TYMCHYSHYN	D	11	(4)	
Volodymyr USHTAN	A		(2)	
Oleh VENCHAK	G		(1)	
Volodymyr VILCHYNSKYI	D	22	(3)	
Lyubomyr VOVCHUK	M	18	(7)	
Serhiy YEVHLEVSKYI	M	4	(10)	
Olexandr YEVTUSHOK	D	6		
Mykola ZAKOTYUK	D	11	(3)	
Roman ZUB	M	3	(2)	

LEAGUE RESULTS 1999/2000

12/07/99	Nyva Ternopil	A	2-1	Pokladok, Hetsko
16/07/99	CSCA Kyiv	H	1-0	Mizin
20/07/99	Metalist Kharkiv	A	0-1	
24/07/99	Dynamo Kyiv	A	0-3	
01/08/99	Chornomorets Odesa	H	5-0	Mizin 2, Khoma, Semochko, Kovalets
07/08/99	Metalurg Donetsk	A	1-2	Tanasyuk
15/08/99	Zirka Kirovohrad	H	3-0	Kovalets, Tanasyuk, Semochko
21/08/99	Tavriya Simferopol	A	1-4	Pokladok
29/08/99	Dnipro Dnipropetrovsk	H	4-0	Hetsko 4
25/09/99	Kryvbas Kryvyi Rih	A	1-2	Hetsko
16/10/99	Metalurg Zaporizhzhya	A	1-3	Hetsko
24/10/99	Shakhtar Donetsk	H	1-0	Pokladok
28/10/99	Vorskla Poltava	H	3-1	Mizin 2, Hetsko
01/11/99	Prykarpattya Ivano-Frankivsk	A	1-3	Sharan
07/11/99	Metalurg Mariupol	H	3-1	Sharan, Hetsko 2
18/03/00	Metalurg Mariupol	A	0-1	
25/03/00	Prykarpattya Ivano-Frankivsk	H	0-1	
02/04/00	Shakhtar Donetsk	A	0-4	
08/04/00	Metalurg Zaporizhzhya	H	1-0	Nazarov
16/04/00	Vorskla Poltava	A	0-1	
22/04/00	Kryvbas Kryvyi Rih	H	1-0	Lutsyshyn
06/05/00	Tavriya Simferopol	H	0-1	
10/05/00	Dnipro Dnipropetrovsk	A	1-1	Luchkevych
14/05/00	Zirka Kirovohrad	A	2-0	Tolochko, Makovei
21/05/00	Metalurg Donetsk	H	1-1	Pavlyukh (p)
26/05/00	Chornomorets Odesa	A	0-0	
04/06/00	Dynamo Kyiv	H	2-3	Makovei, Pokladok
08/06/00	Metalist Kharkiv	H	1-1	Lutsyshyn
16/06/00	CSCA Kyiv	A	3-2	Nazarov (p), Pokladok, Makovei
20/06/00	Nyva Ternopil	H	0-1	

KRYVBAS KRYVYI RIH

CLUB DIRECTORY

Kryvbas Kryvyi Rih
Av. Metalurgiv 5
320 070 Kryvyi Rih
tel - (0564) 281838/284912/400725
fax - (0564) 400726/236161
website - www.krivbas.dp.ua
email - fck@krcrme.dp.ua
Year of Formation - 1966
President - Serhiy Polishchuk
Secretary - Svyatoslav Azarkin
Coach - Oleh Taran
Stadium - Metalurg (30,170)

APPEARANCES 99/00

	P	Ap	(s)	Gls
Andriy ANISHCHENKO	D	16	(1)	
Serhiy DATSENKO	D		(4)	
Ihor DOROSHENKO	D	14		
Olexandr GRANOVSKYI	M	29		1
Ivan HETSKO	A	9	(1)	9
Olexandr HREBYNYUK	A	1	(2)	1
Andrius JOKSAS (LIT)	M	8	(7)	1
Alexandr KAIDARASHVILI (GEO)	A	3	(6)	1
Denys KOLCHIN	D	3	(2)	
Stanislav KRIULIN	M	4	(4)	
Olexandr LAVRENTSOV	G	27		
Serhiy MIZIN	M	13		4
Anton MONAKHOV	D	10		
Roman MONAREV	A	10	(4)	5
Hennadiy MOROZ	A	26		10
Andriy OKSYMETS	D	3	(1)	
Olexandr PALYANYTSYA	A	27	(1)	6
Valentyn PLATONOV	M	19	(2)	3
Volodymyr PONOMARENKO	M	27		
Serhiy PRAVKIN	G	3		
Andriy RUSOL	D		(3)	
Yevhen RYMSHIN	A	5	(18)	3
Oleg SIMAKOV (RUS)	M	29		5
Serhiy SUKHORUCHENKO	D	3	(6)	
Olexiy YAKYMENKO	M	6	(7)	2
Olexandr YEVSYUKOV	M		(3)	
Volodymyr YEZERSKYI	D	8	(1)	
Olexandr ZOTOV	M	27	(1)	2

LEAGUE RESULTS 1999/2000

12/07/99	Dynamo Kyiv	H	1-1	Rymshin
16/07/99	Vorskla Poltava	H	4-0	Simakov, Palyanytsya, Platonov, Moroz
20/07/99	Metalurg Zaporizhzhya	A	2-1	Rymshin, Simakov
24/07/99	Shakhtar Donetsk	H	1-0	Granovskyi
01/08/99	Prykarpattya Ivano-Frankivsk	A	3-1	Yakymenko, Moroz 2
07/08/99	Metalurg Mariupol	H	2-1	Moroz (p), Simakov
21/08/99	CSCA Kyiv	H	2-1	Monarev 2
25/08/99	Karpaty Lviv	H	2-1	Platonov 2
12/10/99	Nyva Ternopil	A	3-3	Monarev, Palyanytsya, Zotov
16/10/99	Metalurg Donetsk	H	0-0	
24/10/99	Zirka Kirovohrad	A	3-0	Palyanytsya, Monarev, Yakymenko
28/10/99	Chornomorets Odesa	A	0-2	
01/11/99	Tavriya Simferopol	H	2-1	Monarev, Moroz (p)
07/11/99	Dnipro Dnipropetrovsk	A	0-1	
20/11/99	Metalist Kharkiv	A	1-1	Simakov
18/03/00	Dnipro Dnipropetrovsk	H	2-2	Hetsko 2
25/03/00	Tavriya Simferopol	A	4-2	Simakov, Mizin 2, Kaidarashvili
02/04/00	Zirka Kirovohrad	H	3-1	Zotov, Moroz, Hetsko
08/04/00	Metalurg Donetsk	A	0-0	
16/04/00	Chornomorets Odesa	H	2-0	Mizin, Rymshin
22/04/00	Karpaty Lviv	A	0-1	
29/04/00	Metalist Kharkiv	H	2-0	og (Tofan), Palyanytsya
06/05/00	CSCA Kyiv	A	2-1	Moroz 2 (1p)
14/05/00	Nyva Ternopil	H	5-1	Hetsko 4 (1p), Mizin
21/05/00	Metalurg Mariupol	A	2-0	Hetsko, Palyanytsya
04/06/00	Shakhtar Donetsk	A	1-3	Moroz (p)
08/06/00	Metalurg Zaporizhzhya	H	1-0	Moroz (p)
12/06/00	Prykarpattya Ivano-Frankivsk	H	3-0	Palyanytsya, Hetsko, Hrebynyuk
16/06/00	Vorskla Poltava	A	0-3	
20/06/00	Dynamo Kyiv	A	1-2	Joksas

METALIST KHARKIV

CLUB DIRECTORY

Metalist Kharkiv
vul. Plekhanivska 65, 61001 Kharkiv
tel - (0572) 277646/278646
fax - (0572) 277936
website - www.vostok.net/sport/fotball/
Year of Formation - 1925
President - Valeriy Buhai
Secretary - Yuriy Lander
Coach - Mykhailo Fomenko
Stadium - Metalist (25,000)

MAJOR HONOURS
Domestic Cup (USSR) - (1) 1988.

APPEARANCES 99/00

	P	Ap	(s)	Gls
Dmytro CHUPRYN	M		(2)	
Valentyn GOLDIN	M	24		4
Olexandr GORYAINOV	G	30		
Viktor IVANENKO	D	29		10
Olexandr KARABUTA	M	1		
Vadym KHARCHENKO	M	18	(7)	4
Oleh KOLESOV	G		(1)	
Serhiy KOSTYUKOV	M	21		2
Oleh KUCHER	M	26	(1)	1
Andriy KYRLYK	M	29		4
Vitaliy LOTS	D	13	(4)	
Oleh LUKASH	D	2	(2)	
Roman PETS	D	27		1
Ihor PLAKHITIN	M	18	(5)	
Dmytro RUDNYAK	A	21	(5)	5
Serhiy RYZHYKH	A	3	(10)	1
Volodymyr SERIKOV	M		(6)	
Oleh SHEVCHENKO	A	1	(6)	
Yan SHKOLNIKOV	M	29		4
Ihor SHOPIN	M	19	(6)	
Olexandr SIMONOV	A	2	(8)	1
Vasyl TOFAN	D	17	(4)	4
Vitaliy ZAYETS	A		(1)	

LEAGUE RESULTS 1999/2000

12/07/99	CSKA Kyiv	A	1-0	Shkolnikov
16/07/99	Dynamo Kyiv	A	1-2	Ivanenko (p)
20/07/99	Karpaty Lviv	H	1-0	Tofan
24/07/99	Chornomorets Odesa	A	1-0	Pets
01/08/99	Metalurg Donetsk	H	2-1	Goldin, Ivanenko
07/08/99	Zirka Kirovohrad	A	2-2	Kyrlyk, Simonov
15/08/99	Tavriya Simferopol	H	2-1	Rudnyak, Kyrlyk
21/08/99	Dnipro Dnipropetrovsk	A	0-1	
25/08/99	Vorskla Poltava	A	1-3	Goldin
03/10/99	Metalurg Zaporizhzhya	H	0-0	
16/10/99	Shakhtar Donetsk	A	1-3	Goldin
24/10/99	Prykarpattya Ivano-Frankivsk	H	2-0	Goldin, Kharchenko
31/10/99	Metalurg Mariupol	A	1-3	Shkolnikov
07/11/99	Nyva Ternopil	H	5-2	Tofan, Ivanenko 2, Kharchenko 2
20/11/99	Kryvbas Kryvyi Rih	H	1-1	Kharchenko
18/03/00	Nyva Ternopil	A	1-2	Kostyukov
25/03/00	Metalurg Mariupol	H	2-0	Ivanenko, Kostyukov
02/04/00	Prykarpattya Ivano-Frankivsk	A	1-2	Tofan
08/04/00	Shakhtar Donetsk	H	0-1	
16/04/00	Metalurg Zaporizhzhya	A	1-1	Rudnyak
22/04/00	Vorskla Poltava	H	2-1	Ryzhykh, Rudnyak
29/04/00	Kryvbas Kryvyi Rih	A	0-2	
06/05/00	Dnipro Dnipropetrovsk	H	2-1	Kyrlyk 2
14/05/00	Tavriya Simferopol	A	2-2	Rudnyak, Ivanenko
21/05/00	Zirka Kirovohrad	H	4-0	Ivanenko (p), Shkolnikov 2, Rudnyak
26/05/00	Metalurg Donetsk	A	1-1	Ivanenko (p)
04/06/00	Chornomorets Odesa	H	1-1	Ivanenko
08/06/00	Karpaty Lviv	A	1-1	Kucher
16/06/00	Dynamo Kyiv	H	0-5	
20/06/00	CSCA Kyiv	H	2-0	Ivanenko, Tofan

METALURG DONETSK

THE EUROPEAN FOOTBALL YEARBOOK 2000-2001

CLUB DIRECTORY

Metalurg Donetsk
vul. Kuibysheva
Sportkomplex Metalurg
83062 Donetsk
tel - (062) 3329354/2616094/2613041
fax - (062) 2612208
email - postmaster@metallurg.donetsk.ua
Year of Formation - 1995
President - Mykhailo Lyashko
Secretary - Ihor Klykov
Coach - Mykhailo Sokolovskyi; Semen Altman
Stadium - im 125 richchya DMK (10,000)

APPEARANCES 99/00

	P	Ap	(s)	Gls
Olexiy BULGAKOV	D	6	(4)	
Yuriy DANCHENKO	A	15	(1)	
Olexandr DOROKHOV	D	23	(2)	
Serhiy DRANOV	A	12	(12)	6
Viktor DYAK	D		(1)	
Ihor KOROL	D	2	(4)	
Olexandr KOVAL	D	10		
Olexandr KOVALENKO	M	20	(1)	1
Albert KOVALEV	D	28		2
Yakiv KRIPAK	A	8	(4)	1
Vadym KROKHAN	M		(5)	
Andriy KUPTSOV	M	2	(2)	
Andriy KURAYEV	G	27		
Ihor LEONOV	D	2	(4)	
Olexandr MARTYUK	D	1	(1)	
Vitaliy MINTENKO	A	2	(4)	
Olexiy MORGUNOV	M	2	(8)	
Andriy MUKHIN	M		(3)	
Andriy NIKITIN	G	3		
Serhiy OSADCHYI	D	26		1
Volodymyr PYATENKO	D	21		1
Roman PYLYPCHUK	A	10		4
Olexandr SEVIDOV	A	9	(3)	8
Oleh SHELAYEV	M	12	(1)	3
Serhiy SHYSHCHENKO	M	25		8
Denys SOKOLOVSKYI	M	4	(4)	
Vadym TALOVEROV	M	1	(1)	
Mykola VOLOSHYN	D	3	(2)	
Olexandr VOSKOBOINIK	A	19	(2)	2
Volodymyr YAKSMANYTSKYI	D	22		1
Andriy ZAVYALOV	M	12	(9)	
Sergei ZHUNENKO (RUS)	M	3		1

LEAGUE RESULTS 1999/2000

12/07/99	Prykarpattya Ivano-Frankivsk	A	1-1	Sevidov
16/07/99	Metalurg Mariupol	H	2-1	Shyshchenko, Sevidov
20/07/99	Nyva Ternopil	A	0-3	
24/07/99	CSCA Kyiv	H	0-0	
01/08/99	Metalist Kharkiv	A	1-2	Shyshchenko
07/08/99	Karpaty Lviv	H	2-1	Shyshchenko 2
15/08/99	Chornomorets Odesa	A	1-0	Shyshchenko
21/08/99	Dynamo Kyiv	A	0-1	
29/08/99	Zirka Kirovohrad	H	2-0	Voskoboinik, Dranov
25/09/99	Tavriya Simferopol	A	1-1	Kovalev
03/10/99	Dnipro Dnipropetrovsk	H	5-1	Shyshchenko (p), Kovalenko, Dranov, Savidov 2
16/10/99	Kryvbas Kryvyi Rih	A	0-0	
24/10/99	Vorskla Poltava	H	2-3	Savidov 2
31/10/99	Metalurg Zaporizhzhyu	A	1-1	Sevidov
07/11/99	Shakhtar Donetsk	H	2-3	Zhunenko, Sevidov (p)
18/03/00	Shakhtar Donetsk	A	0-2	
25/03/00	Metalurg Zaporizhzhya	H	2-1	Voskoboinik, Shelayev
02/04/00	Vorskla Poltava	A	0-0	
08/04/00	Kryvbas Kryvyi Rih	H	0-0	
16/04/00	Dnipro Dnipropetrovsk	A	1-0	Shyshchenko
22/04/00	Tavriya Simferopol	H	0-0	
29/04/00	Zirka Kirovohrad	A	2-0	Kripak, Pylypchuk
06/05/00	Dynamo Kyiv	H	0-4	
14/05/00	Chornomorets Odesa	H	4-0	Pylypchuk 2, Pyatenko, Shelayev
21/05/00	Karpaty Lviv	A	1-1	Kovalev
26/05/00	Metalist Kharkiv	H	1-1	Yaksmanytskyi
04/06/00	CSCA Kyiv	A	0-1	
08/06/00	Nyva Ternopil	H	3-2	Pylypchuk, Shyshchenko, Dranov
16/06/00	Metalurg Mariupol	A	1-4	Shelayev
20/06/00	Prykarpattya Ivano-Frankivsk	H	4-1	Dranov 3 (1p), Osadchyi (p)

METALURG MARIUPOL

CLUB DIRECTORY

FC Metalurg Mariupol
vul. Yevpatoriiska 45A
341 015 Mariupol
tel - (0629) 331240/530017/371264
fax - (0629) 333363/336124
Year of Formation - 1994
President - Lyubomyr Palyi
Secretary - Serhiy Katrych
Coach - Mykola Pavlov
Stadium - Azovstal (9,000)

APPEARANCES 99/00

		P	Ap	(s)	Gls
Volodymyr ANIKEYEV	D	27			2
Kostyantyn BABYCH	A	29			12
Volodymyr BRAILA	M	11	(2)		1
Serhiy DIRYAVKA	D	21			
Anatoliy DUKHNO	A		(2)		
Vitaliy FENIN	D	1			
Olexandr GAIDASH	A	14			5
Danylo HANYTSKYI	A	4	(12)		1
Serhiy HONCHARENKO	M	13	(2)		
Serhiy KOLESNYK	M	7	(4)		
Andriy KOTYUK	M	4	(10)		1
Olexiy LEVCHENKO	M		(2)		
Olexandr MEKHANOSHYN	M	7	(8)		
Serhiy MITIN	D	2	(1)		
Stepan MOLOKUTSKO	M	11	(12)		2
Vitaliy PANTILOV	M	17	(7)		4
Ihor PLOTKO	M	25			5
Vitaliy PUSHKUTSA	A	15	(2)		1
Roman RUSANOVSKYI	D	8	(1)		
Olexandr RYKUN	M	23	(2)		6
Kostyantyn SAKHAROV	M	28	(1)		4
Ihor SHUKHOVTSEV	G	30			
Oleh SYZON	D	2	(2)		
Andriy TARAKHTIY	G		(1)		
Yevhen TARAN	D	1	(2)		
Mykola VOLOSYANKO	D	27	(1)		3
Vitaliy ZALIZNYAK	D	3	(4)		

LEAGUE RESULTS 1999/2000

12/07/99	Chornomorets Odesa	H	5-0	Molokutsko, og (Matyushenko), Pushkutsa, Sakharov, Volosyanko
16/07/99	Metalurg Donetsk	A	1-2	Plotko
20/07/99	Zirka Kirovohrad	H	3-0	Kotyuk, Sakharov, Babych
24/07/99	Tavriya Simferopol	A	0-1	
01/08/99	Dnipro Dnipropetrovsk	H	3-2	Volosyanko, Molokutsko, Plotko
07/08/99	Kryvbas Kryvyi Rih	A	1-2	Babych
15/08/99	Vorskla Poltava	H	2-1	Pantilov (p), Babych
21/08/99	Metalurg Zaporizhzhya	A	1-2	Plotko
25/09/99	Prykarpattya Ivano-Frankivsk	A	0-3	
03/10/99	Dynamo Kyiv	H	2-3	Braila, Babych
16/10/99	Nyva Ternopil	H	2-1	Babych 2
20/10/99	Shakhtar Donetsk	H	1-2	Pantilov
24/10/99	CSCA Kyiv	A	1-1	og (Ulyanytskyi)
31/10/99	Metalist Kharkiv	H	3-1	Pantilov (p), Hanytskyi, Babych
07/11/99	Karpaty Lviv	A	1-3	Pantilov
18/03/00	Karpaty Lviv	H	1-0	Gaidash
25/03/00	Metalist Kharkiv	A	0-2	
02/04/00	CSCA Kyiv	H	2-0	Plotko, Sakharov
08/04/00	Nyva Ternopil	A	1-2	Gaidash
16/04/00	Dynamo Kyiv	A	1-6	Rykun
22/04/00	Prykarpattya Ivano-Frankivsk	H	2-0	Rykun, Gaidash
29/04/00	Shakhtar Donetsk	A	0-3	
06/05/00	Metalurg Zaporizhzhya	H	1-1	Rykun
14/05/00	Vorskla Poltava	A	1-1	Gaidash
21/05/00	Kryvbas Kryvyi Rih	H	0-2	
26/05/00	Dnipro Dnipropetrovsk	A	0-1	
04/06/00	Tavriya Simferopol	H	4-1	Gaidash, Babych 2, Anikeyev (p)
08/06/00	Zirka Kirovohrad	A	2-1	Anikeyev (p), Rykun
16/06/00	Metalurg Donetsk	H	4-1	Babych 2, Rykun 2
20/06/00	Chornomorets Odesa	A	4-3	Plotko, Sakharov, Babych, Volosyanko

METALURG ZAPORIZHZHYA

CLUB DIRECTORY

Metalurg Zaporizhzhya
vul. 12 April 2
69037 Zaporizhzhya
tel - (0621) 326672/571433/126645
fax - (0621) 326672/326887
website - www.reis.zp.ua/fcmetallurg
Year of Formation - 1949
President - Viktor Mezheiko
Secretary - Ihor Pavlenko
Coach - Myron Markevych
Stadium - Metalurg (25,000)

APPEARANCES 99/00

		P	Ap	(s)	Gls
Armen AKOPYAN	M	22	(3)	1
Olexandr BATRACHENKO	D		(6)	
Yuriy BENIO	D	13		
Oleh BERESKYI	G	21		
Ivan BOHATYR	D	3	(9)	
Roman BONDARENKO	A	21	(5)	4
Serhiy BUHAI	D	19	(3)	
Andriy CHEREVAN	M	2	(1)	
Olexandr CHORNYAVSKYI	D	5	(7)	
Olexandr CHYZHEVSKYI	D	13		
Andriy DEMCHENKO	A	24	(1)	3
Yuriy DUDNYK	M		(5)	
Taras HREBENYUK	G	9		
Andriy KONYUSHENKO	D	28	(1)	6
Serhiy KLYUCHYK	M		(8)	
Yuriy MARKIN	D	2	(2)	1
Ivan OLEXIYENKO	D	3	(6)	
Olexandr OSTASHOV	A		(4)	
Valentyn POLTAVETS	M	29		9
Oleh RATIY	D	27		1
Vyacheslav SHEVCHUK	D	12	(9)	1
Andriy SHPAK	A	2	(5)	1
Vitaliy SKYSH	D	14		2
Denys SMIRNOV	M	5	(7)	2
Olexandr SPIVAK	M	21	(2)	3
Dmytro TOPCHIYEV	M	17		
Aco VASILJEVIC (YUG)	A	6	(4)	5
Vladyslav ZUBKOV	M	12	(1)	4

LEAGUE RESULTS 1999/2000

12/07/99	Tavriya Simferopol	H	3-2	Demchenko, Spivak, Markin
16/07/99	Dnipro Dnipropetrovsk	A	2-0	Ratiy, Poltavets
20/07/99	Kryvbas Kryvyi Rih	H	1-2	Spivak
24/07/99	Vorskla Poltava	A	0-3	
06/08/99	Shakhtar Donetsk	H	1-0	Konyushenko
15/08/99	Prykarpattya Ivano-Frankivsk	A	0-0	
21/08/99	Metalurg Mariupol	H	2-1	Bondarenko 2
29/08/99	Nyva Ternopil	A	3-0	Bondarenko, Poltavets 2
25/09/99	CSCA Kyiv	H	2-2	Poltavets, Skysh (p)
03/10/99	Metalist Kharkiv	A	0-0	
16/10/99	Karpaty Lviv	H	3-1	Konyushenko 2, Poltavets
24/10/99	Chornomorets Odesa	A	0-1	
31/10/99	Metalurg Donetsk	H	1-1	Skysh (p)
07/11/99	Zirka Kirovohrad	A	1-1	Poltavets
21/11/99	Dynamo Kyiv	A	0-2	
18/03/00	Zirka Kirovohrad	H	2-0	Bondarenko, Demchenko
25/03/00	Metalurg Donetsk	A	1-2	Spivak
02/04/00	Chornomorets Odesa	H	2-0	Zubkov, Demchenko
08/04/00	Karpaty Lviv	A	0-1	
16/04/00	Metalist Kharkiv	H	1-1	Vasiljevic
22/04/00	CSCA Kyiv	A	0-1	
29/04/00	Nyva Ternopil	H	4-0	Zubkov 2 (1p), Vasiljevic 2
06/05/00	Metalurg Mariupol	A	1-1	Konyushenko
14/05/00	Prykarpattya Ivano-Frankivsk	H	2-2	Poltavets (p), Vasiljevic
21/05/00	Shakhtar Donetsk	A	0-4	
04/06/00	Vorskla Poltava	H	3-1	Vasiljevic, Konyushenko, Shevchuk
08/06/00	Kryvbas Kryvyi Rih	A	0-1	
12/06/00	Dynamo Kyiv	H	0-3	
16/06/00	Dnipro Dnipropetrovsk	H	6-1	Konyushenko, Akopyan, Poltavets, Zubkov, Smirnov, Shpak
20/06/00	Tavriya Simferopol	A	2-1	Poltavets (p), Smirnov

NYVA TERNOPIL

CLUB DIRECTORY

Nyva Ternopil
pr. Stepan Bandera 5
46002 Ternopil
tel - (0352) 223153/220752/246407/251837
fax - (0352) 220752/254742
Year of Formation - 1983
President - Olexandr Kryvyi
Secretary - Ivan Hresko
Coach - Valeriy Bohuslavskyi
Stadium - Central (17,000)

APPEARANCES 99/00

	P	Ap	(s)	Gls
Muslim AGAYEV (TRK)	A	8	(4)	1
Serhiy BOHORODYCHENKO	D		(1)	
Olexandr BOITSAN	D	19	(1)	
Ihor BISKUP	D	13	(3)	1
Shota CHOMAKHIDZE (GEO)	M	10	(3)	2
Mykhailo DEMYANCHUK	M		(2)	
Kakhaber DGEBUADZE (GEO)	M	9	(9)	1
Pavlo FILIPENKO	D	18	(1)	1
Avtandil GVIANIDZE (GEO)	A	21	(3)	
Serhiy HONCHARENKO	M	9	(1)	1
Aleksandre KAIDARASHVILI (GEO)	A	8	(5)	4
Avtandil KAPANADZE (GEO)	A	21	(1)	12
Tariel KAPANADZE (GEO)	M	30		3
Serhiy KHOMENKO	A	8	(3)	1
Serhiy KRYVYI	M	11	(7)	2
Mykola LAPA	D	25		
Yevhen LASHUK	A	5	(2)	
Kostyantyn LEMISHKO	M	13		2
Hennadiy LOSEV	G	21	(1)	
Yuriy MAGDIYEV (TRK)	M	10	(1)	3
Dmytro MAZUR	D	21	(4)	2
Konstantine METREVELI (GEO)	A		(1)	
Oleh MISHENIN	D	5	(1)	
Yuriy NIKITENKO	G	9	(1)	
Matviy NYKOLAICHUK	M	5	(2)	
Andriy SHPAK	A	2	(6)	
Serhiy SHYMANSKYI	D	4	(3)	
Avtandil SIKHARULIDZE (GEO)	A	9	(8)	3
Ivan SOPRONYUK	D		(2)	
Ihor SUSHKO	D	8	(5)	
Valentyn ZAYETS	D	8		

LEAGUE RESULTS 1999/2000

Date	Opponent		Score	Scorers
12/07/99	Karpaty Lviv	H	1-2	Honcharenko
16/07/99	Chornomorets Odesa	A	0-1	
20/07/99	Metalurg Donetsk	H	3-0	Magdiyev, Kaidarashvili, Kapanadze T.
24/07/99	Zirka Kirovohrad	A	1-1	Sikharulidze
01/08/99	Tavriya Simferopol	H	1-1	Kaidarashvili
07/08/99	Dnipro Dnipropetrovsk	A	1-1	Magdiyev
21/08/99	Vorskla Poltava	A	2-4	Agayev, Kryvyi (p)
29/08/99	Metalurg Zaporizhzhya	H	0-3	
25/09/99	Shakhtar Donetsk	A	0-5	
06/10/99	Prykarpattya Ivano-Frankivsk	H	3-1	Kryvyi (p), Magdiyev, Sikharulidze
12/10/99	Kryvbas Kryvyi Rih	H	3-3	Kapanadze A. 2, Sikharulidze
16/10/99	Metalurg Mariupol	A	1-2	Kapanadze A.
23/10/99	Dynamo Kyiv	H	0-1	
01/11/99	CSCA Kyiv	H	2-2	Kaidarashvili 2 (1p)
07/11/99	Metalist Kharkiv	A	2-5	Kapanadze A. 2
18/03/00	Metalist Kharkiv	H	2-1	Mazur (p), Kapanadze A.
25/03/00	CSCA Kyiv	A	0-0	
02/04/00	Dynamo Kyiv	A	1-4	Dgebuadze
08/04/00	Metalurg Mariupol	H	2-1	Mazur, Kapanadze T.
16/04/00	Prykarpattya Ivano-Frankivsk	A	1-2	Kapanadze A.
22/04/00	Shakhtar Donetsk	H	1-1	Khomenko
29/04/00	Metalurg Zaporizhzhya	A	0-4	
06/05/00	Vorskla Poltava	H	1-1	Chomakhidze
14/05/00	Kryvbas Kryvyi Rih	A	1-5	Kapanadze A.
21/05/00	Dnipro Dnipropetrovsk	H	1-1	Lemishko
26/05/00	Tavriya Simferopol	A	1-1	Kapanadze A.
04/06/00	Zirka Kirovohrad	H	3-0	Chomakhidze, Kapanadze A., Kapanadze T.
08/06/00	Metalurg Donetsk	A	2-3	Kapanadze A., Filipenko
16/06/00	Chornomorets Odesa	H	3-1	Lemishko, Kapanadze A., Biskup (p)
20/06/00	Karpaty Lviv	A	1-0	og (Pavlyukh)

PRYKARPATTYA IVANO-FRANKIVSK

CLUB DIRECTORY

Prykarpattya Ivano-Frankivsk
vul. Taras Shevchenko 47
76000 Ivano-Frankivsk
tel - (0342) 25222/25303/552432
fax - (0342) 552432
Year of Formation - 1981
President - Anatoliy Revutskyi
Secretary - Orest Babiy
Coach - Ihor Yavorskyi; Anatoliy Boiko;
Serhiy Morozov
Stadium - Rukh (15,000)

APPEARANCES 99/00

		P	Ap	(s)	Gls
Orest ATAMANCHUK	A	10	(4)	3
Yuriy CHUMAK	G	12		
Yuriy FOKIN	D	10	(4)	
Olexiy GORODOV	A	13	(2)	2
Valentyn GREGUL	D	28		5
Ihor HOHIL	M	5		1
Olexandr HONCHAR	M	14	(1)	
Pavlo IRYCHUK	A	13	(1)	3
Andriy KHOMYN	D	4		
Olexiy KHRAMTSOV	D	9		
Ivan KORPONAI	A	1		
Taras KOVALCHUK	M	9	(5)	
Volodymyr KOVALYUK	M	18	(8)	2
Serhiy KOZYR	M	1	(4)	1
Ihor KRIL	M	13	(7)	
Volodymyr LARIN	A	17	(5)	
Stepan MATVIIV	M	4	(5)	
Matviy NYKOLAICHUK	M	1	(5)	1
Vitaliy PERVAK	D	24		
Serhiy POLISHCHUK	G	18		
Serhiy PTASHNYK	M		(4)	1
Oleh RAK	A	1	(5)	
Anatoliy REDUSHKO	A	6	(6)	
Dmytro SEMCHUK	D	8		
Kostyantyn SOSENKO	D	20		
Andriy SPIVAK	M	29		6
Yaroslav VATAMANYUK	D	5	(6)	
Olexandr VENHLYNSKYI	M	24	(2)	
Ruslan ZABRANSKYI	A	4	(3)	1
Mykola ZUYENKO	D	9	(1)	

LEAGUE RESULTS 1999/2000

12/07/99	Metalurg Donetsk	H	1-1	Ptashnyk
16/07/99	Zirka Kirovohrad	A	1-1	Gregul
20/07/99	Tavriya Simferopol	H	0-2	
24/07/99	Dnipro Dnipropetrovsk	A	1-1	Atamanchuk
01/08/99	Kryvbas Kryvyi Rih	H	1-3	Kovalyuk (p)
07/08/99	Vorskla Poltava	A	0-2	
15/08/99	Metalurg Zaporizhzhya	H	0-0	
21/08/99	Shakhtar Donetsk	A	0-1	
25/09/99	Metalurg Mariupol	H	3-0	Kovalyuk (p), Nikolaichuk, Atamanchuk
06/10/99	Nyva Ternopil	A	1-3	Spivak
16/10/99	CSCA Kyiv	H	0-0	
24/10/99	Metalist Kharkiv	A	0-2	
10/11/99	Karpaty Lviv	H	3-1	Zabranskyi, og (Tanasyuk), Atamanchuk
07/11/99	Chornomorets Odesa	A	0-0	
03/12/99	Dynamo Kyiv	A	0-6	
18/03/00	Chornomorets Odesa	H	1-0	Gregul
25/03/00	Karpaty Lviv	A	1-0	Irychuk
02/04/00	Metalist Kharkiv	H	2-1	Gregul (p), Gorodov
08/04/00	CSCA Kyiv	A	1-2	Hohil
16/04/00	Nyva Ternopil	H	2-1	Irychuk, Gregul (p)
22/04/00	Metalurg Mariupol	A	0-2	
29/04/00	Dynamo Kyiv	H	1-2	Spivak
06/05/00	Shakhtar Donetsk	H	0-2	
14/05/00	Metalurg Zaporizhzhya	A	2-2	Spivak, Irychuk
21/05/00	Vorskla Poltava	H	0-1	
04/06/00	Dnipro Dnipropetrovsk	H	1-1	Gregul
08/06/00	Tavriya Simferopol	A	0-1	
12/06/00	Kryvbas Kryvyi Rih	A	0-3	
16/06/00	Zirka Kirovohrad	H	4-2	Gorodov, Spivak 3 (1p)
20/06/00	Metalurg Donetsk	A	1-4	Kozyr

SHAKHTAR DONETSK

CLUB DIRECTORY

Shakhtar Donetsk
vul. Artema 86A, 83050 Donetsk
tel - (062) 3358828/3354694/3373271/
3353961
fax - (062) 3357899
website - www.shakhtyor.donbass.com
email - postmaster@shakhtyor.donbass.com
Year of Formation - 1946
President - Rinat Akhmetov
Secretary - Vyacheslav Sharafutdinov
Coach - Anatoliy Byshovets; Olexiy Drozdenko;
Viktor Prokopenko
Stadium - Shakhtar (40,483)

MAJOR HONOURS
Domestic Cup (USSR) - (4)
1961, 1962, 1980, 1983.
Domestic Cup - (2) 1995. 1997.

APPEARANCES 99/00

	P	Ap	(s)	Gls
Vitaliy ABRAMOV (RUS)	M	7	(3)	2
Marian ALIUTA (ROM)	M	2	(4)	
Serhiy ATELKIN	A	8	(1)	1
Alexei BAKHAREV (RUS)	M	18	(6)	1
Olexiy BELIK	A	2	(6)	4
Yuriy BENIO	D	8		1
Olexandr CHYZHEVSKYI	D	9		
Dainus GLEVECKAS (LIT)	D	13		1
Yevhen KOTOV	D	10	(2)	
Olexandr KOVAL	D	3	(1)	
Serhiy KOVALEV	M	25	(3)	1
Yakiv KRIPAK	A	1	(2)	
Valeriy KRIVENTSOV	A	7	(5)	
Viktor MATSYUK	A	1	(1)	
Oleh MATVEYEV	M	7	(5)	1
Volodymyr MYKYTYN	M	9	(3)	
Serhiy NAHORNYAK	M	6	(2)	1
Hennadiy ORBU	M	19	(3)	7
Oleh PESTRYAKOV	M	5	(2)	1
Serhiy POPOV	D	24	(1)	6
Yuriy SELEZNEV	M	9	(5)	1
Oleh SHELAYEV	A		(4)	
Alexandr SHMARKO (RUS)	D	6	(3)	
Andrey SHTOLCERS (LAT)	A	11	(4)	4
Dmytro SHUTKOV	G		(1)	
Mykhailo STAROSTYAK	D	27		
Anatoliy TYMOSHCHUK	M	18	(5)	
Yuriy VIRT	G	30		
Andriy VOROBEI	A	22	(2)	15
Hennadiy ZUBOV	M	23	(3)	12

LEAGUE RESULTS 1999/2000

12/07/99	Zirka Kirovohrad	H	1-0	Matveyev
16/07/99	Tavriya Simferopol	A	3-0	Benio, Orbu, Popov
20/07/99	Dnipro Dnipropetrovsk	H	2-0	Popov, Zubov
24/07/00	Kryvbas Kryvyi Rih	A	0-1	
01/08/00	Vorskla Poltava	H	0-0	
06/08/00	Metalurg Zaporizhzhya	A	0-1	
21/08/99	Prykarpattya Ivano-Frankivsk	H	1-0	Seleznev
25/09/99	Nyva Ternopil	H	5-0	Popov 2, Nahornyak, Shtolcers 2
16/10/99	Metalist Kharkiv	H	3-1	Vorobei 2, Orbu
20/10/99	Metalurg Mariupol	A	2-1	Popov, Vorobei
24/10/99	Karpaty Lviv	A	0-1	
28/10/99	CSCA Kyiv	A	0-1	
02/11/99	Chornomorets Odesa	H	0-1	
07/11/99	Metalurg Donetsk	A	3-2	Shtolcers 2, Zubov (p)
29/11/99	Dynamo Kyiv	H	0-0	
18/03/00	Metalurg Donetsk	H	2-0	Vorobei, Pestryakov
25/03/00	Chornomorets Odesa	A	3-0	Zubov 2, Vorobei
02/04/00	Karpaty Lviv	H	4-0	Atelkin, Bakharev, Zubov (p), Vorobei
08/04/00	Metalist Kharkiv	A	1-0	Vorobei
16/04/00	CSCA Kyiv	H	3-0	Zubov 2 (1p), og (Yevtushok)
22/04/00	Nyva Ternopil	A	1-1	Vorobei
29/04/00	Metalurg Mariupol	H	3-0	Zubov 2, Vorobei
06/05/00	Prykarpattya Ivano-Frankivsk	A	2-0	Popov, Abramov
14/05/00	Dynamo Kyiv	A	1-2	Vorobei
21/05/00	Metalurg Zaporizhzhya	H	4-0	Orbu 2 (2p), Zubov, Vorobei
26/05/00	Vorskla Poltava	A	3-0	Orbu, Belik, Vorobei
04/06/00	Kryvbas Kryvyi Rih	H	3-1	Vorobei, Orbu (p), Kovalev
08/06/00	Dnipro Dnipropetrovsk	A	2-1	Belik 2
16/06/00	Tavriya Simferopol	H	2-0	Vorobei, Zubov
20/06/00	Zirka Kirovohrad	A	6-2	Orbu, Abramov, Vorobei (p), Gleveckas, Belik, Zubov

TAVRIYA SIMFEROPOL

CLUB DIRECTORY

Tavriya Simferopol
vul. A. Pushkin 46, 95000 Simferopol
tel - (0652) 255383/276083
fax - (0652) 270147
email - fct@pop,cris.net
Year of Formation - 1963
President - Ruvin Aronov
Secretary - Borys Levin
Coach - Anatoliy Korobochka; Volodymyr Muntyan
Stadium - Lokomotyv (23,612)

MAJOR HONOURS
League Championship - (1) 1992.

APPEARANCES 99/00

	P	Ap	(s)	Gls
Denys ANDRIYENKO	D	5	(6)	
Olexiy ANTYUKHIN	A	17	(5)	7
Serhiy AVERIN	M	4	(17)	1
Oleh BOHOMOL	M	5	(4)	
Dmytro DEMYANENKO	D	6		
Yuriy DONYUSHKIN	D	26		
Olexandr GAIDASH	A	13	(2)	5
Olexiy HRYSHCHENKO	M	1	(3)	
Serhiy KLYUCHYK	M	14	(1)	
Mykhailo KONOPELKO	M	7	(2)	
Hennadiy KUNDENOK	M	11	(3)	1
Olexandr KUNDENOK	M	26	(4)	3
Pavlo KUTSYI	D	5	(2)	
Olexiy KUZNETSOV	D		(3)	
Gennadiy MARDAS (BLS)	M	11	(2)	
Yuriy MARKIN	D	14	(1)	1
Olexandr MITROFANOV	D	29		3
Dmytro NAZAROV	D	25	(1)	
Andriy OPARIN	M	27	(1)	1
Olexiy OSIPOV	M	14		5
Volodymyr POLISHCHUK	D	12		3
Vsevolod ROMANENKO	G	10		
Viktor SMIGUNOV	D	12	(1)	1
Olexandr SOKORENKO	G	2		
Ruslan TABACHUN	A	4	(8)	
Serhiy VELYCHKO	G	18		
Serhiy VETRENNIKOV	M		(2)	
Roman VOINAROVSKYI	M	1	(4)	
Serhiy YESIN	D	11	(12)	1

LEAGUE RESULTS 1999/2000

12/07/99	Metalurg Zaporizhzhya	A	2-3	Gaidash, Oparin
16/07/99	Shakhtar Donetsk	H	0-3	
20/07/99	Prykarpattya Ivano-Frankivsk	A	2-0	Gaidash, Osipov
24/07/99	Metalurg Mariupol	H	1-0	Antyukhin
01/08/99	Nyva Ternopil	A	1-1	Osipov
07/08/99	CSCA Kyiv	H	1-2	Gaidash
15/08/99	Metalist Kharkiv	A	1-2	Osipov
21/08/99	Karpaty Lviv	H	4-1	Kundenok O., Osipov 2 (1p), Averin
29/08/99	Chornomorets Odesa	A	2-1	Mitrofanov, Antyukhin
25/09/99	Metalurg Donetsk	H	1-1	Smigunov
03/10/99	Zirka Kirovohrad	A	2-2	Gaidash 2
15/10/99	Dynamo Kyiv	A	0-2	
24/10/99	Dnipro Dnipropetrovsk	H	1-1	Kundenok H.
01/11/99	Kryvbas Kryvyi Rih	A	1-2	Yesin
07/11/99	Vorskla Poltava	H	0-3	
18/03/00	Vorskla Poltava	A	0-4	
25/03/00	Kryvbas Kryvyi Rih	H	2-4	Mitrofanov (p), Kundenok O.
03/04/00	Dnipro Dnipropetrovsk	A	0-1	
08/04/00	Dynamo Kyiv	H	1-3	Polishchuk
16/04/00	Zirka Kirovohrad	H	2-0	Antyukhin, Mitrofanov (p)
22/04/00	Metalurg Donetsk	A	0-0	
29/04/00	Chornomorets Odesa	H	1-1	Polishchuk
06/05/00	Karpaty Lviv	A	1-0	Kundenok O.
14/05/00	Metalist Kharkiv	H	2-2	Antyukhin, Markin
21/05/00	CSCA Kyiv	A	0-3	
26/05/00	Nyva Ternopil	H	1-1	Antyukhin
04/06/00	Metalurg Mariupol	A	1-4	Polishchuk
08/06/00	Prykarpattya Ivano-Frankivsk	H	1-0	Antyukhin (p)
16/06/00	Shakhtar Donetsk	A	0-2	
20/06/00	Metalurg Zaporizhzhya	H	1-2	Antyukhin (p)

VORSKLA POLTAVA

CLUB DIRECTORY

Vorskla Poltava
Nezalezhnosti square 16
36003 Poltava
tel - (0532) 222668/229598/229623
fax - (0532) 224833
Year of Formation - 1987
President - Volodymyr Artemov
Secretary - Ihor Romanov
Coach - Anatoliy Konkov
Stadium - Vorskla (28,000)

APPEARANCES 99/00

	P	Ap	(s)	Gls
Serhiy BALANCHUK	D	30		1
Vyacheslav BOGODELOV	G	1	(1)	
Serhiy CHERNYAK	D	22		1
Viktor DOTSENKO	D	30		3
Andriy HOLOVKO	A	2	(16)	4
Olexandr Mykolayovych HOLOVKO	D	11	(4)	1
Andriy HUZENKO	M	7	(11)	1
Vitaliy KOBZAR	M	28		9
Olexiy KOSENKO	M		(3)	
Ihor KOSTYUK	M	15		4
Andriy KOVTUN	G	29		
Serhiy LEZHENTSEV	D	7	(4)	1
Ihor MACHOHAN	D	9	(10)	
Mikhail MAKOVSKIY (BLS)	M	20	(2)	1
Vladimir MAKOVSKIY (BLS)	M	15		2
Volodymyr MAZYAR	A	20	(5)	10
Olexandr MELASHCHENKO	M	4	(15)	6
Olexandr OMELCHUK	M	30		2
Serhiy ONOPKO	M	23	(6)	3
Olexandr PERSHIN	D	19		
Yordan PETKOV (BUL)	D	7		
Serhiy SILETSKYI	A	1		

LEAGUE RESULTS 1999/2000

12/07/99	Dnipro Dnipropetrovsk	H	4-0	Holovko A., Lezhentsev, Mazyar, Onopko
16/07/99	Kryvbas Kryvyi Rih	A	0-4	
20/07/99	Dynamo Kyiv	H	1-2	Kobzar
24/07/99	Metalurg Zaporizhzhya	H	3-0	Kobzar, Mazyar, Holovko A.
01/08/99	Shakhtar Donetsk	A	0-0	
07/08/99	Prykarpattya Ivano-Frankivsk	H	2-0	Kostyuk, Onopko
15/08/99	Metalurg Mariupol	A	1-2	Kobzar
21/08/99	Nyva Ternopil	H	4-2	Kobzar 2, Mazyar, Kostyuk
25/08/99	Metalist Kharkiv	H	3-1	Kostyuk (p), Mazyar, Melashchenko
29/08/99	CSCA Kyiv	A	1-1	Kobzar
16/10/99	Chornomorets Odesa	H	4-0	Dotsenko, Mazyar 2, Melashchenko
24/10/99	Metalurg Donetsk	A	3-2	Mazyar 3
28/10/99	Karpaty Lviv	A	1-3	Dotsenko
01/11/99	Zirka Kirovohrad	H	1-1	Melashchenko
07/11/99	Tavriya Simferopol	A	3-0	Makovskiy M., Kostyuk, Huzenko
18/03/00	Tavriya Simferopol	H	4-0	Makovskiy V., Mazyar, Omelchuk, Holovko A.
25/03/00	Zirka Kirovohrad	A	2-0	Kobzar, og (Shapovalov)
02/04/00	Metalurg Donetsk	H	0-0	
08/04/00	Chornomorets Odesa	A	1-1	Kobzar
16/04/00	Karpaty Lviv	H	1-0	Dotsenko
22/04/00	Metalist Kharkiv	A	1-2	Melashchenko
29/04/00	CSCA Kyiv	H	2-0	Chernyak, Omelchuk
06/05/00	Nyva Ternopil	A	1-1	Holovko O.
14/05/00	Metalurg Mariupol	H	1-1	Balanchuk
21/05/00	Prykarpattya Ivano-Frankivsk	A	1-0	Makovskiy V.
26/05/00	Shakhtar Donetsk	H	0-3	
04/06/00	Metalurg Zaporizhzhya	A	1-3	Holovko A.
08/06/00	Dynamo Kyiv	A	0-3	
16/06/00	Kryvbas Kryvyi Rih	H	3-0	Kobzar, Melashchenko, Onopko
20/06/00	Dnipro Dnipropetrovsk	A	1-2	Melashchenko

ZIRKA KIROVOHRAD

CLUB DIRECTORY

Zirka Kirovohrad
vul. Yuriy Gagarin 1A, PO Box 342
25050 Kirovohrad
tel - (0522) 222457/240824
fax - (0522) 223430
Year of Formation - 1922
President - Olexandr Nikulin
Secretary - Mykola Kovalev
Coach - Olexandr Ishchenko; Yuriy Koval
Stadium - Zirka (18,000)

APPEARANCES 99/00

	P	Ap	(s)	Gls
Ihor BAZHAN	G	5		
Borys BILOSHAPKA	G	5		
Olexandr BILOZERSKYI	D	13	(1)	
Yuriy BOGDANOV	M		(14)	
Viktor BOHATYR	M		(1)	
Olexandr BONDARENKO	D	14		1
Yevhen BURKHAN	A	3	(11)	
Volodymyr CHALYI	M	22	(2)	
Olexiy CHORNOIVAN	A		(1)	
Leonid FEDOROV	M	8	(1)	
Volodymyr GASHCHIN	A	8	(3)	2
Andriy HLUSHCHENKO	G	20		
Volodymyr HRYN	M	6	(1)	
Ihor KISLOV	A	19		4
Yaroslav KOMAR	M	2	(3)	
Volodymyr KOSSE	A	9	(4)	4
Denis KOVBA (BLS)	A	24	(1)	
Yuriy KUDINOV	A	3	(6)	
Ihor LAHOIDA	M		(1)	
Serhiy LAVRYNENKO	D	13	(7)	
Ihor MAKOHON	D	4		
Yuriy MARKIN	D	7		
Andriy MARTYNENKO	M	3	(2)	
Yuriy MARTYNOV	M	5	(3)	
Yuriy MYKOLAYENKO	A	2	(1)	
Andriy NIKIFOROV	M	5	(1)	
Vladyslav NOSENKO	D	10	(2)	
Maxym PETRUNYA	M	4	(1)	
Ihor PRODAN	A	1		
Hennadiy PRYKHODKO	D	8		
Olexandr ROMASHOV	D	5	(1)	1
Valeriy SHAPOVALOV	D	26		3
Serhiy SHCHASLYVYI	D	5		
Vladyslav SHUBIN	M	2	(2)	
Olexandr SOBOL	D	17	(5)	
Olexandr TOLKACH	D	2	(1)	
Bohdan YESYP	A	6	(2)	
Vadym ZAYETS	M	19	(2)	1
Oleh ZHILIN	D	25		

LEAGUE RESULTS 1999/2000

12/07/99	Shakhtar Donetsk	A	0-1	
16/07/99	Prykarpattya Ivano-Frankivsk	H	1-1	Shapovalov
20/07/99	Metalurg Mariupol	A	0-3	
24/07/99	Nyva Ternopil	H	1-1	Gashchin
01/08/99	CSCA Kyiv	A	0-3	
07/08/99	Metalist Kharkiv	H	2-2	Kislov, Gashchin
15/08/99	Karpaty Lviv	A	0-3	
21/08/99	Chornomorets Odesa	H	0-0	
29/08/99	Metalurg Donetsk	A	0-2	
25/09/99	Dynamo Kyiv	A	0-3	
03/10/99	Tavriya Simferopol	H	2-2	Kislov 2
16/10/99	Dnipro Dnipropetrovsk	A	0-2	
24/10/99	Kryvbas Kryvyi Rih	H	0-3	
01/11/99	Vorskla Poltava	A	1-1	Zayets
07/11/99	Metalurg Zaporizhzhya	H	1-1	Kislov
18/03/00	Metalurg Zaporizhzhya	A	0-2	
25/03/00	Vorskla Poltava	H	0-2	
02/04/00	Kryvbas Kryvyi Rih	A	1-3	Shapovalov
08/04/00	Dnipro Dnipropetrovsk	H	1-1	Kosse
16/04/00	Tavriya Simferopol	A	0-2	
22/04/00	Dynamo Kyiv	H	1-4	Shapovalov (p)
29/04/00	Metalurg Donetsk	H	0-2	
06/05/00	Chornomorets Odesa	A	0-1	
14/05/00	Karpaty Lviv	H	0-2	
21/05/00	Metalist Kharkiv	A	0-4	
26/05/00	CSCA Kyiv	H	0-0	
04/06/00	Nyva Ternopil	A	0-3	
08/06/00	Metalurg Mariupol	H	1-2	Kosse
16/06/00	Prykarpattya Ivano-Frankivsk	A	2-4	Kosse, Romashov
20/06/00	Shakhtar Donetsk	H	2-6	Bondarenko, Kosse

WALES

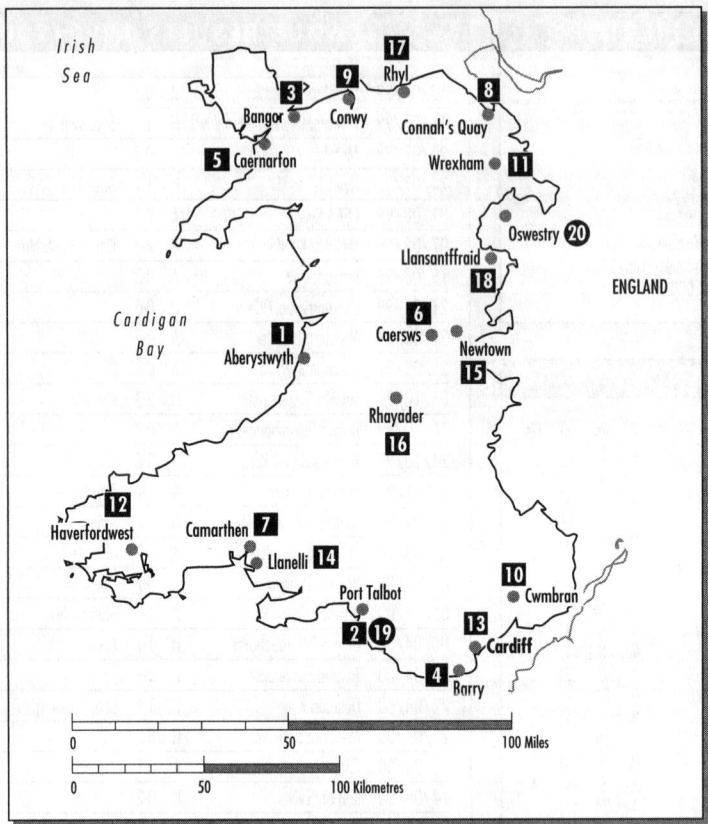

Irish Sea

Bangor **3** **9** Conwy **17** Rhyl **8**

Connah's Quay

5 Caernarfon Wrexham **11**

Oswestry **20**

Llansantffraid **18** ENGLAND

Cardigan Bay

1 Aberystwyth **6** Caersws Newtown **15**

Rhayader **16**

12 Haverfordwest Camarthen **7** Llanelli **14**

Port Talbot **10** Cwmbran

2 **19** **13** Cardiff

4 Barry

0   50   100 Miles

0   50   100 Kilometres

1	ABERYSTWYTH TOWN	1064	12	HAVERFORDWEST COUNTY	1075
2	AFAN LIDO	1065	13	INTER CARDIFF	1076
3	BANGOR CITY	1066	14	LLANELLI	1077
4	BARRY TOWN	1067	15	NEWTOWN	1078
5	CAERNARFON TOWN	1068	16	RHAYADER TOWN	1079
6	CAERSWS	1069	17	RHYL	1080
7	CARMARTHEN TOWN	1070	18	TOTAL NETWORK SOLUTIONS	1081
8	CONNAH'S QUAY NOMADS	1071	**Promoted clubs**		
9	CONWY UNITED	1072	19	PORT TALBOT ATHLETIC	
10	CWMBRAN TOWN	1073	20	OSWESTRY TOWN	
11	FLEXSYS CEFN DRUIDS	1074			

FANS FLOCK TO MILLENNIUM STADIUM

TNS release Barry Town stranglehold

FEDERATION DIRECTORY

The Football Association of Wales
Plymouth Chambers, 3 Westgate Street, Cardiff CF10 1DP
tel - (02920) 372325
fax - (02920) 343961
website - www.faw.org.uk
Year of Formation - 1876
Chairman - John Hughes
Secretary - David Collins
Stadium - Millennium Stadium, Cardiff (73,000)

Total Network Solutions may not sound like a football club, but it is the name of the new champions of Wales. Formerly known as Llansantffraid, TNS (the popular abbreviation of the team's sponsors) claimed the National League title in dramatic fashion to end the four-year monopoly of Barry Town, a team most fans in Wales had believed to be invincible.

It was the most exciting conclusion to the League in its brief eight-year history. Everything hinged on Barry Town's final match. TNS had already completed their schedule, winning each of their final five matches and dropping only four points from the last 42 available. But clumsy fixture planning had left Barry with a game in hand, away to their *bête noire* Connah's Quay Nomads, and they knew that if they won it, they would be champions for the fifth year in a row.

But there was to be no final-day glory for the South Wales Dragons. A goal in each half from Nomads striker Stuart Rain sent Barry slumping to a 2-0 defeat... and led to wild celebrations in the tiny mid-Wales village of Llansantffraid.

The champions deserved their title for their superb unbeaten run at the end. Even though they were well beaten in their two meetings with Barry, TNS kept their nerve when they had to. The signing of striker John Toner from Conwy United proved to be a masterstroke. He was one of a number of Englishmen in a team managed by Dr. Andy Cale, who, aside from his full-time duties at TNS, was also employed as the coach to the England U-17 side.

Barry's consolation for surrendering their title was a fourth consecutive League Cup triumph, which they sealed with a 6-0 thrashing of Bangor City in the final. Barry's

LEAGUE CHAMPIONSHIP RESULTS 99/00

		1	2	3	4	5	6	7	8	9	10	11	12	13	14	15	16	17	18
1	Aberystwyth Town		2-0	2-1	3-1	6-0	1-1	2-1	2-1	1-1	1-2	3-0	4-0	1-2	3-1	3-2	3-1	2-1	4-1
2	Afan Lido	2-1		4-0	0-2	4-0	3-0	0-0	1-1	3-0	0-0	2-2	4-3	3-0	0-0	2-1	3-0	0-1	0-0
3	Bangor City	1-3	4-1		3-3	1-0	1-3	0-1	0-2	8-0	1-1	3-3	1-0	3-1	1-3	3-2	1-0	3-2	0-2
4	Barry Town	3-3	5-0	5-2		3-0	1-0	3-1	3-3	4-1	3-1	7-0	3-1	5-1	4-2	4-0	2-0	1-1	5-1
5	Caernarfon Town	0-0	0-3	1-2	0-3		1-3	0-0	0-2	0-2	0-2	2-3	0-4	0-0	0-2	1-1	3-0	2-3	2-3
6	Caersws	0-3	3-0	2-5	1-2	2-2		2-1	0-2	3-3	0-1	3-0	1-0	0-3	0-2	0-1	1-1	0-1	0-1
7	Carmarthen Town	4-3	3-0	0-1	3-2	3-1	3-2		2-0	4-1	3-1	3-0	0-3	0-1	2-1	5-3	1-1	1-0	2-1
8	Connah's Quay Nomads	0-1	1-1	0-1	2-0	2-1	1-1	0-2		10-0	1-2	1-0	2-2	2-1	1-0	2-0	0-0	2-0	2-4
9	Conwy United	4-2	0-0	0-2	0-4	4-0	0-4	0-2	3-2		0-5	1-2	1-0	0-2	0-2	0-1	0-3	0-2	4-5
10	Cwmbran Town	2-1	3-2	6-0	1-0	4-0	1-1	3-1	0-2	3-1		2-1	1-0	3-1	3-1	3-2	1-2	5-0	0-2
11	Flexsys Cefn Druids	2-0	1-0	1-2	0-1	3-0	1-3	0-2	0-2	3-1	3-2		2-3	2-1	2-1	2-1	0-2	4-0	0-1
12	Haverfordwest County	0-5	0-2	2-1	0-6	1-1	0-0	1-6	1-4	1-1	1-1	3-0		2-1	1-1	1-1	0-1	2-2	1-1
13	Inter Cardiff	0-1	1-1	1-0	1-5	1-1	2-7	0-4	2-0	2-0	1-4	0-1	0-0		0-3	0-0	1-1	2-1	1-2
14	Llanelli	5-0	4-2	4-1	2-1	1-1	3-2	7-2	2-0	3-2	1-3	2-1	3-2	3-1		0-4	2-0	7-0	0-2
15	Newtown	2-0	0-0	2-0	1-0	5-0	2-3	0-2	0-1	1-2	2-0	4-1	0-0	2-0	1-2		2-1	1-0	0-1
16	Rhayader Town	0-3	0-1	1-3	0-0	2-1	0-1	1-2	1-2	5-0	1-1	3-1	2-0	1-0	1-3	0-2		2-2	0-1
17	Rhyl	1-0	1-0	1-0	0-5	2-1	2-0	0-1	1-4	1-1	1-1	2-0	3-1	2-0	1-3	2-3	1-0		2-4
18	Total Network Solutions	4-1	3-0	2-1	0-2	4-0	0-0	2-1	1-0	7-0	1-3	0-3	4-1	2-0	2-0	0-0	3-1	2-1	

LEAGUE CHAMPIONSHIP FINAL TABLE 99/00

			Home					Away					Total					
		Pd	W	D	L	F	A	W	D	L	F	A	W	D	L	F	A	PT	GD
1	Total Network Solutions	34	12	2	3	37	14	12	2	3	32	23	24	4	6	69	37	76	32
2	Barry Town	34	14	3	0	61	17	9	2	6	37	17	23	5	6	98	34	74	64
3	Cwmbran Town	34	13	1	3	41	17	8	5	4	30	20	21	6	7	71	37	69	34
4	Carmarthen Town	34	13	1	3	39	21	9	2	6	29	21	22	3	9	68	42	69	26
5	Llanelli	34	13	1	3	49	24	8	2	7	27	22	21	3	10	76	46	66	30
6	Aberystwyth Town	34	13	2	2	43	16	6	2	9	27	30	19	4	11	70	46	61	24
7	Connah's Quay Nomads	34	8	4	5	29	16	9	2	6	28	19	17	6	11	57	35	57	22
8	Newtown	34	9	2	6	25	13	5	4	8	24	28	14	6	14	49	41	48	8
9	Bangor City	34	8	3	6	34	27	7	0	10	22	34	15	3	16	56	61	48	-5
10	Afan Lido	34	9	6	2	31	11	3	4	10	13	31	12	10	12	44	42	46	2
11	Rhyl	34	9	2	6	23	24	4	3	10	17	36	13	5	16	40	60	44	-20
12	Caersws	34	4	3	10	18	28	7	5	5	31	22	11	8	15	49	50	41	-1
13	Flexsys Cefn Druids	34	9	0	8	26	22	4	2	11	18	41	13	2	19	44	63	41	-19
14	Rhayader Town	34	5	3	9	20	23	4	4	9	14	24	9	7	18	34	47	34	-13
15	Haverfordwest County	34	3	8	6	17	34	3	3	11	20	31	6	11	17	37	65	29	-28
16	Inter Cardiff	34	4	5	8	15	31	4	1	12	15	31	8	6	20	30	62	29	-32
17	Conwy United	34	4	1	12	17	38	2	4	11	16	59	6	5	23	33	97	20	-64
18	Caernarfon Town	34	1	4	12	12	33	0	4	13	9	48	1	8	25	21	81	11	-60

N.B. Inter Cardiff - 1 point deducted; Conwy United - 3 points deducted.

DOMESTIC CUP 99/00

SECOND ROUND
Ely Rangers 1, Garden Village 2
Blaenrhondda 2, BP Llandarcy 1
AFC Rhondda 1, Afan Lido 2
Ton Pentre 1, Haverfordwest County 2
Garw Athletic 6, Goytre United 1
Maesteg Park Athletic 1, Caerleon 3
Llanelli 6, Briton Ferry Athletic 0
Rhayader Town 3, Tredegar Town 1
Hoover Sports 2, Port Talbot Athletic 2
(aet; 4-5 on pens.)
Llanwern 2, Ammanford 1
Bridgend Town 0, UWIC 1
Treowen Stars 1, Porth Tywyn Suburbs 2
Corwen Amateurs 1, Bangor City 2
Buckley Town 1, Rhydymyn 3
Oswestry Town 0, Rhyl 1 (aet)
Llandyrnog United 0, Total Network Solutions 7
Newtown 11, Holywell Town 0
British Aerospace 3, Llandudno 5 (aet)
Flexsys Cefn Druids 2, Flint Town United 0
Ruthin Town 0, Amlwch Town 0 (aet; 2-4 on pens.)
Halkyn United 6, Prestatyn Town 2 (aet)
Guilsfield 3, Connah's Quay Nomads 3
(aet; 5-4 on pens.)
Llanidloes Town 0, Penrhyncoch 1 (aet)
Lex XI Wrexham 0, Caernarfon Town 5

Denbigh Town 1, Llangefni Town 2
Caersws 5, Llandudno Junction 0

THIRD ROUND
UWIC 0, Afan Lido 2
CPD Penrhyncoch 2, Blaenrhondda 1 (aet)
Llanelli 7, Porth Tywyn Suburbs 1
Llanwern 0, Amlwch Town 1
Aberystwyth Town 3, Garw Athletic 1
Cwmbran Town 0, Caernarfon Town 0
(aet; 5-3 on pens.)
Inter Cardiff 5, Garden Village 0
Rhyl 1, Guilsfield 0
Port Talbot Athletic 0, Carmarthen Town 1
Total Network Solutions 2, Newtown 0
Caersws 1, Flexsys Cefn Druids 0
Llangefni Town 1, Caerleon 3
Barry Town 2, Rhydymwyn 0
Conwy United 2, Rhayader Town 4 (aet)
Bangor City 5, Llandudno 0
Haverfordwest County 0, Halkyn United 1

FOURTH ROUND
Afan Lido 1, Total Network Solutions 0
Bangor City 4, Inter Cardiff 0
Barry Town 3, Rhayader Town 0
Caersws 1, Cwmbran Town 2

Carmarthen Town 4, Aberystwyth Town 1
Halkyn United 2, Caerleon 3
Llanelli 3, Rhyl 0
CPD Penrhyncoch 6, Amlwch Town 1

QUARTER-FINALS
Afan Lido 3, Llanelli 1 (aet)
Barry Town 5, CPD Penrhyncoch 0
Caerleon 1, Bangor City 4
Carmarthen Town 2, Cwmbran Town 3

SEMI-FINALS
Barry Town 1 (Ince 75),
Cwmbran Town 1 (Summers 66) (aet; 2-4 on pens.)
Afan Lido 2 (Patton 44, 85p), Bangor City 4 (Bird 7, Coady 88, Roberts 110, Comley-Excell 117) (aet)

FINAL
07/05/2000, Wrexham
BANGOR CITY 1 Roberts (29)
CWMBRAN TOWN 0
referee - Lawlor
BANGOR CITY - Mulliner, Johnson, Rowlands, Brett, Bird, Williams S., Williams R. (Comley-Excell 83), Coady, Roberts, Allen, Williams E..
CWMBRAN TOWN - Wager, Carter (Davies 45), Wigley (Powell 87), Aizlewood, Blackie, O'Brien, Summers, Moore, Graham, Futcher (Pattimore 67), James.

excuse for not winning the league again was a succession of injuries, which left them at times with only a skeleton squad. Player-manager Richard Jones, who replaced Gary Barnett at the start of the campaign, was voted the League's Player of the Season, but he decided to step down from the manager's role at the end of the campaign, to to be replaced subsequently by former Wales international midfielder Peter Nicholas.

Bangor City made a quick recovery from their League Cup final mauling. A week later they were a team transformed as they deservedly beat Cwmbran Town 1-0 to win the Welsh Cup final. The victory enabled Bangor to claim a UEFA Cup place and send Cwmbran, the league's third-placed team, into the InterToto.

Bangor's success contrasted with the misery that

TOP SCORERS

28	Chris SUMMERS (Cwmbran Town)
22	Danny BARTON (Rhyl)
21	Mark DICKESON (Llanelli)
20	Paul EVANS (Barry Town)
19	Glyndwr HUGHES (Aberystwyth Town)
18	Richard PARKER (Carmarthen Town)
16	Richard JONES (Barry Town)
	Justin PERRY (Barry Town)
	John TONER (Conwy United/ Total Network Solutions)
14	Paul ROBERTS (Bangor City)

engulfed the other two clubs from the north-west, Caernarfon Town and Conwy United. Both clubs were relegated, having each used a massive contingent of players. Caernarfon's entire first-team squad was sacked at one stage, while Conwy suffered through the winter months after drainage problems rendered their home pitch unusable. Inter Cardiff avoided the drop, but they, too, had a season to forget. They had to contend with a mass player walk-out over unpaid wages and by the summer the club had been forced to merge with Division One outfit University of Wales Institute.

It was not all doom and gloom in the capital, however. The unveiling of the new Millennium Stadium on the site of the old Arms Park brought great pride to the citizens of Cardiff and to the people of Wales. Inaugurated for the

NATIONAL TEAM APPEARANCES 99/00

Manager - Mark HUGHES	BLS	SUI	QTR	FIN	BRA	POR	Cps	Gls
Paul JONES (18/04/67) - Southampton (ENG)	G	G	G				14	-
Robert PAGE (03/09/74) - Watford (ENG)	D	D	D	D	D	D	13	-
Andy MELVILLE (29/11/68) - Fulham (ENG)	D		D	D	D	D	39	3
Chris COLEMAN (10/06/70) - Fulham (ENG)	D	D	D	D			28	4
Darren BARNARD (30/11/71) - Barnsley (ENG)	D	D	D89	D66	s84	D68	12	-
John ROBINSON (29/08/71) - Charlton Athletic (ENG)	M	M	M	M	M	M	22	3
Mark PEMBRIDGE (29/11/70) - Everton (ENG)	M80		M	M86			36	5
Gary SPEED (08/09/69) - Newcastle United (ENG)	M	M	M	M	M	M31	58	3
Ryan GIGGS (29/11/73) - Manchester United (ENG)	M			A			26	7
Dean SAUNDERS (21/06/64) - Bradford City (ENG)	A	A67		s79	A84		73	22
Nathan BLAKE (27/01/72) - Blackburn Rovers (ENG)	A	A77	A	A79			15	2
Carl ROBINSON (13/10/76) - Wolverhampton Wanderers (ENG)	s80					s68	2	-
Mark DELANEY (13/05/76) - Aston Villa (ENG)		D	M		D	D	4	-
Robbie SAVAGE (18/10/74) - Leicester City (ENG)		M		M79	M75		16	1
John OSTER (08/12/78) - Sunderland (ENG)		M67					4	-
John HARTSON (05/04/75) - Wimbledon (ENG)		s67					18	2
Matthew JONES (01/09/80) - Leeds United (ENG)		s67	M		M75	M	4	-
Neil ROBERTS (07/04/78) - Wrexham		s77					1	-
Kit SYMONS (08/03/71) - Fulham (ENG)			s89				32	1
Mark CROSSLEY (16/06/69) - Nottingham Forest (ENG)				G			3	-
Gareth ROBERTS (06/02/78) - Tranmere Rovers (ENG)				s66	D	D84	3	-
Andy JOHNSON (02/05/74) - Nottingham Forest (ENG)				s79	s75	s31	7	-
Iwan ROBERTS (26/06/68) - Norwich City (ENG)				s86	A	A	10	2
Roger FREESTONE (19/08/68) - Swansea City					G		1	-
Craig BELLAMY (13/07/79) - Norwich City (ENG)					s75	A	9	2
Darren WARD (11/05/74) - Notts County (ENG)						G	1	-
Rhys WESTON (27/10/80) - Arsenal (ENG)						s84	1	-

Rugby World Cup in the autumn, the stadium opened its gates to the national football team in the spring, and, with ticket prices set at a sensible level, a record crowd of 66,500 flocked to see Wales take on Finland in a friendly.

That record was broken two months later when the mighty Brazil came to town. A capacity crowd of 72,500 watched that game, with all tickets having been snapped up within 24 hours of going on sale.

Despite all the enthusiasm, the Welsh team were unable to give their fans what they had come to see. They lost 1-2 to Finland and 0-3 to Brazil. There was some encouragement to be gained from the latter performance as Wales, even without the injured Ryan Giggs, matched the Brazilians for an hour before eventually succumbing to the class of Rivaldo and co.

Earlier in the season Welsh hopes of reaching the Euro 2000 finals died a predictable death, although it was unfortunate that the final nail in their coffin should have been hammered in just a few days after they had put themselves back on track with a splendid 2-1 win in Belarus.

Denmark's shock 3-2 victory in Italy made it impossible for Wales to qualify, and there was a distinct feeling of "why are we here?" when Wales went down 0-2 at home to fellow victims Switzerland in their final qualifier in Wrexham.

Those qualifying games had been played with Mark Hughes acting as a caretaker coach. But although the results did not go to plan, the former Manchester United idol was handed a four-and-a-half-year contract, with the added bonus that he was allowed to continue playing at club level in the English Premiership for half of the term.

NATIONAL TEAM RESULTS 99/00

04/09/99	Belarus (ECQ)	A	Minsk	2-1	Saunders (42), Giggs (85)
09/10/99	Switzerland (ECQ)	H	Wrexham	0-2	
23/02/00	Qatar	A	Doha	1-0	Robinson J. (10)
29/03/00	Finland	H	Cardiff	1-2	Giggs (61)
23/05/00	Brazil	H	Cardiff	0-3	
02/06/00	Portugal	A	Chaves	0-3	

PLAYER OF THE SEASON

ROBBIE SAVAGE

Robbie Savage has come a long way since the day Manchester United told him he wasn't good enough and showed him the door. He was a trainee then, but now he is an established member of the Welsh national side and one of the team's brightest hopes for the foreseeable future. He is a player driven by passion and the will to win. What he lacks in natural skills he makes up for with his phenomenal work-rate and his undying loyalty to the cause. Easily recognisable by his flowing blond locks, the 26-year-old midfielder has earned himself something of a reputation for occasionally taking his fiery enthusiasm too far, but fans of English Premiership side Leicester City are well aware of the immense contribution the Welshman made to the club's best season ever in 1999/2000. A fixture in Martin O'Neill's side, Savage helped the East Midlanders to victory in the League Cup and a very respectable eighth place in the Premiership.

INTERNATIONAL HONOURS

World Cup Finals appearances: 1958 (qtr-finals)
European Championship appearances: 1976

EUROPEAN CUPS 99/00

CHAMPIONS' CUP
● **BARRY TOWN**
Preliminary round 1 VALLETTA (MLT)
H 0-0
Wells, Evans, Davies D., Jones, York, Barrow, Barnett, Carter, Mitchell, Sloan, Ince (Perry 62).
A 2-3
Sloan (44, 56)
Wells, Evans, Davies D., Jones, York, Barrow, Barnett (Jenkins 84), Carter, Mitchell, Perry, Ince (Sloan 46).

UEFA CUP
● **CWMBRAN TOWN**
Qualifying round CELTIC (SCO)
H 0-6
O'Hagan, Wills, John, Blackie, O'Brien, Dyson, Wigley (Aizlewood 72), Moore, Evans (Thomas A. 59), Graham D., Summers (Hughes C. 84).
A 0-4
Morris, Aizlewood, Wills, John, Futcher, O'Brien (Graham B. 79), Blackie, Summers (Pattimore 88), Moore, Graham D., Wigley (Goodridge 88).

● **INTER CARDIFF**
Qualifying round HIT GORICA (SLO)
A 0-2
Wager, Poretta, Mardenborough (Evans 60), Wile, Murray, David, Davies, Williams, Brazil, Misbah, Philpott.
H 1-0
Mainwaring (57)
Wager, David, Davies, Tyler (Dyer 80), Giles (Murray 80), Brazil, Misbah, Hewitt, King (Wile 88), Philpott, Mainwaring.

Although Hughes is a well-loved figure in Wales, it has to be remembered that he is unqualified as a coach and a complete novice at management. His bid to rescue Wales from the wilderness is unlikely to be successful as long as the players available to him continue to be of such modest quality. There is eager talk that youngsters like Craig Bellamy, Matthew Jones and Mark Delaney could help the team turn the corner, but the truth remains that Ryan Giggs is the only Welsh player currently available who possesses genuine international class.

Until that situation changes, it will continue to be a case of: nice stadium, shame about the team...

PROMOTED CLUBS 99/00

SECOND DIVISION FINAL TABLES
SOUTH (WELSH LEAGUE DIVISION ONE)

		Pd	W	D	L	F	A	Pt	GD
1	Ton Petre	34	25	5	4	111	34	80	77
2	**Port Talbot Athletic**	**34**	**22**	**9**	**3**	**85**	**33**	**75**	**52**
3	Maesteg Park Athletic	34	18	11	5	67	41	65	26
4	BP Llandarcy	34	17	5	12	96	57	56	39
5	Cardiff Civil Service	34	15	9	10	70	49	54	21
6	AFC Rhondda	34	17	3	14	67	61	54	6
7	Bridgend Town	34	15	5	14	67	72	50	-5
8	Briton Ferry Athletic	34	14	6	14	47	55	48	-8
9	Gwynfi United	34	14	5	15	73	79	47	-6
10	Penrhiwceiber Rangers	34	13	6	15	61	65	45	-4
11	Goytre United	34	13	6	15	64	70	45	-6
12	Porth Tywyn Suburbs	34	12	7	15	60	70	43	-10
13	Treowen Stars	34	12	6	16	61	74	42	-13
14	Pontardawe Town	34	11	8	15	56	63	41	-7
15	UWIC	34	10	8	16	50	82	38	-32
16	Ammanford	34	10	6	18	41	54	36	-13
17	Cardiff Corinthians	34	9	7	18	45	71	34	-26
18	Aberaman Athletic	34	2	2	30	47	138	8	-91

N.B. Ton Pentre declined promotion; Port Talbot Athletic promoted instead.

NORTH (CYMRU ALLIANCE)

		Pd	W	D	L	F	A	Pt	GD
1	**Oswestry Town**	**32**	**21**	**4**	**7**	**64**	**43**	**67**	**21**
2	CPD Glantraeth	32	18	7	7	82	39	61	43
3	Cemaes Bay	32	17	8	7	74	44	59	30
4	Welshpool Town	32	17	6	9	60	41	57	19
5	CPD Porthmadog	32	17	5	10	64	40	56	24
6	Flint Town United	32	16	8	8	65	43	56	22
7	Llandudno	32	16	5	11	70	57	53	13
8	Rhydymwyn	32	15	5	12	55	54	50	1
9	Llangefni Town	32	13	10	9	60	43	49	17
10	Buckley Town	32	13	8	11	53	44	47	9
11	Ruthin Town	32	13	7	12	55	45	46	10
12	Holyhead Hotspur	32	9	6	17	52	70	33	-18
13	Lex XI Wrexham	32	9	3	20	55	90	30	-35
14	Brymbo Broughton	32	7	8	17	32	51	29	-19
15	Denbigh Town	32	8	5	19	36	79	29	-43
16	Holywell Town	32	7	4	21	41	69	25	-28
17	Corwen Amateurs	32	5	3	24	25	91	18	-66

CLUB DIRECTORIES
Port Talbot Athletic FC
28 Morrison Road
Sandfields
Port Talbot
tel - (01639) 897912
fax - (01639) 882465
Year of Formation - 1901
Chairman - Andrew Edwards
Secretary - John Dawkins
Manager - David Rees

Oswestry Town FC
22 Victoria Road
Oswestry
SY11 4DS
tel - (01691) 653786
Year of Formation - 1876
Chairman - Ivor Davies
Secretary - Malcolm Lashbrook
Manager - Ken Swinnerton

ABERYSTWYTH TOWN

CLUB DIRECTORY

Aberystwyth Town FC
31 Maes Gogerddan, Penglais, Aberystwyth
SY23 2EY
tel - (01970) 623520
fax - (01970) 617939
Year of Formation - 1884
Chairman - Donald Kane
Secretary - Rhun Owens
Manager - Barrie Powell
Stadium - Park Avenue (5,500)

MAJOR HONOURS
Domestic Cup - (1) 1900.

APPEARANCES 99/00

	P	Ap	(s)	Gls
Shaun BEDWARD (ENG)	A	1	(6)	1
David BLAIR	M	2	(6)	
Nathan CADETTE	A	3		
Mark DAVIES	A		(4)	
Simon DYER	A	6	(10)	5
Andy EVANS	A	6		7
Gary FINLEY (ENG)	D	19	(1)	
Mike FOSTER	D	25	(5)	
Martyn GRIFFITHS	M	15	(6)	3
Chris HAMMOND (ENG)	M	16	(6)	1
Wayne HEWITT	D	14	(5)	2
Gareth HUGHES	M	28	(2)	1
Glyndwr HUGHES	M	33	(1)	19
Llyr HUGHES	D		(8)	
Huw JONES	A		(7)	
Martin JONES (ENG)	G	22		
Donald KANE (SCO)	D	1	(1)	
Gari LEWIS	D	34		1
Steve MARDENBOROUGH (ENG)	A	19		9
Ricky MARSHALL (ENG)	A	1	(1)	
Simon MELLOR (ENG)	M		(8)	
Richard MORGAN	G	12		
Kevin MORRISON (SCO)	A	19	(3)	8
Gavin O'TOOLE (ENG)	D	33		3
Dean PHILPOTT	D	13	(2)	
Craig SHAKESPEARE (ENG)	M	2		
Dean SMITH	A		(2)	
Nicky SMITH	M		(2)	
Jonathan TAPPIN (ENG)	M	3	(15)	
Aneurin THOMAS	D	31		1
Carwyn THOMAS	M		(1)	
Jonathan WILLIAMS	A	16		7

LEAGUE RESULTS 1999/2000

20/08/99	Total Network Solutions	H	4-1	Evans 2, Williams, O'Toole
24/08/99	Llanelli	A	0-5	
28/08/99	Rhayader Town	A	3-0	og (Morris), Evans, Hughes Gl.
04/09/99	Barry Town	H	3-1	Evans 2, Williams
11/09/99	Bangor City	A	3-1	Evans, Hammond, Hughes Gl.
17/09/99	Cwmbran Town	H	1-2	Evans
26/09/99	Flexsys Cefn Druids	A	0-2	
01/10/99	Newtown	H	3-2	Dyer, Morrison (p), Hughes Ga.
23/10/99	Conwy United	A	2-4	Dyer, Morrison
30/10/99	Haverfordwest County	H	4-0	Hughes Gl., Morrison, Williams, Griffiths
13/11/99	Afan Lido	H	2-0	Hughes Gl., Williams
27/11/99	Caernarfon Town	A	0-0	
17/12/99	Caersws	H	1-1	Griffiths
27/12/99	Carmarthen Town	A	3-4	Williams, Morrison, Thomas A.
11/01/00	Llanelli	H	3-1	Williams 2, Morrison
14/01/00	Rhayader Town	H	3-1	Hughes Gl. 2, Mardenborough
22/01/00	Barry Town	A	3-3	Morrison, Hughes Gl., Mardenborough
29/01/00	Bangor City	H	2-1	O'Toole, Hughes Gl.
05/02/00	Cwmbran Town	A	1-?	Dyer
08/02/00	Rhyl	H	2-1	Griffiths, Hewitt
19/02/00	Flexsys Cefn Druids	H	3-0	Lewis, Dyer, Mardenborough
25/02/00	Newtown	A	0-2	
03/03/00	Conwy United	H	1-1	Mardenborough
07/03/00	Connah's Quay Nomads	A	1-0	Hughes Gl.
11/03/00	Haverfordwest County	A	5-0	Hughes Gl. 2, Mardenborough, Hewitt, Dyer
25/03/00	Afan Lido	A	1-2	Mardenborough
01/04/00	Caernarfon Town	H	6-0	Hughes Gl. 2, Morrison 2 (1p), Mardenborough, og (McNeil)
04/04/00	Inter Cardiff	H	1-2	Bedward
08/04/00	Inter Cardiff	A	1-0	O'Toole
11/04/00	Total Network Solutions	A	1-4	Hughes Gl.
15/04/00	Rhyl	A	0-1	
22/04/00	Connah's Quay Nomads	H	2-1	Hughes Gl., Mardenborough
24/04/00	Carmarthen Town	H	2-1	Hughes Gl. 2
29/04/00	Caersws	A	3-0	Mardenborough, Hughes Gl. 2

AFAN LIDO

CLUB DIRECTORY

Afan Lido FC
56 Abbeyville Avenue
Sandfields
Port Talbot
SA12 6PY
tel - (01639) 885638
fax - (01639) 881432
Year of Formation - 1967
Chairman - David Dale
Secretary - Phil Robinson
Manager - Mark Robinson
Stadium - Afan Lido Sports Ground (5,000)

APPEARANCES 99/00

	P	Ap	(s)	Gls
Dahi AL-WADI	M		(1)	
Scott CONATY	D	1		
Michael COOK	D	19	(10)	1
Stephen COOK	D		(1)	
Gareth DEENEY	M	2	(2)	
Paul EVANS	D	34		1
Shaun GALSWORTHY	M	11	(7)	
Greg HURLEY	D	25		3
Gary ISAAC	M		(2)	
Dean JOHNSTON	M	25		5
Leighton JONES	D	20	(5)	2
Karl LEWIS	M		(3)	
Stephen LLEWELLYN	M		(7)	
Phil LYONS	A	4	(5)	
Michael NICHOLAS	M		(2)	
Shaun O'LEARY	M	25	(2)	5
Stephen PARRY	D	29	(1)	1
Mitch PATTON	A	31		9
Andrew PEARSON	A	24	(4)	5
Chris PIPER	A	10	(1)	
Andy PITMAN (ENG)	M	8		1
Darrell RICHARDS	G	1		
Andrew RICKARD	D	34		1
Morys SCOTT	A	7	(12)	1
James TAYLOR	A	19	(14)	8
Brian THOMAS	G	33		
Edward TOBIN	M		(2)	
Ian VAUGHAN	D	11	(8)	
John WAKLEY	M	1	(10)	
Justin WILLIAMS	D		(1)	

LEAGUE RESULTS 1999/2000

21/08/99	Conwy United	A	0-0	
24/08/99	Haverfordwest County	H	4-3	Taylor, Patton, Hurley, Evans
28/08/99	Carmarthen Town	A	0-3	
04/09/99	Rhayader Town	H	3-0	Pearson, Johnstone, Patton
11/09/99	Caernarfon Town	H	4-0	Patton, O'Leary, Rickard, Johnstone
17/09/99	Inter Cardiff	A	1-1	Patton
25/09/99	Connah's Quay Nomads	H	1-1	Pearson
02/10/99	Caersws	A	0-3	
10/10/99	Newtown	A	0-0	
30/10/99	Total Network Solutions	A	0-3	
13/11/99	Aberystwyth Town	A	0-2	
04/12/99	Bangor City	A	1-4	Pearson
18/12/99	Flexsys Cefn Druids	A	0-1	
27/12/99	Barry Town	H	0-2	
08/01/00	Conwy United	H	3-0	Taylor 2, Pearson
15/01/00	Carmarthen Town	H	0-0	
22/01/00	Rhayader Town	A	1-0	Parry
29/01/00	Caernarfon Town	A	3-0	Cook M., Pearson, O'Leary
05/02/00	Rhyl	H	0-1	
19/02/00	Connah's Quay Nomads	A	1-1	O'Leary
22/02/00	Newtown	H	2-1	Patton, Hurley
26/02/00	Caersws	H	3-0	Johnston, Patton, Taylor
04/03/00	Rhyl	A	0-1	
14/03/00	Cwmbran Town	H	0-0	
17/03/00	Llanelli	A	2-4	O'Leary, Taylor
21/03/00	Inter Cardiff	H	3-0	Jones, Patton, Hurley
25/03/00	Aberystwyth Town	H	2-1	Taylor, Patton (p)
28/03/00	Haverfordwest County	A	2-0	Taylor, Jones
01/04/00	Total Network Solutions	H	0-0	
08/04/00	Bangor City	H	4-0	Taylor, Scott, Patton, O'Leary
11/04/00	Llanelli	H	0-0	
21/04/00	Cwmbran Town	A	2-3	Johnstone 2
24/04/00	Barry Town	A	0-5	
29/04/00	Flexsys Cefn Druids	H	2-2	og (Richards), Pitman

BANGOR CITY

CLUB DIRECTORY

Bangor City FC
12 Lôn y Bryn, Menai Bridge, LL59 5LL
tel - (01248) 712820   fax - (01248) 372132
Year of Formation - 1875
Chairman - Gwyn Pierce Owen
Secretary - Alun Griffiths
Manager - Mairion Appleton
Stadium - Farrar Road (10,000)

MAJOR HONOURS
League Championship - (2) 1994, 1995.
Domestic Cup - (5)
1889, 1896, 1962, 1998, 2000.

APPEARANCES 99/00

	P	Ap	(s)	Gls
Gavin ALLEN	A	27	(2)	11
Mark ALLEN (ENG)	D	2		
Steve BIRD (ENG)	D	28		2
Matthew BISHOP (ENG)	D	2	(13)	
Graham BRETT (IRL)	D	25	(1)	
Lewis COADY (ENG)	M	25	(6)	4
Nathan COMLEY-EXCELL (ENG)	A	8	(5)	2
Matt CROSS (ENG)	D	22	(11)	
Brian DAVIES	G	2		
Jamie DAVIES	A	3		1
Lee DIXON	M		(2)	
Sean HAZELDEN (ENG)	D	28	(5)	4
George HORAN (ENG)	D	2		
Phil JOHNSON (ENG)	M	34		3
Paul MOONEY (ENG)	D	1	(5)	
Nigel MOORE	A	1	(1)	1
Andy MULLINER (ENG)	G	27		
Tommy MUTTON	A	2	(3)	1
Richard OWEN	D	1	(2)	
Gareth PARRY	M	1	(6)	
Andy RICHARDS	M			
Paul ROBERTS	A	24	(2)	14
Aled ROWLANDS	M	29	(5)	3
Richie SEMPLE (ENG)	M	2	(2)	1
Anthony SMITH (ENG)	M		(2)	
David SWEET	A		(1)	
Aaron THOMAS	A		(9)	
Jason TURNER	G	5		
Emrys WILLIAMS	D	14	(10)	3
Robbie WILLIAMS	M	26	(3)	5
Scott WILLIAMS	D	30		1
Stephen WILLIAMS	A	3	(3)	

LEAGUE RESULTS 1999/2000

21/08/99	Caersws	A	5-2	Allen G. 3, Roberts 2
24/08/99	Rhyl	A	0-1	
28/08/99	Total Network Solutions	H	0-2	
04/09/99	Llanelli	A	1-4	Allen G.
11/09/99	Aberystwyth Town	H	1-3	Mutton
18/09/99	Barry Town	A	2-5	Coady, Davies J.
25/09/99	Rhayader Town	A	3-1	Williams E. 2, Semple
02/10/99	Cwmbran Town	H	1-1	Johnson
23/10/99	Flexsys Cefn Druids	A	2-1	Bird, Coady
30/10/99	Newtown	H	3-2	Hazelden, Coady, Roberts
13/11/99	Haverfordwest County	H	1-0	Roberts
27/11/99	Carmarthen Town	A	1-0	Allen G.
04/12/99	Afan Lido	H	4-1	Roberts, Coady, Allen G., Williams R.
11/12/99	Caernarfon Town	A	2-1	Bird, Roberts
18/12/99	Inter Cardiff	H	3-1	Hazelden, Roberts, Williams R.
27/12/99	Connah's Quay Nomads	A	1-0	Roberts
08/01/00	Caersws	H	1-3	Allen G.
15/01/00	Total Network Solutions	A	1-2	Roberts
18/01/00	Rhyl	H	3-2	Roberts, Hazelden, Williams S.
22/01/00	Llanelli	II	1-3	Roberts
25/01/00	Conwy United	H	8-0	Williams R. 3, Rowlands 2, Roberts, Johnson, Allen G.
29/01/00	Aberystwyth Town	A	1-2	Hazelden
05/02/00	Barry Town	H	3-3	Allen G. 2, Comley-Excell
26/02/00	Cwmbran Town	A	0-6	
03/03/00	Flexsys Cefn Druids	H	3-3	Roberts 2, Allen G.
17/03/00	Conwy United	A	2-0	Rowlands, Johnson (p)
21/03/00	Rhayader Town	H	1-0	Moore
25/03/00	Haverfordwest County	A	1-2	Comley-Excell
01/04/00	Carmarthen Town	H	0-1	
04/04/00	Newtown	A	0-2	
08/04/00	Afan Lido	A	0-4	
22/04/00	Caernarfon Town	H	1-0	Williams E.
24/04/00	Connah's Quay Nomads	H	0-2	
29/04/00	Inter Cardiff	A	0-1	

BARRY TOWN

CLUB DIRECTORY

Barry Town AFC
Jennar Parl, Barry Road, Barry, CF62 9BG
tel - (01446) 735858   fax - (01446) 701884
Year of Formation - 1912
Chairman - Paula O'Halloran
Secretary - Alan Whelan
Manager - Gary Barnett; Richard Jones
(00/01 - Peter Nicholas)
Stadium - Jenner Park (6,000)

MAJOR HONOURS
League Championship - (4)
1996, 1997, 1998, 1999.
Domestic Cup - (3) 1955, 1994, 1997.

APPEARANCES 99/00

	P	Ap	(s)	Gls
Lee BARROW (ENG)	D	34		3
Nicky BURKE (IRL)	M	1	(10)	2
Darren DAVIES	D	16	(7)	2
Lawrence DAVIES	M	26	(7)	6
Paul EVANS	A	32		20
Paul EVANS	G	1		
Terry EVANS	D	22	(7)	2
Chris FRY	M	32	(2)	9
Morten HILDEGAARD (DEN)	G	3		
James INCE (ENG)	M	30	(3)	3
James JENKINS	A	17	(17)	3
Jodie JENKINS	A	14	(20)	9
Richard JONES	M	30	(1)	16
Gary LLOYD	M	26	(6)	4
Ian LOVELESS	G	2		
Paul MITCHELL (ENG)	D	7		
Pat MOUNTAIN	G	1		
Justin PERRY (ENG)	A	21	(13)	16
Chris PRIDHAM	M	1	(2)	
John ROBERTS	G	3		
Dave WELLS (NIR)	G	24	(3)	
Andrew YORK	D	31	(3)	1

LEAGUE RESULTS 1999/2000

21/08/99	Rhyl	H	1-1	Jones
24/08/99	Total Network Solutions	A	2-0	Perry, Fry
27/08/99	Llanelli	H	4-2	Perry 2, Fry, Lloyd
04/09/99	Aberystwyth Town	A	1-3	Jones
11/09/99	Rhayader Town	A	0-0	
18/09/99	Bangor City	H	5-2	Evans P. 2, Fry, Evans T., Perry
25/09/99	Cwmbran Town	A	0-1	
02/10/99	Flexsys Cefn Druids	H	7-0	Perry 2, Fry, Evans P., Jenkins Jo., York, Davies L.
07/10/99	Caersws	A	2-1	Evans P., Jenkins Jo.
22/10/99	Newtown	A	0-1	
30/10/99	Conwy United	H	4-1	Jenkins Jo. 2, Evans P., Jenkins Jo.
06/11/99	Haverfordwest County	A	6-0	Evans P. 2, Jones 2 (2p), Davies D., Jenkins Jo.
13/11/99	Carmarthen Town	H	3-1	Jenkins Jo. 2, Davies L.
04/12/99	Caernarfon Town	H	3-0	Jones (p), Lloyd, Evans P.
10/12/99	Inter Cardiff	A	5-1	Lloyd 2, Perry, Evans P., og (Morgan)
18/12/99	Connah's Quay Nomads	H	3-3	Jenkins Jo., Evans P., Perry
27/12/99	Afan Lido	A	2-0	Jones (p), Davies L.
08/01/00	Rhyl	A	5-0	Barrow 2, Perry 2, Evans P.
11/01/00	Total Network Solutions	H	5-1	Jones 2, Perry, Barrow, Fry
14/01/00	Llanelli	A	1-2	Jones
22/01/00	Aberystwyth Town	H	3-3	Jones, Ince, Evans P.
29/01/00	Rhayader Town	H	2-0	Jones, Davies L.
05/02/00	Bangor City	A	3-3	Evans P. 2, Fry
18/02/00	Cwmbran Town	H	3-1	Perry 2, Davies L.
22/02/00	Caersws	H	1-0	Ince
26/02/00	Flexsys Cefn Druids	A	1-0	Evans P.
04/03/00	Newtown	H	4-0	Perry, Ince, Jones, Evans
18/03/00	Haverfordwest County	H	3-1	Jones, Perry, Davies L.
21/03/00	Conwy United	A	4-0	Jones, og (Holton), Evans, Burke
25/03/00	Carmarthen Town	A	2-3	Jenkins Jo., Davies D.
08/04/00	Caernarfon Town	A	3-0	Fry, Jenkins Jo., Burke
22/04/00	Inter Cardiff	H	5-1	Evans P. 3, Jones 2
24/04/00	Afan Lido	H	5-0	Fry 2, Perry, Evans T., Jenkins Ja.
29/04/00	Connah's Quay Nomads	A	0-2	

CAERNARFON TOWN

CLUB DIRECTORY

Caernarfon Town FC
20 South Penrallt, Caernarfon
Gwynedd LL55 1NS
tel - (01286) 674045
Year of Formation - 1876
Chairman - Geraint Lloyd Owen
Secretary - John Watkins
Manager - Paul Rowlands; Dixie McNeil
Stadium - The Oval (3,000)

APPEARANCES 99/00

	P	Ap	(s)	Gls
Lee ALLEN	M	1	(2)	
Paul ALLEN	D	10	(2)	2
Aaron BAILEY	D	2	(1)	
Ryan BAKER (ENG)	D	8	(6)	
Nicky BROOKMAN (ENG)	M	5	(5)	
Peter BYRNE (ENG)	D	12		1
Ian CLARKE (ENG)	M	1		
David CLEGG (ENG)	D	1		
Ray CLIFTON (ENG)	G	16		
Dave COCKRAM (ENG)	A	2	(3)	
Matt CORCORAN	A	6	(2)	
Phil DALEY (ENG)	A	11	(1)	2
Mark DEEGAN (ENG)	G	4		
Neil DOHERTY (ENG)	M	4	(1)	
Mark EDWARDS (ENG)	D	8	(1)	1
Darren EMMETT (ENG)	A	6		2
Richard EVANS	M	12	(6)	2
Steve FISHER (ENG)	A	12		
John GARNELL (ENG)	D	1		
Anthony GODFREY (ENG)	D	4		
Ronnie GOULDBOURNE (ENG)	M	7		
Eiddon GRIFFITHS	D		(2)	
Kevin HAGAN (ENG)	A	2	(5)	1
Graham HALL	D	6	(1)	
Geoff HINCHCLIFFE (ENG)	D	27	(1)	1
Ian HORRIGAN (ENG)	M	6	(2)	1
Carl HOUGHTON (ENG)	M		(1)	
Colin HUGHES	M		(1)	
Darren HUGHES	D		(2)	
Neil JAT	D	1		
Jonathan JONES	M	2		
Steve C. JONES (ENG)	A	1		
Chris JOYCE	D	4	(5)	
Jason JOYCE	D	7		
Robbie LAWTON (ENG)	M		(1)	
Steve LLOYD	M	1	(1)	
Paul McANDREW (ENG)	D	7	(1)	
Gary McCOSH (ENG)	D	6		
Dave MACDIARMID (ENG)	M	1	(4)	
Damien McKEOWN	D	15		
Richard McNEIL (ENG)	A	14		2
Paul MOONEY (ENG)	A	3	(1)	1
Rob MORRIS (ENG)	D	4		
Chris OWEN	M		(1)	
Gavin OWEN	D	1	(2)	
Rhys OWEN	D	2	(1)	
Gwyn PETERS	A	7	(6)	1
Mark PHILLIPS (ENG)	D	7	(1)	
Chris PICKERING (ENG)	D	9	(3)	1
Mike PIMBLETT (ENG)	G	1		

LEAGUE RESULTS 1999/2000

21/08/99	Newtown	H	1-1	Pickering
25/08/99	Conwy United	H	0-2	
28/08/99	Haverfordwest County	A	1-1	Horrigan
04/09/99	Carmarthen Town	H	0-0	
11/09/99	Afan Lido	A	0-4	
18/09/99	Rhayader Town	H	3-0	Hinchcliffe, Byrne (p), Sadler
25/09/99	Inter Cardiff	H	0-0	
02/10/99	Connah's Quay Nomads	A	1-2	Edwards
23/10/99	Caersws	H	1-3	Daley
29/10/99	Rhyl	A	1-2	Mooney
13/11/99	Llanelli	A	1-1	Hagan
27/11/99	Aberystwyth Town	H	0-0	
04/12/99	Barry Town	A	0-3	
11/12/99	Bangor City	H	1-2	Daley
18/12/99	Cwmbran Town	A	0-4	
27/12/99	Flexsys Cefn Druids	H	2-3	Williams D., Peters
08/01/00	Newtown	A	0-5	
15/01/00	Haverfordwest County	H	0-4	
22/01/00	Carmarthen Town	A	1-3	Sadler
29/01/00	Afan Lido	H	0-3	
05/02/00	Rhayader Town	A	1-2	Allen P.
09/02/00	Conwy United	A	0-4	
19/02/00	Inter Cardiff	A	1-1	Allen P.
23/02/00	Total Network Solutions	H	2-3	Evans R. 2
26/02/00	Connah's Quay Nomads	H	0-2	
04/03/00	Caersws	A	2-2	Emmett, McNeil
11/03/00	Rhyl	H	2-3	Emmett, McNeil
18/03/00	Total Network Solutions	A	0-4	
25/03/00	Llanelli	H	0-2	
01/04/00	Aberystwyth Town	A	0-6	
08/04/00	Barry Town	H	0-3	
22/04/00	Bangor City	A	0-1	
24/04/00	Flexsys Cefn Druids	A	0-3	
29/04/00	Cwmbran Town	H	0-2	

APPEARANCES 99/00 (CONT.)

	P	Ap	(s)	Gls		P	Ap	(s)	Gls
Kevin RHONE (ENG)	M	1	(3)		Andy TAYLOR (ENG)	M	2		
Gari ROBERTS	M	1	(2)		Matthew THURNSON (ENG)	M	1	(4)	
Neil ROBERTS	M	14	(2)		Jason TURNER	G	9		
Karl ROBINSON (ENG)	A	9	(4)		Robbie TYNAN (ENG)	M	9	(2)	
Richard ROBINSON	G	4	(2)		Tony UNGI (ENG)	A		(4)	
Chris ROSCOE (ENG)	M	5			David WILLIAMS	M	2	(1)	1
Paul ROWLANDS (ENG)	D	10			Steve WILLIAMS	D	1	(2)	
Jason SADLER	A	22	(3)	2	Tom WINGROVE (ENG)	D	10		
Chris SHORT (ENG)	D	7							

CAERSWS

Caersws FC
3 Hafren Terrace
Caersws
SY17 5ES
tel - (01686) 688103
fax - (01686) 688103
Year of Formation - 1887
Chairman - Garth Williams
Secretary - Mike Jones
Manager - Mickey Evans
Stadium - Recreation Ground (4,000)

APPEARANCES 99/00

	P	Ap	(s)	Gls
Nicky BEDDOES	D	1	(1)	
Hugh CLARKE	A	30	(2)	4
Simon COOK (ENG)	A	13	(2)	
Andy DAVIES	M	31	(2)	5
Phil DAVIES	A		(2)	
Steven EDWARDS	A		(1)	
Graham EVANS	A	10		6
Paul EVANS	G	32		
Alex FLETCHER	D	3	(8)	
Antony GRIFFITHS	D	27	(1)	
David GRIFFITHS	D		(3)	
Robert HAMER	A	19	(6)	1
Lee HARDING	M	5	(10)	1
Mark HOWELLS	D	16	(13)	1
Marc HUGHES	M	33		1
Sean JEHU	M	33		7
Gary JONES	A		(7)	
Wyn JONES	M	2	(7)	
Geraint LEWIS	M	29	(2)	6
Marc LEWIS	M		(1)	
Neil LEWIS	D		(2)	
Gary POWELL	D		(1)	
John SILLITOE (ENG)	G	2		
Tim STEEL	A	13	(9)	4
Andy THOMAS	D	31	(1)	1
Dave TIMMS (ENG)	D		(1)	
Mark TOBIN	M		(1)	
Jason WEETMAN (ENG)	D	6	(2)	1
Andrew WHITTICASE	A	28	(4)	10
Gwyn WILLIAMS	D	10	(12)	

LEAGUE RESULTS 1999/2000

21/08/99	Bangor City	H	2-5	Lewis G. 2
28/08/99	Flexsys Cefn Druids	H	3-0	Jehu, Thomas, Hughes
01/09/99	Cwmbran Town	A	1-1	Davies A.
11/09/99	Conwy United	H	3-3	Jehu 2 (1p), Whitticase
18/09/99	Haverfordwest County	H	1-0	Weetman
25/09/99	Carmarthen Town	A	2-3	Clarke, Whitticase
02/10/99	Afan Lido	H	3-0	Howells, Hamer, Jehu
07/10/99	Barry Town	H	1-2	Davies A.
23/10/99	Caernarfon Town	A	3-1	Harding, Clarke, Steel
30/10/99	Inter Cardiff	H	0-3	
06/11/99	Connah's Quay Nomads	A	1-1	Steel
12/11/99	Rhayader Town	H	1-1	Jehu
27/11/99	Rhyl	H	0-1	
04/12/99	Total Network Solutions	A	0-0	
17/12/99	Aberystwyth Town	A	1-1	Steel
27/12/99	Newtown	H	0-1	
03/01/00	Llanelli	H	0-2	
08/01/00	Bangor City	A	3-1	Whitticase, og (Brett), Jehu
11/01/00	Cwmbran Town	H	0-1	
15/01/00	Flexsys Cefn Druids	A	3-1	Whitticase, Jehu (p), Steel
05/02/00	Haverfordwest County	A	0-0	
19/02/00	Carmarthen Town	H	2-1	Clarke, Whitticase
22/02/00	Barry Town	A	0-1	
26/02/00	Afan Lido	A	0-3	
04/03/00	Caernarfon Town	H	2-2	Whitticase, Evans G.
11/03/00	Inter Cardiff	A	7-2	Evans G. 3, Lewis G. 2, Davies A., Clarke
18/03/00	Connah's Quay Nomads	H	0-2	
24/03/00	Rhayader Town	A	1-0	Evans G.
01/04/00	Rhyl	A	0-2	
05/04/00	Conwy United	A	4-0	Davies A. 2, Whitticase, Evans G.
08/04/00	Total Network Solutions	H	0-1	
21/04/00	Llanelli	A	2-3	Lewis G. 2
24/04/00	Newtown	A	3-2	Whitticase 3
29/04/00	Aberystwyth Town	H	0-3	

CARMARTHEN TOWN

CLUB DIRECTORY

Carmarthen Town FC
3 Maesdolau
Idole
Carmarthen
SA32 8DQ
tel - (01267) 232432
fax - (01267) 222783
Year of Formation - 1948
Chairman - Malcolm Williams
Secretary - Alan Latham
Manager - Tomi Morgan
Stadium - Richmond Park (3,000)

APPEARANCES 99/00

	P	Ap	(s)	Gls
Richard ADAMS (ENG)	A		(1)	
David BARNHOUSE	D	32		
David BURROWS	D		(4)	
Paul BURROWS	A	16	(4)	2
Matthew CABLE	D	23	(1)	3
Matthew DELICATE (ENG)	A	12	(19)	11
Craig EVANS	M	6	(2)	1
Steve EVANS	D	5	(3)	1
Andy FISHER (ENG)	G	1		
Robert FITZGERALD	G	32		
Pat JENNINGS (ENG)	G	1		
Gethin JONES	M	8	(9)	2
Wayne JONES	D	19	(14)	3
Sion MEREDITH	M	20	(7)	5
Tommi MORGAN	A	2	(11)	1
Nigel NICHOLAS	D	26	(5)	2
Ryan NICHOLLS	A	27	(2)	4
Richard PARKER (ENG)	A	32		18
Gavin REES	D	17	(6)	4
Dean ROSSITER	M	27	(1)	2
Carwyn THOMAS	M		(2)	
Wyn THOMAS	M	34		6
Malcolm VAUGHAN	M	13	(8)	1
Paul WALKER	D	21	(3)	2

LEAGUE RESULTS 1999/2000

21/08/99	Haverfordwest County	A	6-1	Delicate 3, Parker 2, Thomas W.
25/08/99	Rhayader Town	H	1-1	Cable
28/08/99	Afan Lido	H	3-0	Burrows P., Parker, Delicate
04/09/99	Caernarfon Town	A	0-0	
10/09/99	Inter Cardiff	H	0-1	
18/09/99	Connah's Quay Nomads	A	2-0	Burrows P., Meredith
25/09/99	Caersws	H	3-2	Nicholls, Cable (p), Parker
02/10/99	Rhyl	A	1-0	Nicholas
10/10/99	Conwy United	A	2-0	Delicate 2
23/10/99	Total Network Solutions	H	2-1	Jones W., Delicate
29/10/99	Llanelli	A	2-7	Delicate, Parker
13/11/99	Barry Town	A	1-3	Meredith
27/11/99	Bangor City	H	0-1	
11/12/99	Flexsys Cefn Druids	H	3-0	Meredith, Parker, Vaughan
18/12/99	Newtown	A	2-0	Thomas W., Delicate
27/12/99	Aberystwyth Town	H	4-3	Cable, Thomas W., Parker, Jones W.
08/01/00	Haverfordwest County	H	0-3	
12/01/00	Rhayader Town	A	2-1	Thomas W., Morgan
15/01/00	Afan Lido	A	0-0	
22/01/00	Caernarfon Town	H	3-1	Parker 2, Meredith
28/01/00	Inter Cardiff	A	4-0	Rees 2, Jones W., Parker
05/02/00	Connah's Quay Nomads	H	2-0	Nicholls, Parker
19/02/00	Caersws	A	1-2	Parker
26/02/00	Rhyl	H	1-0	Rees
04/03/00	Total Network Solutions	A	1-2	Evans C.
22/03/00	Cwmbran Town	A	1-3	Delicate
25/03/00	Barry Town	H	3-2	Nicholas, Walker, Meredith
01/04/00	Bangor City	A	1-0	Parker
04/04/00	Llanelli	H	2-1	Jones G., Nichols
07/04/00	Cwmbran Town	H	3-1	Rossiter 2, Parker
15/04/00	Conwy United	H	4-1	Walker, Thomas W., Parker 2
22/04/00	Flexsys Cefn Druids	A	2-0	Parker, Jones G.
24/04/00	Aberystwyth Town	A	1-2	Evans S.
29/04/00	Newtown	H	5-3	Nicholls, Parker, Thomas W., Delicate, Rees

CONNAH'S QUAY NOMADS

CLUB DIRECTORY

Connah's Quay Nomads FC
40 Brookdale Avenue
Connah's Quay
CH5 4LU
tel - (01244) 831212
Year of Formation - 1946
Chairman - T.R. Morris JP
Secretary - Rob Hunter
Manager - Nev Powell
Stadium - Halfway Ground (3,000)

APPEARANCES 99/00

		P	Ap	(s)	Gls
Mike CARROLL (ENG)	M	13	(21)	
Phil COLLISTER (ENG)	G	28		
Kevin DAVIES (ENG)	A	25	(4)	13
Andy GRIFFITHS (ENG)	M	29	(1)	5
Gareth HANSON	D		(1)	
Nicky HENDERSON (ENG)	D		(11)	
Jamie HOLMES (ENG)	M	10	(21)	2
Steve HOPKINS	D	24		
Phil HUGHES	A		(2)	
Craig HUTCHINSON (ENG)	M	28		2
Jamie JARDINE (ENG)	D	29		1
Paul JONES (ENG)	D	20	(2)	2
Jon KENWORTHY	M	34		8
Ben McKENZIE	M		(1)	
Richard McNEIL (ENG)	A		(4)	
Paul MAZZARELLA	M	29	(3)	2
Julian PEPPER (ENG)	A	19	(12)	4
Nathan POPE	G	1		
Stuart RAIN (CYP)	A	24	(7)	13
Jamie RENSHAW	D		(2)	
Carl SMYTH (ENG)	D	34		4
Andy THOMAS (ENG)	D	20		
David WALSH	G	5		
Darren WYNNE	M	2	(8)	

LEAGUE RESULTS 1999/2000

21/08/99	Cwmbran Town	H	1-2	Davies
24/08/99	Flexsys Cefn Druids	A	2-0	Griffiths, Davies
28/08/99	Newtown	H	2-0	Jones, Smyth (p)
04/09/99	Conwy United	A	2-3	Kenworthy, Pepper
11/09/99	Haverfordwest County	A	4-1	Kenworthy, Pepper, Davies, Rain
18/09/99	Carmarthen Town	H	0-2	
25/09/99	Afan Lido	A	1-1	Hutchinson
02/10/99	Caernarfon Town	H	2-1	Kenworthy, Pepper
23/10/99	Inter Cardiff	A	0-2	
30/10/99	Rhayader Town	H	0-0	
06/11/99	Caersws	H	1-1	Griffiths
12/11/99	Rhyl	A	4-1	Griffiths, Pepper, Kenworthy, Davies
27/11/99	Total Network Solutions	H	2-4	Mazzarella, Holmes
04/12/99	Llanelli	A	0-2	
18/12/99	Barry Town	A	3-3	Kenworthy 2, Rain
27/12/99	Bangor City	H	0-1	
08/01/00	Cwmbran Town	A	2-0	Rain, Kenworthy
11/01/00	Flexsys Cefn Druids	H	1-0	Hutchinson
15/01/00	Newtown	A	1-0	Rain
22/01/00	Conwy United	H	10-0	Davies 5, Jardine, Rain, Smyth, Griffiths, Holmes
29/01/00	Haverfordwest County	H	2-2	Davies, Mazzarella
05/02/00	Carmarthen Town	A	0-2	
19/02/00	Afan Lido	H	1-1	Rain
26/02/00	Caernarfon Town	A	2-0	Griffiths (p), Smyth
04/03/00	Inter Cardiff	H	2-1	Kenworthy, Smyth
07/03/00	Aberystwyth Town	H	0-1	
11/03/00	Rhayader Town	A	2-1	Jones, Davies
18/03/00	Caersws	A	2-0	Rain 2
25/03/00	Rhyl	H	2-0	Davies, Rain
04/04/00	Total Network Solutions	A	0-1	
08/04/00	Llanelli	H	1-0	Davies
22/04/00	Aberystwyth Town	A	1-2	og (Philpott)
24/04/00	Bangor City	A	2-0	Rain 2
29/04/00	Barry Town	H	2-0	Rain 2

CONWY UNITED

CLUB DIRECTORY

Conwy United FC
1 Tan-y-Maes, Glan Conwy, Conwy LL28 5LQ
tel - (01492) 573243 / fax - (01492) 573243
Year of Formation - 1977
Chairman - Joe Davies
Secretary - Graham Rees
Manager - Stan Allen; Dave Lloyd
Stadium - Morfa Conwy (4,000)

APPEARANCES 99/00

	P	Ap	(s)	Gls
Chris ADAMSON (ENG)	M	14		2
Steve BACCIMO (ENG)	A	1	(3)	
Matthew BISHOP (ENG)	D	8		
Dave BLACKALL	G	2		
Chris BOULTON (ENG)	A	1	(3)	
Terry BROWN (ENG)	M	8	(4)	4
Adam CAIN (ENG)	M		(1)	
Lee CARROLL	M	12	(3)	
Bobby COLVILLE	D	1		
Matt CORCORAN	A	9	(4)	1
Lee DIXON	M	12		
Joe DONNELLY (ENG)	M	13		
Danny EMBLETON (ENG)	G	13		
Daren EMMETT (ENG)	M	13		7
Gary FINLEY (ENG)	D	4		
Anthony GODFREY (ENG)	D	5	(4)	
Daren GORMAN (ENG)	D	3		
Greg HARDIE	M	2		
John HARGREAVES	A	6	(2)	
Paul HAWKINS	M	10	(3)	1
Peter HAYES (ENG)	M	4	(3)	2
Daren HILDITCH (ENG)	A	6		1
Steven HILDITCH (ENG)	A	8	(1)	2
Alex HILL (ENG)	G	14	(1)	
Paul HOLLAND	M	2	(4)	
Ross HOLTON (ENG)	D	8		
Shane HOWARD (ENG)	M	2	(1)	
Eifion HUGHES	M	1		
Phil HUGHES	M	4	(2)	
Bevan HUMPHRIES	D	9	(2)	
Barry JONES (ENG)	A	2	(1)	
Simon KENDRICK (ENG)	M	2	(2)	
Michael LENNON (ENG)	M	13	(1)	2
Paul LLOYD	D	12	(6)	
Danny McGOONA	M	2		
Mike MALONEY (ENG)	M	12		1
Craig MICKLEBURGH	M	1	(1)	
Anthony MITCHELL (ENG)	M	2	(6)	2
Mark ORME	D	2	(1)	
David OWEN (ENG)	D	2	(3)	
Alan PEASE (ENG)	M	14		
Mark PHILLIPS (ENG)	D	10		
Paul PHILLIPS (ENG)	M	12	(1)	1
Joe QUINN (ENG)	D	13		
Alfie ROBERTS	D		(1)	
Martin ROBERTS	G	3	(1)	
Stephen ROBERTS	D	10	(5)	
Steve ROBERTS	M	6	(1)	
Damien RODEN (ENG)	D	2		
Richie SEMPLE (ENG)	M	5	(1)	

LEAGUE RESULTS 1999/2000

21/08/99	Afan Lido	H	0-0	
25/08/99	Caernarfon Town	A	2-0	Toner 2
04/09/99	Connah's Quay Nomads	H	3-2	Emmett, Corcoran (p), Smith A.
11/09/99	Caersws	A	3-3	Emmett 2, Toner
25/09/99	Total Network Solutions	H	4-5	Hayes 2, Brown, Hilditch S.
02/10/99	Llanelli	A	2-3	Brown 2
10/10/99	Carmarthen Town	H	0-2	
23/10/99	Aberystwyth Town	H	4-2	Mitchell 2, Hilditch D., Emmett (p)
30/10/99	Barry Town	A	1-4	Emmett
13/11/99	Cwmbran Town	A	1-3	Brown
27/11/99	Flexsys Cefn Druids	H	1-2	Emmett
04/12/99	Newtown	A	2-1	Hilditch S., Phillips P.
08/01/00	Afan Lido	A	0-3	
22/01/00	Connah's Quay Nomads	A	0-10	
25/01/00	Bangor City	A	0-8	
05/02/00	Inter Cardiff	H	0-2	
09/02/00	Caernarfon Town	H	4-0	Emmett, Maloney, Williams, Stirk
19/02/00	Total Network Solutions	A	0-7	
26/02/00	Llanelli	H	0-2	
03/03/00	Aberystwyth Town	A	1-1	Stirk (p)
15/03/00	Rhyl	H	0-2	
17/03/00	Bangor City	H	0-2	
21/03/00	Barry Town	H	0-4	
25/03/00	Cwmbran Town	H	0-5	
28/03/00	Flexsys Cefn Druids	A	1-3	Hawkins
01/04/00	Haverfordwest County	H	1-0	Adamson
05/04/00	Caersws	H	0-4	
08/04/00	Newtown	H	0-1	
15/04/00	Carmarthen Town	A	1-4	Lennon
19/04/00	Rhayader Town	A	0-5	
22/04/00	Rhayader Town	H	0-3	
24/04/00	Rhyl	A	1-1	Adamson
29/04/00	Haverfordwest County	A	1-1	Lennon
06/05/00	Inter Cardiff	A	0-2	

APPEARANCES 99/00 (CONT.)

	P	Ap	(s)	Gls		P	Ap	(s)	Gls
Chris SHORT (ENG)	D	10			Matthew THURSTON	M	4		
Antony SMITH (ENG)	M	9	(1)	1	Molly TIDSWELL	D	2		
Colin SMITH (ENG)	A		(6)		John TONER (ENG)	A	7	(1)	3
Joe SPENCER	M		(2)		Jason TURNER	G	2	(1)	
Scott STIRK (ENG)	M	6		2	Nathan WATSON	M	2		
Kevin THELWELL (ENG)	D	11	(5)		Lee WILLIAMS	A	1	(1)	

CWMBRAN TOWN

CLUB DIRECTORY

Cwmbran Town AFC
19 Duffryn Close
Roath Park
Cardiff, CF23 6HT
tel - (029) 20764381
fax - (029) 20764381
Year of Formation - 1955
Chairman - John Colley
Secretary - Roy Langley
Manager - Tony Wilcox
Stadium - Cwmbran (13,200)

MAJOR HONOURS
League Championship - (1) 1993.

APPEARANCES 99/00

	P	Ap	(s)	Gls
Mark AIZLEWOOD	D	14	(10)	
Jim BLACKIE	D	33	(1)	
Richard CARTER	D	18	(4)	
Eston CHIVERTON (ENG)	M	5	(8)	
Richard DAVID	D	17	(2)	1
Mattie DAVIES	A		(6)	4
Lee DYSON (ENG)	D	3	(9)	
Mark EVANS	D	15	(9)	1
Steve FUTCHER (ENG)	M	24	(6)	4
Ben GRAHAM	D	1	(5)	
Deiniol GRAHAM	A	20	(8)	12
Carl HUGHES (ENG)	A	1		
Jamie HUGHES (ENG)	A	13		4
Phil JAMES	M	13	(4)	
Ray JOHN	D	7	(1)	
Gary McPHEE (SCO)	M	8		5
Adam MOORE	M	32	(1)	5
Steve MORRIS	G	4		
Neil O'BRIEN	D	30	(2)	4
Pat O'HAGAN	G	20		1
Michael PATTIMORE	M	8	(5)	
Kevin PAYNE	M	2	(2)	
Raith PLANT	A	1	(2)	
Darren PORRETTA	M	2		
John POWELL	M	6	(11)	
Gary STURCH	M		(3)	
Chris SUMMERS	A	30		28
Andy THOMAS (ENG)	D	2	(1)	1
Gary WAGER	G	10		
Russ WIGLEY	A	18	(2)	
John WILLS (ENG)	M	17		

LEAGUE RESULTS 1999/2000

21/08/99	Connah's Quay Nomads	A	2-1	Graham D., Moore
01/09/99	Caersws	H	1-1	Thomas
04/09/99	Total Network Solutions	A	3-1	O'Brien 2, Evans
11/09/99	Llanelli	H	3-1	Summers 2, Graham D.
17/09/99	Aberystwyth Town	A	2-1	Graham D. 2
25/09/99	Barry Town	H	1-0	Summers
02/10/99	Bangor City	A	1-1	O'Hagan
10/10/99	Rhyl	A	1-1	McPhee
22/10/99	Rhayader Town	A	1-1	Graham D.
30/10/99	Flexsys Cefn Druids	H	2-1	McPhee, Moore
06/11/99	Newtown	A	0-2	
13/11/99	Conwy United	H	3-1	O'Brien, Moore, Graham D.
27/11/99	Haverfordwest County	A	1-1	McPhee
18/12/99	Caernarfon Town	H	4-0	McPhee 2, Summers, Graham D.
27/12/99	Inter Cardiff	A	4-1	Summers 4
08/01/00	Connah's Quay Nomads	H	0-2	
11/01/00	Caersws	A	1-0	Summers (p)
15/01/00	Rhyl	H	5-0	Summers 2, David, Futcher, O'Brien
22/01/00	Total Network Solutions	H	0-2	
29/01/00	Llanelli	A	3-1	Hughes J. 2, Summers
05/02/00	Aberystwyth Town	H	2-1	og (O'Toole), Summers
18/02/00	Barry Town	A	1-3	Summers (p)
26/02/00	Bangor City	H	6-0	Summers 4, Moore, Graham D.
03/03/00	Rhayader Town	H	1-2	Summers
14/03/00	Afan Lido	A	0-0	
18/03/00	Newtown	H	3-2	Summers 2, Futcher
22/03/00	Carmarthen Town	H	3-1	Summers, Futcher, Hughes J.
25/03/00	Conwy United	A	5-0	Summers 3, Moore, Graham D.
01/04/00	Flexsys Cefn Druids	A	2-3	Graham D., Hughes J.
07/04/00	Carmarthen Town	A	1-3	Davies
12/04/00	Haverfordwest County	H	1-0	Davies
21/04/00	Afan Lido	H	3-2	Futcher, Summers, Davies
24/04/00	Inter Cardiff	H	3-1	Summers, Davies, Graham D.
29/04/00	Caernarfon Town	A	2-0	Summers, Graham D.

FLEXSYS CEFN DRUIDS

CLUB DIRECTORY

Flexsys Cefn Druids FC
7 Lancaster Terrace, Acrefair, Wrexham, LL14 3HP
tel - (01978) 823027
fax - (01978) 823027
Year of Formation - 1869
Chairman - Brian Beesley
Secretary - Ron Davies
Manager - Gareth Powell
Stadium - Plaskynaston Lane (2,500)

MAJOR HONOURS
Welsh Cup - (8) 1880, 1881, 1882, 1885,
1886, 1898, 1899, 1904.

APPEARANCES 99/00

		P	Ap	(s)	Gls
Mark ALLEN (ENG)	D	17	(3)	1
Tim ALLEN	A	7	(4)	2
Konye AMONECHI (NIG)	A	1		
Richard BEAN (ENG)	M	4		
Kevin BREEZE	D	3		
René BRUCE-PINARD (CIV)	A	25	(3)	6
Andy DAVIES	M	34		1
Jay DAVIES	A	1	(3)	
Mike DAVIES	A	27	(1)	13
Leigh EDWARDS	G	34		
Alan GOODWIN	D		(4)	
Huw GRIFFITHS	D	23	(4)	4
Andrew HARPER	A		(5)	
Ross JEFFRIES	A	15	(14)	3
Phil JONES	D	9	(10)	
Grant MONTGOMERY (NIR)	A	2	(3)	
Paul MORRIS (ENG)	D	22	(2)	
Lee PHELAN (ENG)	A	2	(14)	
James PIERCE	A	10	(9)	1
Gareth POWELL	M		(1)	
Danny PURDIE	A		(1)	
Simon RICHARDS	M	26	(1)	2
Llion ROBERTS	M	7	(2)	
Damien RODEN (ENG)	D	1	(3)	
Aled ROWLANDS	D	34		4
Mark RUTTER	D	30	(1)	3
Eddie SHIELDS (ENG)	M		(3)	
Dave TAYLOR	A		(5)	
Craig WILKINSON (ENG)	A	7	(4)	2
Alan WILLIAMS	D	33		1
Geraint WILLIAMS	A		(2)	1

LEAGUE RESULTS 1999/2000

21/08/99	Inter Cardiff	A	1-0	Davies M.
24/08/99	Connah's Quay Nomads	H	0-2	
28/08/99	Caersws	A	0-3	
04/09/99	Rhyl	A	0-2	
11/09/99	Total Network Solutions	H	0-1	
18/09/99	Llanelli	A	1-2	Davies A.
26/09/99	Aberystwyth Town	H	2-0	Davies M. 2
02/10/99	Barry Town	A	0-7	
23/10/99	Bangor City	H	1-2	Davies M.
30/10/99	Cwmbran Town	A	1-2	Griffiths
06/11/99	Rhayader Town	A	1-3	Davies M.
13/11/99	Newtown	H	2-1	Davies M., Bruce-Pinard
27/11/99	Conwy United	A	2-1	Rowlands 2 (2p)
04/12/99	Haverfordwest County	H	2-3	Williams A., Jeffries
11/12/99	Carmarthen Town	A	0-3	
18/12/99	Afan Lido	H	1-0	Wilkinson
27/12/99	Caernarfon Town	A	3-2	Davies M. 2, Jeffries
07/01/00	Inter Cardiff	H	2-1	Davies M. 2
11/01/00	Connah's Quay Nomads	A	0-1	
15/01/00	Caersws	H	1-3	Griffiths
21/01/00	Rhyl	H	4-0	Rowlands 2 (2p), Richards, Bruce-Pinard
29/01/00	Total Network Solutions	A	3-0	Bruce-Pinard 2, Wilkinson
05/02/00	Llanelli	H	2-1	Rutter, Griffiths
19/02/00	Aberystwyth Town	A	0-3	
26/02/00	Barry Town	H	0-1	
03/03/00	Bangor City	A	3-3	Davies M. 2, Bruce-Pinard
18/03/00	Rhayader Town	H	0-2	
25/03/00	Newtown	A	1-4	Jeffries
28/03/00	Conwy United	H	3-1	Richards, Davies M., Rutter
01/04/00	Cwmbran Town	H	3-2	Rutter, Pierce, Allen T.
08/04/00	Haverfordwest County	A	0-3	
22/04/00	Carmarthen Town	H	0-2	
24/04/00	Caernarfon Town	H	3-0	Allen T., Allen M., Williams G.
29/04/00	Afan Lido	A	2-2	Griffiths, Bruce-Pinard

HAVERFORDWEST COUNTY

CLUB DIRECTORY

Haverfordwest County AFC
Trem y Gorwel, Chapel Lane
Keeston
Haverfordwest
SA62 6HL
tel - (01437) 710805
fax - (01437) 767203
Year of Formation - 1899
Chairman - Roger Cottrell
Secretary - Barry Vaughan
Manager - Mike Ellery; Jason Jones
Stadium - Bridge Meadow (2,000)

APPEARANCES 99/00

	P	Ap	(s)	Gls
Tom BILLING	M		(2)	
Derek BRAZIL (IRL)	D	18		2
David BURROWS	M	16	(4)	2
Paul BURROWS	A	13		2
Adam COLLINS	D	1		
Alex DAVIES	M	18	(10)	
Simon DAVIES	M	5	(4)	1
Phil EVANS	D	26	(2)	3
Steve EVANS	D	6		1
Neil FREDERICKSON	G	2		
Richard GAY	A	12	(2)	2
Mickey GEORGE	M	19	(6)	
Martyn JAMES	A	17	(10)	1
Andy JONES	A	4	(11)	
Jason JONES	M	20	(3)	3
Paul JONES	A	6	(1)	
Lee KISSICK	D	5	(3)	
Carl MAINWARING	A	17	(3)	5
Ben MILES (ENG)	G	32		
Mark OTTEN	D	27	(2)	3
Chris PIPER	A	8	(1)	
Chris PRIDHAM	M	26		4
Jamie RICKARD	M	30	(1)	3
Neil SIMON	D	15	(10)	1
Nigel STEVENSON	D	5	(4)	
Chris THOMAS	D	2	(1)	
Billy TIMOTHY	A	6	(21)	2
John WILE	M	18	(1)	1

LEAGUE RESULTS 1999/2000

21/08/99	Carmarthen Town	H	1-6	Otten
24/08/99	Afan Lido	A	3-4	Rickard, Davies S., James
28/08/99	Caernarfon Town	H	1-1	Evans S.
04/09/99	Inter Cardiff	A	0-0	
11/09/99	Connah's Quay Nomads	H	1-4	Rickard
18/09/99	Caersws	A	0-1	
25/09/99	Rhyl	H	2-2	Pridham, Otten
02/10/99	Total Network Solutions	A	1-4	Evans P.
10/10/99	Rhayader Town	H	0-1	
30/10/99	Aberystwyth Town	A	0-4	
06/11/99	Barry Town	H	0-6	
13/11/99	Bangor City	A	0-1	
27/11/99	Cwmbran Town	H	1-1	Burrows D.
04/12/99	Flexsys Cefn Druids	A	3-2	Otten, Gay, Mainwaring
11/12/99	Newtown	H	1-1	Simon
27/12/99	Llanelli	H	1-1	Pridham
08/01/00	Carmarthen Town	A	3-0	Mainwaring, Jones J., Pridham
15/01/00	Caernarfon Town	A	4-0	Jones J., Gay, og (Joyce J.), Mainwaring
22/01/00	Inter Cardiff	H	2-1	Jones J., Wile (p)
29/01/00	Connah's Quay Nomads	A	2-2	Mainwaring, Burrows D.
05/02/00	Caersws	H	0-0	
19/02/00	Rhyl	A	1-3	Burrows P.
26/02/00	Total Network Solutions	H	1-1	Mainwaring
11/03/00	Aberystwyth Town	H	0-5	
18/03/00	Barry Town	A	1-3	Burrows P.
25/03/00	Bangor City	H	2-1	Timothy, Evans P.
28/03/00	Afan Lido	H	0-2	
01/04/00	Conwy United	A	0-1	
08/04/00	Flexsys Cefn Druids	H	3-0	Brazil, Pridham, Evans P.
12/04/00	Cwmbran Town	A	0-1	
15/04/00	Rhayader Town	A	0-2	
22/04/00	Newtown	A	0-0	
24/04/00	Llanelli	A	2-3	Timothy, Rickard
29/04/00	Conwy United	H	1-1	Brazil

INTER CARDIFF

CLUB DIRECTORY

Inter Cardiff AFC (now - UWIC Inter Cardiff)
18 Clos Nant Glaswg, Cardiff, CF2 7NB
tel - (01222) 549038
Year of Formation - 2000
Chairman - Max James
Secretaries - Clive Harry
Manager - Phil Holme; Phil Lewis
(00/01 - Jonathan Magee)
Stadium - Leckwith (6,000)

MAJOR HONOURS
Domestic Cup - (1) 1999.

APPEARANCES 99/00

		P	Ap	(s)	Gls
Gavin BEDDARD (ENG)	A		12	(8)	5
Jason BEKKER	A		1	(3)	1
James BEVAN	D		5		
Derek BRAZIL (IRL)	D		9		
Chris BRENNAN (ENG)	D		5	(3)	
Lee BRIDGEMAN	A			(1)	
David BROADBENT	A		11	(4)	
Neil BUCHANAN (ENG)	M		19		
Marc BURROW (ENG)	D		16	(1)	
Ben BURROWS	D		1		
Ross CASEY (ENG)	M		2	(3)	
Rob CHESTERS	A		17		6
Eston CHIVERTON (ENG)	M		4		
Phil CLARKE	D		5	(2)	
Mark COLMAN (ENG)	D		11		1
Mull CROCKER	M			(4)	
Craig DALE	D			(1)	
Richard DAVID	D		9	(1)	
Gareth DAVIES	D		15	(6)	
Neil DAVIES	M		2		
Tomas DAVIES	D		10	(1)	
Jason DONOVAN	M		5	(2)	1
Simon DYER	A		3		
Ian EDWARDS	M		19	(3)	1
Paul GILES	M		7	(3)	
Warren GREEN (ENG)	D		8	(2)	
Jarred HARVEY	D			(2)	
Wayne HEWITT	D		5	(1)	1
Jason HISLOP	D		3	(5)	
Alun HUGHES	D		10	(7)	
Craig HUGHES	A		1		
Pat JENNINGS (ENG)	G		4		
Ray JOHN	D		1	(1)	
Chris JONES	M			(1)	
Ian JONES	A		1	(2)	1
Rob KING	D		4		
Daniel LOCK (ENG)	D		5	(1)	
Carl MAINWARING	A		4	(3)	
Steve MARDENBOROUGH (ENG)	A		8	(1)	2
Samir MISBAH	D		12	(5)	3
Chris MORGAN	D		4		
Joel MORGAN	D		3	(6)	
Jamie MURRAY	M		2	(1)	
Christian OWEN	M		6	(3)	
Dennis PERRETT	M		1		
Dean PHILPOTT	D		5		
Adam PITCAIRN (SCO)	A			(3)	
Logan PLANT (ENG)	M		15	(1)	
Darren PORRETTA	M		4		1
Matt RAMADAN	M			(1)	

LEAGUE RESULTS 1999/2000

21/08/99	Flexsys Cefn Druids	H	0-1	
31/08/99	Newtown	A	0-2	
04/09/99	Haverfordwest County	H	0-0	
10/09/99	Carmarthen Town	A	1-0	Hewitt
17/09/99	Afan Lido	H	1-1	Porretta
25/09/99	Caernarfon Town	A	0-0	
02/10/99	Rhayader Town	H	1-1	Donovan
23/10/99	Connah's Quay Nomads	H	2-0	Mardenborough, Tyler
30/10/99	Caersws	A	3-0	Tyler 2, Williams C.
06/11/99	Rhyl	H	2-1	Misbah, Mardenborough
13/11/99	Total Network Solutions	A	0-2	
10/12/99	Barry Town	H	1-5	Sanderson
18/12/99	Bangor City	A	1-3	Jones I.
27/12/99	Cwmbran Town	H	1-4	Watts
07/01/00	Flexsys Cefn Druids	A	1-2	Edwards
11/01/00	Newtown	H	0-0	
22/01/00	Haverfordwest County	A	1-2	Bekker
28/01/00	Carmarthen Town	H	0-4	
05/02/00	Conwy United	A	2-0	Chesters 2
19/02/00	Caernarfon Town	H	1-1	Chesters
26/02/00	Rhayader Town	A	0-1	
04/03/00	Connah's Quay Nomads	A	1-2	Beddard
11/03/00	Caersws	H	2-7	Beddard, Chesters
18/03/00	Rhyl	A	0-2	
21/03/00	Afan Lido	A	0-3	
25/03/00	Total Network Solutions	H	1-2	Chesters
31/03/00	Llanelli	A	1-3	Chesters
04/04/00	Aberystwyth Town	A	2-1	Beddard 2
08/04/00	Aberystwyth Town	H	0-1	
22/04/00	Barry Town	A	1-5	Smothers
24/04/00	Cwmbran Town	A	1-3	Misbah
29/04/00	Bangor City	H	1-0	Misbah
01/05/00	Llanelli	H	0-3	
06/05/00	Conwy United	H	2-0	Colman, Beddard

APPEARANCES 99/00 (CONT.)

		P	Ap	(s)	Gls			P	Ap	(s)	Gls
James ROBINSON (ENG)	G		20			Matthew TREVETT	A		1	(2)	
Paul SANDERSON (ENG)	D		1		1	Simon TYLER	M		8	(1)	3
Ryan SHUGAR	M			(3)		Gary WAGER	G		10		
Gavin SMITH	D		1			David WATTS	D		2		1
Neil SMOTHERS	M		16		1	John WILE	M		10	(1)	
Carl STEPHENS	M		1			Chris WILLIAMS (ENG)	M		8	(2)	1
Paul STEPHENS	D		1			Thomas WILLIAMS	M		1		

LLANELLI

Llanelli AFC
Stebonheath Park
Llanelli
SA12 1HF
tel - (01544) 756176
fax - (01544) 772973
Year of Formation - 1896
Chairman - Robert Jones
Secretary - Roger Davies
Manager - Leighton James (00/01 - John Leary)
Stadium - Stebonheath Park (3,700)

APPEARANCES 99/00

	P	Ap	(s)	Gls
John ANDERSON	A	5	(18)	3
Jamie BOWEN	M	28	(3)	3
Wayne BOWEN	M		(2)	
Nathan CADETTE	A		(1)	
Jan CEGIELSKI	A	1	(5)	1
Richard CLEVERLEY	D	1	(1)	
Phil DAVIDSON	D	1	(1)	
Gary DAVIES	D	33	(1)	1
Jamie DAVIES	D	10		6
Mark DICKESON	A	30		21
Steve DYER	A	6	(11)	4
Paul FOWLER	M	8	(21)	3
Neil FREDERICKSON	G	6		
Glyn GARNER	G	28		
Andy HILL	M	24	(2)	5
David HUGHES	A		(6)	
Richard JENKINS	D	23	(6)	
Jason JONES	M	4		
Lee JONES	M	27	(1)	8
Scott JONES	D	20	(13)	1
Raymond MICHAEL	M		(1)	
Andrew MUMFORD	M	22	(6)	2
Mark PARFITT	D	28	(3)	1
Thomas RAMASUT	D	8		1
Chris WATKINS (ENG)	A	34		6
Anthony WRIGHT	M	27		5

LEAGUE RESULTS 1999/2000

Date	Opponent		Score	Scorers
21/08/99	Rhayader Town	A	3-1	Watkins, Jones L., Dickeson
24/08/99	Aberystwyth Town	H	5-0	Jones L., Dyer, Hill, Cegielski, Dickeson
27/08/99	Barry Town	A	2-4	Dickeson, Hill
04/09/99	Bangor City	H	4-1	Anderson 2, Fowler, Dickeson
11/09/99	Cwmbran Town	A	1-3	Dickeson
18/09/99	Flexsys Cefn Druids	H	2-1	Dickeson, Parfitt
25/09/99	Newtown	A	2-1	Wright, og (Reynolds)
02/10/99	Conwy United	H	3-2	Mumford, Dickeson, Jones L. (p)
10/10/99	Total Network Solutions	A	0-2	
29/10/99	Carmarthen Town	H	7-2	Dickeson 3, Jones L. (p), Davies J., Wright, Anderson
13/11/99	Caernarfon Town	H	1-1	Dickeson
04/12/99	Connah's Quay Nomads	H	2-0	Dickeson, Davies J.
18/12/99	Rhyl	H	7-0	Dickeson 2, Bowen J., Watkins, og (Thomas B.), Davies J., Hill
27/12/99	Haverfordwest County	A	1-1	Wright
03/01/00	Caersws	A	2-0	Jones L., Davies J.
08/01/00	Rhayader Town	H	2-0	og (Morgan), Dickeson
11/01/00	Aberystwyth Town	A	1-3	Watkins
14/01/00	Barry Town	H	2-1	Dickeson, Hill
22/01/00	Bangor City	A	3-1	Davies G., Watkins, Fowler
29/01/00	Cwmbran Town	H	1-3	Jones L. (p)
05/02/00	Flexsys Cefn Druids	A	1-2	Dyer
19/02/00	Newtown	H	0-4	
26/02/00	Conwy United	A	2-0	Davies J., Watkins
07/03/00	Total Network Solutions	H	0-2	
17/03/00	Afan Lido	H	4-2	Wright, Davies J., Dickeson, Dyer
25/03/00	Caernarfon Town	A	2-0	Fowler, Jones L.
31/03/00	Inter Cardiff	H	3-1	Jones S., og (Green), Watkins
04/04/00	Carmarthen Town	A	1-2	Wright
08/04/00	Connah's Quay Nomads	A	0-1	
11/04/00	Afan Lido	A	0-0	
21/04/00	Caersws	H	3-2	og (Thomas), Dickeson, Mumford
24/04/00	Haverfordwest County	H	3-2	Hill, Dickeson, Bowen J.
29/04/00	Rhyl	A	3-1	Dickeson 2, Bowen J.
01/05/00	Inter Cardiff	A	3-0	Dyer, Jones L., Ramasut

NEWTOWN

CLUB DIRECTORY

Newtown AFC
Latham Park, Newtown
Powys SY16
tel - (01686) 622666
fax - (01686) 623813
Year of Formation - 1875
Chairman - Keith Harding
Secretary - Howard Ellis
Manager - Brian Coyne
Stadium - Latham Park (4,000)

MAJOR HONOURS
Domestic Cup - (2) 1879, 1895.

APPEARANCES 99/00

		P	Ap	(s)	Gls
Phil BATES (ENG)	D	19	(2)	2
Romily BROWN	M	6	(5)	
Paul BYWATER (ENG)	M	9		
Steve CLIFFORD (ENG)	A	3	(7)	2
Dean CRAVEN (ENG)	M	9		
Lee DAVIES (ENG)	D		(5)	
Steve DAVIES (FNG)	A		(2)	
Steve ECCLESTONE (ENG)	D	7		
Steve EDWARDS (ENG)	M	4	(6)	
Gareth EVANS	D	34		
Dean GARDNER (ENG)	A		(7)	1
Pat JENNINGS (ENG)	G	8		
Danny JONES (ENG)	G	2		
Paul LINE (ENG)	M	24	(7)	3
Phil MORRIS (ENG)	M		(10)	
Robyn ONIONS (ENG)	A		(4)	
Richard PIKE (ENG)	M		(11)	
Colin REYNOLDS	D	31		4
Mark ROBERTS	M	29	(5)	3
Scott RUSCOE (ENG)	M	32	(1)	6
Chris TAYLOR (ENG)	D	7	(1)	1
Mark THOMAS	D	22	(9)	
Dave TIMMS (ENG)	D		(2)	
Nicky WARD	A	10		4
David WATKINS	A		(2)	
Colin WEBSTER (ENG)	D	12		1
Justin WICKHAM (ENG)	A	33	(1)	7
Mark WILLIAMS	A	28	(2)	6
Andy WITHINGTON (ENG)	G	24		
Jason YATES (ENG)	A	21	(13)	7

LEAGUE RESULTS 1999/2000

Date	Opponent		Score	Scorers
21/08/99	Caernarfon Town	A	1-1	Ward
28/08/99	Connah's Quay Nomads	A	0-2	
31/08/99	Inter Cardiff	H	2-0	Williams, Ward
11/09/99	Rhyl	H	1-0	Line
18/09/99	Total Network Solutions	A	0-0	
25/09/99	Llanelli	H	1-2	Williams
01/10/99	Aberystwyth Town	A	2-3	Ward, Reynolds
10/10/99	Afan Lido	H	0-0	
22/10/99	Barry Town	H	1-0	Ward
30/10/99	Bangor City	A	2-3	Webster, Wickham
06/11/99	Cwmbran Town	H	2-0	Ruscoe, Line
13/11/99	Flexsys Cefn Druids	A	1-2	Yates
27/11/99	Rhayader Town	A	2-0	Taylor, Yates
04/12/99	Conwy United	H	1-2	Gardner
11/12/99	Haverfordwest County	A	1-1	og (Otten)
18/12/99	Carmarthen Town	H	0-2	
27/12/99	Caersws	A	1-0	Williams (p)
08/01/00	Caernarfon Town	H	5-0	Wickham 3 (1p), Bates, Line
11/01/00	Inter Cardiff	A	0-0	
15/01/00	Connah's Quay Nomads	H	0-1	
29/01/00	Rhyl	A	3-2	og (Taylor), Roberts, Williams
04/02/00	Total Network Solutions	H	0-1	
19/02/00	Llanelli	A	4-0	Ruscoe 2, Clifford, Williams
22/02/00	Afan Lido	A	1-2	Yates
25/02/00	Aberystwyth Town	H	2-0	Bates, Reynolds
04/03/00	Barry Town	A	0-4	
18/03/00	Cwmbran Town	A	2-3	Wickham, Yates
25/03/00	Flexsys Cefn Druids	H	4-1	Yates, Wickham, Roberts, Ruscoe
31/03/00	Rhayader Town	H	2-1	Roberts, Yates
04/04/00	Bangor City	H	2-0	Ruscoe, Williams
08/04/00	Conwy United	A	1-0	Wickham
22/04/00	Haverfordwest County	H	0-0	
24/04/00	Caersws	H	2-3	Clifford (p), Reynolds
29/04/00	Carmarthen Town	A	3-5	Ruscoe, Reynolds, Yates

RHAYADER TOWN

CLUB DIRECTORY

Rhayader Town FC
9 Glangwy, Station Road, Rhayader, LD6 5BW
tel - (01597) 811286 / fax - (01597) 826260
Year of Formation - 1890
Chairman - M.A. Pugh
Secretary - Paul Rowe
Manager - Steve Elwell; Gary Proctor
Stadium - Y Weirglodd (2,000)

APPEARANCES 99/00

		P	Ap	(s)	Gls
Mike BARTON	G	31			
Shaun BEDWARD (ENG)	A	2		(13)	
David BLAIR	M	3		(4)	
Romily BROWN	M	8			
Andrew CAREE	D	5		(1)	1
Gavin CHESTERFIELD	D	5		(2)	
Neil COOPER	M	10		(2)	
Steve CORRIERRI (ENG)	D	16		(6)	
Nathan COTTRELL	D	14			1
Martin CROMPTON (ENG)	D	13		(1)	
Ryan DURHAM	D	2			
Simon DYER	A	4		(1)	
Carl GITTINS	M	3		(4)	
Ben GRAHAM	D	5			
Edward HARE (ENG)	M	2		(3)	
Jarred HARVEY	D			(1)	
Darren HILDITCH (ENG)	M	4			1
Mark HUGHES	D	9		(3)	
Ray JOHN	D	13			2
Huw JONES	A	10		(8)	3
Ian JONES	M	5		(1)	
Richard JONES	A	9		(7)	
Stuart JONES (ENG)	M	18			3
Rob KING	D	3			
Ian LANCASTER (ENG)	M	3			
Paul LANGLEY (ENG)	M	1			
Tony McCARTNEY (ENG)	A			(1)	
Dylan McPHEE	M	20		(8)	3
Lee MATTHEWS	M	9			1
Paul MOONEY (ENG)	M	4			
Chris MORGAN	D	13		(2)	
Richard MORGAN	G	1			
John MORRIS	D	12		(8)	1
Steve MORRIS	G	2			
Lyn OWEN	M	12		(2)	
Gavin PERRY	D	1		(3)	
Chris PIKE	A	14			6
Damon RUSSELL (ENG)	A	27		(2)	10
Anthony THOMAS	D	2			
Tim TURNER	M	4		(7)	
Geraint TWOSE	M	3			
Leigh VICK	D	3		(3)	1
Chris WILLIAMS	M	1			
Craig WILLIAMS	M	11		(7)	
Stephen WILLIAMS	A	10		(1)	1
Glen WILLIS	D	27			

LEAGUE RESULTS 1999/2000

Date	Opponent		Score	Scorers
21/08/99	Llanelli	H	1-3	Caree
25/08/99	Carmarthen Town	A	1-1	Williams S.
28/08/99	Aberystwyth Town	H	0-3	
04/09/99	Afan Lido	A	0-3	
11/09/99	Barry Town	H	0-0	
18/09/99	Caernarfon Town	A	0-3	
25/09/99	Bangor City	H	1-3	Russell
02/10/99	Inter Cardiff	A	1-1	Vick
10/10/99	Haverfordwest County	A	1-0	Jones S.
22/10/99	Cwmbran Town	H	1-1	Jones S.
30/10/99	Connah's Quay Nomads	A	0-0	
06/11/99	Flexsys Cefn Druids	H	3-1	Jones H., Jones S., Russell
12/11/99	Caersws	A	1-1	Jones H.
27/11/99	Newtown	H	0-2	
04/12/99	Rhyl	A	0-1	
27/12/99	Total Network Solutions	A	1-3	Jones H.
08/01/00	Llanelli	A	0-2	
12/01/00	Carmarthen Town	H	1-2	Hilditch
14/01/00	Aberystwyth Town	A	1-3	Morris J.
22/01/00	Afan Lido	H	0-1	
29/01/00	Barry Town	A	0-2	
05/02/00	Caernarfon Town	H	2-1	Russell, Pike
26/02/00	Inter Cardiff	H	1-0	Pike
03/03/00	Cwmbran Town	A	2-1	Pike, Russell
11/03/00	Connah's Quay Nomads	H	1-2	Russell
18/03/00	Flexsys Cefn Druids	A	2-0	Pike, Russell
21/03/00	Bangor City	A	0-1	
24/03/00	Caersws	H	0-1	
31/03/00	Newtown	A	1-2	Pike
08/04/00	Rhyl	H	2-2	Russell, McPhee
15/04/00	Haverfordwest County	H	2-0	John, McPhee
19/04/00	Conwy United	H	5-0	Cottrell, Pike, Russell, McPhee, John
22/04/00	Conwy United	A	3-0	Russell 2, Matthews
24/04/00	Total Network Solutions	H	0-1	

RHYL

CLUB DIRECTORY

CPD y Rhyl FC
3 Maes Rhosyn, Rhuddlan
Rhyl
LL18 2YW
tel - (01745) 591287
Year of Formation - 1883
Chairman - David Simmons
Secretary - Dennis McNamee
Manager - Adie Jones; Steve Jones
Stadium - Belle Vue (4,000)

MAJOR HONOURS
Domestic Cup - (2) 1952, 1953.

APPEARANCES 99/00

	P	Ap	(s)	Gls
Mark ANTROBUS (ENG)	D	30	(1)	2
Danny BARTON (ENG)	A	31		22
James BREWERTON	D	15		
Andy CAIRNS (ENG)	M	6	(2)	1
Damien CURRIER (ENG)	A	6	(3)	1
Gary CURTIS (ENG)	D	34		1
Danny EMBLETON (ENG)	G	19		
Karl EVANS	M	15	(1)	1
Peter EVANS	M	10	(5)	
Steve FISHER (ENG)	A	4		
Jon FISHER-COOKE	A	9	(5)	3
Dave FULLER (ENG)	D	32	(1)	2
Brian HATTON (ENG)	M	4		
Ian HORRIGAN (ENG)	M		(1)	
Lee HUGHES (ENG)	G	5		
Dave JOHNSON (ENG)	G	6		
Rob JONES	M	6	(4)	
Steve B. JONES (ENG)	A	8		
Steve C. JONES (ENG)	A	13	(4)	1
Neil MARSH (ENG)	M	8	(6)	
Andy MULLINER (ENG)	G	2		
Liam MURRAY (ENG)	M	6	(8)	1
Phil PARRY	M	1	(3)	
Stuart PICKTHALL	D	25	(6)	1
Paul POMFORD (ENG)	M		(16)	1
Chris ROSCOE (ENG)	M	6		1
Mark RUTTER (ENG)	D	9	(17)	
David SAVAGE (ENG)	M	1		
Chris TAYLOR (ENG)	D	4		
Aaron THOMAS	A	15	(2)	1
Barry THOMAS	D	10	(3)	
Tony UNGI (ENG)	A	3	(10)	
Gary URQUHART	A		(3)	
Jamie WEBSTER (ENG)	D	6		
Gareth WEST (ENG)	D	5		
Lee WILLIAMS (ENG)	G	2		
Darren WYNNE	M	18		1

LEAGUE RESULTS 1999/2000

21/08/99	Barry Town	A	1-1	Barton
24/08/99	Bangor City	H	1-0	Barton
04/09/99	Flexsys Cefn Druids	H	2-0	Fisher-Cooke 2
11/09/99	Newtown	A	0-1	
25/09/99	Haverfordwest County	A	2-2	Curtis, Cairns
02/10/99	Carmarthen Town	H	0-1	
10/10/99	Cwmbran Town	H	1-1	Barton
29/10/99	Caernarfon Town	H	2-1	Barton, Currier
06/11/99	Inter Cardiff	A	1-2	Jones S.C.
12/11/99	Connah's Quay Nomads	H	1-4	Barton
27/11/99	Caersws	A	1-0	Pomford
04/12/99	Rhayader Town	H	1-0	Barton
11/12/99	Total Network Solutions	H	2-4	Barton, Roscoe
18/12/99	Llanelli	A	0-7	
08/01/00	Barry Town	H	0-5	
15/01/00	Cwmbran Town	A	0-5	
18/01/00	Bangor City	A	2-3	Fuller (p), Thomas A.
21/01/00	Flexsys Cefn Druids	A	0-4	
29/01/00	Newtown	H	2-3	Barton 2
05/02/00	Afan Lido	A	1-0	Antrobus
08/02/00	Aberystwyth Town	A	1-2	Fisher-Cooke
19/02/00	Haverfordwest County	H	3-1	Murray, Barton 2
26/02/00	Carmarthen Town	A	0-1	
04/03/00	Afan Lido	H	1-0	Antrobus
11/03/00	Caernarfon Town	A	3-2	Barton 3
15/03/00	Conwy United	A	2-0	Barton, Wynne
18/03/00	Inter Cardiff	H	2-0	Barton, Pickthall (p)
25/03/00	Connah's Quay Nomads	A	0-2	
01/04/00	Caersws	H	2-0	Barton, Evans K.
08/04/00	Rhayader Town	A	2-2	Barton 2
15/04/00	Aberystwyth Town	H	1-0	Barton
22/04/00	Total Network Solutions	A	1-2	Barton
24/04/00	Conwy United	H	1-1	Fuller
29/04/00	Llanelli	H	1-3	Barton

TOTAL NETWORK SOLUTIONS

CLUB DIRECTORY

Total Network Solutions FC
Birchlea, Portywaen, Oswestry, SY10 8LY
tel - (01691) 828645
fax - (01691) 828645
Year of Formation - 1959
Chairman - Edgar Jones
Secretary - Gwynfor Hughes
Manager - Dr. Andy Cale
Stadium - Recreation Field (2,000)

MAJOR HONOURS
League Championship - (1) 2000.
Domestic Cup - (1) 1996.

APPEARANCES 99/00

	P	Ap	(s)	Gls
Tim ALEXANDER (ENG)	D	32		7
Tim ALLEN	A	1	(1)	
Andy CALE (ENG)	M		(1)	
Lee COATHUP (ENG)	D	19		
Steve COOPER	D	4		1
Ian COX (ENG)	A	4		
Chris EDGE (ENG)	M	27	(1)	2
Tim EDWARDS	D	30		3
Gary EVANS	M	16	(1)	1
Ricky EVANS	M	26	(4)	2
Steve EVANS	D	12	(2)	4
Mick GALLAGHER (ENG)	D	3		
Leon GIERKE	A	14	(8)	7
Ben HATTON (ENG)	A	9	(2)	4
Glyn HODGES	M	3	(1)	
Pat JOHNSON (ENG)	D		(1)	
Arwel JONES	D	17		2
Ken McKENNA (ENG)	A	5	(24)	4
Mike MALONEY (ENG)	M	2	(1)	
Scott MILLINGTON (ENG)	M	13	(9)	
Rob MORRIS (ENG)	D	5	(6)	
Dewi PARRY	D	25	(3)	
Darren POWELL	G	2	(1)	
Gary POWELL	A	13	(18)	
Darren RYAN (ENG)	M	1	(3)	
Paul SMITH	G	5	(1)	
John TONER (ENG)	A	18		13
Nicky WARD	A	7	(1)	4
Colin WEBSTER (ENG)	D	9	(3)	1
Lee WILLIAMS (ENG)	G	27		3
Gareth WILSON	A	15	(10)	3
Anthony WRIGHT	M	10		6

LEAGUE RESULTS 1999/2000

20/08/99	Aberystwyth Town	A	1-4	Edwards
24/08/99	Barry Town	H	0-2	
28/08/99	Bangor City	A	2-0	Hatton, Evans R.
04/09/99	Cwmbran Town	H	1-3	Gierke
11/09/99	Flexsys Cefn Druids	A	1-0	Gierke
18/09/99	Newtown	H	0-0	
25/09/99	Conwy United	A	5-4	Alexander 2, Hatton, Edwards, Gierke
02/10/99	Haverfordwest County	H	4-1	og (George), Wilson, Gierke, Alexander
10/10/99	Llanelli	H	2-0	Jones, Edge
23/10/99	Carmarthen Town	A	1-2	Williams (p)
30/10/99	Afan Lido	H	3-0	Hatton 2, Gierke
13/11/99	Inter Cardiff	H	2-0	Alexander, McKenna
27/11/99	Connah's Quay Nomads	A	4-2	Toner 2, Ward, Wilson
04/12/99	Caersws	H	0-0	
11/12/99	Rhyl	A	4-2	Ward 2, Williams (p), McKenna
27/12/99	Rhayader Town	H	3-1	Wilson, Alexander, Toner
11/01/00	Barry Town	A	1-5	Edge
15/01/00	Bangor City	H	2-1	Jones, Cooper
22/01/00	Cwmbran Town	A	2-0	Webster, Alexander
29/01/00	Flexsys Cefn Druids	H	0-3	
04/02/00	Newtown	A	1-0	Evans S.
19/02/00	Conwy United	H	7-0	Toner 3, Gierke 2, Ward, Evans R.
23/02/00	Caernarfon Town	A	3-2	McKenna 2, Evans S.
26/02/00	Haverfordwest County	A	1-1	Evans S.
04/03/00	Carmarthen Town	H	2-1	Williams (p), Wright
07/03/00	Llanelli	A	2-0	og (Jenkins), Wright
18/03/00	Caernarfon Town	H	4-0	Toner 2, Wright 2
25/03/00	Inter Cardiff	A	2-1	Edwards, Evans G.
01/04/00	Afan Lido	A	0-0	
04/04/00	Connah's Quay Nomads	H	1-0	Toner
08/04/00	Caersws	A	1-0	Toner
11/04/00	Aberystwyth Town	H	4-1	Toner 3, Wright
22/04/00	Rhyl	H	2-1	Alexander, Evans S.
24/04/00	Rhayader Town	A	1-0	Wright

YUGOSLAVIA

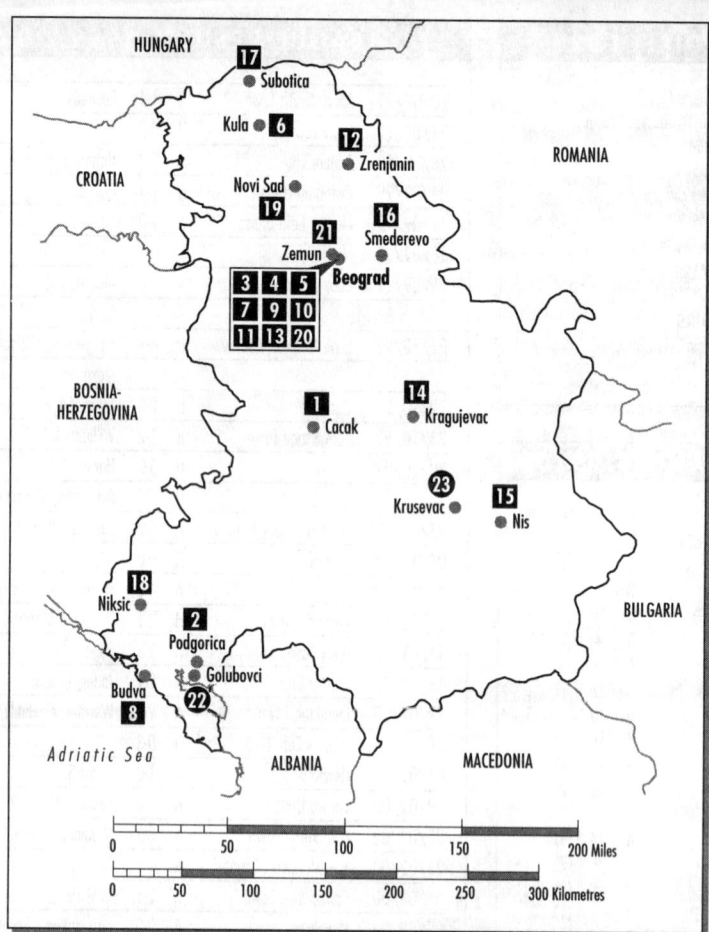

1	**BORAC CACAK**	1090
2	**BUDUCNOST PODGORICA**	1091
3	**CRVENA ZVEZDA BEOGRAD**	1092
4	**CUKARICKI BEOGRAD**	1093
5	**HAJDUK BEOGRAD**	1094
6	**HAJDUK KULA**	1095
7	**MILICIONAR BEOGRAD**	1096
8	**MOGREN BUDVA**	1097
9	**OBILIC BEOGRAD**	1098
10	**OFK BEOGRAD**	1099
11	**PARTIZAN BEOGRAD**	1100
12	**PROLETER ZRENJANIN**	1101
13	**RAD BEOGRAD**	1102
14	**RADNICKI KRAGUJEVAC**	1103
15	**RADNICKI NIS**	1104
16	**SARTID SMEDEREVO**	1105
17	**SPARTAK SUBOTICA**	1106
18	**SUTJESKA NIKSIC**	1107
19	**VOJVODINA NOVI SAD**	1108
20	**ZELEZNIK BEOGRAD**	1109
21	**FK ZEMUN**	1110
Promoted clubs		
22	**ZETA GOLUBOVCI**	
23	**NAPREDAK KRUSEVAC**	

RED STAR BACK IN CHARGE AT HOME

Eventful Euro 2000 for Boskov's boys

FEDERATION DIRECTORY

Fudbalski Savez Jugoslavije
Terazije 35, 11000 Beograd

tel - (011) 3233447
fax - (011) 3233433
website - www.fsj.co.yu

Year of Formation - 1919
President - Miljan Miljanic
Secretary - Branko Bulatovic

Never a dull moment. That was the most appropriate summation of Yugoslavia's Euro 2000 adventure. Every match they played was incident-packed. There were sensational comebacks, brilliant goals, red cards, pitch invasions - the lot.

On balance there were probably more bad things than good. The manner of the team's departure was certainly one of them. Holland had eliminated the Yugoslavs from the 1998 World Cup with a last-minute goal but this time the Dutch slaughtered them. It finished 6-1, but so over-run were Vujadin Boskov's team that the final scoreline might have been even more damaging.

The Yugoslav defence had already conceded seven goals in the first round, so it was perhaps not surprising that the co-hosts should slice through them so readily. But, for a top international team, Yugoslavia's lack of shape and organisation at the back was desperately poor.

Yugoslavia were utterly outplayed for an hour by Slovenia in their opening match but they rescued themselves with a stunning late fightback, scoring three goals in six minutes despite having been reduced to ten men following the senseless dismissal of Sinisa Mihajlovic. Clearly the team preferred it when the Lazio man was absent because when he was suspended, Yugoslavia

LEAGUE CHAMPIONSHIP RESULTS 99/00

#	Team	1	2	3	4	5	6	7	8	9	10	11	12	13	14	15	16	17	18	19	20	21
1	Borac Cacak		2-1	2-2	1-2	0-1	1-3	0-5	0-1	0-2	0-2	0-1	0-1	2-3	0-1	0-2	1-0	1-0	0-2	2-3	2-1	3-2
2	Buducnost Podgorica	2-0		0-2	0-0	2-0	0-2	2-1	4-1	0-2	3-1	1-4	2-0	1-0	2-0	1-0	1-1	4-0	0-0	4-0	1-0	1-0
3	Crvena zvezda Beograd	4-0	3-0		1-0	3-0	2-0	3-2	2-0	2-0	3-1	2-1	4-0	1-0	1-0	1-0	2-0	4-0	5-0	4-0	0-0	1-1
4	Cukaricki Beograd	2-0	1-1	0-1		1-0	0-0	1-1	1-0	1-2	3-3	0-2	2-0	1-1	2-0	2-0	2-1	2-1	2-2	0-1	0-0	1-2
5	Hajduk Beograd	3-0	0-2	0-3	1-0		1-1	5-1	1-0	0-3	1-2	1-2	2-1	2-2	2-1	4-1	3-0	3-2	2-0	2-2	2-1	2-1
6	Hajduk Kula	4-0	0-3	1-3	2-0	3-1		2-0	1-0	0-2	2-0	0-5	1-1	2-1	0-1	1-0	0-0	3-0	0-0	1-1	1-0	3-1
7	Milicionar Beograd	7-4	2-1	1-2	2-0	2-0	1-0		5-0	1-0	1-1	0-1	0-0	0-3	1-0	0-0	1-1	2-0	2-1	0-0	0-2	1-0
8	Mogren Budva	3-1	1-1	0-2	1-3	3-0	1-0	3-1		4-0	1-1	0-7	2-0	1-2	2-1	2-0	1-0	1-1	2-1	0-0	2-1	1-2
9	Obilic Beograd	6-0	3-1	1-1	0-1	3-2	1-0	1-0	2-0		2-2	3-0	3-1	1-0	3-0	2-1	1-0	2-0	2-1	2-0	2-0	1-0
10	OFK Beograd	1-4	2-1	1-2	3-1	2-1	1-0	2-1	3-1	4-2		2-2	3-0	0-0	1-1	1-0	0-1	3-0	2-3	2-0	1-1	1-1
11	Partizan Beograd	8-1	4-1	2-0	2-1	4-2	3-0	2-1	2-0	0-1	3-0		1-0	1-0	4-0	5-2	4-0	7-2	2-0	4-1	1-1	4-1
12	Proleter Zrenjanin	1-1	1-0	0-1	0-0	2-0	1-0	3-0	1-2	0-2	0-2	0-2		1-1	2-1	0-1	1-0	1-3	2-1	1-0	1-0	5-1
13	Rad Beograd	3-0	1-0	1-1	2-0	2-1	2-0	1-1	3-1	2-3	0-1	1-2	2-2		1-1	2-1	0-1	0-1	2-1	1-0	1-0	5-1
14	Radnicki Kragujevac	1-1	0-0	1-1	1-3	3-1	2-0	1-0	0-0	0-0	0-0	1-1	0-0	1-2		2-0	1-0	3-1	3-0	2-1	0-0	1-0
15	Radnicki Nis	4-1	1-0	1-2	3-0	2-0	1-0	1-0	4-2	2-1	4-0	0-1	1-3	3-0	0-0		2-1	2-0	2-0	2-1	2-0	2-3
16	Sartid Smederevo	2-0	2-0	1-2	1-1	4-2	4-0	0-2	3-1	2-3	1-0	1-3	2-0	1-1	1-2	1-0		2-0	0-0	1-0	3-2	1-2
17	Spartak Subotica	1-1	2-2	0-2	2-3	2-0	1-3	3-2	3-0	0-0	1-2	0-6	1-3	2-3	2-0	1-1	1-0		0-2	1-0	1-0	2-1
18	Sutjeska Niksic	2-1	1-0	0-1	0-0	4-3	1-0	2-0	2-0	1-2	3-2	2-2	3-1	1-0	0-1	3-1	4-1	1-0		1-0	2-1	0-0
19	Vojvodina Novi Sad	4-0	2-0	1-2	2-0	5-1	1-2	0-1	3-0	1-1	3-0	2-2	2-1	3-2	2-0	2-0	0-1	4-1	1-1		1-0	3-3
20	Zeleznik Beograd	5-3	1-0	1-3	1-2	3-1	2-0	2-2	4-0	0-3	4-3	0-1	3-0	2-2	3-1	3-1	1-0	3-0	3-1	1-0		2-1
21	FK Zemun	2-1	2-0	0-4	0-1	0-3	1-1	2-2	2-0	3-1	2-1	0-3	2-0	2-1	2-0	1-0	0-0	1-0	1-1	2-1	1-1	

LEAGUE CHAMPIONSHIP FINAL TABLE 99/00

		Pd	Home W	D	L	F	A	Away W	D	L	F	A	Total W	D	L	F	A	PT	GD
1	Crvena zvezda Beograd	40	18	2	0	48	5	15	4	1	37	14	33	6	1	85	19	105	66
2	Partizan Beograd	40	18	1	1	63	14	14	4	2	48	16	32	5	3	111	30	101	81
3	Obilic Beograd	40	17	2	1	41	10	11	3	6	30	23	28	5	7	71	33	89	38
4	Sutjeska Niksic	40	14	3	3	33	16	3	6	11	17	33	17	9	14	50	49	60	1
5	Rad Beograd	40	12	4	4	33	17	5	5	10	23	29	17	9	14	56	46	60	10
6	Cukaricki Beograd	40	8	7	5	24	18	7	4	9	18	25	15	11	14	42	43	56	-1
7	OFK Beograd	40	11	5	4	35	22	4	5	11	23	39	15	10	15	58	61	55	-3
8	FK Zemun	40	11	5	4	26	21	4	4	12	22	36	15	9	16	48	57	54	-9
9	Zeleznik Beograd	40	14	2	4	44	24	1	7	12	11	23	15	9	16	55	47	54	8
10	Vojvodina Novi Sad	40	12	4	4	42	18	3	4	13	12	32	15	8	17	54	50	53	4
11	Buducnost Podgorica	40	13	3	4	31	14	2	4	14	14	31	15	7	18	45	45	52	0
12	Radnicki Nis	40	15	1	4	39	15	1	3	16	10	34	16	4	20	49	49	52	0
13	Radnicki Kragujevac	40	9	9	2	23	14	4	4	12	11	30	13	13	14	34	41	52	-7
14	Hajduk Kula	40	11	4	5	27	19	4	3	13	12	27	15	7	18	39	46	52	-7
15	Milicionar Beograd	40	11	5	4	29	16	3	4	13	23	36	14	9	17	52	52	51	0
16	Sartid Smederevo	40	11	3	6	33	21	3	5	12	9	26	14	8	18	42	47	50	-5
17	Proleter Zrenjanin	40	9	6	5	21	13	3	4	13	14	36	12	10	18	35	49	46	-14
18	Hajduk Beograd	40	12	3	5	37	25	2	0	18	19	50	14	3	23	56	75	45	-19
19	Mogren Budva	40	11	4	5	31	24	2	1	17	9	46	13	5	22	40	70	44	-30
20	Spartak Subotica	40	8	4	8	26	31	0	1	19	8	52	8	5	27	34	83	29	-49
21	Borac Cacak	40	5	1	14	17	35	1	3	16	19	65	6	4	30	36	100	22	-64

N.B. Where two or more teams are level on points, classification is determined by the results of the matches between them.

NATIONAL TEAM RESULTS 99/00

18/08/99	Croatia (ECQ)	H	Belgrade	0-0	
01/09/99	Republic of Ireland (ECQ)	A	Dublin	1-2	Stankovic D. (59)
05/09/99	Macedonia (ECQ)	H	Belgrade	3-1	Stojkovic (36, 54), Savicevic (77)
08/09/99	Macedonia (ECQ)	A	Skopje	4-2	Milosevic (1), Babunski (4og), Stankovic D. (14), Drulovic (38)
09/10/99	Croatia (ECQ)	A	Zagreb	2-2	Mijatovic (25), Stankovic D. (31)
23/02/00	Macedonia	A	Skopje	2-1	Mijatovic (21, 38)
28/03/00	China	H	Belgrade	1-0	Mijatovic (8)
25/05/00	China	A	Beijing	2-0	Kezman (20), Kovacevic (73)
28/05/00	South Korea	A	Seoul	0-0	
30/05/00	South Korea	A	Seoul	0-0	
03/06/00	Hong Kong	A	Hong Kong	2-4	Kezman (67), Mihajlovic (90)
13/06/00	Slovenia (ECF)	N	Charleroi	3-3	Milosevic (67, 73), Drulovic (70)
18/06/00	Norway (ECF)	N	Liège	1-0	Milosevic (7)
21/06/00	Spain (ECF)	N	Bruges	3-4	Milosevic (32), Govedarica (51), Komljenovic (76)
25/06/00	Holland (ECF)	A	Rotterdam	1-6	Milosevic (90)

claimed their only victory of the tournament, beating Norway 1-0 thanks to Savo Milosevic's freak early goal. The Yugoslavs deserved their win but for all the skilful technique they showed, they were not afraid to dish out the violence or lie on the turf feigning agony. Substitute Mateja Kezman's quickfire red card just sec-

TOP SCORERS

27 Mateja KEZMAN (Partizan Beograd)
22 Mihajlo PJANOVIC (Crvena zvezda Beograd)
21 Petar DIVIC (OFK Beograd)
19 Sasa ILIC (Partizan Beograd)
   Vladimir IVIC (Partizan Beograd)
17 Dragan DJUKANOVIC (Mogren Budva)
16 Nenad MIROSAVLJEVIC (Proleter Zrenjanin)
15 Gabrijel RADOJCIC (Obilic Beograd)
14 Zoran JANKOVIC (Vojvodina Novi Sad)
   Bogic POPOVIC (Hajduk Beograd)

onds after his arrival was more a case of the referee finally losing his patience than the young Partizan Belgrade striker being the game's worst aggressor.

The final group game, against Spain, will long be remembered. It had everything. Three times Yugoslavia led, but each time the Spaniards came back, eventually winning 4-3 with two stoppage-time goals. The Yugoslav fans were incensed, and a couple of them even tried to attack the match officials, but they were unaware that because of Norway's 0-0 draw with Slovenia their team had still made it into the last eight.

The only pleasant memory that those fans had to take home from the quarter-final in Rotterdam was Milosevic's consolation goal in the the final minute. In fact, it was more than a consolation because it enabled the big striker to earn a share of the Golden Boot with Holland's Patrick Kluivert, Yugoslavia's chief tormentor on the day.

Vujadin Boskov, who had been drafted in to replace Milan Zivadinovic as coach a year earlier, quit shortly after the team's return to Belgrade. He was entitled to feel satisfied with a job well done. First of all, he had succeeded in taking Yugoslavia to the Low Countries, which was no mean feat given that they had to play five of their eight fixtures within a short period at the end of the qualifying campaign as a result of earlier politically-induced postponements. Reaching the last eight

Ljubinko Drulovic of FC Porto.

was probably about the best that Yugoslavia could hope for at the finals.

While Milosevic was undeniably Yugoslavia's outstanding individual, other plusses were Ljubinko Drulovic, the chief architect of the fightback against Slovenia, and veteran Dragan Stojkovic, who enjoyed an impressive swansong to his outstanding international career, demonstrating that he had lost none of his elegant craft, despite the advanced years. Stojkovic was purported to be first in line to take over from Boskov after the finals, but the Yugoslav FA decided that, with important World Cup qualifiers around the corner, the time was not right and handed the job instead to former assistant coach Ilija Petkovic.

The mere presence of Yugoslavia at the European finals - their first appearance at the tournament for 16 years -

DOMESTIC CUP 99/00

1/16 FINALS
Zeleznik Beograd 3, CSK Celarevo 2
Obilic Beograd 3, Radnicki Jugopetrol Beograd 1
Zeleznicar Lajkovac 2, FK Zemun 3
Sloboda Uzice 0, Sartid Smederevo 2
Vojvodina Novi Sad 2, FK Becej 1
Zeta Golubovci 5, Buducnost Podgorica 4 (aet)
Partizan Beograd 4, Spartak Subotica 2
Buducnost Beograd 1, OFK Beograd 0
Borac Cacak 1, Milicionar Beograd 3
Celik Niksic 3, Radnicki Nis 2 (aet)
Balkan Bukovica 2, Hajduk Rodic MB 1
FK Bor 0, Crvena zvezda Beograd 3
Napredak Krysevac 3, Rad Beograd 1
OFK Kikinda 0, Radnicki Kragujevac 0
(aet; 2-4 on pens.)
Cukaricki Beograd 2, Proleter Zrenjanin 0
Mogren Budva w/o FK Pristina

1/8 FINALS
Zeta Golubovci 1, Obilic Beograd 2
Napredak Krusevac 2, Mogren Budva 0
Balkan Bukovica 0, Milicionar Beograd 2
FK Zemun 0, Partizan Beograd 0 (aet; 4-3 on pens.)
Sartid Smederevo 0, Crvena zvezda Beograd 3
Buducnost Beograd 2, Celik Niksic 4 (aet)
Radnicki Kragujevac 1, Cukaricki Beograd 0
Zeleznik Beograd 1, Vojvodina Novi Sad 0

QUARTER-FINALS
Crvena zvezda Beograd 1, Radnicki Kragujevac 0
Celik Niksic 0, FK Zemun 5
Napredak Krusevac 0, Zeleznik Beograd 0
(aet; 3-1 on pens.)
Milicionar Beograd v Obilic Beograd 1
(aet; 5-4 on pens.)

SEMI-FINALS
Milicionar Beograd 0, Crvena zvezda Beograd 3
Napredak Krusevac 0, FK Zemun 0
(aet; 5-4 on pens.)

FINAL
10/05/2000, Belgrade
CRVENA ZVEZDA BEOGRAD 4 Pjanovic (13p, 38), Ilic (55), Vukomanovic (58)
NAPREDAK KRUSEVAC 0
referee - Cokanica
CRVENA ZVEZDA BEOGRAD - Kocic, Dudic, Ivic, Vukomanovic, Glogovac, Bunjevcevic, Gvozdenovic (Vitakic 55), Lerinc, Drulic, Pjanovic (Micic 72), Boskovic (Gojkovic 59).
NAPREDAK KRUSEVAC - Krnjinac, Atanackovic, Antic, Krstic, Mijatovic, Zajic, Vidojevic, Dragnjevic, Stefanovic, Kojicic, Filipovic (Petrovic 59).

NATIONAL TEAM APPEARANCES 99/00

Coach - Vujadin BOSKOV	CRO	IRL	MAC	MAC	CRO	MAC	CHN	CHN	KOR	KOR	HKG	SLO	NOR	ESP	HOL	Cps	Gls
Aleksandar KOCIC (18/03/69) - Crvena zvezda Beograd	G	G						s46								17	-
Zoran MIRKOVIC (21/09/71) - Juventus (ITA)	D		D	D40	D	s58										39	-
Goran DJOROVIC (11/11/71) - RC Celta (ESP)	D46					D50	D46	D36		D35			D	D15		44	-
Miroslav DJUKIC (19/02/66) - Valencia CF (ESP)	D	D	D	D	D	D	D46		D		s46	D	D	D	D	42	1
Sinisa MIHAJLOVIC (20/02/69) - Lazio (ITA)	D	D68		D		D	D46	D46			s46	D		D	D	48	6
Dejan STANKOVIC (11/09/78) - Lazio (ITA)	M	M	M74	M	M		M46	s46	M46	M46	M36				s51	23	6
Slavisa JOKANOVIC (16/08/68) - RC Deportivo (ESP)	M		M	M		M46	M46	M46	M46	M		M	M86	M		55	8
Albert NADJ (29/10/74) - Real Oviedo (ESP)	M	M76			M56			s46	M46	s60	D46		D	s83		35	3
Jovan STANKOVIC (04/03/71) - RCD Mallorca (ESP)	M						M46	M		M				s15	s61	10	-
Predrag MIJATOVIC (19/01/69) - Fiorentina (ITA)	A	A	A	A	A74	A46	A46	s46	A46	A46	A46	A83	A85	A	A	54	22
Darko KOVACEVIC (18/11/73) - Juventus (ITA)	A62	s76	s83	s83		A	s46	s46	A46	A46	A46	A52			s69	40	6
Ljubinko DRULOVIC (11/09/68) - FC Porto (POR)	s46	s53	M	M	s56	M		M60			M	M	M	M	M69	31	3
Savo MILOSEVIC (02/09/73) - Real Zaragoza (ESP)	s62	A	A83	A83	A	s46	A	A46	s46	s46	s46	s52	A	A	A	52	25
Slobodan KOMLJENOVIC (02/01/71) - 1.FC Kaiserslautern (GER)	D		s40				s46	s46	s46		s46		D	D	D	23	3
Drazen BOLIC (12/09/71) - Salernitana (ITA)		D			s53	s55										7	-
Dejan GOVEDARICA (02/10/69) - RKC Waalwijk (HOL)		M	s74				s46	s46	s46		s46		s86	s46	M	31	2
Dejan SAVICEVIC (15/09/66) - SK Rapid Wien (AUT)	M53	s66	s46	s74												56	20
Nisa SAVELJIC (23/03/70) - Girondins de Bordeaux (FRA)	s68	D				s46	s46	D	D	D	D46		D	s68	D61	34	1
Ivica KRALJ (26/03/73) - PSV (HOL)		G	G		G	G46	G46	G46	G46	G46	G46	G	G	G	G	39	-
Mladen KRSTAJIC (04/03/74) - Partizan Beograd		D	D			s50	s46	s36	D	s35						7	-
Dragan STOJKOVIC (03/03/65) - Nagoya Grampus 8 (JPN)		M66	M46	M53			M46	s60	M60		M	s36	M83	M68	M51	83	15
Nenad SAKIC (15/06/71) - Sampdoria (ITA)						D55	D46									3	-
Nenad GROZDIC (03/02/74) - Vitesse (HOL)							M	M	s46		s46					10	-
Vladimir JUGOVIC (30/08/69) - Inter (ITA)						M46	M58		s46		M	M	M	M46	M	39	3
Zeljko CICOVIC (16/09/70) - UD Las Palmas (ESP)						s46	s46		s46	s46	s46					5	-
Predrag DJORDJEVIC (04/08/72) - Olympiakos (GRE)						s46	s46									4	-
Goran BUNJEVCEVIC (17/02/73) - Crvena zvezda Beograd						s46	s46	D	D	D	D					7	-
Ivan DUDIC (13/02/77) - Crvena zvezda Beograd								D46	D46	D46	D46	D				5	-
Mateja KEZMAN (12/04/79) - Partizan Beograd								A46	s46	s46	s46	s83	s85			6	2

was a source of celebration for the people back home. The various political and military crises of the 1990s, and the subsequent bans and suspensions, had hit Yugoslav hard, and its international profile had suffered accordingly.

There was still a legacy of the war in Kosovo at the start of the 1999/2000 season as Red Star Belgrade, Partizan Belgrade and Vojvodina Novi Sad were all forced to play the home legs of their European ties on neutral territory. Perhaps directly as a result of this the trio all bowed out of the UEFA Cup in the first round.

Partizan had missed out on Champions' League qualification following a comprehensive defeat by Spartak Moscow, and they were no match either for Leeds United in the UEFA Cup, beaten 4-1 on aggregate after the first leg had been switched to the northern Dutch town of Heerenveen. Red Star chose a venue rather closer to home, Bulgarian capital Sofia, for their tie with Montpellier but it made no difference as they lost 0-1. They gave it their best shot in the return, but a 2-2 draw in Montpellier was insufficient to save them from elimination by a French club for the second season running.

With European interest at an end by October, Yugoslavia's top clubs settled down for a long grind on the domestic front. Because the previous season's

EUROPEAN CUPS 99/00

CHAMPIONS' CUP
● **PARTIZAN BEOGRAD**
Preliminary round 1 FC FLORA TALLINN (EST)
H 6-0   Ilic S. (12), Pekovic (25, 71), Ivic (37, 75), Kezman (56)
Ilic R., Rasovic, Stanojevic (Duljaj 20), Krstajic (Miskovic 40), Stojanoski,
Trobok, Ivic (Ilijev 85), Ilic S., Tomic, Pekovic, Kezman.
A 4-1   Kezman (10, 69), Ilic S. (20), Tomic (82)
Ilic R., Rasovic, Duljaj, Stanojevic, Stojanoski (Savic 43), Trobok, Ivic
(Miskovic 84), Ilic S., Tomic, Pekovic, Kezman (Obradovic 75).

Preliminary round 2 RIJEKA (CRO)
H 3-1   Ilic S. (10), Krstajic (22, 87)
Damjanac, Stanojevic, Duljaj, Rasovic, Krstajic (Miskovic 89), Trobok, Ivic
(Ilijev 67), Tomic, Ilic S. (Vukovic 77), Kezman, Pekovic.
A 3-0   Kezman (7, 82), Ivic (19)
Damjanac, Rasovic, Duljaj (Savic 71), Krstajic, Stanojevic, Trobok, Ivic,
Ilic S., Tomic, Pekovic (Ilijev 79), Kezman (Vukovic 83).

Qualifying round SPARTAK MOSKVA (RUS)
A 0-2
Damjanac, Rasovic, Krstajic, Duljaj, Stanojevic (Sabo 88), Trobok
(Gerasimovski 65), Ivic (Ilijev 71), Ilic S., Tomic, Kezman, Pekovic.
H 1-3   Kezman (73)
Damjanac, Rasovic, Duljaj, Krstajic, Stanojevic, Trobok, Ivic
(Gerasimovski 65), Ilic S., Tomic, Kezman, Pekovic (Ilijev 71).

UEFA CUP
● **CRVENA ZVEZDA BEOGRAD**
Qualifying round NEFTCHI BAKU (AZB)
A 3-2   Boskovic (68), Pjanovic (69), Pantelic (70)
Kocic, Dudic, Vukomanovic (Boskovic 46), Glogovac, Bunjevcevic,
Pantelic, Vitakic, Gojkovic (Micic 46), Ilic (Acimovic 46), Pjanovic, Bajcetic.
H 1-0   Pantelic (76)
Kocic, Dudic, Glogovac, Bunjevcevic, Pantelic, Boskovic (Lerinc 46),
Vitakic, Gojkovic, Ilic (Acimovic 75), Pjanovic (Micic 60), Bajcetic.

1st round MONTPELLIER HSC (FRA)
H 0-1
Kocic, Dudic, Bjegovic, Glogovac, Bunjevcevic, Pantelic (Acimovic 74),
Vitakic, Gojkovic, Ilic, Pjanovic (Ilic 64), Bajcetic (Baskovic 46).
A 2-2   Jelic (48), Boskovic (55p)
Kocic, Dudic, Bjegovic, Bunjevcevic, Boskovic, Vitakic, Gojkovic, Pjanovic,
Lerinc (Pantelic 77), Georgijevski (Acimovic 79), Jelic.

● **PARTIZAN BEOGRAD**
1st round LEEDS UNITED (ENG)
H 1-3   Tomic (21)
Damjanac, Rasovic, Savic, Stanojevic, Trobok, Tomic, Kezman, Ilijev
(Pekovic 70), Ivic (Stojakovic 89), Krstajic, Ilic (Gerasimovski 82).
A 0-1
Damjanac, Savic, Sabo, Gerasimovski, Stanojevic, Trobok (Duljaj 68),
Tomic, Stojisavljevic, Obradovic (Baljak 63), Ivic (Stojakovic 86), Pekovic.

● **VOJVODINA NOVI SAD**
Qualifying round ÚJPEST FC (HUN)
H 4-0   Suskavcevic (5), Jankovic (18p, 47), Jovic (62)
Zilic, Suskavcevic, Ristic, Tanasijevic (Jovic 58), Vranjes, Jankovic,
Krivokapic (Seckovic 67), Bogdanovic, Bratic, Aleksic (Vasic 84), Belic.
A 1-1   Bratic (87)
Zilic, Dragic, Suskavcevic (Mudrinic 74), Vasic, Ristic, Tanasijevic,
Jankovic, Krivokapic, Bogdanovic (Habi 84), Bratic, Belic (Jovic 63).

1st round SLAVIA PRAHA (CZE)
H 0-0
Zilic, Suskavcevic, Vasic (Jovic 63), Ristic, Tanasijevic, Jankovic,
Krivokapic, Bogdanovic, Bratic, Aleksic (Habi 84), Belic (Vranjes 63).
A 2-3   Belic (18), Bogdanovic (47)
Zilic, Dragic, Suskavcevic, Ristic, Vranjes (Vasic 58), Krivokapic,
Bogdanovic, Bratic, Aleksic, Mudrinic (Vaskovic 74), Belic (Jovic 68).

championship had been cut short by the NATO bombing campaign and subsequently abandoned, the league authorities decided that it would be unfair to subject the teams at the bottom of the suspended table to relegation. However, they did permit the promotion of four new teams. The end-product was a bloated First Division of 22 clubs.

The total number was immediately reduced by one when FK Pristina, from war-torn Kosovo, decided to withdraw. But that still left a marathon campaign of 40 matches, which all had to be squeezed in by mid-May in order to assist with the national team's Euro 2000 preparations.

It proved to be an exhausting ordeal, particularly for defending champions Partizan. Despite the departure of their long-serving coach Ljubisa Tumbakovic to AEK Athens, the club were successful in forestalling the exodus of their best players such as Kezman, Sasa Ilic, Mladen Krstajic and Vladimir Ivic. Yet despite possessing the strongest squad in the country, Partizan were unable to claim a sixth championship victory in eight years. They

scored plenty of goals and also led handsomely in the autumn. But when the matches came thick and fast in the spring they began to run out of gas and effectively surrendered their title on April Fool's Day when arch-foes Red Star beat them 2-1 in the 'Marakana'.

Obilic, the 1998 champions, dropped off the pace even more dramatically in the second half of the season. They were the leaders by two points at the halfway juncture but the assassination in January of their patron and president, the infamous warlord known as 'Arkan', was to send them into inevitable decline.

While Partizan and Obilic eased off, Red Star put together a storming run in the spring to come through and collect their first title in five years. The former champions of Europe ended the campaign with 17 straight wins, which enabled them to overhaul the previous front-runners and amass a spectacular final total of 105 points.

Red Star won 33 of their 40 matches and were beaten just once - 0-2 away to Partizan at the end of October,

PLAYERS OF THE SEASON

SAVO MILOSEVIC

When Savo Milosevic scored his fifth and final goal at Euro 2000 late in the quarter-final mauling by Holland, there was precious little celebration. But with Patrick Kluivert having one of his four goals in the same match chalked off and then missing a penalty in the Holland v Italy semi-final, the big Yugoslav striker ended up with a share of the tournament's Golden Boot. Milosevic's five goals took his international total to an impressive 25 in 52 games, enabling him to surpass the tally of his strike-partner Predrag Mijatovic. It was no great surprise that he should find his form so spectacularly in the Low Countries. He had just completed a superb season in Spain with Real Zaragoza, helping the club to the brink of Champions' League qualification with a steady supply of memorable goals, including two in a 5-1 win away to Real Madrid. The ex-Aston Villa striker did enough for club and country to earn himself a dream move to

Italy in the summer, with Parma signing him as the replacement for Lazio-bound Hernán Crespo at a cost of £16m.

GORAN BUNJEVCEVIC

The sweeper and skipper of Red Star Belgrade's Yugoslav 'double'-winning team, Bunjevcevic was born in Croatia but has chosen to play international football for Yugoslavia and received a deserved call-up for the national squad at Euro 2000. Tall, elegant and classy in possession, the left-footed libero has been dubbed the "Serb Beckenauer" by the Yugoslav press - a comment on the way in which he appears to glide effortlessly through matches. A Red Star player since 1997, when he joined from Rad Belgrade, Bunjevcevic is seen as a natural replacement for Miroslav Djukic at the heart of the Yugoslav national team defence. Now 27, it is only a matter of time before a foreign club steps in to shower him with the riches his talent deserves.

a match which was shrouded in tragedy as a Red Star supporter was killed when struck by a flare thrown by opposing fans. Hooliganism was a common theme of the season, with the tone being set in Red Star's opening fixture, away to Borac, which was so blighted by violence that the original 10,000 crowd was reduced to just a few hundred by the end of the match, which finished 2-2. Red Star were forced to play their next two home games behind closed doors, and in the first of them, against Zeleznik, they dropped another two points.

After the team's UEFA Cup elimination, Red Star changed coach. Miloljub Ostojic, who had been recruited during the summer from Obilic, was sacked and replaced by Slavoljub Muslin, an experienced coach who had spent most of his career in France, advancing the careers of such famous names as David Ginola, Zinedine Zidane and Christophe Dugarry. It proved to be an inspired move, because under Muslin the performances and the results greatly improved.

Red Star were not as free-scoring as Partizan, but they knew how to control games and get the desired result. Although a relatively young team, they had an experienced goalkeeper in Aleksandar Kocic and an outstanding team-leader in libero Goran Bunjevcevic, both of whom contributed to the team's outstanding defensive record of less than one goal conceded every two games. The key match was the 2-1 victory at home to Partizan, attended by a capacity crowd of over 50,000. That win

came in the midst of Red Star's unstoppable run, which lasted all the way through to the end of the season. The team's outstanding player during this period was 23-year-old striker Mihajlo Pjanovic, who not only opened the scoring against Partizan but also struck both goals in the 2-0 win over Sartid Smederevo that clinched the title one round from the end.

A week earlier Pjanovic had also bagged a brace to fire Red Star to an easy 4-0 victory over Second Division Napredak Krusevac in the Yugoslav Cup final - the first leg of the sixth 'double' in the club's history. It was plain sailing all the way for Red Star in the Cup. With Partizan and Obilic both exiting early after penalty shoot-out defeats, they met no major opponents and came through each of their five matches without conceding a single goal. No trophy defence had ever been more straightforward.

Napredak's consolation for losing the final was a place in Europe. They also won promotion to the First Division, comfortably winning their regional group, as did Zeta Golubovci, who reached the top flight for the first time. The third group winners, FK Belgrade, should have joined Napredak and Zeta in promotion but their modest facilities were deemed inadequate for the First Division so they remained where they were, enabling Sartid Smederevo, 16th in the First Division, to do likewise. Five teams did, however, go down as the First Division was mercifully restored to its familiar 18-team complement for the new 2000/01 season.

PROMOTED CLUBS 99/00

SECOND DIVISION FINAL TABLES

NORTH		Pd	W	D	L	F	A	Pt	GD
1	FK Beograd	34	22	6	6	65	35	72	30
2	FK Novi Sad	34	19	5	10	62	41	62	21
3	Radnicki/Jugopetrol Beograd	34	19	4	11	64	45	61	19
4	Zvezdara Beograd	34	19	4	11	54	37	61	17
5	FK Vrbas	34	17	8	9	45	37	59	8
6	Mladost Apatin	34	15	6	13	55	32	51	23
7	BSK Borca	34	15	6	13	53	42	51	11
8	Kolubara Lazarevac	34	14	9	11	43	38	51	5
9	Cement Beocin	34	14	8	12	42	34	50	8
10	CSK Celarevo	34	15	5	14	41	37	50	4
11	Teleoptik Zemun	34	15	5	14	57	55	50	2
12	Zeljeznicar Beograd	34	14	7	13	52	52	49	0
13	FK Becej	34	12	8	14	39	53	44	-14
14	Big Bull Bacinci	34	12	7	15	47	45	43	2
15	Kabel Novi Sad	34	12	4	18	40	54	40	-14
16	Dinamo Pancevo	34	8	9	17	33	51	33	-18
17	OFK Kikinda	34	5	7	22	28	65	22	-37
18	Palilulac Beograd	34	4	2	28	17	84	14	-67

N.B. FK Beograd declined promotion.

WEST		Pd	W	D	L	F	A	Pt	GD
1	**Zeta Golubovci**	**34**	**26**	**6**	**2**	**91**	**25**	**84**	**66**
2	Mladost Lucani	34	23	6	5	70	26	70	44
3	FK Novi Pazar	34	19	4	11	61	28	61	33
4	Bane Raska	34	16	13	5	54	31	61	23
5	Sloboda Uzice	34	16	9	9	59	34	57	25
6	Zlatibor Uzice	34	16	4	14	50	42	52	8
7	Rudar Pljevlja	34	14	10	10	39	37	52	2
8	Bokelj Kotor	34	15	6	13	38	33	51	5
9	Sloga Kraljevo	34	13	7	14	23	46	46	-23
10	Javor Ivanjica	34	11	11	12	50	47	44	3
11	Mladost Podgorica	34	12	5	17	41	49	41	-8
12	Sumadija Kragujevac	34	11	6	17	27	45	39	-18
13	Celik Niksic	34	11	5	18	47	41	38	6
14	Jedinstvo Bijelo Polje	34	9	10	15	31	45	37	-14
15	Lovcen Cetinje	34	9	10	15	34	48	37	-14
16	Grbalj Kotor	34	10	6	18	25	61	36	-36
17	Ibar Rozaje	34	7	8	19	34	74	29	-40
18	FK Berane	34	3	4	27	22	84	13	-62

N.B. Mladost Lucani 5 pts deducted.

EAST		Pd	W	D	L	F	A	Pt	GD
1	**Napredak Krusevac**	**32**	**23**	**3**	**6**	**70**	**28**	**72**	**42**
2	Zeljeznicar	32	17	9	6	58	27	60	31
3	Buducnost Valjevo	32	16	6	10	59	38	54	21
4	Jedinstvo Paracin	32	15	8	9	54	28	53	26
5	OFK Nis	32	14	7	11	41	31	49	10
6	Radnicki Svilajnac	32	15	4	13	45	40	49	5
7	Trajal Krusevac	32	14	5	13	36	45	47	-9
8	ZSK Valjevo	32	13	6	13	41	37	45	4
9	FK Loznica	32	11	9	12	38	39	42	-1
10	Mladi Radnik Pozarevac	32	11	7	14	39	54	40	-15
11	Dubocica Leskovac	32	10	8	14	30	42	38	-12
12	Temnic/Lipa Varvarin	32	11	5	16	30	52	38	-22
13	FK Bor	32	9	9	14	33	35	36	-2
14	FK Vucje	32	10	5	17	46	59	35	-13
15	Rudar Kostolac	32	11	2	19	39	54	35	-15
16	Rudar Aleksinacki Rudnici	32	9	8	15	36	65	35	-29
17	Radjevac Krupanj	32	9	7	16	31	52	34	-21

N.B. Crvena zvezda Gnjilane withdrew.

BORAC CACAK

CLUB DIRECTORY

FK Borac
Gradski bedem 6
3200 Cacak
tel - (032) 25458
fax - (032) 22302
Year of Formation - 1926
President - Dragan Kuzmanovic
Coach - Bozo Vukovic
Stadium - Gradski (12,000)

PLAYERS 99/00

	P	Gls
Nebojsa ALEMPIJEVIC	M	
Ivan BABIC	D	
COSIC	M	1
Milenko DJEDOVIC	M	1
Zoran DJURICIN	D	
Dragan DRAGUTINOVIC	D	3
Mijo GARDASEVIC	M	1
Boban GOCANIN	D	3
Branko JELIC	A	3
Branko JOVANOVIC	D	
nenad KOVACEVIC	A	1
Emanuel LAZOVIC	D	
Zoran MARICIC	M	4
Slobodan MARKOVIC	D	3
Mirko MIJAILOVIC	M	
Milan MIJAJLOVIC	A	3
Borislav MIKIC	D	1
Drasko MILEKIC	D	2
Nebojsa MILEKIC	G	
Dejan MILICEVIC	D	
NIKOLIC	M	
Marko OBRADOVIC	A	
Predrag PLAZINIC	A	5
Mirko POLEDICA	D	1
Ilija PRODANOVIC	A	
Srdjan RAICEVIC	D	
Radisa RUZIC	M	
Ivan SARIC	M	
Vladimir STAMATOVIC	D	
Vasilije STANISIC	D	1
Miodrag STARCEVIC	D	
Indir TOSKIC	M	3
Dragan VESELINOVIC	A	
VIDOJEVIC	M	
Vladan ZLATKOVIC	G	

LEAGUE RESULTS 1999/2000

31/07/99	Crvena zvezda Beograd	H	2-2	Plazinic, Jelic
07/08/99	Zeleznik Beograd	A	3-5	Maricic, Jelic 2
21/08/99	FK Zemun	H	3-2	Milekic D. (p), Gocanin, Maricic
11/09/99	Buducnost Podgorica	A	0-2	
18/09/99	Rad Beograd	H	2-3	Plazinic, Gocanin
21/09/99	OFK Beograd	A	4-1	Toskic 2, Plazinic, Gardasevic
25/09/99	Radnicki Kragujevac	H	0-1	
02/10/99	Spartak Subotica	A	1-1	Poledica
13/10/99	Radnicki Nis	H	0-2	
16/10/99	Sutjeska Niksic	A	1-2	Toskic
23/10/99	Partizan Beograd	H	0-1	
31/10/99	Cukaricki Beograd	A	0-2	
06/11/99	Hajduk Beograd	H	0-1	
13/11/99	Proleter Zrenjanin	A	1-1	Milekic D.
17/11/99	Vojvodina Novi Sad	H	2-3	Mijajlovic, Stanisic
20/11/99	Hajduk Kula	A	0-4	
27/11/99	Obilic Beograd	H	0-2	
04/12/99	Mogren Budva	A	1-3	Maricic
11/12/99	Sartid Smederevo	H	1-0	Mikic
15/12/99	Milicionar Beograd	A	4-7	Mijajlovic, Plazinic, Dragutinovic, Maricic (p)
12/02/00	Crvena zvezda Beograd	A	0-4	
16/02/00	Zeleznik Beograd	H	2-1	Plazinic, Markovic
19/02/00	FK Zemun	A	1-2	Mijajlovic
26/02/00	Buducnost Podgorica	H	2-1	Markovic, Dragutinovic
01/03/00	Rad Beograd	A	0-3	
04/03/00	OFK Beograd	H	0-2	
11/03/00	Radnicki Kragujevac	A	1-1	Djedovic
15/03/00	Spartak Subotica	H	1-0	Cosic
18/03/00	Radnicki Nis	A	1-4	Markovic
22/03/00	Sutjeska Niksic	H	0-2	
25/03/00	Partizan Beograd	A	1-8	Gocanin
01/04/00	Cukaricki Beograd	H	1-2	Dragutinovic
08/04/00	Hajduk Beograd	A	0-3	
15/04/00	Proleter Zrenjanin	H	0-1	
22/04/00	Vojvodina Novi Sad	A	0-4	
29/04/00	Hajduk Kula	H	1-3	Kovacevic
03/05/00	Obilic Beograd	A	0-6	
06/05/00	Mogren Budva	H	0-1	
13/05/00	Sartid Smederevo	A	0-2	
17/05/00	Milicionar Beograd	H	0-5	

BUDUCNOST PODGORICA

CLUB DIRECTORY

FK Buducnost
Vaka Djurovica bb
81000 Podgorica
tel - (081) 41955/41560
fax - (081) 51651
Year of Formation - 1925
President - Mikan Zec
Coach - Bozidara Vukovic
Stadium - FK Buducnost (15,230)

PLAYERS 99/00

	P	Gls
Ognjen BRAJOVIC	G	
Aljbino CAMAJ	M	1
Zeljko CVETKOVIC	M	
Zeljko DAMJANOVIC	M	1
Hasim DJOKOVIC	M	
Goran DJUROVIC	M	2
Igor DRAGICEVIC	M	
Branimir IVANISEVIC	A	1
Radovan KAVAJA	D	
Zlatko KOSTIC	M	5
Darko LUBARDA	G	
Zarko LUCIC	G	5
Davor MARAS	A	5
Dragan MARAS	M	1
Miroslav MESTER	M	
Zeljko MRVALJEVIC	D	
Aleksandar NEDOVIC	M	7
Nikola NIKEZIC	M	
Srdjan NIKIC	A	
Radenko NOVOVIC	M	
Dejan OGNJENOVIC	D	
Sanibal ORAHOVAC	A	9
Zvonko PAVICEVIC	M	
Rade PETROVIC	A	
Milos PRODANOVIC	M	
Dejan RABRENOVIC	D	2
Blazo RAOSAVLJEVIC	D	
Djordjije RAZNATOVIC	D	
Vladimir STANIC	A	
Milan VRANJES	A	
Miodrag VUKICEVIC	M	3

LEAGUE RESULTS 1999/2000

31/07/99	Mogren Budva	A	1-1	Nedovic
07/08/99	Sartid Smederevo	H	1-1	Maras Dr.
21/08/99	Milicionar Beograd	A	1-2	Orahovac
11/09/99	Borac Cacak	H	2-0	Orahovac, Nedovic
18/09/99	Crvena zvezda Beograd	A	0-3	
21/09/99	Zeleznik Beograd	H	1-0	Nedovic
25/09/99	FK Zemun	A	0-2	
13/10/99	Rad Beograd	H	1-0	Djurovic
16/10/99	OFK Beograd	A	1-2	Nedovic
23/10/99	Radnicki Kragujevac	H	2-0	Damjanovic, Orahovac
30/10/99	Spartak Subotica	A	2-2	Maras Dr. 2
06/11/99	Radnicki Nis	H	1-0	Rabrenovic
13/11/99	Sutjeska Niksic	A	0-1	
17/11/99	Partizan Beograd	H	1-4	Orahovac
20/11/99	Cukaricki Beograd	A	1-1	Orahovac
27/11/99	Hajduk Beograd	H	2-0	Nedovic, Vukicevic
04/12/99	Proleter Zrenjanin	A	0-1	
11/12/99	Vojvodina Novi Sad	H	4-0	Vukicevic, Lucic 2 (2p), Maras Dr.
15/12/99	Hajduk Kula	A	3-0	(w/o)
18/12/99	Obilic Beograd	H	0-2	
12/02/00	Mogren Budva	H	4-1	Kostic 2, Maras Dr. 2
16/02/00	Sartid Smederevo	A	0-2	
19/02/00	Milicionar Beograd	H	2-1	Djurovic, Kostic (p)
26/02/00	Borac Cacak	A	1-2	Nedovic
01/03/00	Crvena zvezda Beograd	H	0-2	
04/03/00	Zeleznik Beograd	A	0-1	
11/03/00	FK Zemun	H	1-0	Rabrenovic
18/03/00	Rad Beograd	A	0-1	
22/03/00	OFK Beograd	H	3-1	Orahovac 2, Lucic (p)
25/03/00	Radnicki Kragujevac	A	0-0	
01/04/00	Spartak Subotica	H	4-0	Lucic 2 (2p), Kostic 2
08/04/00	Radnicki Nis	A	0-1	
15/04/00	Sutjeska Niksic	H	0-0	
22/04/00	Partizan Beograd	A	1-4	Nedovic
29/04/00	Cukaricki Beograd	H	0-0	
03/05/00	Hajduk Beograd	A	2-0	Orahovac 2
06/05/00	Proleter Zrenjanin	H	2-0	Vukicevic, Camaj
13/05/00	Vojvodina Novi Sad	A	0-2	
17/05/00	Hajduk Kula	H	0-2	
20/05/00	Obilic Beograd	A	1-3	Ivanisevic

CRVENA ZVEZDA BEOGRAD

CLUB DIRECTORY

FK Crvena zvezda
Ljutice Bogdana 1a, 11000 Beograd
tel - (011) 668213/660216
fax - (011) 661753
website - www.fc-redstar.com
Year of Formation - 1945
President - Dragan Dzajic
Secretary - Vladimir Cvetkovic
Coach - Miloljub Ostojic; Slavoljub Muslin
Stadium - Crvena zvezda (56,000)

MAJOR HONOURS
League Championship - (21)
1951, 1953, 1956, 1957, 1959, 1960, 1964,
1968, 1969, 1970, 1973, 1977, 1980, 1981,
1984, 1988, 1990, 1991, 1992, 1995, 2000.
Domestic Cup - (18) 1948, 1949, 1950, 1958,
1959, 1964, 1968, 1970, 1971, 1982, 1985,
1990, 1993, 1995, 1996, 1997, 1999, 2000.
European Champions' Cup - (1) 1991.
World Club Cup - (1) 1991.

APPEARANCES 99/00

	P	Ap	Gls
Milenko ACIMOVIC (SLO)	M	21	4
Srdjan BAJCETIC	M	23	1
Nikoslav BJEGOVIC	D	12	
Branko BOSKOVIC	M	31	9
Goran BUNJEVCEVIC	D	40	7
Ivan DUDIC	D	38	
Blaze GEORGIJEVSKI (MAC)	M	25	3
Stevo GLOGOVAC	D	24	
Jovan GOJKOVIC	M	30	7
Ivan GVOZDENOVIC	M	34	1
Dejan ILIC	M	32	2
Branko JELIC	A	18	7
Aleksandar KOCIC	G	39	
Nenad LALATOVIC	D	14	
Leo LERINC	M	25	2
Marjan MARKOVIC	D	7	2
Dragan MICIC	D	7	
Nenad MILJKOVIC	M	3	1
Vladislav MIRKOVIC	A	15	3
Miodrag PANTELIC	A	19	7
Dejan PESIC	G	1	
Mihajlo PJANOVIC	A	27	22
Dalibor SKORIC	M	2	
Dragan STEVANOVIC	A	15	6
Boban STOJANOVIC	A	7	
Milivoje VITAKIC	D	19	
Ivan VUKOMANOVIC	M	23	

LEAGUE RESULTS 1999/2000

31/07/99	Borac Cacak	A	2-2	Pantelic, Bunjevcevic
21/08/99	Zeleznik Beograd	H	0-0	
11/09/99	FK Zemun	A	4-0	Jelic, Boskovic 2, Pantelic
18/09/99	Buducnost Podgorica	H	3-0	Boskovic, Pjanovic (p), Acimovic
21/09/99	Rad Beograd	A	1-1	Pjanovic (p)
25/09/99	OFK Beograd	H	3-1	Gojkovic, Bunjevcevic, Jelic
02/10/99	Radnicki Kragujevac	A	1-1	Pantelic
13/10/99	Spartak Subotica	H	4-0	Pantelic 2, Gvozdenovic, Gojkovic
16/10/99	Radnicki Nis	A	2-1	Gojkovic, Pantelic
23/10/99	Sutjeska Niksic	H	5-0	Boskovic, Pjanovic 2, Bunjevcevic, Jelic
30/10/99	Partizan Beograd	A	0-2	
06/11/99	Cukaricki Beograd	H	1-0	Pjanovic
13/11/99	Hajduk Beograd	A	3-0	Pjanovic 2, Jelic
20/11/99	Vojvodina Novi Sad	A	2-1	Bunjevcevic 2
27/11/99	Hajduk Kula	H	2-0	Acimovic (p), Mirkovic
01/12/99	Proleter Zrenjanin	H	4-0	Pjanovic 2, Jelic, Bunjevcevic
04/12/99	Obilic Beograd	A	1-1	Bunjevcevic
11/12/99	Mogren Budva	H	2-0	Jelic, Pantelic (p)
15/12/99	Sartid Smederevo	A	2-1	Gojkovic, Jelic
18/12/99	Milicionar Beograd	H	3-2	Boskovic, Acimovic 2 (1p)
12/02/00	Borac Cacak	H	4-0	Pjanovic, Lerinc, Miljkovic, Mirkovic
19/02/00	Zeleznik Beograd	A	3-1	Pjanovic 2, Ilic
26/02/00	FK Zemun	H	1-1	Boskovic (p)
01/03/00	Buducnost Podgorica	A	2-0	Georgijevski, Stevanovic
04/03/00	Rad Beograd	H	1-0	Pjanovic
11/03/00	OFK Beograd	A	2-1	Georgijevski, Stevanovic
15/03/00	Radnicki Kragujevac	H	1-0	Gojkovic
18/03/00	Spartak Subotica	A	2-0	Stevanovic 2
22/03/00	Radnicki Nis	H	1-0	Boskovic
25/03/00	Sutjeska Niksic	A	1-0	Stevanovic
01/04/00	Partizan Beograd	H	2-1	Pjanovic, og (Savic)
08/04/00	Cukaricki Beograd	A	1-0	Lerinc
15/04/00	Hajduk Beograd	H	3-0	Boskovic, Gojkovic, Mirkovic
22/04/00	Proleter Zrenjanin	A	1-0	Pjanovic
29/04/00	Vojvodina Novi Sad	H	4-0	Markovic, Stevanovic, Ilic, Gojkovic
03/05/00	Hajduk Kula	A	3-1	Pjanovic 2, Georgijevski
06/05/00	Obilic Beograd	H	2-0	Pjanovic 2 (1p)
13/05/00	Mogren Budva	A	2-0	Pjanovic (p), Boskovic
17/05/00	Sartid Smederevo	H	2-0	Pjanovic 2
20/05/00	Milicionar Beograd	A	2-1	Markovic, Bajcetic

CUKARICKI BEOGRAD

CLUB DIRECTORY

FK Cukaricki Beograd
Beogradskog bataljona 25
11000 Beograd
tel - (011) 551302/558627
fax - (011) 545646/544091
Year of Formation - 1926
President - Aleksandar Mihajlovic
Coach - Zvonko Radic
Stadium - Cukaricki (8,000)

PLAYERS 99/00

	P	Gls
Goran ALEKSIC	A	9
Slaven BOROVIC	M	2
Vojislav BUDIMIROVIC	A	6
Nemanja COROVIC	A	11
Srbo DIMITRIJEVIC	D	
Milan DUDIC	D	2
Ivan GAJIC	M	
Goran GAVRANCIC	D	
Panco GEORGIJEVSKI(MAC)	A	1
Srdjan GOLOVIC	M	
Rudi GUSNIC	D	1
Saudin HUSEINOVIC	A	1
Nenad KATAVIC	D	
Dejan MAKSIC	G	
Dusko MATIJEVIC	D	
Dragan MILENKOVIC	D	
Momir MILETA	M	
MIRKOVIC	D	
Dejan MUSOVIC	D	
Ajzadin NUHI	A	3
Dragan PAUNOVIC	D	
Nenad PAVLOVIC	D	
Srdjan PECELJ	A	1
Resad PEPIC	M	2
Petar PERISIC	M	
Nikola PJEVIC	G	
Ivan POPOVIC	D	
Denis PRTENJACA	M	2
Igor STOJAKOVIC	M	1
Vladimir SUBERT	D	

LEAGUE RESULTS 1999/2000

31/07/99	Sutjeska Niksic	H	2-2	Nuhi, Budimirovic (p)
07/08/99	Partizan Beograd	A	1-2	Borovic
11/09/99	Hajduk Beograd	H	1-0	Budimirovic (p)
18/09/99	Proleter Zrenjanin	A	0-0	
21/09/99	Vojvodina Novi Sad	H	0-1	
25/09/99	Hajduk Kula	A	0-2	
02/10/99	Obilic Beograd	H	1-2	Aleksic
10/10/99	Milicionar Beograd	A	0-2	
13/10/99	Mogren Budva	A	3-1	Corovic 2, Prtenjaca
16/10/99	Sartid Smederevo	H	2-1	Budimirovic (p), Aleksic
31/10/99	Borac Cacak	H	2-0	Pepic, Aleksic
06/11/99	Crvena zvezda Beograd	A	0-1	
13/11/99	Zeleznik Beograd	H	0-0	
17/11/99	FK Zemun	A	1-0	Aleksic
20/11/99	Buducnost Podgorica	H	1-1	Budimirovic
27/11/99	Rad Beograd	A	0-2	
04/12/99	OFK Beograd	H	3-3	Corovic, Aleksic, Dudic
11/12/99	Radnicki Kragujevac	A	3-1	Corovic 2, Prtenjaca
15/12/99	Spartak Subotica	H	2-1	Pepic, Pecelj
18/12/99	Radnicki Nis	A	0-3	
12/02/00	Sutjeska Niksic	A	0-0	
16/02/00	Partizan Beograd	H	0-2	
26/02/00	Hajduk Beograd	A	0-1	
01/03/00	Proleter Zrenjanin	H	2-0	Dudic, Budimirovic (p)
04/03/00	Vojvodina Novi Sad	A	0-2	
11/03/00	Hajduk Kula	H	0-0	
15/03/00	Obilic Beograd	A	1-0	Georgijevski
18/03/00	Mogren Budva	H	1-0	Stojakovic
22/03/00	Sartid Smederevo	A	1-1	Corovic
25/03/00	Milicionar Beograd	H	1-1	Borovic
01/04/00	Borac Cacak	A	2-1	Corovic 2
08/04/00	Crvena zvezda Beograd	H	0-1	
15/04/00	Zeleznik Beograd	A	2-1	Nuhi, Corovic
22/04/00	FK Zemun	H	1-2	Aleksic (p)
29/04/00	Buducnost Podgorica	A	0-0	
03/05/00	Rad Beograd	H	1-1	Gusnic
06/05/00	OFK Beograd	A	1-3	Corovic
13/05/00	Radnicki Kragujevac	H	2-0	Corovic, Aleksic
17/05/00	Spartak Subotica	A	3-2	Aleksic 2, Huseinovic
20/05/00	Radnicki Nis	H	2-0	Budimirovic, Nuhi

HAJDUK BEOGRAD

CLUB DIRECTORY

FK Hajduk Beograd
Milana Rakica 48
11000 Beograd
tel - (011) 3406706
fax - (011) 417338
President - Stojak Golic
Coach - Djordje Gerum
Stadium - Hajduk (4,000)

PLAYERS 99/00

	P	Gls
Sead BAJRAMOVIC	D	
Vladimir BAKRAC	A	4
Milorad BRANKOVIC	M	
Dusan DAVIDOVIC	M	1
Milos DJOLOVIC	D	
Goran DRAGICEVIC	D	1
Marko FILIPOVIC	D	2
Radomir GOJKOVIC	M	
Mladen GOLIC	D	
Ljubisa IVIC	M	5
Ivan JEVIC	M	1
Zeljko JOKSIMOVIC	M	5
Viborg KOCEIC	G	
Zoran LONCAR	A	
Vladimir MADZAREVIC	D	
Srdjan MAKSIMOVIC	G	
MARINKOVIC	A	
Aleksandar MARUNOVIC	D	1
Oliver MERDOVIC	M	
Dejan NIKOLIC	M	2
Bogic POPOVIC	A	14
Dragan POPOVIC	A	12
Ognjen RADOVIC	G	
Bojan RASOVIC	D	
Zvonko RMANDIC	M	
Nebojsa SELAKOVIC	A	1
Bojan SIMIC	D	1
Alen SOSO	D	
Goran STEFANOVIC	D	
Vladimir TERZIC	M	
Mirko TODOROVIC	M	4
TUCOVIC	D	1
Aco VASILJEVIC	A	
Aleksandar VESELINOVIC	D	
Dejan ZDRAVKOVIC	D	1

LEAGUE RESULTS 1999/2000

Date	Opponent	H/A	Score	Scorers
01/08/99	Radnicki Nis	H	4-1	Ivic, Popovic B. 3 (1p)
07/08/99	Sutjeska Niksic	A	3-4	Popovic B. 2 (1p), Marunovic
21/08/99	Partizan Beograd	H	1-2	Popovic B.
11/09/99	Cukaricki Beograd	A	0-1	
21/09/99	Proleter Zrenjanin	H	2-1	Davidovic, Nikolic
25/09/99	Vojvodina Novi Sad	A	1-5	Popovic B.
02/10/99	Hajduk Kula	H	1-1	Popovic D.
13/10/99	Obilic Beograd	A	2-3	Popovic B. 2
16/10/99	Mogren Budva	H	1-0	Popovic B.
23/10/99	Sartid Smederevo	A	2-4	Popovic D., Popovic B.
30/10/99	Milicionar Beograd	H	5-1	Popovic D., Ivic 2, Popovic B., Zdravkovic
06/11/99	Borac Cacak	A	1-0	Ivic
13/11/99	Crvena zvezda Beograd	H	0-3	
17/11/99	Zeleznik Beograd	A	1-3	Popovic B.
20/11/99	FK Zemun	H	2-1	Popovic B., Ivic
27/11/99	Buducnost Podgorica	A	0-2	
04/12/99	Rad Beograd	H	2-2	Todorovic, Joksimovic
11/12/99	OFK Beograd	A	1-2	Popovic D.
15/12/99	Radnicki Kragujevac	H	2-1	Joksimovic, Popovic D.
18/12/99	Spartak Subotica	A	0-2	
12/02/00	Radnicki Nis	A	0-2	
16/02/00	Sutjeska Niksic	H	2-0	Simic, Filipovic
19/02/00	Partizan Beograd	A	2-4	Filipovic, Todorovic
26/02/00	Cukaricki Beograd	H	1-0	Todorovic
04/03/00	Proleter Zrenjanin	A	0-2	
11/03/00	Vojvodina Novi Sad	H	2-2	Dragicevic, Popovic D. (p)
15/03/00	Hajduk Kula	A	1-3	Nikolic
18/03/00	Obilic Beograd	H	0-3	
22/03/00	Mogren Budva	A	0-3	
25/03/00	Sartid Smederevo	H	3-0	Popovic D. (p), Joksimovic, Bakrac
01/04/00	Milicionar Beograd	A	0-2	
08/04/00	Borac Cacak	H	3-0	Jevic, Popovic D., Tucovic
15/04/00	Crvena zvezda Beograd	A	0-3	
22/04/00	Zeleznik Beograd	H	2-1	Todorovic, Joksimovic
29/04/00	FK Zemun	A	3-0	Popovic D. 2, Joksimovic
03/05/00	Buducnost Podgorica	H	0-2	
06/05/00	Rad Beograd	A	1-2	Popovic D.
13/05/00	OFK Beograd	H	1-2	Bakrac
17/05/00	Radnicki Nis	A	1-3	Bakrac
20/05/00	Spartak Subotica	H	3-2	Selakovic, Popovic D., Bakrac

HAJDUK KULA

CLUB DIRECTORY

FK Hajduk
Svetozara Markovica 8
25230 Kula
tel - (025) 722812/723569/723045
fax - (025) 722814
Year of Formation - 1925
President - Bogdan Rodic
Coach - Risto Pavic
Stadium - Hajduk (10,000)

PLAYERS 99/00

	P	Gls
Zoran ANTIC	M	1
Slobodan BACIC	M	1
Milos BOGDANOVIC	A	
Dragan CIRIC	G	
Drazen CVJETKOVIC	G	
Bratislav DIKLIC	A	
Srdjan DJURDJEVIC	A	10
Predrag GAJIC	A	4
Nenad JEVTIC	M	
Aleksandar KIRKOV	M	
Nebojsa KLJESTAN	D	
Igor KOZOS	M	1
Zoran KULIC	M	
Ognjen LAKIC	M	
Nikola MALBASA	D	
Dragan MANDIC	D	
Bojan MARKOVIC	D	
Aleksandar MARKOSKI	M	2
Ivica MILIVOJEV	M	1
Dragan MOJIC	D	
Dejan OSMANOVIC	A	11
Blazo PESIKAN	M	
Ivan RADIVOJEVIC	D	3
Ljubomir RISTOVSKI	A	
Uros STAMATOVIC	M	3
Aleksandar STOJAKOVIC	A	
Dusan SVEDIC	M	
Dragan VUKSANOVIC	D	1
Velimir ZDRAVKOVIC	G	
Nenad ZECEVIC	M	

LEAGUE RESULTS 1999/2000

31/07/99	OFK Beograd	H	2-0	Osmanovic, Djurdjevic
07/08/99	Radnicki Kragujevac	A	0-2	
21/08/99	Spartak Subotica	H	3-0	Gajic 2, og (Zebic)
11/09/99	Radnicki Nis	A	0-1	
18/09/99	Sutjeska Niksic	H	0-0	
21/09/99	Partizan Beograd	A	0-3	
25/09/99	Cukaricki Beograd	H	2-0	Radivojevic, Bacic
02/10/99	Hajduk Beograd	A	1-1	Djurdjevic
13/10/99	Proleter Zrenjanin	H	1-1	Djurdjevic
16/10/99	Vojvodina Novi Sad	A	2-1	Djurdjevic, Radivojevic
30/10/99	Obilic Beograd	H	0-2	
06/11/99	Mogren Budva	A	0-1	
13/11/99	Sartid Smederevo	H	0-0	
17/11/99	Milicionar Beograd	A	0-1	
20/11/99	Borac Cacak	H	4-0	Gajic 2, Milivojev, Djurdjevic
27/11/99	Crvena zvezda Beograd	A	0-2	
04/12/99	Zeleznik Beograd	H	1-0	Djurdjevic
11/12/99	FK Zemun	A	1-1	Radivojevic
15/12/99	Buducnost Podgorica	H	0-3	
18/12/99	Rad Beograd	A	0-2	
12/02/00	OFK Beograd	A	0-1	
16/02/00	Radnicki Kragujevac	H	0-1	
19/02/00	Spartak Subotica	A	3-1	Osmanovic 2, Kozos
26/02/00	Radnicki Nis	H	1-0	Markovski
01/03/00	Sutjeska Niksic	A	0-1	
04/03/00	Partizan Beograd	H	0-5	
11/03/00	Cukaricki Beograd	A	0-0	
15/03/00	Hajduk Beograd	H	3-1	Osmanovic 2, Djurdjevic
18/03/00	Proleter Zrenjanin	A	0-1	
22/03/00	Vojvodina Novi Sad	H	1-1	Vuksanovic
01/04/00	Obilic Beograd	A	0-1	
08/04/00	Mogren Budva	H	1-0	Osmanovic
15/04/00	Sartid Smederevo	A	0-4	
22/04/00	Milicionar Beograd	H	2-0	Osmanovic 2 (1p)
29/04/00	Borac Cacak	A	3-1	Osmanovic 2, Stamatovic
03/05/00	Crvena zvezda Beograd	H	1-3	Djurdjevic
06/05/00	Zeleznik Beograd	A	0-2	
13/05/00	FK Zemun	H	3-1	Osmanovic, Djurdjevic 2
17/05/00	Buducnost Podgorica	A	2-0	Stamatovic 2
20/05/00	Rad Beograd	H	2-1	Antic, Markovski

MILICIONAR BEOGRAD

CLUB DIRECTORY

FK Milicionar
Stari obrenovacki put 1A
11000 Beograd
tel - (011) 3547302/3548032
fax - (011) 556688
President - Stojan Misic
Coach - Slavko Radovanovic
Stadium - Milicionar (5,000)

PLAYERS 99/00

	P	Gls
Sasa ANTIC	M	
Aleksandar BOGDANOVIC	D	1
Nenad CIRKOVIC	D	
Bojan COSIC	M	
Nemanja DANCETOVIC	M	10
Miodrag DJERISILO	M	
Zivorad DJORDJEVIC	D	
Goran DJUKIC	D	3
Ivan ILIC	D	
Goran JEZDIMIROVIC	M	
Predrag KATIC	A	1
Marko KNEZEVIC	D	
Oliver KOVACEVIC	G	
Boban KRISANOVIC	D	3
Djordje KUNOVAC	A	
Marinko MARKOVIC	G	
Uros MARKOVIC	M	1
Sinisa MULINA	A	8
Vladimir PANTELIC	A	2
Vladimir PETROVIC	M	
Milan RADOJICIC	A	11
Goran RADOVANCEVIC	M	
Ivan RANDJELOVIC	G	
Darko SPALEVIC	A	2
Mladen STANISIC	D	1
Dejan STOJKOVIC	D	2
Vladan STOJKOVIC	M	3
Perica STOJILJKOVIC	A	
Sasa TESIC	A	2
Nebojsa ZIVKOVIC	D	2

LEAGUE RESULTS 1999/2000

31/07/99	Zeleznik Beograd	H	0-2	
07/08/99	FK Zemun	A	2-2	Radojicic 2
21/08/99	Buducnost Podgorica	H	2-1	Stojkovic V., Dancetovic (p)
11/09/99	Rad Beograd	A	1-1	Pantelic
18/09/99	OFK Beograd	H	1-1	Dancetovic
21/09/99	Radnicki Kragujevac	A	0-1	
25/09/99	Spartak Subotica	H	2-0	Djukic, Radojicic
02/10/99	Radnicki Nis	A	0-1	
10/10/99	Cukaricki Beograd	H	2-0	Dancetovic 2 (1p)
13/10/99	Sutjeska Niksic	H	2-1	Stojkovic D., Dancetovic
16/10/99	Partizan Beograd	A	1-2	Mulina
30/10/99	Hajduk Beograd	A	1-5	Dancetovic
06/11/99	Proleter Zrenjanin	H	0-0	
13/11/99	Vojvodina Novi Sad	A	1-0	Radojicic
17/11/99	Hajduk Kula	H	1-0	Dancetovic (p)
20/11/99	Obilic Beograd	A	0-1	
27/11/99	Mogren Budva	H	5-0	Radojicic 3, Markovic, Mulina
04/12/99	Sartid Smederevo	A	2-0	Stojkovic V., Dancetovic
15/12/99	Borac Cacak	H	7-4	Radojicic 2, Pantelic, Djukic,
				Mulina 2, Dancetovic (p)
18/12/99	Crvena zvezda Beograd	A	2-3	Radojicic, Mulina
12/02/00	Zeleznik Beograd	A	2-2	Krisanovic, Radojicic
16/02/00	FK Zemun	H	1-0	Dancetovic
19/02/00	Buducnost Podgorica	A	1-2	Stojkovic D.
26/02/00	Rad Beograd	H	0-3	
01/03/00	OFK Beograd	A	1-2	Zivkovic
04/03/00	Radnicki Kragujevac	H	1-0	Stojkovic V.
11/03/00	Spartak Subotica	A	2-3	Stanisic, Zivkovic
15/03/00	Radnicki Nis	H	0-0	
18/03/00	Sutjeska Niksic	A	0-2	
22/03/00	Partizan Beograd	H	0-1	
25/03/00	Cukaricki Beograd	A	1-1	Djukic
01/04/00	Hajduk Beograd	H	2-0	Spalevic, Bogdanovic
08/04/00	Proleter Zrenjanin	A	0-3	
15/04/00	Vojvodina Novi Sad	H	0-0	
22/04/00	Hajduk Kula	A	0-2	
29/04/00	Obilic Beograd	H	1-0	Mulina
03/05/00	Mogren Budva	A	1-3	Mulina
06/05/00	Sartid Smederevo	H	1-1	Mulina (p)
17/05/00	Borac Cacak	A	5-0	Katic, Krisanovic 2, Tesic 2
20/05/00	Crvena zvezda Beograd	H	1-2	Spalevic

MOGREN BUDVA

CLUB DIRECTORY

FK Mogren
Jadranski put bb
81310 Budva
tel - (086) 51126/52580/51613
fax - (086) 52487
Year of Formation - 1945
President - Miroslav Ivanovic
Coach - Slobodan Halilovic
Stadium - Mogren (4,000)

PLAYERS 99/00

	P	Gls
Zarko BELADA	D	3
Boris BERKULJAN	A	1
Dejan DIMIC	M	1
Dragan DJUKANOVIC	A	17
Zlatko DJURISIC	M	
Aleksandar JOKIC	M	
JOLOVIC	A	
Dragan KLJAJEVIC	A	
Milos KRSTAJIC	G	
Djeto LJUCOVIC	D	
Bojan MAGAZIN	D	
Sasa MARAS	M	
Nenad MIRKOVIC	D	
Ivica MOMCILOVIC	D	
Miodrag NIKOLIC	M	
Ranko NOVOVIC	M	
Dusko PRIJOVIC	M	1
Milko PUSONJA	A	
Ilija RADJENOVIC	M	1
Dusan RADOJEVIC	A	3
Ranko RADONJIC	A	1
RADOVIC	D	
STANJEVIC	M	3
Ivan STANKOVIC	A	2
Dejan SUSKAVCEVIC	G	
Dusan VLAISAVLJEVIC	D	
Nebojsa VOJVODIC	A	1
Srdjan VUKOJE	D	
Miodrag VUKOTIC	A	
Darko VUSUROVIC	M	1
Obrad ZIROJEVIC	M	2
Milija ZIZIC	D	1

LEAGUE RESULTS 1999/2000

31/07/99	Buducnost Podgorica	H	1-1	Dimic (p)
07/08/99	Rad Beograd	A	1-3	Djukanovic (p)
21/08/99	OFK Beograd	H	1-1	Prijovic
11/09/99	Radnicki Kragujevac	A	0-0	
18/09/99	Spartak Subotica	H	1-1	Djukanovic (p)
21/09/99	Radnicki Nis	A	2-4	Djukanovic 2 (1p)
25/09/99	Sutjeska Niksic	H	2-1	Zirojevic, Radonjic
03/10/99	Partizan Beograd	A	0-2	
13/10/99	Cukaricki Beograd	H	1-3	Djukanovic
16/10/99	Hajduk Beograd	A	0-1	
23/10/99	Proleter Zrenjanin	H	2-0	Zirojevic, Zizic
30/10/99	Vojvodina Novi Sad	A	0-3	
06/11/99	Hajduk Kula	H	1-0	og
13/11/99	Obilic Beograd	A	0-2	
20/11/99	Sartid Smederevo	H	1-0	Radojevic
27/11/99	Milicionar Beograd	A	0-5	
04/12/99	Borac Cacak	H	3-1	og, Djukanovic, Belada
11/12/99	Crvena zvezda Beograd	A	0-2	
15/12/99	Zeleznik Beograd	H	2-1	Djukanovic 2 (2p)
18/12/99	FK Zemun	A	0-2	
12/02/00	Buducnost Podgorica	A	1-4	Djukanovic
16/02/00	Rad Beograd	H	1-2	Djukanovic
19/02/00	OFK Beograd	A	1-3	Radojevic
26/02/00	Radnicki Kragujevac	H	2-1	Belada, Djukanovic
01/03/00	Spartak Subotica	A	0-3	
04/03/00	Radnicki Nis	H	2-0	Djukanovic 2
11/03/00	Sutjeska Niksic	A	0-2	
15/03/00	Partizan Beograd	H	0-7	
18/03/00	Cukaricki Beograd	A	0-1	
22/03/00	Hajduk Beograd	H	3-0	Stankovic, Berkuljan, Vusurovic
25/03/00	Proleter Zrenjanin	A	2-1	Radojevic, Belada
01/04/00	Vojvodina Novi Sad	H	0-0	
08/04/00	Hajduk Kula	A	0-1	
15/04/00	Obilic Beograd	H	4-0	Djukanovic 3, Vojvodic
29/04/00	Sartid Smederevo	A	1-3	Stanjevic
03/05/00	Milicionar Beograd	H	3-1	Stankovic, Radjenovic, Djukanovic (p)
06/05/00	Borac Cacak	A	1-0	Stanjevic
13/05/00	Crvena zvezda Beograd	H	0-2	
17/05/00	Zeleznik Beograd	A	0-4	
20/05/00	FK Zemun	H	1-2	Stanjevic

OBILIC BEOGRAD

CLUB DIRECTORY

FK Obilic
Gospodara Vucica 189
11000 Beograd
tel - (011) 412085/412945
fax - (011) 412085
Year of Formation - 1924
President - Svetlana Raznjatovic
Coach - Dragoslav Sekularac
Stadium - Obilic (3,000)

MAJOR HONOURS
League Championship - (1) 1998.

PLAYERS 99/00

	P	Gls
Mirko ALEKSIC	M	4
Kuzman BABEU	D	2
Mirko BABIC	D	
Veselin BOJIC	D	
Igor DIMITRIJEVIC	G	
Nenad DJORDJEVIC	D	
Bojan FILIPOVIC	M	2
Sasa KOVACEVIC	A	2
Igor KOZOS	A	2
Nikola LAZETIC	M	7
Igor MANOJLOVIC	A	2
Goran MARKOVIC	D	
Predrag MARKOVIC	G	
Dejan MILICEVIC	D	
Vladan MILOSAVLJEVIC	D	
Miroslav MILOSEVIC	M	
Nesko MILOVANOVIC	M	1
Goran MLADENOVIC	M	
Nenad NONKOVIC	M	
Darko NOVIC	D	1
Milan OBRADOVIC	D	
Predrag OCOKOLJIC	D	2
Gabrijel RADOJCIC	A	15
Zoran RANKOVIC	A	4
Sead SALAHOVIC	A	2
Dragan SARAC	M	1
Miroslav SAVIC	D	
Sasa SIMONOVIC	A	5
Mirko TEODOROVIC	M	
Darko VARGEC	D	1
Markica VAZIC	D	
Sasa VICIKNEZ	D	3
Igor VUJANOVIC	A	
Sasa ZIMONJIC	M	5
Sasa ZORIC	M	9

LEAGUE RESULTS 1999/2000

31/07/99	Rad Beograd	H	1-0	Milovanovic
07/08/99	OFK Beograd	A	2-4	og (Sandulovic), Zoric
21/08/99	Radnicki Kragujevac	H	3-0	Rankovic 2, Zoric
11/09/99	Spartak Subotica	A	0-0	
18/09/99	Radnicki Nis	H	2-1	Lazetic, Radojcic
21/09/99	Sutjeska Niksic	H	2-1	Radojcic, Kozos
25/09/99	Partizan Beograd	H	3-0	Rankovic, Viciknez (p), Radojcic
02/10/99	Cukaricki Beograd	A	2-1	Rankovic, Radojcic
13/10/99	Hajduk Beograd	H	3-2	Filipovic, Radojcic, Kozos
16/10/99	Proleter Zrenjanin	A	2-0	Lazetic, Viciknez
23/10/99	Vojvodina Novi Sad	H	2-0	Simonovic, Viciknez
30/10/99	Hajduk Kula	A	2-0	Lazetic, Radojcic
13/11/99	Mogren Budva	H	2-0	Radojcic, Simonovic
17/11/99	Sartid Smederevo	A	3-2	Lazetic 2, Zoric
20/11/99	Milicionar Beograd	H	1-0	Radojcic
27/11/99	Borac Cacak	A	2-0	Novic, Filipovic (p)
04/12/99	Crvena zvezda Beograd	H	1-1	Babeu
11/12/99	Zeleznik Beograd	A	3-0	Radojcic, Ocokoljic, Aleksic
15/12/99	FK Zemun	H	1-0	Lazetic (p)
18/12/99	Buducnost Podgorica	A	2-0	Simonovic, Aleksic
12/02/00	Rad Beograd	A	3-2	Salahovic 2, Lazetic
16/02/00	OFK Beograd	H	2-2	Radojcic, Aleksic
19/02/00	Radnicki Kragujevac	A	0-0	
26/02/00	Spartak Subotica	H	2-0	Sarac, Zoric (p)
01/03/00	Radnicki Nis	A	1-2	Radojcic
04/03/00	Sutjeska Niksic	A	2-1	Aleksic, Radojcic
11/03/00	Partizan Beograd	A	1-0	Zimonjic
15/03/00	Cukaricki Beograd	H	0-1	
18/03/00	Hajduk Beograd	A	3-0	Zimonjic 2, Radojcic
22/03/00	Proleter Zrenjanin	H	3-1	Radojcic, Simonovic, Zoric (p)
25/03/00	Vojvodina Novi Sad	A	1-1	Simonovic
01/04/00	Hajduk Kula	H	1-0	Babeu
15/04/00	Mogren Budva	A	0-4	
22/04/00	Sartid Smederevo	H	1-0	Kovacevic
29/04/00	Milicionar Beograd	A	0-1	
03/05/00	Borac Cacak	H	6-0	Zoric 3, Ocokoljic, Manojlovic 2
06/05/00	Crvena zvezda Beograd	A	0-2	
13/05/00	Zeleznik Beograd	H	2-0	Zimonjic, Radojcic
17/05/00	FK Zemun	A	1-3	Zimonjic
20/05/00	Buducnost Podgorica	H	3-1	Vargec, Zoric (p), Kovacevic

OFK BEOGRAD

CLUB DIRECTORY

OFK Beograd
Mije Kovacevica 10
11000 Beograd
tel - (011) 765425/767045
fax - (011) 762364
Year of Formation - 1945
President - Momcilo Minic
Coach - Zvonko Varga
Stadium - Omladinski (25,000)

MAJOR HONOURS
Domestic Cup - (4) 1953, 1958, 1962, 1966.

PLAYERS 99/00

	P	Gls
Miodrag ANDJELKOVIC	A	9
Nikola ANDRIC	D	
Nenad BEGOVIC	M	1
Milan BOSANAC	M	1
Aleksandar BRATIC	D	
Srdjan DIMITRIJEVIC	A	1
Petar DIVIC	A	21
Dejan DJURDJEVIC	M	1
Dusko DJURICIC	D	1
Bozo DJURKOVIC	A	7
Milan DRAGELJEVIC	D	
Dragan DRASKOVIC	G	
JESIC	D	
Srdjan KARANOVIC	G	
Sasa KLJAJIC	M	
Stevica KUZMANOVSKI	D	
Zoran LUKIC	M	
Slavko MATIC	M	
Djordje MRDJANIN	M	
Srdjan OBRADOVIC	D	
Kostantin OGNJANOVIC	A	2
Cedomir PAVICEVIC	M	
Milorad PEROVIC	A	
Dusan PETKOVIC	D	2
Vladimir PETKOVIC	M	
Drazen PODUNAVAC	A	
Milorad POPOVIC	D	2
Dejan RADJENOVIC	M	7
Miftar RAMA	D	
Vladimir SANDULOVIC	D	2
Zlatko TODOROVSKI	D	1
Sasa TRIFUNAC	M	

LEAGUE RESULTS 1999/2000

Date	Opponent		Score	Scorers
31/07/99	Hajduk Kula	A	0-2	
07/08/99	Obilic Beograd	H	4-2	Divic 2, Radjenovic, Dimitrijevic
21/08/99	Mogren Budva	A	1-1	Divic
11/09/99	Sartid Smederevo	H	0-1	
18/09/99	Milicionar Beograd	A	1-1	Sandulovic
21/09/99	Borac Cacak	H	1-4	Ognjanovic
25/09/99	Crvena zvezda Beograd	A	1-3	Andjelkovic
02/10/99	Zeleznik Beograd	H	1-1	Ognjanovic
13/10/99	FK Zemun	A	1-2	Radjenovic
16/10/99	Buducnost Podgorica	H	2-1	Radjenovic (p), Divic
23/10/99	Rad Beograd	A	1-0	Radjenovic (p)
06/11/99	Radnicki Kragujevac	H	1-1	Sandulovic
13/11/99	Spartak Subotica	A	2-1	Andjelkovic 2
17/11/99	Radnicki Nis	H	1-0	Andjelkovic
20/11/99	Sutjeska Niksic	A	2-3	Petkovic, Divic
27/11/99	Partizan Beograd	H	2-2	Djurkovic 2
04/12/99	Cukaricki Beograd	A	3-3	Djurkovic, Petkovic, Andjelkovic
11/12/99	Hajduk Beograd	H	2-1	Andjelkovic 2
15/12/99	Proleter Zrenjanin	A	1-2	Djurdjevic
18/12/99	Vojvodina Novi Sad	H	2-0	Divic, Radjenovic
12/02/00	Hajduk Kula	H	1-0	Todorovski
16/02/00	Obilic Beograd	A	2-2	Andjelkovic, Popovic
19/02/00	Mogren Budva	H	3-1	Divic 3
26/02/00	Sartid Smederevo	A	0-1	
01/03/00	Milicionar Beograd	H	2-1	Djurkovic, Divic
04/03/00	Borac Cacak	A	2-0	Andjelkovic, Divic
11/03/00	Crvena zvezda Beograd	H	1-2	Divic (p)
15/03/00	Zeleznik Beograd	A	3-4	Divic 2, Begovic
18/03/00	FK Zemun	H	1-1	Popovic
22/03/00	Buducnost Podgorica	A	1-3	Bosanac
25/03/00	Rad Beograd	H	0-0	
08/04/00	Radnicki Kragujevac	A	0-0	
15/04/00	Spartak Subotica	H	3-0	Radjenovic, Divic 2 (1p)
22/04/00	Radnicki Nis	A	0-4	
29/04/00	Sutjeska Niksic	H	2-3	Divic 2
03/05/00	Partizan Beograd	A	0-3	
06/05/00	Cukaricki Beograd	H	3-1	Divic (p), Radjenovic, Djurkovic
13/05/00	Hajduk Beograd	A	2-1	Djurkovic, Divic
17/05/00	Proleter Zrenjanin	H	3-0	Divic, Djuricic, Djurkovic
20/05/00	Vojvodina Novi Sad	A	0-3	

PARTIZAN BEOGRAD

CLUB DIRECTORY

FK Partizan
Humska 1
11000 Beograd
tel - (011) 3227181/3229793
fax - (011) 3229906
website - www.partizan.co.yu
Year of Formation - 1945
President - Ivan Curkovic
Secretary - Stojance Ristevski
Coach - Miodrag Jesic (00/01 - Ljubisa Tumbakovic)
Stadium - Partizan (31,300)

MAJOR HONOURS

League Championship - (16) 1947, 1949, 1961, 1962, 1963, 1965, 1976, 1978, 1983, 1986, 1987, 1993, 1994, 1996, 1997, 1999.
Domestic Cup - (8) 1947, 1952, 1954, 1957, 1989, 1992, 1994, 1998.

APPEARANCES 99/00

	P	Ap	Gls
Milivoje CIRKOVIC	D	12	
Nikola DAMJANAC	G	12	
Andrija DELIBASIC	D	16	2
Igor DULJAJ	M	32	1
Marjan GERASIMOVSKI (MAC)	D	19	3
Radisa ILIC	G	28	
Sasa ILIC	M	32	19
Ivica ILIJEV	A	29	8
Vladimir IVIC	M	30	19
Mateja KEZMAN	A	32	27
Mladen KRSTAJIC	D	29	2
Goran OBRADOVIC	A	21	6
Milorad PEKOVIC	A	26	2
Ljubisa RANKOVIC	M	12	1
Vuk RASOVIC	D	18	
Zoltan SABO	D	17	1
Branko SAVIC	D	29	
Aleksandar STANOJEVIC	D	23	
Milan STOJANOSKI (MAC)	D	24	4
Dragan STOJISAVLJEVIC	A	16	
Djordje TOMIC	M	30	11
Goran TROBOK	M	37	3
Zvonimir VUKIC	M	6	1
Aleksandar VUKOVIC	M	5	

LEAGUE RESULTS 1999/2000

Date	Opponent	H/A	Score	Scorers
07/08/99	Cukaricki Beograd	H	2-1	Sabo (p), Gerasimovski
21/08/99	Hajduk Beograd	A	2-1	Ilic S., Pekovic
11/09/99	Proleter Zrenjanin	H	1-0	Ilijev
18/09/99	Vojvodina Novi Sad	A	2-2	Tomic, Gerasimovski
21/09/99	Hajduk Kula	H	3-0	Tomic (p), Ilijev, Ilic S.
25/09/99	Obilic Beograd	A	0-3	
03/10/99	Mogren Budva	H	2-0	Gerasimovski, Ilic S.
13/10/99	Sartid Smederevo	A	3-1	Ilic S. 2, Ivic
16/10/99	Milicionar Beograd	H	2-1	Kezman 2 (2p)
23/10/99	Borac Cacak	A	1-0	Tomic (p)
30/10/99	Crvena zvezda Beograd	H	2-0	Ilic S., Kezman
06/11/99	Zeleznik Beograd	A	1-0	Ilic S.
13/11/99	FK Zemun	H	4-1	Obradovic 3, Kezman
17/11/99	Buducnost Podgorica	A	4-1	Kezman 3, Obradovic
20/11/99	Rad Beograd	H	1-0	Ivic
27/11/99	OFK Beograd	A	2-2	Kezman (p), Ivic
04/12/99	Radnicki Kragujevac	H	4-0	Ilic S. 3, Trobok
11/12/99	Spartak Subotica	A	6-0	Kezman 3, Ivic 2, Ilic S.
15/12/99	Radnicki Nis	H	5-2	Ivic, Obradovic, Ilic S. 2 (1p), Delibasic
18/12/99	Sutjeska Niksic	A	2-2	Ivic, Kezman
16/02/00	Cukaricki Beograd	A	2-0	Tomic 2
19/02/00	Hajduk Beograd	H	4-2	Ivic 2, Ilijev, Trobok
26/02/00	Proleter Zrenjanin	A	2-0	Ilic S., Ivic
01/03/00	Vojvodina Novi Sad	H	4-1	Stojanoski, Kezman 2, Ivic
04/03/00	Hajduk Kula	A	5-0	Ivic 2, Ilic S., Kezman, Ilijev
11/03/00	Obilic Beograd	H	0-1	
15/03/00	Mogren Budva	A	7-0	Ilic S., Ivic 2, Ilijev 3, Obradovic
18/03/00	Sartid Smederevo	H	4-0	Kezman 2, Ilic S. 2
22/03/00	Milicionar Beograd	A	1-0	Stojanoski
25/03/00	Borac Cacak	H	8-1	Tomic, Stojanoski, Kezman 2, Ivic, Krstajic, Pekovic, Rankovic
01/04/00	Crvena zvezda Beograd	A	1-2	Kezman
08/04/00	Zeleznik Beograd	H	1-1	Tomic
15/04/00	FK Zemun	A	3-0	Ilic S., Kezman, og (Djurovic S.)
22/04/00	Buducnost Podgorica	H	4-1	Ivic 3, Tomic
29/04/00	Rad Beograd	A	2-1	Kezman, Krstajic
03/05/00	OFK Beograd	H	3-0	Ilijev, Tomic, Delibasic
06/05/00	Radnicki Kragujevac	A	1-1	Kezman
13/05/00	Spartak Subotica	H	7-2	Kezman 3, Trobok, Tomic 2 (1p), Vukic
17/05/00	Radnicki Nis	A	1-0	Duljaj
20/05/00	Sutjeska Niksic	H	2-0	Stojanoski, Kezman

PROLETER ZRENJANIN

CLUB DIRECTORY

FK Proleter
Karadjordjev trg 100
23000 Zrenjanin
tel - (023) 564856/66550/30430
fax - (023) 66550
Year of Formation - 1947
President - Borko Kovac
Coach - Radivoje Draskovic; Miljoljub Ostojic
Stadium - Gradski (20,000)

PLAYERS 99/00

	P	Gls
Aleksandar RODIC	M	
AMIDZIC	A	
Nikola BOGIC	M	
Stanoje DJOKIC	M	
Ivan DJUROVIC	D	
Dragan JANJATOVIC	M	
Dragan JOLOVIC	M	
Dusko KLINDO	A	
Zoran LISICA	D	
Nenad LJUBENOVIC	M	2
Predrag LUBURIC	D	
Predrag MACANOVIC	D	
Borko MARINKOVIC	M	3
Nenad MIROSAVLJEVIC	A	16
Dejan MILJKOVIC	M	
Goran MLADENOVIC	A	
PEKOVIC	M	
Sasa PESIC	G	
Srdjan PJEVAC	D	
Danilo PUSTINJAKOVIC	G	
Jovo SIMANIC	D	1
Vlada SNEGIC	D	
Sasa TODIC	G	
Nenad TRAJKOVIC	M	1
Svetozar VUKASINOVIC	M	1
Srdjan ZAKIC	D	2
Milorad ZECEVIC	A	7
Marko ZORIC	M	1
Djordje ZUZA	D	

LEAGUE RESULTS 1999/2000

Date	Opponent	H/A	Score	Scorers
31/07/99	Spartak Subotica	H	3-0	og, Lubenovic, Zakic
07/08/99	Radnicki Nis	A	3-1	Zecevic, Mirosavljevic, Trajkovic
21/08/99	Sutjeska Niksic	H	2-1	Mirosavljevic, Marinkovic
11/09/99	Partizan Beograd	A	0-1	
18/09/99	Cukaricki Beograd	H	0-0	
21/09/99	Hajduk Beograd	A	1-2	Marinkovic
03/10/99	Vojvodina Novi Sad	H	0-1	
13/10/99	Hajduk Kula	A	1-1	Simanic
16/10/99	Obilic Beograd	H	0-2	
23/10/99	Mogren Budva	A	0-2	
30/10/99	Sartid Smederevo	H	1-1	Zakic
06/11/99	Milicionar Beograd	A	0-0	
13/11/99	Borac Cacak	H	1-1	Vukasinovic
20/11/99	Zeleznik Beograd	H	0-0	
27/11/99	FK Zemun	A	0-2	
01/12/99	Crvena zvezda Beograd	A	0-4	
04/12/99	Buducnost Podgorica	H	1-0	Ljubenovic
11/12/99	Rad Beograd	A	2-2	Mirosavljevic, Zecevic
15/12/99	OFK Beograd	H	2-1	Mirosavljevic 2
18/12/99	Radnicki Kragujevac	A	0-0	
12/02/00	Spartak Subotica	A	3-1	Mirosavljevic 2, Zecevic
16/02/00	Radnicki Nis	H	0-0	
19/02/00	Sutjeska Niksic	A	1-3	Zecevic
26/02/00	Partizan Beograd	H	0-2	
01/03/00	Cukaricki Beograd	A	0-2	
04/03/00	Hajduk Beograd	H	2-0	Mirosavljevic 2
15/03/00	Vojvodina Novi Sad	A	1-2	Marinkovic (p)
18/03/00	Hajduk Kula	H	1-0	Mirosavljevic
22/03/00	Obilic Beograd	A	1-3	Zecevic
25/03/00	Mogren Budva	H	1-2	Zoric
01/04/00	Sartid Smederevo	A	0-2	
08/04/00	Milicionar Beograd	H	3-0	Zecevic, Mirosavljevic 2
15/04/00	Borac Cacak	A	1-0	Zecevic
22/04/00	Crvena zvezda Beograd	H	0-1	
29/04/00	Zeleznik Beograd	A	0-3	
03/05/00	FK Zemun	H	1-0	Mirosavljevic
06/05/00	Buducnost Podgorica	A	0-2	
13/05/00	Rad Beograd	H	2-0	Mirosavljevic 2
17/05/00	OFK Beograd	A	0-3	
20/05/00	Radnicki Kragujevac	H	1-1	Mirosavljevic

RAD BEOGRAD

CLUB DIRECTORY

FK Rad
Crnotravska bb
11000 Beograd
tel - (011) 663039/666884/664377
fax - (011) 662169
Year of Formation - 1958
President - Milos Mandic
Coach - Cedomir Djoincevic
Stadium - Rad (13,000)

PLAYERS 99/00

	P	Gls
Mirko BUNJEVCEVIC	D	
Sasa DJORDJEVIC	M	
Darko DREC	D	
Jane GAVALOVSKI	A	1
Uros GOLUBOVIC	G	
Aleksandar GRUBER	M	
Saudin HUSEINOVIC	A	5
Goran JERINIC	D	2
Ivan JOVANOVIC	A	1
Mile KNEZEVIC	D	2
Stevica KUZMANOVSKI	D	2
Milan MARTINOVIC	D	
Zeljko MIJOVIC	D	
Zeljko MITIC	A	
Goran MLADENOVIC	M	
Nedeljko PEROVIC	A	
Uros PREDIC	M	1
Ozren RADANOVIC	D	1
Dejan RADIC	G	
Aleksandar RANKOVIC	M	1
Milan SEVO	G	
Borislav STEVANOVIC	A	10
Dragan STEVANOVIC	A	9
Dragan TOMIC	M	2
Nebojsa TOPALOV	M	3
Dusan VIDOJEVIC	A	4
Nebojsa VIGNJEVIC	M	
Ede VISINKA	D	2
Aleksandar ZIVKOVIC	M	9

LEAGUE RESULTS 1999/2000

Date	Opponent		Score	Scorers
31/07/99	Obilic Beograd	A	0-1	
07/08/99	Mogren Budva	H	3-1	Kuzmanovski 2 (1p), Zivkovic
21/08/99	Sartid Smederevo	A	1-1	Stevanovic B.
11/09/99	Milicionar Beograd	H	1-1	Zivkovic
18/09/99	Borac Cacak	A	3-2	Stevanovic B., Radanovic, Stevanovic D.
21/09/99	Crvena zvezda Beograd	H	1-1	Stevanovic D.
25/09/99	Zeleznik Beograd	A	2-2	Stevanovic D. 2
02/10/99	FK Zemun	H	5-1	Stevanovic B. 2, Predic, Zivkovic 2
13/10/99	Buducnost Podgorica	A	0-1	
23/10/99	OFK Beograd	H	0-1	
30/10/99	Radnicki Kragujevac	A	2-1	Stevanovic D., Stevanovic B.
06/11/99	Spartak Subotica	H	1-0	Visinka
13/11/99	Radnicki Nis	A	0-3	
17/11/99	Sutjeska Niksic	H	2-1	Visinka, Huseinovic
20/11/99	Partizan Beograd	A	0-1	
27/11/99	Cukaricki Beograd	H	2-0	Knezevic, Vidojevic
04/12/99	Hajduk Beograd	A	2-2	Topalov, Huseinovic
11/12/99	Proleter Zrenjanin	H	2-2	Huseinovic, Stevanovic B.
15/12/99	Vojvodina Novi Sad	A	2-3	Huseinovic, Knezevic
18/12/99	Hajduk Kula	H	2-0	Huseinovic, og (Malbasa)
12/02/00	Obilic Beograd	H	2-3	Topalov (p), Vidojevic
16/02/00	Mogren Budva	A	2-1	Tomic, Stevanovic B.
19/02/00	Sartid Smederevo	H	0-1	
26/02/00	Milicionar Beograd	A	3-0	Stevanovic B. 2, Zivkovic
01/03/00	Borac Cacak	H	3-0	Zivkovic, Jerinic, Stevanovic B.
04/03/00	Crvena zvezda Beograd	A	0-1	
11/03/00	Zeleznik Beograd	H	1-0	Zivkovic
15/03/00	FK Zemun	A	1-2	Zivkovic
18/03/00	Buducnost Podgorica	H	1-0	Zivkovic
25/03/00	OFK Beograd	A	0-0	
01/04/00	Radnicki Kragujevac	H	1-1	Rankovic
08/04/00	Spartak Subotica	A	3-2	Stevanovic D. 3
15/04/00	Radnicki Nis	H	2-1	Jerinic, Stevanovic D.
22/04/00	Sutjeska Niksic	A	0-1	
29/04/00	Partizan Beograd	H	1-2	Vidojevic
03/05/00	Cukaricki Beograd	A	1-1	Tomic
06/05/00	Hajduk Beograd	H	2-1	Vidojevic, Jovanovic
13/05/00	Proleter Zrenjanin	A	0-2	
17/05/00	Vojvodina Novi Sad	H	1-0	Topalov
20/05/00	Hajduk Kula	A	1-2	Gavalovski

RADNICKI KRAGUJEVAC

CLUB DIRECTORY

FK Radnicki
17 udarne divizije 21
34000 Kragujevac
tel - (034) 332974/331937
fax - (034) 762364
Year of Formation - 1924
President - Petar Arandjelovic
Coach - Slobodan Stasevic
Stadium - FK Radnicki (10,000)

PLAYERS 99/00

	P	Gls
Dalibor ANTONIJEVIC	D	2
Srdjan BALJAK	A	
Zeljko BUZIC	A	8
Radojica DESPOTOVIC	D	
Darko DIMITRIJEVIC	D	2
Budimir DJUKIC	M	4
Milos FILIPOVIC	M	
IGNJATOVIC	D	
Zoran JEREMIC	D	1
Nebojsa JESIC	M	1
Milorad JOVANOVIC	A	1
Dragan MILJKOVIC	M	
Dragan MILOSAVLJEVIC	D	1
Nebojsa PANTOVIC	D	
Goran PELEMIS	A	
Radovan RADAKOVIC	G	
Goran RADOSAVLJEVIC	M	5
Milan RISTIC	M	1
Dragan SPASIC	D	1
Goran SRETENOVIC	G	
Aleksandar STANKOVIC	M	
Darko STANOJLOVIC	M	1
Zoran STEVANOVIC	D	4
Zoran TANASIJEVIC	A	
Dragan VELJOVIC	A	
Goran VRANIC	G	
Dejan ZERADJANIN	D	

LEAGUE RESULTS 1999/2000

31/07/99	Vojvodina Novi Sad	A	0-2	
07/08/99	Hajduk Kula	H	2-0	Spasic, Djukic
21/08/99	Obilic Beograd	A	0-3	
11/09/99	Mogren Budva	H	0-0	
18/09/99	Sartid Smederevo	A	2-1	Djukic, Dimitrijevic
21/09/99	Milicionar Beograd	H	1-0	Djukic
25/09/99	Borac Cacak	A	1-0	Buzic
02/10/99	Crvena zvezda Beograd	H	1-1	Djukic
13/10/99	Zeleznik Beograd	A	1-3	og
16/10/99	FK Zemun	H	1-0	Stevanovic
23/10/99	Buducnost Podgorica	A	0-2	
30/10/99	Rad Beograd	H	1-2	og (Visinski)
06/11/99	OFK Beograd	A	1-1	Antonijevic
17/11/99	Spartak Subotica	H	3-1	Buzic 2, Stevanovic
20/11/99	Radnicki Nis	A	0-0	
27/11/99	Sutjeska Niksic	H	3-0	Milosavljevic, Stevanovic, Ristic
04/12/99	Partizan Beograd	A	0-4	
11/12/99	Cukaricki Beograd	H	1-3	Buzic
15/12/99	Hajduk Beograd	A	1-2	Antonijevic
18/12/99	Proleter Zrenjanin	H	0-0	
12/02/00	Vojvodina Novi Sad	H	2-1	Buzic, Jeremic
16/02/00	Hajduk Kula	A	1-0	Buzic
19/02/00	Obilic Beograd	H	0-0	
26/02/00	Mogren Budva	A	1-2	Dimitrijevic
01/03/00	Sartid Smederevo	H	1-0	Radosavljevic
04/03/00	Milicionar Beograd	A	0-1	
11/03/00	Borac Cacak	H	1-1	Buzic
15/03/00	Crvena zvezda Beograd	A	0-1	
18/03/00	Zeleznik Beograd	H	0-0	
22/03/00	FK Zemun	A	0-2	
25/03/00	Buducnost Podgorica	H	0-0	
01/04/00	Rad Beograd	A	1-1	Buzic
08/04/00	OFK Beograd	H	0-0	
22/04/00	Spartak Subotica	A	0-2	
29/04/00	Radnicki Nis	H	2-0	Stevanovic, Radosavljevic (p)
03/05/00	Sutjeska Niksic	A	1-0	Jesic
06/05/00	Partizan Beograd	H	1-1	Radosavljevic
13/05/00	Cukaricki Beograd	A	0-2	
17/05/00	Hajduk Beograd	H	3-1	Radosavljevic 2, Jovanovic
20/05/00	Proleter Zrenjanin	A	1-1	Stanojlovic

RADNICKI NIS

CLUB DIRECTORY

FK Radnicki
Sportska hala Cair
18000 Nis
tel - (018) 22016/25030
fax - (018) 24445
Year of Formation - 1923
President - Dragan Pantelic
Coach - Radmilo Ivancevic
Stadium - Cair (25,000)

PLAYERS 99/00

	P	Gls
Zoran ANTIC	D	1
Boban CENTIC	D	
Petar DJENIC	D	5
Srdjan GOLOVIC	A	1
Boban IGNJATOVIC	D	
Ivan ILIC	D	5
Ivan KRSTIC	M	4
Ivan LAZIC	G	
Dragan LJUBISAVLJEVIC	D	1
Dejan MANJENCIC	A	
Miodrag NIKOLIC	M	
Aleksandar PAJIC	M	1
Ivan POLIC	M	1
Zarko RADONJIC	M	
Mladen RISTIC	M	
Goran SIMOV	G	
Bojan STAMENKOVIC	M	
Nenad STAMENKOVIC	M	
Predrag STAMENKOVIC	D	2
Dragan STANKOVIC	D	
Zoran STOJANOVIC	A	1
Sasa TAGI	M	2
Aleksandar TRAJKOVIC	D	2
Martin TRAJKOVIC	D	
Dejan TRICKOVIC	M	
Kristijan TUCAKOVIC	D	2
Dragan VASILJEVIC	D	2
Zoran VASKOVIC	G	
Malesija VOJVODA	A	13
Mihajlo VUJACIC	A	2
Obrad ZIROJEVIC	A	3

LEAGUE RESULTS 1999/2000

01/08/99	Hajduk Beograd	A	1-4	Djenic
07/08/99	Proleter Zrenjanin	H	1-3	Antic
21/08/99	Vojvodina Novi Sad	A	0-2	
11/09/99	Hajduk Kula	H	1-0	Vojvoda
18/09/99	Obilic Beograd	A	1-2	Djenic
21/09/99	Mogren Budva	H	4-2	Vojvoda 2, Pajic (p), Vasiljevic
25/09/99	Sartid Smederevo	A	0-1	
02/10/99	Milicionar Beograd	H	1-0	Vujacic
13/10/99	Borac Cacak	A	2-0	Vujacic, Krstic
16/10/99	Crvena zvezda Beograd	H	1-2	Vojvoda
23/10/99	Zeleznik Beograd	A	1-3	Djenic
30/10/99	FK Zemun	H	2-3	Vojvoda 2
06/11/99	Buducnost Podgorica	A	0-1	
13/11/99	Rad Beograd	H	3-0	Polic, Vojvoda, Vasiljevic
17/11/99	OFK Beograd	A	0-1	
20/11/99	Radnicki Kragujevac	H	0-0	
27/11/99	Spartak Subotica	A	1-1	Tucakovic
11/12/99	Sutjeska Niksic	H	2-0	Vojvoda, Tagi
15/12/99	Partizan Beograd	A	2-5	Trajkovic A., Stamenkovic P.
18/12/99	Cukaricki Beograd	H	3-0	Ilic 2 (1p), Vojvoda
12/02/00	Hajduk Beograd	H	2-0	Tucakovic, Ljubisavljevic
16/02/00	Proleter Zrenjanin	A	0-0	
19/02/00	Vojvodina Novi Sad	H	2-1	Ilic (p), Krstic
26/02/00	Hajduk Kula	A	0-1	
01/03/00	Obilic Beograd	H	2-1	Vojvoda, Djenic
04/03/00	Mogren Budva	A	0-2	
11/03/00	Sartid Smederevo	H	2-1	Stamenkovic P., og (Mrdak)
15/03/00	Milicionar Beograd	A	0-0	
18/03/00	Borac Cacak	H	4-1	Zirojevic 2, Tagi, Trajkovic A.
22/03/00	Crvena zvezda Beograd	A	0-1	
25/03/00	Zeleznik Beograd	H	2-0	Zirojevic, Vojvoda
01/04/00	FK Zemun	A	0-1	
08/04/00	Buducnost Podgorica	H	1-0	Vojvoda
15/04/00	Rad Beograd	A	1-2	Golovic
22/04/00	OFK Beograd	H	4-0	Ilic, Vojvoda, Djenic, Krstic
29/04/00	Radnicki Kragujevac	A	0-2	
03/05/00	Spartak Subotica	H	2-0	Ilic, Krstic
13/05/00	Sutjeska Niksic	A	1-3	Stojanovic
17/05/00	Partizan Beograd	H	0-1	
20/05/00	Cukaricki Beograd	A	0-2	

SARTID SMEDEREVO

CLUB DIRECTORY

FK Sartid 1913
Goranska 55
11300 Smederevo
tel - (026) 223319/224509
fax - (026) 223030
President - Radoslav Djordjevic
Coach - Bosko Antic
Stadium - FK Sartid (10,000)

PLAYERS 99/00

	P	Gls
Miodrag ANDJELKOVIC	A	7
Bojan ANDREJEVIC	D	
Sasa ANTUNOVIC	M	8
Dejan BATOS	M	
Goran BOGDANOVIC	M	1
Radoslav BULIC	D	
Damir CAKAR	A	
Dalibor CORLUKA	D	1
Igor DJOKIC	G	
Vladislav EFIMOV (RUS)	M	3
Dragan GLOGOVAC	M	2
Branislav JEVTIC	A	
Goran JEVTIC	M	
Dragan JOVIC	A	1
Milan JOVIC	M	
Predrag KATIC	A	3
Dusan KLJAJIC	D	
Sasa KOCIC	M	1
Goran MIHAJLOVIC	A	
Milorad MRDAK	D	1
Vladimir MUDRINIC	A	2
Aleksandar PANTIC	M	
Mladen RANITOVIC	D	
Darko SAVIC	D	1
Sasa STEFANOVIC	G	
Marko STOJIC	D	1
Dragan VASIC	G	
Srdjan VASILJEVIC	D	1
Boris VASKOVIC	M	
Dejan VILOTIC	D	
Darko VOJVODIC	M	9
Goran VUCIC	D	

LEAGUE RESULTS 1999/2000

31/07/99	FK Zemun	H	1-2	Katic
07/08/99	Buducnost Podgorica	A	1-1	Glogovac
21/08/99	Rad Beograd	H	1-1	Stojic
11/09/99	OFK Beograd	A	1-0	Vasiljevic
18/09/99	Radnicki Kragujevac	H	1-2	Katic (p)
21/09/99	Spartak Subotica	A	0-1	
25/09/99	Radnicki Nis	H	1-0	Vojvodic
02/10/99	Sutjeska Niksic	A	1-4	Savic
13/10/99	Partizan Beograd	H	1-3	Antunovic
16/10/99	Cukaricki Beograd	A	1-2	Vojvodic
23/10/99	Hajduk Beograd	H	4-2	Vojvodic 3 (2p), Jovic D.
30/10/99	Proleter Zrenjanin	A	1-1	Kocic
06/11/99	Vojvodina Novi Sad	H	1-0	Vojvodic
13/11/99	Hajduk Kula	A	0-0	
17/11/99	Obilic Beograd	H	2-3	Vojvodic (p), Katic
20/11/99	Mogren Budva	A	0-1	
04/12/99	Milicionar Beograd	H	0-2	
11/12/99	Borac Cacak	A	0-1	
15/12/99	Crvena zvezda Beograd	H	1-2	Vojvodic
18/12/99	Zeleznik Beograd	A	0-1	
12/02/00	FK Zemun	A	0-0	
16/02/00	Buducnost Podgorica	H	2-0	Efimov, Vojvodic
19/02/00	Rad Beograd	A	1-0	Bogdanovic
26/02/00	OFK Beograd	H	1-0	Mrdak
01/03/00	Radnicki Kragujevac	A	0-1	
04/03/00	Spartak Subotica	H	2-0	Efimov, Andjelkovic
11/03/00	Radnicki Nis	A	1-2	Antunovic
15/03/00	Sutjeska Niksic	H	0-0	
18/03/00	Partizan Beograd	A	0-4	
22/03/00	Cukaricki Beograd	H	1-1	Antunovic
25/03/00	Hajduk Beograd	A	0-3	
01/04/00	Proleter Zrenjanin	H	2-0	Efimov, Andjelkovic
08/04/00	Vojvodina Novi Sad	A	1-0	Corluka
15/04/00	Hajduk Kula	H	4-0	Andjelkovic 2, Antunovic 2
22/04/00	Obilic Beograd	A	0-1	
29/04/00	Mogren Budva	H	3-1	Glogovac, Antunovic, Andjelkovic
06/05/00	Milicionar Beograd	A	1-1	Andjelkovic (p)
13/05/00	Borac Cacak	H	2-0	Mudrinic, Andjelkovic (p)
17/05/00	Crvena zvezda Beograd	A	0-2	
20/05/00	Zeleznik Beograd	H	3-2	Andjelkovic, Antunovic, Mudrinic

SPARTAK SUBOTICA

CLUB DIRECTORY

FK Spartak
Lenjinov Park 10
24000 Subotica
tel - (024) 551035/551979
fax - (024) 555016
Year of Formation - 1945
President - Milorad Stavljanin
Coach - Slobodan Kustudic
Stadium - Gradski (28,000)

PLAYERS 99/00

	P	Gls
Srdjan AJDARIC	G	
Nikola BASTA	A	
Zoran BOGESIC	A	
Sead BRUNCEVIC	M	
Novo CUJOVIC	A	3
Sasa DJURASOVIC	D	1
Milos DROBNJAK	D	
DULIC	M	
Ivica FRANCISKOVIC	M	5
Caba HANDJA	A	3
Dragan ILIC	M	
Rade IVLJANIN	M	3
JEVRIC	M	1
KEKEZOVIC	M	
Aleksandar KOPUNOVIC	A	2
Ognjen KOROMAN	M	2
Zoltan KUJUNDZIC	G	
Zoran KUNTIC	A	1
LJUBINKOVIC	D	
Goran MARINKOVIC	M	4
Slobodan MAZIC	D	
Dejan MRVALJEVIC	D	
Sead MURATOVIC	M	
Vladimir PAVICEVIC	M	
Perko PEROVIC	D	
Dusan PETKOVIC	A	1
Dejan POLJAKOVIC	M	1
Antal PUHALAK	A	4
Nemanja RAICEVIC	M	
Dejan RONCEVIC	D	
Goran SOMODJI	D	
Zoran STJEPANOVIC	M	3
Davor STOJANOVIC	G	
Flórián URBÁN (HUN)	M	
Zlatko ZEBIC	A	

LEAGUE RESULTS 1999/2000

31/07/99	Proleter Zrenjanin	A	0-3	
07/08/99	Vojvodina Novi Sad	H	1-0	Puhalak
21/08/99	Hajduk Kula	A	0-3	
11/09/99	Obilic Beograd	H	0-0	
18/09/99	Mogren Budva	A	1-1	Djurasovic
21/09/99	Sartid Smederevo	H	1-0	Marinkovic
25/09/99	Milicionar Beograd	A	0-2	
02/10/99	Borac Cacak	H	1-1	Kopunovic (p)
13/10/99	Crvena zvezda Beograd	A	0-4	
16/10/99	Zeleznik Beograd	H	1-0	Kopunovic
23/10/99	FK Zemun	A	0-1	
30/10/99	Buducnost Podgorica	H	2-2	Koroman, Marinkovic
06/11/99	Rad Beograd	A	0-1	
13/11/99	OFK Beograd	H	1-2	Puhalak
17/11/99	Radnicki Kragujevac	A	1-3	Franciskovic
27/11/99	Radnicki Nis	H	1-1	Puhalak
04/12/99	Sutjeska Niksic	A	0-1	
11/12/99	Partizan Beograd	H	0-6	
15/12/99	Cukaricki Beograd	A	1-2	Ivljanin
18/12/99	Hajduk Beograd	H	2-0	Kuntic, Puhalak
12/02/00	Proleter Zrenjanin	H	1-3	Jevric
16/02/00	Vojvodina Novi Sad	A	1-4	Marinkovic
19/02/00	Hajduk Kula	H	1-3	Cujovic
26/02/00	Obilic Beograd	A	0-2	
01/03/00	Mogren Budva	H	3-0	Marinkovic, Koroman, Franciskovic
04/03/00	Sartid Smederevo	A	0-2	
11/03/00	Milicionar Beograd	H	3-2	Stjepanovic, Poljakovic, Ivljanin
15/03/00	Borac Cacak	A	0-1	
18/03/00	Crvena zvezda Beograd	H	0-2	
22/03/00	Zeleznik Beograd	A	0-3	
25/03/00	FK Zemun	H	2-1	Stjepanovic, Petkovic
01/04/00	Buducnost Podgorica	A	0-4	
08/04/00	Rad Beograd	H	2-3	Cujovic, Franciskovic
15/04/00	OFK Beograd	A	0-3	
22/04/00	Radnicki Kragujevac	H	2-0	Cujovic, Handja
03/05/00	Radnicki Nis	A	0-2	
06/05/00	Sutjeska Niksic	H	0-2	
13/05/00	Partizan Beograd	A	2-7	Handja, Franciskovic
17/05/00	Cukaricki Beograd	H	2-3	Franciskovic, Ivljanin
20/05/00	Hajduk Beograd	A	2-3	Stjepanovic, Handja

SUTJESKA NIKSIC

CLUB DIRECTORY

FK Sutjeska
Trg Marsala Tita 1
81400 Niksic
tel - (083) 213426
Year of Formation - 1944
President - Brana Micunovic
Coach - Giljen & Nikolic
Stadium - Gradski (18,000)

PLAYERS 99/00

	P	Gls
Vojislav BAKRAC	M	
Zoran BANOVIC	G	
Savo BARAC	A	1
Goran BOSKOVIC	D	2
Ivan BOSKOVIC	M	
Sasa BRANEZAC	A	12
Milos BURSAC	A	2
Novo CUJOVIC	A	7
Slobodan DJUKIC	D	
Mijo GARDASEVIC	M	
Goran GILJEN	G	
Milinko ILIC	D	
Ziko KOJIC	A	2
Zeljko KONTIC	M	
Boris KOPRIVICA	A	1
Vladan KOSTIC	M	2
Aleksandar KRESOJA	M	
Darko KRSTEVSKI (MAC)	D	
Bojan LAZIC	D	1
Nenad LUKIC	G	
Bojan MAGAZIN	M	1
Drazen MEDJEDOVIC	M	
Semjon MILOSEVIC	D	1
Predrag NIKCEVIC	A	
Boban NIKOLOVSKI	M	
Milos OGNJENOVIC	D	
Zeljko PEROVIC	M	3
Igor RADOVIC	D	1
Miljan RADOVIC	M	7
Miljan SAVIC	D	1
Milan STANJEVIC	A	2
Rade TODOROVIC	D	1
Vukoslav VELICKOVIC	D	
Mirko VUCINIC	A	3
ZEKOVIC	M	

LEAGUE RESULTS 1999/2000

31/07/99	Cukaricki Beograd	A	2-2	Cujovic 2 (1p)
07/08/99	Hajduk Beograd	H	4-3	Perovic, Lazic, Cujovic 2 (1p)
21/08/99	Proleter Zrenjanin	A	1-2	Perovic
11/09/99	Vojvodina Novi Sad	H	1-0	Radovic M.
18/09/99	Hajduk Kula	A	0-0	
21/09/99	Obilic Beograd	A	1-2	Koprivica
25/09/99	Mogren Budva	A	1-2	Radovic M.
02/10/99	Sartid Smederevo	H	4-1	Branezac 2, Cujovic, Vucinic
13/10/99	Milicionar Beograd	A	1-2	Barac
16/10/99	Borac Cacak	H	2-1	Cujovic, Radovic M.
23/10/99	Crvena zvezda Beograd	A	0-5	
30/10/99	Zeleznik Beograd	H	2-1	Radovic M. (p), Cujovic
06/11/99	FK Zemun	A	1-1	Milosevic
13/11/99	Buducnost Podgorica	H	1-0	Branezac
17/11/99	Rad Beograd	A	1-2	Branezac
20/11/99	OFK Beograd	H	3-2	Kostic, Stanjevic (p), Branezac
27/11/99	Radnicki Kragujevac	A	0-3	
04/12/99	Spartak Subotica	H	1-0	Stanjevic
11/12/99	Radnicki Nis	A	0-2	
18/12/99	Partizan Beograd	H	2-2	Boskovic G., Branezac
12/02/00	Cukaricki Beograd	H	0-0	
16/02/00	Hajduk Beograd	A	0-2	
19/02/00	Proleter Zrenjanin	H	3-1	Kostic, Kojic, Radovic I.
26/02/00	Vojvodina Novi Sad	A	1-1	Branezac
01/03/00	Hajduk Kula	H	1-0	Radovic M. (p)
04/03/00	Obilic Beograd	H	1-2	Branezac
11/03/00	Mogren Budva	H	2-0	Magazin, Todorovic
15/03/00	Sartid Smederevo	A	0-0	
18/03/00	Milicionar Beograd	H	2-0	Perovic, Savic
22/03/00	Borac Cacak	A	2-0	Branezac, Radovic M.
25/03/00	Crvena zvezda Beograd	H	0-1	
01/04/00	Zeleznik Beograd	A	1-3	Bursac
08/04/00	FK Zemun	H	0-0	
15/04/00	Buducnost Podgorica	A	0-0	
22/04/00	Rad Beograd	H	1-0	Boskovic G.
29/04/00	OFK Beograd	A	3-2	Vucinic, Branezac, Bursac
03/05/00	Radnicki Kragujevac	H	0-1	
06/05/00	Spartak Subotica	A	2-0	Vucinic, Branezac
13/05/00	Radnicki Nis	H	3-1	Radovic M., Kojic, Branezac
20/05/00	Partizan Beograd	A	0-2	

VOJVODINA NOVI SAD

CLUB DIRECTORY

FK Vojvodina
Zarka Zrenjanina 8, 21000 Novi Sad
tel - (021) 25481/421688
fax - (021) 20270
website - www.fkvojvodina.co.yu
Year of Formation - 1914
President - Zivko Sokolovacki
Secretary - Nestor Sremcev
Coach - Tomislav Manojkovic; Dragan Okuka
Stadium - Gradski (22,000)

MAJOR HONOURS
League Championship - (2) 1968, 1989.

PLAYERS 99/00

	P	Gls
Mirko ALEKSIC	M	1
Sasa ANTIC	D	
Vlada AVRAMOV	G	
Radoslav BATAK	A	
Milan BELIC	A	7
Igor BOGDANOVIC	A	7
Dejan BOGUNOVIC	G	
Vidak BRATIC	M	2
Milorad BUKVIC		3
Milan CAKIC	A	3
Sasa CILINSEK	D	2
CIMESA	D	
Dalibor DRAGIC	D	
Dragoljub GAJEVIC	M	
Miroslav GRUJIC	M	
Ronald HABI	M	1
INJAC	M	
Zoran JANKOVIC	A	14
JOVANOVIC	A	
Milan JOVIC	M	
Radovan KRIVOKAPIC	M	3
Dejan KUVALJA	D	
Dragan MILADINOVIC	D	1
Milorad MRDAK	D	
Vladimir MUDRINIC	M	1
Sabolc PALDJI	A	
Milan RAKIC	M	5
Ivan RISTIC	D	1
Milislav SECKOVIC	M	
Darko SUSKAVCEVIC	D	
Jovan TANASIJEVIC	D	1
Sreten VASIC	D	
Boris VASKOVIC	M	
Mico VRANJES	M	1
Dragan ZILIC	G	

LEAGUE RESULTS 1999/2000

31/07/99	Radnicki Kragujevac	H	2-0	Aleksic, Bogdanovic
07/08/99	Spartak Subotica	A	0-1	
21/08/99	Radnicki Nis	H	2-0	Jankovic, Bratic
11/09/99	Sutjeska Niksic	A	0-1	
18/09/99	Partizan Beograd	H	2-2	Krivokapic, Jankovic
21/09/99	Cukaricki Beograd	A	1-0	Bogdanovic
25/09/99	Hajduk Beograd	H	5-1	Ristic, Jankovic, Belic, Mudrinic, Vranjes
03/10/99	Proleter Zrenjanin	A	1-0	Bratic
16/10/99	Hajduk Kula	H	1-2	Belic
23/10/99	Obilic Beograd	A	0-2	
30/10/99	Mogren Budva	H	3-0	Belic, Rakic 2
06/11/99	Sartid Smederevo	A	0-1	
13/11/99	Milicionar Beograd	H	0-1	
17/11/99	Borac Cacak	A	3-2	Cilinsek, Bukvic, Rakic
20/11/99	Crvena zvezda Beograd	H	1-2	Bukvic
27/11/99	Zeleznik Beograd	A	0-1	
04/12/99	FK Zemun	H	3-3	Bukvic, Belic, Jankovic
11/12/99	Buducnost Podgorica	A	0-4	
15/12/99	Rad Beograd	H	3-2	Jankovic, Rakic, Miladinovic
18/12/99	OFK Beograd	A	0-2	
12/02/00	Radnicki Kragujevac	A	1-2	Bogdanovic
16/02/00	Spartak Subotica	H	4-1	Jankovic 2, Belic, Rakic
19/02/00	Radnicki Nis	A	1-2	Krivokapic
26/02/00	Sutjeska Niksic	H	1-1	og (Milosevic)
01/03/00	Partizan Beograd	A	1-4	Habi
04/03/00	Cukaricki Beograd	H	2-0	Bogdanovic, Belic
11/03/00	Hajduk Beograd	A	2-2	Cakic, Cilinsek
15/03/00	Proleter Zrenjanin	H	2-1	Jankovic 2
22/03/00	Hajduk Kula	A	1-1	Jankovic
25/03/00	Obilic Beograd	H	1-1	Jankovic
01/04/00	Mogren Budva	A	0-0	
08/04/00	Sartid Smederevo	H	0-1	
15/04/00	Milicionar Beograd	A	0-0	
22/04/00	Borac Cacak	H	4-0	Bogdanovic 2, Cakic 2
29/04/00	Crvena zvezda Beograd	A	0-4	
03/05/00	Zeleznik Beograd	H	1-0	Tanasijevic
06/05/00	FK Zemun	A	1-2	Krivokapic
13/05/00	Buducnost Podgorica	H	2-0	Jankovic 2
17/05/00	Rad Beograd	A	0-1	
20/05/00	OFK Beograd	H	3-0	Belic, Bogdanovic, Jankovic

ZELEZNIK BEOGRAD

CLUB DIRECTORY

FK Zeleznik
Avalska bb
11250 Beograd
tel - (011) 577164
fax - (011) 577164
Year of Formation - 1930
President - Aca Bulic
Coach - Sasa Ciric
Stadium - Zeleznik (10,000)

PLAYERS 99/00

	P	Gls
Srdjan ALEKSIC	D	
Nebojsa BABIC	D	
Branko BOZOVIC	D	2
Aleksandar CIRIC	D	
Igor CVETKOVIC	D	
Antonio FILEVSKI (MAC)	G	
Radoslav GLAVARDANOV	M	
Sead GORANI	A	
Dragan ILIC	M	3
Vladan ISAILOVIC	D	
Slavoljub KIZIC	D	8
Sinisa LUCIC	D	
Bojan MARTIC	M	
Ilija MILOSEVIC	A	
NIKOLIC	M	1
Sinisa NINKOVIC	D	
Slobodan PANIC	A	2
Vladan PASIC	D	
Dragan PERISIC	M	1
Dalibor PESTERAC	D	
Boban PETKOVIC	M	3
Vladimir POPOVIC	D	
Sinisa PRERADOVIC	A	1
Vojin PROLE	G	
Vladimir RANDJELOVIC	M	1
Slobodan SLOVIC	M	6
Srdjan SOLDATOVIC	G	
Sladjan SPASIC	A	12
Igor STANISAVLJEVIC	M	2
Vladimir SUBASIC	A	
Ivan TASIC	M	1
Milovan TODOROVIC	A	
Slobodan ZIVKOVIC	A	12

LEAGUE RESULTS 1999/2000

Date	Opponent	H/A	Score	Scorers
31/07/99	Milicionar Beograd	A	2-0	Panic, Preradovic
07/08/99	Borac Cacak	H	5-3	Spasic, Zivkovic 2, Kizic, Tasic
21/08/99	Crvena zvezda Beograd	A	0-0	
18/09/99	FK Zemun	H	2-1	Slovic, Bozovic
21/09/99	Buducnost Podgorica	A	0-1	
25/09/99	Rad Beograd	H	2-2	Zivkovic, Panic
02/10/99	OFK Beograd	A	1-1	Bozovic
13/10/99	Radnicki Kragujevac	H	3-1	Zivkovic 2, Spasic
16/10/99	Spartak Subotica	A	0-1	
23/10/99	Radnicki Nis	H	3-1	Kizic, Zivkovic, Ilic
30/10/99	Sutjeska Niksic	A	1-2	Perisic
06/11/99	Partizan Beograd	H	0-1	
13/11/99	Cukaricki Beograd	A	0-0	
17/11/99	Hajduk Beograd	H	3-1	Slovic, Nikolic, Randjelovic
20/11/99	Proleter Zrenjanin	A	0-0	
27/11/99	Vojvodina Novi Sad	H	1-0	Ilic
04/12/99	Hajduk Kula	A	0-1	
11/12/99	Obilic Beograd	H	0-3	
15/12/99	Mogren Budva	A	1-2	Ilic
18/12/99	Sartid Smederevo	H	1-0	Spasic
12/02/00	Milicionar Beograd	H	2-2	Spasic, Slovic
16/02/00	Borac Cacak	A	1-2	Slovic
19/02/00	Crvena zvezda Beograd	H	1-3	Kizic
01/03/00	FK Zemun	A	1-1	Kizic
04/03/00	Buducnost Podgorica	H	1-0	Zivkovic
11/03/00	Rad Beograd	A	0-1	
15/03/00	OFK Beograd	H	4-3	Kizic, Zivkovic, Spasic, Petkovic
18/03/00	Radnicki Kragujevac	A	0-0	
22/03/00	Spartak Subotica	H	3-0	Spasic 3
25/03/00	Radnicki Nis	A	0-2	
01/04/00	Sutjeska Niksic	H	3-1	Petkovic, Zivkovic 2
08/04/00	Partizan Beograd	A	1-1	Kizic
15/04/00	Cukaricki Beograd	H	1-2	Kizic
22/04/00	Hajduk Beograd	A	1-2	Spasic
29/04/00	Proleter Zrenjanin	H	3-0	Zivkovic (p), Petkovic, Zivkovic
03/05/00	Vojvodina Novi Sad	A	0-1	
06/05/00	Hajduk Kula	H	2-0	Spasic, Slovic
13/05/00	Obilic Beograd	A	0-2	
17/05/00	Mogren Budva	H	4-0	Spasic 2, Kizic, Stanisavljevic
20/05/00	Sartid Smederevo	A	2-3	Slovic, Stanisavljevic

FK ZEMUN

CLUB DIRECTORY

FK Zemun
Ugrinovacka 80
11080 Zemun
tel - (011) 612949/618889
fax - (011) 666197
Year of Formation - 1946
President - Dusan Celar
Coach - Milan Milanovic
Stadium - Gradski (15,000)

PLAYERS 99/00

	P	Gls
Milos ADAMOVIC	G	
Vladimir ANOKIC	D	
Branislav BAJIC	D	
Aleksandar BOJANIC	M	2
Sinisa BRANKOVIC	M	1
Dejan CELAR	M	
Goran CELAR	A	10
Bosko CVORKOV	M	
Sinisa DJURIC	A	5
Sreten DJUROVIC	D	
Milos DOBRIJEVIC	D	1
Ranko GOLIJANIN	D	1
Goran GRKINIC	D	
Djordje INDJIC	A	4
Sasa JELOVAC	A	2
Nikola JOLOVIC	D	2
Milos KRUSCIC	D	2
Igor MATIC	M	
Dragoslav MILENKOVIC	D	
Zoran MILJKOVIC	D	
Dragan MLADENOVIC	M	
Uros NIKITOVIC	D	
Sasa RACA	M	4
Milos RADULOVIC	D	
Predrag RISTOVIC	G	
Dejan SARIC	A	5
Ivan STEFANOVIC	D	
Ilija STOLICA	M	4
Dejan TOMIC	M	1
Djordje TOPALOVIC	G	
Jovan VESELINOVIC	M	1

LEAGUE RESULTS 1999/2000

Date	Opponent		Score	
31/07/99	Sartid Smederevo	A	2-1	Dobrijevic, Raca
07/08/99	Milicionar Beograd	H	2-2	Celar G. 2
21/08/99	Borac Cacak	A	2-3	Saric 2
11/09/99	Crvena zvezda Beograd	H	0-4	
18/09/99	Zeleznik Beograd	A	1-2	Djuric
25/09/99	Buducnost Podgorica	H	2-0	Saric, Celar G.
02/10/99	Rad Beograd	A	1-5	Stolica
13/10/99	OFK Beograd	H	2-1	Brankovic, Celar G.
16/10/99	Radnicki Kragujevac	A	0-1	
23/10/99	Spartak Subotica	H	1-0	Tomic
30/10/99	Radnicki Nis	A	3-2	Stolica, Saric, Jolovic
06/11/99	Sutjeska Niksic	H	1-1	Indjic
13/11/99	Partizan Beograd	A	1-4	Indjic
17/11/99	Cukaricki Beograd	H	0-1	
20/11/99	Hajduk Beograd	A	1-2	Saric
27/11/99	Proleter Zrenjanin	H	2-0	Veselinovic, Djuric
04/12/99	Vojvodina Novi Sad	A	3-3	Stolica, Raca 2
11/12/99	Hajduk Kula	H	1-1	Kruscic
15/12/99	Obilic Beograd	A	0-1	
18/12/99	Mogren Budva	H	2-0	Raca, Celar G.
12/02/00	Sartid Smederevo	H	0-0	
16/02/00	Milicionar Beograd	A	0-1	
19/02/00	Borac Cacak	H	2-1	Celar G., Jelovac
26/02/00	Crvena zvezda Beograd	A	1-1	Djuric
01/03/00	Zeleznik Beograd	H	1-1	Stolica
11/03/00	Buducnost Podgorica	A	0-1	
15/03/00	Rad Beograd	H	2-1	Jolovic, Bojanic
18/03/00	OFK Beograd	A	1-1	Celar G.
22/03/00	Radnicki Kragujevac	H	2-0	Djuric, Bojanic
25/03/00	Spartak Subotica	A	1-2	og (Dulic)
01/04/00	Radnicki Nis	H	1-0	Golijanin (p)
08/04/00	Sutjeska Niksic	A	0-0	
15/04/00	Partizan Beograd	H	0-3	
22/04/00	Cukaricki Beograd	A	2-1	Kruscic (p), Djuric
29/04/00	Hajduk Beograd	H	0-3	
03/05/00	Proleter Zrenjanin	A	0-1	
06/05/00	Vojvodina Novi Sad	H	2-1	Celar G. 2
13/05/00	Hajduk Kula	A	1-3	Indjic
17/05/00	Obilic Beograd	H	3-1	Celar G., Jelovac, og
20/05/00	Mogren Budva	A	2-1	og, Indjic

MAJOR SUMMER TRANSFERS 2000

PLAYER	OLD CLUB	NEW CLUB
● **AUSTRIA**		
Georg BARDEL	SK Sturm Graz	VfB Admira Mödling
Kliton BOZGO (ALB)	NK Maribor (SLO)	VfB Admira Mödling
Harald GÄRTNER (GER)	Hannover 96 (GER)	VfB Admira Mödling
Dejan MARKOVIC (YUG)	CA Osasuna (ESP)	VfB Admira Mödling
Armando MLINAR (CRO)	NK Domzale (SLO)	VfB Admira Mödling
Aljosa ASANOVIC (CRO)	Panathinaikos (GRE)	FK Austria Wien
Dirk Jan DERKSEN (HOL)	FC Zwolle (HOL)	FK Austria Wien
Martin HIDEN	Leeds United (ENG)	FK Austria Wien
Adam LEDWON (POL)	Fortuna Köln (GER)	FK Austria Wien
Timo ROST (GER)	VfB Stuttgart (GER)	FK Austria Wien
Dragan SARAC (YUG)	Obilic Beograd (YUG)	FK Austria Wien
Mirsad VARESANOVIC (BOS)	Bursaspor (TUR)	FK Austria Wien
Franz WOHLFAHRT	VfB Stuttgart (GER)	FK Austria Wien
Thomas AMBROSIUS (DEN)	FC Midtjylland (DEN)	SW Bregenz
Frank BAZZANO (ITA)	Melbourne Knights (AUS)	SW Bregenz
Armand BENNEKER (HOL)	SC Austria Lustenau	SW Bregenz
Daniel BOGOJEVIC (BOS)	FC St. Gallen (SUI)	SW Bregenz
Mladen POSAVEC (CRO)	Varteks Varazdin (CRO)	SW Bregenz
Mika PULKKINEN (FIN)	SC Heerenveen (HOL)	SW Bregenz
Jiri ROSICKY (CZE)	Atlético Madrid (ESP)	SW Bregenz
Ronald BRUNMAYR	SV Ried	Grazer AK
Adolf HÜTTER	SV Salzburg	Grazer AK
Zeljko MILINOVIC (SLO)	LASK Linz	Grazer AK
Herbert WIEGER	VfB Admira Mödling	Grazer AK
Wolfgang FEIERSINGER	Borussia Dortmund (GER)	LASK Linz
Geir FRIGÅRD (NOR)	Tennis Borussia Berlin (GER)	LASK Linz
Thomas GRÖBL	SK Sturm Graz	LASK Linz
Sladjan NIKOLIC (YUG)	SV Salzburg	LASK Linz
Johannes WOLDEAB (GER)	SK Vorwärts Steyr	LASK Linz
Jürgen KAUZ	LASK Linz	SK Rapid Wien
Florian SCHWARZ	SV Salzburg	SK Rapid Wien
Gaston TAUMENT (HOL)	OFI (GRE)	SK Rapid Wien
AKAGÜNDÜZ Muhammet	FK Austria Wien	SV Ried
Amir BRADARIC	LASK Linz	SV Salzburg
Juan CARCAMO (HON)	CD Platense (HON)	SV Salzburg
Armin HOBEL	FC Tirol Innsbruck	SV Salzburg
Julio SUAZO (HON)	CD Victoria (HON)	SV Salzburg
Maynor SUAZO (HUN)	CD Marathón (HON)	SV Salzburg
Ramiz MAMEDOV (RUS)	Dynamo Kyiv (UKR)	SK Sturm Graz
Jerzy BRZECZEK (POL)	Maccabi Haifa (ISR)	FC Tirol Innsbruck
Markus HOCHENBURGER	SW Bregenz	FC Tirol Innsbruck
Jürgen PANIS	LASK Linz	FC Tirol Innsbruck
Michael STREITER	FK Austria Wien	FC Tirol Innsbruck

PLAYER	OLD CLUB	NEW CLUB
● **BELGIUM**		
Besnik HASI (YUG)	KRC Genk	RSC Anderlecht
Aleksandar ILIC (YUG)	Club Brugge KV	RSC Anderlecht
Yves VANDERHAEGHE	R Excelsior Mouscron	RSC Anderlecht
Tristan PEERSMAN	KSK Beveren	RSC Anderlecht
Aruna DINDANE (CIV)	ASEC Abidjan (CIV)	RSC Anderlecht
Emmanuel PIRARD	RAA La Louvière	RSC Anderlecht
Kris MAMPAEY	Dunfermline Athletic (SCO)	Royal Antwerp FC
Gert PEELMAN	K Lierse SK	Royal Antwerp FC
Iyenemi FURO (NIG)	FC Sion (SUI)	Royal Antwerp FC
Kurt MERTENS	K St.-Truidense VV	Royal Antwerp FC
Jurgen DE NEYS	KV Mechelen	Royal Antwerp FC
Benoît THANS	KVC Westerlo	KSK Beveren
Khalid FOUHAMI (MAR)	Dinamo Bucuresti (ROM)	KSK Beveren
Olivier SURAY	Adanaspor (TUR)	KSK Beveren
Timmy SIMONS	KFC Lommelse SK	Club Brugge KV
Peter VAN DER HEYDEN	KSC Eendracht Aalst	Club Brugge KV
Dejan NEMEC (SLO)	Mura Murska Sobota (SLO)	Club Brugge KV
Pascal DIAS	R Standard Liège	RSC Charleroi
Ronald FOGUENNE	KAA Gent	RSC Charleroi
Gauthier REMACLE	R Standard Liège	RSC Charleroi
Enzo SCIFO	RSC Anderlecht	RSC Charleroi
Marc VANGRONSVELD	KRC Genk	RSC Charleroi
Roberto BISCONTI	R Standard Liège	RSC Charleroi
Rade MOJOVIC (YUG)	Royal Antwerp FC	KSC Eendracht Aalst
François RIGAUX (FRA)	RC Lens (FRA)	KSC Eendracht Aalst
Dejan MRVALJEVIC (YUG)	Spartak Subotica (YUG)	KSC Eendracht Aalst
Raphaël MICELI (FRA)	Le Havre AC (FRA)	KSC Eendracht Aalst
Tim DE KEYSER	K Lierse SK	KSC Eendracht Aalst
Emest ETCHI (CMR)	RC Lens (FRA)	KSC Eendracht Aalst
Dejan MITROVIC (YUG)	KVC Westerlo	R Excelsior Mouscron
Kurt VANDOORNE	KRC Harelbeke	R Excelsior Mouscron
Nenad JESTROVIC (YUG)	FC Metz (FRA)	R Excelsior Mouscron
David PAAS	KRC Harelebeke	KRC Genk
Fritz EMERMAN	KV Mechelen	KRC Genk
Wesley SONCK	Germinal Beerschot Antwerpen	KRC Genk
Jan MOONS	Germinal Beerschot Antwerpen	KRC Genk
Thomas CHATELLE	KAA Gent	KRC Genk
Blessing KAKU (NIG)	KRC Harelebeke	KRC Genk
Akran ROUMANI (MAR)	MAS Fes (MAR)	KRC Genk
Didier ZOKORA (CIV)	ASEC Abidjan (CIV)	KRC Genk
Bernd THIJS	R Standard Liège	KRC Genk
Geri ÇIPI (ALB)	NK Maribor (SLO)	KAA Gent
Jacky PEETERS	Arminia Bielefeld (GER)	KAA Gent
Vital BORKELMANS	Club Brugge KV	KAA Gent

MAJOR SUMMER TRANSFERS 2000

PLAYER	OLD CLUB	NEW CLUB
Alexandros KAKLAMANOS (GRE)	RSC Charleroi	KAA Gent
Aldo OLCESE (PER)	Sporting Cristal (PER)	KAA Gent
Martin LAAMERS (HOL)	KRC Harelbeke	KAA Gent
Robby VAN DE WEYER	K Lierse SK	Germinal Beerschot Antwerpen
Dirk HUYSMANS	K Lierse SK	Germinal Beerschot Antwerpen
Bert DHONT	KSK Beveren	Germinal Beerschot Antwerpen
Miklós LENDVAI (HUN)	KFC Verbroedering Geel	Germinal Beerschot Antwerpen
Vilson KNEZEVIC (AUS)	Adelaide City (AUS)	Germinal Beerschot Antwerpen
Steve COOREMAN	KSC Eendracht Aalst	Germinal Beerschot Antwerpen
Sébastien NOTTEBAERT	RAA La Louvière	KRC Harelbeke
Franky FRANS	KVC Westerlo	KRC Harelbeke
Jan VAN STEENBERGHE	KSC Eendracht Aalst	RAA La Louvière
Jean-Jacques MISSE-MISSE (CMR)	Ethnikos Astir (GRE)	RAA La Louvière
Geoffrey CLAEYS	KSC Eendracht Aalst	K Lierse SK
PEPA (POR)	SL Benfica (POR)	K Lierse SK
Yves VAN DER STRAETEN	CS Marítimo (POR)	K Lierse SK
Gonzague VANDOOREN	R Excelsior Mouscron	K Lierse SK
Oleg VERETENNIKOV (RUS)	Aris (GRE)	K Lierse SK
Axel SMEETS	Sheffield United (ENG)	K Lierse SK
Arnar GRÉTARSSON (ISL)	AEK (GRE)	KSC Lokeren
Nenad VANIC (SLO)	Albacete Balompié (ESP)	KSC Lokeren
Emeka MAMALE (CON)	Kaizer Chiefs (SAF)	KSC Lokeren
Eddy DIERICKX	K St.-Truidense VV	KV Mechelen
José DEL SOLAR (PER)	Universitario de Lima (PER)	KV Mechelen
Luis GUADELUPE (PER)	Universitario de Lima (PER)	KV Mechelen
Masahiro ENDO (JPN)	Shimizu S-Pulse (JPN)	KV Mechelen
Peter MEEUSSEN	KFC Verbroedering Geel	KV Mechelen
Søren HERMANSEN (DEN)	Lyngby FC (DEN)	KV Mechelen
Rudi SMIDTS	Germinal Beerschot Antwerpen	KV Mechelen
Zeljko BABIC (AUS)	Marconi Stallions (AUS)	K St.-Truidense VV
Sésiré MBONABUCYA (RWA)	Gaziantepspor (TUR)	K St.-Truidense VV
Jacky MATHIJSSEN	KFC Lommelse SK	K St.-Truidense VV
Stijn MEERT	RSC Anderlecht	K St.-Truidense VV
Ole Martin ÅRST (NOR)	KAA Gent	R Standard Liège
Ivica DRAGUTINOVIC (YUG)	KAA Gent	R Standard Liège
FOLHA (POR)	FC Porto (POR)	R Standard Liège
Harold MEYSSEN	SV Salzburg (AUT)	R Standard Liège
Petr VLCEK (CZE)	Slavia Praha (CZE)	R Standard Liège
Frank DAUWEN	KAA Gent	KVC Westerlo
Jef DELEN	KFC Verbroedering Geel	KVC Westerlo
Dalibor MITROVIC (YUG)	Club Brugge KV	KVC Westerlo

● CZECH REPUBLIC

PLAYER	OLD CLUB	NEW CLUB
Marek SPILAR	1.FC Kosice (SVK)	Banik Ostrava
Kamil MATUSZNY	Slovan Liberec	Bohemians Praha

PLAYER	OLD CLUB	NEW CLUB
Michal HRBEK	Slovan Liberec	Bohemians Praha
Libor JANACEK	Slovan Liberec	Bohemians Praha
Stanislav MAREK	Slovan Liberec	SK Ceske Budejovice
Karel VACHA	FC Tirol Innsbruck (AUT)	SK Ceske Budejovice
Tomas KLINKA	Viktoria Zizkov	SK Ceske Budejovice
Marek MECIAR (SVK)	Banik Prievidza (SVK)	SK Ceske Budejovice
Martin VOZABAL	Slavia Praha	SK Ceske Budejovice
Zbynek HAUZR	Slovan Liberec	SK Ceske Budejovice
Martin PETRAS (SVK)	Banik Prievidza (SVK)	FK Jablonec 97
Michal NEHODA	Petra Drnovice	Marila Pribram
Damir GRLIC (CRO)	Cakovec (CRO)	Marila Pribram
Fábio Luís GOMES (BRA)	Spartak Trnava (SVK)	Petra Drnovice
Marek UJLAKY (SVK)	Spartak Trnava (SVK)	Petra Drnovice
Dusan SNINSKY (SVK)	HFC Humenne (SVK)	Petra Drnovice
Pavel HAPAL	Sparta Praha	Sigma Olomouc
Pavel KAMESCH (SVK)	VTJ KOBA Senec (SVK)	Sigma Olomouc
Daniel KASPRIK (SVK)	VTJ KOBA Senec (SVK)	Sigma Olomouc
Radek SPILACEK	SFC Opava	Sigma Olomouc
Radim NECAS	FK Jablonec 97	Slavia Praha
Jindrich SKACEL	Sigma Olomouc	Slavia Praha
Darko SUSKAVCEVIC (YUG)	Vojvodina Novi Sad (YUG)	Slavia Praha
Lumir SEDLACEK	SFC Opava	Slavia Praha
Petr SVANCARA	Stavo Artikel Brno	Slavia Praha
Roman JUN	Bohemians Praha	Slovan Liberec
Jan NEZMAR	SFC Opava	Slovan Liberec
Marian KLAGO	Bohemians Praha	Slovan Liberec
Marek KINCL	Viktoria Zizkov	Sparta Praha
Petr PAPOUSEK	FK Jablonec 97	Sparta Praha
Zdenek GRYGERA	Petra Drnovice	Sparta Praha
Martin KOTULEK	Sigma Olomouc	Stavo Artikel Brno
Libor DOSEK	Chmel Blsany	Stavo Artikel Brno
Petr DROBISZ	FK Jablonec 97	Synot Stare Mesto
Tomas POLACH (SVK)	ZTS Dubnica (SVK)	Synot Stare Mesto
Vladimir LEITNER (SVK)	Spartak Trnava (SVK)	FK Teplice
Pavol PIATKA (SVK)	Tatran Presov (SVK)	FK Teplice
Robert SEMENIK (SVK)	Gençlerbirligi (TUR)	FK Teplice
Vaclav PECHOUCEK	FC Basel (SUI)	Viktoria Plzen

● DENMARK

PLAYER	OLD CLUB	NEW CLUB
Michael JOHANSEN	Bolton Wanderers (ENG)	AB
Erik BOYE	Vejle BK	AGF
Jens MADSEN	Vejle BK	AGF
Ulrik KRISTENSEN	AGF	Haderslev FK
Jens JESSEN	AaB	FC Midtjylland
Mogens LAURSEN	Randers Freja FC	FC Midtjylland

MAJOR SUMMER TRANSFERS 2000

PLAYER	OLD CLUB	NEW CLUB	PLAYER	OLD CLUB	NEW CLUB
Urmas ROOBA (EST)	FC Flora Tallinn (EST)	FC Midtjylland	Martijn REUSER (HOL)	Vitesse (HOL)	Ipswich Town
Jesper SØGAARD	Vejle BK	FC Midtjylland	John SCALES	Tottenham Hotspur	Ipswich Town
Johnny HANSEN	Esbjerg FB	Silkeborg IF	Olivier DACOURT (FRA)	RC Lens (FRA)	Leeds United
Per OTTOSEN	Køge BK	Silkeborg IF	Mark VIDUKA (AUS)	Celtic (SCO)	Leeds United
Karim ZAZA	FC København	Silkeborg IF	Dominic MATTEO	Liverpool	Leeds United
			Ade AKINBIYI (NIG)	Wolverhampton Wanderers	Leicester City
● ENGLAND			Gary ROWETT	Birmingham City	Leicester City
LAUREN Etamé Mayer (CMR)	RCD Mallorca (ESP)	Arsenal	Callum DAVIDSON (SCO)	Blackburn Rovers	Leicester City
Robert PIRES (FRA)	Olympique Marseille (FRA)	Arsenal	Trevor BENJAMIN	Cambridge United	Leicester City
Sylvain WILTORD (FRA)	Girondins de Bordeaux (FRA)	Arsenal	Simon ROYCE	Charlton Athletic	Leicester City
ALPAY Özalan (TUR)	Fenerbahçe (TUR)	Aston Villa	Richard CRESSWELL	Sheffield Wednesday	Leicester City
David GINOLA (FRA)	Tottenham Hotspur	Aston Villa	Nick BARMBY	Everton	Liverpool
Luc NILIS (BEL)	PSV (HOL)	Aston Villa	Bernard DIOMEDE (FRA)	AJ Auxerre (FRA)	Liverpool
David HOPKIN (SCO)	Leeds United	Bradford City	Pegguy ARPHEXAD (FRA)	Leicester City	Liverpool
Ashley WARD	Blackburn Rovers	Bradford City	Markus BABBEL (GER)	FC Bayern München (GER)	Liverpool
Dan PETRESCU (ROM)	Chelsea	Bradford City	Gary McALLISTER (SCO)	Coventry City	Liverpool
Peter ATHERTON	Sheffield Wednesday	Bradford City	Christian ZIEGE (GER)	Middlesbrough	Liverpool
Ian NOLAN (NIR)	Sheffield Wednesday	Bradford City	Paulo WANCHOPE (CRC)	West Ham United	Manchester City
Benito CARBONE (ITA)	Aston Villa	Bradford City	Alf Inge HÅLAND (NOR)	Leeds United	Manchester City
Claus JENSEN (DEN)	Bolton Wanderers	Charlton Athletic	Steve HOWEY	Newcastle United	Manchester City
Jonatan JOHANSSON (FIN)	Rangers (SCO)	Charlton Athletic	George WEAH (LIB)	Milan (ITA)	Manchester City
Radostin KISHISHEV (BUL)	Lovech (BUL)	Charlton Athletic	Paul RITCHIE (SCO)	Rangers (SCO)	Manchester City
Ben ROBERTS	Middlesbrough	Charlton Athletic	Fabien BARTHEZ (FRA)	AS Monaco (FRA)	Manchester United
Jimmy Floyd HASSELBAINK (HOL)	Atlético Madrid (ESP)	Chelsea	Joseph Desiré JOB (CMR)	RC Lens (FRA)	Middlesbrough
Mario STANIC (CRO)	Parma (ITA)	Chelsea	Alen BOKSIC (CRO)	Lazio (ITA)	Middlesbrough
Eidur GUDJOHNSEN (ISL)	Bolton Wanderers	Chelsea	Noel WHELAN	Coventry City	Middlesbrough
Carlo CUDICINI (ITA)	Castel di Sangro (ITA)	Chelsea	Christian KAREMBEU (FRA)	Real Madrid (ESP)	Middlesbrough
Christian PANUCCI (ITA)	Inter (ITA)	Chelsea	Mark CROSSLEY (WAL)	Nottingham Forest	Middlesbrough
Winston BOGARDE (HOL)	FC Barcelona (ESP)	Chelsea	Paul OKON (AUS)	Fiorentina (ITA)	Middlesbrough
Craig BELLAMY (WAL)	Norwich City	Coventry City	Carl CORT	Wimbledon	Newcastle United
David THOMPSON	Liverpool	Coventry City	Christian BASSEDAS (ARG)	Vélez Sarsfield (ARG)	Newcastle United
Giorgi KINKLADZE (GEO)	Ajax (HOL)	Derby County	Daniel CORDONE (ARG)	Racing Club (ARG)	Newcastle United
Danny HIGGINBOTHAM	Manchester United	Derby County	Mark DRAPER	Aston Villa	Southampton
Bjørn Otto BRAGSTAD (NOR)	Rosenborg BK (NOR)	Derby County	Uwe RÖSLER (GER)	Tennis Borussia Berlin (GER)	Southampton
Youl MAWENE (FRA)	RC Lens (FRA)	Derby County	Julio ARCA (ARG)	Argentinos Juniors (ARG)	Sunderland
Simo VALAKARI (FIN)	Motherwell (SCO)	Derby County	Don HUTCHISON (SCO)	Everton	Sunderland
Alex NYARKO (GHA)	RC Lens (FRA)	Everton	Stanislav VARGA (SVK)	Slovan Bratislava (SVK)	Sunderland
Duncan FERGUSON (SCO)	Newcastle United	Everton	Jürgen MACHO (AUT)	First Vienna FC (AUT)	Sunderland
Alessandro PISTONE (ITA)	Newcastle United	Everton	Emerson THOME (BRA)	Chelsea	Sunderland
Niclas ALEXANDERSSON (SWE)	Sheffield Wednesday	Everton	Serhiy REBROV (UKR)	Dynamo Kyiv (UKR)	Tottenham Hotspur
Thomas GRAVESEN (DEN)	Hamburger SV (GER)	Everton	Ben THATCHER	Wimbledon	Tottenham Hotspur
Steve WATSON	Aston Villa	Everton	Neil SULLIVAN (SCO)	Wimbledon	Tottenham Hotspur
Paul GASCOIGNE	Middlesbrough	Everton	Frédéric KANOUTE (FRA)	Olympique Lyonnais (FRA)	West Ham United
Idan TAL (ISR)	Maccabi Petach-Tikva (ISR)	Everton	Nigel WINTERBURN	Arsenal	West Ham United
Hermann HREIDARSSON (ISL)	Wimbledon	Ipswich Town	Davor SUKER (CRO)	Arsenal	West Ham United

MAJOR SUMMER TRANSFERS 2000

PLAYER	OLD CLUB	NEW CLUB	PLAYER	OLD CLUB	NEW CLUB
● **FRANCE**			Franck JURIETTI	SC Bastia	AS Monaco
Pierre DEBLOCK	CS Sedan Ardennes	AJ Auxerre	Xavier GRAVELAINE	Le Havre AC	AS Monaco
Jean-Alain BOUMSONG	Le Havre AC	AJ Auxerre	André BIANCARELLI	FC Metz	AS Monaco
Oumar DIENG	CS Sedan Ardennes	AJ Auxerre	MÁRIO SILVA (POR)	Boavista FC (POR)	FC Nantes
Khalilou FADIGA (BEL)	Club Brugge KV (BEL)	AJ Auxerre	Nicolas LASPALLES	Paris Saint-Germain	FC Nantes
Demétrius FERREIRA (BRA)	AS Nancy-Lorraine	SC Bastia	Stéphane ZIANI	Girondins de Bordeaux	FC Nantes
Yann LACHUER	Paris Saint-Germain	SC Bastia	Viorel MOLDOVAN (ROM)	Fenerbahçe (TUR)	FC Nantes
BRUNO BASTO (POR)	SL Benfica (POR)	Girondins de Bordeaux	Stéphane DALMAT	Olympique Marseille	Paris Saint-Germain
Bruno DA ROCHA	Toulouse FC	Girondins de Bordeaux	Peter LUCCIN	Olympique Marseille	Paris Saint-Germain
Frédéric ROUX	AS Nancy-Lorraine	Girondins de Bordeaux	Nicolas ANELKA	Real Madrid (ESP)	Paris Saint-Germain
Aleksei SMERTIN (RUS)	Lokomotiv Moskva (RUS)	Girondins de Bordeaux	Lionel LETIZI	FC Metz	Paris Saint-Germain
David SOMMEIL	Stade Rennais FC	Girondins de Bordeaux	Sylvain DISTIN	FC Gueugnon	Paris Saint-Germain
Marc WILMOTS (BEL)	FC Schalke 04 (GER)	Girondins de Bordeaux	Frédéric DEHU	FC Barcelona (ESP)	Paris Saint-Germain
Bruno RODRIGUEZ	RC Lens	En Avant Guingamp	Philippe DELAYE	Montpellier HSC	Stade Rennais FC
Romain FERRIER	Montpellier HSC	En Avant Guingamp	CÉSAR Augusto (BRA)	Paris Saint-Germain	Stade Rennais FC
Morten NIELSEN (DEN)	RC Strasbourg	En Avant Guingamp	Olivier ECHOUAFNI	RC Strasbourg	Stade Rennais FC
Hubert FOURNIER	Olympique Lyonnais	En Avant Guingamp	Bernard LAMA	Paris Saint-Germain	Stade Rennais FC
Antoine SIBIERSKI	FC Nantes	RC Lens	LUCAS Severino (BRA)	Atlético Paraná (BRA)	Stade Rennais FC
Mickaël DEBEVE	Le Havre AC	RC Lens	Mario TURDO (ARG)	RC Celta (ESP)	Stade Rennais FC
Esteban FUERTES (ARG)	Colon Santa Fé (ARG)	RC Lens	Laurent HUARD	CS Sedan Ardennes	AS Saint-Etienne
Franck DUMAS	Olympique Marseille	RC Lens	Aleksandr PANOV (RUS)	Zenit Sankt-Peterburg (RUS)	AS Saint-Etienne
El Hadji DIOUF (SEN)	Stade Rennais FC	RC Lens	Allan OLESEN (DEN)	AB (DEN)	AS Saint-Etienne
Radek BEJBL (CZE)	Atlético Madrid (ESP)	RC Lens	Maxym LEVYTSKYI (UKR)	Chernomorets Novorossiisk (RUS)	AS Saint-Etienne
Teddy RICHERT	Girondins de Bordeaux	Lille OSC	Christophe SANCHEZ	Girondins de Bordeaux	AS Saint-Etienne
Christophe PIGNOL	AS Monaco	Lille OSC	Patrice CARTERON	Olympique Lyonnais	AS Saint-Etienne
Sylvain N'DIAYE	Girondins de Bordeaux	Lille OSC	Salif DIAO (SEN)	AS Monaco	CS Sedan Ardennes
Edvin MURATI (ALB)	Paris Saint-Germain	Lille OSC	Moussa N'DIAYE (SEN)	AS Monaco	CS Sedan Ardennes
Mikkel BECK (DEN)	Derby County (ENG)	Lille OSC	Toni BROGNO (BEL)	KVC Westerlo (BEL)	CS Sedan Ardennes
Jean-Marc CHANELET	FC Nantes	Olympique Lyonnais	Corentin MARTINS	Girondins de Bordeaux	RC Strasbourg
Marc-Vivien FOE (CMR)	West Ham United (ENG)	Olympique Lyonnais	Danijel LJUBOJA	FC Sochaux	RC Strasbourg
Patrick MÜLLER (SUI)	Grasshopper-Club Zürich (SUI)	Olympique Lyonnais	Jean-Christophe DEVAUX	Olympique Lyonnais	RC Strasbourg
Steve MARLET	AJ Auxerre	Olympique Lyonnais	Yannick FISCHER	Olympique Marseille	RC Strasbourg
Eric DEFLANDRE (BEL)	Club Brugge KV (BEL)	Olympique Lyonnais	NUNO MENDES (POR)	GD Chaves (POR)	RC Strasbourg
Zoumana CAMARA	Inter (ITA)	Olympique Lyonnais	Christophe EGGIMANN	FC Metz	RC Strasbourg
Daniel MONTENEGRO (ARG)	Huracán (ARG)	Olympique Marseille	Christophe REVAULT	Stade Rennais FC	Toulouse FC
Michaël MARSIGLIA	RC Strasbourg	Olympique Marseille	Victor BONILLA (COL)	Real Sociedad (ESP)	Toulouse FC
Manuel DOS SANTOS	Montpellier HSC	Olympique Marseille	Jean-Christophe ROUVIERE	Girondins de Bordeaux	Toulouse FC
Bruno NGOTTY	Milan (ITA)	Olympique Marseille	Dario CABROL (ARG)	Union Santa Fé (ARG)	Toulouse FC
Klas INGESSON (SWE)	Bologna (ITA)	Olympique Marseille	Alfredo CASCINI (ARG)	Independiente (ARG)	Toulouse FC
Carlos ADRIANO (BRA)	Atlético Paraná (BRA)	Olympique Marseille	Bruno CAROTTI	Paris Saint-Germain	Toulouse FC
Farid MONDRAGON (COL)	Independiente (ARG)	FC Metz	Cédric URAS	Olympique Lyonnais	Toulouse FC
Patricio D'AMICO (ARG)	Belgrano Córdoba (ARG)	FC Metz	Stéphane LIEVRE	FC Nantes	Toulouse FC
Shabani NONDA (DRC)	Stade Rennais FC	AS Monaco	Nicolas GOUSSE	FC Metz	A Troyes AC
Stéphane PORATO	Olympique Marseille	AS Monaco	Fabio CELESTINI (ITA)	Lausanne-Sports (SUI)	A Troyes AC
Ousmane DABO	Parma (ITA)	AS Monaco	Mehdi MENIRI	AS Nancy-Lorraine	A Troyes AC

MAJOR SUMMER TRANSFERS 2000

PLAYER	OLD CLUB	NEW CLUB
● **GERMANY**		
MARQUINHOS (BRA)	Inter Limeira (BRA)	Bayer 04 Leverkusen
Seyedali MUSAWI (IRN)	Fortuna Köln	Bayer 04 Leverkusen
Andreas NEUENDORF	Hertha BSC Berlin	Bayer 04 Leverkusen
Pascal OJIGWE (NIGF)	1.FC Köln	Bayer 04 Leverkusen
Pascal ZUBERBÜHLER (SUI)	FC Basel (SUI)	Bayer 04 Leverkusen
Willy SAGNOL (FRA)	AS Monaco (FRA)	FC Bayern München
Ciriaco SFORZA (SUI)	1.FC Kaiserslautern	FC Bayern München
Berkant GÖKTAN (TUR)	Arminia Bielefeld	FC Bayern München
Ante COVIC	Hertha BSC Berlin	VfL Bochum
Sergei MANDREKO (TAD)	Hertha BSC Berlin	VfL Bochum
Zoran MAMIC (CRO)	Bayer 04 Leverkusen	VfL Bochum
Damir MILINOVIC (CRO)	Rijeka (CRO)	VfL Bochum
Jörg HEINRICH	Fiorentina (ITA)	Borussia Dortmund
Philipp LAUX	SSV Ulm	Borussia Dortmund
Sunday OLISEH (NIG)	Juventus (ITA)	Borussia Dortmund
Sasa CIRIC (MAC)	Tennis Borussia Berlin	Eintracht Frankfurt
János HRUTKA (HUN)	1.FC Kaiserslautern	Eintracht Frankfurt
Olaf JANSSEN	AC Bellinzona (SUI)	Eintracht Frankfurt
Markus LÖSCH	1.FC Nürnberg	Eintracht Frankfurt
Gerd WIMMER (AUT)	SK Rapid Wien (AUT)	Eintracht Frankfurt
Ferenc HORVÁTH (HUN)	KRC Genk (BEL)	FC Energie Cottbus
Andrzej KOBYLANSKI (POL)	Hannover 96	FC Energie Cottbus
Toni MICEVSKI (MAC)	Pelister Bitola (MAC)	FC Energie Cottbus
Laurentiu REGHECAMPF (ROM)	Steaua Bucuresti (ROM)	FC Energie Cottbus
Vilmos SEBÖK (HUN)	SV Waldhof Mannheim	FC Energie Cottbus
Ronny THIELMANN	FC Hansa Rostock	FC Energie Cottbus
Ismail COULIBALY (MLI)	El Zamalek (EGY)	SC Freiburg
Régis DORN (FRA)	RC Strasbourg (FRA)	SC Freiburg
Sebastian KEHL	Hannover 96	SC Freiburg
Sergej BARBAREZ (BOS)	Borussia Dortmund	Hamburger SV
Marek HEINZ (CZE)	Sigma Olomouc (CZE)	Hamburger SV
Marcel KETELAER	Borussia Mönchengladbach	Hamburger SV
Roland MAUL	Arminia Bielefeld	Hamburger SV
Stig TØFTING (DEN)	AGF (DEN)	Hamburger SV
Milan FUKAL (CZE)	Sparta Praha (CZE)	Hamburger SV
Andreas JACOBSSON (SWE)	Helsingborgs IF (SWE)	FC Hansa Rostock
Rene RYDLEWICZ	Arminia Bielefeld	FC Hansa Rostock
Rayk SCHRÖDER	FC Energie Cottbus	FC Hansa Rostock
Stefan BEINLICH	Bayer 04 Leverkusen	Hertha BSC Berlin
Rui Manuel MARQUES (POR)	SSV Ulm	Hertha BSC Berlin
Piotr REISS (POL)	MSV Duisburg	Hertha BSC Berlin
Petr GABRIEL (CZE)	Sparta Praha (CZE)	1.FC Kaiserslautern
Dimitrios GRAMMOZIS (GRE)	Hamburger SV	1.FC Kaiserslautern
Vratislav LOKVENC (CZE)	Sparta Praha (CZE)	1.FC Kaiserslautern
Murat YAKIN (SUI)	FC Basel (SUI)	1.FC Kaiserslautern
Ibrahim SAMIR (EGY)	Bursaspor (TUR)	1.FC Kaiserslautern
Lajos SZÜCS (HUN)	Ferencváros (HUN)	1.FC Kaiserslautern
Archil ARVELADZE (GEO)	NAC (HOL)	1.FC Köln
Alexander BADE	Hamburger SV	1.FC Köln
Miroslav BARANEK (CZE)	Sparta Praha (CZE)	1.FC Köln
Jens KELLER	VfB Stuttgart	1.FC Köln
Markus KREUZ	Hannover 96	1.FC Köln
Alassane OUEDRAOGO (BFA)	RSC Charleroi (BEL)	1.FC Köln
Ivan VUKOMANOVIC (YUG)	Crvena zvezda Beograd (YUG)	1.FC Köln
Markus BEIERLE	MSV Duisburg	TSV 1860 München
Uwe EHLERS	FC Hansa Rostock	TSV 1860 München
Erik MYKLAND (NOR)	Panathinaikos (GRE)	TSV 1860 München
Achim PFUDERER	Stuttgarter Kickers	TSV 1860 München
Jörg BÖHME	Arminia Bielefeld	FC Schalke 04
Mike BÜSKENS	MSV Duisburg	FC Schalke 04
Tomasz HAJTO (POL)	MSV Duisburg	FC Schalke 04
Andreas MÖLLER	Borussia Dortmund	FC Schalke 04
Stefan BLANK	Hannover 96	VfB Stuttgart
Ales CHVALOVSKY (CZE)	Chmel Blsany (CZE)	VfB Stuttgart
Alexandr GLEB (BLS)	FC BATE Borisov (BLS)	VfB Stuttgart
Silvio MEISSNER	Arminia Bielefeld	VfB Stuttgart
Jochen SEINTZ	SpVgg Unterhaching	VfB Stuttgart
Alexander BUGERA	MSV Duisburg	SpVgg Unterhaching
Dietmar HIRSCH	MSV Duisburg	SpVgg Unterhaching
Guido KOLTERMANN	VfL Wolfsburg	SpVgg Unterhaching
David ZDRILIC (AUS)	SSV Ulm	SpVgg Unterhaching
Ivica BANOVIC (CRO)	Zagreb (CRO)	SV Werder Bremen
Fabian ERNST	Hamburger SV	SV Werder Bremen
Mladen KRSTAJIC (YUG)	Partizan Beograd (YUG)	SV Werder Bremen
Frank VERLAAT (HOL)	Ajax (HOL)	SV Werder Bremen
Mike BUSCH	Hannover 96	VfL Wolfsburg
Dietmar KÜHBAUER (AUT)	Real Sociedad (ESP)	VfL Wolfsburg
Tomislav MARIC (CRO)	Stuttgarter Kickers	VfL Wolfsburg
Andreas VOSS	MSV Duisburg	VfL Wolfsburg
Martin WAGNER	1.FC Kaiserslautern	VfL Wolfsburg
● **HOLLAND**		
André BERGDØLMO (NOR)	Rosenborg BK (NOR)	Ajax
Cedric VAN DER GUN	FC Den Bosch	Ajax
Tomas GALASEK (CZE)	Willem II	Ajax
Bogdan LOBONT (ROM)	Rapid Bucuresti (ROM)	Ajax
Andy VAN DER MEYDE	FC Twente	Ajax
Olaf LINDENBERGH	De Graafschap	AZ
Paul MATTHIJS	FC Groningen	AZ

MAJOR SUMMER TRANSFERS 2000

PLAYER	OLD CLUB	NEW CLUB
Robin NELISSE	SC Cambuur Leeuwarden	AZ
Kenneth PEREZ	MVV	AZ
Henk TIMMER	FC Zwolle	AZ
Johan ELMANDER (SWE)	Örgryte IS (SWE)	Feyenoord
Arco JOCHEMSEN	Vitesse	Feyenoord
Zbigniew MALKOWSKI (POL)	Stomil Olsztyn (POL)	Feyenoord
Pascal AVERDIJK	FC Groningen	Fortuna Sittard
Jo GEERINCKX	KFC Verbroedering Geel (BEL)	Fortuna Sittard
Stijn HAELDERMANS (BEL)	KFC Lommelse SK (BEL)	Fortuna Sittard
Jochem VAN DER HOEVEN	Vitesse	Fortuna Sittard
Marco APOLLONI (ITA)	Vicenza (ITA)	De Graafschap
Kostas DEDELETAKIS (GRE)	OFI (GRE)	De Graafschap
Stefan POSTMA	FC Utrecht	De Graafschap
Dejan CUROVIC (YUG)	Vitesse	FC Groningen
Mustapha EL IDRISSI (MAR)	CD Santa Clara (POR)	FC Groningen
Roel JANSSEN	MVV	FC Groningen
Erwin VAN DE LOOI	Stuttgarter Kickers (GER)	FC Groningen
Ignacio TUHUTERU	FC Zwolle	SC Heerenveen
Ian CLAES (BEL)	K St.-Truidense VV (BEL)	SC Heerenveen
Gábor BABOS (HUN)	MTK Hungária FC (HUN)	NAC
Arno DOOMERNIK	Roda JC	NAC
Patrick AX	Vitesse	NEC
Pieter COLLEN	Vitesse	NEC
Georgi HRISTOV (MAC)	Barnsley (ENG)	NEC
Peter WISGERHOF	Vitesse	NEC
CLÁUDIO de Oliveira Pedeira (BRA)	Vitória Bahia (BRA)	PSV
Robert FUCHS	De Graafschap	PSV
Kevin HOFLAND	Fortuna Sittard	PSV
John DE JONG	FC Utrecht	PSV
Mateja KEZMAN (YUG)	Partizan Beograd (YUG)	PSV
Theo LUCIUS	FC Utrecht	PSV
Adil RAMZI (MAR)	Willem II	PSV
Martijn KUIJPER	Vitesse	RBC Roosendaal
Sander KELLER	FC Utrecht	RBC Roosendaal
Peter VAN DEN BERG	AZ	RKC Waalwijk
Johan GUDJÓNSSON (ISL)	MVV	RKC Waalwijk
Ivar VAN DINTEREN	FC Groningen	RKC Waalwijk
John VAN LOENHOUT	RBC Roosendaal	RKC Waalwijk
Bas ROORDA	NEC	Roda JC
Sven VANDENBROECK (BEL)	KV Mechelen (BEL)	Roda JC
Ellery CAIRO	Feyenoord	FC Twente
Nick HOEKSTRA	Feyenoord	FC Twente
Tom VAN DER LEEGTE	RKC Waalwijk	FC Twente
Boudewijn PAHLPLATZ	SC Heerenveen	FC Twente
Dave VAN DEN BERGH	Rayo Vallecano (ESP)	FC Utrecht

PLAYER	OLD CLUB	NEW CLUB
Tibor DOMBI (HUN)	Debreceni VSC (HUN)	FC Utrecht
Stefaan TANGHE	R Excelsior Mouscron (BEL)	FC Utrecht
Matthew AMOAH (GHA)	Fortuna Sittard	Vitesse
Tim CORNELISSE	RKC Waalwijk	Vitesse
Didier MARTEL (FRA)	FC Utrecht	Vitesse
Patrick POTHUIZEN	NEC	Vitesse
Remco VAN DER SCHAAF	Fortuna Sittard	Vitesse
Marian ZEMAN (SVK)	Grasshopper-Club Zürich (SUI)	Vitesse
Edwin ZOETEBIER	Feyenoord	Vitesse

● ITALY

PLAYER	OLD CLUB	NEW CLUB
Maurizio GANZ	Milan	Atalanta
Nicola VENTOLA	Inter	Atalanta
Massimo PAGANIN	Bologna	Atalanta
Jaime GONZALEZ (CHL)	Colo Colo (CHL)	Bari
Oscar AYALA (PAR)	Tacuary Asunción (PAR)	Bari
Hany SAID (EGY)	AC Bellinzaona (SUI)	Bari
Emanuele BRIOSCHI	Venezia	Bologna
Giacomo CIPRIANI	Lecce	Bologna
Tomas LOCATELLI	Udinese	Bologna
Francisco LIMA	Lecce	Bologna
Pasquale PADALINO	Fiorentina	Bologna
Luís OLIVEIRA (BEL)	Cagliari	Bologna
Renato OLIVE	Perugia	Bologna
Marcello CASTELLINI	Sampdoria	Bologna
Aimo DIANA	Verona	Brescia
Pierpaolo BISOLI	Perugia	Brescia
Pavel SRNICEK (CZE)	Sheffield Wednesday (ENG)	Brescia
Fabio PETRUZZI	Roma	Brescia
Pierluigi ORLANDINI	Milan	Brescia
Max ESPOSITO	Perugia	Brescia
Francesco MARINO	Lecce	Brescia
Alejandro CORREA (URU)	Deportivo Maldonado (URU)	Brescia
Kubilay TÜRKYILMAZ (SUI)	AC Bellinzona (SUI)	Brescia
Alessandro CALORI	Perugia	Brescia
Roberto BAGGIO	Inter	Brescia
Alexandre AMARAL (BRA)	Vasco da Gama (BRA)	Fiorentina
Marco ROSSI	Salernitana	Fiorentina
LEANDRO (BRA)	Portuguesa (BRA)	Fiorentina
Saliou LASSISSI (FRA)	Parma	Fiorentina
NUNO GOMES (POR)	SL Benfica (POR)	Fiorentina
Paolo VANOLI	Parma	Fiorentina
Domenico MORFEO	Verona	Fiorentina
HAKAN Sükür (TUR)	Galatasaray (TUR)	Inter
Francisco FARINOS (ESP)	Valencia CF (ESP)	Inter

MAJOR SUMMER TRANSFERS 2000

PLAYER	OLD CLUB	NEW CLUB	PLAYER	OLD CLUB	NEW CLUB
Sébastien FREY (FRA)	Verona	Inter	Rabiu AFOLABI (NIG)	R Standard Liège (BEL)	Napoli
Andrea PIRLO	Reggina	Inter	Stephen APPIAH (GHA)	Udinese	Parma
Matteo FERRARI	Bari	Inter	Johan MICOUD (FRA)	Girondins de Bordeaux (FRA)	Parma
Marco BALLOTTA	Lazio	Inter	Matias ALMEYDA (ARG)	Lazio	Parma
Robbie KEANE (IRL)	Coventry City (ENG)	Inter	Sabri LAMOUCHI (FRA)	AS Monaco (FRA)	Parma
Cristian BROCCHI	Verona	Inter	Patrick MBOMA (CMR)	Cagliari	Parma
Corrado COLOMBO	Atalanta	Inter	SÉRGIO CONCEIÇÃO (POR)	Lazio	Parma
Stefano LOMBARDI	Lazio	Inter	Savo MILOSEVIC (YUG)	Real Zaragoza (ESP)	Parma
Bruno CIRILLO	Reggina	Inter	JÚNIOR (BRA)	Palmeiras (BRA)	Parma
Anselmo ROBBIATI	Napoli	Inter	Emiliano BONAZZOLI	Brescia	Parma
Sixto PERALTA (ARG)	Racing Club (ARG)	Inter	Gianluca FALSINI	Verona	Parma
Fabio MACELLARI	Cagliari	Inter	Pietro STRADA	Genoa	Parma
VAMPETA (BRA)	Corinthians (BRA)	Inter	ALEX (BRA)	Palmeiras (BRA)	Parma
Michele PARAMATTI	Bologna	Juventus	Emanuele BLASI	Roma	Perugia
Marco ZANCHI	Udinese	Juventus	AHN JUNG-HWAN (KOR)	Puzan Icons (KOR)	Perugia
Fabian O'NEILL (URU)	Cagliari	Juventus	Christian BUCCHI	Vicenza	Perugia
David TREZEGUET (FRA)	AS Monaco (FRA)	Juventus	MA MING-JU (CHN)	Sichuan Quanxine (CHN)	Perugia
ATHIRSON (BRA)	Flamengo (BRA)	Juventus	Davide BAIOCCO	Vieterbese	Perugia
Claudio LOPEZ (ARG)	Valencia CF (ESP)	Lazio	Riccardo ZAMPAGNA	Catania	Perugia
Angelo PERUZZI	Inter	Lazio	Massimo MARAZZINA	Chievo	Reggina
Roberto BARONIO	Reggina	Lazio	Andrea ZANCHETTA	Chievo	Reggina
Hernán CRESPO (ARG)	Parma	Lazio	Massimo TAIBI	Manchester United (ENG)	Reggina
Francesco COLONNESE	Inter	Lazio	Ivan FRANCESCHINI	Genoa	Reggina
Emanuele PESARESI	Sampdoria	Lazio	MAMEDE (POR)	Vitória Setúbal (POR)	Reggina
Davor VUGRINEC (CRO)	Trabzonspor (TUR)	Lecce	Gabriel BATISTUTA (ARG)	Fiorentina	Roma
Dimitar BERBATOV (BUL)	CSKA Sofia (BUL)	Lecce	Walter SAMUEL (ARG)	Boca Juniors (ARG)	Roma
Alberto MALUSCI	Cosenza	Lecce	Gianni GUIGOU (URU)	Nacional (URU)	Roma
Dario DAINELLI	Fidelis Andria	Lecce	Jonathan ZEBINA (FRA)	Cagliari	Roma
Diego MATEO (ARG)	Newell's Old Boys (ARG)	Lecce	ÉMERSON (BRA)	Bayer 04 Leverkusen (GER)	Roma
Aldo OSORIO (ARG)	Argentinos Juniors (ARG)	Lecce	Abel BALBO (ARG)	Fiorentina	Roma
Davide OLIVARES	Bari	Lecce	Giuseppe DI MASI	Foggia	Roma
Gianni COMANDINI	Vicenza	Milan	Johan WALEM (BEL)	Parma	Udinese
DIDA de Jesus (BRA)	Corinthians (BRA)	Milan	Christian DIAZ (ARG)	Independiente (ARG)	Udinese
ROQUE JÚNIOR (BRA)	Palmeiras (BRA)	Milan	Luis HELGUERA (ESP)	Real Zaragoza (ESP)	Udinese
Luca SAUDATI	Empoli	Milan	Maurizio BEDIN	Monza	Udinese
Fernando REDONDO (ARG)	Real Madrid (ESP)	Milan	Alessandro MAZZOLA	Piacenza	Verona
Francesco COCO	Torino	Milan	Alfredo AGLIETTI	Chievo	Verona
Drazen BRNCIC (CRO)	Monza	Milan	Mario CVITANOVIC (CRO)	Venezia	Verona
Nicola AMORUSO	Juventus	Napoli	Adrian MUTU (ROM)	Inter	Verona
Abdelilah SABER (MAR)	Sporting CP (POR)	Napoli	Fabrizio FERRON	Inter	Verona
Fabio PECCHIA	Juventus	Napoli	Massimo ODDO	Milan	Verona
Francesco MORIERO	Inter	Napoli	Emiliano SALVETTI	Cesena	Verona
Salvatore FRESI	Inter	Napoli	Giorgio STERCHELE	Perugia	Vicenza
Marek JANKULOVSKI (CZE)	Banik Ostrava (CZE)	Napoli	Luca TONI	Treviso	Vicenza
VIDIGAL (POR)	Sporting CP (POR)	Napoli	Stjepan TOMAS (CRO)	Dinamo Zagreb (CRO)	Vicenza

MAJOR SUMMER TRANSFERS 2000

PLAYER	OLD CLUB	NEW CLUB
Raffaele LONGO	Parma	Vicenza
Giuseppe CARDONE	Parma	Vicenza
Mohammed KALLON (SRL)	Inter	Vicenza
● **PORTUGAL**		
CORREIA	FC Porto	Alverca FC
RICARDO ESTEVES	Vitória Setúbal	Alverca FC
RICARD CARVALHO	Vitória Setúbal	Alverca FC
TITO	Vitória Guimarães	Alverca FC
MARCO FREITAS	SL Benfica	Alverca FC
PEDRO MARTINS	Boavista FC	Alverca FC
Juan Francesco VIVEROS (CHL)	Sporting CP	Alverca FC
CHIQUINHO CONDE (MOZ)	Vitória Setúbal	Alverca FC
TÓ LUIS	Rio Ave FC	Desportivo Aves
JOSÉ SOARES	SC Campomaiorense	Desportivo Aves
NUNO AFONSO	CS Marítimo	Desportivo Aves
ABÍLIO	SC Campomaiorense	Desportivo Aves
NILTON	Boavista FC	Desportivo Aves
Rudolph DOUALA (CMR)	Boavista FC	Desportivo Aves
RUI LIMA	Boavista FC	Desportivo Aves
LUÍS MANUEL	Boavista FC	SC Beira Mar
MARCELO PASSOS (BRA)	Ala Araby (QTR)	SC Beira Mar
GAMBOA	CD Santa Clara	SC Beira Mar
PEDRO HENRIQUES	Vitória Setúbal	CF Os Belenenses
VERONA (BRA)	CF Estrela Amadora	CF Os Belenenses
ELIEL (BRA)	Coritiba (BRA)	CF Os Belenenses
GUGA (BRA)	Gil Vicente FC	CF Os Belenenses
Ivan DUDIC (YUG)	Crvena zvezda Beograd (YUG)	SL Benfica
Alejandro ESCALONA (PER)	Torino (ITA)	SL Benfica
FERNANDO MEIRA	Vitória Guimarães	SL Benfica
Carlos MARCHENA (ESP)	Sevilla FC (ESP)	SL Benfica
CARLITOS	Gil Vicente FC	SL Benfica
LUÍS MIGUEL	CF Estrela Amadora	SL Benfica
Pierre VAN HOOIJDONK (HOL)	Vitesse (HOL)	SL Benfica
FRECHAUT	Vitória Setúbal	Boavista FC
MARÇAL (BRA)	União Leiria	Boavista FC
RUI ÓSCAR	CS Marítimo	Boavista FC
GOUVEIA	Montpellier HSC (FRA)	Boavista FC
PEDRO SANTOS	Gil Vicente FC	Boavista FC
PETIT	Gil Vicente FC	Boavista FC
DUDA (BRA)	Alverca FC	Boavista FC
SILVA (BRA)	SC Braga	Boavista FC
ANDRADE	SL Benfica	SC Braga
EDMILSON (BRA)	Vitória Guimarães	SC Braga
Vedran PELIC (BOS)	KVC Westerlo (BEL)	SC Braga

PLAYER	OLD CLUB	NEW CLUB
RIVA (BRA)	Vitória Guimarães	SC Braga
Srdjan ZAHARIEVSKI (MAC)	VfB Stuttgart (GER)	SC Campomaiorense
Srecko RISTIC (CRO)	VfB Stuttgart (GER)	SC Campomaiorense
HUGO ALVES	Vitória Setúbal	CF Estrela Amadora
FONSECA	Vitória Guimarães	CF Estrela Amadora
Jorge CADETE	Bradford City (ENG)	CF Estrela Amadora
DJALMA (BRA)	Recife FC (BRA)	CF Estrela Amadora
JEAN PAULISTA (BRA)	Desportivo Aves	SC Farense
SÉRGIO GAMEIRO	CD Santa Clara	Gil Vicente FC
VÍTOR VIEIRA	CF Estrela Amadora	Gil Vicente FC
BAKERO	Sevilla FC (ESP)	CS Marítimo
QUIM	Dundee United (SCO)	CS Marítimo
ALFREDO BÓIA	União Leiria	FC Paços Ferreira
ZÉ NANDO	Gil Vicente FC	FC Paços Ferreira
BETO (BRA)	Rceife FC (BRA)	FC Paços Ferreira
FORMOSO	CD Santa Clara	FC Paços Ferreira
GLAUBER (BRA)	Recife FC (BRA)	FC Paços Ferreira
LEONARDO (BRA)	ABC Natal (BRA)	FC Paços Ferreira
Sergei OVCHINNIKOV (RUS)	Alverca FC	FC Porto
PEDRO ESPINHA	Vitória Guimarães	FC Porto
JORGE ANDRADE	CF Estrela Amadora	FC Porto
Dmitriy ALENICHEV (RUS)	Perugia (ITA)	FC Porto
Silvio MARIC (CRO)	Newcastle United (ENG)	FC Porto
Carlos PAREDES (PAR)	Olimpia (PAR)	FC Porto
PAULO ASSUNÇÃO (BRA)	Palmeiras (BRA)	FC Porto
Miran PAVLIN (SLO)	Karlsruher SC (GER)	FC Porto
Juan Antonio PIZZI (ESP)	Rosário Central (ARG)	FC Porto
PENA (BRA)	Palmeiras (BRA)	FC Porto
Diego TROTTA (ARG)	Vélez Sarsfield (ARG)	SC Salgueiros
Ivan LITERA (YUG)	Velbazhd Kiustendil (BUL)	SC Salgueiros
Phil BABB (IRL)	Tranmere Rovers (ENG)	Sporting CP
DIMAS	Fenerbahçe (TUR)	Sporting CP
HUGO	Sampdoria (ITA)	Sporting CP
Pavel HORVATH (CZE)	Slavia Praha (CZE)	Sporting CP
PAULO BENTO	Real Oviedo (ESP)	Sporting CP
Alan MAHON (IRL)	Tranmere Rovers (ENG)	Sporting CP
JOÃO PINTO	SL Benfica	Sporting CP
Jovan KIROVSKI (USA)	Borussia Dortmund (GER)	Sporting CP
SÁ PINTO	Real Sociedad (ESP)	Sporting CP
BRUNO CAIRES	RC Celta (ESP)	Sporting CP
COSTINHA	CD Tenerife (ESP)	União Leiria
TIAGO	CD Tenerife (ESP)	União Leiria
CANDIDO	Desportivo Aves	Vitória Guimarães
NUNO CLARO	FC Paços Ferreira	Vitória Guimarães
AURI (BRA)	Gil Vicente FC	Vitória Guimarães

MAJOR SUMMER TRANSFERS 2000

PLAYER	OLD CLUB	NEW CLUB
FONSECA	CF Estrela Amadora	Vitória Guimarães
PAULÃO (BRA)	FC São Paulo (BRA)	Vitória Guimarães
ROGÉRIO MATIAS	SC Campomaiorense	Vitória Guimarães
WILLIAM (BRA)	SCD Compostela (ESP)	Vitória Guimarães
FANGUEIRO	Gil Vicente FC	Vitória Guimarães
HUGO CUNHA	SC Campomaiorense	Vitória Guimarães
MAURÍCIO (BRA)	Juventude Caxias (BRA)	Vitória Guimarães
MANOEL (BRA)	Vitória Bahia (BRA)	Vitória Guimarães

● SCOTLAND

PLAYER	OLD CLUB	NEW CLUB
Chris SUTTON (ENG)	Chelsea (ENG)	Celtic
Joos VALGAEREN (BEL)	Roda JC (HOL)	Celtic
Alan THOMPSON (ENG)	Aston Villa (ENG)	Celtic
Marco DE MARCHI (ITA)	Vitesse (HOL)	Dundee
Jamie BUCHAN	Aberdeen	Dundee United
Danny GRIFFIN (NIR)	St. Johnstone	Dundee United
Grant JOHNSON	Huddersfield Town (ENG)	Dundee United
Hasney ALJOFREE (ENG)	Bolton Wanderers (ENG)	Dundee United
Marco RUITENBEEK (HOL)	Go Ahead Eagles (HOL)	Dunfermline Athletic
Youssef ROSSI (MAR)	Stade Rennais FC (FRA)	Dunfermline Athletic
Rob McKAY	Motherwell	Dunfermline Athletic
Audrius SKERLA (LIT)	PSV (HOL)	Dunfermline Athletic
Didier AGATHE (FRA)	Raith Rovers	Hibernian
Ulrik LAURSEN (DEN)	OB (DEN)	Hibernian
John O'NEIL	St. Johnstone	Hibernian
Paul FENWICK	Raith Rovers	Hibernian
Ian WESTWATER	Dunfermline Athletic	Hibernian
Gary SMITH	Aberdeen	Hibernian
Andy McLAREN	Reading (ENG)	Kilmarnock
Craig DARGO	Raith Rovers	Kilmarnock
Greg STRONG	Bolton Wanderers (ENG)	Motherwell
Allan JOHNSTON	Sunderland (ENG)	Rangers
Bert KONTERMAN (HOL)	Feyenoord (HOL)	Rangers
Peter LØVENKRANDS (DEN)	AB (DEN)	Rangers
Kenny MILLER	Hibernian	Rangers
Paul REID (ENG)	Carlisle United (ENG)	Rangers
Fernando RICKSEN (HOL)	AZ (HOL)	Rangers
Ronald DE BOER (HOL)	FC Barcelona (ESP)	Rangers
Paul HARTLEY	Hibernian	St. Johnstone
Tommy LØVENKRANDS (DEN)	AB (DEN)	St. Johnstone
Craig RUSSELL (ENG)	Manchester City (ENG)	St. Johnstone
Ricky GILLIES	Aberdeen	St. Mirren
Jamie McGOWAN	Motherwell	St. Mirren

● SPAIN

PLAYER	OLD CLUB	NEW CLUB
Vlatko DJOLONGA (CRO)	Hrvatski dragovoljac Zagreb (CRO)	Deportivo Alavés
Delfín GELI	Albacete Balompié	Deportivo Alavés
Ivan TOMIC (YUG)	Roma (ITA)	Deportivo Alavés
Jurica VUCKO (CRO)	Hajduk Split (CRO)	Deportivo Alavés
IVAN ALONSO (URU)	River Plate (URU)	Deportivo Alavés
Jordi CRUIJFF (HOL)	Manchester United (ENG)	Deportivo Alavés
Carlos MERINO	Nottingham Forest (ENG)	Athletic Bilbao
Domingo NAGORE	CD Numancia	Athletic Bilbao
Pablo ORBAIZ	CA Osasuna	Athletic Bilbao
Richard DUTRUEL (FRA)	RC Celta	FC Barcelona
Iván DE LA PEÑA	Lazio (ITA)	FC Barcelona
GERARD López	Valencia CF	FC Barcelona
Marc OVERMARS (HOL)	Arsenal (ENG)	FC Barcelona
Emmanuel PETIT (FRA)	Arsenal (ENG)	FC Barcelona
ALFONSO Pérez	Real Betis	FC Barcelona
Pablo CAVALLERO (ARG)	RCD Espanyol	RC Celta
DORIVA (BRA)	Sampdoria (ITA)	RC Celta
JESULI Mora	Sevilla FC	RC Celta
CATANHA (BRA)	Málaga CF	RC Celta
VAGNER (BRA)	Roma (ITA)	RC Celta
José Francisco MOLINA	Atlético Madrid	RC Deportivo
CÉSAR SAMPAIO (BRA)	Palmeiras (BRA)	RC Deportivo
HÉLDER Cristovão (BRA)	Newcastle United (ENG)	RC Deportivo
Aldo DUSCHER (ARG)	Sporting CP (POR)	RC Deportivo
ÉMERSON (BRA)	CD Tenerife	RC Deportivo
Juan Carlos VALERON	Atlético Madrid	RC Deportivo
DIEGO TRISTAN	RCD Mallorca	RC Deportivo
Walter PANDIANI (URU)	Peñarol (URU)	RC Deportivo
RENALDO (BRA)	UD Las Palmas	RC Deportivo
Angel MORALES	Deportivo Alavés	RCD Espanyol
NAN RIBERA	Deportivo Alavés	RCD Espanyol
OSCAR García	Valencia CF	RCD Espanyol
David AGANZO	Real Madrid	RCD Espanyol
BAIANO (BRA)	Santos (BRA)	UD Las Palmas
EDO ALONSO	Athletic Bilbao	UD Las Palmas
Thórdur GUDJÓNSSON (ISL)	KRC Genk (BEL)	UD Las Palmas
OKTAY Derelioglu (TUR)	Gaziantepspor (TUR)	UD Las Palmas
Martin RIVAS (URU)	Inter (ITA)	Málaga CF
Sebastián Fernández "BASTI"	Albacete Balompié	Málaga CF
Júlio César DELY VALDES (PAN)	Real Oviedo	Málaga CF
ISMAEL Marchal	CA Osasuna	Málaga CF
Carlos ROA (ARG)	unattached	RCD Mallorca
FINIDI George (NIG)	Real Betis	RCD Mallorca
Albert LUQUE	Málaga CF	RCD Mallorca
GUSTAVO de la Parra	Atlético Madrid	CD Numancia
MANEL Menéndez	RC Deportivo	CD Numancia

MAJOR SUMMER TRANSFERS 2000

PLAYER	OLD CLUB	NEW CLUB
Laurentiu ROSU (ROM)	Steaua Bucuresti (ROM)	CD Numancia
JOSE MANUEL Colmenero	RC Deportivo	CD Numancia
ANGEL Rodríguez	Sevilla FC	CA Osasuna
Sergei SHUSTIKOV (RUS)	Racing Santander	CA Osasuna
Milan MARTINOVIC (YUG)	Rad Beograd (YUG)	Real Oviedo
Djordje TOMIC (YUG)	Partizan Beograd (YUG)	Real Oviedo
Maximiliano ESTEVEZ (ARG)	Racing Club (ARG)	Racing Santander
Leider PRECIADO (COL)	Colon Santa Fé (ARG)	Racing Santander
Sergio BALLESTEROS	CD Tenerife	Rayo Vallecano
Francisco FERREIRA	Athletic Bilbao	Rayo Vallecano
IVAN IGLESIAS	Real Oviedo	Rayo Vallecano
José María QUEVEDO	Sevilla FC	Rayo Vallecano
Gustavo BARTELT (ARG)	Roma (ITA)	Rayo Vallecano
Elvir BOLIC (BOS)	Fenerbahçe (TUR)	Rayo Vallecano
César SANCHEZ	Real Valladolid	Real Madrid
Albert CELADES	RC Celta	Real Madrid
FLÁVIO CONCEIÇÃO (BRA)	RC Deportivo	Real Madrid
Claude MAKELELE (FRA)	RC Celta	Real Madrid
Santiago SOLARI (ARG)	Atlético Madrid	Real Madrid
Manuel CANABAL	Rayo Vallecano	Real Madrid
Edwin CONGO (COL)	Real Valladolid	Real Madrid
Luís FIGO (POR)	FC Barcelona	Real Madrid
Pedro MUNITIS	Racing Santander	Real Madrid
Alberto RIVERA	CD Numancia	Real Madrid
RODRIGO Fabri (BRA)	Real Valladolid	Real Madrid
Mattias ASPER (SWE)	AIK (SWE)	Real Sociedad
Stéphane COLLET (FRA)	RC Lens (FRA)	Real Sociedad
TAYFUN Korkut (TUR)	Fenerbahçe (TUR)	Real Sociedad
ARIF Erdem (TUR)	Fenerbahçe (TUR)	Real Sociedad
Frédéric PEIREMANS (BEL)	FC Twente (HOL)	Real Sociedad
Rubén VEGA	Albacete Balompié	Real Sociedad
Carlos PEREZ	Villarreal CF	Valencia CF
Rubén BARAJA	Atlético Madrid	Valencia CF
Didier DESCHAMPS (FRA)	Chelsea (ENG)	Valencia CF
Livero PARRI	Villarreal CF	Valencia CF
Zlatko ZAHOVIC (SLO)	Olympiakos (GRE)	Valencia CF
John CAREW (NOR)	Rosenborg BK (NOR)	Valencia CF
Diego ALONSO (URU)	Gimnasia y Esgrima (ARG)	Valencia CF
Pablo RICHETTI (ARG)	Colón Santa Fé (ARG)	Real Valladolid
Dragan CIRIC (YUG)	AEK (GRE)	Real Valladolid
FERNANDO Fernández	Real Madrid	Real Valladolid
Cuauhtemoc BLANCO (MEX)	América (MEX)	Real Valladolid
Jaime Iván KAVIEDES (ECU)	RC Celta	Real Valladolid
Rodolfo ARRUABUENA (ARG)	Boca Juniors (ARG)	Villarreal CF
Guillermo AMOR	Fiorentina (ITA)	Villarreal CF
Bruno MARIONI (ARG)	Independiente (ARG)	Villarreal CF

PLAYER	OLD CLUB	NEW CLUB
VICTOR Fernández	Real Valladolid	Villarreal CF
ALVARO Rubio	Albacete Balompié	Real Zaragoza
Miguel REBOSIO (PER)	Sporting Cristal (PER)	Real Zaragoza
Alen PETERNAC (CRO)	Real Valladolid	Real Zaragoza

● SWITZERLAND

PLAYER	OLD CLUB	NEW CLUB
Marc FIECHTER	FC Baden	FC Aarau
Levan KHOMERIKI (GEO)	Dinamo Batumi (GEO)	FC Aarau
Romain CREVOISIER	SC Kriens	FC Basel
Yao AZIAWONOU (TUG)	FC Sion	FC Basel
Feliciano MAGRO	Udinese (ITA)	FC Basel
Jean-Michel TCHOUGA (CMR)	Yverdon-Sports	FC Basel
Carlos VARELA (ESP)	Servette FC Genève	FC Basel
Ivan ERCIG (AUS)	Perth Glory (AUS)	FC Basel
Peter JEHLE (LIE)	FC Schaan (LIE)	Grasshopper-Club Zürich
Andres GERBER	Lausanne-Sports	Grasshopper-Club Zürich
Elvir MELUNOVIC	Servette FC Genève	Grasshopper-Club Zürich
Daniel JOLLER	FC Luzern	Grasshopper-Club Zürich
Patrick DE NAPOLI	Karlsruher SC (GER)	Grasshopper-Club Zürich
Rainer BIELI	Neuchâtel Xamax FC	Grasshopper-Club Zürich
Remo MEYER	FC Luzern	Lausanne-Sports
Olivier BAUDRY (FRA)	FC Sochaux (FRA)	Lausanne-Sports
David HELLEBUYCK (FRA)	Olympique Lyonnais (FRA)	Lausanne-Sports
Olivier BIAGGI	Yverdon-Sports	FC Lugano
Badile LUBAMBA	FC Luzern	FC Lugano
Ludovic MAGNIN	Yverdon-Sports	FC Lugano
Sylvain MOUKWELLE (CMR)	FC Sion	FC Lugano
Yannick GORDIEN (FRA)	RC Lens (FRA)	FC Luzern
Rouven FEUZ	BSC Young Boys Bern	FC Luzern
Martin LENGEN	BSC Young Boys Bern	FC Luzern
Christophe OHREL	Lausanne-Sports	FC Luzern
Zemun SELIMI (ALB)	BSC Young Boys Bern	FC Luzern
Blaise N'KUFO	Grasshopper-Club Zürich	FC Luzern
Timothée ATOUBA (CMR)	Union Douala (CMR)	Neuchâtel Xamax FC
Marco TSCHOPP	FC Basel	Neuchâtel Xamax FC
Jan BERGER (CZE)	FC Baden	FC St. Gallen
Christophe JAQUET	Yverdon-Sports	Servette FC Genève
Oscar LONDONO (COL)	Lausanne-Sports	Servette FC Genève
Bertrand FAYOLLE (FRA)	AS Saint-Etienne (FRA)	FC Sion
Florent DELAY	Neuchâtel Xamax FC	Yverdon-Sports
Ricardo IGLESIAS (ESP)	Lausanne-Sports	Yverdon-Sports
Steve GOHOURI (FRA)	Bnei Yehuda (ISR)	Yverdon-Sports
Tihomir IVANOWSKI	Lausanne-Sports	Yverdon-Sports
Fabien MARGAIRAZ	Servette FC Genève	FC Zürich
Marcel HELDMANN	FC Aarau	FC Zürich